Age	Milestone	Age	Milestone
13 months	Pats toy in imitation Vocalizes four different vowel-consonant combinations Stands alone Walks alone	31 months	Builds tower of eight cubes Swings leg to kick ball Jumps distance of 4 inches
16 months	Scribbles spontaneously Imitates single words Walks alone with good coordination Throws ball while standing	34 months	Imitates vertical and horizontal strokes Poses question Walks on tiptoe for four steps
19 months	Builds tower of two cubes Uses word(s) to make wants known Walks up stairs or down stairs with help	37 months	Understands concept of one Understands two prepositions Walks up stairs, alternating feet
22 months	Combines word(s) and gesture(s) Points to three of doll's body parts Stands on right foot or left foot with help	42 months	Names four colors Understands four prepositions Copies a circle, a plus sign, or a square
25 months	Uses a two-word utterance Imitates a two-word sentence Runs with coordination	48 months	Goes to toilet alone Hops on one foot Throws ball overhand Climbs well
28 months	Builds tower of six cubes Uses a three-word sentence Walks up stairs or down stairs alone, placing both feet on each step	60 months	Skips Ties shoes Follows three commands Dresses and undresses self

Source: Ages 1 month through 42 months from N. Bayley (1993), *Bayley Scales of Infant Development,* Copyright © 1993 by The Psychological Corporation. Reproduced by permission. All rights reserved. Ages 48 months and 60 months from M. Lewis (1991), Northern and Downs (1991), and Shapiro (1991).

Clinical and Forensic Interviewing of Children and Families

Guidelines for the Mental Health, Education, Pediatric, and Child Maltreatment Fields

Jerome M. Sattler
San Diego State University

Jerome M. Sattler, Publisher, Inc.
San Diego

Editorial Services: Sally Lifland and Jeanne Yost, Lifland et al., Bookmakers
Interior Design: Jerome M. Sattler and Sally Lifland
Cover Designer: Jerome M. Sattler
Proofreaders: Denise Throckmorton and Gladys Moore
Indexers: Madge Schworer and Andrea Deibler-Gorman
Production Coordinators: Sally Lifland and Jerome M. Sattler
Compositor: Omegatype, Champaign, Illinois
Cover Printer: Phoenix Color
Printer and Binder: Maple-Vail Book Manufacturing Group

This text was set in Times Roman and Helvetica, printed on Highland Book, Smyth sewn, with Type 2 mylar lamination and
photoembossed cover stock.

Cover: Latin American fabric art, artist unknown

Library of Congress Catalog Card Number: 97–67148

ISBN 0-9618209-4-2

16   15   14   13   12   11   10   9   8   7   6   5   4   3   2   1   06   05   04   03   02   01   00   99   98   97

Printed in the United States of America

To my wife,
Bonnie Jeanne Sattler
for her love, devotion, and support

To my friend and colleague,
William A. Hillix
for his wise counsel and generosity

To my children,
Heidi Beth Philips, David Nathen Sattler, Deborah Elaine Hendrix, and *Keith Richard Sattler*
to my son- and daughter-in-law,
Walter Edwin Philips and *Sudie Back Sattler*
to my grandchildren,
Nicole Marie Philips and *Justin Lewis Philips*
to my father-in-law,
Richard McIntyre
to my brother-in-law,
Paul McIntyre
for their love, continued support, and friendship

To the memory of
my brother,
Paul Sattler
my mother-in-law,
Marjorie McIntyre
my parents,
Nathan and Pearl Sattler
for their love and affection that will always endure

CONTENTS

LIST OF TABLES

LIST OF FIGURES

PREFACE

There are only two lasting bequests we can hope to give our children. One of these is roots; the other wings.

—Hodding Carter

Clinical and Forensic Interviewing of Children and Families is designed to help students and professionals in human services fields become competent clinical assessment and forensic interviewers. The impetus for writing this text was my renewed appreciation of the importance of the interview as an assessment tool. The human services field is evolving rapidly. More and more children are being referred for custody evaluations, maltreatment, depression, suicide attempts, and health-related conditions. Homelessness, AIDS, substance abuse, and crisis intervention have become extremely important areas for mental health professionals. The increase in managed–health care programs places greater demands on all clinicians to provide time-limited, focused, and cost-effective service. There is less time and money for intense diagnostic study, despite the potential benefits. A text that addressed these topics was clearly needed.

This book is based on the philosophy that one cannot be a competent clinical assessment or forensic interviewer unless he or she has the relevant information about the child's presenting problem, as well as knowledge of the interventions that might help the child and family. Therefore, in this text, you will find information about the major problem areas encountered by children and their families and about interventions, along with suggestions for conducting interviews. You should consult additional references about the child's problem areas, as needed.

This book will benefit students and professionals in all human services fields, including social work, clinical psychology, counseling psychology, school psychology, rehabilitation psychology, health psychology, pediatric psychology, psychiatry, education, and speech therapy. In addition, professionals in such allied fields as medicine, nursing, law, and law enforcement have much to gain from reading it. This text provides both theoretical and practical guidelines to help students and professionals develop skills in interviewing children, adolescents, parents, families, and teachers.

Clinical and Forensic Interviewing of Children and Families contains several study aids. Each chapter begins with a list of the major headings, followed by chapter objectives. Within the chapters are exercises designed to give you feedback about your understanding of the material and to help you explore related areas. I encourage you to do these exercises. Each chapter ends with an in-depth summary, followed by a list of key terms, concepts, and names, as well as study questions. You can use this list and the questions that follow it to evaluate which parts of the chapter you have mastered and which parts require further study. The *Thinking Through the Issues* section of each chapter will guide you in reflecting on important issues related to clinical assessment and forensic interviewing. Finally, the glossary at the end of the book will help you review key terms contained in the text, as well as related terms not found in the text.

One entire section of the book is devoted to the assessment of child maltreatment. Two considerations led me to give extensive coverage to this area. First, child maltreatment is of increasing concern to human services workers, as billions of dollars are being spent by governmental agencies for the investigation, care, and treatment of children who are alleged to have been maltreated or who have been maltreated. Second, the interview plays a critical role in the assessment of child maltreatment. The more you know about the pitfalls of interviewing in cases of child maltreatment, the more effective you will be in interviewing children and in presenting your findings in any criminal proceedings, in which interview techniques are sometimes challenged. The material in Section V will give you a foundation for understanding child maltreatment and a foundation for conducting child maltreatment interviews.

To conduct effective clinical assessment or forensic interviews with children and adolescents, you need to know about normal children and their families and about children who have developmental or behavioral problems or special needs. Although this book presents normal developmental landmarks and reviews features associated with several behavioral and medical problems found in children, I encourage you to read appropriate texts in normal child development and child psychopathology if you are unfamiliar with these areas.

There are many excellent behavioral checklists, psychological tests, and observational systems useful for evaluating children with psychological disorders. Because the focus of this text is on interviewing, most of these assessment tools are not discussed here. You can obtain information about behavioral checklists, psychological tests, and observational systems by consulting, for example, Adams, Parson, Culbertson, and Nixon (1996), Breen and Feidler (1996), Kamphaus and Frick (1996), and Sattler (1992).

Clinical assessment and forensic interviewing are dynamic and challenging fields. As an interviewer, you are in a unique position to help children and their families. I hope this text plays a part in your development as a skilled clinical assessment or forensic interviewer of children and families.

Note to Instructors: An *Instructor's Manual* accompanies *Clinical and Forensic Interviewing of Children and Families.* The manual contains primarily multiple-choice questions useful for objective examinations.

ACKNOWLEDGMENTS

Two broken down old men sat on a park bench. One said,
"I'm here because I never took advice from anybody."
"Shake," said the other man, "I'm here because I took
everybody's advice."

—Bill Adler

I have been fortunate in receiving the wisdom, guidance, and suggestions of several individuals, who willingly gave of their time and energy to read the manuscript. Because of their efforts, the book is more thorough, comprehensive, and up to date than it might have been.

The following people read the entire manuscript. I wish to express my thanks and appreciation to

Dr. Harvey Clarizio, Michigan State University
Dr. Larry Hilgert, Valdosta State University
Dr. William A. Hillix, San Diego State University
Dr. Loring Jones, San Diego State University
Dr. Vanessa Malcarne, San Diego State University
Dr. Eric J. Mash, University of Calgary
Bonnie J. Sattler, MS, RD, Kaiser Permanente, San Diego
Inta M. Sellars, J.D., St. Paul, Minnesota
Dr. Steven Sparta, University of California Medical School, San Diego
Dr. Audrey Spindler, San Diego State University

I also have been fortunate in having the following individuals read one or more selected chapters of the manuscript. Their excellent feedback was extremely helpful in making the manuscript more scholarly and accurate. Thanks go to

Jean Maria Arrigo, MA, Clairmont Graduate University
Dr. Vernon D. Avila, San Diego State University
Dr. Chris Bagley, University of Calgary
Dr. Angela O. Ballantyne, University of California, San Diego
Genevieve Bromley, MSW, Department of Social Services, County of San Diego
Detective Michele Bustamante, San Diego Sheriff's Department
Jonathan Butterfield, J.D., Williamsport, Pennsylvania

Dr. Jan Culbertson, University of Oklahoma Health Sciences Center
Deborah Daro, DSW, National Committee to Prevent Child Abuse, Chicago
Dr. Gwen Dean, private practice, Orange County, California
Barbara Duddle, MSW, San Diego
Dr. Marc Everson, University of North Carolina
Dr. Kathleen Coulborn Faller, University of Michigan
Dr. Jeannine Feldman, San Diego State University
Dr. Larry Fenson, San Diego State University
Investigator Dana Gassaway, Office of the District Attorney, County of San Diego
Kristine Gist, MS, Children's Hospital, San Diego
Dr. Linda Saylor Gudas, Children's Hospital, Boston and Harvard Medical School
Dr. Robert G. Harrington, University of Kansas
Toni Haynes, MSW, San Diego County Adoptions
Dr. Bob Heaton, University of California, San Diego
Dr. Steven Henderson, San Diego State University
Lori Holmes, MA, LISW, CornerHouse Interagency Child Abuse Evaluation Center, Minneapolis
Barbara Huntington, MBA, San Diego State University
Dr. Teresa LaFromboise, Stanford University
Dr. Phil Langalis, San Diego State University
Dr. Myra Liefer, Illinois School of Professional Psychology
Larry Leik, Department of Social Services, State of Michigan
Dr. Martha Lequerica, Montclair State University
Charlotte Lilliedah, MA, NCC, LaPalta County Department of Social Services, Durango, Colorado
Dr. Paula K. Lundberg-Love, University of Texas at Tyler
Dr. William M. McQueen, Jr., Biola University
Detective Walter Parsons, Arvada Police Department, Arvada, Colorado
Walter E. Philips, MSW, Union of Pan Asian Community, San Diego
Dr. Robert Pinta, University of Virginia
Dr. John Richards, Kaiser Permanente, San Diego
Dr. Michael C. Roberts, University of Kansas
Dr. Kjell Rudestam, Fielding Institute
Dr. James F. Sallis, Jr., San Diego State University
Barry Salovitz, MSW, New York State Department of Social Services
Dr. David N. Sattler, College of Charlestown
Susan Sattler, RN, Miami, Florida
Dr. Richard Schulte, San Diego State University
Dr. William J. Sieber, University of California, San Diego

Catherine Stephenson, J.D., Deputy District Attorney, County of San Diego

Dr. Melvin Swartz, private practice, San Diego

Baxter Venable, Lawrenceville, NJ

Sgt. William Walkup, San Diego Sheriff's Department

Judith Weigman, MA, LICSW, CornerHouse Interagency Child Abuse Evaluation Center, Minneapolis

Dr. Deborah Whitcomb, Education Development Center, Newton, Massachusetts

Dr. Diane Willis, University of Oklahoma Health Sciences Center

A number of students at San Diego State University read and commented on the manuscript, checked references, and helped in other invaluable ways. Thanks go to

Louis Alvarez	Sandara C. Lopez
Annmarie K. Baker	Kelly McIntyre
Sylvia Bigatti	Michael E. Musgrove
Darlene Braasch	Colleen O'Connell
Valerie Brew	Rebecca J. Poage
Janice Cochran	Michael Ricks
Anna D. Dotran	Allana C. Shelton
Lynn Fonacier	Dana Smith
Deane Fulbright	Shannon Swanson
Elana Gichon	Michelle Tenen
Meah Graves	Deborah A. Walker
Wendy Hester	Ellen G. Weinstein
Catherine Hill	Kelli Wright
Debra James	Jefferson Young
Jill Kattelman	

My able secretary, Jennifer Williams, spent six years typing and retyping the manuscript, references, and abstracts and performing related duties. Together, we learned enough about WordPerfect to master the fundamentals of typesetting. Jennifer, thanks for being so special. Your dependability and dedication to getting this book published is much appreciated.

Brenda Pinedo, office manager at Jerome M. Sattler, Publisher, Inc., has been an exceptional staff member. Thanks, Brenda, for keeping the company office going and helping with the various details involved in getting the book into production.

I could never have completed this book without the assistance of the Interlibrary Loan staff at the San Diego State University Library. Thank you, Kelley Martin, Teri Roudenbush, Cathy Cook, Darlene Sperling, Edward Di Bella, and the student assistants for being so helpful and finding those books and articles that were so critically needed. Wendy Schmidt and Joan Goodwin, from the Circulation Department at the San Diego State University Library, also were helpful in obtaining books and journals. Thank you, Wendy and Joan.

Rachael Litonjaa-Witt and James F. Edwards from Instructional Technology Services at San Diego State University were invaluable in helping me with computer problems. Thanks, Rachael and Jim, for your knowledge and expertise. It is comforting to know that you are available when I get into trouble with the computer, which sometimes seems to be a weekly occurrence.

I also wish to thank the able secretarial staff at the Psychology Department at San Diego State University for relaying messages, notifying me of faxes, and helping me in innumerable other ways. Thank you, Darlene Pickrel, Linda Corio, Romina Pacheco, and Rebecca Smith. Deborah Walker, Janice Genovese, Andrew Koopmans, Kathleen Mayes, Laurie Palmer, John Philips, Jane Via, Lowell Waxman, Deborah Hendrix, and Nora Dresser also deserve thanks for helping with the preparation of the book.

Part of the manuscript for the book was written while I was an exchange professor at the Department of Applied Psychology at University College Cork in Cork, Ireland, during the 1989–1990 academic year. Thank you, Professor Max Taylor, Dr. Jurek Kirakowski, and Mary Corbett for your wonderful hospitality, friendship, and intellectual stimulation.

I also want to acknowledge Roy A. Wallace, West Coast representative from Maple-Vail Book Manufacturing Group. Roy, thank you for your help in getting this book printed. It has always been a pleasure working with you. My relatives have been supportive throughout this eight-year project. Thank you, Susan Sattler, Robert Sattler, Robin Sattler, Aaron Sattler, Wesley Sattler, Taylor Sattler, Florence Sattler, and Ester Newman for your encouragement and support.

I have been fortunate in having a superb copyediting and production staff help get this book ready for publication. The staff at Lifland et al., Bookmakers are craftpersons and, as the title of their firm indicates, truly "bookmakers." Thank you, Sally Lifland and Jeannie Yost for your patience and tolerance and for working with me during an 11-month period to make the manuscript clear, grammatically correct, well organized, coherent, as free from error as possible, a delight to read, and a work that we can be proud of.

I also want to thank Yoram Mizrahi and the staff at Omega-type for putting my galleys into pages with exceptional expertise. Thank you, Yoram, for doing such an excellent job.

Finally, I wish to acknowledge the role that San Diego State University has played in my life. For almost 32 years, this great university has given me the support and academic freedom needed to pursue my interests in teaching, research, writing, and consultation. Thank you, San Diego State University, for all that you have given me. I hope that in my small way I have returned something to my students and to the university community at large.

ABOUT THE AUTHOR

I grew up in the East Bronx of New York City during the 1930s and 1940s in an immigrant family. I began my study of psychology at the City College of New York and obtained my BA in 1952. I then obtained my master's degree in 1953 and my Ph.D. in 1959 from the University of Kansas (KU). While at KU, I was fortunate to be introduced to gestalt and existential psychology and to participate in the Veterans Administration clinical psychology training program. My mentors, Fritz Heider and John Chotlos, were extraordinarily gifted and creative psychologists and teachers. In 1954, I was drafted into the U.S. Army and worked as a psychologist in an outpatient mental health clinic.

After graduation, I began teaching and working in a child guidance clinic at Fort Hays Kansas State College. In 1961, I accepted a position at the University of North Dakota. In 1965, I joined the staff at San Diego State University (SDSU), where I taught for 29 years. I retired from SDSU in 1994. Currently, I hold the positions of Professor Emeritus and Adjunct Professor. Also, I am a Diplomate in Clinical Psychology and a Fellow of the American Psychological Association. Finally, I am the author of *Assessment of Children (Revised and Updated Third Edition)* and one of the coauthors of the *Stanford-Binet Intelligence Scale: Fourth Edition.*

I had three excellent international experiences. The first was as a Fulbright lecturer at University of Kebangsaan in Kuala Lumpur, Malaysia in 1972. The second was as an exchange professor at Katholieke Universiteit in Nijmegen, The Netherlands, in 1983. And the third was as an exchange professor at University College Cork in Cork, Ireland in 1989. When I'm not working on an assessment text, I enjoy listening to jazz, watching movies, reading, participating in my youngest son's Boy Scout troop, and spending time with my family, including my two grandchildren.

Writing this book has been an extremely rewarding experience. It has put me in touch with several critical issues facing our nation's children and families. With knowledge and understanding and with faith in the basic integrity of our fellow human beings, we all will be in a better position to make a difference.

SECTION I

GENERAL PRINCIPLES AND TECHNIQUES OF INTERVIEWING AND REPORTING

Section I provides the background information that you will need to conduct the initial clinical assessment and post-assessment interviews with children, parents, families, and teachers and to write the interview report. To conduct effective interviews with children, you will need to use a developmental focus in asking them questions and in understanding their replies. To conduct effective interviews with parents, you will need to enlist their cooperation in sharing with you what they know about their children. And to conduct effective interviews with families, you will need to be aware of both family and individual dynamics. A knowledge of psychological disorders in children also will be valuable in interviewing children with special needs and their parents and teachers.

The general interviewing techniques that you will learn will help you conduct effective interviews in many different situations. The interview may be the most personal of all clinical assessment procedures. You, as the interviewer, serve a function somewhat like that of a psychological test. Your questions, comments, and mannerisms are the stimuli. However, unlike a psychological test, you cannot be exactly the same each time you conduct an interview. This variability is both an asset and a liability. It allows you to tailor the interview to the specific needs of each interviewee, but it creates difficulties in standardizing the situation. Interviews require you to rely on your personal skills in getting the needed information. To complete the interview process, you need to write a report. The guidelines for report writing in this section will help you in this effort.

1

INTRODUCTION TO CLINICAL ASSESSMENT INTERVIEWING

Co-authored by Eric J. Mash

The meaning of life is felt through relationship...
Relationship with others and with one's own self.
From what it is at birth to whom we become as a child,
Adult, parent grand parent and ultimately, as ancestor.
The meaning of life flowers through relationship...
Parenting teaching serving creating.
Learning from nature, the sages, our peers,
From our emerging selves in a state of becoming.
— Jonas Salk and Carol Anne Bundy

Goals and Objectives

This chapter is designed to enable you to:

- Describe the goals of the clinical assessment interview
- Discuss the important factors in conducting an evaluation
- Understand several theoretical perspectives for conducting clinical assessment interviews, including the developmental, normative-developmental, cognitive-behavioral, humanistic-phenomenological, psychodynamic, family-systems, and eclectic perspectives
- Describe how a clinical assessment interview differs from a conversation, a psychotherapeutic interview, a survey research interview, and a forensic interview
- Discuss the strengths and weaknesses of the clinical assessment interview
- Describe a preferred model for the interviewer-interviewee relationship
- Compare unstructured, semistructured, and structured clinical assessment interviews
- Describe the usual steps in a clinical assessment interview
- Assess your potential as an effective interviewer
- Understand the factors that place children at risk for developing psychological disorders and adjustment problems
- Understand the factors that may help children withstand aversive environments
- Describe intervention programs that may reduce the stressors that children face in society

Clinical assessment interviews with children come about because children, their parents, or other interested parties are concerned about the children's development and welfare. Clinical assessment interviews are unique situations where highly able and skilled professionals devote their exclusive attention to one child and that child's parents and other family members. This may never have happened before in the lives of the child, the parents, and the family members, and it may never happen again. The relationship is based on trust and collaborative problem solving. An implied contract exists between the interviewer and interviewee: "I'll ask you questions, and you try to do your best to answer truthfully. The results will help us work together to try to make things better for you."

This text is designed to help you become an effective clinical assessment interviewer. Clinical assessment interviewing is a critical part of the assessment process. And even more than other assessment techniques, it places a premium on your personal skills, such as your ability to communicate effectively and your ability to establish a meaningful relationship. As in all clinical assessments, the relationship you establish with the children and their families is critical.

Occasionally, the clinical assessment interview may be part of a clinical evaluation in which children also are administered psychological tests and medical examinations.

In addition, parents are likely to be interviewed, and sometimes other family members are interviewed as well. In other cases, the clinical assessment interview may be the only assessment performed. This may happen when the information obtained in the interview is sufficient to answer the questions posed by the individual making the referral.

The following terms are related to clinical assessment:

- *Clinical assessment or evaluation*—any procedure involving the assessment of an interviewee's behavior, temperament, and personality
- *Clinical assessment interview*—an interview designed to obtain information about an interviewee's behavior, temperament, and personality
- *Psychological evaluation*—a procedure usually consisting of a clinical assessment interview and the administration of a battery of psychological tests or neuropsychological tests
- *Neuropsychological evaluation*—a procedure usually consisting of a clinical assessment interview and the administration of a battery of neuropsychological tests
- *Diagnostic workup*—a procedure consisting of a clinical assessment interview and, at times, the administration of a battery of psychological tests or neuropsychological tests, designed to obtain a diagnosis, usually one associated with the *Diagnostic and Statistical Manual of Mental Disorders, Fourth Edition* (*DSM-IV*) or later edition (American Psychiatric Association, 1994) or with the *Diagnostic Classification: 0–3* (National Center for Clinical Infant Programs, 1994)

GOALS OF THE CLINICAL ASSESSMENT INTERVIEW

The primary goal of the clinical assessment interview is to obtain relevant, reliable, and valid information about the interviewees and their problems. This includes information about their personality, temperament, motor skills, cognitive skills, study habits, work habits, interpersonal behavior, daily living skills, interests, and difficulties in living. Important sources of information are the *content of the interview* (that is, what interviewees tell you) and the *interviewees' style* (that is, how they speak, behave, and relate to you). The information you obtain will depend on how interviewees perceive you, the atmosphere you establish, your interviewing style, and, with children, your success in gearing the interview to their developmental level.

Clinical assessment interviews with children may serve several clinical or educational purposes, including (a) conducting a screening evaluation, (b) making a diagnostic classification, (c) designing an intervention, (d) evaluating the intervention, and (e) evaluating the effectiveness of programs that the children are participating in. *Screening evaluations* may involve assessing children's risk for suicide or for being maltreated, the reasons children fail to adhere to a medical regimen, the credibility of the children's statements, or the readiness of children to enter kindergarten programs. Assessments for *diagnostic classification* may involve deciding which *DSM-IV* classification best reflects a child's current difficulties or deciding which educational classification best accounts for the child's functioning in school. Diagnostic classification is important for obtaining payment for services needed by children. Assessments contribute to *designing interventions* by clarifying the nature and severity of the problem and proposing the most appropriate therapy or intervention procedure. Assessments also help in *evaluating the effectiveness of the interventions* once they are begun. Finally, assessments contribute to *evaluating the effectiveness of specific programs* designed to improve children's skills, performance, or behavioral functioning.

Following are the major goals of the initial clinical assessment interview:

1. To establish rapport with the child and parents
2. To identify the child's major problem areas (including a description of problem, antecedent events and consequences, and factors that may have caused or made a problem worse)
3. To obtain the child's developmental history (including physical, intellectual, emotional, educational, and social development)
4. To find out about any prior assessments and treatments that the child has had, including dates and treatment outcomes
5. To learn about the child's current family situation (including the child's relationship with parents, siblings, and relatives and the relationship between the parents)
6. To obtain information about the child's experiences and behavior at home, at school, and in the community (including interests, activities, hobbies, jobs, and relationships with others)
7. To evaluate the child's (and family's) need and motivation for help, as well as coping skills
8. To generate hypotheses about the development and maintenance of the child's problem behaviors
9. To evaluate the extent to which the child's other problems (or familial factors) make it difficult to assess the child's primary problem. (For example, significant medical problems may make it difficult to evaluate a behavior problem; a parent's own problem, such as alcoholism, may make it difficult for the parent to discuss the child's problem.)
10. To arrive at a tentative formulation of the child's problem
11. To develop a more formal assessment plan for the child (and family), if needed
12. To clear up any misconceptions the child and family may have about the assessment process
13. To convey information to the parents and child (where relevant) about policies related to the assessment or treatment (either your policies or those of the clinic regarding fees, unkept appointments, treatment of child and parents, frequency of visits, types of treatment, and related matters)
14. To answer the referral question
15. To develop treatment recommendations, where relevant

Illustration of a Clinical Assessment Interview

The following interview segment will give you a glimpse of what an effective clinical assessment interview is like. It illustrates how the interviewer (IR) used several interview techniques, such as probing questions, reflection, and listening skills, to obtain information about the problems of an adolescent (IE) (Spitzer, Gibbon, Skodol, Williams, & First, 1989, pp. 309–312).

IR: Tell me about when things were the hardest for you. When was that?

IE: It was around Christmas time last year.

IR: And you were how old then?

IE: 13.

IR: You're 14 now, right?

IE: Yes.

IR: When things were really at their worst, can you tell me what it was that was disturbing to you at that time?

IE: Well, the major part about it was that, like all these things that I did, they were really stupid, and they didn't make any sense; but I'm still gonna have to do it and, it was sort of like being scared of what would happen if I didn't do it.

IR: What were the things that you were doing?

IE: In the morning when I got dressed, I was real afraid that there'd be germs all over my clothes and things, so I'd stand there and I'd shake them for half an hour. I'd wash before I did anything—like if I was gonna wash my face, I'd wash my hands first; and if I was gonna get dressed, I'd wash my hands first; and then it got even beyond that point. Washing my hands wasn't enough, and I started to use rubbing alcohol. It was wintertime and cold weather, and this really made my hands bleed. Even if I just held them under water, they'd bleed all over the place, and they looked terrible, and everyone thought I had a disease or something.

IR: And when you were doing that much washing, how much time every day did that take if you added up all the different parts of it?

IE: It took about six hours a day. In the morning I didn't have a whole lot of choice, because I had to get up at 6:00 and get ready for school. All I'd do was get dressed as best I could. I didn't even have time to brush my hair. At the time I never ate breakfast, so all these things—it was just so complex that I didn't have time to do anything.

IR: You also told me about other things in addition to the washing and worrying about dirt: that you would have plans about how you would do other things.

IE: Okay, well, they were like set plans in my mind that if I heard the word, like, something that had to do with germs or disease, it would be considered something bad and so I had things that would go through my mind that were sort of like "cross that out and it'll make it okay" to hear that word.

IR: What sort of things?

IE: Like numbers or words that seemed to be sort of like a protector.

IR: What numbers and what words were they?

IE: It started out to be the number 3 and multiples of 3 and then words like "soap and water," something like that; and then the multiples of 3 got really high, they'd end up to be 124 or something like that. It got real bad then....

IR: At any time did you really believe that something bad would happen if you didn't do these things? Was it just a feeling, or were you really scared?

IE: No! I was petrified that something would really happen. It was weird, because everyone would always say how sensible I was and intelligent. But it was weird because I tried to explain it in order to really make them understand what I was trying to say and they'd go, you know, like, "Well, that's stupid," and I knew it; but when I was alone, things would be a lot worse than when I was with this group, because if I was around friends, that would make me forget about most of this. But when I was alone it... like, my mind would wander to all sorts of things and I'd get new plans and new rituals and new ideas, and I'd start worrying more and more about people that could get hurt that I cared about and things that could really go bad if I didn't.

IR: Who were the people you'd worry most would get hurt?

IE: My family, basically my family.

IR: Any particular people in your family?

IE: Well, like my grandmother—she's 83, and you know, I was just worried that... I know that she's old and she's not gonna be around much longer, but I was worried that maybe something I did could cause her to get really, really sick or something.

IR: Had anything like this ever been on your mind before you were 13, when this started?

IE: Well, let's see... my mother, her family has always been mostly real neat people and extremely clean and so that could have affected it, because I was growing up in that sort of background. But I always like to be clean and neat, and I was never really allowed to walk around the house with muddy shoes or anything like that, so....

IR: But your concerns about clean, about how many times you did things—have they ever gotten in the way of your doing things that you wanted to do?

IE: Uh-huh. Many times. Like, I was supposed to go somewhere with a friend, and we were gonna leave at 11:00 and I wanted to take a shower before I left. So I had to get up about 6:00 in the morning, and sometimes I just won't even make it with five hours to do it....

IR: And that was since you were 13. But what about any time in your life before that—had anything like this ever happened? Or as far as you know was this the first?

IE: It was the first time.

IR: Have you at any time felt that you had some other special idea about forces beyond you... about your being able to control things magically or be in control?

IE: I'm really scared of supernatural things. I don't like to say that I believe in superstitions and things, but I guess I really do 'cause they frighten me. When I was little they weren't really bothering me or anything, but now I avoid it as much as I can. Like, the number 13 now, if it came up, you know, it wouldn't bother me, but I'd rather have the number 7 instead.

IR: So you are superstitious, but you've never heard any special voice talking to you or....

IE: Yeah, I have. It's like... if I tried to describe it, people would think that I saw little people dancing around or something, and that was wrong because all it was, it wasn't like a voice, it was just like a thought.

IR: More like being able to hear yourself think?

IE: Right.

IR: Have you ever seen things that other people couldn't see?

IE: No.

IR: I know you are doing very well here in school and on the ward here at the hospital. Do you have any signs left of the problems that you used to have with your rituals and compulsions?

IE: Well, everyone is compulsive to a point. I can see little things that I'll do. Like I will go over something twice or three times, because that's a special number. Like, if I read something and I really don't understand it, maybe I would go over it one more time and then, say, one more time will make three. But nothing really big. It's been really good, because I have gotten out and taken a shower, and gotten dressed, and washed my face and brushed my teeth, and all that stuff in like half an hour! That's really good for me because I wasn't able to do that before.

IR: So, in general it's fair to say it's things that just you would notice now, and probably someone sharing the room with you wouldn't be able to tell the other things you are doing even though you know these little things are there. Good.... Well, thank you very much.

Professions Using Clinical Assessment Interviewing

The focus of the clinical assessment interview is related to your professional role and the task at hand. For example, the task of a *mental health system interviewer* of children is to elicit information about their feelings, thoughts, and experiences (both objective and subjective); with parents, the task is to obtain information about the children's problems and concerns, the children's developmental history, the parents' concerns about their children, and information about their families. The task of an *educational system interviewer* is to learn about factors contributing to children's school performance by interviewing children, teachers, and parents. The task of a *pediatric health system interviewer* is to obtain health-related information, including information about stress, life style, and adherence to medical regimens from children and their parents. And the task of a *criminal justice system interviewer* is to obtain from children and their parents objective, truthful, and relevant information that will stand up in a court of law and that will help in deciding what interventions are needed.

Different professions, then, may be involved in clinical assessment interviewing. Table 1-1 shows the missions and roles of 12 different professional fields that offer educational, psychosocial, and medical services to children. Each profession has an important role to play in working with children and their families.

Values of the Clinical Assessment Interview

Clinical assessment interviews allow you to establish trust and rapport with interviewees; to gain information about their experiences and behavior and attitudes underlying that behavior; and, if appropriate, to give them information about applicable agencies or services. The information you obtain in clinical assessment interviews may be helpful in determining the nature of the interviewees' problem, including the frequency, severity, chronicity, and pervasiveness of the problem; what has been done to solve the problem; what attempts have been successful or unsuccessful; and what environmental or cultural factors may be contributing to the maintenance of the problem.

Interviews will help you place children's problems in a historical-developmental context, which, in turn, will promote better diagnostic precision and intervention strategies. For example, the type of recommendation you make for remediation for a 9-year-old boy with defiant behavior may depend on the chronicity of the boy's problem or on whether the problem is related to a recent illness or to his parents' divorce.

Clinical assessment interviews deserve special care. They often serve as the first contact with children and their families, and they are an appropriate place to discuss the entire assessment process. They may have a significant influence on how children and their families perceive the entire assessment process and subsequent interventions. And, if conducted properly, they can motivate children and their families to continue seeking help, as needed.

As a clinical assessment interviewer, you must appreciate the worth and dignity of each interviewee. The interview represents a mutual engagement between you and the interviewee, and it should be a collaborative effort; it is not something done *to* the interviewee. It will entail your following ethical guidelines for informed consent and informed refusal. This means that you must fully inform families (and children, where applicable) about the assessment process and what will happen to the information you obtain and give them the opportunity to decide whether they want to participate. However, when the court refers them, they may have less choice about their participation. If they refuse to participate in such cases, there may be consequences associated with their refusal.

FACTORS TO CONSIDER IN PERFORMING CLINICAL ASSESSMENT INTERVIEWS

A clinical assessment interview of children and parents should consider the following factors: (a) developmental level of children, (b) gender, (c) race, culture, and ethnicity, (d) family background and parental reactions, (e) health history and current health appraisal, (f) educational history and current performance in school, (g) behavioral patterns and possible psychological disorders, (h) personality and temperament, (i) psychological and psychoeducational test results, (j) contextual or ecological factors, and (k) nature of referral problems.

Developmental Level of the Children

The assessment must be sensitive to the children's level of development. When interviewing children of average intelligence, you will find that their age usually provides a general index of their developmental level. Awareness of developmental level is particularly important during the infant and preschool periods and during pre-adolescence. Infants and young children experience rapid developmental changes in their nervous systems. Infants who are developmentally below average for their age may have, for example, a delay in development, a neural dysfunction, a sensory impairment, or an impoverished environment. Deciding which explanation best accounts for their below-average development will not be easy. It may take repeated evaluations by several professionals before you can make this determination. For pre-adolescents, there will be physical changes, social and peer pressures, and increased need for independence. The assessment should focus on these factors as they affect each child's functioning. In cases in which children's level of intelligence is below average, you will need to consider their mental age in conducting the interview. Information about intelligence and mental age may be available from school records and psychological reports.

Gender

Rates of physical, verbal, and motor maturation differ in girls and boys, and you will need to consider these differences in the assessment. Girls and boys also differ in the types of problems they have and the expectations society holds for them. These expectations will affect how their family, parents, school, and society treat them. Girls and boys also may differ in the importance they ascribe to certain interviewer

Table 1-1 (*Continued*)

Discipline	Primary mission	Major roles
Nursing	To diagnose, treat, and help children with medical illnesses and disabilities and help their families cope with changes in their lives resulting from the children's medical illnesses and disabilities	1. Develop medical plans to treat underlying cause or help parents to carry out treatment plan 2. Work with parents to meet basic needs of child (for example, health needs, daily care, and feeding) 3. Recommend, plan, and carry out interventions to improve child's developmental status 4. Enhance child's and family's ability to cope with child's disabilities 5. Serve as case managers 6. Evaluate effectiveness of treatments and interventions 7. Refer to and consult with other programs or professionals
Audiology	To provide and coordinate services to children with auditory handicaps, including detection of problems and management of existing communication disabilities	1. Assess children's auditory acuity 2. Identify types of hearing loss 3. Recommend hearing aids or assistive listening devices as needed 4. Evaluate the effectiveness of the hearing aids or assistive listening devices 5. Recommend, plan, and carry out interventions 6. Consult with families and with other professionals 7. Reassess children periodically
Optometry/ ophthalmology	To provide and coordinate services for children with visual handicaps, including detection of problems and management of existing visual disabilities	1. Assess children's visual acuity 2. Identify types of visual difficulties 3. Recommend corrective lenses or assistive visual procedures as needed 4. Evaluate the effectiveness of the corrective lenses or assistive visual procedures 5. Recommend, plan, and carry out interventions 6. Consult with families and with other professionals 7. Reassess children periodically
Criminal justice, juvenile justice, and child protection	To evaluate children's functioning to help the criminal and juvenile courts take appropriate actions or make appropriate placements	1. Assess psychological and behavioral characteristics of children 2. Evaluate reasons for children's referral to juvenile court or criminal court 3. Evaluate, when children are delinquent, their degree of psychopathy, dangerousness, rehabilitation potential, educational issues, and whether substance abuse is a concern 4. Evaluate, in cases of child maltreatment, the parent's suitability as a parent, degree of psychopathy, treatment needs, future abuse potential, and whether substance abuse is a concern 5. Assess children's environment as a contributing factor 6. Recommend possible interventions 7. Advise court about findings and recommendations

Note: Not all professions that offer services to children are shown in this table.

Source: Reprinted and adapted, with permission of the publisher and author, from D. B. Bailey, Jr., "Issues and directions in preparing professionals to work with young handicapped children and their families," in J. J. Gallagher, P. L. Throhanis, & R. M. Clifford (Eds.), *Policy Implementation & PL 99-457: Planning for Young Children with Special Needs*, copyright 1989 by Paul H. Brookes Publishing Company (P.O. Box 10624, Baltimore, MD 21285-0624), pp. 109–116.

qualities. For example, compared with boys, girls may attach proportionately greater weight to interviewers' relational skills than to their status or expertise. Gender differences in psychological problems and medical illnesses of children, when relevant, are pointed out in several chapters of this book.

Race, Culture, and Ethnicity

You must consider the racial, ethnic, and cultural backgrounds of the interviewees. This is especially important in establishing rapport, in conducting the interview, in interpreting the information you obtain, in applying normative standards, and in formulating treatment and intervention recommendations. Types of problems individuals have, their perceptions of mental health professionals and other health professionals, and the interventions they will accept may be related to their culture and ethnicity. Chapters 8 and 9 discuss ethnic and cultural factors related to the interview.

Family Background and Parental Reactions

Children's families play a critical role in their development. You will learn much about children by interviewing their parents or caregivers, siblings, and other persons who are close to them. Elicit information that will help you understand how the family members view the child, their concerns and problems, and what they have done to alleviate their concerns and problems. Ideally, you should visit a child's home to gain additional information about her or him and the family.

Within one family, there may be differences in the way the mother and father perceive the child's problem. Mothers typically report more problems for their children than do fathers (Mash & Johnston, 1983). Therefore, you will want to interview both parents to get a thorough picture of how each views the child.

Parents in individual families will differ in how they react to their children's problems. Some parents genuinely want help, whereas others may be uncertain about wanting help, may fear receiving help, or may not want help at all. When parents resist getting help, they may deny that their children have problems, disagree with teachers' reports that their children have problems, feel embarrassed or guilty because they believe that their children's problems reflect poorly on them, become defensive because they believe that a mental health professional will uncover their own problems, or prefer to have problems handled within their families rather than by outsiders.

Some parents, unable to tolerate any undesirable behavior in their children, will immediately seek professional help when any misbehavior occurs. These parents may have neither the tolerance for undesirable behavior nor an understanding of normal developmental patterns. Other parents are able to tolerate a wide range of behavior in their children and will not seek professional help until their children's behavior is seriously disturbed.

Health History and Current Health Appraisal

Parents' genetic backgrounds and mothers' health and health-related behaviors influence development of fetuses. Several developmental disabilities are directly linked to genetic factors, such as Down Syndrome and Klinefelter's Syndrome, which are forms of mental retardation associated with chromosomal abnormalities. Similarly, mothers' alcohol or drug usage may affect the development of the fetus (see Chapter 10).

You also will need to consider children's physical health history, including illnesses, accidental injuries, and hospitalizations, and incorporate the medical findings in your evaluation. Physical health factors are considered further in Chapters 15 through 19.

Educational History and Current Performance in School

Children's performance in school over several years may be a key indicator of their adjustments. Fluctuations in grades or test scores, for example, may indicate the presence of stress. And the timing of a severe or sudden drop in school performance may give you clues about when the stress occurred. Also, absences, tardiness, and the number of relocations noted in children's school records may give you clues to account for changes in their performances. Interviewing children's teachers to obtain information about how they view the children and their families also may be valuable.

Behavioral Patterns and Possible Psychological Disorders

It is important to identify children's usual behavioral patterns and to note when deviations from these patterns occur. For example, an older child who is confident, outgoing, and sociable and then becomes withdrawn, anxious, and depressed may be at risk for suicide. Section III of this book discusses behavioral patterns and psychological disorders.

Personality and Temperament

Children's coping mechanisms, values, interests, interpersonal relationships, problem-solving styles, and ability to withstand stress are important areas to evaluate in interviews. For example, a moderately anxious child with limited coping skills may exhibit behavior problems when faced with stress, whereas a highly anxious child with strong coping skills may show no outward behavior problems when faced with the same stress. Information about personality and temperament will help you understand child-parent relationships, develop interventions, and formulate prognoses. Several chapters (see, for example, Chapters 10, 11, and 12) focus on children's personality and temperament.

Psychological and Psychoeducational Test Results

It is important to review the results of any psychological and psychoeducational evaluations administered previously to the children or administered during the present assessment.

Contextual or Ecological Factors

Your findings and intervention plans must have *ecological validity*. This means that you must consider the children's environment—including their immediate families, extended families, peers, cultures, homes, neighborhoods, schools, and larger communities—in evaluating the interview findings and in planning the interventions.

Nature of Referral Problem

Although the reason for referral may be of prime importance, it may not be the most important issue. Children rarely present a single problem, and problems may be much more complex than referral sources recognized. You will need to clarify the *referral question* when it is vague. Referral questions are the "tickets" into a clinical assessment interview where other important issues also may emerge. Identifying the critical issues and arranging them in order of importance become a critical part of clinical assessment interviews.

CLINICAL ASSESSMENT INTERVIEWS IN RELATION TO OTHER ASSESSMENT PROCEDURES

Other procedures for assessing children include norm-referenced tests, behavior rating scales, questionnaires, systematic behavioral observations, informal tests, role playing, sociometric procedures, and psychophysiological and physical measurements and examinations. These assessment procedures provide information primarily about children's present functioning. In contrast, clinical assessment interviews may provide information about children's past *and* present functioning and about their future hopes and aspirations. Information obtained in clinical assessment interviews provides a unique historical portrait of the children's, parents', and families' lives.

Clinical assessment interviews, like observations, tests, and behavior rating scales, are behavior sampling tools. Clinical assessment interviews, with additional assessment procedures used in a multidimensional assessment battery, will help you

- determine children's and parents' strengths and weaknesses
- understand the nature, presence, and degree of disabling conditions
- evaluate whether children are at risk for psychopathology or other types of behavioral disturbance
- determine the conditions that inhibit and support the acquisition and maintenance of appropriate skills
- provide baseline information prior to an intervention program
- develop useful intervention and instructional programs
- guide individuals in selecting appropriate intervention, educational, and vocational programs
- monitor changes in children and their parents
- measure the impact of the intervention and instructional programs

Frank and Ernest

THEORETICAL PERSPECTIVES FOR THE CLINICAL ASSESSMENT INTERVIEW

Several theoretical perspectives in developmental and clinical psychology are useful in guiding clinical assessment interviews with children, parents, families, caregivers, teachers, and others who have relevant information. These perspectives include the developmental, normative-developmental, cognitive-behavioral, humanistic-phenomenological, psychodynamic, family-systems, and eclectic theoretical perspectives. Although these theoretical perspectives share a common emphasis, there also is diversity among them. Each theoretical perspective has something to offer in helping you formulate questions, interpret the information you obtain, and develop interventions. These theoretical perspectives may deal with similar issues, but each looks at the issues in different ways. We first consider each theoretical perspective briefly and then draw propositions from each to form an eclectic perspective.

Developmental Perspective

A developmental perspective proposes that the ongoing interplay between genetic disposition and environmental factors gives development a definite, nonrandom form and direction. This interplay also assures that development proceeds toward specific goals: learning to walk and talk, developing complex coordinated movements, developing thinking skills, and reaching sexual maturity. However, there are individual differences in the rate and timing of development. Newly developed skills bring challenges to children, especially at critical points in development such as puberty.

The developmental perspective also emphasizes that biological, psychological, and social factors constantly interact to shape and modify children's development. The environments that play a role in children's development—including family, peer, school, and work environments—are each dependent in part on the effects of the other ones (Compas, Hinden, & Gerhardt, 1995). Children "evoke differential reactions from the environment as a result of their physical and behavioral characteristics, and environments contribute to individual development through the feedback they provide [children]" (Compas et al., 1995, p. 270). Developmental problems come about, in part, when there is a mismatch between children's needs and the opportunities afforded them by their environments. This may happen, for example, when the expectations or demands of the environments either exceed the children's capacities or are conflicting.

Growth is seen as both qualitative and quantitative. For example, as development proceeds, organizational and adaptational changes emerge. At first, children's thoughts are dominated by what they can see. By 2 years of age, they begin to develop expressive language and can recall some prior actions and responses; thinking tends to be egocentric. By age 7, thought processes become more systematic and

skills needed to solve concrete problems develop. By age 11, children can think abstractly and make logical deductions without the necessity of direct experience.

A developmental perspective focuses on individual changes that occur during development. It views the distinctions between maturation and learning and between cognition and socioemotional components of behavior as arbitrary.

The interviewer following a developmental perspective would focus on the following:

- genetic factors that might be affecting the child's development by looking at, in part, traits of the child's relatives
- the child's individual and unique pattern of development
- the interaction of environmental factors with biological factors that might be influencing the child's development
- the child's perceptual ability (for example, the ability to see, hear, and feel)
- the child's awareness of his or her sensory experiences
- the child's comprehension of his or her experiences

Normative-Developmental Perspective

A normative-developmental perspective evaluates children's cognitions, affect, and behavior in relation to a reference group, usually composed of children of the same age and gender as the referred child, and attempts to account for changes as the referred child matures (Edelbrock, 1984). *Cognitions* refer to mental processes, including perception, memory, and reasoning, by which children acquire knowledge, solve problems, and make plans. *Affect* refers to the experience of emotion or feeling. The normative-developmental perspective considers (a) *demographic variables,* such as the child's age, grade, gender, ethnicity, and socioeconomic status (SES); (b) *developmental variables,* such as language, motor, social, and self-help skills; and (c) the influence of prior development on current and future development. (Chapter 3 discusses typical developmental sequences found in children and adolescents.)

Normative data are useful in various ways (Edelbrock, 1984). First, normative data provide information about how a particular child's development compares with that of average children. Norms allow you to establish reasonable treatment goals and to evaluate the clinical significance of changes resulting from interventions. Second, normative data guide you in selecting appropriate target areas and behaviors that need change—for example, deciding that a child is not growing normally or is not developing age-appropriate skills. Third, normative data allow you to compare information acquired from different sources. Thus, for example, comparing information from parents and teachers will help you learn about the consistency of children's behavior. Fourth, normative data may help you to identify behaviors with unusually low or high rates (that is, behaviors that occur at levels different from expected levels), transient behaviors, behaviors that are relatively normal for a particular age group (for example, fear of strangers in very young children), and situational variables that may place the child at risk for developing problem behaviors (for example, adverse home environments or classrooms). Finally, normative data assist in research investigations by allowing investigators to form relatively homogeneous groups and to compare subject samples across investigations.

The interviewer following a normative-developmental perspective would focus on the following:

- looking at the child's behavior in relation to similar behavior of children of the same age and gender
- examining the child's level of development in such areas as language, motor skills, social skills, self-help skills, and interpersonal skills
- interviewing a parent or caregiver to obtain information about the child's developmental history and relevant current behaviors and interests

Cognitive-Behavioral Perspective

A cognitive-behavioral perspective focuses on the importance of (a) cognitions as major determinants of emotion and behavior, including the child's thoughts and how she or he processes information; (b) the role that cognitions—such as beliefs, self-statements, problem-solving strategies, expectancies, and images—play in the development of maladaptive behavior; and (c) the individual and environmental influences that may shape and control the child's and family's thoughts, feelings, and behavior. The cognitive-behavioral perspective emphasizes the importance of empirical validation throughout the assessment and treatment. Quantitative measures—such as frequency counts, measures of duration, and time of occurrences—are used to document the relevant thoughts, feelings, and behavior of the child.

The cognitive aspect of a cognitive-behavioral approach proposes that cognitions, although private, mediate behavior and learning. Cognitions and behavior also are functionally related—a change in one can cause changes in the other. The concern is with how behavior varies as a function of changes in a child's cognitions and environment, and how cognitions, behavior, and the environment in which the behavior occurs can be modified.

The behavioral aspect of a cognitive-behavioral approach proposes that environmental contingencies, such as setting factors, natural reinforcers, and distractors, also mediate behavior and learning. Particular attention is given to the antecedents and consequences of a particular behavior—that is, the events that precede and the events that follow a behavior. This is termed *behavioral analysis,* or *functional analysis,* and can be represented as follows: antecedents → behavior → consequences.

The interviewer following a cognitive-behavioral perspective would focus on the following:

- encouraging the child and parents to give concrete examples of the problems and, when possible, specify related

thoughts, feelings, and actions occurring at the time of the problems
- exploring the frequency, duration, and intensity of each problem and how the problems affect the child
- looking at the relationship between environmental events, the child's thoughts, and the problems, seeking to learn what precipitates the problems and what maintains them
- assessing the child's (and parents') motivation for change
- interviewing family members to learn about their perception of the problems
- measuring behavior where appropriate, by self-monitoring, by parent-monitoring, or by observing the child (and parents) in a clinic setting, school setting, or natural setting such as the home

Humanistic-Phenomenological Perspective

A humanistic-phenomenological perspective emphasizes the child's perception of the world. Behavior is viewed as a response to how the child views the world at a particular moment in time. The emphasis is on the here and now, with children seen as active, thinking people who are responsible for their behavior and who can make choices. Behavior, in part, is determined by children's expectations about the consequences of their actions. Further, children are seen as behaving to achieve their fullest potentials, which is called *self-actualization.* Problematic behaviors occur when needs are not fully satisfied.

The interviewer following a humanistic-phenomenological perspective would focus on the following:

- the way the child and parents see themselves, others, and their environments
- the expectations the child has about the consequences of his or her behavior
- the assumptions the child has about his or her life
- the needs the child has that are not being met
- the way the child views his or her choices

The interviewer following this perspective would not independently make recommendations but would work with the child (particularly an older child) and family to identify viable interventions. Some humanistically oriented interviewers, however, believe that assessment is not needed or should be de-emphasized. They maintain that assessment may impede the therapeutic process by placing the interviewer in an authoritative, superior role in relation to the interviewee.

Psychodynamic Perspective

A psychodynamic perspective emphasizes intrapsychic factors that influence behavior, such as thoughts, feelings, impulses, desires, motives, and conflicts. Early childhood experiences in particular—such as relationships with parents, siblings, other relatives, caregivers, and peers—play a critical role in the formation of behavioral patterns. Individuals use various *defenses* (or defense mechanisms) to help them avoid thinking about certain feelings and thoughts. Defenses serve to alleviate the pain and anxiety that would be present if individuals acknowledged undesirable feelings and thoughts. However, there are costs associated with the use of defenses, such as constricted affect, limited spontaneity, increased rigidity, and interpersonal distance. Defenses can be thought of as a form of cognitive style.

Attachment theory, which has evolved from both psychodynamic and cognitive-behavioral perspectives, also is valuable in understanding parent-child relations. According to attachment theory, infants develop internal working models of their self and their caregiver (or attachment figure) (Ainsworth, Bell, & Stayton, 1974; Bowlby, 1958, 1969). These models, which have both cognitive and affective components, help infants forecast and interpret their caregivers' behavior and plan their own behavior in response to that of the caregivers. Attachments help ensure infants' safety and survival through access to the care, nurturance, and protection of the caregivers.

Models may develop in the following ways. Infants whose caregivers are responsive to their needs will develop secure attachments (Dozier, 1990). When distressed, infants with secure attachments will seek out their caregivers because they have confidence that their caregivers will reduce their distress. When they are not distressed, their sense of security allows these infants to explore their environment.

Infants whose caregivers are not attuned to their needs, however, are likely to become insecure (Dozier, 1990). To deal with their insecurity, they may use various coping strategies. One strategy is to look for their caregiver to come and attend to their needs, although they have been disappointed in the past. A second is to suppress the need for their caregiver as a way of reducing their distress. Unfortunately, both strategies may leave infants more vulnerable to disturbances in development.

Newer interactions between infants and caregivers are then superimposed on the existing models or patterns (Bretherton, 1993).

For this reason, old patterns of relating are not readily relinquished, even when a partner's behavior begins to change. An infant who has frequently been rebuffed by the caregiver and has consequently become more reluctant to seek or accept comfort is not likely to respond in kind when a previously unresponsive caregiver suddenly becomes responsive. . . . [The infant's reluctance] is likely to make it more difficult for a caregiver to remain responsive. The converse is also likely to be true. If the caregiver has been consistently responsive, the infant is not likely to change his or her expectations because of fairly infrequent parental lapses. (pp. 281–282)

One key factor in how caregivers relate to their children is how they view their own experiences. Caregivers who have (a) coherent, well-organized views of their experiences, (b) experiences easily accessible to awareness, and (c) minimal defensiveness are in the best position to form secure attachment relationships with their children (Bretherton, 1993). In contrast, caregivers who have (a) incoherent, disorganized views of their experiences, (b) experiences not easily accessible to awareness, and (c) much defensiveness are likely to have difficulty reading their infants' signals. This difficulty likely will interfere with their ability to form attachments and may lead them to neglect their children.

Other key factors in how caregivers relate to their children are how the children respond to the caregivers and the characteristics of the children (Darling, 1991). Caregiver-child attachments will be more difficult to achieve when the child has an atypical appearance, responds negatively to being handled (that is, stiffens, tenses up, or lacks responsiveness), cries incessantly, is hyperactive or listless, has feeding difficulties, fails to maintain eye contact, fails to vocalize, behaves unpleasantly, or is under intense medical care and needs special medical equipment, such as feeding tubes or oxygen masks. When children fail to stimulate their caregivers, caregivers, in turn, may fail to stimulate their children.

A psychodynamic perspective postulates two interlinked *maturational processes.* One process involves the development of the self (or *ego*). As children develop, the more global personality of the infant shifts to a more specific identity of self. Similarly, instinctual processes give way to those that are more reality based, and preoccupation with self shifts to an understanding of interpersonal relations. The second process involves *psychosexual development.* During such development, the source of gratification shifts from the mouth to the genitals, accompanied by changes in socialization patterns. For example, socialization during infancy is passive-dependent, whereas during adolescence the focus is on autonomy and independence. Early experiences are seen to have lasting consequences for later personality development.

The interviewer following a psychodynamic perspective would focus on the following:

- the child's thoughts, feelings, motives, fears, early experiences in the family, intrafamilial relationships, and symptoms
- behavioral patterns suggesting defense mechanisms (such as denial, rationalization, or projection)
- the mother/child relationship and the father/child relationship
- the child's (and parents') motivation for treatment
- dreams, particularly for older children
- play for younger children, as a way to understand their conflicts

Family-Systems Perspective

A family-systems perspective focuses on the structure and dynamics of the family. From this perspective, a well-functioning family can be characterized as follows (Turk & Kerns, 1985):

The members are related to one another in a network of interactions. The four basic characteristics of a family system are (a) it is an open, rather than a closed, system and has a continuous interchange with the external social and physical environment; (b) it is complex, with an intricate organizational structure; (c) it is self-regulating, in the sense of containing homeostatic mechanisms to restore balance; and (d) it is capable of transformation. The family system, confronted with continuous internal and external demand for change, may be able to respond with growth, flexibility, and structural evolution.... Consequently, the family is a powerful determinant of behavior and can foster adaptive as well as maladaptive activities. (pp. 6–7)

Factors such as the family's structure, functions, assigned roles, modes of interacting, resources, history, life cycle, and the individual members' unique histories are important elements of a family-systems perspective (Turk & Kerns, 1985, pp. 3–4, with changes in notation):

1. *Structure.* The structure or configuration of a family refers to characteristics of the individual members that make up the family unit including gender, age distribution, spacing, and size or number of members.

2. *Function.* Function refers to the tasks the family performs for society and its members (such as educational, economic, and reproductive functions).

3. *Assigned roles.* Assigned roles concern the prescribed responsibilities, expectations, and rights of the individual members. Thus one family member may be designated the role of breadwinner, another the overseer of health care, and still another the manager of household operations. Roles do not have to be mutually exclusive and they seldom are. For example, in most families the mother is the custodian of health as well as the manager of the household.

4. *Mode of interaction.* Mode of interaction relates to the style adopted by the family members to deal with the environment and with one another in both problem solving and decision making.

5. *Resources.* Resources include general health of the family members, social support and skills, personality characteristics, and financial support. These resources will influence the way that the family interprets events.

6. *Family history.* Family history refers to sociocultural factors as well as prior history of illness and modes of coping with stress. The history of the family will affect the ways families interpret and respond to various events.

7. *Life cycle.* Families also have a life cycle that changes over time. In brief, the family progresses through a reasonably well-defined set of phases of development beginning with a courtship phase and ending with the death of parents or parent figures. Each phase is associated with certain developmental tasks in which the successful completion leads to somewhat different levels of family functioning.

8. *Individual members.* Families are composed of individual members who have unique experiences beyond the family. Thus they have their own unique conceptions and behavioral repertoires that account for a substantial portion of what is observed within the family contexts. Considerable

information is acquired by both children and adults from peers, coworkers, the media, and so forth. Thus it should not be assumed that the family comprises all the individuals' experiences or is the exclusive shaper of individuals' conceptions of themselves and the world. The unique characteristics of individual family members need to be considered in our thinking about families and family functioning.

The key assumptions of a family-systems perspective are that (a) the parts of the family are interrelated, (b) one part of the family cannot be understood in isolation from the rest of the family, (c) family functioning cannot be fully understood by simply understanding each part, (d) changes in one part of the family will affect the other parts, (e) the family is greater than the sum of its parts, (f) the family's structure and organization are important factors determining the behavior of family members, and (g) interactions among family members shape the behavior of the family members (Epstein & Bishop, 1981).

During all phases of childhood development, the family *ideally* provides the food, shelter, and safety needed for the child to survive and develop. During infancy, the family helps the child develop a sense of trust and acquire a sense of others as being reliable and nurturing. During preschool years, the family encourages the child to explore his or her environment and to develop skills needed for school. During the middle childhood years, the family encourages the child to learn about the wider culture, to distinguish himself or herself from others, and to gain a sense of competence and skill. During adolescence, the family helps the adolescent to establish a positive sense of self-identity and to accept increased responsibility.

The interviewer following a family-systems perspective would focus on the following:

- the family's problem-solving style, communication patterns, roles, boundaries, affective responses and involvement, and values and norms
- the way the family members interact (using both verbal and nonverbal cues)
- the type of conflict expressed by the family members
- the family members' judgment about issues affecting the family
- the way the family members handle issues of autonomy and identity and the family members' interactions within the wider community
- the family's rules
- how the family recognizes the rights of its members

Eclectic Perspective

An eclectic perspective, which is based on individual elements from other perspectives, emphasizes that (a) individual, familial, and environmental determinants are critical factors in children's development, (b) children are shaped by their environments and by their genetic constitutions, (c) what can be observed in children may not always reflect their potentials, and (d) children also shape their environments.

An eclectic perspective is not a new perspective, nor does it offer an in-depth interpretive system that replaces other systems; it does offer, however, a meaningful approach for *gathering information*. If you gather a sufficient range and quantity of information during the interview by using an eclectic perspective, you may still want to apply a specific perspective to interpret the problem at hand.

This text favors an eclectic perspective because a wide spectrum of information will be useful for the clinical assessment interview. Even if you favor one specific perspective, you still will want to consider elements of other perspectives as they relate to the particular child and family. The propositions that follow are based on an eclectic perspective. They serve as an important foundation for interviewing children and their parents, although they are hardly exhaustive (Bretherton, 1993; Campbell, 1989; Edelbrock, 1984; Luiselli, 1989; Masten & Braswell, 1991; Millon, 1987; Turk & Kerns, 1985). Propositions 1 through 19 deal with the normal development of children and normal family functioning; propositions 20 through 32 deal with children's developmental problems and with family problems.

1. Children are rapidly changing and evolving individuals, showing changes that are both quantitative and qualitative.
2. Children's temperaments and early experiences simultaneously interact to affect the development and nature of their emerging psychological structures and functions.
3. Children possess relatively enduring biological dispositions that give a consistent coloration and direction to their experiences.
4. Children develop deeply ingrained behaviors, cognitions, and affects.
5. Children's cognitions are major determinants of emotion and behavior.
6. Children replace primitive, sensory-bound, and concrete behavior during their development with more conceptual, symbolic, and cognitively mediated behavior.
7. Children's motives and emotions become more refined, civilized, and controlled during their development.
8. Children's unique learning histories and cultural backgrounds play major roles in determining behavior.
9. Children display an internally consistent pattern of characteristics that, in part, stems from generalized learning and from similarities that exist among related situations.
10. Children engage in behaviors and seek situations that are rewarding.
11. Children's behavior that is appropriate at one age may be inappropriate at another age.
12. Children may develop abilities that are not fully expressed.
13. Children's environments during their formative years are closely controlled by parents and other caregivers. However, children also help shape their environments.

14. Children's sense of self and capacity for relatedness to others develops from the parent-child relationship.
15. Children's physical maturation plays an especially important role in influencing their behavior during infancy and childhood.
16. Children's behavior can be influenced by anatomical, biochemical, and neuromuscular factors.
17. Children can be stimulated by sensory events, such as pleasant sounds or sights, to continue a behavior that they are engaged in.
18. Children's chronological age, developmental status (that is, the level at which they are functioning), and familial and social influences affect their behavior.
19. Children's interactions with their family will shape their behavior.
20. Normative data provide useful information about children's degree of deviance; serve to establish reasonable goals; serve to evaluate the clinical significance of changes resulting from interventions; and help identify unusually low or high rates of behavior, transient behaviors, behaviors that are relatively normal for a particular age group, and situational variables that may place the children at risk for developing problem behaviors.
21. Children's problems are influenced by complex interactions of biological and environmental factors.
22. Children's maladaptive behavior may be related to their cognitions (for example, emotional problems may be caused by distortions or deficiencies in thinking).
23. Children's problems that occur early, express themselves in several forms, are pervasive across settings, and persist throughout their development are likely to have the most serious long-term consequences.
24. Children with similar psychological disorders may have different behavioral symptoms, and children with different psychological disorders may have similar behavioral symptoms.
25. Children's referral for assessment and treatment in part depends on their caregivers' perceptions and interpretations of difficult behavior and on their caregivers' psychological and emotional states.
26. Children may have transient problems (such as fears and worries, nightmares, bedwetting, and tantrums) characteristic of a particular developmental period; these problems also can serve as a warning signal for the development of more serious problems and, therefore, must be handled skillfully.
27. Children may have developmental problems that reflect (a) an exaggeration or distortion of age-appropriate behaviors (for example, attachment problems in infancy), (b) difficult transitions from one developmental period to the next (for example, noncompliance in toddlers and preschoolers), or (c) age-related, but maladaptive, reactions to environmental, particularly familial, stress (for example, school difficulties among older children).
28. Children's families function on a continuum from highly functional to highly dysfunctional.

29. The families of children who function well before stress occurs may continue to function adequately once the stress occurs. (For example, the families may handle the stress, protect their members, adjust to role changes within their families, and continue to carry out their functions.)

30. The families of children not functioning well before stress occurs may make their members more susceptible to stress. (For example, they may induce maladaptive behavior or illness in their members, induce persistent problems in their members, be unable to protect their members from breakdown, and induce problems that are more likely to require treatment.)

31. Parents who have distorted thought processes likely will have difficulty communicating with their children, which, in turn, may restrict the children's ability to adapt flexibly and appropriately to new situations.

32. Children must receive interventions geared to their developmental level.

The interviewer following an eclectic perspective would focus on the following:

- taking a history from the child, parents, teachers, and other relatives
- genetic factors that might be affecting the child's development
- the interaction of environmental and biological factors to account for the child's development
- the child's behavior in relation to normative data
- a broad range of behaviors, cognitions, and affects related to the child's development, including the development of language, motor skills, social skills, self-help skills, and interpersonal skills
- the frequency, duration, and intensity of the problem behaviors and the situational contexts in which the behaviors occur
- how the problem behaviors affect the child, the parents, and the family
- the child's and parents' motivation for change and treatment
- ways to measure the child's problem behaviors, such as self-monitoring or systematic observation
- the ways in which the child, parents, and family members see themselves, others, and their environment
- the family's structure and dynamics, including the family's decision-making style, communication patterns, roles, affective responses and involvement, values and norms, patterns of interaction, means of conflict resolution, and ways in which the family meets the needs of its members

---

Exercise 1-1. Identifying Perspectives

Read each question and identify the theoretical perspective most closely identified with it. Each question represents one of the following perspectives: developmental, normative-developmental, cognitive-behavioral, humanistic-phenome-nological, psychodynamic, family-systems, and eclectic. Recognize, however, that assigning each question to one perspective is a matter of relative emphasis because there is considerable overlap among the perspectives. Compare your answers with those following the questions.

1. How is the child handling feelings of anxiety, and what has been the consistency of the caregiver's responses?
2. How does the child view herself, her parents, and her choices?
3. Have the child's size and level of maturity affected how his peers relate to him?
4. What role does the child have in the family, and what is the family's structure?
5. How does the child's behavior compare with that of other children of the same age?
6. How does the child's self-concept affect the frequency of her acting-out behavior and the roles she assumes in the family?
7. What were the child's thoughts and feelings at the time the problem was occurring, and what environmental contingencies are related to the problem behavior?

Suggested Answers
1. Psychodynamic 2. Humanistic-phenomenological
3. Developmental 4. Family-systems 5. Normative-developmental 6. Eclectic 7. Cognitive-behavioral

---

CLINICAL ASSESSMENT INTERVIEWS COMPARED WITH CONVERSATIONS AND OTHER TYPES OF INTERVIEWS

Clinical Assessment Interviews and Ordinary Conversations

There are several key differences between the clinical assessment interview and ordinary conversation (Kadushin, 1983). First, we consider the main characteristics of a clinical assessment interview, and then we take a look at ordinary conversation.

1. The clinical assessment interview is usually a formally arranged meeting.
2. The interviewer is usually obliged to accept the interviewee's request for an interview. Sometimes children and parents also are obliged to come for an interview.
3. The clinical assessment interview has a definite purpose.
4. The interviewer and interviewee, in theory, have a well-defined relationship—the interviewer questions, the interviewee answers.
5. The interviewer plans and organizes his or her behavior.
6. The interviewer attempts to direct the interaction and choose the content of the interview.
7. The interviewer must keep attuned to and focused on the interviewer-interviewee interaction.
8. The interviewer accepts without undue reaction unpleasant facts and feelings that the interviewee reveals.

9. The interviewer makes explicit what might be left unstated in ordinary conversation.
10. The interviewer follows guidelines concerning confidentiality and privileged communication.

Ordinary conversation, in contrast, is more spontaneous, less formal, and less structured and may have few, if any, of the characteristics associated with formal interviews. *Essentially, the difference between the clinical assessment interview and ordinary conversation is that the interview involves an interpersonal interaction that has a mutually accepted purpose, with formal, clearly defined roles and a set of norms governing the interaction.*

Clinical Assessment Interviews and Psychotherapeutic Interviews

Clinical assessment interviews and *psychotherapeutic interviews* are part of an ongoing process, with clinical assessment continuing throughout. There is continuity between the two types of interviews, with changing and evolving goals rather than different goals; still, there are important differences. Some of the differences between clinical assessment interviews and psychotherapeutic interviews follow.

1. *Goals.* The purpose of the clinical assessment interview is to obtain relevant information in order to make an informed decision about the interviewee—for example, whether there is a problem and what type of treatment, advice, or services the interviewee may need. The clinical assessment interview is not an open-ended, client-centered counseling session; there is an agenda to be covered. The function of the psychotherapeutic interview, in contrast, is to relieve the emotional distress of the client, foster insight, and enable changes in behavior and life situations.

2. *Direction and structure.* In the clinical assessment interview, the interviewer may cover a specific set of topics or questions in order to obtain a developmental history, a social history, or a detailed description of a specific problem or to conduct a mental status evaluation. The interviewer uses probing techniques to get information and to clear up misconceptions. In the psychotherapeutic interview, the interviewer uses specialized techniques to reach therapeutic goals. The focus may be on problem solving, cognitive assignments, or perceiving shades and degrees of feeling and on responding to the expressions of feeling.

3. *Contact time.* The clinical assessment interview usually lasts 50 to 60 minutes, although its length may vary. Often, there is no expectation that the interviewer will see the interviewee again. Psychotherapeutic interview sessions, in contrast, usually run a specific length of time, and there is an expectation that the therapist will see the interviewee for several interviews.

Now let's take a look at some of the similarities between the two types of interviews.

1. *Rapport.* In both types of interviews, interviewers must establish an accepting atmosphere in which interviewees feel comfortable talking about themselves. This requires interviewers to be respectful, genuine, and empathic.

2. *Skills.* In both types of interviews, interviewers must have a sound knowledge of child development and psychopathology and good skills in listening, attending, and reflecting feelings and content.

3. *Goals.* In both types of interviews, interviewers gather information and continuously assess the interviewees' thinking, affect, perceptions, and attributions.

Clinical assessment interviewing and psychotherapeutic interviewing, as we have seen, are not mutually exclusive. (See Figure 1-1 for an outline of objectives in the two types of interviews.) In psychotherapeutic interviews, you should be continually assessing the interviewee; in clinical assessment interviews, you should be using a psychotherapeutic strategy to deal with the interviewee's anxiety, especially if the interviewee is distraught.

Clinical Assessment Interviews and Survey Research Interviews

Survey research interviews usually focus on interviewees' opinions about various topics or their preferences for particular issues. To obtain this information, techniques similar to those used in clinical assessment interviews are used. There are, however, major differences between the two types of interviews. In survey research, interviewers usually initiate the interviews in order to obtain the interviewees' opinions about particular topics. Interviewees are encouraged to give short answers or to choose answers from those offered by the interviewer (for example, "disagree," "somewhat agree," or "strongly agree"). Additionally, the consequences of the survey research interview for the interviewees are minimal. In contrast, in clinical assessment interviews, interviewees or their families initiate the interview because they may be motivated to address problems, relieve symptoms, or seek changes. Interviewees are encouraged to provide in-depth responses, focusing on personal experiences and behavior. Additionally, *the consequences of the clinical assessment interview for the interviewees are significant, no matter who initiates the interview.*

Clinical Assessment Interviews and Forensic Interviews

Both clinical assessment interviews and *forensic interviews* usually involve obtaining a case history and evaluating the mental status of the interviewee. However, clinical assessment interviews involve developing an intervention plan to help children and families, whereas forensic interviews involve providing an objective opinion to the referral source, *independently of whether it helps the children and families.*

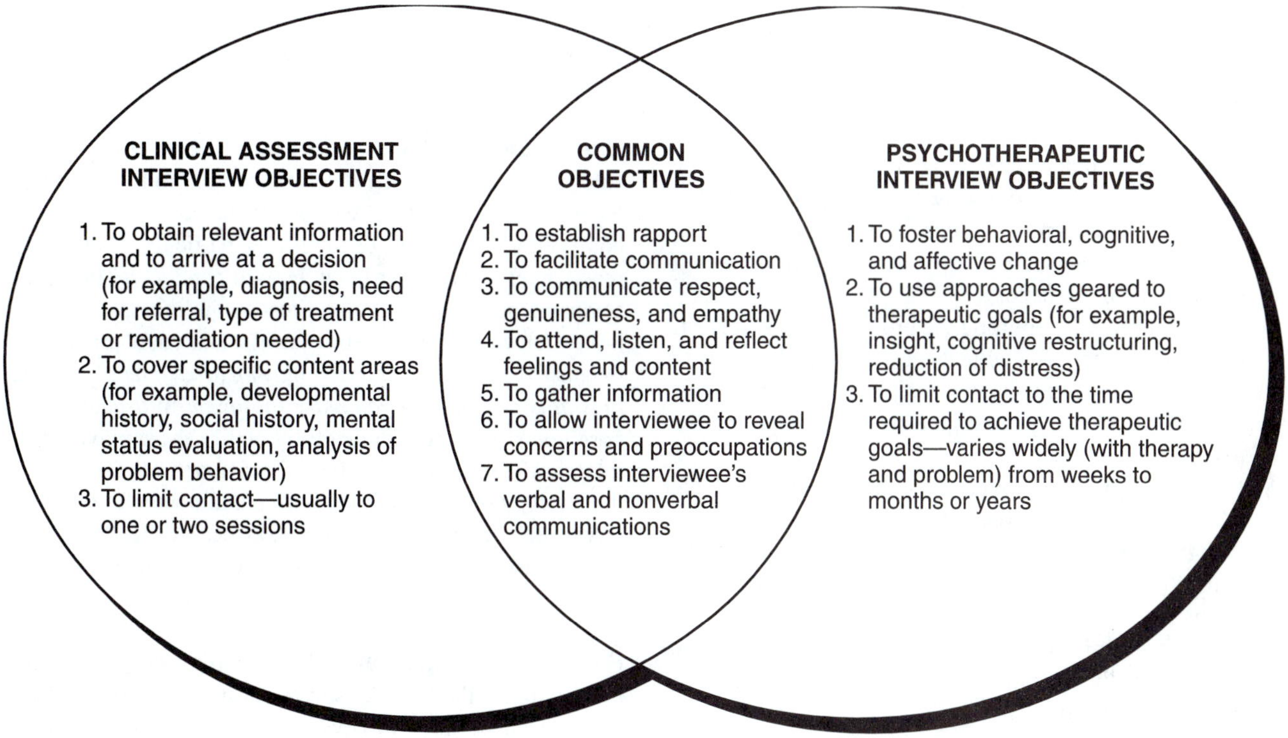

CLINICAL ASSESSMENT INTERVIEW OBJECTIVES

1. To obtain relevant information and to arrive at a decision (for example, diagnosis, need for referral, type of treatment or remediation needed)
2. To cover specific content areas (for example, developmental history, social history, mental status evaluation, analysis of problem behavior)
3. To limit contact—usually to one or two sessions

COMMON OBJECTIVES

1. To establish rapport
2. To facilitate communication
3. To communicate respect, genuineness, and empathy
4. To attend, listen, and reflect feelings and content
5. To gather information
6. To allow interviewee to reveal concerns and preoccupations
7. To assess interviewee's verbal and nonverbal communications

PSYCHOTHERAPEUTIC INTERVIEW OBJECTIVES

1. To foster behavioral, cognitive, and affective change
2. To use approaches geared to therapeutic goals (for example, insight, cognitive restructuring, reduction of distress)
3. To limit contact to the time required to achieve therapeutic goals—varies widely (with therapy and problem) from weeks to months or years

Figure 1-1. Differences and similarities between clinical assessment interviews and psychotherapeutic interviews.

Forensic interviews, however, also can be therapeutic for children and their families, especially in cases of maltreatment where safety plans are initiated or where the children feel relieved after revealing their maltreatment. (Some of the material in this section is courtesy of Steven Sparta, personal communication, May 1994, and Melvin Schwartz, personal communication, June 1994.)

Purposes of forensic interviews. Following are some purposes of forensic interviews. In legal cases involving personal injury, the aim is to arrive at a judgment about how a specific event—such as an accident, exposure to a chemical or a toxic substance, malfunctioning equipment, medical negligence, or situational stress—may have contributed to any psychological or medical problems of the interviewee. In child custody evaluations, the aim is to assist the court in learning about the strengths and weaknesses of each parent and about the factors that will promote the best interests of the child. In civil litigation for psychiatric hospitalization, the aim is to help decide whether the child's commitment should be voluntary or involuntary, that is, at the parents' request. In child maltreatment evaluations, the aim is to evaluate the child's functioning and to recommend needed interventions. In addition, those who work in Child Protective Services or law enforcement will evaluate whether the child was maltreated, whether the child's report and the

reports of others of the maltreatment are credible, whether the child is at risk for further maltreatment, and what steps are needed to protect the child (see Chapters 20 through 23).

The courts might ask clinical assessment interviewers to answer questions such as the following (Koocher & Keith-Spiegel, 1990): Was the child abused sexually? Which parent should be given custody of the child? Was the adolescent competent to waive his *Miranda* rights (the right of a person accused of a crime to have counsel and the right not to incriminate himself or herself) when he was arrested?

Clinical assessment interviews with children usually are conducted at the request of parents, schools, or health care providers. Forensic interviews, in contrast, are requested by attorneys, courts, or insurance companies but also may be requested by parents or by adolescents directly; in cases of child maltreatment, forensic interviews usually are required by law.

Questions asked in a personal injury case. When the forensic interview involves a personal injury case in which a child is involved, the referral source usually would like the following questions answered:

1. Does the interviewee have psychological problems? If so, what are the type and extent of the interviewee's psychological problems?

2. Did the interviewee have any psychological problems before the event? If so, what were they?

3. Did the event exacerbate the interviewee's psychological problems? If so, what proportion of the interviewee's psychological problems might be associated with the event?

4. Are the reported problems the interviewee is having commonly observed following similar types of events?

5. Are there other factors not related to the event that contribute to the interviewee's psychological problems? If so, what are these factors?

6. Is the interviewee reporting the problems accurately? If not, what is interfering with the accuracy of the reports?

7. Are the interviewee's parents reporting the problems accurately? If not, what might be the reasons for the inaccuracies?

8. Is the interviewee exaggerating the problems? If so, what might be the reasons for the exaggerations?

9. Are the parents exaggerating the interviewee's problems? If so, what might be the reasons for the exaggerations?

10. To what extent will the interviewee recover from the event? How much confidence do you have in your estimate of recoverability?

11. What type of treatment does the interviewee need?

12. For how long will the interviewee need treatment?

13. What re-evaluations will the interviewee need in the future and how often will they be needed?

Explaining a forensic interview. The forensic interviewer will usually inform the interviewee about the nature and purpose of the interview, including how the interview will be conducted and what the interviewee's role will be. Here is an example of what might be said to an adolescent and his or her family regarding a personal injury case.

"I am Dr. (Mr., Ms.) _____. I have been retained by _____ to evaluate you in connection with your recent automobile accident.

"I will ask you questions about your past and current life and about the accident. I want to learn about you, your interests, how you think and feel about things in general, and about other things as well." (In some cases, the interviewer might add, "I also may recommend that you complete some psychological tests.")

"You may not want to answer some of my questions and that is your right. However, if you don't want to answer some questions, I will advise the attorneys about which questions you did not answer. OK?

"You can telephone your attorney at any time during the evaluation, and I'll arrange for you to make your call in private if you want to.

"Please remember that the results of my evaluation will be given to your attorney (or other referring party) and also will be read by the other party in the dispute. You also should keep in mind that I may be asked to testify in court about the things we talk about or do today. This means that the results of my evaluation are not private or confidential."

You would, of course, have to modify these statements for a younger child.

Use of the results of a forensic interview. The results of the forensic interview will be used in litigation (in a legal proceeding that takes place either in court or out of court) either to support or to refute a particular claim. A forensic interviewer must know how to conduct a clinical assessment interview and also must know the specific legal issues relevant to the referral and formal court procedures. *Because the forensic interview may be used in legal proceedings, it is critical that you make thorough, well-documented case notes.* Be sure you carefully clarify the purpose of the interview (for example, an investigation or a mediation) with the attorney or other referral source and obtain all of the interviewee's relevant records (Koocher & Keith-Spiegel, 1990). Also consider any potential conflicts of interest, and apprise the referral source of your areas of competence.

Rendering an opinion. Because forensic interviewers must evaluate their findings in relation to the possible questions posed by the attorneys, they may render an opinion, such as "There is a reasonable certainty that the accident contributed to the interviewee's psychological problems" or "In my opinion, his memory problems were present before the injury and no additional memory problems developed after the injury." Opinions should be supported by or based on the data obtained in the evaluation. Because the forensic interview is part of an adversarial system, the forensic interviewer usually will be cross-examined by the opposing attorney. Forensic interviewers must be prepared to defend their opinions, to maintain clear and complete records, and to justify their procedures and conclusions. (Also see Chapter 6 on testifying as an expert witness and Adams and Rankin [1996] for more information about conducting forensic psychological evaluations.)

Precariousness of dual roles. Mental health professionals who become involved in cases of child maltreatment are in a precarious role when they both investigate the allegation of maltreatment and treat either the child victim or the perpetrator (Melton, 1994). Melton advocates that mental health professionals focus on clinical evaluation (for the purpose of treatment planning, not for legal investigation) and treatment. Furthermore, Melton believes that "mental health professionals should not offer an opinion about whether a particular child was abused or whether he or she told the truth, and courts should not admit such an opinion . . . [because] such opinions are inherently misleading and prejudicial, and . . . they should be excluded from evidence" (pp. 111–112). These opinions, Melton argues, involve commonsense inferences—not specialized knowledge—and are within the province of the judge and the jury.

However, we believe that mental health professionals can make a unique contribution in cases of child maltreatment by conducting diagnostic evaluations, as well as by focusing on treatment and planning. Thus, the legal system will need to define the role of mental health professionals in cases of child maltreatment.

We hope our colleagues will step forward as ethical professionals, as thoughtful experts, and as wise advocates in cases in which their knowledge and expertise can legitimately inform decision makers and advance the well-being of children.

—Gerald P. Koocher and Patricia C. Keith-Spiegel

STRENGTHS AND WEAKNESSES OF THE CLINICAL ASSESSMENT INTERVIEW

Strengths of the Clinical Assessment Interview

The clinical assessment interview serves several functions as an assessment procedure for children and their families (Edelbrock & Costello, 1988; Gorden, 1975; Gresham, 1984). It allows the interviewer to

- communicate and clarify the nature and goals of the assessment process to the child and parents
- understand the child's and parents' expectations regarding the assessment
- obtain information about the child's past and current life events
- document the context, severity, and chronicity of the child's problem behaviors
- use flexible procedures to ask the child questions
- resolve the child's ambiguous responses
- clarify misunderstandings that the child may have
- compare the child's verbal and nonverbal behavior
- verify previously collected information about the child and family
- formulate hypotheses about the child and family that can be tested using other assessment procedures
- learn about the child's understanding of his or her situation and how the child perceives others
- learn about the beliefs, values, and expectations that the parents and other adults hold about the child's behavior
- assess the child's and parents' receptivity to various intervention strategies and willingness to follow recommendations

The interview, as previously noted, is a flexible assessment procedure, useful in pursuing leads or in changing the focus of the discussion as needed. The interviewee's verbal responses and nonverbal behavior (for example, posture, gestures, facial expressions, and voice inflection) will serve as valuable guides for understanding and evaluating the interviewee. Sometimes, the interview may be the only direct means of obtaining information from children or parents—particularly those who are illiterate or severely depressed or those unwilling to provide information by other means.

Overall, the interview is one of the best techniques for obtaining information because it allows interviewees to express in their own terms their views about themselves and events that are relevant in their lives. The interview allows great latitude for the expression of concerns, thoughts, feelings, and reactions, with a minimum of structure and coercion.

Weaknesses of the Clinical Assessment Interview

The clinical assessment interview has some weaknesses as an assessment tool because of the following reasons:

- reliability and validity may be difficult to establish (see Chapter 6 for information about reliability and validity)
- the freedom and versatility offered by the interview sometimes result in lack of comparability of one interview with another
- the information obtained by one interviewer may differ from that obtained by another interviewer
- interviewers may fail to elicit important data or fail to interpret the data accurately
- interviewees may provide inaccurate information (for example, their memory for long-term events may be fallible, they may distort replies, they may be reluctant to reveal information, they may deliberately conceal information, or they may be unable to answer the queries)
- interviewees, especially young children, may have difficulty describing events and their thoughts and feelings
- interviewees may feel threatened, inadequate, or hurried and thus fail to respond adequately
- interviewees may be susceptible to subtle, unintended cues from the interviewer that may lead them to distort their replies
- interviewees and interviewers may have personal biases, resulting in selective attention to and recall of certain information, inaccurate associations, and faulty conclusions

Later chapters in this book explore these and other problems more fully.

A PREFERRED MODEL FOR THE INTERVIEWER-INTERVIEWEE RELATIONSHIP

The Preferred Model

An open and responsible collaborative partnership should characterize the interviewer-interviewee relationship. The interviewer shows respect and concern for the interviewee, recognizing that the interviewee must maintain freedom and control over his or her life; this holds even with young children. The interviewee, in turn, shows respect for the interviewer, sharing his or her concerns with the interviewer and providing the requested information.

Restrictive Models

The above model contrasts with more *restrictive interviewer-interviewee models,* which include (a) an *active-interviewer, passive-interviewee model*—the interviewer believes she or he is responsible for everything that goes on in the interview; (b) a *"pure" scientist model*—the interviewer is concerned with facts only; (c) an *autocratic model*—the interviewer assumes an autocratic role, removing all decision-making power from the interviewee; and (d) a *collegial model*—the interviewer tries to become a colleague or buddy of the interviewee, despite differences in interests and values. Because elements of restrictive models may intrude in the interview, it is important for you to recognize when they are occurring and change focus as needed.

Difficulties in Establishing the Preferred Model

The preferred model may be difficult to establish when interviewees fear you, fear the results of the interview, or fear appearing foolish or ignorant. Even when interviewees desire to please you, to have successful outcomes, to unburden themselves, to confirm opinions, or to learn better ways of doing things, the clinical assessment interview may still arouse anxiety. Interviewees may be reluctant to talk with you about highly personal matters, particularly in cases of child sexual abuse. They may recognize that there is a problem but not be ready to face it. And they may not want you to make judgments about their competency or fitness. Consequently, be prepared for some awkward moments in the interview, and be prepared to reduce any anxiety, fear, or embarrassment that interviewees may have.

Mutual trust and respect may be more difficult to achieve when the interviewees' educational or ethnic background differs from yours. Differences in language and customs may hamper communication. In such situations, you should exercise even more patience and attempt to understand interviewees from their perspective (see Chapters 8 and 9).

When interviewees endow you with magic powers and see you as all-powerful—perhaps thinking that you can provide miracle cures—an ideal relationship will be difficult to establish. Because these beliefs may foster dependency and limit the interviewees' involvement, try to mitigate them when they are present. You also don't want to encourage interviewees, either overtly or subtly, to be unduly influenced by your ideas and attitudes or to express extreme gratitude to you for your help. *You should want to help interviewees, not win their gratitude.*

He must be a humble man to resist the temptations of a position with so much built-in authority. The more he becomes identified with his profession and the more he views himself as the representative of a trained elite, the less likely he may be to see his client as someone who is similar to him.

—Robert Katz

STAGES OF CLINICAL ASSESSMENT INTERVIEWS

We can distinguish three stages of clinical assessment interviews: the initial interview, the post-assessment interview, and the follow-up interview.

Initial Interview

The *initial interview* is designed to obtain information relevant to diagnosis, treatment, remediation, or placement in special programs, and to inform the interviewee about the assessment process. The initial interview may be part of an assessment process that includes psychological testing or it may be the sole assessment procedure. When psychologists administer tests, the initial interview usually precedes the testing.

During the initial interview, you will form impressions of the interviewee, including his or her ability to establish a relationship, general attitude, attitude toward answering questions, attitude toward himself or herself, and need for reassurance. You also will receive a host of other impressions that will be tested and evaluated as the interview progresses. You will want to obtain as much information as possible during the initial interview, both because your workload may impose time constraints and because the interviewee may not be available for further questioning. The goal is to gather information to arrive at a diagnostic impression and to generate recommendations for treatment.

Post-Assessment Interview

The *post-assessment interview* (also known as the *exit interview*) is designed to discuss the assessment findings and recommendations with the interviewee's parents, with the interviewee, and sometimes with the interviewee's teachers or the referral source. The post-assessment interview is covered more fully in Chapter 5.

Follow-Up Interview

The *follow-up interview* is designed to assess outcomes of treatment or intervention and to gauge the appropriateness of the assessment findings and recommendations. The treatment or intervention plan will need to be altered when it isn't working properly. Techniques described for the initial interview and post-assessment interview also are useful for the follow-up interview (see Chapters 2, 3, 4, and 5).

DEGREES OF STRUCTURE IN INITIAL CLINICAL ASSESSMENT INTERVIEWS

Initial clinical assessment interviews vary from unstructured interviews to structured interviews. We focus on three types—namely, unstructured interviews, semistructured interviews, and structured interviews. Unstructured interviews allow the interview to unfold without a preset agenda. Semistructured interviews provide general and flexible guidelines for conducting the interview and for recording information. Structured interviews specify the exact order and wording of each question, with little opportunity for follow-up questions not directly related to the specified questions.

Each type of interview format also may vary as to its degree of structure, the scope of the material covered in the interview, and the depth of the information gathered. This means that some unstructured interviews may cover one area in depth or superficially touch on several areas. Similarly, some semistructured interviews may be tailored to a single area, whereas others may cover several areas. And structured interviews may differ in how much coverage they give to a particular area. Let us now look more closely at these three forms of initial interviews. (This section is based in part on Edelbrock and Costello, 1988.)

Unstructured Interviews

Unstructured interviews place a premium on allowing interviewees to tell their stories with minimal guidance. "Unstructured" doesn't mean, however, that there is no agenda. You will still be guiding interviewees to talk about issues and concerns relevant to your clinical task. This guidance requires clinical sophistication. Unstructured interviews offer more versatility than either semistructured or structured interviews. You are free to follow up leads as needed and to tailor the interview to the specific interviewee. You can ask parents, teachers, friends, neighbors, or other interviewees different questions, depending on their relationship to the interviewee and the contribution they can make to the assessment task. You also can use unstructured interviews initially to identify general problem areas, after which you can use a semistructured interview or a structured interview.

Semistructured Interviews

Semistructured interviews also are designed for clinically sophisticated interviewers. These types of interviews do provide a guideline to follow; however, they allow latitude in phrasing questions, pursuing alternative lines of inquiry, and interpreting responses. They are especially useful when you want to obtain detailed information about specific psychological or physical problems or concerns.

The semistructured interviews shown in Appendix F are most useful for children 6 years of age and older. This text contains semistructured interviews for many clinical, developmental, and forensic areas, such as behavior disturbances, suicide, family interviewing, developmental disabilities, brain injury, medically related illnesses, learning disabilities, homelessness, child maltreatment, and child custody.

The semistructured interviews presented in Appendix F orient you to areas that you may want to cover in a specific interview. They are meant to be used not rigidly or inflexibly, but merely as templates or guides. Use only those portions you think you need, and feel free to modify the wording and order of questions to fit the needs of the situation. Be sure to follow up leads. Each semistructured interview will help you target specific areas needing inquiry. (The inside back cover contains an index of the semistructured interviews in Appendix F.)

The Semistructured Clinical Interview for Children and Adolescents Aged 6–19 (SCICA, McConaughy & Achenbach, 1994) also provides a flexible procedure for interviewing children. After the interview is completed, the interviewer rates the symptoms reported by the interviewee on a four-point scale (no occurrence, very slight or ambiguous occurrence, definite occurrence of mild to moderate intensity, and definite occurrence of severe intensity). The resulting scores are plotted on a profile that provides standardized scores for the following areas: anxious/depressed, anxious, family relations, withdrawn, aggressive behavior, attention problems, strange, and resistant. McConaughy and Achenbach (1994) emphasize that the SCICA should be used together with other assessment procedures. This advice is important, because reliability studies in the manual indicate that neither interrater reliability (the extent to which information obtained from one rater is comparable to the information obtained from another rater) nor test-retest reliability reaches acceptable levels for making diagnostic decisions about children.

Your focus during the semistructured interview must always be on the interviewee; this, of course, is true for all types of interviews. The focus on the interviewee is needed because the interviewee may not want to talk to you, may be hesitant to discuss some topics, may speak so quietly or quickly that you will not understand him or her, may be upset over some remark made, may be unable to recall some details because of memory difficulty or other reasons, may be physically sick and unable to concentrate on the questions, may be recovering from an illness that interferes with the ability to converse, and so on. In each case, deviate from the suggested list of questions to handle the problem. Also deviate from the suggested list of questions when you need to probe, to follow up leads, or to check some point of interest.

Structured Interviews

Structured interviews aim to increase the reliability and validity of traditional child diagnostic procedures. Such interviews usually are available for both children and parents.

Structured interviews differ in the types of information they provide. Most structured interviews yield information about the presence, absence, severity, onset, and duration of symptoms, but others yield quantitative scores in symptom areas or global indices of psychopathology. (Table 1-2 shows some questions contained in a structured psychiatric interview schedule.)

Structured interviews minimize interview bias and the role of clinical inference in the interview process. They require specialized training in the use of the specific interview schedule. Even individuals without professional degrees can be given this specialized training. The following is a list of some structured interviews.

1. Child and Adolescent Psychiatric Assessment (CAPA): Version 4.2—Child Version (Angold, Cox, Rutter, & Simonoff, 1996)
2. Child Adolescent Schedule (CAS) (Hodges, 1997)
3. Diagnostic Interview for Children and Adolescents—Revised (DICA-R) 8.0 (Reich, 1996; see Table 1-2)
4. Diagnostic Interview Schedule for Children (DISC-IV) (Shaffer, 1996)
5. Schedule for Affective Disorders & Schizophrenia for School-Age Children (K-SADS-IVR) (Ambrosini & Dixon, 1996)
6. Revised Schedule for Affective Disorders and Schizophrenia for School Aged Children: Present and Lifetime Version (K-SADS-PL) (Kaufman, Birmaher, Brent, Rao, & Ryan, 1996)
7. Schedule for Affective Disorders and Schizophrenia for School-Age Children, Epidemiological Version 5 (K-SADS-E5) (Orvaschel, 1995)

Table 1-2
Examples of Questions Used in Structured Psychiatric Interviews

---

DIAGNOSTIC INTERVIEW FOR CHILDREN AND ADOLESCENTS—REVISED (DICA-R) 8.0

Coding

No 1
Rarely 2
Sometimes or somewhat 3
Yes 5

Mood Disorders
All the questions so far have been about the kinds of things that young people can do. Now I'm going to ask you some questions about your feelings. We'll start with happy and sad.

Major Depressed Episode:

Standard Probes
"Is (Was) this a big problem for you?"
"Is (Was) this *a lot* different from the way you usually are (were)?"

A. **Dysphoria**
    I1a. Are you the kind of person who gets sad or down, or in bad moods a lot of the time?
    I2a. During the past month, have you felt sad, miserable or unhappy a lot more than usual?

IF NO, SKIP TO I2d.
IF YES, CONTINUE.

    b. Have you been feeling that way (sad, miserable or unhappy) for more than a day or two?
    c. On days when you feel sad, miserable or unhappy, do the bad feelings last most of the day?
    d. Do you remember any (other) time when you felt sad, miserable or unhappy *a lot* more than usual?
    I3a. During the past month, have there been times when you felt tearful or felt like crying?

IF NO, SKIP TO I3d.
IF YES, CONTINUE.

    b. Have you been feeling tearful or like crying for more than a day or two?
    c. On days when you feel tearful or feel like crying are you like that for most of the day?
    d. Do you remember any (other) time when you felt tears coming into your eyes, or felt like crying *a lot* of the time?

Source: Reprinted with permission of Wendy Reich.

All of these structured interviews can be used for children with psychological disorders, and most can be used for survey interviews. All of the structured interviews have either parent versions or parent and child versions that are contained within the same interview. Table C-1 in Appendix C lists sources for these interviews. Structured interviews are constantly being changed to conform with changes in accepted diagnostic systems, such as those reported in the most recent edition of the *Diagnostic and Statistical Manual of Mental Disorders*. Use the most up-to-date version of these measures to obtain a diagnosis, especially one that you will use for billing.

Structured interviews generally use the same questions for each interviewee. This procedure is especially valuable when the primary goal is to make a psychiatric diagnosis or to obtain data in research studies. The standardization provided by structured interviews ensures that each interviewee is asked the same questions (unless their responses require follow-up questions asked of some but not all interviewees) and no topics are overlooked.

Hodges (1993), in her review of the available literature, offered the following conclusions about structured interviews for children:

1. Children "can respond to direct questions aimed at inquiring about their mental status" (p. 50).
2. Asking direct questions about their mental status has no negative effects on children.
3. The reports of the parent and child "cannot be considered interchangeable, nor can the parent report be considered the 'gold standard' to which the child's report is compared" (p. 50).
4. In research studies, diagnostic interviews need to be supplemented with measures that evaluate children's level of functioning and degree of impairment.
5. Interviewers, even professional ones, need to be adequately trained in using structured interview schedules reliably.
6. Continued research is needed to evaluate the reliability and validity of structured interviews for children.

Potential difficulties with structured interviews.
Structured psychiatric interviews also have several disadvantages (Kleinmuntz, 1982). The rigid format may interfere with rapport. Answers may be short and supply minimal information, making meaningful leads difficult to follow up. Structured interviews primarily tell you whether a disorder is present, and they are designed to produce diagnoses associated with the *Diagnostic and Statistical Manual of Mental Disorders* (Mash & Terdal, 1988). They neither address specific family or individual dynamics needed to design intervention programs nor focus on a functional analysis of behavior problems. And, unless they are revised, they may become obsolete for diagnostic purposes when commonly used diagnostic systems are revised.

Reliability may be a problem with structured interviews (McConaughy, 1996). First, young children may not be reli-

able informants. Second, reliability fluctuates depending on the diagnosis. Third, scoring on a present-versus-absent format (that is, whether a problem is or is not present) may be difficult. Fourth, agreement between the responses of children and parents may be low. Finally, lengthy interviews may challenge children's attention span.

A structured interview does not guarantee that the interview will be conducted in a standardized way or that all interviewees will understand the questions in the same way. First, interviewers ask questions in different ways, using various vocal inflections, intonations, rhythms, and pauses. Second, interviewers have unique nonverbal behaviors and vocalizations (for example, clearing the throat, making guttural sounds), use idiosyncratic words (for example, "you know," "like," "that's fine"), and make clarifying remarks (for example, "Can you repeat what you said?"). Third, interviewers may follow up responses differently, depending on their interpretation of the interviewees' responses. Fourth, interviewees may not understand the questions or may interpret the same questions in different ways (for example, research shows that some children and mothers will have difficulty understanding questions related to obsessive and compulsive symptoms and to delusions; Breslau, 1987). Fifth, interviewees' level of anxiety or distress may be related to the number of symptoms they report (for example, research shows that mothers who were highly anxious or distressed reported that their children had more symptoms than did mothers who were less anxious or distressed; Frick, Silverthorn, & Evans, 1994). Finally, interviewers and interviewees give subtle unintended cues to each other—associated with language and communication patterns, attitudes, prejudices and stereotypes, cultural practices, social and interpersonal patterns of relating, and personal likes and dislikes—that will color the interaction. These are some ways variability is introduced into the interview, even when interviewers use a set of standard questions.

We recommend that you study one or more of the structured interviews. They not only are valuable in themselves but also provide questions that you can incorporate into the traditional unstructured or semistructured assessment interview.

Computer-generated interviews. The ultimate in structured interviewing may be *computer-generated interviewing* (see Exhibit 1-1). Computers ask the same questions of all interviewees who are assigned to a particular interview schedule, ask every question in the same manner, never fail to ask a question (unless there is a glitch in the program), and, for some interviewees, may provide a more comfortable and less embarrassing situation. However, computers are impersonal and usually do not reword questions, follow up meaningful leads, use clinical judgment to introduce questions, or make judgments about the interviewee's nonverbal behavior.

Computers may miss subtle cues and reactions noticeable to an interviewer. To be maximally effective, computer programs should adjust to the age and ability of the interviewee.

Exhibit 1-1
Will Computers Replace Interviewers?

Interviewers may soon be obsolete: Computers are now interviewing people.

Techniques and equipment vary. A person seated at a computer keyboard may be asked to type simple responses to questions posed on a video screen or a telephone caller may be asked to punch numbers in response to questions asked by a mechanical voice at the other end of the line. Often, all that's needed is a personal computer with adequate memory, a color monitor to heighten appeal, and appropriate software.

Limitations

There are limits to what machines can do. They can't win over respondents with social chitchat or explain questions that are misunderstood. Unless the interviewees are good typists, the computers can't solicit lengthy responses. They can't recognize fuzzy or superficial answers and prod respondents to elaborate. They can't ask follow-up questions of interviewees who drop unexpected leads.

Strengths

Backers of computer interviewing say it's the very inanimateness of the machine that gives the method its strength. The computer is unbiased, and it lets the respondent ponder a question as long as necessary without feeling pressured by an interviewer with pencil poised in hand.

Computers, furthermore, put the same question to each respondent in precisely the same way. At the same time, they can be somewhat flexible; responses to questions can trigger new sets of questions attuned to the interests and earlier answers of each interviewee.

The answers don't have to be coded for computer tabulation and analysis; the responses are transcribed automatically on a computer disk. And perhaps most important, people are more willing to disclose sensitive information to an impersonal machine than to other people or a paper questionnaire.

John Greist, a psychiatrist at the University of Wisconsin in Madison, came

to that conclusion after interviewing—with computers and trained professionals—a group of people waiting to be treated or waiting for others at a general medical clinic. People, he found, "prefer giving private, personal or sensitive information to a computer rather than a human, be it a nurse, physician or psychotherapist."

For example, when asked about exercise, a nonsensitive area for most people, individuals are equally frank with computers and people, he says. But when it comes to questions about sexual activity, people are more open with the machines, "disclosing more sexual dysfunction to a computer than to well-trained psychiatrists, even of the same sex," Dr. Greist says.

"Computers are perceived as less judgmental," he explains. "We've had all kinds of negative experiences with people." Thus, computer interviews may allow us to gather data faster and obtain more truthful answers.

Source: Adapted from S. Feinstein, "Computers Are Replacing Interviewers for Personnel and Marketing Tasks," *The Wall Street Journal,* October 9, 1986, p. 37.

As the fields of artificial intelligence and expert systems advance, computers are gaining increased flexibility. Computer interviewing may be the trend of the future. Perhaps computers will be used as a preliminary assessment tool, followed by an interview with a clinician who will focus on areas needing further study.

complementary techniques that can be used independently of each other or together in the same interview.

The term interview *was derived from the French* entrevoir, *to have a glimpse of, and* s' entrevoir, *to see each other.*

—Arthur M. Wiens

Comparison of Unstructured, Semistructured, and Structured Interviews

All three types of interviews are valuable and play a role in the clinical assessment process. In some types of situations, unstructured interviews are preferred, especially in crises when the interviewee's concerns must be dealt with or an immediate decision made about the interviewee. Semistructured interviews can be tailored to almost any problem area or situation and can elicit spontaneous information. Structured interviews are valuable when you want to cover systematically several clinical areas. It is best to view unstructured, semistructured, and structured interviews as

STEPS IN THE CLINICAL ASSESSMENT PROCESS

You can think of the clinical assessment process as involving nine steps (see Figure 1-2).

1. *Review referral information.* Review the referral information when you receive it. If the referral is not clear or if you need further information, check with the referral source. Clarify ambiguous or vague information, and consider what the referral source expects you to accomplish. The interview will be off to a good start when you understand the referral question and the expectations the referral

source has about what you can accomplish. Aim to establish a good working relationship with the referral source. In cases of self-referral, follow similar procedures. Always determine the appropriateness of the referral, and refer elsewhere if your skills are not appropriate for the task.

2. *Obtain and review previous evaluations, if they were performed.* Obtain and review previous medical, psychiatric, psychological, psychosocial, educational, and police reports to learn about the child. Be sure to have the parents or caregivers sign a release-of-information consent form.

3. *Interview the child.* When you receive a referral, make an appointment as soon as possible to interview the child. How quickly you should see the child depends on the problem. Cases of suspected physical or sexual abuse, for example, need prompt attention, whereas those involving toilet training may not. If possible, interview the child alone; in cases of possible maltreatment, never allow a *suspected perpetrator,* such as a suspected parent, to be in the room when you conduct the initial interview (see Chapter 22). Determine the child's preferred language and use an interpreter as needed (see Chapter 8).

4. *Interview the parents, other relevant adults, and siblings.* To evaluate the child's problems fully, it is critical that you interview the parents or caregivers, and other relevant adults and siblings as needed. Determine each parent's or caregiver's preferred language and use an interpreter as needed. Carefully explain to the parents the policies of the clinic, the school, or your own practice, the fees, the time constraints, and what you think you can accomplish. Give them the opportunity to ask questions, and answer their questions as simply, clearly, and directly as possible. Help the parents prepare the child for her or his visit with you. For example, you can ask them to say to their child, "We're going to see Dr. Smith, who will help us with your...."

5. *Observe the child at home, at school, or in other relevant settings, if possible.* If you have the opportunity to visit the child's home, school, or other settings, observe how the child interacts with children and adults. For example, observe how the child communicates with his or her parents, communicates with other children, relates to the teacher, handles requests from his or her parents and teacher, handles class assignments, and behaves during recess and on the playground or playing field. Attend carefully to the child's language and motor skills. Home and classroom visits provide added benefits—the opportunity for you to establish rapport with the child, parents, and teachers and to observe the physical characteristics of the child's environments, such as the layout and structure of the home and the classroom. If you are visiting a home or classroom, avoid interfering with regular home routines or classroom procedures, and avoid stigmatizing the child under study (for example, do not stare at or point to the child). Although you should make every effort to reduce the parents' or teacher's anxiety about your visit, parents and teachers must understand that their behavior may be part of the problem and that changes in their behavior may be part of the solution. The behaviors of the

child and parents or the child and teacher are usually so intertwined that it is almost impossible to examine one without the other. Chapter 4 describes procedures for observing the home and classroom in more detail.

6. *Formulate hypotheses and recommendations.* You will need to formulate hypotheses about the child's problems and concerns and to develop recommendations by reviewing and analyzing the information you have gathered. Chapter 7 describes how you can do so. This process also will involve taking into consideration cultural factors (see Chapters 8 and 9).

7. *Write a report.* The interview report, which includes the assessment findings and recommendations, is a crucial part of the assessment process and deserves your careful attention. A careful study of the material in Chapter 7 will help you master some fundamentals of report writing.

8. *Meet with parents, the child, and others involved in the case after the assessment is completed, if appropriate.* Discussing the assessment results and recommendations with interested parties also may be part of the assessment process. Chapter 5 provides guidelines for conferring with parents.

9. *Follow up on recommendations.* You (or a colleague) should closely monitor the interventions. Both short- and long-term follow-up are important parts of the clinical assessment process. We strongly recommend short-term follow-ups—within two to six weeks after the beginning of an intervention program. If the interventions prove to be ineffective, either because the child's situation changes or because the interventions were inadequate from the beginning, revise them or develop new ones. Follow-ups also may reveal other issues that require additional assessment.

You may not necessarily carry out the nine-step clinical assessment process in the sequence depicted in Figure 1-2. Observations may lead to questions that require further contact with the child, parents, or other individuals. And as you formulate hypotheses, you may want to obtain additional information to help you decide which hypotheses are most appropriate.

Clinical assessments are not once-and-for-all matters. Some childhood problems reflect chronic conditions that require ongoing assessment to monitor changes and progress. Children change because of development, life experiences, and treatment. An assessment conducted when the child is 2 years old may have little meaning a year later, except as a basis for comparison. Continued assessment is an important means of monitoring the child's response to an intervention, the progression of a disease, or the course and rate of recovery. Repeated assessments are especially important when a clinical intervention procedure has been recommended—such as medical treatment (for example, chemotherapy or surgery) or a cognitive-behavioral program (for example, a cognitive rehabilitation program). Repeated assessments also are required by federal law when children are placed in special education programs (Public Law 94-

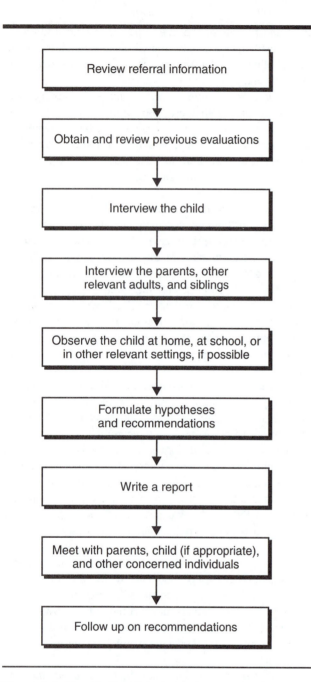

Figure 1-2. Steps in the clinical assessment process.

142 and Public Law 101-476) and when preschool children are classified as having a developmental disability (Public Law 99-457). Exhibit 5-1 in Chapter 5 discusses these laws in more detail.

The recommendations you develop may need to be modified as the child's needs change or when the interventions fail. Additional assessments may be needed at these times. All too often, clinicians perform assessments, make recommendations, and then vanish. Effective consultation and delivery of services requires continuous monitoring by short-term and long-term follow-up contacts.

LEARNING TO BE AN EFFECTIVE INTERVIEWER

Personal Interviewer Qualities

You should carry out clinical assessment interviewing with sensitivity and concern for the child, the parents, and the family, treating them with courtesy, giving them your full attention, and acknowledging and respecting their problems. As you conduct the interview, consider the interviewee's expectations about the interview; how your dress, appearance, ethnicity, and other personal attributes may affect the interviewee; and how your expectations, biases, and cultural values will affect your interview techniques. You must be realistic about yourself and what you have to offer and aware of your strengths and weaknesses. You also will need to acknowledge and accept the differences between yourself and the interviewee without making value judgments. You want to understand the interviewee from his or her perspective. Finally, you want to maintain enthusiasm for your work; see the interviewee's problems clearly and not deny or minimize them, even if they are remote from your experience; admit your ignorance or mistakes; and not mislead the interviewee and his or her family.

As an interviewer or interviewer-in-training, you must carefully examine your attitudes toward children and families, particularly those with serious problems and concerns. Consider how you feel, for example, about children who have been physically or sexually abused, children with physical deformities, children who are antisocial, children who come from multiproblem families, and children who have abused other children. Not every interviewer can work with every type of child with special needs or with every type of parent and family. Some of you, for example, may find it difficult to work with children who have been physically or sexually abused, with children who have severe developmental delays, or with adult offenders who have maltreated children. You need to learn what types of children and parents you can and cannot work with comfortably. You can, of course, try to learn to work with children and parents whom you initially thought you could not work with.

For those children and parents with whom you find it difficult to work, you will either have to learn to master your reactions—such as anxiety, anger, disgust, fear, intolerance, or revulsion—or forgo working with these children and parents. For example, if you find that you are feeling pity for interviewees, avoiding certain topics, or getting impatient, consider why you are feeling so (Cobb, 1989). Similarly, if you feel anger and disgust toward an abusive parent, you must recognize these feelings and suppress them; if you do not, your effectiveness as an interviewer will be limited.

Recognize that you have likes and dislikes, attractions and repulsions, periods of happiness and sadness, illnesses, and a host of emotions and reactions common to all human beings. However, when your moods and reactions adversely affect your objectivity or competency as an interviewer, the interview will suffer.

Developing Effective Interviewing Skills

Three key concepts relate to your role as a clinical assessment interviewer—*objectivity, understanding,* and *goal directedness.* Each contributes to effective interviewing skills.

- *Objectivity* means that you will be open to what you see, hear, and feel, that you will not prejudge the interviewee, and that you will carefully consider your responses. Being objective, however, doesn't mean being aloof or disregarding your feelings.
- *Understanding* means that you will need to be knowledgeable, helpful, and empathic. You do care, and you should convey this caring to the interviewee.
- *Goal directedness* means that you will be aware of the purpose of the interview. You want to gather relevant information pertinent to the referral—whether it be to make a tentative diagnosis, to arrive at a placement decision, or to decide the appropriateness of a discharge from a treatment center, for example.

This text contains graphic descriptions of child maltreatment, domestic violence, suicide, AIDS, homelessness, and other problems that children face in our society. If you find that reading about this material is upsetting, consider seeing someone to talk to about your feelings. It may help to talk to a counselor or therapist, to professionals in the field, to your supervisor, or to a mentor. Mastering your anxiety and becoming familiar with the serious problems that children may face will better prepare you to function as a clinical assessment interviewer.

Exercise 1-2. Evaluating Your Communication Style

These exercises are designed to help you become aware of factors that can facilitate or hinder effective communication in your interviews. Becoming aware of these factors is an important step in becoming an effective clinical assessment interviewer. Parts 1 and 2 were adapted from Zima (1983).

Part 1. Evaluating Conversations

First, think about the conversations you have had with people during the past 24 hours. List 10 factors (or as many as possible) that *helped* you converse effectively. Then list 10 factors (or as many as possible) that *hindered* effective communication. What else might you have done to facilitate the conversations? After you have listed the factors, compare your lists with those at the end of the exercises.

Part 2. Self-Analysis of Communication Behaviors

Answers to the following questions may give you some insight into your interviewing strengths and weaknesses.

1. How effective am I in face-to-face communications?
2. Do people understand what I am saying?
3. What are my strengths in face-to-face communications? (For example, am I warm, friendly, articulate, sincere, sympathetic, receptive to others' ideas, direct in my responses, and comfortable when meeting strangers? Do I speak clearly, listen carefully, put others at ease, use good grammar, give others time to speak, follow through promptly, make sure that I understand what others say, and dress appropriately?)
4. What are my weaknesses in face-to-face communications? (For example, am I cold, impersonal, self-conscious about how I look or sound, disorganized, suspicious of others, easily shocked, impatient, preoccupied, or nervous? Do I monopolize conversation, interrupt, avoid others, jump to conclusions, become argumentative, get angered easily, take criticism poorly, and avoid conflict or problem situations?)
5. In what situations do I have difficulty talking with others?
6. What kinds of people do I sometimes avoid?
7. What kinds of people do I enjoy being with?
8. What kinds of behavior do I find annoying in others?
9. What kinds of outward appearances do I find distracting in others?
10. What are my most apparent prejudices?
11. What are some of my stereotypes about people?
12. What types of people do I have difficulty listening to?
13. In what situations do I find it difficult to listen to others?

Part 3. Responding to Problematic Situations

Read each scenario and then answer the following three questions for each one: (a) What would you say? (b) How would you feel? (c) How might the other person perceive your response? Your answers to each question may give you some understanding of how you react to problematic situations.

1. You are having coffee with a friend and someone you really don't like sits at your table.
2. An acquaintance tells you that her spouse was recently killed in an auto accident.
3. Someone asks to borrow your notes before an examination.
4. You are walking down the street and meet a blind person who asks you for directions.
5. You are talking with two other people and one of them is monopolizing the conversation.
6. Your friend introduces you to Bill, the conversation turns to ethnic groups, and Bill then makes prejudicial remarks about an ethnic group.

Factors That Facilitate and Hinder Communication

Following are factors that usually *facilitate* conversations (or interviews or discussions): being friendly, articulate, sincere, sympathetic, receptive to ideas, direct in response, positive, and receptive to the other person; speaking clearly; listening carefully and empathically; putting the other person at ease; using simple, plain language; using good grammar; giving the other person time to speak; following through on comments; and making sure that you were understood.

Following are factors that usually *hinder* conversations: being impersonal, disorganized, suspicious, easily shocked, impatient, critical, argumentative, preoccupied, anxious, and inattentive to the other person's verbal behavior and nonverbal behavior; monopolizing conversations; interrupting; jumping to conclusions; getting angered easily; avoiding problem situations; using poor grammar; using stereotyped thinking; and letting preconceived ideas influence your responses.

ETHICAL CONSIDERATIONS FOR CLINICAL ASSESSMENT INTERVIEWERS

Clinical assessment interviewers are obligated to follow the *ethical guidelines* of their profession. The following ethical guidelines serve as a minimum for clinical assessment interviewing of children and their families (adapted from the American Psychological Association, 1994a).

1. *Training.* The clinical assessment interviewer who works with children and their families has sufficient education, training, expertise in child and family development, child psychopathology, and adult psychopathology to conduct interviews. Those working in a specialty area, such as behavioral medicine, visitation and custody proceedings, or child maltreatment, need additional training in that area. The clinical assessment interviewer also keeps abreast of the latest developments in the field.

2. *Consultation.* The clinical assessment interviewer consults with other professionals when in doubt about assessment findings.

3. *Knowledge of federal and state law.* The clinical assessment interviewer is knowledgeable about the relevant federal and state laws concerning assessment, such as laws governing children with disabilities, child maltreatment, family violence, and custody evaluations.

4. *Awareness of personal and societal biases and non-discriminatory practice.* The clinical assessment interviewer is aware of any personal biases regarding age, gender, race, ethnicity, national origin, religion, sexual orientation, disability, language, culture, and socioeconomic status that may interfere with an objective evaluation and recommendations. The clinical assessment interviewer recognizes and strives to overcome any such biases or withdraws from the evaluation if the biases cannot be overcome.

5. *Avoidance of multiple relationships.* The clinical assessment interviewer avoids potential conflicts of interest. For example, he or she would not take on a new client to conduct a child custody evaluation, a child abuse evaluation, or an assessment affecting any other legal matter, if the assessment would affect the relationship the interviewer has with a present client.

6. *Informed consent.* The clinical assessment interviewer obtains informed consent from parents (or caregivers) to conduct the interview and discusses the assessment procedures with the child, where appropriate.

7. *Confidentiality and disclosure of information.* The clinical assessment interviewer informs the children and their parents about the limits of confidentiality and the situations in which information must be revealed (also see Chapter 2).

8. *Multiple methods of data gathering.* The clinical assessment interviewer uses several sources to gather information about the interviewee, including clinical interviews, observation, psychological and psychiatric reports, and records from schools, hospitals, and other agencies and sources when these are available.

9. *Interpretation of data.* The clinical assessment interviewer interprets data cautiously and appropriately, considers alternative interpretations, and avoids overinterpreting data.

10. *Explanation of assessment findings.* The clinical assessment interviewer explains the results of the assessment and the recommendations in a clear and understandable manner to the parents, and to the child, where appropriate.

11. *Records and data.* The clinical assessment interviewer maintains raw data, written records, and copies of all audiotapes and videotapes.

CHILDREN AT RISK

What leads children to develop psychological disorders or to have adjustment difficulties? There are no easy answers to this question. In some cases, it may be genetic predisposition; in others, family dysfunction or poverty; and in still others, combinations of several factors. In later chapters, you will be reading about individual and family dynamics that contribute to children's maladjustment. Here let's consider some of the risk factors within our society that contribute to children's maladjustment and how children rise above adversity.

Risk Factors

The concepts of *"at risk" children* and *developmental risk* refer to the probability that children who have certain types of life experiences or who come from certain ethnic or socioeconomic groups may be vulnerable to psychological, physical, or adaptive difficulties during their developmental years and later in life as well. These difficulties include increased risk of dropping out of school, drug and alcohol abuse, delinquency, suicide, and psychiatric and behavioral problems (Athey & Ahearn, 1991). Note that "risk" refers to outcomes as well as to psychological disorders.

The same factors that place children "at risk" can be viewed as "outcome" factors, depending on whether you look at a problem's cause or its outcome—that is, where in the cycle the factors are considered. For example, poor prenatal care (a risk) can lead to low birthweight in infants (an outcome), low birthweight (a risk) can lead to medical illness (an outcome), medical illness (a risk) can lead to problems in school (an outcome), problems in school (a risk) can lead to dropping out of school (an outcome), dropping out of school (a risk) can lead to a poorly paid job (an outcome), a poorly paid job (a risk) can lead to poverty (an outcome), and poverty (a risk) can lead to poor prenatal care (an outcome). The cycle is now complete (see Figure 1-3).

Let's look at some statistics, obtained from national surveys and reports, on 10 major risk or outcome factors. When they are available, the statistics for Black American, Hispanic American, and White American children will also be considered (see Table 1-3; also see American Psychological Association, 1996; Annie E. Casey Foundation, 1993; Carnegie Corporation of New York, 1994; Tarnowski & Rohrbeck, 1993).

1. *Low birthweight.* Babies who weigh less than 5.5 pounds at birth are considered to have low birthweight. Low birthweight babies have a greater chance of dying at birth, and those who survive are more likely than normal birthweight babies to have medical and school problems. In 1990, 7% of all babies born were of low birthweight. For Black Americans, 13% of the babies were of low birthweight, whereas 6% of White American and Hispanic American babies were of low birthweight. Low birthweight may be associated with lack of prenatal care in pregnant women.

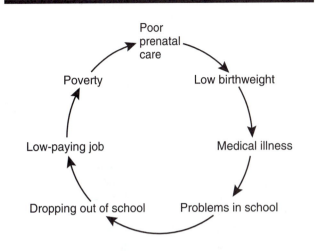

Figure 1-3. An example of a cycle of risk and outcome factors. The diagram illustrates that factors can be risk factors or outcome factors depending on where in the cycle the factors are considered.

2. *Infant mortality.* Infant deaths are commonly associated with complications during pregnancy and often occur within 28 days after birth. In 1990, approximately 9.2 infants

Table 1-3
A Profile of Children "at Risk" in the United States: 1988–1992

Indicator	White American	Black American	Hispanic American	Total U.S. population
1. Percentage of low birthweight babies	5.7	12.9	6.1	7.0
2. Infant mortality rate (per 1,000 live births)	7.7	17.0	7.8	9.2
3. Child death rate, ages 1–14 (per 100,000 children)	29.5	47.6	NA	30.5
4. Percentage of all births that are to single teens	6.1	20.8	10.1	8.7
5. Juvenile violent crime arrest rate, ages 10–17 (per 100,000 youths)	283.0	1456.0	NA	466.0
6. Percentage of teenagers graduating from high school	73.4	60.7	41.6	68.7
7. Percentage of teenagers not in school and not in labor force, ages 16–19	3.7	9.2	7.8	5.0
8. Teen violent death rate, ages 15–19 (per 100,000 teens)	70.0	104.6	NA	70.9
9. Percentage of children in poverty	11.4	44.1	37.9	19.8
10. Percentage of children in single-parent families	16.8	57.7	30.2	24.7

The "Ethnic group" heading spans the White American, Black American, and Hispanic American columns.

NA = not available.
Source: Adapted from *Kids Count Data Book,* published by the Center for the Study of Social Policy, Annie E. Casey Foundation, 1993, p. 21.

died per 1,000 live births. The death rate for Black American babies was more than 50% higher than that for White American or Hispanic American babies. The infant mortality rate in the United States in 1990 was higher than that in 19 other developed nations.

3. *Child mortality.* Approximately 30 per 100,000 children ages 1 to 14 years died in 1990. The highest percentage of child deaths was associated with accidents (over 40%), and almost one-half of those deaths were due to motor vehicle accidents. Black American children had a death rate that was almost 1½ times that of White American children. Parents who are disadvantaged socially and economically are less likely than their nondisadvantaged counterparts to use infant car seats, follow safety precautions around the home, and engage in other prevention-related activities.

4. *Teenage parenthood.* In 1990, the United States had one of the highest teenage pregnancy rates in the developed world—double the rate of England and seven times that of the Netherlands. Almost 9% of all births in 1990 were to single teenage mothers. Black American teenagers have the highest rate of pregnancy, 20%, compared to 10% for Hispanic American teenagers and 6% for White American teenagers. Becoming a teenage parent may lead to dropping out of school, limited job prospects, poverty, poor prenatal care, and giving birth to vulnerable babies. "The price of out-of-wedlock teen births to mothers, babies, and communities is great. One out of three female-headed families is started by a teen mother. Over three-fourths of unmarried teen mothers receive welfare at some time within the first five years of giving birth. Children of early child bearers are more likely to have developmental delays and behavioral problems; by high school they are more likely to fail academically or become delinquent" (Annie E. Casey Foundation, 1993, p. 14).

5. *Arrests of juveniles for violent crimes.* The juvenile violent crime arrest rate in 1990 was 466 youths per 100,000 in the population. The rate of violent crime arrests for Black American youths was five times that for White American youths. Male juveniles were seven times more likely than female youths to be arrested for a violent crime. In 1991, there were 1,668 arrests for juvenile homicide (Cornell, 1993; also see the statistics shown in Table 1-3). Of this number, 311 arrests were of White American youths (22.4%), 1,024 of Black American youths (73.9%), 25 of Hispanic American youths (1.8%), and 26 of other youths (1.9%). Male youths were 14 times more likely than female youths to be arrested for homicide. In 1984, the number of juvenile homicide arrests was 732; thus, the overall incidence has more than doubled in seven years. The increase was primarily due to the use of handguns by minority males to kill acquaintances (Cornell, 1993).

6. *Dropping out of school.* In 1990, approximately 69% of all American youths graduated from high school. About one-fourth of students who entered high school graduated on time. Ethnic status is a strong predictor of school dropout. In 1990, Hispanic American youths had the lowest graduation rates at 42%, followed by Black American

youths at 61% and White American youths at 73%. Because of chronic school failure, adolescents may lose the "hope of attaining a secure and challenging job with economic security and a moderate degree of status" (Kagan, 1991, p. 3).

7. *Teenage unemployment.* In 1990, approximately 5% of American teenagers ages 16 to 19 were not in school or in the labor force. The rate for Black American youths was almost 2½ times that for White American youths, and the rate for Hispanic American youths was twice that for White American youths.

8. *Violent deaths of teenagers.* The teenage violent death rate in 1990 was approximately 71 per 100,000 youths between 15 and 19 years of age. The leading cause of death for White American youths was motor vehicle accidents, whereas the leading cause of death for Black American youths was murder. Children are at risk for violent death when they live in neighborhoods that encourage violence and other forms of antisocial behavior or that provide few, if any, positive support networks.

9. *Poverty.* Approximately 20% of all children lived in poverty in 1990. Almost 44% of Black American children lived in poverty, followed by 35% of Hispanic American children and 11% of White American children.

10. *Single-parent families.* Close to 25% of all children in 1990 were living with only one parent. Almost 58% of Black American children lived in single-parent families, followed by about 30% of Hispanic American children and 17% of White American children. "The increase in single-parent households is a result of both a rise in divorce rates and an increase in out-of-wedlock births. Many single-parent families succeed. But finding the time to parent, run a household, and work is difficult. Paying for a child's needs on a single salary is also hard, particularly for women. The average income of single-mother families is 60 percent of single-father families' income. Only 31 percent of mother-headed households receive any child support or alimony" (Annie E. Casey Foundation, 1993, p. 14). Children living in single-parent households are five times more likely to be poor than children living with both parents (also see Exhibit 1-2).

Low socioeconomic status (SES) is probably the single most significant factor placing children at risk for developing problems and for maladjustment. Poverty does not directly cause children to have problems; rather, it exposes children to risk. Children from low SES backgrounds have been called "economically disadvantaged children," "disadvantaged children," or "poor children." In comparison to nondisadvantaged children, disadvantaged children are more likely to have, for example, growth retardation and anemia, high levels of lead in the blood because of exposure to lead from old paint and from the air, developmental and behavioral problems, developmental delays, learning problems, mild mental retardation, injuries, asthma, dental problems, and childhood diseases because of lack of vaccinations. Many of these problems may be due to poor

Exhibit 1-2
Rate of Poverty in Relationship to Parental Living Arrangement and Ethnicity

According to the U.S. Bureau of the Census (1993c), "The poverty rate for children in 1990 was 18 percent, but it was 3 or 4 times larger for Blacks and Hispanics than for Whites. Nine percent of children in two-parent families were poor, but children in father-only families were more than twice as likely to be poor, and children in mother-only families were more that 5 times as likely to be poor. Among children in two-parent families, the Hispanic poverty rate was more than 3 times greater than the rate for White children, and the rate for Blacks was about twice the rate for Whites. The poverty rate for Hispanic and Black children in mother-only families was much greater than for Whites in mother-only families [also see Figure 1-A below]" (p. 14, with changes in notation). Thus, there is a direct relationship (a) between poverty and being raised in a single-parent home and (b) between poverty and ethnic minority status.

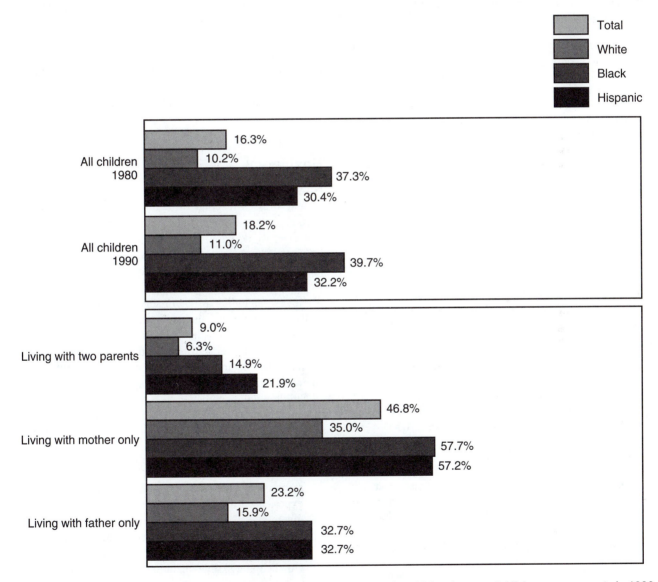

Figure 1-A. Poverty rates for children in 1980 and 1990, and poverty rate for children by parental living arrangements in 1990 (percentage in poverty).

Source: Adapted from U.S. Bureau of the Census (1993). "We the American...Children," p. 14.

nutrition and poor health care. Homeless children are at even greater risk for many of these problems (Tarnowski & Rohrbeck, 1993; also see Chapter 14).

Research suggests that "low SES status coupled with membership in a minority group is the strongest predictor of school dropout.... [It] is related to juvenile delinquency... and is the strongest predictor of teenage pregnancy" (McWhirter, McWhirter, McWhirter, & McWhirter, 1993, p. 37). Low SES adolescents may engage in delinquent activities because they see little hope of finding a good job or of being accepted in society. Becoming pregnant may ensure that a female adolescent receives welfare and perhaps gives her a sense of responsibility and belonging. Low SES leads to educational difficulties because

the socio-cultural context of poverty and the life circumstances with which it is typically associated make it difficult for the young child to acquire the skills and values that are prerequisites for success in education settings.... Considering the limited financial resources and lack of effective programs, schools responsible for educating large populations of children in poverty are faced with a nearly impossible task....

Raising a child in poverty makes it extremely difficult for a parent to provide a background that is conducive to success in school. The stressors encountered as a part of everyday life often result in parents having to focus their energies on the attainment of short-term outcomes (e.g., providing adequate food and shelter, achieving immediate compliance) with little time to concentrate on facilitating the development of skills and attitudes that will allow the child to function well outside of the family. (Egeland & Abery, 1991, pp. 283–284)

Here are some examples of how poverty adds to a family's level of stress (Peter Digre, Los Angeles County Director of Children's Services, reported by Terry, 1995, in an interview published in the *Los Angeles Times*):

When a family's economic assistance is curtailed, people start to get their utilities cut off. They can't pay their rent so they are forced from their housing and end up homeless.

As people go into that downward spiral from poverty to destitution, we start to see an increase in physical abuse. When AFDC [Aid to Families with Dependent Children] was cut about 6% in 1992 [in Los Angeles County], in the year after that we saw a bump of about 10% more kids in the child welfare system, and about 20% more child abuse reported.... As families come under increased stress, they become more desperate—and they become more violent. So we saw a big jump in physical abuse directed at children.

As families are unable to provide the necessities for their children, namely food, clothing and shelter, we see a lot of children being reported for neglect. They don't have food. They don't have a place to live. They don't have medical care. They don't have adequate clothing.... As families hit on this downward spiral, we see a lot more kids in the foster-care system. (p. M3)

Evaluating Children Who May Be at Risk

The following questions may be useful when you evaluate children from a risk perspective:

1. What factors associated with the child, parents, family, and community place the child at risk?
2. What factors associated with the child, parents, family, and community will help the child cope with the risks?
3. What informal supports—such as grandparents, older siblings, relatives, day care providers, nursery school teachers, and neighbors—are available for the family if a parent is incapacitated or unavailable?
4. What can be done to enlarge the child's repertoire of problem-solving skills?
5. What can be done to enhance the child's sense of self-esteem, competence, and confidence?
6. What can be done to make the environment more organized, predictable, warm, and caring?
7. What can be done in the environment to establish more explicit limits that are consistently enforced?
8. What can be done to encourage the parents, caregivers, and teachers to help the child become more independent, flexible in solving problems, self-confident, and willing to help others?

Resiliency

No one knows why children exposed to the same environmental stresses respond differently—some become criminals, for example, and others become productive citizens. However, we do know that how children cope with stress is influenced by their developmental level, relationships with parents, relationships with other family members, type of stress, perception of the stress, social and psychological resources (including problem-solving skills, interpersonal skills, temperament, and self-esteem), prior experiences with stress, level of adjustment, and availability of a supportive social network. Coping with stress is thus influenced by individual factors, stress factors, familial factors, and environmental factors (also see Chapter 10).

Children will cope better with stress and be better able to master and overcome adversity when they have the following *protective factors* (McWhirter et al., 1993; Werner, 1990; Wright & Masten, 1997):

1. A healthy infancy, during which they were active, alert, responsive, and sociable; had an easy temperament; experienced nurturance; and learned to trust their caregivers
2. A sense of self-esteem and self-confidence and close, trusting relationships
3. Good coping skills—including an internal locus of control (that is, an ability to use their experiences as guides to their behavior), a willingness to plan, and a sense of humor—that help them deal with change and make adaptations
4. Good intellectual skills, an ability to solve problems, and an ability to communicate well with others
5. An ability to exercise some control over decisions and over their future

6. An achievement-oriented focus and persistence in achieving goals
7. A family that provides warmth, cohesion, support, and good communication and parents who allow age-appropriate autonomy, make themselves available at the time of the children's failures or distresses, buffer and protect the children against excessive stress, and set reasonable and consistent rules
8. A middle or upper SES family
9. Membership in the majority group
10. A community with good schools, good day care facilities, supportive teachers, positive role models, supportive social networks, and opportunities to learn and master new skills and challenges

The more of these protective factors present in a child, the greater is the likelihood that the child will be able to cope with adversity. We don't know, however, which combination of protective factors will lead to better adjustment. And "what works for the child in one situation may not work for a different child in the same situation, the same child in another situation, or the same child at another point in development" (Masten, 1994, p. 21).

Masten (1994), from her review of research on risk, vulnerability, adversity, and psychopathology, came to the following conclusions:

Studies of resilience suggest that nature has provided powerful protective mechanisms for human development. Children have a remarkable capacity for adaptation. Only organic illness, damage, and major interference in the early nurturing system appear to permanently affect that capacity.... When motivation, self-esteem, and competence are crushed or dampened by relentless oppression, atrocities, or maltreatment, the capacity for recovery may not be evident. When adversity is relieved and basic human needs are restored, then resilience has a chance to emerge. Rekindling hope may be an important spark for resilience processes to begin their restorative work. (pp. 20–21)

Improving Resiliency in Children

In order to help children who may be at risk for developing psychological disorders or adjustment problems, society must find ways to increase protective factors and to reduce risk factors in children and their families. We can increase resilience in children and reduce the occurrence of psychological disorders (and physical disorders as well) by using the following strategies (Masten, 1994):

1. *Reduce children's vulnerability and risk.* The aim is to reduce exposure to "malnutrition, toxic substances, illnesses, accidents, and other preventable risk factors" (Masten, 1994, p. 15). This can be done by (a) promoting and establishing "programs to reduce childbirth in early adolescence and to promote healthy pregnancies and child development" (Masten, 1994, p. 15) and (b) reducing poverty and homelessness, which in turn is likely to, for example, reduce

risks for chronic illnesses, emotional and behavioral problems, and academic delays.

2. *Reduce stressors and the pileup of multiple stressors.* The aim is "to reduce exposure to adversity of the piling up of multiple stressors" (Masten, 1994, p. 16). This can be done by (a) reducing the stress associated with going from elementary school to junior high school by establishing middle schools, (b) stabilizing the school environment for highly mobile families by establishing magnet schools, district-wide school choice, and open enrollment policies, and (c) improving public safety in dangerous urban areas.

3. *Increase available resources.* The aim is "to increase the availability of resources to children at risk" (Masten, 1994, p. 17). This can be done by (a) increasing personal resources (for example, improving children's social and problem-solving skills), (b) increasing material resources (for example, providing breakfast at school to help children learn better) and increasing community resources (for example, providing tutors and encouraging teachers to give additional attention to children), (c) establishing health clinics in schools, and (d) helping children and their families who are at risk take advantage of available resources. Providing income, food, education, job training, and child management skills to parents also can increase children's resources. Similarly, helping teachers improve their skills will benefit children.

4. *Mobilize protective resources.* The aim is to mobilize protective resources in order to foster resilience. This can be done by (a) establishing programs designed to improve parent-child relationships, (b) offering children relationships with adults (such as in the Big Brother/Big Sister organizations) and encouraging children to participate in other mentoring programs, and (c) promoting children's social and intellectual development (such as in the Head Start program).

Parents and other caregivers can help children become more competent individuals by doing the following (Masten, 1994, p. 14):

- Make a person feel worthwhile and valued through their consistent nurturing behavior and engender trust in people as resources. Children who are turned off to adults as resources and social references may lose opportunities and valuable sources of information.
- Model competent behavior.
- Provide information and access to knowledge.
- Coach competent behavior, providing guidance and constructive feedback.
- Steer children away from wasteful or dangerous pitfalls, both by advice and by proactive buffering.
- Support the undertaking of new challenges that they feel reasonably confident a young person can handle or can stretch to meet.
- Function as advocates, opening doors.
- Provide opportunities for competence- and confidence-building experiences.

At the individual level, interventions with children and families at risk need to deal with the risk factors these children and families face and the protective factors available to them. Families at risk will need health care, family support services, and treatment for specific problems. Even resilient children and families may have times in their lives during which they cannot cope with overwhelming life events. The key to intervention efforts is to reduce the risk factors and increase the protective factors to restore a favorable balance between the two.

At the city and state level, schools need to establish programs designed to prevent school dropout, substance abuse, delinquency, pregnancy, and suicide (McWhirter et al., 1993). Within the classroom, teachers need to encourage open discussion, tolerance of ideas, cooperative activities, acceptance of others' viewpoints, weighing of options, and making decisions based on reasoning (McWhirter et al., 1993). Schools should not only provide knowledge and teach problem-solving skills but also "provide a setting where children can become connected with caring, competent adults. Effective schools usually have high expectations, combined with high positive regard and support.... They also provide a variety of opportunities for efficacy-enhancing achievements, either academic or extracurricular. A given school's actions will vary according to context, culture, and the needs of its children. Good schools vary, just as good parents do. However, some of the basic strategies of effective schools may be similar" (Masten, 1994, p. 15).

At the national level, to reduce risks to children, we must (a) promote responsible parenthood, (b) guarantee quality child-care choices, (c) ensure good health and protection to children and their families, and (d) mobilize communities to support young children and their families (Carnegie Corporation of New York, 1994). To achieve these goals, all sectors of society must cooperate, including federal, state, and local agencies; private philanthropic groups; educators, health care providers, and human service workers; business, media, and community leaders; and individual citizens.

Case Illustration

The following case illustrates how two of the three children in a family at risk made a relatively good adjustment despite chronic maltreatment at home (Herrenkohl, Herrenkohl, & Egolf, 1994).

CASE 1-1. THE BROWN FAMILY

The oldest of three siblings, a 19-year-old girl, was in her first year of college, where she was working her way through school. The youngest, a 17-year-old girl, was a junior in high school. The middle child, an 18-year-old boy, had dropped out of school in the ninth grade; he was living at home and was unemployed, in trouble with the law, and constantly threatening suicide. The parents had been abusive—physically, emotionally, and sexually—to all three children. The father had sexually abused the two girls and the mother had sexually abused the boy. Both parents had used severe physical punishment on all three children, including beatings that resulted in broken bones. The parents also had been physically explosive toward each other. Both parents were alcoholics and drug abusers who spent most of the family income on drugs and alcohol, leaving little for food and clothing for the children.

The paternal grandparents had been the source of much of the physical sustenance for the family, providing food for the children when necessary. They also had provided a refuge from the parental home for the two girls, who had spent frequent weekends and vacations with their grandparents, though not for their brother, who had been too active and difficult for the grandparents to manage. The two girls also had attracted support from such members of the larger community as a Girl Scout leader and school counselors. During their high school years, the two girls left the parental home of their own volition—the older sister moved to her grandparents' home, and the younger one to the home of a neighbor for whom she babysat. Neither girl would have any contact with their father during most of that time, pinpointing him as the major source of violence in the home. Their brother, however, remained at home, unable and unwilling to escape as his sisters had done.

The girls, reinforced by their teachers, grandparents, and counselors, had developed high expectations for themselves and, most important, were determined to become self-sufficient, in contrast to their extremely dependent mother, a high-school dropout. The oldest girl assumed a protective, nurturing role toward her younger siblings. Although both girls exhibited goal-oriented behavior and determination, their brother was lacking goals, had low self-esteem, and felt hopeless about his future. Instilled with the notion that passivity and nonaggressiveness were unacceptable in males, at the age of 14 the boy had been convicted of raping an 8-year-old girl, a repetition of the physical violence displayed by the parents. The sisters were not themselves violent but revealed a propensity to become involved with physically abusive boyfriends. (p. 305, with changes in notation)

No government policy can love a child and no policy can substitute for a family's care. [But] government can either support or undermine families as they cope with the moral, social, and economic stresses of caring for children.... The undeniable fact is that our children's future is shaped both by the values of their parents and the policies of our nation.

—National Conference of Catholic Bishops, 1992

OVERVIEW OF THE TEXT

This chapter has discussed the goals of the clinical assessment interview, its relationship to other assessment procedures, several perspectives that can guide the clinical assessment interview, the basic components of the clinical assessment interview, its strengths and weaknesses, different types of clinical assessment interviews, and personal and ethical considerations in interviewing. It also has introduced the concepts of "at risk" children and resilient children. The chapters that follow further discuss the skills and strategies needed to conduct the interview; procedures used in the initial and post-assessment interviews with children, parents, families, and teachers; techniques for closing the interview; techniques for reporting the interview findings; strategies useful in interviewing children and adults who are from ethnic minorities; specific procedures for interviewing children with psychological disorders, with special needs, and with medical problems; and responsible ways to conduct child maltreatment interviews.

The interviewing guidelines presented in this text are *guidelines,* not fixed and unalterable procedures. *Always be guided by the child's age and abilities, the nature of the referral, background information, and what develops during the interview. No set of guidelines can prepare you for every situation that you will face.* The semistructured interview questions in Appendix F, for example, may need to be modified in order to follow up leads given by the interviewee. The questions cannot cover the countless situations that may arise in each interview. Therefore, you will need to use judgment in deciding what to probe and how much to deviate from the suggested questions. The beauty of the clinical assessment interview is that it allows you to follow up leads as they develop during the interview. This means that you can adapt the interview to the unique needs of the interviewee and to the purpose of the interview.

In preparing to become a clinical assessment interviewer, you may be concerned about the following issues.

1. *How much information should I obtain?* This may be one of your initial concerns; however, there are no simple answers. You want to obtain, as a minimum, the information needed to answer the referral question. The semistructured interviews in Appendix F provide useful guidelines for areas to cover. Feedback from supervisors, peers, and self-study should help you acquire the clinical skills needed to pace the interview properly and to cover the appropriate areas.

2. *How many interviews are necessary and how long should they be?* The number of interviews and the length of each interview you hold will be determined by such factors as the seriousness and the nature of the referral, the interviewee's age, the amount of time the interviewee can spend without feeling fatigued or stressed, and the time available to you to conduct the interview(s). Again, there are no firm or absolute guidelines about these issues. You will need to use clinical judgment in each case.

3. *How broad should the assessment be?* You or other members of the clinical staff will need to decide the type of assessment needed for each case. You will want to consider, for example, whether some or all of the family members should be interviewed, whether teachers should be interviewed, whether psychological testing or neuropsychologi-

cal testing is needed, whether self-monitoring procedures are necessary, or whether other types of evaluation are needed. Sometimes, these decisions may not be made until *after* the initial interview.

4. *What procedures are appropriate?* Throughout this text, you will find suggestions for conducting interviews with children, their parents, and their families. Sometimes, several procedures will be described, such as procedures for obtaining information from reluctant children or procedures for getting family members to interact with each other. The intent of the text is to serve as a source to which you can turn for ideas to facilitate the interview. With experience, you will learn to judge when to use a specific technique and which technique is most useful. For example, if the child is open and willing to share his or her thoughts with you, you may not need to probe much. However, if the child is reluctant to talk to you, you may have to consider play procedures—such as the use of a play telephone or drawings—to encourage the child to speak. Similar considerations hold for a family assessment interview. The best strategy is to let the interview unfold naturally, but to lend a guiding hand when necessary. If the interview does not unfold naturally, you will need to assume a more directive role to obtain the needed information.

Everyone has acquired a vast amount of knowledge from her or his interactions with children, parents, family, and others. You can use this knowledge, coupled with the guidelines offered in this text, when you begin to interview children and their parents. The best way to use this book is to become familiar with its contents and then review the section of the text covering the specific referral question. The intent of this book is not for you to memorize every step of every interview with every type of interviewee for every purpose. Your common sense and knowledge, coupled with what you learn as a student, will help you whenever unforeseen circumstances arise in the interview.

After you have completed studying this text, the major components of the clinical assessment interview should be clear to you. *It will take considerable training and supervised experience, however, to master clinical assessment interviewing.*

CONCLUDING COMMENTS

This text provides guidelines designed to promote the usefulness and fairness of clinical assessment interviews. We believe that clinical assessment and psychoeducational assessment can promote the mental health and educational needs of children from all ethnic backgrounds. Each child and his or her parents will represent a separate challenge for you; this text aims to increase your ability to rise effectively to the challenge.

Assessment plays a critical role in all fields that offer services to children and families with special needs. Assessment is critical because you cannot even begin an intervention until you know what problems the child and family are having and what resources are available to them. And once the intervention begins, you can judge its effectiveness only by monitoring and assessing changes in the child's problems. The initial assessment serves as a baseline by which to evaluate future changes and interventions.

We close this chapter with a poem of Ina J. Hughs that expresses the varied experiences that children face in this world ("A Prayer for Children" from *A Prayer for Children*, pp. xiv, xv [revised version obtained from William Morrow], text copyright © 1995 by Ina J. Hughs. Reprinted by permission of William Morrow & Company, Inc.).

A Prayer for Children

We pray for children
    who give us sticky kisses,
    who hop rocks and chase butterflies,
    who stomp in puddles and ruin their new pants,
    who sneak Popsicles before supper,
    who erase holes in their math workbooks,
    who can never find their shoes.
And we pray for those
    who stare at photographers from behind barbed wire,
    who've never squeaked across the floor in new sneakers,
    who never "counted potatoes,"
    who are born in places we wouldn't be caught dead,
    who never go to the circus,
    who live in an X-rated world.
We pray for children
    who bring us fistfuls of dandelions and sing off key,
    who have goldfish funerals, build card-table forts,
    who slurp their cereal on purpose,
    who put gum in their hair, put sugar in their milk,
    who spit toothpaste all over the sink,
    who hug us for no reason, who bless us each night.
And we pray for those
    who never get dessert,
    who watch their parents watch them die,
    who have no safe blanket to drag behind,
    who can't find any bread to steal,
    who don't have any rooms to clean up,
    whose pictures aren't on anybody's dresser,
    whose monsters are real.
We pray for children
    who spend all their allowance before Tuesday,
    who throw tantrums in the grocery store
    and pick at their food,
    who like ghost stories,
    who shove dirty clothes under the bed
    and never rinse out the tub,
    who get quarters from the tooth fairy,
    who don't like to be kissed in front of the car pool,
    who squirm in church and scream in the phone,
    whose tears we sometimes laugh at and
    whose smiles can make us cry.

And we pray for those
    whose nightmares come in the daytime,
    who will eat anything,
    who have never seen a dentist,
    who aren't spoiled by anybody,
    who go to bed hungry and cry themselves to sleep,
    who live and move, but have no being.
We pray for children
    who want to be carried,
    and for those who must.
    For those we never give up on,
    and for those who don't get a second chance.
    For those we smother,
    and for those who will grab the hand of anybody
    kind enough to offer.

THINKING THROUGH THE ISSUES

You can use clinical assessment interviews for different purposes. What are some common issues in all clinical assessment interviews?

How easy might it be for you to forget that you are conducting a clinical assessment interview and fall back into your ordinary mode of conversation?

To what extent will the disadvantages associated with the clinical assessment interview affect the information you obtain?

How might you go about achieving an open and responsible relationship with the interviewee?

When do you think you would use an unstructured interview, a semistructured interview, and a structured interview?

What do you see as the role for computer-generated interviewing? What are some advantages and disadvantages of computerized interviewing? When might computerized interviewing replace interviewers in clinical assessment? What are the ethical issues involved in using computers for interviewing?

You can think of the clinical assessment interview as having nine interrelated steps. What problems can occur at each step that might interfere with your ability to complete the interview? What might you do to prevent such problems? Is there anything you could do to recover and continue the interview if problems arose? What effects might such actions have on the interviewee?

Do you have a preference for any of the theoretical perspectives presented in the chapter, or do you favor another one? Do you agree with the proposition that an eclectic perspective is most useful for the clinical assessment interview? Defend your answer.

What information will you need to arrive at a diagnostic impression? And what will it take for you to have confidence in your impression, once reached?

How would you be able to know if you had any biases that might interfere with your role as an interviewer? And, if you did recognize some biases, how would you go about altering them so they didn't interfere with your ability to conduct an interview?

Can you explore the intimate details of other people's lives without feeling squeamish or embarrassed, or like a voyeur or an intruder? And can you keep their confidences without feeling overburdened?

Are you willing to spend the time needed to gain the child's and parents' confidence and trust?

Can you work with members of the same sex and with members of the opposite sex, with young people and with old people, and with other racial, ethnic, and religious groups?

Are you tolerant of other people's attitudes, values, and beliefs?

How difficult do you think it will be for you to remain objective when you learn that a child was sexually molested, physically abused, psychologically abused, or neglected?

How will you feel when you interview parents who have had different life experiences than you have had?

If someone were to interview your parents about you, how would you want the interview to proceed?

What are some ethical issues that you believe may affect the clinical assessment interview? How do these issues relate to your personal life and to your professional career?

What are the obligations of our society to provide for the basic needs of its citizens?

How can society protect those who can't protect themselves, without subverting personal responsibility and initiative?

If you were designing a program for children "at risk," what would you do?

Can poverty be eliminated in our society? If so, how?

SUMMARY

1. Clinical assessment interviews are unique situations where highly able and skilled professionals devote their exclusive attention to one child and that child's parents and family.

Goals of the Clinical Assessment Interview

2. The primary goal of the clinical assessment interview is to obtain relevant, reliable, and valid information about the interviewees and their problems.

3. Important sources of information are the content of the interview and the interviewee's style.

4. Purposes of the clinical assessment interview include screening, diagnostic classification, designing interventions, evaluating the effectiveness of interventions, and evaluating the effectiveness of specific programs.

5. Clinical assessment interviewing may be done by individuals in several different professions that offer educational, psychosocial, and medical services to children. These professions include special education, psychology/psychiatry, speech/language pathology, occupational therapy, medicine, social work, nutrition/dietetics, physical therapy, nursing, audiology, optometry/ophthalmology, and criminal justice/juvenile justice/child protection.

6. The clinical assessment interview allows you to establish trust and rapport with interviewees; to gain information about their experiences, behavior, and attitudes underlying that behavior; and, if appropriate, to give them information about applicable agencies or services.

7. The information you obtain in clinical assessment interviews may be helpful in determining the nature of the interviewees' problem, including the frequency, severity, chronicity, and pervasiveness of the problem; what has been done to solve the problem; what attempts have been successful or unsuccessful; and what environmental or cultural factors may be contributing to the maintenance of the problem.

8. Interviews will help you place children's problems in a historical-developmental context, which, in turn, will promote better diagnostic precision and intervention strategies.

9. Because the clinical assessment interview may be the first contact that the child or family has with a mental health clinician, it should be carried out with special care.

Factors to Consider in Performing Clinical Assessment Interviews

10. A clinical assessment interview of children should consider their developmental level (including age), gender, race, culture, and ethnicity; family background and parental reactions; health history and current health appraisal; educational history and current performance in school; behavioral patterns and possible psychopathology; personality and temperament; psychological and psychoeducational test results; contextual or ecological factors; and the referral question.

11. You should evaluate the reasons for referral. Recognize that children often have more than one problem and that problems may be more complex than the referral source recognized.

12. You should identify the critical areas of concern and arrange them in order of importance.

Clinical Assessment Interviews in Relation to Other Assessment Procedures

13. Other valuable assessment procedures that complement interviews are norm-referenced tests, behavior rating scales, questionnaires, systematic behavioral observations, informal tests, role playing, sociometric procedures, and psychophysiological and physical measurements and examinations.

14. Interviews are behavior sampling tools.

15. Interviews, together with additional assessment procedures used in a multidimensional assessment battery, will help you determine the children's and parents' strengths and weaknesses; understand the nature, presence, and degree of any disabling conditions; evaluate whether children are at risk for psychopathology or other types of behavioral disturbances; determine the conditions that inhibit and support the acquisition and maintenance of appropriate skills; provide baseline information prior to an intervention program; develop useful intervention and instructional programs; guide individuals in selecting appropriate educational and vocational programs; monitor changes in children and their parents; and measure the impact of the intervention and instructional programs.

Theoretical Perspectives for the Clinical Assessment Interview

16. Several theoretical perspectives in developmental and clinical psychology are useful in guiding the clinical assessment interview with children, parents, families, caregivers, teachers, and

others who have relevant information. These perspectives include the developmental, normative-developmental, cognitive-behavioral, humanistic-phenomenological, psychodynamic, family-systems, and eclectic theoretical perspectives. Although these perspectives share a common emphasis, there also is diversity among them. Each theoretical perspective has something to offer in helping you to formulate questions, to interpret the information you obtain, and to develop interventions.

17. A developmental perspective proposes that the ongoing interplay between genetic dispositions and environmental factors gives development a definite, nonrandom form and direction. This interplay also assures that development proceeds toward specific goals: learning to walk and talk, developing complex coordinated movements, developing thinking skills, and reaching sexual maturity. However, there are individual differences in the rate and timing of development. Newly developed skills bring challenges to children, especially at critical points in development such as puberty.

18. The interviewer following a developmental perspective would take a careful history, focusing on genetic factors that might be affecting the child's development by looking at, in part, traits of the child's relatives; the child's individual and unique pattern of development; the interaction of environmental factors with biological factors to influence the child's development; the child's perceptual ability; the child's awareness of his or her sensory experiences; and the child's comprehension of his or her experiences.

19. A normative-developmental perspective evaluates children's cognitions, affect, and behavior in relation to a reference group, usually composed of children of the same age and gender as the referred child. It also attempts to account for changes as the referred child matures.

20. The interviewer following a normative-developmental perspective would look at the child's behavior in relation to similar behavior of children of the same age and gender; examine the child's level of development in such areas as language, motor skills, social skills, self-help skills, and interpersonal skills; and interview a parent or caregiver to obtain the child's developmental history and relevant behaviors and interests.

21. A cognitive-behavioral perspective focuses on the importance of cognitions as major determinants of emotion and behavior, the role that cognitions play in the development of maladaptive behavior, and the individual and environmental influences that may shape and control the child's and family's thoughts, feelings, and behavior. The cognitive-behavioral approach emphasizes the importance of empirical validation throughout the assessment and treatment.

22. The interviewer following a cognitive-behavioral perspective would encourage the child and parents to give concrete examples of the problems and, when possible, specify related thoughts, feelings, and actions occurring at the time of the problems; explore the frequency, duration, and intensity of each problem and how the problem behaviors affect the child; look at the relationship among environmental events, the child's thoughts, and the problems, seeking to learn what precipitates the problems and what maintains them; assess the child's (and parents') motivation for change; interview the family members to learn about their perception of the problems; and measure behavior where appropriate, such as by self-monitoring, parent-monitoring, or observing the child (and parents) in a clinic setting and a natural setting such as the home.

23. A humanistic-phenomenological perspective emphasizes the individual's perception of the world. Behavior is viewed as a response to how the individual views the world at any particular moment in time. The emphasis is on the here and now, with individuals seen as active, thinking people who are responsible for their behavior and capable of making choices. Behavior, in part, is determined by individuals' expectations about the consequences of their actions. Further, individuals are seen as behaving to achieve their fullest potential, which is referred to as *self-actualization.*

24. The interviewer following a humanistic-phenomenological perspective would focus on the way the child and parents see themselves, others, and their environments; the expectations the child has about the consequences of his or her behavior; the assumptions the child has about his or her life; the needs the child has that are not being met; and the way the child views his or her choices. The interviewer following this perspective would not independently make recommendations but would work with the child (particularly an older one) and family to identify viable interventions. Some humanistically oriented interviewers, however, believe that assessment is not needed or should be de-emphasized. They maintain that assessment may impede the therapeutic process by placing the interviewer in an authoritative, superior role in relation to the interviewee.

25. A psychodynamic perspective emphasizes intrapsychic factors that influence behavior, such as thoughts, feelings, impulses, desires, motives, and conflicts. Early childhood experiences, in particular, play a critical role in the formation of behavioral patterns. Attachment theory proposes that infants develop internal working models of their self and their caregiver. These models help infants forecast and interpret the caregiver's behavior and plan their own behavior in response to the caregiver. Early relationships with parents, siblings, other relatives, caregivers, and peers play a critical role in the formation of behavioral patterns.

26. The interviewer following a psychodynamic perspective would focus on the child's thoughts, feelings, motives, fears, early experiences in the family, intrafamilial relationships, and symptoms; material related to defense mechanisms; the mother/child relationship; the child's (and parents') motivation for treatment; dreams, particularly for older children; and play, particularly for younger children as a way to understand their conflicts.

27. A family-systems perspective focuses on the structure and dynamics of the family. Factors such as the family's structure, functions, assigned roles, modes of interacting, resources, history, life cycle, and the individual members' unique histories are important elements of a family-systems perspective.

28. The interviewer following a family-systems perspective would focus on the family's problem-solving style, communication patterns, roles, affective responses and involvement, and values and norms; the way the members interact (using both verbal and nonverbal cues); the type of conflict expressed by the family members; the members' judgment; the way the members handle issues of autonomy and identity; their interactions within the wider community; the family rules; and the way the family recognizes the rights of its members.

29. An eclectic perspective, which is based on individual elements from other perspectives, emphasizes that individual, familial, and environmental determinants are critical factors in children's development; that children are shaped by their environ-

ments and by their genetic constitutions; that what we observe in children may not always reflect their potentials; and that children also shape their environments.

30. The interviewer following an eclectic perspective focuses on taking a history from the child, parents, teachers, and other relatives; the genetic factors that might be affecting the child's development; the interaction of environmental and biological factors to account for the child's development; the child's behavior in relation to normative data; a broad range of behaviors, cognitions, and affects related to the child's development, including language, motor skills, social skills, self-help skills, and interpersonal skills; the frequency, duration, and intensity of the problem behaviors and the situational context in which the behaviors occur; how the problem behaviors affect the child, the parents, and the family; the child's and parents' motivation for change and treatment; ways to measure the child's problem behaviors, such as by self-monitoring or systematic observation; the ways in which the child, parents, and family members see themselves, others, and their environment; and the family's structure and dynamics, including the family's decision-making style, communication patterns, roles, affective responses and involvement, values and norms, patterns of interaction, ways of conflict resolution, and ways in which it meets the needs of its members.

Clinical Assessment Interviews Compared with Conversations and Other Types of Interviews

31. The clinical assessment interview, in contrast to ordinary conversation, is formally arranged, requires the interviewer to accept the interviewee's request for a meeting, has a definite purpose, has a well-defined relationship between the interviewer and interviewee, and is planned. It is directed by the interviewer, requires the interviewer to keep attuned to and focused on the interviewer-interviewee relationship, acknowledges unpleasant facts and feelings, makes explicit what might be left unstated in ordinary conversation, and requires the interviewer to follow guidelines concerning confidentiality.

32. Clinical assessment interviews and psychotherapeutic interviews are part of an ongoing process, with clinical assessment continuing throughout. There is continuity between the two types of interviews, with each having changing and evolving goals rather than different goals.

33. Clinical assessment interviewing and psychotherapeutic interviewing both involve establishing rapport, facilitating communication, communicating respect, attending, gathering information, allowing the interviewee to reveal concerns and preoccupations, and assessing verbal and nonverbal communications. Because the goal of the assessment interview is to make decisions, you should obtain detailed information, cover specific content, and limit contact to a brief period. Because the goal of the psychotherapeutic interview, in contrast, is to foster behavioral, cognitive, and affective change, you should use therapeutic approaches and maintain contact over time.

34. The clinical assessment interview differs from the survey research interview, particularly in that it has more significant consequences for the interviewee.

35. Clinical assessment interviews and forensic interviews share many features. They both usually involve obtaining a case history and evaluating the mental status of the interviewee. In addition, in the clinical assessment interview, an important goal is to develop an intervention plan, with the aim being to help the child and family. In the forensic interview, however, the goal is to provide an objective opinion, independent of whether it helps the interviewee. The results of the forensic interview may be used in litigation, either to support or to refute a particular claim.

Strengths and Weaknesses of the Clinical Assessment Interview

36. The strengths of clinical assessment interviews are that they allow interviewers to communicate and clarify the nature and goals of the assessment and treatment process; to understand the child's and parents' expectations regarding the assessment; to obtain information about the child's past and current life events; to document the context and chronicity of the child's problem behaviors; to be flexible in questioning; to resolve ambiguous responses; to clarify misunderstandings; to compare the child's verbal and nonverbal behavior; to verify previously collected information; to formulate hypotheses that can be tested using other assessment procedures; to learn about children's understanding of their problems and their perceptions of others; to learn about the beliefs, values, and expectations that parents (and other adults) hold about the children's behavior; and to assess interviewees' receptivity to various intervention strategies and willingness to follow recommendations.

37. The weaknesses of clinical assessment interviews include difficulty in establishing reliability and validity; possible lack of comparability of one interview with another; possible differences in the information obtained by different interviewers; difficulty in eliciting important information; difficulty in interpreting data accurately; difficulty some interviewees have in providing accurate information; difficulty in interviewing young children; difficulty in obtaining information from interviewees who feel threatened, inadequate, or hurried or who show susceptibility to subtle, unintended cues from interviewers; difficulty in cross-cultural interviews; and susceptibility to judgmental bias on the part of interviewees or interviewers, resulting in selective attention and recall of information.

A Preferred Model for the Interviewer-Interviewee Relationship

38. The preferred interviewer-interviewee relationship is one in which each party is open and responsible. The interviewer recognizes the interviewee's individuality and shows respect and concern for the interviewee, and the interviewee shares his or her concerns with the interviewer and shows respect for the interviewer.

39. Restrictive interviewer-interviewee relationships include an active-interviewer, passive-interviewee model; a "pure" scientist model; an autocratic model; and a collegial model.

40. The preferred model may be difficult to establish when the interviewees fear the interviewer, the results of the interview, or appearing foolish or ignorant.

Stages of Clinical Assessment Interviews

41. The initial interview is designed to obtain information relevant to diagnosis, treatment, remediation, or placement in special programs and to inform the interviewee about the assessment process.

42. The post-assessment interview is designed to discuss the assessment findings and recommendations with the inter-

viewee's parents, with the interviewee, and sometimes with the interviewee's teachers or the referral source.

43. The follow-up interview is designed to assess outcomes of treatment or intervention and to gauge the appropriateness of the assessment findings and recommendations.

Degrees of Structure in Clinical Assessment Interviews

44. The clinical assessment interview can vary from unstructured to structured. Unstructured interviews allow the interview to unfold without a preset agenda. Semistructured interviews provide general and flexible guidelines for conducting the interview and for recording information. Structured interviews specify the exact order and wording of each question, with little opportunity for follow-up questions not directly related to the specified questions.

45. Each type of interview format may vary as to its degree of structure, the scope of the material covered in the interview, and the depth versus breadth of the information gathered.

46. Unstructured interviews place a premium on allowing the interviewee to tell his or her story with minimal guidance. "Unstructured" doesn't mean, however, that there is no agenda. You will still be guiding the interviewee to talk about issues and concerns relevant to your clinical task.

47. Semistructured interviews also are designed for clinically sophisticated interviewers; they allow latitude in phrasing questions, pursuing alternative lines of inquiry, and interpreting responses. They are especially useful when you want to obtain detailed information about specific psychological or physical problems or concerns.

48. Structured interviews minimize interviewer bias and the role of clinical inference in the interview process but require that the interviewer have specialized training in the use of the specific interview schedule.

49. Structured interviews have disadvantages. These disadvantages include a rigidity that may interfere with rapport, getting unelaborated answers, and restricted range of coverage. Answers may be short and include minimal information. The format makes it difficult to follow up meaningful leads. And structured interviews do not address specific family or individual dynamics needed to design intervention programs.

50. A list of specific questions does not guarantee that each interviewer will conduct the interview in the same way or that all interviewees will understand the questions in the same way.

51. The ultimate in structured interviewing may be computer-generated interviewing.

52. It is best to view unstructured, semistructured, and structured interviews as complementary techniques that you can use independently of each other or together in the same interview.

Steps in a Clinical Assessment Interview

53. We can perceive the clinical assessment interview as having nine steps: review referral information; obtain and review previous evaluations, if they were performed; interview the child; interview the parents, other relevant adults, and siblings; observe the child at home, at school, or in other relevant settings, if possible; formulate hypotheses and recommendations; write a report; meet with parents, the child, and others involved in the case after the assessment is completed, if appropriate; and follow up on recommendations.

54. Clinical assessments are not once-and-for-all matters, because some conditions may require ongoing monitoring.

55. Continued assessments are especially important when a clinical intervention has been recommended; they also may be required to comply with various federal laws.

56. Effective consultation and delivery of services require continuous monitoring by short-term and long-term follow-up contacts.

Learning to Be an Effective Interviewer

57. As a clinical assessment interviewer, you need to be sensitive to the child, the parents, and the family.

58. As an interviewer (or interviewer-in-training), you must carefully examine your attitudes toward children and families, particularly those with serious problems and concerns. Learn about your preferences for working with various groups.

59. Recognize that when your moods and reactions adversely affect your objectivity or competency as an interviewer, the interview will suffer. You must strive to be objective, even though it may not always be easy.

Ethical Considerations for Clinical Assessment Interviewers

60. Clinical assessment interviewers are obligated to follow the ethical guidelines of their profession.

Children at Risk

61. The concepts of *"at risk" children* and *developmental risk* refer to the probability that children who have certain types of life experiences or who come from certain ethnic or socioeconomic groups may be vulnerable to psychological, physical, or adaptive difficulties during their developmental years and later in life as well.

62. The same factors that place children "at risk" can be viewed as "outcome" factors, depending on whether you look at a problem's cause or its outcome—that is, where in the cycle the factors are considered.

63. Low birthweight babies have a greater chance of dying at birth, and those who survive are more likely than normal birthweight babies to have medical and school problems.

64. In 1990, 7% of all babies born were of low birthweight.

65. Approximately 30 per 100,000 children ages 1 to 14 years died in 1990. The highest percentage of child deaths was associated with accidents (over 40%), and almost one-half of those deaths were due to motor vehicle accidents.

66. Almost 9% of all births in 1990 were to single teenage mothers.

67. The juvenile violent crime arrest rate in 1990 was 466 youths per 100,000 in the population.

68. In 1990, approximately 69% of all American youths graduated from high school. About one-fourth of students who entered high school graduated on time.

69. In 1990, approximately 5% of American teenagers ages 16 to 19 were not in school or in the labor force.

70. The violent death rate in 1990 was approximately 71 per 100,000 youths between 15 and 19 years of age. The leading cause of death for White American youths was motor vehicle accidents, whereas the leading cause of death for Black American youths was murder.

71. Approximately 20% of all children lived in poverty in 1990.

72. Close to 25% of all children in 1990 were living with only one parent.

73. Low socioeconomic status (SES) is probably the single most significant factor placing children at risk for developing problems and for maladjustment.

74. Research suggests that low SES status coupled with membership in a minority group is the strongest predictor of school dropout, is related to juvenile delinquency, and is the strongest predictor of teenage pregnancy.

75. How children cope with stress is influenced by their developmental level, relationships with parents, relationships with other family members, type of stress, perception of the stress, social and psychological resources (including problem-solving skills, interpersonal skills, temperament, and self-esteem), prior experiences with stress, level of adjustment, and availability of a supportive social network.

76. Children will be in the best position to cope with stress when they had a healthy infancy; have a sense of self-esteem and self-confidence and close trusting relationships; have good coping skills; have good intellectual skills; have some control over decisions and over their future; are achievement-oriented and persistent in achieving goals; have families that provide warmth, cohesion, support, and good communication; have families in the middle or upper SES classes; are from the majority group; and live in communities with good supportive services.

77. We can increase resilience in children and reduce the occurrence of psychological disorders (and physical disorders as well) by reducing children's vulnerability and risk, reducing stressors and the pileup of multiple stressors, increasing available resources, and mobilizing protective resources.

78. At the individual level, interventions with children and families at risk need to deal with the risk factors these children and families face and the protective factors available to them.

79. At the city and state level, schools need to establish programs designed to prevent school dropout, substance abuse, delinquency, pregnancy, and suicide.

80. At the national level, to reduce risks to children, we must promote responsible parenthood, guarantee quality child-care choices, ensure good health and protection to children and their families, and mobilize communities to support young children and their families.

Overview of the Text

81. The interviewing guidelines in the text are *guidelines,* not fixed and unalterable procedures. Always be guided by the child's age and abilities, the nature of the referral, background information, and what develops during the interview.

Concluding Comments

82. This text provides guidelines designed to promote the usefulness and fairness of clinical assessment interviews.

83. Each child and his or her parents will represent a separate challenge for you; this text aims to increase your ability to rise effectively to the challenge.

KEY TERMS, CONCEPTS, AND NAMES

Clinical assessment or evaluation (p. 3)
Clinical assessment interview (p. 3)
Psychological evaluation (p. 3)
Neuropsychological evaluation (p. 3)
Diagnostic workup (p. 3)
Content of the interview (p. 3)
Interviewee's style (p. 3)
Screening evaluation (p. 3)

Diagnostic classification (p. 4)
Mental health system interviewer (p. 5)
Educational system interviewer (p. 5)
Pediatric health system interviewer (p. 5)
Criminal justice system interviewer (p. 5)
Ecological validity (p. 11)
Referral question (p. 11)
Developmental perspective (p. 12)
Normative-developmental perspective (p. 12)
Cognitions (p. 12)
Affect (p. 12)
Demographic variables (p. 12)
Developmental variables (p. 12)
Cognitive-behavioral perspective (p. 13)
Behavioral analysis (Functional analysis) (p. 13)
Humanistic-phenomenological perspective (p. 13)
Self-actualization (p. 13)
Psychodynamic perspective (p. 13)
Defenses (Defense mechanisms) (p. 14)
Attachment theory (p. 14)
Maturational processes (p. 14)
Ego (p. 14)
Psychosexual development (p. 14)
Family-systems perspective (p. 14)
Structure (family) (p. 15)
Function (family) (p. 15)
Assigned roles (family) (p. 15)
Mode of interaction (family) (p. 15)
Resources (family) (p. 15)
Family history (p. 15)
Life cycle (family) (p. 15)
Eclectic perspective (p. 15)
Ordinary conversation (p. 17)
Psychotherapeutic interviews (p. 18)
Survey research interviews (p. 18)
Forensic interviews (p. 18)
Preferred interviewer-interviewee model (p. 21)
Restrictive interviewer-interviewee model (p. 22)
Active-interviewer, passive-interviewee model (p. 22)
Pure scientist model (p. 22)
Autocratic model (p. 22)
Collegial model (p. 22)
Initial interview (p. 22)
Post-assessment interview (Exit interview) (p. 22)
Follow-up interview (p. 22)
Unstructured interview (p. 23)
Semistructured interview (p. 23)
Structured interview (p. 24)
Computer-generated interviewing (p. 25)
Steps in a clinical assessment interview (p. 26)
Interviewer qualities (p. 28)
Objectivity (p. 29)
Understanding (p. 29)
Goal directedness (p. 29)
Ethical guidelines (p. 30)
"At risk" children (p. 30)
Developmental risk (p. 30)
Low birthweight (p. 31)
Infant mortality (p. 31)
Child mortality (p. 32)
Teenage parenthood (p. 32)

Arrests of juveniles for violent crimes (p. 32)

Dropping out of school (p. 32)

Teenage unemployment (p. 32)

Violent deaths of teenagers (p. 32)

Poverty (p. 32)

Single-parent families (p. 32)

Low socioeconomic status (SES) (p. 32)

Resiliency (p. 33)

Protective factors (p. 34)

STUDY QUESTIONS

1. What are some of the goals of the clinical assessment interview?

2. Discuss some of the professions involved in clinical assessment interviewing.

3. The text lists 11 factors related to performing a clinical assessment interview. Discuss 5 of these factors.

4. Compare and contrast the following theoretical perspectives: developmental perspective, normative-developmental perspective, cognitive-behavioral perspective, humanistic-phenomenological perspective, psychodynamic perspective, family-systems perspective, and eclectic perspective. Include in your discussion their similarities and differences. Which perspective do you prefer for a clinical assessment interview and why?

5. How would an interviewer using each of the following perspectives conduct a clinical assessment interview: developmental perspective, normative-developmental perspective, cognitive-behavioral perspective, humanistic-phenomenological perspective, psychodynamic perspective, family-systems perspective, and eclectic perspective?

6. The text lists 32 propositions reflecting an eclectic perspective. Discuss 5 propositions that deal with normal development and family functioning and 5 that deal with developmental problems and family difficulties.

7. How is a clinical assessment interview different from an ordinary conversation?

8. Discuss the similarities and differences between a clinical assessment interview and a psychotherapeutic interview.

9. Discuss the similarities and differences between a clinical assessment interview and a survey research interview.

10. Compare and contrast the clinical assessment interview with the forensic interview.

11. What are the strengths and weaknesses of the clinical assessment interview?

12. Discuss a preferred model for the interviewer-interviewee relationship.

13. Compare and contrast the initial interview, the post-assessment interview, and the follow-up interview.

14. Compare unstructured, semistructured, and structured interviews. In your comparisons, comment on the advantages and disadvantages of each.

15. Discuss the benefits and limitations of computer-generated interviewing.

16. Discuss the nine steps in a clinical assessment interview.

17. Discuss how the personal qualities of an interviewer may affect the interview.

18. Discuss some ethical considerations in being a clinical assessment interviewer.

19. Discuss the concept of "at risk" children. Include in your discussion specific risk factors, ethnic differences related to the risk factors, resilient children, evaluating children who may be at risk, and improving resiliency in children.

2

CONDUCTING THE INTERVIEW

A question rightly asked is half answered.

—G. J. Jacobi

An answer is invariably the parent of a great family of new questions.

—John Steinbeck

Goals and Objectives

This chapter is designed to enable you to:

- Develop listening skills
- Develop observational skills
- Develop rapport with the interviewee
- Formulate appropriate questions
- Avoid ineffective questions
- Use structuring statements
- Encourage appropriate replies
- Use probing techniques
- Time questions and change topics appropriately
- Deal with difficult situations in the interview
- Recognize your emotions
- Explain confidentiality and privileged communication as they relate to the interview

INTRODUCTION TO INTERVIEWING GUIDELINES

As noted in Chapter 1, underlying all successful interviews are the ability to communicate clearly and the ability to understand the communications of the interviewee; this is true for interviewing both children and adults. Although this text emphasizes interviewing children, much of the material also applies to interviewing adults. A thorough assessment of children's problems and concerns will require you to interview parents, caregivers, and teachers, for example. This chapter presents general interviewing principles, Chapter 3 discusses strategies particularly useful for interviewing children, and Chapter 4 provides guidelines for interviewing parents, teachers, and families. The interviewing guidelines in this book cannot cover every possible contingency. However, once you have mastered the material in the book, you can generalize your knowledge to new situations.

During the interview, you will be asking questions, following up and probing responses, moving from topic to topic, encouraging replies, answering questions, gauging the pace of the interview, and formulating impressions of the interviewee. Following are important guidelines for conducting the interview, many of which are further elaborated in the chapter (Gratus, 1988, adapted from pp. 91–93).

1. Prepare for the interview by considering the purpose of the interview, the physical setting, the structure of the interview, and the possible issues that may arise. Have a broad outline of the topics you want to cover. If you want to, you also can have a set of detailed questions ready. Be sure that you know what information you want to obtain and frame your questions accordingly.

2. Learn as much as you can about the interviewee *before* the interview. Consider how the interviewee's health and situational factors may affect the interview. The more you know about the interviewee beforehand, the better position you will be in to anticipate problems and to conduct the interview.

3. Be sure that any equipment you plan to use is in good working order and that the interview room is available. Make arrangements so that you are not likely to be interrupted and so that the interview room is free from distractions.

4. Consider the interviewee's cognitive and developmental levels and what intellectual demands the interview will make on his or her ability to report factual information and feelings.

5. Be prepared to explain confidentiality, and have the interviewee sign a consent form to release information, as needed.

6. Greet the interviewee in a friendly, polite, open manner, and put him or her at ease. Speak clearly at a normal volume, using a friendly, reassuring tone. Establish rapport and a productive climate, and then probe carefully.

7. Recognize that you may have difficulty obtaining information when interviewees are anxious, upset, resistant, or unable to concentrate. Adjust your techniques to overcome their problems.

8. Be prepared to explain or expand on the questions you ask. Few interviewees will understand every question the first time you ask.

9. Develop the art of good listening. This means concentrating on what interviewees say, showing them that you are doing so, and "hearing" what they convey by their gestures and expressions. Remind yourself to *listen*.

10. Answer the interviewee's questions as clearly and directly as possible.

11. Judge how the interview is proceeding and make adjustments as needed.

12. Do not be frightened of silences. Pauses between questions may indicate that interviewees have more to say. Do not rush them. Give them the chance to answer you in full.

13. Check periodically to see that your understanding of the interviewee's problems and situations is correct by offering a concise summary of the essential details.

14. Summarize, toward the end of the interview, the salient aspects of the information you have obtained.

15. Record the information you obtain accurately, either during the interview proper or shortly thereafter. This is necessary because short-term memory is unreliable. Keep your notes brief, and try not to lose eye contact with the interviewee for too long if you take notes during the interview.

16. Evaluate the information you obtain and decide whether you need follow-up interviews.

17. End the interview in the same friendly manner in which it began, and, no matter what the nature of the interview, always try to leave the interviewee with his or her dignity and self-esteem intact.

No matter how well you have planned the interview, each interviewee will present a new challenge. No individual is predictable. Even the most carefully laid plans may need to be changed. You must be flexible and prepared to deal with unanticipated problems. You also must judge how much information to obtain during an interview session and whether to schedule additional interview sessions. Recognize that there is no one absolute way to conduct the interview, as alternative ways of asking questions can be equally effective in soliciting information.

Listen carefully to what the interviewee says. Interpret and assess what is significant, but do not accept everything as literal truth; remember, however, that it may be the interviewee's truth (Stevenson, 1960). Let the interviewee's values, culture, attitudes, and developmental level guide your interpretations.

Sometimes the interviewee's emotions are congruent with his or her words and sometimes they are not. *What interviewees say is important, but how they act and speak are equally important.* Consequently, you will need to attend to both the interviewee's verbal and nonverbal communications.

You will have difficulties as an interviewer if you fail to express interest and warmth, uncover the anxieties of the interviewee, recognize when the anxieties of the interviewee are being exposed too rapidly, or understand the cognitive level and culture of the interviewee. *However, failures are more likely to arise from defects in attitude than from technical difficulties* (Stevenson, 1960). Interviewees usually are forgiving, unless interviewers show lack of interest or lack of kindness.

To be successful as an interviewer, you must know yourself, trust your ideas, be willing to make mistakes, and, above all, have a genuine desire to help the interviewee (Benjamin, 1981). You must be careful not to present yourself as all-knowing; instead, reveal your humanness to the interviewee. This means being honest with the interviewee and with yourself. Let the interviewee know that you don't have all the answers and that solutions may be difficult to find.

A good interview takes careful planning, skillful execution, and good organization; it is purposeful and goal-oriented. The success of the interview ultimately rests on your ability to guide the interview successfully. For this, you need practice, which is best acquired by interviewing volunteer children and adults before interviewing clients. Videotape and study yourself conducting interviews. Also ask skilled interviewers to review the videotapes and give you feedback about your interviewing techniques. Role play various types of interviews. Also observe how skilled interviewers conduct interviews, and study their techniques. These activities will help you develop good interviewing skills.

FACTORS INFLUENCING THE INTERVIEW

The interview is affected by *interviewer and interviewee characteristics* (for example, physical, cognitive, and affective factors), *message components* (for example, language, nonverbal cues, and sensory cues), and *interview climate* (for example, physical, social, temporal, and psychological factors), as shown in Figure 2-1. Your task is to consider how these factors interact when you conduct the interview and when you evaluate the information you obtain in the interview.

EXTERNAL FACTORS AND ATMOSPHERE

Conduct the interview in a private, quiet room that is free from distractions. Select furniture that fits the interviewee. For example, use a low chair and table for a young child, and arrange the space so that there is no barrier between you and the child. For an older child, you can use standard office furniture.

Keep interruptions to a minimum or avoid them entirely. Because telephone interruptions are particularly troublesome, arrange to have calls held at the switchboard or reception desk, or unplug your phone. If you must answer the phone, inform the caller that you are busy and will call back. Obviously, you should not be glancing at your mail, eating lunch, or constantly looking at your watch during the interview. Begin the interview at the scheduled time. If you need another session to complete the interview, tell the interviewee. You might say "Mrs. Smith, we have about 5 minutes left. Since we need more time, let's schedule another meeting next Tuesday at the same time, if that is convenient for you." Interview the parent(s) without small children in the room. Small children can be distracting, and you need to have the full attention of the parent. Ask the parent(s) to arrange for child care, or arrange for someone to watch the child while you interview the parent.

FORMING IMPRESSIONS

When you and the interviewee first meet, both of you will form initial impressions of each other. These impressions will blend into other ones as the interview progresses. The ebb and flow of the interaction will continually modify the impressions both of you have. Be aware of signs of psychological disturbance and signs of psychological health that the interviewee shows and of how the interviewee affects you (such as by bringing out compassion, pity, attraction, irritation, or discomfort). Recognizing these factors will help you regulate the pace of the interview and give you some appreciation of how the interviewee affects others. You can form accurate impressions of the interviewee by being a skilled listener and observer and by remaining objective.

LISTENING

Good listening skills are not easy to acquire. Sometimes the interviewer becomes so preoccupied with what should be asked next that she or he fails to listen to what the inter-

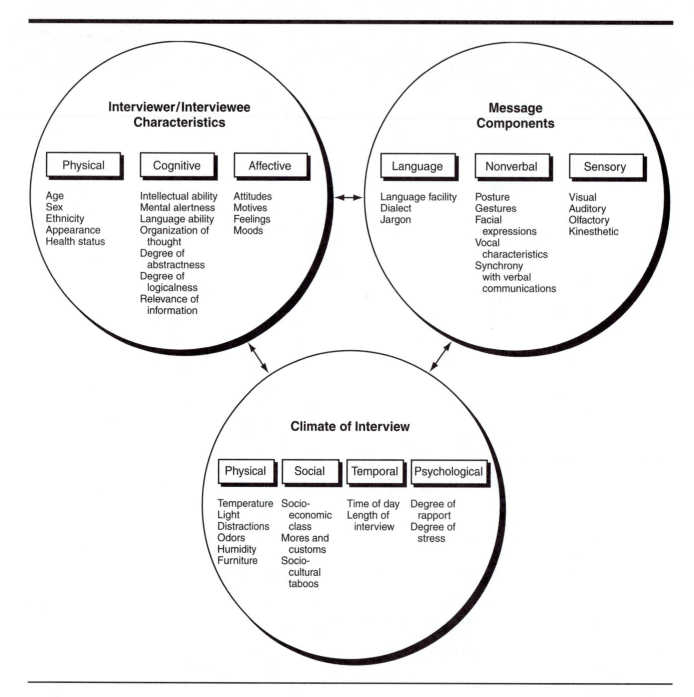

Figure 2-1. Factors influencing the interview.

viewee is saying. This is especially true of novice interviewers. Effective listening is hampered when the interviewer prematurely evaluates and judges everything the interviewee says, interrupts the interviewee before he or she has enough time to develop an idea, is preoccupied and fails to respond to the interviewee's concerns, and is uncomfortable with silence (Downs, Smeyak, & Martin, 1980).

Following are some steps you can take to become an effective listener:

1. Make sure that you have no auditory or visual deficits that will interfere with your ability to conduct an interview.
2. Attend to your personal needs, such as eating and drinking properly and going to the toilet.
3. Maintain interest in and involvement with the interviewee.
4. Concentrate on the interviewee's communications.
5. Link the information you obtain from the interviewee.

Here are some some characteristics of effective listeners and ineffective listeners (adapted from Gratus, 1988).

EFFECTIVE LISTENERS

1. They have sufficient empathy to create the best surroundings, which permit the interviewees to give their best.
2. They have prepared themselves so that they have the freedom and confidence to devote time and energy to listening to what is being said by the interviewee rather than worrying about whether they are asking the right questions to get the information they require.
3. They have worked out in advance the main questions they intend to ask and the order in which to ask them so that they can impose on the interview a structure to which the interviewee can respond and with which the interviewee feels at ease.
4. They have cultivated the ability to listen behind the words to catch nuances of meaning, words emphasized, hesitations, uncertainties, omissions, and inconsistencies that tell them more than just the words do.
5. They have the persistence and patience to probe the interviewee with further questions until the interviewee understands that the omissions and evasions have been noted and that further information must be forthcoming to satisfy the interviewer.
6. They have the maturity and insight to remain objective and not to impose their own views on what the interviewee is saying, while recognizing that the events and experiences related by the interviewee have been subjectively interpreted by the interviewee.
7. They talk as little as possible, concentrate as much as possible, and show the interviewee by expressions and gestures that they are taking everything in.

INEFFECTIVE LISTENERS

1. They hear what they want to hear, not what the interviewee is saying.
2. They listen only to those details that interest them and switch off for the rest.
3. They are unable to put themselves in the interviewee's shoes and cannot really understand what feelings the interviewee is expressing.
4. They are too sympathetic to the interviewee's point of view and so cannot listen objectively to what the interviewee is saying.
5. They are too involved with their own thoughts and problems to concentrate on those of the interviewee.
6. They have not prepared themselves well enough in advance, and so they are thinking up the next question while they should be listening.
7. They are easily distracted by the interviewee's mannerisms, dress, accent, and so on.
8. They are uncomfortable with silence, lack patience, and will not let the interviewee begin or finish answering properly.

Listening to the Interviewee

Much of the art of interviewing lies in the ability to listen creatively and empathically and to probe skillfully beneath the surface of the communication. *The ability to listen is the key factor in the interview* (Benjamin, 1981). Being a good listener means being free of preoccupations and able to give the interviewees your full attention. A good listener is attentive not only to *what* the interviewee says but also to *how* she or he says it—such as the interviewee's tones, expressions, and gestures—and to physiological cues, such as pupil dilation, tremors, and blushing. A good listener is aware of what is *not* said—feelings or facts lurking behind what is spoken. This requires use of the "inner ear" as well as the outer one. A good listener also uses empathic skills to judge when to say something that will relieve the interviewee's discomfort.

Listening to Yourself

Being a good listener also means listening to yourself. Become attuned to your thoughts, feelings, and actions, and learn how to deal with them appropriately during the interview. Often you will need to suppress your reactions so that you can remain objective. If you have videotaped the interview, study the videotape to see how your needs, values, and standards emerged during the interview and how they affected your interview techniques and the hypotheses you formed about the interviewee.

Following are some questions you might ask yourself about your role as an interviewer:

- Do you recognize how your standards affect the judgments you make? For example, do you think that it is acceptable for an adolescent to be lazy because you were lazy as a 12-year-old? If so, do you say to yourself "Why can't these parents be like my parents and leave her alone?"
- Can you determine the basis for your hypotheses? For example, if you hypothesize that a mother is hiding some facts about an issue, is your hypothesis based on what she said, the way she looked when she said it, the way she reacted to your questions, or a combination of these factors?
- Are you aware of the style or tone of your communications? For example, if are you speaking more rapidly with one interviewee than with others, why are you doing so? Or if you are speaking in a condescending manner to an interviewee, why are you doing so?
- Are you aware of your emotional blindspots, such as sensitive words or concepts that may distract you from listening in an unbiased manner? For example, do you flinch when you hear the term *homosexual*? Do you panic when you hear the word *rape* because you have been raped? What can you do about these reactions so that they don't interfere with your ability to listen effectively?

A good listener is not only popular everywhere, but after a while he knows something.

—Wilson Mizner

SENDING NONVERBAL MESSAGES

Body Language

Be aware of your body language, including your facial expressions; gestures; the way you sit, hold your head, and direct your eyes; the small vocal sounds you make; and other nonverbal mannerisms, such as frowning, puckering lips, biting fingernails, cracking knuckles, tapping a foot or finger, twisting hair or a paper clip, rocking, scratching, or shaking your head. Interviewers often do these things when they are anxious or uncomfortable, and they may be unaware that they are doing them. *Your body language conveys meaning to the interviewee.* Monitor it and use it to promote your aims (see Table 2-1). A well-timed smile or nod of the head conveys to the interviewee your interest and attention. You also want to avoid body language that sends negative messages. For example, frowning or shaking your head may impede the interviewee from talking further. Also avoid distracting mannerisms, such as cracking knuckles, as they may

Bent Offerings   by Don Addis

By permission of Don Addis and Creators Syndicate.

cause the interviewee to lose track of what he or she wants to say. Because idiosyncratic mannerisms may distract interviewees and usually serve no purpose during the interview, eliminate them or at least reduce their occurrence.

Eye Contact

Eye contact is important. It helps interviewees gauge the extent of your interest. You want to maintain eye contact with the interviewees but not stare or gaze intently at them. By occasionally looking away and then resuming your eye contact, you give interviewees some breathing room, especially when they are having trouble responding to a question.

Appearance

Dress appropriately and maintain acceptable grooming. You do not want to be too formal or too casual, or to present an unkempt appearance.

ANALYTICAL LISTENING

The ability to analyze the responses of the interviewee critically as you listen—termed analytical listening—*is an important interviewing skill.* Your questions are designed to obtain information from the interviewee. As the interviewee gives a response, immediately evaluate it and follow it up with an appropriate comment or question. For example, your evaluation may tell you that the interviewee's response was unintelligible, irrelevant, inadequate, minimally appropriate, or appropriate. Based on your evaluation, you decide what to say next. The sequence is

questioning → listening → analyzing → further questioning or clarifying

Purposes Served by Analytical Listening

Analytical listening serves several purposes (Downs et al., 1980). It will help you understand the frame of reference of the interviewee, reduce the interviewee's emotional tension, convey to the interviewee a sense of his or her importance, give the interviewee time to refine his or her thoughts, and relate effectively to the interviewee. Good analytical listening skills include getting the main ideas, facts, and details; understanding the connotative meanings of words; identifying affect and attitudes appropriately; discriminating between fact and imagination; recognizing discrepancies; judging the relevancy of communications; and making valid inferences.

Recognizing Interviewees' Response Sets

Interviewees have certain ways or patterns of answering questions, or what is called *response sets* (or *response*

Table 2-1
Illustrations of Positive and Negative Interviewer Nonverbal Behaviors

Positive nonverbal behavior	Negative nonverbal behavior
Facial expressions	
Warm, inviting smile	Cold, frowning, frozen, rigid, or "poker-faced" expression
Good eye contact (be aware that some cultures find this particular behavior offensive)	Avoidance of or poor eye contact: eyes downcast, peering, staring, darting around the room, fixating
Eyes at same level as interviewee's eyes	Eyes at level higher or lower than interviewee's eyes
Appropriately varied and animated facial expressions	Lifting eyebrow critically, nodding head excessively, yawning
Mouth relaxed; occasional smiles	Inappropriate slight smile, pursing or biting lips
Body posture	
Body posture oriented to encourage interpersonal interaction	Body posture oriented to discourage interpersonal interaction
Leaning slightly toward the interviewee	Laid-back, or "propped-up cadaver," look, feet on desk
Facing the interviewee squarely	Not facing the other squarely, giving the cold shoulder
Relaxed active movement, conveying interest in the interviewee	Rigid posture, communicating cold, impersonal attitude
Settling back in chair, indicating willingness to listen	Sitting on the edge of chair as if ready to jump to feet
Sitting with arms and legs uncrossed, communicating openness	Sitting with arms and legs crossed, communicating closedness
Establishing optimal comfort zone between interviewer and interviewee (3–4 feet in the United States, although there are cultural differences about the preferred space)	Distance between interviewer and interviewee too close or too far (comfort zone violated)
Vocal behaviors	
Warm, interesting, natural voice	Cold, impersonal, lacking interest in the interviewee, mumbling, monotonic voice, halting speech
Appropriate volume and pitch	Voice too loud or too quiet
Appropriate rate of speech	Speech too fast, too abrupt, too terse, too animated, or too slow
Fluency in language use	Stammering, halting speech, hesitant speech
Receptive noises ("umm hmm," "ah ha," etc.)	Clearing throat repeatedly, nervous laughter
Silence suggesting the interviewee has time to think or elaborate	Silence causing undue anxiety
Interrupting when appropriate to clarify, summarize, or reflect meanings	Interrupting frequently and inappropriately
Gestures, mannerisms, and motor behavior	
Outstretched arm or welcoming wave (culturally dependent)	Cold, impersonal greeting; brusque seating gesture
Firm handshake	Limp or crushing handshake
Cessation of activity when interviewee enters	Continuing to look at papers on desk or to write when interviewee enters
Closing door to indicate privacy	Allowing door to be open
Unplugging phone	Not unplugging phone
Engaging in no distracting gestures	Looking repeatedly at watch, chain-smoking cigarettes, chewing gum, playing or fidgeting with objects, cracking knuckles, clicking ballpoint pen, running hands through hair, rubbing or scratching body, yawning, constantly shifting body position, swinging legs, crossing and uncrossing legs or arms, nodding head continuously, twitching nervously
Taking minimal notes and continuing to look at interviewee	Taking excessive notes and seldom looking at interviewee

Note. Positive and negative nonverbal behaviors do not apply to all cultural groups.
Source: Adapted from Zima (1983).

styles). Some response sets simply reflect interviewees' preferred styles of responding to specific questions or to open-ended questions; these styles may not affect the accuracy of the information. Examples are giving short answers, giving long answers, giving answers only when one is very certain of the answers, answering questions only when one fully understands the questions, and thinking about the answers before giving them.

Other response sets, however, may affect the accuracy of the information. Examples include the following:

- agreeing with all or most questions (that is, saying "yes" to "yes-no" questions, called *acquiescent response style*)
- disagreeing with all or most questions (that is, saying "no" to "yes-no" questions)
- picking the last alternative when presented with two or more alternatives
- picking the first alternative when presented with two or more alternatives
- slanting answers in a negative direction
- slanting answers in a positive direction
- answering in a socially desirable manner
- answering in a socially undesirable manner
- giving answers even when one is uncertain of the answers in order to please the interviewer
- answering questions even when one does not understand the questions in order to please the interviewer
- answering questions impulsively and then recanting the answers

You should question the accuracy of the information when interviewees disregard the content of the questions or when they seriously distort their responses.

Be alert to the interviewee's response set. When you have a hunch that the interviewee's response set may be affecting the accuracy of his or her replies, introduce questions that will help you determine whether this is so. Here are some suggestions (Horton & Kochurka, 1995).

1. If the interviewee always answers "yes" to "yes-no" questions, introduce questions to which you know that "yes" is the wrong answer. For example, ask "Do both your parents live at home?" when only one parent lives at home, or ask "Do you have a sister?" when the interviewee has one brother.
2. If the interviewee always selects the last alternative in a series of alternatives, frame questions with an incorrect response as the last alternative. For example, if you know the interviewee was hit on the face, ask "Did he hit you on the hand, the face, or the arm?", or after the interviewee says a woman touched her but she can't say where, and you know she was touched on her privates, ask "Did she touch you on your privates, your back, or your arm?"

Be wary of interviewees' replies when they always select the same response alternative. When you interview children with developmental disabilities, be particularly alert to response sets that may affect the accuracy of the information (Horton & Kochurka, 1995). Children with developmental disabilities may be deficient in assertiveness skills and may be more prone to acquiesce by answering "yes" to "yes-no" questions.

Evaluating Whether You Can Get All the Information

You must judge whether you have obtained all the information the interviewee is willing to tell you and whether the interviewee's responses tell you all you need to know (Gorden, 1975). For example, if you ask an interviewee to tell you about his family and he simply says that they are "okay," you might want to probe further: "Well, can you tell me about how you get along with them?" Usually, you will need to ask follow-up questions.

The following example illustrates the importance of flexibility in the interview. The interviewer tried to learn about the interviewee's ability to concentrate but appeared to reach a dead end. However, by shifting focus, the interviewer learned some facts (Mannuzza, Fyer, & Klein, 1993, pp. 160–161, with changes in notation).

IR: What has your concentration been like recently?
IE: I don't understand what you're asking.
IR: Can you read an article in the paper or watch a TV program right through?
IE: I don't read the papers, and my television has been broken for several months.
IR: Do your thoughts drift off so that you don't take things in?
IE: Take things in? Maybe. I'm not sure if I know what you mean.
IR: Well, let's turn to something else. What do you do in your spare time?
IE: I play a lot of baseball.
IR: What position?
IE: Left field.
IR: Do you ever have difficulty focusing on the ball as it's coming toward you?
IE: Not too often.
IR: How often do you drop the ball, or let it get past you?
IE: Well, that happens a lot. It's usually because I'm thinking about other things when I'm out in the field.
IR: Do you have any problem keeping your mind on the game, or remembering the score from one inning to the next?
IE: Yes. I have to keep on looking at the score board. My teammates always complain that I'm not paying attention. They think that I don't care about the game, but that's not true.

Interviewees must recognize that you are evaluating their communications and organizing them into some coherent theme. *By conveying an attitude of critical evaluation—interest in precise facts, concern for correct inferences, and desire to establish an accurate sequence of events—you show interviewees that you want to get beneath the surface of the communications and away from vague, superficial, and incomplete responses.* Analytical listening also is involved in formulating probing questions, a topic discussed later in the chapter.

Staying Attuned

Toward the end of the interview, you can ask about important areas you did not discuss, clarify previously discussed material, make other needed comments, or invite questions that the interviewee might have. Listening analytically will help you recognize when there are gaps in the information you have. For example, when interviewing recent immigrant parents, you may realize that you have failed to ask whether the referred child was born in the United States or how old the referred child was when the family arrived in the United States. To know what information is missing, you will need to be attuned to what you learned during the interview and what information you still need to obtain. You don't want to wait until the interview is over to evaluate what you have learned, because if you do you won't know what you still need to ask; instead, continuously evaluate the information you obtain.

Treat every word as having the potential of unlocking the mystery of the subject's way of viewing the world.
—Robert C. Bogdan and Sari K. Biklen

OBSERVATION GUIDELINES

Besides attending to what the interviewee says, you will want to attend to his or her appearance and nonverbal and verbal behavior. The observational guidelines that follow do not allow for the interviewee's ethnicity or culture; you also should consider how ethnic and cultural factors may affect your observations (see Chapters 8 and 9 for information about culture and ethnicity). Note that some behaviors are difficult to classify. For example, vocal behaviors can be considered nonverbal or verbal, depending on one's preference.

Observing Personal Appearance

Make note of the interviewee's height, weight, clothing, hairstyle, grooming, and general appearance. For example, observe whether the interviewee's dress is clean, neat, disheveled, dowdy, dirty, atypical, or appropriate; whether the interviewee's breath smells ordinary or from alcohol or another substance; whether the interviewee has body odors; whether there are abrasions or needle marks on the inter-

viewee's forearms or inside his or her elbows; or whether there are signs of malnutrition, such as being underweight, having stunted growth, being lethargic, having limited attention span, or having eyes that lack luster.

These observations may give you clues about various conditions, such as bulimia, anorexia, substance abuse, medical illness, and neglect. The impressions you receive will guide you in conducting the interview, in formulating hypotheses, and in determining possible areas to probe. For example, if an interviewee reeks from alcohol, but he or she denies drinking, consider probing the inconsistency further. By attending to the interviewee's physical appearance, you also may gain clues about his or her attitude toward himself or herself and the group he or she belongs to or emulates. The way children dress may be a reflection of their parents' values.

Observing Nonverbal Behavior

You have recently read about body language that you, as an interviewer, might show during the interview. You also, of course, need to be aware of the interviewee's body language (see Table 2-2). Body language may tell you about the interviewee's (a) moods, (b) openness for communication or distance from you, (c) amount and range of expressive gestures, and (d) idiosyncratic or symptomatic patterns of body movements (Atakan & Cooper, 1989). Things to look for in the interviewee's body language are

- *facial expressions* (for example, alert, angry, anxious, averting eye contact, bland, calm, distressed, drooping eyelids, grimacing, habitually perplexed, making eye contact, sad, scowling, seductive, sleepy, smiling, staring into space, tic, vacant)
- *posture* (for example, crossing and recrossing legs, erect, legs and arms drawn close to trunk, legs and arms outstretched, recumbent, relaxed, rigid, slouched, stooped, tense)
- *gestures, mannerisms, and motor behavior* (for example, abnormal staring; agitation; aimless movements or odd stylized movements or acts suggesting special meaning or purpose; biting lips; clumsiness; clutching; finger pointing; fist clenching; flapping hands; frowning; gaze avoidance; grimacing; hyperactivity; hypoactivity; inappropriate posturing; licking lips; lip pouting; nodding head; nose twitching; pacing; picking at or touching parts of body; playing with clothing or jewelry; pounding fists; rapid movements; repetitive movements; responses related to autonomic activity reflecting tension, such as changes in skin color, sweating, breathing noises, sounds of intestinal action, smacking of lips, and pupil dilation; rituals such as touching or counting things or staying still with arms folded to avoid germs, dirt, and so forth; rocking; rolling eyes to ceiling; rubbing; scratching; screaming; self-stimulation; shrugging shoulders; slow movements; squirming; stereo-

Table 2-2
Examples of the Meanings of Nonverbal Behaviors

Nonverbal behavior	Possible meaning
1. Direct eye contact	Readiness for interpersonal communication, attentiveness, staring
2. Staring at or fixating on a person or object	Confrontational defiance, preoccupation, possible rigidness or anxiety
3. Tight lips (pursed together)	Stress, determination, anger, hostility
4. Shaking head from left to right	Disagreement, disapproval, disbelief
5. Slouching in chair, turned away from interviewer	Sadness, discouragement, resistance to discussion
6. Trembling, fidgety hands	Anxiety, anger, fear of self-disclosure
7. Foot-tapping	Impatience, anxiety
8. Whispering	Difficulty in revealing material, hoarse throat
9. Silence	Reluctance to talk, preoccupation, shyness, fear, waiting
10. Clammy hands, shallow breathing, pupil dilation, paleness, blushing, rashes on neck	Fearfulness, arousal—positive (excitement, interest) or negative (anxiety, embarrassment), drug intoxication

Note. These meanings do not hold for all cultural groups. Also note that some nonverbal behaviors may suggest more than one thing.
Source: Adapted from Cormier and Cormier (1979).

typic motion; stumbling movements; tics; tremors; trying to touch you; twitches; yawning; waving arms; winking or eye blinking)
• *vocal behaviors* (for example, saying "ah-uh"; barking; clacking; coughing; saying "eeee"; grunting; gurgling; hawking; hissing; saying repetitive or meaningless words, phrases, or statements; screeching; sniffling; spitting; sucking; saying "uh-uh"; whistling)
• *senses* (for example, looking closely at things; straining to see; straining to hear)

Here are some specific *voice and speech qualities* that you should note (Nay, 1979):

• *loudness or speech intensity* (appropriate or inappropriate—too loud, too soft, too unvarying)
• *tone* (appropriate or inappropriate—expressionless/dull)
• *pitch of voice* (appropriate or inappropriate—too low, too high, monotonous)
• *pace* (appropriate or inappropriate—too slow, too fast, monotonous, jerky)
• *ease of speech* (relaxed, hesitant, stumbling, or blocked)
• *spontaneity* (spontaneous or guarded)
• *reaction time* (appropriate, too slow, or too quick)
• *relevance of speech production* (relevant or irrelevant)
• *manner of speaking* (relaxed, pedantic, formal, or too familiar)
• *organization of speech* (organized or disorganized)
• *clarity of speech* (clear, mumbled, slurred, or too clipped)
• *voice quality* (pleasant, harsh, hoarse, hypernasal, or hyponasal)
• *fluency* (smooth; consistent; repetitious; revises; uses incomplete phrases, broken words, or prolonged sounds)

Signs of speech (and language) difficulties include

• failure to utter any sounds
• a delay of more than a year in the appearance of individual speech sounds
• use of vowel sounds to the exclusion of most other sounds
• being embarrassed or disturbed by speech
• a consistently monotonous, inaudible, or poor-quality voice
• consistent use of a pitch inappropriate for the child's age
• noticeable hypernasality or lack of nasal resonance
• unusual confusions, reversals, or telegraphic speech (a type of speech in which connectives, prepositions, modifiers, and refinements of language are omitted)

When you observe any of these deviations, refer the child for a speech evaluation.

If you observe voice or speech deviations, consider why they occurred and whether you need to recommend a speech, medical, psychological, or neuropsychological evaluation. Deviations such as omitting sounds (for example, saying "ing" for "thing"), substituting sounds (for example, saying "den" for "then"), or distorting sounds suggest an articulation disorder. Other deviations, such as saying "dad" for "pad" or "run" for "bun," suggest difficulty in distinguishing sounds. In still other cases, voice or speech deviations may suggest anxiety, inattention, auditory sensory difficulties, or brain injury.

In observing nonverbal behavior, be aware of any changes in the interviewee's facial expressions, posture, gestures, mannerisms, motor behavior, and vocal behavior. For example, is the interviewee first alert and later sleepy or first tense and later relaxed? Or does the interviewee speak in a low-pitched voice sometimes and a high-pitched voice at other times? And what content might be associated with the changes in the interviewee's nonverbal behavior? For example, did any topics result in changes in the interviewee's voice or tempo of speech?

Read each statement and describe what the gestures might mean. Then compare your answers with the suggested answers that follow and with those of your classmates. The first 10 examples, with minor adaptations, are from Okun (1982).

1. A father walks into your office, takes off his coat, loosens his tie, sits, and puts his feet up on a chair.
2. An adolescent walks into your office, sits erect, and clasps her arms across her chest before saying a word.
3. An adolescent rests her cheek on her hand, strokes her chin, cocks her head slightly to one side, and nods deeply.
4. A father walks into your office, sits as far away as he can, folds his arms, crosses his legs, tilts the chair backwards, and looks over your head.
5. A child refuses to talk and avoids eye contact with you.
6. A child gazes at you and stretches out her hands with her palms up.
7. A child quickly covers his mouth with his hand after revealing some sensitive material.
8. An adolescent holds one arm behind her back and clenches her hand tightly while using the other hand to grip her wrist or arm.
9. A mother crosses her legs and moves her foot in a slight kicking motion, while simultaneously drumming her fingers.
10. An adolescent sits forward in his chair, tilting his head, and nodding at intervals.
11. An adolescent rubs the back of her neck.

Suggested Answers

1. Relaxed, comfortable, confident, feels in control of the situation, not taking situation seriously, situation not important, may not care, trying to intimidate
2. Uncomfortable, anxious, hostile and defiant, defensive, upset, it has taken some effort to come to talk with you
3. Listening, thinking, paying attention, eager to please, seductive, reflective, looks interested
4. Uncomfortable, avoidant, resistant, anxious, fearful, defensive, doesn't want to be there, forced to come, feels intimidated
5. Uncooperative, hostile, angry, negative, intimidated, fearful, shy, anxious, doesn't want to be there, forced to come, may be showing sign of respect (For example, if the child is Native American or Hispanic American, he or she may avoid eye contact but not necessarily refuse to talk.)
6. Helpless, wants help, feels at a loss, shows trust, wants to be comforted
7. Regret, trying to take back what he said, wishes he hadn't said it, perhaps embarrassed, told not to say something and said it, realizes it was inappropriate or dangerous
8. Extremely anxious and tense, keeping herself there
9. Bored, somewhat anxious, impatient, not in agreement, wants to finish

10. Attentive, interested, eager to please, might be listening, wants your trust
11. Soreness, muscle tension, stress, conflict, tired, wants to leave

---

Observing Verbal Behavior

As you listen to the interviewee, note such things as the following:

- the type of communications (see Figure 2-2)
- the content of the speech
- where hesitations occur
- the style and eloquence of the language
- the logic of the communications
- how questions are responded to
- how often the interviewee asks to have questions repeated
- what material is spontaneously brought forth
- how the interviewee refers to herself or himself and to other persons
- whether any topics distract the interviewee or cause her or him to attempt to distract you or to have you change to another topic
- any unusual remarks
- whether the communications are consistent with those of the average interviewee of the same age, level of development, ethnicity, and culture

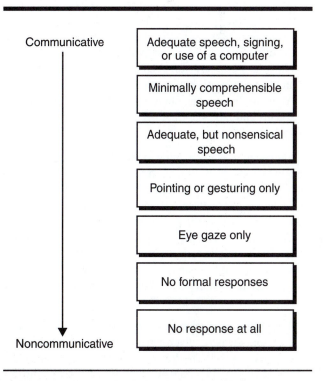

Figure 2-2. A continuum of communicative language.

You will want to note, for example, whether the interviewee talks at all, babbles, uses simple words, imitates isolated words, spontaneously uses isolated words to communicate needs or desires or to name objects, spontaneously uses phrases to communicate needs or desires, imitates complete sentences, or spontaneously uses sentences to communicate needs or desires.

Language distortions may be related to psychological disorders or to brain damage. For example, interviewees who cannot complete a train of thought (blocking) or who often repeat what you say (echolalia) may have a disturbance in thinking; even slightly unusual remarks may suggest lapses in judgment, self-control, or thinking. Other indications of disturbed processing include confabulations (for example, bizarre stories), stereotyped phrases (for example, repeating a pet phrase over and over), misnamings, digression (caused, for example, by accidental associations), mispronunciations, or difficulties in initiating a conversation. It is unusual, for example, for an interviewee to refer to himself or herself as "we," "he," "she," "they," or "it." In all instances, you will need to consider the entire case history before you arrive at a diagnostic impression.

As children develop, language skills should be developing. Following are some possible indicators of language problems:

1. At about 18 months, the child makes no attempt to say meaningful words.
2. At about 24 months, the child fails to use phrases communicatively, has unintelligible speech, and uses language inappropriately.
3. At about 3 to 5 years, the child shows lack of speech, uses unintelligible speech, and fails to speak in sentences.
4. At about 5 to 6 years, the child substitutes easy sounds for difficult ones, consistently drops word endings, uses faulty sentence structure, exhibits noticeable nonfluency, and has abnormal rhythm, rate, and inflection of speech.
5. At about 7 years, the child distorts, omits, or substitutes sounds and has abnormal rhythm, rate, and inflection of sounds.

Language usage is a guide to the interviewee's personality and thought processes, as are the tempo, quality, and content of the interviewee's verbal responses. To help you evaluate the interviewee's language style and communication skills, look over the questions in Table 2-3.

Communication patterns also may give you valuable leads. These include association of ideas, shifts in conversation, opening and closing sentences, recurrent references, inconsistencies and gaps, and concealed meanings (Garrett, 1982).

- *Association of ideas* refers to when the interviewee deviates from the particular topic under discussion and begins to free associate. The free association may provide clues about feelings or concerns that the interviewee did not express directly.

- *Shifts in conversation* may be best understood by examining what the interviewee was saying just before the topic changed. The shifts may provide clues about what is troubling the interviewee or reveal personal preoccupations.
- *Opening and closing sentences* may be of special significance. Initial remarks may reveal how the interviewee feels about being interviewed, and closing remarks may reveal what the interview meant to the interviewee. Occasionally, the initial topic discussed by the interviewee may be of special importance in his or her life.
- *Recurrent references* or themes that run throughout the interview may provide clues about a major source of concern or significant attitudes of the interviewee.
- *Inconsistencies and gaps* may suggest guilt, confusion, ambivalence, or avoidance.
- *Concealed meanings,* which the interviewee may reveal by slips of the tongue, rationalizations, or ambivalent questions, may suggest areas that need to be explored further.

Following are examples of unusual remarks made by adolescents that may suggest some form of thinking difficulty (Weiner, 1982, pp. 80, 82–83, with changes in notation).

Example 1. The interview was with a 17-year-old high school senior.

IR: What are your future plans?
IE: I plan to enter college with a football scholarship.
IR: Did you play football in high school?
IE: No, I never played football because I wanted to avoid risk of injury and save myself for the big time.

Comment: Expecting to play college football on a scholarship without having had any prior experience with the sport reflects poor judgment and possibly delusional thinking.

Example 2. The interview was with a 13-year-old girl.

IR: If you had three wishes, what would they be?
IE: A motorcycle, an eagle, and a hawk.
IR: Tell me about your wishes.
IE: Well, the motorcycle is nice. I could use the eagle to stop the school bus if I ever wanted to get someone off. And I could use the hawk for delivering messages.

Comment: The uselessness of a motorcycle to a 13-year-old who could not be licensed to drive it suggests the unusual quality of her first wish. Her explanations of her wishes for an eagle and a hawk are strange and unrealistic.

Example 3. The interview was with a 14-year-old boy.

IR: How are you?
IE: I'm going on 14.

Comment: The response might be irrelevant or tangential, or it could indicate that he didn't hear the question appropriately.

Table 2-3
Evaluating Interviewees' Language Styles and Communication Skills

1. Does the interviewee seem to understand what you are saying?
2. Does the interviewee understand gestures?
3. Does the interviewee use gestures or mime to communicate?
4. Does the interviewee appropriately use nonverbal behaviors when speaking?
5. Does the interviewee attend to your face or watch your lips when you speak?
6. Does the interviewee understand verbal communications when his or her back is turned to you?
7. Does the interviewee talk?
8. Does the interviewee have normal vocalizations?
9. Does the interviewee have normal articulation?
10. What is the usual tempo of the interviewee's responses (for example, quick or slow)?
11. Does the interviewee grope for words?
12. Does the interviewee substitute descriptions for precise words?
13. Does the interviewee avoid certain topics?
14. Is the interviewee sometimes enthusiastic and at other times despondent?
15. What is the output of the interviewee's communications (that is, approximate number of words spoken per minute)?
16. How much effort does the interviewee need to produce speech? (For example, note any visible struggles, facial grimaces, body posturing, deep breathing, or hand gestures.)
17. What is the interviewee's typical phrase length (for example, single words, short phrases, or complete sentences)?
18. If the interviewee makes errors, what can the errors be attributed to? (For example, do they reflect problems with memory, remembering what you asked, expressive language, receptive language, fluency, organization, pronunciation, or sentence structure?)
19. Is the interviewee's speech melodic?
20. Does the interviewee take time before responding?
21. Does the interviewee think aloud, or does he or she give only the final answer?
22. How competent is the interviewee in the use of words and grammar? (For example, does the interviewee's language contain objects, actions, and events in a variety of relationships?)
23. Does the interviewee echo what you say or use words inappropriately?
24. Are the interviewee's utterances appropriate for the context?
25. Does the interviewee use words for social communication?
26. Does the interviewee express ideas clearly?
27. Does the interviewee distinguish between relevant and irrelevant information?
28. Does the interviewee verbalize several possibilities and perspectives?
29. Does the interviewee make self-critical responses?
30. Can the interviewee assume the role or viewpoint of another?
31. Does the interviewee (if a child) use imitation and symbolization in play?
32. Does the interviewee (if a child) while playing respond appropriately to the speaker?
33. What spoken language difficulties does the interviewee show, if any?
34. If the interviewee has language difficulties, do they affect reading, writing, and speaking?
35. Does the interviewee take turns appropriately in conversations?

Note. You must consider the interviewee's age in making your evaluation.

Example 4. The interview was with a 15-year-old boy.

IR: What kinds of things do you like to do?
IE: I like to play basketball; I'm a good aimer.
IR: You're a good shot?
IE: Yes, last summer at camp we shot at targets with real bullets.

Comment: This is a concrete answer that shows possible confusion in thinking.

Example 5. The interview was with a 13-year-old boy.

IE: The kids at school tease me and call me all kinds of names.
IR: Like what?

IE: Oh, like "stupid" and "mental" and "retarded" and like that.
IR: Do they also call your brother those names? (Reference is to interviewee's younger brother in the same school.)
IE: No, no one calls me "brother."

Comment: This is a concrete answer that shows possible problems in thinking or in hearing.

Observing Mood, Affect, and Attitude

Your observations of the interviewee's nonverbal and verbal behavior also will provide you with information about his or her mood, affect, and attitude. You will want to note, for example, whether the interviewee was cooperative or uncooperative, hostile or friendly, active or passive, calm or agitated, fearful or accepting, happy or sad, withdrawn or expansive, or attentive or inattentive. You will also want to note to what degree the interviewee attends to things in his or her environment and for how long; whether the interviewee stops talking or changes the subject when he or she is distracted by trivial noises; whether the interviewee seems to have blank spells (that is, suddenly stops speaking for a few seconds or longer); whether the interviewee asks to have questions repeated; and whether the interviewee withdraws his or her attention from the interview by moving lips soundlessly, looking around, giggling, or making other gestures that suggest hallucinations.

Also consider how the interviewee's mood and affect relate to the contents of the communications.

1. Observe whether the interviewee's tone is congruent with the content. For example, does the interviewee seem depressed, anxious, or angry but give responses that suggest a lack of concern about matters that would trouble other people more deeply?

2. Observe the interviewee's activity level and how it changes as the interview proceeds. For example, is the interviewee active initially but later inactive?

3. Observe whether the interviewee's affect is appropriate to the content of the communication. For example, is the interviewee frowning while discussing how happy she or he feels?

Observing Behaviors Related to Physical and Neurological Development

Observing the posture, gait, fine and gross motor coordination, handedness, speech, and quality and tone of voice of the interviewee will provide you with information about his or her physical and neurological development. When you observe motor behavior, be especially aware of the possible causes of any abnormalities. If the interviewee has motor problems, consider their frequency and how the interviewee reacts to them. You also will want to watch for any visual or auditory problems. In addition, by observing the height, weight, skin tone, and general appearance of the interviewee, you will obtain clues about his or her physical development, especially when the interviewee is a child.

Observing Behaviors Suggesting Psychological Problems

Table 2-4 provides a useful list of some psychological problems that you might observe during the interview. Each problem can vary as to its *intensity* (absent, mild, moderate, or severe) and *duration* (none, infrequent or brief, frequent or prolonged, permeating behavior).

The Far Side   by Gary Larson

How to recognize the moods of an Irish setter

Exercise 2-2. Listening for Feelings

For each of the following statements, describe what you think the interviewee is feeling. Ask yourself "What is the underlying feeling here?" Compare your answers with those following the statements and with those of other students. The items were adapted from Okun (1982, pp. 52–53).

1. Seven-year-old boy: "Two big boys were picking on me when I was coming home from Boy Scouts today" (said in a trembling voice).
2. Seventeen-year-old male adolescent: "The doctor told me to come over here and have all these tests. I'll sit over here and wait until you're ready for me."
3. Lenny's wife: "Poor Lenny! He works so hard, and he never gets home for dinner anymore."
4. Fifteen-year-old female student: "I can't wait until final exams are over."
5. Mother: "I think people are out to get what they can for themselves."

Table 2-4
Indicators of Possible Psychological Difficulties Observed in the Interview

Relation to Interviewer

1. *Withdrawn*—Preoccupied; avoids eye contact; aloof; distant; mechanically responsive; exhibits no sustained emotional relatedness
2. *Negative*—Actively opposes and resists interviewer's initiative; makes guarded, evasive replies or is deliberately silent; exhibits teasing, manipulative, or hostile refusal to cooperate
3. *Clinging*—Actively clings, physically or verbally; seeks physical contact; demands constant attention and direction
4. *Overcompliant*—Goes along with interviewer passively; does not assert self reasonably
5. *Unspontaneous*—Does not initiate or sustain social or verbal interchange; lacks spontaneity; inhibited
6. *Confused*—Bewildered; perplexed; puzzled

Motor Behavior

7. *Motor compliance*—Melts into interviewer's lap
8. *Inappropriate posturing*—Maintains uncomfortable or inappropriate postures of trunk or extremities
9. *Odd mannerisms*—Exhibits odd, stylized movements or actions; engages in complex motor rituals, usually idiosyncratic; darts and lunges peculiarly
10. *Grimacing*—Makes bizarre facial movements
11. *Deviant locomotion*—Walks on toes; whirls on own longitudinal axis or runs in small circles
12. *Flapping*—Flaps or oscillates hands; wiggles fingers or positions them bizarrely
13. *Flaccidity*—Slumps; lets arms dangle limply; has slack facial muscles
14. *Motor retardation*—Sits unusually still; sluggish; has slow, feeble or labored movements; walks slowly; delays in performing movements
15. *Poor gross motor coordination*—Awkward; stiff; clumsy; stumbling
16. *Peculiar rhythmic movements*—Rocks; sways; bangs head; rolls; engages in repetitive jumping
17. *Hyperactive*—Has difficulty staying seated; gets up; moves fast; exhibits vigorous, impulsive bursts of locomotion
18. *Squirming*—Wriggles; squirms; moves or shifts restlessly in chair
19. *Tense*—Has generally taut, strained, or tense musculature; keeps body rigid; clenches jaws; grips arms of chair; hands are tremulous
20. *Nervous habits*—Taps; "drums" with hands or feet; grinds teeth; sucks tongue; bites lips, nails, hands, or cuticles; sucks body parts (fingers, hair, etc.); picks on skin, scabs, or nose; twists hair
21. *Facial tics*—Shows tic-like movements of eyes, lips, or cheeks

Affect

22. *Incongruous affect*—Expresses affect, but not in keeping with concurrent verbal content or context of interview; changes in content are precipitated by minimal or no external stimulus
23. *Blunted affect*—Has restricted range and intensity of emotional expression, immobile facial expression, or monotonous voice
24. *Irritable affect*—Screams; cries; agitated; excited
25. *Labile affect*—Changes suddenly from one mood to another
26. *Silly affect*—Engages in excessive clowning; giddy; playfully silly; facetious; makes silly jokes and flippant remarks
27. *Angry affect*—Angry; hostile; touchy; erupts easily
28. *Suspicious affect*—Wary; guarded; distrustful of interviewer; constantly questions intentions or goodwill of interviewer in a suspicious manner
29. *Anxious affect*—Fearful; apprehensive; overconcerned; tense; worried; speaks in a frightened tone of voice; has tremor, has sweaty palms
30. *Depressed affect*—Sad; has mournful look; breaks into tears; speaks in a gloomy tone of voice; sighs deeply; voice chokes on distressing topic

Vocal Production

31. *Abnormal prosody*—Uses "question-like melody" (rising inflection) for statements; chants; uses sing-song melody; has hollow-sounding or scanning speech; exhibits other manneristic changes in pitch, intonation, stress, phrasing, and rhythm
32. *Underproductive speech*—Fails to answer questions; monosyllabic; has to be pressured for an answer; doesn't elaborate
33. *Slow speech*—Leaves long pauses before answering and long pauses between words
34. *Voice low*—Has weak, soft, whispering, almost inaudible voice
35. *Voice loud*—Boisterous; shouts; sings loudly; shrieks; squeals
36. *Pressured speech*—Speech is abundant, accelerated, loud, or difficult to interrupt

Language and Thought

37. *Unintelligible speech*—Speaks no recognizable words, only babbling or jargon
38. *Immediate echolalia*—Repeats interviewer's words
39. *Delayed echolalia*—Repeats interviewer's words after a delay
40. *Neologisms*—Uses complex idiosyncratic words
41. *Incoherence*—Statements are incomprehensible; sentences are confused; syntax is distorted

(Continued)

Table 2-4 (*Continued*)

42. *Irrelevant language*—Speech is out of context, unrelated to theme of play or conversation; speech shows partial reference to topic; "triggered" stereotyped sequences are off the point
43. *Derailment*—Associations are derailed (loose) or obliquely related; shifts of topic are obscure, idiosyncratic, or unexplained; connections are illogical
44. *Poverty of content*—Speech is adequate in amount but conveys little information because it is vague, over-abstract, or over-concrete (for child's age), repetitive, or stereotyped
45. *Blocking*—Train of thought stops abruptly, even in mid-sentence, in the absence of apparent anxiety
46. *Odd communication*—Speech is tangential, digressive, vague, over-elaborate, circumstantial, or metaphorical
47. *Perseveration*—Repeats the same statement or returns to the same topic over and over
48. *Distractible*—Distracted by trivial or irrelevant stimuli; shifts topics or interrupts speech or actions abruptly

Attention
49. *Primitive attention to objects, environment*—Stares; ignores objects; holds object in undifferentiated fashion with no visual fixation on it; mouths or sucks object; taps; engages in repetitive banging
50. *Aberrant attentional behaviors*—Clearly preoccupied with listening to self-induced, nonvocal sounds such as scratching or tapping; visually preoccupied with hand or finger movements; bangs, rubs, or flicks; covers ears or eyes
51. *Aberrant responses to toys*—Lets objects passively fall on and off hand; flicks at objects; feels, strokes, rubs, or scratches objects; preoccupied with trivial specks, breaks, points, and the like in objects; uses objects in a bizarre, idiosyncratic manner; spins objects
52. *Pathologically repetitive play behaviors*—Exhibits "light-switching" or other repetitive behavior; remains preoccupied with same object; uses object(s) ritualistically; remains preoccupied with same activity
53. *Self-mutilation*—Bites or hits self; bangs head
54. *Disorganized behavior*—Engages in inconsistent behavior that changes abruptly; shifts intentness and focus of attention abruptly; exhibits fragmented behavior, without coherent goal-direction
55. *Eccentric/odd behavior*—Preoccupied with odd objects or activities; engages in other peculiar or inappropriate behavior

Source: Adapted from *Children's Psychiatric Rating Scale—A* by Fish (1985).

6. Ten-year-old male student: "Only two more weeks until vacation!"
7. Wife: "My husband is out of work, and I don't know how we're going to pay the rent next month."
8. Mother: "All children steal at that age, don't you think?"
9. Eleven-year-old student: "Why should I stay in school? I don't know what I want to do. What do you think?"
10. Nine-year-old female: "No one ever picks me to be on a team at school."

Suggested Answers

When you read the suggested answers, note that usually there is more than one possible explanation. It is difficult to interpret precisely the interviewee's feelings from remarks made out of context. When you interpret the interviewee's feelings in the interview, consider *what* is said, *how* it is said, *when* it is said, and in *what context* it is said, and ask additional questions as needed.

1. Scared
2. Afraid of illness, pleased at attention from doctor, frustrated with wait, polite, unassertive
3. Sympathy for Lenny or anger at Lenny for never getting home
4. Anxiety about coming exams or anticipation of vacation after exams
5. Fear of being hurt or anger at others' selfishness, cynicism
6. Anticipation, relief
7. Desperation, anxiety
8. Fear that something is wrong with child, denial that child has a problem, uncertainty
9. Confusion, fear, indecision
10. Anger at rejection, loneliness, sadness

ESTABLISHING RAPPORT

The success of an interview, like that of any other assessment procedure, depends on the rapport you establish with the interviewee. Your aim is to create a comfortable and safe atmosphere that will allow the interviewee to talk openly and without fear of judgment or criticism. *Rapport is based on mutual confidence, respect, and acceptance.* It is your responsibility to engage the interviewee and to bring her or him to see you as a trusting and helping person.

The climate you establish should ensure that the interviewee experiences freedom to give information and to express feelings. You must show the interviewee that you are willing to accept whatever information she or he wants to give, within the aims and goals of the interview. Establishing an appropriate climate is not a matter of attending only to the opening minutes of the interview. Because shifts in feelings and attitudes occur throughout the interview, you will need to stay keenly aware of how the interviewee responds to you and adjust your techniques accordingly to maintain an open and productive climate.

Facilitating Rapport

You can facilitate rapport by

- making the interview a joint undertaking between you and the interviewee
- giving the interviewee your undivided attention
- conveying to the interviewee that you want to listen and can be trusted
- giving the interviewee reassurance and support
- listening to the interviewee openly and nonjudgmentally
- speaking slowly and clearly in a calm, matter-of-fact, friendly, and accepting manner
- interrupting the interviewee only when necessary
- using a warm and expressive tone
- maintaining a natural, relaxed, and attentive posture
- maintaining appropriate eye contact
- asking tactful questions
- timing questions and comments appropriately

All these actions convey your interest and respect for the interviewee.

The following suggestions also will be helpful in establishing rapport (Dresser, 1996a). If the interviewee has several names, ask the interviewee which name she or he prefers to use. If you have difficulty pronouncing the interviewee's name, ask the interviewee to help you say it correctly. Finally, the way you dress may affect rapport. Some interviewees may respond positively to "professionals who are formal in dress and demeanor" (p. 62).

Getting Started

Interviewees are likely to be anxious to tell you their story as soon as possible. Therefore, it may not be necessary to engage in small talk—such as talk about the weather, baseball, or current news—to establish rapport with the interviewee. Sometimes a general opening question such as "How are you today?" may be all that you need to ask. This type of question gives interviewees an opportunity to talk about themselves and helps build rapport.

As soon as possible, focus on topics related to the referral questions, to the interviewee's concerns, or to your concerns. However, you may have to take a slight detour at times. For example, if the interviewee is anxious and you know about his or her interest in sports or movies, you might want to talk about one of these topics early in the interview. Although such talk is likely tangential, it may be just what is needed to relax the shy, inhibited interviewee and help him or her talk about more relevant issues.

Showing Interest

Showing interest in the information given to you by the interviewee is crucial in establishing rapport. Interviewees need to sense that you want to understand how they see the world; appreciate their experiences; share in their struggle to recall, organize, and express their experiences; appreciate their difficulties in discussing personal material; and reflect accurately their opinions, feelings, and beliefs (Gorden, 1975). You can show your interest by the things you say, by the way you say them, and by your actions. You want to be responsive, empathic, and sensitive.

Handling Anxiety

You will need to reassure anxious interviewees. For example, older children may wonder what will happen to them because of the assessment. Some children and their parents may be too embarrassed to discuss their reasons for being at the interview. And most parents will be anxious to learn how serious their children's problems are and what can be done about the problems.

How anxiety may be expressed. Interviewees may express their anxiety through verbal channels, nonverbal channels, or both. Verbal indices of anxiety include sentence corrections, slips of the tongue, repetitions, stuttering, intruding or incoherent sounds, omissions, and frequent use of "uh" expressions. Nonverbal indices of anxiety include sweating, trembling, fidgeting, restlessness, hand clenching, twitching, scowling, and forced smiling.

Encouraging the interviewee to talk about anxiety. When you sense that the interviewee's anxiety is interfering with rapport, encourage him or her to talk about it. Following are some possible leads (Shea, 1988; Stevenson, 1974):

- "Bill, I know that it's difficult to talk at first. I'm wondering what some of your concerns are about being here today?"
- "Bill, it's hard to talk about personal feelings. Is there anything I can do to make things easier for you?"
- "This one is tough, huh, Bill?"
- "Something makes it hard for you to talk about this matter; can you tell me what it is that makes it hard?"
- "Are you afraid of what I will think of you?"

If you believe that the interviewee does not feel that he or she can trust you, you might say "I know it's difficult to talk to a stranger, and it may take time for you to trust me. That's natural. I don't expect you to say anything that makes you uncomfortable unless you're ready" (Shea, 1988). Similarly, if the interviewee appears anxious when talking about threatening material, you might say "It's all right if you don't feel like talking about that yet." This gives the interviewee permission to wait but also establishes the expectation that the interviewee may be ready to discuss the topic later and that you might inquire about the topic again (Kanfer, Eyberg, & Krahn, 1992).

Pointing out the interviewee's responsibility. When all else fails and the interviewee will still not talk with you, you may need to point out gently his or her responsibility as an interviewee: "We have to work together; we can't accomplish very much unless you can tell me more about yourself." When interviewees still are not ready to discuss sensitive or anxiety-provoking material, return to the topic at a more opportune time. By being attentive to the interviewee's distress, you can help him or her experience what a therapeutic relationship might be like. This knowledge might serve as a valuable starting point for therapeutic interventions, if they are needed.

Young children may not understand that you expect them to share information with you or even that they have a problem. They may not understand their role as an informant. In such cases, be patient and encourage them to talk with you by playing games or doing other activities (see Chapter 3).

Complimenting the interviewee's sharing. If you sense that the interviewee is anxious about some material that he or she shared with you, you can probably reduce his or her anxiety by saying "What's it been like for you to share these experiences with me?" You also can praise the interviewee for sharing. For example, you might say "You've done an excellent job of sharing difficult material. It's really helping me to understand about what you've been experiencing" (Shea, 1988, p. 47). Direct your compliment to the interviewee's *sharing* and not to the content of the statement. You don't want to reinforce certain responses or hint that certain responses are either right or wrong.

Handling Agitation and Crying

Interviewees may become agitated during the interview, especially when they recently have faced traumatic experiences. As they relive the experience, they may lose control for a few minutes, cry, or express deep personal feelings. Give them time to work through their feelings and acknowledge their feelings; this should help make a difficult situation easier.

An interviewee who is sad and on the verge of tears may feel especially vulnerable. You might say "You seem sad now" or "Are you trying not to cry?" or "It's all right to cry. We all cry at times. It's our body's way of telling us we're hurting. [Pause] Maybe you can tell me a little more about what is hurting you" (Shea, 1988, p. 259). However, if an adult interviewee's crying is uncontrollable, you may have to be more firm and say "Mr. Jones, this is obviously very upsetting and would be to anybody. Take a moment to collect yourself. It's important for us to talk more about what is bothering you" (Shea, 1988, p. 259). This comment, though firm, still should be said gently. Also, always have a box of tissues within easy reach of the interviewee.

Facilitating Communication

Use language suitable to the age, gender, and education of the interviewee. Be sure that your questions are concrete and easily understood and that you do not unintentionally bias them toward a particular response (Gorden, 1975). You don't want to say, for example, "School isn't that bad, so why don't you like going to school?" Avoid ambiguous words, psychological jargon, and repeating the interviewee's slang or idioms that are unnatural to you. When interviewing children about parts of the body, *always* use their words for the body parts (and get comfortable using these sometimes uncomfortable-to-use words). Recognize when the interviewee's speech is figurative, and don't respond to it as the literal truth. For example, if an interviewee says "I feel like my insides are coming out," you don't want to say "Show me where they are coming out." Use of an appropriate vocabulary also will facilitate rapport.

Attending to Actions That May Diminish Rapport

The following list presents actions likely to diminish rapport. We all engage in them at times, but an interviewer should attempt to reduce their occurrence.

* Don't tell the interviewee about the people you've helped or about the important people who refer cases to you. It is all right, however, to say that you talk to kids.
* Don't be flippant or sarcastic about statements made by the interviewee.
* Don't use stereotyped phrases or overworked expressions, such as "um," "you know," "like I said," or "well."
* Don't tune in only to the things that interest you.
* Don't disagree or argue with the interviewee.
* Don't verbally attack or belittle the interviewee.
* Don't try to influence the interviewee to accept your values.
* Don't be shocked by life styles that differ from yours.
* Don't lecture the interviewee about having waited too long to come to see you or being wise to have come now.
* Don't constantly interrupt the interviewee (unless the interviewee wanders off aimlessly).
* Don't be distracted by the interviewee's mannerisms, dress, accent, and so forth.
* Don't concentrate on making a good impression instead of focusing on the interviewee.
* Don't concentrate on the next question that you intend to ask instead of on the interviewee's answer to your current question.
* Don't suggest answers if the interviewee hesitates.
* Don't tell the interviewee how others answered the question.
* Don't engage in nonverbal behaviors that send negative messages (see Table 2-1).

- Don't tell the interviewee that you can solve all of his or her problems.
- Don't give the interviewee inappropriate reassurance by telling him or her that there is no cause to worry.
- Don't superficially listen to the interviewee, wait for the interviewee to finish speaking, and then try to make your point by telling the interviewee the way it "really" is.
- Don't minimize the depth of the interviewee's feelings.
- Don't tell the interviewee that you also have your own worries and problems.

Here is an example of how an interviewer's comment led the interviewee to become upset (Bogdan & Biklen, 1982).

During the early part of an interview a mother said that she thought her daughter developed secondary sex characteristics when the daughter was in the third grade. Later she said that it must have been at the end of the fourth grade, to which the interviewer replied "That sounds more like it." This statement may have signified to the mother that the interviewer distrusted her. In fact, later in the interview the mother said that she was having trouble remembering things because she was confused by the interviewer's "doubting." The interviewer's thoughtless remark, which measured the mother against some standard of "normal development," led the mother to distrust the interviewer. (p. 139, with changes in notation)

Regaining self-composure.   Because the clinical assessment interview is a formal, professional relationship, the interviewee should not have to deal with your personal concerns. Most of us as interviewers will let our attention wander, be disturbed by some remark made by the interviewee, or be moved by some remark made by the interviewee that causes us to reflect on our own life and situation. When you have such reactions, redirect your attention to the interviewee.

Finding your way.   Should you find that you have lost your train of thought during the interview, Gratus (1988) offers the following advice:

Return to the point where things started to go wrong, and no harm or loss of face will come from admitting the problem to the interviewee: "I'm sorry, I seem to have lost my way. Now, where was I? Could we go back to…?" In fact, the interviewee might even appreciate your admission, because it will make you appear more human and approachable.

You may not wish to go back but to move the interview on, in which case you should [summarize] before [asking] the next question. Summing up [or paraphrasing] has the immediate effect of getting you back into the flow of the interview and at the same time reinforcing what the interviewee has already told you. (p. 84)

Other barriers to establishing rapport.   Rapport may be difficult to establish when the interviewee does not want to be at the interview or have the information from the interview shared with anyone else. In such cases, show the interviewee what will be gained by cooperating with you. Chapter 3 discusses additional considerations for establishing rapport with children.

TIMING QUESTIONS APPROPRIATELY

The initial part of the interview should focus on areas that are not anxiety provoking or too sensitive. Premature or poorly timed questions may impede the progress of the interview and discourage disclosure of vital information. The way the relationship with the interviewee unfolds should guide you in timing questions and discussing sensitive topics. As you and the interviewee develop a more trusting relationship, you can broach topics that you avoided earlier. Time your comments and questions so that they harmonize with the interviewee's flow of thoughts, while moving the interview toward areas you want to explore.

The following are suggestions on how to pace the interview properly (Gratus, 1988):

1. Have a good idea of the topics you want to cover.
2. Have a strategy, but be prepared to amend it as needed.
3. Focus on one subject at a time and then move on.
4. Keep the interviewee interested.
5. Know approximately how much time has elapsed (or remains) in the interview.

The pace of the interview should be rapid enough to keep the interest of the interviewee, but slow enough to allow the interviewee to formulate good answers. In addition, the interview should not be too long or have many lapses. For school-aged children, 30 to 45 minutes might be appropriate; for parents or caregivers, 50 to 75 minutes is suggested. But you must judge separately the time needed for each interviewee—especially for preschool-aged children, for whom 20 to 30 minutes may be sufficient.

CHANGING TOPICS

I have previously noted that in the interview you should proceed in an orderly manner and finish one area before going on to the next one. Don't constantly go back and forth between topics. However, if you find yourself needing to ask about a previous topic, do so. Introduce the question with an appropriate explanation at a convenient time, such as when the interviewee completes a topic. You may want to make a note of what you want to ask when you first think about it.

It will take practice and sensitivity to judge when you have exhausted a topic and need to change topics. Continuously evaluate how the interview is progressing and how much shifting you believe the interviewee can tolerate. Some interviewees are disturbed by sudden shifts, whereas others become bored with a planned sequence of topics. As a rule, move on to another topic when the interviewee has adequately addressed the previous one. Transitional statements—such as "Let's move on to…" and "Now I'd like to discuss…"—are useful in moving the interview to the next topic and help keep the interview going at a steady pace.

Avoid drastic shifts in questioning (Darley, 1978). For example, a parent may be puzzled if a question about his or her child's school grades is followed immediately by a question about a family member's illnesses. When you want to shift topics, help the interviewee understand what you are trying to do by providing a transitional explanation: "We've covered Tom's schoolwork pretty thoroughly. Let's now turn to another topic that may relate to your concerns."

When the interviewee introduces a topic unrelated to the one under discussion, you must decide whether to explore the new topic and risk losing continuity or stay with the previous topic and risk losing additional information. Sometimes the interviewee will change topics as an evasive tactic to avoid sensitive but relevant material. If this happens, you may want to note that the original topic was changed and return to it later.

WIDENING THE CIRCLE OF INQUIRY

If you want to widen the circle of inquiry (that is, branch out from the topic being discussed), use the communications of the interviewee as a starting point. For example, if a mother reports that her son does not get along with his teacher, you might ask "You said that your son does not get along with his teacher; how did he get along with his previous teachers?" Then, at some later point, you might say "Tell me how you feel about his teachers." When the child is the interviewee, you might say "You mentioned your father earlier; what is he like?" Once the interviewee begins talking, follow up topics in important areas.

FORMULATING APPROPRIATE QUESTIONS

Questions form the heart of the interview. They direct the interviewee to your concerns and elicit information needed for the assessment. Good questions encourage the interviewee to answer freely and honestly about the topic at hand, whereas poor questions inhibit the interviewee from answering freely or may lead to distorted replies (Gratus, 1988). Questions serve many purposes, including drawing out information, amplifying statements, guiding the discussion, bringing out distinctions and similarities, reintroducing a point needing further discussion, encouraging opinions, encouraging relaxation, and checking on your understanding.

The way you ask questions is as important as what you ask. Speak clearly and audibly at a moderate pace in a voice that is not too low, loud, soft, or harsh. When you speak, look at the interviewee. If you find yourself talking too fast, "stop, take a deep breath and let the interviewee take over the talking again, prompted, of course, by a good question from you" (Gratus, 1988, p. 84). The tone of your voice should convey a sense of assurance and confidence and be varied to suit the circumstances of the topic.

Recognize that the way you ask questions can imply the answers you expect. Foddy (1993) provides examples:

- "Are you going to do _____?" implies an expectation.
- "You *are* going to do _____, aren't you?" implies a positive expectation—that is, a "yes" answer.
- "Aren't you going to do _____?" implies a negative expectation.
- "You are going to do _____, *aren't you*?" implies a doubtful expectation.

The words you stress also can change the meaning of what you say (Foddy, 1993). For example, the meaning of the question "How come you went to that friend's house after school?" depends on which words are stressed. Stressing "how come" conveys surprise or disapproval; stressing "that" implies a particular friend rather than any friend; stressing "house" conveys a request for an explanation (for example, for going to the friend's house rather than to another place); and stressing "after school" implies a request for an explanation (for example, why the activity was done after school rather than at another time).

When you formulate a question, the interviewee must understand your words in the same way you understand them. Figure 2-3 illustrates what may occur in a typical interviewer-interviewee interchange. The most accurate

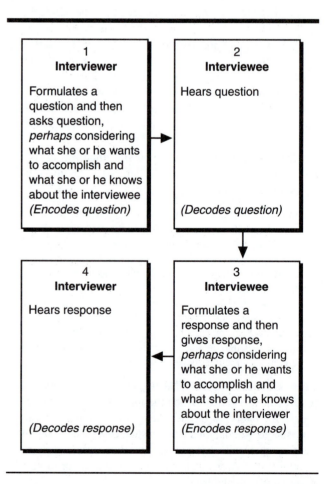

Figure 2-3. An illustration of an interviewer-interviewee interchange.

communication comes about when the speaker (interviewee or interviewer) says what he or she *intends to say* and the listener (interviewee or interviewer) *understands what the speaker means to say* (Clark, 1985). However, speakers may mean more than they say, and listeners may read too much into what a speaker says. Speakers' communications will be more accurately understood when the communications are informative, truthful, relevant, unambiguous, and concise. It is only through cooperation between speakers and listeners that speakers' meanings are clearly understood. When a listener misinterprets (or overinterprets) what a speaker says, the meanings attributed to the speaker may be more a function of the mind of the listener than the intention of the speaker.

Men may be read, as well as books, too much.
—Alexander Pope

A Continuum from Open-Ended to Closed-Ended Questions

Questions vary as to their degree of openness and their focus.

1. *Nonspecific focused questions.* At one end of the continuum are *open-ended questions;* these questions have a nonspecific focus ("Tell me about what brings you here today").

2. *Moderately focused questions.* Toward the middle part of the continuum are *moderately focused questions;* these questions focus on a specific topic but give some latitude to the interviewee ("Tell me about how you get along with your mother").

3. *Highly focused questions.* At the other end of the continuum are *closed-ended questions;* these questions are highly focused ("What subjects does your son like in school?") and may require a "yes-no" answer ("Do you like school?") or the selection of one of the two alternatives presented ("Do you believe that it would be better for you to remain in your regular class, or would you like to be placed in a special class?"). Closed-ended questions of the latter type are called *bipolar questions.*

Figure 2-4 gives additional examples of questions on the continuum.

Open-ended questions are usually preferable, especially at the start of the interview, because they allow the interviewee some responsibility for sharing his or her concerns; they cannot be answered by a simple "yes" or "no." Open-

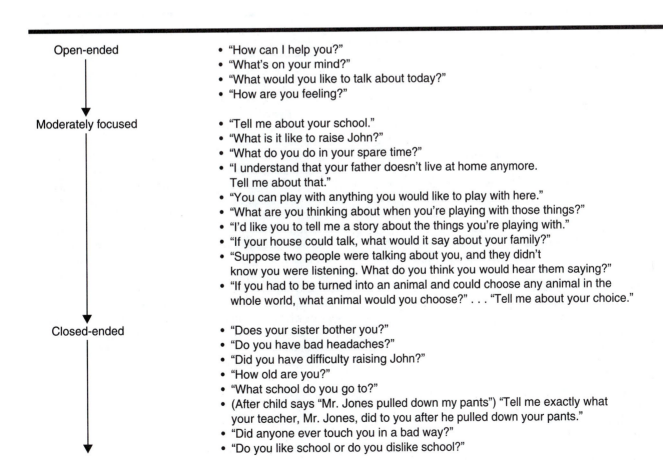

Open-ended
- "How can I help you?"
- "What's on your mind?"
- "What would you like to talk about today?"
- "How are you feeling?"

Moderately focused
- "Tell me about your school."
- "What is it like to raise John?"
- "What do you do in your spare time?"
- "I understand that your father doesn't live at home anymore. Tell me about that."
- "You can play with anything you would like to play with here."
- "What are you thinking about when you're playing with those things?"
- "I'd like you to tell me a story about the things you're playing with."
- "If your house could talk, what would it say about your family?"
- "Suppose two people were talking about you, and they didn't know you were listening. What do you think you would hear them saying?"
- "If you had to be turned into an animal and could choose any animal in the whole world, what animal would you choose?" . . . "Tell me about your choice."

Closed-ended
- "Does your sister bother you?"
- "Do you have bad headaches?"
- "Did you have difficulty raising John?"
- "How old are you?"
- "What school do you go to?"
- (After child says "Mr. Jones pulled down my pants") "Tell me exactly what your teacher, Mr. Jones, did to you after he pulled down your pants."
- "Did anyone ever touch you in a bad way?"
- "Do you like school or do you dislike school?"

Figure 2-4. A continuum from open-ended to closed-ended questions.

ended questions give the interviewee the opportunity to describe events in his or her own words and may help you appreciate his or her perspective.

Moderately focused questions are more directive than open-ended questions and are valuable as the interview proceeds. You will formulate these questions in part in response to the interviewee's answers to your open-ended questions. Bipolar questions are not as constraining as "yes-no" questions, but they still limit the interviewee's responses. Bipolar questions also do not allow the interviewee to express degrees of liking or opinions, can lead to oversimplified responses, and are not suitable for the interviewee who has no opinion at all. However, bipolar questions are useful when you want to find out what the interviewee thinks or feels about specific alternatives related to an issue or when you are helping a reluctant interviewee express his or her thoughts and feelings. After the interviewee chooses one option, you could then say "Tell me about your choice."

Moderately focused questions and closed-ended questions addressed to a specific area are more efficient than open-ended questions in eliciting specific information and in speeding up the pace of the interview. You also can formulate moderately focused questions to obtain *clarification* of a response previously given by the interviewee.

All these questions have their place in the interview. It is only when you use them inappropriately or prematurely that they may bias the interview. For example, a question like "What is the name of the teacher who showed you pictures of naked children?" is specific and directive and may bias the interview if you use it as the initial question in the interview or when you turn to a new topic. It assumes that someone showed the child pictures of naked children. In legal settings, questions like this one are called *leading questions*. Responses to leading questions are sometimes not accepted by the court. However, if the child spontaneously, or in response to an open-ended question or moderately focused question, says "My teacher showed us pictures of naked children," then a follow-up question like "What is the name of the teacher who showed you pictures of naked children?" would be appropriate. Table 2-5 shows the benefits and limitations of open-ended and closed-ended questions. We discuss leading questions in more detail later in the chapter.

Asking Direct Questions

Phrase questions positively and confidently. For example, say "Tell me about..." or "I would like you to tell me

---

Table 2-5
Benefits and Limitations of Open-Ended and Closed-Ended Questions

Open-ended question (Asks for broad or general information)		Closed-ended question (Asks for specific information)	
Benefits	*Limitations*	*Benefits*	*Limitations*
Helps you discover interviewee's priorities	Consumes time and energy	Saves time and energy	Does not allow you to learn how much information interviewee has
Helps you discover interviewee's frame of reference	Makes it more difficult to control interview	Helps when you have many questions and limited time	Does not allow you to learn how strongly interviewee feels about topics
Allows interviewee to talk through ideas	Makes it difficult to record responses, especially with long, rambling responses	Allows you to guide interview	Does not allow you to learn about the interviewee's thoughts about the topic
Gives interviewee freedom to structure an answer	Makes it difficult for interviewee to know how much detail you want	Allows you to focus on many specific areas	Thwarts interviewee's need to explain or talk about answers
Encourages catharsis (that is, the relaxation of emotional tension and anxiety by any kind of expressive reaction)		Allows you to train other interviewers quickly	Allows interviewee to falsify answers easily
Reveals interviewee's emotional state		Helps interviewee reconstruct an event	
Reveals facts about interviewee		Motivates shy and reluctant interviewees	
Reveals how articulate interviewee is		Suffices when you need only brief answers without explanations	
Reveals depth of interviewee's knowledge			

Source: Adapted from Downs, Smeyak, and Martin (1980).

about...." rather than "I wonder if you would be willing to tell me about..." or "Perhaps you might be willing to tell me about...." Also, state your questions clearly. "Avoid starting a question, then qualifying part of it, then going back and reframing it, ending lamely with an ambiguous set of incoherent ideas for the [interviewee] to sort out" (Darley, 1978, p. 45). For example, instead of asking "How old was your child when you began to teach him habits of—uh, well, letting him know that he should go to the bathroom—you know, control his bladder?", ask "When did you begin Eddie's toilet training?" (Darley, 1978, p. 45).

The following are useful questions or statements for inquiring about a symptom, problem, or concern.

- Tell me about _____ (describe problem).
- How often does it happen?
- When does it occur?
- What happens when you feel that way?
- What is it like to feel that way?
- What was it like?
- How old were you the first time you _____?
- When was the last time you _____?
- When you _____, how does it affect your school work?

Animal, vegetable, or mineral?

That's usually the opening question in the game called "Twenty Questions." Then by narrowing down the scope of your questions, you're supposed to determine the object that someone has in mind.

It isn't guesswork that leads to the right answer. It's using the right questions.

—Research Institute of America

MAJOR TYPES OF QUESTIONS TO AVOID

The major types of questions to avoid are "yes-no" questions; double-barreled questions; long, multiple questions; leading questions; random probing questions; coercive questions; embarrassing or sharp questions; and "why" questions. Let's now consider each of these types of questions.

Avoiding "Yes-No" Questions

Do not formulate questions so that a simple "yes" or "no" will suffice, unless you need to ask about a fact (such as whether a child has received help for a particular problem). For example, instead of asking "Do you like arithmetic?" or "Are your headaches severe?", you can ask "What do you think about arithmetic?" or "Tell me about your headaches." The questions "Do you like arithmetic?" and "Are your headaches severe?" may bring the conversation to a halt

because the interviewee may say "yes" or "no" and then remain silent. The question "What do you think about arithmetic?" and the statement "Tell me about your headaches" invite a longer reply, giving the interviewee an opportunity to answer more freely and allowing you to obtain more information.

Similarly, avoid questions that present one alternative only—for example, "Do you get frustrated when you are tired?"—because they may result in invalid replies, as they are restrictive and may be leading. It is better to ask "When do you get frustrated?" or "How do you feel when you are tired?" Another disadvantage of "yes-no" questions is that they may require you to ask additional questions (Darley, 1978). For example, "What illnesses has Bill had?" is a more effective question than "Has Bill been sick much?" A "yes" answer to the last question would require a follow-up question to obtain the needed information. *What, when,* and *how* questions are likely to lead to more open and complete replies than "yes-no" questions. Frame your questions so that there is a good chance of getting the information you want directly. For example, instead of saying "Do you like your teacher?", you might say "What do you think about your teacher?" or "How do you feel about your teacher?" This is a good strategy to get the interviewee to describe a problem, symptom, or situation as fully as possible.

Avoiding Double-Barreled Questions

Double-barreled questions detract from the interview because they confront the interviewee with two questions at once. Here are three examples of double-barreled questions.

1. "How do you feel about your mother and your teacher?" The interviewee may have trouble deciding which part of the question to answer first.
2. "What are the advantages and disadvantages of being in Miss Smith's class?" To get a full discussion of this question, separate the two parts.
3. "At home, do you do any chores and do you like doing them?" A "no" response will be difficult to interpret because there is no way of knowing to what part of the question the reply refers.

Avoiding Long, Multiple Questions

Avoid asking three- or four-part questions. Interviewees may answer part of a long, multiple question and avoid the rest of the question. Examples of these questions include "Tell me about your parents, teacher, and brothers and sisters" and "When did you first notice that you were having trouble with Billy? Was it before or after you moved to your present neighborhood? And what have you been doing to help Billy?" Although all the questions in the latter example may be valuable and in the correct sequence, you should ask each one separately, giving the interviewee time to respond after each question.

Avoiding Leading Questions

Leading questions—questions formulated to direct or control a response—tempt the interviewee to respond in a way you want. The way you ask questions, as noted earlier, also may persuade the interviewee to give the desired response—vocal inflections may give emphasis and direct the interviewee. Because leading questions may bias what the interviewee says, avoid using them, especially suggestive ones, unless necessary.

Here are five types of leading (or suggestive) questions.

1. *Hinting at the expected response.* One example: "He forced you to do that, didn't he?", which directs the interviewee to agree with the response expected by the interviewer. Another example: "What else did he do?", which implies that the person did something else.

2. *Identifying the response you expect from the interviewee in your question.* "Don't you think Miss Smith is a good teacher?"

3. *Using prior statements to cue the interviewee to respond in a certain way.* "It's generally been found that rewarding children for their efforts is helpful in developing good habits. Do you reward Johnny often?"

4. *Persuading the interviewee to agree with your recommendation.* One example: "To aid Jill's emotional development, we need to place her in a therapeutic program. Surely you wouldn't want to hold back her progress?" Another example: "Miss Jones is an exceptionally fine teacher, and I'm sure you will give your consent to allow Bill to attend her class for special children."

5. *Assuming details that were not revealed by the interviewee.* One example: "Tell me the first time it happened" when the interviewee has not mentioned that it happened more than once. A second example: "So after that time, after the last time you were touched, whom did you tell?" when the interviewee has never mentioned that he or she told anybody. A third example: "That was scary, wasn't it?" when the interviewee has never said this but only described the incident.

Avoiding Random Probing Questions

Do not use random probes, such as asking hit or miss questions (Gilmore, 1973). Using *random probing* is like throwing lots of bait in a stream and hoping you will catch one fish. An example: After the child says he gets along well in school, the interviewer says "There must be something that you don't like or that causes you difficulty. How about some of the teachers…or other students…or recess periods…or tests?" Interviewers may use random probing when they do not know what to ask. When you have mastered the techniques of interviewing, you are less likely to resort to random probing.

Avoiding Coercive Questions

Interviewers may use coercive questions to try to force the interviewee to see things as they see them; therefore, avoid using them. Two examples: "You will agree with me that your teacher has some good points, right?" and "Why do you always find fault with your son when he seems to have good points?" Coercive questions inhibit communication. Do not force your opinions on the interviewee.

Avoiding Embarrassing or Sharp Questions

Formulate questions so that they do not embarrass, offend, or put the interviewee on the defensive. For example, instead of saying "How many times have you been expelled from school?", say "What difficulties have you had staying in school?" Likewise, for the question "In what school subjects have you received a failing grade?", you might say "What school subjects are difficult for you?" Finally, instead of the question "Are you telling me the truth?", you can say "Is it possible that other people believe something different?" In these examples, the rephrased questions are potentially less embarrassing than the original questions because of their softened tone, yet they still might elicit the desired information.

Avoiding "Why" Questions

Avoid questions that begin with "why," particularly when they are directed at the child's actions. Children may react defensively to "why" questions, perceiving them as a request "to account for or justify their behavior rather than to describe what led up to the behavior" (Boggs & Eyberg, 1990, p. 93). Rephrase a question like "Why don't you help around the house?" with "What things don't you like about helping around the house?" Both children and adults may respond better to the alternative wording.

Similarly, a question such as "Why do you drink alcohol?" may cause interviewees to think you are judging them. Suitable questions are "When do you drink alcohol?", "How do you feel after you drink?", and "What thoughts do you have when you really want to drink?" Instead of asking "Why are you anxious?", you might say "What makes you anxious?", "What do you do when you are anxious?", or "How long does the anxiety last before it goes away?"

There are times, however, at which "why" questions, when asked carefully, can be helpful and diagnostic. For example, "Why do you think Daddy said that?" might be useful in a case of alleged child maltreatment. You want to avoid any questions that imply the child is guilty.

Exercise 2-3. Identifying Types of Questions

Identify each question or statement used by the interviewer as one of the following: embarrassing or sharp question; "why" question; long, multiple question; double-barreled question; bipolar question; "yes-no" question; coercive question; leading question; open-ended (and direct) question; random probing question; or highly focused question. Suggested answers follow the questions.

1. Would you rather watch TV or play with your friends?
2. Don't you think that your parents can do anything right?
3. What was her behavior like immediately after the accident?
4. How do you feel about your child doing things for herself and getting ready to go to a new school?
5. Why don't you listen to your teacher?
6. Tell me about your family.
7. How have you contributed to your child becoming a delinquent?
8. Although we are here to discuss Tom's reaction to his diabetes, I would like to know what magazines you subscribe to.
9. You know that Mr. Smith is not a nice person. How do you feel about Mr. Smith?
10. Tell me about your neighborhood, then about your family, and then about how you spend your free time.
11. Do you like to read?

Suggested Answers

1. Bipolar question
2. Coercive question
3. Highly focused question
4. Double-barreled question
5. "Why" question
6. Open-ended (and direct) question
7. Embarrassing and sharp question
8. Random probing question
9. Leading question
10. Long, multiple question
11. "Yes-no" question

Exercise 2-4. Rephrasing Questions

Each of the following 15 questions can be improved. Restate each question in a more appropriate form. Suggested answers follow the questions.

1. Do you get along with your brother?
2. Do you like school?
3. Do you argue with your parents often?
4. Is your mother home when you come home from school?
5. Why do you always quit sports?
6. Why have you been sent to the principal's office so many times this year?
7. Why have you been divorced three times?
8. Tell me how you feel about school, your teachers, and your friends.

9. Do you fight with your mother, and how does it make you feel?
10. Kenny is experiencing some learning difficulties, and I believe a special class might be helpful. Surely you wouldn't object to a program that can offer Kenny the extra help he needs?
11. Don't you think Mary tried to be a good friend to you?
12. Many people believe that it is detrimental to punish a child physically. Do you ever punish Bobby physically?
13. Why do you turn to drinking as a way to escape your problems?
14. You've always been treated fairly at school, haven't you?
15. Who could justify a stupid regulation like that?

Suggested Answers

1. How do you and your brother get along?
2. What do you think about school? (Or) How do you feel about school?
3. How do you get along with your parents?
4. Who is home when you come home from school?
5. What sports have you played?
6. How have you been getting along in school?
7. Tell me about your marriages.
8. Tell me how you feel about school. (Then, ask two other separate questions for teachers and friends.)
9. Do you fight with your mother? (If yes) How does it make you feel?
10. What do you think about placing Kenny in a special program?
11. What do you think of what Mary did?
12. How do you discipline Bobby?
13. What do you think are some reasons that you drink alcohol?
14. How do you feel you've been treated at school?
15. What do you think about the regulation?

In interviews, as elsewhere, the value of the answer depends on the quality of the question.

—John Courtis

USING STRUCTURING STATEMENTS

Structuring statements guide the interviewee in talking about a topic (Molyneaux & Lane, 1982). At the beginning of the interview, they may serve to reduce the interviewee's anxiety, although they are valuable at any time during the interview. They are appropriate to begin or end a phase of the interview, to set an objective, and to provide information about the direction of the interview (Evans, Hearn, Uhleman, & Ivey, 1979).

Examples of Structuring Statements Early in the Interview

The following examples offer two different ways to provide structuring statements early in an interview.

Example 1. "The purpose of this interview is to find ways to help your son Bill with his temper. I'm interested in anything you can tell me about him." This structuring statement made early in the interview directs the parent to discuss his or her son who has a problem with his temper. It acknowledges that the parent can give useful information. And it enlists the parent's cooperation and gives the parent the opportunity to discuss material related to his or her son.

Example 2. "We have about an hour to talk, so perhaps we could begin with your telling me the reason you have come to see me today." This structuring statement provides a time limit to the interview, focuses on the perceptions of the interviewee, and invites the interviewee to discuss those perceptions.

Examples of Structuring Statements Later in the Interview

The following examples illustrate three reasons for using structuring statements later in the interview.

Example 1. "Perhaps we can come back to what you are talking about later. But since our time is limited, can you tell me about Jane's…?" This structuring statement can guide a parent to focus on the child's problem rather than on the parent's own problem.

Example 2. "You said that Fred has problems in several different areas. Perhaps we could talk about each in detail. How does that sound to you?" This structuring statement can guide a parent to discuss specific problems.

Example 3. "During last week…" or "Since your headaches began…" or "When you were living with your father…." These structuring statements can guide the interviewee to identify clearly the precise time, place, or situation that you want him or her to respond to.

ENCOURAGING APPROPRIATE REPLIES

The following techniques will help you convey your interest to the interviewee, encourage the interviewee to elaborate on her or his response, or ease the interviewee's anxiety (Stevenson, 1974).

1. Nod your head.
2. Give a verbal prompt such as "uh-huh" and lean forward expectantly.
3. Repeat the last word or phrase of something the interviewee has said in a questioning manner.
4. Use gentle urging, such as "What happened then?" or "Go ahead, you're doing fine" or "I'd like to hear some more about that."
5. Use the name of the interviewee frequently.
6. Maintain eye contact.
7. Maintain a friendly attitude, gentle speech, and a kind expression.

8. Express signs of understanding and empathy by saying, for example, "I can understand how difficult that must have been for you," "That probably made you feel better," "Surely," or "Naturally."

PROBING EFFECTIVELY

Probing is a key to successful interviewing. You need to probe because the interviewee is not likely to respond fully to your questions. Listening *analytically* can help you differentiate adequate from inadequate responses, such as incomplete responses, inconsistent responses, irrelevant responses, poorly organized responses, ambiguous responses, and no responses.

An interviewee may give an inadequate response for various reasons (Downs et al., 1980):

The interviewee does not understand the purpose of the question or how you might use the information; does not understand the kind of answer you want; is uncertain about how much of an answer to give; does not understand the language in the question; is unwilling to give information that is personal, threatening, or endangering to self; may not know the answer; may not remember; finds it difficult to articulate feelings; thinks you will not accept or understand the answer; does not care about you or the interview; fears the results of giving an answer; or has competing thoughts, so concentration lags. By recognizing the possible reason for the inadequate response you can probably determine the kind of probe needed. (p. 88, with changes in notation)

Probing Techniques

There are several types of probing questions and comments that you can use (see Table 2-6). They are elaboration, clarification, repetition, challenging, silence, neutral phrases, reflective statements, periodic summaries, checking interviewee's understanding, and miscellaneous probes (Downs et al., 1980). Let's examine these 10 probing techniques.

Elaboration.   Use elaboration when you want the interviewee to provide additional information. Examples include

- "Tell me more about that."
- "Is there anything else?"
- "Please go on."
- "What happened then?"
- "I suspect that's important. Please expand on it."
- "I guess that means you felt…."
- "What happened before the incident?"
- "And what happened after the incident?"
- "How did you feel about that?"
- "What were you thinking then?"
- "Any other reasons?"

Clarification.   Use clarification when you do not understand what the interviewee is saying or when you are puz-

Table 2-6
Types of Probing Techniques

Technique	Purpose	Example
Elaboration	To get the interviewee to provide additional information	"Tell me more about your family."
Clarification	To get the interviewee to clarify details that are not clear to you	"What do you mean by that?"
Repetition	To get the interviewee to respond when he or she has not answered your question	"Tell me again about the things that get you angry."
Challenging	To get the interviewee to clarify an incongruence in his or her communication	"Just a few minutes ago you said that you didn't like school, but just now you said that the art teacher was nice. How do you explain these different feelings?"
Silence	To get the interviewee to think or reflect about a topic or feeling	Looking interested in the interviewee or nodding your head.
Neutral phrases	To get the interviewee to keep talking	"Uh huh," "I see," or "OK."
Reflective statements	To get the interviewee to tell you more about a topic	"You seem to be saying that it is very difficult for you to talk with your father."
Periodic summaries	To get the interviewee to comment on the adequacy of your understanding and interpretation, to inform the interviewee that what he or she said was what he or she intended to say, to inform the interviewee that you have been listening, to help build transitions from one topic to the next and give direction to the interview, to signal that you are at the end of the interview, and to sum up and clarify what you have covered	"Let's see if I understand what is going on at school. . . ."
Checking interviewee's understanding	To get the interviewee to rephrase your interpretations of his or her situation	"What do you think about what I just said about your family?"
Miscellaneous probes	To get the interviewee to discuss a topic more fully	Echoing the interviewee's last words (for example, "You are really angry with your mother"), or pausing expectantly, or repeating the interviewee's reply and then pausing

zled by some details. Because you are responsible for maintaining effective communication, you need to clarify ambiguous communications when they occur. You don't want to risk getting the meaning wrong by guessing what you think the interviewee means. For example, if a girl says "I study a little every day," find out what she means by "a little." Do not take for granted that your understanding of "a little" is the same as hers.

Here are other examples of how an interviewer clarified ambiguous statements made by an interviewee:

IE: When my son was 12 years old, he had a bad attack of nerves.

IR: What do you mean by a "bad attack of nerves"?
IE: My son is not doing well.
IR: How is he not doing well?
IE: I'm doing OK in my history class.
IR: Tell me more about how you're doing.

Sometimes an interviewer can help the interviewee clarify and describe an indefinite communication (Stevenson, 1960):

IE: When I was younger, I had a nervous breakdown.
IR: Tell me about the nervous breakdown.
IE: I was just nervous then. It was terrible.

IR: Well, can you tell me exactly how you felt?
IE: I was weak all over, and I couldn't concentrate. I felt panicky and would go to bed for hours at a time, and....

Following are examples of probes useful for clarifying communications:

- "So what you're saying is...."
- "Tell me what you mean by that."
- "I'm not sure what you mean. Tell me more about that."
- "Give me some examples."
- "I'm confused. I'm not sure what you meant by...."
- "Did that seem to make a difference to you?"
- "You mentioned that you can't sleep at night. What do you do when you can't sleep at night?"
- "How did you go about toilet training Sally?"
- "Which subjects do you like best?"
- "You mentioned that you like sports. Tell me what kinds of sports you like."
- "You said that you have trouble making friends. What kind of trouble are you having?"
- "Horrible? Tell me about how she is horrible."
- "When did your son do that?"
- "What is it about talking about _____ that makes you anxious?"
- "What were you thinking about when you were crying just now?"
- "Tell me what it is about _____ that makes you angry."

When interviewees tell you about their medical or psychological symptoms, ask them to describe the symptoms in more detail, especially ambiguous ones. Examples of ambiguous symptoms include *spells, blackouts, dizziness, weakness, nervous breakdown, nervousness, tension, anxiety, depression, voices in the head, peculiar thoughts,* and *strange feelings.* Also clarify any terms or phrases that are unfamiliar to you. Finally, probe terms that may have multiple or unique connotations, such as *touching, stroking, physical contact, punished, caressed, hurt, thing,* and *wee wee.* Your goal is to understand what interviewees mean by what they say, and *not* to reject their language.

Repetition. Use repetition when the interviewee has not answered your question. You can repeat the question in the same words or with slight modification. Here are two examples in which the interviewer uses repetition:

IR: How are you doing in school?
IE: I'm taking five subjects.
IR: Tell me how you are doing in these subjects.

IR: What games do you like to play?
IE: I like lots of games.
IR: What are the names of some of the games you like?

Challenging. Use challenging questions to clarify incongruencies in the interviewee's communications. For example, if the interviewee makes a contradictory statement—"I

hate school...but I really enjoy shop"—you might want to call the inconsistency to his or her attention. You might say "Before you said that _____, now you say _____. Can you tell me about what you said?" or "Well, I may have earlier misunderstood what you said about _____." By exploring inconsistencies, contradictions, or omissions with tact, you may learn that the interviewee forgot some important fact, made a mistake, or needed the additional probe to reveal potentially embarrassing material. Challenging may elicit more complete information or give the interviewee an opportunity to elaborate or change statements. Although challenging is potentially unpleasant, it may sometimes be helpful.

Challenging requires particular skill and sensitivity when you observe marked discrepancies between the verbal and nonverbal communications of the interviewee. Incongruence between verbal and nonverbal behaviors suggests that the interviewee may be experiencing conflict or ambivalent feelings. For example, the interviewee may be revealing discomfort when he or she is saying extremely pleasant things—thereby creating a superficial impression of being at ease—and simultaneously rapidly tapping feet and clasping and unclasping hands. You may not know whether the interviewee is aware of the inconsistency, however. You must judge when to call discrepant communications to the attention of the interviewee. If you decide to do so, be cautious, because the interviewee may believe that you are criticizing him or her. When the relationship is on a firm basis, the interviewee may accept challenging more readily.

When you challenge the interviewee with discrepancies, do so nonthreateningly and prepare to explore his or her feelings. Do not challenge to punish, accuse, or judge the interviewee or to suggest solutions to problems (Evans et al., 1979).

Challenging also can be used with interviewees who may be defensive or malingering or who are disengaged from the interview. In these cases, challenging is designed to get information about their motivation. The following probes, designed primarily for adolescents, give interviewees an opportunity to address ambiguities and incongruities that may arise within the interview (adapted from Rogers, 1988a, pp. 302–303).

Interviewees who may be defensive. If interviewees are unwilling to share relevant material with you because of shyness, lack of trust, guilt, or embarrassment, one of these probes may help them relax.

- "Although you are telling me that everything is going fine, when I hear about (description of current problems), I am having some trouble understanding this."
- "I know how much you want me to believe that you have your problems well under control but when I see your (clinical observations of the interviewee) I wonder if this is the case."

- "Life is not all black and white. Whenever someone tells me only good things, I wonder whether anything is being left out...."
- "According to you, you are having no difficulty handling (describe a specific problem), but according to (a reliable informant) it appears that _____."

Interviewees who may be malingering. Interviewees may pretend they can't do something or don't know something because, for example, they are trying to feign illness, to cover up material, or to lie (see Chapter 6 for additional material on malingering). In such cases, the following probes may prove useful:

- "Some problems you describe are rarely seen in teenagers with psychological problems. I am worried that you might see things as worse than they are."
- "Earlier in the evaluation you told me _____; now you are telling me _____. I am having trouble putting this together."
- "Although you have told me about (description of current problems), to me you have not appeared _____."
- "I haven't been able to understand how things are quite as bad as you tell me they are."
- "According to you, you have (current problems), but according to (a reliable informant) you are _____. Can you help me understand this?"

Interviewees who are disengaged. If interviewees fail to cooperate with you, do not seem to care about their responses, or seem remote, you might try one of the following:

- "I don't think we got off on the right foot. Can we start over? Tell me in your words what you see as your problems."
- "I don't think you're listening to what I have to say, and I know that you're not particularly pleased about being here. How can we make sure that this is not a waste of time for you?"
- "I know you took these (psychological tests) for me, but I don't think you paid much attention to how you answered them. What about (specific test items), to which you gave different answers at different times?"

The following excerpt shows how an interviewer called the attention of a 9-year-old boy to a discrepant communication (Reisman, 1973, pp. 60–61, with changes in notation):

IR: You seem to feel very angry.
IE: (Nods, but says nothing.)
IR: Can you tell me why?
IE: The kids at school make fun of me.
IR: Oh, in what way?
IE: They say I don't try in sports, and that I'm no good in baseball.
IR: And this kind of hurts your feelings and makes you feel angry with them.

IE: No, I don't care. They're not my friends so I don't care what they say.
IR: (Pause) Well, then I wonder about why you would like help.
IE: (Pause) I'd like to have more friends in school.
IR: (Pause) On the one hand, you're saying you don't care about them, and on the other, you're saying you would like them to be your friends.
IE: (Begins to cry quietly) I do want them to be my friends.

Silence. Use silence to allow the interviewee more time to reflect or think. Silence expresses that you are willing to wait for her or him to tell you more about the topic. Occasionally, silence increases the interviewee's anxiety and can lead the interviewee to talk more. You can accompany your silence with nonverbal expressions, such as a nod of your head. Silence is discussed in more detail later in the chapter.

Neutral phrases. Use neutral phrases—such as "uh huh," "I see," or "OK"—to encourage the interviewee to keep talking.

Reflective statements. Use reflective statements to get the interviewee to tell you more about a topic. You can do so by paraphrasing a statement that he or she has made. Useful phrases to begin reflective restatements include

- "You feel that...."
- "It seems to you that...."
- "In other words...."
- "As you see it...."
- "What you seem to be saying is that...."
- "You believe...."
- "You think...."
- "I gather that...."

Reflection is a useful technique to guide the interviewee; however, do not restate comments so frequently that you disturb the flow of conversation. Where possible, restatements should be in your words—do not parrot. Reflect the thoughts and feelings of the interviewee rather than the facts he or she presents.

The following dialogue illustrates the use of a reflective statement in an interview with a 12-year-old boy:

IE: My teacher doesn't want to help me. In fact, I think she's got something against me.
IR: You feel she doesn't like you.
IE: Well, she's very unfriendly, ever since I got into trouble last year.
IR: She hasn't liked you since last year?
IE: Yes, well, I think so. When I got into trouble last year, she....

Additional uses of reflection. Reflection and feedback also serve other purposes. By occasionally reflecting and paraphrasing the communications of interviewees, you provide them with valuable feedback, you let them know that you understand them, and you help them verbalize other feelings and concerns more clearly. A statement such as "So you felt that you had no one to turn to" conveys that you are attentive. Additionally, if your understanding of a statement is inaccurate, interviewees can correct what you said. Reflection also can aid you when you aren't sure what question to ask or in what direction you want the interview to go. Reflection not only will buy you some time but may aid interviewees as well. It also serves to change the focus from questioning and probing to a more personal approach. Finally, you can use reflection when interviewees use jargon or terms you believe they do not understand. By repeating their words, you provide a prompt that may lead them to clarify their comments (Boggs & Eyberg, 1990).

Reflection of content and nonverbal behavior. You can use reflection both with the content of the interviewees' communications and with their nonverbal behavior.

In reflecting the content of an interviewee's communication, paraphrase the main ideas of the communication without, as previously noted, parroting the communication. For example, after an interviewee's lengthy description about a fight at school, you might say "What you're saying is that you couldn't go back to school after the fight because everybody would look at you." A summary statement that reflects content should be an integrated restatement of the main ideas of the interviewee's communication about the topic.

Interviewees' nonverbal behavior includes affect, gestures, posture, tone of voice, and facial expressions. By reflecting the interviewees' affect, you not only show understanding but also implicitly give them permission to experience the emotion. For example, when the interviewee is crying, you might say "I can see that it makes you sad to talk about this" (Stevenson, 1974). Remarks such as this may help interviewees experience strong emotions or relive events during the interview. But you must be cautious; otherwise interviewees may become more focused on their feelings than on providing the requested information. Supplement your reflection of feelings with nonverbal behaviors of acceptance, such as a nod of the head.

When interviewees' nonverbal behavior expresses something that they have not yet verbalized, consider making a comment. You can say, for example, "You seem to be fidgety," "You looked frightened when you said that," or "Your fists were clenched when you were talking just now." The interviewee's nonverbal behavior also may be expressing something about the interviewer—"You bore me"—or some need—"I need to go to the bathroom." Reflecting nonverbal behavior may be especially useful when there is an impasse during the interview. However, this technique may make interviewees self-conscious and possibly hinder their communication; therefore, use it with caution.

Rigid and reflecting interviewer styles. The rigid style of interviewing yields information but may make inter-

viewees feel distant and aloof from the interviewer. The reflective style of interviewing, in contrast, not only yields information but also may give interviewees a sense that the interviewer is "with" them and may facilitate a smooth flow of information.

Let's now look at an example of a rigid interviewing style followed by an example of a reflective interviewing style (Shea, 1988, pp. 105–107, with changes in notation).

RIGID STYLE OF INTERVIEWING

IE: The pressures at home have really reached a crisis point. I'm not certain where it will all lead; I only know I'm feeling the heat.

IR: What's your appetite like?

IE: I guess it's okay....

IR: What's your sleep like?

IE: Not too good. I have a hard time falling asleep. My days are such a blur. I never feel balanced, even when I try to fall asleep. I can't concentrate enough to even read.

IR: What about your sexual drive?

IE: What do you mean?

IR: Have you noticed any changes in how interested you are in sex?

IE: Maybe a little.

IR: In what direction?

IE: I guess I'm not as interested in sex as I used to be.

IR: And what about your energy level? How has it been?

IE: Fairly uneven. It's hard to explain; but sometimes I don't feel like doing anything.

REFLECTIVE STYLE OF INTERVIEWING

IE: The pressures at home have really reached a crisis point. I'm not certain where it will all lead; I only know I'm feeling the heat.

IR: Sounds like you've been going through a lot. How has it affected the way you feel in general?

IE: I always feel drained. I'm simply tired. Life seems like one giant chore. And I can't sleep well.

IR: Tell me about the problems you're having with your sleep.

IE: I can't fall asleep. It takes several hours just to get to sleep. I'm wired. I'm wired even in the day. And I'm so agitated I can't concentrate, even enough to read to put me to sleep.

IR: Once you're asleep, do you stay asleep?

IE: Never; I bet I wake up four or five times a night. And about 5 A.M. I'm awake, as if someone slapped me.

IR: How do you mean?

IE: It's like an alarm went off, and no matter how hard I try, I can't get back to sleep.

IR: What do you do instead?

IE: Worry…I'm not kidding…My mind fills with all sorts of worthless junk.

IR: You mentioned earlier that you have problems with concentration. Tell me a little more about that.

IE: Just simply can't function like I used to. Dictating letters, reading, writing notes, all those things take much longer than usual. It really disturbs me. My system seems out of whack.

IR: Do you think your appetite has been affected as well?

Non Sequitur

by Wiley

IE: No question. My appetite is way down. Food tastes like paste; really very little taste at all. I've even lost weight.

IR: About how much and over how long a time?

IE: Oh, about five pounds, maybe over a month or two.

Exercise 2-5. Selecting the Appropriate Reflective Response

This exercise is designed to check on your ability to give appropriate replies. It contains statements made by mothers of disabled children. Each statement is accompanied by two possible interviewer replies. Select the interviewer reply you prefer, and give a justification for your selection. Then check your choices against those following the items. This exercise was adapted, with permission of the author, from P. J. Winton (1992), *Communicating with Families in Early Intervention: A Training Module,* Frank Porter Graham Child Development Center, pp. 9–10.

1. IE: I try, honestly, to do the physical therapy exercises, but I don't get anywhere. Working hard doesn't seem to make any difference; he's still so far behind.

   IR-1: I guess you're depressed.

   IR-2: You sound frustrated.

2. IE: What can I do? I don't know anything about babies with problems. I know I should do something, but I don't know what.

   IR-1: You sound as if you've given up all hope.

   IR-2: It's hard to know which way to turn.

3. IE: (Showing interviewer a snapshot of her son) You should have seen him at his party. He was really something…sitting up like a big boy with all of the other children.

   IR-1: That's cute. You really enjoyed seeing him have so much fun.

   IR-2: That's cute. But don't get your hopes up. You know he's not always going to be able to participate with normal kids.

4. IE: (With head down, speaking in a low tone of voice) I was going out of town, but now my mother-in-law is coming for the weekend.

   IR-1: You don't look too happy about that.

   IR-2: It sounds as if that will be just as enjoyable.

5. IE: Jesse is going to be evaluated at the clinic next week. I'm eager to find out more about his condition, but I know it's going to be a long, hard day.

   IR-1: You're looking forward to getting more information, but you're anxious about the long evaluation process?

   IR-2: It's really going to be great to get more information about Jesse.

6. IE: (Said with tears in her eyes) I'm really glad Jason has gotten into the developmental center.

   IR-1: (Looking briefly at her notes) Oh, I know you're happy about that.

   IR-2: You say you're glad, but you look kind of sad too.

7. IE: (Fidgeting, looking anxious, biting nails, etc., and not talking)

   IR-1: Surely, it can't be that difficult to talk about this; I can't help you unless you talk.

   IR-2: (Silence) You seem uncomfortable going on with this discussion.

Suggested Answers

1. IR-2's response is preferable. It reflects the mother's feelings. IR-1's response is an overinterpretation.

2. IR-2's response is preferable. It reflects the mother's confusion. IR-1's response suggests that the mother has given up all hope, an interpretation that may not be accurate.

3. IR-1's response is preferable. It reflects the mother's feelings. IR-2's response puts a damper on the mother's joy; the admonition is not necessary.

4. IR-1's response is preferable. It reflects the mother's nonverbal communication. IR-2's response fails to recognize *how* the response was said.

5. IR-1's response is preferable. It reflects both messages conveyed in the mother's statement. IR-2's response fails to recognize both messages.
6. IR-2's response is preferable. It considers both the mother's verbal and nonverbal behavior. IR-1's response fails to note the two types of behavior.
7. IR-2's response is preferable. It conveys to the mother that silence is acceptable, and it reflects her feelings. IR-1's response fails to recognize the value of silence or to respect the mother's discomfort at talking.

Periodic summaries. Use periodic summaries for several purposes, including to convey your understanding of the problem, to allow interviewees to comment on the adequacy of your interpretation, to inform interviewees that you have been listening, to help build transitions from one topic to the next and give direction to the interview, to signal that you are at the end of the interview, and to sum up and clarify what you have covered (Downs et al., 1980).

You can use different ways to begin a summary (either a periodic one or an ending one), such as "Let's see if I understand what is going on at home" or "Let me see, as I understand things so far.... Is that right?" or "If I understand you correctly, you are saying.... Have I got it right?" or "So...." Here is an example of what a summary statement to an adolescent might be: "So, you're concerned about your relationship with your father and how your stress is affecting your school work, and you're trying to find some help for your problem."

Checking interviewee's understanding. Use a check of the interviewee's understanding to learn about the clarity of your communications. Here is an example: "It would help me if you could tell me what I just said about (ways we can help Jim, what the major findings were, or any other topic). This will help me make sure that I said what I meant to say." By putting these statements in the context of helping you, rather than whether the interviewee was listening to you or understanding what you said, you may reduce pressure on him or her.

Miscellaneous probes. Use other types of probes to get the interviewee to discuss a topic more fully. Examples are echoing the last words of the interviewee; pausing expectantly, with a questioning facial expression; and repeating the reply of the interviewee and then pausing. An example of echoing can be found in the following exchange:

IR: How are you getting along in school?
IE: I'm not getting along too well.
IR: You're not getting along too well?

Do not confuse echoing with parroting. Echoing is a probing technique in which you rephrase the interviewee's statement in the form of a question to get the interviewee to expand on his or her remark. In contrast, parroting is merely repeating

the interviewee's statement verbatim and, as noted, is not a preferred technique.

Guidelines for Probing

Decide on what statements to probe by keeping in mind your interview goals. For example, if statements made by the interviewee convey two or more possible leads, consider your goals before choosing which lead to follow up.

IE: I'm really upset with my teacher. She never gives us a clear assignment. I'm about ready to explode.
IR-1: How are the assignments unclear?
IR-2: You're pretty upset about this.

Either of these responses is good. The first response would be appropriate to keep the conversation at an informational level. The second response would be useful for exploring the feelings of the interviewee. You also have the option of using both responses by first discussing content and then discussing feelings (or first discussing feelings and then discussing content). For example, if you initially asked about how the assignments were unclear but also wanted to explore the interviewee's feelings about the assignments, you could say "A while ago, you said that you were ready to explode about the way your teacher hands out assignments. Tell me more about the way you feel."

We have seen that probes allow you to direct, organize, and focus the interview. You will want to consider the needs of the interviewee when you use probes. Some interviewees may need to hear about your reasons for asking certain questions, to see that you are willing to listen when they express feelings, or to have help in expressing feelings. In any event, be sensitive to the needs of interviewees and also to your assessment goals.

The following example illustrates several options available for responding to statements made by an 11-year-old girl. Each option is followed by a brief comment. Note that some options are preferable to others.

IR: I know you're having problems at home, Sara. Tell me about them.
IE: Yes, I am. I am planning to leave home and go and live with my aunt. It's impossible to live with my mother.
IR-1: What kinds of problems are you having? (This is an open question that essentially repeats the original question. It could be useful because it gives the interviewee a chance to be more specific.)
IR-2: So you're having trouble with your mother. I'm particularly interested in hearing about the kinds of problems you're having at home. (This comment is similar to the probing question by IR-1 but contains an empathic introductory comment as well.)
IR-3: Is your aunt's house a better place to live? (This is a closed-ended question that is tangential, especially if you want to find out about the problems the interviewee is facing at home.)

IR-4: In what way is your mother impossible to live with? (This is a focused question asking about the interviewee's feelings about her mother.)

IR-5: You've reached your limits at home. (This is a reflective comment, but it may be premature. It is, nevertheless, a useful option because it may reflect the interviewee's feelings about her situation.)

IR-6: Don't you like it at home? (This is a poor closed-ended question. Obviously, the interviewee doesn't like it at home. There is little reason to ask this question.)

IR-7: When do you plan to leave home? (This is a closed-ended question that asks for useful information. However, it is premature at this point in the interview. It assumes that the decision of the interviewee is final, which it may not be. Also, it directs the interviewee away from the original question.)

The following interview segment with the father and mother of a 6-year-old boy who has a language delay shows the use of active listening and the use of clarification and reflection (Andrews, 1986). The abbreviations are IE-F = father, IE-M = mother, IR = interviewer, and IE-MF = mother and father.

IE-F: I get pretty mad when he won't talk to me.

IR: You feel upset and angry when your son doesn't use words to communicate.

IE-F: Yes, very upset, and I get angry with him even though I know that's not going to help a bit.

IR: You know the anger won't help, but you're so upset that you just can't help expressing it.

IE-F: You got it.

IR: It's pretty frustrating for you when you try to get Tony to use words and he just can't.

IE-F: You bet, I get mad and blow up, and then Carol (wife), if she's around, asks me what's wrong and I tell her that Tony refuses to say "car" when I *know* he knows how and then *she* blows up at me and everyone's upset.

IR: Your concern about Tony's inability to use words seems to create turmoil in the whole family.

IE-F: Yep—everyone gets so upset that I mostly have just given up and try now to say as little as possible.

IR: At this point, you're pretty discouraged and really don't know what to try next.

IE-F: Yes, Carol and I are both very discouraged.

IR: Mrs. Smith, can you recall the last time you tried to get Tony to say a word?

IE-M: Not really, it happens a lot, but it's hard to remember an exact time...

IE-F: What about when he wants a drink or something to eat?

IE-M: Oh yeah, that happens quite often. I'll be in the kitchen trying to make supper and hurrying, and he'll start to pull on my jeans and he says "uh—uh—uh—."

IR: What do you do when he pulls on you and says "uh—uh—uh?"

IE-M: Oh, it varies...but usually I'll say "What do you want? Please quit tugging at me!"

IR: It sounds like Tony pulls on you when you're feeling rushed and hurried. Are you usually working in the kitchen when this happens?

IE-M: Yes! He always seems to want my attention when I'm the busiest!

IR: Well, it's difficult and frustrating to have to cook and also figure out what he wants when you don't understand what he's saying.

IE-M: Yes, very hard....

IR: What usually happens after you tell him to say the word for you?

IE-M: He just keeps tugging at me. He's very persistent. Finally, I'll say "What do you want? Milk? Water? Juice? Say the word for mommy!"

IR: Does he try to say the word then?

IE-M: No, I think he can tell that I'm upset, and he just tugs at me more and might start to cry; then we're both upset, so I usually give him some juice or something so he'll stop crying.

IR: Is this how it usually goes when you're feeling hurried and tired and you want Tony to use a word?

IE-M: Yes...(sighs dejectedly).

IR: Do you have any better luck when things are less rushed?

IE-M: No, things are always rushed. If Tony isn't wanting something, then the baby's crying or Tom (husband) is looking hungry and unhappy.

IE-F: I'm not unhappy; I just try to stay out of your way. Sometimes I try to help and you won't let me near you (jokingly).

IR: (To Mr. Smith) You'd be willing to help out when Carol's feeling rushed?

IE-F: Sure, of course!

IR: Tell me, Mr. Smith. Do you ever try to get Tony to talk to you?

IE-F: Not really, he doesn't want to be around me much. He seems to cling to Carol.

IR: Does he ever want to just play with you?

IE-F: No...I've tried to get him to play ball or watch T.V. with me, but he usually ignores me.

IR: What does he do to show you that he's ignoring you?

IE-F: He walks away or throws the ball in an opposite direction or just acts disinterested.

IR: So what do you do then?

IE-F: I give up and go do something else...watch T.V. alone or bother Carol!

IE-M: (Laughs) You really are quite a pest!

IR: It seems then that you both feel pretty discouraged when you try to get Tony to talk or pay attention to you.

IE-MF: (In unison) Yes!

Sometimes, no matter what you do, there will be a communication breakdown. The following humorous dialogue, written anonymously, illustrates this point. (*Note:* The IE is a farmer and the IR is an attorney.)

IE: I'm here to get one of them devorces.

IR: Do you have grounds?

IE: Yup, I got 30 acres.

IR: No, that's not what I mean; do you have a case?

IE: Nope, I got a John Deere; that's what I farm them 30 acres with.

IR: No, no. You're not understanding me; do you want to bring suit? Have you got a grudge?

IE: Well, I've got a suit hanging in the closet. The grudge, that's where I keep my John Deere.

IR: Oh, we're not communicating at all. Let's talk about your wife for a minute. Do you beat her up?

IE: Nope, she gets up about 4:30, about the same time I do.

Exercise 2-6. Probing Techniques

This exercise has three parts. The instructions are presented at the beginning of each part.

Part 1. Identifying Probing Techniques

This part has six interview segments. For each segment, identify the probing technique used by the interviewer. In items 4 and 5, identify the probing technique used in the statement followed by an asterisk. Select from the following techniques: repetition, reflective statement, probe used for elaboration, use of neutral phrases, clarification probe, and challenging probe. Suggested answers follow the interview segments.

1. IE: The other day at school I got into a fight with my best friend.
   IR: What happened to cause the fight?

2. IE: My mother is always on my back.
   IR: What does she get on your back about?

3. IR: What sports do you enjoy playing?
   IE: We are playing soccer in P.E. at school.
   IR: Do you enjoy playing soccer?

4. IE: I get so uptight when the kids are around the house all day.
   IR: Do they ever go play at a friend's house?
   IE: I'd really rather that they have their friends over at our house, so then I don't have to worry about what they are doing.
   IR: You say that it makes you very uptight when the children are at the house all day, but you prefer to have them at home. Can you tell me more about this?*

5. IE: Sometimes I get so mad.
   IR: Uh huh.
   IE: Well, I get so angry that I can hardly see straight.
   IR: I see.*

6. IE: I tell my father the reasons why I want to do something, and he still says I can't do it.
   IR: So, as you see it, your father isn't understanding your needs because he doesn't let you do what you want.

Suggested Answers

1. Probe used for elaboration
2. Clarification probe
3. Repetition
4. Challenging probe
5. Use of neutral phrases
6. Reflective statement

Part 2. Formulating Probing Questions

Read each statement. Then formulate two different probing responses you believe are appropriate. Check your answers with those following the statements. The exercise in this part was adapted from Hepworth and Larsen (1990).

1. My mother doesn't like my friends.
2. The work is too hard in school.
3. Other children pick on him all the time because he is retarded.
4. My husband and I disagree about how to discipline her.
5. I think my brother is a dodo.
6. My 10-year-old has a terrible temper. She'll never change.
7. My mom is 45 years old but still acts like she is 16. She just has no patience.
8. The kids don't appreciate me. I have a full-time job and also prepare meals and do the laundry. No one cares.

Suggested Answers

1. a. Tell me more about that.
   b. What reasons does your mother have for not liking your friends?
2. a. In what way is the work too hard?
   b. Give me some examples of how your schoolwork is hard.
3. a. What do they do?
   b. How do you feel when this happens?
   (You might want to ask both questions.)
4. a. In what ways do you disagree?
   b. Tell me about your disagreements.
5. a. I'm not sure what you mean by "dodo." Tell me what that word means.
   b. What is a "dodo"?
6. a. Could you tell me what happens when she loses her temper?
   b. You sound like you don't have much hope she'll ever get control of her temper. What makes you think she'll never change?
   (You might want to ask both questions.)
7. a. Tell me about an instance when she was like that recently.
   b. How does her behavior affect you?
   (You might want to use both responses.)
8. a. You must feel very unappreciated and taken for granted. I'd like to get a picture of exactly what happens between you and the children. Tell me about some recent times when you've had these feelings.
   b. How long have you felt this way?
   (You might want to use both responses.)

Part 3. Evaluating Interviewer Replies

Your task is to evaluate replies that an interviewer may give to the statements of an interviewee (a mother). Read the interviewee's statement, and then evaluate the nine possible replies offered here. First, decide whether the reply is acceptable or unacceptable. Then, describe the message the reply might send to the interviewee or what the reply represents. Check your answers with the suggested answers. The exercise in this part was adapted from Sincoff and Goyer (1984).

IE: Yesterday, I really ran into a problem with my son.
IR-1: (Silence)

IR-2: Hmm.

IR-3: Isn't he the one who was arrested six months ago?

IR-4: He's always having problems, isn't he?

IR-5: You ran into a problem with your son?

IR-6: When do you plan to place him in a youth home?

IR-7: How do you know what the problem is?

IR-8: He caused you some difficulty?

IR-9: Your son?

Suggested Answers

IR-1: Acceptable. Silence shows that you want the interviewee to keep talking.

IR-2: Acceptable. This response tells the interviewee that you want her to keep talking.

IR-3: Unacceptable. This is a closed-ended question.

IR-4: Unacceptable. This is a leading question.

IR-5: Acceptable. This comment tells the interviewee that you want her to tell you more.

IR-6: Unacceptable. This is a leading question.

IR-7: Unacceptable. This is a challenge.

IR-8: Acceptable. This comment informs the interviewee that you understand her comment and want to probe the cause of the problem.

IR-9: Acceptable. This comment tells the interviewee that you want her to tell you more about it.

"Then you should say what you mean," the March Hare went on.

"I do," Alice hastily replied; "at least—at least I mean what I say—that's the same thing, you know."

"Not the same thing a bit!" said the Hatter; "why, you might just as well say that 'I see what I eat' is the same thing as 'I eat what I see!'"

—Lewis Carroll

DEALING WITH DIFFICULT SITUATIONS

Some interviews will be more challenging than others. For example, blocks in the interview will arise when interviewees are uncommunicative, impatient, closed-minded, extremely hyperactive, dogmatic, argumentative, excessively anxious, opinionated, hostile, angry, uncooperative, highly agitated, disoriented, extremely depressed, or confused. (Table 2-7 offers information on additional interviewee styles that may create problems during the interview.) The material in this section will help you deal with these and other difficult interview situations.

Handling Interviewees Who Try to Take Control

When you lack confidence, feel intimidated by interviewees, or are poorly prepared for the interview, interviewees might try to take control of the interview (Gratus, 1988). Interviewees may sense that you are not in control during the

opening minutes of the interview. If you show confidence and appear friendly, helpful, and encouraging, they are less likely to try to assume control. If they still try to control the interview, despite all your efforts, remain calm, detached, and objective, evaluate where the interview has strayed, and refocus on the area of concern.

Handling Difficult Behavior

If interviewees engage in disruptive play or behave in other ways that evoke discomfort in you, do not stop their behavior prematurely (Greenspan & Greenspan, 1981). They may need time to work through their discomfort. By giving them time, you can learn more about their behavior. Dealing with such situations, of course, requires clinical judgment. *You do not want to allow a situation to develop in which interviewees become too disorganized, frightened, or aggressive.* You must develop some tolerance for anxiety-provoking behavior yet know when to step in to reduce or change the behavior if it becomes too intense or is on the verge of becoming out of control.

In extreme cases, interviewees may become abusive. They may disparage your training, sex, ethnicity, or other personal qualities. When this happens, consider the possible reasons for the comments, such as whether the interviewees have a thought disorder or simply are frightened. Although verbally abusive comments may make you anxious and angry, do not respond in kind. *You must rise above the occasion and help interviewees calm down and return to the task at hand. To do so, you must remain calm, objective, and detached.*

Handling Emotional Upsets

When interviewees show strong emotions, again remain calm, objective, and detached. You should *not* show excessive sympathy and concern, react critically or judgmentally, or pry too deeply. As a clinical assessment interviewer, you want to obtain information, not to uncover traumas. If you believe that uncovering the trauma will be useful, refer the interviewee to another source or deal with the trauma in a therapeutic relationship. Often, however, interviewees will feel better simply from talking to someone who is caring and willing to listen to them. Interviewees who break down during the interview are likely to feel embarrassed and awkward. When this happens, reassure them through words, facial expressions, and gestures. Show them that it is all right to show their feelings, that you can accept their feelings, and that you are interested in understanding how they feel. However, once they recover their composure, continue the interview in the direction you had planned.

Occasionally, interviewees may inundate you with their innermost feelings and concerns. When this occurs, you may not grasp everything they say. In such cases, make a mental or written note of the questions to which you might want to return.

Table 2-7
Difficult Interviewee Styles

Interviewee style	Description	Suggestions
Apprehensive	Has unsteady voice, has anxious gestures, constantly shifts body, has frozen facial expressions	Help interviewee see that fears about you are unfounded, give constant reassurance, smile and nod frequently, be calm and relaxed, don't rush questions
Arrogant	Answers each question as concisely and sharply as possible, acts insolent or cute, gives impression that the interview is beneath him or her	Help interviewee see how answering your questions will benefit him or her or someone else who is close to interviewee, probe with increasing directness
Crafty	Acts as if he or she has something to hide, tries to play games with you or outwit you	Let interviewee know that his or her ploy is not working, confront interviewee
Defensive	Says "I don't know," is hesitant, exaggerates or conceals unfavorable facts	Don't hurry interviewee; praise honest responses; ask simple, narrow questions at first
Disorganized	Seems confused or distracted	Be patient; use short, directed questions; summarize frequently
Hostile	Appears angry, will not cooperate, withholds information, presents information hurriedly	Remain calm and interested, reassure interviewee that cooperation can be rewarding, touch on topics that are at first neutral
Nontalkative	Gives one- or two-word answers, provides little or no elaboration	Help interviewee explore reason for silence; spend more time developing rapport; ask easy questions and open-ended questions; relate anecdotes about similar experiences; convey interest by a nod, an encouraging smile, and a voice that indicates interest
Overeager	Talks too much because of a desire to aid you as much as possible	Help interviewee realize that you want an accurate and complete answer, don't be too flattered by interviewee's willingness to talk
Stolid	Appears impassive, unemotional, or slow	Ask questions slowly, be patient, help interviewee dig out facts, use ingenuity and perseverance
Tenacious	Doesn't admit the possibility of error; is bold, aggressive, or stubborn	Use polite, indirect, and tactful approaches; don't lose patience
Too talkative	Says too much; gives roundabout, long-winded answers	Phrase questions in a way that limits the scope of the response, tactfully bring interviewee back to topic

Source: Adapted from Donaghy (1984) and Zima (1983).

Handling Sensitive Topics

You can introduce potentially sensitive topics by pointing out that the problem is not a unique one. For example, if the referral question or reports from others lead you to suspect that the interviewee has a problem controlling his or her temper, you might say "Sometimes people have difficulty controlling their temper. Have you ever lost your temper?" If the answer is affirmative, you might fol-

low it up by asking for examples. You also could ask "Have you ever done anything you regretted when you lost your temper?"

With a parent who may have difficulty restraining his or her own aggressive behavior, you might say "Sometimes parents can be pushed to their limit, and they're so upset they just feel like hitting their kid if the kid acts out one more time. Have you ever felt like that yourself?" (Shea, 1988, p. 323, with changes in notation).

If the interviewee is extremely reluctant to talk about sensitive topics, such as sexual difficulties, you have some options. You can ask a same-sex interviewer to conduct the interview, allow the interviewee to write out his or her concerns, or ask persons whom the interviewee trusts to get the needed information. Chapter 3 discusses other techniques that you can use to obtain information from children who are reluctant to talk about themselves.

Handling Inadequate Answers

It will not always be easy to learn why interviewees give inadequate answers or why they do not talk much. For example, interviewees may be shy or embarrassed to talk about themselves or frightened about the outcome of the interview, or they may not like the way you are conducting the interview. Try to find out why they are not responding and what you can do to make the situation more comfortable for them. You may have to redouble your efforts to establish rapport—be even more friendly, encouraging, warm, accepting, and nonjudgmental. You want to convey to the interviewee that you both are engaged in a cooperative enterprise from which you both will benefit.

If the interviewee still fails to respond to you after your attempts to be supportive, examine your behavior with the aid of the following questions.

1. Are your questions more like interrogations than like open-ended questions designed to allow the interviewee to talk about himself or herself?
2. Are you asking questions too rapidly?
3. Are your questions too leading?
4. Do you convey the impression that you are in a hurry to get the interview over?
5. Are you speaking in a dull, plodding manner that bores the interviewee?
6. Are you asking the same questions that the interviewee already answered?
7. Did you establish rapport before exploring intimate topics?
8. Can the interviewee understand your questions?

Handling Uncooperative Interviewees

Interviewees may be uncooperative because they were coerced to come to the interview; they are shy; they resent you because of your ethnicity, gender, or some other factor; or they are unable to attend or concentrate on your questions. Uncooperative interviewees may maintain silence, show anger or hostility, give superficial answers, or want to end the session early. Although you should make every effort to establish rapport and reduce the interviewee's stress or anger, your efforts may not always be successful. Also, remember that interviewees may not understand what role you have envisioned for them. For example, interviewees may appear oppositional when, in reality, they do not have the social orientation or the cognitive maturity to know what to expect.

Handling Memory Difficulties

Interviewees may have memory difficulties for various reasons, including (a) the events occurred in the remote past and were not particularly meaningful, (b) the events are too painful to recall, or (c) the interviewees have amnesia associated with neurological deficits or acute trauma. Memory lapses may serve defensive purposes, such as protection against further pain. The pressure to recall by itself also may be a barrier to recall. To help interviewees recall information, give them time to recall an event without pressure; switch topics, and then come back to the topic later in the interview; or ask direct questions about the topic to help them structure the sequence of events (Downs et al., 1980).

Handling Silences

Occasionally, conversation may halt. Learn to recognize different silences. A pause may mean one of several things—that the interviewee has finished giving information about the topic, needs time to recall more information or consolidate thoughts, senses that she or he has been misunderstood, recognizes that you have touched on a sensitive area, or doesn't know what else to say.

Silence also may be a sign of mourning or deep reflection over some past tragedy; in such cases, do not feel compelled to say something to get the interviewee to talk. An empathic smile or a nod of the head is all that may be needed to show that you understand and are waiting for the interviewee to continue. If you do decide to speak, you might say "Do you want to just sit and think for a while? That's fine."

Note the interviewee's posture for possible clues about what the silence might mean. For example, crossed arms or crossed legs may suggest resistance. (The following discussion of extreme silences pertains particularly to older children and adults. Chapter 3 discusses the implications of silence for younger children.)

Statements to make when silence is extreme.   When progress is stifled or when the interviewee is extremely reluctant to continue, you might discuss the difficulty with him or her. Following are useful statements to make at these times (Stevenson, 1960):

• "During the last few minutes, you've become pretty quiet. I'm wondering what you are feeling."
• "It's hard to go on talking about this, isn't it?"
• "It seems hard for you to talk to me about yourself. Is there anything I can do to make it easier for you?"
• "What are you thinking about right now?"
• "Something seems to be preventing you from talking. Could you tell me a little about what it is?"

- "I've been wondering if the difficulty you're having in talking comes from your wondering how I'll react to what you tell me."
- "We do not seem to have made much progress. Tell me what we can do differently."
- "We don't seem to be making a lot of progress. What do you think is the reason?"

Statements such as these will likely cause the interviewee to respond with renewed interest. If they do not, why might the interviewee still be irritated or anxious? Interviewees may be reluctant to talk because of distrust or dislike of you, fear of you, fear of their own emotions, fear of examining themselves too closely, or uncertainty about the confidentiality of the interview (Stevenson, 1960). Do not pressure interviewees to talk, and do not get into an argument about their silence. Instead, deal with their possible concerns sensitively and reassuringly.

Statements to make when silence suggests guilt. If you believe that the silence may be associated with guilt or depression, you might say "I can see that this is something that is very difficult for you to talk about, but it's important that we talk about it sometime. Should we do it now or come back to it later?"

Techniques to use when silence suggests resistance. Silence can indicate resistance. When you judge this to be the case, the following techniques may be useful (Shea, 1988):

1. Follow up on topics when interviewees give the slightest hint that they want to discuss them.
2. Temporarily avoid sensitive topics, such as the use of drugs and alcohol, sexual matters, or suicidal thoughts.
3. Choose topics that are neutral ("Tell me about your neighborhood" or "Tell me about your hobbies"), that interviewees may have a strong opinion about ("What are some things your teacher does that you think are unfair?"), or that are meaningful or important to the interviewees.
4. Use phrases with gentle commands. For example, use "Tell me about…" or "Let's discuss…" instead of "Can you tell me…" or "Would you tell me…." Interviewees might answer the latter phrases with even more silence or frowns.
5. Increase eye contact and positive verbal comments—say "You're doing fine," "Go on," or "That's fine" along with positive nonverbal gestures, such as head nodding. However, with hostile interviewees, these techniques may not be appropriate because they may be misinterpreted.
6. Avoid long pauses between your questions.

Appreciating silence. At first, silences may seem to be interminably long, but in time you will learn to appreciate them. Silences can give you some time to think, help reduce the tempo of an interview that is too intense, or press interviewees to assume responsibility for what they are discuss-

ing (Reisman, 1973). You will want to avoid silences, however, when they are causing stress for the interviewees.

Handling Irrelevant Material

Occasionally, interviewees have difficulty knowing when to stop talking and may produce a stream of irrelevant material. When this happens, redirect them; otherwise, you will waste time and get useless information. Here are some techniques you can use to redirect interviewees who wander off course (Gratus, 1988; Shea, 1988):

1. Comment on what they said and refocus the direction of the interview. Say, for example, "Yes, that's very interesting, and we may come back to it later, but right now I'd like to discuss…." This statement lets interviewees know that they might have a chance to get back to the topic at some later stage and that you're not dismissing them completely. It allows you to regain control.
2. Use more narrow questions that require relatively short and pinpointed answers.
3. Avoid positive nonverbal gestures, such as head nodding or any other behaviors that reinforce the behavior of the interviewees.
4. Use structuring statements to introduce topics. Say, for example, "We need to discuss how you're doing at home. This is an important area, so let's focus on it for a few minutes."
5. Use structuring statements to inform interviewees about how you want to conduct the interview, if the above techniques fail. Say, for example, "We have a limited amount of time. So let's focus on one important area at a time, because I need to understand each area as clearly as possible."
6. Confront interviewees with the behavior itself. Say, for example, "I notice that when I ask a question, we wander off the topic. What do you think is happening?"
7. Guide interviewees back to the topic as firmly as possible. Say, for example, "Let's focus on how you're doing in school this semester. Please don't discuss other things right now. It's important that we learn about how you're doing in school this semester. If we wander off, I'll bring you back to the topic. Okay? Let's start with how you're getting along with your teacher."

Handling Derogatory Remarks

Occasionally, interviewees make remarks about other people that get you upset. This can happen when they make racist comments, belittle groups, or make other insulting remarks. In such situations, you must control your reactions. Remind yourself that the purpose of the interview is to learn about the interviewees and not to instruct them or to confront them about your feelings. Although you may have value conflicts with the views you hear, you want to encourage interviewees to tell you what they feel, think, and believe. You are not there to change their views, but to learn what their views are and, if possible, how they developed those views (Bogdan & Biklen, 1982).

Handling Violence

Occasionally, interviewees may become violent. (This section is adapted from Shea, 1988.) This is a distinct possibility in emergency wards of mental hospitals or clinics. Signs of potentially violent behavior are primarily nonverbal, but they also can be verbal.

An interviewee may be exhibiting a sign of potentially violent behavior when he or she begins to speak more quickly in a subtly angry tone of voice; makes statements such as "You think you're a big shot, don't you?"; paces and refuses to sit down; makes rapid and jerking gestures, such as pointing a finger at the interviewer to make a point; stares with increased intensity; shows signs of paranoia, disorganization, or other psychotic processes; clenches fists, grasps objects in a way that causes knuckles to whiten; snarls with lips pulled back, showing front teeth; raises a closed fist over the head; shakes a fist; assumes a boxing stance; gestures as if strangling an opponent; pounds a fist into the opposite palm; or makes verbal threats that he or she is about to strike.

Here are some suggestions for dealing with potentially violent behavior:

1. The first thing you should consider is taking preparatory measures, when deemed reasonable, such as having help available and having a buzzer signal for emergencies.
2. Arrange chairs so that you have an unobstructed path to the doorway, especially with an interviewee you do not know.
3. When you recognize the potential for violent behavior, defuse the behavior.
4. Give a gentle request for the interviewee to return to his or her seat when the interviewee paces: "It might help you to relax if you sit there" or "I'd like you to sit over there so we can talk." You may quietly add a comment such as "It's difficult to have to keep staring up. I think things will go more smoothly if you sit over there."
5. Compliment the interviewee when she or he says something positive.
6. Change to a more neutral topic if the topic under discussion is too stressful.
7. Avoid the appearance of aggressive actions. You don't want to raise your voice, speed up your movements, make angry remarks, or do anything that may increase the level of agitation of the interviewee. Instead, you want to appear calm in order to help an angry or frightened interviewee calm down. Speak in a normal and unhurried voice.
8. Assume a submissive posture: Decrease eye contact, avoid raising your hands in any gesture that may signify attack, avoid placing your hands behind your back as this may arouse suspicion that a weapon is being hidden, avoid pulling your shoulders back and appearing powerful and confrontational, and remain in front of the interviewee as an approach from behind or the side may startle him or her.
9. Give the interviewee sufficient space—getting too close may result in being hit.
10. Be prepared to seek help if your actions fail. If you become fearful, consider leaving the room and returning with another staff member or a security guard. You can say "I want to help you, but I will need some help. Please excuse me for a few minutes."

Confronting violent behavior is a scary experience. Knowing signs of possible violence and ways to prevent it from occurring will help you deal more effectively with this most difficult situation. You will need to suppress your natural tendencies to run away or to react with violence; instead, use your clinical skills to help the interviewee regain a sense of control.

You also should consider your personal safety when you interview children and parents in their homes, particularly when you are in unfamiliar locations or when you are in dangerous neighborhoods. Consider notifying a friend or colleague of your location and what time you expect to return or having a friend or colleague go with you. Work closely with law enforcement personnel when your visit involves interviewing the family for possible child maltreatment (see Chapters 20 and 21).

Handling Questions about Your Clinical Competence

Interviewees occasionally may wonder about your competence and may directly confront you with questions about your ability to help them (Anderson & Stewart, 1983). They may ask you questions about your professional qualifications and credentials, such as "Are you a student?" or "What kind of professional training have you had?"

Challenges to the interviewer's competence usually arise out of interviewees' concern about whether the interviewer can help them and mistaken notions of what qualities and qualifications a good interviewer should have. Some interviewees rely on advanced degrees while others think that if the interviewer is similar to them in race, culture, sex, or other attributes, he or she will automatically be a better interviewer for them. Interviewers and interviewees alike often make the mistaken assumption that only an interviewer who has successfully negotiated all stages of marriage, parenthood, and life is qualified to assess other people's problems. (Anderson & Stewart, 1983, pp. 149–150, with changes in notation)

Other forms of challenges include "I don't need to see a social worker; I have no financial problems"; "I need a medical doctor and not a psychologist"; and "You can't help me because you're [too young, too old, Black, White, male, female, married, single, childless, too problem-free, too different, too much like us" and so forth] (Anderson & Stewart, 1983, p. 130, with changes in notation). These remarks reflect some resistance by the interviewees—that is, interviewees may not be ready to talk with you and reveal intimate details of their lives. In such cases, do not become defensive and engage in a power struggle with the interviewee. If you do, the interview may fail.

Here are some suggestions on how to deal with challenges to your competence.

1. *Don't be defensive.* Recognize that it is perfectly acceptable for interviewees to wonder about your competence (Anderson & Stewart, 1983). Accept their concerns. To help you become less defensive, focus on their concerns. Find out exactly what their concerns are. As they see that you are interested, caring, and trustworthy, they may become less resistant. You can accept their concerns with such statements as "That is a good question" or "Your point is a good one, which is one of the reasons we are closely supervised in our work" (Shea, 1988, p. 527).

If interviewees are concerned about your professional qualifications, you can briefly explain your background in social work, psychology, counseling, psychiatry, or any other relevant field of training. You can say "I'm a professional who works with children and their families." If you are licensed or certified, you also can mention this to the interviewee.

2. *Be prepared.* Be aware of your own vulnerabilities and be prepared to deal with them. For example, if you are an interviewer-in-training or look very young, be prepared to discuss these issues (Anderson & Stewart, 1983).

3. *Evaluate the context.* Determine when during the interview the interviewee challenged your competence. Was it at the beginning of the session or when a sensitive topic was being raised? Consider what the interviewee's challenge may mean, what you may have done to provoke it, and whether the interviewee was trying to get the focus away from himself or herself to avoid answering questions.

4. *Answer the question.* Answer directly any questions interviewees have about your professional background and training; do not say "Why do you ask?" Answering their questions directly in a nondefensive way may show the interviewees that you take their concerns seriously (Anderson & Stewart, 1983).

5. *Admit that differences may be a problem and appeal for the interviewees' help.* Interviewees may be caught off guard by an appeal for their help: "No, I've never had a child with a drug problem; in fact, I have no children. Do you think that's a problem?" (Anderson & Stewart, 1983, p. 136). The request for feedback about what you might be missing may enlist their cooperation.

6. *Use humor.* If you judge that the interviewee would respond favorably to banter, you might say, if your age is questioned, "I'm only 25, but some days I feel a lot older.

Does that qualify?" (Anderson & Stewart, 1983, p. 138, with change in notation). Follow a remark such as this with an offer to discuss the issue seriously. However, be cautious: "The use of humor demands some skill in knowing when it will be effective and appropriate rather than offensive.... A good rule is 'When in doubt, don't'" (Anderson & Stewart, 1983, p. 138).

7. *Use the team approach.* Those of you who are in training can say, for example, "Yes, I am a first-year social work graduate student in training. My work here will be supervised by Mr. Smith, one of the members of the staff." You also can introduce the supervisor to the interviewee, stressing that the supervisor will be reviewing the interview.

8. *Admit that you will never know the depth of the interviewees' distress.* When interviewees have faced a severe crisis and say that you cannot understand them, admit that you do not know what they have experienced. However, you can reassure them that you want to listen to them and to understand how they are feeling. By listening carefully to what they have experienced, you will be helping establish rapport.

Handling Requests for Your Opinion

Interviewees may try to get your opinion about some personal matter or may try to get you to side with them. For example, they might ask you if you support their position. Remain neutral in such situations. Simply reflect what they have told you and ask for further information, as needed.

IE: Mrs. Brown shouldn't have placed me on probation. Don't you agree with me?
IR: You seem to feel that she made the wrong decision. How come?

Occasionally, interviewees become more persistent.

IE: It seems that physical punishment is the only way I can get Johnny to mind. Now what's wrong with hitting him once in a while?
IR: You seem to be uncertain about whether physical punishment is okay.
IE: Well, that is not what I asked you. What do you think of physical punishment?
IR: What would you like me to say?
IE: I want you to agree with me.
IR: I'm not sure how my agreeing with you would help you. Have you found much support from your husband?
IE: Not too much. I don't get much support from anyone.

In the above incident, the interviewer tried to sidetrack the interviewee but was not successful initially. After directly confronting the question, the interviewer managed to get the interviewee to talk about her feelings.

Handling Self-Disclosures

Interviewees may ask you questions about yourself. Be tactful in responding to such questions. Share information about yourself if you believe it will be helpful. However, you do not want to allow a situation to develop in which you are doing most of the responding and the interviewees are doing most of the questioning. Although some self-disclosure may be helpful, keep it to a minimum.

REMAINING OBJECTIVE

Distinguishing Between Acceptance and Endorsement

Consider the distinction between accepting the communications of the interviewees and endorsing their communications. *Accepting* their communications means that you acknowledge and appreciate their point of view; it does not mean that you agree or approve of it. *Endorsing* their communications means that you agree that their perspective is accurate. When they discuss a particular event, accept their viewpoint but do not endorse it. For example, if an interviewee tells you how angry he or she is about what another child did, you can acknowledge his or her feeling by saying "You were hurt when he did that." However, it would be inappropriate to say "That was an awful thing he did to you." The goal in such situations is to express that you appreciate their point of view, without endorsing it.

Recognizing Your Emotions and Keeping Them Under Control

Every interview represents a unique interpersonal encounter. Your ability to conduct an effective interview will be determined not only by your interviewing skills but also by personal factors in your life. You must be sensitive to how you are feeling as the interview begins. Do you have any personal concerns that might interfere with the conduct of the interview? Did anything happen shortly before the interview to make you anxious (for example, a death in the family, too little sleep, recovery from an illness, a harrowing experience on the ward, confrontation with an angry interviewee)? Do you feel tired, rushed, angry, or depressed? You must ensure that these and similar feelings don't interfere with the interview.

During the interview, you will react to many things the interviewee says. You may feel sorrow, disgust, embarrassment, anger, pleasure, or humor, for example. Recognize these feelings, but keep them under control. Again, you don't want them to interfere with the interview. You do not have the luxury you have in personal relationships of responding to disagreement or anger in kind. If you express anger or disgust, for example, you might inhibit inter-

viewees from talking further about intimate details in their lives. *Also, if something is humorous, you can laugh with the interviewee, but never at him or her!*

If you believe that your feelings hampered the interview, look for the source of the difficulty. For example, were you too sympathetic, indifferent, cold, or overprotective; angry when the interviewee was rude or uncooperative because of your need to be liked; too reassuring because the interviewee's problems reminded you of your own similar problems; or too talkative to impress the interviewee with your knowledge? *Self-awareness is an important step in becoming an effective clinical assessment interviewer.*

RECORDING INFORMATION AND SCHEDULING

Recording Information

It is important to record what the interviewee says. However, it is difficult, if not impossible, to record every word unless you are skilled at shorthand, use a tape recorder, or videotape the interview. Therefore, if you do take notes, jot down only the most important remarks made by the interviewee. You can paraphrase the communications of the interviewee or use various formal or informal shorthand techniques. Notes serve as a way of record keeping. However, if they are subpoenaed, you may have to make them available to an attorney. You can make note taking easier by telling the interviewee "I'm taking notes so that I can remember important things you say, because what you say is so important."

Student interviewers frequently use video or audio recordings during training. Audiotape recorders also are used by skilled clinicians, and videotape recording is highly recommended, if not a necessity, in child maltreatment cases (also see Chapter 22). Be sure that you have the written consent of adult interviewees to use an audiotape or videotape recorder. With children, written consent may not be necessary in all circumstances. In child maltreatment cases, some agencies routinely tell children about the video recording, whereas others do not, unless the children ask.

If you take notes, do not let note taking interfere with your listening. Do not hide behind your notes ("Let me see my notes about that matter") or use them in a secretive way. Also, maintain eye contact with the interviewee. If the interviewee speaks too quickly and this interferes with your note taking, you might say "Please talk more slowly so that I can write down your important ideas." A remark like this, however, may interfere with the flow of conversation.

Scheduling

If you have a heavy interview schedule, take a few minutes between sessions to write notes and relax. Unless there is a break, you may be thinking about the past interview when you should be thinking about the present one.

Second Interviews

Occasionally, you may need more than one session to obtain the needed information. In such cases, schedule additional sessions as necessary. Here are some suggestions for ways to begin the second interview (Stevenson, 1960):

- "How have you been since our last meeting?"
- "What's been happening since we last met?"
- "Last time, we had to stop before we covered everything. Perhaps we could continue where we left off."
- "You may have thought of some things that you didn't have a chance to say last time. Let's talk about those things now."

If these inquiries are not productive, you can turn to specific areas of the interviewee's history or current situation that you need to inquire about. If you also administered psychological tests and the second interview occurs after you have completed the formal testing, you can ask questions related to the testing *and* to the interview. For example, you can ask questions about particular responses on the tests, pursue unclear details that were in the interview, and resolve incongruities in the interview, in the observations, and in the test findings. Also, if you gave the interviewee a self-monitoring task, you can look over her or his self-monitoring record and discuss it with her or him (see Chapter 3). Finally, you may want to give a brief summary of what you covered or learned during the prior interview.

CONFIDENTIALITY OF THE INTERVIEW MATERIAL AND ASSESSMENT FINDINGS

The issues of confidentiality and privileged communication play an important role in the interview. Interviewees need to understand what will happen to the information you obtain and who will have access to it. This section provides guidelines for dealing with these issues.

The best sources of information about the confidentiality of the interview material and assessment findings are the ethical principles of your profession and the laws of your state. There is a subtle distinction between confidentiality and privileged communication.

- *Confidentiality* is an ethical practice—the obligation never to reveal information obtained in the assessment (or through any professional relationship) without specific consent from the client. It protects the client from unauthorized disclosures of information given in confidence to a clinician.
- *Privileged communication* is a legal right granted by a law of a state. It protects clients from having their disclosures to certain professional groups—such as social

workers, psychologists, marriage and family counselors, attorneys, clergy, and physicians, including psychiatrists—revealed during legal proceedings without their informed consent. (Check your state law to learn whether your profession is bound by privileged communication prohibitions.) Privileged communication protects clients from having their confidences revealed in public unless they give their permission.

The Supreme Court of the United States in 1996 ruled in a federal court case (Jaffee vs. Redmond, 950-266) that the confidential notes of a psychotherapist or social worker are private and need not be revealed. The ruling brought federal courts into line with standard practice in the courts of all 50 states. Justice John Paul Stevens noted that effective psychotherapy depends on an atmosphere of confidence and trust and that the bond will be broken if there is even a possibility that a confidential discussion will be disclosed in court.

Minors generally are entitled to the same confidential relationship as are adults. Federal regulations define a minor as "a person who has not attained the age of majority specified in the applicable State law, or if no age of majority is specified in the applicable State law, the age of eighteen years" (42 C.F.R., Part 2, 1993). State laws may require social workers and other government officials to preface interviews with warnings that tell interviewees how the information collected will be used.

Exceptions to Confidentiality and Privileged Communication

There are occasions when you must suspend confidentiality and privileged communication (Federal law, 42 C.F.R, Part 2, 1993). Check your state law regarding these exceptions. The following are examples of laws suspending confidentiality and privileged communication:

1. *When there is suspicion of child maltreatment (that is, child abuse or neglect), you are legally obliged to report it to the authorities.*
2. *When the interviewee poses a physical threat to another person, you must warn the prospective victim.*
3. *When the interviewee is a minor and poses a threat to himself or herself (for example, any situation that places the minor in danger of death, where the delay of medical treatment would pose a health risk to the minor, or when treatment is needed to decrease physical pain), you are required to notify those responsible for the child.*

These three exceptions involve the principle that *when there is a clear and imminent danger to another individual, to society, or to the child directly, you must breach confidentiality.* You must use considerable judgment in determining when a dangerous situation exists. Strict confidentiality also cannot be maintained within schools, clinics, hospitals, prisons, and other agencies because agency personnel involved in the case usually have access to the child's records. You must tell interviewees of this fact. Again, check your state law.

If children ask about parental rights to their records, check your state law to learn whether you are legally obligated to inform the parents of the assessment results. Parents often have a right to assessment information, depending on the child's age and whether the child is emancipated (discussion to follow).

Confidentiality of School and Other Institutional Records

The Federal Educational Rights and Privacy Act (Public Law 93-830), which was passed in 1974, and its modifications address the issue of confidentiality of school records (see also Exhibit 5-1 in Chapter 5). State laws may have other requirements or modifications. Some highlights of the Federal Educational Rights and Privacy Act follow:

1. Parents have access to official educational records of their children. (Note, however, that state law may have certain exceptions.)
2. Parental consent must be obtained for release of records to other agencies, except in certain limited circumstances such as school transfer, requests by state educational authorities, requests by accrediting agencies, and so forth.
3. These rights transfer to students at the age of 18 years or to any student attending a post-secondary educational institution.
4. Schools must provide a hearing, when requested by parents or students, in which records may be challenged.
5. Schools have the responsibility to inform parents of their right to access to the records.
6. Schools must release records if a subpoena is issued and must notify the parents and student that the records will be released pursuant to the subpoena.
7. Failure to follow these guidelines may result in removal of federal funding for the school.

State of California Civil Law and Education Code Concerning Confidentiality of Records of Minors

Let's examine the State of California civil law and education code regarding confidentiality of minors' records as an example of how state laws may operate.

Civil law. Parents hold the privilege of withholding information about their children. This means that you must obtain their permission to obtain or release the child's records and that parents have the legal right to the child's records. There are certain exceptions, however.

1. Emancipated minors hold the privilege or the exclusive right to release their own records and to grant access to others. Emancipated minors are those who are legally married, are on active duty with the armed forces of the United States, or have had an emancipation petition granted by the courts. The petition usually will be approved if they are over 14 years of age, living separate and apart from their parents or guardians with their consent, managing their financial affairs, and receiving income that is not illegal.
2. Parents may not have access to their child's records "where...[a] health provider determines that access to the patient records requested by the representative would have a detrimental effect on the provider's professional relationship with the minor patient or the minor's physical safety or psychological well-being" (Health and Safety Code 1795.14). Thus, although parents have the legal right to access the records of their minor children, mental health professionals have a legal and ethical right to deny them access if it would have a detrimental effect on the child.
3. If the minor is being evaluated or treated without the consent of the parent, the minor holds control over the release of information. Legally, any minor over 12 who is sufficiently mature may request an evaluation or outpatient mental health treatment when (a) the treatment is needed to prevent serious physical or mental harm to the minor, (b) the minor has been the alleged victim of incest or child maltreatment, or (c) the minor has a substance abuse problem. In addition, all minors may request medical help for the prevention or treatment of pregnancy. Minors under the age of 12 may not receive evaluation or treatment without parental consent, except for pregnancy.

In carrying out California law, the clinician must balance the child's right to privacy against the parents' right to information to help and protect their child. Similar considerations apply to laws in other states regarding minors.

Education code. The education code of the State of California specifies that "any information of a personal nature disclosed by a pupil 12 years of age or older in the process of receiving counseling from a school counselor...is confidential.... The information shall not become part of the pupil record...without the written consent of the person who disclosed the confidential information" (California Education Code 49602, p. 723). Information of a personal nature does not include objective information related to academic or career counseling.

Again, there are certain exceptions to confidentiality in a counseling relationship in an educational setting. Exceptions for the clinician include holding discussions with other health care providers for referral for treatment; reporting information to the principal or parents of the pupil when there is reasonable cause to believe that disclosure is necessary to avert a clear and present danger to the health, safety, or welfare of the pupil or to other people in the school community; reporting information to the principal, parents, or other persons when the pupil says that a crime has been committed; reporting information when the pupil signs a written waiver granting the release of information; reporting information when ordered by a court of law, when requested by law enforcement in the investigation of a crime, or when ordered for an administrative or judicial proceeding.

Discussing Confidentiality with Children and Parents

Children and parents must be informed about confidentiality and its limits. Clinicians may be reluctant to discuss confidentiality because they believe that it may hamper rapport. And there are some agencies that do not have clear-cut policies about discussing confidentiality with children and parents. Yet children and parents need to be told about confidentiality, particularly about its limits. In addition, discussing confidentiality is an ethical obligation and shows that you have followed proper procedures if you are sued. I suggest that, in carrying out this recommendation, you follow your agency's policy, which in turn should be based on your state laws, the ethical principles of your profession, the child's age, the child's level of comprehension, the parents' level of comprehension, and clinical considerations.

Following are some suggestions about how you might handle the issue of confidentiality in the interview. None of these suggestions should be carried out unless they are approved by your supervisor or agency and unless they follow your state regulations and laws. Raising the issue of confidentiality may protect you and the agency and even help build rapport because interviewees might regard you as honest and open when you do so.

1. *Present statements about confidentiality on a consent form.* It's good practice to inform the parents (and older children) about confidentiality and its limits on a form that they read and sign before the interview begins. This form would follow your state laws and any agency policy that is more specific than state laws. The statement about the limits of confidentiality might read as follows (with additions as needed): "I understand that if the interviewer has reason to believe that a child or any other client (a) is being physically, emotionally, or sexually abused or neglected, (b) intends to hurt someone else, or (c) intends to hurt himself or herself, the proper authorities will be notified."

2. *Discuss the issue of confidentiality directly with the child.* To children older than 5 years who you believe can understand what you say to them, you might say "I want you to know that there are some things you might say that I must share with your parents or other people. This could happen if you tell me that someone has hurt you, if you plan to hurt someone else, or if you plan to hurt yourself in some way. OK? Do you understand?" To adolescents, you might say "I will share with your parents what we talk about today. It is important that they know how you are feeling because they want to help you. OK?"

3. *Discuss the issue of confidentiality with parents who have control of the information about their minor children.* In this situation, you might say "I will release no information unless I have your consent or am compelled to do so by the courts. However, I am legally obligated to report to the proper authorities if I learn that your child has been physically, emotionally, or sexually abused or neglected; if you plan to hurt someone; or if your child plans to hurt someone. I also will try to get you help if you are planning to hurt yourself or your child. OK?"

4. *Meet with the child and the parents to ask the parents to waive their rights to some information.* You may want to meet with the child and parents for a few moments during the initial contact. Then, you might say "In order for me to help [child's name], I need to be able to have his [her] trust. That means that nearly everything I talk about with [child's name] will be confidential, unless [child's name] tells me that it is okay to share things with you. However, I will tell you about my general findings and recommendations. Also, I will tell you if [child's name] is planning to hurt himself [or herself]. And I must notify the proper authorities if I learn that [child's name] has been hurt by someone; or has been physically, emotionally, or sexually abused or neglected; or is planning to hurt someone else. OK? Do you have any questions about this?"

5. *Discuss confidentiality when the issue of maltreatment, self-harm, or harming others is raised.* If the child or parent says that abuse or neglect occurred or talks about suicidal ideations, or harming others, you might say "Remember what I told you about sharing what you say when we first started talking? After hearing what you just told me, I must tell [law enforcement, Child Protective Services, and so forth]." Then, continue to explain why you are going to do so.

Failure to discuss confidentiality can have serious consequences (Mapes, 1995).

A court-appointed social worker conducted a very thorough and professional assessment in a child sexual abuse case that basically was to determine whether the child or the alleged perpetrator was more credible. During the assessment, one statement made by the alleged perpetrator significantly tipped the credibility scale in favor of the child. Realizing that the social worker's testimony would be harmful to his client, the defense attorney asked the social worker whether she discussed the limits of confidentiality with the client before the evaluation. The social worker said she had not done so. As a result, the defendant's statements to the social worker could not be admitted, and lacking other evidence the defendant was found not guilty. (p. 7, with changes in notation)

Releasing Information in Cases of Divorce

When parents are divorced, ask the custodial parent for permission before you release any information to the other parent. When the custodial parent does not want to give permission to share the assessment findings with the other parent, check your state law. *State law generally gives a noncustodial parent the right to request a psychological evaluation and to receive a report as long as he or she has visitation rights* (Overcast, Sales, & Kesler, 1983). If the law is not clear about this matter, check with your state professional association and with your local school administration if you are working at a school.

Exercise 2-7. Selecting the Appropriate Response

This exercise is designed to sharpen your ability to give appropriate responses in an interview. It contains statements made by interviewees, each of which is accompanied by two possible interviewer responses. Select the interviewer response you prefer and justify your selection. Then, check your choices against the suggested answers.

1. IE: I feel I need affection and can't get any.
   IR-1: Well, we all need affection and you're not alone in this.
   IR-2: What interferes with your getting affection?

2. IE: I'm afraid that I may lose control of myself.
   IR-1: What do you think would happen if you did?
   IR-2: Would that be bad?

3. IE: I was afraid of my parents when I was younger.
   IR-1: What about them made you afraid?
   IR-2: Yes, many young children are afraid of their parents.

4. IE: Doctor, I think that I'm going crazy.
   IR-1: Oh, no, you're not. You don't have any symptoms.
   IR-2: Tell me what you mean by "crazy."

5. IE: My teacher is mean to me.
   IR-1: Can you give me an example of that?
   IR-2: I'm sorry that he is.

6. IE: My headaches are getting worse, and my mother says that she can't stand it much longer.
   IR-1: Does your mother have headaches too?
   IR-2: What can't your mother stand?

7. IE: Yesterday I had a big quarrel with my Dad.
   IR-1: Again?
   IR-2: What happened?

8. IE: I don't think this will help me at all.
   IR-1: Let's talk about that; what do you think is happening?
   IR-2: If you don't cooperate, I'll have to notify the school principal.

9. IE: You look tired.
   IR-1: This headache is killing me.
   IR-2: I've had a touch of sinus congestion, but that won't interfere with our session.

10. IE: I refuse to give in to my mother.
    IR-1: What do you mean by "give in"?
    IR-2: How can you expect your mother to do anything for you if you don't do anything for her?

11. IE: Well, I liked school a lot. I was on the swim team and had lots of friends. I had a good figure then, too. That was before I gained all this weight. My boyfriend liked me better when I was thin. Then, when I was a senior, my mother died from cancer. All of my girlfriends got steady boyfriends. That's when I gained weight. Things just weren't the same.
    IR-1: So things were going pretty well for you until your senior year, when many difficult changes occurred.
    IR-2: Tell me about your mother.

12. IE: My marriage was not exactly good. You see, my husband and I used to get into these huge fights, and he'd get really violent. One time, he shoved me so hard I flew through the sliding glass doors. I had to have all kinds of stitches. It was a real mess.
    IR-1: How long were you and your husband married?
    IR-2: That must have been very frightening for you. What kinds of things did you fight about?

13. IE: I'm not going to be able to finish my senior year in high school.
    IR-1: If you graduate, you'll have a better chance of getting a job.
    IR-2: Tell me about that.

14. IE: (In a hospital) At home, my mom lets me eat whatever I want.
    IR-1: You're unhappy that you can't always eat what you want when you're in the hospital.
    IR-2: Wow! Your mom sure spoils you. She lets you eat anything you want.

Suggested Answers

1. IR-2's response is preferable. It acknowledges the interviewee's statement and also explores possible reasons for not receiving affection. IR-1's response tends to close off the remark, halting further exploration.

2. IR-1's response is preferable. It gives the interviewee room to comment on a range of possible feelings and actions. IR-2's response is less constructive because it is too specific, pointing to the "badness" and loss of control, and the interviewer doesn't even know what "lose control" means to the interviewee.

3. IR-1's response is preferable. It opens up the area to further discussion, whereas IR-2's response tends to close the discussion and provide false reassurance.

4. IR-2's response is preferable. It allows the interviewee to say what he or she means by "crazy." Although it is reassuring, IR-1's response assumes that the interviewer knows what the interviewee means, and this assumption may not be accurate.

5. IR-1's response is preferable. It leads the interviewee to focus on a specific event and to document the statement. IR-2's response, although somewhat sympathetic, tends to close off discussion and imply endorsement of the interviewee's perception. The interviewer could say "I'm sorry you feel that way. Could you tell me *how* he is mean to you, though?"

6. IR-2's response is preferable. It attempts to clarify what the interviewee meant by saying "can't stand it much

longer." IR-1's response is somewhat tangential at this time.

7. IR-2's response is preferable. It asks the interviewee to comment on the quarrel. IR-1's response, which simply recognizes that the quarrel is a recurring event, is not likely to facilitate further discussion.

8. IR-1's response is preferable. It asks the interviewee to explore his or her feelings about the reason for coming to the interview. A punitive response such as the one given by IR-2 should not be used under any circumstances.

9. IR-2's response is preferable. It acknowledges the interviewee's comment but reassures the interviewee that the interviewer is in control. Comments that burden the interviewee with the interviewer's own difficulties, such as IR-1's response, should be avoided.

10. IR-1's response is preferable. It is a clarifying probe. Argumentative comments such as IR-2's response should be avoided.

11. IR-1's response is preferable. It acknowledges the interviewee's statements and allows her to comment further on her difficulties. IR-2's response focuses on one specific area. Although it might be valuable to explore this area at another time during the interview, such a focus is premature.

12. IR-2's response is preferable. It is an empathic response, followed by a request for more information about an important area. IR-1's reply is not as responsive to the interviewee's statements. It is a useful information-gathering probe, but it seems out of place after the interviewee's statements.

13. IR-2's response is preferable. It is a good probing response, which informs the interviewee that the interviewer wants to know about the interviewee's reasons for not going back to school. IR-1's response gives advice—advice the interviewee likely has heard before and knows.

14. IR-1's response is preferable. It is a reflective/interpretive comment, which shows the interviewee that the interviewer understands how the interviewee feels. IR-2's response is somewhat inappropriate because it makes a generalization that may or may not be true.

Exercise 2-8. Evaluating an Interview

Obtain an audiotape or videotape of an actual interview or a transcript of an interview if these are not available. You might borrow a tape from an interviewer you know (but be sure that the client has signed a release form indicating that the tape can be used for instructional purposes), record an interview from radio or television, listen to an interview recommended by your instructor, or look at a transcript of an interview such as the ones found in Chapter 1 and Chapter 22. Carefully evaluate the way the questions are asked and answered. If necessary, play the recording a second or third time (or reread the transcript) until you can answer the questions below. If there are no examples of statements or questions in the interview that satisfy the task, simply put "No example." This exercise was in part adapted from Donaghy (1984).

1. How much talking, including both questions and statements, did the interviewer do in comparison to the interviewee? (If possible, time the interviewee's total speaking time and subtract that time from the total interview time. If that is not possible, give a rough approximation.)
2. Identify a statement or question made by the interviewer that
   a. helped the interviewer maintain control
   b. helped shape a response
   c. encouraged participation
   d. helped maintain the formality level
   e. helped improve rapport
   f. helped clarify what the interviewee meant
   g. reassured or supported the interviewee
   h. redirected the interviewee
3. Give examples of any *words* used by the *interviewer* that you think were too abstract, ambiguous, subjective, or jargonistic.
4. Give examples of any *words* used by the *interviewee* that you think were too abstract, ambiguous, subjective, or jargonistic.
5. Identify a statement or question made by the interviewer that you think was
   a. open-ended
   b. direct
   c. bipolar
   d. an elaboration
   e. a clarification
   f. a repetition
   g. a challenge
   h. a reflection
   i. a summary
   j. overly long
   k. double barreled
   l. leading
   m. coercive
   n. too embarrassing or sharp
6. Identify a statement or question made by the interviewee that
   a. was vague
   b. was clear
   c. was rambling
   d. was too detailed
   e. suggested good insight
   f. suggested a desire to help the interviewer understand him or her
   g. suggested a language problem
   h. suggested a thought disorder
   i. suggested any other problem
7. If you are observing a videotape, identify (and describe) one nonverbal behavior of the *interviewer* that showed a positive facial expression, positive body posture, positive vocal behavior, positive gesture or mannerism, or negative gesture or mannerism.
8. If you are observing a videotape, identify (and describe) one nonverbal behavior of the *interviewee* that showed a positive facial expression, positive body posture, positive vocal behavior, positive gesture or mannerism, or negative gesture or mannerism.
9. Evaluate the *interviewer's* style, including personality, sincerity, maintenance of control, pace, and repetition.

10. Evaluate the *interviewee's* style, including personality, sincerity, naturalness, accuracy, and pace.
11. What suggestions do you have for improving the interview? Consider interviewer talking time; alterations in words, phrases, or questions; style changes; and anything else you think could have been improved.

For just when ideas fail, a word comes in to save the situation.

—Goethe

THINKING THROUGH THE ISSUES

During an interview, what clues might you use to guide you in evaluating the extent to which the interviewee is being open and honest?

How might the interviewee judge your openness and honesty?

What can you do to become a good observer of behavior?

Why might you have difficulty establishing rapport?

How will you know when your questions are effective?

Which probing techniques do you think you will use most frequently as an interviewer? Why did you make these choices?

To what extent does the use of probing techniques reflect an invasion of privacy?

How can you tell whether silence reflects a pause or an impasse in the interview?

How would you deal with interviewees who become emotionally upset?

How would you prepare for an interview?

If your emotions interfered with the flow of the interview, what steps would you take to regain control?

Imagine that you were an interviewee. How would you know whether the interviewer liked you, understood you, and respected you? What would the interviewer have to do to convey this information to you?

What is your opinion about discussing issues of confidentiality in the interview?

SUMMARY

Introduction to Interviewing Guidelines

1. Prepare for the interview by considering the purpose of the interview, the physical setting, the structure of the interview, and the possible issues that may arise. Have a broad outline of the topics you want to cover.
2. Learn as much as you can about the interviewee *before* the interview.
3. Be sure that any equipment you plan to use is in good working order and that the interview room is available. Make arrangements so that you are not likely to be interrupted and that the interview room is free from distractions.
4. Consider the interviewee's cognitive and developmental levels and what intellectual demands the interview will make on his or her ability to report factual information and feelings.
5. Be prepared to explain confidentiality, and have the interviewee sign a consent form to release information.
6. Greet the interviewee in a friendly, polite, open manner, and put him or her at ease. Speak clearly, at a normal volume, using a friendly, reassuring tone. Establish rapport and a productive climate, and then probe carefully.
7. Recognize that you may have difficulty obtaining information when interviewees are anxious, upset, resistant, or unable to concentrate.
8. Be prepared to explain or expand on the questions you ask.
9. Develop the art of good listening.
10. Answer the interviewee's questions as clearly and directly as possible.
11. Judge how the interview is proceeding and make adjustments as needed.
12. Do not be frightened of silences.
13. Check periodically to see that your understanding of the interviewee's problems and situations is correct by offering a concise summary of the essential details.
14. Summarize, toward the end of the interview, the salient aspects of the information you obtain.
15. Record the information you obtain accurately, either during the interview proper or shortly thereafter.
16. Evaluate the information you obtain and decide whether you need follow-up interviews.
17. End the interview in the same friendly manner in which it began, and, no matter what the nature of the interview, always

---

Peanuts   by Charles Schulz

try to leave the interviewee with his or her dignity and self-esteem intact.

18. In planning the interview, know the purpose of the interview and be prepared to tell it to the interviewee, identify the main areas you wish to cover, formulate questions that will cover these areas, structure the interview so that you can cover the important areas, and anticipate possible questions or problems.

19. Listen carefully to the interviewee and interpret and assess what is significant, but do not accept everything as literal truth.

20. What interviewees say is important, but how they act and speak are equally important.

21. You will have difficulties if you fail to express interest and warmth, to uncover the anxieties of the interviewee, to recognize that the anxieties of the interviewee are being exposed too rapidly, to recognize the interviewee's level of understanding, or to understand the interviewee's culture.

22. Interviewing failures are more likely to arise from defects in attitude than from technical difficulties.

23. To be successful as an interviewer, you must know yourself, trust your ideas, be willing to make mistakes, and, above all, have a genuine desire to help the interviewee.

24. A good interview takes careful planning, skillful execution, and good organization; it is purposeful and goal-oriented.

Factors Influencing the Interview

25. Factors that affect the interview include interviewer and interviewee characteristics (for example, physical, cognitive, and affective factors), message components (for example, language, nonverbal cues, and sensory cues), and interview climate (for example, physical, social, temporal, and psychological factors).

External Factors and Atmosphere

26. Conduct the interview in a private, quiet room that is free from distractions; select appropriate furniture, keep interruptions to a minimum, and begin on time.

Forming Impressions

27. Both you and the interviewee will form impressions of each other. Be attentive to any signs of psychological disturbance shown by the interviewee—including cognitive, affective, and psychomotor disturbances—as well as to signs of psychological health. Also, be attentive to the feelings invoked in you by the interviewee.

Listening

28. Following are some steps you can take to become an effective listener. Make sure that you have no auditory or visual deficits that will interfere with your ability to conduct an interview; attend to your personal needs, such as eating and drinking properly and going to the toilet; maintain interest in and involvement with the interviewee; concentrate on the interviewee's communications; and link the information you obtain from the interviewee.

29. The ability to listen is a key factor in conducting the interview.

30. Being a good listener also means listening to yourself. Become attuned to your thoughts, feelings, and actions, and learn how to deal with them appropriately during the interview.

Sending Nonverbal Messages

31. Be aware of your body language.

32. Show your interest through good eye contact.

Analytical Listening

33. The ability to analyze the responses of the interviewee critically as you listen—termed *analytical listening*—is an important interviewing skill. Analytical listening will help you understand the frame of reference of the interviewee, reduce the interviewee's emotional tension, convey a sense of importance to the interviewee, give the interviewee time to refine his or her thoughts, and relate effectively to the interviewee.

34. Interviewees have certain ways or patterns of answering questions, or what is called *response sets* (or *response styles*). Some response sets may affect the accuracy of the information.

35. Carefully evaluate whether the information you get meets your objectives.

36. Convey an attitude of critical evaluation—interest in precise facts, concern for correct inferences, and desire to establish an accurate sequence of events—and you'll show the interviewee that you want to get beneath the surface of the communication and away from vague, superficial, and incomplete responses.

37. Toward the end of the interview, ask about important areas you did not discuss, clarify previously discussed material, make other needed comments, or invite questions that the interviewee might have.

Observation Guidelines

38. Observe the appearance, nonverbal and verbal behavior, and voice and speech of the interviewees to obtain valuable diagnostic clues.

39. Obtain useful leads from the interviewees' communications by attending to association of ideas, shifts in conversation, opening and closing sentences, recurrent references, inconsistencies and gaps, and concealed meanings.

40. Obtain useful information about the interviewees' physical and neurological development by observing their posture, gait, fine and gross motor coordination, speech, and quality and tone of voice.

Establishing Rapport

41. Establishing rapport is critical for the success of the interview. It is based on mutual confidence, respect, and acceptance. Facilitate rapport by both verbal and nonverbal behaviors, including making the interview a joint undertaking between you and the interviewee; giving the interviewee your undivided attention; conveying to him or her that you want to listen and can be trusted; giving him or her reassurance and support; listening to him or her openly and nonjudgmentally; speaking slowly and clearly in a calm, matter-of-fact, friendly, and accepting manner; interrupting the interviewee only when necessary; using a warm and expressive tone; maintaining a natural, relaxed, and attentive posture; maintaining appropriate eye contact; asking tactful questions; and timing questions and comments appropriately.

42. Focus on topics relevant to your assessment goal as soon as possible.

43. Show interest in the information given to you by the interviewees to establish rapport.

44. Accompany any statements you make with appropriate nonverbal behaviors.

45. Reassure interviewees when they show anxiety.

46. Point out gently the interviewee's responsibility when all else fails and the interviewee will still not talk with you.

47. Compliment the interviewee when she or he shares material with you.

48. Give interviewees time to work through their difficult feelings and acknowledge their feelings.
49. Use language suitable to the age, sex, and education of the interviewee.
50. Several verbal and nonverbal behaviors can diminish rapport. Do not boast and brag; be flippant or sarcastic; use stereotyped phrases or overworked expressions; tune in only to the things that interest you; argue, attack, or belittle the interviewee; try to influence the interviewee to accept your values; be shocked by life styles that differ from yours; lecture the interviewee; interrupt the interviewee; be distracted by the interviewee's mannerisms; concentrate on impressing the interviewee; concentrate on the next question; suggest answers; tell the interviewee how others answered the question; engage in nonverbal behaviors that send negative messages; tell the interviewee that you can solve all of his or her problems; give the interviewee inappropriate reassurance; superficially listen to the interview and then try to make your point; minimize the depth of the interviewee's feelings; or tell the interviewee about your problems.

Timing Questions Appropriately
51. Time your questions so that they are in harmony with the interviewee's thoughts and in the direction you want the interview to move.
52. Keep the pace of the interview rapid enough to keep the interest of the interviewee, but slow enough to allow the interviewee to formulate good answers. In addition, the interview should not be too long or have many lapses.

Changing Topics
53. Change topics in an orderly manner, recognize that it will take practice and sensitivity to judge when you have exhausted a topic and need to change topics, and avoid drastic shifts in questioning.

Widening the Circle of Inquiry
54. Widen your circle of inquiry to obtain additional information.

Formulating Appropriate Questions
55. Formulate appropriate questions. Good questions encourage the interviewee to answer freely and honestly about the topic at hand, whereas poor questions inhibit the interviewee from answering freely and may lead to distorted replies.
56. Formulate good questions to draw out information, to amplify statements, to guide the discussion, to bring out distinctions and similarities, to reintroduce a point needing further discussion, to encourage opinions, to encourage relaxation, and to check on your understanding.
57. Remember that the way you ask questions is as important as what you ask.
58. Realize that questions fall on a continuum from open-ended to closed-ended, with moderately focused questions toward the middle part of the continuum.
59. Use open-ended questions, especially at the start of the interview.
60. Phrase questions positively and confidently.

Major Types of Questions to Avoid
61. Avoid "yes-no" questions; double-barreled questions; long, multiple questions; leading questions; random probing questions; coercive questions; embarrassing or sharp questions; and "why" questions.

Using Structuring Statements
62. Use structuring statements throughout the interview to guide the interviewee in talking about a topic.
63. Use structuring statements to begin or end a phase of the interview, set an objective, or provide information about the direction of the interview.

Encouraging Appropriate Replies
64. Encourage appropriate replies by using both verbal and nonverbal behaviors.

Probing Effectively
65. Learn when to probe. Probe when interviewees give incomplete responses, inconsistent responses, irrelevant responses, poorly organized responses, ambiguous responses, or no responses.
66. Learn how to use the following probing techniques: elaboration, clarification, repetition, challenging, silence, neutral phrases, reflective statements, periodic summaries, checking interviewee's understanding, and miscellaneous probes.
67. Decide on what statements to probe by keeping in mind the interview goals.
68. Use probes to direct, organize, and focus the interview.

Dealing with Difficult Situations
69. Be prepared to handle difficult situations, including interviews where interviewees try to take control or where interviewees show difficult behavior, become emotionally upset, become embarrassed by sensitive topics, give inadequate answers, fail to cooperate, show memory difficulties, become silent, give irrelevant material, make derogatory remarks, become violent, ask questions about your clinical competence, request your opinion, and request you to give personal information.

Remaining Objective
70. Accept the interviewees' communications without endorsing them.
71. Recognize your emotions and keep them under control.
72. Increase your self-awareness and effectiveness by becoming aware of your behavior.

Recording Information and Scheduling
73. Record what the interviewee says as accurately as possible.
74. When you use an audiotape or videotape recorder, usually inform the interviewee that you are doing so.
75. Schedule breaks between interviews to write notes and relax.
76. Second interviews may focus on areas needing further inquiry or on pursuing leads discovered through psychological testing.

Confidentiality of the Interview Material and Assessment Findings
77. Confidentiality is an ethical practice—the obligation never to reveal information obtained in the assessment (or through any professional relationship) without specific consent from the client. It protects the client from unauthorized disclosures of information given in confidence to a clinician.
78. Privileged communication is a legal right granted by a law of a state. It protects clients from having their disclosures to certain

professional groups—such as social workers, psychologists, marriage and family counselors, attorneys, clergy, and physicians, including psychiatrists—revealed during legal proceedings without their informed consent.

79. Generally, there are three occasions when you must suspend confidentiality and privileged communication: when there is suspicion of child maltreatment, when the interviewee poses a physical threat to another person, and when the interviewee is a minor and poses a threat to himself or herself.

80. The Federal Educational Rights and Privacy Act (Public Law 93-830), which was passed in 1974, gives parents certain rights to their child's school records. The law also protects the release of children's school records.

81. Inform children and parents about confidentiality and its limits.

82. When parents are divorced, tell the custodial parent before you release any information to the other parent.

KEY TERMS, CONCEPTS, AND NAMES

STUDY QUESTIONS

1. Seventeen guidelines were presented for conducting an interview. Discuss seven of these guidelines.
2. What are some factors that may influence the interview? In your answer, discuss interviewer and interviewee characteristics, components of the message, and climate of the interview.
3. What are some factors involved in effective listening?
4. Discuss the importance of nonverbal messages.
5. Discuss the concept of analytical listening. Include in your discussion purposes served by analytical reasoning, response sets, and obtaining relevant information.
6. Describe how you would observe the interviewee's personal appearance, nonverbal behavior, verbal behavior, mood, behaviors related to physical and neurological development, and behaviors suggesting psychological problems.
7. What are some factors to consider in establishing rapport?
8. What are some factors to consider in timing questions?
9. What are some factors to consider in changing topics?
10. How would you go about widening the circle of inquiry?
11. What are some factors to consider in formulating appropriate questions?
12. Discuss the major types of questions to avoid in an interview.
13. What are some factors to consider in using structuring statements?
14. What are some factors to consider in probing effectively? Include in your discussion several useful probing techniques.
15. Describe several difficult situations that you may encounter in an interview and give suggestions for dealing with them.
16. Distinguish between acceptance and endorsement of an interviewee's communications.
17. Discuss some issues involved in recording information and scheduling.
18. Discuss confidentiality of the interview material. Include in your answer a discussion of the difference between confidentiality and privileged communication, as well as information on the confidentiality of school and other institutional records.

3

THE INITIAL INTERVIEW WITH CHILDREN

Children live in a world of imagination and feeling.... They invest the most insignificant object with any form they please, and see in it whatever they wish to see.
                    —Adam G. Oehlenschlager

Goals and Objectives

This chapter is designed to enable you to:

- Identify the goals of the initial assessment interview with children
- Consider the child's age in developing interview strategies
- Describe specialized interview techniques that are useful with children
- Develop self-monitoring procedures

GENERAL CONSIDERATIONS IN AN INITIAL INTERVIEW WITH CHILDREN

Interviews with children will give you information about problems as they perceive them, their thoughts and feelings about themselves, and their impressions of their situation and their relationships. How you obtain this information depends on their developmental level and on their linguistic and conceptual abilities (Bierman, 1983). You will need to support and encourage them to get them to reveal their thoughts and feelings to you.

Children are sometimes more difficult to interview than adults because they may have limitations in language comprehension, language expressions, conceptual abilities, and memory. They may not know the words to describe their symptoms, particularly the subjective experience associated with their feelings. For example, because of their limited vocabulary, they may have difficulty distinguishing a *throbbing* pain from a *dull* one. They may identify an emotion as a physical sensation—for example, feeling anxious may be expressed as a stomachache—especially if they are young. They also can be led to make inaccurate statements with poorly worded questions. For these reasons, you must be especially careful about how you word questions with young children.

Children may not be aware that they have problems. If they come to see you, it will usually be because someone tells them to do so or because someone brings them to you. If they come under protest, you must gain their trust. With older children, a brief sentence or two that provides them with some understanding of the reason for the interview may help. With younger children, you will have to judge how to get them to relax. Suggestions for working with reticent children are provided later in the chapter.

Children may give you hints or leads that they have been maltreated. In such cases, convey to them that you are interested in what they might want to tell you. *You want them to know that you can accept them no matter what they tell you.* If you disregard or dismiss their hints about possible maltreatment, they probably will not say anything about it.

In conducting the interview, always consider the child's age, experiences, level of cognitive development, and ability to express himself or herself, as well as the extensiveness of any psychological disturbance. Each of these factors will affect the interview, and some may not become apparent until after the interview has begun. You also want to be aware of the child's attention and concentration, level of distractibility, and any physical impediments that might affect the interview. Several interviewing techniques discussed in Chapter 2 also are discussed in this chapter, with particular emphasis on their application to children.

I cannot emphasize enough the importance of considering the *child's level of linguistic and conceptual development.* Imagine an interviewer asking an 8-year-old girl if she ever had any delusions. The child, not understanding what the word means, wants to please the interviewer and says "Yes, all the time." The interviewer records the response, continues the interview, and reaches a tentative diagnosis that the child has a thought disorder. The interviewer could have averted this situation by telling the child the ground rules, such as "Say 'I don't understand' when you don't understand a question and I'll try to ask it better."

Children are more dependent than adults on their immediate environments, as they have less power to shape them. Children have little first-hand knowledge about the opportunities that exist beyond their immediate familial and physical environments. Because of restricted resources, they usually have fewer opportunities than adults to make significant changes that might help them reduce stress.

Children also differ from adults in that they are in the process of developing. In comparison to adults, they may be more open to new ways of behaving, thinking, and feeling, and their personality patterns may be less rigid or set. They also may be more open in expressing their feelings, thoughts, and concerns.

Strangeness of the Interview Situation

Because the interview setting is unfamiliar and because the interviewer is a stranger, children's behavior in the interview may not be typical of their behavior in other settings (Bierman, 1990). Even so, there is still a good chance that you can establish rapport and learn about their feelings, beliefs, and concerns. The first 10 or 15 minutes of the interview may give you useful information about their initial reactions to new and perhaps stressful situations. You can follow up on information obtained from children in interviews with their parents and teachers.

Interviewer-Initiated Interviews

In school settings, and particularly in juvenile detention settings, you may initiate interviews when the children or parents have not sought help for a problem. In these cases, you must exercise special care on first contact with the children. Inform them simply and directly why you asked them to come to see you. Be prepared to spend additional time establishing rapport. With parents who have not initiated the interview, also be prepared to work harder to gain their trust and to respond to their concerns.

Goals of the Initial Interview with Children

The goals of the initial interview with children will depend on the referral question, as well as the children's age and communication skills. Generally, the initial interview with children is designed

1. to obtain informed consent to conduct the interview (for older children) or agreement to be at the interview (for younger children)
2. to evaluate the children's understanding of why they are at the interview and how they feel about being at the interview
3. to gather information about the children's perception of the situation
4. to identify antecedent and consequent events related to the children's problems
5. to estimate the frequency, magnitude, duration, intensity, and pervasiveness of the children's problems
6. to identify the circumstances in which the problems are most or least likely to occur
7. to identify potentially reinforcing events related to the problems
8. to identify factors associated with the parents, school, and environment that may contribute to the problems
9. to gather information about the children's perceptions of their parents, teachers, peers, and other significant individuals in their lives
10. to assess the children's strengths, motivations, and resources for change
11. to evaluate the children's ability and willingness to participate in formal testing
12. to estimate what the children's level of functioning was *before* an injury
13. to discuss the assessment procedures and possible follow-up procedures

Preparing for the First Meeting

As noted in Chapter 1, in preparing for the first meeting, you should study the referral question and review available background material. If the parents have completed the Background Questionnaire (see Table C-2 in Appendix C), review it. Also review teacher reports, medical reports, police reports, and prior evaluations of the child and the parents. Make sure that the interview room is ready. If your knowledge of the presenting problem is rusty, review relevant literature. As noted earlier, if the referral question is beyond your competence, refer the case to someone else.

The First Meeting

Observations begin when you first meet the child in the waiting room. If a parent brought the child, watch how the parent and child interact. (These guidelines also pertain to situa-

tions in which a caregiver other than a parent brings the child or when both parents are present.) As noted in Chapter 2, you will want to observe the child's appearance, dress, grooming, physical features, and any indications of neglect or abuse.

Observing parent and child.   The following questions should be addressed during your initial observations of parent and child:

- Do the parent and child talk?
- Does the parent yell at, scold, or reprimand the child?
- Does the parent sit close to or far away from the child?
- Does the parent maintain eye contact with the child?
- Does the child cling to the parent?
- What are the child's and parent's facial expressions?
- How does the child respond to the parent's requests?
- How does the parent respond to the child's requests?
- Is the parent or child eating?
- If other siblings are present, how do their appearance and behavior differ from those of the referred child?
- If other siblings are present, does the parent treat them differently than the referred child? (If so, how?)
- Is the child playing or doing homework?
- If the child is playing, what is the nature of the play?
- Does the child seek help from the parent?
- Does the parent help or ignore the child?
- Does the child look relaxed or tense? (If the child looks tense, does she or he cry, kick, verbalize fear or distress, or withdraw by remaining silent and immobile?)
- If the child is distressed, how does the parent react to the child?
- Does the parent look relaxed or tense? (If the parent looks tense, does she or he cry or sob, pound fists, drum fingers, chew fingers, tap feet, or verbally express anger or dismay?)
- Do the parent and child seem preoccupied or estranged?
- Are the parent and child caring and affectionate?
- Does the parent reassure the child if the child is anxious?
- How does the child make the separation from the parent to come with you?

Even a brief period of observation—say, 30 seconds—may provide you with useful information about the child (for example, how the child communicates and interacts and how the child deals with the anxiety-arousing situation of seeing an interviewer), the parent, and the parent-child interaction.

Introducing yourself.   After your initial observation, introduce yourself to the parent, and then introduce yourself to the child. You might say to the child "Hello, I'm Ms. _____, the staff social worker. We're going to be talking in my office for about 40 minutes while your mother waits out here for us." This simple introduction serves several functions (Reisman, 1973). First, it emphasizes through use of the interviewer's formal title that the relationship is a professional one. Second, it makes clear that communication is a major activity in which they are to engage. Finally, it tells the child where the parent will be during the meeting, thus helping to alleviate any anxiety that the child may have about separation.

Calming children down. Sometimes, however, children will scream and cry in the waiting room, and sometimes they will not want to separate from their parents. In such cases, pause a few minutes before you enter the waiting area to see if the child's distress is brief and to see if the parents can calm the child (Kanfer, Eyberg, & Krahn, 1992). If the child continues to cry, try "to distract the child by offering him or her a toy and engaging briefly in play. If this too fails, suggest beginning the session with a joint family interview" (Kanfer et al., 1992, p. 56). As you talk with the parent(s) in the family interview, most children are likely to calm down, especially if there are appropriate toys in the room (see Chapter 4).

Bringing child and parent into the interview room. Another useful procedure is to bring the child and the parent into the interview room together to explain what will be happening: "Hello, I'm Ms. _____, the staff social worker. You must be Tom, and this is your mother, Mrs. _____. I'd like to talk to both of you in my office. Please come in (follow me)." This procedure may reduce the anxiety of both the child and the parent, gives them both time to ask questions, allows you to go over confidentiality with both of them present, lets the parent see where the child will be, and lets the child get ready to say goodbye to the parent as the child becomes comfortable in the setting. It also means that you don't have to make introductions in the waiting room in front of other people; if the child is going to cry or protest over the separation, the child can do so in the privacy of your office (or interview room) rather than in the waiting room.

Children under the age of 6 years, and sometimes older children, may not want to separate from their parents. In such cases, allow the parent to come into the room. Then, depending on your goals, you may request that the parent be an observer only or leave after a few minutes, or you may not make any specific request. The latter is preferred when you want to keep the situation as natural as possible, noting the spontaneous interactions between the parent and child. *However, if one parent (or both) is suspected of having abused or neglected the child, interview the child alone* (see Chapter 22). For children who have separation anxiety, show them where their parent will be waiting. Offer your hand to the child and say "Come with me to the playroom...." Or you could ask "Would you like to leave your dolly here with your mother, or would you like to bring it with you?" (Kanfer et al., 1992, p. 56). The question gives the children some choice and control and may help reduce their anxiety. You can coax hesitant children by showing them a toy and encouraging them to go into the playroom to play with it. If these strategies fail, you can ask the parent to come into the room with the child. As the child relaxes, you can ask the parent to leave, reassuring the parent and the child that everything will be fine.

Children's Initial Apprehensions

When you first meet children, they are likely to be apprehensive. Typical concerns center on such issues as *medical treatment* ("Will I get needles?"), *removal from home* ("Am I going to be 'put away'?"), *competency* ("Will I have my head examined? How?"), *self-concept* ("Will they find that I am crazy or 'dumb'?"), and *being singled out* ("Why am I the only one in the family to come?", "How come the other kids at school don't come?", or "What will I tell my classmates about why I had to leave school today?") (Swanson, 1970). To deal with these and other concerns, you will need to establish rapport, allay their apprehensions, and reduce their anxiety.

At the beginning of the interview, you usually will want to inform the child about the reason for the evaluation: "Your parents are concerned about your schoolwork. I'm here to find out how we can help you." By allaying the apprehensions of the child through questions and comments, you convey to the child that you will treat him or her professionally, with decency, safety, and respect (Swanson, 1970). Be honest with the child, and tailor your comments to his or her age and level of understanding.

Older children may be curious about what you are going to do with the information you obtain; how much of the information you are going to share with parents, guardians, school, or court (see Chapter 2); and what will happen to them after you complete the evaluation. What you say about these matters will depend on the referral question, what you learn about the child during the interview, your agency policy, your state law, or some combination of these factors. Even if children are not curious about these matters, share with them the steps in the evaluation procedure and, if feasible, tell them that you will meet with them to discuss the results and recommendations. Anything you can do to allay their anxiety and concerns will be helpful.

Here are two examples of what you might say:

1. "After we finish today, I'll review the information and consult with other members of the staff. Then, I'll ask you and your parents to join me at a meeting so that we can plan what to do next."

2. "As you know, you are having problems with your studies. After we finish today, I'm going to recommend that you see a member of our staff who will give you some tests to find out more about why you are having problems. OK?"

Children (and adults) may wonder about you. They may wonder about who you are, your competency (especially if you are an interviewer-in-training), what you know about them, whose side you are on, and how your actions will affect what will eventually happen to them. Be prepared to encounter these and other apprehensions. Children may not express them directly, so watch for their presence. It may help to let children know that you recognize their apprehensions: "Bill, I know how difficult it is for many children to come to a new place and talk with new people."

It also is helpful to learn what the child thinks the reason is for the interview. You might ask "What did your parents tell you about coming to see me?" or "What kind of place did you think this would be?" Clarify any misperceptions. If you think it would reduce the child's anxiety, explain that you do not give shots and that after the session is over she or he can go home. Evidence of some toys in the room may be reassuring, although too many toys can be distracting.

Despite your efforts, children may not want to speak with you. They may be wary of strangers, uncertain of why you want to interview them, resentful of having been coerced to come to the interview, reluctant to confide anything that may get back to their parents, or fear talking about painful or frightening material (Kessler, 1988). If a child won't talk openly with you, use alternative procedures such as drawings, play materials, or sentence completion techniques (discussion to follow). With reluctant children, drawings may be especially useful and can serve as an ice-breaker. With wary children, empathize with their fears and resentments and offer them support and reassurance (Kessler, 1988). Other techniques for handling resistance and anxiety in children are discussed in the sections that follow.

DEVELOPMENTAL CONSIDERATIONS IN INTERVIEWING CHILDREN

In each developmental period, children face various tasks. Mastering these tasks will likely facilitate the children's development (Masten & Braswell, 1991).

1. *Infants.* Tasks include attaining smooth physiological regulation (such as eating and sleeping), making the transition from reflex to voluntary behavior, becoming attached to a caregiver, and separating self from others.

2. *Preschool children.* Tasks include mastering toileting and other self-care activities, developing language, developing self-control and compliance, and achieving gender identity formation.

3. *Children in middle childhood.* Tasks include adjusting to school (including attendance, appropriate behavior, and peer acceptance), achieving academically (including learning to read, write, spell, and master basic mathematics), establishing friendships with peers and peer acceptance, and learning moral development (including following rules of home and school).

4. *Adolescents.* Tasks include adjusting to pubertal changes, making the transition to secondary schooling, establishing friendships and dating, and achieving identity formation, such as a coherent sense of self.

The following case illustrates how a child's failure to reach a developmental milestone led a health care provider to make a referral for psychosocial services (Rounds, 1991).

CASE 3-1. MRS. M.
Mrs. M. suspected that "something was wrong with her two-year-old daughter" because she was not talking yet, seemed "very clumsy, and was always walking into things," and at times "didn't seem to connect" with her. On the advice of the pediatrician, Mrs. M. adopted a "wait and see approach." After several months her anxiety about her daughter's lack of progress escalated and the pediatrician finally made a referral to a clinic for a multidisciplinary assessment. The social worker on the team met with Mrs. M. to prepare her for the assessment. Because Mr. M. thought that there was nothing wrong with his daughter and refused to participate in the assessment process, Mrs. M. requested that her mother be allowed to attend. At times Mrs. M. believed that if she quit her job to stay at home with her daughter, "she would begin to talk." The social worker, with the mother's consent, contacted the day care teacher for additional information and to schedule an observation of the child at day care as part of the assessment process. During the assessment, the social worker asked Mrs. M. to talk about her daughter's strengths and needs and what her goals were for her. Mrs. M.'s highest priority was to "get her daughter to talk"; she identified family needs to include "helping her husband understand that there was a problem, so that they wouldn't fight about it so much" and finding a better day care for her child so that she wouldn't have to quit her job. (pp. 493–494, with changes in notation)

Table 3-1 provides examples of factors that may lead to developmental problems for children from birth to 18 years. Areas covered are sensory-motor and neurological functioning; communication behaviors; temperament, affect, and interpersonal relations; and family stressors.

Infants

Although you cannot interview infants, you can learn about them by observing them and by interviewing their parents. Table 3-2 presents guidelines for observing nine facets of an infant's behavior: the infant's interactions with play materials and involvement in play, affect in play, attention span in play, temperament and motivation, auditory responsiveness, expressive language, motor behavior, eating patterns, and general behavior. Chapter 4 presents guidelines for observing parent-infant interactions at home.

The parent's description of the infant may give you information about the infant's temperament. *Temperament* refers to the style in which infants (or any individuals) react to their environment. Chess and Thomas (1986) identified the

Table 3-1
Possible Indicators of Disturbances in Physical and Psychological Development from Birth to 18 Years

Ages	Indicators of disturbance			
	Sensory-motor and neurological functioning	Communication behaviors	Temperament, affect, and interpersonal relations	Family stressors
Birth to 6 months	Birthweight low Quiet or fussy Startles frequently and/or is nonresponsive to stimuli Sleep cycles unusual Scores on developmental tests show delays	Does not vocalize Crying not related to needs Does not turn to voice Does not startle at loud noises	Anticipatory social responses absent (e.g., smiling response) Eye-to-eye contact poor or absent Fails to respond to mother's attention and crib toys Temperament difficult Passive, low energy, quiet, inhibited	Parental stress Parental substance abuse (prenatally for mother and postnatally for mother and father) Poor parental care Clash in child/parent temperaments Parent insensitive to infant's moods, overstimulates infant, unable to comfort infant
6 to 12 months	Sleep and eating cycles fail to develop Motor development uneven Transition to table foods difficult Fails to hold objects Forms attachments to unusual objects Appears to be deaf Is preoccupied with fingers Over- or underreacts to sensory stimuli	Babbling may stop Does not imitate sounds, gestures, or expressions Does not take turns vocalizing Does not look at objects mentioned by adults	Unaffectionate Difficult to engage in baby games Does not wave "bye-bye" Shows no interest in toys Forms insecure attachments Affect flat Relates poorly to people	Parental stress Parental substance abuse Poor parental care Clash in child/parent temperaments
12 to 24 months	Has problems with sleep cycle Loses previously acquired skills Sensitive to stimuli Seeks repetitive stimulation Makes repetitive motor movements Has unusual mannerisms (e.g., handflapping, whirling)	Does not speak or says only occasional words Stops talking Gestures do not develop Repeats sounds noncommunicatively Does not respond to name Does not respond to simple requests	Withdrawn Shows no separation distress Uses toys in unusual ways (e.g., spins, flicks, lines up objects) Has little impulse control Comforts self by excessive rocking or thumb sucking Relates poorly to people	Parental stress Parental substance abuse Poor parental care, including excessive criticism and overcontrol Clash in child/parent temperaments Parent withdrawn because he or she thinks infant/toddler doesn't need him or her anymore Unrealistic parental expectations

(Continued)

Table 3-1 (*Continued*)

Ages	Indicators of disturbance			
	Sensory-motor and neurological functioning	Communication behaviors	Temperament, affect, and interpersonal relations	Family stressors
24 to 36 months	Gross and fine coordination poor Sleep cycle problems continue Appears to be able to do things but refuses Self-care skills delayed Unusually sensitive to stimuli Has repetitive motor mannerisms Hyperactive and/or hypoactive Performance variable on intelligence tests	Mute or talks intermittently Echolalia (e.g., repeats TV commercials exactly) Cognitive abilities good in some areas but poor in others (e.g., good rote memory, superior puzzle skills, but poor language skills) Leads adult by hand to communicate needs Shows no interest in other person's conversations	Does not play with others Prefers to be alone Unusual use of toys continues Flicks objects away Depressed Disposition angry and hostile Anxious, irritable Emotionally flat Withdrawn, passive Distractible Negativistic	Poor parental care Parental stress Parental substance abuse Separation from parents
3 to 5 years	Gross and fine coordination poor Sleep cycle problems continue Appears to be able to do things but refuses Self-care skills delayed Hyperactive and/or hypoactive Performance variable on intelligence tests	Does not speak Echolalia Reverses pronouns Speech has abnormal tone and rhythm Expresses unusual thoughts	Unusual use of toys continues Flicks objects away Depressed Disposition angry and hostile Anxious, irritable Emotionally flat Withdrawn, passive Distractible Negativistic Upset by changes in environment	Poor parental care Parental stress Parental substance abuse Separation from parents
5 to 12 years	Gross and fine motor coordination poor Exhibits attention impairment Performance variable on intelligence tests	Does not speak Associations loose Tangentiality Speech incoherent Speech illogical Speech circumstantial Pressure of speech Speech distractible Clang associations Blocking of speech	Emotionally unstable Aggressive, disruptive, hyperactive, impulsive Interpersonal relationships poor Immature Fearful Inhibited, withdrawn Affect inappropriate School adjustment poor	Death of a parent Poor parental care Parental stress Parental substance abuse Poor discipline Father not involved Poor family relationships Marital discord Poor family communication

(Continued)

Table 3-1 (Continued)

| Ages | Indicators of disturbance | | | |
	Sensory-motor and neurological functioning	Communication behaviors	Temperament, affect, and interpersonal relations	Family stressors
12 to 18 years	Gross and fine motor coordination poor Exhibits attentional impairment Performance variable on intelligence tests	Does not speak Associations loose Tangentiality Speech incoherent Speech illogical Speech circumstantial Pressure of speech Speech distractible Clang associations Blocking of speech	Emotionally unstable Aggressive, disruptive, hyperactive, impulsive Interpersonal relationships poor Immature Fearful Inhibited, withdrawn Affect inappropriate School adjustment poor Substance abuse Heterosexual relationships poor	Death of a parent Poor parental care Parental stress Parental substance abuse Poor discipline Father not involved Poor family relationships Marital discord Poor family communication

Source: Adapted, in part, from Asarnow (1988) and Freeman and Ritvo (1984).

following nine major temperament characteristics in infants (also see Medoff-Cooper, Carey, & McDevitt, 1993; Willis & Walker, 1989).

1. *Activity level*—the amount of physical motion during sleeping, eating, playing, dressing, bathing, and so forth. An active infant is characterized by much movement and fitful sleep; the caregiver is likely to feel that she or he cannot leave the infant alone for even a few seconds for fear that the infant will move or fall.

2. *Rhythmicity*—the regularity of physiological functions such as hunger, sleep, and elimination. An infant with rhythmicity has regular feeding times, sleeping times, and times for bowel movements.

3. *Approach or withdrawal*—the nature of initial responses to new stimuli, including people, situations, places, foods, toys, and procedures. An infant with an approach tendency reacts well to new people, approaches people eagerly, and reacts well to new surroundings.

4. *Adaptability*—the ease or difficulty with which reactions to stimuli can be modified in an appropriate way. An adaptable infant adjusts easily to unexpected company, warms up to new people, and tries new foods with interest.

5. *Threshold of responsiveness*—the amount of stimulation, such as sound or light, necessary to evoke discernable responses in the infant. An infant with a good threshold of responsiveness adjusts well to noises, textures of clothing, heat, cold, and environmental sounds such as the telephone and a siren.

6. *Intensity of reaction*—the energy level of responses, whatever the quality or direction. An infant with a high level of intensity displays a vigorous reaction to pleasure or displeasure.

7. *Quality of mood*—the amount of pleasant, joyful, and friendly behavior or the amount of unpleasant, crying, and unfriendly behavior. An infant with a joyful quality of mood is happy and content overall and displays this mood in varied situations.

8. *Distractibility*—the effectiveness of extraneous environmental stimuli in interfering with or altering the direction of ongoing behavior. An infant who is not distractible can carry out her or his activities, such as eating, despite some noise or people entering the room.

9. *Attention span and persistence*—the length of time particular activities are pursued by the child and the extent to which activities are continued in the face of obstacles. An infant with a good attention span and persistence can stay with an activity for a period; when such a child drops a toy, he or she looks for the toy, tries to retrieve it, and persists at getting it.

These nine characteristics, in turn, lead to three temperamental types: "(1) the *easy child,* who is mild, predominantly positive in mood, approachable, adaptable, and rhythmic; (2) the *difficult child,* who is predominantly negative and intense in mood, not very adaptable, and arrhythmic; and (3) the *slow-to-warm-up child,* who is low in activity, approach and adaptability; variable in rhythm; and somewhat negative..." (Willis & Walker, 1989, p. 35).

Preschool Children

Although you usually will not formally interview preschool children, try to get them to talk about themselves. Preschool children are often shy and timid and have difficulty verbaliz-

Table 3-2
Guidelines for Observing Infants

Guideline 1. Observe the infant's interactions with play materials and involvement in play. Note, for example:

- how the infant looks at, touches, and manipulates objects (for example, active, passive)
- what objects hold special interest for the infant (for example, those that make sounds; those made of wood, plastic, or cloth; those that can be used as containers)
- how the infant plays with toys that can be used in several ways (for example, small boxes with tops, nesting toys, cubes and containers with lids, including pots and pans)
- how the infant approaches new things (for example, with anticipation, fearfully)
- how much encouragement the infant requires to become involved in play (for example, little encouragement, much encouragement)
- how the infant shows interest in a toy (for example, looks at the toy, makes grasping movements toward the toy)
- how the infant's interest varies with different activities
- the intensity of the infant's play
- how much time it takes the infant to become involved in playing with a toy
- how the infant's behavior changes when the infant is given time to explore an object or use materials
- how often the infant achieves goals in play
- what the infant does after being interrupted in an activity (for example, goes back to the activity, goes to a new activity)

Guideline 2. Observe the infant's affect in play. Note, for example:

- what emotions the infant shows during play (for example, happiness, anger, tension, irritability, sadness)
- how the infant expresses likes and dislikes, enjoyment, distress (for example, smiles, whines, shows distress, laughs, cries)
- how the infant reacts when he or she is given a new object, discovers a new way to use a toy, or is given just enough help to succeed in an activity
- what activities frustrate the infant
- what the infant does when frustrated (for example, cries, reacts stoically, looks for caregiver)

Guideline 3. Observe the infant's attention span in play. Note, for example:

- what activities hold the infant's attention the longest
- how the infant explores objects (for example, attends briefly, attends for long period of time, turns object frequently)
- how long the infant plays with an object
- what toys the infant selects (for example, those that keep the infant involved and interested for a reasonable time, those that are nearest)

Guideline 4. Observe the infant's temperament and motivation. Note, for example:

- what kind of temperament the infant has (for example, active or passive, content or fussy, relaxed or tense, engaging or unfocused, sleepy or alert, cuddly or rigid, easy to comfort or difficult to comfort)
- what activities cause the infant to be distressed and how the infant shows distress (for example, frowning, turning away, making sounds, kicking)
- what cues the infant gives that she or he is overstimulated, bored, frustrated, happy, or involved
- how consistent the infant's tempo is across several activities
- how persistent the infant is in pursuing a goal in play in the face of obstacles
- how interested the infant is in activities
- how the infant's tempo compares with that of the infant's parent(s)
- what changes in temperament the infant shows during the observation

Guideline 5. Observe the infant's auditory responsiveness. Note, for example:

- how the infant responds to the spoken language of others (for example, becoming attentive, animated, quiet)
- what the infant does when someone calls his or her name (for example, looking up, attending to the face of the person talking, not looking up, not attending)
- what the infant does when adults talk to each other in his or her presence
- how the infant seems to understand and attend to words (for example, looks at a ball when it is mentioned, touches his or her nose when it is named, attends to words or phrases contingent on his or her activity)
- what cues the infant gives that indicate some interest in language spoken (for example, looks at a speaker when language is not directed to him or her, turns to see who is speaking)
- what is required to get the infant's attention (for example, clapping hands, talking loudly, using dramatic gestures)
- how the infant attends to language when there is background noise

Guideline 6. Observe the infant's expressive language. Note, for example:

- what sounds the infant makes
- how the infant babbles or uses jargon (for example, as if participating in others' conversation, making playful sounds without semblance of participation in others' conversation)

(Continued)

Table 3-2 (*Continued*)

- what vocalizations the infant makes in various situations (for example, when excited, when a parent is on the telephone, when a parent watches, when engaged in solitary play)
- how the infant reacts to his or her vocalizing (for example, becomes more animated, shows no particular reaction)
- what the infant does when making certain sounds (for example, looks consistently at the same object when making a specific sound, such as *baba* for blanket or *ga* for cracker; makes sounds without specific referents)
- how the infant expresses wants (for example, makes sounds, kicks feet, points, crawls to place)
- how the infant communicates without using vocal language
- how the infant reacts when he or she keeps making a certain sound and does not get a response

Guideline 7. Observe the infant's motor behavior. Note, for example:

- what fine and gross motor behaviors the infant shows (for example, ability to handle various objects of different sizes and shapes, ability to throw a ball, ability to move)
- the quality of the infant's motor behaviors (for example, normal motor development, delayed motor development, disturbed motor development)
- how the infant reacts when staying in one place for long periods
- how the infant's motor behavior changes in different situations
- how the infant shows newly acquired or emerging skills (for example, persists in repeating skills, performs skill only once or a few times)
- what the infant does when encouraged to perform a motor movement for which he or she is not developmentally ready

Guideline 8. Observe the infant's eating patterns. Note, for example:

- what cues the infant gives indicating a readiness to eat (for example, reaches for bottle, spoon, or food, opens mouth eagerly)
- how the infant is fed (breast fed, bottle fed, breast and bottle fed, fed with solid food and finger foods)
- how the infant feeds herself or himself (for example, with fingers, utensils)
- what foods the infant eats (for example, liquids, solids, soft foods, chewable foods)
- how the infant reacts to being fed and to feeding (for example, sucks, swallows, or chews food eagerly; pushes food or bottle away; holds food in mouth without chewing or swallowing; talks to avoid eating; becomes easily distracted from feeding)

Guideline 9. Observe the infant's general behavior. Note, for example:

- what the infant's best-developed skills are
- how the infant's behavior varies in different activities (for example, when engaged in play, in social behavior, in language, in motor activities)
- how the infant reacts to people (for example, to familiar adults, children, strangers)
- atypical behaviors displayed by the infant (for example, fails to cuddle, cries excessively, rocks constantly, bangs head)
- in what situations the behaviors are displayed (for example, with mother, with father, with both parents, with babysitter, with stranger present along with caregiver, with siblings, with other relative)
- how the infant indicates readiness for some independence (for example, plays alone, sits on floor alone)

Note. Record specific instances of each behavior, where appropriate, and the conditions under which the behavior occurred.

ing their feelings and thoughts. Seldom will they make a remark such as "I was very angry at my mother for not letting me have a large ice cream cone." Instead, they may convey this feeling with a remark such as "Don't like mommie" or "Bad mommie."

Here are some other characteristics of preschool children (Bierman, 1990). They tend to

- confuse temporal and sequential aspects of events and may mix wishful thinking with fact
- be concrete and specific in their emotional, interpersonal, and conceptual reasoning
- be rigid and inflexible in their social conceptions
- see people in all-or-none categories, failing to appreciate that people have both positive and negative qualities

- be too egocentric to consider perspectives other than their own
- highlight events that emphasize pleasures and sorrows rather than a broader range of emotions

Thus, "the cognitive limitations of young children result in social and emotional concepts that are more limited and unidimensional, more concrete and behavioral, and more externalized and inflexible than the conceptions of older children and adults" (Bierman, 1990, p. 207).

On the other hand, preschool children are "not self-conscious about their fears and fantasies, and, through play and game-like tasks, will reveal much about their social perceptions and current concerns" (Bierman & Schwartz, 1986, p. 269). They also will respond to short, concrete probing questions designed to help them expand on and clarify their ideas. If you keep these characteristics in mind, talking with young children can provide valuable information about their feelings, interests, and concerns.

Establishing rapport with preschool children. One way to establish rapport with young children is to play a game or show them an interesting toy before the interview begins (Yarrow, 1960). Another way is to visit the children's nursery school or home before the interview. Rapport may be easier to establish when preschool children have previously met you.

Using a free-play setting.   With children younger than 5 years of age, you can hold the clinical or forensic assessment interview in a playroom. In the playroom, you might have paper, pencils, crayons, paint, paintbrushes, an easel, clay, blocks, balls, dolls, a doll house, puppets, animals, dress-up clothes, and a sink. Pictures, toys, and stories may help stimulate young children to think and talk about their own immediate concerns. If you relate your own ideas, thoughts, and memories in relation to these props, you can probably draw the children into a discussion. Note, however, that you may not need to follow a free-play strategy to conduct interviews to investigate acknowledged or alleged child maltreatment. In such cases, you can interview children aged 3 to 5 years in a room without many toys (see Chapter 22).

Using observational guidelines in a free-play setting. If you hold the interview in a playroom, you will find the guidelines in Table 3-3 useful for observing children's play. The guidelines emphasize observing the children's entrance into the playroom, initiation of play, energy expenditure, manipulative actions, tempo of play, body movements, verbalizations, affect and tone of play, integration of play, creativity, products of play, attitude toward adults, and departure from the playroom.

Your observations may provide information about the children's ability to assume and change roles; thoughts and fantasies; spontaneity, creativity, and organization, as related to play; ability to solve or adopt new solutions to a problem; tolerance for frustration; language; and interpersonal interactions. Play also may help children verbalize the thoughts and feelings that they are unable to express in a traditional one-to-one interview.

Useful techniques in a free-play setting.   You might begin the play session by saying "Let's play with some toys. You can play with anything you like." Then, as the child plays, record her or his behavior, using the guidelines shown in Table 3-3. Answer questions as necessary to build rapport. Consider using some of the following techniques.

1. If the child asks "What are you writing?", you can say "I'm writing about what you are playing with."

2. If the child gives a major lead, pursue it. For example, if the child says "Mommie is mean," you can repeat the phrase as a question: "Mommie is mean?" You can then follow up by asking "How is Mommie mean?" You also can follow up specific play behavior with questions based on that behavior. For example, you might say "What does Mommie do when you don't eat?" or "What did the baby do before Daddy spanked him?"

3. If a child begins to act out excessively, such as by trying to break toys, hit you, or draw on the walls, decide what limits should be set. You always will need to set firm limits regarding not hitting a person or destroying property. You might say, for example, "You can hit the punching doll, but you can't hit me" or "You can draw on the paper but not on the wall." In other cases, the limits you set will depend on the child's age and behavior and the goals of the interview.

4. If the child's parent or caregiver is present in the playroom, you can, in a quiet voice, call certain behaviors to her or his attention and ask for clarification (Swanson, 1970): "Does he frequently pull his hair at home?" "Is this her natural walk?" "Can he stack blocks at home?" "Is she usually this active?"

The experiences of the first three years of life are almost entirely lost to us, and when we attempt to enter into a small child's world, we come as foreigners who have forgotten the landscape and no longer speak the native tongue.

—Selma Fraiberg

"I FEEL PRETTY SILLY PUTTING PEGS IN HOLES WHEN I HAVE A PERSONAL COMPUTER AT HOME."

Table 3-3
Guidelines for Observing Children at Play

Guideline 1. Observe the child's entrance into the playroom. Note, for example:

- how the child goes into the playroom (for example, goes alone; refuses to go without parent; asks to hold the mother's, father's, or interviewer's hand)
- the child's reactions to the playroom (for example, happy, excited, fearful, hesitant, calm)
- how the child approaches the toys (for example, warily, with conviction, forcefully)

Guideline 2. Observe the child's initiation of play. Note, for example:

- how long it takes the child to begin to play
- whether the child needs help to get started in play
- how long it takes the child to become involved in play
- how the child plays (for example, needs continuous encouragement to keep playing; directs own play; plays alone or needs assistance; shows initiative, resourcefulness, and curiosity; plays impulsively; initiates many activities but seldom completes them; maintains interest in a single activity)
- the toys or materials the child chooses (for example, dolls, moving toys, building toys, kitchen utensils, doctor kit)

Guideline 3. Observe the child's energy expenditure in play. Note, for example:

- the pace at which the child plays (for example, hurriedly, slowly, carefully)
- the child's level of energy (for example, highly energetic, listless, lethargic, lacking in vitality)
- how much energy the child uses in different activities (for example, in manipulating the play materials, in moving body, in making verbalizations)
- the child's play patterns (for example, pursuing an activity to the point of tiring, starting to work slowly and then gaining momentum until actions are energetic, gradually losing momentum)

Guideline 4. Observe the child's manipulative actions (operations with hands) in play. Note, for example:

- how the child uses the play materials (for example, in conventional ways, in unconventional ways)
- how skillful the child is in play (for example, shows great aptitude, is awkward)
- what the child does with the play materials (for example, looks at materials, touches materials, explores materials)

Guideline 5. Observe the child's tempo of play. Note, for example:

- the child's rate of play (for example, rapid tempo, leisurely tempo, slow tempo)
- how the child's tempo varies with different activities

Guideline 6. Observe the child's body movements in play. Note, for example:

- the quality of the child's body movements (for example, tense, relaxed, constricted, free, smooth and coordinated, jerky and uncoordinated)
- which hand the child uses predominantly

Guideline 7. Observe the child's verbalizations. Note, for example:

- the quality of the child's verbalizations (for example, sings, hums, uses nonsense phrases, uses meaningful phrases)
- the quality of the child's vocal tones (for example, loud, shrill, excitable, soft, aggressive, tense, enthusiastic, matter-of-fact)

Guideline 8. Observe the child's affect and tone of play. Note, for example:

- the affect displayed by the child (for example, angry, aggressive, happy, satisfied, hostile, friendly, impatient, patient)
- how the child handles play materials (for example, protects play materials; throws, tears, or attempts to destroy play materials)
- how the child controls his or her behavior (for example, always in control of behavior; somewhat in control of behavior; loses control of behavior to the point that it poses a threat to him or her, to other children, to the interviewer, or to the materials in the playroom)
- quality of the child's involvement in play (for example, mild, moderate, intense)
- how noise affects the child's productivity (for example, no effect, some effect, much effect)
- the evolution of the child's play (for example, from appropriate to inappropriate or vice versa)
- the child's reactions to frustration (for example, becomes angry, looks to adults for assistance, shouts, becomes depressed)

Guideline 9. Observe the child's integration of play. Note, for example:

- what goals the child pursues in play
- what the child does when interrupted in an activity (for example, goes to another activity, is frustrated, is agitated)
- how the child reacts to new materials (for example, shows delight and interest, shows no reaction and disinterest)
- the age-appropriateness of the child's play (for example, appropriate, inappropriate)
- the quality of the child's play (for example, goal directed, fragmentary, organized, haphazard, mostly normal, filled with peculiar elements)
- the quality of the child's attention span (for example, sustained, fleeting)

(Continued)

Table 3-3 (*Continued*)

- how long the child plays with an object or stays with an activity
- how the child's play changes over time (for example, becomes more integrated, becomes less integrated)
- the child's level of interest in different forms of play (for example, high, low)
- whether the child plays with an object long enough to explore its possibilities
- whether the child shows increased attention when given toys that can be used in several ways, such as small boxes with tops or nesting toys
- how often the child becomes distracted

Guideline 10. Observe the child's content and creativity of play. Note, for example:

- the dominant themes in the child's play
- the quality of the child's creativity in play (for example, improvises play, constricts play, plays imaginatively, plays in a stereotyped manner, plays in a more complex way when given time to decide how to use play materials)
- the type of toys or objects the child plays with creatively (for example, blocks, dolls, sand, clay, animals, household objects)
- what roles the child assumes in play
- how the child represents others in play
- what the child's concerns, wishes, and conflicts are

Guideline 11. Observe the child's products of play. Note, for example:

- what play materials the child prefers (for example, blocks, dolls, sand, clay, animals, household objects)

- what the child creates during play (for example, designs, block buildings, objects, drawings)
- the quality of the child's products (for example, recognizable form, unrecognizable form, neat, careless, aligned, not aligned, balanced, unbalanced)
- how the child interacts with the products (for example, shows interest in the product, tells a story about the product, shows the interviewer or parent the product, wants to save the product, wants to give the product to someone, uses the product for protective or aggressive purposes)

Guideline 12. Observe the child's attitude toward adults reflected in play. Note, for example:

- how the child interacts with an adult during play (for example, waits for an adult to initiate the play, shows changes in play when an adult plays with him or her, complies with the adult's requests, does what he or she thinks the adult expects of him or her, imitates the adult's manners accurately, avoids the adult, attempts to obtain tender responses from the adult, refuses help from the adult, is hostile toward the adult, follows own ideas independently of those of the adult)

Guideline 13. Observe the child's departure from the playroom. Note, for example:

- the child's emotions toward the end of the session (for example, anxious to leave, reluctant to leave)
- reactions to comments that play time is over (for example, ignores, accepts)
- how the child greets the caregiver (for example, happily, warily, sadly)

Note. These guidelines represent various facets of children's play behavior; they are not meant to cover all contingencies.
Source: Adapted from Goodman and Sours (1967); Hartley, Frank, and Goldenson (1952); Lerner and Murphy (1941).

Children in Middle Childhood

During middle childhood (about 5 to 11 years of age), children make great strides in their language and conceptual development (Yarrow, 1960). They can consider relationships among concepts, describe concepts in relational terms, and consider part-whole relationships. "Lawfulness, logic and rules enter the social-emotional world as children become able to combine, integrate, and organize concepts and events along temporal and hierarchical dimensions" (Bierman, 1990, p. 207).

Because of these new-found abilities, children in middle childhood can do the following:

- provide longer descriptions of themselves
- make distinctions between themselves and others
- use a temporal perspective
- use norms as a basis for making comparisons between themselves and others

- construct more stable perceptions of themselves and others
- accept conflicting behaviors in themselves and others
- emphasize relational and normative functioning of social roles (for example, a person becomes a father when he has children and his role remains, whatever his occupation)
- understand emotions as "multidimensional, internally determined, and internally controlled" (Bierman, 1990, p. 208)

Children in the middle childhood period (and younger), however, may have difficulty telling you when a symptom was at its worst, making comparative judgments about the severity of their symptoms, or describing their symptoms using long-term memory (Clarizio, 1994). Therefore, in interviewing children younger than 12 years, be as concrete as possible, especially when you discuss problem areas. Provide a context for your questions or use situationally related statements where possible, such as "How do you get along with your sister at dinner?"

Children in middle childhood may be reluctant to share their feelings, concerns, and attitudes with adults who are unfamiliar to them. To help build rapport, you can use competitive board games, such as checkers or 4-in-a-row, which have special appeal for children in this age group.

Bierman and Schwartz (1986) observed that children in middle childhood are more likely than younger children to

approach the interview as a task to accomplish. Some children view this task positively, hoping to do it well and do it right, while others only hope to endure it and be finished as soon as possible. Grade-school children are usually aware that the interviewer wants to ask them personal questions, but realize that they can keep their feelings secret if they wish to. Typically, they take offense at simple invitations to play and are suspicious of an adult who acts like a peer. At the same time, they are often not prepared to deal with the verbal onslaught of adult-style, open-ended interview questions, and they respond with short, concrete statements (e.g., "I don't know") or blank stares. (p. 270)

When to consider a play period. It usually isn't necessary to structure the interview as a play situation with children older than 5 years of age. It sometimes may be valuable, however, to have a short period of play observation, particularly with hyperactive children, developmentally disabled children, or children who have problems handling aggression. You also can use the guidelines presented in Table 3-3 for observing the free play of children in middle childhood.

Case illustration of a play observation. The following case illustrates how observing the free play of a 7½-year-old boy provided clues about how he handled aggression (Simmons, 1987).

CASE 3-2. JOHN

John, age 7½, was referred for aggressive behavior at home and at school. He rushed to the playroom the instant he was invited. He quickly took the guns and shot wildly around the room with vivid sound effects and descriptive phrases such as "I got 'em! He's dead!" He tried to shoot the interviewer but was easily persuaded to direct his fire at the targets and the doll figures. As the intensity of his play subsided, he began to talk about his father and of the fun they had fishing, boat riding, and playing ball together last summer.

John appeared acutely anxious and showed that he handles anxiety by overactivity. He further showed that his behavior can be controlled by mild prohibitions when he acquiesced to the request to shoot inanimate targets rather than the examiner. He also evidenced inner control by gradually stopping the aggressive play. This contrasts with the behavior of some children, whose aggressive actions tend to snowball in intensity and will cease only with strong external prohibitions. (p. 18, with changes in notation)

This face in the mirror
stares at me
demanding Who are you? What will you become?
And taunting, You don't even know.
Chastened, I cringe and agree
and then
because I'm still young,
I stick out my tongue.

—Eve Merriam

Adolescents

Adolescents (about 12 to 18 years of age) face several challenging developmental tasks. These include accepting their physical and sexual roles, working through peer relationships with both sexes, achieving independence from parents, testing parental roles and authority, preparing for an occupation, becoming aware of social and political forces, acquiring socially responsible behavior, preparing for family life, and establishing values that are in harmony with their immediate environment. These challenges may lead adolescents to a heightened preoccupation with self; an active fantasy life; activities involving self-expression ("doing your own thing"); preoccupation with philosophical abstractions, theories, and ideals; and increased embarrassment. In addition, adolescence may bring with it *hedonism* (pursuing instant gratification) or *asceticism* (renouncing pleasures); heightened conformity to peer group values and pressures; and heightened sensitivity, mood swings, acting-out behavior, or withdrawn behavior. They may take on the values, dress, and codes of their peer group. Their increased embarrassment may be associated with their understanding that they may be judged by others and by the changes taking place in their physical growth and development.

Examples of stresses that adolescents *may* face are

- *problems of self-esteem* (for example, concerns with weight, height, size, appearance, clothes, body image, and peer relations)
- *problems of independence* (for example, concerns with rules at home, peer pressure, leisure time, and money)
- *problems with academic and physical competence* (for example, concerns with grades, homework, academic plans, relationships with teachers, sports ability, and health)
- *distresses arising from family relations* (for example, concerns with parents divorcing, spending time with parents, parents arguing, sibling relations, and feeling pressured to get good grades)
- *distresses with moving* (for example, concerns with having to change schools and move to a new neighborhood)

Adolescents need to understand that they have input into the decisions that will be made about them and that it is in their best interest to voice their feelings, desires, and wishes.

They need to feel respected and to understand that their opinions are important. Your goal is to enlist their cooperation without undue coercion. You can accomplish this in part by assurances of confidentiality (when appropriate) and open, honest communication. As noted in Chapter 2, adolescents should be told that confidentiality promises do not hold when there are indications of possible suicide, self-harm, harm to others, or child maltreatment.

Adolescents have an increasing command of language concepts, a more developed capacity for abstract thinking, and a more complex social world. They can "generate and consider multiple solutions or perspectives for a given problem or situation" (Bierman, 1990, p. 208). Because of these advances in their thinking, adolescents can

- describe themselves more clearly, making fine distinctions between themselves and others
- establish relationships based on values
- view others by their motivations, intentions, and mutual interests
- question their own thoughts and feelings, as well as those of others

Because they have a more complete sense of personal and historical time than younger children, they can report more accurately the duration of their symptoms (Clarizio, 1994). Thus, adolescents can tell you about previous episodes of their symptoms and about the time of onset of long-lasting symptoms. However, they still may not be able to articulate their feelings clearly or reflect on their experiences.

Using a personal data questionnaire. For adolescents who can read and write, a personal data questionnaire, completed before the interview, can be useful as part of the assessment. The personal data questionnaire allows you to obtain information economically and quickly in a standard format. You can probe selected responses from the personal data questionnaire in the interview.

Questions on a personal data questionnaire may cover identifying information, school information, activities, hobbies, work experience, information about the family and home, health history, stress factors, relationship with parents, and plans (see Table C-3 in Appendix C). Administering the questionnaire may have an added benefit—helping adolescents collect their own thoughts and gain some insights. However, if the adolescent has a reading difficulty, you may not want to use a personal data questionnaire.

Many items on a personal data questionnaire have normative characteristics. You can compare adolescents on such characteristics as the number of magazines they read, jobs they have held, school activities they have participated in, situations that cause them stress, and so forth. If you want to make these comparisons, you will need to establish informal norms for the groups with which you work. These norms, if established, will apply to your setting but may not apply to other settings. An example of informal norms is "60 percent of the eighth-graders in _____ school participate in zero extracurricular school activities, 30 percent in one activity, and 10 percent in two or more activities."

You should consider the accuracy of the information given by adolescents on a personal data questionnaire. In some situations, such as when an adolescent is inhibited, you may want to complete a personal data questionnaire with him or her. The personal data questionnaire can be a helpful tool in gathering information; however, do not rely on it as the sole procedure. You usually will need to obtain more details on their problems and information about possible etiological factors related to the problems. Use the personal data questionnaire as one source of information, not as a replacement for the interview.

Dealing with adolescents who show resistance. In the interview, adolescents may be impatient and uncommunicative—they may not want to talk to you.

Picture a 16-year-old male sitting in your office, slouched in a chair, a cap and long hair covering his averted eyes. His first words and only complete sentence for the next hour are: "I don't want to talk to no f—king shrink." A reflective statement on your part noting that he must be upset about something only brings a muffled grunt. Your best open-ended questions elicit only a series of unelaborated "Yes's," "No's," "I don't know's," "Maybe's," and "It's the damn teachers." Your feeble attempts at humor or to discuss "safe" topics bring only more grunts, a few eye rolls, or no response at all. His posture throughout the seemingly never-ending hour remains essentially unchanged. (Prout, 1989, p. 20)

In such cases, it may be nearly impossible to complete the clinical or forensic assessment interview during the first meeting; you may not be able to obtain any information at all. In any event, when you work with adolescents, you will need to put them at ease, explaining what you want to accomplish and how working together will help. You might want to begin by obtaining factual information, leaving sensitive topics for the end of the interview or for a second interview. You will need to be nonjudgmental, avoiding comments that might be perceived as personal criticism. With adolescents who are resistant, don't allow long silences to develop or make too many noncommittal responses. You may have to be more direct, concrete, explicit, and active than you prefer to be, but such directness may be the only way to obtain information from resistant adolescents.

To adolescents (and perhaps younger children as well) who are reluctant to speak to you, you might say "I want to respect your privacy and if there are things you don't want to talk about today I will understand" or "Sometimes people who come to see me don't feel comfortable talking about certain subjects when they first meet me and that's fine" (Barker, 1990, p. 58). Comments like these may relieve pressure on adolescents and open conversation.

I think that what is happening to me is so wonderful and not only what can be seen on my body, but all that is taking place inside. I never discuss myself with anybody; that is why I have to talk to myself about them.

—Anne Frank

Sequences of Normal Development

The table on the inside front cover shows milestones in development from birth to 60 months. In Appendix C, Tables C-4 through C-10 show broad normal developmental sequences in the following areas: cognitive development, language acquisition, concept of self, person perception, moral judgment, temporal concepts, and recognition of emotion. These tables are useful in understanding children's development. Refer to them when you have questions about typical, or normal, developmental sequences. However, you should view the information in these tables simply as approximate norms. There is much variability among normal children in reaching milestones. Consequently, do not consider children as delayed or advanced if they are only a few months behind or ahead of the expected age for the development of a skill.

Tables C-11 and C-12 in Appendix C show height and weight percentile rank growth norms from birth through 18 years of age. These norms were compiled in the 1970s and may not be completely accurate for the 1990s and later.

TECHNIQUES FOR INTERVIEWING CHILDREN

General Techniques

The most common way to help young children remember, think, and tell you about themselves is to ask them questions. Unskilled use of questions, however, may inhibit their responses. If you use questions extensively and relatively few acknowledging or accepting statements (such as "I see," "Oh," or "Really"), children are more likely to give brief replies. Continual questioning also may inhibit children from asking questions or volunteering information.

In asking questions, recognize that you are making demands—you are directing the attention of the children to memories or ideas that they might not have otherwise considered. Children need more time than adults to think about the questions and to think about their answers. If you want to get only specific information from children and are confident that they understand the questions, then a direct question-and-answer format may be acceptable (Wood, 1982). However, you should avoid a strict question-and-answer format if you are unsure of exactly what information you want; if you want the child to take an active, constructive role in the interview; or if you are unsure whether the child understands your questions, particularly with young children. In these cases, use a more conversational style.

You can become a more effective interviewer of children by learning about their current interests. Look at Saturday morning television programs, talk with parents, visit toy stores, look at children's books, and visit day care centers and schools to observe children in their natural habitat. Familiarity with children's interests will help you establish rapport with children and will give you insight about them.

Chapter 2 presented general suggestions for conducting interviews. This chapter focuses on interview strategies particularly useful in establishing rapport with and maintaining the cooperation of children. You always will need to adjust your interviewing strategy depending on how children respond (Bierman & Schwartz, 1986). Following is an amusing example of how the interviewer heard the child's response but ignored the implications of the response.

Baby Blues   by Rick Kirkman and Jerry Scott

Reprinted with special permission of King Features Syndicate.

IR: Do you have any fears?
IE: I have a terrible fear of deadlines.
IR: Tell me everything about your fear of deadlines. You have until 10:50.

Specific Techniques

Here are 21 techniques useful for interviewing children.

Use appropriate language and intonation, and do not lead children. Use simple vocabulary and short sentences tailored to the developmental and cognitive levels of the children. For example, instead of saying "What things are reinforcing for you?", say "What things do you like?" Be sure that the children understand the questions. Use simple terms in exploring the children's feelings. For example, use *sad* instead of *depressed*. Be friendly and enthusiastic, and show interest in the children.

You especially want to avoid leading children to give a particular response. For example, in a case of alleged child maltreatment, do not tell the child that the alleged offender is bad or that the child should tell you the bad things the offender has done. Similarly, phrase your questions so that the children do not receive any hint that one response is more acceptable than another. Be sure that the manner and tone of your voice do not reveal any personal biases.

Ask for examples. Ask children to give examples of how they behave or how other people behave when they are feeling a certain way (for example, how they behave when they are sad).

Be open to what children tell you. You want to convey to children that you are open and accepting of what they want to tell you. This means that you must not ignore information that does not support your expectations or beliefs.

You want to take a more active role with children than you would with adults. Get as complete a story as possible from the children, but do not interpret for the children what happened to them.

Formulate appropriate opening statements. The opening statement that will help put the child at ease will depend on the child's age, ability level, and behavior and the reason for the referral. After introducing yourself and establishing rapport, you might say

- "This is a place where moms and dads and kids come to talk with a helper like me. Sometimes they tell me they wish things could go better at home or at school. I help them figure things out so that they can feel better" (Bierman, 1990, p. 212).

or

- "Your teacher has told me about some problems you've been having, but I'd like to hear about them from you."

or

- "I understand that you are having some problems at home."

To older children, it may be useful to say

- "What brings you here today?"

or

- "We could begin by your letting me know what is bothering you."

To children in school, an appropriate comment might be

- "I'm Mr. Smith, the school social worker. I understand from Ms. Jones that you are not doing too well in school. I'd like to talk to you about your schoolwork."

To children in a juvenile detention center, you might say

- "I'm Dr. Brown, a clinical psychologist here at the center. I'd like to talk to you about why you are here at the center."

Make descriptive comments. When you comment on the child's appearance, behavior, or demeanor, you are making a descriptive comment (Kanfer et al., 1983; 1992). Descriptive comments provide a simple way of giving attention to the child and encouraging the child to continue with appropriate behavior. An added benefit of descriptive comments is that you can use them to maintain communication with the child while you are formulating other questions. Examples of descriptive comments include "Your shirt is nice," "I see that you are feeding the doll," and "You look cheerful today." Descriptive comments are nonthreatening, focus the child's attention, and encourage the child to elaborate further (Boggs & Eyberg, 1990).

Use reflection. Reflective statements rephrase what the child has said or done, retaining the essential meaning of the communication or behavior (Kanfer et al., 1992). These statements provide clarity and help organize the child's behavior. For example, in response to the statement "My brother is a brat," you might say "Your brother doesn't act the way you want him to, is that right?"

Give praise frequently. Praise and support serve to guide children to talk about areas that you consider important (Kanfer et al., 1983). Younger children will need more praise than older children. Examples of praise are "I'm glad you can tell me about these things" and "Some of these things are hard to talk about, but you are doing fine." Praise children's efforts, not *what* they say. For example, do not reward children (either verbally or nonverbally) for making responses that they think you want to hear. Similarly, do not use coercion, pressure, or threats—such as telling children that they can't play with toys, go to the bathroom, go home, or get to see their parents soon—to get them to respond in the way you want them to.

Avoid critical statements.   Criticism is likely to generate anger, hostility, resentment, or frustration—reactions that will interfere with your ability to establish and maintain rapport (Kanfer et al., 1992). Examples of critical statements are "You are not trying very hard" and "Stop tearing the paper." When the child is behaving negatively, focus on more appropriate behavior to turn the attention of the child away from the negative behavior or invoke rules that govern the playroom or office. For example, when a child is throwing blocks, say "Let's throw the ball," or when a child is tearing paper inappropriately, say "One of the rules is that you can't tear this paper." If you are forewarned, you can have available paper that the child can tear. In that case, you can say "One of the rules is that you can only tear this paper." This may help children redirect their inappropriate behavior.

Sometimes you can ignore inappropriate behavior, make a mental note to watch for positive behavior, and reinforce the positive behavior. Here are two examples of how this can be done (Kanfer et al., 1992, pp. 52–53, with changes in notation):

EXAMPLE 1

IE: (Climbs on table)
IR: (Ignores climbing)
IE: (Gets off table)
IR: It's safer when you stand on the floor.

EXAMPLE 2

IR: Tell me a story about this picture.
IE: I can't think of anything.
IR: (Ignores statement) What is this girl doing?
IE: She's sitting.
IR: She is sitting. I'm glad you told me about part of this picture. What else is going on in this picture?

Use simple questions and concrete referents. You can increase children's responsiveness and elicit more coherent and complete responses by simplifying the questions, adding concrete referents, and simplifying the responses required (Bierman, 1983). For example, you can say "Tell me one thing that you like about your teacher," "When was the last time you felt that way?", or "What happened yesterday morning when you woke up?"

Following are six techniques that use concrete referents to help children talk about their feelings. These techniques are especially useful with children who are reluctant to talk about themselves.

1. *Ask for affect labels.* Show the child simple line drawings that depict emotional expressions, such as happy, sad, and angry (Bierman, 1990; also see Figure 3-1). First, ask the child to describe each face. As you point to each face, say "Tell me how this face looks." Then, ask a series of

Figure 3-1. Line drawings depicting three emotional expressions.

questions, such as "How do you look when you go to school?", "How do you look when you go to bed?", and "How do you look when your daddy (or mommy) comes home?" After each question, ask the child to point to a face if he or she has not described his or her feelings or has not pointed to one. The pointing technique is especially useful for young children because they do not have to make a verbal response.

If the child is reluctant to tell you about the faces, consider saying "How would a child feel if he (she) had a time out? Point to a picture that shows how he (she) would feel." If the child points correctly, say "That's right, a child would feel sad (or angry) if he (she) was punished. What do you think he (she) did to get punished?" Follow up by asking "Who punished him (her)?" and "What was the punishment?" To learn the child's feelings about a positive event and about an aggressive event, you first might say "How would a child feel if he (she) got a special toy? Point to a picture that shows how he (she) would feel." Follow up with appropriate questions. You then might say "How would a child feel if he (she) had a fight with another child? Point to a picture that shows how he (she) would feel." Again, follow up with appropriate questions.

A more difficult version of this procedure is to point to each face in turn and say "Tell me something that makes you feel like this" (Bierman, 1990, p. 213). For children who are willing to talk about their feelings, you can then probe their response to the faces. For example, if a boy says that he is angry when he fights with his brother, you can ask "What about fighting with your brother makes you angry?" You can follow up with "What do you do when you fight with your brother?" If the child seems threatened by the questions or simply refuses to answer, stop probing. (See Bierman, 1990, for a discussion of other techniques useful in eliciting affect-laden material.)

2. *Use the picture question technique.* Select pictures that you think will engage the child, show the child the pictures one at time, and then ask the child to tell a story about each picture. The picture question technique, although similar to thematic projective techniques, is not used as a personality test or projective test (Bierman, 1990). Rather, it

simply is a way of getting children to talk about their feelings. Pictures may serve as a less intrusive and more concrete way of getting information about children's feelings than questions alone.

You may select pictures that relate to specific themes in the child's life. For example, if you want to find out about how a girl feels about a new baby in the family, show her a picture that contains a girl, a mother, and a baby. First, ask "What do you think is happening?" Then, say "How does the girl feel about the baby?" Then, ask "What is going to happen?"

Another example: If you want to learn about a boy's feelings about his parents' divorce, show him a picture of a boy (about the child's age), a mother, and a father. Then, you might say "Here are a mom and dad and a boy about your age. The mom and dad got divorced. What do you think happened?...What did the mom say?... What did the dad say?... What did the boy say?...How did the mom feel?... How did the dad feel?...How did the boy feel?...What will happen next?... Did that ever happen to you?...What did you do?... How did you feel?" (Bierman, 1983, p. 234, with changes in notation).

If you use the picture question technique, it might affect how children respond to a projective story-telling test, like the Children's Apperception Test, if the test is to be administered later. Therefore, you should weigh the advantages and disadvantages of using this procedure. You might want to try other techniques to get reluctant children to talk to you before you use the picture question technique, especially if they will be referred for psychological testing.

3. *Have the child draw a picture and tell about it.* Ask the child to draw a picture of a child or an adult, and then ask him or her about the picture (Bierman, 1983). Following is a brief list of questions that you might ask as you point to the pictures; add additional questions as needed.

- "What an interesting drawing. Now we're going to do something special. Tell me three things that this child likes to do."
- "Tell me three things that this child doesn't like to do."
- "What does this child like about school?"
- "What doesn't this child like about school?"
- "What does this child like about her family?"
- "What doesn't this child like about her family?"
- "What does this child do that gets her into trouble?"
- "What gets this child mad?"
- "What makes this child sad?"
- "What makes this child happy?"
- "What makes this child angry?"
- "What makes this child frightened?"
- "How do other children feel about this child?"

You can repeat the procedure by asking the child to draw a picture of an adult, substituting the word "woman" or "man" for "child" in the above questions. The drawing-a-picture technique allows you to encourage and praise the

"You must be Mr. and Mrs. Smith. I'd recognize you anywhere from Henry's drawings."

Courtesy of Jerome M. Sattler and Jeff B. Bryson.

child for his or her efforts and gives the child a way of expressing his or her hopes, fears, and frustrations (Bierman, 1983).

4. *Use the story completion technique.* First, ask the child to complete sentence stems that you have constructed about the child's life situation. Here is one way of introducing the task (Bierman & Schwartz, 1986).

Okay, now I have this story that we're supposed to fill out together. I'll read the story, and then you think of an answer to fill in the blanks, okay? This first story is about the way kids act at school. At school, some kids act really _____. How should I say they act? (Child replies, "mean.") OK, good answer! One mean thing that they do is _____. (Child replies, "fight.") Fight, yeah, that's a mean thing. Another mean thing they do is _____. (p. 271)

Then, use follow-up questions to obtain additional information.

As children become more comfortable answering these structured sentence completions, the interviewer can introject personal probes, such as: "Wow, do kids do that in your school, too?" or "Has that ever happened to anyone you know?" Using this flexible story-completion approach, the interviewer can get a basic sense of the social perceptions and reasoning level of the child, and, depending upon the child's responsivity, can also pursue themes of personal relevance to the child. (pp. 271–272)

5. *Have the child respond to a hypothetical problem.* Ask the child to respond to a hypothetical problem that addresses relevant issues (Bierman & Schwartz, 1986); for example,

I know of a girl who has a problem that you might be able to help with. Her parents have been talking about getting a divorce, and she's scared about it. She doesn't really know what it will be like, or how she will feel, or what she can do about it. What do you think I can say to help her? (p. 272, with changes in notation)

The technique may be less anxiety-provoking and make fewer demands on the child's conceptual and verbal skills than open-ended questions.

6. *Model the interview after a school-type task.* You can model the interview after a more familiar school-type task (Bierman & Schwartz, 1986).

The interviewer might introduce some papers with a comment such as: "There are some questions I need to ask you," and go on to write notes periodically during the interview. This approach enables the interviewer to become an ally of the child—working with the child to get the necessary questions answered. Interviewer comments, such as: "Oh, here's a tough one—see what you think of this one," can soften the impact of difficult questions; and praise can be directed toward the child's task mastery attempts (for example, "Neat answer! That one seemed kind of hard to me, but you've clearly thought about it"). Additionally, focusing on the paper enables the interviewer to avoid extended, intensive eye contact with the child. (p. 270, with changes in notation)

Formulate questions in the subjunctive mood (hypothetical) when necessary.

Questions formulated in the subjunctive mood (or hypothetical questions) may be useful in getting reticent children to speak. Useful leads that employ a subjunctive mood include "Suppose you were…," "What if you…," and "Let's pretend that…." For example, you might say "Suppose you were to take a friend to your house. Suppose you were going to show your friend some things there—what kinds of things might your friend see?" This type of syntactical structure "allows the child some degree of emotional distance by adding a game-like quality to the question" (Goodman & Sours, 1967, p. 29). For some children, this type of question is preferable to a question such as "What is your house like?"

The following case illustrates the use of hypothetical situations in helping a young girl discuss her feelings toward her mother.

CASE 3-3. SALLY
Sally, an 8-year-old girl referred for outbursts of crying and temper tantrums, seemed resigned to the interview as she came into the office. Her head was bent and her eyes avoided direct contact. Her verbal responses were at first stereotyped. She answered most questions "I don't know," or "because just because," while looking at her feet. She seemed to be struggling to control her feelings. This was most apparent as she spoke of coming to the interview "because my mother says I'm a problem."

Until that point, the interview had been labored, slow, and unproductive. Sally had no inclination to play or to talk spontaneously about herself. The interviewer told her that he once knew "a little girl who did a lot of worrying and felt she couldn't find grown-ups who could understand these worries." Sally made no verbal response but looked directly at the interviewer for a moment. Taking the cue, the interviewer

went on: "Sometimes this little girl would worry so much that she couldn't eat." "Oh, that's not me," said Sally. "What might you do?" asked the interviewer. Sally started fidgeting with the sash on her dress. The interviewer again asked: "What might you do if the worries get real big?" After further fidgeting and biting her lip, she said: "Nothing." Now more sure of his ground, the interviewer continued: "Well, I sense that you must be pretty worried right now." "How do you know?" she said. "Because you seem to be like this girl—maybe sad and holding back your feelings." Tears rolled down Sally's cheeks. The interviewer then said: "Maybe you can talk a little about what it's like to feel sad." Sally regained her composure, wiped the tears away, and said she would like to play. She then expressed some of her feelings about her mother. (Goodman & Sours, 1967, pp. 71–72, with changes in notation)

Be tactful. Phrase questions tactfully to avoid causing children anxiety or discomfort. An ineffectively worded question may lead to discomfort. For example, after a child complained about a teacher, it would be tactless to say "Do you always have trouble with teachers?" You might get a more responsive answer if you said "Have you found other teachers as upsetting as this one?" or if you simply acknowledged the child's feelings about his or her teacher. Instead of asking "Did you quit school?", which may require an admission of having done so, say "What was the last grade you were in?"

Recognize children's discomfort. Recognize children's discomfort and make the situation as free of stress as possible. Recognize that children may have additional discomforts if family members are actively responsible for the children's problems. Be ready to change topics if children become too distressed.

Use props, crayons, clay, and toys to help young children talk. You will need special skills to help young children talk. One method is to use props during the interview—such as having the children talk through dolls or puppets or carry on a conversation via a toy telephone (Yarrow, 1960). A second method, which may reduce children's self-consciousness, is to allow them to use crayons or clay while they talk to you. Do not allow the use of crayons or clay to become a convenient escape from talking, however. A third method is to allow young children to express themselves by using toys. Observe carefully the play of the children—including motor, language, and fantasy elements.

Props may be particularly valuable when children are unable to converse freely:

A common method is the use of props to stimulate memory, to supplement language ability, or to facilitate communication in the interview setting. Props can be used to recreate the setting of an event, permitting the child to [re]enact the event itself. A doll house and dolls, for instance, can be used to help describe a domestic event that is either too complex or too traumatic to describe in words. Pretending to talk on the telephone may act as a vehicle for talking with the interviewer (and may also help the child feel a sense of control over the interview, since he [she] can stop the conversation at any time by hanging up). (Garbarino & Stott, 1989, p. 191)

Use a sentence completion technique.   Another way to elicit information from middle childhood–aged children and from adolescent children who are reticent to talk with you is by use of a sentence completion technique. This technique consists of giving sentence stems orally and then recording the children's answers. You then can use their answers to probe further about an area. Table 3-4 shows examples of sentence stems that you can use.

Table 3-4
Sentence Completion Technique

Directions: Say to the child "I am going to start a sentence. I'd like you to finish it any way you want. Here is an example. If I say 'A car...,' you can say 'is fun to go in,' 'is nice to have,' 'is good when it works,' 'costs a lot of money,' or anything else that you can think of. OK? Let's try the first one."

1. My favorite TV show _____ .
2. At night _____ .
3. My teacher _____ .
4. The scariest thing is when _____ .
5. My mother _____ .
6. At school, I usually feel _____ .
7. I hate it when _____ .
8. When I wake up, I usually _____ .
9. I dislike _____ .
10. My father _____ .
11. I am happiest when _____ .
12. My favorite subjects are _____ .
13. I worry about _____ .
14. My friends _____ .
15. I need _____ .
16. My life would be better if _____ .
17. I feel angry when _____ .
18. My neighborhood is _____ .
19. Animals are _____ .
20. It is wrong to _____ .
21. The best thing about being me _____ .
22. I like _____ .
23. The saddest time is when _____ .
24. The best thing about my home _____ .
25. My favorite book _____ .
26. I feel ashamed when _____ .
27. My worst subjects are _____ .
28. I am proud of _____ .
29. If I could change one thing about my family, it would be _____ .
30. (If appropriate) My sister(s) _____ .
31. (If appropriate) My brother(s) _____ .

Use fantasy techniques.   For middle childhood–aged children and for adolescent children who are reluctant to speak with you, consider using fantasy techniques, such as the three wishes technique or the desert island technique (Barker, 1990).

1. *Three wishes technique.* To use the three wishes technique, say "If you could have any three wishes, what would they be?" An alternative phrasing is "If you could wish for any three things to happen, what would they be?" Listen carefully to what the child says. Children's wishes may give you some leads to their feelings about their parents, siblings, friends, insecurities, and so forth. You can then follow up on their answers. The three wishes technique may not be appropriate for younger children because they may come up with concrete answers, such as wanting a bike, a toy, or something to eat.

2. *Desert island technique.* To use the desert island technique, you ask the child whom he or she wants to be with on a desert island. Say "Here's a pretend question. Imagine you were shipwrecked on a desert island. There's no one else there, but you've got plenty of food to eat and water to drink. If you could have just one person to be with you on the island—anyone in the whole world—I wonder whom you would most want to have?" (Barker, 1990, p. 66, with changes in notation).

After the child has selected someone, say "Now if you could have another person—[the person first named] and somebody else—whom would you choose next?" Then ask "And if you could have one more—and this would be the last one you could have—whom would you choose for your third person?" You also can ask "Is there anyone you wouldn't want to have on the island with you?" If the child says "Yes," say "Who would that be?" (Barker, 1990, p. 66).

Help children express their thoughts and feelings.   You can help children express their thoughts and feelings in several ways. First, let them speak in whatever words they choose. Second, encourage them to speak freely and openly, and follow up leads that they give you. Third, convey to them that you are willing to listen to any of their feelings and thoughts, even those that may be *culturally unacceptable.*

The following techniques may help children talk about things that might not be considered culturally acceptable, such as things they don't like (Yarrow, 1960, p. 580, with changes in notation and additions from Bierman & Schwartz, 1986, p. 271).

1. *Present two alternatives.* Examples:

- "If your little brother writes on the wall, do you punish him so he won't do it again, or do you see that your mother finds out about it?"
- "Do you ever wish that you could be someone else, or are you happy being yourself?"

- "Do you ever wish that your dad spent more time with you, or do you think he spends enough time with you?"

If the child says "yes" to any question that has two alternatives, follow up the response by saying "How would you punish him?" or "Who would you like to be?" or "How much time does he spend with you?" or whatever else would be appropriate.

2. *Give children an opportunity to express a positive response before presenting a question that will require a negative response.* Examples:

- "What things do you like best about school?"… "What things aren't so good?"
- "What is one thing that you like best about your sister?"… "What is something she does that you don't like very much?"

You may combine these approaches in a question.

- "There are some things most boys like about school and other things they don't like at all. First, tell me about the things you like best about school." After the child responds, say "What are some things that aren't so good about school?"

You can extend these techniques with specific probes.

Follow-up probes that provide concrete structure are usually more effective in helping children expand their answers to initial questions. For example, a child might respond to the question, "What kinds of things don't you like about school?" with a one-word answer or "I don't know." A structured probe might be: "Well, let's just try to think about one thing first. Tell me one thing you don't like at school." If the child answers simply "math," a structured probe might also be: "What happens in math that you don't like very much?" Or, if that does not work, you could offer a choice: "Well, is it more the work you don't like or the teacher?" These probes are all preferable to options such as "Can you tell me anything else?" This almost invariably receives a negative response. (Bierman, 1983, p. 235)

Clarify an episode of misbehavior by recounting it.
When you want to obtain further information from children about an episode of misbehavior, ask them to recount the details of the episode, as illustrated in the following dialogue (Karoly, 1981, p. 102, with changes in notation).

IR: Your teacher tells me that yesterday a bunch of kids in your class "went wild" with paints, throwing them around the room and at other kids.
IE: Yeah.
IR: That really happened?
IE: Yeah. So?
IR: What led up to it?
IE: The kids were bored.
IR: Were you bored?
IE: Yeah, I guess.
IR: Did you throw the paints too?
IE: Yeah.

IR: Did you enjoy throwing the paints?
IE: What do you mean?
IR: Was it a way to be less bored?
IE: Sure…for a while.
IR: Then what happened?
IE: We had to clean the place up. It took all afternoon.
IR: Did you think you would have to clean up?
IE: I don't know.
IR: Was it unfair for her to make you clean up?
IE: The janitor should do it.
IR: But the kids made the mess.
IE: Mrs. Masters [the teacher] is supposed to give us stuff to do.

In this case, the recounting technique brought to light the child's perception that the teacher is responsible for keeping the students occupied.

Clarify interview procedures for children who are minimally communicative.
Some children may respond to your questions with "Yes," "No," "I don't know," or "I guess." Handle these responses with comments like the following:

- "What I'd like to have you do rather than just saying 'Yes' or 'No' is to try to tell me as much as you can about what I ask you."
- "Sometimes it is hard to talk about things. But I'd really like to you try. It will help me get to know you better."

On the rare occasion when a child simply refuses to participate in the initial interview, it probably is best to reschedule the interview, as illustrated in the following case (Reisman, 1973).

CASE 3-4. SUZIE
Suzie, a 7-year-old girl, had refused to attend school. When first seen by the interviewer she was clutching tightly to her mother and refused to accompany the interviewer to his office. When brought to the office by her mother, she began kicking and biting her mother, crying and screaming because her mother wished to go to her own appointment. After her mother left, Suzie retreated to a corner, where she wept angrily, hurling curses at the interviewer, demanding to see her mother, and refusing to cooperate. In such cases it may be best to go along with the child's behavior and allow the behavior to run its course. Arrange to see the child again for another meeting. It may take a few sessions before you obtain the child's trust, acceptance, and cooperation.

Understand and use silence.
Because the clinical and forensic assessment interview depends primarily on conversation, children who are silent are a challenge. Silence may indicate one of several possibilities. Determine which possibility is most applicable, because what you decide may have a direct bearing on how you proceed. Possible reasons for children's silence are (a) they resent being at the interview, (b) they are frightened, (c) they may want to talk but don't know what to say, (d) they prefer to sit quietly and do nothing else, or (e) they may need time to collect

their ideas in order to express them (Reisman, 1973). Chapter 2 presented other possible reasons for silence. For some children, silence is comfortable at first but later becomes stressful. Other children find silence stressful from the beginning but do not know how to break it. Recognize when children are experiencing stress and when it is becoming more pronounced, and then try to reduce the stress.

Younger children (under 5 or 6 years of age) usually have more difficulty with silence than do older children. If silence leads to resistance, it can be detrimental to the interview. Therefore, try to keep silences to a minimum with young children.

Observing the nonverbal communications of children may help you understand the meaning of silence. For example, children who are angry about coming for the interview may be silent at first. They will likely talk to you once they begin to accept you and understand the purpose of the interview. However, if they wish to remain silent, accept their decision. For young children and for middle childhood–aged children who are silent, point out that they can play with the toys and play materials if they want to. As the silence continues, you can comment from time to time about what they are doing and about how much time is left. You also can play with some toys as they play. These activities may serve as a way to break the silence and to build rapport.

What you don't want to do is to assume that the children's silence (or failure to respond to a question) means that they are ashamed of talking about the topic. Failure to respond may simply mean that they have nothing to say about the question, that the situation is strange, or that other unknown factors are operating.

Handle resistance and anxiety by giving support and reassurance. Older children may be reluctant to reveal their feelings and thoughts to a stranger, especially when they are concerned about the reason for and outcome of the evaluation. They may show their anxiety by hesitancy in speaking, sadness, hostility, or other means (Jennings, 1982).

If you observe that a child is anxious, you may want to help the child express his or her anxiety directly. You could say "How do you feel about being here today?" or "You look a little nervous about talking to me." You might want to respond to the child's answers with encouragement or support, with a statement that asks for further exploration, or with a comment that acknowledges his or her feelings (Jennings, 1982). Matter-of-factly accepting everything children say, helping them understand the reasons for the evaluation, and helping them work through their feelings also may help reduce their anxiety. Possible things you can say are

- "Many children feel as you do at the beginning. But in a little while, most feel more relaxed. You probably will too."
- "I'd like to understand why you don't want to talk to me."
- "You do seem to feel hesitant about talking with me."

Consider the child's age and needs in setting the tempo and length of the interview. You need to be alert to how tired the child is becoming. Take short breaks of about 5 minutes each during a lengthy interview. Provide a brief period of free play or nonintense activity at any time, if needed. Leave some time toward the end of the interview to allow the child to regain composure, especially if the child reveals strong feelings during the interview.

Exercise 3-1. Rewording Questions

Reword each of the following questions so that it will be more comprehensible to an elementary school–aged child. Then, compare your answers with those following the questions.

1. What are your dreams and aspirations?
2. What is your relationship like with your peers?
3. How do you respond to your negative emotions?
4. How do you feel about your current life style?
5. What is your father's occupation?

Suggested Answers
1. What do you want to be when you grow up?
2. How do you get along with your friends?
3. What makes you angry?
4. How do you feel about how things are going in your life?
5. What is your father's job?

AREAS COVERED IN THE INITIAL INTERVIEW WITH CHILDREN

The typical sequence in an interview with children is as follows:

1. Introduce yourself to the parent (or caregiver or guardian) and to the child.
2. Greet the child.
3. Give your name and professional title.
4. Open the interview with an introductory statement.
5. Continue the interview as appropriate.
6. Review the issues with the child as you see them.
7. Describe what will happen to the child after you complete the interview.
8. Express appreciation for the child's effort and cooperation.
9. Close the interview.

Typical areas covered in the initial interview with children follow:

1. identifying data/reason for coming
2. confidentiality and other possible ethical concerns
3. school (including perception of teachers, peer group, and school environment)
4. home (including perception of parents, siblings, and home environment)

5. interests (including leisure time activities, hobbies, recreation, clubs, and sports)
6. friends
7. moods/feelings
8. fears/worries
9. self-concept
10. somatic concerns
11. obsessions and compulsions
12. thought disorder
13. memories/fantasies (recollections about their infancy and early childhood [what parents told them], including developmental milestones, if known)
14. aspirations (including plans and career possibilities)
15. other information voluntarily supplied by the children

Additional areas covered in the initial interview with adolescents include

16. jobs
17. sexual relations (including sexual identity and peer relationships)
18. eating habits
19. drug/alcohol use (including use and type of drug)
20. pregnancy (for females)
21. impregnation of a female (for males)

In discussing these areas, attend to the child's ability to relate to you, ability to discuss relevant information, thought processes, language, affect, nonverbal behaviors, temperament and personality, and possible psychological disturbances.

The questions presented in Table F-13 in Appendix F will aid you in obtaining information about the areas noted. The questions in Table F-13 are only sample questions meant to illustrate the areas most frequently covered in interviews of children; do not use the questions mechanically. Include follow-up and probing questions and reassuring comments, as needed. You may need to alter the wording of some questions in Table F-13, depending on the child's age.

Reinforcers

In some situations (such as when you are planning a therapeutic behavioral intervention), you may want to identify, during the interview, reinforcers important to the children. The positive reinforcement sentence completion technique shown in Table 3-5 is useful for this purpose.

Children's Environment

If you believe that the physical layout of the child's home may be contributing to her or his difficulties, you can ask the child to draw a picture of her or his room and other rooms in the house, as needed. This technique also is helpful in establishing rapport and getting children used to the question-

Table 3-5
Positive Reinforcement Sentence Completion for School-Aged Children

Directions: Read all the sentence stems to the child, following up on the child's responses as necessary. Then, state all the reinforcers named by the child, and ask the child to rank them in order of their importance.

1. My favorite grown-up is _____ .
2. My favorite thing to do with him (her) is _____ .
3. The best reward anybody can give me is _____ .
4. The two things I like best to do are _____ .
5. My favorite adult at school is _____ .
6. When I do something well, what my mother does is _____ .
7. I feel terrific when _____ .
8. When I have money, I like to _____ .
9. Something I really want is _____ .
10. The person I would like most to reward me is _____ .
11. I would like (person's name) to reward me by _____ .
12. The thing I like best to do with my mother is _____ .
13. On Saturday or Sunday, my favorite thing to do is _____ .
14. The thing I like to do most is _____ .
15. My two favorite TV programs are _____ .
16. The thing I like best to do with my father is _____ .

Child's Ranking of Reinforcers

_____
_____
_____
_____
_____

Source: Adapted from Tharp and Wetzel (1969).

and-answer flow of the interview. The following case illustrates the value of this technique (Gutheil, 1992).

CASE 3-5. SANDY

Sandy, a severely depressed 17-year-old girl who had a history of substance abuse and a past suicide attempt, was admitted to a private psychiatric hospital. She lived at home with her parents and her 16-year-old brother. After an aggressive episode with another patient in the hospital, Sandy was required to remain in her room. She went into the closet and covered herself with a blanket. Sandy's social worker sensed the importance to her client of having a safe place to hide when she was upset. In exploring this with Sandy, she learned that Sandy would go into her closet at home to hide when she felt she needed to escape the pressures of the world for a while.

The social worker knew that Sandy had her own room at home and believed it was important to explore why going into her room was not safe enough for her. The social worker explained that she would like to see Sandy's room through her eyes and asked her to draw a picture of her room.

There was a good deal of clutter on the floor, bed, dresser, and mirror. This confirmed the worker's sense that Sandy experienced her life as disordered. The curtains were drawn in the picture, leading Sandy to explain that she kept her room darkened most of the time, a poignant reflection of her depression. Sandy had drawn a door inside her room. This door led to her brother's room. Her brother must walk through her room to get to his own room. Her parents do not allow her to lock her door, so Sandy could never be certain that someone would not walk into her room. The social worker gained a much clearer understanding of Sandy's need to go into a closet to ensure that she would be in a truly private place. (p. 393, with changes in notation)

Exercise 3-2. Becoming More Aware of Environments

This exercise was adapted from Gutheil (1992).

Part 1. Your Home Environment

Draw a diagram of your home or apartment. Note the layout of the rooms. Then describe the layout of your bedroom, including colors of walls; placement, condition, and type of furniture; pictures and plants; and so forth. Comment on the following: How is space arranged in your home? What private space is available to each member of your family? What do you consider your personal space to be? How do the family members respect each other's need for personal space? What do the other family members think about the layout of the home? What is the noise level of the home, and is this level acceptable to you? What do the other members of the family think about the noise level? Compare and contrast your diagram and your description and commentary with those of four other class members.

Part 2. Your Work Environment

If you are working in an agency ("agency," as used here, refers to any professional center), draw a diagram of the layout of the entrance, waiting room, and office. Then describe the setting in as much detail as possible. Sit in the interviewee's seat and see how the setting looks from this perspective. What aspects of the agency's physical environment are conducive to establishing rapport and facilitating the interview climate? How do the surroundings influence you? For example, do you avoid certain areas of the agency because they are depressing and crowded? What is the general noise level in your office and in the agency? Is this level acceptable to you? Compare and contrast the physical environment of your home with that of your agency. How do they differ and how are they similar? Which environment do you prefer and for what reasons? Is one environment suitable for certain activities and the other environment suitable for other activities?

Mental Status Evaluation

As part of the initial interview with children, you may want to conduct a mental status evaluation. A mental status evalu-

ation may be particularly helpful in cases of brain injury, when children appear confused, or when you simply want to obtain some indication of their general mental functioning. Table F-25 in Appendix F offers a brief mental status examination for older children. This type of evaluation is especially important when children appear to have problems in orientation to time, place, or person or in memory or attention or show signs of confused thinking. Interpret all areas in a mental status evaluation within a developmental framework, using age-appropriate norms or age-appropriate expectations. For adolescents, difficulties in answering the questions in Table F-25 in Appendix F may suggest disturbed functioning.

Evaluation of the Child's Interview

The questions in Table 3-6 will help you evaluate the information you obtained from the child in the interview. The questions cover background information, appearance and behavior, speech and communications, perception of the problem, content of thought, sensory and motor functioning, cognitive functioning, temperament and emotional functioning, insight and judgment, attitudes toward home and school, and intervention considerations. You may not always be able to answer all of the questions, but do your best. Occasionally, you may need more than one interview to obtain the information you need. Chapters in Sections III, IV, and V present guidelines for evaluating children with specific problems or concerns.

Exercise 3-3. Formulating an Appropriate Response

This exercise contains descriptions of phases of an initial interview conducted in a school. After you read each one, formulate a response. Then, check your responses with those following the statements. (This exercise was adapted from K. France and M. Kish [1995], *Supportive Interviewing in Human Service Organizations: Fundamental Skills for Gathering Information and Encouraging Productive Change.* Charles C Thomas, Publisher, Springfield, Illinois.)

1. In the waiting area, you have just introduced yourself to a 9-year-old boy whom you are meeting for the first time.
2. Pleasantries have been exchanged, and it is time to discuss the matter at hand. The student was referred by his teacher for inappropriate behavior, such as running and screaming.
3. Having explained the reason for the meeting, you are ready to solicit comments from the student.
4. The student has just said "I scream and run around when the other kids are doing the same thing. We do it in class, going to the cafeteria, and on the bus. But I'm the only one who ever gets in trouble."
5. The student has just said "When it's time to go to lunch, they don't line up, they don't get their coats on, and she gets mad. By the time we get to the cafeteria, she's yelling

Table 3-6
Evaluating the Child's Interview

Background Information

1. Who referred the child?
2. What was the reason for the referral?
3. What is the composition of the family (including age of children, parents, and extended family members living at home)?
4. What grade is the child in at school?
5. What is the socioeconomic status of the family?

Appearance and Behavior

6. How did the child present himself or herself?
7. How did the child look generally? (Note, for example, height, weight, personal hygiene, grooming, facial appearance, clothes, special adornments, physical handicaps.)
8. How did the child act during the interview? (Note, for example, normal behavior or problematic behavior, such as bizarre gestures or actions, repetitive movements, abnormal posture, disruptive behavior, tantrums, poor eye contact, inappropriate facial expressions, inappropriate laughter, abnormally slow movements, excessive movements, wildly excited behavior, special mannerisms, unusual preoccupation with special activities, unusual sensory interest in play materials or persons, attempts at self-injury.)
9. Was the child's behavior appropriate for his or her age and education?
10. How did the child relate to you? (For example, was he or she cooperative, wary, submissive, attentive, friendly, manipulative, approval seeking, excessively conforming, hostile, superficial, trusting, guarded, resistant, fearful, suspicious, cautious, warm, cold, sullen, indifferent?)
11. What was the child's range of facial expressions? (Note whether the facial expressions were appropriate to the situation.)
12. How did the child respond to your behavior? (For example, did he or she show interest in working with you to solve problems?)
13. Did the child's behavior change during the interview? (If so, when did the behavior change and in what way?)

Speech and Communications

14. What was the child's primary mode of communication?
15. How was the general flow of the child's speech? (For example, was it rapid, controlled, hesitant, slow, pressured?)
16. Did the child have any speech impediments?
17. How intelligible was the child's speech?
18. How was the general tone and content of the child's speech? (Note, for example, normal tone and age-appropriate content or problematic speech such as over- or under-productivity of speech, flight of ideas, paucity of ideas, loose associations, clang associations, rambling, circumstantiality, tangentiality, non sequiturs, blocking on certain content, perseveration, irrelevance, vagueness, neologisms, bizarre use of words, incoherence of speech, repetitive speech, and misleading responses, such as answering "yes" to all questions. See the glossary for definitions.)
19. What were the child's gestures like? (For example, were they graceful, clumsy, tense, open, compulsive?)
20. Was there congruency between the child's verbal and nonverbal communications?
21. What was the relationship between the tone and the content of the child's communications?
22. How interested was the child in communicating? (For example, was the child evasive, or did the child avoid certain questions, refuse to talk, change topics?)

Perception of Problem

23. What did the child discuss? (Note especially content that he or she brought up spontaneously.)
24. What problems did the child mention?
25. How well did the child describe the problem?
26. How does the child's perception of the problem compare with the parents' perceptions?
27. How does the child's perception of the problem compare with the teacher's perceptions?
28. Were there any recurrent themes in the child's communications?

Content of Thought

29. Were there any signs of psychopathology in the child's communications? (For example, were delusions, hallucinations, phobias, obsessions, compulsions, depersonalization experiences, flight of ideas, confused thinking, racing thoughts, grandiose reasoning, paranoid ideation, ideas of reference, or unusual thought content present?)

Sensory and Motor Functioning

30. How intact were the child's senses—hearing, sight, touch, and smell?
31. How adequate was the child's gross motor coordination? (For example, was the child awkward, clumsy, or graceful?)
32. How adequate was the child's fine motor coordination?
33. Did the child show any signs of motor difficulties? (For example, did he or she show exaggerated movements, repetitive movements [tics, twitches, tremors], bizarre postures, grimaces, slow movements, or rituals? To what extent were these signs, if present, associated with mood-altering substances?)

Cognitive Functioning

34. Was the child oriented as to time, place, and person? (For example, did he or she know time of day, date, place where interview was being conducted, name of city, own name, birthdate?)
35. Was the child able to concentrate and follow instructions?

(Continued)

Table 3-6 (*Continued*)

36. Was the child alert? (For example, was he or she responsive to changes in your questions?)
37. How good was the child's memory for immediate, recent, and remote events?
38. Did the child's vocabulary and general fund of information reflect his or her educational and familial background?
39. Could the child read, write, and spell appropriately for his or her age group?

Temperament and Emotional Functioning
40. What was the child's temperament? (For example, was he or she excited, lethargic, active, passive?)
41. What was the general mood of the child? (For example, was he or she sad, cheerful, elated, indifferent, angry, energetic, irritable, changeable, anxious, tense, distressed, suspicious, perplexed?)
42. What was the child's range of emotional expressions? (For example, was it broad, expansive, restricted, blunted?)
43. Were there fluctuations in the child's mood during the interview? (For example, did the child show rapid changes from laughter to tears?)
44. Were the child's emotions appropriate to his or her age and life circumstances?
45. Was the child's affect appropriate for the speech and content of his or her communications?
46. What did the child say about his or her mood and feelings?
47. Was the child's self-report congruent with his or her behavior during the interview?

Insight and Judgment
48. What was the child's belief about why he or she was coming to the interview?

49. Was the child's belief appropriate and realistic?
50. Was the child aware of his or her problem and the concerns of others?
51. Did the child have ideas about what caused the problem?
52. Did the child have ideas about how the problem could be alleviated?
53. How good was the child's judgment in carrying out everyday activities?
54. How does the child solve problems of living? (For example, does the child solve problems impulsively, independently, responsibly, or through trial and error?)
55. Does the child make appropriate use of advice or assistance?
56. How much does the child desire help for his or her problems?

Attitudes Toward Home and School
57. What is the child's attitude toward his or her parents and siblings?
58. What is the child's attitude toward his or her home and neighborhood?
59. What is the child's attitude toward the school?
60. What is the child's attitude toward the teachers?
61. What is the child's attitude toward other children in the school?
62. What is the child's attitude toward the principal?

Intervention
63. What help does the child want?
64. What are the child's resources for overcoming the problem?
65. How open is the child to change?

Source: Adapted from Crary and Johnson (1975) and Sundberg, Taplin, and Tyler (1983).

---

that I will have to go to detention or something like that. Then I get mad at her. While we're waiting to get our food, the other kids play around in line. They act like clowns to get people's attention."
6. The student has just said "Sometimes I act up. I might get wild at times. But when I need to, I just tell myself to chill out. I know that if I go on yelling and stuff, I'll get in trouble, which I'm not going to do."

Suggested Responses

1. "We're going to talk in my office, which is the first room on the left." (This comment directs the student to the interviewing room; it should be made in a firm, cordial way that assumes the student will be cooperative.)
2. "Your teacher asked that we talk. She says she is concerned about your running around and screaming during times when such behavior can be disruptive and dangerous." (This comment describes the reason for the meeting in a way that the student should understand. The comment does not indicate either agreement or disagreement with the teacher, but it does imply that the teacher is interested in the student's welfare.)
3. "Tell me about a time when you were screaming and running around." (The comment requests a description of a specific event in the expectation of getting a productive answer.)
4. a. "You've named a number of places where it might be important to stay in control. Which one would you like to talk about first?" (The first sentence is a factual reflection that casts the issue in the positive light of staying in control; the second sentence gives the student an opportunity to choose what to discuss.)
   b. "So, you get involved with commotion that goes on in several different places. Tell me about one of those." (This comment combines a reflection with a probe that requests a concrete description of a relevant scene in order to obtain more information from the student.)

5. "So, you're in the cafeteria feeling angry, and you're with other students who are cutting up. What are you doing?" (This first sentence reflects the student's feeling and is followed with a question that focuses on the student's behavior.)
6. "There are times when you yell and act up, but you believe you are able to calm down and control yourself." (This comment reflects what the student said.)

SELF-MONITORING ASSESSMENT

If your initial interview extends beyond one session, you may want the child to conduct a self-monitoring assessment to obtain more information about a particular behavior. In a self-monitoring assessment, the child observes and records specific overt or covert aspects of his or her behavior and, sometimes, the circumstances associated with the behavior over a specified period. (I use the term *behavior* to include the child's actions, thoughts, and feelings.) To perform a self-monitoring assessment, the child must discriminate the presence or absence of a particular response (for example, a thought, an action performed by self, or an action performed by another) and record the response in a behavioral log, diary, or other form. The goal is to have the child make a systematic record of the behaviors of interest, gain awareness of his or her behavior, and participate in resolving the problem.

Self-monitoring assessment has several advantages (Bornstein, Hamilton, & Bornstein, 1986; Tunks & Bellissimo, 1991). First, it minimizes the use of retrospective reporting, thereby diminishing the chance of errors of memory or other possible distortions. Second, it can aid the child in answering questions about his or her behavior. Third, it may sensitize the child to his or her problem behavior and to the situations in which the problem behavior occurs. Fourth, it may reduce the power of the interviewer, present in face-to-face interactions, to influence the child's responses (such as by nods of the head, smiles, and reinforcing comments). Fifth, it provides information about the child's behavior in different settings and over a period of time. Sixth, it provides a relatively objective picture of the child's behavior because it tends to minimize defensiveness and the withholding of information. Finally, it provides "a baseline of the frequency, intensity, duration, and other characteristics of the presenting problem" (Tunks & Bellissimo, 1991, p. 32). (The remainder of this section on self-monitoring assessment is based in part on Bornstein et al., 1986.)

Rationale of Self-Monitoring Assessment

Following is the rationale behind self-monitoring assessment:

- Children have control over their behavior.
- Children receive feedback about their behavior in several settings.

- The procedure is portable and cost effective.
- The procedure provides an in-depth picture of the behaviors under study, including access to private data at the time the behaviors are occurring.
- The procedure, depending on the task and the child's ability, has good reliability and validity.
- The procedure reduces but does not eliminate reactive effects; these effects refer to the changes that children may make in their behavior simply because they know that they are being observed or that their products will be looked at.

Setting Up a Self-Monitoring Assessment

Setting up a self-monitoring assessment involves selecting the appropriate target behaviors, identifying the variables that may relate to those behaviors, and selecting a recording procedure that is easy to use and provides adequate and accurate information. You may want the self-monitoring assessment to give you information about the

- *frequency of the behavior* (how often the behavior occurs)
- *onset of the behavior* (when the behavior occurs)
- *quality of the behavior* (for example, how good or bad the behavior is)
- *intensity of the behavior* (for example, how severe or mild the behavior is)
- *duration of the behavior* (how long the behavior lasts)
- *situation in which the behavior occurs* (for example, at home, at school, or on the playground)
- *antecedent events associated with the behavior* (what events preceded the behavior)
- *consequent events associated with the behavior* (what events followed the behavior)

Two Examples of Self-Monitoring Assessment Forms

Table 3-7 offers an example of a self-monitoring form that you can give to older children to record stressful situations and other events as well. An example of a daily exercise log is shown in Table 3-8. Chapter 18 contains additional examples of self-monitoring forms.

Factors to Consider in Selecting a Self-Monitoring Procedure

In selecting a self-monitoring procedure, consider the child's age, motivation, and cognitive level and how these factors may affect his or her ability to do the recording. The child should understand fully how to use the recording procedure and how to recognize the targeted behaviors. Show the child, step by step through example, how to use the

Table 3-7
Example of a Self-Monitoring Questionnaire for Recording Stressful Situations

SELF-MONITORING QUESTIONNAIRE

Name _____

Directions: Complete the following items for each situation that made you uncomfortable or unhappy.

Date	Describe situation	What happened before?	What happened after?	Who else was there?	How did you feel and think?	Stress rating[a]

[a]Rate how much stress you were feeling on a scale from 1 to 10, with 1 = the least intense stress and 10 = the most intense stress.

Table 3-8
Example of a Daily Exercise Log

EXERCISE LOG

Name _____

Directions: Complete the following items about your daily exercise.

Date	What kinds of exercise did you do?	What time of day did you exercise?	How many minutes did you exercise?	Who else was there?	How much did you exert yourself?[a]	How much did you enjoy yourself?[b]	What problems did you have while exercising?

[a]Use a scale from 1 to 10, with 1 = no exertion and 10 = completely exhausted.
[b]Use a scale from 1 to 10, with 1 = did not enjoy at all and 10 = really enjoyed.

recording procedure. For example, if the targeted behavior is the child's making a positive statement to his or her parents, provide the child with examples of such statements. Sometimes you may want to evaluate the accuracy of the child's recordings by having an observer also record the child's behavior or by examining by-products associated with the behavior of interest (for example, number of problems completed on the assignment sheet). With some children, you may want to use mechanical means, such as counters or tokens and plastic boxes, instead of written records of behavior. Be sure that the child can read if the self-monitoring form requires reading ability.

Self-monitoring assessment may cause the child to become anxious. For example, the child's anxiety level may increase when she or he records failures or lack of progress. Consequently, you will need to monitor whether the procedure induces excessive anxiety. If you find that it does, alter it as needed. For self-monitoring to be effective, significant others in the child's environment must be supportive of the procedure and encourage the child to record the needed information.

The following case illustrates the use of a self-monitoring procedure to assess a problem behavior before a behavior change program was designed. The initial and subsequent self-monitoring records served to evaluate the effectiveness of the treatment program (Evans & Sullivan, 1993).

CASE 3-6. PAUL

Paul, a 12-year-old boy, was referred because of excessive thumbsucking. His dentist had informed his parents that this behavior was having a destructive effect upon his teeth. Paul and his parents said that his friends had begun to tease him more frequently about sucking his thumb.

Excessive thumbsucking appeared to be Paul's only major problem. A psychological report indicated that he had above-average intellectual functioning and adequate social skills. He had friends who often came to his house, and he enjoyed playing soccer and other games.

Because Paul was eager to stop sucking his thumb, a self-control program was initiated after the first interview. To assess the frequency of thumbsucking and the antecedent events for this behavior, a self-monitoring program was instituted. Paul was instructed to record the number of times he sucked his thumb before school, during morning time in school, during afternoon time in school, and after school. In addition, Paul recorded where he was and what he was doing when he sucked his thumb. To estimate the accuracy of Paul's self-recordings, his father recorded the number of times Paul sucked his thumb during the periods when Paul was not in school. Whenever Paul's recordings for the day matched his father's within two instances, he was rewarded. (adapted from pp. 79–80)

Problems in Self-Monitoring Assessment

Limitations associated with self-monitoring assessment include reactive effects and difficulty in keeping accurate records. Let's examine each of these in more detail.

Reactive effects.   Reactive effects are possible with self-monitoring assessment because the children know that someone will be looking at their recording sheet. If the child changes his or her behavior because of reactive effects, the changes may distort or modify the behaviors to be studied. Reactive effects may be beneficial in intervention programs if they *reduce* the frequency of negative behaviors or *increase* the frequency of positive behaviors. You need to monitor reactive effects to learn whether they are interfering with the assessment goals.

Accuracy effects.   The accuracy of the recordings may be affected by the child's age, degree and type of pathology, and degree of cooperativeness and interest; the type of behavior targeted (for example, verbal or nonverbal, on task or goal related); the length of time it takes to record the behavior; whether the behavior is positive or negative; the number of behaviors to be monitored; other activities occurring contemporaneously; the type of recording device; and the presence of observers who also are recording the behavior. Children who are not well motivated, for example, may not do daily recordings. In such cases, children should be encouraged to turn in their recordings every day and possibly be rewarded for their efforts.

Children under 5 or 6 years of age will likely have difficulty making self-monitoring recordings (Shapiro, 1984). Therefore, limit the target behaviors to one or two behaviors and use a simple and clear recording procedure. Also use visual or verbal-auditory cues whenever possible to prompt the self-observation and recording. Finally, you may want to give the children appropriate rewards for accurate recordings.

Even for children in the middle years of childhood, the procedure must be simple and readily comprehensible. You can enhance children's accuracy by giving immediate feedback about how their recording agreed with that of an external judge, carefully defining the target behaviors, providing examples, selecting behaviors that are readily discriminable, modeling the process, giving several trials, and keeping the procedure short (for example, less than 5 minutes). Occasionally, when children are completing a self-monitoring assessment for specific symptoms, prompts from parents or teachers at the appointed or critical times may increase the children's compliance with the procedure.

Comment on Self-Monitoring Assessment

In setting up a self-monitoring assessment, tailor the techniques and instructions to the comprehension level of the child. Consider role playing the self-monitoring procedure *before* you end the interview. Obviously, self-monitoring assessment, like any self-report measure, is open to distortion if the child wants to deny problems, exaggerate symptoms to gain attention, or withhold sensitive information. Make every effort to enlist the child's cooperation and interest in the procedure.

When self-monitoring assessment is part of an intervention program, you may use the data as an index of change, for evaluating the effectiveness of the intervention plan and for carrying out changes in the plan. Self-monitoring assessment also may help children focus on the behavior of interest and may help them understand the relationship among situational events, the occurrence of the behavior, and possible consequences associated with it.

CASE HISTORY REPORT

Exhibit 3-1 presents a brief case history report of a 14-year-old adolescent who was in a long-term treatment facility. He volunteered for the interview so that the interviewer could practice her interviewing skills. The report includes referral information, behavioral observations, a short case history, and a summary and impressions. It is well written and illustrates how various elements of the interview can be incorporated in the report. The report describes the adolescent's behavioral patterns; it was not written, however, to offer treatment recommendations.

Exercise 3-4. Evaluating Segments of an Initial Interview with a School-Aged Child

---

This exercise contains part of an initial interview with a 9-year-old girl who was repeating the second grade and still having problems mastering her school subjects. The interview is divided into three segments in order to facilitate evaluating the interview. Evaluate each segment. Describe the subject matter covered in the segment, and evaluate the interviewer's techniques. Consider such issues as the following: Are the interviewer's questions helpful in obtaining information that might be related to the child's problems in school? What other areas need to be inquired about? What generalizations can you make from these interview segments about interviewing school-aged children? Compare your comments with those that follow the interview segments.

Interview Segment 1
IR: Patricia, let me get some information from you. How old are you now?
IE: Nine.
IR: Nine. And your birthday is?
IE: September 24th.
IR: What year were you born?
IE: I don't know.
IR: Do you know? I think you were born in 1986. That makes you 9 years old. Where do you live, Patricia?
IE: 587 Travel Blvd.
IR: You live with your mom and your dad?
IE: My stepdad.
IR: Your stepdad. And your mom. Who else lives in your family?
IE: My brother and my sister.
IR: How old is your brother?
IE: I don't know.

IR: What's his name?
IE: Gerald.
IR: Is he older than you or younger?
IE: Gerald is older than me.
IR: Is he all grown up?
IE: Well, he's still living there.
IR: Is he in—does he go to junior high school or high school? Where does he go to school?
IE: I'm not sure. He goes to Merrymount School, but he's in a higher grade.
IR: Is he pretty good to you? Or…
IE: He's good to me. He's good to me.
IR: He is good to you.
IE: My sister's name is Alice.
IR: How old is Alice?
IE: I don't know.
IR: Is she bigger than you or smaller?
IE: She's bigger than me.
IR: Does she go to Merrymount School?
IE: Uh huh.
IR: Is she a teenager?
IE: Not yet.
IR: Not yet. What does your stepdad do? What is his job?
IE: He delivers newspapers.
IR: And your mom, does she work too?
IE: She works at the Forrest Medical Care Facility.
IR: When does she go to work, what time?
IE: In the morning, I'm not sure, but she gets home at four o'clock.
IR: And do you go to your house when you get out of school, or do you…
IE: My sister gets off at our house and watches me.
IR: So your sister watches over you.
IE: My sister has a real mom. Her name is Beatrice. My mom is Alice's stepmom.
IR: I see.
IE: My mom is Gerald's stepmom.
IR: That's why you don't know how old they are. How long has your stepdad been your stepdad? Has it been a long time, or just…
IE: I think about a short time.
IR: Okay.
IE: I'm not sure though.
IR: Do you have another dad someplace too?
IE: He lives—my other dad lives in Clairmont.
IR: Do you go see him at times?
IE: No. Cause my mom doesn't want me to.
IR: Okay.
IR: How long has it been since you've seen him?
IE: I don't know.
IR: Since you were a baby, do you remember seeing him at all?
IE: Yeah.
IR: When did you see him?
IE: Once when I was a little baby.

Interview Segment 2
IR: Do you like school?
IE: Yeah.
IR: What do you like about school?
IE: I like to do a lot of stuff.

Exhibit 3-1
Case History

CASE HISTORY

Name: John
Date of Birth: April 18, 1980
Chronological Age: 14 years
Site of Interview: Beckman House

Interviewer: Jane Roberts
Date of Interview: April 12, 1994
Date of Report: April 16, 1994

Reason for Referral

John volunteered to be interviewed to help the interviewer fulfill a requirement for an interviewing course at _____ State University.

Behavioral Observations

John is a 14-year-old, muscular, tan-complexioned, Caucasian male of average height for his age. He had neatly groomed black hair, and he wore a T-shirt, blue jeans, and tennis shoes.

John sat straight in his chair and made frequent eye contact with the interviewer. His voice was low pitched, but not excessively loud or soft. At times he spoke rapidly and slurred his words together. His thoughts were organized, and his vocabulary appropriate for his age. He frequently used slang words such as "nosey-doze" and "booze" when referring to drugs and alcohol.

John's affect was flat and indifferent throughout the interview, except on two occasions: once when he talked excitedly about his drug use, and another time when he laughed while he described aiming guns at people in a local canyon. After he reported that he had attacked his mother, he was asked what made him threaten her. He turned and faced the wall for about 30 seconds and then said that he had not heard the question. The question was repeated, and he abruptly said he did not remember. John did not discuss why he currently resides at Beckman House, an inpatient treatment center for severely disturbed adolescents.

Interview Findings

John was born in Tennessee. When he was 2 years old, his parents divorced. Shortly afterwards, he was placed in a foster home because his mother could not support him. When John was 7 years old, he was reunited with his mother, and he moved to Albany, New York with her and his 6-year-old sister.

John described his relationship with his mother as confused, fluctuating among the roles of husband, brother, and son. However, there apparently has been no incestuous contact.

John attended public schools until the age of 12 years. In sixth grade, he received therapy for a speech impediment. At school, he played with cap guns and wore trench coats and wing-tipped shoes to be different and to attract attention. In addition, he slept during class and talked back to his teachers. His classmates responded by laughing or becoming shocked or scared. John sometimes shot guns in a local canyon with his friends, and he threatened people by aiming his gun at them. John believed he was participating in the Vietnam War while in the canyon.

John said he frequently argued with his mother about staying out late at night and wearing his dirty boots in the house. He and his sister fought over the television and the radio. At age 13, John began drinking alcohol and using cocaine, LSD, and amphetamines. He and his mother argued about his drug use, and she reported him to the police several times. John said he attacked his mother with a machete; this was verified by the director of Beckman House. John subsequently was hospitalized at County Mental Health, El Monte Hospital, and Pinecrest New Alternatives. In October, 1993, John was referred to Beckman House for violent ideation, assault, and drug abuse. John reported that he had a close friend who died at about the time he came to Beckman House. Shortly after arriving, John made a serious suicide attempt by jumping through a plate-glass window. Two months later, his grandfather, with whom he had a close relationship, died. John frequently fantasizes becoming a hero by killing people who are hurting others. He hopes to return home and return to school.

John's records show that he was previously diagnosed as having a schizo-affective disorder. His current treatment includes medication for depression and aggression, individual therapy, and group therapy. Currently, he is functioning well at Beckman House. However, his future remains uncertain.

Summary and Impressions

John is a 14-year-old Caucasian male of muscular build and medium height. At times he spoke rapidly and slurred his words together. John was indifferent throughout the interview, except when he excitedly talked about his drug use and when he laughed while describing aiming guns at people. John's history is filled with instability. His relationships with his mother and sister have been marked with conflict and confused roles. His school adjustment also has been poor. He has had several episodes of violent behavior and has used illegal drugs. He entered several hospitals before coming to Beckman House, where he was referred for violent ideation, assault, and drug abuse. John has also attempted suicide and has fantasies of killing people. He says he wants to return home and to school. John's treatment includes medication for depression and aggression, individual therapy, and group therapy. John is an adolescent obsessed with thoughts of violence. His impulse control is weak, and at times he acts out. John displays anger toward others through both verbal and physical means. His suicide attempt suggests that some of his anger may be directed toward himself. He appears to be in continued need of treatment.

(Signature)

Jane Roberts, B. S., Interviewer

IR: Give me some examples. What do you like to do?

IE: Math…

IR: What else do you like?

IE: Spelling.

IR: What else?

IE: English, gym, recess.

IR: You like a lot about school then, don't you?

IE: Uh huh.

IR: Anything you don't like?

IE: There's nothin' I don't like.

IR: So you like it all. Anything that's hard for you to do in school? What do you have the most trouble with?

IE: Math.

IR: What else?

IE: Nothin' else.

IR: Do you have a lot of friends at school?

IE: Yeah.

IR: Give me some names of your friends. Who are your friends?

IE: Florence, Virginia, Jennifer, and Keith, he's a boy.

IR: It's nice to have friends who are boys as well.

IE: Bonnie.

IR: So you have lots of friends in school. Have you always gone to this school, or did you go to another school?

IE: I went to Dixon School when I was little.

IR: Like in kindergarten? Or first grade?

IE: I think I started kindergarten there.

IR: But you went to Dixon before?

IE: Yeah.

IR: And you're in second grade now, right?

IE: Uh huh.

IR: Who's your favorite teacher you've ever had?

IE: Mrs. Fureness.

IR: Why? Why was she your favorite?

IE: Well, I was in her class, and then I got put back in second grade 'cause I was having so much trouble with math.

IR: I see. So you're taking second grade over this year, are you?

IE: Uh huh.

Interview Segment 3

IR: At home if you have a problem or if you need help with something…

IE: I don't.

IR: Whom would you go to, though, if you wanted to talk to somebody about a problem?

IE: My mom.

IR: You'd go to your mom and talk to her.

IE: And my dad.

IR: Either one of them you'd go to?

IE: Or I would go to my brother or sister.

IR: What do you like to do with your family? What is fun for you to do?

IE: All sorts of things.

IR: Such as? Give me an idea of what you enjoy doing with your mom.

IE: Going shopping.

IR: With your dad? What do you like to do?

IE: Going shopping.

IR: Do you have friends around home?

IE: There's this lady that lives next door and she has a little girl, her name is Tilly. She's only a baby. I like to go there and play with her.

IR: Okay.

IE: Outside. We play with wagons and things.

IR: Do you have any kids your age around home that you play with?

IE: Only Tilly. All the other ones, except Kim Green. I don't play with her because they're real mean to me and my mom doesn't want me going over there.

IR: Is Kim your age or older?

IE: I don't know.

IR: Patricia, now I'd like to ask you whether you have ever been in the hospital because you got real sick or had an accident?

IE: I had spinal meningitis. I've been in there.

IR: When did you have that? Do you know?

IE: When I was a little baby.

IR: I see.

IE: When I was first born.

IR: And how do you know? Do you remember being in the hospital, or did your mom tell you?

IE: I remember 'cause my mom told me.

IR: Any other times you've been in the hospital and you've been real sick?

IE: I can't remember.

IR: Do you ever have trouble with your ears? Like do you have earaches, or do you have tubes in your ears or anything?

IE: Uh uh.

IR: Do you ever have trouble with your eyes?

IE: Uh uh. I have 20/20 vision with my eyes.

IR: Have you had them checked by a doctor?

IE: (Nods head "yes")

IR: Do you get headaches and stomachaches very much?

IE: (Shakes head "no")

IR: No. So you're pretty healthy. What do you worry most about? What things do you think about and worry about?

IE: Nothing.

IR: You never worry?

IE: Uh uh.

IR: Not even when…

IE: Unless when I let my dog out to go to the bathroom, I think she'll get ran over by a car.

IR: So you worry about your dog. You never worry about anything else, or think about it and kind of worry about it?

IE: I worry about my mom and dad when they go to work.

IR: Sure. Do you ever have nightmares?

IE: Uh uh.

IR: No?

IE: I never had them since I was 3 years old.

IR: Do you remember them when you were 3? Did you used to get up and your mom would have to come and calm you down or anything?

IE: Uh uh.

IR: No. They would just—you would go back to sleep, would you?

IE: (Nods head "yes")

IR: When you were little, or even now, what things were you afraid of? Like scared of?

IE: I was scared of snakes.

IR: Snakes? I'm still scared of snakes. Anything else? What else are you scared of? Things that scare you, people…

IE: Bears.

IR: What makes you mad? People or things or situations that make you really feel angry?

IE: Like when my dog chews up one of my favorite toys.

IR: Your dog is important to you.

IE: Ya.

IR: How old is he?

IE: It's a girl. She's only about 4 months old, I think.

IR: A puppy?

IE: (Nods head "yes")

IR: Is it a big puppy or a little puppy?

IE: Well, that little (makes a gesture). Oh wait, this little (makes a smaller gesture).

IR: Kind of a little puppy. Is that the only thing that makes you mad? Do you never get mad at other kids or at your brother or your sister or…

IE: Yeah, I sorta get mad at my brother.

IR: For doing what?

IE: Because he—he takes my stuff out of my room and I get mad.

IR: And when you're mad what do you do?

IE: Well, I used to turn my stereo up real loud.

IR: And how would that help?

IE: That would make him mad.

IR: That would make him mad. But you don't do that anymore?

IE: (Shakes head "no")

IR: Why not?

IE: Because if he gets mad at me and I get mad at him, alls I have to do is go in his room and take one of his tapes and hide it in my room somewhere and don't give it back.

IR: So you have your ways of getting even. Do you ever get in trouble at home?

IE: No. Sorta sometimes.

IR: What happens if you get in trouble? Like with your mom or dad?

IE: Well, one time me and my brother were playing around downstairs. I took his coat and wouldn't give it back. I threw it up on them bars on top of our stairs and he couldn't get it down, and I got it down 'cause I was jumping up and down and I reached it and got it down, ran upstairs, and threw it on his waterbed. He got mad.

IR: He got mad?

IE: And told my dad.

IR: Then what happened?

IE: I didn't get in trouble.

IR: You didn't get in trouble? Have you ever really done anything that was bad and you did have to get punished?

IE: (Shakes head "no")

IR: You don't tend to do things that are bad.

IE: Not since I remember.

IR: What are your favorite activities to do at home, or your hobbies? You know, things you love to do on your own time.

IE: Eat ice cream.

IR: What else?

IE: Eat dinner and stuff.

IR: Aside from eating.

IE: I play with my Barbie dolls.

IR: You like Barbie dolls?

IE: And I like to play with my little puppy dog Damie.

IR: Anything else you like to do for fun? Your favorite activities.

IE: In school, I like to do art.

IR: Art, okay. Do you have jobs you have to do? What are your jobs at home?

IE: Sometimes, when my mom's at work, I have to clean up the living room and stuff.

IR: Do you have to do that every day or just when your mom wants you to?

IE: Just when my mom wants me to.

IR: Do you have any jobs you have to do every day?

IE: (Shakes head "no") Except make my bed.

IR: You make up your bed. Who gets you ready for school?

IE: I do.

IR: All by yourself?

IE: Uh huh.

IR: Do you do a pretty good job of it?

IE: Yeah.

IR: Okay.

IE: Except when I didn't make my bed this morning. I forgot. I was late.

IR: I think you can be excused for once anyway. Do you get enough help in school, or do you need more help?

IE: I get enough.

IR: What kind of help does Mrs. Black give you? How does she help you?

IE: Well, they teach me how to do times and stuff and math. (Interview continues.)

Comment

Interview Segment 1

The interviewer inquires about the child's background, including her family. The questions and comments are short and to the point and comprehensible to the child. Most of the questions are factual. The child seems to be at a loss, not knowing her complete birthdate, the ages of her stepbrother and stepsister, and the length of time her mother has been married. Many 9-year-olds would know this information. The interviewer moves from topic to topic, accepting the child's failure to give the requested information. This matter-of-fact approach is good because it does not place undue stress on the child.

Interview Segment 2

The interviewer lightly touches on the child's attitude toward school and the child's favorite subjects. The probing comment and question "Give me some examples. What do you like to do?" are excellent. However, the interviewer accepts the child's statement that there is nothing she doesn't like. Instead of probing for further information about not liking anything, the interviewer asks about "hard" things at school. Even though the child says that she likes math, she also says that math is hard. It might have been helpful to ask the child about this seeming paradox. In addition, the interviewer fails to probe about why math is hard for the child. The interviewer focuses briefly on the child's friends at school but learns little about what she does with her friends. We do learn that the child is repeating the second grade, but we never learn why Mrs. Fureness is the child's favorite teacher because the child fails to answer the question and the interviewer fails to probe further. The interviewer also asks a "why" question that should be rephrased—for example, "What makes Mrs. Fureness your favorite teacher?" Finally, the interviewer fails to inquire about the child's feelings about her current teacher and class.

Interview Segment 3
The interviewer focuses on the child's family, friends outside of school, illnesses, worries, feelings, hobbies, and chores at home. Transitions between topics are relatively smooth. The child seems to comprehend the questions, and she answers openly and willingly. However, most answers are short, with minimal details.

Possible Generalizations
Following are some possible generalizations that can be made about school-aged children from these interview segments. First, some school-aged children may not know or remember details of their background and current situation or those of family members. Second, they may give short, non-detailed answers. Third, they may give tangential replies. Fourth, they may use denial. Fifth, they may give answers that are not informative. Sixth, they may answer questions with nonverbal gestures rather than with a verbal reply. And last, but not least, their language may not be polished. Although these generalizations may hold for some older children and adults as well, they appear to be more applicable to many school-aged children. They also, of course, apply to many younger children.

The Childhood shows the man,
As morning shows the day.

—John Milton

THINKING THROUGH THE ISSUES

How do interviews with children differ from interviews with adults?

How difficult do you believe it will be for you to interview young children?

Do you think that you can get into the psychological framework of a young child?

How accurate do you find the reports of young children?

What clues might you use to distinguish temporary delays in development from those due to more chronic problems?

What other kinds of problems might you encounter in interviewing children, besides those discussed in the text?

How will you reconcile information given by a child that conflicts with information given by his or her parents and by other adults?

How can observing a child's play reveal possible emotional, behavioral, familial, or medically related problems?

How useful do you believe knowledge of developmental milestones will be in interviewing children and their families?

When do you think you might use a self-monitoring procedure? In what situations do you believe that self-monitoring will be especially useful?

SUMMARY

General Considerations in an Initial Interview with Children
1. Interviews with children will give you information about problems as they perceive them, their thoughts and feelings about themselves, and their impressions of their situation and their relationships.
2. You will need to support and encourage young children to get them to reveal their thoughts and feelings to you, and you will need to adjust interview strategies to the linguistic, developmental, and conceptual abilities of the children.
3. It is more difficult to interview children than adults because children may have limitations in language comprehension, language expressions, conceptual abilities, and memory.
4. Children often are not aware that they have problems.
5. In conducting the interview with a child, always consider the child's age, experiences, level of cognitive development, and ability to express himself or herself, as well as the extensiveness of any psychological disturbance.
6. Children's behavior in the interview may not be typical of their behavior outside the interview.
7. The goals of the initial interview with children will depend on the referral question, as well as the children's age and communication skills.
8. In preparing for the interview, study the referral question and review available background material.
9. Observe how the children and parents interact in the waiting room.
10. If the children refuse to come with you, wait a few moments to see if their distress will diminish.
11. If absolutely necessary, allow the parents of children younger than 6 years to come into the interview room but request that they only observe. In cases of alleged child abuse or neglect in which the parent(s) may be a perpetrator, interview the child alone.
12. Children are likely to be apprehensive when you first meet them; your job is to reduce their apprehensions.

Developmental Considerations in Interviewing Children
13. Children face various tasks in each developmental period. In infancy, these tasks include attaining smooth physiological regulation (such as eating and sleeping), making the transition from reflex to voluntary behavior, becoming attached to a caregiver, and separating self from others. In toddlerhood and preschool, the tasks include mastering toileting and other self-care activities, developing language, developing self-control and compliance, and achieving gender identity formation. In middle childhood, the tasks center on adjustment to school. In adolescence, tasks include adjusting to pubertal changes, making the transition to secondary schooling, establishing friendships and dating, and achieving identity formation, such as a coherent sense of self.
14. Although you cannot interview infants, you can learn about them by observing them and by interviewing their parents.

15. The nine major temperament characteristics of infants (or any individuals) are activity level, rhythmicity, approach or withdrawal, adaptability, threshold of responsiveness, intensity of reaction, quality of mood, distractibility, and attention span and persistence.

16. Although you may have difficulty formally interviewing preschoolers, try to get them to talk about themselves.

17. Some useful ways to establish rapport with preschool children include playing a game and showing them an interesting toy before the interview begins.

18. When you observe children in a free-play setting, note other children's entrance into the playroom, initiation of play, energy expenditure, manipulative actions, tempo of play, body movements, verbalizations, affect and tone of play, integration of play, creativity, products of play, attitude toward adults, and departure from the playroom.

19. During middle childhood, children make great strides in language and conceptual development and can engage in meaningful conversations. However, they still may have difficulty in describing their symptoms and talking about themselves.

20. To help build rapport with children in middle childhood, consider using competitive board games.

21. Adolescents face several challenging developmental tasks that in part focus on their accepting their physical and sexual roles, working through peer relations with both sexes, achieving independence, preparing for an occupation, becoming aware of social and political forces, acquiring socially responsible behavior, preparing for family life, and establishing values that are in harmony with their immediate environment.

22. Adolescents' command of higher-level concepts and language provides them with the means of mature communication. However, they still may not be able to articulate their feelings or reflect on their experiences.

23. When adolescents show resistance, be prepared to be more direct, concrete, explicit, and active than you prefer to be.

Sequences of Normal Development

24. It is important for you to be familiar with normal sequences of development in such areas as cognitive development, language acquisition, concept of self, person perception, moral judgment, recognition of emotion, and temporal concepts.

Techniques for Interviewing Children

25. The best way to get children to remember, think, and tell you about themselves is to ask them questions.

26. The following strategies are useful for interviewing children: use appropriate language and intonation, and do not lead children; ask for examples; be open to what children tell you; formulate appropriate opening statements; make descriptive comments; use reflection; give praise frequently; avoid critical statements; use simple questions and concrete referents; formulate questions in the subjunctive mood (hypothetical) when necessary; be tactful; recognize children's discomfort; use props, crayons, clay, and toys to help young children talk; use sentence completion techniques; use fantasy techniques; help children express their thoughts and feelings; clarify an episode of misbehavior by recounting it; clarify interview procedures for children who are minimally communicative; understand and use silence; handle resistance and anxiety by giving support and reassurance; and consider the child's age and needs in setting the tempo and length of the interview.

Areas Covered in the Initial Interview with Children

27. The typical sequence in interviewing a child is to introduce yourself to the parent (or caregiver or guardian) and to the child, greet the child, give your name and professional title, make an introductory statement, continue the interview as appropriate, review the issues with the child as you see them, describe what will happen to the child after you complete the interview, express appreciation for the child's effort and cooperation, and close the interview.

28. Typical areas covered in the initial interview with children include identifying information about the child, the reason for coming to the interview, confidentiality, school, home, interests, friends, moods and feelings, fears and worries, self- concept, somatic concerns, obsessions and compulsions, thought disorder, memories and fantasies, aspirations, and other information voluntarily supplied by the children. In addition, for adolescents, typical areas include jobs, sexual relations, eating habits, possible drug and alcohol use, and pregnancy or impregnation.

29. You may want to ask about reinforcers important to the children if you are planning a therapeutic behavioral intervention.

30. If you believe that the physical layout of the child's home may be contributing to her or his difficulties, you can ask the child to draw a picture of her or his room and, if needed, other rooms in the house. This technique also serves to establish rapport.

31. In every interview, you should evaluate such things as the child's appearance and behavior, speech and communications, content of thought, sensory and motor functioning, cognitive functioning, temperament and emotional functioning, and insight and judgment.

Self-Monitoring Assessment

32. In self-monitoring assessment, children systematically observe and record aspects of their behavior over a specified period.

33. Setting up a self-monitoring assessment involves selecting the appropriate target behaviors, identifying the variables that may relate to those behaviors, and selecting a recording procedure that is easy to use and provides adequate and accurate information.

34. In a self-monitoring assessment, you will want to obtain information about the frequency, onset, quality, intensity, duration, situation, antecedent events, and consequent events associated with the behavior.

35. In selecting a self-monitoring procedure, consider the child's age, motivation, and cognitive level and how these factors affect the accuracy of his or her recording.

36. Problems with self-monitoring assessment include reactive effects and difficulty in keeping accurate records.

37. When self-monitoring assessment is part of an intervention program, the data can serve as an index of change, for evaluating the effectiveness of the intervention plan, for carrying out changes in the plan, for helping the children focus on the behavior of interest, and for helping the children understand the relationship among situational events, the occurrence of the behavior, and possible consequences associated with it.

KEY TERMS, CONCEPTS, AND NAMES

STUDY QUESTIONS

1. Discuss some general considerations in interviewing children. Include in your discussion why children are more difficult to interview than adults.

2. What are some goals of the initial interview with children?

3. When you initially meet a child and his or her parents, what should you observe?

4. What are some initial apprehensions that children might have about the interview?

5. What are some of the tasks that children face in each developmental period?

6. Give some guidelines for observing infants, and discuss what things you would look for under each guideline.

7. Chess and Thomas identified nine major temperament characteristics in infants. List the characteristics, and give examples for each one.

8. Briefly describe why it is difficult to interview preschool children.

9. Describe some useful guidelines for observing preschool children in a free-play setting.

10. What are some abilities of middle childhood–aged children that can assist them in an interview?

11. Discuss some qualities of adolescents that can help or hinder them in an interview.

12. Discuss some milestones in development from birth to 60 months of age.

13. There are important developmental sequences in such areas as cognitive development, language acquisition, concept of self, person perception, moral judgment, recognition of emotion, and temporal concepts. Discuss three of these developmental sequences.

14. Twenty-one specific techniques for interviewing children are discussed in the text. Describe seven of them.

15. What are the typical areas covered in the initial interview with children?

16. Discuss the mental status evaluation. In your discussion, comment on the areas typically covered in a mental status evaluation and on some important factors to evaluate in each area.

17. Describe self-monitoring assessment. In your discussion, consider its rationale, how to set up the procedure, factors to consider in selecting a procedure, and the assets and limitations of the procedure.

4

INITIAL INTERVIEWS WITH PARENTS, TEACHERS, AND FAMILIES

No matter how many communes anybody invents, the family always creeps back.

—Margaret Mead

Goals and Objectives

This chapter is designed to enable you to:

- Understand and conduct interviews with parents
- Understand and conduct interviews with teachers
- Understand and conduct interviews with families
- Learn techniques for closing the initial interview
- Evaluate the initial interview findings
- Evaluate your role as an interviewer

INTERVIEWING PARENTS

The interview with parents is an important part of the assessment process. Parents have a wealth of knowledge about their children. A well-conducted parent interview will serve to establish rapport and a positive working relationship with the parents, will help focus the perception of the parents on the issues, will serve as a valuable source of information about the child and family, will help the parents organize and reflect on the information, will contribute to the formulation of a diagnosis, will provide a basis for decisions about treatment and further investigation, and will lay the groundwork for parental efforts to be a part of intervention efforts (Barkley, 1981; Canino, 1985; La Greca, 1983).

You want the parents to participate actively in the interview (Kessler, 1988). To encourage them to do so, you need to treat them with respect, consider their cultural and ethnic backgrounds and practices, use language they understand, be honest with them, establish a working relationship with them, and respect their privacy and confidentiality, unless confidentiality must be broken (see Chapter 2).

Parents not only serve as an important source of information but also will play a key role in any proposed intervention. If they feel threatened by the initial interview, such as by your probing questions, demands they cannot fulfill, or unempathic responses, they may prematurely terminate contact with you and find excuses to avoid coming for further help. They may say that they have transportation difficulties, babysitting difficulties, or difficulty in scheduling appointments; sometimes, however, these may be real concerns. You want to lessen any anxiety parents may have and make every effort to show them that you are interested in them and their child and are concerned about the child's welfare.

Goals of the Initial Interview with Parents

Following are the main goals of the initial clinical assessment interview with parents (Mash & Terdal, 1981):

1. to gather information about parental concerns and goals
2. to assess parental perceptions of the strengths and weaknesses of the child
3. to obtain a case history of the child from the parents, including the child's medical, developmental, educational, and social histories
4. to identify the child's problems and related antecedent and consequent events
5. to determine how the parents have dealt with the problems in the past, including whether they sought prior treatment, who provided the treatment, and the dates and outcomes of the treatment
6. to identify events that reinforced the problem for both the child and the parents
7. to obtain a family history (where relevant)
8. to assess the parents' motivation and resources for change and their expectations for the child's treatment
9. to obtain informed consent from the parents to conduct an assessment of the child
10. to discuss the assessment procedures that may be used with the child
11. to discuss what follow-up contacts they and their child may need

If all these goals are reached, you can probably construct a picture of the life experiences of the child and arrive at some preliminary judgments about the child's difficulties, the child's strengths and weaknesses, and the parents' reactions, concerns, coping abilities, strengths, and weaknesses. You also can probably arrive at a picture of the family's life style and its prevailing values, mores, and concerns.

Age of the Child

The age of the child will, in part, determine the content of the interview with the parents. If you are interviewing the parents of a young child, the focus will be on the mother's pregnancy and delivery, the child's early developmental milestones, and the nature of the problem. With parents of elementary school–aged children, you also will need to ask about language and motor skills, peer and social relations, and educational progress. With parents of adolescents, additional areas of inquiry will include the adolescent's peer group, sexual relations, academic progress, vocational plans, interests, and use of alcohol, drugs, and cigarettes.

Concerns of Parents

Parents may be apprehensive about their child's evaluation. They may be concerned about a variety of issues, depending on the type and severity of the child's problems, their cultural subgroup and ethnicity, and their religious affiliation. They may be interested in knowing about or be concerned about several of the following issues:

1. *Etiology.* What is the cause of the child's problem? How serious is the child's problem?
2. *Interventions.* What can they do about the child's problem? What treatments are needed, and will the treatments cure the problem? Where can they get treatment? How long will the treatment last? How much will it cost? Will their insurance cover the cost of treatment (if they are

insured)? What special services will their child need? Will they also need to be seen for treatment? What can they do at home to help their child? Where can they get more information about their child's condition? Will the authorities try to take their child away?

3. *Family issues.* Will other children in the family also have these problems? What should they tell their other children about their sibling's condition? How will the other children in the family react to their sibling being seen by a mental health professional? What secrets will the child reveal about the family? Will these secrets, if revealed by the child, damage the family in any way?

4. *Parental responsibility.* Are they responsible for their child's problems? Have they exaggerated the problem or put ideas into their child's head? Will other people think that they are incapable of taking care of their child?

5. *Stigma.* Will their child resent them for taking him or her to a mental health professional? What will it mean that their child has a record of visiting a "shrink"? Will other people think that their family is crazy? What will their relatives, neighbors, friends, the child's peers, the peers' parents, and the child's teachers think about the child going to see a mental health professional?

Parents may ask you how to prepare their child for the interview. Tell them to be straightforward. Suggest that they tell the child who is going to be seen, the reason for the appointment, and what will happen. Explanations should, of course, be consistent with the child's level of comprehension. For children between 3 and 6 years, the parents should emphasize that there will be toys to play with in the office and that the children will be talking to someone. For children between 6 and 10 years, the parents should emphasize that the children will be talking with someone and possibly playing some games. For children older than 10 years, the parents should emphasize that the person they will see is someone who knows how to help children (or teenagers) and families, that the children (or teenagers) will be talking with that person, and that it often helps to get the advice of someone outside the family.

Potential Negative Feelings of Parents

By the time parents seek an evaluation for a school-aged child (and sometimes for a preschool child as well), they may have already experienced much frustration and anguish. They may have seen other professionals but still may be seeking a magic solution. They may know that their child has a problem but may be tired of feeling that they are to blame. If they feel this way, they may displace on you the anger that has developed from prior encounters with medical and mental health professionals. Because parents may feel inadequate—as a result of their inability to work with their child and of their impatience and irritability with him or her—they also may have a diminished sense of self-esteem and feelings of guilt.

Parents sometimes deny that there is a problem, reacting angrily to being interviewed about a problem they do not wish to recognize. At a school-initiated interview, for example, they may make comments (a) *reflecting anger or denial* ("We didn't know he was having any problems. No one told us before." "We don't see any problems like that at home."), (b) *implying blame* ("Do you think it's because my wife works?" "Do you think it's because my husband spends so little time with him?"), (c) *reflecting rationalization* ("Perhaps it's because his older brother is like that." "You know, we are divorced. That could be the reason."), (d) *reflecting disbelief* ("How can you tell from just a few weeks in class?" "Aren't all the children his age like that?"), and (e) *reflecting the school's responsibility* ("If you would give her special help, it would help the problem." "I think he should see a counselor. That will straighten everything out.").

Deal with any negative feelings the parents may have about themselves or others during their initial contact with you; otherwise, their feelings may interfere with the interview. Give them an opportunity to talk about their feelings. Help them recognize that together you can work to understand and improve the behavior and functioning of their child. If necessary, tell them that you are aware of the discomfort they may feel in discussing personal topics and that you welcome their questions. *However, keep in mind that the focus of the interview is on the child, not on the parents' problems.*

Occasionally, you will find that the parents have problems, such as depression, stress, marital conflict, or substance abuse. If so, refer them for appropriate treatment services. In many clinics, children will not be seen for treatment unless their parents also are involved in treatment.

Clinical Skills Needed for Interviewing Parents

Clinical skills needed for interviewing parents include the abilities

- to become attuned to the parents' anxieties
- to listen carefully to what they are saying
- to give them an opportunity to talk without giving them advice or suggestions
- to convey your understanding of their needs and perceptions
- to establish a meaningful relationship with them
- to communicate your findings, suggestions, and recommendations clearly (in the post-assessment interview)
- to convey a sense of collaborative partnership between you and them

The foundation is one of empathic understanding, diagnostic skill and acumen, and communication skills.

Useful Interview Formats with Parents

Three useful formats for interviewing parents are the unstructured (open-ended) interview, the semistructured interview, and the structured interview. When parents are extremely anxious or resistant, it is best to use an open-ended format at the initial stage of the interview before moving on to a semistructured interview or another interview format.

Semistructured interview. A semistructured interview is useful in assessing what is important to the parents, what they hope to accomplish from the evaluation, what their concerns are, and how they view their own role in helping the child. The semistructured interview allows parents the leeway to discuss anything that they believe is relevant.

We now consider three types of semistructured interviews with parents: (a) a developmental history interview, (b) a screening interview with parents of preschool children, and (c) a typical-day interview.

1. *Developmental history interview.* If the parents do not complete a background questionnaire (see next section), you will need to obtain a history of the child's development. The history should give you some perspective on the current situation of the child, what interventions have been tried and with what success, and clues to what might benefit the child in the future.

Following are typical areas covered in a developmental history (Nay, 1979):

- *description of child's birth and events related to the birth* (including mother's health; mother's use of drugs, alcohol, or cigarettes during pregnancy; and pregnancy and birth complications)
- *child's developmental history* (including important developmental milestones—such as age of sitting, standing, walking, use of functional language, bladder and bowel control, self-help skills, and personal-social relationships)
- *child's medical history* (including types and dates of injuries, accidents, operations, and significant illnesses, as well as prescribed medications)
- *characteristics of family and family history* (including age, ordinal position, sex, occupation, employment status, and marital status of family members and significant medical, educational, and mental health history of siblings and parents)
- *child's interpersonal skills* (including child's ability to form friendships and relationships with others, child's play activities, and how other children and adults relate to the child)
- *child's educational history* (including schools attended, grades, attitude toward schooling, relationships with teachers and peers, and special education services received)
- *child's sexual behaviors* (including relationships with those of the same and opposite sex)
- *child's occupational history, if any* (including types and dates of employment, attitude toward work, and occupational goals)
- *description of presenting problem* (including a detailed description of the problem, antecedent events, consequences, and how the parents have dealt with the problem)

- *parental expectations* (including the parents' expectations and goals for treatment of their child and of themselves)

Table F-36 in Appendix F provides a semistructured interview for obtaining a detailed case history from parents. The parents are asked to describe the following areas: child's problem behavior, home environment, neighborhood, and sibling relations; child's peer relations, relationship with parents, interests and hobbies, daily activities, cognitive functioning, academic functioning, biological functioning, affective life, and abilities in comparison with those of siblings; and parents' concerns and related issues. Exhibit 4-1 shows a report based on an interview with the mother of a "normal" 4½-year-old boy.

2. *Screening interview with parents of preschool children.* Table F-38 in Appendix F provides a brief semistructured screening interview for use with parents of preschool children. It focuses on the parents' concerns about their child's development. It is useful when you want an overview of how a preschool child is functioning.

3. *Typical-day interview.* Sometimes you may want to ask a parent or caregiver about how his or her preschool or elementary school–aged child spends a typical day (see the semistructured interview in Table F-39 in Appendix F). This information may help you better understand how the child functions in his or her family and social and interpersonal environment. For preschoolers who are not attending school, you might ask about any day of the week. For preschoolers who are attending school and for school-aged children, you might ask about a typical Saturday or Sunday if you want to know about a full day at home, or you might ask about any Monday through Friday if you want to know about a typical school day, or you might ask about both a typical school day and a typical weekend day.

Structured interview. In a structured interview, the questions are designed to cover various areas of psychopathology systematically. Chapter 1 describes several structured interviews. They are useful when you need to arrive at a specific diagnosis.

Background Questionnaire

Another way to obtain information about the child and family is to have the parents complete a background questionnaire before the interview (see Table C-2 in Appendix C for an example of a background questionnaire). A background questionnaire is useful in obtaining a detailed account of the child's developmental, social, medical, and educational history, as well as information about the family. You can send the background questionnaire to the parents a week or two before the interview is scheduled and have them send it back a few days before the interview. If necessary, they can bring it with them to the interview. However, it is beneficial to

Exhibit 4-1
Developmental History

DEVELOPMENTAL HISTORY

Informant: Helen Blue
Child's Name: Keith Blue
Child's Date of Birth: March 15, 1992
Child's Chronological Age: 4–6

Interviewer: Barbara Smith
Date of Interview: October 16, 1996
Date of Report: October 22, 1996

Reason for Referral

This interview was done to fulfill an assignment for a class in assessment at Manchester University. Helen Blue, the mother of a child enrolled in Manchester University's Campus Lab School, volunteered to be interviewed about her child's development.

Behavioral Observations

Helen Blue is a tall, slender, attractive, 39-year-old mother of two children (Debbi, age 13 years, and Keith, age 4½ years). Mrs. Blue started the interview by saying that she did not feel well and had considered canceling the appointment. However, these feelings did not seem to interfere with her behavior, as she was lively, responsive, cooperative, and frequently humorous during the interview. Mrs. Blue also seemed tense. She sat quite straight in her chair and frequently clenched her hands. Occasionally, when the content of her conversation was emotion laden, Mrs. Blue turned away from the tape recorder. She spoke rapidly, and her movements were sometimes abrupt. Nevertheless, she was articulate and expressed herself clearly, though sometimes in a roundabout way. Mrs. Blue maintained good eye contact with the interviewer and seemed to speak freely and without hesitation. The information obtained in the interview appears to be accurate.

Developmental History

According to his mother, Keith is a tall, active, physically strong, and healthy boy. His birth and subsequent development were normal, although he does have exceptional large-muscle coordination for his age. Keith walked before he was 10 months old. At 3 years, 10 months of age, he could hit a plastic baseball with a plastic bat and throw and catch a frisbee. His balance also is excellent. He is enrolled in a kindergym class, where he does tumbling and works out on a balance beam.

Keith's mother notes that his small-muscle coordination is less well developed than was his older sister's at the same age. He is, for example, not as adept at writing or drawing as was his sister. His mother added that differences in Keith's large- and small-muscle coordination seem to be related to his preferred activities. Keith's favorite activities are riding his bike and playing ball. At nursery school, he prefers being outside on the playground or building with large blocks over coloring or cutting and pasting.

Keith loves nursery school and is disappointed when he learns that it is the weekend and he cannot go to school for two days. This is in spite of the fact, his mother explained, that most of his friends from last year's class were older and have gone on to kindergarten and he has not yet developed new friendships in this year's class.

Keith was described as a relaxed and easygoing child, yet extremely sensitive to disapproval. He responds to a verbal reprimand with tears but usually requires no other discipline. On the few occasions when he has had his hand slapped, however, Keith responded not with tears but with anger and defiance. Generally, there are no discipline problems with Keith, and the only behavior that worries his mother is his lack of fear. From infancy, he has climbed whatever he could climb. He likes to balance on the edge of the bathtub and walk along ledges where a long fall is possible. He seems, however, to respond reasonably to explanations of the potential danger of such activities.

Keith exhibits compassion and sympathy for those around him. For example, when he notices that people on television are sad, he is sorry. In nursery school, Keith tries to comfort a new girl who cries every day. In addition, he often asks to spend time with his grandfather, who is quite ill. He sits close to his grandfather, with his arm around him, or pats his hand.

Summary and Impressions

To fulfill the interviewer's assignment for an assessment class, Helen Blue, the mother of a preschool child, was interviewed about her son's development. Mrs. Blue was cooperative, cheerful, and articulate. Although she displayed some signs of tension, the tension did not appear to be related to her discussion of Keith, about whom she spoke freely. Keith's birth and development were normal. He is a strong, healthy, and active 4½-year-old boy. His large-muscle coordination is especially good, and his favorite activities are riding a bike and playing ball. Keith enjoys preschool. He is an easygoing child who is sensitive to disapproval and who exhibits sympathy and compassion for others. His fearlessness is of some concern to his mother.

(Signature)

Barbara Smith, B. A., Interviewer

Quality Time by Gail Machlis

I'm perfectly capable of getting ready for school on my own, but it makes my parents feel needed.

© Chronicle Features 1995

Copyright © 1995, Chronicle Features. Reprinted with permission.

have the questionnaire returned before the interview so that you can review it.

Sometimes you may prefer to complete a background questionnaire jointly with the parents, especially if they have reading or writing difficulties or cannot complete it for some other reason. Completing the background questionnaire together serves as a type of structured interview. However, time constraints or agency policy may not allow you to complete the background questionnaire together.

Major Components of the Initial Interview with Parents

A list of the major components of the initial interview with parents follows:

1. *Greet the parents.*
2. *Give your name and professional title.*
3. *Open the interview with an introductory statement.* Useful introductory statements include the following (Lichtenstein & Ireton, 1984):

- "Tell me what brings you here today."
- "How can I help you?"
- "Tell me about your child."

- "Please tell me your concerns about your child."
- "Please tell me what [child's name] has been doing lately."
- "How well do you think your child is doing?"
- "How do you get along with your child?"
- "I understand that your son is having some difficulties in school. I'd like to discuss his difficulties with you and see whether we can work together to develop a plan to help him."

4. *Ask parents about items on the background questionnaire.* If the parents have completed a background questionnaire, you will not have to cover most of the areas covered in a developmental history interview. Allow them, however, to describe in their own words their concerns about their child. Also ask the parents about any items on the background questionnaire that need to be clarified. For example, "I see that John is having problems at home. Would you tell me more about these problems?" If the parents have not completed a questionnaire, ask them about the typical areas covered in a developmental history. These areas, as we have just seen, are (a) the child's developmental, medical, educational, and social histories, (b) the family's medical and psychiatric histories, (c) previous treatments for the child, (d) the child's strengths and weaknesses, (e) the child's interests and play activities, and (f) related information. As previously noted, you might want to use the semistructured interview in Table F-36 in Appendix F.

5. *Review problems.* Review the child's problems as presented by the parents, and ask the parents whether they would like to comment further on any problem.

6. *Describe the assessment procedure.* If the child will be administered psychological tests, tell the parents about the tests and why they will be administered. Inform the parents about who will have access to the assessment information and how the information will be used. Discuss confidentiality of the assessment results, including the conditions under which confidentiality will need to be broken. (See Chapter 2 for further discussion of confidentiality.) In some cases, this also would be an appropriate time to offer the parents information on services available through the clinic, school, or hospital. In other cases, you may want to offer this information in the post-assessment interview.

7. *Arrange for a post-assessment interview.* Arrange to discuss the results of the assessment with the parents. In some cases, the results will be presented to the parents at an interdisciplinary staff conference (see Table 1-1 in Chapter 1 for a list of the disciplines that may be involved in assessing the child). In other cases, one clinician may present the overall results of the assessment based on reports provided by all the professionals involved in the case. In still other cases, only the one clinician who conducted the evaluation will present his or her results to the parents.

8. *Close the interview.* Escort the parents from the room and make appropriate closing remarks, such as "Thank you for coming. In case you have any other questions, here is my phone number."

The major components of the interview presented above did not include obtaining biographical information from the parents. You usually will obtain this information by having the parents complete an application form (or questionnaire) that asks them to list their name, address, phone number, child's teacher's name, child's grade, family structure (for example, number of people in family, ages, sexes, and occupations), and other important identifying information. The background questionnaire shown in Table C-2 in Appendix C has a section for obtaining biographical information.

Guidelines for Interviewing Parents

Following are 20 guidelines for interviewing parents:

1. Listen carefully to the parents' concerns.
2. Explain what lies ahead, what may be involved in the assessment process, and what interventions are possible.
3. Adopt a calm, nonjudgmental approach to reduce the parents' stress.
4. Help the parents understand that many children have problems at times and that emotional problems or physical problems may develop in a child from events beyond the parents' control.
5. Reassure parents that the records will be kept confidential, unless the law requires that the records be disclosed or agency policy requires that the records be shared by others (see Chapter 2).
6. Help parents who are having problems in managing their child understand that child rearing is a complex and difficult activity and that a child with special problems may be especially difficult to cope with.
7. Take special care to convey respect for the parents' feelings.
8. Avoid any suggestion that parents are to blame for their child's difficulties. (This and the following points do not apply when the parents have maltreated their child or are alleged to have maltreated their child.)
9. Emphasize their constructive and helpful parenting skills rather than their destructive or harmful approaches.
10. Enlist their cooperation in the diagnostic and remediation program; do not be authoritarian.
11. Schedule more than one meeting (if needed) to gain the cooperation of parents who are uncooperative.
12. If working with a two-parent family, try to get both parents to come to the interview. Having both parents at the interview may help you get a more thorough picture of the family.
13. Plan to interview both parents together. Or consider interviewing them separately, especially in cases of custody evaluations or maltreatment or when they are hostile to each other.
14. Help the parents clarify vague, ambiguous, or incomplete statements.
15. Encourage the parents to discuss fully their child's problem and how the problem affects the family.
16. Use follow-up and probing questions to learn the specific conditions that may serve to instigate, maintain, or limit the child's behavior and to learn about the parents' resources and motivation to change.
17. Determine the areas in which parents agree and disagree about child management.
18. Guide the parents back to the topic in an appropriate and gentle manner if they give many irrelevant details.
19. Have the parents check their recollections against baby books, medical and school records, and other formal and informal records if they cannot recall events or the dates of the events.
20. If you schedule a second interview, ask the parents to keep a record of the occurrences of the problem if you believe that such a record would be helpful. The record should include where the problematic event occurred, when it occurred, what preceded it, what followed it, their reactions to it, their manner of dealing with it, and who else was involved in it. You can use a form similar to the one shown in Table 3-7 in Chapter 3, deleting the term *self-monitoring* from the heading.

When parents have difficulty recalling the child's developmental milestones, you can provide a time frame to help them. Rudel (1988) suggests the following:

"Was he walking on his first birthday?" If this fails, you can discuss family history (moves from one place of residence to another, holidays, family celebrations, or visits to relatives) and, by estimating the child's age on these occasions, can relate developmental data to these events. "Was he toilet-trained when you visited your in-laws? Did you have to change diapers en route? Did he speak to your mother when he met her? Do you recall what they said? Was your mother surprised that he was not talking in sentences at that time?" By providing an event-related context, you sometimes can obtain a more reliable estimate of the child's developmental history. (p. 90, with changes in notation)

If parents cannot recall developmental events, this may mean that the child's development was normal; the parents would likely remember unusual or deviant behavior (Rudel, 1988).

Two Examples of an Initial Interview with Parents

The first example is part of an initial interview with a mother. The interviewer inquired about a problem and learned that the problem behavior was occurring frequently and had been a problem for some time (McMahon & Forehand, 1988, p. 118, with changes in notation).

IR: Do you have any problems with Mark at bedtime?
IE: Oh my gosh, yes. It takes forever for him to go to sleep. He gets out of bed again and again.
IR: Tell me about your family's routine during the half-hour before Mark's bedtime.
IE: At 7:30 I help Mark with his bath. After he brushes his teeth and goes to the bathroom, I read him a story. Then Bob and I kiss him goodnight.

IR: OK. Then what happens?

IE: Well, things are quiet for about 10 to 15 minutes. Then Mark is up. He gets out of bed and comes into the den where Bob and I are watching TV.

IR: What does Mark do when he gets up?

IE: He usually comes in and climbs in either Bob's or my lap and complains that he can't sleep.

IR: What do you do then?

IE: Sometimes we let him sit with us for a while, but usually I take him back to bed and tell him goodnight again.

IR: What happens then?

IE: Mark stays there for a while, but he's soon out again.

IR: And then what do you do?

IE: I may tell him he's being a bad boy. Then I take him back to bed. Usually I read him another story—hoping he'll get sleepy this time.

IR: Does that work?

IE: No, he's up again before I have time to get settled in my chair.

IR: What happens then?

IE: The whole thing repeats itself. I put him in bed, read him another story, and he gets up again.

IR: How long does this go on?

IE: For about 2 or 3 hours—until Bob and I go to bed.

IR: What happens when you and your husband go to bed?

IE: Mark still gets up, but we let him get in bed with us and he goes to sleep then.

IR: How many nights a week does this happen?

IE: Every night! I can't think of a night's peace in the last few months.

IR: How long has Mark been doing this?

IE: Oh, I would guess for about a year.

IR: Have you or your husband tried any other ways of handling Mark at bedtime?

IE: Sometimes I get angry and yell at him. Sometimes Bob tries spanking him, but then Mark just ends up crying all evening. At least my way, we have a little peace and quiet.

The second example is part of an initial interview with the father and stepmother of a 9-year, 9-month-old boy named Frank. It is divided into three segments for discussion purposes. Frank's special education teacher referred him because of his hyperactive behavior and poor school performance. The interview segments are followed by extensive notes written by the interviewer about Frank and his family. Abbreviations are as follows: IR = interviewer, IE-F = father, and IE-M = mother.

IR: Hi. I'm Ms. Marilyn Brown. I'm a social worker at the clinic. And you are Mr. and Mrs. Hardway? I'd like to talk to you about your son Frank. I have looked over the questionnaire that you completed, and I appreciate your taking the time to complete it. What I'd like to do now is review some of this information and hear from you both what your current concerns are and what help you would like. Why don't you all just start by telling me what you are most concerned about?

IE-F: Well, one of our main concerns is that we have to tell him to do the same things repeatedly. We have to stay on him all the time, and again I feel like, oh, what's that word I'm looking for? Being mean to him I have to constantly ride him to get him to do something simple like clean your room, do your homework, that's to remind him every day to do the same things every day.

IR: What's your impression about why he's not doing these things? Do you have an idea why he's not doing these things?

IE-F: My theory is it doesn't interest him. He's not, he just don't. I understand when you're a kid you don't do something that doesn't interest them, they don't want to do it, it's going to take them longer. You may have to tell them a couple extra times to get it done, but with Frank here, it's every day, it's five, five and six times, sometimes more depending on what it is to get him to do things.

IR: So it sounds as if you think he understands what you want him to do and he's just choosing not to do it. He's ignoring you, or he's refusing…

IE-F: He'll start, he'll start, he'll start to do it.

IR: Oh, he will?

IE-F: Okay, but on his homework, for example, he knows the rules from day one, it's not something I just started. I did it with my oldest girl, I done it with Sandra and I've done it with him. As soon as you walk through that door, you hang your coat up, you get, you sit down at the dining room table, do your homework, and after that the evening belongs to you. Because I want the homework done first thing. You have to tell him, every day the same, "do your homework." Once he gets in there and starts it, he might do one or two questions. He just gets up and goes off.

IE-M: Or he just sits there.

IE-F: Yeah. He'll just sit there like…

IE-M: He'll just stare at it.

IR: Do you think he can do the work?

IE-M: Oh, he can do it if he wants to.

IE-F: Yeah.

IR: So the problem is not that he doesn't understand how to do the homework.

IE-M: Some of it he does, the math, he can do it.

IE-F: Yeah, the math he can do. He does have a reading problem, and he's in lab for that.

IR: I understood he had some testing for his reading difficulty.

IE-F: Right.

IR: Is he also getting some other help in writing or spelling?

IE-F: Spelling and math, I think.

IE-M: Yeah. Mr. Franklin has him for spelling, math…

IE-F: And reading.

IE-M: And reading. And a little bit of science because he does not have a regular science class. He don't have science.

IR: So how long does he spend in the lab every day?

IE-F: He's in there…

IE-M: About half and half.

IE-F: About half the day, yeah. It used to be when he first started, a few hours a day, and they increased it because they felt that the 2 hours a day was not enough. And based on his progress and the type of progress I would like to see him make, in 2 hours is not enough, so I had no problem with them increasing it.

IR: When did they increase it?

IE-M: At the beginning of this year.

IE-F: Yeah.

In this first segment, the interviewer, after a brief introduction, uses an open-ended comment, "Why don't you all just start out by telling me what you are most concerned about?" The father responds to the first four inquiries and then the stepmother speaks. The interviewer asks questions to clarify what the parents are saying and makes several interpretive and reflective comments in an attempt to understand the parents' concerns. The parents seem to complement each other. As one is speaking, the other steps in to continue the thought. In several segments, each parent provides some information before the interviewer makes a response.

IE-M: Well, he's the only person I know that takes 25 minutes to take a shower. From the time you tell him the first time, it takes him 25 minutes to get in the shower.

IE-F: But he's only actually in the shower like 2 or 3 minutes.

IE-M: In like 5 minutes, he's in and out. It takes 45 minutes just to get there.

IR: Are you saying he gets distracted? Is that why it takes him so long? Or…

IE-M: I have no idea.

IR: Is he stalling and not wanting to take a shower so he's just taking his time?

IE-F: I think it's a little of both myself. I think it's something that…

IR: Do you think he may get distracted?

IE-F: Yeah. He'll go in there and he'll start to take a shower, but then he'll say he sees a toy he had that he wants to play with, he'll play with that.

IR: So he gets sidetracked.

IE-F: He gets sidetracked; he doesn't stay focused on what he's supposed to be doing.

IE-M: Or, if his TV is on, he'll see something he wants to see on TV and he'll sit and watch it, so he don't take a shower. It takes about 45 minutes every day. He's lucky to have a shower by 7:30 when he starts…

IE-F: Around 6:00.

IR: So it's hard to get him to clean his room, it's hard to get him to take a shower, and it's hard to get him to finish his homework, even though you've set rules about doing homework before his other things.

IE-F: Right.

IR: Other things that it's hard to get him to do?

IE-M: The only thing he does real good is take the kitchen trash out.

IR: Well that's good. So what other things are hard for him to do?

IE-M: He can't stand still.

IE-F: It's like he's bouncing, he's constantly wanting to bounce off the walls. He's running constantly, wanting to do something. He's also a very slow eater. It takes him forever to eat. But anyway…

IR: Is he up and down a lot from the table?

IE-F: No, he'll, he'll sit…

IE-M: He'll touch his fork and put one pea on it. And that's what we mean. One green bean.

IE-F: At a time.

IE-M: At a time.

IE-F: I understand you don't take big bites, but come on.

IE-M: An hour and a half at the dinner table is a bit long. Isn't it?

IR: Is that how long it takes?

IE-F: Sometimes.

IR: Does he end up staying there by himself after everybody else is done?

IE-M: No. I always sit there with him.

IE-F: One of us. One of us will sit there with him.

IR: What is he doing during dinner? Is he talking a lot?

IE-F: Nope. No, he's just, he's just…

IR: He's just eating slower.

In this second segment, the interviewer tries to learn what might account for Frank's procrastination. She raises the possibility that Frank might be distracted or that Frank might be stalling. She nicely summarizes the difficulties Frank is having—"So it's hard to get him to clean his room, it's…."—and follows this summary statement with a probing question about other possible areas of difficulty—"Other things that it's hard to get him to do?" But the stepmother responds to the probing question by offering what Frank does well. Several of the interviewer's comments are designed to obtain information about the frequency of the behavior of concern and the length of time the behavior of concern takes.

IR: What is the teacher telling you about his attention span?

IE-F: He doesn't.

IE-M: Mrs. Jones, that's his other teacher, says all he does is sit and play and daydream.

IR: Is that his regular teacher?

IE-M: Yeah, Mrs. Jones, that's his regular teacher. And he'll start his work and then, but he won't finish it.

IE-F: Yeah. He'll do homework, and then I will know for a fact that homework is done because he gets it on a Monday and he…

IE-M: Turns it in on Friday.

IE-F: Turns it in on Friday along with the spelling test.

IE-M: If you're lucky.

IE-F: Yeah, that's if you're lucky. He'll do it, he'll bring it, you'll have to remind him bring it home on Monday, every day, every Monday—"Don't forget your homework, Frank." He comes in, as soon as he walks in the door Monday, "Frank, go do your homework." About 20 to 30 percent of the time he'll say he forgot it at school.

IR: So he only gets homework on Monday?

IE-M: He gets a packet.

IE-F: It's a packet.

IE-M: And it has, let's see, he doesn't have nothing on Monday because that's Mrs. Jones's math class, but he has to do Tuesday, Wednesday, and Thursday. And he has the first six spelling words for his test on Friday. And that's the existence of his homework. Sometimes he'll have it in his book bag, but he don't have homework.

IR: So you'll find it in his book bag and he's telling you he doesn't have any.

IE-M: Yeah. And then when he does do it, getting him to take it back to school…

IE-F: And turn it in, is something else.

IR: What happens to it?

IE-M: He forgets, or he leaves it at home.

IR: Does he lose it or…?

IE-M: No, he's never lost any. No, I find them all in his bedroom. 'Cause he just got finished turning in three months of homework. And he's only getting half a credit for it. Because most of it was all for the first nine weeks; and you can't get credit over that. He made three F's for the first semester.

IE-F: As far as his grades go, even his last labs never looked this bad. It's like he…

IE-M: His lab is usually A's.

IE-F: It's like he's just throwing up his hands and saying the heck with it, I quit.

IE-M: He's pushing a C in math.

IE-F: And that used to be one of his stronger…

IE-M: And that was his lab the first nine weeks.

IR: Is this primarily due to his not turning in the homework?

IE-M: Mrs. Jones says it is. Because he's got English and his science and his social studies. That's the three classes he made F's. In the first nine weeks, they were B's and C's. And she told him that if he would just turn his homework in, because that is 90% of his grade.

In this third segment, the interviewer asks about what the teacher has told the parents about Frank's attention span. Frank's homework assignments are discussed and why he fails to complete them. The parents do most of the talking.

The interviewer wrote the following notes based on the entire interview, the background questionnaire filled out by the father, and the questionnaire filled out by the teacher.

Frank was referred to Children's Center by his special education teacher at Patrick Elementary School because of her concerns about his overactivity, poor work habits, and difficulty in getting along with his peers. The interview was conducted on March 7, 1996.

Frank was accompanied to the Children's Center by his father and stepmother, Justin and Helen Hardway, who provided a background history. Frank's teacher, Mr. Ted Alonzo, also filled out a questionnaire about Frank.

The history provided by the father indicated that he has had physical custody of Frank and Frank's two older siblings, Shirley who is 15 years old and Sandra who is 11 years old, since his divorce from Frank's mother on September 10, 1993. Frank's father has since remarried, and the home now includes the stepmother's 19-year-old daughter and 3-month-old grandson, as well as Mr. Hardway's three children. Frank reportedly visits his natural mother on a sporadic basis.

Past medical history provided by the father revealed that Frank weighed 6 pounds, 8 ounces at birth. The pregnancy was complicated by the mother having increased blood pressure and swelling during the final trimester, as well as treatment of a kidney infection during pregnancy. The father reported maternal alcohol use occasionally during the pregnancy, but no binge drinking, no use of nonprescription drugs, and no smoking during pregnancy. Delivery was breeched with the aid of forceps but was otherwise unremarkable. Approximately two weeks after Frank was discharged from the hospital, he had to be readmitted for treatment of neonatal jaundice.

Subsequent medical history indicates that Frank has been healthy. He has had only occasional ear infections and no severe illnesses or injuries that would be expected to affect his development. His hearing and vision are normal, but he does have dental cavities in need of care. He is reported to have an "underactive colon" that is controlled by diet at the present time. Frank was enuretic [a bedwetter] until the summer of 1995, but he no longer has this problem.

Frank reached developmental milestones within the expected age range. He sat independently at 5 to 6 months, crawled at 6 months, and walked alone at 13 to 15 months. He was slow in cutting teeth and slow in beginning to talk. Frank was approximately 18 months old when he began to use meaningful single words, and 24 months old before he began combining words into phrases. Frank was described as always having been very active and distractible. These problems have persisted as he has grown older, and they now are considered to be interfering with his school performance. He has never been evaluated for a possible attention-deficit/hyperactivity disorder.

Frank is currently in the third grade at Patrick Elementary School. He attends a learning disability laboratory for two periods per day (10 hours per week). In addition, he receives speech/language management twice weekly for 30 minutes each session. Frank repeated kindergarten and began attending the learning disability laboratory during his second year in kindergarten, from 1993 to 1994. He began receiving speech therapy at age 4 years while he was in Head Start and has received these services continually since then through the public school system.

Frank's current Individualized Educational Plan indicates instructional objectives in mathematics, basic reading, and expressive language. His teacher, Mrs. Alma Jones, indicated that Frank is severely overactive, inattentive, impulsive, and has difficulty concentrating in the classroom. He sometimes daydreams and has staring spells and sometimes makes inappropriate responses. His academic skills are at the first-grade level in reading, math, spelling, and penmanship. Mrs. Jones's concerns that Frank may have an attention-deficit/hyperactivity disorder led to the referral.

The interview with Frank's father and stepmother revealed primary concerns about Frank's behavior and getting him to mind, in addition to the possible attention-deficit/hyperactivity disorder. Mr. Hardway complained that he must tell Frank repeatedly to do things, and that Frank is noncompliant. There is a constant battle at home getting Frank to clean his room, to take a shower, and to do his homework. Frank is reported to be constantly active and distractible. Frank cannot watch a 30-minute television show unless he is moving around and getting up and down. Frank is reportedly left under the supervision of his older siblings to do his homework. The parents complain that his work is not completed when they get home from work. Even when he does complete his homework, he sometime forgets to take it back to school. The problems with Frank's noncompliance were reported to be apparent even when Frank was a preschool child. Disciplinary strategies used by the father include "whipping" and occasionally removing privileges, both of which are described as being ineffective.

Socially, Mr. Hardway described Frank as being a loner. He plays with only one or two friends. Other children tease Frank because of his speech and language problems, attention-span difficulties, and overactivity. Mr. Hardway could not report anything that reflects Frank's strength or for which Frank would be proud of himself. Frank is described as an extremely sensitive child who cries easily. The family environment is reported by the father to be chaotic and stressful due to behavior problems among all of the children and the crowded living conditions. Frank's 11-year-old sister, Sandra, is described as having serious conduct problems, including aggression, stealing, and frequent suspensions from school. The background information suggests that Frank should be referred for a psychological evaluation.

[*Editorial note.* Frank was seen by a psychologist and was administered a battery of psychological tests. On the Wechsler Intelligence Scale for Children—III, he obtained a Verbal Scale IQ of 73 (4th percentile rank), a Performance Scale IQ of 93 (32nd percentile rank), and a Full Scale IQ of 81 (10th percentile rank), which places him in the Low Average range. On the Wechsler Individual Achievement Test, he obtained the following percentile ranks: basic reading, 5th percentile rank; reading comprehension, 8th percentile rank; spelling, 8th percentile rank; and written expression, 5th percentile rank. On the Bender-Gestalt, he obtained a score that was at the 55th percentile rank. Based on these and other test scores and personality tests, plus the information obtained from the parents and teachers, the psychologist came to the following diagnostic impressions: (a) attention-deficit/hyperactivity disorder, (b) reading disorder, (c) disorder of written expression, (d) mixed receptive-expressive language disorder, and (e) phonological disorder. The psychologist recommended continued placement in the special education program, curriculum modifications, medical consultation to consider possible psychostimulant medication for treatment of the attention-deficit/hyperactivity symptoms, family therapy, and behavior management training for the parents.]

Evaluating the Parent Interview

The questions in Table 4-1 will help you evaluate the information you obtain from parents. If you want more specific information about how a child with special needs affects a family, ask a parent to complete the questionnaire shown in Table 4-2.

Recognize that not all parents will be reliable informants. Expect to find some distortions, biases, and memory lags in the information you collect from parents. Developmental milestones are difficult to remember, and relating particular events to particular behavioral responses may be even more difficult. Research on the accuracy of parental reports suggests the following (Canino, 1985): Variables such as the child's weight, height, and health are recalled more accurately by parents than information about the child's personality and temperament. Discrete symptoms that the child had—such as nightmares, stuttering, bedwetting, stealing,

Pepper...and Salt

" I WOULD HAVE BROUGHT MY HUSBAND, BUT WE'D JUST END UP ARGUING ! "

From the Wall Street Journal—Permission, Cartoon Features Syndicate.

and temper tantrums—are recalled better than less well-defined symptoms, such as the child's activity level, feeling states, and social relationships. Questions and dates regarding major events in the family—such as deaths, weddings, moves, financial reversals, and births—are recalled relatively accurately. Mothers usually are more reliable informants in answering questions about the child's development than are fathers.

Before I got married, I had six theories about bringing up children; now I have six children and no theories.

—John Wilmot

Exercise 4-1. Formulating an Appropriate Response in an Interview with a Mother

This exercise describes phases of an initial interview with a mother. Some items set the scene; others give statements made by the mother. After you read each one, formulate a response. Then compare your responses with the suggested responses. (This exercise was adapted from K. France and M. Kish [1995], *Supportive Interviewing in Human Service Organizations: Fundamental Skills for Gathering Information and Encouraging Productive Change.* Courtesy Charles C Thomas, Publisher, Springfield, Illinois, pp. 232–247, and Reprinted with Permission.)

1. You are on the phone talking to the mother of a 16-year-old girl. The mother wants to arrange an appointment with you. Presently, you have ongoing commitments that

Table 4-1
Evaluating the Parent Interview

Background
1. Who referred the child?
2. What is the composition of the family? (Include ages of children, parents, and extended family members living at home.)
3. What are the occupations of the parents?
4. What is the socioeconomic status of the parents?
5. What is the physical health status of the parents?
6. What is the mental health status of the parents?

Perception of Problem
7. How do the parents perceive the child's behavior?
8. What are the parents' perceptions of the child's problem and feelings about the problem?
9. How well did the parents describe the problem? (Include your assessment of how objective they were.)
10. How do the parents' perceptions of the problem compare with the child's perception?
11. How do the parents' perceptions of the problem compare with the teacher's perception?
12. How do the parents' estimates of the child's intellectual ability and achievement level compare with the child's scores on objective tests and school grades? (If there are discrepancies, are they overestimates or underestimates? What might account for the discrepancies?)
13. Are the parents more preoccupied with their own problems, failures, and difficulties than with their child's problem?
14. How have the problems of the child affected the parents (and the family as a whole)?

Quality of Information
15. Did the parents give a reasonable account of the development of the child?
16. Were the parents open or guarded?
17. What is the quality of the parents' memory?
18. Was each parent consistent in his or her statements?
19. Were the parents in agreement about their child's problems?
20. Was there any evidence that the parents gave distorted or evasive replies or withheld information?

Attitudes of Parents
21. What are the parents' attitudes toward the school?
22. Toward the teachers?
23. Toward other children in the school?
24. Toward the principal?
25. Toward the neighbors?
26. Toward other children in the neighborhood?

Background Questionnaire (if used)
27. How thorough and consistent was the parent in completing the background questionnaire?
28. What is the quality of the parent's writing and spelling on the background questionnaire? (For example, did the parent understand the questions, answer them to the point, and spell correctly? Was the handwriting legible or childish? [Rudel, 1988, p. 89])

Involvement of Parents
29. How well do the parents respond to their child's needs?
30. How well do the parents support their child?
31. What kind of supervision do the parents provide for the child?
32. How do the parents discipline the child?
33. Do the parents reinforce their child's problem?
34. How do the parents treat their child? (For example, do they treat the child in a mature manner, overprotect the child, infantilize the child, neglect the child, or reject the child?)
35. How do the parents treat the referred child in comparison to the other children in the family?
36. How much are the parents involved in the child's free-time activities? (That is, do the parents take the child to Little League, gymnastics, and other similar activities?)
37. (If the parents are heavily involved in the child's free-time activities) Why might the parents be so heavily involved in the child's free-time activities? (For example, are the parents trying to compensate for the child's poor social skills, or are the parents trying to find an activity at which the child can excel? [Rudel, 1988])

Coping (if the child has a psychological or medical disorder)
38. What emotional state were the parents in after learning that their child has a psychological or medical disorder?
39. How is each parent coping with the child with a psychological or medical disorder?
40. How are the siblings coping with the child with a psychological or medical disorder?
41. (If relevant) How is the extended family coping with the child with a psychological or medical disorder?
42. Can the parents cope with the increased financial obligations necessitated by their child's psychological or medical disorder?
43. Can the parents cope with the increased time demands required by their child's psychological or medical disorder?
44. Can the parents meet the needs of the other children in the family who do not have a psychological or medical disorder?
45. Can the parents continue to work and also take care of their child with a psychological or medical disorder?
46. What adjustments does the family need to make in order to take care of the child with a psychological or medical disorder?

Intervention
47. What do the parents want from the interview?
48. What are the parents' resources for overcoming the problem?
49. How much do the parents know about support services?
50. Are the parents capable of raising their child?
51. How open are the parents to change?
52. Are the parents willing to participate in a treatment program for themselves?
53. How do the parents see the child's future?

Table 4-2
A Short Form of the Questionnaire on Resources and Stress

This questionnaire deals with your feelings about a child in your family. There are many blanks on the questionnaire. Imagine the child's name filled in on each blank. Give your honest feelings and opinions. Please answer all of the questions, even if they do not seem to apply. If it is difficult to decide between true (T) and false (F), answer in terms of what you or your family feel or do most of the time. Sometimes the questions refer to problems your family does not have, but even then they can be answered true or false. Please remember to answer all of the questions. Circle T or F for each item. Thank you.

T F 1. _____ doesn't communicate with others of his/her age group.

T F 2. Other members of the family have to do without things because of _____ .

T F 3. Our family agrees on important matters.

T F 4. I worry about what will happen to _____ when I can no longer take care of him/her.

T F 5. The constant demands for care for _____ limit growth and development of someone else in our family.

T F 6. _____ is limited in the kind of work he/she can do to make a living.

T F 7. I have accepted the fact that _____ might have to live out his/her life in some special setting (for example, institution or group home).

T F 8. _____ can feed himself/herself.

T F 9. I have given up things I have really wanted to do in order to care for _____ .

T F 10. _____ is able to fit into the family social group.

T F 11. Sometimes I avoid taking _____ out in public.

T F 12. In the future, our family's social life will suffer because of increased responsibilities and financial stress.

T F 13. It bothers me that _____ will always be this way.

T F 14. I feel tense whenever I take _____ out in public.

T F 15. I can go visit with friends whenever I want.

T F 16. Taking _____ on a vacation spoils pleasure for the whole family.

T F 17. _____ knows his/her own address.

T F 18. The family does as many things together now as we ever did.

T F 19. _____ is aware of who he/she is.

T F 20. I get upset with the way my life is going.

T F 21. Sometimes I feel very embarrassed because of _____.

T F 22. _____ doesn't do as much as he/she should be able to do.

T F 23. It is difficult to communicate with _____ because he/she has difficulty understanding what is being said to him/her.

T F 24. There are many places where we can enjoy ourselves as a family when _____ comes along.

T F 25. _____ is overprotected.

T F 26. _____ is able to take part in games or sports.

T F 27. _____ has too much time on his/her hands.

T F 28. I am disappointed that _____ does not lead a normal life.

T F 29. Time drags for _____, especially free time.

T F 30. _____ can't pay attention for very long.

T F 31. It is easy for me to relax.

T F 32. I worry about what will be done with _____ when he/she gets older.

T F 33. I get almost too tired to enjoy myself.

T F 34. One of the things I appreciate about _____ is his/her confidence.

T F 35. There is a lot of anger and resentment in our family.

T F 36. _____ is able to go to the bathroom alone.

T F 37. _____ cannot remember what he/she says from one moment to the next.

T F 38. _____ can ride a bus.

T F 39. It is easy to communicate with _____.

T F 40. The constant demands to care for _____ limit my growth and development.

T F 41. _____ accepts himself/herself as a person.

T F 42. I feel sad when I think of _____.

T F 43. People can't understand what _____ tries to say.

T F 44. Caring for _____ puts a strain on me.

T F 45. Members of our family get to do the same kinds of things other families do.

T F 46. _____ will always be a problem to us.

T F 47. _____ is able to express his/her feelings to others.

T F 48. _____ has to use a bedpan or a diaper.

T F 49. I rarely feel blue.

T F 50. I am worried much of the time.

T F 51. _____ can walk without help.

Note. The 51-item Questionnaire on Resources and Stress, Short Form (QRS-SF), is useful for assessing the resources, coping and adaptation mechanisms, and stress reactions of families with children with special needs. The original form of the QRS was published by Holroyd (1974). Four distinct factors are found on the QRS-SF: Parent and Family Problems, Pessimism, Child Characteristics, and Physical Incapacitation. The QRS-SF has acceptable reliability and validity. The current copyright holder is Pro-Ed.

Item numbers for the factors and scoring directions are as follows: Factor I, Parent and Family Problems (2T, 3F, 5T, 9T, 10F, 12T, 15F, 16T, 18F, 20T, 24F, 31F, 33T, 35T, 40T, 42T, 44T, 45F, 49F, 50T); Factor II, Pessimism (4T, 7T, 13T, 22T, 25T, 27T, 28T, 29T, 32T, 46T); Factor III, Child Characteristics (1T, 6T, 11T, 14T, 17F, 19F, 21T, 23T, 30T, 34F, 37T, 39F, 41F, 43T, 47F); and Factor IV, Physical Incapacitation (8F, 26F, 36F, 38F, 48T, 51F).

Source: Reprinted, with minor changes, with permission of the publisher and authors, from W. N. Friedrich, M. T. Greenberg, and K. Crnic, "A Short-Form of the Questionnaire on Resources and Stress," *American Journal of Mental Deficiency, 88,* 1983, pp. 47–48.

end at 3:45 P.M. or shortly thereafter. "It's hard for me to leave work during the day. But I get off at 3:00, and a 3:30 appointment would be great for me."

2. "That sounds good. About how long will the appointment last?"

3. It is now the appointed time on Tuesday. You greeted the mother in the waiting area, then made your way to your office, where you both have just taken a seat.

4. You have engaged in some social conversation, and the mother has a clear understanding of both your role and the purpose of the interview. It is now time to begin discussing what led to the appointment.

5. "I guess I'm embarrassed about being here. But I really need some help in controlling my 16-year-old daughter. I want to be a better parent, but I don't want other people to know that I'm getting this kind of help. When would be a time that you would break confidentiality without my permission?"

6. "I've never been to a place like this before. I hope what you do isn't going to be like some of those magazine articles I've seen where an expert lists five magic steps I'm supposed to take and says that if I follow them, everything will be fine. I don't think that's going to do it. A prepackaged program is not what I want. I need to feel that what we do is going to work in my particular situation."

7. "I need some help. But I only want to do things that I feel right about. I've heard about parents being told that they *had* to do this thing or that thing, so I guess I'm hoping that won't happen here. I want to have input in what is decided."

8. "So, I guess I should tell you what's happening with Patti. She seems to be getting wilder by the day. She just got her driver's license, and she is an incredibly reckless driver. Even when I'm in the car, she's squealing around turns and screeching to stops. She never slows down for a yellow light. Instead, she just barrels on through the intersection. It's got me very worried about her safety."

9. "She's also been staying out too late. Even before she got her license, she was missing her curfew. Sometimes she stays out all night, and I have no idea where she is or who she's with. She's starting to hang around with friends I don't know or I don't approve of. There are guys who call on the phone for her, and when I ask who it is, they hang up on me. I don't know what she is getting involved in, but she is developing a very bad temper. And when I confront her about any of this, she just blows up. I'm really upset, and I don't know what I'm going to do."

10. "I'm very worried. She could easily be killed in an accident because of the way she drives. And with these kids she's hanging around, for all I know she's using drugs and doing who knows what else. I really have no idea what she's getting into. I don't know how serious it is because she won't talk to me. If she were your daughter, what would you do?"

11. "Well, the communication between us has really gone downhill. I can't even get her in the house for more than 15 minutes without her running out the door. If I try to put my foot down and say 'No, you are not going out,' she

blows up and takes off anyway. On the few occasions that we actually have tried to talk, she just gets defensive, clams up, or makes some excuse that she has to leave."

12. You have completed the exploration phase of problem solving with the mother, and you now want to begin considering alternatives.

13. "I've tried confronting her, especially when she comes home past her curfew. When I've had no idea who she's been with or what they've been doing, I'll ask her to tell me. But I have to be very careful. There have been times when she's just turned around and taken off again. Recently, I've tried to communicate to her how serious this is by taking away her car keys. But that doesn't seem to matter because she usually can get a ride with one of her friends. I guess mostly I've just tried confronting her."

14. In response to your last comment, the mother is silent.

15. "I was thinking about difficulties I had with my parents when I was a teenager."

16. "When you're 16 years old, who do you think should be the boss, you or your parents?"

17. You have considered alternatives and have developed a plan with the mother. It is now near the end of the interaction.

18. The interaction is over, and the mother has just left. What should you do then?

Suggested Responses

Note that some items have more than one suggested response. In such cases, either one is acceptable.

1. "Right now I have other commitments at 3:30, but 4:00 would be OK. How would 4:00 on Tuesday be for you?" (The 4:00 time is realistic and probably will be acceptable to the mother.)

2. "We will plan to talk for about 45 minutes." (This is a simple factual response to the mother's question.)

3. "How was it finding our office?" (This open question on a nonthreatening topic provides an opportunity for light social conversation. A few moments of such interaction will allow the mother to become acclimated to the setting.)

4. "Tell me your reason for coming in today." (This is an open, neutral probe; it focuses the interaction on the task at hand while also giving the mother wide latitude in how to respond.)

5. "Unless you give permission for release of information, the only time we would break confidentiality would be in order to prevent suicide, in order to protect someone who is about to be harmed, and in cases of child abuse or neglect." (This response gives a straightforward account of the issue of confidentiality.)

6. a. "Although you're looking for a source of support that will help you deal with your daughter, you want to feel comfortable with any strategies you attempt." (This summary is on target.)

   b. "Rather than simplistic answers, you want a full airing of issues. And it seems like you also want to be sure you're the one who decides that what you try is really right for you." (This statement reflects what is on the mother's mind.)

7. It sounds to me like you want us to discuss important issues, to think about possible options, then to come up with a plan you feel good about. And that is exactly what I would like to help you do." (This response reflects the mother's concern and also conveys the idea that the mother should retain the decision-making authority.)

8. a. "Her driving really scares you." (This reflection is a good option if the interviewer would like more discussion relevant to the issue of driving.)
   b. "So, your daughter's driving is *one* area that's troubling you." (This reflection is good if the interviewer is interested in hearing about other topics that may be of concern to the mother.)

9. a. "So, staying out too late is another area of friction between you." (This is a good response to encourage the mother to continue surveying the situation.)
   b. "You're frightened about what she might be getting into with her late hours and her new friends." (This response reflects a feeling component. It increases the likelihood that the mother will continue to explore the topic under discussion.)

10. "If she were my daughter, I probably would try to communicate my concern to her, and I might try to use any leverage I had. But what's important for us to do is to figure out what options are realistic for you." (This is a brief reply to the question and returns the focus to the mother.)

11. "Improved communication with her is something you'd like to achieve, but your recent efforts have been frustrating." (This is an accurate reflection.)

12. "Your daughter's behavior is exasperating for a number of reasons: her possible high-risk activities, the unknown nature of her new friends, her driving, and the difficulty in having a conversation with her. In addition to your attempts to talk with her, what else have you tried with Patti?" (This transition comment recognizes the mother's past efforts and uses them as a bridge for taking the topic in a new direction.)

13. "In addition to initiating conversations, two other efforts you've made are speaking with Patti when she arrives home late and taking away her driving privileges. What else have you tried?" (This comment recognizes the mother's efforts and moves the focus to other past attempts. This is a good response for surveying a range of material.)

14. "We were talking about your efforts to influence Patti. What are you thinking?" (The first sentence summarizes what has been discussed, and the second sentence questions the silence.)

15. "Mmhmm." (This nonverbal expression of interest gives the mother freedom to decide where to go with the interaction.)

16. "I think that depends in part on the 16-year-old. It seems to me you're wondering if Patti is ready to make and be responsible for her own decisions." (This comment provides a brief reply to the mother's question, then looks behind it to focus on the interaction in a productive direction.)

17. "Review for me one more time the steps you've decided to take." (This comment asks the mother to describe the plan that was negotiated.)

18. You write an account of the interview that has just ended. (Barring emergencies, this is a good procedure to follow routinely.)

INTERVIEWING TEACHERS

In the initial interview with teachers, you can cover many of the same topics that you cover with parents. The focus, however, is somewhat different in the two interviews. In interviewing a teacher, your concern is not only with the teacher's perception of the problem, the antecedents and consequences of the problem behavior, and what the teacher has done to alleviate the problem, but also with how other children and other teachers react to the child and to his or her problems and how the child performs academically. If the child's problem occurs in specific situations or settings, inquire about what the teacher considers appropriate behavior in that situation or setting. To help you interview teachers, see Table F-43 in Appendix F.

You also can use a teacher-completed questionnaire as part of the assessment (see Table C-13 in Appendix C). Ask the teacher to complete it before the interview, and then review it before you see her or him. Like the parent background questionnaire, it may give you some useful leads for further inquiry during the interview proper.

Areas Covered in the Initial Interview with Teachers

Following are the areas usually covered in the initial interview with teachers: the teacher's perception of the child's problem behavior, reactions to the child's problem behavior, opinion of the child's relationship with peers, assessment of the child's academic performance, assessment of the child's strengths and weaknesses, view of the child's family, expectations of the child, and suggestions for helping the child.

Two Examples of an Initial Interview with Teachers

The following two examples illustrate statements made in an initial interview with a teacher. The examples show how you can use the initial interview with a teacher to develop a plan for obtaining further assessment information about the child's problem. (The examples are from Bergan, 1977, pp. 97–99, reprinted, with changes in notation, with permission of the author.)

CHILD WITH BEHAVIOR PROBLEM

1. "Tell me about Alice's problem in the classroom."
2. "What does Alice do when she annoys you?"
3. "How often during the week does she talk out of turn?"

4. "You have said that Alice talks without permission. She does this about three times a week. Is that right?"
5. "What is generally going on right before Alice talks out of turn?"
6. "What are you usually doing just before Alice talks out of turn?"
7. "What do you do when Alice talks out of turn?"
8. "When does she talk out of turn during the day?"
9. "On what days of the week does she talk out of turn?"
10. "You have said that Alice usually talks out of turn when your back is turned and you are writing on the blackboard. Is that right?"
11. "Afterwards, the other kids giggle and laugh and sometimes treat her as though she had really done something great. Is that correct?"
12. "Will you be able to make a record of when Alice talks out of turn?"
13. "The record will help us to establish a baseline against which to evaluate the success of our intervention plan."
14. "Throughout the rest of this week, would you record on this form the number of times Alice talks out of turn?"
15. "If you have the time to do it, you also could make a note of what happens before and after she talks out of turn."
16. "Do these suggestions meet with your approval?"
17. "We agreed that you would record the number of times that Alice talks out of turn during the rest of this week."
18. "You're going to use this form."
19. "If you have a chance, please note what happens before and after she talks out of turn."
20. "Did I summarize our recording plans accurately?"
21. "Could we meet Monday or Tuesday of next week?"
22. "Shall we meet in the teacher's lounge or in your classroom?"
23. "If it is okay, I'll give you a call sometime this week to see how the data collection is going."

CHILD WITH READING PROBLEM
1. "Tell me about Ted's reading problem."
2. "Give me some other examples of Ted's reading difficulties."
3. "About how many errors does Ted make during an oral reading session?"
4. "You said that Ted continually misreads and omits words during oral reading. Is that correct?"
5. "How do you introduce oral reading?"
6. "How do the other children react when Ted makes errors while reading?"
7. "What is the sequence of steps that you go through in teaching reading in the oral reading groups?"
8. "You said that when you call on Ted to read, he reads eagerly and that after he has finished, you always go over all of his mistakes with him. You pronounce the words for him and have him say the words correctly. Is that an accurate review of what happens?"
9. "If you could record the number of errors that Ted makes during reading for the rest of the week, it would

help us to establish a baseline against which we can measure improvement in his reading."
10. "You could use this form for recording."
11. "And if you have a chance, note the other children's reactions and your own reactions when Ted makes a mistake."
12. "Would these plans be okay with you?"
13. "To summarize, we said that you would record the number of errors that Ted makes during oral reading on this form for the rest of the week and that if you have the chance, you'll note your own reactions and those of the other children to Ted's mistakes. Is that right?"
14. "Could we meet Monday or Tuesday of next week?"
15. "Shall we meet in the teacher's lounge or in your classroom?"
16. "If it is okay, I'll give you a call sometime this week to see how the data collection is going."

Working with the Teacher

During the interview, allay the teacher's anxiety about his or her responsibility for the child's problem behaviors. Inform the teacher that children's problems likely stem from several factors. Also tell the teacher when the assessment results will be ready. Do not leave the impression that immediate changes for the better will occur automatically.

Visiting the Classroom

A visit to the classroom may give you valuable information about the child and the teaching environment. Be careful not to be obtrusive or single the child out; you don't want your visit to stigmatize the child.

As you observe the classroom, note anything in the classroom that may affect the child adversely (see Table 4-3). For example, observe the features of the physical environment, other children, possible distractions inside the classroom, possible distractions outside the classroom, and the teacher's style of teaching. Be sensitive to things such as noises associated with activities going on in the hallway or street and odors coming from the cafeteria. Note the space allotted for various activities, the period of the day when the activities occur, the equipment used for the activities, the seating arrangements, the classroom displays, and the atmosphere in the room. Be sensitive to both verbal and nonverbal cues, patterns of interactions and group formations, and other features that will help you understand how the classroom functions, and try to determine how these features may affect the child's functioning.

Evaluating the Teacher Interview

Based on your interview with the teacher (and on classroom observations and interviews with the child and parents), you

Table 4-3
Guidelines for Observing the Classroom

1. How many students are in the classroom?
2. How many teachers and aides are in the classroom?
3. Is the classroom open-spaced or self-contained?
4. What is the atmosphere in the classroom? (For example, is the classroom organized or disorganized, pleasant or unpleasant, disciplined or undisciplined?)
5. What is the level of sound in the classroom?
6. Is the level of sound distracting?
7. What distractions, if any, are present in the classroom?
8. What distractions, if any, are present outside of the classroom?
9. Where do the students sit? (For example, does each student sit at a single desk or at a table with other children?)
10. If students work in small groups, do they help each other?
11. Do any children receive individualized instruction?
12. (If so) How many?
13. Do all the children work on the same activity at the same time?
14. What teaching methods are used? (For example, does the teacher use lectures, cooperative groups, learning centers, or hands-on activities?)
15. Are the lessons clearly presented, well sequenced, and well organized?
16. Are the explanations clear?
17. If the teacher lectures, do the students listen carefully to the lectures?
18. Do the students ask questions and participate in discussions?
19. If so, how does the teacher respond to the questions?
20. Are students given appropriate feedback for their performance?

21. How would you describe the teacher's behavior? (For example, does the teacher give praise, prompts, criticism, constructive feedback, approval for academic performance, disapproval for academic performance, approval for social performance, or disapproval for social performance?)
22. Is the teacher's approval/disapproval appropriate?
23. How do the students get along with the teacher?
24. How do the students get along with each other?
25. What equipment is available for the students to use? (For example, are there computers, maps, books, audio-visual equipment, and so forth?)
26. Does the teacher use any special reinforcers to motivate the students? (For example, does the teacher use tokens for achievement; self-recording or charting of academic progress; time to spend in a game center or recreational activity; time to play tapes or records; the opportunity to schedule when academic lessons take place; a "bank account" to buy privileges or free time; tangible reinforcers, such as fast food coupons, magazines, and movie tickets; exemption from additional assignments or homework; or extra time for lunch or for a break?)
27. Are the students' works displayed in the classroom?
28. What type of tests are given? (For example, does the teacher give multiple-choice, short-answer, or essay tests?)
29. Is sufficient time allotted for the tests?
30. Does the teacher allow children with special needs to ask questions when they do not understand, photocopy other students' notes, tape record lectures, do examinations orally, or obtain time limit extensions on examinations?

can probably come to some understanding about the following matters:

1. What does the teacher see as the major problems?
2. How effective is the teacher?
3. Is the child's class placement appropriate?
4. Is a placement change needed for the child?
5. What insights does the teacher have about the child?
6. What techniques have proved to be successful (or partially successful) in helping the child?
7. What techniques have proved to be unsuccessful in helping the child?
8. How do other children contribute to the problem?
9. What stressors exist in the classroom?
10. If stressors are present in the classroom, can they be diminished?
11. How does the teacher's account of the child agree with that of the parent and child?
12. What are the teacher's recommendations for interventions?

Children need models rather than critics.

—Joseph Joubert

INTERVIEWING THE FAMILY

Value of the Family Interview

A family interview has certain advantages in the assessment process (Kinsbourne & Caplan, 1979). (In this text, a family interview is assumed to be an interview of the child and parents, but occasionally you may want to include siblings and other family members as well. In single-parent families, the child and one parent are a family unit.) One advantage of the family interview is that it informs the child and the parents that you prefer to be open about the problem—that you want to include the child in some discussions. Another advantage is that it allows you to observe how the parents and child interact when discussing the problem and other matters. Sometimes this may be the family's first attempt as a family unit at discussing the perceived problem. It may be a turning point in the child's life when you say to the family "Let's go into my office and discuss why you are here today."

A family interview allows you to gather information about the child's problem; family dynamics, family communication patterns, and family social and cultural values; how well the family accepts the child; what impact the child's difficulties have on the family, on the parents' relationship, and on other family members; and the extent to which the family is using functional or dysfunctional strategies to cope with the child's problems.

The following represent *functional family strategies* that families may use to cope with a child with a psychological or medical disorder (DePompei, Blosser, & Zarski, 1989):

1. *Reacting.* Family members have initial reactions of grief, anger, disappointment, guilt, anxiety, frustration, and a sense of loss.

2. *Mobilizing.* Family members draw on internal and external support systems to respond to the needs of the child.

3. *Recognition.* Family members perceive the strengths and weaknesses of the child in a realistic light.

4. *Understanding.* Family members gain an understanding of what may be accomplished in a rehabilitation program.

5. *Continuing.* Family members continue with other aspects of their lives.

6. *Hoping.* Family members maintain hope for the future for their child and for themselves.

7. *Appreciating.* Family members develop a new appreciation for many aspects of life for themselves and for their child.

8. *Reasoning.* Family members engage in adequate reasoning and do not make faulty assumptions.

The following represent *dysfunctional family strategies* that families may use to cope with a child with a psychological or medical disorder (DePompei et al., 1989; also see Exhibit 4-2):

1. *Blaming.* Family members criticize actions of the child, threaten the child and accuse the child of acting to embarrass them, and blame the child for other unrelated family problems. Parents also may blame each other or themselves for the child's problems.

2. *Taking over.* Family members assume responsibility for the child by speaking for the child and by performing tasks that the child could do or should do.

3. *Employing power.* Family members use authority to direct the behaviors of the child, to rely heavily on the use of guilt, and to cling to old roles to maintain their position and authority.

4. *Avoiding.* Family members use work, medications, food, and blaming the child to remove themselves from direct involvement in the family; they also fail to accept responsibility for family disharmony.

5. *Denying.* Family members try to return to how the family was before the child developed problems, failing to recognize the severity of the child's deficits.

6. *Controlling.* Family members select what the child should do rather than allowing the child to choose for himself or herself.

7. *Rescuing.* Family members remove the child from situations that the child created so that the child does not have to suffer the consequences of his or her actions.

8. *Faulty reasoning.* Family members engage in rationalizing—if the child could just come home from the hospital or clinic and return to school or work, everything would return to normal—and assume that the child has behavioral controls that the child actually does not have.

Families may cope with stress in adaptive or maladaptive ways (Turk & Kerns, 1985). A key factor in coping with stress—whether the stress is psychological, environmental, or physical—is how the family was functioning *before* the stress occurred. A family that was functioning well before the stress occurred may continue to function adequately, although with some problems. The family may handle the stress, protect its members, adjust to role changes within the family, and continue to carry out its functions. A family that was not functioning well before the stress may break down in the face of stress, which, in turn, may lead to maladaptive behavior or illness in its members.

When you interview the family, a healthy sibling also may be present. In such cases, you may find that the healthy child who has a sibling with a psychological or medical disorder also is under stress. Healthy siblings may dislike their increased responsibilities at home, be unhappy about decreased parental attention and increased parental tension, feel guilty and ashamed, be upset with having to deal with negative reactions of others outside the family, feel resentful toward the sibling with a psychological or medical disorder and be concerned and worried about their sibling's disorder. Be prepared to deal with these and similar reactions.

The family interview, like the interview with the child or parents alone, may be the initial encounter that the family has with a mental health professional and may serve as the beginning of a family therapy intervention program as well. (See Chapter 1 for a review of the family systems perspective.)

Exercise 4-2. Describing Your Family

Write your answer to each question or statement after you read it. Then compare your answers with those of your classmates. This exercise is designed to enhance your understanding of how families function. The questions are from Fine (1991, p. 10), with minor changes and additions.

1. Who are the members of your family?
2. Describe your family's cultural and ethnic background. Include a discussion of your family's values, behaviors, attitudes, and customs, and give a description of one family tradition or holiday ritual.

Exhibit 4-2
Dysfunctional Family Patterns

1. *Loud, chronic complaining* is exhibited by some families. These families may

(a) literally scream and create crises out of every minor concern, even when special efforts have been made to meet their needs. They seem preoccupied with the way agencies and professionals "should" and "must" provide quality and expanded services with little appreciation for large caseloads, high staff turnover, and dwindling agency budgets.

(b) telephone staff at home any hour of the day or night with minor problems, even when asked to call only during office hours.

(c) sometimes turn to lawyers, agency executives, local legislative representatives, special interest groups, or the mass media with complaints about service delivery, without first trying to resolve problems themselves or with direct service professionals.

(d) verbally attack professionals along racial, age, gender, religious, or personal lines, and demand other more suitable staff be provided to them.

2. *Program sabotage* is a trait of some families who tend to see professionals and agencies as adversaries. These families may

(a) block attempts to provide treatment approaches (for example, restrictions on family visits, timeout procedures, or pharmacotherapy) necessary for assisting behaviorally disturbed children.

(b) refuse to support plans to place their institutionalized child in a community setting, or demand a disabled child be "discharged against advice" from a residential setting at the first sign of behavioral improvement.

(c) repeatedly break scheduled appointments with professionals, or appear an hour too early or too late for an appointment and demand immediate attention.

(d) have unrealistic or impossible expectations for their disabled child, or at the other extreme impede program success by being overly pessimistic concerning the disabled child's prognosis.

3. *Extreme overprotectiveness* is displayed by some families who seem overpowered by a ubiquitous sense of guilt. These families may

(a) infantilize and create dependency in otherwise capable, mildly disabled children. For example, parents may insist on still bathing their marginally retarded adolescent; demand a mature female wear an adolescent undershirt rather than a brassiere; drive an older adolescent everywhere rather than allowing him or her to use public transportation; and insist on a hair style for the disabled child or adolescent that is not age appropriate.

(b) refuse to spend time away from their disabled child (for example, "During the first 18 years of Tom's life, I never was away from him for more than 3 hours at a time"). Family "martyrs" who devote their whole life to their disabled child often secretly resent the life-long cost in time and money of caring for their child.

(c) take great personal risks when their disabled child meets with a minor catastrophe to prove their undying love (for example, parents driving 30 miles through a blinding snowstorm after learning their institutionalized daughter had developed a minor physical ailment).

(d) tolerate seemingly intolerable behavior (for instance, carrying out ridiculous requests from a disabled child to go for a car ride at 3:00 a.m. or to screw out every light bulb in the house, refusing to say "no" to a disabled child's compulsive eating of 14 chocolate bars at one time, or failing to seek assistance for a physically violent child who has repeatedly injured family members).

4. *Hypochondriac obsessions* are found in some families. Family members often talk incessantly about their own somatic problems and may

(a) "shop around" from one specialist to another to find some miracle cure for their child's disability. They may even demand that physicians perform unnecessary surgery or change the disabled child's treatment to some "medical breakthrough" described in sensationalized publications.

(b) request that unnecessary laxatives or vitamins be given to their disabled child, or constantly censure physicians for not finding undetectable ailments. They may also stockpile psychotropic medication when their disabled child is quiet and then overdose the child when behavior problems appear.

(c) stubbornly deny the functional basis for many behavioral problems, while insisting their disabled child's difficulties are caused entirely by some vague "brain disease" or obscure physiological problem.

(d) continually ruminate about the probable etiology for their child's disability (for example, "She was developing normally until she had her tonsils out at age 2").

5. *Open warfare* is observed in some families. Overt hostility is the hallmark here. In these families,

(a) parents seldom show warmth and closeness toward each other. Their marriage is characterized by sarcastic exchanges, violent arguments, extramarital affairs, and often untimely divorce.

(b) intense sibling rivalry occurs that lasts into adulthood. Brothers and sisters vacillate between displacing enormous anger onto their disabled sibling, and competing to prove who loves the person more (for example, over-indulgent gift-giving).

(c) "shared family secrets" create considerable tension. These secrets involve knowledge the family is forbidden to talk about concerning incest, physical or sexual abuse, alcohol or drug problems.

(d) physical violence is common. Yet, the ever-present hostility can easily be projected onto professionals or

(Continued)

Exhibit 4-2 (*Continued*)

agency officials who provoke family members in even minor ways. Professionals may be verbally threatened, sexually propositioned, or physically attacked by irate family members.

6. *Symbiotic relationships* are encountered in some families, involving a pathologically close relationship between the disabled child and one or both parents, uncanny sensitivity for each other's pain, and double-bind communication. [This is a form of faulty communication in which the child receives contradictory messages from the parent. The parent communicates warmth, but when the child approaches, the parent is cold and withdraws. The child is thus caught in a "double bind."] "Folie famille" refers to cases where symbiotic fusion and a commonly shared delusion permeate the entire family. Three such delusions may be found in severely dysfunctional families:

(a) delusions of persecution in which the family socially isolates itself and develops a paranoid distrust of outsiders, be they neighbors or helping professionals.

(b) delusions of grandeur in which one family member, sometimes the disabled child, is idolized beyond any realistic dimensions (for example, the family may believe one member has magical healing powers, can forecast future events, or deserves most of the family's attention).

(c) delusions of wish-fulfillment in which the family inaccurately believes their relative has been deliberately malingering ("He puts on a fake retarded act in public"), or in which families feel finding the right faith healer will cure their disabled relative.

7. *Avoidance of the disabled child* is demonstrated by other families. Sometimes,

(a) family members completely terminate contact with the disabled child after placing the child in a residential setting. They may never visit, write, or even acknowledge their child's existence. Such total rejection can destroy the disabled child's self-worth, precipitate severe depression, and leave the child fantasizing about family that never comes. Other families may keep contact only until money from an inheritance or other source "runs dry."

(b) family members make grand promises to disabled children (for example, vow to visit them in the institution or promise gifts) that are never kept.

(c) one parent will withdraw completely into vocational or spare-time activities, leaving the other parent to deal almost singlehandedly with their disabled child.

(d) family members withdraw into severe depressions which effectively lead to little or no contact with the disabled child (for example, escape through psychiatric hospitalization, or alcohol and drug abuse).

8. *Psychosocial deprivation* characterizes some families in isolated rural or urban slum areas. In these multideficit families,

(a) little attention is paid to the special needs of the disabled child because all family members face day-to-day struggles meeting basic needs. A child's disability may never even be diagnosed, unless the degree of handicap is extreme or a major crisis arises. In some cases, environmental deprivation or genetic influences may result in limited intellectual capacities in several or all family members.

(b) there is often a distrust of professionals and helping agencies. Many of these socioeconomically disadvantaged families are frustrated after long-term contact (sometimes involving more than one generation) with welfare and social service establishments.

(c) incest and unwanted pregnancies sometimes run rampant. The disabled child may be vulnerable to sexual exploitation by other family members.

(d) disabled children may still, even in this day and age, be found locked or hidden away in the home to minimize embarrassment or facilitate behavioral management.

Source: Reprinted, with changes in notation, with permission of the publishers and author from J. Dale Munro, "Counseling Severely Dysfunctional Families of Mentally and Physically Disabled Persons," *Clinical Social Work Journal, 13,* pp. 20–24, copyright 1985 by Human Sciences Press.

3. What was happening in your family at the time of your birth (for example, economic status of your family, type of housing where your family lived, employment of parents)?

4. What was the significance of your birth (for example, long-awaited child, financial burden, birth order, etc.)?

5. What role(s) did you assume within your family as compared to other family members (for example, the studious child role, the helpful child role, etc.)?

6. What subgroups existed in your family (for example, parents subgroup, children subgroup, younger children subgroup, older children subgroup)?

7. What rules and expectations (implicit and explicit) existed in your family?

8. What alliances existed in your family and how did they shift (for example, mother and son versus father on discipline, mother and father versus daughter on school issues)?

9. How and by whom were decisions made about money, child management, vacations, and other issues?

10. Was affection expressed? If so, was it expressed physically or verbally, by whom, to whom, etc.?

11. How did the family members communicate?

12. Were there family secrets?

13. In what ways and in what areas were you (and your siblings) able to establish independence?
14. How did your family interact with its extended family?
15. How did your family interact with the community?
16. How was spirituality or religion treated in the family?
17. Was there an active church affiliation?
18. How did family patterns shift as the children got older?
19. How did your family respond to crises? If possible, describe how your family responded to one crisis.
20. How do you think your family would have reacted to a child with a psychological or medical disorder? You might speculate in terms of which child (oldest or youngest) and the nature and severity of the problem.

Necessity of Individual Interviews

The family interview is not a substitute for individual interviews—you should still see the child and the parents separately. You also may have to see each parent separately. Parents and children may be more open in an individual interview than in a family interview. Observing how they behave in both an individual and a family interview may be helpful. If you begin the assessment with a family interview, obtain the child's developmental history from the parents during an interview at which the child is not present.

Goals of the Family Interview

The goals of the family interview are to obtain historical and current details of family life relevant to the problems of the child and to observe patterns of family interaction, noting the family's strengths and weaknesses. The interview should clarify the family structure, along with details of the family's makeup, such as names, ages, relationships, and occupations of members (unless the family has previously supplied this information on a questionnaire). In a family interview, you will want to learn about the child's problem, the family members' understanding of the child's problem, the family's motivation to help the child, and what interventions are possible given the family's resources.

Help every family member feel at ease and involved. You want the family members to interact freely, to contribute ideas about the problem, to describe the conditions that they find most troublesome, and to discuss what changes they would like to see and what might be done to resolve the problem. *Recognize that your questions and probes may result in potentially painful confrontations among family members and may elicit feelings that have not been previously articulated.* When confrontations occur, offer support to the family members who need it.

Table F-17 in Appendix F provides an example of a semistructured family interview. It covers the presenting problem and issues related to the family's image, perceptions of its members, organization, communication patterns, relationships, activities, conflicts, and decision-making style.

Guidelines for Conducting the Family Interview

Before beginning the family interview, consider who referred the family to you, the reason for the referral, and whether the family came voluntarily or under coercion (for example, at the insistence of the court, the school, or one family member). Following are useful guidelines for conducting the family interview (Kinston & Loader, 1984):

1. Encourage open discussion among the family members.
2. Make the interview no more stressful than absolutely necessary.
3. Support any family member who is on the "hot seat."
4. Do not create guilt or loss of face for any family member.
5. Create a safe and supportive atmosphere so that the family members can interact in a way that they find most comfortable and natural.
6. Use praise and approval to ease the family members' acceptance of the interview.
7. Help family members clarify their thoughts.
8. Be objective but understanding in your evaluation of the family members.
9. Maintain a balance between formality and informality, while promoting informality among the family members.
10. Encourage the family members who are children to participate in the discussion.
11. Encourage family members to give specific examples of concerns and problems.
12. Do not provoke the family members. Ask, for example, "How do arguments arise?" rather than "Who is the troublemaker in the family?"
13. Be aware of the dynamics among the family members.

You want to create a setting in which the family members can risk sharing their feelings and problems and can seek information about the referred child's problems and also their problems as they relate to the child. You can do this by creating a sense of trust and safety and by minimizing anxiety and fear of negative evaluations. When the family members see that you are interested in each member's point of view and that you want to understand them, they may be more willing to engage in a free discussion of the personal and intimate details of their lives.

Table 4-4 presents some guidelines for observing the family. Note, for example, which members talk, in what sequence, at whom each member looks, and who speaks first, interrupts, clarifies, registers surprise, remains silent, disagrees, assumes a leadership role, expresses emotional warmth, and accepts responsibility. Also, observe how the parents discipline their child, whether the child misbehaves, how the parents view the child and her or his problems, how the family resolves anger, how members are encouraged to speak, how they support and cooperate with each other, and how they make physical contact.

Table 4-4
Guidelines for Observing the Family

Early Moments of the Interview
1. How did the family enter the room?
2. Were the family members resistant or cooperative?
3. If the child was resistant, how did the parents deal with him or her?
4. How were the family members dressed?
5. How did they seat themselves?
6. Who replied first to the interviewer's initial comment?
7. What was the tone of voice of each family member?
8. What was the demeanor of each family member? (For example, did they appear anxious, distressed, or comfortable during the early moments of the interview?)

Intrafamily Relations
9. How did the parents treat the referred child?
10. How did the parents treat the other children (if present)?
11. Were all the children treated similarly (if more than one child was present)?
12. How did the children treat their parents?
13. What pairings occurred between family members?
14. Who talked to whom and in what manner?
15. What was the sequence of talking?
16. Were the family members sensitive to one another?
17. Did one family member speak for another member without taking into account the latter's feelings?
18. Did one family member ask another member about what a third member said in the presence of the third member?
19. Did family members interrupt each other?
20. Did one family member attempt to control, silence, or intimidate other family members?
21. Did two family members engage in nonverbal activities together? (For example, did they cry together, laugh together, roll eyes together, or make certain facial expressions together?)
22. Were there times when there was a chain reaction between pairs of family members that distracted them from their task?
23. Did one family member disregard other members' feelings?

24. Did the family members describe each other in clear terms?
25. Did one family member intercede in a dialogue between two other members?
26. If so, how did the pair accept the intercession?

Affect Displayed by Family Members
27. What type of affect was displayed by the family members during most of the interview? (For example, were the family members anxious, depressed, angry, sullen, or hopeful?)
28. What degree of curiosity did the family members show about the problem and its possible resolutions?

Relationship with the Interviewer
29. How did the family members relate to you? (For example, did one member try to get too close to you? Were the members distant and aloof from you?)

Background Factors
30. What was happening in the family that might be contributing to the child's problem?
31. Was there someone missing from the interview who might furnish important information about the problem?
32. Who in the family thought it was a good idea to come to see you, and who did not think so?
33. What did the family expect from the interview?
34. Did the parents share the same view of the child's behavior and problem?
35. (If not) How do the parents' views differ?

Causes and Interventions
36. What did the parents think is the cause of the child's problem?
37. What did the child think is the cause of his or her problem?
38. What can be done to change the situation?
39. What did the parents want to do about the problem?
40. What did the child want to do about the problem?

If you touch upon an emotionally charged area that upsets family members and makes it difficult to continue the interview, consider moving on to a more neutral subject. You can schedule a second session, if needed, to explore more sensitive areas. You want to obtain as much information as possible during the initial evaluation, but you don't want to cause undue anxiety. In crises, instead of conducting a standard intake assessment interview, you might need to focus on what can be done about the problem. For more information on crisis interviewing, see Chapter 11.

When a child who is at the family interview seems unable to answer a question and is uncomfortable about it, do not prolong the discomfort. It is best to take the child off the hook

(Karpel & Strauss, 1983). Consider rephrasing the question, switching to another topic, or questioning another family member. You might even consider saying that the question was "too fuzzy," as a way of reassuring the child. Finally, you can "encourage the child to bring up the topic later if he or she gets any new ideas" (Karpel & Strauss, 1983, p. 204).

You want to be aware of how the family members perceive you. For example, note at what points they ask you to give your opinion, to intercede, to solve problems, or to give them support. Key interviewing skills are listening to one family member while simultaneously observing other family members, being aware of your role in the interactions, and being aware of your reactions to the family members.

Strategies for Working with Resistant Families

When you meet families who have *not* come to see you voluntarily, you may have to clarify your role by informing them of your goals. One way to begin is to say "The school [or other referral source] has asked me to meet with you. I understand that Bill is [describe problem]. I'm here to help you and Bill with the problem."

Interviewing a family ordered to come to see you will require patience. Tell the family you need to obtain information to make the most appropriate recommendations or to obtain the best services possible for the child.

You also will meet individual family members who will deny the problem or resist your efforts to obtain information. Your patience will be tried when this happens. Be patient, however; show the family that you are a good listener and genuinely interested in its problems and that you are willing to wait until the reluctant members are willing to participate.

Here are some useful strategies for handling various types of resistance in the family interview (Anderson & Stewart, 1983):

1. *Parents say that the child is the problem, not the parents or the family.* Leave the focus on the child, at least initially. If the child is old enough and mature enough to handle the confrontation, ask the child whether the parents' position is accurate: "Is what they are saying about you really true?"

2. *Family denies there is a problem.* Be supportive of the family so that family members may come to trust you. Allow the family members to say that they are there because of someone else's referral ("We're doing this only because the doctor told us to come").

3. *One member dominates the discussion.* Reward the family member who is talking, but move on to other family members. Inform them that the family member who is doing all the talking is getting the other members off the hook. Tell the family member who is talking that what he or she is saying is important, but that you want to hear from everyone.

4. *The child won't talk.* One strategy is to inform the family of the importance of having everyone talk: "I really need to hear what everyone thinks of all this" or "It will help me to understand what's going on in this family if you all tell me what you think." A second strategy is to give the child permission to be silent: "Okay, Henry, it's okay if you don't want to be here and even if you don't want to talk. Maybe if you just listen while your parents and I talk, it will be helpful. If you change your mind and want to join in, let us know." A third strategy is to take the avenue of least resistance and focus on those members who will speak. As the child sees that the interviewer listens and is fair, he or she may begin to talk.

5. *Family insists that the focus be on historical information.* Ask the family why the information is relevant: "Okay, so Helen was 5 when she entered kindergarten and had two teachers. How's that going to help us now?"

6. *Family refuses to focus on historical information.* Provide the family a rationale for what you want to learn. "I think it's important to get a picture of the family members' health and illnesses, both physical and psychological" or "We don't want to make any assumptions about what the problem is until we look at your past history so that we can get a good perspective on what is happening now."

7. *Family can't find the time for all members to meet.* Be flexible in scheduling appointments because some families can meet only in the evenings or on weekends. You can give the family members the job of finding available times, you can make home visits, and you can arrange for transportation.

8. *Family disagrees about the problem.* Find a new definition of the problem with which all the family members agree. Inform the family that everybody's feelings are important and legitimate in evaluating what the problem might be.

Opening Phase of the Family Interview

Here are some techniques that you can use during the opening phase of the family interview.

1. After introducing yourself, you might say "We are all here today to work out the problems you're having as a family. I'd like to hear from each of you about what is going on." Then you might say "Who would like to begin the discussion?"

2. Or, looking at no one in particular but addressing the family as a whole, you might say "Would you like to tell me why you are here today?" or "How can I help you?"

3. Another possibility is to say "I asked you all to come here today so that I can find out how you all feel about your family." Then pause and see if anyone begins to speak. If you need to, you can say "Perhaps you all can tell me what you see as the problems you are having as a family."

4. Encourage reluctant members to speak in the interest of being helpful.

5. Foreclose lengthy or excessive responses by such comments as "We have much ground to cover. Let's hear what Mr. Smith thinks."

6. In working with families that have been coerced to see you because their child misbehaved, you might say to the family early in the interview "You know, raising a child is difficult for many families today. How has it been for you?" This comment recognizes that the family is struggling with issues common to many families with children and invites their participation.

7. In cases of a court or school referral, you also might consider saying "I know that the [court/school, etc.] has asked all of you to come to see me. But I also believe, [say the child's name and look at him or her], that your parents care about what happens to you and that you also care about what happens to you. I'm interested in how I can help all of you [looking at the entire family] get through this." These comments recognize that the parents

have complied with an order or referral, and the comments may help reduce the family's defensiveness (Oster, Caro, Eagen, & Lillo, 1988).

8. Pay special attention to the way each family member describes the problem.

Here is an example of the early part of an initial family interview. The interviewer tried to get the family members to discuss the presenting problem. Note how the interviewer tried to clarify the discussion and to empathize with and understand the family (Catherall, 1988, pp. 53–56, with changes in notation). Abbreviations are as follows: IR = interviewer, IE-F = father (Mr. A.), IE-M = mother (Mrs. A.), IE-C = child (Jack).

IR: I would like to hear from each of you about how you see the problem. Would you like to begin, Mr. A.? What do you see as the problem you are here to work on?

IE-F: Well, the problem is our son, Jack. He is always mouthing off to his mother and won't do anything she tells him. The two of them are always arguing.

IR: How does that make you feel?

IE-F: It makes me angry. And it frustrates me that I can't get him to obey her.

IR: Are you angry with anyone in particular?

IE-F: Yes, at Jack! There would be no problem if he would just do what he's told.

IR: And what have you done to try and solve this problem?

IE-F: I tell Jack I will give him a whipping when I get home if his mother says he's been mouthing off to her. And we have grounded him and taken away the use of the car.

IR: What about the whippings? Have you given him a whipping?

IE-F: Several times.

IR: Have these things changed Jack's behavior in any way?

IE-F: Nope, he's still arguing with her all the time.

IR: I see. Mrs. A., what about you, what do you see as the problem?

IE-M: Like my husband said, Jack just won't do anything I tell him. He's disrespectful, and he does as he pleases. If I try to appeal to him, all I get is smart-mouth answers.

IR: So how are you feeling about this problem?

IE-M: I'm fed up. At first, I wanted Jack to be happy with what I asked him to do; now I don't care, I just want cooperation.

IR: What have you done to try and get cooperation?

IE-M: I've tried everything. I tried to talk to him about why he is always talking back to me, but it didn't make any difference. I ask him to do things very politely, and he says he doesn't have the time. He's always running off with his friends. Then we said he couldn't go out until he was more respectful. It didn't make any difference. He's always sarcastic.

IR: All right, Mrs. A., let me speak to Jack. Jack, what do you feel is the problem? Your parents both say you are disobedient and have a smart mouth. I want to know how you see it.

IE-C: I'm not disobedient. Ask them. I haven't gone out once since they grounded me. And other people don't think I'm a smart aleck. It's just my mom. She's always on my case about something. She never lets up. She's always asking questions about my friends and what I do with them. I do what she asks, too, when it's reasonable. But she's always wanting me to do stupid stuff like go to the grocery store with her so I can carry the bags. I tell her that they'll put the bags in the car for her and I'll come out and get them when she gets home. But she insists that I have to go with her, so we end up arguing. Even if I go, we argue the whole time.

IR: So you think the problem is just between you and your mom.

IE-C: That's right. My dad and I don't fight, except about what I've done to make Mom mad. When Dad's around, I do whatever he tells me. If I think it's unreasonable, I can tell him and he listens.

IR: How about that, Dad?

IE-F: Well, sort of. I'm firmer than Alice, and Jack knows I mean business when I say I want something done. But there's always a fight going on when I get home. I feel like a referee at a boxing match.

IR: Jack, how do you feel about this constant bickering between you and your mom?

IE-C: I hate it. I feel like I'm at war and there's nobody else on my side.

IR: Does your dad ever take your side?

IE-C: No. Sometimes he just tries to stay out of it; other times he comes down on me and says I have to do whatever Mom says. But he never says she's wrong.

IR: What have you done to try and get along better with your mom?

IE-C: I just try and be reasonable with her, but it doesn't work. She doesn't listen to me when I explain something. I know I get sarcastic sometimes, but it's because she's not listening to me.

IR: All right, Jack, thank you. Mom, Jack says that he's not disrespectful or disobedient in general. He feels that the problem is mostly between him and you. What do you think about that?

IE-M: It's true that I'm the one he's always mouthing off at, but then I'm the one who has to deal with him the most.

IR: Have you heard of him having similar difficulties at school or elsewhere outside the home?

IE-M: He has been kept after school for talking back to his teacher.

IE-C: That was only in Mrs. Smith's class last year. Everyone has trouble with her. I haven't had any trouble this year, and I have kept my grades up.

IR: What about that, Mrs. A.?

IE-M: He does okay in school. I guess he saves his smart remarks for me.

IR: All right then. It sounds like we are agreed that the problem occurs primarily between Jack and Mom. Mom feels Jack is disrespectful and won't cooperate with her. And Jack feels that Mom doesn't listen to him and asks unreasonable things of him. And everyone agrees that Jack and Mom are arguing too much.

Middle Phase of the Family Interview

After each family member has had time to share his or her views about the presenting problems (say for a total of 15 to 20 minutes), you can turn to a discussion of the family (see questions 15 through 54 in Table F-17 in Appendix F). In addition to what the family members say, be alert to the nonverbal cues that they give (for example, knowing glances, fidgeting), how they talk to each other (for example, friendly, hostile, neutral), their power maneuvers (for example, who tries to control the discussion), their provocative behaviors (for example, who tries to start an argument), and their ability to send and receive messages (for example, clarity of communications, clarity of responses). Encourage all the family members to participate in the discussions.

Family assessment tasks. To study family interaction patterns, you might want to give the family one or more of the following tasks. The middle phase of the interview may be the most appropriate time to give one of these tasks, but you can give it in any phase of the interview. The first three tasks are from Szapocznik and Kurtines (1989, p. 35, with changes in notation).

Task 1. Planning a Menu
"Suppose all of you had to work out a menu for dinner tonight and would like to have your favorite foods for dinner. But you can only have one main dish, one vegetable, one drink, and one dessert. Discuss this together; however, you must choose one meal you would all enjoy that consists of one main dish, one vegetable, one drink, and one dessert. Go ahead."

Task 2. Commenting on Things Others Do in the Family That Please or Displease the Members
"Each of you tell about one thing everyone in the family does that pleases you the most and makes you feel good, and one thing each one does that makes you unhappy or mad. Everyone try to give his or her own ideas about this. Go ahead."

Task 3. Discussing a Family Argument
"In every family, things happen that create a fuss now and then. Together, discuss an argument you have had—a fight or argument at home. Discuss what started it, who was part of it, what happened, and how it ended. See if you can remember what it was all about. Go ahead."

Task 4. Planning a Family Vacation
"What would your family like to do for a vacation? Discuss this together. However, you must all agree on the final choice. Go ahead."

Task 5. Allocating Lottery Winnings
"If a member of your family won $500,000 in a lottery, what would your family do with it? Discuss this together. However, you must all agree on the way the money will be handled. Go ahead."

Task 6. Planning an Activity
"Plan something together as a family. The plan you come up with should be one that everyone agrees to. Go ahead."

Task 7. Using Descriptive Phrases to Characterize the Family
"Say as many phrases as you can that would describe your family as a group. Select one member to record your answers. All of you must agree with the phrases that describe your family before they are written down. Go ahead."

Task 8. Making Up a Story
Select a picture from a magazine or from some other source that you think would be useful for this task. Say "Here is a picture. Make up a story about the picture. Select one member to record the story. The story should be one that you all agree with. In the story, tell what is happening in the picture. Include a beginning, a middle, and an end to the story. Go ahead."

Task 9. Discussing Specific Issues
For a family that is shy or hesitant to discuss issues or for a family that needs more structuring, consider using the following procedure (Olson & Portner, 1983). Say "I'm going to name some issues one at a time. I'd like you to tell me whether the issue is or is not a problem in your family. OK? Here is the first one." You can then name each of the following issues or select only the ones you believe are most pertinent for the family: money, communication, sharing feelings, expressing feelings, physical intimacy, recreation, friends, alcohol, drugs, raising the children, handling parental responsibility, sharing responsibilities for raising children, jealousy, personal habits, resolving conflicts, taking disagreements seriously, leisure time, vacations, making decisions, time spent away from home, careers, moving to a new place, sharing household duties, putting clothing away, and having time to be alone. Probe any problem area mentioned by the family, "In what way is _____ a problem?" Try to get each member to respond. If there are disagreements, say "It seems that you have different ideas about whether _____ is a problem. Let's discuss why you have different ideas."

Task 10. Participating in Miscellaneous Activities
Ask a parent to request that the child perform some action, such as writing a sentence, doing an arithmetical problem, or solving a puzzle. Observe the interaction. For example, observe how the parent asks the child to perform the task, how the child does it, how other members react as the child performs the task, and how the child presents the finished task.

These 10 tasks might help you learn about the family's negotiation style; ways of resolving conflicts; pattern of alliances; decision-making style; patterns of parent-child, parent-parent, sibling-child, and parent-sibling interactions; roles; communication and language patterns; beliefs and expectations; and affective reactions. If a task becomes too stressful for the family, do not continue with it.

Additional areas to probe in a family interview. Besides the questions in Table F-17 in Appendix F and the family assessment tasks, you also might want to explore several areas of family life. These include the layout of the home; a typical day in the life of the family; rules, regulations, and limit setting within the family; alliances and coalitions with the family; family disagreements; changes that the family members want to make; and previous family crises. We now consider each of these areas in more detail. (Sample instructions are from Karpel & Strauss, 1983, pp. 137–147, with changes in notation.)

1. *Layout of home.* After the initial discussion of the problem, a useful way to get the family to talk is to ask them about the layout of the home: "I want to take a little bit of time to pull back from discussing the immediate problem, just to get a better idea about your family. You've mentioned some things already, but maybe one way to start would be for you to give me a description of your home, the layout of the rooms, who sleeps where, and anything you want to tell me about your home." Ask follow-up questions as needed.

2. *A typical day.* A useful probing question for this area is "I also want to get a description from all of you of what a typical day consists of for your family. Start from the first thing in the morning, beginning with who gets up first. Go ahead." If the family tells you about an atypical day, redirect them to discuss a typical day, usually a weekday. You also can ask them how they spend a typical weekend day. You may want to ask about the following issues (Karpel & Strauss, 1983, p. 139, with changes in notation):

- Do any family members have breakfast at home?
- Do they eat together?
- Which members, if any, are home during the day or return home from school or work for lunch?
- At what time do different family members arrive home from school or work?
- Who usually prepares dinner, and who is usually home for dinner?
- Does the family eat together?
  (If so, answer questions 7 through 10)
- Do they have an established seating arrangement at a table?
- What is the atmosphere around the table at a typical family meal?
- Are things quiet or noisy?
- If noisy, is it the sound of animated conversations and joking, or is it a time of petty arguments or major conflicts?
- How does each family member spend the evening?

3. *Rules, regulations, and limit setting.* A useful question for this area of family life is "All families have certain kinds of rules and regulations for people in the family: chores, curfews, and that kind of thing. What are some rules and regulations in your family?" Valuable follow-up questions include asking what happens if chores are not done; how discipline is managed by the parents; whether both parents play active roles in discipline; whether the parents work together, independently, or at cross purposes in using discipline; what role each parent plays in disciplining the children; and whether the discipline is consistent with the children's behavior and age.

4. *Alliances and coalitions.* Several different probing statements may reveal the family's alliances and coalitions without creating undue stress on the family. For example, you might say "I'd like to get a better idea of who spends time with whom in the family." After they discuss this, you can say "I'd like to know whom each of you is most likely to talk to when something is on your mind." You can direct these probes to each member of the family. Other useful questions are "Who sticks up for whom?", "Who worries about whom in the family?", and "Who do you worry about the most?"

5. *Family disagreements.* One useful question (as you look at each family member) is "Every family has areas they frequently disagree about, but these areas differ from one family to another. I wonder if you could fill me in on the kinds of disagreements your family has most often?" Another version is "Most families have some kind of disagreement every once in a while about something or some gripes about something once in a while. What kinds of gripes have there been from time to time in your family?" After someone describes an event, ask follow-up questions to obtain more detailed information, such as "What was said first?" "What happened next?" "What was everyone doing at the time?" "How did it end?"

6. *Desired changes.* Useful questions are "Can any of you think of any changes you'd like to see made in your family?", "If you could change anything you wanted about your family or about life in the family, what kinds of changes would you make?", and, directed at the children, "If you had magic powers and could change anything you wanted, what would you change about your family?"

7. *Previous family crises.* A useful statement is "It will help us in dealing with the present problem to learn something about any previous problems your family has experienced or that any members of the family have gone through. Any past situation that has been especially upsetting to the family or put stress on it would help me better understand your family, as would any previous problems that required professional help." Or you can substitute for the second sentence "Have there ever been times that have been really rough for the family?" Ask follow-up questions as needed. The way the family managed past crises may help you learn about the family's organization, judgment, flexibility, mutual trust, and internal resources.

Closing Phase of the Family Interview

Toward the end of the interview, summarize the salient points of the interview, including those family dynamics most related to the child's problem. Then ask the family

Suburban Cowgirls   by Janet Alfieri and Ed Colley

members to respond to your formulation. After that, give your initial recommendations and ask the family what they think about them. Gauge the family's willingness to change and the suitability of its members for treatment.

Here are three examples of summary statements made during the closing phase of family interviews (Karpel & Strauss, 1983):

EXAMPLE 1

It's certainly clear that you are all concerned for each other and have all been very upset over Peter's [the identified patient] recent symptoms. Peter, you have been described by everyone as the "sensitive" one in the family, "the worrier," and you have all mentioned several recent family pressures that have caused worry—like Mrs. S.'s mother's recent surgery and problems in the family's grocery business. It makes sense then that Peter was worried about such things, along with dealing with the normal pressures of being in the last year of high school and facing graduation. And being worried about each other's welfare, while it's a good thing, a sign of caring, can also take its toll on people, especially in combination with other pressures or factors.

Because you are all naturally involved in each other's lives and care about each other and react to each other's good and bad times, I think it would be helpful to continue meeting for a time as a family to discuss these family-wide pressures and Peter's recent problems. Peter, I think individual meetings will also help you maintain the progress you have been making. How does that sound to all of you? (p. 183, with changes in notation)

EXAMPLE 2

As you know, our primary purpose in seeing you is to help Margaret [the identified patient] continue to make progress toward solving problems. It has been found in cases like these that family tensions or pressures can contribute to the child's symptoms and that family members can be very helpful to each other in dealing with the problems. I am impressed with your willingness to come in together and work on the problem, and you obviously care a good deal about each other. So I think it makes good sense to con-

tinue the work you all started in the hospital and for you all to come in as a family on a weekly basis. (p. 191, with changes in notation)

EXAMPLE 3

You have all clearly been under a lot of strain recently, and Mr. and Mrs. Q, things have clearly been very rocky between both of you and Tommy [the identified patient]. Tommy, you said your individual treatment sessions really didn't accomplish much, and I think it's fair to say that both you and your folks need to be seen together in order to help with this problem. I hear how angry everybody has been, but in my experience what lies behind a good deal of anger is hurt, and I think you are all hurting at this point. I would like to try to be of help to you with the problem, because it seems to me that you do all care about each other, even if that doesn't come out too directly. I think it has been very helpful getting together with all of you for these first few sessions, and I would like to feel able to meet with any of you individually again, but for the next several weeks I would like to see Mr. and Mrs. Q. and Tommy together to focus in on the recent problems. (p. 191, with changes in notation)

It also may be useful toward the end of the family interview to ask whether there is anything else you should know about how the family is functioning. Ask about any recent changes, problems, or stressors that the family members think are noteworthy.

Following is an example of an interview segment that illustrates this technique. The M. family was seen for an initial evaluation session several days after 17-year-old Ken was treated in a hospital emergency room for signs of acute psychotic episode. The M. family consists of parents (IE-F = father, IE-M = mother), 17-year-old Ken (IE-K = Ken), and 20-year-old Susan (IE-S = Susan). (Karpel & Strauss, 1983, pp. 131–132, with changes in notation):

IR: Let me ask all of you again. In recent weeks, recent months, have there been any other changes for people in the family or the family as a whole or any other problem areas besides the situations you've mentioned? Susan, you were nodding before.

IE-S: Yes. Well, Dad drinks. Okay, and I think it has a lot to do with everything that goes on. He escapes by having a drink when he comes home at night. I don't know how much otherwise he drinks, but to me that is an escape, just as it is to go out and smoke a joint, or, for me, some nights, just to go out and have a few drinks. Only I feel for myself that, especially recently, you can't escape it, you can't just go out and have a drink or go out and smoke pot, 'cause it catches up to you. It goes, it's still there the next day, whether you face it or not, and I think that has a lot to do with a lot of our problems.

IR: How does that affect the family, you or other people in the family, from your point of view?

IE-S: Well we don't really talk. We're hardly together as a family as a whole very often, even for supper. You never know who's gonna be there…I think that…

IR: Okay. Mr. M., any thoughts about what your daughter's been saying?

IE-F: She's saying I have a drinking problem. Well, I suppose I do, I've been drinking for thirty years and it's an out. I go to bed at night, and the next morning it's like nothing happened. I'm talking about the problems, and I try to go to work and forget 'em. There was times that I didn't.

IR: The problems…

IE-F: Through the years, like I say, he (Ken) didn't work and we decided that he should work or whatever or help around the house…it would bother me, there was times, I worked eighteen years in one job and I think maybe not altogether but I stayed out of work a few days because of him and different things related. I left that job after 18 years.

IR: What were the reasons for that?

IE-F: I really don't know. I'd get upset, thinking about my problems, and then at work I'd get into an argument or get upset with them, and then one time I just decided to get out.

IE-S: But that didn't, it didn't…

IE-F: Well I say, you say I have a drinking problem, it isn't just drinking, it's…

IE-S: It didn't start just yesterday.

IE-F: No it started…

IE-S: I can remember…when you wanted your keys to take a ride…

IE-K: That's when I remember the first time I saw you drunk. I was only, what, 8 or 9 years old.

IE-S: I remember that too…

IE-K: You know how much that hurts when you're a little kid?

IR: Okay, Mrs. M., you seem to be reacting to what was being said.

IE-M: I honestly feel that my husband doesn't think it's so much of a problem. He's a good provider, does his work, does his job, he's a good father, it's that he doesn't realize that this is a problem, being a father also means you're there when I need you, you're not just sleeping because you've drunk too much. He doesn't see this side I guess. I really don't think he thinks it's such a problem.

[The interviewer then would add appropriate closing comments.]

Illustration of the Phases of a Family Interview

The following interview is an edited version of the three phases of a family interview that took place in a hospital. Toward the end of the interview, the interviewer summarized some important family dynamics. You will need considerable experience to make this type of summary. (The case and commentary have been edited and reprinted from *Journal of Adolescence, 14,* P. Reder, C. Lucey, and G. Fredman, "The Challenge of Deliberate Self-Harm by Young Adolescents," 135–148, 1991, by permission of the publisher, Academic Press Limited, London.)

CASE 4-1. ANNA'S FAMILY

A pediatrician referred Anna, a 15-year-old girl, for evaluation. Anna had been admitted the previous day because of an overdose of aspirin. She had told the pediatrician that she wanted to die. Anna's parents were divorced, and she was their only child. She is currently living with her mother (the pediatrician was unsure which parent was legally responsible for Anna). Anna and both of her parents were requested to attend the interview. Initially, Mr. E., the father, appeared hostile and answered the questions curtly; however, he later became more engaged in the exploration. Mrs. E., the mother, seemed emotionally brittle. She sat upright in her chair and made little eye contact with anyone. Anna entered the room unsteadily and sat between her parents. Although she was fully conscious, her speech was slightly slurred. She showed no evidence of a depressive disorder or of another psychological disorder. Outwardly, she was self-confident, assertive, and articulate. The interviewer introduced himself and explained his method of working. (Abbreviations are as follows: IR = interviewer, IE-F = father, IE-M = mother, IE-C = child.)

IR: I am Dr. Brown from the Child Psychiatry Department. Our department has an arrangement with the pediatric staff that if someone comes in having taken pills they ask us to see the person. They would like to know whether Anna can be discharged and whether anything else should happen after that. So that is why I am seeing you. I understand that you are divorced. What is the legal arrangement about Anna?

IE-F: We have joint custody.

IR: What does that mean in practice?

IE-F: (Frostily) The decisions are a joint responsibility.

IR: Anna, I was told that you came in yesterday after taking some pills. What happened?

IE-C: I swallowed 41 aspirins…yesterday morning.

IR: Who was the first to know?

IE-C: Mom.

IR: How did she find out?

IE-C: I came down and told her.

IR: And who second…after her?

IE-C: Dad.

IR: So what was your mother's reaction?

IE-C: She can tell you. (Pause)

IR: And your dad's?

IE-C: I don't know.

IR: Can you guess?

IE-C: I expect he was surprised.

IR: (To Mr. E.) Is that so?

IE-F: (Abruptly) Of course.

(Pause)

Initially, the interviewer tries to track the communication implicit in Anna's overdose—that is, for whom it was intended and that person's response. However, the family members signal their difficulty discussing emotional and relationship issues. Therefore, the interviewer changes to a different topic—how the family feels about receiving help.

IR: If there had been no arrangement between Child Psychiatry and Pediatrics, would you have thought you needed a meeting like this…with a person like me?

IE-F: Anna has been seeing a child psychiatrist…

IE-C: I stopped six months ago….It made no difference.

IE-F: (To Anna) No?

IE-C: No.

IE-M: She may need help. She has to feel it is helpful herself.

(Pause)

IR: Do you think there is a need now?

IE-F: Yes.

IR: For what?

IE-F: For a decision about any action.

(Mrs. E. nods agreement. Anna remains silent.)

IR: How come now? How come you think there's a need for help now?

IE-M: Anna is depressed. She gets bullied at school. There's this unkind girl who's rejected her…. They had become very close. Also we have split up…. Anna's been on an emotional seesaw and suffering for some time.

IR: So Anna's been suffering for some time. Has anyone else been suffering?

IE-M: (Tersely) No.

IE-F: (Impatiently) It's Anna that needs help. She suffered because of our separation.

IR: (To Mr. E.) In what way did she suffer? How particularly?

IE-C: (Interrupts) I'm almost over it.

Anna's parents offer "her depression" as the problem that needs treating, even though they acknowledge that her emotional state is responsive to other difficulties. Anna seems both to accept and to reject her parents' insistence that the problem resides in her.

IR: How long had you been suffering, before you started to get over it?

IE-C: My friend, she hurt me. I didn't do anything.

IR: What happened between you and your friend?

IE-C: She was my best friend, we talked a lot, were really close. Then suddenly she changed, she wasn't interested anymore.

IR: Has there been anybody to replace her?

IE-C: A best friend?

IR: What about anybody in the family, whom you could talk to?

IE-C: Well, she replaced my grandmother. When I was little, I used to talk to my grandmother. But then it wasn't so good…. She used to get involved in "the things." Anyway, she's old and frail now, and I see a lot less of her.

Having lost the confiding relationship with her grandmother, Anna then lost her best friend.

IR: "The things"? How do you mean?

IE-C: (Glancing uncomfortably at each parent) I feel tired…. I think I'm going to be sick.

Although sympathetic to Anna, the interviewer implies that these areas can be explored.

IR: If you need it, we can get you a bowl…. It seems your parents have a problem.

IE-C: Yes.

IR: How have they tried to solve it?

IE-C: They kept pushing me to see Dr. D.

(Dr. D. is an experienced adolescent psychiatrist.)

IR: Well, what about your parents? Can you talk to them?

IE-C: I'm not sure of it.

IE-M: Anna used to visit an osteopath for cranial massage, and then she saw Dr. D.

IR: When was that?

IE-M: When she was 14. She saw him every two weeks…for about nine months. She stopped about six months ago.

IR: (To Anna) What was the reason for your seeing Dr. D.?

IE-C: My mother wanted me to…because of my depression.

IR: Why did you agree to go?

IE-C: My mother was keen. She wanted me to talk to someone.

IR: She was more keen than you? Why was she more keen than you?

IE-C: (Shrugging) I couldn't see the point of help…I just wanted to die.

IR: But you told your mother.

IE-C: I realized that it might not have worked…I might not actually die and I didn't want to end up a vegetable.

The family's attempted solutions to its relationship problems have been for Anna to receive treatment. Anna communicates a sense of helplessness—she has wanted to change but it has seemed impossible. She also has rendered everyone else helpless. The interviewer tracks the effect of her behavior to reveal its hidden communication.

IR: If it had worked…if you had died…what do you think might have happened?

IE-C: People would have felt guilty.

IR: Who?

IE-C: My parents.

IR: Who would have felt the most guilty?

IE-C: Equally.

IR: Would anything else have happened?

IE-C: They would have spoken together.

IR: And said what?

IE-C: (Facetiously) "Nice day!" I don't think it would have brought them together.

IR: Who would have missed you the most…if you had died?

IE-C: Mom would miss me a lot. Dad too. They'd never get over it.

IR: Who do you think would get over it first?

IE-C: My friends.

IR: In what way would your mother's life be different…if you had died?
(Mrs. E. began to cry.)

IE-C: Do we have to do this? Can't you see? (pointing to her mother)…But if I had managed it, it would have been worth it.

Anna gives two contradictory messages, "I'm glad I did not expose my mother to this hurt" and "I wish I had," which reflect the conflict she experiences. Her resolution is to attribute responsibility for her mother's suffering to the interviewer.

IR: Does it happen often, Anna, that you are somehow part of the reason for everyone to be upset, but then you work hard to try to calm them down again?

IE-M: Yes. She feels she must protect us both. Like, when she has a good time with me, she keeps quiet about it. Also with her grandmother, she keeps this quiet too. Look, my mother and her other grandmother, they've never liked each other…more like hate. It's made worse because my mother looked after Anna a lot when she was a baby and Anna often visited in the holidays. My mother claims credit for rearing Anna, and the two mothers are always arguing. Anna is torn between the two women.

IR: (To Mrs. E.) Is that how you see it?

IE-M: Yes, in the past. But now the difficulty for Anna is hearing about her father's new wife and their child. But I'm also under pressure.

IR: Do you think that you are under the greatest pressure at the moment?

IE-M: (Crying) No. I hadn't thought so. I just want Anna better.

IE-C: (Looking first to her mother and then to the interviewer) Her brother died last year, and she has been trying to sort out the arrangements. She had to go up to Oxford to sort out the memorial.

It emerges that Anna's overdose may be a metaphor for unresolved loss.

IR: Do you think she's got over it yet?

IE-C: No.
(Mrs. E. shook herself as though trying to pull herself together.)

IR: (To Mrs. E.) Have you turned to anybody for help?

IE-M: It's more or less sorted out.

IR: (To the family) So whom do people tend to turn to?

IE-C: I can't discuss anything with mom…she is so biased.

IE-M: I turned to Anna…in the past, not now.

IR: (To Mrs. E.) What about Anna's grandmother?

IE-M: She used to turn to Anna, but not now.

IR: (To Mr. E.) And you?

IE-F: I think things through myself.

IR: It seems that these days nobody turns to anybody. What would have to happen to allow any of you to turn to each other again?

IE-C: Well, mom and gran need someone.
(Pause)

Anna's self-harm may be an attempt to increase the connectedness among members of the family. However, the belief that the "two mothers" cannot get together and her father's undeclared loyalty conflict between his mother, his ex-wife, and his second wife make this impossible. Anna feels involved but hopeless, so she declines to define relationships by making ambiguous or contradictory statements.

IR: It seems that at this point we should look at two things. First of all, about discharge and who will decide it; and second, what help, if any, is needed after that. Anna, do you think any help is needed for anything?

IE-C: Don't know…. Maybe just time.
(Interviewer looks to Mr. E.)

IE-F: My mother is so isolated at the moment. I'm trying to buy a house for her to live near us…. I could talk to Anna more (looking at her questioningly).

IR: (To Mrs. E.) What about you, do you think any help is needed for anything?

IE-M: Maybe at the school. I'm not sure if I should remove her and put her in a different one.

IR: Do you think there's a role for us…for our Department?

IE-M: Don't know. Psychotherapy perhaps?

IR: Anna?

IE-C: Something's got to be done about my depressions. It could help…but why bother?

IE-F: (Imploringly to Anna) It couldn't hurt. It might help.

IR: (To both parents) The decision about Anna's going home is yours, because you have joint custody. What do you want to happen?

IE-C: (Interrupts) I'm not sure I want to go home.

IE-M: I'm worried about her being left on her own. Do we need immediate steps?

IE-F: I could enlarge the house. (To Anna) What do you think?

IE-C: If mom can cope, I'll go home.
(Mrs. E. says nothing.)

IE-C: I want to go back to school quickly. I don't want anyone there to know…. They'll get suspicious if I miss any more time.

IE-F: (To the interviewer) I want your advice. What should we do?

IR: It's very hard for me to advise. As I see it, it's important for you, as Anna's parents, legally responsible for her, to reach a satisfactory decision…that you both agree with. If you can't decide, I can think about the alternatives with you.

Mr. and Mrs. E. spend the next 15 minutes discussing this but are unable to reach a decision. They turn to Anna repeatedly, asking her to make their decision for them, and whenever a resolution seems possible, Anna maintains ambiguity by offering a reason why it cannot work.

IR: I'll leave you to think about those two things…discharge and help. I'll come back in a few minutes.

It seems that the family members have become organized by an unspoken belief that resolving their interpersonal problems would involve considerable suffering. Instead, they give ambiguous messages to each other so that their relationships remain undefined. They also draw in one person as a mediator between two others with the conflicting injunctions "Try to sort this out…" and "…but nothing can change." Similarly, the family wants the interviewer to take responsibility for solving its dilemmas but also indicates that resolution is impossible. This mirrors Anna's position in the family system. Anna has learned to give contradictory messages that prevent her from defining her position too closely.

IR: I have some ideas, which you may not agree with. I think that Anna does have a problem, but it's not so much about depression. More, that you are all caught up in the middle of complex relationship problems that you're still in the middle of sorting out. These are between you, Mrs. E., you, Mr. E., Anna's grandmother, and Anna. Anna, you are right in the middle of it. (She nods agreement.) You keep hoping that people outside will…sort of… "take the heat" off you and sort it out for you. We could meet with you as a unit…all four, including Mr. E.'s mother, to look at the relationship issues. This might allow the grown-ups to sort out the things that belong to them, and for Anna to deal with her bits.

IE-F: My mother couldn't face it.

IE-C: Yes. It would be too much for her.

IR: The invitation is to all of you, whoever comes.

IE-F: We're looking to you to tell us what should happen. You're a psychiatrist. Wouldn't it be better for you to see Anna on her own?

IE-C: Look, maybe we should try.

IR: So that's my offer of help. You need to decide what happens. Do you want Anna discharged? I'm sure the pediatric staff will ask us if Anna can go home.

IE-M: I can't take her home.

IE-F: Maybe she could stay here for the night… have a good rest.

IE-C: I want to go to school. I don't want them to know.

IE-F: You could come home to me.

IE-C: You've got no room.

IE-F: (To the interviewer) You said you could tell us the alternatives. Where could she go, if not here?

IR: What occurs to me are she could go home to you, Mrs. E.; she could go home to you, Mr. E.; she could go home to someone else's house; she could stay here; or go into care; or to an adolescent psychiatry unit…an in-patient unit.

IE-F: What do you want, Anna?

IE-C: Definitely not care, or the last one. Maybe I'll stay in the hospital tonight.

IE-F: Yes. How about another day at the hospital, until you're stronger.

IE-C: But I need constant company and I wouldn't be able to sleep here.

Eventually, Anna's parents decided that she should stay in the hospital for one more night and the next afternoon would go home with her father. They agreed as a family to attend therapy. They came for two of the three sessions offered in the Child and Family Psychiatry Department. During the sessions, they repeated many interactions described above. By the time they decided to stop treatment, Anna was expressing more hope about her future.

Tasks in Preparation for a Second Family Interview

If you plan to ask the family to return for a second interview, you may want the family to record information about a problem area. This information may help both you and the family understand the problem better. For example, you might give each member the same task, such as recording disagreements that occur between family members or recording positive statements, or both. When they bring this information to the second session, you can study, for example, the types of disagreements that occurred or positive statements made, the extent to which the family members agree and disagree about what happened during the week, whether there is more agreement between the child and one parent than between the child and the other parent, and whether there is more agreement about certain types of behaviors than others (for example, pleasing versus displeasing behaviors, passive versus active behaviors, cognitive behaviors versus affective behaviors).

Visiting the Home

Whenever possible, consider visiting the child's home to obtain a more comprehensive picture of the family. You can observe family members interacting, environmental stressors, and the physical characteristics of the home. However, do not visit the home without the permission of the parents. In general, you will want to respect the family's wishes if it does not want you to visit the home. However, there are exceptions to this guideline. For example, in cases of alleged child maltreatment, Child Protective Services workers may enter the home without the permission of a parent or caregiver to check out the allegation (check your state laws). In such situations, a law enforcement officer also may be present. Law enforcement personnel can enter the home without the family's permission under certain circumstances, such as when they have obtained a warrant or when they have requisite knowledge that a child may be in danger. Case workers in social agencies can make unannounced visits to evaluate foster homes. Parental permission to enter a home isn't needed when an agency has a court order to enter the home.

Observing the home.   Your observations should help you to answer such questions as the following (Besharov, 1990; Garbarino, Guttman, & Seeley, 1987; Kropenske & Howard, 1994; Polansky, Borgman, & De Saix, 1972):

1. Is the home located in a safe area?
2. What is the comfort level of the home?
3. What is the safety level of the home?
4. Are there any safety or health hazards?
5. What is the state of repair of the home (including electrical system, gas lines, water supply, and sanitary facilities)?
6. What is the condition of family possessions?
7. What are the sanitary conditions of the home?
8. Are there rodents or other infestations?
9. Is the food supply adequate, both in quantity and in nutritional content?
10. What play equipment is present?
11. What are the sleeping arrangements?
12. What is the quality of the sleeping areas?
13. If there is a newborn child, what supplies do the parents have for the baby?
14. How are the children dressed?
15. How are the children groomed?
16. What educational and recreational possessions are available?
17. Do they have a phone?
18. Do they have a car?
19. Do they use public transportation?
20. Are mature theme videos or pornographic materials accessible to the children?
21. How do the children interact with the parents?
22. How do the parents interact with the children?
23. How do the children get along with each other?
24. Who is living in the home?
25. What are their relationships to the children?
26. What are their occupations?
27. How do the parents interact with each other?
28. Is there evidence of domestic violence?

To help you to answer these and related questions, complete the Home Environmental Checklist in Table 4-5. (See Chapter 20 for a discussion of domestic violence.)

Observing parent-child interactions. Three sets of guidelines follow for observing parent-child interactions. These guidelines are relevant for observing interactions either in the home or in a clinic. The first is for observing parent-infant interactions (Baird, Haas, McCormick, Carruth, & Turner, 1992; Hirshberg, 1993), the second, for observing parent-toddler interactions (Hirshberg, 1993; Zahn-Waxler, Iannotti, Cummings, & Denham, 1990), and the third, for observing interactions between a parent and a school-aged child (Mahoney, Powell, & Finger, 1986; Stein, Gambrill, & Wiltse, 1978).

Overall, with any age child, you will want to observe whether the parent (a) can relax and be comfortable with his or her child, (b) is accepting and affectionate with his or her child, (c) is sensitive to the child's needs, wants, and desires, (d) seems able to take the child's perspective, (e) is alert to issues of safety and protection while allowing the child freedom to explore his or her environment within the limits of the child's age and ability, and (f) helps the child acquire new skills. Similarly, in all interactions with the parent, you will want to observe how the child responds to the parent's behavior or lack thereof.

You are not expected to keep all of the guidelines in mind during an observation. Rather, the guidelines are designed to help you prepare for your observations and to remind you of things to include in your report.

PARENT-INFANT INTERACTIONS

1. *Social interactions.* Note, for example, whether the parent and infant interact socially. Does the parent look and smile at the infant as the infant looks and smiles at the parent? How does the infant respond to physical contact with the parent?

2. *Responsiveness.* Note, for example, whether the parent responds to the infant's interpersonal signals and whether the infant responds to the parent's interpersonal signals. Does the parent take a toy offered by the infant? How does the infant respond to the parent's actions and presence? Does the infant take a toy offered by the parent?

3. *Directing.* Note, for example, whether the parent directs the infant in an attempt to lead the pace, content, or form of the infant's behavior. Does the parent say "Put them on your arm" to an infant who is playing with beads or direct the infant in similar ways? How does the infant respond to the parent's directions?

4. *Intrusiveness.* Note, for example, whether the parent's intrusiveness leads to breaks in the infant's attention. Does the parent offer a rattle to an infant who is playing with beads or break the infant's attention in similar ways? How does the infant respond to the parent's intrusiveness?

5. *Joining.* Note, for example, whether the parent joins the infant's play. Does the parent pat an object similar to the one the infant patted? How does the infant respond when the parent joins him or her in play?

6. *Imitation.* Note, for example, whether the parent responds to a behavior initiated by the infant. Does the parent kiss the infant after the infant kisses the parent or imitate the infant's coos in response to the infant's cooing? How does the infant respond to the parent's imitation?

7. *Affect and attitude.* Note, for example, whether the parent and infant display affect and, if affect is displayed, the type displayed. Do the parent and infant show (a) pleasure, enjoyment, and a happy mood, (b) warmth, tenderness, and affection, (c) irritability, anger, impatience, or hostility, or (d) approval or disapproval? Does the parent (a) hold and comfort the infant, (b) use affectionate statements, such as "You're Mommy's friend, sweetie," (c) use positive statements such as "That's great!" about the infant's behavior, or (d) display affection in expressions or behavior, such as smiling with eye contact, holding, or hugging the infant? How does the infant respond to the parent? Does the infant hug the parent or express other signs of warmth and affection?

8. *Safety and protection.* Note, for example, whether the parent is alert to protecting the physical safety of the infant. Is the parent continuously monitoring the infant's

Table 4-5
Home Environmental Checklist

HOME ENVIRONMENTAL CHECKLIST

Name of family _____   Date _____

Date of visit _____   Name of rater _____

Directions: Circle Y (yes), N (no), or ? (can't evaluate) for each item.

Neighborhood
Y N ?   1. Outside of home in good condition.
Y N ?   2. Other homes and apartment buildings in neighborhood in good condition.
Y N ?   3. Neighborhood free of garbage and litter.
Y N ?   4. Sidewalks and streets in good repair.

Utilities
Y N ?   5. Water in home.
Y N ?   6. Electricity/gas in home.
Y N ?   7. Heating in home.

Layout of Home
Y N ?   8. Room sufficient for inhabitants.

Safety of Home
Y N ?   9. Exits adequate.
Y N ?   10. Electric wiring in good condition and unexposed.
Y N ?   11. Heating appliances in good condition.
Y N ?   12. Cooking appliances properly vented.
Y N ?   13. Poisons, dangerous sprays, cleaning fluids, and open medication bottles stored out of child's reach.
Y N ?   14. Play area and inside of home free from broken glass and dangerous items, such as rusting metal and sharp objects.
Y N ?   15. Floors and stairs free of hazards.
Y N ?   16. Tools safely stored.
Y N ?   17. Guns and rifles safely stored.
Y N ?   18. Gates at top of stairs (if toddler in home).
Y N ?   19. Decals on glass doors at child's eye level (if toddler in home).
Y N ?   20. Yard-gate latch secure (if toddler in home).
Y N ?   21. Electrical outlets covered or unexposed (if toddler in home).

State of Repair
Y N ?   22. Roof in good condition.
Y N ?   23. Windows in good condition.
Y N ?   24. Plumbing in good condition.
Y N ?   25. Screens in good condition.
Y N ?   26. Floors in good condition.
Y N ?   27. Walls in good condition.
Y N ?   28. Paint in good condition.
Y N ?   29. Furniture in good condition.
Y N ?   30. Play equipment in good condition.
Y N ?   31. Fence in good condition.
Y N ?   32. Automobile in good condition.

Hygienic Conditions
Y N ?   33. Toilet in good condition.
Y N ?   34. Odors satisfactory in bathroom.
Y N ?   35. Kitchen in good condition.
Y N ?   36. Odors satisfactory in kitchen.
Y N ?   37. Other rooms in good condition.
Y N ?   38. Odors satisfactory in other rooms.
Y N ?   39. Yard in good condition.
Y N ?   40. Food properly stored.
Y N ?   41. Garbage properly stored.
Y N ?   42. No signs of rodents or insects, such as mice or roaches.
Y N ?   43. Pets adequately cared for (adequately fed and feces adequately disposed of).

Physical Properties
Y N ?   44. Noise level acceptable.
Y N ?   45. Lighting satisfactory.
Y N ?   46. Temperature satisfactory.

Health
Y N ?   47. Physical health of child appears good.
Y N ?   48. Physical health of other children appears good.
Y N ?   49. Physical health of parents appears good.
Y N ?   50. Child appears to have adequate dental care.
Y N ?   51. Other children appear to have adequate dental care.
Y N ?   52. Parents appear to have adequate dental care.

Food and Nutrition
Y N ?   53. Child appears to be adequately fed.
Y N ?   54. Other children appear to be adequately fed.
Y N ?   55. Parents appear to be adequately fed.
Y N ?   56. Meals appear to provide well-balanced diet of nurturing food.

Clothing, Linens, and Furniture
Y N ?   57. Child dressed appropriately.
Y N ?   58. Other children dressed appropriately.
Y N ?   59. Clothing clean and mended.
Y N ?   60. Bedding in good condition.
Y N ?   61. Bed or mattress in good condition.
Y N ?   62. Furniture adequate for family.

Grooming
Y N ?   63. Child adequately groomed.
Y N ?   64. Child washes before meals.
Y N ?   65. Child brushes teeth before going to bed.
Y N ?   66. Child washes hands after using toilet.

(Continued)

Table 4-5 (Continued)

Y N ?   67. Soap available.
Y N ?   68. Towels available.

Sleeping Arrangements

Y N ?   69. Child has place for sleeping at bedtime away from family living and recreation space.
Y N ?   70. Child 5 years old or older sleeps in separate room from parents.
Y N ?   71. Members of the family do not sleep more than two to a bed.
Y N ?   72. Child appears to be well rested.

Educational and Recreational Materials

Y N ?   73. Educational toys in home.
Y N ?   74. Educational books in home.
Y N ?   75. Tape recorder in home.
Y N ?   76. Computer in home.
Y N ?   77. Typewriter in home.
Y N ?   78. Camera in home.

Communication and Transportation

Y N ?   79. Telephone in home.
Y N ?   80. TV in home.
Y N ?   81. VCR in home.
Y N ?   82. Radio in home.
Y N ?   83. Automobile available.
Y N ?   84. Public transportation nearby.
Y N ?   85. Newspaper in home.
Y N ?   86. Magazines in home.

Parenting

Y N ?   87. Parent supervises child—in and outside the home—appropriately for child's age.
Y N ?   88. Parent enforces traffic rules about going into the street.

Y N ?   89. Parent follows through on rewards.
Y N ?   90. Parent follows through on punishment.
Y N ?   91. Parent listens to child.
Y N ?   92. Parent comforts child when child needs it.
Y N ?   93. Parent uses appropriate punishment.
Y N ?   94. Parent uses appropriate rewards.
Y N ?   95. Parent and child comfortable with demonstrations of affection.
Y N ?   96. Parent cautions child about potential dangers in home (such as flaking paint).
Y N ?   97. Parent sensitive to child's feelings and needs.
Y N ?   98. Parent treats child in a manner consistent with child's age and level of ability.

Interpersonal Relations

Y N ?   99. Parent doesn't get drunk in presence of child.
Y N ? 100. Parent doesn't use drugs in presence of child.
Y N ? 101. Parent doesn't argue with someone else excessively in presence of child.
Y N ? 102. Parents do not expose child to domestic physical violence.
Y N ? 103. Parents do not expose child to pornographic materials.
Y N ? 104. Parents do not expose child to prostitution.
Y N ? 105. Child shows no fear of parents.
Y N ? 106. Child shows no fear of siblings.
Y N ? 107. Child shows no fear of any other relative.
Y N ? 108. Child goes to parent for comfort or assurance.
Y N ? 109. Child gets along well with parents.
Y N ? 110. Child gets along well with siblings.
Y N ? 111. Child gets along well with other relatives.
Y N ? 112. Child gets along well with other children.
Y N ? 113. Parents interact well with each other.
Y N ? 114. Parents interact well with other relatives.
Y N ? 115. Parents interact well with neighbors.

Other comments_____

_____

_____

_____

safety and taking action to protect him or her when necessary? Is the parent appropriately vigilant and protective, or either overprotective and highly anxious about the baby's safety on the one hand or careless and lacking in awareness or concern on the other? Does the infant show either excessive caution and timidity, or recklessness? (Sample questions are from Hirschberg, 1993, p. 183.)

9. *Physiological regulation.* Note, for example, whether the parent is alert to the infant's needs for food, warmth, stimulation, elimination, and sleep. Does the parent recognize when the infant is hungry or when the stimulation should be reduced or increased? How does the infant respond to the parent's attempt at regulation?

10. *Teaching and learning.* Note, for example, whether the parent tries to help the infant learn new skills and how the parent goes about teaching the infant those skills. Does the parent show flexibility in helping the infant and keep the infant focused on the task? How does the infant respond to the parent's teaching?

11. *Power and control.* Note, for example, how the parent presents himself or herself to the infant. Is the parent calm, confident, and in control of himself or herself, of the

infant, and of the situation he or she is in, or does the parent appear passive, overwhelmed, disorganized, confused, tense, or potentially explosive? How does the parent manage the challenges the infant may present to him or her during the observation, such as refusal to clean up, constant interruptions, or acting-out behavior? How does the infant respond to the parent's attempt to control (or parent's failure to control) the situation?

PARENT-TODDLER INTERACTIONS

1. *Attunement to toddler's needs and to parent's needs.* Note, for example, whether the parent is attuned to the toddler's needs. Does the parent (a) simplify or provide more information when the toddler apparently does not understand what to do, (b) show sensitivity to the toddler's visual perspectives by moving objects into or out of the toddler's field of vision or by giving information about the location of the objects, or (c) indicate awareness of the toddler's wants, needs, or feelings without the toddler explicitly expressing these? Note whether the toddler is attuned to the parent's needs. Does the toddler push the parent to his or her limits? Does the toddler recognize when the parent is happy, sad, tired, angry, and so forth?

2. *Promotion of prosocial behaviors.* Note, for example, whether the parent verbally encourages prosocial behavior. Does the parent (a) state "It's her turn" or something similar when the toddler is playing with another child or (b) share, help, or show compassion to the toddler or to another child or adult who is present?

3. *Perspective-taking or self-awareness.* Note, for example, whether the parent encourages perspective-taking or self-awareness. Does the parent (a) direct the toddler's attention to the feelings of others in the room by making a comment such as "Why is John so sad?", (b) direct the toddler's attention to the toddler's own thoughts by saying "You thought that this was the big block" or something similar, or (c) use another person as a point of reference by saying "It's the one in front of Paul" or something similar?

4. *Affect and attitude.* Note, for example, whether the parent and toddler display affect and, if affect is displayed, the type displayed. Do the parent and toddler show (a) pleasure, enjoyment, and a happy mood, (b) warmth, tenderness, and affection, (c) irritability, anger, impatience, or hostility, or (d) approval or disapproval. Does the parent (a) use affectionate statements, such as "You're Mommy's big girl," (b) use positive statements such as "That's great!" about the toddler's behavior, or (c) display affection in expressions or behavior, such as smiling with eye contact, holding, or hugging the toddler? Does the toddler hug the parent or express other signs of warmth and affection?

5. *Modulated control.* Note, for example, whether the parent modulates his or her behavior. Does the parent (a) use qualified commands or questions to direct the toddler's behavior, such as "Would you like to…," "Why don't you…," "How about if we…," "Maybe you could…," or (b) bargain or cajole by saying "You can have juice if you finish cleaning up" or something similar?

6. *Power and control.* Note, for example, how the parent presents himself or herself to the toddler. Is the parent calm, confident, and in control of himself or herself, of the toddler, and of the situation he or she is in, or does the parent appear passive, overwhelmed, disorganized, confused, tense, or potentially explosive? How does the parent manage the challenges the toddler may present to him or her during the observation, such as refusal to clean up, constant interruptions, or acting-out behavior? Does the parent use unqualified, power-assertive methods such as direct commands, prohibitions, yelling, or physical control methods? How does the toddler respond to the parent's attempt to control (or parent's failure to control) the situation?

7. *Physiological regulation.* Note, for example, whether the parent is alert to the toddler's needs for food, warmth, stimulation, elimination, and sleep. Does the parent recognize when the toddler is hungry or when the stimulation should be reduced or increased? How does the toddler respond to the parent's attempt at regulation?

8. *Teaching and learning.* Note, for example, whether the parent tries to help the toddler learn new skills and how the parent goes about teaching the toddler those skills. Does the parent show flexibility in helping the toddler and keep the toddler focused on the task? How does the toddler respond to the parent's teaching?

INTERACTIONS BETWEEN A PARENT AND A SCHOOL-AGED CHILD

1. *Affect and attitude.* Note, for example, whether the parent and child display affect and, if affect is displayed, the type displayed. Do the parent and child show (a) pleasure, enjoyment, and a happy mood, (b) warmth, tenderness, and affection, (c) irritability, anger, impatience, or hostility, or (d) approval or disapproval?

2. *Responsiveness.* Note, for example, whether the parent is responsive to the child and the child responsive to the parent and the type of responsiveness displayed. Does the parent (a) respond to the child's distress, (b) make suggestions to the child, or (c) respond to the child's questions with caring and sensitivity? How does the child respond to the parent's needs and requests?

3. *Stimulation of the child and parent.* Note, for example, whether the parent stimulates the child and the child stimulates the parent and the type of stimulation displayed. Does the parent (a) provide toys for the child, (b) play with the child, (c) make physical contact with the child, (d) talk to the child, or (e) encourage the child? Does the child introduce new ideas to the parent?

4. *Power and control.* Note, for example, whether the parent controls the child's behavior and the child controls the parent's behavior and the type of control used. Does the parent (a) protect the child, (b) control the child's play and behavior by ordering, by demanding compliance, by threats, or by other means, (c) restrict the child's activities, or

(d) criticize or punish the child? Does the child demand certain things from the parent or criticize the parent? Note also how the parent deals with issues of child management—for example, (a) what behavior of the child evokes praise or punishment from the parent, (b) the length of time that elapses before the parent responds to the child's behavior, (c) whether the parent ignores certain behaviors, (d) whether the parent is consistent in following through on the promised reward or punishment, (e) what the reward or punishment is (a hug or a positive statement, physical punishment or a demeaning statement), (f) whether the promised punishment is realistic ("You can't go out for the next two months"), (g) whether the parent makes threatening statements ("If you aren't good, I'll leave you" or "I won't love you anymore if you do that again"), (h) whether the parent tells the child why he or she is being punished, (i) whether the parent metes out punishments and rewards uniformly to all the children involved in the behavior, (j) whether verbal communications accompany punishments or rewards, (k) whether, in two-parent families, both parents mete out the punishments and rewards, (l) whether the parents agree or disagree about the punishments and rewards, (m) whether the parent bribes the child ("If you leave me alone, I'll give you such and such later on"), and (n) whether the parent sets limits for the child ("You may go as far as the street corner, but you cannot cross the street").

Conditions affecting home observations. Your ability to do a home observation may be influenced by the conditions you meet in the home. You may be fortunate and find parents who are grateful for your help, cooperative, and desirous of your services. If this is the case, you can probably spend time with the family and make your evaluation. On the other hand, you may find hostile parents who resent your presence or you may find frightening conditions, such as a filthy house with brutalized children. In such cases, you must exercise caution and good judgment. You can probably perform only a cursory inspection and may need to leave quickly. *If you suspect that your visit may be dangerous because of conditions in the home or neighborhood, don't go to the house unless accompanied by a police officer.*

In evaluating the child's home, remember that poverty will affect the family's material possessions. For example, if there is no phone or car or if the home lacks toys, it doesn't mean that the family is worse than a family that can afford those things. *Poverty shouldn't bias your observations.*

When children and parents know that they are being observed, their behavior may change; such changes in behavior are referred to as *reactive effects.* For example, they may feel conspicuous or anxious, sweat profusely, stammer, or talk more quickly than usual, or they may appear relaxed, talk more slowly and distinctly than usual, censor swear words, or behave in other ways that show their best behavior. It is safe to assume that when you observe children and their parents, reactive effects are usually present. However, unless the children or parents tell you that

their behavior was atypical, you will have difficulty evaluating how representative the observed behaviors were.

Case illustration. Here is a case that shows the value of a home visit (Grevious, 1985).

CASE 4-2. TODD

Todd was acting out in school and falling behind in his work. Mrs. B. complained of feeling overwhelmed and out of control and cited her son's behavior as proof of her difficulties. During a home visit, the interviewer observed that the family lived in a run-down building in a declining neighborhood. Despite these conditions, the apartment was immaculate. In addition, Mrs. B. had arranged for Todd to have his own sleeping and working space in the tiny apartment. The family's deep religious convictions also were evident in the presence of Bibles and several religious pictures and art work.

The home visit also yielded important information about the maternal grandmother's role in the family. Until recently, the grandmother had worked and maintained her own apartment. But an operation (amputation of a leg) had made her completely dependent on her daughter and grandson. Also, her chronic diabetic condition added considerable stress to the household environment. The interviewer spoke with the grandmother and observed the power struggle that was occurring between the grandmother and Mrs. B. Despite her ill health, the grandmother appeared to be the "power broker" in the family. The information obtained during the visit proved invaluable in clarifying problem areas and family strengths. The interviewer identified dysfunctional family patterns and moved to change them. Identifying family strengths helped Mrs. B. mobilize the energy necessary for change. (adapted from p. 118)

Evaluating the Family Interview

Table 4-6 lists questions for you to consider in evaluating six major areas of family functioning—namely, problem-solving style, communication patterns, roles and structure, affective responses and involvement, control mechanisms, and values and norms. The suggested questions are just a few of the many questions that you could ask about the family. You do not have to go through these questions item by item each time you complete a family interview. Rather, they are designed to sensitize you to family dynamics.

After you answer these questions, you can quantify your evaluations by completing the Family Rating Checklist (see Table 4-7). Finally, you can rate the family along a continuum from optimally healthy functioning to severely disturbed functioning in these six areas (see Table 4-8).

You also should consider the following questions in your evaluation of the family:

1. Who referred the family?
2. What is the composition of the family?
3. Who was at the interview?
4. How does the family provide models for its members; handle its successes and failures; recognize the talents, skills, and interests of its members; and use resources in the community?

Table 4-6
Questions for Six Major Areas of Family Functioning

Problem-Solving Style

1. How does the family solve problems and respond to conflict, stresses, and crises? (For example, do family members deny conflict, avoid conflict, skirt conflict, allow conflict to emerge but fail to bring it to any resolution, or allow conflict to emerge and bring it to resolution? Different styles may be appropriate on different occasions.)
2. Does the family have adequate problem-solving skills?
3. Does each family member have input into family decisions?
4. Do the parents have appropriate parenting skills?
5. Does the family engage in preventive health practices?
6. Does the family have enough money for basic home and child-care needs?
7. Does the family have access to preventive and medical services and to child-care services?
8. Do the parents' work schedules allow for solving problems with the entire family together?
9. What stresses is the family facing? (For example, what is the child's problem, disorder, or disability? Do any of the family members have a substance abuse problem? Are any family members in trouble with the law? Have any children been physically or sexually abused or neglected? Is there domestic violence?)
10. What environmental stresses are there outside of the immediate family?
11. Does the family have a supportive social network, such as an extended family, neighbors, friends, and co-workers?
12. To what extent is the family isolated?
13. What are the family's resources?
14. Is the family able to meet the educational, social, psychological, and physical needs of the child?
15. What are the help-seeking patterns of the family? (For example, do they seek help from doctors, ministers, relatives, friends, or the mental health system, or do they wait to be referred by schools, juvenile court, or the social welfare system?)

Communication Patterns

16. How do the family members exchange information and communicate their thoughts, feelings, and desires both verbally and nonverbally? (For example, are exchanges democratic, supportive, bidirectional, and accepting, or are they authoritarian, critical, unidirectional, and confrontational?)
17. What is the quality of the family's communications? (For example, are they clear and direct or vague and ambiguous?)
18. What is the quality of the family members' vocabulary, vocal tone, facial expressions, eye contact, and body language?
19. Does the family have any rules about what can and cannot be discussed?

20. Is there a family member who controls or directs the flow of communication?
21. Is there a family member who speaks for other members of the family (spokesperson)?
22. Do the family members listen to each other?
23. Do the family members interrupt one another during conversation?

Roles and Structure

24. Who are the members of the family, including their ages and genders?
25. What are the occupations of the family members?
26. What roles do the family members have?
27. Have there been any recent events in the family that have necessitated role changes?
28. What is the socioeconomic status of the family? (For example, what are the family's life style and material resources, and what educational opportunities does the family provide for its members?)
29. What are the living arrangements in the family, including individual space, basic amenities, and study facilities?
30. Who assumes the leadership roles?
31. Is the leadership appropriate?
32. Which family members make decisions?
33. How are disagreements between parents and children and between parent and parent settled?
34. Are the family members satisfied with the decisions?
35. Who keeps order in the family?
36. Are the attempts to keep order successful?
37. Who provides advice and suggestions?
38. Who assumes the follower roles?
39. Who supports whom?
40. Are these supports successful?
41. Who pairs with whom?
42. Which child, if any, functions as a parent surrogate?
43. Is the family cohesive and committed to its members?
44. How are the daily responsibilities handled by the family members?
45. How effective is the family in accomplishing its tasks?
46. Are the parents treating their children in a manner consistent with the children's developmental age?
47. What roles does each parent play in raising the children?
48. How is the community involved in the structure of the family?
49. Do the parents encourage expression of feelings and thoughts in the children?
50. Do the parents encourage social, intellectual, political, and cultural pursuits?
51. Do the parents encourage independence?
52. At what developmental level are the children functioning?
53. If there is an extended family, what roles do the other members play in raising the children?

(Continued)

Table 4-6 (*Continued*)

54. What is the family's understanding of the child's disability?
55. What types of changes have taken place in the family as a result of having a child with a psychological or medical disorder?
56. How is the family coping with the changes that have taken place?
57. How is the family reacting to its altered life style?
58. How does each family member cope with the changes?
59. How does the family assist in the child's rehabilitation? (If the disorder developed after the child was born, answer questions 60 to 62.)
60. What role in the family did the child with a psychological or medical disorder have *before* the disorder occurred?
61. What role in the family does the child with a psychological or medical disorder have *after* the disorder occurred?
62. Is the family more anxious now than before the child developed a psychological or medical disorder?
63. How has the presence of the child with a psychological or medical disorder affected the family's sense of well-being?
64. What is the family doing to restore its sense of well-being?
65. Does the family use the child with a psychological or medical disorder as a scapegoat for any of its failures?
66. (If yes) Does the family fail to help the child with a psychological or medical disorder improve because of a need to have a scapegoat?
67. To what extent are the child's symptoms "used" by the family?
68. What purposes do the child's symptoms serve, particularly in maintaining the family dynamics?
69. How do the child's symptoms fit into the family patterns?
70. How would the family dynamics change if the child's symptoms were alleviated?
71. Is the family relatively stable?
72. What activities do the family members share?
73. What family stresses are present, such as unemployment, parental psychopathology, marital problems, domestic violence, or other children with a psychological or medical disorder?
74. Do family members change their patterns of interaction with each other as the need arises?
75. How flexible is the family in meeting stress and crises?
76. Have family members' roles changed as a result of a new addition to the family, death of a family member, pending divorce, divorce, a member's leaving home, or other factors?
77. (If yes) In what way?
78. At what stages in the life cycle are the family members? (For example, are children in the family in the early childhood years, school-age years, or young adult years? Are the parents working, or are they retired?)

79. What roles do family members have outside of the family?
80. What is the quality of relationships that family members have with people outside of the family?

Affective Responses and Involvement
81. How do the family members express their emotions?
82. How do the family members respond to each other?
83. How do the family members respond to events that occur in their life?
84. What is the quality of the interest and investment that family members have in each other? (For example, are they hostile, angry, pleasant, positive, empathic, aloof, disengaged, enmeshed, or overinvolved?)
85. What type of affect and mood do the family members display? (For example, are they relaxed, tense, angry, hostile, cooperative, hopeful, depressed, anxious, thoughtful, detached, impulsive, mobilized, immobilized, motivated, trusting, or suspicious? Do they have a sense of humor?)
86. What are the family dynamics? (For example, do the family dynamics suggest a nurturing home environment, positive reinforcement, reasonable rules for peer interaction, and reasonable general discipline procedures, or do they suggest a nonnurturing home environment, negative reinforcement, unreasonable rules, and discipline given without explanation?)
87. Does the family mutually support its members?
88. How do the parents describe the children? (For example, do they make positive remarks or negative remarks?)

Control Mechanisms
89. How does the family handle the biological needs, social needs, and behavioral needs of its members?
90. Do any family members have excessive or dangerous biological, social, or behavioral needs?
91. How does the family influence the behavior of its members? (For example, does the family use rewards, punishment, guilt, shame, silence, or obligation?)
92. How do the parents supervise their children?
93. What is the style and consistency of the parents' supervision?
94. What discipline techniques do the parents use?
95. How consistent are the parents in applying discipline?
96. Who in the family assumes responsibility for discipline?
97. Are family members rigid, flexible, or laissez-faire?
98. What is the capacity of the family members for change?

Values and Norms
99. What are the family values and norms? (For example, do the family norms and values suggest mutual aid, adaptability, natural goodness, respect, responsibility, unconditional love, cooperation, work orientation, religion, and kinship networks, or do they suggest selfishness, materialism, paranoia, individualism, manipulativeness, and distress?)

(*Continued*)

Table 4-6 (*Continued*)

100. What is the quality of the friendships between family members and those outside the family?
101. What are the moral and religious values of the family?
102. How do these values affect how the family members function?
103. In what way is the family concerned about societal and political issues?
104. What is the ethnic background of the family?

105. What subcultural issues, if any, are the family concerned about?
106. What is the family's degree of acculturation (especially for ethnic minority groups)?
107. Can the family function independently (that is, without supervision)?
108. What interventions can the family handle?

Note. Your evaluation of family functioning also should consider cultural factors in more depth than this table shows (see Chapters 8 and 9).
Source: Adapted, in part, from Garbarino, Guttman, and Seeley (1987), Haley (1987), and Szapocznik and Kurtines (1989).

Table 4-7
Family Rating Checklist

FAMILY RATING CHECKLIST

Directions: Circle the number that best characterizes the family. Circle DK (don't know) if you don't have sufficient information to make the rating. Preface each item with "Given the family's cultural/ethnic heritage..."

Rating key:　　1 = not characteristic of the family
　　　　　　　2 = occasionally characteristic of the family
　　　　　　　3 = usually characteristic of the family
　　　　　DK = don't know (or insufficient information)

		Rating		

Problem-Solving Style

1. There is little conflict in family	1	2	3	DK
2. Family is able to adapt to developmental changes in the children	1	2	3	DK
3. Family copes well with stressful events	1	2	3	DK
4. Members are able to voice dissension	1	2	3	DK
5. Members are flexible and explore different alternatives	1	2	3	DK
6. Members do not blame another family member for all problems (that is, they avoid scapegoating)	1	2	3	DK
7. Members are able to monitor the impact of stressful events	1	2	3	DK
8. Members are able to evaluate how other members are managing stress	1	2	3	DK
9. Members accept help from non-family members	1	2	3	DK
10. Family welcomes community members who offer help	1	2	3	DK
11. Family is able to ward off destructive environmental influences	1	2	3	DK
12. Family interacts with neighbors	1	2	3	DK
13. Family interacts with wider community	1	2	3	DK
14. Members show self-determination	1	2	3	DK
15. Family does not rely too much on outside help	1	2	3	DK
16. Family retains privacy	1	2	3	DK
17. Rules are clear and understood or supported by all members	1	2	3	DK
18. Rules change with circumstances or with the stage of family development	1	2	3	DK
19. Rule changes are made by consulting family members	1	2	3	DK

Communication Patterns

20. Members engage in open and effective communication	1	2	3	DK
21. Members give clear messages	1	2	3	DK
22. Members understand and do not distort the messages they receive	1	2	3	DK

(Continued)

Table 4-7 (*Continued*)

23. Members care whether their messages are clearly addressed	1	2	3	DK
24. Members ask clear questions and answer them in direct ways	1	2	3	DK
25. Transactions among members have a clear ending	1	2	3	DK
26. Members' messages are expressed so that affect is almost always congruent with the verbal content	1	2	3	DK
27. Members act as messengers for other members	1	2	3	DK
28. Members clearly convey messages they are expected to convey	1	2	3	DK
29. Members express opinions, hopes, and fears freely	1	2	3	DK
30. Members share information	1	2	3	DK
31. Members have few secrets	1	2	3	DK

Roles and Structure

32. Members have defined roles	1	2	3	DK
33. Members experience little internal conflict about their family roles	1	2	3	DK
34. Members are assigned to specific tasks	1	2	3	DK
35. Members are able to assume other roles when one member is unable to play a particular role	1	2	3	DK
36. Parents share power	1	2	3	DK
37. Parents are in control of their children	1	2	3	DK
38. Members make suitable adjustments when required by developmental pressures or changes in circumstances				
39. Members do not isolate other members by forming separate alliances	1	2	3	DK

Affective Responses and Involvement

40. Members have warm and close relationships with one another	1	2	3	DK
41. Members identify with the family as a whole	1	2	3	DK
42. Members have a sense of family pride	1	2	3	DK
43. Members provide each other with support or guidance and listen to one another	1	2	3	DK
44. Members do not misconstrue the motives of other members	1	2	3	DK
45. Members have autonomy	1	2	3	DK
46. Members have their own identity	1	2	3	DK
47. Family does not experience increased difficulties when older children wish to become independent	1	2	3	DK
48. Members feel a sense of togetherness	1	2	3	DK
49. Parents make positive comments about children	1	2	3	DK

Control Mechanisms

50. Members are realistic in judging themselves, other family members, or the family as a whole	1	2	3	DK
51. Family checks its assessment of a problem against professional opinion	1	2	3	DK
52. Members' grasp of relevant facts is sound	1	2	3	DK
53. Members do not allow one member with eccentric views to exert a disproportionate influence on other members	1	2	3	DK
54. Members believe that they have control over events	1	2	3	DK
55. Family maintains realistic confidence in its ability to face hardship	1	2	3	DK
56. Family takes a realistic view of the likely outcome of problematic situations	1	2	3	DK
57. Family's assessments of problematic situations are based more on judgment than on hope	1	2	3	DK
58. Family does not create myths that conceal the truth about important family matters	1	2	3	DK

Values and Norms

59. Family respects need for privacy	1	2	3	DK
60. Family recognizes issues of conflict and tackles them constructively	1	2	3	DK
61. Family discusses issues openly, and members negotiate or compromise	1	2	3	DK
62. Members attempt to bring about reconciliation when disputes arise	1	2	3	DK

Note. The lower the score, the more dysfunctional the family. Thus, ratings of 1 indicate less optimal functioning than ratings of 3. A large number of 1 ratings suggests a dysfunctional family.
Source: Adapted from Frude (1991).

Table 4-8
Checklist for Evaluating Six Areas of Family Functioning

	Level of functioning				
Area	Optimally healthy	Adequately healthy	Neither healthy nor unhealthy	Borderline disturbed	Severely disturbed
Problem-solving style	Willing to engage in problem solving	Usually willing to engage in problem solving	Not sure about how to solve problems	Most of the time can't solve problems	Incapable of solving problems
Communication patterns	Clear	Generally clear	Minimally adequate	Poor	Confused and distorted
Roles and structure	Very clear and accepted	Generally clear and accepted	Not clear	Poorly defined	Very poorly defined
Affective responses and involvement	Respect, warmth, and intimacy	Some respect, warmth, and intimacy	Some anxiety, anger, and ambivalence	Anger, rage, depression, and aloofness	Anger, rage, despair, cynicism, and overinvolvement
Control mechanisms	Individual choice	Some control struggles	Constant effort at control	Poor control	Loss of control
Values and norms	Many moral and ethical values	Some moral and ethical values	Moral and ethical values not clear	Some amoral and unethical values	Many amoral and unethical values

Note. Your evaluation of family functioning also should consider cultural factors (see Chapters 8 and 9).

5. Overall, what are the strengths and weaknesses of the family?
6. What prior interventions has the family received, and how successful were these interventions?
7. What are the family's resources?
8. What types of services does the family need?
9. What short-term and long-term goals can be formulated?

What you achieve in the initial family interview in part will be related to your interview style and the idiosyncracies of each family. You may not obtain all the information you want, but do your best to evaluate the family. For more information about family assessment, see Beavers and Hampson (1990).

Exercise 4-3. Evaluating a Family

Read the following family case study. Then answer the questions. Compare your answers with those at the end of the exercise. The material in this exercise is from Friedman (1986).

Mrs. Ruby Nichols, a 34-year-old obese woman, came to the mental health clinic because, she said, "I just don't know what

to do." She was crying hysterically and unable to respond to further questioning. She told the interviewer that her 5-year-old foster daughter, Ann, was removed from her home last week per court order. Welfare funds, her only support for herself, her husband, and their five children, were being stopped in a week because they had received financial assistance for the maximum time allowed by their state, leaving her unable to pay the bills or buy enough food for her family.

Ruby and John Nichols had been married 15 years. Four children were born of the marriage: Priscilla, 13; Cindy, 10; John Jr., 6; and Lisa, 4. Their foster daughter, Ann, was 5. The couple had known each other a year before their marriage in their hometown of Smithfield, Louisiana. John was an unskilled laborer but had always been employed. Ruby had attended business school before their marriage and was employed as a bookkeeper until the first child was born. She described her early marriage as fine except for frequent moves caused by John's "meddling mother." The family would move to get away from his mother, but she would always manage to locate them and "appear on the scene." According to Ruby, "We were a healthy, happy family and everything was fine as long as John's mother stayed away." This source of conflict between Ruby and John was resolved each time by a new move. However, she and John never really discussed their mother-in-law problem. Following each new move, Ruby would join clubs and organizations to make new friends and John's work provided a similar opportunity for him to make friends. John also spent several evenings a week in the local bar, "shooting the bull" with the "boys" from work.

The last move was 6 months ago. After 2 months, John lost his job and was unable to find another one. The family went on welfare, but Ruby and John were ashamed of this; they had always prided themselves on paying their own bills. Shortly after they received welfare, John's mother found the family and moved into town. After a recent visit by John's mother, Ruby and John had a bitter argument about the visit. Since the argument, John avoided coming home and began to drink excessively. About 3 months ago, Ruby had abdominal surgery, followed by complications and a prolonged hospitalization. During her absence from home, Priscilla assumed the mothering role and managed well with help from the next door neighbor, Mrs. Law.

When Ruby came home from the hospital 3 weeks ago, she saw that the children had functioned well in her absence. She thought that they did not need her and even seemed to resent her. During her hospitalization, John remained away from the family most of the time. He continues to be minimally involved in the family.

Last week, Ruby learned of the court's decision to remove her foster child, Ann, from the home. Ruby felt less and less able to manage herself and experienced depression and suicidal thoughts. However, her concern for her children prevented her from doing anything self-destructive. The next-door-neighbor, Mrs. Law, realizing the gravity of the family's situation, encouraged Ruby to go to the mental health clinic for help.

A visit to the family home revealed that the children were having problems and that Ruby did not know how to handle their difficulties. The interviewer observed that the children and parents did not discuss their problems or their concerns with each other, and there was no movement toward sharing their feelings about Ann's leaving, the mother-in-law's disruptive influence, or Ruby's health problems.

Priscilla, age 13, seemed to resent Ruby's return, because it meant the loss of her "mothering" role. She and her mother have had arguments over the discipline of the younger children, what they should wear, and how they should act. The arguments usually ended with Priscilla leaving the house for long periods without telling Ruby where she was going. This caused Ruby to worry. Priscilla was not interested in school; her main interest was to grow up as quickly as possible and emulate her mother. She also wanted desperately to be independent and make her own decisions in life. Ruby had "weaned" Priscilla early in life to make her self-sufficient at home, and from age 6 on, Priscilla was caring for her younger siblings and helping her mother.

Cindy, age 10, seemed unaffected by the situation. She was involved with her school activities and Campfire Girls and spent much time in these activities and at her friends' homes. Priscilla and Cindy evidently have a closer sibling relationship than the other siblings do. Cindy tells "all her secrets" to Priscilla when she is upset or worried or needs someone to talk to.

John Jr., a first-grader, was refusing to go to school. Each morning it was a struggle to get him off to school. He would cry and hang on to his mother. His teacher reported poor schoolwork and lack of attentiveness when he was present.

Lisa, age 4, displayed clinging behavior similar to that of John Jr. She seemed frightened when her mother left the house and was wetting the bed after having been toilet trained for 2 years. Both John Jr. and Lisa frequently questioned their mother about the recent absence of Ann. They asked if Ann went away because she was "bad."

In discussing Priscilla, the parents recognized her need to care for her younger siblings and to be independent, but they were not open to her avoiding the family or developing a set of friends outside the family. The mother recognized that Lisa was attached to and dependent on her and needed reassurance that she would be back when she left for the hospital. Both parents thought Ann's leaving threatened the younger children, who feared this might happen to them if they misbehaved. Ruby was trying to spend more time with Lisa to help her with her fears over the mother's separation and Ann's leaving. John showed interest in "comforting" and being involved with Lisa also, since Lisa always responded "in such a cute, loving way to her daddy," according to the mother.

Both parents can show affection and warmth to the younger children (John Jr. and Lisa) but do not feel that it is appropriate to be so "physical" when children get older. The interviewer observed that the parents were not physically affectionate to each other and seemed emotionally distant during the interviews. Ruby said that they seldom share their personal concerns with each other. "It takes another woman to understand my feelings. I used to confide in Priscilla a lot, but since she is upset with me, I haven't been able to talk with her."

1. To what extent does each family member perceive and meet the needs of other family members? (Evaluate each member separately.)
2. Do the family members mutually respect each other's feelings and needs?
3. Do the family members provide mutual nurturance to each other, and do they support each other?
4. Is there a sense of closeness and intimacy in the family relationships?
5. How compatible and affectionate are the family members toward each other?
6. Do the family members identify with each other, and is there a sense of bonding?
7. How does the family deal with the issues of independence and relatedness?
8. What short-term stressors are impinging on the family?
9. What long-term stressors are impinging on the family?
10. What family strengths counterbalance these stressors?
11. Can the family realistically and objectively appraise their situation?
12. How does the family react to stressful situations? Consider both functional and dysfunctional strategies.

Suggested Answers

1. a. *John (father).* His behavior—staying away and drinking excessively—suggests that he is not meeting his family's needs. The family may or may not be meeting his needs.
   b. *Ruby (mother).* The mother's depression and suicidal thoughts suggest that she is not meeting her family's needs. The family may or may not be meeting her

emotional needs. Priscilla, her former confidant, is focused on her own needs and is unable to meet Ruby's need for a close relationship.

c. *Priscilla (age 13)*. Because Ruby feels threatened by Priscilla's ability to manage the younger siblings when she was gone, Ruby is now unable to reinforce positively Priscilla's parenting efforts and meet Priscilla's needs. Neither parent encourages or facilitates Priscilla's need to become less involved with the family and more involved with her peer group.

d. *Cindy (age 10)*. Her behavior, especially staying away from the home for long periods, may reflect the family's inability to meet her socioemotional needs. Priscilla does serve as Cindy's confidant, meeting some of Cindy's emotional needs.

e. *John Jr. (age 6)*. There is no evidence that John's socioemotional needs are being met, as noted by his school phobia, clinging to his mother, and poor schoolwork.

f. *Lisa (age 4)*. Although both parents evidently spend more time with Lisa than with the other children, her clingingness, her fear when her mother leaves, and her bedwetting (after 2 years of being toilet trained) suggest that some of her needs are not being met.

2. There is no specific information about whether mutual respect exists. However, we can infer that the family members are insensitive to each other's needs and have limited respect for each other.

3. Mutual nurturance may be limited. Family members do not share their feelings with each other in the face of difficulties. Lisa seems to be comforted and nurtured by the parents more than the other family members are. Priscilla also provides nurturance to Cindy.

4. Three sets of relationships in the family show closeness and intimacy: Cindy and Priscilla, Lisa and Ruby, and Lisa and John. Also, Priscilla and Ruby had a close relationship in the past. The parents believe that affectionate feelings should be expressed only to the two younger children.

5. The degree of compatibility and affection is difficult to evaluate. No open conflict was described between the children and parents, except the arguments between Priscilla and Ruby. John and Ruby show signs of incompatibility. John handles his feelings by withdrawal—staying away from home and drinking—and both parents fail to discuss important issues. The failure to discuss important issues and feelings, however, may be due to social class and cultural role expectations; that is, the spouses do not see this as one of the expected roles in marriage.

6. There is evidence that (a) the spouses are staying together, although marital bonds need to be strengthened; (b) Priscilla emulates her mother's mothering behaviors and role; and (c) the two younger children show separation anxiety when the mother leaves.

7. The information in the areas of independence and relatedness is limited. However, the parents place more emphasis on being with Priscilla and the other children than on being with each other. The parents do not stress individuality, independence, and personal growth among the family members.

8. Short-term stressors include John's being unemployed; the family's being on welfare and threatened with termination from welfare; Ann's removal from the home; and Ruby's recent ill health, hospitalization, convalescence, depression, and suicidal thoughts.

9. Long-term stressors include the perceived interference of John's mother; emotional distance and limited communication between the spouses and other family members; the family's continual moves, which prevent the family from establishing a stable social network; and the father's minimal participation in family life and excessive and frequent drinking bouts.

10. The family's strengths are the presence of a social support system, although small, such as the mental health clinic and Mrs. Law, the neighbor; Ruby's caring for and commitment to the children; the parents' staying together; the father's interest in Lisa and potential for greater participation in family life; the parents' motivation to find employment and be financially self-sufficient; and Priscilla's interest in and ability to care for the children.

11. The parents' ability to act based on an objective and realistic appraisal of a situation is limited. They simply ignore issues regarding John's mother. They do not seem to understand that to solve this problem they will need to discuss it with each other and with the mother-in-law. The case does not give information about how the parents felt about why Ann was removed. Ruby showed some distorted thinking in believing that her children did well without her and did not want her back.

12. Functional strategies include seeking help from a mental health clinic and accepting the help of the neighbor, Mrs. Law. Dysfunctional strategies include the failure of the spouses to communicate with each other; withdrawal of the father from the family, including increased drinking; use of denial to avoid the family's problems; and use of the mother-in-law as a scapegoat for the family's problems.

A family was seated in a restaurant. The waitress took the order of the adults and then turned to their young son. "What will you have, sonny?" she asked. The boy said timidly, "I want a hot dog." Before the waitress could write down the order, the mother interrupted. "No hot dog," she said. "Give him potatoes, beef and some carrots." But the waitress ignored her completely. "Do you want some ketchup or mustard on your hot dog?" she asked of the boy. "Ketchup," he replied with a happy smile on his face. "Coming up," the waitress said, starting for the kitchen. There was a stunned silence upon her departure. Finally, the boy turned to his parents, "Know what?" he said. "She thinks I'm real."

—Bill Adler

CLOSING THE INITIAL INTERVIEW

The final moments of the interview are as important as any other period in the interview. They give you a chance to summarize to the interviewee what you have learned, to get feedback from the interviewee about whether you have understood her or him, to ask any remaining questions, to inform the interviewee of any other assessments needed and about possible interventions, and to give the interviewee time to share any remaining thoughts and feelings.

Don't rush the ending of the interview. Budget your time so that there is enough remaining to cover what you need to cover. You want to leave the interviewee feeling that he or she has made a contribution and that the experience was worthwhile. Be courteous and friendly; inform the interviewee of what the future course of action will be and what you might expect of her or him. You don't want the interviewee to feel dismissed or used for your own purposes. A statement such as "Thank you for coming" might be all that you need to say to convey a sense of respect to the interviewee. If you discuss possible interventions and a prognosis, be careful not to create false hopes or expectations. You want to be as realistic as possible, recognizing what the intervention program may or may not accomplish.

How you close the interview is especially important when the interviewee is expressing some deeply felt emotion. Try not to end the interview abruptly; allow enough time for the interviewee to regain composure before she or he leaves. Allow an interviewee who is in the middle of a communication to finish. Gauge the time and, when necessary, provide some indication to the interviewee that the interview will soon be over (say, in 5 minutes). When the interviewee recognizes that the interview will soon be over, she or he may begin to move away from the subject at hand and regain composure.

What you say, of course, will depend on whether you plan to see the interviewee again. If you do not, you might say "You have some deep feelings about…. However, since our time together is about up, I would be glad to give you names of some professionals that you could contact. I am sure they will be able to help you. I do appreciate your cooperation." If you plan to see the interviewee again, you might say "I can see that this is extremely important to you, and we need to talk about it some more. But our time is just about up for today. We can continue next time." Then arrange another appointment while continuing to express support, understanding, and confidence that you can help the interviewee find a solution.

Planning for Enough Time at the Close of the Interview

It is easy to continue the main body of the interview to a point where there is little time left to end it appropriately, especially if you are on a tight schedule. Be aware of how much time has passed, what important areas you need to discuss, and how much time the interviewee may need to discuss any remaining concerns so that you don't have to rush at the end. When you are first learning to interview, have a clock in a visible location so that you don't lose track of

time. However, don't let the clock distract you. Plan the areas you want to cover before you begin the interview. In the time remaining, attempt to cover the most important areas that you haven't yet addressed.

Issues to Consider Near the Completion of the Interview

Here are some issues you will want to consider near the close of the interview:

1. Have you covered everything you wanted to cover?
2. Does the interviewee know what other assessments he or she will be given?
3. Does the interviewee know how he or she will get the results of the assessment?
4. Have you and the interviewee had the opportunity to correct misperceptions?
5. Does the interviewee know how you will use the assessment findings? (For example, will they be used to make recommendations, to give to a court, to give to school officials, and so forth?)
6. Is the interviewee aware of the clinic's, school's, or your policies regarding fees and procedures?
7. Have you treated the interviewee with respect and concern?

You will want to consider these and similar issues as you approach the close of the interview and when you reflect on the interview as a whole. If you find that you cannot recall some important information that was covered, you can say "I know you told me about [describe topic], but I didn't note it fully. Can you tell me more about…?" You can make this type of statement at any time during the interview.

Giving the Interviewee the Opportunity to Ask Questions

Use the last minutes of the initial interview to summarize, evaluate, and plan and to give the interviewee an opportunity to ask any remaining questions that he or she might have.

Recognizing the Interviewee's Concerns

Toward the close of the interview, the interviewee may wonder how the interview went, how serious the problem is, whether you can help him or her, what you thought of him or her, whether he or she told you all you needed to know, and what will happen next. Be prepared to deal with these and similar concerns. Here are some useful questions to ask:

• "Is there anything else you would like to tell me?"
• "Is there anything else you think I should know?"
• "I have asked you many questions. Are there any questions that you would like to ask me?"

Following are examples of interviewees' concerns and some possible interviewer responses. The interviewer's response, of course, depends on the specific situation.

1. IE: Did I say the right things?
   IR-1: Yes, you did. There are no right or wrong answers. You told me about yourself, and that was helpful.
   IR-2: Your responses have been helpful, and I believe we can help you.

2. IE: Do you think you can help me?
   IR: Yes, I do, but it will take time to work things out.

3. IE: Well, am I crazy?
   IR-1: (If there is no evidence of psychosis) No, you are not crazy. Sometimes teenagers think that things are not under their control, but this is only natural.
   IR-2: (If there is evidence of psychosis) You seem to have some problems in your thinking, and that concerns you.

4. IE: Am I going to be sent away?
   IR-1: (If no such plans are being considered) No, you are not going to be sent away. You will be going home when we finish.
   IR-2: (If you are not sure whether the child is going to be sent away) We should wait until all the results are in before we make any decisions. But whatever we decide, we will let you know, and we will always try to do what is best for you.

5. IE: So what happens now?
   IR: First, we need to study what we have learned about you and your family. Then we will talk about how to make things better.

Summary Statement

A summary statement should identify the main points of the problem for the interviewee's confirmation or correction. Following is an example of a summary statement: "You believe that Helen's major problem is her inability to read. Emotionally, you see her as well adjusted. However, her frustration in learning how to read does get her down at times."

Toward the close of the initial interview with a parent or teacher, you might say something like "We met today so that I could learn about Bill. Do you believe that I have most of the important information?" Or you could say "I think we have accomplished a great deal today. The information you have given me is very helpful. I appreciate your cooperation and look forward to seeing you again after we have completed the evaluation." These statements are not mutually exclusive; they can be used together at the close of the interview. Where relevant, make an appointment with the interviewee to discuss the assessment findings and recommendations.

Acknowledging your satisfaction with cooperative interviewees.   It may be helpful, especially with children, to acknowledge their openness and willingness to share their problems, concerns, hopes, and expectations. Comments such as the following may be appropriate (Jennings, 1982):

- "I appreciate your sharing your concerns with me."
- "It took a lot of courage to talk to me about yourself, your family, and your school."
- "It took a lot of trust to tell me what you just did, and I'm proud of you for doing that."
- "You took this interview seriously, and that will help me do my job to help you."

Acknowledging your disappointment with uncooperative interviewees.   When the interviewee has been uncooperative and you need to schedule another appointment, you may want to express your concern about how the interview went: "We didn't get too much accomplished today. Perhaps next time we can cover more ground."

EVALUATING THE INITIAL INTERVIEW

Considering Factors Affecting the Interviewee's Replies

After the interviews with the child, parents, teachers, offender, or other informants have been completed, estimate the extent to which the interviewees could report accurately their behaviors, thoughts, and feelings, and also events. For example: How did intellectual, developmental, and situational factors affect the replies of the interviewees? Were the interviewees cooperative, evasive, or hostile? How reliable and valid was the information you obtained from the interviewees (see Chapter 6)? These and similar questions should guide your evaluation.

Comparing Information from Multiple Informants

You will want to compare the information you obtained from different informants. What were the similarities and differences in the information obtained from the child, parent, and teacher about the child's problems and concerns? How does each interviewee describe the child's behavior? For example, what were the trends evident in the developmental history, observational findings, parental reports, teacher reports, medical reports, psychological and psychiatric reports, and police reports (if applicable), and how consistent were the trends?

Don't be surprised to find differences in the information given to you by children, parents, and teachers. For example, they may agree about external symptoms but not about internal ones. If there are differences between the accounts of the parents and child, parents and teacher, or parent and parent, what might account for the differences?

1. Do the parents and teacher differ in their ability to observe, evaluate, and judge the behavior of the child?
2. Could differences be associated with different standards for judging deviant behavior or different tolerances for behavioral problems? Thus, what the parents consider hyperactive, the teacher may consider normal, or vice versa.
3. Or could differences in how the parents and teacher view the child's behavior be due to situational factors? For example, when parents report *fewer* problems than does the teacher, it may reflect overindulgence at home but normal treatment at school (Rudel, 1988). When parents report *more* problems than does the teacher, it may reflect a stressful environment at home (for example, unsympathetic parents, poor structure and discipline, conflicts with siblings) but a normal environment at school (for example, evenhanded discipline, more consistency, clearer and more reasonable expectations).

Thus, the discrepancies between informants may suggest that the behaviors of concern are not pervasive or generalizable—the child may behave differently at home than at school (Clarizio, 1994). Consider all the information you have before arriving at an explanation for the discrepancy between informants.

When information is available to you from several sources, you will need to organize and interpret it to arrive at a systematic understanding of the child. You will need to consider the child as a whole, given his or her family, culture, and environment. Although the information may not always be clear, you still must sort out the findings, establish trends, arrive at a diagnostic impression, and sometimes formulate an intervention plan. When you do formulate an intervention plan, consider what interventions are feasible, given the assessment findings, available facilities and personnel, and familial resources. These steps are a critical part of the appraisal process. The answers to the questions in Table 4-9 will help guide you in evaluating the child.

Evaluating Your Reactions

Consider your reactions to the interviewee and the feelings the interviewee evoked in you:

1. Did you feel exhausted, frustrated, disappointed, indifferent, angry, satisfied, or pleased after the interview?
2. Do you believe that the interview went well? If not, why not?
3. Do you believe that you came to some understanding of the interviewee?
4. Do you think that you need another interview to gain vital information?
5. Do you have biases that affected the evaluation?

The answers to these and similar questions will provide information about how the interviewee functions in a structured interpersonal relationship. Your personal reactions also will aid you in formulating a more comprehensive picture of the child, family, and school (where applicable).

THINKING THROUGH THE ISSUES

How would you handle a situation in which the information given by the child and parents, or child and teacher, or parents and teacher differed?

Do you think that you will be more comfortable in individual or in family interviews or equally comfortable in both? What is the basis for your answer?

What stresses will family interviews place on you that are different from those that occur in an individual interview?

What problems do you foresee in handling the group dynamics of the family interview?

Is the family interview simply interviewing individuals in a group, or does it have its own dynamics? What is the basis for your answer?

What do you think you can learn in a family interview that you can't learn in individual interviews with each family member?

How are you going to handle a family member who wants to dominate the family interview?

How would you get a family together for an interview if the members didn't want to be together?

How have your beliefs changed because of reaching adulthood?

How have you adopted or assimilated values that differ from those of your family?

What stresses might you face when you visit a child's home?

How do you think you might react when you find deplorable living conditions in a child's home?

If you see that you are running out of time in the interview, what is the best strategy to follow? Explain your reasoning.

Under what conditions would you want to see the interviewee for a second interview?

What problems do you foresee in bringing the interview to an end?

SUMMARY

Interviewing Parents
1. A well-conducted parental interview will serve to establish rapport and a positive working relationship with the parents, will help focus the perception of the parents on the problem, will serve as a valuable source of information about the child and family, will help the parents organize and reflect on the information, will contribute to the formulation of a diagnosis, will provide a basis for decisions about treatment and further investigation, and will lay the groundwork for parental efforts to be a part of intervention efforts.

Table 4-9
Questions to Consider About the Child at the Completion of the Assessment

Early History
1. What was the mother's pregnancy like?
2. Did the mother receive prenatal care?
3. Were there any problems with the birth, and if so, what were the problems and what treatments did the child receive?
4. What was the relationship like between the parents and the child during the child's early development?

Problem
5. Does the child have any problems?
6. If a problem is present, what is the nature of the problem (for example, its severity, etiology, and pervasiveness), and what are the antecedent, intervening, and consequent events associated with the child's problem?
7. What is the evidence of psychological difficulties, such as confused thinking or inappropriate affect?
8. What are the major stressors in the child's life?
9. What is the evidence that the child has or does not have specific kinds of difficulties?
10. To what degree do the child's problems interfere with her or his growth and development?
11. What behaviors of the child are of concern to the parents, teachers, and significant others?
12. How do the child, family, and teachers perceive and deal with the problem?

Physical Development
13. When were developmental milestones reached for walking, talking, toilet training, self-feeding, and eating solid foods?
14. What are the child's sleep patterns like?
15. What are the child's fine and gross motor movements like (normal or clumsy, coordinated or uncoordinated)?
16. What serious illnesses or accidents or hospitalizations (including head injuries, seizures, major infections, psychophysiological illness) has the child had?
17. Is the child's height and weight normal?
18. What are the child's eating patterns like (for example, normal or peculiar, binge eating, disgorging food unobtrusively, engaging in food fads, eating non-food material, hoarding food, secreting food)?
19. What is the child's build like (thin or obese, muscular or nonmuscular)?
20. Is there any evidence of visual, auditory, or other types of deficits?
21. Are there any unusual facial features, such as open mouth, drooling, or sores?
22. Is the child on any medications?
23. If so, what medications and for what conditions?
24. If the child has a medical disorder of disability, how does it affect the child's language, motor skills, self-concept, interpersonal relations, and related areas?

Behavior, Personality, Affect, Abilities, and Performance
25. How would you describe the child's behavior, personality, temperament, affect, language, communication skills, speech, interpersonal behavior, memory ability, cognition, ability to concentrate, motor skills, social and self-help skills, and other relevant behavioral factors?
26. What is the child's level of social and emotional maturity as revealed by her or his ability to cooperate with peers, parents, and teachers; to play fair and understand rules; to develop a conscience; to play constructively; and to play alone?
27. What was the major theme presented by the child?
28. What topics did the child avoid, if any?
29. How does the child feel about her or his parents, siblings, relatives, school, friends, community, and other relevant individuals or sources?
30. How does the child spend her or his leisure time?
31. What is the child's self-concept?
32. Does the child have adequate coping skills?
33. Does the child's family have adequate coping skills?
34. Have there been any recent changes in the child's behavior (for example, mood shifts, attentional deficits, memory loss, motor or sensory changes, sleep disturbances, speech abnormalities) or deviations from normal development?
35. What are the child's strengths and weaknesses?
36. How much control does the child have over her or his behavior?
37. Does the child seem to learn from the consequences of her or his behavior?
38. How does the child handle frustration?
39. Is the child's ability to care for herself or himself commensurate with her or his age?

Social Development
40. How does the child relate to her or his parents, siblings, other adults, and other children (for example, relates well to others, quiet and shy, inhibited, withdraws from others, suspicious of others, flustered by people, muddled and confused when with others, fails to take part in group activities, cooperative, stubborn, quarrelsome, bossy, argumentative, defies authority, wary in presence of adults, challenges authority, hostile, shows need to be accepted)?
41. How does the child get along with other children at school (for example, accepted, taunted, picked on, rejected, neglected, ignored, popular, unpopular, liked, disliked, bullied, butt of practical jokes, called derogatory names, teased frequently, antagonistic, disruptive, argumentative, cruel, provocative, leader, follower, easily led, gullible, crafty, tricked into doing things)?

(Continued)

Table 4-9 (*Continued*)

42. Has the child joined any organized groups (for example, Boy or Girl Scouts, Little League, YMCA)?
43. If so, what group(s)?
44. What is the child's play like (for example, imaginative or unimaginative, responsive or unresponsive to others)?
45. How does the child spend her or his free time?

Schooling
46. How is the child performing in school?
47. Are the child's grades commensurate with her or his ability level?
48. How is the child performing in reading (oral and silent), arithmetic, spelling, and other subjects?
49. What is the child's handwriting like (legible, illegible, tremor)?
50. What is the child's speech like (normal, stutters)?
51. Is the child in a special class or receiving special services?
52. Does the child have difficulties in any specific academic area?
53. What is the child's level of interest in school?
54. Are the child's parents interested in her or his school performance?
55. Does the child complete her or his assignments on time?
56. What are the child's favorite subjects?
57. What is the child's school attendance like?
58. Has the child ever been expelled from school?
59. How does the child's behavior compare in school and at home (and in other situations)?

Environmental Factors
60. What role do environmental factors—including family, school, and neighborhood—have in affecting the child? (Consider the kinds of environmental demands typically placed on the child, the presence of environmental supports, and the types of stressors present.)
61. Is there any evidence of child abuse or neglect?
62. (If child abuse or neglect is in question) What was the alleged offender's role in the child abuse or neglect, and what role did the nonoffending parent have?
63. Is the child in any danger in her or his present environment?

Diagnosis
64. How reliable and valid is the information you obtained?
65. What is your overall impression of the child and the family?

Treatment/Intervention
66. What are the child's resources for change and for coping with stress?
67. What is the most appropriate educational program and setting for the child?
68. What realistic goals can be set for the child?
69. What would happen if the problem behavior continued without change?
70. What would happen if the problem behavior was changed as a result of some intervention?
71. What interventions are most feasible?
72. What expectations do the child and family have for change?
73. What would be the effects—positive or adverse—on the parents and significant others if the child's problem behavior were changed?
74. What new problems would successful intervention pose for the child, the parents, and significant others?
75. What persons or groups are most effective in controlling the child's problem behavior?
76. What reinforcers (for example, social approval, food, money, watching TV, avoidance of punishment) are most effective in controlling the problem behavior?
77. Does the problem behavior occur in all or only some settings (for example, child behaves acceptably at school but not at home, or vice versa)?
78. What consequences have followed from the problem behavior in each setting?
79. Has the child acquired some measure of self-control in avoiding situations conducive to performing the problem behavior?
80. If the child said that he or she will try to control the problem behavior, how successful do you think the child will be?
81. What has been done to help the child?
82. What seems to help the problem behavior?
83. How can the school and family deal more effectively with the child's problems or handicaps?
84. How does the information you obtained from the child agree with other sources of information, such as the parents, school, siblings, relative, and so forth?
85. What is the prognosis (likely outcome)?

Additional Questions for Adolescent Children
86. Does the adolescent have a substance abuse problem?
87. How is the adolescent learning to become independent?
88. How is the adolescent handling her or his sexual development?
89. What future plans, if any, does the adolescent have?

Note. Adapted, in part, from Hoghughi (1992) and Kanfer and Saslow (1969).

2. The main goals of the initial clinical assessment interview with parents are to gather information about parental concerns and goals, to assess parental perceptions of the strengths and weaknesses of the child, to obtain a case history of the child from the parents, to identify the child's problems and related antecedent and consequent events, to determine how the parents have dealt with the problems in the past, to identify events that reinforced the problem for both the child and the parents, to obtain a family history (where relevant), to assess the parents' motivation and resources for change, to obtain informed consent from the parents to conduct an assessment of the child, to discuss assessment procedures that may be used with the child, and to discuss what follow-up contacts they and their child may need.

3. The age of the child will, in part, determine the content of the interview with the parents.

4. Parents will likely have several questions to ask you about their child, depending on the type and severity of the child's problems. Their questions may relate to the causes of the child's problem, what they can do about the problem and the cost of treatment, how the problem relates to other members of the family, what their responsibility is for the problem, and whether there will be a stigma associated with going to see a mental health professional.

5. If parents ask you what they should say to their child about coming to see you, advise them to be straightforward with their child.

6. By the time the parents seek an evaluation for their child, they may have already experienced much frustration and anguish. Expect some possible negative feelings from the parents. Deal with these feelings during their initial contact with you.

7. Clinical skills needed for interviewing parents include the abilities to become attuned to the parents' anxieties; to listen carefully to what they are saying; to give them an opportunity to talk without giving them advice or suggestions; to convey your understanding of their needs and perceptions; to establish a meaningful relationship with them; to communicate your findings, suggestions, and recommendations clearly (in the post-assessment interview); and to convey a sense of collaborative partnership between you and them.

8. Several formats are useful for interviewing parents. They include an unstructured (or open-ended) interview, a semistructured interview, and a structured interview.

9. A semistructured interview is useful in assessing what is important to the parents, what they hope to accomplish from the evaluation, what their concerns are, and how they view their own role in helping the child.

10. A structured interview is useful when you want to cover systematically various areas of psychopathology.

11. A background questionnaire is useful in obtaining a detailed account of the child's developmental, social, medical, and educational history, as well as information about the family.

12. The major components of the initial interview with parents include greeting the parents, giving your name and professional title, opening the interview with an introductory statement, asking the parents about items on the background questionnaire that are of interest (if they have completed a background questionnaire) or covering similar content areas, reviewing problems, describing the assessment procedure, arranging for a post-assessment interview, and closing the interview.

13. The following guidelines will be useful for interviewing parents. Listen carefully to the parents' concerns. Explain what lies ahead, what may be involved in the assessment process, and what interventions are possible. Adopt a calm, nonjudgmental approach to reduce the parents' stress. Help the parents understand that many children have problems at times and that emotional problems or physical problems may develop in a child from events beyond the parents' control. Reassure parents that records will be kept confidential, unless the law requires that the records be disclosed or agency policy requires that the records be shared by others. Help parents who are having problems in managing their child understand that child rearing is a complex and difficult activity and that a child with a psychological or medical disorder may be especially difficult to cope with. Take special care to convey respect for the parents' feelings. Avoid any suggestion that parents are to blame for their child's difficulties (except if they are the alleged perpetrators in cases of child maltreatment). Emphasize their constructive and helpful parenting skills rather than their destructive or harmful approaches (except if they are the alleged perpetrators in cases of child maltreatment). Enlist their cooperation in the diagnostic and remediation program; do not be authoritarian. Schedule more than one meeting (if needed) to gain the cooperation of parents who are uncooperative. If working with a two-parent family, try to get both parents to come to the interview. Usually plan to interview both parents together. Help the parents clarify vague, ambiguous, or incomplete statements. Encourage the parents to discuss fully their child's problem and how the problem affects the family. Use follow-up and probing questions to learn the specific conditions that may serve to instigate, maintain, or limit the child's behavior and to learn about the parents' resources and motivation to change. Determine the areas in which parents agree and disagree about child management. Guide the parents back to the topic in an appropriate and gentle manner if they give many irrelevant details. Have the parents check their recollections against baby books, medical and school records, and other formal and informal records if they cannot recall events or the dates of the events. If you schedule a second interview, ask the parents to keep a record of the occurrences of the problem if you believe that such a record would be helpful.

14. After you complete the interview with the parents, evaluate the findings. Consider such issues as the referral source, the parents' perception of the problem, the quality of the information you received, the attitudes of the parents, information from the background questionnaire (if completed), how involved the parents are in parenting, how the parents are coping (if their child has special needs), and their resources and desire for intervention.

15. Recognize that not all parents will be reliable informants. Expect to find distortions, biases, and memory lags in the histories you collect from parents. Developmental milestones are difficult to remember, and relating particular events to particular behavioral responses may be even more difficult.

Interviewing Teachers

16. Many topics covered in the initial interview with parents also are pertinent to initial interviews with teachers. The focus is different, though. You want to inquire about the teacher's perceptions of the child, the antecedents and consequences of the problem behavior, what the teacher has done to alleviate the

problem, how other teachers and students react to the child, and the child's academic progress.

17. The areas usually covered in the initial interview with teachers include the teacher's perception of problem behavior, reactions to the problem behavior, opinion of the child's relationship with peers, assessment of the child's academic performance, assessment of the child's strengths and weaknesses, view of the child's family, expectations of the child, and suggestions for helping the child.

18. During the interview, allay the teacher's anxiety about her or his responsibility for the child's problem behaviors. Inform the teacher that children's problems likely stem from several factors. Also tell the teacher when the assessment results will be ready. Do not leave the impression that immediate changes for the better will occur automatically.

19. A visit to the classroom may give you valuable information about the child and the teaching environment.

20. Based on your interview with the teacher (and on classroom observations and interviews with the child and parents), you can probably come to some understanding about what the teacher sees as the major problems, how effective the teacher is in handling the child's problems, the appropriateness of the child's class placement, whether a placement change is needed, what insights the teacher has about the child, what techniques have proved to be successful and what techniques unsuccessful in helping the child, how other children contribute to the problem, the stressors that exist in the classroom, whether the stressors in the classroom can be diminished, how the teacher's account of the child agrees with that of the parent and the child, and what recommendations the teacher has for interventions.

Interviewing the Family

21. A family interview is valuable because it informs the child and the parents that you want to include the child in some discussions; it allows you to observe how the parents and child interact when discussing the problem and other matters; it allows you to gather valuable information about the child's problem and about family dynamics, family communication patterns, and family social and cultural values; it may enable you to learn how well the family accepts the child and how much of an impact the child's difficulties have on the family, on the parents' relationship, and on other family members; and it may give you some information about the extent to which the family is using functional or dysfunctional strategies to cope with the child's problems.

22. Functional family strategies for coping with a child with a psychological or medical disorder include reacting, mobilizing, recognition, understanding, continuing, hoping, appreciating, and reasoning.

23. Dysfunctional family strategies for coping with a child with a psychological or medical disorder include blaming, taking over, employing power, avoiding, denying, controlling, rescuing, and faulty reasoning.

24. Families may have adaptive or maladaptive ways of coping with stress. A key factor in coping with stress—whether it be psychological, environmental, or physical—is how the family was functioning *before* the stress occurred.

25. The family interview should not be a substitute for individual interviews.

26. The goals of the family interview are to obtain historical and current details of family life relevant to the problems of the

child and to observe patterns of family interaction. The interview should clarify the family structure, along with details about family members.

27. Recognize that your questions and probes may result in potentially painful confrontations among family members and may elicit feelings that have not been previously articulated.

28. The following are useful guidelines for conducting the family interview. Encourage open discussion among the family members. Make the interview no more stressful than absolutely necessary. Support any family participant who is on the "hot seat." Allow the family to defend itself and maintain its status quo without guilt or loss of face. Create a safe and supportive atmosphere so that the family members can interact in a way that they find most comfortable and natural. Accept the family the way it is. Use praise and approval to facilitate the family's acceptance of the interview. Help family members clarify their thoughts. Be objective, empathic, and supportive of the family. Maintain a balance between formality and informality, while promoting informality among the family members. Encourage the children to participate in the interview. Encourage family members to give specific examples of concerns and problems. Do not provoke the family. Be aware of family dynamics.

29. Create a setting in which the family members feel that they can risk sharing their feelings and problems and can seek information about the referred child's problems and their problems as they relate to the child.

30. If you touch upon an emotionally charged area that upsets family members and makes it difficult to continue the interview, consider moving on to a more neutral subject.

31. Interviewing a family ordered to come to see you will require patience.

32. You can use different strategies during the three phases of the family interview. In the opening phase, encourage the family members to talk about their concerns. During the middle phase, focus on general family dynamics and issues. In the closing phase, summarize the salient points of the interview.

33. There are several family assessment tasks that you can use to get the family to interact. These include planning a menu, commenting on things others do in the family that please or displease the members, discussing a family argument, planning a family vacation, allocating lottery winnings, planning an activity, using descriptive phrases to characterize the family, making up a story, discussing specific issues, and participating in miscellaneous activities.

34. The family assessment tasks might help you learn about the family's negotiation style, ways of resolving conflicts, pattern of alliances, decision-making style, patterns of interactions, roles, communication and language patterns, beliefs and expectations, and affective reactions.

35. Other areas of family life that you might want to explore include the layout of the home; a typical day in the life of the family; rules, regulations, and limit setting within the family; alliances and coalitions with the family; family disagreements; changes that the family members want to make; and previous family crises.

36. A home visit may lead to a more comprehensive and accurate assessment. You can observe family members interacting, environmental stressors, and the physical characteristics of the home.

37. A home visit may help you obtain information about whether the home is located in a safe area, the comfort and safety level

of the home, the state of repair of the home, possessions in the home, the hygienic conditions of the home, the extent of disease prevention, the adequacy of the food supply, the adequacy of the play equipment, the sleeping arrangements, the adequacy of supplies for an infant, the adequacy of the children's clothes, the adequacy of the children's grooming, the availability of educational and recreational possessions, the availability of communication and transportation, whether the children are exposed to parental "immorality," the interactions of the children with the parents, the interaction of the parents with the children, how the children get along with each other, who is living in the home, and how the parents interact with each other.

38. Overall, with any age child, you will want to observe whether the parent can relax and be comfortable with his or her child; is accepting and affectionate with his or her child; is sensitive to the child's needs, wants, and desires; seems able to take the child's perspective; is alert to issues of safety and protection while allowing the child freedom to explore his or her environment within the limits of the child's age and ability; and helps the child acquire new skills. Similarly, in all interactions with the parent, you will want to observe how the child responds to the parent's behavior or lack thereof.

39. In observing parent-child interactions, look at such things as whether the parent and child interact and how they interact, whether the parent and child are attuned to each other's needs, whether the parent is responsive to the child and regulates the child's physiological needs, whether the parent directs the child, whether the parent is intrusive, whether the parent is concerned with the child's safety and protection, whether the parent teaches the child, and, for preschool and older children, whether the parent promotes prosocial behaviors and perspective taking and whether the parent modulates his or her behavior.

40. If you suspect that your visit may be dangerous, don't go to the house unless accompanied by a police officer.

41. The six major areas to consider in evaluating a family are problem-solving style, communication patterns, roles and structure, affective responses and involvement, control mechanisms, and values and norms.

42. You also should consider the following in your evaluation of the family: Who referred the family? What is the composition of the family? Who was at the interview? How does the family provide models for its members; handle its successes and failures; recognize the talents, skills, and interests of its members; and use resources in the community? Overall, what are the strengths and weaknesses of the family? What prior interventions has the family received, and how successful were these interventions? What are the family's resources? What types of services does the family need? What short-term and long-term goals can be formulated?

Closing the Initial Interview

43. The final moments of the interview are as important as any other period in the interview. They give you a chance to summarize to the interviewee what you have learned, to get feedback from the interviewee about whether you have understood her or him, to ask any remaining questions, to inform the interviewee of any other assessments needed and about possible interventions, and to give the interviewee time to share any remaining thoughts and feelings.

44. Don't rush the ending of the interview. Budget your time so that there is enough remaining to cover what you need to cover. You want to leave the interviewee feeling that he or she has made a contribution and that the experience was worthwhile. Be courteous and friendly; inform the interviewee of what the future course of action will be and what you might expect of her or him. You don't want the interviewee to feel dismissed or used for your own purposes.

45. How you close the interview is important, especially when the interviewee is expressing some deeply felt emotion. Try not to end the interview abruptly; allow enough time for the interviewee to regain composure before she or he leaves.

46. Be aware of how much time has passed so that you don't have to rush at the end of the interview.

47. Toward the close of the interview, reflect on the interview as a whole, and consider whether you have covered everything you want to cover, whether the interviewee has any remaining questions, and similar issues.

48. Use the last minutes of the initial interview to summarize, evaluate, and plan and to give the interviewee an opportunity to ask any remaining questions.

49. Be prepared to deal with any concerns that the interviewee may have about the interview.

50. A summary statement should identify the main points of the problem for the interviewee's confirmation or correction.

51. Use appropriate comments to acknowledge the interviewee's openness and willingness to share problems, concerns, hopes, and expectations.

52. If the interviewee has not been cooperative, you may want to express your concern about what occurred in the interview.

Evaluating the Initial Interview

53. Integrate the information you obtain from a child with information you obtain from parents, teachers, physicians, psychologists, psychiatrists, and other sources. You will need to collect, organize, and interpret the assessment data to arrive at a systematic understanding of the child. Interpret the data in relation to the child as a whole, given his or her family, culture, and environment.

54. In evaluating the initial interview, you will want to consider factors affecting the interviewee's replies, compare information from multiple informants, evaluate your reactions, review the information you obtained, and consider diagnostic questions.

55. When you find differences in the accounts of the informants, consider all the information you have before you arrive at an explanation for the differences.

56. Evaluate the feelings and reactions the interviewee evoked in you.

KEY TERMS, CONCEPTS, AND NAMES

Goals of the initial interview with parents (p. 134)
Concerns of parents (p. 134)
Potential negative feelings of parents (p. 135)
Semistructured interview (p. 136)
Developmental history interview (p. 136)
Screening interview with parents of preschool children (p. 136)
Typical-day interview (p. 136)

STUDY QUESTIONS

1. What are the goals of the initial interview with parents?
2. What are some typical concerns parents may express in the interview?
3. How can you go about reducing parental resistance during the initial interview?
4. What are some useful formats for interviewing parents?
5. What are some major areas covered in a developmental history interview?
6. Describe the major components of the initial interview with parents.
7. Describe some guidelines for interviewing parents.
8. How would you evaluate the parent interview?
9. How would you go about interviewing teachers? Include in your discussion the typical areas covered in the initial interview with teachers.
10. What should you observe when you visit a classroom to obtain information about a referred child?
11. How would you evaluate the teacher interview?
12. Discuss the family interview. Include in your discussion the value of the family interview, goals of the family interview, guidelines for conducting the family interview, phases of the family interview, family assessment tasks, and evaluating the family interview.
13. Compare and contrast functional and dysfunctional family strategies in coping with a child with a psychological or medical disorder.
14. What should you be aware of when you visit the home?
15. Present guidelines for observing parent-infant interactions, parent-toddler interactions, and interactions between a parent and a school-aged child.
16. Discuss the closing phase of the initial interview. What factors need to be considered at the close of the interview?
17. Discuss how you would evaluate the findings of the initial interview with the child, parents, family, teachers, offender, and other informants as relevant. Include in your discussion how you would compare information from multiple informants, how you would account for differences in accounts from several informants, and factors you should consider in evaluating the information obtained in the interview. Give examples in your discussion.

5

THE POST-ASSESSMENT INTERVIEW

Many individuals have, like uncut diamonds, shining qualities beneath a rough exterior.

—Juvenal

Goals and Objectives

This chapter is designed to enable you to:

- Describe the major components of the post-assessment interview
- Understand the reactions of parents when they learn that they have a child with special needs

This chapter primarily describes the *post-assessment interview* (also called the *interpretive interview*) with children and with parents. Much of the discussion of the post-assessment interview centers on parents because they play a crucial role in deciding how to carry out the assessment findings and recommendations. The chapter ends with a discussion of the follow-up interview.

The post-assessment interview with children and with parents serves several purposes. These include presenting the findings, presenting possible interventions, helping children and parents understand the findings and the suggested interventions, allowing children and parents to express their concerns, and following up on hypotheses. When you plan the post-assessment interview, consider what information you want to discuss with children and parents, how much detail you want to give, and how you want to present the information. During the post-assessment interview, leave plenty of time for the children and parents to ask you questions; whenever possible, encourage them to ask questions. In your presentation, be sure to discuss the family's strengths and also its weaknesses. Although this chapter focuses on the post-assessment interview with children and with parents, the procedures discussed are generally applicable to any post-assessment interview—with teachers, physicians, attorneys, or other interested parties. Like the interview proper, the post-assessment interview will be most successful when the children and parents see you as competent, trustworthy, understanding, and interested in helping them.

Two cautions are in order about the post-assessment interview. As a clinical assessment or forensic interviewer, you will be making important decisions about children's lives. *You should never make a diagnosis, a recommendation concerning the child's treatment or placement, or a decision about whether an alleged event took place unless you are fully qualified to do so.* Also recognize that if you are discussing with the parents and child results from examinations performed by other professionals, you might not be able to answer their questions about these results.

GUIDELINES FOR THE POST-ASSESSMENT INTERVIEW

We can look at the post-assessment interview with children and parents as having five aspects—cognitive, interactive, affective, ethicoreligious, and ethnocultural.

1. The *cognitive* aspect refers to how the parents and child understand the information given to them.
2. The *interactive* aspect refers to the interaction between the interviewer and the parents and child, with the interviewer encouraging the parents and child to participate and helping them to accept the treatment recommendations.
3. The *affective* aspect refers to the feelings of the parents and child about the information presented.
4. The *ethicoreligious* aspect refers to how the parents' and child's ethical and religious views affect their beliefs about their responsibility for the problem and their willingness to follow the treatment recommendations.
5. The *ethnocultural* aspect refers to how the parents' and child's ethnic background and cultural practices affect their reactions to the information they receive and their willingness to follow the treatment recommendations.

Children and parents need time to express their feelings and reactions to the information they receive. They may feel threatened by the results, they may express doubts about the accuracy of the results, or they may express such feelings as anger, embarrassment, disappointment, or even satisfaction. You will need to cope with their feelings and reactions.

In discussing your findings, experiment with terms that you feel comfortable with and that are easily understood by children and parents. Ask them if they understand what you said and whether they would like to discuss any matters more fully. Questions such as "Is that clear?", "Would you like me to go over that again?", or "Do you have any other questions?" will be helpful.

As in the initial interview, you will want to actively listen to the children and parents; treat the children and parents with respect and dignity; recognize family values, customs, beliefs, and cultural practices; communicate openly and honestly with the children and parents; build on the children's and parents' strengths; and acknowledge and address the children's and parents' concerns and needs. Also be aware of their nonverbal behavior, such as "a shaking of the head, a scowl or frown, a sigh, a low whistle, raised eyebrows, or tears" (Miller & Rollnick, 1991, p. 98). For older children and parents, be prepared to offer such comments as the following:

- "This is hard for you to hear."
- "It must be good to hear that the problems were not as bad as you expected."
- "This is a lot of information to understand, and it may be confusing for you."
- "Do you want to get another opinion?"
- "You may be thinking 'Where do we go from here?'"
- "What would you like to do now?"
- "What do you think about what I told you?"
- "Is that clear?"
- "Would you like me to go over that again?"
- "Were the results similar to what you expected?"
- (If not) "In what way were they different?"
- (If child has been examined before) "How do these findings compare with those you have received before?"

- "What do you think you should do, based on what I've just told you?"

In addition, for parents, you might say:

- "It is difficult to learn that your child is having these problems."
- "Perhaps you're wondering what can be done to help your child."

Keep the post-assessment interview to about a 1- to 1½-hour period. Longer sessions may tax the abilities of the children or parents to comprehend all that has happened. If needed, schedule a second session. For example, you might discuss the results in one session and the intervention plan in a second session.

Confidentiality. A potentially troubling issue in the post-assessment interview with parents is the confidentiality of the information obtained from the child. Specifically, what role do children have in limiting information parents receive? Unfortunately, there are no clear legal guidelines about the extent to which information received from children is confidential; the courts and legislatures continue to define the rights of children and their parents. Although parents are responsible for their children, there is an increasing tendency toward protecting the rights of children to make their own decisions, especially when children can make competent ones (also see Chapter 2).

Release of information. It is preferable to get children's permission to release information to their parents, but you may not be legally required to do so. Obviously, you should consider the children's age and their ability to give the required permission. Any release of information must follow your state law (also see Chapter 2).

Post-Assessment Interview with Children

If possible, you should hold the post-assessment interview with children soon after the initial interview. However, you may have to hold the interview at a later time, depending on what other assessment procedures were used. The post-assessment interview may allay their fears about the assessment. The assessment results are beneficial to children who can understand the information. Children need this information as much as anyone else because they make many important self-appraisals. For example, some children wrongly estimate their abilities, and a face-to-face conference may give them information needed for self-corrective or esteem-building purposes.

Post-Assessment Interview with Parents

In the post-assessment interview with parents, your role is (a) to provide a thorough presentation of the children's learn-

ing or emotional problems (description, etiology [refers to the study of the causes of disease], severity, and prognosis), (b) to plan a specific program geared to the children's needs and capabilities, (c) to recognize and deal with the personal problems of the parents as they affect the children or as they are affected by their children's condition, and (d) to plan for future meetings as needed. Review the presenting problem, report and explain the assessment findings, and discuss the recommendations in a professional, caring, and thoughtful manner.

Four phases of the post-assessment interview with parents. Four phases characterize the post-assessment interview with parents: the establishment-of-rapport phase, the communication-of-results phase, the discussion-of-recommendations phase, and the termination phase.

FIRST PHASE: ESTABLISHING RAPPORT

1. *Arrange to meet with the parents in a private setting, and avoid interruptions.*

2. *Allow enough time for the meeting.*

3. *Make every effort to have both parents at the interview.* This will help you obtain a more objective picture of their reactions and enable them to share in the decisions that need to be made about their child. It will also relieve one parent of the burden of having to convey to the other parent the results of the evaluation.

4. *Find out if the parents want to bring other people to the meeting, such as a relative or an interpreter, and allow them to do so.*

5. *Greet the parents, giving them your name.*

6. *Establish rapport.* Help the parents feel comfortable during the interview. Encourage them to talk and to ask questions freely. Recognize the frustration and hardships that they may have faced and may face in the future. Convey to them that they have something important to contribute to the discussion. Avoid making them feel defensive, avoid fault finding and accusations, and avoid pity and condescension. Point out how they have been helpful (for example, bringing their child to the evaluation and participating themselves) and the positive qualities of the family and of the child. Your respect for the parents and your appreciation of their problems will go a long way in facilitating the post-assessment interview.

7. *Review what the parents have told you about their primary concerns, what they hope to learn from the evaluation, what they think are the causes of the problem, and what they think should be done about the problem.* If you have not seen the parents before the post-assessment interview, ask them to comment on each of these areas. You want to encourage the parents to take an active role in the interview.

8. *Never be afraid to say "I don't know."*

9. *Start and end the session with something positive about the child.*

SECOND PHASE: COMMUNICATING
THE ASSESSMENT RESULTS

10. *Summarize the assessment results and their implications as clearly as possible.* Be relaxed and unhurried in your presentation, and speak clearly, gently, and slowly. Explain your findings in a straightforward, detailed, and unambiguous manner so that the parents will understand them. Use simple, comprehensible, and nontechnical language. Avoid jargon, explain technical terms, and do not talk down to the parents. Provide illustrations and analogies as needed. Point out the significance of the findings, their treatment implications, and areas of uncertainty. Reiterate that you encourage their participation. Prepare them for information that may arouse conflicts. Be alert to how the parents understand your presentation, and make adjustments as needed to ensure, as much as it is possible, that they understand you. Give parents the opportunity to respond to the findings and to ask questions about the findings. You also may wish to tell the parents about the diagnostic procedures used in the assessment and the reasons for their selection. Allow them time to process the information. Answer their questions as honestly as possible, admit ignorance or uncertainty, and make prognostic statements with caution.

11. *Focus the interview on the child.* Tell the parents which of the child's problems are major and which are minor. Include information on the child's competencies and also his or her limitations. Help the parents understand that children with psychological or medical disorders have the same needs as all children and also some unique needs of their own. Stress the strengths and potentials of the child, keeping in mind, of course, the nature of the child's problems and the limitations associated with them. Parents especially need help so as not to be overwhelmed by their child's disorder. Inform the parents that your primary concern is the welfare and happiness of the child and that you want to work with them to achieve this goal. This focus might help reduce the personal frustration of the parents. If the parents discuss their personal problems, bring back the discussion to the child's problems. It is not that the parents' problems are unimportant, but rather that your focus *now* should be on the child. You or another professional can address their problems on another occasion.

12. *Be prepared, if the results suggest that the child has a serious problem, to deal with such parental reactions as anxiety and emotional distress, grief, disbelief, shock, denial, ambivalence, anger, disappointment, guilt, despair, and even relief.* Some parents may feel cheated because they did not produce a "perfect" being, and others may feel guilty and make self-deprecating remarks. Help the parents express their feelings, and acknowledge the feelings they express. You may have to be especially patient and understanding at these times. If the parents cry, tell them that it is OK and that many parents cry when they are given bad news.

13. *Raise the issue of etiology.* Parents often are concerned about the source of their child's problem, even if they don't ask about it. They may have misperceptions about what caused the child's problem and may feel guilty about the problem. Discuss the issue of etiology, even if you don't know the answer. Discussing the possible etiology gives you the opportunity to correct their misperceptions and relieve their guilt when it is inappropriate.

14. *Use the diagnostic findings to help the parents give up erroneous ideas and adopt a more realistic approach to the child's problems.* Give them copies of the reports, and discuss the assessment results. Some diagnoses are easier for parents to understand than others. A known genetic disorder that has predictable consequences may be easier to discuss than conditions that are not clear-cut, such as mental retardation in a very young child. Use labels cautiously whenever there is any doubt about the diagnosis. Help the parents understand that the problems are only one aspect of their child's life and that they should deal with difficulties, not avoid them. Also help them set realistic expectations for their child and shift from searching for the cause of the problems to determining what they can do for the child. Encourage them to view their child as a unique individual with rights and potentials.

15. *Evaluate how the parents understand the results throughout this second phase.* Occasionally, you may have difficulty helping the parents understand the assessment findings and recommendations. This may happen, for example, because parents have feelings of guilt that interfere with their ability to accept the information and conclusions, are embarrassed to admit that they do not understand the information, or are frustrated at not being able to solve the problem themselves and resent your interference. A calm, encouraging, and supporting manner should help parents accept the results and the recommendations better. Some parents may consider it impolite to interrupt you, to ask you questions, or to reveal that they did not understand what you said. You cannot be sure from their manner that they understood you. You may wish to check the parents' understanding of their child's disorder by saying "Please tell me in your own words what you understand about your child's condition." Use follow-up comments as needed.

16. *Be aware of your attitude toward the parents and the child.* You do not want to show pity or condescension. Instead, you want to be empathic and respectful and show an appreciation of the parents' and child's problems. Do not hide your feelings, because the parents will value them as showing your concern and your humanity.

17. *Be aware of potential pitfalls in discussing the results.* You don't want to be hasty, hurried, or rushed; lecture; get sidetracked by tangential issues; offer premature interpretations of the child's behavior or motivation; be vague and overgeneral; be too definitive based on limited findings; ignore parents' views or become defensive when they challenge your views; criticize or blame the parents; show pity or sorrow; appear irritated at questions; or give too much or too little information.

THIRD PHASE: DISCUSSING THE RECOMMENDATIONS

18. *Try to let the parents formulate a plan of action.* Allow some time for parents to assimilate the findings. Help them plan how much information about the child to give to other individuals, such as siblings, grandparents, friends, and neighbors, and how to share this information with others. Do not try to bring about fundamental changes in the parents' philosophy about child rearing or educational practices. Instead focus on the immediate, concrete issues at hand.

19. *Present your recommendations and alternatives for consideration, and discuss possible courses of action.* Develop the intervention plans with the parents, and ask for their opinions about the options. If you recommend additional diagnostic procedures, tell the parents why they are needed.

20. *Encourage the parents to assume responsibility, not to be dependent.* Some parents superficially may appear attentive, but they may not want to hear what you tell them. They may fear the future and not want to take responsibility for their child's problem. They may want to put all their faith in you and fail to assume any responsibility: "We're in your hands, doctor. Anything you say we will do. You know best." They may deny that there is a problem or express anger about the results. They may not want to appear vulnerable or to bother you with their concerns. They may attribute magic curative powers to you—as all powerful and all knowing. They may prefer that *you* deal with their child's problems. You may feel flattered by their dependence on you, but this is not what they need. They need to assume responsibility and work through their dependency feelings.

21. *Give the parents the opportunity to ask questions about the recommendations.* Evaluate what the parents think and feel about the recommendations. Some parents simply want to hear that everything will work out well without their having to put forth any effort, or they may fear that nothing will change and that the problems will continue. Help the parents see that you recognize their concerns.

22. *Be prepared to discuss possible treatment or remediation strategies, length of treatment, and financial costs, if you recommend a treatment.* Present possible treatment options, as needed. Give parents all the options that could help their child. If appropriate, let them know that competent professionals are available to work with their child and with them. If the child needs a special treatment, describe the benefits of the treatment and how the treatment will contribute to the development of the child. Deal with any concerns that the parents may have honestly and nondefensively. If you recommend placement in a special class, give the parents the opportunity to visit the class (or other facility) and to discuss the program with the teacher (or staff) before they make their final decision about the placement of their child.

23. *Carefully consider everything you know about the case before offering an opinion about prognosis, especially when dealing with young children.* Include appropriate precautions about the tentativeness of any prognosis. You want to leave the parents with some hope, even when their child is severely disabled; however, do not mislead them or give them false expectations. Parents need to know that their child will change with time, although the change may be slow when compared with changes in children who do not have a disability. Focus on the most appropriate means to obtain short-term rehabilitation goals. This will give the parents direction and motivation.

24. *Inform the parents of their legal rights, and be sure they understand them.* Discuss their rights under applicable federal laws and relevant state and local policies (see Exhibit 5-1).

25. *Recommend books, pamphlets, materials, and organizations that will aid parents in learning about their children's problems.* Ask the parents if they are interested in reading about their child's disorder, illness, or situation (see Appendix B for recommended readings for parents and children). Also, ask them if they are interested in contacting local or national organizations to learn more about their children's problems or in joining a support group or an advocacy group; if so, tell them how to do so (see the list of national organizations in Appendix A).

FINAL PHASE: TERMINATING THE POST-ASSESSMENT INTERVIEW

26. *Evaluate the parents' understanding and feelings about the results and recommendations toward the end of the post-assessment interview.* You could say, for example, "We met today so that we could discuss the results of the evaluation. What is your understanding of the findings?… How do you feel about the recommendations?"

27. *Encourage the parents to ask any additional questions, especially if you believe that they still have some concerns about the results or recommendations.* They may ask about obtaining second opinions, who else will have access to the assessment results, how long treatment may take, what role they will have in the intervention plan, what community resources are available, and the cost of treatment. Answer their questions to the best of your ability.

28. *Inform the parents that you are available for later meetings, especially if you think that you need to clarify the findings or recommendations or that they might want to see you again.* Make it easy for them to arrange subsequent meetings. You want to have an open-door policy. Encourage them to contact you or other professionals any time they have questions—even weeks, months, and years after the initial diagnosis has been made.

29. *Convey to the parents your understanding of their difficulty, especially if they are unable to accept the results of the evaluation.* Describe referral services. Provide the parents with the names of other agencies or professionals, should they want other opinions.

30. *Find out what the parents want to do immediately after the interview is over.* Ask the parents what they would like to do, such as sit in the waiting room for a while, talk to another professional if one is available, or go home.

Exhibit 5-1
Public Laws Pertinent to Children with Disabilities

The major law covering children with disabilities is Public Law 101-476, the Individuals with Disabilities Education Act (IDEA), passed by Congress in 1990 (20 USC, Sections 1401–1491). This is one of a series of laws designed to ensure that all children with disabilities, from birth to 21 years, receive a free and appropriate public education that emphasizes special education and related services designed to meet their unique needs. Public Law 101-476 incorporates and extends prior laws designed to provide services for disabled children, including (a) Public Law 94-142, the Education for All Handicapped Children Act (EAHCA or EHA), which passed in 1975 and covers ages 3 to 21, and (b) Public Law 99-457, the Infants and Toddlers with Disabilities Act (ITDA), which passed in 1986 and covers birth to age 3.

Section 504 of the Rehabilitation Act of 1973 (29 UCS, Section 706; 30 CFR Part 104) also affects the educational rights of children with disabilities (Guernsey & Klare, 1993). This law prohibits discrimination in general and covers programs or activities receiving federal assistance. Section 504 provides a broader definition about who qualifies for services than does the Individuals with Disabilities Education Act. Under Section 504, qualifying conditions include any physical or mental impairment that substantially limits one or more of life's "normal" activities; under the Individuals with Disabilities Education Act, qualifying conditions are the specific ones listed in the statute (see the list of conditions following). The statutes overlap, and both pertain to children with disabilities.

Following is a summary of children's and parents' rights under the Individuals with Disabilities Education Act and Section 504 of the Rehabilitation Act:

Nondiscriminatory Assessment
The assessment procedures used to evaluate children with disabilities must be nondiscriminatory and carried out in the child's native language or, where appropriate, by some other means of communication. Areas assessed should include health, vision, hearing, social and emotional status, general intelligence, academic performance, communicative status, and motor abilities.

Use of Trained Personnel and Multiple Procedures
The assessment procedures must be administered by trained personnel and validated for the specific purposes for which they are used. No decision should be made based on a single procedure. Observations of the child should be carried out by someone other than the child's teacher.

Qualifying Conditions
The physical or mental conditions that qualify children as "disabled" include

- developmental delay (in cognitive development, physical development, language and speech development, psychosocial development, and self-help skills)
- any condition that has a high probability of resulting in developmental delay
- mental retardation
- hearing impairments or deafness
- speech impairments
- visual impairments
- serious emotional disturbances
- orthopedic impairments
- other health impairments (including heart condition, tuberculosis, rheumatic fever, nephritis, asthma, sickle cell anemia, hemophilia, epilepsy, lead poisoning, leukemia, and diabetes)
- specific learning disability
- autism
- traumatic brain injury
- multiple disabilities

Under Section 504, children with acquired immune deficiency syndrome and attention-deficit/hyperactivity disorder also might qualify for services (Guernsey & Klare, 1993). States have the option of extending services to infants who are at risk for developmental problems, such as those with low birthweight or those who have been exposed to drugs.

Individualized Plans
A multidisciplinary team, including the parents, should formulate an individualized family or education plan. For developmentally delayed or disabled infants or toddlers, the plan used is an Individualized Family Service Plan (IFSP). It includes information about the infant's or toddler's level of development and unique needs, the family's ability to help the infant or toddler, the interventions needed by the infant or toddler, the services needed by the family to meet the infant's or toddler's needs, and the outcomes to be achieved. For preschool and school-aged children with disabilities, the plan used is an Individualized Education Program (IEP). It includes information about the disabled child's present level of educational performance, the short-term educational objectives, the annual educational goals, the specific educational services needed by the child, and the evaluation procedures for determining whether the instructional objectives are achieved.

Least Restrictive Environment
Children identified as disabled should be educated in the least restrictive environment. Placement in special classes or separate schools should be made only when the children cannot be educated satisfactorily in the regular classroom.

Needed Services
Children with developmental delays or disabilities should be provided with needed services to help them benefit from special education. These services include medical and educational assessment, physical and occupational therapy, speech and language intervention, parent counseling and training, counseling and social work services, and transportation. Services may take place in classrooms, at home, or in hospitals and institutions.

Transition Services
Schools must provide services to help students with disabilities make the transition from school to work. Transition

(*Continued*)

Exhibit 5-1 (*Continued*)

services include vocational training, continuing and adult education, adult services, independent living–skills training, and community participation training. The transition services should be included in the IEP beginning no later than age 16.

Parental Permission
Parents must give their permission for both the assessment and the placement. However, some states have provisions for overcoming parental refusal. Parents can revoke their consent to assessment or services at any time.

Keeping Parents Informed
Parents should be given a description of each evaluation procedure, test, record, or report involved in the assessment of their child and notified if there are significant changes made in the child's educational placement. These changes include transfer from a private to a public school, transfer to a more restrictive environment, returning a student to special education after a placement in regu-

lar education, initiation or termination of homebound education, and a change in the number of hours per week spent in special education classes (Guernsey & Klare, 1993).

Privacy and Confidentiality of Records
Parents have (a) the right to privacy and confidentiality of all educational records, (b) the right to receive, inspect, and review copies of all educational records before meetings, (c) the right to initiate a request for an educational assessment, (d) the right to be involved in educational planning and placement decisions, and (e) the right to an independent educational assessment at their own expense if they disagree with the assessment conducted by the school. The school must consider the independent evaluation in developing the IEP or IFSP.

Accuracy of Records
Parents have the right to request that information contained in their child's records be changed or removed if they

believe that the information is inaccurate, misleading, or in violation of their child's right to privacy.

Right of Due Process
Parents have the right of due process, meaning that parents can appeal any decision regarding the assessment, eligibility, placement, or designated instruction and services. Parents can ask for an informal meeting, a mediation conference, or a state level hearing, for example. They also have the right to be accompanied and advised by an attorney and by individuals with special knowledge or training related to the problems of disabled children. They also have other due process rights, such as the right "to present evidence, confront and cross-examine witnesses, compel attendance of witnesses, and obtain verbatim records of the hearing" (Underwood & Mead, 1995, p. 159). Parents are entitled to have their attorney's fees reimbursed if they prevail in a court action arising from a due process hearing.

---

31. *Close the interview by giving the parents your business telephone number (if they don't have it) and inviting them to call you if they have further questions.* Again, you might want to compliment the parents on their participation in the assessment and encourage them to follow the recommendations. Escort the parents from the room, thank them for their cooperation, and say goodbye.

Two examples follow that illustrate some features of the post-assessment interview. The first example shows how it can be helpful to share with the parents the child's performance on a psychological test (Pollak, 1988; J. M. Pollak, personal communication, October 1989).

CASE 5-1. TIM
Tim, a 10-year-old boy, was performing poorly in school. He appeared anxious and compulsive and seemed to be rejected by both parents. When the clinician tried to describe some positive features about the child, the father rebuffed the clinician. The clinician then decided to share a story that the child composed for Card 16 (the blank card) of the Thematic Apperception Test. The story contained the following content as rephrased by the psychologist: "A baby bird is abandoned by his family because he is unable to learn to fly. He falls out of the nest and miraculously survives a score of predators due to a series of fortuitous meetings with benevolent mice.

Because of their support and faith in him, the little bird grows up to be a leader, a 'captain of a band of birds,' and is eventually reunited with his family" (pp. 149–150). After the father heard the story, his anger and sullen demeanor changed. He was on the verge of tears and began talking about what he and his wife could do to help their son.

The second example illustrates the value of raising the issue of etiology and shows the benefits that may result from a sensitive discussion of the issue (J. Culbertson, personal communication, November 1995).

CASE 5-2. HELEN
Helen broke into tears when the interviewer discussed the etiology of her daughter's profound brain damage. The child had spastic cerebral palsy, cortical blindness, and deafness and was profoundly mentally retarded secondary to birth asphyxia because of a compressed cord at delivery. When the interviewer spoke with her, Helen had believed for seven years that she caused her child's brain damage because she had a cold at the time of delivery. She believed that she had transmitted her "cold" to the child, which caused respiratory problems and ultimately brain damage. She was relieved to hear that she did not cause her daughter's brain damage and that in all likelihood the brain damage could not have been prevented.

Sample post-assessment interview with a parent.
Let's now look at some segments of a post-assessment interview with the mother of an 8-year-old boy. The child's history and the highlights of the psychological evaluation precede the interview segments. A social worker initially interviewed the mother, and a psychologist performed the psychological evaluation and conducted the post-assessment interview. William's mother and his teacher filled out questionnaires about the child.

CASE 5-3. WILLIAM

William was referred by his pediatrician for evaluation of possible attention-deficit/hyperactivity disorder. His second-grade teacher also is concerned about his behavior in school. William is 8 years, 1 month old and is the oldest of three children. His two sisters are 6 years and 2 years old. The parents are currently separated, although the children see their father frequently. No problems have been reported for the siblings.

William reached developmental milestones at the expected times. He has had no serious illnesses or accidents. He is described as well coordinated and good at athletics. As a young child, he would not listen to stories being read by his mother, and currently his short attention span is reported to interfere with his classroom performance. He is easily distracted and has difficulty completing his work. William also is enuretic nightly but does not have toileting accidents during the day. Various interventions have been tried to help him develop bladder control, but none have been successful. He receives tutoring for reading and spelling at the parochial school that he attends, but he has never been formally evaluated for a possible learning disability or for an attention-deficit/hyperactivity disorder.

Behaviorally, William is described as a pleasant youngster who gets along well with other children his age. He is not aggressive, and he has close friends. At home, his mother has difficulty getting him to follow through on her directions, but he is not excessively defiant. She believes that he "tunes her out" and gets distracted when he tries to follow instructions. Homework is a "battle" every night according to the mother, and she must sit next to William in order to get him to complete his work. His teacher also reported that she has difficulty getting William to complete his work in class, unless she works with him on a one-to-one basis.

The results of the psychological evaluation indicated that William has average intellectual ability (IQ = 102), with relative strengths in perceptual organization abilities and relative weaknesses in verbal comprehension abilities. There was a severe discrepancy between expected and actual achievement in reading comprehension and written expression, including spelling. His reading comprehension was at the 13th percentile rank, written expression at the 13th percentile rank, and spelling at the 7th percentile rank. However, his arithmetical reasoning was average, at the 55th percentile rank. His visual-motor integration ability also was below average, at the 5th percentile rank. These results suggest that William has a learning disability in the areas of reading, written expression, and spelling. He also meets the criteria for an attention-deficit/hyperactivity disorder, with symptoms of inattention, impulsivity, and hyperactivity. Other difficulties involve expressive communication (primarily related to the

fluency of his oral expression), word-finding and labeling problems, vocabulary, and syntax. These language difficulties likely underlie his learning disability.

It is recommended that William be considered for special education services to address his learning disabilities in reading and written expression. He needs remedial assistance to reinforce and teach basic skills in reading and written expression. He also needs help with his attention-deficit/hyperactivity disorder. This would include helping him organize his work and develop study habits and providing him a quiet place to study that is relatively free from distractions. A behavioral management program should be considered that emphasizes rewards for appropriate behavior and nonphysical types of punishment for inappropriate behavior. William also should be referred to a pediatrician for possible medical management of his attention-deficit/hyperactivity disorder. Finally, William should be evaluated by a speech-language pathologist to determine appropriate remediation for his oral-expressive problems.

SEGMENTS FROM THE POST-ASSESSMENT INTERVIEW

[Introductions]

IR: Well, what I'd like to do is just go over the test results that we got on William and try to address them around the questions that you came in asking—that you were concerned about his learning.

IE: Mmm-hmm.

IR: The first thing on your list, though, was whether he has attention-deficit/hyperactivity disorder. You're really worried about his attention and his activity level and how that gets in the way of his school performance.

IE: Yes.

IR: But also about his learning ability.

IE: Right.

IR: His reading, his writing, and so forth, spelling.

IE: Mmm-hmm.

IR: So we looked at all of that. We tried to pay close attention to language, to writing abilities, to all the things that go into school performance.

IE: Mmm-hmm.

IR: And William was very cooperative so I feel like we got a very good, valid look at what he knows and what he doesn't know.

IE: Mmm-hmm.

IR: He did everything I asked him to do....

[Discussion of behavior and test results.]

IR: When I say I think he has a learning disability, what I mean is he's got normal intelligence. Kids with learning disabilities do have normal intelligence. But there are some things that block the way they understand certain types of information. We think it's related to how his brain is functioning, but if we were to do brain scans or EEGs we wouldn't see any area probably that was damaged on his brain.

IE: Mmm-hmm.

IR: These are very, very subtle things that have to do with the way information is transmitted in his brain. They usually don't show up on medical tests. But we know that they have a big effect on the way that he's able to learn his basic reading and writing skills. And children with learning disabilities generally can learn, but they may need a special type of teaching. We need to find out what are his strengths in learning and use those strengths to help him learn.

IE: Mmm-hmm.

IR: And we also need to be very careful that we don't have expectations that are above what he can do right now, because his learning is going to be slower because of this learning disability. And I think that William's feeling a lot of pressure because he knows he's struggling.

IE: Right.

IR: And it's showing up as he works. He looks frustrated, and he acts frustrated. And it's hard for him.
[Further discussion of William's test performance and what his teachers might do at his parochial school.]

IR: Another option might be to just go visit the school that he would be allowed to go to, the public school, and see for yourself. Just see what the classrooms would be like. Get a feel for it. You could tell a lot by being there.

IE: Do you think he would be in a special education class?

IR: Well, I think that he would benefit from special education for his learning disability. And I haven't talked about the other area that you were concerned about, but I do think William has an attention-deficit/hyperactivity disorder. From talking to you, from looking at the behavioral checklists that you and his teacher filled out, and from working with him all day long myself, I really think that he's struggling with the attention problems. He's very fidgety, and he's impulsive.

IE: Mmm-hmm.

IR: When I was working with him in a very quiet room without distractions, I noticed that in trying to give him instructions for a test, that he kept starting before I finished the instructions.

IE: Mmm-hmm.

IR: And it was like he had such trouble holding back.

IE: Mmm-hmm.

IR: So I really think that it is probably a problem, too—that he has trouble with attention and staying focused. All this activity level gets in the way of his learning.

IE: Mmm-hmm.

IR: He developed two different disabilities that he has to perform with—one being the learning disability and the other being the attention-deficit/hyperactivity problem.

IE: Mmm-hmm.

IR: And I think both of those things together make it very, very difficult for him to stay focused on his work at school, to get it finished. That's why I think William's not getting his work done. And I don't think this is any motivation problem. And I don't think it's a behavior problem, where William's just not hearing.

IE: Because he does want to do it.

IR: Yeah.

IE: He really does want to do it.

IR: My impression was that he really does care, but he just feels defeated and he's giving up, some of the time. Now we can encourage him again to try again, but even when he tries hard, he struggles.

IE: Mmm-hmm.

IR: And he's bright enough to make it. I think that's where the stress is coming from for William.

IE: Mmm-hmm.

IR: He knows he's smart and he knows that he still can't do it, in some areas.

IE: So what do we do about his attention-deficit disorder?

IR: Well, there are options there, too. The behavioral options are, number one, we inform his teacher that this is a disorder he has. This is something he can't help. And I've suggested in the report several things that the teacher might want to consider trying to do in her classroom. Let me just show you what I wrote. I try to think of practical recommendations that would be helpful to the teacher. Curriculum modifications that we often recommend include things like helping William develop study skills that would help his organization. This is maybe not as big a deal in second grade as it's going to be in third grade and fourth, and on up.

IE: Mmm-hmm.

IR: But, just remembering to write down all of his assignments and bring them home is a big first step.

IE: Right.

IR: Once he's home, you can monitor things and make sure he gets it done.

IE: Right.

IR: But then the teacher's going to have to check him in the next morning and make sure he turns it in, because that's probably going to be difficult for William.

IE: Mmm-hmm.

IR: We need to make sure he has a notebook to carry his papers in, and we might buy a notebook that has dividers for each subject area. So once the homework's done it goes right back in the notebook in that area, and his assignments get written down in that area. Children who have an attention-deficit/hyperactivity disorder are going to have difficulty organizing themselves, and William's going to need help from you and from his teacher to get better organized. And that's about half the battle, right there, just getting him all organized. What we want to work on in the classroom, then, is to help him with his problem staying focused and to teach him to work in short bursts. In other words, we might set a 5-minute span where we want him to work just solidly for 5 minutes and then we're going to give him a break. At home, what we often recommend is if you have a little kitchen timer that you can set, and it will go for 5 minutes and a little bell will ring. Try to get him to do work bursts at home also, for homework.

IE: Mmm-hmm.

IR: "William, if you work for 5 minutes, the bell's going to go off, and something nice will happen." Either he gets a special hug from you or he gets a treat or he gets a break—he can stand up and run around the kitchen two or three times.

IE: Mmm-hmm.

IR: And then he'll come back and work for another 5 minutes.

IE: Mmm-hmm.

IR: But we realize that he can't work for prolonged periods. He needs to work in short bursts and then take a break. And what we want to do by setting that procedure up for him is we want to train him to do that himself. We want him to learn to really focus in for short periods and then take a break. And then focus back in for short periods, and then take a break. And when he learns to do that himself, then he'll be able, we hope, to lengthen the time that he works.

IE: Mmm-hmm.

IR: But right now those periods of work have to be pretty short. Because he can't sustain…What he's doing now is he's just sitting there, and he's on task a few seconds and he's looking around and he's back on.

IE: So he's automatically taking those little breaks himself.

IR: And he's frustrated and you're frustrated because you don't see him getting his work done.

IE: Mmm-hmm.

IR: We want him to be really focused during that 5 minutes, and if he can't make it for 5 minutes, we've got to bring it down to 2 minutes.

IE: Mmm-hmm.

IR: I mean, whatever length of time he can work without getting distracted. We've got to set it real short and then let him take a break. But we want to train him to work diligently during that short period of time. And if the teacher's doing that also, then that's going to be helpful.

IE: Mmm-hmm.

IR: The bottom line there is that he needs feedback about how he's doing after he's worked for that short period of time. "William, you got five problems done! That's terrific!" And he needs to hear of the good: "We're real proud of you because you got five problems done!"

IE: Mmm-hmm.

IR: It takes more effort from him; it doesn't come naturally because he has this disorder. And so he has to work harder than you and I would to maintain his attention. He could use an awful lot of praise to help him gear up and get more motivated and put that extra energy into doing that.

IE: Mmm-hmm.

IR: And we need to find incentives for him to work in these short bursts with a brief rest period. Think of things that maybe you could come up with around the house. Each evening is kind of a battle for him to remember homework. So if there could be some kind of special incentive like—don't know—special time with you or with his dad. Five minutes of special time, where the girls aren't allowed—it's just you sitting with him doing a fun game that he could choose. It might be a reward for getting his homework done. And if homework is frustrating, it's a nice way to finish the day, to have some positive play time with mom or with dad.

IE: Mmm-hmm.

IR: And 5 minutes wouldn't be a really big amount of time, but it might make a big difference for William if it's done consistently.

IE: Mmm-hmm.

IR: But any kind of little incentives that you could come up with would be helpful to try to think of. So these were things we could do behaviorally. Another option for dealing with this is to consider a referral for possible medical management of the attention-deficit/hyperactivity disorder. Now this becomes your choice once you hear about what medications have been used, how well they work, and what potential side effects are.

IE: Mmm-hmm.

IR: Some parents choose to give a trial of medications—Ritalin is one that's commonly used—to see if it helps

their child calm down his or her activity level and stay focused in a little better. For about 70 to 80 percent of children who do have an attention-deficit/hyperactivity disorder, these medications work.

IE: Mmm-hmm.

IR: And parents and kids are pleased with them. There are then 20 to 30 percent of children where it does not work—it is not effective. And I'm not sure which group William would fall in.

IE: Mmm-hmm.

IR: So when we say consideration of medical management, we're realizing you need more information. You need to talk to a physician who's experienced in using these medications to tell you what the benefits would be and the potential side effects. One of the side effects has to do with decrease in appetite in some children, and we wouldn't want William to slow down his growth or to be losing his appetite and losing his opportunity to grow because he's already small.

IE: Mmm-hmm.

IR: So the physician would have to work with you about how to time the dosage after a meal, rather than before a meal, so you don't affect his appetite.

IE: Mmm-hmm.

IR: There are a lot of ways to work around it.

IE: Mmm-hmm.

IR: These are medications that if they're going to work, they work quickly. And you know it pretty well at the beginning. But that's the other option that you have to consider. We could work with the teacher. We could try to structure things in the classroom and at home, or the best thing might be to consider both options.

IE: Mmm-hmm.

IR: Some parents have pretty strong feelings about medications and don't like that idea. Whatever you feel about that, the recommendation is that we try to help you get some more information so you can make a decision about whether you want to try that.

IE: Mmm-hmm.

IR: Because medication is helpful to so many children, it's important for you to know about it.…

[More discussion of William's difficulties and how they may affect his school performance and concluding remarks.]

Evaluation of the post-assessment interview with parents.   Questions to consider in the post-assessment interview with parents include the following:

1. How much information did the parents hear and absorb?
2. Did the parents understand the results?
3. Did they accept the results?
4. Did they understand the recommendations?
5. Did they accept the recommendations?
6. What areas did they question, if any?
7. What kinds of interventions did they want?
8. Did they understand their rights under relevant federal laws and state and local policies?
9. Did they want another evaluation of their child from an independent source?

10. What would they consider successful treatment or remediation?
11. How willing are they to change their own expectations and behavior?
12. Are they willing to involve themselves in parent-training programs or in other skill programs?
13. What are their resources for making changes and for cooperating with the intervention plans?
14. What resources do the parents have to hospitalize or institutionalize their child if they want to do so?

When handled poorly, the initial diagnostic phase will remain as a bitter memory whose details linger in the minds of the parent for many years thereafter. When handled with sensitivity and technical skill, this experience can contribute to a strong foundation for productive family adaptation and for constructive parent-professional collaboration.

—Michael Thomasgard and Jack P. Shonkoff

Parents' Ability to Cope with the Diagnosis

A five-stage coping model. It is a traumatic experience for most parents to learn that they have a child with special needs when they were not aware or only slightly aware that the child had problems. In coming to terms with the diagnosis, families tend to go through five stages: impact, denial, grief, focusing outward, and closure (Fortier & Wanlass, 1984; also see Table 5-1). However, not all families (or individuals) go through stages or do so in the same way. Here are some parents' reactions as they went through the five stages (Drotar, Baskiewicz, Irvin, Kennell, & Klaus, 1975, pp. 712–713; Leff & Walizer, 1992, pp. 148–149):

1. *Impact.* During the impact phase, parents may be agitated, feel anxious, seek support, and be somewhat disoriented.

- My most painful experience was the initial evaluation that our son was impaired neurologically. The grief, crying, pain, anxiety, *loss* were awful. There are still times when waves from those first few days of formally knowing return. However, I feel that no professional could or should have cushioned these feelings. Support, yes; cushioning, no. Our distress was a necessary human reaction that helped us push forward to investigate appropriate programs. I must add that the bad news was coupled with specific recommendations for treatment and programs. We were able to focus our grief and anger in ways that helped our child.
- It was a big blow. It just shattered me.

2. *Denial.* During the denial phase, parents may shop for new cures, have mood swings, seek people who support their views, and have distorted expectations.

- I knew Rochelle had problems, but I couldn't face up to the fact that this could be a life-long disability for many months—at no fault of the many doctors, friends, family, and professionals that tried to help me. I just wasn't ready.
- I found myself repeating "It's not real" over and over again.
- I just couldn't believe it was happening to me. I thought it was unreal and I would soon wake up.

3. *Grief.* During the grief phase, parents may be sleepless, feel angry and helpless, have anxiety-related physical symptoms, be distant from others, and question the meaning of life.

- Shocked, angry; I was so careful before and during my pregnancy. We were tortured by his sufferings. I longed to put him back inside me where he belonged. No one is so naked as a premature baby. I was angry at science's ineffectual interference; my baby was saved to be tormented.
- I felt terrible. I couldn't stop crying. Even after a long while, I still cried about it.
- I never hated the baby, I hated what she was. I didn't care if she died.
- I just wanted to kick someone.
- Holding him with the tube distressed me. Initially, I held him only because it was the maternal thing to do.
- I asked, Why me? Why him? Why us? What did we do wrong? What did I do wrong? Am I being punished? Is he being punished? For what? What did he do? He didn't do anything, he's just a kid. How come? What is the reason for all this? There is no reason. I sat out there last summer in the swing in the middle of the night wondering all about God and religion and the church with no real answer.

4. *Focusing outward.* During the focusing-outward phase, parents may seek information, regain some confidence, have renewed energy, consider options with others, and have a sense of increased reality.

- When they gave her to me and put her in my arms, then she was mine.
- We had been conjuring up all kinds of things—that there could be something wrong with every organ. But then what I saw was a relatively normal baby.

5. *Closure.* During the closure phase, parents may return to the precrisis behavior, feel more at ease and relaxed, work toward new goals, and accept the child and the situation.

- I realized that it was nothing I had done.
- We worried more about each other than the baby. We needed each other more during this time.
- He's [husband] the only way I'm holding up still. We couldn't have gotten through this without each other.

Further exploration of the impact phase. Now let us look at the impact phase in more detail.

Children with special needs identified at birth. As noted in Table 5-1, parents who give birth to a child with special needs may be in a state of shock when they learn that their child is disabled (Frude, 1991). They may experience a sense of failure or humiliation because they did not produce a normal child. They also may experience a feeling of loss—loss

Table 5-1
Characteristics of Crisis Stages over Five Modalities

Stage	Behavior	Affect	Sensation	Interpersonal relations	Cognition
Impact	Agitation, pacing, fidgeting; or lethargy, moving in slow motion, appearing dazed	Feelings of anxiety or shock	Physiological changes of anxiety or shock; nausea, diarrhea, fainting, muscle tenseness	Seeking support of others, needing to talk; or isolation, withdrawal	Disorientation, confusion, circular thinking
Denial	Shopping for cures or new diagnoses, going through motions of pre-crisis behavior; or selective attention to acceptable data only	Alternating between hope, despair, and avoidance of feelings	Controlled anxiety	Seeking the company of those who support current view of problem and avoiding those who disagree	Disbelief, imagining situations where problem disappears or cure is found, fictionalized explanations, distorted expectations, not hearing
Grief	Sleeplessness, crying, spurts of activity alternating with lethargy, changes in behavior due to care of child	Anger, helplessness, sense of loss, self-pity, self-doubt, sense of isolation, guilt, revival of dormant or unresolved feelings	Anxiety-related physical symptoms, tears, fatigue	Loss of interpersonal warmth	Questioning "how?" and "why?", death wish toward child as possible solution, reliving of prior events that might be "reason for this punishment," thoughts of what it will be like in future
Focusing outward	Information seeking, increased friendliness and contact with others	Relief, confidence	Renewed energy	Talking options over with others, seeking out those who have knowledge	Reconsidering options, increased awareness of reality, formulating plans
Closure	Beginning to meet needs of child and family, returning to precrisis behavior where possible	Calm	Relaxed muscles, decrease in physical symptoms	Emergence of family solidarity as work toward new goals begins, increased closeness with similar others	Acceptance of child and situation

Source: Copyrighted (1984) by the National Council on Family Relations, 3989 Central Ave. NE, Suite 550, Minneapolis, MN 55421. Reprinted with changes in notation by permission. From L. M. Fortier and R. L. Wanlass, "Family Crisis Following the Diagnosis of a Handicapped Child," *Family Relations*, 1984, *33*, p. 18, with changes in notation.

of the child they expected and loss of a healthy infant. The feeling of loss may lead to an acute bereavement reaction. They also may feel revulsion, embarrassment, guilt, and anger. They may worry about bonding with their infant.

The following examples illustrate how interviewers reflected parents' feelings in order to keep lines of communication open during the post-assessment interview (Krehbiel & Kroth, 1991, p. 117, with changes in notation):

1. IE: It might be better if Janey just dies.
   IR: Today, your pain for Janey is very strong.

2. IE: People will always stop to stare at him, all of his life.
   IR: It seems that people are not always aware of the harm they can do.

3. IE: Is this what people call "quality of life"? I don't think so.
   IR: You're taking another look at the meaning of life now.

4. IE: Right now, I hate everyone connected with "special children."

   IR: Right now, everyone reminds you that there is something not right with Jess.

5. IE: I feel like everyone is rejecting me and our family.

   IR: Just when you need support, people don't come through for you.

6. IE: I am going to kill somebody before this is over.

   IR: You feel on fire thinking about the injustices your daughter suffers.

7. IE: I know it is my fault. I am the one who gave birth to this child.

   IR: It's painful when you believe you caused your child to be disabled.

Children with special needs identified later in life. Parents may be less shocked when their child is identified as being disabled later in life (Frude, 1991).

The disability is likely to be less serious…and the parents will probably have developed a strong attachment to the infant.

The indication that all is not well may come gradually, and in many cases it will be the parents themselves who first suspect that there is something amiss. At first their fears may remain unspoken, and they may strongly dismiss any suggestions from others that the child has some handicapping condition. Later they may be forced to acknowledge that something could indeed be wrong, although at first their anxieties may be hesitatingly expressed….

[However,] confirmation that their child is suffering from a lifetime disabling condition is always profoundly disheartening for parents. They need to adjust their view of the child's future and their own. Critical to the impact made by such a diagnosis is the way in which the process of informing the parents is handled. This is a task calling for the utmost sensitivity, and many parents are able to recall, long afterwards, precise details of how the news was communicated to them. (pp. 128–130)

Sometimes, however, parents have as much difficulty accepting the disability or illness of an older child as they do that of an infant. Parents' image of normal existence and faith in an orderly and just world may be called into question (Chesler & Barbarin, 1987).

Further exploration of the denial phase. Parents may use several defensive methods, which in the examples to follow are all variants of denial, to cope with the diagnosis (Cutter & Miller, 1971). One method that parents use is to believe that their child is normal and then reject the diagnosis. This denial mechanism may subject their child to extreme pressure because they will expect their child to perform like other children. A second method is to recognize that something is wrong but to hold out for the most acceptable diagnosis. The parent might say "My child is only emotionally disturbed," when, in reality, the child is brain damaged and functioning in the mentally retarded range. A third defensive method used by parents is to deny the clinician the opportunity to discuss the child's condition by being overly accepting of the diagnosis—for example, "We know all about the condition and are doing everything possible to accept it, and we do not need any help or suggestions." This method insulates the parents from considering the implications of the diagnosis.

When a child is diagnosed as having a serious disability such as mental retardation or an autistic disorder, parents are behaving realistically if they want to seek a second opinion, given the tremendous impact of the diagnosis. However, some parents of children with special needs *shop around*— that is, they visit several different professionals or clinics in the hope of obtaining an acceptable diagnosis. Once they get an acceptable diagnosis, they may look endlessly for new treatments or educational programs to "cure" the disorder. This shopping behavior is frequently maladaptive. It is costly in time, parental energy, and money. It is disruptive of family life and sometimes involves making long trips or even relocating. It also takes the parents' focus away from constructive efforts to work with their child. To reduce the possibility of shopping behavior, help the parents work through their feelings when they learn about their child's disability.

Parental differences in learning about their child's disability. A mother and a father may react differently to learning that their child has a disability, as the following case illustrates (Miller, 1979):

CASE 5-4. MR. & MRS. C.
Mr. and Mrs. C. brought their son, 5-year-old Jim, for an evaluation because he seemed to be a slow learner. Testing revealed that Jim was moderately retarded, functioning on the level of about a 3-year-old. The father's initial reaction was overt grief. Stunned by the diagnosis, he cried openly during the initial and later interviews and later became depressed and withdrawn at home. Mrs. C. showed little overt emotion and questioned the test results because Jim was shy with the examiner. After the evaluation, she became highly overprotective of Jim.

After six sessions with the therapist, Mr. C. became mobilized and began actively seeking resources. He took Jim to join Special Olympics and signed up as a coach. Mrs. C. became extremely angry with her husband, saying that in so doing he had admitted the child was retarded and had given up hope. Mr. C. thought that his wife was denying reality and that her overprotectiveness was preventing Jim from having many normal daily experiences. She asserted that if she didn't watch Jim's every move, he would surely die—by drowning in the bathtub or experiencing some other calamity.

Mr. and Mrs. C. reacted in highly different ways to their son's diagnosis, both according to their own coping styles, needs, and fears. As the parents were increasingly able to accept the reactions of the other and to discuss their own feelings of loss, anger, and depression, they began working together for Jim's benefit. Mrs. C.'s involvement in a mothers' group was an important intervention, where she felt comfortable expressing feelings she could not yet expose to her husband. (p. 300, with changes in notation)

Post-Assessment Interview with Parents as a Staff Conference

In some settings—such as schools, mental health clinics, and hospitals—several professionals may evaluate the child and the family (see Table 1-1 in Chapter 1). In such cases, a staff conference may be helpful when each member of the team can make a unique contribution to the presentation or when it is important for the parents or child to hear the views of each professional directly. When the post-assessment interview with parents is in the form of a staff conference, the following guidelines complement those presented previously (Greenbaum, 1982):

1. *Prepare for the conference carefully.* The *team leader* (sometimes called the *case manager*) should review all case history information, medical reports, test results, and recommendations.

2. *Set specific goals for the conference.* The team leader should prepare goals before the meeting. The team members should reach a unified position before the conference.

3. *Be organized.* The team leader should start and end the conference on time, follow the agenda, and allow enough time to cover the agenda. Team members should introduce themselves. If each member presents his or her findings, the presentations should be organized and orderly.

4. *Individualize the conference.* The team members should focus on material relevant to the concerns of the child and family.

5. *Appear confident.* The team members should choose their words carefully and maintain their composure.

6. *Don't be defensive.* The team members should recognize that they do not have all the answers. They should not get involved in power struggles with the parents or with each other.

7. *Form an alliance with the parents.* The team members should see the parents as part of the team, help the parents to see themselves as part of the team, and encourage the parents to work with the team in carrying out the recommendations. Parents should be encouraged to address questions to any team member.

8. *Explore the needs of the parents.* The team members need to understand the feelings and reactions of the parents and switch from the agenda, if necessary, to help the parents work through their special concerns.

9. *Tell it like it is.* The team members should be direct and honest and avoid technical jargon. They should discuss relevant public laws and state and local policies that pertain to the child and family (see, for example, Exhibit 5-1 presented earlier in the chapter).

10. *Explain the recommended interventions.* The team leader or another team member should explain the interventions. Parents should not be pressured to follow a plan they believe is inappropriate for their child.

11. *Make a closing statement.* The team leader should summarize the findings and decisions, arrange for future appointments, and tell the parents how they can reach each member of the team.

Holding a staff conference may not be the best way to conduct a post-assessment interview, however. Sitting at one end of a table watching six or seven professionals give reports is an intimidating experience for many parents. An alternative is to have a designated case manager who meets with the parents and summarizes the findings and recommendations of the staff or to have each professional individually meet with the parents.

Comment on the Post-Assessment Interview with Parents

The way in which each post-assessment interview unfolds will depend on the needs of the parents and on your orientation. *Always show warmth, understanding, and respect.* Children and parents are especially appreciative when they see that you are listening to them and are understanding of their concerns. Help parents become less defensive by telling them that you appreciate the effort they are making to help their child (where appropriate). The crucial test of the effectiveness of the post-assessment interview is whether the parents act based on what they have learned.

What you don't want to do in the post-assessment interview is to be brusque, to present the findings and leave little or no time for discussion, or to disregard the needs of the parents.

I felt the way I was told and the circumstances in which I was told caused me a greater shock than the news of [my son's] condition did...The first words uttered to me by a total stranger in a totally strange room in the absence of any other human being whom I knew by sight even were, "Mrs X, what do you know about Mongolism?" I was not invited to sit down, he did not introduce himself to me, nothing came before the words I quote above...And the preparation would have been so easy—"please sit down", "how are you?", "how was the birth?", "what's his name?" My husband might have been asked to be present (later I had to scrounge money for the phone box); where was my lovely doctor who had seen me through 10 years of trying to get pregnant after a still-birth? Perhaps my baby could have been there? Maybe we could have looked at those little straight lines on his hand palm together? (Nursey, Rohde, & Farmer, 1991, p. 51)

Parents holding erroneous beliefs about their child's condition before the interview will probably not give them up after one interview. These beliefs may be protecting them from unpleasant consequences. Therefore, you may need several interviews with the parents. You also may want to visit their home in such cases.

In working with families of children with special needs, recognize that the family has considerable influence on the ability of the child to deal with the disability and to profit from an intervention program. Help the family members understand how the child can cope with the disability so that they can become part of the rehabilitation team and help the rehabilitation staff by working with the child at home.

Parents will be reacting to the entire assessment process from the beginning of the initial interview to the end of the post-assessment interview. This experience with professionals may be positive, negative, or somewhere in between (Boyer & Chesteen, 1992). Parents will especially resent professionals who fail to include them in the decision-making process, who view them as objects, who talk down to them, or who fail to consider their needs. Parents will appreciate professionals who answer their questions honestly, give understandable explanations, respect their self-determination, solicit their participation, give them support,

offer understandable and realistic recommendations, provide information about the best possible care, and are knowledgeable about community resources. Table 5-2 lists negative and positive experiences that families may have with mental health professionals. If you want to, you can ask the parents to evaluate the services they received by filling out a questionnaire such as the one shown in Table 5-3. It contains 13 items and can be completed in a few minutes' time.

The following comments also will help you understand the feelings and concerns that parents of children with special needs may face in their interactions with professionals. (Reprinted, with permission, from S. M. Duwa, C. Wells,

Table 5-2
Negative and Positive Experiences That Families of Children with Special Needs May Have in Their Contacts with Mental Health and Medical Professionals

Negative experiences	Positive experiences
The professional	The professional
• resented the family's questioning his or her recommendations or disagreeing with him or her • did not seem interested in listening to the family's opinions and ideas • did not know community resources that might be helpful to the family • talked down to the family and made the members feel incompetent • gave advice too quickly without learning important information about the family or child • lacked empathy for the family • did not answer the family's questions • used technical jargon • tended to gloss over the family's concerns and offer inappropriate reassurance • rushed the family • did not explain recommended treatments or procedures • offered the family little hopeful or positive information • made recommendations for treatments without taking the family's time and monetary resources into account • did not clearly explain his or her findings and recommendations • made the family members believe that many of the child's problems were their fault • was negative about other community resources • seemed uncomfortable with the child and family • kept the family waiting for unreasonable periods of time or frequently changed or canceled appointments • communicated poorly with other team members and had goals that differed from those of other team members • failed to describe follow-up services adequately at the time of discharge	• gave the family members ideas of how to deal with their problems but left the final choice of action up to them • listened to the family members and answered their questions • was interested in the family members' observations and opinions about the problem • gave the family members enough time to discuss their concerns • supported the family members' efforts to deal with their problems • did not make the family feel guilty about the child's problems • gave the family reasons for the recommendations • was generally on time for appointments and did not change or cancel them • had empathy for the family's feelings and concerns • seemed to like and want to help the family • respected the family's abilities and competencies • was respectful of the family's resources in recommending treatments, procedures, or other services • had a good knowledge of other resources available to help the family • explained the findings and observations in an understandable way • welcomed the family's questions and was not threatened by disagreements • was honest yet hopeful about the child • appeared to have good working relationships with other professionals in the community • encouraged all family members to come to the interviews • respected the family's other responsibilities and time commitments in recommending treatments, procedures, and other services

Source: Adapted from Boyer and Chesteen (1992).

Table 5-3
Assessment of Parent Satisfaction

ASSESSMENT OF PARENT SATISFACTION

Please help us improve our program by answering some questions about the services you have received. We are interested in your honest opinions, whether they are positive or negative. *Please answer all of the questions.* We welcome your comments and suggestions, and we appreciate your help. Place a check in the appropriate space for Questions 1 through 11, and write your comments for Questions 12 and 13. Thank you.

1. How long did you wait to get an appointment after your initial request?

   _____ 0–2 weeks   _____ 2–4 weeks   _____ 4–8 weeks   _____ more than 8 weeks   _____ don't know

2. This waiting time seemed   _____ short   _____ acceptable   _____ somewhat long   _____ very long.

3. What did you think about the total length of the visit?   _____ too short   _____ all right   _____ too long

4. The staff was   _____ very helpful   _____ somewhat helpful   _____ not very helpful   _____ not helpful at all.

5. The staff was   _____ late   _____ somewhat late   _____ mostly on time   _____ on time.

6. The staff was   _____ easy to understand   _____ somewhat easy to understand

   _____ somewhat hard to understand   _____ hard to understand.

7. The information you received was   _____ confusing   _____ not very clear   _____ somewhat clear   _____ clear.

8. The recommendations you received were   _____ useful   _____ somewhat useful   _____ not very useful   _____ useless.

9. To what extent has our program met your needs?

   _____ none met   _____ only a few met   _____ most met   _____ almost all met

10. Overall, how satisfied are you with the service you received?

    _____ very satisfied   _____ mostly satisfied   _____ indifferent/mildly dissatisfied   _____ quite dissatisfied

11. If you were to seek help again, would you return to our program?

    _____ no, definitely not   _____ no, I think not   _____ yes, I think so   _____ yes, definitely

12. What did you like best about the clinic or agency?

13. What did you like least about the clinic or agency?

Source: Adapted from Krahn, Eisert, and Fifield (1990).

and P. Lalinde [1993]. Creating Family-Centered Programs and Policies. In D. M. Bryant and M. A. Graham [Eds.], *Implementing Early Intervention: From Research to Effective Practice,* pp. 92–123, New York: Guilford.)

- I called the social worker to let her know I could not make it to the parent meeting that morning. I started crying. I didn't mean to.... I was just worried they would think I didn't care about Maria if I couldn't make it to every meeting.
- Some professionals sound like car salesmen with all of their promises of what they are going to "do" for us. I don't want promises, I don't want them to "DO" for me, I want to learn how to get my family back to where we are in control again.

- Nolan wasn't eligible for their program but definitely needed some help. They gave me a stack of books and papers to use as guides to work with him myself until his next evaluation. After she left, I took the papers home and put it on top of the stuff the other places had given me; the stack was already 3 feet high and he isn't even 2 years old yet.
- I don't want to go someplace else for services for Cedrick. I don't know those people. They don't know us. They will never have to look us in the eye if they make a mistake. I don't like maps. What if the car breaks down? What if we can't find the place? How will I know if they are doing the right things?
- The professionals begin to get uneasy when we start to get emotional. They want us to focus on Katrina's future. Can't they

understand that we are talking about what is left of our dreams and the impact it will have on our family forever? Forever is a long time....Who can see beyond forever?

- You can't even begin to imagine what it is like in our home. We have to deal with a lot more than Courtney's problems. If we can't get the other things done, we can't take care of her.
- By the time Janell was 2 years old, we had weekly contact with 14 doctors, 11 nurses, 2 home health agencies, 4 case managers, 4 state agencies, 3 therapists, 2 insurance companies, 2 pharmacies, 3 tertiary care centers, 2 durable medical equipment companies, and special education teachers.
- I didn't agree with some of the ways that our family was treated so I asked to talk to someone at the main office. I found out that they were really interested in helping, but they were so far away that they didn't always know what we needed.
- This is a very important but difficult job I am doing. I am human and possess all of the wonderful and not so wonderful emotions that go with it. There will be times when I will cry, when I will laugh, when I will be angry, sad, or when I just won't care. Please don't overreact or read too much into my human emotions. I have as much right to them as you do.
- She stops breathing several times a night, her heart rate drops to 40 or soars into the 300s, she shakes all the time and throws up most of what I feed her. I am sorry I don't remember how old she was when she rolled over for the first time.
- When they wrote the program, it never occurred to them that it just doesn't work that way in a home. The phone rings, brothers and sisters get hurt and need bandages, there are Cub Scout meetings, the never-ending advice of grandparents, and, of course, someone has to feed the family. The plan never considered someone has to cook.
- I knew we needed some help so I started to call around. Each person I spoke with had the name and number of another person for me to call. Ten phone calls later I still didn't have the information I needed.
- On most days I am an occupational therapist, physical therapist, nurse, teacher, case manager, taxi driver, social worker, and dietitian. Some days I just want to be her mom; nothing else, just her mom. Please don't make me feel wrong for that.

The post-assessment interview with parents requires sensitivity and understanding of their feelings, needs, and desires. It is not a matter of simply reciting results or reading a report. Rather, you should make every effort to enlist the cooperation of the parents in working toward an effective intervention plan. You want to establish a collaborative partnership with the parents so that together you can come to a better understanding of the needs of the child and work toward solving the problems.

Families that adopt a positive, coping strategy—because of their own resources, the help that you have offered them, or some combination of the two—ideally can accomplish the following (from Marsh, D. T., FAMILIES AND MENTAL RETARDATION: NEW DIRECTIONS IN PROFESSIONAL PRACTICE [Praeger, an imprint of Greenwood Publishing Group, Inc., Westport, CT 1992]. Copyright © 1992 by D. T. Marsh. Reprinted with permission of Greenwood Publishing Group, Inc.; all rights reserved, p. 58):

- accept the disability and its consequences for the family
- focus on individual and family capabilities rather than on limitations
- seek information about the disability and available services
- develop skills to help them with the child's disability
- understand the cognitive, behavioral, emotional, and social components of family adaptation
- develop realistic expectations for the child with special needs and for other family members
- achieve a balance that meets the needs of all family members
- maintain cognitive and behavioral flexibility
- strive to maintain a normal family life style
- understand and strengthen the family system
- improve communication, conflict resolution, problem solving, assertiveness, behavior management, and stress management skills
- seek informal and formal sources of social support
- share feelings and coping strategies with other families
- seek outlets outside the family
- develop collaborative relationships with professionals
- seek professional counseling when appropriate
- move into advocacy roles

The post-assessment interview represents an important part of the assessment procedure. It can be particularly rewarding, because it allows you to present the results of the evaluation in a purposeful way. It also can be frustrating and sometimes heartbreaking. Understanding your attitudes toward children with special needs is especially important in working with them and their parents. By following the

"I SAID, 'YOUR SON DOESN'T SEEM TO LISTEN VERY WELL.'"

guidelines presented in this chapter, you can alleviate some anxieties in communicating the assessment results to parents and children.

Exercise 5-1. Evaluating Two Interview Excerpts

This exercise contains two interview excerpts. Read the first excerpt, evaluate it, and then compare your evaluation with the comments following the excerpt. Then, follow the same procedure for the second excerpt.

Excerpt 1

This excerpt is from an interview between a staff worker in a child development clinic and the mother of a 4-year-old developmentally disabled boy. How sensitive do you believe this interviewer was? How could this interview be improved? The excerpt is from Molyneaux and Lane (1982, pp. 128–129, with changes in notation).

1. IR: We are recommending placement of Ronnie in the Developmental Center preschool program.
2. IE: I won't agree to that. Ronnie is just fine, and you people are making some big deal out of these tests. First the pediatrician, then my in-laws, and now you!
3. IR: We're all just trying to find out what would be best for Ronnie—to give him the best possible chance to develop.
4. IE: You act like he's some kind of moron. My husband didn't talk until he was almost 2 years old and there's nothing the matter with him! Taking him around to these places, sitting and waiting until somebody gets good and ready to see us—it's damned annoying!
5. IR: Well, you had to wait because there are several parts to the tests and different people administer them.
6. IE: I hope they know more than that pediatrician does. With all the shots and vaccines and vitamins and now these tests—before you know it, there *will* be something the matter with Ronnie!
7. IR: Mrs. Monner, your son is mentally retarded. There's no doubt about that. But if he's going to get the best possible training, we want to have as much information about his condition as we can.
8. IE: What do you mean, retarded? That's a terrible thing to say about a little fellow only 4 years old. He's a lot smarter than some of the people we've come across in the last six months!
9. IR: It's foolish for you to act this way about the situation. People are trying to help, and you refuse to face the facts.
10. IE: Nobody has given me any facts. They're too busy playing God!

Comments on Excerpt 1

In this excerpt, the interviewer did not deal with the mother's grief, frustration, and defensiveness. Instead, the interviewer almost matter-of-factly related the diagnosis (no. 7) and then went on to berate the parent for not accepting it (no. 9). The interviewer not only failed to prepare the mother for the findings but also became argumentative. Instead of informing the mother of the recommendation directly (no. 1), the interviewer might have asked the mother what treatment she thought would be beneficial for her child *after* the assessment findings were explained to her. The interviewer's second comment (no. 3), although it may be accurate, failed to deal with the mother's anger. Perhaps a comment such as "You seem to be upset with the test results" might have been more appropriate. This interview could have been improved by active listening, acceptance of the feelings of the parent, and empathic responses.

Excerpt 2

This excerpt is the opening dialogue of a post-assessment interview between the mother of a 9-year-old boy and an interviewer who is reporting on the child's test results. How sensitive do you believe this interviewer was? How could this interview be improved? What differences do you see between this excerpt and the first one?

1. IR: As you know, Mrs. A., Dr. Allen, our staff psychologist, recently examined Bill. During the evaluation Dr. Allen had Bill do several things, like draw pictures, tell stories, and answer questions. He was cooperative and tried to do everything Dr. Allen asked. But he seemed to get frustrated when he didn't do something as well as he would like to, and he gave up easily.
2. IE: Yes, I know. He gives up even when he can do something. He just doesn't try.
3. IR: Well, in fact, there are many things he can't do yet, no matter how hard he tries. His score on the intelligence test places him at the 10th percentile. This means that he is intellectually behind most other children his age. About 90 out of 100 children score higher. He will learn, but at a much slower pace than other children his age.
4. IE: So it will take him a while to catch up to the other kids in his class. That's all right, as long as I know he'll be normal.
5. IR: This may take some time for you to accept. Bill probably will always be behind most children his age. It's going to take him longer to learn to read and to learn some things, and he may never catch up completely.
6. IE: Oh.
7. IR: I suspect that he is aware of his limitations. He knows what he can and cannot do. He wants so badly to do well that when he gets frustrated about what he can't do, he tries to distract people by doing something cute, and that often gets him in trouble in school.
8. IE: Yeah. He's always acting like a clown. He's really funny.
9. IR: It's his way of keeping others from finding out that he's having difficulty understanding how to do something.
10. IE: So what can we do to help him?

Comments on Excerpt 2

In this excerpt, the interviewer informs the mother about how Dr. Allen evaluated her son (no. 1). The interviewer then describes the intelligence test results in a way that should be comprehensible to the mother (no. 3). The interviewer tries to help the mother accept findings that suggest the child may have academic difficulties (no. 5). The interviewer also relates the behavior patterns of the child to the child's level of cognitive and academic performance (nos. 7 and 9). I have no suggestions for improving this interviewer's technique.

Thank you for letting me know by your voice
and your expression that you cared when you told me
the diagnosis.

—Anonymous

FOLLOW-UP INTERVIEW

This text is primarily focused on the initial clinical assessment interview and the post-assessment interview, but much of the material that you have read regarding the post-assessment interview also applies to the follow-up interview. The follow-up interview is designed to obtain information about how the child and family are functioning and to evaluate the intervention efforts, where applicable. For example, follow-up interviews with parents may focus on the following areas (Krehbiel & Kroth, 1991):

* changes in the child's functioning
* the child's performance at home
* the child's progress in school (where appropriate)
* the parents' concerns about whether they are doing the right thing for their child or expecting too much or too little
* the family's adjustment to the child's problem
* the parents' efforts toward normalization of the child
* the family's stress level
* the family's social and community supports
* the parents' attitudes toward professionals who are treating the child
* the parents' satisfaction with the intervention program
* the family's plans for the future

When the parents show that they are taking adequate care of their child, you should acknowledge their progress. Such comments reinforce the parents' efforts in raising a child with special needs. Some examples follow (Krehbiel & Kroth, 1991, p. 118, with quotation marks added):

* "You've come a long way in learning medical terminology."
* "You have discovered the roots of Paul's refusal to maintain his diet. Tell me how you did that."
* "So things are still frustrating and difficult, but you have gotten the routine under control."
* "There are some new parents that I see who would like to talk with another parent. Would you be willing to talk with them?"

THINKING THROUGH THE ISSUES

What are the problems involved in explaining the results of clinical evaluations to children, parents, and other laypeople?

How do you think you would handle informing children and parents about diagnoses that imply serious pathology?

How would your approach to children differ from your approach to parents in the post-assessment interview?

What problems do you think you might have in explaining to children and parents the assessment results obtained by other professionals?

SUMMARY

Post-Assessment Interview

1. The post-assessment interview with children and parents serves several purposes. These include presenting the findings, presenting possible interventions, helping them understand the findings and the suggested interventions, allowing them to express their concerns, and following up on hypotheses.

2. When you plan the post-assessment interview, consider what information you want to discuss with children and parents, how much detail you want to give, and how you want to present the information. During the post-assessment interview, leave plenty of time for the children and parents to ask you questions; whenever possible, encourage them to ask questions. In your presentation, be sure to discuss the family's strengths and also its weaknesses.

3. We can look at the post-assessment interview with children and parents as having five aspects—cognitive, interactive, affective, ethicoreligious, and ethnocultural. You need to consider each aspect when you conduct a post-assessment interview.

4. Give the interviewee time to express his or her feelings and reactions to the information.

5. Keep the post-assessment interview to about a 1- to 1½-hour period. Sessions longer than this may tax the abilities of the children or parents to comprehend all that has happened. If needed, schedule a second session.

6. In conducting a post-assessment interview with parents, the confidentiality of the information received from the child presents a troubling issue. There are no clear legal guidelines about whether this information is confidential. It is preferable to get the child's permission to release information to the parents, but it may not be legally required.

7. It is desirable to hold a post-assessment interview with children because it allows you to allay their fears about the assessment results.

8. In the post-assessment interview with parents, your role is to provide a thorough presentation of the children's learning or emotional problems, to plan a specific program geared to the children's needs and capabilities, to recognize and deal with the personal problems of the parents as they affect the children or as they are affected by their children's condition, and to plan for future meetings as needed.

9. The four phases of the post-assessment interview with parents are the establishment-of-rapport phase, the communication-of-results phase, the discussion-of-recommendations phase, and the termination phase.

10. During the first phase, establish rapport and review what the parents have told you about their primary concerns, what they hope to learn from the evaluation, what they think are the causes of the problem, and what they think should be done about the problem.

11. During the second phase, summarize the assessment results and their implications as clearly as possible and focus the interview on the child. Be prepared, if the results suggest that the child has a serious problem, to deal with such parental reactions as anxiety and emotional distress, grief, disbelief, shock, denial, ambivalence, anger, disappointment, guilt, despair, and even relief. Raise the issue of etiology. Use the diagnostic findings to help the parents give up erroneous ideas and to adopt a more realistic approach to the child's problems. Evaluate how the parents understand the results throughout the second phase.

12. During the third phase, try to let the parents formulate a plan of action. Present your recommendations and alternatives for consideration, and discuss possible courses of action. Encourage the parents to assume responsibility, not to be dependent. Give parents an opportunity to ask questions about the recommendations. Be prepared to discuss possible treatment or remediation strategies, length of treatment, and financial costs, if you recommend a treatment. Carefully consider everything you know about the case before offering an opinion about prognosis, especially with young children. Inform the parents of their legal rights, and be sure they understand them. Recommend books, pamphlets, materials, and organizations that will aid parents in learning about their children's problems.

13. During the final phase of the post-assessment interview, evaluate the parents' understanding and feelings about the results and recommendations. Encourage the parents to ask any additional questions, especially if you believe that they still have some concerns about the results or recommendations. Inform the parents that you are available for subsequent meetings, especially if you think that you need to clarify the findings or recommendations or that they might want to see you again. Convey to the parents your understanding of their difficulty, especially if they are unable to accept the results of the evaluation. Find out what the parents want to do immediately after the interview is over. Close the interview by giving the parents your business telephone number (if they don't have it) and inviting them to call you if they have further questions.

14. Evaluate the parents' understanding of the information presented in the post-assessment interview and their reactions to the interview.

15. When parents learn that they have a child with special needs, they tend to go through five stages: impact, denial, grief, focusing outward, and closure.

16. Parents may be less shocked when their child is identified as being disabled later in life.

17. Parents may use several defensive methods, all variants of denial, to cope with an unacceptable diagnosis. They may believe that their child is normal and reject the diagnosis; recognize that something is wrong, but hold out for the most acceptable diagnosis; or deny the clinician the opportunity to discuss the child's condition by being overly accepting of the diagnosis.

18. Some parents of children with special needs shop around—that is, they visit several different professionals or clinics in the hope of obtaining an acceptable diagnosis. This shopping behavior is frequently maladaptive. To prevent or alleviate such behavior, help the parents work through the feelings they experience on learning about their child's disability.

19. A mother and father in the same family may react differently to learning that their child has a disability.

20. When the post-assessment interview with parents is in the form of a staff conference, prepare for the conference carefully, set specific goals for the conference, be organized, individualize the conference, appear confident, don't be defensive, form an alliance with the parents, explore the needs of the parents, tell it like it is, explain the recommended interventions, and make a closing statement. Recognize that holding a staff conference may not be the best way to conduct a post-assessment interview.

21. The way in which a particular post-assessment interview unfolds will depend on the needs of the parents and on your orientation. Always show warmth, understanding, and respect.

22. In working with families of children with special needs, recognize that the family has considerable influence on the ability of the child to deal with the handicap and to profit from an intervention program.

23. Parents will especially resent professionals who fail to include them in the decision-making process, who view them as objects, who talk down to them, or who fail to consider their needs.

24. Parents will appreciate professionals who answer their questions honestly, respect their self-determination, solicit their participation, give them support, offer understandable and realistic recommendations, provide information about the best possible care, and are knowledgeable about community resources.

25. The post-assessment interview with the parents requires sensitivity and understanding of their feelings, needs, and desires. It is not a matter simply of reciting the results or reading the report. Make every effort to enlist the cooperation of the parents in working toward an effective intervention plan.

26. The post-assessment interview represents an important part of the assessment procedure. It can be particularly rewarding, because it allows you to present the results of the evaluation in a purposeful way. It also can be frustrating and sometimes heartbreaking.

Follow-Up Interview

27. Much of the text material on the post-assessment interview also applies to the follow-up interview. However, the follow-up interview with parents may focus on changes in the child's functioning, the child's performance at home, the child's progress in school (where appropriate), the parents' concerns about whether they are doing the right thing for their child or expecting too much or too little, the family's adjustment to the child's problem, the parents' efforts toward normalization of the child, the family's stress level, the family's social and community supports, the parents' attitudes toward professionals who are treating the child, the parents' satisfaction with the intervention program, and the family's plans for the future.

KEY TERMS, CONCEPTS, AND NAMES

Post-assessment interview (interpretive interview) (p. 186)
Cognitive aspect of the post-assessment interview (p. 186)
Interactive aspect of the post-assessment interview (p. 186)
Affective aspect of the post-assessment interview (p. 186)
Ethicoreligious aspect of the post-assessment interview (p. 186)
Ethnocultural aspect of the post-assessment interview (p. 186)
Confidentiality of information (p. 187)
Release of information (p. 187)
Four phases of the post-assessment interview (p. 187)
Public laws pertinent to children with disabilities (p. 190)
A five-stage coping model (p. 195)
Impact stage of coping (p. 195)
Denial stage of coping (p. 195)
Grief stage of coping (p. 195)
Focusing-outward stage of coping (p. 195)
Closure stage of coping (p. 195)
Shop around (p. 197)
Differences in parents' responses on learning about their child's disability (p. 197)
Post-assessment interview as a staff conference (p. 198)
Team leader (case manager) (p. 198)
Follow-up interview (p. 203)

STUDY QUESTIONS

1. Discuss the post-assessment interview. Include in your discussion (a) the purposes of the post-assessment interview, (b) general guidelines for the post-assessment interview, (c) the issue of confidentiality, (d) the post-assessment interview with children, and (e) the post-assessment interview with parents.

2. Discuss the four phases of the post-assessment interview with parents. In your discussion, focus on key points that should be attended to in each phase of the post-assessment interview with parents.

3. What are some important questions to consider in evaluating the post-assessment interview with parents?

4. Discuss the possible reactions parents may have on learning that their child has a disability. Include in your discussion the five stages of coping that parents may go through on learning that their child has a disability.

5. Discuss the post-assessment interview as a staff conference.

6. Discuss the follow-up interview. Include in your discussion what areas you should focus on and how you would acknowledge the progress of the child and parents, if appropriate.

6

RELIABILITY, VALIDITY, AND OTHER CONSIDERATIONS RELATED TO THE INTERVIEW

Convictions are the greater enemies of truth than lies.
—Nietzche

Goals and Objectives

This chapter is designed to enable you to:

- Discuss the reliability and validity of the interview
- Recognize malingering
- Evaluate your interview techniques
- Function as an expert witness
- Recognize and deal with interviewer stress

The chapter first focuses on evaluating the interview findings by considering issues of reliability and validity. The chapter then turns to evaluating your interview techniques, which is especially critical during your training period. The chapter ends with a discussion of the challenges of being an expert witness and of dealing with interviewer stress and burnout.

RELIABILITY AND VALIDITY OF THE INTERVIEW

Obtaining reliable and valid information from the interviewee is critical in clinical assessment interviewing. Therefore, you must evaluate the interview, like any other assessment technique, for reliability and validity. Following are several types of reliability related to the interview (Mash & Terdal, 1981, p. 46, with changes in notation):

- *test-retest reliability*—whether the information obtained from the interviewee on one occasion is comparable to the information that was or would have been obtained from the same interviewee on other occasions
- *interinterviewee agreement*—whether the information obtained from the interviewee agrees with the information obtained from another interviewee
- *internal consistency*—whether the information given by the interviewee is consistent with other information given by the interviewee in the same interview
- *interinterviewer reliability or method error*—whether the information obtained by one interviewer is consistent with that obtained by another interviewer from the same interviewee

The two major types of validity related to the interview are as follows (Mash & Terdal, 1981, p. 47, with changes in notation):

- *concurrent validity*—the extent to which the information obtained in the interview corresponds to the information obtained through other methods
- *predictive validity*—the degree to which information obtained in the interview predicts the treatment outcome

You may have difficulty determining the overall reliability and validity of an interview because interviews yield several types of information, including demographic, developmental, observational, and diagnostic data (Bellack & Hersen, 1980). Ideally, you should have independent estimates of the reliability and validity of each type of information. In addition, interviews are highly dependent on the specific interviewer and interviewee characteristics, type of interview, and conditions under which the interview takes place. These factors interact, not only among themselves, but also with the different types of information, to affect the reliability and validity of the obtained information. Despite these difficulties, you need to evaluate the reliability and validity of information obtained in the interview as you would information obtained from other types of assessments.

Bias Associated with the Situation

The interview situation itself may be a source of unreliability, in which case we say that *situational bias* exists. Situational factors that may lead to an unreliable interview include external noise, delays in starting the interview, the location of the interview, the time of the interview, the chance assignment of an interviewee to an interviewer, and temporary fluctuations in the behavior of the interviewer and interviewee. Thus, for example, interviewing a child before naptime or when the child is sleepy or hungry may lead to an unreliable interview, as may interviewing a child after you have had a sleepless night.

Bias Associated with Interviewees

A reliable and valid interview is possible only if the interviewee is willing and able to give you accurate information. Consequently, when you evaluate the interviewee's responses, you will need to consider the interviewee's age, intellectual ability, cognitive development, emotional and social development, receptive and expressive language competence, self-awareness, degree of psychological disturbance, and culture and ethnicity.

Some potential sources of error associated with interviewees are the interviewee's attitudes; understanding of questions; memory; interpretation of events; language; affect; personal likes, dislikes, and values; and behavior. Let's examine these potential sources of interviewee error in more detail.

1. *Errors associated with interviewees' attitudes.* Interviewees who are angry or uncooperative, who want to give socially desirable answers, or who want to please you and say things you want to hear likely will not give useful information. The validity of the information also will be compromised if interviewees are under stress, are resistant, lack trust, feel pressured to give certain responses, or fear reprisal or punishment if they are truthful. Those who come voluntarily for help are likely to give more accurate information than are those who are coerced to come (Bellack & Hersen, 1980).

2. *Errors associated with interviewees' understanding of the questions.* When interviewees fail to understand questions and yet do not ask you to rephrase the questions or do not say "I don't understand," they usually will give misleading information. Such misunderstandings are likely to occur, for example, when interviewees have hearing difficulties that have not been corrected, have cognitive limitations, have language comprehension difficulties, or are embarrassed to tell you that they do not understand the questions.

3. *Errors associated with interviewees' memory.* Interviewees may have difficulty recalling information, including important developmental milestones, and may have memory lapses. Sometimes, rather than saying they don't know, they may guess or make up information.

4. *Errors associated with interviewees' interpretation of events.* Interviewees may distort what happened to them or to others. For example, what interviewees say occurred may not be what actually occurred because people tend to interpret their own behavior in a manner consistent with the image they have of themselves. Interviewees also may exaggerate or minimize the significance of events.

5. *Errors associated with interviewees' language.* Interviewees may have difficulty finding the correct words to describe their thoughts, feelings, or previous events. They may misuse words and thereby unintentionally give wrong information.

6. *Errors associated with interviewees' affect.* The fears and anxieties that some interviewees have may impede their ability to give accurate replies. For example, withdrawal, overtalkativeness, giggling, and loss of voice are possible manifestations of fear or anxiety and possible manifestations of coping and defensive behaviors; these reactions, if present, likely will contribute to the unreliability of the interview.

7. *Errors associated with interviewees' personal likes, dislikes, and values.* Interviewees may fail to cooperate simply because you belong to an ethnic, economic, age, or gender class that differs from theirs. Reactions to the interviewer that are not objective are called *reactive effects.*

8. *Errors associated with interviewees' behavior.* Interviewees may behave in the interview—or when they are observed in the playroom or at home—in a way that differs from their usual behavior. For example, they may be more cooperative, use more polished language, or treat people with more respect than they usually do. This change in behavior, associated with the knowledge that they are being evaluated, also is referred to as a reactive effect. Interviewees also may intentionally try to distort their behavior in order to convince you that they have some type of disturbance. These behaviors, which may suggest malingering, are discussed in more detail later in the chapter. Finally, interviewees may be too distraught or preoccupied to talk coherently.

You are likely to find that children and parents differ in their reports and that younger children differ from older children in the reliability of their reports. Here are some findings.

1. Children and parents agree *least* often about covert and private symptoms such as anxiety, fear, and obsessions and agree more often about overt, easily observable behaviors such as behavior problems and conduct problems (Edelbrock, Costello, Dulcan, Conover, & Kalas, 1986; Thompson, Merritt, Keith, Murphy, & Johndrow, 1993).
2. Agreement between children and parents is moderate for depressive symptoms (Klein, 1991).
3. Generally, parents are more reliable than children in reporting the symptoms that children have (Klein, 1991).
4. Adolescents are more reliable than younger school-aged children in reporting symptoms (Edelbrock, Costello, Dulcan, Kalas, & Conover, 1985; Schwab-Stone, Fallon, Briggs, & Crowther, 1994; Schwab-Stone, Fisher, Piacentini, Shaffer, Davies, & Briggs, 1993). Younger school-aged children have particular difficulties with questions about duration and onset of symptoms but not with questions about fears.

Reports of symptoms by young children should be confirmed by other sources. Reports by adolescents are more reliable because their improved cognitive, memory, and language skills enable them to respond more accurately to questions that require self-awareness, perspective taking, recall, reasoning ability, and expressive skill. But even adolescents' reports may show poor agreement with parents' reports (Klein, 1991). *Whenever you get conflicting information, you need to inquire further.*

Bias and Errors Associated with Interviewers

Potential sources of bias and errors in the interview include your techniques and style; personal needs; personal likes, dislikes, and values; understanding of the interviewee; attention to the physical environment; selective perceptions and expectancies; ethnicity; recording techniques; interpretations; and theoretical position. Let's first examine each of these sources and then look at ways to reduce potential bias and errors.

1. *Errors associated with the interviewer's techniques and style.* You can influence the interviewee's responses by the way in which you word a question, your choice of follow-up responses, the tone of your voice, your facial expressions (particularly those following responses from the interviewee), your posture, and other verbal and nonverbal behaviors. Errors may occur, for example, if you fail to establish rapport, use ambiguous or vague questions, ask more than one question at a time, use complex and abstract words, use biased wording, time questions poorly, ask "why" questions, ask many leading questions, are insensitive to the interviewee's mood, or fail to monitor your verbal and nonverbal behavior. In addition, you will make errors if you fail to probe adequately or fail to gather enough information to reach valid conclusions.

Interviewer bias occurs when your actions influence, directly or indirectly, the interviewee (a) to respond in a way that he or she did not intend or (b) to distort his or her communications to please you. Sometimes you may not even recognize that you are influencing the interviewee to give certain responses. Kleinmuntz (1967) provides examples of statements made by an interviewer that may bias the interview. The statement "Well, I guess we beat that subject to death" can effectively limit further discussion. A loaded question such as "I take it that you are happy to accept your new class schedule" may leave the interviewee with little choice but to agree. Similarly, the interviewee is not likely to contest a statement that begins with "A good kid like you would think...."

2. *Errors associated with the interviewer's personal needs.* Your personal needs may affect the way you conduct the interview and the topics you approach and avoid. If you are anxious about sexual orientation, for example, you may fail to probe this area or you may avoid it altogether. Similarly, if you have strong feelings about certain issues such as abortion or religion, you may have difficulty discussing these topics.

Excessive questions about a topic are improper when the questions further your needs rather than the needs of the interviewee or the goals of the interview. For example, excessive probing of the interviewee's sexual behavior, when there are no indications of any problems in this area, may be a reflection of the needs of the interviewer, rather than a reflection of good interviewing techniques.

3. *Errors associated with the interviewer's personal likes, dislikes, and values.* Your personal likes, dislikes, and values may influence how you relate to the interviewee. For example, if you like attractive interviewees, or those who dress well, or those who have a rich voice, or those who belong to a specific ethnic group, you may conduct interviews with these interviewees differently than you do interviews with those who do not have these characteristics. You may unknowingly send signals showing your pleasure or displeasure to interviewees you are attracted to or not attracted to, respectively. Diagnostic impressions also may be tainted in these cases.

You may be susceptible to the interviewee's nonverbal behavior. For example, interviewees who make eye contact, smile, have an attentive posture, or show interest in you may encourage you to probe topics and ask follow-up questions. In contrast, you may be hesitant to probe and ask follow-up questions when interviewees fail to make eye contact, frown, have an inattentive posture, or fail to show interest in you.

Another type of error occurs when you constantly compare your values with those of the interviewee and find the interviewee's values lacking; in such cases, you are making a *contrast and similarity error.* Your goal as an interviewer is to understand the interviewee's values, not to measure him or her against your personal standards. The way you perceive similarities and differences between you and the interviewee also may affect how you conduct the interview.

You may be attracted by odors some interviewees have and be repelled by others. Nevertheless, you must not let your attitude toward the odors influence either the length or the direction of the interview. Awareness of odors is subtle and often preconscious. By recognizing your preferences for odors, you will be in a better position to guard against allowing these preferences to bias the interview.

In general, reactions to the interviewee that are not objective are called reactive effects. Errors will occur if you fail to recognize your biases and attend to them.

4. *Errors associated with the interviewer's understanding of the interviewee.* You are likely to make errors when you fail to consider the interviewee's age, cognitive level, or culture or when you misunderstand what the interviewee says. These errors may occur, for example, when you have difficulty understanding the interviewee's speech or language, are preoccupied with other thoughts, are distracted, or have hearing difficulties that have not been corrected.

5. *Errors associated with the interviewer's failure to attend to the physical environment or to other situational factors.* If you fail to prepare the interview room properly—by failing to minimize distractions, keeping the room too hot or too cold, having poor lighting, failing to disconnect the phone, or having uncomfortable seats, for example—the interview may suffer. Other situational factors that may bias the interview include conducting the interview (a) with the child and the alleged perpetrator in the same room, (b) in a police station or in another stressful environment, or (c) shortly after a traumatic event.

6. *Errors associated with the interviewer's selective perceptions and expectancies.* Bias occurs when you have selective perceptions and expectancies that diminish your ability to listen to the interviewee. One example: You may miss important communications if you have preconceived notions about the interviewee and allow these preconceptions to influence what you attend to. Another example: You may distort information if you listen only to things that you believe are impor-

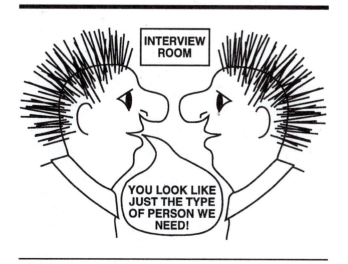

Courtesy of Brendan Mulcahy.

tant or that confirm your expectancies. When you excuse behaviors shown by the interviewee because of your preconceived views, you are making a *leniency effect error*. The tendency to be lenient also can shape your questions and probes.

When you have a narrow or prejudicial view of the interviewee (for example, because of expectancies developed from the referral information or knowledge of prior records or because of personal prejudices), you are making a *halo effect error*. Such errors diminish the validity of the interview. For example, a referral of a child for aggressive behavior may lead you to describe marginally aggressive actions as aggressive because of your mindset. If the mindset were not operating, you might not have noticed the marginally aggressive behavior.

7. *Errors associated with the interviewer in cross-ethnic, cross-cultural, or cross-class situations.* Bias can occur when you distort replies or make inaccurate inferences simply because of racial or class differences or antagonisms (also see Chapters 8 and 9). One example: It is wrong to infer that an Asian American or Native American interviewee is evasive because he or she won't look you in the eye; for these interviewees, such behavior is a sign of respect. The errors discussed previously under the interviewer's personal likes, dislikes, and values (no. 3) and the interviewer's selective perceptions and expectancies (no. 6) also pertain to cross-ethnic, cross-cultural, or cross-class situations.

8. *Errors associated with the interviewer's recording of data.* You may make recording errors simply because of careless notations or because you omitted, added, or subtly changed details. Or you may make recording errors because of your preconceived ideas—you hear what you want to hear or what you expect to hear. These errors may occur when you are making notes either during the interview proper or after the interview is completed.

9. *Errors associated with the interviewer's interpretation of observations and information.* If you make inferences beyond your observations or beyond the information you obtain, you may lose objectivity. For example, the speech of an interviewee may be characterized as "deliberate" by one interviewer, as "slow and dull" by another interviewer, and as "depressed and despondent" by still another interviewer. To be objective, your notes should reflect the interviewee's behavior—for example, that the interviewee "spoke slowly" or "paused several seconds before responding." Use adjectives that best describe the behavior of the interviewee. Don't draw inferences unless you have sufficient information. Interpretation errors are more likely to occur when the behavior of the interviewee is ambiguous.

When you are unable to form judgments about the interviewee's behavior, you may opt for the middle ground. That is, you may take a neutral position—for example, "the interviewee's behavior was neither aggressive nor passive." This statement is fine if your observation was accurate. However, if it was not, and you failed to observe some important behavior, your error would be called a *central tendency error*. This error may lead you to fail to probe valuable leads.

When you generalize from one behavior to others with little evidence to support the generalization, you are making a *generalization effect error*. The generalization effect error is a type of halo effect error in that the interviewer allows the judgment of the interviewee in one area to color judgments in other areas. The generalization effect error also is a *logical rating error* in that the interviewer believes that it is permissible to rate one area as being like another one because the two might be logically related. For example, an interviewer might think that because the interviewee hits his sister, he is likely to steal things as well.

10. *Errors associated with the interviewer's theoretical position.* These errors come about when you interpret all behavior from a preconceived position. Not all of the child's behaviors are likely to be due to having an unresolved Oedipus complex, being an oldest child, or having an inappropriate reinforcement history.

Ways to Reduce Interviewer Bias and Errors

Here are some strategies for improving the reliability and validity of the interview:

1. *Plan and use guidelines.* Have a plan for the interview. Use semistructured or structured interview schedules as a guide.

2. *Relate to the interviewee.* Word questions so that they do not lead the interviewee toward an answer. Listen carefully to the interviewee. Give your undivided interest and attention to the interviewee. Show your acceptance of the interviewee. Maintain an attitude of professional interest and concern. When interviewees are fearful and anxious, try even harder to establish rapport. For example, make frequent supportive comments, show them that you are understanding of their fears and anxieties and can accept them even if they are fearful and anxious, listen carefully to them, and take the pressure off by interjecting light conversation. If you still detect anxiety or defensiveness, stay relaxed and try to get them to relax by making small talk before broaching or returning to anxiety-laden topics. When interviewees will not cooperate simply because of who you are, you can do nothing to change your status. You can, however, show them that you can be trusted and want to help them.

3. *Develop self-awareness.* Become aware of personal needs that may adversely affect how you conduct the interview, and find ways to suppress them. Recognize your attitudes, values, and objectives and how they relate to interviewees from different ethnic, cultural, or socioeconomic groups. Develop an awareness of your nonverbal and verbal behavior. Be aware not only of the communications of the interviewee and your reactions to them, but also of your communications and how the interviewee may perceive them. Minimize selective perceptions, theoretical preconceptions, and expectancies that may distract you from eliciting information and from making appropriate decisions.

4. *Gather additional information.* When you have doubts about the reliability of the information you obtain, ask questions in different ways or at different times, or ask both the interviewee and someone else about the same areas. You can evaluate the validity of the information you obtain by checking against baby books, school and medical records, and other formal and informal records, where applicable.

5. *Attend to recordings.* Check your notes for accuracy shortly after the interview is over. If you do not take notes, record (by writing or tape recorder) the information you have obtained and your impressions soon after the interview.

6. *Develop hypotheses.* Study all sources of information about the interviewee for corroborating facts. Cross-validate inferences and predictions. Closely review the data before you make inferences. Recognize the limitations of your theoretical approach. Be open to alternative explanations. Principle 4 of report writing in Chapter 7 discusses this strategy in more detail.

You must strive to overcome any conditions that will impede your effectiveness as an interviewer. In case of substantial doubts about your findings, arrange to have the interviewee interviewed by another interviewer, and then compare the results of the two interviews. Your goal is to be vigilant and objective, yet always caring.

Exercise 6-1. Recognizing Interviewer Errors

Identify the type of error illustrated in each of the following descriptions. Each description reflects one of the following sources of error: interviewer bias, error associated with the interviewer's personal needs, error associated with the interviewer's personal likes and dislikes, contrast and similarity error, error associated with cross-ethnic or cross-cultural situations, error associated with recording data, leniency effect error, central tendency effect error, generalization effect error, halo effect error, and error associated with theoretical bias.

1. The interviewer becomes especially alert and attentive with interviewees who speak with a southern accent.
2. The interviewer fails to follow up the interviewee's statements because she thinks that the statements don't indicate anything significant.
3. The interviewer, who is from a lower socioeconomic class, loses interest in talking with an interviewee who is from the upper class.
4. The interviewer interprets all fears as stemming from family communication problems.
5. The interviewer believes that it is no problem, or at least only a minor problem, that the interviewee hit a classmate.
6. The interviewer frowns as he says in a questioning tone "Are you *sure* about that?"
7. The interviewer believes that the interviewee will be aggressive toward the interviewee's friends because the interviewee fights with her sister.
8. The interviewer fails to record on his notepad that the interviewee said positive things about her father.

9. The interviewer changes topics as quickly as possible when the interviewee begins to talk about airplanes because the interviewer has a fear of flying.
10. The interviewer, who is a member of the majority group, interprets the minority interviewee's statements as hostile to the majority group when the interviewee only was ambivalent in his remarks about the majority group.
11. The interviewer believes that the child was likely abused because her sister was abused.

Suggested Answers

1. Error associated with interviewer's personal likes and dislikes
2. Central tendency error
3. Contrast and similarity error
4. Error associated with theoretical bias
5. Leniency effect error
6. Interviewer bias
7. Generalization effect error
8. Error associated with recording data
9. Error associated with interviewer's personal needs
10. Error associated with cross-ethnic or cross-cultural situations
11. Halo effect error

ASSESSMENT OF MALINGERING

Another factor that directly affects the reliability and validity of the interview is *malingering* by the interviewee. *Malingering can be defined as a conscious fabrication or gross exaggeration of physical or psychological symptoms in pursuit of a recognizable goal.* Malingering includes deliberate distortions or misrepresentations of psychological symptoms, attempts to distort or misrepresent a self-report, and outright dishonesty (Rogers, 1988b). Almost any psychological or physical disorder is open to malingering. Malingering is difficult to identify because subjective symptoms are hard to verify.

Degrees of Malingering

There are gradations of malingering (Rogers, 1988a). In *mild malingering,* the distortions or variations present in the interviewee's report have little or no bearing on the diagnosis or disposition. In *moderate malingering,* there is a clear pattern of exaggeration or fabrication of symptoms, making it difficult to arrive at a diagnosis or a disposition. In *severe malingering,* the pattern of fabrication is overwhelming, with the interviewee appearing severely psychologically disturbed, producing rare and improbable symptoms, or having symptoms uncorroborated by clinical observations.

Reasons for Malingering

Reasons for malingering include efforts to reduce personal accountability, escape the consequences of antisocial or immoral actions, avoid punishment by pretending to be incompetent to stand trial, avoid military service, seek financial gain for alleged psychological illness, seek a transfer to another setting, and gain admission to a psychiatric hospital. The case of an adolescent girl who malingered to obtain hospitalization follows (Greenfield, 1987).

CASE 6-1. 14-YEAR-OLD GIRL

A 14-year-old girl feigned hallucinations and other psychotic symptoms to obtain hospitalization; she desperately wanted to escape from the sexual harassment of her mother's boyfriend. The girl previously had observed a cousin's psychotic episode and learned how to mimic the symptoms. Only when the hospital staff told her that they were planning to place her infant with the baby's father did she reveal that she had faked the psychotic symptoms.

This case illustrates an important constellation of factors that may lead to malingering—namely, an intolerable living condition or intolerable stress, awareness of alternatives to one's present dilemma, and knowledge of how a psychiatric or medical disorder can be simulated. In other cases, a different constellation of factors may exist.

Malingering and Conduct Disorder

Children with a *conduct disorder* (see Chapter 11)—that is, a repetitive and persistent pattern of conduct in which the major rights of others or major age-appropriate societal rules are violated—may be particularly prone to presenting false or grossly exaggerated symptoms. Insincerity or untruthfulness is an essential characteristic of some children with a conduct disorder. Children with a conduct disorder tell lies at rates two and one-half times greater than those for normal children (Stouthamer-Loeber, 1986). The unlikely expression of strong remorse or depression in a child with a conduct disorder should raise some suspicion about the child's credibility. However, for the most part, "the form of malingering, its frequency, and its duration may have far more to do with the context of the malingering than with personality variables" (Clark, 1988, p. 57).

Age and Malingering

Malingering is more likely to occur in older elementary school–aged children and adolescents than in younger children. "Malingering requires considerable skill in role-playing, impression-management, and deception; these skills are simply not available to younger children" (Quinn, 1988, p. 115).

Evaluation of Malingering

Evaluate malingering by considering the interviewee's past and current functioning, test performance (if available), clinical records, and reports from others. Sometimes symptoms

may be so exaggerated (for example, extremely severe confusion, disorientation, and attention-concentration deficits) that they strain credibility. The interviewee who cannot recall even simple word pairs or the day of the week may be malingering because only in the most severe cases of amnesia, dementia, or delirium would this occur. Other clues to malingering are lack of internal consistency in presented deficits, apparent inconsistencies in performance, implausibility of explanations, evasiveness and uncooperativeness, attempts to avoid examination, and discrepancies between ability to study (or work) and ability to play. When possible, monitor (by observing or recording on videotape) the interviewee's alleged symptoms (for example, fainting spells, sleeplessness, exaggerated startle reactions).

Following are guidelines for evaluating possible malingering (Quinn, 1988):

1. Does the interviewee have the capacity to deceive? Children under 6 years of age usually are not able to lie deliberately and be successful.
2. Does the interviewee have a pattern of persistent lying? If so, the information presented by the interviewee may not be reliable.
3. Does the interviewee have psychological problems that would severely distort communications? If so, the interviewee's behaviors may be a reflection of the psychological problems and not a manifestation of malingering.
4. Are there stressors in the interviewee's environment that may lead to lying? If so, consider these stressors in evaluating the interviewee's behavior.
5. Are the interviewee's symptoms consistent with a well-recognized illness or syndrome? If so, there is less possibility of malingering.

The following signs should alert you to the possibility that the interviewee might be malingering (Cunnien, 1988). The more signs present, the stronger the possibility of malingering. Still, the presence of these signs only suggests—but does not prove—malingering.

POSSIBLE SIGNS OF MALINGERING

- Interviewee is involved in a legal action.
- Interviewee's symptoms worsen when she or he is observed.
- Interviewee's symptoms are bizarre or ridiculous.
- Interviewee's symptoms wax and wane, depending on what is going on in her or his environment at the time.
- Interviewee's symptoms fail to respond to customary treatment.
- Interviewee's complaints are grossly in excess of physical findings.
- Interviewee's symptoms cannot be explained by a known mental or physical disorder.
- Interviewee is uncooperative during the examination and with the recommendations.
- Interviewee's symptoms give her or him some advantages, such as avoidance of school, avoidance of incarcer-

ation, financial gain, avoidance of prosecution, or acquisition of drugs.

- Interviewee's self-report cannot be verified by independent observers.

Overall, you can be certain that the interviewee is malingering only (a) when the interviewee voluntarily confesses—convincingly—to the deception or (b) when the interviewee confesses when you confront him or her during an obvious lie. In summary, look for incongruities in the interviewee's behavior, observe the interviewee's reaction when confronted with the incongruities, evaluate the interviewee's motivation for the possible deception, and consider both the interviewee's cognitive level *and* moral level of development in assessing malingering (Quinn, 1988).

EVALUATING YOUR INTERVIEW TECHNIQUES

This book has presented guidelines that should help you become a successful clinical or forensic assessment interviewer. However, you should not follow the guidelines rigidly or expect them to cover every possible contingency. Human relationships are unique, and a "cookbook" of techniques is neither possible nor desirable. You must be the judge of how, when, and where to use a particular procedure.

You should continuously evaluate your interview techniques, particularly when you are first learning to interview or when you haven't conducted an interview for some time. One way is simply to think about the interview and then evaluate it shortly after its completion. Or you can record some interviews that you conduct on either audiotape or videotape (with proper consent) and then study the recordings. Both audiotapes and videotapes give you the opportunity to study your interview techniques and your diction, speech intensity, and other voice and speech characteristics. Videotapes, in addition, allow you to evaluate your eye contact, posture, gestures, and other nonverbal behaviors. If possible, review your tape recordings with a classmate or, better yet, someone who has expertise in interviewing.

Questions to Consider in Your Self-Evaluation

You can evaluate your interview techniques by answering the questions in Table 6-1 and then rating the competencies shown in Table 6-2. During your training, you should answer the questions and do the ratings after each interview. Table 6-2 also can be used by your supervisor to rate your interview techniques.

As you review your answers to the questions in Table 6-1 and Table 6-2, what themes emerge? What were the strengths and weaknesses of your interviewing style? What can you do to improve your interview techniques? After you

conduct several interviews, does any pattern emerge in your interviewing style? Have you improved your skills in subsequent interviews?

If you have a rating of 4 or 5 ("poor demonstration of this skill" or "very poor demonstration of this skill") on any of the items in Table 6-2, determine why, when, and where the difficulty occurred and what you can do to improve your interview techniques. One example: If you daydreamed, try to determine why. During what part of the interview did the daydreaming occur? What content was being covered? Did you have other problems with similar content? Was the content of your daydream related to the communications of the interviewee in some way? Another example: Did you convey to the interviewee such personal needs as wanting respect from him or her or wanting to be liked? If so, these messages may have interfered with the relationship. The interviewee may have felt guilty if he or she didn't satisfy your needs. Furthermore, why was it necessary for you to have these needs fulfilled in a professional relationship? Evaluate thoroughly every problem you find with your interview techniques. Practice situations involving the problem areas with colleagues, friends, and family.

Here are two cases from the child custody field that illustrate how interviewers may conduct a biased interview (Freedman, Rosenberg, Gettman-Felzien, & Van Scoyk, 1993).

CASE 6-2. MS. A

Ms. A divorced her husband after 12 years of marriage and now seeks sole custody of the couple's two young children. She describes her former husband as controlling and wanting a marriage in which her career goals were subjugated to the needs of her husband and children. The female custody evaluator, who had begun her professional career later in life, identified quickly with Ms. A's dilemma, without being entirely aware of her identification, and began making favorable remarks about her even before much of the evaluation had begun. Then, as the evaluation went on, the female evaluator tended to disregard negative information about Ms. A, while highlighting her strengths. Only when the male member of the custody team noted her consistent dismissal of negative psychological test data, an unusual stance for this seasoned evaluator, did she begin to realize how her feelings toward the female client had clouded her perceptions. (p. 61, with changes in notation)

CASE 6-3. MR. B

Mr. B sought a divorce after 7 years of marriage. He had remained at home with his 4-year-old daughter while his physician wife financially supported the family. Mr. B's wife was more and more unavailable because of her work, and he now wanted both a divorce and sole custody of the daughter. The male custody evaluator found himself making derogatory remarks about Mr. B to his co-evaluator. Upon reflection, it became apparent to him that because Mr. B stayed at home with his daughter, rather than working at a career, he saw Mr. B as a weak, ineffective person, lacking in self-confidence. Furthermore, he became aware of envious feelings toward Mr. B for being able to stay at home with his daughter while

Table 6-1
Evaluating Your Performance in the Interview

Background Influences

1. What assumptions did you make as an interviewer?
2. Were any of them stereotyped?
3. Were your understanding and interpretations of what you saw, heard, and said biased in any way? If so, in what way?

Factors Occurring During the Interview

4. How did environmental conditions—such as degree of privacy, comfort, placement of furniture, noise level, temperature, and so forth—affect the interview?
5. Did you subtly influence the interviewee to give certain responses? If so, what did you do, and were you aware that you were doing it?
6. How were you affected by the interviewee's appearance, voice, audibility, articulation, projection of interest, rate of speech, pauses, facial expressions, and other characteristics?
7. Were you able to suspend judgment about the interviewee until the interview was over?
8. As the interview progressed, what thoughts did you have about your role and about how things were going in the interview?
9. What did the interviewee say or do that led you to form opinions of him or her?
10. What type of questions did you mostly ask (for example, open-ended or closed-ended)?
11. Did you have a chance to probe and follow up leads?
12. How did you begin the interview?
13. And how did you end the interview?
14. How do you feel about the interviewee?
15. Were you aware of your verbal behavior? If so, what was it like?
16. Were you aware of your nonverbal behavior? If so, what was it like?
17. Did your nonverbal behavior change as the interview progressed? If so, in what way did it change?
18. What role did your appearance, eye contact, and facial expressions play in the interview?
19. How do you think the interviewee reacted to your appearance, voice, audibility, articulation, projection of interest, rate of speech, pauses, facial expressions, and other characteristics?
20. To what degree did your verbal and nonverbal behavior coincide?
21. Did your verbal behavior change as the interview progressed? If so, in what way did it change?
22. Were you distracted? If so, what distracted you from listening more carefully?
23. Did you daydream or let your mind wander? If so, when did this happen during the interview?
24. What did you do to reduce the distractions and become a more effective listener?
25. What can you do to prevent these distractions from occurring in interviews in the future?

26. How well did you understand the interviewee's verbal communications?
27. Were you aware of the interviewee's nonverbal behavior?
28. Were you aware of any changes in the interviewee's verbal and nonverbal behavior?
29. Were you a good listener?
30. How effectively were you able to listen to the interviewee when he or she presented a viewpoint that differed from your own?
31. Did you tune out the interviewee? If so, how easily and how often did you do so and why?
32. How effective were you in spotting the major themes in the interviewee's communications?
33. How effective were you in noticing discrepancies between the interviewee's verbal and nonverbal communications?
34. How did you handle the times in the interview when the interviewee may have been exaggerating, contradicting himself or herself, misinterpreting situations, holding things back, feeling extremely emotional, and so forth?
35. How did you feel during silences?
36. How did you handle silences?
37. What communication problems developed in the interview?
38. Were any of the communication problems associated with your and the interviewee's assigning different meanings to the same words?
39. What role did "technical talk" or jargon play in communication difficulties?
40. How did you react to questions posed by the interviewee about you?
41. If there were any personal rebuffs, how did you take them?
42. To what extent were you aware of your feelings about what was going on during the interview, including feelings about the interviewee and feelings about yourself?
43. Was there any material discussed by the interviewee that made you anxious? If so, what was the material and why did it make you anxious?
44. What risks were involved in saying some of the things you said?
45. What did you hope to bring about by saying some of the things you said?
46. Were your hopes borne out?
47. What role did power and status play in the interview?
48. Did you have trouble formulating questions? If so, why? And was it obvious to the interviewee?
49. How did you want the interviewee to see you?

Evaluation of the Interview

50. What did you learn about the interviewee?
51. How motivated was the interviewee to talk with you?
52. How easily was the interviewee able to recall information?

(*Continued*)

Table 6-1 (*Continued*)

53. How accurate do you believe the interviewee was in recalling experiences?
54. How did the interviewee react to your questions?
55. How do you think the interviewee perceived you (for example, trusting, accessible, understandable, competent, cold, distant, aloof, marginally competent)?
56. Do you think that the interviewee believed that you were an effective interviewer?

57. Did you accomplish your goals?
58. What did you learn about your interviewing techniques?
59. Which techniques were most successful?
60. How could you have been a more effective interviewer?
61. What would you do differently if you had to do it again?
62. How satisfied, overall, were you with your performance in the interview?

Table 6-2
Interview Techniques Checklist

INTERVIEW TECHNIQUES CHECKLIST

Name of interviewer: _____   Date of interview:_____

Name of interviewee: _____   Rater's name: _____

Rating key:

Excellent demonstration of this skill	Good demonstration of this skill	Fair demonstration of this skill	Poor demonstration of this skill	Very poor demonstration of this skill	Not applicable
1	2	3	4	5	NA

Skill	*Rating*
1. Made a smooth transition from opening greeting to serious topic	1 2 3 4 5 NA
2. Created a positive interview climate	1 2 3 4 5 NA
3. Showed respect for interviewee	1 2 3 4 5 NA
4. Gave undivided attention to interviewee	1 2 3 4 5 NA
5. Established an environment free from distractions	1 2 3 4 5 NA
6. Used good diction	1 2 3 4 5 NA
7. Spoke in a clear audible voice with warmth	1 2 3 4 5 NA
8. Spoke in a modulated voice that reflected nuances of feelings	1 2 3 4 5 NA
9. Spoke at a moderate tempo	1 2 3 4 5 NA
10. Used vocabulary understandable to interviewee	1 2 3 4 5 NA
11. Formulated appropriate general questions	1 2 3 4 5 NA
12. Formulated appropriate open-ended questions	1 2 3 4 5 NA
13. Formulated appropriate follow-up questions to pursue issues	1 2 3 4 5 NA
14. Used nonleading questions	1 2 3 4 5 NA
15. Used relatively few "yes-no" questions	1 2 3 4 5 NA
16. Used few, if any, multiple-choice questions	1 2 3 4 5 NA
17. Used appropriate structuring statements	1 2 3 4 5 NA
18. Encouraged appropriate replies	1 2 3 4 5 NA
19. Used probes effectively	1 2 3 4 5 NA

(Continued)

Table 6-2 (*Continued*)

Skill	Rating
20. Allowed interviewee to express feelings and thoughts in his or her own way	1 2 3 4 5 NA
21. Followed up leads effectively	1 2 3 4 5 NA
22. Was alert to interviewee's nonverbal behavior	1 2 3 4 5 NA
23. Conveyed to interviewee a desire to understand him or her	1 2 3 4 5 NA
24. Conveyed to interviewee an interest in obtaining relevant facts and not in confirming a pre-existing hypothesis	1 2 3 4 5 NA
25. Rephrased questions appropriately	1 2 3 4 5 NA
26. Used reflection appropriately	1 2 3 4 5 NA
27. Used feedback appropriately	1 2 3 4 5 NA
28. Handled a minimally communicative interviewee appropriately	1 2 3 4 5 NA
29. Handled interviewee's resistance and anxiety appropriately	1 2 3 4 5 NA
30. Showed sensitivity to interviewee's emotional state	1 2 3 4 5 NA
31. Clarified areas of confusion in interviewee's statements	1 2 3 4 5 NA
32. Intervened appropriately when interviewee had difficulty expressing thoughts	1 2 3 4 5 NA
33. Handled rambling communications appropriately	1 2 3 4 5 NA
34. Dealt with difficult behavior appropriately	1 2 3 4 5 NA
35. Used props, crayons, clay, or toys appropriately	1 2 3 4 5 NA
36. Timed questions appropriately	1 2 3 4 5 NA
37. Handled silences appropriately	1 2 3 4 5 NA
38. Used periodic summaries appropriately	1 2 3 4 5 NA
39. Asked questions about all relevant areas without avoiding potentially stressful ones	1 2 3 4 5 NA
40. Made clear transitions	1 2 3 4 5 NA
41. Paced interview appropriately	1 2 3 4 5 NA
42. Self-disclosed only when necessary	1 2 3 4 5 NA
43. Established and maintained appropriate eye contact	1 2 3 4 5 NA
44. Maintained appropriate facial expressions	1 2 3 4 5 NA
45. Used nonverbal behavior appropriately	1 2 3 4 5 NA
46. Demonstrated consistency between nonverbal and verbal behavior	1 2 3 4 5 NA
47. Responded in nonjudgmental manner (without moralizing, sermonizing, advising prematurely, persuading, criticizing, blaming, labeling, prejudging, or making glib interpretations)	1 2 3 4 5 NA
48. Resisted distractions	1 2 3 4 5 NA
49. Avoided overreacting	1 2 3 4 5 NA
50. Avoided getting into arguments	1 2 3 4 5 NA
51. Handled interviewee's questions and concerns appropriately	1 2 3 4 5 NA
52. Allowed interviewee to express remaining thoughts and questions at close of interview	1 2 3 4 5 NA
53. Arranged for post-assessment interview	1 2 3 4 5 NA
54. Used summary statements as needed	1 2 3 4 5 NA
55. Used appropriate closing statements	1 2 3 4 5 NA
56. Conducted an appropriate interview overall	1 2 3 4 5 NA

Comments: _____

_____

_____

_____

he needed to obtain child care for his 3-year-old son. When he realized that his perceptions of Mr. B were clouding his judgments, he began to view Mr. B as a person with an important investment in raising his child, rather than just an impotent, dependent father. (pp. 65–66, with changes in notation)

Obtaining Feedback from the Interviewee

During your training (and even periodically during your career), you may want to obtain feedback from interviewees about your performance. If you decide to do so, you can use the checklist shown in Table 6-3. It contains 18 "yes-no" questions and space for additional comments.

Recognizing the Interviewee's Limitations

If you were unsuccessful in obtaining information from the interviewee, don't be too hard on yourself. There are children and parents who simply will not cooperate or who won't disclose for various reasons. Children with an autistic disorder, those with a severe conduct disorder, or those who are severely developmentally disabled, for example, may be uncooperative. Parents who have been coerced to come to the interview also may be uncooperative. In such cases, note their behavior and schedule another appointment. Your failure to obtain information may be related more to the dysfunctions of the interviewee than to your clinical skills. However, as your clinical skills improve, you may become

---

Table 6-3
Checklist for an Interviewee's Evaluation of an Interviewer

EVALUATING THE INTERVIEWER

Client's name: _____   Name of interviewer: _____

Date of interview: _____

Directions: Please rate the interviewer on each item. Use the following rating scale:

Y = Yes
N = No
? = Not sure

For each item, circle the choice that best describes your rating. Be sure to respond to each item. Thank you!

Item	Rating	Item	Rating
1. The interviewer saw me at approximately the scheduled time.	Y N ?	10. The interviewer asked about my feelings and responded to them.	Y N ?
2. The interviewer put me at ease during the interview.	Y N ?	11. I was able to talk about problems and issues that were important to me.	Y N ?
3. The interviewer greeted me in a way that made me feel comfortable.	Y N ?	12. The topics covered by the interviewer were appropriate.	Y N ?
4. The interviewer appeared interested in me.	Y N ?	13. The interviewer seemed organized during the interview.	Y N ?
5. The interviewer appeared to be confident.	Y N ?	14. The interviewer was thorough in asking me relevant questions.	Y N ?
6. The interviewer spoke clearly and was easily understood.	Y N ?	15. The interviewer summarized the problems as he or she saw them.	Y N ?
7. The interviewer asked questions in a way that allowed me time to think about my answer.	Y N ?	16. The time spent with the interviewer was adequate for my needs.	Y N ?
8. The interviewer asked relevant questions about my personal and social life.	Y N ?	17. I felt nervous during the interview.	Y N ?
9. The interviewer seemed to understand what I said.	Y N ?	18. Overall, I felt satisfied with the interview.	Y N ?

Any other comments are welcome. _____

_____

_____

Source: Adapted from Brockway (1978).

more successful in interviewing difficult children and parents, or children and parents who are in difficult situations.

THE CHALLENGES OF BEING AN EXPERT WITNESS

As a mental health professional (or other human service provider), you may be called on to testify in court or at special hearings conducted in schools and agencies. For example, you may be asked to give your opinion about the interviewee's need for special programs, mental status, adaptive skills, or general adjustment. Testifying as an expert witness can be a difficult experience, especially in court or court-like settings. Court procedures are radically different from those used in mental health settings, medical settings, and schools. A witness in court may be expected to answer many questions with a simple one-word response. "Isn't it true that..." is a form that questions often take, and little opportunity is afforded to qualify responses. The courtroom is a place for decision-making—not a place to debate or to resolve complex issues.

The Clash Between Two Systems

There is a clash between professional or scientific practice and the *adversarial system* (Newman, 1991).

When [mental health professionals] serve as expert witnesses, a clash exists between two very different conceptual systems for viewing the world and ordering events: the scientific method or hypothesis testing versus the adversarial system. The scientific method seeks to determine the factors that influence a certain behavior, and to evaluate the extent and direction of their influence. More specifically, various hypotheses about an individual's behavior, emotions, personality, and cognitive functioning are developed while simultaneously collecting and analyzing data. This data collection and analysis, whether by clinical interview, history taking, or psychological testing, takes place in order to test hypotheses, and to arrive at data-based inferences as to what, how, and with what probability various factors influence an individual. Social scientists answer clinical and behavioral questions in this manner.

The adversarial system, by contrast, seeks to answer moral and legal questions in an absolute ("yes" or "no") fashion. The trier of fact, either the judge or jury, must consider both sides to every argument. Each side is presented in its most positive light and then the two sides are weighed against each other. No matter how convincing both sides may be, only one side can prevail. In this system there is little room for qualifiers or contingencies. The defendant, for example, is either guilty or not guilty, competent or incompetent, morally responsible or irresponsible, negligent or not liable. The trier of fact can—and actually must—consider all relevant factors and circumstances. The ultimate answer, however, to any question must be an unequivocal "yes" or "no." (pp. 242–243)

The goal of the mental health system is to promote mental health, whereas the goal of the legal system is to promote justice. These goals can clash when the two systems come into contact. Yet, the two systems also share similar values, particularly in rejecting deceit and exploitive use of power; emphasizing fairness, honesty, and competence in expert testimony; recognizing limitations in current scientific knowledge; and stressing the advancement of human welfare (Melton, 1994).

Testifying as an Expert Witness

Before the trial—that is, during the information-gathering period known as the *time of discovery*—you may be asked to give a *deposition*. At the deposition, the opposing attorney will want to learn about your involvement in the case, your findings, how you arrived at your conclusions and recommendations, and related matters. The attorney is likely to refer to your report and any other related materials. Questions at the deposition tend to be phrased in an open-ended manner, which invites the witness to expand on his or her responses, whereas at the trial the cross-examination questions tend to be closed-ended and require short, specific answers (Pope, Butcher, & Seelen, 1993).

When you testify as an expert witness, expect to answer questions similar to those asked at the deposition, including questions about (a) your professional background, credentials, and experience (see Table 6-4), (b) the amount of contact you have had with the child, (c) the history of the child's difficulties, and (d) the procedures you used to evaluate the child, to draw conclusions, and to arrive at the recommendations. Many of these questions about the child can be answered by referring to your report. An expert witness can and should rely on notes or other materials for information that cannot be readily recalled. This process, called *refreshing recollection,* is both an acceptable and an accurate means of providing information to the court. However, you don't want to read from your notes; use them only to verify facts or for other information. A key to being an expert witness is to stick closely to the data, to be familiar with current research findings in your field, and to make interpretations cautiously.

Your role as an expert witness is to provide information to the court so that the court can reach an appropriate decision. In your testimony, present your findings and observations, the implications of the findings, and whatever conclusions you reached. A logical, carefully reasoned presentation will help the court come to a proper decision.

As an expert witness, you may be asked to predict whether the individual on trial may engage in dangerous behavior in the future. This is an area fraught with difficulty. You will need to be aware of the current research literature before giving an opinion. In the early 1990s, long-term predictions of violence by expert witnesses have had rather low accuracy (Poythress, 1992).

Table 6-4
Examples of Questions Asked of an Expert Witness

Background
1. Please state your name.
2. What is your present occupation?
3. For those unfamiliar with the term (social worker, psychologist, counselor, speech therapist, etc.), please explain to us what a (social worker, psychologist, counselor, speech therapist, etc.) is.
4. How does a (social worker, psychologist, counselor, speech therapist, etc.) differ from (other professionals)?
5. By whom and where are you employed?
6. How long have you been so employed?
7. Do you have a particular specialty in your work?
8. What services are provided at your organization?
9. What are your specific duties?
10. Describe your prior work history.
11. What education have you had to allow you to do this work? Tell me about your undergraduate degree and institution, graduate degree and institution, and specialized training in the field while you were in school.
12. (If pertinent to testimony) Did you have to write a thesis or research paper to obtain your graduate degree?
13. What is a thesis?
14. What was the topic of your thesis?
15. How long was your thesis?
16. How many hours of research were involved?
17. Have you had any other specialized training in your field, such as on-the-job training and seminars and continuing education?
18. (If yes) Tell me about this specialized training.

Publications and Professional Experience
19. In the state where you reside, what are the licensing procedures for people in your profession?
20. What licenses have you obtained?
21. Have you published any books or articles that deal with your work?
22. (If yes) Please describe each publication, including title, topic, publisher, length, and approximate amount of time spent on the publication.
23. Are you presently on the teaching staff of any college or university?
24. (If yes) What classes do you teach?… How long have you been teaching?… Do you have other teaching experience?
25. Have you presented any papers on the subject of _____ to professional symposiums?
26. (If yes) When?… Where?… What specific subjects?
27. Are you a member of any professional organizations?
28. (If yes) What organizations?… Have you ever served as an officer or in any special capacity for that organization?… (If yes) In what capacity did you serve?
29. Have you received any honors or prizes for your work in the field of _____?
30. (If yes) Tell me about them.

31. Have you appeared on local or national television concerning your work in this area?
32. (If yes) Tell me about your appearance.
33. Have there been newspaper or magazine articles written concerning your efforts in the field of _____?
34. (If yes) Tell me about these articles.
35. Have you received any national recognition for your work?
36. (If yes) Tell me about that.

Experience as an Expert Witness
37. Have you previously testified as an expert in the superior courts of this state regarding (reason for lawsuit or prosecution)?
38. (If yes) Tell me about that.
39. Have you testified as an expert in the courts of any other states?
40. (If yes) Which states?
41. How many times have you testified as an expert on the topic of (reason for lawsuit or prosecution)?

Familiarity with Subject Matter
42. Are you familiar with recent literature/articles/research in the area of (reason for lawsuit or prosecution)?
43. Do you subscribe to any professional journals that deal with (reason for lawsuit or prosecution)?
44. (If yes) What journals?
45. Do you routinely keep up with the current literature in this field?
46. What is the present state of knowledge in your profession on the characteristics of the (sexually abused child, brain-injured child, learning-disabled child, etc.)?
47. Can you give any examples? (Produce a comprehensive bibliography that can be used in court.)
48. Do you devote all of your professional time to this field, or do you do work in other areas?
49. (If other areas) Tell me about these other areas.
50. Please explain how you came to be involved in your area.
51. Can you estimate the number of children you have talked to who have been (type of child cited)?
52. What services do you offer these children?

Research on Subject Matter
53. Have you participated in any research regarding these children?
   (If yes, go to question 54; if no, go to question 74.)
54. In what way did you participate?
55. Was anyone else involved in this research? If so, who?
56. What were the goals of your study?
57. How many children were involved in the study?
58. Did you use accepted scientific methodology in conducting your research?
59. Did you follow approved and established statistical methods in compiling your data?

(Continued)

Table 6-4 (*Continued*)

60. Please explain those methods.
61. What verification procedures were followed to ensure the authenticity of your data?
62. Have other similar studies been conducted?
63. Can you give us some examples?
64. Have you compared the information you gathered with information obtained from the work of other experts in your field?
(If yes, go to question 65; if no, go to question 67.)
65. How do they compare?
66. Is their information consistent with yours?
67. What use is made of this information within your profession?
68. Have these characteristics gained general acceptance in your profession?
69. How can you know that to be true?
70. Are these characteristics and responses relied on by members of your profession in forming opinions or in making inferences regarding diagnosis and treatment of these children?
71. Are they helpful to you in other ways?
72. In your experience, is the information revealed by your studies and those of other researchers in your field known to the average person?
73. On what do you base that opinion?

Compliance with Subpoena
74. Have you complied fully with each and every element of the subpoena to produce material?
75. Are there any items that you did not make available to me?
76. Were any of these documents altered in any way?
77. Were any of them recopied, erased, written over, enhanced, edited, or added to in any way since the time each was originally created?
78. Are the photocopies you gave me true and exact replicas of the original documents without any revision?
79. Have any documents falling within the scope of the subpoena or otherwise relevant to the case been lost, stolen, misplaced, destroyed, or thrown away?
80. Are any documents you made, collected, handled, or received that are within the scope of this subpoena or otherwise relevant to the case absent from the documents made available to me?

Evaluation of Child
81. How many times do you normally like to see a child to make an evaluation?
82. Did you have an opportunity to interview/evaluate (child's name)?
83. Who contacted you for an evaluation of (child's name)?
84. Before meeting with (child's name), what did you do to familiarize yourself with the case?
85. Before meeting with (child's name), did you talk with anyone?
(If yes, go to question 86; if no, go to question 88.)

86. With whom?
87. What type of information did you hope to obtain from (person met with)?
88. Did you look at any reports in this case before meeting with (child's name)?
(If yes, go to question 89; if no, go to question 92.)
89. From whom did you get the reports?
90. How did you use the information that you obtained from (persons or reports)?
91. How much weight did you attribute to information learned from sources other than the child?
92. Is meeting with an adult before talking to the child an accepted practice within your profession?
93. How long were your meetings with (child's name)?
94. Were your interviews an acceptable length of time, considering the child's age and level of development?
95. How many times did you see (child's name)?
96. How much time would you estimate that you spent with (child's name) in total?
97. How much time would you estimate that you have spent on this case?
98. Where did your meetings with (child's name) take place?
99. When evaluating a child for (reason for referral), what procedures do you typically use for your evaluation?
100. Why do you use these procedures?
101. Do you typically follow the same protocol?
102. Are all of these procedures accepted by professionals in your field?
(If no, go to question 103; if yes, go to question 105.)
103. Which procedures are not accepted?
104. Why aren't they accepted?
105. How many children have you evaluated using this protocol?
106. Are the procedures you have just described accepted means of assessment in your profession?
107. Do you regularly keep records of what was found during your evaluation?
(If yes, go to question 108; if no, go to question 110.)
108. Please describe what is kept in these records.
109. When are these records completed?
110. Is there anything you can do or attempt to do to ensure that what a child is telling you is not something that was related to the child by a third person?
111. (If yes) Tell me about that.
112. Please describe how (child's name) appeared during your evaluations and how (he, she) acted during the interview.
113. During the course of your evaluation, did (child's name) express any reluctance to talk about anything?
(If yes, go to question 114; if no, go to question 116.)
114. What was the child reluctant to talk about?
115. How did you respond to the child's reluctance?
116. Did you arrive at a diagnosis?
(If yes, go to question 117; if no, go to question 119.)
117. What was it?

(*Continued*)

Table 6-4 (*Continued*)

118. How confident are you of your diagnosis?
119. Why didn't you arrive at a diagnosis?
120. Would other evaluators arrive at the same (diagnosis, conclusions/recommendations)?
121. (If no) Why not?
122. Do you have any doubts about the reliability or validity of the assessment findings?
123. (If yes) Tell me about your doubts.
124. What recommendations did you make?
125. What was the basis for your recommendations?

126. Is there anything else you want to tell us about your findings?
127. (If yes) Go ahead.
128. After meeting with (child's name), did you offer (him, her) any further services?
129. (If yes) What services did you offer the child?
130. Did you offer or suggest any referral services to (child's name)?
131. (If yes) What referral services did you offer the child?

Source: Questions 1 to 73 reprinted and adapted, with permission of the American Prosecutors Research Institute of the National Center for the Prosecution of Child Abuse, *Investigation and Prosecution of Child Abuse* (2nd ed.), pp. 353–395, copyright 1993 by the American Prosecutors Research Institute. Questions 74 to 80 adapted from Pope, Butcher, and Seelen (1993). Questions 81 to 115 and 128 to 131 adapted with permission of the author, from M. Zehnder, *Using Expert Witnesses in Child Abuse and Neglect Cases,* copyright 1994 by the Minnesota County Attorney's Association, pp. 28–29.

The Cross-Examination

Be prepared for the opposing attorney to scrutinize your credentials and question your expertise and credibility. The opposing attorney may ask you about

- *your education* (if you do not have a master's or doctoral degree: "Isn't it true that a master's in social work is the accepted degree for the practice of social work?" or "Isn't it true that a Ph.D. is the accepted degree for the practice of psychology?")
- *your experience* ("You're not a medical doctor, are you? Then, how can you tell us about the effects of brain damage?")
- *the amount of time that you spent with the child* ("Do you mean that you spent only two hours interviewing the child?")
- *your ability to make recommendations* ("Do you think that you know the child well enough to make a recommendation based on two hours of interviewing?")
- *the type of recommendations that you made* ("How can you be sure that the child should be placed with the mother/has been abused/needs a classroom for learning-disabled children rather than a special tutor?")
- *your publications* (if you have published a book or an article: "Isn't it true that on page 17, you wrote that children are not reliable informants?")

The opposing attorney may try to discredit you by trying to show that your assessment procedures were faulty, that you are a "hired gun," that you have a bad character, that your testimony conflicts with testimony you gave in prior trials, that your publications are inconsistent, or that you lack knowledge about the subject matter (Schultz, 1990). In addition, the opposing attorney may do anything within the legal limits of courtroom procedure to impeach your testimony. Because court hearings are based on the adversarial process, there are few absolute truths; the verdict or decision often depends on which party presents a more convincing case.

Suggestions for Testifying as an Expert Witness

The following suggestions may help you better prepare for those occasions when you testify as an expert witness. You want to assume responsibility for ensuring that the attorney calling you as an expert witness presents you in the best possible light (American Prosecutors Research Institute of the National Center for the Prosecution of Child Abuse, *Investigation and Prosecution of Child Abuse* [2nd ed.], pp. 387–389, copyright 1993 by the American Prosecutors Research Institute, adapted and reprinted with permission).

PREPARATION

1. Be prepared. Always know the pertinent facts of the case better than anyone else in the courtroom. Determine the key legal issues. Also be up-to-date on the empirical findings in the area. You don't want to rely only on in-depth knowledge of a single case.
2. Request a pre-trial conference with the attorney calling you as a witness to learn what he or she wants from you and to educate him or her about the subject matter of your testimony. Review with him or her other cases in which you have given similar testimony.
3. Discuss with the attorney calling you as a witness potential cross-examination questions and answers.
4. Avoid using professional jargon. Review your testimony with the attorney calling you as a witness and identify any difficult words. Use a thesaurus to find simple and clear alternative words that the judge and/or jury will understand.

5. Provide the attorney calling you as a witness with a list of qualification and foundation questions—that is, questions asked to establish your credentials. You will be more at ease knowing the questions you will be asked, and the attorney will be grateful to you for making his or her job easier.

6. Provide the attorney calling you as an expert witness with an up-to-date resume of your professional credentials and educational background.

7. Dress professionally and conservatively.

8. Maintain a ready file of literature, including monographs, articles, and books, about the specialty area in which you will be offering expert testimony. Make these available to the attorney calling you so that he or she will be more educated on your subject. Also, be sure that the attorney is aware of anything you have written about the subject of your testimony.

9. If you are going to be interviewed by opposing counsel, avoid doing so in your office. By meeting in your personal office, you give the attorney a chance to look around at the various reference books and texts and then challenge you in court with one of your own reference books. A neutral place like a restaurant, a conference room, or even an attorney's office is a better place for your meeting.

10. Avoid sitting for an interview or for a deposition with opposing counsel until you are fully prepared, know the facts of your case, have spoken to the attorney calling you as a witness, and have reviewed the relevant references to the professional literature.

11. Segregate your personal notes and work products from the case file. Do not show them to the opposing counsel without either the permission of the attorney calling you as a witness or a court order.

12. At an interview with the opposing counsel or at a deposition, have a "game plan." One plan is to impress the other attorney with *all* the facts that support your position to encourage settlement of the case. If you expect the case to go to trial, then another plan is to answer the questions honestly but narrowly. Discuss the "game plan" with the attorney calling you as a witness.

13. Always tell the truth, and strive to be fair and objective.

14. If you anticipate that the opposing attorney also will be calling an expert witness, suggest to the attorney calling you as a witness that you spend time preparing him or her to deal with the other expert witness. You can even sometimes sit with the attorney in court and suggest methods of cross-examination to him or her.

COURTROOM BEHAVIOR

15. Remember, when you are approaching the courthouse or are inside it, anyone you pass may be a judge, juror, hostile witness, or opposing attorney. Always conduct yourself accordingly.

16. When you enter the courtroom, do not do anything that will draw attention to your behavior. Before sitting down in the witness stand, make brief eye contact with the judge and/or jury. Adjust the chair and microphone so that you don't have to lean forward to answer questions.

17. Before answering each question, control the situation by consciously pausing. This allows the judge and/or jury to mentally shift from hearing the attorney's question to listening to your answer. For example:

Q: State your name and occupation.
[Three-count pause]
A: My name is _____. I am a social worker for the _____.

Q: How long have you been employed?
[Three-count pause]
A: I have been working there for _____ years.

18. Answer each question with a declarative statement rather than a word or phrase. The opposing attorney may want the judge and/or jury to hear only his or her question. By using the three-count pause, the declarative sentence, and the spatial positioning, you will take psychological control away from the opposing attorney.

19. When answering questions, don't guess. If you don't know, say you don't know, but don't let the cross-examiner get you in the trap of answering question after question with "I don't know."

20. Understand the question before you attempt to give an answer. If necessary, ask that it be repeated. You can't possibly give a truthful and accurate answer unless you understand the question.

21. Listen and try to avoid asking the attorney to repeat the question. Keep a sharp lookout for questions with a double meaning and questions that assume you have testified to a fact when you have not done so.

22. Answer the question asked and then stop, especially on cross-examination. Don't volunteer information not called for by the question you are asked.

23. Choice of words is important. Develop your ability to use words that not only depict what happened but also convey the impression you intend. Here are some examples of positive "soft" words, followed by negative "hard" words in parentheses: *mother* (woman, respondent, abuser), *father* (subject, suspect, defendant), *child* (juvenile, youth), *cut* (laceration, open wound), *molest* (rape, sexually assault), and *bruise* (contusion). Note how the hard and soft words leave different impressions.

24. Talk loudly enough so that everyone can hear you, yet softly enough so that you can suddenly raise your voice to emphasize a point. This is especially important if the proceedings are being audiotaped or videotaped.

25. Avoid distracting mannerisms such as eating mints, chewing gum, or fumbling through a file.

26. Give an audible answer so that the court reporter can hear it. Don't nod your head; say "yes" or "no" instead. The court reporter is recording everything you say.

27. Don't look at the attorney who called you as a witness or at the judge for help when you are on the witness stand. You are responsible for your testimony.

28. Beware of questions involving distances and time. If you make an estimate, make sure that everyone understands that you are estimating. Think clearly about distances and intervals of time. Be sure your estimates are reasonable.

29. Don't be afraid to look the jurors in the eye. Jurors are naturally sympathetic to witnesses and want to hear what they have to say. Look at them most of the time and speak to them as frankly and openly as you would to a friend or neighbor.

30. Don't argue with the attorney cross-examining you. He or she has every right to question you. The attorney who called you should object if the other attorney asks an inappropriate question. Don't answer a question with a question unless the question you are asked is not clear.

31. Don't lose your temper, no matter how hard you are pressed. If you lose your temper, you have played right into the hands of the cross-examiner.

32. Be courteous. Being courteous is one of the best ways to make a good impression on the court and/or on the jury. Address the judge as "Your Honor."

33. If asked whether you have talked to the attorney calling you as a witness or to an investigator, admit it freely. If you are being paid a fee, admit without hesitation that you are receiving compensation.

34. Avoid joking, wisecracks, and condescending comments or inflections. A trial is a serious matter.

EXPERT TESTIMONY

35. Most people learn visually. Use blackboards, diagrams, charts, etc., liberally. At the blackboard or easel, turn around and talk to the judge and/or jury. Almost inevitably, witnesses not following this instruction get into an inaudible conversation with the blackboard. Remember spatial positioning.

36. Draw in proportion. Before drawing anything—think! Don't start with the old cliché "Well, I am not much of an artist." Draw in proportion, and never refer to "here" and "there." A reviewing court will not understand what you mean. Describe what you draw orally, and number each relevant representation.

37. Never read from notes unless absolutely necessary. If you must, announce the fact that you are doing so and state your reason—that is, refreshing memory, need for specificity, etc. The attorney cross-examining you will most likely have a right to see the notes that you are referring to during your testimony.

38. An opposing attorney may cross-examine you using articles, books, other people's opinions, or things you have said. You may be confronted with something that appears contradictory in an effort to show that your opinion is inconsistent with these other sources. Ask to see the book or article the opposing attorney refers to. Read it, and compare what you read with what the attorney has said. Often, you will find that something has been taken out of context or misinterpreted by the attor-

ney. You can then demonstrate not only that you are right, but that the article or book agrees with you.

CONCLUSION

39. When you finish testifying, nod to the judge and/or jury, and say "thank you."

40. After each appearance as an expert witness, check with the attorney or others present for a critique of your performance. Use the critique to improve or modify the way you testify.

Effectiveness of Testimony

Your effectiveness as an expert witness will be judged on the following issues (Myers, 1993): Did you consider all relevant facts? How much confidence can be placed in the accuracy of the facts underlying your opinion? Did you show an adequate understanding of the pertinent clinical and scientific principles involved in the case? Did you use methods of assessment and analysis recognized as appropriate by professionals in your field? Were the inferences you drew logical? Were your assumptions reasonable? Were you reasonably objective? Thus, your testimony will be judged on whether it was "logical, consistent, explainable, objective, and defensible" (Myers, 1993, p. 179). See Brodsky (1991) for more information about testifying in court as an expert witness.

INTERVIEWER STRESS

You may find clinical assessment interviewing stressful, and you may have difficulty dealing with the stress. If the stress becomes too great, you are likely to experience burnout, and you may want to leave your job. *Burnout* is a state of physical, emotional, and mental exhaustion resulting from emotionally demanding situations. It is primarily associated with mental and behavioral symptoms that are usually work-related (Maslach & Schaufeli, 1993). The key symptoms are emotional exhaustion, inability to get close to others, and feelings of reduced personal accomplishment. Other, more specific symptoms of burnout include tiredness and fatigue, low energy, anxiety, loss of appetite, frequent headaches, sleeplessness, irritability, losing temper more easily, carelessness, sudden weight loss or gain, increase in blood pressure, increase in minor illnesses, muscle aches and backaches, feeling run down, depression, apathy, boredom, cynicism, not looking forward to going to work, frequent absences, being less productive, making more mistakes, increased interpersonal conflicts, increased alcohol consumption, and use of drugs. These symptoms occur in normal persons who may have had no history of mental disturbance, and the "decreased effectiveness and work performance occur because of negative attitudes and behaviors" (Maslach & Schaufeli, 1993, p. 15).

The uncomfortable feelings associated with burnout at times "can and do give way to transient feelings of irritation

Us & Them   by Wiley Miller & Susan Dewar

and repugnance, anger, and even revulsion" (Lederberg, 1989, p. 632). Individuals who experience burnout may be upset and even surprised at themselves. Consequently, they may feel guilty or suppress negative feelings that, in turn, may lead to over-sacrificing behavior. You will soon be reading about burnout in more detail, but first let's look at some of the reasons for interviewer stress.

Reasons for Interviewer Stress

As an interviewer, you may experience stress for several reasons (Kash & Holland, 1989; Lederberg, 1989; Tracy, Bean, Gwatkin, & Hill, 1992):

1. You may find it difficult to deal with children or parents who are excessively dependent, angry, or uncooperative; issues involving terminal care; suicidal ideations; third-party conflicts; legal issues; debilitation and disfigurement; and other issues involving the care of children and work with their parents and families.
2. You may not be able to tolerate how children are treated by their parents or others.
3. You may become over-involved in your cases. This may happen when you identify with the children or parents or when they remind you of an important person in your life.
4. You may disagree with the intervention plans, such as the choice of treatments or placements made for the children and families, and feel hampered when your judgments aren't accepted. This is particularly a problem when legal issues are involved.
5. You may have stress in your personal life (for example, conflict with spouse or children, personal illness, per-

sonal grief associated with loss of a family member or friend, or personal financial problems) that affects your professional work.
6. You may have stresses associated with the agency, clinic, or hospital that you work for. These include "low pay, long hours, excessive paperwork, little opportunity for advancement, powerlessness, and unresponsive and unappreciative bureaucratic environments" (Oktay, 1992, p. 432). In addition, there may be stress because of conflicts with the staff, peers, and supervisors; lack of feedback; working with multiproblem families; working with children and parents who have chronic and complex problems; and professional isolation.
7. You may have stresses associated with the clinical demands of your job. Sources of such stresses include answering phone calls at night, handling crisis calls, making visits in rural or isolated areas, visiting homes of clients who are violent or suspected of being violent, receiving threats of bodily harm, visiting clients during bad weather conditions, recommending removal of children from their homes, appearing in court, recommending termination of parental rights, and seeing clients' difficult living conditions.
8. You may experience a sense of helplessness in dealing with severely ill children.
9. You may feel stress if you work in a medical setting because of a sense of low status and limited power (particularly if you are a social worker, psychologist, counselor, nurse, or dietician) and a need to "sell" the importance of your efforts.
10. You may feel alienated from your job but have to continue to work in the setting because you have limited job mobility.

Here are some comments made by professionals when they were experiencing symptoms of burnout (Larson, 1993, pp. 32–33, with changes in notation):

- I feel upset about my physical symptoms of anxiety—muscle tension, rapid pulse, diarrhea, loss of appetite, difficulty sleeping. Sometimes I feel trapped and just want to get outside. And I ask myself: Who takes care of me?
- Sometimes I feel I deserve more because I give more. I get tired of trying. I'm so sick of patients' draining every ounce of energy out of me. Mostly, lately, I feel like I have no more to give anyone. I need all my energy for me. I can't get over being "tired" all the time. My mental acuity is poor. Recall is almost zero.
- I wear a mask. I work so hard at being "up" for others and getting others "up"—and no one really knows how tired I am. I want out.

Example of Stress in Working with Maltreated Children

Seeing children who have been maltreated may make you angry, depressed, and nauseated and leave you with an empty feeling in the pit of your stomach. Because of your work with maltreated children, you may experience nightmares, intensive and repetitive images, and somatic complaints, such as headaches, nausea, and sleeplessness—reactions similar to those experienced by individuals with a post-traumatic stress disorder (Lyon, 1993; also see Chapter 11). You also may feel "contaminated" by the descriptions of abuse, isolated and alienated from other staff members and from friends, and confronted by issues of good and evil.

Here are some comments made by professionals about their work with maltreated children (Lyon, 1993, pp. 412–413, with changes in notation):

- You think about this material as something toxic and don't have a way to consciously shut it out.
- I find myself wanting to share with friends…but I feel a terrible sense of guilt.
- I can't talk to anyone else about the images because then I'll pollute *them*.
- I'm feeling resentful that I now have terrible memories that are a part of who I am…that I now carry these ghosts with me as part of my legacy.
- I had difficulty sleeping last night after hearing Gail's story. Did anyone else feel that way?
- I guess when I hear what Mary's mother did to her, I realize I might have the capacity to be sadistic too, in some way. That's pretty scary!

The following describes why work with maltreated children may be so stressful (Walker, 1992):

Most [of us] have been trained to be neutral, to control our feelings, and sometimes even to deny our feelings. But working with abused children brings out intense emotions in adults, from stimulating memories of one's own maltreatment as a child to personal sexual discomfort with some issues raised, as well as identification with the client whether it be the child, the adult offender, or maybe the also-battered mother. Feelings of anger toward the offender, helplessness and frustration with the often-ineffective legal and child protection system, dismay with the parent who does not seem to be able to protect the child, concern with the…colleague who does not appear to view the case in the same way, and self-deprecation for not being more powerful to fix things all may interfere with treatment at some time. Consultation, supervision, and even referral at appropriate times are important resources for those who treat violated children. (p. 48)

Examples of Stress When a Suicide Occurs

When one of your clients commits suicide, you may experience feelings of astonishment, grief, anger, incredulity, guilt, and failure—feelings similar to those experienced by the relatives of the deceased (Moritz, Van Nes, & Brouwer, 1989). Your professional competence may be undermined, and your thoughts may be haunted by questions of whether the suicide might have been prevented and whether you bear responsibility for the suicide. The suicide of a young child may be particularly difficult to accept. Not all of you may experience these reactions, however. Some of you, as a way of protecting yourself emotionally, may see the suicide as the responsibility of the interviewee alone or of his or her family (Moritz et al., 1989).

Here are two accounts of how clinicians reacted to their client's suicide (Moritz et al., 1989):

CLINICIAN 1

I didn't talk to the team about the suicide, I only spoke to a colleague, on her initiative. I told her of my doubts. I work here in a fairly independent fashion, I have to sort out the problems on my own. We do have sessions to discuss clients, but I wouldn't bring this up there. I did cry in the department, with team members around, they all came to comfort me, but talking about it at any length there's just no time, everybody is rushed off their feet. I would like to talk about it at more length but it takes too much time. Furthermore, if I admit to making certain errors in judgment, I will be making myself vulnerable. Perhaps I will be blamed then, they might think I don't do my work properly. There is only the one colleague that I trust. It is not just a question of having no time but of anxiety about the consequences too. (p. 207)

CLINICIAN 2

We, as a team, wondered whether we had not made a mistake in our judgment of the situation. We went through the case with a fine-tooth comb and looked at each step again. We are supportive of one another in the team. The week afterwards, we talked about it again, rounding the whole thing off, all together. If I had not had my team, I would have gone sick. I have the feeling that it was well resolved through the support [we] gave to one another. If I had had to go through it alone, I would have had a very difficult time. (p. 207)

In cases of suicide, it is a good idea that the whole team discuss the case (Moritz et al., 1989). The team can play an important role in supporting clinicians.

Stages of Burnout

Burnout can be viewed as a five-stage process (Kash & Holland, 1989; Lederberg, 1989):

Stage 1. Job demands exceed emotional or physical resources.

Stage 2. Somatic complaints develop, including tension, irritability, tiredness, aches, and difficulty getting up.

Stage 3. Attempts are made to cope with the stress, such as becoming emotionally detached, withdrawn, or cynical; developing a negative or suspicious outlook; and developing feelings of alienation.

Stage 4. Disturbances develop in job performance, such as absenteeism, decreased satisfaction with work, and work slowdown. Disturbances also develop in personal life, such as feelings of disgust or substance abuse.

Stage 5. Severe physical and psychological disturbances develop, including anxiety, depression, withdrawal, collapse, and possibly risk of suicide.

Be alert to the early phases of burnout, and take action to prevent your reactions from reaching chronic proportions (see the next part of the chapter for suggestions).

Exercise 6-2. Evaluating a Case of Burnout in a Social Worker

---

Read the case, and then answer the questions following it. Compare your answers with those following the questions. This exercise was adapted from Grosch and Olsen (WHEN HELPING STARTS TO HURT: A New Look at Burnout Among Psychotherapists by William N. Grosch and David C. Olsen. Copyright © 1994 by William N. Grosch and David C. Olsen. Reprinted by permission of W. W. Norton Company, Inc., pp. 96–97).

Cliff, a social worker and team leader at a mental health center, came to the interview complaining of chronic fatigue and burnout. He reported feeling numb and said that he is only going through the motions on his job. He described staring into space in the mornings while at his desk and dreading all the clients he has to face the rest of the day. He is not at all sure that going back into therapy will help, but feels he has to do *something*. He is beginning to wonder whether he is in the right position, even in the right profession.

Cliff was the oldest of five children in a close-knit, perfectionistic family. His father was demanding and difficult to please. In childhood, even when he would bring home a good report card, his father would point out how it could have been better. He felt pressured by both parents to be the one who excelled in the family, and he had a sense that his mother lived vicariously through him. She went to work on a factory assembly line at an early age to help her family and always

regretted not going to college herself. He could not recall being able to relax, even play much with friends in the neighborhood, because he was always striving to get high grades.

Now he sees his parents infrequently and feels like a child when he is with them. He acknowledged that he is still trying to earn his father's approval. He usually asks his father if he needs any help with household repairs, though his dad has always been the better repairer. He also feels estranged from his wife and two adolescent children and says that his wife neither understands nor appreciates him and is constantly critical of him. He feels distant from his kids.

On the other hand, he relates that for at least the first 10 years in his present position he loved the work and even put in hours way beyond what was expected. He says it gave him a sense of meaning and purpose to be of help to people and admits that he is a people pleaser and enjoys getting people to like him. Lately, however, many of his staff have been calling in sick, while his director has been complaining about his team's decline in units of service and rate of collecting fees. He recently was criticized because several members of his team have been delinquent in their record keeping. He has always hated checking charts to see if his staff were keeping up with their workload.

Cliff thought his hard work (and that of others as well) was primarily a matter of ideals and professionalism, but the real engine that drove him was wanting to be liked. When he turned to his wife, Martha, and children, Jenny, 17, and Michael, 15, for support, he found them cold and critical. This left him hurt and frustrated, but he was unable to realize how he contributed to their detached attitude. His long hours at the clinic, along with an expanding part-time private practice, had left his family bitter and distant. The more he gave to his work, the more it seemed to consume him. His current fantasies were to meet another woman who would understand him and give him the affection he "deserved" and to find a new agency that would "appreciate" him. At the same time, he realized that the problem is more complex.

1. What symptoms of burnout was Cliff exhibiting?
2. How might Cliff's upbringing have affected his feelings about his job?
3. How has Cliff's current family contributed to his burnout?
4. What changes in Cliff's workplace might have contributed to his burnout?

Suggested Answers

1. Chronic fatigue, feeling numb, loss of meaning and purpose, distractibility, feelings of hopelessness, and doubts about his competence and choice of career
2. Being brought up in a family that was not nurturing and accepting led Cliff to seek approval from his job and to need to be appreciated by others.
3. Cliff does not realize that he has distanced himself from his family by working long hours. In turn, his family's critical attitudes and lack of response have made him feel insecure, leading him to work longer and harder to achieve feelings of self-worth.
4. Cliff's work environment became less supportive. Because of his need to be liked, he had not learned how to supervise the staff that reported to him, and this shortcoming led to further disappointment.

Dealing with the Stress of Being a Clinical Assessment or Forensic Interviewer

Your ability to deal with the stress of being a clinical or forensic assessment interviewer will in part depend on how you have coped with stress in the past. If you were successful in coping in the past, you may be able to conquer your present stress. However, you will have a more difficult time coping with the stress of being a clinical assessment or forensic interviewer if you avoid talking about your stress; feel shame, guilt, and anger at having to recognize that you are vulnerable; think that experiencing job stress is incompatible with your professional image; and think that if other professionals learn of your self-doubts and vulnerability, your reputation will be diminished.

One common way individuals deal with work stress is to discuss problems associated with their work with family and friends. This outlet may not be available to clinical assessment or forensic interviewers because their family and friends may not want to hear about their work. It may be painful for them to listen to problems dealing with child abuse and neglect, domestic violence, terminal illness, substance abuse, mentally or physically disabled children, custody disputes, or potential suicide, for example. Family and friends may find these areas depressing, or they may be frightened by these areas because of their own fears, vulnerabilities, or misconceptions. *Obviously, if you discuss cases with family members or friends, you must maintain confidentiality of client information.* This means that you never use names or discuss anything that may reveal the client's identity. Chapter 2 discusses issues associated with confidentiality in more detail.

Here are some useful strategies to help you cope with stress (Corey, Corey, & Callanan, 1993; Holland, 1989b; Lederberg, 1989):

- recognize and monitor any symptoms
- change pace
- exercise
- eat a balanced diet
- spend time on your hobby
- decrease overtime
- maintain a sense of humor
- attend interesting lectures, seminars, and conferences
- clarify ambiguous work assignments
- work toward obtaining a manageable work load
- don't volunteer for additional work and responsibility
- keep your work goals realistic
- vary the type of client you work with, if possible
- vary your work activities
- keep lines of communication open with other staff members (this will be especially helpful in defining problems, working out solutions, ventilating feelings, providing information, clarifying misunderstandings, and negotiating partial solutions)

The following Irish prayer also provides some valuable guidelines for handling stress (and perhaps life in general):

Take time to work,
It is the price of success.
Take time to think,
It is the source of power.
Take time to play,
It is the secret of perpetual youth.
Take time to read,
It is the foundation of wisdom.
Take time to be friendly,
It is the road to happiness.
Take time to love and be loved,
It is the privilege of the gods.
Take time to share,
Life is too short to be selfish.
Take time to laugh,
Laughter is the music of the soul.

—Author unknown

The Rewards of Being a Clinical Assessment or Forensic Interviewer

There are many rewards associated with being a clinical assessment or forensic interviewer (Lederberg, 1989).

Many of the features that make work with…[clients] special can cut either way, because they can make a staff member feel stress or they can make him or her feel valuable and worthwhile. For example, one can repress anger or one can feel strong enough to be generous. One can feel numb or one can feel capable of tolerating the human condition. One can flee from overemotional encounters or feel privileged to share extraordinary moments. One can feel guilty or one can feel a special gratitude and refined appreciation for life. One can feel intellectually overwhelmed or intellectually challenged. One can feel useless or proud of one's unique personal contribution. One can feel alienated or anchored in a valuable human enterprise. (p. 639)

Sources of job satisfaction include seeing clients reach their goals; making a difference in clients' lives; working intensively with clients and seeing them progress; establishing satisfying relationships with clients; receiving expressions of gratitude from clients; improving skills in working with clients; working outside an office; having a flexible schedule; having small caseloads; having a good salary, benefits, and promotion opportunities; receiving recognition from other professionals in the community; receiving support and recognition from clients; receiving support and recognition from coworkers; receiving support and recognition from the supervisor; having personal feelings of accomplishment; increasing one's knowledge and skills about human behavior, social problems, and so on; and having opportunities for personal growth and development (Tracy et al., 1992).

Our society needs competent clinical assessment and forensic interviewers to help children and families in need of services. Handling stresses as they arise, finding daily satisfactions in your work, no matter how small, and feeling proud of your contributions as a professional (or professional-in-training) will help you in your work and perhaps reduce or prevent burnout.

The art of caregiving is the art of interdependence. It's a delicate [and] often precarious balance: being involved and keeping perspective: caring and yet being objective; spending time together and taking time to be alone; giving to ourselves and setting limits.

—Kairos House

THINKING THROUGH THE ISSUES

In actual practice, how do you think you would go about evaluating the reliability and validity of the information you obtain in an interview?

Do you believe that you can detect malingering?

How effective do you think you can be in evaluating your interview techniques?

How do you think you will feel when someone evaluates your interview techniques?

How do you think you will react to constructive criticism?

How will you know if you are conveying to the interviewee that you want respect from him or her or want to be liked? And if you find that you are doing this, what can you do to change your behavior?

How do you think you will handle the role of an expert witness? Can you withstand the cross-examination of the opposing attorney? How will you prepare for your day in court?

How do you think you will deal with a work environment that is unresponsive and bureaucratic? Do you think, for example, that you will work for change in the organization, tolerate the organization but accept the satisfactions from helping clients, or look for another place to work?

If the level of stress you faced as an interviewer became overwhelming to you, how would you go about reducing the stress?

SUMMARY

Reliability and Validity of the Interview

1. Evaluate carefully the reliability of the interview findings. Types of reliability are test-retest reliability, interinterviewee agreement, internal consistency, and interinterviewer reliability or method error.

2. Test-retest reliability is evaluated by determining whether the information obtained from the interviewee on one occasion is comparable to the information that was or would have been obtained from the same interviewee on other occasions.

3. Interinterviewee agreement is evaluated by determining whether the information obtained from the interviewee agrees with the information obtained from another interviewee.

4. Internal consistency is evaluated by determining whether the information given by the interviewee is consistent with other information given by the interviewee in the same interview.

5. Interinterviewer reliability or method error is evaluated by determining whether the information obtained by one interviewer is consistent with that obtained by another interviewer from the same interviewee.

6. Evaluate the concurrent validity and predictive validity of the interview findings.

7. Concurrent validity refers to the extent to which the information obtained in the interview corresponds to the information obtained through other methods.

8. Predictive validity refers to the degree to which information obtained in the interview predicts the treatment outcome.

9. It may be difficult to determine the overall reliability and validity of an interview because of the many types of data that are obtained.

10. Bias in the interview can be associated with situational factors, with the interviewee, and with the interviewer.

11. Sources of interviewee error are associated with the interviewee's attitudes; understanding of questions; memory; interpretation of events; language; affect; personal likes, dislikes, and values; and behavior.

12. Research suggests that children and parents differ in their reports and that younger children differ from older children in the reliability of their reports. Children and parents agree *least* often about covert and private symptoms such as anxiety, fear, and obsessions and agree more often about overt, easily observable behaviors such as behavior problems and conduct problems. Adolescents are more reliable than younger school-aged children in reporting symptoms. Younger school-aged children have particular difficulties with questions about duration and onset of symptoms but not with questions about fears.

13. Seek confirmation of the symptoms reported by young children from other sources.

14. Sources of interviewer error are associated with the interviewer's techniques and style; personal needs; personal likes, dislikes, and values; understanding of the interviewee; attention to the physical environment; selective perceptions and expectancies; ethnicity; recording techniques; interpretations; and theoretical position.

15. Excessive questions about a topic are improper when the questions further your needs rather than the needs of the interviewee or the goals of the interview.

16. A contrast and similarity error occurs when you constantly compare your values with those of the interviewee and find the interviewee's values lacking.

17. Reactions to the interviewee that are not objective are called reactive effects.

18. A leniency effect error occurs when you tend to excuse behaviors shown by the interviewee because of your preconceived views.

19. A halo effect error occurs when you develop expectancies that lead you to have a narrow or prejudicial view of the interviewee.

20. Errors occur in cross-ethnic, cross-cultural, or cross-class situations when you distort replies or make inaccurate inferences simply because of racial or class differences or antagonisms.

21. A central tendency error occurs when an inability to form judgments about the interviewee's behavior causes you to opt for the middle ground.

22. A generalization effect error occurs when you generalize from one behavior to others with little evidence to support the generalization.

23. A logical rating error occurs when you rate one area like another one simply because the two seem to be logically related.

24. You can increase the reliability and validity of the interview by having a plan and using guidelines; wording questions so that they do not lead the interviewee toward an answer; listening carefully to the interviewee; giving your undivided interest and attention to the interviewee; showing your acceptance of the interviewee; maintaining an attitude of professional interest and concern; becoming aware of your personal needs and finding ways to suppress those that may adversely affect how you conduct the interview; recognizing your values and objectives; developing an awareness of your nonverbal and verbal behavior; being aware not only of the communications of the interviewee and your reactions to them, but also of your communications and how the interviewee may perceive them; minimizing selective perceptions, theoretical preconceptions, and expectancies that may distract you from eliciting information and making appropriate decisions; becoming aware of cross-ethnic, cross-cultural, and cross-class dynamics and being willing to work through them; gathering additional information as needed; checking your notes for accuracy shortly after the interview is over; recording (by writing or tape recorder) the information you have obtained and your impressions soon after the interview if you do not take notes; studying all sources of information about the interviewee for corroborating facts; cross-validating inferences and predictions; closely reviewing the data before you make inferences; recognizing the limitations of your theoretical approach; and being open to alternative explanations.

Assessment of Malingering

25. Malingering can be defined as a conscious fabrication or gross exaggeration of physical or psychological symptoms in pursuit of a recognizable goal.

26. Malingering ranges from mild to severe.

27. Reasons for malingering include efforts to reduce personal accountability, escape the consequences of antisocial or immoral actions, avoid punishment by pretending to be incompetent to stand trial, avoid military service, seek financial gain for alleged psychological illness, seek a transfer to another setting, and gain admission to a psychiatric hospital.

28. Children with a conduct disorder may be particularly prone to presenting false or grossly exaggerated symptoms.

29. Malingering is more likely to occur in older elementary school–aged children and adolescents than in younger children.

30. Evaluate malingering by considering the child's past and current functioning, test performance, clinical records, and reports from others.

31. Possible signs of malingering include the following: interviewee is involved in a legal action; interviewee's symptoms worsen when she or he is observed; interviewee's symptoms are bizarre or ridiculous; interviewee's symptoms wax and wane, depending on what is going on in her or his environment at the time; interviewee's symptoms fail to respond to customary treatment; interviewee's complaints are grossly in excess of physical findings; interviewee's symptoms cannot be explained by a known mental or physical disorder; interviewee

is uncooperative during the examination and with the recommendations; interviewee's symptoms give her or him some advantages, such as avoidance of school, avoidance of incarceration, financial gain, avoidance of prosecution, or acquisition of drugs; and interviewee's self-report cannot be verified by independent observers.

32. In the final analysis, you can be certain that the interviewee is malingering only when the interviewee voluntarily confesses—convincingly—to the deception or when the interviewee confesses when you confront him or her during an obvious lie.

Evaluating Your Interview Techniques

33. Particularly during training, an interviewer should evaluate his or her interview techniques after completing each interview.

34. During training, you may want to obtain feedback from the interviewee about your performance.

35. Your failure to obtain information from an interviewee may be related more to the dysfunctions of the interviewee than to your clinical skills.

The Challenges of Being an Expert Witness

36. Testifying as an expert witness can be a difficult experience, especially in court or court-like settings, because the structure of the courtroom is radically different from that of the staff conference room or classroom.

37. The goal of the mental health system is to promote mental health, whereas the goal of the legal system is to promote justice.

38. When you testify as an expert witness, expect to answer questions about your professional background, credentials, and experience; the amount of contact you have had with the child; the history of the child's difficulties; and the procedures you used to evaluate the child, to draw conclusions, and to arrive at the recommendations.

39. Your role as an expert witness is to provide information to the court so that the court can reach an appropriate decision.

40. Be prepared for the opposing attorney to scrutinize your credentials and to question your expertise and credibility.

41. You should assume responsibility for ensuring that the attorney calling you as an expert witness presents you in the best possible light.

42. There are several things that you can do to increase your effectiveness as an expert witness. Perhaps the most important ones are to be prepared; to dress conservatively; to be absolutely fair and objective; to understand the question before you give an answer; to choose your words carefully; to keep your temper, be courteous, and avoid joking and wisecracks; and to use notes sparingly.

43. Your opinion as an expert witness will be judged on whether it was logical, consistent, explainable, objective, and defensible.

Interviewer Stress

44. Burnout is a state of physical, emotional, and mental exhaustion resulting from emotionally demanding situations.

45. Symptoms of burnout include tiredness and fatigue, low energy, anxiety, loss of appetite, frequent headaches, sleeplessness, irritability, losing temper more easily, carelessness, sudden weight loss or gain, increase in blood pressure, increase in

minor illnesses, muscle aches and backaches, feeling run down, depression, apathy, boredom, cynicism, not looking forward to going to work, frequent absences, being less productive, making more mistakes, increased interpersonal conflicts, increased alcohol consumption, and use of drugs.

46. Reasons for stress include finding it difficult to deal with demanding clients, not being able to tolerate how children are treated, becoming over-involved in your cases, disagreeing with the intervention plans, facing stress in your personal life, having conflicts with staff, handling the demands of the job, feeling helpless in dealing with some problems, having low status in some settings, and feeling alienated from the job but not being able to seek other employment.

47. Seeing children who have been maltreated may make you angry, depressed, and nauseated and leave you with an empty feeling in the pit of your stomach.

48. When one of your clients commits suicide, you may experience feelings of astonishment, grief, anger, incredulity, guilt, and failure—feelings similar to those experienced by the relatives of the deceased. Your professional competence may be undermined, and your thoughts may be haunted by questions of whether the suicide might have been prevented and whether you bear responsibility for the suicide.

49. Burnout can be viewed as a five-stage process: excessive job demands, development of somatic complaints, coping attempts, disturbances in job performance, and development of severe physical and psychological disturbances.

50. Your ability to deal with the stress of being a clinical or forensic assessment interviewer will in part depend on how you coped with stress in the past.

51. Useful strategies to help you cope with stress include recognizing and monitoring symptoms, changing pace, exercising, eating a balanced diet, spending time on your hobby, decreasing overtime, maintaining a sense of humor, attending interesting lectures, clarifying ambiguous work assignments, obtaining a manageable work load, not volunteering for additional work and responsibility, keeping your work goals realistic, varying the type of client you work with, varying your work activities, and keeping lines of communication open with other staff members.

52. Sources of job satisfaction include seeing clients reach their goals; making a difference in clients' lives; working intensively with clients and seeing them progress; establishing satisfying relationships with clients; receiving expressions of gratitude from clients; improving skills in working with clients; working outside an office; having a flexible schedule; having small caseloads; having a good salary, benefits, and promotion opportunities; receiving recognition from other professionals in the community; receiving support and recognition from clients; receiving support and recognition from co-workers; receiving support and recognition from the supervisor; having personal feelings of accomplishment; increasing your knowledge about and skills in dealing with human behavior, social problems, and so on; and having opportunities for personal growth and development.

KEY TERMS, CONCEPTS, AND NAMES

Reliability of interview (p. 207)
Test-retest reliability (p. 207)
Interinterviewee agreement (p. 207)
Internal consistency (p. 207)
Interinterviewer reliability or method error (p. 207)
Validity of interview (p. 207)
Concurrent validity (p. 207)
Predictive validity (p. 207)
Situational bias (p. 207)
Sources of interviewee bias (p. 207)
Reactive effects (p. 208)
Sources of interviewer bias (p. 208)
Contrast and similarity error (p. 209)
Leniency effect error (p. 210)
Halo effect error (p. 210)
Central tendency error (p. 210)
Generalization effect error (p. 210)
Logical rating error (p. 210)
Malingering (p. 211)
Mild malingering (p. 211)
Moderate malingering (p. 211)
Severe malingering (p. 211)
Conduct disorder (p. 212)
Self-evaluation (p. 213)
Expert witness (p. 218)
Adversarial system (p. 218)
Time of discovery (p. 218)
Deposition (p. 218)
Refreshing recollection (p. 218)
Cross-examination (p. 221)
Effectiveness of testimony (p. 223)
Interviewer stress (p. 223)
Burnout (p. 226)

STUDY QUESTIONS

1. Discuss the reliability and validity of the interview. Include in your discussion situational factors, interviewee factors, interviewer factors, and ways to reduce errors.
2. Discuss malingering. Include in your discussion degrees of malingering, reasons for malingering, malingering and conduct disorder, age and malingering, and evaluation of malingering.
3. What factors should you consider in evaluating your interview techniques?
4. Describe the challenges of being an expert witness.
5. Give 10 suggestions for testifying as an expert witness.
6. What are some reasons why interviewers experience stress?
7. Discuss the stages of burnout.
8. Describe some ways in which interviewers can deal with stress.
9. List five rewards associated with being a clinical assessment or forensic interviewer.

7

WRITING THE INTERVIEW REPORT

The difference between the right word and the almost right word is the difference between lightning and a lightning bug.
—Mark Twain

Goals and Objectives

This chapter is designed to enable you to:

* Write a clinical assessment or forensic interview report
* Understand the sections of a clinical assessment interview report
* Develop appropriate skills for communicating your findings and recommendations

This chapter covers the writing of a clinical assessment or forensic interview report. It first discusses the qualities of a good report and then describes what goes into each section of the report. The final section of the chapter presents 11 principles that serve as guidelines for writing the report. After you complete this chapter, you should know the fundamentals of clinical assessment or forensic report writing. However, the final test of your skills will be your ability *to write* a good report.

You may write a clinical assessment or forensic report based on, for example, (a) an interview alone, (b) interviews with several individuals, including the child and his or her parents, (c) an interview plus psychological test findings, or (d) an interview plus any related findings and information, such as medical findings, psychiatric findings, psychological test findings, school records, prior reports, and other information. Sometimes a clinical assessment or forensic report does not include an interview and is simply based on psychological tests. Although the information in this chapter holds for any type of clinical assessment or forensic report, the chapter focuses specifically on writing a clinical assessment or forensic report based on an interview. Note that when the interview is *one component* of the clinical or forensic assessment, the interview material then is *one component* of the report.

INTRODUCTION TO WRITING THE INTERVIEW REPORT

The interview is complete only after you have synthesized, integrated, and organized the information you obtained. The traditional medium for presenting information is a report, although you may use other formal and informal means of presentation. The preparation and writing of the report are integral parts of the clinical or forensic assessment. The report should clearly and concisely convey the information you obtained, your findings, your clinical impression (where applicable), and any recommendations. A report may influence the child and family for years to come; it deserves much care and consideration. (This chapter is designed primarily for writing clinical assessment or forensic reports for children. However, with minor modifications, it can be used for adults as well.)

Qualities of a Good Report

Your report should be well organized and solidly grounded. A good report does not merely present facts. It brings together case history material (which includes prior social, psychological, psychiatric, and medical findings), behavioral observations, and other assessment findings obtained during the interview. In some settings, depending on your professional role, you may want to integrate the interview findings with the current psychological test findings. In short, the report should present what you have learned about the interviewee in a way that shows respect for the interviewee's individuality. This respect for individuality should permeate the entire interview process: You should view the interviewee as an individual and not simply as a stimulus for gathering statistics. (Substitute "family" for "interviewee" when the report focuses on the family.)

Formulating the Report

In formulating and constructing your report, first consider the primary audience for the report, such as a parent, teacher, health care provider, attorney, judge, or colleague. Second, consider the circumstances under which the interview took place, the limited opportunities for observation and interaction, and the behavioral basis for the judgments you make about the interviewee. Third, include examples to illustrate or document selected statements you make in the report. Fourth, make your recommendations with an appreciation of the needs and values of the interviewee, the family, the extended family, the interviewee's ethnic group, the school, and society. Finally, consider how your values affect the way in which you conduct interviews, how you arrive at recommendations, and what you emphasize in reports.

Purposes of the Report

Following are some purposes of a clinical assessment or forensic interview report:

1. It provides accurate assessment-related information (for example, developmental highlights, interpersonal skills, and information about the interviewee's language, motor skills, speech, attention, and memory) to the referral source and other concerned parties.
2. It provides a source of information for testing clinical hypotheses, developing appropriate treatment recommendations, and conducting program evaluation and research.
3. It serves as a record of (a) historical, observational, and other information gathered in the interview and (b) recommended interventions.
4. It may serve as a legal document.

Subjective Elements in the Report

Although you should strive for objectivity and accuracy in writing the report, no report can be completely objective. Every report has elements of subjectivity because interviewers may interpret the same information differently. Recognize that *you choose* which words to use to describe the interviewee, which behaviors to highlight, which elements of the history to cite, and which sequence to follow in presenting the information. By recognizing that your personal viewpoint is a part of any report, you are in a better position to reduce bias associated with your personal viewpoint.

Promptness in Writing the Report

Write the report as soon as possible after you complete the interview. You want to record all important details and not forget any. The referral source needs a prompt reply. Unfortunately, in some settings, there is often a delay between the time someone makes a referral and the initiation of the interview. You, as the interviewer, should not contribute to further delay by failing to write the report promptly.

Contents of the Report

The interview report should describe adequately the interviewee's history, current problems, assets, and limitations. The value of the interview report, with other assessment information, lies, in part, in the degree to which it is responsive to the referral question. The report also provides meaningful baseline information for evaluating the interviewee's progress in an intervention program. Let's now turn to the major components of an interview report.

A naturalist's life would be a happy one if he had only to observe and never to write.

—Charles Darwin

SECTIONS OF AN INTERVIEW REPORT

A typical interview report will have the following sections:

1. Identifying Information
2. Reason for Referral
3. Behavioral Observations
4. Case History Information
5. Clinical Impressions
6. Recommendations
7. Summary
8. Signature

Identifying Information

The first part of the report presents relevant identifying information. Include, as a minimum, the interviewee's name, date of birth, gender, chronological age, and grade in school (if applicable); date of interview; date of report; and interviewer's name. You also may want to include the teacher's name (if applicable), parents' names, and names of other significant persons interviewed or in the interviewee's life.

Reason for Referral

The second section of the report usually consists of a brief summary of the referral source's questions regarding the interviewee. Citing the reasons for the referral helps document why you conducted the evaluation.

The Referral section may include the following information: (a) name, position, and affiliation (if applicable) of the referral source, (b) why the referral source asked for the assessment, (c) specific questions the referral source has about the interviewee, and (d) a brief summary of the specific behaviors or symptoms that led to the referral.

Behavioral Observations

One of the challenges in writing a report is to communicate what you have observed during the interview. A good report carefully describes the interviewee's behavior during the interview and any observations that you made in the interviewee's classroom, home, or hospital setting. Your observations help the reader understand what you consider to be important features of the interviewee's behavior. They also lend some objectivity to the report by providing information about what the interviewee did that led you to form specific impressions. Finally, behavioral descriptions may tie in with the intervention plans.

In writing about your observations, recognize the differences between statements that *describe* behavior and those that *interpret* behavior. A statement that the child was tapping his or her feet during the interview is one that describes the child's behavior. A statement that the child was anxious is one that interprets the child's behavior. Both descriptive and interpretative statements are valuable to include in the report. Sometimes it is useful to include a descriptive statement that is followed by a statement interpreting the behavior.

The child's behavior during the interview may differ from his or her behavior in other settings. Consequently, you must be careful in making generalizations about the child's behavior in other settings from the child's behavior during the interview. Obtain information about how the child behaves in other settings before making any generalizations about the child's behavior.

In the Behavioral Observations section of the report, you can comment on the interviewee's physical appearance, reactions to being interviewed, reactions to you, general behavior, activity level, language style, general response style, mood, response to inquiries, response to encouragement, attitude toward self, motor skills, and unusual habits, mannerisms, or verbalizations. You also can include your reaction to the interviewee. Four examples of a Behavioral Observations section follow:

William is a 5-year, 2-month-old child with blond hair and brown eyes. He was friendly and animated and appeared eager to talk. He was curious about the toys in the room, and he examined each cabinet. During the interview, he often squirmed in his seat, exhausting nearly every position possible while remaining on his chair. William maintained a high degree of interest throughout the interview. He was attentive and followed the questions well, and he established excellent rapport with the interviewer.

Regina is a 16½-year-old adolescent whose cosmetics and hairstyle make her look older than she is. She appeared anxious and somewhat depressed throughout the interview. Her wide-eyed look and clenched hands underscored her anxiety and tension and suggested fearfulness. Although Regina seemed able to relax after talking with the interviewer, she was extremely tense when some topics were discussed. In discussing her school performance, for example, she made many self-deprecating remarks, such as "I can't do well in most subjects" and "I'm terrible at that subject." She also responded with "I don't know" rather than attempting to answer difficult or personal questions. Despite Regina's anxiety, she occasionally smiled and laughed appropriately.

Karl is a bright-eyed amiable, 6-year, 3-month-old child of above average height. He was eager to begin the interview and immediately took a seat when I asked him to do so. Initially, he chatted easily with me. However, when I gave him an opportunity to play with the toys in the room, he seemed unsure of himself. He wandered from activity to activity, never staying with any one toy or game. He seemed to be unable to focus his attention. His initial attitude of confidence and self-composure seemed to deteriorate. When we talked again, he whispered his answers. It appeared that he was afraid to respond in the event that I might disapprove of his answers. He was concerned about and sensitive to my opinion of his responses and frequently asked "Was that OK?" or "Is that right?"

Karl appeared disappointed when he could not talk about some things that I asked him to discuss. Even when I gently encouraged him to tell exactly what he meant, he continued to use the same words or added "I don't know."

Karl appeared to relax somewhat as the interview progressed. When he realized that I was not critical of responses, he gave his answers in a normal voice and became more assertive. Karl was given a short break because of his restlessness, after which he seemed considerably more relaxed and comfortable.

Frank, a 17-year, 4-month-old adolescent, avoided eye contact with me and at times seemed to have difficulty finding the right words to express himself. He showed some signs of anxiety, such as heavy breathing, sniffling a great deal, mumbling, and making short, quick movements with his hands and head. He seemed to answer some questions impulsively, but he also occasionally would say quietly "No, wait" and then give another answer.

Case History Information

In the Case History Information section, you can include material obtained from interviews with the child, parents, and teacher(s); the interviewee's educational file; and previous psychological, psychiatric, and medical reports. Acknowledge the sources of the information, and report relevant dates when the reports were written. You may include the child's age (repeated from the Identifying Information section); grade in school (if applicable, repeated from the Identifying Information section); educational history; present level of academic functioning; prior psychological test results (including major findings, diagnostic impressions, recommendations, and follow-up contacts); response to previous interventions (if any) and outcomes (including what progress has been made and which interventions have been effective); family makeup; significant health history (including types of illnesses and injuries, treatments, and extent of recovery); developmental history (including events in the child's life that may have a bearing on his or her psychological or educational problems); current family situation; and social interactions and peer relationships.

You also can include information about the parents' statements about the child's developmental history (including the child's symptoms and prior treatments) and relevant family history (including pertinent information about the parents' occupations, education, views on discipline and on the child's responsibilities, and involvement with the child). Finally, you can include information about the teacher's observations of the child's behavior and attitudes (where applicable), report of the child's academic performance, and report of the child's relationships with peers and teachers.

The sample Case History Information section that follows provides information on the interviewee's life-situation that may help the reader understand his current level of functioning. The interviewee was admitted to a psychiatric hospital on an emergency basis because of bizarre, unpredictable, and out-of-control behavior. His mother reported that he had been talking to himself and that he was having possible delusions and hallucinations.

Henry, a 12-year, 9-month-old adolescent, is the youngest of five children. He lives with his mother, who has been married three times. He last saw his father when he was 5 months old and just beginning to crawl. He first walked alone at 15 months and achieved bowel control at 2 years of age. However, he never achieved bladder control, and he remains enuretic.

He attended a Head Start program at the age of 4 years and was referred to a child guidance clinic because of behavioral problems. He received a diagnosis of hyperactivity at this time. When Henry was 5 years old, his maternal grandmother died of a stroke, and Henry became extremely depressed. His mother noted that shortly afterward Henry told her that he knew in advance that his grandmother was going to die; he claimed that he had psychic abilities.

At 6 years of age, Henry attempted suicide by throwing himself in front of a car after his mother had been hospitalized for hypertension; however, he was not seriously injured. Henry told her that he believed that she was going to die and he wanted to die, too. This incident resulted in Henry's referral to County Mental Health, where he was treated for the suicide attempt and for hyperactivity and enuresis.

When Henry was 9 years old, his youngest sister, who was then 16 years old, attempted suicide by a drug overdose. Henry was upset for several months. At the age of 10 years, he was expelled from school for alleged sexually inappropriate behavior, including touching other children's genitalia. He was subsequently transferred to another school, where he currently attends special education classes. Academically, he has always performed poorly.

According to Henry's mother, their relationship has always been close, although recently he has become "difficult to get along with." She described Henry as a social isolate—having no friends and preferring to spend his time alone or only with her. He has had no serious medical problems.

Clinical Impressions

In the Clinical Impressions section, you should discuss the implications of the information obtained in the interview, taking into consideration the entire case history. Evaluate the reliability and validity of the information; you should have a reasonable supporting basis for any impressions you offer. In fact, state in the report any concerns you have about the reliability and validity of any information and the reasons for your concerns.

In reporting assessment results you believe are valid (in which case they must be reliable), you might say "The information presented in the report appears to be valid because Jim's motivation, attention, memory, and language appeared to be satisfactory." An appropriate way to report results that have questionable validity might be "Rebecca often appeared confused and unable to discuss many facets of her life. Consequently, it is doubtful that the information she gave was either reliable or valid."

When you develop hypotheses about an interviewee's functioning, consider all the sources of information you have. These may include your observations about the interviewee's attitude, language, speech, motor skills, and temperament; information obtained from interviews with the interviewee and the interviewee's parents and teachers; case history information; prior and present psychological and medical test results; and other background information.

You are on firmer ground for making interpretations when you have consistent findings from several sources. *Use extreme caution in making any interpretations or diagnostic formulations when you have inconsistent data.* Inconsistent data pose questions that you might want to explore

further. In any case, *never make diagnostic statements based on insufficient data.*

Here is an example of a Clinical Impressions section of a report that emphasizes a mental status evaluation.

Judy, a 15-year-old adolescent female, is tall and slender. She was casually dressed, and it seemed that she had not taken much time with her appearance because her hair was uncombed. Judy was referred to the clinic by her mother because of a recent history of fatigue, crying spells, and refusal to attend school. Upon introduction, Judy presented herself as shy, withdrawn, and reserved. She had difficulty making eye contact and often stared out the window even when she was answering questions. Periodically, Judy's attention seemed to wander, as she often asked for questions to be repeated. Although Judy generally tried to answer the questions, she gave brief responses. Frequently, the interviewer had to probe further to learn the full meaning of her responses. Judy spoke slowly and hesitantly. She often was tearful and sighed between her statements. Throughout the interview, Judy maintained emotional distance from the interviewer, and she seemed preoccupied with her own thoughts.

Initially, Judy was vague about both the duration and the intensity of her presenting symptoms. Although she maintained that she was unsure about any precipitating event for the symptoms, it seemed that there was a specific crisis that had led to them. Judy, however, was hesitant and feared revealing the specific crisis. Because it appeared to the interviewer that Judy displayed many symptoms consistent with adolescent sexual abuse, questions regarding any recent abuse were posed. At first, Judy admitted to replaying an event repeatedly in her mind but refused to give details about the event. When questioned about her specific concerns, Judy said that she was worried about hurting her parents by making them think that she was a "bad girl." With the interviewer's support, Judy briefly described being sexually molested by a male peer at school. Her initial ambiguity regarding these recent events did not therefore appear to be a memory difficulty but more a function of extreme fearfulness about revealing the trauma she had experienced. Judy acknowledged that her everyday functioning deteriorated after the "incident." She feared retribution by the perpetrator if she revealed the molestation. The limited information Judy provided agreed with her mother's reports of Judy's decrease in adjustment and overall functioning. Her mother had said that Judy had been a "straight A" student who was interested in school until a month ago, when she had insisted on staying home due to illness and had not completed any schoolwork.

Throughout the interview, Judy was anxious and depressed. She had great concern about her future. Both her emotional expressions (for example, tearfulness) and the content of her responses suggested a youngster who was overwhelmed by sadness and anxiety. Judy said that she had sleep disturbances, always felt fatigued (but had difficulties falling asleep), and had a decreased appetite. Judy also said that she felt helpless and hopeless. Although she said that she had recently considered suicide, she was vague regarding the way she would harm herself. Judy said she was preoccupied with being harmed and being considered by others as a "bad girl." However, she was hesitant to elaborate on why she felt this way. Judy denied any homicidal ideation and any disturbances of perception, including auditory or visual hallucinations. There was no evidence suggesting circumstantiality, tangentiality, or looseness of associations in her thinking processes. Judy did seem "paranoid" about being attacked again, but, given the recent trauma, this seemed fairly normal. Reality testing therefore appeared largely intact.

She was oriented to time, place, and person, even though she took a considerable amount of time to answer questions. However, she had difficulty concentrating, and, as already noted, she was somewhat distractible throughout the interview. Her difficulties seemed to begin after her recent trauma because until recently she had had an outstanding scholastic record. Judy did seem to have some insight into her problems. Additionally, there was no observable evidence that her recounting of events was anything but accurate and reliable.

In summary, Judy appears to be a depressed and anxious youngster. The inception of her difficulties was clearly marked by an incident of sexual molestation by a school peer. She had been hesitant and fearful to share this incident with family members and school officials because she was concerned about retribution by her assailant. Her clinical picture is consistent with a diagnosis of post-traumatic stress disorder. The severity of her symptoms, including pervasive anxiety, persistent sleep and appetite disturbance, and thoughts of self-harm indicate that a short-term hospitalization may be beneficial to help her recover. Judy and her family agree with the need for a short hospitalization, because they think they need some assistance in dealing with her acute distress. Her level of insight, degree of perceived distress, and accurate reality testing indicate that the prognosis is favorable. (*Source:* G. D. Oster, J. E. Caro, D. R. Eagen, and M. A. Lillo, *Assessing Adolescents,* pp. 34–36, copyright 1988 by Allyn and Bacon. Adapted by permission.)

Recommendations

Recommendations are an important part of a clinical assessment or forensic report. As with the Clinical Impressions section, base your recommendations on all information available. If you believe that further assessment is needed before you make a diagnosis or recommend a treatment plan, you may recommend, for example, psychological testing, a neuropsychological workup, further medical evaluation, a psychiatric evaluation, or additional interviews with other informants. When you have sufficient information, you will be in a better position to recommend a treatment plan, a trial placement, or other intervention.

Developing effective recommendations. Recommendations should describe realistic and practical intervention goals and treatment strategies. When you make recommendations, consider the following:

- the nature and degree of the child's problems
- the family's internal resources
- the family's external resources
- the way in which transition periods in the child's development (such as entering school, beginning adolescence, and entering young adulthood) may bring new stresses

- the stresses that the family may experience over time
- the interaction of all sources of stress

If the child has a serious problem, there will be increased caretaking demands, the need to find and coordinate services for the child, increased financial strain, and uncertainty about the child's progress, future needs, and availability of services. Recommendations should take into account that the presence of a child with a psychological or medical disorder in the family may call for a restructuring of family roles, rules, and goals and the adoption of new coping strategies.

Questions to consider in developing the recommendations include the following:

1. How accurate are the interview findings?
2. Were all relevant factors considered in arriving at the recommendations, including observations, parental reports, teacher reports, interviewee's self-report, medical evaluations, school grades, prior history, present and previous psychological test results, and response to prior interventions (if applicable)?
3. What is the interviewee's eligibility for special programs?
4. What type of intervention program does the interviewee need (for example, behavioral, academic, or counseling)?
5. What are the goals of the intervention program?
6. How can the interviewee's strengths be used in an intervention program?
7. How might family members become involved in the treatment plan?
8. Can the recommendations be implemented, given the family's, community's, and school's resources?
9. Who is willing to be involved in carrying out the recommendations?
10. Are the recommendations written clearly and understandably?
11. Are the recommendations sufficiently detailed that they can be easily followed?
12. Is there a need for further evaluation?
13. Are follow-up interviews necessary?
14. If so, when and by whom?

You might want to list the specific recommendations in order of priority. The highest priority recommendations usually should address the referral question. However, if you find more pressing problems and have recommendations to alleviate these problems, emphasize them in this section of the report.

Involving children, parents, and teachers in the recommendations. An important aim in making recommendations (and carrying out the assessment as a whole) is to find ways to help the interviewee help himself or herself and to involve parents and teachers directly in any therapeutic and educational efforts. The emphasis is on the interviewee, on the interviewee's situation, and on identifying avenues for growth and enrichment. You want to encourage the interviewee to become actively involved in influencing his or her own life. Your suggestions for change should be practical, concrete, individualized, and based on sound social work practice, psychological practice, and educational practice.

Using caution in making long-range predictions.
Making predictions about future levels of functioning is difficult and risky. You don't want to lull the reader of the report into thinking that a course of development is fixed or unchangeable. Although you should indicate the interviewee's present level of functioning and make suggestions about what can be expected of him or her, any statements dealing with the interviewee's performance in the distant future should be made cautiously.

Write the recommendations so that the reader clearly recognizes your degree of confidence in any predictions. Cite behavioral data, when needed, to help the reader better understand the recommendations. Your recommendations should individualize the report, highlighting the major findings and their implications for intervention.

Summary

A summary, which reviews and integrates the information in the prior sections of the report, is optional. Besides being repetitious and unnecessarily lengthening the report, a summary may detract from the report by giving readers the idea that they can ignore the main body of the report. Ideally, the report itself should be a summary: precise and concise. In settings where the reader expects a summary (such as in medical settings), however, include one in the report.

When you write a summary, limit it to one or two short paragraphs. Consider including in the summary one key idea (or more as needed) from each part of the report. *Do not include new material in the summary.* The summary might include the reason for referral, behavioral observations, highlights of the case history, highlights of the information you obtained, clinical impressions, and recommendations.

Signature

Your name, professional title, and degree should be typewritten at the end of the report, and your signature placed above your typewritten name.

Comment on Sections of an Interview Report

The preceding discussion on organizing a report is a good guide. However, there is no fixed, unalterable way to organize a report. The way you organize a report depends on your preference, which is governed partly by the users of the report. The organization of the report should be logical and convey as clearly as possible the interview findings, other relevant information, interpretations, and recommendations. Sometimes you may want to place the Recommendations section after the summary rather than before it. The summary would then focus on the interview and case history findings—not on the recommendations.

PRINCIPLES OF REPORT WRITING

Eleven principles designed to help you write better reports are offered in this part of the chapter. They cover how to

---

Calvin and Hobbes   by Bill Watterson

organize, interpret, and present the interview findings. Exercises are included to help you evaluate your understanding of the principles. For the exercises, evaluate each statement, and then compare your evaluations with those that follow in the Comment section of the exercise.

These 11 principles of report writing are as follows:

Principle 1. Organize interview findings by detecting common themes that run through the case history.

Principle 2. Include in the report relevant material and delete potentially damaging material not germane to the evaluation.

Principle 3. Be extremely cautious in making interpretations based on observations of a limited sample of behavior.

Principle 4. Use all relevant sources of information about the interviewee—including behavioral observations, interview data, and the case history—in generating hypotheses, formulating interpretations, and arriving at recommendations.

Principle 5. Be definitive in your writing when the findings are clear; be cautious in your writing when the findings are problematic.

Principle 6. Cite specific behaviors and sources to enhance the report's readability.

Principle 7. Communicate clearly, and do not include unnecessary technical material in the report.

Principle 8. Eliminate biased terms from the report.

Principle 9. Write a report that is concise but presents your findings and recommendations adequately.

Principle 10. Attend carefully to grammatical and stylistic points in your writing.

Principle 11. Develop appropriate strategies to improve your writing, such as using an outline, rereading your rough draft, using a word processor, and proofreading your final report.

Organizing Findings

Principle 1. Organize interview findings by detecting common themes that run through the case history.

As a beginning student or practitioner, you may have difficulty making sense out of the information you obtain, especially when it comes from several sources. Some findings may be clear-cut, others murky. You may get conflicting information from different interviewees about the same topic. Base your judgment of the accuracy of the information on what you know about each interviewee. Let the interviewee's age, mental status, and communication ability and your observations guide you. Occasionally, you may have to report that you have no way of evaluating the accuracy of the information. With experience, you will be able to detect more easily the common themes that run through the case history.

Before you write the report, look over all of the available information. Consider the following questions:

1. What are the reasons for the referral?
2. What are the major findings you want to report?
3. How do the present findings compare with the previous ones?
4. What are the major themes you want to develop?
5. What are the major recommendations you want to present?
6. How have the findings helped answer the referral question?
7. What questions remain unanswered?
8. What is the background of the persons for whom the report will be written?

Once you have a general understanding of the information, you are ready to undertake the following three-step process of organizing and interpreting the information.

Step 1. Detect common themes. The first step is to detect the common themes and trends that appear in the information you obtained. The information may have come from the interviewee and other informants (such as parents and teachers); social work, medical, and psychiatric reports; psychological reports; and the developmental history.

The following questions may help you detect common themes:

1. What are the consistent themes?
2. What are the divergent findings?
3. Which divergent findings are major, and which are minor?
4. What do the themes suggest to you about the interviewee's present problems, strengths, weaknesses, coping mechanisms, and possibilities for remediation or change?
5. How do significant others fit in? (For example, do anxiety attacks occur only when the interviewee's mother is present?)
6. What are some important environmental contingencies? (For example, does the child have trouble eating in the cafeteria but not at home?)

Step 2. Integrate main findings. The second step is to consider all the information you have, even information that may be contradictory, as you develop your clinical impressions and recommendations. Recognize, however, that you cannot expect anyone to show the same behavior in every situation. Suppose, for example, that the child has a general pattern of memory difficulty, but not a consistent one. Note this variability and consider it in evaluating the child. The child may have sufficient memory in some areas to capitalize on a rehabilitation program. Similarly, the child may behave differently at home, at school, or at friends' homes. This information also may shed light on the child's resources and ability to change.

Be aware of two potential sources of error in understanding the findings (Nay, 1979). One source of error is forming hypotheses prematurely, which may lead you to ignore information that conflicts with your initial conceptualization. A second source of error is overgeneralizing based on limited findings. It is inappropriate to draw conclusions about a child's everyday school behavior from a limited observation period or to generalize from the child's behavior in the interview to how the child may behave in other settings.

It may not always be possible to resolve discrepant findings. Discuss them in the report and provide alternative explanations, if you can. For example, if you observe a behavior that is not consistent, describe the inconsistency in the report and attempt to explain it. If you cannot explain it, say that there is no apparent explanation for the inconsistent findings. Caution the reader about the results where appropriate.

Step 3. Use a theoretical perspective to assimilate findings. The third step is to integrate the material using a specific theoretical focus or an eclectic theoretical perspective. The major theoretical perspectives are the developmental, normative-developmental, cognitive-behavioral, humanistic-phenomenological, psychodynamic, and family systems (see Chapter 1). If possible, use a theoretical perspective that not only sheds light on the interviewee's behavior but also offers some strategies for remediation and treatment. Often, it may be useful to use an eclectic perspective—that is, interpret findings from more than one theoretical perspective (see Chapter 1).

Including Relevant Material

Principle 2. Include in the report relevant material and delete potentially damaging material not germane to the evaluation.

When you are deciding what material to include in the report, consider its accuracy, relevance, fairness, and ability to augment the reader's knowledge of the interviewee. No matter how interesting or true it is, information that does not contribute to an understanding of the interviewee and the referral question is irrelevant; consequently, you should leave it out of the report. Weigh the value of each statement; do not make statements simply to fill space. Critically evaluate how the information will contribute to an understanding of the interviewee. If you leave a controversial sentence in the report, make its relevance clear and present supporting data.

Also discuss how much weight you gave to various factors in arriving at your clinical impressions, conclusions, and recommendations. This will help the reader understand your reasoning.

What information does the reader really need? The reader wants your opinion about the referral question, about the seriousness of the interviewee's problems, and about possible interventions. In most cases, do not include tangential information. For example, information about the father's sex life usually is tangential in a report about a child referred for learning problems. In exceptional cases, however, where such information has a direct bearing on the problem, think carefully about the most professional way to phrase the information so that it does not become simply an item of interesting gossip. When is it worthwhile to note in a report such information as whether the interviewee is right handed or left handed or whether the interviewee is well groomed? A discussion of the interviewee's handedness is worthwhile if there is a question of mixed dominance, and a discussion of the interviewee's grooming is useful if it helps the reader understand the interviewee's self-concept, attitudes, or familial environment (for example, parental care and guidance). In other cases, neither handedness nor grooming may be important.

The following are examples of irrelevant or potentially damaging statements (Drake & Bardon, 1978):

1. "James told the examiner that his mother frequently invited different men over to the house." This information is unlikely to add to the understanding of the child or the test results, and it is potentially damaging to the child and his mother. *Suggestion:* Delete it, or, if you are convinced that this statement is relevant, replace it with a statement that may give some insight about the child's feelings—for example, "James expressed resentment about frequent male visitors to his house" or "James's mother's frequent male visitors may keep her from meeting James's emotional needs."

2. "Ted is in excellent health but does have food allergies. Some researchers have posited an association between learning disabilities and allergies." The last sentence is controversial. *Suggestion:* Delete the last sentence; however, you can recommend that Ted be referred to a health care provider, if he is not already under treatment.

3. "Joe appeared disheveled and dirty at times because his family is on welfare." Don't assume a strong relationship between grooming and limited income. This statement is prejudicial toward people who receive welfare aid. *Suggestion:* The problem here could be corrected by making separate statements about Joe's appearance and family income, without assuming a relationship between them.

4. "Jeffrey's mother has been seen leaving the house at odd hours." This statement may be irrelevant to the case. *Suggestion:* If this statement is potentially relevant, say why it is relevant, cite the source, use the qualifier *reportedly,* or convey the information verbally to the referral source; otherwise delete it.

Focusing on the *presence* of a behavior rather than on its absence will promote clarity in the report. You can cite many adjectives that did *not* characterize the interviewee's behavior (for example, not sad, not anxious, not impulsive), but such citations are not illuminating. Instead, emphasize how the interviewee behaved. Occasionally, the referral source may ask you to comment on a specific problem or symptom. In such cases, include a statement about the problem or symptom, even if it did not occur.

Evaluate each of the following statements. Then, compare your evaluations with those in the Comment section.

1. "Eileen did much better than expected in her communications with me, given the fact that she lives in an impoverished neighborhood."
2. "At one time, she wanted to use my pencil to write out a response, but I explained to her that she should try to talk about herself."

Comment

1. The assumptions here reveal the writer's prejudices. First, the writer labeled the neighborhood "impoverished." A more effective way of presenting information about the child's living conditions would be to describe what was observed in the neighborhood rather than simply labeling it. Second, the writer has made the assumption that poor living conditions lead to poor communications skills, which is probably an erroneous assumption. Thus, the writer made a value-laden judgment that the child did much better than expected without presenting a reasonable explanation for this interpretation.
2. Unless this statement illustrates a point, why include it? If left in, it may distract the reader. The interviewer's failure to allow the interviewee to write out a response also may reveal an unwise attitude because the interviewee may have wanted to divulge sensitive material that she was unwilling to say aloud. Interviewers should try to be flexible in the way they allow interviewees to express difficult things.

Making Interpretations Carefully

Principle 3. Be extremely cautious in making interpretations based on observations of a limited sample of behavior.

Observations conducted during a short period usually yield a small sample of behavior. Consequently, be careful about the generalizations and inferences you make from this limited sample. Make inferences about underlying traits or processes only with extreme caution, if at all. For example, "Johnny refused to be interviewed and ran away from the office in tears" is better than "Johnny is a negative child who shows hostility toward those who wish to help him." If the latter statement were based only on the observation that the child ran away from the office in tears, it would be unacceptable because it was an undue generalization. If, however, you believe that you have enough information to support an interpretation, go ahead and make it. Also avoid the temptation to assume that a behavior demonstrated in one setting will occur in another setting. For example, do not assume that an interviewee who is hyperactive in the classroom also is hyperactive at home. Other errors associated with inter-

pretation of data are discussed in Chapter 6 in the section on reliability and validity.

The following are examples of statements that make incorrect inferences:

1. "From the start, Derek tended either to repeat questions to himself or to ask the interviewer to repeat the questions for him. This appeared to be Derek's attempt to structure or clarify the questions for himself." This behavior could reflect the child's attempt to structure the question, but it is not clear how repeating the question helped him to clarify it. It also could be a means of controlling the situation, or it could suggest inattention. In addition, the behavior may reflect a delay tactic, a need for additional support, or a coping pattern associated with a possible hearing deficit. Examine all you know about the child to arrive at the best interpretation, if you need to make one. *Suggestion:* Leave out the last sentence ("This appeared to be…") unless you have other supporting information.
2. "As the interview progressed, he tended to sit with his arms folded or to pick at and scratch his arm when responding to questions. Although, at first, these behaviors made John seem less interested, it appears that he was compensating for his low self-confidence." This interpretation seems to have little merit. In what way do folding arms and scratching arms reflect compensation for low self-confidence? Could these actions simply be a habit or a response to frustration? *Suggestion:* Keep the first sentence and eliminate the second one. Then, describe comments the child made about himself, if any, and note how cooperative he was.
3. "She responded impulsively to some questions and gave detailed replies to others. This behavior may simply reflect an impulsive personality." This interpretation may or may not be correct. Responding impulsively to some questions but not others may *not* be a sign of an impulsive personality. Perhaps there are tendencies in this direction, but the generalization may be inappropriate. Also consider whether there was anything about the questions that led her to respond impulsively. *Suggestion:* Keep the first sentence and eliminate the second one. Then, describe what content was being discussed when she gave impulsive replies and nonimpulsive replies.
4. "Harry's statements about his inadequacies resulted in an increase in feelings of inferiority and self-deprecating behavior, as shown by an increase in nervous laughter and by impulsive answers." This inference is conjectural. It implies a cause-and-effect relationship between verbal expressions and behavior. There is no way of knowing what the interviewee's statements resulted in. *Suggestion:* Limit the statements to a description of his verbalizations and behavior—for example, "When he was asked about his school work, Harry answered impulsively, laughed anxiously, and made self-deprecatory remarks."

5. "Perhaps she played independently because other children could not or did not want to keep up with her." This inference may or may not be correct. To make this statement, you must have supporting information about the other children's behavior. *Suggestion:* Omit it unless information is available about the behavior of the other children.

**Exercise 7-2. Evaluating Statements
That May Contain Incorrect Inferences**

Evaluate the following statements. Then, compare your evaluations with those in the Comment section.

1. "The child is small for his age and may feel a need to achieve."
2. "Her physical appearance suggested no behavioral problems."

Comment

1. Without additional information, these two thoughts are unrelated—a non sequitur. If the only bit of data available to you about the child's achievement needs is that he is small, do not make this inference.
2. Rarely will a child's physical appearance denote a behavioral problem. Additionally, this is an example of stating positive information in the negative. *Suggestion:* "Her appearance was ordinary. She was dressed in a loosely fitting sweater and skirt. Her height and weight are normal for her age."

Making Generalizations

Principle 4. Use all relevant sources of information about the interviewee—including behavioral observations, interview data, and the case history—in generating hypotheses, formulating interpretations, and arriving at recommendations.

Conclusions and generalizations should follow logically from the information in the report. Support your conclusions with reliable and sufficient data, and avoid undue generalizations. You can base your inferences and conclusions on several factors, including the quality of the interaction between you and the interviewee, the case history, the medical history, and previous assessment results. Consider all relevant sources of information, and make generalizations only when you have a clear, consistent pattern of behavior. Consider definite cause-and-effect relationships only when the data are substantial and clear. When you make a generalization, cite supporting data, particularly if the generalization has important consequences for the interviewee.

Consider the following questions:

1. Are there consistent trends in the information you obtained from the developmental history; prior medical, psychological, and psychiatric evaluations; interview findings; teacher reports; observational findings; and informal and formal test results?

2. Does the child's behavior in the interview correspond with his or her behavior in the classroom and at home?
3. To what extent do the child, parents, teachers, and other informants agree in reporting on the child's assets, limitations, problems, and concerns?
4. Do the findings point to a clear diagnostic impression?
5. What interventions are likely to be both effective and feasible, given the assessment findings, available facilities and personnel, and familial resources?

After you answer these questions, formulate hypotheses and look for confirming evidence. Entertain alternative hypotheses and revise them as needed. Regard as tentative or drop hypotheses supported by only one piece of minor evidence. Retain for further consideration those hypotheses supported by more than one piece of evidence—especially if the supporting data come from several sources (for example, from the child, parents, *and* health care provider or from the child, parents, *and* teacher). Also review any evidence that may disconfirm hypotheses. Advance those hypotheses that receive support. Although these latter hypotheses are tentative and unproved explanations of a complex situation, they may help you in working with the referral source, the child, and the parents and in formulating treatment recommendations.

You can view statements in reports as reflecting one of three levels of clinical inference (Goldenberg, 1983).

First level. Take the assessment data at face value and keep interpretations to a minimum. *Example:* "Bill spoke rapidly throughout the interview."

Second level. Present clinical assessment or forensic findings, draw generalizations, and present hypotheses about the causes of the behavior. *Example:* "Sylvia's parents and teacher report that she has mood changes, and several changes in her mood were observed during the interview. This behavior suggests that Sylvia may have difficulty controlling her emotions, which, in part, may contribute to her interpersonal difficulties."

Third level. Make the most inclusive interpretations, including explanatory speculations about the interviewee's behavior; this level involves clinical hunches, insights, and intuitions. *Example:* "A pervasive pattern of neglect during his formative years, coupled with feelings of self-doubt, suggests a negative self-concept. His negative self-concept may, in part, contribute to his poor school performance."

You may use all three levels of clinical inference in the report. However, as you move up the inferential chain, carefully weigh the data before you decide to offer broad explanatory speculations. Label any speculations as such in the report.

Conveying Degree of Certainty

Principle 5. Be definitive in your writing when the findings are clear; be cautious in your writing when the findings are problematic.

Phrases and words such as *probably, it appears, perhaps,*and *it seems* are often used in reports when the writer is not completely sure about his or her conclusions, inferences, or predictions. When the data are definitive, however, present them confidently. When you do use qualifiers, do not use them redundantly: "It appears as though he has a tendency toward sometimes saying the wrong thing."

The degree of certainty you convey in your statements should relate to the adequacy of your information: The more current, reliable, complete, and valid the information, the greater the certainty. The degree of certainty also should relate to the type of data you are considering: Observed data (what you observed an interviewee doing) have a greater degree of certainty than prognostic statements (what the interviewee may do under other conditions or in the future). For example, you usually are certain that the interviewee has brown eyes, spoke clearly, or has adequate gross motor skills. You are only reasonably certain that the interviewee can engage in most sports appropriate for his or her age. You are less certain that the interviewee will improve his or her performance if transferred to another teacher.

Enhancing Readability

Principle 6. Cite specific behaviors and sources to enhance the report's readability.

When you describe the interviewee's behavior, draw inferences, or make conclusions, add carefully selected examples of the interviewee's behavior to illustrate your points. For example, if you say that the interviewee gave overly detailed replies, provide an example. Give sources for any information you did not obtain personally. Statements such as "his mother reported," "according to his classroom teacher," "according to the report prepared by the school psychologist," or "according to the police report" provide documentation for the source of your information.

The following are examples of undocumented statements:

1. "Billy has uncontrolled temper tantrums." The source of the statement should be cited. *Suggestion:* "According to Billy's classroom teacher, he cries and stomps his feet when she denies him a privilege. All methods tried by the teacher to prevent these tantrums have proved unsuccessful" (Drake & Bardon, 1978).
2. "The father is an alcoholic." Either a source should be cited for this statement or the statement should be eliminated. Be careful about accepting such information from sources other than persons likely to have firsthand knowledge of the situation. *Suggestion:* "The father said that he is an alcoholic and a member of AA" (Drake & Bardon, 1978).

Communicating Clearly

Principle 7. Communicate clearly, and do not include unnecessary technical material in the report.

Good writing is essential if you want the report to be useful. Present your ideas in a logical and orderly sequence, with smooth transitions from thought to thought. You will impede clear communication if the report contains sentences with unfamiliar words, an excessive number of words, highly technical words, or irrelevant material. You will improve communication if you write clearly, cut words where possible, follow rules of grammar and punctuation, use a consistent style, make clear transitions between different ideas or topics, and give examples of the interviewee's abilities and behavior.

Here are some suggestions to help you communicate more effectively.

1. *Use clear and accurate statements.* Write so that you will be understood. Make your statements as direct and concrete as possible; abstract ideas and terms often are difficult to follow. As noted in Principle 3, behavioral descriptions usually are preferable to interpretive statements. Describe the interviewee's behavior accurately. Choose the term that best says what you want to say. For example, was the interviewee *anxious, eager, uninterested,* or *depressed*? Did the interviewee *walk, stomp, prance, saunter,* or *race* around the room? Do not say that an interviewee *lacks* an ability when you mean that the interviewee's ability is *weak*. Use *limited, restricted, weakness,* or *less well developed* rather than *lack of,* unless *lack of* is literally correct.

Make sure that all statements are as precise as possible. For example, the statement that an interviewee's "enthusiasm was slightly off track" is vague, and the statement that an interviewee "cultivated a recalcitrant pose" forces the reader to work too hard to understand the sentence.

The word *only,* as in "John raised his hand only twice," may be misleading. If this behavior was the norm, the reader might be led to believe incorrectly that John did not raise his hand as frequently as the other students. Use of the word *just* has similar problems. The words *very* and *quite* usually add little meaning to a sentence and are best left out.

Be careful with words that connote special meanings, such as *intelligent, bright, average,*and *psychopathic.* Use these words only when you have objective information to support what they convey.

Use the word *thinks* or *believes* when you refer to a person's thoughts and the word *feels* when you refer to a person's feelings or emotions.

In professional writing, be precise when you discuss numbers. For example, the statement "Most children were age three" is vague. *Three* could refer to months or years or even days. Although the context of the report will likely clear up the meaning, be precise. For example, add *years* if that is what you mean.

Be as specific as possible in your descriptions. For example, instead of saying "There was a small group of children," note the exact size of the group. More detail would enhance the following description: "Joseph is a somewhat apprehensive child, with brown eyes and brown hair." Although the term "apprehensive child" may be accurate, it would be helpful to cite the behaviors that led to this description. Don't use *tends to* or *has a tendency to* to describe a behavior when you have observed the specific behavior. For example, instead of saying "Tommy tends to hit other children," describe what you observed: "Tommy hit his younger brother three times during my visit to their home."

2. *Use transition words.* Transition words help achieve continuity in the report. Some transition devices are time links (*then, next, after, while, since*), cause-effect links (*therefore, consequently, as a result*), addition links (*in addition, moreover, furthermore*), and contrast links (*however, but, conversely, nevertheless, although, whereas, similarly*). Although the transition word *while* often is used in informal writing and conversation to refer to connections other than time (for example, *while* is used when *whereas* is meant), in scientific and professional writing *while* should be used only to reflect time (American Psychological Association, 1994b). Similarly, use *since* to refer to time and use *because* when it is appropriate for transitions.

3. *Use standard terms.* Avoid the following:

- informal meanings of terms (for example, *feel* for *believe* or *think*)
- terms of approximation (for example, *quite a few* or *lots of* for a specific number) because they can be interpreted in different ways
- stylistic phrases (for example, *in terms of*)
- unnecessary jargon (for example, *structural methodology*)
- colloquial expressions (for example, *right away, long-distance relationship, kids* for *children,* or *lots of* for *many*) and expressions that imply more than you mean (for example, *gang* for *peer group*)

You weaken your presentation when you use informal meanings of terms, terms of approximation, stylistic phrases, and colloquial expressions to describe your observations and interpretations. These terms and expressions diminish the professional quality and readability of the report. Use these terms, of course, when you are quoting the interviewee.

4. *Avoid technical terms.* Whenever possible, use common expressions to present the information you have gathered. Technical terms may confuse the reader.

5. *Avoid confusing and inappropriate devices.* You may be tempted to inject excitement into your writing by using grammatic devices appropriate in creative writing—namely, shifts in topic, tense, or mood; or surprising or ambiguous statements. However, these devices may confuse the reader and should be avoided (American Psychological Association, 1994b). Also do not use creative embellishments or language that attracts undue attention to itself, such as heavy alliteration (repetition of unusual initial consonant sounds in two or more neighboring words or syllables), rhymes, and clichés. If you do, you may distract readers and diminish the focus of your ideas. Use metaphors with care, and avoid mixed metaphors. For example, do not use "She tends to get

on bandwagons, go off in all directions, and end up clear out in left field" for "She is impetuous." Use figurative or colorful expressions (like "tired as a dog") sparingly to avoid sounding labored or unnatural. When you use synonyms to avoid repetition of terms, choose your words carefully so that you do not unintentionally suggest a different meaning. The use of pronouns sometimes can reduce repetitions without creating ambiguity.

The following are examples of statements that are not clear:

1. "A review of his school records suggests that his performance is a submaximal representation of his intellectual ability." The word "submaximal" is a poor choice. *Suggestion:* "His scores may underestimate his ability."
2. "He had a tendency to elicit heavy sighs and become visibly frustrated when he was having to discuss his home life." "Elicit" is incorrect. *Suggestion:* The writer likely means "emit heavy sighs" and not "elicit heavy sighs."
3. "There was no evidence of abnormality in her conversation." The term "abnormality" is likely to be confusing to most readers and potentially misleading. *Suggestion:* If you do use the term "abnormality," define it.
4. "The seizure impacted his behavior." The seizure is a behavior; therefore, the statement is not clear. Also, the word "impacted" is jargon. *Suggestion:* "He was unable to complete the examination because he had a seizure."
5. "The classroom, consisting of nine students, was observed while having a snack for 10 minutes." The statement implies that the classroom was having a snack instead of the students *in* the classroom. *Suggestion:* "There were nine students in the classroom who were having a snack for 10 minutes."
6. "Jim was interviewed to provide training experience for students in the interview course at _____ University." It is not clear from the sentence whether the training experience was for Jim, who also could be a student in the assessment class, or for the interviewer. *Suggestion:* "A graduate student at _____ University interviewed Jim to get training experience."
7. "His behavior and even speech seemed to deteriorate toward the end of the interview." The term "deteriorate" in this statement is not clear; it carries connotations of possible impairment and must be used with caution. Also, the word "even" gives misplaced emphasis to the child's speech. *Suggestion:* "His behavior and speech became more erratic, and he had difficulty listening to my questions."
8. "During the interview, Jill engaged in reactive behavior." The term "reactive behavior" is not clear. The sentence forces the reader to guess what the writer means. Instead, the child's behavior should be described. *Suggestion:* "During the interview, Jill became upset when she discussed her parents' divorce."
9. "She was observed in the outdoor, free-play period." This sentence sounds strange. Be careful how you mod-

ify terms. *Suggestion:* "She was observed outdoors during a free-play period."

10. "When approached by a child whom he appeared to dislike, however, Albert threw a swing at the child with one fist." This sounds like the other child has one fist. *Suggestion:* "When approached by a child whom he appeared to dislike, Albert, using one hand, tried to punch the child."

The following "politically correct" report was constructed to show humorously how language can greatly reduce the clarity of a report and the reader's understanding of issues. In your reports, you should use conventional terms that are accepted by your profession and not those that are simply "PC" (politically correct terms obtained, in part, from Beard and Cerf, 1992).

A POLITICALLY CORRECT REPORT

John is a *cerebrally challenged* child (slow learner) who is *uniquely coordinated* (clumsy) in his movements. In school, he *achieved deficiencies* (failed) in several subjects because of *differently logical* (wrong) answers. He has an *alternative body image* (obese) and is *vertically challenged* (short). Occasionally, he *engages in negative attention getting* (misbehaves) and is *temporally challenged* (late) in getting to his classes. His teacher says he is *differently honest* (untrustworthy) at times and *motivationally deficient* (lazy). He has been caught committing an *ethically different act* (stealing).

John's parents are *domestically incarcerated* (married) and have a *passive income system* (are on welfare). His father is *visually inconvenienced* (blind), *involuntarily leisured* (unemployed), *follicularly challenged* (bald), and a *person of differing sobriety* (alcoholic). John's mother is a *human ecologist* (housewife) who keeps a *nontraditionally ordered* (sloppy) house. John's brother has been hospitalized for having a *pharmacological preference* (addiction) and for *socially misaligned* (psychotic) behavior. Once, his brother was wrongly jailed for *ethically impaired* (criminal) behavior. And a 6-year-old sister is *developmentally inconvenienced* (mentally retarded). There also is a baby in the family who engages in *precommunicative vocalizations* (babbles), is *orally challenged* (messy eater), wears *temporary waste containment devices* (diapers), and is *periodontically oppressed* (teething). A grandfather who is *chronologically gifted* (old) lives at home.

In summary, this appears to be a *uniquely functioning* (dysfunctional) family.

Exercise 7-3. Rephrasing Unclear Statements

Rephrase the following statements. Then, compare your rephrased statements with those in the Comment section.

1. "Exact verbal interaction was difficult to ascertain."
2. "When I observed the child in the classroom, he was engaged in focused work behavior."
3. "His father was in an orderly transition between career changes."
4. "Mrs. Jones is an unwaged laborer."

5. "Jill was randomly referred for the interview by her teacher."

Comment

1. This is an awkward sentence. *Suggestion:* "It was noisy, and this interfered with my ability to hear what the child was saying."
2. The term "focused work behavior" sounds like jargon. Limit the use of adjective modifiers for nouns. *Suggestion:* "The child was focused on the task."
3. The phrase "in an orderly transition between career changes" may be politically correct but potentially misleading. If the father planned the period of unemployment, then the sentence is acceptable. However, if the unemployment was not planned, the sentence is less acceptable. *Suggestion:* "His father was unemployed" (in the second case).
4. The phrase "unwaged laborer" may be politically correct, but it is not clear. *Suggestion:* "Mrs. Jones is a homemaker."
5. It is possible, but highly unlikely, that the teacher randomly referred the child for the interview. The statement would be correct if the teacher put all names in a hat and drew one name or if the teacher used a table of random numbers to select the child. *Suggestion:* "Jill was referred for the interview by her teacher."

Avoiding Bias

Principle 8. Eliminate biased terms from the report.

Your report should avoid implications of bias. This may be difficult, as biased language is well established in our culture. The use of *man* to denote *humanity* and the use of *he* as a generic pronoun are common examples of gender bias. These terms may convey an implicit message to the reader that women are not included in the reference or that females are unimportant. Where possible, eliminate the use of gender-referenced nouns, pronouns, and adjectives in sentences, replacing them with terms that refer to people in general.

Implications of bias also may arise from the use of nonparallel terms. *Woman* and *husband,* for example, are not parallel, and using them together may imply differences in the roles of women and men. The terms *husband* and *wife* are parallel, as are *man* and *woman* (American Psychological Association, 1994b). Guard against expressions and clichés that imply inappropriate roles or inequalities between men and women.

Refer to members of ethnic groups with nouns and adjectives that are acceptable given the current social trends, the preferences of members of the group being referred to, and the preferences of readers of the report. Consider carefully whether ethnic designations are needed in the report. For example, reporting that a child's teacher is Hispanic American or Black may be important if you are discussing the child's response to the teacher, but not if you are merely citing the teacher as an informant about the child. Generally, the ethnicity of the *subject* of the report is useful information for the reader.

Look for signs of stereotyping or prejudice in your writing. For example, do not assume that all welfare clients have limited intellectual ability or that all obese people are happy. Do not make inferences about the interviewee's family or friends based on knowledge of the interviewee's social class or ethnic group. Comparing two ethnic groups may result in irrelevant, negative evaluations of one of the ethnic groups. *Never make evaluative statements about social, ethnic, or gender groups or members of these groups in a report.*

Writing Concisely

Principle 9. Write a report that is concise but presents your findings and recommendations adequately.

The following guidelines will help you write more concise reports.

1. *Avoid wordy sentences, trite phrases, useless repetitions, and abstract words.* Here are some examples of *wordy sentences:* (a) "Although it cannot be definitely established, it is quite probable that the patient, in all likelihood, is suffering some degree of aphasia." *Suggestion:* "The patient is probably aphasic." (b) "The patient was positioned in bed in such a way that he could not move his left leg sideways or bend it at the knee." *Suggestion:* "The patient's left leg was immobilized." (c) "His weight was beyond the norms of a typical child." *Suggestion:* "He was overweight."

The following examples illustrate *trite phrases:* "It has come to my attention" for "I learned" and "up to this writing" for "now." (Item 15 in Table 7-1 lists some wordy expressions and trite phrases and shows their concise equivalents.)

Examples of *useless repetitions* follow, with the redundant phrase in italics: "The twins were *exactly* identical." "He was small *in size*." "The family needs to make *new* changes."

Here are two examples of *abstract words* or phrases: (a) "She manifested overt aggressive hostility." *Suggestion:* "She punched a younger child in the nose." (b) "A minority of the class was misbehaving." *Suggestion:* "Five of the 30 children were misbehaving."

2. *Avoid either too long or too short sentences.* The length of sentences is an important factor in readability. A lot of short, choppy sentences may make the text sound disjointed and dull, but many long, complicated sentences may render the text difficult to follow. You can vary the sentence length as a way of maintaining the reader's interest and aiding comprehension. When you need long sentences to communicate a difficult concept, use the simplest possible words and sentence construction.

3. *Avoid long paragraphs.* The content and length of paragraphs in a report contribute to the report's readability. A paragraph should contain a cohesive and unifying theme and usually should run about four or five sentences. Ordi-narily, a paragraph that runs longer than one-quarter of a page strains the reader's attention span and ability to recognize the unifying themes and ideas. If you have written a long paragraph, break it down and reorganize it.

4. *Avoid writing a report without adequate explanation.* A report should be long enough to adequately present the information you obtained, your conclusions, and your recommendations. Although clinicians may have no difficulty in understanding a brief account, the interviewee's parents, teachers, health care providers, or attorneys may have difficulty in comprehending a report written without adequate explanations and illustrations or without headings that highlight the major areas of discussion.

If it is possible to cut a word out, always cut it out.

—George Orwell

Attending to Grammar

Principle 10. Attend carefully to grammatical and stylistic points in your writing.

You must follow conventional grammatical rules in report writing. A good general source for technical writing is the *Publication Manual of the American Psychological Association* (1994b). Consult a dictionary, a thesaurus, a text on grammar, as needed. You also might want to use the grammar-checking function of your computer's word processing program. The following discussion highlights some important grammatical, stylistic, and structural aspects of report writing.

1. *Abbreviations.* Generally, in a report do not use abbreviations or terms such as *etc.,* because they may be unfamiliar to the reader or misleading. If you do use abbreviations, anticipate problems the reader might have in understanding them. It is permissible to abbreviate the names of commonly used tests (for example, WISC-III for Wechsler Intelligence Scale for Children—Third Edition). However, the first time you refer to a test, use its complete name, followed immediately by the accepted abbreviation in parentheses.

2. *Hyphens.* The rules for hyphenation are complex. It is helpful to consult a dictionary or other sources, such as *The Chicago Manual of Style* published by the University of Chicago Press (1993). A term such as *7-year-old* is usually hyphenated, both as a noun (the 7-year-old) and as a compound adjective (a 7-year-old child). Whatever style you use, be consistent throughout the report.

3. *Punctuation.* Effective punctuation will help clarify what you write and will enhance the report's readability. Punctuation cues the reader to the relationship between ideas, as well as to the normal pauses and inflections that help emphasize the main ideas and concepts in the report.

The placement of quotation marks sometimes presents a problem. Always place a period or comma *before* the closing quotation mark. Place a colon, semicolon, or question mark *after* the closing quotation mark, unless it is part of the quoted material. Again, use a style manual or similar source to check your punctuation.

4. *Tense.* The major problem you may encounter with tense is how to determine when to use the past tense and when to use the present tense. In general, refer to interviewee's *enduring traits*—such as ethnicity, intelligence, sex, and physical characteristics—that exist at the time you write the report in the present tense. For example, in the following sentence, the present tense is more appropriate than the past tense: "Leah *is* a dark-haired, 18-year-old female." However, describe behavior you observed during the interview in the past tense, because the child displayed the behavior on a specific past occasion: "John *is* a muscular, overweight adolescent who *was* cooperative during the interview."

In the following sentence, the past tense is more appropriate than the present tense: "The classroom *was* brightly lit and *had* paintings by many children on the wall." The past tense is more appropriate because the room might not always be brightly lit or have children's paintings on the wall. Finally, the past tense is appropriate in the following sentence: "Martin *held* his pen in a firm grip." Here, the past tense is appropriate because the statement describes an action that was previously observed.

5. *Spacing.* When you are planning to send a report to an agency, use single spacing. During your training, however, double space your reports to allow for corrections and for the instructor's comments.

The following are examples of statements with grammatical difficulties:

1. "John goes to HMMS." This statement will not be clear to readers who are unfamiliar with the abbreviation. *Suggestion:* "John goes to Horace Mann Middle School."
2. "His mother said, that Fred is lazy". There is no need for a comma after the verb, and the placement of the period is incorrect. *Suggestion:* "His mother said that Fred in lazy."
3. The teacher reports that Elaine is distractible." The past tense probably is more appropriate for the word "report" because it refers to a past event. The present tense is an appropriate way to describe the child's distractibility. *Suggestion:* "The teacher reported that Elaine is distractible."

Exercise 7-4. Evaluating Grammar

Evaluate each statement. Then, compare your evaluation with those in the Comment section.

1. "Phil constantly kept finding things in a drawer of the desk he was being interviewed at to play with throughout the interview, ie. paper clips, rubber bands, pens, etc."
2. "Virginia's behavior when she discussed her love of sports seemed to be more confident and less anxious."

Comment

1. This is an awkward sentence. There also are punctuation mistakes, such as a period missing after the "i" in "i.e." and a comma missing after the "i.e." *Suggestion:* "Throughout the interview, Phil played with paper clips, rubber bands, and pens that he found in the desk drawer."
2. The sentence needs a reference point. In addition, grammatically speaking, "behavior" cannot be more confident or less anxious; only Virginia can be. Behavior is a manifestation of the person. *Suggestion:* "Virginia was more confident and less anxious when she spoke about her love of sports than when she discussed her home life."

Improving Writing Style

Principle 11. Develop appropriate strategies to improve your writing, such as using an outline, rereading your rough draft, using a word processor, and proofreading your final report.

You should develop a writing strategy that suits your needs and style. Four effective ways of improving the quality of your writing are using an outline, rereading and editing your first draft, using a word processor to write a report, and proofreading your report.

1. *Using an outline.* Writing from an outline will help you maintain the logic of the report because, at the outset, you identify the main ideas and subordinate concepts (American Psychological Association, 1994b). An outline also may help you write more precisely and ensure that you include all pertinent data. You can use the report outline shown earlier in the chapter as the basis for a more detailed report outline tailored to each case.

2. *Rereading and editing your first draft.* Look at your draft for errors and for ways to clarify your meanings. Revise vague, ambiguous, or potentially misleading material. Everything in the report, including the information you present and your interpretations and recommendations, should be clear. You want to write a succinct report that deals with relevant issues and avoids undue generalization and speculation. A guiding theme that underlies the 11 principles in this chapter is that reports should be written so that an intelligent layperson can understand them.

The following checklist may help you assess the quality of your report:

- Are the identifying data correct? Be sure to check the accuracy of the interviewee's name, date of birth, chronological age, and sex; the date of the interview; your name; and the date of the report.
- Is the referral question stated succinctly?
- Does the background material contain relevant historical data, such as developmental history, family history, medical evaluations, psychiatric evaluations, and prior test results and recommendations (if available)?

- Do the behavioral observations enable the reader to form a clear impression of the interviewee and his or her behavior?
- Is there a statement about the reliability and validity (or accuracy) of the interview findings?
- Is the information you obtained from various sources clearly organized, succinct, and integrated, and is the source of the information noted?
- Does the report answer the referral question?
- Are themes about the interviewee's functioning clearly delineated?
- Are illustrative examples and descriptions provided?
- Are any doubts you might have about the information, findings, or conclusions stated clearly?
- Does the report say which questions remain unanswered or answered incompletely?
- Are your clinical impressions clearly stated?
- Do your recommendations clearly follow from the findings?
- Are the recommendations clear and practical?
- Are speculations clearly labeled as such?
- If there is a summary, is it accurate, concise and specific, self-contained, coherent, and readable?
- Is the writing style professional and grammatically correct?
- Is the report free of jargon?
- Is the report free of biased wording?
- Is the report free of ambiguities?
- Is the report straightforward and objective?
- Does the report focus on both weaknesses and strengths—pathology as well as adaptive capabilities?
- Is the report a reasonable length?
- Has the report been proofread carefully?

When someone evaluates and corrects your report, I hope he or she isn't like the reader described in Exhibit 7-1.

3. *Using a word processor to write a report.* Word processors can facilitate the writing of a report (Matthews, Bowen, & Matthews, 1996). If your word processor has a thesaurus, you can use it to help make your writing more varied and interesting. The spell-check and grammar-check functions contained in many word-processing programs also are useful, but they can lull you into thinking that a report is in better shape than it really is. In the first-draft stage of development, grammar-checkers are most helpful for picking up simple mechanical problems, such as a missing parenthesis or quotation mark, and for picking up writing quirks, such as too many short sentences or overuse of "to be" verbs. However, they cannot evaluate the meaningfulness of your writing. You must still make those judgments yourself.

When you use a word processor, save your work frequently and make a backup copy of the file on a second disk as a safeguard against inadvertently erasing the file. Remember to update the backup file each time you make revisions. When you are not working on the computer, store the backup disk in a safe place.

Some writers prefer to make a printout of the draft and then make changes by hand, which they later enter into the computer. Use the spell-check function as one of the last steps after you have revised and edited the report and have made the necessary changes in the computer. As the last step, always proofread your report.

4. *Proofreading your report.* As you proofread your report, look for spelling errors, grammatical errors, omitted phrases, and other typing errors. You will need to make major revisions less often as you gain experience, but you will always need to proofread carefully. Even if you use the spell-checker of a word-processing program, don't assume that your word usage is correct: You may have *spelled* the words correctly, but you may not have *used* them correctly. If you have any questions about word usage, consult a dictionary. If you have used a word-processing program to write the report, check the final copy to see that it is formatted properly.

The preceding strategies may require you to invest more time in a report than you had anticipated, but these strategies will result in greater accuracy, thoroughness, and clearer communication.

Spelling Checker
I have a spelling checker.
It came with my PC.
It plainly marks four my revue,
Mistake I cannot see.
I've run this poem threw it,
I'm sure your please too no.
It's letter perfect in it's weigh,
My checker tolled me sew.

—Poem circulating at Coastal Corp.
in Houston, Texas, in August 1992

Here are some humorous examples of what may happen when writers fail to proofread and correct their work:

- Proofread carfully!
- Lost: small apricot poodle. Reward. Neutered, like one of the family.
- Dinner Special—Turkey $6.35; Chicken or Beef $6.25; Children $4.00.
- Now is your chance to have your ears pierced and get an extra pair to take home, too.
- Have several very old dresses from grandmother in beautiful condition.
- Tired of cleaning yourself? Let me do it.
- Dog for sale: Eats anything and is fond of children.
- Stock up and save. Limit: one.
- For Rent: 6-room hated apartment.
- Man, honest. Will take anything.
- Three-year-old teacher needed for preschool. Experience preferred.
- Our experienced Mom will take care of your child. Fenced yard, meals, and smacks included.

Exhibit 7-1
The Sky Is Blue by Daniel R. White

THE SKY IS BLUE

Every law partner fancies himself a grammarian. He would edit Strunk and White. There is no sentence so straightforward and simple that he will not happily torture it beyond recognition.

Take the sentence "The sky is blue."

No junior associate would be so naive as to think this proposition could pass muster in a big firm. If he made it through law school, he knows enough to say, "The sky is *generally* blue."

Better yet, "The sky generally *appears* blue."

For extra syllables, "The sky generally appears *to be* blue."

A senior associate seeing this sentence might take pity on the junior associate and explain that before showing it to a partner the junior associate should put it in a more "lawyerly" form. At the very least the sentence should be revised to say, "In some parts of the world, what is generally thought of as the sky sometimes appears to be blue."

Armed with these qualifiers, the junior associate thinks himself protected. His conversation with the reviewing partner will proceed thus:

Partner Carter: You say here that in some parts of the world, what is generally thought of as the sky sometimes appears to be blue. I assume this is just an early draft. Could I see the final version?

Associate Williams: Uh, that's all I have right now...what exactly do you mean?

Partner Carter: Well, it's a bit bald, don't you think? I mean, just to come right out and assert it as fact.

Associate Williams: I beg your pardon? Are we talking about the same thing?

Partner Carter: Well, this business about "the sky"—what did you mean by "the sky"?

Associate Williams: Well, I meant what I see when I look up...at least, when I'm outside. Isn't that what everyone sees?

Partner Carter: Okay, if you mean *only* when you're outside, you have to say so. Our opponents in this case would love to rip us apart on that kind of error. And what about at night? Even at night? I see stars at night—are they blue? Do you mean everything *but* stars, or do you mean when there are no stars out?

Associate Williams: I meant during the day, I guess.

Partner Carter: You *guess.* Williams, this is serious business. We can't go around guessing at things. Besides, what about the sun? If it's daytime, the sun will be out—or do you know something I don't?

Associate Williams: Well, sure...I mean, no, I don't.... But no one in his right mind looks at the sun. You'd go blind.

Partner Carter: What support do you have for this comment about "some parts of the world"? *Which* parts? Do we need to state it so broadly? Can't we just say "in Cleveland" or wherever we mean?

Associate Williams: That sounds fine to me. I just never thought anyone would challenge...that is, who would disagree with...

Partner Carter: And what do you mean by "generally thought of"? Thought of by whom? Lawyers? Scientists? Morticians? Dammit, Williams, this piece has more holes in it than Swiss cheese. I haven't seen such sloppiness in all my years at Cavil, Quibble & Quiver. Take it back and see if you can't do a little better this time around.

PRINCIPLES OF LEGAL WRITING

1. Never use one word where ten will do.
2. Never use a small word where a big one will suffice.
3. Never use a simple statement where it appears that one of substantially greater complexity will achieve comparable goals.
4. Never use English where Latin, *mutatis mutandis,* will do.
5. Qualify virtually everything.
6. Do not be embarrassed about repeating yourself. Do not be embarrassed about repeating yourself.
7. Worry about the difference between "which" and "that."
8. In pleadings and briefs, that which is defensible should be stated. That which is indefensible, but which you wish were true, should merely be suggested.
9. Never refer to your opponent's "arguments"; he only makes "assertions," always "bald."
10. If a layperson can read a document from beginning to end without falling asleep, it needs work.

Source: Reprinted, with changes in notation, with permission of the author, from Daniel R. White, *The Official Lawyer's Handbook,* copyright 1983, by Daniel R. White, pp. 176–179, and published by Wallaby Books.

- Illiterate? Write today for free help.
- And now, the Superstore—unequaled in size, unmatched in variety, unrivaled inconvenience.
- Semi-Annual Clearance Sale! Savings like these come only once a year.
- Dinner special—Lack of Ram.
- Police begin campaign to run down jay walkers.
- Safety experts say school bus passengers should be belted.
- Drunk gets nine months in violin case.

Calvin and Hobbes

by Bill Watterson

- Squad helps dog bite victim.
- Enraged cow injures farmer with ax.
- Juvenile court to try shooting defendant.
- We will oil your sewing machine and adjust tension in your home for $40.00.

Table 7-1 will help you avoid some common pitfalls in report writing; study it carefully. Accompanying each guideline are examples of sentences that fail to meet acceptable standards of communication. Try to figure out the error in the sentence before you read the *Appropriate Statement* column. You also can improve your report-writing skills by studying the content and style of reports written by other interviewers who are good writers. A well-written sample report based on an interview with an adolescent can be found in Chapter 3 (Exhibit 3-1, page 127), and a similar report based on an interview with the mother of a 4½-year-old boy can be found in Chapter 4 (Exhibit 4-1, page 137).

Exercise 7-5. Evaluating and Rewriting Sentences

Evaluate the following statements to determine why they are inadequate, and then rewrite them. Check your evaluations and revisions with those in the Comment section.

1. The teacher reported that an academic weakness for Bill is in arithmetic computation. His spelling ability is below average. Word recognition was also poor.
2. When discussing the future, it became apparent that John's parents have unusually high expectations.
3. Ted appeared to be curious about his environment.
4. This interview with Helen just flew by in terms of time, because the subject answered quickly and without any hitch.
5. He tapped his foot nervously on the floor.
6. In comparison, his view of school is better.
7. This subject is a small girl with a pleasant disposition and rapport.
8. The child frequently said "I don't know".
9. The mother currently shares an apartment with another woman which she doesn't get along with.
10. He generally answered quickly while malingering over questions about his home.
11. Since there is no evidence of Oedipal conflict in Gunnar's behavior, he must have completely repressed it.
12. Most of our LDs are resourced, but Mark is in a self-contained class because he's both LD and EMH.
13. Hector's mother is on welfare, so it's no wonder he often comes to school dirty or hungry.
14. Although her parents are concerned about her and try to aid her in any way possible, their own lack of education and verbal abilities has an effect on the child's learning process.
15. Because of her family's size and income, she has been exposed to too little cultural and social enrichment.
16. Richard's obnoxious mannerisms tend to irritate adults.
17. He should receive direct help (counseling) with hypothesized emotional issues.

Comment

Poor Writing

1. These sentences would read more smoothly if they were expressed in a more conversational and concise manner. *Suggestion:* "The teacher reported that Bill has academic weaknesses in arithmetic computation, spelling, and word recognition."
2. This sentence is ambiguous because the subject of the sentence is not clear. We do not know who was discussing the future—John or his parents—or what kind of expectations the parents have. *Suggestion:* "In discussing plans for his future, John said that his parents expect him to attend college and to pursue a professional career."

Table 7-1
Some Guidelines for Good Report Writing

Guideline	Inappropriate statement	Appropriate statement
1. *Use language that is specific rather than general, definite rather than vague, concrete rather than abstract.*	"The child appeared to be mentally retarded."	"Tom obtained an IQ of 62 ± 5 on the Wechsler Intelligence Scale for Children—Third Edition. This level of intelligence falls within the Mentally Retarded range."
2. *Make the verb of a sentence agree with the subject.* Use singular verb forms with singular subjects and plural verb forms with plural subjects.	"All of the students in the class was able to answer the question but Joey." "Lisa's grades are below average but is an accurate reflection of her abilities."	"All of the students in the class except Joey were able to answer the question." "Lisa's grades are below average but appear to be an accurate reflection of her abilities."
3. *Avoid unnecessary shifts in number, tense, subject, voice, or point of view.*	"When he heard about his grade, he complains." "Tom was born in California, but New York was his home in later years."	"When he heard about his grade, he complained." "Tom was born in California but lived in New York in later years."
4. *Avoid sentence fragments.* Fragments often occur when syntax becomes overly complicated.	"Not being sure of himself, several items which should have been easy for him, though he said they were difficult."	"Not being sure of himself, James said that several items were difficult, even though they should have been easy for him."
5. *Avoid redundancies and superfluous material.*	"His confidence was congruent with his abilities, and although he realized he was intelligent, he did not appear to undervalue it or overvalue it but rather seemed to accept it without evaluating it." "He did not appear to be anxious or concerned but was willing to try to succeed within his normal pattern of motivation." "The client complained of numbness and loss of feeling." "The client was excited and agitated." "The client is doing well without problems."	"He displayed a great deal of confidence in his abilities." "His motivation was satisfactory." "The client complained of numbness." "The client was agitated." "The client is doing well."
6. *Make the phrase at the beginning of a sentence refer to the grammatical subject.*	"Administering the Vineland Adaptive Behavior Scales, the mother admitted that enuresis was still a problem." "Analyzing the results of the two tests, the scores indicated below-average functioning." "After climbing the mountain, the view was nice."	"Replying to questions on the Vineland Adaptive Behavior Scales, the mother said that the child was enuretic." "The results of the two tests indicated below-average functioning." "After climbing the mountain, we enjoyed a nice view."
7. *Use verb forms of words rather than noun forms whenever possible.* Using verb forms puts life into reports and helps shorten sentences.	"The principal suggested the implementation of a point system for the improvement of Ricky's playground behavior." "The child is negligent in the details of her work."	"The principal suggested using a point system to improve Ricky's playground behavior." "The child neglects her work."

(Continued)

Table 7-1 (*Continued*)

Guideline	Inappropriate statement	Appropriate statement
8. *Do not overuse the passive voice.* Although use of the passive voice is acceptable, its overuse can make a report sound dull. To change a sentence from passive to active voice, make the actor the subject of the sentence.	"Authorization for the absence was given by the teacher." "The previous testing was completed during her former hospitalization."	"The teacher authorized the absence." "Bonnie underwent assessment during her hospital stay earlier this year."
9. *Provide adequate transitions.* Each sentence in a report should follow logically the prior one. The first sentence in a paragraph should prepare the reader for what follows.	"Richard is above average on memory items. He failed a memory test at a level below his chronological age."	"Richard's memory ability is above average relative to that of his age peers, even though he failed a memory test at a level below his chronological age."
10. *Express coordinate ideas in similar form.* Keep elements that are parallel in thought parallel in form. The content, not the style, should protect the interview report from monotony.	"The patient sat alone at 6 months. At 8 months, crawling began. Walking was noted at 12 months." "The recommendations are to learn a phonics approach and attending an individualized reading class."	"The patient sat alone at 6 months, crawled at 8 months, and walked at 12 months." "The recommendations are to learn a phonics approach and to attend an individualized reading class."
11. *Combine or restructure sentences to avoid repeating the same word, phrase, or idea.* Consecutive sentences with the same subject, or ones that describe the same process, often require revision.	"Jim's mother said that he had been in an automobile accident last year. His mother also told me that Jim has had memory difficulties since the accident." "Hyperactivity characterized Jim's behavior. He was hyperactive in class and hyperactive on the playground, and he was also hyperactive in the interview."	"Jim's mother said that he has had memory difficulties since his automobile accident last year." "Jim was constantly in motion in the classroom, on the playground, and during the interview."
12. *Keep related sentence elements together, and keep unrelated elements apart.* Express new thoughts in new sentences.	"Mrs. James has not attended any teacher conferences this year, and she has been married four times."	"Mrs. James has not attended any teacher conferences this year. She has been married four times."
13. *Do not use too many prepositional phrases in one sentence.*	"The teacher reported that John slept poorly the night before the test session, which resulted in his being too tired to stay awake in class."	"The teacher reported that John slept poorly the night before the test and was too tired to stay awake in class."
14. *In formal writing, do not end sentences with a preposition.*	"Eric could not decide which hand he wanted to do the block design with."	"Eric could not decide which hand to use to complete the block design."
15. *Omit needless words and phrases. Make every word count.* Cut out words that duplicate information.	"the question as to whether" "whether or not" "he is a man who" "call your attention to the fact that" "due to the fact that" "in order to" "for the purposes of" "in the event that" "in an effort to" "by means of"	"whether" "whether" "he" "remind you (notify you)" "because" "to" "to" or "so that" or "for" "if" "to" "with"

(*Continued*)

Table 7-1 (*Continued*)

Guideline	Inappropriate statement	Appropriate statement
	"in connection with"	"with"
	"for the length of time that"	"while"
	"with the result that"	"so"
	"is supportive of"	"supports"
	"to be of great benefit"	"beneficial"
	"in such a state that"	"so" or "such"
	"pertains to the problem of"	"concerns"
	"at this point in time"	"now"
	"am (or are) in agreement with"	"agree"
	"insofar as"	"so"
	"with reference to"	"regarding"
	"many in number"	"many"
	"round in shape"	"round"
	"audible to the ear"	"audible"
	"tasted bitter to the tongue"	"tasted bitter"
	"second time in my life"	"second time"
	"quickly with haste"	"quickly"
	"there were several members of the family who said"	"several family members said"
	"they were both alike"	"they were alike"
	"four different teachers said"	"four teachers said"
	"absolutely essential"	"essential"
	"one and the same"	"the same"
	"room was juxtaposed to hers"	"room was next door" or "room was across the hall"
	"in close proximity"	"in proximity" or "close"
	"period of time"	"time"
	"the reason is"	"because"
	"summarize briefly"	"summarize"
	"in the near future"	"soon"
	"in view of the fact that"	"because"
	"with regard to"	"about"
16. *Avoid misplaced modifiers.* Misplaced modifiers add to confusion and occasionally create unintended humor in the report. Be sure that modifiers qualify the appropriate elements in the sentence. Modifiers should be placed (a) close to the words they modify and (b) away from words that they might mistakenly be taken to modify.	"In response to my instructions, Aaron picked up the ball and walked around the room with his left hand." "Dr. Jones instructed the patient while in the hospital to watch his diet carefully."	"In response to my instructions, Aaron picked up the ball with his left hand and then walked around the room." "While visiting her patient in the hospital, Dr. Jones told him to watch his diet carefully."
17. *Avoid the use of qualifiers.* Words such as "rather," "very," "little," "pretty" are unneeded and are best left out of the report.	"The patient was very attentive." "She was a pretty good student." "a pretty important rule"	"The patient was attentive." "She was a good student" or "She was a mediocre student" or "She had a grade-point average of 3.4." "an important rule"
18. *Use words correctly.* Misused words reflect unfavorably on the writer and discredit the report. Two commonly misused words are "affect" and "effect."	"The behavior modification approach used by the teacher seems to have had a favorable affect on Edward."	"The behavior modification approach used by the teacher seems to have had a favorable effect on Edward" or "The behavior modification approach used by the teacher seemed to affect Edward favorably."

(Continued)

Table 7-1 (*Continued*)

Guideline	Inappropriate statement	Appropriate statement
19. *Avoid fancy words.* The line between fancy words and plain words is sometimes alarmingly fine. The wise writer will avoid an elaborate word when a simple one will suffice. The interview report must not become a two-page exhibition of the writer's professional vocabulary. The best writers use vocabulary true to their own experience.	"The patient exhibited apparent partial paralysis of motor units of the superior sinistral fibers of the genioglossus, resulting in insufficient lingual approximation of the palatoalveolar regions. A condition of insufficient frenulum development was noted, which produced not only sigmatic distortion but also obvious ankyloglossia."	"The patient was tongue-tied."
20. *Do not take shortcuts at the expense of clarity.* Acronyms should be avoided unless they will be understood by all readers. (Even sophisticated readers appreciate having test names written out initially.)	"The PPVT-R, VABS, and WISC-III were administered."	"The following tests were administered: Peabody Picture Vocabulary Test—Revised (PPVT-R), Vineland Adaptive Behavior Scales (VABS), and Wechsler Intelligence Scale for Children—Third Edition (WISC-III)."
21. *Capitalize proper names of tests.*	"In a previous assessment, he was given the bender and the motor-free test."	"In a previous assessment, he was given the Bender Visual Motor Gestalt Test and the Motor-Free Visual Perception Test."
22. *Put statements in positive form. Make definite assertions. Avoid tame, colorless, hesitating, noncommittal language.* The reader may be dissatisfied with being told only what did not happen; he or she wishes to be told what did happen as well.	"The child did not know his colors." "The child did not have good motor control."	"The child did not name the colors of the red and blue blocks. However, he did separate the blocks by color and matched them to other red and blue objects in the room." "The child stacked two blocks but was unable to stack three blocks."
23. *Do not affect a breezy manner.* Be professional, avoid pet ideas and phrases, and cultivate a natural rather than a flippant style of writing.	"Would you believe, Ma and Pa had a fuss right in the middle of the interview over when the child began to walk." "Mom said her child was sad."	"The child's parents disagreed as to when the child had first walked." "Mrs. Smith said her child was sad."
24. *Do not overstate.* If you overstate, the reader will be instantly on guard, and everything that precedes your overstatement, as well as everything that follows it, will be suspect in the reader's mind.	"There is no tension in the home." "The client is absolutely brilliant."	"Bill's father reported no tension in the home." "The student scored 141 on the Stanford-Binet Intelligence Scale: Fourth Edition, presented a report card with all As, and was voted 'most intelligent' by the high school faculty."

Source: Adapted from Bates (1985), Gearheart and Willenberg (1980), Kolin and Kolin (1980), and Moore (1969).

3. The word "environment" should be clarified. Does it refer to the child's immediate environment (that is, the interview room and building) or to the larger environment? *Suggestion:* "Ted appeared to be curious about his immediate environment and asked the interviewer several questions about objects in the room."

4. The colloquial expressions "just flew by in terms of time" and "without any hitch" are not appropriate. *Suggestion:* "Helen was cooperative and well motivated and answered questions quickly."

5. A term such as "rapidly" is preferable to the word "nervously," which is subjective.

6. It is unclear what comparison the writer has in mind.

7. This sentence is awkward. *Suggestion:* "The child is a small girl who has a pleasant disposition. Rapport was easily established."

8. The final quotation marks should be placed *after* the period.

9. "Which" is not the correct pronoun for "another woman." The proper pronoun is "whom" (with whom). Also, generally do not place prepositions such as "with" at the end of a sentence. *Suggestion:* "The mother currently shares an apartment with another woman with whom she doesn't get along."

10. "Malingering," which means pretending to be ill, is used incorrectly in this sentence. "Lingering" was probably intended.

Unwarranted Inference

11. The interpretation may or may not have merit, depending on your theoretical orientation. Avoid making such interpretations, especially when they are based on the *absence* of data.

Inappropriate Abbreviations

12. Many readers will not know what these abbreviations mean. They are best left out; if they are needed, they should be described fully. *Suggestion:* "Mark is in the classroom for children with learning problems."

Inappropriate Value Judgments

13. This statement is based on hearsay and should be verified. It may be best to omit the reference to the family's source of income. The sentence also contains a colloquial expression ("it's no wonder") that should be eliminated.

14. This type of interpretation should be made only when there is sufficient evidence. Has the interviewer observed the family? If so, a statement of their observed behavior should be included and then a possible interpretation of the implications of this behavior offered. The report could say, for example, "In a meeting with the family, I observed that little verbal interaction took place between Joanne and her parents. Perhaps this pattern has hindered the development of Joanne's verbal skills." Recognize that parents with limited education and limited verbal abilities may have children who have excellent learning abilities.

15. The writer's prejudice or stereotypes may be showing in this sentence. No such interpretation should be made

simply based on family size and income. Large families with low income may provide adequate cultural and social enrichment for their members.

16. This statement represents a value judgment, because the behavior in question may not necessarily be irritating to all adults. *Suggestion:* "Richard's mannerisms tended to irritate me" or "Richard's snorting, popping of gum, and wriggling in his chair were irritating" or "Richard's teacher reported that he has mannerisms that irritate her."

Inappropriate Recommendations

17. This is a vague and awkwardly written sentence. *Suggestion:* "He may benefit from counseling to help him accept the difficult family situation that he described during the interview."

CONCLUDING COMMENT ON WRITING THE INTERVIEW REPORT

In formulating the interview report, consider all sources of information, the possible implications of the information, and the possible interventions. As you work through this material carefully and logically, recognize which statements are based on observations and which are based on inferences. Clearly acknowledge those findings that are substantial and those that are inconclusive. Also acknowledge uncertain or incongruous findings. Don't come to conclusions prematurely. Write a report that clearly informs the reader of your findings and recommendations—not a report that becomes an assessment of the reader's ability to understand your language.

Report writing is a process of refining ideas, establishing clarity of expression, and using expertise in decision making. The ability to write a clear and meaningful report is an important skill. A good report will contribute to both the assessment and the treatment of the child and his or her family.

THINKING THROUGH THE ISSUES

What should be the function of a report based on an interview?

How might a teacher, a health care provider, and an attorney differ in the kinds of information they want in a report?

Why do you think report writing is so difficult for many students?

How would you avoid writing a report that may be misunderstood by the reader?

What type of information might you wish to communicate to the referral source that you would not include in the report? Is it appropriate for such communications to take place?

Besides this book, what sources can you consult to help you in writing better interview reports?

Calvin and Hobbes   by Bill Watterson

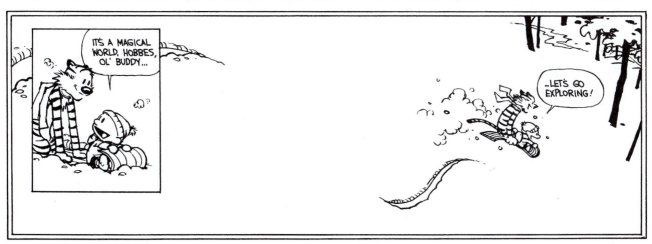

SUMMARY

Introduction to Writing the Interview Report

1. The interview is complete only after you have synthesized, integrated, and organized the information you obtained. The traditional medium for presenting information is a report, although you may use other formal and informal means of presentation.

2. The report is a key part of the clinical assessment or forensic interview. It conveys the information you obtained, your findings, interpretations, and recommendations and serves as a record that you and others can use in the future. The report deserves careful preparation.

3. Your report should be well organized and solidly grounded.

4. In formulating and constructing your report, consider the primary audience for the report, the circumstances under which the interview took place, the need to include examples, needs and values of the interviewee and others, and how your values affected what you say in the report.

5. Reports provide accurate assessment-related information to the referral source and other concerned parties; serve as a source of information for testing clinical hypotheses, developing appropriate treatment recommendations, and conducting program evaluation and research; serve as a record of historical, observational, and other information gathered in the interview and recommended interventions; and may serve as legal documents.

6. Strive for objectivity and accuracy in the report, but recognize that all reports have elements of subjectivity, including those deriving from your value system.

7. Write the report as soon as possible after the interview.

Sections of an Interview Report

8. A typical report based on a clinical assessment or forensic interview usually includes eight sections: Identifying Information, Reason for Referral, Behavioral Observations, Case History Information, Clinical Impressions, Recommendations, Summary, and Signature.

9. The Identifying Information section presents relevant information to identify the interviewee, interviewer, and date of report.

10. The Reason for Referral section summarizes the concerns of the referral source.

11. The Behavioral Observations section describes the child's behavior during the interview and attempts to capture the child's unique style.

12. The Case History Information section provides information obtained from those you have interviewed and from the interviewee's records, including the educational file and past psychological, psychiatric, and medical reports.

13. The Clinical Impressions section synthesizes the major findings. Use extreme caution in making any interpretations or diagnostic formulations when you have inconsistent data. In any case, never make diagnostic statements based on insufficient data.

14. The Recommendations section usually provides possible intervention strategies; develop your recommendations based on all available information. If possible, be specific in your recommendations. Your suggestions for change should be practical, concrete, individualized, and based on sound social work practice, psychological practice, and educational practice (for children). Make long-range predictions cautiously, if at all, and use words that appropriately convey your degree of confidence in any predictions.

15. The Summary presents a concise picture of the findings and recommendations. It generally includes one or more major findings (or points) from each section.

16. The Signature section presents your name, degree, and professional title.

Principles of Report Writing

17. Organize the interview findings by detecting common themes that run through the case history.

18. Include in the report relevant material and delete potentially damaging material not germane to the evaluation.

19. Be extremely cautious in making interpretations based on observations of a limited sample of behavior.

20. Use all relevant sources of information about the interviewee—including behavioral observations, interview data, and the case history—in generating hypotheses, formulating interpretations, and arriving at recommendations.

21. Be definitive in your writing when the findings are clear; be cautious in your writing when the findings are problematic.

22. Cite specific behaviors and sources to enhance the report's readability.

23. Communicate clearly, and do not include unnecessary technical material in the report.

24. Eliminate biased terms from the report.

25. Write a report that is concise but presents your findings and recommendations adequately.

26. Attend carefully to grammatical and stylistic points in your writing.

27. Develop appropriate strategies to improve your writing, such as using an outline, rereading your rough draft, using a word processor, and proofreading your final report.

Concluding Comment on Writing the Interview Report

28. Your goal is to write a report that will clearly inform the reader of your findings and recommendations.

29. Report writing is a process of refining ideas, establishing clarity of expression, and using expertise in decision making. The ability to write a clear and meaningful report is an important skill.

KEY TERMS, CONCEPTS, AND NAMES

Sections of an interview report (p. 233)
Identifying information (p. 233)
Reason for referral (p. 233)
Behavioral observations (p. 233)
Case history information (p. 234)
Clinical impressions (p. 235)
Recommendations (p. 236)
Long-range predictions (p. 237)
Summary (p. 237)
Signature (p. 237)
Principles of report writing (p. 237)
Organizing findings (p. 238)
Including relevant material (p. 239)
Making interpretations carefully (p. 240)
Making generalizations (p. 241)
Conveying degree of certainty (p. 241)
Enhancing readability (p. 242)
Communicating clearly (p. 242)
Avoiding bias (p. 244)
Writing concisely (p. 245)
Attending to grammar (p. 245)
Improving writing style (p. 246)

STUDY QUESTIONS

1. What are the qualities of a good report?

2. What purposes are served by a report based on an interview?

3. Compare and contrast the various sections of an interview report.

4. What strategies can you use to organize the assessment findings in a report?

5. What guidelines should you use to decide which material to include in a report?

6. What are some guidelines for making generalizations, interpretations, and diagnoses?

7. What are some important factors to consider in communicating your findings in a report?

8. How can you eliminate biased language in a report?

9. Describe some useful strategies for writing reports.

10. Develop a checklist for evaluating the quality of an interview report.

11. Discuss seven common pitfalls in report writing.

SECTION II

INTERVIEWING CHILDREN AND FAMILIES OF ETHNIC MINORITY GROUPS

Section II focuses on issues pertinent to interviewing Black Americans, Hispanic Americans, Asian Americans, Native Americans, and refugees or immigrants. These issues include majority-minority group relations, acculturation, and language fluency. When you interview ethnic minority children and their families, it will be helpful if you know, for example, about the problems they face in society; about how they view mental and physical illnesses; about the roles of children, male and female adults, and extended family members in their culture; and, if they are recent immigrants, the problems they have in adjusting to a new culture.

Although the two chapters in this section contain several generalizations about specific ethnic minority groups, you always must consider each child and family as unique. Unfortunately, society often stereotypes members of ethnic minority groups and fails to recognize their individuality. This is an error that you must guard against. Cultures, as well as individuals, are rich in diversity.

8

ETHNIC MINORITY GROUPS: AN OVERVIEW

"First of all," he said, "if you can learn a simple trick, Scout, you'll get along a lot better with all kinds of folks. You never really understand a person until you consider things from his point of view—"

"Sir?"

"—until you climb into his skin and walk around in it."
—Harper Lee

Goals and Objectives

This chapter will enable you to:

- Discuss the concept of culture and value orientations and the concept of acculturation
- Describe cross-ethnic and cross-cultural interviewing
- Recognize problems involved in using interpreters

This chapter emphasizes the need to consider cultural variables when you interview ethnic minority children and their parents. By considering cultural variables, you will be in a better position to establish rapport, obtain valid information, arrive at an accurate diagnosis, and formulate meaningful intervention plans. It will not always be easy to evaluate the role that cultural variables play because members of ethnic minority groups differ in their adherence to their group's cultural traditions and practices. Great diversity exists within ethnic minority groups, especially between recent immigrants and those who are acculturated. Even among those who are acculturated, differences exist in patterns of acculturation. However, members of ethnic minority groups do not need to reject their cultural heritage to adapt to the new culture; they can choose to value their old traditions and practices while also valuing those of the new culture. *Our society must recognize and preserve cultural diversity and promote culturally sensitive and culturally relevant clinical services.*

Broad generalizations about cultural practices do not do justice to regional, generational, socioeconomic, and idiosyncratic variations in life styles. However, when you know about the cultural mores and customs that influence the child's and family's development and organization and are aware of how the migration experience and acculturation may have affected the child and family, you will be in a better position to conduct an effective interview (Falicov, 1982). The generalizations in this chapter about different ethnic minority groups and the majority group must remain generalizations; do not apply them indiscriminately to each child and family. For example, although White Americans may be more individualistic than Hispanic Americans, you "cannot predict with any certainty the level of individualism of a particular person" (Okazaki & Sue, 1995, p. 368). Instead, use what you know about ethnic minority groups and the majority group as a background for the interview, but treat each child as an individual and each family as unique. Chapter 1 also discusses ethnic minority children, focusing on those who are at risk.

The concept of culture is closely intertwined with the concepts of race, ethnicity, and social class. Definitions of these terms will help you in understanding the material in this chapter (Betancourt & López, 1993, pp. 630–632):

Culture is the human-made part of the environment, consisting of highly variable systems of meanings that are learned and shared by a people or an identifiable segment of a population. Culture represents designs and ways of life normally transmitted from one generation to another.

Race refers to the physical characteristics, such as skin color, facial features, and hair type, common to a population.

Ethnicity refers to groups characterized by a common nationality, culture, or language.

Social class refers to designations, usually based on occupation, education, or both, that are given to groups in a society.

BACKGROUND CONSIDERATIONS

The 1990 U.S. census reported that there were 63,604,432 children under 18 living in the United States (U.S. Bureau of the Census, 1993c). The ethnic affiliation of the children was as follows (also see Figure 8-1): White (67%), Black (15%), Hispanic (12%), Asian and Pacific Islander (3%), and Native American (less than 1%). The Hispanic children traced their origins to Mexico, Puerto Rico, Cuba, El Salvador, Colombia, Guatemala, Nicaragua, Ecuador, Peru, Honduras, and other Central and South American countries. The Asian and Pacific Islander groups included Chinese, Filipino, Japanese, Asian Indian, Korean, Vietnamese, Laotian, Cambodian, Thai, and Hmong.

The U.S. Bureau of the Census projected that Hispanic Americans and Asian Americans will account for more than half the growth in the U.S. population every year for the next half-century and beyond. As a result, the ethnic portrait of America will change dramatically: The population of White Americans, which in 1996 was three-quarters of all Americans, will shrink to a bare majority by the year 2050 (Rosenblatt, 1996). Because the Hispanic American population is young and has a high fertility rate, it will become the nation's largest ethnic minority group in 2009.

It is estimated that by 2050, Hispanic Americans will form 24.5% of the population, up from the current 10.2%, and Asian Americans will make up 8.2%, an increase from the current 3.3%. The Black American population will remain relatively constant, rising to about 13.6% from the current 12%. The Native American population will stay about the same, showing a small rise from 0.7% to 0.9%. The population as a whole, it is estimated, will rise from 263 million in 1995 to 394 million in 2050.

Problems Faced by Ethnic Minority Groups

In the United States, ethnic minority groups may face (a) racism and discrimination, (b) poverty, (c) conflicts associated with acculturation and assimilation, especially when children begin to identify more closely with the majority culture and reject their ethnic culture, (d) problems in dealing with medical, educational, social, and law enforcement organizations, and (e) problems in using standard English. These underlying

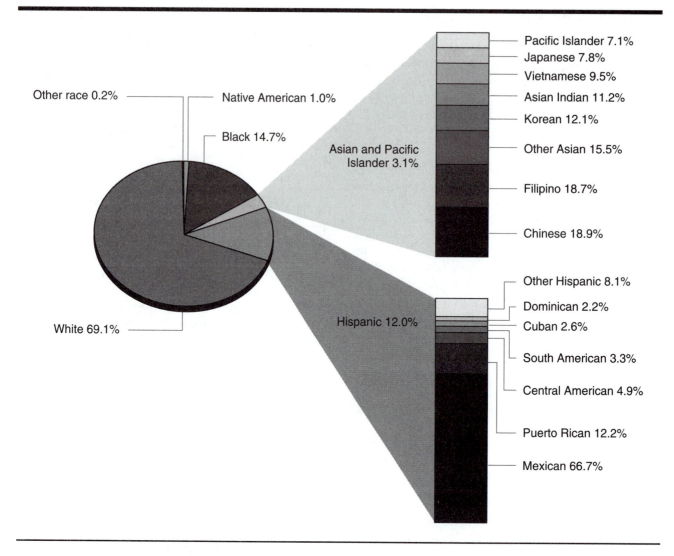

Figure 8-1. Distribution by race of U.S. children in 1990 (percent distribution of children under 18 years old). From U.S. Bureau of the Census (1993), *We the American…Children*, p. 3.

problems may affect the clinical assessment and forensic interview.

Prejudice.   A common thread in the experience of ethnic minority groups in our society is confronting prejudice. Prejudice is an insidious process that ethnic minorities face at all socioeconomic levels. Prejudice can lead to segregation in housing, inequality before the law, discrimination in employment, and other kinds of social and political discrimination. The experience of prejudice may make ethnic minority clients wary of help offered by the majority group.

Here is an example of prejudice experienced by an interracial family (Scheer, 1993):

I have an 8-year-old son and he was told by an African American boy in his class that he wouldn't play with him because he was told he had Japanese germs. I am Anglo American and my husband is Japanese-American. My husband was born in a[n internment]

camp in California. And my daughter, when she was in the first grade, had a White boy call her with so much disdain "Chinatown," and after a while she didn't want to go to school. She wouldn't tell me why. She thought there was something wrong with her. Racism is alive and well. (p. B5, with changes in notation)

Exhibit 8-1 offers several other accounts of prejudice occurring in the United States.

Poverty.   Let's look at the *poverty rate* for families in 1995 for four ethnic groups. White Americans had the lowest poverty rate, followed by Asian Americans, Black Americans, and Hispanic Americans. Over one-quarter of Black American and Hispanic American families were below the poverty level (see Figure 8-2). The median family income was $40,884 for White American families, $24,698 for Black American families, $28,658 for Hispanic American families, and $46,106 for Asian American families. Infor-

Exhibit 8-1
The Many Faces of Prejudice in the United States

The following excerpts poignantly illustrate incidents of racism, stereotyping, and discrimination in the United States in the 1990s. Incidents such as these may make the victims of prejudice suspicious of people from ethnic groups different from their own and distrustful of institutions run by the majority group, such as police departments, social welfare agencies, mental health clinics, hospitals, and schools. Sometimes, ethnic minority interviewees' suspicions of people in a position of authority are completely justified. The excerpts also reveal that ethnic minorities may suffer discrimination at the hands of individuals from their own ethnic group because they are newcomers to the United States or differ in certain ways from the majority group.

Example 1. Black American
Female College Student
A female college student in California wrote the following letter (which has been edited) to a school newspaper in November 1995. "When I go shopping a sales clerk follows me or older White women look at me with fear in their eyes. Every time I use my MasterCard I get put through the third degree or am considered incompetent because my skin is of the darker shade. I am from the suburbs near a large city and have an upper-middle-class upbringing. But despite my background or upbringing, to White America I'll always be just another 'n----.' And when I graduate and eventually obtain my Ph.D. and I have a six-digit salary, to White America I'll always be just another 'n----.'"

Example 2. Black American
Adult Male
A 29-year-old Black maintenance man, who works for a church in Beverly Hills, has been stopped eight times by the Beverly Hills police since August 1993 when he began his employment. In a lawsuit filed in November 1995, he reported an incident in which he was followed by police for several blocks into the church parking lot where an officer demanded that he lie on the ground as

horrified parishioners looked on. "There was no reason for me to get on the ground. I had done nothing wrong," said the man. Many church members wrote the city to complain and to demand that officials review police policies, but they never received an official response.

Example 3. Black American Male
Adolescent
Two Black teenagers were stopped while visiting an Eddie Bauer store outside Washington, D.C. Two moonlighting police officers asked them to produce a receipt for the shirt one teenager was wearing. One of the teenagers had purchased the shirt a day before at the store. Because the teenager could not produce the receipt, the police demanded that he take it off and he did so. The cashier recalled selling the youth a shirt but could not remember if it was the particular shirt in question. The teenager went home in his tee shirt, found the receipt, returned to the store, and obtained the shirt he had purchased the previous day. Neither the police nor the store offered an apology. The police had no proof that the shirt had been shoplifted, and the teenager was under no legal obligation to carry a receipt for every article he was wearing.

Example 4. Black American Males
Black men face many educational obstacles. As early as elementary school, teachers often have low academic expectations of Black males and relegate them to inferior classes. Teachers also are threatened by Black male students and view them as having chronic disciplinary problems. In college, Black male students face a persistent attitude that they owe their success to affirmative action instead of to merit. One Black college student recalled that in the fourth grade he was assigned to a low-level reading group. "I felt like I was reading preschool books; I felt really held back. The teachers had an opportunity to plant a huge seed of doubt in my mind." Another Black male college student recalled that he was the only male in his class in the honor society.

Yet, when he told his counselors of his aspirations to go to Georgetown, Harvard, or Columbia, they scoffed and said "That's nice, but it's not realistic. Don't waste your time." He did enroll in Georgetown and, by his senior year, achieved an overall grade point average close to 3.0. While in college, he believed that "people will assume I am stupid until I prove otherwise. When they realize you're smart they think you must be a genius and that you are the ultimate exception to Black people. I wake up every morning knowing I have to prove myself every day. Is it offensive, is it annoying? Sure."

Example 5. Black Americans
Black churches are on fire just as they were 30 years ago. A Black 9-year-old in South Carolina was recently tied to a tree and terrorized by a White playmate and his parents. A 300-unit apartment building in Ohio refused ever to rent to African Americans. In Alabama recently, we caught a landlord racially coding his applications. A 6-foot cross was burned in front of a neighborhood auto repair shop in Florida because the White shop owner hired two Black workers. Not far from there, a police department routinely threw applications from Blacks in the trash.

Example 6. Black Immigrants
West Indian Black immigrants often face hostility in their interactions with native-born African Americans. The tension appears to stem from the strange blend of contempt and envy the two groups exhibit toward each other. One source of contention is workplace competition. African Americans and West Indians may be rivals for the menial positions available at the bottom rung of the employment ladder. Some West Indians say African Americans don't want to work hard and are too quick to use racism as an excuse for their failure to advance. African Americans resent West Indians because they say they are too eager to take their jobs or too willing to work with Whites at the expense of African Americans. Uncertain where

(Continued)

Exhibit 8-1 (*Continued*)

they stand with either African Americans or White Americans, many West Indian Blacks prefer to stick close to their tightly knit families in their adopted country. That feeling goes both ways, as many African Americans say they avoid contact with West Indian Blacks for the same reasons they avoid contact with White Americans—a sense of being out of place in a racially stratified society. One African American said "Often African Americans feel there is a disrespect for what they had to go through for West Indian Africans to come over here and get the benefits.... African Americans need to hear that their struggle is respected."

Example 7. Hispanic Immigrants
American-born Hispanic teenagers are ridiculing Hispanic immigrant teenagers from Mexico. They make fun of the immigrant boys who dress in white buttoned shirts instead of tee shirts and high-water cotton trousers instead of oversized jeans. They ridicule the immigrant girls in their ruffled starched blouses and pleated skirts and braids tied with bows. They make fun of the immigrant children's shyness, respectfulness, and dedication to academics. They make fun of the immigrants' "nerdy" Micky Mouse–adorned backpacks and have even coined a term for them: "Wetpacks." They call the immigrant students other names—"beaner" and "Wehac" (a derogatory term for a Mexican immigrant of Indian descent)—and tell them to "go back where you come from."

Example 8. Asian American Adolescent
A 17-year-old high school girl who was brought as an infant from a refugee camp in Thailand to a small Northern California town decided to drop out of school and finish her senior year (in 1996) at home. She is one of the school's few students of color and one of only two Asian students. She has found swastikas scratched into her desk, felt students spitting at her, and found the words "demon girl," "White pride," and "hippy dink" scrawled in the dust that coated her pickup truck. The harassment was too much. The girl said "It was very painful, I couldn't stand it anymore." One parent said "I think it's terrible that she should feel that way in this community where she grew up." A teacher said "It's probably only one or two kids who are responsible, but those one or two kids can cause a lot of problems and a lot of heartache." And her father said "There has been enough damage. We've already gone through the 'tough-it-out, let's-go-back' scenario."

Example 9. Interracial Families
There is an emerging new face among America's "traditional" families: the ethnically/racially mixed couple representing different backgrounds—White, Black, Hispanic, Asian-Pacific, and so forth. Many of these spousal unions produce children of mixed heritage. These children are lucky because they are enriched by two different cultures. Nevertheless, much to the horror and

chagrin of these children and their parents, they often face a new type of discrimination. They are asked, for demographic identification purposes, to choose the parent with whom they most identify when they fill out test and application forms. Failure to include a multi-ethnic option reflects a bureaucracy insensitive and indifferent to the needs of these students and their families. The face of America is changing, and city, county, state, and federal officials should not be the last to realize it.

Example 10. The Invisible "Glass Ceiling"
A 20-member, bipartisan commission created by Congress reported that as of November 1995, 30 years after the passage of the federal Civil Rights Act guaranteeing equal employment opportunities to all Americans, the invisible "glass ceiling" has kept women and minorities out of the top management ranks of most major U.S. corporations. Only 5% of senior managers are women, and almost all of them are White. African American men with professional degrees earn 21% less than their White counterparts holding the same degrees in the same job categories. Hispanic Americans account for only 0.4% of corporate managers, although they make up 8% of the work force. The glass ceiling continues to deny untold numbers of qualified people the opportunity to compete for and hold executive-level positions in the private sector of our nation.

Source: Adapted, in order of the examples, from Porcher (1995), Helfand and Steinberg (1995), Cohen (1995), Arnett (1995), Patrick (1996), Fulwood (1995b), Quintanilla (1995), Associated Press (1996b), Jenkins (1995), and Swoboda (1995).

mation about Native American families is available for 1990. Their poverty rate was 27.2% and their median family income was $21,619. As noted in Figure 8-2, the income amount at the poverty level for a family in 1995 was $15,569. Poverty can raise individuals' stress levels and place them at increased risk for health problems such as obesity, suicide, and alcoholism.

Schooling. When we look at data for 1995 on the *years of school completed* by persons 25 years of age and older, we find that Asian Americans as a group had the highest percentage of individuals with at least four years of high

school or more (83.6%), followed by White Americans (83.0%), Black Americans (73.8%), and Hispanic Americans (53.4%); for Native Americans in 1990, the figure is 65.6% (see Figure 8-3).

Terminology

In this chapter, I use the terms *ethnic minority group, minority group,* and *minority* to refer to "a group subordinated in terms of power and privilege to the majority group" (Kumabe, Nishida, & Hepworth, 1985, p. 9). Minority groups

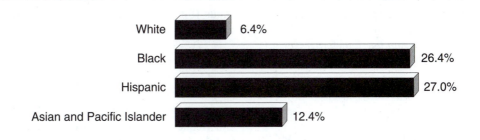

Figure 8-2. Percentage of families below the poverty level in 1995 for four ethnic groups. The income amount at the poverty level for a family in 1995 was $15,569. In 1990, the latest year for which data are available, 27.2% of Native American families were below the poverty level. From Baugher and Lamison-White, U.S. Bureau of the Census (1996), *Poverty in the United States: 1995*, p. vii, and U.S. Bureau of the Census (1996), *Statistical Abstracts of the United States: 1996* (116th Edition), p. 50.

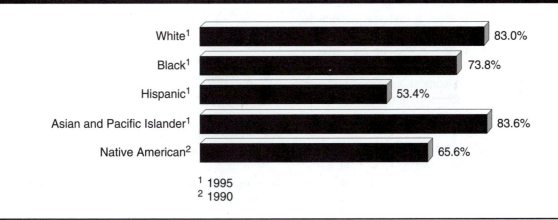

Figure 8-3. Percentage of persons 25 or over completing 4 years of high school or more for five ethnic groups. From U.S. Bureau of the Census (1996), *Statistical Abstracts of the United States: 1996* (116th Edition), pp. 48–51.

usually are referred to in terms of race, ethnicity, nationality, religion, or sex. I use the terms *majority group, White Americans,* and *Anglo Americans* interchangeably, depending on the context, although Anglo Americans may not be the majority group in a specific geographical area.

Civil rights today is, as it has always been in human history, a struggle for the human conscience, and…we all have a stake in that struggle.… Let history record that we in our time faced our challenges remembering who we are and believing finally in that old adage that we are more than our brother's keeper; that is on this earth, we are his savior and he is ours.

—Deval Patrick

Culture and Value Orientations

Ethnic minority groups and the majority group may differ in their value orientations about human nature, the relationship between person and nature, time, activity level, and social

relations. Let's look at some value orientations associated with each of these areas (Kluckhohn, 1958; Spiegel, 1982).

- *Human nature: evil orientation* (people are born with evil inclinations that must be controlled) versus *good orientation* (people are born good) versus *mixed orientation* (people are born with both evil and good inclinations)
- *Relationship between person and nature: subjugation orientation* (people are subjected to natural forces and cannot control them) versus *mastery orientation* (people can gain mastery over nature) versus *harmony orientation* (people can achieve a partnership with nature)
- *Time: past orientation* (traditions, ancestors, and the wisdom of the elderly are valued) versus *present orientation* (life is lived in the here and now) versus *future orientation* (life is planned for tomorrow with an emphasis on newness and youth)
- *Activity level: being orientation* (emphasizes cooperation, seeking harmony with nature, concern with what the person is, and spontaneous self-expression) versus *doing orientation* (emphasizes achievement, competitiveness, striving for upward mobility in jobs, and controlling

feelings) versus *being-in-becoming orientation* (emphasizes what the person is and developing aspects of the self in an integrated manner)

• *Social relations: lineal orientation* (emphasizes clearly established lines of authority) versus *collateral orientation* (emphasizes collective decision making) versus *individual orientation* (emphasizes individuality and autonomy over group goals)

You will be reading more about these value orientations in connection with Black American, Hispanic American, Native American, and Asian American groups in Chapter 9.

Acculturation

Acculturation is a process of cultural change that occurs in individuals when two cultures meet; it leads the individuals to adopt elements of another culture, such as values and social behaviors. The process of acculturation may involve several stages, including (a) initial joy, relief, and idealization of the new culture, (b) disillusionment associated with the adjustment, and (c) gradual acceptance of the good and bad aspects of the new culture (Arredondo-Dowd, 1981).

Factors affecting acculturation. The extent to which individuals have maintained or departed from their traditional cultural practices or have allowed prior cultural practices to coexist with new ones depends on several variables (Kumabe et al., 1985).

1. *History of migration experience.* The nature of the migration experience may influence individuals' self-concepts and how they acculturate to the resettlement country. Consider whether ethnic minority groups view themselves as *forced to come against their will* (for example, Black Americans who were forced to come to the United States as slaves), *conquered* (for example, Native Americans or Mexican Americans), *displaced* (for example, Vietnamese), *oppressed* (for example, Cubans who were oppressed in Cuba), or *voluntary immigrants* (for example, individuals who migrated for professional or personal reasons).

2. *Temporal and geographic distance from the country of origin and its indigenous culture.* Individuals' degree of acculturation may be influenced by their length of residence in the United States, the extent to which they maintain ties with the indigenous culture, and how often they return to their native land. Acculturation is more likely under the following conditions: long residence, minimal ties with the indigenous culture, and limited returns to the native land.

3. *Place of residence and socioeconomic status in the homeland.* Individuals' acculturation may be influenced by where they lived in the homeland (for example, in an urban or rural area) and their status in the homeland (for example, their economic, occupational, and educational strata). Individuals with rural backgrounds and low socioeconomic status may have more difficulty adjusting to U.S. culture than

those who have urban backgrounds or high socioeconomic status (for example, rural Cambodians versus urban Vietnamese).

4. *Type of neighborhood in the resettlement country.* Individuals who live in a neighborhood with others of the same ethnicity and who have primary ties with their ethnic minority group are more likely to keep their indigenous traditions than those who live in an integrated neighborhood and frequently interact with other ethnic minority groups and the majority group.

5. *Close ties with immediate and extended family.* Individuals may have difficulty becoming acculturated when they have close ties to their immediate and extended families.

6. *Role of the family's power and authority.* Individuals will have difficulty deviating from family norms when their families insist that they maintain indigenous traditions.

7. *Language and customs.* Individuals may have difficulty acculturating when they speak primarily the language of their homeland, celebrate the holidays of their homeland, and follow the traditions and customs found there. In addition, acculturation may be difficult when individuals had limited exposure to Western culture in their homeland.

Tables 8-1 and 8-2 provide questions that will help you determine children's and parents' degree of acculturation (including language preference).

Dealing with acculturation. Individuals may deal with acculturation in different ways.

1. *Traditionalism.* Individuals maintain and practice mainly the traditions of their culture of origin. "People put me down because I'm Mexican, but I don't care anymore. I can accept myself more" (Mexican American female; Phinney, 1989, p. 44).

2. *Transitional period.* Individuals partake of both the old and the new culture but question basic traditional values and also those of the new culture. "It will take some time, but eventually I'll know what group is best for me" (Asian American female).

3. *Marginality.* Individuals develop anxiety by partially, but unsuccessfully, meeting the demands of both the old and the new culture. In the process, they may become isolated both from the culture of origin and from the new culture. "There are a lot of non-Japanese people around me, and it gets pretty confusing to try and decide who I am" (Asian American male; Phinney, 1989, p. 44).

4. *Assimilation.* Individuals embrace traditions of the new culture and reject practices and customs of their culture. "My past is back there; I have no reason to worry about it. I'm American now" (Mexican American male; Phinney, 1989, p. 44).

5. *Biculturalism.* Individuals integrate practices of both the old and the new culture by selectively adapting new customs and maintaining former ones without losing a sense of identity. "I have been born Filipino and am born to be Filipino.... I'm here in America, and people of many differ-

Table 8-1
Interview Questions for Determining an Adolescent's Degree of Acculturation

1. What language do you usually use when you talk with your mother?
2. What language do you usually use when you talk with your father?
3. (If applicable) What language do you usually use when you talk with your sisters and brothers?
4. (If applicable) What language do you usually use when you talk with your grandmother and grandfather?
5. What language do you usually use when you talk with your friends?
6. What language do you usually use when you talk in school?
7. In what language are the television programs you usually watch?
8. In what language are the radio station programs you usually listen to?
9. In which language do you usually think?
10. What language do you use for reading?
11. What language do you use for writing?
12. What cultural or ethnic groups live in your neighborhood?
13. What is the cultural or ethnic background of your close friends?
14. What type of foods do you eat at home?
15. What is the ethnic background of your father?
16. What is the ethnic background of your mother?
17. What ethnic or cultural holidays and traditions do you celebrate?
18. What culture do you feel the most proud of?

Note. Items 1 through 11 will not be applicable to groups that speak and write in English only.

Table 8-2
Interview Questions for Determining a Parent's Degree of Acculturation

1. What language do you usually use when you talk with your (husband, wife)?
2. What language do you usually use when you talk with your child?
3. (If applicable) What language do you usually use when you talk with your (brothers, sisters)?
4. What language do you usually use when you talk with your friends?
5. What language do you usually use when you shop at the grocery store?
6. In what language are the television programs you usually watch?
7. In what language are the radio station programs you usually listen to?
8. In which language do you usually think?
9. What language do you use for reading?
10. What language do you use for writing?
11. What language did you use as a child?
12. What cultural or ethnic groups live in your neighborhood?
13. What is the cultural or ethnic background of your close friends?
14. What type of foods do you eat?
15. What ethnic or cultural holidays and traditions do you celebrate?
16. What culture do you feel the most proud of?

Note. Items 1 through 11 will not be applicable to groups that speak and write in English only.

ent cultures are here, too. So I don't consider myself only Filipino, but also American" (Asian American male; Phinney, 1989, p. 44).

Here is an example of acculturation as reported by a Cambodian father. He describes how his views toward women changed after he emigrated to the United States. His daughters were ages 8 to 17 when they came to the United States (Yarborough, 1996a, with permission of Trin Yarborough who conducted the interview).

CASE 8-1. RIEM MEN

In Cambodia, it was always taught that women must obey and respect men. Many of the old books that some Cambodians still read set out rules for a "good woman." She should always go to bed later than her husband and get up earlier than him, so she can attend to all household tasks. If he is a drunkard or adulterer or gambler, he is still always right. And even if he curses her, she should be quiet and respectful. If she follows these rules she'll be considered the best woman in the community and when she dies she'll go to heaven.

When I grew up in Cambodia no one had any different ideas about that, so it all seemed natural and right. In my mind, women were a group of people who were there to take care of the house and raise children. They were regarded as very weak people, and they certainly had no chance to express opinions on such matters as politics.

Therefore you can imagine my surprise when I first landed in San Francisco with a group of 350 other Asian officers and at our orientation an American girl [who looked] about 19 years old got on stage and talked in front of hundreds of high-ranking officers. She didn't even seem nervous, just normal, and I thought: Oh, my God! I've never seen anything like this before! Yet it was exciting to see a woman taking that kind of role and I felt admiration for her. Suddenly, it seemed appropriate. And as time went on, all my ideas began to change....

When my daughters were little girls I never imagined they would grow up to be educated or to run businesses. I thought that would be only for my sons. But my thinking changed as I saw women here go to school and have good jobs. All my daughters are independent in the American way. I taught them to respect their husbands if their husbands respected them, but to respect themselves first.

Many Cambodians, even the mothers, value sons more than daughters. Sometimes when Cambodians come here and the wives see other ways, it even can lead to divorce. The husband might say: "Get me a drink of water." And the wife might say: "Get your own water." And he might say: "Oh, you've got freedom now, you're American now!" I tell fathers who come from old ways that if they want their children to respect them, they must earn it. Otherwise the father will end up alone. The old traditions were OK 100 years ago, but not now. This is true not just for the United States or for Cambodia but for the whole world. (p. B7)

Stresses associated with acculturation.   The stresses associated with acculturation are many. Difficulties faced by children include leaving relatives and friends behind when moving from their homeland to the United States, being exposed to customs and mores that differ from those they are accustomed to, having difficulty understanding English, being taunted because of their ethnic origin, being ridiculed because of the way they dress or speak English, feeling lonely because they have few friends from their ethnic minority group, speaking in one language and having their friends answer in another, feeling pressured to speak only the ethnic language at home, being teased at home about not knowing how to speak their ethnic language, feeling pressured to speak only English at home, and having to act as mediators, negotiators, or translators for their parents who do not speak English (Zambrana & Silva-Palacios, 1989).

Ethnic Identity and Identification

Ethnic identity refers to "one's sense of belonging to an ethnic group and the part of one's thinking, perceptions, feelings, and behavior that is due to ethnic group membership" (Rotheram & Phinney, 1986, p. 13). Ethnic minority youth may have difficulty in developing a clear identity if they must choose between the values of the larger society and those of their own group (Spencer & Markstrom-Adams, 1990). For example, do they choose competition or cooperation? Do they value the family over the individual? Do they celebrate the holidays of their group and miss school, or do they attend school and anger their family?

Stereotypes of children's ethnic minority groups also may impede their identity formation (Spencer & Markstrom-Adams, 1990). If the majority group, for example, views their ethnic minority group negatively (say, as powerless and primitive), how are they to perceive themselves? In addition to hindering identification with the majority group, stereotypes may create in children anxieties and doubts about their own group. Children may internalize negative portrayals by the majority culture, which, in turn, may lead to low self-esteem and behavioral problems.

In the following passages, five adolescents, representing four ethnic minority groups and a biracial heritage, tell what stereotyping means to them. Their comments appeared in the *Los Angeles Times* in November 1992. (Adapted from p. B7, Copyright © 1992, *Los Angeles Times*. Reprinted by permission. "The Stereotyping Habit..." November 30, 1992. By LA Times Staff.)

BLACK AMERICAN ADOLESCENT

There are 365 days in a year and each and every day I must confront my blackness. Many Black people on TV are portrayed through White people's eyes; portrayed as violent, negative people. However, my life is surrounded by positive Black male role models: my dad, my brother, uncles, grandfathers, and godfather. Physical proof that television portrayals are wrong, or at least unbalanced. Television influences a lot of viewers' impressions of Black people. Newscasters many times choose to run criminal stories about Black people. They make gang members seem like a typical group of Black youths instead of the small minority they really are. Not all of the negative images of Black people are generated by Whites. Some come from within our own race. Some youths falsely claim membership in gangs because they think it's cool. I will reject these negative influences no matter where they came from.

—Darryl Meigs, Age 12

HISPANIC AMERICAN ADOLESCENT

Everyone thinks that my ultimate goal is to be married and be a baby-maker. That's the stereotype. My mom had eight children. Just because I'm Mexican, they think I want to be barefoot and pregnant. That's not what I want. In my English class last semester, we saw a play written by a 17-year old Latina. Her family just wanted her to be married. But she wanted to go to school. I found myself being stared at. I spoke out, and tears came out. They kind of wanted to know, "Is that true, Antonia? Is that you?" They figured that was me. Even though there were other Latinas in the class—they didn't ask them—they asked me....

—Antonia Villalobos, Age 17

AMERICAN INDIAN ADOLESCENT

I'm a full-blooded American Indian; half Sioux, one-quarter Navajo and one-quarter Chickasaw. People will say things like, "How!" They'll shake your hands and make that weird noise come out. I think that's racist. [People] make fun of what they don't understand. People call me a *savage*. And they ask me stuff like: "Do you pray to God?" They might say, "Is it true that you people really sacrifice yourselves to the sun god?" I usually don't do anything about it. I just walk away. I'm glad that Native Americans are getting into the movie business. Finally. For too long, everyone was making films about Native Americans that didn't show the truth at all. They showed us as killers. But it's not true. We're very spiritual. [To avoid stereotyping] learn about it. Don't just put it out of your mind.

—Sundance Bekinnie, Age 13

ASIAN AMERICAN ADOLESCENT

Yeah, I stereotype people, but not seriously, not putting them in a box to stay forever. I couldn't or wouldn't do that because I know it's wrong, also because it has happened to me too often. Most people think that Asians are nerds or that all of us are smart. People stereotype me because of the color of my skin, and no one ever thinks I speak English or that I speak English well. Those are some of the stereotypes we [Asians] feel. People make fun of us all the time. It makes me feel awful. Sometimes awful sad, sometimes awful pissed off. I don't know how you can surpass this, it's been going on for years and I see no end in sight. I don't know about solutions; I don't think there are any solutions. Parents teach you prejudice and bias before you are out of the house and then you pass them on or use this information to judge people yourself.

—Raymond Carpio, Age 18

BIRACIAL AMERICAN ADOLESCENT

My mother is White and my father is Black. I've experienced stereotyping [when I've had] discussions about being Black. A lot of people feel my opinions are less valid than theirs because I'm not a "full" Black. You still get called names like *half-breed*. I used to get my hair done at this lady's house. She always used to say, "A lot of people like you think that they're better because your hair is like this—you have good hair, better hair than Black people." One day I said I thought my hair made me look like a *pickaninny*. She said, "You shouldn't say that kind of thing." But it was OK for her to call other Blacks n---- if she wanted to, because she was Black. But since I was mixed, I wasn't allowed to say that. I think mixed kids are left out. They're not thought of as a separate group. You're thought of as Black if you're mixed and that's it. These kids go through identity problems. [We] need more recognition. [We] feel a lot of rejection. I think there should be more groups, like Black heritage groups, biracial camps or self-help groups.

—Aburée Duggan, Age 16

Identity formation is impeded when the family fails to discuss ethnic or racial issues with children (Spencer & Markstrom-Adams, 1990). This is likely to happen when the parents are uncomfortable with issues related to race or ethnicity.

Interviewees from the same ethnic background may have different levels of identification with their ethnic group, reflected, in part, by how they wish to be addressed. For example, some prefer to be identified as African American rather than Black, others prefer Latino or Chicano over Hispanic, and still others prefer no specific ethnic minority group designation and simply want to be called American. In an interview reported in the *Los Angeles Times,* actress Whoopi Goldberg had this to say about being called African American:

"I don't hear people calling themselves Russian Americans. Everybody calls themselves American. My family and their grandparents and their grandparents built this country. This is mine. Four generations, five generations. I have a huge root that goes to the core. I've been to Africa. Completely different culture. This is my culture. And if I am only to be identified by what you see, which part of me are you seeing? The Chinese in me?" she asks, gesturing toward her eyes. "The Black?" Her hands go to her nose. "The Indian?" She touches her smile. (cited by Winer-Bernheimer, 1994, p. F5, with changes in notation)

Ethnic identification becomes particularly complex when individuals have a biracial heritage (Herring, 1992). One issue involves the transmission of a cultural heritage and an ethnic identity from the parents to their children. Parents may emphasize their children's membership in one or both groups, or they may simply consider them members of the human race and not focus on race or color.

A second issue involves how the larger community treats biracial children and their families—with acceptance or discrimination, for example.

CASE 8-2. MOLLY BYRD

I am a Heinz-57 American of Irish/Scandinavian/French descent and my husband is African American. We have raised six children. The issues that have arisen during our 20-plus years are far outweighed by questions we have been asked like: "What's it like being married to a Black man?" "Do these children belong to both of you?" "Did you meet your husband in the U.S.?" etc. I often tell people that love sees no color. I did not go out searching for someone Black to marry. I fell in love with a beautiful, wonderful and caring person with whom I have shared many things—from the birth of a child to the tragic death of a child. This man is our tower of strength, source of wisdom and always gives us his unconditional love.

I'll tell you what it's like being married to a Black man. It's heartbreaking when we go into a restaurant and the waiter refuses to look at my husband but asks me instead what we want to eat. It hurts when we're standing in line at the grocery store and the checker smiles and speaks to everyone except my husband. It was agonizing when my 17-year-old son asked us to sell his [new] truck because he was sick of being stopped by the police and asked, "Where did you get this car, boy?"

Interracial marriages can be wonderful and also heartbreaking. Let me offer this word to your readers. When you see someone who looks different than you, please try to do as Martin Luther King Jr. advised—judge him by the content of his character instead of the color of his skin. (Molly Byrd, 1994, p. B6, with changes in notation)

A third issue involves how biracial children integrate dual racial or cultural identifications.

CASE 8-3. SUE

Sue, the 9-year-old daughter of a Black mother and a White father, was from a wealthy eastern family. After growing up in a Black neighborhood and attending an exclusive primary school, she was enrolled in a West Coast public elementary school. Her first year was difficult because she preferred to socialize with the White students from similar backgrounds and felt that the Black students were very hostile to her. Eventually, she became very depressed and her academic productivity declined. She was referred to the counselor's office by her homeroom teacher after she did not respond to the teacher's questions about her poor attitude and interest. Sue confided to the counselor that she felt as if she was split between two worlds but belonged in neither. She expressed considerable anger at her parents "for treating me like I was White and not preparing me for the real world as a Black person." (Herring, 1992, p. 126)

I have a dream that my four little children will one day live in a nation where they will not be judged by the color of their skin but by the content of their character.

—Martin Luther King, Jr.

Health Care Practices

Depending on their degree of acculturation, members of ethnic minority groups in the United States may use both traditional and Western methods of healing. Those who use traditional healing methods may be reluctant to reveal their practices to Western health professionals for fear of being misunderstood or deprecated (Kumabe et al., 1985).

You will need to gain the family members' trust to learn about their attitudes toward health and illness and about their health and medical care practices. A key question is *What does the family believe causes illness or disease?* (Kumabe et al., 1985). For example, does the family view illness and disease as punishment from God for unacceptable behavior, as an invasion of the body by evil spirits, as a test of their religious faith or courage, or as a challenge to be overcome? Does the family accept illness as part of the life process, seek medical care, and follow medical prescriptions? Does the family have any folk beliefs or practices that conflict with tenets of Western medicine? These issues are discussed in Chapter 9 in connection with Black American, Hispanic American, Native American, and Asian American groups. The family's interpretation of why the child has an illness, disease, or problem will have a direct bearing on what is considered an appropriate intervention (Coll & Meyer, 1993). In addition, some healing practices may lead others to think that a child was maltreated (see Chapter 20).

Some ethnic minority groups, such as Asian Americans and Hispanic Americans, follow the "hot-cold theory" of health and diet (U.S. Department of Agriculture, 1986). These groups believe that diseases can be prevented and cured by balancing the body fluids, or "humors," between hot and cold.

These practices stem from the Greek theory of disease that considers illness to be the result of humoral imbalance causing the body to become too hot or too cold.... The "hot-cold theory" describes intrinsic properties of a food, beverage, or medicine and its effect on the body. It is not necessarily related to the spiciness or temperature of the substance. The classification of foods, beverages, and medicines as "hot" or "cold" varies within each cultural group. In general, warm or hot foods are believed to be easier to digest than cold or cool foods. Illnesses are treated with substances having the opposite property of the illness in order to achieve balance. Conditions thought to be caused by exposure to cold or chilling are cured by "hot" medicines as well as by ingesting "hot" foods and beverages. The reverse is true of illnesses brought about by exposure to heat. (p. 5)

Ethnic Minorities' Use of Mental Health and Medical Services

Ethnic minority groups' use of mental health and medical services may be affected by the following issues, several of which apply to all people:

1. What are the group's cultural values? For example, does the group prefer to solve or treat its problems within the family or extended family?
2. What is the group's attitude toward mental health and illness, physical health and illness, psychological treatment, and medical treatment? For example, does the group accept the need for treatment of medical illnesses but not for treatment of psychological illnesses? Does the group view mental illness as carrying a stigma? Do members of the group fear being ostracized if other members find out that they are receiving treatment for mental health problems?
3. What is the availability of medical and mental health services? For example, does the group face a long waiting list to obtain required services?
4. How accessible are the medical and mental health services? For example, where are the facilities, and what transportation services are available?
5. Who is providing the services? For example, are the practitioners professionals, paraprofessionals, or recent graduates? Will the group accept help from practitioners who are members of another ethnic group or who are females or who are young?
6. How culturally relevant are the treatment programs? For example, are the treatment programs willing to recognize and use the group's cultural practices?

Factors that may make it difficult for members of ethnic minority groups to use the mainstream health care system include the following (Kumabe et al., 1985): perceptions of health and illness that differ from those of the majority culture, unfamiliarity with the clinic or hospital setting, fear of Western medical practices, distrust of Western health care providers because of the prejudice they have experienced, and fear of being discovered and deported if they are illegal immigrants. Some ethnic minority group members will seek treatment from the mainstream health care system *only* when they have exhausted their own traditional remedies. At times of stress, it may be comforting to turn to familiar cultural and religious roots.

Some ethnic minority families (and majority families as well) may wonder whether an interviewer who is a female or young or not a "doctor" or who is from another ethnic group possesses sufficient skill and training to help them. If you have any of these characteristics, you may have to show the family that you are a competent professional (or professional-in-training).

If the family subscribes to mainstream medical and psychological practices *and* to traditional methods, *consider encouraging them to seek help from both services.* A combined treatment approach may be the most beneficial for these families (Kumabe et al., 1985).

Culture and Communication Styles

Let's now consider how verbal and nonverbal communication styles may lead to difficulties in cross-cultural interviews.

Verbal communication difficulties. You may encounter communication barriers when you work with ethnic minority clients (Kumabe et al., 1985). Ethnic minority clients, as well as majority clients, may be mystified by complex medical or psychological terminology. They may be reticent about discussing a personal or family problem with an outsider because it "may be perceived as a reflection of personal inadequacy and as a stigma upon the entire family" (Kumabe et al., 1985, p. 130). This is especially true for some Asian American groups. Consequently, be sensitive to any subtle cues that interviewees give you about their willingness to talk about personal issues. If you fail to recognize their preferences and mistakenly urge them to be open and direct, they may resent your suggestion and become silent.

Communication difficulties arise when ethnic minority clients view health care professionals as authority figures. In the presence of authority figures, they may become passive and inhibited in their communications and reluctant to ask questions or express disagreement (Kumabe et al., 1985).

Ethnic minority clients may respond at their own pace to your questions (Tharp, 1989). Some Native American children, for example, prefer to wait before responding to questions. If they feel hurried, they may resent your intrusion. Do not perceive this hesitation as refusal to talk to you or as resistance. Rather, respect their need for silence between your question and their answer (see discussion of silence in Chapters 2 and 3). In contrast, some Native Hawaiians may interrupt your questions or comments because they want to show their involvement; in such cases, don't interpret their interruptions as a sign of rudeness.

Problems also may arise when interviewers misinterpret the interviewee's communications. The following amusing fictional excerpt shows how misinterpretations can occur when an interviewer is not familiar with the interviewee's jargon. The exaggerated excerpt illustrates the danger of making interpretations and diagnoses when you do not fully understand the interviewee's language.

IE: I was at home and this cat I know came in and asked to borrow some lettuce from me so he could buy some tickets to the show. (IR quickly writes in his notebook "Delusions that cats can talk and that lettuce can be used as money.")

IE: Then, I was shooting the breeze with my chick and the pigs came along and took us to jail. (IR jots "Fantasies of using a chicken to shoot breezes and delusional thinking that pigs can take people to jail.")

IE: I didn't have on my best rags, and they wouldn't let me use a wire to call. (IR jots "Claims to wear rags of various quality and believes wires can be used to make phone calls. Definite signs of delusions.")

IE: Before the pigs came, I smoked some horse while my chick got high on snow. (IR jots "Bizarre ideation in thinking that he could smoke a horse and misperceptions that people can use snow to change their mood. Continues to make references to pigs and chicks in his fantasies. Signs of distorted thinking and confusion.")

(*Diagnosis:* Paranoid schizophrenia with delusional material, distorted thinking, and confusion. Psychological treatment needed. Prognosis is guarded.)

Here is the translation in standard English of what the interviewer should have heard:

I was at home and a guy I know asked to borrow some money to buy tickets to the show. Then, I was talking to my girlfriend and the police came along and took us to jail. I didn't have on my best clothes, and they wouldn't let me use a phone to call. Before the police came, I smoked some heroin while my girlfriend got high on cocaine.

Interviewers and interviewees may give symptoms different interpretations, depending on their group membership. For example, behavior viewed as hypersensitive or paranoid by a middle-class Anglo American interviewer may be viewed as reality-oriented coping by a non–Anglo American interviewer or interviewee.

Language may pose a problem in the initial family interview, particularly when the family members have different levels of language proficiency in their native language and in English. If the parents prefer to speak Spanish and the child prefers to speak English, for example, you may have difficulty knowing which language to use and whether to use an interpreter. When the child's command of English is better than that of the parents, the child may take advantage of the parents' limited language skills to control the flow of information to the parents. In such situations, the child becomes powerful, thus reversing the usual parent-child relationship. Later in the chapter, we discuss working with an interpreter.

Nonverbal communication difficulties. Nonverbal communications are another potential source of communication difficulties in cross-cultural interviews. Areas of difficulty may involve perception and use of personal and interpersonal space (*proxemics*); bodily movements (such as facial expressions, posture, and gestures), characteristics of movement, and eye contact (*kinesics*); and vocal cues used in talking (*paralanguage*). Misunderstandings of nonverbal communication contribute to sustaining stereotypic interpersonal judgments. Examples of difficulties in nonverbal communication follow. (This material was adapted primarily from Sue, 1990.)

Proxemics. Hispanic Americans and Black Americans tend to stand closer when conversing with others than do White Americans. When interviewing members of these ethnic minority groups, White American interviewers may back away from the interviewees. If they do so, their behavior may be misinterpreted as aloof, cold, haughty, or as expressing a desire not to communicate, or as a sign of superiority. White American interviewers, in turn, may mistakenly view the ethnic client's behavior as inappropriately intimate or as a sign of pushiness or aggressiveness.

Some ethnic minority groups will be sensitive to the spatial arrangements in the interview. "Chinese people feel more comfortable in a side-by-side or right-angle arrangement and may feel uncomfortable when placed in a face-to-face situation. [Anglo] Americans prefer to sit face-to-face or at right angles to each other" (Giger & Davidhizar, 1991, p. 363).

Kinesics. Cultures may interpret the same gestures in different ways. For example, some cultures interpret the "thumbs-up" gesture as obscene, and the American "bye-bye" gesture means "come here" to people from Southeast Asia. Cultural upbringing also shapes how people move their bodies. For example, people from Northern Europe tend to hold their torsos rigidly, whereas those from the Caribbean tend to move their bodies more fluidly (Dresser, 1996a).

White Americans usually view smiling as an indication of positive affect. However, to Asian Americans, smiling may suggest weakness. They consider restraint of feeling to be a sign of maturity and wisdom. Thus, White American interviewers may assume that Asian American interviewees are out of touch with their feelings when, in reality, they are following cultural patterns. Many Native Americans and Japanese avoid eye contact as a sign of respect or deference. In such cases, it is wrong to assume that avoidance of eye contact indicates "inattentiveness, rudeness, aggressiveness, shyness, or low intelligence" (Sue, 1990, p. 426).

Black Americans tend to make greater eye contact when speaking than when listening. The reverse is true of White Americans—they tend to make more eye contact when listening than when speaking. For Black Americans, attentiveness is signaled by mere physical proximity. When Black listeners do not look at the speaker, it is wrong to interpret their behavior as sullen, resistant, or uncooperative. And when White listeners look at the speaker, it is wrong to interpret their behavior as unduly scrutinizing the speaker.

Japanese people tend to present a blank, nearly motionless facial expression that reveals little of their inner feelings to the Western observer. Westerners, in contrast, tend to keep their forehead and eyebrows constantly in motion as they speak. Thus, "simply because of the greater stillness of the Japanese face there tends to be a large amount of Japanese-Western miscommunication: The Japanese are regarded as noncomprehending or even antagonistic" (Morsbach, 1988, p. 206).

Paralanguage. Silence, for Asian Americans, is traditionally a sign of respect for elders. When an Asian American speaker becomes silent, it may not be a cue for the listener to begin talking. "Rather, it may indicate a desire to continue speaking after making a particular point. At other times, silence may be a sign of politeness and respect, rather than a lack of desire to continue speaking" (Sue, 1990, p. 426). Native Americans also may prefer to remain silent in some situations as an act of patience and respect. Thus, for some ethnic minority groups, do not interpret reticence in speaking out as a sign of ignorance or lack of motivation. Sometimes, if you break the silence, you may discourage further elaboration.

Asian Americans, Native Americans, and some Hispanic Americans value indirectness in communications. Use of euphemisms and ambiguity serves as a way of not hurting the feelings of or embarrassing the other person. Native Americans perceive the asking of direct questions (as occurs when you are taking a social history) as rude or incompetent or as an invasion of individual privacy. They prefer that the interviewer share personal information about himself or herself (self-disclosure) or deduce the problem by instinct. In contrast, White Americans accept direct interrogation and an impersonal interviewer style (Everett, Proctor, & Cartmell, 1983).

Comment on Background Considerations

When you interview children and parents who are members of ethnic minority groups, be prepared to cover issues that go beyond those covered by a traditional psychosocial history. You will need to consider issues related to ethnic and racial identity, acculturation, language, changing family patterns, sex roles, religious and traditional beliefs, customs for dealing with crisis and change, racism, poverty, social class, health care practices, and the interactions among these factors. Children and parents who maintain strong ties to their culture, particularly recent refugees or immigrants, may be influenced by indigenous cultural beliefs and practices that affect the symptoms they develop, how they understand the symptoms, their coping mechanisms, their help-seeking behavior, their use of services, and their satisfaction with services and clinical outcomes (Chung & Lin, 1994). What you learn about these and related issues will help you formulate a diagnosis, develop an intervention plan, and conduct interviews.

Interviewers have the difficult task of evaluating whether behaviors that suggest personality or temperament problems in the majority group reflect similar problems in ethnic minority groups. For example, when ethnic clients remain silent, speak softly, or avoid extended eye contact, are they revealing shyness, weakness, or reluctance to speak or are they exhibiting politeness and respect? Does expressing emotions in an indirect, understated way with little emotion suggest denial, lack of affect, lack of awareness of one's feelings, deceptiveness, or resistance, or do such expressions suggest a wish to sustain interpersonal harmony (Uba, 1994)? The failure to understand cultural practices can lead to incorrect diagnoses and ineffective interventions.

DYNAMICS OF CROSS-ETHNIC AND CROSS-CULTURAL INTERVIEWING

Let's now look at what may happen in cross-ethnic and cross-cultural interviewing. In these situations, interviews will suffer if interviewers display patronizing attitudes, fail to recognize the value of interviewees' traditional customs and mores, or are obsessed with the interviewees' cultures (LaFromboise, Trimble, & Mohatt, 1990). Interviewers are patronizing when they expect the worst from interviewees or lower their expectations for interviewees. Trust will be difficult to establish when interviewees fear that interviewers will try to influence their value structure, thereby separating them from their own people and traditions. They want help with their problems, not help in giving up cultural traditions. Alienation is the likely result when interviewers focus too much on interviewees' customs, mores, and traditions.

Majority Interviewer with Minority Interviewee

Difficulties in a majority interviewer–minority interviewee relationship stem from several sources. Because of racial antagonism, minority interviewees may find it difficult to react to majority interviewers as individuals, and vice versa. Minority interviewees may view majority interviewers with suspicion and distrust, as part of the hostile majority world. And, because interviewers who are from majority groups may have been encouraged through education and training to view prejudice as unacceptable, they may deny or suppress negative reactions toward interviewees who are from minority groups. When majority interviewers begin to feel guilty about their own racial and class identity and allow these feelings to intrude on the relationship, difficulties may arise. For example, majority interviewers may miss subtle cues given by minority interviewees, may be too accepting of behaviors, or may fail to probe sensitive topics.

Misinterpretations in intercultural communication will occur when minority interviewees view majority interviewers as immature, rude, and lacking in finesse because they want to get to the point quickly. Similarly, majority interviewers should not view minority interviewees as evasive and afraid to confront their problems because they communicate indirectly.

Majority interviewers must recognize that minority interviewees will be judging their behavior. If majority interviewers speak bluntly and directly, some minority interviewees (such as Asian Americans) may view this behavior as socially disruptive, embarrassing, or even hurtful (Uba, 1994). Minority interviewees also will be frustrated when the social cues they give are not noticed by majority interviewers.

Minority Interviewer with Majority Interviewee

Interviewers who are from minority groups may experience difficulties in their relationship with interviewees who are from majority groups because of the sociocultural aspects of minority-majority interpersonal relations. Conflicts may arise if majority interviewees avoid the race issue, deprecate the interviewer, have special admiration for the interviewer, or view the interviewer as all-forgiving or uncritical. Minority interviewers, on the other hand, may be unsympathetic or punitive because of hostility toward nonminorities, or they may overcompensate by being too permissive (denying their

hostility toward nonminorities or over-identifying with them). Any of these dynamics can affect the interview process.

Minority Interviewer with Minority Interviewee of the Same Group

Interviewers who are from the same minority group as interviewees may be in the best position to obtain reliable and valid information. Middle-class minority interviewers, however, may have some difficulties with lower-class minority interviewees. Difficulties arise when interviewers (a) cannot accept interviewees because of the interviewees' class, (b) become defensive, (c) over-identify with interviewees, or (d) view work with minority interviewees as lower in status and priority than work with majority interviewees. Similarly, difficulties arise when minority interviewees perceive minority interviewers as (a) collaborators with the majority community, (b) objects of jealousy because of their success in the majority community, (c) less competent than majority interviewers, or (d) too removed from their problems.

If minority interviewers believe that minority interviewees' problems primarily stem from sociopolitical or economic factors, interviewers may dismiss the interviewees' psychological problems and instead deliver lectures about social-class oppression (Hunt, 1987). Minority interviewers walk a fine line between over-identification and objectivity when interviewing minority interviewees of the same ethnic background.

Minority Interviewer with Minority Interviewee of a Different Group

Interviewers who are from a minority group may experience difficulties in their relationship with interviewees who are from a different minority group. Problems may be associated with racial antagonism, depending on how the groups have been getting along in society at large. Interviewees may be envious of the interviewers, believing, for example, that the interviewers have been given special treatment because of their group membership. Interviewers might have similar feelings about the interviewees. However, because they are likely to have had similar experiences with racism and discrimination, ethnic minority interviewers may have increased empathy for ethnic minority interviewees' situations and problems.

Exercise 8-1. Do You Agree with Forest Whitaker?

In an interview reported in the *Los Angeles Times* on November 12, 1995, Forest Whitaker, the movie actor and director, was quoted as saying:

It's a difficult time, race-wise, emotionally and psychologically, for people. As a result, many people are acting violent or turning apathetic.... This society is one big dysfunctional family, with the parents—those who are more financially in charge—beating up on the children—those who aren't financially in charge. They, in turn, beat up on themselves and others. All the minority races are in the position of this abused child. (p. 70)

Do you agree with Forest Whitaker? Was the racial climate at the time the article was written dramatically different from that in other decades in the last half of the twentieth century? If so, in what way was it different? Is American society dysfunctional? Do people with wealth abuse those who are poor? Should people from minority groups be equated with children who are abused? Compare your answers with those of other students in your class.

No oppressive White person can hurt me as much as a Black sister, for no oppressive White person knows me so well where to hurt me. Turn this around and it is a Black sister's love and support that can allow me to soar because her power and strength is a reflection of my own strength and power.

—Anonymous (Cited by J. van Heeswyk and J. Hibbert)

Possible Distortions in Cross-Ethnic and Cross-Cultural Interviews

Preoccupation with and heightened sensitivity to ethnic differences may lead to distortions, guardedness, and evasiveness on the part of interviewees, and to guardedness, failure to probe, defensiveness, and feelings of intimidation on the part of interviewers. Because responses given by both interviewees and interviewers require subtle forms of cognitive activity—such as summarizing one's opinion to oneself, estimating the listener's probable reaction, and then deciding whether to convey the opinion accurately to the listener—there is always the potential for both interviewees and interviewers to distort opinions, attitudes, and even facts.

Do some interviewees replace genuine feelings with a facade of submissiveness, pleasure, impassivity, or humility? Can interviewers be genuine and avoid patronizing? Is any form of social distance between interviewers and interviewees likely to create difficulties with rapport and communication? These and similar questions are a matter of special concern in cross-ethnic, cross-cultural, and cross-class interviews.

Comment on Cross-Ethnic and Cross-Cultural Interviewing

Mental health professionals are not immune to racism and to harboring *stereotypes. It is your responsibility to ensure that any such views you may have do not adversely affect the information you obtain from children and parents.* Stereotypes change, and you must monitor them constantly lest they interfere with your ability to conduct a meaningful interview.

No matter what generalizations are made about ethnic relations and about the interviewer-interviewee relationship in particular, each interview involves two unique individuals. It is their specific attitudes, values, experiences, and behavior that will determine whether racism and bias enter the interview. Even interviewers and interviewees from the same ethnic minority group or majority group may be mismatched if they have different values. And, conversely, interviewers and interviewees from different ethnic minority groups or from the majority group can work cooperatively when they have similar values and speak the same language. Usually, interviewers will be effective when they are tolerant and accepting of interviewees, despite value differences. Your goal is to establish a professional relationship characterized by trust and acceptance with people of all ethnic groups.

Exercise 8-2. Confronting Prejudice

Read the following vignette. Then, answer the questions that follow. Compare your answers both with those suggested in the exercise and with those of your classmates. This exercise was adapted from Kavanagh and Kennedy (1992).

Helen Lafty is a Black American social worker assigned to a private medical floor of a hospital and is a supervisor of an Anglo American social work student. Ms. Lafty and the student entered a patient's room. She introduced herself and the student to the patient by giving their names only. After a few minutes, both Ms. Lafty and the student left the room. Later, Ms. Lafty returned to the room to ask the patient how she was doing. The patient asked Ms. Lafty to "go get the real social worker so she can talk to me."

1. What assumptions did the patient make?
2. How would you feel if you were Ms. Lafty?
3. How could Ms. Lafty effectively manage this situation with minimal risk to the social worker–patient relationship and to her personal integrity?

Suggested Answers
1. The patient assumed that the Anglo American student was the social worker.
2. Some of you may feel angry, frustrated, or upset because of the patient's insensitivity. Others may feel no strong emotion and excuse the patient's remark.
3. She could say "I believe you misunderstood. I am the social worker. The person you met earlier with me is a student-in-training at the hospital."

Exercise 8-3. Understanding Your Culture

Cultures have different attitudes about child care, discipline, eating, gender roles, decision making, support networks, influential sources, family values and beliefs, handling illness, economic and career choices, education, and so forth.

As you read the following questions, think about how your family dealt with each area when you were a child. How do you think your answers compare with those of other people in your culture and with those of people in other cultures? How could failure to recognize cultural differences lead to misunderstandings or misjudgments about other people? And how will an understanding of your values and traditions help you in understanding the values and traditions of other cultures? (The material in this exercise was reprinted, with changes in notation and with additions, with permission of the publisher and authors, from J. S. Rycus, R. C. Hughes, and J. K. Garrison, *Child Protective Services: A Training Manual,* pp. 199, 201, copyright 1989, Child Welfare League of America.)

Child Care

1. Who took care of you when your mother or father had to go out?
2. At what age were you first left alone?
3. At what age were children in your family given responsibility to take care of the other children in the family?
4. At what age were you allowed to take care of younger children in your family when your parents weren't at home?

Discipline

5. What form of discipline did your family use most often?
6. Did this form of discipline affect how you felt about your parents?
7. In what way did this discipline affect your feelings toward your parents?
8. Were there any forms of discipline that your parents wouldn't use because your parents thought they would be harmful to you?
9. (If yes) What were these forms of discipline?

Eating

10. What were the family rules about meals?
11. Did everyone sit as a group to eat together?
12. Did your mother or father cook meals?
13. Did the children cook?
14. Did the children serve food to the other family members?
15. Could you eat whatever you wanted, when you chose?
16. What foods did you frequently eat?

Roles

(For questions 17 through 19) Did your family have different expectations:
17. for different children in the family?
18. for older as opposed to younger children?
19. for boys as opposed to girls?

Decision-Making

20. How were decisions made in your family?
21. Which decisions did your mother make?
22. Which decisions did your father make?
23. Which decisions did your mother and father make jointly?
24. Which decisions were children allowed to make for themselves?
25. (If relevant) What influence did your extended family, grandparents, or other relatives living in the home have on decision making?

Support Networks

(For questions 26 through 32) In times of need or trouble:
26. did your family help itself?
27. did your family turn to your immediate, close, extended family?
28. did your family turn to a wide range of extended family and friends?
29. did your family turn to a church group?
30. did your family turn to the larger community?
31. did your family turn to mental health professionals?
32. did your family turn to another group not mentioned above?
33. If so, what group did your family turn to?

Influential Sources

34. Did adults other than your parents sometimes care for you or have a strong influence on your development? (If yes, go to question 35; if no, go to question 37.)
35. Who were these adults?
36. How did you feel about being cared for by people other than your parents?
37. What was your relationship with your relatives?
38. What part did aunts, uncles, cousins, grandparents, non-blood family, godparents, etc., play in your life?

Family Values and Beliefs

(For questions 39 through 46) What were your family's attitudes about:
39. respecting your elders?
40. sex outside marriage?
41. pregnancy outside marriage?
42. people who didn't have regular jobs?
43. people on welfare?
44. talking to people outside the family about family matters?
45. money and finances?
46. other ethnic and religious groups?
47. What were the major life goals your parents had for you?
48. Which of your family's values and patterns of behavior do you still follow?
49. Which of your family's values and patterns of behavior do you not follow?

Illnesses

50. Who took care of you when you were sick?
51. What was your family's attitude toward health care providers?
52. What was your family's attitude toward taking medicine?
53. What is your attitude toward health care providers?
54. What is your attitude toward taking medicine?

Economic and Career Choices

55. Who was the breadwinner in the family?
56. What was your family's attitude toward women working outside the home?
57. What influence did your family have in deciding the careers of family members?

Education

(For questions 58 through 62) What were your family's attitudes about:
58. attending open houses at school?

59. the value of a formal education?
60. helping children with their homework?
61. children going to college?
62. girls and boys going to school and studying for a profession?

Human beings are more alike than unalike, and what is true anywhere is true everywhere, yet I encourage travel to as many destinations as possible.... Perhaps travel cannot prevent bigotry, but by demonstrating that all peoples laugh, cry, eat, worry, and die, it can introduce the idea that if we try to understand each other, we may even become friends.

—Maya Angelou

INTERPRETERS

When you interview a child or parent who speaks a language you do not speak, you must use an interpreter. Be careful, however, when you use an interpreter, particularly during clinical assessment or forensic interviews where sensitive issues are involved, such as child sexual abuse or child physical abuse and neglect (see Chapters 20 through 23, for example). Language usage can vary depending on economic status, geographical differences, and so forth. Although it may not be intentional, interpreters may delete information or make other changes and embellishments in the translations that distort what you and the interviewee say. These distortions may lead to inaccurate information.

Before you use an interpreter, ask the child about his or her language preference. Also, ask the parents and, if possible, the child's teacher the questions shown in Table 8-3. *Recognize that no matter how carefully the interpreter makes the translation, the interview is likely to be ineffective if you and the interpreter are not familiar with the interviewee's culture, values, and ideology.*

If you use an interpreter, ask the interpreter to inform the child and parents about her or his role, that she or he is acting as your agent, and that she or he will keep all information confidential. Also have the interpreter tell them that you want to get accurate information, to explain the services clearly, and to make them comfortable in the interview. Use of an interpreter will increase the time needed to complete the interview; you must schedule accordingly and should consider having more than one session.

Even if the family members speak English as a second language, offer them the services of an interpreter because they may have minimal proficiency in English. Sometimes interviewees switch languages during the interview, in a process called "code switching." For example, interviewees may change from their primary language to English to discuss topics that would be upsetting if discussed in their primary language (Bond & Lai, 1986).

Table 8-3
Informal Assessment of Language Preference

Questions for Parents
1. In what language do you speak to (child's name)?
2. In what language does your (husband, wife) speak with (child's name)?
3. In what languages do you speak with your (husband, wife)?
4. In what languages does (child's name) speak to you?
5. In what language does (child's name) speak to (his, her) (father, mother)?
6. In what language does (child's name) speak to (his, her) (sisters, brothers)?
7. What language does (child's name) prefer to speak at school?
8. In what language are the television programs that (child's name) watches?
9. In what language do you read stories to (child's name)?
10. In what language does (child's name) prefer to be given psychological or educational tests?

Questions for Teacher
11. What language does (child's name) use in the classroom?
12. In what language can (child's name) read?
13. In what language does (child's name) speak with (his, her) classmates?
14. What language does (child's name) use on the playground?
15. In what language does (child's name) write?
16. Overall, how competent is (child's name) in English?
17. Overall, how competent is (child's name) in (preferred language)?

You should be sure to obtain permission from the child and parents to use an interpreter. *Also, when you write your report or make notes in the interviewee's chart, always note that you used an interpreter.* This is especially important if you quote the interviewee.

Difficulties in Using an Interpreter

The following difficulties may arise when interpreters are used:

1. *Failure to reveal symptoms.* Interpreters may not reveal symptoms they believe portray the child or parent in an unfavorable light. Taboo topics for Asian American interpreters, for example, are sexual matters, financial information, suicidal thoughts, homicidal thoughts, and material disrespectful to the interviewer. An interpreter hearing information about these topics may omit details, substitute details, reformulate details, or change the focus of the communication. For example, the interpreter may try to make

sense out of disorganized statements made by the interviewee and thus prevent you from getting a clear idea of the interviewee's mental state.

2. *Mistrust of interpreter.* Some children and parents may be uncomfortable because of the interpreter's age, sex, level of education, relationship to them, or mere presence. They also may distrust the interpreter, fear being judged by the interpreter, fear that they will be misinterpreted, or fear loss of confidentiality.

3. *Preaching to interviewees.* Some interpreters, if they believe that the child has strayed from their culture, may preach to the child and parents about the need to follow traditions.

4. *Unequivalent concepts.* Some concepts either have no equivalent in other languages or are difficult to translate. Thus, the meaning of important phrases may be lost in translation.

5. *Dialectical differences.* Translations usually are made into a standard language, as translators necessarily have only a limited ability to provide for dialectical or regional variations. For example, the appropriate translation of the word *kite* in Spanish may be *cometa, huila, volantin, papalote,* or *chiringa,* depending on the speaker's country of origin.

6. *Mixture of two languages.* The language familiar to children from ethnic minority groups may be a combination of two languages. For Spanish-speaking children, this combination may be "Pocho," "pidgin," "Spanglish," or "Tex-Mex." In such cases, a monolingual translation may be inappropriate. Here are some examples of words that combine English and Spanish: *raite* (ride), *raiteros* (drivers), *lonche* (lunch), *dompe* (dump), *yonke* (junk), *dame un quebrazo* (give me a break), and *los baggies* (baggy jeans).

7. *Regional variations.* Some words have different meanings for various ethnic minority groups that share a similar language. For example, *toston* means a half-dollar to a Mexican American child but a squashed section of a fried banana to a Puerto Rican child or Cuban child. Some words differ in meaning not only across countries but within a country as well. For example, the word *guila* means sunny in Sonora, Mexico, but in Mexico City it means prostitute.

8. *Change in difficulty level.* The level of difficulty of words may change because of translation. For example, *animal domestico,* the Spanish equivalent of the common English word *pet,* is an uncommon phrase in Spanish.

9. *Alteration of meaning.* Translation can alter the meanings of words. For example, seemingly harmless English words may translate into Spanish profanity. *Huevos* is the literal translation of the word *egg,* but the Spanish term *huevon* has more earthy connotations. The context determines the meaning of the word.

10. *Use of colloquial words.* Translators may use colloquial words for more formal words and, in the process, inadvertently offend some interviewees. For example, use of the Spanish words *pata* for foot and *espinizo* for back, which are more appropriate for animals than for humans, may offend interviewees who prefer the more formal words *pie* and *espalda,* respectively.

Examples of an Interpreter's Incorrect Paraphrasing

Here is an example of an interpreter, working with a Chinese-speaking interviewee, who incorrectly rephrased both the interviewer's question and the interviewee's reply (Marcos, 1979, p. 173, with changes in notation; IT = Interpreter).

IR: What kind of moods have you been in recently?
IT: How have you been feeling?
IE: No, I don't have any more pain, my stomach is fine, and I can eat much better since I take the medication.
IT: He says that he feels fine, no problem.

In the following example, the interpreter tended to normalize the thought processes of the interviewee, thereby preventing the interviewer from obtaining an accurate picture of the interviewee's thoughts (Marcos, 1979, p. 173, with changes in notation).

IR: What about worries, do you have many worries?
IT: Is there anything that bothers you?
IE: I know, I know that God is with me. I'm not afraid, they cannot get me. (Pause) I'm wearing these new pants and I feel protected. I feel good; I don't get headaches anymore.
IT: He says that he is not afraid, he feels good, he doesn't have headaches anymore.

Suggestions for Working with an Interpreter

Here are some suggestions for working with an interpreter:

1. *Selecting interpreter.* Select an interpreter who is thoroughly familiar with the interviewee's language and with the linguistic variations or dialect used by the child's ethnic group.

2. *Briefing interpreter.* Brief the interpreter thoroughly on issues that may affect his or her role. For example, discuss with the interpreter *before* you begin the interview the (a) goals of the evaluation, (b) areas you want to cover, (c) need for addressing sensitive topics, (d) level of competence the interpreter has in both languages, (e) attitude of the interpreter toward the interviewee and possible problem areas, and (f) need for accurate translations. Stress the importance of neutrality, not reacting judgmentally to what the interviewee says or to what you say, transmitting all the information between the parties, and the confidentiality of the proceedings. With some interpreters, you may need to

deal with their feelings and reactions, especially when you discuss extremely sensitive issues such as child maltreatment or rape. Also, the gender of the interpreter may be an issue if there are cultural taboos against males and females discussing certain topics. This issue should be discussed before the interview.

3. *Discussing technical terms.* Discuss beforehand any technical terms and concepts that may pose a problem for translation. Ideally, the interpreter should be familiar with terms related to psychological disorders and medical disorders. Encourage the interpreter to conduct a sentence-by-sentence interpretation to ensure that each translated phrase is equivalent to the phrase in the original language, to refrain from giving explanations that you did not ask him or her for, and to mirror your affective tone as closely as possible.

4. *Practicing with interpreter.* Practice with an interpreter *before* the interview to help the interpreter develop good skills as an interpreter.

5. *Selecting nonfamily member as interpreter.* Use an interpreter who is not a family member, a family friend, or someone the family knows because of possible sensitive subject matter or conflicts of interest.

6. *Using interpreter as an assistant.* Use the interpreter as an assistant, not as a co-interviewer. You don't want the interpreter to formulate his or her own questions, unless the interpreter is a qualified mental health professional and you give him or her permission to do so.

7. *Positioning interpreter.* Face the interviewee when you talk to him or her. Position the interpreter at your side, speak as though the interviewee can understand you, speak in a normal tone of voice, use facial expressions that are not forced or faked, use short sentences, and be attentive to the interviewee's reactions, gestures, and facial expressions. If the interviewee looks confused or puzzled, try to determine at what point the translation may have gone wrong or whether other factors have interfered with the communication. Do not interrupt the interpreter.

8. *Talking to interpreter.* Avoid talking to the interpreter about the family in the presence of family members.

9. *Encouraging attention to details.* Encourage the interpreter to tell you about the paralinguistic aspects of the interviewee's speech—such as cries, laughter, sighs, stuttering, and melodic voice changes—and where these occurred.

10. *Rephrasing words.* Ask the interpreter to alert you to specific translated words that might be too difficult for the interviewee to understand. You then can rephrase as needed.

11. *Summarizing and confirming.* Summarize what you have learned at appropriate points, and ask the interviewee to confirm your understanding.

12. *Reviewing interpreter's performance.* Meet with the interpreter after you complete the interview to discuss problems that he or she encountered and to review his or her performance. Include in your report the name and qualifications of the interpreter and any reservations about the reliability and validity of the information you obtained.

13. *Using interpreter in future sessions.* Use the same interpreter in any future sessions with the interviewee and in the post-assessment interview, assuming that the interpreter performed adequately.

After you complete the interview, evaluate the adequacy and the quality of the information. Does the information make sense? Do you believe you have obtained all of the relevant information you need? Are you puzzled by any details? Do you think the interpreter left out some information? Do you believe that the interpreter did her or his job well?

In the post-assessment interview, also evaluate the family's understanding of the results and the planned intervention program. Do they seem puzzled? If so, why? Ask them to repeat the major findings and recommendations.

Here is an example of how bilingual parents had difficulty understanding their son's medical diagnosis and how their problem was resolved (Holden & Serrano, 1989).

CASE 8-4. JOSÉ'S PARENTS

During rounds in the Pediatric Intensive Care Unit, the nurse asked the child psychiatrist to see the parents of José, a 2-year-old boy with a tracheotomy. José was irritable, combative, clinging, and had to be sedated or restrained. The parents were very concerned about his behavior. When the psychiatrist met with José's parents, who were bilingual (marginally fluent in English and fluent in Spanish), they talked of feeling somewhat frightened and of being confused about José's behavior: "He isn't like this normally." The parents wondered if he was angry or depressed about being in a strange place and being away from home. When the psychiatrist discussed her conversation with the pediatric resident, the resident stated that he had explained to the parents that José's behavior was secondary to hypoxia and other problems associated with the illness. He was surprised and angry that the parents could not understand or accept his explanation.

The parents did not feel comfortable requesting additional information or clarification, as they believed it would be disrespectful to ask "too much." The psychiatrist recommended that a bilingual pediatric resident join the pediatric resident in reviewing Jos's condition with the parents. During the meeting, the parents experienced considerable relief; being more informed, they could participate more fully in their child's care. (adapted from p. 194)

Exercise 8-4. Evaluating an Interpreter

Read the following case, which contains an interview segment, and evaluate the interpreter's performance. Did the interpreter make any errors? If so, what were they? Compare your answers with those in the Comments section. This exercise was adapted from Vasquez and Javier (1991).

A 40-year-old Hispanic American woman requested assistance in handling her difficulties with her 14-year-old mildly retarded son. He had just been hospitalized for an acute psychotic condition. After an argument with his younger brother, he had destroyed several items in their home.

The mother appeared anxious and tense as she talked about her son. She spoke in a loud voice and with pressured speech, as if in great need to talk to someone. Her mood was depressed, and she cried frequently. The following is an excerpt of the interview that took place through an interpreter. The interpreter's comments to the mother were in Spanish.

IR: Can you tell me about your son's problems?

IT: The doctor has already read your record, but could you tell him how are things with your son? Explain to him a bit more about your relationship with your son.

IE: What is it that happened?

IT: Aha! Yes, tell him what happened, what upsets you or makes you anxious.

IE: Well, I have a 14-year-old son who gives me a great deal of trouble at home. Anything makes him upset and next thing you know, the whole house is a mess. Right now…I don't want to even remember. He also hangs around with the wrong crowd at the hotel where we live…has picked up vices from them and gets himself in trouble with the neighbors. The worst thing is that he does not show any respect—he does not pay attention. In the meantime, my nerves have gotten bad, out of control.

IT: She has a 14-year-old son who has been giving her a hard time. He has been hanging out with the wrong people. He is now into drugs. She lives in a hotel, and he has been giving problems there.

IR: You are unhappy with how your son is treating you?

IT: The doctor wants to know if you feel sad.

IE: Yes. I feel like crying almost every night. Sometimes I wonder if it is better to be dead. I have not been able to sleep for two nights because of my son. I just need to sleep for a while.

IT: She said yes and has thought that it was better killing herself. She said that only in this way she was going to be able to rest.

IE: When was the last time you had these thoughts?

IT: And when was the last time you felt this way?

IE: Last night.

Comments

Vasquez and Javier (1991) pointed out that the interpreter lost perspective of his role and assumed the role of the interviewer. He introduced his own questions and condensed and distorted the mother's statements. Here are several examples of his errors. First, the mother said that her son has "vices," not that he uses drugs. Second, the interpreter omitted some important material, such as the mother's statement that the son does not show respect. Third, the interpreter changed "I wonder if it is better to be dead" into "She…has thought that it was better killing herself." This change may have led the interviewer to believe that the mother was suicidal when, in fact, the mother may have had no suicidal wish at all. The mother's comment is typical of the reaction of many Hispanic American individuals when they are faced with stressful situations and likely reflects her feelings of exhaustion and a wish to withdraw from the interaction, rather than an active decision to terminate her life.

THINKING THROUGH THE ISSUES

With what ethnic or cultural group do you identify?

What are your ethnic group's attitudes toward children with behavioral problems, physical disabilities, or medical illnesses?

What are your ethnic group's attitudes toward homelessness, divorce, welfare, and other social issues?

How does your ethnic or cultural identity relate to your self-view and self-esteem?

How do you feel about members of other ethnic or cultural groups?

If you are aware of your personal biases toward an ethnic minority group, how would you try to conduct an unbiased interview?

How might your cultural practices and traditions interfere with your ability to understand and relate to interviewees from other cultural and ethnic backgrounds?

What personal qualities do you have that would be helpful in interviewing ethnic minority groups? What personal qualities do you have that would be detrimental?

Do you believe that to be an effective interviewer you must be of the same ethnic group as the interviewee? If so, what would you do if you were scheduled to interview someone of a different ethnic group?

If you were scheduled to be interviewed for your personal problems by someone of an ethnic group different from your own, how would you feel? Would you take any actions to arrange for another interviewer? If so, why?

Do you believe that many problems faced by ethnic minority interviewees are a direct result of an oppressive society? If you answered "yes," then what role do mental health practitioners have in working with ethnic minority groups?

Have you ever experienced prejudice? What form of prejudice did you experience and how did you feel during the experience and afterwards?

SUMMARY

1. You will need to consider cultural variables when you interview ethnic minority children and their parents. However, the role that cultural variables play will not always be easy to evaluate.

2. Our society must recognize and preserve cultural diversity and promote culturally sensitive and culturally relevant clinical services.

3. Culture is the human-made part of the environment, consisting of highly variable systems of meanings that are learned and shared by a people or an identifiable segment of a population. Culture represents designs and ways of life normally transmitted from one generation to another.

4. Race refers to the physical characteristics, such as skin color, facial features, and hair type, common to a population.

5. Ethnicity refers to groups characterized by a common nationality, culture, or language.

6. Social class refers to designations, usually based on occupation, education, or both, that are given to groups in a society.

Background Considerations

7. In 1990, the population of the United States was distributed in the following way: 69.1% White, 14.7% Black, 15.0% Hispanic, 3.1% Asian and Pacific Islander, 1% Native American, and 0.2% other races.

8. It is estimated that by 2050, White Americans will be the majority group (about 51% of the population), followed by Hispanic Americans (about 24.5%), Black Americans (about 13.6%) Asian Americans (about 8.2%) and Native Americans (about 0.9%).

9. In the United States, ethnic minority groups may face racism and discrimination; poverty; conflicts associated with acculturation and assimilation (especially when children begin to identify more closely with the majority culture and reject their ethnic culture); problems in dealing with medical, educational, social, and law enforcement organizations; and problems in using standard English.

10. In 1995, White Americans had the lowest poverty rate, followed by Asian Americans, Black Americans, and Hispanic Americans. Over one-quarter of Black American and Hispanic American families were below the poverty level. The poverty rate for Native Americans in 1990 was 27.2%.

11. When we look at data for 1995 on the years of school completed for persons 25 years of age and older, we find that Asian Americans as a group had the highest percentage of individuals with at least four years of high school or more (83.6%), followed by White Americans (83.0%), Black Americans (73.8%), and Hispanic Americans (53.4%). In 1990, similar data for Native Americans was 65.6%.

12. Three orientations can characterize a group's attitude toward human nature: evil orientation, good orientation, and mixed orientation.

13. Three orientations can characterize a group's attitude toward the relationship between person and nature: subjugation orientation, mastery orientation, and harmony orientation.

14. Three orientations can characterize a group's attitude toward time: past orientation, present orientation, and future orientation.

15. Three orientations can characterize a group's attitude toward activity level: being orientation, doing orientation, and being-in-becoming orientation.

16. Three orientations can characterize a group's attitude toward social relations: lineal orientation, collateral orientation, and individual orientation.

17. Acculturation is a process of cultural change that occurs in individuals when the two cultures meet; it leads the individuals to adopt elements of another culture, such as values and social behaviors.

18. Factors affecting acculturation include the history of the person's migration experience, temporal and geographic distance from the country of origin and its indigenous culture, place of residence and socioeconomic status in the homeland, type of neighborhood in the resettlement country, affiliative ties with immediate and extended family, role of the family's power and authority, and language and customs.

19. Individuals may deal with acculturation by adhering to the traditions of their culture (traditionalism), by partaking of both the old and the new culture (transitional period), by unsuccessfully meeting the demands of both the old and the new culture (marginality), by embracing the traditions of the new culture and rejecting the practices of the old culture (assimilation), and by integrating practices of both the old and the new culture (biculturalism).

20. Children may face several stresses dealing with acculturation.

21. Ethnic identity refers to one's sense of belonging to an ethnic group and the part of one's thinking, perceptions, feelings, and behavior that is due to ethnic group membership.

22. Stereotypes of children's ethnic minority groups may impede their identity formation.

23. Ethnic identification becomes particularly complex when individuals have a biracial heritage.

24. Depending on their degree of acculturation, members of ethnic minority groups in the United States may use both traditional and Western methods of healing.

25. The interviewer should inquire about what the family believes causes illness or disease.

26. Ethnic minority groups' use of mental health and medical services may be affected by their group's cultural values; the group's attitude toward mental health and illness, physical health and illness, psychological treatment, and medical treatment; the availability of medical and mental health services; how accessible the services are to the group; who provides the services; and how culturally relevant the treatment programs are.

27. Factors that may make it difficult for members of ethnic minority groups to use the mainstream health care system include perceptions of health and illness that differ from those of the majority culture, unfamiliarity with the clinic or hospital setting, fear of Western medical practices, distrust of Western health care providers because of the prejudice they have experienced, and fear of being discovered and deported if they are illegal immigrants.

28. If the family subscribes to mainstream medical and psychological practices *and* to traditional methods, consider encouraging them to seek help from both services. A combined treatment approach may be the most beneficial for these families.

29. You may encounter communication barriers when you work with ethnic minority clients.

30. Problems may arise when interviewers misinterpret the interviewee's communications.

31. Interviewers and interviewees may give symptoms different interpretations, depending on their group membership.

32. Nonverbal communications are a potential source of communication difficulties in cross-cultural interviews.

33. Proxemics refers to the perception and use of personal and interpersonal space.

34. Kinesics refers to bodily movements (such as facial expressions, posture, and gestures), characteristics of movement, and eye contact.

35. Paralanguage refers to the vocal cues used in talking.

36. When you interview children and parents who are members of ethnic minority groups, be prepared to cover issues related to ethnic and racial identity, acculturation, language, changing family patterns, sex roles, religious and traditional beliefs, customs for dealing with crisis and change, racism, poverty, social class, health care practices, and the interactions among these factors.

37. Interviewers have the difficult task of evaluating whether behaviors that suggest personality or temperament problems in the majority group reflect similar problems in ethnic minority groups.

Dynamics of Cross-Ethnic and Cross-Cultural Interviewing

38. Cross-ethnic and cross-cultural interviewing will suffer if interviewers display patronizing attitudes, fail to recognize the value of interviewees' traditional customs and mores, or are obsessed with the interviewees' cultures.

39. Misinterpretations in intercultural communication will occur when minority interviewees view majority interviewers as immature, rude, and lacking in finesse because they want to get to the point quickly. Similarly, majority interviewers should not view minority interviewees as evasive and afraid to confront their problems because they communicate indirectly.

40. Conflicts may arise if majority interviewees, when they are interviewed by minority interviewers, avoid the race issue, deprecate the interviewer, have special admiration for the interviewer, or view the interviewer as all-forgiving or uncritical. Minority interviewers, on the other hand, may be unsympathetic or punitive because of hostility toward nonminorities, or they may overcompensate by being too permissive (denying their hostility toward nonminorities or over-identifying with them).

41. Interviewers who are from the same minority group as interviewees may be in the best position to obtain reliable and valid information. Minority interviewers walk a fine line between over-identification and objectivity when interviewing minority interviewees of the same ethnic background.

42. Interviewers who are from a minority group may experience some difficulties in their relationship with interviewees who are from a different minority group because of problems associated with racial antagonism, depending on how the groups have been getting along in society at large.

43. Preoccupation with and heightened sensitivity to ethnic differences may lead to distortions, guardedness, and evasiveness on the part of interviewees and to guardedness, failure to probe, defensiveness, and feelings of intimidation on the part of interviewers.

44. It is your responsibility to ensure that any stereotypical views you may have do not adversely affect the information you obtain from children and parents.

45. Interviewers usually will be effective when they are tolerant and accepting of interviewees, despite value differences. Your goal is to establish a professional relationship characterized by trust and acceptance.

Interpreters

46. When you use interpreters, recognize that they may delete information or make other changes and embellishments in the translations that distort what you and the interviewee say. These distortions may lead to inaccurate information.

47. Before you use an interpreter, learn about the child's language preference.

48. Recognize that no matter how carefully the interpreter makes the translation, the interview is likely to be ineffective if you and the interpreter are not familiar with the interviewee's culture, values, and ideology.

49. When you write your report or make notes in the interviewee's chart, always note that you used an interpreter. This is especially important if you quote the interviewee.

50. There are several potential difficulties in using interpreters. Interpreters may not reveal symptoms they believe portray the child or parent in an unfavorable light. Some interviewees may be uncomfortable with having an interpreter. Some interpreters will preach instead of being neutral. Some concepts are difficult to translate. Translations sometimes are made with limited provision for dialectical or regional variations. The language familiar to ethnic minority children may be a combination of two languages. Some words have different meanings for various ethnic minority groups that share a language. The level of difficulty of words may change because of translation. Translations can alter the meaning of words. Translators may use colloquial words for more formal words and, in the process, inadvertently offend some interviewees.

51. Here are some suggestions for working with an interpreter. Select an interpreter who is thoroughly familiar with the interviewee's language and with the linguistic variations or dialect used by the child's ethnic group. Brief the interpreter thoroughly on issues that may affect his or her role. Discuss beforehand any technical terms and concepts that may pose a problem for translation. Practice with an interpreter *before* the interview to alleviate some problems associated with translations. Because of possible sensitive subject matter or conflicts of interest, use an interpreter who is not a family member, a family friend, or someone the family knows. Use the interpreter as an assistant, not as a co-interviewer. Face the interviewee when you talk to him or her. Avoid talking to the interpreter about the family in the presence of family members. Encourage the interpreter to tell you about the paralinguistic aspects of the interviewee's speech. Ask the interpreter to alert you to specific translated words that might be too difficult for the interviewee to understand. Summarize what you have learned at appropriate points, and ask the interviewee to confirm your understanding. Meet with the interpreter after you complete the interview to discuss problems that he or she encountered and to review his or her performance. Use the same interpreter in any future sessions with the interviewee and in the post-assessment interview, assuming that the interpreter did his or her job well.

KEY TERMS, CONCEPTS, AND NAMES

Culture (p. 259)
Race (p. 259)
Ethnicity (p. 259)
Social class (p. 259)
Projections of the U.S. Census Bureau (p. 259)
Poverty rate (p. 260)
Years of school completed (p. 262)
Ethnic minority group (minority group, minority) (p. 262)
Culture and value orientations (p. 263)
Human nature (p. 263)
Evil orientation (p. 263)
Good orientation (p. 263)
Mixed orientation (p. 263)
Relationship between person and nature (p. 263)
Subjugation orientation (p. 263)
Mastery orientation (p. 263)
Harmony orientation (p. 263)
Time (p. 263)

STUDY QUESTIONS

1. Discuss why it is important to consider cultural variables when you interview children and families.
2. How do the concepts of culture, race, ethnicity, and social class differ?
3. What is the ethnic distribution of minorities in the United States, as discussed in the text?
4. Describe some of the problems faced by ethnic minority groups in the United States.
5. What are some key value orientations of ethnic groups?
6. Discuss acculturation. In your discussion, examine factors affecting acculturation, strategies for dealing with acculturation, and stresses associated with acculturation.
7. Discuss ethnic identity and identification.
8. Discuss some of the factors that may affect ethnic minorities' use of mental and medical health care services.
9. Discuss culture and communication styles. Include in your discussion both verbal and nonverbal communication difficulties. Touch on issues related to proxemics, kinesics, and paralanguage.
10. Discuss cross-ethnic and cross-cultural interviewing. Include in your discussion issues related to the following relationships: majority interviewer–minority interviewee, minority interviewer–majority interviewee, minority interviewer–minority interviewee of the same group, and minority interviewer–minority interviewee of a different group.
11. Discuss issues involved in using an interpreter. Include in your discussion some of the difficulties that may arise when an interpreter is used and suggestions for working with an interpreter.

9

SPECIFIC ETHNIC MINORITY GROUPS

In the history of human thinking, the most fruitful developments frequently occur at those points where different lines of thought meet. These lines may have their roots in different cultures, in different times, in different religious traditions. If these are allowed to meet…a new and interesting way of being will emerge.

—Werner Heisenberg

Black Americans
Hispanic Americans
Asian Americans
Native Americans
Refugees
Intervention Considerations
Semistructured Interviews
Recommendations for Interviewing Ethnic Minority
    Children and Their Families
Thinking Through the Issues
Summary

Goals and Objectives

This chapter will enable you to:

- Discuss subcultural considerations within the Black American, Hispanic American, Asian American, and Native American communities
- Understand the problems in interviewing refugee children and their families
- Carry out guidelines for effective cross-ethnic and cross-cultural interviewing

This chapter focuses on four ethnic groups: Black Americans, Hispanic Americans, Asian Americans, and Native Americans. Each group is discussed in terms of its culture, language, and traditional medicine practices. (To get the most from this chapter, you should read Chapter 8 first.)

BLACK AMERICANS

According to the 1990 U.S. census, there are approximately 30 million Black Americans in the United States, representing about 12% of the population. About one-third of Black Americans are under 18 years of age. Most Black Americans live in the South (53%), followed by the Midwest (19%), Northeast (15%), and West (9%).

Black American Culture

Black Americans in the United States tend to be bicultural, incorporating aspects of mainstream culture and Black culture. The roots of Black culture in the United States include not only an African heritage but also a survival strategy developed by people required to deal daily with institutional racism and personal discrimination. Black cultural patterns are

also a means of dealing with the bicultural situation of the group, which requires people to learn to live in two worlds, to coordinate the elements of the two traditions borne by the parents, to learn the conventions of two cultures, and to manage the contradictions between them. (Young, 1974, p. 411)

To be Black in the United States is to be more than simply a person of dark color. The Black experience incorporates the collective experiences unique to Black Americans, encompassing racism, language, child-rearing practices, role expectations, socioeconomic status, and kinship bonds. To survive in the United States, Black Americans must size up potentially difficult situations and deal with persons who may be prejudiced against them and who perform discriminatory actions. They must interpret conflicting sets of messages and respond to them. Black-oriented music, religion, and speech patterns are some means by which Black children are socialized into Black American culture.

Black culture usually does not emphasize status and authority positions. Rather, it is a pragmatic culture, with highly varied content and values (Young, 1974). It also is a remarkably adaptive culture. The various African American cultures that exist in the United States attempt to retain their identity and interpersonal cohesion while continually responding to the forces exerted by the dominant culture.

Black American adolescents face several problems (Gibbs, 1990; also see Exhibit 9-1). Many Black youth have become convinced that traditional society has no place for them; schoolwork in particular, they believe, is for White Americans (Pearson, 1994). Black students "tell of being made to feel uncomfortable [by other Black students] if they apply themselves and get good grades" (Pearson, 1994, p. A14). High-achieving Black students in inner-city schools may be ridiculed and socially excluded by their peer group. Black students who excuse their poor school performance by saying "It's a Black thing; you wouldn't understand" need to recognize that ambition and industry will help them achieve success, both personally and in business.

Following are some historical and cultural forces that have played a role in the identity development of Black Americans (Mays, 1986):

History and ethnicity are important in the identity development of Black Americans who have lived among Whites promulgating their own superiority over the Black American subculture. Slavery objectified Blacks as pieces of property; it had the psychological effect of making Blacks both fearful and angry towards the majority population, leading them to engage in adaptive survival strategies, such as adopting assigned stereotypes or modeling Whites' behaviors and finding self-expression in religion, language, and music. During the Reconstruction, the master-slave relationship changed; many free Blacks became individualistic and lost their sense of community with other Blacks. Jim Crowism created ghettos and led to a greater sense of community among Blacks. The Jim Crow period marked the beginning of the loss of individuality for the sake of group survival. During the Black Renaissance of approximately 1915 to 1930, group pride and cohesiveness continued to grow, culminating in the Civil Rights movement of the 1950s and 1960s and the Black Power movement of the 1970s. Sense of self was submerged in ethnic group pride. During the 1980s, to achieve a definitive experience of self, Black Americans struggle with the ambivalences surrounding their identities. (pp. 592–593)

And here is a view of why assimilation poses difficulties for Black Americans (Bates, 1996):

The fact is, no matter how well we do or how high we fly, we will be glaringly apparent on the great assimilation landscape. Our sheer physicality sets us apart. What does an Irish American look like? An American whose parents came from Lithuania 60 years ago? Because we are part of the African diaspora, we look different from our citizen-peers. And we alone have been subjected to the ravages of American slavery and its haunting aftereffects.

Black is not the only thing I am, but it is the thing people see—and react to—for better or worse, first.... In order [for Black Americans] to be woven into the great American tapestry, there will have to be some acceptance from the mainstream that the addition of

Exhibit 9-1
A Portrait of Black Adolescents

Introduction

Black adolescents occupy an unenviable position as one of the most vulnerable and victimized groups in American society. As the largest group of minority youth, they frequently have been misdiagnosed by the mental health system, mislabeled by the educational system, mishandled by the juvenile justice system, and mistreated by the social welfare system. In the last decade of the twentieth century, the problems of Black adolescents have become so severe that these children have been called an "endangered species" and a population "at risk" for social and psychological dysfunction.

Generations of discrimination, prejudice, and economic deprivation have contributed to high rates of psychological and behavioral disorders and also several problematic psychosocial behaviors among Black adolescents, with a disproportionate impact on those from low-income families. It is a tribute to the resiliency and adaptability of the Black family that most of these youth develop into competent and well-functioning adults.

Attitude Toward Self

Black adolescents have the same levels of positive self-esteem as White adolescents. Black adolescents tend to place a high value on verbal skills (for example, rapping), assertiveness, physical attractiveness (especially for females), and athletic ability (especially for males). High-achieving Black adolescents may feel caught between the low expectations of their White teachers and the anti-intellectual attitudes of their peers. Physical characteristics such as height and weight also can be sources of anxiety for Black males who are small in stature and Black girls who are precociously mature, exposing them to sarcasm, humor, and aggressive or sexual behaviors. Skin color and socioeconomic status can lead to invidious social distinctions that damage the adolescents' self-esteem.

Affect

Black adolescents typically are described as expressive, lively, and extroverted. However, they often are portrayed as angry and hostile or sullen and withdrawn in treatment situations. While these teenagers may appear uncommunicative and uncooperative, their unresponsive demeanor is often a facade masking underlying depression and feelings of helplessness over multiple personal and family problems.

Speech and Language

The prestige norms within the culture of the Black inner-city child place a high premium on the ability to use words. The channel through which this ability is promoted and developed and through which recognition is given is oral-aural. Expertise via this channel is more highly regarded and developed in Black culture than in White middle-class culture. On the other hand, expertise via the written channel, by virtue of the cultural aesthetic that motivates achievement through this channel, is more highly regarded and more extensively developed in White middle-class culture than in Black culture.

The prestige attached to men of words—preachers, storytellers, tellers of toasts and jokes, signifiers, "dozens" players [a rhyming game of clever insults, often aimed at the relatives of the players]—within the Black community is unrivaled. A rich and colorful oral tradition is an integral part of the Black cultural aesthetic.

Status on the street is not inherited or conferred but has to be earned. Acquiring status is a prime motivation for the Black street youngster. Verbal ability, like the ability to dance, fight, sing, or run, is highly prized in the Black community because such ability helps to establish one's "rep." At the same time, life on the streets is full of hazards, and control over events is desirable. While one is often secure within one's group, intergroup transactions are often filled with uncertainties. Verbal ability helps the Black child maximize control in those contexts, especially expert development of the directive function that permits him or her to establish control over people through the art of persuasion, manipulation, deception, and a developed sensitivity to what motivates others. Since status is often achieved by this directive use of words, there is generally a high correlation in Black street culture between high status and this kind of ability.

Interpersonal Relations

Black adolescents often form same-sex peer groups with strong bonds and group norms that provide a sense of social identity and social cohesion. These strong bonds also can foster group conflicts, gang rivalries, and pressures to participate in antisocial activities. In some neighborhoods, males who are not gang members are at risk for verbal and physical harassment.

Coping and Adaptive Behaviors

To compensate for their marginality in American society, Black adolescents have developed a repertoire of adaptive behavioral patterns. For example, many Black males have focused on developing athletic abilities, one of the limited number of routes to upward mobility for low-income adolescents. Black females have been rewarded for developing their social and interpersonal skills, yet they have not always been able to translate these skills into educational and career opportunities.

Family Structure and Roles

Black teenage females in single-parent families may become parent-substitutes with detrimental effects on their educational and occupational outcomes. Alternatively, teenagers in extended families are more likely to experience conflicts over discipline and autonomy in relating to several adult caregivers. Those adolescents from nontraditional family structures may express shame or embarrassment about their home environments to middle-class clinicians.

Educational Issues

Black adolescents may attend schools with fewer facilities, lower teacher morale, greater disciplinary problems,

(Continued)

Exhibit 9-1 (*Continued*)

and lower achievement scores than schools in middle-income areas. Responses of Black adolescents to these school environments range from apathy and alienation, anger, and hostility to fear and anxiety, leading to high rates of truancy, vandalism, and dropping out. High-achieving adolescents often are ridiculed and excluded socially in inner-city schools.

Experiences in the Greater Community

Adolescence may signal the first introduction to overt racial discrimination and prejudice for Black youths who enter an integrated high school, seek employment, or participate in community-wide sports and recreational activities. As they perceive barriers to their full participation in American society, they also learn more about the effects of poverty, drugs, and crime in their neighborhoods. These experiences foster feelings of cynicism, anger, alienation, and despair in many adolescents, increasing their risk for involvement in antisocial or self-destructive activities such as drug abuse, unwed teenage pregnancy, homicide, and suicide.

Source: Reprinted and adapted, with permission of the publisher and author, from J. T. Gibbs, Mental health issues of Black adolescents: Implications for policy and practice. In A. R. Stiffman and L. E. Davis (Eds.), *Ethnic Issues in Adolescent Mental Health,* pp. 21–52. Pages cited are 21, 22, 34, 37, 39, 40. Copyright 1990 by Sage Publications. Section on speech and language from Kochman (1972), pp. 239, 241, 242.

these African-hued threads will change the look of the cloth. You do not, after all, drip chocolate syrup into milk and expect it to remain White, do you? (p. B9, with changes in notation)

Black American family structure. The Black American family is more likely than the Anglo American family to be headed by a female. "Within the Black family structure, the wife and/or mother is often charged with the responsibility of protecting the health of the family members.... Some Black families are composed of large networks and tend to be very supportive during times of crisis and illness" (Giger & Davidhizar, 1991, p. 156). The prevalence of female-headed families may be directly associated with slavery, when Black men were separated from their families and were not allowed to provide for their families. However, in Black families there appears to be more role flexibility between the spouses than in White families (McGoldrick, 1993). Black families frequently have extended family members living with them. They also tend informally to adopt children of relatives or babies born out of wedlock (Friedman, 1986). There is no standard or typical Black American family structure; family structures are very similar to Anglo American family structures.

African perspective. Black Americans have cultural traditions based, in part, on those found in traditional African societies (Boykin, 1983). The African perspective emphasizes spiritualism in the universe; harmony with nature and other people; feelings, expressiveness, and spontaneity; and duty to the group and group property. The Euro-American perspective, in contrast, emphasizes materialism, efficiency, and task centeredness; mastery over nature and individualism; control of impulses, self-discipline, and dispassionate reason; and individual rights and private property. Black Americans are at a disadvantage in American society because they do not subscribe to the Euro-American perspective completely, because they typically develop a stylistic repertoire that arises out of their African heritage and is at odds with mainstream ideology, and because they are victimized by racial and economic oppression (Boykin, 1983).

Racism. The withering effect of racism may lead to major psychiatric problems among Black individuals. Family patterns developed in the inner city, which may be conducive to occupational and economic survival, are likely to be unsuitable for socializing children to achieve in middle-class mainstream culture. This quandary is part of the psychological experience of many Black Americans.

Even Blacks who have become successful in the United States may feel that they are in a no-win situation, out of place in both Black and White worlds. Other Blacks may make them feel guilty for succeeding, and Whites may make them feel that it was only luck or affirmative action, not their ability, that led to their success. Leanita McClain's essay, in Exhibit 9-2, poignantly describes this dilemma.

The following case illustrates the struggles of a Black American adolescent who, at the time, was having an identity crisis (Jones, 1992).

CASE 9-1. MARK

At the time he entered treatment, Mark was 15 years old. He was referred by an African American school counselor who viewed him as a bright, talented boy with a great deal of potential if he could get help with his emotional problems. Mark was president of a districtwide Black student organization in a suburban school district. He was highly regarded by his peers but was having serious academic problems and was seen by many of his teachers as hostile and provocative. Mark had developed a good relationship with a school counselor, and she became concerned one day when he confessed to her that he sometimes had suicidal thoughts. She convinced him to cooperate with her plan for referral to an African American psychologist.

In the clinical evaluation it became clear that Mark was experiencing a major depression. An important part of Mark's history was the fact that his father had died in an alcohol-related automobile crash when Mark was 3 years old. Mark

Exhibit 9-2
The Middle-Class Black's Burden

I am a member of the Black middle class who has had it with being patted on the head by White hands and slapped in the face by Black hands for my success.

Here's a discovery that too many people still find startling: when given equal opportunities at white-collar pencil pushing, Blacks want the same things from life that everyone else wants. These include the proverbial dream house, two cars, an above-average school and a vacation for the kids at Disneyland. We may, in fact, want these things more than other Americans because most of us have been denied them so long.

Meanwhile, a considerable number of the folks we left behind in the "old country," commonly called the ghetto, and the militants we left behind in their antiquated ideology can't berate middle-class Blacks enough for "forgetting where we came from." We have forsaken the revolution, we are told; we have sold out. We are Oreos, they say, Black on the outside, White within.

The truth is, we have not forgotten; we would not dare. We are simply fighting on different fronts and are no less war weary, and possibly more heartbroken, for we know the Black and White worlds can meld, that there can be a better world.

It is impossible for me to forget where I came from as long as I am prey to the jive hustler who does not hesitate to exploit my childhood friendship. I am reminded, too, when I go back to the old neighborhood in fear—and have my purse snatched—and when I sit down to a business lunch and have an old classmate wait on my table. I recall the girl I played dolls with who now rears five children on welfare, the boy from church who is in prison for murder, the pal found dead of a drug overdose in the alley where we once played tag.

My life abounds in incongruities. Fresh from a vacation in Paris, I may, a week later, be on the milk-run Trailways bus in Deep South backcountry attending the funeral of an ancient uncle whose world stretched only 50 miles and who never learned to read. Sometimes when I wait at the bus stop with my attaché case, I meet my aunt getting off the bus with other cleaning ladies on their way to do my neighbors' floors.

But I am not ashamed. Black progress has surpassed our greatest expectations; we never even saw much hope for it, and the achievement has taken us by surprise.

In my heart, however, there is no safe distance from the wretched past of my ancestors or the purposeless present of some of my contemporaries; I fear such fate can reclaim me. I am not comfortably middle class; I am uncomfortably middle class.

I have made it, but where? Racism still dogs my people. There are still communities in which crosses are burned on the lawns of Black families who have the money and grit to move in.

What a hollow victory we have won when my sister, dressed in her designer everything, is driven to the rear door of the luxury high rise in which she lives because the cab driver, noting only her skin color, assumes she is the maid, or the nanny, or the cook, but certainly not the lady of any house at this address.

I have heard the immigrants' bootstrap tales, the simplistic reproach of "why can't you people be like us." I have fulfilled the entry requirements of the American middle class, yet I am left, at times, feeling unwelcome and stereotyped. I have overcome the problems of food, clothing and shelter, but I have not overcome my old nemesis, prejudice. Life is easier, being Black is not.

I am burdened daily with showing Whites that Blacks are people. I am, in the old vernacular, a credit to my race. I am my brothers' keeper, and my sisters', though many of them have abandoned me because they think that I have abandoned them.

I run a gauntlet between two worlds, and I am cursed and blessed by both. I travel, observe and take part in both; I can also be used by both. I am a rope in a tug of war. If I am a token in my downtown office, so am I at my cousin's church tea. I assuage White guilt. I disprove Black inadequacy and prove to my parents' generation that their patience was indeed a virtue.

I have a foot in each world, but I cannot fool myself about either. I can see the transparent deceptions of some Whites and the bitter hopelessness of some Blacks. I know how tenuous my grip on one way of life is, and how strangling the grip of the other way of life can be.

Many Whites have lulled themselves into thinking that race relations are just grand because they were the first on their block to discuss crab grass with the new Black family. Yet too few Blacks and Whites in this country send their children to school together, entertain each other or call each other friend. Blacks and Whites dining out together draw stares. Many of my coworkers see no Black faces from the time the train pulls out Friday evening until they meet me at the coffee machine Monday morning. I remain a novelty.

Some of my "liberal" White acquaintances pat me on the head, hinting that I am a freak, that my success is less a matter of talent than of luck and affirmative action. I may live among them, but it is difficult to live with them. How can they be sincere about respecting me, yet hold my fellows in contempt? And if I am silent when they attempt to sever me from my own, how can I live with myself?

Whites won't believe I remain culturally different; Blacks won't believe I remain culturally the same.

I need only look in a mirror to know my true allegiance, and I am painfully aware that, even with my off-white trappings, I am prejudged by my color.

As for the envy of my own people, am I to give up my career, my standard of living, to pacify them and set my conscience at ease? No. I have worked for these amenities and deserve them, though I can never enjoy them without feeling guilty.

These comforts do not make me less Black, nor oblivious to the woe in which many of my people are drowning. As long as we are denigrated as a group, no one of us has made it. Inasmuch as we all suffer for every one left behind, we all gain for every one who conquers the hurdle.

Source: From Leanita McClain, "The Middle-Class Black's Burden," *Newsweek,* October 13, 1980.

had only sketchy memories of his father, but conversations over the years with several extended family members had produced an impression of Mark's father as a creative man whose achievements were eclipsed by a serious drinking problem. After his death, Mark's mother had used money from a life insurance policy to return to school for a master's degree in public health administration and was now the administrator of a major regional medical facility.

Mark's mother was determined to balance her career and parenting responsibilities and felt proud of her ability to remain involved in family life despite intense professional demands. Mark, as he entered adolescence, seemed ungrateful, and his mother was puzzled about this. Mark openly accused her of "selling out" in choosing a prestigious life style that included living in a predominantly White suburban community. His mother's strong professional commitments to several health projects with direct implications for Black patients appeared to Mark as irrelevant to his expressed anger with his mother.

Treatment required unraveling complicated underlying dynamics involving Mark's blaming of his mother for his father's death, an idealized picture of his father as a Black hero, and an identity crisis fueled in large part by attempts to live out his father's unfulfilled life, all exacerbated by the family's life style in a largely White suburban environment. A focus on grief work helped Mark and his mother release some of the tension that had mounted in their relationship. Mark began to separate his genuine commitment to social causes from behavior motivated primarily by unresolved personal issues. Still, it was only after several years of intermittent therapy (punctuated by problems with substance abuse) that Mark could commit himself to working on a college degree in political science, with a grade point average to match his professed passion for political issues. (pp. 38–39, with changes in notation)

Distrust of the environment. Some Black children and parents have learned to distrust their environment. Distrust develops when individuals are placed in inferior positions or when they are singled out simply because they are Black. For example, when the majority culture tends to associate criminal behavior with Black Americans, Black Americans feel defensive and distrustful. Similarly, when Black Americans see that they have high unemployment rates and minimal social and educational opportunities, they become distrustful and resentful of the majority culture. Black Americans are likely to become less distrustful when they can control their environment and influence the way others use information about them. This, of course, is true for members of any group.

In the last third of the twentieth century, some Black Americans, in part because of their distrust and resentment of White America and in part because of their desire to control their environment, have begun to distance themselves from Anglo Americans. The following excerpt from the *Los Angeles Times* describes how attitudes of Black Americans are shifting away from the goal of inclusion (Fulwood, 1995a):

Hundreds of thousands of Black Americans, their patience worn thin by the lingering indignities of racism, are turning away from the centuries-old quest for inclusion in the mainstream of White society. Like an ocean tide swelling and ebbing in reaction to gravitational forces, Black Americans' commitment to the ideas of integration and a colorblind America has historically risen and fallen in tandem with their perception of whether the struggle against racism was making progress. As of November 1995, a growing body of evidence suggests that in the wake of a series of tense incidents that have highlighted racial disparities, the willingness of many African Americans to work as hard as they once did for a colorblind society is receding.

An increasing number of middle-class Blacks, for example, have the financial means to live almost anyplace, but many are choosing to create predominantly Black residential neighborhoods instead of settling in White communities. Further, although nearly all Black Americans support the idea of racially diverse public education, increasing numbers are losing faith in local schools. They are especially turning away from busing plans that require their children to travel across metropolitan areas to sit next to White children. And though most employed Blacks share work spaces with Whites, many say their greatest frustration stems from what they believe is lack of commitment by America's corporate and political leaders to provide jobs for Black people.

In these and other ways, many middle-class Blacks are putting distance between themselves and the cultural, social, economic, and political norms of White America in order to insulate themselves from the uncertainties of interracial pioneering. Rather than feel alone in largely White communities, "they want to find a comfortable space for their family, themselves, and their children," said David Dent, a journalism and history professor at New York University. "They're saying to themselves 'I'm not going to set myself up in a hostile world for the sake of integration.' Black people are aggressively looking for comfortable spaces to breathe and be themselves." Similar trends are visible in public education. (pp. A1, A16, with changes in notation)

When a Black interviewee distrusts a non-Black (or Black) interviewer, it will be difficult to conduct a valid clinical assessment or forensic interview. Cooperative behavior may be replaced by hostility, and silence substituted for openness. Although interviewers who are distrusted are likely to be frustrated, they must make every effort to establish rapport with Black children and parents and to gain their trust. Rapport is more likely to be established when Black interviewees see interviewers (regardless of their ethnicity) as competent, caring professionals who are interested in helping them.

I'd like to think that I'd have my problems no matter what I was, and sometimes I believe it. But sometimes I think it's all because I'm Black. I can't be sure. I just don't know. Maybe you could tell me what it really means to be Black.

—Bertram P. Karon

Language Considerations for Black Americans

Some Black children and their parents speak a variant of English that linguists call *Black English, nonstandard Black*

English, Black dialect, or *Ebonics.* The term *Ebonics* is a combination of the words "ebony" and "phonics." Black English tends to be used by urban Black Americans and by Black Americans who remain isolated racially and economically in poor Black communities ("Mainstream English...," 1996; "Ebonics at a glance," 1997; Lynch & Hanson, 1992). It is primarily used in informal settings, such as at home and among friends, rather than in business or professional settings.

Here are comments from two Black American students about their use of Black English (Boykin, 1996):

EIGHTH GRADER—AGE 13

When I am around friends, I speak in the dialect, but when I am in the classroom, I speak plain king's English because I am in a different mindset. In the classroom, I pay attention and learn. But when I am around my friends, I am relaxed and loose.

—Richard Post

SENIOR—AGE 18

I do find that among some of us African Americans, there is a greater rejection of those who have no traces of the dialect. You can put a group of us together who have never met before, and just by the way an African American teen from the Valley or another place says hello, someone will say, "He talks white." That person is not accepted well and has to work his way to fit in.

But I think the ultimate goal is to be able to communicate both with and without the dialect.

—Terrence Braggs

Black English shares many language features with standard English, but it has several distinguishing pronunciational and grammatical features (see Table 9-1). "Among the most common speech markers are its use of 'be' to denote an ongoing action ('he be going to work'), its dropping of linking verbs ('you crazy'), its shortened plurals 'twenty cent'), its dropping of some final consonants ('firs' instead of 'first' or 'des' instead of 'desk'), and its substitution for some pronouns ('that's the man got all the money')" ("Ebonics at a glance," 1997, A22). Black English is a fully formed linguistic system with its own rules of grammar and pronunciation; it has a rich repertoire of forms and usages.

Black English has contributed to American society in the following ways (Emmons, 1996):

It has enriched the fabric of American English. Black English is in jazz. Among the hundreds of the jazz world's words that have fil-

Table 9-1
Some Differences Between Black English and Standard English

Black English		Standard English	
Usage	*Example*	*Usage*	*Example*
1. Uses *got*	The girls got a cat.	1. Uses *have*	The girls have a cat.
2. Omits *is* and *are*	The cat in the wagon.	2. Uses *is* and *are*	The cat is in the wagon.
3. Omits the third-person singular ending *-s* from some verbs	The man ask the boy what to wear.	3. Uses the *-s* ending on verbs	The man asks the boy what to wear.
4. Omits the *-ed* ending from verbs	The dog get chase by the cat.	4. Uses the *-ed* ending on verbs	The dog is chased by the cat.
5. Uses *do*	The girl do pull the wagon to the boat.	5. Uses *does*	The girl does pull the wagon to the boat.
6. Uses *be* in place of *am, is,* and *are*	The big ball be rolling down the hill.	6. Uses *am, is,* and *are* in place of *be*	The big ball is rolling down the hill.
7. Uses *he be, we be,* and *they be*	They be going home.	7. Uses *he is, we are,* and *they are*	They are going home.
8. Pronounces "*th*" at beginning of a word as "*d*"	Des boys kick de ball.	8. Pronounces "*th*" at the beginning of a word as "*th*"	These boys kick the ball.
9. Pronounces "*th*" at end of word as "*f*"	In the baf, he washed his mouf and played wif a toy.	9. Pronounces "*th*" at the end of a word as "*th*"	In the bath, he washed his mouth and played with a toy.
10. Drops the final *r* and *g* from words	My fatha and motha were talkin and laughin.	10. Pronounces the final *r* and *g* in words	My father and mother were talking and laughing.

tered into the American lexicon are "hip," "cool," "gig," "jiving around," "get high" and "gimme five." Black English is in blues and soul, giving America expressive, often sensual, words and phrases like "hot," "baby," "mojo," "fine," "mess with," "thang" (as doin' my), "take it easy," "slick," "rip-off," "cool out," and "bad." Black English is in Negro spirituals ("Dat Ole Man River," "Ah Got Shoes"). It is in gospel ("Ain't No Devil in Hell Gonna Walk on the Jesus in Me") and through these mediums of expression has found home in the vernacular of the black church. (p. B9)

Black English has its roots in the oral traditions of the African ancestors of Black Americans. "Black English evolved from West African languages and slave traders who used a form of pidgin English to communicate with African slaves who were allowed neither to speak their tribal languages nor to learn English in a classroom" ("Mainstream English...," 1996, M4, with changes in notation). In many African groups, the history and traditions of the group were transmitted orally, and the elder who kept this information was a revered member of the community. Black American culture maintains the tradition of orality. To *rap, sound,* or *run it down* is a prized oral skill. This holds not just for the street culture, but for every level of Black culture. Sources of prestige among inner-city Black youth include skill in using language in ritual insults, verbal routines, singing, jokes, and storytelling.

In school, teachers may tell Black children that their dialect is "wrong" and that standard English dialect is "right." By extension, Black children may feel that they are inadequate and inferior to other children who speak standard English. These feelings may extend to the interview and lead to reticence and even withdrawal. Regardless of your ethnicity, there may not be much you can do to alleviate such feelings immediately, but children may begin to talk to you if you are supportive and encouraging. Black children who speak both Black English and standard English have a highly developed skill. Do not view Black English as inferior to standard English.

Schools have failed to appreciate that Black American children have spoken and written language skills that are extremely useful, such as "keen listening and observational skills, quick recognition of nuanced roles, rapid-fire dialogue, hard-driving argumentation, succinct recapitulation of an event, striking metaphors, and comparative analyses based on unexpected analogies" (Heath, 1989, p. 370). Schools make little effort to help Black American children use these skills in the classroom.

The following example illustrates an interviewer's attempt to understand an adolescent who was using Black English (adapted from Russell, 1988):

IE: It be's that way...you know...don't nobody care nothin' about you except if they somethin' in it for them.
IR: So you feel that nobody cares about you as a person?
IE: Yeah, I guess you could say it like that.
IR: It sounds like I might understand a part of what you meant, but I think there's something there that I'm miss-

ing. I'm not sure I understand the whole meaning when you say "It be's that way."
IE: Well, you know—it be's that way...ain't nobody cared about me, not my mom, my family, my wife...sometimes I just feel like it ain't never gonna be no different.
IR: So you mean *nobody* cares, *nobody's* there that you can count on, not even the least little bit. That's what you mean when you say "It be's that way today and it be's that way tomorrow," isn't it?
IE: Yeah.

Russell (1988) noted that

the interviewer sensed that he was not grasping a facet of the interviewee's original statement. The phrase "It be's that way" means more than "It is that way." A more complete translation would be "It continually is that way," a meaning much closer to the last paraphrasing. Also, the interviewer was careful not to paraphrase in a way that might be correcting the interviewee. It was important for him to use parts of the interviewee's language to show respect. (p. 58, with changes in notation).

Black Americans continue to use Black English because of habit, ease of usage, peer pressure, and group identification and because it provides a sense of protection, belonging, and solidarity. For example, Maya Angelou (1969) noted that, in school,

we all learned past participles, but in the streets and in our homes, the Blacks learned to drop s's from plurals and suffixes from past tense verbs. We were alert to the gap separating the written word from the colloquial. We learned to slide out of one language and into another without being conscious of the effort. At school, in a given situation, we might respond with "that's not unusual." But in the street, meeting the same situation, we easily said, "It be's like that sometimes." (p. 191)

The social distance between Black and White Americans contributes to the maintenance of Black English. Encouraging Black American children to speak in their natural language may enable them to speak more freely about themselves and, thus, may give you a better sample of their language skills. Recognize, however, that some Black children and adults may be comfortable using either Black English or standard English, depending on the situation. And use of standard English by Black Americans may be important for their social and economic mobility. You must attend carefully to the communications of interviewees who speak Black English if you are not familiar with the language.

If, as our folk theories maintain, schools are in the business of improving benefits for society, they have much to learn from the oral and literate traditions of Black American family and community life.

—Shirley Brice Heath

Traditional Medicine Among Black Americans

The roots of Black American traditional medicine.
When slavery was abolished after the end of the Civil War, there was a rise in the use of traditional medicine and of midwives among Black Americans. It was common for older women to administer traditional remedies (Friedman, 1986).

Black American traditional medicine has its roots in African society (Spector, 1991).

To the African, life was a process rather than a state. The nature of a person was viewed in terms of energy force rather than matter. All things, whether living or dead, were believed to influence each other. Therefore, one had the power to influence one's destiny and that of others through the use of *behavior,* whether proper or otherwise, as well as through *knowledge* of the person and the world. When one possessed health, one was in harmony with nature; illness was a state of disharmony. Traditional Black belief regarding health did not separate the mind, body, and spirit. (p. 190, with changes in notation)

Africans attributed illness primarily to demons and evil spirits. They saw illness as resulting from one of three areas: environmental hazards (for example, a hurricane or an insect bite), divine punishment (for example, illness because of sin), or impaired social relationships (for example, a spouse leaving). Also, Africans espoused the belief that everything has an opposite. "For every birth, there must be a death; for every marriage, there must be a divorce; for every occurrence of illness, someone must be cured" (Giger & Davidhizar, 1991, p. 159). The goal of treatment was to remove the spirits from the body of the ill person (Spector, 1991). "For example, in West Africa,…man was perceived as a… being from which body and soul could not be separated.… Since life was centered around the entire family, illness was perceived as a collective event and subsequently a disruption of the entire family system" (Giger & Davidhizar, 1991, pp. 158, 159). Therefore, the entire family was involved in the care of a sick individual.

Traditional medicine beliefs and treatments.
Black American traditional medicine takes the form of voodoo, witchcraft, magic, herbal medicine, and spirituality (Spector, 1991).

Voodoo came to [the United States]…about 1724, with the arrival of slaves from the West African coast.… The people who brought voodoo with them were "snake worshipers." *Vodu,* the name of their god, became with the passage of time *voodoo*…, an all-embracing term that included the god, the sect, the members of the sect, and priests and priestesses, and rites and practices, and the teacher.… *Gris-gris,* the symbols of voodoo, were used to prevent illness or to give illness to others. (pp. 191, 192)

Examples of gris-gris are powders and oils that are highly and pleasantly scented or have a vile odor and colored candles designed for special intentions (Spector, 1991).

Followers of Black American traditional medicine see health as a gift from God and illness as a punishment from God or as retribution for sin and evil. This fatalistic perception affects their attitudes regarding children with disabilities: The child's disability is retribution from God for some sin of the parents. "In the system of Black traditional medicine, illness is perceived as a natural or unnatural occurrence. A natural illness may occur because of an exposure to the elements of nature without protection (such as a cold, the flu, or pneumonia)" (Giger & Davidhizar, 1991, p. 161). An unnatural illness may occur because of punishment from God or the work of the devil. Thus, for example, among followers of Black American traditional medicine, there may be no motivation to stop smoking because they see no relation between smoking and lung cancer (Giger & Davidhizar, 1991).

Examples of preventive measures Black Americans may use to ward off illness include (a) a proper diet, rest, and a clean environment, (b) *asafetida,* a rotten flesh that looks like a dried-out sponge, worn around the neck to prevent the contraction of contagious diseases, (c) a sulfur-and-molasses preparation, rubbed up and down the back in the spring to prevent illness, and (d) copper or silver bracelets, worn by girls around the wrist to protect them as they grow (Spector, 1991).

For treatment of illness, Black traditional medicine uses prayer with the laying on of hands and magic rituals. Other remedies are poultices (a mixture of several substances) of various kinds to treat infections, earaches, and other maladies; herb teas to treat pain, reduce fevers, and cure colds; and clay in a dark leaf to treat sprained ankles (Spector, 1991).

Comment on traditional medicine among Black Americans.
Black Americans, primarily those of lower socioeconomic status, may use home remedies and secure advice from community healers before seeking conventional medical care. Unfortunately, relying on home remedies even when the condition is *not* improving may delay standard treatment until the condition becomes much more serious (Friedman, 1986).

Black traditional medicine…took roots not only as an offshoot of African cultural heritage, but as a necessity when Black Americans could not gain access to the traditional health care delivery system [because of segregationist practices]. Furthermore, some Black Americans turned to Black traditional medicine because they either could not afford the cost of medical assistance or were tired of the insensitive treatment of caregivers in the health care delivery system.… (Giger & Davidhizar, 1991, p. 164)

In the 1990s, some Black Americans still refuse to use the mainstream health system for the reasons cited above. And, even if they want to use mainstream medicine, their access may be limited because of lack of health insurance. However, as Western medical care has become more accessible to Black Americans, the use of traditional medicine and lay practitioners has declined.

Know where you came from and you'll always know where you're going.

—African American saying

HISPANIC AMERICANS

Hispanic Americans currently are the third-largest ethnic group, after Anglo Americans and Black Americans. According to the 1990 U.S. census, approximately 23 million people of Hispanic origin live in the United States, representing roughly 9 percent of the total population. The Hispanic American populations in the United States are not homogeneous. The major groups are Mexican Americans (Chicanos), Puerto Ricans, Cubans, and people from Central and South America (see Figure 9-1). Many Hispanic Americans speak Spanish, but some speak Portuguese or French. Some children of Hispanic heritage who were born in the United States speak English only.

Hispanic Americans comprise the fastest-growing ethnic minority in the United States (U.S. Bureau of Census, 1993d).

The Hispanic population grew by 53 percent between 1980 and 1990 and by 61 percent between 1970 and 1980. Several factors contributed to the tremendous increase in the Hispanic population since 1970. Among them are a higher birth rate than for the rest of the population and substantial immigration from Mexico, Central America, the Caribbean, and South America. The Mexican population nearly doubled between 1970 and 1980, and nearly doubled again by 1990. Both the Cuban and the Puerto Rican populations grew at least four times as fast as the rest of the nation. Other Hispanic populations grew dramatically between 1980 and 1990, partly because of the large influx of Central and South American immigrants during the period [see Figure 9-2]. (p. 2, with changes in notation)

According to the 1990 U.S. census, most Hispanic Americans live in the West (45%), followed by the South (30%), Northeast (17%), and Midwest (8%). Approximately 11 million Hispanic Americans are concentrated in two southwestern states—California (33%) and Texas (19%). Approximately

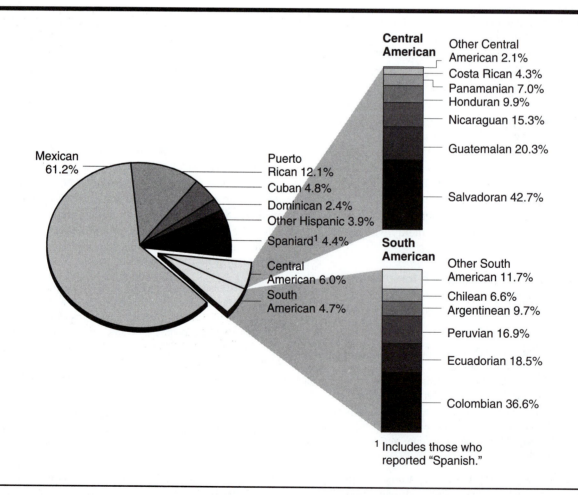

Figure 9-1. Origins of the Hispanic American population in the United States in 1990 (percent of the total Hispanic American population reporting each origin). From U.S. Bureau of the Census (1993), *We the American...Hispanics,* p. 4.

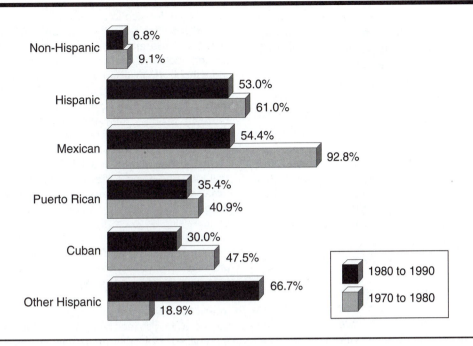

Figure 9-2. Hispanic American population growth in the United States: 1970 to 1990 (percent increase). From U.S. Bureau of the Census (1993), *We the American…Hispanics,* p. 2.

35% of the Hispanic American population is under 18 years of age; this fact suggests that the Hispanic American population is likely to increase substantially in the next several decades.

Mexican Americans are the largest group of Hispanic Americans in the United States. Most of the approximately 13.5 million persons of Mexican American heritage reside in California (45%) and Texas (28%), perhaps because these were once Mexican territories. After the Mexican War between Mexico and the United States, Mexico recognized the U.S. annexation of Texas and in 1848 ceded California and New Mexico (including all present-day states of the Southwest) to the United States.

Puerto Ricans are the second-largest group of Spanish-speaking persons in the United States. Spain ceded the island of Puerto Rico to the United States in 1898. It was a territory until 1948 and then became a commonwealth. Puerto Ricans became citizens of the United States in 1917 with the passage of the Jones Act. In 1990, there were approximately 2.7 million Puerto Ricans on the mainland, compared with 3 million inhabiting the island of Puerto Rico. On the mainland, they reside mostly in the Northeast (particularly New York, New Jersey, Connecticut, Pennsylvania, and Massachusetts); many also live in Illinois. New York State accounts for about 40% of the total Puerto Rican population in the United States. Puerto Ricans are an economically deprived group, being at a great disadvantage with respect to income, employment, and education.

Most of the approximately 1 million Cubans who live in the United States reside in Florida (62%). Approximately 5 million other Hispanic Americans live in the United States, with the largest numbers coming from the Dominican Republic, Colombia, and Chile.

Hispanic American Culture

Most Hispanic American groups share a similar language, Spanish heritage, and Roman Catholic religious orientation, but they maintain their autonomy and are clearly distinguishable from one another. "Hispanic culture developed as a result of the fusion of Spanish culture (brought to the Americas by missionaries and conquistadors) with American Indian and African (the result of the slave trade) cultures in Mexico, South America, and the Caribbean Basin" (Lee & Richardson, 1991, p. 141). Although Hispanic Americans have a similar language, there are dialectal variations. Differences also exist between the lower and middle classes and between those born in the United States and those born in other countries. Keeping these differences in mind, let's now turn to some cautious generalizations about Hispanic American culture.

Hispanic American family structure. The foundation of the Hispanic community is the nuclear family. The father has the dominant role and is responsible for making decisions; the mother is responsible for keeping the family together. Members of the extended family or other relatives also may live in the same household, especially if elderly members of the family are not self-sufficient (Giger & Davidhizar, 1991). This is especially true for new immigrants who have come to the United States for social or economic reasons. Sometimes it is more important for children to attend family functions than to go to school.

The Catholic practice of *compadrazgo,* or godparenthood, is important in the Hispanic family. Godparents accept responsibility for a child along with the child's parents (Giger & Davidhizar, 1991). This relationship usually lasts throughout the child's life.

In Hispanic communities, the extended family unit comes first, the individual second. "People are valued more for their character than for their level of success alone" (McGoldrick, 1993, p. 341). When an individual is dishonored or shamed, it reflects on the entire family. Many Hispanic Americans use the extended family network to solve problems; they seek outside professional help only if necessary.

Hispanic American values. Hispanic Americans tend to value human relations and person-centeredness and are open to displays of emotion, temperament, and affection. They emphasize strong identification with the nuclear and extended family. There is a sense of fatalism running through Hispanic cultures ("Whatever will be, will be"), with the belief "that one is at the mercy of the environment and has little control over what happens. [Hispanic Americans also may believe] that personal efforts are unlikely to influence the outcome of a situation [and therefore they are not] personally responsible for future successes or failures" (Giger & Davidhizar, 1991, p. 195).

Hispanic American socialization practices emphasize clear norms, responsibility training, and pressure to conform to adult standards. The traditional values are continually undergoing change, however, because of increased urbanization and higher levels of assimilation. For example, many Hispanic Americans believe that people can actively control their fate, that planning brings rewards, that they can place trust in people other than family and friends, and that family ties should not hamper a person's individual career. When children have these beliefs, friction may arise between them and their parents. Because traditional values still exert a powerful force, you will need to consider their importance when you work with Hispanic American children and families.

Hispanic Americans may experience value conflicts associated with cultural clashes. They may want to be seen as Americans and dissociate themselves from the traditional culture, or they may want to identify closely with their traditional culture and dissociate themselves from American values and symbols.

The following case illustrates how cultural values and the stress of acculturation affected a Hispanic American family (Canino & Canino, 1980).

CASE 9-2. MARIA PEREZ

Maria Perez, 14 years old, was referred to our mental health clinic by her school for occasional truancy and defiant behavior in the classroom. The school had previously requested a parents' conference to discuss this problem, and Maria had served as the translator between the English-speaking school officials and her Spanish-speaking parents. Maria's parents [believed], as do many Puerto Rican parents, that the school, as an extension of the family, should discipline her. The school [thought] otherwise. Mr. and Mrs. Perez perceived the school as hostile and intrusive. They fluctuated between severely punishing Maria and siding with her against the school. The problems were compounded when Mr. Perez was told that Maria's truancy was due to her "escapades" to meet a boyfriend. Mr. Perez reacted by demanding that Maria be home earlier than before, by withdrawing permission for his daughter to leave the household unless accompanied by a family member, and by accusing his wife of not raising her correctly.

Maria openly rebelled, citing the behavior of her peer group and accusing her father of ridiculous and old-fashioned attitudes. The once normally enmeshed, culturally acceptable pattern, whereby young girls are overly protected and discouraged from becoming independent, had broken down. In addition, Maria was bilingual and had become the family translator in its relations with outside institutions. As a "parentified" child with many responsibilities, it was difficult for her to assume a more submissive, dependent, and "respectful" role. In response to her increasing protestations and lack of respect, Mr. Perez forced Maria to stay at home and eventually did not even trust her to go to school. Mr. Perez became increasingly overprotective toward his daughter and developed difficulties with his wife concerning child-rearing practices. Maria's need to differentiate and express autonomous behavior had been curtailed. From the family's perspective, Maria had brought *verguenza* (shame) to her family and had broken the prescribed mores of *respeto* and *dignidad* (self-worth of the family). (p. 539)

Interventions would have to support the parents' authority to decide family rules *and* the child's right to autonomy (Canino & Canino, 1980).

Attitudes toward mental health. Hispanic Americans tend to be more tolerant than Anglo Americans of deviant behavior. They generally prefer to solve emotional problems within a family context. The pride of the Hispanic American family—manifested, for example, by a family's not wanting to lose face by admitting that a child is disabled—may make it extremely difficult even to arrange for a mental health evaluation. Hispanic Americans also are more likely to resist hospitalization of their children or to resist placing their children in institutions. Because of these attitudes, they tend to underuse organized mental health services.

When Hispanic American parents recognize that their child has a disability, they may give the child special treatment—showing the child excessive sympathy, overindulging the child, or placing few demands on the child. They may mistrust special education classes because they believe such classes are for "sick" or "crazy" children. Their most immediate concern may be "How long will it take to make the child well?"

The following case illustrates how misunderstanding of the child's culture initially led to an improper diagnosis and how the diagnosis was changed after the child's culture was considered (Ramos-McKay, Comas-Dias, & Rivera, 1988).

CASE 9-3. TOMÁS

Tomás, a 15-year-old Puerto Rican male, was brought to a clinic in New York City because of bizarre ideation and behavior. Tomás, who had arrived 6 months earlier from Puerto Rico, had been in school for 3 months on the mainland. During those 3 months, his behavior had deteriorated and he had become increasingly disruptive and aggressive. Before he came to the clinic, Tomás said that he saw the devil, who spoke to him. The devil, according to Tomás, was trying to get him to do "bad things."

An Anglo American psychiatrist evaluated Tomás and made a diagnosis of schizophrenia. However, the psychiatrist's lack of knowledge about Puerto Rican culture and about the socioeconomic conditions in the youngster's home, coupled with a lack of rapport with Tomás, apparently led to a more severe diagnosis than was indicated.

Tomás then was evaluated by a Hispanic American psychiatrist. Tomás told her that he had not wanted to come to the mainland to live, particularly because his father was still in Puerto Rico (the parents had been divorced for several years). Tomás, his mother, and five brothers and sisters were living in a slum area of New York City in a run-down three-room apartment and relied solely on welfare assistance. In Puerto Rico, Tomás's mother had had a job, although low paying, and the extended family had helped them to meet their needs so that no welfare assistance was necessary. In addition, Tomás saw his father from time to time when he lived in Puerto Rico. Tomás was experiencing stress with which he was not coping adaptively.

Tomás's auditory and visual "hallucinations" coincided with his mother's religiosity. When he told the school personnel about his hallucinations, it brought him a great deal of attention. Tomás did not present other symptomatology that suggested a thought disorder. He said that he felt fine when he was away from his home, family, and school.

The interviewer believed that Tomás was experiencing culture shock, material deprivation due to reduced financial circumstance, trauma over separating from his father, and humiliation over his living situation. The diagnosis made was of an adjustment disorder with mixed emotional features.

Tomás was sent to an adolescent facility for short-term treatment. During his stay in the facility, Tomás's hallucinations disappeared. Any discussion about returning home, however, increased his level of anxiety.

Tomás was discharged to a relative's home where living conditions were better and Tomás could still see his own family. No symptoms recurred, and Tomás returned to school successfully. Had the diagnosis of schizophrenia been maintained, Tomás would have been medicated with a major tranquilizer and hospitalized in a long-term treatment facility, possibly resulting in the development of a more chronic emotional problem. (adapted from pp. 26–27)

Language Considerations for Hispanic Americans

Linguistically, Hispanic American children and their families are a heterogeneous group, with wide variations in their degree of mastery of English and Spanish. Some Hispanic American children have difficulty in both languages. When Hispanic American children speak Spanish as their primary language, the Anglo American interviewer may have difficulty talking with them without an interpreter. Speech patterns of bilingual Hispanic American children often are a complex mixture of English and Spanish. This complexity may make it difficult for some Hispanic American children to become proficient in either language.

Spanish-speaking children may encounter three types of difficulties when they speak their own language.

Sibling Revelry   by Man Martin

1. *Borrowing from English.* Because their Spanish vocabulary may be limited, they may borrow from their English vocabulary to complete expressions begun in Spanish. For example, they may say "Yo estaba leyendo cuando it started to rain" (I was reading when it started to rain).

2. *Anglicizing words.* They may "anglicize certain words or…borrow English words to develop specific linguistic patterns (e.g., '*Está reinando*' for 'It's raining' [instead of '*Está lloviendo*'], calling a grocery store a '*groceria*' [instead of '*una tienda de abarrotes*'], or using '*carpeta*' for 'rug' instead of '*alfombra*')" (Marin & Marin, 1991, p. 86). English words given Spanish pronunciations and endings are called *pochismos.* Examples of pochismos include the word *huachar* (from the English verb "to watch"), used instead of the correct Spanish verb *mirar,* and the word *chuzar* (from the English verb "to choose"), used instead of the correct Spanish word *escoger.*

3. *Pronunciation problems.* They may have difficulties in pronunciation and enunciation in both the Spanish and the English language.

Traditional Medicine Among Hispanic Americans

As with other cultural practices, differences exist among Hispanic Americans in their health care practices. The following discussion of the health care practices of Hispanic Americans focuses on Mexican Americans and, to a lesser extent, Puerto Ricans.

Curanderismo. *Curanderismo* is the health care belief and practice system followed by some Mexican Americans. This system combines elements of European Roman Catholicism with beliefs and practices of native Indians of Mexico.

The concept of balance dominates much of the Mexican American world view regarding the cause and treatment of illness. Good health infers that one is in proper balance with God, as well as the family, fellow men, and the church…. Illness is often believed to be an imbalance in the social or spiritual aspects of life. (Giger & Davidhizar, 1991, p. 198)

Within curanderismo, there is a hierarchy of practitioners, beginning with a family member who is the recipient of family cures passed from generation to generation. Next is the *yerbero,* who specializes in using herbs and spices for healing and prevention. Then there is the *curandero,* who treats serious illnesses with prayers, teas, poultices and herbs. The primary focus of the curandero is to relieve individuals of their sins. Mexican Americans believe that the curandero has a gift from God for healing.

In addition, there are other traditional healers. One is the *espiritualisto,* a traditional healer who can analyze dreams and fears, foretell the future, and treat some supernatural or magical diseases. Another is the *brujo,* a traditional healer who practices witchcraft and uses hexes to solve problems of love and illness often motivated by hatred, jealousy, or envy (Friedman, 1986). Mexican Americans may prefer their traditional healers to conventional medical practitioners because the healers may be less dehumanizing, know the family, are part of the community, and may have a close, personal relationship with the patient.

Mexican American traditional medicine addresses specific ailments in children and adults. Here are some examples of such ailments:

1. *Caida de la mollera.* This condition is caused by some trauma to the infant, such as a fall or blow to the head. The infant's anterior fontanelle (a membrane-covered opening between bones in the head) is depressed below the contour of the skull. Symptoms include the inability of the infant to grasp firmly with his or her mouth when eating or drinking, diarrhea, crying spells, and restlessness. Local healers apply different unconventional treatments such as "prayers, pushing the palate from inside the infant's mouth, application of different substances such as eggs to the skull with subsequent pulling of the hairs, holding the child from the feet, and the like" (Ruiz, 1985, p. 67). These treatments are ineffective, and, if babies are not brought to the hospital in time, many may die (Spector, 1991).

2. *Mal de ojo.* This means "evil eye" or "powerful eye." The illness is caused when one person glances or stares at another person. Certain persons in the community can cause the illness, and women and children are particularly vulnerable to it. Symptoms include general malaise, sleepiness, fatigue, high fever, and severe headache. The treatment is to find the person who caused the illness and have that person touch the afflicted individual. If the person can't be found, special rituals are performed by the brujo, including saying prayers as the afflicted individual is brushed with eggs (Trotter, 1991). The afflicted area is located where the yolk of the egg settles.

3. *Susto.* This refers to illness from fright, and results from a stressful event or traumatic experience. It is believed that a person's soul or spirit leaves the body. Symptoms include restlessness during sleep, anorexia, depression, listlessness, and lack of interest in personal appearance (Hautman, 1979). Herbal teas and supernatural rituals are used to treat the illness (Trotter, 1991).

4. *Empacho.* This illness is caused by undigested food. Common symptoms are stomach pains, diarrhea, and vomiting. The illness is treated by body massages, such as rubbing and gently pinching the spine, laxatives, and saying prayers (Ruiz, 1985; Spector, 1991).

5. *Envidia or envy.* This misfortune happens to a person when his or her success provokes the envy of friends and neighbors. Thus, to succeed can be perceived as a failure by others in the culture (Spector, 1991). As a result, some Hispanic Americans would rather not be successful—they don't want to cause *envidia.*

The following example shows how a social worker's understanding of *envidia* helped her intervene in a case involving recovery from surgery.

CASE 9-4. CARMEN

A Mexican American female adolescent was recovering in a hospital from a successful operation. Before the operation, Carmen was friendly and cooperative with the nursing staff. However, after surgery, she became highly anxious and withdrawn. Carmen told a social worker that her mother had convinced her that her physical problems were due to a neighbor's *envidia* (envy) and that more problems would develop. The girl's family practiced *espiritism*. The social worker received permission from the girl and her family to contact the family's spiritual leader. He came to the hospital, performed the ritual of *despojo* (exorcism), and Carmen became her former gregarious self.

Diseases indigenous to the Hispanic American culture, such as those previously mentioned, are usually seen and treated first by the curandero. When the treatment is not successful, patients will probably turn to Western-style medical practitioners (Giger & Davidhizar, 1991). Curanderos may be particularly effective in treating those indigenous conditions that have significant psychological components.

The following excerpt illustrates the use of a culturally sensitive perspective in working with Mexican American families in a medical setting (López, Blacher, & Shapiro, 1998, who based their presentation on the work of Anderson, Toledo, and Hazam, 1982 and Toledo, Hughes, and Sims, 1979).

As a pediatric cardiologist, I encountered several Mexican American families who did not follow up with the recommended medical regimen of cardiac catheterization or heart surgery. They either stopped coming to their scheduled appointments or they did not agree to have the procedures. The parents had been told that if these medical procedures were not performed their children would likely become significantly impaired and in some instances die. Despite this information, they failed to follow the treatment regimen. Cost was not usually a factor as financial assistance was provided by the state.

Over a period of several years we studied what led to their noncompliance, and based on this information, we developed an intervention to increase compliance. The first two steps of this intervention were (a) to establish rapport with the family, sometimes meeting the families at their homes, and (b) to let them know that the purpose of the visit was to listen to their views, not to force them to make a decision.

Another important step was to elicit their beliefs about the heart, what might happen with heart surgery, and their child's heart condition. Religious and spiritual themes often came up. Some stated that with an operation the Holy Ghost (Spirit) would escape from the child's heart. Others were concerned that the surgeon would see the child's sins when the heart was exposed. Still others were concerned that the child might die with such procedures. In terms of the child's health status, many found it difficult to believe that the child was indeed ill. As far as they could tell, there were no obvious signs that their child's heart was any different from any other child's heart.

We listened to their views about the heart and surgery. We respected their religious beliefs. What we tried to do was help them "see" the problem. In contrast to past efforts which used x-rays and medical terminology, we described and explained the problem in their terms. To do so, we had them compare their child's impaired heart to…another child's normal heart. We had the parents place their hand over the child's heart and feel the distinctive heaving of the impaired heart. We also had them listen to the child's heart to hear the trill created by the heart's abnormal anatomy. When noticeable, we showed them the subtle but observable signs of heart disease, such as deformity in the chest. We also used the analogy of a pump or motor locked up in a closet. One can't see that something is wrong with the motor, but by feeling different vibrations, by hearing different sounds, and by doing a test (a catheterization) one can "open the door and see" that something is indeed wrong. They understood this.

It was also important to know who made the decisions in the family. Prior efforts to obtain the parents' consent sometimes, due to scheduling problems, resulted in obtaining only the mother's consent. Some of the fathers disliked the fact that they were not included. On other occasions, the "abuelita" (grandmother) played a key role in the decision making and needed to be included. We made sure to assess who made the important decisions and to include them all.

Health practices. Mexican Americans may turn first to their families for help and support. Separation of patients from their families and kin runs counter to Mexican American culture. Often, Mexican Americans will not make medical decisions until they have consulted with their families (Friedman, 1986).

Magico-religious practices are common among Mexican Americans, especially when illnesses become severe. These include making promises to God, visiting shrines, offering medals and candles, and saying prayers. Many homes have special shrines with statues of saints where candles are lit and prayers are offered. These shrines may hold prominent places in the homes (Spector, 1991). These practices usually are done at the same time as any medical treatment and are not likely to interfere with the treatments. Exhibit 9-3 describes how the failure to recognize cultural traditions may lead to an incorrect interpretation.

Puerto Ricans. Puerto Ricans perceive health and illness in many of the same ways as Mexican Americans do. They share beliefs in spirits and spiritualism (*espiritismo*), they encourage the acceptance of having visions and hearing voices, and they usually have faith in traditional healers. In addition, Puerto Rican traditional healers treat other maladies such as *fatigue* (asthma-like symptoms), *pasmo* (paralysis-like symptoms of the face or limbs), and *ataque* (screaming, falling to the ground, and wildly moving arms and legs).

Puerto Ricans turn to traditional medicine for the same reasons as Mexican Americans—language barriers, religious beliefs, and poverty. Also, both groups may turn away from the majority health care systems because of differences in time orientation. For example, both groups tend to give little attention to the exact time of day. When they are given an early appointment, they may come late or fail to come at all because it is not important to them to adhere to time demands (Spector, 1991).

Cubans. Some health care practices of Cubans have "their roots in Africa and came to Cuba during the slavery

**Exhibit 9-3
Multicultural Manners:
Recognizing Death as a Part of Life**

The hospital oncology department holds meetings for doctors to ease the emotional toll of treating dying children. At one session, Dr. Kent relates his concern about the family of Estela Ramirez, an 8-year-old patient who has recently died. He has visited the Ramirez home and discovers an altar with incense, candles, yellow flowers, fruit, plates of food and Estela's photo. He notices more disturbing articles: candied skulls with eyes of rhinestones and sequins, small round breads decorated with skulls and crossbones, tiny toy coffins with pop-up cadavers and skeleton puppets. Dr. Kent finds these objects morbid. Since Estela died more than three weeks ago, he believes the Ramirez family is behaving inappropriately, that they are obsessed with death. He advises, "You must get on with your life." The Ramirez family believes that is what they are doing.

What Went Wrong?
Dr. Kent should have checked the calendar. He arrived at the Ramirez house on Nov. 2, All Soul's Day. For Mexicans living across the border and here, it is also Dia de Los Muertos, or Day of the Dead. Rather than discovering a macabre memorial for Estela, the doctor had stumbled into an annual event where families offer flowers and favorite foods to the recently deceased. This Aztec-based holiday, with ties to Halloween, recognizes—even celebrates—the reality that death is a part of life.

Rule: Before making assumptions, check the cultural traditions of the people with whom you are involved.

Source: Reprinted, with permission of the author, from N. Dresser, "Recognizing Death as a Part of Life," in *Los Angeles Times,* October 24, 1994, p. B6, copyright by N. Dresser.

ments section. The material in this exercise was adapted from López, Grover, Holland, Johnson, Kain, Kanel, Mellins, and Rhyne (1989).

A 5-year-old Hispanic American girl at a summer camp refused to take showers at night and had difficulty dressing and undressing in the presence of other people. She was throwing huge tantrums and required considerable individual attention from her female counselors. She seemed terrified that someone would hurt her if they saw her naked.

Comments
The staff at the camp initially considered a behavior modification program to get her to take showers and dress in the morning, because they thought she was emotionally disturbed. However, a supervisor wondered whether her symptoms might be related to her cultural background and upbringing. The supervisor called the parents. They told the supervisor that the child was raised to be modest about her body and not to expose herself to anyone except her mother. One can imagine the terror that she must have been feeling when her counselors tried to get her to shower with other people. The staff was asking her to violate her parents' code of honor and to act in ways that previously would have resulted in punishment. A behavior modification plan would have been disastrous. Instead, the staff considered cultural issues and modified the camp rules. They allowed her to shower with one adult and to dress quickly after the other children had left the bunk. The child's tantrums stopped after the staff began the new procedure.

No hay mal que por bien no venga. (There is nothing bad out of which good cannot come.)

—Hispanic American saying

---

era of the Spanish colonization period" (Ruiz, 1985, p. 70). Cubans may see illnesses as being caused by natural or supernatural causes. Even illnesses such as colitis, colds, or headaches may be seen as stemming from supernatural causes. Treatment may include the use of "prayer, animal sacrifice, special baths, perfumes, oils, candles, herbs, weeds, plants, and the like" (Ruiz, 1985, p. 70). These health care practices are called *santeria* (saintcraft) and *brujeria* (witchcraft). Cubans who are members of the lower social classes are more likely to follow these health care practices than are those from the middle and upper classes.

**Exercise 9-1. Using a Culturally Sensitive
Approach in Case Management**

Read the following case. What do you believe are the reasons for the child's tantrums? What interventions would you recommend? Compare your ideas with those in the Com-

ASIAN AMERICANS

Asian Americans are one of the fastest-growing populations in the United States, numbering, according to the 1990 U.S. census, over 7.3 million people. About 29% of Asian Americans are below 18 years of age. Most Asian Americans live in the West (56%), followed by the Northwest (18%), South (15%), and Midwest (11%). Figure 9-3 shows selected groups of the Asian American population.

Between 1971 and 1993, the United States admitted 1,077,242 refugees from Asia. Asian American communities in the United States are made up of individuals who emigrated mainly from China, Japan, Korea, the Philippines, Thailand, Vietnam, Cambodia, and Laos. However, most of the refugees came from Vietnam (approximately 52%) and Laos (approximately 18%). "Of the major Southeast Asian groups, Vietnamese are the most likely to have been exposed to Western life before migration, while Cambodians have suffered the most severe trauma under the Pol Pot regime, and many Laotians, especially the highland tribal people, are from strictly agricultural and nonliterate societies. These

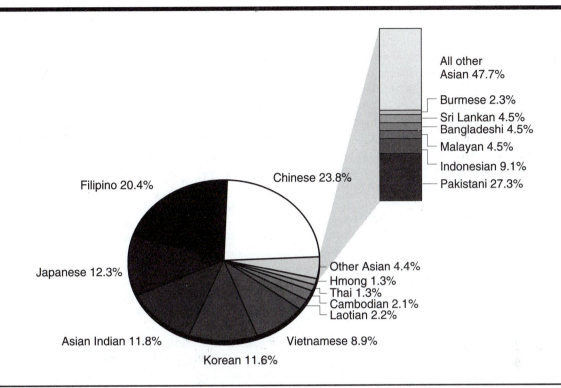

Figure 9-3. Origins of the Asian American population in the United States in 1990 (percent of the total Asian American population reporting each origin). From U.S. Bureau of the Census (1993), *We the American…Asians,* p. 2.

differences are likely to mediate differential mental health needs, service use, and outcome patterns" (Ying & Hu, 1994, p. 454).

Table 9-2 shows the demographic characteristics of the major Asian groups living in the United States in 1990. Southeast Asians, having recently fled from wars in their countries, were the least acculturated group and had the lowest per capita income.

Asian American Culture

Asian immigrant groups have special problems associated with language competency, unemployment, education, racism, and discrimination. Within the Asian American population, there are at least 29 distinct subgroups, which differ in language, religion, and customs. Thus, generalizations about Asian Americans are difficult because of differences in subcultural backgrounds, demographic variables, life style, socioeconomic status, and degree of acculturation. (The material in this section in part is based on Sue & Sue, 1987.)

A bimodal distribution of wealth exists among Asian Americans, with some families living close to the poverty level and others enjoying economic success. In 1995, approximately 12.4% of Asian American families were living below the poverty level (U.S. Bureau of the Census, 1996b). (This compares with 6.4% of White families and 26.4% of Black families.) Educationally, Asian Americans tend to do well in the physical sciences but poorly in subjects requiring mastery of the English language. Their degree of difficulty in understanding and speaking English is similar to

Table 9-2
Demographic Characteristics of Major Asian Groups in the United States

Characteristic	Chinese	Japanese	Korean	Filipino	Southeast Asian
Speaks English well	76%	90%	75%	91%	53%
Born in United States	37%	72%	18%	35%	9%
Graduated high school	71%	82%	78%	74%	56%
Per capita income	$7,500	$7,800	$5,200	$6,700	$2,900

Source: U.S. General Accounting Office (1990).

that of Hispanic Americans. Also, the two groups are similar in their underutilization of mental health services.

Asian American family structure. Asian Americans tend to carry on the traditions and customs of their forefathers, one of which is to view ancestors and elders with great respect. The father is the traditional head of the household, and his authority is unquestioned. Male and female children have different allegiances after they marry—the male to the family in which he was born, the female to the family into which she marries. The younger generation is expected to care for the older generation, although this practice is changing with acculturation.

Asian American families tend to be conservative, to resist change, and to stress high achievement. Family roles are rigidly defined. Asian Americans tend to confront problems indirectly and avoid offending others. They emphasize the restraining of emotions, particularly in Chinese culture. The family has great importance, and the reputation of individual family members reflects on the entire family. The family uses various techniques, such as the induction of guilt and shame and appeals to obligation, to keep family members in line. Family members are expected to subordinate their own interests to the interests of the family. Parents may insist that girls marry individuals chosen by the parents (arranged marriages). Finally, many Asian Americans view the role of the female as subservient to that of the male, a view that may be difficult for non-Asian clinicians and acculturated Asian American females to accept.

The strong sense of obligation to the family may be foreign to non-Asian clinicians, who may value autonomy and independence. However, for Asians, *interdependency is encouraged and autonomy and independence are discouraged.* Interdependency refers to relationships among family members in which support and assistance are provided for each family member, who, in turn, provides support and assistance for the entire family. When children become adults, they are expected to continue to be involved with the family and to be active in maintaining its status, welfare, and integrity. For example, it is common for Asian adult children to live at home, for several extended families to live in the same home or near each other, and for family members to help with the family business. Although these patterns exist in all cultures, they are seen to a greater extent in many Asian cultures.

In Asian American groups, parents expect children to (a) obey authority figures, (b) avoid overt signs of conflict and get along with others, (c) be humble, obedient, and not outspoken, (d) speak only when spoken to, and (e) say nothing rather than upset someone. Failure to follow these practices may cause shame for the family. You will need to decide to what extent these generalizations hold for a particular case. (Also see Exhibit 9-4 about the myth of the so-called model minority and Exhibit 9-5 about a tradition in Chinese culture that, if violated, can cause some Chinese people to become upset.)

In some Asian American families, when the parents have not learned English, children may take on a parental role because of their knowledge of English. This may create problems in families that have a traditional family structure. The parents may have difficulty allowing their children to assume a position of power and control, even in limited interactions.

In the passage that follows, an Asian American adolescent female describes her conflict with her parents about dating (Uba, 1994):

When I was sixteen, I felt I was ready [to start dating], but my parents didn't think so. They told me that it wasn't time yet and that if I had a boyfriend, it would interfere with my education. I fought with my parents telling them all my friends are dating and I didn't see how it could interfere with school. This only made matters worse and then my mom would start with her life story of how she wasn't even allowed to talk to boys when she was my age. I would argue back, telling her that it is different in Thailand than in America, and then she would really get furious leaving the problem unsolved. That was how most of our arguments ended. (p. 126)

Problems of assimilation. As Asian Americans begin to assimilate, they may experience cultural conflicts. For example, they may be confused about how they should behave because Anglo Americans tend to view their traditionally accepted restraint of feelings in a negative light—that is, as passive and inhibited. The way Asian Americans resolve such conflicts plays an important role in their adjustment. Elders and male adults may experience loss of status if they are not successful in obtaining high-paying or prestigious jobs. To add to the confusion and possible maladjustment, clashes with the dominant society, such as the internment of Japanese-Americans in concentration camps in the United States during World War II, have led to the further suppression of self-expression among some Asian Americans. They have come to value silence and inconspicuousness as a shield against abuse when dealing with the Anglo American culture. Their conflict with the dominant culture may explain why some Asian American youths seek out and join Asian gangs.

Here are two examples of how Asian American adolescents describe the problem of integrating two cultures (Uba, 1994).

I can't decide which culture I can relate myself to. There are some situations that I ran into, I don't know if I listen to the American voice or the Chinese voice inside my head. I do not know which culture [is] suitable for me. Being caught between two cultures is not a good place to be in. When you approach a problem or situation that needs to be solved, there are two voices in your head—one tells you to do [it] the American way and the other tells you to do it the Chinese way. (p. 116)

I'm only part Thai. I have some Chinese in me and the rest of me is American. I don't think I can ever be fully Thai as my parents would like, because almost everything I do I do using some parts of each culture. I eat some American food with chopsticks and a spoon. When I pray to the Buddha, I speak to him in English. When

Exhibit 9-4
Asian Americans Find Being Ethnic "Model" Has Downside

Youth

Many young Asian Americans complain that the stereotype that they are a "model minority"—quiet, hard-working, and whizzes at mathematics and science—is too narrow and often confining. They find it difficult to live up to the expectations of their parents and feel hemmed in by the attitudes of the larger society.

The stereotype that they are introverted has led, they believe, to their being discouraged from going into fields such as art, acting, and management. And the stereotype that they are whizzes at mathematics and science has occasionally led non-Asian students to transfer out of classes that have many Asian students for fear that the Asian American students will inflate the grading curve. The success image also prevents people from recognizing psychological problems that develop among Asian Americans students.

Severity of Problems

Problems may become so severe that some Asian American students will even consider suicide.

At age 17, Kio T. Konno seemed to fit the stereotype perfectly. Hard-charging, industrious and bright, she was destined for stardom, like so many of her Asian American "whiz kid" peers. A senior at prestigious Lowell High School, she pulled a B-plus average, spoke fluent Japanese, and snagged national swimming awards. Her Japanese parents cared so much about her education that they moved closer to the school to ease her commute. Brown University was actively recruiting her. But last October, a week before her 18th birthday, Miss Konno walked into her closet and hanged herself. Miss Konno's parents decline to comment on their daughter's death. But people familiar with the case, as well as a friend, say Miss Konno was distraught over the pressure to succeed—from her parents, from Asian and non-Asian society and even, in a sense, from Asian history.

Though Asian Americans have been in the United States for generations, they stand out from other cultural groups, and White Americans view them as outsiders.

Influence of Parents

Cultural factors to some extent encourage Asian American students to pursue careers in math and science. Asian culture encourages children to work alone quietly and not to express themselves in public. However, some Asian American children say that their parents press them to go into math and science because these fields are more financially stable. First-generation Asian Americans are heavily influenced by their parents.

The influence of Asian American parents on the lives of their children can be so great that it borders on almost complete control of their social life and educational careers.

In many respects Crystal Hul, 16, is more American than Cambodian. The daughter of a well-known leader in Southern California's Cambodian refugee community, she has been in the United States since the age of 4. She speaks fluent English, gets good grades, was recently nominated for sophomore princess by her classmates, and hopes to pursue a career in political science. Yet when Crystal walks through the front door of her Long Beach home, she enters a different world. Here she must never allow her head to rise above that of her father's. She must continually refill his rice bowl until he finishes dinner and signals that she may eat. She must never leave the house alone. She is not allowed to date, drive a car, enter a movie theater, or attend any party not also attended by her brothers. And she fully expects her parents eventually to choose a husband for her—whom she is unlikely even to speak with before the wedding.

Pressure from Two Opposing Cultural Forces

The struggle to balance the strain of living in two worlds—the world of tradi-

tional Asian culture, with its concern with family harmony, and the world of contemporary American culture, with its emphasis on individuality—is becoming increasingly difficult for countless Asian American children. And some are breaking down under the strain.

Attitudes Toward Professional Help

What can make all this especially difficult for Asian American youths is that they are generally less likely to seek professional psychological help than other youths. Families may seek counseling only when their children have a mental breakdown. Asians believe that you are not supposed to tell people your personal business.

Adults

The myth of the affluent "model minority" also pertains to Asian American adults and families. Here are some statistics released in 1994:

1. *Rate of poverty.* Asian Americans in Los Angeles, San Francisco, and New York have a rate of poverty twice as high as that of Anglo Americans.

2. *Welfare.* Southeast Asians—Vietnamese, Cambodians, and Laotians—have the highest welfare dependency rate of any racial or ethnic group within the Asian community.

3. *Business opportunities.* Asians are engaged in low-margin, low-profit businesses, with one-third of Asian Americans employed in the highly competitive retail section; they most commonly operate restaurants.

4. *Jobs.* A disproportionate number of Asian Americans are in low- and mid-level jobs. They have little opportunity to advance into management, encountering a "glass ceiling" that prevents Asian Americans and other minorities from becoming managers.

Source: Adapted from "Asian Girls: A Cultural Tug of War," by D. Haldane, *Los Angeles Times,* September 24, 1988, pp. 1, 22, 23; "Asian American Youth Suffer a Rising Toll for Heavy Pressures," by J. E. Rigdon, *Wall Street Journal,* July 10, 1991, pp. A1, A5; "Asian Americans Find Being Ethnic 'Model' Has Downside," by J. Toth, *Los Angeles Times,* May 21, 1991, p. A5; "Study of Asians in U.S. Finds Many Struggling," by N. R. Brooks, *Los Angeles Times,* May 19, 1994, pp. A1, A25.

Exhibit 9-5
Multicultural Manners: Sweeping Away the Luck

Janet's grandmother is an elderly Chinese lady from Vietnam who holds on to tradition. On the eve of the Chinese New Year, all the relatives come over for dinner. The children play games and are given red envelopes with money inside by the married adults. The next day, Janet wants to do something nice and sweeps the floor. Grandmother becomes so infuriated she ignores Janet for the whole day.

What Went Wrong?
What Janet didn't know was that, according to her grandmother's belief, wealth and good luck were swept away along with crumbs and dust. Similarly, many Chinese people do not shower on New Year's Day for fear of washing away good luck. This year [1995], the Chinese Year of the Boar begins Jan. 31. Vietnamese people celebrate their new year at the same time but call it Tet. They hope to attract good luck by placing food offerings on home altars to invite spirits of deceased family members to share the holiday. Janet's misunderstanding is typical of problems caused by generational differences. As younger members of an immigrant family become more Americanized, they become less familiar with traditions of their elders.

Rule: Chinese people skip some cleaning routines on New Year's Day to avoid undoing good fortune in the coming year.

Source: "Sweeping Away the Luck" in *Multicultural Manners,* N. Dresser, Copyright © John Wiley & Sons, Inc. 1996, p. 114. Reprinted by permission of John Wiley & Sons, Inc.

I speak to my sisters or Thai friends, I blend the two languages together (but they still understand me). I mix both cultures so much, sometimes I think I've started my own new culture. (p. 116)

Contrasts between Anglo American and Asian American character traits. In comparison with Anglo Americans, Asian Americans tend to (a) be more practical in approaching problems, favoring concrete and well-structured ideas that have immediate practical application, (b) be less autonomous and more dependent, conforming, and obedient to authority, (c) be more inhibited and reserved, and therefore, more withdrawn from social contacts and responsibilities, often experiencing social alienation, (d) be more formal in interpersonal relationships, (e) view outsiders with more suspicion, (f) value silence more, and (g) make more effort to avoid disagreeing or criticizing, keeping their voices low because raising one's voice is seen as a sign of anger.

Asians tend to view time differently than Westerners do. They perceive time as a reflection of the eternal, not in terms of past, present, and future. Consequently, they may not adhere to fixed schedules, may arrive late for appointments, and may insist on completing one task before moving on to another (Giger & Davidhizar, 1991).

Use of mental health and medical services. Asian Americans may seek treatment for psychological disorders *only* when the disorders are relatively severe (Sue & Sue, 1987). They usually treat milder disturbances within the family structure. Asian Americans may differ from the majority group in their ability to pay for services, in their degree of familiarity with available mental health services, and in their attitude toward mental health clinics. They may view mental health clinics with suspicion. If they go to a mental health clinic, they may be reluctant to share personal problems with a clinician, whom they view as a stranger. Thus, the low rates of psychiatric hospitalization and juvenile delinquency among Asian Americans likely reflect cultural values and not low rates of psychological disorders.

Asian Americans may be reluctant to discuss their feelings and problems openly for several reasons (Uba, 1994). They may believe that (a) discussing feelings and problems with a stranger is immodest, boring, dominating, indicative of a lack of character, and likely to bring shame to the family, (b) complaining has no purpose because problems are a natural, unavoidable aspect of life, (c) displaying emotions is a sign of weakness (distress is hidden out of a sense of stoicism and pride), (d) talking about problems may bring out hostility in the listener, (e) refusing to talk about their traumas will protect them and their families from memories of the traumas, or (f) a mental health professional cannot be trusted. Another obstacle for some Asian Americans is that being interviewed in a small room may bring back memories of being interrogated.

Because Asian Americans attach more stigma or shame to mental or emotional problems than do Anglo Americans, they may be hesitant to seek treatment. The entire family unit may feel stigmatized when one member of the family has mental or emotional problems. This loss of face is called "mentz" by the Chinese, "haiji" by the Japanese, "hiya" by Filipinos, and "chaemyum" by Koreans. The stigma may be so great that Asian Americans may be extremely reluctant to admit to any psychological problems. When they do admit to them, they may see the problems as having an organic or somatic basis. Southeast Asian Americans may view psychological services as a business transaction in which one remains aloof and avoids private revelations or the expression of feelings (Nashio & Bilmes, 1987).

Their reluctance to discuss family relationships, criticize their parents, or make any comments that might reflect poorly on themselves, their family, or their ethnic community may interfere with the clinical assessment (Uba, 1994). Asian Americans may talk around the issues or not talk at all; their behavior may lead mental health professionals to make erroneous inferences. Reluctance to speak about feelings and problems does not mean that Asian Americans lack affect, are unaware of their feelings, or are deceptive. Rather, as you have read, these are functional patterns and coping mechanisms that must be understood from their cultural perspective.

The communication styles of Asian Americans may differ from those found in Anglo American culture in the following ways (Uba, 1994). Asian Americans may (a) make self-deprecating remarks out of modesty, not because they believe their statements or because they have low self-esteem, (b) prefer "to employ indirect styles of communicating, to avoid direct confrontations, and to deflect unpleasantness that can lead to disagreements and embarrassment..." (p. 230), (c) talk about their emotional difficulties in an oblique, understated way with little obvious emotion to sustain interpersonal harmony, (d) expect listeners "to be sensitive to indirect verbal and nonverbal social cues, read between the lines, and infer the attitudes and sentiments of the speaker" (p. 231), (e) speak softly and interpret the loud speech of others as indicative of aggressiveness or poor self-control, and (f) avoid extended eye contact.

You can establish rapport with Asian Americans by being gracious—such as by warmly welcoming them, offering tea or soft drinks, encouraging them to remove their coats, or offering a comfortable chair—and helping them feel welcome; greeting family members in the proper order, with the elder person first; using the clients' proper names (do not use nicknames, and recognize that in many Asian groups the order of the first and last names is reversed); pronouncing clients' names properly; and not calling attention to or praising children in public (Uba, 1994). Some Asian Americans feel uncomfortable and embarrassed if they are praised. "They may even consider praise as a form of subtle criticism" (Dresser, 1996, p. 159).

In medical facilities, some particular problems also may arise in the treatment of Asian Americans (Giger & Davidhizar, 1991).

Chinese Americans experience a great amount of stress when they are in health care facilities. The language barrier and different cultural background often cause these people to experience confusion, depression, frustration, helplessness, and powerlessness. However, they feel that they would inconvenience the health care worker and thus are often embarrassed to ask questions when no healthcare workers speak their language.... These emotional experiences are often not verbally expressed but may be indicated by nonverbal cues. Frequently, observing nonverbal behaviors and encouraging patients to verbalize will help identify these psychological problems. (p. 362)

The following case illustrates how a family turned to a mental health clinic only when other sources of help had been exhausted (adapted from Huang & Ying, 1989).

CASE 9-5. ROSE

Rose was an 18-year-old adolescent who had emigrated from China with her parents as a young child. She was brought to an inpatient mental health crisis unit by her mother with the assistance of a mental health outreach worker. At intake, she was hostile and belligerent and needed to be restrained. She was disheveled and unkempt, disoriented, and angry at her parents for "incarcerating" her; she claimed she had important appointments to keep.

The mother had noted a gradual deterioration in Rose's behavior following completion of high school about one and a half years earlier. At that time, she had become sullen and withdrawn, lost all friendships, and had difficulty maintaining a job in the family's small restaurant. She began using makeup in a garish fashion, staying out late at night, and verbally abusing her mother. The precipitating incident for admission to the crisis unit was increasingly bizarre behavior in the home, followed by a physical assault on her mother.

During the first six months of Rose's deterioration, the mother had sought help from an acupuncturist, relatives, the family doctor, and a minister. When nothing seemed to relieve the problem, the family, ashamed and desperate, began to lock Rose in her room. It was during this eight-month period that she would escape at night and wander the streets. Her brother would find her, usually quite delusional, and bring her home. Rose's mother was quite tearful as she provided this history.

Huang and Ying (1989) noted that the "family had lived with their daughter's deteriorating condition for over a year with limited resources and no formal assistance. It was not until she became unmanageable that they sought help. By that time, the daughter had become so psychotic that inpatient treatment was required" (pp. 52–53). The case illustrates that when Asian American families come to a crisis unit, they may have a profound sense of failure and shame and may have feelings of guilt and uneasiness for exposing family problems. Conversely, they also may be yearning for relief and a close supportive relationship. It is important to appreciate this possible ambivalence.

Language Considerations for Asian Americans

Anglo American clinicians may have language and communication problems when they interview Asian Americans. Misunderstandings may result because of the ways Asian Americans use language or pronounce English words. For example, some Asian Americans tend to avoid using the word "no" because they consider it rude to do so. "The word 'yes' can mean 'no' or 'perhaps.' A direct 'no' is avoided because it may cause the same individual to lose face. Hesitance, ambiguity, subtlety, and implicity are dominant in Chinese speech" (Giger & Davidhizar, 1991, p. 361).

Asian languages also are context bound: "Most of the meaningful information is either in the physical context or internalized in the person who receives the information, while relatively little is contained in the verbally transmitted part of the message.... The speaker or sender's true intent is thus often camouflaged in the context of the situation.... Nonverbal communication thus conveys significantly more information in high-context Asian cultures, wherein silence is particularly valued" (Lynch & Hanson, 1992, pp. 232, 233).

Traditional Medicine Among Asian Americans

Chinese traditional medicine is based on a view that health is a state of spiritual and physical harmony with nature. The following discussion focuses primarily on Chinese traditional medicine, which serves as the prototype for Asian American traditional medicine; differences, however, exist among Asian American cultures in their practice of traditional medicine. The foundation of Chinese traditional medicine rests in the religion and philosophy of Taoism (Spector, 1991). Taoism maintains that people have no control over nature; therefore, they must adjust to the physical world and not attempt to control or change it. "The concepts of *yin* and *yang* represent the power that regulates the universe and that exists also within the body, as well as food. *Yang* represents the positive, active, or 'male' force, and *yin* represents the negative, inactive, or 'female' force" (Giger & Davidhizar, 1991, pp. 367–368). In addition, yang reflects light, warmth, and fullness, and yin reflects darkness, cold, and emptiness (Spector, 1991).

Some Chinese believe that an imbalance of the forces of yin and yang is responsible for illness, as their balance is responsible for good health. They classify body systems and food as either yin or yang (Giger & Davidhizar, 1991).

Chinese medicine includes disease prevention and treatment. Amulets are used to drive out evil spirits (Spector, 1991).

These consist of a charm with an idol or Chinese character painted in red or black ink and written on a strip of yellow paper. These amulets are hung over a door, pasted on a curtain or wall, worn in the hair, or placed in a red bag and pinned on clothing.... Jade is believed to be the most precious of all stones because jade is seen as the giver of children, health, immortality, wisdom, power, victory, growth, and food. Jade charms are worn to bring health, and should they turn dull or break, the wearer will surely meet misfortune. (p. 176)

Treatment procedures include acupuncture, herbal medicines, massage, coining, spooning, cupping, and moxibustion (Giger & Davidhizar, 1991). Let's look at some of these practices.

Acupuncture. Acupuncturists cure illnesses or relieve pain by puncturing the skin with needles. Specific points known as *meridians* extend internally throughout the body in a fixed network. "Since all of the networks merge and have their outlets on the skin, the way to treat internal problems is to puncture the meridians, which are also categorically identified in terms of yin and yang, as are the diseases" (Spector, 1991, p. 178).

Herbal medicines. Healers prescribe herbal medicines based on the yin-yang properties of the illness. The gathering season of an herb is important for its effect. A popular herb used to treat several conditions is ginseng root. Proper preparation is needed to release all of its therapeutic properties (Spector, 1991).

Other treatments. Other treatments include (Giger & Davidhizar, 1991):

- *massage,* which stimulates circulation, increases joint flexibility, and improves resistance to illnesses
- *coining,* which involves the application of oil and rubbing of the affected area with the edge of a coin; the treatment may result in bruises
- *spooning,* which involves the application of saline or water to the back, neck, shoulders, chest, or forehead, after which the area is pinched or massaged until it reddens, and then scratched with a porcelain spoon until bruises appear
- *cupping,* which consists of creating a vacuum by burning a material in a cup and immediately placing it on the selected area; the treatment leaves 2-inch circular burns
- *moxibustion,* which involves igniting the moxa plant and placing it near specific areas of the body; the treatment leaves tiny craters on the skin

Comment on traditional medicine among Asian Americans. Chinese Americans may find many aspects of Western medicine distasteful. They may be most upset by blood tests, because they see blood as an irreplaceable source of life for the entire body. They will not react well to diagnostic workups that include blood tests if they believe that a physician can make a diagnosis from a physical examination only. Chinese Americans have a great respect for the body, and they prefer to die with their bodies intact; therefore, they may refuse surgery (Spector, 1991).

Because some Chinese Americans are fatalistic, they may hesitate to seek conventional medical treatment. Instead, they may attempt to treat themselves according to the principles of yin-yang. Even when they do seek conventional medical treatment, they may continue to treat themselves. The Western medical practitioner needs to be aware of the possible double treatments to prevent complications (Giger & Davidhizar, 1991).

A journey of a thousand miles begins with the first step.

—Chinese saying

Better to cover the fish than to chase the cat.

—Japanese saying

Birds have nests. People have roots.

—Vietnamese saying

NATIVE AMERICANS

According to the 1990 U.S. census, there are about 2 million Native Americans, including Eskimos and Aleuts, constituting less than 1% of the U.S. population. About 35% of Native Americans are below 18 years of age. Most Native Americans live in the West (48%) and the South (29%), fol-

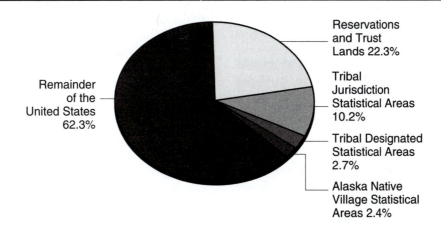

Reservations and Trust Lands 22.3%

Tribal Jurisdiction Statistical Areas 10.2%

Tribal Designated Statistical Areas 2.7%

Alaska Native Village Statistical Areas 2.4%

Remainder of the United States 62.3%

Figure 9-4. Types of areas inhabited by American Indians, Eskimos, and Aleuts in 1990 (percent of the total Native American population inhabiting each type of area). From U.S. Bureau of the Census (1993), *We the…First Americans,* p. 7.

lowed by the Midwest (17%) and Northeast (6%). Figure 9-4 shows the areas in which Native Americans live.

The term *Native American* is a broad, almost arbitrary category covering 552 federally recognized tribes in the United States. These groups speak 252 language dialects (perhaps representing only six language families) and represent many tribal nations, such as the Cherokee, Navajo, Chippewa, and Sioux. Figure 9-5 shows the populations of the 10 largest Native American tribes.

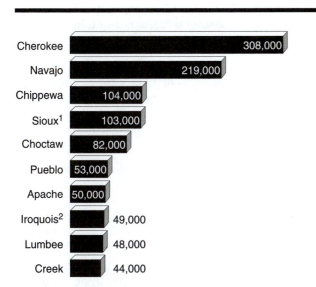

Cherokee 308,000
Navajo 219,000
Chippewa 104,000
Sioux[1] 103,000
Choctaw 82,000
Pueblo 53,000
Apache 50,000
Iroquois[2] 49,000
Lumbee 48,000
Creek 44,000

[1] Any entry with the spelling "Siouan" was miscoded to Sioux in North Carolina.
[2] Reporting and/or processing problems have affected the data for this tribe.

Figure 9-5. Populations of the 10 largest Native American tribes in 1990 (in thousands of people). From U.S. Bureau of the Census (1993), *We the…First Americans,* p. 2.

Native Americans have a long history of oppression and discrimination. Anglo Americans forced them to live on reservations and give up property rights and required some of their children to live in boarding schools. Many Native Americans have few economic opportunities—especially those living on reservations, most of whom live in poverty. As noted in Chapter 8, approximately 27.2% of Native American families lived below the poverty level in 1990. However, the emergence of gambling casinos on Native American property has brought prosperity to a few Native American groups and, depending on the distribution of casino profits, to some individual Native Americans as well. In addition, Alaskan Native Americans have seen remarkable economic changes in the second half of the twentieth century, resulting from "(a) the discovery of oil; (b) the passage of the Alaska Native Claims Settlement Act…which created Alaska Native corporations; (c) the modernization of villages with water and sewer; (d) locally controlled schools; (e) publicly subsidized housing; (f) the cash economy; (g) the introduction of commercial and educational television; and (h) the development of implementation of the most sophisticated methods of communication through teleconferencing, slow-scan television, electronic bulletin board, and micro-computers" (Mohatt, McDiarmid, & Montoya, 1988, p. 327).

Native American Culture

The Native American identity is complex (Everett et al., 1983).

The search for a Native American identity goes in many directions and is compounded by the immediate difficulty of defining a Native American. There is no single definition of a Native American. Individuals vary in degree of blood and level of acculturation. For some purposes one may be a Native American but not for others, and one may be accepted as a Native American by some individuals but not by others. This search for a definition involves both legal and emotional issues. The primary identification that Native Americans make is with their particular nation, band, or clan, such as Navajo, San Juan Pueblo, or Eastern Band Cherokee. Because there is great cultural diversity among Native American groups, you should not treat them as homogeneous. You must learn about the history and traditions of the particular Native American communities that you are serving if you are to achieve success. (p. 601, with changes in notation)

Native American family structure. The Native American family is frequently composed of extended family members and of nonfamily members of the same band or tribe, who may encompass several households (Giger & Davidhizar, 1991). In some Native American tribes, elders are viewed as the family leaders, and respect for individuals increases with age. Also, there is a strong role for women. The family is viewed as important, particularly in periods of crisis, when family members are expected to serve as sources of support and security. Some Native Americans tend to place great emphasis on the extended family as a unit; therefore, you should solicit the opinions of the family members in deciding treatment options.

Failure to consider the role of the extended family in Native American children's culture may result in a wrong decision, as the following case illustrates (Red Horse, 1982).

CASE 9-6. LINDA
Linda, a 17-year-old Native American girl, was performing well in high school. At the age of 14 years, she chose to move out of her home. The county social worker allowed her to choose her foster placements because her parents had problems with alcohol. And since she moved out, she has lived with five different relatives. The county social worker concluded that her frequent moves indicated irresponsibility on Linda's part. At the age of 17 years Linda requested a place of her own. The county social worker resisted the request because of Linda's presumed pattern of irresponsibility. Indian professionals interceded on Linda's behalf. They noted that Linda was doing well in school, and that many members of her extended family lived within an 8-block radius of her apartment. She also had the support of her peers and the school counselors. Her pattern of living with several relatives and the community's role in raising children were not uncommon in her group.

Cultural values and beliefs. Traditional Native American values and beliefs have been described in the following way (Everett et al., 1983; Zintz, 1962):

NATURE AND SPIRITUALITY
1. Desiring harmony with nature instead of mastery over nature
2. Attaching importance to religion (belief in a supreme force and deep reverence for nature, with much mysticism, including beliefs in spirits, spells, hexes, and anthropomorphism [attribution of human motivation,

characteristics, or behavior to inanimate objects, animals, or natural phenomena])
3. Explaining natural phenomena by mythology, by the power of nature, and by spirituality (also see Exhibit 9-6)

FAMILY
4. Attaching importance to the extended family and tribal relationships
5. Using a noncoercive and noninterfering parenting style (allowing children to develop freely)
6. Providing children with warmth and support
7. Ignoring or shunning children who misbehave or correcting them quietly or verbally rather than by using physical punishment
8. Valuing childhood and old age

INTERPERSONAL RELATIONS
9. Respecting individuality by observing a principle of noninterference while still being sensitive to group values
10. Valuing modesty and humility in the presence of others (for example, not talking about assets or things done well, not readily identifying strengths and assets during an interview)
11. Emphasizing giving, sharing, and cooperating (holding a nonmaterialistic view of life and eschewing competition)
12. Aspiring to follow in the ways of old people and to cooperate and maintain the status quo rather than to compete and climb the ladder of success
13. Preferring community and "nonself-promotion" over individuality and aggression
14. Wanting to focus on the present and satisfy present needs, rather than worry about getting ahead
15. Valuing a wry sense of humor and use of analogy

TEMPORAL ORIENTATION
16. Viewing time in a spatial rather than a linear way (time moves not by the hands of a clock but by natural phenomena, the occurrence of events, the location in space of these events, and internal feelings of synchronicity)
17. Orienting oneself toward the present rather than the future

Beliefs about traditional medicine are discussed later in this chapter.

Changes are occurring in the traditional cultural values of Native Americans. Over one-half of all Native Americans now live in urban areas (Fixico, 1986). Economic development programs on reservations, although minimal, and modern technology have brought changes in many areas. For example, Alaskan Native Americans have made changes in the way they hunt and fish (Mohatt et al., 1988):

[Alaskan Native Americans] use high-powered rifles, shotguns, outboard motors, aluminum boats, snow machines, three-wheelers, and other modern conveniences to subsist. Some Native technology, such as walrus skin boats, mukluks [boots], parkas, and so on have been retained because of superior effectiveness. Villagers have, however, been quick to change their subsistence methods to incorporate modern tools for greater efficiency. (pp. 330, 331)

Exhibit 9-6
Multicultural Manners:
Remaining Safe from the Remains

A 16-year-old girl brings a heart-shaped box to her Arizona high school English class. The box contains the cremated remains of the girl's mother, who died two years before. While showing the ashes to a girlfriend, the teenager inadvertently spills some of the ashes on the floor. The next day, 100 students are absent from the school.

What Went Wrong?

The students whose families boycotted the school were Native Americans, from the Hopi and Navajo nations, which represent about half of the school's 800 students. According to their beliefs, they could not enter a room where the remains of the dead had been spilled. They believed that if the classroom were not spiritually cleansed, the spirit of the deceased would remain in the area, posing a threat to them. Subsequently, a traditional Navajo medicine man and a Hopi spiritual leader conducted a cleansing ceremony that returned the spirit of the student's mother to its resting place and allowed students to come back to school.

Generally, Native Americans do not cremate their dead, preferring the burial tradition. In preparing for burials, Navajos wash the deceased and afterward, many will not touch the body lest they leave their handprints or fingerprints on it. Older Navajos won't go near the grave after a person is buried, but many in the younger generation will visit veterans' cemeteries and other grave sites on memorial holidays.

Source: Reprinted with permission of the author, from N. Dresser, "Remaining Safe from the Remains," in *Los Angeles Times,* April 20, 1996, p. B7, copyright by N. Dresser.

Although many Native Americans favor formal education, it has caused conflict between the younger and older generations (Mohatt et al., 1988). Whereas in the past elders were accorded prestige because of their storehouse of knowledge, today younger, more educated Native Americans sometimes have more status. Education also has caused other changes for Alaskan Native Americans, as illustrated in the following passage (Mohatt et al., 1988):

Along with formal education comes the acquisition of a new language and world view. Many young people no longer speak or clearly understand their native language. Because of this they are unable to freely converse with elders in their own villages [and learn their culture and history]. Many Native groups recognize the importance of speaking one's native language since many concepts are not easily translated into English or vice versa. As a result there are numerous efforts to ensure that young people learn their native language. (p. 334)

Other Native American groups are likely undergoing similar struggles.

Native Americans traditionally perceive individuals "as being more important than possessions, wealth, or other material things. If something is perceived as good, it is only as good as its value to other people" (Giger & Davidhizar, 1991, p. 226). However, for many Native Americans, the "rapid breakdown of organized traditional values, religion, and life style, as well as social relationships, has led to an inability to find a meaningful role in the modern world" (Giger & Davidhizar, 1991, p. 283).

Part of the cultural conflict between Native Americans and the majority culture involves differences in values. Cultural conflict poses special problems for Native American children and families, particularly when children enter Anglo American schools and when they reach adolescence.

One of the most important health problems facing Native Americans is alcoholism. "Indeed, five of the ten leading causes of death among Native Americans are directly related to alcoholism: accidents, cirrhosis of the liver, alcohol dependency, suicide, and homicide" (Young, 1993, p. 41). Alcohol and drug abuse also are problems for Native American adolescents (LaFromboise & Low, 1989).

A fundamental problem for Indian youth continues to be the high incidence of alcohol and drug abuse. Alcohol abuse alone has critical consequences for young children in the form of fetal alcohol syndrome, which can lead to mental and psychosocial retardation.... Indian youth come into contact with both legal and illegal drugs at an early age. They continue to sustain utilization rates for alcohol up to three times that of adolescents in the population at large and for marijuana and amphetamines twice that of their White counterparts. Substance abuse is a widely modeled means of coping with depression, anxiety, hostility, feelings of powerlessness, and stress reactions among Indian youth.... For adolescents, this coping mechanism exacerbates, rather than solves, the problems that contribute to educational underachievement, teen pregnancy, self-destructive behavior patterns, and high delinquency and arrest rates. (pp. 119, 120)

In working with Native Americans, consider the extent to which the children and families are acculturated into Anglo American culture. Be open to children's and parents' presentation of spiritual issues (LaFromboise, Choney, James, & Running Wolf, 1995). Because Native Americans may state their needs indirectly without asking for help, you should gently probe to find out their needs and wishes. Anglo American interviewers may be scrutinized to determine whether they are trustworthy. Suspicions about Anglo interviewers stem from a history of oppression by Anglo Americans and by the U.S. government. Native American mistrust of Anglo interviewers is rooted in the reality of their history.

Anglo American interviewers need to gain the trust of Native Americans by being flexible and supportive and by showing goodwill and self-awareness. Native Americans will especially appreciate interviewers who are flexible about appointment times, allow a third party to be present at the interview, keep promises, have no hidden agendas, show acceptance without stereotypic beliefs, self-disclose in the spirit of openness and reciprocity, and interpret nonverbal behavior correctly (LaFromboise et al., 1995).

Chapter 8 discussed some nonverbal behaviors of Native Americans. These behaviors include a tendency to avoid eye contact during some kinds of interpersonal interactions (avoidance of eye contact is a sign of respect and not a reaction of guilt or shame; it may result in a preference to sit side by side rather than face to face), to use a mild handshake (because a firm handshake may be considered rude), to delay in responding in order to interpret communications or decide on responses, and to seek somewhat more personal space than the three- to four-foot comfort zone of middle-class Anglo Americans (LaFromboise et al, 1995).

The following legend captures some important cultural values of Native Americans:

Long ago, there was a young woman whom we would call in our language "aiyaiyesh" meaning "stupid" or "retarded." While all the other young people of her age helped their elders, the aiyaiyesh girl would sit beneath the Cedar Tree, day after day and all day long, watching the world go by. Finally, the Cedar Tree could not stand it any longer, and spoke to her.

"You're so aiyaiyesh" the Tree said "now watch and I will show you how to do something." The Tree showed her how to take its roots, coiling their cool moist paleness into circle upon circle, fashioning the first hard-root cedar basket in the Pacific Northwest. Circles are very sacred to Native people…the wind moves in its strongest power in a circle…the circle represents the world, which turns in a circle. When she completed this first basket, the Cedar Tree approved of it but pointed out that it was naked and that a basket to be really finished required patterns—designs.

The aiyaiyesh girl began crying for she knew no patterns. The Cedar Tree told her to start walking, keeping her eyes, her ears, and her heart open, and she would discover all sorts of patterns for her basket. And so it was she traveled, and different beings would speak to her…the rattlesnake showed her its diamond-shaped designs; the mountains showed her the shape of triangles; the salmon showed its gills…all around her were the designs of shadows and leaves and colors. And when she had learned to put all of these designs into her baskets, she returned to the village where she taught her relatives and her friends how to make these baskets. And she wasn't aiyaiyesh anymore.…

—Traditional Sahaptin legend

The following two cases illustrate the importance of taking into account cultural factors in evaluating and treating Native Americans.

CASE 9-7. GERALD

Gerald, a 7-year-old boy, was referred by his teacher to a psychologist because of his withdrawn, sullen behavior. Gerald seldom raised his hand in class and avoided eye contact with teachers. He was also reportedly not as competitive in recess play as the teacher thought he should be. The teacher perceived this behavior as depressed and as a sign of psychological disturbance. Such behaviors were not interpreted within the context of this child's more traditional rearing in a rural area of Oklahoma. Fortunately, the psychologist appreciated the role that culture played in this child's behavior. Although Gerald was not clinically depressed, he was clearly unhappy about the many demands on him that were inconsistent with his culture. Consultation with the teacher was an important part of the intervention, and changing the teacher's expectations and reactions improved this Native American child's affect and school performance and behavior. (Everett et al., 1983, p. 597, with changes in notation)

CASE 9-8. HENRIETTA

Henrietta, a 12-year-old Indian girl, is admitted to the hospital with a history of school difficulties and seeing "spirits." The elders in her tribe feel that she is a gifted individual because of her visions. Her family is quite traditional and appreciates the special nature of her gift, but nevertheless her relatives are troubled because she becomes so engrossed in the visions that she neglects friends, family, and schoolwork. She has no history of substance abuse, and there is no history of substance abuse or mental disorder in her family. On being given a mental status exam, she is revealed to be a friendly and happy child, of average intelligence, who easily relates the above history. She is not disturbed by her visions, which she describes as elders appearing before her to give advice about her daily activities. She exhibits no other signs of psychosis, except that some of her explanations seem verbose and do not closely hang together.

Although seeing visions may well be viewed as normal in Henrietta's culture, and, indeed, may receive support from her tribal members, nevertheless, her schoolwork is impaired. It is not clear whether she is in fact dissociating while having the visions and therefore cannot concentrate on schoolwork, or whether she is not confident about her academic abilities and uses a culturally acceptable method of avoiding the work. This distinction would be important diagnostically. If possible, treatment would be aimed at dealing with the school problem, rather than removing the hallucinations per se, because the hallucinations may well serve an important function for her in her society. It would also be important to encourage her parents to seek out the traditional healers in their community and for them to discuss the problem as they see it with both the Western and traditional healers. (Thompson, Walker, & Silk-Walker, 1993, pp. 223–224, with changes in notation)

When I was a child I was taught certain things: don't stand up to your elders, don't question authority, life is precious, the earth is precious, take it slowly, enjoy it. And then you go to college and you learn all these other things, and it never fits.

—Native American high school girl
(quoted by Wright and Tierney, 1991)

Language Considerations for Native Americans

There is no universal, traditional Native American language (Everett et al., 1983). Each tribe is likely to have its own language, and within a tribe different dialects may exist. Native Americans differ in their command of the English language: "As with any bilingual group, these abilities range from a very articulate command of English to...a limited receptive vocabulary and little or no expressive vocabulary" (Everett et al., 1983, p. 592).

Because Native American children's and parents' command of English may be limited, they may have difficulty understanding your questions. If you speak only English, you may experience difficulties in communicating with Native American children and their parents who speak a native language and have limited knowledge of English. In addition, you will need to consider that Native Americans are more likely than Anglo Americans to be hesitant to speak, to speak softly, to give short responses that lack important details, to fear making a mistake, to be nonassertive, and to be reluctant to offer self-disclosures.

[American] Indians are sort of an invisible people. There are a lot of [American] Indians in this country, and people have no idea of what to expect from us.

—Sheila Tousey

Traditional Medicine Among Native Americans

Although the traditional beliefs of Native Americans about health and illness vary with different tribes, they center on the idea that illness can result from natural causes; from an imbalance of spiritual and environmental forces, caused by breaking taboos or coming into contact with taboo products; or from supernatural activity (Locust, 1988; Spector, 1991). In addition, some Native Americans with traditional orientations believe that there is a reason for every sickness and pain and that illness is the price individuals pay for something that has happened in the past or for something that will happen in the future.

The Native American concept of health is broad. It encompasses not only physical well-being but also congruency with family, the environment, supernatural forces, and the community. Traditional healing ceremonies play an important role in treatment (Giger & Davidhizar, 1991).

Traditional healers spend many years learning their skills. One becomes a traditional healer by inheriting the gift from the family, having a vision, or serving a lengthy apprenticeship. Healers fall into three categories: *diagnosticians,* who diagnose illness or disharmony; *singers,* who perform or direct the ceremonies; and *herbalists,* who use herbs to treat and diagnose patients (Giger & Davidhizar, 1991). These categories are not necessarily distinct because some traditional healers perform all three functions. The Indian Health Service and healers make an effort to work together. For example, traditional healers often refer serious cases of injury to hospitals, and physicians may send patients to traditional healers, particularly in cases of psychological or behavioral disorders (Giger & Davidhizar, 1991).

A traditional healer may assume the roles of doctor, counselor, priest, historian, and safekeeper of ancient legends. "The healer uses the wisdom of spiritual legends for insight into human behavior and to explain emotional and behavioral problems" (LaFromboise, 1988, p. 392).

Native Americans may handle psychological problems in the following way (LaFromboise, 1988):

When problems arise in Indian communities, they become not only problems of the individual but also problems of the community. The family, kin, and friends coalesce into a network to observe the individual, find reasons for the individual's behavior, and draw the person out of isolation and back into the social life of the group. The strong social and symbolic bonds among the extended family network maintain a disturbed individual within the community with minimal coercion....

Disturbed individuals in certain tribes are encouraged to attend peyote meetings [or sweat lodges or herb-burning ceremonies] that involve confession of a ritualized rather than personal nature and collective discussions.... The cure may involve confession, atonement, restoration into the good graces of family and tribe, and intercession with the spirit world. Treatment usually involves a greater number of individuals than simply the client and healer; often the client's significant others and community members are included.... Thus, the collective treatment of psychologically troubled individuals in tribal groups not only serves to heal the individual but also to reaffirm the norms of the entire group.... (p. 392)

You can incorporate some of these practices when you evaluate a Native American child and his or her family. For example, you can obtain information about how the child's presenting problem affects not only the child and his or her family but members of the extended family as well. You also will want to learn about the cultural fit between the family and the surrounding community (LaFromboise & Low, 1989).

One cannot for long have one's feet placed in two canoes.

—Iroquois saying

Exercise 9-2. Experiences Associated with People of Other Racial or Ethnic Groups

---

This exercise is designed to help you recall personal, familial, and environmental experiences that may have negatively (Part 1) or positively (Part 2) influenced your perceptions and attitudes about people of ethnic or racial groups different from yours. Read each statement in Part 1, and circle the number of the item if it applies to you. Follow the same procedure for Part 2. After you finish, read the Comments section. The items in this exercise were adapted, in part, from Creighton and Kivel (1992).

Part 1. Negative Experiences Associated with People of Different Racial or Ethnic Groups

1. You (or your family) were refused housing, were discouraged from applying for housing, or had to move because of your race or ethnicity by a person of another racial or ethnic group.

2. You heard people of another racial or ethnic group say that people from your racial or ethnic group should go back to where they came from.

3. You were called names or otherwise ridiculed by a stranger of another racial or ethnic group because of your race or ethnicity.

4. You were ridiculed by a teacher, employer, or supervisor of another racial or ethnic group because of your race or ethnicity.

5. You were treated discourteously by a public official or professional of another racial or ethnic group because of your race or ethnicity.

6. You were discouraged or prevented from pursuing academic or work goals or were tracked into a lower vocational level by a teacher or a counselor who was a member of another racial or ethnic group because of your race or ethnicity.

7. You were mistrusted or accused of stealing, cheating, or lying by a person of another racial or ethnic group because of your race or ethnicity.

8. You were aware that someone of another racial or ethnic group was afraid of you because of your race or ethnicity.

9. You were stopped by police officers of another racial or ethnic group and treated discourteously because of your race or ethnicity.

10. You were paid less, treated less fairly, or given harder work than a person from another racial or ethnic group in a similar position by a person of another racial or ethnic group.

11. You were refused employment by a person of another racial or ethnic group because of your race or ethnicity.

12. You were treated discourteously by a person of another racial or ethnic group in a restaurant where most of the customers were members of another racial or ethnic group.

13. You felt the threat of violence or were a victim of violence from a person of another racial or ethnic group because of your race or ethnicity.

14. You were not allowed to join an organization, such as a fraternity or sorority, because of your race or ethnicity.

15. You saw your racial or ethnic group portrayed on television or in the movies in a derogatory way.

16. You heard your parents make derogatory remarks about other racial or ethnic groups.

17. You heard your neighbors make derogatory remarks about other racial or ethnic groups.

18. You heard your friends make derogatory remarks about other racial or ethnic groups.

19. You were told by your parents not to play with children of a racial or ethnic group different from yours when you were a child.

20. You went to a high school where all or most of the students of one racial or ethnic group were in the college preparatory track and students of other racial or ethnic groups were in other tracks.

21. You were encouraged by your parents not to join an organization that had members of racial or ethnic groups different from yours.

22. You were encouraged by your parents or friends not to go to a dance where there were members of other racial or ethnic groups.

23. You grew up in a neighborhood where people of several racial or ethnic groups lived in disharmony.

Part 2. Positive Experiences Associated with People of Different Racial or Ethnic Groups

24. Your family was made to feel welcome by a person of another racial or ethnic group when the family wanted to rent an apartment or buy a house.

25. You heard people of another racial or ethnic group saying that people from your racial or ethnic group made good contributions to society.

26. You were treated courteously by a stranger who was a member of another racial or ethnic group.

27. You were treated courteously by a teacher, employer, or supervisor who was a member of another ethnic or racial group.

28. You were treated courteously by a public official or professional who was a member of another racial or ethnic group.

29. You were encouraged to pursue academic or work goals according to your level of ability by a teacher or a counselor who was a member of another racial or ethnic group.

30. You never felt that you were mistrusted by a member of another racial or ethnic group solely because of your race or ethnicity.

31. You never thought that someone was afraid of you because of your race or ethnicity.

32. You were stopped by police officers who were members of another racial or ethnic group and were treated courteously.

33. You were paid the same, treated the same, or given the same type of work by a person of another racial or ethnic group as people from other racial or ethnic groups in a similar position.

34. You were hired for a job by a person of another racial or ethnic group.

35. You were treated courteously in a restaurant where most of the customers were members of another racial or ethnic group.

36. You never felt the threat of violence or were a victim of violence because of your race or ethnicity.

37. You joined an organization, such as a fraternity or sorority, that had members of other racial or ethnic groups.

38. You saw your racial or ethnic group portrayed on television or in the movies in favorable ways.

39. You heard your parents make favorable remarks about other racial or ethnic groups.

40. You heard your neighbors make favorable remarks about other racial or ethnic groups.

41. You heard your friends make favorable remarks about other racial or ethnic groups.

42. You were encouraged by your parents to play with children of other racial or ethnic groups when you were a child.
43. You went to a high school where students of several racial or ethnic groups were in the college preparatory track and also in other tracks.
44. You were encouraged by your parents to join an organization that had members of other racial or ethnic groups.
45. You went to a dance where people were from several racial or ethnic groups and everyone got along.
46. You grew up in a neighborhood where people of several racial or ethnic groups lived in harmony.

Comments

Look over your answers. What do they suggest? For example, do they suggest that you have been (a) a target of prejudice (items 1–14), (b) exposed to situations that have negatively influenced your attitudes about other racial and ethnic groups (items 15–23), (c) accepted by people of other racial or ethnic groups (items 24–37), or (d) exposed to situations that have positively influenced your attitudes about other racial and ethnic groups (items 38–46)? Or do your answers suggest that you had little exposure to members of other ethnic groups or to issues of race and ethnicity? Do your answers suggest other patterns in your interactions with other racial or ethnic groups? What is the balance of the negative and positive influences that have shaped your perceptions and attitudes about people from other racial and ethnic groups?

What did you learn about yourself by doing these exercises? If you have been a target of prejudice, how did you feel when the incident(s) occurred? What happened? What did you do about the incident(s)? Are you still angry or upset about any incidents? Do you think that you are prejudiced now? If you learned to be prejudiced in your youth, what can you do to become more accepting of people from other ethnic and racial groups? What suggestions do you have for eliminating or, at least, reducing prejudice and racism in our nation?

People often protect themselves against negative self-evaluations, either by forgetting aspects of themselves (like a tendency to be prejudiced) and remembering the times when they showed unbiased behaviors or by believing that other people were racist in making some negative decision about them when in fact the decision had nothing to do with race. Do you see either of these tendencies in yourself? You might want to keep a record of your interactions with people of other racial or ethnic groups to get a more accurate evaluation of where you stand with respect to prejudice.

Finally, if you are from the majority group, answer the questions again as you think a person of your age and sex from an ethnic minority group would. If you are from an ethnic minority group, answer the questions again as you think a person of your age and sex from the majority group would. In either case, instead of circling the number of an item if it applies to you, place an "X" over the item number that applies to you when you read the statements a second time. Compare the responses you gave the first time with those you gave when you considered the statements from the perspective of a person of another ethnic or racial group. What does the comparison indicate?

REFUGEES

Because ethnic minority groups may begin their journey to the resettlement country as refugees (or emigrants), it is important to have some understanding of how refugee status affects children and families. *Refugees* are individuals fleeing corrupt political regimes, war, famine, religious persecution, violence, or economic deprivation. Emigrating to a new country results in the loss of natural ties and social supports. Even the migration experience itself may cause considerable stress. Children represent nearly one-half of the world's refugees, who, at the end of 1994, numbered slightly over 16 million (Famighetti, 1995). Between 1987 and 1990, a total of 1,031,752 children (under 20 years of age) from other countries came to the United States (U.S. Bureau of the Census, 1993a). Most came from Mexico, Central and South America, and Asia (particularly Vietnam, Cambodia, and Laos). "Immigrant children and their families come to live in the United States permanently via one of three modes of entry: legal immigration, humanitarian admission (as refugees and asylees, statuses that are also legal), or illegal entry (as either visa overstayers or undocumented immigrants). The vast majority (85%) of the foreign-born living in the United States are in the country legally" (Board on Children and Families, 1995, p. 75). Note that much of the material in this section also pertains to immigrant children and their families who are not refugees.

Types of Stress Faced by Refugee Children and Their Families

Because of their experiences, refugees may have physical, social, and emotional traumas. Arriving in a new country may cause additional adjustment problems associated with a disruption in normal cultural patterns and traditions, loss of possessions, worries about family members left behind or otherwise separated, and dealing with strange customs, language, mores, and traditions. They may have symptoms associated with posttraumatic stress disorder (PTSD; see Chapter 11). PTSD-like symptoms, however, may not necessarily be maladaptive. They can be understood as a form of "cultural bereavement," and individuals may experience them as part of the rehabilitative process (Eisenbruch, 1991).

The following case illustrates stresses that refugee children may face.

CASE 9-9. MARIO

Mario, who was living in Chile, was 5 years old when his peaceful life was suddenly interrupted by civil security agents who knocked on his door in the middle of the night. They dragged his father out of his bed and carried him away in his underwear into a waiting van. When his father was released after a week of torture, the family escaped to Sweden within another week.

Six months later Mario was examined in Sweden. He was an anxious boy who was upset by anything unexpected. A knock on the door triggered a hasty escape under the bed. The grocery store was his favorite scene for violent outbursts of rage when his will was crossed. In the hotel where he was lodged he did not play with the other children; instead he followed his father around, never letting him out of sight. Mario slept with his father and they often woke each other up with nightmares. Mario's main occupation during this time was eating and drinking. He gained 30 pounds during the first six months in Sweden. (Hjern, Angel, & Höjer, 1991, p. 7, with changes in notation)

Refugee children may face loss of parental support and protection and may experience pressures to assume adult responsibilities (De Monchy, 1991). They may need to take care of their younger siblings and find food and shelter. In the resettlement country, refugee children often become the critical link between their parents and the new culture, serving to communicate with authority figures. If separated from their parents, older children often will assume the burden of parenting younger siblings. Conflicts develop when children and parents cannot uphold the traditions of their native culture in the resettlement country. Such conflicts may lead adolescents to join gangs.

Refugee children may experience stress in school (Athey & Ahearn, 1991). Flight disrupts the continuity of the socialization process and interrupts normal learning. Different schooling practices in the resettlement country and unfamiliarity with the language will add to their stress. Religious practices also may be called into question because of differences between practices in their homeland and those of the resettlement country (Athey & Ahearn, 1991).

Refugee families may be unfamiliar with procedures for filling out forms and validating documents, as required by schools, mental health facilities, and medical facilities. Undocumented immigrants may feel especially vulnerable; living in constant fear of deportation, they may refrain from seeking help.

Refugee families often face racism in their new country. Racism robs them of trust, makes them feel bewildered, and prevents them from entering community life by isolating them from others (Athey & Ahearn, 1991). They may deal with racism by seeing only members of their immediate and extended family, which further isolates them from the larger community.

Finally, refugee families may have problems associated with changes in class and social status, unemployment or underemployment, low wages and poor work conditions, vulnerability to employer victimization, substandard and crowded living conditions, limited social supports, poor health care, immigration status, marital tension, and intergenerational conflict (Zayas, 1992).

Despite the available research, much remains to be learned about refugee children's adaptation to the United States (Board on Children and Families, 1995).

Why do some immigrant children succeed in school and others fail? Why do some impoverished immigrant groups show strikingly low rates of infant mortality compared with U.S.-born groups

with similar background characteristics? Under what conditions and for whom do development and schooling outcomes deteriorate over time, for whom do they improve, and why? What role does self-selection play among immigrants and how do the personal characteristics that immigrant children and families bring with them help or hinder their adjustment to life in the United States? How do the economic or political factors motivating parents' immigration, and their status as legal or illegal immigrants, affect the developmental challenges and adaptation strategies of children? (p. 84)

When immigrants are disoriented in a strange new world they understandably rely heavily on their heritage. Bewilderment can prompt excessive pride. It can sadly degenerate into hostility toward others. At the same time, recent arrivals more often than not infuse our society with family loyalties. And the new friendships they provide replace the frayed relationships in our neighborhoods and the deteriorating trust at work. Their get-up-and-go, can-do spirit consistently revives the best values in our democracy, including a new birth of freedom.

—Bishop Roy I. Sano

Case Study

The following case provides a glimpse of the tremendous stress a Cambodian girl endured as a refugee and how she adjusted to it (Kinzie & Sack, 1991).

CASE 9-10. V.

When first seen, V. was a 17-year-old high school sophomore. She had been living with a Cambodian foster mother. Before coming to the United States, she had lived in a large city, where she attended school for four years. She was unsure what her father did, but she knew he earned a good living. There were nine other children in the family.

When Pol Pot came to power, her father was captured and apparently committed suicide. V. was with him when he died. Her mother was in another camp, and V. never saw her again. V. learned that her mother was executed. V. and three siblings were spared execution. V. was placed with a group of other young people who were building dikes. She never saw any other family members for four years. She was never physically beaten. Pol Pot cadres, besides killing her mother, probably killed five brothers and sisters. Three younger siblings were killed as they were escaping, hit with a mortar. She saw many people executed, "too many to count." An older sister was severely beaten, and she refused to escape when the Vietnamese invaded. The sister might still be in Vietnam, but no word was ever received from her.

V. did forced labor, building dikes, from morning to night. She lost so much weight during that time that she could not sit up. She said she looked like a skeleton. She tried to steal enough food to live and work so they would not kill her. Recalling her escape in 1979, she said there were thousands who tried to get to the border, "corpses all over the place," starving, but she just kept going. She lived in a refugee camp for three years.

After she came to the United States, she reported many posttraumatic stress disorder (PTSD) symptoms including nightmares and difficulty falling asleep; she jumped and startled easily even at small noises. She had to be on guard and check the house security multiple times each day. She woke up frequently with nightmares and had been irritable for the past year. She had difficulty concentrating on her homework. She said she did not want to be around her friends, but wanted to live alone and take care of only herself. She lost interest in most activities and did not want to do anything, feeling irritable and angry at times. She tried hard to avoid anything that reminded her of Cambodia, saying it was unbelievable that she was still alive. She also had many symptoms of generalized anxiety and depressive and panic disorders.

In appearance V. was an attractive young woman who seemed older than 17. She was serious and thoughtful throughout the interview, with little emotional expression but obviously engaged with the questions, and she found some relief talking about her experiences. Her concentration was good throughout. It was surprising, in view of her symptoms, that she could function moderately well and complete regular school activities.

Four years later she was seen at a follow-up interview. She was a strikingly beautiful 21-year-old woman. She had spent two years going to secretarial school, and had a fiancé whom she had met in a Thai refugee camp. She said her major symptoms were better than they were before, but intrusive and startle symptoms were still present and occurred sometimes "too often." More than 50 percent of the time she had depressive symptoms, but there were days when she was "okay." She also had panic attacks. Despite multiple symptoms she functioned well at work and had many friends and even taught classical Cambodian dance to students.

This young woman, with severe traumas and multiple symptoms, could continue school and was working at the time of the second interview, but still had severe symptoms with a diagnosis of PTSD and depression with minimal overt behavioral impairment. (pp. 99–101, with changes in notation)

INTERVENTION CONSIDERATIONS

The information you obtain from the interview and from other sources will be helpful in designing intervention programs for members of ethnic minority groups. You will need to consider the child's and family's culture, including their attitudes toward treatment and toward the child's problem, illness, or disability; gender roles; religious views; and the role of the extended family. These factors, of course, should be considered for all children and families, regardless of their ethnicity. In addition, you need to consider sociopolitical factors, such as the majority's view and treatment of ethnic minority groups. But, even more important, you will need to consider the needs and cultural values of the *specific* child and family. *The intervention program must not be designed to change, either subtly or overtly, the child's and family's values to match those of the dominant culture or to*

pacify and eliminate legitimate anger and political initiative (LaFromboise et al., 1990).

The following case illustrates the importance of considering cultural factors in understanding the child's school behavior and in formulating an intervention plan. Failure to consider cultural factors in this case might have resulted in an educational misclassification (Rosado, 1986).

CASE 9-11. MARISOL

Marisol, a relatively soft-spoken but alert 9-year-old female Hispanic student in the fourth grade, was referred to the special services department in mid-November by her teacher. The referral centered on the sudden appearance of a pattern of academic underachievement, incomplete homework, and marked increase in shyness. Marisol was born in a rural setting in Puerto Rico and was raised there up to the age of 4 in an extended-family setting. When she was 4 years old, the extended family, including an aunt and uncle, moved to an urban area in the northeastern United States. School reports indicated that despite some early language problems in kindergarten and first grade, Marisol's overall academic achievement up to third grade was average to slightly above average.

Preliminary physical and medical examination results were unremarkable. A learning evaluation was complicated by Marisol's extreme introversion, long response latency, lack of eye contact, and generalized reticence, and was thus deferred. A bilingual school psychologist was contacted. A teacher interview and observations of Marisol's behavior in the classroom, lunchroom, and playground indicated that she was socially inhibited only in the classroom. She interacted age-appropriately with all of her peers, primarily during recreational periods.

The school psychologist decided to visit the home, not only to interview the parents but also to establish rapport, trust, and mutual respect with the family. Señora H., Marisol's mother, was an unemployed single female parent with three children—a 19-year-old male college student, a 13-year-old daughter, and 9-year-old Marisol. Señora H. had completed elementary school, had limited proficiency in English, and was receiving federal assistance. She attended church twice weekly and held traditional cultural beliefs with a strong value on education for her children. Señora H. was divorced when Marisol was 2½ years old; her support systems were the church/religious group and Marisol's godparents, who also were Marisol's uncle and aunt.

For the second home visit, the school psychologist requested Señora H. to have the godparents present. As mother and godparents grew to trust the school psychologist, they shared their worry and fear that Señora H.'s mother—who was 70 years old and living in Puerto Rico—might die because she was quite ill. Señora's fears and worries also appeared to affect Marisol, who still remembered the "good play times" she had with her grandmother. News of her grandmother's illness came in late October, 2½ weeks before the referral. Señora H. was not aware of the changes displayed by Marisol in the classroom.

Marisol, who was relatively bilingual, was then interviewed. She recognized the school psychologist from home visits. Initially, she was slow to warm up and often cast her eyes downward. Through various figure drawings, use of the Children's Apperception Test, and assessment of play with a toy house and family figures, Marisol revealed a sense of sadness and hopelessness about her grandmother. In addition, she expressed fear of disapproval from the teacher because of her incomplete homework. She felt shame and embarrassment in asking for help from her teacher. At home, she would start her assignments, but fail to complete them because thoughts of her grandmother intruded and decreased her concentration and motivation. Marisol also feared that her classmates would ridicule her if they found out she did not complete her assignments. Her silent despair and preoccupation with her grandmother's health caused and perpetuated her shyness and incomplete assignments that underlay the sudden academic underachievement.

Full-scale multidisciplinary team evaluations were postponed in favor of the following interventions. The godparents were willing to support her mother emotionally and to tutor Marisol at home with her assignments. Señora H. and the godparents met the classroom teacher, who gave them materials for tutoring. In addition, the mother was asked to hold a special Mass in behalf of her grandmother's recovery, to recite the rosary, and, with Marisol and her sister, to light candles for hope and recovery for the grandmother. The school psychologist worked with Marisol, using modified play therapy, projective story-telling, and supportive and expressive counseling twice a week for 20 minutes a session for 3 months. Señora H. and the godparents were contacted every 2 weeks for support and updates. They planned to visit her grandmother during the Easter vacation, which helped to allay some of Marisol's worries and fears. Her older brother and cousin were willing to volunteer as tutors for Marisol during the Easter vacation and summer, if necessary.

A follow-up conference 3 months later with the teacher found that Marisol completed assignments, spoke in class more frequently and confidently, and was not in danger of repeating her grade. Señora H. and the godparents talked with Marisol about the play times with her grandmother and maintained tutoring into late May. Before Easter, the grandmother improved but did not fully recover. A visit to Puerto Rico during the summer was still planned. (p. 195, with changes in notation)

Several different types of intervention efforts may be needed to help refugee children in the resettlement country. These include "providing adequate nutrition, mitigating the effects of acute loss through social support and other procedures, providing good prenatal care, improving schooling and child-rearing practices, developing coping skills of individuals at risk for problems, bolstering social networks, family planning, and genetic counseling" (Williams, 1991, p. 210).

Prevention programs in refugee camps also should be considered. These include "providing toys and athletic equipment; establishing centers to provide infant care, preschool programs, school programs, and adolescent activities within the camp; establishing central obstetrical and pediatric care; placing families as quickly as possible; maintaining the integrity of large families when resettling; and keeping any unaccompanied minors with 'unofficial foster families,' rather than separating them from the adults in the camp and placing them with [resettlement host] families" (Williams, 1991, p. 211).

The above intervention efforts rest on the willingness of the resettlement country and other countries to provide assistance. Unfortunately, such assistance is not always forthcoming.

Finally, it is important to emphasize that the growth and development of refugee children are also associated with community systems beyond the neighborhood where decisions are made and policies implemented that greatly affect their lives and those of their parents. Economic and political systems, over which individuals have little if any influence, largely determine the conditions of refugee life. Day-to-day economic security, personal safety, and personal freedom are typically dependent on these outside forces—in the country of origin, the refugee camp, and the settlement country. Decision-making in these larger systems is rarely designed to enhance the growth and development of children. (Athey & Ahearn, 1991, p. 16)

The following case illustrates how an alert social worker discovered that an adolescent's traditional beliefs about his ancestors were interfering with his medical treatment (adapted from De Monchy, 1991).

CASE 9-12. BORAMY

Boramy, a 17-year-old Cambodian adolescent, with some knowledge of English, was hospitalized one week after his arrival in the United States as an unaccompanied minor. He was diagnosed as having severe sclerosis of the liver because of untreated hepatitis B and immediately placed in isolation with the requirement that all staff and visitors must wear gowns, gloves, and masks when entering his room. On the third day following admission, Boramy suddenly became unmanageable. He was found cowering under his bed, pulling his intravenous line out of his arm, and wrapping the tubing around his neck as if to strangle himself.

Unfortunately, there were no bilingual, bicultural staff members available at the hospital. Still, the adolescent was referred for psychological testing, which further agitated him and produced no indication of the cause of his behavior. A staff social worker then spoke with him. She learned that he was "seeing" his mother, grandmother, and four friends, all of whom had died during the Pol Pot regime, surround his bed and call him to join them. He also saw many white ghosts in the room. This was terrifying to him and an indication that he would die soon.

A Cambodian paraprofessional [a trained worker who is not a member of a given profession but who assists a professional] also assisted in future interviews. Boramy said that he believed strongly in the power of ancestors and in the protection offered by blessings from the monks. A Cambodian monk was contacted, came to the hospital room, and performed a ceremony of protection around the patient. A knotted string, blessed by holy water, was tied around his waist and an altar was set up next to his bed. Following this ritual, Boramy was compliant with treatment and responsive to medication.

While the courage and resilience of refugee children are often formidable and demonstrate the power of their spirit, and while policies and programs should explicitly build on these strengths, it is incumbent on us to recognize that even the strongest child can be overwhelmed when the stresses are too great and the supports unavailable. When refugee children receive adequate support, assistance, and nurturing, however, they can and do develop into loving and competent persons, productive and secure.

—Jean L. Athey and Frederick L. Ahearn, Jr.

SEMISTRUCTURED INTERVIEWS

In interviewing ethnic minority children and their parents, use the same procedures as you would with nonminority children and their parents (see Chapters 2, 3, and 4). In addition, you should follow the guidelines discussed in this chapter.

In Appendix F, Table F-29 presents a semistructured interview for use with immigrant children, and Table F-42 presents one for use with immigrant parents. Use these tables with other tables in Appendix F designed to elicit a more in-depth history (such as Table F-13 and Table F-36). You can use Tables F-29 and F-42 to obtain information about how the child and parent, respectively, are adjusting to a new culture.

After you complete interviews with an ethnic minority child, her or his parents, and other family members, you will want to evaluate the interviews in the way you would any other interview (see Chapters 3 and 4). In addition, you should consider ethnic and cultural factors in evaluating the family (see Table 9-3).

RECOMMENDATIONS FOR INTERVIEWING ETHNIC MINORITY CHILDREN AND THEIR FAMILIES

In working with ethnic minority children and their families, show them that you are sensitive to and respect their culture's perspective and value systems and that you are willing to help them. Also convey to them an acceptance of their culture (Manio & Hall, 1987). Allow the parents and child to consult other family or community members if they request to do so.

With ethnic minority children and their parents, you may need to spend more time establishing rapport than you would with children and parents from the majority culture, as ethnic minority interviewees may feel particularly vulnerable or distrustful (Kumabe et al., 1985). Take time to understand the fears, hopes, and aspirations of ethnic minority interviewees, especially those who are refugees or immigrants. The process of acculturation often carries with it stresses caused by a loss of autonomy and feelings of shame and doubt.

The following guidelines will help you conduct more effective interviews with ethnic minority children and their families.

LEARN ABOUT THE INTERVIEWEES' CULTURE

1. Learn about the child's, family's, and community's cultural values, attitudes, and world view. (For example, learn about the family's structure and family roles, including distribution of power and authority; marriage customs; mutual obligations; and how the family handles shame. You can learn about the family's structure by reviewing information about the family's size and composition, ages of members, and living arrangements; education and employment of family members; and frequency and nature of contact with family members who are living outside the home. Consider whether the family's cultural practices are related to any of the child's symptoms.)

2. Learn about the child's and family's ethnic identification. (For example, do they perceive themselves as (a) African American, Black American, or American or (b) Latin American, Hispanic American, Mexican American, or American?)

3. Learn about the family's specific cultural patterns related to child rearing. (For example, what are the family's attitudes concerning dating among adolescents, age of independence from the family, and the differential importance of education for males and females?)

4. Consider the family's socioeconomic status and how it may affect the family's values, attitudes, and world view.

5. Learn how the family's community is organized, supported, and developed, including the role of the family in the community, the place of traditional healers, and the role of community leaders.

6. Learn how the sociopolitical system in the United States influences the way ethnic minorities are treated.

7. Recognize your ignorance about some details of the family's culture.

8. Recognize that if you are not a member of the ethnic group, you may be viewed as "the stranger."

9. Do not be afraid to let the child and family know that you are not aware of some aspects of their value system, world view, or life style—not only will you learn, but they will appreciate your interest and honesty.

LEARN ABOUT THE INTERVIEWEES' LANGUAGE

10. Determine the child's and family's preferred language *before* beginning the interview.

11. Ideally, learn the language spoken by the child and family.

12. Do not assume that because the child and family speak some English, they can fully understand you.

13. Do not assume that just because you have some speaking knowledge of the family's language, you can ask

Table 9-3
Questions to Consider in Working with Ethnic Minority Groups

Acculturation

1. What is the family's cultural group?
2. What is the family's national origin?
3. What is the family's native language?
4. How much English is spoken at home?
5. (If applicable) How long has the family been in the United States?
6. (If applicable) Why did the family come to the United States?
7. To what degree is the family acculturated to American culture?
8. How strongly does each member of the family follow traditional cultural practices?
   (Questions 9 through 16 are primarily for recent immigrants.)
9. How did the family get to the United States?
10. How far is the home country from the United States?
11. How often do family members visit their home country?
12. Where did the family live in the home country?
13. What was the socioeconomic status of the family in the home country?
14. Where does the family live in the United States? For example, does the family live in culturally homogeneous community or in a heterogeneous setting, and does the family live in a safe community?
15. What is the socioeconomic status of the family in the United States?
16. Has there been any role change for the parents after coming to the United States? For example, is the father who formerly was a physician now working as a gardener?

Beliefs About Causes of Present Illness

17. What role do cultural or religious factors have in guiding the family's beliefs about the child's illness or disability? For example, does religion play a part in how the family defines the illness or disability, responds to the illness or disability, and accepts the illness or disability? Do family members view the illness or disability as stemming from natural causes, environmental causes, or supernatural causes? Do they view the illness or disability as a punishment for some unnamed wrong? Do they view the illness or disability as divine punishment for sin? Do they see intervention as thwarting God's will or as playing the role of God?
18. What does the family believe caused the child's illness? For example, does the family believe that illness is caused by natural causes, by God giving punishment for wrongdoing, by evil forces, or by an externally induced curse or hex?
19. How does the family view the role of fate in the child's illness and treatment?

Indigenous Cultural Resources

20. Does the family follow traditional health healing practices, and, if so, which ones? For example, does the family believe in the power of shamans or healers, the potency of culturally prescribed rituals, the power of religious or other ethnic leaders, or the power of family members with authority?

Family Structure and Intrafamily Relationships

21. What is the family structure (for example, matriarchal or patriarchal)?
22. What are the culturally prescribed rules governing family transactions?
23. What family roles are the members expected to fulfill?
24. What is the family's attitude about sex roles?
25. What is the family's work ethic?
26. How does the family express emotions and religious beliefs?
27. What influence does the extended family have on the family? For example, how important are members of the extended family? Do you need to include members of the extended family in designing the interventions? Do you need to conduct a home visit to become acquainted with the members of the extended family and members of the community? Does the family have multiple caregivers and authority figures who need to be included in the intervention plan?
28. What are the family's attitudes and beliefs about sexual matters, exposure of body parts, surgery, use of prescription drugs, discussions of death, and discussions of fears?
29. What customs or beliefs does the family have about child rearing, including ideas about acceptable and unacceptable child behaviors, disciplining and rewarding children, differential expectations for girls and boys, adolescent independence, and appropriate ways for children to show courtesy and respect for adults, and what is the family's attitude toward education and careers?
30. What customs or beliefs influence the way the family takes care of infants, including feeding, skin care, hair care, and other areas of personal hygiene?
31. How authoritarian are the parents and other adult authority figures?
32. Who takes care of the children?

Role of Family Members During Illness and Treatment

33. What is the attitude of family members toward the child's illness?
34. How does the family treat the child with a problem, illness, or disability? For example, do family members encourage the child to become independent and self-sufficient, or do they foster dependency and isolation? Do they keep the child at home and not allow him or her to go to school? Do they allow the child to go to school but not to play with friends?
35. What role does the family play when and if the child is hospitalized?

(Continued)

Table 9-3 (*Continued*)

36. What role does the family play in following the treatment regimen?
37. What changes take place in family roles and functioning because of the child's illness or problem?

Attitude Toward Medical and Mental Health Professionals and Treatment
38. From whom does the family seek help for the child's illness?
39. Does the family rely on cultural healers, and, if so, in what way and for what problems or illnesses?
40. What is the family's attitude toward medical and mental health professionals and toward treatment? For example, do family members believe that they can do little about their problems? Do they have an attitude of resignation and acceptance, believing that fate has decreed that misfortunes are a part of life? Do they delay treatment until the illness has become severe? Do they seek traditional healers to help them before contacting mainstream practitioners? Do they view mental illness as a sign of weakness of character? Do they view treatment as disgraceful, carrying with it shame and a loss of pride?
41. How open is the family in its communication with medical and mental health professionals?

42. Does the family distrust medical and mental health professionals who are from other ethnic groups?
43. Is the family too compliant and dependent on medical and mental health professionals?
44. Does the family covertly try to undermine medical and mental health professionals?
45. What are the family's views about the need for treatment for male and female members? For example, do male members have a more difficult time accepting a disability (considering it a weakness) than female members? Will male members stop treatment when they have some symptom relief because they view longer-term treatment as socially unacceptable? Do male and female members of the family view the disability in the same way?

Ability to Communicate
46. What is the family's proficiency in English?
47. Do family members have adequate receptive but not expressive ability, or vice versa?
48. What is the chance that family members will be misunderstood?
49. If an interpreter was used, did the interview go smoothly?

Note. The questions in Table 9-3 complement those in Tables 4-1, 4-4, and 4-6 in Chapter 4. The questions in this table pertain to interviewees who may be referred for different types of problems or concerns, including mental health problems, physical health problems, and child maltreatment. Therefore, consider only those questions that are applicable for the particular case.
Source: Adapted from Bloch (1983) and from Kumabe, Nishida, and Hepworth (1985).

meaningful questions in that language or fully understand the family's communications.
14. Use an interpreter, if needed, and recognize the limitations of using an interpreter.

ESTABLISH RAPPORT
15. Make every effort to encourage the child's and family's motivation and interest.
16. Take time to enlist the child's and family's cooperation.
17. Be diplomatic and tactful. Avoid confrontation, arguments, and kidding because the child and family may see such actions as disrespectful, rude, or offensive.
18. Write your notes after the interview is over if taking notes during the interview will offend the child or family.

IDENTIFY STEREOTYPES
19. Recognize any stereotypes and prejudices that you have about the family's ethnic group.
20. Take precautions to ensure that your stereotypes and prejudices do not interfere with your work.
21. Do not assume that the family follows the ethnic group's traditional medicine healing practices or uses traditional healers. Some ethnic families will be offended if you

assume that they believe in traditional healers. Ask them about these matters as needed.

PROMOTE CLEAR COMMUNICATION
22. Speak clearly, and avoid idioms, slang expressions, and statements with implied or double meanings.
23. Ask the parents and the child whom they want at the interview. Some families prefer to invite extended family members, whereas others do not.
24. Address all family members present at the interview, not just the child and parents.
25. Call children by their proper names. (Hispanic Americans, for example, are often given two last names, one from each parent.)
26. Monitor your verbal and nonverbal behavior to eliminate words, expressions, and actions that may offend the child and family. (Monitoring your nonverbal behavior will not be easy.) You must learn whether your behavior changes with members of different ethnic groups. (For example, if you are a majority interviewer and work with both minority and majority interviewees, examine your behavior with both groups. Do you find that you place yourself farther away from interviewees who are from minority groups than you do from interviewees

Frank and Earnest   by Bob Thaves

who are from majority groups, spend less time with them, or make more speech errors with them? If so, you may be revealing signs of anxiety or avoidance behavior. Videotape your interviews and study them carefully for subtle signs of altered communications with different ethnic groups.)

27. Evaluate whether ethnic group differences between you and the child and family may be hampering the interview; if so, try to rectify the problems.

28. Be flexible, and use innovative interviewing strategies tailored to the needs of the family's ethnic group.

IDENTIFY FAMILY NEEDS

29. Determine the material resources and physical health of the child and family. (For example, do they have adequate food, water, clothing, bedding, shelter, and sanitation and proper immunizations? What unmet needs do the child and family have that can affect treatment?)

30. Determine the psychological and social needs of the child and family. (For example, does the child have adequate time for play? What is the child's level of self-esteem? Has the child established friendships? Does the family have adequate leisure time? Are family members able to practice their religious beliefs? Does the child have adequate schooling? Does the home offer a place to study free from distractions? Are the parents able to supervise the child? Is the child forced to assume adult responsibilities prematurely? Is the child vulnerable to corruption on the streets of the resettlement country?)

IDENTIFY ATTITUDES TOWARD HEALTH AND ILLNESS

31. Learn about the child's and family's traditional concepts of illness and healing, traditional rituals, and religious beliefs, and how they differ from those of the majority culture. (For example, healing practices that produce bruises on a child may not indicate child abuse, and the shaving of one's head and eyebrows, performed as a

sacrifice to wronged ancestors, may not be a sign of mental illness.)

32. Learn what the child's and family's expectations are of medical or psychological treatment. (For example, when they take medicine, do they expect immediate relief, and, if they do not get it, will they discontinue taking the medicine? Do they believe that only a pill will make them well?)

33. Learn what prescribed drugs, over-the-counter drugs, traditional remedies, and illicit drugs the child is taking.

RECOGNIZE THE EXTENT OF ACCULTURATION

34. Recognize that acculturation will take different forms among different ethnic groups. Learn about the extent to which the child and the parents are acculturated.

35. Expect to find large differences among children and families from the same ethnic group in their values and level of acculturation and in the problems they face.

36. Learn about stresses associated with acculturation, particularly for refugee and immigrant groups. (For example, do they feel depressed, angry, or guilty about those left behind in their home country? Do they have any symptoms associated with posttraumatic stress disorder? If you hold the interview after a period of adjustment in the resettlement country, do they complain that nobody cares about them, do they express fear of failure or feelings of isolation, or do they have delayed grief reactions? Do they have conflicts in transition periods, such as when the children enter adolescence? Do other refugee or immigrant families reject them when they try to identify with the new culture? How great are the cultural differences between the resettlement country and the home country? Because children tend to acculturate faster than adults, to what extent is there intergenerational conflict between the child and parents? Does the child feel alienated—rejected both by his or her culture of origin and by the resettlement culture? Is the child

accepted by one culture but not the other? Or is he or she accepted by both cultures? Does the family need help in interpreting laws and regulations of the resettlement country?)

37. Obtain information about how the child and family were functioning *before* leaving their home country. (For example, children and families who had serious problems before their migration may find their unresolved problems exacerbated in the resettlement country.)

ACCEPT THE INTERVIEWEE'S PERSPECTIVES

38. Show a willingness to (a) accept cultural perspectives other than your own, (b) see the strengths and values of the coping mechanisms of ethnic groups other than your own, and (c) appreciate and respect the viewpoint of each ethnic group with which you work. (For example, recognize how your own culture—its values, customs, mores, traditions, and standards—differs from other cultures. Be tolerant of family norms that may have developed as responses to stress and prejudice. Include extended family members in the intervention if they are highly involved with the child and family. Also consider contacting traditional healers and practitioners as needed, and work with the established power structures within the child's and family's community.)

39. Do not violate the child's and family's culture and traditional beliefs during the interview or in formulating intervention plans.

40. Build on the child's and family's strengths, use the family's natural support systems, and help the child remain in his or her natural community in the least restrictive environment.

41. Fully support the premise that society must give each child in the nation an equal opportunity to achieve to the limits of his or her capacity.

42. Recognize that members of ethnic minority groups (and members of the majority group as well) often face major social issues. Major social issues include changes in women's roles, changes in the concept of the family, role conflict and its impact on children, substandard schools, unequal pay scales, dilapidated housing, high dropout rates from school, a shortage of relevant mental health services in the community, prejudice and discrimination, accessibility of mental health services, and relevance of treatments.

43. Recognize that families at a low socioeconomic status level can provide a healthy, strong, and nurturing environment for their children; *do not equate low socioeconomic status with dysfunction.*

44. Recognize how the sociopolitical system in the United States treats ethnic minorities and how institutional barriers affect ethnic minorities' use of mental health facilities and medical facilities.

45. Consider each child and family as unique, but use what you know about the child's and family's ethnic background to guide you in the interview.

46. Do not use your knowledge of the family's ethnic background to make sweeping generalizations based on stereotypes you hold, or to probe into cultural practices not relevant to the child's and family's difficulties.

47. Learn about any stresses experienced by immigrant children and their families before they came to the resettlement country. (For example, how have traumatic experiences, if any, affected the child's development and the child's and family's perceptions of the world and view of the future?)

48. Avoid attributing all the child's and family's problems solely to their ethnic minority group status.

49. Have the case reassigned if you find yourself unable to be objective or unwilling to learn about the family's culture.

The above suggestions will help you become a *culturally skilled interviewer* and help you establish trust with the child and parents. Trust, in turn, will improve the quality of the communications. For trust to develop, children and parents must perceive that you have expert knowledge and good intentions and that they can rely on you. *Unless mutual trust develops, the clinical assessment or forensic interview is doomed to failure.*

You can become more credible in the eyes of ethnic minority families by conducting several informal interviews initially and by visiting the child's home (see Chapter 4 for a discussion of home visits). Be sure to obtain the permission of the parents *before* you visit the child's home. Some ethnic minority families are distrustful of a stranger coming to their home, especially if the person is employed by a city, county, state, or federal agency. Ethnic minority parents may need time to accept the need for evaluation and treatment. Explain program objectives so that the parents—and the child, where applicable—understand them fully. Repeatedly stress that the welfare of the child is important. Give the parents as much support as they need. Resolve value conflicts to their satisfaction. If the child has a disability, help the parents accept the child's disability and be realistic about it. Recruit parents with children in special programs from the same ethnic group as the new families to orient the new families to the program.

Honesty and reliability can be effective in changing negative opinions about mental health and medical services and about practitioners. By being patient, understanding, competent, and tolerant, you can probably mitigate any hostile feelings that the parents have and help them see that the child's welfare is the concern of all involved.

Improved intercultural communication will ultimately depend on changes in the sociopolitical system. Until our society eliminates racism and discrimination, there will always be vestiges of suspicion and mistrust between people of different ethnicities. As an interviewer (and health care provider), you can improve race relations. You can strive to eliminate social inequalities and prejudice from our society by (a) helping children develop pride in their native language and culture, (b) improving families' attitudes toward learning, and (c) helping society and the educational system be more responsive to the attitudes, perceptions, and behaviors of different ethnic groups. These and similar actions will improve the quality of life of the children and families with whom you work.

A culture must be created that allows us to see that one person's gain means the advancement of us all. Over the last 15 years [1980–1995], the concept of the common good has been tragically corrupted. Children grow up in homes where individualism is preeminent and human solidarity is unknown. God has created us to be one family. We can never eradicate racism that corrodes the soul of the nation unless we affirm our membership in that one human family, brothers and sisters, all sacred. I believe this is the central issue of our time. Our lives and destinies are wrapped up together.

The Greeks have a saying that there is no justice in Athens until the uninjured are as indignant as the injured parties. Religious leaders, civil rights leaders, politicians, academics, educators, lawyers, doctors, writers, editors must be committed to creating this culture of the common good.

What an incredible gift to families raising children in these troubled days if we could create a moral vision for America where the affluent are tied to the poor, the secure ones are bound together with the homeless and the well-being of my children and grandchildren is dependent on the health of all children. If a nation could not survive half-slave and half-free, no nation will be blessed if it is half-rich and half-impoverished.

There is something decadent about a city or a nation that denies this human solidarity. There is something corrupting about the assumption that a few have the right to good health, dignified jobs, fine education and decent housing— while others live in misery. It is my deepest conviction that any hope of racial healing is found in this renewed commitment to the common good and creating a culture in which this texture is unmistakably clear.

—George Regas

Exercise 9-3. Thinking About Culture

This exercise contains several questions about culture. First, answer the questions, and then, if possible, compare your answers with those of other students in your class.

1. How would you define culture?
2. Is culture synonymous with ethnicity?
3. How do the concepts of race and ethnicity differ?
4. How does the notion of a "melting pot" (that is, a place where immigrants of different cultures or races form an integrated society) fit in with the recommendation that it is important to learn about other cultures to be a knowledgeable interviewer?
5. How do your cultural practices differ from those of other groups?
6. Think about members of an ethnic group that you know fairly well. How do the members differ from each other, and how are they similar?
7. As you were growing up, do you remember noticing that another family did things differently than your family? If so, how old were you and what do you remember about the experience?
8. Are initiation rights for preadolescents in some cultures—such as beatings, genital mutilation, and withholding of food—forms of child maltreatment? What is the basis for your answer?
9. Which aspects of culture are passed on by the family and which by the society?
10. Describe what you would consider rituals in your culture. Do the same for another culture, if you can. How do the rituals in the two cultures differ, and how are they similar? What purposes do rituals serve?
11. What are some child-rearing practices in different cultures aimed at achieving the same or similar goals?

THINKING THROUGH THE ISSUES

What problems do you foresee in interviewing members of ethnic groups different from yours? How would these problems interfere with the interview? What can you do about these problems?

If you were planning to visit the home of a (Black American, Hispanic American, Asian American, Native American, Anglo American) middle-class family, what expectations would you have for your first visit? (Answer this question separately for each ethnic group.)

If you were working at a school and a 12-year-old (Black American, Hispanic American, Asian American, Native American, Anglo American) middle-class (male, female) was referred to you for truancy, what expectations would you have for the adolescent's first visit? (Answer this question separately for each ethnic group and for each sex.)

What would your response be to an interviewee who wanted to be interviewed by a person of his or her ethnic group?

How would you know whether the interviewee's problems stemmed from ethnic identity conflicts or from other reasons?

How would a knowledge of different cultures help you conduct a more effective interview with ethnic minority interviewees?

What are some ways in which failure to recognize cultural differences might lead to misunderstandings and misjudgments in interviews with ethnic minority interviewees?

Have you ever been in a situation where you felt out of place because of your ethnic identity? If yes, what was the situation? What did you do about your feeling of being out of place? How long did the feeling last? Do you think you would still feel out of place if the situation occurred again?

If you are a member of the majority group, think of a specific ethnic minority group. What would it be like for you to be a member of that minority group? If you are a member of an ethnic minority group, think of the majority group. What would it be like for you to be a member of the majority group?

SUMMARY

Black Americans

1. Black Americans comprised about 12% of the population in 1990.
2. Black Americans in the United States tend to be bicultural, incorporating aspects of mainstream culture and Black culture.
3. The Black experience incorporates the collective experiences unique to Black Americans, encompassing racism, language, child-rearing practices, role expectations, socioeconomic status, and kinship bonds.
4. Black adolescents occupy an unenviable position as one of the most vulnerable and victimized groups in American society. As the largest group of minority youth, they frequently have been misdiagnosed by the mental health system, mislabeled by the educational system, mishandled by the juvenile justice system, and mistreated by the social welfare system.
5. The Black American family is more likely than the Anglo American family to be headed by a female.
6. Black Americans have cultural traditions based, in part, on those found in traditional African societies. The African perspective emphasizes spiritualism in the universe; harmony with nature and other people; feelings, expressiveness, and spontaneity; and duty to the group and group property.
7. The withering effect of racism may lead to major psychiatric problems among Black individuals.
8. Even Blacks who have become successful in the United States may feel that they are in a no-win situation, feeling out of place in both Black and White worlds.
9. Some Black children and parents have learned to distrust their environment. When distrust exists, it is difficult to conduct a valid clinical assessment interview.
10. Some Black children and their parents speak a variant of English that linguists call Black English, nonstandard Black English, or Black dialect. Black Americans may use Black English because of habit, ease of usage, peer pressure, and group identification and because it provides a sense of protection, belonging, and solidarity.
11. Black American traditional medicine takes the form of voodoo, witchcraft, magic, herbal medicine, and spirituality.

Hispanic Americans

12. The major Hispanic groups in the United States are Mexican Americans (Chicanos), Puerto Ricans, Cubans, and people from Central and South America. Many Hispanic Americans speak Spanish, but some speak Portuguese or French. Some children of Hispanic heritage who were born in the United States speak English only.
13. Most Hispanic American groups share a similar language, Spanish heritage, and Roman Catholic religious orientation, but they maintain their autonomy and are clearly distinguishable from one another.
14. The foundation of the Hispanic community is the nuclear family. The father has the dominant role and is responsible for making decisions; the mother is responsible for keeping the family together. Members of the extended family or other relatives also may live in the same household, especially if elderly members of the family are not self-sufficient.
15. Hispanic Americans tend to value human relations and person-centeredness and are open to displays of emotion, temperament, and affection. They emphasize strong identification with the nuclear and extended family. There is a sense of fatalism running through Hispanic cultures.
16. Hispanic American socialization practices emphasize clear norms, responsibility training, and pressure to conform to adult standards. The traditional values are continually undergoing change, however, because of increased urbanization and higher levels of assimilation.
17. Hispanic Americans may experience value conflicts associated with cultural clashes.
18. Hispanic Americans tend to be more tolerant than Anglo Americans of deviant behavior. They generally prefer to solve emotional problems within a family context.
19. When Hispanic American parents recognize that their child has a disability, they may give the child special treatment—showing the child excessive sympathy, overindulging the child, or placing few demands on the child. They may mistrust special education classes because they believe such classes are for "sick" or "crazy" children.
20. Linguistically, Hispanic American children and their families are a heterogeneous group, with wide variations in their degree of mastery of English and Spanish.
21. Curanderismo is the health care belief and practice system followed by some Mexican Americans. This system combines elements of European Roman Catholicism with beliefs and practices of native Indians of Mexico.
22. Mexican Americans may turn first to their families for help and support. Separation of patients from their families and kin runs counter to Mexican American culture. Often, Mexican Americans will not make medical decisions until they have consulted with their families.

Asian Americans

23. Between 1971 and 1993, the United States admitted 1,077,242 refugees from Asia. Asian American communities in the United States are made up of individuals who emigrated mainly from China, Japan, Korea, the Philippines, Thailand, Vietnam, Cambodia, and Laos. However, most of the refugees came from Vietnam and Laos.
24. Asian immigrant groups have special problems associated with socioemotional stress, language competency, unemployment, education, racism, and discrimination. A bimodal distribution of wealth exists among Asian Americans, with some families living close to the poverty level and others enjoying economic success.
25. Asian Americans tend to carry on the traditions and customs of their forefathers, one of which is to view ancestors and elders with great respect. The father is the traditional head of the household, and his authority is unquestioned. The younger generation is expected to care for the older generation, although this practice is changing with acculturation.
26. In Asian American groups, parents expect children to obey authority figures; avoid overt signs of conflict and get along

with others; be humble, obedient, and not outspoken; speak only when spoken to; and say nothing rather than upset someone. Failure to follow these practices may cause shame for the family.

27. As Asian Americans begin to assimilate, they may experience cultural conflicts.

28. In comparison with Anglo Americans, Asian Americans tend to be more practical in approaching problems, favoring concrete and well-structured ideas that have immediate practical application; to be less autonomous and more dependent, conforming, and obedient to authority; to be more inhibited and reserved and, therefore, more withdrawn from social contacts and responsibilities, often experiencing social alienation; to be more formal in interpersonal relationships; to view outsiders with more suspicion; to value silence more; and to make more effort to avoid disagreeing or criticizing, keeping their voices low because raising one's voice is seen as a sign of anger.

29. Asian Americans may seek treatment for psychological disorders *only* when the disorders are relatively severe. They usually treat milder disturbances within the family structure and may be reluctant to discuss their feelings and problems openly. They attach more stigma and shame to mental or emotional problems than do Anglo Americans.

30. Anglo American clinicians may have language and communication problems when they interview Asian Americans. Misunderstandings may result because of the ways Asian Americans use language or pronounce English words.

31. Chinese traditional medicine is based on a view that health is a state of spiritual and physical harmony with nature. Treatment procedures include acupuncture, herbal medicines, massage, coining, spooning, cupping, and moxibustion.

Native Americans

32. The term *Native American* is a broad, almost arbitrary category covering 552 federally recognized tribes in the United States. These groups speak 252 language dialects, perhaps representing only six language families.

33. Native Americans have a long history of oppression and discrimination. Anglo Americans forced them to live on reservations and give up property rights and required some of their children to live in boarding schools. Many Native Americans have few economic opportunities—especially those living on reservations, most of whom live in poverty.

34. There is no single definition of a Native American, as individuals vary in degree of blood and level of acculturation.

35. The Native American family is frequently composed of extended family members and of nonfamily members of the same band or tribe, who may encompass several households. In some Native American tribes, elders are viewed as the family leaders, and respect for individuals increases with age. Also, there is a strong role for women. The family is viewed as important, particularly in periods of crisis, when family members are expected to serve as sources of support and security.

36. Traditional Native American values and beliefs may be characterized as follows: desiring harmony with nature instead of mastery over nature; attaching importance to religion; explaining natural phenomena by mythology, by the power of nature, and by spirituality; attaching importance to the extended family and tribal relationships; using a noncoercive and noninterfering parenting style; providing children with warmth and support; ignoring or shunning children who misbehave or correcting them quietly or verbally rather than by using physical punishment; valuing childhood and old age; respecting individuality by observing a principle of noninterference while still being sensitive to group values; valuing modesty and humility in the presence of others; emphasizing giving, sharing, and cooperating; aspiring to follow in the ways of old people and to cooperate and maintain the status quo rather than to compete and climb the ladder of success; preferring community and "nonself-promotion" over individuality and aggression; wanting to focus on the present and satisfy present needs, rather than worry about getting ahead; valuing a wry sense of humor and use of analogy; viewing time in a spatial rather than a linear way; and orienting oneself toward the present rather than the future.

37. Changes are occurring in the traditional cultural values of Native Americans, as over one-half of all Native Americans now live in urban areas.

38. One of the most important health problems facing Native Americans is alcoholism.

39. Anglo American interviewers need to gain the trust of Native Americans by being flexible and supportive and by showing goodwill and self-awareness.

40. There is no universal, traditional Native American language. Each tribe is likely to have its own language, and within a tribe different dialects may exist. Native Americans differ in their command of the English language.

41. The traditional beliefs of Native Americans about health and illness center on the idea that illness can result from natural causes; from an imbalance of spiritual and environmental forces, caused by breaking taboos and coming into contact with taboo products; or from supernatural activity.

42. Traditional healers spend many years learning their skills. One becomes a traditional healer by inheriting the gift from the family, having a vision, or serving a lengthy apprenticeship. A traditional healer may assume the roles of doctor, counselor, priest, historian, and safekeeper of ancient legends.

Refugees

43. Refugees are individuals fleeing corrupt political regimes, war, famine, religious persecution, violence, or economic deprivation.

44. Arriving in a new country may cause additional adjustment problems associated with a disruption in normal cultural patterns and traditions, loss of possessions, worries about family members left behind or otherwise separated, and dealing with strange customs, language, mores, and traditions. Refugees may have symptoms associated with posttraumatic stress disorder.

45. Refugee children may face loss of parental support and protection and may experience pressures to assume adult responsibilities. They also may experience stress in school.

46. Refugee families often face racism in their new country. Racism robs them of trust, makes them feel bewildered, and prevents them from entering community life by isolating them from others.

47. Refugee families may have problems associated with changes in class and social status, unemployment or underemployment, low wages and poor work conditions, vulnerability to employer victimization, substandard and crowded living conditions, limited social supports, poor health care, immigration status, marital tension, and intergenerational conflict.

Intervention Considerations

48. In designing intervention programs for members of ethnic minority groups, you will need to consider the child's and family's culture, including their attitudes toward treatment and the child's problem, illness, or disability; gender roles; religious views; and the role of the extended family. For any particular case, you will need to consider the needs and cultural values of the *specific* child and family.

49. The intervention program must not be designed to change, either subtly or overtly, the child's and family's values to match those of the dominant culture or to pacify and eliminate legitimate anger and political initiative.

Semistructured Interviews

50. In interviewing ethnic minority children and their parents, use the same procedures as you would with majority children and their parents, as well as specific procedures that are relevant for the particular ethnic minority group.

Recommendations for Interviewing
Ethnic Minority Children and Their Families

51. In working with ethnic minority groups, show them that you are sensitive to and respect their culture's perspective and value systems and that you are willing to help them. Also convey to them an acceptance of their culture. Allow the parents and child to consult other family or community members if they request to do so.

52. Learn about the child's, family's, and community's cultural values, attitudes, and world view; the child's and family's ethnic identification; the family's specific cultural patterns related to child rearing; the family's socioeconomic status; how the family's community is organized, supported, and developed; and how the sociopolitical system in the United States influences the way ethnic minorities are treated.

53. Determine the child's and family's preferred language *before* beginning the interview. Ideally, learn the language spoken by the child and family. Do not assume that because the child and family speak some English, they can fully understand you. Do not assume that with some speaking knowledge of the family's language, you can communicate in a meaningful way. Use an interpreter, if needed, and recognize the limitations of using an interpreter.

54. Make every effort to encourage the child's and family's motivation and interest, and take time to enlist the child's and family's cooperation. Be diplomatic and tactful; avoid confrontation, arguments, and kidding. Write your notes after the interview is over if note taking might offend the child or family.

55. Recognize any stereotypes and prejudices that you have about the family's ethnic group. Take precautions to ensure that your stereotypes and prejudices do not interfere with your work. Do not assume that the family follows the ethnic group's traditional medicine healing practices or uses traditional healers. Ask them about these matters as needed.

56. Speak clearly, and avoid idioms, slang expressions, and statements with implied or double meanings. Ask the parents and the child whom they want at the interview. Address all family members present at the interview, not just the child and parents. Call children by their proper names. Monitor your verbal and nonverbal behavior to eliminate words, expressions, and actions that may offend the child and family. Videotape your interviews and study them carefully for subtle signs of altered communications with different ethnic groups. Evaluate whether ethnic group differences between you and the child and family may be hampering the interview; if so, try to rectify the problems. Be flexible, and use innovative interviewing strategies tailored to the needs of the family's ethnic group.

57. Determine the family's material resources, the physical health of the child and family, and their psychological and social needs.

58. Learn about the child's and the family's traditional concepts of illness and healing, traditional rituals, and religious beliefs; their attitudes toward the treatment of mental and physical illnesses; their expectations of medical or psychological treatment; and what prescribed drugs, over-the-counter drugs, traditional remedies, and illicit drugs the child is taking.

59. Recognize that acculturation will take different forms among different ethnic groups. Learn about the extent to which the child and the parents are acculturated and about stresses associated with acculturation. Expect to find large differences among children and families from the same ethnic group in their values and level of acculturation and in the problems they face. In working with refugees, obtain information about how the child and family were functioning *before* leaving their home country.

60. Show a willingness to accept cultural perspectives other than your own, to see the strengths and values of the coping mechanisms of ethnic groups other than your own, and to appreciate and respect the viewpoint of each ethnic group with which you work. Do not violate the child's and family's culture and traditional beliefs during the interview or in formulating intervention plans. Build on the child's and family's strengths, use the family's natural support systems, and help the child remain in his or her natural community in the least restrictive environment. Fully support the premise that society must give each child in the nation an equal opportunity to achieve to the limits of his or her capacity. Recognize that major social issues are often faced by members of ethnic minority groups (and by members of the majority group as well). Recognize that families at a low socioeconomic level can provide a healthy, strong, and nurturing environment for their children; *do not equate poverty with dysfunction.* Recognize how the sociopolitical system in the United States treats ethnic minorities and how institutional barriers affect ethnic minorities' use of mental health facilities and medical facilities. Consider each child and family as unique, but use what you know about the child's and family's ethnic background to guide you in the interview. Do not use your knowledge of the family's ethnic background to make sweeping generalizations based on stereotypes you hold or to probe into cultural practices not relevant to the child's and family's difficulties. Learn about any stresses experienced by immigrant children and their families before they came to the resettlement country. Avoid attributing all the child's and family's problems solely to their ethnic minority group status. Have the case reassigned if you find yourself unable to be objective or unwilling to learn about the family's culture.

61. Improved intercultural communication will ultimately depend on changes in the sociopolitical system. Until our society eliminates racism and discrimination, there will always be vestiges of suspicion and mistrust between people of different ethnicities.

62. As an interviewer (and health service provider), you can improve race relations. You can strive to eliminate social ine-

qualities and prejudice from our society by helping children develop pride in their native language and culture; improving families' attitudes toward learning; helping society and the educational system be more responsive to the attitudes, perceptions, and behaviors of different ethnic groups; encouraging parents to become more involved in their children's lives; and helping parents learn more effective ways of reinforcing their children's achievements.

KEY TERMS, CONCEPTS, AND NAMES

Black Americans (p. 282)

African perspective (p. 284)

Racism (p. 284)

Black English (nonstandard Black English, Black dialect, Ebonics) (pp. 286, 287)

Voodoo (p. 289)

Gris-gris (p. 289)

Asafetida (p. 289)

Hispanic Americans (p. 290)

Compadrazgo (p. 292)

Pochismos (p. 294)

Curanderismo (p. 294)

Yerbero (p. 294)

Curandero (p. 294)

Espiritualisto (p. 294)

Brujo (p. 294)

Caida de la mollera (p. 294)

Mal de ojo (p. 294)

Susto (p. 294)

Empacho (p. 294)

Envidia (p. 294)

Fatigue (p. 295)

Pasmo (p. 295)

Ataque (p. 295)

Santeria (p. 296)

Brujeria (p. 296)

Asian Americans (p. 297)

Interdepency (p. 298)

Yin (p. 302)

Yang (p. 302)

Acupuncture (p. 302)

Meridians (p. 302)

Herbal medicines (p. 302)

Massage (p. 302)

Coining (p. 302)

Spooning (p. 302)

Cupping (p. 302)

Moxibustion (p. 302)

Native Americans (p. 302)

Diagnosticians (p. 307)

Singers (p. 307)

Herbalists (p. 307)

Refugees (p. 309)

Intervention considerations (p. 311)

Recommendations for interviewing ethnic minority children and their families (p. 313)

STUDY QUESTIONS

1. For Black Americans, discuss cultural considerations, language considerations, and traditional medicine practices.
2. For Hispanic Americans, discuss cultural considerations, language considerations, and traditional medicine practices.
3. For Asian Americans, discuss cultural considerations, language considerations, and traditional medicine practices.
4. For Native Americans, discuss cultural considerations, language considerations, and traditional medicine practices.
5. Discuss considerations for interviewing refugees.
6. What are some critical interventions in working with ethnic minority groups?
7. Discuss 10 recommendations for working with ethnic minority groups. Include one recommendation in each of the following areas: culture, language, rapport, stereotypes, communication, family needs, attitudes toward health and illness, acculturation, and perspectives.
8. Compare and contrast Anglo American, Black American, Hispanic American, Asian American, and Native American cultures.

SECTION III

INTERVIEWING CHILDREN WITH PSYCHOLOGICAL DISORDERS AND CHILDREN AND FAMILIES FACING LIFE STRESSORS

Section III focuses on children with psychological disorders and on those who face life stresses. Children with psychological disorders may have difficulties in thinking, feeling, behavioral control, interpersonal relations, and language. Psychological disorders may be associated with genetic factors, environmental factors, or some combination of the two. Psychological disorders (such as autistic disorders or severe mental retardation) may stem primarily from genetic or biological factors, whereas disorders (such as separation anxiety disorder or posttraumatic stress disorder) may be associated primarily with environmental factors.

Children who face life stresses may or may not have psychological disorders—much depends on their level of adjustment, their coping skills, and the support they receive from their family and others. The psychological disorders that some of these children have may simply be a reaction to crisis. In most cases, when the crisis passes, their symptoms will diminish or disappear. When the symptoms persist, the children may need treatment.

Chapter 10 provides an overview of children with psychological disorders. Chapter 11 focuses on children who have behavioral or emotional disorders; Chapter 12 discusses children with developmental, learning, or sensory disorders; and Chapter 13 deals with children and families who face life stresses, such as bereavement, suicide, adoption, divorce, and homelessness.

As the Preface noted, this text is not a substitute for texts about abnormal psychology or exceptional children. You are encouraged to read such texts and also the latest edition of the *Diagnostic and Statistical Manual of the American Psychiatric Association.* And, as Chapter 1 noted, a supervised internship or supervised practicum training is essential for those of you who want to become mental health professionals. Some areas of interviewing, such as custody adoptions and evaluations, will require additional specialized training.

10

CHILDREN WITH PSYCHOLOGICAL DISORDERS: AN OVERVIEW

All children need:
To be free from discrimination
To develop physically and mentally in freedom and dignity
To have a name and nationality
To have adequate nutrition, housing, recreation, and
  medical services
To receive special treatment if handicapped
To receive love, understanding, and material security
To receive an education and develop [their] abilities
To be the first to receive protection in disaster
To be protected from neglect, cruelty, and exploitation
To be brought up in a spirit of friendship among people
                              —United Nations' Declaration
                                  of the Rights of the Child

How Psychological Disorders Develop in Children
Living with a Child with a Psychological Disorder
Interviewing Issues
Interventions
Thinking Through the Issues
Summary

Goals and Objectives

This chapter is designed to enable you to:

* Understand how children develop psychological disorders
* Recognize factors that protect children from developing psychological disorders
* Evaluate facilitated communication and augmentative communication
* Understand families' needs associated with raising children with psychological disorders
* Understand interventions useful for children with psychological disorders

Children who have psychological disorders are a heterogeneous group. They may have problems involving *cognitive functions* (such as impaired ability to reason or learn), *affect* (such as anxiety or depressive reactions), or *behavior* (such as socially inappropriate behavior, hyperactivity, or violence toward self and others). In addition, they may have physical disabilities and medical problems. See Table 10-1 for a sampling of symptoms and behaviors found in children and adolescents with psychological disorders.

Generalizations about children with psychological disorders must be made with caution because each child has unique temperament and personality characteristics, cognitive skills, social skills, adaptive-behavior skills, and support systems. *Approach each child as a unique individual and never only as a child who represents a psychological disorder.* If you approach the child in a stereotyped way, your ability to obtain accurate information will be impaired. You want to learn as much about the child's positive coping strategies and accomplishments and the protective factors in her or his life—including those provided by the immediate and extended family—as you do about the symptoms, negative coping strategies, and other factors that hinder her or his development.

Children who have one psychological disorder may have another one as well, a phenomenon referred to as *co-occurring disorders* or *comorbid disorders*. Disorders that commonly occur together are conduct disorder and attention-deficit/hyperactivity disorder, autistic disorder and mental retardation, and childhood depression and anxiety (Mash & Dozois, 1996). Children with co-occurring disorders are likely to have more problems and longer-lasting problems than children with only a single disorder. Nottelmann and Jensen (1995), for example, found that sixth-grade boys with both conduct problems and depressive symptoms were more likely to continue to have problems in eighth grade than boys with only one disorder. Always consider whether children have more than one type of psychological disorder because psychological disorders in childhood may not be "pure."

Children with a psychological disorder *usually* will go through the same developmental sequences as normal children, although sometimes at a different rate. Some may be delayed in reaching developmental milestones (see the table on the inside front cover), and some, particularly those with severe psychological disorders such as an autistic disorder or mental retardation, may never reach more mature stages of language development or conceptual thinking. Advise parents to obtain a detailed assessment if their children have significant developmental delays. For example, children may have a significant motor delay if they are not walking by 18 months of age or a significant language delay if they are not speaking by 3 years of age. Table 3-1 in Chapter 3 provides possible indicators of disturbance in physical and psychological development of children from birth to 18 years.

Children with psychological disorders form their *self-concepts* in ways similar to those used by normal children. Parents are the primary source of feedback, followed by siblings and other relatives, friends and neighbors, and teachers and other professionals. You will want to learn about children's self-concepts, how their self-concepts affect their relationships with others, their feelings about having problems, and their future aspirations. You also will want to learn how parents view their child and their child's disorder and about the parents' future aspirations for their child (see Chapter 4). Children with psychological disorders are likely to have more negative self-concepts and to experience more frustration, rejection, teasing, prejudice, depression, anxiety, and motivational deficiencies than children without psychological disorders (Cobb, 1989).

Children with psychological disorders who also have physical impairments may be limited in their ability to obtain a full range of sensory information, to socialize, to engage in sports and other physical activities, and to reach expected height and weight (see Tables C-11 and C-12 in Appendix C). These limitations may interfere with the development of cognitive, affective, and interpersonal skills. Multiple physical impairments, together with a psychological disorder, pose even greater challenges for children's development and care. Let's now examine some factors that contribute to the development of psychological disorders in children.

HOW PSYCHOLOGICAL DISORDERS DEVELOP IN CHILDREN

Psychological disorders in children develop from the interaction of children's (a) genetic characteristics, (b) biological features, (c) family experiences and cultural background, (d) individual characteristics (such as personality, emotional reactions, self-concept, coping strategies, motivations, and beliefs), (e) interpersonal relations (such as interpersonal competence and environmental supports), and (f) life stresses (Hammen & Rudolph, 1996; also see Figure 10-1). Let's now consider how genetic and biological factors as well as environmental factors influence the development of psychological disorders.

Table 10-1
Symptoms and Behaviors Found in Children and Adolescents with Psychological Disorders

Amnesia and Memory Problems
Tends to wander off
Gets lost easily
Loses things easily
Has general amnesia
Has amnesia for traumatic experiences
Has amnesia for specific situations
Has a loss of time

Anxiety and Phobic Behaviors
Has generalized anxiety
Has separation anxiety
Has phobias
Has panic attacks

Attention and Concentration Problems
Is easily distracted
Has difficulty concentrating on task
Has difficulty sustaining attention
Fails to listen
Fails to follow through on instructions
Has difficulty organizing tasks and activities
Is impulsive and hyperactive
Often fidgets with hands and feet
Often leaves seat in classroom
Runs about or climbs excessively
Talks excessively
Frequently blurts out answers
Frequently has difficulty waiting turn
Interrupts or intrudes on others

Conduct Problems
Is disruptive
Shows aggression
Has an explosive temper
Fights often
Lies often
Steals often
Sets fires
Is cruel to animals
Runs away from home
Is truant
Sexually assaults others
Has homicidal ideation
Destroys property
Stays out late at night
Show a lack of remorse

Depression
Is sad
Has low self-esteem
Expresses hopelessness
Blames self

Is irritable
Shows affective lability
Has suicidal ideation
Has made a suicide attempt
Shows fatigue

Dissociative Symptoms
Has alter personalities
Shows age regression
Displays rapid changes in personality
Has poor body boundaries
Has spontaneous trance states
Shows involuntary movements
Displays conversion symptoms
Has fluctuating somatic complaints
Has pseudoseizures

Eating Problems
Has anorexia
Has bulimia
Compulsively overeats
Has many appetite changes
Is obese
Eats nonnutritive substances
Regurgitates and rechews food

Elimination Disorders
Lacks bladder control
Lacks bowel control

Hallucinations
Has auditory hallucinations
Has command hallucinations
Has aggressive hallucinations
Has hallucinations that urge self-injury
Has visual hallucinations
Has tactile hallucinations
Has somatic hallucinations
Has imaginary companions (for adolescents)

Interpersonal Problems
Fails to develop peer relationships
Fails to share things with people
Lacks social or emotional reciprocity
Displays indiscriminate sociability

Language Problems
Has a delay in or lack of spoken language
Has difficulty initiating or sustaining a conversation
Shows stereotyped or repetitive use of language
Has idiosyncratic language
Displays echolalia

Has a deficit in expressive language
Has a deficit in receptive language

Motor Problems
Has tics (vocal or motor)
Displays nonfunctional motor movements

Obsessive and Compulsive Behaviors
Has obsessions
Has rituals
Has compulsions

Oppositional Symptoms
Loses temper often
Argues with adults often
Actively defies adults or refuses to comply with adult requests
Deliberately annoys people
Frequently blames others for mistakes
Is often touchy or easily annoyed by others
Is often angry and resentful
Is often spiteful
Is often vindictive

Posttraumatic Stress Symptoms
Has traumatic nightmares
Has intrusive thoughts
Has flashbacks
Is hypervigilant
Has exaggerated startle reaction
Avoids traumatic stimuli
Is fearful
Shows disorganized or agitated behavior
Engages in repetitive play

School Problems
Has a learning disability
Has a reading disability
Has a mathematics disability
Has a spelling disability
Has an oral language disability
Has a written expression disability
Is truant
Has been suspended from school
Has been expelled from school

Separation Problems
Shows distress when separated from attachment figures
Worries excessively about losing attachment figures

(Continued)

Table 10-1 (*Continued*)

Refuses to go to school
Is fearful of being alone without attach-
    ment figure
Is reluctant to go to sleep without
    attachment figure
Has nightmares involving separation

Sexual Behavior Problems
Shows inappropriate sexual behaviors
Masturbates compulsively
Displays genitals in public
Engages in inappropriate sexual play
Perpetrates sexual abuse
Is promiscuous

Sleep Problems
Has nontraumatic nightmares
Has night terrors
Has insomnia
Has hypersomnia
Sleepwalks

Speech Problems
Stutters
Makes errors in sound production

Stereotyped Behaviors
Shows stereotyped or restricted
    behavior

Has inflexible routines
Has repetitive motor mannerisms
Is persistently preoccupied with parts
    of objects

Thought Disorder Symptoms
Is confused
Is disoriented
Shows disorganized thinking
Expresses delusions
Displays paranoia
Displays grandiosity

Source: Adapted, in part, from Hornstein and Putnam (1992).

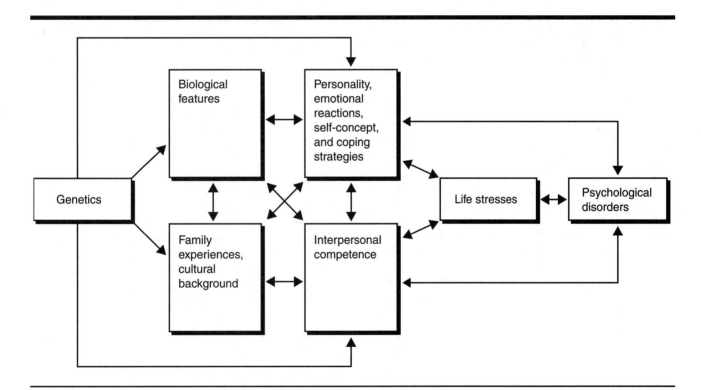

Figure 10-1. A model showing the development of psychological disorders in children. Adapted from Hammen and Rudolph (1996).

Genetic and Biological Factors

Several hereditary disorders affect both physical and psychological development. Examples are disorders associated with *chromosomal abnormalities* (such as translocations found in Down syndrome [Trisomy 21] and fragile X syndrome) and *inborn errors of metabolism* (such as phenylketonuria [PKU] and Tay-Sachs disease). (See the Glossary for definitions of these and other conditions noted in the book.) Other factors that can affect the fetus (*prenatal factors*) and lead to physical and psychological disorders include *infections* (such as rubella, toxoplasmosis, cytomegalovirus, syphilis, and human immunodeficiency virus [HIV; see Chapter 17]), *teratogens* (such as alcohol and radiation), *toxins* (such as cocaine, lead, and maternal phenylketonuria), and *placental dysfunction*. Genetic or biological vulnerabilities may limit children's development and may make it more difficult for them to acquire needed competencies and to cope with stress.

A critical factor affecting children's development is whether their mothers used drugs or alcohol during pregnancy. Children born to mothers who abuse substances are at risk for birth defects as well as for motor, cognitive, language, social, and emotional deficits (Cunningham, 1992; Phelps & Cox, 1993). As *infants,* they may tremble or be agitated, restless, hyperactive, or rigid, and they may have sleep and respiratory difficulties or be difficult to console. As *toddlers and preschoolers,* they may have subtle cognitive delays and may show deficits in fine motor control, self-organization and initiation, activity level, and attention, speech, and language. As *school-aged children and adolescents,* they may exhibit mild mental retardation, developmental learning disorders, attention difficulties, hyperactivity, and conduct disorders. Children born to drug- or alcohol-abusing mothers will need a comprehensive assessment of their physical and psychological functioning. (Also see Chapter 12 for a discussion of fetal alcohol syndrome.)

The following case deals with a toddler who was exposed to drugs prenatally and who displayed deficits in emotional stability, attention, speech, and activity level (Cohen & Erwin, 1994).

CASE 10-1. T.

T. was observed in a preschool when she was 49 months old. Her moods shifted from being happy—smiling, laughing, and engaging in playful teasing with other children—to crying, screaming, and being sad and depressed. She usually screamed when she could not get something she wanted immediately or when she was asked to stop an activity. T. showed anger and aggressiveness toward other children and toward the teaching staff. She attempted to hit the teacher in the face with Playdough, threw plates, hit and kicked a classmate, knocked over chairs, and swore at an assistant teacher. T. also showed affection toward staff members at times and eagerly accepted affection from them. She also was friendly with other children and displayed affection toward one girl in particular.

T. usually was extremely active, although on occasion she just lay still on the floor. Most of the time her attention was fleeting or she appeared preoccupied. She had difficulty making transitions. For example, she went from painting a picture on paper to painting her face, from playing with shaving cream on a table to rubbing shaving cream along the lengths of her arms, and from coloring on her own paper to coloring across both her paper and that of the child next to her. T. frequently used gestures instead of words. There were long periods during which she sucked her thumb and did not talk to anyone. When she spoke, her sentences were short (two to five words) and her attention was poor.

Environmental Factors

The primary way in which infants and young children learn about themselves and others is through familial experiences.

These experiences probably are encoded in memory as a set of beliefs about themselves and others and about expectations for future relationships with others. Children's adjustment likely will be adversely affected if their parents (Bagley & Shewchuk-Dann, 1991; Cunningham, 1992; Kendziora & O'Leary, 1992)

- are cold and insensitive and reject or neglect them
- have inappropriate developmental expectations for them
- are inadvertently attentive to their inappropriate behavior
- are vague in communicating with them
- are unable to establish reasonable expectations and limits for them
- are inconsistent with them and have difficulty handling situations that call for discipline
- are tardy in dealing with their misbehavior
- use overly harsh or overly lax disciplinary procedures
- physically, psychologically, or sexually abuse them
- have psychological disorders (for example, if they are anxious or depressed; show unexpected changes in mood, energy, or self-esteem; or have deficient reality testing— that is, difficulty determining their relationships with the external world and with social environments)
- are substance abusers
- are experiencing chaotic living arrangements
- are unable to obtain social supports
- are under considerable stress (for example, from domestic violence, work pressures, financial pressures, low socioeconomic status, legal matters, or criminal matters)

Effects of poor caregiving. Children whose caregivers are insensitive or rejecting may come to think of themselves as incompetent or unworthy, to think of others as hostile or unresponsive, and to think of relationships with others as aversive or unpredictable (also see the discussion of attachment theory in Chapter 1). These negative thoughts about self and others may interfere with the development of their emotions and behavior-regulation skills. Children may find it particularly difficult to cope with parental rejection, which can arise when a parent is absent physically or emotionally from the child. Children may experience loss of love, care, protection, guidance, and a model to emulate. Under such conditions, children are at risk for depression and other forms of psychological disorders (LaRoche, 1986).

Parents with psychological disorders or with drug habits. Parents who have psychological disorders may have difficulty helping their children feel emotionally secure, gain an understanding of social causes and effects, develop planning ability, or learn the importance of delayed gratification and the ability to take responsibility for their own actions (Clarke & Clarke, 1994). They also may have difficulty coping with developmental changes in their children and will be more likely to be thrown into a crisis by stressful events (Frude, 1991).

Although children whose parents become addicted to drugs *after* the children are born are not considered "drug

Calvin and Hobbes   by Bill Watterson

exposed," this exposure to drugs or alcohol nevertheless places them at risk for developing psychological difficulties. Preoccupation with alcohol or drugs or organic deficits sustained as a result of excessive use of substances can interfere with the parents' ability to raise their children (Cunningham, 1992). Parents who are substance abusers may have various problems—such as depression, anxiety, somatoform disorders, temper tantrums, aggressiveness, and hyperactivity—and be at risk for neglecting their children or for physically, sexually, or emotionally maltreating their children.

Other environmental stresses faced by children.
Children may face stresses associated with any of several events or conditions, such as

- the birth of a sibling
- moving to a new home or apartment
- changing schools
- failing classes in school
- being suspended from school
- having poor proficiency in English
- being exposed to cultural clashes
- being a victim of violence (such as maltreatment, mugging, or sexual assault)
- becoming involved with drugs or alcohol
- being overweight or underweight
- being rejected by peers
- being poor at sports
- going to jail
- attempting suicide
- running away from home
- having a best friend move
- losing a job
- having a parent lose a job
- having a relative or close friend die

- becoming pregnant (for females)
- impregnating a female (for males)

Stress is a key factor that contributes to the development of psychological disorders in children. Stress can exacerbate problems that children face and bring about new problems—by, for example, leading to acting-out behavior or a breakdown in behavior and producing changes in various neurochemicals in the body.

Effects of violence on children. *Exposure to violence* may affect children's psychological adjustment. In a national survey of a representative sample of 2,000 American children (1,042 boys and 958 girls) aged 10 to 16 years, one-third (33.3%) of the children reported having been the victim of an assault (Boney-McCoy & Finkelhor, 1995). Assaults were characterized as aggravated assault (12.3%), simple assault (11.5%), sexual assault (10.5%), genital violence (7.5%), attempted kidnapping (6.1%), nonparental family assault (5.1%), and parental assault (2.2%). The *victimized children* reported more psychological and behavioral symptoms than did the nonvictimized children. The increased number of symptoms was associated with experiencing (a) more symptoms of posttraumatic stress disorder (PTSD) during the previous week (such as frightening thoughts and images, trouble falling asleep, and temper outbursts that could not be controlled; see Chapter 11 for a discussion of PTSD), (b) increased sadness in the past month, and (c) more trouble with teachers in the past year. Extrapolating these results to the entire nation suggests that over 6.1 million youths ages 10 to 16 have suffered some form of assault.

Boney-McCoy and Finkelhor (1995) concluded that the "evidence suggests that violent victimization is a major traumagenic [an event that causes trauma to the individual] influence in child development, and it may account for a substantial portion of mental health morbidity in both childhood and later adult life. These are powerful arguments for the need to quell the tide of violence in society and to protect children from its consequences" (p. 735). They also noted that the experience of being victimized and its associated trauma may interfere with or distort several developmental tasks of childhood. For example, victimized children may have impaired attachment to a caregiver or impaired self-esteem, adopt highly sexualized or highly aggressive modes of relating to others, fail to acquire competence in peer relations, or deal with anxiety in dysfunctional ways, such as by using drugs, dissociating, or engaging in self-injurious behavior (Finkelhor, 1995). The developmental effects of being victimized are likely to be more severe when the victimization is repetitive and ongoing; changes the nature of the child's relationship with her or his caregivers; adds to other serious stressors, such as when a child is simultaneously suffering from bereavement, parental divorce, or racial discrimination; and interrupts a crucial developmental transition, such as when an adolescent is sexually abused.

Comment on the Development of Psychological Disorders

Psychological disorders may lead children to experience a diminished sense of mastery and control, affect family interactions as well as biological functioning, and compromise children's future development by disrupting important social bonds, undermining their existing competencies, inducing stress, and reaffirming their negative views of themselves and the world (Hammen & Rudolph, 1996). Let's now look at how families cope with children with psychological disorders.

LIVING WITH A CHILD WITH A PSYCHOLOGICAL DISORDER

Not only do families experience initial trauma associated with learning that a child has a psychological disorder; they also have the continuing burden of responsibility for the care and education of the child. How well the family copes with raising the child will depend on the severity of the child's disorder, the family's resources, and the types of stressors the family faces.

Familial Life-Span Issues

Families raising a child with a psychological disorder may face various issues at different stages during the child's life span, depending on the severity of his or her disorder. (Marsh, D. T., FAMILIES AND MENTAL RETARDATION: NEW DIRECTIONS IN PROFESSIONAL PRAC-

TICE [Praeger, an imprint of Greenwood Publishing Group, Inc., Westport, CT 1992]. Copyright © 1992 by D. T. Marsh. Reprinted with permission of Greenwood Publishing Group, Inc.; all rights reserved; p. 110.)

1. *Early childhood.* The issues include clarifying the diagnosis, informing other family members, locating and accessing services, locating and accessing community resources and supports, fulfilling general family functions, resolving the emotional burden, redefining the family in meaningful and constructive ways, and dealing with the larger society.

2. *Middle childhood.* The issues include easing school entry, learning about educational policies and procedures, participating in educational conferences, dealing with peer issues, and locating and accessing extracurricular activities.

3. *Adolescence.* The issues include adjusting to puberty and sexuality, dealing with peer issues, formulating vocational plans, undertaking transitional planning, and developing recreational and leisure opportunities.

4. *Young adulthood.* The issues include carrying out vocational plans; making residential choices when needed; dealing with sexuality, marriage, and family; maintaining recreational and leisure activities; and undertaking long-term planning.

5. *Late adulthood.* The issues include planning for caregiving and supervision following the death of the caregiver, setting up residential plans when needed, transferring parental responsibility, and balancing the rights and responsibilities of all family members.

Parents of children with psychological disorders are faced with more issues of dependence and independence throughout their children's development than are other parents. They may overprotect their children because they do not want them to experience frustration or rejection. However, limiting their children's experiences may increase their children's dependency, discourage them from coming to grips with their problems, and keep them from developing effective coping strategies. You will need to explore with both children and their parents issues of independence, considering the children's ages and capabilities. Parents should allow their children to assume whatever responsibilities they can handle and provide them with as rich and stimulating an environment as possible.

Determinants of Families' Responses to Children with Psychological Disorders

Families' responses to children with psychological disorders will depend on the following (Frude, 1991; Minnes, 1988):

- type and extent of the disorder
- how often the disorder occurs
- intensity of the children's symptoms
- level of care needed by the children

- situational factors, including suddenness of onset of the disorder and when the problems are most severe
- personality and temperament of the children and family members
- resources of the family members
- role structure and organization of the families
- support received from the health care staff
- support received from other members of the community, including extended family, friends, neighbors, agencies, and self-help groups

Families are best able to cope with stress when they are intact and well integrated, when channels of communication are open, when authority and role structures are flexible, and when they have successfully dealt with crises in the past (Minnes, 1988).

Following are some sources of stress that parents of a child with a psychological disorder may face (Duwa, Wells, & Lalinde, 1993; Krehbiel & Kroth, 1991; Weiss, 1991; Wikler, Wasow, & Hatfield, 1981):

1. *Collaborating with several professionals and arranging for support services.* Parents may need to work with several different professionals, including psychiatrists, psychologists, social workers, pediatricians, speech and language pathologists, and special education teachers. When parents obtain conflicting information from professionals, they may become upset and angry. If the child also has medical problems, there may be additional stresses associated with performing medical or nursing tasks. Difficulty in finding adequate educational programs, day care centers, babysitters, respite workers, or other support services also may cause stress.

2. *Strain among family members.* Parents may experience stress from having to care for the child, readjust family priorities, cope with household disruptions, accept the child's slow progress, work out differences in opinion on the appropriate treatment or placement for the child, and cope with siblings who resent the increased attention given to the child. The parents' ability to cope with the child's psychological disorder will be impaired if marital satisfaction is reduced and marital turmoil is increased.

3. *Stigmatization from the child's disorder.* Parents may feel embarrassment and shame as a result of the negative reactions of relatives, neighbors, community members, and health professionals to their child with a psychological disorder. They may believe that some people and professionals blame them for their child's disorder.

4. *Dealing with the extremes of the child's behavior.* Parents of a child with a severe psychological disorder may be anxious if they are not able to predict or control the child's behavior. When they can't handle the child's behavior, parents may have a sense of fear or shame and feelings of incompetence. Examples of severe behavior problems include screaming and hand flapping, explosive or violent attacks on other people, self-stimulating or self-destructive behavior, releasing and smearing of feces in public places, and destruction of property. But even milder behavior problems, such as bedwetting or hyperactivity, may be stressful to parents.

5. *Concerns by parents about their own mental health.* Parents may be concerned about their own mental health. This is especially true for parents who frequently feel angry, guilty, depressed, or anxious. They may feel unable to cope with the child's special problems or behavior. If the child does not respond to them in the expected or desired way, they may feel that parenting is not rewarding.

6. *Concerns with the child's developmental progress.* Parents may experience heightened stress and depression at developmental transition points, such as when their child is supposed to walk or talk, enters school, graduates from elementary school, reaches puberty, graduates from high school, or reaches her or his 21st birthday. They also may experience stress when their child is initially diagnosed (see Chapter 5) and when the child falls behind other children in growth and development.

7. *Concerns about the child's future.* Parents may have concerns about the child's future, such as whether the child can work, whether they will need to institutionalize the child if his or her behavior becomes bizarre or uncontrollable, who will take care of the child when they die, and how to handle specific developmental issues such as an adolescent's emerging sexuality.

Raising a child with a psychological disorder may be both a burden and a strength to families. It may help put things in proper perspective, bring family members closer, provide a fuller understanding of love, and bring new realizations and joys. Occasionally, parents mourn the "loss" of the child they knew *before* the disorder and rebound with their acceptance of the child as he or she is *after* the disorder is diagnosed.

Parents may cope with the stress of raising a child with a psychological disorder in several different ways. They may seek information; use wish-fulfilling fantasies; blame themselves; seek support from relatives or friends; engage in counseling or therapy; join support groups; turn to religion; partake in yoga, meditation, or other forms of stress reduction; use antidepressive drugs or other drugs to reduce anxiety; and use alcohol or illegal drugs. To reduce their stress, they will need help in identifying appropriate schools, competent respite caregivers, behavioral specialists, and support groups.

INTERVIEWING ISSUES

As discussed in Chapter 3, it may be difficult to obtain accurate information from children. Children may be unable to recognize or verbalize their feelings, mood changes, or thoughts; depending on their age, they may not realize that their feelings (such as fears) or thoughts (such as delusions) are out of proportion to the demands of the situation. Interviewers, in turn, may have difficulty deciding which behaviors are problematic and which are normal. Interviewers may attribute some behaviors, such as irritability, defiance, and changes in mood, to normal childhood development (for example, identifying such behaviors as "adolescent turmoil") and fail to recognize that these behaviors may not be normal or typical for the child. Interviewers also may have difficulty in arriving at an accurate diagnosis because of overlapping symptoms.

When you interview children with psychological disorders, you can generally use standard interviewing techniques. However, their application is likely to be more demanding because the children may have expressive or receptive difficulties or attention difficulties or they may feel self-conscious, ill at ease, or at a disadvantage in the interview. You will need to be patient and encourage them to talk to you and to attend to your questions.

Before you interview children who may have psychological disorders, have their vision, hearing, physical condition, and health status screened. If you know before you interview them that they have communication difficulties, ask their parents about the signs, signals, or gestures that the children understand or use to communicate.

The following suggestions should help you interview children with psychological disorders (Ramirez, 1978; Shontz, 1977; Wright, 1983):

- Do not allow their disorder in one area to bias your perception of how they may function in other areas. For example, children who are mentally retarded may have excellent motor skills.
- Keep the interview short because the children may become fatigued easily if they are unaccustomed to concentrating for long periods. If you need to, schedule more than one interview.
- Be prepared to work hard to establish rapport and to ensure that they understand your questions.
- Position the children in your office to make them comfortable and to accommodate any physical disabilities they may have.
- Be sure the children use in the interview the adaptive equipment that they always use (for example, eyeglasses or hearing aids).
- Say to children who may need assistance "Do you need help?" or "How should I help you?"
- Do not "talk over" or provide the words for children who have difficulty speaking. Be patient, listen, and let them speak for themselves. Don't try to outguess them or assume that you know what they are trying to express.
- Do not direct your conversation to an attendant, assistant, or nearby companion as though the children were not present.

Other chapters in this section of the book, as well as in Sections IV and V, contain suggestions for interviewing children with specific types of disorders or problems.

Evaluating the Findings of the Interview

To evaluate the findings from interviews with children with psychological disorders, follow the guidelines presented in Chapter 3 (see Table 3-1, for example). In addition, use Table 10-2 for a framework useful for evaluating children, and use Table 10-3 to evaluate children's cognitive skills, communication skills, social skills, self-help skills, emotional skills, behavioral skills, motor skills, physical status, and sensory development.

Facilitated Communication

Some children with severe communication disorders—such as those with a severe autistic disorder, severe mental retardation, or profound mental retardation—cannot communicate by normal channels. To help them find alternative ways to communicate, several procedures have been developed. In this part of the chapter, we will consider facilitated communication; in the next part, we will look at augmentative communication.

In *facilitated communication,* a *facilitator* guides the disabled individual's hand, wrist, or arm across a keyboard or keyboard facsimile to help the individual type a message or point to letters. This technique has generated much controversy because the facilitator, rather than aiding the disabled individual in communicating, is likely to be the one actually communicating.

The theoretical justification for facilitated communication is based on beliefs about individuals with an autistic disorder. Proponents of facilitated communication believe that people with an autistic disorder do not have cognitive impairments but, instead, have motor apraxia, or the "neurologically determined inability to voluntarily initiate behavior or movement" (Mulick, Jacobson, & Kobe, 1993, p. 277). This impairment supposedly prevents individuals with an autistic disorder from oral or written expression without the aid of a facilitator (Biklen, Morton, Gold, Berrigan, & Swaminathan, 1992). Biklen et al. (1992) believe that this is the explanation for the surprisingly advanced communication skills and general knowledge of individuals who, before using facilitated communication, could barely communicate and were considered developmentally delayed.

Four examples of claims about the performance of disabled individuals under facilitated communication follow:

1. "Without facilitation, Mark [a 7-year-old boy] has no effective means of communicating, save to grab objects, pull people to objects or events that might be of interest to him, or throw tantrums. With facilitation, he can say what is on his mind, he can converse with other students, and he is doing school work at and above the grade level norm for his age" (Biklen, 1992, p. 15).

2. With the aid of facilitated communication, an adolescent with an autistic disorder and an IQ of 50 was transferred

**Table 10-2
A Framework for Assessment of Children**

1. Individual Characteristics and Psychological Adjustment
   a. child's age
   b. child's sex
   c. child's physical appearance
   d. child's health status
   e. child's affect
   f. child's cognitive ability
   g. child's sensory and motor functioning
   h. child's self-concept and self-esteem
   i. child's relationship with family members
   j. child's interpersonal competence
   k. child's degree of independence
   l. child's management of aggression and impulse control
   m. child's coping and defense mechanisms
   n. child's use of alcohol and drugs
   o. child's symptoms

2. Family Relations
   a. family structure
   b. family size
   c. family's health status
   d. family's traditions
   e. family's communication patterns
   f. family's expectations
   g. family's disciplinary practices
   h. family's relationship with child
   i. family's treatment of boys and girls
   j. child's birth order

3. School Adjustment and Achievement
   a. child's adjustment to school
   b. child's academic achievement
   c. child's relationship with peers in school

4. Relationship with Peers in the Community
   a. child's relationship with peer group in the community
   b. adolescent's dating practices
   c. adolescent's involvement in sexual activities
   d. adolescent's attitudes toward contraception
   e. adolescent's knowledge about sexually transmitted diseases

5. Adaptation to the Community
   a. older child's/adolescent's areas of interest in the community
   b. older child's/adolescent's participation in community activities
   c. older child's/adolescent's behavioral adjustment outside the home
   d. older child's/adolescent's quality of relationships with adults other than family members

Source: Adapted from Gibbs and Huang (1989).

from her special school to a regular high school, where she is handling an 11th-year program successfully (Crossley, 1992).

3. Individuals who previously had been unable to read or write are attending college classes and typing out their examinations with the aid of their facilitators (Dillon, 1993).

4. "A child with severe retardation and spastic quadriplegia who had been considered 'untestable' was estimated to be functioning in the severe to profound range of mental retardation. Testing using FC [facilitated communication] was said to reveal receptive language skills indicating an IQ of over 140 and prompted his parents to request full time regular education placement and revised academic goals" (Meinhold, 1994, p. 4).

Validity of facilitated communication. *There is no scientific evidence that facilitated communication works.* If the presence of motor apraxia is used to explain the success of facilitated communication and the success of facilitated communication is used to confirm the presence of motor apraxia, this circular reasoning undermines all efforts to assess the validity of facilitated communication. Controlled experiments and single-subject studies almost universally report that severely disabled individuals cannot solve even the simplest problem unless the facilitator also knows the answer or has been given the questions or stimuli. In fact, *"studies have consistently shown that facilitators are virtually controlling what is typed"* (Jacobson & Mulick, 1994, p. 97, italics added). When facilitators don't know what stimulus has been shown to the disabled individuals, there is almost no chance that the individuals' "answers" will be correct. In one study (Szempruch & Jacobson, 1993) that illustrates this conclusion, 23 severely to profoundly mentally retarded adult subjects were shown pictures and then given the words for the pictures when the facilitators were absent. When the facilitators were present, the subjects were asked to write, through facilitated communication, the words for or a description of the pictures. However, only the subjects could see the pictures. Three pictures were shown during a session. The subjects (or, more likely, the facilitators) were not successful in any of the trials.

Besides the experimental findings, which fail to support the validity of facilitated communication, other factors raise questions about how the technique is used.

1. Facilitators typically hold their hand around the disabled individual's hand, thereby creating doubts about who is actually doing the typing.
2. When individuals with severe disabilities "type," they often do not look at the keyboard; it is the facilitator who looks at the keyboard.
3. Individuals with an autistic disorder who are using facilitated communication express themselves in sophisticated language highly superior to their level of education or

Table 10-3
Evaluating the Skills of Children with Psychological Disorders (or Other Developmental Disorders)

Evaluation of Cognitive Skills

For Infants and Preschool Children

1. Does the child recognize objects?
2. Does the child recognize pictures?
3. Does the child seem to want to control his or her environment?
4. Does the child show anticipatory behaviors? (For example, does the child reach out when the caregiver holds out hands?)
5. Does the child avoid situations that previously caused pain?
6. Does the child ask for help in difficult situations?
7. Does the child recognize familiar people in his or her environment?
8. Is the child's attention span developmentally appropriate?
9. Is the child aware that some items are needed to perform daily tasks? (For example, that a towel is needed after a bath?)
10. Does the child understand cause and effect relationships? (For example, that pulling a string will cause a toy to move?)
11. Does the child recognize the functions of objects in his or her environment? (For example, that a bottle is used for feeding, diapers for wearing, and so forth?)
12. What other indications are there of cognitive skill development?

For School-Aged Children

13. What academic skills does the child have? (For example, can the child read, write, spell, perform arithmetic tasks, and so forth, commensurate with his or her age?)
14. What is the level of the child's comprehension, reasoning, and problem-solving skills?
15. How does the child handle complicated tasks?
16. What is the child's ability to solve puzzles?
17. What other indications are there of cognitive skill development?

Evaluation of Communication Skills

Expressive Skills

18. What means does the child typically use to express himself or herself verbally?
19. Does the child understand the concept of choice?
20. How does the child communicate about things that are not physically present?
21. With whom does the child typically communicate—when, where, and under what circumstances?
22. Does the child spontaneously communicate or only respond to others' communications?
23. What communication aids does the child use, if any?

Receptive Skills

24. Does the child recognize auditory communication in general?
25. Does the child respond to his or her name?

26. Does the child understand information presented verbally?
27. Does the child understand information presented by signing, gestures, facial expressions, and so forth?
28. What level of sound does the child need in order to respond?
29. How long can the child attend to other people's communications?
30. How much time elapses between a communication from another person and the child's response?

Evaluation of Social Skills

31. How does the child interact with parents?
32. How does the child interact with siblings?
33. How does the child interact with other children?
34. How does the child interact with staff members (if appropriate)?
35. Is the child able to differentiate himself or herself from others?
36. Does the child display appropriate social behavior at home, at school, and in other settings?
37. Does the child display appropriate social behavior alone, in small groups, and in large groups?

Evaluation of Self-Help Skills

Eating Skills

38. What kinds of food can the child eat?
39. To what extent can the child eat independently? (For example, can the child obtain food, put it in his or her mouth, remove it from the utensil or bite off a piece, chew it, swallow it, and so forth?)
40. What position is the child in when he or she eats? (For example, upright or reclining?)
41. What utensils does the child use without undue spillage?
42. What specific behaviors interfere with the child's eating? (For example, does the child eat too fast, put too much food in his or her mouth, attempt to eat all foods with fingers, and so forth?)
43. To what extent are the child's eating skills commensurate with his or her age?
44. In what way are the child's eating skills similar at home and in other settings?
45. How does the child chew his or her food? (For example, only an up/down chewing motion or a rotary motion or no chewing at all?)
46. Does the child show any abnormal reflexes of muscle tone associated with eating? (For example, does the child show abnormal gag reflexes [gagging too easily or not gagging at all], clamp teeth together at inappropriate times, thrust tongue and push out food, or drool so badly and close lips so poorly that the food is lost?)
47. What kind of drinking skills does the child have?
48. What is the quality of the child's teeth? (Are teeth aligned well enough to chew, or are gums swollen so that chewing is painful?)

(Continued)

Table 10-3 (*Continued*)

49. Are there any inappropriate behaviors associated with eating, such as pica (eating inedible food), rumination (swallowing food and bringing it back up for more chewing), and voluntary vomiting (vomiting without cause in a self-stimulatory manner)?

Toileting Skills

50. Is the child toilet trained?
51. If the child is not toilet trained, what is the reason?
52. If the child is not toilet trained, how long can the child stay dry?
53. Is the child brought to the toilet at a set time, or does the child ask to go to the toilet?
54. Does the child display any behavior problems associated with toileting? (For example, does the child flush clothing down the toilet, dip hands in toilet, splash water, and so forth?)
55. Does the child use any adaptive toileting devices?
56. At what level of independence is the child for toileting skills?

Dressing Skills

57. Can the child dress himself or herself independently?
58. If the child cannot dress himself or herself independently, what steps in the dressing process can he or she accomplish?
59. Does the child display any inappropriate behaviors while dressing? (For example, does the child chew, tear, or pull on clothing?)

Hygienic Skills

60. Can the child wash his or her hands and face, brush teeth, bathe, shave (if male adolescent), wash hair, and take care of feminine hygiene (if female adolescent) when needed?
61. Does the child display any inappropriate behavior while engaging in hygienic tasks?

Evaluation of Emotional Skills

62. What emotions does the child show at home, at school, on the playground, and in other settings?
63. How do the child's emotions change as a function of the setting?
64. Are the child's displays of emotions appropriate to the setting and his or her age?
65. Are there any warning signs that the child may have a "bad day"?
66. Does the child's behavior change as a function of medication (if applicable)?

Evaluation of Behavioral Skills

67. What is the child's typical behavior at home, at school, on the playground, and in other settings?

68. Is the behavior appropriate for the setting and the child's age?
69. If not, in what ways is it inappropriate? (For example, does the child show noncompliance, aggression, self-abuse, socially inappropriate or age-inappropriate behavior, or withdrawn behavior?)
70. If not, what are the antecedents and consequences of the behavior?
71. What reinforcers work best for the child?
72. What prompts does the child need to learn a task?

Evaluation of Motor Skills, Physical Status, and Sensory Development

Gross Motor Skills

73. What is the child's duration of head control, trunk control, sitting balance, and standing balance?
74. How much assistance does the child need, if any, to perform daily gross motor tasks?
75. What is the child's preferred mode of moving about in the environment?
76. What is the child's ability to perform gross motor tasks without supervision?
77. What adaptive equipment does the child use to help him or her with gross motor movements?

Fine Motor Skills

78. What is the quality of the child's fine motor skills?
79. Can the child use her or his upper extremities for fine motor skill tasks?
80. What is the child's ability to grasp and release objects of various sizes?
81. What is the child's ability to transfer objects from one hand to the other?
82. What is the child's ability to bat/push/pull objects?
83. What is the child's ability to reach or point?
84. What is the child's ability to use fine motor skills encountered in everyday activities, such as twisting, cutting, buttoning, winding, stacking, threading, and so forth?
85. What adaptive equipment, if any, does the child use to help her or him with fine motor skill tasks?

Physical Status

86. What is the child's range of motion in feet, fingers, arms, neck, legs, and hips?
87. What evidence is there, if any, of body deterioration?

Sensory Development

88. What is the quality of the child's sensory ability, including vision, hearing, smell, taste, and touch?
89. Does the child explore his or her environment using appropriate senses?
90. What sensory aids does the child use, if any?
91. If the child wears sensory aids, how effective are they?

Source: Adapted from Reavis (1990).

training. Even individuals who have not previously shown any interest in reading, writing, or the alphabet—including individuals classified as profoundly mentally retarded—appear to write in complex, grammatically correct sentences soon after beginning to use facilitated communication.

4. Ability and fluency vary within the same individual, depending on the facilitator helping the individual.

5. Facilitators-in-training are told that they will not be effective unless they believe in the effectiveness of the technique—"this is tantamount to emotional blackmail, which pushes students 'to read' messages out of loosely held hands" (Schopler, 1992, p. 337).

The results of empirical investigations and observational reports suggest that what happens with facilitated communication is similar to what happens with a Ouija board—it is the facilitator who subtly controls the hand movements (Calculator & Singer, 1992; Dillon, 1993; Moses, 1992; Mulick, 1993). Because experimental results fail to support the validity of facilitated communication, Shane (1993) concluded that *facilitated communication appears to be a pseudoscientific procedure and a hoax.*

Despite the lack of empirical evidence, proponents continue to support facilitated communication. For example, Haskew and Donnellan (1993) believe "There is no further need to see academics embarrass themselves by reporting that they cannot document or make predictable a procedure that thousands of people are using with profit every day" (p. 3). Biklen (1992) says that the procedure does not lend itself to rigorous experimental testing because testing undermines the confidence and motivation of the person who is typing and that laboratory settings are not conducive to facilitated communication. Finally, Andrews (cited by Seligmann & Chideya, 1992) says "We've determined we're not going to stop facilitating with children just because we're hearing things we wish we didn't hear" (p. 5).

Harmful consequences of facilitated communication.

Unfortunately, harmful consequences are associated with the use of facilitated communication (Shane, 1993).

- Time and money are being diverted from other proven communication methods.
- Individuals with an autistic disorder are being placed in classrooms and educational settings far exceeding their intellectual abilities, resulting in a waste of time and effort and loss of valuable training for these individuals.
- Vulnerable families, seeking a cure for autistic disorder, are given false hopes and are investing their financial resources for training, purchase of equipment, and facilitators' salaries.
- Accusations of sexual abuse are arising out of facilitated communication.

Following is a case in which allegations of sexual abuse arose during facilitated communication (Shane, 1993).

CASE 10-2. DONNA

Jim, a 14-year-old boy, was accused of raping his developmentally delayed 15-year-old sister Donna. Jim's indictment came just 24 hours after his father had been accused similarly. Their mother was charged as a co-conspirator, since it was alleged she witnessed and participated in these sexual encounters. Donna was interviewed by means of facilitated communication. During the interview, allegations of sexual abuse surfaced.

Following the first allegation of sexual abuse, Donna was removed from her home and placed in a foster home. Medical examination did not find any physical evidence to corroborate the allegations. Social services records indicate that Donna was noticeably happy and affectionate when she was in the supervised company of her family. This behavior was in marked contrast to the facilitated communications that revealed a hate for her family, a tremendous fear for her safety, and a wish that her father be killed.

Nevertheless, the allegations of sexual abuse made via facilitated communication were sufficient to separate Donna from her family. A review of Donna's educational history reveals that she has a dual diagnosis of severe mental retardation and autism. She has never been exposed to a reading curriculum and had shown no particular interest in letters, sight words, or even pictures. A former teacher indicated that Donna had never shown any interest in printed matter. The teacher was convinced that she was incapable of spelling.

When Donna made similar statements that her brother also was abused, he too was moved to a foster placement. Under intense interrogation by the state police (who admitted that such a confrontation often facilitates a confession) and his school guidance counselor (who indicated that he believed Jim to be innocent of the charges), Jim denied vehemently any sexual misconduct. He became confused and distraught in the new living arrangement, and his school performance deteriorated. Before the matter was resolved, Jim was separated from his family for a total of 4 weeks.

Jim and Donna's father stood accused of a horrible crime, all based on a written transcript created through the assistance of another individual. The father was reportedly severely depressed and missed a great deal of work. His friends and neighbors, while publicly supporting the parents, undoubtedly harbored some feelings that perhaps what they perceived to be a well-adjusted, pleasant and happy family were in fact sexual deviants.

Almost 5 weeks following the indictments, I was asked to evaluate the validity of the technique, not the veracity of her testimony. Testing was conducted in Donna's school using her familiar facilitator. Donna showed no signs of agitation regarding the procedures and was cooperative. She was given frequent opportunities to terminate testing if she felt threatened by the procedures or believed that she was treated unfairly or without dignity. No requests to cease testing were made, nor were there any facilitated statements indicating that she was uncomfortable, annoyed, or insulted by the evaluation. Her facilitator also cooperated and was pleasant throughout the evaluation. Donna rarely looked at the letter board while being facilitated. For more than 25% of the time she held a teddy bear in front of her eyes. The letter display was located at the level of her belt, which seemed to mitigate the argument that she was viewing it through her peripheral vision. The obvious disregard for the letter display was noted by two independent observers. The facilitator never seemed to divert her own gaze from the display while supporting Donna's wrist. These subjective impressions were paired with a variety of validation procedures in reaching a conclusion about the validity of facilitated communication in this case. The results revealed two objective findings and one subjective impression. The principal results of the validation testing were: (a) no evidence of any ability by Donna to communicate via facilitated communication, and (b) the facilitator not only influenced the communication, she controlled it completely. It was my impression from observations of and discussions with Donna's facilitator that she was unaware of her control over message creation.

Jim and Donna have been reunited with their parents and all charges have been dropped. One can only hope that this 14-year-old boy will receive adequate counseling and guidance and will not be scarred permanently by this tragedy. Their father is not back to work. Hopefully, the small community in which they reside will recognize that facilitated communication is the villain here and not this innocent family. (pp. xi, xii, with changes in notation)

The views of one parent about facilitated communication follow (Mark S. Painter, Sr., cited in Dillon, 1993):

Professionals are very quick to dismiss the abilities of autistics. Our children are often tagged with the additional label of "mentally retarded." Parents know better. We live with autistics. We see their sly smiles, the gleam of intellect in their eyes, and their astute problem-solving skills. We see when the "nonverbal" autistic child perks up at the mention of the word "cookie," or spontaneously breaks out into song.

So when Facilitated Communication (FC) proponents say they have found a way around the wall, parents are quick to believe. FC confirms our faith in our children. But...

The workshops and sessions can cost $250. The equipment $800 more. And what do we get for our money? Parents themselves "can't facilitate," they tell us. Our children will require FC for life, they say, and will never communicate on their own. If a parent has the temerity to ask the child a question the facilitator does not already know the answer to, the parent may be told that "autistics don't like to be tested," or that testing is against the FC "philosophy."

In short, the price we are asked to pay in an effort to communicate with our children is to allow strangers into our families to mediate our relationships with our own kids and to accept everything the stranger tells us on blind faith. (p. 286)

A communication technique that evidence suggests does not help severely developmentally delayed individuals communicate is now being used to accuse family members, teachers, and others of sexual abuse. Unfortunately, as of the mid-1990s, the courts have no set policy about accepting evidence obtained by facilitated communication, although they usually have ruled against such evidence (B. Rimland, personal communication, July 1994). How could something like this have happened? And what will happen to facilitators if they are sued for contributing to false allegations? (See Chapter 21 for a discussion of false allegations.)

Role of the facilitator. Facilitators do not appear to be purposely faking communication. The cursory training they receive, the faith they are told to have in the procedure, and the effort and interest they put into their role may lead them to believe that the communications have come from the individual with a disorder. Some facilitators are surprised to see their thoughts being typed by the individuals they are helping. To explain this, they attribute to the disabled individuals a sixth sense—namely, *extrasensory perception (ESP)*—with which the individuals can read the mind of their facilitator and communicate what they are reading (Haskew & Donnellan, 1993).

Comment about facilitated communication. Why is facilitated communication used when children with an autistic disorder or with another severe communication disorder have the motor skills needed to type or point? Why can't the children simply type out their responses or point to letters without help if they can spell or even spell poorly? Why can't they use the reliable and valid augmentative communication procedures discussed in the next section? And, if they can't spell, how can they spell when a facilitator merely guides their hands?

If you are reviewing a report based on information obtained by means of facilitated communication, I recommend that you not use this information for any purpose at all. The information likely is contaminated and probably reflects the facilitator's communications rather than those of the child.

If you have the opportunity to observe a session in which facilitated communication is being used, watch carefully the entire process. If you see that (a) the child is not looking at the keyboard, (b) the facilitator is holding one of the child's fingers and touching the keyboard with that finger, and (c) the words typed are accurately spelled and meaningful, you will know that the communication is not that of the child. It is almost impossible—if not completely impossible—for anyone to type accurately with one finger without looking at the keyboard. Just try it yourself. If you observe the child looking at the keyboard, inquire why the child can't touch the keys without someone's steadying (and probably directing) his or her hand.

Why has facilitated communication become such a powerful fad? Several reasons have been offered (Mulick, 1993)—namely, that it "is part of a historical rejection of biomedical and behavioral sciences by many in the disabilities field in favor of an evolving system of social and political beliefs" (p. 3), that it is consistent with the current popular ideology of total inclusion of children with special needs in the regular classrooms, and that it fills a demand for new and amazing breakthroughs in the developmental disabilities field. If scientists are too slow in making progress, others will show the way.

Facilitated communication is no longer a harmless tool used to create the illusion of intelligence and normalcy in individuals with an autistic disorder or with other severe developmental disabilities. *It is a dangerous, ineffective procedure that is inadvertently being used to disrupt families, ruin reputations, and waste the time, energy, and money of all those involved in helping communicatively handicapped individuals.* "If the rhetoric and media hype boosting 'facilitated communication' without research accountability continues, it may succeed in setting autism back 40 years" (Schopler, 1992, p. 6). Like all procedures used for educational or therapeutic purposes, facilitated communication needs to be rigorously tested and validated before it is used. The American Psychological Association (APA) at its Spring 1995 Council meeting approved the following resolution: *Therefore, be it resolved that APA adopts the position that facilitated communication is a controversial and unproved communicative procedure with no scientifically demonstrated support for its efficacy.*

Augmentative Communication Procedures

Children with severe expressive communication disorders can compensate for their motor or sensory deficits by using several widely accepted procedures known as *augmentative communication procedures,* or *alternative communication procedures* (Beukelman & Mirenda, 1992). *Unlike facilitated communication, augmentative procedures allow children to communicate without someone's directing their movements.* For example, children can use hand signals (such as those used in American Sign Language), pantomime, Morse code, pictures or symbols (such as photographs, line drawings, or phonemic symbols) on communication handboards or footboards, electrical or electronic equipment that registers movements of various parts of the body (such as from the finger, hand, foot, voice, head, or eye), Braille, fingerspelling, portable amplifiers, enlarged keyboards on typewriters, splints with pencil attachment or modified pencil holder, and mouthsticks or headsticks for pointing. They also can respond with scanning devices that systematically point to words or symbols.

Perhaps the most significant advance in augmentative communication is the computer. For children with severe motor impairments who cannot use standard computer keyboards, adaptive keyboards are available with switches that can be activated by eye movements, breath control, or any other reliable muscle movement; the children need to push one key only. Computer programs also can be activated with a mouse, with a head-pointing device that uses light or sound, with a touch screen (for selecting letters, words, or symbols), and with a touch-sensitive pad.

If you are not familiar with the procedure the child uses for communication (such as sign language), you will need to use an interpreter. If you do so, follow the guidelines in Chapter 8.

The following case illustrates how augmentative communication devices allowed a child who is severely physically disabled to communicate in a relatively independent manner (Vanderheiden & Lloyd, 1986).

CASE 10-3. FRANK

Frank is a 7-year-old boy of normal intelligence who has severe athetoid cerebral palsy. He is in the first grade, where he spends part of his time in a regular room and part of his time in a special education program. Although he is unable to use his arms, he can use a lightbeam mounted on his head to point to squares of approximately 1" x 1". His speech is sufficient for a few words understandable by his parents and some, but not all, of his siblings.

Frank's communication system is designed around a communication board, but it also involves speech, eye gaze, and gesture. Speech is his first choice, because it is quick and convenient and allows him to communicate even if others are not paying close attention. Often, he will use his speech even when it is not intelligible to attract attention and to initiate more intelligible communication. He has been taught to use his eyes extensively and can often communicate basic needs through vocalization in combination with an eye gaze toward an object, person, or place. For those familiar with him, he has worked out an idiosyncratic communication technique, whereby he can communicate many common thoughts by gazing at objects in his environment. For example, to ask "When do we go?" he looks at his watch and then at the door.

He has several communication boards. One is made out of a piece of paper covered with clear contact paper and small enough for him to keep tucked into the waistband of his pants. It remains with him at all times, even as he moves or is carried about the house. A second manual board, which is mounted to a piece of wood, is his primary communication board at home. Most of the time, he uses it with the lightbeam pointer mounted on his head. The board contains words and phrases that can be easily changed. He also can direct his feeding activities so that he can eat the items on his plate in the order and at the time he wishes.

When he does homework and his work at school, he has an electronic aid that allows him to use the lightbeam pointer to point to items on a selection panel. As he points to them, they are spoken or printed out for him. This ability to print out his messages allows him to complete his work, take tests, and participate in the classroom activities where other children use pencil and paper.

His school system uses computer-based drill-and-practice programs. A special adaptation lets him hook up his lightbeam pointer aid to the computer so that it can function as the standard computer keyboard. Because he can use all of the computer programs that his class uses, he can continue to participate in the regular education program. (adapted from pp. 141–143)

INTERVENTIONS

As part of the clinical assessment interview, you will want to consider what services a child with a psychological disorder and her or his family need (see Table 10-4). For example, you may refer the child and her or his family to an agency, suggest that the child be hospitalized, recommend place-

Table 10-4
Examples of Services Needed by Children with Psychological Disorders and Their Families

Outpatient services	Residential or inpatient services	Services to the family	Other services
Outpatient therapy	Foster family homes	Family-support groups	Supervised after-school activities
Case management	Group home placement	Family-to-family networking	Transportation to needed services
School-based mental health services	Inpatient alcohol/drug treatment	Family counseling	Recreational services
Psychological testing	Residential treatment center	Respite care	Therapeutic camps
Intensive in-home therapy	Psychiatric hospitalization	Financial assistance	Special education
Psychiatric evaluation	Supervised independent living arrangements	Family-preservation services	Child Protective Services
Outpatient alcohol/drug treatment		Home-visiting programs	In-home education
Day treatment		Parent-education programs	Training in independent living skills
Therapeutic schooling			Vocational services
Medication evaluation			Child care/specialized child care
Nutritional support			Legal and advocacy services
			Adoptive services

Source: Adapted from Trupin, Forsyth-Stephens, and Low (1991).

ment of the child in a residential facility or in an institution, or recommend special services in the school for the child. What you recommend will be determined in part by the severity of the child's disorder and the family's needs and competencies. Outpatient therapy is preferred to inpatient treatment when the child's disorder is not too severe. For children who cannot be protected or treated at home, it is better to recommend a foster family home or a therapeutic group home than a residential treatment facility. And recommending parent-education programs is a less severe alternative to recommending family-preservation services. Ideally, family-support programs should be available to all families *before* crises develop. As family needs grow in intensity, so do the number of services required to meet those needs. Other chapters in Section III discuss interventions for children with specific psychological disorders.

The greatest revolution of our generation is the discovery that human beings, by changing the inner attitudes of their minds, can change the outer aspects of their lives.
—William James

Referral to an Agency

If you need to refer the family to an agency or to another service, consider the following suggestions (Gilliland & James, 1993, pp. 57–58, with changes in notation):

1. Keep a handy, up-to-date list of frequently used agencies and the personnel in those agencies.

2. Have a good working relationship with agency personnel with whom you are in contact.

3. Know the agencies' hours, basic services, modes of operation, limitations, and, if possible, policies on insurance, sliding scale fees, and conditions for service.

4. Encourage a family member to make the call to the agency. If no family member wants to call, obtain permission from an adult family member before you call the agency for them.

5. Don't assume that all families have the skills to get the services they need. Be prepared to help them avoid runarounds and bureaucratic red tape.

6. Accompany the family to the agency to help them, if needed.

7. Consider the family's needs for transportation and child care and how these needs will affect their ability to obtain services.

8. Keep accurate records on the families you have referred, and follow up on any referrals you make to ensure that the families receive the expected services.

9. Ask family members about their experiences with agencies from which they are currently obtaining services.

10. Use courtesy and good human relations skills when dealing with agency personnel.

Recommending Hospitalization

Although making the decision to hospitalize children is complex and difficult, you may have to recommend that children be hospitalized when they are in an acute crisis, are in danger, cannot be successfully treated on an outpatient basis, or require a more thorough evaluation than can be performed on an outpatient basis. Consider recommending hospitalization if one or more of the following conditions are present (Costello, Dulcan, & Kalas, 1991):

- The child presents a clear and imminent danger to himself or herself.
- The child has exhibited extreme aggressive outbursts toward other people, animals, or objects.
- The child has a rapidly deteriorating condition.
- The child has an acute physical condition or a psychotic disorganized state that requires treatment or diagnostic procedures that cannot be done on an outpatient basis.
- The child has a dysfunctional family that makes treatment without hospitalization impossible.
- The child has a disordered state that creates severe difficulties for the family.
- The child has a condition requiring 24-hour observation that only a hospital can provide, including stabilization or reevaluation of medication or treatment of drug or alcohol dependence.

Hospitalization should be as brief as possible, and efforts should be made to keep the child current with his or her schoolwork (Weiner, 1992).

Recommending a Residential Facility

When children have not responded to an outpatient program or when they have not improved sufficiently during a period of acute-care inpatient treatment, consider recommending a residential facility (Stout, 1993). A residential facility is usually appropriate for children who need continued care, but not in an acute-care inpatient facility. A residential facility that offers a 24-hour structured and supervised setting may be needed to stabilize a condition, to resolve symptoms, or to maintain the stability achieved in an acute-care setting. Candidates for a residential facility include children with chronic behavior problems, chronic substance abuse problems, or chronic or severe school phobias. Candidates also include children who engage in self-destructive acts that cannot be managed by their family, as well as children whose parents have severely impaired parenting skills. Residential facilities usually are not considered a permanent placement for children—the aim is to return the children to their families once the condition has been stabilized.

Families Seeking an Institutional Placement

An institutional placement is usually considered a permanent placement for children with severe and profound psychological disorders. Although a majority of children with severe developmental disabilities live at home, the decision to seek institutional placement will depend on several factors associated with the child and the family (Blacher,

1994). These factors include the economic, social, psychological, and physical costs associated with raising a child with a severe and profound psychological disorder. Such children are more likely to be institutionalized when they need nursing care because they are unable to take care of personal hygiene, feeding, routine medical needs, and other personal needs; need constant supervision because of their unpredictable or destructive behavior; or need regular attention at night (Seltzer & Krauss, 1984).

In some cases, parents care for a child for several years and then reach a point where the tremendous burden associated with the child's care becomes too great. In general, these parents have a strong attachment to the child and have established a loving bond. It can take as long as two years or more before parents complete the process of placing their child in an institution (Blacher, 1994). This process is traumatic for many families.

In other cases, parents may seek to place their child in an institution when they are not strongly attached to the child; have little concern about the child's school activities; view the child's progress as negative; have little hope for gains in the child's development; lack supportive social networks and a supportive extended family; are recently married, divorced, or single; have an erratic life style, including frequent relocations, alcoholism, and unemployment; do not have the mental stability to take care of the child; are elderly; or have poor health (Blacher, 1984, 1994).

In exploring with parents the possibility of placing their child in an institution, consider differences among available institutions, the degree and type of their child's needs, and the situation of the family. Some institutions have excellent training programs that focus on self-help habit training, motor skills development, and language acquisition programs, whereas others are less comprehensive in their approach.

Although institutional placements for children with severe and profound psychological disorders are out of favor because they isolate children from normal interactions with others, institutions serve an important role for children whose families have trouble caring for them at home. Families with a child who has a severe and profound psychological disorder may experience a high degree of stress, personal tension, financial concerns, work concerns, and intrafamilial conflict. High stress levels may lead to pessimism, poor self-esteem, anxiety, depression, feelings of isolation, and poor physical health among family members (Seltzer & Krauss, 1984). High stress levels also may interfere with the ability of families to give appropriate care to children with special needs.

Every effort, however, should be made to support families who want to keep their children with severe disabilities at home. Families will be better able to do so when they have *informal support services*—such as support from friends, immediate family members, other relatives, and even professionals—and *formal support services*—such as support from schools, parent-training programs, respite care, homemaker services, and financial aid supplements (Blacher, 1994).

The following case describes why a mother selected an institutional placement for her son (Blacher & Bromley, 1990). Unfortunately, not all parents continue to be so involved with their children who are placed in an institution.

CASE 10-4. STEVE

Steve is a 12-year-old boy who is severely retarded and non-ambulatory. He has seizures that are under control with medication. Steve has no self-help skills; he must be fed, bathed, and toileted. Although blind, he can hear well and can make some vocal sounds. Steve is able to reach and grasp objects.

Steve's parents were divorced shortly after his birth. His mother, Ann, raised Steve at home for several years. Perhaps because she spent so much time with Steve, Ann developed a very strong attachment to her son. However, she could not work and keep Steve at home, so at the age of 5 years, Steve was placed in an institution. Steve currently lives in a large, privately operated facility for severely and profoundly handicapped individuals.

Since Steve's placement, Ann has been able to complete her M. S. in special education, and she is currently enrolled in a Ph.D. program. She is of upper socioeconomic status and owner/director of her own company. She has remarried, and her new husband gets along well with Steve. Ann also is involved in developmental disabilities organizations in the local community.

Ann says that she is still strongly attached to Steve, despite the fact that he has been placed for about seven years. She either visits the facility or brings Steve home every weekend, and she calls once or twice a week to see how he is doing. There are some things about the facility that Ann does not like, such as residents not always having their own hairbrushes; she does not hesitate to talk to the staff about these problems. She commented that the staff do not like to see her coming because they know she will complain about something. Ann stated that although her son will remain in the institution, she is the only advocate Steve has and she will remain strongly involved with his care until he dies. (pp. 31–32, with changes in notation)

The natural desire of parents to nurture their children during their growing years should be especially encouraged for children whose progress is measured in centimeters.

—Arnold Birenbaum and Herbert J. Cohen

Special Services in Schools

Children with psychological disorders (or with physical disorders) may benefit from special programs in school. Table 10-5 shows the number of children with psychological and

Table 10-5
Students Ages 6 through 21 Served Under the Individual Disabilities Education Act (IDEA) in 1993–94

Disability	Number of children ages 6–21	Percentage of IDEA population				Percentage of all children ages 6–17[e]	Percentage of all children ages 6–21[e]
		Ages 6–11[a]	Ages 12–17[b]	Ages 18–21[c]	Ages 6–21[d]		
Specific learning disabilities	2,444,020	41.40	62.60	50.20	51.10	5.28	4.19
Speech or language impairments	1,009,379	36.30	5.30	1.80	21.10	2.29	1.74
Mental retardation	553,992	9.00	12.90	26.50	11.60	1.09	0.93
Serious emotional disturbances	414,279	5.70	12.10	9.40	8.60	0.89	0.71
Multiple disabilities	109,746	2.20	2.00	5.20	2.30	0.22	0.19
Hearing impairments	64,249	1.30	1.40	1.80	1.30	0.13	0.11
Orthopedic impairments	56,616	1.30	1.00	1.60	1.20	0.12	0.10
Other health impairments	83,279	1.80	1.70	1.60	1.70	0.18	0.14
Visual impairments	24,935	0.50	0.60	0.70	0.50	0.05	0.04
Autism	18,903	0.40	0.30	0.80	0.40	0.04	0.03
Deaf-blindness	1,372	0.02	0.03	0.09	0.00	0.00	0.00
Traumatic brain injury	5,295	0.08	0.10	0.30	0.10	0.01	0.01
All disabilities	4,786,065	100	100	100	100	10.31	8.19

[a]Based on 2,464,237 children ages 6–11.
[b]Based on 2,079,475 children ages 12–17.
[c]Based on 242,353 children ages 18–21.
[d]Based on 4,786,065 children ages 6–21.
[e]Based on estimated number of children in the population.
Note. There were 587,012 children from birth through age 5 also receiving services. The total number of children receiving services was 5,373,077, which represents an increase of 1,664,476 children since the program began in 1976.
Source: Adapted from U.S. Department of Education (1995), pp. 11, A6–A11, A32, A33.

physical disorders, from ages 6 through 21, who received services in schools in the United States during the 1993–94 academic year under the *Individuals with Disabilities Education Act* (IDEA; for information about the IDEA, see Exhibit 5-1 in Chapter 5). The largest number of children receiving services were those who had specific learning disabilities (51.1%), followed by children with speech and language impairments (21.1%), mental retardation (11.6%), and serious emotional disturbances (8.6%). These four categories contained 92.4% of all children receiving services. The remaining 7.6% of the children had multiple disabilities, hearing impairments, orthopedic impairments, other health impairments, autism, hearing and visual problems, or traumatic brain injury.

The program selected for children who need special services will depend on the type and extent of their problem and their ability to function in a regular classroom. Many schools try to include children with psychological disorders in regular classes, a program called *full inclusion* or *mainstreaming*. The school placements of children covered by the Individuals with Disabilities Education Act for the 1992–93 school year were as follows (U.S. Department of Education, 1995, adapted from pp. 13, 14, 17).

- 39.8% were in a *regular class*. (This placement includes students who receive most of their education program in a regular classroom and receive special education and related services either outside the regular classroom for less than 21% of the school day or within the regular classroom.)

- 31.7% were in a *resource room*. (This placement includes students who receive special education and related services outside the regular classroom for at least 21% but not more than 60% of the school day. It may include students placed in resource rooms with part-time instruction in a regular class.)

- 23.5% were in a *separate class*. (This placement includes students who receive special education and related services outside the regular classroom for more than 60% of the school day. Students may be placed in self-contained special classrooms with part-time instruction in regular classes or placed in self-contained classrooms full-time on a regular school campus.)

- 3.7% were in a *separate school*. (This placement includes students who receive special education and related services in separate day schools for students with disabilities for more than 50% of the school day.)

- 0.8% were in a *residential facility*. (This placement includes students who receive special education and related services in a public or private residential facility, at public expense, for more than 50% of the school day.)

- 0.5% were *homebound* or in a *hospital environment*. (This placement includes students who receive special education and related services in a hospital or a home-based program.)

Coordinating Services

In school settings, a school-aged child with a psychological disorder may be treated by more than one mental health professional, such as a school counselor (or school social worker or school psychologist) *and* a private psychologist (or social worker, marriage and family counselor, or psychiatrist). If the services are not integrated or coordinated, the child, the family, the teacher, other school officials, and the therapists may be confused by inconsistent advice and information. Whenever possible, a case manager (one of the mental health professionals on the staff) should be designated to coordinate services and attempt to avoid conflicting messages and redundant services. This advice holds for other settings as well.

Helping Parents Cope

Parents will be better able to cope with a child who has a psychological disorder when they have adequate cognitive ability, social support from friends and other family members, good physical health, a prior history of successfully coping with stress, an optimistic view of life, a sense of personal control over life's demands, a sense of self-worth, and good parenting skills (Matheny, Aycock, Pugh, Curlett, & Cannella, 1986). One of the best predictors of how a family with a child with a psychological disorder will function is the quality of the parents' marriage and the extent of spousal support (Abbott & Meredith, 1986).

Following are some specific suggestions for helping parents of children with psychological disorders. Encourage the parents

1. to accept their child as a whole unique individual despite the child's psychological disorder.
2. to see the child's strengths but not ignore her or his deficits.
3. to learn as much as they can about the disorder.
4. to learn about their child's feelings, thoughts, hopes, and aspirations.
5. to be realistic about their child's future but not to foreclose prematurely areas or tasks that may prove manageable.
6. to be flexible and to help their child function in their family.
7. to encourage their child to partake in normal family social experiences and also in social experiences outside the family.
8. to support their child's independence.
9. to recognize age-appropriate behaviors.
10. to allow their child to make choices and to experience the consequences of making correct as well as incorrect ones.
11. to seek an educational placement most appropriate for their child.

The following "alphabet" of child-raising ideas will be helpful to parents of children with psychological disorders and parents of other children as well (reprinted with permission of Jo Frisbie von Tiehl):

A is for Accountability. Hold your children accountable for their behavior.

B is for Boundaries. Set specific limits, and make clear the repercussions if those limits are exceeded.

C is for Consistency. Hold to the same principles and practices.

D is for Discipline. Make the punishment fit the crime. Never discipline in anger.

E is for Example. Children are in greater need of models than critics. Set a good example.

F is for Forgiveness. Practice it, and teach the importance of forgiving.

G is for Giving. Teach the joy of giving, not only to family and friends, but to strangers in need.

H is for Humor. Keep your sense of humor and promote laughter with your children.

I is for Imagination. Be creative, and play with your children. Make up stories or songs when you read and sing with them.

J is for Justice. Be fair, and insist that they be fair.

K is for Knowing your children's friends and their parents as well as their teachers.

L is for Listening. Listen to your children. It will teach them how to listen to others, and their thoughts will give you insights.

M is for Morals. Be sure your own standard of conduct is sound.

N is for No. Use it, and mean it.

O is for Outdoors. Provide as much outdoor activity as possible. Teach respect for nature.

P is for Pressure. Reduce the pressure on your children, but insist they maintain high standards.

Q is for Questions. Pay close attention to their questions, and give simple answers unless they demand more.

R is for Respect. Show respect, teach respect and earn respect.

S is for Source of Strength. Share your own faith or beliefs with your children. Faith can be their port in the storms of life later.

T is for Togetherness. Have special, designated times to be together as a family—but know when to let go, too.

U is for Uniqueness. Understand the uniqueness of each child, and let that child be who he or she is.

V is for Voice. Be mindful of your tone of voice. It conveys more to a child than the words spoken.

W is for Words. Keep your word. Promises broken destroy trust.

X is for eXamine. Examine constantly, and be aware.

Y is for You. Take care of yourself mentally, physically and spiritually.

Z is for Zowie! Who would have thought they would grow up so quickly?

—Jo Frisbie von Tiehl

Suggestions for Parents for Working with Siblings of Children with Psychological Disorders

Parents should be open and honest with the siblings of a child with a psychological disorder, considering the siblings' ages and levels of understanding. Siblings who have a brother or sister with a psychological disorder may be concerned about their role in the family, the extent of their brother's or sister's disorder, the prognosis, and the changes taking place in the family dynamics and structure.

Siblings should not be expected to compensate for what the child with a psychological disorder lacks or to become a "baby sitter, automatic playmate, or inappropriate parent substitute.... Parents need to provide help, direction, understanding and explanation. They need to inspire in their non-disabled offspring a sense of compassion and care without depriving or isolating these children from the experiences of everyday life or exposures to neighbors, classmates and others in the world outside the family" (Schreiber, 1993, p. 38). Exhibit 10-1 contains guidelines that you can give parents to help them work with siblings of children who have psychological disorders.

Following are examples of siblings' concerns about a brother or sister who has a psychological disorder (Schreiber, 1993, pp. 39–40).

CONCERNS AS CHILDREN AND ADOLESCENTS

- You'll see kids making fun of him within the neighborhood, and I can feel myself tense right up. I want to go over and smash the kid. I think that's really something you have to deal with within yourself.
- Normal children do want to see if a handicapped person is real.
- My peers were very important to me right then and that was that—I just didn't want to have any little tag-alongs.
- And though you were younger, how do you explain this to people who come over to the house?
- At times we thought we were tied down in certain instances in our lives.
- When I got to be about dating age and boys came to the house, if there were inquiries about my mother, my father, my sister, I told them about my family. Donny is a member of the family, and that was the perfect time for me to go on and tell them these things about his disability.

CONCERNS AS YOUNG ADULTS

- If I were married or got married later on and my parents die, I will have to take him in.
- If we have to, we'll take him in. But I would rather know that he could stand up alone—well, not alone, but be able to go through life.

Exhibit 10-1
Guidelines for Parents for Helping Siblings of Children with Psychological Disorders

1. Don't expect your nondisturbed children to compensate for the child with a psychological disorder and make all your dreams come true.

2. Be sure that your expectations for your nondisturbed children are realistic. It's easy to forget sometimes that they are children first; you cannot expect them to handle difficult situations like little adults. For example, it would be unrealistic to expect a young child alone to be able to supervise a disruptive sibling in public.

3. Don't allow your nondisturbed children to assume excessive chores and responsibilities, because this may lead to feelings of resentment toward you and the sibling with a psychological disorder.

4. Let your nondisturbed children know that you also get upset and sometimes wish you could have done some things differently. Sharing an account of your own shortcomings can ease the sense of shame and guilt that the nondisturbed children might feel over some incident of their own.

5. Praise your nondisturbed children whenever they do something you want them to do more often. Let them know specifically what it was that you liked—for example, "I liked the way you played with your brother today while I was fixing dinner."

6. Don't expect too much too soon from your nondisturbed children when they interact with their sibling who has a psychological disorder. Progress often comes in short, sometimes halting steps. Don't be surprised by occasional setbacks, but be sure to give corrections in a gentle, positive manner.

7. Keep the lines of communication open, paying attention to the feelings underlying what your children tell you. Let them know that their observations, concerns, and suggestions are valued and worthy of discussion.

8. Remember that your nondisturbed children will have occasional negative feelings toward the child with a psychological disorder and that these feelings are normal and best

approached with understanding, not with shame or guilt.

9. Most importantly, show your nondisturbed children how you want them to behave. There is no substitute for a positive example, especially when it is coupled with the opportunity to practice appropriate behavior under the watchful eye of a warm, supportive parent.

10. If your nondisturbed children begin to obtain lower school grades, be ill more frequently than usual, have tantrums, or show regressive behavior, explore with them the possible reasons for the changes and try to improve the situation. Obtain professional help, if needed.

11. Finally, help establish a sibling program in your community by encouraging organizations for those with special needs, schools, and early intervention programs to have a "sibling day" or sponsor a sibling workshop. Parents also can establish informal sibling support groups through their own networks.

Source: Adapted from Pendler (1993, pp. 85–86).

- I thought that if it was going to make any difference to my fiancé, it was a very important thing to bring up.
- I told them about my family and that it was a package deal.
- I got a different outlook on life, and I really think that I'm lucky to have my brother.
- I could still be the parent of a handicapped child and I have very positive feelings about this, that it can work, that a family can stay together.
- I think that since there is a handicapped child we have grown as people.

Here is an essay written by a sibling of a child with mental retardation. (Originally published in Klein and Schleifer, eds., IT ISN'T FAIR! SIBLINGS OF CHILDREN WITH DISABILITIES [Bergin & Garvey, an imprint of Greenwood Publishing Group, Inc., Westport, CT, 1993], pp. 107–108. Copyright © 1993 by Exceptional Parent Press. Reprinted with permission of Greenwood Publishing Group, Inc. All rights reserved.)

The titles are endless: mental retardation, autism, Down syndrome, cerebral palsy. People. Sheltered from our world, they are shunned by society, all but forgotten by our communities. The world they know is theirs, and theirs alone. As people not afflicted with any

mental or physical disability, we may push them aside, unwilling to accept them, yet willing to avoid the burden they present to us. Because they are harder to deal with, because they do strange things, things that are not "normal," we are unwilling to accept them as part of our society. Dealing with special children is difficult and, so, many people don't. If any one of those people that ignore the situation would gather the courage to spend even a short amount of time with a retarded child, they would immediately sense the many needs of the child.

As the sibling of a mentally retarded child, I felt cheated because my brother was not the same as other kids. I was waiting for the day he would wake up and be like me, a day that will never come. So many times he pleaded for the affection he desperately needed and so many times I turned my back and ignored his appeal. I did not understand.

Finally, I came to accept his condition, and from there I was able to help him. Acceptance leads to understanding, which in turn leads to helping, assisting.

Like all special children, my brother's love for everyone and everything around him is wholly genuine. He has no ulterior motive attached to his smiles and hugs. All of the kids, from the highest functioning independent child, to the lowest functioning who is dependent for all his or her needs, sense attention and respond to it. The value of the return outweighs the investment.

When they respond, we do not see sadly deformed or mentally disabled people. We see regular human beings, happy to be alive.

We are the ones that shower pity on them while they enjoy life, regardless of their disability. They don't have the worries and complexities of normal life. Often we express our desire to become children again to escape, which is exactly how they live their lives. Seeing them perform and progress holds an indescribable gratification. Adjectives written on a page are inadequate to describe the lives of these wonderful beings. How, in a land booming with technology, can we turn our backs? We must further our involvement, in every fashion, and strive to make better the conditions in which they, and we, function.

THINKING THROUGH THE ISSUES

Do you think that you can interview children with psychological disorders?

How will an understanding of psychological disorders help you interview children who may have psychological disorders and their families?

With which type of children with psychological disorders do you think you will have the most difficulty establishing rapport?

How will your expectations about psychological disorders affect how you interview children who may have psychological disorders and their families?

Do you know any children with psychological disorders? If so, what disorders do they have? What have you observed?

Why do you think facilitated communication became popular? What can be done to get professionals and the lay public to accept the scientific evidence showing that severely disabled individuals do not communicate through facilitated communication?

"If you were to become intellectually disabled and unable to speak or write as a result of injury or disease, would you agree to someone taking your hand and helping you type, without evidence that you were in fact communicating through typing? Furthermore, would you want decisions about your children, estate, or future made with such a process?" (Smith & Belcher, 1994, p. 73).

What factors might help families stay involved with their children who are placed in institutions?

How do you think families feel after they place their children in an institution?

Do you believe that the schools are doing an acceptable job of teaching children with psychological disorders? What is the basis for your answer?

Have you experienced any severe personal or family stressor in the past year? If so, what was the nature of the stressor? How did you react to it? How did the stressor affect your overall adjustment? How did the stressor affect your relationships with your family and friends? How did the stressor affect your ability to go to school or to work? What helped you with the healing process? How long did it take you to recover from the stressor? If the stressor was a family stressor, how were other family members affected? How were your reactions similar to and how were they different from those of other family members? What helped other family members with the healing process? How long did it take other family members to recover from the stressor? Did you experience a severe stressor prior to any you experienced in the past year? If so, answer the same questions as previously posed for a stressor experienced in the past year. How will your understanding of your personal or family stressor help you in interviewing children and families who have experienced stressors?

SUMMARY

1. Make generalizations about children with psychological disorders with caution because each child has unique temperament and personality characteristics, cognitive skills, social skills, adaptive-behavior skills, and support systems.
2. Approach each child as a unique individual and never only as a child who represents a psychological disorder.
3. Children who have one psychological disorder may have another one as well, a phenomenon referred to as co-occurring disorders or comorbid disorders.
4. Children with co-occurring disorders are likely to have more problems and longer-lasting problems than children with only a single disorder.
5. Always consider whether children have more than one type of psychological disorder because psychological disorders in childhood may not be "pure."
6. Children with a psychological disorder usually will go through the same developmental sequences as normal children, although sometimes at a different rate.
7. Advise parents to obtain a detailed assessment if their children have significant developmental delays.
8. Children with psychological disorders form their self-concepts in ways similar to those used by normal children. Parents are the primary source of feedback, followed by siblings and other relatives, friends and neighbors, and teachers and other professionals.
9. Children with psychological disorders who also have physical impairments may be limited in their ability to obtain a full range of sensory information, to socialize, to engage in sports and other physical activities, and to reach expected height and weight.

How Psychological Disorders Develop in Children

10. Psychological disorders in children develop from the interaction of children's genetic characteristics, biological features, family experiences and cultural background, individual characteristics, interpersonal relations, and life stresses.
11. Several hereditary disorders affect both physical and psychological development, such as disorders associated with chromosomal abnormalities and inborn errors of metabolism.
12. Other prenatal factors that can lead to physical and psychological disorders include infections, teratogens, toxins, and placental dysfunction.
13. Genetic or biological vulnerabilities may limit children's development and may make it more difficult for them to acquire needed competencies and to cope with stress.

14. A critical factor affecting children's development is whether their mothers used or abused drugs or alcohol during pregnancy.

15. Children born to mothers who abuse substances are at risk for birth defects, as well as for motor, cognitive, language, social, and emotional deficits.

16. Children born to drug- or alcohol-abusing mothers will need a comprehensive assessment of their physical and psychological functioning.

17. The primary way in which infants and young children learn about themselves and others is through familial experiences. These experiences probably are encoded in memory as a set of beliefs about themselves and others and about expectations for future relationships with others.

18. Children's adjustment will likely be adversely affected if their parents are cold and insensitive and reject or neglect them; have inappropriate developmental expectations for them; are inadvertently attentive to their inappropriate behavior; are vague in communicating with them; are unable to establish reasonable expectations and limits for them; are inconsistent with them and have difficulty handling situations that call for discipline; are tardy in dealing with their misbehavior; use overly harsh or overly lax disciplinary procedures; physically, psychologically, or sexually abuse them; have psychological disorders (are anxious or depressed; show unexpected changes in mood, energy, or self-esteem; or have deficient reality testing); are substance abusers; are experiencing chaotic living arrangements; are unable to obtain social supports; or are under considerable stress from domestic violence, work pressures, financial pressures, low socioeconomic status, legal matters, or criminal matters.

19. Children whose caregivers are insensitive or rejecting may come to think of themselves as incompetent or unworthy, to think of others as hostile or unresponsive, and to think of relationships with others as aversive or unpredictable.

20. Parents who have psychological disorders may have difficulty helping their children feel emotionally secure, gain an understanding of social causes and effects, develop planning ability, or learn the importance of delayed gratification and the ability to take responsibility for their own actions.

21. Although children whose parents become addicted to drugs after the children are born are not considered "drug exposed," their exposure to drugs or alcohol after their birth nevertheless places them at risk for developing psychological difficulties.

22. Children may face stresses associated with the birth of a sibling, moving to a new home or apartment, changing schools, failing classes in school, being suspended from school, having poor proficiency in English, being exposed to cultural clashes, being a victim of violence, becoming involved with drugs or alcohol, being overweight or underweight, being rejected by peers, being poor at sports, going to jail, attempting suicide, running away from home, having a best friend move, losing a job, having a parent lose a job, having a relative or close friend die, becoming pregnant (for females), or impregnating a female (for males).

23. A key factor that contributes to the development of psychological disorders in children is stress. Stress can exacerbate problems that children face and bring about new problems.

24. Victimized children report more psychological and behavioral symptoms than do nonvictimized children.

25. Evidence suggests that violent victimization is a major traumagenic influence in child development and may account for a substantial portion of mental health morbidity in both childhood and later adult life.

26. The developmental effects of being victimized are likely to be more severe when the victimization is repetitive and ongoing, changes the nature of the child's relationship with her or his caregivers, adds to other serious stressors, or interrupts a crucial developmental transition.

Living with a Child with a Psychological Disorder

27. Not only do families experience the initial trauma associated with learning that a child has a psychological disorder; they also have the continuing burden of responsibility for the care and education of the child.

28. Families raising a child with a psychological disorder may face various issues at different stages during the child's life span, depending on the severity of his or her disorder.

29. In early childhood, family life-span issues include clarifying the diagnosis, informing other family members, locating and accessing services, locating and accessing community resources and supports, fulfilling general family functions, resolving the emotional burden, redefining the family in meaningful and constructive ways, and dealing with the larger society.

30. In middle childhood, the issues include easing school entry, learning about educational policies and procedures, participating in educational conferences, dealing with peer issues, and locating and accessing extracurricular activities.

31. In adolescence, the issues include adjusting to puberty and sexuality, dealing with peer issues, formulating vocational plans, undertaking transitional planning, and developing recreational and leisure opportunities.

32. In young adulthood, the issues include carrying out vocational plans; making residential choices when needed; dealing with sexuality, marriage, and family; maintaining recreational and leisure activities; and undertaking long-term planning.

33. In late adulthood, the issues include planning for caregiving and supervision following the death of the caregiver, setting up residential plans when needed, transferring parental responsibility, and balancing the rights and responsibilities of all family members.

34. Parents of children with psychological disorders are faced with more issues of dependence and independence throughout their children's development than are other parents.

35. Families' responses to children with psychological disorders will depend on the type and extent of the disorder; how often the disorder occurs; intensity of the children's symptoms; level of care needed by the children; situational factors, including suddenness of onset of the disorder and when the problems are most severe; personality and temperament of the children and family members; resources of the family members; role structure and organization of the families; support received from the health care staff; and support received from other members of the community, including extended family, friends, neighbors, agencies, and self-help groups.

36. Families are best able to cope with stress when they are intact and well integrated, when channels of communication are open, when authority and role structures are flexible, and when they have successfully dealt with crises in the past.

37. Sources of stress that parents of a child with a psychological disorder may face include collaborating with several profes-

sionals and arranging for support services, strain among family members, stigmatization from the child's disorder, dealing with the extremes of the child's behavior, concerns by parents about their own mental health, concerns with the child's developmental progress, and concerns about the child's future.

38. Raising a child with a psychological disorder can help strengthen family ties.

39. Parents may cope with the stress of raising a child with a psychological disorder in several different ways. They may seek information; use wish-fulfilling fantasies; blame themselves; seek support from relatives or friends; engage in counseling or therapy; join support groups; turn to religion; partake in yoga, meditation, or other forms of stress reduction; use antidepressive drugs or other drugs to reduce anxiety; and use alcohol or illegal drugs.

Interviewing Issues

40. When you interview children with psychological disorders, you can generally use standard interviewing techniques; however, their application is likely to be more demanding because the children may have expressive or receptive difficulties or attention difficulties or they may feel self-conscious, ill at ease, or at a disadvantage in the interview.

41. Before you interview children who may have psychological disorders, have their vision, hearing, physical condition, and health status screened.

42. If you know before you interview them that they have communication difficulties, ask their parents about the signs, signals, or gestures that the children understand or use to communicate.

43. When you interview children with psychological disorders, do not allow their disorder in one area to bias your perception of how they may function in other areas. Keep the interview short because the children may become fatigued easily if they are unaccustomed to concentrating for long periods. Be prepared to work hard to establish rapport and to ensure that they understand your questions. Position the children in your office to make them comfortable and to accommodate any physical disabilities they may have. Be sure the children use in the interview the adaptive equipment that they always use. Say to children who may need assistance "Do you need help?" or "How should I help you?" Do not "talk over" or provide the words for children who have difficulty speaking. Do not direct your conversation to an attendant, assistant, or nearby companion as though the children were not present.

44. In facilitated communication, a facilitator guides the disabled individual's hand, wrist, or arm across a keyboard or keyboard facsimile to help the individual type a message or point to letters. This technique has generated much controversy because the facilitator, rather than aiding the disabled individual in communicating, is likely to be the one actually communicating.

45. Proponents of facilitated communication believe that people with an autistic disorder do not have cognitive impairments but, instead, have motor apraxia, or the neurologically determined inability to initiate behavior or movement voluntarily. This impairment supposedly prevents individuals with an autistic disorder from oral or written expression without the aid of a facilitator.

46. There is no scientific evidence that facilitated communication works. Studies have consistently shown that facilitators are controlling what is typed. The results of empirical investigations and observational reports suggest that what happens with facilitated communication is similar to what happens with a Ouija board—it is the facilitator who subtly controls the hand movements.

47. If you are reviewing a report based on information obtained by means of facilitated communication, do not use this information for any purpose at all.

48. Facilitated communication is a dangerous, ineffective procedure that is inadvertently being used to disrupt families, ruin reputations, and waste the time, energy, and money of all those involved in helping communicatively handicapped individuals.

49. Children with severe expressive communication disorders can compensate for their motor or sensory deficits by using several widely accepted procedures known as augmentative communication procedures, or alternative communication procedures. Unlike facilitated communication, augmentative procedures allow children to communicate without someone's directing their movements. Perhaps the most significant advance in augmentative communication is the computer. For children with severe motor impairments who cannot use standard computer keyboards, adaptive keyboards are available with switches that can be activated by eye movements, breath control, or any other reliable muscle movement.

Interventions

50. As part of the clinical assessment interview, you will want to consider what services a child with a psychological disorder and her or his family need.

51. You may refer the child and his or her family to an agency, suggest that the child be hospitalized, recommend placement of the child in a residential facility or in an institution, or recommend special services in the school for the child.

52. Ideally, family-support programs should be available to all families before crises develop.

53. Recommend that children be hospitalized when they are in an acute crisis, are in danger, cannot be successfully treated on an outpatient basis, or require a more thorough evaluation than can be performed on an outpatient basis. Hospitalization should be as brief as possible, and efforts should be made to keep the child current with his or her schoolwork.

54. Recommend a residential facility when children have not responded to an outpatient program or when they have not improved sufficiently during a period of acute-care inpatient treatment.

55. Children with severe and profound special needs are more likely to be institutionalized when they need nursing care because they are unable to take care of themselves, need constant supervision because of their unpredictable or destructive behavior, or need regular attention at night.

56. Children with psychological disorders or with physical disorders may benefit from special programs in school. In the 1993–94 academic year, the largest number of children receiving services under the Individuals with Disabilities Education Act were those who had specific learning disabilities (51.1%), followed by children with speech and language impairments (21.1%), mental retardation (11.6%), and serious emotional disturbances (8.6%).

57. Many schools try to include children with psychological disorders in regular classes, a program called full inclusion or mainstreaming.

58. Children covered by the Individuals with Disabilities Education Act were in regular classes (about 40%), a resource room (about 32%), a separate class (about 24%), a separate school (about 4%), a residential facility (about 1%), and a hospital environment or homebound (0.5%).

59. In school settings, a case manager (one of the mental health professionals on the staff) should be designated to coordinate services and attempt to avoid any conflicting messages and redundant services.

60. Parents will be better able to cope with a child who has a psychological disorder when they have adequate cognitive ability, social support from friends and other family members, good physical health, a prior history of successfully coping with stress, an optimistic view of life, a sense of personal control over life's demands, a sense of self-worth, and good parenting skills.

61. One of the best predictors of how a family with a child with a psychological disorder will function is the quality of the parents' marriage and the extent of spousal support.

62. To help parents of children with a psychological disorder, encourage them to accept their child as a whole unique individual despite the child's psychological disorder; to see the child's strengths but not ignore her or his deficits; to learn as much as they can about the disorder; to learn about their child's feelings, thoughts, hopes, and aspirations; to be realistic about their child's future but not to foreclose prematurely areas or tasks that may prove manageable; to be flexible and to help their child function in their family; to encourage their child to partake in normal family social experiences and also in social experiences outside the family; to support their child's independence; to recognize age-appropriate behaviors; to allow their child to make choices and to experience the consequences of making correct as well as incorrect ones; and to seek an educational placement most appropriate for their child.

63. Parents should be open and honest with the siblings of a child with a psychological disorder, considering the siblings' ages and levels of understanding.

64. Siblings who have a brother or sister with a psychological disorder may be concerned about their role in the family, the extent of the brother's or sister's disorder, the prognosis, and the changes taking place in the family dynamics and structure.

KEY TERMS, CONCEPTS, AND NAMES

Cognitive functions (p. 325)
Affect (p. 325)
Behavior (p. 325)
Co-occurring disorders (comorbid disorders) (p. 325)
Self-concepts (p. 325)
Genetic and biological factors (p. 327)
Chromosomal abnormalities (p. 327)
Inborn errors of metabolism (p. 327)
Prenatal factors (p. 327)
Infections (p. 327)
Teratogens (p. 327)
Toxins (p. 327)
Placental dysfunction (p. 327)
Environmental factors (p. 328)
Exposure to violence (p. 329)

Victimized children (p. 329)
Stress (p. 329)
Facilitated communication (p. 332)
Facilitator (p. 332)
Extrasensory perception (ESP) (p. 337)
Augmentative communication procedures (alternative communication procedures) (p. 338)
Referral to an agency (p. 339)
Recommending hospitalization (p. 339)
Recommending a residential facility (p. 340)
Institutional placement (p. 340)
Informal support services (p. 340)
Formal support services (p. 340)
Full inclusion (mainstreaming) (p. 342)
Individuals with Disabilities Education Act (IDEA) (p. 342)
Regular class (p. 342)
Resource room (p. 342)
Separate class (p. 342)
Separate school (p. 342)
Residential facility (p. 342)
Homebound (p. 342)
Hospital environment (p. 342)
Coordinating services (p. 342)
Suggestions for parents for working with nondisabled siblings (p. 343)

STUDY QUESTIONS

1. Discuss how psychological disorders develop in children. Include in your discussion genetic and biological factors and environmental factors, including the effects of poor caregiving, stressors, and violence.

2. Discuss some critical issues faced by families raising a child with a psychological disorder. Include in your discussion (a) life-span issues in raising a child with a psychological disorder, (b) high-risk periods, (c) determinants of a family's response to a child with a psychological disorder, (d) sources of stress in the family, and (e) how parents may cope with a child with a psychological disorder.

3. Discuss issues involved in interviewing children with psychological disorders. Include in your discussion how you would evaluate the interview findings.

4. Discuss facilitated communication. Include in your discussion the theoretical basis for facilitated communication, the validity of facilitated communication, harmful consequences of facilitated communication, the role of the facilitator, and your evaluation of facilitated communication.

5. Compare and contrast facilitated communication with augmentative communication procedures.

6. Discuss interventions with children with psychological disorders. Include in your discussion referral to an agency, hospitalization, need for a residential facility or an institutional placement, and need for special services in schools.

7. Describe some ways to help parents cope with their child who has a psychological disorder.

8. Describe some ways to help parents cope with the sibling of a child with a psychological disorder.

11

CHILDREN WITH BEHAVIORAL OR EMOTIONAL DISORDERS

That energy which makes the child hard to manage is the energy which afterward makes him a manager of life.
—Harriet Ward Beecher

Goals and Objectives

This chapter is designed to enable you to:

- Understand and appreciate the concerns that family members may have in raising a child with a behavioral or emotional disorder
- Develop skills in interviewing children who may have an attention-deficit/hyperactivity disorder, a conduct disorder, an oppositional defiant disorder, a depressive disorder, an anxiety disorder, a posttraumatic stress disorder, or a dissociative identity disorder

This chapter offers a description of children who have behavioral or emotional disorders. Its coverage of disorders is selective rather than comprehensive. All of the disorders discussed in the chapter are described in the *Diagnostic and Statistical Manual of Mental Disorders—Fourth Edition* (*DSM-IV*) (American Psychiatric Association, 1994). For each disorder, a brief description is presented, followed by interviewing issues, intervention considerations, and one or two case illustrations.

ATTENTION-DEFICIT/HYPERACTIVITY DISORDER

Description

Attention-deficit/hyperactivity disorder (ADHD) is a behavioral syndrome marked by inattention, hyperactivity, and impulsivity (American Psychiatric Association, 1994). In the past, this disorder also was called minimal brain damage, minimal brain dysfunction, hyperkinetic reaction of childhood, and attention deficit disorder with or without hyperactivity. According to *DSM-IV*, the symptoms of ADHD must be present for at least six months to a degree that is maladaptive and inconsistent with the child's developmental level to receive the diagnosis.

DSM-IV cites the following symptoms associated with inattention, hyperactivity, and impulsivity:

INATTENTION

1. Often fails to give close attention to details or makes careless mistakes in schoolwork, work, or other activities
2. Often has difficulty sustaining attention in tasks or play activities
3. Often does not seem to listen when spoken to directly
4. Often does not follow through on instructions and fails to finish schoolwork, chores, or duties in the workplace
5. Often has difficulty organizing tasks and activities
6. Often avoids, dislikes, or is reluctant to engage in tasks that require sustained mental effort (such as schoolwork or homework)

7. Often loses things necessary for tasks or activities (for example, toys, school assignments, pencils, books, or dolls)
8. Often is easily distracted by extraneous stimuli
9. Often is forgetful in daily activities

HYPERACTIVITY

10. Often fidgets with hands or feet or squirms in seat
11. Often leaves seat in classroom or in other situations in which remaining seated is expected
12. Often runs about or climbs excessively in situations in which it is inappropriate
13. Often has difficulty playing or engaging in leisure activities quietly
14. Often is "on the go" or acts as if "driven by a motor"
15. Often talks excessively

IMPULSIVITY

16. Often blurts out answers before questions have been completed
17. Often has difficulty awaiting turn
18. Often interrupts or intrudes on others (for example, intrudes into conversations or games)

Children with ADHD "spend disproportionate amounts of time attending to task-irrelevant stimuli and engaging in task-irrelevant activities" (Whalen, 1989, p. 129). Most children with ADHD either are academic underachievers or have a learning disability (DuPaul & Stoner, 1994). Children with ADHD also may have low self-esteem, lability of mood (that is, quickly shifting from one emotion to another), low tolerance for frustration, and temper outbursts. The disorder becomes most evident when children reach school age and have difficulty meeting the demands of the classroom. Overactivity is a major part of ADHD in early childhood. The syndrome is more common in boys than in girls, with estimates of the boy-girl ratio ranging from 3:1 in nonreferred samples to 6:1 in clinic-referred samples (Rapport, 1994).

Like many learning-disabled children, children with ADHD may have information-processing deficits. Such deficits may include inefficient use of time, superficial analyses of written or spoken material, premature stopping of processing information, inadequate evaluation of promising strategies to help with learning or recalling information, poor rehearsal strategies, and limited awareness of problem-solving strategies (Whalen, 1989). Information-processing deficits thus may involve, in part, *poor task analysis* and *poor strategic planning*.

Children with ADHD also may have a deficit in *self-regulation*, which means that they may have difficulty with organization and planning, with the mobilization and maintenance of effortful attention, and with the inhibition of inappropriate responding (Douglas, 1988). Consequently, they may show considerable variability in different situations. Their variability may depend on the task requirements, the presence and type of environmental distractors, the support they receive from others, and their ability to regulate their behavior.

Etiology.   ADHD appears to have a genetic component, although the mode of inheritance and the types of specific genetic abnormalities are yet to be learned (Hechtman, 1994). In addition, ADHD may be associated with an *imbalance of or deficiency in one or more of the brain neurotransmitters,* and several areas of the brain may be involved, particularly the frontal lobes (Hechtman, 1994). Other theories about the causes of ADHD involve *environmental toxins,* such as lead, food additives, sugar, and cigarette smoking or alcohol consumption by the mother during pregnancy. These theories remain speculative because none have received wide-ranging support (Rapport, 1994).

A mother's description of her child with ADHD. The following account illustrates some hardships faced by parents in raising a child with ADHD (Richard, 1993).

CASE 11-1. MRS. DEVILLE

I'm the mother of nine-year-old twin boys who have (finally) been diagnosed with ADD [attention-deficit disorder] through our school. It has been a rough nine years. They were out of their cribs before they could even crawl. They could open any childproof lock ever made and slept less than any human beings I have ever known. No baby-sitter has ever been willing to come more than twice. No child care center or after-school program has even been willing to keep them, so I quit my part-time teaching job and have stayed home with them since they were three. My husband has to work a second job, so most of the supervision of the boys falls on me. I almost never have any relief. Their grandparents work full-time and live in another state. Over the last few years my health has begun to fail. Although my doctor cannot find anything wrong with me, I am constantly catching colds [and] exhausted, and have frequent headaches. I'm losing weight. I sleep very poorly. Are there other mothers of children with ADD who feel this way? Is there anything I can do about it? (p. 10)

An adult's description of growing up with ADHD. The following interview is with a 37-year-old woman who describes some of her experiences growing up with ADHD (Rief, 1993, pp. 57–58, with changes in notation).

IR: What are your memories of elementary school?
IE: My family was one of avid readers. I grew up surrounded by books. I loved to be around books, but I couldn't read them. I remember how much I loved hearing my teacher read *Charlotte's Web* to the class in third grade. Hearing the stories was so powerful. My biggest frustration was not being able to get further in my reading.
IR: Tell me how your attentional difficulties affected you in school.
IE: One of the pitfalls with ADD is that I would have my good days and my bad days. I never knew when the trap door would open and I'd lose my train of thought. For example, in class I would want to ask a question. I would raise

my hand and repeat in my head over and over the question I wanted to ask, so I wouldn't forget. In the meantime, I would miss everything in between the waiting and getting called on. I lost a lot, and it was very frustrating. I spent hours on homework. Reading, processing, and writing were very difficult for me.
IR: What about junior high and high school?
IE: One of my survival skills was being "Miss Goody Two Shoes." I wasn't popular, but that didn't matter much to me. Friends came second to my wanting to do well. Teachers always liked me. I would always tune in to what the instructors wanted and did what I could to please them. I had some very good teachers. A lot of my trauma was self-inflicted. I used to have teachers so fooled. I fooled everybody, but in fooling people (i.e., hiding that I couldn't read), I thought I was cheating. In speaking with a lot of other adults who have learning disabilities, many of us felt that we were cheating by not doing what was expected of us the traditional way. We might have squeaked through the system, but we had to find our own methods. Most of us knew when we were very young that something was wrong, but we just didn't know what. In junior high I remember being the last to get started. I would sit down to write something, but I just couldn't get started. I would get so frustrated, and my anxiety level would go up and up, making it worse. I often felt that my body and I were separate. My body was next to me. My brain and body weren't coordinated with each other.
IR: How did you cope with your difficulties?
IE: I had trouble coping. In fact, I went through periods of serious depression. I saw psychiatrists when I lived back East. No one ever figured out that I couldn't read. I have learned how to accommodate myself. In class I sit up front, close to the teacher, and do as much one-to-one with the teacher as possible. In college I never missed a single class. I am a very disorganized person, but I have an office that I am responsible for organizing. I can do this successfully by setting up visual cues for myself. I set things up in neat little boxes and color code them all. I use tools to help me compensate, like my Franklin Language Master, and I take advantage of Recordings for the Blind, which will record books and texts on tape for individuals with learning disabilities. If I can't reach the top shelf, I can with a ladder—so what if you need aids to compensate! I can do a lot of things that others can't do. I'm very creative. I'm learning to pat myself on the back now, so I don't go back into that black hole I was in for 30 years.

Diagnostic difficulties.   Arriving at a diagnosis of ADHD is not easy. Restlessness and overactive behavior are common in normal children, especially in boys between 6 and 12 years of age. Some "problem" children are never referred for hyperactive behavior because they have parents who are tolerant of their behavior, teachers who do not perceive their behavior as a problem, or optimal environments that provide structure for their behavior. Conversely, essentially normal but active children are referred for evaluation because of less tolerant environments, either at home or at school.

Children with ADHD also may have behaviors and symptoms associated with oppositional defiant disorders, learning disability, depressive disorders and mania, anxiety disorders, and communicative disorders (American Psychiatric Association, 1994). The overlapping-symptom picture sometimes leads to diagnostic difficulties. The ADHD population is heterogeneous, displaying a diversity of behavior despite the underlying attention problems (Weinberg & Emslie, 1991).

Children with a dual diagnosis of oppositional defiant disorder (or conduct disorder) and ADHD (or who show behaviors associated with oppositional defiant disorders and ADHD) may exhibit greater problems during adolescence and adulthood than those who have either diagnosis alone. These problems include delinquency and substance abuse in adolescence and criminality in adulthood (DuPaul & Stoner, 1994).

The occurrence of ADHD is estimated at 3% to 5% in the school-aged population (*DSM-IV*, American Psychiatric Association, 1994). Estimates of ADHD in *clinical populations* of children range from 23% to 50%, depending on the criteria used to define hyperactivity (Whalen, 1989). Hyperactivity appears to account for many problems treated at child mental health clinics.

Attention-deficit/hyperactivity disorder in adolescence.   Children who have ADHD in early childhood usually continue to have difficulties in adolescence, but the manifestations of the disorder may change. Although restlessness, distractibility, and poor concentration may diminish, they still remain problems for some adolescents. The major shift is in the emergence of difficulties associated with social behavior and interpersonal relationships. Particularly evident are rebelliousness, antisocial behavior, and low self-esteem.

Difficulties with academic achievement and problem solving also remain (Whalen, 1989). Adolescents with ADHD repeat more school grades, perform more poorly in academic subjects, and obtain lower intelligence test scores on group-administered tests than do normal children. In the classroom, adolescents with ADHD continue to show problems in attention and concentration, but these problems are less disruptive than in earlier years. During adolescence and young adulthood, individuals who had ADHD as children are more at risk than normal children for behavioral problems, particularly in the area of conduct problems and antisocial personality disorder (after age 18). Little is known about what variables predict long-term adjustment in individuals with ADHD (Whalen, 1989).

Interviewing Issues

You will want to interview the child referred for the assessment of ADHD, as well as his or her parents or caregivers and teachers. In addition, I highly recommend that you observe the child at school, at home, and in a clinic play-

room. Use the semistructured interview in Table F-13 in Appendix F for interviewing children who may have behavioral difficulties such as ADHD. Also, you should ask older children to complete the *Personal Data Questionnaire* (see Table C-3 in Appendix C), if they can.

To interview parents, first use the questions in the semistructured interview in Table F-36 in Appendix F. These questions will give you information about the child's development and possible behavioral difficulties. If you want to conduct a more detailed inquiry with a mother about the child's early development, use the semistructured interview questions in Table F-21 in Appendix F. Also have the parents complete the *Background Questionnaire* (see Table C-2 in Appendix C).

To interview teachers, I recommend that you use the semistructured interview in Table F-43 in Appendix F. It contains questions that will help you evaluate the child's attention span, degree of impulsiveness, possible learning problems, and possible behavioral problems. Also have the teachers complete the *School Referral Questionnaire* (see Table C-13 in Appendix C). As noted in the Preface, the text edited by Adams, Parsons, Culbertson, and Nixon (1996), *Neuropsychology for Clinical Practice: Etiology, Assessment, and Treatment of Common Neurological Disorders,* has references to several excellent behavioral checklists for parents and teachers to complete.

The *Classroom Observation Code* (Abikoff & Gittelman, 1985, reproduced in Sattler, 1992) is a formal procedure useful for observing children who may have ADHD in a school setting, and the *Restricted Academic Playroom Situation* (Barkley, 1988) is a useful formal procedure for observing children who may have ADHD in a clinic playroom. When you observe the child during the interview, at school, or at home, you will want to look at her or his ability to stay focused on a task without becoming distracted. Also be aware of the extent of the child's repetitive purposeless motions, ability to remain in her or his seat, vocalizations, aggressive behavior, and negativistic behavior. The questions in Table 11-1 will help you evaluate and compare the information given to you by the child, parents, and teacher.

Interventions

A popular and usually first-line treatment for ADHD is *stimulant pharmacotherapy,* which may involve the use of *methylphenidate* (*Ritalin*), *d-amphetamine* (*Dexedrine*), or *pemoline* (*Cylert*) (Swanson, McBurnett, Christian, & Wigal, 1995). *Tricylic antidepressants* also have been used with some success (Spencer, Biederman, Wilens, Harding, O'Donnell, & Griffin, 1996). Children with ADHD who take stimulant medication often show dramatic behavioral changes, with noticeable improvement in motor behavior, attention, and impulse control. In addition, they show increased compliance and less physical and verbal hostility. Thus, in what is commonly called a "paradoxical effect," stimulant pharmacotherapy

Table 11-1
Evaluating the Findings from Interviews of the Child, the Parents, and the Teacher
in Cases of Attention-Deficit/ Hyperactivity Disorder[a]

The Child
Problem
 1. How does the child view the referral?
 2. What are the child's concerns?
 3. Does the child believe that he or she has a problem?
 4. If so, how does the child describe his or her problem?
 5. How does the child's description of his or her behavior, feelings, and problems agree with the parents' and teacher's descriptions?
 6. Can the child control his or her behavior?
 7. If yes, in what situations and how does the child control his or her behavior?

Learning Style
 8. Does the child seek information before undertaking an assignment?
 9. Does the child keep notes of the class lecture?
10. Does the child review the test results?
11. Does the child have a place to study at home that is free from distractions?
12. Does the child study the material by reviewing it several times and rehearsing the answers?
13. Does the child seek help with his or her school work from peers, teachers, siblings, parents, or other adults?
14. Does the child read the textbook, study it, reread notes, or review prior tests in preparing for a new test?
15. Does the child receive rewards from the parents if performance in school is good?

School
16. How does the child perceive his or her relations with teachers and other school personnel?
17. If interventions were tried at school, what is the child's opinion of them?
18. How does the child feel about his or her present class placement?
19. What changes in the family and at school might lead the child to experience greater happiness?
20. What services would the child like to receive?

Observations During Interview
21. What are the child's appearance, behavior, motor skills, attention level, activity level, and degree of cooperativeness during the interview?
22. What is the quality of the child's expressive language and receptive language? For example, did the child understand the questions, make appropriate and coherent replies, seem to understand nonverbal messages, use correct grammar, listen appropriately, and understand idioms presented in the conversation?
23. What social skills did the child exhibit in interacting with the interviewer?

Health
24. What is the child's health history?
25. Are there any indications of visual or auditory difficulties?
26. If the child has visual or auditory difficulties, have glasses or hearing aids been prescribed?
27. If so, does the child have these appliances and wear them?
28. Does the child take any medicine that might affect school performance?
29. If so, what are the medications that the child is taking?

Social Skills and Interests
30. How does the child perceive his or her relations with other family members?
31. How does the child get along with other children?
32. Have the child's interpersonal relations changed as he or she developed?
33. If so, in what way?
34. What responsibilities does the child have at home and how does he or she fulfill these responsibilities?
35. Has the child shown any aggressive behavior during development?
36. If so, what type of behavior and during what ages?
37. What are the child's general interests, academic interests, and hobbies?

The Parents
Problem
 1. How do the parents describe the child's problems?
 2. What are the frequency, duration, and magnitude of the child's problems?
 3. Where does the child display his or her problems (such as at home, at school, and at other places)?
 4. How old was the child when the parents became aware of the child's problems?
 5. How do the parents handle the child's problems?
 6. Which interventions have been successful and which have been unsuccessful in helping the child?
 7. What was the child's temperament as an infant?
 8. Were there any signs of irritability?
 9. As a toddler, did the child overreact to stimuli and have difficulty settling down?
10. Did the child's behavior problems emerge only after he or she entered school?
11. Does the child have frequent temper tantrums?
12. How do the parents describe the child's strengths and weaknesses?
13. What do they believe might contribute to the child's problems, such as biological predispositions, deficiencies or delays in basic skill areas, personality and temperament, familial influences, environmental influences, or the interaction of any of these factors?
14. How do the parents handle the child's problems?

(Continued)

Table 11-1 (*Continued*)

15. What are the parents' greatest concerns?
16. How do the parents' reports differ from the child's and the teacher's reports?
17. Do the parents agree with each other about the child's problems?
18. If they do not, in what areas do they disagree?
19. What information have the parents been given by teachers, psychologists, or physicians about the child's problems?

Developmental Considerations
20. How did the mother's pregnancy progress, and was there any unusual exposure to drugs or any unusual event?
21. Did the child have hypoxia, neonatal jaundice, head trauma, meningitis, epilepsy, or other illnesses or conditions at birth or shortly thereafter?
22. If so, what did the child have, what treatment did the child receive, and what was the outcome of treatment, including any residual symptoms?
23. Did the child reach developmental milestones at the ages expected, or were there delays?
24. If there were delays, in what areas did they occur?
25. Has the child had any problems in fine and gross motor development (such as mixed dominance—right handed, right footed, left eyed, or other such combinations), in sensory functions (such as in hearing and vision), in language development, in cognitive thinking, in affective or emotional expression, in social adjustment, in academic functioning, or in family relations? For example, with respect to motor and cognitive functions, did the child have difficulty learning to ride a bicycle, skate, tie shoes, remember addresses, recognize familiar routines, tell time, recite the alphabet, count to more than five, or follow single instructions?
26. If so, what problems did the child have, what treatments did the child receive, and what was the outcome of the treatments?

Social Skills
27. How do the parents perceive the child's relationships with other family members?
28 How does the child get along with other children?
29. Have the child's interpersonal relations changed as he or she developed?
30. If so, in what way?
31. What responsibilities does the child have at home and how does he or she fulfill these responsibilities?
32. Has the child shown any aggressive behavior during development?
33. If so, what type of behavior and at what ages?
34. What are the child's general interests, academic interests, and hobbies?

School
35. How do the parents describe the child's schooling?
36. How do the parents describe the child's teachers?

37. What schools has the child attended?
38. If the child has attended more than one school, what were the reasons for the changes?
39. What has been the child's attendance record at school?
40. Has the child repeated any grades and, if so, what grades?
41. What letter grades did the child receive for his or her schoolwork since he or she began elementary school?
42. Has the child shown a consistent pattern in letter grades and, if so, what is the pattern?
43. Have the letter grades changed and, if so, in what way?
44. Has the child received any special education services?
45. If so, what were the services, what was the individualized educational plan, and what do the parents think about the services?
46. Has the child ever been suspended or expelled from school?
47. If so, when did this take place and for what reason?
48. What, if any, interventions have been attempted?
49. If interventions have been attempted, which have been successful and which unsuccessful in helping the child?
50. What suggestions do the parents have for needed interventions?

Family History
51. Have any family members had a history of learning disabilities, attention-deficit/hyperactivity disorder, or other developmental disorders?
52. If so, who had the disorders and what disorders did they have?
53. Are there any factors in the family that might affect the child's ability to learn, such as dysfunctional family environment, limited economic resources, hunger, lack of privacy for studying, health problems, and so forth?

The Teacher
Problem
1. How does the teacher describe the child's problems?
2. How does the teacher describe the child's strengths and weaknesses?
3. What does the teacher believe is the cause of the child's problems?
4. How does the teacher describe the child's family?
5. How well does the teacher's description of the child agree with those of the child and the parents?
6. If there are disagreements, in what areas are they?
7. What is the child's current level of academic functioning (including letter grades and test scores), social functioning, and general classroom behavior?
8. How does the teacher describe the child's ability to sit still, make friends, get along with other children, listen to stories, follow oral and written directions, skim reading selections, locate information in a textbook, take notes from a discussion, sustain attention over a protracted period, understand age-appropriate rule-governed behavior, take turns when playing with other children, understand and manipulate symbols, count, spell, read,

(*Continued*)

Table 11-1 (*Continued*)

carry through a series of goal-oriented moves, maintain appropriate spatial direction, understand the complexities of a short story, and understand the complexities of a long story?

9. If the child has a reading problem, how does the teacher describe the problem? For example, does the child have difficulty reading new words or nonsense syllables (phonological problem), have difficulty in comprehension, show reluctance in trying to read different words, have a tendency to lose his or her place while reading, read quickly without close inspection, have a tendency to repeat words, hold a book close to his or her face, become bored or distracted while reading, become easily tired or fatigued, become restless and fidget, follow word by word with finger, or use an aid (such as a ruler) to underline what is being read?

10. If the child has a writing problem, how does the teacher describe the problem? For example, does the child have problems in capitalization, punctuation, and syntax; write in an incomprehensible manner with poor sentence structure or with poor word choice; fail to use notes; fail to outline; fail to use a dictionary or use other resources; or fail to rewrite or revise?

11. If the child has a spelling problem, how does the teacher describe the problem? For example, does the child reverse letters, substitute incorrect letters, omit letters, add letters, spell the wrong word, or make incomprehensible errors, or does the child not even try to spell the word?

12. What specific examples does the teacher give of the child's attention to tasks, impulse control in various situations, and activity level?

13. Does the child's behavior change as a function of the academic subject, teacher, class size, time of day, or other factors?

14. How does the child obey the classroom rules?

15. What is the quality of the assignments completed by the child in the classroom and at home?

16. Does the teacher have any opinion of the family and, if so, what is her or his opinion?

17. What is the child's current attendance record?

18. What is the frustration level of the teacher when interacting with the child?

19. If the child was given psychological tests, what were the results of the evaluation?

20. What teaching methods are used in the classroom?

Interventions

21. What interventions have been tried?

22. And with what success?

23. What suggestions does the teacher have for needed interventions?

[a] These questions also can be used in evaluating the interview findings in cases of other types of learning disabilities.
Source: Adapted, in part, from Barkley (1991) and Voeller (1991).

---

decreases behavioral excesses or disruptive behaviors. However, "stimulant pharmacotherapy does not typically correct social or academic deficits. These drugs do not improve learning, increase positive peer interactions, or enhance learning and achievement. Stimulants…may act to decrease inappropriate behavior, but they are unlikely to act to increase appropriate behavior" (Swanson et al., 1995). There is some evidence that stimulant medication improves adolescents' school performance on study hall assignments and quizzes, although more research is needed to learn whether short-term improvements in academic performance lead eventually to greater academic success (DuPaul & Stoner, 1994). Unfortunately, once the medication is withdrawn, the gains associated with behavioral control often disappear.

Approximately 60% to 90% of hyperactive children respond positively to stimulant medication (Whalen, 1989). However, stimulant medication may have adverse side effects, including appetite suppression, sleep disturbance, headaches, stomachaches, weight loss, decrease in growth rate, hypersensitivity, and tremors (Hinshaw, 1994; Voeller, 1991). Methylphenidate is not particularly useful in the treatment of hyperactivity in preschoolers. When hyperactive children are not responsive to stimulants, the physician should seek alternative forms of therapy and end the medication.

Stimulant medications may restore central nervous system arousal levels and inhibitory levels to normal, thereby providing children with ADHD better control and allowing a wider range of behaviors. The use of chemotherapy does not mean that the child does not need special services. *All children who have serious academic deficiencies need remediation.* In addition, cognitive retraining, social skills training, parent training, and family and individual child therapy should be considered for children with ADHD to help them with their interpersonal problems and other adjustment difficulties (Weiss, 1991). Parent-training programs can help parents to increase the child's compliant behaviors and to change the child's noncompliant behaviors (Barkley, 1995). For example, parents need to understand what factors lead to noncompliant behavior, how to attend and reinforce the child's positive behaviors in and out of the home, and how to use time-outs. Combining pharmacological and psychological treatments may be more effective than pharmacological treatment alone. Table 11-2 summarizes some behavioral interventions helpful in managing ADHD.

The principal aim in treating children with ADHD or with similar problems is to help them focus and sustain their

Table 11-2
Behavioral Interventions Helpful in Managing ADHD

1. Provide as much individual attention as possible, involving directed teaching: highly structured, step-by-step methods, with ample opportunities for practice; targeting of goals; and regular monitoring of performance.

2. Modify work demands to increase success rate, break tasks into manageable segments, set task priorities, establish fixed work periods, intersperse breaks of high-interest activities to maintain motivation, and promote consistent study habits and the sense of responsibility for completing tasks.

3. Present directions in parts, use demonstrations and models of what is to be done, monitor understanding by asking for evidence of understanding (samples of work, verbal repetition), and ensure mastery of initial elements before proceeding.

4. Incorporate as much routine as possible in home and school environments, and establish clear guidelines and limits for behavior, understood and consistently maintained consequences, rewards for achieving goals, and positive expectations for success.

5. Devise ways to test what the student knows by permitting completion of alternative assignments (such as by completing a project, making a diorama, or making a poster instead of taking a test), modifying examinations (such as by using multiple-choice questions instead of short-answer questions or by using oral examinations instead of written examinations), and modifying the examination process (such as by testing in a quiet environment or under untimed conditions).

6. Reduce distractions by seating the student toward the front of the classroom (preferably with other quiet students), encouraging the student to use an index card when reading to minimize visual distractions, and using study carrels (a small enclosure for individual study), if possible.

7. Plan or restructure situations that tend to lead to failure or noncompliance.

8. Allow and even encourage participation in high-interest activities and appropriate social interactions, setting aside time irrespective of ability to keep up with schoolwork.

9. Have a special staff member at school serve as "case manager" to help troubleshoot, provide counseling and support, check work, serve as a liaison between teachers and between school and home, and help in the carrying out and overseeing of any behavioral interventions.

10. Encourage the use of organizational aids, such as assignment logs or memory and study strategies.

11. Encourage parents' participation in support groups and the involvement of the child and family in counseling or therapy as indicated.

Source: Reprinted with permission from D. Rich and H. G. Taylor, "Attention Deficit Hyperactivity Disorder," in M. I. Singer, L. T. Singer, and T. M. Anglin (Eds.), *Handbook for Screening Adolescents at Psychosocial Risk*, p. 362. Copyright © 1993 Jossey-Bass, Inc., Publishers. First published by Lexington Books. All rights reserved. Two items from Busch (1993).

attention and keep impulsive responding under control. Children can be taught to verbalize to themselves effective problem-solving strategies, such as planning ahead, stopping to think, and being careful. Self-verbalizations of these kinds may help them bring their behavior under their own control and make it possible for them to reinforce themselves for employing appropriate strategies. A structured and predictable environment with clear, consistent verbalized expectations and immediate feedback also can help. Chapter 5 includes an example of a post-assessment interview with the parent of a child with an attention-deficit/hyperactivity disorder.

Case Illustration

The following case of a child with ADHD illustrates how an eclectic perspective was used to obtain information and to formulate a treatment plan (Black, 1993).

CASE 11-2. FRED

Fred, a 7-year-old boy, was referred because of difficulties in concentration and aggressive behavior at school. At home, his behavior has always been more difficult than that of his 13-year-old brother. His parents, however, were not concerned about his behavior until he started school. At home, they always could cope with him by isolating him and by not attending to his disruptiveness. However, when he entered school, they were critical of his young and inexperienced teacher's ability to cope with him, but they did recognize that he was a handful. Their concern was mainly that he was not progressing as well at school as his older brother. The father was inclined to make light of Fred's aggressive behavior— "Boys will be boys."

Fred was born after a long labor. As an infant, he had difficulty establishing a normal sleep pattern and was extremely active. As a toddler, he had more than his share of accidents because he was fearless and adventurous. He had been excluded from nursery school because he was aggressive. He enjoyed staying at home with his mother because she had enjoyed his being there. However, Fred's mother felt frustrated at not being able to follow her career.

The family history was well within normal limits. The older boy was described as normal and helpful, but had mild asthma. The marriage was satisfactory, except for the mother's stress about her career and the parents' different views about Fred.

When seen with the family, Fred was extremely active and engaged in dangerous behavior. He began to throw objects that nearly hit his brother. When that happened, his father laughed, but his mother became sad and subdued. Because neither parent acted to stop this behavior, the interviewer had to step in and redirect Fred's behavior.

The results of a psychological assessment indicated that Fred was of superior intelligence, but he had low scores in reading, spelling, and math. His low scores suggest deficits in attention and concentration. Fred also revealed a poor self-image. He believed that he was bad and that he could not be good. He had few friends at school, and he thought that everyone hated him. He was often bullied and teased, and he hated school.

Fred appears to have an attention-deficit/hyperactivity disorder. Generally, the parents have managed to cope with his difficult behavior because they are competent and their older son poses no problems. Still, Fred's behavior has caused tensions within the family, particularly his poor academic and social performance at school. Some of Fred's behavior has been reinforced by his father, who does not recognize the extent of Fred's difficulties. The mother's loneliness, which has led to her wanting a companion at home, has prevented her from recognizing the problem earlier.

The following intervention program was devised for Fred and his family. First, he was placed on methylphenidate by a physician. Second, he began a behavioral training program to bolster his low self-esteem. Third, the parents began family therapy aimed at (a) helping them teach Fred how to cope with his disability, (b) changing their ways of reacting to Fred, (c) encouraging the mother to develop her career, and (d) addressing marital tensions. The medication improved Fred's concentration and lessened his distractibility, and the behavioral treatment improved his self-esteem. Fred began to make progress at school. His teacher and peers started to treat him more positively, which also improved his self-concept and self-esteem.

Courtesy of Jerome M. Sattler and Jeff B. Bryson.

CONDUCT DISORDER AND OPPOSITIONAL DEFIANT DISORDER

Description

Children with a *conduct disorder* have a pattern of antisocial behavior, rule breaking, or aggressive behavior that creates difficulties for themselves, their families, their school systems, and their communities (Forness, Kavale, & Lopez, 1993; Gardner, 1992). Conduct disorder can be defined as "a repetitive and persistent pattern of behavior in which the basic rights of others or major age-appropriate societal norms or rules are violated" (American Psychiatric Association, 1994, p. 85). It is a condition regarded by others as unmanageable.

DSM-IV cites the following behaviors associated with a conduct disorder:

1. Aggressive conduct that causes or threatens physical harm to other people or animals (examples include bullying, threatening, or intimidating others; initiating physical fights; using a weapon that can cause serious harm to others; physical cruelty to people or animals; stealing while confronting a victim; and forcing someone into sexual activity)
2. Nonaggressive conduct that causes property loss or damage (examples include deliberately engaging in fire setting and deliberately destroying others' property by other means)
3. Deceitfulness or theft (examples include breaking into someone else's residence or car; lying to obtain goods or favors or to avoid obligations; and stealing items of nontrivial value without confronting a victim)
4. Serious violation of rules (examples include staying out at night despite parental prohibitions, running away from home overnight, and missing school)

Children with a conduct disorder also may have impairments in social, academic, and occupational functioning.

DSM-IV describes other features associated with children and adolescents who have a conduct disorder. These features include little empathy and concern for the feelings, wishes, and well-being of others; minimal feelings of guilt or remorse; poor frustration tolerance; irritability, temper outbursts, and recklessness; early onset of sexual behavior, drinking, smoking, and use of illegal substances; school suspension or expulsion; problems in work adjustment; legal difficulties; acquiring sexually transmitted diseases; unplanned pregnancy; promiscuity; and physical injury from accidents or fights. The prevalence rates are estimated to range from 6% to 16% for males and from 2% to 9% for females.

Another type of disruptive behavior disorder described in *DSM-IV* is *oppositional defiant disorder*. The major characteristic of oppositional defiant disorder is a recurrent pattern of negativistic, defiant, disobedient, and hostile behavior toward authority figures. Typical behaviors include arguing with adults, actively defying or refusing to comply with the requests or rules of adults, deliberately doing things that will annoy other people, blaming others for one's own mistakes or misbehavior, being touchy or easily annoyed by others, being angry and resentful, or being spiteful or vindictive. Children with this pattern of behavior also may have impairments in social, academic, or occupational functioning.

Oppositional defiant disorder is distinguished from conduct disorder by the *lack of conduct that seriously violates others' rights or violates age-appropriate society norms and rules.* Children with an oppositional defiant disorder typically do *not* show aggressive behavior toward people or animals, destroy property, steal, or deceive people.

The features associated with oppositional defiant disorder depend on children's age and gender (American Psychiatric Association, 1994). In *preschool years,* the disorder is more prevalent among children who have problematic temperaments, such as high reactivity, difficulty being soothed, or high motor activity. "During the *school years,* there may be low self-esteem, mood lability, low frustration tolerance, swearing, and the precocious use of alcohol, tobacco, or illicit drugs. There are often conflicts with parents, teachers, and peers.... The disorder is more prevalent in males than females before puberty, but the rates are probably equal after puberty. Symptoms are generally similar in each gender, except that males may have more confrontational behavior and more persistent symptoms" (American Psychiatric Association, 1994, p. 92, italics added). It is estimated that between 2% and 16% of children receive an oppositional defiant disorder diagnosis. Note that all of the features of the oppositional defiant disorder are usually present in children with a conduct disorder.

The typical age of onset of symptoms for conduct disorder and oppositional defiant disorder, as noted in the reports of parents, are as follows (Lahey & Loeber, 1994):

- *Conduct disorder:* lies (8 years), fights (8½ years), bullies (9 years), sets fires (9 years), uses weapon (9½ years), vandalizes (10 years), is cruel to animals (10½ years), engages in physical cruelty (11½ years), steals (12 years), runs away from home (12 years), is truant (12½ years), mugs (12½ years), breaks and enters (12½ years), and forces sex (13 years).
- *Oppositional defiant disorder:* acts stubborn (3 years), defies adults (5 years), has temper tantrums (5 years), is irritable (6 years), argues (6 years), blames others (6½ years), annoys others (7 years), is spiteful (7½ years), and is angry (8 years).

For conduct disorder, symptoms usually appear between 8 and 13 years, whereas for oppositional defiant disorder, they usually appear between 3 and 8 years.

Conduct disorders represent a major class of childhood difficulties, including the commission of crimes. Children with conduct disorders have the highest rate of referral to mental health facilities, with estimates ranging from one-third to two-thirds of the referrals (Baum, 1989). Figure 11-1

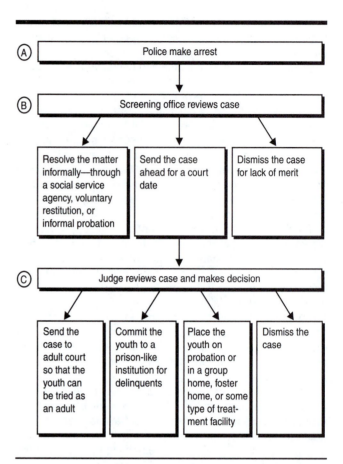

Figure 11-1. Options available for juvenile offenders.

illustrates what may happen if children are arrested for committing a crime.

Etiological considerations.   Biological, behavioral, and familial factors have been proposed to account for the development of conduct disorders; however, there is no firm evidence to support any one etiological theory (American Psychiatric Association, 1994; Baum, 1989; Frick, 1993; Gardner, 1992).

- *Biological factors* include children's genetic makeup and constitutional factors.
- *Behavioral factors* include difficult infant temperament, sensation seeking, learning deficits, academic underachievement, immaturities in moral reasoning, maladaptive peer relationships, association with a delinquent peer group, and poor interpersonal problem-solving skills.
- *Familial factors* include parental marital conflict and divorce, depression, substance abuse, antisocial behavior, social isolation, rejection of child, failure to supervise the child properly, harsh or inconsistent discipline, ineffective communication with the child, and failure to become involved in the child's activities.

The following developmental model is useful for understanding how children develop a conduct disorder (Conduct

Problems Prevention Research Group, 1992; Shaw & Bell, 1993). At each developmental stage, genetic factors either may be involved in the children's behavior problems or may exacerbate the problems related to parental attachment and neglect. *Thus, parents may be victims of the children's behavior problems as well as contribute to the children's problems.* The developmental model emphasizes that there is an interaction between genetic and familial/environmental conditions that places children at risk for developing a conduct disorder.

1. *Infancy.* From birth to 24 months, infants who later develop a conduct disorder may be neglected by their caregivers, who are indifferent to them and who fail to comfort them (also see discussion of attachment theory in Chapter 1). When this happens, infants may become demanding, which, in turn, may make caregivers even more nonresponsive. By 24 months, infants who are insecure may become more bold, noncompliant, and negative. Caregivers, in turn, are likely to continue to be indifferent to them and to try to control the infants' behavior. Caregivers might prefer not to interact at all with infants who show unpleasant behavior (Shaw & Bell, 1993).

2. *Preschool years.* By 2 years of age, "the basic pattern of interaction and emotional attachment between the parent and child has been formed. The child has developed an internal working model of expected responsiveness from the caregiver and she or he has developed her or his own expectations and standards of appropriate responsiveness concerning the child's most common reactions to her or his interventions" (Shaw & Bell, 1993, p. 512, with changes in notation). Caregivers begin to demand more things from the toddler. When physical contact has been negative and infrequent in the first two years, it is likely to continue this way during the next two years. In such cases, there is little opportunity for the caregiver to negotiate goals and plans with the child. When the relationship is secure, these negotiations can take place successfully. As early as ages 2 and 3, children may show irritability, inattentiveness, and impulsivity and have discipline problems. When there is a coercive caregiver-child relationship, the caregiver may provide only low levels of stimulation and support so the child fails to develop needed emotional control, social skills, and academic readiness (Conduct Problems Prevention Research Group, 1992).

The conflict between preschool children and their caregivers has ramifications for the development of later antisocial behavior (Shaw & Bell, 1993). The children may not internalize parental or societal standards. Parents may give rewards infrequently and, if rewards are given, use them as a means of controlling the child's behavior. When children comply, it may be only because of perceived threats to their freedom or to their physical safety. They develop an extrinsic motivation system, doing things because they have to—they do not independently pursue complex and challenging activities.

3. *Middle-childhood years.* During 6 to 12 years of age, children who develop conduct disorders may show deficiencies in critical social-cognitive skills (Conduct Problems Prevention Research Group, 1992). Compared with their peers, they may fail to attend to relevant social cues, to interpret peers' intentions accurately, and to assume a friendly attitude toward others. They may have limited skills in solving social problems, and, instead of using competent verbally assertive social strategies, they may respond aggressively in social situations. Aggression may be their preferred way of interacting with others.

The following picture emerges during the middle-childhood years for children who develop a conduct disorder (Conduct Problems Prevention Research Group, 1992):

During the grade school years, negative school and social experiences further exacerbate the adjustment difficulties of children with conduct problems. Children who are aggressive and disruptive with peers quickly become rejected by their peers.... Because of their noncompliant and disruptive behavior, high-risk children develop poor relations with their teachers and are less supported and nurtured in the school setting.... Parents' negative encounters with teachers, coupled with continued and escalating aversive interactions with their children in the home, lead some parents to reject their own highly aggressive children and show less interest in them as they enter adolescence. Several consequences follow from this spiraling pattern of aversive behavior, rejection, and reactivity. One is that high-risk children perform more poorly in school and become alienated from the goals and values of [school].... A second consequence is that some of these children become depressed and develop negative self-concepts in the cognitive, social, and behavioral domains. A third consequence is that rejected, aggressive children drift into deviant peer groups in early adolescence. (p. 513)

4. *Adolescent years.* Adolescents need to establish a strong bond, consisting of attachment, commitment, and positive beliefs, with the family and other social institutions to prevent deviant behavior and delinquency from developing. The following picture emerges during adolescence of children with a conduct disorder (Conduct Problems Prevention Research Group, 1992):

By early adolescence, alienation from the mainstream culture and association with deviant peers may play a particularly critical role in promoting adolescent delinquency.... It is the deviant peer group in adolescence that appears to be a major training ground for delinquency and substance abuse.... Parents of high-risk adolescents are relatively unlikely to monitor their children's activities adequately..., and teachers at this level cannot consistently monitor contact with adolescents.... In fact, dropping out of school seems to be predictable from deviant peer group membership in middle school. (p. 513)

Parents' perceptions of their children with conduct problems. The following accounts of parents will help you understand what it is like to raise a child with a conduct disorder. These accounts are from parents of children between 3 and 8 years of age (Webster-Stratton & Herbert, 1994, pp. 44–53, 56, 57, reprinted with permission of the author and publisher from C. Webster-Stratton and M. Herbert, *Troubled families—problem children: Working with parents: A collaborative process,* copyright 1994 by John Wiley & Sons Limited).

1. *Aggression against parents.* Parents may feel victimized and tyrannized by their child.

Just a few weeks ago, he threw his booster seat in my face and hit my jaw. And he thought it was funny!…He was acting up, and I think he had already had one Time Out for yelling and screaming and interrupting us at the table. And I said, "Fine, you are going upstairs now. You are not having dessert." And he just flew into a rage. He picked up a metal fork and threw it with all his force, and hit me—barely missed my eyes. There was blood on my forehead. I was screaming, I was hysterical. And I was terrified, I mean, to see that type of behavior, that type of rage.

2. *Aggression against siblings.* Parents may be concerned that the child will show aggression toward siblings and toward other family members.

He is so violent with his sister. He split her lip a couple of times. And he almost knocked her out once when he hit her over the head with a five-pound brass pitcher. He's put plastic bags over her head. Even things that you wouldn't think could be dangerous, you have to make sure and keep out of his reach.

3. *Aggression against animals.* Parents may be concerned that the child will harm pets.

He is just real violent with animals. And I have repetitively taught him how to stroke animals nicely. He can't help himself. I caught him holding the cat in the toilet with the lid shut.

4. *Aggression against other children.* Parents may be concerned that the child will show aggression toward other children in day care settings, in their home, or in public places.

He is aggressive around other children. We can't really trust him not to walk up and wallop the smaller ones. He pokes them in the eyes or pushes them down…. I understand a lot of children go through this thing with aggression—but again, it seems so exaggerated, it's almost like he seeks out other children to hurt them. If you take him to the zoo, here we are in a situation where we could be having fun, talking about animals, walking…and he's seeking out little children in strollers and picking up handfuls of sand and throwing it in their faces.

5. *Dismantling the house.* Parents may be concerned that the child will attempt to destroy parts of the house or household objects.

I have really tried to value the children more than I value the house, but it's been incredibly painful to watch our brand new house—brand spanking new—be destroyed. And we've told ourselves, it's all fixable, but he has caused an incredible amount of destruction which has been painful to watch. When you work and personally invest yourself in your home, when other people don't respect it or take care of it, it's painful.

6. *Noncompliance and defiance.* Parents may be concerned about the child's refusal to comply with their requests.

He's the most stubborn child or person I have ever met, because he won't stop. His power is that he won't stop. He usually ends up crying and he gets like a mule—he kind of digs his heels in, and doesn't want to do it.

7. *Sleep problems.* Parents may be concerned about the child's resistance to going to bed.

You have to follow them every step of the way to get them to go to bed. And then, once they are in bed, they're either turning on the light and getting up and playing with their toys, or else sneaking around the house. They won't stay put. I found the only thing that I can do to really control that is: I take a chair down at the end of the hall, park it in front of their door, and sit and read a book. Then they'll settle down and go to sleep.

8. *Eating problems.* Parents may be concerned about the child's inability to sit still long enough to eat a meal.

A meal at our house is like a circus. It's like two rats out of a sack. One goes one way and one goes the other. He'll run around the table. He'll take a bite of food, he'll sit down half on the chair, take another bite of food and then run off and chew it and run around.

9. *Transition difficulties and poor adaptability.* Parents may be concerned about how the child will handle changes in routines or react when new activities are introduced.

Transitions are really hard for him. We try to give him warning like, bedtime is in ten minutes. And then sometimes you get a temper tantrum getting his teeth brushed. Because even though he's had warnings, it hasn't assimilated that we mean, you are going to bed, we're going to turn the light off. He thinks he can still play.

10. *Fears and talk of suicide.* Parents may be concerned about the child's fears and suicidal thoughts.

He often talks about wanting to die and how he wants to kill himself. Like the other day he was angry because he got pulled out of swim lessons for not keeping his hands to himself and he said, "It's so terrible, I should just die."

11. *Hyperactivity, distractibility, and high intensity.* Parents may be concerned about the child's high rate of activity, being "wound up," and having difficulty listening and concentrating.

He's mentally fine, but his emotions are twisted in some ways—he doesn't seem to have the normalities that a lot of kids have. I look at my nieces and nephews and, while they have their moments, most of the time they can listen and talk. But with Keith he goes off into outer space and won't come back—he's not even on this planet! He's crazy, running around the house screaming, jumping on the bed, and goes into a fit of hyperactivity trying to accumulate as many things wrong as possible in that time. To get him under control we have to restrain him until he's so worn out, he's exhausted.

12. *Difficulty learning from experience or parental instructions.* Parents may be concerned about the child's inability to learn from experience.

I'm concerned because he makes a mistake and we talk about it, but there is no carryover to the next situation. He still makes the same mistake. Then when I try to talk about it with him, he has this blank face with rolling eyes and I get scared that a kid this young is tuning me out.

13. *Variable temperament.* Parents may be concerned about the child's alternating between negative and positive behaviors.

He is like a "Jekyll and Hyde." Sometimes he can be sweet, charming, loving, easy to get along with, he's a very good-natured child. But then there's the other side of him which emerges—an angry, hostile, aggressive, hurting child, who will do violent things to try to get his way. He is rough with animals and mean with little children, and he is very noncompliant. By the time he is ready to be loving again, you are fed up.

14. *Impact on marital relationship.* Parents may be concerned about the need to monitor and discipline the child continually.

One of the things that is so frustrating is that he has consumed our lives. Since he's been born, 99% of our conversation is about Matthew and what we are going to do to deal with his behavior problems. We don't have a life—everything revolves around Matthew.

15. *Impact on siblings.* Parents may be concerned about having little time or energy for the "good sibling," developing unrealistic expectations about the good sibling, and fearing that the good sibling will exhibit the same behavior problems as the child with a conduct disorder.

What happens in our family dynamic is that our nonproblem child always has to be responsible. Wrongly, but you know, because life with his brother is so incredibly complicated, he is expected to act like a 40-year-old and think like a 40-year-old. The consequences for him are great. I expect too much of him, I expect him to act, to use his head every minute of every day about dangers for his brother—that's more than an eight-year-old should have to contend with. Because life with his brother is so dangerous for everybody and because we try to control his brother's behavior, we are constantly on to him to control his. And that is hard…he never gets to have a bad day, he never gets to throw a tantrum, he never gets to do anything because we are so maxed out on his brother, there's nothing left for him. He has to shut up, behave, and not talk to us about any of his concerns and problems.

16. *Impact on extended family relations.* Parents may be concerned about the tension the child's problems create with grandparents and with other relatives.

When Grandma comes to visit about once a month, he (child) just goes ape. He starts terrorizing the cats, he starts throwing his toys, he starts going ape. And he has a real hard time when Grandpa is there and Grandpa likes him. But Grandma thinks we should "nail the little sucker a good plant a couple of times on the rear end."

Interviewing Issues

The general interviews in Tables F-13 and F-36 in Appendix F are useful for children referred for conduct problems and for their parents, respectively. After you complete the interviews with the child and parents, evaluate issues concerning the child's development, family history, and other relevant

areas as you would for any other case. Give the following questions your close attention (Snyder, Rains, & Popejoy, 1988):

CHILD

1. What are the child's behavior problems?
2. When do the problems occur, such as in the morning, in the afternoon, at night, before bed, before meals, before homework, when a parent returns from work, or after a marital dispute?
3. What occurs before the problem begins (antecedents), and what occurs after the problem ends (consequences)?
4. Who is involved in the confrontations, such as siblings, mother, father, other relatives, peers, or teachers?
5. What is the child's temperament?
6. What is the child's overall level of adjustment?
7. What age-appropriate self-care skills does the child have?
8. How does the child relate to peers and siblings?
9. How does the child perform and behave in school?
10. How does the child respond to the parents' discipline?
11. Is the child responsive to parental requests?
12. Is the child "difficult" or minimally responsive?
13. How does the child respond to positive social attention?

PARENTS

14. What is the adjustment level of the parents?
15. If the child has violent episodes, are they associated with drug use or intoxication by the child or the parents?
16. Do the parents have realistic expectations about the child's behavior given the child's age?
17. How do the parents feel about the child?
18. Do the parents communicate appropriately with the child?

DISCIPLINE

19. How do the parents discipline the child?
20. Do the parents control their anger when they discipline the child?
21. Does parental discipline stop aversive child behavior, at least for a short time?
22. What is the reaction of each parent and each sibling when the child is disciplined?
23. How do the parents discipline the siblings?
24. Do all the children in the family receive the same type of discipline?
25. (If not) How does the discipline differ among the siblings?

If you are interested in evaluating an adolescent's views about morality, the following questions, which are from the Social Reflection Questionnaire, may be useful (Gibbs, Basinger, & Fuller, 1992; see Gibbs et al. for a quantitative method for scoring responses to the questions).

1. Think about when you've made a promise to a friend of yours. How important is it for people to keep promises, if they can, to friends?

2. Think about keeping a promise to anyone. How important is it for people to keep promises, if they can, even to someone they hardly know?

3. Think about keeping a promise to a child. How important is it for parents to keep promises, if they can, to their children?

4. In general, how important is it for people to tell the truth?

5. Think about when you've helped your mother or father. How important is it for children to help their parents?

6. Let's say a friend of yours needs help and may even die, and you're the only person who can save him or her. How important is it for a person, without losing her or his own life, to save the life of a friend?

7. Think about saving anyone's life. How important is it for a person, without losing her or his own life, to save the life of a stranger?

8. How important is it for a person to live even if that person doesn't want to?

9. How important is it for people not to take things that belong to other people?

10. How important is it for people to obey the law?

11. How important is it for judges to send people who break the law to jail?

Interventions

Children with conduct disorders are difficult to treat (Quay, Routh, & Shapiro, 1987). Pharmacological agents, behavioral approaches, social learning approaches, and parent-training approaches have been attempted. Pharmacological agents in use include the following (Gadow, 1991; Klein & Slomkowski, 1993): lithium, stimulants (such as Ritalin), and neuroleptics (such as thioridazine, chlorpromazine, and haloperidol). Some success has been achieved, but long-term outcome research is needed. Neuroleptics have several side effects, including impairment of adaptive behavior, increased mood and behavioral disturbances, weight gain, drowsiness, gastrointestinal upsets, and movement disorders that may not abate following drug withdrawal (Gadow, 1991). Medication alone will rarely suffice in the treatment of children with conduct disorders (Lewis, 1991a).

Behavioral interventions are used to increase children's coping behavior; improve their peer interactions, cooperative behavior, self-esteem, and frustration tolerance; and reduce their aggressive behavior (Quay et al., 1987). Behavioral and social learning approaches also are used to teach parents and children better ways to communicate and to respond to each others' needs in order to alter maladaptive family patterns. Parent training helps parents learn ways to improve family management practices. Although some immediate gains have been realized through the use of behavioral, social learning, and parent-training approaches, long-term gains are questionable (Frick, Strauss, Lahey, & Christ, 1992).

The following are some implications of the developmental model (presented earlier) for interventions with children who have conduct disorders (Conduct Problems Prevention Research Group, 1992):

[The first strategic point in development for preventive intervention is at school entry. At this point in development] high-risk children need help in learning to control anger, in developing social-cognitive skills, and in generating more socially acceptable and effective alternatives to aggression and oppositional behavior. Many high-risk children need concentrated assistance in getting ready for the academic tasks of school. Their parents need to acquire more consistent, more positive, and less punitive discipline methods. Parents also need to learn how to provide support for their children's cognitive growth. Many parents need support in learning to relate to teachers and to provide support at home for the goals of the school for their children. Teachers may need help in preparing their classrooms for these high-risk children, especially classrooms with a high concentration of high-risk children. Finally, a case management approach may be necessary to assist highly stressed and disorganized families in providing a more stable and supportive atmosphere for child rearing.

A second logical point for intervention is at the transition into middle school. High-risk children are clearly identifiable at this age. The key issues for these children seem to be the control of aggressive behavior, the acquisition and use of prosocial skills for integrating themselves into the mainstream peer culture, and concentrated assistance with academic skills. They may also profit from individual competency-enhancing experiences to maintain or restore self-esteem and positive affect. Parents of these preadolescents need to establish effective and nonpunitive disciplinary control of their children and to maintain or regain an active interest in their activities so that reasonable monitoring of adolescent behavior can occur. Furthermore, some effective partnership between parents and the schools must take place if the monitoring of homework, school attendance, and resistance to deviant peer group involvement is to take place. (p. 514, with changes in notation)

Perhaps the best approach to intervention with children who have conduct disorders is to address individual, familial, and environmental vulnerabilities of the child and parents. Treatment will likely need to be ongoing, focusing on medical, psychological, and educational supports to the child and family (Lewis, 1991).

Case Illustration

The following case describes a child with a conduct disorder. Familial factors appear to have contributed to his disturbed behavior (Weiner, 1982).

CASE 11-3. MARTIN
Martin was 13 when his school principal recommended professional help for him. The referral was precipitated by the latest episode in a long history of aggressive behavior, which included numerous unprovoked beatings of younger children. Martin also had been disruptive in class and had recently begun to yell out, "I hate everyone." According to the principal, Martin was "the worst boy we've ever seen at his age."

Martin's father, Mr. Brown, did most of the talking during an initial interview with the parents, both of whom were high school teachers. Mr. Brown said he was very upset by his son's aggressive and unruly behavior in school. He described Martin as a lazy, easily frustrated boy who wanted to achieve without working, who could not tolerate losing in anything, and who lied constantly. Mr. Brown could offer no explanation for Martin's misconduct, except to say, "Maybe he was just born bad." He also reported that he was a stern disciplinarian and had no trouble with Martin at home. He went on to suggest that perhaps Martin's teachers, by not being sufficiently firm and by picking on him whenever there was a class disturbance, were at least partly responsible for his record of poor conduct.

In a later meeting alone, Martin's mother, Mrs. Brown, painted a quite different picture. She said that she had kept this to herself during the previous joint interview because she was afraid of arousing her husband's anger. As far as she was concerned, Mrs. Brown volunteered, Mr. Brown's description of their son was as true of her husband as of her son. Mrs. Brown said that although her husband was highly successful in impressing other people with his maturity, competence, and sincerity, he was an irresponsible, lazy, dishonest man who paid little attention to family affairs and who frequently absented himself from the home for days at a time without explanation. Much of his self-description, she added, especially about his stern disciplining, was a bald-faced lie: "He likes to think of himself as a big man, but he's never done anything constructive to discipline Martin; when he is home, which isn't often, he can't be bothered."

This new information, supplemented by later evaluation of Martin himself, clarified the likely relation of his behavior problems to his relationship with his father. In retrospect, the father's blaming the school for his son's problems could be seen as his way of evading any personal responsibility. Mr. Brown's attitudes also probably suggested to Martin the appropriateness of denying guilt and externalizing blame for difficult situations. (p. 410, with changes in notation)

DEPRESSION

Description

Depression can refer to a symptom, such as a sad affect, that is a common experience of everyday life or to a syndrome or disorder in which a group of symptoms go together (Kazdin, 1990). *DSM-IV* (American Psychiatric Association, 1994) cites the following symptoms associated with a major depressive episode:

1. Irritable or depressed mood most of the day and nearly every day
2. Markedly diminished interest or pleasure in all, or almost all, activities most of the day and nearly every day
3. Failure to make expected weight gain, significant weight loss when not dieting, weight gain, or decrease or increase in appetite nearly every day
4. Insomnia or hypersomnia nearly every day
5. Psychomotor agitation or retardation nearly every day
6. Fatigue or loss of energy nearly every day
7. Feeling of worthlessness or excessive or inappropriate guilt nearly every day
8. Diminished ability to think or concentrate, or indecisiveness nearly every day
9. Recurrent thoughts of death, recurrent suicidal ideation without a specific plan, or a suicide attempt or a specific plan for committing suicide

The symptoms of depression from a developmental perspective include the following (Edwards & Starr, 1996; Gotlib & Hammen, 1992; Kazdin, 1988, 1990; Pataki & Carlson, 1990; Schachter & Romano, 1993):

1. *Infants and preschool children.* Although infants during the first year of life may not have "depression" in the clinical sense, they do experience depressive symptoms.

Non Sequitur by Wiley Miller

These symptoms include sleep disturbances, increased clinging, aggressive behavior, crying, sadness, apprehension, decreased contact with parents or caregivers, stupor, loss of appetite, and refusal to eat. The prevalence rate for depression in preschool children is low—about 1% of children in the 2- to 3-year age range are depressed.

2. *Middle childhood–aged children.* Besides the symptoms noted for infants, children between 6 and 12 years of age may show such symptoms as loss of weight, temper tantrums, concentration difficulties, and sleeplessness. Approximately 2% of the children in middle childhood meet the criteria for diagnosable depression.

3. *Adolescents.* Besides the symptoms noted for infants and middle childhood–aged children, symptoms include loss of feelings of pleasure and interest, low self-esteem, excessive fatigue and loss of energy, inability to tolerate routines, overinvolvement with pets, aggressive behavior, somatic complaints, restlessness, loneliness, irritability, running away, stealing, guilt feelings, feelings of worthlessness, weight loss or gain, and suicidal preoccupations. In adolescence, the prevalence rate for depression is about 6%: 2.6% in boys and 10.2% in girls. Adolescent females, thus, are at greater risk than males for depression or depressive symptoms. In early adolescence, rates of depression increase, and the first episode of depression is likely to occur. When adolescents who are depressed reach adulthood, they may continue to exhibit depressive symptoms.

Because many of these signs occur in children who are developing normally, a depressive disorder should be considered primarily when the symptoms (a) reflect a change in the children's behavior maintained over time and (b) are detrimental to the children's functioning. Additionally, children and adolescents may have psychotic depression or melancholic depression, both of which are subtypes of depression also found in adults. Children and adolescents initially diagnosed as having depression sometimes develop a bipolar reaction—that is, both depression and mania (Gotlib & Hammen, 1992).

Coexistence with other disorders. Depressive disorders in children often coexist with other disorders (Gotlib & Hammen, 1992). These other disorders include conduct or oppositional disorders, anxiety disorders, and, less often, attention-deficit/hyperactivity disorder. In older children, depressive disorders often coexist with eating disorders and with drug or alcohol abuse. Children with depressive disorders frequently have academic difficulties and low achievement in school, as well as interpersonal difficulties, particularly with their parents. Depression, then, often disrupts children's cognitive, academic, and interpersonal functioning. When children are depressed, they are likely to "construe themselves, their worlds, and futures in negative ways that likely contribute to and sustain their dysphoria" (an emotional state characterized by anxiety, depression, and restlessness) (Gotlib & Hammen, 1992, p. 46).

Etiology. The etiology of depression is uncertain. Both biological and psychosocial causes have been proposed (Kazdin, 1990). Biological theories of causation include a deficit in or imbalance of neurotransmittors (substances found in the brain) and genetic transmission (for example, a family history of depression). Psychosocial theories of causation propose that depression results from limited rewards or satisfactions received from interactions with the environment, parental resentment or rejection of the child, deficits in self-regulatory skills in coping with stress, negative thinking about oneself, failure of behavior to influence events in one's life, deficits in interpersonal problem-solving skills, and reactions to major and minor forms of stress. Stressful events include illness, significant losses such as the death of a parent, minor daily hassles, remarriage of a parent, child maltreatment, and pregnancy.

Views about adolescent depression. One adolescent described his depression in the following way (McKnew, Cytryn, & Yahraes, 1983):

It's a coming-and-going thing. I don't feel depressed all the time. Usually it takes something, no matter how minor, to really set it off, and I start feeling bad about something and I can't do anything, and so today everything's been going pretty well, so I don't feel bad at all. But on another day, you know, I might just not want to get up in the morning or do anything at all.... Just like everything's worthless, like it's just not worth it to even be. That's about the best I can do. It's—it seems like it's a silly thing to even go through life and exist. And from one day to the next you're always wondering if you're going to make it to the next day if it's—if you can stand it, if it's worth trying to get to tomorrow.... It's just—just, I feel like—I feel mostly like I'm worthless, like there's something wrong with me. It's really not a pleasant feeling to know that you're a total failure, a complete nothing, and I get the feeling that I didn't do nothing right or worthwhile or anything. (p. 17)

Following are two views about the problem of adolescent depression. The first is from Elizabeth Felton, a social worker, and the second is from Han Phung, a student (Blair, 1995).

Generally, students aren't referred due to "depression." Something else gets the attention of a teacher or a dean, or a parent says, "I don't know what's going on with my child. All of a sudden they're breaking curfew."

What we usually notice in school is that they're acting out—having trouble with teachers, grades are dropping. Sometimes they report not sleeping or that they're sleeping from the time they get home until the next day when it's time to come to school. They're not eating or they're overeating. Some admit to using drugs or alcohol—getting high a lot—and isolating themselves.

Initially, the major concern is to assess how depressed they are. If we determine suicide is a possibility, we would have them evaluated to see if they need to be hospitalized, ask about past attempts, notify the parents and give them resources.

If it's not that serious, we offer them support. We're available on an individual basis, offer peer counseling, get the parents involved. We have hotlines they can call 24 hours a day. And sometimes we have to refer to outside agencies. (p. B7)

I've seen students with high grade point averages, great parents that have high expectations for them, have depressions because they can't meet those expectations. But I've also seen students with depression when they live in a household where their mother is never there or they are just not well cared-for. And I've seen depression where students don't have high self-esteem and think that no one loves them. I've seen them cry. I've seen them on the edge of being ready to give up.

I think they feel lonely because they don't really think there are people out there for them. They think that they have to deal with their problems by themselves. (p. B7)

Interviewing Issues

The semistructured interview in Table F-24 in Appendix F is designed to help you interview children who may be depressed. For children who may have suicidal preoccupations, also review the material in Chapter 13. In evaluating depression in children, consider whether the symptoms (a) represent a change in behavior, (b) are consistent in behavior, (c) lack a clear precipitant, or (d) significantly affect the children's everyday behavior (Kazdin, 1988). This will help you evaluate whether the symptoms are situationally based or are of a long-standing nature. Also consider how the following familial factors contribute to the depression (Reynolds, 1992): marital discord, child maltreatment, poor family cohesion, poor family communication, father absence, mother absence, parental resentment, and parental rejection of children. Because depression in children involves both internalizing and overt symptoms, comprehensive evaluation will involve obtaining information from the child, parents, teacher, and possibly peers (Clarizio, 1994).

Interventions

Treatment of depression may involve use of tricylic antidepressant medications, serotonin-specific reuptake inhibitors, and psychotherapy, including cognitive-behavioral approaches. If parents ask for help with their daughter or son who is depressed, consider giving them the following suggestions (Oster & Montgomery, 1995):

- Treat your daughter or son as you normally would.
- Encourage your daughter or son to share her or his thoughts and feelings.
- Show that you care about and value your daughter or son.
- Share with your daughter or son similar unpleasant experiences that you had that ended positively to provide a basis for hope.
- Offer your daughter or son praise and compliments.
- Do not criticize or blame your daughter or son for her or his bad feelings.
- Acknowledge your daughter or son's pain and suffering. It is easy to get impatient and angry with someone who is depressed. Make it clear that you are genuinely concerned about her or his feelings.

- Take seriously any talk or threats about suicide that your daughter or son makes or any attempts that your daughter or son makes to hurt herself or himself.

Interventions will be complicated if the parents also are depressed or have other forms of psychological disturbance (Reynolds, 1992). Depressed parents, for example, may reinforce their children's depressive cognitions and behaviors.

Case Illustrations

The following case offers an example of depression in an adolescent (Compas & Hammen, 1994). It illustrates that depression in adolescents sometimes is accompanied by symptoms associated with other disorders (co-occurring or comorbid disorders).

CASE 11-3. RAYMOND

Raymond is a 16-year-old adolescent boy who lives alone with his single mother. Both he and his mother report that he is experiencing emotional and behavioral problems. For the past few months he has been persistently sad and unhappy, overcome with feelings of personal worthlessness. He is socially withdrawn from others, spending most of his time alone at home or avoiding contact with his peers on those days when he manages to attend school. He is constantly tired but still finds it difficult to sleep, lying awake at night and then struggling to drag himself from bed in the morning. Both he and his mother are concerned about his weight, which has increased substantially due to his inability to control his appetite for chips, candy, and soda. Even if he makes it to school, he finds he is unable to concentrate on his work.

Raymond's listlessness and withdrawal are countered, however, by his frequent outbursts of anger and aggression. He frequently lashes out in rage at his mother, recently punching his fist through a wall and a door at home. He also has been involved in several fights with other students at school as a result of being teased by his peers. He rarely complies with rules and limits either at home or at school, resulting in frequent conflicts with his mother and with school authorities. Finally, the event that precipitated the current referral was Raymond's arrest for shoplifting at a local store. (pp. 225–226, with changes in notation)

ANXIETY DISORDERS—AN OVERVIEW

Description

DSM-IV (American Psychiatric Association, 1994) describes 10 types of anxiety disorders in children. Following are the essential features of the anxiety disorders:

1. *Separation anxiety disorder* is characterized by excessive anxiety concerning separation from the home or from those to whom the child is attached, anxiety beyond that which is expected for the child's developmental level, and anxiety that causes clinically signifi-

cant distress or impairment in social, academic, occupational, or other important areas of functioning.

2. *Panic attack* is characterized by "a discrete period in which there is the sudden onset of intense apprehension, fearfulness, or terror, often associated with feelings of impending doom. During these attacks, symptoms such as shortness of breath, palpitations, chest pain or discomfort, choking or smothering sensations, and fear of 'going crazy' or losing control are present" (p. 393).

3. *Agoraphobia* is characterized by anxiety about being in places or situations from which escape might be difficult or embarrassing.

4. *Panic disorder* is characterized by the presence of recurrent, unexpected panic attacks, worry about the possible implications or consequences of the panic attacks, or a significant behavioral change related to the attacks.

5. *Specific phobia* is characterized by "clinically significant anxiety provoked by exposure to a specific feared object or situation, often leading to avoidance behavior" (p. 393).

6. *Social phobia* is characterized by "clinically significant anxiety provoked by exposure to certain types of social or performance situations, often leading to avoidance behavior" (p. 393).

7. *Obsessive-compulsive disorder* is characterized by "obsessions (which cause marked anxiety or distress) and/or compulsions (which serve to neutralize anxiety)" (p. 393). *Obsessions* are persistent ideas or thoughts that an individual recognizes as irrational but can't get rid of. *Compulsions* are irrational and repetitive impulses to perform some act.

8. *Posttraumatic stress disorder (PTSD)* is characterized by "the reexperiencing of an extremely traumatic event accompanied by symptoms of increased arousal and by avoidance of stimuli associated with the trauma" (p. 393).

9. *Acute stress disorder* is characterized by symptoms similar to those of posttraumatic stress disorder and covers the period immediately following an extremely traumatic event.

10. *Generalized anxiety disorder* is characterized by "at least 6 months of persistent and excessive anxiety and worry" (p. 393).

After some features of the anxiety disorders are considered, separation anxiety disorder and posttraumatic stress disorder will be discussed in more detail in the next two parts of the chapter.

Anxiety disorders are considered *internalizing disorders,* along with depressive disorders, social withdrawal, psychophysiological disorders, eating disorders, gender identity disorder, and schizoid disorders. Internalizing disorders are inner-directed (directed toward self); the symptoms are primarily associated with overcontrolled behaviors. These disorders contrast with *externalizing disorders,* such as conduct disorder, oppositional defiant disorder, attention-deficit/hyperactivity disorder, aggressive reactions, and adjustment disorder. Externalizing disorders are outer-directed (directed toward others); the symptoms are primarily associated with undercontrolled behaviors. Children with anxiety disorders also may have a diagnosis of depression, perhaps in one-third to one-half of the cases (Frick, Strauss, Lahey, & Christ, 1992).

From a developmental perspective, the major types of fears and anxiety during normal childhood development and the adult years are as follows (Reed, Carter, & Miller, 1992):

- *Birth to 6 months:* fears of excessive or unexpected sensory stimuli, loss of support, and loud noises
- *6 to 9 months:* fears of strangers and novel stimuli, such as masks and heights
- *1 year:* fears of separation, injury, or toilets
- *2 years:* fears of monsters, imaginary creatures, loss of a loved object or person, and robbers
- *3 years:* fears of dogs, large animals, and being alone
- *4 to 5 years:* fears of the dark, parental separation, and abandonment
- *6 to 12 years:* fears of school (including fears of taking tests and getting poor grades), injury, natural events, parental punishment, and rejection by peers
- *13 to 18 years:* fear of injury (especially injuries that may disfigure the body), anxiety about feelings of social alienation and rejection, and fear of the macabre
- *19 years and older:* fears of injury and natural events and anxiety about sexual issues (including personal adequacy, sexually transmitted diseases, pregnancy, having a defective child, and abortion), economic issues, moral issues, and religious issues

Among children with an obsessive-compulsive disorder, certain specific obsessions and compulsions are common (Rapoport, Swedo, & Leonard, 1992). *Obsessions* primarily center on (a) dirt, germs, or environmental toxins and (b) concerns that something terrible is going to happen, such as fire, death, or illness of self or loved ones. *Compulsions* primarily center on (a) excessive or ritualized handwashing, showering, bathing, toothbrushing, or grooming, (b) repeating rituals (such as going in or out the door or getting up from or sitting down in a chair), (c) excessive checking of things (such as doors, locks, stove, appliances, emergency brake on car, and homework), and (d) miscellaneous rituals involving writing, moving, or speaking. Chapter 1 includes part of an interview with a child who has an obsessive-compulsive disorder.

Among children with agoraphobia, common anxiety reactions include fear of open spaces or of other places, including closed spaces, low places, and underwater. What follows is a description of a woman's first experience with agoraphobia as a child (Zane & Milt, 1984).

CASE 11-4. ANN

I was on a bus, all the way in the back and it was packed. All of a sudden, I panicked. I had to get to the front, where I could breathe. But no one moved. I felt like I was lost.... After the bus incident, I didn't want to be in any crowded place because I couldn't breathe. I was afraid I wouldn't get enough oxygen, and die. I used to miss a lot of time from school so I wouldn't have to go through the halls with all the kids; I was afraid I wouldn't be able to breathe.… I went to all sorts of doctors and got all sorts of hospital tests and they all told me there was nothing wrong with me, but that didn't make me any less afraid. (pp. 84–85)

Interviewing Issues

The semistructured interview in Table F-13 in Appendix F is useful for children who may have an anxiety disorder. More specifically, Table F-12 in Appendix F is useful for children who may have an obsessive-compulsive disorder.

Following is an illustration of how an older adolescent described the onset of a panic attack (Craske & Barlow, 1993, p. 23, with changes in notation):

IR: In what situations are you most likely to panic?
IE: Crowded restaurants and when I'm driving on the freeway. But sometimes I am driving along, feeling OK, when all of a sudden it hits. And other times I can be sitting at home feeling quite relaxed and it just hits. That's when I really get scared because I can't explain it.
IR: So, when you are driving on the freeway, what is the very first thing you notice that tells you you're about to panic?
IE: Well, the other cars on the road look as if they are moving really slowly.
IR: And what is the first thing you notice when you're at home?
IE: An unreal feeling, like I'm floating.
IR: So, it sounds like the panic attacks that seem to occur for no reason are actually tied in with the sensations of unreality or when things look as if they are moving in slow motion.
IE: I guess so. I always thought the physical feelings were the panic attack, but maybe they start the panic attack.

The interview excerpt illustrates that prior to a panic attack adolescents may experience an alteration in perception and feeling, with feelings of fear and anxiety.

Interventions

Several different methods of treating anxiety disorders are available, including behavior therapy approaches, cognitive-behavioral procedures, and pharmacological treatments. The behavior therapy approach uses principles of learning to reduce anxiety: "Cognitive-behavioral approaches include a variety of procedures designed to alter perceptions, thoughts, images, and beliefs by manipulating and restructuring maladaptive cognitions" (Hagopian & Ollendick, 1993, p. 129). Pharmacological treatments include the use of anti-anxiety medications and antidepressant medications, but not all types of anxiety respond to medication (Hagopian

& Ollendick, 1993). See Barlow (1993) for more information about the treatment of anxiety disorders.

Case Illustrations

Following are four cases that describe anxiety disorders (Eisen & Kearney, 1995). Cases reflecting separation anxiety disorder and posttraumatic stress disorder can be found in the next two parts of the chapter.

CASE 11-5. LAURIE—PANIC ATTACK
Laurie was a 15-year-old white female referred for recent panic-like symptoms and avoidance of public places. Laurie reportedly began to experience hyperventilation, increased heart rate, and dizziness while driving during a practice lesson for an upcoming driving permit test. The physical changes were severe enough to force Laurie to pull over to the side of the road and wait several minutes for the symptoms to subside. She was unable to complete the lesson. Subsequently, Laurie began to avoid many methods of transportation out of fear of experiencing a similar attack and that "something terrible will happen." One month later, she experienced four panic attacks in a three-week period while riding the bus to school. Since that time, Laurie attended school only when her mother drove her there. In addition, Laurie refused to attend social gatherings due to the possibility of an embarrassing attack. Laurie's parents reported no other behavioral problems. (p. 13)

CASE 11-6. JOHN—SPECIFIC PHOBIA
John was a 13-year-old white male referred for an evaluation of fear of dogs. John reported that he was unable to approach or pet a large dog even if the animal was familiar to him. John experienced marked distress during exposure and on two recent occasions his movements were restricted because of the proximity of a dog. A recurring cognition associated with his distress was, "It will bite me and I'll get sick." John's fear of dogs could be traced to an incident three years earlier when he was attacked and bitten by a dog while retrieving a ball inadvertently thrown into a neighbor's yard. John's mother indicated that her son's fear of dogs significantly interfered with his daily activities (e.g., staying outside alone, playing sports). (p. 11)

CASE 11-7. ANDREW—SOCIAL PHOBIA
Andrew was a 12-year-old white male referred for acute school refusal behavior. Andrew had entered a new school building following his entry into seventh grade and subsequently became distressed over the presence of new classrooms, teachers, peers from other elementary schools, and a rotating class schedule. In particular, he avoided initial social interactions and disliked performing in front of others. As a result, his most distressful periods involved physical education classes, hallways, and oral presentations before classmates and teachers. He refused to go to school intermittently during the initial four weeks of the school year, after which worsening somatic complaints (i.e., headaches, stomachaches) forced him to remain home most days. Andrew's parents indicated great difficulty getting Andrew to school but no

problems in other interactions with close friends or on days when Andrew was not supposed to attend school. (p. 10)

CASE 11-8. CAROLYN—OBSESSIVE-COMPULSIVE DISORDER
Carolyn was a 16-year-old white female referred for evaluation of separation anxiety and obsessions/compulsions. Carolyn had reportedly experienced persistent and intrusive thoughts involving themes of harm to herself (e.g., going blind and deaf) and her parents (e.g., car accident, death) for the past five years. The former obsession contains elements of truth. For example, Carolyn suffered from progressive myopia that required her to strengthen her prescription lenses every few months. Her impaired hearing, which was the result of spinal meningitis during infancy, also continued to deteriorate. Situations that could potentially alter her limited visual and auditory mechanisms thus produced tremendous anxious apprehension and obsessive thoughts. Carolyn also reported that she performed compulsions to neutralize her anxiety. These involved cleanliness (e.g., organizing her room, cleaning the bathroom) and touching rituals (e.g., touching everything an even number of times). Carolyn's parents indicated that their daughter's rituals required an inordinate amount of time (i.e., two hours per day) and that her obsessions disturbed family life. (pp. 13–14)

SEPARATION ANXIETY DISORDER

Description

Separation anxiety disorder refers to developmentally inappropriate and excessive anxiety concerning separation from home or from those to whom the child is attached. Symptoms of separation anxiety disorder include excessive distress about harm to self or to attachment figures when separated from them, worry that something will happen to attachment figures, school refusal, reluctance to sleep alone or sleep away from home without the presence of an attachment figure, repeated nightmares involving themes of separation, and physical complaints and signs of distress in anticipation of separation or at the time of separation (American Psychiatric Association, 1994). The prevalence of separation anxiety disorder is estimated to be about 4% in children and young adults (American Psychiatric Association, 1994).

The onset of separation anxiety disorder typically occurs during the early and middle school years and before adolescence; symptoms vary with age. Note that "separation anxiety is a normal developmental phenomenon from approximately age 7 months to the early preschool years" (Bernstein & Borchardt, 1991, p. 520).

1. *Young school-aged children.* Young school-aged children (between 5 and 8 years) with separation anxiety disorder may worry about unrealistic harm coming to attachment figures, refuse to go to school, or have nightmares.

2. *Middle childhood–aged children.* Middle childhood–aged children (between 9 and 12 years) with separation anxiety disorder may have excessive distress at the time of separation and become withdrawn, apathetic, or sad and have difficulty concentrating.

3. *Adolescence.* During adolescence, the most frequently reported symptoms may be refusing to go to school and physical complaints.

Separation anxiety disorder "most often occurs following a major stressor, such as the start of school, death of a parent, or move to a new school or neighborhood.... The onset of [separation anxiety disorder] has been tied to developmental transition periods, such as entering kindergarten or making the change from elementary school to junior high school" (Albano, Chorpita, & Barlow, 1996, p. 217). Note that school refusal is a symptom of several possible disorders, including separation anxiety disorder and social phobia.

Interviewing Issues

You can use the semistructured interview in Table F-13 in Appendix F for children who may have a separation anxiety disorder. Allow the child's parent to be in the room with him or her while you conduct the interview if he or she is too fearful of separating from the parent.

Interventions

Behavioral interventions have been used to help children overcome school refusal (Bernstein & Borchardt, 1991). The focus is on "rearranging contingencies in the family and school environments to facilitate the child's attendance at school (e.g., child is positively reinforced for school attendance or receives negative consequences for nonattendance)" (Bernstein & Borchardt, 1991, p. 527). Cognitive therapy coupled with behavioral therapy may be used to teach children positive coping self-statements. Parents also can be taught to restructure cognitively any distorted perceptions that they may have about their children (Bernstein & Borchardt, 1991). Pharmacological treatment also has been tried, such as the use of antidepressants, but the results have been inconclusive (Bernstein & Borchardt, 1991).

Case Illustration

The following case concerns a child with a separation anxiety disorder (Ollendick & Huntzinger, 1990).

CASE 11-9. LACY
Lacy, an 8-year-old White third-grade elementary school girl, was evaluated because her parents were concerned about her fears that they might be injured and possibly die. Because of her worries, she refused to go to sleep and had thoughts of suicide. Her mother had undergone successful back surgery about seven months before the interview. Lacy has one older sister, who is 19. Her parents said that Lacy

complained frequently of headaches and stomachaches on school days, that she recently stayed home from school on at least four occasions because of her complaints, that she stopped spending weekend nights at her friends', and that she did not invite any of her friends to stay with her. Her teachers reported that she is well liked, a class leader, hard-working, and a good student.

During the interview, Lacy appeared more anxious than depressed. She fidgeted in her chair, clasped and unclasped her hands, swung her feet, bit her lips, and stammered as she spoke. She said that she was very afraid that her mother might get sick again, even though her mother had returned to work. She wondered aloud "Who will take care of her? Daddy is always at work and Sissy is at work too, you know." In talking about her nighttime fears, she said that "zombies" come into her room, that she really saw them, and that they might kill her. She also stated "I can't be happy. I used to be but not now. Even my friends don't like me now."

Lacy's primary problem appeared to center on separation anxiety. She had exaggerated and unrealistic worries that harm would come to her mother and herself and that she would be separated from her mother. She complained of physical distress on leaving for school, was reluctant to have friends over or to stay with friends, and refused to sleep alone. Furthermore, social withdrawal and depression were evident.

Weekly treatment sessions over a 13-week period consisted of relaxation training, self-instruction training, and reinforcement for sleeping in her own room. Within three weeks, Lacy was sleeping in her own bed seven nights a week and reported having much less anxiety. At six months posttreatment, the treatment gains continued, and, in addition, she no longer expressed concerns about her mother's or her own well-being and expressed positive statements about herself. (adapted from pp. 140–142)

POSTTRAUMATIC STRESS DISORDER

Description

Posttraumatic stress disorder (PTSD) is a clinical label for a traumatic reaction following any serious event or life-threatening crisis involving actual or threatened death or serious injury, such as a natural or human-induced disaster, accident, suicide, or violent crime involving child abuse (American Psychiatric Association, 1994; Eth, 1990). The reactions may affect children's cognitions, affect, and behavior. Even infants and toddlers may develop PTSD with symptoms similar to those of older children and adults, but with unique symptoms as well (Drell, Siegel, & Gaensbauer, 1993).

Following are the symptoms associated with PTSD in children:

1. *Reexperiencing the trauma.* These symptoms include "recurrent, intrusive, and markedly dysphoric memories [*dysphoric* refers to an emotional state characterized by anxiety, depression, and restlessness] and dreams of the trauma

…and traumatic play, which reenacts elements of the event in a repetitive, stereotyped, and joyless fashion" (Eth, 1990, p. 264).

2. *Psychic numbing.* These symptoms include inability to remember parts of the event, erosion of interest in life, loss of interest in school, constricted affect, interpersonal detachment, pessimism about the future, and suppression of thoughts, feelings, and actions associated with the event (Eth, 1990).

3. *Pathologic psychophysiologic arousal.* These symptoms include disorganized or agitated behavior, regressive behavior (in young children, this may be seen in loss of acquired skills such as expressive language and toileting skills), irritability, hypervigilance, exaggerated startle reactions, poor concentration, sleep disturbances, and night terrors (American Psychiatric Association, 1994; Eth, 1990).

4. *Interpersonal difficulties.* These symptoms include feelings of humiliation, feelings of being singled out, failure to trust people, fearfulness of strangers, oversensitivity, and withdrawnness (Dunne-Maxim, Dunne, & Hauser, 1987).

From a developmental standpoint, posttraumatic stress disorder has the following features (Eth, 1990, pp. 270–272, with changes in notation; also see Table 11-3):

1. *Preschool children.* They may have changes in personality, play, and fears that reflect the traumatic event; they may be particularly helpless when confronted with great danger. They may be withdrawn, subdued, or even mute and are prone to regression in the wake of a traumatic experience.

2. *School-aged children.* They may exhibit a wider range of cognitive, behavioral, and emotional responses to psychic trauma than do preschool children. They may no longer be bound to the passive role of spectators but can become participants in the traumatic event, if only in fantasy. They may display a diversity of behavioral alterations in the aftermath of trauma and, on occasion, seem both different and inconsistent.

3. *Adolescents.* They may have symptoms that resemble those of adults. Because of their access to automobiles and weapons, the combination of poor impulse control, bad judgment, and reenactment behavior can be life threatening for adolescents.

DSM-IV (American Psychiatric Association, 1994) describes three phases of PTSD: (a) *acute,* if the duration of symptoms is less than three months, (b) *chronic,* if the duration of symptoms is three months or more, and (c) *delayed onset,* if the onset of symptoms is at least six months after the stressor.

1. *Acute phase.* Children in the acute phase may have symptoms such as nightmares, distressing dreams, distress on real or symbolic exposure to the stressor, difficulty falling asleep, hypervigilance, exaggerated startle response, and generalized agitation/anxiety.

Table 11-3
Examples of Children's Reactions to Crises at Three Developmental Stages

Developmental stage	Reactions
Preschool	Thumb-sucking, bed-wetting, fears of the darkness or animals, separation and stranger anxiety, clinging to parents, whining, moaning, crying, temper tantrums, self-stimulation, night terrors and other sleeping problems, play with reenactment of traumatic theme, loss of or lapses in bladder or bowel control, loss of other previously attained skills, speech difficulties (for example, stammering), and loss of or increase in appetite
School-aged	Irritability, whining, clinging, regressive behavior, anxiety, depression, fear, lack of emotion, hypervigilance, aggressive behavior at home or school, overt competition with younger siblings for parents' attention, loss of self-esteem and self-confidence, redramatizations of event, night terrors, nightmares, fear of darkness, school avoidance, withdrawal from peers, loss of interest in school, poor concentration, intrusion of traumatic memories, fantasies of rescuing those injured in the trauma, amnesia for event, and psychophysiological symptoms (for example, stomach pains, headaches, and other bodily complaints)
Adolescent	Anger, guilt, shame, betrayal, rage, despair, poor impulse control, startle reaction, anxiety, hopelessness, helplessness, depression, constricted affect, hypervigilance, sleep disturbance, appetite disturbance, rebellion at home, refusal to do chores, loss of interest in school, loss of interest in peer social activities, amenorrhea or dysmenorrhea, agitation or decrease in energy level, apathy, decline in interest in opposite sex, irresponsible and/or delinquent behavior, loss of self-esteem and self-confidence, decline in emancipatory struggles over parental control, poor concentration, intrusion of traumatic memories (such as quick, intrusive unwelcome flashbacks), sensitivity to imperfections, amnesia for event, and psychophysiological symptoms (for example, headaches, rashes, vague aches and pains, skin eruptions, bowel problems)

Source: Adapted from Eth (1990) and Pitcher and Poland (1992).

2. *Chronic phase.* Children in the chronic phase may have symptoms such as detachment or estrangement from others, restricted range of affect, thinking life will be difficult, sadness, unhappiness, and dissociative episodes (Famularo, Kinscherff, & Fenton, 1990).

3. *Delayed-onset phase.* Children in the delayed-onset phase may have symptoms similar to those in the acute phase. The number, severity, and duration of the symptoms may be directly related to the intensity of the traumatic experience.

Now that you have read about the definition and the symptoms of PTSD, let's consider how the disorder may come about. A crisis is a state of extreme psychological discomfort and can be viewed as *"an important and seemingly unsolvable problem with which those involved feel unable to cope"* (Pitcher & Poland, 1992, p. 10). In a crisis, children may feel vulnerable, and their normal coping mechanisms may not work. It is the children's reaction to the event that defines the crisis, not the event itself (Pitcher & Poland, 1992). For example, a teenage pregnancy may create a crisis for one adolescent, but for another adolescent it may be a welcome event.

As a mental health professional, you will usually focus on the psychosocial aspects of crises. *However, in some cri-* *ses, it is far more important that you first evaluate children's and families' basic needs—such as the needs for food, shelter, clothing, and medical treatment—and then help them obtain the needed services.* After these needs have been met, you can then focus on their need for psychosocial services. It will be difficult to provide psychosocial services when children and families lack the necessities of living or when they need immediate medical care.

Extrafamilial and intrafamilial crises. Crises can be either extrafamilial or intrafamilial.

Extrafamilial crises are associated with major hazardous events that happen outside the family and that are not under the family's control (Steele & Raider, 1991). Examples are war, terroristic activity, economic recession, violence, kidnapping, natural disasters (such as hurricanes, tornadoes, fires, earthquakes, and floods), and people-made disasters (such as plane crashes, mine disasters, and shipwrecks). A parent's loss of a job is a more individual type of extrafamilial crisis. Extrafamilial crises usually are sudden, with the stresses shared by the community. The reactions usually last between six and seven weeks, although sometimes adverse reactions—such as sleep problems, depression, anxiety, recurrent memories, loss of energy, and somatic disturbances—may last for several months or even years.

"*Intrafamilial crises* are those events that take place within the family, such as physical abuse, sexual abuse, abandonment, substance abuse, suicide, teen pregnancy, or divorce" (Steele & Raider, 1991, p. 32, with changes in notation). Intrafamilial crises usually emerge gradually, with the stresses shared among the family members primarily, and may last a long time, depending on the child, the family, and the type of crisis.

In both types of crises, children may wonder "What happened? Why did it happen? [Is it my fault?] Why did I act as I did then and since? Will I be okay if it happens again?" (Figley, 1983, p. 13).

Extrafamilial crises further explored. Stresses associated with extrafamilial crises are different from those associated with ordinary life transitions. The following attributes apply to victims of extrafamilial crises (McCubbin & Figley, 1983).

- They usually have little or no time to prepare—the onset is sudden, without warning.
- They usually fail to plan and rehearse a survival strategy because the event occurs without anticipation.
- They usually have limited experiences with extrafamilial crises to draw upon for guidance and strength.
- They usually have few sources of guidance to help them cope with the stress.
- They sometimes feel estranged from others because they believe that others cannot understand their experiences.
- They often have adverse reactions that are more intense than reactions to ordinary crises or stresses.
- They sometimes feel a sense of loss of control and feel totally helpless.
- They sometimes experience acute and chronic emotional problems, including "sleep disorders, social isolation and conflict, depression, distorted perceptions of self and others, phobia, paranoia, sexual dysfunction, and other potentially impairing reactions" (p. 226).
- They sometimes are left with lasting changes in their personalities.
- They sometimes experience medical problems—such as headaches, hypertension, heart disease, asthma, skin disorders, and influenza.

Victims of extrafamilial crises may feel extreme discomfort and powerlessness because their existence has been disrupted and because they barely had any influence on the occurrence of the event. Acts of war, natural disasters, horrendous accidents, and sudden deaths may be so overwhelming that individuals feel completely helpless (Kleber, Brom, & Defares, 1992).

Children may be traumatized not only by directly experiencing a traumatic event but also by observing the event (Lyons, 1988). Unfortunately, parents may not always recognize this and may downplay the effects that witnessing traumatic events has had on their children.

Following is an example of one family's experience immediately after an extrafamilial crisis (Smith, 1983).

CASE 11-10. THE FLORES FAMILY

It was all gone. In less than 40 seconds a killer tornado had completely destroyed a home the Flores family had built and lived in for 18 years. But they were unharmed; they had sufficient insurance (they thought), and the neighbors, friends and family would pitch in. That was for later. Now they had to think about salvaging a lifetime's belongings. Everywhere they looked were personal belongings—photographs, clothing, a matchbook from a local restaurant, pieces of furniture. It was the first house Ramon and Mary had owned and the only one their children, Bennie and Sue, ever knew. Eighteen years of memories were strewn everywhere for neighbors and insensitive sightseers to see. They would gather the most important items together in plastic garbage bags and store them in a neighbor's garage. And only then would they seek refuge at the National Guard Armory set up by the Red Cross for survivors who were displaced by the freak May storm.

The four huddled together with their ration of food, clothing, and bedding. Slowly they met and talked with other survivors—first with those they knew, then with total strangers. But very shortly they would be friends for life: fellow survivors. (pp. 120–121)

Coping with an extrafamilial or intrafamilial crisis. Children in either an extrafamilial or an intrafamilial crisis may go through four phases (Pitcher & Poland, 1992):

1. *Impact phase.* The child may experience shock, trauma, heightened affect, confusion, and other symptoms.

2. *Recoil phase.* As the immediate crisis passes, reactions set in that may include fearfulness, denial, and anger.

3. *Resolution or adjustment phase.* The child begins to get over the aversive emotional reactions.

4. *Postcrisis functioning level phase.* The child begins to adjust to the crisis and the changes it may have brought. Occasionally, this adjustment takes several months or even years.

Children may be unable to cope with a crisis when they have the following characteristics (Pitcher & Poland, 1992):

1. They deny or ignore the crisis, hoping it will go away.
2. They are overwhelmed by the crisis, and the stress depletes their resources.
3. They are unable to cope with the new demands created by the crisis because the crisis exacerbates prior unresolved difficulties.
4. They have inadequate or underdeveloped capabilities and resources to meet the demands of the crisis.
5. They make changes that lead to further difficulties.

Children who can quickly master crises or who are resilient to crises may have the following characteristics (Pitcher & Poland, 1992):

1. They prepare for the crisis (when forewarned) and deal with it when it comes.

2. They have active, socially engaging, and autonomous personalities that can deal with crises.
3. They have family members who offer genuine support and emotional closeness.
4. They have good peer and extrafamilial support, such as support from friends, teachers, clergy, or neighbors.
5. They have problem-solving skills, physical and emotional health, adaptive personality traits, and good coping skills.

In a crisis, children usually have difficulty continuing with normal daily living routines and often feel tense and panic stricken. Rationally working through the problem may not be possible. Note, however, that children's symptoms in a crisis reflect their reactions to situational stress; the symptoms usually do not reflect long-standing psychological difficulties (Pitcher & Poland, 1992).

Both extrafamilial crises and intrafamilial crises often result in changes in the family. Families that thought they were invulnerable now may see themselves as vulnerable. They may see the world as a threatening place and feel guilty for not having avoided the crisis or for not having been better prepared. If one member of the family is suffering greatly, other members may suffer as well. Because of the crisis, several things may happen to the family. The members' roles may change, members may avoid responsibilities, or members may begin to use or increase their use of alcohol and other drugs, for example (Craine, Hanks, & Stevens, 1992). Sometimes, family members have difficulty accepting available services, such as those offered by social service agencies, the Red Cross, mental health clinics, or individual mental health clinicians.

Families successful in coping with crises may use some of the following strategies (McCubbin & Patterson, 1983):

1. The family will coordinate efforts among its members.
2. The family members will pull together to cope with the crisis by trying to meet each other's needs and by using the resources of each member.
3. The family will accept its circumstances realistically and will accept less than a perfect solution.
4. The family will try to maintain the morale and self-esteem of its members during the stressful periods, especially by helping its members understand that the family is worth saving.

Children will be affected by the reactions of others around them and, in particular, by the reactions of other family members. Children may pick up other members' feelings of uncertainty, anxiety, and grief. Family members' reactions can either smooth or exacerbate children's reactions to a crisis. If the other family members break down and must be consoled, children are likely to experience additional anxiety and stress. If the family members exhibit their stress but are still able to console the children, the children will feel more secure. Adult members of the family should not huddle together in a way that signifies that they do not want the children to hear what they are talking about; doing so only will cause the children to become more anxious. Preferably, older family members should not talk to each other about deeply disturbing negative feelings about the crisis when children are present.

Interviewing Issues

The following guidelines for an initial crisis interview will help you interview a child who may be experiencing an extrafamilial or intrafamilial crisis (Adams, 1991; Pitcher & Poland, 1992). To carry out some of the suggestions, you may need more than one interview.

1. *Determine whether the child is in a crisis.* Determine whether the child is experiencing a crisis by reviewing the referral information and by examining the child's specific dysfunctions and symptomatology, including the nature and severity of the child's symptoms and the ability of the child to carry out routine tasks, such as going to school. Evaluate whether the child is at risk for suicide (see Chapter 13). Also consider the precipitating events that may have led to the crisis. If you decide that the child is in a crisis, carry out the guidelines that follow.

2. *Determine whether the child is in danger.* Consider whether there are any threats to the child's safety. If so, take the steps needed to ensure the safety of the child.

3. *Determine the meaning of the event for the child.* Ask the child how she or he perceives the event, and then evaluate whether the child's perceptions are realistic.

4. *Determine how the child copes with the crisis.* Learn about how the child is coping with the crisis and evaluate whether the coping patterns are maladaptive or adaptive.

5. *Determine affective connections to the child's experiences.* Evaluate how the child's feelings generated by the crisis relate to her or his prior experiences. Look for possible unresolved feelings about matters that the crisis may have brought to the surface.

6. *Determine the relevant past coping resources of the child.* Ask the child how she or he coped with past crises to estimate how the child may cope with the present crisis.

7. *Determine the family's support of the child.* Learn about how the child feels about her or his family and whether the family can help the child.

8. *Determine the family's coping resources.* Learn about how the family is coping with the crisis and how the family's coping ability affects the child's coping ability.

9. *Determine the help wanted and needed by the child and family.* Consider what help the child wants, what help the child needs, whether the child is ready to receive help, how treatment may help the child, what help the family wants for the child and for itself, and what the family's resources are.

Table F-23 in Appendix F presents a semistructured interview for a child who is experiencing either an extrafamilial or an intrafamilial crisis. Table 11-4 presents a useful PTSD symptom checklist that you can complete after the interview. The checklist simply is a way to record what you learn in the interview; it has not been standardized or normed.

If you are observing the child in a play situation (see Table 3-3 in Chapter 3), especially attend to any indications of behavior "typically associated with trauma, such as evidence of intrusive imagery, repetitive play enactments, avoidance of certain play materials or themes, constriction of mood, and the like" (Drell et al., 1993, p. 299). The case of Anna in Chapter 4 illustrates an intrafamilial crisis interview. For further information about crisis interviewing, see Haley (1987), Pitcher and Poland (1992), and Steele and Raider (1991).

In evaluating a child who is in a crisis, consider everything going on in the child's and the family's life, not just the crisis alone (see Table 11-5). The crisis, for example, may lead to additional stressors, such as parental separation or divorce, financial hardships, foster placement, family relocation, and changed alliances within the family. The crisis also may be embedded in a long series of family stressors (Lyons, 1987).

Interventions

In developing interventions for a child in a crisis, consider the following (Green, Korol, Grace, Vary, Leonard, Gleser, & Smitson-Cohen, 1991):

- *characteristics of the stressor* (for example, extrafamilial or intrafamilial, life threatening, type and degree of loss, physical disruptions, and crisis stage)
- *individual characteristics of the child* (for example, age, sex, coping style, intelligence, temperament, personality, adjustment, and cognitive style)
- *familial characteristics* (for example, reactions of other family members to the crisis and to the child and family support for the child)
- *environmental characteristics* (for example, child's peer support and school support systems and any other support systems)

Initially, instead of conducting a standard clinical assessment interview with a child in a crisis, you may have to deal with the immediate effects of the crisis. For example, if the child is in an acute crisis, you will want to reduce the child's anxiety or panic feelings and prevent withdrawal and isola-

---

Table 11-4
PTSD Symptom Checklist

Name _____ Date _____

Sex _____ Age _____ Interviewer's name _____

☐ 1. Is afraid when thinks of event	☐ 12. Feels alone	☐ 27. Withdraws from peers
☐ 2. Is tense or upset in response to reminders of event	☐ 13. Dreams of event	☐ 28. Engages in self-injurious behavior
☐ 3. Sees intrusive images and hears sounds of event	☐ 14. Has bad dreams	☐ 29. Has suicidal tendencies
☐ 4. Avoids reminders of event	☐ 15. Has disturbed sleep	☐ 30. Has death fantasies
☐ 5. Has decreased interest in activities	☐ 16. Has nightmares	☐ 31. Has lessened interest in play or other usually enjoyable activities
☐ 6. Avoids knowing own feelings	☐ 17. Feels guilty	
☐ 7. Fears repeat of event	☐ 18. Is enuretic	☐ 32. Feels distant from parents or friends
☐ 8. Has reduced impulse control	☐ 19. Has difficulty paying attention	
☐ 9. Has intrusive thoughts about event	☐ 20. Has somatic complaints	☐ 33. Shows anxious attachment behavior
	☐ 21. Is too upset to talk or cry	☐ 34. Shows general mistrust of others
☐ 10. Is more jumpy or nervous (startles easily)	☐ 22. Has thoughts of event that interfere with learning	
	☐ 23. Fears for personal survival	☐ 35. Other _____
☐ 11. Shows little affect	☐ 24. Has separation anxiety	_____
	☐ 25. Is hyperactive	
	☐ 26. Is depressed	

Child's level of anxiety during the interview, on a continuum from (1) no anxiety during interview to (5) severe anxiety during interview: 1 2 3 4 5
Child's level of depression during the interview, on a continuum from (1) no depression during interview to (5) severe depression during interview: 1 2 3 4 5

Source: Adapted from Pynoos and Nader (1989) and Steele and Raider (1991).

Table 11-5
Evaluating the Interview Findings in Cases of Crises

1. How long after the crisis is the interview being held?
2. What was the crisis?
3. Did the crisis have a sudden or gradual impact?
4. How does the family understand the crisis?
5. What role did each family member have in the crisis?
6. How have the individual family members' roles within the family changed since the crisis?
7. How has the crisis changed the family, including their life style, schedules, and place of residence?
8. Which members of the family were affected by the crisis?
9. Was the child directly or indirectly involved in the crisis?
10. How well does the child remember the crisis?
11. What symptoms or problems does the child have?
12. How does the family view the child's adjustment?
13. How do the family members view their problems?
14. Is there more tension in the family than before the crisis?
15. Are there more arguments and fights in the family than before the crisis?
16. Do the family members use drugs or alcohol more than they did before the crisis?
17. Do the family members have problems that they didn't have before the crisis, such as sleeplessness, hypertension, headaches, skin disorders, colds, sexual dysfunctions, distorted perceptions of self and others, phobias, or paranoia?
18. Do the family members have a sense of loss of control or feelings of helplessness?
19. Does the family provide support for its members, such as love, affection, comfort, and sympathy? If so, how are these expressed?
20. Does the family provide encouragement to its members, such as praise and positive statements?
21. Does the family provide advice to its members to help solve problems?
22. Does the family provide companionship to the child, such as spending time with the child and participating in activities with the child?
23. Does the family provide direction, guidance, support, and tangible aid to the child, such as helping the child with homework, money, needed transportation, and leisure activities?
24. Are the family members affectionate, warm, willing to communicate, able to recognize conflict, and involved in decision making, taking into account each member's ability?
25. Do the family members accept responsibility?
26. Do the parents and child have a healthy relationship, such as open communication, trust in each other, and willingness to discuss conflicts?
27. Do the family members believe that they can solve the crisis?
28. What help does the family need?
29. Are the family members willing to ask for help?

tion. Focus on the child's recent traumatic experiences, the normalcy of his or her reactions, and the expectation that the child will resume her or his usual roles soon (Vernberg & Vogel, 1993). You will need to help the child (and family) devise a plan for handling the crisis, emphasizing the steps needed, the services available, and how to reduce the potential for dangerous or self-destructive behavior (Steele & Raider, 1991). How you go about developing the interventions will depend on the child's developmental level.

Consider interventions that build on the family's strengths and reduce its vulnerabilities, such as helping the family improve its communication skills and group problem-solving skills, helping parents support each other and their children, and helping the family accept changes and develop ways of coping with the altered situational demands (Craine et al., 1992). Mental health professionals should be available following disasters to help parents "to understand and meet their children's needs and to establish relationships directly with the child victims and survivors" (Gudas, 1993, p. 81). Exhibit 11-1 presents guidelines that you can give to parents to help them cope with a child who is in a crisis.

Here are some strategies that you can use for short-term interventions designed to facilitate children's adaptive coping.

1. *Accepting the situation.* Share with the child what you know about his or her coping style, affect, and skills in interpersonal relations and how these traits relate to the present crisis. Be as simple and as clear as possible in your presentation. Help the child accept the events that have occurred. Offer young children more environmental support and structure than you would offer older ones (Pitcher & Poland, 1992).

2. *Working through feelings.* Help the child identify, label, and express emotions appropriately. Then help the child work through feelings of anxiety, fear, worry, self-blame, guilt, helplessness, and similar emotions. Some children will recognize the cognitive aspects of the crisis but be unable to deal with the affective ones. In such cases, they will need help in accepting the "painful emotions evoked by past experiences, as well as those related to the current situation" (Adams, 1991, p. 118). Reassure the child that he or she was not to blame for the disaster. Tell preschool children, for example, that they did not start the earthquake by stomping on the ground; reassure teenagers that they used good judgment in not attempting to attack the assailant (Gillis, 1993).

3. *Evaluating the situation.* Help the child realistically evaluate his or her situation, explore alternative methods of coping with the situation, understand that strong emotional reactions are normal in such crises, regain a sense of mastery and control, and establish realistic goals for the near future (Pitcher & Poland, 1992). You can help mobilize the child's coping resources by supporting his or her efforts to resolve the crisis (Adams, 1991). Find out what social supports are available to the child. Encourage an older child (or adolescent) to seek support from friends, self-help groups,

Exhibit 11-1
Parental Guidelines for Helping a Child in a Crisis or a Disaster

HELPING YOUR CHILD IN A CRISIS

Children who have experienced a crisis or a disaster may have problems. The following information is designed to help you with your children who may be having problems.

Introduction

Disasters strike quickly and without warning. These events can be traumatic for adults, but they are frightening for children if they don't know what to do.

During a disaster, children may have to leave their homes and change their daily routines. They may become anxious, confused, or frightened. As an adult, you'll need to cope with the disaster and also give your children crucial guidance about how to respond.

Children depend on daily routines: They wake up, eat breakfast, go to school, and play with friends. When emergencies or disasters interrupt this routine, children become anxious.

In a disaster, they'll look to you and other adults for help. How you react to an emergency gives them clues about how to act. If you react with alarm, a child may become more scared. They see your fear as proof that the danger is real.

Children's fears also may stem from their imagination, and you should take these feelings seriously. A child who *feels* afraid *is* afraid. Your words and actions can provide reassurance.

Feelings of fear are healthy and natural for adults and children. But, as an adult, you need to keep control of the situation. When you're sure that danger has passed, concentrate on your child's emotional needs by asking the child to explain what's troubling her or him. Your response during this "problem time" may have a lasting impact.

General Suggestions

1. Think of your child as a normal child who has experienced great stress.

2. Listen carefully to what your child tells you.

3. Let your child know that you are interested in her or him and want to help.

4. Talk to your child about what has happened, and provide as much information as you think she or he can understand. This will be helpful because children are fearful when they do not understand what is happening around them.

5. Encourage your child to ask questions; then answer honestly.

6. Check with your child to make sure that she or he understands what you are saying and that you understand what she or he is saying. You can do this, for example, by asking your child to repeat what you said.

7. Praise your child when she or he does something positive for herself or himself or for someone else.

8. Relax some family rules, and allow your child to do more "babyish" things if she or he needs to.

9. Explain to your child that adults also feel pain and show it in their own way, if your child wonders why you (or other adults) have been showing your frustration by crying or banging fists, for example.

10. Promise only what you can do.

11. Reassure your child by your words and by your actions that things will work out. Be prepared to do this again and again.

Dealing with Problems

12. Accept your child's fears as very real to her or him. Fear is a common reaction to a disaster. Your child may have fears about another disaster coming, about someone being injured or killed, and about being separated from the family and being left alone.

13. Recognize that if your child shows excessive clinging and doesn't want to leave you, it might mean that she or he fears being separated from you. Once the threat of danger has gone, this fear should diminish.

14. Develop a familiar bedtime routine, and plan some calming, prebedtime activity if your child has trouble falling asleep. You also can do the following: Allow your child to sleep on a mattress in your room if she or he asks to do so, but set a time limit on this arrangement. Or, at bedtime, plan to spend more time with your child in her or his bedroom, or leave a night light on, or leave the door ajar, or do anything else that will comfort your child. Sleep disturbances are among the most common problems that children have after a crisis

or a disaster. By following the above suggestions, you may diminish your child's problems associated with going to sleep.

15. Reassure your child that she or he was not to blame if someone close to your child died, such as a parent or other close relative. Sometimes children think that what they did or thought might have caused someone to die.

16. Tolerate your child's asking questions about a loss over and over again if she or he has lost, for example, a relative, a pet, property, valuables, or a treasured sentimental object. This is your child's way of adapting to the loss.

17. Take seriously any feelings that your child expresses, especially those conveying helplessness, hopelessness, or worthlessness. If your child expresses these feelings and also shows signs of withdrawal, loss of interest, agitation, sleep disturbance, loss of appetite, or poor judgment or expresses thoughts of suicide, seek professional help.

18. Also seek professional help if your child shows signs of extreme confusion, such as being disoriented, being extremely agitated, or appearing out of control.

Keeping Routines Normal and Encouraging Your Child to Be Active

19. Make every effort to allow your family to remain together—your child needs all the support and comfort she or he can get. When your child sees you act with strength and calmness, she or he will see that it is possible to act courageously, even in times of stress and fear.

20. Encourage your child to go to school, even if she or he doesn't want to. School is a major source of activity, guidance, direction, and structure for your child.

21. Encourage your adolescent to participate in community activities, such as clean-up activities after a disaster, helping elderly people, or babysitting for families. These activities will help her or him feel a sense of belonging.

Requesting Help

If you need more help, contact:

_____

at the following number: _____

Source: Adapted from Farberow and Gordon (1981) and Federal Emergency Management Agency (1992).

and other social or religious groups. Ask the child to review what he or she has learned during the interview(s).

4. *Resuming normal activities.* Encourage the child to resume normal activities as soon as possible. This will help the child establish routines and give the child a sense of connection with his or her precrisis way of life (Vernberg & Vogel, 1993).

5. *Joining a support group.* Encourage the child to join a group composed of other children who experienced the crisis or who witnessed the traumatic event, particularly during the impact phase of an extrafamilial crises. The focus of the group should be on ventilation, acknowledging feelings, and providing information about the disaster (Vernberg & Vogel, 1993). Ideally, the group leader should want to learn how each individual in the group copes with the crisis and how to help him or her prepare better for future crises.

Case Illustrations

Let's now turn to several cases that describe the reactions of children to various types of crises. The first case concerns an acute episode of PTSD (Jones & Peterson, 1993).

CASE 11-11. TERESA

The 3-year-old daughter of a recently immigrated Spanish-speaking family was riding with her father in their car and was buckled into her car seat in the right rear seat. As the father drove through a residential intersection, the car was struck on the left side by a large truck. The child was the first to see the truck approaching and screamed to her father, "Watch out!" but the father did not see the truck until impact. The left side of the car was destroyed, and the father sustained bruised ribs and a dislocated vertebra. The child was covered with shattered glass and debris but sustained no physical injuries and was therefore not evaluated medically at the time of the accident.

After the accident, the child experienced nightmares every 3 or 4 nights and would repeatedly scream "Watch out!" until she was awakened and consoled. In an awake state, the child would cry and tremble whenever she saw large trucks, cars, or motorcycles. She demonstrated reluctance to get into a car, especially when required to sit in the right rear seat. She would often tell her father to drive carefully. When a television program contained car chases or violence, the child would immediately ask her parents to change the channel. The parents also noted that the child's play was more violent: she would occasionally run at her 5-year-old sister and hit her repeatedly. She had never exhibited these behaviors prior to the accident. These symptoms had persisted for 28 days before the parents sought help. (p. 223)

The next four cases illustrate how crisis interviews helped families resolve children's immediate behavioral problems (Farberow & Gordon, 1981, pp. 33–35, with changes in notation).

CASE 11-12. THE H. FAMILY

The H. family—a mother, a father, and an 8-year-old daughter—was awakened at 6 a.m. by an earthquake violently shaking their home. The mother had difficulty reaching her daughter because of a large bookcase that had fallen across the threshold to the child's room. Fortunately, the home received only minor damage. However, problems appeared a few days later when the child refused to return to her room for fear of being trapped there. The mother began to suffer severe headaches. In reaction to her daughter's fears, she was not allowing her out of her sight. The father, a police officer, had to go on duty for several days and was unavailable to the family during the first several days following the quake.

Mrs. H. called the crisis line and was invited to come to the crisis center to talk about her own and her daughter's fears. She felt reassured when told that her child's fears would diminish as time went on. She was advised to let her daughter sleep with her or in a sleeping bag in a nearby room for a while and to give her much warmth and attention. Mrs. H. also was able to become more permissive with her daughter, once her own fears for the child's safety were alleviated by discussing them. She was interviewed with her husband and was able to express her anger and frustration at being "abandoned" by him because of his work responsibility. Mr. H. had found himself under additional stress when family needs came into conflict with his job responsibility. Mrs. H. was encouraged to seek more actively the comfort of the community support system of family and friends in order to reduce her feelings of isolation and abandonment.

CASE 11-13. LORRAINE

Ms. Jones, mother of an 18-month-old daughter, called the crisis line for advice. The family had been evacuated in a flood and had just returned home. Her baby was clinging to her and refusing to sleep in her crib. Ms. Jones was advised to stay with the toddler for longer periods at bedtime and to be comforting to her. Moving the crib to another wall in the same room also helped. Understanding that the baby's reaction was "normal" was reassuring to the mother.

CASE 11-14. JOAN

Eight-year-old Joan refused to return to school after a tornado had devastated a nearby area. Her mother, Mrs. P., was reluctant to force her to go because she might cry in school. Mrs. P. was encouraged to volunteer at the school for a few days. Joan's refusal behavior stopped in a few days. Her mother was helped by being advised about how to be firm and at the same time to be supportive to the child. She was encouraged to recognize and accept Joan's fears and to share her own with her daughter. As the mother learned to feel secure in separating from her daughter, her child's fears lessened and disappeared.

CASE 11-15. TODD

The mother of Todd, a deaf boy, told a social worker that her son was showing regressive behavior since a tornado had forced the family to evacuate their home. Todd seemed confused and unable to stay in one place. He did not seem to understand why his family had moved and what had caused the destruction around him. The family was urging a housing advisor to return them to their former home or at least to the same neighborhood because Todd needed a more familiar routine and environment. A mental health consultant was called in to help. She explained to the family and the housing advisor the psychological reasons for the child's reaction. She also devised a plan that included providing the boy with an explanation of the events of the tornado, what a tornado is, and how the family planned to resume its normal life. The parents were advised that their son's needs for attention at this time were greater than usual; that this was a transitory situation. Once Todd's fears were alleviated by parental support, his regressive behavior was reduced.

DISSOCIATIVE IDENTITY DISORDER

(This part of the chapter was co-authored with Maria Arrigo.)

Description

Dissociative identity disorder (formerly called *multiple personality disorder* or *MPD*) is one of four principal types of dissociative disorders. The common theme of the dissociative disorders is an alteration in the normal, integrated functions of a person's identity, memory, or consciousness. Dissociative identity disorder is a condition in which the individual develops two or more distinct identities or personality states that recurrently take control of his or her behavior. There is usually a primary or main personality, which is the name the person goes by. In the other personality states, the individual is unable to recall important personal information, which cannot be explained by ordinary forgetfulness or by direct physiological effects of a substance or a medical condition (American Psychiatric Association, 1994). *Dissociative identity disorder cannot be attributed to children simply because they have imaginary playmates or engage in fantasy play.*

A second dissociative disorder is *depersonalization disorder,* a condition in which the individual loses a sense of reality and feels estranged from the self and perhaps separated from the body. A third dissociative disorder is *dissociative amnesia,* a condition in which the individual has memory loss of psychological origin. It may occur as a reaction to an intolerable traumatic situation in which there is a loss of memory for devastating personal information. A fourth dissociative disorder is *dissociative fugue,* a condition in which the individual not only is amnesic but also wanders away from home, often assuming a completely new identity.

Let's now focus on dissociative identity disorder, which is the most severe of the dissociative disorders. The distinct personalities of individuals with a dissociative identity disorder are called *alters,* which is short for "alternative personalities." Each alter is individually complex and has its own unique behavior and social relationships. Frequently, alters are not aware of the existence or activities of the other alters. The transition from one alter to another is often precipitated by stress, by feelings of impending danger, or by some identifiable social or environmental cue. Different alters may govern the person's behavior in different situations. For instance, the child with a dissociative identity disorder who spends nights locked in an automobile trunk but attends school during the day may have alters that help him or her adapt to the extreme environments.

DSM-IV provides no special criteria for diagnosing dissociative identity disorder in children. Clinicians have noted that many children with dissociative identity disorder do not clearly meet the adult criteria of two or more distinct alters that repeatedly take full control of the individual's behavior. Nevertheless, classical dissociative identity disorder has been documented in children as young as 3 years of age (Riley & Mead, 1988). The main features of childhood dissociative identity disorder are as follows (Peterson, 1991, p. 6, with changes in notation):

1. recurrent amnesic periods or missing blocks of time
2. frequent trance-like states or appearing to be in a daze
3. major fluctuations in behavior, which may include dramatic changes in school or work performance or variations in apparent social, cognitive, or physical abilities

Peterson and Putnam (1994) have proposed that the following criteria—which differ from those used in *DSM-IV*—be used for the diagnosis of dissociative disorder of childhood (p. 213, with changes in notation and permission):

A. A disturbance of at least six months during which either one or two of the following are present:
  1. Recurrent amnesic periods or missing blocks of time
  2. Frequent trance-like states or appearing to be in a daze or in another world
B. Perplexing, major fluctuations in behavior, which include at least two of the following:
  1. Dramatic fluctuations in school or work performance and behavior
  2. Variations in apparent social, cognitive, or physical abilities
  3. Sudden, recurrent shifts in friendship patterns
  4. Changes in language, accent, and voice tone
  5. Perplexing changes in preferences for clothes, food, toys, games, etc.
C. At least three of the following:
  1. Refers to self in third person or uses another name to refer to self or parts
  2. Has vivid imaginary companionship
  3. Frequently disavows observed behavior
  4. Exhibits frequent inappropriate sexual behaviors or is sexually precocious
  5. Has intermittent depression
  6. Has auditory hallucinations from inside the head
  7. Has frequent sleep problems
  8. Exhibits unprovoked explosive anger and violent behavior
  9. Exhibits other antisocial behaviors

Prevalence. An increase in reported cases of childhood dissociative identity disorder has followed advances in the field of dissociative disorders and closer monitoring of child maltreatment; however, the prevalence of children with dissociative identity disorder in the general population is unknown. One children's inpatient unit at a large metropolitan hospital has reported an incidence of 3% of cases of dissociative identity disorder and 2% of other dissociative disorders over a three-year period (Hornstein & Tyson, 1991). All these children had been severely maltreated, and over 60% of those with dissociative identity disorder had been removed from their homes because of the maltreatment. Adult psychiatric units have reported slightly higher percentages of individuals with dissociative identity disorder (Ross, Anderson, Fleisher, & Norton, 1991).

Dissociative experiences in normal childhood.

Dissociative experiences are common in normal childhood development. They include playing with imaginary companions and ascribing intentions to inanimate objects. For example, the 6-year-old cartoon character Calvin, of *Calvin and Hobbes,* calls to life his stuffed toy tiger, Hobbes, to accompany him on intergalactic adventures. In adolescence, common dissociative experiences are deep absorption in a novel, obliviousness to calls to the dinner table, and unconcern with pain during athletic competition. Stronger forms of dissociation are a sense of unreality in a dangerous situation or amnesia for a car accident or injury. In extreme cases of dissociation, there may be no recall of a parent's death or of a pregnancy. Dissociative experiences usually peak at 9 or 10 years of age and decline through adolescence and adulthood (Putnam, 1991).

Conditions that may lead to a dissociative identity disorder.

In Western society, children with a dissociative identity disorder typically are victims of chronic and severe sexual abuse or physical abuse within the family (Ross, 1989). In a vast majority of cases, dissociative identity disorder "appears to be a response to a chronic trauma originating during a vulnerable period in childhood" (Ross, Miller, Bjornson, Reagor, Fraser, & Anderson, 1991, p. 97). Less common causes are long-term medical/surgical trauma, exposure to deaths of family members, cultural dislocation, and the carnage of war. Large-scale clinical studies indicate that chronic and severe child maltreatment is a primary cause in about 97% of cases of dissociative identity disorder (Kluft, 1987).

Infants and small children are relatively helpless in coping with trauma. They cannot, for example, run away or seek help. Dissociation is a major self-protective mechanism available to them (Yates & Musty, 1993). An adaptive response to an extremely painful event, dissociation temporarily changes the normal processes of encoding memory so that knowledge of the traumatic event is dissociated from everyday consciousness. For ongoing trauma, alter personalities may organize around the memories and situational demands of the traumatic event (Whitman & Munkel, 1991).

CASE 11-16. BEN

Consider the predicament of a 2-year-old boy, Ben, whose mother sometimes lovingly nurtures him and sometimes suffocates him to the point of unconsciousness. If this toddler rejects his mother, he rejects also the source of food and care. Instead he may develop three alters: one alter has no memory of punishment and is warmly responsive to the nurturing mother; another alter is stoically mute and rigid under torture, enduring the terror; and another alter shows angry and vengeful behavior in periods of safety.

If the parents (or other caregivers) are not responsible for the trauma to the child—as in natural disasters, sexual abuse outside the family, or long-term illness—then the child ordinarily does not require different alters ignorant of each other to cope with the trauma. The parents of a child with life-threatening asthma, for example, help the child integrate her or his knowledge of the asthmatic attacks with other life experiences. The parents teach the child to watch for warning signs, and they notify babysitters and teachers of the child's medical condition. Outsiders acknowledge the child's affliction and respond appropriately.

CASE 11-17. MELISSA

In contrast to Ben's case (Case 11-16), consider the case of 9-year-old Melissa, whose father has pimped for her at truckstops for five years. Her father conceals his actions by threatening Melissa to maintain secrecy and by treating her as a princess among his business associates. This environment is likely to help the girl dissociate. To be safe, she has no awareness of her conflicting roles. The many perpetrators and witnesses who disregard the girl's plight reinforce her adaptive amnesia between alters.

Certainly, not all severely traumatized children dissociate. Children are more likely to develop a dissociative identity disorder when a parent or another primary caregiver uses unusually severe forms of treatment that have a bizarre and sadistic tone (Whitman & Munkel, 1991).

Manifestations of dissociative identity disorder.

Let's now look at the distinctiveness of alters; the subjective ages of alters; gender, promiscuity, and aggression of alters; and the social competence of alters.

Distinctiveness of alters. During early and middle childhood, a diagnosis of dissociative identity disorder is difficult because normal children also have dissociative experiences. The different alters of children with dissociative identity disorder may be indistinct to those who do not observe the children during traumatic episodes. Young children with dissociative identity disorder have less freedom and fewer resources than do adolescents for expressing themselves— less accessibility to clothes, friends, and activities. The alters of adolescents with dissociative identity disorder become more distinctive, as do the single personalities of normal adolescents (Putnam, Guroff, Silberman, Barban, & Post, 1986).

Some alters are fully elaborated, with well-developed talents, responsibilities, and personal relationships and with distinct names. Other alters may be fragmentary, with a limited range of memory, affect, and function—such as the bleak, silent alter of the child that emerges when his mother locks him in a car trunk as a way of babysitting. Generally, the number of distinct personalities increases with the duration, severity, and variety of traumatic situations (Putnam et al., 1986).

Alters are often completely unaware of each other, but sometimes they may be protective of other alters who may not be aware of them. For example, the "truckstop prostitute" alter of Melissa (Case 11-17) may diligently protect the school-girl alter from knowledge of the maltreatment, while the school-girl alter is oblivious to the alter who is a prostitute. Less commonly, alters may be mutually aware of each other or possibly "co-conscious."

Subjective ages of alters.   Alters range in age from infancy to ages older than the child's chronological age. Each alter displays developmental characteristics congruent with her or his subjective age. For example, a 9-year-old may thumb-suck or scribble in a toddler personality while experiencing an alter. Usually, at least one personality alter has a subjective age much younger than the child's biological age (Lowenstein & Putman, 1990).

Gender, promiscuity, and aggression of alters.   Children with a dissociative identity disorder commonly have alters of both genders; some alters may be homosexual, while others may be heterosexual. Male alters in biological females often serve as "bodyguards" or result from identifying with a male perpetrator (Bloch, 1991). Adolescents with a dissociative identity disorder typically have promiscuous, delinquent, or criminally aggressive alters of whom the other alters are unaware (Kluft, 1985; Van der Hart, Faure, Van Gerven, & Goodwin, 1991). The following case of a 16-year-old boy who was arrested for setting fires illustrates these points.

CASE 11-18. FRED
Fred's father had rented him out to a troop of "boy lovers" since early childhood. Fred has a female alter with a self-perceived age of 8 years. "Her" plan is to escape from juvenile hall by seducing a male custodian. This plan conflicts with the heroic knife-point escape envisioned by another of his alters, a violent male who is the same age as Fred's chronological age.

Social competence of alters.   Despite the many dysfunctional behaviors associated with children who have dissociative identity disorder, it is not unusual for them to behave in a socially competent manner. "Children who develop dissociative identity disorder become quickly alerted to acceptable and unacceptable behavior and often times may be seen as academically, musically, or athletically superior in an effort to maintain an acceptable, highly rewarded personality that is not subject to punitive or abusive actions of oth-

ers" (G. Dean, personal communication, January 1993). Also, perpetrators may "force" the child to develop alters who perform well socially to conceal the perpetrators' wrongdoing.

Signs of dissociative identity disorder in children.
Children with dissociative identity disorder are more likely to complain of physical problems than of psychological or family problems, so a medical examination is critical. Common symptoms include headaches and gastrointestinal and genito-urinary difficulties (Kluft, 1985). The Child/Adolescent Dissociation Checklist is useful in recording the symptoms or signs that suggest dissociative identity disorder in children (see Table 11-6).

The psychological problems of children with dissociative identity disorder mimic other traumatic conditions and psychiatric and neurological disorders. These include dissociative disorders in general, reactions to child maltreatment, conduct disorder, attention-deficit/hyperactivity disorder, posttraumatic stress disorder, oppositional defiant disorder, separation anxiety disorder, schizophrenia, seizure disorder, and bipolar disorders. Table 11-7 shows the symptoms and signs of dissociative identity disorder that may overlap with these other conditions.

The behavioral signs shown in Table 11-7 principally apply to children with dissociative identity disorder whose maladaptive behavior has alerted authorities. The needs of other children with dissociative identity disorder who have socially competent alters may not be as obvious to teachers, health professionals, and police.

Clinicians agree that the most prominent characteristic of childhood dissociative identity disorder is the bewildering array of symptoms (Hornstein & Tyson, 1991). There is no typical behavioral profile of children with dissociative identity disorder, perhaps because of the variety, duration, and intensity of the traumatic contexts that underlie the disorder.

The following case is an account of a woman who describes a childhood of abuse and psychological torture that led her to develop a dissociative identity disorder. (THE FAMILY INSIDE: Working with the Multiple by Doris Bryant, Judy Kessler, and Lynda Shirar. Copyright © 1992 by Doris Bryant, Judy Kessler, and Lynda Shirar. Reprinted by permission of W. W. Norton & Company, Inc.)

CASE 11-19A. JUDY (AS A CHILD)
I was born uncelebrated. I was not often held or nurtured. As a result, I lay in my crib most of the day, surrounded by the dismal iciness of gray walls. I was cold, hungry and dirty most of the time. In addition, I was not called by a name. I was an object that was discarded and dumped in the corner of a room, only to be used and abused for the pleasure of others. I did not know I existed.

From the time I was two years old and out of the crib until the age of five or six, I lived locked in my room, a prisoner isolated from the world outside. Only on special occasions was I taken from my room—to be used in rituals or pornographic movies.

Table 11-6
Child/Adolescent Dissociation Checklist

CHILD DISSOCIATION CHECKLIST

Name _____ Age described _____ Sex _____ Birthdate _____

Interviewer's name _____ Date _____

Circle the answer that best describes the child at the time (within the last two years) you knew the most about him or her. Also use information from primary caregivers, teachers, counselors, social service workers, etc. Circle "?" if you are unsure or if the child showed only suggestive signs; "Y" if signs were clear or strongly suggestive; or "N" if there were no signs of clinical significance.

Y N ? 1. SEXUAL ABUSE: rape, attempted rape, or unwanted sexual touching or fondling.

Y N ? 2. PHYSICAL ABUSE: hitting, biting, beating, burning, hurting with objects or weapons.

Y N ? 3. EMOTIONAL ABUSE: tricking, harassing, abandoning, blaming, shunning, etc.

Y N ? 4. SERIOUS ILLNESS/INJURY: may or may not be due to abuse.

Y N ? 5. SERIOUS LOSS: may or may not be due to abuse.

Y N ? 6. EXTREME INCONSISTENCIES IN ABILITIES, LIKES, DISLIKES: dramatic fluctuations in behavior/performance, unexpected changes in preferences for food/clothing/social relationships.

Y N ? 7. DENIAL OF BEHAVIOR OBSERVED BY OTHERS: perceived as lying when confronted re behavior witnessed by credible adults, often fierce sense of injustice if punished.

Y N ? 8. EXCESSIVE DAYDREAMING/SLEEPWALKING: trance-like behaviors, "spacey," extreme concentration/attention difficulties, sleep disturbances.

Y N ? 9. PERPLEXING FORGETFULNESS: loss of time, unexpected test failure, confusion re names of teachers and peers, inability to use or acknowledge prior experience, loss of familiarity with well-known objects.

Y N ? 10. INTENSE ANGRY OUTBURSTS: often without apparent provocation; may involve unusual physical strength; brief or persistent, often followed by amnesia.

Y N ? 11. PERIODIC INTENSE DEPRESSION: may include suicidal gestures/attempts, often without clear precipitation or focus; psychomotor slowing or agitation.

Y N ? 12. REGRESSIVE EPISODES: often followed by amnesia; dramatic reductions in language or motor skills when exposed to trauma-related stimuli (for example, frightened thumb-sucking at age 12).

Y N ? 13. IMAGINARY COMPANIONS (beyond age 6): imaginary quality may be denied by client.

Y N ? 14. AUDITORY HALLUCINATION-LIKE EXPERIENCE: friendly or unfriendly; content related to "imaginary companions" or to traumatic experience; voices arguing or commenting, usually inside head.

Y N ? 15. PHYSICAL COMPLAINTS/INJURIES OF VAGUE ORIGIN: may be self-inflicted, accidental, or abuse related; fluctuating degrees of discomfort expressed; often uncertain medical basis.

Y N ? 16. POOR LEARNING FROM EXPERIENCE: normal discipline/guidance/therapeutic measures have little or no lasting effect; corrective experience may be denied by client.

Y N ? 17. FAMILY HISTORY OF DISSOCIATIVE IDENTITY DISORDER OR OTHER DISSOCIATIVE DISORDER: may not have been formally diagnosed as such.

TOTALS: _____ Y; _____ N; _____ ?

A total score of 10 or more "Ys" suggests a need for thorough evaluation for dissociative identity disorder.

Note. A score of 9 or less does not rule out dissociative identity disorder. Some behaviors on the checklist simply may not be observed, especially if a child with dissociative identity disorder has a socially competent alter.
Source: Reprinted, with changes in notation, with permission of the authors and publisher, from P. A. Reagor, J. D. Kasten, and N. Morelli, "A Checklist for Screening Dissociative Disorders in Children and Adolescents," *Dissociation, 5*, 1992, p. 5. Copyright 1992.

Table 11-7
Overlapping Symptoms or Signs Seen in the Histories of Children with Dissociative Identity Disorder and Other Conditions

Other condition	Overlapping symptoms or signs
Dissociative disorder in general	Truancy, rejection by peers, disruptive behavior, depression, suicidal gestures and attempts, self-harm, physical complaints, hypochondriacal complaints, conversion disorder symptoms (for example, sudden blindness, epileptic-like seizures, paralysis, loss of sensation), disturbed sleep (for example, sleepwalking, frequent repeated nightmares, sleep terror), amnesia, loss of sense of time, denial of behavior
Maltreatment	Headaches, gastrointestinal and genito-urinary difficulties, injuries of which the child denies knowledge (such as genital bleeding), traumatic history (for example, sexual abuse, physical abuse, emotional abuse, serious illness or injury, serious loss), repeated maltreatment, amnesia for maltreatment (if occurred), maltreatment that occurred before 12 years of age
Conduct disorder	Theft and forgery, cruelty to people or animals, destruction of property, breaking and entering, lying, aggressive behavior, intensive angry outbursts, thrill seeking, fire setting, use of a weapon, argumentative conduct, truancy
Attention-deficit/hyperactivity disorder	Attention and concentration difficulties, distractibility, shifting from one incomplete task to another with no recollection of having done previous task, difficulty playing quietly, difficulty understanding instructions, frequently accused of manipulating
Posttraumatic stress disorder	Intensive angry outbursts, attention and concentration difficulties, distractibility, shifting from one incomplete task to another with no recollection of having done previous task, regressive behavior, physical complaints, hypochondriacal complaints, frequent repeated nightmares, amnesia, auditory hallucinations
Oppositional defiant disorder	Intensive angry outbursts, disruptive behavior, strong protestations of innocence or stoical detachment when disciplined, fierce sense of injustice
Separation anxiety disorder	Intensive angry outbursts, physical symptoms, hypochondriacal complaints, frequent nightmares
Schizophrenia	Hallucinations, imaginary companions, flashback memories, variability in personality (or changes in identity), referring to self in third person
Seizure disorder	Lapses of awareness, staring spells or trance-like states, amnesic periods, missing parts of lesson in school
Bipolar disorders	Extreme mood swings, heightened energy, depression, elation

Source: Reprinted, with adaptations and changes, with permission of the authors, from Dean, Dean, Giem, Guerra, and Leark, copyright 1989; also from Lewis (1991b).

My room was located at the top of a staircase, and I could hear if anyone approached my bedroom door. Most of the day I strained to listen for the old wooden steps that creaked and cried with the footsteps of those invading my world. In my confusion, I believed that my abusers thought I liked their intrusions; I often heard them say, "Are you ready for a little love?" Their love hurt.

My days were filled with lonely play. I craved companionship. As my need to be with people increased, I created an inside friend called "Little Judy"; she began to talk to me and I to her. I liked to hear her voice, and I could play with her whenever I wanted. I felt so glad she was my friend; she made me feel good in my upside-down world. We were inseparable. My secluded and lonely world was now filled with laughter and hope. I knew better than to tell anyone of my secret friend, for they would take her away, just as they had taken away everything else.

As the darkness of each night crept into my room and the light of day subsided, the shadows on the wall grew more monstrous. I hated the night. Often I would cry out for help, screaming, "Do you know where I am?" It was not safe for a little girl to be alone at night in her room. I experienced the cries of other children inside my head as I sat in the corner of my room, terrified of the approaching darkness and straining to hear the footsteps of the invaders. When I heard their steps, and they reached the top of the stairs, my heart began to pump so hard I thought it would explode. Every breath was so hard; I gasped for air. I wheezed and shook as I heard the intruders unlatch my bedroom door. The doorway would then be filled with enormous, towering figures. . . .

Years went by during which I didn't know I was human, didn't know who I was. I lived in a world of silence, shattered only by the screaming voices of other personalities. The abusers raped my body, tortured me and took my body from me. They raped my soul and tried to take my spirit as well. They assaulted me with objects that pierced and cut and tore from me any belief I might have had that I was anything human. I was a thing, no better than a chair or a rock, or dirt. I was the filth that constantly covered my body. They had taken everything from me, including my "self." Thrown around like a rag doll that had no feelings, I was given to others to be used and I was carefully instructed to give them pleasure. I thought I was rotten and evil, that this could happen only to bad little girls. I was not sure of anything in this crazy world I lived in except that I was an awful and ugly "thing" and must deserve these awful, bad things that happened to me.

I began school around the age of six or seven. School for me was like an abstract dream running in slow motion. I tried so hard to follow the rules at school. And, as instructed by the abusers, I never talked about the abuse or said anything about my life at home. I knew better than to tell the awful secrets. Almost daily I was sent home from elementary school for not wearing panties (they hurt), or for fighting with other kids on the playground, or for not listening in class, or for lying, or for just not being "a good girl."

I was not allowed to be involved in any outside activities other than school and I was not allowed to have any friends. My isolation continued, as did the secret abuse during the nights. From this time on the lies were well hidden behind the false facades that the abusers began to create. The abusers involved themselves in community activities such as Boy Scouts and attended church on Sundays. They were considered good upstanding people by others.

Life was not real. I was not real. I was only this "thing," waking each day so I could be used and abused each night. Time no longer existed for me; I hid inside, covered by layer upon layer of created personalities. I lay dormant inside myself, still and unformed. I was not a person. I had no hope, no unity, no life at all. I felt ugly and dead. I still to this day cannot comprehend how I survived, even though I know it was my ability to dissociate that brought me through. (pp. 2–4)

Judy now describes what it is like to have a dissociative identity disorder.

CASE 11-19B. JUDY (AS AN ADULT)

Walking on the edge of life, never knowing when you may appear in a place you know nothing about or how you got there; being called by a name that is not yours; voices, broken families, suicide attempts, confusion, incongruent feelings of laughter and depression; unspeakable nightmares, cold chilling memories that don't belong to you; more voices, intense feelings of shame, guilt and anguish—this is what it's like to be a multiple. Life lacks continuity, strung along a time frame you have no control over; normal environmental stimuli

are overwhelming, resulting in switching from personality to personality. And still there are the voices.

For a child, being a multiple is like giving life to an already dead thing, hidden away under the pressures of unspeakable tragedies: incest, beatings, emotional abuse, neglect, torture, paradoxical anger and love; tricks, always devious and cruel. These are demoralizing experiences that take away your childhood—forever.

Growing up under truly intolerable circumstances, my feelings became too intense for me to bear, especially when the abusers warned against telling the "secrets." Their intensity grew as the abuse continued, all the way up to the age of 18. I began to seal off from my awareness the child who experienced the pain of those horrendous experiences. I began to create personalities in my inner family who could serve as a means for me to survive. If I had not become a multiple, I would have either died or gone completely crazy. The struggle to survive the abuse was so overwhelming that the child-self hid away inside. Her existence was denied, and therefore she lived—but at a great psychological cost. (p. 41)...

I learned how to disguise the loss of time I experienced; in fact, I learned how to manipulate time and use it to accomplish life's everyday tasks. In almost every situation I learned how to maintain an outward appearance that everything in my life was great, even when chaos was running rampant on the inside. I learned not to show the pain which constantly pounded in my heart. But in reality there was not an ounce of my life that was not affected by the abuse which caused me to become a multiple; it permeated everything. I became even more trapped inside. (p. 42)...

When I was a child I had to play mostly in my imagination—I played in my head. I don't remember using my body at all for play, in the way kids usually play—using their hands in mud, or skipping, or just moving freely. Even to this day I feel stifled within my own body, unable to make it move freely. When a child's experience is only in her mind, it leaves her frozen, unable to move about freely with the body. Other multiples I know also look stiff; they too are still locked up in their bodies. (p. 58)...

As an abused child, my whole life has been taken out of my control. So the one thing I might have in my control is the ability not to feel, through dissociation. (p. 164)...

So much objectification occurred when I was a child that I thought of my body as a "thing." The "thing" is what got abused sexually or physically, and the "thing" was something I had to leave because I could not bear the pain that was placed on or within it. I was able to dissociate from the shame, guilt and pain by seeing my body as the thing that was abused, rather than myself. To this day it is hard not to see my body as a "thing," but as a part of me. Even though my awareness now is that this is my body, it's hard for me to stay in contact with it. (p. 239)

Controversy over diagnosis. Some professionals question whether dissociative identity disorder exists (Gleaves, 1996; North, Ryall, Ricci, & Wetzel, 1993; Spanos, 1994). Spanos (1994), for example, maintained that the disease perspective of dissociative identity disorder is flawed. Rather, individuals assume multiple identities for purposes geared to social interaction, and "neither childhood trauma nor a history of severe psychopathology is necessary for the development or maintenance of multiple identities" (p. 143). Gleaves (1996), in contrast, argued that dissociative identity disorder is a valid diagnostic category and that the arguments of Spanos and others that dissociative identity disorder is a creation of psychotherapy and the media are based on false assumptions about psychopathology, assessment, and treatment. Ignoring the posttraumatic symptomatology of individuals with a dissociative identity disorder can be harmful to patients. North et al. (1993), in their review of literature, also concluded that "to doubt the existence of dissociative identity disorder would require believing that every single patient ever diagnosed with the disorder was consciously malingering.... Dissociative identity disorder is a syndrome that cannot simply be considered nonexistent, even if its diagnostic status has not been adequately validated..." (p. 162, with changes in notation).

Exercise 11-1. Evaluating a Child with a Dissociative Identity Disorder

---

Read the following case, and then list the child's risk factors for developing a dissociative identity disorder. The case was obtained from Tyson (1992).

Lyle was a 9-year-old male whose mother was seeing me for treatment of dissociative identity disorder. When she began to describe her son's emotional and behavioral adjustment, I suggested that Lyle be psychologically assessed. Lyle was described by his mother as a hyperactive and emotionally immature young boy who had been previously diagnosed and treated for seizure-like behavior. A series of neurological evaluations failed to reveal a clear-cut source for his seizure-like behavior. The parents were divorced, and Lyle had been largely raised in the home of his maternal grandparents where the mother also resided for several years. The family unit was described as highly dysfunctional. The grandfather, a retired police officer with a felony conviction and a history of drug and alcohol abuse, was alleged to have sexually abused Lyle's mother throughout much of her childhood. The mother asserted that the grandparents controlled every aspect of Lyle's early life and seemed especially focused on his eating and elimination patterns. His mother believed that the grandfather had sexually abused Lyle. She also was aware of a rejecting and possibly emotionally abusive alter personality of her own who did not relate well to Lyle. Lyle was described by his mother as having several animal alters who growled and made other animal noises, but did not speak. Their function apparently was to protect Lyle. Lyle talked openly about his animal personalities at times, but, at other times, totally denied their existence or insisted that they were just "make believe." (p. 23, with change in notation)

Suggested Answers

The notable risk factors for developing dissociative identity disorder are a parent with dissociative identity disorder, multigenerational child abuse, multiple perpetrators, excessive control of the boy's eating and elimination patterns, and seizure-like behavior. Even without his mother's report of

Lyle's animal alters, the possibility of dissociative identity disorder should be explored.

The existence of significant dissociative psychopathology related to physical and sexual abuse suffered in childhood was known to Pierre Janet and other 19th-century clinicians. However, it is only recently that implications of this forgotten linkage have begun to be appreciated by modern mental health practitioners.

—Frank W. Putnam

Interviewing Issues

Preparation.   Before the interview, review the child's prior records, including school, medical, and court records and psychosocial evaluations. Consider the following questions: Does the child have a history of maltreatment? Were the parents maltreated as children? Do one or both parents have a dissociative disorder?

When you interview the child's parents, teachers, nurses, and other caregivers, pay close attention to any information that suggests inconsistencies in the child's behavior and abilities, amnesia, or trances. Ask about variations in test scores and handwriting; variability in visual acuity; and wide shifts in sports skills, artistic abilities, use of tools, food preferences, speech habits, and moods. For example, does the child have mood swings from prim to seductive or from timid to belligerent; temperament changes from feminine to masculine or vice versa; or speech changes from halting speech to bold and fluent speech? Is the child described as "possessed" because the child's aggressive personality is so different from her or his usual docile personality (Lewis, 1991b)?

Parents may try to convince you that the problem lies with the child rather than with themselves. Parents who maltreat their children will try to appear normal or even ideal. If you attempt to challenge the parents, they may dismiss your efforts or rationalize the situation (Kluft, Braun, & Sachs, 1984). The child's trust in you will depend heavily on your ability to resist deception, charm, or intimidation by any adults who have maltreated the child.

Interviewing strategies.   The extensive role-playing skills of children with dissociative identity disorder, coupled with their amnesia, will likely prevent you from obtaining a complete history. They may have long periods for which they are amnesic, they may be unable to discuss trauma, and they may even misinterpret current experiences. For example, they may naturally assume that all children hear voices inside their heads, are scared to go home, or have discontinuous experiences of time. In addition, they may accept what adults say about their inconsistent behavior—namely, that they are lying or malingering.

With children younger than 5 years of age, use a play interview (see Chapter 3). Young children with dissociative identity disorder may express traumatic memories in their play nonverbally, such as by injuring small animals or by violating dolls (Baldwin, 1990). This is illustrated in the case of a 2-year-old boy who saw his mother's head crushed in an automobile accident. In a play interview at the age of 4 years, he slammed the head of a doll into the wall, shouting "Daddy, I'll beat your brains out." Older children with dissociative identity disorder who may be unwilling to talk with you may, however, be willing to share their drawings or writings (Doyle & Bauer, 1989). Their artistic work may depict repulsive or horrific themes, such as mutilated genitals. If they talk to you about traumatic experiences, they may describe a brutal rape or beating matter-of-factly (Baldwin, 1990).

For children older than 5 years and adolescents, you can use the semistructured interview questions in Table F-16 in Appendix F. Be supportive and informal in your interviewing style. When the child mentions signs or symptoms that suggest dissociative identity disorder—for example, periods of lost time, amnesia for events or periods of life, flashbacks, and other intrusive images—inquire further. If alters appear during the interview, respond to them matter-of-factly. Use their different names if the child gives them, and do not force the view that "You are only one person"; be careful not to be voyeuristic (Hornstein & Tyson, 1991).

It is prudent not to hypnotize a child during the initial interview. If alters emerge during the hypnotic state, critics reviewing the interview may attribute these alters to hypnotic fantasy. Furthermore, information obtained in a hypnotic trance cannot be used in court. *Despite the difficulties encountered in interviewing children who may have dissociative identity disorder, do your best—you may be their only resource.*

Concealing dissociative identity disorder. Children with dissociative identity disorder are skilled in concealing their circumstances from others and are not likely to display their several personalities in an interview. You may be able to interview only one alter, usually the primary personality. If so, this personality is likely to be a schoolchild personality who is unaware of the existence of other alters and perhaps amnesic for traumatic experiences.

Unlike the Hollywood stereotype of the flamboyant and opportunistic individual with dissociative identity disorder, only 6% to 10% of adults with dissociative identity disorder are exhibitionistic (Kluft, 1987). Children who live in danger are even more secretive. Adolescents with dissociative identity disorder will usually dress and act appropriately in the interview and may even appear shy, introverted, and bland. In public situations, these adolescents may appear depressed or anxious and may show poor adaptive skills. Others may appear superficially well adjusted during the interview, but, on closer examination, you may find striking inconsistencies or peculiarities in their behavior or beliefs.

Distrust. Because of the trauma that children with dissociative identity disorder likely have faced, they may be guarded in disclosing material that makes them vulnerable to further hurt. Adults may disbelieve severely maltreated children about the causes of their problems. You must be willing to tolerate vagueness in children's communications until you can establish trust. Children with dissociative identity disorder who are hospitalized may need a month or more of building trust before they will allow their therapist to "meet" their alters (Hornstein & Tyson, 1991).

Maltreated children may believe that disclosure will endanger them. They may accurately perceive that authorities cannot protect them, especially in cases of victimization by cults or organized crime. Abusers may have convinced the children that they or their family members or pets will be hurt if they reveal any secrets. Also, some alters may be intensely loyal to their abusers and fear punishment from authorities.

Focus on imaginary companions and hallucinations. Be sure to ask all children and adolescents who are at risk for dissociative identity disorder whether they have (or had) imaginary companions or hallucinations, and explore any positive responses. Do not automatically consider hallucinations and voices speaking to each other as indicators of schizophrenia; these signs also are characteristic of dissociative identity disorder (Lewis, 1991b). Individuals with schizophrenia may not only have hallucinations, but they also may have delusions, disorganized thinking, grossly disorganized behavior, dysphoric mood and withdrawal (such as loss of interest in previously pleasurable activities), inappropriate affect, and abnormalities in psychomotor activity (such as pacing and rocking movements, grimacing, and odd mannerisms). Misdiagnosis of dissociative identity disorder as schizophrenia may lead to psychologically and physiologically damaging drug treatments. Medications are even less effective with children with dissociative identity disorder than with adults with dissociative identity disorder (Putnam, 1991).

Interventions

All severely traumatized children should be screened for dissociative disorders, as well as for the related posttraumatic stress disorder (see discussion of posttraumatic stress disorder earlier in the chapter). Treatment for children with dissociative identity disorder—once they are in a safe environment—is remarkably brief and usually successful, compared to the years of arduous and uncertain therapy undertaken by adolescents or adults with this disorder (Kluft, 1985). In fact, Ross (1989) said that "no other disorder in psychiatry could be [treated] on such a scale with the methods already available" (p. 202). Finally, Whitman and Munkel (1991) give a strong mandate for screening for dissociative identity disorder: "Continued failure to diagnose and treat this disorder in childhood supports a charge of professional neglect against those entrusted with the management of these abused children" (p. 427).

Case Illustration

The following case of dissociative identity disorder illustrates the importance of obtaining prior records and conducting interviews with several sources (Bowman, Blix, & Coons, 1985).

CASE 11-20. DEBRA

Debra, a 14½-year-old, was brought to a university child psychiatric clinic by her prospective adoptive parents, Mr. and Mrs. K, who requested help with "adjusting as a family" and with "Debra's problems from the past."

Little is known about Debra's early childhood. At age 6, her mother taught her to have sexual intercourse with her father and subsequently the mother abandoned the family. For three years, Debra's alcoholic father sexually abused her and her siblings in bizarre ways, beat them, and neglected them. Debra's sister, Kim, complained to a neighbor, the children testified in court against their father, and he was sentenced to life imprisonment. Debra passed through a series of six temporary homes and again was sexually abused at one of the homes. At age 14, she was placed with Mr. and Mrs. K, her second pre-adoptive family.

Diagnostic information was obtained from family and individual interviews, from welfare department records, transcripts of Kim's court testimony, and police descriptions of her father's home.

Welfare records showed previous evaluations of Debra at 9½ years; 13 years, 3 months; and 13 years, 11 months. Information from the first evaluation was not available. The second evaluation took place just after termination of the first adoptive placement. Unresolved anger toward her natural and adoptive parents was noted, but she impressed the evaluating psychiatrist as "not being a seriously disturbed girl." The third evaluator, also a psychiatrist, believed that she did not warrant psychiatric diagnosis and was "quite sound psychologically."

At the time of our evaluation Debra had completed the ninth grade, was maintaining a B+ average, and was involved in several musical organizations in which she performed well. She presented no blatant behavior problems at school, participated in church activities, maintained friendships with peers, and helped care for Mr. and Mrs. K's young children. Her health was good and her physical development normal.

Mr. and Mrs. K were having difficulty understanding Debra and were openly ambivalent about adopting her. Debra habitually sucked her thumb at home and would not function alone, demanding attention from peers and the family. She tended to "grab at people," monopolizing their time and feeling devastated when they spent time with someone else. Mrs. K noted that at times Debra seemed totally unaware of dinner-time conversations that had just occurred around her. She and Debra had read a book together, but while discussing it Debra could not remember reading major portions that Mrs. K had observed her reading. Debra also frequently stated she had no memory of being told to do household tasks. Mrs. K also noted Debra's abrupt changes in affect, including times when she suddenly stared mutely at Mrs. K with a "spine-chilling hatred" that occurred for no apparent reason, lasted only several minutes, and was markedly different from her usual affect. Debra never told Mr. or Mrs. K

about her amnesic episodes and they attributed her memory difficulties to "poor concentration."

During the initial interview, Debra initially appeared anxious but quickly warmed up and talked freely. She was dressed casually in age- and sex-appropriate clothing and was cooperative with the interviewer. Her affect ranged appropriately from smiles to tears and her thought processes were logical, well-focused, and productive of relevant material. No evidence was found of psychosis. Her insight was good, her judgment adequate for her age, and her intelligence appeared to be average. Debra, her foster parents, and the welfare department said that she did not use or abuse drugs.

The diagnosis of dissociative identity disorder was first suspected during the diagnostic interviews when Debra casually mentioned that she used the name Karen while living in her first pre-adoptive home where she was sexually abused. She first characterized Karen as a part of her that wanted to be "bad and resentful," but on further questioning stated that Karen was really a different person. Later in therapy, full dissociation occurred and Debra had amnesic episodes while Karen, who was coconscious with Debra, was in full control. (pp. 110–111, with changes in notation)

If the interviewer in this case had relied only on her immediate clinical impression of Debra, she would have missed the diagnosis of dissociative identity disorder, as had the other two clinicians who had evaluated Debra earlier. Debra's alter, Karen, did not reveal herself until after several interviews. Nevertheless, the history of severe and bizarre sexual abuse, which was obtained from court and placement records; the inconsistencies between school and home behavior; and her pre-adoptive parents' observations of Debra's trances and amnesia would have suggested a follow-up evaluation for childhood dissociative identity disorder.

THINKING THROUGH THE ISSUES

How difficult do you think it will be to distinguish children with an attention-deficit/hyperactivity disorder from children with a learning disorder?

What do you think about giving drugs to young children to help them with a behavior disorder, such as attention-deficit/hyperactivity disorder?

How can you distinguish behavior that reflects normal childhood acting out or testing of limits from behavior that reflects a psychological disorder?

Do you think that you can work with children who have a conduct disorder?

How effective do you think you can be in helping children with a conduct disorder and in helping their parents?

How will you distinguish normal depression from depression that may suggest a psychological disorder? What are your thoughts about giving children antidepressant medications for depression instead of counseling or psychotherapy?

How difficult do you believe it will be for you to distinguish normal anxiety from anxiety beyond that expected for the child's developmental age?

Do we live in an age of anxiety? What is the basis for your answer?

How would you prepare children and their families for an extrafamilial crisis, such as a possible earthquake, tornado, flood, or other natural disaster? What can you do to emphasize the importance of preparation for an impending disaster?

How would you distinguish between a child's normal reactions to a crisis and reactions that may suggest a psychological disorder? How will you know when to conduct a standard, initial information-gathering interview instead of a more therapeutically oriented interview when you interview a child who may be in a crisis or who may be experiencing posttraumatic stress disorder?

Do you think that a dissociative identity disorder is a valid diagnostic category, or is it simply a type of role-playing or some other type of behavior that is under the complete control of the child? What is the basis for your answer?

How easy do you think it is to distinguish between a child with a dissociative identity disorder and one who has a pervasive developmental disorder?

SUMMARY

Attention-Deficit/Hyperactivity Disorder

1. Attention-deficit/hyperactivity disorder (ADHD) is a behavioral syndrome marked by inattention, hyperactivity, and impulsivity.

2. Most children with ADHD either are academic underachievers or have a learning disability.

3. Children with ADHD also may have low self-esteem, lability of mood, low tolerance for frustration, and temper outbursts.

4. ADHD becomes most evident when children reach school age and have difficulty meeting the demands of the classroom.

5. Overactivity is a major part of ADHD in early childhood. The syndrome is more common in boys than in girls, with estimates of the boy-girl ratio ranging from 3:1 in nonreferred samples to 6:1 in clinic-referred samples.

6. Information-processing deficits associated with ADHD may include inefficient use of time, superficial analyses of written or spoken material, premature stopping of processing information, inadequate evaluation of promising strategies to help with learning or recalling information, poor rehearsal strategies, and limited awareness of problem-solving strategies.

7. Children with ADHD also may have a deficit in self-regulation, which means that they may have difficulty with organization and planning, with the mobilization and maintenance of effortful attention, and with the inhibition of inappropriate responding.

8. ADHD appears to have a genetic component, although the mode of inheritance and the types of specific genetic abnormalities are yet to be learned.

9. ADHD also may be associated with an imbalance of or deficiency in one or more of the brain neurotransmitters, and several areas of the brain may be involved, particularly the frontal lobes.

10. Other theories about the causes of ADHD involve environmental toxins, such as lead, food additives, sugar, and cigarette smoking or alcohol consumption by the mother during pregnancy; these theories remain speculative because none have received wide-ranging support.

11. Arriving at a diagnosis of ADHD is not easy. Restlessness and overactive behavior are common in normal children, especially in boys between 6 and 12 years of age. Some "problem" children are never referred for hyperactive behavior because they have parents who are tolerant of their behavior, teachers who do not perceive their behavior as a problem, or optimal environments that provide structure for their behavior.

12. Essentially normal but active children are referred for evaluation of ADHD because of less tolerant environments, either at home or at school.

13. Children with ADHD also may have behaviors and symptoms associated with oppositional defiant disorders, learning disability, depressive disorders and mania, anxiety disorders, and communicative disorders.

14. The overlapping-symptom picture between ADHD and several other conditions sometimes leads to diagnostic difficulties.

15. The ADHD population is heterogeneous, displaying a diversity of behavior despite the underlying attention problems.

16. Children with a dual diagnosis of oppositional defiant disorder (or conduct disorder) and ADHD may exhibit greater problems during adolescence and adulthood than those who have either diagnosis alone.

17. The occurrence of ADHD is estimated at 3% to 5% in the school-aged population and at 23% to 50% in clinical populations.

18. Hyperactivity appears to account for many problems treated at child mental health clinics.

19. Children who have ADHD in early childhood usually continue to have difficulties in adolescence, but the manifestations of the disorder may change.

20. Although restlessness, distractibility, and poor concentration may diminish in children with ADHD, they still remain problems for some adolescents.

21. The major shift in adolescents with ADHD is in the emergence of difficulties associated with social behavior and interpersonal relationships. Particularly evident are rebelliousness, antisocial behavior, and low self-esteem. Difficulties with academic achievement and problem solving also remain.

22. During adolescence and young adulthood, individuals who had ADHD as children are more at risk than normal children for behavioral problems, particularly in the area of conduct problems and antisocial personality disorder (after age 18).

23. Little is known about what variables predict long-term adjustment in individuals with ADHD.

24. You will want to interview the child referred for the assessment of ADHD, as well as his or her parents or caregivers and teachers. You should also observe the child at school, at home, and in a clinic playroom.

25. A popular and usually first-line treatment for ADHD is stimulant pharmacotherapy, which may involve the use of methylphenidate (Ritalin), d-amphetamine (Dexedrine), or pemoline (Cylert). Tricylic antidepressants also have been used with some success. Children with ADHD who take stimulant medication often show dramatic behavioral changes, with noticeable improvement in motor behavior, attention, and impulse control. In addition, they show increased compliance and less physical and verbal hostility.

26. In what is commonly called a "paradoxical effect," stimulant pharmacotherapy decreases behavioral excesses or disruptive behaviors. However, stimulant pharmacotherapy does not typically correct social or academic deficits.

27. Unfortunately, once the medication is withdrawn in cases of ADHD, the gains associated with behavioral control often disappear.

28. Approximately 60% to 90% of hyperactive children respond positively to stimulant medication.

29. Stimulant medication also may have adverse side effects, including appetite suppression, sleep disturbance, headaches, stomachaches, weight loss, decrease in growth rate, hypersensitivity, and tremors.

30. The use of chemotherapy does not mean that the child with ADHD does not need special services. All children who have serious academic deficiencies need remediation. In addition, cognitive retraining, social skills training, parent training, and family and individual child therapy should be considered for children with ADHD to help them with their interpersonal problems and other adjustment difficulties.

31. The principal aim in treating children with ADHD or with similar problems is to help them focus and sustain their attention and keep impulsive responding under control.

32. Children can be taught to verbalize to themselves effective problem-solving strategies, such as planning ahead, stopping to think, and being careful.

Conduct Disorder and Oppositional Defiant Disorder

33. Children with a conduct disorder have a pattern of antisocial behavior, rule breaking, or aggressive behavior that creates difficulties for themselves, their families, their school systems, and their communities.

34. Conduct disorder is a repetitive and persistent pattern of behavior in which the basic rights of others or major age-appropriate societal norms or rules are violated.

35. Children with a conduct disorder also may have impairments in social, academic, and occupational functioning.

36. The major characteristic of the oppositional defiant disorder is a recurrent pattern of negativistic, defiant, disobedient, and hostile behavior toward authority figures.

37. Children with an oppositional defiant disorder also may have impairments in social, academic, or occupational functioning.

38. Oppositional defiant disorder is distinguished from conduct disorder by the lack of conduct that seriously violates others' rights or violates age-appropriate society norms and rules.

39. Children with conduct disorders have the highest rate of referral to mental health facilities, with estimates ranging from one-third to two-thirds of the referrals.

40. Biological factors that may contribute to the development of conduct disorders in children include genetic makeup and constitutional factors.

41. Behavioral factors that may contribute to the development of conduct disorders in children include difficult infant temperament, sensation seeking, learning deficits, academic underachievement, immaturities in moral reasoning, maladaptive peer relationships, association with a delinquent peer group, and poor interpersonal problem-solving skills.

42. Familial factors that may contribute to the development of conduct disorders in children include parental marital conflict and divorce, depression, substance abuse, antisocial behavior, social isolation, rejection of child, failure to supervise the child properly, harsh or inconsistent discipline, ineffective communication with the child, and failure to become involved in the child's activities.

43. Children with conduct disorders are difficult to treat. However, pharmacological agents, behavioral approaches, social learning approaches, and parent-training approaches have been attempted.

44. Perhaps the best approach to intervention with children who have conduct disorders is to address individual, familial, and environmental vulnerabilities of the child and parents.

45. Treatment for children with a conduct disorder will likely need to be ongoing, focusing on medical, psychological, and educational supports to the child and family.

Depression

46. Depression can refer to a symptom, such as a sad affect, that is a common experience of everyday life or to a syndrome or disorder in which a group of symptoms go together.

47. The symptoms of depression in infants and preschool children include crying, sadness, apprehension, decreased contact with parents or caregivers, stupor, loss of appetite, and refusal to eat.

48. The symptoms of depression in middle childhood–aged children, in addition to those noted for infants and preschool children, include loss of weight, temper tantrums, concentration difficulties, and sleeplessness.

49. The symptoms of depression in adolescents, in addition to those noted for infants and preschool children, and middle childhood–aged children, include loss of feelings of pleasure and interest, low self-esteem, excessive fatigue and loss of energy, inability to tolerate routines, overinvolvement with pets, aggressive behavior, somatic complaints, restlessness, loneliness, irritability, running away, stealing, guilt feelings, feelings of worthlessness, weight loss or gain, and suicidal preoccupations.

50. Depressive disorders in children often coexist with other disorders, such as conduct or oppositional disorders, anxiety disorders, and, less often, attention-deficit/hyperactivity disorder.

51. In older children, depressive disorders often coexist with eating disorders and with drug or alcohol abuse.

52. The etiology of depression is unclear.

53. In evaluating depression in children, consider whether the symptoms represent a change in behavior, are consistent in behavior, lack a clear precipitant, or significantly affect the children's everyday behavior.

54. Also consider how familial factors, such as marital discord, child maltreatment, poor family cohesion, poor family communication, father absence, mother absence, parental resentment, and parental rejection of children, contribute to the depression.

55. Treatment of depression may involve use of tricylic antidepressant medications, serotonin-specific reuptake inhibitors, and psychotherapy, including cognitive-behavioral approaches.

56. Interventions for depression will be complicated if the parents also are depressed or have other forms of psychological disturbance. Depressed parents, for example, may reinforce their children's depressive cognitions and behaviors.

Anxiety Disorders—An Overview

57. Separation anxiety disorder is characterized by excessive anxiety concerning separation from the home or from those

to whom the child is attached, anxiety beyond that which is expected for the child's developmental level, and anxiety that causes clinically significant distress or impairment in social, academic, occupational, or other important areas of functioning.

58. Panic attack is characterized by a discrete period in which there is the sudden onset of intense apprehension, fearfulness, or terror, often associated with feelings of impending doom.

59. Agoraphobia is characterized by anxiety about being in places or situations from which escape might be difficult or embarrassing.

60. Panic disorder is characterized by the presence of recurrent, unexpected panic attacks, worry about the possible implications or consequences of the panic attacks, or a significant behavioral change related to the attacks.

61. Specific phobia is characterized by clinically significant anxiety provoked by exposure to a specific feared object or situation, often leading to avoidance behavior.

62. Social phobia is characterized by clinically significant anxiety provoked by exposure to certain types of social or performance situations, often leading to avoidance behavior.

63. Obsessive-compulsive disorder is characterized by obsessions and/or compulsions. Obsessions are persistent ideas or thoughts that an individual recognizes as irrational but can't get rid of. Compulsions are irrational and repetitive impulses to perform some act.

64. Posttraumatic stress disorder (PTSD) is characterized by the reexperiencing of an extremely traumatic event accompanied by symptoms of increased arousal and by avoidance of stimuli associated with the trauma.

65. Acute stress disorder is characterized by symptoms similar to those of posttraumatic stress disorder and covers the period immediately following an extremely traumatic event.

66. Generalized anxiety disorder is characterized by at least six months of persistent and excessive anxiety and worry.

67. Anxiety disorders are considered internalizing disorders, along with depressive disorders, social withdrawal, psychophysiological disorders, eating disorders, gender identity disorder, and schizoid disorders.

68. Internalizing disorders are inner-directed (directed toward self); the symptoms are primarily associated with overcontrolled behaviors.

69. Conduct disorder and oppositional defiant disorder are externalizing disorders, along with attention-deficit/hyperactivity disorder, aggressive reactions, and adjustment disorder.

70. Externalizing disorders are outer-directed (directed toward others); the symptoms are primarily associated with undercontrolled behaviors.

71. Methods of treating anxiety disorders include behavior therapy approaches, cognitive-behavioral procedures, and pharmacological treatments.

Separation Anxiety Disorder

72. Symptoms of separation anxiety disorder include excessive distress about harm to self or to attachment figures when separated from them, worry that something will happen to attachment figures, school refusal, reluctance to sleep alone or sleep away from home without the presence of an attachment figure, repeated nightmares involving themes of separation, and physical complaints and signs of distress in anticipation of separation or at the time of separation.

73. Behavioral interventions have been used to help children overcome school refusal.

Posttraumatic Stress Disorder

74. Posttraumatic stress disorder (PTSD) is a clinical label for a traumatic reaction following any serious event or life-threatening crisis involving actual or threatened death or serious injury, such as a natural or human-induced disaster, accident, suicide, or violent crime involving child abuse.

75. The three phases of PTSD are acute, chronic, and delayed onset.

76. Extrafamilial crises are associated with major hazardous events that happen outside the family and that are not under the family's control.

77. Intrafamilial crises are those events that take place within the family, such as physical/sexual abuse, abandonment, substance abuse, suicide, teen pregnancy, or divorce.

78. Children in either an extrafamilial or an intrafamilial crisis may go through four phases: impact phase, recoil phase, resolution or adjustment phase, and postcrisis functioning level phase.

79. In the initial interview with a child in a crisis, determine whether the child is in a crisis or in danger, determine the meaning of the event for the child and how the child copes with the crisis, determine affective connections to the child's experiences and the relevant past coping resources of the child, determine the family's support of the child and the family's coping resources, and determine the help wanted and needed by the child and family.

80. In evaluating a child who is in a crisis, consider everything going on in the child's and family's life, not just the crisis.

81. In developing interventions for a child in a crisis, consider characteristics of the stressor, individual characteristics of the child, familial characteristics, and environmental characteristics.

82. Initially, instead of conducting a standard clinical assessment interview with a child in a crisis, you may have to deal with the immediate effects of the crisis.

83. Consider interventions that build on the family's strengths and reduce its vulnerabilities, such as helping the family improve its communication skills and group problem-solving skills, helping parents support each other and their children, and helping the family accept changes and develop ways of coping with the altered situational demands.

84. Short-term interventions designed to facilitate children's adaptive coping include accepting the situation, working through feelings, evaluating the situation, resuming normal activities, and joining a support group.

Dissociative Identity Disorder

85. Dissociative identity disorder (formerly called multiple personality disorder or MPD) is one of four principal types of dissociative disorders. The common theme of the dissociative disorders is an alteration in the normal, integrated functions of a person's identity, memory, or consciousness.

86. Dissociative identity disorder is a condition in which the individual develops two or more distinct identities or personality states that recurrently take control of his or her behavior. There is usually a primary or main personality, which is the name the person goes by. In the other personality states, the individual is unable to recall important personal information,

which cannot be explained by ordinary forgetfulness or by direct physiological effects of a substance or a medical condition.

87. Dissociative identity disorder cannot be attributed to children simply because they have imaginary playmates or engage in fantasy play.

88. Depersonalization disorder is a condition in which the individual loses a sense of reality and feels estranged from the self and perhaps separated from the body.

89. Dissociative amnesia is a condition in which the individual has memory loss of psychological origin. It may occur as a reaction to an intolerable traumatic situation in which there is a loss of memory for devastating personal information.

90. Dissociative fugue is a condition in which the individual not only is amnesic but also wanders away from home, often assuming a completely new identity.

91. The distinct personalities of individuals with a dissociative identity disorder are called alters, which is short for "alternative personalities." Each alter is individually complex and has its own unique behavior and social relationships. Frequently, alters are not aware of the existence or activities of the other alters.

92. Many children with dissociative identity disorder do not clearly meet the adult criteria of two or more distinct alters that repeatedly take full control of the individual's behavior.

93. The main features of childhood dissociative identity disorder include recurrent amnesic periods or missing blocks of time, frequent trance-like states or appearing to be in a daze, major fluctuations in behavior (which may include dramatic changes in school or work performance or variations in apparent social, cognitive, or physical abilities).

94. The prevalence of children with dissociative identity disorder in the general population is unknown.

95. Dissociative experiences are common in normal childhood development.

96. In Western society, children with a dissociative identity disorder typically are victims of chronic and severe sexual abuse or physical abuse within the family.

97. During early and middle childhood, a diagnosis of dissociative identity disorder is difficult because normal children also have dissociative experiences.

98. Alters range in age from infancy to ages older than the child's chronological age.

99. Children with a dissociative identity disorder commonly have alters of both genders; some alters may be homosexual, while others may be heterosexual.

100. Despite the many dysfunctional behaviors associated with children who have dissociative identity disorder, it is not unusual for them to behave in a socially competent manner.

101. Children with dissociative identity disorder are more likely to complain of physical problems than of psychological or family problems, so a medical examination is critical.

102. Common symptoms of dissociative identity disorder include headaches and gastrointestinal and genito-urinary difficulties.

103. The psychological problems of children with dissociative identity disorder mimic other traumatic conditions and psychiatric and neurological disorders.

104. There is no typical behavioral profile of children with dissociative identity disorder, perhaps because of the variety, duration, and intensity of the traumatic contexts that underlie the disorder.

105. Some professionals question whether dissociative identity disorder exists.

106. Before you interview a child for possible dissociative identity disorder, review the child's prior records, including school, medical, and court records and psychosocial evaluations.

107. When you review the records of a child who may have a dissociative identity disorder, determine whether the child has a history of maltreatment, whether the parents were maltreated as children, and whether one or both parents have a dissociative disorder.

108. When you interview the parents, teachers, nurses, and other caregivers of a child who may have a dissociative identity disorder, pay close attention to any information that suggests inconsistencies in the child's behavior and abilities, amnesia, or trances.

109. The extensive role-playing skills of children with dissociative identity disorder, coupled with their amnesia, will likely prevent you from obtaining a complete history.

110. Children with dissociative identity disorder are skilled in concealing their circumstances from others and are not likely to display their several personalities in an interview.

111. Because of the trauma that children with dissociative identity disorder likely have faced, they may be guarded in disclosing material that makes them vulnerable to further hurt.

112. Be sure to ask all children and adolescents who are at risk for dissociative identity disorder whether they have (or had) imaginary companions or hallucinations, and explore any positive responses.

113. All severely traumatized children should be screened for dissociative disorders, as well as for the related posttraumatic stress disorder.

114. Treatment for children with dissociative identity disorder—once they are in a safe environment—is remarkably brief and usually successful, compared to the years of arduous and uncertain therapy undertaken by adolescents or adults with this disorder.

KEY TERMS, CONCEPTS, AND NAMES

Attention-deficit/hyperactivity disorder (ADHD) (p. 350)
Inattention (p. 350)
Hyperactivity (p. 350)
Impulsivity (p. 350)
Task analysis (p. 350)
Strategic planning (p. 350)
Self-regulation (p. 350)
Imbalance of or deficiency in one or more of the brain neurotransmitters (p. 351)
Environmental toxins (p. 351)
Stimulant pharmacotherapy (p. 352)
Methylphenidate (Ritalin) (p. 352)
d-amphetamine (Dexedrine) (p. 352)
Pemoline (Cylert) (p. 352)
Tricylic antidepressants (p. 352)
Conduct disorder (p. 357)
Oppositional defiant disorder (p. 357)
Depression (p. 363)
Separation anxiety disorder (p. 365)
Panic attack (p. 366)
Agoraphobia (p. 366)

Panic disorder (p. 366)
Specific phobia (p. 366)
Social phobia (p. 366)
Obsessive-compulsive disorder (p. 366)
Posttraumatic stress disorder (PTSD) (p. 366)
Acute stress disorder (p. 366)
Generalized anxiety disorder (p. 366)
Internalizing disorders (p. 366)
Externalizing disorders (p. 366)
Obsessions (p. 366)
Compulsions (p. 366)
Acute phase of PTSD (p. 369)
Chronic phase of PTSD (p. 370)
Delayed-onset phase of PTSD (p. 370)
Extrafamilial crises (p. 370)
Intrafamilial crises (p. 371)
Impact phase of a crisis (p. 371)
Recoil phase of a crisis (p. 371)
Resolution or adjustment phase of a crisis (p. 371)
Postcrisis functioning level phase (p. 371)
Poor crisis coping strategies (p. 371)
Good crisis coping strategies (p. 371)
Dissociative identity disorder (Multiple personality disorder
     [MPD]) (p. 377)
Depersonalization disorder (p. 377)
Dissociative amnesia (p. 377)

Dissociative fugue (p. 377)
Alters (p. 378)

STUDY QUESTIONS

1. Discuss attention-deficit/hyperactivity disorder. Include in your discussion the symptoms of the disorder, etiology, diagnostic difficulties, interviewing issues, and intervention considerations.

2. Discuss conduct disorder and oppositional defiant disorder. Include in your discussion a description of the disorders and interviewing and intervention issues.

3. Discuss depression in children. Include in your discussion a description of the condition and interviewing and intervention issues.

4. Briefly describe the 10 types of anxiety disorders.

5. Discuss separation anxiety disorder. Include in your discussion a description of the condition and interviewing and intervention issues.

6. Discuss posttraumatic stress disorder in children. Include in your discussion a description of the condition and interviewing and intervention issues.

7. Discuss dissociative identity disorder in children. Include in your discussion a description of the condition and interviewing and intervention issues.

12

CHILDREN WITH DEVELOPMENTAL, LEARNING, OR SENSORY DISORDERS

A person who is severely impaired never knows his hidden sources of strength until he is treated like a normal human being and encouraged to shape his own life.

—Helen Keller

Autistic Disorder
Mental Retardation
Specific Learning Disability
Visual Impairment
Hearing Impairment
Thinking Through the Issues
Summary

Goals and Objectives

This chapter is designed to enable you to:

- Understand and appreciate the concerns that family members may have in raising a child with a developmental, learning, or sensory disorder
- Develop skills in interviewing children who may have an autistic disorder, mental retardation, specific learning disabilities, visual difficulties, or hearing difficulties

This chapter focuses on children who have developmental, learning, or sensory disorders. The chapter presents guidelines for interviewing children who may have problems in these areas; it does not provide an in-depth review of research or theory about these conditions. You will need to consult other sources to obtain more detailed information about the areas covered in the chapter.

AUTISTIC DISORDER

Description

Autistic disorder is a behavioral syndrome marked by impaired social development and communication and a markedly restricted repertoire of activity and interests (*Diagnostic and Statistical Manual of Mental Disorders—IV,* American Psychiatric Association, 1994). The behavioral characteristics of children with an autistic disorder may include failure to develop normal social relationships, extreme deficits in speech and language, ritualistic behavior and insistence on sameness, abnormalities in response to the sensory environment, self-stimulatory behavior, self-injurious behavior, inappropriate affect, limited intellectual functioning, difficulty generalizing, and behavior problems (such as aggression, noncompliance, tantrums, toileting difficulties, feeding difficulties, and sleeping difficulties) (Schreibman & Charlop, 1989). However, the symptoms of children with an autistic disorder vary from mild to severe, and some children have special skills, such as the ability to dismantle and reassemble a complicated mechanical apparatus and the ability to memorize mathematical tables, bus schedules, and calendars. Although children with an autistic disorder share some characteristics with other groups of exceptional children, there are some important differences, as Table 12-1 points out.

DSM-IV cites the following symptoms—in the areas of social interaction, communication, and behavior—that suggest an autistic disorder:

SOCIAL INTERACTION

1. Marked impairment in the use of multiple nonverbal behaviors—such as eye-to-eye gaze, facial expression, body postures, and gestures—to regulate social interaction

2. Failure to develop peer relationships appropriate to developmental level
3. Lack of spontaneous seeking to share enjoyment, interests, or achievements with other people
4. Lack of social or emotional reciprocity

COMMUNICATION

5. Delay or lack of spoken language, with no attempt to use alternative methods of communication
6. Marked impairment in initiating or sustaining a conversation with others (in individuals with adequate speech)
7. Stereotyped and repetitive use of language or idiosyncratic language
8. Lack of varied, spontaneous make-believe play or social-initiative play appropriate to developmental level

BEHAVIOR

9. Stereotyped and restricted patterns of interest
10. Inflexible adherence to specific, nonfunctional routines or rituals
11. Stereotyped and repetitive motor mannerisms
12. Persistent preoccupation with parts of objects

Children with an autistic disorder often are delayed in their acquisition of speech. Some children who later turn out to have an autistic disorder are initially suspected of having a hearing deficit because they do not respond to sounds. *The most common speech characteristic of children with an autistic disorder is echolalia, either immediate or delayed.* Echolalia refers to the inappropriate repetition of speech previously uttered by another speaker. Other communication deficits that children with an autistic disorder may display are as follows (see the Glossary for definitions of the technical terms): echoing, stereotypic or idiosyncratic speech (saying things in odd ways), circumlocution, rambling, fragmentation, irrelevant speech, bizarreness, neologisms, blocking, automatic phrases, confabulation, circumstantiality, clang association, overelaboration, self-reference, confusion or omission of pronouns and connecting words, mixtures of concrete and abstract words, and unusual intonations.

Let's now look at some ways in which the language deficits of autistic children may be expressed (Baker, 1983):

1. *Receptive language skills may be better developed than expressive language skills.* For example, children with an autistic disorder may understand directions, such as "Give me the pencil," but not say "pencil" when they want the pencil back.

2. *Repetition of rote mechanical phrases or delayed echolalia may not be meaningful language.* For example, children with an autistic disorder who repeat the phrase "Go away" may not use it correctly in context.

3. *Language skills displayed in one setting may not generalize to another setting.* For example, children with an autistic disorder may identify an object correctly at home but not in your office.

Table 12-1
Differential Diagnosis of Autistic Disorder

Category	Similarities with autistic disorder	Differences from autistic disorder
Schizophrenia	Sustained impairment of social relations Resistance to change in environment Speech abnormalities Constricted or inappropriate affect Deviance in language	Period of normal development with onset after 30 months History of mental illness in family more common Poor physical health Poor motor performance Higher IQs Periods of remission and relapse Delusions and hallucinations Involvement in a fantasy or "inner" world
Developmental aphasia	Speech problems, such as echolalia, pronominal reversal, sequencing problems, difficulties in comprehension	Language difficulties less severe and less widespread Good eye contact Meaningful use of gestures Displays of emotional intent Involvement in imaginative play Normal IQs
Mental retardation	Poor intellectual ability that persists through the life span Echolalic speech Self-stimulation Self-injury Attentional deficits	Appropriate social behavior may be exhibited Communication more effective Understandable intentions and motivations Slow physical development Intellectual impairments over a wide range of functioning Few, if any, isolated areas of outstanding functioning (e.g., in music, mechanical ability, rote memory, or mathematics)
Environmental deprivation	Withdrawal from and lack of interest in surroundings Delays in motor skills and language development Unusual motor activity Little interest in toys	Marked improvement once environment is enriched, including gains in language and motor development and in establishing social relationships No display of self-stimulatory behavior, echolalia, or pronominal reversal; no avoidance of social contact

Source: Adapted from Schreibman and Charlop (1989).

4. *Language skills may not follow normal or expected developmental patterns.* For example, children with an autistic disorder who do not talk may read competently.

Etiology, incidence, and prognosis. Autistic disorder appears to have a neurobiological basis, but the exact mechanisms remain unclear (Hooper, Boyd, Hynd, & Rubin, 1993). This disorder is likely to have multiple etiologies, all organic in nature. The best estimates of the prevalence of autistic disorder are about 2 to 5 per 10,000 live births, with boys out numbering girls by 4 or 5 to 1 (American Psychiatric Association, 1994). Autistic disorder is a life-long developmental disability that typically appears during the first three years of life; in only about one-third of the cases is some degree of partial independence possible in adulthood. The best prognosis is associated with children who develop speech before 5 years of age and who function above the mentally retarded range.

Parental concerns. The following quotations illustrate the reactions and concerns of parents raising a child with an autistic disorder (DeMyer, 1979, pp. 27, 34, 36, 37, 45, 62, 75, 91, 104, 109, 112, 116, 138, 163, 182, 220).

1. *The child's first year of life.* Parents usually recall the first year of life as the best year of the child's development.

We thought he was the sweetest and perfectly normal. After his brother was born, we saw some differences. His brother was more demanding and active, but Rinny was cuddly and smiled and sat up and walked well.

2. *The worsening of symptoms.* Parents may worry that their child is seriously different from other children of the same age during the child's second and third years.

Mickey got progressively more withdrawn that year and screamed a great deal. Somewhere around his second birthday, he became very destructive. My husband and I look back on his second and third years with wonder that we didn't go mad or end up divorced.

3. *Reactions to diagnosis.* Parents may be perplexed or devastated when they receive a diagnosis.

When we were told Albie had autism, I was stunned. I didn't know what it meant but I knew it was serious. I don't know—it was just—I was in shock. She explained it again—but I didn't quite get it—I was still stunned. I should have had her write down what was wrong. I remember asking a couple more questions, but she was indefinite about the cause or whether anything could be done. I have come later to realize there are many mental disorders that doctors don't know all about and can't cure, but then I couldn't get anything—I was too shocked.

4. *Social behavior.* Parents usually are concerned about how the child gets along with other children.

Harold won't have anything to do with other children. He ignores them. He simply doesn't understand how to play house. All he wants to do is line toys up in rows. Then he sits down and rocks and stares at his lines of toys.

5. *Destructive activities.* Parents may be concerned about the child's destructive activities.

He doesn't do those things on purpose. He isn't mad. He just pulls on anything that's loose—he'll pull on the drapes or on the tablecloth. He's so active that he'll hit a lamp or stumble over a cord, and there goes another lamp.

6. *Speech and communication.* Parents usually will be concerned about the child's speech and communication problems.

He started at 1 year saying "baba" for bottle and "toast" for breakfast. He also said "mama" and "dada," but he never called us that—these were words he mimicked for a while. These words disappeared and he seldom picked up any more, but he went into jabbering. At 2½ to 3 years, he wasn't talking any better than [he was] at a little past a year.

7. *Eating habits.* Parents usually are concerned about the difficulties they encounter in the child's eating habits.

Wade [an autistic boy nearly 5 years old at interview time] always had a finicky appetite. I plan our meals around what he will eat. His eating manners are about like a small baby who is just learning to feed himself. He loves to spill soupy food over his head and rub milk in his hair. On the whole, I think he does well at the table now that he is feeding himself, which he wouldn't do until the last few months. I don't push him too hard because I recognize that he eats like the other children did before they were 2 years old.

8. *Toilet training.* Parents usually have difficulty toilet training their child.

I know Jane can't learn to toilet train yet; she just doesn't get the idea. I really accept this state for now, and I don't punish except for something extreme like smearing. Since she doesn't learn from punishment, I really have to watch her close and get in there immediately after her nap, or everything is covered. That's a cleanup job I hate.

9. *Sleeping.* Parents usually are concerned about their child's difficulty falling asleep.

Gino [aged 4 years and 3 months] gets hyperexcited. We try to calm him, but once he is in bed he starts laughing hysterically. His big problem is getting too wound up. He just can't let go like a normal child. He almost explodes with laughter. Sometimes he will wake in the middle of the night and be awake for two or three hours. He likes to come out and run and play and eat. He doesn't want to go back to bed and he doesn't want to be held. It didn't do a bit of good to spank and we were getting completely worn out. He would fight sleep. Finally, we tried tying him in bed during the worst period and gradually he would relax and go off to sleep. He is better now, but it has been a problem for a long time. At times we give him medicine for sleep. The medicine works for a short while and then loses its effectiveness, and so we save it for his worst periods.

10. *Emotional expression.* Parents usually are concerned about how the child expresses emotions.

Eddie cried easily, especially if we changed anything around or if he heard a sudden sound. We couldn't go anywhere when he was a baby because he would cry so hard that he couldn't quit; but he was a quiet baby a lot of the time and didn't smile much. He looked bored and unhappy.

11. *Discipline.* Parents usually are concerned about how to discipline the child.

If you don't catch him immediately after he has done something, then you haven't even a small chance of getting him to see the connection between the punishment and the act. I wonder if he gets the connection even then.

12. *Curiosity.* Parents usually are concerned that their child's curiosity is extremely limited.

The only things he is curious about are what is in paper sacks or in people's purses. If he sees us put something up out of his reach on a shelf, he may yell bloody murder to get it. When he gets these things, he just twiddles them or immediately loses interest.

13. *Visitors to the home.* Parents usually are concerned about how their child relates to visitors to the home.

People are puzzled by him. On the one hand, he seems in his own world, but on the other hand, he has no special discipline. He will climb on their backs, crawl over their heads even. This is different from when he was younger and he totally ignored them.

14. *Adolescent sexuality.* Parents usually are concerned about how to handle their adolescent's sexuality.

Mickey [age 18] lives with me now. He has been very affectionate for many years, and it's been no problem. Lately, though, he has started rubbing against some girls and women who come to the house. I am afraid he may do this in a store and get into real trouble. Also, I have a woman friend that Mickey likes a lot. He likes to hug and kiss her, but it gets him too excited. I'm not sure what to do about this.

15. *Guilt.* Parents usually feel guilty about their child's condition or about something they have done or thought in connection with the child.

I often find myself feeling guilty about my child's condition even though I say to myself, "Why, I know I've done nothing to hurt my child."

16. *Doubts about parenting.* Parents may have doubts about their ability to be adequate parents.

I feel on tenterhooks all the time—whether I'm saying the right thing to her, how I should act. The other day I just yelled out something—we were riding in the car. She shrank back in the seat and was quiet. I didn't want to frighten her, but it was good to have her quiet.

17. *Increased tension.* Parents may experience increased physical and psychological tension because of their need to cope with their child's symptoms.

Well—his actions put her [referring to the child's mother] nerves on edge. They do mine too—but her more than me; and things that wouldn't ordinarily bother her, bother her now. He gets out of bed—the day'll go along and the farther into the day we go, the worse it gets. I'd say nine-tenths of the disharmony would stem from him.

Sibling concerns.

Here are two descriptions by siblings of what it is like to live with a brother or sister who has an autistic disorder (Harris, 1994, pp. 25, 73, 74).

1. *Jealousy.* Siblings may be concerned that their sibling with an autistic disorder is getting too much attention.

When I was a kid it seemed to me my brother Rich, who has autism, got the lion's share of attention in our house. Now that I am an adult I can understand the jam my parents were in, but it was tough for me when I was younger. I love Rich, and my wife and I invite him to spend holidays with us, but I try to make sure my own kids understand why Uncle Rich needs so much of Dad's time when he visits. I guess it isn't an accident that I ended up as a pediatrician. All the time I was growing up I kept praying there would be a way to cure Rich.

2. *Concerns about how to act.* Siblings may be concerned about how to behave with their sibling who has an autistic disorder.

I will always be grateful to my parents for how they talked to me when I was kid. They told me about my brother's autism, and they seemed to be able to understand when I teased him or pushed him around a little. I mean they didn't say it was OK, but they didn't do a real guilt trip either. They would punish me the same way my best friend got punished when he would tease his little sister. No more, and no less. Plus, they would help me find things I could do that

would give me a way to play with my brother. It wasn't ideal, and I think they made mistakes like all parents do, but I always knew they would listen to me and try to be fair. I appreciate that all the more now that I'm grown and know how hard it must have been on them raising the two of us and him having autism.

Parental concerns about siblings.

Here are some descriptions of concerns parents may have about the siblings of children with an autistic disorder (Harris, 1994, pp. 26, 49, 97).

1. *Concerns about missing childhood.* Parents may be concerned that the sibling of a child with an autistic disorder is missing out on childhood activities.

Justin is such a terrific kid. Sometimes I think he is almost too good. He spends so much time with his sister, Allie, who has autism. He acts like it is his job to do everything for her. I don't want him to resent that someday. To feel like she stole his childhood. I appreciate his help, but I don't want him to overdo. I'm not sure how much help is too much.

2. *Role reversal.* Parents may be concerned that the sibling of a child with an autistic disorder is assuming too much responsibility or taking on roles beyond his or her capacity.

I think the thing that worries me most about Art is how he is going to feel about Jack as they grow up together. Here is Art, a little guy at age 5, telling his big brother Jack, who is 11, how to do things. I mean, what is he going to think about that as he gets older? Big brothers are supposed to take care of little guys, not the other way around. I'm concerned that it must be confusing to Art.

3. *Concern about what to say.* Parents may not know what to tell the sibling of a child with an autistic disorder about the nature of the disorder.

Zack is only five and Jeff, who is autistic, is seven. Zack asks things like why Jeff won't play with him or why he won't talk. I give him simple answers like "he still has to learn how to talk." I hope that is enough.

4. *Equality of treatment.* Parents may be uncertain about how differently to treat the children in the family.

My seven-year-old daughter who has autism broke one of her brother's favorite toys the other day. He was very upset and wanted me to punish her. At first I thought it wouldn't do any good, but then I realized that even if she didn't learn anything, he would feel that I was standing up for him, and it would make him feel better. So, I sent her to her room.

Living with an autistic child is an exhilarating and humbling experience, an emotional roller coaster without an end—or a seat belt. Michael is frustrating, puzzling, tiring, loving, trusting, and sometimes hilarious. It's like seeing a body turned inside out—a soul exposed. He exposes the souls of others, too.

—Patricia A. Dreier

Interviewing Issues

The inherent disabilities of children with an autistic disorder—such as the difficulty they have establishing social relationships, their impaired communication skills, and their unusual responses to sensory stimuli—may tax your resources as an interviewer. As many as 50% of individuals with an autistic disorder remain mute or nonverbal (Wetherby & Prizant, 1992). In addition, children with an autistic disorder may show little or no desire to interact with you, and your normal methods of encouragement, such as smiling, may be ineffective (Baker, 1983).

Before you interview a child with an autistic disorder, find out as much as possible about the child's communication skills from the parents and teachers; also observe how the child talks in the classroom. Consider the following (Lord & Baker, 1977):

- Can the child follow simple directions?
- Can the child answer "yes" or "no"?
- Does the child understand gestures or pictures or signing?
- Can the child read?
- Does the child have any idiosyncrasies, such as using code words or phrases ("bye-bye" for "no" or "look, look" for a favorite toy)?

Also observe how other people interact with the child (Lord & Baker, 1977):

Watch how people who know the child talk to her or him. Parents or teachers may assure you that the child understands everything they say. However, they may actually use frequent dramatic gestures or physically guide the child through tasks. When working with the child, experiment…with directions or questions of varying complexity. (p. 184)

In interviewing children with an autistic disorder, talk slowly and simply, use short sentences, be concrete, and omit unnecessary words and complex grammatical forms; be prepared to repeat sentences as needed or rephrase sentences to make them simpler (Lord & Baker, 1977). Make sure that you have the children's visual attention when you speak; visual cues help them attend to and process your speech.

Observational guidelines.   When you observe children who may have an autistic disorder, keep the following guidelines in mind (Schopler, Reichler, & Renner, 1986; Schreibman, 1988; also see Table 3-3 in Chapter 3):

1. Observe the child's ability to make eye contact. For example, does the child engage in eye contact either spontaneously or upon a request to do so?
2. Observe the child's interaction with toys. For example, does the child interact with toys? If so, does the child engage in appropriate play or self-stimulation? Note also whether there are restricted repertoires of toy play, long latencies in approaching toys, or repetitive manipulations of toys.

3. Observe the child's interaction with her or his parents. For example, does the child interact with them or avoid them? Does the child notice her or his parents? Is the child cooperative or uncooperative? Does the child initiate any affectionate contact with the parents, such as sitting on a parent's lap or hugging or kissing the parents? If the parents have to ask the child for a hug, does the child respond appropriately or does she or he fuss or turn away and "back into" the parents' arms? How much discipline do the parents need to exert to get the child to comply with their requests?
4. Observe the child's speech. For example, does the child have any speech? If so, what is the nature of the speech? Is it age appropriate? Is it peculiar, bizarre, or unrecognizable? Does the child name toys when asked to do so?
5. Observe the child's affect as noted, for example, in facial expressions, postures, and manners. Is the child's affect appropriate or inappropriate? Is the child's affect inhibited, moderate, or excessive? Does the child show pleasure and displeasure?
6. Observe the child's motor patterns and activity level. For example, are the child's motor patterns age appropriate? Does the child seem driven or apathetic? Is it difficult to get the child to respond to anything? Does the child engage in self-stimulation?
7. Observe the child's interactions with you. For example, is the child cooperative or uncooperative? Does the child seem intensely aloof toward you, avoid you, or seem oblivious to you? Does the child have tantrums?

Semistructured interview.   If the child can speak and attend to your questions, consider using the semistructured interview shown in Table F-13 in Appendix F. For a guide to interviewing parents, see Table F-35 in Appendix F. The questions in Table 12-2 will help you evaluate the information you obtain from parents and teachers (and the child where possible).

Here is a segment from an interview with the parents of a 4-year-old child with an autistic disorder. Notice how the interviewer's questions follow the content of the parents' communications (DeMyer, 1979, p. 30, with changes in notation; IR = interviewer, IE-F = father, IE-M = mother).

IR: When did Albert's problems begin?
IE-F: Well, I guess they have probably always been.
IE-M: But we didn't realize then—but I think in the back of our minds we knew.
IR: You say they have always been.
IE-F: Well, from the time normal children are supposed to do things, he didn't and you couldn't get him to do it. He ignored us.
IE-M: He has never been able to play with children at all, and he has always fiddled with things. And when he was a baby he was almost too good, but he kicked his feet all the time. He tore up things with his feet because of the kicking. Noises scare him—he puts his thumbs in his ears.

Table 12-2
Guidelines for Evaluating Children for a Possible Autistic Disorder

Prior Developmental History
1. Were there any prenatal or perinatal difficulties? If so, what were they?
2. Were there any suspicions of sensory deficits, such as deafness or blindness? If so, what were they based on?
3. When did the child reach developmental milestones, such as sitting unassisted or walking?
4. What was the child's affect during infancy (for example, did she or he mold to the parent's body when held)?

Social Behavior
5. As an infant, was the child responsive to people?
6. As an infant, how did the child react when he or she was held (that is, was the child overly rigid or flaccid, resistant to being held or indifferent to being held)?
7. As an infant, did the child make eye contact with others?
8. As an infant, was the child content to be alone, or did he or she cry or demand attention?
9. Do the parents think that their child is truly "attached" to them?
10. Is the child affectionate with the parents?
11. Does the child seek the parents if he or she is hurt or frightened?
12. What is the child's interest in other children (that is, does the child want to be with other children, or is he or she a "loner")?
13. Does the child interact with other children? If so, what is the quality of the child's interactions?

Speech Development
14. Does the child have speech? If not, has the child ever spoken in the past? If so, when and for how long?
15. If the child speaks, what is the quality of the speech (for example, does the child display echolalia, pronominal reversals, or extreme literalness in comprehension and expression)?
16. In the parents' estimation, what is the extent of the child's language abilities?

Self-Stimulation or Self-Injury
17. Does the child engage in self-stimulation? If so, what kind of self-stimulation?
18. Does the child engage in self-injurious behavior? If so, what behavior leads to self-injury?

19. If the child currently does not engage in self-stimulation or self-injurious behavior, has he or she ever done so? If so, when and what kind of behavior?

Affect
20. Does the child have any irrational fears? If so, what are they?
21. Does the child have appropriate fears, such as fear of moving vehicles on a busy street?
22. Does the child seem to laugh or cry at unusual times or for no apparent reason?
23. Does the child show rapid, typically inexplicable mood swings?

Insistence on Maintenance of Sameness
24. Does the child become upset if furniture is rearranged or if other aspects of the environment are altered?
25. Does the child become upset at changes in routes of travel or routine?
26. Does the child have any compulsive rituals? If so, what are they?
27. Does the child have any unusual food demands (for example, will the child eat only one or two foods, demand to eat out of a particular bowl, or refuse to eat crackers or cookies if they are broken)?
28. Is the child unusually attached to an object or objects (for example, does the child always demand to carry certain objects or refuse to relinquish an outgrown garment)? If so, what are the objects?

Isolated Skills
29. Does the child show particular skill at a certain task? If so, what are the skill and the task?
30. Is the child a whiz at assembling puzzles?
31. Does the child demonstrate unusual ability in music?
32. Does the child have an exceptional memory in one or more areas? If so, in what areas?

Behavior and Behavior Problems
33. What is the child's behavior at home?
34. What is the child's behavior at school?
35. Does the child have severe tantrums?
36. Is the child toilet trained?
37. Does the child eat without assistance?
38. Does the child dress himself or herself?
39. Is the child aggressive, noncompliant, or manipulative?

Source: Adapted from Schreibman (1988).

IR: When did you first notice oversensitivity to noise?
IE-M: I can't remember, but it's been a long time.
  IR: How did you first begin to know something was wrong for sure?
IE-M: My mother and his sister said so.
IE-F: Now, we kind of knew he was slow.

IE-M: Yes, but I know children grow in spurts, and I thought he was in a slow period and would come out of it. I guess you kid yourself. But my mother took me aside and said that she and his sister were sure something was wrong. I was furious at them for a while, but then I finally realized they were really concerned and we went for help. The doctor said he was sure something was wrong too, and we came here. We were surprised and shocked at what we learned.

IR: Even though you had some idea before?

IE-M: It was subconscious, because it was really a shock.

Interventions

Behavioral techniques are often used with children with an autistic disorder to (a) reduce their maladaptive behaviors, such as self-stimulation (for example, rocking and twirling) and self-injurious behaviors (for example, head banging and biting hands or wrists), and (b) teach them skills (for example, sitting and establishing eye contact). If the self-injurious behaviors are life-threatening, physical restraints also may need to be used. There are no complete cures for autistic disorder; the focus usually is on reducing the children's symptoms. In some cases, early and intense interventions have enabled children with an autistic disorder to perform at normal levels and to appear normal to all but the most expert observers.

Here are some suggestions for working with parents of children with an autistic disorder (Morgan, 1984):

1. *Explaining the child's condition.* Give parents a realistic and cautious interpretation of autism, presenting the child as a unique individual with a special set of problems. Parents may have misconceptions about the disorder, perhaps stemming from a stereotypic image of autism derived from television or magazine articles. Help them recognize that symptoms such as bizarre responses to the environment, insistence on sameness, attachments to objects, and deficient and unusual language are part of the syndrome of an autistic disorder.

2. *Explaining the child's level of functioning.* Help parents to understand their child's level of functioning in cognitive and adaptive areas and the possibilities for improvement. Often, parents want to believe that their child's cognitive impairment is only temporary and that their child will return to normal when her or his behavioral and emotional problems are resolved. Caution parents that they should not equate the child's isolated abilities—such as early motor development or good rote memory—with general intelligence. Convey to the parents what their child's strengths and weaknesses are; use age-equivalent scores, where appropriate, if you discuss the results of a psychological evaluation. By interpreting the child's relative skills, you may help parents feel less threatened; as a result, they may become more receptive to your suggestions.

3. *Reassuring parents.* Assure parents that they are not responsible for the child's refusal to interact with the world. Parents of children with an autistic disorder often blame themselves for their children's condition because autism has social and emotional overtones. A prime feature of autism that distinguishes it from other disorders is the child's inability to form affectionate relationships. This is most dis-

turbing to parents. You can best deal with any feelings of guilt by presenting them with information about the diagnosis and the causes of autism. Knowing that they did not cause their child's disorder enables parents to move past their guilt and participate in treatment programs.

4. *Dealing with parental reactions.* Prepare yourself to deal with other parental reactions, such as anger and denial, that may occur when they learn that their child has a severe disorder.

5. *Discussing prognoses.* Phrase statements about prognosis cautiously. Most cases of autism are severe and long term. Parents can play an active role in intervention programs, however.

6. *Helping the family to accept the child.* Prepare yourself to work with the child's siblings to help them understand their brother's or sister's disorder. Families that gain an understanding of autistic disorder will be in a better position to accept and help their child who has the disorder. For more information about interventions and related issues in autistic disorder, see Schopler, Van Bourgondien, and Bristol (1993).

Case Illustrations

The following case illustrates how the parents of a child with an autistic disorder came to terms with their child's disability, grew to understand the diagnosis, and learned to work with the available services (Handleman, 1990).

CASE 12-1. SHAWN

Frank and Rose Penn had been married for six years when their first child, Shawn, was born. Shawn's early months brought joy to everyone. He was a beautiful little boy with a quiet, undemanding disposition. He ate and slept well, seemed to need little attention, and would spend hours contentedly in his crib. Shawn's motor development was on schedule and, by the time he was 1 year old, he had taken his first steps.

Shortly after Shawn's first birthday, Frank and Rose had a growing sense of concern about Shawn because he did not seem interested in them. He also did not babble very much and was often unresponsive when they called his name. The Penns raised their concerns with the family pediatrician, who suggested that they wait another few months and observe Shawn's progress. At 24 months, Shawn still had not spoken his first words; he seemed content to dwell within his own world and had begun to spend long hours each day twirling the wheels of his toy truck. Evidently, something was seriously wrong with their son's development.

Extensive multidisciplinary evaluations at a regional medical center eventually led to the diagnosis of autistic disorder. The news was devastating to Frank and Rose, and the couple felt as though all of their hopes and dreams had been shattered. Questions of "Why?", "How?", and "What do we do?" dominated their every thought.

At the recommendation of the evaluation center, the Penns contacted their local school district about a preschool program for Shawn. At their first meeting with the Child Study

Team, the parents heard from the professionals who examined Shawn. The school psychologist, learning consultant, and speech pathologist all agreed that the assessment was extremely difficult due to Shawn's communication problems and limited attention. Each reported that modifications of testing practices were necessary to obtain meaningful information. Often it was necessary for Mrs. Penn to be present to motivate Shawn and to interpret some of his responses. The Penns struggled to understand all of the details that were being presented and the implications for their son.

The school social worker said that the team members believed Shawn required a structured educational environment, rich in academic and social experiences. Important considerations included small groupings with opportunity for individualized instruction and availability of interactions with students with less severe disabilities. They recommended the use of behavioral teaching strategies.

The Penns visited several schools and reviewed programs with the team coordinator. They compared the advantages and disadvantages of an in-district class with those of a class in a nearby community and in a private school. After some discussion, the parents decided to place Shawn in the private school, because it offered a tightly structured program as well as a family involvement program. They hoped that the experienced staff would help them to understand their son's disability and guide them through the years to come. (adapted from pp. 138–139)

The next case offers a mother's perspective on raising a child with an autistic disorder (Moreno, 1992). The child was 17 years old at the time the mother wrote the essay.

CASE 12-2. BETH

I waited five years before my daughter ever looked at me. That moment, in April of 1977, was absolutely miraculous. It was at bedtime, during her nightly bedtime story, right at the part when I would say, "and Beth went to sleep knowing that her Mommy and Daddy loved her." Then I said, "Oh, Beth, I wish that just once you'd tell me you loved me!" Suddenly, she opened her eyes, looked right into mine, and said, "love Mama." It was the most intensely joyous and miraculous experience that I have ever known in my life. For the first time in her young life, I knew that "someone was home." Only those who have lived with or worked closely with autistic people know exactly what I mean by that. I will never, ever take it for granted when she looks at me, and she does it a lot now.

I will never take for granted my daughter washing her hands. It took me six years to teach her that. Now I think that hand washing is the most amazing and wonderful thing. I am also raising another child, Mandy, who is 11. Through her, because of my experience with Beth, I have been able to see the miracle of normal human development.

I never take peace and quiet for granted. I never take smiles and hugs for granted. I never take laughter for granted. What I am trying to say is that I have learned an exquisite joy in very, very small things.

I have learned about human spirit from living with my daughter and seeing her try to help herself, just as much as we have tried to help her. I have learned a lot more about human dignity. And for all of the cruelty that Beth and our family have experienced, I have learned about human kind-

ness from all of the wonderful people who have befriended Beth and who have been kind to us when we needed it most—people who suddenly and unexpectedly have come to our rescue when she was upset or who have included her in their social plans and outings. And I have learned about caring and commitment from the wonderful teachers who have given so much time and energy to Beth and to us.

I have learned that a few good friends are much more valuable than a long list of superficial friends. My friends have stood by me through the best and worst moments. What I appreciate most is their ability to know when I just need to have a good time instead of talking about deep issues. I have been blessed with bright and caring professional mentors who have made themselves accessible whenever I have needed encouragement, information, or advice.

My husband, Marco, has taught me that although the divorce statistics among parents of handicapped children are horrendous, this experience can instead make a marriage stronger than ever.

Those are good things in my life. If I could do it all over again, of course I would have my daughter be born normal, because she has been through such torture. But if my choice were to not have my daughter at all or to have her as she is, I would still choose to have my daughter and to live with autism. (pp. 102–103)

No problem of human destiny is beyond human beings.
—John F. Kennedy

MENTAL RETARDATION

Description

Two leading professional organizations offer somewhat different definitions of *mental retardation*. The *American Association on Mental Retardation* (*AAMR*; 1992) defines mental retardation in the following way:

Mental retardation refers to substantial limitations in present functioning. It is characterized by significantly subaverage intellectual functioning, existing concurrently with related limitations in two or more of the following applicable adaptive skill areas: communication, self-care, home living, social skills, community use, self-direction, health and safety, functional academics, leisure, and work. Mental retardation manifests before age 18. (p. 5)

Subaverage intellectual functioning is further defined as a score of approximately 70 to 75 or below on an individually administered intelligence test. Adaptive skills should be measured by use of an appropriately normed and standardized adaptive behavior scale. The current classification system of the AAMR does not advocate the use of any categories (such as mild, moderate, severe, and profound) to classify degrees of mental retardation.

DSM-IV (American Psychiatric Association, 1994) defines mental retardation as significantly subaverage intellectual functioning…that is accompanied by significant limitations in adaptive functioning in at least two of the following skill areas: communication, self-care, home living, social/interpersonal skills, use of community resources, self-direction, functional academic skills, work, leisure, health, and safety.… The onset must occur before age 18 years. (p. 39)

Subaverage intellectual functioning is further defined as an IQ of about 70 or below on an individually administered intelligence test, although the IQ can be as high as 75. Information about adaptive functioning can be obtained from informants, developmental and medical histories, and performance on scales to measure adaptive behavior. Finally, *DSM-IV* specifies four degrees of severity of mental retardation:

- *mild mental retardation* (IQ level of 50–55 to approximately 70)
- *moderate mental retardation* (IQ level of 35–40 to 50–55)
- *severe mental retardation* (IQ level of 20–25 to 35–40)
- *profound mental retardation* (IQ level below 20 or 25)

One of these four degrees of severity must be included in the diagnosis of mental retardation, with one exception—when there is a strong presumption of mental retardation but the child's intelligence is untestable by standard tests. In the latter case, the diagnosis according to *DSM-IV* is "Mental Retardation, Severity Unspecified."

The two definitions of mental retardation overlap considerably. In fact, *DSM-IV* follows the 1983 AAMR formulation (H. J. Grossman, 1983). Both approaches emphasize the importance of administering (a) an individual intelligence test to determine children's level of intelligence and (b) an adaptive behavior scale to evaluate adaptive behavior. However, the *DSM-IV* approach is preferable because it provides for the determination of the level of intellectual functioning. These levels are valuable for discussing the assessment results with parents, teachers, and health care providers; for formulating intervention programs; for estimating children's future potential; and for research and data analysis purposes. There is a considerable difference between a child with an IQ of 20 and a child with an IQ of 70, even though both may receive a diagnosis of mental retardation.

Etiology. Mental retardation results from a diverse set of factors (American Psychiatric Association, 1994). Following are the major predisposing factors:

1. *Heredity.* These factors include inborn errors of metabolism inherited mostly through autosomal recessive mechanisms (for example, *Tay-Sachs disease*), other single-gene abnormalities (for example, *tuberous sclerosis*), and chromosomal aberrations (for example, *fragile X syndrome,* which is a physical abnormality on the X chromosome). See the Glossary for explanations of these terms and conditions.

2. *Early alterations of embryonic development.* These factors include chromosomal changes (for example, *Down syndrome*) and prenatal changes due to toxins (for example, maternal alcohol consumption [discussion to follow] and infections).

3. *Pregnancy and perinatal problems.* These factors include *fetal malnutrition,* prematurity, *hypoxia,* viral and other infections, and trauma.

4. *General medical conditions acquired in infancy or childhood.* These factors include infections (for example, *meningitis, roseola, encephalitis,* and *rabies*), trauma (for example, head injuries), and poisoning (for example, lead poisoning).

5. *Environmental influences.* These factors include severe neglect and deprivation of social-linguistic stimulation and other forms of social and cognitive stimulation.

Children who function in the mentally retarded range also may have physical disabilities. For example, infants born to women who abuse alcohol may develop *fetal alcohol syndrome.* This syndrome develops when a sufficient amount of alcohol consumed by the mother crosses the placenta and interferes with neurotransmitter production, cell development, cell migration, and brain growth of the fetus. The main characteristics of this syndrome are low birthweight, growth retardation, organic anomalies (including cleft palate, neural tube defect [a defect caused by the failure of the neural folds to fuse and form a neural tube], hearing loss, and heart defects), and neurobehavioral deficits (including mental retardation, speech and language disorders, and attention-deficit/hyperactivity disorder). Fetal alcohol syndrome is a leading cause of mental retardation in the western world (Abel & Sokol, 1991).

Approximately 1% of the population falls into the mentally retarded range of functioning. Of these individuals, approximately 85% are in the mild classification, 10% in the moderate classification, 3% to 4% in the severe classification, and 1% to 2% in the profound classification (American Psychiatric Association, 1994).

Parental reactions. In the following quotations, parents express various feelings, reactions, and concerns about raising a child who is mentally retarded (Smith, 1993, pp. 4, 84, 86, 93, 105, 119, 147–149, 164, 171, 177, 194, 222, 249, 281, 297, reprinted with permission of the publisher, from R. Smith [Ed.], *Children with Mental Retardation: A Parent's Guide,* copyright 1993 by Woodbine House).

1. *Realization of differences.* Parents may be slow to realize that their child has developmental delays.

Our son had an Apgar score of 9 [this score is well within normal limits; see the Glossary] when he was born, so we had no clue whatsoever. And the doctors didn't either, obviously. It was kind of a gradual depression that whole first year. Two of my girlfriends also had babies. We would get together for these luncheons and we would take our kids, and my son wasn't doing anything that the other two were doing.

2. *Reactions to diagnosis.* Parents react to the diagnosis in different ways.

When our son got into a preschool program, that's when we really found out that he tested in the mentally retarded range. That was the first time that we really knew. It wasn't so much that it was surprising, it was just hard hearing it. I can remember leaving the psychologist's office and crying all the way home. I didn't hear the rest of the hour conversation that we had. I mean, I know that he told me all of these wonderful things about Matthew, but I just couldn't hear that. All I kept hearing was "mentally retarded." I tried to call my neighbor and she wasn't home. Then I called my mother and told her, and the first thing out of her mouth was, "So what? Does that change Matthew?" I just kind of sat down for a minute and said, "She's right."

3. *Awareness of child's functioning.* Parents often are aware of their child's difficulties and strengths.

I don't notice that Scott's different as much when he's by himself. It's when he is with other kids that he seems to be different sometimes. He doesn't talk and they do; he doesn't walk…. I mean, I see another child who's 2½ or 3 years old and walking and talking normally and things like that, and I think, "Well, I guess he *is* slow or he *is* different." But usually we just see the daily progress he makes and don't compare.

Ricky plays so much like other kids—he runs, jumps, throws, shoots a basketball, and catches like other kids. Someone who didn't know that he had mental retardation might not be able to see any differences in how he plays.

4. *Feelings of guilt, anger, grief, betrayal, resentment, stimulation, and acceptance.* Parents experience different emotions, depending on such factors as how and when they learn about the diagnosis, the severity of the child's retardation and associated problems, and their own personality and temperament.

I would get myself into a real depression when I would compare her with other kids, because then I felt that maybe it was something that I missed. I still had a lot of that guilt.

I know this sounds weird, but Cindy has given me the most fascinating education of my life. I find all the information about how mental retardation affects her life, how her brain works, and how she learns tremendously fascinating. I actually look forward to tests and evaluations because I can quiz the teacher, therapist, or psychologist about mental retardation and special education.

5. *Working with professionals.* Parents react to professionals in different ways, depending on the nature of the interactions.

The psychologist tested our son and asked a lot of questions, but she was very careful not to say certain things in front of our son. Then she went over every single bit of information I had collected about him. She sat down and the first thing she said was, "Let me tell you what a learning disability is," and she told me. Then she said, "Now let me tell you what mentally retarded is." She drew me a chart and she told me that he is moderately mentally retarded, not severely retarded. He is working at half of his age level. "Did anyone ever tell you what he is going to do when he's 18?" she asked. I said, "Nobody has ever said to me what he's going to do tomorrow." She said, "Well, let me tell you. The least you can expect

from him…." And I wrote this all down. I walked out of there and I had a head full of information. She explained everything to me in language that I could understand and I felt so much better. Now I knew what we needed to do. I got the answers that I needed and that I had waited all these years to find. I went home feeling like I had lifted this huge weight off my shoulders.

Besides me, the person who knows Janeen best is her teacher. I count what she says more than any other evaluator because, next to me, she spends the most time with my daughter. She knows best how Janeen learns, what works and doesn't work, and what interests her.

6. *Providing input to professionals.* Parents have information and suggestions that may help professionals in working with the child; they also have concerns that professionals need to consider.

I make sure that my input is considered in my child's evaluations. Otherwise, the evaluator gets only a partial picture. Ricky has many skills that he may (on a good day) or may not (on a bad day) show during a test.

To me, it's only fair to give our son a chance to go into his home school kindergarten. I don't know that he can be mainstreamed his whole life long, but I want him to have opportunities that other children have, for many reasons. One reason is that I think it will be best for him. If he is in a situation where certain things are expected of him, he's just that much more likely to do them.

7. *Interacting with other parents who have children who are mentally retarded.* Parents can gain valuable information by talking to other parents who have children who are mentally retarded.

I feel it is good to share some things, like information and energy. I feel that when you're down or someone else is down, you boost each other. You think the same way, you have a lot of things in common. To me, it's very, very helpful to be in a support group, but everybody doesn't feel that way.

8. *Disciplining children.* Parents of children who are mentally retarded have many of the same concerns about discipline that other parents have.

Sometimes when my son's squealing, I get stares because I'm not "correcting" him. But I feel like I can't be telling him to stop all the time—sometimes it's when he's overstimulated. But I don't really know. Maybe I'm making excuses for myself…or for him…or maybe this is the right thing to do. I never know.

If he is being naughty, then he ought to sit in the corner or whatever like some other child would have to do. He ought to be told "no" even if he gets upset.

9. *Daily living skills.* Parents may be concerned about teaching their child daily living skills.

Julie has good days and bad days. Sometimes she could empty that whole dishwasher and put the items on the table. She has the cognitive ability to do that. But if I catch her at a bad time, she starts pounding the dishes and she can't do it. I know to back off, that this is not the right time.

At school he's learned to keep a file of prices of groceries and how to categorize them. It's wonderful. He goes to the store with me, and I'm thinking "Now where is that?" and he finds the thing on his list and knows which aisle to go to.

10. *Concern about other family members.* Parents may be concerned about how other family members will react to the child who is mentally retarded.

It has sometimes been hard for our other two kids that they have a sister who is different from somebody else's older sister. But it is great that they have really kind of ridden along with it. They have never stopped having friends over. She's a puzzle to the friends, too. They know that she has mental retardation—that has never been a question—but they also see her doing these other things. Sometimes I'll overhear our son say, "If you think I'm a good speller, or whatever, then you won't believe how my sister can spell."

11. *Reactions of others in the community.* Parents may be concerned about how to treat their child when they go out and about how other people will judge their behavior.

When we go to a restaurant or something like that and Kyle acts up like any child might act up, my wife especially becomes concerned that people are going to say, "Look at that little retarded boy acting up" as opposed to "Look at that little 2- or 3-year-old acting up," so she's extra careful that he doesn't act up. She's almost overly careful.

12. *Thinking about the future.* Parents have concerns about how their child will function as an adult and what will happen to the child when they die.

Almost everything I do or think about is aimed at Ricky's future—making sure that what he does today builds toward a future in which he is capable and functional. Ricky, on the other hand, lives entirely in the present—he lives for the moment. These two lifeviews often conflict. You can't make Ricky care about the distant future (or even the near future). If you want to teach him skills that he will need for the future, you have to make learning those skills enjoyable to him in the present.

The following poem expresses one parent's feelings about raising a child with mental retardation (Max, 1985, pp. 261–262):

Parenthood of a retarded person…is a kaleidoscope of feeling and experience.

It has its beauty, but it is always changing. It is irritation at ineffectual hands plucking endlessly at a knotted shoelace.…

It is guilt at the irritation.…

It is a surge of love for this person who needs your protection; and a surge of horror that he will always need it.…

It is a glowing admiration for his learning achievements, against such odds.

It is horror at the inexorable ticking of the developmental clock.

It is a prayer that he will painlessly cease to live.

It is the desperate rush to the doctor because he's looking ill.…

It is 365 days a year.

Interviewing Issues

Children who are mentally retarded usually have a slow rate of cognitive development, limited expressive and receptive language abilities, limited adaptive skills, limited experiential background, short attention span, some distractibility, and a concrete and literal style in approaching tasks (Cobb, 1989). Rapport may be difficult to establish because of their "limited verbal abilities, frequent fear of strangers, and distrust of their own ability to communicate effectively" (Ollendick, Oswald, & Ollendick, 1993, p. 49). You must adjust your interview techniques accordingly if you find these qualities present in children suspected of being mentally retarded. Instead of asking open-ended questions, which may be extremely difficult for them to answer, you may need to simplify questions, to be concrete, to ask structured questions, and to prompt frequently. Be prepared to repeat or rephrase your questions or comments. This strategy will require skill and patience (Ollendick et al., 1993). Children who are mentally retarded may be hesitant to ask for breaks in the interview. Therefore, if you see signs of fatigue—such as changes in attentiveness, restlessness, fidgeting, drooping of head, or yawning—take a break. If necessary, schedule several short interview sessions.

Children who are mentally retarded may have higher rates of acquiescence than children who are not mentally retarded; thus, do not rely primarily on asking "yes-no" questions. In fact, uncritical acceptance of responses to "yes-no" questions by children who are mentally retarded may lead you to draw invalid inferences. Children who are mentally retarded may have difficulty recalling when their problems began or other important details of their lives. To improve their recall, link problems to events such as birthdays, holidays, or times of the year based on school projects or summer vacations.

Children who are mentally retarded may have emotional problems unrelated to their intellectual retardation. If they are uncooperative during the interview, evaluate the possible adaptive significance of the uncooperative behavior (as you should for all children who display this or any other significant behavior).

- *Negativistic behavior* may enable them to maintain self-esteem in the face of difficult questions.
- *Aggressive, hyperactive behavior* may represent their emergency reaction to a novel situation involving difficult questions.
- *Echolalia* (inappropriate repetitions of a word or sentence just spoken by another person) may serve as a way for them to establish and maintain a relationship, although it is maladaptive in other ways.
- *Persistent questioning* may represent their effort to ensure stability in the situation.
- *Perseveration* may help them manage the situation.
- *Denial* may be used to cover their feelings of vulnerability.

As with all children, developing a warm, accepting relationship may help to reduce unacceptable behavior.

Children who are *profoundly mentally retarded* may be especially difficult to interview because of self-stimulating behavior, self-injurious behavior, limited attention span, destructive behavior, temper tantrums, seizures, noncompliance with requests, or inability to understand the questions. In such cases, if you can't interview the children, consider simply observing them (see Table 3-3 in Chapter 3).

You will want to obtain from the parents an in-depth developmental, medical, and educational history of their child, their views of the child's problem behaviors, and their feelings and attitudes about raising a child who may be mentally retarded. You will want to evaluate such factors as whether the child's school placement is appropriate, whether the child is receiving adequate environmental stimulation, whether the parents' expectations are realistic, and, for older adolescents, whether plans have been made for future living arrangements and work experiences.

You can use the semistructured interviews in Table F-13 and Table F-36 in Appendix F for interviewing mentally retarded children and their parents, respectively. When you complete the interviews, you will want to consider such questions as the following:

1. Is there any history of mental retardation in the family?
2. Were there any medical complications during the pregnancy? If so, what were the complications?
3. Did the mother have amniocentesis or ultrasound during the pregnancy? If so, what did the test show?
4. Did the child have a normal delivery?
5. When did the child reach specific developmental landmarks, such as smiling, sitting, crawling, walking, saying first words, making simple word combinations, reacting to strangers, becoming toilet trained, and acquiring dressing skills? Were there any delays in the child's reaching developmental landmarks? If so, in what areas were the delays and how long were the delays?
6. Did the parents suspect that something was wrong? If so, when did they first suspect that something was wrong?
7. What were the results of the medical evaluation? In particular, how are the child's vision, hearing, motor skills, and general health? Has the child received any medical treatments? If so, what was the child treated for, what was the treatment, and how effective was the treatment?
8. What were the results of the psychological evaluation? In particular, what were the child's scores on the individual intelligence test, on the test of adaptive behavior, and on other ability tests?
9. Is there any history of brain damage, including seizures or illnesses such as meningitis or encephalitis, that may have had an effect on the child's development?
10. How do the parents describe the child's cognitive level?
11. How do the parents describe the child's behavior?
12. What are the parents' plans for the child?
13. What services does the family need?
14. If the child is attending school, how is the child doing at school? What grades is the child receiving in academic subjects? How does the child get along with other children? Is the child receiving special education services? If so, what types of services is the child receiving?
15. What do the child's teachers report about her or his behavior and academic performance in class?

Interventions

Interventions with children who are mentally retarded may focus on what special services the families need and what help they need in finding the services. Services may begin in the preschool years, and even shortly after the child's birth. Services for children who are mentally retarded may include medical and dental care, special education programs, in-home living assistance programs, employment assistance, sheltered workshops, and places where the children can lead as normal lives as possible when they reach adulthood (Tanguay & Russell, 1991).

Several approaches have been successful in reducing the occurrence of mental retardation (Szymanski & Crocker, 1985). These include

- screening and treating infants for metabolic disorders
- using a low-phenylalanine diet for pregnant women who have *phenylketonuria* (PKU; a condition caused by a recessively inherited deficiency of phenylalanine hydroxylase, which, if untreated, may result in brain damage) and for infants who are born with PKU
- immunizing children
- providing education to adults about the effects of alcohol and drug use during pregnancy
- reducing children's exposure to lead
- constructing safer automobiles
- providing public education about the need to use infant seats and seat belts in automobiles
- using *amniocentesis* (a surgical procedure in which a small sample of amniotic fluid is drawn out of the uterus through a needle inserted in the abdomen of the mother) for prenatal diagnosis of chromosomal disorders; the results of this procedure give the mother (and father) the opportunity to decide whether to continue the pregnancy
- screening parents to identify whether they have genetic conditions or metabolic disorders that could result in retardation in their infants and then encouraging genetic counseling

For children and adolescents who are mentally retarded and who also have behavioral problems, the same interventions used with nonmentally retarded persons can be used. These interventions include environmental change, behavioral treatments, individual psychotherapy, group psychotherapy, family therapy, and pharmacotherapy (under health care provider's guidance). When the behavioral and psychotherapeutic interventions are designed, the child's level of cognitive and social functioning should be considered, as some approaches may need to be modified. For example, sessions may need to be shorter and more frequent, and interventions may need to incorporate more structure, reassurance, problem solving, and constructive feedback (Bregman, 1991).

Case Illustration

The following case illustrates the developmental course of a boy diagnosed as mildly mentally retarded (Weiner, 1982).

CASE 12-3. JORDAN

When Jordan was 6 months old, his mother remembers thinking, "There was something about his eyes, they did not focus correctly; the way he held his spoon seemed different." Comparisons with his older brother emphasized these differences in development, and Jordan's mother suspected he had some problems. However, the family pediatrician reassured her that he was developing normally until age 3½ years, when it became apparent that he was not speaking clearly. The pediatrician then referred the family to an evaluation and treatment center for children with suspected mental retardation. At the center Jordan was evaluated by a psychologist, a pediatrician, and a speech and language pathologist. He obtained an IQ of 64 on the Stanford-Binet Intelligence Scale, which placed him in the Mild Mentally Retarded classification. He also was found to have poor speech patterns that called for special attention to his speech development.

When Jordan was 4 years, 3 months of age he entered a preschool program for mildly and moderately retarded children. He stayed in this preschool for three years until he was 7 years of age. During that time his speech improved considerably, and he developed a friendly, outgoing personality. Jordan then entered the special-education classes in his public school for educable retarded children. He remained in special classes until his graduation from the high school at 20 years of age. Although he was in segregated classes throughout his school years, he participated in school activities by being a manager for the football and wrestling teams. His outgoing personality and willingness to learn managerial tasks enabled him to become well liked in school and popular as a manager. During his school years, Jordan had several IQ tests. His scores ranged from mid-sixties to the mid seventies, thus confirming his intellectual functioning at the mildly retarded range.

Jordan engaged in social activities with his brother and in his role as a manager of the football team, but he never dated or entered a social group outside his family. He attended special programs at the local YMCA for disabled children. He also attended a special camp for intellectually retarded children over the summers. During the latter years of high school, Jordan began work-study programs to prepare him for some type of career. Immediately following his graduation, he was hired as an attendant in the men's department of a local department store, checking the men's fitting rooms. He continued to live at home, take public transportation to and from work, and maintain a regular, although somewhat isolated career role. His social life was restricted to family and special programs available from time to time in local community centers for mildly disabled individuals.

Future problems for him, yet to be encountered, include finding some kind of semiindependent living facility. Jordan will need supervision in basic life skills, such as food preparation and shelter. However, his motivation to work, friendly personality, patience in taking directions, and ability to take responsibility have enabled him to sustain a job in the community, despite his mild mental retardation. (pp. 91–92, with changes in notation)

SPECIFIC LEARNING DISABILITY

Description

Approximately 5% of children in the United States are identified as having some form of learning disability (see Table 10-5, p. 341). Learning disabilities may hinder children's educational progress and adversely affect their self-esteem, social status, and occupational choices. Early identification and effective interventions are therefore needed to help children with learning disabilities get the skills they require for classroom learning.

The term *learning disability* can be used in both a broad and a narrow sense. In the broad sense, it refers to learning difficulties associated with any type of disability, including mental retardation, brain injury, sensory difficulties, or emotional disturbance. In the narrow sense, it refers to the failure, by children who have adequate intelligence, adequate maturational level, appropriate cultural background, and relevant educational experiences, to learn a scholastic skill. This chapter uses the term in the narrow sense. The most common learning disability is reading disorder, followed by mathematics disorder, spelling disorder, and disorder of written expression.

The more specific term used for the narrow meaning of learning disability is *specific learning disability*, defined as follows in Public Law 94-142 (*Federal Register*, December 29, 1977):

"Specific learning disability" means a disorder in one or more of the basic psychological processes involved in understanding or in using language, spoken or written, which may manifest itself in an imperfect ability to listen, think, speak, read, write, spell, or to do mathematical calculations. The term includes such conditions as perceptual handicaps, brain injury, minimal brain dysfunction, dyslexia, and developmental aphasia. The term does not include children who have learning problems which are primarily the result of visual, hearing, or motor handicaps, of mental retardation, of emotional disturbance, or of environmental, cultural, or economic disadvantage. (p. 65083, 121a.5)

Public Law 94-142 provides the following guidelines for determining the presence of a specific learning disability (Federal Register, December 29, 1977):

(a) A team may determine that a child has a specific learning disability if:

(1) The child does not achieve commensurate with his or her age and ability levels in one or more of the areas listed in paragraph

(a)(2) of this section, when provided with learning experiences appropriate for the child's age and ability levels; and

(2) The team finds that a child has a severe discrepancy between achievement and intellectual ability in one or more of the following areas:

(i) Oral expression;
(ii) Listening comprehension;
(iii) Written expression;
(iv) Basic reading skills;
(v) Reading comprehension;
(vi) Mathematics calculation; or
(vii) Mathematics reasoning

(b) The team may not identify a child as having a specific learning disability if the severe discrepancy between ability and achievement is primarily the result of:

(1) A visual, hearing, or motor handicap;
(2) Mental retardation;
(3) Emotional disturbance; or
(4) Environmental, cultural or economic disadvantage. (p. 65083, 121a.541)

The definition of learning disability in Public Law 94-142 has not been universally accepted. First, the discrepancy criteria—that is, the idea that a diagnosis of specific learning disability should be given only when children have a *severe discrepancy* between achievement and intellectual ability in one or more expressive or receptive skills, such as written expression, listening and reading comprehension, or mathematics—may not be valid. Several writers maintain that intellectual ability, as established by a score on an intelligence test, should not be used to decide whether children have a learning disability (see *Journal of Learning Disabilities, 22* [8], 1989).

Second, the term *severe discrepancy* is open to several interpretations. Much depends on which tests psychologists give to the children and how psychologists define a severe discrepancy.

Third, several statements in the federal definition are not clear. For example, how do we identify and define *basic psychological processes*? The statement "the term does not include children who have learning problems which are *primarily* [italics added] the result of visual..." assumes that we can distinguish primary from secondary causes. In practice, however, it is often difficult to decide which condition is primary and which is secondary. For instance, are the emotional problems of children with learning disabilities caused by poor achievement, or do children with emotional problems develop learning problems?

Fourth, the *exclusionary criteria* in the definition of learning disabilities make it difficult, if not impossible, for children with sensory difficulties, with emotional problems, or with environmental disadvantages to receive a learning disability label (Morris, 1988). Neither the definition of learning disability nor the accompanying provisions of PL 94-142 provide any operational criteria for identifying children who have sensory or emotional problems or environmental disadvantages. How much of a sensory loss, for example, is required to exclude a child? Similarly, what are the criteria used to identify children as having an emotional disturbance? The logic behind these exclusionary criteria is hard to understand (Morris, 1988).

Another definition for learning disability, proposed by the National Joint Committee on Learning Disabilities (1987), generally agrees with the one in Public Law 94-142. It deletes the term *basic psychological processes* and specifies difficulties in reasoning in addition to the academic and spoken language problems listed in Public Law 94-142. The committee's definition is as follows:

Learning disabilities is a general term that refers to a heterogeneous group of disorders manifested by significant difficulties in the acquisition and use of listening, speaking, reading, writing, reasoning, or mathematical abilities. These disorders are intrinsic to the individual, presumed to be due to central nervous system dysfunction, and may occur across the life span. Problems in self-regulatory behaviors, social perception, and social interaction may exist with learning disabilities but do not by themselves constitute a learning disability. Although learning disabilities may occur concomitantly with other handicapping conditions (for example, sensory impairment, mental retardation, serious emotional disturbance) or with extrinsic influences (such as cultural differences, insufficient or inappropriate instruction), they are not the result of those conditions or influences. (p. 1)

Children with learning disabilities have difficulty "processing information in a manner that allows them to comprehend, remember, and generalize concepts relevant to the development of oral language, written language, and mathematical skills" (Lyon & Moats, 1988, p. 830). Although the definition of learning disability continues to be elusive and children with this label represent an extraordinarily heterogeneous population, *the common characteristic usually shared by learning disabled children is academic underachievement.* We need to remember that the real task is to determine which children need help, regardless of legal definitions of what constitutes a learning disability or the difficulties and ambiguities of the diagnosis.

A learning disability may reflect a *developmental delay* (that is, the child is functioning at a level below that normally expected for children of her or his age), a *developmental deficit* (that is, the child is deficient in using the specific function), or *both a developmental delay and a developmental deficit.* The combined type of deficit may be characteristic of children with severe learning difficulties. Children with a learning disability are especially vulnerable to the development of severe academic difficulties because once they "have fallen behind academically they are susceptible to still further delays" (Taylor, 1988b, p. 798).

Etiology. Learning disabilities likely have multiple etiologies that are associated with genetic, biological, and environmental factors. Following are three etiological hypotheses that have been offered:

1. *Genetic basis.* There is some evidence, in the form of biological markers, that learning disabilities have a genetic

basis. Children with learning disabilities have been shown to have a greater than expected incidence of (a) family histories of learning problems, (b) prenatal and perinatal complications early in life, (c) electrophysiological abnormalities, and (d) learning difficulties despite good behavioral adjustment and environmental support (Taylor, 1988b). Although the evidence of a genetic basis for learning disabilities is at best suggestive because demonstrable brain disease in children with learning disabilities has not been shown frequently, evidence is accumulating that "phonologically based disabilities are linked to neurobiological and genetic factors…[and] that the phonological deficits observed in reading disability are heritable" (Lyon, 1996, p. 65).

2. *Biological defects.* Learning disabilities may result from biological deficits that affect perceptual systems, perceptual-motor functioning, neurological organization, and oculomotor functioning. Children with a learning disability may have had some minor trauma at birth or during their first year of life or a history of chronic middle ear infection during their first three or four years of life.

Defects in perceptual systems may result in deficiencies in processing auditory and visual information related to language, including listening, speaking, reading, and writing (Lyon & Moats, 1988). Part of the processing difficulty may result from a mismatch between behaviors needed to perform academic tasks and the characteristics of the academic tasks.

A deficit in *phonological processing*—that is, deficiencies in phonological coding and short-term memory for linguistic material—may, in part, account for reading, writing, and spelling disabilities. For example, the primary deficit associated with poor reading may be a "linguistic deficit that interferes with the reader's ability to grasp the concept that words have parts—phonemes, syllables, and morphemes— and that these parts are represented abstractly by the alphabetic code" (Lyon & Moats, 1988, p. 833).

3. *Ineffective learning strategies.* Learning disabilities may result from children's use of ineffective learning strategies (Lyon & Moats, 1988). These include ineffective ways of analyzing the problem, of relating the nature of the problem to previous experience, of developing a strategic plan for operating on the information, and of monitoring and adjusting performance.

Living with a learning disability. The following is a first-person account by an 18-year-old with a learning disability (J. M. Knox, *Encyclopedia of Health: Learning Disabilities* [pages 58–59]. Copyright 1989 by Chelsea House. Reprinted by permission). Tall and thin, with dark hair, Jon had a serious expression as he talked about himself. He had just graduated from a private boarding school that specialized in helping students with learning problems.

CASE 12-4. JON

In elementary school I started having trouble with reading. My eyes would wander. The lines would seem to separate. I had problems with math, too. I can't memorize all the formu-las and what they do. Before sixth grade my Mom would help me. She read to me a lot. But in sixth grade it started getting harder. My Mom couldn't do all the math, and I started having to write more papers. I had trouble getting my ideas down in the right way. My reading wasn't good. I had a lot of trouble pronouncing words.

The public school wasn't any help, so we had to get private tutors. We asked friends whose kids had tutors. Throughout school I've needed an enormous amount of help and tutoring.

There were other factors, too. I've moved around so much that I've had to get used to different kids all the time. I would make a lot of friends and then I'd have to leave them. My stepfather was into real estate, and we had a campground in Florida. Then he thought there was more land in Colorado, so we moved there. Then we traveled to New York City so he could take over his father's business. I would say that moving was 40% of my handicap. I was 15 when we moved to New York. I was angry about that move.

My family is confusing. I was adopted as an infant. My Mom got divorced and she remarried when I was three. Now I have one sister, three stepsisters, and one stepbrother.

I'm a good skier. I started skiing when I was 10 and learned faster than anyone else in my family. I can pick up sports easily. In academics, if I stick to something, I usually get it done. I work hard. I like talking to people and helping them with problems. I'm also pretty neat and organized.

I'm not good at time management. I used to have a lot of trouble with studying. My class participation was poor. I really don't like to read books. Reading with tapes has helped me a lot.

Boarding school has also helped. I had to learn to deal with things on my own because before my Mom had always been there for me. At the boarding school we had a schedule every day and a mandatory study hall from seven to nine every evening. If you weren't studying, they would ask you what was the matter. The students had the same kinds of problems. We were all in the same boat and didn't feel ashamed of it.

I don't want people to think that if they have a learning problem they're stupid. They may just have a slower way of learning. There are people who can help you, but you have to ask for help. You can't expect it to come to you. You have to learn to deal with it and live with it. You have to just accept that it's a problem that you have and be happy with yourself.

Raising a child with a learning disability. In the following excerpt, a mother describes what it was like to raise her child who had a learning disability (J. M. Knox, *Encyclopedia of Health: Learning Disabilities* [pages 36–37]. Copyright 1989 by Chelsea House. Reprinted by permission).

CASE 12-5. CHRIS

Chris was always a sweet kid—considerate. Of all my children, he gave me the least trouble. I returned to work when he was in the second grade. Shortly after that we began to notice that he was having trouble. Spelling was difficult for him; math and reading were not easy either. On my nights off, I would sit with Chris and try to help him with his homework. It was a frustrating experience. By the end of the evening, I would ask him a question, but instead of answering me, he would just say, "I don't know." This would go on for hours. How do you spell this? "I don't know." What is this word? "I don't know!"

His difficulties with math, I thought, were understandable. I had never been very good with numbers, though my husband is. Our two other children grasped it easily, but Chris always struggled with it. I thought it must have been something he inherited from me—this math "dumbness." The rest, though, I began to think was just Chris's way of getting even with me for leaving him each afternoon to go to work. Even though he had an older brother and sister and his father usually came home two hours after school got out, I thought that my working had somehow interfered with Chris's schooling— maybe he wasn't getting enough help at home, maybe he just wasn't trying anymore.

Sometimes when I tried to help him, I would end up screaming, "You're not trying!" and poor Chris would start crying and scream, "I am! I'm just dumb!" and throw his book on the floor and run out.

At the end of that year, the parochial school Chris attended decided to leave him back. I was crushed, and so was Chris. Thank God, Chris's teacher finally spoke up. She told me she thought Chris was very bright—that perhaps he just had a learning disability. I didn't really know that much about learning disabilities, but my husband and I took Chris to be evaluated, and, sure enough, that's what it turned out to be.

In order to get the help he needed, we transferred Chris to a public school. There he worked with other children in a resource room to complete his homework and work out any tough problems. Chris had some trouble learning as fast as the other kids in a normal setting. Fortunately, he also had another wonderful teacher who was willing to stay after school with him and come in early to help with topics they were covering in class.

During high school, Chris attended vocational classes in electricity along with his regular classwork. He soon found that he was really good at electric work—he was bringing home straight A's. Today, Chris is training to be an electrician. He has outgrown his learning disability and is never frustrated by things anymore. His life is really on track.

Correlates of learning disability. Children with learning disabilities have deficits in cognitive-neuropsychological skills and in social-behavioral adjustment (Taylor, 1988a). They also may have some problems that are common to children who have attention-deficit/hyperactivity disorder (see Chapter 11).

Following are representative problems of children with a learning disability:

COGNITIVE-NEUROPSYCHOLOGICAL DEFICITS

- difficulty with verbal material (including poor reading recognition, associated with problems such as confusion in identifying or printing certain letters and numerals and losing one's place frequently when reading printed materials; poor reading comprehension; both poor reading recognition and poor reading comprehension; and poor transfer of learning)

- difficulty with nonverbal material (including poor visual perception, spatial perception, visual organization, revisualization, and perception of figure-ground relationships; difficulty in temporal sequencing; and difficulty interpreting facial expressions)
- deficient information processing skills (including poor cognitive strategies and inadequate study skills)
- poor independent work habits
- poor organizational skills (including sloppy paperwork and a disorganized approach to tasks that involve a sequence of actions)
- auditory or visual memory difficulty
- limited attention span
- poor practical planning skills
- poor fine motor coordination (including poor writing and poor drawing)
- visual acuity difficulties
- auditory perceptual deficits
- cross-modal sensory integration difficulties
- speech articulation problems
- delayed development of consistent hand preference

DEFICITS IN SOCIAL-BEHAVIORAL ADJUSTMENT
- immaturity
- disruptiveness
- impulsiveness
- destructiveness
- hyperactivity
- messiness
- annoying behavior
- mischievousness
- acting-out behavior
- poor self-image
- working slowly
- working poorly under time constraints
- relating better with younger children
- depression

Because children with learning disabilities are such a heterogeneous group, no one child is likely to exhibit all of the problems found among children with learning disabilities. For example, some children with learning disabilities have difficulties with verbal material, and others with nonverbal material; some have adequate information processing and interpersonal skills, while others do not. Impairments may be limited to one special area of functioning, such as reading, arithmetic, spelling, spatial reasoning, or problem solving. Psychosocial problems may stem from learning problems or learning problems may stem from psychosocial problems, or both learning and psychosocial problems may be associated with a common etiology. The appropriate explanation depends on the individual case.

Reading disorder. *Reading disorder* (or reading disability; also referred to as *dyslexia*), the most frequent form of learning disability, is best thought of as being on a continuum, which extends from no reading disability to a severe reading disability (Stanovich, 1988). Dyslexia then is defined in a somewhat arbitrary way by choosing a point on the continuum that identifies individuals with reading problems. This procedure is similar to what occurs in defining obesity, which also is on a continuum and defined somewhat arbitrarily. Unlike obesity, however, which has one critical dimension (weight), dyslexia is best perceived as having at least two important dimensions: *phonetic decoding* (that is, the ability to read phonetically visually presented words) and *whole word reading ability* (that is, the ability to recognize words based on their visual features). Some children have phonological processing deficits, others have visual processing deficits, and still others have deficits in both dimensions.

Following are some major findings from research studies related to children with reading disabilities (Lyon, 1996, adapted from p. 64):

1. Disabled readers with and without an IQ-achievement discrepancy show similar information processing, genetic, and neurophysiological profiles. This suggests that the existence of a discrepancy is not a valid indicator of disability in basic reading skills.
2. Epidemiological studies indicate that as many females as males manifest dyslexia; however, schools identify three to four times more boys than girls.
3. Reading disabilities reflect a persistent deficit rather than a developmental lag that will be remedied with time. Longitudinal studies show that, of those children who are reading disabled in the third grade, approximately 74% continue to read significantly below grade level in the ninth grade.
4. Children with reading disability differ from one another *and* from other readers along a continuous distribution. They *do not* aggregate together to form a distinct "hump" separate from the normal distribution of readers.
5. The ability to read and comprehend depends on rapid and automatic recognition and decoding of single words. Slow and inaccurate decoding are the best predictors of deficits in reading comprehension.
6. The ability to decode single words accurately and fluently is dependent on the ability to segment words and syllables into phonemes. Deficits in phonological awareness reflect the core deficit in dyslexia.
7. The best predictor of reading ability from kindergarten and first-grade performance is phoneme segmentation ability.

Mathematics disorder. Children who have a *mathematics disorder* (also called *dyscalculia*) may have one or more of the following difficulties (American Psychiatric Association, 1994; Rourke, 1993):

- *basic arithmetical skill difficulties* (such as difficulty following sequences of mathematical steps, counting objects, and learning multiplication tables)
- *language difficulties* (such as difficulty understanding or naming mathematical terms, operations, or concepts and difficulty decoding written problems into mathematical symbols)
- *perceptual or spatial difficulties* (such as difficulty recognizing or reading numerical symbols or arithmetical signs, clustering objects into groups, and aligning numbers in columns)
- *attentional skill difficulties* (such as difficulty copying numbers or figures correctly, adding "carried" numbers, and observing operational signs)
- *shifting difficulties* (such as difficulty shifting from one arithmetic operation to another)
- *writing difficulties* (such as writing so poorly that the numbers can't be read)

Mathematics disorder is a heterogeneous condition and may or may not occur with a reading disorder. Harris (1995) hypothesizes that "Math disorder may be associated with right hemispheric dysfunction involving the parietal lobe" (p. 168). The incidence of mathematics disorder is approximately 6% of the school-aged population of children who do not have low intelligence, sensory deficits, or economic deprivation (Lyon, 1996).

Spelling disorder. Children who have a reading disorder also may have a *spelling disorder,* although the processes involved in reading and spelling appear to be different. Spelling requires knowledge of sound-symbol correspondence (phonological skills) as well as linguistic competence, such as an understanding that the way words are spelled may depend on how they are used. Reading, as discussed earlier, likely involves phonetic decoding and whole word reading ability. Some children can memorize the spelling of individual words but have difficult spelling correctly when the words are used in sentences. Achieving skill in spelling also requires knowledge of the correct spelling of irregular words. Children can master spelling by focusing on the sound elements or the meaning and structure of the word. Children who have both reading and spelling difficulties tend to have a more generalized language disorder than those who have either a reading or a spelling disorder alone (Harris, 1995). Children who are good readers but poor spellers tend to have more difficulty manipulating sounds than good readers who also are good spellers (Goswami, 1992).

Disorder of written expression. Children who have a *disorder of written expression* have a disturbance that significantly interferes with their academic achievement or with activities of daily living that require writing skills (American Psychiatric Association, 1994). Their writing may be characterized by "grammatical or punctuation errors within sentences, poor paragraph organization, multiple spelling errors, and excessively poor handwriting" (p. 52). Disorders of written expression are commonly found in combination with reading and mathematics disorders. The child's age must be considered in evaluating the presence of this disorder, as writing skill is one of the last linguistic skills to develop. In addition, the child's vision and hearing should be screened if she or he has trouble with written expression. Writing disorder may be associated with (a) fine motor and linguistic deficits, (b) visual-spatial deficits, (c) attention and memory deficits, and (d) sequencing deficits (Sandler, Footo, Levine, Coleman, & Hooper, 1992). Estimates of written language deficits range from 8 to 15% of the school-aged population, with girls and boys displaying relatively equal rates (Lyon, 1996).

Culturally and linguistically different children. Children who come from cultural and linguistic backgrounds that differ from those of the majority group may perform poorly in school because of, for example, experiential differences, family expectations, limited English proficiency, stresses associated with acculturation and discrimination, and cognitive styles and learning strategies that differ from those of the majority group (also see Chapters 8 and 9). Consequently, ethnic minority children whose achievement is below average may not have a learning disability per se; rather, their achievement level may be related to ethnic and cultural factors. In such cases, it would be improper to label these children as having a "learning disability."

Prognosis for learning-disabled children. Studies do not provide conclusive answers about which children with a learning disability will continue to have problems with reading, mathematics, or spelling after they leave school. However, learning disabilities may persist into adulthood (Spreen, 1988; Taylor, 1988a). The prognosis depends on

- the severity of the child's learning disability
- the age at which the child's disability is recognized
- the types of learning problems the child has
- the child's general level of cognitive ability
- the child's response to intervention efforts
- the types of interventions attempted with the child
- the family's attitude toward the child's disability
- the child's self-concept, level of motivation, expectations, and coping skills
- the teachers' expectations of the child
- the peer group's attitude toward the child

More favorable outcomes tend to be associated with children who have milder forms of learning disability, who are "bright," who are in the middle or upper socioeconomic class, and who have normal neurological structures. Currently, the prognosis for any individual child cannot be determined in a valid way.

Interviewing Issues

Interviewing children. The semistructured interview in Table F-11 in Appendix F is useful in interviewing children who may have a specific learning disability. Your task is to obtain information about

- what learning and behavioral problems the child may be having
- how the child views his or her problems
- whether the learning problems interfere with the child's relationships with other children, teachers, parents, and siblings
- whether emotional problems, if present, are occurring with or in reaction to the learning problems
- the settings in which the emotional problems, if present, are likely to occur
- the child's study patterns
- whether the home environment is conducive to studying
- the child's views of the parents, family, teachers, school, and community

The questions in Table F-11 supplement those in Table F-13 in Appendix F. During the interview, pay close attention to how the child attends to your questions and the child's expressive language, receptive language, motor skills, activity level, and degree of cooperativeness. With respect to language, note, for example, whether the child understood the questions, made appropriate and coherent replies, seemed to understand nonverbal messages, used correct grammar, listened appropriately, and understood idioms presented in the conversation.

In Chapter 3, you read about using a sentence completion technique to elicit information from children who are reluctant to talk with you. You also can use a specialized sentence completion technique with children who may have a learning problem (see Table 12-3). If you use the technique, give the sentences orally and use the child's answers to probe further.

Interviewing parents. In interviewing the parents of a child with a specific learning disability, you will want to ask them about (Taylor, 1988a)

- their views of the child's strengths and weaknesses
- what they see as the problems
- what they believe might contribute to the problems, such as biological predispositions, deficiencies or delays in basic skill areas, personality and temperament, family influences, environmental influences, and the interaction of any of these factors
- which interventions have helped and which have not
- what suggestions they have for interventions

Table F-36 in Appendix F is useful for interviewing parents of a child with a specific learning disability.

Interviewing teachers. In interviewing the teachers of a child with a specific learning disability (see Table F-43 in Appendix F), you will want to ask about (Taylor, 1988a)

- their views of the child's strengths and weaknesses
- the child's academic grades and academic test scores
- the results of any psychoeducational tests administered to the child
- what the teachers see as the child's problems

Table 12-3
Sentence Completion Technique for Children Who May Have Learning Problems

Directions: I am going to start a sentence. Then I'd like you to finish it any way you want. Here is an example. If I say "When I am tired...," you can say "I go to bed," "I take a nap," "I sit down," or anything else that you can think of. OK? Let's try the first one.

Reading

1. When reading in class, I become nervous if _____.
2. Reading is easiest when _____.
3. Jobs that require reading are _____.
4. My favorite reading activity is _____.
5. If I couldn't read _____.
6. My favorite place to read is _____.
7. If I could do any type of reading, I would _____.
8. Reading reminds me of _____.
9. The worst place to read is _____.
10. Jobs that do not require reading are _____.
11. If you asked people what they thought of reading, most would say _____.
12. I would be less nervous about reading if _____.
13. The person with whom I would like to read is _____.

Arithmetic

14. When doing arithmetic in class, I become nervous if _____.
15. Arithmetic is easiest when _____.
16. Jobs that require arithmetic are _____.
17. My favorite arithmetic activity is _____.
18. If I couldn't do arithmetic _____.
19. My favorite place to do arithmetic is _____.
20. If I could do any type of arithmetic, I would _____.
21. Arithmetic reminds me of _____.
22. The worst place to do arithmetic is _____.
23. Jobs that do not require arithmetic are _____.
24. If you asked people what they thought of arithmetic, most would say _____.
25. I would be less nervous about arithmetic if _____.
26. The person with whom I would like to do arithmetic is _____.

Spelling

27. When doing spelling in class, I become nervous if _____.
28. Spelling is easiest when _____.
29. Jobs that require spelling are _____.
30. My favorite spelling activity is _____.
31. If I couldn't spell _____.
32. My favorite place to do spelling is _____.
33. If I could do any type of spelling, I would _____.
34. Spelling reminds me of _____.
35. The worst place to do spelling is _____.
36. Jobs that do not require spelling are _____.
37. If you asked people what they thought of spelling, most would say _____.
38. I would be less nervous about spelling if _____.
39. The person with whom I would like to do spelling is _____.

Source: Adapted from Giordano (1987).

- which interventions have been attempted with the child
- which interventions have or have not helped the child
- their suggestions for further interventions

You also will want to learn from the teachers such things as the child's ability to

- sit still
- make friends
- get along with other children
- listen to stories
- sustain attention over a protracted period
- understand age-appropriate rule-governed behavior
- take turns when playing with other children
- understand and manipulate symbols
- count
- spell
- read
- carry through a series of goal-oriented moves
- maintain appropriate spatial direction
- understand the complexities of a short story
- understand the complexities of a long story
- adapt to different teaching styles and expectations
- accommodate different types of instructional environments (for example, lecture, group discussion, cooperative learning, self-study)
- meet the demands of the assignments in the time allotted
- be an independent and self-directed learner

Evaluating the information. In evaluating the information you obtain from the child, parents, and teachers, consider the child's developmental history and family background, language abilities, motor abilities, social skills, behavior, nonverbal mental abilities, and school performance (see Table 11-1 in Chapter 11). Consider whether the child, parents, and others whom you interviewed reported problems that interfered with the child's cognitive, motor, affective, or behavioral development. If the child had a psychoeducational evaluation, what were the results? Finally, if a medical examination was performed, what were the results? All children referred for a possible learning disability need a comprehensive psychoeducational examination and a medical examination.

Interventions

The most effective interventions with children with learning disabilities involve the use of cognitive, linguistic, and cognitive-behavioral methods. Let's now look at these methods.

Cognitive methods. *Metacognition* refers to awareness of one's own cognitive processes and of one's own self-regulation, or what may be termed "knowing about knowing." Children are taught to use strategies—such as planning, monitoring, self-pacing, alternative ways of approaching tasks, and checking one's work—in order to increase their awareness of task demands, their use of appropriate strategies to ease task completion, and their ability to monitor the success of the strategy (Borkowski, Day, Saenz, Dietmeyer, Estrada, & Groteluschen, 1992; Lyon & Moats, 1988; Taylor, 1988a). Children who acquire these metacognitive skills should become more effective learners. The children must come to believe that effort, ability, and strategy choice are responsible for their success, not just luck.

Here are some examples of situations that children with reading disorders can be taught to recognize and then remedy with metacognitive strategies (Garner, 1987).

- A memory failure occurred. ("I'll have to go back to find the names of the first four presidents.")
- There are discrepancies between a heading in a text and the information the child obtained. ("I only found two economic theories when the text heading indicated that there were three.")
- The material was not completely mastered. ("I think I'll reread the last paragraph.")
- Some parts of the text are more difficult to read than other parts. ("I'll have to read this part more slowly than this part.")
- There is a need to evaluate what he or she learned. ("I'm going to test myself when I finish reading this section.")
- The environment may be distracting. ("I'll have to move to another location because I can't read too well with so much noise.")

Linguistic methods. Children may be given special help, tied to a content-based curriculum, in areas of their weaknesses. If they have a reading disability, for example, they may be given "highly structured programs that explicitly teach application of phonological rules to print...[Research shows that] systematic phonics instruction results in more favorable outcomes for disabled readers than does a context-emphasis (whole language) approach" (Lyon, 1996, p. 65).

Cognitive-behavioral methods. Behavioral interventions may be needed to improve learning disabled children's social and behavioral adjustment, because they tend to be

more anxious and unhappy, to be less liked, and to have lower expectations for academic success than their peers who do not have a learning disability (Casey, Levy, Brown, & Brooks-Gunn, 1992). The interventions are designed to reduce their frustrations both at school and at home. Children also may be taught to recognize their strengths and weaknesses and to adjust their expectations accordingly. They also may be taught how to use their strengths to compensate for their weaknesses.

Case Illustrations

The following two cases describe children who had academic difficulties as well as difficulties in social relations (Ariel, 1992). Note that this combination of difficulties does not occur in all children who have learning disabilities.

CASE 12-6. JIM

Jim is a 9-year-old third-grade student who is behind academically. He can't or won't read, and his writing is illegible. His pencil grasp seems weak, and he has difficulty writing numerals and letters. He is easily distracted and has difficulty attending to a task for any prolonged period. He repeatedly interrupts his classmates and is constantly in and out of his seat.

Jim's sensory-motor functions are markedly impaired. His dominance is confused—he uses his left hand for some activities, such as writing, but uses his right hand for others, such as throwing a ball. He has serious problems with fine motor coordination. His difficulty in grasping a pencil results in slow and shaky writing. Jim's gross motor coordination also is poor. He has trouble jumping and playing handball, and he often appears clumsy.

Jim's ability to memorize is quite strong, enabling him to remember correctly the order in which he has seen and heard information. Although he understands what he hears, Jim exhibits difficulties in verbal expression. His somewhat short sentences are awkward and syntactically incorrect. Overall, he seems to function at the high-average range of intelligence.

Although only 9 years old, Jim is hesitant in his approach to learning. He apparently sees himself as the least successful child in his family and therefore as undeserving of any positive rewards. His self-image is so low that he cannot express any of his positive qualities. Situations in school and life are generally too threatening for him to cope with.

According to his teacher, Jim is unable to discriminate between short and long vowels. He knows all the letters of the alphabet but occasionally confuses the various sounds. He knows some sight words at one time but misses them at another. In written expressive language, Jim becomes quite frustrated when asked to write or even copy from the board. In arithmetic—his stronger area—he functions at about the third-grade level. Emotionally, Jim is anxious about his learning difficulties. (p. 5, with changes in notation)

CASE 12-7. ADAM

Adam is a 14-year-old who is in the ninth grade and functioning at approximately the fourth-grade level in most academic areas. Passive in his approach to school and in his interper-

What A Guy! by Bill Hoest

Reprinted with special permission of King Features Syndicate.

sonal relationships, Adam seems to have given up. His teachers complain that it is impossible to teach him, and his father continuously claims that he is simply lazy. On the playground, Adam always seems to get into trouble. He easily explodes during simple social interactions.

Adam is of average intelligence. His fine and gross motor coordination are age-appropriate. He enjoys sports and would like to participate in his school's athletic program; however, his peers reject him because they think that he "looks strange." His language functions, both expressive and receptive, are impaired. His verbal expression and articulation are not clear, and he sometimes reacts as though he does not understand what is being said to him. Adam has extreme difficulty remembering information presented to him auditorily, but because of his excellent ability to reproduce visual patterns, he easily retains information presented to him visually.

Emotionally, Adam experiences feelings of inadequacy. He is bewildered by his inability to do well in school and claims that he is dumb. Adam is a loner; he has no friends. His social behavior is inappropriate and often awkward. He does not understand why he cannot get along with his peers. He tries his utmost to make friends with them, and consequently they take advantage of him. Adam would easily give his own possessions to others in exchange for their affection. (pp. 5–6, with changes in notation)

VISUAL IMPAIRMENT

Description

People are usually legally defined as blind when they can see no more at a distance of 20 feet than someone with normal vision can see at a distance of 200 feet. People also qualify for legal blindness if the *visual field is severely restricted*—that is, the widest diameter of the field of vision subtends an angle no greater than 20 degrees. Any type of serious visual dysfunction can significantly affect a child's

ability to process visual information. Vision helps in the identification of objects, in acquiring spatial relation concepts, and in integrating disparate elements into a more coherent whole or perceptual unit.

Children who are visually impaired can be classified in three broad groupings (Bauman, 1974):

1. Vision is of no practical use. This group includes the totally blind, those who can differentiate only between light and dark, and those who can distinguish shapes only when the shapes are held between the eyes and the source of light.
2. Vision can be used to handle large objects, to locate test pieces, or to follow the interviewer's hand movements during a demonstration but cannot be used to read even enlarged print effectively. These children are at a great disadvantage if they must read.
3. Vision can be used to read print efficiently only when the type is large, the page is held close to the eyes, or a magnifier or other special visual aid is used.

Children in any of these categories may have difficulty responding to materials requiring adequate vision. Therefore, be especially alert to the adequacy of their vision if you plan to use visual materials in the interview.

Children develop visual impairments because of disease, accidents, or congenital or hereditary disorders. In children from birth to 5 years, the leading causes of visual impairments are *prenatal cataracts, optic nerve atrophy, retrolental fibroplasia, congenital glaucoma,* and *retinoblastoma* (see the Glossary for definitions of these terms). In children from 5 to 10 years, additional causes of visual impairment are trauma, *albinism, myopia,* and *nystagmus* (Freedman, Feinstein, & Berger, 1988).

Signs of visual difficulty. If you see any of the following signs in a child who has *not* been previously referred for possible visual difficulties, recommend to the parents and child that the child have a visual examination.

- Rubs eyes excessively
- Shuts or covers one eye, tilts head, or thrusts head forward
- Has difficulty reading or doing close visual work
- Blinks abnormally or is irritable when doing close visual work
- Moves head excessively when reading
- Holds books too close to or too far from eyes
- Is inconsistent in reading print at different distances (for example, is able to read a book but not material written on the blackboard)
- Is unable to see distant things clearly
- Squints or frowns when using eyes
- Loses place while reading
- Avoids close visual work
- Has poor sitting posture while reading
- Walks overcautiously or runs into objects not directly in line of vision
- Has difficulty judging distances
- Has crossed eyes
- Has red-rimmed, encrusted, or swollen eyelids
- Has inflamed or watery eyes
- Has recurring sties
- Says eyes itch, burn, or feel scratchy
- Says that he or she cannot see well
- Complains of dizziness, headaches, or nausea following close visual work
- Has blurred or double vision
- Tires easily after visual work

Social maturity of children with a visual impairment. Children with a visual impairment tend to have more impaired social functioning than their peers with normal sight. This is so because they have more difficulty seeing meaningful physical gestures and facial expressions, using assertiveness skills, using visual cues to help them in interpersonal relations, receiving adequate feedback about their actions, and receiving positive feedback from others (Sisson & Van Hasselt, 1987).

Parental reactions.   Here are some reactions of parents who were raising blind children (Hancock, Wilgosh, & McDonald, 1990, pp. 411–413):

- I can't really say that you come to an acceptance stage. I am still reliving emotions I had when she was little. There is not one day that goes by that I don't wish she were sighted.
- I see myself more concerned with him now (at school age)… than I was a year or two ago.… I think there will be more issues as we go along that will have an emotional impact on our lives.…
- I feel I have done the best I can, and she seems to be progressing. We'll make it, I guess. I think that is really important.
- I see that we have made it through (a number of years) now and mostly all the things we have experienced have led to positive growth.

- It's so wonderful to see the child progress and do things.… You can say, "See, I don't have to worry, he is doing all right…He is going to make it.…"
- It has always amazed me that I think he is not ready (to do certain things)…but all of a sudden he decides he is ready and then accomplishes so much.
- It made me angry that there were people getting all of these services that I wasn't getting.… There really wasn't anyone around to teach me how to teach him.
- It is hard…to take time to explain things several times. It is easier to say "forget it"…but you can't do that.… You have to bring the experience to her.

Interviewing Issues

There are no special procedures for interviewing children who are visually impaired. However, the following suggestions should be helpful:

- Offer your arm to older children who are visually impaired or even take the hand of young children who are visually impaired to lead them to your office.
- Inform children about the general layout of the room and about other details, such as the presence of a tape recorder, if you are using one.
- Allow children to explore the interview room, provide verbal descriptions as needed, and guide them to where they should sit.
- If you plan to use pictorial materials in the interview, ask the child's parents or teachers how much useful vision the child has.
- Do not shout at children who are blind—these children have a visual problem, not a hearing problem.
- Do not be embarrassed about common expressions that might seem awkward, such as asking blind children whether they have *seen* a specific event. The English language is filled with these terms, and you are likely to be more sensitive to them than the children with whom you are talking. Moreover, children who are blind commonly use the term *see* about themselves.
- Use graphic language when directing older children who are blind. If you do not guide them to the chair, say "From where you are standing now, walk straight ahead about 3 feet; you will find the chair there," instead of saying "The chair is right over there."

Table F-37 in Appendix F is helpful in interviewing parents of a child with a visual impairment.

Interventions

Interventions with children who have visual impairments should focus on developing the children's skills and on helping them become independent and self-reliant. This may require instruction in Braille, help in independent living skills, and making available appropriate audio recordings. Adequate prenatal care and efficient obstetrical procedures may help prevent visual problems from developing in children.

Case Illustrations

The different adjustments made by two children with visual impairments are illustrated in the following cases (Freedman, Feinstein, & Berger, 1988).

CASE 12-8. S. J.

S. J., the product of a normal full-term pregnancy, was found at 6 weeks to have bilateral optic atrophy. He was in all other respects a healthy baby, and his mother, from the beginning, was actively engaging and stimulating. When he was placed on the floor at about 6 months, he would move forward face downward by pushing with his legs. When he was stopped by an obstacle, he would change direction. He sat independently at 9 months and walked at 1 year. At age 5 years, his speech was normal and included use of the first person pronoun. He continued to be a mentally alert, physically vigorous, and socially engaging youngster despite his lack of vision. (p. 872, with changes in notation)

CASE 12-9 FRANK

Frank, a 14-year-old boy with blindness of one year's duration following a long history of congenital, progressive retinal detachment, complained of severe insomnia and depression. He had been born with partial retinal detachment and cataracts and had undergone several corrective surgical procedures as a baby. Although he had a progressive disorder, the prognosis for retaining useful vision into adulthood had been considered good. Frank and his family were informed about the disorder, but no one in his family had anticipated total blindness. Before an accelerating loss of vision beginning at age 10, he had been a superior athlete and an above-average student.

At age 10, he first began waking up in the morning unable to see anything. These periods of blindness initially lasted only a few minutes, but over the next three years they increased in duration, until they lasted up to two hours each time. Frank kept these episodes a secret for many months. During this period, his visual acuity began to deteriorate during the intervals when sight was present.

Although he had more difficulty with schoolwork and lacked sufficient vision to maintain his athletic competitiveness, he tried to conceal these difficulties by making excuses and by being absent from school using made-up illnesses. A final effort at surgery was undertaken, which failed and resulted in near total blindness. Following surgery, Frank continued to insist for some time that he could safely perform activities such as riding his bicycle.

Most of his friendships had been based on his participation in sports programs. When he was forced to withdraw from these, he lost contact with most of his peers. Although special education teachers tried to support his continued mainstream placement, his denial of vision loss and limited cooperation greatly hindered this effort. He became extremely demanding and abusive of his parents, who attempted to placate him by responding to his every request and by failing to confront him about the reality of his blindness. (p. 876, with changes in notation)

HEARING IMPAIRMENT

Description

Hearing impairment is a general term that refers to hearing losses ranging from mild to profound.

- A child who is *deaf* is one whose hearing disability prevents successful processing of linguistic information through audition.
- A child who is *hard-of-hearing* has residual hearing sufficient for successful processing of linguistic information through audition, generally with the use of a hearing aid.
- A child who is *prelingually deaf* (that is, a child whose deafness was present at birth or occurred before the child developed speech and language) is usually unable to acquire speech and language normally.
- A child who is *postlingually deaf* (that is, a child who became deaf after speech and language had developed) has serious problems in acquiring additional language proficiency, but usually not to the same extent as children who are prelingually deaf.

Deafness adversely affects the speech, linguistic, and academic abilities of children (Keane, 1987). In addition, deafness may affect children's personality and temperament. Deaf children tend to be somewhat more impulsive, dependent, and rigid and less motivated and accepting of personal responsibility than normal-hearing children (Keane, 1987).

Hearing impairments occur for the same reasons as visual impairments—disease, accidents, and congenital or hereditary disorders. In infancy, high-risk conditions that may lead to hearing impairments include asphyxia, bacterial meningitis, toxoplasmosis, syphilis, rh incompatibility, rubella, cytomegalovirus, herpes simplex virus, hyperbilirubinemia, and birthweight of less than approximately 3 lb, 5 oz (see the Glossary for definitions of terms; Northern & Downs, 1991). It is estimated that 50% of early childhood hearing impairment is hereditary (Mauk & Mauk, 1992). Later in life, hearing impairments may result from injury or excessive noise, childhood diseases (such as measles, mumps, and chicken pox), and infections accompanied by high fever.

Classification of hearing impairment. Hearing ability is represented by a continuum ranging from very acute perception, such as that of a gifted musical conductor who can detect an out-of-tune instrument in an orchestra, to total deafness, such as that of an individual who can detect only strong vibrations through tactile sensations. The following classification scheme is used by audiologists to evaluate hard-of-hearing individuals. It is based on the extent to which the individual needs a higher than average intensity of sound to hear. (Sound intensity is measured in decibels [dB]. A decibel is 1/10 of a bel—hence the prefix "deci." The bel is a logarithmic unit; a sound that is 10 decibels louder than another is ten times as loud.)

1. *Normal range (0–15 dB loss).*
2. *Slight hearing loss (15–20 dB loss).* Children with a loss of less than 20 dB are the least hard-of-hearing. They hear vowel sounds clearly, but they may miss unvoiced consonant sounds. You should have no difficulty interviewing these children.
3. *Mild hearing loss (20–40 dB loss).* Children with a mild hearing loss may not be recognized as having a problem unless communication problems develop, in which case they may be referred for an audiological evaluation. They may miss soft or whispered speech, and they may have mild speech problems. You should have little difficulty interviewing these children, unless they exhibit communication problems.
4. *Moderate hearing loss (41–60 dB loss).* Children with a moderate hearing loss may have difficulty hearing most speech sounds at normal conversational levels and when there is background noise. They usually have moderate speech problems. You may have difficulty interviewing these children. You may have to talk louder and use special communication procedures (discussion to follow).
5. *Severe hearing loss (61–90 dB loss).* Children with a severe hearing loss hear only the loudest speech sounds; they cannot detect any speech sounds at normal conversational levels. Their articulation, vocabulary, and voice quality will differ from those of normal-hearing children. They usually have severe speech problems. You will need to use special communication procedures (discussion to follow) to interview most, if not all, children in this group.
6. *Profound hearing loss (greater than 90 dB loss).* Children with a profound hearing loss usually hear no speech or other sounds. They also probably have no oral speech at all. This degree of hearing loss has a profound impact on communication. You will need to use special communication procedures (discussion to follow) to interview all children in this group.

Signs of hearing difficulty. If, during an interview with a child who has *not* been previously referred for possible hearing difficulties, you detect any behavior that suggests a hearing deficit, refer the child to an audiologist. General signs of hearing difficulty include the following:

- lack of normal response to sound
- lack of interest in general conversation
- inattentiveness
- difficulty following oral directions
- failure to respond when spoken to
- frequent requests to have the speaker repeat what was said
- mistakes in carrying out spoken instructions
- intent observation of the speaker's lips (lipreading, speechreading) rather than looking at the speaker's eyes in face-to-face encounters
- habit of turning one ear toward the speaker
- cupping hand behind ear

- unusual voice quality (for example, monotonous or high pitched)
- too loud or too soft speech
- faulty pronunciation
- poor articulation
- frequent earaches or discharges from ears

Examples of specific language problems that may indicate hearing difficulties include the following:

- difficulty discriminating consonant sounds; for example, the child hears *mat* for *bat, tab* for *tap*
- difficulty discriminating and learning short vowel sounds
- difficulty sounding out a word, sound by sound; for example, the child has difficulty saying *k-a-t* for *cat*
- difficulty relating printed letters such as "f," "pl,"and "ide" to their sounds
- difficulty separating sounds that make up blends; for example, the child has difficulty determining that "fl" has the sounds f-f…l-l
- better spelling and reading of sight words (using the whole-word method of reading or look-say method of reading) than of phonetic words

Parental reactions. Deafness is an invisible as well as a low-incidence disability; it usually represents a static and irreversible condition (Danek, 1988). Most children who have a hearing impairment have parents with normal hearing. Parents are often unprepared to recognize a hearing impairment in their infant. At first, they may believe that their child is slow, mentally retarded or learning disabled or that something is not quite right. There may be a considerable delay from when the parents suspect some difficulty to when a conclusive diagnosis is reached.

Parents and siblings must learn to communicate with the child who has a hearing impairment. The total communication approach—which entails the simultaneous use of speech, sign language (a manual system of communication such as American Sign Language or Signed English), and fingerspelling—is preferred. The total communication approach seems to improve the social competence of children who have a hearing impairment, promotes more positive attitudes in their parents, and improves parent-child interactions (Danek, 1988). One of the most important things a family can do to help a child with a hearing impairment is to integrate the child into the home by learning about deafness, adapting to the child's hearing loss, becoming interested in the culture of the deaf, and emphasizing the communication process (Danek, 1988).

In the following quotations, parents describe what it is like to raise a child with a hearing deficit (Reprinted with permission of the publisher, from *The Deaf Child and His Family* by S. Gregory, Copyright © 1976 by Routledge [Allen & Unwin], pp. 85, 88, 148–150, 157–160, 162, 163, 178, 180–182, 184, 185, 189, 191, 192, 194, 197, 207).

1. *Learning about the hearing deficit.* Parents learn about their child's deafness in different ways. Some parents believe that their child is deaf before the deficit is officially confirmed, some suspect that there is a problem but are not sure, some are relieved when they find out, some are relieved that the child did not have a "more severe problem," and some are shocked to learn that their child is deaf.

- I had a feeling, yes, because he used to sleep an awful lot, no noise woke him up ever, and if you dropped things like a saucepan lid or anything he never jumped.
- I think I always knew. I think from the time he was born I knew that there was something wrong with him. You know, it was just intuition. I used to say to my husband "There's something wrong with him," and he would say "Oh, you're mad, there's nothing wrong with him," and I would say "Well there is, he either can't hear or he can't see."
- I think it was a relief to hear somebody say—yes she is deaf—it took away the question mark about why she wouldn't talk.
- Well I think the fact I'd realised this before. I think in a way, rather than—I don't know whether it's awful to say this or not, but rather the fact that he should be mentally retarded it was a relief in a way that it was deafness, at least I felt we might get somewhere.
- We knew really, but I was heart-broken, we knew when he was being tested it was a shattering time that was, it was terrible but the thing is you just have to keep telling yourself and make yourself try and accept it. The thing is I don't think you ever really do fully, fully accept it. I'm always waiting you know for one morning I'll get up and Colin will be all right, if I was dead honest about it, but really I know he won't be.

2. *Wanting more information.* Parents may want an explanation for the hearing loss and information on whether there is some cure for their child's deafness.

- I want to have it explained a bit more. I mean I know all about the inner ear and the outer ear, but I want to know why Karl's deaf, whether it's a nerve or what. I mean A _____ [a neighbor's child], she's partially deaf, she's got fluid in the ear but she can have that done. Now I'm wondering whether something like that could be the same with Karl.
- I don't think they know quite whether it can be put right. I'm building my hopes, that it can be put right.

3. *Effects on marriage.* Raising a child with a hearing loss (or any other disabling condition) may change relationships among the family members. For example, it may put a severe strain on the relationship between the parents, it may bring them closer, or it may have little effect on their relationship.

- It's imprisoned us. It's made us do a lot of quarrelling, not that we didn't quarrel before but it's increased horribly.
- I think it brings us closer together in the way that we work together a lot more to help her, but then it's a strain when she plays up, and he's saying "Oh, you've got to go along with her," and I've had it all day so I've had enough of it, you know, it's a strain then.
- I don't know whether it's Samantha but I think we're more in love now than we ever were. I don't know whether love grows in marriage. You see, you don't really know, because you don't

compare anybody else's marriage to your own, do you. I mean we love each other—it's not driven us apart, I'll give it that.

4. *Effects on other children in family.* Having a deaf child in the family may affect the other children.

- I try not to make the difference, but Paul automatically gets more attention from me because he needs me more. You see, Peter's always been very independent—at eight months old he didn't really need me—he was very grown up for his age.
- I don't think she really understands. It's only recently she's said to me "I wish Gary wasn't deaf" and I say "I do as well, Sarah, and we have to help him this way," and this is it. Sarah's very sensitive, she understands, but I don't think she understands fully. We try and include her in everything.
- You can't do the same with a deaf child. You do bring them up differently, you've got to, but at the same time.... It also makes it that you bring the other one up differently, because you've had to give in to Gary a little bit more so I'm probably giving in to Sharon where I wouldn't normally.
- We get feelings of strong resentment against her, but on the whole they've deep affection for her and pity for the fact that she's had to work so hard talking and doing the things that they do normally, they're enough to understand.

5. *Effects on social activities.* Raising a child with a hearing loss may affect the social activities of the family.

- We can't obtain any babysitter, because we would have to have a babysitter who knows or understands him. We can't leave him with anybody.
- Before we had the children we used to have a lot of family get-togethers, and we don't now, and I feel a lot of it is because of Christopher.
- Sometimes when I'm out with Christopher he makes funny noises. It can be embarrassing, but he's my child, so I have to get on with it.
- Anywhere I go, he goes.
- In actual fact I think you make more friends with a handicapped child because everyone wants to know what it's all about. It's a great talking subject.
- Well, people always seem to be stopping and talking to her, and I belong to different associations because she is handicapped, I've met a lot more mothers. Whether it gets worse as she gets older and the handicap becomes more apparent I don't know.

6. *Relationships with other people.* Other people may not realize that deafness may have other consequences as well.

- People are embarrassed. I think they're guilty. You know they feel rotten that you've got a handicapped child and they haven't. They don't want a handicapped child but they wish you hadn't got one.
- They don't like to talk about it to you, I think for fear of upsetting you, but it's never worried me.
- Well I don't think…people don't realise that deaf children can't talk. This is the main thing—they think that they should talk. They don't realise that they can't talk, so of course it makes you embarrassed when you have to tell them she can't talk.

7. *Discipline.* Parents may or may not have special concerns about disciplining their child with a hearing impairment.

- I treated both of mine the same. If they've done anything wrong and it's deserved a smack, that's it. That's all there is to it, he's got to be taught and they've both got to be treated the same. And the more I treat him normal, the better he is. He comes on better.
- Well we could never get it through to her you see, that "If you don't stop you'll go to bed in a minute," so when she was younger and I told her "You'll go to bed if you keep that up" and I followed my word through and put her to bed she'd scream hysterically in the bedroom. It wasn't fair to her. I'd have to go and get her out and think "God, what am I going to do, I just can't explain to the child," so bed as a punishment never meant anything.
- I think knowing where to draw the line about the discipline side of it and not trying to be too soft or too hard on her, because we don't want her to go into a shell, because if she once loses using her voice it's hard for her to get it back, well we don't want to frighten her. It makes you wary of where to draw the line on discipline and other communication.

Interviewing Issues

Before you interview children who have a hearing impairment or who are suspected of having a hearing impairment, consider the type of loss, degree of loss, age of onset, and etiologic components of the hearing impairment. Find out from the parents or an audiologist whether the child's hearing loss affects her or his ability to understand speech sounds. Children who are hearing impaired are not a homogeneous group. If the hearing loss was a result of a neurological disorder (such as meningitis), there may be other concomitant dysfunctions that you will need to consider in the interview. If the child wears a hearing aid, learn when it was last checked, whether it is used consistently, and, at the time of the interview, whether it is turned on. Learn about the child's receptive and expressive skills—that is, the methods by which the child receives and communicates information. You can obtain information about children's preferred modes of communication by interviewing their parents (see Table F-34 in Appendix F) and teachers and by observing them in the classroom. During the interview, encourage children who are hearing impaired to respond in the way in which they are most comfortable.

Interviewing children with a hearing impairment will be more tiring, demand greater attention and concentration, and require more flexibility than interviewing normal-hearing children (Harry, 1986). Both the children and the interviewer may be self-conscious because they will be placing a premium on observation. If you are prepared, you should be able to meet the challenges of interviewing children with a hearing impairment.

Communication skills needed with hearing-impaired children. Those of you who will work with children who are hearing impaired will need special communication skills. If you have not received special training, prepare to interview children who are hearing impaired by observing classes for the hearing impaired and noting how the teachers communicate with their students. Use a total communication approach with children who are deaf if you and they are familiar with this approach.

Effects of visual cues on hearing-impaired children. To properly interview children who are hearing impaired, you will need a high degree of skill and a wide range of experiences with such children. Because sight is the chief means by which children who are hearing impaired receive stimuli, they are likely to seek visual cues from you when you speak—such as from your facial expressions or your hand movements—to gain understanding. You must realize that any movements you make may furnish cues to children who are hearing impaired. Facial expressions, rather than the tone of your voice, will convey your mood. Children who are hearing impaired probably will quickly notice if you make a frown or grimace of impatience and will interpret these gestures unfavorably. Smile to reward their efforts, but not to reward a response. Avoid smiling when they say something that is not comprehensible; you do not want to encourage them to think that they are communicating effectively.

Comprehension problems of hearing-impaired children. Although children who are hearing impaired may give the impression of being able to understand your questions, they may be feigning comprehension in order to obtain your approval. They may have learned how to play a role to avoid confronting potentially embarrassing situations. In turn, you may have difficulty understanding their answers, particularly if they have speech difficulties. If you conduct a mental status evaluation as part of the interview, give credit to responses pantomimed only when you have no doubt about the accuracy of the responses.

Asking questions of hearing-impaired children. If you are to obtain accurate responses from children who are hearing impaired, they must understand your questions. (This is true, of course, for all interviews with children and adults.) If you use pantomime, recognize that the children may not interpret your actions as you intended them. If you routinely interview children who are hearing impaired, learn sign language.

Here are some specific suggestions for interviewing a child who is hearing impaired:

- Use one or a combination of the following techniques: speech, gesture, pantomime, writing, signing, fingerspelling, and drawing. What you use will depend on your skills and on the needs of the interviewee.
- Make sure that you are looking at the child when you speak to him or her and that he or she, in turn, is watching your face.
- Maintain eye contact.
- Maintain a pleasant face.
- Be sure that the light is on your face and hands and that you are in close physical proximity to the child.

- Do not sit with the sun or a bright light behind you because this can create shadows and eyestrain for the child.
- Be sure that the light does not shine in the child's eyes.
- Speak clearly, distinctly, and naturally, at a reduced rate, without exaggerating your lip movements.
- Use short and simple sentences.
- Be sure that there are no obstructions blocking the child's view of your lips.
- Be sure that the room is well lit and free of noise.
- Be sure that the child who wears a hearing aid has it turned on and that he or she brings extra hearing aid batteries to the interview.
- Touch the child gently on the arm or wave your hand in the child's line of vision if the child is looking away.
- Be aware of your facial expressions and gestures because they will provide cues to the child.
- Rephrase misunderstood concepts into simpler, more visible forms rather than repeating them in the same way.
- Consider presenting some questions in written form if the child can read.
- Observe the child's nonverbal behavior.
- Use an interpreter skilled both in sign language and in English, if needed, but do not use a parent or another family member as the interpreter, because the child may not discuss his or her feelings openly in the presence of a family member.

If you use an interpreter, follow the guidelines in Chapter 8. In particular, maintain eye contact and speak directly to the child. Do not speak to the interpreter about the child as if the child weren't there. Your face and mouth and the hands and face of the interpreter should be illuminated by a bright but not blinding light. You and the interpreter should sit near each other and across from the child. Only one of you should talk at a time.

Evaluating the interview. The questions in Table 12-4 will help you evaluate children with a hearing impairment or those suspected of having a hearing impairment.

Interventions

Interventions for children who are hearing impaired should focus on helping the children become independent. This may require instruction in sign language and in speech. Hearing aids should be prescribed when they are helpful. Adequate prenatal care and efficient obstetrical procedures, as well as early treatment of ear infections and high fevers, may prevent auditory problems from developing.

Case Illustration

The following case describes the experiences one family faced in raising a deaf child (Fenster, 1988).

Table 12-4
Evaluating the Behavior of Children Who Are Hearing Impaired or Suspected of Having a Hearing Impairment

---

1. Are the volume and pitch of the child's voice appropriate to the situation?
2. Is the child's pronunciation intelligible, consistent, and age appropriate?
3. Is the child's speech fluent, or are there unusual pauses?
4. Does the child grope for words?
5. Are the child's replies timely, or are there unusual delays?
6. Does the child respond once to a sound and not respond again?
7. Does the child understand your speech?
8. Does the child confuse similar-sounding words?
9. If the child does not speak, how does he or she communicate (for example, pointing, gesturing, shifting eye gaze)?
10. Does the child become frustrated when you do not understand him or her?
11. How does the child behave when he or she is frustrated (for example, withdraws or acts out)?

CASE 12-10. MS. B.'S FAMILY

Ms. B. is a hearing, single 20-year-old mother of two children. Her eldest daughter, Sarah, age 5, is profoundly deaf. Bob, age 1½ years, can hear. The cause of Sarah's deafness is unknown. Ms. B. suspected that Sarah was deaf at age 6 months. She was told by several doctors when she expressed concern that something was wrong that Sarah was too young to be tested; just "give her time." Her suspicions were confirmed when Sarah was about 2½ years old. Sarah was evaluated, given a hearing aid, and referred to a school for the deaf, in a total communication program. According to Ms. B., she just did what she was told to, never asking for any explanations, and if they were given, she cannot remember. She has remained uninvolved in Sarah's schooling. The school has interpreted her noninvolvement as disinterest in her daughter.

Almost 2½ years later, Ms. B. was referred by Sarah's school to our clinic for help with raising Sarah. The school complained that Ms. B. never came to any meetings and that Sarah most often did not have her hearing aid. Also, Sarah knew little sign language.

Ms. B. has not established a productive communication system with Sarah. Sarah makes her desires and needs known through loud vocalizing. She also either brings an object to you or brings you to an object to express what she wants.

Sarah uses a combination of "babble" signs and gestures. Most often, she is not understood. She knows few signs. Ms. B. knows fewer. It is even uncertain whether Sarah knows her name sign.

Although Sarah's deafness has been explained to Ms. B. several times, she reacts by "not hearing" the explanations offered. In essence, the mother, using denial, has become "deaf" to cope with the emotional turmoil inside her. For instance, Ms. B. continues to call Sarah from another room, a dramatic sign of her denial and wishful thinking.

Ms. B. is patient with Sarah. For example, Sarah will vocalize to express that she wants something. When it is time to get dressed, Ms. B. will take out one article of clothing. If Sarah does not want that one, Ms. B. will try another article of clothing, and another, until she comes across the one desired by Sarah. The layout of the home also has been changed to accommodate Sarah. The kitchen area has been rearranged so that Sarah can easily point to the food or drink she wants. This eliminates much of the frustration experienced by both Sarah and her mother. However, when frustration levels are at their limits, Ms. B. gives up and ignores Sarah or just smiles. (pp. 230–232, with changes in notation)

THINKING THROUGH THE ISSUES

What do you think it must be like to raise a child with an autistic disorder? What pressures might parents face from relatives, spouses, and members of the community in raising a child with an autistic disorder? In what way might raising a child with an autistic disorder be different from raising one who is mentally retarded?

Do you know of any families that have a child with a developmental, learning, or sensory disorder? If so, what has it been like for the family to raise the child?

Which system do you prefer for classifying children with mental retardation—the one proposed by the American Association on Mental Retardation or the one proposed by *DSM-IV*? What is the basis for your answer?

What procedures would you use to classify a child as having a specific learning disability?

Which condition do you believe has a more profound effect on a child's ability to function—a visual impairment or a hearing impairment? What is the basis for your answer?

SUMMARY

Autistic Disorder

1. Autistic disorder is a behavioral syndrome marked by impaired social development and communication and a markedly restricted repertoire of activity and interests.

2. The behavioral characteristics of children with an autistic disorder usually include failure to develop normal social relationships, extreme deficits in speech and language, ritualistic behavior and insistence on sameness, abnormalities in response to the sensory environment, self-stimulatory behavior, self-injurious behavior, inappropriate affect, limited intellectual functioning, difficulty generalizing, and behavior problems (such as aggression, noncompliance, tantrums, toileting difficulties, feeding difficulties, and sleeping difficulties).

3. Many children with an autistic disorder are delayed in their acquisition of speech.

4. The most common speech characteristic of children with an autistic disorder is echolalia, either immediate or delayed.

5. Autistic disorder appears to have a neurobiological basis, but the exact mechanisms remain unclear.

6. Autistic disorder is likely to have multiple etiologies, all organic in nature.

7. The inherent disabilities of children with an autistic disorder—such as the difficulty they have establishing social relationships, their impaired communication skills, and their unusual responses to sensory stimuli—may tax the resources of an interviewer.

8. Behavioral techniques are often used with children with an autistic disorder to reduce their maladaptive behaviors, such as self-stimulation and self-injurious behaviors, and to teach them skills (for example, sitting and establishing eye contact).

Mental Retardation

9. The American Association on Mental Retardation (AAMR, 1992) defines mental retardation in the following way: "Mental retardation refers to substantial limitations in present functioning. It is characterized by significantly subaverage intellectual functioning, existing concurrently with related limitations in two or more of the following applicable adaptive skill areas: communication, self-care, home living, social skills, community use, self-direction, health and safety, functional academics, leisure, and work. Mental retardation manifests before age 18" (p. 5).

10. *DSM-IV* (American Psychiatric Association, 1994) defines mental retardation as "significantly subaverage intellectual functioning…that is accompanied by significant limitations in adaptive functioning in at least two of the following skill areas: communication, self-care, home living, social/interpersonal skills, use of community resources, self-direction, functional academic skills, work, leisure, health, and safety…. The onset must occur before age 18 years" (p. 39).

11. Unlike the American Association on Mental Retardation, *DSM-IV* specifies four degrees of severity of mental retardation: mild mental retardation: moderate mental retardation, severe mental retardation, and profound mental retardation.

12. Mental retardation results from a diverse set of factors, including factors associated with heredity, early alterations of embryonic development, pregnancy and perinatal problems, general medical conditions acquired in infancy or childhood, and environmental influences.

13. Fetal alcohol syndrome develops when a sufficient amount of alcohol consumed by the mother crosses the placenta and interferes with neurotransmitter production, cell development, cell migration, and brain growth of the fetus.

14. The main characteristics of fetal alcohol syndrome are low birthweight, growth retardation, organic anomalies, and neurobehavioral deficits.

15. Fetal alcohol syndrome is a leading cause of mental retardation in the western world.

16. Children who are mentally retarded usually have a slow rate of cognitive development, limited expressive and receptive language abilities, limited adaptive skills, limited experiential background, short attention span, some distractibility, and a concrete and literal style in approaching tasks.

17. When you interview children who may be mentally retarded, instead of asking open-ended questions, which may be extremely difficult for them to answer, simplify questions, be

concrete, ask structured questions, and prompt frequently. Be prepared to repeat or rephrase your questions or comments.

18. Children who are mentally retarded may be hesitant to ask for breaks in the interview.

19. Children who are profoundly mentally retarded may be especially difficult to interview because of self-stimulating behavior, self-injurious behavior, limited attention span, destructive behavior, temper tantrums, seizures, noncompliance with requests, or inability to understand the questions.

20. Interventions with children who are mentally retarded may focus on what special services the families need and what help they need in finding the services.

21. Several approaches have been successful in reducing the occurrence of mental retardation, including screening and treating infants for metabolic disorders, using a low-phenylalanine diet for pregnant women who have phenylketonuria, immunizing children, providing education to adults about the effects of alcohol and drug use during pregnancy, reducing children's exposure to lead, constructing safer automobiles, providing public education about the need to use infant seats and seat belts in automobiles, using amniocentesis, and screening parents to identify whether they have genetic conditions or metabolic disorders that could result in retardation in their infants and then encouraging genetic counseling.

22. For children and adolescents who are mentally retarded and with behavioral problems, the same interventions used with non–mentally retarded persons can be used. These interventions include environmental change, behavioral treatments, individual psychotherapy, group psychotherapy, family therapy, and pharmacotherapy.

Specific Learning Disability

23. The term *learning disability* can be used in both a broad and a narrow sense. In the broad sense, it refers to learning difficulties associated with any type of disability, including mental retardation, brain injury, sensory difficulties, or emotional disturbance. In the narrow sense, it refers to the failure, by children who have adequate intelligence, adequate maturational level, adequate cultural background, and relevant educational experiences, to learn a scholastic skill.

24. The most common learning disability is reading disorder, followed by mathematics disorder, spelling disorder, and disorder of written expression.

25. The definition of learning disability in Public Law 94-142 has not been universally accepted, particularly because of questions concerning the discrepancy criteria.

26. A learning disability may reflect a developmental delay (that is, the child is functioning at a level below that normally expected for children of her or his age), a developmental deficit (that is, the child is deficient in using the specific function), or both a developmental delay and a developmental deficit.

27. Learning disabilities likely have multiple etiologies associated with genetic, biological, and environmental factors. Biological deficits may be associated with processing difficulties, and, in particular, with deficiencies in phonological coding. Ineffective learning strategies also may account for some types of learning disabilities.

28. Children with learning disabilities have deficits in cognitive-neuropsychological skills and in social-behavioral adjustment. They also may have some problems that are common to children who have attention-deficit/hyperactivity disorder.

29. Because children with learning disabilities are such a heterogeneous group, no one child is likely to exhibit all of the problems found among children with learning disabilities.

30. Reading disorder (or reading disability; also referred to as dyslexia), the most frequent form of learning disability, is best thought of as being on a continuum. Dyslexia then is defined in a somewhat arbitrary way by choosing a point on the continuum that identifies individuals with reading problems.

31. Disabled readers with and without an IQ-achievement discrepancy show similar information processing, genetic, and neurophysiological profiles. This suggests that the existence of a discrepancy is not a valid indicator of disability in basic reading skills.

32. Epidemiological studies indicate that as many females as males manifest dyslexia; however, schools identify three to four times more boys than girls.

33. Reading disabilities reflect a persistent deficit rather than a developmental lag that will be remedied with time. Longitudinal studies show that, of those children who are reading disabled in the third grade, approximately 74% continue to read significantly below grade level in the ninth grade.

34. Children with reading disability differ from one another and from other readers along a continuous distribution. They do not aggregate together to form a distinct "hump" separate from the normal distribution.

35. The ability to read and comprehend depends on rapid and automatic recognition and decoding of single words. Slow and inaccurate decoding are the best predictors of deficits in reading comprehension.

36. The ability to decode single words accurately and fluently is dependent on the ability to segment words and syllables into phonemes. Deficits in phonological awareness reflect the core deficit in dyslexia.

37. The best predictor of reading ability from kindergarten and first-grade performance is phoneme segmentation ability.

38. Children who have a mathematics disorder (also called dyscalculia) may have basic arithmetical skill difficulties, language difficulties, perceptual or spatial difficulties, attentional skill difficulties, shifting difficulties, and writing difficulties.

39. Spelling requires knowledge of sound-symbol correspondence (phonological skills) as well as linguistic competence, such as an understanding that the way words are spelled may depend on how they are used.

40. The writing of children with a disorder of written expression may be characterized by grammatical or punctuation errors within sentences, poor paragraph organization, spelling errors, and excessively poor handwriting.

41. Children who come from cultural and linguistic backgrounds that differ from those of the majority group may perform poorly in school because of, for example, experiential differences, family expectations, limited English proficiency, stresses associated with acculturation and discrimination, and cognitive styles and learning strategies that differ from those of the majority group.

42. Studies do not provide conclusive answers about which children with a learning disability will continue to have problems after they leave school.

43. In the interview, you should obtain information about what learning and behavioral problems the child may be having; how the child views his or her problems; whether the learning problems interfere with the child's relationships with other

children, teachers, parents, and siblings; whether emotional problems, if present, are occurring with or in reaction to the learning problems; the settings in which the emotional problems, if present, are likely to occur; the child's study patterns; whether the home environment is conducive to studying; and the child's views of the parents, family, teachers, school, and community.

44. In interviewing the parents of a child with a specific learning disability, ask about their views of the child's strengths and weaknesses, what they see as the problems, and what they believe might contribute to the problems, such as biological predispositions, deficiencies or delays in basic skill areas, personality and temperament, family influences, environmental influences, the interaction of any of these factors, which interventions have helped and which have not, and what suggestions they have for interventions.

45. In evaluating the information you obtain from the child, parents, and teachers, consider the child's developmental history and family background, language abilities, motor abilities, social skills, behavior, nonverbal mental abilities, and school performance.

46. The most effective interventions with children with learning disabilities involve the use of cognitive, linguistic, and cognitive-behavioral methods. These methods may involve offering remediation, teaching metacognitive strategies, increasing self-reliance, and increasing social and behavioral adjustment.

Visual Impairment

47. People are usually legally defined as blind when they can see no more at a distance of 20 feet than someone with normal vision can see at a distance of 200 feet.

48. Children develop visual impairments because of disease, accidents, or congenital or hereditary disorders.

49. Children with a visual impairment tend to have more impaired social functioning than their peers with normal sight.

50. You can use the same interviewing techniques with children who are visually impaired that you use with normal-sighted children.

51. Interventions with children who have visual impairments should focus on developing the children's skills and on helping them become independent and self-reliant.

Hearing Impairment

52. Hearing impairment is a general term that refers to hearing losses ranging from mild to profound.

53. A child who is deaf is one whose hearing disability prevents successful processing of linguistic information through audition.

54. A child who is hard-of-hearing has residual hearing sufficient for successful processing of linguistic information through audition, generally with the use of a hearing aid.

55. A child who is prelingually deaf (that is, a child whose deafness was present at birth or occurred before the child developed speech and language) is usually unable to acquire speech and language normally.

56. A child who is postlingually deaf (that is, a child who became deaf after speech and language had developed) has serious problems in acquiring additional language proficiency, but usually not to the same extent as children who are prelingually deaf.

57. Deafness adversely affects the speech, linguistic, and academic abilities of children.

58. Hearing ability is represented by a continuum ranging from very acute perception to total deafness.

59. Deafness is an invisible as well as a low-incidence disability; it usually represents a static and irreversible condition.

60. The total communication approach—which entails the simultaneous use of speech, sign language (a manual system of communication such as American Sign Language or Signed English), and fingerspelling—is the preferred way to communicate with children who are hearing impaired.

61. Before you interview children who have a hearing impairment or who are suspected of having a hearing impairment, consider the type of loss, degree of loss, age of onset, and etiologic components of the hearing impairment. Find out from the parents or from an audiologist whether the child's hearing loss affects her or his ability to understand speech sounds.

62. Children who are hearing impaired are not a homogeneous group.

63. Interviewing children with a hearing impairment will be more tiring, demand greater attention and concentration, and require more flexibility than interviewing normal-hearing children.

64. Mental health professionals who work with children who are hearing impaired need special communication skills.

65. If you have not received special training, prepare to interview children who are hearing impaired by observing classes for the hearing impaired and noting how the teachers communicate with their students.

66. Use a total communication approach with children who are deaf if they are familiar with this approach.

67. Although children who are hearing impaired may give the impression of being able to understand your questions, they may be feigning comprehension in order to obtain your approval.

68. If you routinely interview children who are hearing impaired, learn sign language.

69. If you use an interpreter when you interview children who are deaf, follow appropriate guidelines for use of an interpreter.

70. Interventions for children who are hearing impaired should focus on helping the children become independent. This may require instruction in sign language and in speech. Hearing aids should be prescribed when they are helpful.

KEY TERMS, CONCEPTS, AND NAMES

Autistic disorder (p. 392)
Echolalia (p. 392)
Mental retardation (p. 399)
American Association on Mental Retardation (AAMR) (p. 399)
Mild mental retardation (p. 400)
Moderate mental retardation (p. 400)
Severe mental retardation (p. 400)
Profound mental retardation (p. 400)
Tay-Sachs disease (p. 400)
Tuberous sclerosis (p. 400)
Fragile X syndrome (p. 400)
Down syndrome (p. 400)
Fetal malnutrition (p. 400)
Hypoxia (p. 400)
Meningitis (p. 400)
Roseola (p. 400)
Encephalitis (p. 400)

Rabies (p. 400)
Fetal alcohol syndrome (p. 400)
Phenylketonuria (PKU) (p. 403)
Amniocentesis (p. 403)
Learning disability (p. 404)
Specific learning disability (p. 404)
Severe discrepancy (p. 405)
Exclusionary criteria (p. 405)
Developmental delay (p. 405)
Developmental deficit (p. 405)
Phonological processing (p. 406)
Reading disorder (dyslexia) (p. 407)
Phonetic decoding (p. 408)
Whole word reading ability (p. 408)
Mathematics disorder (discalculia) (p. 408)
Spelling disorder (p. 408)
Disorder of written expression (p. 408)
Metacognition (p. 411)
Visual impairment (p. 412)
Visual field restriction (p. 412)
Prenatal cataracts (p. 412)
Optic nerve atrophy (p. 412)
Retrolental fibroplasia (p. 412)
Congenital glaucoma (p. 412)
Retinoblastoma (p. 412)
Albinism (p. 412)
Myopia (p. 412)
Nystagmus (p. 412)
Hearing impairment (p. 414)
Deaf children (p. 414)
Hard-of-hearing children (p. 414)

Prelingually deaf children (p. 414)
Postlingually deaf children (p. 414)
Slight hearing loss (p. 415)
Mild hearing loss (p. 415)
Moderate hearing loss (p. 415)
Severe hearing loss (p. 415)
Profound hearing loss (p. 415)

STUDY QUESTIONS

1. Discuss autistic disorder. Include in your discussion a description of the disorder, etiology, incidence, and prognosis, interviewing issues, and intervention considerations.

2. Discuss mental retardation. Include in your discussion a description of the condition, problems with the definition, etiology, interviewing issues, and intervention considerations.

3. Discuss specific learning disability. Include in your discussion a definition of the term, problems with the definition, etiology, correlates associated with learning disability, theoretical models of learning disability, prognosis, interviewing issues, and intervention considerations.

4. Discuss children with visual impairments. Include in your discussion a description of the condition, signs of visual difficulty, interviewing issues, and intervention considerations.

5. Discuss children with hearing impairments. Include in your discussion a description of the condition, classifications of hearing impairment, interviewing issues (including observation of signs of hearing impairment and ways to talk to hearing-impaired children), and intervention considerations.

13

CHILDREN AND FAMILIES FACING BEREAVEMENT OR THE THREAT OF SUICIDE

Death ends a life, but it does not end a relationship, which struggles on in the survivor's mind, toward some resolution which it may never find.

—Robert Anderson

Goals and Objectives

This chapter is designed to enable you to:

- Understand the experiences of children and families who face bereavement or the threat of suicide
- Develop skills in interviewing children and families who may be experiencing bereavement or the threat of suicide

The conditions discussed in this chapter do not constitute clinically defined behavioral, social, or emotional disorders of childhood; bereavement represents a reaction to events in a child's life, and a suicide attempt represents an action that poses a threat to a child's self. Like Chapters 11 and 12, this chapter gives you guidelines for interviewing children and their families; it does not provide an in-depth review of research or theory. You are encouraged to read other texts that cover the conditions discussed in this chapter in more detail.

BEREAVEMENT

Description

When a family member or a friend dies, individuals usually experience unique and profound stress. How they cope with the stress is related to the following factors (Rando, 1984, pp. 43–47, with changes in notation):

- *their personal characteristics* (including their age, personality, temperament, mental health, physical health, education, level of maturity, conditioning concerning the expression of feelings, use of alcohol and drugs, and coping behavior)
- *their family and social supports* (including their sociocultural, ethnic, and religious/philosophical background, the funeral rituals their families participate in, and the support they receive from their families, relatives, friends, and neighbors)
- *their past relationship with the deceased* (including whether the relationship was positive or negative and how they were related to the deceased—that is, whether their relationship was that of a child, parent, or other relative)
- *the circumstances of the death* (including the timeliness of the death, their perception of the preventability of the death, whether the death was sudden or expected, whether the dying person was ill and, if so, the length of the person's illness before his or her death, and the way in which they anticipated the death)
- *other stresses that they are experiencing* (such as whether they sustained other losses and what other stresses are in their lives)

When the circumstances of death are traumatic or unusual or when the grief reactions are so overwhelming

that psychological disorders develop, individuals may seek out a mental health professional (Cook & Dworkin, 1992). This section focuses on the initial interview in cases of grief and bereavement.

Although bereavement, grief, and mourning will be defined separately here (Chochinov & Holland, 1989), the three terms are often used interchangeably (Gudas, 1993).

- *Bereavement* refers to the psychological, physiological, or behavioral responses associated with the loss of a loved one through death.
- *Grief* refers to the feeling of sorrow or anguish resulting from the loss of a loved one through death, often accompanied by crying.
- *Mourning* refers to the actions or social expressions of deprivation associated with the loss of a loved one through death. Mourning includes rituals and behaviors specific to an individual's culture and religion.

Reactions of survivors.   Each survivor will experience the loss in his or her unique way. Some survivors experience little grief; others, moderate grief; and still others, overwhelming grief. For some survivors, grief reactions last two to three years or longer (Meshot & Leitner, 1992–1993; Webb, 1993). And some survivors have delayed grief reactions that do not appear until several days, months, or years after the loss. Even after survivors believe they have worked through their grief, certain events—such as birthdays, anniversaries, holidays, or celebrations—may trigger grief reactions. The special case of bereavement associated with suicide will be discussed later in the chapter.

Let's now consider how school-aged children and adults may react to the death of a loved one (Grollman, 1974; Koocher, 1986a).

1. *Denial.* They may look as if they were not affected by the death and pretend that it did not happen.

2. *Questioning.* They may question why the death happened, and they may be confused and perplexed about the death.

3. *Bodily distress.* They may express their anxiety in physical or emotional symptoms.

4. *Hostile reactions toward the deceased.* They may feel deserted, abandoned, and angry.

5. *Hostile reactions toward others.* They may project their anger outward to relieve their own guilt feelings by making someone else responsible for the death.

6. *Replacement.* They may try to win the affection of others as a substitute for that of the deceased person.

7. *Assumption of mannerisms or symptoms of the deceased.* They may adopt mannerisms of the deceased, take on the deceased's role in the family, or take on symptoms of the deceased.

8. *Idealization.* They may become obsessed with the deceased person's good qualities and fail to recognize other qualities of the deceased person.

9. *Anxiety.* They may wonder how they will carry on, who will do all of the duties of the deceased, and who will comfort and take care of them.

10. *Fear.* They may worry about losing another family member, suffering a similar fate, or having less money in the family.

11. *Guilt.* They may feel guilty because they think that the family member's death is retribution for their wrongdoing, or they may wonder whether the death was caused by something they did or failed to do.

12. *Stigmatization or rejection.* They may believe that they will be stigmatized or rejected by others or lose status in the eyes of others because they have lost a loved one (for example, an adult who becomes a single parent or a child who becomes an orphan) or that they will be isolated from their support networks.

13. *Wish fulfillment.* They may hope that the deceased person will return to life.

14. *Drugs and alcohol.* They may either begin to drink alcohol or take drugs (usually adolescents and adults) or increase their usage of these substances.

Depending upon our culture and particular circumstances, we may meet death with equanimity or with anger, rage, and fear. Through the process of grieving we are brought face to face with our own mortality. These culturally defined attitudes toward death may reflect our attitudes toward the value of life.

—Richard J. Preston and Sara C. Preston

Adaptive reactions to death.   Most cultures tolerate a wide range of responses to death (Counts & Counts, 1991). In fact, behavior that might be considered bizarre or pathological under other circumstances often is considered a normal expression of bereavement. Although some reactions are less adaptive than others, even the less adaptive reactions serve a purpose for mourners (Cook & Dworkin, 1992; Crosby & Jose, 1983). It is primarily when the less adaptive reactions are carried to an extreme that they may impede the individual's long-term functioning.

1. *Adaptive reactions to death.* Adaptive reactions include accepting the reality of the loss, experiencing the pain of grief, adjusting to an environment in which the deceased no longer exists, withdrawing emotional energy from the relationship with the deceased and reinvesting it in new relationships, sharing feelings with others, coming to terms with feelings of loneliness and emptiness, seeing the deceased person as he or she *really* was in life, accepting the death without overriding feelings of guilt, and supporting other family members.

2. *Less adaptive reactions to death.* Less adaptive reactions include refusing to talk about the deceased, avoiding thinking about death by keeping busy constantly or by working constantly, avoiding responsibilities by taking a trip or getting away, trying to obliterate the deceased person's prior existence, idolizing the deceased person, endowing the deceased person with a superhuman perfection, blaming others for the death, not sharing feelings with others, not coming to terms with feelings of loneliness and emptiness, having overriding feelings of guilt, and not listening to or supporting other family members.

Pathological grieving may be present when children or adults have prolonged sadness and grief reactions; cannot speak about the deceased without intense sadness and grief; respond to minor events with intense grief reactions; acquire physical symptoms that mimic those of the deceased; assume some personality and temperamental characteristics of the deceased; make drastic changes in their life style after the loss; describe self-destructive tendencies; have prolonged, unaccountable periods of sadness, particularly during activities associated with the deceased; or have phobias related to symptoms of illness or circumstances related to the death (Lazare, 1979).

The following accounts of how children reacted to the death of a parent or sibling illustrate *some* possible reactions of mourners. The death of a loved one, as noted earlier, will affect various children and adults in different ways.

Reactions of children to the death of a parent. Here are some comments that children made about the death of a parent. The themes expressed in these comments include despondency and regret for past behavior and reactions to the funeral.

- Dad, I remember all the good times we used to spend together. I want to know why you had to die suddenly without warning. I wish I had spent more time finding out about you. I didn't really know anything about your childhood. I regret not talking to you that time I saw you in the mall. When you left me, it felt like everything I had to live for went with you. I know now that I can never make you proud of me, so life really doesn't have any purpose. I just don't care about anything anymore. I wish you could come back, but that's not possible. (Oates, 1993, pp. 31–32)

- [She said] that the worst part of the entire experience of her father's death was the funeral. Yet she went on to say "It was really hard. But I am glad I went. I think all kids should go to their parent's funeral…because it's a good way to send them off." (Weller, Weller, Fristad, Cain, & Bowes, 1988, p. 561)

Reactions of children to the death of a sibling. Here are some comments that children made about the death of a sibling (Martinson & Campos, 1991, pp. 59–64; Martinson, McClowry, Davies, & Kuhlenkamp, 1994, p. 22). The themes expressed in these comments include attention given to the dying sibling, effect of the death on the family, and changes in life style because of the death.

- I don't think all the attention she received ever deprived me because she gave me the love I needed in return. Maybe the other kids felt deprived, but I was with P. the most, and I had her extra love and kisses.

- I remember feeling nobody loved me or cared about me [while she was alive]. I was really down…when she was dead…. Now I will have them back [referring to parents] and be normal.
- [My brother's] death brought our family closer. Maybe that is just a feeling I have; it feels as if there's a closer bond. It's not that we do more family-oriented activities. We're still flying every which way, but it's just we're closer because of what we went through. I feel changed. I grew up emotionally quite a bit. Death was something I had to face. I had to accept the reality of it. It wasn't playtime.
- My parents became alcoholics when Amy got really sick. They still are today, probably for the same reason.
- Nothing changed as far as my school grades but I would say that I started using more drugs than I did before. I didn't get really into the hard drugs, but I used marijuana and speed and stuff like that.
- I couldn't stand to be with her. The only time I could be comfortable was with my mother there. Mom would say "go and play with her," but I couldn't.
- Because I talked with Mom about F. that brought us closer. I saw how much she was feeling and I went through that with her.

A child can live through anything so long as he or she is told the truth and is allowed to share with loved ones the natural feelings people have when they are suffering.

—Eda Le Shan

Reactions of parents to the death of a child.

Here are some comments made by parents about the death of a child (Martinson et al., 1994, pp. 20–23). The themes expressed in these comments include the relationship between the parents, fears about other children in the family, and family attitudes about life, death, and survival.

- I think your marriage can go two ways. You can either get drawn together so that the love is what holds you together or you can get pushed apart. Our marital problems started even when Brent was sick and we had to go for bloodwork. My husband would say, "If it's good news, tell me. If it's bad news, don't, because I don't want to know." After a while you think, "If you don't want to know the bad stuff, I'm not going to give you the good stuff either." I started pushing away and feeling resentful.
- There was a time, before Trisha got sick, that we were taking one another for granted. You see a lot of couples in their mid to late thirties who have marital problems. I'm not saying we had marital problems, but we just took one another for granted. Trisha's illness and death brought us closer together. We did talk. We did communicate. We did share because we saw a lot of husbands and wives who did not and consequently they had marital problems afterwards.
- I have an underlying sense of impending doom. I worry that something is going to happen to the kids. Not that I carry it all the time, but I just think things are going to happen and that makes me more controlling which is not healthy for the kids.
- I think I have more compassion for other people who have problems. It brings you closer to death. You're able to talk about it a little bit more. It doesn't bother me to talk to somebody whose

family member died. After our daughter's death I realized that the wake isn't for the person that died. It's for the people who are still living. That's what the funeral is for, a grieving period. You want to grieve then; you want to have your sadness.
- I often wonder why I'm still here. I'm very bitter and angry. Once in a while, I have a good day. I hurt the most when I do for you or others. I feel like everyone's against me, like I'm not an equal anymore. It's easier to stay away. Sooner or later, you find the only thing you have to hold on to is yourself, your own courage. It's the only thing that won't fail you.
- I went to a prayer group. I got my biggest support from that. Before I joined the prayer group, I was at a loss, but after that, I could see things in a better way than I had before. I felt more relaxed, more at ease; I was able to cope with things. I finally opened myself up to the Lord and I think that's what I needed—just to let it be. I am now aware that there is a God and He is merciful in a lot of different ways. He has shown me different things that I never was aware of before. I had taken everything for granted: the sunshine, the beauty of the trees, even the frost on the trees.

Bereaved parents come in all ages. It does not appear to make a difference whether one's child is three, thirteen, or thirty if he dies. The emotion in each of us is the same. How could it be that a parent outlives a child?

—Harriet Sarnoff Schiff

Reactions to suicide.

In cases of suicide, survivors may be emotionally overwhelmed and feel helplessness, shame, and social stigma (see the next part of the chapter for further discussion of suicide). When a loved one commits suicide, children and adults may feel guilty because they didn't do more for the deceased when he or she was alive. They also may feel guilty for being relieved that the deceased is no longer a burden on them. Children may not know what to tell their friends, and adults may not know what to tell their colleagues. Survivors may feel frustrated at not having had the opportunity to say goodbye or to say they were sorry. They also may be anxious about what their neighbors think and fear that their friends will reject them because they may not consider suicide a socially acceptable way in which to die. In some families, there may be a taboo about discussing suicide.

When a child commits suicide, the parents may feel especially guilty. They may believe that they failed to protect their child and that the suicide was a public admission that their love was not enough (Lukas & Seiden, 1987). They may worry that other children in the family also may want to commit suicide. They may blame each other for the suicide and fail to support each other. Some marriages fail because of the guilt, anger, and grief experienced by the parents (Lukas & Seiden, 1987).

When a parent commits suicide, children may see themselves as highly vulnerable and unprotected (Hiegel & Hipple, 1990; McIntosh, 1987). Children may experience guilt because they believe that they caused the death by upsetting the parent, by not being better sons or daughters, by increasing marital tensions, and by not having done something to save the parent, such as coming straight home from school or being at home when the parent was feeling sad. Children may fear that they also might commit suicide. And some children may wish to commit suicide in order to reunite with the deceased parent. Children may have similar feelings when a parent dies of other causes, especially if they have unresolved feelings about their relationship with the parent.

When a parent commits suicide in a two-parent family, the surviving parent may have trouble dealing with the grief process and with the role changes needed to keep the family functioning (Hiegel & Hipple, 1990). The surviving parent may experience shock, anger, denial, guilt, blame, helplessness, shame, physical problems, and thoughts of committing suicide. These reactions may interfere not only with the bereavement process but also with the parent's ability to function as a parent.

If a member of the family committed suicide while he or she was in a hospital or another facility, the survivors may direct their anger at the attending staff. The survivors may reproach the staff for giving the deceased individual too much freedom, for failing to give the deceased individual adequate treatment, or for failing to release the deceased individual soon enough from the facility (Retterstøl, 1993).

Following are the reactions of several survivors whose loved ones committed suicide (Lukas & Seiden, 1987; Van Dongen, 1990, pp. 226–228):

- Her suicide cheated me out of time to say good-bye.
- Guilt was part of the searching. That is, what did we do wrong? We were looking at everything, trying to figure out why it could have happened.
- I'm afraid it will happen to others in our family.
- A big concern was the children. They are not adults. How do you explain something like this to them? I was so worried about what it might do to them.
- If we'd only done something different, she'd be alive today. What did we do wrong?
- Your friends avoid you. No one calls. You're alone.
- Without the support of my family and friends, I don't know how I would have done it. The nice thing is that family and friends still stop by—they've continued.
- I just felt like I had to read or talk to somebody. I went to three support groups. I didn't want to do anything else, I just wanted to find out—about suicide.
- I think I'm doing pretty good and then bang—all of a sudden something happens like some mail comes for him and I get so upset. It's almost like starting over again. I wonder if it will ever end.
- We just need to get it in our minds that there's no answer to "why." There's no way to figure it out, except that he needed to escape and that's the only way he knew how.

In the following poem, a father expresses his grief about the suicide of his 20-year-old son (Bolton, 1987, p. 94).

I don't know why.
I'll never know why.
I don't have to know why.
I don't like it.
I don't have to like it.
What I do have to do is make a choice
about my living.

What I do want to do is accept it and
go on living.

The choice is mine.
I can go on living, valuing every moment
in a way I never did before,
or I can be destroyed by it and,
in turn, destroy others.

I thought I was immortal.
That my family and my children were also.
That tragedy happened only to others.
But I know now that life is tenuous
and valuable.

So I am choosing to go on living,
making the most of the time I have,
valuing my family and friends
in a way never possible before.

Children who lose a close friend through suicide may feel a threat to their self-esteem (Mauk, 1991). The suicide may confront them with the possibility of their own death. They may feel highly vulnerable and uncertain about themselves, may fear that they also might want to commit suicide, and may experience relief that they weren't the person who committed suicide. Death brings an end to the friendship. It deprives the survivor of having someone close to share feelings, secrets, and intimacies with—of having someone to talk to and rely on. The survivor may have difficulty facing the task of finding a new close friend.

Children are usually not prepared for the sudden loss of a close friend by suicide. Coping becomes more difficult under such conditions because of the stigma associated with suicide. Surviving children may have difficulty expressing their bereavement because others fail to provide support.

When a close friend commits suicide, other children in the community may want to imitate the suicidal behavior. Well-functioning children with strong social support networks usually will not commit suicide to imitate their friends or peers (Mauk & Weber, 1991). However, children with emotional problems or those who lack a supportive network are at risk. They may feel anger and guilt at not having read their friend's signals—such as depression, sadness, loneliness, and other feelings of stress and anxiety. They may wonder why it happened, whether they are to blame, and whether they could have done something differently. Later in the chapter, you will find suggestions for helping children better cope with a peer's suicide and helping them understand that they should not view suicide as an alternative choice.

Hindrances to the bereavement process.

The following factors may make the bereavement process more difficult for survivors:

1. *The death is sudden or unexpected.* Survivors sometimes report that a sudden death is "like a devastating emotional blow." The survivor has "no time to work on unfinished relationship issues or to reach a sense of closure" (Hauser, 1987, p. 63).

2. *The death is violent or traumatic, especially in cases of suicide.* "Survivors are blatantly confronted with suicide's destructive nature . . . Family members may feel destructive, lash out at others, and even contemplate taking their own lives" (Hauser, 1987, p. 63). They also may experience guilt and anger and feel stigmatized. When violence was involved in the death, survivors also may develop a posttraumatic stress disorder (see Chapter 11).

3. *The survivors feel responsible for the death.* Survivors may feel heightened guilt if the death occurred while they were in a driving accident, in another type of accident, or through suicide (Hauser, 1987).

4. *The survivors have a developmental disability.* Survivors with a developmental disability may have a difficult time coping with or understanding the death.

5. *The deceased was a young person.* Survivors sometimes report extreme stress when a young person who is close to them dies. First, a young person is not expected to die. Second, the parents of the young person are likely to experience guilt, especially in cases of suicide, because society expects parents to protect their children. Finally, the death of a sibling or close friend or relative of the same age may cause feelings of guilt and confusion in the surviving child—who may identify with the deceased sibling, friend, or relative and may fear that he or she also will die (McIntosh, 1987).

6. *Other stresses are present in the survivors' lives and families.* Survivors may have economic, legal, social, psychological, or medical stresses associated with the death. *Economic stresses* include a decrease in family income and costs associated with the funeral or with distributing the deceased's estate. *Legal stresses* include litigation stemming from a contested estate. *Social stresses* include new role alignments and structures within the family—which may cause considerable disorganization, confusion, and uncertainty—and the need to establish new patterns of authority and decision making (Crosby & Jose, 1983). *Psychological stresses* include guilt stemming from a problematic relationship with the deceased, depression, arguments between the survivors about the death, and failure of family members to share their grief with each other. *Medical stresses* include becoming ill and having substance abuse problems.

7. *The survivors avoid funeral rites.* Survivors who circumvent funeral rites may deprive themselves of community support and closure, which may be needed to help them with the mourning process (Hauser, 1987).

8. *The survivors need to make many arrangements.* Survivors who need to make many arrangements—such as legal, financial, or educational arrangements—may have increased levels of stress (Crosby & Jose, 1983).

9. *The survivors have distorted or inhibited their communications.* Survivors who feel rejected and abandoned by the person who died may look for a scapegoat (Hauser, 1987). They may blame other family members, talk irrationally to each other, or avoid talking about their feelings.

10. *The survivors' support networks fail to provide support.* If survivors' support networks—such as family and relatives, friends, teachers, ministers and rabbis, professional therapists, and acquaintances—make them feel ashamed or isolate them or make them feel different from others, they will interfere with the survivors' bereavement process (Hauser, 1987). When a child commits suicide, relatives may see the parents as partly responsible for the child's death. Similarly, if the death is associated with AIDS, relatives may judge the deceased person harshly and refuse to support the survivors, partly out of fear of contracting the disease themselves (Cook & Dworkin, 1992). Children's grief reactions will be impeded when their grief is not recognized or when they are not allowed to participate in the grief rituals. (This process, referred to as disenfranchised grief, is discussed later in the chapter.)

11. *The surviving child is not told about the reason for the death, particularly in cases of suicide.* Survivors who are children may not be told the reason for the death, particularly when one parent commits suicide. By not telling the child, the surviving parent may be trying to protect the child. However, the "conspiracy of silence" may not work because even older preschool children and young school-aged children may know or suspect the reason for the parent's death. A family that practices denial or distortion and fails to allow open discussion of the death may hinder the child's mourning, perpetuate or exacerbate the child's guilt, and cause psychological problems for the child (McIntosh, 1987).

Anticipatory grief.

Individuals may anticipate the death of a loved one (Rando, 1984). In *anticipatory grief,* individuals, aware of the impending loss, attempt to relinquish their attachment to the dying person. They may become depressed, have heightened concern for the dying person, think about the impending death of the person, and attempt to adjust to the consequences of the person's death. Anticipatory grief allows individuals to (a) absorb the reality of the loss gradually over time, (b) take care of unfinished business with the dying person, such as expressing feelings and resolving past conflicts, (c) begin to change assumptions about their goals in life, and (d) make plans for the future (Rando, 1984).

Individuals experiencing anticipatory grief also may have chronic grief (L. Gudas, personal communication, February 1996). This may happen, for example, when parents must care for a child who has a long-term progressive illness or who is severely impaired (see Chapter 15). Although there may be no definite ending anticipated to the child's life, the parents may think that the child is likely to die in the relatively near future.

Disenfranchised grief.   A form of grief called *disenfranchised grief* occurs when children and adults incur a loss but do "not have a socially recognized right, role, or capacity to grieve" (Doka, 1989, p. 3). In such cases, they are denied the opportunity to grieve or discouraged from grieving because others believe that they cannot comprehend death or that death has little meaning for them. Groups that may be excluded from discussions of death and from participation in death rituals include young children, elderly adults who may be partially senile, and mentally retarded individuals. The failure to recognize that these individuals also experience grief may be due to the fact that those in charge (a) are not aware of the psychological impact of loss on the excluded individuals, (b) want to deny the horror that they, too, are experiencing, or (c) are experiencing conflict in dealing with their grief and, consequently, cannot attend to the needs of the others who are young or who have disabilities (Gudas, 1993).

Phases of grief.   The grief process may involve several phases, particularly for adolescents and adults (Kübler-Ross, 1969; Rando, 1984). These phases are listed here in approximate sequential order, although some individuals may experience more than one phase at the same time, and other individuals may experience the phases in different orders.

1. *Shock and numbness.* Bereaved individuals may be in a state of shock and stunned at the loss. They may try to block out recognition of the loss and any painful feelings.

2. *Yearning and searching.* Bereaved individuals may have an urge to find, recover, and reunite with the deceased person, a condition known as *separation distress.* They may feel anger at the loss and the fruitlessness of the search. They also may experience disbelief, tension, tearfulness, and a desire to keep a clear visual image of the deceased.

3. *Disorganization and despair.* Bereaved individuals may give up the search, experience depression, feel disinclined to look to the future, or fail to see any purpose in life. In the process, they may begin to recognize the reality of the death.

4. *Reorganization.* Bereaved individuals may break down attachments to the lost loved one, establish ties to others, and show a renewed interest in activities and in other people.

Developmental considerations in children's concept of death.   Children's understanding of death will influence the way they react to the deaths of others, as well as to their own forthcoming death. Their reactions to death also will be influenced by how they see others in their environment react to the death. Usually, children's reactions to death will be typical of those associated with other traumas.

1. *Infants.* During the first two years of development, children have little understanding of death, but they do react to the loss of a caregiver (Rowland, 1989a). They may show generalized distress and irritability, lose weight, have feeding and sleeping difficulties, lack interest in pleasurable activities, cry excessively, lose speech, and show increased dependency.

2. *Preschool children.* During preschool years, children are likely to think magically about death. They may view death as reversible—when you die, the doctor (or someone) makes you well again—or they may view the deceased as sleeping (Culbertson & Willis, 1988). They may not understand cause-effect relationships. They may believe, for example, that wishing someone dead can lead to the person's death (Rowland, 1989a). For children between the ages of 2 and 3 years, death is not yet a familiar concept. However, between the ages of 3 and 5 years, children begin to understand that death is something that can happen to others. The concept of death is vague, but preschool children may understand it as the opposite of life and may describe it as remote, dark, and constricted (Schowalter, 1970).

Preschool children's reactions to death may include tearfulness, thumb-sucking and bed-wetting, clinging and dependency behaviors, temper tantrums, aggressive behavior, negativism, sleep problems, frequent nightmares, loss of appetite, concentration difficulties, irritability, withdrawal, decreased interest in play or recreational activities, repetitive play or rituals, and poor school performance (Cook & Dworkin, 1992). They also "may view the death as an abandonment, as punishment, as the realization of unacceptable wishes, or as all three" (Lewis, Lewis, & Schonfeld, 1991, p. 1053).

If it is a parent who has died, children may worry about who will take care of them. They also may ask many questions about their deceased parent, such as "Who will feed daddy?" or "Where is mommy living?" They may cope with the death of someone close to them by identifying with the deceased, such as by wearing an article of clothing of the deceased. Grief responses are often intermittent and show marked affective shifts over time.

Children between the ages of 2 and 3 years who are terminally ill may primarily fear separation from their caregivers (Schowalter, 1970). Preschool children with a fatal illness may view the illness as punishment for real or imagined wrongdoing. Some preschool children who are dying may become angry and rebellious, whereas others may become passive and withdrawn.

3. *School-aged children.* During the early school years, children think more logically about death, particularly focusing on the physical means by which death occurs. Although they begin to understand various dimensions of the concept of death, the concept of death is incomplete and concrete (Rowland, 1989a). Death may be associated with darkness, evil, violence, and sleeping; with grief over anticipated (or actual) separation from loved ones; and with fear when it is seen as punishment for wrong acts. Middle

school–aged children begin to understand death as permanent and nonreversible; this understanding contributes to their fears of mutilation and physical injury.

School-aged children may have various reactions to death, including shock, denial, anxiety, distress, reawakened feelings of childishness and helplessness, inability to share feelings with others, irritability (which may be a symptom of anger), concentration difficulties (which may lead to poor school performance), crying spells, somatic complaints (such as headaches, abdominal pain, listlessness, and fatigue), and difficulty accepting the finality of their personal loss, although they recognize the finality of death in general (Rando, 1984).

School-aged children who are terminally ill may feel responsible in some way for their illness (Schowalter, 1970). They may ask if they are dying, but few want to know the truth. However, they may pick up clues about their condition from the reactions of their caregivers. They may find it difficult to accept when they are told that they are going to die.

4. *Adolescents.* During adolescence, children recognize the implications of death for themselves and for others and gain a perspective toward death similar to that of adults. "Death comes to be recognized as a final and irrevocable biological event, yet it is accompanied by disbelief in the possibility of one's personal death" (Rowland, 1989a). Adolescents' reactions to the deaths of others may include confusion, depression, helplessness, fear, anger, guilt, somatic complaints, difficulties in eating and sleeping, a wish to retreat to childhood, antisocial behaviors, concern about how others will accept their responses, and a denial of feelings (Cook & Dworkin, 1992; Rando, 1984).

Adolescents have particular difficulty enduring the physical ravages of their own terminal illnesses (Schowalter, 1970). Some adolescents who are dying may look to their past for comfort; others may see the time they spent growing up as wasted because there is no future for them.

To lose your parents, you lose your past; to lose your spouse, you lose your present; to lose your children, you lose your future.

—Anonymous (Cited by Therese A. Rando)

Exercise 13-1. Understanding Your Reactions to Death

This exercise is designed to increase your awareness of your experiences with death. It was obtained from Cook and Dworkin (1992, p. 169) and from Rando (1984, pp. 9–12).

1. What was your first encounter with death? How old were you when it happened? Recall your feelings and needs at the time. How did others respond to those feelings and needs? What is your most vivid image associated with this first loss experience? Who died? What was your experience like? How did you cope with the death? How

did other people you knew cope with the death? What did you learn about death, loss, and grief because of this experience?

2. If you had a second death-related experience, how did it compare with your first one? How old were you then? How were your reactions similar to and different from those associated with your first encounter with death?

3. How was the topic of death dealt with in your family? Was it ignored or considered taboo, or was it discussed openly and matter-of-factly?

4. Can you remember the first funeral you attended? How old were you? Who died? How were you prepared for the funeral? What do you remember about it? What feelings did you have about the funeral? How were the funeral and your response influenced by your religion and culture?

5. What significant losses have you had? Which one was the most painful and why? Did you get depressed with any of these losses? If so, how did you act when you were depressed? In what ways has this loss affected your life?

6. What has been your most recent loss by death? How did you react? How did you cope with the loss? How did you know when your grief was resolved, or does it still remain unresolved?

7. How do members of your family act when they have a loss? Does your family have any rituals for handling grief and loss? If so, what are the rituals?

8. What are your current attitudes toward and beliefs about death? How might your beliefs about death affect your work as a mental health professional with individuals who are terminally ill or bereaved?

Interviewing Issues

Table F-31 in Appendix F will be helpful in interviewing older children and adolescents whose loved one has died. Many questions are similar to those covered in cases of depression. You will want to obtain information about the following factors as they relate to the child's bereavement (Webb, 1993): (a) *individual child factors* (age, developmental stage, cognitive level, temperament, and coping skills), (b) *death-related factors* (relationship to deceased, present reactions to the death, meaning of the loss, grief reactions, and past reactions to death), and (c) *family, social, religious, and cultural factors* (family's response to death, support received from others, and religious and cultural traditions).

You will have difficulty obtaining information about the interviewee's perception of the death and her or his worries and concerns when the interviewee is emotionally distraught or fails to discuss the extent of her or his grief reaction or when you fail to probe because you believe the interviewee is too distraught (Cook & Dworkin, 1992). You need to attend to the interviewee's affective state, but you also need to carry out the assessment functions of the interview if you can.

If the interviewee is extremely upset, however, you may have to help her or him overcome shock and grief and forgo the assessment functions of the interview. Here are some of the things you can do when the interviewee is extremely upset (Fremouw, de Perczel, & Ellis, 1990; Rando, 1984).

- Show the interviewee that you can be trusted by exhibiting sympathy, understanding, and warmth.
- Encourage the interviewee to express her or his feelings such as sorrow, guilt, anger, or rejection.
- Encourage the interviewee to engage in activities and reestablish daily routines.
- Help the interviewee formulate plans for her or his immediate future.
- Encourage the interviewee to find supports, such as by joining a bereavement group or starting therapy.
- Provide a reading list of books about suicide and grief to an interviewee who can read (see Appendix B).

The following are some suggestions for maintaining a therapeutic and realistic perspective during the interview:

- Remember that you cannot take away the pain from the interviewee.
- Do not let your own sense of helplessness keep you from reaching out to the interviewee.
- Show the interviewee that you are caring and genuinely concerned.
- Expect to encounter volatile reactions from the interviewee.
- Recognize that your mere presence may be therapeutic for the interviewee.
- View the loss from the interviewee's unique perspective.
- Maintain an appropriate "psychological" distance from the interviewee.
- Do not project your own needs related to mourning on the interviewee.
- Do not try to explain the loss in religious or philosophical terms, but allow the interviewee to explore these areas of her or his belief.
- Do not tell the interviewee to feel better because there are other loved ones who are still alive.
- Do not try to unrealistically "pretty up" the situation.
- Do not encourage responses that will interfere with appropriate grief reactions.
- Hold out the expectation that the interviewee will successfully complete the tasks of mourning and that the pain will subside.
- Remember to plant seeds of hope.

To help you evaluate the interview in cases of bereavement, see Table 13-1. Part of your task in the initial interview is to distinguish normal grief from clinical depression. This is particularly difficult to assess during the first few weeks following a death because symptoms of grief resemble those of clinical depression. In clinical depression, a pervasive pattern of sadness and gloom covers much of the individual's life—the individual has little, if any, enthusiasm for any activity; has feelings of worthlessness, self-blame, and hopelessness; and has difficulty expressing anger (see discussion of depression in Chapter 11). In contrast, in nor-

Table 13-1
Evaluating the Clinical Assessment Interview in Cases of Bereavement

1. How is the interviewee coping with the death?
2. What are the interviewee's expectations?
3. What were the circumstances of the death?
4. What was the interviewee's relationship with the deceased?
5. What is the interviewee's history of loss?
6. Are there secondary losses? (Secondary losses include symbolic losses associated with the death of the loved one, such as loss of hopes and dreams that parents had for their child, failure to receive social invitations, and giving up a role in the family. They also include concrete losses, such as needing to move from the family home.)
7. How does the interviewee express her or his grief?
8. What is the interviewee's developmental status? (The developmental status includes the interviewee's age and understanding of death and how the loss affects the interviewee's development.)
9. Is the interviewee suicidal or homicidal?
10. Does the interviewee have any behavior problems or other psychological difficulties that might suggest poor coping? (Such problems and difficulties include illogical or magical thinking, strong feelings of guilt and responsibility for the death, depression, inability to relax, not caring about how he or she looks, inability to sleep, avoiding friends and social activities, indifference to school and hobbies, feelings of worthlessness, and use of alcohol or drugs.)
11. Does the interviewee have any physical problems that might suggest poor coping? (Physical problems include stress-related problems such as headaches, backaches, muscle aches, stomach upset, and general anxiety.)
12. Is the interviewee under a physician's care? (If so, what type of treatment is he or she receiving, including medications?)
13. What role is the family playing in the interviewee's coping with the death?
14. Does the interviewee have outside support? (Outside support includes friends, extended family, neighbors, teachers, church groups, and other organizations.)
15. What are the interviewee's spiritual and religious beliefs?
16. How do the interviewee's beliefs affect her or his adjustment?
17. What cultural practices are affecting how the interviewee expresses her or his grief?
18. Did the interviewee have a chance to ask questions about the death?
19. (If yes) Were the interviewee's questions answered in terms that were understandable to her or him?

Source: Adapted from Cook and Dworkin (1992).

mal grieving, the individual has an acute reaction; has occasional weeping, confusion, and expressions of anger; and can be responsive to warmth and assurance.

If the interviewee's symptoms—such as not caring about his or her looks, inability to sleep, avoidance of social activities, indifference to school or hobbies, reliance on drugs or alcohol, or not caring for his or her children (in adults)—are impeding his or her functioning, consider referring the interviewee for a more extensive evaluation. Also, because grief reactions may affect the interviewee's health and the health of other family members, recommend a physical evaluation, as needed.

Interventions

Helping families with a dying child.   When a child is dying, there are several things you can do to help the family (Worden & Monahan, 1993).

1. Help them keep in contact with the child. Although it may be difficult for family members to see the child declining, encourage them to be with the child. If they do not spend time with the child, they may have guilt feelings and become depressed.
2. Encourage the family to talk to the dying child.
3. Help family members develop memories of the child that they can hold after the child's death; encourage them to take pictures of the child if they want to.
4. Help family members communicate with the medical staff and negotiate the medical system, if they have difficulty doing so.
5. Provide respite care, especially for overburdened parents; hospital volunteers are a good source of help.
6. Encourage the parents to allow the child some say in how her or his remaining days will be spent.
7. Provide support and comfort to the grieving parents, answer their questions and concerns, and arrange for needed help and services.

Helping survivors.   After the death of a loved one, there are several things you can do to help the survivors. The following suggestions are aimed at helping the family members work through the grieving process, arrive at a sense of closure, and resume a normal life pattern more quickly, when possible (Bolton, 1987; Davies, 1993; Dunne-Maxim, Dunne, & Hauser, 1987; Grollman, 1990; Moody & Moody, 1991; Rando, 1984).

1. *Suggestions for the surviving caregiver(s) to help the surviving child.* Encourage the surviving caregiver(s) to

- physically hold, touch, and hug the child and reassure the child that he or she will be loved, taken care of, and valued as before
- explain that the death was not the child's fault, that it was not the intention of the loved one to die (except in cases of suicide), and that although the deceased will not be returning, he or she loved the child very much
- encourage the child to ask questions; then answer those questions honestly, directly, and simply

- encourage the child to express his or her feelings
- allow the child to express feelings of love for other family members
- model appropriate grieving behavior before the child, such as crying or expression of other feelings
- give the child choices about participating in the grieving process, such as attending the funeral and seeing the deceased
- allow the child space and time to absorb the fact that a loved one died
- recognize that the child's reactions may be related not only to the death of a loved one but also to the additional strains created on the caregiver(s) and the family
- promote open, attentive, and respectful communication between the child and all family members and allow the child to talk with a trusted individual outside the family
- understand that the child's grief may be expressed through play, art, or acting-out behaviors
- be understanding of the child if he or she doesn't outwardly grieve
- be tolerant if the child shows regressive behavior
- not expect from the child adult responses and emotional reactions
- understand that each child in the family will react to the death in his or her own unique way
- allow the child to have responsibilities around the house as a way of "normalizing" life
- encourage the child to be with friends and peers
- avoid comparisons between the surviving child and the deceased individual
- reassure the child that it is not likely that anyone else in the family will die soon (if appropriate)
- make few changes in the child's routines
- recognize that there are no magic words to soothe the child
- allow laughter and fun times, even in the midst of great sadness, and recognize that the child is not being disrespectful when he or she laughs or plays

---

In helping children understand and cope with death, remember four key concepts: be loving, be accepting, be truthful, and be consistent.

—Kathleen McCue

---

2. *Suggestions for the family members.* Encourage or help the family members to

- be patient and not expect too much from themselves or from each other
- find ways to reduce stress in the home, such as engaging in some form of physical activity
- understand that a major loss always requires adjustments and changes and make sure that any new role assignments in the family are appropriate for everyone involved
- spend time with family members and friends in order to avoid being isolated

- resume normal activities as soon as possible, including observing special occasions, although these occasions may cause uninvited reminders of their pain
- use positive strategies to cope with their loss and grief, attend a survivor's support group, and read relevant literature (see Appendix B)
- understand that each family member may grieve differently and try to understand, respect, and talk about how each member is coping with the loss

---

In helping siblings,…the goal of intervention is not for siblings to get over their grief, but rather to acknowledge it and to learn to integrate it into their lives, for it is a memory that they carry with them forever.

—Betty Davies

---

3. *Additional suggestions for children who lose a peer through suicide.* Encourage or help the child to

- talk about the problems the deceased child was having and about the problems she or he is having that may seem overwhelming; then highlight the differences, not the similarities, between the deceased child and the surviving child
- not assume undue guilt for not having acted on clues that might have prevented the suicide from occurring
- realize that the responsibility for the event lies in the deceased child's action and not in the living child's actions
- realize that suicide is not an acceptable coping strategy
- discuss other ways in which the problems could have been solved
- talk about the pain and suffering of those left behind
- express her or his feelings about the suicide in different ways, such as by writing, playing music, and drawing; this will help the child deal with her or his feelings

---

Often the test of courage is not to die but to live.

—Vittorio Alfieri

---

4. *Suggestions for parents who survive the death of their child.* Help the parents understand the following.

- Although the age of the child is inconsequential to their feelings of bereavement, the child's age will determine some issues that arise during the bereavement. Especially try to legitimize grief for parents who grieve for a miscarriage, stillbirth, neonatal death, or SIDS death.
- They have to grieve not only for the loss of their child but also for the loss of their hopes, dreams, and expectations for that child. They must grieve for what they have lost individually, lost as a couple, and lost as a family.
- They will likely differ in how they react to the loss and how they grieve. The individual attributes of the child and

the parents and also specific roles and relationships in the family make each loss idiosyncratic.
- They will never forget the death and the emptiness will remain, but the pain will likely diminish as they learn to live with the tragedy by finding ways to make life meaningful and to channel their intense feelings constructively.
- They will survive, but they will not be the same as before the loss.
- Upsurges of grief are normal, particularly at specific times, such as when the child would have reentered school in the fall, graduated, and gotten married and at other shared family events.
- They may harbor unrealistic expectations about themselves as parents, such as the idea that they could have protected their child from everything. Help them to work through their guilt and to find ways to forgive themselves.
- They cannot overestimate the effects of grief on their relationship, and they must treat each other as fragile people who will require patience and understanding to survive and recover from the loss together. Encourage communication and understanding of problems even as they grieve for the death of their child. Help them cope with unmet expectations. Help them recognize that failure to meet sexual expectations may be due to the grieving process and be unrelated to their feelings of love for one another.
- They must take life one step and one day at a time, and they should postpone major life decisions.
- They can deal with their grief by keeping a journal to help them work through their feelings, by calling a friend who is a good listener, by joining a support group, by calling on personal faith, or by seeking professional help.
- They should express their needs to others and be patient with those who do not understand their feelings and needs.
- They should give themselves permission to take a break from their grief to enjoy their living children and other aspects of their lives. Doing so is not a betrayal of the deceased child, and the willingness to enjoy and to laugh is healing.
- It is common to experience such symptoms as headaches, loss of appetite, and inability to sleep.
- They may feel overwhelmed by the intensity of their feelings and may even experience thoughts of suicide. They need to know that these feelings and thoughts are common and that having them doesn't mean they will act on them. If they feel angry, guilty, confused, and forgetful, it doesn't mean they are crazy; these are common reactions to mourning. They must be patient, give themselves time to heal, and work through their feelings so that they can let go and understand that letting go does not mean forgetting.

You can't prevent birds of sorrow flying over your head—but you can prevent them from building nests in your hair.

—Chinese Proverb

Calvin and Hobbes   by Bill Watterson

5. *Suggestions for a parent whose spouse dies.* Encourage or help the surviving parent to

- support the children, although it may be extremely difficult
- maintain appropriate role expectations for the children
- understand and accept the children's grief reactions
- identify those roles and functions that he or she needs to assume and those that need to be assumed by someone else
- understand that changes in the family's socioeconomic status may result
- accept his or her feelings
- be patient with himself or herself
- monitor his or her health
- avoid the abuse of alcohol and drugs
- share his or her pain with friends
- join a group of others who are grieving
- seek solace from his or her faith (if the parent is religious)

Children will need professional help when they have serious adjustment problems. Signs of possible maladjustment include the following:

- extreme guilt, panic, or despair
- extremely negative view of self
- excessive daydreaming
- marked changes in personality
- serious trouble sleeping
- excessive sleep
- marked eating changes, such as loss of appetite or increased overeating
- fear of going to school
- decrement in school performance
- withdrawal and isolation from others
- excessive acting-out behavior

It will be normal for children to show many of these behaviors and feelings soon after the death, as they attempt to cope with the loss. The key to whether the child's reactions indicate serious adjustment problems is the intensity and duration of these (and other) behaviors and feelings and whether the children are endangered by their reactions. In any case, major depression, thoughts of suicide, excessive use of drugs, anorexia, bulimia, psychotic reactions, and delinquent behavior will require professional assistance.

Case Illustrations

The first case describes a 4-year-old boy's mourning for the loss of his 8-year-old sister, who had died of leukemia (Sourkes, 1987).

CASE 13-1. FRANK

When Frank was told of Katy's death, he immediately said that he wished he had had the chance to say goodbye. Over the next few days, he asked many questions: Why was Katy dead; what did death mean; what did she look like now? The parents told Frank that although Katy could no longer talk to him, he could still tell her things if it would make him feel better. During the first month after Katy's death, Frank asked to go to the cemetery several times. At the grave, he would pose questions to Katy through his mother; for example, "Ask Katy if she really loved me." He would recount anecdotes to Katy about his life, such as his first day of nursery school. When the family dog was found after being lost for a day, Frank insisted on going to the cemetery with the dog so that Katy would know about his return! In school, Frank immediately attached himself to a little girl in his class, and would panic on the days she was absent. About a month after Katy died, while Frank was in the bathtub, he suddenly burst into sobs about how much he missed taking a bath with Katy. Evidently bath time continued to be difficult for about six months, but eventually it became a time for happy recollection about the bath games he and Katy used to play together. Almost a year later, Frank still wakes up some mornings and says that he feels sad because he misses his sister. (pp. 179–180)

The second case illustrates the bereavement process in a brain-injured child (Donders, 1993).

CASE 13-2. EDDY

Eddy, a 3.7-year-old male, sustained a severe traumatic brain injury in a motor vehicle accident. His 5-year-old brother, Ralph (who was his only sibling), was killed in this accident. Approximately 8 weeks after discharge, Eddy began to demonstrate significant mood swings and separation anxiety. His parents had told him that Ralph had gone to "live with Jesus." The mother would take him to Ralph's grave, but tell him that they were just going to "watch flowers." At the site of the tombstone, the mother would then often cry, which Eddy could not understand and which frightened him. At the therapist's suggestion, the mother told Eddy on subsequent occasions that they were going to look at "Ralph's flowers" and that the site of the flowers could be a place to think about Ralph. The parents were also encouraged to use more concrete language with Eddy when talking about Ralph, including the words "died" and "dead." They were also asked to explain to Eddy that Ralph would not be able to come back, and to reassure him that he had done nothing wrong to cause Ralph's death. (pp. 521–522)

The third case illustrates that the grieving process is a series of ups and downs. Lai-Chu resolved her grief when she realized what her mother would have wanted for her future (Roach & Nieto, 1997).

CASE 13-3. LAI-CHU

Lai-Chu, a young girl of 14, was sitting motionless in the Emergency Department waiting room. Her heart felt like it was going to explode. She wanted to cry, but the tears wouldn't come. All she could think about was the picture of her mother lying helpless on the floor when she came home from school. The sound of the ambulance, the questioning, the ride to the hospital all rolled over and over in her head. How could this happen to her? She needed her mother so much. Her dad came and he was frightened too, but Lai-Chu felt so numb. Then the doctor came out and said, "I'm sorry. We did all we could, but it was no use—her heart did not respond." Lai-Chu immediately began crying with uncontrollable sobs. She felt like the floor had fallen out from under her. How could she make it without her mom? What would she do?

Over the next several days, the pain Lai-Chu felt was overwhelming, the sadness unbearable, and a feeling of total helplessness prevailed. She was angry at the doctors for not saving her mother, yet at the same time she felt that, maybe, if she had done something different, her mother would still be alive. "Mom worried so much about me. At times we argued over what time I should come home, my choice of friends, or schoolwork. If only I had not been so selfish, wanting my own way..."

Everyone was there. The church was so crowded. Lai-Chu and the rest of the family sat, crying quietly. Surprisingly, the friends who were present, those who took time to come to the funeral, provided so much comfort. To know that so many

people cared about her mother and the family felt good. Strange how it comforted her. As months came and went, Lai-Chu slowly began to feel again. In fact, the numbness she felt in the beginning gave way to headaches that were only relieved by sleep. Emotions ebbed and flowed. Thoughts of her mother permeated her being all the time, and she talked about her "great mother" in glowing terms. After 10 months of emotional ups and downs, Lai-Chu slowly began to resume living again. Her grades improved, and she began to enjoy social activities and "hanging around" with her friends again. One day, when she was alone and thinking about her mother, she suddenly knew what her mother would want. She would want her to be truly alive and happy. Aloud she said, "I love you, Mom, forever and ever! But I must go on. I can be happy again." (pp. 16–17, with changes in notation)

Healing is a matter of time, but it is sometimes also a matter of opportunity.

—Hippocrates

SUICIDE

Description

Statistics on suicide—the act of intentionally killing oneself—are uncertain because it is often difficult to determine the actual cause of death. For example, a death from an automobile accident may be recorded as a traffic fatality when, in fact, it was a suicide. In addition, statistics may be underestimated because of the social stigma attached to suicide.

Despite possible problems with the data, it is valuable to look at the reported incidence of suicide in children and adolescents. Suicide rates for 10- to 14-year-olds and for 15- to 19-year-olds have increased since 1970 (U.S. Bureau of the Census, 1996b). The rates for 10- to 14-year-olds are as follows:

1970: 0.6 per 100,000
1980: 0.8 per 100,000
1990: 1.5 per 100,000

And the rates for 15- to 19-year-olds are as follows:

1970: 5.9 per 100,00
1980: 8.5 per 100,000
1990: 11.1 per 100,000

Thus, in a 20-year period, suicide rates increased 2½ times for 10- to 14-year-olds and almost doubled for 15- to 19-year-olds. The general increase in adolescent suicide since 1970 may be attributed to several factors, including reduced family influence, economic and peer pressures, alcohol use and abuse, sexual pressures, fear of AIDS, media influences, and gang influences (DeSpelder & Strickland, 1992).

In 1990, the method of committing suicide employed most frequently by children aged 10 to 14 years was use of firearms (55%), followed by strangulation by hanging (36%) and poisoning (6%) (Kachur, Potter, James, & Powell, 1995). In this age group, there were 258 recorded suicides. For children aged 15 to 19 years, use of firearms (67%) was again the method of choice followed by strangulation by hanging (18%) and poisoning (11%). There were 1,979 recorded suicides for this age group in 1990.

Let's consider the ethnic backgrounds and genders of the children and adolescents who committed suicide in 1990 (Centers for Disease Control and Prevention, 1996b; Kachur et al., 1995). Some interesting patterns are shown in Figure 13-1. Among males 10 to 14 years of age, the estimated rate of suicide ranged from 0.7 per 100,000 to 6.0 per 100,000, depending on the ethnic group. The overall rate of suicide for males in this age group was 2.19 per 100,000. The highest rate was among Native American males, followed by White American males, Black American males, Hispanic American males, and Asian American males. The estimated rate of female suicide per 100,000 in these five ethnic groups was much lower and in a narrower range—from 0.4

per 100,000 to 1.1 per 100,000. The overall rate of suicide for females in this age group was 0.81 per 100,000. The highest rate was for Hispanic American females, followed by Native American females, White American females, Black American females, and Asian American females.

Among males 15 to 19 years of age, the estimated rate of suicide ranged from 10.9 per 100,000 to 36.4 per 100,000, depending on the ethnic group. The overall rate of male suicide in this age group was 18.05 per 100,000. The highest rate was among Native American males, followed by White American males, Asian American males, Black American males, and Hispanic American males. The estimated rate of female suicide per 100,000 in these five ethnic groups ranged from 1.9 per 100,000 to 6.5 per 100,000. The overall rate of female suicide in this age group was 3.71 per 100,000. The highest rate was for Native American females, followed by White American females and Asian American females, Hispanic American females, and Black American females.

In both age groups and the five ethnic groups studied, the estimated rate of suicide was much higher for males than for

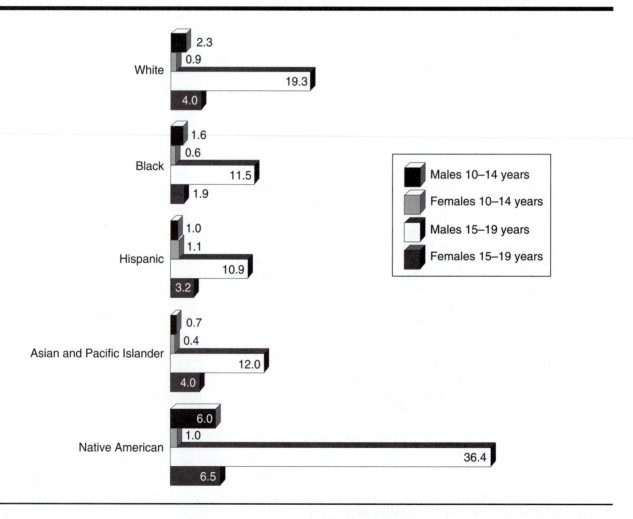

Figure 13-1. Estimated suicide rate per 100,000 population in 1990 for children and adolescents between 10 and 14 and between 15 and 19 years of age in five ethnic groups. From Kachur et al. (1995), pp. 38–43.

females. For example, for adolescents aged 15–19 years, the rate of suicide was about 6.1 times higher for Black American males than for Black American females, about 5.6 times higher for Native American males than for Native American females, about 4.8 times higher for White American males than for White American females, about 3.4 times higher for Hispanic American males than for Hispanic American females, and about 3.0 times higher for Asian American males than for Asian American females. Overall, the suicide rate for males was 2.7 times higher than that for females in the 10–14 age bracket and 4.9 times higher than that for females in the 15–19 age bracket.

It also is interesting to look at the incidence of suicide attempts among adolescents. A national survey of students in grades 9 through 12, conducted in 1995, indicated that 8.7% of the students reported that they had attempted suicide in the 12 months prior to the survey—a rate that translates into approximately 1,270,000 students who made a suicide attempt (Kann, Warren, Harris, Collins, Williams, Ross, & Kolbe, 1996; L. Kann, personal communication, March 14, 1997). Female adolescents (11.9%) were more likely than male adolescents (5.6%) to make suicide attempts. This result contrasts with that for actual rates of suicide, where males outnumber females. One reason for this difference is that males use more lethal methods when attempting suicide than do females. Second, females may be more prone to use suicide attempts as a "cry for help." Of the three ethnic groups studied, Hispanic adolescents had the highest rate of attempted suicide (13.4%), followed by Black adolescents (9.5%) and White adolescents (7.6%). In each ethnic group, the rate of attempted suicide was higher for females than for males (21% vs. 7.0% among Hispanics; 10.8% vs. 7% among Blacks; and 10.4% vs. 5.2% among Whites).

When a child commits suicide, the effects on his or her family and friends can be devastating. Family members of suicide victims are at risk for developing depressive disorders (Brent, Perper, Moritz, Liotus, Schweers, Roth, Balach, & Allman, 1993). Youths exposed to the suicide of a friend or acquaintance also are at risk for developing depressive disorders (Brent, Perper, Moritz, Allman, Liotus, Schweers, Roth, Balach, & Canobbio, 1993), anxiety disorder, and posttraumatic stress disorder (Brent, Perper, Moritz, Friend, Schweers, Allman, McQuiston, Boylan, Roth, & Balach, 1993). Depression is more likely when youths had a close relationship with the victim, were at the scene of death, had a conversation with the victim the day of the suicide, or have a personal and a family history of depression. In addition, anxiety reactions are more likely when youths have a family history of suicide and stressful life events in the year before they were exposed to suicide.

When you evaluate a child's potential for suicide, consider his or her level of language development and understanding of the concept of death. Earlier in the chapter, you read that preschool children have difficulty talking about death, that middle school–aged children's concept of death is incomplete, and that adolescents begin to understand fully that death is final and irreversible. Children who are suicidal, however, often regard death as a temporary and pleasant state that alleviates stress; consequently, there is a need to evaluate their beliefs about death (Pfeffer, 1986).

Psychological disorders, symptoms, and family environment. Studies of adolescents who commit suicide (known as *psychological autopsies*) indicate that 90 to 98% of the victims had a psychological disorder (Ryland & Kruesi, 1992). The disorders, from most to least frequent, are as follows: affective disorder, substance abuse problem, conduct disorder or antisocial personality, major depression, personality disorder, adjustment disorder, and schizophrenic disorder. The most lethal combination might be the coexistence of affective disorder with antisocial behavior, conduct disorder, or alcohol abuse. *The three most prevalent behavioral difficulties are depressive symptoms, behavioral problems, and substance abuse.* The families of adolescent suicide victims are more likely than other families to have intrafamilial turmoil and parental psychological disorders (Ryland & Kruesi, 1992).

Myths about suicide. Table 13-2 shows several myths that are prevalent in our culture about suicide and about those who are likely to commit suicide. A study of these myths will help you understand suicide better and help you work with children (and adults) who are in a crisis.

Escape theory. To help you understand how a person becomes receptive to suicide, let's look at a variant of *escape theory* that I have modified from Baumeister's (1993) work. Children contemplating suicide may not go through each step in the order indicated, may skip a step, or may commit suicide for reasons not included in the theory. Despite these limitations, escape theory provides a useful way of understanding the act of suicide. The theory, as modified, contains nine steps (see Figure 13-2). The examples for each step cited in the following discussion are from Curran (1987), DeSpelder and Strickland (1992), Hafen and Frandsen (1985), and Rich, Sherman, and Fowler (1990).

Step 1. *Major disappointment or stress.* "Suicide attempts follow from recent disappointments that may be triggered by unrealistically high standards and expectations, severe misfortunes and setbacks, or both" (Baumeister, 1993, p. 281). Disappointments and stresses include loss of a loved one (such as a parent, friend, or pet), humiliation or defeat, failure at school, suspension from school, rejection by parents, being called a "sissy" by a coach, rejection by a boyfriend or girlfriend, arguments with father or mother, parents' separating, death of a family member, losing a job, contracting a severe illness, living in an intolerable situation (such as ongoing physical, emotional, or sexual abuse or neglect or a chaotic family situation), starting a new job, having sexual conflict (including pregnancy for adolescent females or impregnating a female for adolescent males), and perceived loss of recognition, status, physical attractiveness, or control.

Table 13-2
Myths and Facts About Suicide

Myth: People who talk about suicide don't commit suicide.
Fact: This fallacy has been called the "grand old myth of suicide," one that excuses the failure to respond to another person's cry for help. Most people who attempt suicide communicate their intentions to others as hints, direct threats, or self-destructive actions or preparations for suicide. Unfortunately, these cries for help often go unheeded by friends, family members, co-workers, and health care personnel.

Myth: Improvement in a suicidal person means the risk of suicide has passed.
Fact: Improvement may be necessary before a severely depressed person can take the steps necessary to carry out the suicidal intention. Many suicides occur within three to six months following apparent improvement. Thus, an apparently positive change in mood can be a danger signal. Making the decision to carry out the suicidal act can be exhilarating and freeing; the person feels "Now that I've made the decision, I no longer have to agonize about what I'm going to do." This relief is subject to misinterpretation by others, who may believe the crisis has passed.

Myth: Once a suicide risk, always a suicide risk.
Fact: The peak of suicidal crisis is generally brief. The simultaneous conjunction of the thought of killing oneself, possession of the means to complete the act, and the lack of help or intervention is a more or less unusual set of circumstances. If intervention occurs, the suicidal person may well be able to put suicidal thoughts behind and lead a productive life.

Myth: Suicide is inherited.
Fact: Although this fallacy gives suicidal behavior an aura of biological fate, the fact is that suicide does not "run in families," in the sense of being a genetically inherited trait. However, dysfunctional family patterns with respect to problem solving or surviving the suicide of a loved one may create beliefs about suicide that influence a person's subsequent behavior. An individual's fear that he or she has a greater potential for suicide may create a self-fulfilling prophecy. Thus, the suicide of a family member may provide an excuse or make it easier to contemplate suicide as a means of escape from a difficult situation.

Myth: Suicide affects only a specific group or class of people.
Fact: Suicide is not the "curse of the poor" or a "disease of the rich." It occurs among all socioeconomic groups and affects individuals with widely divergent lifestyles. Social integration is a more important determinant of suicidal behavior than socioeconomic class.

Myth: Suicidal individuals are insane.
Fact: Although it is true that some suicidal individuals are mentally ill, the planning and carrying out of suicide usually requires careful reasoning and deliberate judgment. Many suicide notes reveal not only ambivalence but also considerable lucidity about the writer's intentions. Despite its devastating effect on the individual's physical being, suicide can be considered a defensive act or a problem-solving technique to preserve the integrity of the self.

Myth: Suicidal individuals are fully intent on dying.
Fact: Actually, most suicidal individuals are undecided about whether to continue to live or end their lives. In their ambivalence, they may gamble with death, leaving the possibility of rescue to fate. Although some attempters do ultimately commit suicide after previously uncompleted attempts, the majority do not. Thus, a suicide attempt may signal that a person's psychological or interpersonal needs are not being satisfactorily met and a change is wanted; it does not necessarily indicate that he or she wants to die.

Myth: The motive for a particular suicide is clearly evident.
Fact: People often try to establish a quick "cause" for suicide, attributing it to economic hardship, disappointment in love, or some other immediate condition. However, there usually is a lengthy sequence of overwhelming accumulated stresses and self-destructive behaviors leading up to the act of suicide. The apparent "cause" may be simply the final step of a complex pattern of self-destructive acts.

Myth: The reported suicide rate for adolescents is accurate.
Fact: The reported suicide rate for adolescents is an underestimate. Many "accidental" deaths among adolescents would be ruled suicides among adults.

Myth: Children's depression is rare and similar to adult depression.
Fact: Children get depressed frequently. Unlike adults, children often mask their depression with other behaviors.

Myth: Suicide happens without warning.
Fact: Of those who attempt suicide, 80% give some warning.

Myth: If you talk with a young person in crisis about suicide, you will put the thought in his or her head.
Fact: Talking honestly, straightforwardly, and empathically about suicide will not create a "suicidal person."

Source: Reprinted with changes in notation from pp. 520–521, from *The Last Dance: Encountering Death and Dying, Third Edition* by Lynne Ann DeSpelder and Albert Lee Strickland. Copyright © 1992 by Lynne Ann DeSpelder and Albert Lee Strickland. Reprinted by permission of Mayfield Publishing Company. The last four items in this table are from James and Wherry (1991), p. 25.

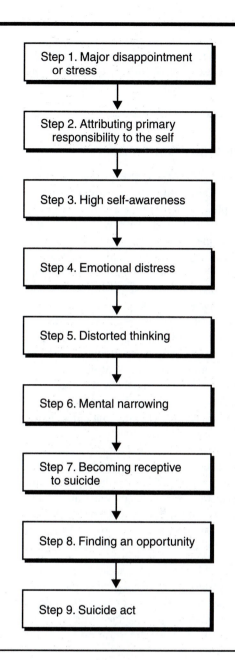

Figure 13-2. Modified escape theory.

Step 2. *Attributing primary responsibility to the self.* The disappointments are blamed on the self, instead of other people.

Step 3. *High self-awareness.* The person begins to think of herself or himself as "incompetent, unattractive, guilty, or inadequate in other ways" (Baumeister, 1993, p. 263).

Step 4. *Emotional distress.* Because of these unfavorable evaluations, "anxiety, depressed mood, anger, and other states of negative affect may arise" (Baumeister, 1993, p. 263). The person is critical of herself or himself, has a negative self-image, or feels that the problems are unbearable. Suicide may be considered in order to escape feelings of despair, depression, worthlessness, pain, or rejection; to escape embarrass-

ment, fear, humiliation, and degradation for poor school performance; to get away from feelings of loneliness and feelings that no one really cares about or understands her or him; to seek help; to gain attention and affection; or to make people understand how she or he is feeling.

Step 5. *Distorted thinking.* In some cases, a person contemplating suicide may have distorted thinking. For example, the person may want to commit suicide in order to manipulate her or his parents, especially if the parents are divorced, separated, or having severe marital conflict; to punish or frighten other people and make them sorry for the way she or he was treated; to get someone to change her or his mind; to find out whether someone really loves her or him; to achieve reunion with a loved one or make things easier for others; or to show how much she or he loved someone.

Step 6. *Mental narrowing.* The person narrows her or his awareness and thinking by focusing on the here and now (such as on movements and sensations and immediate tasks and goals) and by forsaking meaningful thoughts and experiences (Baumeister, 1993).

It can be regarded as a kind of mental and emotional numbness, and as such is preferable to painful distress. Unfortunately,…narrow mental states are generally unstable and hard to sustain…. For people who are unable to reconstruct self and world, however, the remaining choice is between trying to stay numb (which is often an empty, boring state) and acute emotional distress…. People struggle to remain rigidly in this narrow, empty state, which is itself mildly unpleasant but seems preferable to the acute emotional distress that accompanies a meaningful examination of recent events and their unflattering implications about the self. (pp. 263–264, 281)

Step 7. *Becoming receptive to suicide.* "The consequences of [mental narrowing] make the person receptive to suicide, for they include the suspension of normal inhibitions, the suspension of common sense and rational thought, and a reluctance to intervene actively to change life circumstances" (Baumeister, 1993, p. 281).

Step 8. *Finding an opportunity.* The person chooses an available method by which to commit suicide and a private place in which to attempt it.

Step 9. *Suicide act.* The person attempts to commit suicide and is or is not successful.

Risk factors.   Several risk factors associated with child-adolescent suicide, shown in Table 13-3, deserve careful study. The larger the number of risk factors present, the greater the risk for suicide. In addition, in children with a predisposition for suicide, fatigue, lack of sleep, or intoxication with drugs or alcohol may lower the threshold for committing suicide. Five of the most important risk factors are as follows:

1. *The child says he or she wants to die.*
2. *The child has made a prior attempt to kill himself or herself.*
3. *The child is depressed.*
4. *The child shows marked changes in his or her temperament and behavior.*
5. *The child has made final arrangements in preparation for dying.*

Table 13-3
Checklist for Risk Factors for Child-Adolescent Suicide

Historical-Situational Risk Factors

☐ 1. Chronic and debilitating illness
☐ 2. Chronic preoccupation with death and related themes
☐ 3. Fantasies about being immune to death
☐ 4. Romanticizing and glorifying death
☐ 5. Inadequate coping mechanisms
☐ 6. Repeated failures in school
☐ 7. Family pressures to achieve
☐ 8. Poor peer relations
☐ 9. Dysfunctional family (including severe marital discord) and parents with severe emotional distress (for example, psychosis, suicidality, chronic depression)
☐ 10. Severe life stressors (for example, death of a family member or friend, divorce, termination of a significant relationship, family economic hardship, suspension from school, being forced to leave home, failure to get into a college)
☐ 11. Physical, emotional, or sexual abuse or neglect
☐ 12. Family history of suicide
☐ 13. Engaging in deliberately dangerous behaviors
☐ 14. Previous suicide attempts
☐ 15. Peer suicides
☐ 16. Awareness of media attention given to suicide

Psychological Risk Factors

☐ 17. Depression (including flat affect, loss of interest in everyday activities, limited energy, feelings of sadness, worry, poor attention and concentration, difficulty sleeping, excessive feelings of guilt, excessive crying, changes in appetite or weight)
☐ 18. Feelings of hopelessness (for example, saying he or she wants to die)
☐ 19. Feelings of helplessness
☐ 20. Feelings of not being in control of his or her life
☐ 21. Severe anxiety, tension, or irritability
☐ 22. Low self-esteem and poor self-image
☐ 23. Psychosis (especially mood disorders)
☐ 24. Changes in temperament and behavior (for example, sudden displays of disruptive behavior and abrupt changes in school performance and attendance)
☐ 25. Eating disorders (for example, bulimia nervosa or anorexia nervosa)
☐ 26. Substance abuse (including alcohol and drug abuse)
☐ 27. Withdrawal from family and friends
☐ 28. Suicidal plan[a]
☐ 29. Final arrangements (for example, saying goodbye with finality, giving away favored possessions, putting affairs in order, appearing unusually calm and contented)

[a]A suicidal plan would consider means, availability, lethality, and intent. The most common means, in order of lethality from most to least, are gunshot, carbon monoxide, hanging, drowning, suffocation with plastic bag, impact associated with jumping from a high place, fire, poison, drugs, gas, and cutting wrists.
Source: Adapted from DeSpelder and Strickland (1992) and Fremouw et al. (1990).

There is but one truly serious philosophical problem, and that is suicide. Judging whether life is or is not worth living amounts to answering the fundamental question of philosophy.

—Albert Camus

Interviewing Issues

Interviewing a child who may be contemplating suicide. During the interview, remain calm, reassure the child, emphasize alternatives, and be prepared to act quickly to help the child. You don't want to act shocked, argue against suicide, minimize the problem, or leave the child alone. If you suspect that the child is at risk for suicide, discuss your concerns with the child. Children may respond to your questions, often in a surprisingly open and direct manner (Fremouw et al., 1990). However, some children may not volunteer information because of distrust, fear, shame, or confusion. And the information that does become available may be equivocal or contradictory. For example, adolescents may think about committing suicide at home when their father is maltreating them but not when they are at school. The semistructured interview in Table F-30 in Appendix F is useful for evaluating older children or adolescents who have suicidal preoccupations.

For younger children and for children with language difficulties, observe their play behavior for possible clues about suicide risk, particularly when the referral source expresses some concern about suicide. Play may provide the first warning signs of suicidal preoccupations in young children. Young children who are at risk for suicide may show some of the following play behaviors (Pfeffer, 1986):

1. Themes of loss and retrieval, jumping, throwing, and flying that suggest that death may be imminent
2. Engaging repetitively in dangerous and reckless behavior, such as jumping off objects unsafely, darting in and out of traffic on busy streets, or riding bicycles in dangerous areas
3. Repeatedly abusing or misusing playthings, such as aggressively breaking toys, throwing toys around, discarding or abandoning toys
4. Acting out omnipotent fantasies, such as fighting in a way that has the potential for hurting someone or enacting dangerous death-defying maneuvers

Also be alert to messages indicative of suicidal preoccupations in the child's poems, diaries, essays, journals, and artwork (Berman & Jobes, 1991). *Take all suicidal ideas, threats, and actions seriously. "There is no such thing as a meaningless threat or gesture"* (James & Wherry, 1991, p. 27, italics added). *Often, the suicide act may be impulsive, especially in children who feel that they have no other way out of an intolerable situation.* Children may attempt suicide when they no longer want to experience unbearable feelings or problems.

Be especially aware of such comments as the following (Hagerty, 1984, p. 216, with changes in notation).

- I wish I could sleep forever.
- Nothing matters anymore.
- They'll be sorry when I'm gone.
- I want to die.
- I'm afraid I'll drive the car off the road.
- Yes, my father is dead.... I need to be with him now.
- There has to be a better place than this world.
- Take all my clothes. I won't need them anymore.
- The seasons come and go…and so do I.
- I took some pills.
- Yes, I cut my wrists. My mother will feel bad now.
- The angels were calling me to be in heaven.
- Just let me die.

After you complete the interview with a child at risk for suicide or one who has attempted suicide, answer the questions in Table 13-4. Following is a summary of the key issues to consider in your evaluation (Berman & Jobes, 1992; Stelmachers, 1995):

1. *Verbal communication.* Is there an imminent risk of danger to the child (for example, the child says—or others close to the child report—that he or she wants to commit suicide)?

2. *Plan.* Does the child have a suicide plan, and is it concrete, specific, and detailed?

3. *Method.* Has the child selected a method, and is it available and lethal?

4. *Preparations.* Has the child made preparations for death, such as by writing about it?

5. *Stressors.* What are the predisposing conditions and precipitating events in the child's life, including any environmental stressors or critical events that might lead to suicide?

6. *Mental state.* What is the child's degree of depression and other forms of psychological difficulties, such as "despair, powerlessness, self-contempt, murderous rage, feeling alone, having death fantasies, lack of ambivalence, and inability to see alternatives to suicide" (Stelmachers, 1995, p. 374)?

7. *Interventions.* What interventions does the child need, how willing is the child to comply with any interventions, and what resources does the child have in his or her family or community to help with the needed interventions?

Many symptoms found in adolescents who attempt suicide are similar to those found in adolescents who are psychologically disturbed but who do not attempt suicide. *Suicide ideation is the one symptom that distinguishes the two groups* (Trautman, Rotheram-Borus, Dopkins, & Lewin, 1991).

If you decide there is a risk of imminent danger, notify the parents immediately, ask them to come to your office to get their child, and advise them to hospitalize their child. Follow your agency's policies on dealing with psychiatric emergencies. If the parents insist that their child remain at home, check state law regarding the responsibilities of human service providers in such situations. If there are no restraints against the parents' taking their child home, advise them to remove from the vicinity of the child any firearms, drugs, razors, scissors, ropes, and similar items that the child could use as aids to suicide. In addition, tell the parents not to leave the child alone. If you are working in a school or agency, also consider contacting a school administrator when you learn that a student is at risk for suicide.

If you decide that the risk is not imminent, consider what interventions are needed (such as outpatient treatment), give the child a hotline number to call in case you are not available, and make plans to see the child the next day (Peach & Reddick, 1991). Elicit from the child a promise in the form of a contract that he or she will not hurt himself or herself and that he or she will call you (or his or her therapist, if applicable) before doing anything to hurt himself or herself. However, contracts may be only minimally effective because the child may agree to sign a contract just to get away from you. Even if the risk is not imminent, consider asking the parents to come to your office to take their child home. *Recognize, however, that assessing suicide risk in children will not be easy* (Curran, 1987).

The following poem, written by a 17-year-old adolescent three days before her overdose attempt, expresses the depth of her despair (Berman & Jobes, 1991, p. 131):

A Plea

My world is a lonely world
A world devoid of love, laughter, and life
A world full of despair and darkness…
A world in need of a knife

My life is a lonely life
No more friends or happiness do I have
The only thing left in my life
is cold, dark loneliness and sadness

No need for worry
No need for despair
Don't worry for her life
For Cheryl is already dead inside
The job has been done by her knife.

—Anonymous

Exercise 13-2. Evaluating Potential Risk for Suicide

Answer the following questions for each of the two cases. Then compare your answers with those following the case. The material in this exercise was adapted from Motto (1991).

1. Does the adolescent have a low, moderate, or high risk of attempting suicide in the near future?
2. How depressed is the adolescent?
3. To what extent can the adolescent talk about her or his feelings?
4. Is the adolescent asking for help?
5. What supports does the adolescent have?

Table 13-4
Evaluating a Child at Risk for Suicide or a Child Who Has Attempted Suicide

Background
1. What are the child's age and sex?
2. What is the child's health status?
3. What is the child's family like?
4. What are the family's socioeconomic status and environmental circumstances?
5. What is the history of suicide in the family?
6. What is the history of child maltreatment in the family?
7. What is the child's history of accidents and other forms of possibly self-destructive behavior?
8. If there were prior suicide attempts, how serious were they?
9. Has the child ever been treated for mood disorders?
10. (If yes) Were treatment recommendations followed?
11. How did the child become suicidal?
12. How long has the child been preoccupied with suicide or death?
   (Continue the evaluation by going to the "At Risk for Suicide" section or the "Suicide Attempted" section, as appropriate.)

At Risk for Suicide
13. What risk factors are present for this child?
14. Is there a suicide plan?
   (If yes, go to question 15; if no, go to question 17.)
15. What are the specifics of the plan?
16. How lethal is the method?
17. Has the child talked about suicide to other people?
18. (If yes) What did the child say?
19. Does the child have a history of suicidal thoughts and attempts?
20. Has the child given away possessions?
21. How extensive is the child's preoccupation with death?
22. What does the child hope to gain from the suicide attempt?
23. What are the child's thoughts about how other people would react to his or her death?
24. Does the child understand the finality of death?
   (Go to item 42.)

Suicide Attempted
25. What were the precipitating events?
26. How did the child attempt to commit suicide (for example, gunshot, light overdose of nonprescription medicine, cutting wrist in presence of others)?
27. What happened to the child because of the attempted suicide?
28. How potentially lethal was the method?
29. What were the circumstances surrounding the suicide attempt (for example, took precautions against discovery, intervention, or rescue by others; made sure other family members were nearby)?
30. How impulsive was the act?
31. Was a suicide note left?

32. (If yes) What were its contents?
33. Was anyone told about the attempt before it happened?
34. (If yes) Who was told and what was said?
35. What are the child's feelings about the suicide attempt?
36. What did the child hope to gain from the suicide attempt?
37. What is the child's attitude toward death (for example, belief in a wonderful afterlife, reunion with deceased loved ones, relief from suffering)?
38. What is the child's attitude toward his or her suicidal thoughts (for example, accepting, rejecting, or ambivalent)?
39. What are the child's thoughts about how other people would react to his or her death?
40. What was the child's state of mind at the time of the suicide attempt?
41. What was the reaction of the parents and others to the suicide attempt?
   (Go to item 42.)

Affect and Thought
42. What is the child's affect (for example, level of depression; feelings of hopelessness and helplessness; feelings of panic, agitation, and disorganization)?
43. What is the level of the child's stress, including level of panic, disorganization, or agitation?
44. What form does the child's stress take?
45. What situations cause the stress?
46. What is the child's current state of mind?
47. What is the child's level of cognitive functioning?

Coping Mechanisms and Self-Control
48. How well does the child cope with stress?
49. How effective are the child's adaptive strategies (for example, the child's problem-solving strategies, ability to understand self, and ability to seek out other people for help)?
50. What does the child do when faced with difficult situations?
51. How does the child relax?
52. How does the child organize his or her day?
53. What is the child's level of self-control?
54. Does the child have a history of impulsive behavior?
55. (If yes) What is the child's history of impulsive behavior?

Problems
56. What are the type, magnitude, and persistence of the child's problems (including anxiety, loss of interest, diminished concentration, and sleep difficulty)?
57. Does the child have a psychological disorder?
58. (If yes) What is the disorder?
59. Does the child have physical health problems?
60. (If yes) What are the problems?
61. Does the child have a problem with alcohol or drugs or both?

(Continued)

Table 13-4 (*Continued*)

62. (If yes) What is the problem?
63. What losses has the child experienced (for example, loss of parent by death, divorce, separation, or abandonment)?
64. Does the child believe that his or her problems can't change?
65. Can the child wait for his or her problems to change?
66. Can the child formulate a way out of his or her problems?

Treatment and Intervention
67. What help does the child want?

68. Are there any areas of strength that can be used in a treatment program?
69. What help does the child need?
70. What can prevent the child from making other suicide attempts?
71. What support systems are available to the child (for example, family, extended family, school teachers and counselors, peers, clergy, and other adults)?
72. What is the adjustment level of the parents (for example, do they have marital problems, substance abuse problems, physical problems, or mental problems)?

Source: Adapted, in part, from Curran (1987) and Poland (1989).

Part 1. Heather

Heather is a 13-year-old schoolgirl who was referred by her mother after an attempted suicide. She is struggling with issues of low self-esteem, low self-confidence, unsatisfactory peer relations, loneliness, isolation, and emotional turmoil. She acts out many of her feelings in typically adolescent ways, criticizes herself severely, and sums up her dilemma as being "mentally crazy," belonging in a mental hospital, and needing to punish herself and to distance herself from her painful experience, even to the point of suicide. On the other hand, Heather appears to be intelligent, introspective, articulate, and communicative and to retain a sense of humor and whimsy. She explained that cutting her arm was not a suicide attempt, but a way of expressing her upset about a specific situation. Heather's mother is very concerned about her daughter. Although Heather's mother works, she is caring and supportive of her daughter. Heather's father died when she was 8 years old.

Suggested Answers

1. Heather appears to be at low to moderate risk for attempting suicide again soon.
2. She has mild to moderate depression, but no mood disorder.
3. She has good ability to talk about her feelings.
4. Heather is asking for help.
5. Her mother may be a caring adult and an important resource.

Part 2. Ralph

Ralph is a 16-year-old male who was referred by his parents because he has made plans to commit suicide. The case study revealed the following about Ralph: depression, alcohol abuse since age 12, suicidal behavior, instability, delinquency, chronic physical illness, feelings of helplessness, existential despair, and obsession with suicidal ideas, including having a specific plan. In addition, there was a recent suicide in his family and there is a family history of alcoholism. However, these factors have not interfered with his schoolwork to a significant extent, as he has maintained a "B" average. He also has friends that he keeps in contact with. He attributed his suicidal thoughts to an effort to handle anger toward his grandfather, who also lives at Ralph's home. His parents are not at home as often as he would like and he feels estranged from them.

Suggested Answers

1. Ralph is at high risk for attempted suicide in the near future.
2. He has moderate to high depression, but no mood disorder.
3. He has adequate ability to talk about his feelings.
4. Ralph has not asked for help.
5. Ralph's friends may be his primary support network. His parents are concerned about him, but do not appear to offer him the advice and support he needs.

Example of an interview with a child contemplating suicide. The following segment is from an interview with a 7-year-old boy who had been telling his mother that he wished he were dead. His physician had recently informed him that he had a growth hormone deficiency (Fremouw et al., 1990, pp. 76–77).

IR: Mark, have you ever felt very, very sad?
IE: Well, yeah, I feel pretty sad right now.
IR: Have you ever felt so sad that you thought you might hurt yourself?
IE: What do you mean?
IR: Well, sometimes people feel really very sad and they think about doing things to hurt themselves. Have you ever thought about hurting yourself?
IE: Yeah.
IR: When was the last time you thought about hurting yourself?
IE: Last night.
IR: What were you doing when you thought about hurting yourself?
IE: I was in my room.
IR: Where was your mother?
IE: In the kitchen. It was after I finished my homework.
IR: How did you think of hurting yourself?
IE: I wished I was dead.

IR: Did you think of killing yourself?

IE: Yeah.

IR: Did you think about how you would kill yourself?

IE: Yeah, I was going to get a knife from the kitchen drawer and cut my throat.

IR: Did you go to the kitchen to get the knife?

IE: No.

IR: Did something stop you from doing that?

IE: Yeah, my mom was in there and she won't let me get knives out of the drawer.

IR: Did you think of any other ways you might kill yourself?

IE: Yeah, I thought about climbing in the tree just outside my house. It's real high and I thought I could just jump from the very top.

IR: Have you ever climbed to the top of that tree?

IE: No, the lowest branch is way, way high above my head.

IR: Did you think of any other way you might hurt yourself?

IE: Well, yeah, sometimes I go out to the road in front of my house and lay down in the street and wait for cars to come by.

IR: Have you ever done that before?

IE: Yeah, I've done it lots of times. One time I even did it right when it was getting dark and people couldn't really see me.

IR: Have you ever done it when your mother wasn't home?

IE: No.

IR: Mark, have you thought about what would happen if you died?

IE: Yeah, I wouldn't have to worry about going to the hospital or about paying for the hospital bills.

IR: What do you think would happen to your mom?

IE: I don't know.

IR: Do you think she'd miss you?

IE: I don't know. Maybe.

IR: What do you think it's like when people die?

IE: They go to heaven if they've been pretty good.

IR: What's it like in heaven?

IE: I don't know.

IR: Do you think you'd be able to see your mom?

IE: I don't know. (At this point, Mark began to cry.)

IR: Mark, you look like you're thinking about something that upset you. Tell me about what you were thinking just now.

IE: My mom. I'd really miss my mom.

IR: I know your mom would miss you a whole lot.

IE: I know.

IR: Mark, have you had any ideas about hurting yourself today?

IE: No, I really haven't felt like that today.

Interviewing the parents of a child who may be contemplating suicide. You will want to interview the parents of children who have attempted suicide or who are contemplating suicide. Ask the parents and other family members, as needed, about the child's recent behavior, the family's psychiatric history and history of suicides, and how the family is getting along. If you determine that siblings also are severely distressed, consider recommending them for evaluation. You will need to evaluate whether the family can protect, support, and help the suicidal child and

whether family interventions are needed. You don't want to send the child back to a family that is hostile toward her or him, rejects her or him, or shows little concern for her or his welfare.

After you interview the parents, you can probably answer such questions as the following (Barrett, 1985):

1. Do the parents recognize the seriousness of the situation?

2. Do the parents recognize that their child is considering taking her or his life?

3. How do the parents get along with the child?

4. What family dynamics might be contributing to the child's thoughts of suicide? (For example, have there been any unusual changes within the family in the past few months, such as job changes, a death, a move, or a divorce? Have the parents devoted less time to the child because of their own problems? Are there any indications of maltreatment?)

5. How do the parents view their child? (For example, have the parents been disappointed in the child's performance, been critical of the child, or used harsh disciplinary procedures?)

6. How willing are the parents to help their child?

7. What would the parents like to do about their child's attempt at suicide or thoughts of committing suicide?

8. What, if any, psychiatric problems are present in the family members?

9. Is any member of the family suicidal, besides the referred child?

10. If there are siblings, how are they functioning?

11. If there are siblings, how do the siblings get along with the referred child?

12. If there are siblings, how do the siblings get along with the parents?

Suicide can be "infectious." There may be someone else in the family or in the vicinity who harbours such thoughts, where the suicide of one person can trigger suicide in another.

—Nils Retterstøl

Interventions

In working with adolescents who may be suicidal, be patient, listen carefully, avoid a judgmental attitude, talk calmly, explore their problems without belittling them, and show empathy and understanding (James & Wherry, 1991). Help suicidal adolescents see alternatives that can provide hope for their future. Your goal should be to broaden suicidal adolescents' constricted thinking and make options other than suicide appealing. Other interventions include "self-esteem building, dealing with negative thoughts, cognitive restructuring, self-monitoring, confidence training, relaxation training, contracting, and increasing activity levels. Finally, involving the family can be a great asset" (James & Wherry, 1991, p. 31). If the family cannot provide support, which may happen if the parents are themselves depressed or are having other adjustment problems, obtain other support services for the suicidal adolescent. The increased prevalence of psychological symptoms and disorders in families of adolescents who attempt suicide suggests that it may be difficult for some parents in these families to provide support for their suicidal child (King, Segal, Naylor, & Evans, 1993).

The key to intervention is altering the circumstances that preceded the suicide attempt to prevent a repetition of the suicide attempt. You also want to restrict or prevent, if possible, access to available means of self-harm for adolescents who are suicidal. To do this, you may have to consider recommending hospitalization. Hospitalization should be considered when the youth presents a clear and present danger to himself or herself if he or she is not hospitalized, the caregivers are not able to provide sufficient safeguards to prevent an attempt at suicide, or there are no therapeutic interventions or alternative programs that can meet the child's (and family's) needs (Holinger, Offer, Barter, & Bell, 1994). For highly suicidal children, "make frequent risk assessments, realizing that risk fluctuates considerably and unpredictably over time" (Stelmachers, 1995, p. 378).

Other methods of intervention include teaching children in schools about suicide and about death, having response-ready crisis teams available in schools to deal with suicide crises (see Exhibit 13-1), and detecting and treating children who are depressed, anxious, lonely, under stress, experiencing family problems, or having substance abuse problems or affective disorders (McWhirter et al., 1993).

Remove opportunities to commit suicide, especially lethal ones, such as guns. Without an opportunity even an imminently suicidal person cannot commit suicide. This is one of the simplest and most effective methods of suicide prevention.

—Zigfrids T. Stelmachers

Case Illustrations

This section presents three cases. The first case consists of chart notes made by a mental health professional working in a hospital who was asked to consult on a case of attempted suicide (Huszti & Walker, 1991).

CASE 13-4. SUSAN BROWN

Susan Brown, a 16-year-old White female, was referred by Dr. Smith for an assessment of her depression and her risk for suicide. Susan was admitted to the hospital for ingestion of 30 Tylenol tablets. She was interviewed alone for 30 min-utes, and together with Mrs. Brown, her mother, for 15 min-

---

Exhibit 13-1
A School Copes with the Suicide of Two Teenage Girls

Two 14-year-old girls, each carrying a handgun, walked into the desert behind a housing tract in Victorville, California and executed a double-suicide pact that stunned their parents and friends. One victim gave a classmate a suicide note during school the day of the suicide with the admonition that it not be opened until the end of classes. By the time the girl read the note and became frantic, the teenagers were dead. The girls' bodies, dressed in jeans and T-shirts and almost touching each other, were found by children walking through the area. Each was shot in the head, and the weapons were at their sides. The handguns had been taken from the home of one of the girls. Another suicide note was later found at the home of one of the victims. Both notes were signed by both girls and indicated that they "were tired of life," but there was no further elaboration.

The girls had met two years ago in junior high school and were on the honor roll at their high school. One girl was a straight-A student in eighth grade, participated in the junior high student leadership team, and played basketball. The other girl was involved in the school's ROTC program and would have turned 15 three days after the suicide. The assistant superintendent said the girls "had talked with a close cadre of friends about the possibility of suicide, but they weren't taken seriously." He also said that the girl who was a straight-A student "was having difficulties generally in her life, both at school and at home—relationship issues," and that a book found in the girl's locker was marked at a "particularly dark passage that had to do with death."

Counselors spent much of the day after the suicide attempting to assuage the guilt of classmates who believed they should have intervened and could have prevented the tragedy. "We are very concerned about the possibility of copycat suicides," the assistant superintendent said. "Statistics indicate we're more at risk of additional suicides when there are multiple suicides." The father and uncle of one victim met with about 25 of the girls' closest friends at school to address that concern directly. "The father issued a plea to them not to let his daughter's death be in vain, and please, that no one repeat this," the assistant superintendent said. "He said, essentially, 'Let's not have any more tragedy emanate from the loss of my daughter.'" The girl's father told students that she had enjoyed a normal weekend with the family, including a shopping outing with her mother, and that "things were fine" at home. The classmates entered the group counseling session "very depressed, a pall cast about them," the assistant superintendent said. "But as a result of the dad being very upfront with them, very revealing and talking so forthrightly, they left feeling much better about the situation and dealing with their own feelings of ambivalence and guilt."

Source: Adapted from Gorman (1995).

---

utes. Susan was initially reluctant to talk and was fearful. However, by the end of the interview, Susan was more open to discussing her feelings and agreed to meet with the interviewer again to continue the discussion. Mrs. Brown was cooperative and appeared to be worried about her daughter's depression.

Susan is the oldest of four children in the family. Her parents are divorced, and she has not seen her biological father in 10 years or her stepfather in the past 6 months. She reports that she has made one previous suicide gesture when she took 10 aspirins after a fight with her boyfriend. This happened about 9 months ago. After taking the pills, she called her boyfriend; however, she was not hospitalized after this attempt.

Susan reports that she has had several arguments with her mother about her boyfriend, her staying out late, and her poor grades. She is now a sophomore at Central High School. Her grades have dropped from a "B" to a "D" average in the past 9 weeks. She broke up with her boyfriend approximately 1 week ago. Susan has lost 5 pounds and reports problems falling asleep at night in the past few weeks.

Susan reports taking the 30 Tylenol tablets after seeing her boyfriend at a movie with his new girlfriend. She was sad and angry with her boyfriend and thought that she would not "ever have anyone as awesome as he is." Susan returned home and argued with Mrs. Brown about not doing household chores. Susan then went to the bathroom, took the pills, and told her mother. Her mother brought her to Children's Hospital. Susan said that she was upset but did not want to die; she took the pills because she was angry but did not think that taking pills would kill her. Susan was tearful and expressed feelings of helplessness and hopelessness about her relationships with people. She often blames others—such as her mother, her stepfather, her peers, or her teachers—for her problems. Susan does have, however, several close girlfriends and is planning to start a part-time job in 1 week.

The following suggests that Susan has moderate depression: (1) weight loss, (2) sleep disturbance, and (3) feeling hopeless and helpless in relationships. And the following suggests that Susan is a low risk for suicide: (1) She did not view 30 Tylenol as a lethal dose. (2) She denies wanting to die. (3) She was in a situation in which detection was almost certain. (4) She immediately informed Mrs. Brown that she had taken the pills. I do not believe that Susan is a high risk for suicide in the hospital; therefore, she does not require suicidal precautions on the ward.

Susan said that she would not try to kill herself again and was anxious to be discharged from the hospital. She has agreed to a no-suicide contract and to talk with friends or her mother if she feels sad again.

Susan will be referred to the guidance center. Mrs. Brown also has agreed to counseling.

The second case illustrates the role alcohol and drugs may have played in the suicide of an adolescent (Rich et al., 1990).

CASE 13-5. B

B was a tall, good-looking White 17-year-old male student who came to the attention of the school psychologist at age 7 because of his apparent isolation from peers and learning problems. He had mechanical ability, however, and was skillful at building engines and bombs. At age 8, he set the side of his house on fire with a homemade bomb. B attended special education classes where he was labeled "learning disabled," and never learned to read. There was a history of heavy alcohol consumption since age 12 or 13 and a past episode of car theft. He was described by his mother as always having been "nervous and uptight." In the six months prior to his suicide, he had become heavily involved with drug consumption (including cocaine, marijuana, and amphetamines), had stopped attending school, and tended to spend more and more time at home. He lived with his parents and three siblings. B confided to a friend that he always believed that he was a burden to his father. For most of his teen years he was social, had many male and female friends, and for the past few months had a special girlfriend. Four days prior to his death, he saw a suicide depicted on TV. A male friend reported that he appeared excited by it and had commented that he viewed the suicide as a "courageous thing to do." He also spoke of suicide to other friends and family members several days prior to his death.

The day of his death he asked his mother for money, but she refused. He told her that "after tonight I won't need anything." That day he told several family members and his girlfriend that he planned to kill himself. None of them believed him and no one took any action. He drank heavily with friends that night, prior to shooting himself in the head with a rifle. (pp. 859–860, with changes in notation)

In the third case, the child's suicide attempt may have reflected accumulated stress that finally overwhelmed his endurance (Stillion, McDowell, & May, 1989).

CASE 13-6. JOHN

John was an 11-year-old child whose family had a long history of turbulence. There had been frequent threats of separation and many separations throughout the marriage. John's younger brother had been born during one of the many reunions.

Most of the arguments centered on money. John's father's income, as a sporadically employed day laborer, was never enough to support a family of four. John's mother had worked in a department store before marriage but was now forbidden to do so by her husband, who said repeatedly, "A wife's place is in the home with the children."

Although there was only occasional physical violence between the parents, shouting matches occurred weekly. During these emotional arguments—usually witnessed by John—John's parents said terrible things to and about each other. After the arguments, John's mother often tried to persuade him to take her side against his father, to be her protector, and to be her "little man."

As the stress increased in the home, John's mother spent more and more time in bed, abdicating her role as wife and mother. John became more a parent than a sibling to his younger brother. John had to be sure that his younger brother had something to eat for dinner, had a bath, had his lunch packed, and had dressed appropriately for school.

When he was much younger, John had tearfully told a friend that when his parents argued, it "hurt his stomach and made him feel scared." He described running from the house when his parents fought—or hiding in his bedroom and using his pillow to muffle the sound of their shouting. As his parents' fighting accelerated, John spent more and more time away from home, often staying away all night. This resulted in his skipping school to rest during the day. When his teacher questioned him about his absences, her questions were met with stony silence. When she threatened to call his parents, John screamed, "Do it," and ran from the classroom. The teacher's call to the parents provoked a major fight, during which John's father packed his clothes and left the house. Before school the next day, on the school grounds, John set his clothes on fire but he did not die. (pp. 71–72, with changes in notation)

We grow up hating ourselves like society teaches us to. If someone had been "out" about their sexuality. If the teachers hadn't been afraid to stop the "fag" and "dyke" jokes. If my human sexuality class had even mentioned homosexuality. If the school counselors would have been open to a discussion of gay and lesbian issues. If any of those possibilities had existed, perhaps I would not have grown up hating what I was. And, just perhaps, I wouldn't have attempted suicide.

—19-year-old male

Exercise 13-3. Responding to the Statements of a Suicidal Child or the Child's Parents

This exercise contains statements made by suicidal children and their parents. Each statement is accompanied by two possible interviewer responses. Select the interviewer response that you think is preferable, and give a justification for your selection. Then check your choices with the suggested answers that follow the statements. The material in this exercise was adapted from Scully (1990).

1. IE: Sometimes I think I'd be better off dead.
   IR-1: You sound as if you feel pretty desperate. Let's talk about what's bothering you.
   IR-2: When have you felt that way before?

2. IE: I think about death a lot.
   IR-1: Sometimes teenagers think about death as a solution to their problems. What are you thinking about?
   IR-2: What else do you think a lot about?

3. IE: I did it because my parents don't care about me.
   IR-1: When did you start feeling that your parents didn't care for you?
   IR-2: What makes you feel that way?

4. IE: I feel so embarrassed. Everyone will watch to see if I'll try again.
   IR-1: Facing embarrassing situations is difficult, but we're here to help. Let's talk about it.
   IR-2: Well, sometimes embarrassment could be good. How has embarrassment changed your thinking about suicide?

5. IE: When my girlfriend left me, I knew I couldn't go it alone.
   IR-1: No wonder you're so unhappy.
   IR-2: What changed for you when your girlfriend left?

6. IE: How could he disgrace us like this?
   IR-1: You seem to feel disgraced, is that right?
   IR-2: This is a painful situation for both you and your child.

7. IE: This wouldn't have happened if it weren't for those no-good friends of his.
   IR-1: You may be correct, and we probably should consider that matter, but for now let's focus on how to help your child through this crisis.
   IR-2: What can you do about his friends?

8. IE: I'm useless.
   IR-1: Everybody feels that way at times.
   IR-2: Everyone has something he or she can do well. What are some things you enjoy doing?

Suggested Answers

1. IR-1's response is preferable. It shows the interviewee that the interviewer takes the suicide threat seriously. IR-2's response avoids the affective tone of the communication.
2. IR-1's response is preferable. It informs the interviewee that it is permissible to talk about suicide openly. IR-2's response directs the inquiry away from the topic of death and is a premature response.
3. IR-2's response is preferable as the initial response. It is a good probing question. IR-1's response is acceptable, but it should come after the topic is explored.
4. IR-1's response is preferable. It shows that the interviewer respects the child's feelings. IR-2's response goes into a tangential area.
5. IR-2's response is preferable. It is a probing response that may facilitate communication. IR-1's response acknowledges the interviewee's possible feelings, but it may be less appropriate for facilitating communication.
6. IR-2's response is preferable. It acknowledges the interviewee's anger and shame. IR-1's response paraphrases the interviewee's statement in a rather superficial way.
7. IR-1's response is preferable. It directs the interviewee to explore ways of solving the child's problems. IR-2's response is about an issue that little can be done about at the time of a suicidal gesture.
8. IR-2's response is preferable. It is supportive and may help the interviewee identify his or her strengths. IR-1's response may be satisfactory, but IR-2's response focuses on the positive and may better help the interviewee.

The assessment of the adolescent at risk for suicidal behavior has been likened to finding a needle in a haystack. By being alert as to what to observe and by observing alertly, the size and brilliance of that needle increase, thereby correspondingly increasing the likelihood of its discovery.

—Alan L. Berman and David A. Jobes

THINKING THROUGH THE ISSUES

Why do you think people have difficulty talking about death?

When do you think a child's bereavement reaction should come to the attention of mental health professionals?

Do you personally know of anyone who has attempted or committed suicide? If so, what were your reactions to the suicide attempt?

Why do you think suicide has so many negative connotations?

Should people have the right to commit suicide? What is the basis for your answer?

SUMMARY

Bereavement

1. Factors that affect how individuals react to death include their personal characteristics, their family and social supports, their past relationship with the deceased, the circumstances of the death, and other stresses that they are experiencing.

2. Bereavement refers to the psychological, physiological, or behavioral responses associated with the loss of a loved one through death.

3. Grief refers to the feeling of sorrow or anguish resulting from the loss of a loved one through death, often accompanied by crying.

4. Mourning refers to the actions or social expressions of deprivation associated with the loss of a loved one through death.

5. Mourning includes rituals and behaviors specific to an individual's culture and religion.

6. Each survivor will experience the loss in his or her unique way. Some survivors experience little grief; others, moderate grief; and still others, overwhelming grief.

7. School-aged children and adults may react to the death of a loved one by attempting to deny the death; by questioning why the death happened; with bodily distress; with hostile reactions toward the deceased and/or toward others; by trying to win the affection of others; by assuming the mannerisms or symptoms of the deceased; by idealizing the deceased; with anxiety, fear, or guilt; with concern that they will be stigmatized or rejected by others; by wishing the deceased will return to life; and by consuming drugs and alcohol.

8. Behavior that might be considered bizarre or pathological under other circumstances often is considered a normal expression of bereavement.

9. Pathological grieving may be present when children or adults have prolonged sadness and grief reactions; cannot speak about the deceased without intense sadness and grief; respond to minor events with intense grief reactions; acquire physical symptoms that mimic those of the deceased; assume some personality and temperament characteristics of the deceased; make drastic changes in their life style after the loss; describe self-destructive tendencies; have prolonged, unaccountable periods of sadness, particularly during activities associated with the deceased; or have phobias related to symptoms of illness or circumstances related to the death.

10. The bereavement process will be more difficult when the death is sudden or unexpected; when the death is violent or traumatic, especially in cases of suicide; when the survivors feel responsible for the death; when the survivors have a developmental disability; when the deceased was a young person; when other stresses are present in the survivors' lives and families; when the survivors avoid funeral rites; when the survivors need to make many arrangements; when the survivors have distorted or inhibited their communications; when the survivors' support networks fail to provide support; and when the surviving child is not told about the reason for the death, particularly in cases of suicide.

11. In anticipatory grief, individuals, aware of the impending loss, attempt to relinquish their attachment to the dying person.

12. Disenfranchised grief occurs when children and adults incur a loss but do not have a socially recognized right, role, or capacity to grieve.

13. The grief process may involve several phases—particularly for adolescents and adults—including shock and numbness, yearning and searching, disorganization and despair, and reorganization.

14. Children's understanding of death will influence the way they react to the deaths of others, as well as their own forthcoming death.

15. Children's reactions to death also will be influenced by how others in their environment react to the death.

16. Usually, children's reactions to death will be typical of those associated with other traumas.

17. During the first two years of development, children have little understanding of death, but they do react to the loss of a caregiver.

18. During preschool years, children are likely to think magically about death. They may view death as reversible—when you die, the doctor (or someone) makes you well again—or they may view the deceased as sleeping.

19. During the early school years, children think more logically about death, particularly focusing on the physical means by which death occurs. Although they begin to understand various dimensions of the concept of death, the concept of death is incomplete and concrete.

20. During adolescence, children recognize the implications of death for themselves and for others and gain a perspective toward death similar to that of adults.

21. In cases of suicide, survivors may be emotionally overwhelmed and feel helplessness, shame, and social stigma.

22. When a child commits suicide, the parents may feel especially guilty.

23. When a parent commits suicide, children may see themselves as highly vulnerable and unprotected. They may experience guilt because they believe that they caused the death by upsetting the parent, by not being better sons or daughters, by increasing marital tensions, and by not having done something to save the parent.

24. When a spouse commits suicide in a family in which there are children, the surviving parent may have trouble dealing with the grief process and with the role changes needed to keep the family functioning.

25. Children who lose a close friend through suicide may feel a threat to their self-esteem.

26. When you interview a child who may be having a severe bereavement reaction, you will want to obtain information about the child's age, developmental stage, cognitive level, temperament, coping skills, and relationship to the deceased; present reactions to the death, meaning of the loss, grief reac-

tions, and past reactions to death; and the family's response to death, support received from others, and religious and cultural traditions.

27. You will have difficulty obtaining information about the interviewee's perception of the death and her or his worries and concerns when the interviewee is emotionally distraught or fails to discuss the extent of her or his grief reaction or when you fail to probe because you believe the interviewee is too distraught.

28. If the interviewee is extremely upset, you may have to help her or him overcome shock and grief and forgo the assessment functions of the interview.

29. Part of your task in the initial interview is to distinguish normal grief from clinical depression. This is particularly difficult to assess during the first few weeks following a death because symptoms of grief resemble those of clinical depression.

30. When a child is dying, encourage the family to keep in contact with the child, to be with the child, to talk to the child, to develop memories of the child that they can hold after the child's death, to take pictures of the child if they want to, to communicate with the medical staff, to obtain respite care, and to allow the child some say in how his or her remaining days will be spent.

31. Also help the survivors after the death of a loved one.

32. Children will need professional help when they show extreme guilt, panic, or despair; extremely negative view of self; excessive daydreaming; marked changes in personality; serious trouble sleeping; excessive sleep; marked eating changes, such as loss of appetite or increased overeating; fear of going to school; decrement in school performance; withdrawal and isolation from others; or excessive acting-out behavior.

Suicide

33. From 1970 to 1990, the suicide rates increased 2½ times for 10- to 14-year-olds and almost doubled for 15- to 19-year-olds.

34. The general increase in adolescent suicide since 1970 may be attributed to several factors, including reduced family influence, economic and peer pressures, alcohol use and abuse, sexual pressures, fear of AIDS, media influences, and gang influences.

35. The method of choice for adolescent suicide in 1990 was use of firearms, followed by strangulation by hanging and poisoning.

36. The suicide rate is much higher for adolescent males than for adolescent females.

37. Female adolescents are more likely than male adolescents to make suicide attempts.

38. When a child commits suicide, the effects on his or her family and friends can be devastating.

39. Children who are suicidal often regard death as a temporary and pleasant state that alleviates stress; consequently, there is a need to evaluate their beliefs about death.

40. Studies of adolescents who commit suicide (known as psychological autopsies) indicate that 90 to 98% of the victims had a psychological disorder. The disorders, from most to least frequent, are affective disorder, substance abuse problem, conduct disorder or antisocial personality, major depression, personality disorder, adjustment disorder, and schizophrenic disorder.

41. The most lethal combination of psychological disorders might be the coexistence of affective disorder with antisocial behavior, conduct disorder, or alcohol abuse.

42. The three most prevalent behavioral difficulties found in studies of children who have committed suicide are depressive symptoms, behavioral problems, and substance abuse.

43. The families of adolescent suicide victims are more likely than other families to have intrafamilial turmoil and parental psychological disorders.

44. Escape theory is useful in understanding how a person becomes receptive to suicide. The theory has nine steps: (1) the person experiences a major disappointment or stress, (2) the person attributes primary responsibility for the disappointments to the self, (3) the person has high self-awareness, (4) the person experiences emotional distress, (5) the person shows distorted thinking, (6) the person narrows his or her mental processes, (7) the person becomes receptive to suicide, (8) the person finds an opportunity to commit suicide, and (9) the person attempts suicide.

45. Five of the most important risk factors for suicide are as follows: (a) the child says he or she wants to die, (b) the child has made a prior attempt to kill himself or herself, (c) the child is depressed, (d) the child shows marked changes in his or her temperament and behavior, and (e) the child has made final arrangements in preparation for dying.

46. During the interview with a child who may be contemplating suicide, remain calm, reassure the child, emphasize alternatives, and be prepared to act quickly to help the child.

47. For younger children and for children with language difficulties, observe their play behavior for possible clues about suicide risk, particularly when the referral source expresses some concern about suicide.

48. In children who may be contemplating suicide, be alert to messages indicative of suicidal preoccupations in the child's poems, diaries, essays, journals, and artwork.

49. Take all suicidal ideas, threats, and actions seriously, as there is no such thing as a meaningless suicidal threat or gesture.

50. Often, the suicide act may be impulsive, especially in children who feel that they have no other way out of an intolerable situation.

51. In evaluating the interview with a child who may be contemplating suicide, look at the child's verbal communications, whether the child has a plan and a method, whether the child has made preparations, what stressors are present in the child's life, the child's mental state, and what interventions are needed.

52. Many symptoms found in adolescents who attempt suicide are similar to those found in adolescents who are psychologically disturbed but who do not attempt suicide. Suicide ideation is the one symptom that distinguishes the two groups.

53. If you decide there is a risk of imminent danger, notify the parents immediately, ask them to come to your office to get their child, and advise them to hospitalize their child.

54. If you decide that the risk of suicide is not imminent, consider what interventions are needed, give the child a hotline number to call in case you are not available, and make plans to see the child the next day.

55. You will want to interview the parents of children who have attempted suicide or who are contemplating suicide.

56. Ask the parents and other family members, as needed, about the child's recent behavior, the family's psychiatric history and history of suicides, and how the family is getting along.

57. If you determine that siblings also are severely distressed, consider recommending them for evaluation.

58. You will need to evaluate whether the family can protect, support, and help the suicidal child and whether family interventions are needed.

59. In working with adolescents who may be suicidal, be patient, listen carefully, avoid a judgmental attitude, talk calmly, explore their problems without belittling them, and show empathy and understanding.

60. Help suicidal adolescents see alternatives that can provide hope for their future.

61. Your goal should be to broaden suicidal adolescents' constricted thinking and make options other than suicide appealing.

62. The key to intervention is altering the circumstances that preceded the suicide attempt to prevent a repetition of the suicide attempt.

63. Hospitalization should be considered when the youth presents a clear and present danger to himself or herself if he or she is not hospitalized, the caregivers are not able to provide sufficient safeguards to prevent an attempt at suicide, or there are no therapeutic interventions or alternative programs that can meet the child's (and family's) needs.

KEY TERMS, CONCEPTS, AND NAMES

Bereavement (p. 424)
Grief (p. 424)
Mourning (p. 424)
Adaptive reactions to death (p. 425)
Less adaptive reactions to death (p. 425)
Hindrances to the bereavement process (p. 428)
Anticipatory grief (p. 428)
Disenfranchised grief (p. 429)
Phases of grief (p. 429)
Separation distress (p. 429)
Children's concept of death (p. 429)
Suicide (p. 435)
Psychological autopsies (p. 437)
Escape theory (p. 437)
Risk factors for suicide (p. 439)

STUDY QUESTIONS

1. Discuss bereavement. In your discussion, include such issues as factors influencing grief reactions, phases of grief, anticipatory grief, disenfranchised grief, impediments to the bereavement process, functional and dysfunctional coping strategies, interviewing strategies, and interventions. Also include, where possible, developmental considerations in children's bereavement reactions.

2. Discuss children's concepts of death.

3. Discuss suicide in children. Include in your discussion statistics related to suicide, myths about suicide, risk factors, and escape theory.

4. Discuss how you should interview a child who may have tendencies toward suicide.

14

CHILDREN AND FAMILIES FACING ADOPTION, DIVORCE, OR HOMELESSNESS

A society in which more and more people become less and less involved in nurturing their own children will inevitably be less human, less understanding, and less compassionate.
—Alfred Kadushin

Goals and Objectives

This chapter is designed to enable you to:

- Understand the experiences of children and families facing adoption, divorce, or homelessness
- Develop skills in interviewing children and families experiencing adoption, divorce, or homelessness

This chapter describes several life conditions that represent potential stressors for a child: adoption, parental divorce or custody disputes, and homelessness. Like bereavement and suicide in Chapter 13, these conditions do not constitute clinically defined behavioral, social, or emotional disorders of childhood. Like Chapters 11, 12, and 13, this chapter gives you guidelines for interviewing children and their families; it does not provide an in-depth review of research or theory. You are encouraged to read other texts that cover the conditions discussed in this chapter in more detail.

ADOPTION

Description

There is no one profile of who is likely to adopt a child. As Anderson, Piantanida, and Anderson (1993) point out,

adopters may already have one or more biological children, be past their child-bearing years, or may simply have elected to add to their family by adoption for a variety of personal or humanitarian reasons. Some adopt out of a deep sense of caring and moral or religious duty. Others may be members of a helping profession who believe their clinical expertise will facilitate the task of parenting a child with a physical, cognitive, or emotional disability. Many other…adopters are couples in their 30s or 40s who have married late and/or delayed child bearing.… [Infertility is a primary reason why a couple might want to adopt a child. Even parents with a biological child can experience subsequent infertility.]

Since the 1970s, when many social and legal barriers to single-parent adoption began to disintegrate, a growing number of unmarried women and men have joined the ranks of…adopters.… For these individuals, being single is not a transitional life stage, but rather a life style, within which the desire to parent becomes an important goal. (pp. 256–257)

The following case offers a composite portrait of a family that, because of infertility, may want to adopt a child (Glidden, 1994).

CASE 14-1. THE GREERS

The Greers are both 36 years old. They met in college, stimulated into a conversation one day in a sociology course on families and sex roles. They were juniors then, and began to date steadily soon thereafter. They married 3 years after college commencement, when Stephanie had completed a master's degree in personnel administration and Matt had finished law school. The next 4 years were a relatively happy

mix of establishing their careers, settling into their first home, and traveling in Europe and South America. They took their first ski lessons together, quickly became devotees of cross-country treks, and discovered that they enjoyed a similar balance of adventure and relaxation in their leisure activities. They were certainly having fun, just the two of them, but as the Greers approached their 30th birthdays, they began to discuss having a family. They both wanted at least one, and probably two, children, and even though they were mindful of the lifestyle change that would result, they made the decision to start a family and abandoned what had become their normal contraceptive routine.

A year later, with no pregnancy, the Greers began a search for fertility that was to last for the next 4 years. They progressed from sperm count and motility tests to endometrial biopsies, laparoscopy, hormonal analyses, and other sometimes painful, and always psychologically disruptive, procedures. After two in vitro fertilization attempts failed to produce a sustained pregnancy, they started to consider adoption.

It took only a few telephone calls to local adoption agencies and a conversation with one of their friends, an attorney who had handled some adoption cases, to discover that the healthy infant that they had been thinking about in their adoption discussions was in short supply. If they were willing to consider an older child with disabilities or emotional or behavioral problems, or one who was still in foster care status, their local department of social services would work with them. Otherwise, there were two realistic options: adopt internationally or arrange a private or independent adoption. [*Note.* Through newspaper advertisements the Greers found a young woman who, after negotiation, gave up her baby to them for adoption.] (pp. 184–185)

Here is a composite portrait of a couple who already had birth children but still wanted to adopt to increase the size of the family (Glidden, 1994).

CASE 14-2. THE WILSONS

The Wilsons had been married for 13 years and had three birth sons, 5, 7, and 10 years old. They wanted a larger family, and especially at least one daughter, but, after discussion, decided that they did not really want to start over again with another pregnancy, or with sleepless nights or dirty diapers. After all, Cora was 39, would be 40 in a few months, and Robert was already 42. They immediately thought about adoption, because they had heard that there was a shortage of Black parents wanting to adopt, and that there were many Black children to be adopted. It seemed like a perfect solution for them. They could have their daughter, maybe about 5 years old, and also help a needy child, something that was important to them, consistent with their values.

It took about 4 years for this idea to be realized, because they moved across the country temporarily, and were just too unsettled to even think about adding another child. But when they returned to the East, where it seemed as if they would stay for a long while, they came back to the idea. Cora had a part-time job as a pediatric nurse, but she believed that she could do more, especially with an older child who would be in school. Cora and Robert went to a foster care meeting, where they met a social worker from the Department of Social Services. They told her they were really interested in adoption rather than foster care because they wanted a *permanent* member of the family. The worker was quite positive about the possibilities, even when she found out that their income was only $24,000 a year, and that Robert had not even finished high school. That was all right, she said, especially if they were willing to take a child with special needs who would be eligible for an adoption subsidy. That would help considerably with expenses; they would even get a Medicaid card for a child with special needs, so that most of the health care expenses would be paid. The worker mentioned a little girl, 6 years old, who was currently with a foster family. The agency, however, was looking for an adoptive placement for her. [*Note.* The Wilsons adopted the child.] (pp. 185–186)

Making a careful assessment of the prospective adoptive individual or couple (usually called an *adoptive home study*) is a key task in the adoptive placement. Each prospective adoptive individual or couple has a unique history and dynamics. Your goal, in part, is to assess the potential of the prospective adoptive individual or couple to rear an adopted child.

The entire adoption process—which includes waiting, matching, placement, supervision, and finalization—can be lengthy and frustrating for the prospective adoptive individual or couple. Frequently, a couple has spent years trying to have a biological child. By the time they have made the decision to adopt, they may be disheartened and frustrated. They may go through a grieving process for the child they never had (see the section on bereavement in Chapter 13). You need to be sensitive to their feelings.

An individual or couple seeking to adopt a child has several options (White & White, 1993). One is to contact a public agency. A second is to contact a private agency, such as one associated with a religious group or one engaged in international adoptive placement services. However, the cost is likely to be high, and there may be restrictions about where the agency will place the children (for example, an agency may place children only in homes of the same religious denomination as the agency). A third is to work through a physician or a lawyer independently to obtain a child. Again, the costs for this type of adoption may be high. Long waits are inherent in all forms of adoption, unless the prospective adoptive individual or couple is extremely flexible and a child happens to be available.

Phases of adoption. Four phases characterize the adoption process: the uncertainty phase, the adoption phase, the post-adoption phase, and the integration phase (Reitz & Watson, 1992). Let's look at these phases in more detail. (Although the term "parents" will be used in the remainder of this section, note that the same considerations hold for an individual parent who plans to adopt or has adopted a child.)

1. *Uncertainty phase.* The prospective adoptive parents apply to adopt and are screened. A home study of the prospective adoptive parents will be conducted and criminal and child maltreatment records will be checked. Besides carrying out an interview and home observation, the social worker will need to examine such records as birth and marriage certificates, divorce records, medical statements from personal physicians, financial statements, verification of employment, references, and school reports of any children living at home. The qualities sought in prospective adoptive parents include good physical health, good emotional and social adjustment, emotional maturity, a stable relationship, positive feelings for children, appropriate motivation for adoption, ability to accept a child as he or she is, and willingness to seek outside help if the need arises (Steinhauer, 1991).

After all of the information has been collected, their suitability as parents will be evaluated. At this time, the prospective adoptive parents will be asked about the type of child they would like to adopt (for example, an infant, an older child, or a child with special needs). The prospective parents often are concerned about whether a child will be available for adoption.

2. *Adoption phase.* In a public adoption agency, a matching process occurs in this phase. The agency looks for prospective adoptive parents who can best meet the needs of the child, considering what the parents have told the agency about their preferences. When an appropriate child has been identified, the agency tells the prospective adoptive parents everything they know about the child (this step is sometimes called "telling") *before* the parents make a commitment to adopt and *prior to* the parents' meeting the child.

If the child is age 2 or older, the agency will prepare the child to meet the prospective adoptive parents, to visit the prospective parents, and to move into their house. In addition, the social worker should work with the child to help the child understand his or her background. The social worker can facilitate this process by preparing a "lifebook" that provides a chronology of the child's development and placement. It may include the child's birth certificate, weight at birth, pictures of the child as an infant and as a young child, pictures of the biological parents and the foster parents, and other mementoes of the child's life.

After the child is placed, the agency will supervise the family for a time before the adoption is completed. The agency should support the family during this period. If the placement is satisfactory, "the finalization of adoption is made through a court hearing, and a petition to adopt is tendered to a municipal judge. This often takes place in a closed courtroom or the judge's personal chambers. If all investigations and legal documents are in order, the judge orders a decree of adoption. After such a decree, the state issues a new birth certificate for the adopted child, stating his or her new name and the names of the adoptive parents" (White & White, 1993, p. 213).

3. *Post-adoption phase.* In the third phase, which continues throughout the child's development after he or she has been legally adopted, the child and parents must adapt to each other. The parents may be concerned about whether some unforeseen event may force them to give up their

adopted child. For example, they may fear that the birth parents will suddenly reappear or that the child will eventually reject them in favor of his or her birth parents (Anderson et al., 1993).

4. *Integration phase.* The fourth phase overlaps with the post-adoption phase and extends for the rest of the lives of the family members. A central issue for the adoptive parents and family is what it means to have an adopted child in the family. Ideally "the adoptive parents must incorporate the adopted child into their family in a way that recognizes the difference the adoption makes, yet gives full membership to the adopted child and maintains the family as a well-functioning system for all its members" (Reitz & Watson, 1992, p. 119).

Some parents have difficulty accepting that adoption gives them full rights and the same authority over their children as is accorded to biological parents. "Other parents are so grateful to have a child, they can nurture without difficulty but have difficulty providing the discipline so necessary for a child's development and family sanity" (Anderson et al., 1993, p. 264).

In cases of an older-child adoption, it may be difficult for "the child to develop a sense of belonging and attachment within the new family.... The more temporary placements the child has experienced, the more difficult [and longer] this process of attaching will be. [Children who have been in many foster homes] are likely to resist nurturing, because their world view is colored by mistrust, low self-esteem, learned helplessness, and conflicted loyalties toward multiple caretakers" (Anderson et al., 1993, p. 265). With adolescents, who also will be striving for independence, "the tension between nurturing and discipline, the struggle for power and control, can continue for years" (Anderson et al., 1993, p. 265).

Adopting children with special needs. Both normal children and children with special needs may be placed for adoption. If children are in foster care, there is a strong possibility that they were sexually maltreated (Anderson et al., 1993). It will require special efforts by the parents to help these children become integrated into the family. "Adoption represents an important option for community integration of children with multiple and severe disabilities who are given up by their birth parents. If such children are not adopted, the options for their residential care are limited to institutionalization, group homes, and foster care, all of which are considerably more expensive to the service system and less in line with normalization principles..." (Todis & Singer, 1991, p. 11). Children with special needs may be placed with special-needs parents or nontraditional parents (such as single women, single men, gay couples, biracial couples, or people over 35 years) or with couples who have biological children of their own (Brodzinsky, Schechter, & Henig, 1992).

Here are some reasons adoptive parents gave when they were asked why they adopted a child with special needs (Goetting & Goetting, 1993, p. 499, with changes in notation):

- Because of the warmth that I feel for children.
- I wanted to help the child improve.
- This was a foster child of mine whom I adopted because I wanted to keep her.
- To put religious beliefs into action; to do God's work.
- I enjoy the challenge of a difficult task.
- Keeping children in our home makes our marriage work better.
- I knew that caring for this child would make me feel that I am a better person.
- In my past, I learned to love a special-needs child and wanted to bring one into my home.
- I want to have someone who cares about me.
- I felt especially sorry for this child because of his special needs.
- It is a socially good thing to do.
- I looked forward to the respect that others would give to me in this professional role.
- I was needing a constructive way to spend my time.
- To make up for the absence of my own children.

Failure of adoption. Sometimes the adoptive parent-child relationship fails. This may happen when (Steinhauer, 1991)

- the children have a history of severe deprivation and multiple placements
- the children are unable to form a bond with the adoptive family
- the children have a conduct disorder
- the children have been removed from a successful long-term placement with foster parents
- the children have retained strong emotional ties to members of the birth family or the foster family
- the children have personality and temperament traits that interfere with their ability to adjust to the new family
- the parents have personality and temperament traits that interfere with their ability to be effective parents
- the parents have excessive expectations of the adopted child
- the biological children in the family cannot adapt to the changed family environment

Often, when the relationship fails, it is because of a combination of characteristics associated with the child and with the family.

When the adoptive placement fails, the adoption may need to be terminated. "This disruption can occur before or after legal finalization of the adoption. It is important that all parties—parents, child, caseworker, and mental health professionals—have a part in the communication concerning how and why this must occur. Openness will help everyone manage rekindled feelings of failure, anger, loss, and abandonment that accompany this decision" (Anderson et al., 1993, p. 267). The termination of an adoption (that is, a petition to set aside the adoption) is again a legal process involving the court.

Transracial adoption or transcultural adoption. In *transracial adoptions* or *transcultural adoptions,* families will need to face additional issues. These issues include how to help the children maintain a sense of their cultural heritage and how to cope with the treatment they may receive from society—issues that may surface especially when the children reach adolescence. Adolescents may have to cope with racial prejudice, sexual stereotypes, and social biases activated by interracial dating. Physical differences between the adoptive adolescents and the parents—as when dark-skinned adolescents are raised by light-skinned parents or Asian adolescents are raised by Caucasian parents—may cause the adolescents to be embarrassed (Brodzinsky et al., 1992). Issues of identity confusion also may arise. Although every effort should be made to place a child in a family of his or her racial background, it is more important to provide the child with a loving, caring home as early as possible (Glidden, 1994).

Adoptive parents must come to grips with the fact that the biological chain that links one generation to the next, from the past to the future, will have a missing link, and that it will be the psychological relationship that will give continuity to the family history.

—Arthur D. Sorosky

Interviewing Issues

This section focuses on two different sets of issues involved with interviewing in cases of adoption: those involved in the pre-adoption phase and those that may arise after finalization of the adoption. Those of you who will work in adoption agencies will be dealing with the first set of issues, whereas those of you who will work in mental health clinics will be dealing with the second set of issues. Adoption agencies usually provide little support for the child or family after the adoption is finalized.

Pre-adoption phase. The interview with prospective adoptive parents (and family), as part of the home study, is different from an interview in a mental health facility: *"There is no presenting problem, and there is no identified patient"* (Reitz & Watson, 1992, p. 122). In the interview, focus on how the adoption will affect the family and how the family members may cope with a new member. One goal of the initial assessment interview with prospective parents is to find out whether adoption is a good idea, especially when a special-needs child is involved. The semistructured interview in Table F-40 in Appendix F will assist you in interviewing a prospective adoptive parent.

Here are some areas for you to consider:

1. What are the age, sex, genetic history, and medical and behavioral status of the child the parents would like to adopt?
2. What are the placement history and school history of the child they would like to adopt?
3. What is the current composition of the family?

4. What impact will adopting the child have on the family?
5. How will the family accommodate the adopted child?
6. What are the family's resources?
7. Can the family cope with an additional member?
8. What is the life stage of the family?
9. What changes might occur in the family dynamics if a new member were adopted?
10. Will the adoptive parents identify themselves as such or keep the issue of adoption hidden from the child and others?
11. Will the adoptive parents tell the child about his or her birth family?

An indirect goal of the initial assessment interview is to have the family come to a better understanding of its strengths and weaknesses, recognize what kind of child would best fit into the family, and make the appropriate decision about whether to go ahead with plans for adoption. Chapter 4 discusses how to evaluate families in more detail.

Prospective adoptive parents who have any of the following usually will not be eligible for adopting a child (Reitz & Watson, 1992, adapted from p. 123):

* impulse control disorders
* major unresolved issues in personal history, including still fantasizing about an unborn child
* history of certain crimes
* extremely rigid moral or religious beliefs
* significant problems in child rearing
* strong needs and unrealistic expectations
* a history of mental illness or substance abuse
* marital difficulties
* a history of domestic violence
* a history of child maltreatment

You may want to ask whether the prospective parents explored ways to increase fertility and facilitate conception before they decided to adopt a child. The key, then, of the initial assessment interview with prospective adoptive parents is to explore their motivation for the adoption and to evaluate their ability to raise an adopted child.

Post-finalization phase. You may need to conduct interviews with the child and parents after the adoption has been completed if there are difficulties with the placement. Here are some guidelines for preparing for the post-adoption interview.

1. What problems is the family having?
2. What are the child's and family's strengths and weaknesses?
3. Does the child know that he or she was adopted?
4. If yes, how did the child learn that he or she was adopted?
5. How are the child's problems and the adoption related?
6. Is the family open or closed about the adoption with other people?

7. If open, how do they inform others about the adopted child?
8. What are the family dynamics?
9. How have the family dynamics changed since the adoption?
10. What is the adopted child's role in the family?
11. If there is more than one child in the family, what are the children's roles in the family?
12. Are all the children treated equally?
13. If not, how are they treated differently?

Thus, you will want to evaluate the problems the child and family are having as you would evaluate any other difficulties. In addition, you will want to evaluate issues associated with the adoption.

Interventions

Following are several issues that adoptive families face (Reitz & Watson, 1992).

1. *Change.* Adoption makes a difference. The adoptive family must recognize that adoption brings about changes, including shifts in family roles and structures, and must learn how to deal with these changes.

2. *Entitlement.* The adoptive parents must learn to appreciate that they have both the legal and the emotional right to be parents and to see the child as their own.

3. *Claiming.* The adoptive family and child eventually should "come to feel that they *belong* to each other" (pp. 126–127).

4. *Unmatched expectations.* The adoptive family and child must develop realistic expectations about each other.

5. *Separation, loss, and grief.* The adoptive parents may have to cope with the loss of their fantasy of having a biological child and their image of themselves as adults with healthy reproductive systems. The child may have to cope with the loss of the dream of reuniting with her or his birth parents.

6. *Attachment.* The adoptive parents and child will need to become "attached." "Attachment" refers to the psychological process that ties two individuals together in a meaningful way (see Chapter 1). Adopted children can be taught at any age how to make attachments. However, children older than 3 years may need help in overcoming anxiety associated with making attachments because of aversive prior experiences.

7. *Identity formation.* Adoptive parents may need to help the child overcome difficulties understanding who she or he is. The child may have these difficulties because of incomplete information about the birth family history, feelings that she or he is not a full member of the adoptive family, and struggles with the thought that she or he was abandoned by the birth family.

The following letter expresses a mother's concerns about being an adoptive parent, her thoughts about her adopted child's birth parents, and her appreciation of Child Protective Services for protecting her adopted child when he was with his birth parents (Green, 1994):

I am an adoptive parent. Adoption is not always a tidy event in a child's life. Not all children are given up for adoption by a birth parent's "undying" love for them. Nor do most adopted children share a relationship with both their adoptive parents and their birth parents.

Let me tell you about my son. After many calls to Child Protective Services, my son and his siblings were removed from the home of their birth parents, due to severe neglect. The birth parents were given many opportunities to prevent their children from being taken from them.

What happened next was a placement in foster care while the birth parents attempted to comply with their reunification plans. One completed it, one did not. There was drug involvement on the part of both parents. My son's birth father completed all aspects of the plan, but stopped contacting the children, only to rear his head when a court hearing came up.

When my son was placed with me, he was 2 years old. Since that day six years ago, I have been completely honest with him about his adoption and history with his birth parents, to the extent that he could comprehend. This hasn't always been easy. He is aware that he wasn't "given up for adoption," but rather that his birth parents failed at their obligation to care for and nurture him.

My son is a bright, intelligent, witty and charming little boy. My hopes and dreams for him are as any other parent's. He has a family who loves him. My job as a parent will become more intense as he gets older and becomes more cognizant of his early years.

I know that one day he may choose to locate his birth parents. When that time comes, he will have my complete support and love. But it has to be his choice, not his birth parents'. One of my biggest fears is to have contact from them at a time when he is not ready. I do not fear losing him to them.

The point is that not all birth parents are the wonderful people that some stories make them out to be. Not all children are given up for adoption because of birth parents' love for them. I wish it were that simple.

Child Protective Services did a wonderful job protecting my son; it was his birth parents who failed him. He has the love of his "real" family to ensure that contact is kept with his siblings. His birth parents lost that right for contact when they allowed their family to be torn apart. (p. B9)

Even before the adoption takes place, human service workers can help prospective parents by offering adoption preparation classes. These classes can focus on "encouraging prospective parents to carefully examine the possible ramifications of adoption—for example, reactions to infertility, whether or not the dream child has been mourned, differential desires to adopt between spouses, the relentlessness of parenting (especially single parenting), the infant's unknown genetic 'credentials,' and the ramifications of taking a child of another race or culture, or a child who has been neglected or abused" (Anderson et al., 1993, p. 272). Other issues that might be covered include dealing with the possible concerns of biological children about their parents' motivation for adopting and their fears that they might be displaced or neglected.

Families that adopt children with special needs will probably need ongoing services, including "respite care, life planning services, support groups, babysitting for the other children, homemaker services, advocacy training, and ongoing training in how to care for the child" (Marcenko & Smith, 1991, pp. 442–443). (For more information about working with children who have been adopted and their families, see Anderson et al. [1993]. For information about working with teenage girls who are considering giving their child up for adoption, see Lindsay and Monserrat [1989].)

Case Illustration

After representatives of the Department of Social Services investigate parents' suitability to adopt a child, they issue a report based on their findings. Exhibit 14-1 shows a report prepared after such an investigation. It is based on an "independent adoptive petition" rather than an "agency adoptive petition." All names in the report are fictitious, and all dates and places have been changed to protect the privacy of the family.

In recent years, there has been growing a rhetoric of concern about the welfare of our nation's children. These families, particularly those who have taken society's damaged and discarded children into their homes and hearts, have translated the rhetoric into the most personal level of commitment and action. They deserve our gratitude, our respect, and most importantly, our understanding.

—Sherry Anderson, Maria Piantanida, and Carol Anderson

DIVORCE AND CUSTODY EVALUATIONS

Description

In 1990, there were 2.4 million marriages and 1.2 million divorces in the United States (Ahlburg & DeVita, 1992). Consequently, about 40% of children in the United States will spend part of their childhood living with one parent because of divorce (Glick, 1988). Divorce may lead to changes in the family and cause stress, trauma, and disorganization for the parents and children (Shaw, 1991; Sprenkle & Cyrus, 1983). For example, the family will change from a two-parent to a one-parent household, the family income may drop, and the family may move to a new location and possibly lose the family home. Children may change schools, lose contact with friends, live in a lower-quality neighborhood, and spend more time in child-care settings because the custodial parent may work. The custodial parent may have less time to spend with the children and less energy. Other people may begin to move in and out of the children's lives, such as extended family members and new friends of the divorcing parents. The children will probably have less contact with the noncustodial parent and see that parent in a locale different from their home.

Children may have to deal with parental conflict, feelings of anger, issues involving separation from and identification with parents, and perhaps even issues of gender identity. They may think that their friends will not understand them, that their parents might not want to live with them, that they may be abandoned, that their misbehavior caused the divorce, or that their behavior made their parents angry with each other (Hodges, 1991). These beliefs probably will affect how they adjust to the divorce.

The following poem, written by an 11-year-old girl toward the end of her parents' marriage, illustrates some feelings children may have about divorce (Stevenson & Black, 1995, pp. 36–37).

We rake the leaves from the trees
We shovel the snow from the sky
All we do when people we love fight
Is go to our room and cry.

On the positive side, divorce may reduce stress on the parents and children and promote feelings of self-worth, independence, and autonomy in one or both parents. A parent may reenter the work world, feel empowered to make choices, reach out to new friends, undertake new activities, stabilize a new life style and daily routines for the children, explore new interests, take a new job, and make peace with his or her spiritual self (Kaslow, 1991).

Americans, indeed, often seem to be so overwhelmed by their children that they'll do anything for them except stay married to the co-producer.

—Katharine Whitehorn

Stages of children's adjustment to divorce. Children living in a home where divorce has occurred probably have made adaptations over a long period to the existing stresses. Divorce, therefore, is best seen as a "marker event"—that is, the divorce itself is the culmination of a series of events that preceded it (Felner & Terre, 1987). Once the divorce takes place, the children and parents, as noted previously, will need to adapt to a changed family environment (Guttmann, 1993).

Children may go through the following five stages in adjusting to their parents' divorce, although not all children will go through every stage (Ayalon & Flasher, 1993; Grossman, 1986, pp. 81, 82, 102; Hozman & Froiland, 1976):

1. *Denial.* The children may not want to accept the reality of the impending divorce, feeling threatened by the loss of a parent and the changes in their family's status.

I knew he was moving out and I knew they weren't getting along too well, but I didn't think they'd get a divorce.

Exhibit 14-1
Example of an Adoption Report

IN THE SUPERIOR COURT OF THE STATE OF CALIFORNIA IN AND FOR THE COUNTY OF SAN MATEO

In the Matter of the petition of Frank Jeff Taylor and Helen Rebecca Taylor, Adopting Parents

REPORT OF THE SAN MATEO COUNTY DEPARTMENT OF SOCIAL SERVICES NO. A46891

The San Mateo County Department of Social Services, an agency licensed by the State Department of Social Services, in conformity with Section 224 of the Civil Code of California, presents its report in the matter of the petition of FRANK JEFF TAYLOR and HELEN REBECCA TAYLOR, for the adoption of SHAY FRANCIS TAYLOR, also known as BABY GIRL BROWN.

All necessary consents have been obtained, and the San Mateo County Department of Social Services recommends approval.

Minor
The minor, birth registered as Baby Girl Brown, was born on August 25, 1995, in Seattle, Washington (verified). The birth certificate gives the maiden name of the natural mother as Connie Beth Brown and the father's name as Gerald Clifford Hanson.

The petitioners said that placement of the minor was arranged by the natural mother. The petitioners said they did not pay the natural mother's medical and hospital expenses. The minor and the petitioners are related; the male petitioner is the minor's maternal great uncle. The petitioners received the minor from the natural mother on August 25, 1995, and the minor has remained with them continuously since then.

The minor was born at home; therefore, no hospital records were available on the minor's birth.

According to a recent medical report, the minor is in good health. She appears to be responding well in the petitioners' home.

Natural Parents
The natural mother, Connie Brown, was born on March 14, 1981, in Seattle, Washington. She is currently in the 9th grade and resides with her parents in the State of Washington. She reported no known unfavorable family health history. The natural mother reported she had never been married. She said that she has met the petitioners and is satisfied with them as parents for her child.

The natural father, Gerald Hanson, was born on July 21, 1980, in Seattle, Washington. He is currently in the 9th grade and resides with his parents in the State of Washington. The natural father reported an unfavorable family health history of a learning disability. He has not met the petitioners. He said he was not involved in the placement of the minor.

Adopting Parents
The man petitioner, Frank Jeff Taylor, was born on March 25, 1953, in Chicago, Illinois. He received a Bachelor of Arts degree from the University of Illinois. For the past 24 years he has been employed by the U.S. Army where he is a Colonel. The physician who examined him on October 16, 1995, reported no evidence of organic or functional disorder; the physician considered him able to give proper care to a child until the minor reaches majority. The man petitioner reported no previous marriages.

The woman petitioner, Helen Rebecca Taylor, nee Green, was born on October 2, 1952, in Detroit, Michigan. She received a college education from Wayne State University. For the past year she has been employed by the San Mateo City Schools where she is a substitute elementary school teacher. The physician who examined her on October 11, 1995, reported no evidence of organic or functional disorder; the physician considered her able to give proper care to a child until the minor reaches majority. The woman petitioner reported no previous marriages.

The minor is cared for by Patricia Good, who is a licensed daycare provider, when the petitioners are out of the home.

The petitioners were married on June 31, 1983, in Riverside, California (verified). One child has been born to this union, and no children have been adopted by the petitioners. The child in the home appears to accept the minor as a member of the family.

The man petitioner receives $4,642 per month from his employment (verified). The woman petitioner receives $400 per month from her employment (verified). The petitioners are purchasing a home for $160,000 on which they owe approximately $130,000. They have life insurance, savings, and other resources. The petitioners have supplied a financial statement to show they can provide a financially stable home for the minor.

The petitioners appear to have a compatible relationship and a good understanding of the development and needs of children. The petitioners have one child of their own, and are experienced in child rearing. References state they are proper persons to rear a minor child.

A fingerprint clearance on the petitioners through the F.B.I. and the Department of Justice indicated no record.

Consents
The natural mother freely and willingly signed the attached Consent and Consent Statement of Understanding on October 4, 1995 before a Notary Public in King County, Washington. The consents were provided by the petitioners' attorney, Marjorie Delp, who in turn provided them to the Department of Social Services. The signing of the consents was witnessed by the natural mother's attorney, Christine Wilby.

The alleged natural father freely and willingly signed the attached Waiver of Right to Further Notice of Adoption Planning on September 28, 1995, before a Notary Public in King County, Washington. This Waiver was provided by the petitioners' attorney, Marjorie Delp, who in turn provided the Waiver to the Department of Social Services.

(Continued)

Exhibit 14-1 (*Continued*)

Evaluation
It appears to the San Mateo County Department of Social Services that the minor is free for adoption and that the petitioners' home is a proper setting for her.

Recommendation
IN VIEW OF THE FOREGOING FACTS, the San Mateo County Department of Social Services accepts the

Consent and Consent Statement of Understanding of the natural mother provided by the petitioners' attorney and the Waiver of Right to Further Notice of Adoption, and recommends that the petition of FRANK JEFF TAYLOR and HELEN REBECCA TAYLOR for the adoption of SHAY FRANCIS TAYLOR, also known as BABY GIRL BROWN be granted.

DATED THIS ELEVENTH DAY OF JANUARY, 1996

SAN MATEO COUNTY DEPARTMENT OF SOCIAL SERVICES
LESLIE K. FOLD, DIRECTOR BY

_____

LILA BRENDA COLLY, MSW,
ADOPTION WORKER

---

2. *Anger and guilt.* The children may strike out at anyone who they perceive is interfering with their parents' reconciliation. They may be angry at both parents for disrupting their family or at the one parent who sought the divorce. They may feel responsible and therefore guilty about the separation of their parents and feel torn between the parents' demands for loyalty.

We thought he left us. I thought it was because I wasn't doing good in school or wasn't acting right or something.

3. *Bargaining.* The children may recognize that denial, anger, and guilt are not productive. They may try to improve their behavior to create a more favorable environment in the hope that the parents will reconcile.

If I behave myself, maybe they will get together again.

4. *Depression and frustration.* The children may realize that they cannot control the situation. They may give up hope of parental reunification and fear losing the remaining parent. They also may experience frustration because of the actual losses they've experienced or because of the violation of promises made by the parents.

I felt pretty sad 'cause, you know, you live with somebody that long and just real quick he goes away. It just makes you feel bad.

5. *Acceptance.* The children may accept the reality of the impending divorce and come to terms with the new situation. However, they still may have to face new demands associated with the divorce, including visitation, parental remarriage(s), moving to a new home, starting a new school, or new roles within the family.

Well, you kind of feel like a grownup, like you're another lady living with her because she lets you do extra special jobs and special things that your dad used to do.

How divorce may affect children. Several factors may affect how children adjust to divorce (Felner & Terre, 1987).

1. *Individual characteristics of children.* Children's age, coping skills, temperament, personality, and level of adjustment will affect their reactions to the divorce. Every child will react to the divorce in her or his unique way. As children mature, their understanding of and feelings about their parents' separation or divorce will change (Hodges, 1991). When divorce coincides with developmental changes, such as weaning, starting school, or reaching adolescence, children may have additional stresses (Ayalon & Flasher, 1993).

The emotional and behavioral responses of preschool children may include guilt, fear of abandonment, sadness, clinging, eating and sleeping problems, anxiety, bewilderment, and regressive behavior (such as returning to a security blanket, bed-wetting, and soiling) (Morgan, 1994; Sales, Manber, & Rohman, 1992). They have little understanding of the divorce and may fear that the other parent might abandon them.

The emotional and behavioral responses of children aged 6 to 8 years may include sadness, grief reactions, guilt, anxiety, yearning for the return of the departed parent, fear of abandonment, and loyalty conflicts (Morgan, 1994). They have a vague understanding of the divorce.

The emotional and behavioral responses of children aged 9 to 12 years may include sadness, anger, guilt, hostility, and loyalty conflicts. They understand that the divorce represents an emotional/psychological separation of the parents from each other (Morgan, 1994; Sales et al., 1992).

The emotional and behavioral responses of children aged 12 years and older may include sadness, anger, guilt, anxiety, hostility, and loyalty conflicts. They are likely to have "less idealized views of their parents and greater anxiety about their own sexuality, their own eventual marriage, and the postdivorce family's financial situation" (Sales et al., 1992, p. 26).

2. *Level of pre- and post-divorce interparental conflict.* If there is heightened conflict between the parents—such as frequent episodes of interparental conflict and intense forms of marital conflict—children may have increased adjustment

problems (Grych & Fincham, 1990). They may have low self-confidence, low self-esteem, anxiety, depression, and aggressive behavior. Also, when there are pressures associated with interparental conflict, "children may be caught in the middle as they are sometimes asked to carry messages between parents, to inform each parent of the other's activities, to defend one parent against the other's disparaging remarks, or to justify wanting to spend time with the other parent.... Parental conflict provides children with an opportunity to exploit parents and play one off against the other, and when they are older, to escape careful monitoring of their activities" (Hetherington, Law, & O'Connor, 1993, p. 214).

3. *Quality of the relationship between children and each parent, as well as the conditions surrounding the contact between the children and each parent.* A poor relationship between the children and the custodial parent or between the children and the noncustodial parent often will lead to adjustment problems in children. When parental conflict is high, visitation with the noncustodial parent may be stressful. The noncustodial parent may reduce her or his involvement with the children for such reasons as inconvenience associated with visiting, difficulty dealing with the custodial parent when trying to arrange visitation with the children, discomfort surrounding the ambiguity inherent in the visitor role, her or his remarriage or the remarriage of the former spouse, feelings of depression or guilt, and perception of rejection by the children.

4. *Degree of instability and change in the children's daily life surrounding the divorce.* Unstable household routines may interfere with the children's adjustment. This may happen, for example, when a parent who formerly stayed at home goes to work outside the home, starts dating, is not able to help the child with activities such as Girl Scouts or Little League, fails to serve regular meals, and so forth.

5. *Quality of relationship with siblings.* Siblings who share experiences and confide in one another are in a good position to help each other cope with the stress of a divorce (Stevenson & Black, 1995). However, the relationship between the siblings may bring on additional stress if, for example, the siblings disagree about which parent, if any, is to blame for the divorce or if one sibling, who is put in charge, is resented by the other sibling.

6. *Emotional well-being of the parents, particularly the custodial parent.* Children are likely to have more adjustment problems when the custodial parent is not functioning well and is under considerable stress. The custodial parent may face stresses associated with income, the size of the family, the adjustment of the children, interactions with the former spouse, and the overall level of change and demands for readjustment necessitated by the divorce. In addition, the custodial parent's physical or mental health problems will affect her or his adjustment.

7. *Levels of economic stress and deprivation of the household in which the children live.* Children often have adjustment problems when they live in a single-parent family that has experienced a severe drop in income. There also may be problems associated with a parent's failing to pay child support.

Overall, children's adjustment usually will be hindered when the level of conflict between the parents is high, the relationship between the children and the parents is poor, the household routines are unstable, the relationship between the siblings is poor, the custodial parent is under stress, and the family income drops. Children's adjustment may be further hampered when they are not given age-appropriate explanations about the divorce and have limited self-esteem and coping skills (Sprenkle & Cyrus, 1983).

Research on the effects of divorce on children suggests that (a) children of divorce are not a homogeneous group, (b) the differences between children of divorced and nondivorced families are small, (c) the differences between children whose parents have divorced and those whose parents have not divorced can be attributed to paternal absence, family dysfunction, and economic deprivation rather than to divorce per se, and (d) unhappy, conflict-ridden two-parent homes are more harmful to children than are stable single-parent homes (Stevenson & Black, 1995).

We can never know precisely why children behave as they do following the divorce of their parents. It remains "unclear to what extent differences in children *following* divorce reflect predivorce family stress, the actual separation, postdivorce disequilibrium, or even long-standing differences in child behavior that may have contributed to family stress and parental separation" (Zaslow, 1988, p. 356).

How divorce may affect parents. The stresses encountered by the parents in a divorce stem from several sources, although not all divorced parents experience these stresses. The sources of parental stress include (Sprenkle & Cyrus, 1983; Wallerstein, 1983)

- a sense of failure
- the anticipation of negative reactions from children, friends, relatives, and others
- changes in their life style, such as lower or higher socioeconomic status, moving, increased or decreased parental responsibilities, and increased or decreased household responsibilities
- the feelings of guilt associated with spending less time with the children because of the need to work or to seek new relationships
- the anxiety about greater household disorder, poorly enforced discipline, and difficulty enforcing household routines
- the changes in friendship patterns and loss of support from friendship networks
- the feeling of being abandoned, with associated feelings of helplessness, reduced self-esteem, anger, and worry about how the children will be affected by the divorce

The stress of divorce may be so great that some individuals experience symptoms of a posttraumatic stress disorder (see

Chapter 11) or reactions associated with bereavement (see Chapter 13).

Following is a description of how divorce may affect the adjustment of parents, or vice versa (Hetherington et al., 1993):

Separation and divorce place both men and women at risk for psychological and physical dysfunction.... In the immediate aftermath of marital dissolution, both men and women often exhibit extreme emotional lability, anger, depression, anxiety, and impulsive and antisocial behavior, but for most this is gone by 2 years following divorce. However, even in the long run, alcoholism, drug abuse, psychosomatic problems, accidents, depression, and antisocial behavior are more common in divorced than nondivorced adults.... Furthermore, recent research suggests that marital disruption alters the immune system, making divorced persons more vulnerable to disease, infection, chronic and acute medical problems, and even death.... Some of these postdivorce symptoms in adults, such as depression and antisocial behavior, seem likely to have been present before divorce and even to have contributed to a distressed marriage and to marital dissolution. Depression and antisocial behavior are related to irritable, conflictual marital interactions. (p. 215)

Here are some reactions of mothers to their divorce or to an impending divorce (Grossman, 1986, pp. 28, 46, 49, 53, 59, 62, 113):

- It was really hard telling the children that we were going to get a divorce. They both cried and they obviously—two things—one was they felt guilty that it was their fault and the other was they wanted us to get back together and any signs that we were really friendly with each other and stuff they would think oh good, maybe they're going to get back together. And of course there was this long period of several months where that was hard to watch.

- It was a total surprise to me when he told me he wanted a divorce and I was very unhappy and miserable for a complete week and then couldn't eat and couldn't do anything but think about it.... I was lonely and I didn't have any friends to go out with...and I was glad when he came back.... The second time when we finally got—decided to divorce, I was very glad that he was leaving.... I just wanted out, period, and that was it.

- There is nothing good about going through a divorce. It is physically, mentally, and emotionally, at least for me and for the people that I know that have gone through one, exhausting. It's just, regardless of your feelings for the person who you're divorcing, I just, I don't think it can be made easier. It is not a fun thing to go through.... I suppose if you realize that it's going to be a very painful process, you won't be surprised when you get into it.

- It's something that's still ongoing. It's a different kind of loneliness. It's not, your kids can be here all the time and you can have lots of friends and go places and do things. But it's the kind of loneliness for the special companionship that you had, like a relationship that you had with your husband, you know. It's somebody that's here. Somebody that cares, somebody that loves you, somebody you enjoy being with and doing things with.

- There were times when I would have liked to blow him away because of the way I felt, like why did you do this to me, I was

a good wife to you...Yes, you do get angry, very angry sometimes.

- Sometimes I feel just really that I don't ever have any time to myself because I have the kids all the time and if I don't get a break from them I'm going to go absolutely crazy.

- It was gradual but I liked living so much more by myself and with the children. I started to become the mother that I needed to be much more.... I started feeling more like I was relating to them on a new level.

Once the parents realize that the marriage is disintegrating, they may discuss the situation with each other and with the children, seek counseling, consult an attorney, or consult clergy for advice. If the parents cannot resolve their differences, one parent may move out of the home, although this move may be temporary. In some families, parents separate and reconcile briefly and repeatedly. When the parents accept the divorce as final, they need to resolve several issues, including child custody, visitation rights, child support, division of property, insurance, alimony, and living arrangements. Children may be asked about their concerns and wishes. Following the divorce, how the parents relate to each other will depend on how they have handled the divorce, have resolved their feelings, and see their future.

Here is an account of the experiences of one woman who went through a divorce. (Mayer, 1996, © Copyright National Public Radio ® 1996. The news commentary by NPR's Donna Mayer was originally broadcast on National Public Radio's "All Things Considered" on January 18, 1996, and is used with the permission of National Public Radio. Any unauthorized duplication is strictly prohibited.)

CASE 14-3. DONNA

We had been married 20 years when my husband left last winter. At first we called it a trial separation. Every day during those first five months I hoped he would come back. Then on a beautiful Sunday in June, we sat on our back porch and I outlined all my reasons for his return. Actually, I pleaded for it. He listened attentively, and when I was finished he simply said he couldn't do it, it was too late, and I went into the backyard and threw up into an azalea bush.

I knew I had a difficult marriage, but it was my crazy little life, and no matter how challenging it was I never thought it was hopeless. I certainly never thought I would cross over into that 50 percent group that doesn't make it. I couldn't believe that my boys, 16 and 19, so close to adulthood but not quite there, would have to suffer through the breakup of their family. My husband was gone. He wanted more, something intangible, something that I apparently couldn't provide. I loved him right until the end.

There were so many collateral losses that occurred with his exit. Beside the numbing loneliness that came with the actual physical absence, I lost the ability to concentrate for more than five minutes at a time, my appetite, and with that 15 pounds, half a shoe size, and one bra size. I barely slept. Some nights, even though I was exhausted, a terrible vigilance and watchfulness took over and it was as though I had to stay awake to guard against any other awful things that might happen. I roamed my house from room to room, looking, I suppose, for comfort. I didn't find it.

The prefix 'un' took over my life—unloved, unmarried, unattractive, unhappy, uncomfortable, unrecognizable, unglued, undone, unreal. Sometimes I would suddenly become aware of an odd posture that I had adopted, my arms crossed over my chest with a hand clutching each shoulder, some futile attempt to hold myself together. I thought I might die.

Then I came up with some things that I could manage. I could get out of bed. I could get something on the table for Simon, my younger son, to eat for dinner. I could pick up the phone and call my older son Charlie, who was in his first year of college. I could go to work. I could pay the bills on time. I could keep food in the house, even if I couldn't bring myself to eat much of it. I couldn't adjust to buying significantly less food, and the rotting vegetables in my refrigerator seemed to stand as a constant metaphor for my life.

But my friends did both ordinary and extraordinary things that made life bearable. Right at the very beginning, one friend looked me squarely in the eye and said, "You won't die." And another said, "You don't need sympathy, just company," and offered to sleep on the floor next to my bed. Another friend walked miles with me around my neighborhood into the night while I sobbed and kicked fences and street signs. My best friend from childhood came east from Oregon, and my sister and niece came from England.

People showed up unannounced, called constantly, threw me a surprise party, sent flowers, books, CDs, and letters. They invited me out and into their homes. An old friend that had been divorced years ago and is now happily remarried took me out for coffee one night. "There is a strong wind blowing through your house right now," he said, "and there isn't a thing you can do to stop it. But I promise you, the wind will eventually die down and things will look different. But it will be OK."

Although I had lost weight, I refused to buy new clothes or shoes. So, I clomped through the day with my shoes slipping up and down drowning in my hanging clothes. Finally, I faced the reality that I did need smaller bras, and I found myself staring bewildered into the vastness of one of my most hated places—the lingerie department. I'd been the same size for 14 years, and had no idea if I should go down a number or a letter.

Sensing my uncertainty, a very young saleswoman in a leather mini skirt and orange lipstick approached me and helped me figure out my new and reduced size. As she rang up my purchases, she looked at me sympathetically and said, "Wow. Bummer to, like, lose a whole cup size." I wanted to screech, "Wow. Bummer to, like, lose a whole husband, not to mention, like, my whole mind."

Some days when I would see young families, I'd have this urge to go up and say, "Do you know how fragile this all is? Do you know that this seemingly happy man may turn 45 some day and decide that all this is not enough?" I restrained myself. I finally took off my ring. It took a while, and then four out of five mornings I would awake to find a little beaded ring that I wore on my right hand on my left wedding ring finger. I did this in my sleep. Then, one day the beaded ring vanished and now I am ringless.

I miss him still. I miss the day to dayness, the knowledge that someone is home waiting for me. I miss being a family and enjoying our sons together. But I realized I would make it

when I was driving home from work the other day and I heard the Rolling Stones on the radio. I made a u-turn, headed for the record store and bought a double CD of the Stones. My husband hated the Rolling Stones.

I'm spending a little more time with my old friend Mick these days, and he keeps reminding me that I may not always get what I want, but if I try sometimes I'll get what I need.

How divorce may affect parent-child relations. Parents undergoing a divorce may have several concerns about their children (Ayalon & Flasher, 1993). They may wonder, for example, whether their children will be emotionally damaged by the divorce, whether their children can cope with the divorce, and whether there is anything they can do to protect the children against the stresses and strains of the divorce. Before the divorce is final, parents may wonder about when to tell the children about the impending divorce. They may involve the children in struggles over custody, economic support, and visitation rights, or they may be so preoccupied with "their own problems that they barely notice their children's needs" (Ayalon & Flasher, 1993, p. 23).

The following poem expresses some concerns of a divorced mother about her children (Rosenstock, Rosenstock, & Weiner, 1988, pp. 36–37):

To My Son—To My Daughter
Your life is not as
I would
have had it

I wanted you to be
loved
in one house
with
Mommy and Daddy

Instead Daddy lives far away
You go to new schools
Make new friends
Have new people in your family

I ache for your need for
stability
structure
safety and
security

I will try to provide you
with the
love you need
to
garner the
things we
held so dear

Love me
Trust me
as I love you.

Although divorce places children and parents at risk for encountering new challenges and multiple life stressors, it also can offer opportunities for personal growth, more gratifying relationships, and a more harmonious family situation.... It is the diversity rather than the inevitability of outcomes that is notable in response to divorce and remarriage.

—E. Mavis Hetherington, Tracy C. Law, and Thomas G. O'Connor

Custody evaluations. In most divorces, mothers are awarded physical or residential custody of the children; research shows, however, that fathers are no less effective than mothers in raising children (Hetherington et al., 1993). Sometimes there are disagreements about the custody of the children. In these cases, mental health professionals may be asked to evaluate the child and parents. If you are asked to perform a custody evaluation, you usually will give your recommendation to the court. *A judge may rely on your opinion, but the final decision regarding custody and other legal determinations will be made solely by the court.* Custody evaluations are particularly difficult because you are being asked to make predictions about how the child will adapt in the future. Unfortunately, a research base for making such predictions accurately is not available. However, as a mental health professional, you can evaluate the child, parents, and family in a way that may help the court make its decision.

If a court order identifies you as an expert whose role is to assist the court, you may have quasi-judicial immunity (Myers v. Morris, 8th Cir. 1987; 810 F.2d 1437, 1465–1468, cert. den 484 U.S. 828 [98 L. Ed 2d 58]; 108 S. CT 977; this is a federal court ruling—check your state law). This means that you have the freedom to act without fear of liability. However, the actions covered by immunity are only those made in good faith and within your court-ordered role.

Your task as a court-ordered expert will be twofold: to gather information and to make recommendations (Hodges, 1986). *You always should represent the best interests of the child, no matter who is paying for your services.* Because your evaluation will be shared with the court, inform the parents as well as the children about the limits of confidentiality. They must know that you will share the information with the court and that nothing is "off the record."

Custody evaluations are performed within the legal adversarial system rather than within the mental health system. Mental health professionals involved in custody evaluations may face various pressures (Levine, Anderson, Ferretti, & Steinberg, 1992):

An attorney may decline to use unfavorable conclusions or may press a mental health professional to make more favorable statements than the mental health professional may be willing to make. The tendency to identify with the side employing the mental health professional and to see the data in a light most favorable to that side

is strong. Mental health professionals may be perceived as "hired guns," willing to testify on any side of a question for a fee. How does one keep the child's best interests foremost, and not the interest of the parent who is paying? The mental health professional should try to examine all critical parties (for example, mother, father, child) and not just one parent or just a child. Ethically, the mental health professional can be paid by one side, but it requires effort to maintain professional and ethical standards in the evaluation and to keep the child's best interests in mind in communications to attorneys and to the court. (p. 98, with changes in notation)

Section 402 of the Uniform Marriage and Divorce Act (1970) is valuable in guiding courts in determining the best interests of the child; it also may help mental health professionals in making recommendations (Weithorn & Grisso, 1987):

The court shall consider all relevant factors including:

(1) the wishes of the child's parent or parents as to his [or her] custody;

(2) the wishes of the child as to his [or her] custodian;

(3) the interaction and interrelationship of the child with his [or her] parent or parents, his [or her] siblings, and any other person who may significantly affect the child's best interests;

(4) the child's adjustment to his [or her] home, school, and community; and

(5) the mental and physical health of all individuals involved. The court shall not consider conduct of a proposed custodian that does not affect his [or her] relationship to the child. (p. 158)

These guidelines suggest that the following *variables be used for judicial determination of the child's best interests* (Weithorn & Grisso, 1987):

(a) child variables (e.g., age, sex, physical or psychological functioning, individual needs, preference concerning custody); *(b) parent variables* (e.g., age, sex, physical or psychological functioning, history of meeting and capacity to meet the child's physical, educational, moral, emotional, and other needs); *(c) environmental variables* (characteristics of environments offered by each custodial option, e.g., degree to which each environment promotes continuity and stability in child's life); and *(d) interactive variables* (e.g., quality of relationships between child and prospective custodians and significant others).

State statutory and case law typically do not set priorities for these factors in relation to one another. Instead, judges adjudicating individual custody disputes retain significant individual discretion in applying these standards. (pp. 158–159)

Wyer, Gaylord, and Grove (1987) offered the following comment about establishing such standards:

In either the divorce or the child protection context, child custody decisions draw upon the values of the society. The process of establishing criteria for such determinations is still evolving. Historically, the courts were guided by relatively clear presumptions favoring the granting of custody to one parent over another. It is only in recent years that the neutral "best interests of the child" standard has been adopted. This standard has alternately been applauded for its "child-centered" focus, its flexibility, and its minimal a priori bias relative to the parties and criticized for its vagueness and indeterminacy. The vagueness and indeterminacy of this standard often stimulate judges to look to the expertise of psychologists and others to assist in these determinations. (p. 18)

The court will give more weight to the preferences of older children than to those of younger ones (Scott & Emery, 1987). And the court may grant children over 14 years their wishes with respect to a custodial parent. Splitting physical custody of children between parents is a possible decision of the court (Kaplan, Hennon, & Ade-Ridder, 1993). However, the consequences of joint custody arrangements are not always clear. You should evaluate each family carefully before advising a joint physical custody arrangement.

When there is contention over custody or visitation, there is a potential for violent behavior by some family members directed at other family members and at the mental health professional, if one is involved in the case (Poirier, 1991). Concerns over the child's welfare further fuel resentments and unresolved feelings between the parents. Resentment toward the mental health professional will likely increase if the family members see him or her as unfairly favoring one party, as incompetent, as unprofessional, or as arrogant. Consequently, mental health professionals must show the family members that they recognize the dignity of each family member and that they are following the ethical standards of their profession (also see the section on ethical considerations in Chapter 1).

Custody battles might be intense for several reasons (Poirier, 1991).

The circumstances of disputed custody matters can involve the most hurtful, and in the end, the most tragic of distorted allegations being made by the opposing sides. These circumstances also generate very intense feelings of perceived rejection and related anger. In a quick and dramatic manner the care and love of the years of a now lost marital relationship become transformed into the fullest human capacity for hatred. Neither the judicial process nor any clinical effort is an adequate outlet for these powerful feelings. The usual course is for the sum total of feelings from the dissolving marital relationship being displaced into the custody battle. (p. 14)

Interviewing Issues

Conducting the child custody evaluation. In child custody disputes, a thorough evaluation will include (a) *interviewing* the parents (both separately and together), the child, each parent and the child together, and significant people in the child's life (for example, teachers, babysitters, relatives, and neighbors) on one or more occasions as needed and (b) *observing* the child in the home, school, and other settings, as appropriate (Hodges, 1991). The observational guidelines in Chapter 4, particularly those that focus on the parent-child relationship, provide suggestions on what to observe in the home. Note, for example, the responses of the child to each parent, including the child's willingness or reluctance to interact with each one. Ask the

parents to submit any information they wish about their relationship with the child and to recommend other people who may have relevant information. Occasionally, children and their parents may be referred for psychological testing. *When you first meet the parents and the children, you need to inform them that nothing in the interview or psychological evaluation is confidential* (Hodges, 1991). Exhibit 14-2 shows a letter that may be helpful in informing the parents about the interviews.

The following two cases show the value of a home visit in conducting child custody evaluations (Lytle-Vieria, 1987).

CASE 14-3. JEAN
At the court's request, a social worker evaluated a custody question and found her recommendation at odds with that of a clinical psychologist who had been retained by one of the disputants. The psychologist based his testimony on one clinical interview, on projective testing of Jean, a 6-year-old child, and on cursory background information obtained as part of the referral. Based on this one contact, the psycholo-

---

Exhibit 14-2
Suggested Letter to Parents in Cases of Custody Evaluations

Dear Parent:
In conducting a child custody study, my goal will be to determine how each parent can contribute most fully to the emotional and social development of your child(ren). In order to do this, I will be asking for your cooperation and assistance in providing me with information that will help me get to know you and your family. I recognize that this process may be somewhat stressful for you, as I often will be asking personal questions.

I will meet with each parent separately as well as with both of you together. Initially I would like to meet with you in my office, and later I would like to see you at your current residence. I also will see the other parent in my office and then at his or her current residence. In the initial interview, I will have the opportunity to get to know each of your viewpoints. When I see you together, I will try to direct the interview so that arguments are eliminated and so that I hear both of your perceptions on the topics covered. I also would like to interview the child(ren) in my office.

When I visit with each of you and all members of your household at a later date, I will ask you to have the child(ren) at issue with you then. I will talk with you as a family group.

I hope that this information will better prepare you for the child custody process in which you are about to participate. If you have any questions, please feel free to call me at _____.

Sincerely,

_____

Title

Source: Adapted from Bordarampe, Ehrenberg, Foran, and Oksman (1991).

gist gave lengthy and psychologically sophisticated testimony about the "best interests" of this child. The social worker's testimony dealt with the emotional conflict referred to by the psychologist but went further in an attempt to identify for the court the specific ways in which the competing parties could be expected to respond to the child then and in the future.

Because the social worker had made several home visits to each litigant, had contacted the child's teacher and pediatrician, and had seen the child in her actual living situation, her testimony focused on person-in-situation rather than on the psychological aspect exclusively. Apparently, this broader focus was more pertinent to the court, for the judge's decision and accompanying legal opinion paralleled the conclusions reached by the social worker. (adapted from p. 6)

CASE 14-4. FRED

Fred, an uneducated, inarticulate father in office interviews, appeared to be unable to distinguish the different characteristics and needs of his daughters ages 10 and 12. He would have failed miserably any measurement of parental capacity based solely on his answers to the evaluator's questions. However, what he was unable to express verbally to the evaluator, he demonstrated during home visits. During these visits, he cooked elaborate meals based on his daughters' menu requests, revealed his enjoyment of coaching their baseball team, and showed his obvious involvement in their other extracurricular activities. In this way, he showed his commitment to guiding and supporting his daughters' different personalities and individual needs. (adapted from p. 6)

Interviewing parents in cases of child custody disputes. Table F-32 in Appendix F shows a semistructured interview for parents involved in a child custody dispute. It covers the parents' developmental history, work and military history, social-recreational history, criminal history, marital history, present family, custody questions, and future plans.

Listening carefully to the parents is critical to the success of the evaluation (Stahl, 1994).

If we understand their pain, the sources of the conflict through their eyes, and the nature of their fears and beliefs about the other parent, it will assist us in the overall evaluation of the family. Through these interviews we can hope to get a snapshot of the family and the family dynamics that will enable us to see how we can best intervene and solve the custody issues. This is very important psychologically because if parents feel heard, they may be more likely to go along with the evaluator's recommendations even if they do not agree with them. (p. 49)

Here are some suggestions you can give parents about what to tell their children about coming to the interview (Stahl, 1994).

For preschool children, I encourage parents to explain that I am someone who wants to meet them and see them with each parent so that I can help each be a better parent. For older children, if the evaluation is at the beginning of the divorce, I encourage parents to explain to their children that they are in disagreement about how they are going to share the job of parenting now and that they are getting divorced and that I will be talking with them to understand their

thoughts, fears, wishes, and feelings about their parents and their parents' divorce. If the evaluation is significantly postdivorce, I encourage parents to talk openly, without emotion, about the realities of the conflict and to tell the children that I am there to help the parents settle the conflict. At all times, I tell parents to encourage their children to express any feelings they may want and that I am there to listen to them and help them understand and express feelings about the divorce—both good and bad feelings about both parents. (p. 48)

If you decide to hold a joint interview with the parents, the following guidelines will be helpful (Bordarampe, Ehrenberg, Foran, & Oksman, 1991, adapted from pp. 163–164):

1. The purpose of the interview is to gain a better understanding of how the family functions and to determine the best interests of the child. The interview is an evaluation tool and not a mediation or an opportunity for marriage counseling.
2. This is a voluntary approach; if parents do not want a joint interview, then schedule an individual interview only.
3. If one parent lives far away, do not arrange a joint interview unless that parent wants one.
4. Remain neutral and do not enter into disagreements or disputes that may arise during the interview; suppress any temptation to counsel the parents.
5. If there has been a history of domestic violence, consider carefully whether you want to see the parents together.
6. Clearly state the purpose of the interview—for example, to achieve a better understanding of how the parents can work together in the best interest of the child.
7. Set ground rules allowing each parent to complete comments without interruption, and emphasize that each parent will have an additional opportunity to talk to you during the home visit.
8. Gently redirect the parents when they violate the ground rules or when they are not able to focus on the topics.
9. Inform the parents that you may discuss difficult matters when you review the allegations with them.
10. Usually, do not schedule a joint interview when there are allegations of child maltreatment made by one parent against the other.
11. If one parent does not keep a joint interview appointment, arrange for an individual interview.
12. The joint office interview gives you the opportunity to observe how the parents interact and may give you clues about potential obstacles to joint custody arrangements. Although the joint interview may be awkward for parents who have not been in the same room for some time, it may provide a model for future cooperation.

Interviewing the child in cases of child custody disputes. The semistructured interview questions in Table F-8 in Appendix F for a school-aged child will be helpful in cases of a custody dispute. The questions cover the child's affective, cognitive, and interpersonal behaviors and other behaviors as well. When you interview a child in a custody evaluation, don't probe too deeply into issues that the child doesn't want to discuss. If the child shows undue stress, help the child work through the stress. Asking the child to say whom he or she wants to live with can be particularly problematic. If you ask this question, you place the child in the untenable position of having to accept one parent and reject the other and may induce guilt, as the parent who was rejected is likely to feel hurt when he or she finds out (Hodges, 1986). The child may choose the parent who seems more permissive or least punitive, who needs him or her more, or who is least responsible for the divorce, or the child may choose the parent he or she is most attached to at that moment. Any of these reasons may not lead to a wise choice. Some children will refuse to make any choice to avoid guilt. However, if your state law requires you to ask an older child directly which parent he or she wants to live with, then, of course, do so.

You will want to consider the following questions after you complete your interview with the child:

1. What is the child's reaction to the divorce?
2. What is the child's relationship with each of his or her parents?
3. What role does the child see himself or herself as having in the divorce?
4. How does the child view his or her parents as they go through the divorce process (for example, reactions to parental arguments, attorneys, court appearances, and so forth)?
5. How has the divorce affected the child's relationship with his or her parents, siblings, relatives, friends, and so forth?
6. How has the divorce affected the child's living arrangements (for example, financial status, residence, household responsibilities)?
7. How have the parents' new social lives affected the child (for example, parents' dating or remarriage, relationship with stepbrothers and stepsisters)?
8. How has the divorce affected the child's schoolwork?
9. How is the child's mental health?
10. How has the divorce affected the child's adjustment?

In the following case, the child's expression of emotions led the interviewer to believe that someone had coached the child about what he should say (Rosenberg, 1990).

CASE 14-5. ERNIE

Ernie, a 6½-year-old child, announced that he wanted to live with his grandparents because it would be better than living with his mother. The evaluator accepted that statement and did not challenge it. However, the evaluator went on to ask the different ways in which things were good and bad in his grandparents' home and his mother's home. Ernie consistently related many positive experiences in his mother's home as well as some appropriate discomfort associated with things his mother would not give him or with punishment that she would administer. In contrast, Ernie had a great deal of difficulty elaborating on positive experiences in his grand-

parents' home. The original question about where Ernie would rather live was then rephrased in terms of the positive and negative characteristics that he expressed. Ernie began to look tense, stared at the floor, and repeated his original one-sentence preference for living with his grandparents in the manner of a child who has memorized a line for a play. (p. 28, with changes in notation)

Evaluating the results of the child custody evaluation. In arriving at a recommendation for custody arrangements, consider the following questions:

1. Are there charges or indications of child maltreatment, such as physical abuse, emotional abuse, sexual abuse, or neglect? (If yes, go to question 2; if no, go to question 7.)
2. What are the charges or indications of child maltreatment?
3. When did the maltreatment allegedly occur?
4. What symptoms of maltreatment are evident in the child?
5. How did the parent go about making the allegation of child maltreatment?
6. Did the parent see several professionals until she or he found one who was willing to say that maltreatment was occurring?
7. Has there been domestic violence? (If yes, go to question 8; if no, go to question 12.)
8. What happened?
9. How often did it occur?
10. Who was the perpetrator?
11. How did it affect the child (and any other children in the family)?
12. Is there any risk that the child will be maltreated if left with one parent?
13. Does either parent have a history of alcoholism, drug abuse, or psychiatric hospitalization?
14. If so, which parent and what type of difficulty did the parent have?
15. How well adjusted are the children?
16. Is there a custody dispute for some but not all of the children?
17. If so, what accounts for the different children involved in the custody dispute?
18. What are the emotional ties between each parent and child?
19. What are the emotional ties between the siblings?
20. How able is each parent to provide for the emotional and psychological well-being of the child?
21. What setting will provide the child with the most stability and foster her or his potential?

The parent who meets the following criteria is most likely to be the one recommended to have custody of the child (Hodges, 1991, pp. 140–143, with changes in notation):

- fosters visitation rights and cooperates with the other parent
- maintains the best continuity of the child's contacts with relatives, friends, neighborhood, schools, and so forth

- has the best child-rearing skills
- shows the greater humanity, consistency, and flexibility in handling the child
- is the one to whom the child is most deeply attached
- is mentally healthy
- has a good health history
- has concern for conventional cultural values, such as a good education and religious and moral training
- has the capacity to facilitate the child's growth
- has the financial resources to take care of the child

The following list includes some *questionable custody evaluation practices* that you should avoid (Levine et al., 1992):

1. *Saying one parent would be better for the child than the other, especially without examining both parents.* It is better simply to report your findings, without saying that one person would make a better parent than the other.

2. *Completing the evaluation without seeing how the child and parents function outside your office.* You are limiting your ability to make recommendations if you do not see how the child and parents function in their homes.

3. *Using projective tests and questionnaires exclusively to make your decision about custody.* Projective tests and questionnaires have not been validated for making decisions about custody, especially about how an individual will fulfill the parental role. You can use these procedures, however, as a part of the general evaluation if you are trained in their use.

4. *Allowing your personal likes and dislikes to influence your recommendations.* Do not allow your personal likes and dislikes to influence your recommendations. By providing an objective basis for your recommendations, you will reduce this source of error.

Having to fight for custody is like being raped; only it's worse. It never stops. And there is no crisis intervention center for it.

—Anonymous (Cited by P. Chesler)

Interventions

When the parents divorce, children may face several tasks (Wallerstein, 1983). These tasks include acknowledging the reality of the marital rupture, disengaging from parental conflict and distress and resuming customary pursuits, resolving the loss, resolving anger and self-blame, accepting the permanence of the divorce, and achieving realistic hope regarding relationships.

You will want to encourage the parents to work cooperatively for the benefit of the child. The child should understand that both parents still love him or her, "even if they no longer love each other" (Sprenkle & Cyrus, 1983, p. 69). The parents need to understand that they should not use the child as a weapon in their ongoing struggle with each other. They must help the child understand that he or she was not the cause of the breakup. They should not nurture the child's fantasies that they will reconcile. Table 14-1 provides suggestions that parents may find useful in helping their children cope with divorce.

In discussing visitation arrangements, you might want to share the following with the parents (with permission of Neal J. Meiselman):

TWELVE COMMANDMENTS FOR DIVORCED PARENTS (BOTH OF YOU)

1. Never make visitation arrangements directly with children under 12.
2. Never suggest visitation arrangements you have not previously discussed with the other parent. Always confirm with the other parent any visitation arrangements made with children 12 and older.
3. Send and return children who are clean, well-rested and fed. Do not send or return a sack or suitcase full of soiled clothes.
4. Do not use a telephone answering device to screen calls from the other parent or limit telephone access between your children and the other parent—except after your children's ACTUAL bedtime, not the bedtime you would like them to have.
5. Do not discuss divorce disputes with your children or allow them to hear you discussing your differences regarding them.
6. Do not send messages or money with your children.
7. Do not speak ill of the other parent—or of his or her relatives, friends or loved ones.
8. Do not ask your children for information about the other parent's household, friends, income or activities.
9. Do not believe everything you hear from your children.
10. Do not second-guess the other parent regarding discipline, rewards or anything else.
11. Give a sympathetic ear to your children, but affirm and reaffirm as often as necessary that you are not a referee or a mediator between your children and the other parent.
12. Be courteous. Do not honk your horn for your child to come out. Walk to the other parent's door, but don't go inside unless invited. Have the children ready to go. Always be on time. Smile.

If *joint custody arrangements* are being considered, recognize that such arrangements take considerable effort by each parent. Joint custody is not likely to succeed unless all parties involved want to make it work. Here are some considerations for and against joint custody (Coller, 1988; Elkin, 1991).

CONSIDERATIONS FOR JOINT CUSTODY

- Parents are both committed to making joint custody work because of their love for their children and their desire to be involved in their children's lives.
- Parents have a good understanding of their respective roles in a joint custody plan and are willing and able to negotiate differences.

Table 14-1
Pointers for Separated and Divorced Parents

1. Tell your child, in a protective but honest way, what is happening and the plans for him or her. Then answer any questions as calmly and patiently as you can. Some questions will come immediately, others will come later. Reassure the child that it is *not* his or her fault, but a problem between the parents.

2. Provide stability, and try to keep things as much the same as possible for the child. If possible, stay in the same home, neighborhood, and school. Continue to pay special attention to comforting rituals, such as telling bedtime stories, holding special family events (such as holidays or birthdays), participating in favorite activities, playing with favorite toys, or doing other special things that will comfort the child.

3. Recognize that the child needs to respect both parents—don't criticize or berate the other parent in front of the child. Try not to argue in front of the child. This will increase the child's fears and insecurity and ultimately might affect his or her self-esteem.

4. Recognize that the child needs each parent. Don't compete for your child's affection or try to force your child to take sides. If you do, you will cause increased anxiety for the child and, eventually, you might lose your child's respect and affection.

5. Try hard to put aside personal injuries, anger, and grievances and work out with your spouse or ex-spouse reasonable flexible arrangements for custody, visitation, and support. Try to live up to your end of the bargain, even in those difficult times when you feel unsupported or when your ex-spouse is uncooperative.

6. Visitation is critical to a child. Make appropriate arrangements by considering the child's age, developmental stage, and needs. You will need to make changes as the child grows older. Regular, dependable visitation is

important if the child is to have confidence in the noncustodial parent. Thus, visitation commitments should be kept unless there is an emergency to justify cancellation. If changes are made, the parent making the changes should explain to the child the reasons for such changes. If a child refuses to go on visits or seems upset after visits, explore the reasons with him or her. Try to work out a solution or seek counseling assistance.

7. Divorce requires a substantial period of adjustment. Visitation schedules must be made considering work schedules, school and child care facilities, as well as the activities of the child.

8. The noncustodial parent should maintain regular contact with the child via the telephone when not visiting. This parent should be aware of how the child is doing in school and in after-school activities and have a sense of the child's daily life. The custodial parent should be cooperative with the noncustodial parent's access to the child. If the noncustodial parent was involved in child maltreatment, these suggestions may not be applicable.

9. Turn to your friends or family, not your children, for consolation. This is the time to use any support network you have—family, friends, or community organizations. Try to reduce your stress, as this will ease the stress on the child, too.

10. Allow the child to discuss his or her feelings. Be more sensitive to his or her behavior than you usually would be. Either being "too good" or "acting up" may be a sign that professional help is needed. Don't hesitate to get professional help for either yourself or your child. This is a difficult period, and professional support can help ease the transition. It is wiser to act preventively than to wait for acute distress.

Source: Reprinted, with changes in notation, with permission of the publisher and authors, from B. A. Weiner, V. A. Simons, and J. L. Cavanaugh, Jr. (1985). The Child Custody Dispute. In D. H. Schetky and E. P. Benedek (Eds.), *Emerging Issues in Child Psychiatry and the Law*, pp. 66–67, copyright 1985 by Brunner/Mazel.

- Parents have maintained some objectivity through the divorcing process, at least in relation to the children.
- Parents give priority to their children's needs and are willing to arrange their life styles to accommodate their children's needs.
- Parents have a reasonable level of communication, a willingness to cooperate, a firm belief that the other parent is competent, and a firm belief that the other parent is important to the child.
- Parents have the potential flexibility to make changes in the joint custody arrangement as the developmental needs of their children change.
- Parents live in close geographic proximity.
- Children prefer joint custody.

CONSIDERATIONS AGAINST JOINT CUSTODY

- One or both parents have a history of substance abuse.
- One or both parents have engaged in family violence, child abuse, or child neglect.
- One or both parents are extremely emotionally disturbed.
- Parents have shown that they disagree regarding the rearing of their children.
- Parents are unable to differentiate between their needs and the needs of their children.
- Parents live far from each other (particularly problematic when small children are involved).
- Parents constantly display overt hostility to each other.
- One or both parents do not want to participate in joint custody arrangements.

- Children are likely to be unresponsive to joint custody arrangements or to rebel against joint custody.

The following comments illustrate how some children were affected by joint custody arrangements (Ayalon & Flasher, 1993, p. 19, with changes in notation):

- Sleeping one night on the closed balcony at mother's and the next night on the couch in my father's living room.
- Having a bath at my father's and taking a shower at my mother's.
- It's sausage sandwiches for lunch at my father's and vegetarian health food at my mother's.
- On Tuesdays I do my math lessons with my father, and my history homework with my mother every Thursday.
- My problem is that my running shoes are always left behind at my mother's when I sleep at my father's, and at my father's when I sleep at my mother's!
- When I invite friends over to my house, I always have to explain whether by "my house" I mean at my mother's or my father's.

Case Illustrations

The first case illustrates how a divorce may come about (Grossman, 1986).

CASE 14-6. MRS. GREEN

It was about five years before I filed for a divorce. I knew that I was going to do it. It was just a matter of doing the specific things that I felt I should have done before.... When I first noticed that I was really unhappy with my husband was when my little one was just a baby, three or four months old. I thought "well here I am, I've got a baby, what can I do?" So I would think about it and think about it and I thought well, I really felt I owed Bobby as much of myself as I had given to John [the older child]. I felt that I should be home with him during a good portion of his formative years. But then I really didn't have any type of way to support myself because I had been to college for three years and was a drama major and then dropped out when I got married. So I didn't have a degree and really wasn't trained to do anything and I thought "Oh I have to do something to be able to support us" so I decided to go to nursing school. So I put in my application and waited a year and a half and went and got my nursing degree and then worked part time until Bobby was in kindergarten and then I filed for a divorce. So there was a lot of things—there were times within those five years when I would say "oh today wasn't so bad, I really shouldn't do this" but most of the time I knew that I was just waiting until Bobby was older and I had a career and then I would file. And that's what I did. (pp. 23–24)

The second case describes some stresses a family may experience when faced with an impending divorce (Wertlieb, 1991).

CASE 14-7. MS. M.

Ms. M. sought consultation to insure that her recent decision to divorce her husband of 15 years was the "right" one for her and her two children, ages 7 and 10. A sophisticated and educated woman, she was distraught in her understanding from the popular literature that even under the best circumstances, divorce would likely exert an untoward influence on the lives of her children. Another goal of the consultation was "damage control," how could she best minimize the risks and maximize the children's short-term and long-term adjustment.

The initial interview highlighted the uniqueness of each individual's divorce experience. The 10-year-old boy focused his concerns on missing his best friend whom he had to leave behind when the family relocated to more affordable housing several towns away from where he grew up. His anger at both parents was explicit, with part of it manifest in his refusal to get involved in his new school, as evident in his declining grades. In contrast, the younger sister spoke longingly of the lost and idealized father, often blaming the mother as the main provocateur in the continuing parental marital conflict.

Mother's sense of being abandoned and overwhelmed by these family dynamics was only accentuated by the day-to-day dread she experienced as she reentered a professional career ladder, discovering how deep and far-reaching changes in her field had been while she was off raising her family. (p. 39)

Above all, humility and caution must characterize the involvement of psychologists in custody cases. There is much we do not know, such as what is "best" for children. Our assessment tools are limited: they can neither predict the future nor substitute for the wisdom of the court.

—L. Weithorn

HOMELESS FAMILIES AND CHILDREN

Description

Homeless persons can be defined as those who lack a fixed, regular, and adequate nighttime residence (The Stewart B. McKinney Homeless Assistance Act, 1987). It is difficult to arrive at accurate estimates of how many individuals are homeless in the United States. The National Alliance to End Homelessness (1995) estimated that on any given night 750,000 Americans are homeless. The National Alliance estimated that between 1.3 million and 2 million persons will experience homelessness over the course of a year. Figure 14-1 shows the composition of the homeless population, based on a 29-city survey commissioned by the United States Conference of Mayors (1995); it includes a breakdown of the homeless population by demographic group, ethnic membership, and health factors. The survey revealed the following with respect to the homeless:

- 36.5% were families with children
- 25% were children
- 3.5% were unaccompanied youth

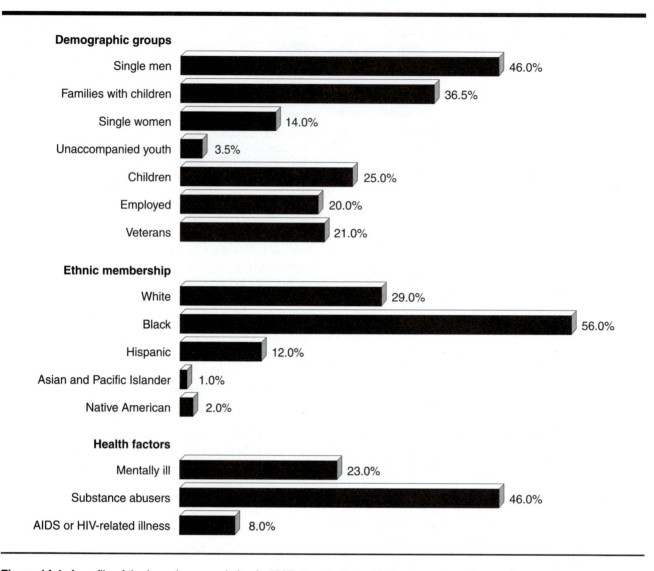

Figure 14-1. A profile of the homeless population in 1995. From the United States Conference of Mayors (1995).

Exhibit 14-3 shows some other major findings of the United States Conference of Mayors' report on hunger and homelessness in America's cities.

Mental health services may be needed by homeless families (Goodman, 1991)

because of the traumatic psychological effects produced by the experience of homelessness itself. Such effects would urgently require psychological aid.... Not to have a room of one's own is a profoundly depersonalizing experience. A home, as well as a family, friends, and work, is part of one's self-definition. Becoming homeless puts one visibly at the bottom of society. No personal touches are available to obscure the starkness of that reality. The status of homelessness severs the present from the past, marking sharp personal discontinuity; it cuts one off from contact with a previous life-style, from the resources necessary to parent one's children adequately, and from the comforting rhythms of everyday routines. Such extreme disruption can cause psychological trauma, as well as feelings of depression and hopelessness. (p. 499)

Homeless children and their parents are deprived of many of the valuable functions provided by a home (Jahiel, 1987).

It provides security against the elements and against crime. It is a place where one can rest and sleep, wash and change clothing. It gives one an address that may be essential in getting certain benefits and very helpful in securing a job. A home of one's own is a place where one can keep one's furniture and other possessions. It provides privacy. It helps in achieving the self-sufficiency that is expected of an adult in the United States. A home may also give people an opportunity to prepare their meals in an inexpensive and convenient way and to meet with friends. Students can study in the home, and some people can engage in their occupation at home. (pp. 99–100)

Homeless families. A profile of a typical homeless family in the 1990s "reveals a single mother in her late twenties or early thirties, living on welfare or minimum-wage income, with one or two small children. She is a member of a minority group, and this is her first experience of being

Exhibit 14-3
Some Major Findings of the Status Report on Hunger and Homelessness in America's Cities

- Requests for emergency shelter increased in 1995 by an average of 11%, with 63% of the cities registering an increase from 1994. Requests for shelter by homeless families alone increased by 15%, with 71% of the cities reporting an increase.

- In 1995, 19% of the requests for emergency shelter by homeless people overall and 24% of the requests by homeless families alone were unmet.

- In the survey cities, people remain homeless an average of six months; 62% of the cities said that the length of time people are homeless increased in 1995.

- During 1995, the number of emergency shelter beds increased overall in the survey cities by an average of 3% from 1994. Transitional housing units increased by an average of 6%. Single-room occupancy units increased by 5%.

- In 64% of the cities, families may have to break up in order to be sheltered. In 54% of the cities, families may have to leave the shelter in which they are staying during the day.

- Requests for assisted housing by low-income families and individuals increased in 73% of the cities from 1994 to 1995.

- Applicants must wait an average of 17 months for public housing in the survey cities.

- Any cuts in housing assistance are expected to produce several negative consequences for low-income families, including increased homelessness, longer waits for public housing, an increased gap between income and rent, increased combining of households, increased incidence of families living in substandard housing, and a reduction in available housing units.

- The survey cities expected requests for emergency food assistance and emergency shelter—by all homeless persons and by homeless families in particular—to increase in 1996.

- The survey cities painted a bleak picture of the cumulative impact of inadequate services, including welfare, Medicaid, housing assistance, the Earned Income Tax Credit, and various social services, on a typical low-income family. That picture includes increased hunger and homelessness, increased stress on families and communities, fewer available housing options, lack of jobs and job readiness, insufficient child care, and reduced social services to address the increased problems. In addition, several cities also stated that they do not believe the private sector can fill in for reduced government assistance or address the increased need for help.

Source: Adapted from the United States Conference of Mayors (1995), "A Status Report on Hunger and Homelessness in America's Cities: 1995," pp. 2–3.

---

homeless" (Seltser & Miller, 1993. p. 7). Homeless women generally face the same social and economic problems as do homeless men. However, because of the treatment of women in our society and the responsibilities of parenthood that they often bear alone, they are even more vulnerable to economic factors (Bassuk, 1993). Thus, "inadequate child-support legislation and enforcement, wage discrepancies, job discrimination, limited child-care options, and family violence render poor women and women of color more vulnerable than men to the crisis in low-income housing" (p. 345).

What leads to homelessness? The following factors may lead to homelessness (Jahiel, 1992):

- *economic factors,* such as living in a community that lacks low-cost or affordable housing, being evicted from home or apartment, or losing a job or job benefits

- *personal factors,* such as being a victim of domestic violence, breaking up a relationship, being a victim of physical or sexual abuse, running away from home, or being thrown out of one's home

- *disability factors,* such as having a substance abuse problem, having a mental disorder, or having a physical disability

- *personal choice factors,* such as liking to move around or preferring not to have a home

Extreme poverty, however, is the primary reason that families become homeless. With approximately 36 million people living below the poverty line in 1995 (or about 14% of the population), homelessness is a danger many Americans face (U.S. Bureau of the Census, 1996a). In 1995, approximately 7.5 million families (or about 11% of all families) were below the poverty level. When a family becomes homeless, it likely has exhausted its financial resources. Although many homeless families receive federal and state aid benefits—such as Aid to Families with Dependent Children (AFDC), Special Supplemental Food Program for Women, Infants, and Children (WIC), and food stamps—these benefits are inadequate (Rafferty & Shinn, 1991). Homeless families also likely have used up the social support they had available from family and friends, making life on the streets the only possibility left (Shinn, Knickman, & Weitzman, 1991).

Here is a description of how families may become homeless (Seltser & Miller, 1993):

Families who become homeless have few resources for buffering their descent onto the streets. They may stay with relatives for a few nights or attempt to borrow money from friends, but these are temporary solutions to a more fundamental problem. With no place to go, a mother bundles her children into their last refuge, a dilapidated car, and here they spend a few uncomfortable nights.

Alternatively, they may make their way to an inexpensive motel where they can pay by the day or week. But because such accommodations seldom have cooking facilities, the family is forced to eat in fast-food restaurants, and very quickly they are penniless. It is at this point that the reality of their situation becomes uncomfortably clear, and if this mother and her children are fortunate, someone refers them to a shelter, which hopefully has room to accommodate them. (pp. 8–9)

Emergency housing and nutrition. The housing options available to homeless families depend on the city and state where the families are located. Emergency shelters in many areas allow homeless people to remain inside during the night, but everyone usually must go outside for some time during the day. This practice exposes homeless children and adults to inclement weather, and, all too frequently, they are not adequately clothed for severe weather conditions. Food served at these facilities may be minimally adequate. During

the night, men are often separated from women and children. Individuals in shelters usually are accommodated in large rooms containing many beds, making any type of privacy impossible (Rafferty & Shinn, 1991). At the end of their stay, they may become understandably bitter if they are sent back to the streets without permanent housing. Exhibit 14-4 describes what it is like to enter a shelter.

Some homeless families prefer to live on the streets rather than go to shelters (Jahiel, 1987).

The streets and parks have their own dangers...but they allow some measure of choice and of control over one's environment. It is possible to choose one's place to sleep where it seems to be safest and to move away when danger appears to be imminent. One can also have a personal space and a measure of privacy that does not exist in many shelters. There is also proximity with other people who are not homeless in contrast with the ghettoized environment of the shelter, which results from the fact that all guests are homeless.

Exhibit 14-4
A Description of What It Is Like to Enter a Shelter

Arriving at the shelter is usually traumatic [for families], even if an opening has already been secured. In spite of the best efforts of shelter staff, these families are coming into a strange and frightening situation, exhausted (and often dirty) from their experiences of the previous few days and surrounded suddenly by people who may appear very different and even intimidating. The check-in areas of these shelters are often crowded and noisy; there are papers to be completed, questions to be answered, rules to be learned, and schedules to be followed. For a disoriented and depressed adult with small children, the first contact with the shelter is usually a very mixed blessing.

However, the other side of the story is equally important. People who arrive at these shelters have been living confusing and often terrifying lives in the immediate past. They have worried about whether they will be able to find a safe place for their children, and many of them are worried that they will actually have their children taken away from them by state authorities. They have usually been looking for a stable residence for days or weeks, often calling shelters to see if there are openings. They are almost always at the end of

their rope, feeling abandoned by family, friends, and society.

In addition, picture their specific living conditions before entering the shelter. In the best of cases, they have been sleeping in small and dingy apartments or motels or sharing crowded living quarters with distant relatives or acquaintances. For others, the past weeks have involved sleeping in cars, on park benches, or on the beach, huddled together for warmth and afraid of being robbed or attacked by passersby. They have usually been bounced around from agency to agency, from advisor to advisor, with little time to reflect on what is happening and even less reason to believe that their situation will improve.

In this context, shelters are a welcome relief from the radical insecurity and terror. The sense of relief is reinforced by the often-friendly voices and faces of the shelter workers, who seem to try to make them feel as welcome as possible. The families arrive, bringing whatever belongings they may have dragged with them across the city, and are provided with necessities that most of us take for granted: a room, a bed, a shower, a meal. Most striking of all, they are told that they do not have to leave

the next day; in most shelters in Los Angeles residents are allowed to stay for one or two months.

It would be hard to indicate how relieved and grateful these people are upon arriving at the shelter. However small their rooms and however limited their privacy, however patronizing and controlling the manner of their treatment, they have been taken into a place that is there for them, which promises to provide their children some respite from the streets, and which will allow them to stay for longer than a day or two. It is small wonder that the shelters are perceived as lifesavers and that these people are eager to stay as long as they can.

Arriving at a shelter represents both success and failure, however. Denial is no longer possible; like the alcoholic forced to stand up and confess "I am an alcoholic," each person now is homeless by definition, living in a shelter with other homeless people. In addition, however friendly and supportive the staff may be, they are explicitly caretakers, counselors, or custodians—people paid to look after, to provide assistance. No one can enter a shelter and fail to appreciate the striking loss of autonomy that suddenly becomes so apparent.

Source: Reprinted with permission of the authors and publisher from B. J. Seltser and D. E. Miller, *Homeless Families: The Struggle for Dignity,* copyright 1993 by University of Illinois Press, pp. 50–51.

Some people are unable to accept the regimentation and institutional aspects of some shelters. For these reasons, many people prefer the streets, parks, benches, or public places to shelters. (p. 107)

Homeless families do not fare much better even if they are fortunate enough to get longer-term housing. These facilities usually are in old hotels, subsidized by government agencies, and often lack refrigerators and stoves, thereby preventing families from cooking less-expensive meals. Families still face hunger even if they are in longer-term accommodations (Rafferty & Shinn, 1991).

The ache for home lives in all of us, the safe place where we can go and not be questioned.

—Maya Angelou

Parental stressors that affect children. Homeless parents spend most of their time and energy trying to obtain food and shelter for themselves and their children. The psychological trauma caused by loss of social support and loss of personal control over their lives can lead to severe stress (Goodman, Saxe & Harvey, 1991). Parents thus have difficulty alleviating the despair and confusion their children may have. Homelessness can disrupt normal relationships between parents and children and exacerbate minor problems that children and their parents might have (Rafferty & Shinn, 1991).

The following portrait of homeless mothers offers insight into why they may have problems raising their children (Bassuk & Weinreb, 1994):

Homeless mothers suffer from every problem specific to their gender and race. The difficulties they experience mirror those of low-income women, but with greater intensity and frequency. Many homeless women have inadequate earning power, poor education, and overwhelming childcare responsibilities. While in shelters, mothers often spend 24 hours a day with their children, sleeping in the same room with the whole family. An alarming number of homeless mothers have other difficulties as well. [They may have been physically or sexually abused at some point in their lives and also have psychiatric and substance abuse problems.]…

At best, life for a homeless family is fraught with peril. Mothers frequently have little energy left to respond adequately to their children's distress and increased neediness. In turn, the children must muster any resources they have and, to a greater degree than usual, fend for themselves. This pattern often sets up a cycle that is harmful both to the individuals and to the mother-child interaction.…

In some states, the mere fact of homelessness is cause to investigate the mother for neglect and to place the children in foster care; the parents are told that, once they have found decent housing, their children will be returned.… Once a mother has lost her child to foster care, she may become ineligible for welfare benefits and food stamps, further decreasing her chances of reuniting her family.… Many mothers never regain custody of their children. (pp. 41–42)

When mothers living in a shelter were asked about their concerns, here are some things they said about their children (Hodnicki & Horner, 1993, pp. 352–354):

1. *Sacrificing for children.* Mothers may be willing to do whatever is necessary to help their children.

- The children are depending on me.
- The only thing I can think of is my kids. I don't have much to say about myself, just my kids.
- I look out more for them than I do for myself because they are number one.

2. *Struggling with limitations.* Mothers may be struggling to provide needed resources for their families.

- By the time you get to see him (a doctor), you have to treat it yourself.
- I pray every night that I will keep my health.
- I don't have the money for health care.
- I try to keep the cold away.
- You have to go to the welfare office and be turned down or get a Medicaid card and then you have to wait on an appointment and it might take months to get in there [health clinic].
- I wouldn't apply [for help]. For just the little things that they give you it is just not worth the trouble. I don't want to be on welfare, period.

3. *Guarding children from harm.* Mothers may be trying to protect their children from danger and from becoming depressed.

- I've got to get my children out of here. I can't have my children in this environment much longer.
- I have to try to make him [son] as happy as I can. I can't fool him no way. He don't like it here. He says, "I don't like it here, no, it's not home, it don't feel like home."

4. *Seeking answers.* Mothers may be trying to cope with homelessness while struggling to become independent.

- I have my kids standing there wondering what is going to happen.
- You can only do so much for such a long time and then after you see that there is no way [it will work out soon], you just live day-to-day.
- It's not really a life [in the shelter], it's just a spot they put you in and that's where you stay.
- You just have to hang in there and help yourself. You have to take [it] a step at a time.

To be rooted is perhaps the most important and least recognized need of the human soul. It is one of the hardest to define.

—Simone Weil

Stresses faced by homeless children living with their parents. Homeless children who live in emergency shelter facilities with their families often suffer from health problems, hunger and poor nutrition, psychological problems, and educational difficulties (Rafferty & Shinn, 1991; also see Exhibit 14-5).

1. *Health problems.* When the mother is homeless during pregnancy, the risk of health problems to the infant

Exhibit 14-5
A Portrait of Bill, a Homeless Child

As morning arrived, Bill Smith, 6 years of age, stirred, homeless and hungry on the floor of a church basement. His two younger sisters slept nearby. Face flat on two inches of foam rubber that separated him from the cold concrete, Bill peeled his eyelids open and, from his peculiar vantage point, glumly watched the usual morning procession. Feet—grimy feet, bare feet, feet in worn-out sneakers, run-over flats, and ragged sandals—shuffled past his face as the 50 or so women who had also slept in the basement the night before arose from their makeshift beds. Almost in slow motion, battered souls gathered the meager snatchings of their lives into garbage bags and backpacks and prepared for another day of homelessness.

Bill dragged his small frame up on one elbow. He looked tired and lost. The acrid smell of bodies wafted up around him. He rubbed his faded blue eyes as though that might magically change the picture. Bill had lived like this for three months. This, however, was a good day. Today, Bill would get to wear his "new" Ninja Turtle sneakers. They were actually obtained from the pile of donated used clothing in a corner. But Bill had proclaimed them new, so everybody agreed that they were. He got up, stuffed sockless feet into the shoes, and pulled on a shirt from the donation pile to match the pants he had slept in that night. Then, off to school he went.

Poverty had taken its toll. Bill is a cute kid, good-looking enough to fit right into a television commercial, but his health is precarious. Numerous black cavities dot his teeth. He is bright, his teachers say, but also an emotionally ravaged child prone to mercurial mood swings. One moment, he is cheerful. Seconds later, he is enveloped by intense anger, sadness, or tears. Particularly painful questions are met with blank stares and nonanswers about ghosts or Peter Pan. Or, he says "I killed the giant and then I ate him. I killed the skeleton." In his quieter moments, he appears worn, tired, blank—the glow of childhood shining ever so dimly. "He's like a toy that has something broken inside," says one of his kindergarten teachers. At school his hair is uncombed, his face is unwashed, and his pants are on backwards. "I don't have on any underwear," he says as though to explain his pants. He yawns incessantly in class. "I feel bad for this boy," says his teacher. "Sometimes his hair isn't combed. I keep an extra comb in here just for him. I comb his hair and wash his face." Most telling, she says, is one of Bill's most persistent habits. "He wants to save anything that you use," she says. "Bill wants to save the paper cups, paper napkins, paper towels. I have to tell him 'No, we don't save those.' But he wants to save them anyway. He doesn't want to throw anything away."

His family moved to a different part of town to live with a relative. Bill became more withdrawn, more distant. Things have changed again for him. His schooling has been disrupted. What little routine there was has disappeared. There are no daily meals, no television, no telephone, no other children to play with.

What the future will bring is unknown, but it does look brighter. His mother plans to marry, she has a job, they have rented an apartment, and there is food at home.

Note. Name has been changed.
Source: Adapted from Harris (1991).

begins even before birth. Infants born to mothers who are homeless have lower birthweights and higher infant mortality rates than infants born to mothers who are not homeless. As infants, they may have limited opportunity for exploration and interactive play, may not receive immunizations, and may be prone to upper respiratory infections, asthma, ear infections, and gastrointestinal disorders; generally, they are at risk for poor health.

2. *Hunger and poor nutrition.* Homeless children are more likely than other children to be malnourished because of a decrease in both the quantity and the quality of their food intake.

3. *Psychological problems.* Homeless preschool children may have developmental problems, such as short attention span, withdrawal, aggressive behavior, speech delays, sleep difficulties, interpersonal difficulties, and motor delays. Homeless elementary school–aged children may have such problems as depression, anxiety, and behavioral difficulties. Homelessness may lead children to mistrust others and to feel apathy and despair.

4. *Educational difficulties.* Homeless children often have educational difficulties for the following reasons. First, they may be hungry and tired, which interferes with their ability to concentrate at school. Second, because shelters usually are in locations away from their original residence, homeless children often are required to leave their neighborhood school. Third, homeless families may have to move from one shelter to another, again requiring a change in schools and preventing children from establishing meaningful relationships with peers and teachers. A homeless mother described why her 8-year-old daughter was in special education: "I think what she really needs is to stop going to a different school every month. She didn't have this 'learning disability' before we lost our home. What she really needs is a permanent home and extra help with her reading and math" (Rafferty & Rollins, 1989, p. i). Homeless children obtain scores on mathematics and reading tests that are, on the average, up to 14 months below their chronological age (Masten, 1992). They also are more likely than other children to repeat a grade or be placed in special education

classes. Finally, they may not attend school regularly or go to school at all.

Here is a description of what it may be like for children to enter a shelter with their family (Masten, 1992):

> By the time they arrive in a shelter, children may have experienced many chronic adversities and traumatic events. More immediately, children may have gone hungry and lost friends, possessions, and the security of familiar places and people at home, at school, or in the neighborhood. Children perceive the strain of frightened parents who do not know what is going to happen. Shelters, which may provide for basic needs of housing, food, and clothing, can be very stressful for parents and children. Locations are usually undesirable, particularly with respect to children playing outside. Moreover, necessary shelter rules may strain child and family life. For example, it is typical for no visitors to be allowed and for children, including adolescents, always to be required to be accompanied by a parent. Some shelters separate fathers and adolescent males from the rest of their families. Children also may be humiliated by other children at school or on the bus knowing where they live. Health care, education, and other services may be difficult to access. (p. 42)

The effects of homelessness on children during their formative years are devastating and long lasting. Without attention to eliminating homelessness, many more children and their families will be caught in the tragedy of homelessness and its intergenerational devastation.

—Ellen L. Bassuk and Linda Weinreb

Homeless adolescents on their own.   The experiences of homeless adolescents living on their own are different from those of homeless children who remain with their parents (Rotheram-Borus, Koopman, & Ehrhardt, 1991). Many homeless adolescents come from dysfunctional families or from families in which they have been victims of abuse or neglect. Often, the youths are estranged from their parents. There may be conflicts over school, sexual activity, pregnancy, or alcohol and drug use. They are more likely than nonhomeless youths to come from a single-parent family or to have no parental figure at all in their upbringing. Dysfunctional families are particularly vulnerable to breakdown during times of economic stress. The parents of homeless youths tend to be alcoholics, drug addicts, or convicted criminals; ill or injured; welfare mothers; or recently unemployed. Family changes occurring just before adolescents become homeless include the marriage of a parent, a change of residence, or entering a new school. Homeless adolescents include *runaways,* who have left home without parental consent; *throwaways,* who have been thrown out of their home; *system kids,* who leave social service placements; and *street adolescents,* who have left home with the knowledge of their parents or guardians.

Homeless adolescents face several dangers, including being physically assaulted, sexually assaulted, or robbed (Rotheram-Borus et al., 1991). Many homeless adolescents

do not attend school, and many of those in school have learning problems or conduct problems. In comparison to other adolescents of their age, homeless adolescents have more psychological problems, make more suicide attempts, and experience more depression. For babies of homeless teenagers, birthweights are likely to be low, and infant mortality rates are high.

Because homeless adolescents often have difficulty meeting their basic needs, they may become involved in illegal and dangerous activities, such as drug dealing and prostitution. These activities place them at high risk for hepatitis and HIV infection. Many homeless adolescents have suffered sexual abuse, and many abuse drugs. In comparison to nonhomeless adolescents, they have more sexual partners and a higher incidence of sexually transmitted disease. Their teenage pregnancy rate is higher than that of nonhomeless youths (14% versus 1% for females aged 13 to 15 years) (Kiesler, 1991). The average age at which homeless adolescents begin sexual activities is two years younger than the average age for nonhomeless adolescents (12.5 years versus 14.5 years) (Rotheram-Borus et al., 1991). HIV intervention programs will be difficult to carry out when homeless youths have thoughts similar to those expressed by this adolescent: "Why should I care about dying 10 years from now when I do not know where I will sleep and how I will get food tomorrow?" (Rotheram-Borus et al., 1991, p. 1191).

We must accurately perceive the root causes of youth homelessness and not solely attack the symptoms or coping mechanisms of these victimized youth. Importantly, we must view youth homelessness as a social problem, not as an individual problem presented by a number of troubled youth.

—Chicago Coalition for the Homeless

Interviewing Issues

Consider the following points when you interview homeless families and adolescents:

- Homeless families likely have suffered many negative life events in recent months. Parents are likely to suffer from posttraumatic stress disorder (see Chapter 11), and their children are likely to be depressed and anxious (see Chapter 11).
- Many families will be suspicious of your intentions. They may believe that the social service agency is trying to find a reason to deny them shelter or federal or state funds or even trying to take their children away.
- There may be no opportunity for privacy at the shelter facilities, and many families will not cooperate with you unless they have privacy; thus, you will need to find a suitable location to conduct the interview.
- Structure the interview so that it is sensitive to the family members' situation. Do not let your questions diminish

their pride and dignity. Especially avoid any questions that may seem judgmental about their condition.

- Choose the time of the interview carefully so that there is no conflict with shelter curfews. If you conduct the interview away from the shelter, leave sufficient time to allow the family to reach the shelter before it closes its doors for the night.

Tables F-15 and F-41 in Appendix F present semistructured interview questions for homeless children and for homeless parents, respectively. Use these questions with those in the general semistructured interviews for children (Table F-13 in Appendix F) and for parents (Table F-36 in Appendix F).

Homelessness and hunger exist in the face of abundance. Therein lies the outrage.

—Graffito on the sidewalk of East 10th Street in New York City, October 1990 (Cited by René I. Jahiel)

Interventions

The problems faced by homeless children affect their normal development and, therefore, their future success. Making emergency shelter facilities more sensitive to the needs of the homeless could alleviate some of the problems homeless families face. Keeping families together instead of separating men from women and children would reduce the sense of dislocation experienced by many families. Allowing families to remain inside the building during cold winter months might help prevent children from developing upper respiratory infections and other diseases. Avoiding the constant relocation of families would allow children to remain in a single school, thereby helping them gain a sense of security and stability amid the chaos they experience daily. Finally, providing counseling and job placement services would help families psychologically and financially.

In 1987, Congress passed the Stewart B. McKinney Homeless Assistance Act to coordinate the efforts of agencies helping the homeless and to provide additional funds to help the homeless population. The act requires that each state ensure proper public education for homeless children. This provision is important, as homeless children usually miss a great deal of school and are discriminated against because they lack fixed residences. Most importantly, this act recognized the existence of homeless families and the need to help them.

Kondratas (1991) observed that "In a country as rich as the United States, [homelessness] is a manageable problem, even though it is also a disgrace, a national shame, an unforgivable waste of human resources, and an affront to human dignity" (p. 1227). The cost of preventing homelessness and of increasing the quality of life for poor children will be much lower than the future "costs of neglecting children's needs" (Rafferty & Shinn, 1991, p. 1176).

Case Illustrations

The following four cases illustrate how homelessness may develop and some consequences associated with homelessness. The first case describes the events leading to a family's seeking emergency shelter (Maza & Hall, 1988).

CASE 14-8. JIM AND SANDRA'S FAMILY

Jim, Sandra, and their three children under age six were on their way to California from Illinois. Jim had lost his job. Unable to pay the rent, the family was evicted. They moved in with Sandra's mother, who lived in a one-bedroom apartment in a public housing project. The only source of income was Sandra's mother's social security check. Although Sandra's mother loved the children very much, she became nervous around them in the small apartment and disapproved of Jim and Sandra's parenting. Sandra described several heated arguments with her mother. The manager of the public housing project was threatening to evict the family because there were too many people in the small apartment. (p. 9, with changes in notation)

The next case illustrates some problems that homeless children living with their parents may have (Maza & Hall, 1988).

CASE 14-9. MARIA

Maria and her five children, all under ten years old, arrived in Washington, D.C. from Florida. She had been unemployed since the birth of her last child. Since her parents were deceased she had come to Washington to seek help from her former husband's family, but they were unwilling to help her out. Her ten-year-old son was angry and twice agency staff had to stop him from hitting another child in the waiting area. He was a year behind in school and he and his two sisters had already missed 20 days of school this term. The four-year-old was sucking his thumb and clinging to a stuffed bear. The eight-year-old kept asking when they were going to eat. The family had not eaten in 24 hours. (p. 19)

The following two cases depict situations that led adolescents to become homeless (Caton, 1990).

CASE 14-10. RICHARD

Richard is a 16½-year-old Texas-born Hispanic American who was experiencing his first shelter admission, though his first runaway episode was at age 14. He has a history of many different living arrangements in both family and institutional settings, including a group home, a residential school, and a detention center. Most recently, he was living with his grandfather because he does not get along with his mother. Richard went to a youth shelter when his grandfather decided to return to Puerto Rico.

Richard has a long history of antisocial behavior, including car theft and vandalism. He also has a history of heavy alcohol use, during which he drank daily, beginning in the morning. However, he denies that alcohol is a problem now. Other than a girlfriend whom he met while in a group, Richard says that he has no close friends. He admits to being depressed occasionally, but never for more than three days at a time. Richard has thoughts about suicide, but he has never planned it in any way. Despite the unhappiness he has experienced, he is very concerned about making something of himself. His standard reading score is above average, and he says that he likes school and wants to attend college to study computer technology. (p. 57, with changes in notation)

CASE 14-11. DONNA

Donna is an attractive, pleasant 16-year-old who ran away from her parents' home because she was afraid of what her father's response would be when he learned that she was pregnant. This was her second runaway episode. She ran away two years previously when her father made unwanted sexual demands on her while he was intoxicated. As Donna expected that her father would behave violently when he found out about her pregnancy, she went to a youth shelter.

Donna was calm while reporting the details of her history. She said that her best friend was the 21-year-old boyfriend who was the father of her baby. She had seen him twice since she was admitted to the youth shelter.

Donna was well organized in her thinking. She is a good tenth-grade student with reading scores just under twelfth-grade level. Her only noticeable impairment in functioning during the past three months was related to her concerns over her pregnancy and her father's reaction to it. She wants to be sent to a maternity shelter, have her baby, and hopefully go on to finish high school and attend college. She would like to become a social worker, because "I know what I've been through and it would be very interesting to help others with these problems." (pp. 57–58, with changes in notation)

The homeless need to feel that they have dignity, just as the rest of us need to believe that the existence of homelessness does not undermine our moral standing as a people who care about each other. Although their struggle is the harsher one, ours may be equally important, for the answers we find will help define the nature and tone of our national moral sensibility. If we cannot commit ourselves to preventing homelessness, we can at least commit ourselves to recognizing that homeless people are like us in many ways and to acknowledging that our own autonomy can lead us to the sense of solidarity they so desperately seek with us.

—Barry Jay Seltser and Donald E. Miller

THINKING THROUGH THE ISSUES

Do you know of any child who has been adopted? If so, were there any difficulties associated with the adoption or with the child's adjustment to the adopted family?

Why do you think families are willing to adopt a child with a disability?

What are your thoughts about interracial adoptions? Should interracial adoptions be prohibited, encouraged, or simply accepted like any other adoption? In arriving at your answer, consider such issues as the following: (a) Is giving a minority child a loving and caring White family better than

leaving the minority child in a foster home? (b) Do interracial adoptions destroy the racial and cultural identity of minority children? (c) Are the problems of racially blended families daunting and almost impossible to overcome?

What is your opinion of allowing single adults, same-sex couples, or adults with disabilities to adopt children? What are the reasons for your answer?

What do you think about divorce? Are laws that permit divorce too liberal?

Were your parents divorced? If so, what was the experience like for you and the other members of your immediate family?

How many of your close friends come from a family in which there was a divorce? How has the experience affected them?

What are the obligations of our society to provide for the needs of its citizens who cannot find a job or provide for the basic necessities of living?

How can society protect those who can't protect themselves without subverting personal responsibility and initiative?

Does psychotherapy have any role in helping homeless children and their families? What role would this be, and what is the reason for your answer?

SUMMARY

Adoption

1. There is no one profile of who is likely to adopt a child.
2. Making a careful assessment of the prospective adoptive individual or couple (usually called an adoptive home study) is a key task in the adoptive placement.
3. An individual or couple seeking to adopt a child has several options, including contacting a public agency, contacting a private agency, and working through a physician or a lawyer independently to obtain a child.
4. Four phases characterize the adoption process: the uncertainty phase, the adoption phase, the post-adoption phase, and the integration phase.
5. Both normal children and children with special needs may be placed for adoption.
6. Sometimes the adoptive parent–child relationship fails when the children have a history of severe deprivation and multiple placements, are unable to form a bond with the adoptive family, have a conduct disorder, have been removed from a successful long-term placement with foster parents, have retained strong emotional ties to members of the birth family or the foster family, or have personality and temperament traits that interfere with their ability to adjust to the new family.
7. In transracial adoptions or transcultural adoptions, families will need to face additional issues. These issues include how to help the children maintain a sense of their cultural heritage and how to cope with the treatment they may receive from society—issues that may surface especially when the children reach adolescence.
8. The interview with prospective adoptive parents (and family), as part of the home study, is different from an interview in a

mental health facility in that there is no presenting problem and there is no identified patient.

9. In the interview, focus on how the adoption will affect the family and how the family members may cope with a new member.

10. An indirect goal of the initial assessment interview is to have the family come to a better understanding of its strengths and weaknesses, recognize what kind of child would best fit into the family, and make the appropriate decision about whether to go ahead with plans for adoption.

11. Prospective adoptive parents who have various psychological disorders or personality dispositions, such as impulse control disorders, major unresolved issues in personal history, a history of certain crimes, extremely rigid moral or religious beliefs, significant problems in child rearing, strong needs and unrealistic expectations, a history of mental illness or substance abuse, a history of domestic violence, or a history of child maltreatment, usually will not be eligible for adopting a child.

12. Interviews with the child and parents may be held after the adoption has been completed if there are difficulties with the placement.

13. Adoptive families must recognize that adoption makes a difference and that the parents are entitled both legally and emotionally to be parents.

14. Even before the adoption takes place, human service workers can help prospective parents by offering adoption preparation classes.

15. Families that adopt children with special needs will probably need ongoing services.

Divorce and Custody Evaluations

16. About 40% of children in the United States will spend part of their childhood living with one parent because of divorce.

17. Divorce may lead to changes in the family and cause stress, trauma, and disorganization for the parents and children.

18. Children facing divorce in their family may have to deal with parental conflict, feelings of anger, issues involving separation from and identification with parents, and perhaps even issues of gender identity.

19. Divorce may reduce stress on the parents and children and promote feelings of self-worth, independence, and autonomy in one or both parents.

20. Divorce is best seen as a marker event—that is, the divorce itself is the culmination of the series of events that preceded it.

21. Children may go through five stages—denial, anger and guilt, bargaining, depression and frustration, and acceptance—in adjusting to their parents' divorce, although not all children will go through every stage.

22. Children's age, coping skills, temperament, personality, and level of adjustment will affect their reactions to the divorce.

23. Every child will react to the divorce in her or his unique way.

24. The emotional and behavioral responses of preschool children to divorce may include guilt, fear of abandonment, sadness, clinging, eating and sleeping problems, anxiety, bewilderment, and regressive behavior.

25. The emotional and behavioral responses of children between 6 and 8 years of age to divorce may include sadness, grief reactions, guilt, anxiety, yearning for the return of the departed parent, fear of abandonment, and loyalty conflicts.

26. The emotional and behavioral responses of children between 9 and 12 years of age to divorce may include sadness, anger, guilt, hostility, and loyalty conflicts.

27. The emotional and behavioral responses of children 12 years of age and older to divorce may include sadness, anger, guilt, anxiety, hostility, and loyalty conflicts.

28. If there is heightened conflict between the parents—such as frequent episodes of interparental conflict and intense forms of marital conflict—children may have increased adjustment problems.

29. A poor relationship between children and the custodial parent or between children and the noncustodial parent often will lead to adjustment problems in children.

30. Unstable household routines may interfere with children's adjustment to divorce.

31. Siblings who share experiences and confide in one another are in a good position to help each other cope with the stress of a divorce.

32. Children are likely to have more adjustment problems in cases of divorce when the custodial parent is not functioning well and is under considerable stress.

33. Children often have adjustment problems in cases of divorce when they live in a single-parent family that has experienced a severe drop in income.

34. Research on the effects of divorce on children suggests that children of divorce are not a homogeneous group; the differences between children of divorced and nondivorced families are small; the differences between children whose parents have divorced and those whose parents have not divorced can be attributed to paternal absence, family dysfunction, and economic deprivation rather than to divorce per se; and unhappy, conflict-ridden two-parent homes are more harmful to children than are stable single-parent homes.

35. Parents who get divorced may have a sense of failure; may anticipate negative reactions from children, friends, relatives, and others; may make changes in life style; may feel guilty about spending less time with their children; may have anxiety about greater household disorder, poorly enforced discipline, and difficulty enforcing household routines; may make changes in friendship patterns and lose support from friendship networks; and may feel abandoned, with associated feelings of helplessness, reduced self-esteem, anger, and worry about how the children will be affected by the divorce.

36. Once parents realize that the marriage is disintegrating, they may discuss the situation with each other and with the children, seek counseling, consult an attorney, or consult clergy for advice.

37. Parents undergoing a divorce may have several concerns about their children, including whether their children will be emotionally damaged by the divorce, whether their children can cope with the divorce, and whether there is anything they can do to protect the children against the stresses and strains of the divorce.

38. In most divorces, mothers are awarded physical or residential custody of the children.

39. If you are asked to perform a custody evaluation, you usually will give your recommendation to the court.

40. A judge may rely on your opinion, but the final decision regarding custody and other legal determinations will be made solely by the court.

41. If a court order identifies you as an expert whose role is to assist the court, you may have quasi-judicial immunity.

42. You always should represent the best interests of the child, no matter who is paying for your services.

43. The child and the parents must know that you will share the information with the court and that nothing is "off the record."

44. Custody evaluations are performed within the legal adversarial system rather than within the mental health system.

45. In custody disputes, the court will give more weight to the preferences of older children than to those of younger ones.

46. When there is contention over custody or visitation, there is a potential for violent behavior by some family members directed at other family members and at the mental health professional, if one is involved in the case.

47. In custody disputes, it is critical that mental health professionals show the family members that they recognize the dignity of each family member and that they are following the ethical standards of their profession.

48. In child custody disputes, a thorough evaluation will include interviewing the parents (both separately and together), the child, each parent and the child together, and significant people in the child's life and observing the child in the home, school, and other settings, as appropriate.

49. Conducting a joint interview in a custody dispute will require much care; it is an evaluation tool, not a mediation or an opportunity for marriage counseling.

50. In arriving at a recommendation for custody arrangements, look at the entire case study.

51. Custody of the child is likely to be given to the parent who fosters visitation rights and cooperates with the other parent; maintains the best continuity of the child's contacts with relatives, friends, neighborhood, schools, and so forth; has the best child-rearing skills; shows the greater humanity, consistency, and flexibility in handling the child; is the one to whom the child is most deeply attached; is mentally healthy; has a good health history; has concern for conventional cultural values, such as a good education and religious and moral training; has the capacity to facilitate the child's growth; and has the financial resources to take care of the child.

52. When the parents divorce, children may face several tasks, such as acknowledging the reality of the marital rupture, disengaging from parental conflict and distress and resuming customary pursuits, resolving the loss, resolving anger and self-blame, accepting the permanence of the divorce, and achieving realistic hope regarding relationships.

53. Encourage the parents to work cooperatively for the benefit of the child.

54. If joint custody arrangements are being considered, recognize that such arrangements take considerable effort by each parent.

Homeless Families and Children

55. Homeless persons can be defined as those who lack a fixed, regular, and adequate nighttime residence. The National Alliance to End Homelessness estimated that in 1995 on any given night about 750,000 Americans were homeless. The National Alliance estimated that between 1.3 million and 2 million persons will experience homelessness over the course of a year.

56. In the homeless population in 1995, it was estimated that 36.5% were families with children, 25% were children, and 3.5% were unaccompanied youth.

57. Extreme poverty is the primary reason that families become homeless.

58. The housing options available to homeless families depend on the city and state where the families are located.

59. Homeless parents spend most of their time and energy trying to obtain food and shelter for themselves and their children.

60. The psychological trauma caused by loss of social support and loss of personal control over their lives can lead to severe stress in homeless individuals.

61. Homeless children who live in emergency shelter facilities with their families often suffer from health problems, hunger and poor nutrition, psychological problems, and educational difficulties.

62. Many homeless adolescents come from dysfunctional families or from families in which they have been victims of abuse or neglect; often, the adolescents are estranged from their parents.

63. Homeless adolescents face several dangers, including being physically assaulted, sexually assaulted, or robbed.

64. Because homeless adolescents often have difficulty meeting their basic needs, they may become involved in illegal and dangerous activities, such as drug dealing and prostitution. These activities place them at high risk for hepatitis and HIV infection.

65. Structure the interview of homeless families and youths so that it is sensitive to the family members' situation. Do not let your questions diminish their pride and dignity. Especially avoid any questions that may seem judgmental about their condition.

66. It would be helpful to homeless families and children if emergency shelter facilities were more sensitive to their needs, if families were kept together, if they were allowed to remain inside the shelter during cold winter months, if they were not required to constantly relocate and thus children could remain in a single school, and if the adults in the family were provided with counseling and job placement services.

KEY TERMS, CONCEPTS, AND NAMES

STUDY QUESTIONS

1. Discuss adoption. Include in your discussion assessment considerations, stages of the adoption process, reasons why the adoption may fail, interviewing issues, and intervention considerations with adoptive families.

2. Discuss divorce as it relates to children and families. Include in your discussion the divorce process, stages of children's adjustment to divorce, how divorce may affect children, how divorce may affect parents, and how divorce may affect the parent-child relationship.

3. Discuss custody evaluations. Include in your discussion the role of mental health professionals in the custody evaluation, the needs of the court in arriving at an appropriate decision, interviewing considerations, evaluating the results of the child custody evaluation, and interventions.

4. Discuss homelessness as it affects children and their families. Include in your discussion a description of homelessness, the role of the mental health professional in helping homeless adolescents and their families, factors that lead to homelessness, stresses faced by homeless parents that affect their children, stresses faced by homeless children living with their parents, homeless adolescents living on their own, interview considerations, and interventions.

SECTION IV

APPLYING PRINCIPLES AND TECHNIQUES OF INTERVIEWING TO THE PEDIATRIC FIELD

Section IV focuses on children with a medical illness and on families in which there is a medically ill member. Medical illnesses range from mild conditions to chronic, severe, unrelenting, and progressive conditions. Obviously, the types of psychosocial interventions needed by children and families with a medically ill member will vary depending on the type of illness, the age of the ill member, the composition of the family, the resources of the family, the availability of services, and other similar factors. Even healthy children will be affected when a family member becomes ill. This section provides information about several major medical conditions in children. For medical conditions not covered in this section and for more detailed information about the conditions covered in the section, consult appropriate sources.

Chapter 15 introduces the field of behavioral medicine and provides some background considerations relevant to interviewing. Chapter 16 presents considerations for interviewing medically ill children and their families in clinical and hospital settings. Chapters 17 and 18 focus on some major childhood illnesses and conditions, including asthma, diabetes, cancer, HIV infection, headaches, failure to thrive, sleep disorders, substance abuse, and eating disorders. Chapter 19 discusses children with brain injury.

All medical illnesses (or conditions) in children have psychosocial components involving the child, the immediate family, the extended family, and the community. In some illnesses such as pediatric cancer and HIV infection, psychosocial problems, when they develop, may be related directly to the stress brought on by the illness. In other illnesses such as sleep disorders, eating disorders, and substance abuse, psychosocial problems may be key factors in the development of the illness or condition. But even in the latter illnesses, stress also may develop as a reaction to the condition.

Three key concepts run through the chapters in this section: *coping, adherence,* and *stress.* These concepts are central to understanding the psychosocial factors involved in medical illnesses. How children cope with medical illness, how they adhere to treatment regimens, and how they deal with stress will likely depend on the type of illness, their personality and temperament, their family, the health care provider team, and related factors. To understand coping behavior, adherence behavior, and stress reactions, you will need to use an approach that acknowledges the interaction of several psychosocial factors. The family systems approach discussed in Chapter 1 will be particularly helpful.

Information about medical illnesses and their treatments is constantly changing. Therefore, you will need to keep abreast of current treatment and diagnostic procedures for the medical illnesses that you deal with in your work. This recommendation holds for both medical illnesses and psychological disorders.

15

CHILDREN WITH HEALTH-RELATED DISORDERS: AN OVERVIEW

It is more important to know what sort of patient has a disease than what sort of disease a patient has.

—Sir William Osler

Goals and Objectives

This chapter is designed to enable you to:

- Describe how children understand their medical illnesses
- Understand the disruptive effects of medical illness on children's development
- Describe how children and their families cope with medical illness
- Discuss issues involved in adherence to a medical regimen
- Understand the stressors on and concerns of families with a medically ill child
- Describe the stressors on healthy siblings of children with a medical illness
- Understand the effects on healthy children when a parent is medically ill

Behavioral medicine is a multidisciplinary field that integrates behavioral science approaches with biomedical knowledge and techniques. The goal of behavioral medicine is "to promote health and improve disease prevention, diagnosis, therapy, and rehabilitation…" (Rowland, 1989a, p. 519). The field of behavioral medicine applies to all physical illness, not just to disorders that show a strong relationship between psychological factors and physical illness. The growth of behavioral medicine stems in part from the recognition that the course of illness and its prevention are influenced by biological, psychological, and social factors (Engel, 1977). An understanding of the interaction of these factors may help explain, for example, why some children and their families seek immediate medical help for an illness and why other families delay seeking help, how children and their families cope with illness, why stress may adversely affect the immune system (which, in turn, may increase susceptibility to disease and affect recovery from illness), and how the health care provider–patient relationship influences patients' responses to treatment (Kiecolt-Glaser & Glaser, 1992; Maier, Watkins, & Fleshner, 1994). Because social, psychological, and behavioral factors, as well as biological factors, affect illness, health care providers need to consider how these factors interact when they meet with patients and their families, when they make decisions, and when they propose medical interventions.

Health care providers are likely to refer medically ill children to a mental health professional when one or more of the following conditions is present or suspected of being present (Lask & Fosson, 1989; Wickramasekera, 1988): The children

- have poor adherence to the medical regimen
- have severe behavioral or emotional disturbances
- are in families that disagree with the treatment regimen
- are in families that may be dysfunctional
- have learning difficulties
- have physical symptoms that cannot be diagnosed
- have poorly controlled illnesses

- have illnesses in which psychosocial factors are relevant
- have long-term or fatal illnesses

Health care providers also may refer medically ill children to a mental health professional to help the children cope with stressful medical treatment, adjust to hospitalization, and develop healthier life styles.

To best help medically ill children and their families when they are referred to you, you will need to do the following (Baker, 1992):

- Obtain an understanding of the child's illness, its natural progression, its manifestations, its treatments (including medications), and its possible complications.
- Become familiar with the way clinics, hospitals, schools, and social service organizations function in order to help medically ill children and their families obtain needed services.
- Become knowledgeable about the stresses seriously ill children may place on their families.
- Become knowledgeable about how illness may affect children's growth and development.

The following propositions from behavioral medicine underlie work with medically ill children and their families (Bor, Miller, & Goldman, 1993; Roter & Hall, 1992; Shapiro & Koocher, 1996):

1. Medical illnesses are primarily medical problems. However, medical illnesses may have psychological, social, economic, political, and legal implications.
2. Medical illnesses do not invariably lead to psychological or social problems.
3. Problems adjusting to a medical illness can arise at different points during the illness or during children's development.
4. Children facing the extreme stresses of medical illness may react initially with dissociation, denial, anxiety, or depression. These symptoms rarely represent pathology, and they do not warrant the same type of treatment as they would for children without medical distress.
5. Medical illnesses in children have implications for relationships between the children and other family members, peers, other children, teachers, and health care providers. Therefore, children's responses to serious medical illness cannot be understood in a vacuum.
6. Physical symptoms may stem from psychological causes, or what are termed *psychogenic symptoms*. Psychogenic symptoms may cause difficulties similar to those caused by illnesses that stem from medical reasons.
7. Children's families are their most important social systems, particularly when children are young. Therefore, interventions should involve children's families as well as children.
8. The objective reality of a medical illness affects children in different ways along a continuum of social, behavioral, and biomedical functioning. Children with the same illness may have different methods of coping with the illness.

9. How children's illness affects their behavior will depend on the interaction of several factors, including the type of illness, the age of the children, their developmental status, the responses of their families, and the responses of the health care providers (Willis, Elliott, & Jay, 1982).

In a hospital or other medical setting, mental health professionals work closely with other health care providers (see Table 1-1 in Chapter 1 for a description of several professions involved in work with children and their families). The primary medical/psychosocial health care team may be composed of a physician, nurse, social worker, and psychologist. Ideally, all team members should listen to the child's and family's concerns about the illness and treatments and provide reassurance, support, and guidance whenever possible or needed. Their individual contributions to the medical/psychosocial health care team are as follows:

- The *physician's* responsibility is to conduct the medical diagnostic workup, refer the child to other medical specialists as needed, review the medical diagnostic findings, develop medical interventions, and inform the family of the medical findings and recommended interventions.
- The *nurse's* responsibility is to carry out the needed medical interventions, to answer the child's and family's questions about the illness and its treatment, to act as a liaison between the medical staff and the psychosocial staff, and to provide supportive counseling to the child and family.
- The *social worker's* responsibility is to handle concerns that the child and parents may have about the medical diagnosis and medical treatment, to handle family tensions and provide appropriate behavioral and psychological interventions as needed, to help the child adjust to the hospital (or to home care), and to help with planning for discharge from the hospital.

- The *psychologist's* responsibility is to conduct a psychological evaluation of the child, to work with the family as needed, to help the child with problems associated with the hospitalization (or with home care), and to provide appropriate behavioral and psychosocial interventions, particularly when there are problems with adherence to the treatment regimen.

As a mental health professional, it is important that you work closely with the other members of the health care team to coordinate care for the child and information given to the child and family.

CHILDREN'S UNDERSTANDING OF THEIR MEDICAL ILLNESSES AND THE DISRUPTIVE EFFECTS OF MEDICAL ILLNESSES ON DEVELOPMENT

Normal development follows consecutive stages from infancy through adulthood. The child must accomplish a series of tasks in each stage before progressing to the next stage. Illness may disrupt or interfere with this progression. *You should view the developmental guidelines offered in this part of the chapter as guidelines only—each child will respond uniquely to his or her situation.*

Children's understanding of their medical illnesses and the concerns they have about them are directly related to their cognitive-developmental level. Their cognitive-developmental level also may affect the symptoms that result from the disruptive effects of a medical illness. Medical illnesses and their treatments may affect children's ability to acquire skills and carry out developmental tasks. Younger children may have difficulty gaining mobility, learning to communicate and socialize, and learning daily living skills, such as bladder and bowel control. Older children may have difficulty

Momma   by Mell Lazarus

learning to read and write, learning independence, and learning social skills. The type and site of the illness, the extent of the child's incapacities, and the chronicity of the illness will determine the extent to which developmental tasks are disrupted.

Following Piaget (see Sattler, 1992), we can demarcate four major age periods of cognitive development: birth to about 2 years, 2 through 6 years, 7 through 11 years, and 12 through 18 years. Let's see how these age periods relate to children's understanding of their medical illness, their concerns about the illness, and the disruptive effects of medical illness (Bibace & Walsh, 1980; Koocher & MacDonald, 1992; Rowland, 1989a).

Infancy—Birth to About 2 Years

One of the tasks of the infant is to develop trust in a caregiver who provides safety and predictability in the infant's life (see Chapter 1 for a discussion of attachment theory). This task may be interfered with when an infant becomes ill and needs to be hospitalized. The infant cannot understand that being left alone in the hospital does not mean that he or she has been abandoned. Similarly, the infant cannot understand why the trusted caregiver allows others to inflict pain on him or her.

Infants have little understanding of illness; their emotions depend on their immediate sensations. Their anxiety is primarily associated with separation from trusted caregivers. If the illness requires forced feedings, painful procedures, or other unexpected handling, they may experience feelings of helplessness, fear, and mistrust of the environment. The development of their skills may be delayed if they are immobilized for long periods, given treatments that interfere with brain development (for example, cranial irradiation), or placed in isolation rooms.

Early Childhood—2 Through 6 Years

During early childhood, children are unable to separate themselves from their environments and tend to think in magical terms; thus, they are unable to explain in logical terms what causes illness. Because they do not have a good sense of cause and effect, preschool children, for example, may think that they became ill or needed a shot because they were bad to a sibling or because they did not obey their parents. They understand illness in terms of a single external symptom. For example, if you ask a toddler "What causes a cold?", she or he may say "From the sun" (Bibace & Walsh, 1980, p. 914). Or they may describe their experience perceptually, as in "Pain is red." The child sees health and illness as two separate states. More mature children in this stage conceptualize the cause of illness as located in people or in objects in the environment near to them. For example, if you ask such a child "How do people get colds?", the answer

might be "When someone else gets near them" (Bibace & Walsh, 1980, p. 914).

Preschool children experience stress when they are separated from their family and home during hospitalization and during frequent outpatient visits (Rowland, 1989a). They may express anxiety, sadness, and anger about separation from siblings, and they may feel jealous of the good health of siblings. They also may feel guilty about any changes, tensions, or conflicts at home that they think result from their illness and care. Preschoolers have more stable moods than infants, but, unlike infants, they have fantasies and fears that may make them susceptible to mood changes.

If preschool children cannot cope effectively with hospitalization, they may show regressive behavior or other changes in behavior. For example, they may lose previously acquired skills—a child who has not wet his bed for two years may wet his bed or a child who was sleeping through the night now may wake up after a few hours. Such losses can raise doubts in their minds about their ability to control their internal and external environments. Parents, too, are affected by these setbacks and may become anxious that their child's progress toward independence has been thwarted. In some cases, preschool children who need to be hospitalized may initially protest about being hospitalized, then show emotional despair, and then become detached (Adams-Greenly, 1989). *Detachment does not mean good adjustment; in fact, it likely signals distress that needs attention.*

Because preschool children aspire to become independent, they have difficulty accepting the constraints of their illness and the associated treatments. They may become angry, depressed, withdrawn, and stubborn and display tantrums when efforts are made to thwart their autonomy (Rowland, 1989a).

Preschool children may exhibit high levels of distress during medical procedures. Some procedures—such as the placement of intravenous tubes, finger pricks, and lumbar punctures—are confusing, frightening, and painful and may be seen as punishment for misdeeds (Rowland, 1989a). Treatments that produce physical alterations—such as hair loss, surgical amputation, or incisional scarring—threaten preschool children's body image, sense of self-esteem, and sex-role identity (Rowland, 1989a). They may even think that they could die from some medical procedures (Redd, 1989).

Middle Childhood—7 Through 11 Years

During middle childhood years, children tend to think concretely and factually and have a present-time orientation. They have some understanding of the cause of illness and its effects on the body. For example, if you ask a child who is of middle childhood age "How do people get colds?", he or she may answer "You're outside without a hat and you start sneezing. Your head would get cold—the cold would touch it—and then it would go all over your body" (Bibace & Walsh, 1980, p. 914). The more mature children in this stage locate illness within the body, although they may describe the location in vague terms. For example, if they are asked how people get colds, they might say "In winter, they breathe in too much air into their nose and it blocks up the nose" (Bibace & Walsh, 1980, p. 914). When they are asked "How does this cause colds?", they might answer "The bacteria gets in by breathing. Then the lungs get too soft and it goes to the nose" (Bibace & Walsh, 1980, p. 914).

During middle childhood, children may perceive illness as a threat to their competence. They may be fearful and anxious about falling behind in school, restricting their activities, placing additional burdens on the parent or parents who have to take care of them, limiting their contacts with others, and becoming isolated from their peers (Rowland, 1989a). In spite of these potential worries, children in middle childhood do develop skills to help them cope with stress.

Children in middle childhood can understand the seriousness of their illness, and they recognize that death is irreversible. Those who have a chronic life-threatening illness, such as cancer, may become extremely anxious. They may fear that their actions caused the illness or its recurrence (Rowland, 1989a). Hospitalization may lead to fears of separation, but these fears will be more reality based than those of preschool children. Ill children of middle childhood age also may be jealous of their healthy siblings.

Adolescence—12 Through 18 Years

During adolescence, children make the greatest differentiation between their bodies and the environment. They view the source and nature of illness as lying in specific organs of the body. When adolescents are asked how people get colds, they might say "They come from viruses I guess; other people have the virus and it gets into your bloodstream and it causes a cold" (Bibace & Walsh, 1980, p. 915). Older adolescents have the most mature understanding of illness. They recognize that illness can be caused by physical or by psychological factors. For example, when older adolescents are asked "What is a heart attack?", they might say "It's when your heart stops working right." When they are asked "How do people get a heart attack?", they might say "It can come from being all nerve wrecked. You worry too much. The tension can affect your heart" (Bibace & Walsh, 1980, p. 915).

Adolescents' increased cognitive capacities and increased knowledge also may make them more aware of potential complications of treatment and of their personal vulnerability—greater knowledge thus may lead to greater anxiety (Eiser, 1993). Adolescents may worry about their family's not giving them support or sufficient information about their illness. They also likely will be concerned that the illness will lead to loss of privacy and autonomy and affect their interactions with their peers and their ability to continue with school activities. Their ability to be philosophical and to reflect on their illness and situation may affect how they adjust to their illness.

Severe illnesses that result in hospitalization, in physical limitations, and in separation from peers place adolescents at risk for developing behavioral problems. They may feel isolated and anxious, become dependent on their parents, and resort to immature patterns of behavior. However, with appropriate support, they can learn that the dependent role is likely to be temporary and that even in a hospital there are areas in which they can maintain a sense of independence by accomplishing things for themselves. Their dependency on their parents may be appropriate, given the situation they are in. However, once they return to home and school, the same level of dependency may be inappropriate (Rowland, 1989a).

Severe illnesses may not only engender feelings of helplessness but also produce feelings of distrust, alienation, and anger and acting-out and uncooperative behavior. These feelings and behaviors may be exacerbated when the parents and staff overprotect medically ill adolescents.

Severe illnesses may disrupt adolescents' body image, particularly if the illness affects their appearance. Because some adolescents believe that they are invulnerable and that nothing can happen to them, they may not adjust well to illness and may not adhere to treatment regimens. Severe illnesses pose a major threat to their sense of physical invulnerability (Rowland, 1989a). Finally, severe illnesses can precipitate in adolescents a search for life meaning (Rowland, 1989a).

Let's now look at some comments made by adolescents about how their illness affected them and their families (Deasy-Spinetta, 1981, pp. 192, 193; Goldberg & Tull, 1983, pp. 23–25, 27, 36, 37; van Veldhuizen & Last, 1991, pp. 116, 150, 151, 158, 175, 176, 223).

1. *Concerns about changes in body image.* They may be concerned about how the illness affects their ability to participate in activities.

- I used to run cross country all the time. I wasn't that terrific at it, but I enjoyed it. Now when I run I lose my breath faster and everything, and get tired much quicker, so I gave that up and began to do something else that's not as strenuous, like swimming for ten minutes instead of an hour. You know, you can still do the things you like, except you have to watch the time limits on them.

- I want to keep fighting this. I keep saying to myself, "Well, this winter I'm going to lift weights or something to build up my strength, so in the spring it'll be just like it always was." I just can't accept; I just can't give it up yet. I've always been a real fighter, so I'm gonna try to fight this all along. You don't want things to change that are good, that you enjoy. I still have a lot of hope, so I'll keep on trying.

2. *Concerns about peer group membership.* They may be concerned about relationships with peers.

- It was like I was a piece of glass. Nobody wanted to get near me. They were afraid I was going to break. When you have leukemia or some kind of disease most people don't have, there are a lot of things like side effects and drugs, being tired, being sick, not having the energy other people have, having to go for treatments, having to deal with doctors and hospital situations that set you apart from your peers. I guess everybody feels alone, but it seems to me that there is much more that you don't have in common, and that can be lonely.... When I was little, my one wish was to be normal, and I realize now that that was sort of silly because nobody knows what that is, but I guess that's something people try all their lives to accomplish.

- When you're having a hard time coping with everything, you find out who your friends really are. Before I was sick, I used to hang around these kids. Then I went into the hospital. Friends came to visit me, or they came over to see me at my house when I was sick. Some kids, however, you don't see unless you go over to them. So it really singles out who your best friends are. Once I ran into this kid that I hadn't seen since I've been sick, and we were just talking, and he said, "I never hung around with you because you have leukemia." I said, "Why?" He said, "Well, I was scared. I didn't want to say something that would hurt you or anything." So I just told him how good seeing him was and said, "You should talk about it; ask me questions, I don't care." Now we're a lot closer, and it was just because this kid was afraid to speak up that he never hung around me, but we have a lot of good times together now; it's very nice. Talking about it with friends is a lot better. You get things straightened out. It makes you feel less in isolation and just like everybody else, only you have a disease. It's not like you're from some other planet or something.

3. *Concerns about why they became ill.* They may wonder why they became ill.

- The deal of being sick; every time you have to have treatments and you get sick, you think, "Why?" and you know if you don't get the treatments, you're gonna die. So you feel like you're getting the needle. I don't know. I feel cheated. I feel like I'm being punished or something but not by the doctors. It's by somebody higher. The doctors are here to help us.
- When I get up to heaven, I'm gonna ask God why we're all having to go through this, and if he doesn't give me a good answer, I'm gonna punch him right in his face, if I can.

4. *Concerns about their family.* They may be concerned about the effects of their illness on their parents and siblings.

- It is really hard on the family. I think it is harder on my sister, brother, and parents than it is on me because it is happening to me and I know how I feel; they have to guess. After I come home from having chemotherapy, for example, my family walks on ice. It is really tense sometimes. If I'm not feeling well, I don't want to explain to them, and that adds to the difficulty because you need to maintain communication with your family. I understand what I'm going through, but they don't want to show how they feel; they don't want to cry in front of me; they don't want to upset me.
- I have a very close relationship with my sister even though she's only 12. Whenever I am sick we communicate. You don't really have to talk when you have that kind of a relationship. But it is very hard to discuss specifics with her; it's very emotional, very touchy. How do you say to your sister, "Annie, I don't think I'll be around when you go on your first date"?
- You really have to pull together as a family from the very beginning. You must get your lines of communication straight so that you understand and they understand. Frequently, you have to volunteer the information to your brothers and sisters because they are afraid to ask you directly what is really going on.
- My brother is *very* quiet. He doesn't say much at all. So I gently and slowly give him information so that he understands what is going on and is not afraid. Many times I came home really sick, and I think he got scared. I didn't talk at the time because I didn't know what to say. Then it would all come out gradually. I had hepatitis, shingles, or whatever.
- My father and mother have certainly had a shock. They've been very sad. I wasn't really all that sad myself. I don't know...they worry a lot about me and I don't really like that. I don't like it at all that my own parents are so sad about me.

5. *Communicating with parents.* They may have various ways of communicating with their parents.

- Sometimes I'm afraid that if I ask something, my father or mother will also be frightened by it. So I don't ask it.
- I find it easier to ask my parents things than the doctor, but I ask questions anyway. Then I can see what the doctor says and what my parents say and whether it's the same. You can play the funniest tricks on them and then you can see whether they're telling the truth or not. Usually they do say the same thing.
- In the hospital when they were still trying to find out exactly what I had, a girl in the ward said to me: You have cancer because if you didn't, you wouldn't be here. The next day when I was in the elevator with my mother, she was very agitated. She was nervous and stammering and then I said: Before you try to tell me anything, well you don't have to, because I already know I have cancer. I just blurted it out. Later my mother said she thought the elevator had broken down, that it was falling down at a tremendous speed.
- When I feel like talking about it, then I'll start the conversation myself. If they [the parents] start to talk about it and I don't feel like it, I tell them: Let's not bring that up again.
- When I went to the [hospital] they talked about a growth. Kind of strange but I just didn't think about it. During all those tests I just didn't know anything and I didn't ask anything. I didn't really want to know the kind of ward I was in and what was wrong with the other children. After a few weeks I saw my parents coming down the hall and I walked cheerfully towards them but they had just been told the test results by the doctor. Then I asked them if it was serious and they started to cry right away and said I had bone cancer. Then we all cried.
- I was in hospital for treatment at Christmas too. I was very ill and laid there throwing up all the time and it was very hard on my father and mother. Then I decided to cheer them up and began to sing: "Always look on the bright side of life." Well that wasn't such a good idea. Then my mother was really upset.

COPING WITH A MEDICAL ILLNESS

The Challenge of Coping

The typical reaction that older children have when they learn that they have a severe chronic illness is "a period of initial shock and disbelief followed by a period of turmoil accompanied by anxiety and depressive symptoms, irritability, and disruption of appetite and normal sleep.... The ability to concentrate and carry out usual life activities is impaired.... The[y] often experience intrusive thoughts about the diagnosis and its ominous implications for the future [such as fears of death and bodily dysfunction]" (Holland, 1989a, p. 20). When the illness is cancer or AIDS, children may experience additional stress because these are the most stigmatized diseases of our time (Holland, 1989a). You need to distinguish normal or typical reactions when children learn that they have a severe chronic illness from those that are atypical, because children with atypical reactions may need additional help, such as counseling or psychotherapy. Sometimes even children who have normal reactions to abnormal circumstances may require help.

Rowland (1989b) describes how children differ from adults in their ability to cope with illness.

First, children have a more limited repertoire of coping skills and strategies available to them than adults. Second, children are also exquisitely vulnerable to the reactions and behaviors of the adults responsible for their care, in ways that have an enduring impact on future coping, both during [the beginning of their] illness and in later episodes.... the quality of initial experiences with illness takes on added importance; the strategies established or learned early in life are more likely to be used first in future illness situations. (p. 47)

One of your key concerns should be how the child and family cope with and adapt to the child's illness. Although this part of the chapter focuses on how children and families cope with the stress of a medical illness, much of it applies to how children and families cope with any type of stress. *Coping strategies can be defined as the behaviors, cognitions, and perceptions individuals use to maintain equilibrium in the face of illness* (Rowland, 1989b). How the child and family cope with the child's illness will depend on *illness variables, individual variables, familial variables,* and *environmental variables* (Moos, 1977; Rowland, 1989b). Let's look at these variables in more detail.

Illness Variables

Children's and families' ability to cope with a medical illness will depend on the type, severity, site, stage, and course of the illness; the type of treatment; and the type of rehabilitative measures. Coping will be more difficult when illnesses have one or more of the following characteristics:

- They are severe and chronic (such as sickle cell anemia or cystic fibrosis).
- They require constant monitoring (such as renal disease or diabetes).
- They require hospitalization.
- They require confinement to a bed.
- They require frequent visits for treatment or extensive rehabilitative procedures.
- They are *unpredictable* or *episodic* (such as asthma, sickle cell anemia, epilepsy, or bipolar disorders).

- They have a poor prognosis (such as forms of cancer or renal disease).
- They have high visibility (such as illnesses that result in scars, deformations, or loss of hair).
- They involve a social stigma (such as AIDS or physical anomalies).
- They require painful treatments (such as chemotherapy).

Table 15-1 lists stressful medical interventions for several illnesses and possible psychological effects associated with the interventions.

Individual Variables

Children's ability to cope with a medical illness will depend on their age and developmental stage, intelligence/cognitive level, personality and temperament, pre-illness adjustment, values, beliefs, previous experiences with illness, and coping strategies. Children with a chronic illness may feel isolated, angry, guilty, ashamed, lonely, apathetic, bitter, and confused. The loss of health and of ability to plan for the future also may lead to depression (Van Dongen-Melman & Sanders-Woudstra, 1986).

Coping may be more difficult when children have prior adjustment problems, pessimistic beliefs, a predisposition for anxiety, unwillingness to accept psychological factors as contributing to the illness, and prior aversive experiences with illness. Obtaining *secondary gains* from having an illness (that is, benefits that accrue to the child as a function of the illness) also may make coping more difficult. Secondary gains include increased attention from the family and medical community, reduced school work, avoidance of stressful interactions, and lowered expectations from others. Coping also will be difficult for children when parents display anxiety (see the next part of the chapter).

Children may use several strategies in coping with stress, (Lazarus & Folkman, 1984; Weisman & Worden, 1976–1977).

1. *Problem-focused strategies.* Children can use problem-focused strategies to modify the stressors that confront them. These strategies include *rational intellectualizing* (seeking information or advice), *adherence* (seeking direction from an authority and adhering to the direction), *confrontation* (taking action based on their present understanding of the illness, such as trying to change their behavior or that of others in situations they view as solvable), and *alternative rewards* (seeking rewarding activities, relationships, learning experiences, competitions, and other situations involving mastery; improving appearance; spending time with hobbies; and so forth).

2. *Emotion-focused strategies.* Children can use emotion-focused strategies to release, reduce, or manage their emotional tensions. These strategies include *revealing feelings* (crying or yelling when they believe they can do nothing to resolve the situation), *reversal of affect* (laughing off the sit-

Table 15-1
Stressors Associated with Medical Interventions and Their Possible Psychological or Physical Effects

Illness	Stressful medical interventions	Possible psychological or physical effects
Asthma: A respiratory disorder characterized by intermittent and reversible attacks of difficulty in breathing	Repeated hospitalizations Allergy shots Bronchodilators Mist inhalation Corticosteroids Antibiotics for infection Beta-agonists	Fear of dying by suffocation Fear of abandonment Maladaptive use of wheezing to express conflicts Physical and social restrictions Family disruption (sleep interruption, dietary and housekeeping problems) Growth retardation as a secondary effect of steroids
Cancer: A disease in which malignant cells destroy normal cells in various regions of the body[a]	Radiation Chemotherapy Bone marrow aspirations Surgical interventions Hospitalizations for acute episodes	Loss of hair, disfigurement, and other effects of treatment Fear of effects of treatment Fear of death Fear of infection Fear of surgery and hospitalization Pain
Chronic otitis media: Infection of the middle ear with chronic discharge through a perforation of the tympanic membrane	Repeated ear examinations Ear drops Surgical intervention	Hearing loss, with possible subsequent educational disadvantage, learning disability, and reading difficulty Social isolation Developmental delay
Central nervous system infection and its sequelae (meningitis): An inflammation of the membranes surrounding the brain resulting from bacterial or viral infection, which may give rise to chronic brain dysfunction	Lumbar puncture Blood culture Spinal fluid culture Antibiotic therapy Respiratory isolation Treatment of increased intracranial pressure	Fear of death Fear of residual brain damage Residual deficits such as mental retardation, seizures, hydrocephalus, hemiparesis, learning disability, and hearing impairment
Diabetes: A metabolic disease in which there is a lack of insulin or impairment in the insulin mechanism	Insulin injections Diet restrictions Blood and urine testing Hospitalizations for acute episodes	Parent-child control struggle over insulin-food-exercise regimen Adolescent rebellion Pain from daily injections Fear of coma or insulin shock Anxiety over long-term complications
Epilepsy: A condition in which there is continuing proclivity to have seizures	Anticonvulsant medication, which has adverse side effects Regular blood tests Hospitalization Brain surgery	Anxiety over and fear of unconsciousness Loss of sense of control and autonomy Social stigmatization, rejection, and discrimination Parental overprotection or rejection Heightened dependency on parents
Heart defects: Congenital abnormalities of the heart structure	Catheterization for diagnosis and treatment Corrective surgery Palliative surgeries Antibiotics Digitalis for heart failure	Extensive painful procedures Prolonged separation from family during infancy Difficulty on the part of the parent in disciplining the child (for fear of precipitating symptoms) Fear of pain, mutilation, and death Activity restrictions

(Continued)

Table 15-1 (*Continued*)

Illness	Stressful medical interventions	Possible psychological or physical effects
Irritable bowel syndrome: A functional bowel disorder characterized by alternating diarrhea and constipation	Dietary restrictions Stool softeners Antispasmodic medication Exercise program Antidepressant medication Treatment of fecal impaction	Fear of loss of control Feelings of shame and inadequacy Emotional tension, anxiety, and depression Conflicts over holding back versus letting go Difficulty dealing with anger and aggressive feelings
Juvenile rheumatoid arthritis: An inflammatory process affecting the joints	Aspirin Physical therapy Steroids and anti-inflammatory nonsteroids Gold therapy injections Orthopedic intervention (splints and surgery)	Pain and feelings of maltreatment, punishment, and persecution Activity limitation Deformity and disability Depression and mood alteration
Muscular dystrophy: A neuromuscular disorder in which striated muscle progressively deteriorates	Physical therapy Surgery for contractures Calorie-restricted diet Correction of spinal deformity Postural drainage exercises (exercises designed to help patients clear their lungs of accumulated secretions) Orthopedic prosthesis and motorized equipment	Anguish over diagnosis, which brings a prognosis of early crippling and death Chronic physical and mental exhaustion Progressive helplessness and dependency due to loss of strength Isolation and rejection by peers Great difficulty managing anger and aggressive feelings Guilt over sacrifices required by other family members

[a]Symptoms vary depending on site of cancer and type of treatment.
Source: Adapted and reprinted with permission of the authors and publishers from M. O'Dougherty and R. T. Brown, "The Stress of Childhood Illness," in L. E. Arnold (Ed.), *Childhood Stress,* copyright 1990 by John Wiley and Sons Limited, pp. 327–329.

uation or making light of it), *stimulus reduction* (withdrawing from situations), *fatalism* (accepting the inevitable), *self-pity* (feeling sorry for themselves), *tension reduction* (using humor, sharing feelings with others, drinking, overeating, or using drugs or alcohol), and *acting out* (doing something even if it is reckless or impractical).

3. *Appraisal-focused strategies.* Children can use appraisal-focused strategies to evaluate the situation. These strategies include *logical analysis* (putting things in perspective, rationalizing, or reinterpreting the situation), *cognitive redefinition* (redefining the situation by finding something favorable in it and accepting it), and *cognitive avoidance* (trying to forget the situation or put it out of mind, doing other things to distract themselves, or blaming someone else for their predicament).

The most effective coping strategies are those that reflect an acceptance of illness followed by realistic actions that deal with the illness and the problems associated with the illness—that is, having a fighting spirit. Children who be-

lieve they can master the illness may be in a better position to cope with it than those who do not. *How children interpret or appraise situations may be as important as or more important than the situations themselves in determining their responses.* Coping may be difficult, especially for young children who usually do not understand fully their illness, the treatment regimen for their illness, or the long-term implications of their illness. In time, their understanding will improve, but they still may have a difficult time accepting the illness and the limitations it brings. How parents manage their own feelings about the child's illness also can affect how the child copes with the illness.

Familial Variables

A family with a medically ill child, like all families, will need to care for, nourish, and support the child. However, parents of a medically ill child may have concerns about the diagnosis, the treatment, and how the child's illness will affect their family and daily life. For example, they may be concerned (depending on their child's illness) about

- their ability to protect the child from suffering
- how they and their child will cope with hospitalizations and repeated clinic visits
- how the child will cope with absences from school and keep up with schoolwork
- how they will find the extra time needed to prepare special diets
- how they will meet the increased physical burdens associated with caring for their child (including lifting, dressing, feeding, diapering, and washing extra clothes)
- how they will get enough sleep
- how they will manage extra housecleaning duties
- how they will deal with changes in family life
- how they will meet the financial burdens associated with the child's illness
- their leisure time
- their ability to concentrate when they are at work
- their opportunities to pursue their careers
- their having more children
- the possibility that their other children may develop the illness
- the need for housing adaptations—such as fitting their house with special equipment, making the air quality better, or making the climate more optimal

Points of psychosocial stress. Families must continually adjust to their medically ill child. Each new developmental stage may bring with it new adjustments and new problems and also rewards and satisfactions for both children and their families. Following are points at which psychosocial stresses may occur in families with a medically ill child or medically disabled child (Christ & Adams, 1984; Koocher, 1985). (Note that these points are not necessarily in sequential order and that not all families go through each one.)

- Diagnostic evaluation
- Onset of treatment
- Reactions to treatment and side effects of treatment
- End of treatment
- Entry and reentry into school, social, and family life
- Beginning of new developmental stage and educational transitions
- Recurrence of illness
- Instituting of additional treatment or new treatments
- End of active treatment
- Period of terminal illness and death of child
- Period of several months following the death of the child

Family's concerns about health care providers. Parents and older children may have several concerns about the health care providers. For example, they may believe that the health care providers

- do not listen to them
- do not take their concerns seriously

- do not ask their opinion of the treatment process
- do not know their real concerns
- do not ask about their past
- do not have sufficient warmth, acceptance, or humility
- do not give them enough information about their child's illness or disability
- do not recognize that making prognostic statements too early in the treatment process may take away hope or create false hope
- do not recognize that the parents can make valid observations
- do not make a detailed accounting of the cost of the assessment and the treatment
- do not agree among themselves about the child's problems and treatment needs

Unfortunately, in some cases, these concerns may be valid. If you learn that the parents or children are troubled about the health care providers or about any aspect of the treatment regimen, bring up their concerns with the health care providers and work toward effective solutions. When the parents' or older children's concerns show that they do not understand how the health care system works, give them the information they need.

Families from an ethnic minority group may experience additional stressors in coping with the medical regimen. Stressors may include misunderstanding the communications of the medical staff about needed treatments (particularly for parents or children whose primary language is other than English), trying to relate treatment to their cultural or religious orientation, and wondering whether their traditional healing methods will be accepted. Chapter 9 discusses the health beliefs and traditional practices of ethnic minority groups. Exhibit 15-1 offers suggestions for health care providers who work with Asian American children and families. Many of these suggestions also may apply to other ethnic groups.

Factors hindering coping in families. Coping will be difficult in poorly functioning families that are unable to care for, support, nourish, and guide the child, as happens when families are poor, have few resources, have no social supports, and have major stressors. Major family stressors include persistent rejection or abuse of the child by family members, parental ill health, disturbed family relations, life events that require major family changes (for example, moving or the birth of another child), and major traumas (for example, accidents, illness, parental unemployment, or homelessness). Chapter 1 discusses the effects of poverty on families.

If families obtain secondary gains from having a sick child—such as parental power and control over children, attention from the medical community and from the extended family, and rewards for assuming a martyr role, children may have more difficulty coping. This in no way implies that the family and medical community should withhold attention from the ill child; support and help *must* be

Communication

1. *Identify the decision maker and spokesperson in the family.* Note who speaks up in meetings, whom others defer to, and who communicates effectively with the hospital staff and the child. It may not be the child's parents because of limited language and communication skills. Never assume who the family spokesperson will be; always ask the family to choose the person. Also, don't assume that the spokesperson at the hospital is the decision maker at home.

2. *Identify key communicators on the medical team to be family liaisons.* Recognize that identifying and communicating with multiple medical professionals may be especially confusing for Asian families.

3. *Outward appearances may be misleading.* Because Asian cultures emphasize respect for persons in authority, such as the medical team, they may appear to agree with treatment plans. Professionals often mistakenly assume that polite listening means agreement. Maintaining a calm, polite outward demeanor is also a way for Asian families to avoid confrontation. When families do not follow through with instructions, professionals may view them as resistant or noncompliant. In fact, the difficulty may lie with the medical team's lack of awareness that treatment plans conflict with cultural beliefs.

4. *Use a trained interpreter.* When family members are upset over a child's injury or illness, they typically find it difficult to take in a lot of information. Asking a family member to interpret increases the risk that information will not be understood or communicated accurately. Family members may censor information, be unfamiliar with medical terms and be hesitant to deliver bad news. Using children as interpreters can create conflict in family relationships between elders and younger members. [Chapter 8 discusses the use of interpreters in more detail.]

5. *Talk with parents about their understanding of their child's injury or illness, diagnosis and expectations for the future.* Determine how much information the parents wish the health care staff to give their child.

6. *Ask about medicines and herbs used at home.* Asian families often use Eastern and Western medicine simultaneously, particularly after the child returns home from the hospital. It is important for health care professionals to follow up, since medicines and herbs may interact with the prescribed medicines. These questions need to be phrased carefully in order to recognize the importance of Eastern beliefs. Otherwise, these questions may be interpreted as accusatory or derogatory by the Asian family. [Chapter 9 discusses the traditional medical practices of Asian Americans in more detail.]

Hospital Care

7. *Give detailed explanations and reassurance for invasive procedures.* Explain that blood drawing, transfusions, lumbar puncture and surgery are used to help heal the body and not harm the body's balance.

8. *Ask family members about special foods.* These can be prepared in the hospital or brought in from home if they are important to restore the body's harmony. Asian families may not allow some foods if they believe that they prevent or slow down recovery.

9. *Ask whether family members would like to arrange a visit by a religious person.* However, don't assume that religious expressions or customs are comparable to Western beliefs. Religion is integrated into customs and daily life, thus placing less importance on formal visits or places.

10. *If the child has had a head injury, help the family understand differences between brain injury and mental illness or retardation.* It is important to stress that changes in the child's mobility, behavior and learning may result from the injury and are not caused by any wrongful act committed by ancestors. [Chapter 19 discusses brain injury.]

Home Care and Follow Up

11. *Try to give families something tangible when they leave an appointment.* Samples and/or written instruc-

tions will let the family know that something is being done.

12. *Explain the importance of taking medicine for the prescribed number of days.* Even if the child feels better before the medicine is finished, the medicine must be continued in order to restore harmony to the body.

13. *Be sure the family uses standard measures for medicine.* Overdoses occur when a porcelain soup spoon is used. Either demonstrate the exact dosage or give the family a special spoon or measure to use.

14. *Ask what other doctors or clinics are being used.* The use of multiple doctors, clinics, medicines and treatment plans may complicate a child's care and recovery.

Community Relations

15. *Be aware of guilt associated with a disability.* Eastern cultures may see a child with a disability as a punishment or shame to be hidden within the family. This is a common response in an Asian family when a child is born with a disability. Guilt can also result from the belief that the injury was caused by something bad or wrong in the family's ancestral life. Talk with the family about their guilt; however, Asian families may not be familiar with traditional Western interventions such as counseling and consultation.

16. *Encourage families to use community services.* Willingness to accept services in the community can also be linked to feelings of shame about a disability. Western attitudes view services as rights or help that may be paid by insurance. Asian families may resist asking for or receiving services that focus on the child's disability until they are able to resolve their feelings of shame and duty. Explain how these services can help the child adjust and prepare for the future.

17. *Avoid scheduling appointments during cultural holidays.* Find out about holidays that are specific to Asian cultures.

18. *Contact the school nurse or teacher.* Give the child's local school information about any changes in the child or special needs of the child.

Source: Reprinted, with permission, from Marilyn Lash and Vincent Licenziato, *When an Asian Child Needs Health Care: Tips for Health Care Professionals on Cultural Beliefs,* New England Medical Center, Boston, MA, copyright 1995, pp. 3–5.

given to the ill child despite any secondary gains to the family (or to the child). In their most extreme form, secondary gains may become an obsession and result in parental actions that produce or maintain the child's illness (see Chapter 20 for a discussion of Munchausen Syndrome by Proxy).

Marginally adjusted families and single-parent families may be particularly vulnerable when a child develops a chronic or severe illness. In marginally adjusted families, problems that were beneath the surface—such as marital discord—may erupt because of the added stress. The emotional burdens of raising a chronically ill child may be particularly difficult for single parents, because they may have no one with whom to share their feelings and concerns and the demands for increased child care.

All families may experience stress if the expenses for treatment become prohibitive, if paying for the treatment depletes their savings or forces them to sell their home and possessions, if their health insurance is inadequate, or if their health insurer is not willing to pay for the needed services. Parents also have stress if they must miss work or social activities in order to take the child to medical appointments. Sometimes these stresses may result in feelings of resentment toward the sick child, as well as guilt feelings for being resentful.

Families *hinder* the development of a medically ill child when they (Patterson & McCubbin, 1983)

- overprotect the child
- withdraw the family from social involvement with others
- deny the reality of the child's medical illness and ignore his or her special needs
- display anger and resentment about the situation
- become depressed
- become too lenient with the child
- domineer the child
- direct their hostility toward the child or toward each other
- blame each other

The child's development also will be impaired if one parent forms a coalition with the child and excludes the other parent.

Factors facilitating coping in families.   Families *assist* the development of a medically ill child when they (Patterson & McCubbin, 1983)

- support the child
- believe that the child can cope with the illness
- have high self-esteem
- have open, effective communication among their members
- provide mutual assistance and support to their members
- have good problem-solving abilities
- have good physical and emotional health
- have a sense of mastery over events that they are experiencing
- can afford quality respite care

The most effective coping occurs when families use their existing resources and develop new resources to cope with the ever-increasing demands of the child's medical illness.

Coping strategies used by parents.   Here are some coping strategies that parents may use in dealing with their child's severe medical illness (Barbarin & Chesler, 1986).

1. *Information seeking.* Parents may seek information to help them understand the diagnosis, to place their emotional reactions to the illness in perspective, or to reduce uncertainty and fear regarding their child's survival.

2. *Problem solving.* Parents may use behaviorally oriented solutions for specific problems, such as increasing their work hours to raise money to meet medical expenses, rearranging their schedules to be with the child in the hospital, and planning with teachers for the child's return to school.

3. *Seeking informal social support.* Parents may use informal networks of family members and friends for aid and emotional support.

4. *Reliance on religious beliefs/faith.* Parents may use prayer and religion for emotional comfort or to seek an acceptable explanation for the child's illness.

5. *Seeking formal supports.* Parents may seek the services of a counselor or psychotherapist to help them with their adjustment problems.

6. *Maintenance of emotional balance.* Parents may moderate emotional reactions and avoid extreme mood swings; in some sense, parents may try to retain or recapture some degree of normality in their personal life style and social relations.

7. *Optimism.* Parents may hope that things will turn out well, focusing on positive rather than negative possibilities.

8. *Denial.* Parents may not accept the diagnosis, may refuse to focus on illness-related issues, and may withdraw from situations reminiscent of the illness.

9. *Passive acceptance.* Parents may be fatalistic, seeing the child's illness as permanent and irreversible; this may be their way of indirectly coming to terms with the child's illness.

Environmental Variables

Children's and families' ability to cope with a medically ill child will depend on the community's attitude toward illness, the community supports and resources available, the school's attitude toward medically ill children, and physical access to facilities in the community and school. Children's and families' ability to cope with illnesses will be *facilitated* when they have positive and accepting social groups; when they live in hygienic conditions in a safe neighborhood; when the schools accommodate the needs of children who are medically ill; when the physical environment allows children with an illness or disability to be independent—

such as when special ramps are present, light fixtures are arranged in a convenient way, and door openings can accommodate wheelchairs; and when they can afford quality respite care (Lewis, 1994).

Negative attitudes toward children with severe illnesses or disabilities.   Children's ability to cope with severe illnesses or disabilities may be hampered when they come into contact with people who hold negative attitudes toward the ill or disabled. Negative attitudes may stem from several sources, including cultural factors, personal factors, attributions of negative qualities to seriously ill or disabled people, and connotations associated with disability (Livneh, 1984). For example, American culture tends to emphasize youth, health, athletic prowess, and personal appearance while having antipathy toward those who are sick or disfigured.

Nondisabled people may stay away from those who are ill or disabled for the following reasons (Livneh, 1984):

- They don't want to feel guilty about being healthy or able-bodied.
- They believe that if they associate with disabled persons they will be viewed as psychologically maladjusted and therefore ostracized.
- They think that ill or disabled people are dangerous because the illness or disability is an unjust punishment and the ill or disabled person may commit evil to balance the injustice.
- They have feelings of repulsion when they see someone with deformities, believing that they may become contaminated if they interact with him or her.
- They fear recognition of their own mortality when they are confronted with ill or disabled persons.

Teachers' attitudes toward children with medical illnesses or disabilities.   Teachers' interactions with children with medical illnesses may be another source of stress for children and their families. Some teachers are reluctant to have seriously ill children or children with seizures in their classroom (Adams-Greenly, 1989). They may have unresolved feelings about children who are ill, concerns about whether they can meet the needs of sick children as well as the needs of the other children in the class, and concerns about discussing the children's illnesses with other students. Teachers who are ambivalent about having seriously ill children in their classes may subtly withdraw from meaningful interactions with the children; if this happens, the other children may follow the teachers' example. Teachers also may lower academic requirements and behavior standards for sick children. These actions may serve to isolate the sick "child from his or her peers, emphasize the differences due to illness, and increase the child's feelings of hopelessness and helplessness" (Adams-Greenly, 1989, p. 567). Occasionally, however, modifications in the curriculum are needed to help ill children master the academic material.

Educating healthy children about children with severe illnesses or disabilities.   There may be times when health care professionals need to speak to classes about children who have a medical illness or a disability. The following incident highlights the value of a classroom visit (D. J. Willis, personal communication, February 1996).

CASE 15-1. DOMINIC
After Dominic, a 6-year-old child with grand mal seizures, was evaluated, he asked the mental health professional if the professional would write a letter for him to his teacher. The letter read: "Dear Teacher, I have seizures. Don't be afraid. Dominic." When the mental health professional asked him about the letter, Dominic said that he had had a seizure in the classroom and that everyone, including his teacher, seemed to be afraid of him. The mental health professional arranged for a visit to the classroom to talk to the class about children with disabilities and, in particular, children who have epilepsy. The students and teacher learned about seizures, how to help Dominic if and when he had another seizure, that seizures were not "catching," and that Dominic was like everyone else except for one medical problem for which he takes medication.

Comment on Coping with a Medical Illness

A key to *effective coping* with a medical illness is an active approach to problem solving. Active coping strategies are likely to be utilized when the child interprets the illness as a challenge to be overcome. Coping is often more successful when the child has minimal pain or physical impairments, positive beliefs and expectations about her or his abilities, and good family and community supports (Smith & Lazarus, 1990). Serious and chronic illnesses require continual shifts in coping mechanisms, and children (and their families) who are flexible are in a better position to meet these demands (Rowland, 1989b). *Ineffective coping* strategies are those that emphasize inhibition, passivity, stoicism, apathy, and hopelessness (Rowland, 1989b); these strategies may be utilized when the child or parents interpret the illness as a permanent detriment (Smith & Lazarus, 1990).

When children and their families are successful in coping with the stresses caused by illness, they may experience pride in the knowledge that they can conquer adversity. Those who are unsuccessful, however, may experience even greater stress, including feelings of failure and incompetence. You want to make every effort to facilitate children's and families' active participation in managing the challenges imposed by the children's illnesses (Rowland, 1989b).

Exercise 15-1. Evaluating a Child with a Psychogenic Cough

After you read the case, answer the following question: What are the developmental, biological, psychological, social, and familial factors involved in the case? Compare your answers with those following the case. The material in this exercise was adapted from Lask and Fosson (1989, pp. 5–6, with changes in notation).

Adrian, aged 11, developed a persistent, unremitting dry cough about six weeks after changing schools. He had been attending a small, friendly primary school, and his new school was a large secondary school. Detailed physical examination revealed no organic cause, but his general condition is deteriorating. He has no appetite, has lost 11 pounds, and feels exhausted. He can no longer cope with going to school, and he is obviously depressed. The health care provider consulted with a mental health professional, and they arrived at a diagnosis of psychogenic cough.

The psychosocial assessment revealed the following background. Adrian's parents separated two years previously but remain friendly. His father lives with a new partner, and Adrian stays with them on alternate weekends. He feels guilty because he knows that his mother is lonely, having recently ended a brief and violent relationship. One year ago, she was found to have a malignant tumor, for which she had refused surgery but had accepted radiotherapy. She did not want any follow-up treatment and refused to discuss this with anyone. Adrian had been relatively healthy until recently, apart from recurrent upper respiratory infections and a period of separation anxiety when he started school. His mother described Adrian as a sensitive and somewhat anxious child.

Suggested Answers

Developmental, biological, psychological, social, and familial factors may be involved in Adrian's case in the following way:

1. *Developmental.* The transition from a small, friendly primary school to a large secondary school may have been stressful.

2. *Biological.* Adrian's vulnerability to upper respiratory infections may predispose him to recurrent coughing; however, he had been relatively healthy until recently, which is a favorable sign.

3. *Psychological.* Adrian appears to be a sensitive and anxious child who has a history of separation difficulty; however, there was no indication of severe prior psychological problems.

4. *Social.* Adrian may be having difficulty settling in the new school, making friends, and coping with a less friendly school environment.

5. *Familial.* Adrian has had to cope with divided loyalties, wanting to be with both of his parents, who are separated; his divided loyalties and blocked communications may have prevented him from openly discussing his distress; the absence of communication about his mother's potentially fatal illness may have exacerbated his concerns about her; the fact that his parents remain friendly is a favorable sign.

ADHERENCE

Because failure to adhere to a medical regimen is a major reason why mental health professionals become involved with medically ill children, we need to look closely at the factors associated with adherence. (I use the term *adherence* instead of *compliance* because adherence suggests patient involvement, whereas compliance suggests a passive acceptance of a treatment regimen.) Treating a medical illness may require a complex regimen that changes the child's and the family's life style. Adherence to a medical regimen may require taking medication, modifying activity patterns, and going to frequent medical appointments. For younger children, adherence to a medical regimen primarily refers to the parents' behavior because the parents are the persons responsible for carrying out the regimen. Failure to follow the prescribed medical regimen may seriously compromise children's health.

To adequately assess adherence behaviors, you need to know "what behaviors are required of the patient and their relationship to one another" (Johnson, 1991, p. 116). A complex medical regimen that requires several kinds of behaviors may not be easy to monitor because each behavior must be clearly defined (Johnson, 1991). For example, with insulin-dependent diabetes mellitus, a medical regimen may consist of injecting insulin twice a day at appropriate times, eating meals following a defined pattern, avoiding foods with high concentrations of sugars and fats, exercising regularly, and testing blood glucose levels several times a day.

Factors That Affect Adherence

Adherence depends on such factors as the length of time and complexity of the regimen, on the child's and the parents' ability to follow the regimen, on the clarity of the communication from the health care provider to the child and parents, and on the child's and parents' relationship with the health care provider. Adherence to a medical regimen is likely to be lower when the regimen is long term or has several components. The child may believe that she or he is adherent but behave in nonadherent ways because of inadequate knowledge, comprehension, or skill. The health care provider may believe that he or she has adequately instructed the child and parents when, in fact, he or she has used professional jargon or otherwise has not clearly conveyed to them the information they need to implement the treatment regimen. In addition, information from one health care provider may conflict with that given by another health care provider. Children and their parents may not ask for clarification because they do not realize that they need more information or because they prefer not to show their ignorance or to confront the health care provider with questions. In general, a positive relationship with the health care provider is likely to facilitate adherence to the treatment regimen.

Children and their parents may be reluctant to voice their concerns about regimens that do not appear to help the children or that are too difficult to implement. Also, during the meeting with the health care provider they may be tense and anxious, unable to concentrate on what the health care provider is saying, and therefore recall only part of what they were told. *Thus, miscommunication between the health care provider and children and their parents may lead to nonadherence.*

Children or parents may adhere to some aspects of the treatment regimen but not to other aspects. For example, they may keep appointments or take the medications but not follow dietary restrictions. One reason for this pattern is that they may find it more difficult to follow some parts of the treatment regimen than other parts. Responsibility for adherence to a prescribed treatment regimen usually will fall on the parent or on the health care provider, rather than on the child directly. Research suggests that adherence is increased when children and parents perceive the child's illness as serious (Gudas, Koocher, & Wypij, 1991).

Children and parents may find creative ways that are not prescribed to accomplish the treatment goals. For example, children may find ways to exercise without going to physical therapy. Families need to be encouraged to inform health care providers of their ideas and suggestions for an optimally effective regimen.

Children who are anxious or depressed or who experience interpersonal and family conflicts may have more difficulty with adherence than children who are better adjusted and who have supportive and cohesive families (La Greca & Spetter, 1992). Although children's developmental status is important in understanding how they manage their illness, little is known about the relationship between developmental status and adherence (La Greca, 1990). Overall, however, younger children usually require more structure and supervision than older ones.

Factors that affect adherence in adolescents. Let's now look at several factors that affect adherence in adolescents (La Greca, 1990).

1. *Adolescent turmoil.* Adolescents may be concerned about self-esteem, independence, academic and physical competence, sex roles, peer relations, and family relations. These concerns may contribute to adolescent turmoil and rebellion and may affect treatment adherence. (Also see Chapter 3 for more information about adolescents.)

2. *Challenge of some illnesses.* Some illnesses, such as diabetes, "present a greater challenge for adolescents to control, due to the marked physical growth and metabolic fluctuations that accompany the onset and course of puberty" (La Greca, 1990, p. 429). Adolescent children with diabetes tend to underestimate the frequency with which they eat and the amount of food they consume; they also tend to underestimate the strenuousness of their exercise, but not its frequency or duration (Johnson, 1991).

3. *Assuming responsibility for the regimen.* Although adolescents are supposed to assume more responsibility for the management of their illness than younger children, there may be communication breakdowns in some families about who is responsible for carrying out the treatment regimen (Eiser, 1993).

4. *Working independently in following the regimen.* Adolescents working alone in following treatment regimens are expected to be more knowledgeable about their illness than younger children, who are supervised more carefully by their parents. Working alone may lead adolescents to pay greater attention and take on more responsibility, or it may not. Adolescents are likely to function more independently when health care providers explain and demonstrate what needs to be done, check and reinforce what the adolescents have done, and reinforce the adolescents' adherence behaviors.

5. *Type of regimen.* Treatment regimens that are complicated and arduous are especially difficult to follow and may be taxing and exhausting for very sick adolescents (Gudas et al., 1991).

Nonadherence. *Nonadherence* may take several forms including refusing treatment, failing to take medications as prescribed, failing to keep appointments, and choosing alternative, unorthodox treatments to replace the prescribed treatment regimen (Pfefferbaum, 1989). Reasons for nonadherence, as noted earlier, may lie in characteristics of the treatment regimen and in the characteristics and behaviors of the child, parent, or medical provider or in lack of communication between any of the participants (see Table 15-2).

Following are examples of patient and caregiver beliefs that can undermine adherence (Meichenbaum & Turk, 1987, p. 47).

- You need to give your body some rest from medicine once in a while or otherwise your body becomes too dependent on it or immune to it.
- When my child's symptoms go away I can stop using the medicine.
- I don't feel the drug is doing anything.
- I resent being controlled by drugs.
- My pain must have an organic cause; doing the exercises won't make any difference.
- How will I know if I still need them if I keep taking pills?
- Nothing I do seems to help.

In the following interview segments, a family discusses problems associated with the 9-year-old son's adherence to a diabetes regimen (Gross, 1990, p. 159, with changes in notation; IR = Interviewer, IE-M = Mother, IE-F = Father, IE-C = Child).

IE-M: Well, we had quite a fight about doing a blood test this morning.

IR: What happened?

IE-M: I was making breakfast when my son came downstairs. He started getting his insulin ready, and I asked him if he had done his blood test. He said he had and that his blood glucose was 137. Since I had just emptied the trash, I went upstairs while he was eating and checked to see if he had used his test equipment. I found a discarded lancet, test strip, and alcohol swab.

Table 15-2
Possible Reasons for Nonadherence

Child Variables

The child:

- believes the condition is not serious and that it will not get worse; therefore, the regimen doesn't need to be followed.
- is asymptomatic or feels well and doesn't believe she or he needs the treatment.
- believes the illness is incurable.
- believes that her or his religious or cultural faith will cure the illness.
- wants to show her or his autonomy and control or does not want to take the time needed to perform the treatment.
- finds that following the regimen is too inconvenient, painful, or complicated.
- engages in antisocial behavior, which is directed at the physician and health care team because they are authority figures.
- believes the treatment will adversely affect her or his appearance.
- has had a bad experience with the treatment in the past or knows other children who have followed similar treatments and who have not improved.
- has become apathetic or frustrated about the treatment and possibilities of symptom relief or is dissatisfied with some aspect of the treatment.
- does not understand the medical regimen or has a thought disorder that interferes with adherence.
- has inappropriate expectations about treatment.
- believes in traditional healing practices of her or his cultural group that conflict with the medical regimen.
- does not have social supports that encourage adherence to the regimen.
- does not want to lose face with her or his peers by following the regimen.

Parent Variables

The parents:

- don't want or can't stand to be involved in hurting or causing pain to their child.
- believe the illness is incurable.
- refuse to recognize that the child is ill; nonadherence represents a denial of illness and its implications.
- believe that their religious or cultural faith will cure the illness.
- believe the treatment will be too frightening for the child.
- do not understand the medical regimen.
- do not want to take the time needed to comply with the treatment or find that the regimen is too inconvenient or complicated.
- have a thought disorder that interferes with their ability to help the child.

- have severe disagreements with each other or with other caregivers about how to carry out the medical regimen.
- lack resources to comply with the regimen, such as transportation, money, or child care.
- do not support the treatment.
- are overprotective of their child and do not want the child to be bothered with the treatments.
- have inappropriate expectations about the child's ability for self-care.
- fail to clarify with the child who is responsible for following the regimen, especially as the child matures.
- are ambivalent about the treatment, particularly when the child is only marginally motivated to comply or is asymptomatic.
- have inappropriate expectations about treatment.
- have a belief system based on their cultural traditions that conflicts with the medical regimen.
- are angry with the hospital or health care provider staff.

Health Care Provider Variables

The health care provider:

- communicates poorly with the child and parents or is cold, distant, and unempathic.
- fails to give feedback to or solicit feedback from the child and her or his parents.
- fails to gain the trust of the child or parents.
- has given up on the child and the family because of suspected nonadherence.
- communicates poorly with other health care providers on the treatment team.
- provides information that contradicts information already received from other health care providers.

Treatment and Treatment Facility Variables

The treatment:

- is complex, has a long duration, and requires major changes in the child's behavior.
- is aversive, has severe side effects, is expensive, or takes much preparation.
- did not begin until several weeks after the health care provider requested the treatment.
- has not been continuous.
- takes place in a facility that has a poor reputation, has poor services and long waiting times, is poorly located, and has inconvenient hours.
- takes place in a facility that exposes the adolescent to people in advanced stages of illness, which makes her or him uncomfortable.

Source: Adapted from Katz, Dolgin, & Varni (1990) and Meichenbaum and Turk (1987).

However, he simply had opened these up and thrown them into the trash can.

IR: What did you do then?

IE-M: I confronted him about lying to me and told him that he had better get himself upstairs right then and do the test.

IR: Did he obey?

IE-M: He started complaining about how much he hated the test, that it hurt. I lost my temper and started yelling at him.

IR: What happened next?

IE-F: I told him that if he didn't get moving, he couldn't watch TV for the rest of the week.

IR: Did that get him going?

IE-M: He went upstairs but didn't do the test. It was getting late, and we needed to leave to arrive here on time. So we just skipped the test and came here.

IR: Does his behavior usually result in the avoidance of blood testing?

IE-M: Not all the time. Sometimes I simply perform the test on him.

IR: Will you stick to your promise of no TV?

IE-F: Probably not for the entire week.

After obtaining a description of how the parent and child interact in these problem situations, the interviewer met alone with the child. The interviewer attempted to assess the youth's knowledge of why he was in the clinic.

IR: Do you know why you are here?

IE-C: No. Maybe 'cause of my diabetes.

IR: Your Mom and Dad tell me that you don't like doing some of the things that you have to do to control your diabetes. They said that all of you sometimes fight about it and that they want to learn how to get along without yelling and spankings. Would you like that?

IE-C: Yeah.

IR: What could you do to stop the yelling about your diabetes?

IE-C: I could do my blood tests.

IR: What else?

After some discussion, the interviewer tried to learn about rewards that could be used to develop a behavioral intervention program.

IR: Your Dad tells me that you are quite a basketball player. Do you have a favorite team?

IE-C: I like Larry Bird and the Boston Celtics.

IR: Do you ever watch them on TV?

IE-C: Sometimes. Dad says he might take me to see Ole Miss play.

IR: Would you like that?

IE-C: Sure.

Evaluating Adherence

In evaluating adherence, you will want to consider how biological, psychological, and sociological issues influence self-care behaviors (see Table 15-3). You can use some of the questions in Table F-27 and Table F-33 in Appendix F to ask the child and parent, respectively, about adherence to the treatment regimen. *If the child is not improving, do not automatically assume that it is because of his or her failure to follow the treatment regimen.* The child could be following the treatment regimen and still fail to improve because the regimen is ineffective, the diagnosis is wrong, the treatment dosage is wrong, the wrong medicine was prescribed, or because other factors are operating.

Monitoring Adherence

It is not easy to monitor adherence because children and their parents may fail to record or report their behaviors accurately when they are following the treatment regimen or they may record behaviors that they never performed. In addition, unless the child and parents are monitored at frequent intervals, you will have difficulty evaluating whether they are following the treatment regimen consistently. For example, children who initially adhere to the regimen may not do so once they see some improvement. Similarly, parents who initially do everything possible to ensure that their child follows the regimen may not be as attentive when they see some improvement, when the regimen demands are too great or become too time consuming, or when they see no improvement. Thus, children's and parents' beliefs and concerns about the illness may change during the treatment regimen. (Also see Chapter 3 for information about the benefits and limitations associated with self-monitoring.)

Let's examine four ways to monitor adherence, recognizing that each one has some potential difficulties.

1. *Verbal reports from the child and parents.* It is useful to obtain verbal reports from the child and parents about the child's adherence to the medical regimen. However, verbal reports may be inaccurate because the child, the parents, or both may tell you what they believe you want to hear or because they may fail to recall important facts. Also, you may have difficulty deciding which report is accurate if the child's and parents' reports differ. If necessary, encourage the child and parents to make notes about what they have done to follow the regimen. Also, help them recognize that accurate reports are needed for the regimen to be monitored properly and for adjustments in the regimen to be made.

2. *Recordings from the child and parents.* Recordings—on special forms, in a diary, or on a computer—made by the child and parents of the child's daily adherence behavior may be useful (see Chapters 17 and 18 for examples of self-monitoring forms). Note, however, that children and parents may not keep complete records, may complete records inaccurately, and may catch up on their record keeping several days after the fact.

3. *Pill and bottle counts.* Pill and bottle counts serve as an indirect method of assessing adherence, particularly for

Table 15-3
Questions to Consider When the Child or Parent Is Nonadherent

Biological Issues
Medical Condition
1. How long has the child been suffering from this illness?
2. How long can the child expect to be ill?
3. What is the prognosis?
4. Does the child know the prognosis?
5. Are there symptoms of the illness that are particularly problematic for this child?
6. How has the child responded to medical interventions in the past?
7. Are there any other illnesses, either chronic or acute, that may be concurrently affecting the child's condition?

Physiological Make-up
8. Could the age or sex of the child be a factor in her or his nonadherence?
9. What is the family's history of the illness and its response to treatment?
10. Is the child or parent handicapped in any way that would make adherence more difficult (for example, arthritis complicates using child-proof containers, and cognitive impairments complicate remembering to take antibiotics)?

Medication
11. Can the child's family afford the medication?
12. Has the dosage schedule been made as simple and convenient for the child and parent as it can be without sacrificing therapeutic effectiveness?
13. Does either the timing of the dose or the drug itself affect the child's activities in ways that are unacceptable to her or him or to the parent?
14. What is the potential impact of the drug on the child's dietary habits?
15. Is the drug dispensed in a form that is convenient for the child and parent?
16. How many other drugs is the child also taking, and may the quantity of drugs have an effect on adherence?
17. How aversive are the side effects of the drug?
18. Is the treatment worse than the illness (for example, young males may refuse to take phenothiazine because it renders them impotent)?
19. Are the side effects particularly problematic for this child because of life style, vocational, or personal reasons?
20. Is there a less potent medication that would produce similar therapeutic results?

Psychological Issues
Behavioral
21. How does the child's life style affect her or his medication use?
22. Does the child have erratic eating or sleeping habits that may affect her or his medication use?
23. Does the child have any dietary habits that may interfere with drug action or ingestion (for example, insisting on eating milk products despite taking certain antibiotics)?

24. Does the child have any behaviors that may inhibit drug taking (for example, difficulty swallowing pills)?
25. Is the flavor of the drug one that the child dislikes?

Cognitive
26. Is educational level a factor in the child's or parent's noncompliance (for example, can the child or parent read the instructions and measure the appropriate dose)?
27. Can the child or parent make good decisions, if judgment regarding drug use is required?
28. Is the child's or parent's memory sufficiently intact?
29. What is the child's or parent's expectation regarding effects and side effects of the drug?
30. Does the child or parent have any erroneous beliefs about the drug (for example, that the child will become addicted to a nonnarcotic)?
31. What has the child or parent thought about prescribed drugs in the past?
32. How does the child accept the patient role?

Affective
33. Does the child or parent deny that the child is ill?
34. Is the child or parent excessively anxious about either the medical condition itself or aspects of the treatment?
35. Is the child or parent so deeply depressed that the depression might interfere with adherence?
36. Are other emotions in the child or parent (for example, anger, fear, or rejection) maladaptive because they are interfering with treatment?

Sociological Issues
Health Care Provider
37. Did the health care provider adequately explain the rationale for both the medication and the treatment regimen to the child and parent?
38. Did the health care provider take sufficient time with the child and parent?
39. Has the health care provider developed a sense of trust with the child and parent?
40. Have the child and parent complied with the instructions of health care providers in the past?

Environment
41. Are the health care facilities convenient for the child and parent?
42. Does the child have to wait too long to be seen?
43. Is there anything about the child's schooling or job or with the parent's job or other duties that might interfere with making appointments?
44. Are office hours convenient for the child and parent?
45. Are child care facilities available if needed for other family members?

Others' Support
46. Does the health care provider's support staff facilitate adherence?

(Continued)

Table 15-3 (*Continued*)

47. Does the family understand the child's illness?
48. Does the family accept the child's illness?
49. Does the illness or its treatment preclude the child or parent from having social interactions with others?
50. What kinds of experience have family members or friends had with the illness or with the prescribed drug?
51. Have their experiences influenced the child's or parent's beliefs about the illness or its treatment?
52. Do friends or relatives reinforce the child's illness, making it more difficult for her or him to achieve symptom remission?
53. Do friends or family avoid the child since she or he has become ill?
54. Are friends or family more attentive to the child since she or he has become ill?

55. Are friends or family supportive of the prescribed regimen?

Demographic
56. Are there racial, ethnic, or religious factors that may be interfering with the child's or parent's ability to adhere to the regimen?
57. Does the prescribed regimen interfere with the child's schooling (or job) performance or with the parent's work or other duties in significant ways?
58. Can the child's family afford the drug in the dose and amount required?
59. Can the child's family afford follow-up medical care?

Source: Adapted and reprinted with permission of the publisher and authors, from D. J. Moore and E. A. Klonoff, "Assessment of Compliance: A Systems Perspective," in K. D. Gadow and A. Poling (Eds.), *Advances in Learning and Behavioral Disabilities* (Supp. 1), copyright 1986 by JAI Press Inc., pp. 239–241.

adolescents and adults. The counts are only partially useful, however, because complex medical regimens require more than taking medication, and the medication may be taken in the wrong dosage, taken at the wrong time, or thrown away.

4. *Twenty-four-hour recall interview.* The focus of a 24-hour recall interview is specific regimen-related behaviors that the child engaged in during the preceding 24 hours. You can interview children (even as young as 6 years) and their parents separately and then compare their reports as a reliability check. Here are two examples of instructions for a 24-hour recall. The first is for a child with diabetes mellitus: "I'd like you to think about yesterday. Tell me about all the things you did to take care of your diabetes. What was the first thing you did yesterday? What was next? And what was after that?" The second is for a child who has an eating disorder: "I'd like you to think about yesterday. Tell me about what you ate. First, what time did you get up? When did you first eat? What did you eat? And when did you eat next?"

After the child and parents share their recollections with you, you may need to give them prompts to elicit more details about the behaviors related to the illness. For example, for a child with insulin-dependent diabetes mellitus, you may need to ask whether the child took injections, exercised, ate properly, and did glucose tests. For a child with an eating disorder, you may need to ask about quantity of food, liquids, or snacks consumed. If the child and parents did not report on these areas, you will need to probe about each one that was not discussed.

Although the 24-hour recall interview is useful, the information may be misleading, as any one day may not be typical of the child's usual pattern. You may want to interview the child and his or her parents on several different days to get a more accurate record.

Improving Adherence

Encouraging children and their parents to participate actively in the children's health care is a key to improving adherence. Involving both children and their parents in treatment planning and in making decisions will give them an opportunity to voice their concerns about the treatment regimen, set realistic goals, indicate their priorities, and consider possible barriers to adherence (Haynes, Wang, & Da Mota Gomes, 1987). Another key to improving adherence is to evaluate the perceptions that children and parents have of their ability to follow the treatment regimen and then to help them do what is needed to follow the plan.

Children with little hope, few social supports, negative self-esteem, and poor problem-solving skills are at risk for not following the regimen (Gudas et al., 1991). Look for ways to improve their self-management skills and to foster self-esteem, mastery over life events, and hopefulness. This can be achieved, in part, by helping the children and their families share responsibility for treatment management, encouraging family members and friends to give the children support, and increasing the children's understanding of their illness and the treatment regimen (Gudas et al., 1991).

Adherence also can be improved by encouraging children and their parents to inform the health care provider when they believe that the regimen can be improved or when they think that there is a better way to accomplish the treatment goals. Health care providers should act as facilitators, encouraging children and parents to ask questions and give suggestions. Encouraging children and parents to be active participants in the regimen will improve their adherence and empower them at a time when they may feel anxious and depressed (L. Gudas, personal communication, February 1996).

For Better or For Worse   by Lynn Johnston

Finally, children and their parents are more likely to adhere to a regimen when they have rapport with and respect for the health care provider, have their questions answered clearly and honestly by the health care provider, see the illness as curable or at least as becoming more manageable, understand how the illness developed and how it is maintained, recognize the costs and rewards of entering treatment, understand the time and effort required to adhere to the regimen, know an approximate timetable for getting relief of symptoms, and recognize the obstacles that may occur and ways of dealing with them (Tunks & Bellissimo, 1991). Table 15-4 gives specific suggestions for improving adherence.

In an area where efficacious therapies exist or are being developed at a rapid rate, it is truly discouraging that one-half of patients for whom appropriate therapy is prescribed fail to receive full benefit through inadequate adherence to treatment.

—R. B. Haynes

FAMILIES OF MEDICALLY ILL CHILDREN

Earlier you read about familial variables related to coping. Some other issues related to families with a medically ill child follow.

Parents' Concerns in Raising a Medically Ill Child

Let's now look at how parents of medically ill children voice their concerns about raising their children (Chesler & Bar-

barin, 1987, p. 48; Diehl, Moffitt, & Wade, 1991, pp. 177–178; K. Gist, personal communication, July 1995; Martinson & Cohen, 1988, pp. 84–89, 91–94; van Veldhuizen & Last, 1991, pp. 116, 130–131, 141, 170–171, 202).

1. *Unpreparedness for the diagnosis or failure to receive an adequate diagnosis.* Parents may not have considered the possibility that their child's symptoms represent a serious illness; they wanted to think that the problem was minor. They may be frustrated if they have not received an adequate diagnosis or sufficient information about their child's condition.

- She had diarrhea for three weeks. It was really bad. I thought about bringing her to the doctor, but I thought I was being a hypochondriac, so I just waited and kept giving her stuff like crackers and no milk. I just don't understand how something like this [leukemia] can happen to a little baby.
- We didn't know. Babies, when they are born—a lot of things look different until they get a little older. I thought maybe she needed a patch over her eye or something, because when I was little, I had a patch over my eye because I was cross-eyed. I thought it [the diagnosis] was ridiculous. How can a 3-month-old baby have to have her eye removed because she's got crossed eyes. I just couldn't believe that. It was like a nightmare.
- At the hospital I was calm the entire day, but when I got home I just kept on crying. I didn't break down in front of her. Once she said to my wife: I never see daddy cry. Doesn't he care? My wife explained that I cried too, but that I preferred to do this when I was alone.
- Cerebral palsy is so broad. I don't know what it means.
- I just never get a diagnosis.
- It was a terrible blow for me when I heard what was wrong with him. It was like someone threw a stone through a window which cannot be repaired anymore. It made me cry. It's so unfair to the boy. Later on I managed to leave it all to science and to Our Heavenly Father.

Table 15-4
Suggestions for Improving Adherence

The following suggestions must be tailored to the child's age, ability to comprehend the regimen, type of illness, and culture and to the parents' culture, ability to comprehend the regimen, and resources that will allow them to follow the regimen. To carry out these suggestions, you should have as many answers as possible to the questions shown in Table 15-3.

Information Management

1. Organize and present information regarding the causes of the illness, expected outcome, reason for treatment, expectations and collateral effects of treatment, and consequences of inadequate treatment.
2. Entertain questions from the child and parents about the illness and treatment in order to deal with fears, misunderstandings, misconceptions, and needed clarifications. Be available if doubts or questions arise later.
3. Use clear, age-appropriate, and straightforward language.
4. Present information gradually and in a rational way, recognizing that the child and parents may be distressed and that there are limits to their ability to process information.
5. Break down a complicated or long-term regimen into smaller segments.
6. Present information both orally and in written form, and use visual aids to increase retention.
7. Emphasize the "how-to" aspects, and avoid esoteric explanations.
8. Use adjunctive personnel, such as a health educator, dietician, or pharmacist when necessary.
9. Encourage the child and parents to tell the primary care provider when they believe that part of the regimen could be improved or does not work or that there is a better way to accomplish the treatment goal.

Behavior Management

10. Tailor the instructions to the child's and parents' daily routine.
11. Use procedures designed to help the child and parents remember and develop a habitual routine. For example, recommend the use of pill containers that have each pill in a slot for a given day and the use of written reminders to be posted in a convenient place by the child or parents.
12. Introduce components of the regimen gradually, especially when the regimen is complex.
13. Give the child and parents a specific appointment time and the name of the health care professional to be seen; use reminders, such as cards sent by mail or telephone calls; schedule the appointment in the near future; ensure continuity of care; keep an active follow-up appointment file; and discuss reasons for previously missed appointments to ensure that appointments are kept.

Self-Management

14. Be sure that the child and parents understand the rationale behind the treatment regimen and the evidence that it will work. Create positive expectations about its efficacy and about the child's and parents' ability to carry out the treatment regimen.
15. Clearly define the steps that the child and parents need to follow in the treatment regimen. Have the child (and parents, where relevant) repeat the instructions or state them in her or his own words.
16. Use self-monitoring procedures for measuring progress toward following the treatment regimen.
17. Give skill training when necessary to help the child and parents follow the treatment regimen. This training may include oral and written instructions, modeling by the professional, and practice by the child. Assess the child's and parents' ability to carry out the regimen. Also have the parents (and child when she or he is capable) write down the instructions, and have the parents (or child when she or he is capable) call the health care provider if they have any questions.

Incentive Management

18. Evaluate carefully the problem in its context.
19. Eliminate unnecessary hassles in the regimen or in the treatment setting, such as in time scheduling or in a clinic organization.
20. Avoid treatment routines that could be interpreted as demeaning.
21. Keep the regimen simple. If, for example, several behavioral steps are required, tie them into a sequence that is logistically straightforward and similar from time to time.
22. Prepare the child and parents for any inconvenience, discomfort, pain, and the like. Give the child and parents specific instructions on how to cope with these potential problems. Use modeling and rehearsal as needed.
23. Develop regimens that do not make the child appear different from his or her peers or highlight differences, if possible.
24. Build natural reinforcement into the treatment system. For example, increasing the throwing tolerance of a child who has shoulder pain may be tied to the number of innings she or he can play in a baseball game.
25. Use other systems of reward—such as rebates, awards, or recognition by a peer group—to improve the child's adherence. This can be done, in part, by contingency contracting, in which the child and the health care provider negotiate a series of treatment activities and goals and specify the rewards the child will get for succeeding.

Support Management

26. Introduce the child's family to the treatment program to enlist their support, and modify their responses where

(Continued)

Table 15-4 (*Continued*)

their behavior could pose obstacles to the child's behavioral changes. For example, teach parents to distinguish legitimate complaints from those that are used to avoid the treatment, to reinforce the child for cooperation, and to use discipline strategies to minimize nonadherence. For an older child, encourage the parents to support, as much as possible, the child's self-management and to improve parent/child communication.

27. Build in a regular system of review so that you can verbally reward adherence to the regimen.
28. Build a good child/parents–clinician relationship by being warm, empathic, and understanding of the child, the parents, and their culture.
29. Arrange for the child to have the same treatment personnel consistently, if possible.
30. View the child and the parents as key members of the treatment team, without whose cooperation you can accomplish nothing.
31. Encourage the parents to inform the teacher about the child's medical condition.
32. Contact the teachers and discuss with them how they can help the child follow the treatment regimen when you have the child's and parents' permission to do so.
33. Follow up continuously on how the child and parents adhere to the regimen. Do not, however, monitor to the point where it impairs your relationship with them. For example, you may want the parents to monitor the child's behavior to corroborate the child's self-report. However, insisting on it against the child's wishes might produce nonadherence.

Medication Management

34. Encourage the parents to call the child's physician if the child has trouble taking the medication. Perhaps the child's physician can prescribe an alternative product or form of the medication.
35. Encourage the parents to call the child's physician if the parents think the medication is causing the child to have an adverse reaction; the physician can probably diagnose the cause of the problem.
36. Encourage the parents to give their child the medication at the same time every day so that it becomes routine. Tell the parents to tape a reminder on the refrigerator or in another convenient location about when the medication is to be given. Inform the parents that some pharmacies sell containers with compartments for storing the medication by days of the week and times of day.
37. Tell the parents not to double the dose the next scheduled time if they forget to give the child a dose, unless doing so is approved by the child's physician.
38. Tell the parents to continue to give the medication to their child even if they believe it is not working. Some medications need time to take effect. Encourage the parents to contact the child's physician if they have any questions about discontinuing the medication.
39. Tell the parents not to assume that once symptoms go away it's okay to stop giving their child the medication. Encourage the parents to give their child the medication for the entire time noted on the prescription or as recommended by the child's physician.
40. Tell the parents to ask the child's physician if a less expensive medication is available if the prescribed medication is too expensive. Also encourage the parents to check with their health care provider to learn whether there are programs available to help them in the purchase of the medication.
41. Encourage the parents to keep all medications out of the reach of young children.

Source: Adapted and reprinted with permission of the authors and publishers, from E. Tunks and A. Bellissimo, *Behavioral Medicine: Concepts and Procedures*, copyright © 1991 by Allyn & Bacon, pp. 24–26. Other sources are Dunbar and Waszak (1990); Kaiser Permanente (1995); Rapoff, Lindsley, and Christophersen (1985); Sarafino (1994); and Sheridan and Radmacher (1992).

---

2. *Initial relinquishing of control.* Parents may initially try to cope with the diagnosis by relinquishing control of the situation.

- You reach a certain point where everything comes to a head, and you've worried and cried so much that you can't do it anymore. And all of a sudden, it was just like this burden was gone. All of a sudden I realized it wasn't all on me, and then I felt a lot better. It was like a transformation. I could hear in my mind—it wasn't really a voice, it was just a thought that things were being taken care of, and whatever would happen was going to happen…. It was such a comfort to know you weren't [responsible]; I mean, it was out of your hands.
- We had complete confidence in the doctors. It's "Here's my son—fix him!" you know, like a car. I just felt whatever [the doctor] thought should happen should happen.

- I turned it over to God when it first happened because it was something I couldn't control. There was nothing I could do other than give her love and attention and the things she needs as a human being.

3. *Need for information.* Some parents appreciate being given complete information about the child's condition, whereas others do not.

- They told me the good side and the bad side. I was really impressed with their honesty.
- [The doctors] have been very good about laying everything out and dealing with it the way it is. I wish more people could be that way. It's really good because…. Why lie to us? Why keep something from us? We're going to have to deal with it eventually, so maybe [it] gives us a little more time to deal with it. That's how I see it.

- We didn't want anything held back from us [but] they were talking about the radiation, and I just said: Is it absolutely necessary for her to have the radiation? And [the doctor] turned around to me and said: "Do you want her to be dead?" So that answered my question, but it was a little abrupt.
- [My wife] didn't want to be so well informed. She said, "I wish they wouldn't say so much to us."

4. *Self-blame and guilt.* Parents may be concerned about their not having done things that might have helped the child's illness, their being too late in noticing that something was seriously wrong with their child, their having to see their child suffer, and their being helpless to do anything about the situation.

- Why didn't I take her to the doctor sooner?
- He got sick because I didn't feed him the proper foods.
- I know that I can do something more to help her but I'm just not sure what that could be.

5. *Ability to cope with the situation.* Parents may be concerned about their ability to work through their feelings of helplessness, anxiety, fear, anger, guilt, and sadness and feelings that they are going to break down.

- I had to learn to relax and say "If my child is alive when I get home, then my husband has done the job [of taking care of our child]."
- Who is going to take over if I get sick?
- I had quite a problem with my stomach. It bothered me. In fact, I was close to having ulcers afterwards, but I had always had some problems with a nervous stomach. When he was in the hospital, I had quite a time with my stomach…nervous problems I think.
- I was very hurt and hopeless and I didn't know what to do. I had a lot of depression and anger during certain periods, and a lot of frustration. I lost a lot of sleep and didn't eat for the longest time.
- During her illness, my problem was patience. I was very impatient. I got upset with her even though I knew she was in a lot of pain, but I wanted her to keep it to herself. The medication made her cranky and that was hard for me to tolerate. I was upset because she hurt. I didn't want her to hurt but I didn't want her to tell me about it either.

6. *Strategies for managing probabilistic information.* Parents who receive information about the *probability* of their child's survival will interpret this information from their own perspective.

- I don't think we could be more happy unless it was not having [cancer] at all. [Our daughter's] chances of complete, total recovery are better than 90 percent.
- There's still a 10-to-15-percent chance that [our daughter] will have some other kind of tumor in the field of radiation. To me, the chances are a lot different when something's really happened to you. The chances of 10 to 15 percent seem high to me. Humongous!
- I'd like to ask about his chances, about survival rate, but I don't do that when he's in the room. I think its o.k. for him to believe that the worst trouble is behind him. What's more, the questions don't help anyway because you know it's only a statistic.

7. *Dealing with hospitalization.* Parents may have concerns about how the child will be treated in the hospital.

- Get a good rapport with the nurse right away.
- Hospital is like a trauma scene when you go in there. She's so tense and upset.

8. *Uncertainty about communicating with the child.* Parents may not be sure about how to communicate with their sick child.

- I keep on trying to find out what he's thinking. I think this is important. He himself is convinced he'll get better. Of course I'll get better, he says. I think this is a dilemma. He has a very malignant tumor so I can't be so optimistic myself. On the one hand, you want to be as realistic as possible with him. Try to reduce his optimism a bit. On the other hand, it's also very important to help him bear up. If he would all of a sudden go to the other extreme and would say: I don't believe in it anymore, I don't want to go on, then I'd find that terrible too.
- When everything was going alright it was easier. Then you could talk freely in his presence. But now that it's come back, I really don't think I can handle it anymore. Now you know that his chances are much worse. Now the big issue is whether he'll get better. I don't think you should talk about this when he's there. You try to protect him from everything and still be honest. That can be very trying at times.
- My husband and I wanted to tell him together, but I couldn't. I was too upset. So my husband told him but I was there at the time. Later I asked him: If we hadn't told you then and you would have learned it from another person later, what would you have thought? Then I would've thought you were very mean, he said. From that moment on I've always been honest with him. In time I found it less difficult.
- You have this feeling of doubt. Am I doing the right thing by telling her all this? She was so optimistic…then if you say there's a chance she might die…I was afraid she would lose her courage so I didn't tell her that. In time everything gradually became clear to her. She's seen so much misery around her.

9. *Fears about bringing the child home from the hospital.* Parents may fear bringing the child home from the hospital.

- It scares me to think [that] once we get out of the hospital, as much as I look forward to it, I'm not gonna have this daily boost of someone telling me: "Things are getting better. Things are looking good." I want a doctor to live in with me and tell me she's just fine.
- Once I got her home, I was really feeling like I was bringing home a time bomb.
- I think it will be harder after we bring her home, to be honest with you, because I think I will worry more than I do right now, knowing that she's in such good care—whereas at home, it will be my responsibility.

10. *Concerns about interactions with professionals.* Parents may be concerned about their ability to communicate with the health care provider staff.

- Professionals think parents are ignorant. You're the only one, nasty or nice, that's going to be an advocate for that kid.

- I had to keep saying, "wait a minute," because the doctor wanted to walk out on me.
- I'm always gonna be with her. You guys might only last a year or two.
- I'd love someone to devise a little notebook to concisely organize all the information that we have to keep track of, because doctors do not talk to other doctors.
- I had to feed her every hour on the hour and my doctor said, "Why are you doing that?" and I said, "That's the only way she'll eat." He thought I was making it up.
- They said, "Can't you make her behave?" They stick her five times and then became all upset because I couldn't make her sit still.

11. *Concern about the medical management of their sick child.* Parents may be concerned about their ability to assume additional responsibilities, such as providing special diets, cleaning equipment, providing daily therapy, and keeping medical appointments.

- There was 10 months between my equipment request and the needed home assessment. Then the person who came to assess the situation had no knowledge or background to make an assessment.
- I was following her around with the pump. All day long all I was doing was following her around with the pump. She kept pulling it out and it was spilling it everywhere. It wasn't working.
- They wanted the braces on my child 24 hours a day, but I can't listen to my child scream 24 hours a day.

12. *Financial burdens.* Parents may be concerned about their ability to meet the increased financial burdens associated with their child's illness.

- Everyone talks of money but nobody knows what's available to who, for what.
- Their answer was to have another baby because the more people in your family the easier it is to qualify.
- We've been double billed on our monitor for a year and a half. We sent the insurance company a certified letter but the bills just keep coming.
- You have to stand your ground and know you have rights. The first person you talk to is not the bottom line. I went through three case workers before I got SSI [Supplemental Security Income].
- Sometimes I just feel like giving up and going on welfare.
- No matter how much money we made, we could not subsidize these kinds of bills.

13. *Need to normalize family life.* Parents may be concerned about their ability to maintain a normal family life, including caring for their ill child and siblings, handling marital stresses, and handling strained family relationships.

- My main concern is to bring [our daughter] home and try to lead as normal a lifestyle as we possibly can, knowing at the same time that it will never be the same. But I would like to try, very hard, just to have it as close [to normal] as I can.
- I don't let myself get too hopeful. I just try to enjoy her day to day.
- I avoid thinking about two months from now—two years from now. I think about today—that we're handling it today. And that's just about the *only* way we can handle it.

- My wife deals with this differently than I do. I want to talk about it often. But she doesn't. I need people around me. She doesn't. We often drive to Amsterdam in silence; go the whole way without saying anything to each other. We aren't able to help each other with emotional problems because we cope so differently. That causes tension. It's changing our marriage.
- She [the healthy sibling] could not sleep for quite awhile. She would lie in her bed at night crying. She was also jealous of the attention that her sister received. Then we told her how ill her sister was and then it became clear that she had not been able to sleep because she was afraid her sister would die.

14. *Concern about educational needs.* Parents may be concerned about whether the school can cope with their sick child, including whether school personnel can recognize symptoms and take appropriate actions when needed.

- They have their little programs set up, your child is labeled for one of them and is supposed to fit in.
- The teachers and aides think I'm a pest but it's the only way my child gets service.
- They sell you a bill of goods and then say they're only responsible for "educational therapy."
- No preschool will take a child with a trach [tracheotomy] and she doesn't qualify for any placement. I didn't know what I needed until I knew what was viable.
- I'm torn between keeping her protected in her special class or giving her the advantages of mainstreaming.
- The individualized education plan looks great on paper, but implementation is another story. The aide is the only one providing direct service.

15. *Physical appearance, treatment, and social isolation.* Parents may be concerned about the child's physical appearance, teasing from peers, absences from school, social isolation, and any side effects of treatment, such as fatigue and weakness.

- You can't blend into any crowd. She's too obvious. No matter how you look, everyone is gonna be looking.
- It's like an invisible handicap. She looks normal so everyone expects she should act normally. Sometimes I wish she had cerebral palsy so everyone would give her a break.
- He is beginning to lose his hair and that makes me sad.
- I think it's not so much the side effects but what are the long-term side effects of the medication.
- How will the other children treat her when they see her scars?

16. *Developmental needs.* Parents may be concerned about how to protect their child who is chronically ill and yet meet his or her needs for increased autonomy, how to get the child to become more responsible for his or her care, how to get the child to realize that he or she is valued and has worthwhile future possibilities, and how to balance medical management and the child's psychosocial needs (including determining what risks are acceptable, weighing the pros and cons of various activities, and deciding whether to include the child in the decision making).

- When will he be ready to play ball with his friends?
- She seems ready to take her medicine by herself twice a day, but I'm just not sure.

17. *Fear of recurrence.* Parents may fear recurrence of the illness.

- [The fear] is still there. If he gets sick or something, it still crops up. Could this be it? He was complaining his stomach hurt, and it was on the other side of where he had his surgery. So it would be his other kidney. And we thought right away that's what it was.
- It's made me insane. There's times of absolute terror in the middle of the night when you just sit there and think about that whole thing all over again. Boy, as soon as she got sick [with a viral infection] in the back of my mind I thought, "It's back! Oh, it's back."…That unknown terror that hangs over your head; I don't know any other word to describe it other than just terror. You beat it once, but it's hiding and it's waiting. What I would like is for God to come down and tell me, "This is how it's going to go. You're never going to have any more problems."

18. *Dissatisfaction with information as death approaches.* Parents may be dissatisfied with the information they receive from health care providers about the impending death of their child. They also may be concerned about how to talk to their child about these matters if death is a strong possibility.

- The only indication he gave me that he thought Jerry—he really didn't say die, he didn't use that word; he couldn't say Jerry wasn't going to make it either. But he told me on the phone he didn't think he would be able to control Jerry's disease. I think that was his way to tell us that Jerry wasn't going to pull through, but I don't think he ever [really] told us.
- I'm not faulting the nurses particularly, but a friend of mine who's a nurse told me, "Remember, the last thing they lose is their hearing." Well, no one had told me that. I think, in this situation, it would be extremely important to be able to give parents advice without their asking for it.
- I don't want her zipped up in a body bag and taken out the door. You don't want that to be your last memory.
- Most people don't want to talk about it with you but you need to.
- I went to a funeral of a friend's child and I saw them taking this little casket out of the back of a station wagon. It reminded me of a picnic cooler. I don't want that for my child.

19. *Relief through death.* Parents may react to the death of their child as a mixed blessing.

- She had a dramatic case of shingles. [It] went to her brain and liver, and she suffered a great deal. It really brought us to the point where we realized there were definitely things that were worse than death. After [she died], I had a tremendous sense of relief.
- There's more of a constantness in our family now. Things aren't quite as erratic as they were. You plan more. Everything isn't so from-one-minute-to-the-next. We're essentially a normal family now.
- There's a certain stress that left when Donna died. You don't have the constant anxiety from 6 o'clock when the doctors' offices closed until they were opened at 9 the next morning—or when it got light outside. That's how bad it was. I almost hated to see it get dark.

20. *Anniversaries.* Parents may become especially aware of their loss on the date of the child's death, on the date of the child's birthday, during holiday seasons, and on other special occasions.

- I have flowers put on the altar in May in church to commemorate her death. [My husband] said, "This is the last year we're going to put flowers on the altar at that time. I'd rather put flowers on the altar on her birthday." May will always be a bummer. It's not so bad now, but Mother's Day is the 13th [this year], and that's the day she died.

The following case illustrates how conflicts with the medical staff may cause stress for the family (Shuster, Guskin, Hawkins, & Okolo, 1986).

CASE 15-2. TIM

My son, Tim, is now 18 months old. Right after he was born, the doctors knew something was wrong. By the time he was 2 weeks old, he had had two surgeries and a good portion of his bowel had been removed. Specialists then inserted an intravenous line to provide his nutrition and fluids. For the next 9 months, he was very sick. The line would become infected, the doctors would replace it, send him home, and then we would be right back in the hospital needing another line. It was terrible to see my son suffer and gain so very little weight. I cried a lot during those 9 months; I was constantly grieving.

I stayed with my son at all times, even in the hospital. My husband was wonderful; he also stayed in the hospital with me. I was amazed and often angry at the way I was treated by the doctors. When I would call them from home or alert them in the hospital that something seemed very wrong, they would put me off, tell me I was wrong, and even make me feel like something was wrong with me.

After a particularly negative experience I decided I had to do something to change the situation. We changed to a local doctor. Our new doctor told us that "you're the ones that know your son best." That was the best visit we ever had.

My son is better now. Although I'm glad, I still get depressed when I remember all my bad experiences. Why was it that some physicians had a way of making me feel like everything I did was wrong? (pp. 20–21, with changes in notation)

The next case illustrates stresses that families may face when their normal family routines are disrupted by the demands of the treatment regimen (Adams-Greenly, 1991). The case also shows the contributions that health care providers can make to the rehabilitation effort.

CASE 15-3. WARREN

Warren was the 8-year-old son of Mr. and Mrs. B. During the initial phase of his outpatient treatment, he and his mother spent 8 to 10 hours together every day. Mr. B. worked and then made a makeshift dinner each night for himself and Warren's older brother, Sam. Because he had no one to drive him, Sam dropped out of basketball. When Mrs. B. and Warren arrived home each evening, they expected to be greeted with support and concern; in turn, Mr. B. and Sam expected the same for themselves. Mrs. B. resented what she perceived as her husband's escape into his job; Mr. B. felt unappreciated for his ability to continue working and being productive. When he did come to the outpatient department, he felt left out and bewildered by his wife's ease in talking with the staff about medical matters. Even on days when Warren felt well, he was relieved of his chores and responsibilities, which Sam was forced to assume and resented. When Warren began his maintenance therapy and was ready to return to school, his family found that they had grown apart.

The B. family was initially reluctant to meet with the hospital social worker and nurse practitioner, with Mrs. B. voicing the opinion that there isn't much to talk about. At the meeting, each family member's perception was elicited. They had been so absorbed in their own struggles during the past 3 months that they had not even considered how they were affecting each other. During the meeting, they began to appreciate that they all had suffered and needed each others' support to continue. This family that had not much to talk about became animated, highly interactive, and even humorous during this meeting. In the words of Sam, "My whole family didn't even know what was happening to us until we talked!" Because of the meeting, each child's chores and responsibilities were redefined to allow for Warren's side effects of treatment but still require his active participation in family life. Because Warren's treatments were now less frequent, it was possible for Mr. B. to accompany him at times, which enhanced their relationship, allowed Mrs. B. and Sam some time together, and helped Mr. B. better relate to hospital staff and procedures. (adapted from p. 7)

Health care providers should help families with an ill child "accept the realities of the disease and its treatments, communicate openly with one another, and begin to implement adaptive coping behaviors" (Altmaier & Johnson, 1992, p. 324). This process can begin in the initial interview. Families that have a child with cancer, for example, will need to come to recognize that "the diagnostic phase is only the beginning of a long period of stress and coping; the medical treatment and its side effects, prognostic uncertainty, and general disruption of family life goes on for years" (Chesler & Barbarin, 1984, pp. 113–114). The family members need to be realistic with the child; provide emotional support for her or him; inhibit the expression of their feelings of anger, guilt, and possible confusion about the diagnosis to the child; and help each other (Rait & Lederberg, 1989). They need to do these things although they may feel powerless in the face of the diagnosis.

Communication Between the Parents and the Medically Ill Child

Encourage the parents to give the child a reasonable explanation of the illness, the needed treatment, and the possible side effects of the treatment, gearing the explanation to the child's developmental level. At times, the parents may not want to talk to the child about the illness or to inform the child about the diagnosis because they want to protect him or her from worries and anxieties. Their child, however, may soon realize the serious nature of his or her illness by observing the reactions of parents, siblings, and other family members (Altmaier & Johnson, 1992). Additionally, the child may feel isolated and wonder why other people's behavior is changing. As a result, the child may imagine that the situation is worse than it is. Consequently, it is best that the parents make an attempt to be honest with their child about his or her condition.

The following case illustrates what might happen if parents withhold information from a child (Adams-Greenly, 1991).

CASE 15-4. KATRINA

Eight-year-old Katrina's parents wanted to protect her from the upset of knowing she had leukemia; they answered her questions by saying "You're going to be fine." At the same time, they themselves were visibly tearful, whispered on the phone, and deluged Katrina with presents. Katrina became very demanding and provocative. Katrina was overheard saying to another child, "Everybody buys me presents and nobody even yells at me anymore, no matter what I do. I bet I'm going to die." Once educated about her disease and treatment, Katrina became cooperative; intellectually challenged, she did her science project for school on leukemia. (pp. 6–7)

Sometimes a medically ill child may not ask his or her parents questions about the illness. The child may not want to hear alarming information, see the parents cry, or confront the parents' emotions.

HEALTHY CHILDREN IN A FAMILY WITH A MEDICALLY ILL MEMBER

Healthy Siblings of Children with a Medical Illness

Healthy siblings of children with a medical illness may experience guilt, shame, low self-esteem, jealousy, depression, anxiety, periods of daydreaming, social difficulties, withdrawal, preoccupation with their sibling's illness, resentment toward and conflicts with their parents, impaired academic and social functioning, and somatic complaints (Adams-Greenly, 1989). At first, they may experience relief that they did not get sick, but this soon may turn to guilt over having been spared and feeling good about having been spared. Also, if they must assume more responsibilities at home and act more grown up than before their sibling became ill, they may come to resent the sibling who is ill and again feel guilty about harboring anger (Miller, 1991).

Healthy siblings may be concerned about their ill sibling's physical pain or ability to cope with the illness and treatment, about the cause of their sibling's illness, and about the possibility that they also might get sick (Chesler, Allswede, & Barbarin, 1991). They may develop symptoms to get attention. They may sense that their parents are anxious and worried and, therefore, make fewer demands on the parents. If the parents give most of their attention to the ill child, the healthy siblings may feel overlooked or left out, rejected, jealous, resentful, and guilty about their anger and jealousy. "One four-year-old who had a baby sister with cystic fibrosis solved the problem by demanding physiotherapy [physical therapy] twice a day for himself" (Eiser, 1993, p. 175). These sources of anxiety put healthy siblings at risk for developing school-related problems, becoming socially maladjusted, and developing depression.

How the healthy siblings react will depend on several factors, including their age, their sex, and the type of illness their sibling has; their relationship with their sibling before the sibling became ill; their relationship with their parents; their coping skills; the supports they receive from their family, relatives, and peers; and the changes in the family since their sibling became ill. For example, healthy infants may be at risk because mothers, preoccupied with their sick child, may fail to respond to the healthy infants' cues. Healthy toddlers and preschool children may interpret family changes as rejection because they are unable to comprehend what is happening. And healthy school-aged children, although they likely understand the added family stresses, still may be angry and resentful if their parents give them limited attention.

Parents need to be open in their communications with their healthy children in order to help them cope with their sibling's illness and its possible ramifications. Healthy children need information about the illness and recognition and understanding of their feelings by their parents. Later in the chapter, you will read about how to help parents work with the healthy siblings of medically ill children.

The following case describes the difficulties that an adolescent had when his sibling became seriously ill (Adams & Deveau, 1987).

CASE 15-5. SUZIE

"We can live with Suzie's illness, but we cannot tolerate Jim's failure to help us," were Jim's father's words as he became increasingly exasperated with his son's behavior. Jim was nearing his 16th birthday and had experienced continued difficulty managing the changes that had affected his sister and his family during the two years since she had been diagnosed with leukemia. Suzie, who was 16 at the onset of her illness, was an outgoing and vibrant teen—an athlete and a scholar. At the beginning, Suzie had a difficult battle with infections before entering remission and spent considerable time in hospital. After 17 months in remission, her illness returned and her physical condition deteriorated rapidly as she became increasingly resistant to chemotherapy.

Prior to her illness, Jim and Suzie went to the same high school and had a close, friendly relationship. When Jim experienced difficulties in school subjects, Suzie helped him. She also taught him how to play tennis and helped him to improve his basketball. Jim's initial reaction to Suzie's illness was characterized by sympathy and a willingness to go to the homes of relatives for meals or to cook for himself when his parents were at the hospital. During Suzie's remission, Jim changed. He seemed to be disappointed at his sister's lack of energy, he flatly refused to go to relatives at any time and demanded that his mother leave his meals prepared when she took Suzie to the hospital for her late afternoon appoint-

ments. He also became very angry when his father paid special attention to Suzie's academic achievements.

When Suzie relapsed, she again required periodic hospitalization for chemotherapy and treatment of infections. Her parents became more attentive to her needs and more demanding of Jim. In response, Jim became more volatile and less communicative. Eventually, he refused to help out at home and neglected even his usual duties. He avoided his sister, came home as little as possible and, if asked about his activities, remained silent or gave a curt reply. As Suzie deteriorated, Jim's behavior became more pronounced and he presented as a sad, irritable, unkempt, and depressed adolescent. (pp. 285–286)

In the following quotations, healthy children describe what it is like to live with a sibling who is medically ill (Adams-Greenly, 1991, p. 8; Chesler et al., 1991, pp. 24–25, 27, 29, 34–35; Koch, 1985, p. 68; Koch-Hattem, 1986, p. 114; Schreiber, 1993; Wiener, Fair, & Pizzo, 1993, p. 98).

1. *Concerns about not knowing about the illness.* They may be concerned about their limited knowledge of the illness and about their parents' reluctance to be open with them.

- I understood it from the beginning. My parents would go behind closed doors to talk about it.... My parents didn't really come right out and say it to me—I guess we don't communicate that well.
- I just couldn't see in my mind when I grew up why they weren't exactly telling me what it was.
- You ask, when you are younger, about what his disability is and you are confused. You'll never really get a direct answer.

2. *Concerns about the sibling who is ill.* They may worry about how the illness is affecting their sibling and about the pain that the sibling is experiencing.

- When he was in intensive care, I was really upset. When he has his treatments, I feel sorry for him.
- Sometimes when I'm in there with him taking shots, I'll just say, "Why couldn't it be me instead of him?" 'Cause he's so little and so young that I probably could take shots better than he could.
- I worry about her adjusting to life and friends. It's pretty rough on them. Her friends have reacted well, but they don't come around as much because it's hard on them, which makes it hard on C.
- I spend more time with him because I'm afraid he might die.
- I used to tease my sister all the time, and my mother said I would wear her down. Is that why she got cancer?
- I think my brother has become a very strong person inside and keeps on getting stronger with every battle against the AIDS virus he wins. Someday I know he won't be able to win a battle, and he'll go to heaven, but that doesn't mean that he got tired of fighting. I know I'll miss him when he goes, but I also know that he won't hurt anymore.

3. *Concerns about self.* They may worry about contracting the illness and about their relationship with their sibling who is ill.

- I used to think I had all kinds of things.... I used to sit and think, "Oh no, what if I have...." I really thought I had something. I was afraid to tell anybody 'cause they'd think I was silly. But it was very real to me for awhile.

- Sometimes I feel bad and sometimes I feel a little jealous. I feel sad when I hear that he had all these needles and stuff stuck into him, and I get jealous when he comes home and gets all the attention and don't have to clean and make his bed.

- I think it's helped me to mature and accept things faster. I've been taking care of the boys, taking care of the family, baby-sitting.

4. *Concerns about family relations.* They may worry about what is happening to their family as a result of their sibling's illness.

- Since my sister got lymphoma, my father has gotten quieter. He isn't home a lot; he goes to the library. When he is home, he stays in the basement working.

- My mother has gotten a hot temper, so she yells at me a lot. Then, the other day, I saw her crying. I didn't know what it meant. I think I'd rather have her yelling.

- I got mad because my brother got all the attention, so one day I put my face in front of the heater and made my mom worried because my face was red and hot. Then, when she took my temperature, it was normal, so she got more worried. Then I told her the truth, and she said my feelings are important to her, and I should talk to her when I'm upset.

- If I blew up, it gets the whole family uptight. And I don't like to do that. They can't handle it.... It's hard enough already on them, having to worry about what's going to happen with this.... I take care of it myself. I just try to get it out somehow, without bothering them. I do it for them.

- It brought us closer together.

- At first, it tore each of us apart. Everyone in the family, individually. But because of it, we've gotten a little closer.

- If my mother would cry, I would try to comfort her and say that she should think of better things.

- Sometimes when things aren't going well, you can't misbehave because they have too much on their minds to worry about you.

5. *Advice to others experiencing a similar situation.* Many have suggestions for others who have a sibling who is ill.

- Just be nice and help out if he's feeling bad.

- Don't feel sorry for them, treat them the same. It will make it a lot easier. Also, make it easier for your parents by doing what you're told.

- There are a lot of changes, and a lot of them aren't that bad. There are a lot of times you need to spend time with your friends and you need a lot of attention.

- You have to understand that there's a lot of tension in the patient and that he's going through a lot. So understand when he gets edgy. Don't get mad at him when he yells at you; don't get hurt. Don't feel jealous because he gets everything he wants—it's only because he's sick and that makes him feel better.

- It's going to be hard. You have to have a lot of patience and time. Try to be understanding, and spend time with the sick person. Let them know that you care, but don't get so caught up in it that you're completely changed. Talk to someone if you need to, because you have to get your frustration out. Talk about your feelings to someone close.

- Try to find someone you can talk to because you're going to need someone to talk to for sure. You have to let your feelings

out, and talk it over with the patient. A lot more responsibility will be thrown at you—chores in the house. Continue to get good grades in school, help more with the patient, keep everybody in good spirits. You must act older, and you may feel that nobody cares about you. Just try to help. Talk things out at home, communicate more so that everyone knows what's going on.

Siblings may struggle to find meaning in a time of emotional crisis and may begin to develop philosophical views of life and death. The following letter was written by a 15-year-old whose brother was hospitalized for AIDS (Wiener et al., 1993, p. 99).

It's Hard…
It's hard going hour by hour, day by day seeing your brother get weaker and weaker, sicker and sicker. It's hard knowing that your brother is going to die from a horrible disease like AIDS and you have no control over anything.
It's hard saying good-bye or good night and not knowing if it is the last good-bye or good night that you're going to say to him.
It's hard not knowing where he is going next. But God has good reasons for doing everything that he does and we will just have to learn to accept them.

The semistructured interviews in Table F-18 and Table F-33 in Appendix F will help you in interviewing siblings of chronically ill children and their parents, respectively.

Healthy Children of a Medically Ill Parent

Let's now consider some of the issues that arise when healthy children have a medically ill parent. Life may be particularly stressful when a parent becomes ill or disabled (Florian, Katz, & Lahav, 1989; Urbach & Culbert, 1991). Much, of course, depends on the type of illness or disability the parent has and how the children and other family members react to the situation. Each member of the family will need to adjust to the changes in the family and in the family dynamics in his or her unique way.

1. *Disturbances in the bonding process.* Young children may not realize the extent of the parent's illness or disability, but they usually will recognize that something is wrong. They may experience a disruption in the bonding and attachment process with their ill parent (see Chapter 1 for a discussion of attachment theory). School-aged children will have a greater appreciation of their parent's illness or disability and how it will affect the family, but they also may experience a disruption in their relationship with the ill parent.

2. *Interacting with an ill parent.* Children may have to deal with a parent who has changed in ways that they do not understand. The parent, for example, may be less receptive to the children because of preoccupation with the illness, may be more impatient with the children, may have altered mental functioning or emotional control, or may behave in inappropriate ways and be especially difficult to relate to.

3. *Family changes.* Children may have to deal with several family changes, including a decline in family income, a move to another residence, and alterations in family roles and routines. Depending on their age, children may have to assume more responsibility in the home and may even need to work to supplement the family income.

4. *Relationship with the healthy parent.* Children's relationship with their healthy parent in two-parent families also may change, depending on the healthy parent's adjustment and ability to deal with the spouse's illness. The healthy parent, for example, may feel socially isolated, overwhelmed with increased responsibilities, torn between attending to the ill spouse and meeting the needs of the healthy children, concerned about economic security, resentful about a decrease in personal time, depressed if the ill spouse fails to recover or gets worse, and guilty if he or she considers getting a divorce. If the healthy parent becomes depressed, he or she may argue with the children, become impatient with them, or feel overwhelmed by them (Pessar, Coad, Linn, & Willer, 1993). These difficulties may not arise as easily when there is flexibility and good communication and mutual decision making between the spouses.

5. *Adjustment problems.* Children may have increased adjustment problems (Pessar et al., 1993). For example, children may have physical, emotional, or interpersonal problems, such as headaches, bad dreams, or difficulty getting along with their friends. Young children, in addition, may display regressive behavior and have tantrums, and school-aged children may engage in acting-out behavior, have behavioral problems in school and at home, be truant from school, have temper outbursts, or disobey parents.

Children should be given information about their parent's illness commensurate with their age, level of understanding, and maturity. If the parent is hospitalized or in a rehabilitation center and if the child is mature enough, arrange for the child to spend time with the parent to share thoughts, experiences, and feelings (Carlton & Stephenson, 1990). Help the child understand and deal with any changes in the parent. Arrange for the child to meet the parent's health care providers—including his or her physical therapist, occupational therapist, and speech and language therapist—to learn about how the parent is functioning and about any adaptive equipment needed by the parent. Permit the child, if possible, to observe the parent as he or she remasters specific skills. Answer any what-why-how questions that the child may have about the parent's illness, and prepare the child for the parent's return home.

In two-parent families in which one parent is disabled, each parent is likely to experience anxiety and pressure. The disabled parent is likely to be concerned about how he or she will adjust to the disability and how the disability will affect the economic security of the family, his or her ability to take care of the children, and his or her relationships with other members of the family. These concerns may occur in addition to those associated with the disability itself. The healthy

parent may worry about similar issues and also worry about managing to continue his or her career and also take care of the disabled spouse as well as the children in the family.

If the disabled parent does not have impaired mental faculties, the parents can probably work through many of their concerns. However, when the disability affects the disabled parent's mental faculties, both parents are likely to have more difficulty working through their problems. If the parents cannot work out their problems, the healthy parent may experience frustration, irritability, anger, and depression, particularly if the disabled spouse becomes more dependent and shows regressive behavior. The disabled parent may have similar feelings. Both parents also may resent the decline in their social activities (which may be accompanied by loneliness and social isolation), the reduction in personal time, and the anxiety associated with possible economic insecurity. The healthy parent also may resent the pressures associated with the need to assume almost total responsibility for running the family, and the inability to consult with the disabled parent about important family matters.

The disabled parent will probably play less of a role in parenting. In addition, he or she may compete with the children for the attention and love of the healthy parent. If this happens, the family members may be angry and upset. The healthy parent is confronted with dual loyalties—namely, who needs him or her more, the disabled spouse or the children? If the healthy parent considers divorce, feelings of guilt and fear of social condemnation may lead him or her to remain in the relationship although he or she wants to leave. See McCue (1994) for more information on how to help children who have a parent with a serious illness.

The following case illustrates some changes that may take place in a healthy adolescent when a parent becomes ill (Urbach & Culbert, 1991).

CASE 15-6. MARK

Mark, a 15-year-old adolescent, was referred for adjustment difficulties following his father's severe head trauma. When Mark was in the fourth grade, he was diagnosed as having an attention-deficit/hyperactivity disorder and was given methylphenidate. Despite an IQ in the Superior range, he was doing below average work in school.

Mark's father was comatose for over a month at the time of referral, during which time he was only minimally responsive to commands. He showed some improvement after 6 months of rehabilitation but still had severe mental impairment. The treatment unit recommended that he be transferred to a nursing facility because recovery prospects were poor.

Mr. E. was a retired military officer, which guaranteed at least a minimum standard of living for the family. Mrs. E. spent most of her days at the hospital helping with Mr. E.'s care; she was determined that her husband would eventually gain back almost full functioning. Mark and his sister remained alone at home with responsibility for most of the chores previously performed by Mr. E.

Mark appeared increasingly angry and argumentative toward his mother. He failed several school subjects, because he refused to do his homework. Mark's anger appeared to be a displacement of feelings about his father's injury. Mark's new role of "man of the household" also created conflicts between mother and son, especially when Mark performed responsibilities differently than his father would. In psychotherapy, as he better understood his reactions, his hostility toward his mother diminished. Mrs. E. also worked on the guilt she felt regarding the decreased attention she was giving her children, but she persisted in the belief that her husband would recover.

By helping the family members understand the role shifts that had been taking place, they began to resolve conflicts. Although Mark continued to have difficulties in school, he did show more responsibility and participated in efforts to remediate his school difficulties. (adapted from p. 27)

In a single-parent family, there may be additional concerns when the parent becomes ill. The child and the parent, for example, may be concerned about who will take care of the child, long-range plans for the child's care if the parent's illness continues, increased financial burdens associated with the parent's illness, and how much responsibility to give the child in managing household tasks, depending on the child's age.

Exercise 15-2—Evaluating Two Families with a Chronically Medically Ill Child

---

In evaluating the two cases below, consider the following questions (and whether there is sufficient information to answer the questions):

1. How did each mother accept the child's illness?
2. What did each mother do to maintain control?
3. What was each child's relationship with other people?
4. What supports were available to each mother?
5. How did each mother communicate and interact with professionals?

Compare your evaluation with the discussion in the Comments section. The two cases are from Paluszny, DeBeukelaer, and Rowane (1991, adapted from pp. 19–21, from "Families Coping with the Multiple Crises of Chronic Illness," *Loss, Grief & Care, 5,* 15–26, and reprinted with permission of The Haworth Press, Binghamton, New York, copyright 1991).

Peter, a 2-year-old boy and the only child in a one-parent family, had multiple admissions for problems related to progressive kidney failure. While on dialysis, he had recurrent infections. He also had hypertension, which resulted in a stroke that caused temporary partial paralysis. After a renal transplant, he had clotting problems; the transplant had to be removed hours after the surgery. Throughout these crises, Peter's mother remained concerned about his welfare but managed to provide affection and set limits when necessary to get Peter to cooperate with the staff. Peter's mother had several sources of support. First, she had a good relationship with Peter. She viewed Peter as the one worthwhile aspect of

her life, someone who needed her and returned unquestioned love. Peter is a bright and charming boy and, even after the stroke, made remarkably rapid progress. Despite his problems, he is rarely irritable and is usually happy and outgoing. Second, she had help from her extended family. Even though her extended family lived out of state, her father, mother, or brother came to be with her each time Peter was hospitalized. Finally, the mother herself was such an open and pleasant lady that the hospital staff was eager to spend time with her. Even after discharge, the mother sometimes came to the ward just to visit old friends. In addition, the mother called the psychosocial staff when she felt overwhelmed and followed their suggestions.

In contrast to Peter, Cheryl, a 9-year-old girl, had fewer medical problems but more psychological difficulties. Cheryl, the older of two children from a two-parent family, was diagnosed as having a prune-belly syndrome at birth. [A prune-belly syndrome is a congenital disorder in which one or more layers of the abdominal musculature may be absent at birth.] She also had multiple urinary anomalies and progressive renal failure. At the age of 9, she was evaluated prior to a renal transplant. During the evaluation, Cheryl was serious but somewhat immature and expressed concerns about school. She was having problems with her homework, which she and her mother worked on for hours each day. In addition, she was repeatedly teased by her peers, who found out she was enuretic and had to wear diapers. At times, they also called her fatso because of her prune belly. Because of work commitments, the father could not come for the evaluation. At first, the mother wanted to know if it was safe for Cheryl to wait alone in the lobby because she feared that Cheryl could be kidnapped from the waiting room. She said that professionals had told her that Cheryl would never walk because of her prune belly. Nevertheless, she spent hours daily with Cheryl strengthening her muscles so that eventually Cheryl had no problems walking. She also described how she tried to help Cheryl with her problem with bedwetting. However, she could not understand why we thought that it was so important to teach Cheryl to put on her own diapers. The mother insisted that she had to do this as she believed that Cheryl, despite her age, could not manage on her own. The mother described her husband as being invested in both children, and she said that he spent time with them when he was not working. However, she also gave the impression that he was unavailable to her as a source of support. Her extended family lived some distance away and rarely visited them. When the issue of a kidney transplant was raised, the mother was interested in being the donor. When psychotherapy for Cheryl was recommended, the mother initially was reluctant to give her consent, but she eventually agreed to have someone from school work with Cheryl about school and peer issues.

Comments

1. How did each mother accept the child's illness? Peter's mother appears to have fully accepted Peter with his handicap. She could be empathic and also set limits for him. We do not have enough information about Cheryl's mother to answer this question.

2. *What did each mother do to maintain control?* Peter's mother maintained control by setting limits when necessary to get Peter to cooperate with the staff and by dealing with each crisis appropriately. Cheryl's mother was, perhaps, too involved and controlling to the point of worrying about leaving Cheryl alone in the lobby, insisting that Cheryl couldn't manage to put on her own diapers, and hesitating to allow psychotherapeutic intervention. This level of overinvolvement may have interfered with the development of Cheryl's age-appropriate independence. Cheryl's mother may be temperamentally more closed and anxious than Peter's mother.

3. *What was each child's relationship with other people?* Peter's relationship with his mother was one of mutual support and unquestioned love. Although he was rarely irritable and usually happy and outgoing, he apparently needed occasional limits set to get him to cooperate with the medical staff. Cheryl is known to have problems with her peers' frequent teasing; however, the case description provides no insight as to her relationships with her parents, teachers, or the health care professionals.

4. *What supports were available to each mother?* Peter's mother finds support in Peter's unquestioned love for her and in her extended family that manages to be there for each of Peter's hospitalizations. Cheryl's mother believes her husband is unavailable. There also seems to be little support from her family, as they rarely visit (other types of contact are unknown).

5. *How did each mother communicate and interact with professionals?* Peter's mother is open with the hospital staff and is, therefore, assumed to be communicative and cooperative about the medical procedures. She also calls the psychosocial staff when the need arises and uses their suggestions. Cheryl's mother prefers to challenge the information or advice offered to her by the health care providers. For example, she did not understand the necessity for Cheryl to change her own diapers and was reluctant to accept psychotherapy for Cheryl.

THINKING THROUGH THE ISSUES

Are there childhood illnesses or disabilities that would make you feel uneasy and consequently interfere with your ability to help seriously ill children and their families? If so, how could you overcome your uneasiness? And if you can't, what options do you have?

How do you feel when you are visiting a patient in a hospital?

If you have ever been hospitalized, how did you feel about the experience?

How did you feel when you were sick as a child?

How did your parents treat you when you were sick?

Did you get any special favors or treats when you were sick as a child? If so, how did your siblings feel about the special treats you received?

What is your attitude toward health care providers?

What is your attitude about taking medicine when you are sick?

Do you take your prescriptions for the recommended amount of time? If not, why do you not follow the recommendations of your physician?

If you were sick and were given a special regimen to follow, like special exercises, did you follow it? If not, why did you not follow it?

If you had a sibling who had a serious illness, how did you feel?

When one of your parents was sick, how did it change the family organization? What were your responsibilities at those times?

If your family experienced a severe illness, adversity, or loss, how did the event affect you and the other family members? How did the experience affect your beliefs about such things as normality, mastery, control, optimism/fatalism, value of family efforts, and so forth? Did issues of blame, shame, or guilt surface in the family during this experience? If so, how were they handled? Were they resolved? If so, what helped resolve them? How does the experience affect your philosophy and work as a prospective clinician or as a practicing clinician? (This paragraph adapted from Rolland, 1994, p. 270.)

SUMMARY

1. Behavioral medicine is a multidisciplinary field that integrates behavioral science approaches with biomedical knowledge and techniques.

2. The goal of behavioral medicine is to promote health and improve disease prevention, diagnosis, therapy, and rehabilitation.

3. Health care providers are likely to refer medically ill children to a mental health professional primarily when the children have poor adherence to the medical regimen, have severe behavioral or emotional disturbances, are in families that disagree with the treatment regimen or are dysfunctional, have learning disabilities, have physical symptoms that cannot be diagnosed, have poorly controlled illnesses, have illnesses in which psychosocial factors are relevant, or have long-term or fatal illnesses.

4. To best help medically ill children and their families when they are referred to you, you will need to obtain an understanding of the child's illness, its natural progression, its manifestations, its treatments (including medications), and its possible complications; become familiar with the way clinics, hospitals, schools, and social service organizations function in order to help children and their families obtain needed services; become knowledgeable about the stresses seriously ill children may place on their families; and become knowledgeable about how illness may affect children's growth and development.

5. In a hospital or other medical setting, mental health professionals work closely with other health care providers.

6. The physician's responsibility is to conduct the medical diagnostic workup, refer the child to other medical specialists as needed, review the medical diagnostic findings, develop medical interventions, and inform the family of the medical findings and recommended interventions.

7. The nurse's responsibility is to carry out the needed medical interventions, to answer the child's and family's questions about the illness and its treatment, to act as a liaison between the medical staff and the psychosocial staff, and to provide supportive counseling to the child and family.

8. The social worker's responsibility is to handle concerns that the child and parents may have about the medical diagnosis and medical treatment, to handle family tensions and provide appropriate behavioral and psychological interventions as needed, to help the child adjust to the hospital (or to home care), and to help with planning for discharge from the hospital.

9. The psychologist's responsibility is to conduct a psychological evaluation of the child, to work with the family as needed, to help the child with problems associated with the hospitalization (or with home care), and to provide appropriate behavioral and psychosocial interventions, particularly when there are problems with adherence to the treatment regimen.

Children's Understanding of Their Medical Illnesses and the Disruptive Effects of Medical Illness on Development

10. Children's understanding of their medical illnesses and the concerns they have about them are directly related to their cognitive-developmental level.

11. Infants have little understanding of illness; their emotions depend on their immediate sensations.

12. During early childhood, children are unable to separate themselves from their environments and tend to think in magical terms; thus, they are unable to explain in logical terms what causes illness.

13. During middle childhood years, children tend to think concretely and factually and have a present-time orientation. They have some understanding of the cause of illness and its effects on the body.

14. During adolescence, children make the greatest differentiation between their bodies and the environment. They view the source and nature of illness as lying in specific organs of the body.

Coping with a Medical Illness

15. The typical reaction that older children have when they learn that they have a severe chronic illness is a period of initial shock and disbelief followed by a period of turmoil accompanied by anxiety and depressive symptoms, irritability, and disruption of appetite and normal sleep. The ability to concentrate and carry out usual life activities is impaired. The children often experience intrusive thoughts about the diagnosis and its ominous implications for the future, such as fears of death and bodily dysfunction.

16. You need to distinguish normal or typical reactions when children learn that they have a severe chronic illness from those that are atypical, because children with atypical reactions may need additional help, such as counseling or psychotherapy.

17. Coping strategies can be defined as the behaviors, cognitions, and perceptions individuals use to maintain equilibrium in the face of illness.

18. How the child and family cope with the child's illness will depend on illness variables, individual variables, familial variables, and environmental variables.

19. Children's and families' ability to cope with a severe or chronic medical illness will depend on the type, severity, site, stage, and course of the illness; the type of treatment; and the type of rehabilitative measures.

20. Coping will be more difficult when illnesses are severe and chronic, require constant monitoring, require hospitalization, require confinement to a bed, require frequent visits for treatment or extensive rehabilitative procedures, are unpredictable or episodic, have a poor prognosis, have high visibility, involve a social stigma, or have painful treatments.

21. Children's ability to cope with a medical illness will depend on their age and developmental stage, intelligence/cognitive level, personality and temperament, pre-illness adjustment, values, beliefs, previous experiences with illness, and coping strategies.

22. Children with a chronic illness may feel isolated, angry, guilty, ashamed, lonely, apathetic, bitter, and confused.

23. Children can use problem-focused strategies to modify the stressors that confront them.

24. Children can use emotion-focused strategies to release, reduce, or manage their emotional tensions.

25. Children can use appraisal-focused strategies to evaluate the situation.

26. The most effective coping strategies are those that reflect an acceptance of illness followed by realistic actions that deal with the illness and the problems associated with the illness.

27. How children interpret or appraise situations may be as important as or more important than the situations themselves in determining their responses.

28. Parents of a medically ill child may have concerns about the diagnosis, the treatment, and how the child's illness will affect their family and daily life.

29. Psychosocial stresses may occur in families with a medically ill or medically disabled child at the following points: diagnostic evaluation; onset of treatment; reactions to treatment and side effects of treatment; end of treatment; entry and reentry into school, social, and family life; beginning of a new developmental stage and educational transitions; recurrence of illness; instituting additional treatment or new treatments; end of active treatment; period of terminal illness and death of a child; and period of several months following the death of the child.

30. Parents and older children may believe that the health care providers, for example, are not attentive to their concerns, are not warm, and are not giving them sufficient information about the illness or disability.

31. Families from an ethnic minority group may experience additional stressors in coping with the medical regimen.

32. Coping will be difficult in poorly functioning families that are unable to care for, support, nourish, and guide the child.

33. If families obtain secondary gains from having a sick child—such as parental power and control over children, attention from the medical community and from the extended family, and rewards for assuming a martyr role, children may have more difficulty coping.

34. Marginally adjusted families and single-parent families may be particularly vulnerable when a child develops a chronic or severe illness.

35. All families may experience stress if the expenses for treatment become prohibitive, if paying for the treatment depletes their savings or forces them to sell their home and possessions, if their health insurance is inadequate, or if their health insurer is not willing to pay for the needed services.

36. Families hinder the development of a medically ill child when they overprotect the child, withdraw the family from social involvement with others, deny the reality of the child's medical illness and ignore his or her special needs, display anger and resentment about the situation, become depressed, become too lenient with the child, domineer the child, direct their hostility toward the child or toward each other, and blame each other.

37. Families assist the development of a medically ill child when they support the child; believe that the child can cope with the illness; have high self-esteem; have open, effective communication among their members; provide mutual assistance and support to their members; have good problem-solving abilities; have good physical and emotional health; have a sense of mastery over events that they are experiencing; and can afford quality respite care.

38. Coping strategies that parents may use in dealing with their child's severe medical illness include information seeking, problem solving, seeking informal social support, reliance on religious beliefs/faith, seeking formal supports, maintenance of emotional balance, optimism, denial, and passive acceptance.

39. Children's and families' ability to cope with a medically ill child will depend on the community's attitude toward illness, the community supports and resources available, the school's attitude toward medically ill children, and physical access to facilities in the community and school.

40. Children's and families' ability to cope with illnesses will be facilitated when they have positive and accepting social groups; when they live in hygienic conditions in a safe neighborhood; when the schools accommodate the needs of children who are medically ill; when the physical environment allows children with an illness or disability to be independent; and when they can afford quality respite care.

41. Children's ability to cope with severe illnesses or disabilities may be hampered when they come into contact with people who hold negative attitudes toward the ill or disabled.

42. American culture tends to emphasize youth, health, athletic prowess, and personal appearance; people who are sick or deformed tend to be stigmatized.

43. Teachers' interactions with children with medical illnesses may be another source of stress for the children and their families.

44. Some teachers are reluctant to have seriously ill children or children with seizures in their classroom.

45. There may be times when health care professionals need to speak to classes about children who have a medical illness or a disability.

46. A key to effective coping with a medical illness is an active approach to problem solving.

47. Coping is often more successful when the child has minimal pain or physical impairments, positive beliefs and expectations about her or his abilities, and good family and community supports.

48. The least effective strategies are those that emphasize inhibition, passivity, stoicism, apathy, and hopelessness; these strategies may be utilized when the child or parents interpret the illness as a permanent detriment.

49. When children and their families are successful in coping with the stresses caused by illness, they may experience pride in the knowledge that they can conquer adversity.

Adherence

50. A complex medical regimen that requires several kinds of behaviors may not be easy to monitor because each behavior must be clearly defined.

51. Adherence depends on the length of time and complexity of the regimen, on the child's and the parents' ability to follow the regimen, on the clarity of the communication from the health care provider to the child and parents, and on the child's and parents' relationship with the health care provider.

52. Miscommunication between the health care provider and children and their parents may lead to nonadherence.

53. Children and parents may find creative ways that are not prescribed to accomplish the treatment goals.

54. Children who are anxious or depressed or who experience interpersonal and family conflicts may have more difficulty with adherence than children who are better adjusted and who have supportive and cohesive families.

55. Factors that affect adherence in adolescents include adolescent turmoil, the challenge of some illnesses, assuming responsibility for the regimen, working independently in following the regimen, and the type of regimen.

56. Nonadherence may take several forms including refusing treatment; failing to take medications as prescribed; failing to keep appointments; and choosing alternative, unorthodox treatments to replace the prescribed treatment regimen.

57. It is not easy to monitor adherence because children and their parents may fail to record or report their behaviors accurately when they are following the treatment regimen or they may record behaviors that they never performed.

58. Four ways to monitor adherence are verbal reports from the child and parents, recordings from the child and parents, pill and bottle counts, and a 24-hour recall interview.

59. Encouraging children and their parents to participate actively in the children's health care is a key to improving adherence.

60. Children with little hope, few social supports, negative self-esteem, and poor problem-solving skills are at risk for not following the regimen.

61. Look for ways to improve children's self-management skills and to foster self-esteem, mastery over life events, and hopefulness.

62. Adherence also can be improved by encouraging children and their parents to inform the health care provider when they believe that the regimen can be improved or when they think that there is a better way to accomplish the treatment goals.

63. Children and their parents are more likely to adhere to a regimen when they have rapport with and respect for the health care provider, have their questions answered clearly and honestly by the health care provider, see the illness as curable or at least as becoming more manageable, understand how the illness developed and how it is maintained, recognize the costs and rewards of entering treatment, understand the time and effort required to adhere to the regimen, know an approximate timetable for getting relief of symptoms, and recognize the obstacles that may occur and ways of dealing with them.

Families of Medically Ill Children

64. Health care providers should help families with an ill child accept the realities of the disease and its treatments, communicate openly with one another, and begin to implement adaptive coping behaviors.

65. Encourage the parents to give the child a reasonable explanation of the illness, the needed treatment, and the possible side effects of the treatment, gearing the explanation to the child's developmental level.

Healthy Children in a Family with a Medically Ill Member

66. Healthy siblings of children with a medical illness may experience guilt, shame, low self-esteem, jealousy, depression, anxiety, periods of daydreaming, social difficulties, withdrawal, preoccupation with their sibling's illness, resentment toward and conflicts with their parents, impaired academic and social functioning, and somatic complaints.

67. Healthy siblings may be concerned about their ill sibling's physical pain or ability to cope with the illness and treatment, about the cause of their sibling's illness, and about the possibility that they also might get sick.

68. How the healthy siblings react will depend on several factors, including their age, their sex, and the type of illness their sibling has; their relationship with their sibling before the sibling became ill; their relationship with their parents; their coping skills; the supports they receive from their family, relatives, and peers; and the changes in the family since their sibling became ill.

69. Parents need to be open in their communications with their healthy children in order to help them cope with their sibling's illness and its possible ramifications.

70. Life may be particularly stressful for children when a parent becomes ill or disabled.

71. Young children may not realize the extent of the parent's illness or disability, but they usually will recognize that something is wrong.

72. When a parent gets sick, children may have to deal with a parent who has changed in ways that they do not understand.

73. When a parent gets sick, children may have to deal with several family changes, including a decline in family income, a move to another residence, and alterations in family roles and routines.

74. When a parent gets sick, children's relationship with their healthy parent in two-parent families also may change, depending on the healthy parent's adjustment and ability to deal with the spouse's illness.

75. When a parent gets sick, children may have increased adjustment problems.

76. In two-parent families in which one parent is disabled, each parent is likely to experience anxiety and pressure.

77. If the disabled parent does not have impaired mental faculties, the parents can probably work through many of their concerns, particularly when there is open communication, flexibility, and mutual decision making between the two parents.

78. The disabled parent will probably play less of a role in parenting.

KEY TERMS, CONCEPTS, AND NAMES

Behavioral medicine (p. 483)
Psychogenic symptoms (p. 483)
Detachment (p. 485)
Coping strategies (p. 488)
Illness variables (p. 488)

Individual variables (p. 488)
Familial variables (p. 488)
Environmental variables (p. 488)
Unpredictable illness (p. 488)
Episodic illness (p. 488)
Secondary gains (p. 488)
Problem-focused strategies (p. 488)
Rational intellectualizing (p. 488)
Adherence (p. 488)
Confrontation (p. 488)
Alternative rewards (p. 488)
Emotion-focused strategies (p. 488)
Revealing feelings (p. 488)
Reversal of affect (p. 488)
Stimulus reduction (p. 490)
Fatalism (p. 490)
Self-pity (p. 490)
Tension reduction (p. 490)
Acting out (p. 490)
Appraisal-focused strategies (p. 490)
Logical analysis (p. 490)
Cognitive redefinition (p. 490)
Cognitive avoidance (p. 490)
Information seeking (p. 493)
Problem solving (p. 493)
Seeking informal social support (p. 493)
Reliance on religious beliefs/faith (p. 493)
Seeking formal support (p. 493)
Maintenance of emotional balance (p. 493)
Optimism (p. 493)
Denial (p. 493)
Passive acceptance (p. 493)
Effective coping (p. 494)
Ineffective coping (p. 494)
Adherence (p. 495)
Nonadherence (p. 496)
Verbal reports from the child and parents (p. 498)
Recording from the child and parent (p. 498)
Pill and bottle counts (p. 498)
Twenty-four-hour recall interview (p. 500)
Improving adherence (p. 500)
Concerns of families of medically ill children (p. 501)
Concerns of children in a family with a medically ill member (p. 507)

STUDY QUESTIONS

1. What is behavioral medicine?
2. For what reasons might health care providers refer a medically ill child to a mental health professional?
3. Discuss six propositions from behavioral medicine that underlie work with medically ill children.
4. Briefly describe the roles of the physician, nurse, social worker, and psychologist as members of a medical/psychosocial health care team.
5. Discuss children's understanding of medical illness and the disruptive effects of medical illness from a developmental perspective, covering four age periods from birth through adolescence.

6. Discuss coping with a medical illness. Include in your discussion illness variables, individual variables, familial variables, and environmental variables. Also describe strategies that children and families might use to cope with stress, as well as factors that hinder coping and factors that facilitate coping in children and families.

7. Discuss stressful medical interventions and possible psychological effects associated with *four* different medical illnesses of your choice.

8. Discuss adherence to a medical regimen. Include in your discussion a definition of adherence, factors that affect adherence and nonadherence, how to evaluate adherence, how to monitor adherence, and how to improve adherence.

9. Discuss some concerns that parents of medically ill children may have.

10. Discuss some concerns that healthy siblings of children with a medical illness might have.

11. Discuss some concerns that healthy children of a medically ill parent might have.

16

CHILDREN AND FAMILIES WITH HEALTH-RELATED DISORDERS—INTERVIEWING AND FORMULATING INTERVENTIONS

Inferior doctors treat the disease of a patient
Mediocre doctors treat the patient as a person
Superior doctors treat the community as a whole
                              —Huang Dee (2600 BC)

Goals and Objectives

This chapter is designed to enable you to:

- Develop techniques for interviewing medically ill children and their parents
- Describe useful techniques for preparing children for hospitalization
- Help children and their families deal with terminal illness
- Evaluate the results of the interview with medically ill children and their families
- Develop interventions with medically ill children and their families
- Develop interventions for helping a parent work with healthy children when a family member is ill

INTERVIEWING CHILDREN WITH MEDICAL ILLNESSES

Interviewing children with medical illnesses is similar to interviewing children with other problems. As in all interviews, you will need to adjust your interviewing strategies—such as questioning, reflection, and feedback about the illness—to the child's level of comprehension. During the interview, assess the child's understanding of the referral for psychosocial services. Clarify your role as a mental health professional and the role of the health care provider in the assessment and treatment program. Explain to the child that your concerns are the health care provider's concerns: "Dr. _____ asked me to talk to you about how you are getting along" or "Dr. _____ is concerned about how you are following her treatment recommendations." One goal of the interview will be to identify the possible psychosocial stressors that accompany the medical illness in order to make medical treatment work better and to prevent serious psychosocial problems from developing. To accomplish this goal, you will need to identify what meaning the illness has for the child and for the child's family.

Older medically ill children who can communicate should be considered experts about their condition. They may have valuable insights about their physical state, functional status, and quality of life (Roter & Hall, 1992).

With medically ill children who are reluctant to speak with you, consider using the sentence completion technique shown in Table 16-1 as an "ice breaker." Do not use it as a projective technique. If you decide to use the sentence completion technique and see that the child is becoming distraught because the questions are too personal, discontinue using it and find some other way to engage the child.

During the interview, help the medically ill child maintain his or her dignity and self-respect. You can do this, in part, by actively listening, reflecting, and asking the child what he or she wants and thinks. If the caregiver is present, address the child directly instead of addressing the caregiver (except when needed). Each child and each family will have unique

Table 16-1
Sentence Completion Technique for Medically Ill Children

Say "I'm going to say the first part of a sentence; then, I want you to complete it. For example, if I say 'In winter...,' you might complete the sentence by saying '...it is fun to ride a sled' or '...it is very cold' or anything else that you would like to say. OK? Here is the first one."

1. When I feel good, I like _____.
2. When I am sick, I _____.
3. I became sick because _____.
4. If I am sick, I am supposed to _____.
5. My favorite TV show is _____.
6. I feel sick when _____.
7. The best thing my father does when I am sick is _____.
8. When I eat ice cream, I _____.
9. Hospitals _____.
10. If I am sick, I miss _____.
11. Doctors are _____.
12. My favorite sport is _____.
13. I like this sport because _____.
14. I get mad when _____.
15. People who are disabled _____.
16. When I am sick, I like my mother to _____.
17. My favorite thing to do is _____.
18. I pretend to be sick by _____.
19. I know when I am starting to be sick because _____.
20. Sickness is _____.
21. What I like about my best friend is _____.
22. If I am sick, it is wrong to _____.
23. The best thing about being sick is _____.
24. If a close friend is sick, I _____.
25. My sickness is serious if _____.
26. In order to keep healthy, I _____.
27. The worst sickness I've had is _____.
28. The sickness I fear most is _____.
29. When I grow up, I want to be _____.

Source: Adapted from Wilkinson (1988, p. 268).

needs and unique methods of coping with the illness; children who are chronically ill and their families especially need support. Take your cues from the child and the family about how you can best help them and ensure respect for their cultural values and traditions (see Chapters 8, 9, and 15).

Obtaining Information

You can obtain information about the child's biological, developmental, psychological, and social functioning from several sources, including the following:

1. Background Questionnaire completed by the parent (see Table C-2 in Appendix C)

2. Personal Data Questionnaire completed by an older child or adolescent (see Table C-3 in Appendix C)
3. School Referral Questionnaire completed by the teacher (see Table C-13 in Appendix C)
4. Initial clinical assessment interviews with the child, parents, and teachers (see Tables F-13, F-36, and F-43, respectively, in Appendix F)
5. Medical reports about the child's current and past medical conditions, treatment, and use of medications

Review all of the information you obtain and note areas of agreement and disagreement in the reports. A good working relationship with the health care provider team during the information-gathering period and at other times as well will be useful.

If you are not familiar with the child's illness, before you interview the child study relevant sources (such as the latest edition of *The Merck Manual* and the *Handbook of Pediatric Psychology*). Focus on the etiology of the illness, the symptoms and usual course of the illness, the manner in which the illness impairs the child, and the potential psychosocial stressors associated with the illness.

When you interview a medically ill child, in addition to covering standard interview topics (see Table F-13 in Appendix F), you will want to obtain information about the impact of the illness on the child, the child's reaction to previous illnesses, and the child's prior treatments (see Table F-27 in Appendix F). Allow the child to document his or her past medical history, including diagnostic medical tests and surgeries, and to tell his or her story in his or her own way. Encourage the child to reflect on any feelings of disappointment, frustration, anger, isolation, and hopelessness associated with his or her illness. Any unrealistic expectations the child has, such as visions of a speedy or complete recovery, also should be addressed (Wickramasekera, 1988). Similar considerations hold for interviewing the child's parents (see Table F-33 in Appendix F). Covering these areas will give you the "opportunity to correct misperceptions, provide reassurance when necessary, and design treatment regimens that are sensitive to the feelings and expectations of the child" (Mash & Terdal, 1990, p. 61). Table 16-2 (presented later in the chapter) shows a list of topics and questions that you should consider in interviewing medically ill children and in evaluating the interview.

Information about the impact of the illness.
When you ask about the impact of the illness on the child and family, you will want to cover, depending on the child's age, such areas as the following (Adams-Greenly, 1989):

- pain or incapacitating physical symptoms
- psychological symptoms, such as anxiety, fear, embarrassment, withdrawal, aggression, or depression
- effects of the illness on the child's body image, family life, friendships, self-concept, independence, and ability to assume responsibility at home, at school, and at work

- conflicts with parents
- conflicts with medical staff
- impact of the illness on sexuality
- concern about the future, including schooling, career plans, marriage, and childbearing (for a female) or child siring (for a male)

When you ask the child about her or his symptoms, focus on the onset, frequency, duration, and severity of the symptoms. This focus is similar to that for any problem. Obtain examples of the symptoms and the events, situations, and occurrences that induce the symptoms and contribute to changes in the symptoms. As with any problem behavior, seek information about the antecedents and consequences of the symptoms. Determine how psychological problems relate to the child's medical illness. Some of the child's medical problems may be alleviated if one or more of the associated psychological problems can be relieved.

If you are visiting the child at her or his home or in a hospital, observe the child's behavior (see Chapters 2 and 3). The child's level of activity is one factor indicating how well she or he is coping with the illness. The continuum shown in Figure 16-1, which ranges from fully active to unresponsive, can help you in your observations of a child's activity level (Lansky, List, Lansky, Ritter-Sterr, & Miller, 1987).

If you plan to conduct a second interview with an older child or adolescent, consider asking her or him to keep a diary between the interviews to record information about each major problem (or symptom). For each occurrence of the problem, have the child record the time of day, the duration, the intensity, where the problem occurred or in what situation, what the child was doing at the time, who else was present, what events preceded the episode, what events followed the episode, what was done for the problem, and what the child's perception of the outcome was (for example, successful, partially successful, or unsuccessful). If the child has several problems, focus on the major ones or on those of greatest concern to the child or the parents.

Information about the child's reactions to previous illnesses.
When you inquire about the child's reactions to previous illnesses, focus on, for example, how the child reacted to colds, measles, and minor injuries. Did the child react with withdrawal, with acting-out behavior, with his or her usual behavior, or with other behaviors?

Information about treatments.
When you inquire about what treatments have been recommended for the present illness, also note whether the recommendations have been followed, whether the child or parents made suggestions for alternative treatments or for changes in the treatment regimen, and whether there were any side effects from the treatments. Possible adverse reactions to drugs include depression, irritability, euphoria, psychosis, delirium, ataxia, confusion, paranoia, altered sensations, muscle weakness,

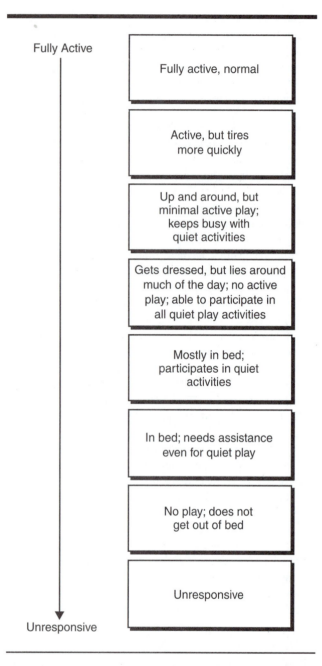

Figure 16-1. A continuum of activity. From Lansky, List, Lansky, Ritter-Sterr, and Miller (1987).

Information about cognitive, educational, interpersonal, and affective factors.   Obtain information about the child's intellectual functioning, problem-solving ability, social skills, educational history, and relationship with parents and siblings. If there are periods of psychological distress, determine whether there is a relationship between these periods and periods of somatic complaints. For example, when the child is lonely or in need of attention, do somatic complaints and visits to physicians increase? If you interview the child's teachers, review the guidelines presented in Chapter 4.

Interviewing Medically Ill Children in a Hospital

When children are hospitalized, they are likely to experience stress—their daily schedule is disrupted, familiar people and activities are missing, and they have little control over what happens to them (Koocher & MacDonald, 1992). While they are in the hospital, children may cry, cling to their parents, be fearful, withdraw from people, become aggressive or destructive, eat and sleep poorly, be uncooperative in the treatment process, express heightened bodily concerns, and show regressive behavior (Willis et al., 1982). The stress of *hospitalization* also may cause "physiological changes, such as elevated pulse rate, blood pressure, and temperature" (Willis et al., 1982, p. 50). The parents also will feel a loss of control, and both the child and the parents must adapt to the hospital staff; in the process, they may begin to lose their feelings of competence (Lewis, 1994).

Hospitalization also can have positive effects beyond improving the children's physical health (Willis et al., 1982).

Seriously abused, neglected, emotionally deprived children often thrive on the emotional care and attention they receive while in the hospital. Infants admitted to the hospital for nonorganic failure-to-thrive begin to gain weight and thrive from the cuddling and regular feeding given them by the nursing personnel. Children from unbearable home situations may find the hospital to be a safe haven where the hospital routine, the regular nutritious meals, and personal attention offer a relief from the chaotic home environment. Children from low-income, multiproblem families, who experience the adverse effects of poverty, can also find hospitalization a positive experience. (p. 54)

While the child is in the hospital, the health care provider staff can do the following:

- arrange to have a thorough assessment of the child's development
- observe parent-child interactions
- recommend appropriate interventions
- provide services to help stabilize the family (such as welfare services, food stamps, housing aid, and nutritional education)
- provide therapeutic play experiences (depending on the child's age) to allow the child to express his or her feel-

weight gain, fatigue, anorexia, weight loss, and agitated depression. Consult the *Physician's Desk Reference* to find out about the side effects associated with the medications that the child is taking. Determine the child's understanding of the treatment regimen and his or her desire and ability to follow it. If the child (or a parent) has not followed the regimen, is it because of forgetfulness, irresponsibility, carelessness, lack of understanding, or active decision or choice, or is a parent responsible for the nonadherence? (Also see Chapter 15 for a discussion of adherence.)

ings about the illness and hospitalization, to enhance the child's sense of mastery, and to foster adaptive behavior

A medically ill child's adjustment to a hospital will depend on several factors, including the following (Adams-Greenly, 1989; Yap, 1988):

- age of the child
- child's level of cognitive development
- type of illness
- severity of the illness
- level of pain
- type of treatment
- level of risk for death
- length of the hospitalization
- family dynamics
- family resources
- child's temperament and personality
- extent of the child's separation anxiety
- child's coping mechanisms
- extent to which the child misses school, sports, and social events
- hospital layout, including roommates and access to preferred rooms, television, radio, and personal items from home
- hospital staff's ability to relate to and comfort the child

It is also important that hospitals follow the bill of rights for children, shown in Exhibit 16-1. In England, these rights form the charter of the National Association for the Welfare of Children in Hospital.

Preparing Children for Hospitalization and for Threatening Medical Procedures

When you prepare children for hospitalization and for *threatening medical procedures,* consider their level of development.

1. *Preschool children.* Preschool children are likely to have limited understanding of illness and health, and, as noted in Chapter 15, they may think in magical terms. They may perceive hospitalization as rejection or punishment, see treatment as hostile or punitive, and have concerns about body penetration aroused by surgery or injections (Magrab, 1984). They may fear separation from their parents. On the other hand, they may perceive hospitalization as special positive attention. You will need to deal with their beliefs about illness. For example, preschool children may fail "to understand that one cannot bleed to death from a venipuncture, that being 'put to sleep' before the operation is not the same treatment their injured dog received, and that their illness is not punishment for wrongdoing" (Peterson, Farmer, Harbeck, & Chaney, 1990, p. 353). (Also see Chapter 15.)

2. *School-aged children.* Hospitalization and threatening medical procedures may generate feelings of inadequacy in

Exhibit 16-1
The National Association for the Welfare of Children in Hospital (NAWCH) Charter

1
Children shall be admitted to the hospital only if the care they require cannot be equally provided at home or on a day basis.

2
Children in hospital shall have the right to have their parents with them at all times provided this is in the best interests of the child. Accommodation should therefore be offered to all parents, and they should be helped and encouraged to stay. In order to share in the care of their child, parents should be fully informed about ward routine and their active participation encouraged.

3
Children and their parents shall have the right to information appropriate to their age and understanding.

4
Children and their parents shall have the right to informed participation in all decisions involving their health care. Every child shall be protected from unnecessary medical treatment, and steps taken to mitigate physical and emotional distress.

5
Children shall be treated with tact and understanding and at all times their privacy shall be respected.

6
Children shall enjoy the care of appropriately trained staff, fully aware of the physical and emotional needs of each age group.

7
Children shall be able to wear their own clothes and have their own personal possessions.

8
Children shall be cared for with other children of the same age group.

9
Children shall be in an environment furnished and equipped to meet their requirements, and which conforms to recognised standards of safety and supervision.

10
Children shall have full opportunity for play, recreation and education suited to their age and condition.

Source: Belson (1993), p. 208.

school-aged children. They may become demanding or rebellious in order to maintain a semblance of control. And they, like their younger counterparts, may fear separation (Magrab, 1984).

3. *Adolescents.* Adolescents may see hospitalization and threatening medical procedures as threats to their independence. There may be conflicts over control. They may fear separation and be concerned about how hospitalization may affect their status in their peer group (Magrab, 1984).

Successful preparation of children and their parents for hospitalization and threatening medical procedures can reduce their anxiety before, during, and after the hospitalization, minimize posthospitalization behavior disturbance, and facilitate coping during the hospitalization (Peterson et al., 1990).

Helping parents prepare their child for hospitalization. Encourage the parents to help the child cope with hospitalization, and stress the importance of parental presence and support. Parents can help their child with the impending hospitalization in the following ways (Sarafino, 1994, p. 342, with changes in notation and additions). The parents should

- explain to the child the reason for going to the hospital and what it will be like. (A doll or stuffed animal can be used to help explain what will happen—parents can undress the doll, put pajamas on the doll, take the doll's blood pressure and temperature, put the doll in a bed and wheel the bed around, offer the doll food on a tray, give the doll an opportunity to watch television, talk to the doll as a nurse or doctor would, and so forth.)
- tell the child the truth, but without going into detail (for example, "The shot may hurt for a little while, and it is ok to say 'ouch'").
- give the child opportunities to ask questions, and then answer them carefully in a way that the child can understand.
- read with the child a children's book that describes a child's hospital experience.
- explain to the child any medical terms that he or she may need to know (for example, "stool collection" doesn't mean a collection of small chairs).
- take the child to the hospital for an orientation and to meet some of the staff (if allowed by the hospital), and explain to the child some hospital routines, such as what to do about going to the bathroom and how he or she will be awakened in the morning and have breakfast in bed.
- describe when they will be with the child and where they will stay, especially if they plan to stay overnight.
- encourage the child to bring a favorite stuffed animal, Walkman radio/tape player, or other favorite thing from home (as long as it is small and replaceable).
- maintain a calm and confident manner, thereby conveying the message that there is no need to be frightened.

Informing children and parents about the hospitalization. Give the child and parents information about what to expect in the hospital, taking into consideration the child's age and level of comprehension. With younger children, use simple words, be repetitive and slower in your speech, and emphasize vocal inflections. With all children, look for signs that they understand and follow what you are saying. They may try to block out the information you want to give them. They may do so, for example, by "changing the subject, becoming fascinated with the bottom of their shoe, or unraveling the carpet edge when a medical instrument is shown" (Peterson et al., 1990, p. 354).

Here are some specific suggestions useful for working with adolescents (and older elementary school–aged children) who will be hospitalized (Denholm, 1991).

1. *Understanding and responding to concerns.* Find out why the adolescent will be hospitalized and what treatments he or she will receive. Discuss with the adolescent his or her concerns about the illness and the treatments.

2. *Privacy.* Discuss with the adolescent any fears and concerns he or she may have about exposure of his or her body while in the hospital. Inform the adolescent that the hospital provides (as appropriate) adequate screening between beds, bathroom facilities, quiet areas for patient use, telephones, televisions, and a library.

3. *Peer visitation and contact.* Encourage the adolescent to tell his or her friends about the hospitalization. Inform the adolescent that he or she can invite friends to visit him or her in the hospital, if allowed by the hospital.

4. *Mobility.* Explain to the adolescent that he or she will be encouraged to walk, move, and do as much for himself or herself physically as is appropriate. Inform the adolescent about the limitations and necessary restrictions that he or she will face in the hospital. Acknowledge the adolescent's frustrations about any physical restrictions. Suggest how the adolescent might help promote faster recovery for himself or herself and how progress might be impeded. Help the adolescent develop realistic expectations about the results of the medical or surgical procedure and about the resumption of previous activities.

5. *Personal items.* Inform the adolescent about his or her possible room assignment. Encourage the adolescent to take suitable, comfortable clothes and a bathrobe, along with personal grooming and hygiene accessories. Suggest that the adolescent bring appropriate personal effects to the hospital but not bring valuable items. This might include items that will make him or her comfortable, such as photographs, a favorite game, a stuffed animal, or other mementos.

6. *Independence.* Acknowledge how being in a hospital may bring about a loss of control, a lack of independence, and changes in the adolescent's relationship with parents, siblings, and friends. For example, the health provider staff rather than the parents will assume primary responsibility for the adolescent's care, the parents may be more tolerant of the adolescent's behavior, and siblings may become jealous about the favors given to the adolescent who is ill. Explain to the adolescent the usual reactions and feelings—including anxiety, loneliness, and uncertainty—that other adolescents have to the planned medical procedures.

7. *Schoolwork.* Discuss with the adolescent how long he or she might be in the hospital and how this stay might affect his or her schoolwork. Encourage the adolescent to take adequate schoolwork to the hospital, to maintain regular contact with his or her teachers and the school counselor during the hospitalization and the recovery, to arrange for his or her parents or others to facilitate these contacts, and to plan for tutoring services, where available and/or necessary. Explore any concerns the adolescent might have about the effect of

the illness (or accident) on his or her physical ability to do schoolwork and to participate in extracurricular activities (such as athletics and band).

Helping the child develop ways to cope. Assist the child in developing coping strategies to deal with the anxiety and stress associated with the medical procedures and with the hospitalization. Most medical procedures, including lumbar punctures, cardiac catheterizations, anesthesia induction, and physical therapy, will be more effective when children are relaxed and cooperative.

Working with the staff. Have a good working relationship with all the staff members who will have contact with the child. You want to ensure that the staff knows what information you are giving to the child and parents and what expectations the child and parents have about the medical procedures. *You also want to ensure that what you tell the child and parents is compatible with what the other health care providers are saying and doing.* Parents and their medically ill children will lose trust in you if significant inconsistencies arise in the information they receive from you and others. You don't want the following to happen: "Many parents have complained that they had effectively prepared their child to deal with an injection cooperatively and calmly, only to have two nurses enter the room, and one of them physically restrain the child while the injection is given by the other" (Peterson et al., 1990, p. 358). If you work in a facility where you can negotiate such issues with the staff beforehand, do so, and prepare the child for what to expect from the staff. If possible, also prepare the staff for what they can expect from the child. (See Johnson, Jeppson, and Redburn, 1992, for more information about how professionals who come into contact with medically ill children can improve the psychosocial environment in the hospital.)

Case illustration. This case illustrates the importance of recognizing behavioral problems and the possible effects of these problems on treatment of children who are hospitalized (Adams-Greenly, 1989).

CASE 16-1. REBECCA

Rebecca was 5 years old when she was admitted to the hospital for a bone marrow transplant. Psychosocial intervention was requested because of her serious behavioral problems, including enuresis, rocking, shrieking, food refusal, and intractability. If frustrated, she quickly regressed into impulsive, aggressive behavior. Her mother was described as anxious, depressed, inhibited, and unable to set any limits with Rebecca. There were four other children at home; the oldest, age 7, had many responsibilities for the care of the younger three children.

The staff believed that Rebecca's behavioral problems were life threatening because of her limited ability to tolerate the frustrations and demands of isolation, skin and mouth care, and other aspects of the transplant procedure. The transplant was postponed until Rebecca became more manageable. Interventions included the use of medication and psychotherapy to lessen her anxiety; supportive counseling with the mother that focused on helping her set limits with Rebecca, follow the care plan developed by the nursing staff, and reorganize responsibilities for Rebecca at home; and play therapy with Rebecca and her 7-year-old sibling. After 15 sessions of treatment, Rebecca successfully participated in the transplant procedure. (adapted from p. 569)

Working with Children Who Are Hospitalized

Despite adequate preparations (or when there are no preparations), children may feel lonely, frustrated, bored, and helpless in the hospital. When they feel this way, they may need help to keep them from becoming depressed, hostile, or fearful; from withdrawing; from regressing; or from having other undesirable reactions (Bowen, 1985).

Here are some useful things that you can do to help children who are hospitalized:

- Minimize their anxiety as much as possible.
- Give them some control in the planning of their treatments, timing of procedures, daily scheduling, and other similar matters.
- Encourage them to talk about their concerns, needs, fears, plans, and dreams.
- Encourage their families and their friends to visit them as much as possible.
- Help them establish realistic, achievable goals.
- Help them identify the progress that they have made.
- Focus on the positive aspects of their hospitalization and treatment.
- Encourage them to do their schoolwork.
- Encourage them to read, draw, play games, and join an established support group in the hospital (if one is available) when they are ready.
- Encourage them to talk with other children who have the same problem when they are ready.

The following two cases illustrate various facets of mental health consultation in a hospital setting (O'Malley & Koocher, 1977). The cases demonstrate that consultation can be effective or ineffective.

CASE 16-2. JIM

Jim, a 13-year-old, was referred for psychosocial consultation by his nurse, who was concerned about his possible psychotic behavior. There was nothing in Jim's history to suggest psychosis. His nurse was concerned about his refusal to have his cancer medication delivered through an intravenous tube (IV). It was not conceivable to the nurse that anyone would refuse potential life-giving treatment. A brief interview with Jim suggested that he needed to feel that he had some control over his own destiny and that this control had been taken away by his cancer and by his hospitalization. The social worker met with the nurse and discussed ways to allow Jim to have some control. Together they agreed that Jim should be allowed to choose the time at which the medicine would be given and the site of the IV and should be encouraged to keep track of the flow, reporting it to the nurse if any deviation occurred. After these changes were made, the nurse reported that no further difficulties arose. (adapted from p. 55)

CASE 16-3. JANE

Jane, a lovely 15-year-old girl with advanced Hodgkins disease, was referred for a psychosocial consultation because she was depressed. Prior to the first interview with Jane, Jane's parents informed the social worker that they expected Jane to be happy and not to talk about morbid things. During the interview, Jane said that she was furious with her parents for not allowing her to talk about death, her sadness, or her grief. She repeated what her parents said to her: "Don't talk like that! Everything will be fine." Jane shared these feelings with the social worker and experienced some relief. However, when Jane shared the content of the interviews with her parents, they became angry and summarily dismissed the social worker. The parents were unable to deal with the finality of the illness and wanted their daughter to help maintain their denial. Because the social worker did not maintain the denial and failed to clarify the parents' expectations, the parents stopped the counseling sessions. (adapted from p. 56)

Preparing Older Adolescents for Transition to Adult Services

As chronically ill adolescents reach young adulthood, they may need to transfer from a pediatric facility to an adult facility for continued care (Eiser, 1993). This may cause stress for them and their families for the following reasons. First, the transition is likely to involve a change in physicians—from a pediatrician to a specialist in adult medicine. Second, the young adult may see patients in the clinic's waiting room who have highly visible complications of their diseases, such as blindness and amputations associated with diabetes. If they feel uncomfortable in the new setting, they may not want to continue with their treatments. Third, the transition to adult services may elicit feelings of anxiety and depression with the thought that the disease will not be outgrown; in such cases, the young adult may need to reach a new level of acceptance. Thus, older adolescents may need help in making the transition from pediatric care to adult care.

Let's now see how an older adolescent described his first experience at an adult clinic (Eiser, 1993).

CASE 16-4. JOEY

My first visit to the [adult] clinic really frightened me. The only reason for this was on this particular day while waiting to see the doctor, there appeared to be a large number of elderly patients with problems such as amputations, inability to walk very well, and very poor eye-sight. Although I realise that these are problems that can happen to a very badly diagnosed diabetic, I felt thoroughly depressed and hated my diabetes. Since that time I have got over my hatred, but still feel anxious coming to clinic. (p. 88)

INTERVIEWING PARENTS OF MEDICALLY ILL CHILDREN

In interviewing parents of medically ill children, you will want to ask about the following:

- their knowledge of the child's illness
- their communications with the health care provider staff
- their feelings about and reactions to the child's illness
- their communications with the child about the illness
- their communications with the child's siblings about the illness (if applicable)
- their communications with each other about the illness
- their ability to manage the disease
- their resources and needs concerning their child's illness

This information can be useful in designing intervention plans, monitoring the treatment program, and helping with adherence.

During the interview, you may learn that the parents are extremely anxious about their child's illness or extremely overprotective toward their child. If you believe, for example, that they will be unable to support their child during a painful medical procedure, give them permission to leave the hospital room (Redd, 1989). Reassure them that it is acceptable for them to remain in the waiting room until the procedure is over and then return to the child's room to comfort and support the child. You want to reduce parental guilt and provide the parents with a means to be effectively involved (Redd, 1989). If they choose to leave the room, they should inform their child that they will be close by.

In addition to seeing the parents at the time of the child's initial diagnosis, you may want to see them at times of remission and relapse of the child's illness, as well as at other critical times during the child's development. These times, as noted in Chapter 15, also can be anxiety-provoking.

The following poem expresses some of the concerns of parents of medically ill children.

Where Can I Go?

If this is not a place where tears are understood,
Where do I go to cry?
If this is not a place where my spirits can take wing,
Where do I go to fly?
If this is not a place where my questions can be asked,
Where do I go to seek?
If this is not a place where my feelings can be heard,
Where do I go to speak?
If this is not a place where you'll accept me as I am,
Where can I go to be?
If this is not a place where I can try and learn and grow
Where can I just be me?
If there is not a place where tears are understood,
Where can I go to cry?

—Ken Medina

INTERVIEWING IN CASES OF TERMINAL ILLNESS

When you interview a child who has a terminal illness, it will be useful for you to have an understanding of the child's conception of death (see Chapter 13). A child and her or his parents may have worries about death even when the child's illness is not terminal. If death is approaching, allow children to express their anger, grief, fear, and other feelings. Talking about their feelings may relieve some of the pain associated with the impending death.

Health care professionals face several tasks in dealing with children who are terminally ill and their families. One task is to help the family "normalize the life of the child and family as much as possible within the constraints of the child's illness" (Siegel, 1993, p. 489). Another task is to facilitate effective coping with stressful events associated with the disease and its treatment. As in the case of a medical illness, you will want to facilitate communication among the family members, encourage them to express their feelings and concerns, and foster a sense of mastery and control (Siegel, 1993). By carrying out these tasks successfully, you will help terminally ill children adjust better to their impending deaths and also help families cope better after a child's death.

Among the special needs of children who are terminally ill (Johansen, 1988; Spinetta, 1980) are the need

- to be treated the same way as they were before they were ill by their family and friends, whenever possible
- to be told the truth about their disease and the treatment they are receiving
- to be allowed to maintain contact with their peers, especially if they cannot go to school
- to be allowed to talk about their feelings whenever they want to
- to have their parents sleep in their hospital room or hospice room, if this is allowed
- to be with relatives as the time of death approaches
- to know that they have done all they could with their lives
- to be told that when death comes it will not hurt and that after death there will be no pain
- to know that they will be remembered for the good times they and their family had together

Terminally ill children who do not yet understand the concept of death (see Chapter 13) are likely to be more worried about being in the hospital and suffering from pain than about dying. However, those who do understand the concept of death may be depressed, anxious, and angry and express their feelings in various ways.

In cases of impending death, find out what the family wants for the terminally ill child. For example, do they want home care, a hospice, a hospital, or another facility, or do they want to make other arrangements (Katz, Dolgin, & Varni, 1990)? Each family member will react in his or her own way after the child dies, and some may need help in coping with their grief. The need for help may arise even after a considerable amount of time has elapsed after the child's death (Katz et al., 1990). See Chapter 13 for further discussion of bereavement.

Suggestions for Health Care Providers Who Work with Children Who Are Terminally Ill

The following suggestions will be useful to health care providers who care for a terminally ill child in a hospital (Brown, 1989, p. 257, with changes in notation). *These suggestions are primarily for physicians, physician's assistants, and nursing personnel.*

1. Do not make *critical decisions* without the parents' consent, except in emergency situations.
2. Have both parents present, whenever possible, when you give any news about the child's progress.
3. Do not change staff members' assignments, unless necessary, when the child is in terminal care; children and their families need familiar faces.
4. Do not whisper when you are in the room when the child is awake, unless the parents ask you to do so.
5. Do not always be pessimistic. Find something positive to tell the child and parents.
6. Do not stop touching the dying child when you previously had touched him or her.
7. Do not avoid the child or parents.
8. Give the child and parents, where applicable, choices regarding medication, treatment, and care. Tell them what you are going to do and why you are going to do it *before* you do it. Let them participate in the decisions, as much as this is possible.
9. Let the child and parents speak to the attending physician whenever they want to, when the physician is available.
10. Do not be judgmental about how the parents act either before the child dies or at the time the child dies.
11. Prepare the parents for what might happen at the time of the child's death.
12. Anticipate the parents' questions and give them the information they might need because they may not have the energy, knowledge, or courage to ask appropriate questions.
13. Anticipate what medical information might be confusing, and give explanations geared to the child's and parents' levels of understanding.
14. Be sensitive to the parents' intellectual level and level of literacy when offering written material or directions for care of the child.
15. Allow the parents and other family members, as much as it is feasible, to participate in caring for the dying child.
16. Treat each parent equally. Do not always talk directly to one parent and ignore the other one.

17. Let the parents spend some time alone with the child after he or she dies.

18. Call the family and keep in touch. The staff has been a significant part of the family members' lives, often for years, and the family would like to know that the staff cares and has not forgotten them. Also, over time, the family may have new concerns that you can address.

Going "gentle into that good night" with one's dignity and sense of self intact is certainly as morally acceptable as raging "against the dying of the light."

—Timothy Quill

Healthy Children Who Have a Terminally Ill Family Member

Healthy children who have a terminally ill sibling, parent, or other relative are likely to experience great stress (Johansen, 1988). They have to cope with an emotionally charged household, and they are likely to receive less attention from healthy family members because of the increased attention given to the ill or dying relative, who may be at home, in a hospital, or in another setting. If the healthy children are still too young to understand illness and death, they may fear that they also may get sick and die, or they may see the illness or death of their sibling, parent, or other relative as punishment or as the fulfillment of a thought that they had had but didn't really mean.

Healthy children who have a terminally ill sibling may feel guilty because they think that the terminally ill sibling resents them for being healthy (Sourkes, 1987). Also, because fighting and rivalry usually are involved in sibling relationships, the death of a sibling may elicit in the surviving siblings feelings of guilt about these interactions, which may affect their mourning.

The stresses experienced by healthy children who have a terminally ill parent place them at increased risk for social impairment and for psychological disorders (Christ, Siegel, Freund, Langosch, Hendersen, Sperber, & Weinstein, 1993; Urbach & Culbert, 1991). They may have "an acute sense of impending doom and the expectation of a complete loss of their normal life" (Christ et al., 1993, p. 418). Their fears may center on getting the same symptoms as their ill parent; worrying that their ill parent may die; feeling guilty for causing or exacerbating their ill parent's illness; feeling responsible for their ill parent's anger, withdrawal, and lack of affection; worrying that the healthy parent might get sick or die; worrying that the parents may divorce; and worrying about changed family roles and expectations.

The following examples illustrate some of these worries (Christ et al., 1993).

During his father's terminal illness, Frank, aged eight, developed a tic that seemed to mimic his father's facial spasm from his brain tumor progression. (p. 419)

Ruth, aged nine, believed that her mother's difficult labor at Ruth's birth (five years before the cancer was diagnosed) had caused too much stress and led to her mother's brain tumor. Ruth's belief that she was responsible for her mother's terminal illness made her intensely guilty and sad. (p. 420)

Ben, aged eight, was quite uncharacteristically withdrawn from peers. He explained that it was difficult for him to talk about his mother's leukemia with his father because his father "cries all the time," and consequently he has to judge his father's mood before asking him for something. He was worried about how fragile his father seemed and didn't want him to "fall apart, because who would be there to take care of me then?" (p. 421)

Charles, aged eight, who had recently lost his grandfather and now faced the imminent death of his father, stated: "I began to think that maybe grandma will die, and then mother will die, and then everybody on the planet Earth will die. And nothing will be there." (p. 418)

The worries and concerns of children about a critically ill parent may affect how they function at home, at school, and in the community (Christ et al., 1993). At home, the children may complain that the healthy parent seems distracted, impatient, or irritable. If they had a close relationship with the ill parent, they may feel particularly abandoned and vulnerable. Tension and anxiety may mark their relationship with their siblings, particularly when family roles are changed.

The following two examples illustrate some of these family dynamics (Christ et al., 1993).

Melissa, aged eight, said she was afraid to ask questions about her father's illness because she thought her parents would yell at her or punish her. (p. 422)

Ed, aged eight, remarked (angrily) that when his mother became ill, his 13-year-old sister, Ellen, became "a little mother to me…she bosses me around, never lets me do what I want and nags me more than Mom ever did." Ellen and Ed fought, teased, and provoked each other constantly. (p. 423)

At school, the children may have difficulty concentrating on their work, perform poorly on tests, and engage in inappropriate behavior. In the community, the children may be less able to partake in extracurricular activities or maintain peer contacts outside the classroom because the family is directing its resources to the ill parent; for example, there may be no adult available to transport the children to their former activities.

Children of a terminally ill parent may have outbursts of anger, sadness, and anxiety; suicidal thoughts; severe conflict with both parents; and somatic symptoms (Christ et al., 1993). They are at greater risk for developing psychological disorders when their family has closed communication patterns, severe financial problems, and changed family roles and life styles (for example, the healthy mother has to start working or work longer hours). They also are more at risk when they have had a parent whose disease was severe and had a rapid course, multiple recent experiences of loss, recent severe stress, or a history of multiple illness-related deaths in the family.

The following case illustrates what may happen when a family cannot make the transition from the chronic phase to the terminal phase of a parent's illness (Rolland, 1994).

CASE 16-5. THE SMITH FAMILY

A family with three children, aged 18, 12, and 9, had seemingly coped with the mother's breast cancer for five years; they had steadfastly believed in their ability to conquer cancer. Mom had become disease-free, and the family never mentioned her illness. In general, the family seldom talked about feelings. When metastatic spread was discovered, the family become emotionally paralyzed. While new treatments were tried and failed, no one could discuss the next phase. The children, particularly the two younger ones, were emotionally shielded and not prepared for Mom's impending death. The 9-year-old was excluded from the funeral; she became severely withdrawn and depressed within a year. The 18-year-old moved away and limited her contact with the family. The 12-year-old became overfunctional and watched over Dad and her younger sister. Dad, the family wage earner, was ill prepared to provide the nurturing side of family life, especially under such emotionally difficult circumstances. (p. 51)

Rolland (1994) pointed out that "this family's somewhat rigid style and lack of communication about emotional issues made them vulnerable to a terminal illness. They could live with a chronic condition in which the threat of loss was in the background. When a recurrence of the cancer heralded the next phase, they were unable to adapt" (p. 51).

All life is terminal. Even if one's own timetable is tragically shortened by a medical diagnosis, the end is not yet. There is still time, time for children and parents who love each other to make the most of it. Don't try to shield your children from making the most of that time.

—Kathleen McCue

EVALUATING THE INTERVIEW

Table 16-2 and Table 16-3 will help you in evaluating the interview with a medically ill child and with his or her parents, respectively. With the child, you will want to evaluate the following areas: knowledge of the illness, symptoms, ability to cope with illness, ability to implement treatment, family and support systems, stress, and knowledge of events related to any accidents. With the parents, you will want to evaluate these areas: knowledge of the illness, ability to cope with the illness, parent-child relations, marital functioning, and support systems, significant stressors, and ability to implement treatment.

As part of your evaluation, you should examine the child's hospital charts and medical records, as they may provide valuable information about the child's illness, including the type of symptoms, the frequency of visits to the hospital and to physicians, the medications prescribed, the laboratory results, and other diagnostic test results. Charts and records also may contain staff observations about the child, family involvement, and family members' interactions with each other and with the hospital staff. You can compare information in the child's hospital charts and medical records with behavioral information—such as changes in life style, school performance, friendships, and temperament—to discover relationships between changes in the child's medical illness and behavioral events.

THE POST-ASSESSMENT INTERVIEW WITH MEDICALLY ILL CHILDREN AND THEIR PARENTS

When children are told that they have a chronic, serious, or potentially fatal illness, they may be stunned. Soon afterward, they "may develop increased anxiety, loss of appetite, insomnia, social isolation, emotional withdrawal, depression and apathy, and marked ambivalence toward adults who are providing primary care" (Koocher & MacDonald, 1992, p. 76). If you give them information about their illness, you also want to help them work through their feelings and see that there are still rewards in living.

Parents may react to a diagnosis that their child has a chronic medical illness with feelings of helplessness, fear, anger, guilt, or sadness; with a combination of several of these feelings; or, occasionally, with relief at getting closure. Your task, in part, will be to encourage them to focus on ways to help their child. This may entail getting them to accept the treatment, even though the treatment may be toxic, potentially disabling, or even life-threatening (Adams-Greenly, 1991). When the parents are extremely anxious and have limited information about the illness or medical procedures, they may have difficulty understanding or absorbing what you tell them. In such cases, you will need to be even more patient and find ways to get across the information. (See Chapter 5 for more information on the post-assessment interview.)

The following two cases illustrate communication problems between the health care provider staff and the parents of medically ill children.

CASE 16-6. MRS. G.

Mrs. G. appeared at her social worker's office, sobbing and shaking with fear. The attending physician had told her that her son had developed a blood infection that would require intravenous antibiotics. She had been appropriately concerned, but calm, until the intern had used the words "septicemia" and "therapy." Mrs. G. had concluded her son had been diagnosed with a second cancer and would be starting an additional protocol. (Adams-Greenly, 1991, p. 6)

CASE 16-7. MRS. D.

Mrs. D. called the hospital to inquire about her son's condition. She was told by the intensive care unit that he was on the ventilator and was paralyzed. Mrs. D. became hysterical.

Table 16-2
Evaluating the Interview with Medically Ill Children

Knowledge of the Illness

1. What type of illness does the child have?
2. What is the natural course of the illness?
3. What does the child know about his or her illness?
4. How did the child learn about his or her illness? (For example, what information did the child receive from his or her parents, physician, nursing staff, psychosocial staff, siblings, other relatives, friends, classmates, and fellow patients [if hospitalized]?)

Symptoms

5. What are the child's symptoms?
6. What events exacerbate the symptoms?

Coping with the Illness

7. What is the child's level of emotional, social, and cognitive development?
8. What is the child's reaction to the diagnosis?
9. How does the child adapt to the illness?
10. What experiences has the child had with illness?
11. How has the child coped with prior illnesses?
12. How is the child coping with the illness (for example, acceptance, denial, anxiety, fear, projection)?
13. What is the impact of the illness on the child's life (including impact on family, friends, and school)?

Implementing Treatment

14. What is the child's treatment (including medicines, physical therapy, exercise, diet, injections, etc.)?
15. Is the child adhering to the treatment? (If not, why not?)
16. How effective is the treatment?
17. What are the child's feelings about the treatment?
18. How does the child accept restrictions placed on him or her?
19. Does the treatment have any side effects?
20. What medical specialists has the child seen?
21. What other professionals has the child seen?
22. What needs does the child have that are not being met?

Family and Support Systems

23. How does the child feel about his or her family?
24. How does the child feel about his or her family's reaction to the illness?

25. How does the child feel about his or her family's help with the medical regimen?
26. How does the child communicate with his or her family about the illness and about his or her concerns? (For example, does the child actively inquire about the disease, express his or her worries or grief, talk about the illness, or initiate conversation about the illness?)
27. What was the relationship between the child and the parents and between the child and the siblings before the illness?
28. Does the child receive support from other individuals in the community, including relatives other than those in the immediate family, friends, classmates, pastor, physician, social worker, psychologist, or psychiatrist?

Stress

29. Are there any factors in the child's life that might explain why the illness is now occurring?
30. Has the child experienced any recent stress?
31. Does the child have any behavioral problems? (For example, does the child show problems such as bed-wetting, sleep problems, withdrawal, eating problems, acting-out behavior, problems in school, problems getting along with peers, or problems getting along with parents?)
32. If so, are they a result of the illness or were they present before the child got sick?

Additional Questions If Disability or Injury Was Caused by an Accident

33. What were the circumstances surrounding the accident?
34. Have previous accidents occurred?
35. If so, when did they occur and what happened?
36. What role did the child play in the accident? (For example, was child negligence involved in the accident?)
37. What role did the family play in the accident? (For example, was parental negligence involved in the accident?)
38. What was going on in the child's life when the accident occurred? (For example, for adolescents and young adults [and adults as well] who sustained orthopedic injuries, burn injuries, or automobile accident injuries, note whether drugs or alcohol was involved.)
39. What was going on in the family when the accident occurred?

Source: Adapted in part from Koocher and MacDonald (1992).

She did not understand (and was not told) that the paralysis was temporary and was induced by drugs to keep her son still while he was on mechanical ventilation. The nurse failed to anticipate what the patient's mother might or might not know about the procedure. (K. Gist, personal communication, July 1995)

Suggestions for establishing a collaborative relationship with families of medically ill children follow (also see

Chapter 4 on ways to conduct family interviews). They assume that you are working in a facility—such as a hospital, a clinic, or another center or agency—and are in a position to coordinate services for the child and family. These suggestions hold not only for the post-assessment interview, but for the initial interview as well as for all interactions with families (Spano, 1994, pp. 33, 34, 37, 38, 40, 41, 43, 44, 46, with changes in notation).

Table 16-3
Evaluating the Interview with Parents of Medically Ill Children

Knowledge of the Illness
1. What did the parents know about the child's illness?
2. How did the parents learn about the child's illness?
3. How many different medical providers did the parents consult?
4. What members of the family and extended family have been told about the child's medical illness?

Coping with the Illness
5. How have the parents accepted the child's diagnosis?
6. In what stage of the adjustment process are the parents (for example, shock, denial, sadness, anger, adaptation, reorganization)?
7. What information-seeking behaviors have the parents engaged in (for example, reading books, magazines, newspapers, medical journals, or medical encyclopedias)?
8. How has the family adapted to the child's illness? (For example, what is the mood of the family members? How do they communicate with each other? How have their relationships been affected? How have their roles changed within the family?)
9. How will the family's culture affect its approach to the child's illness and treatment?
10. How much support will the family offer the medically ill child?
11. What experiences has the family had with illness?
12. How has the family coped with the child's prior illnesses and with illnesses of other family members?
13. Have the parents received help in coping with their child's illness?
14. Who has primary responsibility for taking care of the child?
15. How do the parents feel about this arrangement?
16. Do the parents talk with the child's siblings and relatives about the child's illness?

Parent-Child Relations
17. How do the parents and medically ill child get along?
18. Do the parents and medically ill child agree about following the treatment regimen?
19. How has the illness affected the way the parents treat the medically ill child?
20. How do the parents treat the other children in the family?
21. How have the siblings been affected by the child?
22. How will the parents handle sending the child to school during periods of minor flare-ups?
23. How do the parents talk to the child about the illness? (For example, do the parents tell the child about the severity and possible course of the illness? Do they try to control the flow of information? Do they answer the child's questions honestly? Do they reassure their child about the outcome of the disease and give the child hope for the future?)

Marital Functioning and Support Systems
24. How do the family members communicate with each other about the child's illness and treatment regimen?
25. Are both parents involved in the child's treatment program?
26. In divorced or separated families, are both parents aware of the treatment regimen and are changes needed in the treatment regimen?
27. What sources of support does the family have?
28. What is the quality of the marital relationship?
29. What needs do the parents have that are not being met?
30. What needs do the siblings have that are not being met?

Significant Stressors
31. Besides the stressors associated with the child's illness, what other stressors are present in the family (for example, economic, social, or health problems)?
32. Do the parents have any behavioral manifestations of stress? (For example, do they have sleep problems, problems on the job, short temper, or sleep difficulties? Are there more arguments in the family? Do the parents use sedatives or tranquilizers? Have they increased their visits to a physician for their own difficulties? Have they consulted a psychotherapist?)
33. How has the family changed because of the child's illness?
34. How will the family manage the stress of the child's illness?

Implementing Treatment
35. Do the parents understand the illness?
36. What are the parents' concerns about their child, the illness, and the treatment regimen?
37. Do they understand the treatment regimen needed to manage the illness?
38. Do they have beliefs or attitudes that may interfere with their ability to follow the treatment regimen?
39. Do they have any difficulty communicating with hospital staff, school personnel, or friends and relatives about the child's illness?
40. What services does the family need?
41. Do the parents have an adequate support system to help them with the treatment regimen?
42. What problems are there that can interfere with the family's ability to follow the treatment regimen?
43. How much responsibility does the child assume in following the treatment regimen?
44. How will the child's responsibility for following the treatment regimen change as the child grows older?
45. How much credibility can you give to the parents' statements about following the treatment regimen?
46. What is the parents' relationship with the health care providers?
47. Are the parents' expectations for improvement congruent with those of the health care providers?

Source: Adapted from Koocher and MacDonald (1992) and Mash and Terdal (1990).

BUILDING MUTUAL TRUST AND RESPECT

- Listen actively to the concerns and priorities of the family.
- Be open and honest with the family in sharing information.
- Follow through on coordinating the recommended plans for caring for the child, if you were assigned this task by the health care team or facility.
- Do not speak to family members condescendingly.
- Do not assume that only the health care provider team knows what is best for the child.
- Acknowledge that parents can contribute to health care decisions about the child and that they should be respected for their expertise.
- Offer support and encouragement to the family.
- Allow time for the family members to talk openly about their concerns and worries for the child, and give them choices about how to best meet those challenges.
- Answer questions from the family clearly and concisely, using appropriate language. When you do not know the answers, say so, and tell the family that you will find out the answers to the extent possible or suggest how they can contact other sources to get answers.
- Remember that the family members are struggling to balance their day-to-day living with the complexities of the medical community they now must deal with. Dignify their efforts by assuming that each family member is doing the best that he or she can do.
- Do not impose your life choices or judgments on the family.
- Refer the family to local support organizations, and acknowledge the positive efforts of the family and the successes of the child.
- Offer the family options for early intervention supports and services.
- Acknowledge the family's cultural patterns in dealing with illness and consider these patterns in formulating treatment plans. (Also see Chapters 8, 9, and 15.)

CLARIFYING ROLES AND EXPECTATIONS

- Identify your role as a health care provider, and clarify how you fit in with the health care team.
- Clarify for the family all important information about the health care team.
- Ask the family members relevant questions that will determine their expectations for the child and their expectations of the health care team.
- Determine the role of each family member in the care of the child.
- Establish for the family a contact person at your facility.
- For your records, report and file all information about the child and family, determining what has already taken place, what will happen next, and which member of the health care team is responsible for each action.
- Restate the care coordination plan at the end of the meeting with the family.
- Allow the family to exercise its choice in determining which health care providers should be involved in the care of the child. Minimize anxiety for the family by providing available options before decisions are made and by openly discussing the role of each health care provider.

COMMUNICATING WITH THE FAMILY

- Listen to the family without preconceived notions or judgments.
- Explain medical terminology clearly and concisely.
- Openly share information about the health care of the child to help the family in making informed choices.
- Offer medical recommendations as options for the family, and support the family in its decision, even if members select a recommendation less preferred by the health care team.
- Consider differing abilities of families to understand and process given information.
- Create an environment for open communication, and express medical recommendations clearly without denying the needs and rights of the family.
- Listen to the concerns of the family, and respond appropriately to those concerns.
- Choose your words carefully. Remember that the manner in which you give information and the words you use will stay in the hearts and memory of the family. A caring attitude helps.

SOLVING PROBLEMS AND RESOLVING CONFLICTS

- Help the family recognize that each family member has a right to his or her own opinion when there are disagreements.
- Establish each family member's interests, goals, and priorities as they relate to the problem. Identify common goals and desired outcomes for the well-being of the child.
- Generate options that can result in a win/win situation, if possible. Try to get family members to remain flexible and open to compromise, and have each member explore options for the child before making a final decision.
- Strive for agreement among the family members. Recognize that they may need more time to consider and review the options before making a final decision. Encourage the family members to seek a second opinion if they are ambivalent or uncertain about how to proceed.
- Remember that as a health care provider you are working with a child and a family—not just a "case." The family members may bear lifelong emotional scars from the actions they take in resolving issues of conflict.
- Acknowledge the family members' right to know the truth, even if the truth is painful. Deception only serves to rob them of their dignity and self-esteem.

If you interview the child and parents some time after the initial diagnosis and the initiation of the treatment plan, consider the following questions (Rait & Lederberg, 1989):

1. Have the child and parents followed the treatment plan?
2. Do the child and parents concur on the surface but remain ambivalent about the treatment plan?

3. Do the child and parents argue and disagree at every step or just sometimes?
4. Have the child and parents sought alternative treatments?
5. Have the child and parents sought opinions from several doctors?
6. Are the parents prepared to answer the child's questions about his or her illness and the treatment plan?
7. If not, what additional information do the parents need to answer their child's questions?
8. Do the parents prefer that a third party discuss illness and treatment issues with the child?

INTERVENTIONS WITH MEDICALLY ILL CHILDREN AND THEIR FAMILIES

Chronic illnesses (and injuries and disabilities) are likely to create adjustment problems for the child and for her or his family throughout the child's life. Therefore, the initial clinical assessment interview may be one of many interviews needed during the child's development. You may need several meetings with the family members to help them learn how to adapt to and manage the child's illness.

An important intervention goal is to maintain the quality of life for the medically ill child. In setting realistic goals, consider the following factors:

1. child's age
2. child's developmental level
3. type of illness the child has
4. treatments available for the child's illness
5. limitations the illness and treatment impose on the child and on the family
6. family support available to the child
7. other family, community, and school resources available to the child
8. child's prognosis

Services Needed by Medically Ill Children and Their Families

The services that medically ill children and their families need may include the following (Bristol & Schopler, 1984; Walker, Epstein, Taylor, Crocker, & Tuttle, 1989):

- an appropriate diagnosis, accompanied by detailed information about the illness and its course
- adequate medical services for the ill child
- adequate physical therapy, speech and language therapy, and occupational therapy for the ill child
- adaptive equipment for the ill child
- appropriately designed educational programs for the ill child
- regular communication with the school nurse, teacher, and ancillary school personnel
- social and recreational opportunities for the ill child, including summer camp

- work opportunities for the ill child if he or she is an older adolescent
- training in sexuality for the ill child if he or she is a teenager or young adult
- counseling for the ill child
- a good residential facility for the ill child if he or she is severely impaired (see Chapter 5)
- education on the child's entitlements for the parents (see Exhibit 5-1 in Chapter 5)
- child care and after-school care for both ill and healthy children
- financial assistance
- community acceptance
- contact with other parents of medically ill children
- counseling for the healthy family members, including genetic counseling
- contact with knowledgeable and concerned professionals
- information on community resources
- social/recreational opportunities for the ill child and for healthy family members
- training for the parents on the ill child's health needs
- transportation
- legal services
- help with the ill child's behavior problems
- support groups for siblings
- help in making changes in the physical layout of the home
- home health/nursing care
- respite care

For most families, taking care of a chronically ill child is a demanding task and may be all-consuming, depending on the type of illness. The family's primary concerns may be how to ensure the survival of the child and how to conquer the illness. Part of the focus of an intervention program is to help family members balance "their emphasis on illness-related issues with an equal emphasis on growth and wellness" (Maul-Mellott & Adams, 1987, p. 208).

Health care providers may need to inform parents about how to administer the child's medications, injections, and other treatments; formulate a diet; carry out the rehabilitation program; use special equipment; handle seizures; and recognize signs of worsening or recurring of illness and signs of medication toxicity. If the family does not have adequate psychological, physical, and economic resources to care for the child, you may need to arrange for visiting health care providers, for economic assistance, or, in extreme cases, for a residential facility. When possible, families also need information about the child's expected rate of progress.

If the family is not satisfied with the medical services, you will need to deal with their concerns. If the child is hospitalized, the parents or child, for example, may have disagreements with the health care providers about over- or under-treatment, room assignment, medications, length of hospital stay, diagnostic procedures, type of food served, recreational opportunities, changing of bed linens, number of visitors, visiting hours, availability of reading materials, and so forth. If these issues are not resolved, they may interfere with the child's treatment and recovery.

Planning the discharge from the hospital. Prior to the child's discharge from a hospital, if you are the health care provider conducting the discharge interview, be sure that the parents have been given the information they need to take care of their child and that they understand what needs to be done for their child after she or he leaves the hospital. If you give them written instructions, be sure that they can read and understand the instructions. As noted earlier, if they don't understand the written instructions, you will need to explain the instructions in a way that is comprehensible to them.

Additional topics to cover in the discharge interview may include arranging for follow-up visits, arranging for the child to return to school, arranging for special educational services for the child if she or he cannot return to school, and arranging for any other needed services. The semistructured interview in Table F-7 in Appendix F contains questions that you may find useful in conducting the discharge interview with a child who is leaving a hospital. This semistructured interview also contains follow-up questions.

Evaluating the physical layout of the home. Occasionally, physical alterations in the home—such as modification of doors, installation of railings, or construction of ramps—may be sufficient to enable the chronically ill child to live at home. You or another staff member may need to visit the home to assist in determining what modifications are needed there.

The following guidelines will be useful in evaluating the home (Schmitz, 1988):

- Note the type of home; entrances to the building or home; the width of hallways, door entrances, and stairs; and features of the bedroom, bathroom, living room, dining room, kitchen, laundry area, and any other areas that the child uses.
- Note how accessible each area is for a child who is chronically ill and physically handicapped. For example, considering the child's age and abilities, note whether the child can manage stairs, unlock doors, move safely from one part of the house to another, turn on light switches, get into bed, get clothes, use the toilet and sink, use the bath or shower, transfer from a wheelchair to a chair, turn on the television and radio, open the refrigerator door and take food, open and close cabinets, light the stove, use the oven, use appliances, use outlets, manage laundry facilities, use cleaning utensils, use the phone, and escape in case of emergency.
- Determine whether the parents understand the level of care required to help their child.
- Note whether the parents can provide a safe environment, and especially note any areas that pose a danger.

See Schmitz (1988) for a detailed checklist useful for evaluating the suitability of a home for a physically handicapped child.

Guidelines for Working with Medically Ill Children and Their Families

Psychotherapeutic techniques can be used to help medically ill children and their families cope better with the children's illnesses. These techniques include

- *education* (such as information on how to follow the treatment regimen and how to handle stress)
- *positive and negative reinforcement* (procedures used to obtain desirable responses or to inhibit undesirable responses)
- *systematic desensitization* (procedures used to teach the child how to relax or to behave in ways that are inconsistent with anxiety)
- *contracts* between the child and the mental health professionals (such as an agreement between the child and the health care provider that certain behaviors will be performed each day)
- *family management* (such as providing information on how to coordinate the child's schooling with medical appointments)

Let's now look at some specific guidelines useful in working with medically ill children and their families (Creer & Reynolds, 1990; Davis & Wasserman, 1992; Rosenthal & Young, 1988).

Provide general information. After determining the parents' level of understanding and literacy level, provide basic information about the illness or injury through brochures, articles, books, the media, the Internet, computer data, or referral to classes or lectures. Similarly, provide information about the specific routines of the intervention program, including scheduling, rest periods, types of therapies (including behavioral and cognitive approaches), and nutritional requirements. Help the child and parents understand the illness, how it was diagnosed, and its management.

Provide specific information. Provide specific information that will help the child and parents learn ways to monitor the child's condition (including what precipitates an attack or makes the condition worse) to prevent the illness from becoming worse, and to use any needed medical equipment effectively. Inform the child and parents about the mode of action, use, and side effects of the prescribed medications. Give the family information on how to help the child manage activities of daily living, including feeding, dressing, and toileting. Provide families with concrete, detailed responses to questions. Work with the other health care providers to facilitate communication with the child and parents.

Arrange for psychotherapy. Arrange to have the family members receive psychotherapy if they experience too much confusion, uncertainty, and emotional distress. Psychotherapy, in part, should be directed toward helping them adapt and cope with the child's illness or injury.

Encourage normal routines. Encourage the family with a seriously ill child to maintain (or return to) its regular routine. This means having the child attend school, if possible, and resume or maintain friendships and normal activities. School provides social contacts and opportunities for play, boosts morale, counters boredom, maintains dignity, provides career training and skills, and normalizes life (Klopovich, Vats, Butterfield, Cairns, & Lansky, 1981).

A child's return to school allows family members to return to work and to resume more normal routines. However, it may not be possible for very sick children to attend school. Children who are absent for some time may experience additional stress when they return to school. If they are chronically ill or disabled, they may have problems with their schoolwork and peer relationships. They may fear being "socially ostracized, ridiculed, and teased because of the illness, appearance, or absences" (Pfefferbaum, 1989, p. 555). If they have fallen behind, they may have to repeat a grade and be separated from their peers. And they will have to contend with teachers who may hold negative stereotypes toward children with chronic illnesses or disabilities.

Help the parents understand that giving a sick child inordinate attention and privileges may foster undue dependency and, in the end, increase behavioral problems (Katz et al., 1990). Help the child and parents understand that they should avoid letting the child's illness become the center of their lives or dictate the quality of their lives, as much as this is possible given the extent of the child's illness. Encourage the parents to integrate their medically ill child *and* the treatment regimen into their normal family patterns without neglecting the needs of the other family members.

Parents need to recognize, however, that there are limits to their attaining a normal routine (Eiser, 1993). Chronically ill children may not partake in all games and activities with their peers, and they may need to keep away from other children who are acutely ill to reduce the risk of infection. Chronically ill children also may need to leave school or miss other activities for treatments or medical appointments. Thus, the family with a chronically ill child will have challenges and demands that other families do not have.

Encourage self-reliance. When the illness has been stabilized or is in remission, encourage the family to become more self-reliant and independent from health care personnel (Katz et al., 1990). However, in certain cases, you may need to encourage the family to obtain frequent medical checkups for the child (Katz et al., 1990). Frequent checkups are especially necessary when the child's illness makes him or her vulnerable to learning and emotional problems

and places him or her at risk for developing other medical problems.

Encourage adherence. Help the child and parents adhere to the medical regimen, and encourage the parents to supervise the child's adherence, as needed. Help the child correct any behavioral deficits—such as poor medication adherence—that may cause the illness to become worse (see Chapter 15). Also, bolster the child's self-confidence, emphasizing (as relevant) that he or she can perform the needed self-care routines.

Parents can do several things to help their child cope with painful medical procedures (Redd, 1989).

- They need to convey to the child that he or she has to have the medical procedure.
- They need to maintain a sense of control over the situation and show the child that they expect him or her to do the same. However, they also may need to give the child some control over the options. For example, they can say to their child "You can cry big tears if you want, but you must hold still" or "If it hurts, squeeze my hand or yell but don't move."
- They need to tell their child that they know the procedure will hurt but that other children have managed the pain and they know their child also will be able to do so.
- They need to give the child treatment options, where possible. For example, they should let the child decide which arm an injection should be given in or choose the time of day to receive treatment.
- They need to compliment the child after the procedure is over. They should tell the child that they are pleased with what he or she did and say something like "I knew you could do it."

Encourage self-monitoring. Self-monitoring procedures may help children with medical problems become good observers of their own behavior, discriminating changes in their symptoms and seeing how symptoms change over time and across situations. Self-monitoring also lets medically ill children feel that they are doing something constructive and that they are not helpless.

Self-monitoring of symptom changes, activity level, mood ratings, and situational contexts will give you information about the antecedent events and consequences associated with the child's symptoms. With this information, you are in a better position to formulate hypotheses about the relationship between social-psychological variables and the child's medical illness. For example, you may find a relationship between settings and the child's symptoms (for example, symptoms appear at school but not at home) or a relationship between stressful events and symptom expression (for example, symptoms appear before a test but not before a picnic).

Self-monitoring procedures include the use of diaries, rating scales, counters, daily charting, and portable monitoring devices (such as a blood pressure cuff or pulmonary function test useful for recording physiological changes). The procedure chosen depends on the ease of detection of the targeted symptom, symptom frequency, the age and intellectual ability of the child, and ease of use. See Sattler (1992) for further information about observational techniques that can be used in self-monitoring procedures.

For children with severe pain, self-recordings of activity level and medication usage are helpful. Children can keep a diary of daily activities (for example, amount of time on an hourly basis spent standing, walking, sitting, and reclining) and medication usage (for example, type and amount of medication and at what time medication was taken). Chapters 17 and 18 give examples of forms that can be used for a child's self-monitoring of several different illnesses or conditions.

In all self-monitoring procedures, carefully evaluate the child's willingness to record data, the reliability of the data, whether the child's recording depends on whether he or she is observed (called *reactive effects*), and the accuracy of the self-reports over an extended period (also see Chapter 6 for more information about reliability). Select a recording procedure appropriate to the child's age and ability to record data (also see Chapter 3 for more information about self-monitoring).

Make services for the family available continuously. Offer the child and parents continuous consultation with the health care providers, and encourage them to seek such consultation whenever they need to.

The following three cases illustrate the use of some of these guidelines. The first case (Tracy) offers an example of the need to consider physical, developmental, social, and psychological factors in formulating a treatment program for a child whose medical problems may have psychological components (Lask & Fosson, 1989). Occasionally, you may have difficulty convincing children and parents of the need for an interdisciplinary treatment approach, especially when the children's problems are primarily physical in their manifestations. When you meet resistance, you will need to be especially patient and empathic. The second case (Greg) focuses on how an elementary school teacher accepted the child's disability and worked with the students to teach them not to fear people with disabilities. The third case (Molly) illustrates what might happen to a sick child who, on return to school, is given an incorrect school placement.

CASE 16-8. TRACY

Tracy's severe eczema clearly has allergic origins but appears to be exacerbated by the following stresses: Tracy is teased at school and has few friends; she has difficulties with both reading and spelling, although her intelligence is well within the normal range; she is distressed by her illness and feels hopeless about the future; her parents are unable to help her express her distress, which remains suppressed but intense; her mother feels guilty that she seems unable to protect Tracy from exposure to allergens; her father is irritated by

his wife's over-involvement with Tracy, believing that Tracy should be encouraged to do things and forget her eczema; and her older brother tries to stop Tracy from scratching herself, leading to arguments between them and more determined scratching by Tracy with consequent worsening of the eczema.

The following interventions were recommended and carried out: (a) Tracy's school was contacted and encouraged to offer her remedial help for her learning difficulties and help with how to handle peer group teasing. The school agreed and began programs to remediate her learning difficulties and to help her with her social difficulties. (b) Tracy began counseling and was given relaxation training to help her find relief from her itching and ways to express her feelings outwardly rather than holding them in. (c) Tracy was given social skills training to help her develop skills needed to respond to teasing. (d) Family therapy began that focused on ways to help family members identify and share their distress, to help the parents adopt a consistent approach to managing Tracy's response to her illness, and to help diminish arguments between the siblings. (e) Tracy continued with medical management of her eczema.

Tracy's eczema improved as a result of the interventions. Her family became more responsive to her emotional needs, her reading and spelling improved, and she gained confidence in herself as she learned self-relaxation to control the itching and learned how to handle the teasing. At the one-year follow-up, she had required no further hospitalization and was on a reduced dose of medication. (Lask & Fosson, 1989, adapted from pp. 89–90)

CASE 16-9. GREG

Seven-year-old Greg was understandably anxious about returning to school following amputation of part of his arm. Before his return, he, his mother, and the hospital social worker met with his teacher and school nurse one afternoon after the school day had ended. He was assured that he was an important part of his class. He saw that his desk was still in the same place and that his name tag was still above his coat hook and his cubbyhole. He was encouraged to talk about his experience and to answer the other children's questions.

On the day of his return, his classmates' first reaction was to deny that his arm had been amputated, saying "It's still there; you just have it tied down inside your shirt." Enraged, Greg jumped up and stripped off his shirt, to the great dismay of his teacher. At first, the other children were shocked; then they began to gather around Greg. Although worried, the teacher recognized that to stop the children from investigating would give them the impression that Greg's amputation was too horrible to talk about and to make them even more anxious. She also recognized that the situation gave Greg an opportunity to master his own trauma and to educate his classmates.

As Greg proudly displayed his incision, the class looked closely and, with awe and respect, counted every suture mark. They asked questions such as "Why did this happen?", "How did they cut it off?", "What did they do with it?", and "How will you tie your shoes?" The teacher helped Greg answer some of their questions, and Greg described life in the hospital in great detail. The teacher reinforced his positive feelings about his experience and knowledge. She then developed a plan to teach the children about cancer and its treatment and about the many ways in which disabled people can live normal lives. (Adams-Greenly, 1991, p. 9, with changes in notation)

CASE 16-10. MOLLY

Fifteen-year-old Molly, diagnosed with leukemia during the summer, was eager to return to school that September and coped with her hair loss by wearing a wig and a trendy headband. She was a bright student, who had always done well academically and socially. Surprisingly, her grades began to drop, and she became a management problem in the classroom because of her inattentiveness and constant chatting.

Molly's guidance counselor and two of her teachers met with the hospital staff and asked many questions about childhood cancer. The hospital staff emphasized the advances in treatment, improved survival rates, and the importance of normalizing life at school. Some time after the meeting, Molly's counselor wrote a letter to the hospital staff: "Our meeting enlightened me and made me aware that I have made a serious mistake. When I found out that Molly had leukemia I assumed she would die. I did not want to add to her stress, so I scheduled her for classes below her academic potential. I realize now that her behavior problems are due to boredom and that I may have unwittingly limited her chances of being accepted at a good college. Thank you for helping me help her better."

Molly's classes were changed, her behavior problems ceased, and her grades and her spirits dramatically improved. She continued to do well and later graduated from college and prepared for a career as a high school teacher. (Adams-Greenly, 1991, p. 9, with changes in notation)

Guidelines for Helping Parents Help Healthy Children When a Family Member Is Ill

The following guidelines may help you in working with parents of a healthy child who has a medically ill or terminally ill family member (Adams & Deveau, 1987; Christ et al., 1993; Johansen, 1988; Lewis, Lewis, & Schonfeld, 1991; Wiener, Fair, & Pizzo, 1993, p. 102; also see Chapter 13).

1. *Enlist cooperation.* The parents should enlist the cooperation of the healthy child in the care of the family member who is ill, as much as this is feasible, so that the healthy child can feel useful and appreciated.

2. *Offer explanations.* The parents should offer the healthy child careful and detailed explanations about the illness and the medical treatment, keep the child informed of any changes in the family member's status, and ask a health care provider to help in this task as needed so that the child feels part of the team.

3. *Encourage communication.* The parents should be available to listen to and talk to the healthy child at any time. The parents should allow the healthy child to talk as much as she or he wants to about her or his feelings associated with

having an ill family member. The parents should show the child that they understand the child's fears and concerns.

4. *Encourage understanding.* The parents need to understand the feelings and emotions that the healthy child is experiencing (see the earlier part of this chapter).

5. *Encourage honesty.* The parents should be honest with the healthy child and establish trust, respect, and open lines of communication.

6. *Support the healthy child.* The parents should help the healthy child understand that the child was not responsible for the family member's illness.

7. *Encourage pacing of information.* The parents should give the healthy child information about the illness at a rate comprehensible to the child and commensurate with the stage of the family member's illness.

8. *Encourage a review of family roles.* The parents need to understand the changes that are taking place in the family and need to discuss these changes with the healthy child on an ongoing basis.

9. *Relieve guilt.* The parents need to understand that they are not entirely responsible for the healthy child's being under stress because illness in one family member often causes stress in other family members.

10. *Encourage normal activities.* The parents should encourage the healthy child to spend time with her or his friends, to keep up with school activities, and to lead as normal a life as possible.

11. *Involve the healthy child in decision making.* The parents should involve the healthy child in decisions about the care of the ill family member, as much as this is possible.

12. *Inform teachers.* The parents should inform the healthy child's teachers of the family member's illness and how the illness has affected the healthy child.

13. *Encourage visits.* The parents should encourage the healthy child, if possible, to visit the ill family member when the ill family member is hospitalized.

14. *Encourage sharing.* The parents should encourage the healthy child to call the ill family member when the ill family member is hospitalized. The healthy child can send the ill family member photographs, handmade presents, and artwork if visitors are not permitted. These things can be presented in person if the healthy child visits the ill family member in the hospital.

15. *Recognize modeling.* The parents should understand that some reactions of the healthy child may involve modeling of the parents' behavior; consequently, the parents should be aware of their behavior and how it may affect the healthy child.

16. *Encourage joining of support groups.* The parents should encourage the healthy child to join a support group for children with a family member who is hospitalized or to participate in activities sponsored by the hospital or clinic for family members. The parents also may choose to join a support group.

17. *Allow grieving.* The parents, in the case of the death of a family member, should allow the healthy child to grieve at

her or his own pace and to attend the funeral if deemed appropriate (also see the discussion of bereavement in Chapter 13). The parents should allow the healthy child to visit the cemetery, view photo albums, watch family videos, and share memories with those who knew the family member who died.

THINKING THROUGH THE ISSUES

Can you work with physicians and other medical personnel?

What are your feelings about working with terminally ill children?

Can you work with medically ill children who have terminal illnesses?

Can you work with medically ill children and their family members who may have feelings of anger, frustration, sadness, and depression?

Can you actively involve the medically ill child and family in the treatment program?

Can you work with children who have catastrophic illnesses, including illnesses that may involve debilitation and disfigurement?

Can you work in a setting in which there may be disagreements among the health care team about which treatment may be most effective?

Can you handle being on a health care team that may have to inflict pain as part of the treatment?

Do you believe that you would feel completely helpless working with chronically ill children?

SUMMARY

Interviewing Children with Medical Illnesses

1. Interviewing children with medical illnesses is similar to interviewing children with other problems.
2. One goal of the interview will be to identify the possible psychosocial stressors that accompany the medical illness in order to make medical treatment work better and to prevent serious psychosocial problems from developing.
3. During the interview, help the medically ill child maintain his or her dignity and self-respect.
4. Review all of the information you obtain and note areas of agreement and disagreement in the reports.
5. A good working relationship with the health care provider team during the information-gathering period and at other times as well will be useful.
6. When you interview a medically ill child, in addition to covering standard interview topics, you will want to obtain information about the impact of the illness on the child, the child's reaction to previous illnesses, and the child's prior treatments.
7. When you ask the child about her or his symptoms, focus on the onset, frequency, duration, and severity of the symptoms.
8. If you plan to conduct a second interview with an older child or adolescent, consider asking her or him to keep a diary between the interviews to record information about each major problem (or symptom).
9. When you inquire about what treatments have been recommended for the present illness, also note whether the recommendations have been followed, whether the child or parents made suggestions for alternative treatments or for changes in the treatment regimen, and whether there were any side effects from the treatments.
10. When children are hospitalized, they are likely to experience stress—their daily schedule is disrupted, familiar people and activities are missing, and they have little control over what happens to them. However, hospitalization also can have positive effects.
11. While the child is in the hospital, the health care provider staff can arrange to have a thorough assessment of the child's development, observe parent-child interactions, recommend appropriate interventions, provide services to help stabilize the family, and provide therapeutic play experiences to allow the child to express his or her feelings about the illness and hospitalization, to enhance the child's sense of mastery, and to foster adaptive behavior.
12. A medically ill child's adjustment to a hospital will depend on the age and level of cognitive development of the child; type and severity of the illness; level of pain; type of treatment; level of risk for death; length of the hospitalization; family dynamics; family resources; child's temperament and personality; extent of the child's separation anxiety; child's coping mechanisms; extent to which the child misses school, sports, and social events; hospital layout, including roommates and access to preferred rooms, television, radio, and personal items from home; and hospital staff's ability to relate to and comfort the child.
13. When you prepare children for hospitalization and for threatening medical procedures, consider their developmental level.
14. Preschool children may perceive hospitalization as rejection or punishment, see treatment as hostile or punitive, and have concerns about body penetration aroused by surgery or injections.
15. Hospitalization and threatening medical procedures may generate feelings of inadequacy in school-aged children.
16. Adolescents may see hospitalization and threatening medical procedures as threats to their independence.
17. Encourage the parents to help the child cope with hospitalization, and stress the importance of parental presence and support.
18. Give the child and parents information about what to expect in the hospital, taking into consideration the child's age and level of comprehension.
19. Help the child develop ways to cope with the anxiety and stress associated with the medical procedures and with the hospitalization.
20. Have a good working relationship with all the staff members who will have contact with the child.
21. Despite adequate preparations (or when there are no preparations), children may feel lonely, frustrated, bored, and helpless in the hospital.
22. When children feel lonely or frustrated, help them avoid becoming depressed, hostile, or fearful; withdrawing; regressing; or having other undesirable reactions.
23. As chronically ill adolescents reach young adulthood, they may need to transfer from a pediatric facility to an adult facility for continued care; the transfer may cause stress for them and their families.

Interviewing Parents of Medically Ill Children

24. In interviewing parents of medically ill children, you will want to ask about their knowledge of the child's illness, their communications with the health care provider staff, their feelings

about and reactions to the child's illness, their communications with the child about the illness, their communications with the child's siblings about the illness (if applicable), their communications with each other about the illness, their ability to manage the disease, and their resources and needs concerning their child's illness.

25. In addition to seeing the parents at the time of the child's initial diagnosis, you may want to see them at times of remission and relapse of the child's illness, as well as at other critical times during the child's development.

Interviewing in Cases of Terminal Illness

26. Health care professionals face several tasks in dealing with children who are terminally ill and their families. One task is to help the family normalize the life of the child and family as much as possible within the constraints of the child's illness. Another task is to facilitate effective coping with stressful events associated with the disease and its treatment.

27. Terminally ill children who do not yet understand the concept of death are likely to be more worried about being in the hospital and suffering from pain than about dying.

28. In cases of impending death, find out what the family desires for the terminally ill child.

29. Healthy children who have a terminally ill sibling, parent, or other relative are likely to experience great stress.

30. Healthy children who have a terminally ill sibling may feel guilty because they think that the terminally ill sibling resents them for being healthy.

31. The stresses experienced by healthy children who have a terminally ill parent place them at increased risk for social impairment and for psychological disorders.

32. The worries and concerns of children about a critically ill parent may affect how they function at home, at school, and in the community.

33. Children of a terminally ill parent may have outbursts of anger, sadness, and anxiety; suicidal thoughts; severe conflict with both parents; and somatic symptoms.

Evaluating the Interview

34. After you interview a medically ill child, evaluate the child's knowledge of the illness, symptoms, ability to cope with the illness and implement treatment, family and support systems, stress, and knowledge of events related to any accidents.

35. After you interview the parents of a medically ill child, evaluate the parents' knowledge of the illness and ability to cope with the illness; the parent-child relations; and the parents' marital functioning and support systems, significant stressors, and ability to implement the treatment.

The Post-Assessment Interview with Medically Ill Children and Their Parents

36. When children are told that they have a chronic, serious, or potentially fatal illness, they may be stunned.

37. Parents may react to a diagnosis that their child has a chronic medical illness with feelings of helplessness, fear, anger, guilt, or sadness; with a combination of several of these feelings; or, occasionally, with relief at getting closure.

38. Your task, in part, will be to encourage the parents to focus on ways to help their child.

39. You can establish a collaborative relationship with families of medically ill children by building mutual trust and respect, clarifying roles and expectations, communicating with the family, and solving problems and resolving conflicts.

Interventions with Medically Ill Children and Their Families

40. Chronic illnesses (and injuries and disabilities) are likely to create adjustment problems for the child and for her or his family throughout the child's life; therefore, the initial clinical assessment interview may be one of many interviews needed during the child's development.

41. The services that medically ill children and their families need may include an appropriate diagnosis, accompanied by detailed information about the illness and its course; adequate medical services for the ill child; adequate physical therapy, speech and language therapy, and occupational therapy for the ill child; adaptive equipment for the ill child; appropriately designed educational programs for the ill child; regular communication with the school nurse, teacher, and ancillary school personnel; social and recreational opportunities for the ill child, including summer camp; work opportunities for the ill child if he or she is an older adolescent; training in sexuality for the ill child if he or she is a teenager or young adult; counseling for the ill child; a good residential facility for the ill child if he or she is severely impaired; education on entitlements for the parents; child care and after-school care for both ill and healthy children; financial assistance; community acceptance; contact with other parents of medically ill children; counseling for the healthy family members, including genetic counseling; contact with knowledgeable and concerned professionals; information on community resources; social/recreational opportunities for the ill child and for healthy family members; training for the parents on the ill child's health needs; transportation; legal services; help with the ill child's behavior problems; support groups for siblings; help in making changes in the physical layout of the home; home health/nursing care; and respite care.

42. For most families, taking care of a chronically ill child is a demanding task and may be all-consuming, depending on the type of illness.

43. Health care providers may need to inform parents about how to administer the child's medications, injections, and other treatments; formulate a diet; carry out the rehabilitation program; use special equipment; handle seizures; and recognize signs of worsening or recurring of illness and signs of medication toxicity.

44. If the family is not satisfied with the medical services, you will need to deal with their concerns.

45. Prior to the child's discharge from a hospital, the health care provider conducting the discharge interview should be sure that the parents have been given the information they need to take care of their child and that they understand what needs to be done for their child after she or he leaves the hospital.

46. Occasionally, physical alterations in the home—such as modification of doors, installation of railings, or construction of ramps—may be sufficient to enable the chronically ill child to live at home.

47. Psychotherapeutic techniques can be used to help medically ill children and their families cope better with the children's illnesses.

48. If you use these techniques, you may provide general information, provide specific information, answer questions, arrange for counseling, encourage normal routines, encourage self-

reliance, encourage adherence, encourage self-monitoring, and make services for the family available continuously.

49. Encourage parents of a healthy child who has a medically ill or terminally ill family member to enlist the child's cooperation, to offer explanations to the child, to encourage the child to communicate, to be understanding of the child's feelings, to be honest with the child, to support the child, to pace carefully the information given to the child, to review changes in family roles with the child, to relieve their own guilt, to encourage the child to continue with normal activities, to involve the child in decision making, to inform the child's teachers about what is happening at home, to encourage the child to visit the ill family member, to encourage the child to share his or her feelings and thoughts, to recognize that the child might be modeling the parent's behavior, to encourage the child to join support groups, and to allow the child to grieve if the family member dies.

KEY TERMS, CONCEPTS, AND NAMES

Hospitalization (p. 521)
Threatening medical procedures (p. 521)
Transition to adult services (p. 524)
Terminal illness (p. 525)
Evaluating the interview (p. 527)
Post-assessment interview (p. 527)
Interventions with medically ill children (p. 531)
Education (p. 532)
Positive and negative reinforcement (p. 532)
Systematic desensitization (p. 532)
Contracts (p. 532)

Family management (p. 532)
Self-monitoring procedures (p. 533)
Reactive effects (p. 534)

STUDY QUESTIONS

1. Discuss the factors involved in interviewing a child with a medical illness. In your discussion, compare and contrast interviewing a child with a medical illness to interviewing a child with a psychological disorder.
2. What special issues are involved in interviewing medically ill children in a hospital?
3. How would you go about preparing children for hospitalization and for threatening medical procedures?
4. How would you go about helping children who are not adjusting well to the hospital?
5. Discuss interviewing parents of medically ill children.
6. What are some important issues in evaluating the interview with medically ill children and their parents?
7. What are some considerations in conducting the post-assessment interview with medically ill children and their parents?
8. What suggestions would you give health care providers who are working with children who are terminally ill?
9. What are some services that medically ill children and their families may need?
10. What are some specific guidelines for working with medically ill children and their families?
11. If a parent asked you for some help in working with a healthy child in a family with an ill member, what advice would you give him or her?

17

INTERVIEWING AND INTERVENTIONS FOR SPECIFIC PEDIATRIC HEALTH-RELATED DISORDERS, PART 1

She was a great doctor; she really knew what she was doing with our daughter. But she also knew what she was doing with us. She always listened to what we had to say. She treated us like adults, made us feel involved. She told us what was going on. She made us feel important, and that we could manage. We came away feeling we could make decisions for ourselves and do things.

—Anonymous (Cited by Hilton Davis)

Goals and Objectives

This chapter is designed to enable you to:

- Interview children and their families who need assistance with behavioral management of pain, asthma, diabetes, childhood cancer, HIV infections and AIDS, pediatric headaches, and failure to thrive
- Apply the general principles of interviewing discussed in Chapter 16 to the conditions discussed in this chapter and to other medically related conditions
- Understand the reactions of children and their families to chronic medical illnesses and appreciate their struggles and their ability to overcome adversity

This chapter covers several medical illnesses and medically related conditions. The coverage is designed to serve at least three purposes. First, it will allow you to apply the information you learned about medically related issues in Chapters 15 and 16 to specific medical illnesses or problems. Second, it will help you conduct clinical assessment interviews with children who have these illnesses or problems. Third, it will help you generalize to other medical illnesses and medically related problems. If you plan to work in the pediatric field, you should read texts that discuss medical illnesses in more detail.

In Chapter 1, you read that poverty places children at risk for behavioral problems. There also is a direct relationship among the prevalence of severe chronic medical conditions, health care utilization, and socioeconomic status: Children who are poor have a higher prevalence of chronic health conditions and use outpatient services less frequently than do children who are more affluent (Newacheck, 1994). Poor children, however, are hospitalized more often, perhaps because they have more serious health disorders or because of their reduced use of outpatient services.

The semistructured interviews referred to in this chapter are designed to obtain information from school-aged children about their medical illness. If you want to interview parents about their children's medical illness, you can use the same semistructured interviews, with minor alterations. For example, instead of saying "I'd like to talk to you about the problems you are having," you can say "I'd like to talk to you about the problems [child's name] is having" (or "your son is having" or "your daughter is having"). You will want to learn about the parents' concerns, their perceptions of the child's behavior, the conditions under which the child's problems occur, what the parents consider to be acceptable behavioral alternatives for the child, what the potentially reinforcing stimuli are for the child, how much the parents know about the disease and its treatment, how family problems affect the child's adjustment, and how the child's illness affects the family (Gross, 1990).

After you complete the interview with the child and parents, you will need to evaluate the information you obtained. Tables 17-1 and 17-2, designed for children and their parents, respectively, will assist you in this effort.

Table 17-1
Evaluating the Interview Findings Obtained from Children with a Medical Disorder

1. What is the child's understanding of his or her illness?
2. Does the child understand the treatment regimen?
3. Who manages the regimen?
4. If the child manages the treatment regimen, does he or she understand all components of the treatment regimen?
5. Do the child and the parents have similar expectations for the management of the illness?
6. Does the child adhere to all aspects of the treatment regimen or to some only?
7. Does the child avoid taking medications as prescribed, use less of the medications than required, or overuse the medications?
8. Can the child recognize when the illness is going to flare up?
9. Can the child ask for help when needed?
10. How does the child communicate with his or her parents about the illness?
11. What peer pressures does the child face that interfere with his or her adherence to the treatment regimen?
12. What other illnesses does the child have?
13. What reinforcers are available to the child?
14. How do these reinforcers reflect the child's preferences for reinforcers?
15. What complications have been associated with the child's illness?
16. What have been the effects of the illness on the child's normal activities?
17. How has the illness affected the child's eating patterns?
18. What is the child's attitude toward the illness?
19. Is the illness the center of the child's life?
20. Does the child show any negative reactions to his or her illness, such as frustration, anger, fears and phobias, malingering, use of illness for personal gain, denial, body preoccupation, other excesses, depression, nonassertiveness, isolation, or immaturity?
21. How does the child see his or her future in relation to the illness?
22. How much does the family help the child?
23. Is the child's family cohesive?
24. What conflicts are there in the child's family?
25. How much does the family encourage the child to be independent?
26. How do the family members communicate?

As noted in Chapter 15, mental health practitioners need to have ongoing communication with the child's primary health care provider (and other health care providers, as needed) to share findings, philosophy, treatment regimens, and psychosocial interventions. As stressed throughout this text, the child should have a physical examination for any presenting complaint that may have a physical basis. Mental

Table 17-2
Evaluating the Interview Findings Obtained from Parents of Children with a Medical Disorder

1. What is the parents' understanding of the child's illness?
2. Do the parents understand the treatment regimen?
3. Who manages the child's treatment regimen?
4. Do the parents and the child have similar expectations for the management of the illness?
5. Do the parents supervise the child's adherence to the treatment regimen?
6. How do the parents communicate with their child about the illness?
7. Do the parents respond in a manner that allows any attacks associated with the illness to be managed quickly and efficiently?
8. Do the parents share responsibilities for the treatment regimen?
9. Do the parents disagree over how to implement the treatment regimen?
10. Does either parent ever panic when the child has an attack associated with the illness? (If so, who is it?)
11. Do the siblings respond in a manner that allows any attacks associated with the child's illness to be managed quickly and efficiently?
12. How do teachers and school personnel respond to the child's illness?
13. Are the parents satisfied with the responses of medical personnel when a flare-up of the child's illness requires emergency treatment?
14. Do family activities center on the child's illness?
15. Do the family members exhibit any negative reactions to the child's illness—such as anger, anxiety, resentment, jealousy, overprotectiveness, reinforcement of socially inappropriate behaviors, other types of behavioral excesses, withdrawal from community activities, ignorance of the illness, or denial of the illness?
16. What pressures do the parents face that interfere with their ability to help their child?
17. What reinforcers do the parents use for the child?
18. How do these reinforcers reflect the child's preferences for reinforcers?
19. What complications have been associated with the child's illness?
20. How has the child's illness affected the parents' work and social activities?
21. How has the child's illness affected the other children in the family or extended members of the family?
22. What are the parents' attitudes toward the child's illness?
23. How do the parents see their future in relation to the child's illness?
24. How much do the parents help the child?
25. Is the child's family cohesive?
26. What conflicts are there in the child's family?
27. How much does the family encourage the child to be independent?
28. How do the family members communicate?

health professionals then need to know the results of the physical examination before beginning any psychological interventions.

PAIN

Description

Pain is an unpleasant sensation or emotional experience that may be acute, recurrent, or chronic (McGrath & Hillier, 1989). *Acute pain* may be associated with anything from "superficial bumps, cuts, burns, and scrapes that cause minimal tissue damage to deeper wounds that cause moderate to severe tissue damage" (p. 10). *Recurrent pain* may occur in the absence of a well-defined organic etiology and may be triggered by external or internal factors, particularly events that provoke stress; between episodes, the child may be healthy and pain free. *Chronic pain* may be associated with several diseases (such as arthritis, hemophilia, and sickle cell anemia), with accidents, and with severe burns.

Because pain is so pervasive, prevalence rates are difficult to discuss in the abstract. Certain medical illnesses are more painful than others, particularly pediatric cancer and pediatric headaches. These and other conditions are considered later in the chapter. Some medical treatments also may be painful.

Recognize that pain has value. It alerts us to problems, motivates us to seek help, and tells us when treatments may not be working properly.

Children, like adults, differ in their pain reactions. Some will report the slightest pain, others only severe pain. Some will reduce their activities and see themselves as disabled, while others will try to continue with their activities and see themselves as normal. How the child reacts to pain will depend on the following (Maron & Bush, 1991):

- the amount, type, and location of tissue damage
- the child's physiological response to the pain, including her or his pain threshold and tolerance
- the child's age, sex, and cognitive-developmental level
- the child's temperament and personality, including her or his level of anxiety and depression
- the child's previous pain experiences
- the attitudes of parents and other family members toward pain, their reactions to the child's pain, and their strategies for dealing with it
- situational factors
- the adequacy of treatment

Thus, children's experience of pain is multidimensional (McGrath, 1989). It may be difficult to determine whether it is the pain alone or fear and anxiety or a combination of pain, fear, and anxiety that causes behavioral or physiological changes (Savedra & Tesler, 1989). In any case, children's experience of pain can be heightened by fear or anxiety.

The way children react to pain is heavily dependent on what they learn in their culture. For example, girls and boys differ in their response to pain (McGrath, 1989): "Girls may express more fear and anxiety, whereas boys express the need to be stoic and brave. Similarly, girls and boys may be taught to cope with pain differently, so that girls learn to rely on parents for reassurance while boys learn to rely more on themselves" (p. 36). Children of both sexes learn when it is permissible to cry, to ask for help, or to use analgesics. Children also learn by observing how others react to pain.

You will need to consider the *operant components* of a chronic or recurring pain problem—that is, under what circumstances does the pain occur and what consequences follow from the pain? To do this, you will need to answer such questions as the following:

1. Is there positive reinforcement of the pain behavior? For example, does the child receive positive rewards, such as attention from parents or special treats?
2. Is there positive reinforcement of the pain behavior in the form of avoidance of aversive consequences? For example, do the parents remove the child from negative situations, such as stresses at home or school?
3. Are well behaviors reinforced? That is, do the parents reinforce alternatives to sick behaviors?

Here are some examples of how school-aged children describe their pain (Gaffney & Dunne, 1986, pp. 111–112).

1. *Concrete definitions—approximately ages 5–7 years.* Pain is…

- in your tummy, it hurts you.
- sore…hurting you.
- a thing what you don't like.
- sickness…sick.
- when you have a sore head.
- when you eat too much things.

2. *Semiabstract definitions—approximately ages 8–10 years.* Pain is…

- something that can hurt any part of your body.
- a thing you get when you are sick.
- annoying and very dreadful; at times it is very sore. It makes people angry.
- a thing you feel inside you; it makes you feel ill.
- a sort of feeling that hurts you.
- you would have a feeling like knives and forks stabbing into you.

3. *Abstract definitions—approximately ages 11–14 years.* Pain is…

- a very sore sensation in any part of your human body.
- the way the body reacts when hurt.
- something we get every so often; sometimes it can show up serious illness.
- a particular disturbing aspect of life.
- suffering mentally or physically.
- an internal pressure on the body.

Children may cope with pain by doing one or more of the following (Ross & Ross, 1984; Siegel & Smith, 1989):

1. Diverting attention from the pain by focusing on some aspect of the immediate environment or part of the body unrelated to the pain or by thinking about some pleasant event, activity, or situation
2. Reinterpreting the painful sensations
3. Imagining that they are some character who does not feel pain (for example, Superman)
4. Inhibiting feelings
5. Engaging in relaxation activities
6. Asking someone for comfort or help
7. Asking for medication
8. Reducing discomfort by changing body positions
9. Suffering in silence
10. Crying, gritting teeth, or clenching fist
11. Engaging in other activities, such as watching television or reading

We need to consider the following factors when a child appears unable to cope with pain (Holland, 1989a):

- the organic etiology of the pain
- the attributes associated with the pain, such as its intensity, location, and quality
- the child's emotional and behavioral reactions to the pain, such as acute anxiety, depression, despair, agitation, irritability, uncooperativeness, anger, inability to sleep, and fear that the disease is getting worse
- how the pain influences the child's thought processes and self-concept
- what the child does to control the pain, including behaviors and the use of analgesics
- what the family does to help the child control the pain

Interviewing Issues

The following developmental considerations will be useful in interviewing children about their pain (McGrath & Brigham, 1992).

1. *Infants and toddlers.* Very young children and children of any age who have inadequate communication skills cannot report their pain experiences clearly. In such cases, you will need to observe the child's facial and bodily gestures to obtain clues about how the child experiences pain or anticipates pain. You also can benefit from parents' reports about the infant's pain. Changes in drinking, eating, or elimination patterns may suggest that a small child is experiencing discomfort. Parents may report that an infant cries differently when in pain.

2. *Kindergarteners, school-aged children, and adolescents.* "By the age of five, most children can differentiate a wider range of pain intensities and they can use quantitative scales to rate their pain intensity. Children can also understand and communicate other aspects of their pain perceptions (sensory and emotional) in more abstract concepts as they mature" (McGrath & Brigham, 1992, p. 298).

A thorough assessment of a child's pain includes an examination of behavioral, cognitive-affective, and physiological factors (Jay, Elliott, & Varni, 1986).

1. *Behavioral factors.* Observe the child's verbal and nonverbal behaviors that suggest that he or she is experiencing pain (Tarbell, Cohen, & Marsh, 1992). These include complaints of pain, groans, moans, grunts, deep sighs, sobbing sounds, grimacing, bodily expressions of pain (such as rubbing or touching a painful area), facial expressions of pain (such as opening the mouth and pulling the lips back at the corners; squinting and closing the eyes; and bulges, creases, or furrows above or between the eyebrows), and frequent changes in position while sitting. Use behavioral observation scales as needed (Jay & Elliott, 1984; also see Table 17-3). You may want to observe the child on more than one occasion because the quality, type, and amount of pain can vary in different situations and at different times of the day. Table 17-4 contains a list of possible pain descriptors.

2. *Cognitive-affective factors.* Ask the child about the location of the pain (see Figures 17-1 and 17-2) and how he or she feels about the pain. Table 17-5 describes four *visual-graphic procedures* you can use to obtain ratings of pain intensity: poker chips; a *word-graphic scale;* happy-sad faces, which are especially useful for young children (Hester, Foster, & Kristensen, 1990); and a pain thermometer. You also can use an oral scale, by saying "Rate how you feel on a scale from 1 to 10, with 0 equaling no pain and 10 equaling the worst pain you can imagine."

3. *Physiological factors.* If the information is available, look at measures of heart rate, blood pressure, sweat gland activity, and respiration to obtain information about physiological factors that may be related to the pain.

As in every interview, you will want to establish rapport. Obtain information about the strength, quality, location, duration, and affective component of the pain *and* about the situational, familial, and emotional factors pertinent to the child's pain. The semistructured interview in Table F-27 in Appendix F covers these and related areas. Answers to the questions in Table 17-6 will help you evaluate the information you obtained in the interview. *Any information you obtain from the child should be corroborated by the parents or by a knowledgeable caregiver.*

There is no simple way to evaluate whether a child's pain is primarily or totally due to organic or nonorganic factors. Consider the medical findings, the child's history, the presence of reinforcers that may encourage pain behavior, and the nature and consistency of the child's statements and behavior (Chapman, 1991). Do not conclude that the child has no physical basis for pain simply because the child reacts in a way that differs from what would be expected based on the medical findings. There is no one-to-one relationship between medical findings and the child's experience of pain.

Following is an interview segment with a child who was in pain (Wells, Benson, & Hoff, 1985, p. 185, with changes in notation):

Table 17-3
Checklist for Observing Pain Behavior

CHECKLIST FOR OBSERVING PAIN BEHAVIOR

Child's name: _____ Sex: _____

Rater's name: _____ Date: _____

Rating key:
1 = Never observed   4 = Frequently observed
2 = Seldom observed   5 = Almost always observed
3 = Occasionally observed   NA = Not applicable

Behavior	Circle one
1. Is tense	1 2 3 4 5 NA
2. Falls asleep during the day	1 2 3 4 5 NA
3. Is quiet and withdrawn	1 2 3 4 5 NA
4. Mentions having more pain after therapy	1 2 3 4 5 NA
5. Appears drowsy and sleepy	1 2 3 4 5 NA
6. Says that she or he is tired	1 2 3 4 5 NA
7. Takes a nap after lunch	1 2 3 4 5 NA
8. Is restless and nervous	1 2 3 4 5 NA
9. Moves rigidly and stiffly, with stretched limbs	1 2 3 4 5 NA
10. Rubs painful parts of the body	1 2 3 4 5 NA
11. Changes from one buttock to the other while sitting	1 2 3 4 5 NA
12. Groans, moans, or sighs	1 2 3 4 5 NA
13. Gives lively descriptions of the pain	1 2 3 4 5 NA
14. Isolates herself or himself	1 2 3 4 5 NA
15. Walks with abnormal gait	1 2 3 4 5 NA
16. Stands in unusual posture	1 2 3 4 5 NA
17. Worries	1 2 3 4 5 NA
18. Has bad mobility	1 2 3 4 5 NA
19. Drags feet when walking	1 2 3 4 5 NA
20. Walks guardedly and carefully	1 2 3 4 5 NA
21. Appears sad	1 2 3 4 5 NA
22. Complains about pain	1 2 3 4 5 NA
23. Says that the pain has not diminished	1 2 3 4 5 NA
24. Changes positions frequently while sitting	1 2 3 4 5 NA

Note. Factors are as follows: Distorted mobility: items 9, 15, 16, 18, 19, 20; Verbal complaints: items 4, 6, 13, 22, 23; Nonverbal complaints: items 10, 11, 12, 24; Nervousness: items 1, 8, 17; Depression: items 3, 5, 14, 21; Day sleeping: items 2, 7.
Source: Adapted from Vlaeyen, Pernot, Kole-Snijders, Schuerman, Van Eek, and Groenman (1990).

Table 17-4
Pain Descriptors Used by Children

Sensory Descriptors

Temporal aspects: Beating, hitting, pounding, punching, throbbing

Spatial aspects: Shocking, shooting, splitting

Incisive pressure: Biting, cutting, like a pin, like a sharp knife, pinlike, sharp, stabbing

Constrictive pressure: Cramping, crushing, like a pinch, pinching, pressure

Thermal aspects: Blistering, burning, hot

Tightness: Numb, still, swollen, tight

Brightness: Itching, like a scratch, like a sting, scratching, stinging

Dullness: Aching, hurting, like an ache, like a hurt, sore

Affective Descriptors

Fear: Crying, frightening, screaming, terrifying

Sensory aspects (miscellaneous): Dizzy, sickening, suffocating

Punishment: Awful, deadly, dying, killing

Evaluative Descriptors

Evaluative aspects: Annoying, bad, horrible, miserable, terrible, uncomfortable

Control: Never goes away, uncontrollable

Source: Adapted from Melzack and Torgerson (1971) and Wilkie, Holzemer, Tesler, Ward, Paul, and Savedra (1990).

IE: So the pain is with me all the time.
IR: You must feel pretty discouraged.
IE: Oh yes!
IR: Can you tell me more about your feelings about the pain?

IE: It's hard. It's there all the time. Sometimes I want to cry or find something to throw or break.
IR: So the pain is on your mind a lot and sometimes you feel pretty despairing or angry.
IE: Both. It's pretty hard.
IR: It sounds very hard. How have you coped with the pain?

If the child does not reply to the semistructured interview questions, you might want to use a sentence completion procedure. Tell the child: "I'm going to start a sentence, and you complete it. Here is the first one. [Say first item.] Go ahead." The following sentence stems may be helpful:

1. Pain is _____.
2. A child gets pain because _____.
3. A pain sometimes is _____.
4. A pain can make you _____.
5. The worst thing about pain is _____.
6. When I have pain, what makes me feel better is _____.
7. A pain can feel like _____.
8. I had a pain in _____.
9. Children who get pains are _____.
10. You can get pains in _____.

If the child is returning for a second interview, you might want to ask him or her to complete a pain diary, such as the one shown in Table 17-7. Because the pain diary focuses the child's attention on the pain, use it only when you believe that it will serve a definite purpose. You also can use a pain diary as part of an intervention program.

Interventions

Cognitive, behavioral, and pharmacological interventions are useful in the management of pain, whatever its etiology (Smith, Tyler, Womack, & Chen, 1989). Interventions should

Calvin and Hobbes   by Bill Watterson

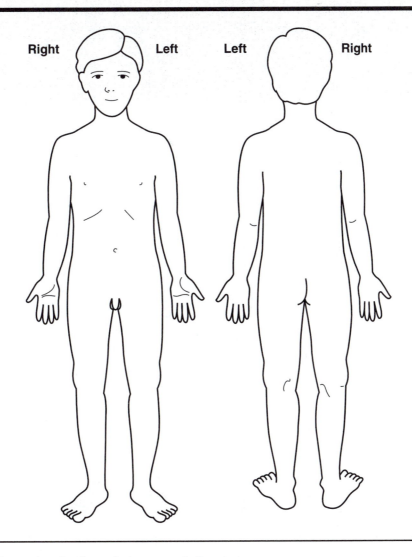

Right   **Left**   **Left**   **Right**

Figure 17-1. Front and rear view drawings of a human male figure.

be tailored to the child's age, cognitive-developmental level, communication skills, and coping abilities. When you give explanations, consider the child's level of anxiety and whether short intervals between explanations would be helpful. Give the information honestly, with reassurance and support.

Following are examples of interventions useful for the treatment of pain (Maron & Bush, 1991; Pain Management Guideline Panel, 1992; L. V. Ross, 1988, cited by Christophersen, 1994; Ross & Ross, 1988):

1. *Cognitive interventions.* First, you can use *attention diversion*—diverting the child's attention by means of external or internal stimuli or a combination of both, such as blowing bubbles, reading story books, telling stories, or counting items in the room. Second, if the pain is associated with a medical procedure, you can tell the child to think of

the procedure not as a continuous process but as a sequence of minor steps and tasks to be mastered one after the other. Teach the child to use *self-instruction,* in which he or she gives hints ("Just relax!"), encouragement ("I'm doing fine!"), and reassurance ("It's nearly over!" or "I can eat lunch soon!") by talking to himself or herself. Third, you can use *incompatible imagery*—asking the child to visualize vivid, pleasant situations or scenery, such as going to an amusement park like Disneyland; playing a game like baseball, soccer, or football; floating or swimming in a pool or ocean; lying on a beach; or lying in bed at home with a favorite blanket or toy.

2. *Behavioral interventions.* First, for infants, you can use pacifiers or swaddle, hold, and rock the infant. Second, for older children, you can use hypnosis; relaxation techniques; music, art, and play therapy; stress management; crisis intervention; supportive therapy; and family support

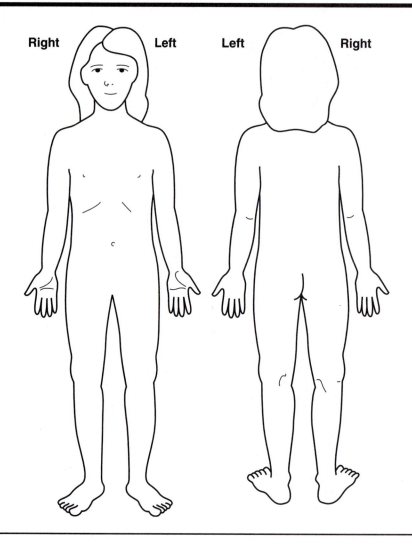

Right   Left   Left   Right

Figure 17-2. Front and rear view drawings of a human female figure.

groups. Third, for children of most ages, you can recommend the application of heat or cold, massage, exercise, rest, or immobilization as needed.

3. *Pharmacological interventions.* Health care providers who are licensed to prescribe medicine can prescribe opiod medications (for example, codeine or morphine) or nonopiod medications (for example, acetaminophen or a nonsteroidal anti-inflammatory drug).

Encourage children to communicate their pain; pain relief is an important part of their treatment. Children and their families should be told that achieving a total absence of pain may not be realistic.

Encourage parents of children who are in chronic pain to do the following (Masek, Russo, & Varni, 1984):

• Give the child frequent approval for maintaining normal activity patterns.

• Encourage the child to stay calm and practice relaxation procedures where feasible.

• Encourage the child to attend school regularly, as much as this is possible.

• Ignore the child's *excessive* complaining, pain gestures, and requests for special treatment and assistance, and encourage other family members to do the same; be careful, however, in determining what is excessive.

• Identify the ways the child's pain is being reinforced— that is, the ways in which the child is getting secondary gains.

• Follow the health care provider's recommendations for administering the medications for relief of pain, including the recommended amounts and times.

• Encourage the child to inform health care providers about whether the pain medications are effective.

• Keep records of when the child's pain occurs, particularly in what situations and at what times during the day.

Table 17-5
Procedures for Evaluating Pain in Children

Poker Chips

Put four red poker chips in a horizontal line in front of the child on the bedside table, a clipboard, or another firm surface. Say "These are pieces of hurt." Beginning with the chip nearest the child's left side and ending with the one nearest her or his right side, point to the chips and say "This [point to the first chip] is a little bit of hurt and this [point to the fourth chip] is the most hurt you could ever have. How many pieces of hurt do you have right now?" Clarify the child's answer with words such as "Oh, you have a little hurt? Tell me about the hurt." Record the number of chips the child selects.

Word-Graphic Scale

Make two copies of the word-graphic scale shown below—one for demonstration and one for the child to use. Show the child the demonstration scale. Say: "This is a line with words to describe how much pain you have. This side of the line means no pain, and over here the line means the worst possible pain. [Point with your finger to where "No Pain" is, and run your finger along the line to "Worst Possible Pain" as you say it.] If you had no pain, you would mark like this. [Make a vertical line on the horizontal line over the words "No Pain."] If you had some pain, you would mark somewhere along the line, depending on how much pain you had. [Make a vertical line on the horizontal line over the words "Little Pain."] The more pain you had, the closer to "large pain" you would mark. The worst pain possible is marked like this. [Make a vertical line on the horizontal line over the words "Worst Possible Pain." Remove the demonstration scale, and give the child the other scale with no marks.] Show me how much pain you have right now by marking with a straight, up-and-down line anywhere along the line to show how much pain you have right now."

Sample scale

No Pain	Little Pain	Medium Pain	Large Pain	Worst Possible Pain

For adolescents, you can use the following instructions: "Place a straight up-and-down mark on this line to show how much pain you have. Go ahead."

Happy-Sad Faces

Instruct the child by saying "Look at these faces. Point to the one that shows how you are feeling now. Go ahead."

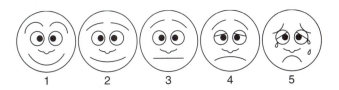

Pain Thermometer

Instruct the child by saying "Look at this picture. The number at the bottom, 0, means no pain at all. The number at the top, 100, means the worst possible pain. The number in the middle, 50, means a medium amount of pain. You can use any number you want. Do you have any questions about what the numbers mean? . . . [Answer any questions.] Now point to the number that shows how much pain you are having now. Go ahead."

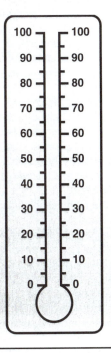

Source: Adapted, in part, from Hester, Foster, and Kristensen (1990) and Savedra, Tesler, Holzemer, and Ward (1989).

If the child is hospitalized and scheduled for a potentially painful medical procedure, let the child see the room in which the medical procedure will be performed beforehand to alleviate anxiety. Informing the child about how much time he or she needs to prepare for the medical procedure also may be helpful. However, it may be better to say too little rather than too much—giving the child too much information may be disconcerting to him or her.

Case Illustration

The following case illustrates the importance of a multidisciplinary approach to pain assessment.

CASE 17-1. MARIA

Maria, a 15-year-old promising gymnast, had fallen off a balance beam during practice, badly spraining her left ankle. After consultation with an orthopedist, X-rays, and the place-

Table 17-6
Evaluating the Interview Findings Obtained from Children Who Are in Pain and Their Families

Quality, Severity, Location, and Duration of the Pain

1. What type of pain does the child have?
2. How severe is the pain? For example, is the pain mild, moderate, severe, or unbearable?
3. Where is the pain located?
4. Is the pain acute, chronic, or recurrent?
5. How does the child describe the pain? For example, is the pain described as beating, throbbing, shooting, biting, stinging, burning, tight, or hurting (see Table 17-4)?
6. At what times during the day does the pain occur?
7. In what part of the body does the pain occur?
8. How long does the pain last?

Situational Factors

9. In what situations does the pain occur? For example, does the pain occur prior to the start of the school day, after a long day at school, before a difficult task or new situation, during a stressful interpersonal interaction, before a test, before completing an assignment, in the presence of certain persons, or at certain locations?
10. Does the pain become worse in certain situations and, if so, in what situations?
11. How does the child communicate her or his pain? For example, does the child communicate her or his pain verbally, with facial or postural gestures, or through subtle behavioral changes?
12. How does the child react to the pain? For example, does the child complain, seek help, or withdraw?
13. Does the child receive any special favors (called secondary gains) because of the pain? If so, what are the special favors and who gives the favors?
14. How long has the child had the pain?
15. When did the pain start?
16. Was the start of the pain associated with any particular event? If so, what was the event?
17. Is the child too dramatic with her or his report of the pain?
18. What are the medical findings associated with the pain?

Use of Medications

19. What does the child do for the the pain? For example, what medication does the child take for the pain? (If the child takes analgesics, go to question 20; if the child does not take analgesics, go to question 23.)
20. Are the analgesics taken according to a schedule? If so, what is the schedule?
21. How many doses of the analgesics are taken each day?
22. Does the amount of medication vary according to the day of the week? If so, how does it vary?

Consequences of the Pain

23. How has the pain affected the child's activities? For example, has the pain affected the child's ability to go to school, relationships with peers, participation in organizations and sports, and personal and family activities?
24. What makes the child's pain worse?
25. What makes the child's pain better?
26. What activities can the child no longer engage in because of the pain?

Self-Perception

27. To what extent does the child believe that she or he has control over the pain?
28. How does the child feel about herself or himself when she or he experiences pain?
29. How do the pain behaviors shown by the child in the interview relate to the medical findings?
30. How does the child understand the pain?
31. Is the child's understanding of her or his pain accurate?
32. What are the child's expectations about the pain for the future?
33. How open is the child to rehabilitation?

Family's Reaction to the Child's Pain

34. How do the family members know the child is in pain?
35. How do the family members understand the child's pain?
36. Is their understanding of the child's pain accurate?
37. What meaning do the family members ascribe to the child's pain?
38. Do all of the family members feel the same way about the child's pain? If not, how do individual members differ in their feelings about the child's pain?
39. How do the family members cope with the child's pain?
40. What impact does the child's pain have on the health of the other family members?
41. What effect does the child's pain have on family roles and responsibilities?
42. What does the family do to help the child with pain management?
43. What changes do family members make when the child is in pain? For example, do they keep the house quiet, serve the child meals in bed, or take over the child's responsibilities?
44. Do any family members have similar pain? If so, who are they, and what type of pain do they have?
45. Is the family overconcerned with the child's pain? If so, in what way?
46. If the child is taking medication, who assumes responsibility for administering the medication?
47. How open are the family members to the treatment approach recommended by the health care providers for the child's pain?

Source: Adapted from Masek, Russo, and Varni (1984).

Table 17-7
An Example of a Pain Diary

PAIN DIARY

Name: _____ *Age:* _____ *Year:* _____

Instructions: Use this form for a one-week period. Write the month and day of the week at the top of each column. For example, if you are starting on June 1, write 6/1 over the first column and 6/2, 6/3, 6/4, 6/5, 6/6, and 6/7 over the remaining columns. If you have pain any time during the hour listed, note the intensity of the pain. Use the following scale:

1 = barely noticeable pain
2 = mild pain
3 = moderate pain
4 = very bad pain
5 = intolerable pain

Thus, if at 6:30 A.M. on June 1 you had moderate pain, you would put 3 in the first box. Or, if you had barely noticeable pain on 6/7 at 10:45 P.M., you would put 1 in the last box (lower right-hand corner) on the form. If you have no pain, write NP for the day and time.

Dates Recorded

6–6:59 A.M.							
7–7:59 A.M.							
8–8:59 A.M.							
9–9:59 A.M.							
10–10:59 A.M.							
11–11:59 A.M.							
12–12:59 P.M.							
1–1:59 P.M.							
2–2:59 P.M.							
3–3:59 P.M.							
4–4:59 P.M.							
5–5:59 P.M.							
6–6:59 P.M.							
7–7:59 P.M.							
8–8:59 P.M.							
9–9:59 P.M.							
10–10:59 P.M.							

Source: Adapted from Tarnowski and Kaufman (1988).

ment of a soft cast to immobilize the joint, she was assured that the sprain would heal quickly and that she could return to her sport in several weeks. She was advised to rest as much as possible and to interrupt any activity should the pain increase.

Four months later, Maria and her parents arrived in our office. Despite medical assurances that the sprain had completely healed, she had for the past 3 months experienced excruciating, burning pain in the ankle, reported coldness and numbness, and was clearly angry about the unsuccessful treatment she had received at the hands of several specialists. Her parents reported that she spent much time in her room, upset and ambivalent about her return to sports. The parents, themselves athletes, put a great deal of pressure on Maria to excel. This had predated the accident, as Maria's performance had been lacking, and she expressed thoughts of "being more like the other kids" and dropping out of gymnastics. The parents reported that she had become increasingly isolated, moody, and anxious, and her pain always appeared worse during these periods. Maria's medical records indicated good healing of the sprain and no further complications. The parents were clearly upset over the doctor's impression that the pain is "all in her head."

Initially, Maria remained quiet. When a question was directed to Maria, her mother jumped in and answered. She said that her daughter had become increasingly frustrated with telling her story to different experts and with having to answer the same questions repeatedly. Maria's descriptions of her pain were rather vague. She was unable to identify any aggravating factors. She explained that the only measure that would provide some relief from the pain was sleeping.

Maria seemed to have adopted a passive and hopeless attitude about her pain. We asked her to complete a questionnaire and to keep a pain diary. Her parents also were asked to complete a questionnaire. We held a second interview with Maria alone. On the questionnaire, Maria gave much more information about her pain condition than she did in the interview with the parents present. She talked more openly about her anger toward her mother, who asked frequently about her pain and advised her to rest. We learned that Maria had missed a considerable amount of time at school and that she worried about not being promoted to the next grade. Her responsibilities at home had decreased since the onset of her pain. Her pain diary indicated that her pain was not at the same level throughout the day as she had stated during our first meeting. The pain was most likely to be moderate during morning hours, intensifying in the evenings. She noticed that talking to her girlfriend on the phone had distracted her from the pain, and also listening to her favorite music with headphones. Consistent with the parental report, Maria's entries in her diary suggested that at the times when she felt anxious and depressed, her pain might be worse. Interestingly, her mother rated Maria's pain as less intense than did Maria.

Maria also was seen by the anesthesiologist. After a review of her medical history, a physical examination, and laboratory studies to rule out rheumatologic or vascular diseases, the diagnosis of reflex sympathetic dystrophy (that is, pain occurring following injury to bone and soft tissue) was made. Results from a diagnostic lumbar sympathetic nerve block with a local anesthetic were consistent with this diagnosis.

Peanuts  by Charles Schulz

PEANUTS © 1986. United Features Syndicate Reprinted by Permission.

Applying the traditional, purely psychological approach, one might have concluded from Maria's initial presentation that her pain problem was a manifestation of the conflict with her parents about her future as an athlete. This formulation might have focused on the fact that Maria's independence-seeking wishes were blocked by the strong parental investment in her sports career, leading to anxiety regarding her relationship with peers and suppressed anger toward her parents. Although these issues were relevant to the case, this approach would have neglected the physiological dimension of Maria's pain condition. Pharmacologic and physical interventions, such as electrical nerve stimulation and nerve blocks, which would not have been considered otherwise, were used together with behavioral and cognitive methods, resulting in a significant reduction of pain and a return to more normal activities for this patient. (Reprinted, with changes in notation, with permission of the publisher and author from D. C. Russo, B. M. Lehn, & C. B. Berde, "Pain," pp. 432–433, in T. H. Ollendick & M. Hersen [Eds.], *Handbook of Child and Adolescent Assessment,* copyright © 1993 by Allyn & Bacon.)

Because pain is such a complex psychological event, often resulting in such a pervasive reorganization of one's self, it is stressed that the psychological treatment of pain must involve examining behavioral, interpersonal, and cognitive components in the interest of comprehensive holistic health care.

—Roy Grzesiak

ASTHMA

Description

Asthma is a disorder in which the airways of the tracheobronchial passages constrict so that the person feels unable to breathe or to take deep breaths. The disorder is chronic and varies in severity. Asthma is usually diagnosed by clinical symptoms, such as wheezing and coughing, and by exposing the person to allergic substances or exercise to detect changes in airway obstruction.

Asthmatic attacks are usually triggered by such stimuli as cigarette smoke, smog, *allergens* (substances that cause allergic reactions, such as tree, grass, or weed pollen; animal danders [minute scales from hair, feathers, or skin of animals]; airborne molds or fungi; house dust mites and other insects; dust; chemicals; and certain foods), exercise in cold air, respiratory infections, and emotional responses, such as crying and laughing (Creer, Harm, & Marion, 1988). Hospitalization may be required when the child shows such symptoms as blue complexion, tenseness, overbreathing, chattering speech, and a fearful expression in the eyes (Creer, Renne, & Chai, 1982).

Asthma is the most common chronic illness of childhood in the United States, affecting 6 to 7 million children (Fritz & Overholser, 1989). Estimates indicate that between 5% and 15% of children 11½ years of age and younger suffer from asthma (Creer et al., 1982). It is a major cause of emergency room visits and hospitalizations among children and contributes significantly to absences from school. From ages 3 to 14 years, asthma is more frequent in boys than in girls; after 14 years of age, it becomes more prevalent in girls. Black American children have a higher prevalence rate of asthma than White American children (Thompson & Gustafson, 1996). Although both genetic and environmental factors are involved in the development of asthma, its etiology is not well understood (Mrazek, 1991).

The frequency and severity of asthma attacks vary for each child: "A child may experience a burst of attacks over a brief period and then remain free of the disorder for weeks, months, or years. Then, perhaps with the changing of seasons, the child may again suffer an attack or a series of attacks over a short period of time" (Creer et al., 1988, p. 168). Other children may experience asthma attacks throughout the year or have mild asthma symptoms daily. However, "most asthmatic children experience respiratory distress only during attacks; at other times this condition reverses, and their breathing appears normal" (p. 171). Asthma attacks can vary in severity from mild episodes to life-threatening incidents.

Interviewing Issues

The semistructured interview in Table F-6 in Appendix F will help you interview children with asthma. You may find it useful first to use the general semistructured interview for children with medical problems (Table F-27 in Appendix F) and then to use the semistructured interview designed for children with asthma. The asthma diary shown in Table 17-8 is an effective self-monitoring procedure. Answers to the questions in Table 17-1 and Table 17-2, presented earlier in the chapter, will help you evaluate the information you obtain from children with asthma and from their parents, respectively.

Interventions

Several methods are used in the treatment and management of asthma, including environmental management, pharmacologic management, behavioral management, and education and self-management. The aim of *environmental management,* which plays a major part in asthma intervention, is to alter the environment to reduce precipitants of asthmatic attacks. This involves eliminating or controlling allergens—for example, by removing the carpet in the child's bedroom (particularly in warm, moist climates), placing the mattress and box spring in an impermeable zippered casing, removing flowers from the house, vacuuming often but not while the child is at home, installing an air-filtration system, limiting the child's exposure to animals, avoiding any exposure of the child to tobacco smoke, and washing linens, pillows, blankets, and stuffed toys once a week in hot water.

Pharmacologic management may involve the use of several types of drugs, such as the following (Berkow, 1992): (a) *bronchodilators,* which relax and open the airways (such as theophylline and epinephrine); (b) *anti-inflammatory agents* that decrease swelling and allergic reactions in the lungs (such as corticosteroids); and (c) drugs that inhibit the production and release of substances that create an allergic reaction in the lungs (such as cromolyn sodium).

Children may use a *nebulizer* for the delivery of their medicine. This is a device in which a specified dose of the bronchodilating medicine is placed in a canister with a saline solution, creating a mist. The child breathes the mist through a mask for a 10- to 20-minute period.

Some medications have side effects (Creer & Bender, 1995). For example, theophylline may induce changes in mood, behavior, and ability to learn, and corticosteroids may lead to subtle mood and memory changes.

Behavioral management and *education and self-management techniques* are particularly important for asthmatic children because there is no medical cure for asthma (Creer, 1991). These interventions are designed to help children do the following:

- learn self-management skills, such as self-monitoring, information processing and evaluation (to increase, for example, the child's knowledge of asthma and its treatment, ability to discriminate symptoms of attacks, and knowledge of how to avoid conditions that may produce attacks), attack management, and positive self-reactions
- use medications effectively
- relax and follow the prescribed regimen to control the attacks
- reduce hospital overuse
- predict future attacks, particularly through regular use of a peak flow meter (a device that can be used at home to measure breathing capacity)
- prepare, where appropriate, for seasonal asthma

Because asthma occurs when children are young and may be life threatening, parents may become hypervigilant and overprotective of their child (Davis & Wasserman, 1992). They may indulge the child because they do not want the child to cry. Indulgence can be counterproductive because the child learns to cry in order to get her or his way, and, in turn, the crying may trigger an asthma attack. Parents need to learn how to avoid overindulging their child and how to teach the child to behave so that they can help the child manage the asthma.

Rates of adherence to a medical regimen are low for asthmatic children; only about 10% of the children follow their health care provider's advice completely (Creer & Reynolds, 1990). Children with asthma, for example, may not avoid stimuli that trigger attacks and may misuse medications to get "high" instead of to alleviate an asthmatic attack (this applies more to adolescents than to younger children with asthma). A common problem associated with inhalation therapy is that children may not know how to use the equipment properly, and, consequently, they may be unable to gain the maximum benefit from the medication. When this is the case, children should be given additional instruction on how to use the equipment. See Chapter 15 for more information about adherence.

Case Illustration

The following case illustrates the nature of asthma and the effectiveness of an intervention program (Creer & Reynolds, 1990).

CASE 17-2. ZEKE

Zeke Green is a 7-year-old boy who has had asthma since he was 5 years old. Zeke was referred to the behavioral medicine clinic at City Center Hospital following three hospital

Table 17-8
Asthma Diary

ASTHMA DIARY

Patient I.D. #: _____ *Date dispensed:* _____

Please review the instructions for the Asthma Diary before completing the Diary.

Dates

Symptoms

Chest wheezing															
Breathlessness															
Chest tightness															
Cough															

Number of asthma attacks

# of daytime attacks[a]															
# of times awakened[b]															

PEFR

Morning (A.M.)															
Evening (4:00 P.M.)															

Asthma meds

1.															
2.															
3.															
4.															
5.															

INSTRUCTIONS FOR COMPLETING THE ASTHMA DIARY

Symptoms: Enter scores (1, 2, 3, 4, or 5) for your symptoms—record these scores at bedtime.

Mild	0 = No symptoms.
	1 = Symptoms are present but causing little or no discomfort.
Moderate	2 = Symptoms are present and troublesome but not causing interference with either daily activities or sleep.
Severe	3 = Symptoms are troublesome enough to cause interference with either daily activities or sleep.
	4 = Symptoms are troublesome enough to cause interference with *both daily activities and sleep.*
	5 = Symptoms are intolerable and incapacitating.

Number of asthma attacks: [a]Record the number of daytime attacks at bedtime. [b]Upon awakening, record the number of times awakened by asthma last night.

Peak Expiratory Flow Rates (PEFR): Perform peak flow maneuvers in the morning (5 to 10 minutes after awakening) and again in the evening (around 4:00 P.M.) *before* you take your asthma medications. To perform a peak flow maneuver: Inhale as deeply as you possibly can, then blow out as *hard,* as *fast,* and as *long* as you possibly can. Perform three maneuvers, then record the best (the highest) of the three peak flow rates. *Be sure you wait at least one minute between each maneuver.*

Asthma meds:
1. Enter the number of doses (tablets, spoonfuls, suppositories, etc.) taken each day for each drug listed above. (Be sure you list all asthma medications.)
2. Record the total number of doses of your aerosol taken in each 24-hour period. (Each dose = 1 inhalation.) For example, if you take 3 inhalations 6 times, you would record 18 in the space provided.

Source: From T. L. Creer, H. Kotses, and R. V. C. Reynolds, "Living with Asthma: Part II. Beyond CARIH," in *Journal of Asthma, 26,* Marcel Dekker, Inc., N.Y., copyright 1989. Reprinted from pp. 36–37, by courtesy of Marcel Dekker, Inc.

admissions within six months for uncontrolled attacks of asthma. The parents were concerned and frustrated over the apparent unmanageability of Zeke's asthma. Their efforts to control his asthma, such as by removal of all possible allergens from the home, were not successful. In-home observation indicated that Zeke obtained much attention for playing a sick role in the family. Family interactions with the other children centered on their participation in athletics, dance, or school achievement, whereas Zeke's interactions centered on his asthma. Further, the family was overattentive to Zeke's asthma immediately following a severe episode that led to his being hospitalized, but as time passed they became less attentive to his episodes of asthma.

Several factors seemed to play a role in establishing this pattern. First, Mr. and Mrs. Green seemed to feel responsible for Zeke's asthma. They also experienced guilt and fear about their inability to manage his asthma. This led them to be overattentive immediately following an acute episode. However, their gradual awareness that Zeke at times used his asthma to get attention by exaggerating his symptoms led them to be less concerned about his reports of asthmatic symptoms. No doubt, the intermittent and variable nature of the symptoms further promoted the parents' inconsistent response to Zeke's reports.

Several interventions were undertaken to change the course and management of Zeke's asthma. First, Zeke and his parents were trained in the use of a daily asthma diary to monitor changes in asthma symptoms and lung function. The family also was encouraged to limit discussion of asthma until bedtime, unless asthma symptoms were reported or observed. Furthermore, the family was urged to talk to Zeke about issues other than asthma, such as his interests and activities. Also, the parents joined a support group for parents of asthmatic children. Follow-up contact two years later revealed that Zeke had had no recurrence of severe asthma. (adapted from pp. 198–200)

DIABETES

Description

Insulin-dependent diabetes mellitus (IDDM) is a chronic metabolic disease of childhood that affects about 1 in every 600 children under the age of 10 years (Geffken & Johnson, 1994). It also is called *Type I diabetes* or *juvenile-onset diabetes.* Type I diabetes "can occur at any age but typically is diagnosed during childhood or adolescence" (Cox & Gonder-Frederick, 1992, p. 628). Another type of diabetes, *Type II diabetes* or *noninsulin-dependent diabetes mellitus (NIDDM),* occurs mostly in adults, usually after the age of 40. This part of the chapter focuses on insulin-dependent diabetes mellitus, which usually will be referred to simply as *diabetes* or *diabetes mellitus.* The Glossary at the end of the book describes several terms used in the field of diabetes.

The major problem in diabetes is *glucose* (sugar) use and storage. Glucose serves as a fuel for the tissues and organs of the body. When food is consumed, the body converts it to glucose. Glucose cannot enter the tissues and organs without *insulin,* which is a hormone produced by the pancreas. Diabetes in children is caused by destruction of the pancreatic beta cells that produce insulin. When insulin is no longer produced, *hyperglycemia* (called high blood glucose or high blood sugar) occurs. Symptoms of uncontrolled hyperglycemia include fatigue, excessive thirst, frequent urination, weight loss despite increased eating, rapid shallow breathing, abdominal pain, flushed skin, and fruity breath odor (Gross, 1990; Hanson & Onikul-Ross, 1990). Uncontrolled hyperglycemia can lead to *ketoacidosis.* Ketoacidosis occurs when toxic substances build up in the blood. Early symptoms of diabetic ketoacidosis—such as nausea, vomiting, and weakness—can mimic flu symptoms. *Ketoacidosis is extremely dangerous and requires immediate medical attention.* Long-term complications of diabetes include blindness, renal failure, and cardiovascular disease—conditions that may develop 15 to 20 years after the disease begins.

Diabetes regimen. Children with diabetes must follow a complex regimen of daily insulin injections, *blood glucose monitoring,* diet, and exercise. The goal of treatment is to maintain blood sugar levels as near normal as possible. Long-term management of diabetes includes teaching the child to self-administer insulin injections and rotate injection sites, to test his or her blood and urine glucose levels, to follow a diet to meet nutritional requirements, and to compensate for changes in activity level by altering diet or insulin levels.

For infants and young children, parents must assume responsibility for the diabetes regimen. By about 8 to 10 years of age, children can reliably administer insulin injections, and, by about 10 to 12 years of age, they can assume primary responsibility for glucose testing (Geffken & Johnson, 1994). Although adolescents can assume primary responsibility for their diabetes regimen, parents need to monitor their adolescent's adherence to the diabetes regimen, as adherence tends to drop as children reach adolescence (Anderson, Auslander, Jung, Miller, & Santiago, 1990). The child's level of cognitive maturity also must be considered in evaluating his or her ability to follow a diabetes regimen. Family support, cohesion, and organization can enhance diabetes management, whereas family conflict and dysfunction can interfere with diabetes management.

A diabetes regimen may be especially difficult for children and adolescents when they have difficulty resisting peer influence. Estimates of *nonadherence* to a diabetes regimen range from 30% to 90% (Gross, 1990). Children often fail to follow dietary restrictions and to conduct glucose-level testing. *Inadvertent nonadherence* also is a problem because children may make errors when they try to follow the treatment instructions. In addition, some children may conduct the blood glucose tests accurately but deliberately give inaccurate reports so that their blood sugars appear to be better than they actually are.

Adherence will be better when cost for the treatment is reasonable, there is sufficient time to follow the regimen, resources are available to help with the regimen, and competing demands are not overwhelming. In addition, children are more likely to test themselves on days when they have followed the prescribed regimen (Cox & Gonder-Frederick, 1992).

Occasionally, children take too much insulin because they want to hide the fact that they consumed too many carbohydrates (Geffken & Johnson, 1994). Taking too much insulin may result in *hypoglycemia* (low blood sugar). Hypoglycemia also can occur when children fail to eat the right amounts of foods at the right time or when they exercise more than usual. Symptoms of hypoglycemia include tremulousness, cold sweat, low body temperature, heart palpitations, headache, confusion, hallucinations, bizarre behavior, and, ultimately, convulsions, coma, and possible death.

Stresses in the parent-child relationship are likely to arise when children fail to follow the diabetes regimen. The family (or health care provider staff) may ask mental health professionals to intervene when the child does not adhere to the regimen. Children may need to be reminded of the long-term beneficial consequences of their adherence to the diabetes regimen. Sometimes, even though children adhere to the diabetes regimen, blood glucose levels are still unacceptable (Geffken & Johnson, 1994). This can happen if the diabetes regimen is not working properly.

The diabetes regimen can be thrown off course when children contract another illness, such as flu or a stomach virus. Encourage the family to talk to the health care provider about the diabetes regimen whenever the child has another illness (L. Gudas, personal communication, February 1996).

Psychological effects of diabetes on children. Diabetes can affect children in several different ways, including the following:

1. *Diabetes can lead to general psychological disturbance.* Children with diabetes may experience depression, anxiety, and social withdrawal when they are informed of the diagnosis. However, their distress is likely to diminish by the end of the first year. "Parents' psychological response to the diagnosis is an important predictor of the child's adjustment" (Cox & Gonder-Frederick, 1992, p. 630).

2. *Diabetes can contribute to the development of eating disorders.* "The prevalence of eating disorders is higher in adolescent and young adult women with IDDM than in the general population.... [Although] the exact prevalence of eating disorders remains unclear...subclinical levels of eating disorders, such as frequent binge eating, do appear to be prevalent in IDDM and are associated with poorer glycemic control.... In addition, diabetic patients may use insulin reduction or omission to promote glycosuria [the presence of an abnormal amount of glucose in the urine] as a method of purging" (Cox & Gonder-Frederick, 1992, p. 631).

3. *Psychological stress can affect the course of diabetes.* A complex relationship exists between psychological stress and diabetes. "First, relationships between stress and diabetes are bidirectional.... Psychological stress can affect diabetes, *and* diabetes can affect stress levels. In addition, stress can *directly* affect BG [blood glucose] through the release of stress hormones (e.g., epinephrine, which elevates glucose) or *indirectly* affect BG by disrupting self-care behaviors.... Hypoglycemia may indirectly produce stressful consequences such as negative mood states..., fear..., and accidents" (Cox & Gonder-Frederick, 1992, pp. 631–632). Hypoglycemia requires medical attention and, if untreated, will result in poor health.

Interviewing Issues

The semistructured interview in Table F-28 in Appendix F is useful for adolescents with diabetes. You may want to begin with the general semistructured interview for children with medical problems (see Table F-27 in Appendix F) and then use the semistructured interview designed for children with diabetes in particular. As in any interview, you will want to learn why the child has come to the clinic, as well as the nature of the child's social and peer relations and family interactions. You also will want to observe the child's behavior in his or her natural setting, if possible.

Depending on the child's age, you may want to explore the following areas: (a) the child's knowledge of the disease, (b) the child's ability to do blood glucose testing, (c) the child's ability to administer insulin, (d) the support the child receives from his or her parents, and (e) how the child's peer group views his or her illness.

It will be helpful to observe directly how the child administers insulin and performs blood glucose testing, particularly if you are a health care provider or are working in a diabetes clinic as a mental health professional. *Having the child describe the procedures is not sufficient—you will need to learn how to do the necessary procedures yourself to see whether the child can perform them correctly* (Gross, 1990).

If the child, parents, or teachers report that the child is having learning problems, consider recommending that the child be given a psychoeducational evaluation to see whether there are any subtle cognitive impairments that are interfering with the child's learning (Geffken & Johnson, 1994). Research suggests that *some* children with diabetes are at risk for learning disabilities (Rovet, Ehrlich, Czuchta, & Akler, 1993).

Occasionally, you might want to ask the parents to monitor the child's adherence, depending on the child's age and who is responsible for following the diabetes regimen (Gross, 1990). For example, you can give the parents the following homework assignment: "Write down what happens when you ask [child's name] to do a blood glucose test before dinner. Note what [child's name] does and what you do." This assignment will give you some idea of the child-parent relationship and how cooperative the child is in following the diabetes regimen. Monitoring the child's adherence also may help the parents develop a more realistic appraisal of the child's behavior and of their behavior with the child. Depending on the child's age, you also might ask him or her to complete a similar assignment.

After you complete the interview with the child and with the parents, review the questions in Tables 17-1 and 17-2 to help you evaluate the information you obtained. For a more detailed list of questions to consider about the family, see Table 4-7 in Chapter 4.

Interventions

Medical treatment of the diabetic child is designed to control the diabetes. Psychosocial interventions can be directed toward helping the family reduce or manage stress; increasing the family's self-esteem, social supports, and other resources; and opening lines of communication. Adherence to a diabetic regimen may improve when the family's stress is reduced and its resources increased (Auslander, Bubb, Rogge, & Santiago, 1993). Table 17-9 gives an example of a brief intervention program for families with a diabetic child; it consists of two 2-hour sessions scheduled two weeks apart.

Case Illustration

The following case illustrates some problems that diabetic children may have (Geffken & Johnson, 1994).

CASE 17-3. MARY

Mary is a 15-year-old, brown-eyed adolescent, who is slightly overweight. She was admitted to the hospital because of diabetic ketoacidosis. She admitted that she skipped injections, did not monitor her blood glucose levels, frequently ate candy and other concentrated sweets, and did not exercise.

Mary lives with her mother and a 10-year-old brother. Her parents were divorced when she was 3 years old. Mary said that she is responsible for her diabetes care. She has conflicts with her mother about her diabetes management and her failure to keep curfew and do chores at home. Mary's schoolwork is below average—she is receiving grades of Ds and Fs in all her subjects. In the last three months, she has missed 19 days of school, although she said that she enjoys school because of the opportunity to be with friends.

Marks on her body suggested that she engages in minor self-mutilating behavior. Her constant rubbing of an eraser on her hand resulted in places with broken skin. On one of her ankles, she had marked her initials and the initials of her boyfriend with a pen, which again broke the skin.

Mary was evaluated by a psychologist. The psychological report said that she was cooperative and pleasant throughout the evaluation. She had good eye contact, a normal range of affect, no suicidal ideations, and no evidence of a thought disorder. Her scores were in the Low Average range of intelligence and below average in reading, written lan-

---

Table 17-9
Brief Intervention Program for a Family with a Diabetic Child

---

Session 1

Goals
To identify and discuss family responsibilities in diabetes
To change ways in which diabetes tasks are shared

Components
1. Introduction
    Explain goals of the session.
    Discuss demands of diabetes on the family.
    Help family members to identify their strengths.
2. Family members describe their roles/tasks in diabetes care.
3. Family members discuss satisfaction with roles and adherence.
4. Identify possible alternatives in role sharing.
    How might family members change their roles to improve satisfaction and adherence?
5. Choose specific changes to attain.
6. Discuss possible problems or pitfalls.
7. Set up a daily recording system.
8. Practice the agreed-upon plan at home.
9. Follow up with phone calls to evaluate role changes and suggest modifications if needed.

Session 2

Goals
To identify and discuss how family members communicate about diabetes
To increase supportive interactions related to diabetes

Components
1. Discuss family communication about diabetes.
    Who talks about diabetes?
    What is discussed?
    What are the areas of disagreement?
2. Family members discuss dissatisfaction with diabetes-related communication patterns.
3. Identify possible alternatives to diabetes-related communication.
4. Choose specific changes and make a plan.
5. Family members role play specific changes in communicating.
6. Discuss possible problems or pitfalls with the new plan.
7. Practice agreed-upon changes at home.
8. Follow up with phone calls and suggest modifications, if needed.

Source: Reprinted, with changes in notation, with permission of the author and publisher, from W. F. Auslander from "Brief Family Interventions to Improve Family Communication and Cooperation Regarding Diabetes Management" in *Diabetes Spectrum, 6,* p. 332, copyright 1993 by the American Diabetes Association.

guage, and mathematics. Personality test results suggested that Mary is an impulsive, defiant adolescent with interpersonal problems.

Mary and her mother reluctantly agreed that Mary would enter a residential treatment program for diabetic children. Treatment included classes on diabetes management, improving social skills and self-esteem, increasing assertiveness, and decreasing impulsive behavior. Parent training sessions focused on the need for increased parental supervision. Treatment also consisted of helping Mary stabilize her glucose levels, adjust her insulin doses, increase her exercise, and eat properly. After 5 months in the residential program, she was discharged. She made remarkable progress during this period and could follow the diabetes regimen and keep up with her schoolwork. Her relationship with her mother also improved. Two years after discharge, she continued to follow the diabetes regimen and had no episodes of hospitalization because of diabetic ketoacidosis. (adapted from pp. 125–127)

CHILDHOOD CANCER

Description

Each year, approximately 6,000 children under 16 years of age are diagnosed with cancer (Peckham, 1989). The incidence of childhood cancers is approximately 12.1 per 100,000 for White American children and approximately 9.3 per 100,000 for Black American children (Garrison & McQuiston, 1989). The various forms of cancer "have in common the growth of malignant cells in single or multiple sites in the body, leading to destruction of normal cells and associated organs" (Garrison & McQuiston, 1989, p. 51). The etiology of many cancers is unknown, but genetic, environmental, chromosomal, or immunological factors may be involved. Childhood cancers generally arise in "embryonic tissue that persisted, failed to mature, and then reproduced proliferatively" (Peckham, 1989, p. 314). Viral agents also have been implicated in causing human cancers, but the evidence is not definitive (Garrison & McQuiston, 1989).

Following are the common cancers of childhood and adolescence (Manne & Andersen, 1991):

1. *Leukemias. Acute lymphoblastic leukemia* (also referred to as *acute lymphocytic leukemia*) is a condition in which normal bone marrow cells are replaced by malignant cells; it is the most common type of leukemia. Symptoms include lethargy, fatigue, anorexia, abdominal discomfort, signs of hemorrhaging (such as easy bruising), headache, and bone and joint pain.

2. *Central nervous system tumors. Astrocytomas* (tumors composed of fibrous neurological cells) are the form of brain tumor most prevalent in children. Symptoms of central nervous system tumors depend on the area of the brain directly invaded or irritated by the tumor (for example, loss of vision occurs with occipital lobe tumors). Symptoms also may be associated with increased intracranial pressure from the growth of the tumor, from swelling of the surrounding tissues, or from obstruction of the cerebrospinal fluid pathways. Symptoms of increased intracranial pressure include irritability, lethargy, headache, vomiting, decreased appetite, and withdrawn behavior.

3. *Lymphomas. Lymphomas* (a general term applied to any disorder in which there is new or abnormal growth of lymph tissue) are divided into *Hodgkin's disease* and *non-Hodgkin's lymphoma*. In Hodgkin's disease, there is painless lymph node enlargement; symptoms may include fever, sweating, itching, weight loss, and malaise. Non-Hodgkin's lymphomas are a heterogeneous group of malignancies with varied symptoms, such as malaise, cough, dyspnea (difficulty in breathing), and malnutrition with colitis-like symptoms.

4. *Neuroblastomas. Neuroblastomas* (tumors composed of nerve cells) are virulent tumors that can arise anywhere along the sympathetic nervous system, but the most common sites are the adrenal gland and the paraspinal ganglion. The most prominent symptom is a fixed mass in the chest, abdomen, or neck; less common symptoms are fever, weakness, pallor, weight loss, shortness of breath, and cough.

5. *Bone tumors. Osteogenic sarcoma* (a tumor of the bone tissue) is the most common type of bone tumor. Symptoms include bone pain, with or without a palpable overlying mass, as well as pain with increased activity, a limited range of motion, swelling, and, more rarely, a pathological fracture.

6. *Retinoblastomas.* These tumors arise from the tissue within the retina in the eye. Symptoms include eye abnormality (for example, a whitish appearance of the pupil) and strabismus (that is, cross-eyedness).

Several procedures are used to diagnose cancer, depending on the symptoms. They include *bone marrow aspiration, biopsy,* laboratory studies of the blood, *lumbar puncture, x-ray, computed tomography (CT;* see Chapter 19), *magnetic resonance imaging (MRI;* see Chapter 19), *bone scan,* and *ultrasound.* Nearly all of these procedures can be frightening experiences for children.

Table 17-10 shows how children may react at various phases in the diagnosis and treatment of cancer. Children and their parents may regard the diagnosis of cancer with fear and as more of a threat than other diagnoses (Northouse & Northouse, 1987).

In addition to creating fear, cancer is a disease that often involves a high degree of uncertainty regarding its cause, diagnosis, treatment, and prognosis. Patients often do not know why they developed cancer or whether their treatment will result in remission. In addition, patients whose cancer is in remission do not know if their disease-free condition will continue....

Cancer is different from other illnesses such as heart disease and diabetes, which can be directly affected by patient behavior, because patients often perceive cancer and its progression as not easily influenced by their physical or emotional.... They often feel as if their own bodies are out of control...and feel helpless because they are unable to affect the course of their own illness. (p. 19)

Table 17-10
Phases of Cancer and Possible Psychosocial Issues in Children

Phase	Possible psychosocial issues
Prediagnostic phase	Constant overconcern with the possibility of having cancer Denial of the disease's presence and refusal to go to treatment
Diagnostic phase	Shock, disbelief Initial and partial denial Anxiety Anger, hostility, persecutory feelings Depression
Initial treatment Surgery	Grief reaction to changes in body image Postponement of surgery (avoidance) Search for nonsurgical alternatives
Radiation therapy	Fear of x-ray machines and side effects Fear of abandonment during treatment
Chemotherapy	Fear of side effects or changes in body image Anxiety
Follow-up treatment	Return to normal coping patterns Fear of recurrence
Recurrence and retreatment	Shock, disbelief, denial Anxiety Anger Depression
Disease progression	Frenzied search for new information, consultants, and alternative and unproven cures
Terminal phase	Fear of abandonment Fear of dying Loss and anger Anticipatory mourning Acceptance by patient and survivors

Source: Adapted from Rainey, Wellisch, Fawzy, Wolcott, and Pasnau (1983).

Interviewing Issues

The semistructured interview in Table F-27 in Appendix F will be useful for interviewing children with cancer. As with all children with a medical illness, you will want to learn how they are adjusting to their illness. Adolescents with terminal or advanced cancer may be at risk for suicide because of depression, pain, a sense of helplessness, and loss of control. If you believe that suicide is being contemplated, explore the seriousness of the risk with the child and parents (see Chapter 13). Similarly, you need to consider each parent's reaction when she or he learns of the diagnosis, during treatment, during remissions, and during the terminal phase of the child's illness. If you believe that the parent's reaction may adversely affect the child, you may need to monitor the parent's behavior when she or he visits the child at the hospital and offer the parent counseling. Answers to the questions in Table 17-1 and Table 17-2 will help you evaluate the information you obtain from children with cancer and from their parents, respectively.

Interventions

Treatment for cancer, depending on the type, may consist of surgical removal of the tumor mass, radiation, chemotherapy, or a combination of these treatments. Survival rates for some types of cancers in childhood are 70% or better (Peckham, 1989). In chemotherapy, different drugs may be used depending on the type of cancer and the phase of treatment. Unfortunately, chemotherapy and radiation may have several side effects such as nausea and vomiting, mouth sores, pain, weight gain or weight loss, hair loss, sterility, delayed onset of puberty, reduced stature, obesity, skeletal abnormalities, amputations, cardiopulmonary dysfunction, hepatic and renal toxicities, organic brain damage, higher risk for infection, constipation, tiredness, poor coordination, motor restlessness and agitation, anxiety, cognitive difficulties, and learning difficulties (Peckham, 1989; Van Dongen-Melman, 1992). Several of these problems may be temporary, but others may be permanent.

With radiation, the cognitive side effects may not appear until the second or third year after treatments are finished (Peckham, 1989). Because children under 3 years of age have rapidly developing brain structures, they may be the most susceptible to the long-term negative effects of radiation. Chemotherapy is being used to treat brain tumors in children under 3 years of age to avoid the neurocognitive side effects associated with radiation therapy (Thompson & Gustafson, 1996). But even chemotherapy may have some aversive consequences. Following radiation or chemotherapy treatment for brain tumors, young children should have periodic psychological evaluations to assess their intellectual development and academic growth and to determine any special learning needs or school placements.

When children with cancer are treated with chemotherapy, they may develop phobic-like reactions to their chemotherapy sessions. For example, they may vomit when they wake up in the morning on the day of their therapy appointment or feel nausea every time they drive by a hospital. Even magnetic resonance imaging (MRI) and CT scans can be frightening experiences for children. Some children still feel anxious when the treatment ends because they think the disease may recur if they are not being seen frequently by a health care provider (Holland, 1989a).

Short-term psychotherapy may help children with cancer work through their fears and concerns about changes in their physical appearance, their friends' reactions, the treatment's side effects, and the painful medical procedures (Koocher, 1986b). Psychotherapy may reduce their anxiety and provide a heightened sense of self-control as well as hasten their return to school and help them lead as normal a life as possible. The pain interventions discussed earlier in the chapter may be useful in helping children who undergo bone marrow aspirations, spinal taps, and other painful medical procedures.

Case Illustrations

The following two cases illustrate some learning difficulties associated with the treatment of cancer in children (Berkman, 1993).

CASE 17-4. JEFF

When Jeff fell to the bottom of his class in the first and second grades, his parents were bewildered. They refused to believe that Jeff, who had conquered leukemia, lagged behind academically simply because he had missed time from school while receiving chemotherapy treatment. "We thought he was being lazy and not trying," said Helen, Jeff's mother. "He had been a smart baby, very coordinated." But when a neuropsychologist evaluated Jeff last year, he discovered that the boy's learning disabilities, including problems concentrating and memorizing, probably stemmed from the intense chemotherapy he had received for three years, starting when he was 2 years old.

CASE 17-5. JANE

After conquering non-Hodgkin's lymphoma, Jane, aged 10 years, glows with vitality. Her hair, which she lost during chemotherapy, has grown back thick and wavy, and she talks happily about her days at school. But her mother recalled that last year, Jane dissolved in tears because she had forgotten her multiplication tables. "She knew all of her multiplication tables in the second grade, and in the third grade she couldn't even remember two times two." It took 6 months for her and Jane's doctor to persuade the school district that Jane needed a psychoeducational evaluation. The evaluation showed that Jane was a year and a half behind in math. Like other cancer survivors who may be having difficulty in school, Jane has learned to compensate by using memorization aids like flash cards and by putting in more hours of homework.

We lead a life of uneasy ambivalence. Some days we search for miracle cures, other days we celebrate the everyday miracles: support from those who love us, teachers who are amazingly caring and understanding, gifted and compassionate doctors who don't make us wait in waiting rooms. It is these everyday miracles that sustain us on darker days.... And the next time you pass a house with a little boy staring out the window, stop and wave.

—Patricia A. Dreier

HIV AND AIDS

Description

Human immunodeficiency virus type 1 (HIV-1) "is a retrovirus that infects white blood cells, the brain, the bowel, the skin, and other tissues" (Simonds & Rogers, 1992, p. 3). The disease that results from the virus is called *acquired immune deficiency syndrome (AIDS)*. Since statistics became available in 1981, the Centers for Disease Control and Prevention (1996a) report that there were 9,870 confirmed cases of pediatric AIDS in the United States through June 1996. Prevalence rates are highest among Black children, followed by Hispanic children and White children (see Figure 17-3). A majority of the cases (almost 59%) were in children under 5 years of ages (see Figure 17-4). A projected 10 million

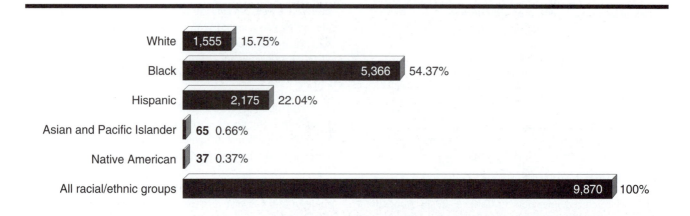

Figure 17-3. Pediatric and adolescent AIDS cases (ages 1 through 19) by race/ethnicity, from 1981 through June 1996. From Centers for Disease Control and Prevention, *HIV/AIDS Surveillance Report,* 1996, *8*(1), p. 13.

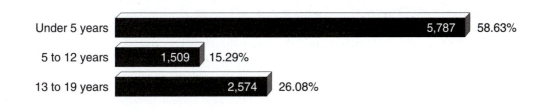

Under 5 years	5,787	58.63%
5 to 12 years	1,509	15.29%
13 to 19 years	2,574	26.08%

Figure 17-4. Pediatric AIDS cases by age groups from 1981 through June 1996. From Centers for Disease Control and Prevention *HIV/AIDS Surveillance Report,* 1996, *8*(1), p. 13.

children will be infected with HIV worldwide by the year 2000 (Mueller & Pizzo, 1992).

Transmission. HIV infection can be transmitted *perinatally* (from mother to child in the period shortly before or after birth), *sexually* (through such means as anal intercourse, vaginal intercourse, anal-genital contact, and oral-genital contact), and *parenterally* (through such means as blood transfusions and sharing of syringes and needles contaminated with the HIV virus). Children are said to be HIV positive when antibodies to the virus are detected in their blood.

Perinatal transmission. Perinatal transmission occurs when an infected mother passes the virus to her baby; this can happen in utero (that is, during pregnancy), during delivery by contact with infected blood or vaginal secretions, and through breast-feeding. However, not all infants born to an infected mother become infected—infection occurs in from 13% to 39% of the cases (Hutto, 1994). Treating HIV-infected mothers with antiretroviral medication during pregnancy appears to reduce the likelihood of transmission to the fetus. Perinatal transmission accounts for approximately 85% of pediatric AIDS cases in the United States (Armstrong, Seidel, & Swales, 1993).

Sexual transmission. HIV infection can occur through exposure to infected blood, semen, or vaginal secretions during sexual activity. Sexually active adolescents are often infected in this manner. The risk of being infected with HIV is highest for individuals who have multiple sexual partners, practice unsafe sex (that is, fail to use condoms during sexual activity), engage in sexual activities with people who are at high risk (for example, individuals who are known to be HIV positive, who have nonmonogamous sex partners, or who are intravenous drug users), and have been sexually abused by someone who is HIV infected.

Parenteral transmission. Parenteral transmission refers to transmission through injection or another route, other than the alimentary canal. There are two major ways in which HIV infection occurs through parenteral transmission (Simonds & Rogers, 1992). One way is through a transplant

or transfusion of infected blood or blood products. Hemophiliacs and those with clotting disorders were initially at risk because of their need for plasma from donors. Most of the adolescents infected in the early stages of the epidemic were hemophiliacs. After 1986, however, better blood tests dramatically reduced the incidence of transmission through blood transfusions. The second way HIV infection occurs through parental transmission is by means of sharing needles among IV drug users.

Transmission in adolescence. Adolescence is the period when risks related to sexual activity and drug activities become more prominent. HIV spreads quickly and silently among teens, and the majority of infected adolescents are unaware of their HIV status until they become symptomatic (sometimes several years after infection). Consequently, they are likely to transmit the virus to other partners unknowingly. It is likely that the number of adolescents contracting HIV will continue to increase because of (a) the high rates of substance abuse in association with sexual behavior among adolescents, (b) the high rates of HIV infection among inner-city youth, and (c) the prevalence of misinformation regarding risk of HIV infection among adolescents (Kalichman, 1996). Some adolescents even believe they are invulnerable to getting the HIV virus. Those adolescents most at risk for becoming HIV infected are runaways, homeless children, prostitutes, and IV drug users. (See Chapter 14 for more information on homeless children.)

Other issues related to transmission. Other issues related to the transmission of the disease include the following (Simonds & Rogers, 1992):

HIV has been cultured from saliva, tears, urine, and spinal fluid, [but] there have been no reports of transmission linked to contact with these fluids.... [In addition,] casual contact such as occurs in home, school, or day care center settings has not been shown to spread HIV infection.... Current recommendations state that most children with HIV infection be allowed to attend school and day care centers, but that more restricted environments be provided for preschool children and children with neurologic disabilities who display aggressive biting behavior or have oozing skin lesions that cannot be covered. (p. 8)

Concern about HIV infection and AIDS led to the formation of the Office of National AIDS Policy, which issued a report to President Clinton in March 1996 about the impact of HIV infection and AIDS on America's youth. Exhibit 17-1 shows a portion of the report, which points out that one-quarter of all new cases of HIV infection occur in adolescents and young adults between the ages of 13 and 21.

The AIDS epidemic has rolled back a big rotting log and revealed all the squirming life underneath it, since it involves, all at once, the main themes of our existence: sex, death, power, money, love, hate, disease and panic. No American phenomenon has been so compelling since the Vietnam war.

—Edmund White

Pediatric Acquired Immunodeficiency Syndrome (Pediatric AIDS). The most severe and the most life-threatening manifestation of HIV infection in children is *pediatric AIDS*. AIDS is the last phase of the HIV infection, when the child's body is unable to fight the infection. The incubation period—that is, the period from infection with HIV to the diagnosis of AIDS—is shorter in children than in adults (Simonds & Rogers, 1992). In children, the incubation period ranges from 12 months (for perinatally acquired infections or infections acquired in utero) to 3 years (for infections acquired through blood transfusion). In adults, the median incubation period is about 8 to 10 years.

AIDS is an autoimmune disease that drastically increases an individual's susceptibility to other illnesses that eventually may lead to death. The virus attacks the body's immune system, leaving it unable to fight infections. The most common illness associated with AIDS is *pneumocystis carinii pneumonia,* a type of pneumonia in which blood appears in the lung tissue. It is most likely to occur in infants and debilitated persons. Other common illnesses associated with AIDS include *recurrent bacterial infections* (from a failing immune system), *esophageal candidiasis* (a fungus infection in the esophagus), and *encephalopathy* (a degenerative disease of the brain).

Pediatric AIDS has a highly variable clinical course, with early symptoms similar to flu symptoms that won't go away, such as the following (Berkow, 1992; Kemper, 1994):

- failure to thrive
- chronic or recurrent diarrhea without definable specific course
- rapid unexplained weight loss
- persistent unexplained fever and night sweats
- swelling of glands in neck, armpits, or groin

As the disease progresses and the immune system deteriorates, other symptoms may appear, including the following (Kemper, 1994):

- unusual sores on the skin or in the mouth
- increased outbreaks of cold sores

- unexplained shortness of breath
- dry cough
- severe numbness or pain in the hands and feet
- unusual cancers and infections
- personality change
- mental deterioration

Because central nervous system involvement occurs in about 50% to 60% of HIV-infected children (Berko, 1992), let's now consider the neurological symptoms associated with HIV infection and pediatric AIDS.

Neurological symptoms. An HIV infection can cause changes in the child's central nervous system that affect language, social and emotional responsiveness, cognitive functioning, attention, memory, visual-motor integration, and gross motor functioning. Neurodevelopmental delays and neuropsychological deficits are exhibited by 75% to 90% of children infected with the HIV virus (Levenson & Mellins, 1992). Infants and toddlers also show neurodevelopmental delays (Mellins, Levenson, Zawadski, Kairam, & Weston, 1994).

AIDS/HIV-1 encephalopathy is a term used to describe changes in motor function and mental status in children with HIV infection. This condition is extremely serious and profoundly affects the child's development and survival. In encephalopathy, symptoms, which can occur singly or in combinations, include the following (Diamond & Cohen, 1992; Wiener, Moss, Davidson, & Fair, 1992):

- *cognitive symptoms* (for example, delays in reaching motor and language milestones, impaired receptive and expressive language, impaired spatial and mathematical abilities, memory loss, comprehension difficulties, and attentional deficits)
- *behavioral symptoms* (for example, depression; anxiety; loss of previously acquired developmental skills; withdrawal; agitated behavior; loss of interest in people, objects, and events; and impassive facial expressions)
- *motor symptoms* (for example, hyperactivity, motor weakness, impaired coordination, writing difficulties, and seizures)

In some cases, the symptoms are stable but then become progressively worse. The cognitive, behavioral, and motor deficits that occur are the primary reasons for referral for medical and neuropsychological evaluations.

Sometimes I have a terrible feeling that I am dying not from the virus, but from being untouchable.

—Amanda Heggs

Mortality. Pediatric AIDS is rapidly becoming a leading cause of death in children. In the period from 1981 through 1995, 3,920 children under the age of 15 years and 7,092 adolescents and young adults from 15 though 24 years of age died of AIDS. The highest percentage of deaths of chil-

Exhibit 17-1
Youth and HIV/AIDS: A Generation at Risk—Part of a Report Issued in 1996
to the President of the United States from the Office of National AIDS Policy

Today's youth are tomorrow's future. Yet, every year in the United States half of all new HIV infections occur among people under the age of 25 and one-quarter of new infections occur among people between the ages of 13 and 21. Based on current trends, that means that an average of two young people are infected with HIV every hour of every day.

While the number of cases of AIDS among teenagers is relatively low, it has grown rapidly from one case in 1981 to 417 cases in 1994. The rate of HIV infection among teenagers becomes more apparent when you examine the number of AIDS cases among people in their 20s. According to the Centers for Disease Control and Prevention (CDC), one in five AIDS cases in the U.S. is diagnosed in the 20–29 year age group. Looking at AIDS cases alone obscures the extent of the epidemic among young people. Since a majority of AIDS cases are likely to have resulted from HIV infections acquired 10 years before, most of these individuals are likely to have been infected as teenagers.

Among adolescents (13–19 years of age), HIV infection is more prevalent among those in their late teens, males, and racial and ethnic minorities. But recent trends also point to a rise in infection and diagnosis among adolescent females—increasing from 14 percent of diagnosed cases of AIDS among adolescents in 1987 to 43 percent in 1994.

What is also clear is that American adolescents are engaging in behaviors that put them at risk for acquiring HIV infection as well as other sexually transmitted diseases, unintended pregnancy, and infections associated with drug injection. According to the CDC, approximately three-quarters of high school students have had sexual intercourse by the time they complete the twelfth grade. About 50 percent of sexually active high school seniors report consistent use of latex condoms and surveys indicate that condom use declines with age. In a recent survey, one in 62 high school students reported having injected an illegal drug. Recent reports indicate an increase in the use of noninjectable drugs, including marijuana, cocaine, and alcohol. The use of alcohol and other drugs impairs judgment and can lead to risky sexual behaviors and practices, particularly for young people in the stage of experimentation.

Also according to the CDC, about 12 million cases of sexually transmitted diseases (STDs) are reported in the U.S. each year. Roughly two-thirds of those cases are reported in individuals under the age of 25 and one-quarter are among teenagers. About 3 million teens contract an STD each year, and many of these young people will suffer long-term health consequences as a result.

Without forceful and focused action, these already troubling trends may worsen. This is a particularly complex challenge. Adolescents are neither large children nor small adults, yet they often are treated as one or the other and their unique characteristics and needs are often overlooked. Adolescents are in a developmental stage that can make them particularly vulnerable—both physiologically and emotionally—to activities that put them at risk of becoming infected with HIV.

Young people are at greatest risk of HIV infection if they have unprotected sex outside of a mutually monogamous relationship between two HIV-negative individuals, use injection drugs, or use alcohol or other drugs that impair their decision-making abilities. Adolescents often do not have the maturity, experience, or range of options that adults usually bring to their decision-making processes. Adolescents are engaged in a developmental process that includes development of decision-making skills, sexual maturation and experimentation, emotional and cognitive changes, and the molding of identity and self-worth.

Adolescents live in a world in which their families, cultural institutions, religious institutions, media, and peers compete to instill values, dictate actions, and impart positive and negative messages to them. The mass media often glamorize youth and sex at the same time that parents and schools are encouraging abstinence. Attempts to turn young people into sex symbols are particularly troublesome because of the message that sends to both young people and adults.

Adolescents, particularly those in their early teens, tend to be short-term thinkers. To many, the present is all important and the future often is perceived in very vague terms. Some adolescents, then, feel invulnerable to harm and often make decisions based on immediate desires rather than after consideration of the long-term consequences of their decisions.

Many young people have an enhanced sense of invincibility and may be unprepared to respond to situations that place them at risk. They may not perceive a need to avoid the risk or be aware that certain behaviors can place them at risk for contracting HIV. At the same time, many young people experience stigmatization and discrimination because of their race, ethnicity, gender, sexual orientation, HIV status, or economic status. Such discrimination hampers their ability to navigate successfully the many challenges and complex situations that they confront.

Set against this backdrop is the fact that young Americans are beginning the physiological and emotional process of puberty earlier in their lives than did previous generations. Yet they are also postponing many traditional adult responsibilities including full-time employment, marriage, or a committed monogamous relationship.

All young people need thoughtful guidance and loving care. The role of parents has never been more important in the successful development of adolescents. But it is a job that has also become much tougher. Parents, too, need assistance in learning how to best communicate with their children about the often difficult subjects of sex, drug use, and death. Many adolescents do not have adults in their lives who can

(Continued)

Exhibit 17-1 (*Continued*)

effectively provide the nurturing and guidance that they need.

Some young people are at particular risk of HIV infection due to circumstances that are often beyond their control. Adolescents who are victims of sexual abuse are at risk for direct transmission from their sexual partners and may also suffer emotional problems that lead them to later engage in high-risk behavior that can lead to HIV infection.

There are also those youth who have left or been kicked out of their homes or who have fled abusive family relationships. They are highly susceptible to risky behavior just to survive. Their sense of self-worth is usually low or nonexistent. They may trade sex for food, housing, drugs, and affection. Adolescents challenged with homelessness rarely view reducing their risk factors for HIV as a high priority in comparison with their daily struggle for survival.

Gay, lesbian, and bisexual youth often are isolated from positive adult role models and peers. Personal, institutional, and societal homophobia can often deny them access to opportunities to address their developing sexuality and contribute to a feeling of worthlessness.

Adolescents need the tools to successfully navigate an increasingly dangerous world. Young people need to hear from parents and other adults that they are loved, valued, and have worth as individuals so they will internalize those feelings and believe they are worth protecting. They must be shown the dangers they may encounter and taught negotiation and decision-making skills. They need to be engaged in activities that will allow them and their peers to practice those skills. And they need to exert personal responsibility to protect both themselves and others from infection.

Adolescent HIV prevention is a job too big for any one segment of society. All parents, adults, leaders, policy-makers, young people, and institutions must become constructively engaged in the important work of preventing HIV infection among our nation's most precious resource.

Source: Reprinted from the Office of National AIDS Policy, *Youth & HIV/AIDS: An American Agenda,* March 1996, pp. 1–3.

---

dren under 15 years of age was among Black children, followed by Hispanic Children and White children (see Figure 17-5). It is estimated that over one-half of the children under 15 diagnosed with pediatric AIDS have died.

Effects of pediatric AIDS on children and their families. Pediatric AIDS can have catastrophic effects on children and their families. Children infected with HIV and their families must deal with the *stigma* attached to the disease, the isolation that occurs once others learn that a family member has the disease, and the limited and fragmented support and services on which the children's survival depends (Boland, Czarniecki, & Haiken, 1992). Because of the fear that their child will be stigmatized, some parents keep the HIV infection a secret from others and from the child as well. They may isolate the child from their extended family, community, and friends (Baker, 1992).

"We keep [our son's] illness a secret as much as possible," said one mother. "We are terribly worried that if his taboo illness becomes generally known our other son will be viewed as a pariah. We have 'vanished' from the eyes of many friends and from much of society. Our life is far more solitary than it was before this awful period of time began." (pp. 152–153)

Parents may keep the diagnosis secret from the child and from other children in the family because they fear that the infected child cannot handle knowing about his or her condition or that the child and other children in the family will reveal the secret. They may wish to protect the child "from painful realities and to preserve and maintain happy childhood experiences for as long as possible" (Tasker, 1992, p. 11). If you are in a situation where the family wants to keep HIV secret, you should respect the family's need to maintain confidentiality. However, parents who fail to be open with their child may leave many unanswered questions in the child's mind. The child may become anxious because of ambiguity.

Sometimes parents may reconsider the issue of not disclosing the diagnosis to the child (Tasker, 1992).

For years I have felt that I could not tell Keesha the diagnosis. Certainly I have a lot of anxiety when I think about answering her questions about death. But in the past I used to think that I would only have Keesha for a few short years. Now I have gone five years over what I thought would be the limit for her life. She is still doing so well. Maybe I will go ten years over the limit with her. I have started to think about her becoming a teenager, and to imagine her going out on dates. What if she became sexually active? No matter what you may feel about it, teenagers sometimes make their own decisions. I cannot be behind her all the time, checking up on her, cautioning her. When she is older she will have to have more freedom, and naturally that means she will have to know her diagnosis. If she did not know it, how would she make responsible and informed decisions? (p. 20)

Children and their families may have initial feelings of shock, hopelessness, anger, shame, and sadness because of the currently inevitable fatal outcome of the disease and the demands on them to adjust to the illness. They may be uncertain about the prognosis, the course of the illness, and the effects of the medications and other treatments. They may be worried about the risk of infection to others and the cost and availability of medicines. They may be depressed because they feel helpless to change their circumstances, guilty about past behavior, and angry about the reduced quality of their lives. Because of their depression, they may

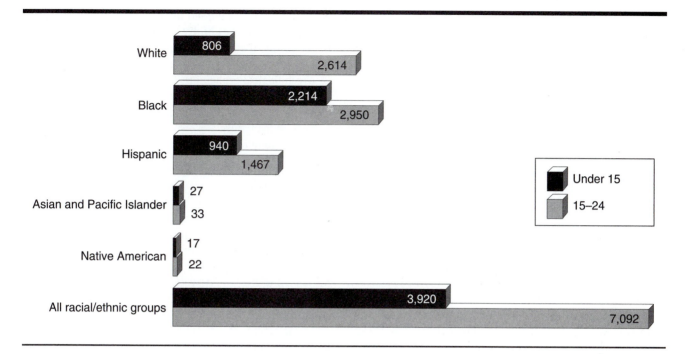

Figure 17-5. Deaths of children, adolescents, and young adults from AIDS by race/ethnicity and age at death, from 1981 through 1995 in the United States. From Centers for Disease Control and Prevention, *HIV/AIDS Surveillance Report,* 1995, *7*(2), p. 20.

want to give up, to stop seeking treatment, or to think of suicide. They may wish to keep the disease a secret from others. However, not all children and families give up; instead, some continue to search for cures and seek new drugs or special diets.

Let's now look at some comments made by children infected with the HIV virus. A 6-year-old dictated the following letter to her school superintendent about her personal struggles (Wiener, Fair, & Granowsky, 1993).

Hi, my name is Tanya. I have AIDS and everyone is different than I am. It feels terrible to have AIDS because my tummy hurts a lot and because, if my friends find out, they wouldn't want to play with me. When I told the kids at school I had AIDS they made fun of me. I told them by accident. Now I want to run away from school. I wish I were not an AIDS patient. I wish I did not have to take medicine.

When you have AIDS you feel bad a lot, even when you don't have a high fever. I am different from everyone. AIDS patients hurt a lot. It is going to take a long time to get rid of [my] AIDS and by the time I do I will be too old to live a long while. I'll only live a little while. In the meantime, my friends only understand I have a catheter. They don't understand my AIDS. I wish they would be my friends forever. But now I am learning to live with my AIDS. If you have AIDS, be proud of who you are. We have to stick together. (p. 112)

A school-aged child said the following about telling others about his having AIDS (Wiener et al., 1993).

Sometimes I want to tell people about my virus, but then I think about the pros and cons. Some pros that I think about are that I wouldn't have to hide anything or lie anymore. I feel bad about

lying, but then again, I can't tell anyone. I like coming to NIH [National Institutes of Health] because I can say it without having to worry about the way that people take it.

But then there's always the cons. People could just forget about the facts and just get away from me. They could tell their parents, but then the parents would maybe want to get me out of the school, but from my point of view, they have nothing to worry about. Another con could be that the people that I tell and that I trust to keep it a secret could tell someone else and then they would tell everyone else so then everyone would get away from me. Even if I tell them and they know the facts, they just wouldn't understand. Then there are always the people who won't believe me or the facts. It just doesn't feel fair. (pp. 112–113)

A 10-year-old boy wrote the following letter about wanting to feel normal and be treated in the same way as his peers (Wiener et al., 1993).

Sometimes you feel sad and you wish your brother and your sister had it. You don't think it is fair that you've got something they don't.

You think, "Why do I have to have it?" but, I, Tim, have it. I wish there was a cure for us that have HIV because we would be well again. I wouldn't have the trouble of carrying this medicine that is going to my heart. Don't you wish that too?

Some people treat you like you can't do this or you can't do that and ALL I want is to do things anybody else can do. Like climb monkey bars or big toys. I want to be normal. Don't you? (p. 113)

Children vary in how they respond to stress and anxiety. Successful coping strategies include dealing with the reality of infection and possible terminal illness, seeking out a health care provider, following up on a prescribed medical regimen, keeping medical appointments, and keeping lines of communication open with the family (Hunter & Schaecher, 1992; also see Chapter 15 on coping).

Despite the legitimate reasons to keep the diagnosis a closely guarded secret, many parents yearn to leave the world of concealment and lies, a world often in conflict with their own moral values. They look forward to a time when they will be free of the tremendously painful existence of living in the shadows with AIDS.

—Mary Tasker

Interviewing Issues

Because the unique epidemiology of pediatric AIDS presents assessment challenges, it is vital to use a multidisciplinary approach to evaluate medical, social, and developmental areas in each case (Cohen & Diamond, 1992). "All staff members who work with HIV-positive patients must be provided with basic knowledge about AIDS, routine medical safety procedures, issues of death and dying, and community resources" (Rotheram-Borus & Koopman, 1992, p. 50). Mental health clinicians will need to coordinate their assessment with other health care providers and agencies to obtain a thorough and comprehensive evaluation of the HIV child and his or her family. An open, frank interview that allows the family members to address their fears and concerns may enhance their ability to cope with the child's disease.

Be especially alert to symptoms that suggest the beginning stages of central nervous system involvement (Bor & Miller, 1989; also see Chapter 19). These include forgetfulness, such as forgetting names and homework assignments and missing appointments; difficulty in locating your office, especially when the child had been there previously; reduced insight; feelings of depression; loss of motor functions, often evidenced by falling; and seizures. Note any changes in the child, particularly changes in his or her behavior, language, insight, and affect.

A thorough assessment of the child with pediatric AIDS and his or her family will be similar to that conducted with other medically ill children, with some changes in focus. The assessment might include the following:

1. Obtaining the child's medical history and current health status, including how the child was infected with the HIV virus, history of other infections, neurological status, nutritional status, cardiopulmonary status, alcohol and drug use, and sexual practices
2. Obtaining the child's developmental history
3. Obtaining a social-psychological history of the family
4. Obtaining a medical history of the family members and their current health status, where relevant, including history of drug use, blood transfusions, sexual practices, and AIDS/HIV status

5. Observing the child and family to see how they interact and observing the child's self-help skills
6. Assessing the child's cognitive, personality, affective, and motor functioning by referring the child for a neuropsychological evaluation
7. Determining parental concerns and goals, including the social, emotional, and financial impact of the child's illness on the family
8. Formulating intervention strategies

Table F-27 in Appendix F presents a semistructured interview that is useful for interviewing HIV-positive children. Answers to the questions in Table 17-1 and Table 17-2, presented earlier in the chapter, will help you evaluate the information you obtain from children who are HIV positive and from their parents, respectively.

The following dialogue illustrates how one interviewer responded to the interviewee's feelings about having AIDS (Bor, Miller, & Goldman, 1993, pp. 45–46, with changes in notation):

IE: I can't believe I have AIDS. It's the end. (Interviewee sobs.)
IR: What is the hardest for you to believe right now?
IE: (Continues to sob loudly)
IR: (Pauses, passes interviewee a box of tissues) What would help you the most right now?
IE: Nothing. Though I wish I could think straight.
IR: Let's talk about the things that are in your mind.
IE: I'll be all right in a minute…(pause)…this is the day I've feared the most. Actually things look a bit clearer now. How is AIDS different to having HIV?…
IR: You said that AIDS means "the end." What would that mean to you?
IE: It's hard to talk about.
IR: Perhaps you could try.
IE: Well, what will it be like being dead? I often wonder.
IR: What do you wonder about?
IE: Whether it's the real end, or just the end of my time on earth.
IR: What would you do differently if it were possible to know whether it was?
IE: (Smiles)

After the assessment, you will need to consider such questions as the following:

1. What are the family's beliefs, attitudes, and expectations about the illness?
2. What family members are aware of the diagnosis?
3. What are the reactions of neighbors, relatives, and friends to the diagnosis?
4. What services does the family need?
5. How is the child coping with the illness?
6. How is the family coping with the illness?

Mental health professionals who work with children who have pediatric AIDS may experience considerable stress, including anxiety, depression, and fear of infection. Maintaining professional reserve is not easy for practitioners who see children die and then must work with their bereaved families. It is extremely difficult to grieve oneself and also help others who are grieving. Some of these issues are covered in Chapter 6 (under stress and burnout) and Chapter 13 (under working with bereaved children and their families). You will have to work through any fears that you might have of contracting AIDS in order to work with children with pediatric AIDS.

Working with children with pediatric AIDS may bring you in contact with families that, because of their child's condition, are experiencing financial hardship, have been targets of violence, or have been discriminated against. In addition, children with pediatric AIDS may face painful medical treatments, hospitalizations, aversive effects of medications, and disruptions in routine because of medical appointments (Armstrong, Seidel, & Swales, 1993). Because of the stigma associated with AIDS, children and their families may be reluctant to talk to you. Also, they may know more about the illness than they think you know, and they may not have confidence in talking to you. Consequently, you will need to show them that you can be trusted and are knowledgeable and that you will listen carefully to them. If society is to cope effectively with the AIDS epidemic, assessment and intervention must go hand in hand.

Interventions

The goals of intervention in cases of HIV infection and pediatric AIDS include the following (Wiener et al., 1992):

1. Ensuring that children and families have access to all needed medical, social, and legal services (see Table 17-11)
2. Helping children with an HIV infection cope with the infection by developing a sense of control, enhancing self-esteem, and finding meaning in life

3. Helping families integrate the various services that they need
4. Helping families obtain adequate financial assistance, housing, psychotherapy, and help with substance abuse (if present)
5. Being an advocate for and a liaison between families and the other services
6. Helping families develop adequate coping skills to deal with any feelings of fear, mistrust, stigma, shame, anger, and hopelessness
7. Helping the children understand how HIV infections can be spread and how to prevent the infections from spreading

To carry out these goals, you will need to provide an inviting, humane, and nonbureaucratic atmosphere if you want children and adolescents to take part in a treatment program (Rotheram-Borus & Koopman, 1992).

To prevent the transmission of HIV infections, individuals should

- avoid using intravenous drugs
- avoid sharing needles if drug abstinence is not possible
- consider carefully whether to engage in sexual intercourse
- practice safe sex by using condoms and spermicides if they engage in sexual intercourse
- avoid high-risk sexual partners by selecting partners carefully
- take blood tests as needed
- openly communicate their sexual history with their current sexual partner
- clean and disinfect all surfaces on which blood or other body fluids have been spilled (a 10% bleach solution is recommended)
- (for women of child-bearing age who are HIV positive) carefully consider the risks of having an HIV-infected infant and, if they give birth to a baby, consider not breast-feeding the baby

---

Table 17-11
Components of a Model Medical and Psychosocial Services Program for AIDS/HIV

Services offered	Participating disciplines	Consulting disciplines	Liaisons
HIV antibody testing and counseling	Infectious disease	Neurology	Chemical dependence
Primary medical care	Clinical psychology	Pulmonary medicine	Home-based case management
Psychological services	Oncology	Psychiatry	Hospice
Social services	Nursing	Dermatology	Inpatient units
Dental services or referral	Phlebotomy (technicians who draw blood)	Hematology	Hemophilia program
Legal services or referral	Laboratory technology	Pharmacy	Health departments
	Social work	Obstetrics/gynecology	Community agencies
	Dentistry	Pediatrics	Community action groups
	Law		

Source: Reprinted, with changes in notation, from K. Sheridan, "Psychosocial Services for Persons with Human Immunodeficiency Virus Disease," in J. J. Sweet, R. H. Rozensky, and S. M. Tovian (Eds.), *Handbook of Clinical Psychology in Medical Settings,* p. 590, copyright 1991 by Plenum Press.

An effective health policy for dealing with the AIDS/HIV epidemic should focus on "(a) protecting people from discrimination; (b) designing testing and screening programs; (c) developing safe and effective antiviral drugs; (d) planning for future vaccine trials; (e) organizing and delivering health care to sufferers of HIV infection; and (f) financing such health care" (Weiss & Hardy, 1990, p. 70).

I was infected with HIV by my first partner when I was 16 years old. Now at 20 I have this virus that's taking my life because everything I heard when I was younger was sugar coated. We need more complete information than what we are being given. Even the pamphlets concerning HIV/AIDS prevention are too basic and bland. We need to know real stuff.

—Ryan

Case Illustrations

Following are two cases illustrating various facets of HIV transmission and AIDS. The first case describes symptoms associated with pediatric AIDS in a young child (Cohen & Diamond, 1992).

CASE 17-6. N.P.

N.P. is a 2-year, 8-month-old Black female child with congenital HIV infection. Her medical history is sketchy. Her mother was an intravenous drug user who gave birth to N.P. at home. N.P. has been in foster care in the home of Ms. S. for the past 8 months. Reportedly, the child had been diagnosed as HIV positive at 5 months of age at another medical center, and follow-up studies confirmed the diagnosis of an HIV infection. No treatment was offered until 2 months before the current visit, when AZT treatment was initiated. AZT appears to have improved N.P.'s general health status and possibly her developmental status as well.

At the time that N.P. came into the S. home she weighed 16 pounds (below the 5th percentile for her age), was not walking independently, and was not speaking any intelligible words. She had previously been in another, reportedly unsatisfactory, foster home.

Since coming into the S. home, her primary developmental advances have been in the area of gross motor skills. She has made little progress in the acquisition of speech and language and can say only "Mommy, ice cream." She can identify parts of her face, such as her eyes, mouth, and nose. Ms. S. noted that because of N.P.'s exposure to abnormal feeding behaviors of another foster child (who also had HIV infection) in the home, she has regressed and occasionally insists on being fed blenderized food, though she can chew and swallow solid food.

Ms. S. notes that N.P. exhibits a pattern of bizarre behaviors. These behaviors often remind Ms. S. of psychiatric patients with whom she once worked as a nurse. She notes that N.P. tends to bite her nails incessantly and pull her hair out. N.P. engages in some ritualistic behavior and tends fre-

quently to stare out into space, which Ms. S. calls "being in limbo." She finds her to be distractible and difficult to focus in play and self-care activities.

In terms of her current adaptive functioning, N.P. can finger feed herself and walk independently, although with great instability. She is unable to walk up or down stairs, has limited self-care skills, and displays no imitative behavior. She often has temper tantrums.

The physical examination revealed an unsteady gait and toe-walking while running. Height, weight, and head circumference were below average. Her spleen was enlarged and there was reduced muscle mass and muscle strength. There was no tremor or sensory abnormalities, and cranial nerves were intact.

Developmental testing showed her fine motor skills were at the 19-month-old level. She could insert pegs into a pegboard slowly and laboriously and place several round and square puzzle pieces into their designated spaces. She appeared to have impaired eye-hand coordination and an immature palmar-type grasp, was easily distracted, and demonstrated motoric slowing in execution of fine motor tasks. Her language functioning is at the 15-month-old level. She could gesture to make her wants known and pointed to shoes, clothing, and parts of her face. However, she was unable to name any simple requested objects.

Socially, she related poorly, with little interest in her environment. She responded to approbation and occasionally established eye contact and sought consolation from Ms. S. She made little attempt to engage in meaningful social interaction.

N.P.'s neurodevelopmental picture appears consistent with mild to moderate mental retardation. She also displays emotional lability and self-stimulatory and repetitive behaviors, such as nail biting and hair pulling. Her poor relatedness suggests a form of pervasive developmental disorder, which should be periodically followed by observation on repeated evaluations. Abnormal tone in her lower extremities, toe-walking, and unsteady wide-based gait might indicate a possible mild diplegia [paralysis of a similar part on two sides of the body]. (pp. 53–54, with changes in notation)

The second case illustrates how an adolescent dealt with the diagnosis of HIV and the effects of AIDS (Hunter & Schaecher, 1992).

CASE 17-7. JOHN

John is a 17-year-old White male from a divorced family. He lived with his father until removed by family court because of physical abuse from his father. He was placed with a foster family at the age of 11 and stayed with them for 5 years.

At age 16 he went to live with his mother, who was a recovering alcoholic at that time. As he became more aware of his homosexual orientation, he felt alone and isolated as a gay person. He was referred to a gay-identified agency with the recommendation that he join an after-school socialization program for gay adolescent males. Up to this point John's efforts to connect with other gay people took place solely through sexual contacts in public places. At the initial assessment interview he expressed a desire to meet a person his own age with whom he could develop a relationship. His mother did not yet know that her son was gay; however, he eventually told her, and she accepted him with much ambivalence.

When family problems developed, John dropped out of his school and was not seen by the agency for a year. Within that year he became HIV positive and returned to the agency for support services. Initially, he denied the seriousness of his infection by avoiding clinic appointments; however, he was already beginning to lose weight. John stated to his counselor that he was "putting his sexuality on hold." When he had sex, he claimed to have safe sex, but he was not informing his sex partners about his health status. The agency was obtaining Medicaid and public assistance for John. The application for benefits was withdrawn by his mother, who wished to keep her address secret. At this point John decided he wanted to get a summer job. However, he began to develop more symptoms, and he was referred to a hospital's adolescent HIV center. He became involved with the hospital program (including a teen theater group), and he also entered an alternative high school program. As school was beginning, he left home because of family problems and got an apartment with a friend. But this arrangement was short lived. His roommate left and he had to support the apartment by himself. He began to come down with other infections and was put on AZT. John had a bad reaction to AZT that finally caused him to confront his fear of illness and death. His defenses were down, and he spoke about being afraid of losing everything he had worked so hard to obtain, and about the sense of helplessness that ensued. When AZT was discontinued, he rebounded and returned to school, work, and the theater group. (pp. 40–41, with changes in notation)

Exercise 17-1. AIDS Risk Behavior Knowledge Test

Read each statement, decide whether it is true or false, and then check your answers with those shown at the end of the exercise. You also can compare your answers with those of a sample of 691 respondents (360 undergraduate students and 331 gay men) who also took the test. The third column ("Norm") in the Correct Answers section shows the proportion of the 691 respondents who answered each statement correctly. The AIDS Risk Behavior Knowledge Test (with adaptations) and norms are from Kelly, St. Lawrence, Hood, and Brasfield (1989).

1. Most people who transmit the AIDS virus look unhealthy.
2. Anal intercourse is high risk for transmitting the AIDS virus.
3. Oral intercourse carries risk for AIDS virus transmission.
4. A person can be exposed to the AIDS virus in one sexual contact.
5. Keeping in good physical condition is the best way to prevent exposure to the AIDS virus.
6. It is unwise to touch a person with AIDS.
7. Condoms make intercourse completely safe.
8. Showering after sex greatly reduces the transmission of AIDS.
9. When people become sexually exclusive with one another, they no longer need to follow "safe sex" guidelines.
10. Oral sex is safe if the partners "don't swallow."
11. Most people who have been exposed to the AIDS virus quickly show symptoms of serious illness.
12. By reducing the number of different sexual partners, you are effectively protected from AIDS.
13. The AIDS virus does not penetrate unbroken skin.
14. Female-to-male transmission of the AIDS virus has not been documented.
15. Sharing toothbrushes and razors can transmit the AIDS virus.
16. Pre-ejaculatory fluids carry the AIDS virus.
17. Intravenous drug users are at risk for AIDS when they share needles.
18. A person must have many different sexual partners to be at risk from AIDS.
19. People carrying the AIDS virus generally feel quite ill.
20. Vaginal intercourse carries high risk for AIDS virus transmission.
21. Withdrawal immediately before orgasm makes intercourse safe.
22. Persons who are exclusively heterosexual are not at risk from AIDS.
23. Healthy persons in AIDS risk groups should not donate blood.
24. Sharing kitchen utensils or a bathroom with a person with AIDS poses no risk.
25. Intravenous drug users become exposed to the AIDS virus because the virus is often contained in heroin, amphetamines, and the injected drugs.
26. A wholesome diet and plenty of sleep will keep a person from becoming exposed to the AIDS virus.
27. A cure of AIDS is expected within two years after 1997.
28. It is more important to take precautions against AIDS in large cities than in small cities.
29. A negative result on the AIDS virus antibody test can occur even for people who carry the virus.
30. A positive result on the AIDS virus antibody test can occur even for people who do not carry the virus.
31. Coughing does not spread AIDS.
32. Only receptive (passive) anal intercourse transmits AIDS.
33. Most present cases of AIDS are due to blood transfusions that took place before 1984.
34. Most persons exposed to the AIDS virus know they are exposed.
35. A great deal is now known about how the AIDS virus is transmitted.
36. Donating blood carries no AIDS risk for the donor.
37. No cases of AIDS have ever been linked to social (dry) kissing as of 1996.
38. Mutual masturbation and body rubbing are low in risk unless the partners have cuts or scratches.
39. People who become exposed to the AIDS virus through needle-sharing can transmit the virus to others during sexual activities.
40. The AIDS virus can be transmitted by mosquitoes or cockroaches.

Correct Answers and Proportion of Sample Responding Correctly to Statement

	Ans.[a]	Norm[b]		Ans.[a]	Norm[b]
1.	F	.90	21.	F	.88
2.	T	.94	22.	F	.97
3.	T	.88	23.	T	.73
4.	T	.95	24.	T	.65
5.	F	.89	25.	F	.80
6.	F	.91	26.	F	.97
7.	F	.88	27.	F	.87
8.	F	.92	28.	F	.80
9.	F	.91	29.	T	.80
10.	F	.90	30.	T	.62
11.	F	.92	31.	T	.88
12.	F	.80	32.	F	.85
13.	T	.59	33.	F	.68
14.	F	.91	34.	F	.89
15.	T	.58	35.	T	.68
16.	T	.87	36.	T	.67
17.	T	.99	37.	T	.89
18.	F	.91	38.	T	.88
19.	F	.76	39.	T	.96
20.	T	.76	40.	F	.76

[a]T = True, F = False.
[b]Proportion of sample who responded correctly to statement.

In pediatric HIV infection, we are all students and we are all teachers—even, and maybe especially, the children.

—Lynn S. Baker

PEDIATRIC HEADACHES

Description

Headaches have functional or organic causes. To determine whether the cause is organic, a thorough medical evaluation of the child should be performed before or concurrent with the clinical assessment interview and *before* any psychological interventions take place. Headache symptoms may be associated with "infections, head traumas, intracranial pressure, toxic conditions, meningitis, and encephalitis" (Williamson, Baker, & Cubic, 1992, p. 280). Infrequent headaches are usually related to acute causes such as fatigue, fever, or alcohol ingestion. Most headaches are functional, involving psychogenic or psychophysiologic factors rather than permanent structural changes in the brain or serious illness.

The most frequent types of headaches in children are *migraine headaches* and *tension headaches* (Williamson, Head, & Baker, 1993). Migraine headaches are recurrent vascular headaches that are commonly preceded by sensory, motor, or mood disturbances. They are more severe and debilitating than tension headaches. About 5% of children are diagnosed with migraine headaches. The primary symp-

toms of migraine headaches in children are unilateral pain (pain that affects only side of the body) and nausea or vomiting. The pain is described as throbbing or pulsating and is relieved by rest. Some children with migraine headaches report warning signs (or prodromal symptoms) that precede the headache, such as "blind spots or flashing lights in the visual field and numbness in the face, lips, and extremities" (Williamson et al., 1993, p. 196). Children with migraine headaches often have a family history of migraine headaches, usually in parents or close relatives.

Tension headaches usually result from sustained tension in the skeletal muscles. "Tension headaches are generally described as a tightness in the forehead, neck, or entire head. The pain is usually constant (i.e., it does not throb, and is episodic, usually lasting only a few hours)" (Williamson et al., 1993, p. 196). Tension headaches are much more common than migraine headaches, accounting for approximately 80% of all headaches in children (Williamson et al., 1992).

Stressors that may precipitate a migraine or tension headache in children may be either environmental/physical or psychological/emotional (Kowal & Pritchard, 1990). "The environmental and physical stressors include: changes in the weather or specific seasons, allergies, vacations or changes in routines, particular foods containing tyramine, hypoglycemia, physical exertion or severe exercise, bright and flashing lights, noise, eyestrain, illness and head trauma.... Psychological stressors...include school problems, family problems and conflicts, sibling competition and family expectations.... Emotional factors [include] anxiety, disappointment, fear of failure and hostile feelings" (p. 639). Headaches commonly increase in number and severity with age. Females tend to have more frequent, more severe, and longer-lasting headaches than males (Williamson et al., 1992).

Interviewing Issues

The interview with a child referred for headaches should cover the following areas (Masek & Hoag, 1990; Williamson et al., 1992):

- description and location of the headache pain
- time of onset of the headaches
- duration of the headaches
- severity of the headaches
- other associated symptoms such as pallor, nausea, vomiting, abdominal pain, *photophobia* (abnormal visual intolerance of light), *sonophobia* (abnormal auditory intolerance of sound), muscle weakness, and speech difficulty
- precipitants, such as sleep deprivation, long intervals between meals, anticipation of an event, emotional factors (such as fear of failing a test), anxiety about social situations, changes in sleeping and eating habits, weather changes, and allergic reactions
- medical and surgical history
- family history of headaches

- success of past treatments, including medications used
- use of drugs such as marijuana, acid, and so forth (see Table 18-4 in Chapter 18)
- consequences of headaches, such as missing school, increased parental attention, missing activities, reduction of responsibilities, and getting special activities

Table F-10 in Appendix F presents a semistructured interview designed to help you learn about children's headaches. As part of the assessment, you may want to have the children (and parents) complete a headache diary and return it when they come back for their next appointment (see Table 17-12). You can ask the children to record when the headache occurred, its duration and intensity, medications used to relieve pain, and activities before and after the onset of the headache (Williamson et al., 1992).

Interventions

In designing an intervention program for children with headaches, consider the following statement: "Regardless of its etiology, effective management of recurrent or chronic pain in [children] involves a balance of cognitive, behavioral and pharmacological interventions" (Smith, Tyler, Womack, & Chen, 1989, p. 85). Many techniques described earlier in the chapter for the management of pain also apply to the management of headaches.

The most successful behavioral treatments for headache include biofeedback and relaxation procedures (Williamson et al., 1993). One type of biofeedback used for tension headaches is *electromyographic (EMG) feedback*. This procedure uses "an electronic amplifier that measures muscle contractions and provides visual or auditory feedback concerning increases or decreases in muscle tension. The patient is taught to relax his or her muscles and [shown] that this leads to improvement in headache pain" (Williamson et al., 1993, p. 197).

Another type of biofeedback procedure, *skin temperature biofeedback,* is frequently used with patients who have migraine headaches. "Skin temperature biofeedback involves the use of a *temperature thermistor* [an electrical resistor made of material whose resistance varies sharply with the temperature] and amplifier to measure small changes in skin temperature, usually of a finger. The patient is taught to warm his or her hands while receiving visual or auditory feedback showing skin temperature changes. Hand warming has generally been associated with a lowered arousal or relaxation state" (Williamson et al., 1993, p. 198).

Several relaxation techniques may be used. In the *progressive relaxation technique,* the patient systematically tenses and relaxes all muscle groups while breathing slowly and deeply. Other examples of relaxation techniques are deep-muscle relaxation training, relaxation through suggestions of heaviness and warmth, and a westernized version of transcendental meditation. Relaxation techniques can be learned by listening to audio tapes.

Table 17-12
Sample Headache Record

HEADACHE RECORD

Name: _____

Day of week	Date	Time	Intensity* (circle one)	Medicines taken (type & amount)	Classes or activities missed	What happened before?	What happened after?
		Start: ___ Stop: ___	Mild Moderate Severe Very Severe				
		Start: ___ Stop: ___	Mild Moderate Severe Very Severe				

*Intensity: Mild = You know the headache is there, but it doesn't bother you much. Severe = The headache bothers you a lot, and you can't do very much.
Moderate = The headache does bother you, but you can still do things. Very Severe = You can't do anything but rest.

Note. This table has space for recording two days. To make space for recording seven days, construct additional rows and use both sides of the paper.
Source: Reprinted, with changes in notation, with permission of Masek and Hoag (1990).

Case Illustration

The following case describes an intervention program for the management of pediatric headaches (Smith et al., 1989).

CASE 17-8. FRAN

Fran, who is a 12-year-old girl, gave a 6-month history of three headaches per week, described as bifrontal, steady, "squeezing," and unassociated with an aura, nausea, or vomiting. The headaches were progressively more intense during the day and often peaked in the late afternoon at 7 out of 10 on the pain intensity scale. Aspirin, acetaminophen, and brief rest brought only partial relief, and headaches occasionally persisted from one day into the next. There was no family history of recurrent headache and no obvious psychosocial stressors in her family or peer relationships. Although she had been an above-average student in elementary school, she was experiencing academic difficulty in several courses in seventh grade. Past medical history, review of systems, complete physical examination, and sinus X-ray films were normal. A review of school records indicated that she had been adequately assessed and found to be of average intelligence without evidence of a learning disability. Tutorial assistance for selected classes and close observation of her academic performance were recommended. In addition, she was taught a 20-minute behavioral technique for headache control using progressive muscular relaxation and mental imagery (self-hypnosis). After sequentially tensing and relaxing muscle groups from her toes to the top of her head, she chose to imagine herself lying on a beach enjoying the warmth of the sunshine with no other obligations. After practicing the relaxation-mental imagery techniques twice daily for 4 weeks, her headache activity abated markedly. Six weeks after the beginning of self-control techniques, she experienced only an occasional headache rated 3 out of 10 on the pain intensity scale. At a 6-month follow-up visit, she was asymptomatic. (pp. 85–86, with changes in notation)

FAILURE TO THRIVE

Description

Failure to thrive (FTT) is a descriptive term, rather than a diagnostic classification, for several disorders that result in poor growth or a significant deceleration in rate of weight gain (Black & Dubowitz, 1991; Drotar & Sturm, 1994). Children with failure to thrive usually weigh below the 5th percentile for their age; it is a disorder of young childhood. Failure to thrive is a potentially life-threatening problem. It is estimated that approximately 5% of infants admitted to pediatric hospitals receive a failure-to-thrive diagnosis (Domek, 1994).

Failure to thrive may be associated with organic causes, nonorganic causes, or a combination of the two (Kelley & Heffer, 1990).

• *Organic causes* include serious pediatric illnesses associated with neurological, gastrointestinal, endocrine, pulmonary, renal, or metabolic disorders. These disorders may result in reduced caloric intake.

• *Nonorganic causes* include situational variables (for example, poverty, stress, or isolation), behavioral deficits of the child or parents (for example, an irritable or passive infant or parental psychological disorders), and dysfunctional parent-child interactions (for example, parental abuse, neglect, or emotional deprivation of the child; parental difficulty in feeding the child; or parental ignorance about the dietary needs and developmental capabilities of infants). The presence of any of these factors also may result in reduced caloric intake. An infant may be so anxious because of a disturbed environment that he or she cannot feed properly, or a parent may put food before the infant and expect the infant to feed himself or herself when the infant is not developmentally ready to do so.

Although failure to thrive occurs among families of all socioeconomic classes, it is more likely to occur in poor families (Black & Dubowitz, 1991). You will need to consider physical, behavioral, and environmental factors as potential causes of failure to thrive.

Infants with nonorganic failure to thrive may show symptoms such as poor weight gain and growth, excessive crying and irritability, expressionless face, crying when approached by others, lack of cuddliness, poor eye contact, minimal response to stimulation, and indifference to separation (Powell & Low, 1983; Powell, Low, & Speers, 1987). These symptoms may directly affect communication and bonding between parents and infants. It is difficult to know whether problems within the family cause the children to have difficulty eating or whether the children's eating problems affect their interactions with others in the family (Denton, 1986). Most probably, the child's symptoms are exacerbated by the family's reactions to the child. Failure to thrive has long-term consequences that may lead to behavioral, academic, and social problems in children afflicted (Black & Dubowitz, 1991).

Children with nonorganic failure to thrive who are taken out of the home and cared for in a nurturing and stimulating environment usually begin to develop normally. This finding substantiates not only the nonorganic diagnosis but also the theory that the problem may lie in families' nurturing of the children (Denton, 1986).

Interviewing Issues

In addition to the questions contained in the standard parent interview (see Table F-36 in Appendix F), ask the parent (or caregiver) to (a) tell you about the child's eating problems, (b) complete a food intake record (see Table 18-9 in Chapter 18), and (c) tell you how he or she has handled the child's problems (Drotar & Sturm, 1994). Also observe parent-child interactions, particularly in feeding situations, and look at such factors as the parent's and child's responsiveness to each other, the parent's and child's affect, and the parent's sensitivity to the child (Drotar & Sturm, 1994). In evaluating the results of the interview and observations, consider the questions posed in Table 17-13.

Table 17-13
Evaluating the Interview with the Parent/Caregiver in Cases of Failure to Thrive

Problem Identification

1. Is the child suffering from a medical condition that can retard growth and, if so, what condition?
2. How severe are the child's medical and nutritional problems?
3. What are the child's psychological deficits, if any?
4. What are the family's resources?
5. What is the parent's/caregiver's understanding of the child's problems?
6. What is the parent's/caregiver's understanding of the child's development?

Background Information

7. Was the child planned, wanted, or unwanted?
8. Were there attempts to terminate the pregnancy or thoughts of doing so?
9. If so, what happened?
10. Who is the father of the child?
11. How were the mother and father getting along when the child was born?
12. Did the mother have physical or emotional problems after giving birth?
13. If so, what were the problems and how were they addressed?
14. What were the mother's feelings toward the baby during and after the birth?
15. What were the father's feelings toward the baby during and after the birth?
16. What are the mother's feelings about the child now?
17. What are the father's feelings about the child now?

Prenatal History

18. Did the mother receive prenatal care?
19. If so, where and how often?
20. Did the mother smoke, drink, or use any kind of drugs during pregnancy?
21. If yes, what did she do, and how much did she smoke, drink, or use drugs?
22. Did the mother have medical conditions that may have affected the pregnancy?
23. If so, what were the conditions?
24. Did the mother have physical or emotional problems during pregnancy?
25. If so, what were the problems and how were they addressed?

Birth History and Early Development

26. Where was the child born, such as at home or in the hospital?
27. Was the child full term or premature?
28. If premature, by how many weeks?
29. What were the child's weight and length at birth?
30. Were there any birth complications?
31. If so, what were they?

32. How long was the child in the hospital after she or he was born?
33. If longer than a few days, did the mother and father visit the child?
34. If so, how often? If not, why not?
35. Did the child have problems after birth?
36. If so, what were the problems and how were they addressed?

Social and Family History

37. Are other caregivers involved with the child besides the mother and the father?
38. If so, who are they and what is their involvement?
39. Are there other siblings?
40. If so, how old are they and what are their sexes?
41. Do the other siblings have medical problems?
42. If so, what are their problems?
43. Is there a support system for the family?
44. If so, who helps the family, what kind of help is offered, and how often is it given?
45. Who else has seen the child within the past few weeks?
46. If anyone has seen the child recently, when and where did he or she see the child, and did the person(s) comment on the child's physical condition?
47. Is the child covered by insurance or by another medical plan?
48. If so, what is the name of the plan?
49. Do any family members have chronic medical problems?
50. If so, who has the problems and what problems do they have?

Medical Follow-Up

51. Did the hospital make referrals for visiting nurses or other home care?
52. If so, why was the referral made and has the referral source visited the home? If not, why not?
53. Who is the child's medical health care provider?
54. Has the child been seen since discharge from the hospital?
55. If so, where, when, and for what purpose?
56. Has the child been hospitalized since discharge?
57. If so, where, when, and for what purpose?
58. When did the parent/caregiver notice a problem with the child's weight?
59. What did they do to resolve the problem?
60. Does the child have a developmental disorder?
61. If so, what is the disorder?
62. What treatment was recommended?
63. Has the family followed through?
64. If not, why not?

Feeding History

65. Did the child have difficulty eating, sucking, or swallowing in the hospital?

(Continued)

Table 17-13 (*Continued*)

66. If so, what were the problems?
67. Has the child had difficulty eating, sucking, or swallowing since discharge from the hospital?
68. If so, what are the problems?
69. Is the child breast- or bottle-fed?
70. If breast-fed, how long does the child suckle?
71. Is the child fed any supplemental formula?
72. If so, how many bottles does the child get each day?
73. Does the parent/caregiver follow the proper way to make the child's formula?
74. Have there been any changes in the child's formula (for example, change in formula due to lactose intolerance)?
75. If so, did the health care provider recommend the change or did the parent/caregiver act on his or her own?
76. Does the child eat or drink anything other than formula or breast milk (for example, whole milk, juices, cereals, solids, etc.)?
77. If so, how often does the child receive supplemental food, and how much does the child eat at a sitting?
78. Does the child have problems nursing, drinking, or eating (for example, spitting up, refusing to take food)?
79. When did the child last eat?
80. How much did the child eat then, and what did she or he eat?
81. Is the parent/caregiver knowledgeable about basic feeding practices and about infant nutritional needs?

Financial History
82. What is the family's income?

83. Are there problems with having enough money to buy food?
84. If yes, what are the problems?
85. Does the family get food stamps?
86. If so, what is the value of the food stamps?
87. Was the mother ever referred to WIC (Supplemental Program for Women, Infants, and Children)?
88. If so, when was she referred and did she go?
89. Is she in WIC now?
90. If not, why not?
91. Is there life insurance on the child?
92. If so, when was it taken out?
93. Has the family contacted the insurance company?
94. When?
95. What is the name of the insurance agent and company?

Home Visit
96. Is there evidence in the home of age-appropriate food for the child?
97. Is the food fresh and stored appropriately?
98. If there are pets, is there food for the pets?
99. If there are other children, is there food for the other children?
100. Is there any evidence that the parent/caregiver spent money on nonnecessities—such as alcohol, drugs, cigarettes, or cable television bills—instead of on food?
101. If there are other children, are they adequately nourished?
102. Is the child who is suffering from failure to thrive treated the same as or differently than the other children?

Source: Adapted from American Prosecutors Research Institute (undated), Drotar and Sturm (1994), and Greer (1995).

Interventions

Several interventions are needed in cases of failure to thrive. First and foremost, *the child's nutritional deficits should be attended to immediately.* Second, parents should be given help in understanding their child's condition. Third, parents should be enrolled in an intervention program designed "to help them stimulate and nurture their child more effectively" (Drotar & Sturm, 1994. p. 33). Finally, parents should be taught about normal sequences of child development and about children's capabilities at each stage of development, particularly during infancy.

Case Illustration

The following case illustrates the effectiveness of an intervention program with an infant with a nonorganic failure to thrive. The child's condition appeared to stem from deficient parenting skills (Drotar & Sturm, 1994).

CASE 17-9. ELISE
When Elise was hospitalized at 5 months of age for failure to thrive, her weight was below the 5th percentile, her length at the 30th percentile, and her head circumference at the 35th percentile. Physical diagnosis revealed no organic cause for her failure to thrive, and she gained weight (.4 kilogram) during a six-day hospitalization on an age-appropriate diet.

Behavioral observations revealed that Elise had age-appropriate interest in food, signaled the nursing staff when hungry, and had no feeding problem. Her developmental status was also within normal limits, as indicated by a Mental Development Index of 96 on the Bayley Scales of Mental Development.

Elise's mother was a 22-year-old single parent with three children—Elise and her two older siblings, ages 2 and 3. She had separated from the child's father and did not have contact with him or much support from her own family. Assessment of the mother-child interaction during Elise's hospitalization indicated several problems that became the focus of subsequent intervention. During one observation, Elise signaled her mother that she was hungry, but her mother consistently ignored these cues. Elise's mother moved the bottle throughout the feeding to see how much Elise was taking. This feeding pattern limited the time Elise spent in feeding. Elise's mother also reported that because Elise did not seem to be hungry or responsive, she did not feed or stimulate her as much as she did her other children.

Intervention took place in the family home and focused on helping the mother set up a feeding schedule for Elise in which she was fed regularly and given enough calories to achieve age-appropriate weight gain and increasing the frequency of interaction between Elise and her mother, especially during feeding. To support this goal, Elise's mother was encouraged to hold Elise during feedings, was strongly discouraged from propping the bottle [that is, leaving the bottle in a position from which the infant can feed himself or herself without being held by the caregiver], and was given education concerning her child's nutritional needs. A final goal of intervention was to encourage Elise's mother to provide the kind of stimulation for Elise that was more in keeping with her developmental needs. To accomplish this, the counselor helped Elise's mother make age-appropriate toys such as a cradle gym and to schedule specific times to play with her.

Elise's progress was monitored by weighing her each week, charting her physical growth, and assessing her cognitive development and attachment. By age 12 months (seven months after intervention had begun), she achieved age-appropriate physical growth. Her weight was now at the 38th percentile, her length at the 65th percentile, and her head circumference at the 48th percentile. In addition, her cognitive development maintained age-appropriate levels, as indicated by a mental age of 13 months and Mental Development Index of 109 on the Bayley Scales of Mental Development. Finally, Elise was observed to have a secure attachment to her mother. Elise maintained her progress in physical growth and cognitive development at the latest follow-up at the age of 3 years. (pp. 37–38, with changes in notation)

THINKING THROUGH THE ISSUES

As a child, did you have any of the medical illnesses described in this chapter? If so, which illness did you have? What was it like to have the illness? What treatment did you receive? Was the treatment effective? How did your illness affect your relationship with your parents and siblings? How did your illness interfere with your life?

Do you know anybody with asthma, diabetes, cancer, AIDS, or headaches? If so, what have you observed about the condition? How does the condition affect the person's life? And how has the illness affected your relationship with this person?

How do you react to pain? How would you describe your current pain threshold? What do you do for pain? Is what you do effective? How did you react to pain when you were a child? What kinds of pain experiences did you have as a child? What did you take for pain when you were a child? Was the treatment effective? What did your parents do for you when you were in pain? Were you given any special favors by your parents when you had pain?

What is your attitude toward AIDS? What thoughts and feelings do you have about AIDS? Can you work with individuals who have AIDS or are HIV positive? Do you believe that individuals with AIDS are responsible for their illness? How do you think persons with AIDS are viewed by society?

How difficult do you think it is to differentiate organic from nonorganic failure to thrive?

SUMMARY

1. The child should have a physical examination for any presenting complaint that may have a physical basis.
2. Mental health professionals then need to know the results of the physical examination before beginning any psychological interventions.

Pain
3. Pain is an unpleasant sensation or emotional experience that may be acute, recurrent, or chronic.
4. Acute pain may be associated with anything from superficial bumps, cuts, burns, and scrapes that cause minimal tissue damage to deeper wounds that cause moderate to severe tissue damage.
5. Recurrent pain may occur in the absence of a well-defined organic etiology and may be triggered by external or internal factors, particularly events that provoke stress; between episodes, the child may be healthy and pain free.
6. Chronic pain may be associated with various diseases, with accidents, and with severe burns.
7. Pain has value. It alerts us to problems, motivates us to seek help, and tells us when treatments may not be working properly.
8. Children, like adults, differ in their pain reactions. Some will report the slightest pain, others only severe pain.
9. Children's experience of pain is multidimensional.
10. The way children react to pain is heavily dependent on what they learn in their culture.
11. Consider the operant components of a chronic or recurring pain problem—that is, under what circumstances does the pain occur and what consequences follow from the pain?
12. Children may cope with pain by diverting attention from the pain; by reinterpreting the painful sensations; by imagining that they are some character who does not feel pain; by inhibiting feelings; by engaging in relaxation activities; by asking someone for comfort or help; by asking for medication; by reducing discomfort by changing body positions; by suffering in silence; by crying, gritting teeth, or clenching fist; and by engaging in other activities, such as watching television or reading.

13. Consider what factors may affect the child's ability to cope with pain.

14. Very young children and children of any age who have inadequate communication skills cannot report their pain experiences clearly. In such cases, you will need to observe the child's facial and bodily gestures to obtain clues about how the child experiences pain or anticipates pain.

15. By the age of 5 years, most children can differentiate a wider range of pain intensities, and they can use quantitative scales to rate their pain intensity.

16. A thorough assessment of a child's pain includes an examination of behavioral, cognitive-affective, and physiological factors.

17. Any information you obtain from the child should be corroborated by the parents or by a knowledgeable caregiver.

18. There is no simple way to evaluate whether a child's pain is primarily or totally due to organic or nonorganic factors.

19. Cognitive, behavioral, and pharmacological interventions are useful in the management of pain, whatever its etiology.

20. Interventions should be tailored to the child's age, cognitive-developmental level, communication skills, and coping abilities.

21. Encourage children to communicate their pain, because pain relief is an important part of their treatment.

22. Children and their families should be told that achieving a total absence of pain may not be realistic.

Asthma

23. Asthma is a disorder in which the airways of the tracheobronchial passages constrict so that the person feels unable to breathe or to take deep breaths. The disorder is chronic and varies in severity.

24. Asthma is usually diagnosed by clinical symptoms, such as wheezing and coughing, and by exposing the person to allergic substances or exercise to detect changes in airway obstruction.

25. Asthmatic attacks are usually triggered by such stimuli as cigarette smoke, smog, allergens, exercise in cold air, respiratory infections, and emotional responses, such as crying and laughing.

26. Asthma is the most common chronic illness of childhood in the United States, affecting 6 to 7 million children.

27. A semistructured interview with the child and a diary completed by the child will be useful in obtaining information about the child's asthma.

28. Several methods are used in the treatment and management of asthma, including environmental management, pharmacologic management, behavioral management, and education and self-management.

29. Parents need to learn how to avoid overindulging their child with asthma and how to teach the child to behave so that they can help him or her manage the asthma.

30. Rates of adherence to a medical regimen are low for asthmatic children; only about 10% of the children follow their health care provider's advice completely.

Diabetes

31. Insulin-dependent diabetes mellitus (IDDM) is a chronic metabolic disease of childhood that affects about 1 in every 600 children under the age of 10 years. It also is called Type I diabetes or juvenile-onset diabetes.

32. Another type of diabetes, Type II diabetes or noninsulin-dependent diabetes mellitus (NIDDM), occurs mostly in adults, usually after the age of 40.

33. The major problem in diabetes is glucose (sugar) use and storage. Diabetes in children is caused by destruction of the pancreatic beta cells that produce insulin; insulin is necessary in order for glucose to enter the tissues and organs of the body.

34. Failure to control diabetes can lead to hyperglycemia or ketoacidosis.

35. Symptoms of uncontrolled diabetes include fatigue, excessive thirst, frequent urination, weight loss despite increased eating, rapid shallow breathing, abdominal pain, flushed skin, and fruity breath odor.

36. Ketoacidosis is extremely dangerous and requires immediate medical attention.

37. Children with diabetes must follow a complex regimen of daily insulin injections, blood glucose monitoring, diet, and exercise.

38. The goal of treatment of diabetes is to maintain blood sugar levels as near normal as possible.

39. A diabetes regimen may be especially difficult for children and adolescents when they have difficulty resisting peer influence.

40. Estimates of nonadherence to a diabetes regimen range from 30% to 90%.

41. Adherence will be better when cost for the treatment is reasonable, there is sufficient time to follow the regimen, resources are available to help with the regimen, and competing demands are not overwhelming.

42. Stresses in the parent-child relationship are likely to arise when children fail to follow the diabetes regimen.

43. The diabetes regimen can be thrown off course when children with diabetes contract another illness, such as flu or a stomach virus.

44. Encourage the family to talk to the health care provider about the diabetes regimen whenever the child has another illness.

45. Diabetes can lead to general psychological disturbance, contribute to the development of eating disorders, and lead to stress.

46. A semistructured interview will be helpful in obtaining information from the child about the child's diabetes. In addition, it will be helpful to observe directly how the child administers insulin and performs blood glucose testing.

47. If the child, parents, or teachers report that the child is having learning problems, consider recommending that the child be given a psychoeducational evaluation to see if there are any subtle cognitive impairments that are interfering with the child's learning.

48. Occasionally, you might want to ask the parents to monitor the child's adherence, depending on the child's age and who is responsible for following the diabetes regimen.

49. Medical treatment of the diabetic child is designed to control the diabetes.

50. Psychosocial interventions in cases of diabetes can be directed toward helping the family reduce or manage stress; increasing the family's self-esteem, social supports, and other resources; and opening lines of communication.

Childhood Cancer

51. Each year, approximately 6,000 children under 16 years of age are diagnosed with cancer.

52. The various forms of cancer have in common the growth of malignant cells in single or multiple sites in the body, leading to destruction of normal cells and associated organs.

53. The etiology of many cancers is unknown, but genetic, environmental, chromosomal, or immunological factors may be involved.

54. The common cancers of childhood and adolescence are leukemias, central nervous system tumors, lymphomas, neuroblastomas, bone tumors, and retinoblastomas.

55. Children and their parents may regard the diagnosis of cancer with fear and as more of a threat than other diagnoses.

56. A semistructured interview will be useful for interviewing children with cancer.

57. Treatment for cancer may consist of surgery, radiation, chemotherapy, or a combination of these treatments.

58. Chemotherapy and radiation may have several side effects.

59. Short-term psychotherapy may help children with cancer work through their fears and concerns about changes in their physical appearance, their friends' reactions, the treatment's side effects, and the painful medical procedures.

HIV and AIDS

60. Human immunodeficiency virus type 1 (HIV-1) is a retrovirus that infects white blood cells, the brain, the bowel, the skin, and other tissues.

61. The disease that results from the HIV virus is called acquired immune deficiency syndrome (AIDS).

62. HIV infection can be transmitted perinatally, sexually, and parenterally.

63. Children are said to be HIV positive when antibodies to the virus are detected in their blood.

64. HIV infection spreads quickly and silently among teens, and the majority of infected adolescents are unaware of their HIV status until they become symptomatic (sometimes several years after infection). Consequently, they are likely to transmit the virus to other partners unknowingly.

65. The most severe and the most life-threatening manifestation of HIV infection in children is pediatric AIDS.

66. Pediatric AIDS is the last phase of the HIV infection, when the child's body is unable to fight the infection.

67. HIV infection can cause changes in the child's central nervous system that affect language, social and emotional responsiveness, cognitive functioning, attention, memory, visual-motor integration, and gross motor functioning.

68. Neurodevelopmental delays and neuropsychological deficits are exhibited by 75% to 90% of children infected with the HIV virus.

69. AIDS/HIV-1 encephalopathy is a term used to describe changes in motor function and mental status in children with HIV infection. This condition is extremely serious and profoundly affects the child's development and survival.

70. Children infected with HIV and their families must deal with the stigma attached to the disease, the isolation that occurs once others learn that a family member has the disease, and the limited and fragmented support and services on which the children's survival depends.

71. Parents may keep the diagnosis secret from the child and from other children in the family because they fear that the infected child cannot handle knowing about his or her condition or that the child and other children in the family will reveal the secret.

72. Children and their families may have initial feelings of shock, hopelessness, anger, shame, and sadness because of the currently inevitable fatal outcome of the disease and the demands on them to adjust to the illness.

73. Because the unique epidemiology of pediatric AIDS presents assessment challenges, it is vital to use a multidisciplinary approach to evaluate medical, social, and developmental areas in each case.

74. A thorough assessment of the child with HIV infection and his or her family will be similar to that conducted with other medically ill children, with some changes in focus.

75. Mental health professionals who work with children who have pediatric AIDS may experience considerable stress, including anxiety, depression, and fear of infection.

76. The goals of intervention in cases of HIV infection and pediatric AIDS include ensuring that children and families have access to all needed medical, social, and legal services; helping children with an HIV infection cope with the infection by developing a sense of control, enhancing self-esteem, and finding meaning in life; helping families integrate the various services that they need; helping families obtain adequate financial assistance, housing, psychotherapy, and help with substance abuse (if present); being an advocate for and a liaison between families and the other services; helping families develop adequate coping skills to deal with any feelings of fear, mistrust, stigma, shame, anger, and hopelessness; and helping children understand how HIV infections can be spread and how to prevent the infections from spreading.

Pediatric Headaches

77. Headaches can have functional or organic causes. To determine whether the cause is organic, a thorough medical evaluation of the child should be performed before or concurrent with the clinical assessment interview and before any psychological interventions take place.

78. Headache symptoms may be associated with infections, head traumas, intracranial pressure, toxic conditions, meningitis, and encephalitis.

79. Infrequent headaches are usually related to acute causes such as fatigue, fever, or alcohol ingestion.

80. Most headaches are functional, involving psychogenic or psychophysiologic factors rather than permanent structural changes in the brain or serious illness.

81. The most frequent types of headaches in children are migraine headaches and tension headaches.

82. Migraine headaches are recurrent vascular headaches that are commonly preceded by sensory, motor, or mood disturbances. They are more severe and debilitating than tension headaches.

83. The interview with a child referred for headaches should cover description and location of the headache pain, time of onset of the headaches, duration of the headaches, severity of the headaches, other associated symptoms, precipitants, medical and surgical history, family history of headaches, success of past treatments, use of drugs, and consequences of the headaches.

84. Effective management of recurrent or chronic pain in children involves a balance of cognitive, behavioral, and pharmacological interventions.

85. The most successful behavioral treatments for headache include biofeedback and relaxation procedures.

Failure to Thrive

86. Failure to thrive (FTT) is a descriptive term, rather than a diagnostic classification, for several disorders that result in poor growth or a significant deceleration in rate of weight gain.

87. Children with failure to thrive usually weigh below the 5th percentile for their age; it is a disorder of young childhood.

88. Failure to thrive is a potentially life-threatening problem.

89. Failure to thrive may be associated with organic causes, nonorganic causes, or a combination of the two.

90. Although failure to thrive occurs among families of all socioeconomic classes, it is more likely to occur in poor families.

91. Infants with nonorganic failure to thrive may show symptoms such as poor weight gain and growth, excessive crying and irritability, expressionless face, crying when approached by others, lack of cuddliness, poor eye contact, minimal response to stimulation, and indifference to separation.

92. In addition to the questions contained in the standard interview, ask the parent (or caregiver) to tell you about the child's eating problems, complete a food intake record, and tell you how he or she has handled the child's problems.

93. Also observe parent-child interactions, particularly in feeding situations, and look at such factors as the parent's and child's responsiveness to each other, the parent's and child's affect, and the parent's sensitivity to the child.

94. Several interventions are needed in cases of failure to thrive. First and foremost, the child's nutritional deficits should be attended to immediately. Second, parents should be given help in understanding their child's condition. Third, parents should be enrolled in an intervention program designed to help them stimulate and nurture their child more effectively. Finally, parents should be taught about normal sequences of child development and about children's capabilities at each stage of development, particularly during infancy.

KEY TERMS, CONCEPTS, AND NAMES

Pain (p. 541)
Acute pain (p. 541)
Recurrent pain (p. 541)
Chronic pain (p. 541)
Operant components of pain (p. 542)
Behavioral factors associated with pain (p. 543)
Cognitive-affective factors associated with pain (p. 543)
Visual-graphic procedures for pain recording (p. 543)
Word-graphic scale for pain recording (p. 543)
Physiological factors associated with pain (p. 543)
Cognitive interventions for pain (p. 545)
Attention diversion for pain (p. 545)
Self-instruction for pain (p. 545)
Incompatible imagery for pain (p. 545)
Behavioral interventions for pain (p. 545)
Pharmacological interventions with pain (p. 546)
Asthma (p. 550)
Allergens (p. 550)
Environmental management of asthma (p. 551)
Pharmacologic management of asthma (p. 551)
Bronchodilators (p. 551)
Anti-inflammatory agents (p. 551)
Nebulizer (p. 551)
Behavioral management for asthma (p. 551)
Education and self-management techniques used for asthma (p. 551)
Diabetes (p. 553)
Insulin-dependent diabetes mellitus (Type I diabetes; IDDM; juvenile-onset diabetes) (p. 553)

Type II diabetes (Noninsulin-dependent diabetes mellitus; NIDDM) (p. 553)
Glucose (p. 553)
Insulin (p. 553)
Hyperglycemia (p. 553)
Ketoacidosis (p. 553)
Diabetes regimen (p. 553)
Blood glucose monitoring (p. 553)
Hypoglycemia (p. 554)
Psychological effects of diabetes on children (p. 554)
Childhood cancer (p. 556)
Leukemias (p. 556)
Acute lymphoblastic leukemia (Acute lymphocytic leukemia) (p. 556)
Central nervous system tumors (p. 556)
Astrocytomas (p. 556)
Lymphomas (p. 556)
Hodgkin's disease (p. 556)
Non-Hodgkin's lymphoma (p. 556)
Neuroblastomas (p. 556)
Bone tumors (p. 556)
Osteogenic sarcoma (p. 556)
Retinoblastoma (p. 556)
Bone marrow aspiration (p. 556)
Biopsy (p. 556)
Lumbar puncture (p. 556)
X-ray (p. 556)
Computed tomography (CT) (p. 556)
Magnetic resonance imaging (MRI) (p. 556)
Bone scan (p. 556)
Ultrasound (p. 556)
Human immunodeficiency virus type 1 (HIV-1) (p. 558)
Acquired immune deficiency syndrome (AIDS) (p. 558)
Perinatal transmission (p. 559)
Sexual transmission (p. 559)
Parenteral transmission (p. 559)
Pediatric AIDS (p. 560)
Pneumocystis carinii pneumonia (p. 560)
Recurrent bacterial infections (p. 560)
Esophageal candidiasis (p. 560)
AIDS/HIV-1 encephalopathy (p. 560)
Cognitive symptoms of encephalopathy (p. 560)
Behavioral symptoms of encephalopathy (p. 560)
Motor symptoms of encephalopathy (p. 560)
Stigma of HIV (p. 562)
Pediatric headaches (p. 568)
Migraine headaches (p. 568)
Tension headaches (p. 568)
Photophobia (p. 568)
Sonophobia (p. 568)
Electromyographic (EMG) feedback (p. 569)
Skin temperature biofeedback (p. 569)
Temperature thermistor (p. 569)
Progressive relaxation technique (p. 569)
Failure to thrive (FTT) (p. 570)
Organic causes of failure to thrive (p. 570)
Nonorganic causes of failure to thrive (p. 570)

STUDY QUESTIONS

1. Discuss pain in children. In your discussion, include types of pain, children's coping with pain, the assessment of pain (including developmental considerations), helping parents cope with children's pain, and interventions.

2. Describe a behavioral-medicine approach to asthma. Include in your discussion a description of asthma, its prevalence, interview considerations, and interventions.

3. Describe a behavioral-medicine approach to diabetes. Include in your discussion a description of diabetes, its prevalence, interview considerations, and interventions.

4. Describe a behavioral-medicine approach to cancer. Include in your discussion a description of cancer, its prevalence, interview considerations, and interventions.

5. Describe a behavioral-medicine approach to pediatric HIV and AIDS. Include in your discussion a description of pediatric HIV and AIDS, their prevalence, interview considerations, and interventions.

6. Describe a behavioral-medicine approach to pediatric headaches. Include in your discussion a description of pediatric headaches, their prevalence, interview considerations, and interventions.

7. Describe a behavioral-medicine approach to failure to thrive. Include in your discussion a description of failure to thrive, its prevalence, interview considerations, and interventions

18

INTERVIEWING AND INTERVENTIONS FOR SPECIFIC PEDIATRIC HEALTH-RELATED DISORDERS, PART 2

The morbidity and mortality rates of Americans are no longer related to infectious diseases prevalent at the turn of the century; instead, they are related to chronic disorders related to our life-styles.

—Thomas J. Stachnik

Goals and Objectives

This chapter is designed to enable you to:

- Interview children and their families who need assistance with behavioral management of sleep disorders of childhood, substance abuse, or eating disorders
- Apply the general principles of interviewing discussed in Chapter 16 to the conditions discussed in this chapter and to other medically related conditions

This chapter continues the presentation begun in Chapter 17. Two of the three conditions discussed in this chapter—substance abuse and eating disorders—are potentially life threatening and may require immediate intervention. As you read about these conditions, think about the role society plays in the formation of these disorders. If you work regularly with children who have the disorders covered in this chapter, you should read additional relevant texts.

SLEEP DISORDERS OF CHILDHOOD

Description

Sleep disorders are common in childhood. They can greatly affect the child's well-being and also affect other family members (Mindell, 1993). Research suggests that about 30% of preschool children, 26% of elementary school children, and 15% of adolescents have sleep difficulties (Morin, 1993). Special populations of children—such as mentally handicapped children, hyperactive children, children who are hospitalized, children with chronic illnesses, and children with acute medical conditions, such as severe burns—often have sleep problems (Mindell, 1993).

Childhood sleep disorders are grouped into two primary categories: *dyssomnias* and *parasomnias*.

- *Dyssomnias,* according to *Diagnostic and Statistical Manual of Mental Disorders, Fourth Edition (DSM-IV)* (American Psychiatric Association, 1994), are sleep disorders characterized by abnormalities in the amount, quality, or timing of sleep, leading to excessive sleepiness or insomnia.
- *Parasomnias* are sleep disorders "characterized by abnormal behavioral or physiological events occurring in association with sleep, during specific sleep stages, or during sleep-wake transitions" (American Psychiatric Association, 1994, p. 551). These disorders reflect a sudden, partial awakening from nondream sleep.

In school-aged children, sleep disorders may be associated with social, behavioral, and learning problems and may predispose children to insomnia during adulthood (Morin, 1993). This part of the chapter follows Mindell's (1993) classifications of sleep disorders. However, you are encour-

aged also to study *DSM-IV* for more information about sleep disorders.

Dyssomnias. Dyssomnias are disorders associated with disturbed sleep at night or with difficulty staying awake during the day (Mindell, 1993). Two types of dyssomnias are physiologically based (narcolepsy and obstructive sleep apnea), and four types are environmentally based (adjustment sleep disorder, limit-setting sleep disorder, sleep-onset association disorder, and nocturnal eating [drinking] syndrome).

1. *Narcolepsy.* Narcolepsy, which is characterized by excessive sleepiness, typically appears in adolescence (Mindell, 1993). It affects approximately 0.03% to 0.16% of the population. Symptoms include excessive napping and inability to stay awake during the day. The disorder is characterized by muscle weakness (*cataplexy*), often associated with emotion-evoking events (Ware & Orr, 1992). Loss of muscle tone occurs in about 68% to 88% of narcoleptics but usually does not develop until years after the disorder first occurs.

2. *Obstructive sleep apnea.* Obstructive sleep apnea is described as follows (Mindell, 1993):

This disorder involves repetitive episodes of upper airway obstruction during sleep, often causing a reduction in blood oxygen saturation.... These apneic episodes cause frequent arousals and brief awakenings throughout the night.... Children with this disorder may be excessively sleepy during the day. They may exhibit daytime mouth breathing, difficulty swallowing, or poor speech articulation.... The mean age at diagnosis for children with sleep apnea is 7 years.... the most common form of treatment involves surgery to remove the airway obstructions. (p. 152)

3. *Adjustment sleep disorder.* "Adjustment sleep disorder is a form of insomnia related to emotional arousal caused by acute stress, conflict, or an environmental change" (Mindell, 1993, pp. 152–153). This type of insomnia is common in children but usually has a short duration. Situations causing heightened emotional arousal include beginning a new school year and moving to a new neighborhood. Once the stressor has been removed or adjusted to, sleep patterns typically return to normal.

4. *Limit-setting sleep disorder.* Limit-setting sleep disorder "involves difficulty in initiating sleep, typically characterized by stalling or refusing to go to bed" (Mindell, 1993, p. 153). It affects about 5% to 10% of children. The disorder in children often is a problem for their parents, who report increased depressive symptomatology, increased marital dissatisfaction, and increased anxiety (Mindell, 1993). However, once the parents set strict limits about bedtime and establish a bedtime routine, the sleep disorder is usually eliminated.

5. *Sleep-onset association disorder.* According to Mindell (1993):

Sleep-onset association disorder occurs when sleep onset is impaired by the absence of a certain set of objects or circumstances, be it the presence of a bottle or a pacifier or being rocked to sleep.... When these objects or circumstances are present, sleep is normal. However, when these objects or circumstances are not present, sleep is disturbed and can result in sleep-onset difficulties and frequent night wakings. (p. 153)

Sleep-onset association disorder occurs in about 15% to 20% of children aged 6 months to 3 years and can be corrected by helping children learn to fall asleep without needing to follow a routine (Mindell, 1993).

6. *Nocturnal eating (drinking) syndrome.* Nocturnal eating (drinking) syndrome occurs in children who wake in the night and cannot go back to sleep without eating or drinking (Mindell, 1993). It is common during infancy and early childhood. Treatment includes gradual reduction of the availability of food and drink.

Parasomnias. Parasomnias are the predominant sleep disorders in children. They "include confusional arousals, sleepwalking, sleep terrors, nightmares, sleep bruxism, and sleep enuresis" (Mindell, 1993, p. 154). Most children experience some type of parasomnia during childhood, usually starting about 18 months of age and the disorder usually disappears with maturation. Parasomnias share the following features: The child cannot remember the event the next morning; the child is difficult to awaken during the episode; the episode is characterized by autonomic arousal; the episode is more likely to occur if the child is overtired or deprived of sleep; and the episode usually occurs during the first hour or two of sleep (Carskadon, Anders, & Hole, 1988).

Let's now examine the six types of parasomnias.

1. *Confusional arousals.* According to Mindell (1993):

Confusional arousals occur almost universally in children before the age of 5 years...and are much less common in older children. Confusional arousals are characterized by confusions during and after arousals from sleep, mainly occurring in the first part of the night.... The child is often disoriented and shows slowed speech and slowed response to commands or questions. This confusional behavior may last from several minutes to hours. Typically, treatment is not recommended, and children outgrow this sleep problem. (p. 154)

2. *Sleepwalking.* Approximately 1% to 6% of children are diagnosed as *sleepwalkers,* with as many as 15% of all children having at least one experience. "The behavior may range from simply sitting up in bed to walking. The child is often difficult to awaken and, on awakening, appears confused" (Mindell, 1993, p. 154). The disorder is most prevalent between the ages of 4 and 8 years and usually disappears after adolescence. Sleepwalking usually is benign, and parents are encouraged to safety-proof the house.

3. *Sleep terrors.* Sleep terrors occur in about 3% to 6% of all children. According to Mindell (1993):

[Sleep terrors are] characterized by a sudden arousal from slow wave sleep with a piercing scream or cry, accompanied by auto-

nomic and behavioral manifestations of intense fear (Diagnostic Classification Steering Committee, 1990, p. 147). Sleep terrors usually happen within 2 hours of sleep onset and are characterized by agitation.... the child is often unresponsive to attempts at soothing and may be confused and disoriented if awakened. Sleep terrors are most common in children ages 4 to 12 and tend to resolve by adolescence.... The use of medications to treat sleep terrors is controversial. (p. 154)

4. *Nightmares.* Between 10% and 50% of children between the ages of 3 and 6 years have nightmares. "Nightmares are typically associated with fears of attack, falling, or death" (Mindell, 1993, p. 155). Generally, they should not be considered signs of a psychological disturbance unless they are frequent and distressing and last a long time. Once nightmares begin, they usually will decrease in frequency over time, particularly by adolescence. Parents should be reassured that nightmares are part of normal development.

5. *Sleep bruxism.* "Sleep bruxism, which involves grinding or clenching the teeth during sleep, occurs in over 50% of normal infants, with the average age of onset at 10 months.... Bruxism may cause dental problems, such as abnormal wear of the teeth or periodontal tissue damage, and may also be related to headaches or jaw pain" (Mindell, 1993, p. 155). Little research has been done on the efficacy of treatment programs for bruxism in children.

6. *Sleep enuresis.* Sleep enuresis, also known as *bedwetting,* affects approximately 5% to 17% of children ages 3 to 15 years (Ware & Orr, 1992). Enuresis has two subtypes—*primary* (the child has always wet the bed) and *secondary* (the child has learned bladder control but then loses control). From 70% to 90% of affected children have primary enuresis (Mindell, 1993). Primary enuresis is most often considered a developmental delay but may be caused by diabetes, urinary tract infections, specific foods, epilepsy, or emotional problems. Secondary enuresis also may have organic causes. Behavioral therapies are popular for the treatment of enuresis. An effective technique, for example, is the bell and pad system, in which a bell sounds when bedwetting occurs, awakening the child and eventually conditioning him or her to waken before bedwetting occurs again.

Interviewing Issues

The semistructured interview shown in Table F-14 in Appendix F will be useful for interviewing children with a sleep disorder. If the child can't answer your questions fully but can write, consider asking the child to keep a diary of his or her sleep patterns (see Table 18-1). The diary will allow you to gain information about the actual occurrences of the sleep disorder. You might ask a parent to keep a diary of the child's sleep patterns if the child can't write or if you want to have a reliability check on the child's diary. Once an older child has completed a diary, schedule another interview with him or her. The questions in Table 18-2 will be useful in assessing a child's sleep problems.

Interventions

Before you begin any intervention with a child with a sleep disturbance, have the child's health care provider examine the child to rule out medical issues, such as colic, recurrent ear infections, urinary tract infections, or any other infections or illnesses.

Because a combination of factors may contribute to a sleep disorder, the evaluation needs to be comprehensive and the treatment often eclectic, keeping in mind that some childhood sleep disorders are best treated by time and reassurance. Certain sleep disturbances, however, may reflect or cause significant medical problems.... The seriousness of problems such as sleep apnea has increased the burden on the clinician to correctly diagnose sleep problems. (Ware & Orr, 1992, p. 277)

Many sleep disorders of childhood can be treated with behavioral techniques such as *stimulus control* (for example, instituting a fixed sleeping place, bedtime, and bedtime ritual), *shaping* (for example, gradually making bedtime earlier), *extinction* (for example, removing any positive reinforcement for bedtime resistance), and, for older children, *positive reinforcement* (for example, praise or star charts for the desired behavior). Sedatives also may be prescribed, though their use is controversial (France & Hudson, 1993).

Referral to a sleep disorder center is usually called for when the child's symptoms suggest narcolepsy, the child's daytime behavior is disturbed because of lack of sleep, or the child's problem has been occurring for over a month and treatments have not been successful.

Management of a sleep disorder includes helping the child maintain a consistent sleep routine, develop a pre-bed ritual, and eliminate daytime naps. The goal of treatment is to improve the child's sleep patterns—for example, by helping the child manage stress, express emotions, and relate to others (Culebras, 1992). Table 18-3 shows suggestions for helping parents manage children's sleep difficulties.

You can help adolescents with insomnia by giving them the following suggestions for improving their sleep (Culebras, 1992):

1. Avoid all dietary forms of caffeine, over-the-counter pills, and medications that contain stimulants.
2. Maintain regular meal schedules.
3. Reduce fluid intake one hour before bed and void before going to bed.
4. Avoid alcohol before going to bed.
5. Establish a regular exercise program, but avoid vigorous physical activity after 6 P.M.
6. Maintain a consistent sleep routine.
7. Develop pre-bed rituals.
8. Avoid stressful activities before going to bed.
9. Eliminate daytime naps.
10. Get out of bed and engage in a relaxing activity if a prolonged wakening occurs.

Case Illustration

The following case describes a child with a sleepwalking disorder.

CASE 18-1. BRIAN

Brian was an 8-year-old boy brought to the clinic by his parents due to their concerns about his unusual events during the night. They said that approximately two to five times each month, they would discover Brian wandering around the house at night or find him in the morning in a different part of the house from where he went to bed. If they found him asleep while he was wandering around, his movements seemed to be semipurposeful, but he was in a "bizarre and possessed-like" state with a far-away look in his eyes. He appeared to be awake to his parents, but he did not recognize them and would not answer questions. Occasionally, he would seem to hear them and could be directed, but he then would suddenly become confused and think they were someone else.

At times, Brian's parents would find him in unusual places, such as in the cellar or in his closet in the morning when they awoke, and no one would have any idea of how he got there. One morning (which had contributed to their coming into the clinic), the entire family panicked when they were unable to find him. After a lengthy search, Brian was found in a small laundry area, covered by clothes.

The sleep history revealed that Brian's "usual" bedtime was 10:00 P.M. on most nights. The bedtime was postponed by several means, however, and often he went to bed at 11:00 P.M. or later. Brian was active at night and had great difficulty winding down, but once he was in bed with the lights out, he seemed to fall asleep quickly. The family's best estimate of when the partial arousal events occurred was around midnight to 1:00 A.M. Except for these events, the rest of the sleep history was negative for disruptions, snoring, or awakenings.

On school days, Brian got up at 6:30 A.M. to catch a 7:00 A.M. bus. It was often difficult to wake him up in the morning, but, once awake, he did not seem to be sleepy during the day. He was an active boy who did well in school, and, except for being a little bit "overactive," there were no other problems described by the family. Brian did not take any structured naps, although the family did note that he occasionally fell asleep during car rides.

On weekends, Brian tended to stay up even later—often until midnight—and usually slept in later, until approximately 9:00 A.M. When asked about any pattern to these events, the parents described an impression that the events were more likely to occur when he came home from spending the weekend with his grandparents, where they knew he tended to be active and get even less sleep at night.

All aspects of the description are consistent with sleepwalking events, including the timing, pattern, and character of the events. In addition, there seems to be at least strong circumstantial evidence that Brian is getting barely adequate sleep and that the sleepwalking events are more likely to occur following sleep deprivation. Although he did not appear sleepy to his parents, he was irritable and sensitive to sleep loss, and whenever he stopped being active (such as during car rides) he fell asleep.

Table 18-1
Sleep Diary for Adolescents

INSTRUCTIONS

In order to better understand your sleep problem and monitor your progress during treatment, we would like you to collect some important information on your sleep pattern. After you get up in the morning, please answer all 10 questions on the sleep diary. It is important that you complete this diary *every morning.* For example, when you get up on a Wednesday morning, complete the column under Tuesday; on a Thursday morning, complete the column under Wednesday; and so forth. It is difficult to estimate how long you take to fall asleep or how long you are awake at night. Please remember, however, that we only want your best *estimates.* If there should be some unusual event on a given night (for example, illness, emergency, phone call), make a note of it. Below are some guidelines to help you answer each question. An example is also provided on the diary.

1. *Napping:* This should include all naps even though they were not intentional. For instance, if you dozed off in front of the TV for 10 minutes, please write this down. Make sure to specify A.M. or P.M.
2. *Sleep Aid:* You should include both prescribed and over-the-counter medications, as well as alcohol used specifically as a sleep aid.
3. *Bedtime:* This is the time you go to bed and actually turn the lights off. If you go to bed at 10:45 but turn the lights off only at 11:15, you should write both times in that space.

4. *Sleep-Onset Latency:* Provide your best estimate of how long it took you to fall asleep after you turned the lights off and intended to go to sleep.
5. *Number of Wakenings:* This is the number of times you remember waking up during the night.
6. *Duration of Wakenings:* Please estimate to the best of your knowledge how many minutes you spent awake for each wakening. If this proves impossible, then estimate the number of minutes you spent awake for all wakenings combined. This should not include your very last wakening in the morning, as this will be logged in number 7.
7. *Morning Wakening:* This is the very last time you woke up in the morning. If you woke up at 4:00 but went back to sleep for a brief period of time (for example, from 6:00 to 6:20), then your last wakening would be 6:20.
8. *Out-of-Bed Time:* This is the time you actually got out of bed for the day.
9. *Feeling upon Arising:* Please use the following 5-point scale:
   1 = Exhausted; 2 = Tired; 3 = Average;
   4 = Rather refreshed; 5 = Very refreshed
10. *Sleep Quality:* Please use the following 5-point scale:
    1 = Very restless; 2 = Restless; 3 = Average quality;
    4 = Sound; 5 = Very sound

(Continued)

The primary component to treatment was explaining what these events were to these concerned parents. The relationship to getting less sleep was pointed out. The need for a physically safe environment also was discussed in detail. The treatment recommendations focused on trying to increase the total amount of sleep that Brian got and regularizing his somewhat erratic schedule. The parents were instructed to put the child to bed 15 minutes earlier each night and have a firm set of rules around bedtime with a point system (with rewards for compliance with this routine and limits). They were further instructed to keep a diary of his sleep times, including bedtime, estimated time to fall asleep, wake-up time, and any pattern of daytime tiredness and the occurrence of the sleepwalking events. The goal was to increase and regularize his sleep.

Brian responded well to a more structured bedtime routine and adjusted easily to early bedtimes. He increased his total amount of night sleep by approximately 45 minutes a night on school nights. He was easier to wake for school in the morning. The frequency of the events decreased dramatically to one event every other month. The parents also noted that he was less irritable and more relaxed.

Brian had a tendency to slip back to late-night schedules when the structure and rewards were discontinued. He also continued to have sleepwalking events following weekends

or camp experiences where he was excited and active and got less sleep. The family motivation to enforce the bedtime decreased as the sleepwalking events were infrequent and of less concern to them. Brian continued to do well, and the sleepwalking events disappeared completely over the next couple of years. (From R. Dahl, "Parasomnias." In R. T. Ammerman, C. G. Last, and M. Hersen [Eds.], *Handbook of Prescriptive Treatments for Children and Adolescents.* Copyright © 1993, by Allyn and Bacon. Adapted from pp. 293–294, with permission.)

Exercise 18-1. Knowledge of Sleep Hygiene and Caffeine

This exercise is designed to test your knowledge of sleep hygiene (Part 1) and caffeine (Part 2). The questions primarily pertain to late adolescents (and adults) because they are more likely to engage in the activities listed than are younger children. Compare your answers to those following the questions. This exercise was adapted from P. Lacks, *Behavioral Treatment for Persistent Insomnia.* Copyright © 1987 by Allyn and Bacon. Adapted by permission of the author. Originally copyrighted in 1987 by Pergamon Books, p. 75. Copyright transferred to author in 1996 by Allyn and Bacon.

Table 18-1 (*Continued*)

SLEEP DIARY

Name: _____   Week: _____ to _____

Questions	Example	Mon	Tue	Wed	Thu	Fri	Sat	Sun
1. I napped from ____ to ____ (note the times of all naps).	*2:00 to 2:45 P.M.*							
2. I took ____ mg of ____ medication and/or ____ oz of alcohol as a sleep aid.	*1 mg ProSom 2 oz*							
3. I went to bed at ____ and turned the lights out at ____.	*10:30 P.M. 11:15 P.M.*							
4. After turning the lights out, I fell asleep in ____ minutes.	*45*							
5. My sleep was interrupted ____ times.	*3*							
6. My sleep was interrupted for ____ minutes	*15, 20, 30*							
7. I woke up at ____ (note time of last Wakening).	*6:15 A.M.*							
8. I got out of bed at ____ (specify the time).	*6:40 A.M.*							
9. When I got up this morning, I felt ____. (1 = exhausted, 5 = refreshed)	*2*							
10. Overall, my sleep last night was ____. (1 = very restless, 5 = very sound)	*1*							

Source: Reprinted, with change in notation, with permission of the publisher and author from C. M. Morin, *Insomnia: Psychological Assessment and Management,* copyright 1993 by Guilford, pp. 209–210.

Part 1. Knowledge of Sleep Hygiene

For the following list of behaviors, indicate your opinion as to the extent of the general effect, if any, that each behavior may have on nightly sleep. Use the following scale for behaviors 1 through 13, circling the appropriate number after each item:

1 = Beneficial to sleep
2 = No effect
3 = Disruptive to sleep

1. Daytime napping   1 2 3
2. Going to bed hungry   1 2 3
3. Going to bed thirsty   1 2 3
4. Smoking more than one pack of cigarettes a day   1 2 3
5. Using sleep medication (prescription or over-the-counter) regularly   1 2 3
6. Exercising strenuously within 2 hours of bedtime   1 2 3
7. Sleeping approximately the same length of time each night   1 2 3
8. Setting aside time to relax before bedtime   1 2 3
9. Consuming food, beverages, or medications containing caffeine   1 2 3
10. Exercising in the afternoon or early evening   1 2 3
11. Waking up at the same time each day   1 2 3
12. Going to bed at the same time each night   1 2 3
13. Drinking alcohol in the evening, such as 2 mixed drinks, 3 beers, or 12 ounces of wine   1 2 3

Part 2. Knowledge of Caffeine

For each product on the following list, indicate whether you believe it contains caffeine or another stimulant by placing a Y (yes) or an N (no) in the space provided. If you are not sure, make your best guess. If you have never heard of a product, place an X in the space.

Table 18-2
Evaluating Sleep Disorders in Children

Description of the Problem
1. How do the parents describe the problem?
2. How does the child describe the problem?

First Occurrence
3. When did the problem begin?
4. What was happening in the child's immediate environment at that time?
5. Had there been any changes in the child's routines?
6. If so, what were the changes?
7. Had there been any stressful events, such as loss of friends, divorce, or a death in the family?
8. If so, what were the events and how did the child and family react to the events?
9. Had the child recently been placed on medication?
10. Had the child recently been taken off a medication?

Time and Frequency of Occurrence
11. When does the problem occur—soon after the child goes to sleep or later in the night?
12. How frequently does the problem occur?
13. Is the problem occurring with increasing frequency?
14. If the problem is occurring nightly, how many times does it occur each night?

Description of Child's and Parents' Behavior
15. What does the child do while awake during the night?
16. What do the parents do when the child is awake?
17. How anxious is the child about the problem?
18. How anxious are the parents about the problem?
19. Has the child's problem significantly increased the amount of attention he or she is receiving?
20. Does the child's level of anxiety over the problem match the parents' level of anxiety?
21. Has the child's problem ever led to an injury?
22. If so, what was the injury and when did it occur?
23. Does the child remember any of the events at the time the problem occurs?
24. If so, what does the child remember?

Other Sleep Parameters
25. Is the problem an isolated sleep event, or are there other sleep problems?
26. If there are other problems, what are they?
27. Does the child settle down normally before going to bed?
28. If not, what does the child do?
29. Is the child's bedtime routine within the normal range for the child's age?
30. If not, how does it differ from the normal range?
31. How easily awakened is the child in the morning?
32. How easily awakened is the child from a nap?
33. What is the temperature of the room, and what is the lighting in the room when the child goes to sleep?

34. What is the quality of the air circulation in the room when the child goes to sleep?
35. What snacks or drinks, if any, does the child have before going to bed?
36. What was the actual event that caused the parents to seek help for the child's sleep problem?

Child's Daytime Performance
37. Have there been changes in the child's attention span, fussiness, school performance, and so on?
38. If so, what are the changes?
39. How many naps does the child take during the day?
40. Does the child regularly exercise?

Family Sleep History
41. Did either of the parents have a similar sleep problem?
42. If so, what was the problem, was its course similar to the course of the child's problem, and how was the problem treated?
43. Does either of the parents currently have a sleep problem?
44. If so, what is the problem and how does the parent react to her or his own sleep problem?
45. (If other children in family) Do the child's siblings have sleep problems?
46. If so, what are their sleep problems and how are their sleep problems being handled by the parents?

Child's Medical History
47. What is the child's medical history?
48. Does the child have any chronic illnesses?
49. If so, what are they?
50. Has the child ever had a brain injury?
51. If so, what was the injury?
52. Are any of the illnesses, if present, related to the sleep problem?

Parents' Response to Sleep Problem
53. What is the parents' response to the child's sleep problem?
54. How do the parents handle the child's sleep problem?
55. What advice have they been given about the child's sleep problem?
56. What have they tried to do to help the child's sleep problem?
57. What has helped in the past with the child's sleep problem?
58. What have they told the child about the child's sleep problems and possible treatments by other professionals?
59. Has the child's sleep problem affected other family members?
60. If so, in what way?

Source: Adapted from Schroeder and Gordon (1991) and Ware and Orr (1992, pp. 276–277, with changes in notation).

Table 18-3
Suggestions for Parents to Help Their Children with Sleep Problems

Problem: Extended periods of crying, sobbing, moaning with wild thrashing during sleep
This problem may occur in children between 6 months and 6 years and occasionally in older children.

What to Do
1. Go in to be sure your child does not injure himself or herself.
2. Let the episode run its course. Keep your distance. Don't forcibly "help." Hold your child only if he or she recognizes you and wants to be held. Do not shake your child or otherwise vigorously try to awaken him or her.
3. Watch for the relaxation and calm that signals the end of the episode. You may then help your child lie down and you may cover him or her. Let your child go back to sleep. Do not awaken your child or try to ask him or her what was wrong or what he or she had been dreaming about. Similarly, don't question your child in the morning. Don't make your child feel strange or different.

General Suggestions
1. Make sure your child gets sufficient sleep. Consider an earlier bedtime. Restart a nap if it was abandoned without good reason.
2. Make sure your child's sleep and daily schedules are fairly regular and consistent.
3. Consider seeking counseling (a) if the sleep problems are frequent and if they began around known stresses, (b) if significant ongoing stresses are present, or (c) if your child is older than 6 years and has extended thrashing during sleep.

Problem: Calm sleepwalking
This problem may occur in children at any age, beginning at the time they learn to crawl or walk.

What to Do
1. Talk quietly and calmly to your child. Your child may follow your instructions and return to bed himself or herself.
2. If your child does not seem upset when you touch him or her, you should be able to lead him or her back to bed calmly. Your child may want to stop at the bathroom to urinate. Although you might be able to awaken him or her, it is better not to.
3. If your child spontaneously wakes after the episode (which older children and adolescents commonly do), he or she will likely be embarrassed. Do not make any negative or teasing comments. Don't mention it in the morning either, unless your child asks. Don't make your child feel peculiar or strange. Treat the sleepwalking matter-of-factly and let your child go back to bed.

General Suggestions
1. For young children, ensure adequate sleep and a normal schedule. Occasionally this will help older children as well.
2. Make the environment as safe as possible to avoid accidental injury. Floors should not be cluttered, objects should not be left on the stairs, and hallways should be lit. If your child's walking sometimes goes unnoticed, put a bell on his or her door so that you will be aware whenever he or she leaves the room. Young children may need a gate by their door or at the top of the stairs. If your child tries to leave the house, an extra chain lock above his or her reach should be installed. If your child sleeps in a bunk bed, the bottom bunk is safer.
3. Consider seeking counseling for the same factors noted for extended thrashing.

Problem: Agitated sleepwalking
This problem may occur during middle childhood and adolescence.

What to Do
1. If the agitation is marked, restraint will only make the event more intense and longer lasting. Keep your distance. Hold your child only if he or she is starting to do something dangerous.
2. When your child becomes calm, treat him or her as you would a calm sleepwalker.

General Suggestions
Follow the same suggestions noted for calm sleepwalking.

Problem: Sleep terrors (including screaming, look of panic and fear, possibly wild running)
This problem may occur during late childhood and adolescence.

What to Do
1. Let the screaming subside and then simply let your child return to sleep. Do not try to awaken him or her. Do not question your child in detail and do not embarrass your child if he or she reaches full waking (as some adolescents may do).
2. If there is wild running and risk of injury, you may have to intercede, but be careful. Both you and your child could get injured. Talk calmly and block your child's access to dangerous areas, but actually holding him or her may be difficult and can lead to even wilder behavior.

General Suggestions
1. Your child may be safer sleeping on the first level of the house or in a finished basement room.
2. If there is a threat of or actual window breakage, consider replacing the glass with Plexiglas.
3. Use the same general precautions as for sleepwalkers.
4. Consult your physician for possible use of medication, especially if there is wild running. If medication is used, view it as a temporary solution used mainly for protection.
5. Consider seeking counseling when arousals are frequent, intense, and dangerous.

14. _____ 7-Up soft drink
15. _____ regular tea
16. _____ Dristan cold remedy
17. _____ aspirin
18. _____ Dr Pepper soft drink
19. _____ Midol menstrual relief medication
20. _____ lemonade
21. _____ root beer
22. _____ chocolate cake
23. _____ regular coffee
24. _____ Excedrin
25. _____ Sudafed decongestant
26. _____ Mountain Dew
27. _____ cola soft drinks
28. _____ Dexatrim diet pills
29. _____ Tylenol
30. _____ Aqua Ban diuretic
31. _____ Sprite soft drink

Answers

1. 3   2. 3   3. 3   4. 3   5. 3   6. 3   7. 1   8. 1   9. 3
10. 1   11. 1   12. 1   13. 3   14. N   15. Y   16. Y
17. N   18. Y   19. Y   20. N   21. N   22. Y   23. Y
24. Y   25. Y   26. Y   27. Y   28. Y   29. N   30. Y
31. N

SUBSTANCE ABUSE

Description

Substance abuse, which includes alcohol and drug abuse, is a major health and social problem among adolescents in the United States. Substance abuse is present whenever use of a drug results in adverse effects to the user. The terms *addiction, dependency,* and *abuse* are often used interchangeably. It is important to distinguish substance *abuse* from substance *use*. Experimental use of substances or occasional use of some substances in moderation is usually considered substance use, not substance abuse.

Experimental Use of Substances

You will soon be reading about the stages in becoming a substance abuser. But first let's consider some reasons that adolescents experiment with and use substances. These reasons involve family and peer group factors, attitudinal factors, cultural factors, and personality and temperament factors (Petraitis, Flay, & Miller, 1995; also see Figure 18-1). These four factors and their interactions affect the probability of substance use. Substance use, in turn, may affect the four factors and their interactions.

FAMILY AND PEER GROUP FACTORS

- inadequate parental warmth, support, or supervision
- negative evaluations from parents
- home strain
- parental divorce or separation
- unconventional values of parents
- unconventional values among peers
- weak attachment to and weak desire to please family members
- strong attachment to and strong desire to please peers
- greater influence of peers than of parents

ATTITUDINAL FACTORS

- weak commitment to conventional values, school, and religion
- social alienation
- weak desire for success and achievement
- hedonic values and emphasis on short-term gratification
- rebelliousness
- desire for independence from parents
- tolerance of deviance
- desire to symbolically reject conventional standards by using drugs

CULTURAL FACTORS

- inadequate schools
- poor career and academic options

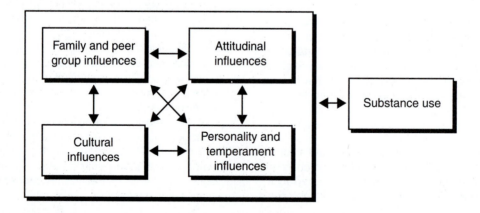

Figure 18-1. Theoretical causes of substance use. Adapted from Petraitis, Flay, and Miller (1995).

- infrequent opportunities for rewards at school
- negative evaluations from teachers
- media glorification of substance use
- availability of substances
- weak public policies on regulating substance use

PERSONALITY AND TEMPERAMENT FACTORS

- impaired cognitive functions
- genetic susceptibility to addiction
- temperamental personality
- impulsiveness
- aggressiveness
- emotional instability
- extroversion
- sociability
- tendencies toward risk taking and thrill seeking
- low self-esteem
- temporary anxiety
- stress
- depressed mood
- poor coping skills
- inadequate social skills
- weak academic skills

Stages in becoming a substance abuser. Adolescents may go through several stages in becoming substance abusers. (Younger children also may use alcohol or drugs, but substance abuse is less common in children under 12 years.) The five-stage continuum described in the paragraphs that follow is useful for classifying an adolescent's degree of substance abuse (Nowinski, 1990; also see Figure 18-2). Note that addiction to drugs or alcohol often starts with experimental or social use and progresses to more serious stages.

1. *Experimental stage—substance use is related to curiosity, risk taking, and, at times, peer pressure.* In this first stage, the mood-altering effects of the substance are *secondary* to the adventure of using the substance. The substance may be used either when the person is alone or in social situations. Experimental substance use is the norm among adolescents in our society. It places adolescents at risk for heavier involvement in drugs, which may occur when they see adults regularly use substances or discover an emotional or physical effect that they find attractive. However, most adolescents who experiment with alcohol or marijuana do not develop dependence on the substance.

2. *Social stage—substance use is social.* The primary motivation at this stage is social acceptance, although curiosity, thrill seeking, and defiance also may play a role. Substance use also serves as a social facilitator and, at this stage, may lead adolescents to experience mood swings and behavioral changes. Adolescents may have difficulty separating from their friends who drink alcohol or use drugs.

3. *Instrumental stage—substance use is designed to manipulate emotions and behavior, such as to suppress or*

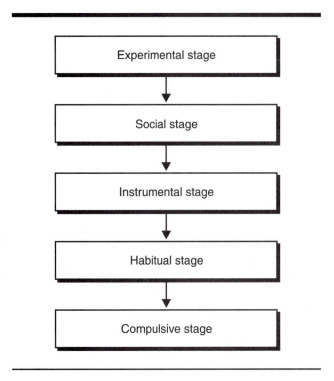

Figure 18-2. Stages in becoming a substance abuser.

embrace feelings or to inhibit or disinhibit behavior. Intoxication and other mood-altering or behavioral effects are sought at this stage. One primary motivation is to seek pleasure (*hedonistic use*)—to get high, to do things that are normally not done, or both. Adolescents aim to discover new ways of feeling good. Another primary motivation for using alcohol or drugs is to cope with stress and uncomfortable feelings (*compensatory use*)—to suppress anger, anxiety, shame, guilt, loneliness, and other negative emotions. The adolescent returns to a state of normality after getting high and experiences little or no discomfort following use of the substance. However, behavioral and personality changes may be noted—erratic performance in school, increased absences, decreased interest in school and other activities, changes in circles of friends, sleeping more than usual, and conflict with parents and siblings.

4. *Habitual stage—substance use becomes habit forming.* Symptoms of dependency on the substance start to appear at this stage. The focus of adolescents' lives is on substance use for coping and being. Former relationships, interests, and activities are neglected. The adolescent is preoccupied with getting high, and the substance is used almost daily. After the substance is used, there is no return to feelings of normality. Users may become anxious, depressed, or irritable, which pushes them toward further use of the substance. Habitual substance users find that they need stronger forms of the substance or new substances to get high.

5. *Compulsive stage—substance use becomes compulsive and addictive.* At this stage, the addict is preoccupied

with thoughts of getting high; other concerns become non-existent or much less important. The use of the substance is out of control. Substance use is necessary to feel normal, but even that feeling is hard to achieve. The addict will now do almost anything to gain access to drugs, including dealing in drugs, stealing, selling valuables, and engaging in prostitution. The addict may feel overwhelmed with shame and hopelessness and may be suicidal, but she or he still may be obsessively self-centered, demanding, defensive, and blaming and attempt to control others.

Problems associated with substance use and abuse.   The use of drugs may result in *physical problems* (impaired growth and physical maturation), *psychological problems* (poor concentration, decreased motivation), and *social problems* (increased involvement in accidents, increased risk-taking activities) (Stout, 1992). In fact, there are strong associations "among a variety of adolescent problem behaviors including alcohol use, cigarette smoking, marijuana use, use of other illicit drugs, delinquent behavior, and precocious sexual intercourse" (Donovan, Jessor, & Costa, 1988, p. 762). Table 18-4 shows more detailed problems that may be associated with major substance abuse. However, moderate, infrequent use of tobacco, alcohol, or marijuana, may not be dangerous (see Exhibit 18-1).

Current trends in substance use and abuse among adolescents.   Table 18-4 lists a number of drugs that have the potential for abuse. The street names of these drugs change frequently; therefore, you will need to keep abreast of current trends and terminology.

Johnston, O'Malley, and Bachman (1995b), in their annual national survey of drug use among 50,000 students in 8th, 10th, and 12th grade in over 400 public and private secondary schools nationwide, reported the following trends for 1995 (also see Table 18-5):

1. A majority of 10th- and 12th-graders surveyed had consumed alcohol on at least one occasion during that year.
2. By 12th grade, almost 74% of the students reported some use of alcohol.
3. About 0.7% of the 8th-graders were drinking alcohol daily; this figure rose to 3.5% by 12th grade.
4. The daily use of marijuana rose from 0.8% in the 8th grade to 4.6% in the 12th grade.
5. The occasional use of marijuana rose from almost 16% in the 8th grade to almost 35% by the 12th grade.
6. For daily use in the 12th grade, tobacco was in the lead, with almost 22% smoking at least one cigarette daily and 12.4% smoking half a pack a day or more.
7. Hallucinogens also were used relatively frequently, with 3.6% of the 8th-graders and 9.3% of the 12th-graders trying them at least once during the year.

Because this is an annual survey, Johnston et al. (1995b) were able to compare the 1995 results with those from past years. They pointed out that the proportion of 8th-graders

taking any illicit drug had almost doubled from 1991 to 1995 (from 11% to 21%). Since 1992, the proportion of high school students using any illicit drug had risen by nearly two-thirds among 10th-graders (from 20% to 33%) and by nearly one-half among 12th-graders (from 27% to 39%).

Marijuana use, in particular, continued the strong resurgence that began in the early 1990s, with increased use at all three grade levels. Among 8th-graders, marijuana use rose to over two times its level in 1992, from 7% in 1992 to 16% in 1995. Among 10th-graders, marijuana use nearly doubled, from 15% in 1992 to 29% in 1995. Among 12th-graders, marijuana use increased by more than half, from 22% in 1992 to 35% in 1995. Use of other illicit drugs, including cocaine, LSD, hallucinogens other than LSD, amphetamines, stimulants, inhalants, tranquilizers, and barbiturates, also continued to drift upward. Alcohol use remained fairly stable over the 1992–1995 period.

Cigarette smoking among adolescents continued to rise. Among 8th-graders, daily use of cigarettes rose from 7.2% in 1991 to 9.3% in 1995; among 10th-graders, from 12.6% in 1991 to 16.3% in 1995; and among 12th-graders, from 18.5% in 1991 to 21.6% in 1995. Cigarette smoking is strongly correlated with the use of marijuana: "Because cigarette smoking usually precedes marijuana use and teaches youngsters how to take smoke into their lungs to secure a drug-induced effect, it provides an excellent training ground for learning how to smoke marijuana" (Johnston et al., 1995b, p. 7). Finally, Johnston et al. (1995a) noted that "Many young lives will be permanently affected by the popularity of cigarette smoking during childhood and adolescence. Many will be foreshortened, and hundreds of thousands of each graduating class may die prematurely as a result of their current smoking rates. More will fall ill with the terrible diseases associated with smoking" (p. 4).

The increase in substance abuse may have occurred because adolescents seem to have softened their beliefs and attitudes about the dangers associated with drug use and relaxed about social disapproval (Johnston et al., 1995b). What adolescents do not consider is that "alcohol related motor vehicle accidents result in 8,000 adolescent deaths and 45,000 injuries each year" (MacKenzie & Kipke, 1992, p. 765). They also do not recognize that habitual cigarette smoking will eventually lead to increased health costs, disease, and premature death. "Because these extraordinary health consequences don't show up for 30 years, we have been able to turn a blind eye to this tragedy" (Johnston, O'Malley, & Bachman, 1994, p. 5).

Alcohol abuse.   Adolescents who abuse alcohol are more likely to be absent from school. If they attend school, they may be intoxicated in class and obtain poorer grades than those who do not abuse alcohol (DeBlassie, 1990). Furthermore,

alcohol, a powerful depressant, can cause both physical and psychological dependence and may lead to brain and liver damage. Alcohol use by adolescents tends to increase dramatically as they

Table 18-4
Major Substances Having Abuse Potential

Substance and method of use	Examples (including substances' street names)	Observable effects of use
Alcohol—swallowed in liquid form	*Beer* (brew); *wine; liquor; mixed drinks* (booze, juice)	Impaired coordination, staggered gait, bloodshot eyes, flushing, slurred speech, impaired judgment, learning and memory deficits
Tobacco—smoked, chewed	*Cigarettes; pipe tobacco; cigars; chewing tobacco; snuff*	Coughing, sore throat, raspy voice, shortness of breath
Cannabis (marijuana/ hashish)—smoked in handrolled cigarettes or pipes	*Marijuana* (grass, pot, smoke, cheeba, joint, weed, ganja, reefer, sinsemilla, bud, endo, boom, blunt [a hollowed out cigar filled with marijuana], Acapulco gold, Colombian, chronic or primo [marijuana mixed with crushed rock cocaine], dime bag [$10 worth of marijuana], dust [marijuana mixed with various chemicals including PCP], frios or lovelies [marijuana dipped in PCP], J [a joint], nickel bag or nick [$5 worth of marijuana]); *tetrahydrocannabinol* (THC); *hashish* (hash, shish); *hashish oil* (hash oil)	Restlessness, relaxation, bloodshot eyes, increased appetite, impaired coordination, dry mouth and throat, impaired short-term memory and comprehension, altered sense of time, reduced concentration and coordination, paranoia, psychosis
Inhalants—inhaled or sniffed, sometimes by using a paper bag, rag, gauze, or ampules	*Nitrous oxide* (laughing gas, whippets, chargers); *amyl nitrite* (poppers, snappers); *butyl nitrite* (rush, bolt, bullet, locker room, climax); *chlorohydrocarbons* (aerosol sprays or cleaning fluids); *hydrocarbons* (solvents, such as cans of aerosol propellants, gasoline, paint thinner); *shoe shine pastes; glue; toluene; adhesives; halothane, ether, or other anesthetics; white-out liquid*	Dilated pupils, runny nose, watery eyes, impaired coordination, slurred speech, headache, weight loss, nausea, sneezing, coughing, nosebleeds, fatigue, loss of appetite, impaired judgment, involuntary passing of urine and feces, disorientation
Cocaine and crack cocaine—snorted, injected, or smoked	*Cocaine* (coke, snow, nose candy, flake, blow, big C, lady, white, snowbirds, snort, toot, white lady, cane); *crack cocaine* (crack, rock freebase)	Increased alertness and energy, dilated pupils, rapid speech, tremors, sweating, runny or irritated nose, decreased appetite, weight loss, depression, nosebleeds
Stimulants—snorted, injected, smoked, or swallowed in capsule, tablet, or pill form	*Amphetamines* (speed, uppers, ups, black beauties, pep pills, bennies, dexies, copilots, bumblebees, hearts, Benzedrine, Dexedrine, footballs, biphetamine); *methamphetamines* (crank, crystal meth, crystal methedrine, speed, ice, ice cream, batu, shabu, water); *other stimulants* (Ritalin, Cylert, Preludin, Didrex, Chlortermine Hydrochloride, Plegine, Tepanil)	Increased alertness, decreased appetite, weight loss, increased respiration and heart rate, dilated pupils, sweating, rash, insomnia, depression, headaches, blurred vision, dizziness, sleeplessness, anxiety
Depressants (or sedatives)—injected or swallowed in capsule, tablet, or pill form	*Barbiturates* (downers, barbs, blue devils, red devils, yellow jackets, yellows, Nembutal, Seconal, Amytal, phenobarbital, secobarbital, pentobarbital, Doriden, Placidyl, Fiorinal, Tuinal); *methaqualone hydrochloride* (quaaludes, ludes, supers); *tranquilizers* (Valium, Librium, Miltown, Serax, Equanil, Tranxene, Halcion, Xanax, Dalmane, Ativan)	Impaired judgment, staggered gait, drowsiness, slurred speech, dilated pupils, shallow breathing, weak and rapid pulse

(Continued)

Table 18-4 (*Continued*)

Substance and method of use	Examples (including substances' street names)	Observable effects of use
Hallucinogens PCP—snorted, injected, drunk, applied to leafy material and smoked, or swallowed in capsule, tablet, or pill form	*Phencyclidine hydrochloride* (PCP, hog, angel dust, loveboat, lovely, killer weed, crystal, superweed, rocket fuel, sherms, embalming fluid, KJ, supergrass)	Drowsiness, excitement, slurred speech, muscle rigidity, unusual eye movements, exaggerated gait, sweating
LSD—swallowed in tablet or capsule form or placed into thin squares of gelatin, paper, sugar cubes, gum, candy, or crackers	*Lysergic acid diethylamide* (LSD, acid, microdot, white lightning, blue heaven, sugar cubes, tab [tiny LSD-soaked bit of paper], blotter acid, cubes, purple haze)	Dilated pupils, elevated body temperature, anxiety, confusion, disoriented sense of direction, distance, and time
Mushrooms or peyote—chewed, smoked, or ground and infused in hot water and drunk as tea	*Psilocybin* (mushrooms, magic mushrooms, 'shrooms); *mescaline* and *peyote* (mesc, STP, buttons, cactus)	Dilated pupils, sweating, hyperventilation, tremors, rambling speech, hyperactivity, depression, muscle tension, vomiting, dilated pupils, dizziness, chills, rapid pulse, sweating, hallucinations
Opiates (or narcotics)—injected, snorted, or smoked	*Heroin* (smack, dope, junk, horse, mud, brown sugar, black tar, big H, China white, Mexican brown); *opium* (paregoric, Dover's powder, parepectolin); *morphine* (Pectoral syrup); *meperidine hydrochloride* (pethidine, Demerol, Mepergan); *other narcotics* (Percocet, Percodan, Tussionex, fentanyl citrate, Darvon, Talwin, Lomotil)	Needle marks, slurred speech, slow gait, sleepy appearance, constricted pupils, decreased pulse and respiration rate, nausea, vomiting, watery eyes, itching
Designer drugs—injected or swallowed in pill form	*Analogues of fentanyl* (synthetic heroin, China white, T's, blues); *analogues of meperidine* (MPTP [new heroin], MPPP [synthetic heroin]); *analogues of amphetamines or methamphetamines* (MDMA [ecstacy, XTC, Adam, essence], MDM, STP, PMA, 2,5-DMA, TMA, DOM, DOB, EVE, methcathinone [cat]); *analogues of phencyclidine* (PCPy, PCE)	Uncontrollable tremors, drooling, impaired speech, blurred vision, chills or sweating and faintness, anxiety, depression, paranoia
Steroids (anabolic)—injected or swallowed in pill form	*Anabolic steroids* (roids, juice)	More than 70 side effects ranging in severity from liver cancer to acne, including extremely aggressive behavior, depression, jaundice, purple or red spots on body, swelling of feet and lower legs, trembling, unexplained darkening of the skin, bad breath odor; in males, withered testicles, sterility, impotence; in females, irreversible masculine traits, breast reduction, sterility

Note. Several over-the-counter drugs, including common compounds for colds and coughs, sleeping aids, weight loss aids, nasal sprays, and alertness medications, also can be abused (Stout, 1992).
Source: Adapted, in part, from Kropenske and Howard (1994) and U.S. Department of Education (1991).

Exhibit 18-1
Newcomb and Bentler's Thoughts on the Consequences of Substance Use and Abuse

Not all drug use is bad and will fry one's brain (as the commercials imply). Such claims, as reflected in the national hysteria and depicted in media advertisements for treatment programs, repeat the failed scare tactics of the past. All drug abuse is destructive and can have devastating consequences for individuals, their families, and society. The difference or distinction lies in the use versus abuse of drugs.

There is little research on the consequences of teenage drug use. The short-term consequences of abuse are obvious: car accidents, fights, and missing school, to name a few. Long-term consequences require lengthy longitudinal studies that follow a group of teenagers from adolescence to adulthood, and results of these studies are only now beginning to reveal meaningful results.

Infrequent, intermittent, or occasional use of drugs by a basically healthy teenager probably has few short-term and long-term negative or adverse consequences. Long-term consequences of abuse, heavy use, or misuse of drugs as a teenager can

potentially affect many areas of life as an adult.

There has been a tendency to focus on the short-term or acute negative consequences of drug abuse, while ignoring the longer term consequences. Although the short-term consequences of abuse are many and can be quite tragic (e.g., a fatal accident if driving while drunk), so too may long term consequences of abuse. One reason that cigarette abuse among teenagers is often not considered a focus of treatment is that there are rarely if ever short-term problems with such behavior, despite the fact that some evidence indicates that cigarettes may be the most deadly drug from a long-term perspective. We found that in the quantities typically used by normal adolescents, cigarettes had more negative health effects and increased health service utilization than use of alcohol, cannabis, or hard drugs over a four-year period....

Most children and teenagers will become drug users in their lives, whether limited to alcohol, caffeine, and cigarettes or extended to marijuana, cocaine, hard drugs, and prescription medica-

tions. The ages at which initiation and, in particular, regular use occur is quite crucial. Childhood and adolescence are critical periods for the development of both personal and interpersonal competence, coping skills, and responsible decision making. Drug use is a manner of coping that can interfere with or preclude the necessary development of these other critical skills if it is engaged in regularly at a young age. For instance, if a young teenager learns to use alcohol as a way to reduce distress, he or she may never learn other coping skills to ameliorate distress. Thus, teenage drug use may truncate, interfere with, or circumvent essential maturational processes and development that typically occur during adolescence. As one result, teenage drug users enter adult roles of marriage and work prematurely and without adequate socioemotional growth and often experience greater failure in these adult roles. Following the area of treatment, consequences of teenage drug use are the second least understood and researched area of child and teenage substance use. They deserve greater attention.

Source: Newcomb and Bentler (1989), pp. 247–248.

---

get older. Beer is by far their favorite beverage of abuse, followed by wine and hard liquor.... Most adolescents are introduced to alcohol by experimenting with beer. Drinking to intoxication, or being "bombed" or "smashed," is a common occurrence among frequent adolescent users of alcohol. Alcohol is a major problem for young drinkers, often leading to the use of other drugs. (p. 355)

Following are warning signs of excessive drinking among adolescents (Towers, 1987, pp. 61–63, with changes in notation):

- truancy, class cutting
- declining interest in extracurricular activities
- dropping old friends or hanging out with new ones
- unexpected mood swings, unprovoked hostility, fighting, or vehement arguments
- vehemently defending the right to drink or get high
- resisting talking or hearing about alcohol
- dramatic changes in physical appearance
- leaving beer or whiskey bottles in room

- slurred or incoherent speech
- always appearing tired
- deterioration of relationships with family members

Marijuana abuse. Research suggests that 18-year-olds who were frequent marijuana users (that is, used it at least once a week) and who also had tried at least one drug other than marijuana were troubled (Shedler & Block, 1990). They were more likely to be interpersonally alienated, emotionally withdrawn, and unhappy than their peers who had only occasionally tried marijuana or one other drug. Even at the early age of 7 years, they were relatively maladjusted. During adolescence, they had difficulty forming good relationships, were insecure, and showed signs of emotional distress. *These findings suggest that the social and psychological problems of adolescents who are frequent drug users may predate adolescence and the initiation of drug use.* Thus, children who have psychological problems may be at increased risk for later alcohol or drug abuse.

Table 18-5
Percentage of Students in 8th, 10th, and 12th Grades Reporting Annual or Daily Use of Drugs in 1995

Drug	Annual use[a]			Daily use[b]		
	8th grade %	10th grade %	12th grade %	8th grade %	10th grade %	12th grade %
Alcohol (any use)	45.3	63.5	73.7	0.7	1.7	3.5
Tobacco						
Cigarettes—any use	—	—	—	9.3	16.3	21.6
Cigarettes—half pack+/day	—	—	—	3.4	8.3	12.4
Smokeless tobacco	—	—	—	1.2	2.7	3.6
Cannabis (marijuana/hashish)	15.8	28.7	34.7	0.8	2.8	4.6
Inhalants	12.8	9.6	8.0	0.2	0.1	0.1
Cocaine (total)	2.6	3.5	4.0	0.1	0.1	0.2
Crack	1.6	1.8	2.1	<0.05	<0.05	0.1
Other cocaine	2.1	3.0	3.4	<0.05	<0.05	0.1
Stimulants	8.7	11.9	9.3	0.2	0.2	0.3
Depressants						
Tranquilizers	2.7	4.0	4.4	<0.05	0.1	<0.05
Barbiturates	—	—	4.7	—	—	0.1
Hallucinogens (total)	3.6	7.2	9.3	0.1	<0.05	0.1
LSD	3.2	6.5	8.4	0.1	<0.05	0.1
PCP	—	—	1.8	—	—	0.3
Other hallucinogens	1.7	2.8	3.8	<0.05	<0.05	0.1
Opiates						
Heroin	1.4	1.1	1.1	<0.05	<0.05	0.1
Other opiates	—	—	4.7	—	—	0.1
Steroids	1.0	1.2	1.5	<0.05	0.1	0.2

[a]Annual use refers to any use in past year.
[b]Daily use refers to use every day.
Source: Adapted from Johnston, O'Malley, and Bachman (1995b).

Although drugs do not necessarily cause the psychological problems seen in drug-abusing adolescents, the abuse of drugs is likely to exacerbate existing problems.

Parental reactions to a child's substance abuse. When parents learn that their adolescent is a substance abuser, they may be concerned about the health and safety of the adolescent, be worried that the adolescent may die, feel guilty about their responsibility for the adolescent's becoming a substance abuser, be concerned that the other siblings also may become drug or alcohol dependent, be annoyed that a member of their family is a substance abuser, and be concerned about the family's reputation in the community (Needle, Glynn, & Needle, 1983). Consequently, you will need to consider the reactions of parents when you interview them about their child's use of substances.

Ethnicity and substance abuse. White American adolescents report higher rates of drug use, both legal and illicit, than do Black American or Hispanic American adolescents (Johnston et al., 1994). Black American youths and Asian American youths have lower-than-average rates of drug use. The reasons for these findings are not clear, but the following hypotheses merit consideration (Wallace & Bachman, 1991). Asian American youths often have a strong commitment to educational advancement and academic success and spend less time in peer-oriented activities than do other youths. And many Black American youths have a strong commitment to religion. These traits may encourage Asian American youths and Black American youths to avoid the use of drugs.

Unfortunately, there are segments of the Black American population in which substance abuse has had tragic consequences. Crack cocaine has affected some Black American families in the following ways (Staples, 1991, p. 259):

1. Adolescents are taking over as heads of their families largely because of their incomes from selling crack.
2. Young, pregnant mothers are risking their lives to secure the drug and, in some cases, exchanging sexual relations for it or the money to buy it.
3. Some adolescent girls are deserting their families and forming violent gangs to sell and buy crack.
4. In some communities, female addicts exceed male users for the first time in the race's history. Because many of them are in their childbearing years, there are increasing reports of drug use or drug addiction among pregnant Black women. The result is the increasing numbers of infants prenatally exposed to drugs and at risk for later developmental problems.
5. Although the extended family network in Black communities has traditionally absorbed needy children, the drug culture has created holes in its safety net. Unlike the individuals ravaged by poverty and racism, the drug-addicted individual is markedly different in behavior, temperament, and willingness to cooperate.

Hispanic American male youths may use drugs because of several cultural traits, such as *machismo* (male role attributes), *personalismo* (emphasis on interpersonal relations), and *cornalismo* (value placed on ethnic unity) (Austin & Gilbert, 1989).

Native Americans have significantly higher rates of alcohol abuse than do other ethnic minorities (Young, 1992). The high prevalence of alcohol abuse may in part be associated with the mortality rate of Native Americans, which is three times the national average (Young, 1992). Seventy-five percent of all Native American deaths are directly or indirectly linked to alcohol. Out of the 10 leading causes of death among Native Americans, five are related to alcohol—accidents, cirrhosis of the liver, alcohol dependency, suicide, and homicide. Drugs other than alcohol also are prevalent in the Native American youth population. The rate of inhalant use among Native American youth is twice as high as the national rate for youths 12 to 17 years old (Young, 1992). Long-term use of inhalants can have substantial deleterious effects on neurocognitive functioning (Filley, Heaton, & Rosenberg, 1990).

Interviewing Issues

In interviewing an adolescent for possible substance abuse, ask about any substances that the adolescent may be taking. The adolescent may not be forthright about his or her sub-

stance use because of fears about disclosure of possible illegal activities. If the adolescent is open about his or her substance use, do not be surprised to learn that he or she has experimented with marijuana; use of marijuana is widespread among adolescents in our culture. One of your major concerns in the interview should be the *frequency of drug use*. A second concern is the different types of drugs that the adolescent is taking because the *interaction effects of the combined use of psychoactive drugs may be lethal* (Tarter, Ott, & Mezzich, 1991). You also need to decide whether the adolescent's pattern of drug use reflects abuse or experimentation.

Be especially alert to the following signs in the child's behavior, which may give you clues to possible drug abuse (Cambor & Millman, 1991):

- impaired family relations
- lying
- stealing
- fighting
- running away from home
- evasion
- unexplained or sudden absences
- changes in daily routines
- recent changes in friends
- social withdrawal
- deterioration in grades
- truancy, class cutting
- declining interest in extracurricular activities
- leaving drug paraphernalia in room

In assessing substance abuse among adolescents, you will need to consider substance variables, individual variables, situational variables, and familial variables (Needle et al., 1983).

SUBSTANCE VARIABLES

- substances used by the adolescent
- doses of substances used
- methods of administration
- purity or strength of substances used

INDIVIDUAL VARIABLES

- the adolescent's age, sex, and ethnicity
- the adolescent's class in school
- the adolescent's school performance
- the adolescent's level of stress
- the adolescent's adjustment to using drugs and alcohol
- the adolescent's expectations about the effects of the drug
- the adolescent's personality, psychological state, and physiological state

SITUATIONAL VARIABLES

- the adolescent's neighborhood, peer group, and peer relationships
- the setting in which the adolescent takes the drug
- the frequency with which the adolescent takes the drug

FAMILIAL VARIABLES

- the parents' use of drugs and alcohol
- the siblings' use of drugs and alcohol
- family communication patterns
- family stresses
- the family's method of dealing with or responding to the adolescent's drug and/or alcohol use

In each case, you should consider the reasons for the drug and alcohol use.

1. Is it a way to avoid problems within the family, at school, or on the job?
2. Is the adolescent imitating peer group, sibling, or parental behavior?
3. Does the family indirectly or directly contribute to the problem?
4. Do the parents focus on the adolescent's problem to avoid their own problems?
5. Have there been any recent changes in the family's level of stress, such as increased arguments between the adolescent and parents, changes in the family's financial status, or increased arguments between the parents?
6. Has the adolescent become drug or alcohol dependent to cope with excessive stress in his or her familial or social environment?
7. Has the adolescent's drug or alcohol use added to the family stress?
8. Have the added stressors created a cycle that can maintain the drug-abusing behavior?

Figure 18-3 shows a possible progression from substance use to substance abuse.

Earlier in the chapter, you read that adolescents who are substance abusers also may engage in illegal activities—such as drug selling, theft, and prostitution—to support their drug-use life style. Therefore, consider asking about possible illegal activities, but be prepared for silence about these issues. *In addition, you should refer the adolescent for a thorough medical examination in cases of substance abuse.* A medical examination is especially needed because chronic drug or alcohol abuse may compromise the adolescent's health.

The following dialogue occurred during an initial interview with a female interviewee who was referred by her health care provider (Beck, Wright, Newman, & Liese, 1993, pp. 172–173, with changes in notation). Note how the interviewer summed up in her last remark what the interviewee said.

IR: Hello, Louise. What would you like to talk about today?
IE: I don't really even know. I was sent here by that doctor at the clinic. I figured I had to be here.
IR: You must have some concerns…some things that are bothering you.
IE: Yeh, I guess. But I don't know what good it will do to talk to you.
IR: You doubt that this will be helpful.

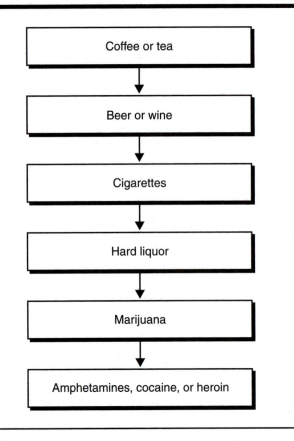

Figure 18-3. Possible progression from substance use to substance abuse.

IE: Yeh, that's right.
IR: What other thoughts do you have about being here?
IE: Well I've been in treatment before, but, as you can probably guess, I'm on the shit again.
IR: What do you mean by "on the shit"?
IE: Oh come on, man! You know what that means! I'm doing drugs!
IR: Does "on the shit" mean that you are doing drugs daily? weekly? monthly?
IE: To me it means doing any drugs at all!
IR: So any slip and you consider yourself "on the shit"?
IE: Yeh! I was clean for a month and then last week I had a really bad time with my old man. I went right out on a two-day binge.
IR: And what have you done since then?
IE: If you mean drugs, I have been clean since then, but I don't suppose it will last.
IR: So when you slip, even once, you see yourself as having a relapse.
IE: Right.
IR: And when you say "I don't suppose it will last" I get the impression that you don't feel fully capable of staying off drugs.
IE: No, not really. Sometimes it seems pretty easy to stay clean and sometimes it's really impossible.
IR: So from what you have said so far, you are skeptical about being here. You doubt that I can be helpful. You

see yourself as having fully relapsed, based on a two-day binge. And generally you see yourself as being somewhat helpless to control your drug use.

IE: Yeh, that's it in a nutshell!

Exercise 18-2. Evaluating Interviewers' Styles

The following examples show a nonpreferred and a preferred way of interviewing adolescents in cases of substance abuse. Evaluate the qualities of each interview, including the interview techniques used and the interviewee's responses. Then compare your evaluation with that in the Comments section. Each statement is numbered to facilitate your evaluation. The dialogue in this exercise was adapted from Miller and Mastria (1977, pp. 18–20).

Part 1. Nonpreferred Style

1. IR: Why did you come here?
2. IE: My mother says that I drink too much.
3. IR: Did you come because you really wanted to, or because your mother made you come?
4. IE: I guess a little of both.
5. IR: You must recognize your alcoholism and want to change, or we will not be able to help you.
6. IE: I understand that.
7. IR: Are you an alcoholic?
8. IE: I'm not sure. I don't think so.
9. IR: You are avoiding your problem. You must admit that you are an alcoholic before we can treat you.
10. IE: I know that I have a problem...that I drink too much ...but I don't drink every day.
11. IR: How often and how much do you drink?
12. IE: I drink about as much as other kids that I know. I overdo it and get drunk about twice a week.
13. IR: And you still say that you're not an alcoholic?
14. IE: I told you that I don't think so!
15. IR: Why do you get so angry when I ask you about your drinking?
16. IE: I'm not angry!
17. IR: You sure sound that way to me. You must be honest with me, or I can't help you.
18. IE: (*Silence*)
19. IR: Your motivation to change seems very poor. I'm not certain that we can help you unless you change your attitude.
20. IE: (*Silence, looking angry*)

Part 2. Preferred Style

1. IR: How can I help you?
2. IE: I'm not sure.
3. IR: Well, maybe we can find out together. What has been bothering you lately?
4. IE: Well, my drinking. My mother says that I drink too much.
5. IR: How has drinking affected your life?
6. IE: Well...my mother and I argue a lot. She nags me all of the time. And...well...my school, too, I guess. I've been drinking a lot on the weekends and missing school on Monday morning.

7. IR: Can you be more specific about your drinking?
8. IE: I drink about as much as other kids that I know.
9. IR: How much would that be?
10. IE: Oh, about 7 or 8 beers at a time.
11. IR: What problems are you having because of your drinking?
12. IE: I overdo it and get drunk about twice a week.
13. IR: Do you drink with your friends?
14. IE: Yes.
15. IR: And how often do they get drunk?
16. IE: Oh, about 2 or 3 times a week.
17. IR: I'd like to learn about how alcohol affects your life. First, what situations cause you to drink?
18. IE: Well...my mother is a problem.... It's her general attitude toward me and my friends.
19. IR: Please be more specific. What does your mother do that bothers you?
20. IE: Well...she nags me a lot. She says that I let people take advantage of me. After the nagging, I start to drink a lot of beer.

Comments

The first interview segment is poor. Most of the questions are either closed questions or confrontational questions. The interviewer's general tone shows a lack of sensitivity. The interview begins with a somewhat confrontational question (1) and then a closed question (3). The interviewee's first remark (2) is not followed up. Several comments are in the form of a lecture (5, 9, 17, 19). One question is blunt (7), and another is a compound question that needs to be divided into two parts (11). Some comments are argumentative and confrontational (13, 15, 17, 19).

The second interview segment is better. There is a mix of open-ended and focused questions, and the interviewer's general tone is caring and thoughtful. Some questions are open-ended (1, 5), one remark is an empathic comment that tries to make the goal of the interview a collaborative effort (3), one question asks for clarification (7), several questions are focused questions (9, 11, 13, 15, 17, 19).

The interviewee in the first interview segment is less responsive and more silent, angry, and hesitant in revealing information than is the interviewee in the second interview segment. The interviewee in the second interview segment reveals more about herself than does the interviewee in the first interview segment.

When an adolescent is abusing illegal drugs, or even alcohol and legal substances, he or she may be guarded or suspicious of you during the interview. One of his or her major concerns may be confidentiality. Usually, you must gain the adolescent's trust before you can obtain the needed information. Table F-1 in Appendix F provides a semistructured interview for interviewing adolescents about drug abuse, and Table F-2 in Appendix F provides a semistructured interview for screening adolescents for alcohol abuse or dependence. After you complete the interview, answer the questions in Table 18-6. Note that a key question is "What is the adolescent's desire for change?"

Table 18-6
Evaluating the Interview Findings for an Adolescent with a Substance Abuse Problem

Background

1. Who referred the adolescent for evaluation?

Drug Use

2. How severe is the adolescent's substance abuse problem?
3. When did the adolescent first begin to use the substance?
4. How long has the adolescent abused the substance?
5. When did the adolescent experience her or his initial "high" with the substance?
6. What method does the adolescent use to take the substance (for example, ingestion, smoking, inhalation, intramuscular or intravenous injection)?
7. How much of the substance does the adolescent take?
8. How often does the adolescent take the substance (for example, daily, weekly, monthly)?
9. How available is the substance?
10. How does the adolescent obtain the substance?
11. Where does the adolescent use the substance?
12. How much money does the adolescent spend on the substance each week?
13. What influence do peers have on the adolescent's substance use?
14. What is the family history of substance use and abuse?

Part Substance Plays in Adolescent's Life

15. What is the perceived importance of the substance in the adolescent's life?
16. What are the reasons that the adolescent takes the substance (for example, to feel good, to have a good time, to be high, to relax, to get along in the world, to see what effect it would have, to be cool, to heighten sexual pleasure, to be in a twilight zone, to lose weight, to escape feelings, to relieve nervousness, to block emotions, to avoid reality, to cope with stress and problems)?
17. What is the adolescent's level of frustration when the substance is not available?
18. How did the adolescent function before she or he started to use drugs?

Problems Associated with Substance Abuse

19. What medical problems does the adolescent have that are associated with the substance abuse?
20. What social problems does the adolescent have that are associated with the substance abuse?
21. What psychological problems does the adolescent have that are associated with the substance abuse?
22. What legal problems does the adolescent have that are associated with the substance abuse?
23. What is the adolescent's overdose history?

Treatment Goals

24. When was the adolescent first concerned about her or his use of the substance (if ever)?
25. What is the adolescent's motivation for changing her or his substance abuse behavior?
26. Why hasn't the adolescent been able to stop use of the substance on her or his own?
27. What is the adolescent's attitude toward receiving treatment for her or his substance abuse problem?
28. Why is the adolescent seeking treatment at this time in her or his life for her or his substance abuse problem (for example, is it because of a genuine desire for change, to get others off her or his back, to alleviate an immediate crisis situation, because the parents are demanding that she or he receive treatment, or because of trouble with the law)?
29. If there were prior treatments for the adolescent's substance abuse problem, what were the results?
30. What does the adolescent expect from treatment for her or his substance abuse problem?
31. What role can the family play in the treatment for the adolescent's substance abuse problem?
32. What community resources are available to the adolescent to support intervention efforts for her or his substance abuse problem?

Source: Adapted from Roffman and George (1988) and Tarter, Ott, and Mezzich (1991).

If you decide that you need more information from the adolescent about his or her substance use or abuse, consider using a self-monitoring procedure. For example, you can ask the adolescent to complete the form shown in Table 18-7 for drugs or the form shown in Table 18-8 for alcohol. Self-monitoring of substance use may help the adolescent become more aware of his or her drug or alcohol pattern and identify the situations in which drug or alcohol use occurs (Sobell & Sobell, 1978). A daily log also may serve as a baseline of substance-use patterns by which to monitor changes if the adolescent enters a treatment program.

Finally, in some cases, adolescents who become more aware of their pattern of substance abuse may begin to try to reduce use of the substance.

A family assessment also may be helpful in cases of substance abuse, particularly in relation to possible family dysfunction (including divorce, marital discord, parent-child conflict, and child abuse) and drug-use behavior (see Chapter 4). A family assessment is important because of the major influence of parents and siblings on adolescents' alcohol consumption and drug use and because of a possible genetic vulnerability. Adolescents who cannot turn to their parents

Table 18-7
Weekly Drug Use Record

DRUG USE RECORD

Name: _____

Item	Day						
	Sun.	Mon.	Tues.	Wed.	Thurs.	Fri.	Sat.
1. Date of drug use							
2. Time of day							
3. Location							
4. People present							
5. Activity while using drug							
6. Name of drug							
7. Amount of drug consumed							
8. Urge to use drug (with 1 = no urge at all, 10 = extremely strong urge)							
9. Other substances being used at the same time							
10. Level of drug high (with 1 = none at all, 10 = extremely high)							
11. Mood states *preceding* use of drug and intensity of mood states[a]							
12. Mood states *following* use of drug and intensity of mood states[a]							

[a]List how you were feeling, such as happy, bored, tense (nervous), calm, sad, depressed, angry, nostalgic, lonely, or emotionally drained. Then, rate the intensity of each feeling you listed from 1 to 10, with 1 = extremely mild and 10 = extremely strong.
Source: Adapted from Roffman and George (1988).

for advice or who are social isolates may be particularly vulnerable to substance abuse (Windle, Miller-Tutzauer, Barnes, & Welte, 1991).

In addition to assessing their substance-abusing behavior, you likely will need to refer adolescents with substance abuse problems for a psychological evaluation. This evaluation may be needed because adolescents who have a substance abuse problem also probably have other types of psychological difficulties (Brown, Mott, & Stewart, 1992).

Interventions

Interventions must consider the part that drugs or alcohol plays in the adolescent's life. The more drugs or alcohol has become an integral part of the adolescent's life, the more difficult it will be for him or her to give the substance up. In working with adolescents who are substance abusers, consider the following (Novacek, Raskin, & Hogan, 1991):

Table 18-8
Weekly Drinking Awareness Record

WEEKLY DRINKING AWARENESS RECORD

Name: _____

Date	Total number and type of standard drinks[a]				Approximate time spent in drinking situation (e.g., if you spent 3 hours at a party where you were drinking put "3 hours")	Feelings while drinking[b]		Drinking context (Check one)				Total number of drinks refused	Estimated total number of drinks to be consumed tomorrow
	Straight	Mixed drinks	Beer	Wine	Total		Emotional	Physical	Alone	With others	Private place	Public place		
1														
2														
3														
4														
5														
6														
7														

Feelings Code—Emotional

A = Happy   F = Depressed
B = Bored   G = Angry
C = Tense, nervous   H = Nostalgic
D = Calm, serene   I = Lonely
E = Sad   J = Emotionally drained

Feelings Code—Physical

A = Headache   E = Simple cold
B = Felt very good   F = Felt ill, very sick
C = Felt OK   G = Tired, sleepy
D = Exhausted   H = Weak, but not ill

[a]One (1) standard drink = 1 oz. of liquor, 4 oz. wine, or 12 oz. of beer.

[b]You may indicate more than one feeling at one time. If your feelings *change* during a drinking situation, indicate this by an arrow. For example, C,G → E means first you felt tense and angry, then you felt sad.

Source: Reprinted, with permission of the publisher, from M. B. Sobell and L. C. Sobell, *Behavioral Treatment of Alcohol Problems: Individualized Therapy and Controlled Drinking,* copyright 1978 by Plenum, p. 200.

598

Drawingboard   by Signe Wilkerson

Signe Wilkerson/Cartoonists & Writers Syndicate

If we want to change these youth, we must (1) acknowledge that their drug experiences are pleasurable; (2) make them aware that being a drug user is an identity choice—a choice that may provide short-term pleasure, but one that will ultimately involve negative health, social, and legal consequences; and (3) provide them with alternative identity options. This latter task will not be easy because drug-using youth have already rejected many of the traditional identities accepted by society. (p. 490)

Adolescent substance abusers and their families can be helped by several methods, including individual and family counseling, group counseling in which individuals share their experiences with others who are experiencing similar problems (including Alcoholics Anonymous, Alateen, and Narcotics Anonymous), and inpatient treatment (also referred to as *detoxification programs*), where needed.

You may need to recommend an inpatient treatment program (or partial hospitalization) if the adolescent is addicted to a substance and one or more of the following are present (Sbriglio, Hartman, Millman, & Khuri, 1988):

- severe abuse of drugs or frequent intoxications
- impaired ability to function at school or at work
- severe psychological disorder or suicidal ideations
- stealing, dealing in drugs, or engaging in other antisocial activities
- failure to benefit from prior outpatient treatment

Keys to successful intervention are identifying the problems within the adolescent and the family and reducing stress. Therefore, family intervention is generally more effective than individual intervention in treating adolescents with a substance abuse problem. However, getting families involved is often difficult because they tend to resist change (Szapocznik, Perez-Vidal, Brickman, Foote, Santisteban, Hervis, & Kurtines, 1988).

Breaking a drug addiction is not easy, as indicated in the following essay, written by the brother of a person with a drug problem (Muñoz, 1996, with permission):

Those of us who daily see the face of drug addiction witness a crushing struggle that illuminates both the remarkable nature of the human spirit and the limits of independent action....

My brother is addicted to crack. Life singled him out early—he flunked first grade for his love of drawing dinosaurs. As he grew older, he could communicate beauty in whatever medium he chose—wood, clay, paint, even movement. It would be a decade later, in my profession as a teacher, that I would find words to describe him: gifted; a kinesthetic learner. He also had a troubled childhood and a case of urban alienation. As to what caused his addiction, who can say? What I do know is that he long ago acknowledged his problem and engaged in a battle against it.

The scope of his struggle became clear to me on the day I encountered him in a corner of his room, glistening in the sweat of his addiction, praying feverishly. I remember him during that phase as resolute in his belief that his faith would bring him to the stable ground of self-possession. But as months passed and his addiction continued he looked elsewhere for hope.

"I can do this alone! I can stop this!" he would shout. "It's just a matter of decision. I just need to win day by day." But my brother continued to lose each day, month after month and year after year. His adamant proclamations of self-reliance were meaningless at 2 in the morning when I would discover his bed empty. A short jail sentence failed to deter him from the seduction of crack. I found him once wandering the streets of South Central Los Angeles, a man with a fractured spirit....

My brother had no chance at a Betty Ford clinic or the other expensive desert getaways available for the rich and famous. Most programs available to the poor are underfunded and many exist in the very neighborhoods where crack is readily available. An incredible demand for rehabilitation overwhelms these scarce resources. One center told us they had a three-month waiting list. Another program asked if my brother had insurance. Still another offered a detox program that lasted only 10 days, and then my brother would be on his own....

"Just don't do it" sounds practical, but it belittles a process that requires participation from the addict himself, key family members, various community agencies and the government. My brother needed rehabilitation, not punishment, to help him reestablish equilibrium and reenter mainstream society....

I'm willing to bet that many if not most crack addicts are presently engaged in an anguished struggle much like my brother's....

The ideals of personal initiative and self-reliance are the engine of the American marketplace and foundation of our culture. But in the realm of drug addiction, they offer little in the way of answers or solutions. (p. B7)

Case Illustrations

The first case that follows provides insight into some general problems associated with substance abuse, and the second case illustrates the effectiveness of an intervention program with an adolescent who was abusing substances.

CASE 18-2. R. W.

R. W. was a 17-year-old, left-handed male referred for neuropsychological assessment by a school psychologist after repeatedly missing classes, fighting with peers, and failing to attend school regularly. R. W. reported a five-year history of extensive alcohol and marijuana abuse. A review of R. W.'s school records revealed a steady decline of his academic performance and an increase in truancy and oppositional behavior since the sixth grade. An interview with his parents indicated that R. W. had always been difficult to discipline but was not openly defiant or disrespectful until recently. The written comments of his grade school teachers indicated that he had difficulty sustaining attention in class and that he had trouble staying in his assigned seat, but his school performance was average until junior high school. Most of the comments of his junior high school teachers indicated that R. W. had more "potential" than was reflected in his resulting grades; furthermore, most of the teachers added that he was not applying appropriate effort in class or on homework assignments.

A neuropsychological evaluation revealed average general intelligence; however, R. W. had significantly lower scores on subtests that required abstract reasoning and nonverbal problem solving. Other neuropsychological test results confirmed that he had difficulty with problem solving as well as difficulty with delayed recall, sustained attention, and visuospatial tasks. Furthermore, R. W.'s behavior during the testing sessions was characterized by impulsivity and concentration and attention difficulties, suggesting that he might be suffering from an attention-deficit/hyperactivity disorder.

Drug use and oppositional behavior appeared to be due in part to difficulties coping with scholastic and interpersonal demands. The pattern and extent of his substance abuse likely exacerbated his cognitive limitations. R. W. was eventually referred to a long-term adolescent inpatient program that stressed coping skills training. (Fals-Stewart & Schafer, 1992, p. 185, with changes in notation)

CASE 18-3. DAVID

David, who was 15 years old when he came to the attention of school personnel, was worried about his parents. He had been close to his mother, but she began to ignore him. Instead, she devoted herself to her alcoholic husband. David began to use marijuana and got into trouble in school. After repeated incidents, he was sent to an inpatient program at a rehabilitation center specializing in drug addiction. Upon his discharge, he immediately returned to drug and alcohol consumption. After a short time, and at the urging of his high school guidance counselor, his parents became involved in weekly family therapy sessions with David. During the sessions, the family learned about how they had been expressing themselves and how they had been communicating with one another. It was pointed out that David had been working at accomplishing two things. First, he was single-handedly keeping his parents' marriage together; second, he was gradually increasing his self-destructive behavior to garner more attention from his mother. In time, David's father became motivated by his son's concern and sought treatment for his own alcoholism. Today, David's father is sober and regularly attends A.A. meetings. David's mother became less obsessed with her husband's problems and therefore had more emotional energy to give to David. The parents' relationship improved. After a final relapse, David remained sober and has been sober for over three years. (Sweet, 1991, p. 7, with changes in notation)

Exercise 18-3. Evaluating Stage of Drug Use

Read the case and then answer the questions that follow it. This exercise is from Nowinski (1990).

Jeff was referred for an evaluation after his parents overheard him on the phone arranging to buy $50 worth of cocaine. During the interview, he admitted that he'd been using cocaine for about four months. Lately, he'd been using cocaine about two or three times a week, in relatively small amounts. His total use was less than a gram every couple of weeks. So far, he has experienced only relatively mild withdrawal symptoms. He said that he sometimes felt a little depressed and jittery after getting high. This was to have been his first independent buy from a dealer; until then, he'd been sharing with friends.

Although Jeff has experimented with alcohol, he didn't enjoy the feeling of alcohol intoxication—not nearly as much as he enjoyed a cocaine high. He liked the feeling of euphoria that cocaine gave him and also the self-confidence it instilled. It made all of his insecurities disappear, at least for a while. The expression on his face and the tone in his voice strongly suggested that he was motivated to seek those feelings. Moreover, he had intended to buy the cocaine and use it alone, not with friends. He wasn't exactly experiencing cravings—yet—but he'd been looking forward with eager anticipation to using the cocaine.

Jeff's parents had already noticed a change in their son's behavior. Always a shy, quiet, and somewhat timid boy, lately he'd been even more withdrawn. Never particularly moody before, he was now. Once reliable and inclined to spend a good deal of time at home working on hobbies, now he was seldom home, and neither parent had seen him at a hobby in months. If they asked him to do something, there was about a fifty-fifty chance of its getting done. Then there was the problem of missing money—at first $5, later $20 or more. On the other hand, some things hadn't changed, like Jeff's school grades, which were still good, and his part-time job, which he still maintained. They were puzzled and concerned, but until they overheard the phone conversation they figured it was just a "phase" that Jeff was going through. (pp. 94–95, with changes in notation)

1. Jeff's addiction represents what stage of the five-stage model of addiction (see discussion earlier in chapter)?
2. What is Jeff's primary motivation for drug use?
3. What factors in the case led you to your answers to questions 1 and 2?
4. What treatment would you recommend for Jeff (and his family) and why?

Suggested Answers
1. The instrumental stage
2. Hedonistic use
3. (a) Jeff used the substance to make his insecurities disappear, to seek out feelings of self-confidence, and to achieve feelings of euphoria. (b) Jeff used the drug with friends, and now Jeff is planning to use the drug privately. (c) Jeff has become more withdrawn from his family and has become moody, unreliable, and uninterested in his hobbies.

4. Outpatient treatment. Jeff has not yet dropped grades in school or jeopardized his job because of drug use. This is his first attempt at treatment, and outpatient care will probably provide the therapy and structure that he needs. It also would be helpful to involve the family in family therapy.

EATING DISORDERS

Description

Children's eating patterns may be related to their biological makeup; their family's eating patterns; the foods available in the home, neighborhood, and school; what they know about the nutritional value of food; what they learn about food in the media; and the eating patterns of their peers (Foreyt & Goodrick, 1988). (The term *children* as used here may refer to children, adolescents, or both, as appropriate.) It is estimated that at least 25% to 35% of children exhibit some type of eating disorder (Linscheid, Tarnowski, & Richmond, 1988). This number may be an underestimate because children or parents may not report eating problems and health care providers may report other conditions that include an eating problem.

There are several types of eating disorders in children—obesity, anorexia nervosa, bulimia nervosa, pica, rumination disorder, and feeding disorder of infancy or early childhood. Each disorder will be discussed briefly. *It is imperative that all children with an eating disorder have a thorough medical examination, because some eating disorders can be life threatening.* In addition, because depression may be found in as many as 50% of children with eating disorders, a psychological evaluation may be needed (DiNicola, Roberts, & Oke, 1989).

Obesity. Obesity is a disorder defined as an excessive accumulation of body fat. *DSM-IV* does not classify obesity as a clinical syndrome. However, when there is evidence that psychological factors are important in the etiology of obesity, obesity can be noted under *DSM-IV's* classification Psychological Factors Affecting Medical Condition. Children may be considered obese if they are 20% or more over ideal body weight. Approximately 14% of children between the ages of 6 and 11 years and approximately 12% of adolescents between the ages of 12 to 17 were termed obese during the 1988–1994 period (Centers for Disease Control and Prevention, 1997). The proportion of overweight children and adolescents has increased about 6% since 1980, which represents almost a doubling of the number of these children and adolescents.

Etiological factors associated with obesity include genetic, biochemical, physiological, and environmental factors. However, we do not know which factor or factors cause obesity or how they interact, especially in individual cases. We do know, however, that obesity is connected to energy intake and energy expenditure and that children who are obese are likely to become obese adults (Bene, Klesges, & Meyers, 1990).

The probability that a child will be overweight is 40% if one parent is overweight and 70% if both parents are overweight (Boeck, 1992). These findings reflect both genetic and environmental components, with heredity accounting for approximately 10% of the variance in weight (Linscheid et al., 1988). In addition, children are more likely to be obese when their parents strongly encourage them to eat, whereas children are less likely to be obese when their parents strongly encourage them to exercise (Bene et al., 1990).

Obese children who remain obese as adults in turn are at risk for developing chronic diseases, including diabetes mellitus, hypertension, and heart disease. In our society—which values thinness and equates it with health, wealth, and beauty—obesity can be associated with social prejudice as well as occupational and college admission discrimination. "Obese children and adolescents suffer from psychological and social problems in the areas of peer acceptance, discrimination from adults, disturbed body image, and self concept" (Linscheid, 1992, p. 465).

Obese children may have irregular eating habits, including skipping meals, snacking, and varying between fasting and overeating. Even skipping meals seems to result in overeating for some obese children. One explanation is that fasting sets the stage for overeating by producing feelings of self-deprivation, hunger, depression, or fatigue. Obese children also may think that they can lose weight in a short time and with little effort.

The following first-person account illustrates how food and eating can become the predominant focus of an individual's existence (Abraham & Llewellyn-Jones, 1992).

I don't want to be like this, but what I eat still rules my life, so that at times every working minute seems occupied with thoughts of food and the day passes in the measured times between when I last ate and when I'll eat again. I'm still plagued with guilt about everything I consume unless I nearly fast. I dream of the perfect day when I have no appetite, no thought, desire, or temptation for food or to eat. I often despair of ever finding a solution. (p. 47)

Anorexia nervosa. Anorexia nervosa is a serious eating disorder that occurs in adolescents and young adults; about 90% to 95% of those affected are females (Coupey, 1992). Between 0.5% and 1.0% of females in late adolescence and early adulthood receive a diagnosis of anorexia nervosa (American Psychiatric Association, 1994). Prevalence rates appear to have increased in recent decades. The mean age at onset is 17 years, with peaks at ages 14 and 18 years. It is a syndrome found primarily in the middle and upper socioeconomic classes.

Anorexia nervosa has four primary features (American Psychiatric Association, 1994):

1. Refusal to maintain a minimally normal body weight, leading to body weight that is less than 85% of that expected

2. Intense fear of gaining weight or becoming fat, although the individual is underweight
3. Disturbance in the perception of body weight and shape
4. In females, amenorrhea (absence of expected menstrual cycles)

Anorexia nervosa has two subtypes: the *restricting subtype* (in which individuals lose weight by restricting food intake or through excessive exercise) and the *binge-eating/purging subtype* (in which individuals attempt to limit food intake and also have episodes of binge eating and/or purging) (American Psychiatric Association, 1994). Individuals with anorexia nervosa may change from one subtype to the other.

There are many medical complications of anorexia nervosa. The long-term mortality rate for individuals with anorexia nervosa who are admitted to hospitals is over 10%. "Death most commonly results from starvation, suicide, or electrolyte imbalance" (American Psychiatric Association, 1994, p. 543). The immediate medical complications include *hypothermia* (body temperature below 98.6°F), *hypoglycemia* (low concentration of glucose in the circulating blood), *hypotension* (reduced blood pressure), slow heart rate, constipation, and dry skin. Long-term complications include reduced fertility as an adult, which is related to the amount of time the individual was amenorrheic, *osteoporosis* (softening of the bones), and increased cardiovascular morbidity.

The etiology of anorexia nervosa is unclear, but it is likely associated with a complex interaction of genetic, biological, personality, familial, and sociocultural factors. Key features include the "pursuit of thinness, preoccupation with body weight and shape, disparagement of body appearance, low self-esteem, and a tendency towards depression and perfectionism" (Lask & Bryant-Waugh, 1992, p. 296). Girls are somewhat at risk for anorexia nervosa when they have such personality traits as "shyness and timidity, social anxiety, obsessiveness, emotional overcontrol, excessive dependency and passivity, compliancy, rigid perfectionism, and self-doubt" (Coupey, 1992, p. 219). Anorexic patients may use the disorder as a way of gaining control of their lives (Linscheid et al., 1988).

The following letter, written to the *Los Angeles Times* by a Southern California honor student with anorexia nervosa, gives us some insight into the thoughts and feelings of an adolescent with the disease.

I'm 15 years old and have anorexia nervosa. I'm not going to tell you that I'm recovering because I'm not. Sure, I'm seeing a psychologist and nutritionist, but I'm still firmly in the grip of this awful disease—still focused on eating little and losing weight.

A couple of months ago, a girl wrote in this column about her worry over a friend who wasn't eating. I'm sure that must be very scary for her, but she has no idea about how scary it is to actually be that person. Every morning, I wake up and tell myself, "This is stupid. Today, I'm gonna go and eat an ice cream or I'm gonna have a nice juicy hamburger." But, no. I usually end up having a small

peach for breakfast, a Cal 70 yogurt for lunch, and something like a bowl of rice or a baked potato for dinner. My "snack" is usually a handful of puffed wheat or a couple of pretzels. I jog a couple of miles a day to try and burn off some of those calories. But it's getting harder to run. I'm getting tired more easily and get the weirdest dizzy spells. It scares me how incredibly hungry I am. Every once in a while I lose control and eat "too much," which is more than 600 calories. (I can depend on my Ex-Lax to rid me of the awful food.)

I don't think of anything except food all day. I purposely look through magazines with pictures of food in them, watch cooking shows and bake delicious-looking goodies for my parents. I'm not going to tell you how it started or when because I'm not really sure. I don't know how this thing is going to turn out, but I want you to try and understand, that's all.

I've dieted from 135 pounds to 105 pounds. At 5-feet-6, I'm not looking too good. I have dark circles under my eyes and I'm pale. Everyone's on my case. As miserable as I am, I still want to lose weight.

Please understand that it's not our fault we have this disease. We are not stubborn, nor are we trying to hurt anybody. We can't "just eat." We need help and support, not insults or pleadings. If you are a victim, know that you're not alone. There are support groups out there that really help.

Thank you for reading this and to my fellow sufferers, good luck. ("Sarah Doe," 1994, p. B5)

Bulimia nervosa. Bulimia nervosa is another serious eating disorder that occurs in adolescents and young adults. It has four primary features (American Psychiatric Association, 1994):

1. Repeated episodes of *binge eating*
2. Episodes followed by inappropriate compensatory behaviors, such as self-induced vomiting; misuse of laxatives, diuretics, enemas, or other medications; fasting; or excessive exercise
3. Episodes occurring at least twice a week for three months
4. Self-evaluation influenced by body shape and weight

Bulimics have concerns about weight similar to those of anorexics. Unlike anorexics, however, bulimics maintain a body weight that may be normal or slightly overweight, thereby masking the disorder. Bulimia nervosa can be a problem for young women of all socioeconomic classes.

Bulimia nervosa has two subtypes: the *purging subtype* (in which individuals regularly engage in self-induced vomiting or misuse laxatives, diuretics, or enemas) and the *nonpurging subtype* (in which individuals use other inappropriate compensatory behaviors, such as fasting or excessive exercise, but do not regularly engage in self-induced vomiting or in the misuse of laxatives, diuretics, or enemas) (American Psychiatric Association, 1994). Approximately 1% to 3% of females in late adolescence and early adulthood receive a diagnosis of bulimia nervosa.

Complications associated with bulimia nervosa include sore throats, abdominal swelling and pain, calluses on the hands from frequent attempts to induce vomiting, scarring on the backs of the fingers from reflexively biting the hand during gagging, and dental problems, such as tooth decay because the regurgitated stomach acid erodes the enamel that protects teeth (Linscheid et al., 1988).

The etiology of bulimia nervosa is similar to that of anorexia nervosa—a combination of biological, psychological, and social factors is likely involved in the disorder. Bulimia nervosa also may be associated with mood disorders, personality disorders, substance abuse, and reactions to sexual abuse or physical abuse (Wonderlich, 1994).

Individuals with bulimia nervosa may be depressed, be unhappy with their body, have low self-esteem, have problems relating to people, be distrustful and suspicious of others, be anxious, strive for thinness, and have impulse control difficulties (Kerr, Skok, & McLaughlin, 1991).

The following first-person account describes how bulimia nervosa took over an adolescent's life for several years (Abraham & Llewellyn-Jones, 1992).

CASE 18-4. KAREN

I find it easy to pinpoint the beginning of my illness. It began with an experience concerning one of my fifteenth birthday presents: a box of chocolates. I was at an age where pressures for social acceptance were, to me, immense, and pencil thinness, to me, was a prerequisite for social acceptance and self-confidence. I ate some of my birthday chocolates and was offered a suggestion by my mother: "If you don't want to get fat, stick your fingers down your throat."

Maybe this statement has more relevance than I'd previously thought. Mum's simple statement triggered off every emotional fear within me: "I'll be fat—socially unacceptable—have no self-confidence—no self-esteem...." The fears were inexpressibly greater than I can even imagine now. My future, with those chocolates in me, appeared what can be plain and simply described as "black." My mother's suggestion seemed the only exit from the "black future" I had prescribed for myself.

Naively I took this exit, which turned out not to be an exit at all but an entrance into hell. If only I'd known!

To induce vomiting was a revolting experience to me, but the fear of the "black future" provided no alternative at all. Physical weakness and psychological euphoria followed my regurgitation. No matter how painful, or revolting, I'd found the key to freedom from that dreaded "black future."

I left school on my fifteenth birthday and found an increase in life's pressures. Coping became difficult, but I still possessed my "key" to confidence and acceptance. I made a habit of vomiting after every evening meal and, as the months progressed, I gradually lost weight, believing that I was becoming more attractive all the while. The fact that my food output by means of regurgitation was almost equal to my food intake allowed me to indulge for longer periods of time in my means of relief from life's pressures—eating—without gaining weight.

I became increasingly aware of my increasing ability to relieve life's pressure through the intake of food. Although the induction of vomiting continued to be traumatic, the relief beforehand, and the euphoria afterwards, were, to me, of no comparison to it. The vomiting became more frequent as the food intake rose and I accompanied my physically strenuous

job with all the exercise I could muster. Some nights I could not sleep due to the immense guilt of either not having done enough exercise or having allowed too much food to digest.

By the age of 16 I found myself unable to cope not only with problems, but with spare time. Anxiety seemed to rule my existence and I could not relax without food. If, even then, I was relaxing, I'm unsure.

Fortunately, my weight only regressed to 111 lbs. at its lowest. But it took its toll on my life. For breakfast I would eat 8–10 slices of toast plus cereal. Then I would do the dishes, eating everyone's scraps in an anxious, embarrassed, hidden hurry. I would then disappear inconspicuously to the toilet, and bring up my breakfast. My nose often bled, as did my stomach, and 10 minutes later (to the dot) I would become very weak, dizzy, and pale.

I suffered malnutrition to the extent that my menstrual periods ceased for six or seven months. My god, I accepted such as being normal!

During the following year, I began to realize that I was too thin so I fought my conscience and established my weight at about 126 lbs.

My eating, cunning and impatience as it was, had increased during this time, and I was spending about $10 per day on food outside the house. This was quite substantial to me, for I was earning only $80 per week. Fortunately I didn't have to pay board....

[After 5½ years of binging and vomiting, Karen went to a psychiatrist. Because she couldn't bear to live with herself, the psychiatrist arranged for her to be admitted to a hospital. Her story continues.]

With the aid of the addiction program, and Alcoholics Anonymous philosophies, I've learnt more about myself and how to cope with life in the past 12 days than I have in the 20 years preceding. I'm gaining confidence, hope and see life as I've only dreamed of seeing it. I have a long way to go to recovery and I accept this. I've told the truth to my family and close friends, who have accepted it well. I'm truly getting there, and I won't give in for I've too much to lose. I've now had a taste of how enjoyable and exciting life can be; so hopefully I will be able to stay in the life I love so much, and hopefully maintain self-control for the rest of my life over my eating and vomiting. (pp. 110–113)

Other types of eating disorders. *DSM-IV* describes three disorders of feeding and eating in infancy or early childhood: pica, rumination disorder, and feeding disorder of infancy or early childhood. Let's examine these eating disorders in more detail.

1. *Pica.* This refers to persistent eating of nonnutritive substances for at least one month. These substances include paint, plaster, string, hair, or cloth for infants and young children and animal droppings, sand, insects, leaves, or pebbles for older children. The behavior is considered developmentally inappropriate and not culturally sanctioned. The prevalence rate is unknown.

2. *Rumination disorder.* This refers to "repeated regurgitation and rechewing of food that develops in an infant or child after a period of normal functioning and lasts for at

least 1 month.... Partially digested food is brought up into the mouth without apparent nausea, retching, disgust, or associated gastrointestinal disorder. The food is then either ejected from the mouth or, more frequently, chewed and reswallowed. The symptoms are not due to an associated gastrointestinal or other general medical condition...and do not occur exclusively during the course of Anorexia Nervosa or Bulimia Nervosa" (American Psychiatric Association, 1994, p. 96). The prevalence rate is unknown, but the condition probably is uncommon.

3. *Feeding disorder of infancy or early childhood.* This refers to "persistent failure to eat adequately, as reflected in significant failure to gain weight or significant weight loss over at least 1 month.... There is no gastrointestinal or other general medical condition (e.g., esophageal reflux) severe enough to account for the feeding disturbance" (American Psychiatric Association, 1994, p. 96). The prevalence rate is approximately 0.5% to 2.5% of all pediatric hospital admissions. This condition also may reflect the nonorganic subtype of failure to thrive (see Chapter 17).

Children may have other types of eating problems that are not classified by *DSM-IV,* including mealtime tantrums; bizarre food habits; obsessive behaviors at mealtime (for example, arranging food in prescribed patterns on the plate); multiple food dislikes; slow eating; food refusal; prolonged subsistence on pureed foods; delay or difficulty in chewing, sucking, or swallowing; and delay in self-feeding (Jaffe & Singer, 1989; Linscheid, 1992).

Interviewing Issues

The focus of the clinical assessment interview with a child who has an eating disorder or is suspected of having an eating disorder should be on obtaining information about the child's current eating patterns, eating problems, attitude toward eating and food, body image, weight, binge eating, purging behavior, other methods used to control weight, exercise and activity patterns, personality and interpersonal relations, health status, family characteristics, and attitude toward interventions.

Anorexics and bulimics may not want to tell you about their symptoms or about their vomiting because they feel shame (McKenna, 1989). *Denial and a need to maintain the secret may be part of anorexia nervosa and bulimia nervosa.* You may be fooled by their behavior into thinking that they have only a minor problem or no problem at all when, in fact, they have a major problem. Bulimics who are well groomed and who have a high need for achievement may be especially difficult to detect. At any rate, you will want to establish rapport and trust with the interviewee.

Carefully attend to statements about the interviewee's self-concept, weight, feelings, and perceptions of self, food, and body weight. For example, note whether there are any statements suggesting that the interviewee has a negative self-image; associates weight with self-worth; feels guilty

about some of his or her behaviors; or has misperceptions about himself or herself, about food, or about body weight (Polivy, Herman, & Garner, 1988). Look for areas of psychological distress and body-image disturbances, both of which can place children and adolescents at risk for eating disorders.

You also will want to obtain information about the previous and current medical and nutritional status of an interviewee with an eating disorder. The interviewee will need a thorough medical examination, particularly to rule out medical conditions that may affect his or her diet or result in weight gain or weight loss. In addition, consider whether any serious illnesses in the interviewee's past are related to his or her present problem. The nutritional assessment of interviewees, which usually is performed by a dietitian, requires assessing food intake in relation to the interviewee's age, height, and weight. Specific deficiencies or excesses in nutrients, vitamins, or calories can be verified through laboratory tests or biochemical analyses. The health care provider team can plan interventions, in part, around the interviewee's nutritional deficits, type of eating problem, and personality and temperament. Table F-9 in Appendix F shows a semistructured interview for interviewing children who may have an eating disorder.

If you interview the child's parents, ask them about the areas mentioned in the previous paragraph. Then ask them about their response to the interviewee's eating disorder, their involvement in the interviewee's eating disorder, their own history of eating disorders, and their nutritional knowledge.

If you think it might be helpful to have the interviewee complete a food diary, schedule a second interview at which to review the diary (see Table 18-9). Instruct the interviewee to keep a record of his or her food consumption over a three- to seven-day period. The food diary will give you information about the interviewee's food preferences and amount of food intake. You also might want to ask the interviewee to keep a more detailed journal about his or her eating behavior and his or her feelings associated with eating (see Table 18-10). Consider referring the interviewee for a psychological evaluation, if warranted, to obtain additional information about his or her personality.

You also might want to ask the child's or adolescent's parent to complete a food diary or journal if you believe the child cannot complete one or if you want to compare the two records as a reliability check. Also discuss with the parent what is happening before, while, and after the child eats. This information is needed because the actual consumption of food is often a small part of a child's eating problem. If possible, it will be helpful if you can observe the child in an eating situation with the person responsible for his or her feedings. This recommendation is especially important for young children with an eating disorder.

Whenever possible, compare the interviewee's reports (that is, subjective information) with observable or objective information. For example, if you are keeping weight records, compare what the child says he or she weighs with

Table 18-9
Three-Day Food Diary

FOOD DIARY

Name: _____

Directions: For each meal, record the time you ate, all of the foods you ate, and the drinks you consumed. Also record the amount of food you ate and how much you drank as closely as possible.

Meal	Day 1: Date: _____ Food/drink · Amount	Day 2: Date: _____ Food/drink · Amount	Day 3: Date: _____ Food/drink · Amount
Breakfast time: _____			
Lunch time: _____			
Dinner time: _____			
Snacks time(s): _____ _____ _____			

his or her scale weight. When the child is weighed, be sure that the child's clothing (pockets, socks, or bra, for example) is not weighted down and that the child is not wearing an excessive amount of clothing. You will know that there is something wrong if the child says that he or she consumed enough calories during the week and yet lost 2 pounds since the previous week.

Questioning interviewees too closely about their eating patterns may make them defensive or evasive or make them distrust you. It is important to establish a nonjudgmental, trusting relationship before using probing questions—otherwise the interviewee may not be truthful. Therefore, do not challenge the interviewee about her or his statements about food or about what she or he eats. Also, you do not want to lecture or persuade the interviewee to change her or his behavior. *Your focus in the clinical assessment interview should be on obtaining information about the interviewee's eating disorder, not on changing her or his behavior.*

Table 18-10
Detailed Food Journal Covering Foods Eaten and Accompanying Feelings

FOOD DIARY

Name: _____   Date: _____   Day of week: _____

What time did you eat?	What did you eat?	How much did you eat?	How fast did you eat?	Where did you eat?	Who else was there?	What else were you doing?	How did you feel while you were eating?	How did you feel after you ate?

Note. This is a portion of the page. A full 8½ ×11 sheet is recommended.

The following dialogue illustrates the predicament that older female adolescents with anorexia nervosa may face (Schwartz & Barrett, 1987; pp. 138–139, with changes in notation):

IR: What would happen if you began to eat regularly and to look and feel better?

IE: It would be too scary. I would have to face everything and it is just too much to face. I would have to decide about schools, about a career, about men, about my family, it is all too much. Plus I know I would get fat.

IR: How do you know that?

IE: I would lose control if I started to eat.

If you find that the interviewee has an eating disorder, consider the possible reasons for the disorder. For example, is it to bolster self-esteem, to handle *depression,* to resolve interpersonal difficulties, or to solve problems? A thorough assessment—which includes a clinical assessment interview, a medical examination, a nutritional assessment, and a psychological evaluation, when needed—should provide the answers to the questions shown in Table 18-11.

Interventions

Any interventions developed for a child with an eating disorder should take into account the child's level of cognitive and emotional maturity and the parents' ability to help in the intervention effort. Interventions should be formulated by a multidisciplinary team—consisting of a primary care physician, a nutritionist, and a mental health professional. The team should assess the child and then institute a treatment plan (Ponton, 1996). Assessments should include a physical examination, laboratory tests, a nutritional assessment, and an evaluation of the child's personality and adjustment and the family's functioning. The goals of treatment include, depending on the condition, "weight restoration or cessation of binging, vomiting, or other unhealthy weight reduction methods; improvement in eating behavior; and improvement in social behavior" (p. 100). The treatment team needs to understand the biological, psychological, social, and cultural components associated with children who have an eating disorder.

Interventions for obesity.   The two most *direct* causes of obesity are over-intake of food and lack of exercise. These causes have cognitive and habit components and may respond to behavioral approaches and to cognitive-behavioral therapy (see Chapter 1). Useful techniques for working with an obese child include having the child avoid stimuli that elicit the desire to eat; family intervention; increased physical activity; modification of eating style, such as slowing the process of eating and eating smaller portions; positive reinforcement for following a diet; and behavioral contracting, with the child agreeing to follow specified actions. Parents who may be contributing to the child's obesity should be helped to learn that there are other ways to be good parents besides overfeeding their child. Changing family eating patterns also may be helpful. Generally obesity is a disorder with a poor prognosis, although success can be achieved with permanent changes in eating and exercise patterns.

Interventions for anorexia and bulimia.   Although pharmacotherapy is useful in treating bulimia nervosa, it appears to be less useful in treating anorexia nervosa (Williamson, Sebastian, & Varnado, 1995). In particular, antide-

Table 18-11
Evaluating the Interview Findings for a Child with an Eating Disorder

Present Complaint

1. What is the reason for the referral?
2. What is the child's present complaint?
3. What physical symptoms does the child have? For example, does the child have such symptoms as obesity, emaciation, sore throat, weakness, fatigue, cavities, swollen glands, diarrhea, constipation, food intolerance, bloating, stress fractures, or amenorrhea (for females)?
4. How have the child's eating problems interfered with school, daily activities, personal relationships, family interactions, feelings about herself or himself, and work (if applicable)?
5. Does the child perceive that she or he has a problem?
6. If so, what does the child think causes her or his problem?

Current Eating Patterns

7. What types of food does the child eat?
8. What amount of food does the child eat?
9. What is the estimated number of calories consumed by the child?
10. When and where does the child eat?
11. How long does it take the child to eat?
12. Who is present when the child eats?
13. What are the child's eating skills?
14. What are the child's eating patterns? For example, are they regular or chaotic? Does the child snack frequently? Does the child wait as long in a day as she or he can before eating anything?
15. What types of forbidden foods does the child have, if any?
16. Does the child keep a running caloric count all day?
17. Can the child tell when she or he is hungry?
18. What would the child consider to be three meals a day?
19. What is the child's dieting behavior? (If the child diets, go to question 20; otherwise, go to question 27.)
20. At what age did the child start dieting?
21. What was the reason the child began dieting?
22. Does the child fast?
23. How often has the child tried dieting?
24. What type of diet does the child have? For example, does the child use fad dieting techniques?
25. Was the dieting begun in relationship to some upcoming event? If so, what event?
26. Is the child always on a diet?

Eating Problems

27. What eating problems does the child have?
28. What foods does the child avoid eating?
29. What foods can't the child eat because of allergies?
30. How tense is the child at mealtimes?
31. Does the child have any food fads?
32. Does the child eat in secret?
33. Does the child dispose of food other than by eating?

34. What is the child's view of a nutritious meal or nutritious daily intake?
35. How does the child know when she or he is hungry or needs to eat?

Attitudes Toward Eating and Food

36. How does the child feel (both psychologically and physiologically) after eating?
37. How does the child feel about eating?
38. Does the child believe that food controls her or his life?

Weight History

39. What is the child's present weight?
40. What have been the child's lowest and highest weights recently or since the problem began?
41. What is the child's desired weight?
42. Is the child's weight stable or fluctuating?
43. Are changes in the child's weight associated with any specific events in her or his life?
44. How does the child feel about her or his weight?

Body Image

45. How does the child feel about how her or his body looks? For example, does the child show dissatisfaction with the shape of her or his body?
46. Does the child avoid activities where her or his body will be seen, such as going to the beach or engaging in sports?
47. How realistic is the child's body image?
48. What is the degree of the child's body-image distortion?
49. How do others perceive the child's body image or weight?
50. Do the child's self-perceptions differ from the way others see her or him?
51. Does the child have an excessive preoccupation with weight or an extreme pursuit of thinness?

Binge Eating

52. Does the child engage in binge eating? (If yes, go to question 53; if no, go to question 66.)
53. What constitutes a binge for the child—how much food?
54. What kinds of food are eaten when the child binges?
55. When do the binges occur? (For example, only after meals or at other times of the day?)
56. How long does a binge last?
57. What triggers a binge? For example, do certain foods, times of day, times of the month, or feelings trigger a binge?
58. What stops a binge?
59. What is the child's mood before, during, and after the binge?
60. At what age did the child start bingeing?
61. How did the child start bingeing?
62. How often does the child binge?

(Continued)

Table 18-11 (*Continued*)

63. Has the child had binge-free periods? If so, when were these periods?
64. Are the binges planned?
65. What rituals are connected with the binges, if any?

Purging Behavior
66. Does the child purge?
    (If yes, go to question 67; if no, go to question 72.)
67. How often does the child purge?
68. What methods does the child use to purge? For example, does the child use vomiting, laxatives, diuretics, or diet pills?
69. When does the child purge?
70. What is the relation between purging and bingeing, if any?
71. Which one is more central to the child, purging or bingeing?

Exercise and Activity Patterns
72. Does the child exercise?
    (If yes, go to question 73; if no, go to question 81.)
73. What type of exercise does the child do?
74. How often does the child exercise?
75. How long does the child exercise?
76. (If exercise involves a distance) How much distance does the child cover when she or he exercises?
77. Have there been any changes in the child's exercise routines? If so, what were the changes?
78. What place does exercise have in the child's life?
79. If the child cannot exercise, how does she or he feel?
80. Does the child keep constantly busy and active?

Personality and Interpersonal Relations
81. How does the child feel about herself or himself? For example, does the child have general feelings of inadequacy, insecurity, or worthlessness, feelings of not being in control of her or his life, or potential for self-destructive behavior? Or does the child have a positive self-image and feel good about herself or himself?
82. Does the child have excessive personal expectations for superior achievement or show signs of perfectionism?
83. What is the quality of the child's interpersonal relations? For example, does the child have a sense of alienation and a reluctance to form close relationships or does the child get along well with others?
84. Does the child lack confidence or have confidence in recognizing and accurately identifying her or his emotions and sensations of hunger and satiety?
85. Does the child desire to avoid psychological maturity by retreating to the security of earlier years or does the child want to assume responsibilities commensurate with her or his age?
86. Has the child told anyone about her or his eating problem? If so, whom has the child told?
87. How does the child get along with family members?

Health Status
88. What is the child's medical history? For example, has the child had thyroid or endocrine disorders, gastrointestinal problems, psychiatric problems, substance abuse problems, food allergies, or other dietary problems?
89. What are the child's current medical findings? For example, are there any medical or growth complications associated with the eating disorder, such as absence of breast buds, absence of menses, emaciation, constipation, skin problems, loss of scalp hair, brittle nails, abdominal pain, cardiac problems, edema, tooth decay, salivary gland enlargement, and so forth?
90. What medications is the child taking, if any?
91. (If the child is taking medications) For what reasons?

Family Characteristics
92. How would you describe the child's family? For example, what are the family dynamics, such as cohesiveness, communication style, methods of conflict resolution, and behavior control?
93. How do the family members feel about the child's eating problem?
94. How do the family members feel about the child's appearance and weight?
95. What attempts have the parents made to encourage appropriate eating?
96. What interactions occur among the family members at mealtime?
97. What are the parents' reactions to the child at mealtime?
98. What are the situational variables related to eating at home? For example, when are meals served, who is present at the table, what room is the meal eaten in, and who feeds the child (if relevant)?
99. What is the family history of eating disorders or other relevant factors? For example, do other children or parents have eating disorders, and what is the level of distress or psychological disturbance among the family members?
100. Does the family encourage the child's symptoms? If so, in what ways?

Intervention
101. What does the child believe caused the eating problem?
102. What does the child know about the eating problem?
103. Has the child received any prior treatment for her or his eating problem?
    (If yes, go to question 104; if no, go to question 108.)
104. What kind of treatment?
105. When did it begin?
106. When did it end?
107. How successful was the treatment?
108. What kind of help does the child want for the eating problem?
109. What kind of help does the family want for the child's eating problem?
110. What external supports are available to the child?

(*Continued*)

Table 18-11 (Continued)

111. What kind of help do you believe the child needs for her or his eating problem?

112. Does the child need to be immediately hospitalized for her or his eating problem?

Note. The term *child* refers to a child or an adolescent.
Source: Adapted from Coupey (1992); Garner, Olmsted, and Polivy, (1983); Garner and Parker (1993); McKenna (1989); Polivy, Herman, and Garner (1988); and Tobin, Johnson, and Franke (1991).

Dennis the Menace   by Hank Ketcham

"ARE WE ALL GONNA HAVE TO GO ON A DIET AGAIN?"

DENNIS THE MENACE ® used by permission of Hank Ketcham and © by North America Syndicate.

pressants decrease bingeing and purging, but long-term studies are needed to learn what happens when medication is discontinued.

Helpful components of an effective treatment regimen for anorexia nervosa and bulimia nervosa include *cognitive-behavioral therapy* (focusing on the individual's beliefs about body weight and shape), *educational intervention* (delivered in a group or individual setting and focusing on appropriate body weight for height, appropriate food choices, and appropriate exercise), and *family therapy* (focusing on the roles the anorexic or bulimic individuals have in the family and helping them gain autonomy from the family if needed). Another intervention to consider is hospi-

talization. *Children whose eating disorder is extremely severe and not responsive to outpatient treatment or whose disorder is life threatening will require hospitalization.* The possible objectives of hospitalization include interruption of weight loss and bingeing, treatment of medical complications, and removing children from families that contribute to their disorder.

At the end of any treatment, individuals who are dissatisfied with their changed body image may be prone to relapse (Martin, 1989). Therefore, they will need to participate in an ongoing therapeutic program. See Barlow (1993) for more information about the treatment of eating disorders.

Case Illustration

The following case describes a female adolescent with anorexia nervosa whose disorder was so severe that she had to be hospitalized (Leon & Dinklage, 1989).

CASE 18-5. WENDY

Wendy was 16 years old when her parents insisted that she be seen by the family pediatrician because of severe weight loss. Wendy was 5 feet, 3 inches tall and weighed 78 pounds. She had been dieting for the past 2 years because she had decided, at a weight of 110 pounds, that she was too fat. Wendy had begun menstruating at age 13, but she had not had a menstrual period for the past 1½ years. She indicated that she was not concerned that her periods had stopped, but she was extremely concerned that she was still too fat. At the time she was seen, Wendy was consuming an average of about 500 calories per day.

Over the course of her past 2 years' dieting efforts, Wendy had become increasingly strict about how much she would eat, and each mealtime ended in a battle with her parents over her food intake. If possible, she tried to avoid eating meals with her parents and her two older brothers, saying that she was not hungry at that time and that she would eat more if she ate alone later. If her parents insisted that she eat with them, she toyed with her food, cut it up into small portions, and piled the leftover food on one part of her plate in order to make it look as if she had eaten more than she actually had. Typically, her daily food consumption consisted of an egg, a small portion of bread, a carrot stick, and some water or diet soda.

Wendy had always been a good student in school. However, both of her brothers had consistently been on the honor roll and had excelled in their academic work and in extracurricular activities. Wendy worked hard to get good grades, but her academic performance was taken for granted by her parents in the context of the superior achievements of her older brothers.

Wendy was described by her parents as having been an obedient child who always complied with her parents' wishes. They indicated that they had been fairly structured in raising Wendy, setting limits on her outside activities, the time she went to bed each night, and the youngsters with whom she played. Wendy was described as agreeable to this structure. Her parents were therefore amazed and helpless in dealing with her intractable stubbornness in relation to eating, given her compliant behavior in all other areas since childhood.

As Wendy grew thinner, she became increasingly preoccupied with planning how much she was going to eat each day, and with how to avoid situations in which she would be pressured to eat more than she had planned to. Wendy had begun an exercise program at the time she started dieting, and her daily exercises, carried out in a strictly ordered routine, became lengthier and more strenuous each day. During the summer, she swam…laps outdoors even in lightning or thunder. Over time, even though feeling exhausted, she added an extra swimming session at night without her parents' knowledge, jumping out of her second story bedroom window to go outside to swim. Wendy felt extremely hungry, tired, and irritable almost all of the time. She was also preoccupied with thoughts of food and how she looked. Her weight continued to drop, and her schoolwork suffered. She stopped interacting with the few girls she had talked to at school and became quite isolated from others.

Despite the efforts of her parents and her pediatrician, Wendy refused to stop dieting. She indicated that she felt extremely good about herself, knowing that she could control her bodily urges to the extent that she would not eat when hungry, and that she could exercise strenuously even though she felt exhausted. Eventually, Wendy was hospitalized for treatment, despite her strong objections that there was nothing wrong with her. Her weight at the time of hospitalization was 68 pounds. (p. 260)

THINKING THROUGH THE ISSUES

Have you ever had a sleep disorder? If so, what was it like? What treatment did you receive? Was it effective? Do you know anyone who had a sleep disorder? If so, what did he or she tell you about the disorder?

Do you know anyone with a substance abuse problem? If so, what kind of problem does he or she have? Has the problem interfered with his or her life? Has the individual received any treatment for the problem? If so, what kind of treatment, and has it been successful?

Do you think drugs should be legalized? If so, which drugs? What would be the effects of legalizing drugs? Should marijuana be approved for individuals with cancer or other debilitating diseases?

Do you know anyone with an eating disorder? If so, what is the disorder? What treatment has the person received for the disorder? Has it been effective?

SUMMARY

Sleep Disorders of Childhood

1. Sleep disorders are common in childhood.
2. The two primary types of childhood sleep disorders are dyssomnias and parasomnias.
3. Dyssomnias are sleep disorders characterized by abnormalities in the amount, quality, or timing of sleep, leading to excessive sleepiness or insomnia.
4. Parasomnias are sleep disorders characterized by abnormal behavioral or physiological events occurring in association with sleep, during specific sleep stages, or during sleep-wake transitions.
5. In school-aged children, sleep disorders may be associated with social, behavioral, and learning problems and may predispose children to insomnia during adulthood.
6. Dyssomnias may be physiologically based (narcolepsy and obstructive sleep apnea) or environmentally based (adjustment sleep disorder, limit-setting sleep disorder, sleep-onset association disorder, and nocturnal eating [drinking] syndrome).
7. Narcolepsy, which is characterized by excessive sleepiness, typically appears in adolescence.
8. Obstructive sleep apnea is characterized by repetitive episodes of upper airway obstruction during sleep, often causing a reduction in blood oxygen saturation.
9. Adjustment sleep disorder is a form of insomnia related to emotional arousal caused by acute stress, conflict, or an environmental change.
10. Limit-setting sleep disorder involves difficulty in initiating sleep, typically characterized by stalling or refusing to go to bed.
11. Sleep-onset association disorder occurs when sleep onset is impaired by the absence of a certain set of objects or circumstances, be it the presence of a bottle or a pacifier or being rocked to sleep.
12. Nocturnal eating (drinking) syndrome occurs in children who wake in the night and cannot go back to sleep without eating or drinking.
13. Parasomnias are the predominant sleep disorders in children. They include confusional arousals, sleepwalking, sleep terrors, nightmares, sleep bruxism, and sleep enuresis.
14. Confusional arousals are characterized by confusions during and after arousals from sleep, mainly occurring in the first part of the night.
15. In sleepwalking, the behavior may range from simply sitting up in bed to walking; the child is often difficult to awaken and, on awakening, appears confused.
16. Sleep terrors are characterized by a sudden arousal from slow wave sleep with a piercing scream or cry, accompanied by autonomic and behavioral manifestations of intense fear.
17. Nightmares are typically associated with fears of attack, falling, or death.
18. Sleep bruxism involves grinding or clenching the teeth during sleep.
19. Enuresis has two subtypes—primary (the child has always wet the bed) and secondary (the child has learned bladder control but then loses control); most affected children have primary enuresis.
20. Before you begin any intervention with a child with a sleep disturbance, have the child's health care provider examine the child to rule out medical issues, such as colic, recurrent ear

infections, urinary tract infections, or any other infections or illnesses.

21. Many sleep disorders of childhood can be treated with behavioral techniques such as stimulus control, shaping, extinction, and positive reinforcement.

22. Management of a sleep disorder includes helping the child maintain a consistent sleep routine, develop a pre-bed ritual, and eliminate daytime naps.

Substance Abuse

23. Substance abuse, which includes alcohol and drug abuse, is a major health and social problem among adolescents in the United States.

24. Adolescents experiment with and use substances because of family and peer group factors, attitudinal factors, cultural factors, and personality and temperament factors.

25. Adolescents may go through several stages in becoming substance abusers.

26. During the experimental stage, substance use is related to curiosity, risk taking, and, at times, peer pressure.

27. During the social stage, substance use is social. The primary motivation at this stage is social acceptance, although curiosity, thrill seeking, and defiance also may play a role.

28. During the instrumental stage, substance use is designed to manipulate emotions and behavior, such as to suppress or embrace feelings or to inhibit or disinhibit behavior.

29. During the habitual stage, substance use becomes habit forming.

30. During the compulsive stage, substance use becomes compulsive and addictive.

31. The use of drugs may result in physical problems (impaired growth and physical maturation), psychological problems (poor concentration, decreased motivation), and social problems (increased involvement in accidents, increased risk-taking activities).

32. Moderate, infrequent use of tobacco, alcohol, or marijuana may not be dangerous.

33. The proportion of 8th graders taking any illicit drug almost doubled between 1991 and 1995 (from 11% to 21%).

34. Between 1992 and 1995, the proportion of secondary students using any illicit drug rose by nearly two-thirds among 10th graders (from 20% to 33%) and by nearly one-half among 12th graders (from 27% to 39%).

35. Cigarette smoking by children increased between 1991 and 1995.

36. The increase in substance abuse may have occurred because adolescents seem to have softened their beliefs and attitudes about the dangers associated with drug use and about related social disapproval.

37. Adolescents who abuse alcohol are more likely to be absent from school. If they attend school, they may be intoxicated in class and obtain poorer grades than those who do not abuse alcohol.

38. Warning signs of excessive drinking among adolescents include truancy and class cutting; declining interest in extracurricular activities; dropping old friends or hanging out with new ones; unexpected mood swings, unprovoked hostility, fighting, or vehement arguments; defending vehemently the right to drink or get high, resisting talking or hearing about alcohol; dramatic changes in physical appearance; leaving beer or whiskey bottles in their room; slurred or incoherent speech;

always appearing tired; and deterioration of relationships with family members.

39. White American adolescents report higher rates of drug use, both legal and illicit, than do Black American or Hispanic American adolescents.

40. In interviewing an adolescent for possible substance abuse, ask about any substances that the adolescent may be taking. The adolescent may not be forthright about his or her substance use because of fears about disclosure of possible illegal activities.

41. One of your major concerns should be the frequency of drug use. A second concern is the different types of drugs that the adolescent is taking because the interaction effects of the combined use of psychoactive drugs may be lethal.

42. Be especially alert to the following signs, which may give you clues to possible drug abuse: impaired family relations, lying, stealing, fighting, running away from home, evasion, unexplained or sudden absences, changes in daily routines, recent changes in friends, social withdrawal, deterioration in grades, truancy, class cutting, declining interest in extracurricular activities, and leaving drug paraphernalia in room.

43. In assessing substance abuse among adolescents, you will need to consider substance variables, individual variables, situational variables, and familial variables.

44. Refer the adolescent for a thorough medical examination in cases of substance abuse.

45. A family assessment may be helpful in cases of substance abuse, particularly in relation to possible family dysfunction and drug-use behavior.

46. A family assessment is important because of the major influence of parents and siblings on adolescents' alcohol consumption and drug use and because of a possible genetic vulnerability.

47. Interventions must consider the part drugs or alcohol plays in the adolescent's life.

48. The more drugs or alcohol has become an integral part of the adolescent's life, the more difficult it will be for him or her to give the substance up.

49. Adolescents who are substance abusers and their families can be helped by several methods, including individual and family counseling, group counseling in which individuals share their experiences with others who are experiencing similar problems, and inpatient treatment.

50. Keys to successful intervention are identifying the problems within the adolescent and the family and reducing stress.

51. Family intervention is generally more effective than individual intervention in treating adolescents with a substance abuse problem.

52. Consider recommending an inpatient treatment program (or partial hospitalization) if the adolescent is addicted to a substance and exhibits one or more of the following symptoms: severe abuse of drugs or frequent intoxications; impaired ability to function at school or at work; severe psychological disorder or suicidal ideations; stealing, dealing in drugs, or engaging in other antisocial activities; and failure to benefit from prior outpatient treatment.

Eating Disorders

53. Children's eating patterns may be related to their biological makeup; their family's eating patterns; the foods available in the home, neighborhood, and school; what they know about

the nutritional value of food; what they learn about food in the media; and the eating patterns of their peers.

54. It is estimated that at least 25% to 35% of children exhibit some type of eating disorder.

55. There are several types of eating disorders in children—obesity, anorexia nervosa, bulimia nervosa, pica, rumination disorder, and feeding disorder of infancy or early childhood.

56. It is imperative that all children with an eating disorder have a thorough medical examination, because some eating disorders can be life threatening.

57. Because depression may be found in as many as 50% of children with eating disorders, a psychological evaluation may be needed.

58. Obesity is a disorder defined as an excessive accumulation of body fat.

59. Etiological factors associated with obesity include genetic, biochemical, physiological, and environmental factors.

60. The probability that a child will be overweight is 40% if one parent is overweight and 70% if both parents are overweight.

61. Obese children who remain obese as adults are at risk for developing chronic diseases, including diabetes mellitus, hypertension, and heart disease.

62. Anorexia nervosa is a serious eating disorder that occurs in adolescents and young adults; about 90% to 95% of those affected are females.

63. Anorexia nervosa has four primary features: refusal to maintain a minimally normal body weight (85% of that expected); intense fear of gaining weight or becoming fat, although the individual is underweight; disturbance in the perception of body weight and shape; and, in females, amenorrhea (absence of expected menstrual cycles).

64. Anorexia nervosa has two subtypes: the restricting subtype (in which individuals lose weight by restricting food intake or through excessive exercise) and the binge-eating/purging subtype (in which individuals attempt to limit food intake and also have episodes of binge eating and/or purging).

65. Individuals with anorexia nervosa may change from one subtype to the other.

66. There are many medical complications of anorexia nervosa.

67. The long-term mortality rate for individuals with anorexia nervosa who are admitted to hospitals is over 10%.

68. The etiology of anorexia nervosa is unclear, but it is likely associated with a complex interaction of genetic, biological, personality, familial, and sociocultural factors.

69. Key features of anorexia nervosa include the pursuit of thinness, preoccupation with body weight and shape, disparagement of body appearance, low self-esteem, and a tendency towards depression and perfectionism.

70. Bulimia nervosa is another serious eating disorder that occurs in adolescents and young adults.

71. Bulimia nervosa has four primary features: repeated episodes of binge eating, episodes followed by inappropriate compensatory behaviors, episodes occurring at least twice a week for three months, and self-evaluation influenced by body shape and weight.

72. Bulimia nervosa has two subtypes: the purging subtype (in which individuals regularly engage in self-induced vomiting or misuse laxatives, diuretics, or enemas) and the nonpurging subtype (in which individuals use other inappropriate compensatory behaviors, such as fasting or excessive exercise, but do not regularly engage in self-induced vomiting or in the misuse of laxatives, diuretics, or enemas).

73. Complications associated with bulimia nervosa include sore throats, abdominal swelling and pain, calluses on the hands from frequent attempts to induce vomiting, scarring on the backs of the fingers from reflexively biting the hand during gagging, and dental problems, such as tooth decay because the regurgitated stomach acid erodes the enamel that protects teeth.

74. The etiology of bulimia nervosa is similar to that of anorexia nervosa—a combination of biological, psychological, and social factors is likely involved in the disorder.

75. Individuals with bulimia nervosa may be depressed, be unhappy with their body, have low self-esteem, have problems relating to people, be distrustful and suspicious of others, be anxious, strive for thinness, and have impulse control difficulties.

76. Other forms of eating disorders in children include pica, rumination disorder, and feeding disorder of infancy or early childhood.

77. The focus of the clinical assessment interview with a child who has an eating disorder or is suspected of having an eating disorder should be on obtaining information about the child's current eating patterns, eating problems, attitude toward eating and food, body image, weight, binge eating, purging behavior, exercise and activity patterns, health status, school performance, personality and interpersonal relations, family, and attitude toward interventions.

78. Anorexics and bulimics may not want to tell you about their symptoms or about their vomiting because they feel shame.

79. Denial and a need to maintain the secret may be part of anorexia nervosa and bulimia nervosa.

80. You will want to obtain information about the previous and current medical and nutritional status of a child with an eating disorder.

81. If you think it might be helpful to have the child complete a food diary, schedule a second interview at which to review the diary.

82. Consider asking the child's parent to complete a food diary or journal if you believe the child cannot complete one or if you want to compare the two records as a reliability check.

83. Whenever possible, compare the child's reports (that is, subjective information) with observable or objective information.

84. Any interventions that you develop for a child with an eating disorder should take into account the child's level of cognitive and emotional maturity and the parents' ability to help in the intervention effort.

85. Useful techniques for working with an obese child include having the child avoid stimuli that elicit the desire to eat, family intervention, increased physical activity, modification of eating style, positive reinforcement for following a diet, and behavioral contracting, with the child agreeing to follow specified actions.

86. Although pharmacotherapy is useful in treating bulimia nervosa, it appears to be less useful in treating anorexia nervosa. In particular, antidepressants decrease bingeing and purging, but long-term studies are needed to learn what happens when medication is discontinued.

87. Helpful components of an effective treatment regimen for anorexia nervosa and bulimia nervosa include cognitive-

behavioral therapy (focusing on the individual's beliefs about body weight and shape), educational intervention (delivered in a group or individual setting and focusing on appropriate body weight for height, appropriate food choices, and appropriate exercise), and family therapy (focusing on the roles the anorexic or bulimic individuals have in the family).

88. Children whose eating disorder is extremely severe and not responsive to outpatient treatment or whose disorder is life threatening will require hospitalization.

89. At the end of any treatment, individuals who are dissatisfied with their changed body image may be prone to relapse. Therefore, they will need to participate in an ongoing therapeutic program.

KEY TERMS, CONCEPTS, AND NAMES

Sleep disorders of childhood (p. 579)
Dyssomnias (p. 579)
Parasomnias (p. 579)
Narcolepsy (p. 579)
Cataplexy (p. 579)
Obstructive sleep apnea (p. 579)
Adjustment sleep disorder (p. 579)
Limit-setting sleep disorder (p. 579)
Sleep-onset association disorder (p. 579)
Nocturnal eating (drinking) syndrome (p. 580)
Confusional arousals (p. 580)
Sleepwalking (p. 580)
Sleep terrors (p. 580)
Nightmares (p. 580)
Sleep bruxism (p. 580)
Sleep enuresis (p. 580)
Primary enuresis (p. 580)
Secondary enuresis (p. 580)
Substance abuse (p. 586)
Substance use (p. 586)
Experimental stage in becoming a substance abuser (p. 587)
Social stage in becoming a substance abuser (p. 587)
Instrumental stage in becoming a substance abuser (p. 587)
Hedonistic use of substances (p. 587)
Compensatory use of substances (p. 587)
Habitual stage in becoming a substance abuser (p. 587)
Compulsive stage in becoming a substance abuser (p. 587)
Alcohol abuse (p. 588)
Cannabis (p. 589)
Hashish (p. 589)
Inhalants (p. 589)

Cocaine (p. 589)
Crack cocaine (p. 589)
Stimulants (p. 589)
Depressants (p. 589)
Sedatives (p. 589)
Hallucinogens (p. 590)
PCP (p. 590)
LSD (p. 590)
Mushrooms (p. 590)
Peyote (p. 590)
Opiates (p. 590)
Narcotics (p. 590)
Designer drugs (p. 590)
Steroids (p. 590)
Marijuana abuse (p. 591)
Ethnicity and substance abuse (p. 592)
Detoxification programs (p. 599)
Eating disorders (p. 601)
Obesity (p. 601)
Anorexia nervosa (p. 601)
Restricting subtype of anorexia nervosa (p. 602)
Binge-eating/purging subtype of anorexia nervosa (p. 602)
Hypothermia (p. 602)
Hypoglycemia (p. 602)
Hypotension (p. 602)
Osteoporosis (p. 602)
Bulimia nervosa (p. 602)
Binge eating (p. 602)
Purging subtype of bulimia nervosa (p. 602)
Nonpurging subtype of bulimia nervosa (p. 602)
Pica (p. 603)
Rumination disorder (p. 603)
Feeding disorder of infancy or early childhood (p. 604)
Eating disorders and depression (p. 604)

STUDY QUESTIONS

1. Describe a behavioral-medicine approach to sleep disorders of childhood. Include in your discussion a description of sleep disorders, their prevalence, interview considerations, and interventions.

2. Describe a behavioral-medicine approach to substance abuse. Include in your discussion a description of substance abuse, its prevalence, interview considerations, and interventions.

3. Describe a behavioral-medicine approach to eating disorders. Include in your discussion a description of eating disorders, their prevalence, interview considerations, and interventions.

19

CHILDREN WITH BRAIN INJURIES

Do not mistake a child for his symptom.

—Eric H. Erickson

Goals and Objectives

This chapter is designed to enable you to:

- Understand some recent findings from the neuroscience field
- Describe lateralization of cognitive, perceptual, motor, and sensory activities
- Describe common causes of brain injury in children
- Describe the cognitive, behavioral, and emotional effects of brain injury on children and their families
- Give examples of neurological and neuropsychological diagnostic techniques
- Observe the symptoms of brain-injured children
- Interview brain-injured children
- Interview parents of brain-injured children
- Identify useful rehabilitation strategies for brain-injured children
- Work effectively with families of brain-injured children

This chapter provides an overview of the issues involved in interviewing brain-injured children and their parents. *Brain injury* refers to any disruption in brain structure (anatomy) or physiology. Preparing to interview brain-injured children requires (a) acquiring knowledge of the types and causes of brain injury and its effects on children's cognitive, behavioral, and affective processes, (b) learning how to talk to brain-injured children and to recognize their cognitive and behavioral limitations, (c) understanding how families react to their brain-injured children, and (d) learning about rehabilitation strategies useful for working with brain-injured children and their families.

This chapter does not cover neuropsychological testing in detail, nor does it present a detailed discussion of brain functioning; rather, the chapter provides background material in these areas and focuses on interviewing, observation, and rehabilitation principles. To get the most out of this chapter, you will need to read or review texts on neuropsychology and physiological psychology.

The assessment of brain damage is a complex and exacting task, requiring extensive specialized professional knowledge and interdisciplinary cooperation. The interview is only one part of the assessment procedure. A multidisciplinary team usually is involved in the assessment of brain-injured children and in the formulation of a rehabilitation program. The multidisciplinary team may include a neurologist, neurosurgeon, orthopedist, neuropsychologist, speech/language pathologist, educator, physical therapist, occupational therapist, and social worker, depending on the setting.

Mental health clinicians can help brain-injured children and their parents, families, and teachers in several different ways. For example, they can point out to all parties involved how brain injury affects children's cognitive functioning, affective reactions, personality, and temperament, and they can help parents, teachers, and children carry out the rehabilitation efforts needed to deal with changes in children's functioning. The aim of consultation, in part, is to delineate brain-injured children's cognitive strengths and deficits in order to understand their neurobehavioral competencies. Although brain-injured children exhibit much individual variability, there are similarities in the ways they function, particularly in their patterns of neuropsychological deficits.

This chapter first provides information about how the brain functions and then describes some possible causes of brain injury. Its focus is on traumatic brain injury, which is the most common cause of brain dysfunction in young children and adolescents. However, the chapter also contains information about brain injuries acquired in other ways.

BACKGROUND CONSIDERATIONS IN UNDERSTANDING BRAIN FUNCTIONS

Recent developments in the neurosciences indicate the following about the human brain and its development (Hotz, 1996a, pp. A20, A22, and 1996b, p. 10, with changes in notation):

1. There is no center of consciousness, no single clearinghouse for memory, no one place where information is processed, emotions generated, or language stored. Instead, the human brain is a constantly changing constellation of relationships among billions of cells. Complex networks of neurons are linked by pathways forged, then continually revised, in response to experience.
2. There is no way to separate the brain's neural structure from the influence of the world that nurtures it. During growth and development, the feedback between the brain and its environment is so intimate that the two are essentially inseparable.
3. There is no single, predetermined blueprint for the brain. More than half of all human genes—about 50,000—are somehow involved in laying the brain's foundations. And they all exert a powerful influence over temperament, learning ability, and personality.
4. No two brains are physically alike, and the complex wiring of each brain is so unique that it is unlikely that any two people perceive the world in quite the same way.
5. Subtle differences in brain anatomy appear to affect the ways men and women process information, even when thinking about the same things, hearing the same words, or solving similar problems.
6. The most efficient brains appear also to be the smartest, with the brains of those with the highest IQs using the least energy. Learning and practice appear to improve brain efficiency.
7. Small structural abnormalities appear to develop in the brains of people with Alzheimer's disease and Huntington's chorea long before any noticeable behavioral symptoms can be diagnosed.

8. Minor alterations in neural circuits for vision and hearing may be responsible for dyslexia; brain abnormalities in regions involved in inhibiting mental activity could be the cause of attention-deficit/hyperactivity disorder.

Now let's discuss lateralization in order to understand the symptoms of brain injury better.

Lateralization of Cognitive, Perceptual, Motor, and Sensory Activities

Lateralization refers to the specialization of the two hemispheres of the cerebral cortex for cognitive, perceptual, motor, and sensory activities. In general, the side of the brain that controls *sensorimotor activities* (activities that combine the functions of the sensory and motor portions of the brain) is opposite to the side of the body that carries out the activity. Consequently, a lesion on the right cerebral hemisphere may result in deficits on the left side of the body, whereas a lesion on the left cerebral hemisphere may produce deficits on the right side of the body. Examples of sensorimotor deficits are weakness, poor coordination, and insensitivity. Subcortical damage, especially involving the cerebellum, may produce deficits on the same side of the body where the damage occurred.

Hemispheric Higher-Level Functions

The two cerebral hemispheres are specialized to varying degrees for *higher-level functions,* such as language, memory, and other cognitive processes (Lezak, 1995).

1. *Left cerebral hemisphere.* In nearly all right-handed individuals and in about two-thirds of left-handed individuals, the left hemisphere is primarily responsible for verbal functions—including reading and writing, understanding and speaking, verbal ideation, verbal memory, and certain aspects of arithmetic ability. Left hemisphere processing has been described as analytic, sequential, serial, and differential.

2. *Right cerebral hemisphere.* The right hemisphere specializes in nonverbal, perceptual, and spatial functions—including spatial visualization, visual learning and memory, arithmetical calculations involving spatial organization of the problem elements, complex visual-motor organization, and nonverbal sequencing. Right hemisphere processing is considered holistic, simultaneous, gestalt-like, parallel, and integrative.

For simple tasks, nonverbal stimuli can be processed holistically by either hemisphere. The right hemisphere is clearly inferior to the left hemisphere in the expressive functions of speech and writing but is less deficient in language comprehension.

Specialized Functions of the Cerebral Hemispheres

Some specialized functions of the cerebral hemispheres include the following (see Figure 19-1).

1. The *frontal lobes* are associated with the planning, initiation, and modulation of behavior and with expressive verbal fluency, control of motor functions, and motor planning.
2. The *temporal lobes* are associated with auditory perception, auditory comprehension, verbal memory, and some forms of visual processing.
3. The *parietal lobes* are associated with somatosensory functions, visual-spatial ability, and the integration of visual, somatosensory, and auditory stimuli.
4. The *occipital lobes* are associated with visual perception, elaboration and synthesis of visual information, and the integration of visual information with the information gathered by the auditory and other sensory systems.

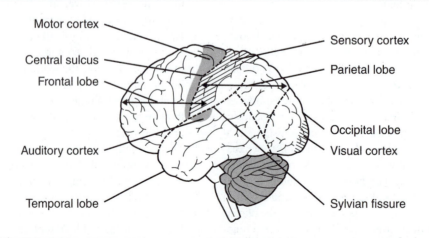

Figure 19-1. Drawing of the surface of the left hemisphere of the cerebrum.

Injuries to the cerebral hemispheres (frontal, temporal, parietal, and occipital lobes) and to subcortical centers (such as the basal ganglia and hippocampal structures) may lead to disorders in cognition, memory, affect, and motivation.

The following case illustrates some problems associated with a closed-head injury that presumably involved the frontal lobe (Mateer & Williams, 1991).

CASE 19-1. SS

SS was injured at the age of 3 years, 2 months when, as a passenger, she was struck in the left side of her face and posterior head in a motor vehicle accident. Unconsciousness lasted approximately 5 minutes. On emergency room examination, she was described as generally lethargic, but extremely agitated when aroused. She was hospitalized for 48 hours. Immediately following discharge, she experienced intense headaches, sleep disturbance, low tolerance for frustration, dramatic and abrupt changes in mood, tantrum behavior, excessive unhappiness, and difficulties with attention and concentration. Before the injury, she had no history of cognitive or behavioral difficulties.

Over the next 5 years, headaches continued but declined in frequency. Her mother noted continued difficulty with sleeping, fussiness about foods, quick and dramatic changes in mood, irritability, and unhappiness. She was described as having a short attention span, poor concentration, problems setting goals and organizing activities to complete tasks, and difficulty remembering instructions. Changes in routine were extremely difficult for her to adapt to.

When she entered school, problems were noted in attention, listening skills, carrying out instructions, finishing assignments, and working independently. Relationships with teachers and classmates were described as strained. (pp. 361–362, with changes in notation)

Development of Lateralization

Lateralization develops gradually in children, as evidenced by the replacement of bilateral movements with unilateral movements. Lateralization begins in utero and continues through childhood until adulthood (Spreen, Risser, & Edgell, 1995). Research suggests that linguistic functions are localized in the left hemisphere at birth for children of both sexes (Hahn, 1987; Paquier & Van Dongen, 1993). Functions lateralized in the right hemisphere, however, are less straightforward—certain abilities are lateralized at birth, whereas others become lateralized with age. For example, at birth, the right hemisphere appears to be specialized for processing nonlinguistic stimuli, whereas its ability to process spatial information is affected by developmental changes. Research on cerebral lateralization in childhood is continuing.

Comment on Lateralization

Lateral specialization for all cognitive, sensory, and motor functions cannot be clearly established for several reasons. First, the role of lateralization is less clear for visuoconstructional skills than it is for language skills. Second, lateralization is difficult to determine for memory tasks that can be encoded either verbally or perceptually (such as those involving easily recognizable figures with familiar names); it is difficult to know the memory processes individuals use in performing these tasks. Third, although the evidence for lateralized cerebral specialization is strong, less cerebral specialization for language may exist in young children than in adults because young children show language disorders even when they have right-sided lesions (Hécaen, 1983). Finally, although language and speech may be lateralized at birth (in the sense that the left hemisphere more readily supports these functions), complex changes in the direction and strength of hemispheric specialization occur as development proceeds (Lewkowicz & Turkewitz, 1982).

Once language develops, the left hemisphere probably is dominant for language for most individuals; the right hemisphere has limited potential for language functions. Lan-

Frank and Earnest   by Bob Thaves

WHILE MY LEFT BRAIN WAS WORKING OUT A SENSIBLE BUDGET FOR THE MONTH, MY RIGHT BRAIN ORDERED A GIANT PIZZA!

E-mail: FandEBobT@AOL.COM

THAVES 10-11

guage disorders in children, as in adults, are associated more frequently with left hemisphere damage than with right hemisphere damage. Although there may be some recovery of the functions mediated by the right hemisphere, deficits may continue to exist in syntactic, reading, and writing skills when there is left hemisphere damage (Moscovitch, 1981).

A primary function of the right hemisphere may be to act as a concrete spatial synthesizer, allowing information to be perceived as a meaningful unit. The right hemisphere does not have the specific analytic skills "required to process linguistic input phonetically or to decode complex syntax" (Moscovitch, 1981, p. 47). The right hemisphere does, however, support communication. Impairments of the right hemisphere may interfere with communication, conceptual skills, memory, and other cognitive functions, especially when a task requires the integration of multiple sources of information or comprehension of nonliteral language, such as metaphor or sarcasm. Additionally, the right hemisphere appears to be important in prosody, allowing for the recognition of emotional expression of speech and of emotional content of the speech of others.

CAUSES OF BRAIN INJURY

Brain injuries result from factors present before birth and from injuries sustained during the birth process, immediately after birth, or some time after birth. Let's examine briefly each of these developmental periods.

Prenatal Period

Prenatal environmental factors (factors existing or occurring before birth) that contribute to brain damage include the following:

- severe maternal malnutrition
- maternal use of alcohol, drugs, or tobacco
- maternal exposure to toxic substances (for example, lead, asbestos, chlorines, fluorides, nickel, and mercury)
- maternal infections due to viruses or bacteria (for example, rubella and syphilis or other sexually transmitted diseases)
- maternal illnesses (for example, hypertension and diabetes)
- radiation

Perinatal Period

Conditions associated with the period shortly before and after birth (*perinatal period*) that may lead to brain damage include the following:

- prematurity
- physical trauma associated with labor and delivery
- *asphyxia* (lack of oxygen or excess of carbon dioxide in the body, which may lead to unconsciousness, seizures, or damage to various sensory systems)

- *hypoglycemia* (low blood sugar)
- infections such as *meningitis* (a brain infection involving an acute inflammation of the membranes that cover the brain and spinal cord and characterized by drowsiness, confusion, irritability, and sensory impairments) or *encephalitis* (acute inflammation of the brain or its meninges, resulting from any of several different infections and toxins)
- *kernicterus* (a condition with severe neurological symptoms, characterized by high levels of bile secretion in the blood and often associated with jaundice)
- maternal sensitization such as *Rh incompatibility* (a condition that occurs when the mother has Rh-negative blood and the fetus has Rh-positive blood; when blood from the fetus mixes in the placenta with the mother's blood, antibodies may be produced that destroy the red blood cells of the fetus in subsequent pregnancies, potentially causing such pathologies as abortion, stillbirth, jaundice, or mental retardation, if not treated)

Postnatal Period

During the *postnatal period* (period after birth), conditions that may result in abnormalities of the nervous system include the following:

- *hydrocephaly* (a condition marked by increased accumulation of fluid within the ventricles of the brain)
- endocrine dysfunctions, such as *hypothyroidism* (a metabolic disorder that may be inherited, in which the child has difficulty producing sufficient levels of the thyroid hormone; if untreated, it can cause delays in brain development) and *Tay-Sachs disease* (a metabolic disorder characterized by degeneration of nervous tissue, blindness, deafness, severe mental retardation, and death by 5 years of age)
- metabolic disorders, such as *PKU* (a genetic condition in which the child is unable to digest phenylalanine, one of the essential amino acids [proteins] in the diet; if untreated, it almost always results in severe mental retardation and may cause convulsions, behavior problems, severe skin rash, and a musty odor of the body and urine) and *galactosemia* (a metabolic disorder caused by a recessive gene, which renders the individual unable to metabolize various forms of sugar and can cause such symptoms as cataracts, mental retardation, jaundice, and poor weight gain)

Metabolic disorders, often a result of hereditary dysfunctions, may be associated with deficient production of particular enzymes.

Period of Infancy, Early Childhood, and Adolescence

During infancy, early childhood, and adolescence, brain damage may be caused by the following factors:

- poor nutrition (for example, iodine deficiency, protein deficiency, or vitamin A, B_1, B_2, or D deficiency)
- trauma (associated, for example, with automobile accidents, falls, or child maltreatment)
- infection (for example, scarlet fever, rabies, Rocky Mountain spotted fever, encephalitis, or meningitis)
- radiation
- drug and alcohol abuse
- exposure to *neurotoxins* (toxic substances such as lead, arsenic, mercury, carbon disulfide, and manganese)

Early signs of brain injury include the following:

- occasions of prolonged nausea and vomiting in the child that are not related to common illnesses
- changes in the child's energy level
- changes in the child's appearance, hygiene, social behavior, temperament, personality, or work habits
- changes in the way the child performs daily routines
- sudden or progressive declines in the child's school performance
- disruptive, aggressive, or confused behavior that interferes with the child's daily living activities, interpersonal relations, or school performance
- significant delays in the child's achieving developmental milestones

Symptoms such as instability, irritability, or lethargy may precede other symptoms of a brain tumor. Sudden and inadequately explained changes in behavior are likely to be associated with acute, as opposed to chronic, brain disorders.

TRAUMATIC BRAIN INJURY

Each year approximately 1 million children in the United States sustain head injuries from falls, child maltreatment, recreational accidents, or motor vehicle accidents (Savage, 1993). Brain injuries to children, it has been estimated, annually result in "7,000 deaths of children, 150,000 hospitalizations, hospital care costing over $1 billion, and 30,000 children becoming permanently disabled" (Savage, 1993, p. 4).

Although many children are surviving head injuries because of advances in medical treatment, brain-injured children still have cognitive, language, somatic, and behavioral difficulties. *Traumatic brain injury* is a threat not only to a child's quality of life—including life style, education, social and recreational activities, interpersonal relationships, freedom to make changes, and control over his or her being and destiny—but also to his or her survival (Hickey, 1992).

Traumatic brain injury is associated primarily with falls and with child maltreatment in children under 5 years of age and with bicycle, motor vehicle, and sports-related accidents and injuries in children over 5 years of age. For older adolescents, traumatic brain injuries often are associated with motor vehicle accidents (including reckless driving, driving

while intoxicated, and being struck by drivers who were driving while intoxicated) or other risk-taking behaviors. Adolescents who are reckless, who have an attention-deficit/hyperactivity disorder, who have other forms of psychological difficulty, or who lack a sense of responsibility may be more prone to traumatic brain injuries than those who do not have these problems or characteristics.

Traumatic brain damage may produce open-head injuries or closed-head injuries. In an *open-head injury,* the skull usually is penetrated by a high-velocity projectile, such as a bullet, and contact occurs between the brain tissue and the outside environment. The physical results, often called *focal effects,* are usually confined to the site of the injury. Examples of focal effects are lacerations, intracranial hematomas, infections, and epilepsy. The latter is particularly likely when an infection is present.

Closed-head injuries may damage the brain severely, although the skull is not penetrated. The force of the trauma affects the brain within the closed, bony space of the skull (Miller, 1992). Motor vehicle accidents are the most frequent cause of closed-head injuries. These injuries produce a range of physical symptoms, often called *multifocal effects* or *diffuse effects,* depending on the type and severity of the injury.

Following are examples of multifocal, or diffuse, effects (Kolb & Whishaw, 1990):

- contusion of the brain tissue at the site of impact
- contusion of the brain tissue at the site opposite where the impact occurred (because the impact forces the brain to rebound against the opposite side of the skull, causing an injury called a *contrecoup*)
- microscopic lesions formed by a twisting or shearing of the nerve fibers (because of the violent movement of the brain within the skull)
- hemorrhage associated with the bruises and strains (which may form a hematoma that places pressure on the surrounding tissue and structures)
- *edema* (a buildup of fluid in and around the damaged tissue that places pressure on the surrounding brain tissue and structures)

According to the *Glasgow Outcome Scale,* children with a traumatic brain injury may experience the following outcomes (Jennett & Bond, 1975):

1. *Good recovery.* The child is able to resume preinjury activities and schooling with minimal neurological deficits.

2. *Moderate disability.* The child is able to function independently, but at a reduced level relative to his or her preinjury status. Special education or rehabilitation services are required.

3. *Severe disability.* The child is unable to function independently and requires substantial assistance with self-care.

4. *Persistent vegetative state.* The child is unable to function without a life-care support system.

5. *Death.* The child dies as a result of the brain injury.

The following case illustrates some problems that resulted from a traumatic brain injury to a preschool child (Lehr, 1990).

CASE 19-2. JONATHAN

Jonathan was 3½ when he fell from a second-floor window through a screen that was not securely fastened. On admission to the emergency room, he was reportedly semicomatose, and a fracture involving the base of his skull was diagnosed. He also had a large collection of blood in the right front part of his brain (right temporal hematoma), which had to be removed surgically 3 days after his injury. He improved markedly after surgery, was able to move his arms and legs 8 days after injury, and was able to follow verbal commands 10 days after injury. When he was admitted to the rehabilitation hospital, he was able to talk but only sparsely, was beginning to feed himself, was taking a few steps by himself, but had not regained bowel and bladder control. By the time of discharge from the rehabilitation hospital, Jonathan was able to talk fluently, would go to the bathroom with reminders, and was able to walk with monitoring for impulsiveness and balance.

Before his injury, Jonathan was described as an angel, who had clearly been a favorite child, not only of his mother and older brother but also of his entire extended family. He and his 10-year-old brother were extremely close and were continually together, sharing a bedroom and toys. After school, they would play with two older boys and their little brothers, building forts and riding their bikes. The accident had occurred while Jonathan was playing with his older brother in their room. His brother was devastated by the accident and blamed himself for it. He refused to sleep in their room and rarely could tolerate visiting Jonathan in the hospital. Because his mother spent much of her time in the hospital with Jonathan, his brother was left alone for long periods.

As Jonathan improved, his mother began to notice changes in his behavior. He was no longer able to wait but wanted things immediately. If he did not get them, he would yell or cry. If not watched carefully, he would impulsively take toys from other children or hit them if they bothered him. He had considerable energy and could easily engage in a full 6-hour day of therapy, but had difficulty channeling his energy in less-structured play-time. When asked to do specific tasks, Jonathan demonstrated difficulty in being able to stay with them longer than 5 minutes without being distracted onto something else. If pushed, he would then refuse to try again. However, he was able to play with toys during supervised play sessions for up to 30 minutes. Jonathan especially liked playing with a dollhouse and repeatedly had the people fall from the roof onto their heads. After they broke their heads, he then had them go to the hospital to get better.

On formal testing 2 months after the injury, Jonathan was functioning about 10 months below his chronological age level. Although he was able to talk fluently in conversation, he had difficulty naming and describing pictures during testing. His verbal responses were slowed, and he substituted closely related words (*shoe* for *foot* and *lock* for *key*). He was not able to copy a circle, and his way of holding a pencil was noticeably awkward. Jonathan especially enjoyed putting puzzles together but could only maintain his attention for puzzles with 4 or 5 pieces.

After he returned home, Jonathan continued to need close supervision. Once when he was hungry, he put a piece of leftover pizza directly on top of a stove burner to heat it. His brother continued to feel very guilty about the accident but began to deal with it by watching out for Jonathan and playing with him again. However, he also was very aware that Jonathan was not as much fun to be with as before injury and that he had to be carefully watched so that he did not get hurt again. (pp. 61–62)

SPECIFIC EFFECTS OF BRAIN INJURY IN CHILDREN

Brain injury may produce the following types of symptoms:

- general deterioration in all or most aspects of functioning
- differential symptoms, depending on the (a) location, extent, and type of injury, (b) child's age, (c) child's premorbid cognitive, temperament, personality, and psychosocial characteristics, and (d) child's familial and environmental supports
- highly specific symptoms when the injury is in certain brain locations
- subtle symptoms detectable only by a careful study of the child's performance
- symptoms not seen until several years later
- no observable symptoms at all

Symptoms of brain injury are usually directly related to the functions mediated by the area where the damage occurred—for example, if the damage is in the occipital lobe, the symptoms likely will include difficulty with visual perception. Occasionally, the symptoms that arise after brain injury disappear quickly; however, subtle impairments may remain (Kolb & Whishaw, 1990).

The following case illustrates some symptoms of an adolescent with a traumatic brain injury (Gans, Mann, & Ylvisker, 1990):

CASE 19-3. T. S.

T. S. is a 16-year-old boy who suffered a severe traumatic brain injury in a motor vehicle accident 6 months ago. He has made excellent progress but still has minor attentional, perceptual, and fine motor deficits. He has had individual tutoring at home, and his academic skills are now at grade level. He is returning to a large high school where each of his classes is in a separate classroom. He arrives at school and has difficulty locating his locker. Once he finds it, he tries the combination several times but is unable to open the lock. He checks the combination in his pocket and realizes that he has reversed the numbers. He succeeds in opening his locker but the bell has rung and he is now late for class. He is unsure of what books he should take with him and whether he will be able to return to his locker before lunch. Arriving at a history class already in session, he finds his seat, dropping his books as he attempts to sit down. Finally he gets settled into the seat but has difficulty in paying attention to the teacher. He has reviewed this material recently with his tutor but finds his attention wandering to the charts on the wall, the noises from the street outside, and the turning notebook pages of his classmates. The bell rings and his teacher gives the assignment for tomorrow. T. S. is distracted by sounds from the hallway and does not note the assignment. After class he stops to ask the teacher to repeat the assignment, but the teacher is talking with another student and becomes impatient when T. S. interrupts. He realizes that he's late for the next class and leaves without his homework assignment. In the crowded hallway, he must concentrate on keeping his balance, becomes disoriented, and is unable to locate his next class.... He returns home from school and his mother asks how his day went. "Fine," he responds. (p. 613)

Cognitive and Behavioral Symptoms of Brain Injury

Much remains to be learned about the long-term effects on cognitive processes of mild, moderate, and severe head injury in children. Minor injuries may cause little or no impairment of higher mental functions, whereas major injuries may cause severe impairment. The effects of brain injury on young children may not be fully known until several years after the injury, when the children are expected to use more complex and higher-level cognitive and behavioral processes. Relatively undeveloped skills at the time of injury may seem to have been spared, but, later in life, these skills may not develop fully or may be impaired (Levin, Ewing-Cobbs, & Fletcher, 1989). Children sustaining brain injury early in life should be reassessed during early adolescence because it is during these years that more complex and higher-level cognitive and behavioral processes emerge.

Some behavioral symptoms present during the early stages of recovery—such as delusions, irritability, hallucinations, and suspiciousness—may result from cognitive changes that interfere with the thinking of brain-injured children (Wood, 1987). These symptoms frequently reflect brain-injured children's difficulty in regulating behavior in response to environmental stimuli. If present, the symptoms probably will reduce children's ability to think adaptively and flexibly and hamper their control over mental processes. Some symptoms may be associated with medications, such as antiseizure medication, which may produce or exacerbate learning or memory disturbances, or antipsychotic medication, which may produce blunted affect; both types of medications may produce psychomotor retardation (Lezak, 1995).

In brain injury, automatic processing may be lost (Wood, 1987). Previously overlearned and automatic sequential activities that were carried out quickly and effortlessly before the injury may require concentration and deliberation and become considerably slower after the injury. With the loss of automatic processing, brain-injured children have less flexibility and less ability to adjust rapidly to environmental changes. Thus, they are placed at a disadvantage in novel situations. In addition, deficits in one area of functioning may impair their performance in other areas. Changes in

cognitive efficiency, vigilance, reaction time, and temperament may make brain-injured children more vulnerable to sustaining a second head injury; those who are accident prone also may sustain repeated head injuries (Levin, Ewing-Cobbs, & Fletcher, 1989).

Let's now examine the major cognitive disturbances and changes in temperament, personality, and psychosocial functioning found in brain-injured children.

Cognitive disturbances. Cognitive disturbances after brain injury may include the following:

- disorders of attention and concentration
- disorders of planning, initiating, and maintaining goal-directed activities (executive functions)
- disorders of judgment and perception
- disorders of learning and memory
- disorders in the speed of information processing
- disorders of language and communication

Table 19-1 shows examples of disorders in each of these areas. Cognitive disturbances also may contribute to a decline in general intelligence.

Some cognitive impairments diminish with time; others are relatively resistant to change but still may diminish with time; and still others are relatively permanent (Prigatano, Fordyce, Zeiner, Roueche, Pepping, & Wood, 1986). The correlation between severity of initial injury and neurodevelopmental outcome is far from perfect; however, if severe damage results in a coma of long duration, there is greater probability of impaired cognitive functioning.

Children with brain injuries may have cognitive impairments that are not evident in the interview. For example, they may have little difficulty during a mental status evaluation but show attentional deficits when left to their own resources. Similarly, although they may be able to converse adequately in the interview, they may easily become distracted when several persons are talking.

Disorders of symbolic processes and language—such as agnosia, apraxia, and aphasia—may be more evident in the interview than other types of disturbances. Let's look briefly at these symbolic and language disturbances.

Agnosia. *Agnosia is a central nervous system disorder manifested through impaired ability to recognize familiar objects perceived via the senses.* The difficulty is not caused by sensory or intellectual impairment, however. Following are some forms of agnosia:

- *visual agnosia,* an impaired ability to name or recognize objects (for example, calling a book "a bunch of papers" or failing to recognize a hat)
- *prosopagnosia,* an impaired ability to recognize familiar faces
- *auditory agnosia,* an impaired ability to identify sounds
- *tactile agnosia,* an impaired ability to identify familiar objects by touch with the eyes closed

Table 19-1
Types of Cognitive Disturbance Observed After Brain Injury

Cognitive disturbance	Examples	Cognitive disturbance	Examples
Disorders of attention and concentration	Trouble sustaining attention Easily fatigued Impaired selective attention and scanning Distractibility Difficulty in shifting attention Trouble initiating activities Poor ability to encode information (difficulty in manipulating information while holding it in memory)	Disorders of learning and memory	Poor rote learning Short-term memory deficits Difficulty in organizing or processing important information Retrograde amnesia (inability to remember events that occurred prior to the onset of the amnesia) Anterograde amnesia (inability to remember events after some disturbance in the brain)
Disorders in planning, initiating, and maintaining goal-directed activities	Limited initiative Impairment of the abstract attitude Difficulty in inhibiting action Slow initiation time Confusion as to where to start in solving a problem Difficulty in ordering or sequencing information Difficulty in knowing when, where, and how to ask for help Difficulty in learning from mistakes and from successes Perseverative errors (difficulty in stopping once activity is begun) Difficulty in shifting cognitive set Difficulty in developing a planning strategy Difficulty in separating out irrelevant bits of information when dealing with moderately complex tasks	Disorders of language and communication	Anomia Reduced word fluency Inefficient word retrieval Tangential thought and speech (for example, problems in word selection, loose connection of thoughts and ideas, impaired abstract thinking, straying from core message or topic) Talkativeness (or verbal expansiveness) Use of peculiar words and phrases (for example, talking about oneself in the third person, using metaphoric expressions) Uninhibited choice of words (for example, using four-letter expletives)
Disorders of judgment and perception	Misinterpretation of actions or intentions of others Confusion on being presented with multiple bits of information at one time Tendency to be socially inappropriate in verbal communications Unrealistic appraisal of self and residual strengths and weaknesses	Disorders in the speed of information processing	Extreme slowness in reaction time and in processing information (for example, poor language comprehension when information is given quickly) Slowness in psychomotor activities (for example, slowness in talking, writing, doing mechanical tasks)

Source: Adapted from Prigatano et al. (1986).

• *visual-spatial agnosia,* an impaired ability to follow directions, to find one's way in familiar surroundings, to understand spatial details such as left-right positions, to describe a floor plan of a house, or to understand other types of visual-spatial characteristics

Apraxia. *Apraxia is a central nervous system disorder manifested through impaired ability to execute learned*

movements or to carry out purposeful or skilled acts. The impairment, however, is not caused by muscle weakness, sensory defects, poor comprehension, or intellectual deterioration. Some forms of apraxia follow:

• *ideomotor apraxia,* an impaired ability to carry out an action on verbal command, although the action can be performed automatically

- *ideational apraxia,* an impaired ability to execute a series of acts, although the steps may be performed separately
- *facial apraxia,* an impaired ability to perform facial movements in response to commands (for example, to whistle, pucker lips, protrude tongue), although the movements may be executed spontaneously
- *limb-kinetic apraxia,* an impaired ability localized to a single limb, resulting in clumsiness or the inability to carry out fine motor acts with the affected limb
- *constructional apraxia,* an impaired ability to construct objects (for example, to construct a pattern with blocks or to draw from a copy)
- *dressing apraxia,* an impaired ability to dress

Aphasia. *Aphasia is a central nervous system dysfunction manifested through disorders in the perception, production, and symbolic use of language.* The following three subgroups of childhood aphasia differ from one another mainly in the severity and age of onset of the language dysfunction:

- *congenital aphasia,* a language dysfunction present at birth, marked by an almost complete failure to acquire language
- *developmental language disorder,* a less pervasive cognitive and developmental impairment, in which language is late in onset and fails to develop fully
- *acquired aphasia,* a language dysfunction resulting from brain injury following normal language development

Aphasia may involve expressive components, receptive components, or both. *Expressive aphasia* reflects impaired ability to use spoken and/or written language. The effects of the disability range from completely losing the ability to speak to simply having difficulty finding the appropriate word. Children with aphasia may have a restricted range of vocabulary, may use words repetitively, and may leave long pauses between words or phrases. Aphasia is primarily a problem in the symbolic use of language. Following are some forms of expressive aphasia:

- *agraphia,* the loss or impairment of the ability to express language in written or printed form
- *agrammatism,* the use of a paucity of adjectives and adverbs in speech, which gives speech a telegraphic quality
- *acalculia,* the inability to carry out simple mathematical calculations

Receptive aphasia reflects impaired ability to understand spoken and/or written language. Forms of receptive aphasia include the following:

- *auditory aphasia,* an impaired ability to comprehend the meaning of spoken words, although the ability to hear remains intact
- *alexia,* a loss of the ability to comprehend written or printed language, despite adequate vision and intelligence

When children have impaired abilities in both expressive and receptive domains, the condition is called *global aphasia* or *mixed-type aphasia.* Children with receptive deficits also are likely to have expressive disturbances, but those with expressive disturbances may not necessarily have receptive problems. Table 19-2 illustrates procedures used to evaluate agnosia, apraxia, and aphasia.

Comment on aphasia in children. Aphasic symptoms of children are similar to those of adults (Paquier & Van Dongen, 1993). Acquired aphasia occurs in children for the same reasons it occurs in adults—as a result of trauma, vascular lesions, tumors, infections, and convulsive disorders. However, the distribution of etiologies in children is somewhat different from that in adults. In children, for instance, brain injury from a traumatic event is the main cause of aphasia, whereas in adults the main cause is cerebrovascular accidents. Traumatic lesions produce fewer clear-cut aphasic symptoms than do cerebrovascular accidents.

The following case illustrates the course of recovery in a young brain-injured child (Cranberg, Filley, Hart, & Alexander, 1987).

CASE 19-4. FRED

Because of a fall, Fred, a 5-year-old, right-handed boy, had a left temporal skull fracture and an acute epidural hematoma (an accumulation of blood below the outer membrane that covers the brain). In the hospital, he was arousable but had limited ability to focus, and the hematoma was removed surgically. On the next day he was more attentive to the environment. He was transferred to a rehabilitation hospital on the 22nd day after he entered the hospital. He had a right hemiparesis and difficulty with vision, did not say any words, and his speech output was limited to occasional mumbles and single syllables. Auditory comprehension was mildly impaired. A computed tomography (CT) scan revealed neurological problems, particularly in the occipital lobe and in the lower brain stem regions.

After a few weeks in the rehabilitation hospital, he was speaking in three- or four-word phrases and repeating three- or four-word phrases. He could count to 10 but could not name colors or body parts, and he had other word-finding difficulties. Three months after the accident he was speaking in five- and six-word phrases. By 9 months, speech was fluent, limited only by mild word-finding difficulty. Auditory comprehension was normal. Motor function of the right arm was normal, but there was residual spasticity of the right leg. He also had focal seizures.

Despite the good oral language recovery, he later did poorly in school. By age 10, he still could not read all the letters or add two-digit numbers. By age 12, although his supply of information (presumably acquired by hearing) was nearly normal, reading skills had progressed to only a third-grade level. (p. 1166, with changes in notation)

Children under the age of 10 years with aphasia are usually alert, attentive, and intent on communicating their thoughts and reactions. The onset of aphasia in later childhood presents a more mixed pattern resembling that of adults, with an increased frequency of disorders involving speech. The prognosis for recovery from aphasia is more favorable

Table 19-2
Procedures Used in Testing for Agnosia, Apraxia, and Aphasia

Disorder	Ability	Procedure
Agnosia	Sound recognition	Ask the child to identify familiar sounds, such as a ringing bell or a whistling sound, with eyes closed.
	Auditory-verbal comprehension	Ask the child to answer questions and carry out instructions.
	Recognition of body parts and sidedness	Ask the child to point to her or his left and right sides and to name body parts.
	Visual object recognition	Ask the child to identify familiar objects, such as a pen or a wristwatch.
	Facial recognition	Observe whether the child recognizes familiar faces.
	Tactile recognition	Ask the child to identify familiar objects placed in her or his hand, such as keys, comb, or pencil, with eyes closed.
	Visual-spatial recognition	(For older child) Ask the child to touch her or his right ear or right hand and to walk to the left side of the room.
Apraxia	Performance of skilled motor acts	Ask the child to complete motor acts, such as drinking from a cup, closing a safety pin, or using common tools.
Aphasia	Visual-verbal comprehension	Ask the child to read a sentence from the newspaper and explain its meaning. If the child is unable to talk, print instructions on a sheet and note whether the child can carry them out.
	Motor speech	Ask the child to imitate several sounds and phrases: "la-la," "me-me," "this is a good book," and others of increasing difficulty. Note abnormal word usage in conversation.
	Automatic speech	Ask the child to repeat one or two series of words that the child has learned in the past, such as the days of the week or the months of the year.
	Volitional speech	Ask the child to answer questions. Note whether the answers are relevant.
	Writing	Ask the child to write (a) her or his name and address, (b) a simple sentence, (c) one word, with eyes closed, and (d) the name of an object that you show her or him, with eyes open.

Note. Some of the activities in the table—such as those requiring reading, writing, and knowledge of right and left—pertain only to children who would be expected to have mastered the skill based on their age.

for children than for adults. When recovery is not complete, brain-injured children may have long-term deficits, including naming disorders, impaired use of syntax, and writing disorders, all of which can disrupt academic performance. The type of aphasic disturbance exhibited and the prognosis for recovery are clearly related to the severity of the injury, including the etiology of the injury and the size and nature of the lesion. The presence of seizures can impede recovery.

The following comments from brain-injured patients (primarily adolescents and adults) describe their experiences with aphasia (Joanette, Lafond, & Lecours, 1993, pp. 23–30, 32). Do not assume, however, that all individuals with aphasia will have these reactions.

DIFFICULTIES WITH ORAL EXPRESSION

- I found that when I wanted to talk, I couldn't recall the appropriate expressions. My thoughts were ready, but I could no longer command the sounds that expressed them. I said to myself *so it's true that I can't speak any more.*

- The speech therapist asked me: *Can you count? How high?* I had no problem counting to thirty, but I couldn't go further. *What time is it?* she continued. It was around 11:15, but I didn't know how to say it.

- I need to visualize the written word in order to pronounce it properly.

- When I sing, the tune or melody will suggest the words, and I feel my nerve pathways become clearer and messages flow easier.

DIFFICULTIES IN AURAL COMPREHENSION

- I heard something, and I didn't understand…. It was like Chinese, or…I don't know…not a foreign language, but more like something meaningless, how shall I put it, I heard vague words.

- At first I heard words and I could only recall that I knew them, the act of hearing them did not reveal their meaning to me.

- I could understand simple things, but complicated instructions—not at all.

- When you speak slowly, it's all right; but if you speak too quickly, it's as if I only hear sounds, I can't understand well. It's the same way if I am with a few people, I can't always follow the conversation. By the time I try to understand what was said, two or three people have already spoken, and I get all confused.

DIFFICULTIES WITH WRITTEN EXPRESSION

- I felt my left hand move.... I tried to write: *Where am I?* But all that I could scribble were a few illegible marks.
- It just doesn't come, you know? It doesn't come from inside, the way you have to form letters.... Sometimes, I say to myself, *Hey, but I can write,* and I try, but then I can't.
- After a few [speech therapy] sessions, I could spell short words; by spelling out loud, it was easier to write.
- It's not the longest and most complicated words that give me the most trouble...instead, it's the small words like "in," "the," "her," "by," especially small invariable words and negatives.

DIFFICULTIES WITH WRITTEN COMPREHENSION

- Reading was impossible for at least a couple of months. I couldn't make sense of what I was reading, all the letters seemed to be jumbled together.
- At the onset of my illness, I had to read out loud.... In order to read, I have to visualize the letter or the word; not only how it looks, but how it sounds.... People would hear me whispering the letter or the word before uttering it out loud. The problem was that I needed not only to see the form of the letter, but also hear how it sounds.
- If the letters are written in large print, I can read and understand well. But small print is just too confusing.
- I read, I understand what I read more or less, but I can't remember the plot. Often, I have to look over the chapter again, or reread the previous paragraph to see where I am. (This may reflect a learning or memory deficit rather than a primary comprehension deficit.)

DIFFICULTIES IN SELF-PERCEPTIONS

- That awful feeling of being a prisoner within myself!
- It's absolutely brutal: You still have the same ideas, the same mind. It takes time to get used to, like the loss of an arm.
- I noticed a change in me, I was another person, someone who was unable to express the little I knew, I was ashamed.
- My life is a mixture of fear and uncertainty. This recent event can only lead to questions, and this terrifies me.

DIFFICULTIES WITH RELATIONSHIPS WITH OTHER PEOPLE

- If you don't know words, you keep quiet.... When it's noisy, you can't talk.... People talk for us.... Anyway, when we talk, it's not the way it used to be...you keep quiet.
- I'm not sure of myself, I feel uncomfortable around other people, I have problems communicating.
- I'm only happy when a person close to me is nearby. I need to feel understood, even if I don't say anything.
- People don't speak to me as much any more.

The following case describes the course of recovery in an aphasic adolescent (Levin, 1981).

CASE 19-5. SARA

Sara, a 17-year-old female student, was involved in a motor vehicle accident in which she received a closed-head injury. Soon after admission to the hospital, she developed right hemiparesis and aphasia. Three days post-injury, the neuro-surgeon performed a partial left temporal lobectomy and removed an intracerebral hematoma. She remained confused for a month after injury but exhibited gradual improvement of receptive language. Two months after the injury, she still had difficulty naming objects or recalling or recognizing names (anomic aphasia). She had many errors of circumlocution (for example, she defined an island as a place where you fish and described a triangle as the thing you use when you play pool) and semantic approximation (for example, she described the trunk of an elephant as a nose). Approximately one year after the injury, she had recovered most of her language facility, except for a subtle residual anomic disturbance evident only during the neuropsychological examination.

Exercise 19-1. Identifying the Type of Language or Symbolic Disorder

Read each statement and identify the type of language or symbolic disorder it illustrates. Each statement reflects one of the following disturbances: acalculia, agraphia, agrammatism, auditory aphasia, alexia, visual agnosia, prosopagnosia, auditory agnosia, tactile agnosia, visual-spatial agnosia, constructional apraxia, facial apraxia, ideational apraxia, ideomotor apraxia, or dressing apraxia.

1. A 9-year-old brain-injured child is shown a baseball bat, and she calls it "a piece of wood."
2. A 16-year-old brain-injured adolescent is asked to touch a doll's right ear and says "I don't know where to touch it."
3. An 8-year-old brain-injured child is asked to put her hands in the air, and she stares out the window.
4. A 9-year-old brain-injured child is asked to put on a sweater and fails in his attempt to do so. However, he can clap his hands when he is asked to do so.
5. An 8-year-old brain-injured child is shown a picture of three blocks that are stacked in a tower from largest to smallest. She is asked to build the same tower. The child puts her three blocks in a row, thus failing to duplicate the pattern shown in the picture.
6. A 13-year-old brain-injured adolescent is shown a picture of his brother, and he calls it "a picture of someone."
7. When asked to write his name, a 10-year-old brain-injured child makes random marks.
8. A 15-year-old brain-injured adolescent is asked to identify a coin placed in her hand without looking at it, and she says "It is something."
9. A 16-year-old brain-injured adolescent with adequate vision, speech, and intelligence is asked to read aloud a paragraph from a third-grade reader and is unable to do so.
10. A 10-year-old brain-injured child is asked to drink out of a cup when it is filled with water and complies with the request. The child is shown another cup, but this time it is empty. When the child is asked to show how he would drink out of it, he simply looks puzzled at the request and does not perform any actions.
11. An 8-year-old brain-injured child is asked to identify the sound of a drum, and she says "I don't know what it is."
12. A 12-year-old brain-injured adolescent says "I go store buy candy."

13. A 9-year-old brain-injured child is asked to add 4 + 3 + 2, and he says "432."
14. A 13-year-old brain-injured adolescent is asked to show her tongue, and she simply stares ahead.
15. A 10-year-old brain-injured child is asked to open the door, pick up a pencil from the table, and then put it on the chair. The child says "I don't know."

Answers

1. Visual agnosia
2. Visual-spatial agnosia
3. Auditory aphasia or ideomotor apraxia
4. Dressing apraxia
5. Constructional apraxia
6. Prosopagnosia
7. Agraphia
8. Tactile agnosia
9. Alexia
10. Ideomotor apraxia
11. Auditory agnosia
12. Agrammatism
13. Acalculia
14. Facial apraxia or auditory apraxia
15. Ideational apraxia (if a comprehension deficit has been ruled out as the cause)

To acquire aphasia is to suddenly lose both an important part of oneself and one's attachment to reality with no readily available means of compensation.

—Pierre Y. Létourneau

Changes in temperament, personality, and psychosocial functioning. The changes in temperament, personality, and psychosocial functioning that brain-injured children may exhibit relate both to their brain injury and to their preexisting personality and temperament. Of particular importance is how they perceive their limitations and the significance of these limitations. As noted earlier, their perceptions, in turn, will be related to their age, cognitive ability, social maturity, family and environmental supports, schooling, ethnicity, and social status.

Here are some symptoms of brain-injured children that are associated with their temperament, personality, and psychosocial functioning (Prigatano et al., 1986):

- *anxiety, irritability, impulsivity, and heightened emotionality* (such as lower tolerance for frustration, rapid mood shifts, temper outbursts, greater dependence on others, making more demands on others, and talkativeness)
- *denial of illness* (or *anosognosia*)
- *paranoid ideation and psychomotor agitation*
- *depression and amotivational states* (such as feelings of worthlessness; feelings of helplessness; feelings of guilt; loss of interest in school, work, or family activities; and decreased libido)
- *psychosocial disturbances* (such as socially inappropriate behavior, saying embarrassing things and performing actions that embarrass others, unawareness of personal impact on others, insensitivity to others, difficulty making friends, social withdrawal, and forgetting school responsibilities)

Some brain-injured children show a pattern of behavior associated with *overarousal* (such as inattentiveness, irritability, hyperactivity, impulsivity, inappropriate behavior, aggressiveness, and, for adolescents, increased sexual drive), whereas others show a pattern of behavior associated with *underarousal* (such as apathy, poor motivation, and social withdrawal) (Filley, Cranberg, Alexander, & Hart, 1987).

Possible Interpretations of Behavioral Symptoms

There is no simple way to interpret the behavioral symptoms of brain-injured children. Behavioral symptoms may (a) be neurologically based, reflecting, in part, impairment of cognitive, emotional, or psychosocial functions directly associated with neurological insult, (b) be emotional reactions to failures or to performance difficulties, (c) reflect preexisting personality patterns, or (d) be a combination of all of the above. You will need to study carefully entire case histories of brain-injured children to arrive at an understanding of the behavioral symptom patterns.

Some possible interpretations of behavioral symptoms follow:

1. *Emotional lability* may be a reaction to failure, may be neurologically based, or may reflect preexisting personality patterns.
2. *Anxiety* may come about as a heightened reaction to increased trouble coping with a difficult environment or because of a decrease in emotional control associated with neurological dysfunction.
3. *Denial of illness* may reflect unwillingness to recognize existing deficits because of a threatening environment, or it may reflect neurological disturbances in awareness and attention.
4. *Paranoid ideation and psychomotor agitation* may be related to preexisting personality difficulties, or they may reflect disturbances in neurological functioning.
5. *Depression and other psychosocial disturbances* may reflect a reaction to repeated performance failures or an attempt to reduce the demands of an insensitive environment, may be neurologically based, or may reflect preexisting personality patterns.
6. *Amotivational states* may be attempts to make the environment simple and predictable to avoid stress, may be neurologically based, or may reflect preexisting personality patterns.

Thus, *many behavioral symptoms of brain-injured children—such as depression, emotional lability, limited motivation, and paranoid ideations—may be as neurologically based as language and motor symptoms, such as aphasia and hemiplegia* (Prigatano et al., 1986).

The following case describes the difficulty of trying to determine whether a particular behavior post-injury is a direct consequence of the brain injury or whether it would have occurred in the normal course of the child's development (Rees, 1988).

CASE 19-6. LY

LY was 13 years old when she fell from her horse and suffered a severe head injury. She was an only child and was loved very dearly. LY was unconscious for many weeks, during which her mother talked and talked, trying by any means to get me [Rees] to tell her that eventually everything would be alright. She spent every waking hour at the hospital, determined to win, and daring visitors to suggest anything different. At last LY went home and was treated [by her family] as normal. Even her physical disability of a "drooped foot" was ignored most of the time, even though each day the mother carried out rigidly the exercises prescribed by the physical therapist. Looking at LY eight years later, it is difficult to detect anything wrong with her, but in fact she is a constant worry to her family. LY will run off with any young lad who shows her what seems to be affection, staying away from home while her parents search endlessly for her. She cannot hold down a job because her memory and concentration are not very good. The mother appears unworried to the outside world and shrugs off the problems, putting them down to "delayed adolescence." But she worries every minute LY is out of her sight; seeming not to worry is just the mother's way of coping. Although things are difficult, this family is a strong one, and even I feel that perhaps mother is right—the problems of running away from home might have happened anyway. Friends have sought my advice and wanted me to intervene somehow, but I find myself pointing out that they may be blaming the head injury for causing LY's trouble, rather than just exaggerating it. (p. 76)

The next case illustrates the continuing problems that follow some traumatic brain injuries (Rees, 1988).

CASE 19-7. HB

HB was 14 years old when she fell from her horse. She was in a coma for many weeks. HB was never docile, and even when she regained consciousness there was a feeling of aggression about her, which gradually increased. She would grit her teeth and refuse to allow food to be put in her mouth; she would take a drink but spit it out at whoever was nearest. HB would swear at the nurses and kick or bite anyone she could get hold of. When she went home it was even more difficult, because there were no longer people around to help and encourage her parents and to act as a buffer. After a month her mother was taking tranquilizers, her father was covered in bruises, and HB had threatened him with a knife. She would not sleep at night but would demand that her father stay at her bedside. All the doors had to be locked in case she tried to get out. The family doctor visited several times but saw nothing wrong, because she behaved quite well while he was there.

When I [Rees] arrived on the scene, after a telephone call from her father, her two brothers were at the point of leaving home, and I anticipated that if the situation continued her mother would be taken to the hospital with a nervous breakdown, and her father would collapse with exhaustion. I telephoned the family doctor, who listened to what I had to say and requested a hospital consultant to arrange HB's admission to hospital for assessment. Drugs were prescribed, which helped somewhat.

Eight years later this family is still trying to cope with a person who, though tremendously improved, still has outbursts of aggression. HB has a job stacking shelves in a supermarket, which is not challenging or satisfying, but she suffers from epilepsy and cannot get any other employer to take her on.

I may not hear from the family for months, but then comes a telephone call for advice, or just for her mother to talk and relieve her feelings. A few months ago I received an invitation to her engagement party. I attended and had the feeling the family might have reached an acceptable balance; perhaps they would find the peace they had been seeking. This was not to be: HB tormented her young man to such an extent that he threatened to jump off a bridge, and the police had to talk him down. The engagement is now off, and the mother and father are back where they were, seeking help again from the mental health professional. (p. 74, with changes in notation)

Differential Effects of Brain Injury in Young Children and in Adults

The effects of brain injury in children under 5 years of age are different from those in adults because young children's brains are still developing. When adults sustain a brain injury, there may be a *loss or dissolution of previously acquired functions,* manifested in impairment of language, memory, perceptual-motor functions, social relations, or general intelligence. In contrast, when children sustain a brain injury, there may be *interference with development* rather than a striking loss of function. If the interference is global, mental retardation may be the result; if it is region-specific, specific difficulties may result, such as difficulties with speech or with the recognition of shapes. Some evidence suggests that children's skills may be more affected by brain damage if they are in the most rapid stage of development than if they are well consolidated (Ewing-Cobbs, Levin, Eisenberg, & Fletcher, 1987).

Acquired brain damage usually produces less specific dysfunctions in young children than in adults. Because cortical specialization has not yet been completed, damage to the immature brain is likely to affect the development of the entire brain rather than produce localized abnormalities. In young children, brain damage may have more than a simple depressing effect on cognitive skills; it may alter the basic pattern of cognitive development. Large unilateral injuries in infants usually produce a more widespread deficit in intellectual functions than do similar injuries in adults. In addition, children's skulls are more flexible than those of adults, and their bones are less fused. Although this incomplete structure and its cushioning effect give children greater resistance to head injury, the incomplete structure also allows for much greater deformation of the brain on impact, leading to greater shearing forces within the cortex.

To understand brain damage in children, it is helpful to consider the principles of behavior development and the relationship between neural structures and behavior (Shaheen, 1984). The first five years of life constitute the period of greatest cortical development. The progress of myelination in various anatomical regions affects behavioral development. *Myelination* refers to the process of insulating, or coating, the axon of the neuron. It is essential in facilitating the speed with which information is passed along an axon.

Myelination occurs at several developmental milestones (Harris, 1995):

1. At 40 weeks' gestation, in the spinal tract areas involved in postural control
2. At 2 to 3 months of age, in the midbrain areas involved in smiling
3. At the end of the first year of life, in the spinal tract areas involved in fine motor control
4. During the second year of life, in the brain areas involved in motor control and coordination
5. During school years and later in life, in the brain areas involved in learning motor programs and higher mental processing

Conceivably, the types of behavioral difficulties that occur in brain-injured children could be related to the neurostructural components undergoing the most rapid development at the time of the brain injury. For example, from a developmental perspective, diffuse brain injuries may affect the development of the following neurostructural components:

1. Speech and language during the second year of life
2. Spatial-symbolic processing during the third year of life
3. Expressive and receptive language functions during the preschool years
4. Written language during middle childhood, particularly between ages 6 and 8 years
5. Verbal processing, nonverbal processing, and visuospatial processing during adolescence

The normal sequences of development, described in Chapter 3, should be reviewed before you evaluate brain-injured children. The development of attention also follows a normal sequence (Passler, Isaac, & Hynd, 1985). For example, young children, in comparison with older ones, are more impulsive, more active, less able to inhibit behavior, and less able to ignore potential distractions in their environment.

Children who sustain severe closed-head injuries may not fully recover from the trauma, as is evident in the case studies presented. They may have not only residual physical defects but also deficits in psychosocial functioning. For example, after the injury, they may show loss of self-esteem, loss of autonomy, loss of independence, impaired academic performance, and lowered job expectations.

The following comments illustrate how children with closed-head injuries and their parents reacted to the injuries (Bergland & Thomas, 1991, pp. 9–16):

COMMENTS BY BRAIN-INJURED CHILDREN ABOUT THEIR GENERAL FUNCTIONING

- I knew I would never be normal.
- I can't do the things I could before.
- Everything came to a halt; little things took forever.
- I got so frustrated and used to hit people. I don't know why; it's not like me.
- I do crazy, inappropriate things.
- I knew I was different because other people acted different toward me. They did things for me that I used to do myself.
- I had trouble remembering, but nobody else seemed to notice, so I said nothing.
- They don't see you as a person; they just don't even give you a chance.
- They expected me to be the same as I was before.
- I don't know what will happen to me. It doesn't look good.

COMMENTS BY PARENTS ABOUT THEIR BRAIN-INJURED CHILDREN'S GENERAL FUNCTIONING

- It was so hard; when you went somewhere, you never knew just what she might do or say.
- He wants to be like he was and can't understand why this can't be.
- You don't get a lot of positiveness from the average person [friends, relatives]. They would come up with a lot of smart-aleck responses, like, "What kind of kid do you have there?"
- They had a lot of free advice that was totally unrealistic; I just thought to myself—what do you know?
- I'm more understanding now; I can really have empathy for other people who are disabled.
- I worry about the future, his ability to fit in.

COMMENTS BY BRAIN-INJURED CHILDREN ABOUT THEIR FAMILIES

- They were just so cautious of me.
- They think I can't take care of myself.

COMMENTS BY PARENTS OF BRAIN-INJURED CHILDREN ABOUT THEIR FAMILIES

- It was just overwhelming. I thought it would never end.
- As a parent, you know, the loss of all the dreams you have for that child is just devastating.
- It was so ongoing.
- I don't think I'll ever get over this.
- The siblings really suffered; I feel that they need counseling just as much as the parents and the person.
- Maybe it would have been better if he had not survived this way.

COMMENTS BY BRAIN-INJURED CHILDREN ABOUT THEIR FRIENDS

- They treated me like I had a disease.
- People didn't want to talk to me.
- I didn't and still don't understand why they didn't like me.
- My thinking is so slow I can't talk to people.
- I lost my boyfriend. He just got tired of my outbursts. I know I was too dependent on him.
- I was no longer a part of the crowd.
- They put me in with the retarded; I'm not retarded.

COMMENTS BY PARENTS ABOUT
THEIR BRAIN-INJURED CHILDREN'S FRIENDS

- He doesn't have any friends.
- No one calls her anymore.
- I feel so badly for him. He used to be included in everything. Now, not very much.

COMMENTS BY BRAIN-INJURED CHILDREN
ABOUT THEIR ACADEMIC WORK

- I tried, but no matter how hard I tried, I still couldn't get my grades back up.
- I would work and work, but I got nowhere, so I finally gave up.
- I had planned to become a nurse, but can't do that, so now I work as a volunteer in the nursing home.
- I'm working every day just breathing, and in school trying to get to know people, and working on patience, which is very hard for me. I don't know if I can ever work.

COMMENTS BY PARENTS ABOUT THEIR BRAIN-INJURED
CHILDREN'S ACADEMIC WORK

- He couldn't keep on schedule or stay with the program. He can't be consistent or follow through.
- He doesn't seem to realize that anything has changed.
- Who will take the time to teach this kid instead of pushing him through classes that he cannot absorb any of the things? He feels a total failure because it went so fast he didn't grasp anything.
- He was rejected by the workshops; they won't take him. There is no place for him to go.

Dear, dear! How queer everything is today! And yesterday things went on just as usual. I wonder if I've been changed in the night? Let me think: Was I the same when I got up this morning? I almost think I can remember feeling a little different. But if I'm not the same, the next question is, "Who am I?" Ah, that's the great puzzle.

—Lewis Carroll

Cerebral Plasticity and Recovery of Function

Cerebral plasticity involves (a) the taking over, by one part of the brain, of functions impaired by lesions in another part of the brain or (b) the functional reorganization of the central nervous system to restore impaired functions. Cerebral plasticity operates primarily between birth and 4 or 5 years of age, but it can occur at any age. However, the assumption that the brain invariably possesses such plasticity has been questioned. How permanent are the effects of brain injuries in children? How easy is it for children to recover from brain injury? How do the effects of *early* brain injuries compare with those of *later* brain injuries? Although there are no simple or definitive answers to these questions, research does suggest some tentative answers.

Overall, studies show that children do not necessarily completely recover all of their functions after brain injury (Johnson, 1992; St. James-Roberts, 1981). Thus, there is little reason to believe that young brain-injured children *always* or *usually* make a better recovery than older brain-injured children. Instead, recovery is variable within each age group, depending on the child's age at the time of the brain injury, congenital makeup, premorbid status, experiential history, education, and the type and severity of the brain damage (including the nature, locus, extent, and progression of the brain lesions). In addition, after injury, some functions may improve more than others, and some anatomical areas may be more susceptible to permanent deficit than others. Research studies need to examine the long-term effects of head injury on cognitive, academic, and psychosocial functions.

Recovery of function depends in part on the ability of the neurons involved in the damaged area to regenerate terminals and to produce new terminals (Taylor, 1990). In this sense, the immature brain has greater plasticity (Rutter, 1982). However, anomalous neuronal connections may impair children's ability to process information (Rutter, 1982; Taylor, 1990). Changes in cognitive development after brain damage may best be viewed as involving cumulative interactions among etiological, recovery period, and experiential variables.

You must be extremely careful when you make prognostic statements about a child's ability to recover from brain injury. It is more difficult to evaluate language, speech, and other functions in children than in adults because young children have developed only rudimentary skills in these areas. The effects of brain injury on a skill yet to be developed will be different from those on an established skill (Rutter, 1982). It is necessary to study not only the child's degree of *recovery* following brain damage but also his or her ability to *learn* and *relearn* cognitive skills.

Those who uncritically accept the notion that children who sustain moderate or severe head injury recover more quickly than adults, and without significant deficits, may be doing a disservice to brain-injured children and their families (Johnson, 1992). The failure to recognize potential deficits may create unrealistic demands on brain-injured children to perform at a level beyond their ability. These unrealistic expectations may result in academic underachievement and emotional and social maladjustment. In addition, if the case goes into litigation with the children or families suing for injuries, the children may receive inadequate financial compensation if the extent of their deficits is not recognized. Brain-injured children should receive a thorough neuropsychological examination to determine their present deficits and strengths.

Absence of evidence is not evidence of absence.

—Hans L. Teuber

DIAGNOSTIC TECHNIQUES FOR BRAIN-INJURED CHILDREN

Children with brain injury should be assessed by both a neurological examination, which may include brain scanning and electrodiagnostic procedures, and a neuropsychological examination, which may include a thorough interview and battery of specialized tests. Let's look at these two procedures in more detail.

Neurological Examination

A neurological examination includes a clinical history, a mental status examination, and a study of cranial nerves, motor functions (including tone, strength, and reflexes), coordination, sensory functions, and gait. Several laboratory procedures may augment the neurological examination, including CT scans (computed tomography), PET scans (positron emission tomography), MRI scans (magnetic resonance imaging), EEGs (electroencephalograms), skull x-rays, lumbar punctures, cerebral angiograms, and single photon emission computed tomography (SPECT).

In the neuropsychological examination, *lower-level functions* (basic biological processes such as motor system functions and reflexes) can be evaluated on the two sides of the body by (a) *motor functioning tests* (measuring such factors as finger-tapping rate, strength of grip, and motor dexterity), (b) *standard neurological techniques* (assessing reflexes and tactile, visual, and auditory senses), (c) *bilateral simultaneous stimulation* (stimulating both sides of the body at the same time), and (d) *dichotic stimulation* (stimulating the two ears with distinctly different stimuli).

Scanning and radiographic methods.
A brief description of scanning and radiography methods follows.

- *Computed tomography* (CT scan) is an imaging technique in which an array of detectors is used to collect information from an x-ray beam that has passed through the brain or another body part. The beam is rotated to produce the equivalent of a slice through the area of interest. A computer reconstructs the internal structure from the information collected and displays it on a screen. CT scans are useful in locating focal pathologies, such as tumors and hemorrhages, and in showing changes in brain structure. However, there are disadvantages to CT scans; they expose children to radiation, the contrast material injected in the blood stream may cause an allergic reaction in a child, and the contrast between grey matter and white matter may be poor.
- *Positron emission tomography* (PET scan) is a scanning method that produces a cross-sectional image of radioactivity in the brain following intravenous injection of a radioactive substance. PET scans provide information about regional metabolic activity by measuring regional

cerebral glucose utilization. The information generated is similar to that produced by CT scans, but PET scans measure blood flow and metabolism in specific regions of the brain more precisely. Disadvantages of using a PET scan are that the technique is expensive and that it exposes children to radiation. Also, the normative standards and clinical correlations are not as well established as they are for structured neuroimaging techniques (such as computed tomography and magnetic resonance imaging).

- *Magnetic resonance imaging* (MRI scan) provides a two-dimensional intensity plot of a cross-sectional slice of any part of the body. The plot is a magnetic resonance image of the anatomy at the cross section. MRI is noninvasive and involves no harmful radiation. An advantage of an MRI scan over a CT scan is the ability to show better contrasts on soft tissue, a feature that makes it particularly suitable for the investigation of tumors, edema, tissue pathology, and small lesions. MRI should not be used with individuals who have a pacemaker, aneurysm clip, or other internal device; are pregnant (because the magnetic field may affect the fetus); have claustrophobia; or have other emotional reactions that may cause anxiety or harmful effects.
- *Electroencephalography* (EEG) is a procedure in which electrodes are placed on the scalp to record the electrical activity of the brain. When a computer is used to collect and analyze data from the electroencephalogram, the procedure is called *computerized electroencephalography* (CEEG). Electroencephalography is easy to perform, is relatively inexpensive, involves no radiation, and is noninvasive. However, the recordings do not necessarily bear a specific relation to any brain structure, and they may pick up artificial signals of noncerebral activity.
- *Cerebral angiography* involves radiographic recordings of internal structures of the vascular system of the brain. The recordings are produced by the action of x-rays or gamma rays on a specially sensitive film after injection of contrast material (for example, iodinated compounds) into the arterial blood system.
- *Single photon emission computed tomography* (SPECT) provides a three-dimensional representation of regional cerebral blood flow. SPECT brings together tomographic techniques for imaging brain structure and methods for measuring brain blood flow. The procedure involves placing the child in a dimly lit room and having her or him inhale a gas (for example, Xenon-133) in an air/oxygen mixture. Breathing the gas produces radioactivity that can be monitored by the machine. The measurement of cerebral blood flow by SPECT is noninvasive, painless, and safe. It has some disadvantages, however. Its use per year must be limited because of radiation exposure, it provides limited spatial resolutions, the representation may be contaminated by background radiation, and detecting lesions in the white matter is difficult. However, progress is being made in dealing with these limitations.

Scanning techniques, overall, provide excellent detail about the gross anatomy of the brain and excel in depicting major structural anomalies of the brain, including hydrocephalus and degenerative effects due to infectious disorders, tumors, and other childhood disorders (Bigler, 1988). Electrodiagnostic procedures provide information about the electrical activity of the brain and can help differentiate seizure type (for example, petit mal vs. grand mal epileptic seizures). However, neither scanning techniques nor electrodiagnostic procedures provide reliable information about levels of cognitive functions or about functional levels of performance—that is, how the child functions in everyday activities and situations.

Neurological signs. The neurological examination may reveal hard signs or soft signs of possible brain damage. *Hard signs* are those that are fairly definitive indicators of cerebral dysfunction (for example, abnormalities in reflexes, cranial nerves, and motor organization and asymmetrical failures in sensory and motor responses) and are usually correlated with other independent evidence of brain damage, such as the results of CT scans or EEGs.

Soft signs are mild and equivocal neurological irregularities in sensorimotor functions. Representative soft signs are poor balance; impaired fine motor coordination; clumsiness; slight reflex asymmetries; *choreiform* (irregular, jerky) *limb movements;* inability to perform rapid, alternating movements of hands and feet in a smooth, fluid, and rhythmic fashion (*dysdiadochokinesia*); inability to detect predisplayed symbols traced on the palmar surface when blindfolded (*dysgraphesthesia*); inability to identify three-dimensional objects in the outstretched hand when blindfolded (*astereognosis*); awkwardness; impaired auditory integration; atypical sleep patterns; visual-motor difficulties; and mental abnormalities. The term *soft signs* applies to behavioral and motor indicators that may not have any systematic relationship to demonstrated neuropathology but may suggest neurological impairment, immaturity of development, or a continuum of dysfunction.

Neuropsychological Examination

The primary aims of the neuropsychological examination are to draw inferences about the organic integrity of the cerebral hemispheres and to specify the adaptive strengths and weaknesses of brain-injured children. An adequate assessment of brain-behavior relationships requires a thorough developmental history and the use of several tests, as no single test can adequately assess the behavioral effects of widely variable cerebral lesions.

A neuropsychological examination complements a neurological examination. It typically includes measures of the following areas and functions (Mapou, 1995):

- *general intellectual skills and academic achievement abilities* (including reading, spelling, writing, and mathematics)

- *arousal and attention* (including level of alertness, focused attention, sustained attention, span of attention, resistance to interference, and mental manipulation)
- *sensory and motor functions* (including visual functions, auditory functions, somatosensory functions [pertaining to bodily sensations, including those of touch, pain, pressure, and temperature], lateral dominance [pertaining to which side of the body is dominant], motor strength, fine motor skills [such as speed and dexterity], and sensorimotor integration)
- *executive functions and problem-solving abilities* (including planning, flexibility of thinking, sequencing and organizational skills, and verbal and nonverbal reasoning abilities)
- *language functions* (including comprehension and production)
- *visuospatial functions* (including perceptual skills, constructional skills, and spatial awareness)
- *learning and memory* (including ability to learn new information, immediate and delayed recall, and recognition)
- *personality*
- *emotional functioning* (including range of expressed affect, lability of affect, and modulation of emotional reactivity)

The neuropsychological examination provides a profile of cognitive ability, sensorimotor functioning, and affective reactions. The results can be useful in the following ways:

- differentiating brain-injured children from those who are not brain injured
- localizing hemispheric involvement
- differentiating static lesions from rapidly growing lesions (particularly with repeated evaluations)
- evaluating the effects of progressive diseases of the central nervous system on adaptive abilities (for example, documenting rate and quality of change with the passage of time)
- differentiating behavioral disturbances that may stem from brain damage from those that may stem from other causes
- planning for rehabilitation (for example, estimating potential for recovery and improvement, describing management implications of the assessment findings, and designing interventions)
- providing essential information regarding changes in children's capabilities and limitations in their everyday functioning

Neuropsychological examinations also may help in evaluating children who have relatively isolated reading or other academic problems, learning disabilities, or an attention-deficit/hyperactivity disorder by providing

- objective behavioral information about children's adaptive functioning
- base-line measures for serially evaluating the course of various neuropathological processes

- indices about the effects of different therapeutic programs on cerebral functions

Base-line measures are those obtained when children are initially evaluated, *before* any treatment begins. Performance on base-line measures is used to assess changes in behavior over time, including those resulting from clinical treatment.

Neuropsychological assessment increases our understanding of the psychological effects of brain damage and, more generally, of brain-behavior relations. A battery of neuropsychological tests provides a comprehensive, objective, and quantified series of measures useful in assessing initial and later effects of various neuropathological conditions, neurosurgical procedures, and drug therapies. Also, in cases of civil liability suits involving head injuries, a neuropsychological examination provides objective measures of adaptive deficits (Schwartz, 1987).

Neuropsychological assessment has been shifting from assisting in the diagnosis of type and location of lesion to assessment of the functional capacities of brain-injured children and development of treatment programs that will help brain-injured children develop better adaptive capacities (Lyon, Moats, & Flynn, 1988). The shift has taken place because brain-imaging techniques have become more widely available and are better able to provide accurate information about the location of brain lesions.

Questions to explore during a neuropsychological assessment include "What type of educational program should this child receive this year or next year?" and "Is the child a good candidate for a visualization-memory training group?" No matter how many improvements are made in brain-imaging techniques, the functional capacities of brain-injured children still need to be evaluated.

Comment on Diagnostic Techniques for Brain-Injured Children

The goal of both the neurological examination and the neuropsychological examination is to assess brain damage accurately. However, the neurological examination focuses primarily on the intactness of lower-level functions, whereas the neuropsychological examination deals more extensively with higher-level cognitive processes, making it more sensitive to higher-level cognitive dysfunction.

A standard neurological examination—coupled with an EEG and other ancillary diagnostic studies—usually is effective in establishing the presence and locus of intracranial disease or damage. Because these procedures are not perfect diagnostic tools, they need to be supplemented with a neuropsychological examination, which can aid in establishing a diagnosis of brain dysfunction, defining the nature and the severity of specific defects in higher (cognitive) and lower (motor and perceptual) cerebral functions, and uncovering possible brain damage when the findings are equivocal or when the effects of cerebral damage are not readily appar-

ent. Thus, a complete assessment of a brain-injured child includes a neurological examination, use of brain-imaging techniques, and a neuropsychological examination, all of which contribute to our understanding of the integrity of the brain.

We are at the brink of enormous breakthroughs in this area—developmental neurobiology—and there is no longer a boundary between biology, psychology, culture and education.

—Benett L. Laventhal

INTERVIEWING BRAIN-INJURED CHILDREN

Children sustaining severe head injury may be difficult to interview, especially if their speech is impaired, they have aphasic disturbances, or they have not fully regained consciousness. If you interview a child shortly after a trauma, look for the child's ability to do the following (Garcia, Garrett, Stetz, Emanuel, & Brandt, 1990):

- maintain alertness
- attend to visual stimuli (such as establishing eye contact with you)
- scan or follow your movements
- respond to sounds (through eye gaze or turning of the head)
- follow your simple requests
- sit, walk, or write with adequate muscle tone
- make purposeful movements
- vocalize

During the interview, be alert to the child's level of consciousness, language, memory, intellectual and cognitive functioning, and sensorimotor functioning. In some cases, children may have amnesia—that is, severe memory difficulties. Two forms of amnesia are (a) *anterograde amnesia* (inability to remember events that occurred *after* the onset of the disorder) and (b) *retrograde amnesia* (inability to remember events that occurred *before* the onset of the disorder).

The semistructured interview for older school-aged children in Table F-26 Appendix F will be useful for interviewing brain-injured children. This interview will help you find out what the child sees as the problem, his or her understanding of the onset and progression of the problem, when he or she first noticed the problem, how the problem developed, what aggravates and diminishes the problem, what type of help he or she has received, and other information that will help you understand his or her background and perceptions. However, you may need to supplement these interview questions with additional ones, depending on the nature of the brain injury. First, you may want to conduct a mental status interview (see Table F-25 in Appendix F) to determine the child's general orientation to time, place, and person; ability to concentrate; alertness; and other relevant characteristics. Second, you may want to use the questions in Table F-13 in Appendix F to ask about (a) the accident (if one occurred), (b) specific problem areas often associated with brain injury, and (c) any changes in the child's behavior or relationships since the injury. The questions that focus on the accident will be useful in cases of traumatic brain injury; the other questions will be useful for children with any type of brain injury. Thus, you can use three tables in Appendix F—Tables F-26, F-25, and F-13—to interview brain-injured children. Although it may be difficult to interview brain-injured children younger than 8 or 9 years, you can ask them some general orientation questions and questions designed to elicit how they are feeling about and coping with the brain injury.

Establishing Rapport with Brain-Injured Children

Brain-injured children will differ in their reactions during the interview. Some may react to your questions without difficulty, whereas others may be fearful, reticent, or emotionally labile (the latter refers to becoming easily aroused and shifting quickly from one emotion to another). If you learn that the child may fear the interview, try to reduce her or his anxieties *before* the formal interview begins. You might try to gain the child's trust and confidence by working with her or him on simple game-like materials. Be sure to conduct the interview in a nonthreatening and casual manner.

Emphasize your use of praise, encouragement, and constructive comments with brain-injured children. Ask them easy questions at the beginning of the interview to help them feel more at ease. In fact, keep the questions as simple as needed throughout the interview.

Occasionally, brain-injured children who know the answer to a question may take a long time to respond, sit quietly for a time before responding, or make a tentative, hesitant response. When this happens, do not pressure them. Let them proceed at their own pace. However, when the delay is excessive (say, over 30 seconds), repeat the question because they may have forgotten it. If they do not answer the question, ask it again later in the interview if it is important.

Before beginning the interview, reduce all potential sources of distraction in the room. The room should be quiet, with all extraneous objects removed. Brain-injured children, when faced with difficult questions, may show perseveration (persistent repetition of the same thought or response), become emotionally labile, display inappropriate anger and hostility, withdraw from the situation, or give irrelevant responses (example, when asked where they live, brain-injured children may say "I go to school"). The behaviors often are not under the willful control of the children but instead are effects of the brain injury. Although these behaviors often interfere with the interview, they may serve as coping mechanisms to help children avoid further stress.

It is important to minimize children's frustration and reduce their fatigue during the interview. To do this, you need to be alert to their reactions. When you notice that they are becoming frustrated or fatigued, change the pace of the interview, change the content of the interview, and make supportive comments as needed.

Handling Perseverative and Avoidance Behaviors with Brain-Injured Children

You can lessen *perseverative and avoidance behaviors* by using the following procedures:

1. Introduce the interview questions slowly and casually, and give the child a toy to play with, if needed.
2. Introduce topics gradually.
3. Avoid sudden movements or noises.
4. Avoid pointing out any inadequacies in the child's responses.
5. Redirect the child to the topic at hand if perseveration occurs.
6. Do not overstimulate the child if he or she overreacts. Simply allow the child to work through his or her moment of anxiety by saying nothing or doing nothing.
7. Treat the child's emotional lability matter-of-factly. The emotional lability is probably caused by the brain injury rather than by the child's being upset.
8. Stop the interview if the emotional lability becomes too severe, and then sit quietly until you believe that the child is ready to continue. Whatever happens, remain calm and take your time.

Techniques for Working with Language-Impaired Brain-Injured Children

You may have difficulty communicating effectively with brain-injured children who have speech or language difficulties. Experiment with different communication methods, rates of communication, and types of content to find the most effective way to communicate. You should find the following guidelines helpful (DePompei, Blosser, & Zarski, 1989; Lubinski, 1981):

1. Face the brain-injured child when speaking with her or him. Eye contact promotes attention and helps the child take advantage of nonverbal cues.
2. Alert the child that communication is about to occur. For example, say the child's name and a few words of greeting before introducing a topic, question, or instruction.
3. Speak slowly and clearly to the child.
4. Talk about concrete topics, such as objects and people in the immediate environment. The child may have difficulty comprehending abstract ideas.
5. Keep related topics together.

6. Use short, grammatically correct complete sentences. A language-impaired brain-injured child may respond more accurately to individual ideas than to a lengthy string of ideas.

7. Pause between sentences to give the child time to comprehend and interpret the message.

8. Verify that the child understood your communication before proceeding. Ask a question based on the information presented to the child, or have the child show her or his understanding of the information.

9. Repeat important ideas several ways; redundancy helps comprehension.

10. Use nonverbal cues to augment spoken communication. Combining speech with nonverbal cues—such as gestures, signing, and pictures—may facilitate comprehension.

11. Ask questions that require short responses or that the child can respond to nonverbally. This will allow the child to have a sense of active participation even if she or he says only single words or gestures.

12. Encourage the child to use nonverbal cues, such as gesturing and pointing, to help her or him communicate.

13. Allow the child to use any means to communicate with you—speaking, writing, typing, using a computer, or pointing to letters.

14. Present the child with a multiple-choice array of responses (if necessary) from which she or he can choose. For example, to get the child to identify how she or he feels, show the child pictures of three faces, each illustrating a different emotion (see Figure 3-1 in Chapter 3). Ask the child to point to the facial expression that is closest to how she or he feels. You may want to point or gesture as you give the directions.

15. Ask the child to repeat a word or statement if it is unintelligible or confusing. The child may become frustrated if you do this often, so use your judgment about how often to ask her or him to repeat a response.

16. Encourage the child to express ideas in several ways if her or his communications are not clear. You can say, for example, "Tell me about that in another way so I can understand it better" or "Give me an example of…." This may help the child express ideas and may help you understand her or him better. Occasionally, a child may be able to sing an answer when she or he cannot express it in any other way.

17. Recognize that the child may become frustrated by her or his communication failures. Be prepared to discuss these difficulties openly. If the child is having communication difficulties, recognize these difficulties and go on to an easier topic, if possible, or to a nonverbal activity.

18. Repeat what the child has said at various intervals to help focus the conversation.

19. Recognize that the child may know what she or he wants to say but be unable to say it because of difficulty in recall or in initiating a task or for some other reason.

20. Recognize that the child may have difficulty in generalizing from one situation to another.

21. Recognize that inappropriate language, self-centeredness, and poor personal hygiene, for example, may be related to the brain injury and be beyond the control of the child.

22. Know what nonverbal cues you are giving the child, because the cues may tell the child how you feel about the effectiveness of her or his communications. Do not show signs of impatience or annoyance. Instead, show that you are interested in and accepting of the child, even though the interview may be difficult.

23. Understand that an in-depth interview is a lengthy and sometimes tiresome process, and that several short interviews may be better than one long interview with a brain-injured child.

OBSERVING BRAIN-INJURED CHILDREN

Observing brain-injured children is an important component of the interview. Ideally, you should observe children in several settings. Observations will give you information about brain-injured children's developmental levels and capabilities, including their language skills, motor skills, social skills, compensatory skills and strategies, temperament, personality, motivation, and interpersonal skills. You can compare your observations with information you obtain from other sources and from more formal assessment evaluations conducted by a neurologist and neuropsychologist. This will give you ample opportunity to cross-validate your observations. You may want to review the observational guidelines in Chapter 2 because they also pertain to brain-injured children.

The following areas are particularly important to observe:

- appearance (for example, dress, hygiene)
- vocabulary and language (for example, variety and complexity of words used, enunciation, grammar and syntax, length of responses)
- ability to carry on a conversation (for example, fluency, length and frequency of pauses, ability to maintain train of thought)
- behavior (for example, social appropriateness of behavior, modulation of behavior)
- attention span (for example, attentive, distractible, variable)
- affect (for example, depressed, blunted, bland [that is, without a normal range of emotional expression], elated, normal)
- tempo of body movements (for example, slow, impulsive, hesitant)
- visual-spatial skills (for example, misreaching, walking into things, getting lost)
- sensory skills (for example, hearing, visual ability, tactile sensation, presence of visual field defect)
- motor skills (for example, style of walking, balance, presence of tremor, presence of tics, degree of muscle tone, degree of muscle activity, degree of restlessness)
- level of consciousness (for example, degree of alertness—in a *coma* [unconscious and not arousable], in a

semicoma or *stupor* [unconscious but able to respond to persistent stimulation], *lethargic* [responding briefly to stimulation but falling back to sleep readily], or *alert* [responding appropriately to environmental stimulation])

Also note whether the child was alone or with parents or caregivers, remembered the appointment, was on time, and could find the office by himself or herself (if applicable). If the child came alone, how did he or she come to your office (such as by public transportation, walking, or driving an automobile [for older adolescents])?

Observing Language and Listening Behaviors

Pay careful attention to the child's language, and consider what is normal for his or her age. For children who have mastered speech, look for possible language processing difficulties such as the following:

- mispronunciations
- difficulty finding the right word
- tangential communications
- omission of syntactical words
- incorrect use of verbs, clauses, or prepositional phrases
- substitutions of incorrect words for correct words
- inappropriate repetition of words
- restricted amount of speech
- unconventional ordering of words
- failure to speak in complete sentences
- monotonic speech

Some of these language difficulties may reflect aphasic disturbances, as described earlier in this chapter.

Observe the quality of the child's listening behaviors in the interview and when he or she speaks with others (Hartley, 1990).

1. Is the child easily distracted by irrelevant noises or movements in the environment?
2. Are the child's facial expressions consistent with the speaker's messages?
3. Does the child maintain reasonable eye contact with the speaker?
4. Does the child refrain from doing things that might distract the speaker?
5. Does the child indicate his or her level of understanding through verbal or nonverbal gestures?
6. Does the child refrain from interrupting the speaker?
7. Does the child wait until the directions have been given before he or she begins a task?
8. Does the child ask for clarification or repetition when he or she is unsure of the instructions or messages?
9. Does the child follow directions without need for excessive repetition or explanation?
10. Do the child's comments indicate understanding of the speaker's intent?
11. Does the child initiate questions or comments about the main topic of discussion?
12. Do the child's comments indicate a good grasp of the main ideas of the discussion?
13. Does the child attend to and understand the speaker's nonverbal communications, such as body positions, facial expressions, and gestures?
14. Does the child remember previous communications after his or her attention has been directed to something else?

Observing Motor Movements

Here are some more detailed questions for observing the quality of children's motor movements.

1. How does the child walk—with ease or with difficulty? When the child walks, note whether her or his feet tend to drop and point toward the ground or remain relatively parallel to the ground, as is normal. Also note whether the child's gait is smooth, hesitant, uncoordinated, or spastic; whether the child walks in a straight line or at an angle; whether the child bumps into furniture; and whether the child demonstrates asymmetrical arm movements.
2. How does the child perform simple motor tasks? Observe how the child jumps, kicks or throws a ball, uses scissors, turns pages, holds a pencil, uses pegs, and so forth. Evaluate the child's performance according to what is expected for her or his age.
3. Does the child exhibit either *at-rest tremors* (tremors that appear when the child is still), *intention tremors* (tremors that appear when the child is to perform an action), or both?
4. Are *tics* present, either constantly or only when the child is asked to perform some action?
5. If tics are present, are they *choreiform movements* (jerky, involuntary movements or spasms of short duration) or *athetoid movements* (slow, recurring, writhing movements of arms and legs)?
6. What is the quality of the child's muscle tone—high muscle tone (*hypertonia*), low muscle tone (*hypotonia*), no muscle tone (*atonia*), or disordered muscle tone and posture (*dystonia*)?
7. What is the level of the child's muscle activity—lowered level of muscle activity (*akinesia*) or motor restlessness shown by pacing or continual movements (*akathesia*)?
8. Does the child have *body asymmetries* (for example, facial asymmetry caused by drooping of one side of the face or weakness in one arm only)?

Observing Brain-Injured Children in Their Natural Environment

Observing how brain-injured children function in their natural environment will add important information to the assessment. Because an interview setting is structured to reduce stress, it avoids demands faced by children in their natural environments. The typical clinical assessment or forensic interview probably is not ecologically valid because it is structured to help brain-injured children compensate for or mask functional impairments. For example, the interview setting deals with (a) attention and concentration difficulties by providing a quiet and structured environment; (b) problems with endurance, perseverance, and fatigue by providing frequent breaks and rest periods; (c) difficulties in task orientation, flexible reorientation to new tasks, problem-solving skills, and memory by providing clear and repetitive instructions; and (d) difficulties in motivation, initiation, and response inhibition by providing active cues, prompts, and encouragement (Sbordone, 1988).

When you observe brain-injured children in natural settings, note how they perform daily activities, use language, use motor skills, cope with different environments, accomplish new learning, and use strategies in different settings. By seeing how they function in different environments—including home, school, playground, and interview settings—you will get a more complete picture of their adaptive and coping abilities, including how they process information, how they behave, and how they handle distractions, information overload, competition, failure, negative feedback for making errors or for misbehaving, and other stressors (Marquardt, Stoll, & Sussman, 1988). These observations also may give you clues about their level of orientation, anxiety, confusion, distractibility, impulsivity, initiative, inhibition, concreteness, flexibility, organization, judgment, and similar behaviors. In addition, a detailed history obtained from parents, teachers, and others may provide ecologically valid information, as described in the next part of the chapter.

INTERVIEWING PARENTS OF BRAIN-INJURED CHILDREN

When parents learn that their child has a brain injury, they may have a variety of reactions, including denial, depression, irritability, anxiety, frustration, feelings of inadequacy, annoyance, anger, feelings of being trapped, and guilt over their having failed to prevent the injury (also see Chapter 5). They may attempt to cope with these reactions by using prayer, becoming more involved in their work or their career, talking with friends, attending support groups, seeking therapy, denying problems, going on vacations, taking tranquilizers or other drugs, or drinking alcohol. Thus, be prepared to deal with depression and guilt in parents of traumatically brain-injured children. These reactions, of course, may apply to parents of children with any form of disability.

Interview one or both parents to obtain a detailed clinical and developmental history of the child (see Chapter 4). Table F-21 in Appendix F provides a semistructured interview useful for obtaining an in-depth developmental history from a mother. In addition, it will be useful to have a parent complete the Questionnaire on Resources and Stress (see Table 4-2 in Chapter 4) and the Background Questionnaire (see Table C-2 in Appendix C). If needed, you also can use Table F-36 in Appendix F to obtain information about problem areas.

With minor modifications, you can use the questions in Table F-26 in Appendix F to interview a parent about her or his brain-injured child's functioning. You especially want to give parents an opportunity to describe their concerns about the child since the injury, including their concerns about the child's physical status, personality, temperament, behavior, and learning ability. If you ask the child the questions in Table F-26 and then ask the parent the same questions about the child, you can compare the responses.

When you interview the child's parents, recognize that they may not always be objective. They may describe the child's premorbid behavior and ability in an overly favorable light. And they may selectively disclose historical information or fail to disclose the child's problems. This may happen for several reasons. For example, they may have forgotten important details, they may have vague recollec-

Frank and Earnest by Bob Thaves

tions, or they may be involved in litigation associated with the child's brain injury.

EVALUATING THE ASSESSMENT FINDINGS FOR BRAIN-INJURED CHILDREN

To evaluate the assessment findings, you ideally will want to review the information obtained from (a) the clinical assessment interview with the child, (b) the mental status evaluation of the child, (c) the interviews with the child's parents, relatives, friends, and teachers about how the child is currently functioning, how the child functioned *before* the injury, and how the family and school are coping with the child's disability, and (d) the formal evaluations conducted by neuropsychologists, neurologists, speech/language pathologists, and other professionals involved in the case.

In reviewing the information obtained by the multidisciplinary health care team in cases of traumatic brain injury, note the following:

- the results of the neurological and neuropsychological evaluations
- how the child was functioning before the injury
- the results of the family study
- any physical, sensory, affective, cognitive, and social/personality problems that the child may have (see Table 19-3 for a listing of symptoms associated with brain injury)
- whether the child has an appreciation of the nature and extent of his or her limitations
- whether the family is able to participate in the rehabilitation efforts

Information about the child's prior functioning is critical in evaluating the results. For example, if a 6-year-old could not read *before* the accident, it's not surprising that he or she cannot read *after* the accident. *You don't want to report a*

Table 19-3
Symptoms Associated with Brain Injury (Obtained from the Interview and from the Child's History)

Physical	Sensory	Affective	Cognitive	Social/Personality
Headaches	Visual disturbances	Depression	Alterations in	Impaired social skills,
Vomiting	Hallucinations and	Blunted affect	consciousness	including mis-
Seizures	other unusual	Anxiety	Confusion	perception of the
Drowsiness	episodic sensory	Apathy	Decreased intellectual	intentions of others,
Psychomotor slowing	experiences (for	Elation	efficiency	unusual remarks,
Hyperactivity	example, smelling	Emotional lability,	Disorientation (for	or inappropriate
Muscle weakness	odd odors or seeing	including mood	example, getting	actions
Stiffness	vision of lights)	shifts, impulsivity,	lost easily)	Subtle changes in
Paralysis	Auditory	excitement,	Impaired judgment	personality (as
Dizziness	disturbances,	agitation,	Poor planning	when a previously
Vertigo	including tinnitus	tearfulness, and	Concentration and	fastidious child
Bowel, bladder, or	(ringing in ears) and	loss of control	attention difficulties	becomes unkempt
genital dysfunction	sensitivity to noise	Reduced frustration	Memory difficulties	and careless)
Abnormal movements,	Pain	threshold	Distractibility	Regression to a more
such as tremors,	Paresthesias	Emotional withdrawal	Failure to learn from	immature level of
jerking, tics,	(abnormal	Guilt feelings	experience	functioning
grimaces, bizarre	sensations)	Mood inappropriate to	Expressive language	Hypochondriacal
gestures	Speech articulation	situation	difficulties	preoccupations
Poor balance and	problems	Anger	Comprehension	Antisocial behavior
coordination	Problems in taste	Hostility	difficulties	(lying, stealing,
Poor fine motor	Problems in smell	Indifference	Rigid and inflexible	truancy, sexual
coordination		Diminished empathy	thinking	offenses)
Blurred vision			Deterioration of	Uncooperativeness
Double vision			academic	Suspiciousness
Fatigue			performance	Impolite speech or
Sleep problems			Inaccurate insight and	coarse language
Appetite problems			self-appraisal	Withdrawal and
			Concreteness	decreased initiative
				Diminished sensitivity

Note. Symptoms of brain damage will vary as a function of lesion type, location, and rate of growth. Additionally, not all symptoms will be present in any individual case.

loss of functioning when the competency was never established in the first place.

When you evaluate the information from the child's case history, use, in part, a normative-developmental framework (see Chapters 1 and 3). For example, recognize that children usually will crawl before they walk, babble before they say meaningful words, draw lines before they draw circles, and read individual alphabet letters before they read whole words. A normative-developmental framework also considers the fact that most children begin to say individual words by 18 months, draw circles by 3 years, and learn to read by 6 to 8 years(see the table on the inside front cover and Tables C-4 through C-10 in Appendix C).

Answers to the questions in Table 19-4 will help you in reviewing the information obtained by the multidisciplinary health care team and working with the multidisciplinary health care team to plan a rehabilitation program. When the multidisciplinary health care team designs a rehabilitation program, the following aspects of the child's functioning will likely be considered (Kay & Silver, 1989):

- *complex attention and speed of information processing* (ability to focus, sustain, shift, and divide attention)
- *learning and memory* (ability to learn and retain new information and recall old information)
- *abstraction and integration of information* (ability to think abstractly, integrate new information, and generalize and apply it flexibly across changing situations)
- *executive functioning* (ability to plan, organize, monitor, modulate, and adjust behavior and awareness of behavior, including awareness of deficit and safety)
- *behavior modulation* (ability to behave in a planned, good-natured, and calm manner)

Although you may not be able to answer all the questions in Table 19-4, they provide a foundation for evaluating the child. If the child has not been seen for a neurological workup and you find symptoms that suggest organic dysfunction, refer the child for a pediatric neurological examination.

Reliability of Information

Corroborate any information obtained from the child—such as the nature of the trauma, length of unconsciousness, perceived changes in functioning, and seizure history—with information obtained from the parents and from the medical records. Compare what the child tells you about herself or himself with what the parents tell you about the child. The extent of agreement between their reports is a useful measure of the validity of the child's report. Brain-injured children sometimes cannot recognize that they are having problems, and they tend to underestimate the severity of their problems and even deny their illness. Because brain-injured children may be unreliable reporters as a result of memory and attention problems, the interview with the par-

ents takes on added importance. Information obtained from the parents also may help you sort out what symptoms were present before the injury and what symptoms occurred after the injury. In rare cases, you may have to question the reliability of the information obtained from the parents, especially, as noted previously, in connection with litigation.

Prognosis

Overall, the *severity* of children's head injuries is the best predictor of long-term outcome (Klonoff, Clark, & Klonoff, 1993). *The poorest prognosis is associated with a long period of unconsciousness, skull fracture, poor neurological status, and the presence of posttraumatic seizures.* For example, severe brain injury, such as hemiplegia (paralysis of one side of the body) and visual field defects (difficulty in seeing parts of the visual field), may show little or no improvement after several years, whereas milder impairments of sensorimotor functions may show excellent improvement. Mental processes, which are more complex than sensory or motor processes and are not as circumscribed or anatomically restricted, may recover more gradually.

Recoverability of intellectual functions is less likely with severe trauma, early damage, frontotemporal area damage, and posttraumatic epilepsy. Rate of recovery is most rapid in the months immediately following injury. Severe cases of brain injury in childhood may limit future learning and subsequent development of higher-level cognitive and behavioral skills. Measured intelligence, for example, could drop over time because of failure to develop and learn rather than because of progressive brain dysfunction.

The factors that affect prognosis, as noted previously, are complex. Some children with significant damage recover many functions, whereas others with minor injuries still show considerable deficits. Whatever else may be involved, recoverability of impaired functions should not be expected automatically in every case. Make prognostic statements tentatively and with caution, subject to revision based on the results of periodic reassessments (Tramontana & Hooper, 1988).

The following case illustrates issues related to prognosis (Yeates, 1994).

CASE 19-8. SCOTT

Scott is a 15-year-old White male who was admitted to Children's Hospital after being struck by an automobile while riding his bicycle. He suffered multiple trauma, including a spinal cord injury, depressed skull fracture in the right frontoparietal region, and closed-head injury. A CT scan showed a small intracerebral hemorrhage in the left frontal region, additional frontal contusions, and cerebral edema. His injury was relatively severe.

Scott's mother reported that he lived with his parents and a younger sister in a local suburb. His father graduated from high school and was employed full time; his mother attended business college and was a homemaker. The family history

Table 19-4
Questions to Consider After the Evaluation of a Brain-Injured Child Is Completed (Based on Interviews with the Child, Parents, and Teacher and Neurological and Neuropsychological Examinations)

Nature of Injury and Problems

1. What were the neurological/medical findings? These findings include the type of brain injury the child sustained, the immediate effects of the injury (including loss of consciousness), treatment (including possible hospitalization), and prognosis.
2. What are the child's presenting problems, including their frequency, intensity, and duration?

Description of the Child

3. What are the child's sex, age, and appearance (including the child's height, weight, posture, facial expression, eye contact, grooming, and personal cleanliness of skin, hair, nails, and teeth)?
4. What is the child's overall adjustment after the injury?
5. What was the child's overall adjustment before the injury?
6. What are the child's temperament and personality like after the injury?
7. What were the child's temperament and personality like before the injury?
8. How does the child's current level of functioning compare to his or her previous level?

Perceptual-Motor Activity

9. What is the quality of the child's fine and gross motor coordination? For example, note whether the child (a) performs the fine and gross motor movements expected for his or her age, (b) has adequate control, balance, strength, and endurance to perform the needed daily living tasks, and (c) has the coordination, depending on his or her age, needed to be responsible for his or her own dressing, feeding, toileting, grooming, and other personal activities.
10. What is the quality of the child's perceptual processes? For example, does the child focus appropriately on selected objects, visually track objects or people appropriately, identify and discriminate among objects and features of objects, or show any abnormal perceptual processes?
11. Does the child display any abnormal motor movements, such as tics, grimaces, bizarre gestures, or other involuntary movements?

Speech and Language

12. What is the quality of the child's speech? This includes speed and quantity, voice quality, prosody, articulation, and any speech disturbances.
13. What is the quality of the child's receptive language? This includes comprehension of questions and directions and any signs of aphasia.
14. What is the quality of the child's expressive language? This includes (a) the quality and amount of automatic

language, spontaneous language, and responsive language, (b) the use of language to express ideas and feelings, and (c) any signs of aphasia.

Complex Attention and Speed of Processing

15. What is the quality of the child's ability to attend to and process information? This includes whether the child can maintain attention long enough to accomplish age-appropriate tasks by focusing on the relevant aspects of a situation and screening out irrelevant visual or auditory background details. It also includes whether the child can process auditory or visual information adequately: (a) Can the child take in information from conversation or reading without losing track of the information? (b) Does the child need to work more slowly or to hear or see one thing at a time in order to stay on track? (c) Can the child sustain attention or concentration when mental processing is required, such as when reading or doing mental arithmetic? (d) Can the child shift back and forth between two or more tasks without becoming overwhelmed or confused? (e) Does the child return to the task at hand spontaneously without losing track when he or she is distracted or interrupted?

Cognition

16. What are the child's level of cognitive functioning; orientation; judgment; level of abstraction; ability to generate ideas, goals, and alternative strategies; and fund of general knowledge? To answer this question, consider whether the child (a) knows who he or she is and where he or she is, (b) recognizes and responds to personal needs, such as hunger and thirst, (c) thinks clearly and identifies and labels thoughts and feelings accurately, (d) shows awareness of his or her deficit, (e) sets goals, formulates a realistic plan of action given his or her limits and capacities, and carries out the practical steps in completing the plan, (f) distinguishes relevant from irrelevant facts, (g) follows the appropriate sequence in completing tasks of daily living, such as dressing, eating, brushing teeth, going to the bathroom, and getting ready for sleep, (h) acts effectively when confronted with problems or circumstances that he or she is not familiar with, (i) asks for clarification of instructions when needed, (j) functions in unstructured situations by assessing what is needed, bringing order and organization, and initiating an appropriate plan of action, (k) demonstrates a capacity to engage himself or herself in productive activities on a regular basis (especially at home) when these are not planned or initiated for him or her by others, (l) stands back from himself or herself and accurately assesses the situation at hand, (m) places himself or herself in the position of others and sees their point of view, (n) identifies the roles of others in his or her environment, (o) applies

(Continued)

Table 19-4 (*Continued*)

what he or she knows about one situation to another (that is, generalizes learning), and (p) gives information that agrees with the information given by his or her parents or caregivers.

Memory and Learning

17. What is the quality of the child's memory? To answer this question, note whether the child (a) recalls events that happened in the recent past (for example, your name, what he or she did yesterday), (b) finds it difficult to remember names of either new or familiar people, (c) fails to keep appointments or do things because he or she forgets, (d) loses his or her way going to familiar places, (e) tends to forget things to which he or she does not pay conscious attention, (f) loses track if he or she has too many things to remember, and (g) remembers how to do activities of daily living.

18. Is the child aware of memory problems, and does he or she compensate by consciously increasing attention or writing things down?

19. What is the quality of the child's learning ability? To answer this question, consider whether the child (a) finds it difficult to learn new procedures or information, (b) benefits from specific training by spontaneously remembering to carry out new procedures, (c) and benefits from cuing such that forgotten routines can be invoked and executed when cued.

Affect and Modulation of Affect

20. What are the child's affect, range of affect, and appropriateness of affect? To answer this question, look at whether the child (a) acts impulsively, (b) becomes angry easily, (c) is irritable most of the time, (d) brings his or her emotions under control if they get out of hand, (e) inhibits inappropriate behaviors or comments, or (f) shows rapid fluctuation in mood without environmental cause, frequent tearfulness, or situationally inappropriate affect (such as laughing at serious subjects or lacking emotional reactions to events that others react to).

21. What factors precipitate, alleviate, or aggravate the child's affect or cause changes in the child's affect?

Social Comprehension and Interpersonal Relations

22. What is the child's understanding of socially acceptable, practical, and appropriate responses to social situations?

23. What is the child's understanding of the reasons and motivations for social behavior?

24. What is the child's ability to understand facial expressions and other nonverbal communications?

25. What is the child's ability to profit from experience?

26. Is the child aware of the effect of his or her behavior on others?

27. What is the quality of the child's interpersonal behavior, including relationships with his or her family, peers, teachers, relatives, and professionals? To answer this ques-

tion, consider whether the child engages in (a) *prosocial behavior* (cooperative, mature, age-appropriate, harmonious, pleasant behavior), (b) *asocial behavior* (passive, withdrawn, defensive, immature, age-inappropriate behavior), (c) *antisocial behavior* (aggressive, disruptive, hostile, dishonest behavior), or (d) *anomalous behavior* (loud vocalizations, grunts, tics, facial twitches, repetitive or compulsive behaviors, picking at or playing with body).

28. Is the child able to perceive the intent and feelings of others?

29. Can the child interpret the actions or intentions of others?

30. Can the child respond to subtle interpersonal cues, such as facial expression, tone of voice, volume, and inferred meaning?

31. Can the child work in groups and conform to changing roles in group situations?

Adjustment to Disability

32. Does the child acknowledge and accept his or her current level of functioning? Consider the child's reaction to the injury, such as reactive depression (including preoccupation with loss, pessimism about the future, or anger about what happened) or acceptance.

33. Is the child taking excessive legal drugs or alcohol or illegal drugs to cope with his or her feelings about the injury?

34. How does the child manage his or her time?

35. To what extent does the child need supervision?

36. What are the child's work habits, rate of learning, learning style, and ability to adapt to new situations?

Developmental History

37. Were there any significant events in the child's prenatal, perinatal, or postnatal development prior to the brain injury? If so, what were these events?

38. Did the child reach developmental milestones at the expected ages?

39. Where there any significant medical problems or indications of psychological problems during the child's development prior to the injury? If so, what were they?

40. Was the child receiving any significant treatments for medical or psychological problems prior to the injury? If so, what were the conditions and the treatments?

Educational History

41. How did the child perform in school before the injury? Consider the child's performance in reading, writing, arithmetic, and spelling and the child's ability to attend, complete assignments, work independently, participate in class discussions, follow class routines, ask for help, use help from adults and peers, and perform other educational tasks. Also consider the child's school attendance, tardiness, and truancy (if any).

42. Did the child have any behavioral difficulties in school before the injury? If so, what were the difficulties?

(Continued)

Table 19-4 (*Continued*)

43. Did the child receive any special services in school before the injury? If so, what were the services and why were they given?

Family History
44. What is the composition of the child's family?
45. What is the quality of the relationships among the family members?
46. What was the child's role in the family prior to the injury?
47. Is there a history of child maltreatment, substance abuse, spouse abuse, medical disorders, psychiatric disorders, or learning disorders among the family members? If so, what were the problems or disorders and which family members had them?

Family's Reaction to Disability
48. How does the family describe the child's functioning?
49. What changes have family members noted in the child's functioning?
50. How have family members reacted to the child's injury? This includes their acceptance of the injury and their reactions to the child, such as acceptance, frustration, or embarrassment because of the child's behavior.

51. What family supports are available?
52. How able is the family to provide for the child's needs?

Treatment and Rehabilitation Program
53. Is the child receiving treatment for his or her problems? If so, what is the treatment and how is the child responding to the treatment?
54. What type of rehabilitation program does the child need?
55. What rehabilitation facilities are available in the community?
56. Is the child willing to cooperate with rehabilitation efforts?
57. What deficits are most likely to interfere with the child's rehabilitation?
58. What deficits are most likely to be the focus of the child's rehabilitation?
59. What strengths does the child have that can assist in the rehabilitation program?
60. What are the child's reward preferences?
61. How willing is the child's family to support rehabilitation efforts?

Source: Adapted in part from Corey (1987), Kay and Silver (1989), Novick and Arnold (1988), and Ylvisaker, Chorazy, Cohen, Mastrilli, Molitor, Nelson, Szekeres, Valko, and Jaffe (1990).

appears to be normal, as was Scott's birth history. He reached developmental milestones at expected times. He sustained a concussion in a fall when he was 9 years, but the concussion appeared to have few, if any, consequences. In school, Scott was an average student.

The initial assessment showed that Scott had reasonably good orientation to person and place, but not to time, and his memory functioning was generally intact. He also was somewhat combative with the staff.

A neuropsychological examination prior to discharge showed that Scott's overall cognitive functioning was in the Average range. However, he had mild deficits in expressive language, problem solving, sequencing, and abstraction of information. It was recommended that Scott return to a regular classroom and receive individual tutoring in study skills and other organizational strategies.

The recommendations were implemented when Scott was discharged from the hospital. He completed tenth grade at his high school with satisfactory performance. He returned for a follow-up evaluation about one year post-injury. His general intellectual functioning was in the High-Average range. Although no specific deficits were apparent in either verbal or nonverbal skills, executive functions, or motor control, he showed mild inattention and impulsivity. Academic achievement was above average in reading and spelling, but below average in arithmetic. He did not have any behavioral or emotional difficulties.

Despite his relatively severe injury, Scott's recovery was rapid, and he appeared to return almost to his premorbid lev-

els of functioning. His recovery appeared to have been facilitated by his good level of premorbid functioning, and by a supportive family, school, and community. (pp. 272–273, with changes in notation)

Assessment and treatment of the neuropsychiatric sequelae [of head injuries] is a complex and challenging process. The mixture of diffuse and focal injuries, the combination of cognitive, language, somatic, and behavioral difficulties do not fit easily into current diagnostic categories.

—Thomas W. McAllister

REHABILITATION PROGRAMS FOR BRAIN-INJURED CHILDREN

Rehabilitation programs are designed to help brain-injured children become more independent by increasing their functional and adaptive skills. The focus is on helping brain-injured children regain former cognitive skills, learn new skills to compensate for lost or impaired abilities, develop more organized behavior, reduce the level of confusion, improve interpersonal skills, and improve their ability to cope with stress. Rehabilitation aims to improve brain-injured children's general adjustment and to help them achieve success in school, in social relationships, and in work.

Rehabilitation Goals

A comprehensive rehabilitation program for brain-injured children may have the following goals:

1. Restoring impaired areas of functioning through application of educational and other intervention procedures, including speech therapy, occupational therapy, and physical therapy
2. Promoting the development of compensatory approaches to help them alleviate difficulties by using remaining intact functions
3. Treating their behavioral problems
4. Altering the physical environment to help them become more mobile and independent in cases of physical disability
5. Creating an environment that is highly organized, contains few distracting stimuli, and provides methods to improve their ability to function, such as the use of timers and lists as reminders.
6. Helping them gradually make the transition back to their natural environments, where things are less structured and more demanding, if they are being discharged from a hospital or rehabilitation center
7. Counseling the family members to help them understand, accept, and learn to cope better with their child's disabilities (by providing them with information about brain-behavior relationships and the child's assets and limitations and by helping parents cope with the increased demands of raising a child with disabilities)

Rehabilitation goals should be appropriate to each brain-injured child's physical and neuropsychological status, including specific dysfunctions, and be geared to his or her readiness and motivation to reach the goals. The goals may change, however, depending on the progress made by the child. For example, in early speech-language therapy the focus may be on structured sensorimotor stimulation and improvement of oral motor skills, whereas toward the end of therapy the focus may be on more practical areas, such as the integration of functional language skills (for example, using the telephone and developing strategies to cope with residual memory impairments) (Milton, 1988).

Some rehabilitation goals may be difficult to achieve because children with acquired brain injury may have limited understanding of their condition (Jacobs, 1993). They may be poorly informed about basic brain functioning, how they sustained their injuries, how their problems developed, and how their injury affects their cognitive processes and social interactions. They may show confusion about the passage of time and believe that their difficulties are primarily physical. To make sense of their injury, they may hold contradictory ideas about their normality—for example, admitting that their injury causes them difficulties but minimizing its effects on their ability to function normally. Holding contradictory ideas may be a way for them to avoid stigmatization and to believe they are like their peers. Part of the

rehabilitation effort should be to improve their understanding of their deficits.

Effects of Alcohol on Rehabilitation Efforts

Consumption of alcohol can complicate both physical recovery from a head injury and the child's response to the head injury (Miller, 1989). Adolescents admitted to hospitals with a positive blood alcohol level have a lower level of consciousness, remain in a coma longer, and have longer hospital stays than those who have not consumed alcohol. In addition, excessive blood alcohol can lead to fluid and electrolyte abnormalities that exacerbate cerebral edema. Excessive alcohol also has other effects, such as altering blood-clotting mechanisms and increasing the risk of brain hypoxia, respiratory depression, and infection.

Chronic abuse of alcohol can produce cognitive deficits that interact with those produced by the traumatic brain injury. The resulting deficits may be compounded and interfere with the recovery process. Adolescents who have a history of alcohol abuse may be less able to compensate for the effects of a head injury and have fewer intact abilities to use in their rehabilitation than those without such a history. Perhaps even more important is their potential for resuming alcohol and other recreational drug use and abuse, which may be greater because of the stresses posed by the brain injury and may interfere greatly with rehabilitation and recovery.

Dimensions to Consider in a Rehabilitation Program

Rehabilitation efforts must simultaneously consider several dimensions, including premorbid level of functioning, current level of functioning, length of time since injury, differential rate of improvement, need for re-examination, and familial issues. Some of these dimensions are similar to those considered in evaluating assessment findings. Recognize that children's post-injury behavior is related to the type of brain injury sustained, their pre-injury development, their post-injury environment, and the treatment and rehabilitation program (see Figure 19-2). Successful rehabilitation is a matter not only of remediating physical disabilities but also of remediating behavioral maladjustments. Let's now look at these dimensions in more detail.

1. *Premorbid level of functioning.* To set realistic goals for the rehabilitation program, consider children's premorbid level of cognitive, perceptual-motor, affective, temperament, personality, interpersonal, and adaptive functioning. For example, children who were functioning at a mildly mentally retarded level before the brain injury have a different prognosis from those who were functioning at an average or superior level. When no prior intelligence test scores

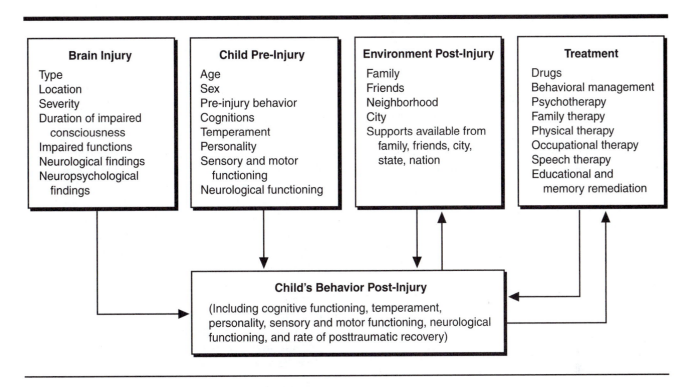

Figure 19-2. Factors that may affect a child's behavior post-injury.

are available, base premorbid intelligence estimates on the children's school grades and academic test scores, parental estimates of the children's intelligence, teachers' estimates of the children's intelligence, and the children's scores on individual or group-administered achievement tests.

2. *Current level of functioning.* Consider children's current (or post-injury) level of cognitive, perceptual-motor, affective, temperament, personality, interpersonal, and adaptive functioning. For example, what are their intact skills and what areas show deficits? What are their cognitive strengths, especially the level of competence that they still retain? How do they compensate for existing deficits? How is their motivation, determination, sense of self, and level of self-awareness? What tasks can they perform? How long can they perform them? How much time do they need to recover from the effort? With what degree of accuracy can they perform the tasks?

3. *Length of time since injury.* Consider the length of time between the injury and the start of the rehabilitation effort. Neuropsychological deficits usually are most prominent the first 6 months after a head injury. Although most of the recovery occurs within the first 12 to 18 months after the brain injury, subtle changes may still occur several years after the apparent recovery. However, temperament and personality changes may persist even after recovery of neurological functions.

4. *Differential rate of improvement.* Consider that different neuropsychological functions improve at different rates, so it may not be appropriate to generalize from one area to another.

5. *Need for re-examination.* Consider recommending relatively frequent neuropsychological re-examinations to map progress and changes. However, interpretation of changes may be complicated by practice effects, especially when alternative forms of neuropsychological tests are not available. If children improve on repeated testing, it will be difficult to know whether the improvement was because they had practiced the items before or because they actually improved their skills.

6. *Familial issues.* Consider the family's ability to carry out the rehabilitation efforts (including having adequate transportation, insurance, and finances), their support of the children, and what environmental supports they and their brain-injured children have and need.

Cognitive-Behavioral Rehabilitation

A cognitive-behavioral orientation, which is useful for remediating brain-injured children's neuropsychologically mediated problems, focuses on ways to help brain-injured children carry out activities of daily living. Its aims are as follows (Prigatano et al., 1986):

- to reduce cognitive confusion by improving brain-injured children's attention, concentration, learning, and memory skills and by gradually helping them process information more efficiently
- to increase their awareness of their residual strengths and deficits and to teach them how to use intact brain functions to solve problems

- to help them develop compensatory behaviors, by first helping them recognize that they have suffered impairments due to a brain injury and then helping them accept their limitations

- to improve their cognitive deficits in interpersonal situations by reducing social withdrawal, interpersonal isolation, paranoid ideation, hyperactivity, and emotionality

From a developmental perspective, the following strategies are useful in improving brain-injured children's information-processing abilities (Ylvisaker, 1986):

1. Preschoolers should be given structured play and manipulative activities. Concrete verbal strategies should be used to help them compensate for word retrieval difficulties.

2. Elementary school–aged children should be helped to improve their attention span, concentration, and selective listening.

3. Adolescents should be helped to improve their metacognitive activities, such as by helping them understand and appraise the effects of their deficits, involving them actively in the design of their treatment plan, and focusing their efforts on realistic goals. It will be problematic working with adolescents when they have difficulty assuming an abstract attitude (for example, difficulty considering situational factors not immediately present) or when they have faulty executive functions (for example, inability to initiate, plan, carry out, and monitor their own activities).

The following example shows how cognitive-behavioral deficits can interfere with activities of daily living (Kay & Silver, 1989).

The head injury patient is likely to have the physical ability to perform any given aspect of ADL's [activities of daily living]. He or she is able to pick up a toothbrush, squeeze the toothpaste tube, execute the requisite motor movements, rinse, and put things away, yet the spontaneous integrated sequencing of these activities into a smooth continuity from beginning to end [may not be possible]. The toothbrush cannot be located. Enormous amounts of toothpaste are squeezed out; the behavior is not terminated at the appropriate point. Brushing is done in a cursory, repetitive, incomplete fashion. Rinsing is forgotten. The brush and toothpaste are left on the sink. And even if brushing one's teeth can be carried out in a reasonable fashion, it does not occur to the head-injured person to do so each morning unless prompted. When questioned, he or she dutifully reports having brushed, with no recollection (or concern) whatsoever if the activity was actually performed that day or not. (p. 146)

Useful rehabilitation strategies. Some prominent symptoms that brain-injured children may show in the early stages of recovery include lethargy; slow mental speed; difficulties in attention, concentration, learning, and memory; confusion; disorientation; agitation; irritability; and fatigue or limited endurance. The following 10 strategies—focusing on involvement, structure, adequate presentation, consis-tency, repetition, specificity, practicality, reward, meaningfulness, and communication—will be useful in helping children improve their functioning (Howard, 1988; Ylvisaker, 1986):

1. *Involvement.* Involve brain-injured children directly in the program to increase their motivation, interest, and self-control. For example, let them decide, when feasible, which activities to work on, how much time they want to spend on an activity, whether they want to share the products of their work with others, where they would like to do the activity, and so forth.

2. *Structure.* Carefully structure their environment, especially in the early stages of recovery, to reduce confusion. Insufficient structure is probably the most common reason for failure of behavior management plans. Brain-injured children cannot deal with nebulous situations; it is better to overstructure than to understructure the program in the early stages of recovery. Avoid overstimulation or overloading the children with information, and keep the immediate environment understandable to them.

3. *Adequate presentation.* In presenting information, observe the following guidelines:

- Take base-line measures of the children's performance in the areas of interest.

- Present information in a controlled and manageable fashion.

- Determine the optimum level of reception of information for each child.

- Provide clear, concrete instructions.

- Keep the children's choices to a minimum on learning tasks.

- Use orientation and memory cues liberally.

- Break complex behaviors down into small, well-defined steps to reduce confusion and to help children compensate for learning and memory deficits.

- Simplify communicative interactions.

- Increase communicative processing activities gradually and systematically.

- Guide the children to listen for specific information in sentences or paragraphs, and gradually increase the amount of information to be processed.

- Focus on activities that the children have a chance to complete successfully, that are neither too easy nor too boring, and that the children like.

- Keep the assignments to a reasonable level based on the children's ability.

- Use frequent rest periods, select simple tasks, present tasks one at a time, and be prepared for delays in the children's responses.

- Use multimodal cuing (that is, use more than one sensory modality), as needed, to help the children learn and consolidate new information.

- Select times of the day at which the children will probably be most alert, keep distractions to a minimum, and keep the length of the sessions within the limits of the children's level of fatigue.

- Allow as much time as needed during each training session to accomplish your goals.

4. *Consistency.* Have each child do the same tasks at the same time with the same people to establish a familiar routine. Consistent daily scheduling helps make the world predictable and reduces confusion and agitation caused by changes in the environment.

5. *Repetition.* Use repetition and drilling on important tasks because brain-injured children usually have attention deficits and difficulties with recent memory. Repetition and drilling will help brain-injured children consolidate previously learned material.

6. *Specificity.* Focus your behavior management program on specific goals relevant for the particular child. Because brain-injured children usually have difficulty mastering generalized problem-solving strategies, focus on the exact behavior that you want in the exact situation in which it will be performed. Do not depend on brain-injured children to generalize from one learning situation to another.

7. *Practicality.* Select rehabilitation goals that will meet the basic needs of the child, that will be pragmatic and comprehensible to the child, and that will be relevant to the long-term outcome goals.

8. *Reward.* Use positive reinforcement to increase desired behavior from children, and make sure that the rewards are appropriate. Reinforce children for cooperation. You are likely to increase motivation and foster independence by establishing a caring, nurturing environment.

9. *Meaningfulness.* Determine goals meaningful to children, their families, and the staff. Children probably will try harder to achieve goals pertinent to their needs when they have the support of their families and the staff.

10. *Communication.* Clarify for the families what you are attempting to accomplish and the methods you are using. Update families about children's progress and problems. Make sure that knowledgeable staff members are available to answer families' questions. Whenever possible, directly involve the families in the rehabilitation program.

The following rehabilitation program was designed to help brain-injured children who have a limited attention span (Wilson, 1991). The program uses principles of behavioral treatment, including reinforcement and feedback, and can be implemented by a teacher, an occupational therapist, or other rehabilitation personnel, often in consultation with a social worker or psychologist. In some cases, under proper supervision, parents can assist in carrying out this rehabilitation program.

1. Ask the teacher/clinician to identify tasks that children can manage on their own, such as looking at baseball or football cards, sorting colors, listening to audiotapes, or coloring in a coloring book.

2. Ask the teacher/clinician to identify tasks that children have difficulty managing, such as completing a simple puzzle or printing their names and addresses.

3. Have children work on a task that they can manage on their own for at least 30 seconds. Sound a timer after 30 seconds to let children know that they were successful in reaching their goal.

4. Increase the interval by 5 seconds every time children succeed in reaching their goal.

5. Each time children achieve the target action, praise them, give them feedback, allow them to get up and walk around for up to 3 minutes, and encourage them to appraise their progress by looking at a wall chart (see Number 9).

6. Once children can work on their own for 5 to 15 minutes, alternate the original tasks with more difficult ones. Use shorter intervals for younger children.

7. Have children work on the more difficult tasks for about 2 to 3 minutes at a time.

8. Teach children the more difficult tasks one step at a time, using prompts, demonstrations, and reinforcement.

9. Monitor children's progress with record sheets or wall charts. Record (a) the date and time of the session, (b) the duration of the interval set for each session, (c) children's success and failures, and (d) any incidents of inappropriate behavior. Show children what you recorded, and encourage them to help record their progress.

Case illustrations of some specific rehabilitation strategies. The following case illustrates the value of taking a base-line measure as a way of learning about the reasons for a brain-injured child's behavior (Deaton, 1987).

CASE 19-9. JASON

Jason, 16, remained in a residential rehabilitation center 3 years after sustaining a severe head injury. Unfortunately, he remained severely cognitively and behaviorally impaired, with aphasia characterized by his being able to articulate clearly but with vacant content. On a multiple-choice measure of receptive vocabulary, Jason scored at chance level because he always chose the one picture of four that was located on the upper left corner of each page. Jason was unable to return to his family and community because of apparently unprovoked physical aggression occurring several times per day. Because Jason was unable to explain why he was aggressive, the staff completed a base-line evaluation to identify the frequency and specifics of Jason's aggression and the circumstances immediately preceding and following each episode of aggression.

During the base-line period, Jason punched or kicked someone an average of 3.5 times per day. A review of the events that occurred just before this behavior showed that Jason never attacked people who did not approach him first. Just before he lashed out, Jason appeared startled. On closer examination, the staff noted that he struck only those who approached him from the right side. Immediately after he attacked someone, the staff typically backed away until

Jason appeared calm and then returned to complete the activity. Following this base-line period, neuropsychological and visual field exams were undertaken. They showed that Jason had a complete right visual field loss consistent with damage to the posterior left hemisphere. It was presumed that Jason struck out because he was startled and frightened when approached from his blind side without warning. This base-line assessment clarified the cause and function of the target behavior and thereby dictated the selection of an appropriate intervention: in this case, approaching Jason from the left side or greeting him aloud before approaching from the right. This intervention decreased the episodes of physical aggression to approximately twice per week, a level that allowed Jason to be transferred to a facility close to his home. (p. 584, with changes in notation)

The case that follows describes how a brain-injured child was helped to generalize from his experiences (Deaton, 1987).

CASE 19-10. EVAN

Evan, a 17-year-old injured in an automobile accident while intoxicated, returned to treatment 2 years after his injury when his parents reported that his behavior could not be managed in their home. Still of average intelligence, Evan had difficulties in the areas of gross motor skills (remained nonambulatory), memory (could remember only two of four objects 5 minutes later), and frustration tolerance. Evan had frequent tantrums in the home when his needs or expectations were not being met. The tantrums consisted of screaming, hitting his fists against nearby objects, and hitting anyone who happened to be nearby. Evan's parents responded to all tantrums immediately with a solicitous attitude, asking him what they could do for him and quickly following his wishes. Evan's homebound teacher had refused to work with him following several such episodes.

Soon after admission to a rehabilitation facility, Evan joined two groups for brain-injured adolescents. One was a high-level social skills group that used videotaped feedback, and the other was a self-assessment group designed to facilitate accurate self-awareness. Initially, Evan expressed his frustration in each of these groups in his usual manner; that is, he had a tantrum. In the social skills group, the response to his tantrum was a brief physical restraint by the therapist to maintain Evan's and others' safety. This was followed by reviewing the videotaped tantrum with Evan, after which he was never observed to have a tantrum in this group while being videotaped. In the self-assessment group, peers did not confront Evan about his tantrums immediately but, rather, reinforced tantrums by letting him have the floor to talk about himself. After several such attention-getting tantrums, however, Evan's peers began to ignore his tantrums or to confront him about interrupting. The incidence of tantrums in this group showed a marked decrease. Generalization of these improvements to the living unit required a separate, unit-based program that used peer feedback in addition to staff feedback and proved effective in decreasing but not eliminating Evan's tantrums. Generalization to home and school settings was expected to require additional training of the significant care providers in these environments. (p. 587, with changes in notation)

The next case illustrates how environmental modifications and a careful selection of prevocational tasks helped a brain-injured adolescent deal with her problems (Deaton, 1987).

CASE 19-11. ANNE

Anne, a 16-year-old, sustained a brain injury as a result of a brain tumor and the subsequent surgery required to remove it. As a result of the surgery, she sustained damage to the temporal lobe, pituitary gland, hypothalamus, frontal lobe, and limbic system. (The limbic system refers to a rim of cortical structures that encircles the top of the brain stem and is involved in emotions and in basic feelings, such as hunger, thirst, sex, and fear.) Although Anne was verbal, she performed in the Borderline range on intelligence measures and learned new information with difficulty and only after much repetition.

Anne had ongoing problems with sudden sleep onset. She also had severe visual deficits, tended to give up on tasks at the first sign of difficulty, and was easily sidetracked. However, she was responsive to positive feedback and willing to attempt new tasks.

To minimize the impact of her sleep disorder on her work performance, she was assigned tasks that were active in nature, requiring her to go from office to office rather than staying in one place and, inevitably, falling asleep. Moving about was difficult for Anne, however, because she was easily distracted from what she was doing and also because her visual limitations made finding the offices difficult. To deal with these problems, Anne's route was made the same each day so that she could establish a visual scanning routine and also an internal map of where she needed to go. Anne performed well in her daily tasks but did not generalize her compensatory skills to novel tasks, suggesting the need for changes in her routine to facilitate generalization. With these changes, Anne's irritability and frustration returned, as did the episodes of sudden sleep onset. She was returned to her original route to reestablish an acceptable level of functioning. Recommendations were made for highly structured, sheltered school and work settings with established routines for work completion. (p. 588, with changes in notation)

The last case in this part describes how a rehabilitation program helped a brain-injured adolescent become more independent (Lehr, 1990).

CASE 19-12. KURT

Kurt, a 15-year-old adolescent boy, had multiple severe physical deficits after traumatic brain injury. Despite his deficits, though, it appeared that he had the capacity to push his wheelchair independently, using one of his feet and one of his hands. This was a major goal for him to accomplish before discharge from a rehabilitation hospital. However, he refused to do so, saying, "It's faster if you do it." The benefits of pushing his wheelchair by himself had been pointed out to him repeatedly, but he persisted in engaging people in verbal reasons why he could not until, to save time, they relented and pushed him.

Physical therapy sessions indicated that Kurt did have the skills to push his wheelchair independently but preferred not to do so. A reinforcement program was designed in which he could play computer games (one of his favorite therapy activities) with the therapist if he pushed his chair from the elevator to the therapy room. The therapist met him at the elevator and timed how long it took for him to push himself to the room. He was told that the longer it took him, the less time he would have to play computer games. She also would not start talking with him if he did not push his wheelchair. She charted how much time it took him to push his wheelchair from the elevator to the therapy room on a graph in the therapy room. During the first week, he took an average of 20 to 25 minutes to get to the therapy room. However, this rapidly decreased, and by the third week he was pushing his chair at the same speed as the therapist was walking, taking about 3 to 4 minutes to get to the room. He was quite proud of his speed and engaged in races with the therapist to see if he could beat his time and go faster than she could walk. He was told that if he pushed himself, he could go to the game room on his own during his free time and down to the cafeteria to pick out his food. Within another week, he was independently moving around the hospital and in his neighborhood on weekend visits without specific reinforcement needed. (pp. 143–144, with changes in notation)

Exercise 19-2. Deciding on Possible Interventions

Read each situation and formulate the most appropriate intervention. Then compare your answers with the Suggested Interventions shown. This exercise was adapted from Blosser and DePompei (1989) and Deaton (1987).

1. A brain-injured child does not understand the task demands.
2. A brain-injured child does not begin the task.
3. A brain-injured child is unable to do the task.
4. A brain-injured child is not motivated.
5. A brain-injured child tries to avoid failure by not complying with the task instructions.
6. A brain-injured child gets out of doing a task by complaining.
7. A brain-injured child receives attention for not doing a task.
8. A brain-injured child is careless about safety.
9. A brain-injured child argues and fights with peers on the playground.
10. A brain-injured child forgets to do homework.

Suggested Interventions

1. Provide clear, concrete instructions, or do the task yourself to show the child how it should be done.
2. Give the child prompts, and reinforce each instance of initiative that the child shows, however minor.
3. Simplify the task, and provide training for the child in the underlying skills required for successful performance.
4. Make the task more interesting, and give the child rewards when he or she completes the task.
5. Alternate difficult with easy and enjoyable tasks, and provide tasks at which the child may succeed.
6. Inform the child that he or she must complete the task before he or she can go on to other activities. Also inform the child that he or she can take as much time as needed to complete the task.

7. Use a time-out procedure when the child is noncompliant, or ignore the child's behavior. Reinforce the child with attention for cooperation. Reinforce other children in the room for their cooperation.
8. Set firm limits on the child's behavior. Establish specific rules for behavior in certain places and at certain times of the day. Work with the child on the activity before allowing him or her to do it independently.
9. Set firm limits on the child's behavior. Select a buddy with whom the child gets along. Encourage the buddy to be with the brain-injured child during recess. Work with the brain-injured child in small groups to encourage sharing.
10. Develop with the brain-injured child a daily written assignment sheet indicating dates and times that assignments are due.

"…because life after head injury may never be the same."
—Logo of the New York State Head Injury Association

Cognitive-behavioral orientation in schools. In formulating rehabilitation strategies for brain-injured children returning to school, consider first what deficits the children have and what effects their cognitive impairments may have on learning experiences (see Table 19-5). Then, before the children return to their classrooms, visit the classrooms and decide, in consultation with the school staff, what modifications are needed to facilitate the children's learning and adjustment. Finally, help the teachers carry out appropriate strategies (a) for modifying, eliminating, and reducing barriers to learning and to reintegrating the children in the classroom and (b) for establishing objectives (see Table 19-6). Review brain-injured children's educational placement periodically, especially during the early stages of recovery, because their needs may change (Savage & Carter, 1988).

When you observe classrooms, consider the following (Ylvisaker, Hartwick, & Stevens, 1991):

1. *Environmental variables,* such as noise level, activity level, consistency in staff, and physical layout of the classroom (especially for mobility issues)
2. *Schedule of activities,* such as length of day, days per week, length of sessions, consistency in schedule, and free time
3. *Cuing systems,* such as lists of tasks on the blackboard, personal contracts, and assignment sheets
4. *Materials,* such as the types of reading materials and worksheets
5. *Instructional aids,* such as computer-assisted instruction, videotapes, and television
6. *Classroom aids,* such as a calculator, tape recorder, and writing aids
7. *Instructional methods,* such as visual, auditory, or multimethod presentations
8. *Work expectations,* such as length of assignments, time spent in independent work, time allowed to complete assignments, and use of self-paced materials

Table 19-5
Influence of Cognitive Impairments on Learning Experiences

Cognitive impairment	Correlated behavior
Poor attention or concentration	Distractibility: fragmented understanding of tasks; problems completing work
Poor orientation to place, person	Confusion: trouble getting around class and building, following schedules, and connecting places, people, materials with activities
Poor retention and retrieval of information	Uncertainty about what is known or has been learned
Impulsivity	Problems with attending, processing information, staying on task, and social interactions; tendency to get into situations where physical safety is compromised
Overload (comprehension breakdown)	Confusion, stress; shuts down when tasks are too long or too complex
Poor organization of thoughts, expression, tasks	Problems with comprehension, reasoning, problem solving, spoken/written expression, and task completion; difficulty planning activities during free, unstructured periods
Poor initiation	Inability to keep up with class; confusion and frustration because others view inactivity as resistance or inability to perform
Slow processing and performing	Poor comprehension of class material; cannot get work done on time
Inflexibility	Resistance, confusion, stress when confronted with changes in activities or variables in reasoning and problem-solving tasks
Inability to think or perform independently	Inability to do tasks that are expected in classrooms
Inability to generalize	Problems connecting old and new information or seeing patterns in processes; need for teacher assistance and cuing to continue learning; cannot learn or work independently as others do
Denial/poor awareness	No recognition that abilities have changed; resistance to participating in new programs; wants to return to former class

Source: Reprinted, with permission of the author and publisher, from S. B. Cohen "Adapting Educational Programs for Students with Head Injuries" in *Journal of Head Trauma Rehabilitation, 6*(1), p. 57, copyright 1991 by Aspen.

9. *Testing methods,* such as timed or untimed tests, multiple-choice tests, essay tests, open-book tests, take-home tests, and grading methods
10. *Motivational variables,* such as types of reinforcers and frequency of use of reinforcers

The following case illustrates how modifications in the structure of the classroom and teaching methods helped a brain-injured preschooler improve his performance (Szekeres, 1989).

CASE 19-13. T. J.

T. J. was a 5-year-old boy who had sustained a head injury when he fell down the stairs at the age of 4 years. (Note that the type of head injury was not described in the published case report.) After a four-month period of hospitalization and recuperation at home, his physical recovery from the injury

was complete, and he began to attend preschool. Before his injury, T. J. had been developing normally. He reportedly had walked at 11 months and was talking fluently at the age of 2 years. He was described as a friendly child who enjoyed playing with his friends. However, after the injury his behavior changed. At the preschool, he now had difficulty adjusting. He was disruptive, did not participate in activities, and often had temper tantrums. However, his self-care skills were good.

After the injury, T. J.'s teacher described him as a highly active, fast-moving, anxious boy who socialized little with the other children and seemed to prefer solitary play. In play, he moved quickly from one object to another and did not create symbolic play sequences or themes with the toys as did the other children. T. J.'s speech was intelligible, but he often repeated what other people said. He made some spontaneous comments when he requested items and when he named objects on a walk or during an activity. Although he

Table 19-6
Strategies and Classroom Adaptations Useful for Brain-Injured Children

1. Plan many small-group activities to facilitate learning of appropriate interaction skills.
2. Clarify verbal and written instructions by (a) accompanying verbal instructions with written instructions, (b) repeating instructions and redefining words and terms, and (c) alerting the student to the important topic or concept being taught ("I'm going to tell a story and then we'll discuss *where* it takes place").
3. Use pauses when giving classroom instructions to allow time for processing information.
4. Provide the student with ample time to respond verbally and complete in-class and home assignments.
5. Avoid figurative, idiomatic, ambiguous, and sarcastic language when presenting lessons. (Example: "You're a ham.")
6. Select a classroom buddy to keep the student aware of instructions, transitions, and assignments.
7. Permit the student to use assistive devices such as calculators, tape recorders, and computers. Allow a student who cannot write to use a typewriter, computer, plastic magnetic letters, or other types of letters, or allow the student to ask a classmate to write for him or her.
8. Help the student formulate and use a system for maintaining organization. Require the student to carry a written log of activities, a schedule of classes, a list of assignments and their due dates, and a list of room locations. Frequently monitor the student's use of the organizational system.
9. Schedule a specific time for rest or emotional release. Encourage the student to share his or her problems with you.
10. Plan extracurricular activities based on the student's physical and emotional capabilities and his or her interests.
11. Privately ask the student to repeat information or answer a few key questions to be sure that he or she understood important information presented. Take care, however, not to cause stress in students who have difficulty responding to direct questions.
12. Structure the physical environment of the classroom to decrease distractions and permit ease of movement by carefully planning seating and furniture arrangements.
13. Modify and individualize the student's assignments and tests to accommodate his or her special needs. Examples of modifications include reducing the number of questions to be answered or amount of material to be read; enlarging printed matter; permitting the student to tape record your lectures or his or her responses to test questions; changing the format of a task, such as giving homework assignments in written form to students who have difficulty with oral comprehension, allowing additional time to complete assignments, using oral presentations for visually impaired students or for those who have visual processing problems, and duplicating course lectures or notes for students who cannot take notes rapidly; and reducing stressful experiences, such as eliminating pop quizzes.
14. Develop resources to accompany textbook assignments. For example, use pictures and written cues to illustrate important information and concepts. Assign review questions at the end of chapters. Write new vocabulary. Present a summary of a chapter on audiotape or on paper. Go over errors made on tests to let the student know where and why errors occurred.
15. Establish a system of verbal or nonverbal signals to cue the student to attend, respond, or alter behavior. (Examples include calling the student's name, touching the student, using written signs, and using hand signals.)
16. Monitor the progress of the student closely so that revisions in the curriculum can be made as improvements in functioning occur.

Source: Adapted from DePompei and Blosser (1987), pp. 298–299, with changes in notation, and Martin (1988).

spoke in sentences, he would repeatedly ask "What's that?" and "What's he doing?" His repetitions, hyperactivity, and anxiety persisted at a high level and interfered with his successful participation in age-appropriate activities.

T. J. had difficulty participating in group activities—such as story time, show-and-tell time, or snack time—for more than two to three minutes at a time. Often, he would leave the group abruptly and move from one area of the room to another, banging toys loudly, or go to another area of the room and sit quietly. T. J.'s peers tended to avoid playing with him because they preferred group activities and playing out real life or fantasy games such as "let's play doctor."

A clinical speech and language evaluation indicated that his articulation was within normal limits and that his vocabulary knowledge and comprehension of simple sentences were both near age expectancy. However, he had difficulty understanding long sentences or short paragraphs.

Based on classroom and clinical evaluations, the following recommendations were made and carried out:

1. The classroom was structured to create small areas that were relatively free from distraction.
2. The length of the activities was shortened. A short story was presented at the beginning of each regular story time that consisted of no more than five pictures, with one statement about each picture. After these mini-stories were finished, T. J. was taken to an area with minimal distractions to play with quiet toys (such as clay or paint) while the other children completed story time. The length of T. J.'s stories was gradually increased so that he was staying longer and longer with the group.
3. Language stimulation during play was reduced in amount and complexity. The teacher said less and spoke in short phrases with pauses between them.

4. The play environment was more highly organized, and the teacher demonstrated simple interactions with the toys.

As T. J. became more familiar with the sets of materials, new objects were introduced into each set by adding objects to his play table. The complexity of thematic play was increased by adding events to the established sequences—for example, "after the airplane landed, he got a car" or "then he got bubble gum at the store."

An adult facilitator was assigned to play with T. J. during play time to promote coherent thematic play interaction. Gradually, the facilitator brought another child into the play, and, as T. J.'s ability to play meaningfully with the other child increased, the facilitator left the situation. T. J. began to experience success with his peers, as the other children could now join his play and understand his interaction with the objects. T. J. also was given free time for exploratory play.

Each modification had a significant and immediate effect on T. J.'s behavior. When distractions were minimized by modifying the physical environment, T. J. could attend for longer periods. As his participation in group activities increased, his peers began to initiate more interactions with him. He could listen to stories of three sentences per picture and stay in the story time group much longer. His echolalia was greatly reduced when the facilitator reduced the amount and complexity of talk during play and kept the talk closely related to the immediate objects and events. T. J. began to talk about the events in play and let his play-people interact with those of other children. When T. J.'s behavior was modified, other children initiated many more positive interactions.

Although T. J. could participate successfully with his peers in many activities, he continued to need more structure than the other children to maintain his attention, and he needed more controlled language stimulation when new items, activities, or people were introduced. (adapted from pp. 167–171)

The next case illustrates what can be accomplished when the school recognizes the problems of a brain-injured adolescent (Savage, 1987).

CASE 19-14. SCOTT

Scott was 16 years old when he sustained a head injury while snow skiing. He was comatose for 7 of the 33 days he spent in a medical center. Although Scott suffered diffuse injury to his brain as the result of a head-on collision with a tree, he sustained major damage in the frontal lobes and the left temporal lobe. When Scott returned home, he had difficulty remembering, following through with initiated plans, understanding the salient points in written and spoken language, engaging in age-appropriate behavior, and performing activities for longer than a few minutes.

When Scott was in the hospital, the speech and language therapist helped him develop some cognitive strategies that he could use to help him organize his thoughts and actions. The school nurse, the special educator, and the speech and language therapist from Scott's school visited him while he was in the hospital and met with his medical team to begin transition services before actual hospital discharge. The social worker worked with the family to discuss his return home and the rehabilitation plans.

During the same period, the school nurse and the special educator also set up three afternoon training sessions on traumatic head injury for Scott's teachers, guidance counselor, and the school administrators. A speaker from the state head-injury chapter worked with the faculty and distributed print and videotape information. During the last training session, several of Scott's friends also were given information on head injury to help them better understand what Scott would be experiencing.

Scott's basic staffing team consisted of his subject area teachers, assistant principal, special educator, speech and language therapist, school nurse, a vocational-rehabilitation counselor, a neuroeducator from the state head-injury chapter, Scott's parents, and the social worker and speech and language therapist from the hospital. The following educational plan was developed for Scott:

1. Scott would reenter school for morning sessions only until it was determined by his health care provider that he could physically handle a full school day.
2. Before his accident, Scott had been a "C" student. The decision was made that Scott should attend the morning classes he was enrolled in before his accident (period 1, English; period 2, history; period 3, study hall; period 4, algebra), with support services provided by the special educator during his third-period study hall.
3. Scott would check in with the special educator before each school day to make sure he had the right materials, books, and supplies for his classes that day. Later, he would check out with the special educator regarding homework assignments, upcoming tests, and any special needs.
4. Three times each week, Scott would meet with the speech and language therapist and continue with the cognitive strategy program that was set up when he was in the hospital.
5. Between classes, Scott would be guided to his next class by one of his friends and peer-tutored in subject area assignments after school and on weekends, as needed.
6. Scott's friends also would informally plan one social activity each weekend (such as an athletic game or school dance) for Scott to attend with them. They also would help Scott monitor and relearn appropriate social behaviors.
7. The following academic strategies were recommended: (a) Scott would keep a daily journal with a calendar of things to do, (b) Scott's teachers would give him a written structured overview of the main points of each of their lessons, (c) Scott would receive textbook study guides to use as he completed his homework with the help of the special educator and/or his peers, and (d) Scott would receive differentiated assignments to decrease the academic load without sacrificing the learning process.

One month after Scott reentered school, he returned to a full school day, and another basic planning meeting was held. An individual education plan (IEP) was written for the remainder of the year, and a five-year long-term plan was outlined that would include Scott's future career goals. The vocational-rehabilitation counselor helped plan Scott's entrance into the area vocational-technical school in the fall and helped assess Scott's present and potential work skills regarding specific vocational training programs.

Two years later, Scott was allowed to graduate with his peers. However, he was not formally awarded a high school diploma so that he could remain in school until age 21 to complete his vocational-technical school program in mechanical arts. Today, Scott works for a local ski resort repairing and renting ski equipment. (pp. 4–5, with changes in notation)

Exercise 19-3. Evaluating a School's Understanding of a Brain-Injured Child

---

Read the following case, answer the questions that follow, and then compare your answers with those in the Suggested Answers section. The material in this exercise was adapted from Savage (1987).

James was 15 years old when he sustained a closed-head injury from a motorcycle accident. He was comatose for 6 days and suffered injury to the right frontal and temporal lobe areas of his brain. After 36 days in the regional medical center, James returned home while still experiencing problems in attention, memory, impulsiveness, and appropriate social and personal behaviors.

Upon reentering school 44 days after his accident, James, who had previously been a "C" to "B" student, was unable to keep up in his previous academic subjects, failed to complete homework assignments, and began to act out aggressively in class. His friends soon began to avoid him because of his weird actions. After an extremely violent fight with a younger student, James was suspended from school for 10 days. Following the suspension period, a special education resource specialist tested James and found his academic skills to be four years below grade level and his emotional stability to be below the norm for his age group. Because he looked good to his teachers, they could not see any reason for his inability to keep up with his school work if he would only just try harder.

The school's staffing team, consisting of a special educator, his primary room teacher, and the assistant principal, decided to place James in a classroom for emotionally impaired students within the school's special education program. However, James continued his outbursts and aggressive acts to the point where residential placement in a school for emotionally disturbed adolescents was initiated. After two weeks in the residential school, James attempted suicide with a drug overdose.

1. After James left the hospital, what plans were made for his rehabilitation or for his returning to school?
2. How was the school prepared to cope with James's return?
3. How did James perform in his initial class?
4. Did placement in a class for emotionally disturbed children meet James's needs?
5. Assuming the basic staffing team was inadequate, who was needed on the team?
6. What were some possible reasons for James's poor school performance?
7. How did the school treat James's aggressive and impulsive behavior?
8. How should the school have treated James?

Suggested Answers

1. As far as can be determined from the case study, no plans were made for James's rehabilitation or for his return to school.
2. As far as can be determined, the school staff was not familiar with children who have traumatic brain injuries and the resulting possible cognitive-behavioral disorders.
3. James could not meet the requirements of a regular classroom. Both his academic work and his social functioning were seriously impaired.
4. No.
5. Besides the three educators, the staffing team should have had, ideally, other teachers, James's parents, the school nurse, the social worker from the hospital medical team (or a school social worker), the school psychologist or guidance counselor, the speech and language therapist, and the vocational rehabilitation counselor. Also, a neuropsychologist trained in rehabilitation should have been consulted and asked to serve on the team.
6. His failure to perform well in school may have been associated with difficulty in integrating new learning with previous learning, memory and organizational problems, language disabilities, concentration difficulties, inappropriate psychosocial behaviors, and fatigue. Because of his right frontal and temporal lobe injuries, he may have had difficulty in organization, in developing study habits, and in controlling his impulsiveness and emotions.
7. The school failed to recognize that James's higher-level functions were impaired. They treated his actions as intentional misbehavior rather than as inappropriate behavioral sequelae resulting from his head injury; therefore, the school used a traditional discipline model and suspended him from school.
8. The school should have begun a special program that considered his cognitive impairments and behavioral difficulties. Such a program would include structured cuing to initiate tasks and to complete assignments, a reduced course load, a shorter day, work with a resource specialist, and provision of a peer tutor.

Psychotherapy

Psychotherapy also can help brain-injured children cope with their feelings and reactions and can help families cope with their own and their brain-injured children's difficulties. Psychotherapy focuses on helping brain-injured children to do the following (Prigatano et al., 1986):

- understand what has happened to them because of the brain injury
- comprehend the meaning and consequences of the brain injury in their life
- achieve a sense of self-acceptance and forgiveness of self and others who may have been responsible for the accident
- make realistic commitments to school (and work, where applicable) and to interpersonal relations
- improve social competence

- develop behavioral strategies to compensate for deficits
- develop realistic goals

In psychotherapeutic work with brain-injured children, keep explanations simple and repeat them whenever you need to, use group therapy together with individual therapy, and use both insight and behavioral strategies. These strategies overlap with those described previously under cognitive-behavioral orientation.

The Family's Role in Rehabilitation Programs

A brain-injured child's recovery will, in part, depend on the level of family support she or he receives and on the family's ability to manage the child's day-to-day problems. You therefore will need to evaluate how the family members function, including their ability to care for the physical, emotional, and behavioral needs of the brain-injured child, and their communication patterns, cohesion, adaptability, and adjustment. You will especially want to learn whether the family has a history of other injuries or accidents, domestic violence, psychiatric disturbances, substance abuse, or child maltreatment. Families that were dysfunctional before the injury are likely to have a more difficult time coping with a child's injuries than families that were not dysfunctional.

When children sustain a brain injury (or have other types of injuries or chronic illnesses), family patterns may change. There may be disruption of family relationships, shifting of social roles within the family, and adjustment problems among the family members. Sometimes, latent family strengths or weaknesses come to the surface. Here are some examples of maladaptive family patterns (Cope & Wolfson, 1994):

- *unrealistic thinking* ("A coma stimulation program will awake my child.")
- *regressive behavior* ("I need several drinks to get by each day.")
- *unjustified blaming* ("It is the hospital staff's fault that my son shows no improvement.")
- *prolonged denial* ("I know that next year she'll be able to apply to college and get a tennis scholarship.")

See Chapter 4 for ways to assess family functioning and Chapter 11 for information on how children's behavioral problems may affect their families.

Family stressors. The effect that a child's brain injury will have on his or her family will depend on (a) the type of onset of the child's injury (sudden or gradual), (b) the severity of the child's injury, (c) the extent of the child's deficits, (d) the length of time the child was hospitalized, (e) the family's ability to pay for the needed treatments, (f) the prognosis, and (g) how the family was functioning before the child's brain injury.

Families of brain-injured children confront several types of stressors, including the following:

1. Handling the shock (in cases of sudden onset) of a traumatic brain injury to a child without having time to prepare for such a devastating event
2. Facing uncertainty about the child's degree of recovery
3. Coping with dramatic changes in the child's cognitive abilities, personality, and temperament
4. Handling the child's increased dependency and the constant struggle with dependence/independence issues
5. Handling the child's symptoms—such as flashbacks, sleeping difficulties, anxiety reactions—associated with posttraumatic stress disorder (especially in cases of traumatic brain injury; see Chapter 11)
6. Facing the dilemma of wanting to foster the child's independence and speedy recovery, yet also wanting to provide control and structure to maintain the child's safety
7. Handling an uninjured sibling's possible jealousy, possible resentment about increased responsibilities, and possible anger at having a "different" family, at not being able to bring friends home, and at not being able to participate in activities because the parents must take care of the brain-injured child
8. Working through possible feelings of blame and/or guilt and personal responsibility for the child's injury
9. Working through grief reactions associated with loss of a normal life for the brain-injured child
10. Working out possible disagreements with professionals about what actions to take to help the child
11. Coping with the financial, time, and energy demands of a long-term rehabilitation program
12. Facing the possibility that the community has poor rehabilitation and educational programs
13. Facing the possibility that the child may need to be placed in a long-term care facility

---

The uninjured sibling can become a potent source of help and support for the patient, or a target for clinical intervention [because of the stress of dealing with the patient]. It is the responsibility of the rehabilitation team to ensure that the former happens and not the latter.

—D. Neil Brooks

Most families will experience stress if their children are hospitalized (see Chapter 15). One parent may have to devote all of his or her time to the brain-injured child while the child is in the hospital. When this happens, additional stress is placed on all family members. If the hospital is located far from home, visiting the child may place further stress on the family members.

The degree of brain-injured children's physical disability typically is *not* the crucial factor in causing stress in families; rather, it is children's behavioral, cognitive, and affective deficits that are likely to influence family harmony. Families may be concerned about children's irritability, inattentiveness, difficulties with social interaction, violence, aggression, immaturity, and dependency.

The following case illustrates the problems parents had in deciding how much autonomy to give to their brain-injured son (Romano, 1989).

CASE 19-15. EC

EC was a 17-year-old high school dropout, the only child of acrimoniously divorced parents. His father, an automobile mechanic, had remarried, and his mother worked full time as a beautician. EC, employed as a delivery boy, fell asleep at the wheel of his panel truck and drove it into a tree. He sustained a brain injury with residual spatial-perceptual deficits, impairment of judgment, and difficulty in initiating behaviors. In preparing EC for a weekend pass to his mother's home, the team set goals for him to work on. His mother was very apprehensive about the pass, however, and hovered over EC, monitoring and cuing him for the entire weekend. The following weekend, with the same learning goals, EC was sent on pass to his father's home. When EC sat staring at the TV, his father threw him the car keys and told him to go for a drive. In the family conference following the second pass, EC's parents berated each other. The father accused the mother of fostering helplessness, and the mother accused the father of wanting EC to get hurt. The parents justified their respective behavior with EC on ethical grounds. EC's mother used beneficence to justify her behavior, while EC's father argued that his behavior fostered autonomy. (p. 36)

The next case describes the pressures a family faced when it had to care for a brain-injured adolescent at home (Romano, 1989).

CASE 19-16. KM

KM, a 16-year-old high school junior, incurred a brain injury in a freak accident in which she was struck by a hockey puck. The eldest of three children, she had brothers aged 12 and 8. Both parents were employed full time, the father as an accountant and the mother as a school librarian, and their families of origin lived many miles away. KM's brothers were involved in sports and other extracurricular activities after school and on weekends, to which her mother drove them, and her father was a volunteer firefighter. Family unit activities centered around the boys' sporting events and weekly Catholic church attendance. KM's injury left her with attentional and memory deficits, impulsivity, and impairment in social judgment. The rehabilitation team believed that she required constant supervision and cuing. During her inpatient rehabilitation stay, KM's parents never questioned their intent to care for her at home, but as the time for discharge approached, it became clear (and anxiety-provoking) to the team that her parents disagreed about who would provide KM's care. Because her income was smaller, KM's mother took a six-month unpaid leave of absence in order to be primary caretaker in the hope that KM would improve sufficiently to allow her mother to return to work at least part time. Unfortunately, KM's discharge home provoked a major crisis for the family. Her mother found herself overwhelmed by

KM's needs and unable to "do it all," while both boys voiced resentment toward KM for the attention she was getting. The 12-year-old said that he wished KM had died, and the 8-year-old said that he wished he'd been brain-injured so that he could get some attention, too. KM's father felt financially pressured and abandoned by his wife, who was preoccupied with KM. Each family member felt guilty and inadequate, and none felt in control of his or her life. Over objections by their priest and their families of origin, they placed KM in a sub acute residential brain injury program. (pp. 39–40)

Suggestions for working with families of brain-injured children. Helping families of brain-injured children may take several years, not just weeks or months (Brooks, 1991). Rehabilitation is best conceived as a process involving different stages: the stage of acute crisis, the stage of prolonged rehabilitation, and the stage of disengagement. At all stages, families need support and accurate information.

1. *Stage of acute crisis.* At this first stage, family members must be ready to accept information about the brain-injured child. If they are in a state of despair or are using denial mechanisms, they may not listen or understand what they hear. Gauge their ability to receive and understand the information, and, if necessary, delay the discussion until they appear ready to listen.

2. *Stage of prolonged rehabilitation.* At this stage, families need information to help them make realistic plans. Involve them in the treatment decisions, if possible.

3. *Stage of disengagement.* At this final stage, families need to disengage from active professional intervention but still have access to professional help for crises or for guidance.

The following list presents some problems that brain-injured children may have and offers suggestions for helping their families deal with these problems (DePompei, Zarski, & Hall, 1988).

1. *Inability to inhibit speaking out or poor social-pragmatic skills.* The family might say "She irritates us by interrupting our conversation, and then she talks about something different." Encourage the family to learn to read the brain-injured child's nonverbal cues that he or she wants to speak, take back the conversational lead if the child does not relinquish it, and return him or her to the conversational topic.

2. *Anomia.* The family might say "He has such difficulty saying the words. Since I know him so well, I know what he wants to say, so I say it for him." Encourage the family to allow the brain-injured child to communicate on his or her own, wait out conversational pauses with patience, and use cues to assist but not to speak for the child.

3. *Tangential speech or poor pragmatic skills.* The family might say "We won't take him to visit our friends anymore. His conversation is irrational and fragmented. He goes from topic to topic." Encourage the family to allow the brain-injured child a choice about participation in social activities and to recognize that the child's behavior is not intended to embarrass them.

4. *Low tolerance for frustration or inability to use logic and reasoning to fight fair.* The family might say "Her temper outbursts are worse. We all try to control her and force her to behave. But we all end up in a fight." Encourage the family to read behavioral signs that the brain-injured child's frustration level is being reached, recognize that his or her outbursts are not deliberate, and decrease stimulation in his or her environment.

5. *Inability to express feelings of rejection.* The family might say "When he gets depressed and doesn't talk to us, we just go out and leave him alone." Encourage the family to accept the brain-injured child's need to be apart and to allow time for the child to share his or her thoughts and feelings with the family.

6. *Poor written expression or poor memory.* The family might say "He's not doing well in writing and often forgets things." Encourage the family to focus on the brain-injured child's remaining strengths, and help the family acknowledge that the child may not be able to do things that he or she did before the injury.

Family support for the brain-injured child is a critical factor in a rehabilitation program (Kay & Silver, 1989).

Families that are enthusiastic, actively involved, and willing and able to make accommodations at home are a great [benefit] to head-injured persons; they open up the range of rehabilitation possibilities. Conversely, a patient who will be returning to a chaotic, conflict-bound family, or whose family does not want him [or her], will encounter an additional set of problems, and the rehabilitation goals must be adjusted accordingly. Consequently, it is absolutely essential in the process of assessment for rehabilitation that the family be intimately involved not only in order to evaluate their level of support but [also] to actively engage them at the very beginning of the rehabilitation process as part of the therapeutic team. (p. 166)

Because the stress of caring for brain-injured children at home can be overwhelming, arrange for home services and for counseling for the family members, if needed. Try to ensure that the home environment is stable and as free of stress as possible to help brain-injured children during their recovery period. Exhibit 19-1 describes the social worker's role in helping families during the various stages of treatment.

The following case illustrates a brother's reaction to his sister's brain injury (Gans, Mann, & Ylvisaker, 1990).

CASE 19-17. R. P.

R. P. is a 5-year-old boy whose 9-year-old sister suffered a traumatic brain injury when she was hit by a school bus when she was crossing the street. He visited her several times during her 2-month hospitalization—the first time while she was still in a coma. At discharge, his sister could walk independently but was still mildly ataxic. She had mild cognitive deficits, emotional lability, and poor endurance. R. P. was extremely overprotective of his sister, assuming the role of an older brother. He hovered over her, offering constant supervision that was not necessary. As her functional skills improved, he was unable to accept her increasing independence, leading to frequent conflicts. Family therapy was helpful in resolving these issues. (p. 609, with changes in notation)

Here are some suggestions for parents to help their brain-injured child during rehabilitation (Lezak, 1978; Miller, 1993; Rollin, 1987; Sachs, 1991):

EDUCATION

1. Give parents accurate information about the nature of the trauma, the brain-injured child's strengths and weaknesses, the types of problems the child may display, and the possible prognosis. Be sure that the information you give is consistent with that of the health care provider.

2. Explain that there may be advances and setbacks during recovery.

3. Explain why the brain-injured child may have behavioral problems during the recovery period, and explain the relationship between behavioral problems and the child's brain injury.

4. Explain the principles of behavioral interventions that will help them work with their brain-injured child at home.

PROBLEM SOLVING

5. Identify the brain-injured child's problems and their possible effects on the family.

6. Help the parents become involved in the education and treatment of their brain-injured child.

7. Help the parents establish goals consistent with their brain-injured child's potential and with their own family values and expectations.

8. Encourage the parents to allow the brain-injured child to become independent, as much as this is possible, and not foster dependence.

9. Encourage the parents to allow the brain-injured child to go at his or her own pace.

10. Elicit from the parents their suggestions for positive reinforcers that can be used with the brain-injured child.

11. Help the parents adjust to the brain-injured child and to the changed roles of family members.

12. Encourage the parents to break up into manageable parts seemingly insurmountable problems that they are having with their brain-injured child and to rehearse and role play potentially stressful activities with the child.

13. Help the parents resolve differences over how to handle the brain-injured child's problems.

SUPPORT AND VENTILATION

14. Help the parents work through their grief, anxiety, guilt, depression, and hopelessness. They must come to recognize that anger, frustration, and sorrow are natural emotions to experience when they have a brain-injured child.

15. Help the parents become organized and focused on the tasks needed to help their brain-injured child.

Exhibit 19-1
The Role of the Social Worker in the Management of Traumatic Brain Injury

The social worker may play an important role during all phases of treatment and rehabilitation with brain-injured children and their families. The focus is not only on the child but also on the family and community. The social worker is in a key position to provide help—using clinical, educational, advocacy/mobilization, and planning skills—with problems that arise over time.

Acute Stage
During the acute stage, the social worker typically meets the brain-injured child's parents in a hospital emergency room or regional trauma center. The social worker is often the first person the family members meet. His or her task is to help the family through the immediate crisis. The social worker may (a) inform the family of the latest information on the brain-injured child's condition and the medical procedures under way; (b) answer questions and deal with the family's immediate concerns; (c) prepare the family for its initial meeting with the brain-injured child; and (d) serve as liaison between the family and the medical staff.

To accomplish these tasks, the social worker must have the most current information available on the brain-injured child's status. When the child is transferred to intensive care following emergency treatment, the social worker tries to facilitate communication between the family and the medical staff and to clarify the course of the brain-injured child's medical treatment. For example, the social worker might clarify what the health care provider has told the family about the child's condition, relay information about the child's condition to the family, correct misconceptions, and clarify inquiries about the purpose and function of the medical equipment and medical procedures.

The social worker also alerts the medical staff to the family's need for explanations, sets up family/staff conferences, and smooths the way for family members to see their brain-injured child, especially if the medical situation becomes critical. The social worker alerts other staff or volunteers, if there is a need for someone to stay with the family, and mobilizes such support when it is needed. Sometimes it is necessary for the social worker to mobilize community resources to meet the practical needs of the family, such as financial and legal assistance or short-term housing if the family does not live nearby.

The social worker encourages the family members to express their feelings and helps family members and friends deal with interpersonal problems. The social worker also tries to find family members or others who can be called on for immediate help, and the social worker may establish support groups for families of children in intensive care.

Rehabilitation Stage
As the brain-injured child moves from the acute to the rehabilitative stage of treatment, the social worker continues to serve as liaison between the medical staff and the family. The social worker must be prepared to deal with such reactions as parental anxiety, depression, tension, fatigue, or denial. The family also may need help with housing, transportation, finances, and medical supplies.

Discharge and
Returning Home Stage
The transition from hospital care to life in the home and the community represents a new adjustment for the brain-injured child and his or her family. As the time of discharge approaches, the social worker helps prepare the brain-injured child and his or her family for the child's return home. The social worker (a) helps the family members express any feelings of anger, frustration, and sorrow and helps them to understand that these are normal reactions, (b) mobilizes family support for the child's parents, (c) encourages the parents to rely on their judgment when conflicts with the brain-injured child or other family members develop, (d) facilitates the adjustment of family members to the new roles and responsibilities that are likely to emerge, and (e) helps the family members to work through divided loyalties and any guilt feelings and to identify and to accept their responsibilities.

When biological sequelae, such as epilepsy, pose special problems, the social worker needs to help the family avoid secrecy, deal with the condition matter-of-factly, avoid overprotection, and learn to discuss the condition with others. Grandparents may need special attention because their unique status in the family gives them special influence on how the brain-injured child's condition is handled. If their influence is beneficial, then the social worker should support the grandparents. If it is not, the social worker needs to help the family find ways to remedy the situation. The social worker may use role-playing techniques, if needed, to help family members develop skills in dealing with anticipated problems.

If training facilities are available in the community, the social worker should arrange for the brain-injured child to attend programs focusing on social skills development and the development of independent living skills and vocational skills, as needed. If training facilities are not available, the social worker should work with community leaders to establish them.

Source: From T. O. Carlton and M. D. G. Stephenson, "Social Work and the Management of Severe Head Injury" in *Social Science and Medicine, 31,* pp. 8–10, copyright © 1990 by Allyn & Bacon. Adapted by permission.

16. Enhance the parents' self-esteem by pointing out that they have control over their lives.
17. Help the parents develop realistic expectations about the length of time needed for their brain-injured child to show improvements so that they can plan accordingly.
18. Support the parents' efforts to set limits on the brain-injured child's behavior.
19. Encourage the parents to continue to pursue activities that they enjoy; they must take care of themselves if they are going to provide the brain-injured child with

good care. They will need to find respite care so that they can have some time alone, with each other, and with any other children in the family.

20. Discourage the parents from making their brain-injured child into a new person.

21. Recognize that some parents of brain-injured children may resist your rehabilitation efforts to foster independence in the child. Caring for a brain-injured child may give purpose to an otherwise meaningless existence. In such cases, you will need to work even harder to help the parents carry out the rehabilitation program.

22. Recommend that the parents seek drop-in counseling; brief, limited therapy to work through specific problems; support groups; or family therapy, as needed.

Exhibit 19-2 presents a mother's account of her experiences in raising her brain-injured child. It shows her turmoil and grief and how the family coped with the accident that led to the child's brain injury. The mother's account also illustrates her struggle to accept the fact that her child has permanent deficits.

Comment on Rehabilitation Programs for Brain-Injured Children

Rehabilitation efforts should be monitored constantly to determine children's progress and to ensure that the programs are not creating undue stress on them or their fami-

---

Exhibit 19-2
A Mother Speaks About Her Experiences with Her Brain-Damaged Child

---

A Mother Speaks
by Rona

"It's never the same child…after a head injury…" one of the doctors said to me several weeks after Ben's accident. I could have killed him. I didn't want to hear it. And, although I am otherwise a reasonable and logical person, I didn't believe it for more than a year. Now, nine years later, I can tell you—it's never the same family after a head injury, either.

Before that day in 1981, we were a typical all-American family. Ben's father had an important career. I, having stayed home until my children were in school all day, had become a "successful" career woman, a Public Relations Director at an area hospital. Ben's brother, age 12, was playing soccer, delivering papers, and goofing his way through junior high school. Ben, age 8, was reading everything in sight and hamming it up in class plays.

The accident happened. The particulars of what happened were gruesome beyond belief. For each family I've met since I have known head injury, the trauma that precipitated the injury was gruesome beyond belief. In one case there may have been a drunk driver, in another a lightning strike in the swimming pool, in another some momentary change in routine which preceded the brain injury and which will haunt the sur-

viving family members for the rest of their lives. I felt that no other grief could supersede what my family felt. And I strongly suspected that one does not recover from a grief of that magnitude.

Then it began. Only I didn't realize for more than a year that it was beginning. In addition to the trauma to Ben's brain, some terrible trauma began to happen to each of us in the family. We were never the same after that trauma. Like Ben, we were left with disabilities and deficits of our own, forced to relearn everything we'd ever known, forced to reshape our lives around unthinkable reality. Parts of the trauma were shared with others, but much of it wasn't. Friends and neighbors couldn't understand Ben's problems and his rehabilitation. They also could not understand what each of us in Ben's family went through over the next few years. Our own extended family members did not even understand what we were going through. The head injury professionals who we were dealing with certainly did not understand.

Ben was in a coma for about a week. We didn't know if he would ever breathe, see, hear, speak, swallow, walk, or talk again. Then he regained consciousness. In addition to our relief, we faced a new realization. Yes, he could breathe.

But could he see? Could he hear? Would any of his other faculties ever work again? Over the next few months, we found that he could see, he could hear, he could read, but again, in addition to our relief, there was horror. What good was hearing or seeing when cognition was faulty? "Please let him see again," we had prayed. We felt guilt over having our prayers answered and being dissatisfied with the answer we were granted.

From the beginning I believed that if I only found the right doctor, therapist, or treatment my son could be Ben again. At the end of the first year of his recovery, however, I began to understand that, no matter what, he would never be the same Ben again. That's when I began to put together the information I had been told in the rehabilitation center with the realization that the world did not operate as I had always assumed it did. Things do not happen in a rational fashion. Our best efforts do not always earn us what we seek.

As any mother would, I was willing to do anything under the sun to restore my child to health. (I had decided that I was willing to accept a dysfunctional limb or two.) I was trying as hard as I could to find the answers to Ben's problems. But as much as I did, the answers weren't to

(Continued)

Exhibit 19-2 (*Continued*)

be found. But, as I found more and more dead ends, I began to see that what needed fixing was my view of the world. Ben, although he continues to this day to surprise me with new skills and insights, was not going to be the old Ben ever again. In order to do the things that Ben now needed of me, I was going to have to accept his head injury as a fact.

I would say that this thrashing and kicking as I struggled to accept Ben's injury took four years. This is the period when I felt so hostile toward professionals. I felt like saying to them, "You are asking me to accept what is unacceptable. You have the help my child needs but in order to access that help I have to be willing to accept my child's permanent disability." Actually, I still get around accepting the injury when I can. An occupational therapist told me Ben's uncoordinated hands would never be able to button shirts, so I should sew Velcro down the front of his shirts. I defiantly found any number of shirts that can be worn without buttoning—rugby shirts, sweaters, sweatshirts. The only time Ben wears a shirt that needs to be buttoned is when he goes to a prom or a wedding.

Through this long period of fighting to the death my old view of a world that was fair, I fought many other things. I continued to negotiate with the system to get things Ben needed: therapies, school programs, tieless shoelaces. All the while I was really angry. I didn't want to be a therapist and a case manager and a parent fighting the system. I didn't have time or energy left after taking care of Ben to do all the extra running and research and politicking. Other mothers weren't called upon to scale these impossible cliffs. But if I didn't get these things for Ben, who would? Probably the pace of things that needed to be done is what kept me sane. The more time there was to think, the worse things seemed.

But I did come out on the other end. Finally one day I gave in and said, "OK, I really loved that other child I had, and I'd still like to have him back, but if I can't have that, then I guess I'll make this child the spunkiest head-injured child on the face of the earth." And I have to admit that although I hated the fighting that I had to do for Ben, I was sometimes quite successful at it.

So that's where we are. My life will never be the same as the result of this head injury. My child may never be independent enough to live on his own. All my plans revolve around first making arrangements for Ben. His evening bath routine takes an hour every night. The further we stray from the usual structure of his day, the more problem behavior we encounter. But more profoundly, I have had to become a person other than the one I was nine years ago in order to traverse this course life dealt me. There are many wonderful things that have come about as a result of this change. I have learned an incredible amount about who I am and how I got to be where I am. I have met people whose patience awes me as they care for and teach Ben and others like him. I have felt unbelievable kindnesses that sometimes offset the hurt the injury caused. And I have a completely altered view of the worth of a person, now that IQ is no longer a measurement that means anything.

It isn't fair of me to speak for the other members of the family except to say that each of us suffered through those painful first days and years in our own (no doubt equally painful) way. Ben's father must have felt even more acutely than I the helplessness at not being able to "provide" recovery for Ben. While I was sleeping in Ben's hospital room each night, totally absorbed in rebirthing this child into wellness, he was discussing technical points with neurologists and rigging mechanical contraptions on wheelchairs. Our communication dwindled and died. Life revolved around Ben's rehabilitation at my emotional level and his factual level. All other facts of our former lives had ceased. When once or twice we tried to get away neither of us had much energy or interest in a life outside of the hospital room. We are now divorced. The tragedy, and I have found it is not unusual among head injury families, is that each of us faced this life crisis without the support of the one person who was most in a position to understand.

Ben's brother, three years older, although he doesn't openly discuss it, has also had a major life change. When his brother was hurt, he was thrust from the world of a goofier-than-most 12 year old into adult realities almost overnight. He learned, as I did, that everything cannot be fixed, that life is incredibly fragile and that even adults don't know what to do sometimes. He experienced the notoriety of his family on the front page of the newspaper. He had friends ask him if his brother was a "vegetable." He suddenly had to relinquish most of our attention while we handled Ben's rehabilitation. He certainly saw the withering of our social life as friends grew weary of our obsession with head injury. His future has changed. In some ways, although I hope not in too burdensome a way, his brother will always be a child for him to watch out for.

Again, these changes have not been without their bright sides. Ben's brother quickly became a charming, helpful, and responsible young man at age 13. His goofiness dwindled and his character rose to the occasion. He caused us few worries—at a time when we would have been admittedly ill equipped to handle them. He learned to ride the bus the twenty minutes to visit his brother on school holidays. He took care of Ben with great humor, and readily absented himself when he'd run out of patience. Because he was so honest, we didn't need to worry that he was being taken advantage of.

One of the fathers in the support group I attend calls it "dashed hopes." Yes, surely our original hopes for Ben have been dashed. Also many of our original hopes for ourselves have been dashed. We have disabilities and deficits—holes in our hearts—where the prior life once was. Now, nine years later, we all have new hopes, possibly even nobler hopes than the first ones. But we are veterans of a battle we wished we never had to fight.

Source: Reprinted, with permission of the author and publisher, from P. R. Sachs, *Treating Families of Brain-Injury Survivors,* pp. 49–52, copyright 1991 by Springer Publishing Company, New York 10012.

lies. If the rehabilitation goals are met, children will be better able to cope with the brain injury and improve the quality of their lives. This means having a more positive attitude toward school, achieving improved school grades, carrying out assignments with minimal help, participating in extracurricular activities, resuming and maintaining friendships, being cooperative and dependable, and assuming increased responsibility at home for personal and household chores. Many brain-injured children can make significant progress even though they may not become fully independent or regain their former level of skills. Rehabilitation efforts will improve as we learn more about how brain injury affects cognitive, linguistic, affective, and behavioral processes and their interactions.

CONCLUDING COMMENT ON INTERVIEWING BRAIN-INJURED CHILDREN AND THEIR PARENTS

As in all clinical cases, you will want to base your interpretations, conclusions, and recommendations on a careful analysis of all available information. Focus on children's deficits and strengths; their awareness and acceptance of their deficits; their motivation; the environmental supports available to them; the degree of accommodation they and their parents have made to any changes in their personality, temperament, cognitive abilities, and social skills; and their goals and future plans (Kay & Silver, 1989). The behavior of brain-injured children must be considered in relation to their organically based neuropsychological deficits (Kay & Silver, 1989)—that is, don't conclude that brain-injured children are lazy, apathetic, and lacking initiative when, in fact, their behavior may be directly related to their organic impairment.

Brain injuries have potentially devastating effects on young children (Johnson, Uttley, & Wyke, 1989).

Trauma to the brain exerts perhaps the highest toll among all injuries, simply because it may dramatically alter the quality of future life for its survivors and their families.... Nonetheless, we as a society continually fail to see the full implications of disability resulting from head injury in childhood...including increased [need for] educational support, lost or diminished careers, poor social and emotional adjustment, and later demands on mental health services.

Accidental head injury is not inevitable; many causes are preventable, given adequate attention to pedestrian safety and playground construction, for example. Yet we continue to accept the carnage resulting from road traffic accidents, fail to implement comprehensive legislation for seat belt restraints and fail to offer adequate protection from nonaccidental injuries. Attention to such factors may help to reduce the probability of an increasingly disabled young population. In the absence of any effective treatments for the consequences of head injury, such preventative measures are urgently needed and may prove substantially cheaper than the increasing demands for continuing care as the true morbidity of this population is recognized. (pp. xv–xvi)

It behooves us as a society to develop safer automobiles, to insist that all children wear seat belts when they are in an automobile, to encourage children to wear safety helmets when they ride a bike and use a skateboard or rollerblades, and to seek other ways to prevent accidental head injuries in children.

THINKING THROUGH THE ISSUES

Do you know a child or an adult who has had a brain injury? If so, what is the child or adult like? In what way has the brain injury affected him or her?

Why is it difficult to evaluate aphasic disturbances in young children?

What behavioral observations are particularly important in interviews with brain-injured children?

After you complete an interview with a child who was referred to you for psychological problems, under what conditions would you refer the child to a neuropsychologist or to a neurologist?

What can you do to educate teachers and others who may work with brain-injured children about the relationship between the brain damage and the brain-injured children's behavior?

Do you think that you have the patience to work with brain-injured children?

Why do you think mental health professionals can play an important role in the rehabilitation of brain-injured children?

Do you believe that it will be possible to reduce the incidence of brain injury in children in the future? What is the basis for your answer?

SUMMARY

1. Brain injury refers to any disruption in brain structure (anatomy) or physiology.
2. The assessment of brain damage is a complex and exacting task, requiring extensive specialized professional knowledge and interdisciplinary cooperation.
3. Mental health clinicians can help brain-injured children and their parents, families, and teachers by pointing out to all parties involved how brain injury affects children's cognitive functioning, affective reactions, personality, and temperament and by helping the parents, teachers, and children carry out the rehabilitation efforts needed to deal with changes in children's functioning.

Background Considerations in Understanding Brain Functions
4. The human brain is a constantly changing constellation of relationships among billions of cells. Complex networks of neurons are linked by pathways forged, then continually revised, in response to experience.
5. There is no way to separate the brain's neural structure from the influence of the world that nurtures it.
6. No two brains are identical, and the complex wiring of each brain is so unique that it is unlikely that any two people perceive the world in quite the same way.

7. The most efficient brains appear also to be the smartest, with the brains of those with the highest IQs using the least energy.

8. Small structural abnormalities appear to develop in the brains of people with Alzheimer's disease and Huntington's chorea long before any noticeable behavioral symptoms can be diagnosed.

9. Minor alterations in neural circuits for vision and hearing may be responsible for dyslexia; brain abnormalities in regions involved in inhibiting mental activity could be the cause of attention-deficit/hyperactivity disorder.

10. Lateralization refers to the specialization of the two hemispheres of the cerebral cortex for cognitive, perceptual, motor, and sensory activities.

11. In general, the side of the brain that controls sensorimotor activities is opposite to the side of the body that carries out the activity.

12. In nearly all right-handed individuals and in about two-thirds of left-handed individuals, the left hemisphere is primarily responsible for verbal functions—including reading and writing, understanding and speaking, verbal ideation, verbal memory, and certain aspects of arithmetic ability.

13. Left hemisphere processing has been described as analytic, sequential, serial, and differential.

14. The right hemisphere specializes in nonverbal, perceptual, and spatial functions—including spatial visualization, visual learning and memory, arithmetical calculations involving spatial organization of the problem elements, complex visual-motor organization, and nonverbal sequencing.

15. Right hemisphere processing is considered holistic, simultaneous, gestalt-like, parallel, and integrative.

16. The frontal lobes are associated with the planning, initiation, and modulation of behavior and with expressive verbal fluency, control of motor functions, and motor planning.

17. The temporal lobes are associated with auditory perception, auditory comprehension, verbal memory, and some forms of visual processing.

18. The parietal lobes are associated with somatosensory functions, visual-spatial ability, and the integration of visual, somatosensory, and auditory stimuli.

19. The occipital lobes are associated with visual perception, elaboration and synthesis of visual information, and the integration of visual information with the information gathered by the auditory and other sensory systems.

20. Injuries to the cerebral hemispheres (frontal, temporal, parietal, and occipital lobes) and to subcortical centers (such as the basal ganglia and hippocampal structures) may lead to disorders in cognition, memory, affect, and motivation.

21. Lateralization develops gradually in children, evidenced by the replacement of bilateral movements with unilateral movements.

22. Research suggests that linguistic functions are localized in the left hemisphere at birth for children of both sexes.

23. Functions lateralized in the right hemisphere are less straightforward—certain abilities are lateralized at birth, whereas others become lateralized with age.

24. Lateral specialization for all cognitive, sensory, and motor functions cannot be clearly established for several reasons.

25. Once language develops, the left hemisphere probably is dominant for language for most individuals; the right hemisphere has limited potential for language functions.

26. A primary function of the right hemisphere may be to act as a concrete spatial synthesizer, allowing information to be perceived as a meaningful unit.

Causes of Brain Injury

27. Brain injuries result from factors present before birth and from injuries sustained during the birth process, immediately after birth, or some time after birth.

28. Prenatal environmental factors (factors existing or occurring before birth) that contribute to brain damage include severe maternal malnutrition; maternal use of alcohol, drugs, or tobacco; maternal exposure to toxic substances; maternal infections due to viruses or bacteria; maternal illnesses; and radiation.

29. In the perinatal period (the period shortly before and after birth), conditions that may lead to brain damage include prematurity, physical trauma associated with labor and delivery, asphyxia, hypoglycemia, infections such as meningitis and encephalitis, kernicterus, and maternal sensitization.

30. During the postnatal period (the period after birth), abnormalities of the nervous system may occur because of hydrocephaly, endocrine dysfunctions, and metabolic disorders.

31. During infancy, early childhood, and adolescence, brain damage may be caused by poor nutrition, trauma, infection, radiation, drug and alcohol abuse, and exposure to neurotoxins.

32. Early signs of brain injury include occasions of prolonged nausea and vomiting not related to common illnesses; changes in energy level; and changes in the child's appearance, behavior, school performance, personality, or development.

Traumatic Brain Injury

33. Each year approximately 1 million children in the United States sustain head injuries from falls, child maltreatment, recreational accidents, or motor vehicle accidents.

34. Traumatic brain injury is a threat not only to a child's quality of life—including life style, education, social and recreational activities, interpersonal relationships, freedom to make changes, and control over his or her being and destiny—but also to his or her survival.

35. In an open-head injury, the skull usually is penetrated by a high-velocity projectile, such as a bullet, and contact occurs between the brain tissue and the outside environment.

36. Closed-head injuries may damage the brain severely, although the skull is not penetrated.

37. Motor vehicle accidents are the most frequent cause of closed-head injuries.

38. Children with a traumatic brain injury may have a good recovery, a moderate disability, or a severe disability; become vegetative; or possibly die.

Specific Effects of Brain Injury in Children

39. Brain injury may produce a general deterioration in all or most aspects of functioning, differential symptoms, highly specific symptoms, subtle symptoms, symptoms not seen until several years later, or no observable symptoms at all.

40. The effects of brain injury on young children may not be fully known until several years after the injury, when the children are expected to use more complex and higher-level cognitive and behavioral processes.

41. Some behavioral symptoms present during the early stages of recovery—such as delusions, irritability, hallucinations, and suspiciousness—may result from cognitive changes that interfere with the thinking of brain-injured children.

42. In brain injury, automatic processing may be lost.

43. Cognitive disturbances after brain injury may include disorders of attention and concentration; disorders of planning,

initiating, and maintaining goal-directed activities; disorders of judgment and perception; disorders of learning and memory; disorders in the speed of information processing; disorders of language and communication; and disorders of spatial analysis and integration.

44. Some cognitive impairments diminish with time; others are relatively resistant to change but still may diminish with time; and still others are relatively permanent.

45. Children with brain injuries may have cognitive impairments that are not evident in the interview.

46. Agnosia is a central nervous system disorder manifested through impaired ability to recognize familiar objects perceived via the senses.

47. Apraxia is a central nervous system disorder manifested through impaired ability to execute learned movements or to carry out purposeful or skilled acts.

48. Aphasia is a central nervous system dysfunction manifested through disorders in the perception, production, and symbolic use of language.

49. Aphasia may involve expressive components, receptive components, or both.

50. Expressive aphasia reflects impaired ability to use spoken and/or written language.

51. Receptive aphasia reflects impaired ability to understand spoken and/or written language.

52. Global aphasia, or mixed-type aphasia, reflects impaired abilities in both expressive and receptive domains.

53. The changes in temperament, personality, and psychosocial functioning that brain-injured children may exhibit relate both to their brain injury and to their pre-existing personality and temperament.

54. Symptoms of brain-injured children include anxiety, irritability, impulsivity, and heightened emotionality; denial of illness; paranoid ideation and psychomotor agitation; depression and amotivational states; and psychosocial disturbances.

55. Some brain-injured children show a pattern of behavior associated with overarousal, whereas others show a pattern of behavior associated with underarousal.

56. There is no simple way to interpret the behavioral symptoms of brain-injured children.

57. Behavioral symptoms may (a) be neurologically based, reflecting, in part, impairment of cognitive, emotional, or psychosocial functions directly associated with neurological insult, (b) be emotional reactions to failures or to performance difficulties, (c) reflect preexisting personality patterns, or (d) be a combination of all of the above.

58. Many behavioral symptoms of brain-injured children—such as depression, emotional lability, limited motivation, and paranoid ideations—may be as neurologically based as language and motor symptoms, such as aphasia and hemiplegia.

59. When children sustain brain injury, there may be interference with development rather than a striking loss of function.

60. If the interference is global, mental retardation may be the result; if it is region-specific, specific difficulties may result, such as difficulties with speech or with the recognition of shapes.

61. Some evidence suggests that children's skills may be more affected by brain damage if they are in the most rapid stage of development than if they are well-consolidated.

62. The progress of myelination in various anatomical regions affects behavioral development.

63. Myelination refers to the process of insulating, or coating, the axon of the neuron.

64. Myelination is essential in facilitating the speed with which information is passed along an axon.

65. The types of behavioral difficulties that occur in brain-injured children could be related to the neurostructural components undergoing the most rapid development at the time of the brain injury.

66. Cerebral plasticity may involve the taking over, by one part of the brain, of functions impaired by lesions in another part of the brain.

67. Alternatively, cerebral plasticity may involve the functional reorganization of the central nervous system to restore impaired functions.

68. Cerebral plasticity operates primarily between birth and 4 or 5 years of age, but it can occur at any age.

69. Studies demonstrate that children do not necessarily completely recover all of their functions after brain injury.

70. Prognostic statements about children's ability to recover from brain injury must be made with caution.

71. It is more difficult to evaluate language, speech, and other functions in children than in adults because young children have developed only rudimentary skills in these areas.

Diagnostic Techniques for Brain-Injured Children

72. A neurological examination includes a clinical history, a mental status examination, and a study of cranial nerves, motor functions, coordination, sensory functions, and gait; several laboratory procedures may augment the neurological examination.

73. Computed tomography (CT scan) is an imaging technique in which an array of detectors is used to collect information from an x-ray beam that has passed through the brain or another body part.

74. Positron emission tomography (PET scan) is a scanning method that produces a cross-sectional image of radioactivity in the brain following intravenous injection of a radioactive substance.

75. Magnetic resonance imaging (MRI) provides a two-dimensional intensity plot of a cross-sectional slice of any part of the body.

76. Electroencephalography (EEG) is a procedure in which electrodes are placed on the scalp to record the electrical activity of the brain.

77. Cerebral angiography involves radiographic recordings of internal structures of the vascular system of the brain.

78. Single photon emission computed tomography (SPECT) provides a three-dimensional representation of regional cerebral blood flow.

79. The neurological examination may reveal hard signs or soft signs of possible brain damage.

80. Hard signs are those that are fairly definitive indicators of cerebral dysfunction and are usually correlated with other independent evidence of brain damage, such as the results of CT scans or EEGs.

81. Soft signs are mild and equivocal neurological irregularities in sensorimotor functions.

82. The primary aims of the neuropsychological examination are to draw inferences about the organic integrity of the cerebral hemispheres and to specify the adaptive strengths and weaknesses of brain-injured children.

83. A neuropsychological examination complements a neurological examination.

84. The neuropsychological examination provides a profile of cognitive ability, sensorimotor functioning, and affective reactions.

Interviewing Brain-Injured Children

85. Children sustaining severe head injury may be difficult to interview, especially if their speech is impaired, they have aphasic disturbances, or they have not fully regained consciousness.

86. If you interview a child shortly after a trauma, look for the child's ability to maintain alertness; attend to visual stimuli; scan or follow your movements; respond to sounds; follow your simple requests; sit, walk, or write with adequate muscle tone; make purposeful movements; and vocalize.

87. During the interview, be alert to brain-injured children's level of consciousness, language, memory, intellectual and cognitive functioning, and sensorimotor functioning.

88. Emphasize your use of praise, encouragement, and constructive comments with brain-injured children.

89. Before beginning the interview, reduce all potential sources of distraction in the room.

90. Minimize children's frustration and reduce their fatigue during the interview.

91. Experiment with different communication methods, rates of communication, and types of content to find the most effective way to communicate with brain-injured children.

Observing Brain-Injured Children

92. Observing brain-injured children is an important component of the interview. Ideally, you should observe children in several settings.

93. Important areas to observe include the brain-injured child's appearance, vocabulary and language, ability to carry on a conversation, behavior, attention span, affect, tempo of body movements, visual-spatial skills, sensory skills, motor skills, and level of consciousness.

94. Pay careful attention to the child's language, and consider what is normal for his or her age.

95. For children who have mastered speech, look for language-processing difficulties.

96. Observing how brain-injured children function in their natural environment will add important information to the assessment.

97. When you observe brain-injured children in natural settings, note how they perform daily activities, use language, use motor skills, cope with different environments, accomplish new learning, and use strategies in different settings.

Interviewing Parents of Brain-Injured Children

98. When parents learn that their child has a brain injury, they may have a variety of reactions, including denial, depression, irritability, anxiety, frustration, feelings of inadequacy, annoyance, anger, feelings of being trapped, fear of further deterioration in their child, and guilt over their failure to prevent the injury.

99. Interview one or both parents to obtain a detailed clinical and developmental history of the child.

100. When you interview the child's parents, recognize that they may not always be objective.

Evaluating the Assessment Findings for Brain-Injured Children

101. To evaluate the assessment findings, you will want to review the information obtained from (a) the clinical assessment interview with the child, (b) the mental status evaluation of the child, (c) the interviews with the child's parents, relatives, friends, and teachers about how the child is currently functioning, how the child functioned before the injury, and how the family and school are coping with the child's disability, and (d) the formal evaluations conducted by neuropsychologists, neurologists, speech/language pathologists, and other professionals.

102. In reviewing the information obtained by the multidisciplinary health care team in cases of traumatic brain injury, note the results of the neurological and neuropsychological evaluations; how the child was functioning before the injury; the results of the family study; any physical, sensory, affective, cognitive, and social/personality problems that the child may have; whether the child has an appreciation of the nature and extent of his or her injuries; and whether the family is able to participate in the rehabilitation efforts.

103. When you evaluate the information from the child's case history, use, in part, a normative-developmental framework.

104. When the multidisciplinary health care team designs a rehabilitation program, the following aspects of the brain-injured child's functioning will likely be considered: complex attention and speed of information processing, learning and memory, abstraction and integration of information, executive functioning, and behavior modulation.

105. Corroborate any information obtained from the child—such as the nature of the trauma, length of unconsciousness, perceived changes in functioning, and seizure history—with information obtained from the parents and from the medical records.

106. Overall, the severity of children's head injuries is the best predictor of long-term outcome.

107. The poorest prognosis is associated with a long period of unconsciousness, skull fracture, poor neurological status, and the presence of posttraumatic seizures.

Rehabilitation Programs for Brain-Injured Children

108. Rehabilitation programs are designed to help brain-injured children become more independent by increasing their functional and adaptive skills.

109. The focus of rehabilitation programs is on helping brain-injured children regain former cognitive skills, learn new skills to compensate for lost or impaired abilities, develop more organized behavior, reduce the level of confusion, improve interpersonal skills, and improve ability to cope with stress.

110. Rehabilitation goals should be appropriate to each brain-injured child's physical and neuropsychological status, including specific dysfunctions, and be geared to his or her readiness and motivation to reach the goals.

111. Some rehabilitation goals may be difficult to achieve because children with acquired brain injury may have limited understanding of their condition.

112. Consumption of alcohol can complicate both physical recovery from a head injury and the child's response to the head injury.

113. Chronic abuse of alcohol can produce cognitive deficits that interact with those produced by the traumatic brain injury.

114. Rehabilitation efforts must simultaneously consider several dimensions, including premorbid level of functioning, current level of functioning, length of time since injury, differential rate of improvement, need for re-examination, and familial issues.

115. A cognitive-behavioral orientation is useful for remediating brain-injured children's neuropsychologically mediated problems.

116. Ten strategies—focusing on involvement, structure, adequate presentation, consistency, repetition, specificity, practicality, reward, meaningfulness, and communication—will be useful in helping brain-injured children improve their functioning.

117. In formulating rehabilitation strategies for brain-injured children returning to school, consider first what deficits the children have and what effects their cognitive impairments may have on learning experiences.

118. When you observe classrooms that brain-injured children are attending, consider environmental variables, the schedule of activities, cuing systems, materials, instructional aids, classroom aids, instructional methods, work expectations, testing methods, and motivational variables.

119. Psychotherapy focuses on helping brain-injured children understand what has happened to them because of the brain injury, comprehend the meaning and consequences of the brain injury in their life, achieve a sense of self-acceptance and forgiveness of self and others who may have been responsible for the accident, make realistic commitments to school (and work, where applicable) and to interpersonal relations, improve social competence, develop behavioral strategies to compensate for deficits, and develop realistic goals.

120. A brain-injured child's recovery will, in part, depend on the level of family support she or he receives and on the family's ability to manage the child's day-to-day problems.

121. When children sustain a brain injury (or have other types of injuries or chronic illnesses), family patterns may change.

122. The effect that a brain-injured child will have on his or her family will depend on the type of onset of the child's injury, the severity of the child's injury, the extent of the child's deficits, the length of time the child was hospitalized, the family's ability to pay for the needed treatments, the prognosis, and how the family was functioning before the child's brain injury.

123. Most families will experience stress if their children are hospitalized.

124. The degree of brain-injured children's physical disability typically is not the crucial factor in causing stress in families; rather, it is children's behavioral, cognitive, and affective deficits that are likely to influence family harmony.

125. Helping families of brain-injured children may take several years, not just weeks or months.

126. Because the stress of caring for brain-injured children at home can be overwhelming, arrange for home services and for counseling for the family members, if needed.

127. Rehabilitation efforts should be monitored constantly to determine children's progress and to ensure that the programs are not creating undue stress on them or their families.

128. Because brain injuries have potentially devastating effects on young children, society must seek ways to prevent accidental head injuries in children.

KEY TERMS, CONCEPTS, AND NAMES

Brain injury (p. 615)
Lateralization (p. 616)
Sensorimotor activities (p. 616)
Higher-level functions (p. 616)
Left cerebral hemisphere (p. 616)
Right cerebral hemisphere (p. 616)
Frontal lobes (p. 616)
Temporal lobes (p. 616)
Parietal lobes (p. 616)
Occipital lobes (p. 616)
Prenatal period (p. 618)
Prenatal environmental factors (p. 618)
Perinatal period (p. 618)
Asphyxia (p. 618)
Hypoglycemia (p. 618)
Meningitis (p. 618)
Encephalitis (p. 618)
Kernicterus (p. 618)
Rh incompatibility (p. 618)
Postnatal period (p. 618)
Hydrocephaly (p. 618)
Hypothyroidism (p. 618)
Tay-Sachs disease (p. 618)
PKU (p. 618)
Galactosemia (p. 618)
Neurotoxins (p. 619)
Traumatic brain injury (p. 619)
Open-head injury (p. 619)
Focal effects (p. 619)
Closed-head injuries (p. 619)
Multifocal effects (Diffuse effects) (p. 619)
Contrecoup (p. 619)
Edema (p. 619)
Glasgow Outcome Scale (p. 619)
Cognitive disturbances (p. 621)
Agnosia (p. 621)
Visual agnosia (p. 621)
Prosopagnosia (p. 621)
Auditory agnosia (p. 621)
Tactile agnosia (p. 621)
Visual-spatial agnosia (p. 622)
Apraxia (p. 622)
Ideomotor apraxia (p. 622)
Ideational apraxia (p. 623)
Facial apraxia (p. 623)
Limb-kinetic apraxia (p. 623)
Constructional apraxia (p. 623)
Dressing apraxia (p. 623)
Aphasia (p. 623)
Congenital aphasia (p. 623)
Developmental language disorder (p. 623)
Acquired aphasia (p. 623)
Expressive aphasia (p. 623)
Agraphia (p. 623)
Agrammatism (p. 623)
Acalculia (p. 623)
Receptive aphasia (p. 623)
Auditory aphasia (p. 623)

Alexia (p. 623)
Global aphasia (Mixed-type aphasia) (p. 623)
Anosognosia (p. 626)
Overarousal (p. 626)
Underarousal (p. 626)
Myelination (p. 628)
Cerebral plasticity (p. 629)
Neurological examination (p. 630)
Lower-level functions (p. 630)
Motor functioning tests (p. 630)
Standard neurological techniques (p. 630)
Bilateral simultaneous stimulation (p. 630)
Dichotic stimulation (p. 630)
Computed tomography (CT scan) (p. 630)
Positron emission tomography (PET scan) (p. 630)
Magnetic resonance imaging (MRI) (p. 630)
Electroencephalography (EEG) (p. 630)
Computerized electroencephalography (CEEG) (p. 630)
Cerebral angiography (p. 630)
Single photon emission computed tomography (SPECT) (p. 630)
Hard signs of possible brain injury (p. 631)
Soft signs of possible brain injury (p. 631)
Choreiform limb movements (p. 631)
Dysdiadochokinesia (p. 631)
Dysgraphesthesia (p. 631)
Astereognosis (p. 631)
Neuropsychological examination (p. 631)
Base-line measures (p. 632)
Anterograde amnesia (p. 632)
Retrograde amnesia (p. 632)
Perseverative and avoidance behaviors (p. 633)
Coma (p. 634)
Semicoma (Stupor) (p. 635)
Lethargic level of consciousness (p. 635)
Alert level of consciousness (p. 635)
At-rest tremors (p. 635)
Intention tremors (p. 635)
Tics (p. 635)
Athetoid movements (p. 635)
Hypertonia (p. 635)
Hypotonia (p. 635)
Atonia (p. 635)
Dystonia (p. 635)
Akinesia (p. 635)
Akathesia (p. 635)
Body symmetries (p. 635)
Prognosis in cases of brain injury (p. 638)
Rehabilitation programs for brain-injured children (p. 641)
Cognitive-behavioral rehabilitation (p. 643)
Psychotherapy (p. 651)
Stresses faced by families of brain-injured children (p. 652)
Anomia (p. 653)

STUDY QUESTIONS

1. Discuss some recent developments in the neurosciences concerning brain functioning.
2. Discuss the causes of brain injury, using a developmental perspective. Include in your discussion factors that may cause brain injury during the prenatal period, the perinatal period, the postnatal period, and the periods of infancy, early childhood, and adolescence.
3. Discuss traumatic brain injury. Include in your discussion incidence of traumatic brain injury, types of traumatic brain injuries, and types of recovery.
4. Discuss the lateralization of cognitive, perceptual, and motor activities.
5. Brain injury produces specific as well as diverse effects. Describe some cognitive and behavioral symptoms of brain injury. Include in your discussion (a) symptoms associated with aphasia, agnosia, and apraxia and (b) possible interpretations of behavioral symptoms of brain injury.
6. Discuss how brain injury may affect children and adults in different ways.
7. Discuss why the assumption of recovery of brain functioning in brain-injured children has been questioned. What position does the text advocate about recovery of functions in brain-injured children, and what reasons does it offer for this position?
8. Describe a neurological examination. Include in your discussion (a) the components of the examination, (b) a brief description of several scanning and radiographic methods, and (c) examples of several of hard and soft signs of possible brain damage that may be found on the neurological examination.
9. Describe a neuropsychological examination. In what way does the neuropsychological examination complement a neurological examination? Include in your discussion how a neuropsychological examination contributes to the diagnostic process.
10. Discuss some techniques for interviewing brain-injured children. Include in your discussion areas to cover in the interview, how to establish rapport, handling perseverative and avoidance behaviors, and techniques for working with language-impaired brain-injured children.
11. What are some important areas to observe when interviewing a brain-injured child? Include in your discussion what you should observe in the child's language, listening behaviors, and motor movements.
12. What are some key areas to focus on in interviewing a brain-injured child for a rehabilitation program?
13. When you interview parents of a brain-injured child, what are some important areas to inquire about?
14. After you have interviewed a brain-injured child and her or his parents and have read the neurological and neuropsychological reports, what information would you want to discuss in your report?
15. What areas are particularly important to cover when you are evaluating a brain-injured child's ability to perform activities of daily living?
16. What factors should you consider in offering a prognosis for a brain-injured child?
17. What are some goals of a rehabilitation program for brain-injured children? Use a developmental framework, in part, in your discussion. Also discuss some important factors in designing the rehabilitation program.
18. The text discusses two general rehabilitation orientations used with brain-injured children: the cognitive-behavioral and the psychotherapeutic. Compare and contrast these two orientations.

19. Discuss several specific rehabilitation strategies that are useful for children with brain injuries.

20. If you were a consultant to a school, what would you tell school personnel about how to work with brain-injured children?

21. Discuss the following proposition: "The brain-injured child's recovery will, in part, depend on the level of family support he or she receives and on the family's ability to manage the child's day-to-day activities." Include in your discussion ways to help family members cope with their brain-injured child.

SECTION V

CHILD MALTREATMENT

Section V covers issues in interviewing in cases of alleged or confirmed child maltreatment. Chapters 20 and 21 present background considerations in interviewing children who have been maltreated or who are alleged to have been maltreated. Chapter 22 deals with techniques for interviewing children, their families, and the alleged offender, and Chapter 23 focuses on evaluating the interview findings and formulating interventions. In this text, the term *maltreatment* refers to physical abuse, sexual abuse, emotional abuse (also referred to as emotional/psychological abuse), and neglect. Individuals who commit child maltreatment are referred to as *offenders, perpetrators,* or *abusers;* all three terms are in current use.

In-depth interviews of children, their parents, and the suspected perpetrators in cases of alleged or known child maltreatment are usually conducted by individuals working in Child Protective Services, law enforcement agencies, or district or county attorneys' offices. Consequently, much of the material in Chapters 22 and 23 will be of primary interest to individuals who plan to work or who do work in these agencies. However, the interviewing principles and techniques described in these chapters also should be of interest to other individuals engaged in human services work.

The material in Section V will sensitize you to issues involved in interviewing children, their families, suspected abusers, and known abusers. After studying the information in this section, you will be in a better position to recognize signs of child maltreatment, establish rapport with interviewees, deal effectively with other professionals and agencies working in the field of maltreatment, and have realistic expectations about possible interventions and their effectiveness.

20

BACKGROUND CONSIDERATIONS IN CHILD MALTREATMENT, PART I

When young lips have drunk deep of the bitter waters of Hate, Suspicion and Despair, all the love in the world will not take away that knowledge.

—Rudyard Kipling

Goals and Objectives

This chapter is designed to enable you to:

- Describe the most prevalent types of child maltreatment
- Discuss factors involved in reporting maltreatment
- Understand child maltreatment as a social problem
- Discuss the reasons why individuals may become offenders
- Understand the relationship between domestic violence and child maltreatment
- Discuss maltreatment in facilities, institutions, and foster homes

The information in this chapter will, first, familiarize you with current definitions of child maltreatment. Second, it will help you understand the extent of the problem and the reasons why children are maltreated. Third, it will familiarize you with laws covering the reporting of child maltreatment. *You should recognize that child maltreatment often represents a repetitive, habitual pattern of behavior carried out by a perpetrator over a period of time with almost complete disregard for the needs, rights, and safety of the maltreated child.* Only when someone notices that something is wrong or when the child notifies someone that he or she is being maltreated can maltreatment be recognized and appropriate actions taken.

You will need to supplement the material in this chapter by studying your state's regulations about your responsibility as a mandated reporter of possible cases of child maltreatment. In addition, you should learn how personnel in public and private agencies in your community conduct child maltreatment investigations and what their roles are in child maltreatment litigation. These individuals include law enforcement personnel, Child Protective Services workers (also referred to as Department of Social Services workers or by other names, depending on the state or county), public welfare workers, child guidance counselors, attorneys, physicians (including psychiatrists), nurses, psychologists, social workers, district attorneys, and judges. Table 20-1 shows the roles and responsibilities of the three major agencies involved in child maltreatment investigation—Child Protective Services, law enforcement, and the district or county attorney's office. Note that numerous legal terms pertaining to the area of child maltreatment can be found in the Glossary.

THE CHALLENGE OF CHILD MALTREATMENT INTERVIEWING

Of all the areas covered in this book, child maltreatment interviewing is the most challenging and has the most serious consequences. The information obtained in child maltreatment interviewing may be used to decide the guilt or innocence of another person or persons. Serious consequences can result if you report inaccurate information or obtain information through methods that jeopardize the credibility of the report: (a) Children may be subjected to continued maltreatment and may even die, (b) parental rights may be terminated, (c) innocent people may be sent to jail, households destroyed, and families ruined, or (d) ethical complaints may be filed with the state licensing board about your professional competency. In some cases, the stigma of being accused of child maltreatment or the pain of being maltreated may be so great that an adult or child will attempt suicide.

Child maltreatment interviewing also is challenging because you may be uncertain of the facts, unable to determine whether maltreatment occurred, and unable to decide whether the child is at risk. Uncertainty occurs because the information may not be clear and convincing and because neither definitions nor symptoms of child maltreatment are precise. Consequently, you will have to rely on your judgment in making decisions and recommendations. Still, the interviews with the child and the alleged perpetrator will play critical roles in the investigation.

You will have more confidence in your decisions and recommendations when the information you obtain is clear and convincing. When the information is ambiguous—that is, when the facts cannot be substantiated, perhaps because of conflicting reports or a hidden agenda behind the communications—your decisions and recommendations will be fraught with uncertainty. You must act on the basis of the information you have, using your best judgment. Be prepared to change your decisions and recommendations if you obtain new information. If you follow the guidelines in this book, you should be able to do your job with a high level of professional skill, a clear conscience, and the knowledge that you are helping children, their families, and society.

THE CHILD ABUSE PREVENTION AND TREATMENT ACT

The Child Abuse Prevention and Treatment Act (CAPTA)—also referred to as Public Law 93-247 and as the Mondale Act—was passed by Congress in 1974 and has been amended and renewed several times. This law has provided the impetus for our nation's current concern with child maltreatment. The reasoning for the continued renewal of the CAPTA was cited in the 1992 amendment to the act (National Center on Child Abuse and Neglect, 1994):

SEC. 1. SHORT TITLE.
This Act may be cited as the "Child Abuse Prevention and Treatment Act."
SEC. 2. FINDINGS.
    Congress finds that—
(1) each year, hundreds of thousands of American children are victims of abuse and neglect with such numbers having increased dramatically over the past decade;
(2) many of these children and their families fail to receive adequate protection or treatment;
(3) the problem of child abuse and neglect requires a comprehensive approach that—

Table 20-1
Roles and Responsibilities of Three Agencies Involved in Child Abuse Investigations

Child Protective Services (CPS)	Law enforcement	District or county attorney's office[a]
The CPS agency/worker	The law enforcement officer generally	The prosecutor
1. accepts reports of abuse	1. responds to calls in an appropriate manner (that is, commensurate with the urgency of the call), stabilizes the crime scene, and takes initial statements as appropriate	1. actively participates in developing the case's overall investigative strategy
2. interviews alleged child victims		2. assesses the evidence collected to determine its potential utility in court
3. interviews siblings or other possible child witnesses		
4. interviews nonoffending parent(s)		3. assists in drafting search warrants
5. interviews other adult witnesses and collateral contacts	2. performs criminal history record checks on alleged offenders	4. participates in interviewing the suspected offender, when appropriate
6. interviews the alleged offender if the team determines this to be appropriate (such an interview is typically performed by law enforcement personnel)	3. collects and preserves physical evidence (for example, trace evidence or instruments used in the assault)	5. gives guidance on legal issues, such as statute of limitations and jurisdictional issues
7. arranges medical examination and psychological examinations of child and parents, if needed	4. interviews child victims or witnesses, consistent with the team's decision	6. determines appropriate charges and the best means of charging the offender (arrest versus grand jury)
8. performs risk assessment (an analytical process to assess the likelihood of future abuse)	5. conducts photo lineups or live lineups to confirm the identification of perpetrators, if necessary	7. negotiates bail or plea agreements and restrictions
9. develops a safety plan to protect the child in his or her home or the home of a relative or family friend	6. interviews adult witnesses in cooperation with CPS	8. prepares witnesses for court or oversees a court school program for children
10. petitions the juvenile or family court (through the attorney representing the agency) for custody in order to place the child in foster care	7. facilitates the use of technological investigative tools, such as equipment to monitor telephone conversations	9. presents the state's case at trial
11. secures a foster home or other appropriate placement for the child	8. interviews alleged perpetrators	
12. develops a case plan to meet the child's needs and reduce the risk of future abuse	9. takes suspects into custody, when and if appropriate	
13. arranges community services to support the plan, such as counseling or financial support for the mother if the offender has moved out of the home	10. presents criminal cases in lawsuits (a) to obtain warrants, (b) to grand juries, if used in jurisdiction, (c) at preliminary hearings, if appropriate, and (d) in criminal court	
14. evaluates the service delivery process and the progress or lack of progress by the involved family member	11. testifies in juvenile or family court, if necessary to ensure the child's protection	
15. testifies in court proceedings (juvenile, family, or criminal court, as well as grand juries if appropriate) and makes recommendations to the court about the long-term plan for permanence for the child, when and if appropriate	12. takes the child into protective custody if the CPS worker assesses that the risks require it (depending on individual state regulations)	

[a]The district attorney or county attorney (prosecutor) will serve in an advisory role, helping guide the field investigators until the case is ready for disposition.

Source: Reprinted, with changes in notation, by permission of Sage Publication Ltd from Donna Pence and C. Wilson, *Team Investigation of Child Sexual Abuse,* Copyright 1994, from pp. 32, 35–38.

(A) integrates the work of social service, legal, health, mental health, education, and substance abuse agencies and organizations;

(B) strengthens coordination among all levels of government, and with private agencies, civic, religious, and professional organizations, and individual volunteers;

(C) emphasizes the need for abuse and neglect prevention, investigation, and treatment at the neighborhood level;

(D) ensures properly trained and support staff with specialized knowledge, to carry out their child protection duties; and

(E) is sensitive to ethnic and cultural diversity;

(4) the failure to coordinate and comprehensively prevent and treat child abuse and neglect threatens the futures of tens of thousands of children and results in a cost to the Nation of billions of dollars in direct expenditures for health, social, and special educational services and ultimately in the loss of work productivity;

(5) all elements of American society have a shared responsibility in responding to this national child and family emergency;

(6) substantial reductions in the prevalence and incidence of child abuse and neglect and the alleviation of its consequences are matters of the highest national priority;

(7) national policy should strengthen families to remedy the causes of child abuse and neglect, provide support for intensive services to prevent the unnecessary removal of children from families, and promote the reunification of families if removal has taken place;

(8) the child protection system should be comprehensive, child-centered, family-focused, and community-based, should incorporate all appropriate measures to prevent the occurrence or recurrence of child abuse and neglect, and should promote physical and psychological recovery and social re-integration in an environment that fosters the health, self-respect, and dignity of the child;

(9) because of the limited resources available in low-income communities, Federal aid for the child protection system should be distributed with due regard to the relative financial need of the communities;

(10) the Federal government should ensure that every community in the United States has the fiscal, human, and technical resources necessary to develop and implement a successful and comprehensive child protection strategy;

(11) the Federal government should provide leadership and assist communities in their child protection efforts by—

(A) promoting coordinated planning among all levels of government;

(B) generating and sharing knowledge relevant to child protection, including the development of models for service delivery;

(C) strengthening the capacity of States to assist communities;

(D) allocating sufficient financial resources to assist States in implementing community plans;

(E) helping communities to carry out their child protection plans by promoting the competence of professional, paraprofessional, and volunteer resources; and

(F) providing leadership to end the abuse and neglect of the nation's children and youth. (pp. 4–5)

DEFINITION AND TYPES OF CHILD ABUSE AND NEGLECT

The Child Abuse Prevention and Treatment Act (42 U.S.C. § 5106g) defines child abuse and neglect as

- the physical or mental injury, sexual abuse or exploitation, negligent treatment, or maltreatment
- of a child under the age of 18, or except in the case of sexual abuse, the age specified by the child protection law of the State in which the child resides
- by a person (including any employee of a residential facility or any staff providing out-of-home care) who is responsible for the child's welfare
- under circumstances that indicate that the child's health or welfare is harmed or threatened thereby

CAPTA defines sexual abuse as

- the employment, use, persuasion, inducement, enticement, or coercion of any child to engage in, or assist any other person to engage in, any sexually explicit conduct or simulation of such conduct for the purpose of producing any visual depiction of such conduct, or
- the rape, molestation, prostitution, or other form of sexual exploitation of children, or incest with children

Strangers and acquaintances who maltreat children are not covered in the definition of child maltreatment. Maltreatment by strangers and acquaintances is a criminal offense and is solely the responsibility of law enforcement. Child Protective Services, however, becomes involved in cases where strangers were allowed by caregivers to maltreat their child; this is considered neglect on the part of the caregivers.

Types of Child Maltreatment

There are four major types of child maltreatment—physical abuse, sexual abuse, emotional abuse, and neglect. (Emotional abuse also is referred to as emotional/psychological abuse.) The following definitions of the four types are from a report provided by the U.S. Department of Human Services, National Center on Child Abuse and Neglect (Peterson & Urquiza, 1993, pp. 17–18, with changes in notation). The information on endangerment, which is included in the definition of neglect, was obtained from Catherine Stephenson, prosecutor from the District Attorney's Office of San Diego County (personal communication, January 1994). Although any type of child maltreatment may occur alone, different types of child maltreatment often occur in combination. Emotional abuse is almost always present when there is physical abuse, sexual abuse, or neglect.

Physical abuse is characterized by inflicting injury by hitting, punching, beating, kicking, throwing, biting, burning, shaking, or otherwise physically harming a child. The injury may be the result of a single episode or of repeated episodes. The physical trauma can range in severity from minor bruising, abrasions, lacerations, burns, eye injuries, and fractures to damage to the brain and internal organs (liver, spleen, abdomen, pancreas, and kidneys) and to death.

Sexual abuse includes a wide range of conduct including genital exposure; masturbation between adult and child;

fondling breasts, genitals, buttocks, and thighs; oral copulation; vaginal or anal penetration by finger, penis, or foreign object; dry intercourse (rubbing penis between child's thighs or anal-genital areas); making a child fondle an adult; and commercial exploitation through prostitution or the production of pornographic materials.

Emotional abuse includes acts or omissions by the parents or other persons that have caused, or could cause, emotional, behavioral, cognitive, or mental disorders. Emotional abuse exists on a continuum of habitual behavioral interactions such as belittling through comments, comparisons, and name-calling; scapegoating; humiliating; isolating; screaming; raging and terrorizing by verbally assaulting the child, threatening the child, and creating a climate of fear; rejecting by refusing to acknowledge the child's worth and the legitimacy of the child's needs; ignoring by depriving the child of essential stimulation and responsiveness; and corrupting by stimulating the child to engage in destructive antisocial behavior.

Child neglect is characterized by failure to provide for the child's basic needs. Neglect can be physical, educational, or emotional. Physical neglect includes refusal of or delay in seeking medical or dental care, abandonment, inadequate supervision, passive drug intoxication with illicit drugs, accidental ingestion of illicit drugs, and expulsion from the home or refusal to allow a runaway to return home. Educational neglect includes permission of chronic truancy, failure to enroll a child of mandatory school age, and inattention to a special educational need. Emotional neglect includes failure to respond to the child's psychological needs for attention, love, and emotional security; emotional deprivation and being psychologically inaccessible; exposure to chronic or extreme spouse or sibling abuse in the child's presence; and permission or encouragement for drug or alcohol use [and illegal activity] by the child. Endangerment, which also can be considered a form of neglect, goes beyond neglect because it may have such immediate tragic consequences. Endangerment includes failing to use a child car seat for the child, driving while intoxicated with a child in the car, and leaving loaded firearms or controlled substances in a young child's reach.

Child Maltreatment Continuum

Child maltreatment can vary on a continuum from mild maltreatment to very severe maltreatment. Table 20-2 describes different points along the continuum for each type of maltreatment. The mild category (1) is not considered to be maltreatment in the legal sense for neglect and emotional abuse, but it is for physical abuse and sexual abuse. However, the moderate, severe, and very severe categories almost always constitute abuse. The continuum does not consider children's vulnerabilities, developmental levels, and reactions, which also are critical to understanding the nature of the maltreatment.

Evidence of Child Maltreatment

Although physical abuse usually results in some observable evidence of the maltreatment, sometimes there are no tangible signs, such as in the cases when someone bangs the child's head, twists the child's arm, punches the child in the stomach, or shakes the child with force. (In infants, the latter is referred to as "shaken baby syndrome.") There also may be behavioral signs—such as fear, anxiety, sleeping difficulties, and other signs of trauma—connected with physical abuse. Sexual abuse seldom yields tangible evidence—such as visible injuries to the child, a sexually transmitted disease, semen residue, or blood stains—but often the abuse leaves behavioral symptoms. Emotional abuse rarely leaves physical evidence but may leave behavioral symptoms of psychological trauma. Neglect, like sexual abuse, may leave behavioral symptoms rather than physical evidence of maltreatment. Observable evidence of maltreatment is unlikely if the child has waited days, months, or years to disclose the maltreatment. Any physical proof—such as bruises or other damage to the body—usually will have healed, and other proof may have been destroyed.

Children may be physically, sexually, or emotionally abused in their home, school, day care center, church or synagogue, residential facility, or any other place. Neglect primarily takes place in the home where the child lives. For all of the above forms of maltreatment, the offender may be a parent, relative, sibling, friend, teacher, or staff member.

The Tragedy of Child Maltreatment

The tragedy of child maltreatment affects all who come in contact with it. The following poem, written by Lorne D. Gilsig of the Los Angeles Police Department, reveals deep feelings about child maltreatment on the part of one who collected the evidence (copyright 1993 by Lorne D. Gilsig and reprinted by permission).

TO A 12-YEAR-OLD WHOSE
NAME I NEVER KNEW
Your mother failed you because
she was a small, bitter woman.
Your father failed you because
his new life was found far away.
Your social worker failed you
because your name was one of many.
I failed you because a badge
and gun do not help me to see.

But death, she did not fail you.

Wearing a soft black dress she
went to the closet where you
lay, passing silently through the
locked door.

Table 20-2
A Continuum of Severity of Physical Abuse, Sexual Abuse, Emotional Abuse, and Neglect

Type of maltreatment	Continuum of severity
Physical abuse	0 = No physical injury 1 = Mild physical mistreatment or injury not requiring medical treatment (for example, slapping, scratches, or bruises) 2 = Moderate physical injury requiring medical treatment but not hospitalization (for example, stitches or minor burns) 3 = Severe physical injury requiring hospitalization but not permanent dysfunction (for example, serious burns or fractures) 4 = Very severe physical injury involving permanent dysfunction, life-threatening injury, torture, or fatal injury (for example, brain injury, internal injuries, or severe/multiple burns)
Sexual abuse	0 = No sexual abuse 1 = Mild sexual abuse (for example, inappropriate stroking or fondling while the child is clothed, adult's undressing the child for the adult's sexual gratification, or voyeurism) 2 = Moderate sexual abuse (for example, inappropriate stroking or fondling when the child is naked, adult's kissing the child for adult's sexual gratification, or adult's exposing self to the child) 3 = Severe sexual abuse (for example, mutual masturbation or exposing the child to pornography) 4 = Very severe sexual abuse (for example, sexual intercourse, sodomy, oral sex, prostitution, creating pornography by photographing or videotaping the child, sadistic sexual abuse, sex with animals, or forcing children to perpetrate sex on younger children)
Emotional abuse	0 = No emotional abuse 1 = Mild instances of unwarranted criticism, hostility, scapegoating, belittling, or rejection 2 = Moderate criticism, hostility, or rejection of the child that results in behavioral problems and need for treatment 3 = Severe criticism, hostility, or rejection of the child that results in the need for medication, special class placement, or out-of-home placement 4 = Very severe criticism, hostility, or rejection of the child that results in the need for placement in a hospital or treatment facility
Neglect	0 = No physical, socioemotional, or cognitive neglect 1 = Mild inattention to the child's (a) nonessential needs (for example, delay in changing soiled diapers), (b) need for supportive interpersonal contact, or (c) cognitive needs (for example, occasional failure to provide an adequate range of stimulating objects) 2 = Moderate (a) physical neglect that leads to potential developmental harm (for example, poor eating or sleeping habits), (b) inattention to the child's socioemotional needs that results in behavioral problems (for example, anxiety, withdrawal, or bed-wetting), (c) inattention to the child's cognitive needs, particularly failure to encourage or reinforce exploration, effort, or achievement, or (d) inattention to the child's medical problems 3 = Severe (a) physical neglect that results in medical treatment or hospitalization, (b) socioemotional neglect that results in the need for medication or placement in a special class, or (c) cognitive neglect that leads to potential developmental delay 4 = Very severe (a) life-threatening or fatal physical neglect, (b) socioemotional neglect that results in the need for out-of-home placement or hospitalization, or (c) cognitive neglect that results in mental retardation, learning disability, or language dysfunction

Note. The continuum does not reflect frequency of maltreatment or degree of coercion. You must consider these factors in evaluating the severity of the maltreatment.
Source: Adapted, in part, from Claussen and Crittenden (1991).

*She placed her pale cool hands
on your wounded brow and said:*

*You will hurt no more, because
I am here.
You will fear no more, because
I am here.
You will never be alone, because
I am here.
Take my hand child, if you will,
and we leave this place together.*

*Offered what you never had
you took her hand. A sigh of
exhaled breath, as if passing
into sleep, and you were gone.*

*You left us behind, behind our
own locked doors. Guilty and
damned we sit in doubt of our
own salvation.*

REPORTING CHILD MALTREATMENT

Responsibility of Professionals to Report Child Maltreatment

With the encouragement of the federal Child Abuse Prevention and Treatment Act, all 50 states in the United States have passed laws about who should report child maltreatment. State laws generally require that individuals working with children—such as child caregivers, teachers, physicians, psychologists, psychiatrists, social workers, marriage and family therapists, counselors, and clergy (in some states)—report child maltreatment when there is *reasonable suspicion*. These individuals are sometimes referred to as *mandated reporters*. *Regulatory statutes use the phrase "reasonable suspicion" to mean that a person should consider the possibility of child maltreatment based on facts that could cause a reasonable person in a like position to come to the same conclusion.* In addition, members of the public can voluntarily notify Child Protective Services or law enforcement if they suspect that child maltreatment has occurred or is occurring.

California Penal Code

The following sections of the California Penal Code offer an example of how laws about mandatory reporting are worded.

Child abuse; duties to report.

(a) Except as provided in subdivision (b), any child care custodian, health practitioner, or employee of a child protective agency who has knowledge of or observes a child in his or her professional capacity or within the scope of his or her employment whom he or she knows or reasonably suspects has been the victim of child abuse shall report the known or suspected instance of child abuse to a child protective agency immediately or as soon as practically possible by telephone and shall prepare and send a written report thereof within 36 hours of receiving the information concerning the incident. A child protective agency shall be notified and a report shall be prepared and sent even if the child has expired, regardless of whether or not the possible abuse was a factor contributing to the death, and even if suspected child abuse was discovered during an autopsy. For the purposes of this article, "reasonable suspicion" means that it is objectively reasonable for a person to entertain such a suspicion, based upon facts that could cause a reasonable person in a like position, drawing when appropriate on his or her training and experience to suspect child abuse. For the purpose of this article, the pregnancy of a minor does not, in and of itself, constitute the basis of reasonable suspicion of sexual abuse.

(b) Any child care custodian, health practitioner, or employee of a child protective agency who has knowledge of or who reasonably suspects that mental suffering has been inflicted on a child or his or her emotional well-being is endangered in any other way, may report such known instance of child abuse to a child protective agency. (Penal Code Section 11166)

A health practitioner is described in the following way:

As used in this article, "health practitioner" means a physician and surgeon, psychiatrist, psychologist, dentist, resident, intern, podiatrist, chiropractor, licensed nurse, dental hygienist, optometrist, or any other person who is currently licensed under Division 2 (commencing with Section 500) or the Business and Professions Code; a marriage, family, and child counselor, any emergency medical technician I or II, paramedic, or other person certified pursuant to Division 2.5 (commencing with Section 1797) of the Health and Safety Code; a psychological assistant registered pursuant to Section 2913 of the Business and Professions Code; a marriage, family and child counselor trainee, as defined in subdivision (c) of Section 4980.03 of the Business and Professions Code; an unlicensed marriage, family and child counselor intern registered under Section 4980.44 of the Business and Professions Code; a state or county public health employee who treats a minor for venereal disease or any other condition; a coroner; a medical examiner or any other person who performs autopsies; or a religious practitioner who diagnoses, examines, or treats children. (Amended by statute 1988, ch. 1530, section 1, effective Jan. 1, 1989)

The penalty for failing to report the abuse is described as follows:

(e) Any person who fails to report an instance of child abuse which he or she knows to exist or reasonably should know to exist, as required by this article, is guilty of a misdemeanor and is punishable by confinement in the county jail for a term not to exceed six months or by a fine of not more than one thousand dollars ($1,000) or by both. (Amended by statute 1987, ch. 1459, section 23)

The law grants immunity in the following way:

No child care custodian, [or] health practitioner...who reports a known or suspected instance of child abuse shall be civilly or criminally liable for any report required or authorized by this article. (Penal Code Section 11172, subdivision a)

As a social policy matter, one might argue that when a child is abused, there is greater urgency or necessity for the legal system to intervene, whether in juvenile, domestic relations, or criminal court; in cases involving child victims, the need to protect the child and make decisions regarding custody or placement of the child requires legal involvement. Moreover, legal intervention, particularly criminal prosecution, is critical not only to prevent further abuse of the victim, but abuse of other children.

—Josephine A. Bulkley and Mark J. Horwitz

Role of Reporting Party

The role of the reporting party is not to determine or to prove that maltreatment did in fact occur; rather, the reporting party's only responsibility is to report a reasonable suspicion of maltreatment. By simply talking with the individual who discloses the possible maltreatment, the reporting party can determine whether there is sufficient reason to report it.

Here are some recommendations to follow when a child wants to disclose that he or she has been maltreated (Connaway, 1996, adapted from pp. 4–5). You might want to share these pointers with other mandated reporters, such as teachers, nurses, school counselors, and health care providers.

1. Pay close attention to your body language. You want to convey interest in what the child says but not shock, horror, or indifference.
2. You may be the only person this child feels comfortable telling about the situation, so you don't want to discourage the child or make him or her think that you are not available to listen.
3. If a child makes a disclosure, don't try to get all the details.
4. Listen attentively, and then ask the child if he or she wants to say anything else.
5. Do not tell the child that you think he or she was or wasn't abused. Your role is to listen carefully, not to make inferences or decisions.
6. When the child is finished, notify the appropriate authorities of what you learned.
7. Write down the exact words used by the child in the disclosure; the date, time, and place of the disclosure; and any other relevant information about the child's behavior and the situation in which the disclosure was made.

Some mandated reporters are ambivalent about reporting suspicions of child maltreatment. They accept the necessity of a law that requires the reporting of possible child maltreatment but see it as a necessary evil or a problematic good and as a potential source of considerable stress. The following quotations describe how two mandated reporters feel about reporting the possibility of child maltreatment.

I find it difficult to report maltreatment. On the one hand, I feel I must report quickly if a child is in danger. But on the other hand,

reporting disrupts treatment, ruins relationships among family members, and the child protection system often acts punitively, even if the family is making therapeutic progress. I often struggle not knowing if maltreatment has occurred, especially when I have young children as clients. (Kalichman, 1993, p. 41)

Oh I hate it.… I feel like a social policeman. I don't want to be a social policeman. I don't want children to be at risk. I truly don't, but…I really hate that part of my job. I mean I do it. I know I have to do it. And I agonize for hours afterwards. Then I say, "I'm going to quit."… It is necessary, but I never like myself after I do it. (Anderson, Levine, Sharma, Ferretti, Steinberg, & Wallach, 1993, p. 337)

What Happens After a Report of Possible Child Maltreatment Has Been Made?

After a report of possible child maltreatment is received, Child Protective Services and law enforcement must investigate the allegation. They are responsible for contacting the parents, neighbors, schools, relatives, and other relevant sources. It is the responsibility of law enforcement to place the child in protective custody if the situation and the recommendations of Child Protective Services justify it. In some states, Child Protective Services has the authority to remove children from the home for an emergency placement for a 48-hour period without a court order. In such situations, the child may be placed in a foster home, may be admitted to a hospital as a social admission, or may be kept in the emergency room until a placement is found. After 48 hours, if the child is still in need of protection, a petition is filed with the court to remove the child from the home for a longer period. The petition, which is filed at the request of Child Protective Services by the county or district attorney, must be approved by a judge; it may be referred to as a *dependency/neglect petition,* or a *child in need of protection or services (CHIPS) petition* or by some similar term.

In some cities and counties, the assessment is conducted by a core multidisciplinary team supported by a supplementary team (Alexander, 1993). The core team may be composed of the following professionals:

- a *physician,* who gathers a medical history and conducts a physical examination of the child
- a *nurse,* who assists in conducting the physical examination
- a *social worker,* who gathers a psychosocial history of the child and family and assists in evaluating family dynamics and in formulating an intervention plan
- a *law-enforcement officer,* who may interview the child, parents, and alleged perpetrator or interview the child jointly with a social worker
- a *psychologist,* who assesses the child's affect, cognitive development, behavior, and family dynamics and assists in formulating an intervention plan

Members of the supplementary team may include an attorney, a speech/language clinician, a nutritionist, a representative from the district attorney's office, a forensic pathologist, a dentist, and an educator.

All members of the core and supplementary multidisciplinary teams *must* be concerned with the safety of the child. However, it is the responsibility of the core team to evaluate the child and develop and recommend a treatment plan. A report of child maltreatment may set off a chain of events, as shown in Figure 20-1.

Representative Situations for Reporting Possible Child Maltreatment

Following are representative situations that caused individuals to report their concerns of possible abuse or neglect to Child Protective Services (National Center on Child Abuse and Neglect, 1989, pp. 7–10, with changes in notation):

CASE 20-1. POSSIBLE CHILD PHYSICAL ABUSE REPORTED BY A PHYSICIAN

An 18-month-old boy was brought to the emergency room with second- and third-degree burns on his legs and buttocks. The doctor noted that the burns extended to a different level on each leg—at mid-calf on the left leg, and mid-knee on the right. In addition, there was an area on the right buttock that was burned. The mother told the doctor that she left her son in the bathtub while she went to answer the telephone. The mother believed that the boy turned on the hot water while she was gone. The doctor did not believe that the mother's explanation was consistent with the injury. The doctor thought that there were two factors which made it unlikely that burns could have occurred as a result of the child turning on the hot water. First, it takes a long time to raise the temperature of normal bath water to the scalding point. Second, if the injuries had occurred as the mother described, the injuries would have been the same. The doctor thought that the injury could have occurred by holding the child and dangling his feet into scalding water.

The physician reported this case to Child Protective Services because (a) the child had sustained a serious injury, (b) the parent's explanation of the cause of the child's injury was inconsistent with the injury and symptoms, and (c) in his clinical opinion, the injury could likely have been caused by the parent.

CASE 20-2. POSSIBLE CHILD PHYSICAL ABUSE REPORTED BY A NURSE

Susan, aged 7, was in her first-grade class when her teacher noticed that she had difficulty sitting and had some unusually shaped marks on her arm. Susan was sent to the school nurse to be examined. The nurse noted approximately 12 linear and loop-shaped marks on her back and buttocks. These marks ranged in length from 6 to 10 inches. The nurse believed that the marks were inflicted by a belt and belt buckle. The marks were purple, blue, brown, and yellow, indicating that the bruises were sustained at different times. Susan said she did not know how she got the bruises. The nurse called Child Protective Services.

Even though the child denied knowing how she got the bruises, the nurse reported this case because (a) the child had sustained a physical injury, (b) the bruises appeared to have been inflicted at different times, perhaps days apart, and (c) the nurse's clinical opinion was that the injuries were inflicted by a belt and belt buckle. The fact that the bruises were in different stages of healing raises greater concern for the child's safety. However, even if the bruises had been inflicted at one time, the nurse still should have reported this case.

CASE 20-3. POSSIBLE CHILD EMOTIONAL ABUSE REPORTED BY A TEACHER

When Cindy was 8 years of age, her teacher called Child Protective Services. Cindy was the only child in her family who wore old tattered clothing to school and was not given the same privileges and opportunities as her brothers and sisters. The other children were allowed to join in after-school activities; however, Cindy was not allowed to participate in any outside activities. Cindy became very withdrawn at school; she stopped speaking in class and would not engage in play activities with her classmates. Her academic performance declined rapidly. Finally, Cindy became incontinent and had "accidents" in class.

The teacher reported this case because (a) Cindy was treated significantly differently from the other children in the family, (b) she showed a marked decline in academic performance and in class participation, and (c) she had become incontinent.

CASE 20-4. POSSIBLE CHILD NEGLECT REPORTED BY A NEIGHBOR

A neighbor called Child Protective Services because a 5-year-old boy wandered around the apartment complex unsupervised, often until 10 or 11 P.M. The child was usually inappropriately dressed for the weather; when it was 45 degrees, the child was wearing a short-sleeved shirt, long pants, and torn shoes. The child was constantly asking neighbors for food. He always had a runny nose and recently had developed a deep cough. In addition, he picked fights with younger children in the neighborhood. The neighbor thought the boy's mother worked at night; however, she rarely saw her at all.

The neighbor reported this case because the child (a) was unsupervised late at night, (b) was not dressed appropriately for the weather, (c) may not have been receiving sufficient nourishment, and (d) had a mother who appeared to be unconcerned about her child's welfare.

CASE 20-5. POSSIBLE CHILD SEXUAL ABUSE REPORTED BY A NEIGHBOR

A neighbor called to report possible sexual abuse of Janise, aged 12. Janise had confided in the neighbor's daughter that her father had been "fooling around" with her for several years. The neighbor talked with Janise before making the report. Janise reported that her dad touched her private parts and made her "do it" with him. When Janise was asked

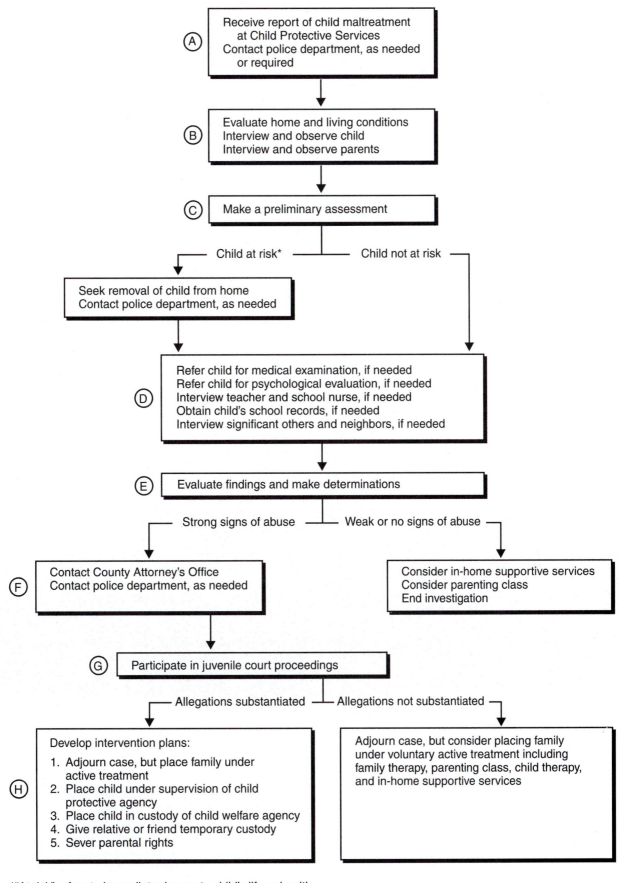

Ⓐ Receive report of child maltreatment at Child Protective Services
Contact police department, as needed or required

Ⓑ Evaluate home and living conditions
Interview and observe child
Interview and observe parents

Ⓒ Make a preliminary assessment

Child at risk* — Child not at risk

Seek removal of child from home
Contact police department, as needed

Ⓓ Refer child for medical examination, if needed
Refer child for psychological evaluation, if needed
Interview teacher and school nurse, if needed
Obtain child's school records, if needed
Interview significant others and neighbors, if needed

Ⓔ Evaluate findings and make determinations

Strong signs of abuse — Weak or no signs of abuse

Ⓕ Contact County Attorney's Office
Contact police department, as needed

Consider in-home supportive services
Consider parenting class
End investigation

Ⓖ Participate in juvenile court proceedings

Allegations substantiated — Allegations not substantiated

Ⓗ Develop intervention plans:

1. Adjourn case, but place family under active treatment
2. Place child under supervision of child protective agency
3. Place child in custody of child welfare agency
4. Give relative or friend temporary custody
5. Sever parental rights

Adjourn case, but consider placing family under voluntary active treatment including family therapy, parenting class, child therapy, and in-home supportive services

*"At risk" refers to immediate danger to child's life or health.
Note. This decision-making model does not cover criminal investigations.

Figure 20-1. Flow chart showing steps taken after a report of child maltreatment.

if her mom knew what was going on between her and her dad, Janise replied, "Yes, she does!" Janise became frightened when the neighbor said she was going to call Child Protective Services. Janise begged her not to call, screaming, "He told me that they'll take me away!" Although the neighbor was horrified that this was happening, she believed that Janise was telling the truth.

The neighbor reported this case because (a) Janise disclosed that her dad had been sexually abusing her and (b) the neighbor was concerned about Janise. Consequently, she felt obligated to call Child Protective Services despite Janise's objections.

Example of a Situation Where Individuals Failed to Report Suspicions of Child Maltreatment

The following case illustrates what can happen to a child when a community chooses to shut its eyes to the strong possibility that the child is being physically abused (U.S. Advisory Board on Child Abuse and Neglect, 1995, p. 131, as reported by Dr. Michael Baden, Director of Forensic Services, New York State Police, in a 1994 New York focus group).

CASE 20-6. A GIRL DIES IN NASSAU COUNTY
The little girl had been bitten on the cheek, and a medical examiner's investigation later showed that she had received severe internal injuries that killed her. Detectives determined that she had been used for karate-kicking practice by the boyfriend of the mother, in front of the rest of the children. She was beaten intermittently for more than a week. Many neighbors in the well-to-do Nassau County, New York, neighborhood saw her badly marked face. But neighbors did not think it was their business, and the family was not reported. Only when the child was killed did the beatings come to the attention of authorities. Caring communities must take action to save children from abuse if this tragedy is to be prevented.

Exercise 20-1. To Report or Not to Report, That Is the Question!

Part 1. Rating Your Tendency to Report Cases of Possible Child Maltreatment

How inclined would you be to report each of the following three cases to Child Protective Services or to a law enforcement agency? Use a 5-point scale to rate your tendency to report after you read each case: 1 = almost certainly would report, 2 = very likely to report, 3 = somewhat likely to report, 4 = not very likely to report, 5 = almost certainly would not report. Then compare your ratings with those in the Comment section. This exercise was adapted from Zellman (1992).

Case 1. When 8-year-old Melanie fails to show up for her first day at your school, you phone to see what happened. Melanie answers the phone and tells you that her mommy and daddy are both at work. When you ask to speak to someone else, she tells you that she is home alone. After she misses the next day, you call and find Melanie at home alone again.

Case 2. The Reeds, a well-dressed middle-class family new to your school, come to see you because neither parent can get their 6-year-old daughter Mara to obey. Mr. Reed tells you that he uses a belt on Mara just as his dad did on him, but lately it isn't working. Mr. Reed admits that he hit Mara yesterday and that the belt left a red mark on her neck. When you ask to see it, you observe several raised welts.

Case 3. James Simmons, a 3-year-old boy, was referred to you by his preschool because he had fondled several children on the playground and masturbates frequently. When you speak with James's mother, Mrs. Simmons angrily states that she is sure that James's male babysitter, whom she hired so that James would have more time with men, has been abusing her son. Physical findings are negative.

Comment on Part 1

Zellman (1992) sent these cases to mental health professionals and almost 1,200 replied. This number represents 59% of those sent the survey. Here are the average ratings.

Case 1. The respondents said they would be *somewhat likely* to report the case of Melanie who stayed home from school.

Case 2. The respondents said they would be *somewhat likely* to report the case of Mara, whose father hit her.

Case 3. The respondents said they would *very likely* report the case of James, who fondled other children.

How do your ratings compare with those of the respondents to the survey? If your ratings differ from those of the respondents, what might account for the differences? What about the cases guided your ratings? Do your own ratings differ for each case? If so, what might account for the differences—the type of abuse, the child's age, or something about the situation? Would your ratings change if the child's age or sex were different? If you knew the ethnicity or socioeconomic status of the family, would that make a difference? Also compare your ratings with those of other class members. In what ways are they similar and in what ways are they different? By understanding the events and circumstances under which you are most likely to report suspicions of maltreatment, you can increase your objectivity and effectiveness as an interviewer.

Part 2. Assessing Possible Cases of Child Maltreatment

Part 2 contains hypothetical cases about four 7-year-old girls referred for psychological evaluation by their schools. After you read each one, answer the four questions preceding the cases. The material in Part 2 was adapted from Finlayson and Koocher (1991). The first portion of each case was obtained from Finlayson (April 1994, personal communication).

1. My clinical impression is that there is (no, little, moderate, substantial) reason to suspect child abuse.
2. I feel _____% certain that child abuse is occurring in this case.
3. I would (definitely not, unlikely, likely, definitely) report this case to the authorities.
4. If the child's mother refused to schedule another appointment, stating that she had decided to handle the child's problems within the family, I would (definitely not, unlikely, likely, definitely) report this case to the authorities.

Case 4. Brenda (age 7) was referred for psychological evaluation by school officials. Brenda's mother reports that about two months ago, Brenda's mood and behavior showed a marked change. She notes that Brenda was previously a happy, well-adjusted child. Brenda's mother now observes that she seems worried and preoccupied, has nightmares every night, and has a diminished appetite. She reports that Brenda's teacher has also noticed the recent change in Brenda's behavior.

Brenda lives with her sister (age 4), mother, and stepfather. Her mother denies any traumatic events or significant life changes in the past year. She reports that Brenda's behavior began to change several months after she started her parttime evening job. She admits that she has less time to spend with Brenda but feels comforted that her husband cares for the children while she works.

During the child's interview, Brenda is nervous and shy. When you ask Brenda about what is worrying her, she says "I can't tell you." When asked if she can show you in a drawing, she proceeds to draw a picture of what appears to be two naked people. You ask Brenda to tell you about the picture, and she says "He's hurting her." You ask her to tell you more and she says "He's peeing on her." Asked to identify the characters in the picture, she states "That's my daddy and that's me, and sometimes my daddy pees on me." She proceeds to cry and is unwilling to talk any more.

Case 5. Tracy (age 7) was referred for psychological evaluation by school officials. Tracy's mother reports that Tracy has become more difficult to manage over the past several months. She states that Tracy has become noncompliant at home and at school and that her behavior seems driven and wild. She also states that she has received reports from other parents that Tracy has forced other children to pull down their pants.

Tracy lives with her sister (age 4), mother, and stepfather. Her mother denies any traumatic events or significant life changes in the past year. She reports that Tracy's behavior began to change several months after she started her part-time evening job. She admits that she has less time to spend with Tracy but feels comforted that her husband cares for the children while she works.

During the child's interview, Tracy is very active and distracted. She erratically explores the room and seems reluctant to talk with you about her school or home life. During her play at the dollhouse, Tracy places a male doll on top of a female doll and says "The man is poking the girl. She's crying." Tracy breaks from the play and begins singing loudly. You ask her to tell you more about the man poking the girl, and she emphatically states that she does not want to talk

anymore. You are unable to elicit any further information by the end of the session.

Case 6. Jean (age 7) was referred for psychological evaluation by school officials. Jean's mother reports that Jean has had a sudden change in behavior over the past month. She notes that Jean has become unusually whiny, clingy, and fearful. In addition, she now wets her bed every night. Jean's teacher has also reported a sudden deterioration in Jean's school performance.

Jean lives with her sister (age 4), mother, and stepfather. Her mother denies any traumatic events or significant life changes in the past year. She reports that Jean's behavior began to change several months after she started her part-time evening job. She admits that she has less time to spend with Jean but feels comforted that her husband cares for the children while she works.

During the child's interview, Jean exhibits significant problems separating from her mother. She insists that the door to the office remain open during the interview. Jean appears frightened and does not interact freely with you. She is reticent about playing or talking with you and asks frequently to return to her mother. Her drawings are disorganized and infantile. You ask Jean to tell you about her drawing, and she states "It's a picture of the bad man." You inquire further about the "bad man," and Jean responds "The bad man is dead." You ask Jean about her worries and fears but she insists on returning to her mother.

Case 7. Anne (age 7) was referred for psychological evaluation by school officials. Anne's mother reports that Anne has complained of stomach pain over the past year, although her physician has been unable to determine any medical cause for the pain. Anne's mother has noticed that in the past year Anne has become more socially withdrawn—for instance, she seldom plays with her friends and often chooses to spend time alone in her room. Anne's grades have fallen, and she seems uninterested in school.

Anne lives with her sister (age 4), mother, and stepfather. Her mother denies any traumatic events or significant life changes in the past year. She reports that Anne's behavior began to change several months after she started her part-time evening job. She admits that she has less time to spend with Anne but feels comforted that her husband cares for the children while she works.

During the child's interview, Anne appears listless and sad. She seems disinterested in the many toys in your office. Anne is polite and compliant. She offers brief responses to your questions about school and home. When you ask Anne about her stomach pain, she responds "It feels like someone is stabbing me." You ask her if she has any worries or concerns, and she states "I worry about what will happen to my sister if I die." When you ask Anne to tell you more about that, she says, "I'm the only one who can take care of my sister." She becomes quiet and withdrawn, and you are unable to elicit further information from her.

Comment on Part 2

Finlayson and Koocher (1991) sent these cases to doctoral-level mental health professionals, and 290 replied. The highlights of their ratings appear in the table.

Question	Response	Case 4 Brenda %	Case 5 Tracy %	Case 6 Jean %	Case 7 Anne %
1. My clinical impression is that there is _____ reason to suspect child abuse.	No Little Moderate Substantial	0 0 8 92	0 3 44 52	5 34 51 10	9 45 43 3
2. I feel _____% certain that child abuse is occurring in this case.	100–75 74–50 49–25 24– 0	85 36 5 0	53 33 10 3	9 29 27 35	6 24 19 52
3. I would _____ report this case to the authorities.	Definitely not Unlikely Likely Definitely	0 3 23 74	2 21 46 31	26 56 14 2	41 48 10 2
4. If the child's mother refused to schedule another appointment stating that she had decided to handle the child's problems within the family, I would _____ report this case to the authorities.	Definitely not Unlikely Likely Definitely	0 1 14 85	1 8 32 59	16 45 29 9	27 48 19 6

How do your ratings compare with those of the respondents to the survey? If your ratings differ from those of the respondents, what might account for the differences? What about the cases guided your ratings? Do your ratings differ for each case? If so, what might account for the differences?

Source of Reports of Child Maltreatment

In 1994, there were 1,508,177 reports of child maltreatment obtained from 44 states. Figure 20-2 shows the sources of the reports. Professionals accounted for almost 53% of the reports; friends, parents, and other relatives, 27%; and victims, self-identified perpetrators, and anonymous and other reporters, 20% (National Center on Child Abuse and Neglect, 1996). Note that a report of child maltreatment may cover more than one child.

U.S. Supreme Court Rules on Immunity

In 1994, in a 7–2 vote, the U.S. Supreme Court let stand a ruling that makes social workers immune from being sued, even if they wrongly accuse a parent of sexually abusing his or her child (Hoffman v. Harris, 93-1044). Mr. Hoffman had charged that his rights were violated by two social workers who worked for an agency in Kentucky. The social workers filed charges of sexual abuse against Mr. Hoffman without speaking to his daughter, on whose behalf they were acting. In addition, a judge, without giving Mr. Hoffman a chance to respond, ordered visitation rights suspended. Based on an allegation by his ex-wife, the father was arrested and indicted on a charge of sexual abuse of his daughter. A jury

later cleared Mr. Hoffman of child abuse charges. In a separate proceeding, he was awarded permanent custody of the child. However, the U.S. 6th Circuit Court of Appeals dismissed Mr. Hoffman's suit, ruling that social workers, like prosecutors, are entitled to "absolute immunity from liability." This rule of immunity "ensures that [social workers] are not deterred from vigorously performing their jobs as they might if they feared personal liability." According to Savage (1994), "While the court's refusal to hear the appeal is not a binding rule, it strongly suggests that the justices support the immunity" (p. A26).

When Does Immunity Stop for Mandated Reporters?

Immunity may apply *only* to the initial reporting of child maltreatment and *not* to all activities associated with the case, as a recent California appellate court in San Diego ruled. The case (James W. et al. v. The Superior Court of San Diego County,…[child's therapist] et al., real parties of interest, 1993) involved parents who alleged that their daughter Alicia's therapist and foster parents had coerced her into naming her father as the man who raped her. A trial court, citing California's reporting act, ruled that the therapist and foster parents were immune. However, the appellate court overturned the lower court's ruling.

According to the appellate court, "The Act is a reporting statute and its protection runs to reporting: it does not apply to activities that continue more than two years after the initial report of abuse by parties who are not acting as reporters." The appellate court also noted the following:

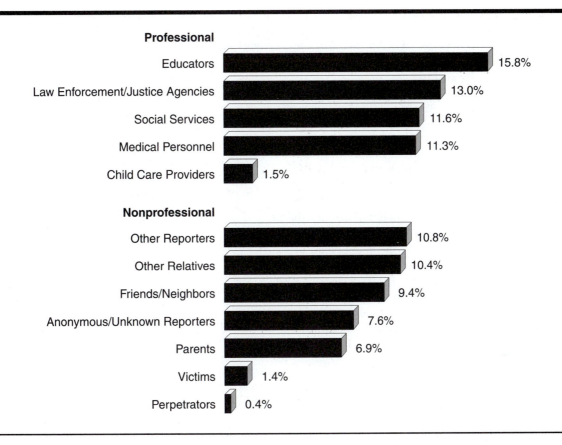

Figure 20-2. Source of reports of child maltreatment in 1994, based on 1,595,701 reports from 49 states. From National Center on Child Abuse and Neglect (U.S. Department of Health and Human Services). *Child Maltreatment 1994: Reports from the States to the National Center on Child Abuse and Neglect* (Washington, DC: U.S. Government Printing Office, 1996), p. 2-2.

The focus of the Act is, as such, directed toward discovering suspected child abuse and, to that end, encouraging reporters to spread the word as quickly as possible without fear of suit so that independent governmental agencies can remove the child from immediate danger and investigate. The Act was satisfied here on May 9, 1989 when officials at the hospital determined eight-year-old Alicia had been raped, filed a report, and enabled the county to file a petition and remove Alicia from her home. The activities of [the therapist] and the [foster parents] for the next two and one-half years went far beyond anything contemplated by statute.

Directing Alicia to say her father was guilty, [the therapist] repeatedly told the child: (1) she knew Alicia's father had molested her; (2) Alicia would feel a lot better if she admitted it; (3) the "story" Alicia had been telling was not believable; (4) Alicia's mother had been assaulted by Alicia's grandfather; and (5) if she wanted to go home, Alicia would have to say her father was the perpetrator. At [the therapist's] direction, [the foster mother] also took Alicia to the bedroom "every night" and said "over and over again" Alicia's father had raped her. [The foster mother] kept telling Alicia she would have to say her father was the perpetrator if she wanted to go home.

[The court also pointed out how important it is to distinguish between those who make the initial report and those who come into a case later. This distinction] discourages family counselors and foster parents from taking on roles they are not adequately pre-

pared to perform. When private citizens become deeply enmeshed in investigatory and prosecutorial activities and take on functions of the police, the DSS [the Department of Social Services], county counsel or district attorney, the system suffers a loss of objectivity, independence, balance and accountability. The combination of private player and public officials all on one side performing the same roles, albeit for different reasons, has a momentum of its own which can, in its own way, overwhelm any family. Such an imbalance leading to grievous injury is precisely the problem, alleged in this complaint.

This ruling, although limited to a specific case, has implications for all clinicians (and others) who work with victims of child maltreatment: Clinicians do not have unlimited immunity if they carry out actions beyond those intended by laws governing the reporting of child maltreatment. In fact, as of January 1996, a law went into effect in California (AB 1355) that holds "that the civil immunity of juvenile court social workers, child protection workers, and other public employees authorized to initiate or conduct investigations or proceedings pursuant to the juvenile court law shall not extend to acts of perjury, fabrication of evidence, failure to disclose exculpatory evidence, or obtaining testimony by duress, fraud, or undue influence if any of these acts are committed with malice…" (Legislative Counsel's digest, February 23, 1995, p. 1).

Credibility of the Reporter

If you work for Child Protective Services or for law enforcement and receive a report of alleged child maltreatment, ask the reporter to give you as much information as possible about the alleged maltreatment. If the reporter prefers to be anonymous, ask why he or she is requesting anonymity. Explain to the reporter that the agency may need his or her name and phone number in order to call back to clarify some details. Assure the reporter that all attempts will be made to maintain confidentiality *unless* court action is required.

You will want to evaluate carefully the initial report of child maltreatment and then determine how to proceed (Jones, 1993). Recognize that families will experience stress and feel stigmatized if they are investigated, especially when they believe that the investigation should never have taken place. Nevertheless, all reports of alleged child maltreatment need to be investigated. It is when agencies continue investigations, despite a lack of evidence to justify the allegation, that they are using their resources improperly and creating legal liabilities. In-depth investigations of reports of child maltreatment should always take place when there is an admission of maltreatment by the offender, a credible witness to the maltreatment, testimony from the child to support the maltreatment, any indication that the child has physical injuries or need of hospitalization, or any signs of neglect or emotional abuse.

CHILD MALTREATMENT AS A SOCIAL PROBLEM

Extent of the Problem

To place the problem of child maltreatment in perspective, it is helpful to reflect on its history (Cicchetti & Carlson, 1989):

History documents that the problem of child maltreatment has existed since the beginning of civilization…. Unfortunately, our understanding of the etiology, intergenerational transmission, and developmental sequelae of this pervasive social problem largely has been the result of relatively recent systematic inquiry. Until a generation ago, modern society had refused to recognize the scope and gravity of child maltreatment. In fact, prior to the 1960s, many sectors of our society (e.g., medical personnel) failed even to acknowledge its existence. (p. xiii)

Reports of child maltreatment in 1994. In 1994, there were 2,935,470 reported cases of child maltreatment in the United States, involving 43 out of every 1,000 children (National Center on Child Abuse and Neglect, 1996). These reported cases represented an increase of 71% over those in 1984 and an increase of 320% over those in 1976, when the

American Humane Association began to report national incidence figures (see Figure 20-3). Between 1992 and 1994, the national rate of reporting child maltreatment appeared to be leveling off. It is not known whether the increased number of reports of child maltreatment from 1976 to 1994 was primarily associated with the rise of professional and public awareness—perhaps stimulated by passage of the Child Abuse and Treatment Act in 1974—and the use of improved data collection methods, or with an increase in the actual incidence of child maltreatment.

Neglect was the type of maltreatment reported most often (53% of the cases), followed by physical abuse (25.5% of the cases), sexual abuse (14% of the cases), and emotional abuse (4.7% of the cases). (See Figure 20-4.) The percentage of children who were victims of neglect was more than twice the percentage of children who were victims of physical abuse. The low reporting of emotional abuse means that it was rarely the *primary* reason for reporting maltreatment. However, as noted previously, emotional abuse may accompany all other forms of child maltreatment. Although sexual abuse is reported less frequently than physical abuse and neglect, it may be the most underreported form of child maltreatment because of the secrecy that so often characterizes sexual abuse cases (National Center on Child Abuse and Neglect, 1991).

Substantiated reports of child maltreatment. In 1994, approximately 1.63 million investigations of alleged child abuse and neglect were conducted (National Center on Child Abuse and Neglect, 1996). As Figure 20-5 shows, 56% of investigated reports were not substantiated, 31% were substantiated, 6% were "indicated or reason to suspect," and 5% had other dispositions. Although more than half of the investigations could not substantiate the reports of child abuse or neglect, failure to substantiate the report does not mean that the report was false. It may be that the report was not thoroughly investigated, the family moved, the child or family refused to talk, corroborating evidence was missing or failed to meet acceptable standards, or the child was unavailable for the interview.

Estimated child maltreatment fatalities in 1994. In 1994, 43 states reported 1,111 child fatalities that resulted from child maltreatment (National Center on Child Abuse and Neglect, 1996). This fatality rate is approximately 2 per 100,000 children younger than 18 years of age in the population at large. However, the fatality rate is estimated to be 110 per 100,000 children who were victims of maltreatment.

Children under 5 years of age were the primary victims of fatalities—46% were under 1 year of age, and 42% were between 1 and 5 years of age (Wiese & Daro, 1995). Physical abuse and neglect accounted for most of the fatalities. In approximately half of the cases, contact had been made with Child Protective Services *prior* to the child's death. The rate of child maltreatment fatalities rose steadily from 1985 to 1994, increasing by approximately 48%. It is not known

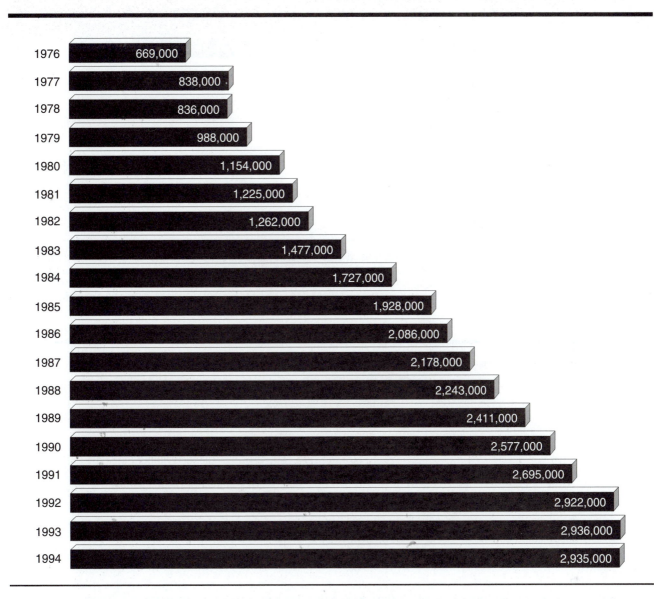

1976	669,000
1977	838,000
1978	836,000
1979	988,000
1980	1,154,000
1981	1,225,000
1982	1,262,000
1983	1,477,000
1984	1,727,000
1985	1,928,000
1986	2,086,000
1987	2,178,000
1988	2,243,000
1989	2,411,000
1990	2,577,000
1991	2,695,000
1992	2,922,000
1993	2,936,000
1994	2,935,000

Figure 20-3. Estimated number of cases of child maltreatment reported from 1976 to 1994. Data for 1990 to 1994 obtained from National Center on Child Abuse and Neglect (U.S. Department of Health and Human Services). *Child Maltreatment 1994: Reports from the States to the National Center on Child Abuse and Neglect* (Washington, DC: U.S. Government Printing Office, 1996), p. 3-2. Data for 1980 to 1989 obtained from National Center on Child Abuse and Neglect (U.S. Department of Health and Human Services). *National Child Abuse and Neglect Data System, Working Paper 2: 1991 Summary Data Component* (Washington, DC: U.S. Government Printing Office, 1993), p. 26. Data for 1976 to 1979 obtained from American Humane Association, *Highlights of Official Aggregate Child Neglect and Abuse Reporting, 1987* (Denver, CO: Author, 1989), p. 5.

whether reports of child maltreatment fatalities increased because of better tracking of cases or because the incidence of fatalities genuinely increased.

Children reported to have been physically abused have a higher probability than nonabused children of dying early in life (Sabotta & Davis, 1992). This conclusion is based on a sample of 11,085 children under the age of 18 who were reported to the child abuse registry in Washington between 1973 and 1986. The children reported to have been physically abused had a risk of death three times greater than that of a comparison group of children matched for sex, county of birth, and year of birth. Children reported to suffer from

neglect or sexual abuse also had an elevated risk of death. Later in the chapter, you will read about the association between domestic violence and child fatalities.

Prosecutors often have a difficult time handling child fatalities (Rainey & Dinsmore, 1994):

The cases are nasty, emotionally draining and filled with procedural frustrations. Victims have often had multiple caretakers who could be suspects. Injuries can be unusual or confusing and may have occurred over a long period. Juries are reluctant to believe anyone would kill a child and judges often loathe to impose severe sentences. Lack of homicide-by-abuse laws may prevent charging suspects with murder even when evidence clearly points to abuse as

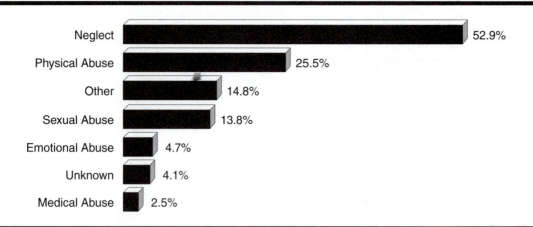

Figure 20-4 Percentage of 1,011,628 victims reporting each type of maltreatment in 1994. Because some states report more than one type of maltreatment per victim, the total does not equal 100. "Other" types of maltreatment include abandonment, congenital drug addiction, and threats to harm the child. From National Center on Child Abuse and Neglect (U.S. Department of Health and Human Services). *Child Maltreatment 1994: Reports from the States to the National Center on Child Abuse and Neglect* (Washington, DC: U.S. Government Printing Office, 1996), p. 2-5.

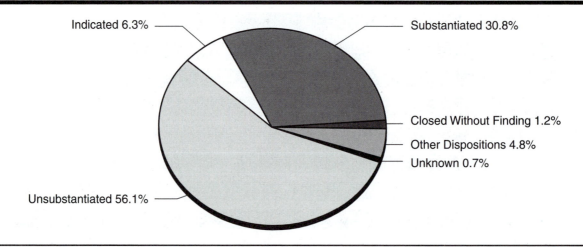

Figure 20-5. Investigated reports by disposition in 1994, based on 1,630,449 reports from 49 states. From National Center on Child Abuse and Neglect (U.S. Department of Health and Human Services). *Child Maltreatment 1994: Reports from the States to the National Center on Child Abuse and Neglect* (Washington, DC: U.S. Government Printing Office, 1996), p. 2-3.

the cause of death. Agency policies and inadequate staff training may undermine timely investigations and bolster a tendency to minimize criminal culpability.... The medical examiner's participation in helping the prosecutor and public understand exactly how a child abuse victim died is important to overcoming barriers to criminal accountability. A good relationship with the medical examiner can also be an important step toward a broader community effort to prevent the torture and killing of children. (p. 2)

Dr. Michael Baden, of the New York State Police Medical Examiner's Office, offers the following case as an illustration of how repeated physical abuse can result in a child fatality (U.S. Advisory Board on Child Abuse and Neglect, 1995).

CASE 20-7. HENRIETTE
Henriette, who was 5 years old, was brought to Lincoln Hospital in the Bronx four times over several months, each time with a different injury: a skull fracture, extensive bruising, cigarette burns on her hands and chest, and severe scalding from hot tapwater. On her final trip, she was DOA [dead on arrival]. An autopsy revealed that she died from a lacerated liver, the result of being severely punched. When the Medical Examiner collected hospital records, he noticed that a different doctor had seen the girl each time, and the seemingly caring family always gave a history of accidents—a clumsy little girl who put her hands in ashtrays, stepped into scalding water, or fell down a flight of stairs. Each time, the new doctor, untrained in the signs of inflicted abuse, believed the story. (p. 49, with changes in notation)

Demographic Information Related to Child Maltreatment

Two major national studies provide information about the incidence of child maltreatment: the annual survey of cases of child maltreatment reported to child protective agencies, conducted by the National Center on Child Abuse and Neglect (1996), and the Third National Incidence Study of Child Abuse and Neglect (NIS-3) (Sedlak & Broadhurst, 1996). Some information from the NIS-3 is presented in this chapter, but more detailed findings from the study can be found in Appendix E. The difference between the two studies is that the National Center on Child Abuse and Neglect study is based only on cases reported to child protective

agencies, whereas the NIS-3 is based on three sources of information: cases reported to child protective agencies, cases known to other investigatory agencies, and cases known to professionals in schools, hospitals, and other agencies. In the latter two instances, the cases may or may not have been reported to child protective agencies.

Age and sex of victims of child maltreatment. In 1994, children of all ages were victims of maltreatment—27% of the victims were 3 years old or younger, 20% were between 4 and 6 years, 17% were between 7 and 9 years, 15% were between 10 and 12 years, and 21% were between 13 and 18 years (see Figure 20-6). Being young and helpless appears to be no barrier to maltreatment, since young chil-

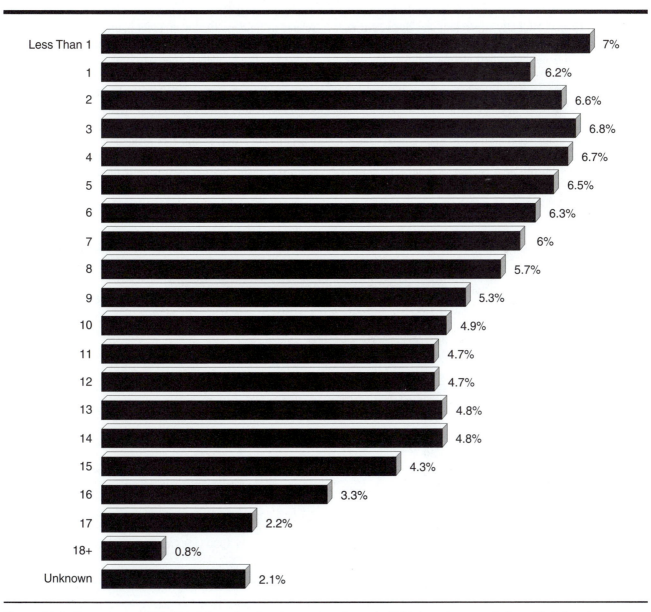

Figure 20-6. Percentage of 901,487 victims of maltreatment at each age in 1994, based on reports from 46 states. From National Center on Child Abuse and Neglect (U.S. Department of Health and Human Services). *Child Maltreatment 1994: Reports from the States to the National Center on Child Abuse and Neglect* (Washington, DC: U.S. Government Printing Office, 1996), p. 2-6.

dren are maltreated more frequently than older ones. Females had a slightly higher rate of victimization than males (52.3% versus 46.7%). In the NIS-3, females were three times more likely to be sexually abused than were males.

Family characteristics associated with child maltreatment. The NIS-3 reported that children had a greater chance of being maltreated when they were members of poor families (income below $15,000 per year), large families (four or more children), or families with a single parent. Sedlak and Broadhurst (1996, p. xviii) offer some specific findings about these three factors:

1. Children from the lowest-income families were 18 times more likely to be sexually abused, almost 56 times more likely to be educationally neglected, and over 22 times more likely to be seriously injured from maltreatment than children from the highest income families (incomes over $30,000).
2. Children in the largest families were physically neglected at nearly three times the rate of those who came from single-child families.
3. Children of single parents had a 77% greater risk of being harmed by physical abuse, an 87% greater risk of being harmed by physical neglect, and an 80% greater risk of suffering serious injury or harm from abuse or neglect than children living with both parents.

Ethnicity and incidents of child maltreatment. In 1994, White American children, Hispanic American children, and Asian/Pacific Islander children were somewhat *underrepresented* in reports of child maltreatment, whereas Black American children and Native American children were somewhat *overrepresented,* given their representation in the population of the United States (see Figure 20-7). The strong relationship between ethnicity and poverty may account, in whole or part, for the overrepresentation of Black American children and Native American children in reports of child maltreatment.

Comment on Incidence of Child Maltreatment

The national statistics just cited indicate that poverty is highly related to child maltreatment. Later in the chapter, you will be reading more about the association of poverty with child maltreatment. The incidence figures from the annual survey conducted by the National Center on Child Abuse and Neglect do not indicate actual rates of child maltreatment, as cases of child maltreatment are inevitably underreported. Middle- and upper-socioeconomic-class families, for example, may go to a health care provider, clinic, or residential facility rather than call Child Protective Services or law enforcement when they learn that their children have been maltreated. And the professionals at these institutions may be more reluctant to report their suspicions of child maltreatment when the family

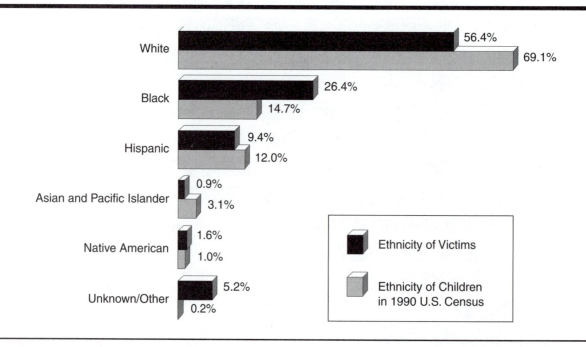

Figure 20-7. Ethnicity of 952,620 victims in 1994, based on reports from 47 states. From National Center on Child Abuse and Neglect (U.S. Department of Health and Human Services). *Child Maltreatment 1994: Reports from the States to the National Center on Child Abuse and Neglect* (Washington, DC: U.S. Government Printing Office, 1996), p. 2-8.

is from a higher socioeconomic class. Similarly, some ethnic minority groups, such as Asian Americans and Hispanic Americans, are more likely to consider child maltreatment a private matter than are Anglo Americans. Consequently, they may not contact Child Protective Services or law enforcement when they learn that their children have been maltreated by family members or by someone else. More research is needed on how socioeconomic class and ethnicity are related to reports of child maltreatment, focusing both on family practices and on the practices of mandated reporters.

Costs of Child Maltreatment

According to the National Committee to Prevent Child Abuse (1994), the estimated minimal annual costs of child maltreatment are as follows:

Costs of Health Care

Hospitalization	$ 792,162,400
Lay person counseling	$ 814,756,800
Subtotal	$1,606,919,200

Cost of Out-of-Home Care

Foster care	$1,908,000,000
Juvenile facilities	$1,945,356,200
In-patient mental health facilities	$2,848,800,000
Subtotal	$6,702,156,200

Costs of Child Protective Services

Investigative services	$504,000,000
Family preservation services	$192,500,000
Subtotal	$696,500,000
Estimated Total	**$9,000,000,000**

Additional costs include those associated with long-term impairment (both physical and mental) of the maltreated children, emergency room care, family reunification services, special education services, and adjudication of child maltreatment cases. And "beyond these costs lie the intangible human costs of emotional stress" (p. 3), lost productivity, and risk for poor parenting in the next generation.

Children Who Are Particularly Vulnerable to Child Maltreatment

Children with physical or intellectual disabilities are about 1.7 times more vulnerable to maltreatment than children without disabilities (National Center on Child Abuse and Neglect, 1993). The following reasons may account for the increased vulnerability of children with disabilities to physical abuse, sexual abuse, emotional abuse, and neglect (Carmody, 1991; Westcott, 1991):

- increased dependency on family and caregivers for basic needs
- limited contact with children of their own choosing

- compliance and obedience instilled as good behavior
- isolation and rejection from others, which increases vulnerability to attention and affection from potential perpetrators
- naive belief in the good intentions of other people
- limited knowledge about sex, misunderstanding of sexual advances, and inability to distinguish when boundaries are being crossed
- difficulty in distinguishing different types of touching
- limited mobility, which impedes their ability to escape from maltreatment
- difficulty in communicating their needs and experiences
- problems in reasoning
- difficulty in predicting the consequences of their actions
- limited impulse control
- limited knowledge of Child Protective Services

The following stressors can increase the likelihood of a caregivers' maltreating a child with a disability (National Committee to Prevent Child Abuse, 1995):

- feeling unable to handle the care of the child with a disability or to simply accept the child as being "different"
- failing to understand the behavioral patterns, communications, and needs of the child with a disability
- having difficulty carrying out the recommended interventions
- having financial or time limits stretched because of the additional medical and educational services needed for a child with a disability
- lacking the necessary social supports or networks to work through the many concerns and situations that arise in providing care for the child with a disability and for the other members of the family

The following case illustrates the vulnerability of an adolescent with a disability (Andrews & Veronen, 1993).

CASE 20-8. MARGARET

Margaret was a 16-year-old female with mental retardation who stayed at home all day throughout summer vacation. She was very lonely and had few friends or social contacts other than her family. Margaret's brother-in-law began to show her special attention. He worked as a yard man, with irregular hours. He began to visit in the middle of the day. Initially, he was nice, but then he began to pressure her to have sex with him. She wanted to please him and eventually gave in. The relationship was discovered only after she became pregnant. (p. 147)

Individuals with developmental disabilities should not be presumed incompetent to disclose maltreatment or to testify in court about the maltreatment (Valenti-Hein & Schwartz, 1993). Rather, they should be assessed in the same way as other witnesses. The presumption of incompetency may result in the failure to prosecute perpetrators, thus placing individuals with developmental disabilities at risk for further maltreatment.

REASONS WHY PEOPLE MALTREAT CHILDREN

Why do people maltreat children? Perhaps there are as many answers as there are offenders. Yet, offenders do share some underlying commonalities. This part of the chapter explores theories of why people become offenders and presents some statistics about offenders.

Child maltreatment does not occur in a vacuum. To understand what may lead people to commit child abuse and neglect, you must look at individual determinants, family determinants, environmental determinants, and child characteristics and how these factors interact (see Figure 20-8). Child maltreatment is primarily a family affair, occurring in the homes where children live. Therefore, you need to study carefully the family and its environment, especially the roles of parents and other caregivers, to understand the forces that lead some family members to hurt, maim, and even kill their children.

Once parents begin to abuse their children, noncompliant or oppositional children may stimulate the parents to continue the maltreatment, particularly physical abuse. *This provocation does not suggest that noncompliant or oppositional children are in any way to blame for the abuse, nor does it suggest that the abuse be condoned.* Sometimes children may be oppositional to gain the attention of caregivers—any attention, even abuse, may be better than no attention. Children with severe disabilities, as noted earlier, may be more prone to maltreatment than children with few or no disabilities.

Do not assume that all parents who have the characteristics shown in Figure 20-8 (or similar ones) will maltreat

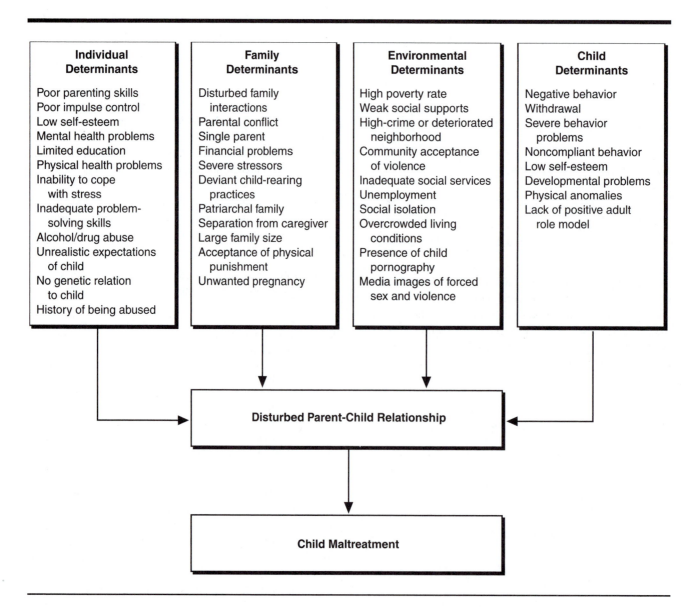

Figure 20-8. Determinants of child maltreatment.

their children. Parents who have some or even many of these characteristics do not maltreat their children. You may find parents who maltreat their children and yet have few, if any, of these characteristics. Although you need to be alert to the major characteristics associated with offenders, your decisions about whether maltreatment occurred must be made on the basis of the evidence available in the specific case.

Child maltreatment may occur when individuals face stressors that outweigh their supports (Belsky, 1993). The following formula illustrates this relationship in the area of child physical abuse:

$$PA = f(V, P) \text{ when } V > P$$

- *PA* refers to physical abuse
- *f* means "function of"
- *V* refers to *vulnerability factors,* such as personal and environmental stressors
- *>* means "greater than"
- *P* refers to *protective factors,* such as *love of children* (for example, wanting to protect, comfort, and nourish children), *social supports* (for example, adequate informal resources, such as relatives and friends, or adequate formal resources, such as mental health or other health care providers and religious leaders who offer counseling and supportive services), *coping skills* (for example, competencies, such as communication skills, problem-solving skills, and skills in handling emotions), and *self-esteem* (for example, the positive perception of personal resources and abilities)

When vulnerability factors exceed protective factors, caregivers may physically abuse their children. Obviously, other outcomes are possible, and physical abuse of children is not inevitable. Unfortunately, few of the above variables have been reliably quantified. However, the formula, rough as it is, reminds us that caregivers do not physically abuse children simply because the caregivers are evil people. A combination of negative personal and environmental variables usually must occur before caregivers physically abuse their children.

It is not in the nature of the mother's back to let the baby fall.

—African Proverb

THE OFFENDER IN CASES OF CHILD PHYSICAL ABUSE AND NEGLECT

Theories of Child Physical Abuse and Neglect

Three major theories have been offered to account for why offenders commit child physical abuse and neglect (Tzeng, Jackson, & Karlson, 1991). The first is the *individual determinants theory,* which focuses on the characteristics of the offender. The second is the *sociocultural determinants theory,* which asserts that social, cultural, economic, and political factors account for the offender's behavior. The third is the *individual-environment interaction theory,* which combines the individual determinants theory and the sociocultural determinants theory. The following material on theories of child physical abuse and neglect is from Tzeng et al. (1991, adapted primarily from pp. 14–20), with additions from Main and Solomon (1986); Pianta, Egeland, and Erickson (1989); and Wolfe (1987).

Individual determinants theory of child physical abuse and neglect. The individual determinants theory suggests that some of the following factors in the offender's development led him or her to commit child physical abuse or neglect:

- *traumatic experiences in early childhood* (for example, the offender was a victim or a witness of child maltreatment or was rejected as an infant)
- *abnormal or deviant characteristics* (for example, the offender has a substance abuse problem, a psychological disorder, antisocial personality traits, poor impulse control, low tolerance for frustration inappropriate expressions of anger, a pattern of displacing feelings, excessive dependency needs, social incompetence, or incompetence as a parent)
- *inadequate affective processes* (for example, the offender has inappropriate or blunted emotions, has a negative affect toward the child, or experiences depression)
- *inadequate cognitive processes* (for example, the offender rationalizes abusive behavior, maintains inaccurate beliefs and expectations regarding the child, maintains inaccurate beliefs concerning discipline, is of low intelligence, has poor judgment, or is poorly educated)
- *inadequate personal resources* (for example, the offender has low self-esteem, poor parenting skills, or inadequate ability to cope with stress)
- *personal stressors* (for example, the offender has family conflicts, a personal illness, a child who engages in disruptive behavior, or difficulty in raising a child with a physical or intellectual disability)
- *removal of inhibitions* (for example, the offender has inhibitions that were reduced by alcohol or drugs)
- *reinforcement for the maltreatment* (for example, the offender obtains relief from tension or satisfaction from the fact that the child becomes quieter and more passive after being beaten)

Sociocultural determinants theory of child physical abuse and neglect. The sociocultural determinants theory suggests that some of the following factors in the offender's environment led him or her to commit child physical abuse or neglect:

- *inadequate family structure* (for example, the offender's immediate family is characterized by harsh norms for punishment; authoritarian child-rearing practices; inadequate family dynamics; disturbed parent-child relationships including inconsistent discipline, inflexibility, and minimal stimulation; poor controls over the child's behavior; or constant crises and chaotic settings, with little organization or structure to daily routines)
- *inadequate support systems* (for example, the offender's community has poor health care, inadequate financial resources, no crisis or social service hotlines, and inadequate child-care education programs, and the offender's family is socially isolated and lacks support from extended-family members, neighbors, and friends)
- *social stressors* (for example, the family is at the poverty level because family members are unemployed, have low incomes, or are poorly educated, or the family has a history of frequent moves, resides in a crime-ridden neighborhood, or maintains deviant subcultural norms)
- *high degree of competition for jobs, promoting intergroup conflict*
- *formal and informal socialization factors and social ideologies that teach selfishness and unconcern for others and thus promote violence*
- *cultural sanctioning of violence as a means of disciplining, solving problems, and expressing authority*
- *cultural attitudes that historically consider children as property*
- *cultural beliefs that assume children are unable to understand and be responsive to nonphysical disciplinary and control tactics*

Individual-environment interaction theory of child physical abuse and neglect. The individual-environment interaction theory suggests that individual determinants and sociocultural determinants interact to contribute to child physical abuse or neglect. For example, a father who physically abuses his child may have had traumatic experiences in his own early childhood and may be authoritarian, of low intelligence, depressed, and in poor health. Such individual characteristics may combine with environmental factors—such as poverty, unemployment, poor and crowded living conditions, social isolation, and marital conflict—to create stress for the father and influence the quality of his caregiving.

Table 20-3 is a chronology of events relating to treatment of children and women in the United States. Until child labor laws were passed in the mid-1880s, children were exploited by society; it would be fair to say that prior to this time society was guilty of maltreating children. It took almost another 100 years before the federal government offered minimally adequate safeguards to protect children. But even the safeguards in the 1990s do not protect immigrant and refugee children and adults who work, for example, in agriculture or the garment industry from exploitation. These children and adults continue to be exploited because

of the difficulty of enforcing labor regulations in general and child labor regulations in particular. Although it is hard to know how society's treatment of children and women affects individual family interactions, cultural attitudes establish the climate in which we interact with each other.

The Theory of the Conflict-Prone Institution

Because maltreatment occurs primarily within the family context, it is useful to examine how the family as an institution can produce an environment in which child maltreatment can grow. Families create climates that may foster violent, nonviolent, or tender and loving behaviors. The *theory of the conflict-prone institution* suggests that family structures and family norms that foster conflict among family members who hold different interests and represent different age and gender groups may encourage violence within families. When violence ensues, family members often cannot easily leave the family, especially if they are children or adults who are not economically independent (Schneider, 1993).

The theory of the conflict-prone institution assumes that family members spend more time interacting with each other than they do with others outside the family. Such interactions are intense and wide ranging, and each family member influences the values, attitudes, and behavior patterns of other family members. Family members know about each other's strengths and vulnerabilities, preferences and dislikes, and assets and fears. They can use this knowledge for mutual support or for devastating attacks on one another. "Families are subject to constant change and transformation: the birth of children, their growing up, the ageing of the parents, their retirements, their deaths" (Schneider, 1993, pp. 38–39). One family member's unemployment, illness, or poor school performance puts pressure on the other family members as well. The insularity of family life makes it difficult for outside forces to intervene in family conflicts.

The social myth of the happy family, as disseminated by the mass media, can intensify family conflicts. When conflicts occur, family members may experience them as highly personal failures and may react to them with violence. For example, parents may believe they have the right to use corporal punishment as a legitimate means of child rearing. Married couples may tolerate violence against each other. Parents and others may wrongly regard violence between brothers or sisters as desirable for the development of the children's conflict-management skills.

The Social Learning and Interaction Theory

The *social learning and interaction theory* helps us understand why the family as an institution sometimes produces violent behavior and sometimes does not. This theory

Table 20-3
Historical Events Affecting the Treatment of Children and Women in the United States

Date	Event	Date	Event
1654	The Massachusetts Bay Colony provided for corporal punishment by whipping of children who behaved disrespectfully and disobediently toward their parents.		child labor laws by this date. Alabama passed a law stating that children needed to be at least 12 years old to work and would be permitted to work a maximum of 66 hours per week.
1710	The New York City Council approved an order that allowed 30 children between 3 and 15 years of age to work in the production of textiles.	1910	New Jersey established a minimum age of 16 years for night work. The U.S. Mann Act prohibited interstate and international traffic of women for immoral purposes.
1790	A cotton mill began operation in Rhode Island, employing children between 4 and 10 years of age.	1912	The Children's Bureau of the U.S. Department of Labor was established.
1813	The Connecticut legislature passed a law requiring factory children to be taught basic literacy and numeracy.	1916	Child labor legislation raised the minimum age for children employed in mills, factories, and mines from 12 years to 14 years.
1834	Married women had few legal rights. They could not sue in their own names or continue contracts made before their marriage. Their property became their husband's upon marriage.		Montana elected the first woman member of the House of Representatives. The U.S. Congress enacted the Federal Child Labor Law, which barred from interstate commerce articles produced by children.
1836	Massachusetts required factory children to have at least three months' education in the preceding year.	1918	The Supreme Court declared the Federal Child Labor Law of 1916 to be unconstitutional.
1839	Mississippi became the first state to grant property rights to women.	1920	The Nineteenth Amendment to the U.S. Constitution, granting women the right to vote, was signed into law.
1842	Massachusetts passed a law restricting the workday of children under 12 years to a maximum of 10 hours a day.	1925	The right of married women to keep their birth names was recognized by the U.S. State Department.
1848	Pennsylvania became the first state to prohibit the employment of children under 12 years in cotton, wool, silk, and flax factories. However, some states in the South continued to employ children as young as 6 or 7 years to work 13-hour days.	1933	Most states had laws requiring that children up to 14 years of age attend school.
		1938	Congress passed the Fair Labor Standards Act, which regulated the employment of children. The law generally set 16 years as the minimum age for employment.
1854	The Children's Aid Society in New York City opened a lodging house for boys.		
1863	Seven states had passed laws limiting the hours of child workers. However, in Massachusetts, the law applied only to children under 12 years and in Connecticut only to those under 14 years.	1962	C. Henry Kempe and his colleagues published a study that introduced the concept of the "battered-child syndrome."
1869	Wyoming became the first state to give women the right to vote.	1963	Thirteen states had laws making the reporting of child maltreatment mandatory.
1871	The Society for the Prevention of Cruelty to Children was established in New York City.	1966	All 50 states had laws making the reporting of child maltreatment mandatory.
1872	The U.S. Supreme Court ruled that the State of Illinois could bar a woman from the practice of law on the grounds that she was married.	1967	The U.S. Supreme Court held that young people in juvenile court were guaranteed many of the constitutional rights granted to adult criminal defendants.
1880s	U.S. laws gave men implicit and explicit permission to beat their wives.		The U.S. Supreme Court extended the Fifth Amendment to juveniles, preventing the State from forcing a young person to testify.
1886	A bill proposed in Pennsylvania to make wife beating a crime failed.		
1890	Illinois allowed married women to practice law.	1970	The U.S. Supreme Court held that the state must prove a child's guilt "beyond a reasonable doubt" in all delinquency hearings. In other types of hearings, such as with children who are in need of supervision or who have committed status offenses, the standard of proof is lower—either a "preponderance of the evidence" or "clear and convincing evidence." Status offenses are actions, performed by children, that parents, guardians, teachers, or custodians consider to be disobedient. Children may be described as
1899	The first juvenile court in the United States was established in Illinois.		
1900	The 1900 U.S. census reported that 1,750,178 children between the ages 10 and 15 years were employed; this represented an increase of over 1,000,000 children in a 30-year period.		
1903	The National Child Labor Committee was formed to promote child labor laws. Fifteen states had passed		

(*Continued*)

Table 20-3 (*Continued*)

Date	Event	Date	Event
	"incorrigible," "beyond control," "habitually disobedient," or truant from school.	1981	Eight million women were raising children alone; only 59% were entitled to child support, and only 72% of those received any payment at all.
	There were 5,600,000 families headed by women, with no husbands present.	1983	There were approximately 500 to 800 battered women's shelters and about 700 rape crisis programs in the country.
1971	The Twenty-Sixth Amendment to the Constitution lowered the voting age in federal elections from 21 years to 18 years.	1985	Only eight states had legally abolished corporal punishment in schools.
1974	The Child Abuse Prevention and Treatment Act was enacted; the act encouraged health care providers and other professionals working with children to report maltreatment.	1987	Ten women were killed every day by their batterers.
		1989	A pregnant Florida cocaine addict was convicted of transmitting drugs to a "minor"—a fetus.
1975	The U.S. Supreme Court ruled that women cannot be excluded from juries on the basis of sex.	1990	The Department of Health and Human Services handled 18 million cases of delinquent child support payments; only 18% resulted in collection.
	U.S. Public Law 94-142 passed, proclaiming the right to equal education for all handicapped children.	1991	More adult women were injured by battery than by any other cause.
1980	Of all births, 18.4% were to unwed women, and 40.8% were to mothers under 20 years.	1992	A court in Florida permitted a 12-year-old boy to "divorce" his parents.
1980s	Legislation emerged affording women protection from their husband's physical assaults; at least 43 states enabled abused spouses to obtain civil protection orders without initiating divorce proceedings, as previously required.	1995	Births among unmarried mothers accounted for 32% of all births, a rate of 44.9 births per 1,000 women. There were 12,200,000 families headed by women, with no husbands present.
	Thousands of homeless children depended on drugs and prostitution to survive		

Source: Adapted, in part, from Carruth (1993), Fyfe (1989), Olsen (1994), Rawlins and Drake (1993), and Sussman (1977).

regards intrafamilial violence as resulting from psychosocial interaction processes, both within the family and between the family and its social environment. "This interaction is conceived as a constant causal chain, a process of action and reaction, with each new action in turn evoking a new reaction" (Schneider, 1993, p. 38). Children who have been maltreated by their parents or who have witnessed the maltreatment of brothers, sisters, or parents may be more likely when they become adults to maltreat their own children or partners or to be maltreated by their partners.

The theory postulates that the roles of the offender and the victim are learned. When violence occurs in a child's family, it is often transmitted to the family the child establishes upon reaching adulthood. Influences outside the family, such as the mass media, also affect what family members learn and how they interact with each other. Both violence and its social and moral justification are learned. For example, corporal punishment may be seen as necessary for the good of the child.

Victims of violence are treated as objects by their abusers. Victims may develop a pattern of learned helplessness, which leaves them unable to defend themselves or remove themselves from intolerable situations. Their failure to act constructively further diminishes their self-esteem and contributes to their social isolation.

Relationship of Socioeconomic Class to Physical Abuse of Children

Families that live in poverty are more likely to abuse their children because they have fewer resources, fewer supports, and more stressors than families that are not living in poverty (see the statistics relating family income and incidence of child maltreatment in Appendix E and the statistics on characteristics of perpetrators later in this chapter). Low-income families

have relatively young parents, with relatively little education, and larger than usual numbers of closely spaced children.... They also tend to have unstable relationships, with many mothers being unmarried, divorced or separated. In addition, many families with abuse depend in part or entirely on public resources for economic support. Finally, most abusive parents were abused or neglected in their own childhood.... Families with physical abuse also resemble families with other forms of violence.... Often, there is spousal and sibling violence as well as abuse of other children.... In addition, abusive parents have difficulty maintaining supportive relationships with friends and relatives. (Crittenden, 1996, p. 159)

Of course, physical abuse also occurs in families from upper socioeconomic classes. These cases may be underreported because of the status of the families, because money has covered the crime, or because professionals may be reluctant to believe that "upper-class" people would be abusive. Physical abuse can and does occur in families of doctors, lawyers, and corporate executives, to take three examples.

Cognitive Models of Child Physical Abuse and Neglect

Let's examine how an offender's distorted cognitive processes may be involved in child physical abuse and neglect.

A cognitive model of child physical abuse. Bugental (1992) proposed that caregivers' responses to the behaviors of their children are mediated by the caregivers' social cognitions, such as their beliefs about their children and about themselves. The cognitive model of child physical abuse, which has received support in several research studies (see Bugental, 1992), contains the following elements:

1. Children behave in a way that makes their caregivers angry.
2. Caregivers believe that the children's behavior is controllable or reflects willful acts on the children's part; the behavior is not seen as stemming from some aspect of the children's environment, from the children's physical state (such as being tired), or from some other factor.
3. Caregivers believe that they can do little to prevent themselves from hurting the children—that is, caregivers believe that they have little control over their actions.
4. Caregivers have elevated physiological reactivity—such as changes in heart rate, skin temperature, skin conductance, and blood pressure (all measures of autonomic arousal)—when they become angry at the children.
5. Caregivers readily interpret the difficult behaviors of the children as posing a threat to the caregivers.
6. Caregivers act to regain perceived control of the situation; these actions may result in their physically abusing the children.
7. Caregivers' actions may maintain or exacerbate the children's actions, and the cycle may elevate to a new level of harm and abuse.

An information-processing model of child neglect. Crittenden (1993) hypothesized that parents who neglect their children may fail to respond to their children's signals. Using information-processing theory, she proposed that parents' failure to respond may occur at any of four stages at which information is processed by the parents.

1. *Stage of perception.* Parents who neglect their children may not be able to perceive essential aspects of their children's states. For example, parents might hear their children's cries but not attend to them. Neglectful parents may have "a systematic bias toward not perceiving signals indicative of children's need for attention.... In many of the most severe cases of neglect, the neglectful parents seem with-

drawn, depressed, and even mentally retarded.... Early neglect of infant signals can have a progressive and deteriorating effect on the development of the parent-child relationship" (pp. 31, 32, 34). Parents with substance abuse problems may have particular difficulty recognizing their infants' signals.

2. *Stage of interpretation.* If the parents perceive their children's states, they may not be able to interpret accurately the meaning of their perceptions or they may interpret what they see as not requiring a response. For example, parents may perceive children's cries but decide that no action is needed. Or parents may believe that children can take care of themselves and need no assistance.

3. *Stage of selection of a response.* If the parents interpret accurately the meaning of their perceptions, they may not be able to determine the appropriate response or they might not have an appropriate response available. For example, a parent may interpret the child's crying appropriately but "knows neither how to respond nor how to elicit help" (p. 31). Parents may believe that there is nothing they can do to help their child.

4. *Stage of implementation of the response.* If the parents are able to determine the appropriate response, they may fail to implement the response. For example, a parent may know what to do to help the crying child but fail to do so because of other priorities or indifference or because the parent is in a crisis.

Neglectful parents probably have most of their problems at the earliest stages of information processing (Crittenden, 1993). The failure to perceive their children's state and the failure to interpret their own perceptions accurately suggests that neglectful parents have a personality disorder that will be extremely hard to treat. It may be difficult to pinpoint at what stage parents fail to process information.

For example, a mother who does not protect her daughters from their father's sexual abuse may (a) have no information to alert her to the problem, (b) not attend to (perceive) available information, (c) believe her daughters can handle the situation, (d) believe she can do nothing useful, (e) know that help is needed, but not know how to help, (f) know what to do, but not do it so as not to jeopardize her relationship with her husband, or (g) know what to do, but not do it because it would evoke feelings of anger, rejection, and so on in herself. (Crittenden, 1993, p. 42)

Signs That New Parents Are at High Risk for Child Maltreatment

When faced with the birth of a child, parents may behave in a manner that suggests the baby is unwanted. Identifying such behavior is helpful in determining which parents may have problems in raising their infant. Table 20-4 offers a list of high-risk signals seen prenatally, in the delivery room, and postnatally.

Some parents are insensitive to their infants' needs because their parents were insensitive to their needs when

Table 20-4
Signals That Parents Are at High Risk for Child Maltreatment

Signals Seen Prenatally

1. Mother or father does not want baby.
2. Mother or father is overconcerned with the unborn baby's sex.
3. Mother or father expresses exceedingly high expectations for the baby.
4. Mother or father tries to deny the pregnancy.
5. Mother or father is depressed over the pregnancy.
6. Mother or father seriously considers an abortion.
7. Mother or father seriously considers giving baby up for adoption.
8. Mother or father has little, if any, support from other people or community agencies.
9. Mother is single and frightened.
10. Mother or father displays excessive emotional withdrawal and mood swings.
11. Mother or father makes no preparation for baby.
12. Mother or father is poorly educated and doesn't understand pregnancy.
13. Mother has poor health.
14. Mother does not keep appointments.
15. Mother or father has poor living arrangements.
16. Neither mother nor father has a stable job.
17. Mother and father have had a disadvantaged upbringing.

Signals Seen in the Delivery Room

1. Mother appears sad, apathetic, disappointed, angry, frightened, or ambivalent.
2. Mother does not talk to baby.
3. Mother does not talk to baby's father.
4. Mother or father does not use baby's name.
5. Mother or father does not establish eye contact with baby.
6. Mother or father does not touch baby.
7. Mother or father does not cuddle baby.
8. Mother or father does not examine baby.
9. Mother or father is hostile toward baby.
10. Mother or father makes disparaging remarks about baby's sex or physical characteristics.
11. Mother or father is disappointed over baby's sex or other physical characteristics.
12. Mother or father refuses to hold baby even when offered the opportunity.
13. Mother does not receive any support from the father or relatives.

14. Mother expresses hostility toward father, who put her "through all this."
15. Father expresses hostility toward mother, who put him "through all this."

Signals Seen Postnatally

1. Mother or father remains disappointed over baby's sex.
2. Mother or father is critical of baby.
3. Mother or father yells or screams at baby.
4. Mother or father hits baby.
5. Other members of family are critical of baby.
6. Mother or father is bothered by baby's crying.
7. Mother or father is at a loss in knowing how to quiet baby.
8. Mother or father views baby as too demanding.
9. Mother or father ignores baby's demands.
10. Mother or father fails to feed baby appropriately.
11. Mother or father is repulsed by baby's messiness, smells, and spitting up.
12. Mother or father has unrealistic expectations for what baby can do.
13. Mother or father easily relinquishes control over care of baby to others.
14. Mother or father does not express any enjoyment about baby.
15. Mother or father does not establish eye contact with baby.
16. Mother or father talks brusquely to baby.
17. Mother or father handles baby roughly.
18. Mother or father speaks negatively about baby.
19. Mother or father does not comfort baby when baby cries.
20. Mother or father fails to dress baby appropriately.
21. Mother or father has complaints about baby that cannot be verified.
22. Mother or father frequently brings the baby to the hospital for unexplained reasons.
23. Mother or father miscommunicates information about baby.
24. Mother or father directs hostile feelings toward baby.
25. Mother or father is lonely or depressed and withdraws from baby.
26. Mother or father doesn't keep medical appointments for baby.

Source: Adapted, in part, from Gray, Cutler, Dean, and Kempe (1976).

they were infants—a phenomenon referred to as *cross-generational effects.* When this happens, the infant and parent may become estranged. However, some parents are able to overcome the rejection they experienced as infants and avoid rejecting their own infants.

Examples of Child Physical Abuse

In the following case of child physical abuse, the abuse came about when the mother's stress level reached a critical point (Kadushin & Martin, 1981).

CASE 20-9. MARTHA

Martha, a 21-year-old single female parent with a 1-month-old child, was alone late in the afternoon caring for her own child and a 2-year-old niece. The infant kept crying, and none of the mother's initial efforts to quiet her were effective. "Everything was building up inside—everything went—my nerves just left—my nerves are very touchy. They went wild—my nerves did—and I didn't know what I was doing." The mother's repeated slappings severely damaged the infant, who needed to be hospitalized. (pp. 158–159, with changes in notation)

In other cases, physical abuse may result from a parent's effort to change the child's behavior, to teach the child a lesson, or to discipline the child. The following is presented in the words of a father who used a belt to discipline his 13-year-old daughter (Kadushin & Martin, 1981).

CASE 20-10. TED

What I was hoping to accomplish was getting her to understand things that when I tell her something, I really mean it. 'Cause I don't think she really believes that you really mean what you say. I don't think she does. And I was trying to get her to understand me that I did believe that, I did mean what I tell her to do. I meant it so that she should take it seriously. Otherwise, anything I say, it don't even register. She blanks herself off from what you're saying. It makes me feel bad to have to spank my kid. I don't feel good doing that. When I do whup 'em, I go to 'em and tell 'em that I am sorry, you know, the thing happened like that, but that's the only way I can get them to understand what I mean—you know, sometimes you just have to throw away your feelings and just whup them. (p. 194)

Here are some reasons perpetrators gave for why they stopped physically abusing their children (Kadushin & Martin, 1981, p. 200, with changes in notation):

What stopped me was my oldest little girl. She was crying and she said, "Please, Mama, Jimmy's bleeding all over, please, Mama, please leave Jimmy alone."

I spanked her hard enough that I broke a blood vessel in my finger. And that stopped me, that amount of pain to myself stopped me and I realized, hey, you know, look what I'm doing.

I finally—I think what really made me stop was, I did see—I think it was blood on his behind where the buckle of the belt—you know, I hit him with the buckle of the belt on the behind, and that—I guess the little point that sticks inside the hole must have punctured his skin. That's really what made me stop, when I seen his blood, I got scared. So I stopped.

Sometimes parents may stop maltreating their child because the school, Child Protective Services, or law enforcement warns them that they may be violating the law. The warning, in some cases, is sufficient to scare the parents or to get them to seek help in order to improve the situation.

Characteristics of Neglectful Parents

Research suggests that the majority of neglectful parents may be characterized in the following ways (Gaudin, 1993; Polansky, Ammons, & Gaudin, 1985):

1. They typically are poor, lack access to resources, or find accessing the services they need to be too complex.
2. They typically are psychologically immature, often as a result of their own deficient nurturing as children.
3. They may be characterized by (a) *apathy*—the belief that nothing is worth doing, evidenced by lack of feeling, (b) *impulsiveness*—lack of self-monitoring and self-control, or (c) *anomie*—distrust of and withdrawal from society.
4. They want to be good parents but do not have the personal or financial resources, or the supportive services needed to raise their children.
5. They have strengths that can be mobilized.
6. They need goals that are positive, relevant, realistic, clearly stated, and achievable.
7. They may need to be ordered by the court to obtain services for their children, especially when they are apathetic.
8. They may need long-term psychological treatment, particularly when the neglect has been chronic.

Following is a characterization of families that neglect their children (Crittenden, 1996):

Child neglect is even more closely tied to poverty than physical child abuse. Indeed, most neglectful families depend on public assistance for their basic life needs. In addition, neglectful families tend to be large, have relatively few adults, and are structured around the mother and her children.... Men often bear a tangential relationship to neglectful families; although some are married, most are boyfriends functioning temporarily as family members. Maternal grandmothers [may], on the other hand, often function in permanent parental roles. Geographic instability appears related to urbanization, with neglectful families in rural areas remaining stable but isolated and neglectful families in cities moving frequently as a result of income and interpersonal difficulties. The only stable social network for most neglectful families consists of relatives who are as impoverished as the neglectful parents and who often reinforce the parents' limited understanding of parental roles. (p. 162)

Exhibit 20-1 is a *Los Angeles Times* reporter's observation of how a social worker handled a case of neglect. In this case, the mother was abusing drugs, had recently given birth, and had a history of neglecting her other children.

The following case illustrates severe neglect (Thornton, 1994).

CASE 20-11. HELENA

A couple were jailed and charged with felonious child endangerment after police found their 21-month-old daughter locked in a closet and near death from malnutrition and anemia. The girl, Helena, weighed only 14 pounds—the average

Background

Dispatched to unfamiliar, sometimes dangerous surroundings, Child Protective Services workers are expected to make instant predictions about a child's safety. They get no public recognition when they are right but are second-guessed, pilloried, and perhaps fired when they make a mistake and a child dies. Part detective, part shrink, and part paper pusher, the social workers respond to hotline reports, assess homes, petition the court if children are to be removed from parents, and then monitor their progress—with the mother and father, relatives, or in foster homes. At best, the social workers encounter overwhelmed parents, without financial or emotional resources but with a sincere desire to be responsible caregivers. At worst, they find adults who abuse drugs, behave violently, live in squalor, and deceive authorities to keep children who are their claim to a larger welfare check. Then the social worker must choose: leave the children in a potentially life-threatening home or push them into the dubious embrace of the foster-care system.

A Report Is Received

Jennifer Garza's day begins when a hotline call comes in to Child Protective Services. A newborn is in the neonatal intensive care unit at a local hospital, born to a mother who shot speed, cocaine, and heroin throughout her pregnancy, had no prenatal care, lives in a notorious welfare motel, and already has four children ages 6 and under scattered among relatives. This is a classic Section B, or "failure to protect," a breach of California's welfare law and grounds for seizing a child. The seasoned social worker moves quickly. She grabs the forms she will need to take custody of five children, along with a cell phone, a beeper, a street guide, a car seat, and a clasp to tie her hair back to avoid catching lice.

Garza's first stop is the hospital, where the drug-abusing mother has already checked out, leaving behind a 6-pound, 5-ounce girl. Garza instructs the nurse not to release the baby to anyone. She is now a ward of the county. A

judge will decide her fate, based on Garza's recommendations.

The original complaint names a motel in Azusa as the mother's home. For Garza it is a bad sign, because the place is well known to social workers as a drug location and the scene of frequent child abuse claims. Attached to the complaint is a computer printout that tells Garza that Child Protective Services social workers have seen this family twice before, another bad sign, although it will be days before the prior case files reach her desk because of antiquated record-keeping.

Garza assumes that the other children, ages 6, 3, 2, and 1, will be at the motel, and she intends to take them into custody. But in Room 119 she finds only Anna Hernandez, 23, and Freddie Alba, 25.

Ms. Hernandez explains that the other children are living with their great-grandmother, leaving the impression that they are normally with her. She does not deny using drugs but downplays the problem. Mr. Alba, shirtless and heavily tattooed, presents himself as outraged at his girlfriend's behavior. He didn't know she was using drugs, he said, and he wants to claim the baby and raise it at his mother's. "So I'm left here by myself?" Ms. Hernandez whines, staring vacantly at the television. Garza notes her indifference to the baby. But Mr. Alba is persuasive: He's taken a Polaroid of the infant and stuck it between the wings of the TV antenna. Perhaps he is a suitable parent.

Garza's next stop is the great-grandmother's Azusa bungalow, which has a tidy garden and several tricycles out front. She finds an extended family that undercuts the couple's version of events. Both Ms. Hernandez and Mr. Alba are heavy drug users, the relatives say. And all of Ms. Hernandez's children, born to a succession of fathers, have been handed off to relatives. "She just dumps them as she has them," wails one of the infant's great-aunts, who has three children of her own as well as Ms. Hernandez's 2-year-old. "Why don't they tie her tubes?"

The 1-year-old was initially fed diluted tea instead of formula, said the

great-aunt who raised him along with her own four children. The 5-year-old has a shunt in his brain as a result of a birth defect but wasn't taken to the doctor for checkups until he was turned over to Ms. Hernandez's father. Ms. Hernandez yanks the children back every once in a while to qualify for a larger welfare check, the relatives say. And previous social workers have visited but closed the case without court intervention.

Garza scowls at what she considers inadequate social work. "This time it's going to be legal," she says. "We want you guys to feel confident." She takes notes, fodder for a court petition. Garza calls her office and asks the secretary to run criminal checks on all adults in this household. She privately interviews Ms. Hernandez's older children about how they are treated. She surveys the home to be sure there is food, fire alarms, no electrical hazards. Her beeper goes off, with results of the criminal checks, all clean.

Three days later, Garza stops at the hospital to see the Hernandez baby, who is ready for discharge. No one has visited, which suggests that the mother is without remorse, the father lying about his intentions, and the paternal grandmother indifferent. Will the maternal relatives take another baby, Garza wonders? Or is this one headed for foster care?

Garza visits the warm circle of relatives caring for the Hernandez children. They have been to court and were awarded temporary custody. Mother and boyfriend were hostile at the hearing, and the great-aunts are nervous about home visits. Now comes the hard part. She tells the family the baby is ready to be discharged and will go to a foster home unless they take her. "You know she'll get pregnant again," one of the aunts says, explaining that they had not gone to the hospital lest the sight of the child melt their hearts. "Let's say we take this baby. Who'll take the next one? And the one after that?" Garza commiserates: "I understand your dilemma and I can't guarantee I won't be back here next year." The family has until morning to decide. The baby winds up in foster care.

---

weight of a 5-month-old child—when police rescued her from the closet of her parents' house. Her parents told officers after their arrests Friday that they put the child in the closet so she would not disturb her 3½-year-old brother and 2½-year-old sister while the couple went out for the evening.

An examining physician determined that Helena was within weeks of death from heart failure due to starvation.

The neighbors said they never knew the baby existed. The mother watched only her other two children playing outside, they said. The neighbors became suspicious when they heard rumors that a baby lived in a closet. They arranged to visit the child without the parents' knowledge. When neighbors saw the child, she wore gloves and bandages that covered swollen fingers and bruises. Despite their fears of retaliation by the child's parents, neighbors reported the abuse to the police. "If we don't do something about it, we'll be as guilty as them," a neighbor said. "We feel good about reporting it." (p. B-3, with changes in notation)

Child endangerment is a form of neglect. In child endangerment, parents may be careless, thoughtless, extremely self-centered and preoccupied with themselves, unable to recognize when they are placing their child in danger, or simply indifferent and uncaring about what happens to their child. The following account from the *Los Angeles Times* describes how parents with methamphetamine laboratories in their homes endanger the lives of their children (Weikel, 1996).

METH LABS IMPERIL YOUNG LIVES

Their parents have turned what should be safe havens into toxic powder kegs. Every day, children in trailer parks, suburban tracts, and cheap motels across California breathe fumes from chemical brews so nasty they can corrode steel.

With alarming frequency, narcotics officers who investigate the manufacture of methamphetamine are encountering hundreds of children whose parents' desires for drugs and fast profits have put them in harm's way. Perhaps no other illegal drug on the market has resulted in more cases of child abuse and endangerment than methamphetamine, a potent stimulant rivaling cocaine as the most prevalent street drug in the state.

The chemicals used to make methamphetamine are some of the most toxic and explosive on the market. Although law enforcement authorities routinely wear hazardous material suits during raids, children living inside the clandestine drug factories sometimes have been found wearing nothing but diapers. Of the 32 chemicals mentioned in recipes for the drug, about a third have been rated extremely hazardous. Fainting, nausea, eye irritations, sore throats and respiratory ailments are the least of the side effects. One key ingredient, hydriodic acid, can cause instant third-degree burns and destroy lung tissue if inhaled.

Not only are the ingredients hazardous, the finished product can have particularly profound effects on juveniles, including irregular heartbeats, seizures, and inflammation and hemorrhaging of the brain. Users can become paranoid, highly irritable, and violent.

Adding to the danger are the deplorable living conditions that characterize homes that have been turned into labs. Some have terrible plumbing because caustic wastes have burned out the drainpipes. Others are filled with trash and spoiled food. Loaded guns sometimes sit on coffee tables. Chemical contamination permeates everything—walls, upholstery, drapes.

Social workers say the children who come out of such poor environments are often withdrawn and distrustful. They have a hard time learning in school. Because their basic needs are rarely met, they stockpile food in hiding places—even when placed in foster care. Others, who were seldom washed by their parents, bathe excessively. In counseling, they draw crank pipes, syringes, and lab equipment such as beakers. Others talk about smoke, fires, and explosions in their homes. (Adapted from pp. A1, A18, A19. Copyright © 1996 *Los Angeles Times*. Reprinted by permission. "How Young Lives Are Put in Peril." April 7, 1996. By Daniel Weikel.)

Munchausen Syndrome by Proxy

Another form of child physical abuse results from a condition known as Munchausen Syndrome by Proxy. Smith (1993) describes this condition in caregivers as follows:

The adult [caregiver], usually the mother, fabricates or induces illness symptoms in a child and presents the child for medical treatment. Medical personnel are presented with a medical mystery, often involving life-threatening incidents, and with a false history. Unwittingly, medical personnel often perform extensive needless and sometimes painful diagnostic procedures in search of an elusive diagnosis.

The medical literature has long recognized Munchausen Syndrome in which a patient presents herself/himself for treatment after fabricating symptoms/illness. Munchausen Syndrome is named after 18th Century Baron Von Munchausen, who was known for telling tall tales. More recently, the term Munchausen Syndrome by Proxy…was introduced by Roy Meadow in 1977 to describe incidents where a [caregiver] induces symptoms/illness in a child and then seeks medical treatment for the child. In some instances, the abusing [caregiver] was herself a Munchausen Syndrome case, and with the birth of a child, the pattern may shift to seeking needless medical care for the child, resulting in Munchausen Syndrome by Proxy. (p. 1)

There are four key elements in Munchausen Syndrome by Proxy (Light & Sheridan, 1990):

1. The child's illness is simulated or produced by a caregiver.
2. The caregiver makes repeated requests for medical evaluation and care of the child.
3. The caregiver denies any knowledge of the cause of the child's symptoms.
4. The child's symptoms quickly cease when the child and the caregiver are separated.

A distinction exists between Munchausen Syndrome by Proxy and medical neglect (Rosenberg, 1995). In *Munchausen Syndrome by Proxy,* the caregiver withholds medication to keep the child ill or to exaggerate the child's illness, uses poisons or manipulates laboratory data, or falsely reports symptoms (Sheridan & Levin, 1995). The caregiver keeps appointments, fills prescriptions, and makes sure that the medicine bottles are empty on schedule, but the child still gets sicker. However, when the child is removed from the caregiver and placed in a foster home, the child improves. In *medical neglect,* the caregiver does not deliberately attempt to make the child sicker. Instead, the caregiver misses appointments, fails to fill or refill prescriptions, or, if the prescriptions are filled, fails to give the child the medicine. When help or transportation is provided for the family, the medically neglected child usually improves.

Although prevalence rates are difficult to establish, Munchausen Syndrome by Proxy may be more common than is often portrayed. The disorder may be present in 0.27% of cases of infants in apnea monitoring programs, 1% of cases of asthmatic patients, and as many as 5% of cases of allergy patients (Schreier & Libow, 1993). These figures should be viewed as tentative until more reliable estimates can be established. Children may be victims of Munchausen Syndrome by Proxy in addition to having genuine illnesses.

The following characteristics should raise suspicions of Munchausen Syndrome by Proxy (Kaufman, 1994; Smith, 1993):

ILLNESS-RELATED FACTORS

1. The child has persistent or recurrent unexplained illnesses.
2. The child's symptoms do not match known medical symptoms or are not consistent with them.
3. The child's symptoms typically have been witnessed only by his or her caregiver.
4. The child's symptoms are resolved each time the child is hospitalized but not when the child is at home.
5. The child has new symptoms at the hospital that have an onset witnessed by the caregiver only.
6. The child's symptoms do not occur when the child is away from the caregiver.
7. The child's symptoms are not consistent with her or his general health, as when the caregiver reports the child has a fever but the child doesn't otherwise appear sick.
8. The child fails to respond to medical therapy.
9. When the child is placed on an apnea monitor (a device to monitor breathing), the device appears to be in good working order but "doesn't work" for unknown reasons.

FAMILY HISTORY FACTORS

10. The child's siblings have or had unusual illnesses or deaths.
11. The caregiver denies knowledge about the etiology of the child's illness.
12. The caregiver is knowledgeable about various aspects of medicine.
13. The caregiver has had illnesses much like the child's.
14. The caregiver was diagnosed as having Munchausen Syndrome in adolescence.

PARENTAL BEHAVIOR FACTORS

15. When the child is hospitalized, the caregiver makes prolonged visits, is very attentive, and won't leave the child's side but doesn't seem as worried about the child as the hospital staff is.

16. The caregiver appears to be enjoying the attention he or she is getting from the hospital staff.
17. The caregiver's level of concern appears to greatly underestimate the gravity of the child's condition.
18. The caregiver welcomes medical tests for the child, even when the tests are painful.
19. The caregiver is more concerned with questioning the medical staff's choice of diagnostic procedures than with attending to the child's condition.
20. The caregiver seems reluctant to have the child discharged, despite assurances that hospitalization is not necessary.
21. The caregiver appears overinvolved with the child and is isolated from the rest of the family.

Here are some examples of unconscionable parental acts of Munchausen Syndrome by Proxy (Toth & Whalen, 1987):

The reported cases typically involve a mother fabricating a history of illness in a child under nine years of age. Some of these mothers …have had prior medical training. Child victims may die or suffer injury as a result of the actions taken by the adult to induce symptoms, which have included repeatedly administering sodium bicarbonate to children, eventually causing one to die and another to be hospitalized with vomiting and diarrhea…; injecting a child with diuretics, causing vomiting, dehydration, high urinary output, low potassium levels and calcium deposits in his [or her] kidneys…; and repeatedly administering laxatives, causing severe diarrhea, blood infection, dehydration and months of hospitalization…. Also described in the literature are cases in which parents have induced seizures or cardiorespiratory arrest by suffocation, injection of contaminated fluid into the child's intravenous tubing, application of caustics to the child's skin to cause a rash, administration of various other poisons, etc. (p. V-54)

The following case illustrates Munchausen Syndrome by Proxy.

CASE 20-12. MRS. STANFORD

A six-year-old child was transferred from another hospital following a three-week history of chronic diarrhea. After one week of hospitalization, it was apparent to the medical staff that the child's diarrhea was not physiologic in nature, given the multitude of normal tests and the cycling nature of the diarrhea. The child was subjected to numerous needle sticks for blood, and numerous IVs were started. She underwent a colonoscopy with a biopsy and a small bowel biopsy, both of which were invasive procedures. A decision was made by the interdisciplinary team to separate the child from the mother to determine the basis of the diarrhea. The mother later admitted to a physician that she had in fact been feeding the child even though she was classified as "nothing by mouth" and that the stools were her own mixed with water. She later recanted this admission. After the mother was prohibited from visiting the child without supervision, the child's diarrhea ceased, and she had to be given a suppository to induce a bowel movement. The family history revealed that there is also a two-year-old child in this family diagnosed as having a seizure disorder and treated with anticonvulsants. His electroencephalogram was normal, but he was treated because of the clinical history given by the mother. The mother had a history of psychiatric problems and was known to fabricate illnesses for herself. This child was discharged home to the care of the grandparents on a voluntary basis. The parents initially cooperated with protective services agencies, and the mother sought counseling. However, the mother began to exhibit abnormal behavior, and family members committed her to the state mental hospital. The parents are in the process of a divorce, and the father has custody of the children. State protective services continues to be active in this case. The hospital social worker and medical staff have been involved with this family for more than a year. (Mercer & Perdue, 1993, p. 76)

It is important that you take a careful history in cases where Munchausen Syndrome by Proxy is suspected. The mother may have gone to many different facilities to get treatment for the child in order to avoid leaving a comprehensive record in one hospital or clinic. Often, it is the social worker who—by making a sustained effort to get an in-depth background history—provides the initial clues about the child's condition.

Domestic Violence— Background Considerations

There is a link between domestic violence and child maltreatment. Children living in a home where domestic violence takes place are vulnerable to physical, emotional, and sexual abuse and also are vulnerable to neglect. Domestic violence degrades and abuses spouses, and it exposes children to situations that make them anxious and fearful and can terrify them. When you learn of domestic violence in a family, if you believe that the battered woman (or man) and the children need protection from the abuser, refer them to services that will offer them that protection.

In the 1990s, the federal government placed increased emphasis on reducing domestic violence. The Violence Against Women Act, passed in 1994, "enables victims to sue in federal court, allows police to pursue offenders across state lines and provides for shelters and counseling for victims of domestic violence" (Associated Press, 1996a, p. A-6).

What is domestic violence? Domestic violence can be defined in the following way (Kaiser Permanente, 1994):

Domestic violence also is known as battering, spousal abuse, family violence, wife beating, and physical violence. Battered women's syndrome refers to the psychological effects of violence, including chronic severe anxiety, depression, panic, insomnia, and associated physical symptoms. It is all of these things, but first and foremost, *domestic violence is a crime*. It is a violent crime.

Even though statistics have been gathered for the last several years, domestic violence is still underreported. Official estimates rely largely on FBI, police, and emergency room reports. But many victims report abuse to friends, family, churches, synagogues, physicians, and nurses. These sources of information are not included in national crime surveys. Also, many reports don't show how many times each battered woman has been abused, or how many instances her children have witnessed.

Domestic violence and spousal abuse refer to the victimization of someone with whom the abuser has or had an intimate or romantic relationship. According to one state penal code, it is "abuse against an adult or fully emancipated minor who is the spouse, former spouse, cohabitant or former cohabitant, or a person with whom the suspect has had a child or has a past or present dating or engagement relationship." Characterized by a pattern of coercive behaviors, domestic violence may take the form of physical, social, emotional, sexual, property, or economic abuse. The violence generally escalates and increases unless intervention occurs.

Physical violence or battering includes hitting, beating, shaking, shoving, pushing, pinching, biting, burning, hair-pulling, throwing things, restraining in any way, physically forcing the victim to do something against her or his will, attacking with objects as weapons, slapping, choking, punching, and kicking. *Forced sexual activity* constitutes sexual violence, while property violence consists of threatened or actual destruction of property. *Psychological and social violence* include threats of harm, physical isolation, extreme jealousy, degradation, economic power, and threats of harm to children. (pp. 10–11, with changes in notation)

Here are some examples of various types of emotional abuse in a domestic relationship. In many cases of domestic violence, all these forms of emotional abuse are present. (Reprinted by permission of Sage Publications Ltd., from C. Kirkwood, *Leaving Abusive Partners: From the Scars of Survival to the Wisdom for Change.* Copyright © 1993.)

1. *Degradation.* Abusers devalue their partners. Partners may be told that they are "stupid, ugly, inadequate mothers, inadequate sexually, and incompetent" (p. 46).

[What was verbally abusive?] Well, name-calling. And picking fault in my appearance. Or even pathetic things like picking fault in the way my underarms smelt, just really ridiculously childish things. That's the thing, they're so childish that, until you realize what state you're in, they do go—not exactly unnoticed—but just a part of the pattern of things. (p. 47)

2. *Fear.* Abusers create fear in their partners so that their partners fear for their physical and emotional safety.

The mental cruelty is a lot worse than the physical cause, I mean with the physical you get a good batterin' or whatever and that's it. But with mental, you see he'll come in at 5 and doesn't want his tea, slap that up against the wall, and have a few drinks. "What's the matter?," "Nothing. You just wait, I've a good one for you." So you sit there from half past 6, 7 o'clock onwards thinkin "Oh my God." And he'll jump quick and you'll jump cause you're nervous and it'll just agitate him and so by half past 10, 11 o'clock when he's well pissed, that's when the good hidin' comes. It might not be then, it might be 2 o'clock in the morning, it might be 6 o'clock the next morning. But you know, cause he's forewarned ya. (pp. 49–50)

3. *Objectification.* Abusers view their partners as objects. They may demand that their partners alter their external appearance to meet the abusers' needs, that they take tranquilizers, or that they account for all their behavior.

I wasn't allowed to get my hair cut. I wasn't allowed to wear skirts, cause men would look at my legs…It was like a regime really. (p. 51)

That's what it was really…I was supposed to be just what he wanted and he could dominate me if he tranquillized me…. It's a way of getting your own way I suppose. (p. 51)

He would just show up at my work—he did this a lot. I used to work graveyard shift, in the middle of the night he'd just be there, accusing me: "Oh, you're flirting with him, he likes you." (p. 52)

4. *Deprivation.* Abusers deprive their partners of money or social interactions.

I was stuck in the house all the time. The only person I got out to see was my mother…he used to *say* "you could go out," but he did it sneakily, you see, he'd only give you enough money to get food and to pay the bills, and then you wouldn't have none left, so you *couldn't* get out. (p. 54)

People weren't allowed to call me at all. *Nobody* could call me *ever.* And if people did call me he would pick up the phone and he'd say "she's busy, she'll call you back, she's busy!"…and he said "you don't have time for friends! The only thing you have time to do is study and take care of *me,* those are the only things you have time to do." At first I'd say "Well, I *need* friends, I need…"—he goes "you don't need that! You need me." So that was about two years we lived together and that's kinda what happened for about two years. (p. 54)

5. *Overburdening with responsibility.* Abusers force their partners "to take exclusive responsibility for the emotional and practical issues of their relationships" (p. 55).

But it was *geared solely* towards *him.* It was constant compensations all the time, I can remember feeling that. Even though we had two small children, we had to do it his way. Again, like having another child, like having to deal with a four year old having a temper tantrum. He *didn't* stand there and scream and shout—it was just a kind of whine, or a moan. (p. 55)

6. *Distortion of subjective reality.* Abusers attack their partners' perceptions and try to create doubts about their partners' ability to perceive and think.

You don't have any sense of reality base. Cause what you see is not what you're told is happening, *constantly.* It's like that whole thing with that jealousy when I *knew* I wasn't doing anything. And yet, after a while I would [think] where there's smoke there's fire—what am I doing? I must be doing something. (p. 56)

Abuse was a *lot* like interrogation and it's a lot like being kidnapped and thrown is a closet and having somebody yell stuff to you every day. After a while the human brain just gives. I mean your *structure* just gives into it. (p. 56)

Women who are victims of domestic violence may have symptoms similar to those seen in a posttraumatic stress disorder, such as feelings of helplessness, reexperiencing of the trauma, intrusive recollections, generalized anxiety, lowered self-esteem, and social withdrawal (Douglas, 1987; Dutton & Painter, 1993; also see Chapter 11). They also may have two apparently opposite emotional responses: (a) psychic

numbing or reduced responsiveness to the environment and (b) generalized hyperarousal, such as exaggerated startle responses, which are reactions thought to be related to the cumulative stress of the abuse. Finally, they may idealize the abuser, deny the danger, or suppress their own anger—reactions that may be coping responses occurring under extreme duress (Dutton & Painter, 1993).

Experiencing violence transforms people into victims and changes their lives forever. Once victimized, one can never again feel quite as invulnerable.

—Mary P. Koss

Some facts about domestic violence.   Although statistics on domestic violence are not complete, here are some important facts (Brasseur, 1994; Bureau of Justice Statistics, 1994; Kaiser Permanente, 1994, p. 12):

- According to the American Medical Association, 25% of the women in the United States, or 12 million women, will be abused by a current or former partner during their lives.
- The incidence of domestic violence is estimated at 4 million cases annually, or one assault every 15 seconds.
- Women in the United States are more likely to be victimized by a current or former male partner than by all other assailants combined. Over 50 percent of all women murdered are killed by male partners, and 12 percent of murdered men are killed by female partners.
- Over half of the defendants accused of murdering their spouse had been drinking alcohol at the time of the offense. Nonfamily murder defendants were even more likely to have been drinking. Also, almost half of the victims of spousal murder had been drinking alcohol at the time of the offense—about the same proportion as for the victims of nonfamily murder.
- Conditions associated with domestic violence include miscarriages, drug and alcohol abuse, attempted suicide and other forms of mental illness, low birthweight babies, pain, injuries, and permanent physical impairment.
- Forty-seven percent of men who beat their wives do so three or more times a year. Battering may start or become worse during pregnancy; more than 23% of pregnant women are abused during pregnancy.
- Twenty-one percent of all women who use hospital emergency and surgical services are battered.
- One in four married couples experience one or more incidents of domestic violence, and repeated severe episodes occur in one marriage out of every four.

Table 20-5 addresses eight myths about domestic violence.

Theories of domestic violence.   The theories of child physical abuse and neglect, presented earlier, also apply, in part, to domestic violence. Individuals who batter their

Table 20-5
Myths About Domestic Violence

1. *Myth:* It doesn't happen to someone like me. It happens to poor and uneducated people.
   Fact: Victims are from all socioeconomic groups.

2. *Myth:* Pregnant women are not battered.
   Fact: Obstetrics and gynecology departments frequently see women who have been battered. Between 25% and 45% of battered women are battered during pregnancy.

3. *Myth:* Battering is a private affair. It isn't appropriate for health care providers to assess or intervene.
   Fact: Health care providers are legally and morally compelled to help by diagnosing victims of battering and informing them of their rights and how to get help.

4. *Myth:* If they wanted the abuse to end, they would leave or seek help.
   Fact: This myth exacerbates the situation. Most women seek outside help from clergy, police, family, and health care providers. A recent Texas study found that women contacted an average of five sources of help, without success, prior to leaving home. Battered women are often encouraged to return home, by people not trained to recognize the signs and ramifications of domestic violence, to keep the family together.

5. *Myth:* The battered woman is masochistic.
   Fact: A woman only stays when she is economically and emotionally dependent, embarrassed, lonely, afraid of retaliation, or guilt-ridden. Many abused women leave as many as seven times before they leave for good. Tragically, 70% of the women killed in domestic violence situations have already left or are in the process of leaving.

6. *Myth:* Only alcoholics and drug addicts abuse their partners.
   Fact: Batterers do demonstrate a high usage of alcohol, but that use is separate from violent behavior. Domestic violence is an issue of control and dominance over another person. Alcohol or drugs do not cause violence or abuse but are contributing factors.

7. *Myth:* Battering only occurs in heterosexual relationships.
   Fact: Battering can occur and has been reported among gay and lesbian couples.

8. *Myth:* Only women are battered.
   Fact: In approximately 5% of the total number of spousal abuse cases, men are battered by women.

Source: Reprinted, with changes in notation, with permission of Kaiser Permanente from "Domestic Violence—What Is Domestic Violence, Really?" copyright 1994 by Kaiser Permanente, *Planning for Health, 2,* 1994, pp. 10–11.

inhibitions; or have received reinforcement for the battering. They also may have an inadequate family structure, inadequate support systems, social stressors, pathological jealousy and possessiveness toward their mate, and a cultural belief that it is permissible to batter their spouse. They may give such excuses as "It somehow got out of hand," "She makes me feel like a child," "I can't talk to her," and "I keep it all inside until...." The family may be geographically or socially isolated, have unruly children, be preparing for the birth of a baby, be dysfunctional, or show an educational disparity between the husband and the wife, with the wife having higher educational or vocational attainment than the husband (Gilliland & James, 1993).

Domestically violent men do not constitute a homogeneous group; they may fall into one of the three following subtypes, as hypothesized by Holtzworth-Munroe and Stuart (1994):

1. *Family-only batterers.* They limit their violence to family members and are not likely to engage in violence outside the home. They are not psychologically disturbed, nor do they have personality disorders. They tend to engage in mild forms of violence.

2. *Dysphoric/borderline batterers.* They engage in moderate to severe wife abuse, including physical, psychological, and sexual abuse. The "violence is primarily confined to the family, although some extrafamilial violence and criminal behavior may be evident. These men are the most dysphoric, psychologically distressed, and emotionally volatile. They may evidence borderline and schizoidal personality characteristics and may have problems with alcohol and drug abuse" (p. 482). Individuals with a *borderline personality* tend to be unstable and impulsive, have drastic mood shifts, and, at times, may appear psychotic. Individuals with *schizoid personality* characteristics tend to be shy, oversensitive, seclusive, and eccentric.

3. *Violent/antisocial batterers.* They engage in moderate to severe marital violence, including physical, psychological, and sexual abuse. They may have a history of extrafamilial aggression and "an extensive history of related criminal behavior and legal involvement. They are likely to have problems with alcohol and drug abuse, and they are the most likely to have an antisocial personality disorder or psychopathy" (p. 482).

As shown in Table 20-3, it was not until the 1980s that women could obtain a restraining order to protect themselves from their spouses without initiating divorce proceedings. Our national goal, and the goal of society in general, should be the removal of all vestiges of unequal treatment of children and women and of all people.

Why women remain in an abusive relationship.
Women may remain in an abusive relationship for the following reasons (Human Resources Administration, 1993; Johann, 1994):

spouse may have had traumatic experiences in early childhood; have abnormal or deviant characteristics, inadequate affective processes, inadequate cognitive processes, inadequate personal resources, or personal stressors; have been under the influence of alcohol or drugs, which removed their

1. They may have no place to go.
2. They may not have enough money to support themselves or skills to obtain employment, and they may believe that they cannot survive alone or support their children.
3. They may be intimidated by the abuser's threats. For example, they may fear that if they leave they might be killed, their children might be killed, or the abuser might kill himself. Or they may have been severely beaten previously when they left the abuser and fear being beaten again.
4. They may believe that it is the woman's role to make the relationship work; consequently, they may feel guilty about the beatings and give the abuser innumerable "second chances."
5. They may believe that their children need a father no matter what—that the family must be kept together at all costs.
6. They may be unable to make long-range plans because they are too busy surviving day to day and protecting the children.
7. They may believe that it is better to remain in a familiar situation than to leave for one in which they would be terrified of the abuser's finding and harming them or of raising the children alone.
8. They may hope that the abuser will change, particularly if they themselves try to improve the relationship.
9. They may be emotionally dependent on the abuser.
10. They may love the abuser.
11. They may have low self-esteem and believe that they deserve the beatings.
12. They may lack the confidence to reach out to people who might help them.
13. They may believe that abuse is a way of life, particularly if they were raised in a violent home.
14. They may believe that they have no social standing without their husbands, particularly if they belong to certain ethnic minority groups.
15. They may believe in the sanctity of marriage.
16. They may fear the American justice system, particularly if they are immigrants or refugees.
17. They may fear, if they are foreign nationals married to U.S. citizens, that they will be deported if they turn in their husbands.

Here are some women's accounts of why they remained in an abusive relationship (Barnett & Lopez-Real, 1985, as cited in Barnett & LaViolette, 1993, pp. 17, 28, 36, 48–49):

HOPE THAT THE PARTNER WILL CHANGE

- That he would change was still a thought in the back of my head.
- I was always hoping since he had gone to A.A.
- I kept making excuses for him.
- After living together for so long without the abuse, I was hoping he would go back to his old self. I don't understand the change in him.
- He's got a lot of pluses. Hopefully he will help himself, and become a better person overall.

RESOURCES AND ECONOMIC DEPENDENCE

- I still feel scared of supporting the kids and bringing home enough money because I can't depend on him.
- I'm facing eviction now. I'm scared.
- I've never worked and have no high school education.
- I am disabled because of his battering.
- I only left once, but I came back because I didn't have any money, but money isn't everything.

REASONS OF PRINCIPLE OR MORALITY

- Divorce is a personal failure.
- I believed you marry forever.
- I wanted to make it because of family pressure.
- I would never leave my children under any circumstances.

FEAR

- He kept seeking me out and finding me.
- I felt other people would die if I left.
- I have left and still have trouble getting out from under abuse and fears and threats. My ex-partner is continuing abuse anyway he can. I now see why it truly is hard to get out and why it took me so long.
- I remember feeling many times afraid to go and afraid to stay. That very real fear of revenge is so powerful a deterrent to doing anything constructive.
- I think that police protection should be questioned a lot.

The following segment is from a crisis interview with a woman who was battered by her husband (Gilliland & James, 1993, pp. 281–282, with changes in notation).

CASE 20-13. MARIANNE

IR: What were you thinking and feeling while he was beating you?

IE: It was like I was standing off to the side watching a movie of this. It was like this can't really be happening, especially to me.

IR: So that's how you cope with it. Kind of separating yourself from the beating, as if it's happening to someone else.

IE: Yes, I guess I've done it that way for a long time. I'd go crazy otherwise.

IR: What is your understanding of why you're being battered?

IE: I don't know. I guess I'm just not a good wife.

IR: You're not living up to his expectations, then. How about your own?

IE: I'm not sure. I mean, I've never thought of that. It's always been what he wants.

IR: How do you cope with the beating other than just kind of separating yourself from the situation when it happens?

IE: I try to do what he wants, but when it starts to build—the tension—I just try to stay out of his way and be nice, although I know sooner or later I'm gonna get it. I dread the waiting. Actually sometimes I push the issue just to get it over with. I know he'll always apologize afterwards and treat me nice.

IR: So you do what he wishes even though you know the bottom line is a beating. Yet because of the anxiety you may even push things to get it over with. Seems like you're willing to pay a steep price to get his love back.

IE: When you say that, I can't believe I'm letting this happen to me. What a fool…a stupid fool!

IR: Then you feel foolish about paying that price. What's keeping you in the relationship?

IE: God! I don't know. Love! Honor! Obey! The kids. The good times. Martyrdom. I don't have a job and I'm pregnant again. Even then, it's no good, but I don't stay. I've got to get out. This is nuts. He'll wind up killing me.

Why women leave an abusive relationship.

Women leave an abusive relationship when it becomes intolerable. Rationalizing the abuse may no longer work, and the batterer may have begun to physically or sexually abuse the children. If women fear for their physical safety, they will likely seek out a battered women's shelter. They also may leave when there is some predictable form of safety. Consequently, in order to help battered women, you must assure them that you can find a safe location for them.

Once in the shelter, battered women may need food and clothing; a security plan; medical attention, particularly if they were recently physically abused; short-term legal assistance, including a temporary restraining order to ensure their safety and to obtain custody of the children; assistance from social service agencies, including Child Protective Services if the children were maltreated; and counseling and emotional support (Somers, 1992).

She has lost her faith in the world's essential predictability, fairness and safety, and approaches even ordinary routines like driving with the hesitancy of an outsider, a foreigner in a hostile land.

—Jeffrey Jay

Case illustration of domestic violence.

The following case illustrates how one woman saved herself and her child from an intolerable relationship; however, the perpetrator continued to abuse another woman (Kaiser Permanente, 1994).

CASE 20-14. MY FRIEND

A friend I've known for almost 20 years was an abused wife. She met her husband when she was 14 years old and they grew up together. They went to college, got married, and started a family. They both worked in Fortune 500 companies. My friend is attractive, smart, funny, and caring. Her husband was very social and on the fast track at work. Everyone thought they were the perfect couple.

This same handsome, enterprising, model husband pushed her down a flight of stairs when she was pregnant—she broke her arm. He drove her miles away from home and pushed her out of the car so she'd have to walk home. She always threatened to leave, he was always sorry. They went to therapy. He cried, said he was sorry, she believed him, and the cycle would begin again. The day she realized he would never change and that the abuse was not her fault, she simply got in the car with her young son, a suitcase, and half

their savings. She drove across the United States and started a new life—she survived. He remarried and abused his second wife. The cycle was broken for my friend. For her husband, it continued. (p. 9)

Domestic violence is prevalent among women on all economic and social levels. Too often, the women are ashamed of being abused, hide their injuries, and do not report the perpetrator.

—Human Resources Administration

Signs of domestic violence.

The following signs should alert you to the possibility of domestic violence (Hatchett-Jones, McClosky, Muzic, Shapiro, Tadros, & Tomita, 1994, based on recommendations for identifying and treating adult domestic violence victims from New York State's Governor's Commission on Domestic Violence):

1. *Central pattern of injuries.* There may be injuries to the head, neck, chest, breasts, and abdomen.

2. *Injuries suggestive of a defensive posture.* There may be forearm bruises or fractures, which are common when an individual tries to fend off blows to the face or chest.

3. *Injuries inconsistent with the interviewee's explanation.* Multiple abrasions and contusions to different anatomical sites are inconsistent with a fall or bump into a cabinet. Fingernail scratches, bite marks, cigarette burns, and rope burns strongly suggest domestic violence.

4. *Multiple injuries in various stages of healing.* Just as x-rays reveal old fractures that aid in diagnosing child maltreatment, evidence of new and old injuries helps diagnose partner maltreatment.

5. *Substantial delay between the time of injury and the presentation for treatment.* Battered individuals may wait several days before seeking medical care. They may see their health care provider at inappropriate times for seemingly minor or resolving injuries. This may occur because they were prevented from leaving the home after they were injured or because they are ambivalent about revealing what has happened.

6. *Frequent visits to a health care provider for vague complaints without evidence of physiologic abnormality.* An individual who has a variety of vague psychosomatic complaints might be a victim of domestic violence.

7. *Alcohol or drug use.* Battered individuals might seek refuge from the pain of battery through excessive use of alcohol, pain pills, or sedatives.

8. *Injury during pregnancy* (for women). Battery might first occur or escalate during pregnancy. Injuries to the breasts or abdomen are typical. Sequelae include miscarriages, fetal injury, and premature labor.

In the following excerpt from an interview with a 31-year-old woman called S., she describes the control and violence in her marriage that eventually resulted in a miscarriage (Yllö, 1993):

CASE 20-15. S.

I didn't even realize he was gaining control and I was too dumb to know any better.... He was gaining control bit by bit until he was checking my pantyhose when I'd come home from the supermarket to see if they were inside out.... He'd time me. He'd check the mileage on the car.... I was living like a prisoner.... One day I was at Zayre's with him...and I was looking at a sweater. He insisted I was looking at a guy. I didn't even know there was a guy in the area, because it got to the point that I, I had to walk like I had horse-blinders on.... You don't look anybody in the eye. You don't look up because you are afraid.

[At one point, S. was insulted by a friend of her husband's and she was furious.] I told him, who the hell was he? And I threw a glass of root beer in his face. My husband gave me a back hand, so I just went upstairs to the bedroom and got into a nightgown. And he kept telling me to come downstairs and I said "No—just leave me alone."...He come up and went right through the door. Knocked the whole top panel off the door and got into the room. Ripped the nightgown right off my back, just bounced me off every wall in that bedroom. Then he threw me down the stairs and...outside in the snow and just kept kicking me and saying it was too soon for me to be pregnant.... His friend was almost rooting him on. (p. 56)

Battering is a pattern *of coercive control.... When a woman is battered, there is a pattern of unfair and unwarranted control being exercised over her life. Even as she resists her abuser's efforts, he continues to use coercion to dominate her. It is essential to understand this dynamic in order to understand why violence against women is so pervasive and powerful.*

—Susan Schechter

The link between domestic violence and child maltreatment. Research shows a clear link between spousal abuse and child maltreatment (McKay, 1994). It is estimated that between 45 and 70% of battered women in shelters report that their children also were abused. Although the mechanisms through which spousal abuse leads to child maltreatment are unknown, the following hypotheses can be valuable:

1. Fathers, thwarted in their attempt to strike their wives, hit their children instead.
2. The stresses that battered women face may lead them to abuse their children.
3. Some battered women give their abusers their full-time attention in a futile effort to control the level of violence in the family and, in the process, neglect their children.
4. "Some battered women are so fearful of their partner's response to the children that they overdiscipline them in an effort to control their behavior and protect them from what they perceive as even greater abuse" (McKay, 1994, p. 30).
5. The batterer uses violence to control everyone in the family, including the spouse and the children.

Effects of domestic violence on children. How domestic violence affects children will depend on several factors, including their age, sex, stage of development, and role in the family; the type, extent, and frequency of the violence; and the effects of the violence, such as economic effects and the need to move and relocate. From a developmental perspective, the symptoms children may exhibit as a result of domestic violence may be described as follows (Jaffe, Wolfe, & Wilson, 1990):

1. *Infants.* When mothers of infants are abused, the attachment needs of infants may be disrupted because of the increased stress on the mothers. Mothers who are fearful may be unable to attend to their infants' needs. Infants, in turn, may have poor health and poor sleeping habits and cry excessively. Infants may be accidentally or purposely hit, pushed, or dropped during a violent episode between their caregivers.

2. *Toddlers and preschoolers.* Toddlers and preschoolers witnessing domestic violence may show typical signs of trauma, including signs of terror, such as yelling, irritable behavior, hiding, shaking, stuttering, and somatic complaints. They, like infants, may be hurt during a violent episode.

3. *School-aged children and adolescents.* School-aged children and adolescents who witness domestic violence may "learn that violence is an appropriate way of resolving conflict in human relationships. Girls may learn that victimization is inevitable and no one can help change this pattern. Suffering in silence is reinforced" (Jaffe et al., 1990, p. 26). School-aged children and adolescents may deny the violence, use aggression as a way to solve problems, blame others for their problems, or show a high degree of anxiety.

Children can witness domestic violence in different ways. They (a) may be physically present and observe the violence directly, (b) may be in their rooms asleep and awaken to overhear part of a violent episode, or (c) may not see or hear anything at the time of the violence, but eventually see the consequences of the violence, such as a parent with physical injuries and visible bruises and broken household possessions (Jaffe et al., 1990). If they observe the violence directly, they may, for example, hide their heads under a pillow to block out the violence, visibly flinch as the sound of hitting occurs, cower in a corner fearing to move, or call the police and report that "daddy put a knife to mommy."

Children witnessing domestic violence may be deeply affected by what they see (Afolayan, 1993). Some school-aged children may believe that they are responsible for the violence in their homes, may change their personality in the hope that their new personality will put an end to the violence, may act as a protector of one of their parents, may keep the violence a secret because of fear that they will be rejected, may assume the role of peacemaker in the home, or may take over caregiving responsibilities for younger siblings.

Living in a violent home may affect children's schooling negatively. "They may either fake illness in order to stay home or they may actually become sick from worrying about the problem" (Afolayan, 1993, p. 55). They may have concentration problems in school. As peacemakers and caregivers, they may miss school in order to pacify their father, protect their mother, and take care of younger siblings.

Children in a violent home may live in shame and be embarrassed by the family secret (Jaffe et al., 1990). Having a diminished sense of self-esteem and a pessimistic view of the future, they may live in fear and anxiety, waiting for the next violent episode to occur. They may find little safety, peace, or security in their home yet be unable to seek an alternative place to live. Some adolescents, in frustration and anger, may engage in delinquent activities or even assault their mother, father, caregiver, or siblings. Finally, some children may run away from home to escape the violence.

A study of 2,402 cases of misdemeanor domestic violence in five U.S. cities provided the following information about the effects of exposure to domestic violence on children (Fantuzzo, Boruch, Beriama, Atkins, & Marcus, 1997):

1. In 74% or more of the cases, children were present in the household when domestic violence was reported.
2. Many of the households had additional risk factors, such as poverty, a single-parent, and low educational levels of the principal caregivers.
3. Children usually were involved in the domestic violence in one of these ways: (a) they literally called for help, (b) they were identified as a precipitating cause of the dispute that led to the violence, or (c) they were physically abused by the perpetrator.

These results indicate that "children in households with family violence are not just 'witnessing' a tragedy; they are involved in various ways in the violent incident" (Fantuzzo et al., 1997, p. 120).

Batterers may be prosecuted not only for spousal but also for child maltreatment when children (a) have observed the assault on one of their parents (or caregivers), (b) have been beaten themselves, or (c) have tried to intervene (American Prosecutors Research Institute, 1996). Sometimes mothers will hold their children during an argument in the hope that the batterer will show mercy. In California, Penal Code § 273a is used as a basis for criminal prosecution. The code refers to mental harm in the following way:

Any person who, under circumstances or conditions likely to produce great bodily harm or death, willfully causes or permits any child to suffer, or inflicts thereon unjustifiable physical pain or mental suffering, or having the care or custody of any child, willfully causes or permits the person or health of that child to be injured, or willfully causes or permits that child to be placed in such a situation that its person or health is endangered,…shall be punished by imprisonment in a county jail not exceeding one year, or in the state prison for…two, four, or six years.

Children of battered women living in shelters face several difficulties. Often, they must leave their home without prep-aration and are wrested "from their schools, friends, and social and sports activities. They're asked not to see friends in case the batterer should try to track down the mother through their connections. They have to leave their pets and toys. And some remain at the mercy of a mother who vacillates about whether or not to go home" (Jameson, 1996, p. E2). Even though their home may have been frightening and the shelter may give them some sense of stability, children may be homesick.

When the mother and children must leave the shelter—usually after 30 to 45 days—the children may have to move to another school and meet yet another circle of friends. Children find their stay ending just as they are getting used to the routine. During their stay at the shelter, mothers are expected to work out a more permanent relocation and survival plan. Although many mothers and children return home, many leave again for good.

Case illustrations of children living in a domestic violence shelter. The following three cases of children living in a domestic violence shelter with their mothers illustrate some of the concerns of children who witness domestic violence (Jaffe et al., 1990).

CASE 20-16. JOHN

John presented himself as a mature adolescent who was very supportive of his mother and younger siblings while they adjusted to the shelter. He appeared to be a positive role model for the younger children in the house by his ability to comply with the rules and help new residents in crisis cope with crowded surroundings. He rarely spoke of his father. When encouraged to discuss his feelings about the violence he witnessed, he expressed his disgust and anger. When asked about his plans to deal with these feelings, he disclosed an elaborate plot "to get even" with his father by poisoning him. (p. 51)

CASE 20-17. LOUISE

Louise was only a few years old but she was very advanced in her social judgment and verbal skills. She demonstrated a wide range of affect, which she utilized to distract her mother and other shelter residents from the pain and sadness that they displayed. She said she knew why she had come to the shelter. Louse claimed that she kept leaving her tricycle on the front walk, contrary to her father's repeated instruction. "One day I got him so mad that he hit mom." Louise was sure she was to blame for the violence. (p. 52)

CASE 20-18. TOM

Tom faced a terrible dilemma. He was only 7 years old, and he had to judge whether or not his father was going to shoot his mother. His father often picked up the shotgun and threatened his mother whenever he was jealous and thought she might leave. His mother could usually talk him into putting away the gun or call his grandmother to come and talk sense into his father. Tonight seemed different. His father seemed more upset than usual and yelled at his mother that he would kill her so nobody else could ever marry her. Tom decided to go to the neighbors to get them to call the police. The police came and used skilled negotiations to avert a tragedy. Tom's father went to jail for six months for threatening his mother and for dangerous use of a weapon. Tom told the shelter staff that he ruined his father's life by calling the police. "If it wasn't for me, he wouldn't have a criminal record, and maybe my mother would have stayed with him." (p. 52, with changes in notation)

The following letter was written by an adult woman who witnessed domestic violence as a child (Landers, 1996. Permission granted by Ann Landers and Creators Syndicate).

CASE 20-19. PHYLLIS

Dear Ann Landers: I would like to address this to battered women everywhere: Please look beyond your own hellish life to the lives of your children. You are not the only one violence will cripple or destroy.

My mother was married for 16 years to a monster we called "Dad." She thought we were safe because he didn't rip off our clothes, threaten us with a gun, choke, kick, stab, punch, shove or scream at us. She didn't realize that he didn't need to do any of those things because we already were paralyzed with fear at the sight of what he did to our mother.

I couldn't concentrate in school, and my grades were terrible. The teachers labeled me lazy and stupid. The only lesson I learned is that I shouldn't count on anyone to help me and that I am on my own.

I seem like everyone else. I smile and am friendly, but no one can get close to me. I know that my underlying hostility and distrust of people is crippling and has prevented me from developing relationships.

To spare other young lives this unhealthy, lonely existence, I beg all battered women—if you don't care about yourself, please care about your children and GET OUT NOW. (p. E-2)

Domestic violence and child maltreatment fatalities. Domestic violence can lead to child maltreatment *fatalities,* particularly when there is a high level of general violence in the home and when "physical violence is the accepted and habitual solution to problems and the response to frustration" (Human Resources Administration, 1993, p. 37, with changes in notation). The following examples illustrate the link between domestic violence and child maltreatment fatalities.

A young mother was abused by her male companion. Allegedly in revenge for some of her actions, the companion scalded the mother's 5-month-old child who was conceived by another man. The child's autopsy revealed signs of prior abuse.

A 3-year-old child died of blunt impact injuries to the head with evidence of child abuse syndrome. The mother said that she beat the child because the child's father had abused her (the mother).

One mother attended a drug rehabilitation program and freed herself from drug addiction, but she continued to be involved with violent men. On several occasions, she entered a battered women's shelter and then returned to her abusive husband. Finally, she left her husband. But she became involved with another violent man. After they had lived together for only three months, the man fatally beat her 15-month-old child.

In the following cases, two mothers describe the events that led them to kill their children (U.S. Advisory Board on Child Abuse and Neglect, 1995, pp. 151–153).

CASE 20-20. ANNE

My terror and rage led to the death of my 6-week-old son. I make no excuses for my acts. What I share with you is an effort to understand myself and others, and perhaps in some way to find even a small degree of forgiveness in myself.

What I want this Board to know is two things: first, that my son's death was tragic; and, second, that it was not until a series of investigations of the events that any meaningful intervention worked for the rest of my five children.

My husband first had sex with me when I was 4 years old, and later he had sex with me and my children. My life and my children's lives have always been hard. On the day my son died, I had gone to a place where I was high on pills and alcohol at least 80 percent of the time. I was disgusted with everything and furious. The more I drank, the angrier I got.

In my craziness that day, I was trying to run away from my husband with my children. The baby's zipper got stuck. I was panicking because I thought he was coming home, and when my son cried, I struck him. I was so out of control I didn't even realize he was dead. He was quiet. I dressed him and put all the kids in the car and started driving around.

I attempted to kill us all by driving over an embankment into Sheepshead Bay. All I succeeded in doing was banging up the car, and my husband found us. I was never arrested for the death of my son or charged, but my husband and I were later charged and found guilty of sexual abuse. The irony is that they thought my son died as a result of whiplash.

I share these things with you because I deeply know that things have to change. At times I am bitter because there were no interventions for me as a child. I was tortured physically and sexually for as long as I can remember. I never knew what normal was or could be. I am a woman and a mother who hurts deeply inside, but I am not a monster. I am a hurting soul. I have a wounded soul, and perhaps the deepest pain is that I became just like all of those people in my life that tortured me.

CASE 20-21. BETSY

It was winter, and for 4½ years of my marriage the abuse escalated. About the time my son was born, 1½ years into the marriage, the abuse became physical. There were words, fists, threats, silence, and isolation.

I lived in constant fear and was always anticipating and trying to avoid the next beating. By the time my daughter was born, it was a nightmare. When she would cry, he constantly threatened that I had better shut her up, and that she had better go to sleep. The baby cried and continued to cry. His hollering, my fear, the craziness of our lives. How could a baby sleep?

I was desperate. I didn't think I wanted to end her life. I only wanted her to be quiet. I'm not sure how sane I was at that point. I have questioned that every year of my imprisonment. I've wondered what his abuse, the postpartum issues also played in my insanity. His threats got severe. They got worse. And the beatings increased. My wrist was broken. He damaged my right eye. He cracked one of my ribs. The bruises, the fear, the terror.

All I know was that somehow I focused on the baby. If only I could get her to quiet down. Every whimper from the baby would send me into a panic, trying to calm her to avoid his anger. But I was angry, terribly angry, and knew her crying was angering him. I was terrified and angry.

I gave her some formula, and I put something in it. I thought it would just help to quiet her down. But what I really did was poison her. When I discovered her quiet in the crib and having difficulty breathing, I took her to the hospital. She was very quiet, and I was very scared. I have relived over and over again the memories of putting that poison in her bottle, and the fact that I killed my innocent child.

When I was sentenced, my husband said to me, you shut her up, and now no one will hear you because you are going to prison.

Failure to recognize effects of domestic violence on children.

Child protective workers "often do not identify the presence of domestic violence in the home or, if noted, minimize its significance. Too often the danger domestic violence poses to children is unrecognized.... Domestic violence presents exceptionally complex issues that challenge the skills of highly trained and experienced professionals" (Human Resources Administration, 1993, p. 37). Child protective workers may believe some of the myths about battered women and assume that these women can't care for their children when, in fact, they can.

The following case describes a situation in which health care providers failed to inquire about injuries that happened as a result of domestic violence (Smith, 1995). (New state laws are gradually changing this situation.)

CASE 20-22. WILLMA

One 41-year-old said she had been treated over the course of her 14-year marriage at various hospitals in Los Angeles for broken ribs, a broken nose and other injuries caused by her husband. Doctors and nurses accepted her stories that she had fallen. Besides, she said, "He would always be there right with me, so I could not say anything right there even if I had wanted to."

She said he even beat her up while she was in a hospital, staying with her children who were being treated for other, unrelated conditions. "We were there so long he didn't like it. We would get into arguments. On two occasions he dragged me into the women's bathroom and beat me. I had black eyes. Not once did any nurses or doctors or social workers ask how this occurred." (p. E2)

The following case, described by Dr. Richard Gelles of the Family Violence Research Program at the University of Rhode Island, illustrates the failure of health care providers to recognize the threat that domestic violence may pose for children (U.S. Advisory Board on Child Abuse and Neglect, 1995).

CASE 20-23. BEATRICE

In Rhode Island, a battered woman appeared at a hospital emergency room with her bruised toddler. None of the doctors or nurses who treated the mother examined the child, and after the woman was patched up, no one thought to notify CPS. Nine months after the mother's visit to the ER [emergency room], the baby was killed by the same violent boyfriend who had been beating the mother. A member of the Child Death Review Team noted, "The child died essentially because of the failure of an emergency room to identify risk, witnessed through the serious abuse of the mother." (p. 50)

As with child abuse in the 1960s, [the United States] has ignored domestic violence because it is a "family affair," largely played out on a very private stage.

—Alvin Poussaint

Exercise 20-2. Evaluating a Case of Domestic Violence

Read the following fictitious newspaper report of a case of domestic violence. Then answer the questions that follow, and compare your ratings with those of a sample of college students. The fictitious newspaper report was obtained from Harris and Cook (1994). The mean ratings were obtained from R. J. Harris, personal communication, February 1995.

Kansas City, KS.—Mike Jones, a 28-year-old male, was arrested last night on charges of domestic abuse. Two police officers arrived at the location of the dispute at 7:05 P.M. Police conducted interviews with Jones (a sales representative for a local furniture store) and his wife, Mary Jones (an interior designer). According to Officer Kevin Smith, of the Kansas City Police Department, he and another officer found Mrs. Jones sitting on the living room couch. She was bleeding and had a black eye.

Mrs. Jones, a 28-year-old female, told the officers that she had arrived home late from work, turned on the television and then made some phone calls. Approximately 10 minutes later, Mr. Jones arrived home and became angry because his wife was on the phone. He then yelled at her that she "had things to do" and "should make sure" that "she gets home on time."

Mrs. Jones became upset, began yelling at her husband, and, as the anger heightened, she began to shout various obscenities at him, calling him a "nagging bastard" and a "miserable excuse for a man." She threatened to leave him if "he didn't shape up."

Mrs. Jones then went into the kitchen to prepare dinner. Mr. Jones followed her, grabbed her by the arm and slapped her, knocked her to the floor, and kicked her. As Mrs. Jones lay there in stunned surprise, Mr. Jones left the house. Upon his return, he was informed by the police that he was being charged with assault.

Directions: Use any number from 1 to 7 for your ratings.

1. As crimes go, how violent was the incident?
   (1 = not violent; 7 = very violent)
2. How responsible was the batterer for the incident?
   (1 = not responsible; 7 = very responsible)
3. How responsible for the incident was the person who was beaten? (1 = not responsible; 7 = very responsible)

4. If you had witnessed this incident from the window next door, how likely would it have been that you would have called the police? (1 = not likely; 7 = very likely)
5. Did the batterer have the right to use physical force? (1 = definitely; 7 = definitely not)
6. In this case, should the batterer be convicted of assault? (1 = definitely; 7 = definitely not)
7. Did the victim fight back when beaten? (1 = definitely; 7 = definitely not)
8. Should the victim leave the batterer for good? (1 = definitely; 7 = definitely not)
9. Do you think the batterer has probably acted this way in the past? (1 = definitely; 7 = definitely not)
10. Overall, how much do you like the batterer? (1 = very much; 7 = not very much)
11. Overall, how much do you like the victim of the beating? (1 = very much; 7 = not very much)

The following ratings were obtained from a sample of 27 male and 34 female college students.

	Men	Women			Men	Women
1.	4.37	4.79		7.	6.15	6.21
2.	6.33	6.47		8.	2.56	2.06
3.	2.26	2.18		9.	2.41	2.38
4.	5.48	5.88		10.	6.67	6.53
5.	6.93	6.85		11.	3.63	3.65
6.	1.85	1.68				

How similar were your ratings to those of the sample? How might you account for any of your ratings that differed by more than one or two points from those of the sample? What do your ratings indicate about your attitude toward domestic violence? How will your attitude toward domestic violence affect how you conduct interviews in such situations? How do your ratings compare with those of your classmates?

THE OFFENDER IN CASES OF CHILD SEXUAL ABUSE

Theories of Child Sexual Abuse

Three major theories of child physical abuse and neglect were offered earlier. Parallel theories have been developed to account for child sexual abuse. Note the similarities in the factors believed to account for different types of maltreatment. Chronic sexual attraction to prepubertal children is called *pedophilia;* if directed toward pubescent children, the offense is called *hebephilia;* if directed toward a family member, the offense is called *incest.* The following material on theories of child sexual abuse is from Tzeng et al. (1991, primarily pages 14–20), with additions from Finkelhor (1984), Powell (1991), Roundy and Horton (1991), and Simkins, Ward, Bowman, Rinck, and DeSouza (1990).

Individual determinants theory of child sexual abuse.
The individual determinants theory suggests that some of the following factors in the offender's development

and current makeup may have led him or her to commit child sexual abuse:

- *history of sexual abuse or of inappropriate sexual experiences as a child* (for example, the offender was a victim of child sexual abuse and tries to master the trauma by assuming the role of the perpetrator through repeating acts that happened to him or her, had an overly seductive parent, or had repressive norms about sexual behavior in his or her family)
- *abnormal or deviant characteristics* (for example, the offender has a drug or alcohol problem, has excessive hostility, has anxiety, has a mental illness or personality disorder, has low tolerance for frustration, has arrested development, suffers from senility, uses mechanisms of dissociation to keep the abuse from awareness, has a psychosexual disorder such as feelings of being sexually deprived or of having normal sexual outlets blocked)
- *inadequate affective processes* (for example, the offender fears mature sexuality, relates poorly to others, confuses sex with love, or experiences jealousy when the child associates with other children)
- *inadequate cognitive processes* (for example, the offender rationalizes to justify the act—"I couldn't help myself because she was wearing a skimpy nightgown," shows irresponsibility in decision making, minimizes the severity of the abusive behavior—"We were just fooling around"—or the number of sexual acts performed with the child—"We only did it a couple of times," engages in self-deception by rationalizing and successfully deceiving himself or herself into believing the distortions—"My daughter wanted me to do it," fails to recognize the pain and suffering he or she causes the child victim and the child's family, or confuses roles by blurring generational and social boundaries and acting as a young suitor to the child victim)
- *inadequate personal resources* (for example, the offender has poor self-esteem, has inadequate social skills, needs to seek out children in order to feel powerful, is unable to get emotional support from other adults, has sexual identity conflicts, has low tolerance for frustration, or has poor stress management skills)
- *personal stressors* (for example, the offender fights with others, has work-related problems, or feels lonely because of rejection by or disinterest of female or male adults)
- *removal of inhibitions* (for example, the offender's inhibitions were reduced by alcohol or drugs)
- *failure to bond with the child* (for example, the offender —stepparent, mother's partner, or other adult—has failed to establish a relationship with the child)
- *manipulative personality* (for example, the offender has the ability to trick, manipulate, or overcome the resistance of the child because the child trusts the offender or because of some other reason)

Sociocultural determinants theory of child sexual abuse. The sociocultural determinants theory suggests that some of the following factors in the offender's environment may have led him or her to commit child sexual abuse:

- *weakening of taboos against sex with children* (for example, movies and advertisements promoting children in sexually provocative roles and child pornography have become more available in society at large)
- *socialization pressures leading to distorted concepts of masculinity* (for example, cultural norms promote the transference of male sexuality into violence, rape, sexual harassment, and abuse; men are socialized to consider sex only as a means of gratification, to view sex partners as objects, to seek partners inferior in size and age, and to be dominant in sexual relations)
- *social isolation* (for example, the offender is socially isolated so friends and neighbors cannot act as a deterrent)
- *inappropriate family norms or living arrangements* (for example, sexual interest in other family members is congruent with the family's beliefs; patriarchal norms are maintained in the home—the offender has chauvinistic attitudes toward his or her mate or treats children as property; nonparticipating mother may be extremely dependent, may have a history of being sexually abused as a child, or may be "blind" to the incest and therefore does not protect the child; mother and daughter roles are reversed; sexual relations between the parents are impaired; the child is poorly supervised; or living conditions are crowded)
- *high divorce and remarriage rates* (for example, the offender is angry and frustrated as a result of divorce and, if remarried, has not bonded with the stepchildren)
- *professional, or job-related, stressors* (for example, the offender has lost his or her job, is unhappy at work, has limited income, or cannot advance in his or her work, which causes him or her to be frustrated, unhappy, and angry)

Individual-environment interaction theory of child sexual abuse. The individual-environment interaction theory suggests that individual determinants and sociocultural determinants interact to contribute to child sexual abuse. For example, a father who sexually abuses his child might have had an overly seductive parent, have excessive hostility and poor self-esteem, view sex only as a means of personal gratification, live in a home where conditions are crowded, and be unable to advance economically because of limited employment opportunities.

An attachment theory model of child sexual abuse. Attachment theory (see Chapter 1) provides a useful means of understanding how child sexual abuse may come about. Children are more at risk for sexual abuse when a biological parent is not present in the family, when the mother is not available to the child, when there is marital conflict and violence, when the child has a poor relationship with the parents, and when a stepfather is present in the family (Alexander, 1992). These conditions can result in insecure parent-child attachments, which, in turn, are likely to diminish the potential abuser's impulse control, reduce the concern of the nonabusive parent(s) with protecting and responding to the child's needs, and increase the child's vulnerability to abuse both inside and outside the home. In addition, conflict and poor cohesion among family members, maternal coldness, paternal dominance, and family isolation increase the risk of adverse long-term effects of child sexual abuse on children. Finally, adults who were sexually abused as children are more likely to have insecure attachments to their children than those who were not sexually abused.

Personality of Individuals Who Sexually Abuse Children

Individuals who sexually abuse children are not a homogeneous group. They show a "range of psychological dysfunction from none to severe and a variety of sexual arousal patterns from normal to quite deviant" (Murphy, Rau, & Worley, 1994. p. 3). The *Diagnostic and Statistical Manual of the American Psychiatric Association—Fourth Edition* (*DSM-IV*; American Psychiatric Association, 1994) describes pedophilia in the following way:

Individuals with Pedophilia generally report an attraction to children of a particular age range. Some individuals prefer males, others females, and some are aroused by both males and females. Those attracted to females usually prefer 8- to 10-year-olds, whereas those attracted to males usually prefer slightly older children. Pedophilia involving female victims is reported more often than Pedophilia involving male victims.... Individuals with Pedophilia who act on their urges with children may limit their activity to undressing the child and looking, exposing themselves, masturbating in the presence of the child, or gentle touching and fondling of the child. Others, however, perform fellatio or cunnilingus on the child or penetrate the child's vagina, mouth, or anus with their fingers, foreign objects, or penis and use varying degrees of force to do so. These activities are commonly explained with excuses or rationalizations that they have "educational value" for the child, that the child derives "sexual pleasure" from them, or that the child was "sexually provocative"—themes that are also common in pedophilia pornography. (pp. 527–528)

Children are easy targets for perpetrators because they are first and foremost children, with all that implies. For example, children may not realize that sexual activity with a parent or another adult is wrong; they may not be able to discriminate affection from purely sexual interest, a line that the perpetrator blurs as part of the "process"; and they may see the perpetrator as an authority figure whom they must obey.

Thus, adult individuals who are truly attracted to children and who engage in sexual activities with them are considered to have a sexual perversion. Although certain factors such as personal inadequacies and loss of inhibitions may contribute to the development of pedophilia, the essential aspects of child sexual molestation are preoccupation with children, grooming of children, and the setting up of conditions for the sexual molestation to take place.

Incest, in particular, often is marked by a pattern of secrecy and addiction. Offenders usually do everything within their power to ensure that the abuse is done secretly and that it remains secret (Furniss, 1991). The sexual act with the child often becomes addictive for the offender.

Incest and other forms of sexual abuse occur because offenders have opportunities to commit the abuse. Victimization may occur when external protections against abuse—such as appropriate supervision or protective care—are missing. For example, a father or other adult male (such as a mother's partner or a neighbor) may sexually victimize girls when their mother is away from home and the girls are left at home with the adult male after school, or a divorced parent may take advantage of being alone with the children when children spend some of their time with each parent.

Children also may be sexually victimized when both parents are present in the home, such as late at night when the father or mother comes into the child's bed or when a parent is bathing the child. The occurrences of these types of victimizations may be chronic or occasional, and they may not be marked by an addictive behavior pattern.

The characteristics associated with sexually abusing families are not well established (Crittenden, 1996); however, several patterns may be found. For example, in some families, members might seek closeness but find intimacy uncomfortable—the sexual abuse satisfies the need for closeness. Or they may resort to the use of alcohol or drugs to lower inhibitions. In other families, members might be disengaged and fearful of showing tender feelings; their sexual abuse might reflect a desperate attempt at establishing a relationship, while allowing them to remain psychologically distant and unavailable.

The following case illustrates how a poor-quality parent-child attachment, difficulty in becoming intimate with other people, and a perverted way of expressing love and caring on the part of the father led to a father's becoming a sex offender (Marshall, 1993).

CASE 20-24. WENDELL
Wendell had been so seriously neglected by his parents that it was at the insistence of Child Protective Services that the court placed Wendell in foster care at the age of five years. A succession of foster home placements followed over the next seven years until Wendell was finally permanently placed into a family. Despite the kindness and warmth this family showed to Wendell, he never allowed himself to become deeply attached to them, and he constantly had nightmares about being taken away again. His insecurity was manifested in all his relationships, and he drove friends away by either being too demanding or trying too hard to please them.

Over time Wendell came to the conclusion that no one was trustworthy, and, not surprisingly, he had few friends.

Wendell had a series of disastrous relationships with peer-aged females during late adolescence and early adulthood, and it was not until he was 26 years old that he met his wife-to-be. They courted for two years before marrying, and, within a year, they had a daughter.

After the child was born, Wendell's wife began to find the responsibilities burdensome, and she started leaving the child with Wendell while she went out with her female friends. Her main complaint, which she voiced often during their courtship and throughout their marriage, was that Wendell had no friends and would not socialize. Furthermore, she felt that he avoided her and, indeed, this seemed to be true. Wendell would always think of reasons to be away from home: He would work extra hours, go fishing alone, go to hockey matches alone, or simply go for long drives in his car. Wendell admitted that he felt uncomfortable spending long hours with his wife. After their daughter was born, however, Wendell became an instantly devoted father. He came home directly from work and gave up all his leisure activities to be with his daughter.

As time went on and the child grew up, Wendell was her constant companion. His wife spent more and more time away from home and eventually, when their daughter was 9, she left Wendell and the child and moved in with another man in a distant city. At this time, Wendell began courting his daughter. He would arrange candlelight dinners for the two of them, he would take her out to various shows and to hockey matches, and he would constantly buy her surprise gifts. Finally, 14 months after his wife left, Wendell initiated sexual relations with his daughter.

When he first attended group therapy, Wendell said that he loved his daughter in more than a fatherly fashion and wished that when she grew up he could live with her as her husband. He realized this was absurd and could not happen, but he declared that she was the only person he had ever trusted and that he had felt emotionally intimate with her in a way he had never been with anyone else. (p. 115, with changes in notation)

Children Who Molest Other Children

Adolescents who commit sexual offenses are mostly males, with a modal age of about 14 years. They tend to have the following characteristics (Aljazireh, 1993):

- a history of having been sexually molested or physically abused
- a history of prior nonsexual delinquent behavior (such as misdemeanors or less serious felonies like trespassing, truancy, and petty theft)
- homes in which some type of family dysfunction is present (such as parental loss through death, divorce, or separation; parents with substance abuse problems; parents who have other psychological impairments; parents who were victims of physical or sexual abuse; or parents with criminal records)
- impaired social skills
- psychiatric disturbances

Young children may be sexually abused by an older sibling who is in a position of authority and has power over the younger sibling (Furniss, 1991). In some cases, the older sibling may have assumed a quasi-parental role and also may have been sexually abused. When sexual activity occurs between siblings who are close in age, it may be difficult to determine responsibility. In such cases, there may be no abuser per se. Again, one or both of the siblings may have been previously abused by a caregiver.

One issue in these situations is whether the parents were neglectful in allowing the abuse to occur. Another issue is what constitutes "normal" sexual activity. You need to be aware of what is normal for children in order to distinguish between siblings "playing doctor" and a sibling sexually abusing another sibling. Similar considerations are involved when nonsiblings play doctor.

Natural and Expected Sexual Behaviors in Children

The following are natural and expected sexual behaviors in (a) preschool children and (b) children in kindergarten through fourth grade (with permission, *Understanding Children's Sexual Behaviors: What's Natural and Healthy,* 1996. T. C. Johnson, 1101 Fremont Ave., Suite 01, South Pasadena, CA 91030).

PRESCHOOL CHILD

- touches or rubs own genitals when diapers are being changed, when going to sleep, and when tense, excited, or afraid
- explores differences between males and females
- touches the genitals and breasts of familiar adults and children
- takes advantage of opportunities to look at nude persons
- asks about genitals, breasts, intercourse, and babies
- has erections (for males)
- likes to be nude and may show others her or his genitals
- shows interest in watching people doing bathroom functions
- shows interest in mother having or giving birth to a baby
- uses "dirty" words for bathroom and sexual functions
- shows interest in own feces
- plays doctor by inspecting others' bodies
- puts something in the genitals or rectum of self or other because of curiosity or exploration
- plays house and acts out roles of mommy and daddy

CHILD IN KINDERGARTEN THROUGH FOURTH GRADE

- asks about genitals, breasts, intercourse, and babies
- shows interest in watching or peeking at people doing bathroom functions
- uses "dirty" words for bathroom functions, genitals, and sex
- plays doctor and inspects others' bodies

- shows interest in mother having or giving birth to a baby
- shows others her or his genitals
- shows interest in urination and defecation
- touches or rubs own genitals when going to sleep and when tense, excited, or afraid
- plays house and may simulate roles of mommy and daddy
- thinks members of the opposite sex are "gross" and chases them
- talks about sex with friends and talks about having a girlfriend or boyfriend
- wants privacy when in bathroom or when changing clothes
- likes to hear and tell "dirty" jokes
- looks at nude pictures
- plays games related to sex and sexuality with same-aged children

THE OFFENDER IN CASES OF CHILD EMOTIONAL ABUSE

Less research has been done on families that emotionally abuse their children than on families that engage in other types of maltreatment (Crittenden, 1996). However, emotional abuse often appears as part of other types of maltreatment, particularly physical abuse and neglect. Therefore, many of the characteristics of families that physically abuse and neglect their children also are found in families that emotionally abuse their children. Among the families that emotionally abuse their children are "middle-income families with both physical and psychological maltreatment who, because of biases protecting middle-income families, are not reported. They may also include families who enter the mental health treatment system rather than the child protection system. In addition, there may be many families who, under the stress of family crises, such as divorce, death, relocation, and unemployment, temporarily psychologically mistreat their children" (Crittenden, 1996, p. 168).

Emotional abuse can occur because the caregiver needs to control the children's lives. The caregiver may constantly demean his or her child by telling the child that he or she is ugly, stupid, fat, and so forth. The caregiver doesn't realize the impact of this behavior on the child's self-esteem, doesn't care about the effect this behavior has on the child, deliberately wants to show who is in control, or carries out the emotional abuse for some other reason.

STATISTICS ON CHARACTERISTICS OF PERPETRATORS OF ALL TYPES OF MALTREATMENT

As you read the material in this chapter, you may have wondered who the perpetrators of child maltreatment are. The

National Center on Child Abuse and Neglect (1996) reported that in 1994 parents were the leading group of perpetrators (79.2%), followed by other relatives (9.9%). Individuals in other caregiving relationships to the child victims (for example, foster parents, facility staff, and child care providers) made up only 2.3% of perpetrators, noncaregivers made up 4.7% of perpetrators, and individuals whose relationship to the victim was unknown made up the remainder (see Figure 20-9).

In the National Committee to Prevent Child Abuse survey for 1995, families in which children were maltreated were likely to have one of more of the following problems: (a) substance abuse, (b) poverty and economic stress, (c) poor parenting skills (because of various mental health problems, poor understanding of a child's normal development, or young maternal age), or (d) domestic violence (Lung & Daro, 1996).

The Department of Justice reported that for offenders who forcibly rape females, the younger the victim, the more likely the offender is to be a family member or an acquaintance (Bureau of Justice Statistics, 1994). As Table 20-6 shows, in 1992, a family member was the offender in 46% of the rapes of female children younger than age 12 but in only 12% of the rapes of female victims 18 or older. A stranger was the offender in only 4% of the rapes of female children younger than age 12 but in 33% of the rapes of female victims 18 or older. In other words, 96% of the rape victims under age 12 knew the offender, whereas 67% of the rape victims over 18 knew the offender. Additional data indicated that fathers raped 20% of the victims under age 12, 11% of the victims aged 12 to 17, and 1% of the victims 18 or older. Appendix E contains information about characteristics of perpetrators, as reported in the NIS-3 survey.

Table 20-6
Relationship Between Age of Victim and Relationship of Offender to Victim in Cases of Forcible Rape in 1992

Victim's age	Relationship of offender to victim		
	Family member (%)	Acquaintance or friend (%)	Stranger (%)
Under 12	46	50	4
12–17	20	65	15
18 or older	12	55	33

Source: Adapted from Bureau of Justice Statistics (1994).

CHILD MALTREATMENT IN FACILITIES, INSTITUTIONS, AND FOSTER HOMES

At least 300,000 children in the United States reside in an out-of-home placement, such as a family foster care home, a group home, a residential treatment facility, or an institution (Rosenthal, Motz, Edmonson, & Groze, 1991). Several factors may lead to child maltreatment in these settings, such as large child-to-staff ratios, frequent staff turnover, and staff that is untrained, uneducated, isolated, underpaid, and overstressed because of difficult job responsibilities, long hours, unscheduled overtime, and double shifts. When these factors are present, the staff may believe that their power over the children is their only source of job significance. This power then may lead to abuse.

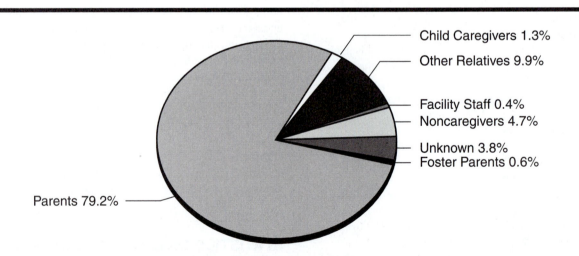

Figure 20-9. Relationship of perpetrators to victims in 1994, based on 678,092 reports from 41 states. From National Center on Child Abuse and Neglect (U.S. Department of Health and Human Services). *Child Maltreatment 1994: Reports from the States to the National Center on Child Abuse and Neglect* (Washington, DC: U.S. Government Printing Office, 1996), p. 2-10.

Here are examples of two incidents of child maltreatment in institutional settings (Rosenthal et al., 1991, pp. 257, 259).

A female resident, 13, returned to the dormitory early from school. When a female counselor attempted to find out why, an argument ensued. The counselor threw the girl onto a bed. The girl got up and picked up a shoe. The counselor threw the girl to the floor, fracturing the girl's nose.

A 14-year-old boy was sexually abused in a residential facility by a female child care staff member. The abuse began with sexual flirtation and love notes. The perpetrator entered the victim's room in the middle of night, fondled the victim's genitals and buttocks, and engaged the victim in sexual intercourse.

The staff in residential facilities can control children through bribes—such as special privileges, furloughs, or special treats—or through threats—such as seclusion, restriction, or delayed release (Andrews & Veronen, 1993). Sexual assaults, in particular, may occur when children are heavily medicated, comatose, or in restraints.

Children in institutional settings may indirectly contribute to incidents of maltreatment, especially when they are angry or difficult to manage (Blatt, 1992). Children placed in these settings may have been maltreated by their parents, may have substance abuse problems, or may suffer from mental illness. *Nonetheless, staff members are never justified in maltreating children in their care.* Other institutional factors that may play a role in child maltreatment include overcrowding, poor guidelines and expectations about how children in residential care should be treated, movement of children to new living areas, poor support systems, and poor programming (Blatt, 1992).

Accurate information on the frequency of child sexual abuse in institutional settings is difficult to obtain because the victims may be afraid to report the abuse, the staff may be hesitant to report the abuse unless there is overwhelming evidence, and the uncovering of problems may have political implications for the staff and directors (Charles, Coleman, & Matheson, 1993). Child sexual abuse is more likely to happen in settings where staff members (a) receive minimal supervision, (b) feel disempowered or maltreated by the administration,(c) were not thoroughly screened before they were hired, and (d) do not have a strong sense of professional identity (Charles et al., 1993).

THINKING THROUGH THE ISSUES

What are your feelings about child maltreatment? Do you, for example, feel revulsion or anger or disbelief when you read about cases of child abuse?

If you were maltreated by a member of your family, how likely would you be to report the maltreatment to authorities? Would you be prepared for the consequences that might follow?

If you were unjustly accused of maltreating a child, how would you respond?

How might your feelings about child maltreatment affect your sensitivity to its possible occurrence, your awareness of potential signs of maltreatment, and your willingness to report suspicion of possible abuse or neglect?

What factors might account for the rapid increase in reports of child maltreatment since 1976?

Why is neglect the most frequently reported form of maltreatment?

How easy is it to distinguish degrees of severity of abuse?

What would you need to know before you would report a case of child maltreatment? Do you have a low threshold (that is, you would make reports even when the facts were meager) or a high threshold (that is, you would make reports only when the facts were substantial) for notifying authorities about possible maltreatment? How did you arrive at your answer?

Do you think that your decision to report child maltreatment will be affected by (a) the possibility that you will be sued for malpractice for accusing someone of maltreating a child on the basis of insufficient evidence, (b) the fear of being wrong, or (c) the belief that the family will drop out of therapy if you report your suspicions of child maltreatment?

If you saw a child being abused by (a) close friend, (b) a neighbor, (c) your brother or sister, (d) your father or mother, (e) your uncle or aunt, or (f) a stranger, how likely would you be to report the abuse in each case? What was the basis for your decision in each case?

How would you feel about telling a stranger (say, the person sitting next to you on the first day of class) about your last sexual experience? What is the basis for your answer?

How familiar are you with your state's laws about the need to report child maltreatment to the appropriate agency?

Are the present laws concerning immunity for reporting child abuse adequate? What changes would you make, if any?

Would you be more likely to report suspicions of child maltreatment about people more like yourself or more unlike yourself? What is the basis for your answer?

Which theory do you believe best accounts for both physical maltreatment and sexual molestation? What is the basis for your answer?

Do you believe that, given the right circumstances, most, if not all, adults have the potential to be abusive toward children? What is the basis for your answer?

How would you go about reducing the incidence of child maltreatment? Can anything significant be accomplished, given our present social-economic-political climate?

Other things being equal, which form of maltreatment has the most serious consequences—physical abuse, sexual abuse, emotional abuse, or neglect? What is the basis for your answer?

What do you think about parents' spanking children and about other types of parental discipline? Where do you draw the line between acceptable and unacceptable forms of punishment? When does unacceptable punishment become physical abuse?

How do you feel about judging other people's child-rearing practices? And how would you feel about other people's judging the child-rearing practices in your family? To what extent are your beliefs about punishment affected by your experiences as a child and/or as a parent?

SUMMARY

1. In-depth interviews of children, their parents, and the suspected perpetrators in cases of alleged or known child maltreatment are usually conducted by individuals working in Child Protective Services, law enforcement agencies, or district or county attorneys' offices.

2. Child maltreatment often represents a repetitive, habitual pattern of behavior carried out by a perpetrator over a period of time with almost complete disregard for the needs, rights, and safety of the maltreated child.

3. The individuals involved in work with child maltreatment include law enforcement personnel, Child Protective Services workers (also referred to as Department of Social Services workers or by other names, depending on the state or county), public welfare workers, child guidance counselors, attorneys, physicians (including psychiatrists), nurses, psychologists, social workers, district attorneys, and judges.

The Challenge of Child Maltreatment Interviewing

4. Child maltreatment interviewing is challenging because the information obtained may be used to decide the guilt or innocence of another person or persons.

5. Serious consequences can result if you report inaccurate information or obtain information through methods that jeopardize the credibility of the report. Children may be subjected to continued maltreatment and may even die; parental rights may be terminated; innocent people may be sent to jail, households destroyed, and families ruined; or ethical complaints may be filed with the state licensing board about your professional competency

6. In some cases, the stigma of being accused of child maltreatment or the pain of being maltreated may be so great that an adult or child will attempt suicide.

7. Child maltreatment interviewing also is challenging because you may be uncertain of the facts, unable to determine whether maltreatment occurred, and unable to decide whether the child is at risk.

The Child Abuse Prevention and Treatment Act

8. The Child Abuse Prevention and Treatment Act (CAPTA)—also referred to as Public Law 93-247 and as the Mondale Act—was passed by Congress in 1974 and has been amended and renewed several times.

Definition and Types of Child Abuse and Neglect

9. The Child Abuse Prevention and Treatment Act defines child abuse and neglect as the physical or mental injury, sexual abuse or exploitation, negligent treatment, or maltreatment (a) of a child under the age of 18, or except in the case of sexual abuse, the age specified by the child protection law of the State in which the child resides, (b) by a person (including any employee of a residential facility or any staff providing out-of-home care) who is responsible for the child's welfare, (c) under circumstances that indicate that the child's health or welfare is harmed or threatened thereby. Sexual abuse is further defined as the employment, use, persuasion, inducement, enticement, or coercion of any child to engage in, or assist any other person to engage in, any sexually explicit conduct or simulation of such conduct for the purpose of producing any visual depiction of such conduct, or the rape, molestation, prostitution, or other form of sexual exploitation of children, or incest with children.

10. Physical abuse of children is characterized by inflicting injury by hitting, punching, beating, kicking, throwing, biting, burning, or otherwise physically harming a child. The injury may be the result of a single episode or of repeated episodes. The physical trauma can range in severity from minor bruising, abrasions, lacerations, burns, eye injuries, and fractures to damage to the brain and internal organs (liver, spleen, abdomen, pancreas, and kidneys).

11. Sexual abuse of children covers a wide range of conduct including genital exposure; masturbation between adult and child; fondling breasts, genitals, buttocks, and thighs; oral copulation; vaginal or anal penetration by finger, penis, or foreign object; dry intercourse (rubbing penis between child's thighs or anal-genital areas); making a child fondle an adult; and commercial exploitation through prostitution or the production of pornographic materials.

12. Emotional abuse of children includes acts or omissions by the parents or other persons that have caused or could cause emotional, behavioral, cognitive, or mental disorders. Emotional abuse exists on a continuum of habitual behavioral interactions such as belittling through comments, comparisons, and name-calling; scapegoating; humiliating; isolating; screaming; raging and terrorizing by verbally assaulting the child, threatening the child, and creating a climate of fear; rejecting by refusing to acknowledge the child's worth and the legitimacy of the child's needs; ignoring by depriving the child of essential stimulation and responsiveness; and corrupting by stimulating the child to engage in destructive antisocial behavior.

13. Child neglect is characterized by failure to provide for the child's basic needs. Neglect can be physical, educational, or emotional. Physical neglect includes refusal of or delay in seeking medical or dental care, abandonment, inadequate supervision, passive drug intoxication with illicit drugs, accidental ingestion of illicit drugs, and expulsion from the home or refusal to allow a runaway to return home. Educational neglect includes permission of chronic truancy, failure to enroll a child of mandatory school age, and inattention to a special educational need. Emotional neglect includes failure to respond to the child's psychological needs for attention, love, and emotional security; emotional deprivation and being psychologically inaccessible; exposure to chronic or extreme spouse or sibling abuse in the child's presence; and permission or encouragement for drug or alcohol use and illegal activity by the child. Endangerment, which also can be considered a form of neglect, goes beyond neglect because it may have such immediate tragic consequences. Endangerment includes failing to use a child car seat for the child, driving

while intoxicated with a child in the car, and leaving loaded firearms or controlled substances in a young child's reach.

14. Child maltreatment can vary on a continuum from mild maltreatment to very severe maltreatment.

15. Physical abuse usually results in some observable evidence of the maltreatment.

16. Sexual abuse seldom yields tangible evidence—such as visible injuries to the child, a sexually transmitted disease, semen residue, or blood stains—but often the abuse leaves behavioral symptoms.

17. Neglect, like sexual abuse, may leave behavioral symptoms rather than physical evidence of maltreatment.

18. Children may be physically, sexually, or emotionally abused in their home, school, day care center, church or synagogue, residential facility, or any other place.

19. Neglect primarily takes place in the home where the child lives.

20. For all forms of maltreatment, the offender may be a parent, relative, sibling, friend, teacher, or staff member.

21. With the encouragement of the federal Child Abuse Prevention and Treatment Act, all 50 states in the United States have passed laws about who should report child maltreatment.

22. State laws generally require that individuals working with children—such as child caregivers, teachers, physicians, psychologists, psychiatrists, social workers, marriage and family therapists, counselors, and clergy in some states—report child maltreatment when there is reasonable suspicion. These individuals are sometimes referred to as mandated reporters.

23. Regulatory statutes use the phrase *reasonable suspicion* to mean that a person should consider the possibility of child maltreatment based on facts that could cause a reasonable person in a like position to come to the same conclusion.

24. Members of the public can voluntarily notify Child Protective Services or law enforcement if they suspect that child maltreatment has occurred or is occurring.

25. The role of the reporting party is not to determine or to prove that maltreatment did in fact occur; rather, the reporting party's only responsibility is to report a reasonable suspicion of child maltreatment.

26. Some mandated reporters are ambivalent about reporting suspicions of child maltreatment.

27. It is the responsibility of Child Protective Services and law enforcement to investigate the alleged child maltreatment.

28. It is the responsibility of law enforcement to place the child in protective custody if the situation and the recommendations of Child Protective Services justify it.

29. In some cities or counties, the assessment of a child who has been allegedly maltreated may be conducted by a core multidisciplinary team composed of a physician, a nurse, a social worker, a law-enforcement officer, and a psychologist.

30. Members of the supplementary team (which supports the core multidisciplinary team) may include an attorney, a speech/language clinician, a nutritionist, a representative from the district attorney's office, a forensic pathologist, a dentist, and an educator. All members of the core and supplementary multidisciplinary teams must be concerned with the safety of the child.

31. The sources of 1,508,177 reports of child maltreatment obtained from 44 states in 1994 were educators (16% of the reports), followed by representatives of law enforcement and justice agencies (13%), social services professionals (12%),

medical personnel (11%), other reporters (11%), other relatives (10%), friends and neighbors (9%), anonymous reporters (7.6%), parents (7%), child care providers (1.5%), victims (1.4%), and perpetrators (0.4%).

32. Professionals accounted for almost 53% of the reports of child maltreatment in 1994; friends, parents, and other relatives, 27%; and victims, self-identified perpetrators, and anonymous and other reporters, 20%.

33. In 1994, in a 7–2 vote, the U.S. Supreme Court let stand a ruling that makes social workers immune from being sued, even if they wrongly accuse a parent of sexually abusing his or her child.

34. Immunity may apply only to the initial reporting of child maltreatment and not to all activities associated with the case.

35. If you work for Child Protective Services or for law enforcement and receive a report of alleged child maltreatment, ask the reporter to give you as much information as possible about the alleged maltreatment.

36. In 1994, there were 2,935,470 reported cases of child maltreatment in the United States, involving 43 out of every 1,000 children.

37. The reported cases in 1994 represented an increase of 71% over those in 1984 and an increase of 320% over those in 1976.

38. Neglect was the type of maltreatment reported most often in 1994 (53% of the cases), followed by physical abuse (25.5% of the cases), sexual abuse (14% of the cases), and emotional abuse (4.7% of the cases).

39. Although sexual abuse is reported less frequently than physical abuse and neglect, it may be the most underreported form of child maltreatment because of the secrecy that so often characterizes sexual abuse cases.

40. Of the approximately 1.63 million investigations of alleged child abuse and neglect conducted in 1994, 56% were not substantiated, 31% were substantiated, 6% were "indicated or reason to suspect," and 5% had other dispositions.

41. In 1994, 43 states reported 1,111 child fatalities that resulted from child maltreatment.

42. Children reported to have been physically abused have a higher probability than nonabused children of dying early in life.

43. An analysis of the ages of the children victimized in 1994 indicates that 27% of the victims were 3 years old or younger, 20% were between 4 and 6 years, 17% were between 7 and 9 years, 15% were between 10 and 12 years, and 21% were between 13 and 18 years.

44. In 1994, females had a slightly higher rate of maltreatment than males (52.3% versus 46.7%).

45. In 1994, the incidence of sexual abuse was three times higher for girls than for boys.

46. In 1994, there was a strong relationship between family income and rate of maltreatment, with children in families with the lowest income level having the highest rate of maltreatment.

47. In 1994, children in families with four or more children had a greater chance of being neglected than children in families with fewer children.

48. In 1994, children of single parents had a greater chance of being maltreated than children with two parents.

49. In reports of child maltreatment in 1994, White American children, Hispanic American children, and Asian/Pacific

Islander children were somewhat underrepresented, whereas Black American children and Native American children were somewhat overrepresented, given the population of the United States in 1990.

50. The national incidence statistics do not indicate actual rates of child maltreatment.

51. The estimated minimal cost of child maltreatment in 1994 was $9 billion.

52. Children with physical or intellectual disabilities are about 1.7 times more vulnerable to maltreatment than children without disabilities.

53. Child maltreatment is primarily a family affair, occurring in the homes where children live.

54. When vulnerability factors exceed protective factors, caregivers may physically abuse their children.

The Offender in Cases of Child Physical Abuse and Neglect

55. The individual determinants theory of child physical abuse and neglect suggests that some of the following factors in the offender's development led him or her to commit child physical abuse or neglect: traumatic experiences in early childhood, abnormal or deviant characteristics, inadequate affective processes, inadequate cognitive processes, inadequate personal resources, personal stressors, removal of inhibitions, and reinforcement for the maltreatment.

56. The sociocultural determinants theory of child physical abuse and neglect suggests that some of the following factors in the offender's development led him or her to commit child physical abuse or neglect: inadequate family structure; inadequate support systems; social stressors; high degree of competition for jobs, promoting intergroup conflict; formal and informal socialization factors and social ideologies that teach selfishness and unconcern for others and thus promote violence; cultural sanctioning of violence as a means of disciplining, solving problems, and expressing authority; cultural attitudes that historically consider children as property; and cultural beliefs that assume children are unable to understand and be responsive to nonphysical disciplinary and control tactics.

57. The individual-environment interaction theory of child physical abuse and neglect suggests that individual determinants and sociocultural determinants interact to contribute to child physical abuse or neglect.

58. Until child labor laws were passed in the mid-1880s, children were exploited by society; it would be fair to say that prior to this time society was guilty of maltreating children.

59. The theory of the conflict-prone institution suggests that family structures and family norms that foster conflict may encourage violence within families.

60. The social learning and interaction theory regards intrafamilial violence as resulting from psychosocial interaction processes, both within the family and between the family and its social environment. The theory postulates that the roles of the offender and the victim are learned.

61. Families that live in poverty are more likely to abuse their children because they have fewer resources, fewer supports, and more stressors than families that are not living in poverty.

62. Cases of physical abuse in families from upper socioeconomic classes may be underreported because of the status of the families, because money has covered the crime, or because professionals may be reluctant to believe that "upper-class" people would be abusive.

63. A cognitive model of child physical abuse suggests that caregivers' responses to the behaviors of their children are mediated by the caregivers' social cognitions, such as their beliefs about their children and about themselves.

64. An information-processing model of child neglect hypothesizes that parents who neglect their children may fail to respond to their children's signals.

65. Some parents are insensitive to their infants' needs because their parents were insensitive to their needs when they were infants—a phenomenon referred to as cross-generational effects.

66. Sometimes parents may stop maltreating their child because the school, Child Protective Services, or law enforcement warns them that they may be violating the law.

67. Research suggests that neglectful parents typically are poor, psychologically immature, apathetic, and impulsive; want to be good parents; have strengths that can be mobilized; need realistic goals; need court-ordered services for their children; and may need long-term psychological treatment, especially when the neglect has been chronic.

68. Munchausen Syndrome by Proxy is a form of child physical abuse characterized by the following elements: (a) the child's illness is simulated or produced by a caregiver, (b) the caregiver makes repeated requests for medical evaluation and care of the child, (c) the caregiver denies any knowledge of the cause of the child's symptoms, and (d) the child's symptoms quickly cease when the child and the caregiver are separated.

69. Major factors that should raise suspicions of Munchausen Syndrome by Proxy include the following: (a) The child has persistent or recurrent unexplained illnesses, (b) the child's symptoms do not match known medical symptoms or are not consistent with them, (c) the child's symptoms typically have been witnessed only by his or her caregiver, (d) the child's symptoms are resolved each time the child is hospitalized but not when the child is at home, (e) the child has new symptoms at the hospital that have an onset witnessed by the caregiver only, (f) the child's symptoms do not occur when the child is away from the caregiver, (g) the child's symptoms are not consistent with her or his general health, (h) the child fails to respond to medical therapy, and (i) the child's apnea monitor "doesn't work" for unknown reasons.

70. There is a link between domestic violence and child maltreatment because children living in a home where domestic violence takes place are vulnerable to physical, emotional, and sexual abuse and to neglect.

71. Domestic violence includes battering, spousal abuse, family violence, wife beating, and physical violence.

72. Battered women's syndrome includes chronic severe anxiety, depression, panic, insomnia, and associated physical symptoms.

73. Domestic violence is a crime.

74. According to the American Medical Association, 25% of the women in the United States, or 12 million women, will be abused by a current or former partner during their lives.

75. Individuals who batter their spouse may have had traumatic experiences in early childhood; have abnormal or deviant characteristics, inadequate affective processes, inadequate cognitive processes, inadequate personal resources, or personal stressors; have been under the influence of alcohol or drugs, which removed their inhibitions; or have received rein-

forcement for the battering. They also may have an inadequate family structure, inadequate support systems, social stressors, pathological jealousy and possessiveness toward their mate, and a cultural belief that it is permissible to batter their spouse.

76. Maritally violent men do not constitute a homogeneous group; they may fall into one of the three following subtypes: family-only batterers, dysphoric/borderline batterers, or violent/antisocial batterers.

77. Women may remain in an abusive relationship for several different reasons. They may have no place to go; they may not have enough money to support themselves or skills to obtain employment, and they may believe that they cannot survive alone or support their children; they may be intimidated by the abuser's threats; they may believe that it is the woman's role to make the relationship work; they may believe that their children need a father no matter what; they may hope the abuser will change; they may love the abuser; and they may believe in the sanctity of marriage.

78. Women leave an abusive relationship when it becomes intolerable. Rationalizing the abuse may no longer work, and the batterer may have begun to physically or sexually abuse the children.

79. Signs that should alert you to the possibility that the interviewee is a victim of domestic violence include a central pattern of injuries, injuries suggestive of a defensive posture, injuries inconsistent with the interviewee's explanation, multiple injuries in various stages of healing, substantial delay between the time of injury and the presentation for treatment, frequent visits to a health care provider for vague complaints without evidence of physiologic abnormality, alcohol or drug use, and injury during pregnancy (for women).

80. It is estimated that between 45 to 70% of battered women in shelters report that their children also were abused.

81. How domestic violence affects children will depend on several factors, including the children's age, sex, stage of development, and role in the family; the type, extent, and frequency of the violence; and the effects of the violence, such as economic effects and the need to move and relocate.

82. Children witnessing domestic violence may be deeply affected by what they see.

83. Living in a violent home may affect children's schooling negatively.

84. In one study, in 74 percent or more of the cases, children were present in the households when domestic violence was reported.

85. Batterers may be prosecuted not only for spousal battery but also for child maltreatment when children (a) have observed the assault on one of their parents (or caregivers), (b) have been beaten themselves, or (c) have tried to intervene in the domestic dispute.

86. Children of battered women living in shelters face several difficulties, such as leaving their home without preparation, losing contact with their schools and friends, and leaving their pets and toys.

87. Domestic violence can lead to child maltreatment fatalities, particularly when there is a high level of general violence in the home.

88. Child Protective Services workers often do not identify the presence of domestic violence in the home or minimize its significance.

The Offender in Cases of Child Sexual Abuse

89. The individual determinants theory of child sexual abuse suggests that some of the following factors in the offender's development may have led him or her to commit child sexual abuse: history of sexual abuse or of inappropriate sexual experiences as a child, abnormal or deviant characteristics, inadequate affective processes, inadequate cognitive processes, inadequate personal resources, personal stressors, removal of inhibitions, failure to bond with the child, and manipulative personality.

90. The sociocultural determinants theory of child sexual abuse suggests that some of the following factors in the offender's development may have led him or her to commit child sexual abuse: weakening of taboos against sex with children, socialization pressures leading to distorted concepts of masculinity, social isolation, inappropriate family norms or living arrangements, and high divorce and remarriage rates.

91. The individual-environment interaction theory of child sexual abuse suggests that individual determinants and sociocultural determinants interact to contribute to child sexual abuse.

92. The attachment theory model suggests that children are more at risk for sexual abuse when a biological parent is not present in the family, when the mother is not available to the child, when there is marital conflict and violence, when the child has a poor relationship with the parents, and when a stepfather is present in the family.

93. Individuals who sexually abuse children are not a homogeneous group. They may or may not have psychological problems, and they vary in their sexual arousal patterns from normal to quite deviant.

94. Children are easy targets for perpetrators because they may not realize that sexual activity with a parent or another adult is wrong, they may not be able to discriminate affection from purely sexual interest, and they may see the perpetrator as an authority figure whom they must obey.

95. Adult individuals who are truly attracted to children and who engage in sexual activities with them are considered to have a sexual perversion.

96. Incest, in particular, often is marked by a pattern of secrecy and addiction.

97. Incest and other forms of sexual abuse occur because offenders have opportunities to commit the abuse.

98. Adolescents who commit sexual offenses are mostly males, with a modal age of about 14 years.

The Offender in Cases of Child Emotional Abuse

99. Less research has been done on families that emotionally abuse their children than on families that engage in other types of maltreatment. However, emotional abuse often appears as part of other types of maltreatment, particularly physical abuse and neglect. Therefore, many of the characteristics of families that physically abuse and neglect their children also are found in families that emotionally abuse their children.

Statistics on Characteristics of Perpetrators of All Types of Maltreatment

100. In 1994, almost 80% of the perpetrators were parents, followed by other relatives. Individuals in other caregiving relationships to the child victims (for example, foster parents, facility staff, and child care providers) made up less than 3% of the perpetrators.

101. Families in which children were maltreated often were found to have one or more of the following problems: substance abuse, poverty and economic stress, poor parenting skills, or domestic violence.

102. For offenders who forcibly rape females, the younger the victim, the more likely the offender is to be a family member or an acquaintance.

Child Maltreatment in Facilities, Institutions, and Foster Homes

103. At least 300,000 children in the United States reside in an out-of-home placement, such as a family foster care home, a group home, a residential treatment facility, or an institution.

104. Several factors may lead to child maltreatment in facilities, institutions, and foster homes, such as large child-to-staff ratios, frequent staff turnover, and staff that is untrained, uneducated, isolated, underpaid, and overstressed.

105. Other institutional factors that may play a role in child maltreatment are overcrowding, poor guidelines and expectations about how children in residential care should be treated, movement of children to new living areas, poor support systems, and poor programming.

KEY TERMS, CONCEPTS, AND NAMES

Child Abuse Prevention and Treatment Act (CAPTA) (p. 667)
Physical abuse (p. 669)
Sexual abuse (p. 669)
Emotional abuse (p. 670)
Neglect (p. 670)
Physical neglect (p. 670)
Educational neglect (p. 670)
Emotional neglect (p. 670)
Endangerment (p. 670)
Child maltreatment continuum (p. 670)
Evidence of child maltreatment (p. 670)
Reasonable suspicion (p. 672)
Mandated reporters (p. 672)
Dependency/neglect petition (p. 673)
Child in need of protection or services (CHIPS) petition (p. 673)
Sources of reports of child maltreatment (p. 678)
Immunity (p. 678)
Child maltreatment as a social problem (p. 680)
Child maltreatment fatalities (p. 680)
National Center on Child Abuse and Neglect (p. 683)
Third National Incidence Study of Child Abuse and Neglect (NIS-3) (p. 683)
Vulnerability factors (p. 687)
Protective factors (p. 687)
Individual determinants theory of child physical abuse and neglect (p. 687)
Sociocultural determinants theory of child physical abuse and neglect (p. 687)
Individual-environment interaction theory of child physical abuse and neglect (p. 688)
Theory of the conflict-prone institution (p. 688)
Social learning and interaction theory (p. 688)
Relationship of social class to physical abuse of children (p. 690)
Cognitive model of child physical abuse (p. 691)
Information-processing model of child neglect (p. 691)

Signs that new parents are at high risk for child maltreatment (p. 691)
Cross-generational effects (p. 692)
Characteristics of neglectful parents (p. 693)
Munchausen Syndrome by Proxy (p. 695)
Domestic violence (p. 697)
Theories of domestic violence (p. 698)
Family-only batterers (p. 699)
Dysphoric/borderline batterers (p. 699)
Violent/antisocial batterers (p. 699)
Why women remain in an abusive relationship (p. 699)
Why women leave an abusive relationship (p. 701)
Link between domestic violence and child maltreatment (p. 702)
Domestic violence and child maltreatment fatalities (p. 704)
Theories of child sexual abuse (p. 706)
Pedophilia (p. 706)
Hebephilia (p. 706)
Incest (p. 706)
Individual determinants theory of child sexual abuse (p. 706)
Sociocultural determinant theory of child sexual abuse (p. 707)
Individual-environment interaction theory of child sexual abuse (p. 707)
Attachment theory model of child sexual abuse (p. 707)
Children who molest other children (p. 708)
Offenders in cases of child emotional abuse (p. 709)
Statistics on perpetrators' characteristics (p. 709)
Child maltreatment in facilities, institutions, and foster homes (p. 710)

STUDY QUESTIONS

1. Discuss the challenges of child maltreatment interviewing.
2. Define the four major types of child maltreatment according to the National Center on Child Abuse and Neglect.
3. Describe the child maltreatment continuum.
4. Who should report child abuse and neglect and under what conditions?
5. Who were the main sources of reports of child maltreatment in 1994?
6. When does immunity stop for mandated reporters?
7. Discuss child maltreatment as a social problem, citing statistics where possible. Include in your discussion the incidence of child maltreatment as a function of (a) age and sex, (b) family income, (c) family size, (d) family structure, and (e) ethnicity.
8. What are the estimated costs of child maltreatment?
9. Discuss which children are particularly vulnerable to child maltreatment.
10. Discuss theories intended to account for child physical abuse and neglect. Include in your discussion the (a) individual determinants theory, (b) sociocultural determinants theory, (c) individual-environment interaction theory, (d) theory of the conflict-prone institution, (e) social learning and interaction theory, (f) cognitive model of child physical abuse, and (g) information-processing model of child neglect. Focus your discussion on offenders.
11. Discuss Munchausen Syndrome by Proxy.
12. Discuss domestic violence. In your discussion, cite some facts about domestic violence; offer theories to account for domestic violence, why women remain in an abusive rela-

tionship, and why women leave an abusive relationship; and describe signs of domestic violence, the link between domestic violence and child maltreatment, and effects of domestic violence on children.

13. What might lead adults to abuse children sexually? In your discussion, refer to the (a) individual determinants theory, (b) sociocultural determinants theory, (c) individual-environ-ment interaction theory, and (d) attachment theory model of child sexual abuse. Focus your discussion on adult offenders.

14. Discuss some statistics on characteristics of perpetrators.

15. How would you answer the question "Who is likely to commit child maltreatment?" Explain fully.

16. Discuss child maltreatment in facilities, institutions, and foster homes.

21

BACKGROUND CONSIDERATIONS IN CHILD MALTREATMENT, PART 2

Being maltreated as a child puts one at risk for becoming abusive but the path between these two points is far from direct or inevitable.

—Joan Kaufman and Edward Zigler

Goals and Objectives

This chapter is designed to enable you to:

- Understand the process of disclosure of child maltreatment
- Describe how child maltreatment may affect the child and family
- Evaluate children's memory, lying, and suggestibility
- Discuss factors involved in evaluating allegations of child maltreatment

This chapter continues the discussion of issues that will help you prepare for interviewing children who are alleged or known to have been maltreated. The disclosure of alleged maltreatment has consequences for the child, for her or his family, for the alleged offender, and for the person making the disclosure. How children are affected by maltreatment depends on the type of maltreatment, their age, their relationship with the alleged offender, the length of time the maltreatment lasted, the threats or rewards used by the offender, and other related factors. To conduct effective interviews with children, you need to understand how memory, lying, and suggestibility affect what children tell you. Finally, you need to know what situational conditions may underlie allegations of child maltreatment.

PROCESS OF DISCLOSURE OF MALTREATMENT

Maltreated Child's Fear of Disclosure of Maltreatment

The dilemma faced by children who have been maltreated by their caregivers is that they are almost completely dependent on their caregivers for survival, especially if they are young. If children disclose the maltreatment, they may lose the very persons they must depend on for their development. If they do not disclose the maltreatment, they must bear continued subjugation or brutality and find some way to cope with an intolerable situation.

Children who have been maltreated may have the following fears:

- fear of retribution and violence because abusers may have threatened to hurt or punish them
- fear of not being believed
- fear of being blamed for the abusive acts
- fear of rejection, humiliation, embarrassment, or social stigmatization by peers, neighbors, and school personnel
- fear of loss of friends
- fear of being abandoned or rejected by their family
- fear that they lack the skills to communicate the maltreatment effectively

Some threats may be overwhelmingly terrifying, such as "If you tell, you will never see your mother again," "I'll kill your dog," or "I'll kill you." Abusers may try to make the children feel guilty and responsible for the maltreatment: "If you tell anyone, it is all your fault if daddy goes to prison" or "It is all your fault if mummy gets upset, and you will have to be sent away" (Furniss, 1991, p. 24).

If children do report the maltreatment, they still may not want to testify in court. Also, some parents will not allow their children to testify in court because of the chance of additional trauma. A conspiracy of silence may exist within the family and the culture. Disclosure of maltreatment has legal, familial, psychological, and social consequences for the child, the abuser, and the nonoffending parent(s).

Children may not want to disclose the maltreatment because of fear that their families will be tarnished by the scandal, that they will be responsible for any destructive actions—such as suicide—committed by the abusers, or that the disclosure will lead to the disintegration of their families. Because of loyalty to the abusers, children may not want to get their abusers in trouble.

In the case of sexual abuse, young children may not disclose the abuse because they are unaware that sexual activity between an adult and a child is wrong. "Without adequate information from parents about sexual development and sexual mores, many young children will have no basis on which to judge what is acceptable and what is unacceptable sexual conduct. Hence, it is obvious that if children possess little knowledge about sexuality, it is relatively easy for parents and trusted adults to use young children to their own sexual advantage" (Bussey & Grimbeek, 1995, p. 181).

Adolescents are more likely to disclose sexual abuse than are young children. This is particularly true when the following conditions are present (Deaton & Hertica, 1993, p. 7):

1. The family is being disrupted as a result of other stresses.
2. The offender has left the home.
3. The adolescent develops the insight that the abuse is not okay or that there are more serious implications than he or she had realized earlier.
4. The adolescent is directly asked about abuse and given assurances of a safe environment.
5. The adolescent finds a safe relationship; i.e., a love relationship or a therapeutic alliance.
6. The offender or another significant other dies.
7. The adolescent becomes aware that other children or siblings are at risk.
8. The abuse becomes intolerable.

Abuser's Fear of Disclosure of Maltreatment

Abusers may resist disclosing their role in maltreatment for the following reasons:

- fear of prosecution and imprisonment
- fear of loss of reputation and stigma
- fear of loss of job or professional license
- fear of rejection by partner, divorce, and loss of family
- fear of loss of support from relatives
- fear of loneliness and isolation
- fear that if the maltreatment is disclosed they will want to commit suicide

If the maltreatment is disclosed, abusers may react in various ways, including the following:

- rationalize or minimize the maltreatment ("I was only cleaning her genitals—she must have thought I was too rough" or "I only gave him a pat on the behind")
- experience low self-esteem and consider their actions as the lowest form of behavior
- experience significant depression
- feel no guilt at all
- exhibit paranoia and feelings of persecution, especially in dealing with helping professionals
- deny that the maltreatment occurred
- blame the allegation on someone else, such as a professional ("The interviewer used leading and subjective questions")
- say that they believe the abuse occurred ("She couldn't lie about such things") but adamantly deny that they perpetrated it
- believe that their actions were appropriate and were provoked by the children's behavior
- show irrational reasoning or behavior, such as expecting complete forgiveness from their spouses and victims in response to simplistic apologies ("I'm sorry, please forgive me")

Nonoffending Parent's Fear of Disclosure of Maltreatment

In some cases, the nonoffending parent (often the mother in cases of child sexual abuse) will deny any knowledge of the child's maltreatment, particularly when the father is involved. The nonoffending parent's denial may be based on the following fears:

- fear of loss of a partner and the family bread-winner, which may result in becoming a single parent and in financial hardship
- fear of loneliness and isolation
- fear of stigmatization and loss of self-esteem, when others find out that he or she is the partner of an abuser, as well as a parent who could not protect his or her child
- fear of the effects the disclosure will have on his or her work and professional career
- fear of loss of social support, particularly from relatives

The nonoffending parent may react in the following ways (Steinmetz, 1996):

- become jealous of the sexually abused child for taking her or his role in the family
- feel anger at herself or himself for not protecting the child
- feel helpless in not knowing what is going to happen to her or his child and fear that the child may be taken away
- feel invisible because most of the attention is on substantiating the allegation of maltreatment
- feel shock, numbness, and repulsion, brought about, in part, by memories of her or his own prior victimization
- experience guilt and self-blame because she or he assumes total responsibility for everything that happens to the child
- feel hurt and betrayal on several counts, including grief over the loss of the child's innocence in cases of sexual abuse and over the loss of a spouse if the spouse was the perpetrator
- experience feelings of sexual inadequacy and rejection if the spouse sexually abused the child, because she or he thinks that the abuse might not have occurred if marital sex had been more satisfactory
- have financial concerns about the family income if the spouse was the abuser and may no longer contribute to the family income
- blame the victim

In some cases, the nonoffending parent genuinely does not know about the maltreatment. It is usually easier for a nonoffending parent to acknowledge child maltreatment if it was committed by someone outside the family.

Failure to Believe the Child

Children who disclose that they were maltreated may not be believed. The following case illustrates what may happen when professionals and the nonoffending parent(s) do not believe a child (Furniss, 1991).

CASE 21-1. MARLENE

A typical example of family members and outside agencies colluding in the denial of sexual abuse is the case of Marlene, a 14-year-old girl who had been sexually abused by her stepfather since the age of 7. Abuse had started when her mother was pregnant again. Although Marlene had tried to tell her mother about the abuse, her mother, instead of believing Marlene and confronting her husband, went to her General Practitioner (GP) for advice. The GP labeled the child as showing signs of jealousy in reaction to the mother's pregnancy. The mother still did not want to confront her husband with Marlene's disclosure. She merely reported the disclosure to him, linking it instantly to the GP's diagnosis of jealousy. The mother's avoidance of confronting her husband and her collusion with the GP's denial of sexual abuse allowed the father to scapegoat Marlene and call her a liar. Marlene was severely punished for her disclosure and was further abused under increased threats of violence. Marlene did not dare repeat the allegation of sexual abuse, which continued until she reached adolescence, when she tried to commit suicide. (p. 23, with changes in notation)

Comment on Disclosure of Maltreatment

Disclosure of child maltreatment often will bring about family stress, especially when the accusations are against a family member. When children disclose that they have been maltreated, they may not realize the consequences of the disclosure; consequently, they may feel responsible for the breakup of their families or resent those to whom they disclosed for not telling them what might happen to them and their families. It is especially poor practice to mislead children to believe that the system will protect their families when, in fact, the system often cannot offer them such protection.

Children's fears associated with disclosure of maltreatment are secondary to the maltreatment itself. But you must deal with these fears if children are going to recover from the trauma. These fears include fear of being socially stigmatized in school and in the community, of having to change schools, and of being scapegoated, rejected, and blamed by the family. If the maltreatment is disclosed but not proven, children may be scapegoated or blamed for all family problems, rejected and punished by the family, and even abused more harshly. In these situations, children need to be monitored closely and protected. Thus, you may have to work with victims of child maltreatment, knowing that the offenders may never be prosecuted or stopped.

There is not a shred of positive evidence to suggest that the majority of sexually abused children disclose immediately after the abuse, nor even that they disclose in childhood at all.

—Anna C. Salter

EFFECTS OF CHILD MALTREATMENT

How Physical Abuse and Neglect May Affect Children

Physical abuse may have devastating effects on a child. The damage inflicted on the child can range from mild bruises to death (see Table 21-1). Children who live to tell the tale may be terrified, cowering in the presence of the abuser. But others may fight back, taunt the abuser, and hope to run away at the earliest possible moment to escape from an intolerable situation. Obviously, most young children have few, if any, options other than to stay and suffer the consequences of the caregiver's actions.

When Child Protective Services workers, health care providers, or law enforcement personnel evaluate a child suspected of being physically abused, they need to evaluate carefully the shape, location, and type of injury; the force needed to produce the injury; and the number of new and old injuries (Besharov, 1990). *They need to be especially alert to children's injuries that are unexplained or that do not make sense, to multiple injuries that are in various stages of heal-ing, to evidence of long bone fractures in infants less than 1 year old, and to repeated visits to the emergency rooms of hospitals.* In all cases of possible physical abuse, the child should be examined by a health care provider, who should write a medical report and send it to the proper investigative authority (such as Child Protective Services or law enforcement agencies).

Most of the physical indicators of possible physical abuse could be associated with injuries due to accidents, illnesses, or natural disasters or to other actions not involved in child maltreatment. *However, a strong suspicion of child maltreatment should be entertained when there are unusual or suspicious patterns of physical abuse or neglect. Similarly, physical injuries that cannot be associated with accidents, illnesses, or natural disasters, with actions taken by the child, or with signs of neglect that are not ordinarily seen in children should raise strong suspicions of child maltreatment.*

Children who have been physically abused may show behavioral problems, emotional disturbance, and inappropriate social responses (see Table 21-1). It is important to recognize that *the behavioral indicators listed in Table 21-1 are not unique to child physical abuse and neglect but also may be associated with other kinds of trauma-related situations (for example, divorce, economic stress, and relocations) or with other forms of psychological disturbance.*

Sometimes child physical abuse or neglect results in the death of the child. The Department of Justice (Bureau of Justice Statistics, 1994) cites several methods that caregivers have used to murder their children, including beating the child (such as by punching the child with fists, kicking the child, throwing the child, pushing the child, slapping the child, and hitting the child with belts, hammers, or wooden brushes), shaking the baby violently, burning the child, disposing of the newborn in a toilet or trash can, drowning the child in a bathtub, using a firearm to kill the child, suffocating or strangling the child, neglecting the child (for example, by dehydration, starvation, or failure to use an infant heart monitor), stabbing the child, poisoning the child with carbon monoxide, giving the child lethal doses of drugs, running over the child with a car, using boiling water on the child, or putting the child in a freezer. In most cases, before these children die, they suffer abuse by the assailant.

Sometimes child physical abuse, child neglect, child sexual abuse, or child emotional abuse (or a combination of forms of maltreatment) may lead to the child's killing the parent (Heide, 1995). For *parricide* (killing of a parent) to occur, the maltreatment usually must take place over a long period and the child must be fairly old.

How Sexual Abuse May Affect Children

This part of the chapter first looks at how children may accommodate to sexual abuse. Then it looks at how child sexual abuse may lead to (a) physical injuries, (b) behavioral problems, emotional disturbance, and inappropriate social

Table 21-1
Physical and Behavioral Indicators of Child Physical Abuse and Neglect

Physical Indicators

1. Skin injuries in various stages of healing
2. Bruises (rupture of small blood vessels and discoloration without break in the skin)
3. Broken bones
4. Fracture associated with hematomas (swelling caused by a collection of blood in the space between the muscle and skin or between the brain and skull)
5. Multiple fractures in various stages of healing
6. Dislocations
7. Burns with unusual patterns
8. Scalded feet and buttocks
9. Cigarette burns
10. Abrasions (scrape or scratch)
11. Lacerations (cuts or jagged openings in the skin)
12. Discolored skin
13. Welts
14. Scars (especially with an unusual shape or location)
15. Whiplash injuries (especially associated with violent shaking)
16. Head injuries (including skull fractures [break in the bone of the skull], depressed fractures [bone fragments pressed into the skull cavity], concussions [a jarring injury to the brain that

results in possible loss of consciousness], and hematomas [internal swelling])
17. Internal injuries (including unexplained rupture of the stomach, bowel, liver, or other organs caused by being hit or kicked)
18. Human bites
19. Malnutrition
20. Unkempt hair
21. Pallor
22. Rashes
23. Cradle cap
24. Headaches
25. Stomachaches
26. Vomiting
27. Injuries to the eyes (including retinal hemorrhaging, black eyes, detached retinas, petechia in eyes [small spots of blood from broken capillaries], cataracts [opacity of the lens or capsule of the eye, causing impairment of vision or blindness], sudden loss of visual acuity, pupils fixed or dilated or unresponsive to light, and eyes not tracking or following motion)
28. Injuries to the ears (including sudden hearing loss, cauliflower ear, bruising to ear, petechia in ear, and blood in ear canal)

29. Injuries to nose (including deviated septum [the thin partition or membrane that divides the two cavities of the nose], fresh or clotted blood in nostrils, and bridge of nose bent or swollen)
30. Injuries to mouth (including chipped, missing, or loose teeth caused by blow to mouth; laceration of lips or tongue; and bleeding of mouth)
31. Intentional poisoning
32. Oral trauma (associated with forced feeding)
33. Unexplained injuries
34. Child appears hungry or asks for food
35. Child is unwashed
36. Child is unattended
37. Child is cared for by sibling
38. Child is left alone for long periods of time
39. Child is improperly dressed for the weather
40. Failure to thrive
41. Exposure to dangerous items or substances (such as guns, poison, defective wiring, and so forth)
42. Failure to seek medical treatment
43. Child is kept out of school
44. Exposure to domestic violence

Behavioral Indicators

1. Anxiety
2. Concentration difficulties
3. Memory difficulties
4. Drop in school performance
5. Irritability or crankiness
6. Depression
7. Sense of unhappiness
8. Anger
9. Loss of trust
10. Fear of separation
11. Intense dislike of being left somewhere or with someone
12. Flashback of the traumatic experience itself
13. Unprovoked crying
14. Changes in appetite or other problems in eating
15. Fear of the dark
16. Regression to more immature behavior (for example, immature play, bedwetting, thumb sucking, excessive

crying, renewed need for "security blanket")
17. Fear of parents
18. Fear of going home
19. Wariness of any physical contact with parents
20. Fear of people in general
21. Protective tendencies toward younger siblings
22. Role reversal in the family
23. Fear of being left with someone
24. Newly manifested clinging behavior
25. Newly manifested changes in behavior
26. Wariness of any physical contact with adults in general
27. Constant alertness for signs of danger
28. Fear of a place
29. Failure to look to parents or guardians for reassurance
30. Anxiety or fear of strangers

31. Aggressive or disruptive behavior
32. Withdrawal
33. Flat affect
34. Reduced responsiveness
35. Detachment
36. Running away
37. Fire setting
38. Cruelty to animals
39. Frequent absences/truancy from school
40. Early arrival at school; remaining after classes rather than going home
41. Delinquent behavior
42. Poor interpersonal relations
43. Altered body image
44. Guilt feelings
45. Feelings of inferiority or poor self-esteem
46. Overly compliant or passive behaviors
47. Extremely dependent behavior
48. Indiscriminately friendly behavior

(Continued)

Table 21-1 (*Continued*)

49. Sense of loss	55. Disturbed sleep patterns	58. Psychosomatic symptoms
50. Suspiciousness	(for example, nightmares,	(for example, headaches,
51. Self-blame	recurrent nightmares,	stomachaches, rashes, stuttering)
52. Secretive behavior	night terrors, sleepwalking,	59. Dissociation experiences
53. Feelings of helplessness	inability to sleep	60. Suicide attempt
54. Excessive self-control	alone)	61. Anorexia/bulimia
(for example, child never cries	56. Hyperactivity	62. Alcohol abuse
or exhibits curiosity)	57. Fatigue	63. Drug abuse

Source: Adapted from American Prosecutors Research Institute (1993), Bentovim and Boston (1988), Besharov (1990), Duquette (1990), Garbarino et al. (1987), and Kendall-Tackett, Williams, and Finkelhor (1993).

responses, and (c) vulnerability to sexually transmitted diseases, including sexually transmitted HIV infection. Finally, the results of empirical studies on the impact of sexual abuse on children are considered.

Children's accommodation to the sexual abuse.
Children involved in sexual abuse may experience conflicting sensations (Furniss, 1991). For some, the sexual abuse may be frightening and painful, but, for others, it may be sexually arousing. When it is sexually arousing, children may describe the sexual acts as "good touches" or as acts that make them "feel good" or "special." This arousal, in turn, may contribute to their loyal behavior to the abuser and to sexual acting-out behavior.

When the sexual abuse is frightening, children may begin to adapt to what is a difficult situation (Furniss, 1991; Summit, 1983). The adaptation may involve coping mechanisms that severely distort their perceptions and emotions. Children may even develop altered states of consciousness to shut off the pain (see dissociative reactions in Chapter 11). They may try to look at the sexual abuse from a distance, pretend to sleep, or during intercourse pretend that the lower part of their body does not exist.

When children accommodate to sexual abuse, they may develop feelings of guilt and question their self-worth. The abuser who is a caregiver not only threatens the child's life and integrity but also, in a perverted way, provides the external care needed for the child's survival and may even be a figure of positive emotional attachment. "This element is crucial in understanding the possibly bizarre attachments and loyalties between victim and perpetrator.... Forms of loyalty and attachment can emerge which can be extremely difficult to understand and to accept" (Furniss, 1991, p. 30). To understand the sexually abused child, you will have to deal with the child's loyalty and attachment to the perpetrator and her or his feelings of guilt.

Physical injuries associated with child sexual abuse.   Children who have been sexually abused may have physical signs of abuse, some of which are shown in

Table 21-2. Most of the physical signs of child sexual abuse are associated with the genital region or with other areas of the body that may be involved in sexual activity, such as the mouth and buttocks. The general physical indicators of child physical abuse and neglect, shown in Table 21-1, also may be present in some cases of child sexual abuse that involve physical abuse as well. However, the majority of children who have been sexually abused show no physical or medical evidence of abuse—absence of findings is the rule rather than the exception.

Behavioral problems, emotional disturbance, and inappropriate social responses.   Children who have been sexually abused, like those who have been physically abused, may show behavioral problems, emotional disturbance, and inappropriate social responses (see Table 21-2). Note that many of the behavioral indicators listed in Table 21-2 are the same as those listed in Table 21-1 for child physical abuse and neglect. Some reflect attempts by children to escape the sexual abuse (for example, running away from home) or to draw attention to the sexual abuse that they are experiencing (for example, depressive symptoms and suicide attempts). Again, it is important to note that *the behavioral indicators listed in Table 21-2 are not unique to child sexual abuse but also may be associated with other kinds of trauma-related situations (for example, divorce, economic stress, and relocations) or with other forms of psychological disturbance.*

Child sexual abuse can have a traumatic impact on children in several different ways.

1. *Sexually abused children may prematurely and inappropriately learn about sex* (Finkelhor, 1988). Such children may come to regard sex as a tool for manipulating people because of the reward they receive for collaborating with adults in sexual acts. They also may acquire distorted ideas of sexual morality and appropriate sexual conduct. Sexually abused children may learn a great deal of inappropriate behavior because of the powerful reinforcement that sexual stimulation provides. Older children may become sexually

Table 21-2
Physical and Behavioral Indicators of Child Sexual Abuse

Physical Indicators

1. Torn or stained clothing
2. Blood or hair of perpetrator on child's body or clothing
3. Semen in oral or anal areas
4. Semen in vaginal area (in females)
5. Vaginal bleeding (in females)
6. Torn or missing hymen (in females)
7. Rectal bleeding
8. Pain with urination or bowel movements
9. Itching
10. Swollen genitals
11. Injury to lips
12. Vaginal discharge (in females)
13. Vaginal infections (in females)
14. Penile swelling (in males)
15. Penile discharge (in males)
16. Rectal infections, irritation, or trauma
17. Foreign bodies in genital or rectal areas
18. Urinary tract infections
19. Unexplained genital injuries
20. Pregnancy (in females)
21. Sexually transmitted diseases or infections (such as gonorrhea, syphilis, chlamydia trachomatis, HIV infection, herpes, trichomonas vaginitis, venereal warts, nonspecific vaginitis, and pubic lice)
22. Bruises and hickeys in the face or neck areas or around the genitals, buttocks, or inner thighs

Behavioral Indicators

1. Anxiety
2. Concentration difficulties
3. Memory difficulties
4. Drop in school performance
5. Irritability or crankiness
6. Depression
7. Sense of unhappiness
8. Anger
9. Loss of trust
10. Fear of separation
11. Intense dislike of being left somewhere or with someone
12. Flashback of the traumatic experience itself
13. Unprovoked crying
14. Changes in appetite or other problems in eating
15. Fear of the dark
16. Regression to more immature behavior (for example, immature play, bedwetting, thumb sucking, excessive crying, renewed need for "security blanket")
17. Fear of parents
18. Fear of going home
19. Wariness of any physical contact with parents
20. Fear of people in general
21. Protective tendencies toward younger siblings
22. Role reversal in the family
23. Fear of being left with someone
24. Newly manifested clinging behavior
25. Newly manifested changes in behavior
26. Wariness of any physical contact with adults in general
27. Constant alertness for signs of danger
28. Fear of a place
29. Failure to look to parents or guardians for reassurance
30. Anxiety or fear of strangers
31. Aggressive or disruptive behavior
32. Withdrawal
33. Flat affect
34. Reduced responsiveness
35. Detachment
36. Running away
37. Fire setting
38. Cruelty to animals
39. Frequent absences/truancy from school
40. Early arrival at school; remaining after classes rather than going home
41. Delinquent behavior
42. Poor interpersonal relations
43. Altered body image
44. Guilt feelings
45. Feelings of inferiority or poor self-esteem
46. Overly compliant or passive behaviors
47. Extremely dependent behavior
48. Indiscriminately friendly behavior
49. Sense of loss
50. Suspiciousness
51. Self-blame
52. Secretive behavior
53. Feelings of helplessness
54. Excessive self-control (for example, child never cries or exhibits curiosity)
55. Disturbed sleep patterns (for example, nightmares, recurrent nightmares, night terrors, sleep walking, inability to sleep alone)
56. Hyperactivity
57. Fatigue
58. Psychosomatic symptoms (for example, headaches, stomachaches, rashes, stuttering)
59. Dissociation experiences
60. Suicide attempt
61. Anorexia/bulimia
62. Alcohol abuse
63. Drug abuse
64. Shame
65. Sexualized play with dolls
66. Compulsive talk about sexual matters
67. Play and fantasy with sexual content
68. Putting objects into the anus or vagina
69. Frequent and overt self-stimulation
70. Seductive behavior
71. Sexual overtures toward other children and adults
72. French kissing
73. Age-inappropriate sexual knowledge
74. Promiscuity
75. Fear of bathrooms and showers
76. Refusal to undress in physical education classes at school
77. Compulsion about cleanliness—wanting to wash or feeling dirty all the time

Source: Adapted from American Prosecutors Research Institute (1993), Bentovim and Boston (1988), Besharov (1990), Duquette (1990), Garbarino et al. (1987), and Kendall-Tackett, Williams, and Finkelhor (1993).

permissive and, in some cases, identify with the aggressor. In the latter case, they may, in turn, abuse young children just as they have been abused: "*Hence the cycle is completed and the victim becomes the offender, creating another victim*" (Bentovim & Boston, 1988, p. 29, italics added). If they victimize other children, their sexual feelings may be inhibited. Later sexual adjustment can be impeded if sex becomes associated with memories of unpleasant incidents. Sexually abused children, when they become young adults, may develop sexual problems, avoid relationships, be anxious and fearful around children, engage in prostitution, commit delinquent acts, experience marital failure due to sexual difficulties, have parenting problems, and have poor self-esteem (Bentovim & Boston, 1988).

2. *Sexually abused children may later discover that society views some acts they performed in the context of a trusting relationship as reprehensible and that the adult they trusted was selfishly motivated* (Finkelhor, 1988). If they make this discovery, children may become dependent and clinging or they may develop a distrust of people and avoid intimacy. Confusion and uncertainty about their relationship with their abuser also may result.

3. *Sexually abused children may experience anxiety because of the furtive quality of the activity and the fear of being blamed if discovered* (Finkelhor, 1988). The anxiety, if experienced, may lead such children to withdraw from social relationships or to engage in self-destructive behavior, such as drug or alcohol abuse, delinquency, and prostitution.

4. *Sexually abused children may develop a negative self-image* (Ochberg, 1988). Sexually abused children may experience shame, embarrassment, and humiliation; feel that they are dirty or "tainted goods"; or believe that they are to blame, despite evidence to the contrary.

5. *Sexually abused children may feel powerless when someone coerces them by force, threat, or deceit to submit to sexual acts* (Finkelhor, 1988). Feelings of powerlessness may develop into anxiety, phobias, sleep disorders, depression, and learning problems in school. Some children may run away, begin to molest other children sexually, or develop sexual aversions later in life.

Children's comments on being sexually abused. In one study, when asked about their experiences of being sexually abused, children reported confusion, mixed feelings, contradictions, and inconsistencies; fear; lingering concerns about the abuse; anger with the law; and relief or ambivalence about having told someone. They also gave advice to others who have been or are being sexually abused. Here are some examples of what they said (Roberts & Taylor, 1993, pp. 26–33).

1. *Confusion, mixed feelings, contradictions, and inconsistencies.* Sexually abused children may be ambivalent about the different parts of the sexual abuse experience, toward the abuser, and toward themselves. Their reactions

express the complex and sensitive nature of child sexual abuse.

IR: How do you feel about the abuse?
IE: I'm angry that I only sat there and froze and didn't do anything to stop it. I feel stupid—that I should have done something. (14-year-old female)

IR: How do you feel about the person who abused you?
IE: He's a little bit nice. He gave me juice. Then he was bad to me. (7-year-old female)
IE: It's difficult to say I miss him. People don't want to hear that. (12-year-old female)
IE: I'm sad about not seeing him. I used to play with him. I want Dad to live with me again. (6-year-old female)

IR: Does the sexual abuse still worry you?
IE: Just at times, when I'm worried—cracking up—it pours into my head—out of control. (16-year-old female)

IR: Do you still think about the abuse?
IE: Yes, I still think about it a lot—when it's in the press or on TV, it flashes back—makes me scared. It's like a black pitch. It's a thing you can't forget. (15-year-old female)

2. *Fear.* Sexually abused children may experience fear and uncertainty connected with the abuse.

IR: What had been the worst part of what happened to you?
IE: He said he would deny it. I was very frightened in case my Mum would batter me for doing it. They gave me money and sweets not to tell. I didn't want it. They made me. (8-year-old female)
IE: Sometimes it comes back—what happened and the fear of it happening again. (12-year-old female)
IE: It's scary—disgusting what he did—what made him do it? I don't know. (15-year-old female)
IE: I can't really describe it...just horrible inside...I did scream once...he said be quiet...I just said to myself, let him do it and then he will go...I dreaded going to bed. (13-year-old female)
IE: I was too scared to tell because X was living with us and he did it lots of times. (8-year-old female)
IE: I was frightened and wanted to cry but I couldn't.... I'm frightened of men. I won't sleep with my light off...he threatened to kill me...he put his hand over my mouth when I tried to scream. (17-year-old female)
IE: I was worried, scared. I had the courage to run, but he'd locked the door. I feel a bit better that he can't come in the house at night. The door's locked. My nightmares are getting better. (11-year-old female)

3. *Feelings that don't go away.* Sexually abused children may feel, for example, anxious and concerned about interpersonal relations and puzzled about their relationship with the nonoffending parent.

IR: What concerns do you have about what happened to you?

IE: I see him from time to time as he lives locally. I saw him the other day. I walked faster. I was scared to walk past him. I walk the other way usually. Will there be a time when I can just walk past him? It should be him who looks down, but he's confident because he's got off with it. (14-year-old female)

IE: I would have grown up different. It did change my life—made me wake up to the violence outside. (15-year-old female)

IE: The whole thing was a nightmare. Police report, investigation and medical just as bad. They didn't consult me about whether I wanted to report it or would have a medical…just turned up. (15-year-old female)

IE: It's causing problems in relationships. Girls give me up when they find out…I think girls are wary of me. Boys tell them about me and they think "danger" and walk. (16-year-old male)

IE: She [my mother] sees him [now] so she must believe him more…it makes me feel funny inside. I can't understand why she says she loves him. It makes me shiver. (13-year-old female)

4. *Anger with the law.* Sexually abused children may be unhappy with the criminal justice system and how perpetrators are punished.

IR: How do you feel about the punishment the abuser received?

IE: [Instead of a fine] he should have been hung. (12-year-old female)

IE: I've seen him. I shall kill him. I felt like it. I feel he should have got jail. I feel angry, hurt, let down. (16-year-old female)

IE: It was not proven. The [prosecutors] told me they knew it was true, but that wasn't any consolation. I was so angry, I couldn't sleep. (15-year-old female)

5. *Satisfaction with having told or ambivalence about having told.* Sexually abused children may feel satisfied or have mixed feelings about having told someone about the abuse. Or they may experience a change in feelings over time about having told about the abuse.

IR: How do you feel about having told someone about the abuse?

IE: I'm glad I told—stopping it was the most important. (16-year-old male)

IE: I'm happy I told. If I hadn't said something, I would have taken my life. Before I told, I was into glue/dope—a cry for help—everything was wrong. Once my mum believed me, it was OK. (15-year-old female)

IE: I was scared at first to tell. I thought I might get shouted at. I feel a lot better having told. I've got it all out now. (12-year-old female)

IE: I would have preferred to tell my teacher in confidence. I did not want it to become public knowledge. I had no feelings of relief. I thought there would have been some. (15-year-old female)

IE: I wish I'd kept my mouth shut. I get on worse with my mum now. She started ignoring me. She was that mad I had to stay at my sister's. She thinks I encouraged him. Confused. Sometimes I wish I was dead. Everything's muddled. Nothing can get sorted out. (12-year-old female)

6. *Advice to other children who have been sexually abused.* Sexually abused children may advise other children who are sexually abused to tell someone about the abuse.

IR: What advice do you have for others who have been sexually abused or are being sexually abused?

IE: Talking about it helped. I regret keeping it to myself. (16-year-old female)

IE: Try to talk it through. Write it down if you can't say it. That's what I did. (13-year-old female)

IE: Tell someone about it straight away. I regret waiting so long before telling. It makes it worse. (14-year-old female)

IE: Tell the nearest person straight away. I know it's hard, but you just do it. Don't back out. I know you go through problems, but it will turn out—but if you don't tell, you go through hell. (15-year-old female)

Case illustrations of child sexual abuse. Let's now look at four cases that illustrate some effects of child sexual abuse. As you read these cases, think about the negative consequences—such as an angry distrust of people, avoidance of intimacy, a negative self-image, and a sense of powerlessness—for children who have been sexually abused.

The case of Sue shows the effects of child sexual abuse into young adulthood and beyond (Witchel, 1991).

CASE 21-2. SUE

Sue was a victim of incest by her stepfather, who began to fondle her when she was eight years old. By age eleven, the maltreatment included oral sex and vaginal penetration and occurred up to five times per week. The abuse continued until Sue left for college, although it was less frequent during her senior year because she often made attempts to be out of the house. Sue had not told anyone about the abuse before entering college, since her stepfather had threatened to kill her and her mother if she did.

Sue had buried herself in her schoolwork throughout high school, never dated, had few close friends, and generally felt depressed and defeated. She had made numerous attempts at suicide during high school, but only one friend knew about them. Sue thought college was her one chance to escape, and she chose a campus about one hour from her home. Sue lived alone in an off-campus residence. One late evening, her stepfather came to visit. He had been drinking, as was often the case. He pressured Sue into having sex with him, leaving her devastated because she had felt that she was finally safe from him. After he left, she felt angry, depressed, and fearful that the abuse was beginning all over again.

Sue's stepfather continued to visit her about once a month, and the pattern of abuse continued. His threats kept her from disclosing the abuse, but finally, out of desperation, she told a faculty member about it. Sue made another suicide attempt, which resulted in an overnight hospital stay. A social worker spoke with her, and she agreed to meet with a counseling center psychologist who specialized in treatment of sexual abuse. Exposing the history of the abuse was painful but brought relief. The most important but most difficult step was meeting with the police and pressing charges against her stepfather. Another important step was revealing the long-term abuse to her mother and her family and managing the aftermath that often comes with such disclosure. As Sue began treatment, stopping her stepfather's behavior was a critical first step in her recovery. (pp. 70–71)

The next case is a first-person account of how child sexual abuse had a lasting effect on a daughter's relationship with her mother (Landers, 1991).

CASE 21-3. ANONYMOUS

Dear Ann Landers: When my mother was 18, she became pregnant and married my father. They stayed together four years and then divorced. Two years later, when I was 6, Mom met a man she liked and he moved in with us. I thought he was wonderful until he began to abuse me sexually. I knew what he was doing was wrong because he gave me candy and little gifts for keeping "our special secret."

The molesting continued for eight years. When I was 14, I felt secure enough to tell my mother. When she accused me of lying I insisted she confront him in my presence. Even though he admitted everything, she stayed with him. From then on Mom was very cold to me, as if I were the one who caused the problem. I moved out the day I turned 16.

I am 20 now and find it difficult to be around my mother. She abandoned me to save her marriage. Her husband will not allow my name to be spoken in their home. I cannot telephone her for fear that awful man will answer. He treats her like dirt, but she refuses to leave him.

Ann, isn't it wrong for my mother to stay married to this animal after what he did to me? (p. E6. Permission granted by Ann Landers and Creators Syndicate.)

The next case shows the devastating consequences that child sexual abuse can have later in life. As an adult female, Priscilla recounts her experience of sexual abuse when she was a child. As a young adult, she began to use alcohol and drugs to help her deal with her feelings and become more social (Miller, Downs, & Testa, 1990).

CASE 21-4. PRISCILLA

As a child, Priscilla was sexually abused by a 17-year-old male who was her babysitter's brother. He had sexual intercourse with her on several occasions, beginning when she was 9 years old. He used her fear of being punished by her parents as a way of ensuring her silence. Priscilla describes her feelings:

I don't know why I kept saying yeah and agreeing to it, but I was scared because he kept saying he was going to tell my mother and she was going to whoop me so I would say ok… not thinking that if he would have told my mother he would have been in trouble too. I wasn't thinking, the only thing I was thinking about was he was going to tell my mother and I was gonna get it.… Afterwards I was so ashamed, nervous, running into things. When his sister came in, I fell over the

table and she asked me what was wrong with me and I told her nothing. I was just real nervous and when I saw my mother my heart just went "boom" like somebody was inside my heart. I couldn't breathe because I knew I was in the wrong. I thought, she is gonna kill me if she found out, and I never told her. To this day, she still don't know.

The initial trauma was followed by a change in her behavior that was subsequently noticed by others. However, she was still unable to overcome her fears about speaking about her victimization. Priscilla continues:

I would get real quiet, and [my mother] would ask me why I was so quiet. I got quiet in school.… I did start smoking when I was 10 because my nerves were so bad. The doctor put me on Valium when I was 14.… I used to have headaches, why I don't know. I would go to the doctor and they never could find anything. I used to just sit there crying and holding my head. … I got quiet, and my nerves were shot.

These feelings were never resolved in her childhood, and she continued to have recurring bad feelings about these experiences in her adult years.

It bothers me a lot now. I get headaches, and I have dreams about it. Like somebody is inside my head beating me with a hammer or something, and I sweat so much I wake up. It is just like I am back to being 9 years old, and I will just wake up.… Sometimes they seem so real. I will get up in the middle of the night, and it seems like I still see it. (pp. 20–21, with changes in notation)

In the following case, a British adult male recalls how he was sexually and emotionally abused as a young child and adolescent and how the abuse affected his adjustment as an adult (Elliott, 1993).

CASE 21-5. ROBERT

I came back home to my mother when I was about 4 years old, having been evacuated to my grandmother's because of the war. My mother used to trap me in her bedroom and get me to do things to her. When I was 14, my mother used to come into my bed in the early hours of the morning, arouse me sexually, and sexual intercourse would take place.

I find it difficult to think about the sexual abuse. I have not evaluated how much damage it did. I do know a lot of damage was done by the emotional abuse—that really screwed me up. I recently went to a counselor recommended by my general practitioner, and we worked out that the emotional abuse was used to rule me and keep me insecure so that I wouldn't tell about the sexual abuse—it worked! Until now.

I am now 52, and I am just beginning to understand myself. I feel that from now on my mistakes are my own, but what a hard and rocky road to get here. I have been to psychiatrists on and off for 35 years. I have been on medication: antidepressants, sleeping pills, "nerve" pills for anxiety of all kinds. Apart from my own unhappiness, I have caused unhappiness to a lot of other people. The cost to society of all those pills and medical treatment, broken marriages, and so on must be enormous.

I think that building a personality is like building a wall. You start off as a child building your wall and if it is not strong and straight it just keeps falling down. I guess as a child when you don't know what normality is, it is impossible to know how to deal with life. To add to my confusion about normality, I was also sexually abused by my mother's boyfriends.

I have been a parent myself, and, as a parent, you seem to develop a sixth sense as to what is going on with your kids, even if they are in the next room. This suggests to me that mothers whose boyfriends go into the child's bedroom "just to go say goodnight to little Jimmy" know or suspect that something else is going on and turn a blind eye. Isn't that also abuse by mothers, even though they are not physically there?

I have never felt better in my life than I do now, but all this has left me with a deep, deep sadness. It isn't just my life that was screwed up. I have been married twice and have generally caused a lot of strife and unhappiness all along the way. If you don't know how to deal with yourself, you don't stand a chance in dealing with other people. I have been very lucky. I am just beginning to form a sound base for my personality. (adapted from pp. 176–177)

Long-term sequelae of child sexual abuse. Studies of adult survivors of childhood sexual abuse indicate that they have adjustment difficulties that include depressive symptoms, anxiety, poor social adjustment, parenting difficulties, substance abuse, suicidal ideation and suicide attempts, revictimization, and problems with sexuality, including fear of sex, low interest in sex, less sexual pleasure, several sexual partners, more compulsive sexual behavior, and more homosexual experiences (Wolfe & Birt, 1995). The degree of their adjustment difficulties may depend on the duration of the abuse, the frequency of the abuse, their relationship with the perpetrator, the severity of the abuse, the degree of force used, the number of perpetrators, the survivors' feelings during the abuse, and the survivor's level of adjustment before the abuse. Also, survivors may make frequent visits to medical providers for complaints of undetermined origin, such as stomachaches, pelvic pain, headaches, and urinary problems (L. Gudas, personal communication, June 1996). Many survivors end up undergoing numerous medical procedures and surgeries to search for the cause of their symptoms.

Adult women's comments on being sexually abused as children. When adult women who were sexually abused as children were asked to comment on the most traumatic aspects of the abuse, they spoke about abandonment, powerlessness, threats of violence, physical injury, loss of childhood, devalued sexuality, betrayal, guilt and shame, and loss of self (Draucker, 1993). The depth of their feelings is obvious in the following comments, which were obtained from interviews with 166 women, who ranged in age from 19 to 56 years. All the women were attending therapeutic groups for adult survivors of childhood sexual abuse. Approximately 60% of the group reported that their abuse lasted over 5 years, 62% reported that their abuse involved intercourse, and 55% reported that their abuse involved more than one offender; the average age of the victim when the abuse began was 5 years, 3 months (Draucker, 1993).

1. *Abandonment.* They were angry because they had not been protected, believed, or supported.

- My father walked in on my grandfather raping me and walked out of the room not saying anything.
- *More* devastating is looking back and knowing how many medical personnel did nothing to report the abuse and/or intervene. This goes for teachers too and others who are now mandated by the state to report. Unfortunately, I don't believe the system works in 1992 any better than it did in 1955.
- No one would/could help, not even God.
- My family disowned me when I brought my father out in the open.

2. *Powerlessness.* They were angry because of their inability to take any action to stop the abuse. As a result, they experienced a great sense of helplessness and felt profoundly vulnerable and trapped.

- I experienced terror and absolute powerlessness… when I was raped around age four.
- I didn't want it to happen but I was powerless to stop it.
- I guess for me it was not knowing when it would happen next.
- There was no place to feel safe. Most of the events occurred in my bed, my "safe" resting place.
- This lack of control over my own body has caused the fears I have of most always wanting to be in control of myself, a lack of spontaneity and joy.

3. *Threats of violence.* They were angry because there were threats of physical harm to themselves or others, such as being beaten, burned, smothered, cut, locked in closets, and denied food.

- I was pushed around and threatened with a knife and told, "I will blow your head off if you tell. I don't care if it's 10 years from now, you better not tell."
- I know for a fact on a lot of my sexual assaults my cousin was stoned and drunk and would tell me if I didn't do what he wanted me to he would hurt my grandmother and he used that threat all the time and it still gets to me a lot even now that she has passed on.

4. *Physical injury.* They were angry because their bodies were injured.

- My insides were first ripped open at age three. I cannot have children due to internal damage from the abuse.
- My first time having sex was rape at age 16. To feel a rough force penetrating into me was terrifying and painful.

5. *Loss of childhood.* They were angry about loss of memory of childhood or loss of innocence.

- The most traumatic aspect of the abuse experience was the fact that I lost my entire childhood. Because I repressed all memory of the abuse, I also lost all pleasant memories of my childhood as well. I feel like I don't have a framework for who I am or where I came from.
- I never felt like a lady. I never felt I was precious. I was never a child nor a lovely young woman.

6. *Devalued sexuality.* They were angry about their exposure to sexual activity, which, in turn, led them to devalue sexuality.

- I learned that sex equals love—that in order to be loved, you had to provide sex.
- I am unable to separate money from sex.
- The abuse led to my becoming a prostitute.

7. *Betrayal.* They were angry about the betrayal of their trust in someone whom they depended on, loved, or admired.

- My pain was the fact that my father, whom I worshipped, could have done this to me.
- The fact that my father was gentle with the abuse and "coaxed" me in the middle of the night. As a result, I felt like his "lover." At four years old—the abuse being the only attention I got from him. As a result, it's nearly *impossible* to be *angry* with him (yet he was my "monster in the night").
- I believe the most traumatic aspect is "trust." I don't have any left for anyone for the rest of my life. I find I cannot trust my husband with my children. Being afraid and looking for mistrust in anything they do or he does. Stripped of my trust, dignity, hope for this relationship....

8. *Guilt and shame.* They were angry about feeling responsible for the abuse at the time it was occurring and about feeling shame associated with specific incidents of humiliation and degradation.

- I must be an awful person.
- Because I was vulnerable I was somehow despicable.
- I was defective, and my only value was sexual.
- I should have stopped it.
- I should have not cooperated with the offender.
- My grandfather bragged to others about our sexual activities.
- The shame I felt when I was 11 years old and told a girl in school that my dad had showed me about sex and the look she got on her face.

9. *Loss of self.* They were angry because the abuse threatened their very being, the core of their identity.

- The most traumatic aspect of the abuse was the subjugation of my personhood, and my femaleness.
- I lost my own person and became an object.
- I felt subhuman and not worthy of life.
- I got lost.
- I was nonexistent.
- My pain stemmed from the rape of my soul.

Other research suggests that women who were sexually abused as children are more likely later in life to have social, interpersonal, and sexual difficulties, as well as depressive symptoms (Hall, Sachs, Rayens, & Lutenbacher, 1993; Mullen, Martin, Anderson, Romans, & Herbison, 1994). The sexual abuse itself did not appear to be solely responsible for their mental health problems; rather, it was the disruption of the development of their capacities for trust, intimacy, sexuality, and self-esteem while they were growing up.

Sexually transmitted diseases and child sexual abuse. Children who have been sexually abused are at risk for getting a sexually transmitted disease, such as syphilis, gonorrhea, chlamydia, genital or anorectal herpes and warts, or the human immunodeficiency virus (HIV). The health care provider who examines a child sexual abuse victim needs to determine whether the child has been exposed to a sexually transmitted disease and to begin appropriate treatments, if needed. Human service providers should work collaboratively with health care providers in this effort.

A sexually abused child is more at risk for getting a sexually transmitted disease when one or more of the following are present (Gellert, Berkowitz, & Durfee, 1993): The perpetrator has a sexually transmitted disease or is HIV seropositive, the perpetrator engages in high-risk behavior, and the sexual abuse occurred in a geographic area where the disease is prevalent. If a child who was not referred for sexual abuse to a health care provider is found to have a sexually transmitted disease and lacks risk factors, such as maternal (perinatal) transmission or a history of blood transfusions, the health care provider should consider referring the child for an assessment of possible sexual abuse.

Empirical studies on the impact of sexual abuse on children. A review of 45 studies of sexually abused children, who ranged in age from preschoolers to adolescents, indicates that there is no one symptom pattern characteristic of all children who have been sexually abused (Kendall-Tackett, Williams, & Finkelhor, 1993). Following are the symptoms that occurred most frequently among sexually abused children:

- *fears and posttraumatic stress disorder reactions* (for example, fear of the dark, nightmares, somatic complaints, guilt feelings, and generalized symptoms of anxiety and stress)
- *behavioral problems* (for example, hyperactivity, regression/immaturity, illegal acts, and running away)
- *sexualized behaviors* (for example, sexualized play with dolls; compulsive talk, play, and fantasy with sexual content; putting objects into the anus or vagina; frequent and overt self-stimulation; seductive behavior; age-inappropriate sexual knowledge; and promiscuity)
- *poor self-esteem*

Equally important is the finding that no clinically observed symptoms were present in approximately one-third of the sexually abused children. Children had more symptoms when the following factors were involved:

- sexual acts that included oral, anal, or vaginal penetration
- high frequency of sexual contact
- long duration of the sexual abuse

- use of force
- a close relationship between the child and the perpetrator
- lack of maternal support at the time of the disclosure
- a negative outlook or coping style on the part of the child

However, the child's age at onset of the sexual abuse, the number of perpetrators, and the time that elapsed between the end of the abuse and the assessment were not clearly related to the presence of symptoms. About two-thirds of the sexually abused children showed recovery 12 to 18 months after the sexual abuse stopped.

Kendall-Tackett et al. (1993) concluded that there is no "specific syndrome in children who have been sexually abused and no single traumatizing process" (p. 164). Overall, the results indicate that sexual abuse produces varied effects in children. These findings are especially important for forensic evaluations (Kendall-Tackett et al., 1993):

The range of symptoms, the lack of a single predominant symptom pattern, and the absence of symptoms in so many victims clearly suggest that diagnosis is complex. Because the effects of abuse can manifest themselves in too many ways, symptoms cannot be easily used, without other evidence, to confirm the presence of sexual abuse. Yet the absence of symptoms certainly cannot be used to rule out sexual abuse. There are too many sexually abused children who are apparently asymptomatic. (p. 175)

However, the two symptoms that appear to distinguish sexually abused children from children in other clinical groups are (a) sexualized behavior and (b) symptoms of posttraumatic stress disorder.

Posttraumatic stress disorder symptoms and child sexual abuse.

Many of the behavioral symptoms associated with child maltreatment are similar to those associated with a traumatic stress disorder. The symptoms can appear while the abuse is occurring or in later years, long after the abuse has stopped. Traumatic stress disorder may be acute, chronic, or delayed. When it is delayed, it is called *posttraumatic stress disorder* (PTSD; see Chapter 11). Symptoms of posttraumatic stress disorder include the following (*DSM-IV*, American Psychiatric Association, 1994): recurrent distressing recollections and dreams of the event, flashbacks of the traumatic experience itself, diminished interests, feelings of detachment from others, restricted range of affect, sense of a foreshortened future, difficulty falling or staying asleep, irritability or outbursts of anger, and difficulty concentrating.

Finkelhor (1990) cautioned that the PTSD model is not necessarily the most appropriate model to account for the symptoms of child sexual abuse for the following reasons. First, although victims of child sexual abuse do show PTSD symptoms, they show other types of symptoms as well. These symptoms include increased sexualization of behavior and distorted cognitions about sex, family, and their self-worth. Second, some victims do not show PTSD symptoms but do show other types of adjustment problems, such as depression and sexual problems. Finally, the classic PTSD theory states that the symptoms arise from an event that overwhelms the individual and results "in helplessness in the face of intolerable danger, anxiety and instinctual arousal" (p. 328). In fact,

much sexual abuse does not occur under conditions of danger, threat, and violence. Many abusers, misusing their authority or manipulating moral standards, act with the child's trust. Sometimes the fact of having been abused is recognized only in retrospect as children learn more about appropriate conduct. The trauma of sexual abuse can result from the meaning of the act ("I am being exploited") as much as from the physical danger.

Even more important, sexual abuse is less of an "event" than a situation, relationship, or process. It often continues for a period of time. The trauma may derive from the distorted socialization in the relationship or in the situation. (pp. 328–329)

Finkelhor's (1990) cautions are excellent. Although you should be aware that the maltreated child may have symptoms of PTSD, don't expect to find these symptoms in each case.

How Emotional Abuse May Affect Children

In Chapter 20, you read that emotional abuse is almost always present when there are other forms of child maltreatment. Emotional abuse may lead to the following problems in children (Hart, Brassard, & Karlson, 1996):

- *problems in learning* (including academic problems and lower cognitive and educational performance)
- *problems in relationships* (including aggressive behavior, social problems, and problems with peers)
- *unusual behaviors and feelings* (including attachment disorders in infancy [not seeking comfort when distressed or not benefiting from parent's presence when distressed], attacking peers in preschool, disruptive behavior in the classroom during elementary-school years, antisocial behavior in adolescence, and behavior problems at all ages)
- *unhappiness or depression* (including low self-esteem or negative self-concept and emotional instability)
- *fears and physical symptoms* (including failure to thrive in infants and poor appetite, encopresis [involuntary passage of feces], enuresis, and somatic symptoms in preschool and later years)

Erickson and Egeland (1996) pointed out the following about emotional neglect in infancy:

It is ironic that the impact of emotional neglect is most profound when it is least likely to be detected—when the child is too young to speak out to others. (It is not surprising that early neglect has such a strong influence, because an infant's whole world revolves around his or her primary caregivers.) It is also ironic that, unless the child shows clear physical signs of neglect (e.g., failure to thrive), intervention is not likely to be mandated in cases of emotional neglect. (p. 15)

Developmental Considerations Related to Child Maltreatment

The following are some important developmental considerations related to child maltreatment (Finkelhor, 1995).

1. *Ability to protect oneself.* One factor in children's ability to protect themselves is their age. Older children, for example, are less likely to be hit by their parents than younger children because they "are better able to run away, to use verbal and intellectual skills to placate, and to fight back" (p. 180). Another factor is their developmental status. As you read in Chapter 20, young children and children with developmental disabilities may be more susceptible to maltreatment because of intellectual or physical limitations that can compromise their ability to protect themselves, including their ability to disclose the maltreatment. A third factor is a history of maltreatment. Maltreatment "itself seems to compromise children's capacities to resist subsequent victimization…, perhaps by undermining their confidence, assertiveness, and ability to assess trustworthiness" (p. 180).

2. *Dependency.* Children are vulnerable to maltreatment because they are dependent on adults for their care. For example, children do not have the economic ability to care for themselves and are therefore susceptible to physical neglect. Adolescents, in contrast, are in a better position to take care of themselves and thus are less susceptible to physical neglect. In addition, younger children are more likely to be maltreated by their caregivers, whereas older children are likely to be maltreated by either their caregivers or other people.

3. *Risk and gender.* Patterns of maltreatment are "less gender-specific for younger children and more so as children grow older" (p. 182). For example, girls are more at risk than boys for sexual abuse in adolescence, whereas, in the younger years, "there is less difference between the sexes in the rates and types of victimization" (p. 182).

The impact of maltreatment on children may differ as a result of the following factors (Finkelhor, 1995):

1. *Developmentally specific effects.* The impact of the maltreatment may depend on the developmental tasks or developmentally critical periods children are facing at the time of maltreatment. Children who are maltreated in infancy by their caregivers may develop insecure attachments to their caregivers. Their insecurity may carry over to subsequent phases of development and to other relationships. Children maltreated during the preschool years may develop a chronic pattern of dissociation as a means of coping. Children maltreated at any age may show disruptions in endocrine functioning and in neurological processes. For example, sexual abuse may hasten the onset of puberty.

2. *Cognitive developmental effects.* The impact of the maltreatment may depend on the children's specific cognitive abilities that affect their appraisal of the maltreatment. For example, young children may not recognize that they are being maltreated because their conceptual abilities are unde-veloped. In adolescence, conceptual abilities are more fully developed; thus adolescents who have been sexually abused may have diminished self-esteem because they are concerned about their sexual desirability or reputation or because they fear losing status with their peers. Recognizing that one is being maltreated may require "knowledge of social norms, conceptions of personal rights and responsibilities, and the ability to make social comparisons" (pp. 187–188).

3. *Developmentally specific symptoms.* The impact of the maltreatment may depend on the forms of symptom expression available to children at their developmental stage. For example, how children describe their reactions to the maltreatment depends on the vocabulary available to them. And symptoms such as depression, self-injurious behavior, running away, and substance abuse are more frequently found among adolescents who have been maltreated than among younger children who have been maltreated. However, even infants and toddlers may show depression.

How Child Maltreatment May Affect the Family

Continuum of family support. Families vary in the support they give to the maltreated child (Burgess, Groth, Holmstrom, & Sgroi, 1978).

- A *supportive family* is loyal to the child victim, shows positive regard and concern, and does not blame the child for the maltreatment.
- An *intermittently supportive family* is ambivalent about the child, the circumstances surrounding the maltreatment, and the child's role in the maltreatment (especially in cases of rape).
- A *nonsupportive family* may feel overburdened with its own crises, have little energy to handle anything besides daily needs, and turn away from any additional crisis. The family may believe that the maltreatment was the child's fault (particularly in cases of rape) and, therefore, not support the child.

In those cases where parental support is intermittent or lacking, gently point out to the parents how much their child needs their support.

The following case describes a mother who did not provide support for her daughter. The mother's behavior may have been influenced by the comments of a police officer and the knowledge that her daughter had been raped before (Burgess et al., 1978).

CASE 21-6. PATRICIA

Patricia, a 16-year-old girl, was brought to a hospital after flagging down a police car and stating that she had been raped by a man who had offered to drive her home. The police called her mother from the hospital, told the mother what had happened, and then added, "I think your daughter is asking for it." Patricia then talked with her mother but did not have any hopes that she would come to the hospital to get her—it was 4 A.M. Patricia said to the counselor after the telephone call: "She doesn't believe me. She did the first time, but she doesn't believe this. I have no car and no money to take a taxi home.... I didn't think she would come down." (p. 79, with changes in notation)

Effects on family members. Earlier in the chapter, you read about how offending and nonoffending parents may react to the child's maltreatment. If one spouse was the abuser, the nonoffending spouse may or may not support the abuser. Spouses who do not support the abusers may threaten divorce or other actions. But if they remain in the relationship and do not carry out their threats, abusers may think that they have been given tacit approval to continue their actions. Spouses who support abusers also may abuse their children or their spouses.

Siblings may live in fear that at any moment they also may be the victim of a parent's abuse. But some siblings, especially the favored ones, may support the abusing parent and even partake in abusing their younger siblings. Thus, the effects of child maltreatment on family members are complex and likely represent the interaction of several variables related to the family dynamics.

A study of mothers whose children had been sexually abused provides some insight into how sexual abuse may affect mothers (Dempster, 1993). Mothers usually bear the burden of caring for their children who have been violated. They need to both pick up the pieces of their own lives and help their children, protecting them from further abuse.

Discovering your child has been sexually abused is devastating for women. They feel shattered, shocked, frightened and isolated. Whether the abuse is by a partner, family member or someone outside the family the women universally experience a struggle to come to terms with the reality. The emotional and behavioural impact which can be long lasting mirrors what is experienced by the victims themselves. (Dempster, 1993, p. 64)

In addition to shock, mothers of victims of child sexual abuse may experience stigmatization, powerlessness, betrayal, and traumatic sexualization. Here are some examples of their feelings and reactions (Dempster, 1993).

1. *Shock.* The discovery can be debilitating.

I was devastated, I was shattered, I went completely to pieces. I just couldn't believe it. I thought "Oh, that's my son. How could he do that to his sister—my daughter?" I was in complete turmoil. When I look back I feel I let my daughter down. I didn't give her enough when all of this came out. I was so shocked I gave too much to my son. He's always been special to me. I love him but I hate him for what he has done to her, to all of us. It's affected the whole family, torn us apart. It was a nightmare that lasted for weeks. I just wanted to wake up and find it wasn't true. (Abuser was the child's older brother.)

2. *Stigmatization.* They may have feelings of shame, guilt, and worthlessness because they think they are bad mothers.

When I walked down the street I felt everyone's eyes on me. I was worried we would draw comments. I was frightened. I felt like shutting myself away. (Abuser was a neighbor.)

3. *Powerlessness.* They may feel that they have no control and were powerless to stop the abuse of their children and undo what had been done.

How was I supposed to know he would abuse the children? He didn't have any previous convictions. We had known him for 11 years. Abusers don't wear badges to tell you who they are. (Abuser was a family friend and godfather to the child.)

4. *Betrayal.* They may experience a loss of confidence in others and thus feel unable to leave their children with a babysitter or to enter into a trusting relationship with a man.

I just don't know who I can trust now. (Abuser was the child's stepfather.)

5. *Traumatic sexualization.* They may feel differently about sex as a result of finding out about their child's sexual abuse.

After it all came out my sex life with my husband was affected. I felt like a victim, like my daughter. If he came anywhere near me I just felt myself recoil. (Abuser was an uncle.)

But there also are cases in which mothers know that paternal incest is occurring and do nothing to intervene. The following dialogue segments, obtained from an interview conducted with a mother whose husband had intercourse with their daughter over a nine-year period, illustrates this phenomenon (deYoung, 1994, p. 26 with additions).

IR: Were you aware of what was going on?
IE: I was suspicious because of the way he touched her and kissed her; it just wasn't normal. Then she told me after two years, I think, and I said, "What do you think I should do?", and she didn't know, so I just didn't do nothing for a year and then he comes to me and asks do I want to join in—my husband, my daughter, and me....
IR: Did you try to do anything about it?
IE: No, I didn't do nothing to stop it. I was always afraid of what he would do to me. I know how violent he could get. He planned it, controlled it, controlled us. I felt like I was being pressured into silence....
IE: How did people find out about what was going on?
IR: She got pregnant from it and she was afraid to tell me, so she told my husband's daughter, she's my daughter's stepsister who lives with my husband's ex-wife. He abused her too when she was a little girl, so she got real upset when my daughter told her, and I guess she called the cops, or maybe her mother did, I don't know....
IR: Did you play a role in what was happening to your daughter?
IE: Yes, I did. I participated in the incest sometimes, I watched. I know what was going on. It was not my fault, and I still believe I couldn't stop it, but I did a wrong thing. I admit it.

The following case illustrates the traumatic effects that the disclosure of child maltreatment may have on a nonsuspect parent (Lipovsky, 1991).

CASE 21-7. KATHY

Kathy disclosed repeated molestation by her stepfather, which he denied. Her mother did not know what to believe, but she recognized that she had to take a protective stance with regard to her daughter. She fled with her daughter to another state and contacted our treatment center. Her mother asked repeatedly in the initial session, "Do you really think this is true?" and clearly knew that the answer was "Yes" but was frightened of believing it. When she allowed herself to believe completely, she became intensely depressed and suicidal, requiring a two-week psychiatric hospitalization. Following the mother's release from the hospital, she started outpatient treatment and maintained her belief in and support of her daughter. (p. 91, with changes in notation)

When a child has been sexually violated, the parents may be concerned about whether their child caught a sexually transmitted disease, how to prevent future violations, how protective they should be of the child, how much damage was done to the child, and how soon the child will recover and resume normal activities. With a daughter, they also may be concerned about her becoming pregnant. In addition, they may ask questions about what will happen to their child, whether the child will be taken from their home, whether the offender will go to jail, whether they can sue the offender, whether the community and the maltreated child's friends will know about what happened, whether their child will have to testify in court and who will be present in court, and why they should put their maltreated child through all of this if there has been no "serious" damage (Wideman, 1990). Sometimes parents wonder whether their child brought on the attack in some subtle way; at other times, they try to avoid the sexual implications of the attack.

Allow the parents to discuss their concerns (including psychological, legal, medical, and sexual concerns), and especially allow them to express their feelings, including any ambivalent ones. Answer their questions to the best of your ability, and try to obtain answers to questions for which you have no answer, but do not give legal advice.

Evaluate how the family members cope with the victim of the maltreatment (Burge, 1983). Do they show *dysfunctional coping methods,* such as *patronization* (for example, guarding the victim's every action and controlling her or his environment), *distraction* (for example, occupying the victim with shopping sprees or vacation trips to keep the victim too busy to think), or *protective silence* (for example, presuming that the victim is too embarrassed or humiliated to talk about the maltreatment)? These methods may interfere with the victim's attempts at recovery. *Functional coping methods* include an *open pattern of communication, directing their anger and blame at the offender, role flexibility* (that is, changing the role alignment of the family members, as needed), and *use of family-oriented support services.*

Exercise 21-1. Personal Reactions to the Topic of Child Sexual Abuse

---

The following exercise on child sexual abuse may make some readers uncomfortable. *Do not do this exercise if you believe it will cause you discomfort.*

Directions: Rate each statement using the following scale:

1 = Strongly agree
2 = Agree
3 = Disagree
4 = Strongly disagree

Compare your ratings with those given by a sample of college students (following the statements) and, if you want to, with those of your classmates. This exercise was adapted from Wellman (1993).

1. Recent publicity about child sexual abuse is blowing things out of proportion.
2. When sexual abuse is discussed, I feel frightened.
3. When sexual abuse is discussed, I feel disgusted.
4. When sexual abuse is discussed, I feel uneasy.
5. When sexual abuse is discussed, I feel sexually excited.
6. Sexual abusers should be given long prison sentences.
7. Fathers who have incest with their daughters should be forced to live in a different residence from their daughters.

Responses of a Sample of College Students

A sample of 734 college students (approximately 80% female and 20% male) gave the following responses to the seven statements. Note that there is a somewhat different pattern of responses for the women and for the men. This pattern (along with responses to 17 other statements) led Wellman (1993) to conclude "that women have stronger beliefs, attitudes, and emotional reactions to the topic of sexual abuse than do men" (p. 545). Do you believe that a similar pattern is present in your class?

No.	Strongly agree (%)		Agree (%)		Disagree (%)		Strongly disagree (%)	
	F	M	F	M	F	M	F	M
1	1	2	5	10	42	57	52	31
2	8	3	30	10	51	63	11	24
3	42	18	43	58	11	23	4	1
4	9	4	36	39	43	48	12	9
5	0	1	1	5	14	29	85	65
6	43	28	35	40	17	26	5	6
7	51	35	39	47	9	14	1	4

CHILDREN'S MEMORY, LYING, AND SUGGESTIBILITY

Children's Memory

What is known about children's memory that can help us understand their ability to provide evidence in legal proceedings, such as in cases of child maltreatment, custody evaluation, and accidents? Research and theory on memory processes point to several generalizations about children's ability to be credible witnesses. The generalizations are based on the assumption that children have stored in memory information that is potentially retrievable, even though they may not immediately volunteer the information when interviewed. (Most of the material on memory in this section was obtained from Ornstein, Larus, and Clubb, 1991, except where noted.)

Although great strides have been made in research on memory processes, more needs to be learned about how memory changes with children's development and about how stress affects memory. More research also is needed on children's suggestibility and on children's lying. Much of the current research is laboratory based and does not include studies on the effects of traumatization on memory. Research should be based on children's real-life experiences and on memory and suggestibility for real-life events over an extended period.

Useful generalizations about children's memory.

Items 1–6 focus on *encoding processes,* which determine how events are registered in memory, and Items 7–20 deal with *retrieval processes,* which determine how events are recalled from memory.

1. Children's memory will be facilitated by long exposures to and many repetitions of the event.
2. Children will have a better memory of the event when they participate in the event than when they observe the event.
3. In comparison with older children, young children (under 5 years of age) have less efficient information-processing skills (such as speed of encoding and retrieving material) with which to recall events.
4. Children will have difficulty encoding events verbally when they do not possess the necessary language skills to describe the event or a framework for interpreting the event (including knowledge of details and the social implications of the event).
5. Complex events are more difficult for children to remember than simple events.
6. Some intervening events can strengthen children's memory, whereas other intervening events can interfere with their memory.
7. "Children between the ages of 3 and 6 years are able to give coherent, detailed accounts of past events even after long delays.... However, their recounts are likely to be highly inconsistent on different recall occasions" (Fivush & Shukat, 1995, p. 22).
8. When children have difficulty remembering some details of an event, it may simply mean that the details were not entered into their memory; it may not indicate a failure in retrieving information.
9. Children will be more accurate in their reports of an event when interviewed shortly after the occurrence of the event because their memories are even more likely than those of adults to fade rapidly.

10. When there is a long delay between the event and the interview, children may embellish or modify their report; consequently, some of the information they give is information that was not stored in memory.
11. Repeated questions from different interviewers—such as parents, social workers, nurses, and police officers—may alter children's memory, even if these individuals did not intend to mislead the children.
12. Statements made spontaneously by children are likely to be more accurate than those made after repeated questioning.
13. The processes of psychotherapy, designed to help victims come to grips with a traumatic experience, may alter their memory of the event.
14. Stress may affect children's memory of an event, but, at present, research is not clear about whether stress interferes with or facilitates memory.
15. Young children are more suggestible than older children, especially when interviewers try to influence them to say certain things.
16. Children may alter statements because they think the interviewer is dissatisfied with the initial report or because they do not understand the questions.
17. Extended discussions about an event with children *before* an interview may influence their recall of the event; in such instances, children's recall can be contaminated.
18. Children's language ability affects their ability to recall information in response to questions. Children will not be able to retrieve information if they fail to understand questions or if they understand words in a way that differs from that intended by the interviewer.
19. Children may give little information because they think the interviewer already has knowledge of the event in question.
20. When there is more than one interview, children, like adults, may change their report because of changes in context (for example, location of the interview, time of the interview, who conducts the interview, types of questions, events that occur between interviews, and other similar factors).

The preceding generalizations about memory in children suggest that you should consider the following factors, as well as others that relate to the individual child, when you interview children who may have been maltreated:

- number of events
- length of event(s)
- whether the child was a participant or observer
- length of time between the event and the reporting of the event
- child's age, developmental level, and intellectual ability
- child's ability to encode and retrieve information
- child's knowledge of anatomy (in cases of sexual abuse or physical abuse)

- child's prior exposure to sexual information, such as pornographic materials in the home, sexually explicit cable programs, educational materials, and nudity within the household (in cases of child sexual abuse)
- child's communication ability
- pressure exerted on the child by peers or adults
- circumstances surrounding the initial report
- effects of repeated questioning on the child's reports
- social context of the interview

Ideally, you should interview the child as soon as possible after the event. Also, minimizing the number of interviews will reduce stress on children.

Memory's usefulness does not lie in its ability to replay the details of our lives with total accuracy, but in its power to recreate and sustain the important emotional experiences of our lives. As such, its power can be a useful survival tool, maintaining a strong link between the lives we have lived and the persons we are now.

—Daniel L. Schacter

The validity of memories of child sexual abuse— the problem of false recollections.

Older children (and adults) who are treated by psychotherapists sometimes report that they were sexually abused when they were younger. However, before beginning psychotherapy, the clients, in some cases, did not remember any abuse. How accurate are reports of child sexual abuse "recalled" after having been forgotten for a long period? There is no simple answer to this question, and much controversy exists about the area of recovered memory (see, for example, Loftus & Ketcham, 1994; Pezdek & Banks, 1996; Pope & Brown, 1996; Reviere, 1996).

Lindsay and Read (1994), who reviewed research studies on both children and adults, came to the following conclusions about errors in everyday memory (Items 1–6), individual differences in the fallibility of memory (Item 7), and memories and the psychotherapeutic process (Items 8–11).

1. Autobiographical memory is imperfect, being "subject to error and distortion, as well as to forgetting" (p. 293).
2. People sometimes believe that suggestions or imagined experiences were real events. These illusory memories may be vivid and detailed, convincing both to the interviewee and to the interviewer.
3. "Memory errors and distortions are more likely to occur if the to-be-remembered events happened long ago than if they happened recently, and…recollections of childhood are especially vulnerable to misleading suggestions and reality monitoring confusions" (p. 293).
4. "Memory suggestibility is heightened by the perceived authoritativeness of the person giving the suggestions, by repetition of the suggestions across sessions, and by the perceived plausibility of the suggestions" (p. 293).

5. "Rehearsing imagined events can make memories of those imagined events similar to memories of actual events" (p. 293).
6. Memory confusions are likely to be increased when people are willing to accept memories as experienced events even when the memories are vague and uncertain.
7. People who rely heavily on environmental cues to make perceptual judgments are more prone to confuse memories of actual and imagined events than are people who rely heavily on personal cues. Similarly, people with psychological problems may be more vulnerable to making memory errors than those without psychological problems.
8. Some survivors of child sexual abuse may not remember the abusive events, but their memories might be recovered, given appropriate cues.
9. Extensive use of particular psychotherapeutic techniques—such as hypnosis, dream interpretation, and guided imagery—may create illusory memories of child sexual abuse among people who were not abused.
10. When memory recovery techniques are used, it is "difficult to discriminate between clients who are remembering accurately and clients who believe they are remembering accurately but are not" (p. 304).
11. There are "no techniques that would provide for the reliable discrimination of illusory and true memories in clients who have been through extensive memory recovery therapy.… Illusory memories can look, feel, and sound like real memories" (p. 325).

Lindsay and Read's conclusions suggest that survivors of child sexual abuse in some cases may forget or repress memories of the abusive event or events and in other cases may recall incidents not based on actual events. To reduce the risk of creating illusory memories, psychotherapists should (a) keep an open mind about what might have caused the client's problems, (b) limit the use of highly suggestive techniques or techniques that provoke false memories, and (c) keep up with contemporary memory research.

Before leaving this area, let's also consider Read and Lindsay's (1994) additional observations about illusory memories:

It may well be that illusory memories are not always made out of nothing. Indeed, we suspect that many false claims have some grounding in reality: actual memories of childhood psychological abuse may contribute to false beliefs about childhood sexual contact abuse; memories of nonabusive but scary and/or painful childhood experiences (e.g., enemas) may underlie illusory recollections of rape; memories of relatively high-frequency forms of sexual contact abuse, such as genital touching, may form the germ of false memories of satanic rituals. It is also quite possible that someone who was abused as a child would later misremember the identity of the perpetrator or make other errors. Therefore, the fact that a person reports false memories does not prove that the person was not sexually abused as a child.… None the less, the existence of demonstrably false recollections provides powerful evidence of the reality of illusory memories of childhood sexual abuse. (pp. 414–415)

Not only does rape hurt everyone, but false memories of rape hurt everyone too.

—Elizabeth Loftus, Maryanne Garry, and Julie Feldman

Can You Tell Whether the Child Is Lying?

Although it is not easy to determine whether a child (or any person) is telling the truth, the presence of one or more of the following factors should alert you to the possibility that the child is lying. Note, however, that no one factor or combination of factors means that the child is lying. *In fact, experts have no more ability than laypersons to judge with certainty whether someone is lying based on the interview alone* (Bussey, 1992).

You should entertain the possibility that a child is lying when one or more of the following factors are present (Quinn, 1988):

- the child has a history of persistent lying
- the child has a psychological disorder that would severely alter his or her perception of reality
- the child is anxious about being caught in a lie
- the child has possible motives for lying, such as anger, revenge, threats, bribes, or wanting more attention
- the child's symptoms are not consistent with a well-recognized psychiatric or medical disorder
- the child has made inconsistent statements in the past or made statements not verified by the reports of others
- the child has been rewarded for lying
- the child has been told that he or she will be punished for telling the truth

Children may lie by omitting or denying events that did happen. If you believe that a child has lied, consider the reason for the lie—that is, whether the lie is deliberate, a result of faulty memory, or an honest difference of opinion (Frank, 1992). In addition, "an important factor governing children's lying and truthfulness is the result they anticipate for either statement. *The more censure children anticipate for telling the truth, such as threat from an adult, the less likely they are to tell the truth.* Children may have more to fear from truth-telling than adults, especially in sexual abuse cases where they might be threatened with dire consequences for disclosure.... Ultimately, there is no guarantee that individuals of any age will be truthful" (Bussey, 1992, pp. 105–106, italics added).

Attending carefully to the way the child presents information about the maltreatment may give you clues about the truthfulness of the disclosure or about whether the child is withholding information. Does the child's report appear to be spontaneous, or does it seem to be rote and prepro-

grammed? Is the child reluctant to share information with you? After you have exhausted other, less confrontational procedures, consider using the following two different approaches.

1. If you *suspect* that the child has made up some of the details about the alleged maltreatment, you might say, depending on the case: "I know you weren't happy at home. Some people might think you made that story up so you could get out of the home. In court, you would have to tell the truth. When the attorney asks you about what happened, would you say anything different from what you told me?" (Nurcombe, 1986, adapted from p. 478).

2. If you *suspect* that the child is withholding information about the alleged maltreatment, you might say, depending on the case: "I know you want everything to be happy at home, but sometimes there are problems at home. In court, you would have to tell the truth. When the attorney asks you about what happened, would you say anything new from what you told me?"

Cases in which the child might not be truthful or might be withholding information present difficult problems, such as how to overcome the child's resistance without using undue suggestion or leading questions.

You should routinely ask the child about other individuals she or he may have spoken with about the alleged maltreatment. If the child spoke with another person or persons, ask what the child told the person and what the person said.

How Suggestible Are Children?

Research suggests that the following factors should be considered in evaluating suggestibility in children (Ceci & Bruck, 1993):

1. *Age.* There are significant age differences in suggestibility. Preschool children are more suggestible than either school-aged children or adults. In fact, "children can be led to make false or inaccurate reports about very crucial, personally experienced, central events.... [There is] compelling evidence that young children do in fact make false claims about actions, central events, and even events that could be construed as being sexually abusive" (pp. 432–433).

2. *Motivational structure.* Children will sometimes lie when it serves some purpose; in this sense, they are probably no different from adults.

3. *Recall ability.* Young children can recollect information that they observed accurately, and much of this information is forensically important. However, in comparison with older children, younger children do not recall as much information, and their reports are more vulnerable to distortion. In addition, "they may be more likely to succumb to erroneous suggestions than older children, but their vulnerability is a matter of degree only" (p. 433).

4. *Credibility of the report.* The conditions under which young children gave the original reports of a criminal event influence the credibility of their reports. It is crucial to know

the circumstances under which the initial report of concern was made, how many times the child was questioned, the hypotheses of the interviewers who questioned the child, the kinds of questions the child was asked, and the consistency of the child's report over a period of time. If the child's disclosure was made in a nonthreatening, nonsuggestive atmosphere, if the disclosure was not made after repeated interviews, if the adults who had access to the child prior to his or her testimony are not motivated to distort the child's recollections through relentless and potent suggestions and outright coaching, and if the child's original report remains highly consistent over a period of time, then the young child would be judged to be capable of providing much that is forensically relevant. The absence of any of these conditions would not in and of itself invalidate a child's testimony, but it ought to raise cautions in the mind of the court. (p. 433)

Ceci and Bruck (1993) concluded the following:

[Research to date] shows that children are able to encode and retrieve large amounts of information, especially when it is personally experienced and highly meaningful. Equally true, however, is that no good will be served by ignoring that part of the research that demonstrates potentially serious social and cognitive hazards to young child witnesses if adults who have access to them attempt to usurp their memories. (p. 434)

Exercise 21-2. Evaluating Children's Ability to Provide Evidence

---

Read the first case. Then evaluate it by considering what factors may assist you and what factors may hinder you in obtaining unbiased information. After you complete your evaluation of the first case, follow the same procedure for the second case. The cases in this exercise and the suggested analyses are from Ornstein et al. (1991).

In this [first] case, a three-year-old girl was [alleged to have been] abused sexually by her stepfather. The girl lived alone with her mother and stepfather and it is thought that she had not been mistreated in any way prior to the incident in question. However, early one morning this girl was found in her nightclothes, somewhat dazed, wandering alone in a parking lot. There was some questionable physical evidence of vaginal penetration, and the child was reported to have said, "Frank did it with his dick." The woman who found the child immediately called the police. During the day the child received an examination by a doctor and was interviewed about what had happened by a female police officer. (p. 147)

[The second case] is more complex than the first...in that nine children, ranging from four to eight years of age, were allegedly abused on multiple occasions at a private school that they attended. Over a period of eight months, the children, both boys and girls, were said to have been frequently victimized individually by an employee of the school. The children's statements indicated that they had been asked to

touch and lick food from [his] penis. In addition, their reports included allegations of penile penetration of the vagina and/or rectum. The children were also threatened with dire consequences (including the deaths of their parents) if they told anyone about the incidents. After observing unusual behaviors in her five-year-old son, a parent contacted a psychologist and then the police regarding possible wrongdoings at the school. The police began their investigation by contacting the parents of other children who attended that school. In order to prevent discussion between the parents and children that could lead to contamination of the children's reports, the police met first with the parents and provided them with information about the symptoms of sexual abuse. The police directed the parents to question their children individually. After this meeting, eight other children indicated that they had been sexually abused. (p. 148)

Suggested Analyses

The first case involves a possible single abuse episode with a 3-year-old girl. If she was abused, her memory may be enhanced by (a) her being an active participant and not merely a bystander with a limited view of the incident and (b) the relatively short interval between the event and the initial report. Her memory may be impeded by the short duration and the nonrepetition of the event, her limited language skills, and the difficulties the interviewer will have in communicating with her. It is possible that many of the details of sexual assault are stored in her memory but cannot be effectively retrieved when she is questioned. What is not clear is her knowledge of sexual anatomy and behavior. If this case lingers, there is an additional source of possible bias: "changes over time in the child's understanding of anatomy and sexuality can lead to reinterpretations and even relabeling of the event" (Ornstein et al., 1991, p. 159). Repeated questioning by a series of different interviewers will confuse her. As a young child, she is extremely susceptible to the social context of the interview, and she may accept interpretations offered to her by the interviewer as her own.

The second case involves possible multiple episodes over a long period with several children. Their memory may be enhanced by (a) the long duration and repetition of the episodes and (b) their ages. Their memory may be impeded by the complex interactions with the alleged offender, making it difficult for them to describe the "stimulus event" precisely. In addition, "there is considerable uncertainty about what the children...have stored in memory.... With the passage of time, it may be difficult for them to differentiate between the memory of a specific episode and their knowledge of what usually happened during these encounters. To complicate matters more, memories of the events could also be distorted by several other factors, including the threats that they received and unmonitored discussions among the several child victims, both during and following the incidents of abuse. Further, because only one child made a spontaneous report of abuse, it is possible that the accusations of the majority were biased by the preconceptions of the initial interviewers, namely their parents.... And finally, during the long interval between the initial reports and the later trial, it is possible that the children's memories could be altered by repeated discussions with a wide range of individuals" (Ornstein et al., 1991, pp. 157–158). As in the first case, repeated questioning by a series of different interviewers may confuse the children. The younger children in this case may be extremely susceptible to the social context of the interview, possibly accepting interpretations offered to them by the interviewer as their own.

There should not be "camps" when it comes to sexual abuse—whether the "witchhunt" or the "children never lie" camp. There should only be a sincere questioning for truth, and the utmost protection of our youngest citizens while we find that truth.

—Ellen Gray

ALLEGATIONS OF CHILD MALTREATMENT

Allegations of child maltreatment made by children or by adults present a thorny problem for those who investigate them. Allegations may be true (a) but unprovable, (b) false, or (c) true and provable. Assessing the validity of allegations of child maltreatment is often a formidable task for the following reasons (Fraser, 1981; Raskin & Steller, 1989; Vizard & Tranter, 1988):

1. There may be limited or no physical evidence, particularly in cases of child sexual abuse or emotional abuse.
2. Young children may have difficulty describing the maltreatment.
3. If there is a long interval between the maltreatment and the report, children (especially those younger than 5 or 6 years of age) may forget important details or may have difficulty describing the maltreatment.
4. If a medical examination is delayed, evidence of maltreatment may be lost.
5. If the maltreatment was done privately, there were probably no eyewitnesses.
6. Children, particularly in cases of intrafamilial maltreatment, may not want to say anything that can get a parent or other relative in trouble. They may deny an original allegation, refuse to talk about possible maltreatment, refuse to testify in court about the maltreatment, remain silent because of pressure or coercion, or fear disclosure because of repercussions. (Parents also may be reluctant to talk about the maltreatment or to accuse the other parent or a relative of maltreatment.)
7. If children are interviewed by several professionals, such as by members of Child Protective Services, a law enforcement agency, a hospital team, a county attorney's office, or another agency, it will be difficult to know which of the several interviews is valid when the findings are not consistent.

There are no firm statistics on the rate of false allegations of child maltreatment (Ceci & Bruck, 1995; National Center on Child Abuse and Neglect, 1996). Much depends on how false allegations are defined. Ceci and Bruck (1995) recommended that the term *false allegations* include (a) adult-instigated false allegations, (b) allegations deliberately concocted by children, and (c) reports by children influenced by the interviewers' (including parents') suggestions. Studies cited by Ceci and Bruck (1995) report a range of false allegations from 6% to as high as 33% of the cases studied. In the 1994 annual survey of reports of child maltreatment conducted by the National Center on Child Abuse and Neglect (1996), 4% of the unsubstantiated reports (see Chapter 20) were intentionally false, as reported by the six states that provided data about false reports. Although, in the 1994 survey, most of the reports of child maltreatment were not intentionally false, more data are needed from other states on the rate of false allegations. The percentage of false allegations reported in the survey probably does not take into account reports by children influenced by the interviewer's suggestions.

Ceci and Bruck (1995) concluded from their review of the research that there is a higher rate of false reports of child maltreatment in families undergoing custody disputes than in families in which custody of children is not an issue. It is important to note that the overall rate of child sexual abuse allegations in families with custody and visitation disputes is low—in one report, it was less than 2% of the 9,000 families studied (Thoennes & Tjaden, 1990). However, even in this study of families engaged in custody and visitation disputes, the rate of reports of allegations of child sexual abuse is six times greater than the rate found in the National Incidence Study, which focused on all families in which there were alleged incidents of child maltreatment.

Let's now look at the types of situations in which false allegations of child maltreatment may occur (Bernet, 1993; Robin, 1991, pp. 93–114).

1. *Situations where children allege maltreatment.* First, children may deliberately lie. They may make false accusations to get out of a troubled family setting or placement, to retaliate against parental figures or teachers for perceived mistreatment, to get more attention or responsiveness from the adults in their lives, or for personal advantage. Children also may make false accusations when they are delusional, confuse dreams or fantasy with reality, tell "white lies," misinterpret acts, or misinterpret communications.

In the following case, an adolescent made a false allegation for personal advantage (Bernet, 1993).

CASE 21-8. WANDA
Wanda, a 14-year-old girl, became pregnant and was very much afraid of the repercussions from her parents. Aiming to shield her relationship with her 18-year-old boyfriend, she accused her stepfather of molesting her. Her accusation served the double purpose of protecting her boyfriend and embarrassing the stepfather. (p. 907)

The following case shows not only how a child misinterpreted her mother's question, but also how the mother misinterpreted the child's response (Yates & Musty, 1988).

CASE 21-9. EILEEN

Eileen, a 5-year-old girl, was asked by her mother about the child's father: "Does he try to make love to you?" Eileen apparently nodded affirmatively to the question. This response led the mother to place Eileen in therapy for treatment of sexual abuse. When the topic was brought up again after several months of therapy, Eileen said that all she meant was that she and her father liked each other a lot, and there was no sexual abuse.

2. *Situations where parents induce their children to allege maltreatment or where parents allege maltreatment.* Parents may induce their children to make false allegations, or they themselves may make false allegations when they have something to gain from the allegations. This may occur, for example, in the context of a custody dispute or when a parent wants to punish another person. Parents also may make false allegations when they are delusional, are influenced by rumors, are caught up in a hysterical climate where accusations are made out of fear or false beliefs, misperceive what the child is saying, or misinterpret the reasons for the child's illness or injury.

In the following case, a child's mother believed that her son's injuries were caused by sexual maltreatment rather than by more benign causes (Bernet, 1993).

CASE 21-10. ROBERT

Robert, who was 8 years old, was the child of divorced parents. He lived with his mother and spent long summer vacations with his father. Robert's mother brought him for a psychiatric evaluation because she thought that he had been physically and perhaps sexually abused by his father during the summer visitation. She had inspected Robert thoroughly on his return and found marks on his back, which she took to be cigarette burns, and also superficial scratches that extended from his umbilicus almost to his pubis, which she thought indicated sexual abuse. She had Robert pose nude so that she could photograph the marks. On investigation, the "cigarette burns" were found to be infected mosquito bites and the abdominal scratches were the result of body surfing at Myrtle Beach, South Carolina. (p. 905, with changes in notation)

3. *Situations where interviewers or therapists coerce children to allege maltreatment.* Interviewers or therapists may use techniques improperly to coerce children to say that (a) a specific person was the perpetrator, even though the children were reluctant to name a person, or (b) they were maltreated, even though the children initially denied being maltreated. Interviewers or therapists also may "unknowingly" obtain allegations of maltreatment when they use facilitated communication with severely disabled children (see Chapter 10).

In the following case, the interviewer coerced the child to make a false allegation (Bernet, 1993).

CASE 21-11. MARGARET

A new staff member of Child Protective Services interviewed Margaret, a 4-year-old girl, and asked her if her father touched her private parts. Margaret said no. The worker asked Margaret again. She said no. The worker told Margaret she would spin her around in the chair, which was a fun activity, if Margaret told her what her father did. Margaret said he didn't do anything. The worker spun Margaret around in the chair, which Margaret enjoyed. The worker said she would spin Margaret again if she said what her father had done. Margaret said her father touched her private parts. (adapted from p. 905)

You need to be alert to the possibility of intentionally false allegations, even though the rate of such reports is low. You need to be equally alert to the possibility that children may be withholding information. *What is even more critical is that each allegation of child maltreatment be carefully assessed, regardless of how the allegation arose. No allegation of child maltreatment should be ignored!* Ignoring allegations of child maltreatment or failing to prove allegations of maltreatment when they are true may lead to continued abuse or neglect and possibly to the deaths of children. In Chapters 22 and 23, you will be reading about cases in which competent interviewers associated with child protective agencies obtained information from children that confirmed allegations of child maltreatment.

I hear so much of people's calling out to punish the guilty, but very few are concerned to clear the innocent.

—Daniel DeFoe

Exercise 21-3. Investigating an Allegation of Sexual Abuse

Read the case. Then answer these questions:

1. How would you investigate the allegation?
2. What specific things would be important to attend to in the interview(s)?
3. List possible conclusions you might reach about the allegation, and then formulate relevant hypotheses, focusing on the roles of the father, the mother, and the child.
4. What clinical recommendations might you consider?

Compare your answers with the suggested answers following the case. The material in this exercise was adapted from Daly (1992).

Jamie, a 5-year-old girl, lives with her mother, father, and a 7-year-old sister. Her parents have been married for 10 years and have an amicable relationship. However, recently they have had several arguments about Mr. Smith's spending considerable time at work. Both parents work, but Mr. Smith has been working overtime lately. He told Mrs. Smith that the overtime is mandatory. When Mrs. Smith called her husband's employer, she learned that Mr. Smith had not been working overtime as he claimed. Mrs. Smith said that during the past few weeks her husband has been coming home with alcohol on his breath. In addition, about three weeks ago, she woke and found her husband naked in bed with Jamie. Since that night, she said that Jamie's behavior has been peculiar.

Yesterday, Jamie told her mother that her father had touched her on the outside of her pajamas in the vaginal area on the evening that he was in bed with her. Jamie woke up when she was touched and then rolled over and went back to sleep. As soon as she heard this information, Mrs. Smith called the police. The police contacted Mr. Smith at work. He denied that he ever sexually touched his daughter and said that the charges were ridiculous.

Suggested Answers

1. To investigate the allegation, you should do the following:

   - Get a copy of the police report.
   - Interview the child.
   - Refer the child for a medical evaluation, and get a copy of the report.
   - Interview the mother.
   - Interview the father.
   - Interview Jamie's sister.
   - Verify the father's current employment, his job performance, and hours spent on the job.
   - Verify the mother's current employment and her job performance.

2. Specific things to attend to in the interviews include the following:

   - In the interview with Jamie, pay particular attention to how she describes the alleged incident, including her vocabulary, affect, and nonverbal behaviors.
   - In the interview with the mother, pay particular attention to her relationship with her two children and her husband, her background (especially prior criminal convictions or allegations and any history of substance abuse, psychiatric problems, or physical or sexual abuse), and her work history.
   - In the interview with the father, pay particular attention to his reaction to the allegation, his relationship with his two children and his wife, his background (especially prior criminal convictions or allegations and any history of substance abuse, psychiatric problems, or physical or sexual abuse), and his work history.
   - In the interview with Jamie's sister, pay particular attention to her relationship with her mother, her father, and her sister and possible disclosures of sexual abuse.

3. Possible conclusions you might reach about the allegations and relevant hypotheses include the following:

   - The father was in bed with Jamie and deliberately touched her.
   - The father was in bed with Jamie but did not touch her.
   - The father was drunk and accidentally touched Jamie.
   - The father wasn't in bed with Jamie and didn't touch her.
   - The mother reported the child's account accurately.
   - The mother made up the allegation to punish her husband because she thinks he is having an affair with another woman.

   - The mother overreacted and misinterpreted what her daughter said.
   - The mother has a psychiatric disorder and misinterpreted what the child said.
   - The mother pressured the child to make the allegation.
   - The mother has legitimate concerns about the father's getting in bed naked with his daughter, whether or not he touched his daughter.
   - The child's story is accurate.
   - The child's story is fantasy.
   - The child made up the story because she is mad because the father spends so little time with her.
   - The child heard about or knows someone else who told a similar story. She wants the same level of attention from her parents, and so she made up the story.
   - The child has reason to be upset because her father was in bed naked with her.

4. You might consider the following clinical recommendations:

   - Regardless of whether the child was touched, the father needs guidance about how to behave properly with his children. This recommendation would not hold if the mother lied about what happened.
   - Marital counseling for the parents.
   - Family therapy, if the children appear to have problems.
   - Individual therapy for each member of the family, if they appear to have problems.

Exercise 21-4. Substantiating Reports of Child Neglect

Read each of the following incidents. Then decide whether there is a *low probability, moderate probability,* or *high probability* that the incident could be substantiated if it was reported to the police or to Child Protective Services. Compare your answers with those of 25 Child Protective Services workers, which follow the list of incidents. Also, consider what additional information you would like to have about the situation to be able to assess it more accurately. This exercise was adapted from Craft and Staudt (1991).

1. A 10-year-old girl is home alone from 3:30 P.M. to 6:30 P.M. Monday through Friday.
2. A parent has drug or alcohol dependence and allows a 12-year-old child to drink from his glass.
3. A child consistently wears clothing that is too small, stained, and has holes in it.
4. An elementary school–aged child is expected to prepare his own meals almost daily.
5. A second-grader goes to school tired daily. She admits to having no set bedtime and sleeps on the living room couch.
6. A child often witnesses his mother's being physically abused by his father.
7. A parent has not taken care of necessary repairs around the house, including leaving broken glass on the front step.

8. Parents who are mentally retarded are unable to rid their infant of diaper rash. The baby's doctor is concerned about the baby's health.
9. A child is often seen outside on a cold winter day with no hat or mittens and only a light jacket.
10. A 13-year-old child does not go to school, and the parents do nothing to encourage the child to attend school.
11. There are no screens in most windows of the home.
12. An 8-year-old child is left at night to baby-sit three younger siblings while the parent works.
13. A parent was to pick up her child from the baby-sitter at 4:00 P.M. but did not return until the next day. There was no call, and this was the second time this had happened.
14. A young mother of three children often trades food stamps for nonfood items such as beer and cigarettes.
15. A parent leaves an infant in an unlocked car while in a store for 15 minutes.
16. A 5-year-old child consistently smells of urine. She does not want to interact with other children in school.
17. A child is often ignored when he tries to tell his parent something and is pushed aside when he shows a need for attention.
18. A parent lost his job and is too proud to go to the local food bank for assistance in feeding three small children.
19. A child does not have toys, and the parents make no effort to obtain them.
20. A parent seems not to follow through on threatened punishments of a child and frequently takes no action when discipline seems necessary.
21. A child suffers from an ongoing illness and is not receiving essential medical care.
22. A parent frequently screams obscenities at the child and the child cries.
23. A family is on public assistance and does not spend money wisely, often running out of food by the end of the month.
24. A 12-year-old child has never been to the dentist.
25. Three children in a family are in special education classes and miss one to two days of school each week.
26. A 12-year-old child is required to do all the housework.
27. A child begs for food. The child has not eaten in a day.
28. An elementary school–aged child eats lunch at school but has no hot meals at home.
29. The child is not bathed for a week at a time.
30. A 9-year-old child is required to provide the discipline for her younger siblings.

Answers from 25 CPS Workers
(Ratings reflect probability of substantiating incident)

1. Low	11. Low	21. High
2. Low	12. High	22. Moderate
3. Low	13. High	23. Moderate
4. Moderate	14. Low	24. Low
5. Moderate	15. High	25. Moderate
6. Moderate	16. Moderate	26. Low
7. Moderate	17. Low	27. High
8. High	18. Moderate	28. Moderate
9. High	19. Low	29. Moderate
10. High	20. Low	30. Moderate

Note. Low, moderate, and high designations are based on the following percentages of child protective workers in the survey who indicated that the incident would likely be substantiated: low—50% or less, moderate—51% to 74%, high—75% or higher.

COMMENT ON THE FEDERAL CHILD ABUSE PREVENTION AND TREATMENT ACT

The Federal Child Abuse Prevention and Treatment Act, designed to protect children and enacted into law in good faith by the U.S. government, may have had unintended consequences. As a result of two major child sexual abuse cases in San Diego in the early 1990s that received national attention (the Dale Akiki case and the Alicia W. case), the San Diego County Grand Jury (1994) issued a controversial report, the conclusions of which (shown in Exhibit 21-1) deserve study. The unintended consequences of the Child Abuse Prevention and Treatment Act, according to the San Diego County Grand Jury, included (a) increasing the number of alleged child maltreatment reports, (b) fueling "sex abuse hysteria," and (c) creating a "child maltreatment establishment" composed of mental health professionals, law enforcement personnel, and medical personnel. (The terms in quotation marks are from the Grand Jury's report.) Thus, the San Diego County Grand Jury believes that a law designed to protect children has had effects that no one anticipated when it was passed. Exhibit 21-1 also contains a rebuttal to the Grand Jury's report from Inta Sellars, Social Services Program Consultant, Family and Children's Services Division, Minnesota Department of Human Services. Sellars maintains that the Grand Jury report misinterprets the Child Abuse Prevention and Treatment Act. Her opinion—that the act never supported frivolous accusations but was and is solely intended to protect children—deserves careful study.

A report in the *Los Angeles Times* offers an example of one possible effect of the Child Abuse Prevention and Treatment Act. Entitled "Fallout from Child Abuse Cases Is Taking Its Toll," the report carries the subtitle "Teachers and Others Are Scared to Reach Out—and Kids Miss Hugs That Used to Come So Freely."

What teacher would deny a hug to a crying child? Or reject a toddler's plea for a moment of closeness? Many would—and do, children's advocates say. A decade of highly publicized child-abuse accusations—from the McMartin preschool case to Michael Jackson—has taken a troubling toll: more parents on the alert for child molestation; more teachers afraid of being wrongly accused. Three million cases of suspected child abuse were reported last year [1992], up from 1 million 10 years ago.

And now, some experts say, the nation's youngsters are paying the price for adults' increased fears. An unwritten edict has been issued at many schools and day-care centers across the nation: Do not touch the little children.

Exhibit 21-1
Some Unintended Consequences Associated with the Mondale Act—
A Report Issued by the San Diego County Grand Jury

Since 1974, the Mondale Act [Child Abuse Prevention and Treatment Act] has been expanded several times, progressively increasing the federal funds allocated to the states. Certain provisions of the original law and its successors worked to encourage people to bring child abuse charges that were frivolous, and sometimes malicious fabrications.

To qualify for federal funds states must pass legislation which provides immunity from prosecution for anyone reporting child abuse. This immunity has its benefits and its problems; many people with legitimate cases gain the confidence to file a charge but the same immunity protects people who make false or malicious charges.

To receive federal funds, states also must pass laws requiring specific people, such as teachers, health-care professionals and law enforcement officials, to report suspected child abuse, backed up by penalties for failure to report. In effect, this provision has made it a criminal offense for such people not to report suspected abuse. The result has been over-reporting of even the most absurd and impossible accusations.

For example, the Grand Jury was informed about a situation involving a North County high school teacher. A 14-year-old special education student, who was pleased to learn that she would not be receiving a failing mark in her woodshop class, hugged her teacher in the presence of several other students. Later she told her family about the incident. By the next day her account included the accusation that she had been touched on her breasts.

She reported the charge to the school administration, who reported it as a charge of fondling. Although there were several other students present when the fondling supposedly happened and, although this teacher had an unblemished record in all respects, he was removed from the classroom and put on unpaid leave while the charges were being investigated.

These charges were brought to the attention of local newspapers and for

months there was publicity about the case. The case went to trial. Fortunately, the jury found the teacher innocent of any wrong doing and expressed astonishment that the case was ever brought to trial.

However, this man's reputation was impugned. His family life was disrupted for months; his teaching career was interrupted and, even when he was allowed to return to school, he was no longer assigned to the woodshop classes which he preferred. Eventually he left teaching for another career, expressing bitterness that the school district assumed he was guilty until he was legally absolved. Some adults falsely accused of molesting children have said they would rather have been accused of murder.

Although the reporting form for suspected child abuse indicates the reporting party needs to check either "occurred" or "observed," accounts relayed to the child care custodian or health practitioner by someone else are also reported. Such hearsay is enough impetus for a report to be filed, so pervasive is the fear of losing one's job or facing criminal charges for *not* reporting.

Evaluators who conclude there has been abuse, set in motion events that bring their offices both state and federal funds. If they conclude there is no abuse, their facilities will receive no funding for further evaluation or treatment.

Federal funding has created a "child abuse establishment." Mental health facilities, child protection services and investigatory agencies all depend on each other. It behooves them to work together because the greater the number of referrals, the greater the justification for the requisite funding.

This fuels a certain amount of sex-abuse hysteria in which an accused individual's constitutional due-process protections are commonly ignored. In other areas immunity from prosecution is generally available only to specific groups essential to the functioning of the legal system, e.g., judges and prosecutors. Immunity under the Child

Abuse Prevention and Treatment Act is incompatible with the basic philosophy of our legal system.

Mandated reporting of any suspicion of child abuse has resulted in the reporting of frivolous and bizarre accusations by children as young as two and three years old, and severely disturbed women against their elderly fathers. Highly skilled examiners who know quite well that the accusation is false, are required by law to report the abuse to individuals who may be predisposed to a prejudicial view toward the guilt of the suspect.

The Grand Jury realizes that child sexual abuse is a deplorable problem, but there must be a balanced approach to the situation. The process that allows anyone to make malicious or vengeful accusations needs to be modified and some degree of accountability provided. The necessary challenge is to strike a balance between the need to protect the children and the need to correct the growing tendency to use the Child Abuse Prevention and Treatment Act as a powerful weapon in the hands of those who misuse it for vengeful or malicious purposes, or to make public accusations.

Counterpoint by Inta Sellars
The Grand Jury report is based on a faulty interpretation of the Child Abuse Prevention and Treatment Act. First, the expansion of the Act has not "progressively" increased federal funding allocated to states. The funding for each state is calculated on a formula based on the population of children under 18 in each state. If a state is not in compliance with the requirements of the Act, the state is not eligible to apply for the funds and those funds allocated to the ineligible states are then distributed proportionately to the eligible states.

Secondly, the Child Abuse Prevention and Treatment Act does not "encourage people to bring child abuse charges that were frivolous and sometimes malicious fabrications." The Act simply requires that, to be eligible to receive the federal funds, states must

(Continued)

Exhibit 21-1 (*Continued*)

have laws for reporting "known and suspected" instances of child maltreatment. People who are mandated to report are not required to report "hearsay" or make "false and malicious charges." "Immunity under the Child Abuse Prevention and Treatment Act" is *not* "incompatible with the basic philosophy of our legal system." In fact, a general principle of law is that immunity doesn't protect those acting in bad faith or maliciously. Additionally, reporters do not make "charges," they make reports. It is not the reporter's responsibility to determine whether maltreatment occurred. It is not the reporter's responsibility to determine whether charges should be brought or whether the reports should

even be assessed. Child Protective Services and law enforcement determine whether maltreatment occurred, whether reports should be assessed, or whether cases should be brought to the county or district attorney for charging decisions.

Finally, despite what the Grand Jury report states, the Child Abuse Prevention and Treatment Act does *not* authorize increases of funding to states because states have increased numbers of child maltreatment referrals. The Child Abuse Prevention and Treatment Act does not require states to show why they should get funding based on having a certain number of reports, investigations, or assessments.

Funding to states isn't contingent on finding that maltreatment occurred. As noted previously, states must only have laws in place that follow the requirements of the act to *be eligible* for this federal funding. Consequently, states that don't define maltreatment as required by the federal law are not eligible for federal money for child maltreatment activities. Despite having the law in place, some states even chose not to get any money via the Child Abuse Prevention and Treatment Act. Ultimately, funding has been decreased. In 1996, Minnesota had an 18% cut in its Child Abuse Prevention and Treatment Act Basic State Grant.

Source: From the San Diego County Grand Jury, *Analysis of Child Molestation Issues,* Report No. 7, June 1, 1994, pp. 29–30, and from Inta Sellars, personal communication, September 1996.

As in: Do not hug, kiss, lift, stroke, offer your lap, rub the back, tuck in the shirt, pat the hair, or be in any way physically responsive to their needs. It has all gone too far, some of the nation's leading child-development experts say.

Such heightened concern may have prevented some acts of "bad touching," they believe, but for many small children it has also removed the essential hugs and snuggles that no words can replace.

"So many children who would never be abused by their caretakers are being deprived of the good, healthy touching they need—especially since they get so little of it from parents they spend less and less time with," said Dr. David Elkind, professor of child study at Tufts University in Boston and author of "The Hurried Child." (Levine, 1993, p. E1–2)

Zimring (1996) observed that "sexual fear is poisoning the atmosphere of child care in the United States and depriving children of warmth and informality in the caregiving settings where they spend many of their waking hours. We are isolating our children in the name of protecting them" (p. B5). Zimring attempts to account for the sexual fear in the following way:

How did it come to pass in the United States of the 1980s and '90s that hugging a 4-year-old is dangerous?...The fixation with child molestation has many characteristics of what sociologists call a moral panic. Two trends have contributed to the reaction. First, the exploitation of children has been more visible in our society, whether or not it is also more frequent. The amount of media attention heightens anxiety, and the public's fear generates the kind of interest that creates even more media attention.

The second factor is the transfer for child-care responsibility from mothers to others in conjunction with the fuller participation of women in the work force. Could it be that we are anxious about leaving our children in the care of others because we are guilty about not being home with them full-time? (p. B5)

Child Protective Services and legal authorities have as their mission the protection of children and their families. But such protection may have its costs. Once someone reports a suspicion of child maltreatment to the appropriate authorities, the report may set off a chain of events that can have devastating effects on the child and family (see Exhibit 21-2). And, once in the "system," the child may be re-victimized.

Cindy's Poem
...a child's view of incest
I asked you for help and you told me you would
if I told you the things my Dad did to me.
It was really hard for me to say all those things,
but you told me to trust you—
then you made me repeat them to fourteen different
*   strangers.*

I asked you for privacy and you sent two policemen
to my school, in front of everyone,
to "go downtown" for a talk
in their black and white car—
like I was the one being busted.

I asked you to believe me,
and you said that you did
then you connected me to a lie detector,
and took me to court where lawyers
put me on trial like I was a liar.
I can't help it if I can't remember times or dates
or explain why I couldn't tell my Mom.
Your questions got me confused—
my confusion got you suspicious.

Exhibit 21-2
"Yes, Abuse Claims Must Be Investigated...But Then What?"

The knock came late one evening in early February. The two children were asleep and the Branches, Anita and Dale, were talking in the family room of their Saugus home. At the door were two strangers. The man was a sheriff's deputy. The woman was a social worker from the Department of Children and Family Services [DCFS]. "They said, 'We want to see your daughter, Christie Branch,'" said Anita, a 39-year-old manicurist. "They said, 'We need to take her into the front yard to look at her.' I said, 'Why?' And the woman said, 'We'll discuss it in a little bit, after we check it out.'"

Anita woke the child, and the deputy took the weeping, disoriented 5-year-old to the front lawn, where he examined the back of her thighs with a flashlight. "Christie was screaming," Anita said. "She wanted me, and I couldn't go with her. That was the hardest part. I asked the social worker, 'What is going on here?' And she said, 'It's been alleged that Dale Branch has been beating Christie on the back of the legs to cause blisters.'"

The Branches were stunned. For more than three years—and it is documented in her medical records—Christie has been treated for eczema that causes a rash on the back of her thighs. Moments later, the deputy returned. Anita thought he looked angry. "He said, 'This is a rash.... I'm leaving.'" The social worker, Anita said, was apologetic and kind. She stayed for a while, asked a lot of questions and observed the family. Eventually, she left, telling the Branches she was sorry, these things happen, and that although the suspicions of abuse were unfounded, by law, she was required to file a report. A report? What kind of report? Where would this report go? Who would know about it? Would it be permanent? Would the Branches receive copies of it? What would happen if Christie fell and hurt herself? Would this incident come back to haunt them?

Already rocked by the earthquake—Dale had been on the Golden State Freeway bridge that collapsed, and the family's home sustained $85,000 in damage—the Branches felt their happy, suburban life coming unglued. Panicked, they took Christie to two doctors the next day to document the rash. Then they went to Christie's school to talk to the principal about how a rash could be misconstrued as abuse. Why didn't someone check the child's school medical records, where the rash was mentioned in a history Anita had filled out? But the principal, the Branches said, was not able to offer much help. And no one seemed to be able to tell the Branches what would happen with the social worker's report.

Dale, 38, who works for a cold storage company and aspires to be a firefighter, wondered if the report would show up somehow in background checks. And what if years from now someone asks the Branches, "Have you ever been investigated for child abuse?" The only honest answer is yes.

Several forces were at work to turn what some saw as an obvious medical condition into an ominous sign of abuse. Anyone who works at a school is a "mandated reporter," required by law to report suspicions of child abuse to the authorities. Failure to do so can result in criminal charges. This mandate can create a hyper-vigilance on the part of some school employees. "If I were a parent," said Howard Friedman, Los Angeles Unified School District assistant general counsel, "I would be absolutely incensed that this happened to me. But if you stand back objectively, I guess you say we look for the best interest of the child...[But] there is a pretty fair paranoia level [on the part of the district personnel]."

From talking with Christie and the social worker, the Branches were able to piece together what probably had occurred. On Feb. 2 [1995], Christie fell while jumping rope at her Granada Hills school, scraping her knee and her head. In the office, someone must have noticed the rash on the back of her legs. Christie told her parents that someone asked, "Does your Daddy spank you here?" The Branches think she dredged up a memory: A year ago, after Christie poked her little sister, Taylor, in the eye with a straw, her dad smacked her on the bottom with the back of his hand and sent her to her room for a time out.

"Yes," she must have replied. Which is probably how the deputy and the social worker came to be on the Branch's porch that night.

These are some of the things the Branches said they have been told by a variety of authorities:

- You cannot see the DCFS report.
- The record stays in DCFS computers indefinitely.
- You cannot have anything in writing that says the suspicion of abuse was unfounded.
- There is a school district registry where abuse allegations are listed.
- You are protected from anyone learning about this information by confidentiality laws.

This is what I learned by making a few calls:

A social worker who answered the phone in the Santa Clarita office of the DCFS (where Anita Branch went to ask questions) told me that "if a report is unfounded, there is nothing to give the parents." (She suggested parents should try to get the police report, which, she added, "would be easier to get" than anything from DCFS.) Not so, said Bill Garcia, the DCFS deputy regional administrator who runs the Child Abuse Hot Line. Parents have the right to know what was reported about their children. And according to DCFS spokesman Schuyler Sprowles, parents have the right to submit a request in writing to their social worker for a form letter called "Notice of Case Closure" stating that a case has been closed because "the allegation of child abuse or neglect was either unsubstantiated or unfounded."

Garcia said that the DCFS, which investigates 7,000 families a month, is required by law to keep case records on file for five years. He said cases deemed "unfounded" are officially closed soon after the paperwork is complete and then put into storage. Friedman, the LAUSD [Los Angeles Unified School District] attorney, said the district

(Continued)

Exhibit 21-2 (*Continued*)

does not maintain any registry of abuse cases. But there is a child abuse office that deals with training employees and advising schools on their legal responsibilities. He said mandated reporters are encouraged—but not required—to provide copies of suspected abuse reports to that office. (An employee in that office told me that the reports are not followed up, and that they are confidential and can be released only if they are subpoenaed.) Promises of confidentiality, though, are hard to keep. This is what keeps the Branches up nights. Indeed, said Sprowles of the DCFS: "These things are confidential and we realize that…things leak out." Friedman said he has seen cases where the identities of mandated reporters, who are legally entitled to anonymity, have been inadvertently revealed. "It is a tremendous dilemma," Friedman said. "You err on the side of protection of kids, but it creates enormous amounts of stress and pressure for everyone involved."

In any case, no one offered the Branches any of this information. They have hired an attorney and are contemplating a lawsuit against the district. The Branches are coping. Sort of. They are in therapy. Anita is afraid to brush 3-year-old Taylor's hair because Taylor screams and Anita is afraid someone will hear. (Could tangled hair signal neglect?) A couple of weeks ago, Taylor pushed Christie into a wall while they were playing and Christie got a bruise on her head. The Branches were terrified. Should they keep her home from school? Anita ended up writing notes for Christie to give to her teacher, her principal and the after-school daycare workers. These days, the Branches are less inclined to let Christie's friends play at their house. "What if they fell and got bruised?" Anita asks. "Can you imagine? Every little bump and bruise I am so paranoid. But that is what I think I need to do. I think the laws need to be changed. It's not common sense to report a rash. The law protects people from using their common sense."

It is true that, in cases such as this, the reporting system errs on the side of protecting children. But in the case of unfounded suspicions, there ought to be some centralized place—a pamphlet, maybe?—disclosing to parents where the information goes, which agencies get the information, which offices receive the reports, how parents can get copies and how they can prove they were exonerated. That's not such a huge request. Surely, it is possible to protect children while treating their parents with dignity and respect.

Note. All names in this exhibit are true.
Source: Adapted from pp. E1, E2. Copyright © 1995, *Los Angeles Times.* Reprinted by permission. "Yes, Abuse Claims Must Be Investigated …But Then What?", April 16, 1995. By Robin Abcarian.

*I asked you for help
and you gave me a doctor
with cold metal gadgets and cold hands
who spread my legs and stared, just like my father.
He said I looked fine—
good news for me, you said, bad news for my "case."
I asked you for confidentiality
and you let the newspapers get my story.
I asked for protection, you gave me a social worker
who patted my head and called me "Honey"
(mostly because she could never remember my name).
She sent me to live with strangers
in another place, with a different school.
I lost my part in the school play and the science fair
while he and the others all got to stay home.*

*Do you know what it's like to live
where there's a lock on the refrigerator,
where you have to ask permission to use the shampoo,
and where you can't use the phone to call your friends?
You get used to hearing, "Hi, I'm your new social worker,
this is your new foster sister, dorm mother, group home."
You tiptoe around like a perpetual guest
and don't even get to see your own puppy grow up.
Do you know what it's like to have more social workers
than friends?*

*Do you know what it feels like
to be the one that everyone blames for all the trouble?
Even when they were speaking to me,
all they talked about was lawyers, shrinks, fees,
and whether or not they'll lose the mortgage.
Do you know what it is like when your sisters hate you
and your brother calls you a liar?
It's my word against my own father's.
I'm twelve years old
and he's the manager of a bank.
You say you believe me—
who cares, if nobody else does.*

*I asked you for help
and you forced my Mom to choose between us—
She chose him, of course.
She was scared and had a lot to lose.
I had a lot to lose too, the difference was,
you never told me how much.
I asked you to put an end to the abuse—
you put an end to my whole family.
You took away my nights of hell
and gave me days of hell instead.
You've exchanged my private nightmare
for a very public one.*

—Cindy, age 12

Cindy's feelings were put into words by Kee MacFarlane (1970, reprinted, with permission of Kee MacFarlane).

The criticisms that have arisen about the Child Abuse Prevention and Treatment Act indicate that professionals working in Child Protective Services and law enforcement (a) must be careful to be responsible but not become overzealous, (b) must know their roles and responsibilities, and (c) must remain accountable to the public. Ways must be found to protect children from maltreatment without intruding on the welfare and rights of individuals.

To this end, the following recommendations for Child Protective Services are useful (Wilson & Steppe, 1994, pp. 67–68, with changes in notation):

1. *Constant and critical internal evaluation.* Child protection administrators must constantly review their training, policy, procedures, supervisory practices, and the nature of their organizational cultures. When CPS is charged with abusing its authority, it is essential to examine the allegation objectively and to face problems head on.

2. *Do not become defensive in the face of criticism.* Respond to criticism in a nondefensive manner. The first rule for swimming with sharks is: Don't bleed. When administrators react defensively to criticism, critics are empowered. By contrast, a calm, objective response minimizes damage. Complaints about training, workload, and performance can be used to garner needed resources.

3. *Policy analysis.* Administrators must guard against "one size fits all" decision making in Child Protective Services. Large bureaucracies often function with strict rules and regulations. However, rigidity can seriously damage child welfare practice, which must operate in a dynamic, ever-changing environment. In child protection the answers are seldom clear-cut. Rather, there are degrees of right and wrong. Child protection workers are required to balance many competing interests, including family preservation versus child protection, parental rights versus child rights, and family privacy versus the need to ask questions. To perform well in the pressure cooker that is child protection, staff must have clear job performance expectations, policy guidance, adequate and ongoing training, objective and supportive supervision, and the freedom to exercise professional judgment. Administrators can structure the decision-making environment, but professionals must ultimately make the difficult decisions.

4. *Support.* CPS judgments cannot be error free, and when mistakes happen staff must understand in advance that they will be supported professionally and personally. Support is most critical when a child dies or is seriously injured. At this tragic moment everyone looks for someone to blame, and the professional responsible for the case deserves and needs support.

5. *Child protection decisions must be based on risk assessment.* Children live in a wide variety of undesirable circumstances ranging from serious poverty and violent neighborhoods to inadequate or inattentive parenting. CPS must not confuse poverty with neglect, discipline with abuse, or less than ideal parenting with maltreatment. Rather, CPS must determine what places a child at risk and how serious the risk is.

6. *Child protection should guarantee alleged perpetrators the protections of due process.* If CPS removes a child from the home or takes other action that adversely affects the rights of an adult, the alleged perpetrator should have a forum *within* CPS to challenge the decision. Conversely, if an accused individual's identity is not made public, and if the individual is not otherwise harmed by a CPS decision, there is little reason to establish a cumbersome bureaucracy within CPS to ensure that everyone involved has an opportunity for a hearing. Such systems push the concept of "due process" to unnecessary limits and drain valuable resources away from protecting children.

An ideal child-oriented child protection system might have the following features (Thompson, 1993, pp. 107–110, with changes in notation):

1. There would be a focus on remedial and treatment efforts that restore the child's functioning to age-appropriate norms and alleviate the consequences of earlier abuse or neglect.
2. There would be respect for the child's family, recognizing the importance of the emotional ties that bind children to family members, even when they are abusive.
3. There would be supportive assistance provided to children and families throughout the various phases of investigation, prosecution, treatment, and remediation. For example, child advocates would accompany the child throughout the various phases of case planning and disposition, informing the child of decisions that have been made and their implications, helping the child anticipate future events, soliciting the child's own preferences and opinions concerning case planning, and communicating the child's views to social service and legal personnel. A special investigative unit within the police or county attorney's office would include well-trained personnel who specialize in investigating child abuse allegations and who would also assist in interviewing children with sensitivity to the child's experience and developmental needs.
4. There would be a recognition that maltreated children are often multiproblem children who each possess a rather unique constellation of vulnerabilities and resiliency owing to their developmental level, intrinsic capabilities, and experiential history. They come to child protection agencies, not only with a history of abuse or neglect, but also often with mental illness, learning disabilities, attention-deficit/hyperactivity disorder, behavioral problems, and other challenges. Moreover, the resources and supports within the family and neighborhood ecology that children can draw upon also are likely to be unique. An individualized treatment, educational, and remediation plan recognizes this, but incorporating this awareness of

individualized needs and resources throughout the system is perhaps the greatest challenge of reforming current child protection efforts.

Finally, Finkelhor (1993) has the following to say about the child welfare system.

[It] needs to do a far better job, not just of detecting child abuse, but of protecting the children who are discovered to be at risk. This means, providing support services for parents, respite care, good foster homes, counseling for parents and children, financial aid, and social work assistance to deal with the crises that put families on the brink of abuse and neglect. If we have nothing to offer when abuse is reported, it is silly to argue about whether we are reporting too little or too much. And if we are truly offering help, rather than stigma, blame, and punishment, what would there be to complain about? (p. 285)

Ultimately, what may most determine the fate of the backlash [against the child protection movement] is not simply rebuttal, but how the child welfare movement responds to what is valid and plausible in the backlash critique. If child advocates improve the quality of investigations, provide more rights for parents reported for abuse, and make other changes, they may deprive the backlash of much of its agenda. Such self-scrutiny and reform should be relatively easy for a movement in as secure a position as the child protection movement is today [1994].

—David Finkelhor

THINKING THROUGH THE ISSUES

How do you think a 5-year-old, an 8-year-old, a 12-year-old, or a 15-year-old would feel if she or he were sexually abused by a family member? What might lead each of them to disclose the abuse?

Do you know anyone who has been maltreated? If so, what was the maltreatment, and how did it affect this person and his or her family?

Do you think that you would be able to know whether a child was lying about an allegation of child maltreatment? What is the basis for your answer?

If you had suspicions that the child was lying, what would you do? What questions would you ask?

Why do you think some children have psychological symptoms as a result of being sexually abused and other children do not have such symptoms? How might children who do not show symptoms react later in life to the sexual abuse they experienced as children?

Should a parent who knowingly allowed or witnessed child maltreatment in his or her home and didn't do anything to stop it (or didn't report it) also be considered guilty? What is the basis for your answer?

Why do you think a parent allows his or her child to be maltreated in the home without doing anything about it?

Do you believe that a nonoffending female parent may be partially responsible for the sexual abuse (in cases of incest) because of her failure to meet the male parent's sexual needs? Do you then partially excuse the offender's actions?

Do you agree with the San Diego County Grand Jury's report that the Child Abuse Prevention and Treatment Act has led to national hysteria? What is the basis for your answer?

SUMMARY

Process of Disclosure of Maltreatment

1. The dilemma faced by children who have been maltreated by their caregivers is that they are almost completely dependent on their caregivers for survival, especially if they are young.
2. Children who have been maltreated may fear retribution and violence because abusers may have threatened to hurt or punish them; not being believed; being blamed for the abusive acts; rejection, humiliation, embarrassment, or social stigmatization by peers, neighbors, and school personnel; loss of friends; being abandoned or rejected by their family; and that they lack the skills to communicate the maltreatment effectively.
3. If children do report the maltreatment, they still may not want to testify in court.
4. Some parents will not allow their children to testify in court because of the chance of additional trauma.
5. Children may not want to disclose the maltreatment because of fear that their families will be tarnished by the scandal, that they will be responsible for any destructive actions—such as suicide—committed by the abusers, or that the disclosure will lead to the disintegration of their families.
6. In the case of sexual abuse, young children may not disclose the abuse because they are unaware that sexual activity between an adult and a child is wrong.
7. Adolescents are more likely to disclose sexual abuse than are young children.
8. Abusers may resist disclosing their role in maltreatment for fear of prosecution and imprisonment; loss of reputation and stigma; loss of job or professional license; rejection by partner, divorce, and loss of family; loss of support from relatives; and loneliness and isolation. They also may fear that if the maltreatment is disclosed they will want to commit suicide.
9. If the maltreatment is disclosed, abusers may rationalize or minimize the maltreatment, experience low self-esteem and consider their actions as the lowest form of behavior, experience significant depression, feel no guilt at all, exhibit paranoia and feelings of persecution, deny that the maltreatment occurred, blame the allegation on someone else, say that they believe the abuse occurred but adamantly deny that they perpetrated it, believe that their actions were appropriate and were provoked by the children's behavior, or show irrational reasoning or behavior.
10. The nonoffending parent may deny that the child is being maltreated because he or she fears loss of a partner and the family breadwinner, loneliness and isolation, stigmatization and the loss of self-esteem, becoming a single parent, the effects the disclosure will have on his or her work and professional career, and loss of social support.
11. The nonoffending parent may become jealous of the sexually abused child for taking her or his role in the family; feel anger

at herself or himself for not protecting the child; feel helpless in not knowing what is going to happen to her or his child and fear that the child may be taken away; feel invisible because most of the attention is on substantiating the allegation of maltreatment; feel shock, numbness, and repulsion, brought about, in part, by memories of her or his own prior victimization; experience guilt and self-blame because she or he assumes total responsibility for everything that happens to the child; feel hurt and betrayal on several counts, including grief over the loss of the child's innocence in cases of sexual abuse and over the loss of a spouse if the spouse was the perpetrator; experience feelings of sexual inadequacy and rejection if the spouse sexually abused the child, because she or he thinks that the abuse might not have occurred if marital sex had been more satisfactory; have financial concerns about the family income if the spouse was the abuser and may no longer contribute to the family income; and blame the victim.

12. Children who disclose that they were maltreated may not be believed.

13. If the maltreatment is disclosed but not proven, children may be scapegoated or blamed for all family problems, rejected and punished by the family, and even abused more harshly. In these situations, children need to be monitored closely and protected.

Effects of Child Maltreatment

14. Physical abuse may have devastating effects on a child. The damage inflicted on the child can range from mild bruises to death.

15. Child Protective Services workers, health care providers, and law enforcement personnel need to be especially alert to children's injuries that are unexplained or that do not make sense, to multiple injuries that are in various stages of healing, to evidence of long bone fractures in infants less than 1 year old, and to repeated visits to the emergency rooms of hospitals.

16. A strong suspicion of child maltreatment should be entertained when there are unusual or suspicious patterns of physical abuse or neglect or when there are physical injuries that cannot be associated with accidents, illnesses, or natural disasters, with actions taken by the child, or with signs of neglect that are not ordinarily seen in children.

17. Children who have been physically abused may show behavioral problems, emotional disturbance, and inappropriate social responses.

18. Children involved in sexual abuse may experience conflicting sensations. For some, the sexual abuse may be frightening and painful, but, for others, it may be sexually arousing.

19. When children accommodate to sexual abuse, they may develop feelings of guilt and question their self-worth.

20. Children who have been sexually abused may have physical signs of the abuse. Most of the physical signs are associated with the genital region or with other areas of the body that may be involved in sexual activity, such as the mouth and buttocks. However, the majority of children who have been sexually abused show no physical or medical evidence of abuse—absence of findings is the rule rather than the exception.

21. Children who have been sexually abused, like those who have been physically abused, may show behavioral problems, emotional disturbance, and inappropriate social responses.

22. Children who have been sexually abused may prematurely and inappropriately learn about sex.

23. Children who have been sexually abused may later discover that society views some acts they performed in the context of a trusting relationship as reprehensible and that the adult they trusted was selfishly motivated.

24. Children who have been sexually abused may experience anxiety because of the furtive quality of the activity and the fear of being blamed if discovered.

25. Children who have been sexually abused may develop a negative self-image.

26. Children who have been sexually abused may feel powerless when someone coerces them by force, threat, or deceit to submit to sexual acts.

27. Studies of adult survivors of childhood sexual abuse indicate that they have adjustment difficulties that include depressive symptoms, anxiety, poor social adjustment, parenting difficulties, substance abuse, suicidal ideation and suicide attempts, revictimization, and problems with sexuality, including fear of sex, low interest in sex, less sexual pleasure, several sexual partners, more compulsive sexual behavior, and more homosexual experiences.

28. When adult women who were sexually abused as children were asked to comment on the most traumatic aspects of the abuse, they spoke about abandonment, powerlessness, threats of violence, physical injury, loss of childhood, devalued sexuality, betrayal, guilt and shame, and loss of self.

29. Children who have been sexually abused are at risk for getting a sexually transmitted disease, such as syphilis, gonorrhea, chlamydia, genital or anorectal herpes and warts, or the Human Immunodeficiency Virus (HIV).

30. A review of 45 studies of sexually abused children, who ranged in age from preschoolers to adolescents, indicates that there is no one symptom pattern characteristic of all children who have been sexually abused.

31. The research showed that the symptoms that occur most frequently among sexually abused children are fears, posttraumatic stress disorder reactions, behavioral problems, sexualized behaviors, and poor self-esteem.

32. The research showed that no clinically observed symptoms were present in approximately one-third of the sexually abused children.

33. The research showed that children had more symptoms when the following factors were involved: sexual acts that included oral, anal, or vaginal penetration; high frequency of sexual contact; long duration of the abuse; use of force; a close relationship between the child and the perpetrator; lack of maternal support at the time of the disclosure; and a negative outlook or coping style on the part of the child.

34. The research also showed that the child's age at onset of the sexual abuse, the number of perpetrators, and the time that elapsed between the end of the abuse and the assessment were not clearly related to the presence of symptoms. About two-thirds of the sexually abused children showed recovery 12 to 18 months after the sexual abuse stopped.

35. The research indicated that there is no specific syndrome in children who have been sexually abused and no single traumatizing process. However, the two symptoms that appear to distinguish sexually abused children from children in other clinical groups are (a) sexualized behavior and (b) symptoms of posttraumatic stress disorder.

36. The PTSD model is not necessarily the most appropriate model to account for the symptoms of child sexual abuse.

37. Emotional abuse may lead to problems in learning, problems in relationships, unusual behaviors and feelings, unhappiness or depression, and fears and physical symptoms.

38. The impact of the maltreatment may depend on the developmental tasks or developmentally critical periods children are facing at the time of maltreatment, the specific cognitive abilities that affect their appraisal of the maltreatment, and the forms of symptom expression available to children at their developmental stage.

39. Families vary in the support they give to the maltreated child.

40. Nonoffending mothers, when they learn that their child was sexually abused, may experience shock, stigmatization, powerlessness, betrayal, and traumatic sexualization.

41. When a child has been sexually violated, the parents may be concerned about whether their child caught a sexually transmitted disease, how to prevent future violations, how protective they should be of the child, how much damage was done to the child, and how soon the child will recover and resume normal activities.

42. In the interview, allow the parents to discuss their concerns (including psychological, legal, medical, and sexual concerns), and especially allow them to express their feelings, including any ambivalent ones.

43. Answer the parents' questions to the best of your ability and try to obtain answers to questions for which you have no answer, but do not give legal advice.

44. Evaluate how the family members cope with the victim of the maltreatment.

Children's Memory, Lying, and Suggestibility

45. Children's memory will be facilitated by long exposures to and many repetitions of the event.

46. Children will have a better memory of the event when they participate in the event than when they observe the event.

47. In comparison with older children, young children (under 5 years of age) have less efficient information-processing skills (such as speed of encoding and retrieving material) with which to recall events.

48. Children will have difficulty encoding events verbally when they do not possess the necessary language skills to describe the event or a framework for interpreting the event (including knowledge of details and the social implications of the event).

49. Complex events are more difficult for children to remember than simple events.

50. Some intervening events can strengthen children's memory, whereas other intervening events can interfere with their memory.

51. Children between the ages of 3 and 6 years are able to give coherent, detailed accounts of past events even after long delays. However, their recounts are likely to be highly inconsistent on different recall occasions.

52. When children have difficulty remembering some details of an event, it may simply mean that the details were not entered into their memory; it may not indicate a failure in retrieving information.

53. Children will be more accurate in their reports of an event when interviewed shortly after the occurrence of the event because their memories are even more likely than those of adults to fade rapidly.

54. When there is a long delay between the event and the interview, children may embellish or modify their report; consequently, some of the information they give is not stored in memory.

55. Repeated questions from different interviewers—such as parents, social workers, nurses, and police officers—may alter children's memory, even if these individuals did not intend to mislead the children.

56. Statements made spontaneously by children are likely to be more accurate than those made after repeated questioning.

57. The processes of psychotherapy, designed to help victims come to grips with a traumatic experience, may alter their memory of the event.

58. Stress may affect children's memory of an event, but, at present, research is not clear about whether stress interferes with or facilitates memory.

59. Young children are more suggestible than older children, especially when interviewers try to influence them to say certain things.

60. Children may alter statements because they think the interviewer is dissatisfied with the initial report or because they do not understand the questions.

61. Extended discussions about an event with children before an interview may influence their recall of the event; in such instances, children's recall can be contaminated.

62. Children's language ability affects their ability to recall information in response to questions. Children will not be able to retrieve information if they fail to understand questions or if they understand words in a way that differs from that intended by the interviewer.

63. Children may give little information because they think the interviewer already has knowledge of the event in question.

64. When there is more than one interview, children, like adults, may change their report because of changes in context.

65. Consider several factors when you interview children who may have been maltreated, such as number of events; length of event(s); whether the child was a participant or observer; length of time between the event and the reporting of the event; child's age, developmental level, and intellectual ability; child's ability to encode and retrieve information; child's knowledge of anatomy (in cases of sexual abuse or physical abuse); child's prior exposure to sexual information; child's communication ability; pressure exerted on the child by peers or adults; circumstances surrounding the initial report; effects of repeated questioning on the child's reports; and the social context of the interview.

66. Survivors of child sexual abuse in some cases may forget or repress memories of the abusive event or events and in other cases may recall incidents not based on actual events.

67. To reduce the risk of creating illusory memories, psychotherapists should keep an open mind about what might have caused the client's problems, limit the use of highly suggestive techniques or techniques that provoke false memories, and keep up with contemporary memory research.

68. It is not easy to determine whether a child (or any person) is telling the truth.

69. Experts have no more ability than laypersons to judge with certainty whether someone is lying based on the interview alone.

70. You should entertain the possibility that a child is lying when the child has a history of persistent lying, the child has a psychological disorder that would severely alter his or her perception of reality, the child is anxious about being caught in a lie,

the child has possible motives for lying, the child's symptoms are not consistent with a well-recognized psychiatric or medical disorder, the child has made inconsistent statements in the past or made statements not verified by the reports of others, the child has been rewarded for lying, or the child has been told that he or she will be punished for telling the truth.

71. Children may lie by omitting or denying events that did happen.

72. If you believe that a child has lied, consider the reason for the lie—that is, whether the lie is deliberate, a result of faulty memory, or an honest difference of opinion.

73. The more censure children anticipate for telling the truth, the less likely they are to tell the truth.

74. Attending carefully to the way the child presents information about the maltreatment may give you clues about the truthfulness of the disclosure or about whether the child is withholding information.

75. Preschool children are more suggestible than either school-aged children or adults.

76. Children will sometimes lie when it serves some purpose; in this sense, they are probably no different from adults.

77. Young children can recollect information that they observed accurately, and much of this information is forensically important. However, in comparison with older children, younger children do not recall as much information, and their reports are more vulnerable to distortion.

78. In evaluating the credibility of a young child's report of a criminal event, examine the conditions under which the child gave the original report.

Allegations of Child Maltreatment

79. Allegations of child maltreatment made by children or by adults present a thorny problem for those who investigate the allegations.

80. Assessing the validity of allegations of child maltreatment is difficult because there may be limited or no physical evidence; young children may have difficulty describing the maltreatment; children may forget important details or may have difficulty describing the maltreatment if there is a long interval between the maltreatment and the report; evidence of maltreatment may be lost if a medical examination has been delayed; there were probably no eyewitnesses if the maltreatment was done privately; children may not want to say anything that can get a parent or other relative in trouble; and the findings of different professionals may not be consistent.

81. There are no firm statistics on the rate of false allegations of child maltreatment; much depends on how false allegations are defined.

82. A reasonable estimate of the rate of intentionally false allegations is 4% of reports.

83. There is a higher rate of false reports of child maltreatment in families undergoing custody disputes than in families in which custody of children is not an issue, although the overall rate appears to be low.

84. You need to be alert to the possibility of intentionally false allegations, even though the rate of such reports is low.

85. You need to be equally alert to the possibility that children may be withholding information.

86. What is even more critical is that each allegation of child maltreatment be carefully assessed, regardless of how the allegation arose.

87. No allegation of child maltreatment should be ignored.

88. Ignoring allegations of child maltreatment, or failing to prove allegations of maltreatment when they are true, may lead to continued abuse or neglect and possibly to the deaths of children.

Comment on the Federal Child Abuse Prevention and Treatment Act

89. The Federal Child Abuse Prevention and Treatment Act, designed to protect children and enacted into law in good faith by the U.S. government, may have had unintended consequences, such as increasing the number of alleged child maltreatment reports, fueling "sex abuse hysteria," and creating a "child maltreatment establishment" composed of mental health professionals, law enforcement personnel, and medical personnel.

90. Inta Sellers said that the Child Abuse Prevention and Treatment Act never supported frivolous accusations but was and is solely intended to protect children.

91. Once someone reports a suspicion of child maltreatment to the appropriate authorities, the report may set off a chain of events that can have devastating effects on the child and family.

92. The criticisms that have arisen about the Child Abuse Prevention and Treatment Act indicate that professionals working in Child Protective Services and law enforcement must be careful to be responsible but not become overzealous, must know their roles and responsibilities, and must remain accountable to the public.

93. Ways must be found to protect children from maltreatment without intruding on the welfare and rights of individuals.

KEY TERMS, CONCEPTS, AND NAMES

Maltreated child's fear of disclosure of maltreatment (p. 719)
Abuser's fear of disclosure of maltreatment (p. 719)
Nonoffending parent's fear of disclosure of maltreatment (p. 720)
Failure to believe the child (p. 720)
Effects of physical abuse and neglect on children (p. 721)
Effects of sexual abuse on children (p. 721)
Long-term sequelae of child sexual abuse (p. 728)
Sexually transmitted diseases and child sexual abuse (p. 729)
Posttraumatic stress disorder symptoms and child sexual abuse (p. 730)
Effects of emotional abuse on children (p. 730)
Developmental considerations related to child maltreatment (p. 731)
Effects of child maltreatment on the family (p. 731)
Supportive family (p. 731)
Intermittently supportive family (p. 731)
Nonsupportive family (p. 731)
Dysfunctional coping methods (p. 733)
Patronization (p. 733)
Distraction (p. 733)
Protective silence (p. 733)
Functional coping methods (p. 733)
Open pattern of communication (p. 733)
Directing anger and blame at the offender (p. 733)
Role flexibility (p. 733)
Use of family-oriented support services (p. 733)
Children's memory (p. 733)

STUDY QUESTIONS

1. Discuss the process of disclosure of child maltreatment. In your discussion, comment on the child's fear of disclosure, the abuser's fear of disclosure, and the nonoffending parent's fear of disclosure.
2. Discuss how physical abuse and neglect may affect children.
3. Discuss how sexual abuse may affect children. Include in your discussion children's accommodation to child sexual abuse, physical injuries associated with child sexual abuse, behavioral and emotional problems associated with child sexual abuse, long-term sequelae of child sexual abuse, sexually transmitted diseases associated with child sexual abuse, empirical studies on the impact of child sexual abuse, and the appropriateness of the posttraumatic stress disorder symptom model to account for child sexual abuse.
4. Discuss developmental considerations related to child maltreatment.
5. Discuss how child maltreatment may affect the family. Include in your discussion a continuum of family support and effects on the family members.
6. What do we know about children's language ability, memory, suggestibility, and lying as related to their ability to give accurate information in cases of child maltreatment and in other forensic areas?
7. Why are allegations of child maltreatment such a thorny problem for mental health workers? Provide several illustrations in your discussion.

22

INTERVIEWING CONSIDERATIONS IN CASES OF CHILD MALTREATMENT

All happy families resemble one another, but each unhappy family is unhappy in its own way.

—Leo Tolstoy

Goals and Objectives

This chapter is designed to enable you to:

- Learn about the preparations needed to interview the child in cases of child maltreatment
- Conduct effective interviews with children, parents, alleged offenders, and known offenders in cases of child maltreatment
- Recognize pitfalls in child maltreatment interviewing
- Learn procedures for interviewing families in cases of child maltreatment
- Learn procedures for interviewing the alleged or known offender in cases of child maltreatment

Interviewing children at risk and parents of children at risk is not an area about which professionals can afford to be complacent. It is more like a mine field: one enters at one's own risk.

—Pittu Laungani

Chapters 20 and 21 presented background information on child maltreatment. This chapter and Chapter 23 are designed for those of you who conduct or are in training to conduct investigatory interviews. Investigatory interviews are usually conducted by Child Protective Services workers (or workers in the Department of Social Services or similar agencies) or law enforcement personnel. This chapter focuses on interviewing children who have been maltreated or who are alleged to have been maltreated, on interviewing their families, and on interviewing the alleged or known offender. Interviewing in cases of child maltreatment is especially challenging because it involves topics usually considered taboo and because it may lead to criminal charges. In addition, young children may not be able to describe the details of the maltreatment clearly, and their families and the alleged offender will likely be reluctant to talk about the maltreatment.

The initial interview in cases of child maltreatment often is not only an information-gathering interview but also an investigative interview. Do not assume the role of a therapist when you are conducting the initial interview—*keep the roles of investigator and therapist completely separate.*

Child maltreatment interviewing will require knowledge of the types of child maltreatment, state laws concerning child maltreatment, law enforcement investigative procedures, available placement facilities in the community, and medical, psychological, and psychiatric evaluative procedures. Chapter 23 discusses how to evaluate the information obtained in the child maltreatment interview.

Two separate organizations are usually involved in child maltreatment investigations: (a) Child Protective Services (or a similar social service agency) and (b) a law enforcement agency (usually a police or sheriff's department). The standards of proof differ in these two organizations. Child Protective Services, whose role is to protect children, makes its decisions on *clear and convincing evidence,* whereas law enforcement, whose role is to uphold laws and protect public safety, aims to obtain a more stringent level of proof—*proof beyond a reasonable doubt.* However, the standard for opening a case is similar in the two systems—*probable cause* or *some credible evidence.*

The following case illustrates some problems in uncovering child maltreatment (Cohen & Mannarino, 1991). As you read the case, consider the following issues: What finally led to the girls' disclosure? What role did the mother play? How did the maltreatment affect the relationship between the girls? What effect will the sexual molestation have on the girls' future adjustment? What other issues does this case raise?

CASE 22-1. ANN AND MARIE

Ann and Marie were sisters, aged 14 and 13, respectively, who were brought for an evaluation by their mother because of the girls' disclosure of sexual abuse by their natural father. The girls were living with their mother (a college-educated housewife) and their 18-year-old sister, Michele. The father, a Protestant minister, had lived with them until his arrest a few weeks prior to evaluation.

Ann had first attempted to tell her mother about the sexual abuse 2 years previously. She did this by asking her mother, "Do you know what sexual abuse is?" The mother apparently did not make anything of Ann's question and did not pursue the subject at that time. Ann let the matter drop. The following year, Marie disclosed the sexual abuse to a counselor at a church camp. Child Protective Services was called to investigate, but Ann was very angry at Marie for telling someone at camp (partly because it was affiliated with the father's church). Consequently, Ann refused to talk to the case-worker. In an attempt to lessen Ann's anger at her, Marie also refused to talk to the worker. Because the girls would not speak to the investigator, the report was not verifiable. Apparently, the mother did not question the girls as to whether they had been maltreated or why Marie had disclosed it. She did, however, confront the father, who was already in individual therapy for treatment of work-related stress. The mother went with the father to see the father's therapist, and he did admit to "inappropriate love and affection" for both girls. (It should be noted that this was the first time his therapist learned about this, after 5 years of ongoing psychotherapy.) Shortly thereafter, the father called the children into his room and, in his wife's presence, praised Marie for her disclosure and apologized for his behavior. He promised it would never happen again, and the mother assumed that it would not.

However, in the last several months, the mother had noted that Marie was frequently fighting with her father and seemed to feel a great deal of hostility toward him. For this reason, the mother brought Marie to a private therapist for individual treatment. During the evaluation by this therapist, Marie again disclosed ongoing sexual abuse by her father. Child Protective Services was called, and this time Marie described the abuse to the investigators. The father was arrested, and both Ann and Marie were referred to our clinic for treatment.

Apparently, abuse of both girls began at about the same time, when Ann was 5 years old and Marie was 4 years old. Each girl was evaluated individually. Ann appeared to be an attractive, well-developed, articulate adolescent. She felt ambivalent about Marie's disclosure, expressing both relief that her father would get some help and anger that Marie had gotten him into trouble by disclosing the abuse.

Ann reported that, most commonly, her father would fondle her breasts and between her legs. At different stages of her life, he would perform different sexual acts on her, which she and Marie would discuss on occasion. The most extensive abuse Ann experienced was what the girls called the "full treatment." This consisted of the father's undressing her, fondling her, and lying down in bed with her back to his chest. He would roll her around his genital area and touch her on her breasts and vaginal area. During the course of the interview, Ann related many incidents of this type being perpetrated against her, almost on a weekly basis during certain periods of her life. She could remember one of many trips out of town with the family, when the mother slept with Michele in one room, and the father slept with Ann and Marie in another room. She stated that while they were sleeping together in the same bed, he attempted to fondle her once again. She asked him to stop and he did. He asked her if she wanted to go in with her mother and she replied yes. Ann related that she felt guilty that she went into the other room with her mother and left Marie alone with her father. She stated that she always knew that the abuse was wrong but did not know how to stop it at the time.

The abuse continued on a regular basis with Ann stating that frequently she would see her father entering Marie's bedroom and would know the abuse was occurring. On several occasions, she attempted to stop her father from abusing Marie by entering the room and beginning a conversation. In her estimation, she was never able to ask him to stop abusing Marie or herself until the first disclosure. Ann stated that she believed that she had given her mother many hints that the abuse was occurring. When she went to her mother and asked her, "Do you know what sexual abuse is?" Ann thought that this should have been a sufficient hint for her mother, but it apparently was not. After the first disclosure, with her father apologizing to her and Marie, she thought that the abuse would no longer continue. Even when he would still attempt to enter her bedroom and give her back rubs, which resulted in his hands moving to her chest, she was able to say no, but she knew in her heart that the abuse was continuing with Marie. She was angry at Marie for disclosing the abuse at camp and believed that it threatened the family. She was "trying to be so good for Mom" so as not to add any additional emotional burdens on her mother. She was unsure that her mother would be able to handle the family without her husband and felt guilty about having "wrecked" their marriage. She said that she needed help to discuss feeling "dirty" about what had happened and what effect this would have on future relationships with the opposite sex. She also was able to express some anger at Marie for acting-out emotionally when she herself was trying to be so good and hold the family together.

Ann expressed fear that Michele, her 18-year-old sister, would be angry at her, although Michele had expressed support for her. What she dreaded the most was having to go to court and face everyone and discuss what had happened to her. She believed that everyone would be looking at her, thinking about the abuse that had been perpetrated against her, and that this made her feel "dirty." She was somewhat angry at her father but expressed more sorrow for him, stating that he "must have problems" and that "he is a sick man." Ann denied any suicidal thoughts or ideation. She reported being sad, angry, and confused and believed strongly that she needed to talk to somebody about this. She thought that her mother was torn between her daughters and her husband and worried about the outcome of their relationship and their marriage.

Marie also was evaluated individually. Like her sister Ann, Marie was attractive, intelligent, and articulate. She was tearful during most of the interview. Marie described the same type of fondling as Ann and also said that she and her sister occasionally discussed the abuse with each other. As Marie got older, the father would perform oral sex on her as well. In describing this, Marie became quite tearful and felt guilty and dirty because of this particular abuse. She wondered if it was her fault and if she should be blamed for not stopping her father sooner. She was angry at him but also sad that he had lost his wife, children, and possibly his job over this disclosure. She also was fearful that he would go to jail and wondered what would become of her mother and the family. She reported difficulty concentrating in school and some sleep disturbance. It took several hours for her to fall asleep at night, and frequently she would awake in the middle of the night or early in the morning. She reported constant sadness and frequent tearfulness since the disclosure as well.

Marie was extremely angry that her father continued to abuse her (and not Ann) even after he promised to stop. She said this was why she began fighting and being noncompliant with her father in the last several months. She was relieved and glad that she had at last followed through on disclosing the abuse, because this would finally make it stop. (pp. 173–175, with changes in notation and with permission of Plenum, from J. A. Cohen and A. P. Mannarino, 1991. "Case of Ann." In R. T. Ammerman and M. Hersen [Eds.], *Case Studies in Family Violence*)

This case illustrates some important elements that may be found in cases of child maltreatment. On the part of the maltreated children, these elements include difficulty in disclosing information, loyalty to the abuser, protecting the sovereignty of the family and failing to disclose the maltreatment in order to keep the family together, feeling powerless about the abusive acts, feeling guilty, protecting siblings, letting siblings substitute for them in the sexual acts, and having conflict with other siblings over disclosure. Other features commonly found in child maltreatment cases are complicity of one parent, efforts by the abuser to keep information from a therapist, and broken promises on the part of the abuser. The presence of any one of these elements may make collection of accurate information difficult in cases of child maltreatment.

A MODEL FOR INTERVIEWING IN CASES OF CHILD MALTREATMENT

Because of the highly sensitive nature of child maltreatment and allegations of child maltreatment and because the investigation of child maltreatment involves individuals from several disciplines, an interdisciplinary model is recommended for interviewing children who have been or who are alleged to have been maltreated.

The Research and Advisory Panel of the California Attorney General's Office (1994) made the following excellent recommendations for establishing *multidisciplinary interview centers* for interviewing children who may have been maltreated (adapted from pp. 8–9). All states should consider implementing these or similar guidelines.

1. Comprehensive interviews in child maltreatment investigations should be conducted by specially trained child interview specialists.
2. Child interview specialists should receive extensive start-up and ongoing training in child development, forensically defensible interviewing, and the informational needs of investigative agencies.
3. Children should be interviewed in a child-friendly setting.
4. Professionals from investigative agencies should (a) coordinate their informational needs prior to the interview conducted by the child interview specialist, (b) observe the interview from behind a one-way glass or on a TV monitor, (c) have an opportunity during a break in the interview to suggest further questions to the interviewer, (d) coordinate the investigation immediately following the interview, and (e) consider the child's needs for mental health and other support services and make appropriate referrals.
5. Investigative agencies should establish protocols for interviewing children in child maltreatment cases.
6. A child advocate should be available at the multidisciplinary interview center to support the child before and after the interview.
7. Investigative interviews conducted at well-run multidisciplinary interview centers should be videotaped. This recommendation does not pertain to therapy sessions with children, which should not be videotaped unless the videotaping is done for therapeutic reasons.
8. Protective orders should be issued by the court to protect the confidentiality of videotaped interviews.
9. A multidisciplinary interview center needs a lead agency; the District Attorney's Office is ordinarily in the best position to assume this role.
10. Each multidisciplinary interview center should have a director to oversee daily operation of the center. The success or failure of a center depends, in large measure, on the skill of the director; therefore, counties should take special steps to employ the most highly qualified and dedicated person to serve as center director.

11. Three multidisciplinary teams should be formed to operate and supervise the multidisciplinary interview center: (a) a policy-level team to set policy for the center, (b) a mid-level management team to work with the director of the center regarding day-to-day operation of the center and to periodically review cases, and (c) a line-level multidisciplinary team to review cases immediately following interviews to make recommendations regarding further investigation, litigation, and provision of appropriate services.
12. Investigative agencies should establish interagency agreements for investigating child maltreatment.
13. Successful operation of a multidisciplinary interview center requires mandatory participation by all investigative agencies. Agreements should be made between agencies requiring that investigators use the center in child maltreatment cases.
14. Medical evaluations should be conducted by medical professionals with expertise in diagnosing and treating cases of child maltreatment.
15. California should certify professionals who complete requirements established by the State for child interview specialists.
16. A child interview specialist classification should be established in county government.
17. California should enact legislation similar to federal legislation that protects the results of state-funded research from discovery in legal proceedings. (See 42 U.S.C. § 37899; 28 C.F.R. Part 22.)
18. A uniform data collection system should be established at multidisciplinary interview centers to track cases and provide case management information.

The San Diego County Grand Jury (1994) independently made similar recommendations.

The victim should be interviewed at the earliest possible moment by a multiple disciplinary evidentiary interview task force. The task force should consist of an interviewer, highly trained in child interviews; a law enforcement officer, preferably the officer investigating the case; a licensed social worker; and a member of the District Attorney's staff. All parties except the interviewer should observe the interview from a remote/obscured location. This interview should be videotaped for future reference. The videotaping should be of high quality, utilizing professional equipment and done by personnel trained in television recording techniques. (p. 32, with changes in notation)

Following these recommendations may reduce the stress that children may experience when they are interviewed repeatedly by different interviewers. The recommendations also are useful in bringing together individuals from several disciplines who can pool their collective talents to arrive at some understanding of what might have happened to the child and of how to proceed further in the investigation.

It may not be possible to implement these recommendations in smaller jurisdictions, where the limited number of cases and limited monetary resources do not permit the hiring of a specialist in interviewing. However, in such jurisdictions, a law enforcement officer or a Child Protective Services worker can serve as the interviewer if he or she is well trained.

Here is an example of how a child alleged to have been maltreated might be interviewed at a multidisciplinary center (California Attorney General's Office, 1994).

CASE 22-2. JENNIFER

Jennifer had a restless night. Over breakfast her mom tried to reassure her that things would be okay. Jennifer knew that her job today was to tell the truth. The truth would be hard to tell. It would be embarrassing. Jennifer hoped someone could help her tell it. After all, she was only eight.

There had been many changes for Jennifer in the last few days. She felt unsure and anxious. Police officers had been to her home, her father was gone, and her mom kept crying all the time.

As they started to leave the house, Jennifer ran back upstairs and grabbed her teddy bear. She held him tight. He would stay with her during the interview.

When they arrived, Jennifer was surprised by the rainbow colors and stuffed animals. A social worker met them at the door and gave Jennifer and her mom a tour of the Interview Center. The social worker showed her the interview room and told her who would talk to her and what to expect.

Later, when all of her questions had been answered and she was ready, the social worker took her to the interview room. A child interview specialist greeted them. When Jennifer appeared comfortable, the social worker left Jennifer and the interviewer alone.

A detective, a child welfare social worker, and a prosecuting attorney had already talked to the interviewer about the case. They would watch the interview from behind a one-way glass. Jennifer knew people were watching. They didn't want her to have to tell her story over and over.

Jennifer sat at a small table and colored as the interviewer asked questions. The interviewer seemed nice and Jennifer could understand her. Jennifer began to tell how her father had touched her. As she talked, the people behind the one-way glass made notes.

Jennifer was given a short break halfway through the interview. During the break the interviewer met with the other professionals for feedback on any additional information they might need. The interview resumed and this information was gathered.

As the interview ended, Jennifer was told she could ask any questions she might have. She also was encouraged to call the interviewer if she remembered anything else or had questions.

After the interview, the professionals discussed their plans for ensuring that Jennifer was protected and her needs met. The child welfare social worker would provide counseling referrals. The detective would contact witnesses. A medical examination would be scheduled. The prosecuting attorney would file charges.

The detective met with Jennifer's mom to discuss the findings and their plans. Jennifer's mother also was given information on how best to support Jennifer. During this time, the interviewer spent time with Jennifer playing a game. When it was time to go, the interviewer gave Jennifer her card, told Jennifer to call her if she wanted to talk to her about anything, and thanked her for her hard work. (p. 1, with changes in notation)

PREPARING FOR THE INITIAL INTERVIEW IN CASES OF CHILD MALTREATMENT

Aims of the Initial Interview

Investigative or assessment interviews in cases of child maltreatment can have one or more of the following aims (Burgess, Groth, Holmstrom, & Sgroi, 1978; MacFarlane & Krebs, 1986; Vizard & Tranter, 1988):

1. To determine whether the alleged maltreatment has occurred by, depending on the case, (a) evaluating all sources of information, including physical evidence, reports of victims, and reports of witnesses, (b) assessing the credibility of the child's report, including whether the child's report can be corroborated, and (c) reconstructing, as much as possible, the events surrounding the alleged maltreatment
2. To assess the child, especially if there has been trauma, including the child's overall functioning and the impact of the alleged maltreatment
3. To assess the family, particularly in cases of known child maltreatment, including the family's overall functioning, the family's relationship to the maltreated child, and the family's reaction to the maltreatment
4. To make recommendations for appropriate interventions, including (a) taking steps to protect the child from further maltreatment, if maltreatment has occurred, (b) developing an intervention program to help the child recover, if needed, and (c) working with the family to protect the child by providing appropriate services, if needed

General Considerations in Preparing for the Child Maltreatment Interview

There are at least two possible strategies for obtaining background information. One strategy is to obtain as many details as possible about the alleged maltreatment *before* you interview the child. For example, you can try to get copies of medical, police, and school reports and any previous interviews—including videotapes and transcripts—with the child, parents, and alleged offender. In addition, you can obtain a thorough developmental and family history from the nonsuspect parent(s). Later in the chapter, there is a discussion of guidelines for conducting interviews with nonsuspect parents or caregivers. A second strategy is to obtain background details *after* you conduct the interview to preclude biasing your questions. In such cases, it is helpful to have at least some minimal details, such as the child's name and a brief description of the allegations.

Answering the following questions will help you prepare for the initial interview and also help you conduct a more effective interview (Burgess et al., 1978):

1. Who first suspected that the child had been maltreated? For example, did the child report the incident(s) to a parent, friend, teacher, neighbor, or police, or did someone else—such as a physician, social worker, teacher, or psychologist—suspect child maltreatment and report it? If the child confided in a friend, did the child ask the friend to promise not to tell anyone else?

2. If the child disclosed the maltreatment, did he or she give full details or only incomplete or partial details? If an individual other than the child disclosed the maltreatment, how confident was the individual about whether the maltreatment occurred?

3. How much time has passed since the first alleged incident of maltreatment occurred?

4. With whom did the original complainant discuss his or her concerns? What was discussed?

5. Did the original complainant or anyone else familiar with the alleged maltreatment discuss his or her concerns with the child? If so, what was discussed, how often did the discussions take place, what did the child initially say, what views about the maltreatment did the other person hold during all of the discussions, and how did the discussions influence the child's reports?

6. Is the interview being conducted shortly after the alleged maltreatment occurred or a long time after the event(s)?

7. Are you the first person to interview the child about the alleged maltreatment, or have other individuals previously interviewed the child?

8. If the child has been interviewed previously, what might he or she have learned from the interviews? For example, did the child learn to say what interviewers expect to hear or what pleases interviewers?

9. Did the child report the alleged maltreatment as a result of a school or television program about maltreatment? If so, when was the program shown and what was the content of the program?

10. What symptoms does the child have? What changes have others noted in the child's behavior, such as bad dreams, bed-wetting, or fearfulness, that may have started when the alleged maltreatment began?

11. What was going on in the child's home at the time of the alleged maltreatment? Was the child exposed to pornography? Was there domestic violence? How were other siblings treated (if relevant)?

12. Did the alleged maltreatment happen to any other children? If so, has the child spoken with these children?

Conduct the interview with the child as soon as possible after the initial report of the alleged maltreatment. Arrange for

the child to have a medical examination, if one has not been done. Obtain photographs of people in the child's life from the caregiver if you think you may need to use them in the interview to identify persons to whom the child is referring.

Videotaping the Child Maltreatment Interview

In cases of child maltreatment, a videotape, as noted earlier, will help you make a detailed record of the interview. If you plan to videotape the interview, be sure, before you begin, that the equipment is in good working order and that the lighting is appropriate. If you cannot videotape the interview, audiotape it. Note, however, that audiotaping is less desirable because it does not give information about the child's nonverbal behavior.

Videotaping may help "demonstrate that the alleged victim has not been subjected to coercive or insistent questioning that induced the child to fabricate allegations simply to please or accommodate the interviewer" (Silcner & Hanson, 1989, p. 62). Videotaped interviews have taken on added importance because some states are allowing videotaped testimony to be presented in court in lieu of in-court testimony in order to shield children from the stress of testifying in open courtrooms (Bottoms & Lantinga, 1995).

Videotaping has its downside. If the case goes to court, it gives the defense attorney the opportunity to question *every* movement, word, and gesture that you made and places you on the defensive. Defense attorneys will try to find some way to discredit you.

In some states, you may need to have a nonsuspect parent sign a consent form that gives you permission to videotape the interview. However, it is a good idea *always* to get permission to videotape or audiotape the interview. Some interviewers routinely inform the child of the videotaping procedure, whereas others tell the child only if the child asks.

If a parent asks to watch the interview from another room, be ready to explain why you prefer that he or she not watch. Risks in allowing a parent to watch include the possibility of the parent's coaching or questioning the child after the interview and the parent's overreacting to the interview. It is preferable to meet with the parent after the interview to give the parent feedback. In rare cases, you might watch the videotaped sessions together. The parent should not be in the room when you conduct the interview because the parent may give subtle—either intended or unintended—cues to the child. Sometimes, however, young children are so frightened that they will not talk unless someone they know and trust also is in the room. In such cases, allow the *nonsuspect* caregiver (or someone else with whom the child feels comfortable) to be in the room. Position that person so that he or she does not look directly at the child; preferably, he or she should sit behind the child, with no face to face contact, and remain quiet during the interview. However, do everything you can to get the child to talk to you alone before you consider having someone else in the room.

Begin the videotape recording by including the purpose, date, time, and location of the interview; the name, address, and date of birth of the interviewee; and your name and affiliation. If this information is not included, the videotape can't be used as evidence.

When you videotape or audiotape the interview, it is valuable to add to the case file such information as the following (Garbarino & Stott, 1989, pp. 197–198, with changes in notation):

- the time, date, and place of the interview
- a description of the setting in which you conducted the interview
- an account of any interactions that occurred immediately before the interview
- an account of who told the child about the interview
- the names of those present (either in the room or waiting outside) and their relationships to the child
- the length of the interview
- a description of the mood of the child
- any other information that would bear on the interpretation of the communication that occurred between you and the child

Document carefully all contacts (including telephone calls) you have with anyone about the case. At a minimum, you want to keep notes about whom you contacted, the date of contact, and the content of the interaction. Careful record keeping is critical because you may be called on to testify in court or to make your records available to attorneys.

Considerations in Interviewing Ethnic Minority Children and Their Parents in Cases of Child Maltreatment

If the child belongs to an ethnic minority group, you may have to consider some additional issues in preparing to interview for child maltreatment (Burgess et al., 1978).

1. *Ability to speak English.* If children and/or their parents do not have a command of the English language and you are not fluent in their language, communication will be difficult. Chapters 8 and 9 discuss language barriers in intercultural communication, the use of translators, and other topics related to ethnic minority groups.

2. *Role of children in the family.* In some ethnic minority groups, children "belong" to the father. Mothers who see their children physically abused by the father may put up with the maltreatment and not report it because they don't want to bring shame to the family or because they do not view such treatment as abuse, especially if the father has the "right" to do as he pleases. If maltreatment is reported, they may be reluctant to talk about it. This, of course, also happens in families that are from the majority group. Female victims in some ethnic groups (such as Asian American and Puerto Rican) may be hesitant to disclose sexual abuse because of the high value their cultures place on a girl's virginity and the taboos that surround the discussion of sex (Fontes, 1993).

3. *Husband and wife relations.* In some ethnic minority groups, as well as in the majority group, husbands may batter their wives in order to "train" them. Battered wives may stay married because they believe they have no status without their husbands and children (see Chapter 20). Battered women who are not American citizens and who are married to American men are especially vulnerable because they may fear being deported if they report their husbands to authorities. This fear also may make them reluctant to talk about the battery. Foreign nationals married to U.S. citizens must be sponsored by their American spouses in order to seek permanent residency.

4. *Role of mythology.* Some ethnic minority groups believe in a mythology that ascribes illness to evil spirits that enter the person's body. The following case illustrates this belief and the importance of understanding traditional healing practices in order to conduct a culturally sensitive interview and to avoid unnecessary removal of a child from a family (Krajewski-Jaime, 1991).

CASE 22-3. JOSÉ

A non-Hispanic caseworker recommended the removal of José, a Mexican-American boy, from his family because of potential physical danger. The assessment indicated that José was ill and in need of medical care, but the mother had obvious emotional problems and appeared to be irrational. The mother had kept on saying in "broken" English that she could not allow any evil spirits to come near her child. She had locked José in his room, hung from the ceiling a pair of sharp scissors just above his head, and would not allow anyone, including the caseworker or the doctor, to enter José's room.

The caseworker's supervisor, who had some knowledge of traditional healing practices, asked a Mexican-American Child Protective Services worker to reinvestigate the case. The worker visited the mother, who, while upset about the child's illness, welcomed someone who spoke Spanish. The mother explained that she had used several home remedies to help her child's fever go away, but evil spirits had already taken possession of her child and the usual remedies no longer helped. The only thing left to do was to prevent new spirits from entering the child's body. The scissors would immediately cut any spirits that would try to enter the child's body. Because evil spirits could attach to anyone who entered the room, she could not allow anyone to enter the room, thus preventing any further harm to her child.

The Mexican-American worker, although familiar with traditional-healing practices, had not seen this particular cure used before. She understood the validity of this belief within the client's cultural context, but to obtain the mother's permission to see José, to remove the dangerous scissors, and to see that José received medical attention, she had to validate the mother's beliefs and gain her trust. She told the mother that although she had not seen anyone use this cure before she had heard her grandmother talk about it. To protect the patient and the entire surroundings, however, the grandmother usually nailed the scissors on the room's entrance door. The worker explained that, should the spirits attach themselves to anyone who wished to enter the room, the scissors on the entrance door would immediately prevent them from doing so and thus provide stronger protection to the patient. The Mexican-American worker went on to ask the mother if this made sense to her. She asked the mother if she thought this would be more beneficial because it would allow José to be seen by the caseworker and by the doctor. The mother agreed and emphasized that she wanted only what was best for her child. She changed the location of the scissors and welcomed the caseworker and the doctor to examine José. (pp. 158–159, with changes in notation)

5. *Cultural views toward child maltreatment.* Child maltreatment has special significance for some ethnic or religious groups. For example, those with certain religious orientations may believe that a child who has been sexually violated has sinned. You want to find out what sexual molestation means to the adolescent and to his or her family and what help the adolescent and family want. Consider what decisions the family makes when an adolescent member becomes pregnant. Is there a preference for abortion, for giving the baby up for adoption, or for keeping the baby? These considerations hold for all families, not only those who are from ethnic minority groups. However, they may have special meaning for families from non-Anglo cultures.

6. *Cultural practices that may mimic physical abuse.* To avoid making false allegations of maltreatment, understand that certain cultural practices may mimic maltreatment. For example, to cure fever, respiratory illnesses, and even convulsions, Vietnamese parents may use a folk practice that consists of scratching, rubbing, and beating the skin (*cao gio*) and pinching around the neck areas (to allow the "bad wind" causing the illness to escape). If you find that a Vietnamese child has multiple bruises around the neck, back, and abdomen, do not automatically assume that the child was physically abused. You must distinguish cultural practices from deliberate physical abuse (see Chapter 9). You can do this by inquiring whether the child was ill and what treatment the child received for the illness.

INTERVIEWING THE CHILD IN CASES OF CHILD MALTREATMENT

A child's response to maltreatment depends on several factors, including (a) the child's sex, age, and level of emotional and cognitive development, (b) the type of maltreatment, including its frequency and duration, (c) the child's relationship to the offender, (d) whether threat or force was used, and (e) the quality of support available to the child (Robin, 1991).

The affect the child shows in the interview may depend on how long ago the abusive incident(s) occurred. If the abusive incident happened recently, the child may be in an acute crisis situation and may be too anxious or numb to talk with you (see Chapter 11 for a discussion of posttraumatic stress disorder). In some cases, the trauma of the maltreatment may exacerbate any symptoms that the child may have previously had. If the maltreatment occurred a long time ago, some children may have adapted to the maltreatment and exhibit little stress, whereas others may show many traumatic symptoms.

General Suggestions for Interviewing Children

Before you begin to interview a child who may have been maltreated, review carefully Chapters 2 and 3. The general interviewing principles discussed in these two chapters also apply to interviews in cases of child maltreatment or suspected child maltreatment.

You must use a developmental perspective in all interviews with children, recognizing age-appropriate cognitive skills, expressive and receptive language skills, and motor skills (see Tables C-4 and C-5 in Appendix C and the table on the inside front cover, for example) *and the children's understanding of morality* (see Table C-8 in Appendix C, for example). Children who are less than 3 years old will be extremely difficult (in many cases, nearly impossible) to interview because they do not have the linguistic capacity to describe events in detail. Children between 3 and 5 years of age may pose challenges for the interviewer because they may not be able to give an organized, or consistent, description of the maltreatment incident(s). They also may have limited capacity to describe events in detail. In addition, they vary greatly in their communication skills (Lamb, Sternberg, & Esplin, 1995). However, children's communicative competence rapidly increases from 3 to 5 years. In some cases, you may need to use play strategies to help preschool children verbalize their thoughts and feelings (see Chapter 3). School-aged children have better verbal capacities but still may resist talking with you. It is with adolescents and adults that verbal reports usually will be more complete.

In investigative interviews when children are reluctant to talk to you, you will have to walk a tightrope, delicately trying to balance two sets of conflicting goals. One goal is to learn whether the child has been maltreated and then get protection for the child. The other goal is to ensure that innocent people are not accused of any wrongdoing. How much do you probe, and what kinds of probes do you use? How much do you prolong the interview? You don't want to use leading or suggestive questions or prolong the interview to the point where children will say anything they think you want to hear simply to end the session or to please you. Yet, failure to uncover child maltreatment may leave the child vulnerable to further maltreatment and possibly to trauma and danger. As you gain competence as a forensic interviewer, you will become comfortable walking this tightrope, but some tension may always remain.

The following guidelines should help you in interviewing a child suspected of being maltreated (Furniss, 1991; Gordon, Schroeder, Ornstein, & Baker-Ward, 1995; Lamb et al., 1995; MacFarlane & Krebs, 1986; Robin, 1991; Saywitz, 1990, 1994; Saywitz, Geiselman, & Bornstein, 1992; Spencer & Flin, 1990). *It is important to emphasize that you should not conduct an investigatory interview unless you have been trained to do so or unless you are directly supervised in this work.* However, many of these interview guidelines also are valuable in situations where you are simply trying to rule out maltreatment.

Guideline 1. Allow sufficient time with the child to obtain relevant information. Discontinue the interview, however, if the child becomes too tired to provide information, and schedule another session. Recognize the limits of the child's attention span and take breaks, if necessary.

Guideline 2. Discuss confidentiality, especially with older children and adolescents, and inform them of your obligation to report any situation in which the child is unsafe. Older children and adolescents need to recognize that what they say is not confidential if there is a possibility of harm to self or to others in what they report or if they have been maltreated. If the interview is being held with a child who has disclosed that she or he was maltreated, inform the child that what she or he says is not confidential. Also inform the child that the interview (and videotape, if one is made) may be used for legal purposes if the case is prosecuted.

Guideline 3. Conduct a nonbiased, noncoercive, and nonrepetitive interview. Do not prejudge the case. Be especially careful not to pressure, coerce, or bully the child into answering questions. Here are several examples of things you *don't* want to say: (a) "If you don't tell, you will feel yucky inside," (b) "All of the other children talked to me and they felt better," and (c) "We need you to tell me so that other children at school don't get hurt." Instead you want say (a) "Please tell me what happened," (b) "Please tell me anything you want to," and (c) "Please tell me about your school." Do not differentially reinforce responses that confirm your expectations. Do not give subtle cues to the child about what she or he should or should not tell you. For example, don't nod your head approvingly when the child says something you like or frown when the child says something you don't like. If you videotape the interview, you should be visible on the video to show that you have not given facial cues to the child.

Guideline 4. Ask open-ended questions, use prompts, and avoid leading questions. Note that some questions may be leading in one context but not in another. Here are some examples of what to say:

- "Is there anything that you would like to tell me?"
- "Did anything else happen?"
- "You mentioned that someone bothered you yesterday. Tell me everything you remember about that."

- Say "Tell me what happened" rather than "Was it your uncle who did it?" when the child never mentioned the uncle.
- Say "How did it feel when she touched you?" after the child mentions that she was touched instead of "Did it hurt when she touched you?"
- Say "How did he look?" instead of "He looked old, didn't he?" when the child never mentioned how the alleged perpetrator looked.
- Say "How was the weather?" instead of "You do remember what the weather was like, don't you?"
- Say "How much did it hurt?" after the child says "It hurt" instead of "I'll bet it hurt a lot."

These examples illustrate that it is better to ask questions that require the child to give information rather than simply answer "yes" or "no." Chapter 2 describes this guideline in more detail.

Guideline 5. Avoid giving the child information given to you by someone else. For example, say "What happened in school that day?" instead of "Amy said that Mr. Smith showed the children in school a snake. Is that right?"

Guideline 6. Ask the child for important information in several different ways if she or he is reluctant to give you the information, especially if you believe the child knows the information. For example, you can use open-ended questions and focused questions to inquire about the alleged maltreatment. You also can use, if necessary, multiple-choice questions and "yes-no" questions. Chapter 3 describes several techniques that are useful for interviewing young children and children who may be reluctant to speak.

Guideline 7. Listen to everything the child says, and follow up on all information the child gives you. For example, if the child hints that a person whom you do not suspect may have been involved in the maltreatment, find out what the child wants to tell you. It is all too easy to tune out information that you do not believe is important.

Guideline 8. Follow up leads by asking the child for more details, using neutral probing questions and prompts as needed. Here are some examples:

- "You mentioned it happened in Grandma's house. Tell me everything that happened from when you got to Grandma's house."
- "Earlier you said something about a bed. Please tell me everything about that."
- "Tell me more about that."
- "Tell me everything that happened."
- "Tell me everything that you can remember."
- "What happened next?"
- "What happened just before he did that?"
- "How did you feel when that happened?"

Guideline 9. Be alert to whether the child answers every question with a "yes" or "no." If the child answers every question with a "yes" or with a "no," you may be phrasing your questions so that only a "yes" or "no" response is acceptable (MacFarlane & Krebs, 1986). Another possibility is that the child is trying to please you or avoid the issues. In such cases, you might want to ask questions that have "yes-no" answers different from the child's previous answers. For example, if the child said "yes" to several questions, say "Did it rain yesterday?" when you know the answer should be "no." This technique may help you obtain more accurate information from the child.

Guideline 10. Help the child find words to express what took place when the child is reluctant to talk about the possible maltreatment or when the child does not know the words to describe the possible maltreatment. This may be especially important in cases of sexual abuse because many families do not discuss sex openly and the child may not have the language to discuss sexual activities. Show the child by example that it is permissible to use explicit language. Ask the nonsuspect parent to give the child permission to "say anything." You must be extremely careful not to lead the child. Your aim is to help the child express what has happened. *But be careful: do not put words in the child's mouth.*

Guideline 11. Give the child who is reluctant to talk directly about the maltreatment opportunities to draw on paper with pencils and crayons and to respond to direct questions. Ask the child to tell you about the drawings and inquire about relevant details (Cage, 1988). When you have evidence that the child may have been abused—such as spontaneous disclosure, suspicious medical evidence, or sexualized behavior inappropriate for the child's age—you may need to ask focused questions if the child is reluctant or refuses to talk about the alleged maltreatment (see Chapter 2 for a discussion of focused questions) (Lyon, 1995).

Guideline 12. Probe any inconsistencies in the child's statements by explaining that you are confused, not by challenging the child. For example, you might say "Gee, I'm confused. You said that Mr. B. was in your room. Tell me again what happened."

Guideline 13. Ask preschool children about multiple incidents of possible maltreatment by asking specific or direct questions about time sequences. Developmentally, preschool children have not yet established a strong concept of time. Therefore, they may have difficulty differentiating time sequences. After you have established that the child has been maltreated, you could say "Did this happen one time or more than one time?" If the child says "more than one time," follow up with questions such as "Tell me about the first time," "Tell me about the time you remember best," or "Tell me about the last time." This approach will yield more information than asking the question "How many times did it happen?"

Guideline 14. Use age-appropriate language. Here are some illustrations of this guideline:

- Say "What were you riding in?" instead of "Was there a vehicle involved?"
- Keep sentences short, and ask one idea per question. For example, say "Where did your mom take you that day?"

followed by, as needed, "Who was there?" and "What room were you in?" Don't say "Where did your mom take you that day, who was there, and what room were you in?"
- Avoid double negatives. For example, say "What did mom say about going there?" instead of "Didn't mom tell you not to go there?"

Guideline 15. Avoid the use of pronouns because of potential ambiguity, unless the referent is clear. For example, say "Then what did Bill do?" instead of "Then what did he do?"

Guideline 16. Use short sentences, few syllables per word, and concrete, visual words with young children. Here are some examples of this guideline.

- Say "Where did it happen?" instead of "I want to know where it happened, if you remember."
- Say "Point to the picture of the person" instead of "Can you identify the individual in the photograph?"
- Say "You said he offered you candy" instead of "You said he offered you a reward."

Guideline 17. Use uncomplicated grammar with all children. For example, say "What did Jake do after he got angry?" instead of "Were you hit by Jake?"

Guideline 18. Use simple and direct questions with all children. For example, say, as a follow-up question, "Did it happen when you went to bed?" instead of "It might have been when you went to bed that day, is that right?"

Guideline 19. Use the active voice with all children. For example, after the child says she was touched by the alleged perpetrator, say "Where did he touch you?" instead of "Where were you touched by him?"

Guideline 20. Use positive phrasing with all children. For example, say "Did it happen when you were in your pajamas or after you were dressed?" instead of "You don't remember whether it happened when you were in your pajamas or after you were dressed, do you?"

Guideline 21. Avoid questions that may imply a child is guilty. For example, say "Tell me what happened when you went to the playground" instead of "Why did you go to the playground with him?"

Guideline 22. Learn about the child's terminology for body parts and for sexual acts, and use the child's terms during the interview, as needed. You can learn about the child's terminology by using drawings of human figures. For example, you can begin to draw a figure and ask the child to help you finish it, or you can have two already drawn figures (one male and one female; see Figure 17-1 and Figure 17-2 in Chapter 17). Ask the child to identify the various parts of the body on each drawing. Accept whatever answers the child gives. For example, if the child calls a penis a "wiener," then that's the term you should use. You don't have to ask the child "Do you have another name for that?" or suggest any other name. When you ask questions, also use the child's terms for body parts. Show the child that you are comfortable talking about private parts of the body and that you will not be shocked by such discussion. It also is helpful to ask a nonsuspect parent what terms the child uses to identify certain parts of the body.

Guideline 23. Consider carefully what it means when a child changes her or his story. Children may change their stories during the interview by retracting their statement that the maltreatment occurred or by saying they were maltreated when they initially denied being maltreated. Why might they do so? Is it because they suddenly realize the possible consequences of their statements, become fearful, want to please you, feel safe enough to talk to you about the maltreatment, or are tired after prolonged questioning? Because there often is no clear-cut answer to why children change their stories, you must judge each case separately. However, take the *change* as an additional piece of information and not as an infallible truth (Haugaard & Reppucci, 1988).

Guideline 24. Accept what the child says when you are inquiring about the maltreatment, and do not offer interpretations. You want to obtain factual information about the maltreatment and not offer interpretations of what the child says.

Guideline 25. Attend carefully to the child's terminology for designating people in her or his world. For example, if the child uses the word "papa," ask the child "Who is papa?" Do not assume that "papa" means father, as the child may use it to designate the grandfather or someone else.

Guideline 26. Determine whom the child is talking about when there are several individuals who may assume similar roles. For example, if a mother, a stepmother, and a girl-friend all assume motherly roles, determine whom the child is referring to when she or he says "mother." Try to get the proper names of the people the child is talking about.

Guideline 27. When you need to clarify whom the child is talking about, show the child photographs or draw faces of people in the child's life. If you have obtained photographs prior to the interview, you can point to each photograph and ask the child to name each person and tell you something about the person. Or, instead of using photographs, you can ask the child to identify the people in her or his family, and then you can draw a small face for each person the child names. Ask the child to point to the person she or he is talking about.

Guideline 28. Take note of the child's concepts (such as knowledge of time and numbers), the child's vocabulary and diction, and other characteristics about the child that may help you in conducting the interview. This information can help you decide what language, inquiries, and questions to use with the child during the interview.

Guideline 29. Determine whether the child knows the difference between the truth and a lie. Here are some questions you can ask to find out:

• "What does it mean to tell a lie?"
• "Would it be a lie if you broke something and you said that you didn't?"
• Show the child a red crayon and say "What does it mean to call this crayon 'blue'?"

• "If your friend broke a toy and you said you broke it, would that be the truth or a lie?"
• "If I said I was the tallest person in the world, would that be the truth or a lie?"
• "Is it a good thing or a bad thing to tell the truth?"
• "Is it a good thing or a bad thing to tell a lie?"

Guideline 30. Ask the child whom she or he has told about the maltreatment. If the child has told anyone else about the maltreatment, also interview him or her (or them). The information you obtain from others may or may not corroborate the child's statement.

Guideline 31. Clarify any terms the child uses that appear to be based on experiences in therapy. Of course, you always need to understand the child's communications. But you must be especially careful when you interview a child who has been in therapy and uses terms that she or he has learned there. In such cases, ask the child to tell you what the terms mean.

Guideline 32. Determine whether a young child or a developmentally delayed child knows basic concepts such as top, under, behind, inside, and outside. You can do this, for example, by asking the child to place a crayon on top of, under, behind, inside, and outside a box or other similar object.

Guideline 33. Keep interruptions to a minimum, allow the child to control the flow of information if at all possible, and take your cues from the child about the speed of questioning and the length of silences. This guideline emphasizes the need to keep the child focused. The interview will proceed more smoothly if you take your cues from the child.

Guideline 34. Help the child get past any fears that she or he may have about revealing the maltreatment. For example, you can ask the child to tell you if there is anybody or anything that has scared her or him or to write a list of people and things that are most scary and then work with the child to figure out why they are scary.

Guideline 35. Give the child permission to break any secrets made between herself or himself and the abuser. You can do this in a number of different ways (Greenberg, 1990, pp. 10–11, with changes in notation):

• "Did he tell you to keep anything a secret?"
• "Is there anything that you are not supposed to tell me?"
• "Is there anything that you might get into trouble for if you told me?"
• "Is there anything that you are afraid to tell me?"

Guideline 36. Take special care to help the child express her or his feelings, reactions, and any painful experiences. A child who has been sexually abused may be reluctant to discuss the maltreatment because of embarrassment or fear of exposure. Give the child time to work through any painful feelings—such as shock, fear, and anger—before she or he talks with you about the incident. In cases in which the child describes a traumatic event, fully acknowledge the impact of the event and be supportive of the child. You must be especially sensitive to the needs of the child in her or his time of crisis. However, be careful. If you give too much support, the defense may accuse you of "leading" the child.

Guideline 37. Help the child be as open as possible in talking about the alleged maltreatment. You can do this by conveying to the child that you will accept anything she or he says, that you want the child's trust, and that you want her or him to feel safe. You also want to show the child that you will not be shocked, dismayed, surprised, or angry, for example, about anything she or he tells you.

This guideline deals with the possibility that some children may think you will not believe what happened; question whether you really want to know or can stand to hear about what happened; think you will become angry, upset, or shocked if you hear about what happened; fear you will view them as bad once the secret is told; think that they did something wrong; or think that you can do nothing to keep them safe from the abuser or from others who will be angry following the disclosure (MacFarlane & Feldmeth, 1988). You will need to overcome the child's anxieties, doubts, and concerns and reassure the child that she or he did nothing wrong. Phrase questions in a way that avoids even the appearance of placing blame or responsibility for the maltreatment on the child.

Guideline 38. Never promise the child what you cannot deliver. You don't want to say "I will make sure that Daddy never hurts you again" or "You will be safe now that you told." You can't say these things because you cannot be sure of their validity.

These guidelines do not cover the use of anatomically detailed dolls or of play materials. Later in the chapter, the controversy surrounding the use of anatomically detailed dolls is discussed. Using play materials in any interview, and particularly interviews for forensic purposes, has advantages and disadvantages. Play materials may be useful with young children who are reluctant to talk to you directly about the alleged maltreatment. Play materials useful in forensic interviews include a doll house with furniture, ordinary dolls representing family members (for example, baby, father, mother, sister, brother) whose clothes can be removed easily, ordinary dolls of different colors representing people of color, hand puppets, paper dolls, telephones, and other devices to help young children express what happened to them. You also might have Legos and similar materials available. However, play materials are potentially distracting; the child may prefer playing with them to talking to you. Still, if the child is reluctant to talk to you and you have difficulty establishing rapport, consider using play materials.

Phases of the Child Maltreatment Interview

Let's now turn to the four phases of the interview—the rapport phase, the free narrative account and nonleading questioning phase, the closed questioning phase, and the closing phase (adapted, in part, from Home Office, 1992). These phases are not necessarily discrete—they may blend into each other, and you may use the same techniques in more than one phase.

Rapport phase. In this first phase, you want to establish a good relationship with the child. Children who have been maltreated or who may have been maltreated may be under considerable stress when you first meet them. Be warm, friendly, supportive, reassuring, and empathic in order to reduce the child's stress and help the child relax. Position yourself so that you are close to the child's level, and sit close to the child without anything (such as a desk) between you and the child.

As in all interviews with children, establishing rapport and a trusting relationship is the first step. In the case of child maltreatment interviews, it is especially critical. However, establishing a trusting relationship may be particularly difficult because such a relationship may be precisely what the child has come to fear the most. Many perpetrators play on the child's emotions and exploit a trusting and caring relationship. Also, parents may have cautioned the child not to trust strangers. Why then should the child trust you, a virtual stranger? Consequently, you will need to show the child that you can be trusted. You must allay the child's fear that you will reject or punish him or her. However, children may still experience rejection, especially when disclosure leads to the breakup of the child's family.

Introduce yourself by stating your name and position. Inform the child that you are there to talk with him or her. Explain the reason for the interview, and show the child the camera or tell the child that you will be videotaping the interview (if you are planning to do so and if your agency follows this procedure). Tell the child that you will be making notes (if you plan to do so) and the reason why. You can say, for example, "It will help me remember what you say." After you introduce yourself and establish rapport, you can make one or more of the following statements, as needed, to children who can understand them. You also can use some of these statements at other times during the interview, as needed (Home Office, 1992; Reed, 1993, pp. 6–8; Saywitz et al., 1992).

- "Well, I talk with children [teenagers] who may be upset. Has anything happened recently that has upset you?"
- (If the child or adolescent is upset) "I can see that you are upset, and I'm interested in hearing about it."
- "I hope that by talking to you I can better understand what is troubling you."
- (If the child mentions an event) "Please tell me all you can remember about [event]. Don't make anything up, and try not to leave anything out."
- "You can tell me anything you want. I don't want you to feel you need to hold anything back. All that matters is that you don't make anything up or leave anything out."
- "Do you know why you are here today?"

- "Is there anything that you would like to talk to me about?"
- (If the child or adolescent is reluctant to speak) "Are there some things you are not very happy about?"
- "Do you need help with anything?"
- "Is anything bothering you?"
- "I understand that something may have happened to you yesterday. Please tell me about it."
- "Now I want you to start at the beginning and tell me what happened, from the beginning, to the middle, to the end. Tell me everything you remember, even little parts that you don't think are very important. Sometimes people leave out little things because they think little things are not important. Tell me everything that happened. Go ahead."
- "There may be some questions that you do not know the answers to. That's okay. Nobody can remember everything. If you don't know the answer to a question, then tell me 'I don't know.' Do not guess or make anything up. It is very important to tell me only what you really remember—only what really happened."
- "If you do not want to answer some of the questions, you don't have to. That's okay. Tell me 'I don't want to answer that question.'"
- "If I ask you a question that you don't understand, never try to guess the answer or say 'yes' just because you think you should. Just tell me 'Hey, I don't understand.'"
- "I wasn't there, so I don't know what happened. I need your help to learn about what happened."
- "Nobody knows everything, do they? I'll be asking you lots of questions today. Some will be easy and some will be hard. Sometimes you may not know for sure what the right answer is. Maybe you forgot or maybe you just don't know. If you don't know what the right answer is for sure or if you forget, please don't guess an answer. Just say 'I don't know' or 'I forget,' because that's the right answer. Only tell me what you know for sure and what you remember."
- "Some of the questions I'll asking you will be tricky, and they might get you mixed up because they get lots of people mixed up. If I ask you something that makes you get mixed up, please just say 'Huh?' or 'I don't know what you mean.' Then I'll say the question with new words to help you understand."
- "Sometimes I get mixed up and don't understand what you said. I need your help if I don't understand. If I do say the wrong thing, will you please tell me? Just say 'That's not right' or 'You made a mistake.' Okay?"
- "I may ask you some questions more than one time. Sometimes I forget that I already asked you that question. You don't have to change your answer, just tell me what you remember the best you can."

You can tell the child about the videotaping (if applicable) in the following way:

- "I want to tell you something special about my room. Behind the mirror is a video camera, and we make video-tapes of all the boys and girls who come in here. That way I can remember everything we talk about. OK?"

The way you establish rapport will depend on the child's age. With preschool children, you might try some activity that you can do together. One possibility is for you to draw a tree and ask the child to color parts of the tree. Another possibility is to ask the child if you can trace an outline of the child's hand. A third is to tell the child that you want to draw a picture of him or her and ask the child for help in completing the drawing. You want to make the activity a cooperative effort. You can ask school-aged children and adolescents how they feel about being at the interview and what they were told about the interview.

You also might want to ask the child to tell you about some recent event, such as a birthday party (Lamb et al., 1995). Or you can ask the child's nonsuspect parent about some recent event—such as a party or vacation—that the child might talk about. This may help the child get accustomed to talking with you and allows you to observe the way he or she relates historical facts to you. In addition, by asking the child to give you as many details as possible and to tell you everything about the event, you may convey to the child your interest in detailed accounts and in his or her experience, not simply in "yes" or "no" responses. In this phase and throughout the interview, attend to the child's language and ability to communicate, and make note of the child's level of conceptual thinking and development.

Free narrative account and nonleading questioning phase. In this second phase, encourage the child to tell you about what happened. Don't interrupt the child's narrative response. When you need to clarify details, ask primarily open-ended questions. Research suggests that open-ended questions (questions that invite children to give as many details as possible) yield longer and richer responses than focused questions (questions that are specific and limited, such as "Who bothered you?" and "What did he do?") (Sternberg, Lamb, Hershkowitz, Esplin, Redlich, & Sunshine, 1996).

If the child says "I don't want to tell anyone about this," you might say "I know it is hard for you to talk about certain things. Let's talk about something else now [or do something else now]." As soon as possible, bring up the topic again. *When you broach the topic of the alleged maltreatment, pay careful attention to any changes in the child's behavior, voice level, and body language, and make note of these changes in the report.* Changes in the child's behavior during the interview may reflect tension associated with having been abused *or* tension over the claimant's (such as a parent's) allegation of maltreatment when no maltreatment occurred. Don't assume automatically that when a child recoils at the mention of maltreatment it means that he or she was maltreated.

Be prepared to have children deny that any maltreatment took place, especially in cases of sexual abuse. When denial occurs, you will have to decide how much further to probe. *In no case should you coerce the child into saying something that you want to hear or into omitting something that you do not want to hear.*

In this second phase, you want to learn more about what happened, but you do not want to pressure the child. Ask focused but nonleading questions after the open-ended questions. Examples of focused questions in this phase of the interview are "What was that like?", "And what happened next?", "How did that happen?", and "How did that make you feel?"

Also inquire about what was happening *before* the event (antecedent conditions) and what was happening *after* the event (consequent conditions). To decrease the child's anxiety after the child has revealed some painful material or toward the end of the interview, say "How do you feel now that you've talked about what happened?" You also can say, if needed, "I can see you are having a hard time talking, but you are being very strong."

When you get to the consequences of a confirmed event of maltreatment, focus on how the maltreatment has affected the child. Inquire about any symptoms the child may have developed and whether there have been changes in the child's eating, sleeping, and play behavior and, where relevant, changes in school performance and work. Also explore whether there have been changes in the child's relationships with parents, caregivers, siblings, other relatives, friends, neighbors, teachers, and the alleged offender.

Closed questioning phase. You may or may not need to use the third phase. If the child tells you what you need to know in the second phase, you can skip this phase. However, with children who are reluctant to answer open-ended questions—particularly preschool children—be prepared to ask more focused and direct questions. The third phase also is helpful when you want to clarify information that the child gave previously.

Now is the time to ask the child for specific information about the alleged maltreatment, if all else has failed. You can consider using "yes-no" questions and/or multiple-choice questions. You might want to start out with a focused question that refers to a specific event or topic, followed by an open-ended question (Lamb et al., 1995). For example, if you suspect that the maltreatment may have occurred in the alleged perpetrator's bedroom, you can say "Did anything happen in [name of the alleged perpetrator mentioned by the child]'s bedroom?" (focused question), followed by "Tell me everything that happened there" (a more open-ended question). However, don't ask about the alleged perpetrator by saying "Did Joe come into your room at night?" when the child never mentioned Joe, because this question may contaminate the child's recollection.

Other focused questions that can be useful during the third phase of the interview include the following:

- "Did you tell anyone about this?"
- "Tell me about how [alleged perpetrator named by the child] looked."
- "Describe the room where it happened."
- "Was there anyone else in the room besides you and [alleged perpetrator named by the child]?"
- "Did [alleged perpetrator named by the child] have any special things that [he, she] used when [he, she] [name of act volunteered by the child]?"

If you learn about any sex aids or other items used in the maltreatment, consider either obtaining a search warrant (if you are in law enforcement) or encouraging law enforcement to do so.

When a child fails to mention certain issues in response to open-ended questions or prompts, you may need to ask somewhat leading questions, particularly when you know details about the alleged maltreatment. However, do not ask leading questions until you have exhausted other strategies to obtain the information from the child. When you use leading questions, phrase the questions so that they are minimally suggestive and don't implicate anyone. For example, when you have reports that the child's vagina was penetrated by her uncle, say "Did anything ever happen to your vagina?" rather than "Did your uncle do anything to your vagina?" or "Did your uncle ever put anything in your vagina?" If the child gives a positive response, follow it with a nonleading statement that attempts to elicit further information, such as "Tell me everything that happened to your vagina" (Lamb et al., 1995).

You also can ask other questions at this time, such as, "Could it have been dark outside when it happened?" If the child says "yes," follow up with a statement such as "Tell me all you remember about what happened when it was dark."

Closing phase. In this fourth phase, you want to summarize what you have learned about the case. As always, use language appropriate to the child's level of comprehension. Attempt to relieve the child of any distress. Sometimes children may make spontaneous corrections or "recant or deny earlier statements that they made....[They may say] that they made it up to get even with their parents or to punish them for something they did to them. Others say that they are confused and wonder if maybe they misunderstood or if it really was their fault" (Walker et al., 1988, p. 122). Evaluate such statements carefully, but do not take them at face value (Walker et al., 1988). Document what the child has said and under what circumstances. At the close of the interview, compliment the child for cooperating with you. For example, say "Thanks for coming to see me today. I really appreciate your talking with me today." Also ask the child if he or she has any questions for you. Give the child your card, and tell him or her (and/or the caregiver) to call you if he or she wants to talk to you again.

Keep the child informed of your progress on the case, if this is your role. In cases of extrafamilial maltreatment, also keep the family informed of your progress. Use your judgment about informing family members in cases of intrafamilial maltreatment.

Children Who Recant Their Statements

After disclosing the maltreatment, some children have second thoughts about what they said. They may regret disclosing the maltreatment, feel pressured and be unhappy about having to talk with professionals, and be unhappy about having their family life disrupted. They may want to forget the whole thing and return to the way the family was functioning before the maltreatment took place. Other children may want the family to return to the way it was functioning before outsiders began intruding into their lives, even though they were being maltreated during this period. Be prepared to have some children recant their statements. When this happens, you will need to explore with the children their reasons for recanting their statements and then decide how to proceed.

Ensuring That the Child Is Never Interviewed with the Alleged Perpetrator in the Room

You should never interview a child suspected of being maltreated in the presence of the alleged perpetrator. The following case illustrates harmful consequences that can occur when a conjoint interview is held in the presence of the alleged perpetrator (Faller, Froning, & Lipovsky, 1991).

CASE 22-4. SUSIE

Susie was a 4-year-old White girl who disclosed the details of sexual abuse by her father to her therapist (clinician A) over a year's time. The sexual abuse was confirmed by another expert (clinician B). After 10 months with no visits with her father, the father was allowed his own evaluator (clinician C), who wished to see the child with her father as part of her assessment. Clinician A wrote to clinician C strongly recommending against a conjoint interview because of Susie's extreme fear of her father and testified to this opinion. However, clinician C testified that she was unpersuaded, despite Susie's spontaneous and direct statement to her that she did not want to see her father. Having spent a little more than an hour with Susie and five minutes speaking with clinician A, clinician C assured the judge that she was in the best position to know the possible effects on Susie and would make the interview safe but would terminate the interview only if she sensed "real terror." The judge ordered the conjoint interview. Susie was to be accompanied by B.

When clinician B told Susie about the conjoint interview, she immediately began to cry and sob, complaining, "I do not

want to see my Daddy; I do not want to see [clinican C]." Clinician B explained that the judge had ordered the interview and that she had to go. According to the affidavit of an accompanying adult, in the car on the way: "Susie said she did not feel well, that she thought she would throw up. She squirmed continuously, kicking at the dashboard. Her various statements about not wanting to see her Daddy were interspersed with long intervals of sobbing and long drawn-out whining sounds similar to those of an injured child."

When they reached the place where the interview was to be held, Susie clung to B's neck, crying and complaining for approximately 15 minutes. Clinician C then asked clinician B to leave. On clinician C's lap, Susie continued to cry for another 15 minutes and said, "I'm sick. I have a fever. I want to go home now to a birthday party." Clinician C nevertheless proceeded with a 2½-hour session in which Susie was confronted with first her paternal grandparents (whom she had also accused of abuse) and then her father. After a few feeble attempts to say she had to leave, Susie gave up and played with everyone.

Near the end of the interview, two things happened to which clinician C gave great weight. First, the father put modeling clay on Susie's nose and she told him no. Second, in front of the three allegedly abusive adults, clinician C asked Susie if any of them had ever hurt her, to which Susie responded no. Clinician C later testified that Susie's no to her father showed "it was very clear that she could stop her father if he was doing something that she didn't want him to do," which left the clear implication that sexual abuse was one of those "things." Susie's denials that the three adults hurt her were also used to buttress clinician C's position that sexual abuse did not occur. Finally, Susie's lack of "real terror" convinced clinician C that the severe abuse Susie described to the other clinicians could not have happened.

Immediately after this interview, Susie was seen by clinician A. On the way she seemed to be in a trancelike state, and she appeared severely traumatized during the session itself, playing out themes of abandonment and demonstrating aggression. At home afterward Susie was violent, destructive, and hostile to her caregivers. She had a flashback of the sexual abuse by her father.

Over the next few weeks, Susie's exhibited regressed behavior, including bedwetting and nightmares and a renewed preoccupation with her sexual victimization, of which she frequently spoke. Her sexual abuse, the trauma of the visit, clinician C's role, and Susie's perception that "judges don't listen to little kids" had to be addressed in treatment. As an indirect result of clinician C's assertions, the father received unsupervised access to Susie and sexually abused her again. This reabuse was documented by Susie's statement to the police, by medical evidence, and by subsequent statements in therapy.

By ignoring the past history and experience of other professionals, as well as Susie's marked reactions before and after the visit, and by focusing on three pieces of information in the parent-child interaction, clinician C grossly misjudged this case. Furthermore, she caused Susie to suffer a serious setback in her recovery and furnished an opinion to the court that ultimately resulted in the child's reabuse. (p. 555, with changes in notation)

Case Illustration of the Use of Direct Questioning

In the following case, direct questioning of a child enabled the interviewer to obtain details about the child's being sexually abused. The case is from Faller (1988, pp. 176–177), but I generated the dialogue from Faller's narrative account.

CASE 22-5. AMANDA

Amanda, who was 8 years old, had told her mother of some scary things that happened when she visited her dad. Her parents were divorced. However, when her mother took her to tell the Friend of the Court [a court-appointed counselor], she refused to say anything. Her mother then brought her for an evaluation by an expert in sexual abuse. After the interviewer asked Amanda about her school, her dog, and her friends, they discussed her relationship with her mother. Then the interviewer raised the subject of her father.

IR: Tell me about your dad.
IE: I don't like to be with him.
IR: Is there any time it is OK?
IE: Yeah, when he takes me to my grandmother.
IR: Did you go to your grandmother the last time you were with your dad?
IE: No.
IR: Could you tell me what happened the last time you were with your dad?
IE: Scary things.
IR: What kind of scary things?
IE: I don't want to talk about it.
IR: What would make it easier for you to talk about it?
IE: Maybe if you would ask me questions about what happened.
IR: Did the scary things happen to someone else or to you?
IE: To me.
IR: Did they happen in the daytime or at night?
IE: At night.
IR: Did the scary things happen before you went to bed or after?
IE: Before I got up in the morning.
IR: What room were you in when the scary things happened?
IE: In my bed.
IR: Who did the scary things to you?
IE: My dad.
IR: What did he do that was scary?
IE: He hurt me.
IR: Where did he hurt you?
IE: (Amanda spread her legs and pointed to her vagina.)
IR: How did your dad hurt you?
IE: With his wiener.
IR: What is his wiener?
IE: What he pees with.
IR: What did he do with his wiener?
IE: He put it in me.
IR: What did it feel like?
IE: Real bad. I begged him to stop. He said in a minute, but he kept on doing it for a long time.
IR: Was that the scary thing that happened to you?

IE: (Amanda nodded vigorously.)
IR: Then what happened?
IE: He pulled it out.
IR: What did you see when he pulled out his wiener?
IE: Blood, there was blood on his wiener when he took it out of me.
IR: What else did you see?
IE: The blood was all from me but it got on his wiener. He wiped it up with his undershirt.

Interviewing Pitfalls That May Lead to Biased Interviews and False Allegations

This part of the chapter presents several interviewing pitfalls that can lead to biased interviews. Biased interviews can lead to actions that damage the child, the family, and the alleged perpetrator. For example, children may feel guilty when they learn that what they said in the interview has put an innocent person in jail. The family may become the target of litigation and be scorned by the community. And an innocent alleged perpetrator may be jailed and, as a consequence, lose his or her family, job, and friends. The damage to all involved may be severe, long lasting, and perhaps irreversible. Biased questions and other biased interview techniques may lead the child to make inaccurate statements because the child (a) wants to please the interviewer, (b) wants to get out of a difficult situation, (c) feels browbeaten, or (d) has some other reason.

Pitfall 1: Failing to recognize your preconceived expectations. Do not enter the interview with preconceived expectations. If you do, you may lead the child to make statements that conform to your expectations. For example, if you have decided *before* you interview the child that the child was abused, you are likely to conduct a biased interview, especially when the evidence is sparse. Furthermore, you may fail to follow up leads that might exonerate the alleged abuser. And if you have decided *before* you interview the child that the maltreatment did *not* occur, you may fail to follow up leads that might implicate the alleged abuser.

When you conduct child maltreatment interviews, you must be (a) aware of your values, needs, prejudices, and moral standards and (b) able to contain your emotions and biases. You also need to know that you have the support of the agency staff behind you. If you are not in control of your personal needs, emotions, and biases and if you are not receiving the support and supervision you need as a professional or professional-in-training, it is extremely difficult to be an effective child maltreatment interviewer. If you have doubts about your ability to interview effectively children who have been or may have been maltreated, have someone else conduct the interview. When you feel more confident of your ability, you can begin to conduct interviews with these children.

Pitfall 2: Failing to distinguish spontaneous statements from those that are simple acknowledgments. Carefully distinguish statements the child makes spontaneously from those the child responds to with "yes," "no," or a nod. You want to be aware of these distinctions when you analyze the information you obtained and when you write your report. Obviously, spontaneous statements that offer new information should be followed up with further questions.

Pitfall 3: Failing to recognize that you are using unintended cues, coercive techniques, or leading questions. Do not give unintended nonverbal or verbal cues or use suggestive or coercive techniques, pressure, or any other tactics that might subtly influence the child to make responses that confirm your expectations or that will shape or mold the child's statements. Your tone of voice, inflections, body movements, posture, smiles, nods of the head, or looks may subtly influence the child. You need to be aware of these aspects of your behavior in the interview.

Here are some examples of *unacceptable* interview techniques (Haugaard & Reppucci, 1988; Wong, 1988).

INAPPROPRIATE USE OF REINFORCEMENTS
1. The interviewer uses nonverbal cues, including smiles, hugs, and nods of the head, to reinforce or reward the child. Cues work because children desire to conform to adults' expectations.
2. The interviewer gives the child candy, food, drinks, toys, and promises of special treats when the child says what the interviewer wants to hear.
3. The interviewer uses verbal cues to reinforce or reward the child. When the child says things the interviewer wants to hear, the interviewer says, for example, "Very good," "That's right," "You're doing very well," "You're doing a very good job," or "Good girl, don't you feel better now?"
4. The interviewer offers to take the child to an ice cream parlor, fast food restaurant, or some other enticing place after the child talks about what happened.

INAPPROPRIATE USE OF AFFECT
5. The interviewer is cold and nondemonstrative and questions the child repeatedly when the child doesn't give the "right" answers. Conversely, the interviewer is warm and demonstrative when the child gives the "right" answers.

INAPPROPRIATE USE OF PROBES
6. The interviewer repeatedly says "And what else?" or tells the child that the interview will be over only when the child responds and answers.

USE OF BADGERING/UNDUE PRESSURE
7. The interviewer badgers the child after the child refuses to say he or she was maltreated: "You told your mother about Dad. You better tell me, or you will still be hurt" or "I know it happened, and you'll have to stay here until you talk." The interviewer also may ask the same question repeatedly until the child relents and gives the "right" answer.
8. The interviewer implies a threat by saying "If you don't talk to me, your mother will be upset."
9. The interviewer puts pressure on the child to conform by saying "Good children tell the truth, and you want to be a good child, don't you?" or "Your mother said that this happened to you. Your mother knows best, so tell me what happened."

INAPPROPRIATE USE OF INCREDULOUSNESS
10. The interviewer uses a statement that implies that he or she doubts the child's story and thus encourages the child to change his or her report: "It isn't that I do not believe you, but if you think of anything else let me know" or "I don't believe that's the only place he touched you. I want you to tell me about the *other* places. You *know* there were other places."

INAPPROPRIATE USE OF QUESTIONS
11. The interviewer uses suggestive or leading questions. For example, soon after the beginning of the interview, the interviewer asks questions such as the following about the alleged perpetrator, who is called Uncle Bill: "What did Uncle Bill do wrong?" or "Has Uncle Bill done anything to you that he shouldn't have done?" Following are other types of suggestive or leading questions (Cage, 1988; DeLipsey & James, 1988): "He hurt you, didn't he?" "You were afraid, weren't you?" "Why didn't you tell us?" "Were you afraid he would hurt you?" "Your mother said that the person who touched you was your stepfather. It was him, wasn't it?" "Did she [referring to the alleged perpetrator] tell you that she would hurt you if you told anyone?" Such questions give children little option except to agree with what the interviewer suggested, leave little room for clarification, may cause children to think that what they did was bad, and may confuse them (Cage, 1988).

USE OF MISLEADING DEMONSTRATIONS
12. The interviewer plants a seed in the child's mind that the event could possibly have taken place. For example, the interviewer shows the child an anatomically detailed doll, puts his or her finger in the doll's vagina, and says "Does your daddy put his fingers in you just like this?"

USE OF FALSE ASSURANCES
13. The interviewer assumes that the maltreatment occurred and offers the child protection to get the child to respond: "Things like this happen to lots of kids. I know many children to whom the same thing happened. Don't worry, I'll protect you if you tell me" or "You can tell me. I'll make sure he'll never do *that* again."

14. In a case involving alleged multiple victims who are interviewed in succession, the interviewer gives one child information provided by another child and lets the child know that he or she expects the child to say the same thing. For example, "Mary said that this happened to her. Mary is a smart girl. Don't you want to be as smart as Mary and tell me that it happened to you, too?" By using other children's revelations, the interviewer tries to convince the child that maltreatment occurred or to make the child feel disloyal if he or she fails to confirm the maltreatment (Lyon, 1995).

WEARING DOWN CHILD

15. The interviewer conducts a lengthy interview, and the child finally succumbs by saying something the interviewer wants to hear.

These techniques are either blatantly coercive and demeaning or suggestive and leading. Even though you want to find perpetrators and protect children, you must allow children to tell their stories without undue pressure. Obviously, you will have to probe and keep the child on task in the interview. But this does not mean that you have to be blunt and coerce the child to find out what happened. When you interview a child, your job is to remain neutral and to obtain reliable and valid information—it is not to judge the guilt or innocence of an alleged offender. *Under no condition should you directly or indirectly lead the child to say things that might never have happened.*

Pitfall 4: Failing to recognize a fabricated story.
If you fail to recognize a fabricated story, you may inadvertently damage the reputation of others and cause undue harm. You need to consider whether someone coerced the child to repeat a fabricated story or whether the child fabricated the story himself or herself. Is the child's story convincing, or is there any evidence that it has been rehearsed and fabricated? Chapter 23 provides more information about evaluating allegations of child maltreatment.

Illustration of an Interview Using Coercive Techniques and Leading Questions

The following excerpt illustrates the coordinated efforts of two interviewers—one a social worker and the other a detective—to manipulate the child victim's responses in a follow-up interview. Whether or not maltreatment occurred in this case, the coercion illustrated in the interview excerpt is completely unacceptable. The excerpt is a verbatim transcript filed as part of the court record submitted to an appellate court in New Jersey in the case of Kelly Michaels (State v. Michaels, Superior Court, Essex County, New Jersey, 1988). In a trial held in 1988, Kelly Michaels was found

guilty of abusing 19 children, ages 3 to 5 years, in a day nursery in New Jersey where she worked. She was sentenced to 47 years in prison. After she served 5 years in prison, an appellate court overturned her conviction in 1993. The appellate court ruled that there was misuse of expert testimony and that the trial judge improperly denied the defense attorney access to the children. The appellate court also was concerned that pretrial interviews may have tainted the children's testimony. The abbreviations in the following excerpt are IR-S = social worker, IR-D = detective, and IE-C = child.

IR-S: Don't be so unfriendly. I thought we were buddies last time.

IE-C: Nope, not any more.

IR-S: We have gotten a lot of other kids to help us since I last saw you.... Did we tell you that Kelly is in jail?

IE-C: Yes. My mother already told me.

IR-S: Did I tell you that this is the guy (pointing to IR-D) that arrested her?... Well, we can get out of here real quick if you just tell me what you told me the last time, when we met.

IE-C: I forgot.

IR-S: No you didn't. I know you didn't.

IE-C: I did! I did!

IR-S: I thought we were friends last time.

IE-C: I'm not your friend any more!

IR-S: How come?

IE-C: Because I hate you!

IR-S: You have no reason to hate me. We were buddies when you left.

IE-C: I hate you now!

IR-S: Oh, you do not, you secretly like me, I can tell.

IE-C: I hate you.

IR-S: Oh, come on. We talked to a few more of your buddies. And everyone told me about the nap room, and the bathroom stuff, and the music room stuff, and the choir stuff, and the peanut butter stuff, and everything. … All your buddies [talked].... Come on, do you want to help us out? Do you want to keep her in jail? I'll let you hear your voice and play with the tape recorder; I need your help again. Come on.... Real quick, will you just tell me what happened with the wooden spoon? Let's go.

IE-C: I forgot.

IR-D: Now listen, you have to behave.

IR-S: Do you want me to tell him to behave? Are you going to be a good boy, huh? While you are here, did he [IR-D] show you his badge and his handcuffs?... Back to what happened to you with the wooden spoon. If you don't remember words, maybe you can show me [with anatomical dolls present].

IE-C: I forgot what happened, too.

IR-S: You remember. You told your mommy about everything about the music room and the nap room, and all that stuff. You want to help her stay in jail, don't you? So she doesn't bother you anymore and so she doesn't tell you any more scary stories.

Exercise 22-1. Rephrasing Questions

Read each question, and then rephrase it in a more acceptable way. Compare your answers with those that follow the questions.

1. Did Mr. Brown threaten you?
2. Why didn't you try to stop him?
3. Did you feel frightened?
4. Was Mr. Jones drinking alcohol?
5. Why did you let her touch you?
6. If you tell me what Mr. Smith did to you in his house, I'll give you some candy.
7. Is that when she hit you?
8. Why did you wait so long to tell anyone?
9. Did he put his hands down your dress?
10. You want to be a good boy and tell me what happened.
11. Did you wear something sexy?
12. Did you enjoy what he did to you?
13. How many times did he hit you?

Suggested Rephrasing

1. What did Mr. Brown do?
2. Did you try to stop him?
3. How did you feel?
4. What was Mr. Jones doing before this happened?
5. How did it happen that she touched you?
6. Let's talk about what happened when you went to Mr. Smith's house.
7. What happened next?
8. Did you tell anyone about it?
9. What did he do?
10. Tell me what happened.
11. What were you wearing?
12. How did you feel when it happened?
13. (After child has said that she was hit) Tell me as much as you can remember about when you were [use words child used].

Use of Anatomically Detailed Dolls in the Interview

You have read about the possibility that children, especially young ones, may be reluctant to talk to you. In addition, they may have difficulty describing what happened to them. To remedy this situation, particularly in cases of alleged child sexual maltreatment, some interviewers use anatomically detailed dolls (also referred to as "anatomically correct dolls," "anatomically explicit dolls," and "anatomical dolls"). This part of the chapter reviews the controversy about the use of anatomically detailed dolls in the assessment of child sexual abuse allegations. Let's first examine arguments in favor of the use of anatomically detailed dolls and then discuss arguments against the use of the dolls. A comment on the two positions closes the discussion.

Arguments in favor of the use of anatomically detailed dolls. Several writers favor the use of these dolls (Everson & Boat, 1994; Jones & McQuiston, 1989; Walker, 1990). Everson and Boat (1994) cite the following advantages:

1. *Dolls may be useful as demonstration aids.* The dolls may serve "as props to help children 'show' rather than 'tell' what happened. This is especially important when limited verbal skills or emotional issues such as fear of telling and embarrassment about discussing sexual activities interfere with direct verbal description" (p. 117).

2. *Dolls may serve as a memory stimulus and a diagnostic screen.* The dolls "may be useful in triggering the child's recall of specific events of a possible sexual nature." In addition, the child's sexual behavior with the dolls may serve "as a possible indication of abuse that warrants careful consideration and further evaluation" (p. 117).

3. *Dolls may serve as anatomical models.* The dolls may help in "assessing the child's labels for parts of the body, understanding of bodily functions, and knowledge of the mechanics of sexual intercourse" (p. 116).

Arguments against the use of anatomically detailed dolls. Several writers argue against the use of these dolls (Ceci & Bruck, 1995; DeLoach, 1995; R. J. Levy, 1989; Skinner & Berry, 1993; Wolfner, Faust, & Dawes, 1993):

1. *Behavior with the dolls may be difficult to interpret.* What the child does with the dolls may have nothing to do with what has taken place in the child's life. The dolls may stimulate fantasy and not recall.

2. *Behavior with the dolls may not provide valid or useful information.* Research suggests that use of the dolls does not help the interviewer determine whether sexual abuse took place. The interviewer may believe that the child's behavior with the dolls is providing additional information useful in decision making, when actually the doll play information is likely to be of little, if any, value. With children under the age of 3 years, "interviews using dolls elicited no more or better information than interviews done without them...[and] the presence of the dolls might even interfere with the memory reports of [very young] children" (DeLoach, 1995, p. 178).

3. *Behavior with the dolls may induce false memories.* Behavior with the dolls, coupled with highly sexualized interview questions, could lead to sexualized doll play and cause the child to form images that alter his or her memory of events. At a later date, the child may not be able to distinguish what happened in the interview from what did or did not happen outside the interview.

Comment on the use of anatomically detailed dolls. Proponents and opponents of the use of anatomically detailed dolls in child maltreatment interviews do have several areas of agreement. Both groups are against the use of the dolls as a diagnostic test—*behavior with anatomically detailed dolls, regardless of its form, should never be used by itself to conclude that sexual abuse took place.* Second, both groups are against the use of coercive questioning. Third, both agree that little is known about how the use of anatomically detailed dolls, coupled with certain types of leading questions, may alter children's memories. However, proponents believe that anatomically detailed dolls serve a useful function, whereas opponents argue against any use of the dolls in child sexual abuse evaluations.

In spite of the potential problems with using anatomically correct dolls, surveys indicate that their use is widespread in interviewing children suspected of being sexually abused (Boat & Everson, 1988; Conte, Sorenson, Forgarty, & Rosa, 1991; Kendall-Tackett & Watson, 1992). A study of 97 videotaped interviews with children between 2 and 12 years of age provides some information about how anatomically detailed dolls are used in practice (Boat & Everson, 1996). The study indicates that (a) the most common uses of anatomically detailed dolls were as anatomical models and demonstration aids, (b) the dolls were used with about the same frequency with children between 2 and 5 years (86% of the cases) and children between 6 and 12 years (80% of the cases), and (c) in many cases, interviewers used the dolls in a way that was questionable (for example, they introduced the dolls when the child was still giving an adequate description); however, the clinical significance of the questionable practices is unknown.

Research does not indicate whether interviewers use anatomically detailed dolls to draw conclusions that sexual abuse has occurred, to aid in the interview, or for both purposes. There is a fine line between using anatomically detailed dolls as an interview aid and using them to make diagnostic decisions and critical recommendations, such as recommending the removal of the suspected abuser or the child from the home. Research suggests that "gender, race, and socioeconomic status of young children may affect the manner in which they interact with anatomical dolls" (Everson & Boat, 1994, p. 124); these variables need to be considered when clinicians interpret children's behavior. However, good norms for these variables do not yet exist, nor is it known whether clinicians consider these variables in their interpretations. It is also important to find out how children who have witnessed sexual abuse, but who have not been themselves sexually abused, would perform in an interview in which anatomically detailed dolls were used.

I recommend that you be extremely cautious if you decide to use anatomically detailed dolls to interview children suspected of being sexually abused. The American Prosecutors Research Institute (1993) recommends that anatomically detailed dolls be used only *after* disclosure to clarify details of the sexual abuse. A working group supported by the American Psychological Association (Koocher, Goodman, White, Friedrich, Sivan, & Reynolds, 1995) indicates that anatomically detailed dolls can "provide a useful communication tool in the hands of a trained professional interviewer [with the understanding that anatomically detailed] dolls are not a psychological test with predictive (or postdictive) validity per se…[and] that definitive statements about child sexual abuse cannot be made on the basis of spontaneous or guided 'doll *play*'" (p. 218). (See the *Practice Guidelines* from the American Professional Society on the Abuse of Children, 1995, and Koocher et al., 1995, for other recommendations and for a discussion of the use of anatomically detailed dolls.)

In no case should you conclude that a child has been abused solely on the basis of his or her behavior with anatomically detailed dolls. You must take into account everything you know about the case in arriving at a conclusion. You may want to try several short open-ended interviews that may build rapport and help the child verbalize what, if anything, happened to him or her before you consider using anatomically detailed dolls. And, if you decide to use anatomically detailed dolls, obtain specialized training in using the dolls, particularly training involving the use of standard protocols (see Everson & Boat, 1994).

Wolfner et al. (1993) believe that the use of anatomically detailed dolls even "as a component in diagnosis violates ethical principles of diagnostic testing" (p. 9), and Skinner and Berry (1993) state that "presently, the use of dolls in validation interviews fails to meet scientific test criteria and, consequently,…AD [anatomical dolls] should not be used as the basis for expert opinions or conclusions" (p. 418). Ceci and Bruck (1995) conclude from their review of the research literature "that this tool [anatomically detailed dolls] has the potential for serious misuse, including misdiagnosis, which could result in removing nonabused children from their homes, the implantation of false memories in therapy, and the imprisonment of innocent adults" (p. 186). Everson and Boat (1994), however, believe that "blanket condemnations of the use of anatomical dolls in sexual abuse evaluations are unjustified…. Evaluators can be confident in their continued, informed use of anatomical dolls in sexual abuse evaluations" (p. 126). Thus, there are no simple answers. Keeping up with current clinical, research, and forensic literature will help you make an informed decision about whether to use anatomically detailed dolls in sexual abuse evaluations of children.

The Cognitive Interview

The cognitive interview is a useful procedure to help children and adults recall information, primarily for forensic purposes and for investigatory interviewing. The procedure includes a collection of techniques designed to enhance witnesses' memories by facilitating the completeness and accuracy of their reports. Here are some examples of techniques used in the cognitive interview (Saywitz, Geiselman, & Bornstein, 1992).

1. The interviewer at the beginning of the interview might say "There may be some questions that you do not know

the answers to. That's okay. Nobody can remember everything. If you don't know the answer to a question, then tell me 'I don't know.' Do not guess or make anything up. It is very important to tell me only what you really remember. Only what really happened" (p. 756).

2. The child is then asked to recall the incident by mentally reconstructing the environmental and personal context that existed at the time of the event. The interviewer might say "Picture the time when you were in the room, as if you were there right now. Think about what it was like. What did the room look like? Tell me out loud.... Were there any smells in the room?... Was it dark or light in the room?... Picture any other people who were there. Who else was there?... What things were there in the room?... How were you feeling when you were in the room? Go ahead" (p. 756).

3. The interviewer asks the child to report everything he or she remembers and not withhold anything, even things that may not seem important. "Now I want you to start at the beginning and tell me what happened, from the beginning, to the middle, to the end. Tell me everything you remember, even little parts that you don't think are very important. Sometimes people leave out little things because they think little things are not important. Tell me everything that happened. Go ahead" (p. 756).

4. After the child has finished with his or her narrative report, the interviewer might ask specific questions to clarify what the child said, as would be done in a standard interview.

5. The interviewer tries to minimize interruptions and changes to easier topics if the child cannot remember some details of the event.

6. After the initial description of the event, the interviewer might ask an older child to recall the event in a different order. "Now I want you to tell me what happened in backward order. Start at the end, then go to the middle, and then the beginning. Again, tell me everything that you remember, even little parts that you don't think are very important."

7. After the initial description of the event, the interviewer might ask the child to try to recall the event from the perspective of someone else who was there and to think about what this other person must have seen. "Put yourself in the body of _____, and tell me what that person saw."

8. The interviewer might ask questions designed to obtain information about the physical appearance of the persons who were at the event, their names, their speech characteristics, and their conversations.

The cognitive interview "is essentially a guided memory search [that] provides explicit retrieval strategies, specific retrieval cues, and strategies for organizing information. Although young children show limited memory strategy usage, they are known to be able to use strategies provided by adults at the moment of retrieval that they cannot spontaneously generate and use on their own" (p. 745). The cogni-

tive interview is useful with people who have a mental age of 7 years or older. Children with a mental age of less than 7 years may not understand the procedures used in this interview. Therefore, you should be sure that the child is cognitively able to do the tasks in the cognitive interview before you use it. For more information about the cognitive interview technique, see Fisher and Geiselman (1992) and Saywitz et al. (1992).

Two Examples of Forensic Interviews

Let's now look at two forensic interviews with children who were allegedly sexually abused. Each interview represents a somewhat different style of interviewing. They both accomplish their goal, but in different ways.

Interview with a 5-year-old boy. The first interview was conducted with a 5-year-old male child who was allegedly sexually assaulted. The interview was videotaped. All names, dates, and locations have been changed to ensure anonymity. What do you think of the interviewer's style? Did he ask appropriate questions? Did he ask inappropriate questions? Did he find out what he needed to know in order to make some decision about the alleged sexual abuse? Compare your evaluation with the comments included in the interview and after the interview.

CASE 22-6. JAMES MCDONALD

Before the child comes into the room, which has a one-way mirror with a closed-circuit television, the interviewer says "My name is Robert Evans. I'm a social worker at the Patrick Center. This morning I'll be interviewing 5-year-old James McDonald. His medical record number is 5957843296. Today's date is June 1, 1996. It's approximately 10:00 A.M., and I'll be bringing James in now."

IR: Hi, James. I'm Robert Evans. I'm a member of the child development staff. How are you today?

IE: OK.

IR: James, let's do something together. I'm going to draw a tree, and I'd like you to help me color it. OK? (Draws an outline of a tree.)

IE: Sure.

IR: Here are some crayons. What color do you want to make the leaves?

IE: I think I'll make them green.

IR: That's a good color. Go ahead and color the leaves.

IE: (Child colors the leaves.)

IR: And now this part, the trunk of the tree (pointing to the trunk). What color do you want to make the trunk?

IE: Black.

IR: Go ahead. You're doing a good job. Is there anything else you want to put on our tree?

IE: No.

IR: James, I want to tell you something special about my room. Behind the mirror is a video camera, and we make videotapes of all the boys and girls who come in here. That way I can remember everything we talk about. OK?

IE: Can I see the room where it is later?

IR: Sure, just remind me. James, I'd like to talk to you about how things are going with you. OK?

IE: Sure.

IR: How old are you, James?

IE: Five (holding up five fingers).

IR: When did you turn five?

IE: November 25th, and I went to Round Table Pizza!

IR: Wow, for your birthday?

IE: (Nods affirmatively.)

IR: What else did you do on your birthday?

IE: I went to school, and I had enough cupcakes for everybody.

IR: So everyone got to celebrate your birthday with you, huh?

IE: Yep.

IR: Well, that's pretty neat.

IE: But I'm the one who got to blow out the candles.

IR: Yeah, 'cause it was your birthday, huh?

IE: Yeah, and we put Power Ranger candies on there.

IR: Was that okay?

IE: Yeah, but one of them broke. I gave Timmy an extra one.

IR: Is he your best friend?

IE: Yeah, but he's in another room. He's in room one.

IR: He's in room one?

IE: Yeah.

IR: Where do you go to school?

IE: Harvest Day School.

IR: What's your teacher's name?

IE: Miss Brenda and Miss Constance, because Miss Brenda's on vacation.

IR: Oh…who lives at your house?

IE: Just me and mom and my sister Sylvia.

IR: Oh…

IE: And dad.

IR: How old is your sister Sylvia?

IE: She's two.

IR: Oh…do you ever…

IE: …and sometimes I have to help take care of her if she's sick, me and my grandma.

IR: Do you know what your address is? That's kind of a hard question…

IE: Three-six-nine-five West 15th Avenue.

IR: Who taught you that?

IE: My mom and dad taught me. I know my phone number too!

IR: What is it?

IE: I forgot.

IR: Do you know what city you live in?

IE: West 15th.

IR: Do you know what state you live in?

IE: Um…Montana, and it's got two parks there, with a playground for big kids and one for little kids. Sylvia can slide down the slide, but my mom has to catch her. But I can do it myself.

IR: And you can go to the big kids' play area?

IE: Uh huh.

IR: That's pretty neat…. How about your colors, do you know your colors?

IE: Uh huh.

IR: (Getting out a box of crayons) One thing I want to tell you, James, is that I am going to be asking you a lot of questions, and I want you to know that if there's something you don't know, you can just say "I don't know," because that's alright, okay?

IE: Okay…you know I could tell you a real good story that I just saw in the movie "Batman Returns" about Batman and Catwoman—Batman and Catwoman both win. And you know Penguin? He's like totally gross.

IR: Really?

IE: Yeah, I saw that movie.

IR: (Holding up a crayon) Do you know what color this is?

IE: Orange. (Interviewer then holds up other crayons, one at a time.) Red…blue…brown…black… purple…green. (Child responds correctly each time.)

IR: Okay! How about counting, can you count?

IE: I can count to 25. (Does so.)

IR: Okay! (Hands a crayon to James.) Can you put this crayon on top of the paper? (Child does so.) Can you put it under the paper? (Child does so.) Can you put it behind your back? (Child does so.) Under the table? (Child does so.) On top of your head? (Child does so.) Inside the box? (Child does so.) Outside the box? (Child does so.)

IE: Red and orange are my favorite colors.

IR: James, what did you do before you came here today?

IE: I watched TV with my dad.

IR: And what are you going to do after you leave here today?

IE: I'm going to McDonald's with my mom and my sister.

IR: Oh, that sounds like fun…. Do you know what this is (holding up a stuffed cat doll)?

IE: It's a cat.

IR: Is it a real cat or a pretend cat?

IE: It's a pretend kitty.

IR: How do you know that?

IE: Because he doesn't move his head or anything.

IR: Can you think of any other reason?

IE: Because his eyes don't move and he doesn't walk or anything. I like kitties, but my mother's allergic to them.

IR: Maybe she wouldn't be allergic to that one, since it's a pretend kitty! James, do you know what a lie is?

IE: If you don't tell the truth.

IR: Could you give me maybe an example of what a lie might be?

IE: A lie is if you don't tell the truth and you tell something that isn't true, that would be a lie.

IR: So, if I told you that this was a red crayon (holding up a black one), would that be the truth or a lie?

IE: A lie.

IR: And if I said this was an orange crayon (holding up an orange crayon), is that the truth or a lie?

IE: The truth.

IR: And if I said that I'm a man, would that be the truth or a lie?

IE: The truth.

IR: One of the things that I do when I talk to kids is always have them promise to tell the truth. Would you promise me to tell me the truth today while we talk, too?

IE: Yep.

IR: Can we shake on it?

IE: (Shakes hands with interviewer.)

In this first segment, the interviewer sets out to determine several things about the child's ability. The interviewer learns that the child knows his age and birthday, the name of his school, the composition of his family, his address, the name of the state he lives in, colors, how to count to 25, the difference between the concepts of real and pretend, and the difference between the truth and a lie. The child, however, does not know his phone number or the name of the city where he lives. The child spontaneously talks about himself. He seems to understand the interviewer's questions well.

IR: James, do you know why you came down here today?
IE: To talk about some stuff.
IR: Okay…what kind of stuff?
IE: Like doing something bad or something…
IR: Okay, what kind of things happened that were bad?
IE: When we were over in Harlowton, Jack, you know, he rubbed my body, you know, my private parts, while we were there.
IR: What else happened?
IE: He just kept doing it until finally I said it didn't feel good and stop, and he did.
IR: And who is Jack?
IE: He's my cousin.
IR: And how old is Jack?
IE: He's 17.
IR: And where does Jack live?
IE: He lives in Harlowton, at Uncle Nathan's.
IR: And you said he touched your body? Your private parts?
IE: Yeah.
IR: (Takes out drawing of a boy.) Could you look at this drawing and take my pen and make a circle around the parts you mean when you say "your body" or "your private parts"?
IE: Yeah (taking the pen).
IR: What did you mean when you said he touched your body?
IE: I meant he rubbed it…(circling the genital area of the male "gingerbread" drawing). (It should be noted that James's outward affect has changed significantly. He is now withdrawn, quiet, and looking down at the table rather than at the interviewer, as he had previously done.)
IR: This part that you circled, is that what you mean when you said he touched your body and he touched your private parts?
IE: Uh huh.
IR: And can you tell me how he touched them?
IE: He squeezed them.
IR: When he touched you there, did he touch you on top of your clothing or underneath your clothing?
IE: Both.
IR: So sometimes when he touched you, his hand touched your skin on your body, your private parts?
IE: Uh huh.
IR: And what part of his body touched your body?
IE: His hands.
IR: I've got another drawing here. Could you take a crayon and put a mark on the parts of his body that touched your body?

IE: Uh huh (placing a crayon mark "X" on both hands of the second drawing).
IR: Did any other part of his body touch any part of your body, James?
IE: Just his hands.
IR: Did he touch you on any other part of your body?
IE: No.
IR: (Points to the drawing.) When he touched you there, how did it feel?
IE: It felt bad…it felt a little bit good, but then it felt bad.
IR: Okay…when Jack touched your private parts there, did he ever touch you like that before?
IE: No.
IR: How many times did this happen, James?
IE: Just once.
IR: Did he do anything else that made you feel kind of uncomfortable?
IE: No…but then he showed me his private parts, too.
IR: The same part that you marked, he showed you that part?
IE: Uh huh.
IR: Did that happen at the same time that he touched yours?
IE: Uh huh.
IR: Where did all this happen?
IE: At my uncle's, in the living room.
IR: You were in the living room?
IE: Uh huh.
IR: Were you standing up or sitting down?
IE: We were laying down under a table. And he called me last night and said he was sorry and he got in trouble. He's grounded.
IR: Oh, James, when this happened, do you remember if it was daytime outside or nighttime?
IE: It was daytime.
IR: Who was at your uncle's when this happened?
IE: Just me and Jack and my uncle.
IR: And where was your uncle?
IE: In the garage working.
IR: Do you remember where your mother and father and sister were?
IE: I'm not sure where my sister was. My mom and dad were skiing.
IR: Was this before Christmas or after Christmas?
IE: It was the day after Christmas.
IR: Did he say anything to you when he was doing that?
IE: He said "Does that feel good?" and I said "Just a little," and I meant just a little (putting his hands over his eyes and covering his face). And then I said "It doesn't feel good, stop."
IR: And then what did he do?
IE: He stopped.
IR: And then what did you do?
IE: And then we played with my monster trucks.
IR: Did he say anything else to you?
IE: He said not to tell anybody because we would get in trouble.
IR: Do you know if he's ever done this to anyone else?
IE: I don't know.
IR: Did he talk about anyone else that he does this with?
IE: No, but my dad talked to him about it.
IR: How did your dad find out?

IE: I told him.

IR: When you told Jack that it didn't feel good anymore, what did he do?

IE: He stopped.

IR: Did anything else like this happen since then?

IE: No. I haven't been around Jack since then. I'm not allowed.

IR: Did he ever do anything like this before?

IE: No.

IR: Was there ever a time that he showed you pictures or movies that had pictures of people with no clothes on?

IE: No.

IR: Do you know if he has any pictures or movies like that?

IE: I don't know.

In the second segment of the interview, the interviewer broaches the topic of the sexual abuse by asking a general question about whether the child knows why he is being interviewed. The interviewer uses the child's word "bad" for referring to what happened to the child. The interviewer systematically inquires about details of the alleged sexual molestation by asking several focused questions.

IR: You remember when we talked about telling the truth?

IE: Uh huh.

IR: Is everything that you've told me today the truth?

IE: Uh huh.

IR: Has anything else happened that you want to talk to me about?

IE: Well…when I went to see the Batman movie, I got a sticker, you can stick it on your window. And I've got Batman shoes (holding a foot up). (Outward affect changes; begins looking at the interviewer and smiling.)

IR: That's pretty cool. I've never seen Batman shoes before.

IE: Yeah. I even have a Batman video at home, too.

IR: Is there anything else that you would like to talk to me about?

IE: Well, I'd like to talk to you about some wild animals that you're not supposed to be around, my dad told me about.

IR: What kind of wild animals?

IE: Well, like wild bears. You're not supposed to go around them, you're supposed to stay away from them.

IR: What should I do if I see one?

IE: Well, you should stay away or stand real still if they come near you.

IR: Well, that's good to know. Thank you…. What should you do if they start chasing you, though?

IE: Well, I think, if they're chasing you, maybe you could pet them and they might feel better.

IR: Well, it might be worth a shot, but maybe it would be better to climb up a tree or get in a car or under a car or something.

IE: Yeah.

IR: Well, I really appreciate you coming in and talking to me today and telling me about what happened. Here's a card for you with my name and phone number on it. If you think of anything else that you need to tell me about, you can give me a call or have your dad or mom call me so that I can talk to you, okay?

IE: Yeah, thanks.

In the third segment, the interviewer inquires about whether the child told the truth, asks the child if he wants to talk about anything else, thanks the child for cooperating, and gives the child his card.

This is an excellent interview. The interviewer had good rapport with the child, used language comprehensible to the child, and learned several important details about the alleged sexual abuse. The probing questions were carefully designed to elicit important information from the child about the alleged molestation. This interview illustrates several features that you may encounter in interviewing older preschool children and kindergarten-aged children. First, you may have to deviate at times from your goal and talk to children about their interests. Second, children may know some important details about their environments but not other details. Third, children's affect may change when details of the maltreatment are disclosed. And fourth, children by the age of 5 years may have good communication skills and recall ability. The report of sexual molestation was corroborated in an investigation by the police—James's cousin admitted that he had fondled James.

Interview with a 4-year, 4-month-old girl. The following interview was with a 4-year, 4-month-old girl who was allegedly sexually molested. As you read the interview, consider the credibility of the child's allegation. Also, what do you think of the interviewer's style? Were there any leading questions? Did the interviewer have good rapport? Did the interviewer elicit enough details to decide on the merits of the allegation? Did the interviewer make the correct decision in continuing the interview in spite of the child's desire to terminate the session? The interviewer's notes, which follow the interview, were based on the interview and on information provided by the police department. The medical report was not available at the time the notes were written. The dialogue was obtained from a videotape interview conducted by one interviewer with the child. The dialogue and the notes have been edited. All names of persons and places are fictitious, and dates have been changed.

CASE 22-7. BETTY TROTH

Before the child comes into the room, which has a one-way mirror with a closed-circuit television, the interviewer says "My name is Diane Jones. I'm a social worker at the Hillman Center. This morning I'll be interviewing 4-year, 4-month-old Betty Troth. Her medical record number is 974860CVY. Today's date is June 14, 1996. It's approximately 9:00 A.M., and I'll be bringing Betty in now."

IR: Hi, Betty. I'm Diane. Why don't you sit here.

IE: OK.

IR: What I want to do first, Betty, is to draw your picture. When kids come in, I like to draw their face. (As she talks, the IR draws a circle and then eyes on a large piece of paper hanging from a clip board on the wall.) You can tell me what these are if you know. (Points to the eyes.)

IE: Eyes.
IR: What color are your eyes, Betty?
IE: Black.
IR: What other color do you have on your eyes?
IE: Hmm.
IR: Do you have blue or green or brown or what?
IE: Hmm.
IR: They look like they might have a little blue.
IE: Hmm.
IR: You have a smile today. Let's draw a smile. (Draws a smile on the face.) What do you have in there? (Points to mouth on the picture.)
IE: Tongue.
IR: (Draws teeth.) What are these?
IE: Teeth.
IR: Lots of teeth. What is this? (Draws ears.)
IE: Ears.
IR: What's that? (Draws hair.)
IE: Hair.
IR: What do you have in your hair today?
IE: Ponytails.
IR: Ponytails, Yeah. (Draws ponytails on the picture.) Does this look like ponytails, Betty?
IE: Yeah.
IR: Does that look like you?
IE: Yeah.

In this first segment, the interviewer uses a drawing technique to establish rapport with the child and to get the child to talk about a picture of a face. This technique helps the interviewer evaluate the child's ability to communicate and prepares the child for questions that will come later in the interview about body parts. The child answers the interviewer's questions readily.

IR: Betty, how old are you?
IE: (Holds up four fingers.)
IR: How many is that?
IE: Four.
IR: Betty.
IE: What?
IR: Betty, who do you live with?
IE: My mom.
IR: Your mom. What's your mom's name?
IE: Susan.
IR: Susan, OK. Your mom is Susan. (Draws on the paper a circle that represents mom.) Do you live with anyone else?
IE: Nope.
IR: Is anyone else in your family?
IE: (Shakes head no.) Just Susan and me. Hey, what are these (looking at coloring markers)?
IR: Those are some of the markers. Do you have someone else in your family, Betty?
IE: Just Julie and Robert and me and mom.
IR: Who is Julie?
IE: (Interrupting) Can I color something?
IR: You know what, if it's OK, could we just talk for a while, and then we can color. Would that be alright?

IE: Hmm…
IR: You could write down here, if you want to, though. (Points to the bottom of the paper.) Could we talk while you write?
IE: Yes.
IR: OK. Who's Julie?
IE: She lives with me.
IR: She lives with you. Is she a girl or a lady or a boy or what?
IE: A lady.
IR: A lady, OK.
IE: A girl.
IR: A girl. OK, how old is Julie?
IE: (Shrugs shoulders.)
IR: Who's Robert?
IE: He's a little boy, like me.
IR: A little boy like you. Does Robert live with you?
IE: Yes.
IR: Ok, he's a little boy like you. Does someone else live with you, Betty?
IE: No.
IR: No, OK. Do you have any brothers or sisters?
IE: I want to color right here.
IR: Betty, do you have any brothers or sisters?
IE: Yeah.
IR: Who are your brothers or sisters?
IE: Susan and Betty and…
IR: Who did you say?
IE: Susan and Betty.
IR: Susan and Betty (points to the pictures she drew), and here's Julie and Robert (draws two more circles that represent Julie and Robert).
IR: Do you have a brother?
IE: (Shakes head no.)
IR: No brother. Do you have a sister?
IE: (Shakes head no.)
IR: No sister. How about a dad? Do you have a dad?
IE: Yes.
IR: Who's your dad?
IE: Frank.
IR: Frank is your dad. Does Frank live with you?
IE: No, no, not Frank. (Pauses.) Phil.
IR: Phil. OK. Does Phil live with you, or does he live somewhere else?
IE: He lives somewhere else.
IR: OK, so your dad is Phil (draws a circle that represents Phil), and he lives somewhere else. Does dad live with anybody?
IE: Hmm.
IR: Who does dad live with?
IE: Doesn't live with nobody.
IR: Doesn't live with nobody. OK. Do you ever go see your dad, or does your dad come to see you?
IE: I go see my dad.
IR: You go see your dad. When you go see your dad, what do you do?
IE: (Draws on the paper…)
IR: Betty?
IE: I don't know.
IR: Do you spend the night at your dad's?
IE: I spend the night.

In the second segment, the interviewer inquires about the child's family. She obtains the names of the child's mother and father. However, she is not successful in identifying who Julie and Robert are or in identifying their relationship to Betty and her mother. Betty shows that she is more interested in coloring than in talking. Allowing children to color during the interview may hinder the interview process, but the tradeoff may be that it allows the interview to be conducted in an informal way and enhances rapport. Betty was somewhat distracted during this segment. She gave her name and the name of her mother when asked about whether she had any brothers and sisters. And she gave a wrong name for her father. Perhaps she wasn't listening or perhaps she was more focused on coloring than on listening to the interviewer's questions. It also may be that the interviewer misunderstood Betty's father's name and Betty corrected the interviewer. Finally, she may have a biological father and a stepfather or someone else living at home and may have gotten confused about who her father is.

IR: You spend the night at your dad's. OK. I have some pictures to show you, Betty. (Reaches for four pictures—two are front and back views of a girl, and two are front and back views of a boy.) That's a nice picture. Who are you drawing?

IE: My dad.

IR: Your dad. OK.

IE: My dad has short hair.

IR: Can you look at these pictures for me, Betty? (Shows pictures.) I have a picture of a girl and a boy. Which one's the girl?

IE: (Points correctly.)

IR: Which one's the boy?

IE: (Points correctly.)

IR: Which one are you, the girl or the boy?

IE: Girl.

IR: Girl. I'm going to put these pictures up, Betty. (Pins front and back pictures of girl on chart on wall.)

IE: OK.

IR: And I want to see what you call the body parts. OK? What's this up here? What's this stuff? (Points to hair.)

IE: Hair.

IR: What's this? (Points to nose.)

IE: Nose.

IR: The nose. What are these? (Points to breasts.)

IE: (Giggling) Boobs.

IR: Boobs. What's this? (Points to hand.)

IE: Hand.

IR: Hand. What's that? (Points to belly button.)

IE: Belly button.

IR: Belly button. What's that? (Points to vagina.)

IE: Pee pee.

IR: Pee pee. What's that? (Points to toes.)

IE: Toes.

IR: Toes. How about this? (Points to buttocks.)

IE: That's a butt.

IR: Butt. How about this, Betty? (Points to back.)

IE: A back.

IR: A back. Good. You know all your body parts. Do you have all of these parts on you?

IE: (Nods yes.)

IR: Let's put your name here. (Writes "Betty" above drawing.)

IR: Betty, who else in your family is a girl, like this?

IE: Uuuh, I have a pee pee.

IR: You have a pee pee.

IE: And a belly button.

IR: Who else has a pee pee and a belly button like this girl?

IE: (No response.)

IR: Are there any girls in your house?

IE: (Shakes head no.) Julie and me.

IR: Julie and you. OK. Who's a boy, like this picture?

IE: My dad.

IR: Your dad. OK. Anybody else?

IE: No.

IR: OK. I'm going to put this picture here, too.

IE: I'm coloring my mom. (Betty is coloring while IR pins a picture of a boy on the chart on the wall.)

IR: You're coloring your mom. What's this on the boy? (Points to breasts.)

IE: Boobs.

IR: Boobs. What's this long part right here? (Points to arm.)

IE: Arm.

IR: What's that? (Points to belly button.)

IE: Belly button.

IR: Belly button. What's this? (Points to penis.)

IE: Pee pee.

IR: Pee pee.

IE: A big pee pee.

IR: A big pee pee. That's a big pee pee. Do you know anyone with a big pee pee?

IE: My dad.

IR: Your dad. OK. What's this here? What's this on the boy? (Points to buttocks.)

IE: Poop.

IR: Poop?

IE: I call it poop.

IR: You call it poop. OK. And what's this? (Points to hair.)

IE: He's going poop in the tub.

IR: He's going poop in the tub? What's this, Betty? (Points to hair again.)

IE: Hair.

In the third segment, the interviewer establishes the child's names for body parts. After almost every question, she repeats the child's answer. This is a useful technique for it allows the child to correct the interviewer if the interviewer misunderstood the child. She also learns about the child's concept-formation ability by asking the child about other people in her family who may be girls or boys. The interviewer is persistent and repeats any questions that the child does not initially answer.

IR: Hair, OK. And you said your dad looks like this picture. Betty, what I want to do now, Betty…

IE: What?

IR: Let's talk about different kinds of touches.

IE: (Draws.)

IR: Do you think we could put these pens down for a couple of minutes?

IE: Yes.

IR: OK, let's put these pens down, right here, and talk about different kinds of touches, Betty. Does anyone ever give you hugs and kisses?

IE: My mom does.

IR: Your mom? Where does your mom kiss you?

IE: But I can't get it off (pointing to coloring marks on her fingers).

IR: You can't get it off? Let me see if I can get a Kleenex for you. If you can't get it now, we can get it off later, because it comes off with soap and water. Here you go. (Hands Betty some Kleenex.) Where does your mom give you kisses, Betty?

IE: (Points to lips.)

IR: Right there. What is that called? What is that?

IE: Lips.

IR: Lips. OK. Do you ever get hugs from anybody, Betty?

IE: My mom.

IR: Your mom. Where does your mom hug you…on your body? Where does your mom hug you on your body?

IE: Hmm…

IR: Where does she hug you on your body?

IE: (Pats her chest.)

IR: Right there (pointing to Betty's chest)?

IE: My heart.

IR: By your heart. How about tickles, Betty? Do you ever get tickles?

IE: (Tickles interviewer.)

IR: (Laughs.) Oh, you're going to tickle me. Do you ever get tickles?

IE: (Nods yes.)

IR: Yeah. Who gives you tickles?

IE: (Points to interviewer.)

IR: Me?

IE: (Nods yes.)

IR: Do I give you tickles, or does someone else give you tickles?

IE: You do. When can I draw?

IR: Betty, do you like to get tickles?

IE: (Shakes head no.)

IR: Do you like to get hugs and kisses from mom?

IE: (Shakes head no.)

In the fourth segment, the interviewer turns to the topic of touches that Betty likes and doesn't like. The child still shows her confusion at times. She first shakes her head no when asked if she ever gets hugs and kisses, and then, when questioned again, she says that her mom does give her hugs and kisses. The interviewer responds to the child's concern about having coloring marks on her fingers but gets back to the topic at hand as soon as possible. Toward the end of this segment, an interesting thing happens. When asked about who gives her tickles, Betty points to the interviewer. As far as I can determine from looking at the videotape, the interviewer never tickled the child. Even when asked again about being tickled by the interviewer, the child said that the interviewer gives her tickles.

IR: Betty, are there places on your body where you don't like to get touched?

IE: (Points to vagina.) I hate that.

IR: Right there? On the pee pee? You hate that?

IE: But Uncle Jason did it.

IR: Uncle Jason did that? What did Uncle Jason do?

IE: He touched my pee pee.

IR: He touched your pee pee.

IE: Like that one. (Points to vaginal area on picture of girl on chart on wall.)

IR: Like that one.

IE: I don't have no big pee pee.

IR: You don't have no big pee pee.

IE: (Shakes head no.)

IR: What did Uncle Jason touch your pee pee with?

IE: His finger.

IR: His finger. What did his finger do when it touched your pee pee?

IE: He poked it.

IR: He poked it. Where did he poke, Betty?

IE: Right inside.

IR: Right inside. What did that feel like, Betty?

IE: It felt bad.

IR: It felt bad. What did it make your pee pee feel like?

IE: Do you have any water?

IR: When we're done, we'll get some water, Ok? Can we just talk for a while first?

IE: I hate talking.

IR: You hate talking. You're doing an OK job talking.

IE: I want to go to my mom.

IR: You want to go to your mom. We're almost done, Betty, OK? When we're done, you can see your mom. Betty, what did that make your pee pee feel like when Uncle Jason poked it?

IE: Felt hurt.

IR: Felt hurt, OK. Where were you when Uncle Jason poked your pee pee?

IE: In the shower.

IR: You were in the shower. Where was Uncle Jason?

IE: He was right by the shower.

IR: Betty, did Uncle Jason poke your pee pee one time or more than one time?

IE: Last night.

IR: Last night, OK. Did he ever do it any other times?

IE: (Shakes head no.)

IR: Betty, did Uncle Jason say something when he poked your pee pee?

IE: (Shakes head no and puts thumb in mouth.) No.

IR: Did you say something to Uncle Jason?

IE: (Nods yes.)

IR: What did you say?

IE: My dad came in. I yelled for my dad. My dad said "Hey, get out of that shower!" And he did. 'Cause he touched my pee pee.

IR: 'Cause he was in there, and he touched your pee pee. So you yelled for your dad, and your dad came in and said "Get out of there!"

IE: (Nods yes.) And he started to beat him.

IR: Who started to beat who?

IE: Uncle Jason.

IR: Who started to beat Uncle Jason?

IE: My dad.

IR: Your dad. OK. Did you see that happen?

IE: (Nods yes.)

IR: OK. What did your dad do for Uncle Jason?

IE: He was laying on the floor for a little while and got up.

IR: Who was laying on the floor for a while?

IE: Uncle Jason.

IR: Uncle Jason was. OK. Did your daddy say something to Uncle Jason?

IE: I just went to the hospital.

IR: You just went to the hospital. Who took you to the hospital?

IE: The police because (unintelligible).

IR: The police because why?

IE: I wasn't bad though, but (mumbles).

IR: I didn't hear you, Betty.

IE: I want to go home.

IR: You want to go home. I know that, Betty. I understand that…. What happened at the hospital?

IE: I want to go with my mom.

IR: OK, can we finish talking, Betty?

IE: (Shakes head no.) I hate talking.

IR: You hate talking. What's Uncle Jason's last name?

IE: (Shrugs, shakes head no.)

IR: You don't know. He's just Uncle Jason. Where does Uncle Jason live?

IE: I don't know.

IR: Does he live at your mom's house or your dad's house or what?

IE: He lives anywhere.

IR: He lives anywhere.

IE: He just lives outside.

IR: He just lives outside. So, whose house were you at when Uncle Jason poked your pee pee?

IE: My dad's.

IR: Your dad's house. OK. Did Uncle Jason say something when he poked you?

IE: No.

IR: Did you say something to Uncle Jason?

IE: No.

IR: Betty, what were you doing when Uncle Jason poked you?

IE: I don't know.

In the fifth segment, the interviewer begins by introducing the topic of places on the child's body where the child doesn't like to be touched. After the first question, Betty informs the interviewer that she "hates that" pointing to her vagina. After the interviewer recounts what Betty said, Betty names "Uncle Jason" as the alleged perpetrator. The interviewer then obtains information about the alleged sexual abuse. She asks about the act, how it was done, on what part of the body it was done, how it felt, where it was done, where the alleged perpetrator was during the act, how frequently the act occurred, what was said during the act, and other events associated with the act. Shortly after the alleged abuse is mentioned, the child appears to become uncomfortable and says that she wants to be with her mother. Betty indicates that she does not know where the perpetrator lives.

IR: You don't know. OK. Betty, has anybody else ever poked you or else touched you on places on your body you didn't like?

IE: No.

IR: Betty, we're almost done. Can I ask you a few more questions?

IE: We're just about done.

IR: Yeah. Has somebody else touched your body in a place you don't like?

IE: (Shakes head, no.)

IR: Has anyone else ever touched you on your pee pee?

IE: (Shakes head, no.)

IR: How about like on your butt?

IE: (Shakes head, no.)

IR: Would that be OK or not OK if someone touched your butt?

IE: No one didn't.

IR: No one didn't. OK. Would that be OK or not OK?

IE: OK.

IR: Is that OK?

IE: If he doesn't touch my pee pee or my butt, that's OK.

IR: OK. Betty, if someone does touch your pee pee again or your butt, what can you do?

IE: I can ask my mom or again my dad.

IR: Ask your dad what?

IE: Ask my dad, he pulled my pee pee again.

IR: OK, so you'd ask for your dad and say he pulled your pee pee again?

IE: (Nods yes.)

IR: Is there anyone else you could tell?

IE: (Shakes head no.)

IR: No, OK. How about mom? Could you tell mom if someone pokes your pee pee? Could you tell mom if someone pokes your pee pee?

IE: (Shakes head, no.)

IR: Betty, can you tell your mom? (Child does not answer but flings ponytails back and forth vigorously.) You're flinging your ponytails, aren't you? Betty, you know what, it's not OK for people to touch your pee pee or your butt or your boobs.

IE: Or your big pee pee.

IR: Or it's not OK for someone to make you touch their pee pee or butt. Did that ever happen, where someone made you touch their pee pee?

IE: (Shakes head, no.)

IR: How about Uncle Jason? Did he make you touch his pee pee?

IE: (Shakes head, no.)

IR: No, ok. Has anyone else made you touch their pee pee?

IE: (Shakes head, no.)

IR: OK. Betty, if that happens, it's good to tell your mom or your dad. Alright. Or another grownup who can help. Like a grandma or a grandpa or somebody like that.

IE: I don't have no grandpa.

IR: No grandpa. Do you have a grandma?

IE: Hmm hmm.

IR: OK, it's good to tell your grandma. Do you go to daycare, Betty?

IE: Yeah.

IR: It's OK to tell your daycare person too, OK? I think we're done talking.

IE: I think so.

IR: I'm going to give you something before you go, Betty.

IE: What is it?

IR: It's a card, and it has my name on it. Here's one for you that's got my name and phone number. You can hang on to that or you can give it to your mom, too.

IE: I want to take my picture (referring to the picture the interviewer drew).

IR: You would like to take your picture.

IE: It's too heavy.

IR: It's not too heavy. I'll roll it up for you. It's pretty light. (Rolls up the picture.)

IE: Yeah.

IR: Thanks for coming in, Betty.

IE: Yeah.

IR: Bye now.

IE: Bye.

In this last segment, the interviewer asks Betty about other experiences involving unwanted touches. The interviewer then asks Betty what Betty can do if she is touched in inappropriate places and tells Betty that it is not right for other people to touch her private parts or to have her touch their private parts. The interviewer also inquires about whether Betty was asked to touch the alleged perpetrator's penis, to which Betty responds "No." The interview ends with the interviewer's giving Betty her card and the picture the interviewer drew of Betty.

The following notes were written by the interviewer after the interview.

NOTES ON THE CASE OF BETTY TROTH

The interview took place on June 14, 1996, at Hillman Children's Center at 9:30 A.M. Betty Troth was referred to Hillman Children's Center by the City of Millville Police Department's Sex Crimes Division. The Division informed us that Betty had told her father that her father's friend, Jason Smith, touched her private parts when she was taking a shower in her father's house. The father reportedly confronted Jason Smith and attacked him. The police were summoned and brought Betty to a shelter because her father was intoxicated and extremely hostile and appeared unable to protect her.

Betty is a 4-year, 4-month-old girl, who was born on February 25, 1992. She appeared to have normal cognitive abilities and development, although her attention span was short. During the interview, she indicated that she does not like to talk; however, she seemed to be comfortable in the interview. She said that she wanted to be with her mother when the alleged molestation was discussed. She had seen her mother prior to the interview for a few minutes for the first time since going to the shelter yesterday.

Betty spontaneously reported that while she was taking a shower at her father's home, "Uncle Jason" (she did not know his last name) "poked" her "pee pee" (vagina) with his finger. She said that this felt bad and that it hurt. Betty said that she was in the shower when "Uncle Jason" touched her and that "Uncle Jason" was close to the shower. Betty said that she yelled for her father, who came into the bathroom and told "Uncle Jason" to "get out of her shower." She said that her father beat "Uncle Jason." Betty also said that the police took her to the hospital and that she wanted to go home.

Her spontaneous report that Jason Smith digitally penetrated her vagina and her behavior during the interview lend credibility to the alleged sexual abuse. Betty also was given safety messages. She appears to have knowledge of what to do if touched inappropriately, as she immediately told her father of this incident. It is recommended that Betty be referred for therapy.

This is an excellent interview. The interviewer had good rapport with the child, used language comprehensible to the child, and did not use leading questions. She systematically inquired about the details surrounding the alleged abusive event. Even though the child was anxious at times, she spoke clearly about the alleged sexual abuse. The interviewer obtained the child's names for body parts and used these names in the interview. I believe that the interviewer was correct in continuing the interview, even though the child wanted to leave. Young children may say they want to leave even when they feel only slightly anxious. Each case must be judged individually. In this case, because the child showed some signs of stress, a brief break to allow the girl to see her mom might have been a good idea. Although some details remain uncertain, which is not unusual when preschool children are interviewed, the interview indicates that *the child appears highly credible.* The conditions surrounding the incident—the involvement of an adult male friend of the father, an altercation between the father and the friend, the presence of the police, the spontaneous nature of the child's report of the molestation, and the child's feelings about the molestation—all suggest that the incident took place as reported by the child. It is highly unlikely that the child was coached to make the allegation, imagined it, or maliciously made it up.

The interview shows several problems that may arise in interviewing preschool children. Many of these problems were alluded to in Chapter 3. Preschool children may

- not always comply with an interviewer's requests
- wish to do other things instead of talking to the interviewer
- have a limited attention span and tire easily
- not know facts about other people that would be useful for identification purposes
- misname people
- misunderstand questions
- give nonverbal replies instead of verbal ones
- engage in nonverbal behavior that contradicts verbal behavior
- be prone to talk about what is on their mind, regardless of how appropriate it is to the interviewer's goals
- attribute to the interviewer actions that, in fact, did not take place in the interview

In spite of these difficulties, this preschool child described the alleged sexual molestation in a way that left little doubt in the interviewer's judgment that the alleged incident occurred.

Examples of Semistructured Interviews

Appendix F provides two semistructured interviews for use with children who may have been or who have been maltreated. Table F-4 is a semistructured interview for a child suspected of being physically or emotionally abused; Table F-5 is for a child suspected of being sexually abused. The questions in both semistructured interviews cover the following areas:

- child's general orientation
- recent events
- similar events
- child's voluntary disclosure
- child's relationship with the alleged offender
- child's sleeping patterns
- child's eating patterns
- child's school
- child's affect
- child's friends
- child's family

In addition, the semistructured interview that focuses on sexual abuse covers sexual activity between the child and the alleged abuser. When the child's maltreatment is associated with domestic violence, the semistructured interview for children in a crisis also may be helpful (see Table F-23 in Appendix F). For school-aged children who have experienced neglect, use the semistructured interview questions in Table F-13 in Appendix F, designed for children who may have adjustment or other behavior problems.

Exercise 22-2. Evaluating the Interviewer's Style

Part 1. Interviewer Techniques

Critically evaluate the following two scenarios. Which scenario illustrates leading questions on the part of the interviewer? Which scenario is better? What are the reasons for your choice? Compare your answers with those in the Comments section.

1. IR: Hi. I'm Dr. Smith. I talk to children who have had something bad happen to them. Something bad has happened to you, right?
   IE: Yes.
   IR: Good. If you tell me about what happened to you, you'll get a special reward.
   IE: OK. Well, something happened at home last week.
   IR: Did your father do anything?
   IE: I don't know.
   IR: Yes, you know. You can tell me.
   IE: Well, he touched me.
   IR: I'll bet he touched you on your private parts, didn't he?

2. IR: Hi. I'm Dr. Jones. Do you know why you're here?
   IE: Yes.
   IR: Tell me why you think you are here today.
   IE: OK. Well, something happened at home last week.
   IR: Tell me about that.

IE: I don't know.
IR: Is it hard for you to talk about what happened?
IE: Well, he touched me.
IR: Touched you?

Comments

The interviewer in Scenario 2 does a much better job than the one in Scenario 1. Nearly every comment made by the interviewer in Scenario 1 is leading or manipulative. Scenario 1 shows poor interviewing techniques and is unlikely to stand up in court; it is a biased interview.

Part 2. Interview Excerpt

The following excerpt from an interview with a child is from a case in which the preschool-teacher defendants were accused of child sexual abuse. The excerpt is from a court transcript (Gorney, 1988, p. D1). The child in the excerpt is an 8-year-old boy who had attended the preschool four years earlier. As the interviewer is speaking, the child is holding a Pac-man puppet in his hand. After you read the excerpt, answer the questions that follow it. Then compare your answers with those in the Comments section.

IR: Here's a hard question I don't know if you know the answer to. We'll see how smart you are, Pac-man. Did you ever see anything come out of Mr. Ray's wiener? Do you remember that?
IE: (No response.)
IR: Can you remember back that far? We'll see how…how good your brain is working today, Pac-man. (Child moves puppet around.)
IR: Is that a yes?
IE: (Nods puppet yes.)
IR: Well, you're smart. Now let's see if we can figure out what it was. I wonder if you can point to something of what color it was.
IE: (Tries to pick up the pointer with the Pac-man's mouth.)
IR: Let me get your pen here. (Puts a pointer in child's Pac-man puppet mouth.)
IE: It was….
IR: Let's see what color is that.
IE: (Uses Pac-man's hand to point to the Pac-man puppet.)
IR: Oh, you're pointing to yourself. That must be yellow.
IE: (Nods puppet yes.)
IR: You're smart to point to yourself. What did it feel like? Was it like water? Or something else?
IE: What?
IR: The stuff that came out. Let me try. I'll try a different question on you. We'll try to figure out what the stuff tastes like. We're going to try and figure out if it tastes good.
IE: He never did that to [me], I don't think.
IR: Oh, well, Pac-man, would you know what it tastes like? Would you think it tastes like candy, sort of trying…
IE: I think it would taste like yucky ants.
IR: Yucky ants, whoa. That would be kind of yucky. I don't think it would taste like…you don't think it would taste like strawberries or anything good?
IE: No.
IR: Oh. Think it would sort…do you think that would be sticky, like sticky, yucky ants?
IE: A little.

This interview segment raises several questions about the interviewer's role and the role of the interview in cases of alleged child sexual abuse. What is your reaction to this interview excerpt? Were the interviewer's probes correct? Why didn't the interviewer accept the child's statement "He never did that to [me], I don't think"? If you were a juror, how would this and similar interviews affect your decision about the guilt or innocence of the alleged perpetrator? How much should an interviewer probe, press, and cajole a child in order to expose a possible child abuser?

Comments

This interview segment does not reflect the interviewing techniques proposed in this book. The interviewer uses leading questions and inappropriate reinforcements and seems to be guiding the child's responses. This segment suggests that the interviewer may have had certain expectations that guided how the interview was conducted. The interviewer should have accepted, at least temporarily, the child's statement about the alleged perpetrator's not doing anything to him. There is little research on how young children remember things over a long period. Jurors might have strong doubts about convicting an alleged offender based on such an interview. Interviewers should not probe, press, or cajole children. Leading children in this way is likely to result in a biased interview and a verdict of "not guilty," regardless of the truth of the matter. In this case, the jury could not arrive at a unanimous decision, and the charges were dismissed.

INTERVIEWING THE FAMILY IN CASES OF CHILD MALTREATMENT

Let's now turn to issues involved in interviewing the family in cases of alleged child maltreatment. As you read this part of the chapter, compare the process of interviewing families with that of interviewing children. What are some similarities and differences? How do the two types of interviews complement each other?

Interviewing the Parents

You want to interview each parent separately, and then you may want to interview them together, depending on the situation. *If possible, do not interview the suspect parent at the same site where the child is being interviewed, especially when the child is aware of where the suspect parent will be interviewed.* The child must know that the child advocacy center is a safe place to be.

What you want to discuss with the parents will depend on whether neither parent or one or both parents were alleged to be offenders. Possible topics include the following (Burgess et al., 1978):

FAMILY COMPOSITION

- a description of the family members

FAMILY DYNAMICS

- family roles and customs (such as who controls the power in the family and the attitude of the family toward nudity and privacy for intimate activities)
- communication patterns among family members

KNOWLEDGE OF THE MALTREATMENT

- parents' explanation of the child's injuries in cases of suspected physical abuse
- their explanation of signs of possible emotional maltreatment or neglect
- what first caused them to suspect maltreatment, if they reported it themselves
- what they did about their suspicions
- a description of the maltreatment as they understand it
- whether they talked with the child about the maltreatment and, if so, how many times they talked about it
- whether they can corroborate the child's story
- whether the child has seen a therapist and, if so, what happened in therapy and whether the child uses the therapist's terminology now about things that allegedly happened to the child
- whether the child has any friends or acquaintances who were maltreated
- whether the parents read to the child stories of child maltreatment
- whether the child has seen any pornographic movies, magazines, or pictures or has seen sexual acts in the parents' presence
- whether the child has witnessed domestic violence or sibling violence
- whether they talked to anyone else about the maltreatment, including other parents, children, relatives, clergy, neighbors, members of their church or synagogue, and so forth
- what type of information, if any, has been given to the child at home and at school about the prevention of maltreatment

VIEW OF THE CHILD AND THE MALTREATMENT

- how the child was functioning *before* the abusive event occurred, particularly if the event was a rape or some other first-time traumatic event (especially any preexisting psychological or physical problems)
- how the child typically handles stress
- names the child uses to refer to all members of the family and family pets
- names of all persons with whom the child has regular contact (such as teachers, babysitters, relatives)
- names the child uses for genitals, as well as for other body parts and for elimination functions (especially needed in cases of possible sexual abuse)
- how the child reacted to the maltreatment
- changes the parents have noted in the child's behavior since the maltreatment occurred, including any unusual behavior (particularly changes in sleeping, eating, acting-

out behavior, and mood; loss of bladder or bowel control; increased anxiety or fear; changes in friendship patterns and school performance; and physical complaints, such as itching or vaginal or rectal pain)
- their relationship with the maltreated child before and since the maltreatment
- their relationship with other children in the family before and since the maltreatment

CONTRIBUTION OF FAMILY TOWARD THE MALTREATMENT
- how responsible the family feels about the maltreatment
- whether the nonsuspect parent supports the alleged offender, particularly in cases of intrafamilial maltreatment

ATTITUDE TOWARD THE ALLEGED OFFENDER
- whether they have observed any inappropriate behavior by the alleged offender
- their past and present attitudes toward the alleged offender

EFFECTS ON THE FAMILY
- how the maltreatment has affected each member of the family
- how the maltreatment has affected the family as a whole

FAMILY BACKGROUND
- any history of mental illness, substance abuse, or criminal activity by the parents
- attitude of parents toward authority, such as the police, district attorney, or Child Protective Services
- how the parents are getting along with each other
- the sexual relationship between the parents, especially in cases of child sexual abuse allegations if one parent is suspect
- whether one parent has accused the other of maltreatment
- whether the father or the mother was maltreated as a child
- whether any siblings were maltreated in the past
- whether there have been incidents of domestic violence
- financial situation of family
- list of addresses lived at and dates (for law enforcement personnel)

FAMILY'S RESOURCES
- how the family plans to cope with the maltreatment
- what supports the family has, such as church, community, and extended family

PROTECTIVE ISSUES AND INTERVENTIONS
- what resources the family has for protecting the child from further maltreatment
- what interventions the parents believe are needed

Often the goals in an initial interview with a parent are to make a preliminary investigation of a report of possible child maltreatment and to evaluate whether the child is in immediate danger. The following case illustrates how an interview might be conducted with a parent in the home after a report of possible maltreatment is received by Child Protective Services. In the following incident, it is assumed that the child, as well as the staff at the preschool, also will be interviewed. The dialogue was adapted from Oppenheim (1992).

CASE 22-8. PETER JONES
IR: Good afternoon, are you Mrs. Jones?

IE: Yes.

IR: I'm Helen Smith, a social worker with Child Protective Services. You'll recall that I called you this morning. As I mentioned on the phone, we received a report that Peter may be having some problems.

IE: What kind of problems? Has something happened to Peter? Who called you? What did they say?

IR: One of the teachers at Kidcare noticed that Peter has some bruises. Do you know anything about that?

IE: No, I didn't notice any bruises, but he might have some. Peter falls down a lot.

IR: Well, I need to find out how Peter got those bruises. May I come in?

IE: Yes, come in. I want to find out what is going on too.

IR: Is Peter still in school?

IE: Yes, I don't pick him up 'til 5 P.M.

IR: You know that children sometimes get bruised or hurt accidentally, but sometimes they get bruises because someone has hurt them. I'd like to find out what happened.

IE: Are you saying someone has hurt Peter?

IR: I don't know. That's why it's so important that we talk. We need to know how Peter got the bruises.

IE: If you're saying I hurt my son, it's just not true.

IR: Is there someone else who might have caused those bruises? Someone else living in the house, for instance?

IE: No one lives here except my George, who is my boyfriend, Peter, and I.

IR: How long has your boyfriend been living here?

IE: Three months.

IR: How do you get along with him?

IE: OK.

IR: How does Peter get along with him?

IE: Not so good. George might have done something the other night when I went out, but I'm sure it would have been an accident. George doesn't like it when Peter acts up.

IR: Tell me about what you mean by "done something."

IE: Well, see, I left Peter with George while I went to do the grocery shopping, and, when I came back, Peter was acting real upset.

IR: Upset?

IE: You know, crying a lot and stuff. George said that Peter was driving him crazy. He said that he couldn't watch television because he was making so much noise. He complains about that a lot. And sometimes he loses his temper.

IR: What does George do when he loses his temper?

IE: I can't say right now.

IR: Does George lose his temper much?

IE: He has a couple of times—not much.

IR: Do you think that he might have done something to Peter last night when he lost his temper?

IE: (Nods affirmatively.)

IR: What might he have done?

IE: Hit Peter.

IR: Did you see any marks on Peter?

IE: (Looks down, but says nothing.)

IR: Kids can be quite a strain sometimes, especially at Peter's age. Does George help out or look after Peter often?

IE: Well, he's not Peter's father, so I really can't expect much.

The interviewer is establishing a partnership with the mother in helping to solve the problem while at the same time getting more information on the habits of the household and the mother's expectations of the boyfriend.

IR: But you'd like him to help more?

IE: Well, yes, but *you* try to make him.

IR: We need to talk to George to hear what he has to say about Peter's bruises. When do you expect him back?

IE: Not until later, about nine o'clock.

IR: How have you been feeling recently?

IE: Not too good. Things have been pretty tense around here lately. Since George moved in things have gotten worse.

IR: How have they gotten worse?

IE: They just have gotten worse. Well, the people at the daycare center don't like me, and now I have you here saying that I'm a rotten mother. I think we would all be better off if I just took Peter out of there.

Here the interviewer is in a difficult dilemma—if she is accusatory, she and the mother will go back to having an adversarial relationship. This would be counterproductive. However, if she denies the accusations, she loses track of the main issue—Peter's safety. While Peter attends daycare, he can be monitored, but the mother's concerns also need to be addressed. To handle this dilemma, the interviewer chooses a neutral response followed by a constructive suggestion, as noted in the following remark.

IR: I'm not saying that you are a bad parent, but you do seem to be having some difficulties here in the household. Peter has been hurt, and that is a serious concern. I think it would be best if Peter continues to go to Kidcare. Why don't we both go down there so you can see how the center is run and so you can get a little more comfortable with the staff?

IE: Well, I don't know what George is going to say about all this.

IR: I think I should talk with you and George tomorrow, perhaps after we've gone to Kidcare. For now though, I'm a little concerned about Peter's safety.

IE: When I'm home, George doesn't pay any attention to Peter. I'll keep a close eye on him all night until he goes to bed.

IR: Good, that'll also give you two some time alone. I think it's important that we find a way to keep this from happening again. Why don't you think about it tonight, and we'll talk some more when we see each other tomorrow. How about if I call at 8 A.M., and we'll arrange to go down to Kidcare together?

IE: OK, I'll talk to you then.

The interviewer decided not to recommend temporary out-of-home placement for the child. This decision raises concern about the child's safety because it leaves the child and the mother unprotected. The decision also means that the mother can talk to George, the suspected perpetrator, about the maltreatment and give George time to make up a story to explain the child's bruises or to convince the mother that he was not responsible for what happened. George could decide to leave the home when Mrs. Jones informs him about the inquiry from Child Protective Services. Safety issues should be discussed with the mother. It is a judgment call on the part of the interviewer whether to leave the child in the home overnight.

Interviewing Other Family Members and Siblings

In interviewing a family in which a child was maltreated, inquire about how other family members get along with the child, whether they have any history of child maltreatment, whether they have emotional difficulties, how the alleged maltreatment has affected them, and what changes in family relationships have occurred since the maltreatment.

The allegedly maltreated child's siblings also are important to interview because siblings are part of the family and will be affected by any family crisis, suffering the consequences of a family's breakdown. They also may have been maltreated, or perhaps they are perpetrators; if so, they may be reluctant to come forward (Furniss, 1991). Siblings who have not been maltreated may know about the maltreatment but may have kept it a secret. They may have feared disclosing the abuse: "Witnessing sexual abuse of a sibling or even only knowing about it can in itself be extremely traumatic and children may for their own emotional protection want to forget what they know" (Furniss, 1991, p. 331). Witnessing any form of maltreatment can be considered a form of emotional abuse in itself. Whenever you interview family members, you will want to compare the child's, parents', and siblings' reports. The material in Chapter 4 on family interviewing is useful for interviewing families in which a child has been maltreated or alleged to have been maltreated.

If you hold a family meeting, invite the siblings to participate. Better yet, interview each sibling individually, as well. You need to inform siblings about what is happening to their family and help them understand how the maltreatment took place. Siblings may blame the maltreated child for the family's problems or may be overprotective of the maltreated child. If they are older siblings, they may feel guilty for not having protected their younger sibling.

Family members may have strong reactions when they learn that a member of their family has been sexually abused, physically or emotionally abused, or neglected. Allow them to vent their feelings before asking many questions. Conduct the interview in private. It is especially important in interviewing victims of child maltreatment that you establish a safe and supportive environment for the victim and his or her family.

Interviewing the Mother and Father Separately

When the father (or another close relative) is the alleged offender, interview the mother separately. You will want to assess the mother's view of the alleged offender, her degree of dependence on the alleged offender, her socioeconomic status, whether she believes her child, what she has done to protect the child, how she has behaved toward the child since learning about the possible maltreatment, and whether she is at risk for abuse (Faller, 1988). If the mother is the alleged offender, you can cover similar areas when you interview the father separately.

Extrafamilial Versus Intrafamilial Child Maltreatment

You may find that how the family talks to you depends on whether the alleged maltreatment is extrafamilial or intrafamilial (Furniss, 1991).

1. *Extrafamilial maltreatment.* In cases of alleged extrafamilial maltreatment, when the alleged abuser is someone outside the family group, the parents may ask many questions about the alleged maltreatment and the alleged abuser, express anger at the alleged abuser, express concern about the physical and psychological consequences of the alleged maltreatment for the child, show concern for the siblings and their possible involvement in the alleged maltreatment, want information and help, express a strong sense of helplessness and desperation, and question their ability to be effective and protective parents.

2. *Intrafamilial maltreatment.* In contrast, in cases of alleged intrafamilial maltreatment, when the alleged abuser is someone inside the family group, the parents may ask fewer questions designed to obtain information or help, show a controlling and aggressive manner, avoid questions about the physical or psychological harm done to the child, avoid talking about siblings, and attack neighbors and professionals. The parents may simply refuse to believe that a member of their family would do such a thing to another family member.

Of course, some families may react to the alleged extrafamilial maltreatment in a manner similar to that described for alleged intrafamilial maltreatment, and vice versa.

When the alleged perpetrator is a family friend, extended family member, or ex-spouse, the parents may be unsure about how to deal with the alleged maltreatment. They may want to know what happened but still have reservations about what to do. Often they have trusted the alleged perpetrator and have a positive relationship with him or her. Extended family members and mutual friends may pressure the parents to suppress the investigation, as silence and denial are more socially acceptable than the scandal that might result from an investigation.

When a family member is definitely involved in the maltreatment, note the following information during the interview (Burgess et al., 1978; Sgroi, 1982):

- How have family relationships changed?
- Which family members side with whom?
- What behaviors, if any, do family members engage in to try to protect the offender or the victim?
- What disruptions have taken place in the family's life style?
- Will the family's finances be affected by the fact that a family member is the perpetrator?
- What does the family do to maintain its equilibrium or life style?
- Have limits been placed on the offending member's behavior?
- Is the child adequately protected from further harm?
- How often did transgressions against the child take place?
- How severe were the prior transgressions (if relevant)?
- Does the offending family member want to change?

Here is an example of a plea for help written by a mother, who was a known offender, shortly before she saw a counselor (Jorgensen, 1990).

To whom it may concern: Please help me. I think I am the worst mother in the world. I have three beautiful children, but I am messing up their lives so bad with my screaming at them and hitting them that I'm afraid they will never be OK and that they will never forgive me.

At night when I think about what I've done, I feel terrible. Sometimes I've thought of suicide but I know that wouldn't help my children.

I make promises that I will do better and be more patient and understanding, but when they make noise or knock something over or do anything, I just lose it.

My life is a disaster. I know I need help, but I'm so afraid that if I talk to someone, the state will take my children away. Maybe that would be better. It would be better for the kids, but I don't know if I could live through it.

I'm afraid I'm going to lose them anyway. How can children love a mother who does what I do? How can I stop? What is wrong with me? Please help me if you can. (p. 52)

Interviewing Guidelines in Cases of Domestic Violence and Possible Child Maltreatment

The fear that battered women have of their abusive partner may be so great that they will refuse to talk freely about anything. Be prepared to have battered women resist talking about child maltreatment, and perhaps about other things as well, for the following reasons (Stacey & Shupe, 1983):

1. They may fear that their children will be taken away, regardless of who maltreated the children.
2. They may fear reprisals from their partner if they disclose that their partner maltreated the children.
3. They may want to protect their partner from going to jail.
4. They may fear loss of financial support.
5. They may fear that if they report the maltreatment their marriage (or relationship) will be over.
6. They may not want their marriage to end, but they do want their partner to stop hitting them and their children.
7. They may believe that by acknowledging the child maltreatment, they will be admitting their failure to care for their children.
8. They may have few job skills and may not be prepared to live an independent life.
9. They may be ashamed to talk about the violence and ashamed of having put up with it for so long.

Therefore, *if you know or suspect that both domestic violence and child maltreatment have occurred, interview the parents or partners separately* (McKay, 1994). If you do not, you may not be able to assess the extent to which the child is at risk in a family in which there is domestic violence.

The following indicators should sensitize you to the possibility that there is domestic violence in the family (McKay, 1994, p. 34, with changes in notation):

The mother
1. offers inconsistent explanations for her own bruises, fractures, or multiple injuries that are in various stages of healing.
2. reports that "accidents" occurred.
3. delays seeking needed medical treatment for herself.
4. has a history of repeated accidents and emergency room visits, often at different hospitals or clinics.
5. is observed to be feeling sad, depressed, or having thoughts of suicide.
6. reports psychosomatic and emotional complaints, such as chest pain, choking sensation, hyperventilation, or sleep or eating disorders.
7. is embarrassed or evasive when questioned about her injuries or about being maltreated.
8. exhibits anxiety and fear in the presence of her partner.
9. offers apologies or explanations for her partner's behavior.

The child (in addition to standard indicators of maltreatment or trauma)
1. is protective of his or her mother or afraid to leave her alone.

2. is abusive toward the mother (presumably modeling the behavior of the father).

The father
1. constantly speaks for his partner during the interview and strongly resists having her interviewed separately.
2. describes his partner with derogatory terms such as "clumsy," "incompetent," "crazy," or "stupid."
3. is overly solicitous and condescending to his partner.
4. admits to the existence of violence but minimizes its frequency and severity. When confronted with the abusive behavior, he blames his partner for provoking it and refuses to accept responsibility for it.
5. holds rigidly to traditional sex roles, expecting or demanding that his partner serve him.
6. is "charming."

When law enforcement personnel respond to a domestic violence call, they need to recognize that women, even if they have obvious injuries, may not want to admit that abuse has occurred. Similarly, children of an abused parent may not be reliable informants, particularly because they do not want to be disloyal to one parent. Authorities may need to use medical records, as well as other sources, to document the abuse associated with domestic violence.

Table F-19 in Appendix F presents a semistructured interview designed for individuals who either may be experiencing domestic violence or have experienced domestic violence. It focuses on such issues as stress, safety, and fears or threats of abuse; in cases of abuse, the interview focuses on a description of the event, the weapon used, reports of the incident, past events, awareness of friends and family of the event(s), a description of the offender, an emergency plan, and prosecution of the offender. If women have been victims of domestic violence and need help, give them a copy of Exhibit 22-1, which describes actions a woman victim should and should not perform.

In addition, social services and law enforcement agencies should (a) offer education, where appropriate, about the illegality of spousal abuse in the United States, (b) inform women and children about the availability of counseling and shelter services, and (c) inform women about how to obtain restraining orders against abusive husbands and boyfriends.

Semistructured Interviews for Parents and Families in Cases of Child Maltreatment

Three semistructured interviews in Appendix F are particularly useful in interviewing parents and families. Table F-22 is useful for interviewing a nonsuspect parent of an allegedly maltreated child; Table F-17, for interviewing families; and Table F-21, for interviewing a mother to obtain a detailed developmental history. Again, parents should be interviewed separately, especially if one of the parents is suspected of being the perpetrator.

Exhibit 22-1
Guidelines for Women Who Are Victims of Domestic Violence

The very first step is to realize that you're being abused. The next step is to realize that you cannot continue to live where you or you and your children are not physically and emotionally safe. If you have family and close friends to confide in, by all means, do that. Talk to them about your situation and your options. Develop a plan of action to escape the maltreatment. *It is vital that you understand that the decisions you make are your responsibility.* You are the one who will have to live with the consequences of your decision. Trust your judgment. You're the expert on you.

1. *Talk to your partner, if it is safe.* Explain how you want to be treated.

2. *Leave, either temporarily or permanently.* Leaving temporarily may send a message to the batterer that you will not allow yourself to be mistreated. He may honestly want to seek help. Unless there is a consequence to his actions (your leaving, in this case), the batterer has no reason to change. If the maltreatment continues, it is your responsibility to protect yourself by leaving permanently. If you need to, you can go for a short period of time to a shelter (or safe house) for women who have been abused. You also can bring your children with you. You may need to consider moving to another part of the city, state, or country if you are being threatened and can't be protected.

3. *Get help.* It is very difficult to extract yourself from a violent situation by yourself. Talk about your situation. Silence about maltreatment is what keeps women trapped in the cycle. Talk to your family, friends, counselors,

Things You Can Do

physicians, clergy, and family violence counselors. You'll get the information you need to make sound decisions about your future and gain control of your life.

4. *Know the law—it's on your side.* Assault is a crime. Arrest and prosecution are known deterrents to continued family violence. Call the police if you have been battered. You also can obtain a restraining order. A restraining order prohibits further maltreatment, prohibits the offender from contacting you, and excludes the offender from your home and place of work or school. However, restraining orders may be ineffective if the offender chooses to ignore them. Laws also can require payment by the offender for spouse support, child support, monetary compensation, or payment for alternative housing for you. Offenders may be required to participate in counseling as part of a protective order. Emergency protective orders can be issued when you fear for your safety, even though violence has not occurred.

5. *Obtain emergency medical treatment.* Many assaults require emergency treatment. Even if you believe your injuries are "not very bad," you may be injured more seriously than you think. A medical report will document your injuries and may help if you decide to seek legal assistance.

6. *Go to any emergency room.* If your injuries are serious, call an ambulance, friend, relative, or the police for help.

7. *Contact your physician or health care provider.* Describe the current and past beatings to your physician or health care provider. This is especially

important if you are pregnant. You might want to obtain a copy of your medical record. This can be important if the District Attorney files charges for the assault.

8. *Develop a safety plan.* Whether it's in the heat of the moment or you've planned ahead of time, you need an organized plan to get you away from danger. Here are a few things to consider:

• Pack an extra set of clothes, toilet articles, and necessary medications for you and your children. Store the suitcase with a friend, relative, or neighbor; include an extra set of keys to your house and car.

• Keep extra cash, checkbook, or savings account hidden or with a friend or relative.

• You'll need identification for you and your children. Keep birth certificates, social security cards, voter registration, marriage or divorce certificates, and your driver's license handy to obtain assistance or to enroll children in school.

• Make sure you have important financial records, such as rent receipts and the title to the car.

• Know exactly where you could go and how to get there, at any time of day or night. Plan various escape routes from inside to outside your home, and from outside your home to the safe place.

REMEMBER: IF YOU BELIEVE YOUR SAFETY IS IN DANGER, GET OUT OF THIS SITUATION, EVEN IF YOU HAVE NOT BEEN ABLE TO FOLLOW ANY OF THE ABOVE SUGGESTIONS.

Things You Can't Do

1. *You can't change your partner's behavior.* You cannot stop your partner's violence toward you. He is in control of his actions, just as you are in control of yours.

2. *You can't stay in an abusive relationship and be safe.* Without intervention, family violence becomes more frequent and severe.

3. *You can't "do the right thing" to please the abuser.* It's not about you. The choice to abuse lies with the abuser.

4. *You can't save the relationship by yourself.* You can go to counseling, you can "be" whatever you think it takes to make things better—but it takes two people to make a relationship work.

5. *Don't blame yourself for your own victimization.* It's not your fault.

6. *You can't forgive and forget.* It only gives the abuser license to strike again. If the abuser suffers no consequences, he has no reason to stop.

7. *You can't shield your partner from the consequences of abusive behavior.* "He didn't really mean it…

(Continued)

Exhibit 22-1 (*Continued*)

this time, officer!" If the abuser doesn't want to change the behavior, it doesn't matter how much he pleads or threatens in order not to face jail. He'll promise anything to avoid consequences.

Don't risk your life to help someone who is hurting you.

8. *You shouldn't respond to violence with violence.* Violence is not an appropriate or helpful response to another

person's actions or words. But remember—if you are in extreme fear for your life, you have the right to defend yourself.

Comment

Regaining self-esteem and leading a meaningful life are attainable for victims of domestic violence. If children are

involved, remove them from the destructive relationship. They need to have role models that allow them to mature into

adults who can handle feelings appropriately, especially anger and stress. Stopping the violence is the ultimate goal.

Source: Reprinted, with changes in notation, with permission of the publisher and authors, from two sources: Kaiser Permanente, "Domestic Violence," pp. 13 and 14, copyright 1994 in *Planning for Health,* 1994, Issue 2; and A. Hatchett-Jones, L. McClosky, J. Muzic, M. Shapiro, W. Tadros, and M. Tomita, "Domestic Violence: Recognizing the Epidemic," p. 24, copyright June 1994, by Kaiser Permanente, Southern California Region. Part of this list was compiled from Kaiser Permanente Colorado Region: Domestic Violence Protocol.

Table F-22 covers the following areas: the maltreatment (one or several incidents), the offender (either a family member or a non-family member), the behavior of the maltreated child, the family's reaction to the maltreatment, the family's reaction to the offender, whether other children were maltreated, a description of the child who allegedly has been maltreated, descriptions of the other children in the family, and social supports. You want to be attentive to any behavioral changes shown by the child since the disclosure or since the maltreatment began.

Interviewer's Notes in a Case of Alleged Physical Maltreatment

The following case consists of notes made by a social worker on the staff of Child Protective Services about a case of alleged physical abuse. The notes are instructive for several reasons:

- They show that the child and the parents initially may deny that any physical abuse took place.
- They show the need to be sensitive to inconsistencies in parental reports.
- They show the importance of a background check of prior reports of maltreatment that are on file for the child or family.
- They show the importance of a team approach to investigation of allegations of child maltreatment. In this case, a social worker, physician, marshal, and school personnel all cooperated in attempting to find the causes of the child's bruises.
- They show the importance of documentation: making careful notes, taking evidence, and persisting in following up hunches.

All names, dates, and locations are fictitious to protect those involved in the case. As you read the case, note that

the children had access to guns. Access to guns is a form of endangerment and can be grounds for filing charges of neglect against the parents.

CASE 22-9. JENNY SMITH

I. *Identifying Information*
Child: Jenny Smith; Date of Birth: 5/6/88; Brother: Jesse, age 4; Parents: Mr. and Mrs. Frank and Elsie Smith; Address: 1235 Main St., Chicago, IL 59326

II. *Nature of Referral*
On 10/17/94, a child maltreatment referral was received from a doctor at Mercy Hospital alleging that a 6-year-old Caucasian female had bruises on her buttocks, bruises on her right upper thigh (towards the back of the leg), and small, almost healed abrasions on her back. The bruises and abrasions seemed consistent with the use of a belt or strap. The child, Jenny Smith, was hospitalized at the time of the investigation for an unknown virus.

III. *Investigative Procedure*
On 10/17/94, I interviewed the reporting party, Dr. Craig Allen. He stated that Jenny Smith had been admitted through the Emergency Room on the previous day (10/16/94). He observed the bruises and abrasions on the evening of 10/16/94. He noted the bruises and abrasions in the medical log. Dr. Allen informed me that he asked the child and family how the injuries occurred. The child told him that she was jumping on the bed and fell against a nearby dresser and crib. Dr. Allen asked the mother about the injuries, and she denied all knowledge of them. However, she stated the injuries could have occurred in the manner described by Jenny. Mrs. Smith also told Dr. Allen that Jenny and her 4-year-old brother play in the bedroom and jump on the bed frequently.

On 10/17/94, I contacted the Cook County Marshal's office and informed Deputy Marshal Jenks of the referral. Deputy Jenks and I agreed that if there were inconsistencies or discrepancies when I spoke to the child and her mother and if Dr. Allen believed that the injuries were inconsistent with the explanation, then I could call the mother back and the Marshal's office would become involved.

On 10/17/94, I interviewed Jenny at the hospital while her mother waited outside the room. Jenny said she remembered hurting herself when she and her brother, Jesse, were doing karate kicks in the bedroom and she fell against the dresser. Jenny was not able to say when she fell or who else was home or if she told anyone. Jenny said she and her brother fight all the time and that they hit each other quite hard. She could not think of any other way that she might have been hurt. She said her parents do not spank her or hit her and when she is in trouble she has to stand in the corner.

On 10/17/94, I interviewed Mrs. Smith in a room at the hospital. She said she had no prior knowledge of the injuries until Dr. Allen informed her of them. When she asked Jenny how they occurred, Jenny said from falling while jumping on the bed. Mrs. Smith said the only physical discipline that occurs in the home is spanking of the children with an open hand, over clothing. She denied the use of any implement to spank the children and can't remember when she last spanked Jenny. Mrs. Smith and I spoke to Jenny together, and Jenny told her mother what she told me. Mrs. Smith said "I thought you said you were jumping on the bed?" Jenny said "No, Jesse and I were karate kicking."

On 10/17/94, I informed the Cook County Marshal's office that I was continuing to investigate the case and would inform them of my progress. On 10/17/94, I spoke with Dr. Allen, who said the child told him that the injuries occurred in the bedroom when she fell against the dresser or the crib. Dr. Allen and I agreed that I would look at the bedroom and again consult with him after I inspected the house. He said the virus Jenny has is still undiagnosed, so she is likely to be in the hospital a number of days. We agreed there were minimal safety concerns for Jenny while she was hospitalized.

On 10/19/94, I spoke briefly to Mrs. Smith at Mercy Hospital. She reported that Jenny had been diagnosed and treated for tonsillitis and would be released the following day.

On 10/20/94, I interviewed Mr. Smith at the Smith residence. I photographed the child's bedroom, including the bed, the dresser, and the crib. Mr. Smith said he recalled that one day, a couple of weeks ago, Jenny came into the living room and said she had scraped her back on a bolt on the crib while she was playing in the bedroom. He denied all knowledge of the bruises. He said his family disciplines by having the kids "put their noses in the corner" or by spanking them with an open hand over their clothing. He can't remember when he last spanked them and said he has never caused them any bruises.

In consultation with my supervisor, Ms. Tyler, we decided that the information provided by the family was inconsistent with a prior unsubstantiated investigation. At that time, the family admitted to using a "paddle" and said they didn't use their hand to spank. A decision was made to consult with Dr. Allen and re-involve the Cook County Marshal's Department. On 10/21/94, I contacted Deputy Marshal Jenks, who agreed to assist in interviewing the family.

On 10/22/94, I consulted with Dr. Allen, who stated that the shape of the bruises was inconsistent with falling against the crib and dresser (as shown to him with evidence of photographs). He believed the bruises were consistent with the use of a strap or a belt.

On 10/26/94, I interviewed Jenny at Harp Elementary School. I told Jenny that I was confused because she told me her parents did not spank her and yet her parents told me they did. Jenny said she does get "whippings" from her father and mother with a belt. Whether Jenny was trying to protect her parents in my previous interview or whether she did not understand my questions clearly is not known.

Jenny said that in the week before her hospitalization (10/16/94), she was "whipped by her mother and father." Jenny also said that Jesse gets more whippings than she does; however, she was not able to say how often she or her brother get whippings with the belt.

On 10/26/94, I spoke with Mrs. Smith and informed her of my interview with Jenny. Mrs. Smith said that she and her husband do use a belt on the children two or three times a week. The belt is kept in the living room armchair where she and her husband can pull it out to threaten the children. I asked Mrs. Smith how this worked. She said that one or two times a night when the children were misbehaving either she or Mr. Smith would pull the belt out and show it to the children. They would tell them they were going to get a whipping with the belt if they did not behave. Mrs. Smith said that often she or her husband would hit the belt against their knee or hand as they would talk to the children.

Mrs. Smith gave me permission to take the brown leather belt for photographing. Mrs. Smith said she could not remember the last time she spanked Jenny nor could she remember whether she spanked Jenny the week prior to Jenny's hospitalization. She remembered coming home one day in the week prior to Jenny's hospitalization and being told by Mr. Smith that Jenny had climbed up on the bureau and had gotten into the guns and ammunition and had gotten into trouble for that behavior. Mrs. Smith said she was under the impression that Jenny had gotten a spanking with the belt from Mr. Smith because of that incident. She thinks it happened on the Tuesday (10/13/94) prior to Jenny's hospitalization. Mrs. Smith continued to state that she did not know how the bruises occurred.

On 10/29/94, I, Deputy Marshal Jenks, and Mrs. Johnson (Social Services Case Aide) interviewed first Mrs. Smith and then Mr. Smith. Mrs. Smith said the children pretty much bathe themselves because she taught Jenny how to. However, she still has to help Jesse. She did see them naked a couple of days ago, but she did not see Jenny's behind or legs because she was sitting in the tub facing the front. When asked about Mr. Smith's temper, Mrs. Smith said that occasionally the kids will just push and push. Mr. Smith will tell them again and again what to do and they keep pushing and then he'll spank their bottoms. She said that the children don't even cry but just look at them when they get their spankings. When asked whether this concerns her, she said "Not usually." Mrs. Smith said the typical spanking is using a belt over clothes and occasionally using a hand. Mrs. Smith gave a number of examples of dangerous behavior that the children had gotten into, such as getting into rat poison and having a knife open on the bed. Those incidents, because the Smiths consider them so serious, resulted in spankings. About Mr. Smith and his anger, Mrs. Smith said that they sometimes get in arguments. When they do, she encourages him to take off and leave the house when he is about to blow. Mrs. Smith knows when he is about to blow by his tone of voice. She will then suggest he go fishing or go see her brother. When asked about the bruises, she said "I really don't know." However, in the week prior to hospitalization, she added that Jenny "very well could have gotten a whipping." She didn't know who could have whipped hard enough to cause bruises.

On 10/29/94, Mr. Smith also was interviewed. Mr. Smith said that most of the time he used his hand, not a belt, to discipline the children. If the kids are into something that can hurt, he will use the belt. When he is very angry with the children, he tries to leave the house instead of hitting them. Mr. Smith denied ever losing his temper with the kids to the point of hurting them. He spanks with his hand and will occasionally use a belt, but never more than two or three hits with the belt. When asked whether he caused Jenny's marks and bruises, he said "I might have caused marks and bruises." He explained that Jenny was in the gun case a few days before she was hospitalized. He struck her several times with the belt. I asked Mr. Smith if the belt lying on the table between us was the belt he used, and he said "I would imagine so."

He said he had caught Jenny doing this before and that it was very dangerous. He had told her to leave the guns alone. He thought to himself when she was up there again "I better enforce this." He believed this happened three or four days prior to Jenny's hospitalization.

Mr. Smith said this was the only time in a month or more that he had had to use the belt on her. I asked if the belt made an impression on Jenny, and he said "Oh yes, she cries even if I use my hand." He was in the house alone with the kids and said that it happened on a weekday. He used the belt two or three times over her clothing. He denied any other hitting or striking of the children. He roughhouses with the kids, and sometimes they have an accident. He said that he never hits the kids on purpose other than spankings. At this time, I left the room, and Deputy Marshal Jenks continued to ask questions. Deputy Marshal Jenks told me that while I was out of the room Mr. Smith admitted to her and Mrs. Johnson that he caused the bruises when he found Jenny climbing on the dresser.

Deputy Marshal Jenks took the belt used for the spanking as evidence.

IV. *Service Plan and Recommendations*
Mr. and Mrs. Smith on 11/2/94 signed a voluntary agreement to attend an ongoing parenting class offered by Head Start. In addition, Mrs. Smith will continue to attend a parenting support group at Head Start. They have signed an agreement to limit spankings to the use of an open hand over clothing on the buttocks with no bruising or marking of the children. They also have agreed to receive Home Based Services to improve their parenting skills.

I recommend that no further steps be taken at this time. However, should Mr. and Mrs. Smith fail to comply, further actions will need to be considered to protect the children.

INTERVIEWING THE ALLEGED OR KNOWN OFFENDER IN CASES OF CHILD MALTREATMENT

Interviews with the alleged or known offender serve several purposes (Faller, 1988):

- to gain an understanding of the maltreatment
- to obtain a direct or indirect admission from the offender
- to make a prognosis
- to obtain information useful in developing an intervention plan

You want to obtain a thorough history of the alleged or known offender. When you know that the alleged offender has committed the maltreatment, inquire about the offense. Recognize, however, that the purpose of the interview is *not* to determine the guilt or innocence of the alleged offender; rather, it is to obtain information about him or her. (The term *offender* in the remainder of the chapter may refer to either the alleged offender or the offender, depending on the context. Sometimes the term *alleged offender* also will be used.)

Evaluations of alleged offenders or offenders, like evaluations of children alleged or known to have been maltreated, should be conducted by highly trained interviewers. Human services personnel should defer to law enforcement personnel regarding who interviews an alleged offender when there are allegations of criminal law violations. This section is designed for those of you in training to work with alleged or known offenders.

Obtain factual information about the offender, as well as information about the offender's attitudes and feelings. Of equal importance is how the offender relates to you and behaves during the interview. A complete forensic assessment may require interviews with the offender's relatives, employers, neighbors, and others acquainted with the offender, depending on the case. You will need to resolve inconsistencies in the information you obtain from the offender and from other sources before you complete the assessment.

In the interview, avoid confrontation, accusations, and punitive statements. Create a comfortable and nonthreatening environment. Depending on your role, you may want to make the offender an ally (Cage, 1988). Focus on information gathering and reflective listening, as in any interview. Inform the offender of the reason for your evaluation and what will be done with your findings. If the offender appears to be violent, use the techniques discussed in Chapter 2 to defuse the situation. *Issues of safety in the interview are extremely important.* Be sure that support is available and that you terminate the interview if the offender becomes angry, threatens you, or frightens you.

You may have difficulty obtaining information from alleged offenders. They may distort information, deny that the alleged offense occurred (when it did, in fact, occur), and say that they cannot remember details concerning the alleged offense. When they want to deny the alleged offense, they may make such statements as the following (Pollock & Hashmall, 1991): "I never laid a finger on her." "The boy is lying." "The cops are out to get me." In addition, offenders may be hostile and antagonistic or present themselves as victims of false accusations. It may be useful after the introductory comments to say "I guess you have been going through some pretty rough times lately" (Walker, Bonner, & Kaufman, 1988, p. 38). Focusing on the alleged offender's feelings may help establish rapport.

In preparing for the interview with the offender, study carefully the information given by the victim and the information about the offender obtained from school, medical, psychiatric, military, and work records. Refer the offender for psychological testing and for physical and neurological evaluations, as needed. Also conduct, as needed, field investigations.

Use Table F-20 in Appendix F to conduct an in-depth interview with a known offender. The questions contained in Table F-20 cover the following areas about the known offender:

- family background
- medical and psychiatric history
- educational history
- military history
- vocational history
- sexual development
- marital history
- family history
- social-recreational history
- criminal history
- offense history, including attitude toward the offense

Some of these areas—such as military history and marital history—are obviously not appropriate for most adolescent offenders.

Discussing Responsibility for the Maltreatment with a Known Offender

When you discuss the issue of responsibility for the maltreatment with known offenders, they may use one of the following tactics (Furniss, 1991; Neidigh & Krop, 1992; Pollock & Hashmall, 1991). These tactics, in part, reflect the ways offenders attempt to overcome their inhibitions (see Chapter 20).

1. *Show superficial acceptance of responsibility for the maltreatment*—"I guess I may have had something to do with it."

2. *Deny responsibility by blaming the child for what happened*—"It was her behavior that started it all," "The kid came on to me," or "She was seductive."

3. *Minimize the severity of the maltreatment*—"I didn't cause her any harm," "Nothing much really happened; it was pretty quick," "There's nothing wrong with it," "She liked it," or "I just gave him a little slap."

4. *Make the consequences of the act positive instead of negative*—"She enjoyed it."

5. *Bargain with you or deny knowledge of the maltreatment*—"I'm really a good father and have done lots of good things for my child, so you can excuse what happened when you look at the whole picture" or "It only happened when I was drunk and I just don't remember."

6. *Plead with you or cite extenuating situational or psychological factors*—"I only did it because I was upset with something that happened to me so I really wasn't responsible for what happened," "I was having money problems," "My wife wouldn't sleep with me," "I don't know what got into me," or "I was physically abused as a child."

7. *Show false remorse in order to be let off quickly*—"I feel bad about what happened."

It also may happen that offenders show genuine acceptance of responsibility for their actions: "I'm guilty for what happened and willing to take my punishment."

The following case illustrates a batterer's attempt to minimize violence in his relationship with his wife. The batterer shows remorse, which is a starting point for change. He was referred to a therapist for possible depression (adapted from Sonkin, Martin, & Walker, 1985, pp. 67–69).

CASE 22-10. EVERETT
IR: Are you married or in a relationship?
IE: I'm married.
IR: How long have you been married?
IE: We've been married 14 years.
IR: Do you have any children?
IE: We have two kids, one 10-year-old boy and a 12-year-old girl.
IR: How are things going in your relationship?
IE: I guess OK, but when I get depressed, I tend to get a lot of flack from my wife.
IR: What kind of flack do you get?
IE: Oh, we just get into arguments about my not wanting to do very much.
IR: Do you argue about other things?
IE: Yes, money, sometimes the kids.
IR: What usually happens when you argue about, let's say, money?
IE: I usually tell her she is spending too much, and she tells me she's not or that she will cut down on her spending.
IR: Do you ever yell at her?
IE: Sometimes.
IR: What do you do at other times?
IE: Sometimes I give up and just leave.
IR: Sometimes when people get angry they may pound their fists on the table or grab or push the other person. Have you ever done that?
IE: I've grabbed her a couple of times to listen to me.
IR: Have you ever slapped her?
IE: A couple of times.

IR: How many times?

IE: Four or five times.

IR: When did you get the most angry with her?

IE: Last year, when she overcharged our credit card.

IR: What happened?

IE: We got into a big fight. She ended up calling the police.

IR: Did you hit her?

IE: Yes, I guess so.

IR: Where did you hit her?

IE: I punched her in the jaw, and it began to bleed. I tried to make up at this point, but it was too late.

IR: And so she called the police?

IE: Yes.

IR: How did you feel about what you did?

IE: Pretty bad.

IR: How have you felt about other incidents of violence in your relationship?

IE: Well, it's not like I want to do it—I just don't feel like I can do anything else at the moment. I really get angry.

IR: Are you curious to know whether there are other ways of dealing with your anger?

IE: I suppose I am.

IR: Did you ever find yourself getting depressed after a violent episode?

IE: Yes, all the time.

IR: Maybe the way you handle your anger and your depression are related?

IE: Could be.

IR: Even if they are not directly tied together, if the violence is stopped, you'll have many fewer times when you'll be depressed. That's a start.

IE: That would be great if you can do that.

Illustration of an Interview with an Alleged Offender

The following case is a transcript of an interview conducted by a detective in a criminal proceeding approximately four days after a 16-month-old child died (all names are fictitious). The detective is (IR) Tom Brown, and the interviewee-suspect (IE) is Jim Gisto, the mother's boyfriend. As you read this interview, keep in mind that the interviewee was an adult suspect who was reluctant to reveal details of the child's death. It is a more coercive interview than that advocated by mental health professionals. Was some coercion necessary? How should a detective investigating the death of a child proceed in an interview with a suspect who is reluctant to speak about the events associated with the child's death? Do you approve of the detective's technique?

CASE 22-11. JIM GISTO

Before the suspect comes into the room, which has a one-way mirror with a closed-circuit television, the detective says "My name is Tom Brown. I'm a detective with the Seattle Police Department. This morning I'll be interviewing Jim Gisto. Today's date is October 20, 1994. It's approximately 1:00 P.M., and I'll be bringing Mr. Gisto in now."

IR: Hi! I'm detective Tom Brown, a member of the Seattle Police Department.

IE: How is she doin'?

IR: Pardon me?

IE: How is she doin'?

IR: Do you mean Jane?

IE: Yes.

IR: She's takin' it hard. I'll explain to you what I explained to her, okay? First of all, it's 1:00 P.M. on Tuesday October 20th, 1994. Spell your last name for me, Jim.

IE: Gisto, G-I-S-T-O.

IR: And your first name is Jim.

IE: Yes.

IR: Okay, Jim. I went to the autopsy Sunday, and I know the injuries that the baby sustained.

IE: Yeah.

IR: The baby was hurt.

IE: Hurt in which way?

IR: Well, there's a lot of different ways, there's a lot of injuries that need to be explained. And Jane couldn't explain any of 'em.

IE: Mm-hm.

IR: The baby apparently was hit in the stomach, or he had been hit with enough force in to the stomach that caused a cut in the liver. And right next to the liver is the pancreas.

IE: Mm-hm.

IR: Which caused the pancreas to hemorrhage or to bleed. The baby had a big cut on the lip.

IE: Mm-hm.

IR: On the bottom and the top. Abrasions on the nose, on the forehead, a cut underneath the right eye. The baby had his ears, both ears were solid purple, but the bruises went down below the skin to the bone.

IE: Mm-hm.

IR: The baby's right testicle was hemorrhaging from the inside.

IE: What do you mean by hemorrhaging?

IR: Hemorrhaging means bleeding.

IE: Okay.

IR: It means—hemorrhage is, you know, the blood vessels break.

IE: Mm-hm.

IR: Caused by some force. The left testicle was fine, but the right one hemorrhaged. The main thing is that the brain hemorrhaged—excuse me, that is called a subdural hematoma. Which means the brain bleeds and swells.

IE: Okay.

IR: And that was the cause of death. Now how it got that way, somehow that's the force of being shaken.

IE: Mm-hm.

IR: Which causes the brain to hit inside the skull. It causes a massive bruising, the bleeding. And because of that, it swells, which causes death.

IE: Mm-hm. That was the cause of death?

IR: That's the cause of death. And it's not accidental. These things do not happen by a baby fallin' down.

IE: Mm-hm.

IR: It does not happen, it's impossible, physically impossible. It doesn't happen when the baby's thrown up in the air, that's not enough force—it's enough force to, to shake violently, rapidly. Now it's not an intentional thing all the time, sometimes it's an accident.

IE: (Clears throat.) Yeah.

In the initial part of the interview, the interviewer explains the autopsy findings. He answers simply and directly any questions asked by the interviewee-suspect.

IR: And that, I don't know what happened. I need to find out. I mean you, you know, you were there, you, just you and Jane are the only ones there.

IE: We were there that night.

IR: What happened?

IE: The baby was fine all day except for vomiting, most of that day. And we put the baby, me and her both put the baby to sleep that night.

IR: About what time?

IE: Must of been about one or two o'clock in the morning.

IR: The baby cry at all?

IE: Huh?

IR: Did the baby cry at all?

IE: Huh?

IR: Did the baby cry at all?

IE: No, he didn't cry. I mean, he cried when, well he didn't cry at all. I think he cried at Target [a department store] when he, he vomited at Target, I mean.

IR: Mm-hm.

IE: He was cryin' then. But other than that, the baby did not cry at all, but he was, his mother said he was gettin' a fever or something and she was givin' him medicine.

IR: Mm-hm.

IE: And we were watchin' a movie and everything but we ate dinner and everything, she made us dinner and we ate like that and everything. And right before we took a shower, the baby started vomiting.

IR: Who took a shower?

IE: Me and the baby—well, a bath, we were about to take a bath.

IR: Uh-huh.

IE: And the baby started vomiting, and I called Jane, the baby vomiting, and she cleaned up the vomit and everything and she gave him some medicine. So we sat him down in front of the TV and we all sat down there and we watchin' TV, and we were watchin' TV, we were watchin' I think the *Bird on a Wire* or something, and once it was over we were gonna put *Grease* on, we were gonna put another movie on. And the baby started, started getting sleepy. So she picked up the baby and she put 'em right, he sleeps right next to us, right, right next to us.

IR: Mm-hm.

IE: And she picked up the baby and put him to sleep right there. The baby started fallin' asleep. You know he fell asleep and everything, he was fine. And then Jane got up and she was gonna take a shower, so I got up with her and we stepped into the shower and you know we were there for a while. And after that we, I got out of the bathroom and everything and the baby was still in his bed where he always sleeps and everything. And me and her were about to lay down and went to go cover up the baby and the baby's lips were kinda purple. The

baby's lips were kinda purple and he had (clears throat) his mouth was like shut on his lips, like on the bottom lip.

IR: Mm-hm.

IE: They were like shut on there. And that's when I seen the baby and Jane was right next to me when I told "Jane, what's wrong with the baby?" And I picked him up and he was real limp, he was real limp. And I immediately took him to the counter and I put him on the counter, and I told her call 9-1-1, but instead of calling 9-1-1 she yelled outside and start calling all the neighbors and everything. And the neighbors walked in, and we tried to give him mouth to mouth and press his stomach.

IR: Mm-hm.

IE: Try to pump 'im. We opened up his mouth 'cause his mouth was shut.

IR: Mm-hm.

IE: We opened up his mouth, and he had a lot of stuff inside of his mouth.

IR: Like what's a lot of stuff?

IE: I, it looked like spit, it looked like blood—well, not blood, it was just like if it was a mixture of soda or tea 'cause he had drinkin' tea that night.

IR: Mm-hm.

IE: Like tea, and he had broccoli and spinach, 'cause we had eaten broccoli and spinach that night. He had broccoli and spinach all around his mouth, and I thought that was the reason he was choking or something. So, some guy named Roger in there you know when we opened his mouth, we stuck our finger inside to take everything that was out, out of his mouth. Started take, takin' stuff out. And he brought a suction thing for, you know, for the baby's nose.

IR: Mm-hm.

IE: And we stuck it in his mouth and we started tryin' to suck stuff up to see if he was you know started breathing again. And by then 9-1-1's already called and they were on their way. While we're doing that, the paramedics came.

In this part of the interview, the interviewer tries to learn how the baby's injuries came about. The interviewer asks many specific questions. Note that once the interviewee begins his narrative, the interviewer largely remains silent, using only minimal prompts to encourage the interviewee to continue.

IR: Okay, now you said that Jane was next to you when you noticed the baby wasn't breathing?

IE: Yeah, no, she was gettin' a glass of water I think, think, I think she was gettin' a glass of water.

IR: Was she in the bedroom with you or not?

IE: Yeah, she was in the bedroom. She was in the bedroom with us at all times, we were gettin' ready to go asleep. We were gonna, we were gettin' ready to watch another movie, when this happened. I was gettin' ready to lay down, I goin' to put the baby in his, with you know he has a blanket right next to him, I put the blanket on him. And when I grabbed him to pick him up, to move him you know on his bed right? 'Cause like he was moved around, he wasn't where we had put 'im, so we usually put him back on his pillow and everything, and he was real limp. And I, when I looked at his face he was like, and his lips were purple.

IR: How do you explain the bruises to the forehead?

IE: I can't explain that. I asked Jane about them, she had said that he had fallen off his toy tractor.

IR: What about the cut to the eye?

IE: I don't know, I didn't, I didn't.

IR: Did you see it that day?

IE: Yeah, I seen it when we went to the hospital.

IR: Did you see it before that?

IE: I hadn't noticed it.

IR: I mean, I mean you're playing with 'im.

IE: Yeah, but I, I didn't notice it.

IR: Yeah, that's a big cut.

IE: Maybe, maybe.

IR: That's a big cut not to notice.

IE: Yeah, I, I noticed it later on. I mean but the baby has cuts everywhere, I mean…

IR: What about his ears?

IE: Oh, his ears, his ears, I was, me and Jane were playing with him and everything and, I was like nibbling on his ears and I had sucked on Jane's eye.

IR: Mm-hm.

IE: And then I was suckin' on his ears. I told Jane that.

IR: Which ear?

IE: I think it was the, the left one I think it was. Well, it was really both of 'em 'cause we were playin' around. I was tossin' him and then I was layin' down, with him on my chest and I was tossin' him in the air.

IR: Was Jane with you then?

IE: Yeah, she was, she was right there with me. She was right next to me, I even told her. I asked her, can I suck on your ear too? She goes yeah. And me and her started playing, and that was it.

IR: Well, she said she never saw you throw him up in the air that night.

IE: Oh no, I didn't say that night. I mean I was, I was playing with him, I was playing with him that night but I mean, she sees me throwin' him all the time.

IR: Well, but night I'm talking about…

IE: No, at night?

IR: I'm talkin' Friday night, Saturday morning.

IE: Then I don't know. I was swingin' him around that night.

IR: How were you swingin' him around?

IE: I was holdin' him by his hands, and I was holdin' him by, on his ankles, I was spinning him.

IR: You were spinning him around and he's got a cast on?

IE: Yeah, well not by his feet, by, by his knees, he likes that.

IR: Well, you said his ankle.

IE: Well, I meant to say his knees, not his ankles 'cause I couldn't get ahold of his ankles 'cause of his cast. I mean I meant to say his knees.

IR: And you swing him around?

IE: Well, not swing him around, I grab him, can I show you how I do it?

IR: Sure.

IE: I would grab him like this, and I grab him by, I grab him by the stomach and I, I go like this to 'im and he starts laughing, okay?

IR: Mm-hm.

IE: I lay him down and then I grab him by his knees, and I pick him up, so now he's upside down with his face out this way.

IR: Okay.

IE: I go like this, shake him like this. And he, he puts his hands down and he likes, he likes to grab onto the, onto the floor or whatever he can touch.

IR: Okay. But you did that Saturday night?

IE: Yeah, I did that night.

IR: Did he hit his head on anything?

IE: I don't think so.

IR: Is it possible?

IE: It is possible but not while I was doin' it to him, but I don't think, I don't think he hit his head that night.

IR: Are you sure?

IE: I'm pretty sure, almost positively sure he did not hit his head. I didn't, I didn't notice him hit his head, he didn't cry that night at all.

In the previous part of the interview, the interviewer tries to get the interviewee's understanding of the baby's specific symptoms. Areas of concern were as follows: How did the symptoms come about? What symptoms did he notice? Who was present? The interviewer also confronts the interviewee with information he obtained in the interview with the baby's mother that appears to contradict the interviewee's statements.

IR: Because see, you know what's confusin' is that there's some neighbors that I've talked to, and the officers there talked to after you guys left for the hospital.

IE: Mm-hm.

IR: They heard Peter cryin' that night. At about 1:30, two o'clock in the morning.

IE: Yeah.

IR: But then he stopped real quick.

IE: Mm-hm.

IR: But it was, he did cry.

IE: I asked Jane "Did the baby cry that night?" and she said no, the baby did not cry at all that night. I don't know, I'm pretty sure he didn't cry. I go but the detectives say that somebody heard the baby crying.

IR: Yeah.

IE: There's maybe 80 babies in that apartment.

IR: But it's from your place. I mean everybody that we've talked to individually before they can get together, talk and said it was from a, it was Peter. 'Cause they recognized Peter's cry.

IE: I'm pretty, I'm…

IR: From your, your condo.

IE: I'm pretty sure that he, he, he didn't, he didn't cry. If he did he, if he did, I didn't, no he had, I don't think he cried.

IR: Do you know about the cuts on the nipples?

IE: Yeah, well, I don't know what happened to his cut nipples but we play with him, me, Jane and him play. That was a new thing that we tell him say ouch, you know, to wherever he gets hurt, you know, we tell him to say ouch.

IR: Mm-hm.

IE: Now we tell 'im, I would tell, I would grab him by the nipple, Peter ouch.

IR: Uh-huh.

IE: We pinch him by the nipple and, so every time we would tell him "Peter ouch," he would grab his nipples and say ouch. Or his legs or anywhere.

IR: But these are not caused by him. These are, you know, these injuries are not caused by Peter. Peter didn't do it. He couldn't of done it to himself.

IE: Mm—okay.

IR: It is physically impossible, he cannot do that. I mean, like, did you ever, were you ever with Jane when she tried to pot, potty train Peter?

IE: Yeah, lots of times.

IR: How would she try to make it, if she got him to the toilet, how would she try to make him go pee?

IE: What do you mean by try to make him go pee?

IR: Well, she says she would have, either standing or sitting on the toilet.

IE: Mm-hm.

IR: And make him go pee.

IE: Yeah.

IR: Do you know how she would make him go pee?

IE: Mm, she would leave him for, for long time. Sometimes we would forget about him. We'd be in the room and all of a sudden, you know, we hear him either stumble or fall and, the baby, and we'd run to the bathroom and be Peter tryin' to get off the toilet and we let him, forget. We shouldn't leave him like that until, you know, we both leave him there until like he'd go to the bathroom or until we would hear him say, ma or pa.

IR: Mm-hm.

IE: You know, we tell him, Peter, say yeah to mean you are done. He'll say yeah and we'd go in, we'd finish with him, pull his pants up or whatever.

IR: Did, do you know if Jane left Peter with anybody else?

IE: That night or ever?

IR: Or the last couple days, before, you know, either Wednesday, Thursday and Friday?

IE: I don't, I don't, I don't know. She, I, I didn't really let her, let her leave. I would tell her, you know, don't leave Peter with nobody.

The interviewer again confronts the interviewee with an apparent contradiction. He points out that what the interviewee is saying conflicts with reports of neighbors. He also points out that the baby's injuries could not have been done by the baby himself. The interviewer tries to find out whether the baby was left with anyone else.

IR: Explain to me, what do you, you know, you spend a few days. What do you think happened to Peter?

IE: Why he died?

IR: Yeah.

IE: I don't, I have no idea. I have no idea. I mean I've, it's been runnin' through my mind, and my I, I can't explain why, why. I'll, all I know that day that he was sick and he was vomiting, that's all that we know.

IR: But that's not goin' to cause any…

IE: Yeah, I know. Well, especially if it's, if you say something to the head.

IR: That's the major…

IE: Espec…

IR: That's the major injury.

IE: But see the doctor had told us that he stopped breathing. Okay, that's what the doctor had told us that he stopped breathing. And he had told us that he had vomit in his lungs.

IR: He…

IE: Okay.

IR: He could have…

IE: That he had vomit, and that's what the doctor had told us that, you know…

IR: That's not why the baby died. See when the brain swells…

IE: It leads to the lack of oxygen to the brain.

IR: Right.

IE: And the lack of oxygen, lack, lack, lack of air.

IR: Right.

IE: That's what the doctor explained to us.

IR: But that doctor didn't do the autopsy. That doctor was, he could not say exactly at that time what, what the baby died of. He could tell why, I mean, you know, because it wasn't breathing they, they did the brain scans, they did CAT scans and all the other tests that they do, and they could tell that the baby had brain damage. They knew that the baby had a, had brain damage. That the brain was swollen and that there was pressure on the brain.

IE: Yeah.

IR: Which causes all the other functions to shut down. So you don't breathe, which cause lacks of, lack of oxygen to the brain.

IE: Mm-hm.

IR: And the brain's gonna quit functioning.

IE: Mm-hm.

IR: I know it's a combination of things, but the major, the main cause of death is because of the brain swelling. Because the brain bled inside the skull, causing the swelling.

IE: Was, was there, was there, what would happen, something happened to his head? He hit himself or…

IR: No, he did not hit himself. No, there's no trauma to the head saying that he was hit blunt, not like a hammer or falling down. It's that this is the type of injury caused by being shaken or some violent acceleration, deceleration to the head, which causes the brain to move inside the skull.

IE: Okay.

IR: Okay? Swinging maybe, maybe could do it. No, I'm not saying this is not an intentional thing.

IE: Oh I, I understand. See but…

IR: But we need to figure out, that's why I need to talk in detail with you and Jane to determine what activity you'd had with the baby.

IE: I understand. Maybe it was swinging, but I doubt it because his ma, I mean if we were to swing him real hard, his mother would of told me to stop. Mm, his mother, we were playing, baby laughs.

Having ascertained that no one else could have injured the baby, the interviewer asks the interviewee for an explanation of the baby's death. The interviewer confronts the interviewee with tests showing that the cause of death offered by the interviewee—vomit in the lungs—was not the actual cause of death. The interviewer then begins to question the interviewee about activities the interviewee was engaged in with the baby.

IR: Mm-hm.
IE: I mean he loved for me to throw him up in the air.
IR: Oh yeah, all babies do.
IE: I would swing him, he would just, he would always, even with his broken leg he would come up to me and ask me to swing'im, and you know I'll turn him around.
IR: Mm-hm.
IE: But what, the baby was never shaken up, never shaken.
IR: Yes, it was.
IE: How do you guys figure it was shaken?
IR: That's, that's how the brain gets in that situation. That's how the brain is injured, because it takes a lot of force to do that. Your body is built and designed to protect itself to a certain point.
IE: Yeah.
IR: And once it passes that point, then you get the damage. Now in lieu of, there was no outer bruising to the head to indicate that it was hit with something.
IE: Mm-hm.
IR: It's some other type of force.
IE: Okay.
IR: It's not falling down. Falling down will not do it. Falling down will cause a bruise.
IE: Like the, like the one on his forehead or nose?
IR: Right.
IE: Yeah.
IR: That's possible for that, but that's also caused by maybe swinging and hitting the head.
IE: No, but his mother seen that, his mother...
IR: Right.
IE: Seen when he fell with the toy tractor.
IR: Right.
IE: I was at work or somewhere, 'cause I wasn't there.
IR: But still I'm sayin' it is, something happened to that baby. Now it could of been done earlier in the day, and it slowly built up the pressure, and that coulda caused the baby to be throwin' up, that's a possibility. Something coulda happened earlier in the day.
IE: I'm tryin' to think back if any...
IR: What time did you get to the house?
IE: I got to the house about nine o'clock that morning 'cause I had to go to work at five in the afternoon. I got there when the baby and the mother were asleep. I knocked on the door, she opened the door for me. They were both asleep, so I went and I cuddled up to Jane and you know we went, we fell asleep. And didn't waken up until like three, about three or two-thirty in the afternoon. I got up and, well, we got dressed and she told me "Can I go to work with you?" and I went "Sure." You know, we got dressed and everything, we started walkin' to Target. She stayed there most of the day at Target, and that's when the baby started vomiting at work.
IR: Mm-hm.
IE: And she told me, she goes "Baby feels kinda hot, Jim" and I go "Does he, well let's buy him medicine." We bought some medicine.

IR: You did, you didn't notice any of the injuries then?
IE: Not there where I was working.
IR: Mm-hm.
IE: I was, I was working at that time.
IR: Well, when you were there sleeping.
IE: Mm-hm.
IR: I mean when you got there and when you woke up during the day, you didn't notice anything unusual about the baby?
IE: Well the, no, yeah. I, I noticed that stuff about the nose but I asked her "What happened to his nose?" Well, he fell off the tractor or somethin'.
IR: When did she say that happened?
IE: When did she say? I didn't, I don't know. I, I can't remember on that. I think it was on, I went to work on Thursday. I think it happened either Wednesday, Tuesday or Wednesday. One of those two days it had to of been.
IR: Uh, um, but, at the, I don't know I'm guessing, I wasn't there, something happened, probably Friday.
IE: Most, yeah.
IR: Something.
IE: Friday night, I mean because I was at work from five to eleven when I came home from work, to, well, she went to go pick me up.
IR: Mm-hm.
IE: She went to go pick me up. We went to Safeway [name of a grocery store].
IR: How was the baby acting?
IE: He was all right. And matter fact and that, yes that Friday night if, if Jane, Jane said that I didn't throw him that night, I did. I remember I grab him, I remember perfectly now. At Safeway when we went to go, went to go buy some, I think sugar and stuff. I don't remember what we bought, we bought soups, Top Ramens and stuff like that. And we're, we're inside of Safeway and the baby kept on bugging me to throw him, so I was throwin' him in Safeway. And we were catchin' him but that was it, I mean we went back into the car and we took off. I put him in the back seat and left him in the back seat and took off home, and, and that was it. That was, that was it and that was Friday night, about 11:30, twelve o'clock.
IR: And, and when you came back to the apartment?
IE: Mm-hm. Oh, when I came back to the apartment?
IR: Mm-hm.
IE: We went inside the apartment, we started cooking dinner. She was gonna make us broccoli. We turned on the TV and we started watchin' TV. We were right there kickin' back watchin' TV until dinner was ready and then we all ate right there in front of the TV. Me, her, and the baby. We ate in front of the TV.

The interviewer probes for specific details about the day before and the day of the baby's death.

IR: Okay. What do you think happened?
IE: I don't know. I wish I did know though. I mean, that about shakin' the baby, I don't know.
IR: There's only two of you there.
IE: Well, I know there's only two.
IR: One of you did it or both of you did it.
IE: I don't, I, I don't believe that.

IR: Somebody did it.

IE: Oh yes, I mean.

IR: Somebody killed the baby.

IE: I don't know, I don't, I don't think, I don't see it that way, somebody killed the baby.

IR: Where do, how do you see it?

IE: I don't know how I see it. I mean, I don't believe that somebody shook the baby 'cause Jane does not.

IR: Somethin' happened to the baby.

IE: Jane never did…

IR: That killed the baby. I'm not talkin' no slap and I'm not saying that it was an intentional act that it was done.

IE: I understand.

IR: To hurt the baby.

IE: I understand what you're saying.

IR: But it's the result.

IE: See but that's what I'm trying to explain to you that we don't, the only physical thing that we do with the baby is, you know, swing him around and throw him up in the air. That's always under Jane's eyes 'cause Jane's always there. Jane don't work, she's always there. I'm the one that works.

IR: Mm-hm.

IE: You know like, and I don't even live there, live there. I live at my uncle's house but I, I spend a lot time there with 'em.

IR: Right.

IE: I don't, I don't think Jane would of shook 'im like that, I mean hard enough for the baby to go through that kind of thing.

IR: Well, the thing is somebody did, and you were the only two there. One of you knows the answer. It boils down to, hey, it was an accident. But the way it is, is somebody's not tellin' me what they know. Either you or Jane. And what it boils down to, the more, the longer it takes for me to find out the truth, the more suspicious I get. Now I understand Jane, she's a young girl, it's very traumatic. But I still need to know the truth. Now if it boils down to where, you know, potentially both of you could be charged. Do you understand that?

IE: I understand.

IR: You know what second-degree murder is?

IE: I understand.

IR: That's 15 years to life in prison.

IE: I understand.

IR: That's the serious part. The other part is, hey, it's an accident, it was an accident, this is what happened. Accidents happen.

IE: I understand that, sir, but see, that's, that's what I don't know I understand. I mean how could of that accident happened?

IR: Exactly, that's what I need to find out. You, you guys were there, I wasn't.

IE: I was there for what, an hour of it? I mean I was, I was at work most of the day.

IR: Right, but you were there, but the baby's fine.

IE: Yeah, but the baby, we put the baby to sleep.

IR: Mm-hm.

IE: Like you said, I mean it coulda happened, you know, a day before or whatever.

IR: Maybe.

IE: Maybe yeah.

IR: But I really don't think so. The baby had too many injuries.

IE: How was the baby shaken?

IR: If, there's a lot of different ways it could be shaken. It could be shaken from holding on to the shoulders, holdin' on to the head, just shaken in a manner that's gonna cause the head to move real fast.

IE: And there was nothin' to indicate what, you know the way he was shaken?

IR: No.

IE: Where he was held from?

IR: Maybe from the back. There's bruises on the back.

IE: Yeah, yeah, I seen a couple bruises on his back. That I asked her about that too.

IR: Did you know that the baby had a broken rib at one time?

IE: Broken rib?

IR: Mm-hm.

IE: Took him to the doctor not that long ago.

IR: Yeah, but the baby had a broken rib, eh, we found it from the autopsy. It was, it was healed.

IE: Oh yeah? How long ago was this?

IR: We're, it's hard to say right now but they're doin' tests to determine how old the injury was. It may be a month or two old. But the baby had a broken rib at one time. And it's broken in a position where it's not from falling down.

IE: Yeah.

IR: There's only one way to break a rib the way this one was broken, and that's from pressure directly, direct pressure to that portion of the rib. There's, there's a lot of questions. Um…

IE: That need to be answered.

IR: Yeah.

IE: Exactly, I understand.

IR: And I'm conducting this in a way I would a murder. Because as far as I'm concerned right now, it's a murder. Unless I'm told otherwise, proved otherwise, we, that's how serious we take it. You know it's not, oh well.

IE: Oh, I know.

IR: It's a freak accident.

IE: No, I'm takin' it seriously too, I mean.

IR: Um.

IE: If it is a murder, I would like, you know, I'll help you in any which way I can. I'm givin' you every, all the information I know, exactly what happened that night, exactly what, you know, what was done.

IR: Well…

IE: From the time I got home to the time I left, till the time you called, everything.

IR: Somebody's holding back. Because this doesn't happen to a baby and somebody's supposedly with this baby 24 hours a day, this doesn't happen.

IE: She was, she was with all, all the times, all the time she was with him. Unless she left him somewhere, which I doubt, because I was at work, I don't you know. She says she was gonna go home.

IR: Okay, Jim, I think that's about it for today. Thanks for comin' on down, appreciate it.

IE: Yeah.

IR: Wonder if I have a card with me.

IE: I, we'll talk, just me and Jane have to talk this over.

IR: Yeah. Like I said, if it's an accident, I need to know. And just because it happened it, it happened. But hiding it or tryin' to make up stories or denying it, which is what, that's the stage we're at now, is denial. You can't deny what happened.

IE: Yeah.

IR: Because it did happen. So let me go get, go back in the office and I'll get you one of my business cards, so.

In the last part of the interview, the interviewer confronts the interviewee with the baby's injuries and the evidence that the baby must have been shaken, which in forensic work is referred to as *shaken baby syndrome*. He also offers the interviewee an alternative explanation that the shaking could have been done unintentionally. The interviewer underscores his view that someone is not telling everything. But he makes no accusations during this interview. [*Editorial note:* A trial was held, and both the mother and the boyfriend were found guilty of second-degree murder.]

Exercise 22-3. Rephrasing Statements to Offender

Rephrase the following statements to make them more acceptable. Compare your responses with those following the statements.

1. "I am removing your daughter because I'm afraid you'll molest her again."
2. "You're sick, and you need treatment right away."
3. "I have no idea when your son will be coming home."
4. "I think there's more to this than what you're telling me."
5. "If you don't come clean, I'll have to tell the court you're not cooperating."

Suggested Rephrasing

1. "I'm removing your daughter for her protection, but also for yours. Until you get the help you need, we want to be sure that your child is not hurt again."
2. "Molesting children is a serious problem. I believe that you should try to get help so that you can have a better relationship with your children."
3. "I know you're eager to have him back. Your high motivation is a step in the right direction. We'll keep assessing the family's progress to decide when he can come home. It may not be for a while."
4. "You have made a good start in talking about this. But I'd like to learn as many details as possible. Let's get to the bottom of it so that we can resolve the problem."
5. "Your daughter really needs your help. If we don't know the whole story, we won't be able to get all of you the help you need."

Interviewing in Cases of Suspected Munchausen Syndrome by Proxy

Not much is known about why parents with Munchausen Syndrome by Proxy intentionally try to keep their children sick (see Chapter 20). Explanations such as their desire to get attention, to find a niche for themselves, or to outwit doctors are not sufficient (Rosenberg, 1987).

To deal effectively with Munchausen Syndrome by Proxy, human services workers and health care providers should be part of a multidisciplinary team (Mian, 1995). This team, ideally, is composed of a pediatrician, social worker, nurse, hospital administrator, hospital legal consultant, and psychologist or psychiatrist. The primary goals of the multidisciplinary team are to protect the suspected victim and to assist in the diagnosis and management of the case.

The team should carry out the following procedures as needed (Rosenberg, 1987):

1. Monitor the child's condition, and recommend that the child receive a thorough medical examination by a health care provider who is an expert in Munchausen Syndrome by Proxy, if possible.
2. Recommend procedures that might detect the cause of the child's illness (for example, assay tests in cases of suspected poisoning), because methods of simulating or producing illness in a child are virtually limitless.
3. Consider recommending hospitalization for the child in order to conduct a thorough diagnostic evaluation. Recognize that the child is not free of risk in the hospital because the parent still has access to the child. Consider installing a video camera in the child's hospital room, if the health care staff agrees.
4. Have the health care personnel supervise all parental visits, if the child is hospitalized, and make sure that the family does not bring food, drink, or medicines into the hospital.
5. Interview the child. Ask the child about foods, medicines, care of medical equipment, secrets between the child and the parents, his or her personal recollections of symptoms, and where and when the symptoms occurred.
6. Interview other people knowledgeable about the child's illness, such as the child's siblings, other relatives, babysitters, and neighbors, and compare their statements about the child's illness with those of the parents.
7. Inform the parents of the team's findings.
8. Review the child's past medical records. Check with all the medical health care facilities and health care providers in the areas where the family has lived.
9. Check out the family medical history from other medical sources. Look for unusual illnesses in the child's siblings or unusual illnesses in the parents.
10. Interview each parent. Cover such areas as the child's illness, the family's background, and each parent's social and work histories.
11. Document carefully all of the information obtained.
12. Arrange for the child to have a thorough psychological evaluation.

13. Contact Child Protective Services or law enforcement if the team believes that there is a reasonable suspicion of Munchausen Syndrome by Proxy.

If you are working in a social services agency and suspect a case of Munchausen Syndrome by Proxy, consider requesting ongoing court-ordered supervision of the case (Rosenberg, 1987). Inform the parents that you want to protect the child and that you want to get help for them. *If there is sufficient proof of Munchausen Syndrome by Proxy, (a) recommend out-of-home placement for the child* (returning the child to the home under the supervision of the other parent is inadequate because the child still may be in danger) and *(b) request a court-ordered review of the child's medical records, examination of all siblings, psychological evaluation of the child and the family, and treatment of the child and the family, as needed.*

When professionals tell caregivers that they suspect that the caregivers have deliberately kept their children ill, the caregivers are likely to deny the allegations (Mian, 1995). Caregivers who have been keeping their children ill may be extremely adept at convincing others of their innocence. Because caregivers may threaten to initiate legal action, professionals may be reluctant to pursue their clinical findings (Mian, 1995).

Most health professionals find the possibility of having to deal with anger, making a mistake, saying the wrong thing, or having to defend their position in a one-to-one confrontation or in a court of law very frightening. The accusation is so horrible that they are reluctant to intervene early for fear of being wrong. The potential for parental decompensation on confrontation cannot be dismissed. It can seem far easier to do more tests than to confront the very real possibility of MBP [Munchausen Syndrome by Proxy] and its perpetrator. Yet the management of MBP requires confrontation of the parent and separation (often as a diagnostic maneuver) of parent and child. (pp. 274–275)

Here are different examples of how two physicians view their role in cases where Munchausen Syndrome by Proxy is suspected (Schreier & Libow, 1993).

PHYSICIAN A
I can also tell you that there have been cases where people have been accused and it hasn't been Munchausen by Proxy syndrome—it's turned out to be a slow-growing brain tumor, or something else causing the vomiting. Then you really have egg all over your face. I haven't personally, but I can tell you that I know people who have done that. That's why we are a little hesitant to make the accusation. Still in our society, that's a heinous accusation to make. To tell somebody that "I think you're doing this to your child," that's not an accusation you make lightly, especially if you happen to like the person or you've gone through this in the past. Maybe a month later you found out you were wrong, it was a brain tumor. So the thing is, you have to work these kids up the wazoo. (p. 69)

PHYSICIAN B
As a physician one of the things you learn early on is to listen to the parents. And what makes Munchausen by Proxy syndrome so difficult to deal with is that your ally in the child's health care is really not your ally. I don't want to use the word "adversary," but in fact I guess it is an adversarial relationship, because they are playing a game with you, except you don't know you're playing a game.

And frankly, I'm not a detective. I'm not Perry Mason and I don't want to be. It's difficult enough to accuse somebody, but for me to have to start snooping around and becoming a detective, and looking through drawers—I don't want to do that. That's not my role…. And I think that that makes it even more difficult because when you finally accuse the person, it's a question of, "Well can you prove it?" Well no, I can't prove it…. If they are looking for hard evidence, it's not going to be there. I'm not going to find a bottle of Milk of Magnesia in the mother's purse with her fingerprints on it, and I'm not going to put a hidden camera or a hidden microphone in a room to try to catch the person…. And the thought of putting cameras in rooms and trying to catch people is repugnant to me. We seek alliances with parents, not adversarial relationships. (p. 35)

CONCLUDING COMMENT ON INTERVIEWING CHILDREN, FAMILIES, AND ALLEGED OFFENDERS IN CASES OF CHILD MALTREATMENT

Although the interviewing guidelines in this book stress open-ended and probing questions, you will encounter children and adults who are reluctant to talk to you. When this happens, you will need to be more active in your questioning. When the interviewee does not respond to your open-ended questions, how direct should your questioning be? What clues can guide you in your questioning? For example, what should you do if you know the child has a sexually transmitted disease but the child will not talk to you about how he or she got the disease? Further research is needed to address these and related issues (Berliner & Loftus, 1992). Meanwhile, each of you must decide, based on your clinical judgment, the best strategy to pursue without violating ethical standards and good professional practice. Exhibit 22-2 presents guidelines for conducting child maltreatment investigations. It is a code of principles for working with children and parents and a set of guidelines for social services agencies. *No matter what strategy you decide to follow, you must safeguard the rights of the child as well as the rights of the alleged offender, and you should never use coercive interviewing techniques.*

How do professionals live with the possibility that as a result of their opinion, a child is returned to an abusive environment or has had a relationship with a nonabusive parent disrupted or severed?

—Lucy Berliner and Elizabeth Loftus

Exhibit 22-2
Guidelines for Conducting Child Sexual Abuse Investigations

In 1989, a commission in England issued recommendations for conducting child sexual abuse investigations. Following are its recommendations for dealing with children and parents and for Child Protective Services.

Children

There is a danger that in looking to the welfare of the children believed to be the victims of sexual abuse the children themselves may be overlooked. The child is a person and not an object of concern.

We recommend that:

1. Professionals recognize the need for adults to explain to children what is going on. Children are entitled to a proper explanation appropriate to their age and developmental level, to be told why they are being taken away from home and given some idea of what is going to happen to them.

2. Professionals should not make promises to a child that cannot be kept, and in the light of possible court proceedings should not promise a child that what is said in confidence can be kept in confidence.

3. Professionals should always listen carefully to what the child has to say and take seriously what is said.

4. Throughout the proceedings, the views and the wishes of the child, particularly as to what should happen to him or her, should be taken into consideration by the professionals involved with the child's problems.

5. The views and the wishes of the child should be placed before whichever court deals with the case. We do not, however, suggest that those wishes should predominate.

6. Children should not be subjected to repeated medical examinations solely for evidential purposes. Where appropriate, according to child's age and understanding, the consent of the child should be obtained before any medical examination or photography.

7. Children should not be subjected to repeated interviews nor to the probing and confrontational type of "disclosure" interview for the same purpose, for it in itself can be damaging and harmful to them. The consent of the child should, where possible, be obtained before the interviews are recorded on video.

8. The child should be medically examined and interviewed in a suitable and sensitive environment, where there are suitably trained staff available.

9. When a child is moved from home or between hospital and foster home, it is important that those responsible for the day-to-day care of the child not only understand the child's legal status but also have sufficient information to look after the child properly.

10. Those involved in investigation of child sexual abuse should make a conscious effort to ensure that they act throughout in the best interests of the child.

Parents

We recommend:

1. The parents should be given the same courtesy as the family of any other referred child. This applies to all aspects of the investigation into the suspicion of child sexual abuse and should be recognized by all professionals concerned with the family.

2. Parents should be informed and, where appropriate, consulted at each stage of the investigation by the professional dealing with the child, whether medical, police, or social worker. Parents are entitled to know what is going on and to be helped to understand the steps that are being taken.

3. Child Protective Services should confirm all important decisions to parents in writing. Parents may not understand the implications of decisions made and they should have the opportunity to give the written decision to their lawyers.

4. Parents should always be advised of their rights of appeal or complaint in relation to any decisions made about them or their children.

5. Child Protective Services should always seek to provide support to the family during the investigation. Parents should not be left isolated and bewildered at this difficult time.

6. Any court order served on the parents should include a written explanation of the meaning of the order, the position of the parents, their continuing responsibilities, and their rights to seek legal advice.

Child Protective Services

We make the following recommendations with regard to Child Protective Services:

1. Place-of-safety orders should only be sought for the minimum time necessary to ensure protection of the child.

2. Records related to the use of statutory powers on an emergency basis should be kept and monitored regularly by Child Protective Services.

3. A code of practice should be drawn up for the administration by social workers of emergency orders for the purposes of child protection including the provision of information to parents defining their rights in clear simple language.

4. Whenever and however children are received into care, social workers should agree on the arrangements for access with parents unless there are exceptional reasons related to the child's interests not to do so. In either event, parents should be notified in writing as soon as possible of the access arrangements and the avenues of complaint or appeal open to them if they are aggrieved.

Source: Levy, A. (1989), pp. 166–168, with changes in notation.

THINKING THROUGH THE ISSUES

How might your feelings about child maltreatment affect the way you conduct an interview with a child who was alleged to have been maltreated?

Do you have any fears about listening to the pain associated with child maltreatment? If you are reluctant to listen to the fear, anger, or hatred that victims may express, will you prematurely cut victims off from talking about their feelings? Can you listen objectively to victims of physical abuse, emotional abuse, sexual abuse, or neglect?

What are your personal resources—such as social, spiritual, and familial resources—for dealing with your emotions in cases of child maltreatment?

What clues might alert you to the possibility that the alleged child maltreatment did or did not occur?

What role do you believe that Child Protective Services and law enforcement should have in cases of child maltreatment?

What skills will you need to develop to communicate effectively with professionals of diverse backgrounds involved in cases of child maltreatment?

Given the controversy surrounding the use of anatomically detailed dolls, would you use them? What is the basis for your answer?

What can you do to get reluctant parents to talk with you about possible child maltreatment?

How might your feelings about offenders who maltreat children affect the way you interview them?

How would you deal with a child who was sexually seductive in the interview?

How would you report borderline cases of physical abuse, emotional abuse, sexual abuse, or neglect? What factors would influence whether you report suspected child maltreatment?

SUMMARY

1. Interviewing in cases of child maltreatment is especially challenging because it involves topics usually considered taboo and because it may lead to criminal charges. In addition, young children may not be able to describe the details of the maltreatment clearly, and their families and the alleged offender will likely be reluctant to talk about the maltreatment.

2. Do not assume the role of a therapist when you are conducting the initial interview—keep the roles of investigator and therapist completely separate.

3. Child maltreatment interviewing will require knowledge of the types of child maltreatment, state laws concerning child maltreatment, law enforcement investigative procedures, available placement facilities in the community, and medical, psychological, and psychiatric evaluative procedures.

4. Child Protective Services, whose role is to protect children, makes its decisions on clear and convincing evidence, whereas law enforcement, whose role is to uphold laws and protect public safety, aims to obtain a more stringent level of proof—proof beyond a reasonable doubt.

A Model for Interviewing in Cases of Child Maltreatment

5. An interdisciplinary model is recommended for interviewing children who have been or who are alleged to have been maltreated.

6. Comprehensive interviews in child maltreatment investigations should be conducted by specially trained child interview specialists.

7. A multidisciplinary interview center should be established in each community where feasible.

8. Investigative interviews conducted at well-run multidisciplinary interview centers should be videotaped.

Preparing for the Initial Interview in Cases of Child Maltreatment

9. Investigative or assessment interviews in cases of child maltreatment have several possible aims: to determine whether the alleged maltreatment has occurred, to assess the child, to assess the family, and to make recommendations for appropriate interventions.

10. There are at least two possible strategies for obtaining background information. One strategy is to obtain as many details as possible about the alleged maltreatment before you interview the child, whereas the other is to obtain background details after you conduct the interview to preclude biasing your questions.

11. Conduct the interview with the child as soon as possible after the initial report of the alleged maltreatment.

12. Arrange for the child to have a medical examination, if one has not been done.

13. Obtain photographs of people in the child's life from the caregiver if you think you may need to use them in the interview to identify persons to whom the child is referring.

14. In cases of child maltreatment, a videotape will help you make a detailed record of the interview.

15. Document carefully all contacts (including telephone calls) you have with anyone about the case.

16. If the child belongs to an ethnic minority group, you may have to consider some additional issues in preparing to interview for child maltreatment. These issues include the ability of family members to speak English, the role of children in the family, husband and wife relations, the role that mythology plays in their lives, cultural views toward child maltreatment, and cultural practices that may mimic physical abuse.

Interviewing the Child in Cases of Child Maltreatment

17. A child's response to maltreatment will depend on the child's sex, age, and level of emotional and cognitive development; the type of maltreatment, including its frequency and duration; the child's relationship to the offender; whether threat or force was used; and the quality of support available to the child.

18. The affect the child shows in the interview may depend on how long ago the abusive incident(s) occurred.

19. You must use a developmental perspective in all interviews with children, recognizing age-appropriate cognitive skills, expressive and receptive language skills, and motor skills.

20. Children who are less than 3 years old will be extremely difficult to interview because they do not have the linguistic capacity to describe events in detail.

21. Children between 3 and 5 years of age may pose challenges for the interviewer because they may not be able to give an

organized or consistent description of the maltreatment incident(s). They also may have limited capacity to describe events in detail. In addition, they vary greatly in their communication skills.

22. In investigative interviews, when children are reluctant to talk to you, you will have to walk a tightrope, delicately trying to balance two sets of conflicting goals. One goal is to learn whether the child has been maltreated and then get protection for the child. The other goal is to ensure that innocent people are not accused of any wrongdoing.

23. Allow sufficient time with the child to obtain relevant information.

24. Discuss confidentiality, especially with older children and adolescents, and inform them of your obligation to report any situation in which the child is unsafe.

25. Conduct a nonbiased, noncoercive, and nonrepetitive interview.

26. Ask open-ended questions, use prompts, and avoid leading questions.

27. Avoid giving the child information given to you by someone else.

28. Ask the child for important information in several different ways if she or he is reluctant to give you the information, especially if you believe the child knows the information.

29. Listen to everything the child says, and follow up on all information the child gives you.

30. Follow up leads by asking the child for more details, using neutral probing questions and prompts as needed.

31. Be alert to whether the child answers every question with a "yes" or "no."

32. Help the child find words to express what took place when the child is reluctant to talk about the possible maltreatment or when the child does not know the words to describe the possible maltreatment.

33. Give the child who is reluctant to talk directly about the maltreatment opportunities to draw on paper with pencils and crayons and to respond to direct questions.

34. Probe any inconsistencies in the child's statements by explaining that you are confused, not by challenging the child.

35. Ask preschool children about multiple incidents of possible maltreatment by asking specific or direct questions about time sequences.

36. Use age-appropriate language.

37. Avoid the use of pronouns because of potential ambiguity, unless the referent is clear.

38. Use short sentences, few syllables per word, and concrete, visual words with young children.

39. Use uncomplicated grammar with all children.

40. Use simple and direct questions with all children.

41. Use the active voice with all children.

42. Use positive phrasing with all children.

43. Avoid questions that may imply a child is guilty.

44. Learn about the child's terminology for body parts and for sexual acts, and use the child's terms during the interview, as needed.

45. Consider carefully what it means when a child changes her or his story.

46. Accept what the child says when you are inquiring about the maltreatment, and do not offer interpretations.

47. Attend carefully to the child's terminology for designating people in her or his world.

48. Determine whom the child is talking about when there are several individuals who may assume similar roles.

49. When you need to clarify whom the child is talking about, show the child photographs or draw faces of people in the child's life.

50. Take note of the child's concepts (such as knowledge of time and numbers), the child's vocabulary and diction, and other characteristics about the child that may help you in conducting the interview.

51. Determine whether the child knows the difference between the truth and a lie.

52. Ask the child whom she or he has told about the maltreatment.

53. Clarify any terms the child uses that appear to be based on experiences in therapy.

54. Determine whether a young child or a developmentally delayed child knows basic concepts such as top, under, behind, inside, and outside.

55. Keep interruptions to a minimum, allow the child to control the flow of information if at all possible, and take your cues from the child about the speed of questioning and the length of silences.

56. Help the child get past any fears that she or he may have about revealing the maltreatment.

57. Give the child permission to break any secrets made between herself or himself and the abuser.

58. Take special care to help the child express her or his feelings, reactions, and any painful experiences.

59. Help the child be as open as possible in talking about the alleged maltreatment.

60. Never promise the child what you cannot deliver.

61. Play materials may be useful with young children who are reluctant to talk to you directly about the alleged maltreatment.

62. In the first phase of the interview, the rapport phase, you want to establish a good relationship with the child. Children who have been maltreated or who may have been maltreated may be under considerable stress when you first meet them. Be warm, friendly, supportive, reassuring, and empathic in order to reduce the child's stress and help the child relax.

63. The way you establish rapport will depend on the child's age. With preschool children, you might try some activity that you can do together. You can ask school-aged children and adolescents how they feel about being at the interview and what they were told about the interview.

64. You might want to ask the child to tell you about some recent event, such as a birthday party. This may help the child get accustomed to talking with you and allows you to observe the way he or she relates historical facts to you.

65. During the second phase of the interview, the free narrative account and nonleading questioning phase, encourage the child to tell you about what happened.

66. When you broach the topic of the alleged maltreatment, pay careful attention to any changes in the child's behavior, voice level, and body language, and make note of these changes in the report.

67. You may or may not need to use the third phase of the interview—the closed questioning phase. If the child tells you what you need to know in the second phase, you can skip this phase. However, with children who are reluctant to answer open-ended questions—particularly preschool children—be prepared to ask more focused and direct questions.

68. The third phase also is helpful when you want to clarify information that the child gave previously.

69. In the fourth phase, the closing phase, you want to summarize what you have learned about the case. As always, use language appropriate to the child's level of comprehension. Attempt to relieve the child of any distress.

70. Be prepared to have some children recant their statements.

71. Never interview a child suspected of being maltreated in the presence of the alleged perpetrator.

72. Interviewing pitfalls that may lead to biased interviews include failing to recognize your preconceived expectations; failing to distinguish spontaneous statements from those that are simple acknowledgments; failing to recognize that you are using unintended cues, coercive techniques, or leading questions; and failing to recognize a fabricated story.

73. Arguments in favor of the use of anatomically detailed dolls include that the dolls may be useful as demonstration aids, may serve as a memory stimulus and a diagnostic screen, and may serve as anatomical models.

74. Arguments against the use of anatomically detailed dolls include that behavior with the dolls may be difficult to interpret, may not provide valid or useful information, and may induce false memories.

75. Both proponents and opponents of the use of anatomically detailed dolls are against the use of the dolls as a diagnostic test—behavior with the dolls, regardless of its form, should never be used by itself to conclude that sexual abuse took place.

76. Interviewers need to be extremely cautious if they use anatomically detailed dolls to interview children suspected of being sexually abused.

77. The cognitive interview is a useful procedure to help children and adults recall information, primarily for forensic purposes and for investigatory interviewing. The procedure includes a collection of techniques designed to enhance witnesses' memories by facilitating the completeness and accuracy of their reports.

Interviewing the Family in Cases of Child Maltreatment

78. You want to interview each parent separately, and then you may want to interview them together, depending on the situation.

79. If possible, do not interview the suspect parent at the same site where the child is being interviewed, especially when the child is aware of where the suspect parent will be interviewed.

80. In interviewing a family in which a child was maltreated, inquire about how other family members get along with the child, whether they have any history of child maltreatment, whether they have emotional difficulties, how the alleged maltreatment has affected them, and what changes in family relationships have occurred since the maltreatment.

81. The allegedly maltreated child's siblings also are important to interview because siblings are part of the family and will be affected by any family crisis, suffering the consequences of a family's breakdown. They also may have been maltreated, or perhaps they are perpetrators; if so, they may be reluctant to come forward.

82. When the father (or another close relative) is the alleged offender, interview the mother separately.

83. You may find that how the family talks to you depends on whether the alleged maltreatment is extrafamilial or intrafamilial.

84. The fear that battered women may have of their abusive partner may be so great that they will refuse to talk freely about anything.

85. Be prepared to have battered women resist talking about child maltreatment, and perhaps other things as well.

86. If you know or suspect that both domestic violence and child maltreatment have occurred, interview the parents or partners separately.

87. When law enforcement personnel respond to a domestic violence call, they need to recognize that women, even if they have obvious injuries, may not want to admit that abuse has occurred.

88. Children of an abused parent may not be reliable informants, particularly because they do not want to be disloyal to one parent.

Interviewing the Alleged or Known Offender in Cases of Child Maltreatment

89. Purposes of interviews with the alleged or known offender are to gain an understanding of the maltreatment, to obtain a direct or indirect admission from the offender, to make a prognosis, and to obtain information useful in developing an intervention plan.

90. You want to obtain a thorough history of the alleged or known offender.

91. Evaluations of alleged offenders or offenders, like evaluations of children alleged or known to have been maltreated, should be conducted by highly trained interviewers.

92. Issues of safety in the interview are extremely important. Be sure that support is available and that you terminate the interview if the offender becomes angry, threatens you, or frightens you.

93. In preparing for the interview with the offender, study carefully the information given by the victim and the information about the offender obtained from school, medical, psychiatric, military, and work records.

94. Refer the offender for psychological testing and for physical and neurological evaluations, as needed.

95. Also conduct, as needed, field investigations.

96. When the issue of responsibility for the maltreatment is discussed with known offenders, they may show superficial acceptance of responsibility for the maltreatment, deny responsibility by blaming the child for what happened, minimize the severity of the maltreatment, make the consequences of the act positive instead of negative, bargain with you or deny knowledge of the maltreatment, plead with you or cite extenuating situational or psychological factors, or show false remorse in order to be let off quickly.

97. It also may happen that offenders show genuine acceptance of responsibility for their actions.

98. Not much is known about why parents with Munchausen Syndrome by Proxy intentionally try to keep their children sick.

99. To deal effectively with Munchausen Syndrome by Proxy, human services workers and health care providers should be part of a multidisciplinary team.

100. If you are working in a social services agency and suspect a case of Munchausen Syndrome by Proxy, consider requesting ongoing court-ordered supervision of the case.

101. If there is sufficient proof of Munchausen Syndrome by Proxy, recommend out-of-home placement for the child and

request a court-ordered review of the child's medical records, examination of all siblings, psychological evaluation of the child and the family, and treatment of the child and the family, as needed.

102. When professionals tell caregivers that they suspect that the caregivers have deliberately kept their children ill, the caregivers are likely to deny the allegations.

Concluding Comment on Interviewing Children, Families, and Alleged Offenders in Cases of Child Maltreatment

103. Although the interviewing guidelines in this book stress open-ended and probing questions, you will encounter children and adults who are reluctant to talk to you. When this happens, you will need to be more active in your questioning.

104. No matter what strategy you decide to follow, you must safeguard the rights of the child as well as the rights of the alleged offender, and you should not use coercive interviewing techniques.

KEY TERMS, CONCEPTS, AND NAMES

Model for interviewing in cases of child maltreatment (p. 755)
Multidisciplinary interview centers (p. 755)
Videotaping the interview (p. 757)
Interviewing ethnic minority children and their parents (p. 758)
Developmental perspective (p. 759)
Guidelines for interviewing in cases of child maltreatment (p. 760)
Phases of the child maltreatment interview (p. 763)
Rapport phase (p. 763)
Free narrative account and nonleading questioning phase (p. 764)
Closed questioning phase (p. 765)
Closing phase (p. 765)
Children who recant their statements (p. 766)
Ensuring that the child is never interviewed with the alleged perpetrator in the room (p. 766)
Interviewing pitfalls that may lead to biased interviews and false allegations (p. 767)
Failing to recognize your preconceived expectations (p. 767)
Failing to distinguish spontaneous statements from those that are simple acknowledgments (p. 768)
Failing to recognize that you are using unintended cues, coercive techniques, or leading questions (p. 768)
Failing to recognize a fabricated story (p. 769)
Use of anatomically detailed dolls (p. 770)
Cognitive interview (p. 771)
Interviewing the family (p. 782)
Extrafamilial maltreatment (p. 785)
Intrafamilial maltreatment (p. 785)
Interviewing guidelines in cases of domestic violence and possible child maltreatment (p. 786)
Interviewing the alleged or known offender (p. 790)
Discussing responsibility for the maltreatment with a known offender (p. 791)
Interviewing in cases of suspected Munchausen Syndrome by Proxy (p. 798)

STUDY QUESTIONS

1. Describe a preferred model for interviewing in cases of child maltreatment.

2. Discuss some considerations in preparing for the initial interview in cases of child maltreatment. Include in your discussion the aims of the initial interview, general considerations in preparing for the interview, videotaping the interview, and considerations in interviewing ethnic minority children and their families.

3. Discuss some factors involved in interviewing children in cases of alleged child maltreatment. Include in your discussion 10 guidelines that you consider basic or fundamental for conducting such interviews.

4. Discuss the four phases of the child maltreatment interview.

5. One clinical student says "I'm not a police officer. I don't need to learn how to investigate allegations of child maltreatment. All I need are good clinical interviewing skills!" Another student says "You must learn about investigatory interview techniques if you want to work in the field of child maltreatment!" Who is right and why?

6. What are some pitfalls in interviewing children in cases of child maltreatment? Discuss each one in detail.

7. What are the advantages and disadvantages of using anatomically detailed dolls?

8. What areas are important to cover in interviewing parents in cases of child maltreatment?

9. Why is it important to interview the siblings in cases of child maltreatment?

10. What differences might you expect to find between an interview with a family in which extrafamilial maltreatment has occurred and an interview with a family in which intrafamilial maltreatment has occurred?

11. Discuss how maltreatment might affect a family.

12. Discuss some interviewing guidelines for cases of domestic violence and possible child maltreatment.

13. If a woman was being battered by her husband, what advice would you give her? Discuss things that she should do and things that she shouldn't do.

14. Discuss some considerations in interviewing an alleged or known offender.

15. Describe some tactics a known offender might use in discussing the issue of responsibility for the maltreatment.

16. Describe some special interview procedures you need to use when you suspect Munchausen Syndrome by Proxy.

17. A commission in England issued guidelines for conducting child maltreatment investigations. It made several recommendations for interviewing children and parents and offered guidelines for social services agencies. Describe three of the recommendations for children, three for parents, and three for social services agencies.

23

EVALUATION AND INTERVENTION IN CASES OF CHILD MALTREATMENT

The hearts of small children are delicate organs. A cruel beginning in the world can twist them into curious shapes.
—Carson McCullers

Goals and Objectives

This chapter is designed to enable you to:

- Evaluate the findings obtained in interviews with children, families, alleged offenders, and known offenders in cases of child maltreatment
- Evaluate the child's credibility, the caregivers' credibility, and the alleged offender's credibility in cases of child maltreatment
- Evaluate facilities, institutions, and foster homes in cases of child maltreatment
- Formulate interventions in cases of child maltreatment

In cases of child maltreatment, if you are working or in training in Child Protective Services or in a law enforcement agency, you will need to evaluate the findings and make decisions after you have completed your interviews and reviewed relevant records and reports. This chapter provides guidelines to help you with these tasks. One of the most critical decisions you will need to make is whether the child is at risk for further abuse or neglect or in danger of being killed. You also may need to consider possible interventions. Interventions can include assistance to parents, supervised home visits, temporary placement of the child with a relative or in a foster home, reunification with the family at a later time if the child was removed from the home, assigning legal guardianship of the child to another relative, placing the child for adoption, and so forth. Although the material in this chapter is geared toward workers who will be employed in child protective agencies or law enforcement agencies, it is relevant to all who have contact with children.

Here are some of the specific critical questions that you may need to decide (DePanfilis & Salus, 1992, pp. 9, 25, with changes in notation):

- Is the source of information credible?
- Does the alleged maltreatment constitute child maltreatment as defined by state statute?
- Is the child at risk for further maltreatment, and what is the level of risk?
- If the child is at risk, what type of agency or community response will ensure the child's safety?
- If the child's safety cannot be ensured within the family, what type and level of care does the child need?
- How quick must the response be to ensure the safety of the child?
- Does the family have emergency needs that must be met?
- Should ongoing agency services be offered to the family?

Your decisions about a case may be based on (a) your interview with the child or with the alleged or known offender, (b) your interviews with the caregivers, (c) your interviews plus some combination of medical reports, psychiatric or psychological reports, law enforcement reports, parental reports, school records, reports of prior interviews with the child, or reports from those who suspected the child maltreatment, or (d) your observations of the setting in which the alleged maltreatment took place, such as the family home, the facility or institution, the foster home, or the school or day care facility. Ideally, you should not make any decisions unless you have sufficient information about the case. There are times, however, when you must act immediately to protect the child. These are discussed later in the chapter when risk assessment is considered.

When you evaluate what the interviewee tells you, consider such issues as the interviewee's cognitive and developmental level; the content of the interviewee's communications; the interviewee's language, affect, and nonverbal behavior; the quality of the interviewee's relationship with you; and other factors related to the interview (see Chapters 2 and 3). You will have to judge, for example, the accuracy and truthfulness of what the interviewee tells you, whether distortions are present, and whether the interviewee was influenced or pressured to make certain statements. Making judgments about the interviewee's credibility is an important part of the evaluation.

Evaluating cases of alleged child physical abuse or neglect is somewhat different from evaluating cases of child sexual abuse. The signs of child physical abuse or neglect often will be evident to you or to those who reported the maltreatment. Evaluating cases of alleged child sexual abuse may be particularly difficult if there are no physical signs of sexual abuse. In such cases, you will have to base your decision about whether the alleged sexual abuse occurred primarily on the child's statements (and the statements of other informants, as applicable). Evaluation of alleged emotional abuse also can be difficult because signs associated with this type of maltreatment are difficult to verify.

There are two types of errors that you can make in your evaluation of allegations of child maltreatment. First, you may conclude that *no* maltreatment occurred when, in fact, maltreatment *did* occur; this is referred to as a *false negative error.* Second, you may conclude that maltreatment *did* occur when, in fact, *no* maltreatment occurred; this is referred to as a *false positive error.* A false negative error means that a child will remain in a home (or situation) in which maltreatment has occurred (or is occurring)—the perpetrator may continue to victimize the child and also other children. A false positive error means that an innocent person has been wrongly accused—the lives of the child, family members, and the accused may be irreparably damaged, and the accused may face a ruined reputation, loss of parental rights, and possibly a prison term.

Interviewers often develop their own standards for making decisions. If their primary concern is to *prevent child maltreatment,* they may decide that a child has been victimized when there is only a suspicion of maltreatment. If their primary concern is to *prevent false accusations,* they may decide that a child has been victimized only when the evidence is overwhelming, establishing guilt beyond a reasonable doubt. A standard geared to preventing child maltreatment may lead interviewers to make false positive errors, whereas a standard geared to preventing false accusations may lead interviewers to make false negative errors. Try to be as fair as possible. You want to avoid making false allegations of maltreatment as much as you want to identify the perpetrator of the maltreatment if maltreatment, in fact, has occurred and to protect the child from further maltreatment. *In all cases, you always must consider the need to protect children from harm and to ensure that innocent people are not wrongly accused.*

EVALUATING ALLEGATIONS OF CHILD MALTREATMENT

Let's now consider guidelines for evaluating the information you obtain from children, from their families, and from the alleged offenders. Although the information available to you usually will be obtained separately from each source, your task will be to integrate the information from all sources into a coherent picture. You also want to review any other information about the case, including medical reports, police reports, and teachers' reports.

It is useful to think of *gradations of certainty about child maltreatment,* unless you are *absolutely* positive that maltreatment has or has not occurred. There is no litmus test that always can be used. Thus, in evaluating allegations of child maltreatment, consider using the following continuum:

- strongly convinced that maltreatment occurred
- moderately convinced that maltreatment occurred
- weakly convinced that maltreatment occurred
- not sure whether maltreatment occurred
- weakly convinced that maltreatment did not occur
- moderately convinced that maltreatment did not occur
- strongly convinced that maltreatment did not occur

Sometimes you may not be able to arrive at a decision about the allegation of child maltreatment. In such cases, you still should be concerned about the child's safety and seek services that will protect the child and help the family.

Basic Information Needed for the Evaluation

In preparing for your evaluation of a case, review the following (Peterson & Urquiza, 1993, pp. 23–25, with additions): (a) information obtained from the interviews with the child, family, and alleged perpetrator, (b) physical evidence, photographs, and information from other individuals about the abuse or neglect obtained by law enforcement personnel, and (c) the medical report. Pay particular attention to the following details:

1. *Description of the victim:* name, address, phone number, age, sex, race and ethnicity, birth date, school informa-

tion, psychological and behavioral symptoms, physical signs of maltreatment, medical condition, current level of psychological functioning, and general adjustment level.

2. *Description of the family:* size and membership, siblings' ages and genders, occupation or means of financial support of parent(s), description of all persons living in the home, description of all persons responsible for the child's care, family relationships, family roles, family communication patterns, and general adjustment level of the family members.

3. *Description of the alleged maltreatment:* specific information about who reported the alleged maltreatment, what occurred, when and how often it occurred, duration of the maltreatment (days, weeks, months, years), events that occurred before and after the maltreatment, whether siblings or other children were maltreated, and, for sexual abuse, whether photographs were taken, videotapes made, or any other evidence collected.

4. *Description of the suspected perpetrator:* name, address, age, relationship to the victim (for example, parent, friend, babysitter, relative), psychological and behavioral symptoms, physical evidence connecting him or her to the maltreatment (for example, stained clothing, semen, blood, pornographic photos of child), photographs (for example, photographs of any physical abuse or of conditions in home), perpetrator's explanations about the maltreatment, and general adjustment level.

5. *Description of any witnesses:* name, address, and phone number of any persons who might have observed or participated in the alleged maltreatment, who might have been involved as additional victims, or who might have information about the abuse or neglect.

Guidelines for Evaluating Children

The information you obtain from the child should help you answer the questions shown in Table 23-1, which cover the following areas:

- background information
- type of alleged maltreatment
- details of disclosure
- child's feelings about the alleged abusive event
- child's credibility
- alleged offender
- conditions under which the alleged maltreatment occurred
- medical examinations
- behavior, affect, personality, and temperament of the child
- future actions and needs

To answer the questions in Table 23-1 (and other relevant questions), consider the following:

- the history of the child's symptoms
- the child's verbal report
- the child's phenomenological experience (the child's perception of the events or how the child experienced the events)

Table 23-1
Questions to Consider About the Child in Cases of Alleged Child Maltreatment

Background Information

1. What are the child's age, sex, and grade in school?
2. Who lives at home, including parents, siblings, relatives, and pets?
3. Where does the child live?
4. What are the characteristics of the neighborhood the child lives in?
5. What are the characteristics of the child's family?
6. At what point in time is the child being evaluated, relative to the maltreatment?

Type of Alleged Maltreatment

7. What type of maltreatment is alleged?
8. Were there any signs of physical abuse?
9. (If yes) What were the signs?
10. Were there any signs of neglect?
11. (If yes) What were the signs?
12. Were there any signs of sexual abuse?
13. (If yes) What were the signs?
14. When did the alleged maltreatment start?
15. When did the alleged maltreatment stop?
16. What was the duration of the alleged maltreatment?
17. How frequent was the alleged maltreatment?
18. How violent was the alleged maltreatment?
19. What was the interval between the alleged maltreatment and the disclosure?
20. Were there any witnesses?
21. (If yes) Who are they?
22. Were there alleged multiple victims?
23. (If yes) Who are they?
24. Were there alleged multiple perpetrators?
25. (If yes) Who are they?

Details of Disclosure

26. How did the authorities learn about the alleged maltreatment?
27. Did the child try to inform someone else about the alleged maltreatment?
28. (If yes) Who is this person, and what did this person do on learning about the alleged maltreatment?
29. (If applicable) Why did the child tell at that time?
30. Did the child fear that he or she would not be believed if he or she reported the alleged maltreatment?
31. Did the child fear that revealing the alleged secret would cause catastrophic results for himself or herself or others?
32. What did the child say about the alleged maltreatment?
33. What did the child say about the alleged perpetrator?
34. How long after the disclosure did Child Protective Services become involved?

Child's Feelings About the Alleged Abusive Event

35. Did the child know that the alleged maltreatment was taking place?

36. What are the child's feelings about the alleged event (for example, anger, anxiety, fear, terror, guilt)?
37. Is the child reluctant to reveal the maltreatment because of a feeling that he or she caused the maltreatment, that he or she deserved the maltreatment, or that he or she is a bad person?
38. How does the child's behavior change when the topic of the alleged maltreatment is introduced in the interview?
39. Was the alleged maltreatment physically painful or pleasurable to the child?
40. Did the child think that it was all right to engage in the alleged activity because an adult sanctioned it?

Child's Credibility

41. Does the child understand the difference between the truth and a lie?
42. Does the child understand the difference between fact and fantasy?
43. Are there any indications that the child is lying?
44. (If yes) What are the indications?
45. Are there any indications that the child was coached, pressured, or coerced?
46. (If yes) What are the indications, and who may have coached, pressured, or coerced the child?

Alleged Offender

47. Who is the alleged offender?
48. What relationship does the alleged offender have with the child, such as natural parent, stepparent, live-in boyfriend or girlfriend of natural parent, other relative, teacher, neighbor, or stranger?
49. How does the child feel about the alleged offender?
50. Does mention of the alleged offender's name or seeing the alleged offender make the child anxious?
51. Does the child still feel attached to the alleged offender?
52. Where were the child's caregivers when the alleged maltreatment happened?
53. Has the child been maltreated by anyone else?
54. (If yes) Who was the offender, what did he or she do, and when did the maltreatment take place?
55. How did the alleged offender engage the child?

Conditions Under Which the Alleged Maltreatment Occurred

56. Was the child pressured or coerced (for example, with threats of physical harm or rejection or violence) into the activity?
57. Did the alleged offender bargain for physical contact with the child, by offering rewards to the child (for example, material possessions, social activities, drugs, adult approval, or human contact)?
58. (If applicable) How did the child feel about the pressure used by the alleged offender to get him or her to participate in the activity?

(Continued)

Table 23-1 (*Continued*)

59. Was the child aware of the implications of the alleged offender's actions?
60. Did the alleged offender pledge the child to secrecy?
61. Were there any other people present?
62. (If yes) Who are they, and did any other adults (or older children) help the alleged offender?
63. Were there any other children involved?
64. (If yes) Who are they, and what was done with the other children?

Medical Examinations
65. Was a medical examination conducted?
66. (If yes) What were the findings and conclusions (for example, what physical symptoms were present, and what did the health provider staff conclude about the nature of the injuries)?

Behavior, Affect, Personality, and Temperament of the Child
67. What is the child's behavior?
68. What is the child's affect?
69. What are the child's personality and temperament?
70. Is the child's affect congruent with his or her reports?
71. What changes have taken place in the child since the alleged maltreatment?

72. What changes have taken place in the child's relationship with family members, other relatives, friends, peers, neighbors, strangers, and teachers since the alleged maltreatment?
73. How has the alleged maltreatment affected the child's
    a. school performance or behavior in a child care setting?
    b. affect?
    c. sleep?
    d. eating patterns?
    e. health status?
    f. vulnerability to stress?
    g. play?
74. What other stressors are present in the child's life?
75. If the child has symptoms, what are they and do they fall into any pattern?

Future Actions and Needs
76. What would the child like to see done about the alleged maltreatment?
77. What would the child like to see done about his or her present living arrangements?
78. What additional information do you need to obtain a more thorough understanding of the case?
79. What other assessments need to be performed?
80. What interventions do you recommend?

Source: Adapted, in part, from Burgess et al. (1978).

- the child's presentational style (how the child described the events, the behaviors and affect that accompanied the child's descriptions, and the relationships among the child's descriptions, behaviors, and affect)
- corroborating evidence (such as information obtained from other activities engaged in by the child during the interview, like drawing or play activity)
- family dynamics (including level of stress, custody proceedings, and substance use and abuse among family members)

Indices of credibility. Use everything you know about the case to evaluate the child's credibility. The indices in the following lists, in particular, will help you evaluate credibility (Conte, Sorenson, Fogarty, & Rosa, 1991; Fontana & Besharov, 1996; McGraw & Smith, 1992; Steller & Boychuk, 1992). The indices in the first group (items 1 to 24) refer to all types of maltreatment. These indices are followed by additional indices of credibility for each of the four major types of maltreatment. All of them must be viewed in relation to the entire case history and to the child's age and developmental level. Research is needed to determine the validity of these indices—for example, how many indicators are needed before it can be concluded with a high degree of certainty that the child was maltreated. Many of these indices do not pertain to children under 5 years of age.

You need to use your judgment in each case. However, you will be on firmer ground in substantiating allegations of child maltreatment if several of these indices are present or even if one major one is present.

GENERAL INDICES OF CREDIBILITY
1. The child had physical signs of maltreatment.
2. The child described the maltreatment spontaneously.
3. The child, rather than someone else, disclosed the maltreatment.
4. The child's report was clear, logical, and detailed.
5. The child gave unique or distinguishing details of the setting where the maltreatment occurred.
6. The child gave information about the maltreatment consistent with information from one or more other credible sources.
7. The child's report was not contradicted by information from other sources or by other findings.
8. The child volunteered that she or he was told to keep the maltreatment a secret.
9. The child was interviewed in an unbiased manner.
10. The child knew the difference between the truth and a lie.
11. The child had no known reason to lie.
12. The child was not pressured or coerced to give false or misleading information about the maltreatment by her or his caregivers or by anyone else.

13. The child may have given misleading information because of a memory distortion, an honest difference of opinion, or a misunderstanding of the questions.
14. The child's report of the maltreatment was consistent with her or his developmental level.
15. The child's report of the maltreatment contained important features that were consistent over time.
16. The child's affect was appropriate and congruent with the content of the report of the maltreatment.
17. The child's report overall did not contain strong fantasy elements.
18. The child answered questions based on their content—that is, the child did not have a response set that led her or him to give inaccurate replies.
19. The child had clinical depression or other features associated with posttraumatic stress disorder.
20. The child was wary, apprehensive, or frightened of caregivers, strangers, or other people.
21. The child showed no expectation of being comforted and was wary of physical contact initiated by the parents or anyone else.
22. The child seemed to be constantly alert for signs of danger.
23. The child's maltreatment was witnessed by other people.
24. The child had been the subject of several reports of maltreatment.

ADDITIONAL INDICES OF CREDIBILITY IN ALLEGATIONS OF PHYSICAL ABUSE

25. The child had injuries, such as unusual unexplained bruises in various stages of healing, unexplained fractures or multiple fractures (particularly in a young child who has not started walking), unexplained burns, or other unexplained injuries (see signs of physical abuse in Table 21-1 in Chapter 21).
26. The child's caregiver(s) gave improbable explanations for the injuries or explanations inconsistent with the injuries.
27. The child had several "accidents" that occurred within a short period.
28. The child has a history of unexplained accidents.
29. The child's injury appeared to be older than stated.

ADDITIONAL INDICES OF CREDIBILITY IN ALLEGATIONS OF NEGLECT

30. The child was hungry, underweight for height, inappropriately dressed for the weather, dirty, and frequently tired; often slept in class or in child care; lacked supervision for long periods of time; was always searching for food or anything that might have some value or use; had unattended physical or dental problems; and overall seemed to be poorly cared for (see signs of neglect in Table 21-1 in Chapter 21).
31. The child's caregiver ignored the child.
32. The child's caregiver was unaware of the seriousness of the child's condition.

ADDITIONAL INDICES OF CREDIBILITY IN ALLEGATIONS OF EMOTIONAL ABUSE

33. The child had an impaired sense of self-worth and was withdrawn; showed extremes in behavior, such as overly aggressive or overly passive behavior; and showed delayed emotional development (see other signs of emotional abuse in Table 21-1 of Chapter 21).
34. The child's caregiver had unrealistic expectations of the child.
35. The child's caregiver either had rejected the child or was overly harsh and impatient with the child.

ADDITIONAL INDICES OF CREDIBILITY IN ALLEGATIONS OF SEXUAL ABUSE

36. The child had physical indicators suggestive or indicative of having been sexually abused (for example, sexually transmitted disease; pregnancy in females; tears in and/or enlargement of the vaginal area in females; tears in and/or enlargement of the anal areas; evidence of ejaculation in the vaginal area in females; evidence of ejaculation in the oral and/or rectal orifices; or other medical problems) (see other signs of child sexual abuse in Table 21-2 in Chapter 21).
37. The child's statement related a progression of sexual activity.
38. The child's description of sexual abuse contained elements of pressure or coercion.
39. The child had age-inappropriate sexual knowledge.
40. The child showed age-inappropriate sexual play, excessive masturbation, excessive preoccupation with genitals, precocious sexual behavior, or seductive behavior.

Here are some other considerations in evaluating allegations of child maltreatment.

- Some injuries may be due to medical conditions, birth defects, accidents, falls, fights with other children, and cultural healing practices, for example, rather than to physical abuse.
- When the information from several sources is not consistent, try to account for the discrepancies.
- When the child is reluctant to speak about the maltreatment, consider the possible reasons for the reluctance.
- When the child's report is disorganized, inconsistent, or lacking in details or when it contains inaccurate statements or fantasy elements, consider why this is so and how these elements affect the credibility of all the information the child gave you.

Note, however, that the presence of any of these elements in the child's report does not invalidate the entire report. You must judge which aspects of the report are accurate and which aspects reflect fantasy on the part of the child. You also must recognize that some parts of the child's report may be true, even though other parts may be false.

Statement Validity Analysis.   A potentially useful way to evaluate allegations of child sexual abuse is a method called *Statement Validity Analysis* (Steller & Boychuk, 1992). This method of systematically examining the case material and the content of the interview provides a formal way of looking at the child's statements. Parts of this method were incorporated in the criteria previously described under indices of credibility. Insufficient research at present precludes the use of the method in forensic work, so it is not discussed in detail in this book. Statement Validity Analysis, however, does appear to be promising, particularly with further refinements that incorporate a developmental framework and more field testing that focuses on the reliability and validity of the method.

Evaluating Sudden Infant Death Syndrome. When an infant dies suddenly—a condition referred to as Sudden Infant Death Syndrome (SIDS)—it may be difficult to distinguish between death due to unexplained causes and death due to fatal child abuse. The following guidelines may assist you in this effort (Reece, 1994).

1. *History surrounding death.* In SIDS, an apparently healthy infant, usually between 2 and 4 months of age, dies in his or her sleep. In fatal child physical abuse, the infant may be older than 4 months, and the death may occur at any time during the day or night.

2. *Physical examination.* In SIDS, the infant appears well cared for, and there is no trauma to the infant's body. In fatal child physical abuse, the infant may have traumatic injuries to the body, including fractures, bruises, and signs of malnutrition and neglect.

3. *History of pregnancy, delivery, and infancy.* In SIDS, the mother may have smoked cigarettes during pregnancy, and the infant may have been premature, had subtle feeding problems, or had pneumonia or other respiratory problems that required hospitalization. In fatal child physical abuse, the mother may have had an unwanted pregnancy, had little or no prenatal care, used alcohol or drugs during the pregnancy, and, after the baby was born, smoked cigarettes and also used alcohol or drugs. The mother may describe the baby as having been hard to care for. She may have improperly fed the child (by starving the baby, failing to give the baby, sufficient nutrients, or failing to give the baby solid foods when the baby was ready).

4. *Death scene investigation.* In SIDS, the infant's crib usually is in good repair, and no dangerous objects are found near the crib at the time of death. Room temperature usually is normal, and ventilation and heating usually are adequate. In fatal child physical abuse, living conditions may have been chaotic and unsanitary. The mother may have been high on alcohol or drugs. There may be signs of a terminal struggle in the crib or bed, and blood-stained clothing may be discovered. Caregivers may show hostility toward the investigators and discord among themselves; they may accuse each other of the infant's death.

5. *Previous infant injuries or deaths.* In SIDS, the death usually is the first unexplained death in the family. In fatal child physical abuse, there may have been prior unexplained infant injuries or deaths in the family.

6. *Autopsy findings.* In SIDS, the autopsy usually reveals no adequate cause of death. All findings are essentially normal. In fatal child physical abuse, the autopsy findings may indicate a traumatic cause of death—including external bruises, hematomas, abrasions, burns, or fractures on the infant's body—and abnormal medical laboratory findings.

7. *Previous involvement of Child Protective Services or law enforcement.* In SIDS, the family usually has had no prior involvement with Child Protective Services or law enforcement. In fatal child physical abuse, there may have been one or more prior occasions when either Child Protective Services or law enforcement was called to the home, or someone in the family may have been arrested for violent behavior.

There has been a remarkable decline of 30% in SIDS deaths between 1993 and 1995; the rate among children in the United States went from 1.1 per 1,000 children to about 0.75 per 1,000 children ("Infant care livesaver," 1996). The decline has been attributed to educating caregivers to put infants to sleep on their backs instead of on their stomachs.

When the crime is child sexual abuse, … a conviction hinges on the words of children.

—Ninth Circuit U.S. Court of Appeals, 1993

Evaluating an interview segment. The following interview segment is an edited version of a forensic interview. The interviewer was part of a Child Protective Services team. Names, dates, and locations were changed to ensure anonymity. Much of the transcript deals with how the interviewer sought to obtain information about the sexual molestation. What do you think of the interviewer's style? Did she ask any inappropriate questions? If so, note them as you read the interview and check your notes with the comments included within the interview. What do you think of the credibility of the child's allegation?

CASE 23-1. BILL SMITH
Before the child comes into the room, which has a one-way mirror with a closed-circuit television, the interviewer says "My name is Jane Jones. I'm a social worker at the Children's Center. This morning I'll be interviewing 7-year-old Bill Smith. His medical record number is 1249C91340. Today's date is July 10, 1993. It's approximately 11:00 A.M., and I'll be bringing Bill in now."

IR: Hi, Bill. I'm Jane Jones. No one will bother us while we're in here, okay? You can play with these Legos or the doll house or draw some pictures—what would you like to do?
IE: Are these markers?

IR: Are you a good artist?
IE: Kind of.
IR: Kind of. Well, I can't wait to see. Bill, you can call me Jane. Do you have a nickname, or does everyone call you that?
IE: Bill.
IR: Bill, okay, you have very colorful clothes on today.
IE: Thank you.
IR: Did you pick out that outfit?
IE: No.
IR: Your mom dress you?
IE: No.
IR: Who dressed you today?
IE: Nobody but me.
IR: You did, and you picked that out, good for you. How old are you?
IE: Seven.
IR: Do you know when your birthday is?
IE: Yeah, I know when my birthday is.
IR: When?
IE: January the 2nd, '86.
IR: Oh, you sure do know, you know your name and everything. So you're gonna be eight not too long from now. Seven and a half already. Do you go to school?
IE: Yes.
IR: Yeah, are you in the second grade?
IE: (Nods head.)
IR: Yeah. Good for you. What school do you go to?
IE: Hillside.
IR: And do you like school?
IE: Yeah.
IR: That's good. What do you like best to do at school?
IE: Do homework.
IR: Is there a subject that you like the best? Math or reading or…?
IE: Both.
IR: Good for you—get pretty good grades?
IE: Yeah.
IR: How'd you lose your teeth?
IE: Take 'em out. (Conversation about losing teeth.)
IR: I want to tell you something special about my room, okay? 'Cause behind that mirror there's a video camera, and we make videotapes of all the boys and girls that come in here.
IE: (Laughs.)
IR: That way I can remember everything we talk about.
IE: There really is?
IR: There really is. You can't see it, but it's back there. Bill, it's not a videotape that can be in school or on TV or anything like that.
IE: Oh.
IR: It's just for us to look at, and it takes real special permission from a judge for anyone else to see it. You don't have to worry about friends or people seeing what we talk about. Okay, when we're all done, I'll show it to you, okay? Remind me to show it to you. We'll go back there, and you can look at the camera. You want to ask me any questions about that? All right. Do you have a favorite color?
IE: Yeah.
IR: What is it?
IE: Red.

IR: And red, where's red in the room?
IE: There's some.
IR: What's that thing?
IE: A crab, a sea crab.
IR: It is. What if I told you that that color was purple, would I be right or wrong?
IE: Wrong.
IR: Would that be the truth or a lie?
IE: A lie.
IR: What happens if kids tell lies, Bill?
IE: Get in trouble.

In this first part of the interview, the interviewer showed an interest in the child. Note the way she attempted to make him feel comfortable with her by asking him questions about himself. She tried to determine whether the child knows right from wrong. However, she also asked many closed-ended questions.

IR: Okay. Who lives with you at your house?
IE: My brother and my sister and my mom.
IR: Do you have your own room there?
IE: No, my brother takes over in our room a lot. (Conversation about his brother, his room, and the house.)
IR: Do you know where we are, Bill?
IE: Central City.
IR: We sure are. Do you know the name of this place where we are?
IE: Nope.
IR: This is part of Children's Center. Do you know why your mom brought you here today?
IE: Yeah, my sister.
IR: What about your sister?
IE: She got molested.
IR: Where'd you learn that word?
IE: At school.
IR: At school?
IE: Uh-huh.
IR: What did they tell you about it, what does that mean?
IE: Some kids get like, mess with girls and stuff.
IR: Do you know who messed with your sister?
IE: Yeah.
IR: Yeah, who did that?
IE: My dad.
IR: Oh, how do you know about it? Did you see it, or did someone tell you?
IE: No, but nobody told—my mom, mom told me.
IR: Your mom told you.
IE: But I was asleep. I don't know, he might have the door closed.
IR: Oh.
IE: I would of heard though.
IR: You would of heard?
IE: Yeah.
IR: If what?
IE: The door was open.
IR: If the door was open.
IE: But the door wasn't open when I was asleep.
IR: Mm.
IE: She, oh, now can I get the Legos?

IR: Sure you can. You don't have to put those away 'cause you might want to use them again—let's just leave 'em here just in case you decide to use 'em.

IE: I use this, this one.

IR: Bill, how do you feel about what your dad did to your sister? How's it make you feel?

IE: Sad.

IR: Yeah, I can understand that. I wonder if you ever got molested or messed with?

IE: Yeah.

IR: Yeah? Who did that to you?

IE: My dad.

IR: Your dad? I'm sorry he did that. That's not somethin' he should be doin'. Is that something that happened one time or more than one time?

IE: More than one.

IR: More than once? How old were you the first time that happened?

IE: I think four or five.

IR: Where were you when that happened?

IE: What happened?

IR: When your dad molested you.

IE: When he did it, when he did it?

IR: When, when, you said when you were four or five you think it happened the first time? Right?

IE: Yeah, but…

IR: Yeah but what? Is that hard to talk about?

IE: Yeah.

IR: Yeah, what makes it hard?

IE: (Shrugs shoulders.)

IR: Bill, you know you and your sister didn't do anything wrong. Do you know that?

IE: Yeah.

IR: That you're not in trouble. What did he do when you were four or five? What did he do?

IE: Molest me like he did my sister.

IR: Did you get touched somewhere?

IE: Yeah.

IR: Where did you get touched?

IE: My private part.

IR: What touched you there?

IE: His finger.

IR: Anything else? Do you know what kind of touching did his finger do? Can you show me like here? (Holds doll.)

IE: (Points to penis on doll.)

IR: OK. Where were you when he did that the first time?

IE: In my mom's room—my mom was gone.

IR: Bill, did he touch your private part on your clothes or on your skin?

IE: Skin.

IR: Did you have clothes on?

IE: Yeah, when I was in the tub once he did it, and then he did it lots of times.

IR: He did it lots of times?

IE: And once he did it with my clothes on.

IR: Did he touch on your clothes that time or under your clothes when you had them on?

IE: On.

IR: He touched on your clothes that time. Were all the other times on your skin?

IE: Yes.

IR: And that happened in your mom's room and in the bathtub?

IE: Yeah.

IR: Did it happen anywhere else?

IE: No, I can't remember the other ones.

IR: Can't remember the other ones? Did anyone ever see your dad touch your private parts?

IE: No, my mom has once.

IR: She did what once? She saw once?

IE: Yeah, and then my mom—boom with a fork.

IR: Boom with a fork? What happened?

IE: She hit him on the arm. She was mad then.

IR: Yeah, I guess she was. Where did he, where were you when he touched you and she saw that happen? Where did she see that happen?

IE: When I was in my room and my mom's room.

IR: In your mom's room.

IE: She said "What the hell you…" She tipped open the door, and she came in and she said "Mike?"

IR: Okay.

IE: And then he went like that and jumped back and made like he was asleep.

IR: When was the last time he touched your private part, how old were you?

IE: Five or six.

IR: Do you think you were in kindergarten or were you in the first grade the last time?

IE: Kindergarten and then first grade.

IR: He did do it when you were in first grade too?

IE: Yeah.

IR: How many times when you were in first grade do you think he did that?

IE: Three.

IR: Three times? How many times do you think when you were in kindergarten?

IE: Twice.

IR: Twice. Do you think he ever did it before you started kindergarten, before you ever started going to school?

IE: I think so but I don't know.

IR: Okay, that's a hard question, huh? Did you ever see him touch your sister?

IE: Yeah, lots of times.

IR: Lots of times. Where did you see him touch her, where on her body?

IE: Her back and the front.

IR: The back and the front?

IE: Yeah.

IR: Do you have other names for those places?

IE: Private and, oh, I forgot the one the teacher told me, the P. E. teacher—gluteus maximus.

IR: Oh.

IE: Something like that.

IR: That's a very sophisticated word—this place, is that where you mean? (Points to vaginal area on doll.)

IE: Yeah.

IR: What did he touch your sister with?

IE: His fingernails.

IR: Was that on her skin or on her clothes?

IE: Skin and clothes once.

IR: Where was your mom when you saw him touching your sister?

IE: She was there.

IR: Did she see Mike touch your sister?

IE: No, she was cooking then.

IR: Oh.

IE: But I just went in to watch T.V.

IR: Yeah.

IE: And I went in there and there he was.

IR: What room?

IE: Her room.

IR: Her room. What was your sister doin' when he did that touching to her?

IE: Hollering.

IR: Uh-huh.

IE: My mom thought I was doing it, but I didn't.

IR: I wonder if your dad ever did touching to you with his mouth. Did his mouth touch anywhere on you?

IE: Yeah.

IR: Where did his mouth touch you?

IE: Private part.

IR: Your private part? Lots of boys tell me that happens to them. Did that happen one time or more than one time?

IE: Only once.

IR: Once? And how old were you when that happened?

IE: Six.

IR: Just last year when you were six?

IE: Yep.

IR: And where did that happen?

IE: In my room.

IR: What were you doing before that happened, do you remember?

IE: Say that over.

IR: What were you doing before your dad did that? Were you sleeping?

IE: Playing my Nintendo.

IR: Playing Nintendo. And was anyone playing with you?

IE: No.

IR: Was it daytime or nighttime when he did that touching with his mouth?

IE: The day, I like to play my Nintendos in the day.

IR: In the day. And did you have clothes on while you were playing Nintendo?

IE: No, yeah.

IR: Yeah? What happened to those, did they stay on or come off?

IE: He made me get up, and he broke my pants.

IR: He ripped your pants?

IE: He split'em straight through the middle. He took'em off of me.

IR: Yeah. Bill, is that the only time he did touching with his mouth?

IE: Yeah.

IR: Did he say something to you when he did that?

IE: Yeah, he said "Don't, you better not tell your mamma."

IR: Did he say something would happen if you told? Did he say that?

IE: Yeah.

IR: Or did he just do that?

IE: Yes, he said it.

IR: What did he say?

IE: He said "I'm gonna scratch you if you tell your mamma."

IR: Oh-huh.

IE: And then when I told, he scratched me real hard and blood was comin' off me.

IR: How did it feel?

IE: It was red and sore, and I got a scar.

IR: Oh, I'm sorry. Do you have any other scars on you?

IE: No.

IR: Bill, did you ever have to do touching to your dad?

IE: No.

IR: Has he ever asked you to?

IE: Yeah.

IR: What did he ask you to do?

IE: Touch my stuff and then, once he told my sister that he said, he go like this, pull his pants down and pull them up and go like this. (Touches pants but doesn't pull them down.)

IR: Did he say something when he did that?

IE: No, he did it to my sister, he never did it to me.

IR: You mean he pulled his pants down in front of her?

IE: Yeah.

IR: Were you there or did you see it?

IE: Yeah.

IR: Did you say that he did ask you to touch him?

IE: No.

IR: He just asked your sister to?

IE: Mm-hm.

IR: When your dad would do the touching to you, did he have clothes on or clothes off?

IE: Say that over?

IR: When your dad did touching to you all those different times, did he have clothes on or clothes off? Were his clothes ever off or were they on?

IE: On, sometimes off.

IR: Sometimes off?

This second segment of the interview focused on gathering information from the child about the alleged maltreatment and about his understanding of why he is being interviewed. It contained some focused questions that should have been preceded by nonfocused questions and shows some inappropriate assumptions made by the interviewer. First, when the child said "Private and, oh, I forgot the one the teacher told me, the PE teacher—gluteus maximus," the interviewer said "That's a very sophisticated word—this place, is that where you mean?" and pointed to the vaginal area on the doll. Why did she point to that area on the doll? What was her assumption? Second, a less focused question such as "How were you dressed while you were playing Nintendo?" or "What were you wearing while you were playing Nintendo?" would have been preferable to the focused question "And did you have clothes on while you were playing Nintendo?" A less focused question such as "Did your dad ever touch you with any other part of his body?" would have been preferable to the focused question "I wonder if your dad ever did touching to you with his mouth. Did his mouth touch anywhere on you?"

It is difficult to understand why the interviewer repeatedly asked how many times and in what grades the maltreatment occurred. If the maltreatment happened over time and was frequent, a child may become confused if the issue is pressed. Because the maltreatment began when the child was young, it would be difficult for him to have a clear conception of time. The interviewer also asked multiple questions, which is a poor technique. Finally, why did the interviewer say "Lots of boys tell me that happens to them"? What purpose did this comment have? Did it contaminate the interview in some way?

IE: Yeah. Is my sister gonna be in here?

IR: She's talking to Helen, a social worker, in the room over there.

IE: Right now?

IR: Right now.

IE: How long we got left?

IR: About three more minutes—I'm almost done.

IE: One, two, three.

IR: Not seconds, minutes. Are you gettin' tired of answering questions?

IE: Yeah.

IR: You're being a really good talker.

IE: It's been three seconds already.

IR: Can I get you to sit down, and we can finish up real fast, how's that?

IE: Hm-um.

IR: Bill, did you ever see your dad do touching to himself anywhere?

IE: Yeah.

IR: Where would he touch himself?

IE: Private.

IR: His private? Would he say anything to you when he did that?

IE: No.

IR: Where would he do that?

IE: In the living room, he goes and looks at the pictures in the magazine.

IR: Did you ever see anything come out of his private when he touched it?

IE: Yeah.

IR: What would come out? What'd it look like?

IE: Yellow, sometimes red.

IR: Sometimes red?

IE: Yeah.

IR: Where would that go?

IE: Into his hand.

IR: And then what would he do?

IE: Said that I did it, and then I get in trouble.

IR: He said you did it?

IE: Yeah.

IR: Mm. Would anyone else be there when he did that touching to himself?

IE: Would anybody else be there?

IR: Yeah, you and your dad, would anyone else be there?

IE: No.

IR: Yeah. Did your dad ever show you pictures or movies or books?

IE: No, my mom does that.

IR: What kind of things does she show you?

IE: Reading books and stuff and…

IR: Mm-hm.

IE: And shows us movies and then she let us stay up late sometimes.

IR: Mm.

IE: When it's not school time.

IR: Well, that's nice. Did anyone ever show you pictures of people with no clothes on?

IE: My dad?

IR: Did anybody?

IE: No.

IR: Bill, do you know if your dad drinks or uses medicines or drugs?

IE: He drinks, smokes, and uses medicine.

IR: What does he drink?

IE: Beer, wine, all that stuff.

IR: Do you ever see him get drunk?

IE: Yes.

IR: Yeah, how often?

IE: All the time, every night.

IR: Oh, every night. Did he, do you know if he was drinkin' when he did the touching stuff?

IE: No, he never drinks when he touched us.

IR: Oh, okay. What kind of medicine does he use?

IE: Don't know.

IR: Don't know? What does he smoke?

IE: Cigarettes and green stuff—what's that stuff called? I don't know what the green stuff is called.

IR: What does he smoke the green stuff in?

IE: Paper.

IR: Paper? Does he do that alone or with somebody?

IE: Alone.

IR: He ever want you to drink or smoke that stuff?

IE: Nope.

IR: Bill, I just have one more question for you. Has anybody else ever tried to do touching to you?

IE: No.

IR: That's good. I wonder if you'd like to ask me something?

IE: Three minutes are up.

IR: I know, but you know what, I thought of one more question, it's important. Did you ever get touched back here? (Points to anus on picture of a child.)

IE: No.

IR: Would you be able to tell me if that happened?

IE: Yeah.

IR: Yeah, you've been a really big help today. I just wonder if anything else happened with your dad that I should know about. Did he do anything else that you didn't like?

IE: Yeah.

IR: What?

IE: Try to mess with my mom.

IR: What kind of messing?

IE: Fighting with her when I don't want him to.

IR: Oh.

IE: I call the police.

IR: Uh-huh.

IE: My sister and me gets out the house quick.

IR: Uh-huh. Have you had to run out of the house lots of times?

IE: Yeah.

IR: Because of fighting?

IE: Yeah.

IR: And where do you go?

IE: To my grandma's house 'cause we don't have a tele-phone.

IR: Do you think your dad's gonna come home?

IE: No, I hope he don't.

IR: I don't think your mom's gonna have him come home, that's what she said. She doesn't want to let him come back.... Did you know that you would see the doctor today too?

IE: Doctor?

IR: Doctor? Yeah, the doctor.

IE: I don't want to stay here.

IR: Oh, well, they're just gonna give you a quick checkup.

IE: Right now?

IR: Yeah, in a couple of minutes. They're gonna check you out, Bill, from head to toe and make sure that you're healthy, and everything's okay.

IE: I weigh 50 pounds now.

IR: Is that right?

IE: I'm worried about the doctor.

IR: What are you worried about?

IE: I'll be taken.

IR: That you'd be taken?

IE: Yeah.

IR: Taken where?

IE: To Juvenile Hall.

IR: Oh, Bill, no one's gonna take you, and you can have your mommy in the checkup with you if you want.

IE: Oh goody, mommy.

IR: Yeah. No one's gonna take you away from your mommy today, I promise.

IE: Nobody, ever?

IR: Not today, there's no reason for them to take you, okay?

IE: OK.

IR: Thanks for comin' in, Bill.

IE: OK.

In the final segment of the interview, the interviewer tried to broach topics that she had not yet covered. When the interviewer asked about "pictures or movies or books," the child understood this to mean any books or movies, not solely pornographic ones. She had to follow up her question with a more direct one that mentioned "pictures of people with no clothes on." She tried to alleviate the child's anxiety about his father's coming home and the possibility that he might be removed from the home. Her comment that "you've been a really big help today" followed by a request for more information about his dad might be viewed as a suggestive remark. However, there is little doubt that the child was sexually molested.

Three case evaluations. Let's now look at how three cases of alleged child sexual abuse were evaluated. In the first two cases, the interviewer used several sources of information to decide whether the alleged child sexual abuse occurred (Heiman, 1992).

CASE 23-2. BRENDA

A 4-year-old female was alleged to have been abused by her father on visitation. The allegation occurred when Brenda spread her legs and asked her mother to play the "making love" game. When Brenda was asked where she learned such a game, she said that her father taught her.

History of symptoms. The mother reported that Brenda, who is normally vivacious and verbally precocious, was withdrawn and spent hours underneath the kitchen table when she returned from her visits with her father. Although she had been toilet trained since the age of 2, with few nighttime accidents since age 3, she recently had begun to wet the bed regularly. Furthermore, she said she had itching and burning of her vagina, and medical reports confirmed vaginitis [inflammation of the vagina]. On several occasions, Brenda's mother observed her enacting elaborate sexual scenes with her Barbie dolls. On one occasion, Brenda was found asking neighborhood children to touch her on the vagina. During the interview, Brenda appeared to be sexually precocious.

Verbal report. Brenda described several games that she played with her father. For example, she said "He takes off his underwear and says 'I love you' and then I take off my clothes and we play the making love game." When asked what this game was, she said "I do my legs like this (demonstrates spreading her legs), and he puts his pee pee here" (and pointed to her thigh region outside the vagina). When she was asked "What else can you tell me about this game?" she said "He goes up and down and then he runs to the bathroom." Thus, she described specific sexual acts that were beyond knowledge expected for her age, and she provided information about how she engaged in sexual activities. She also said that the activities occurred in the living room and bedroom, and she denied that they had anything to do with bathing or helping her with hygiene: "No, I'm a big girl. I don't need help."

Phenomenological experience. Brenda reported feeling confused about these activities: "Is it okay to play the making love game?" At one point, she asked the interviewer "Does your daddy touch you? Does it feel funny inside?" She did not appear to understand fully the sexual nature of the activities, and she did not have the vocabulary to describe the experience. She appeared to be anxious and sexually overstimulated.

Presentational style. Brenda was hesitant to talk about the sexual activities. For example, on several occasions, she took a play baby bottle and lay down on the couch, stating "It's too bad to say. I can't tell you. I'm tired. I need a nap." She gave the details of the sexual abuse slowly. First, she agreed to give some details if she whispered and the interviewer didn't look at her. She said "I'll show you what daddy did, if you cover your eyes. It's okay to peek" and then took a Barbie doll and kissed it on the breast. Then she became more comfortable and described the sexual games and activities in more detail. Her affect was often sad. She would describe events in a low voice, looking at the floor, and sucking her thumb. Sometimes she appeared overstimulated, and a glazed look came over her, accompanied by a smile, when she demonstrated certain actions.

Brenda seemed to use her own words and showed no signs of being rehearsed or coached. She also was confident of what she said had happened and did not change her story.

Corroborating evidence. Besides vaginitis, which is not specific to sexual abuse, there was no specific medical evidence documenting trauma. There would be no reason to expect medical evidence associated with such activities described as fondling, rubbing of the labia and the penis, masturbation, or oral sex. Brenda, however, described the sexual abuse in several ways. She described the sexual games. She demonstrated these same activities with dolls. And she drew pictures in which she and her father's mouth and genital areas were enlarged.

Dr. Heiman concluded that Brenda had been sexually abused by her father based on the following analysis:

1. She had a history of acute symptoms.
2. She gave verbally rich descriptions of events that included contextual and affective details of the alleged sexual abuse.
3. She had advanced sexual knowledge.
4. She displayed anxious behavior when she described the alleged sexual abuse.
5. She gave consistent demonstration of the alleged sexual abuse in several different ways.

Subsequently, Brenda's father was indicted on criminal charges and pleaded guilty. (adapted from pp. 322–324)

CASE 23-3. SAM

Sam, a 4-year-old male, was alleged to have been sexually abused by his father. The allegation was made by Sam's maternal grandmother when he said to her that his cousin's baby food smelled like his father's penis.

History of symptoms. Sam was an oppositional child who had a history of behavioral problems. He had a high energy level, a short attention span, and difficulty listening to authority figures. He often cursed and destroyed toys. After his visits with his father, he was more uncontrollable and his difficult behaviors escalated. Since the allegation, he has not had any additional symptoms.

Verbal reports. Sam denied ever being touched on his penis or being asked to touch his father's penis. He did relate smelling his father's penis when they showered together. His father said that he took showers with his son in order to accomplish quickly the bathing task and "head off" any problem behavior. He reported that Sam rarely complied independently with a request to do something. Sam denied any secrecy surrounding his relations with his father.

Phenomenological experience. Sam did not express being uncomfortable or anxious when he discussed with the interviewer his activities with his father. There was no unusual affect when he discussed his or others' private parts, dressing, bathing, or bathroom activities.

Presentational style. Sam laughed when he described taking a shower with his father. His affect throughout the interview remained constant, and there was no significant change in his mood, affect, or behavior when the topic of sexual abuse was raised.

Corroborating evidence. None.

Dr. Heiman concluded that the probability that Sam had been sexually abused by his father was low, based on the following analysis:

1. He had no specific symptomatology. His increased agitation after visits with his father appeared to be related to his behavioral problems and was indicative of the difficulty he encounters making transitions and changes, especially with respect to his parents' divorce.
2. There was no verbal description or demonstration of abuse. Although Sam did make an unusual statement to his maternal grandmother, he denied ever being touched by his father.
3. He did not display behavior or affect that suggested that he was sexually abused.
4. There was nothing unusual in his presentational style. His presentational style did not reveal signs of denial, an aversion to discussing events, or a need to hide information.
5. There was no corroborating evidence.

Sam remained in therapy for two years to decrease his behavioral problems. During that time, no other allegations or concerns about possible abuse arose. In a follow-up one year later, the family did not express any concerns about the alleged abuse. (adapted from pp. 324–325)

The next case shows an interviewer's notes made in a case of alleged child sexual abuse. Note the careful documentation by the interviewer, including direct quotes from the child. The interviewer's conclusions reflect the careful application of reasoning and judgment. All names are fictitious.

CASE 23-4. DONNA

Donna Brown, who is 8 years old, was interviewed on October 15, 1994. She accompanied me to the interview room at National Hospital. She was advised that the interview was being videotaped. Donna appeared somewhat reluctant to speak when the topic of molestation was introduced. However, after rapport was established, she said she was at the hospital because of what her stepgrandfather, whom she refers to as "Mr. Fred," did. She later said that Fred's last name was "Harris." Donna reported that Fred was "doing stuff to me and my brother." She was aware of her brother's molestation because she observed the molestation in Fred's house, stating it "was stuff that kids should not do." Henry, her brother, is 10 years old.

Donna indicated she witnessed "stuff" happening to her brother in the living room, dining room, pool, and other rooms of the suspect's house. Donna stated "things" also happened to her in the same places. Her brother also had "seen stuff happen to her."

When asked specifically about what had occurred between Fred and her, she said that Fred touched her in the "private spots," pointing to her vagina and buttocks. Donna labeled her vagina as a "private." She said that Fred would pull down her clothes while she was asleep. She would wake up, and, when she attempted to get up, Fred would push her back down with his hand. Fred would pull down her pants and underwear to approximately her knees and then would pull her shirt up to her neck. Fred told Donna not to tell, otherwise he would "do something" to her. Fred, however, never explained to her exactly what he would do.

Donna also stated that Fred's "private" would touch her on her "private," and his clothes would be "down" when this occurred. She said the touching was both on the inside and on the outside of her "privates," and it "hurt." She said that Fred touched her on the inside and outside of her vagina with his hand and touched her buttocks, both on the inside and on the outside, and it "hurt"; Fred also put his penis in her buttocks. When asked if anything came out of Fred's privates, Donna said "white stuff," but she could not remember where the substance may have gone. Donna said this would happen when Fred would do touching to her and Henry. It also would occur when she and her brother would be made to touch Fred with their hands on his privates; she indicated an up and down motion with her hand. She said that these activities occurred more than once. Fred also would make them touch his buttocks with their hands, then rub him both over and under his clothes, while he touched them.

When the subject of touching with mouths was broached, Donna stated that she and Henry were made to "suck his private" but that no ejaculation occurred. Donna also indicated that Fred made them kiss him on the lips, buttocks, and privates. She explained that Fred would kiss them on the same areas, as well as kissing her on her "boobs" both over and under her clothes.

Donna stated that the touching started when she was approximately 5 years old, and it occurred at Fred's house and in his pool. When asked whether Fred showed her any videotapes, she said that he showed them to her and her brother. In the videos, children and adults were touching each other, and, at times, they were nude.

Donna further added that Fred made Henry and her touch each other: "He'd make us touch private spots, and he'd make us get on each other, and he'd make us kiss each other's privates, and that's what he'd make us do."

The touching occurred during the daytime and at nighttime. Her grandmother, Mrs. Harris, would be asleep or at work. She cited as an example that her grandmother would be in the same room but sitting on a separate couch from Fred. While the grandmother was in the room, Fred would have Donna and Henry lie with their heads in his lap, covering them and his lower body with a blanket, and would make the children orally copulate him. Fred would have his pants pulled down part way when this occurred.

Donna could only approximate the time the last incident of molestation occurred. It was several weeks prior to this interview. She thought it had occurred in late August, on a Saturday, when she and her brother were at home. This incident of molestation took place in the living room with Henry witnessing the touching.

Donna stated that the first person she disclosed to was her best friend, Virginia Peters. Virginia told her mother, who reported it to Child Protective Services.

Donna's report indicates that the probability that sexual abuse occurred over a three-year period is very high. Both she and her brother Henry were victims. There is no reason to doubt the veracity of Donna's statements. Her descriptions of several events were clear, her knowledge of details was excellent, and her descriptions of several sexual acts suggest that she was personally involved in these acts. She is being referred for a medical examination. In addition, we plan to interview her brother Henry.

To doubt everything or to believe everything are two equally convenient solutions; both dispense with the necessity of reflection.

—Jule Henre Poincaré

Guidelines for Evaluating the Family

You want to evaluate the family in cases of child maltreatment in order to learn about the following areas:

- personality and temperament of the family members
- family environment
- family members' reactions to the possible maltreatment, including whether they can corroborate the child's story
- strengths and weaknesses of the family
- family members who may be called on to help in the intervention

As a result of your evaluation of the family, you should be able to answer the questions shown in Table 23-2. The questions cover the following areas:

- family composition
- family dynamics
- knowledge of the alleged maltreatment
- view of the child and the alleged maltreatment
- contribution of the family to the alleged maltreatment
- attitude toward the alleged offender
- effects of the alleged maltreatment on the family
- family background
- family resources
- interventions
- overall evaluation of the family

When the family has been involved in a case of domestic violence, you will want to evaluate the results of the interview by answering the questions in Table 23-3. These questions cover the following areas:

- nature of the domestic violence
- involvement of children
- support systems available to the victim
- needed services
- available options

Guidelines for Evaluating the Alleged or Known Offender

In evaluating the alleged or known offender in cases of child maltreatment, you will want to answer the questions shown in Table 23-4. They cover the following areas:

- alleged or known offender's general background
- background of current alleged or known offense
- current alleged or known victim
- mental status, temperament, and personality of alleged or known offender

Table 23-2
Questions to Consider About the Family in Cases of Alleged Child Maltreatment

Family Composition
1. What members are in the family?
2. Who is living at home?

Family Dynamics
3. What is the affective climate of the family (for example, warm, cold, hostile, friendly)?
4. What is the family style (for example, rigid, flexible, disorganized, organized)?
5. Do family members share power or abuse power?
6. How do family members view authorities?
7. Are family members active in society or withdrawn from society?
8. Do family members deny negative aspects of their family or acknowledge them?
9. Are family members empathic or lacking in empathy?
10. How do family members communicate?
11. Are they emotionally expressive or emotionally withdrawn?
12. Do family members have adequate or inadequate controls?
13. Do they share a realistic outlook, or are they looking for magical solutions?
14. What activities do family members participate in together?
15. What extended family members are important to the family?
16. What emotional ties do family members have to each other?
17. What responsibilities does each member have in the family?
18. How do family members carry out their responsibilities?
19. To what extent are family members satisfied with their roles in the family?
20. Are the roles in the family clear among the members?
21. Are there marital problems?
22. (If yes) What kinds of problems are there?

Knowledge of the Alleged Maltreatment
23. What do the family members know about the child's alleged maltreatment?
24. What words do they use to describe the child's alleged maltreatment?
25. What type of affect do they show in discussing the child's alleged maltreatment?
26. What types of explanations do they give to account for the child's alleged maltreatment (if applicable)?
27. What, if anything, did the child say to them about the alleged maltreatment?
28. Did the family members notice any changes in the child's behavior or unusual behavior before or after the disclosure of the alleged maltreatment?
29. Do they believe that the child was maltreated?

30. Do they corroborate the child's story about the alleged maltreatment?
31. How consistent are the reports of the family members about the alleged maltreatment?
32. Were any of the family members suspicious that someone might possibly be maltreating the child?
33. (If yes) Which family members, and what led them to be suspicious?
34. Has any family member observed inappropriate behavior on the part of the alleged offender?
35. (If yes) What was observed and by whom?

View of the Child and the Alleged Maltreatment
36. What is each family member's understanding of the child's reaction to the alleged maltreatment?
37. What did the family members do when they learned about the alleged maltreatment?
38. Does the nonsuspect parent feel guilty about not having protected the child from the alleged maltreatment?
39. Does the nonsuspect parent believe that he or she has the child's trust?
40. If the nonsuspect parent knew of the alleged maltreatment, why did he or she allow it to continue?
41. Is there rivalry between the nonsuspect parent and the child?
42. How much blame does the nonsuspect parent attribute to the child for what has happened?
43. How did the disclosure of the alleged maltreatment affect the nonsuspect parent's conception of his or her parenting role?
44. How do family members feel about the alleged maltreatment (for example, denial, anger, acknowledgment, shock, betrayal)?
45. How did the family members get along with the child before the alleged maltreatment?
46. How have they reacted to the child since the alleged maltreatment has been reported (for example, supportive, blaming, angry, rejecting, ambivalent)?
47. Can they talk with the child about the alleged maltreatment?
48. How do cultural factors influence family members' attitudes toward the alleged maltreatment and toward working with outside agencies?
49. What is the current risk to the child?
50. Is there a need to remove the child from the family?

Contribution of the Family to the Alleged Maltreatment
51. Did poor supervision of the child contribute to the child's alleged maltreatment?
52. Did poor choice of a caregiver or babysitter contribute to the child's alleged maltreatment?
53. Did inappropriate caregiving contribute to the child's alleged maltreatment (for example, inappropriate sleep-

(Continued)

Table 23-2 (*Continued*)

ing arrangements, genital exposure, or lack of privacy for intimate activities)?

Attitude Toward the Alleged Offender

54. What are the family members' attitudes toward the alleged offender?
55. What do they want done about the alleged offender?
56. Was any family member involved in the maltreatment? (If yes, consider questions 57–59.)
57. How did the disclosure of the alleged maltreatment affect the nonsuspect parent's feelings about the spouse, if the spouse was the alleged offender?
58. How have the family members treated the alleged offender?
59. Will the alleged offender continue to remain in the home?

Effects of the Alleged Maltreatment on the Family

60. How has the child's alleged maltreatment affected each family member?
61. How have family members reacted to each other since the alleged maltreatment of the child was reported?

Family Background

62. Does either parent have a history of mental illness, substance abuse, or criminal activity?
63. (If yes) Which parent and what problem did he or she have?
64. What crises have family members experienced in the past?
65. How have they dealt with these crises?
66. What is the general stress level of family members?
67. Are family members currently experiencing any additional crises (in addition to having a member of their family allegedly maltreated)?
68. How does each family member add to the stress level of the family?
69. Was either parent subjected to maltreatment as a child?
60. (If yes) Which parent and what type of maltreatment was he or she subjected to?
71. (If there are other children in the family) Were any other members of the family maltreated?

72. (If yes) Who was maltreated, and how were they maltreated?
73. What is the cultural and ethnic background of the family?
74. What role does the cultural and ethnic background of the family play in the alleged maltreatment, if any?

Family Resources

75. What are the family's resources?
76. Have the family's resources been affected by the child's alleged maltreatment?
77. (If so) In what way?
78. What environmental supports does the family have?
79. Can the family provide for the child's needs (and the needs of the other children in the family, as well)?
80. What types of support do the other family members offer the child?
81. How do the family members differ in their ability to support the child?
82. How does the cultural and ethnic background of the family help it cope with crises and stressful situations?

Interventions

83. What would the family like done about the situation?
84. Would the family be willing to accept professional help?
85. (If a family member is involved or the family is in part responsible for the maltreatment) What is the family's potential for change?

Overall Evaluation of the Family

86. What is the level of adjustment of the family?
87. What are the strengths of the family?
88. What are the weaknesses of the family?
89. Who are the strong, supportive members of the family?
90. What happy events has the family experienced?
91. What sad events has the family experienced?
92. What is the degree of acculturation of the family?
93. How responsible are the parents in taking care of their child's needs?
94. How will the family be able to protect the child from further maltreatment?
95. How might the family respond to the suggested interventions?

Note. Also see Chapter 4 for information on family assessment.
Source: Adapted, in part, from Burgess et al. (1978), Cage (1988), and Sgroi (1982).

- reasons alleged or known victim participated
- alleged or known offender's reaction to the alleged or known offense
- alleged or known offender's reaction to his or her children (if alleged or known offender is a parent)
- prognostic signs for known offender

Recognize that *alleged offenders only become offenders in the eyes of the court when they confess or are judged to be*

guilty. You must not assume that everyone alleged to have maltreated a child has, in fact, committed an offense. In some cases, there may have been no maltreatment at all, and, in other cases, the actual abuser may be someone other than the alleged offender. Note that most of the questions in Table 23-4 also are useful in evaluating offenders in confirmed incidents of domestic violence.

Don't use the interview to decide whether the alleged offender committed the offense. *Neither the interview nor*

Table 23-3
Evaluating the Interview in Cases of Domestic Violence

Background Information

1. What are the victim's name, age, sex, ethnicity, address, phone number, place of employment, and business phone number?
2. What are the abuser's name, age, sex, ethnicity, address, phone number, place of employment, and business phone number?
3. How is the abuser related to the victim?

Type of Alleged Maltreatment

4. What was the nature of the maltreatment? (Include a description of the maltreatment, when and where it happened, injuries, weapons used, and so forth.)
5. Has the maltreatment been escalating?
6. (If yes) In what way has it been escalating?

Victim's Actions

7. Did the victim try to defend herself or himself?
8. (If yes) What were the results?
9. Did the victim report the current maltreatment to any agency?
10. (If yes) What agency and what was the agency's response?
11. Has the victim in the past been in contact with any agencies?
12. (If yes) With what agencies has the victim been in contact, when was the contact made, and what were the results?

Involvement of Children and Others

13. Were any children involved in the maltreatment?
14. (If yes) In what way?
15. Were there any witnesses?
16. (If yes) Who are they, and what are their relationships to the victim and to the abuser?

History of Domestic Violence

17. Have there been prior incidents of maltreatment?
18. (If yes) What happened, who was involved, where did the incidents happen, and what help did the victim receive?

Interventions

19. How does the victim feel about what happened? (For example, does she or he blame herself or himself, blame the abuser, or blame others for the incident?)
20. How much does the victim fear the abuser?
21. What support systems does the victim have?
22. What services would benefit the victim?
23. Is the victim safe going back home, or does she or he (and the children, if relevant) need to go to a shelter?
24. Does the victim need a restraining order against the abuser?
25. How does the victim feel about leaving the abuser?
26. What options are available for the victim?

Source: Adapted from Johann (1994).

psychological tests can tell you whether someone is an offender. This determination is best left to law enforcement agencies and to the courts (Quinsey & Lalumière, 1995).

In evaluating alleged or known offenders, you want to review all sources of information to arrive at a clinical impression of their temperament, personality, and adjustment. This includes information about the alleged or known offender's physical and behavioral traits; self-image; needs, attitudes, and values; sense of personal worth; perception and judgment; social skills; predominant mood states; ability to cope with stress and manage his or her life; ability to communicate effectively; ability to establish and maintain positive relationships with others; emotional expressiveness; and sense of humor (Groth, 1979). Consider indications of maladjustment, as well as of adaptive strengths.

In evaluating the known offender's personality, you also will want to consider the following areas (Groth, 1979):

1. At the time of the maltreatment, what were the known offender's frame of mind, precipitating stressors, motivational intent, perception of the victim, reasons for selecting the victim, style of maltreatment, type of maltreatment, physiological response, and attitude toward the victim?

2. How can the offense be understood in light of the known offender's developmental and family history, the social-environmental context of his or her early life, the environmental-situational context of the maltreatment, and the known offender's current psychological and emotional life?

Indices in caregiver of possible child maltreatment. Let's look at some caregiver behaviors that should raise suspicions of child maltreatment (Briggs, 1991; Warner & Hansen, 1994; also see discussion of Munchausen Syndrome by Proxy in Chapter 20). These behaviors also may be seen in caregivers who are not alleged to be offenders; however, they represent behaviors that should alert human service workers, mental health professionals, educators, and health care providers to the possibility that a child may have been maltreated.

1. Caregiver shows little concern for the child.
2. Caregiver denies that the child has problems or blames the child for the child's problems.
3. Caregiver delays getting an injured child medical attention.

Table 23-4
Questions to Consider About the Alleged or Known Offender in Cases of Child Maltreatment

Alleged or Known Offender's General Background

1. What are the age, sex, and ethnicity of the alleged or known offender?

2. What is the alleged or known offender's family history? (For example, was there disruption in family unity, such as abandonment, death, divorce, separation, illness, foster placement, or institutionalization of parents; poor or ineffective parenting, such as child abuse or neglect, inadequate role models, family violence, substance abuse, mental illness, criminal behavior, or inappropriate sexual behavior; or behavioral problems, such as running away, chronic rebelliousness, intense sibling rivalry, or temper tantrums?)

3. What is the alleged or known offender's medical, psychiatric, and treatment history? (For example, were there major illnesses or accidents; serious injuries, disabilities, impairments, or handicaps; or hyperactivity, encopresis/enuresis, organic insult, persistent nightmares, blackouts, psychogenic complaints, suicide gestures/attempts, or mental illness? If any of these conditions were present, what treatments were attempted and how successful were they?)

4. What is the alleged or known offender's educational history? (For example, consider his or her school adjustment, academic performance, level of intellectual functioning, cognitive skills, scholastic interests, aptitudes, abilities, achievements, grades completed, letter grades, classroom behavior, study habits, attitude toward education, and relationships with teachers, administrators, and classmates. Did he or she have school phobias, learning problems or disabilities, changes in intelligence test scores, dramatic shifts in grades, or behavioral or disciplinary problems [such as truancy, fighting, or suspensions]? Did he or she repeat grades, receive special classes or services, or drop out of school?)

5. What is the alleged or known offender's military history (if applicable)? (For example, consider the nature and quality of his or her military service, branch of service, military adjustment and performance, type of discharge, attitude toward military service, and combat experiences. Was his or her application for enlistment rejected? Were there infractions [AWOL], disciplinary actions [reprimands, court-martial], or a less than honorable discharge? Did he or she experience a service-connected disability or traumas [violence or risk of injury or death]?)

6. What is the alleged or known offender's social history? (For example, consider the nature and quality of his or her interpersonal relationships, type of friendships and relationships established, number of friends, social interests, activities, and memberships in organizations or groups. Did he or she have superficial or unstable relationships, poor associates, a tendency to relate mostly to people much younger or older than himself or herself, or excessively controlling or competitive behavior? Was he

or she socially isolated; susceptible to the influence of others; self-centered; or intimidated, exploited, or manipulated by others? Did he or she keep others at a distance? Did he or she use religion as a justification for physical abuse, sexual abuse, or neglect?)

7. What is the alleged or known offender's sexual history? (For example, consider the nature and quality of his or her sexual development, experiences, habits, and interests; sexual education; types of sexual encounters; types and number of partners; sexual fantasies; sexual attitudes, values, and orientations; sexual performance and subjective reactions; and frequency of sexual activity. At what age did he or she have a first sexual experience? Has he or she been influenced by alcohol and drugs? Have there been premarital, marital, and extramarital relationships? Does his or her background include sexual trauma or victimization, sexual dysfunctions, sexual offenses, unconventional sexual interests and behaviors, or sexual violence?)

8. What is the alleged or known offender's marital or current family history (if applicable)? (For example, consider the quality of his or her relationship with spouse, number of times married, sexual compatibility and fidelity of spouse, number of offspring, relationship with children, attitudes and expectations regarding marriage, and success with marriage. Was there marital discord, spouse abuse, infidelity, dissolution of the marriage [divorce, separation, or abandonment], child maltreatment, psychological problems on the part of the spouse [mental illness, addiction, or criminal activity], or psychological problems on the part of the children [school problems, behavioral problems, emotional problems, substance abuse, or delinquency]?)

9. What is the alleged or known offender's occupational history? (For example, consider his or her work history, job performance, stability of employment, vocational skills, types of jobs held, job satisfaction, relationships with co-workers and supervisors, advancements and achievement, and salary. Was there a history of unstable employment [dismissal, quitting, suspension, unemployment, welfare assistance, work-related disabilities, or economic hardship]?)

10. What are the alleged or known offender's recreational interests? (For example, consider his or her leisure-time interests and activities, sports activities, hobbies, and memberships in organizations or clubs. Does he or she engage in solitary, high-risk activities; drinking; gambling; or speeding? Does he or she have an obsession with weapons, an interest in physical violence, or a habit of overspending?)

11. What is the alleged or known offender's criminal history? (For example, consider his or her arrest record, age at time of first offense, types of crimes committed, prison terms, and probation or parole record. Did he or she

(Continued)

Table 23-4 (*Continued*)

engage in preadolescent delinquent behavior [stealing, property damage, fire setting, cruelty to animals/ children, or felonies], crimes against persons, crimes of violence [arson, murder, or sexual assault], prostitution, or pornography? Consider the number of prior convictions for sex offenses, the number of allegations of or arrests for sexual offenses that did not result in convictions, the total number of victims of alleged or known sexual offenses that did not result in conviction, the number of convictions—both juvenile and adult—for nonsexual crimes, and any history of violence not including the present offense.)

12. (If more than one child maltreatment offense) What characteristics are shared by the children who have been victimized (for example, age, sex, ethnicity, hair color, or other distinguishing characteristics)?

Background of Current Alleged or Known Offense

13. What type of offense was alleged or known to have been committed?
14. How long is the offense alleged or known to have been going on?
15. What is the relationship of the alleged or known offender to the child?
16. What degree of secrecy is alleged or known to have been maintained by the accused and the child?
17. What is the degree of attachment between the alleged or known offender and the child?
18. How is the accused alleged or known to have gotten the child to comply (for example, bribes, threat of physical harm, or threat that family would be ruined, especially in cases of child sexual abuse)?
19. How much physical force is the accused alleged or known to have used, if any?
20. What affect is the accused alleged or known to have shown during the maltreatment?
(Questions 21 through 27 are primarily for alleged or known offenders involved in child sexual abuse.)
21. Did the accused allegedly involve the child in the production of pornographic movies?
22. Did the accused allegedly show the child pornographic materials?
23. Did the accused allegedly involve the child in acts of bestiality (sexual relations between a human being and animal) or sadistic rituals?
24. Did the accused allegedly have the child wear special clothing or make-up?
25. Did the accused allegedly constrain the child in any way?
26. Did the accused allegedly use any sexual aids or instruments during the offense?
27. What, if any, deviant arousal patterns does the alleged or known offender have?
28. What was the reason for the alleged or known offense (for example, personal gratification, loss of control, act of vengeance, hatred, fear, desire, impulsive act, act gener-

ated by some other past or present interpersonal relationship, intentional harm by a sociopathic personality, anger triggering a violent outburst, ignorance, or overuse of substances)?

29. What purpose did the alleged or known maltreatment serve (for example, release of tension, way to avoid reality, or part of an addiction)?
30. Was there a personal ritual associated with the alleged or known maltreatment?
31. (If yes) What was the ritual?
32. In what surroundings was the maltreatment alleged or known to have taken place? (For example, if it was a sexual act, did it take place in silence, without eye contact, or in total darkness, as if the offender was trying to disconnect himself or herself from the child?)
33. Were there other adults present during the alleged or known maltreatment?
34. (If yes) Who are they?
35. Were other children involved in the alleged or known maltreatment?
36. (If yes) Who are they?
37. To what extent does the alleged or known offender have access to children?
38. To what extent do the alleged or known offender's statements agree with those of the child and others?

Current Alleged or Known Victim

39. What are the age and sex of the alleged or known victim?
40. What is the relationship of the alleged or known offender to the alleged or known victim(s) (for example, relative, friend, or stranger)?
41. What was the physical and psychosocial trauma to the alleged or known victim?

Mental Status, Temperament, and Personality of Alleged or Known Offender

42. What was the mental status of the alleged or known offender when the offense was allegedly committed? (For example, was he or she under the influence of drugs or alcohol, psychotic, reacting to stress, goaded on by others, or influenced by pornographic materials?)
43. What stresses were operating in the alleged or known offender's life at the time of the alleged or known offense (for example, economic difficulties, joblessness, interpersonal frustrations, marital disharmony, sexual frustrations, poor relationship with other children, divorce, illness, unmet and unreasonably high expectations for the child's behavior given the child's age and level of development, or inability to use nonviolent management techniques to control the child's misbehavior)?
44. What particular stresses are currently operating in the alleged or known offender's life?
45. (In cases of child sexual abuse) To what extent is the alleged or known offender's sexual interest in children a persistent orientation or a new interest?

(Continued)

Table 23-4 (*Continued*)

46. What are the alleged or known offender's characteristic mood, degree of impulse control, tolerance for frustration, level of emotional stability, degree of contact with reality, aptitude for of interpersonal relations, empathic ability, self-image, and adaptive strength?
47. Does the alleged or known offender exhibit any suicidal or homicidal tendencies?
48. Does the alleged or known offender have a drug or alcohol problem?
49. (If yes) What type of problem does the alleged or known offender have, and how severe is it?

Reasons Alleged or Known Victim Participated
50. What was the degree of participation on the part of the child in the alleged or known act (for example, no cooperation, fear-ridden reluctance, some anxiety, or some cooperation)?
51. (In cases of child sexual abuse) What did the accused allegedly do to get the child to perform the act (for example, enticed or bribed the child to perform the act by offering a reward such as money, candy, toys, human contact, or adult approval; used persuasion; physically forced the act on the child; or used violence or threats to get the child to perform the act)?

Alleged or Known Offender's Reaction to the Alleged or Known Offense
52. What is the alleged or known offender's reaction to the alleged or known offense (for example, remorse, shame, guilt, acceptance of responsibility, attribution of blame to someone else ["It was her fault" or "My wife's attitude led me to do it"], distress over being discovered, denial of act, minimizing act ["I didn't hit him hard enough to do any damage"], invoking alcoholic blackout ["I don't remember what happened"], attribution to some external factor ["I was drunk when she came over to me"], or rationalization ["She kicked me"])?
53. What kind of fantasies, if any, did the alleged or known offender have when carrying out the alleged or known maltreatment?
54. During the abusive act, is the accused alleged or known to have behaved differently from his or her usual self, using different gestures, voices, facial expressions, or other physical behaviors?
55. Did the alleged or known offender get sexually excited before, during, or after the alleged or known maltreatment?

Alleged or Known Offender's Reaction to His or Her Children
(Questions 56 to 58 are for alleged or known offenders who have one or more children in their family.)
56. To what extent does the alleged or known offender describe his or her children as individuals?
57. How does the alleged or known offender describe his or her relationship with his or her children?
58. How accurate is the alleged or known offender's description of his or her children, based on what you know about the children from other reports (or your own interviews)?

Additional Questions to Consider for Known Offenders
59. What is the degree of chronicity of the abusive acts performed by the offender?
60. Was the abusive act committed by an individual with sociopathic tendencies or other personality problems?
61. What is the extent of drug or alcohol abuse on the part of the offender?
62. What is the level of the offender's overall psychological functioning?
63. Does the offender understand that his or her behavior was wrong?
64. To what extent does the offender accept responsibility for his or her act?
65. Does the offender understand the impact of the offense on the child?
66. Does the offender understand the reason(s) why he or she committed the maltreatment?
67. Does the offender show remorse for the offense?
68. What changes have occurred in the offender's life as a result of his or her being identified as an abuser?
69. What type of help, if any, does the offender want?
70. What resources, including social supports, does the offender have for getting help for himself or herself (for example, spouse, other family members, clergy, friends, agencies, or private therapists)?
71. What resources does the offender have for getting help for his or her family (such as when there is a financial problem, when there is a problem with one of the children, or when someone is sick)?
72. Does the offender pose a continuing threat to the victim(s) or to other potential victims in the future?
73. To what extent does the offender want help to enable him or her to stop maltreating children?

Source: Adapted from Burgess et al. (1978), Faller (1988), Groth (1979, 1982), Jones and McQuiston (1989), Kelly (1983), and McGovern and Peters (1988).

4. Caregiver's report of the injury does not accord with the injury observed in the child.
5. Caregiver provides no explanation for the injury.
6. Two or more caregivers give different explanations for the injury.
7. Caregiver describes behavior inconsistent with the child's developmental level, such as a 6-month-old's turning on the hot water.
8. Caregiver's report of the injury differs from that of the child.

9. Caregiver changes the report about the child's injury or gives inconsistent reports.
10. Caregiver does not provide information voluntarily about the child's injury.
11. Caregiver is the only one who had access to the child at the time of the injuries.
12. Caregiver attributes the injuries to the child's sibling when there is little likelihood that the sibling could have carried out the behavior.
13. Caregiver does not show concern about the child's injury, treatment, or prognosis.
14. Caregiver does not follow medical advice about the child (for example, caregiver refuses to admit the child to a hospital for observation, refuses to sign for additional tests, or refuses to agree to necessary treatment for the child).
15. Caregiver does not bring the child in for routine medical health checks, such as immunizations.
16. Caregiver brings the child to different medical providers for different injuries.
17. Caregiver gives limited, if any, physical or emotional support to the child or shows inappropriate or no response to the child when the child is crying.
18. Caregiver is not available for questioning about the alleged maltreatment.
19. Caregiver is involved in domestic violence.
20. Caregiver says that he or she knows little about basic child care and child development.
21. Caregiver says that he or she has little patience with the child.
22. Caregiver is constantly criticizing the child.
23. Caregiver says that he or she fears that he or she might hurt the child or cannot take care of the child.
24. Caregiver says that he or she is frequently drunk or high on drugs.
25. Caregiver says that he or she has little energy to take care of the child.
26. Caregiver says that he or she has violent temper outbursts.
27. Caregiver makes excuses for the child's condition—such as bruises, burns, or other injuries—or minimizes the child's condition.

As a practical matter in cases of physical abuse involving infants and toddlers, if there isn't a confession or eyewitness, it will be difficult to identify the offender. Evaluating the family and protecting the victim can be especially challenging when no one accepts responsibility for the physical abuse. However, if you are conducting an investigation, eliminate those who could not be offenders and further narrow the list by a process of elimination.

Caregiver behaviors that should raise suspicions of child sexual abuse are much more difficult to identify than those associated with child physical abuse. If the alleged perpetrator denies all knowledge of child sexual abuse in the interview, look for other ways to investigate the possible sexual abuse, such as reports from the child, a physical examination of the child, and reports from others.

Neglect will be identified primarily by observing the child and the child's surroundings. Emotional abuse usually will be difficult to identify unless others observe the abuse or the offender confesses to the abuse.

Sample Reports

Let's now consider two sample reports. Exhibit 23-1 is an unsubstantiated report of neglect; it shows the value of a home visit and how careful observations of the home, child, and mother helped the social worker arrive at her decision to close the case. Exhibit 23-2 is a report of a social worker who investigated a complaint of child physical abuse. It provides background information and statements by the child and parents. The recommendations are useful, directed to protecting the child and obtaining further information about the family.

Exercise 23-1. Evaluating the Offender and the Offense

Read the case. Then answer the questions using the 7-point rating scale after each item. After you complete your ratings, compare them with those given for a sample of college students. This case was adapted from Drugge (1992).

James Simpson, a 30-year-old man, has pleaded guilty to charges that he sexually molested Lisa R., an 8-year-old girl who lived next door to him. According to police reports, Simpson approached the girl as she was playing near his home and asked her if she would like to come to his house "for a drink of juice." Once inside, Simpson sat the child on his lap and asked her if she would like to "play a game." The "game" involved Simpson and the girl fondling each other's genital area; at first, through their clothing and then, at Simpson's request, underneath it. This continued for several minutes. When the child got up to leave, Simpson asked her not to tell anyone about the incident, saying that he might "get into trouble." A few weeks later, the girl told her parents, who contacted the police. Simpson was arrested shortly thereafter and pleaded guilty.

1. In your opinion, how serious a crime is the offense you have just read about? (1 = not at all serious, 7 = extremely serious)   1 2 3 4 5 6 7
2. In your opinion, how likely or common is the kind of situation you have just read about? (1 = not at all common, 7 = extremely common)   1 2 3 4 5 6 7
3. How harmful do you think this kind of situation would be for the child involved? (1 = not at all harmful, 7 = extremely harmful)   1 2 3 4 5 6 7
4. How likely is this offender to commit a similar offense in the future? (1 = not at all likely, 7 = extremely likely)   1 2 3 4 5 6 7
5. To what extent would you say that this offender is psychologically disturbed? (1 = not at all disturbed, 7 = extremely disturbed)   1 2 3 4 5 6 7

Exhibit 23-1
Example of an Unsubstantiated Report of Neglect

FALLEN COUNTY
DEPARTMENT OF SOCIAL SERVICES

Name: Harold Dembo
Date of Birth: May 14, 1984
Age: 12   *Sex:* M

Parent(s): Mrs. Elsie Dembo
Address: 1489 Els St., Albany, NY 12260
Social Worker: Helen Smith

Referral Summary

10-19-96
Case received and reviewed. The referral alleged general neglect of the minor by the mother. The mother reportedly doesn't buy enough food for the minor and spends her AFDC money on drugs. She and her boyfriend supposedly lock themselves in their room all day and get high, leaving the minor locked out. According to the referral, the mother and her boyfriend slept in the same room with the minor, and the minor was exposed to sexual activity until the reporting party told them to stop. The referral indicates that the mother would then leave the minor alone while she spent the night with her boyfriend.

10-19-96
Phone call to the Brown School District. Harold is enrolled at Central Junior High.

10-20-96
Phone call to Central Junior High School. Harold is in attendance today.

10-20-96
School visit. Harold opted not to have school personnel present during the interview. The minor was clean and well dressed, and I saw no marks or bruises on him. The minor stated that he and his mother do share a room that she rents in a boarding house but said that there is a divider curtain and that he has his own bed and his mother has her own bed. He denied knowing of anyone who used drugs. He stated that he knew what drugs looked like because he saw them when he went through a D.A.R.E. program. The minor described eating a variety of nutritious meals at home and denied ever having to miss any meals because there was no food. He denied that anyone ever slept in the room with himself and his mother. He denied ever being locked out of the room. The minor denied that anyone has touched him sexually or that he has been involved in any sexualized activity.

10-20-96
Home visit. The mother and her landlady were at home. The house was clean. The mother stated that she had smoked pot when she was in high school but denied any other drug use. She is a very thin woman, but I could not see any crystal sores or track marks. Her eyes appeared to be normal. The mother showed me her room, and there was a curtain hung in the middle of the room to divide it. Her son's bed was on one side of the room, and there was a model airplane hanging over the bed and posters were on the wall. The mother's bed was on the other side of the room, and she had pictures of herself and her family on the headboard. The beds were made. I observed a freezer that was well stocked with meats and vegetables. There were eggs, milk, and other nutritious foods in the refrigerator. There were potatoes, soups, canned vegetables, cereal, and other items in the pantry. When I asked the mother what they had for dinner last night, she said that she fixed spaghetti. (Minor had told me the same thing when I interviewed him at school.) The mother stated that no one else has ever been in the room with her when her son was there. She denied leaving him alone at night.

Relevant Family History
Harold and his mother live in a rented room in a boarding house in Albany. Harold's father lives in St. Louis with Harold's older sibling.

Assessment of Family Strength
The mother appeared to be cooperative.

Replacement Preventative Services
I suggested to the mother that it would be better if she and Harold did not have to share such a small room. The mother agreed and said that she would be moving as soon as she was able to find an apartment that she could afford. She said that a friend of hers has told her about an apartment that may become available in a couple of months.

Need for In-Home Caregiver Emergency Shelter Care Services
N/A

Social Worker Evaluation
The referral alleged general neglect of Harold by the mother. Both Harold and his mother deny any current drug use in the home. They both deny that anyone has slept in the room that the minor and mother share when the minor was present. They both deny that there has ever been a lack of food. They both deny that the mother has locked the minor out of the room and that she has left the minor alone at night. The minor was clean and well dressed when I saw him. The home the mother lives in was clean, and the beds were made. There was plenty of nutritious food in the home at the time of the home visit. Other than the fact that the mother is extremely thin, I saw nothing in the home to indicate that the mother uses drugs. The mother and minor do share a room together, but there is a curtain hung between the beds to divide the room. I was unable to substantiate the allegations in the referral. While it is possible that the mother may have been less than honest with me about her using drugs, it does not appear that there is no food for the minor because the mother spends all her money on drugs. Although the mother is extremely thin, the minor appears to be well fed. When I suggested that it would be better if the mother and minor did not have to share such a small room, the mother agreed and stated that she is planning to move into an apartment as soon as she can find one that she can afford.

Plan
Close case. Case closed.

(Signature)

Helen Smith, Social Worker

Exhibit 23-2
Social Worker's Report of a Child Who Allegedly Had Been Physically Abused

SOCIAL STUDY

Name: Johnnie S.
Age: 6 years
Born: October 2, 1990

Pet. No: 419C65W96
Date of Report: October 7, 1996

Jurisdictional Facts

On October 2, 1996, Officer William Black, from the Main Street Police Department, after observing deep and infected welts on the minor's back, transported the child to Cresthaven Receiving Home. The police took pictures, and we are told the pictures should be available within the next couple of days.

On October 3, 1996, I contacted the school nurse, Karen T., and she said that she observed the injuries on October 2, 1996. She added that a routine medical exam turned up "10 huge welts, some very deep and infected," on the minor's back. She also stated that "the minor was in considerable pain and he also complained of being dizzy and lightheaded." Johnnie told her "Daddy hit me yesterday." In her medical opinion, the injuries sustained were caused by a "terrible beating." She had called the Main Street Police Department on October 2, 1996.

On October 3, 1996, I made contact with Johnnie at the Cresthaven Receiving Home. He told me "My daddy spanked me with his belt, and he hit me a lot." He said "He hits me every day."

On October 3, 1996, Mr. S. stated to this worker "I do spank Johnnie about once per week; I don't remember using a belt on him. I'm not sure how he got those welts; maybe I did it; I usually don't hit him hard enough to leave bruises."

There have been previous complaints of child maltreatment relating to Johnnie. On September 5, 1996 and September 15, 1996 the Hot Line received complaints by anonymous callers that Johnnie was being beaten. One complaint said "Johnnie is in danger of being hurt badly." A social worker made a home visit on September 16, 1996, could find no bruises, and the case was closed.

Also, I followed up on a notation in the case record about a possible active Child Protective Services case history in Case County, Toledo. On October 5, 1996, a Social Services Supervisor in that department found a closed file on Johnnie. The supervisor provided the following information by phone: "Two years ago, Case County medical authorities discovered suspicious past fractures of Johnnie's pelvis and thigh. However, the parents moved out of the county before anything could be done."

The supervisor stated that Case County could release the medical reports if we sent a signed authorization. (If the parents refuse to sign, a blank Release of Information Form is attached to this report for the Court's authorization.)

Social Assessment

I was able to visit with the parents on October 3, 1996. The family consists of William and Ann S. and their three children: Johnnie, age 6; Billy, age 5; and Nancy, age 4. The family resides in a well-kept, clean, two-bedroom apartment in San Francisco. The boys sleep in one bedroom, the girl sleeps in the other, and the parents sleep in the living room.

The parents have been married for 12 years. Mr. S. is an enlisted man in the Navy. He stated that he was recently released from the brig for being AWOL. Mr. S. indicated the couple may separate. Mrs. S. stated that her husband "used to drink a lot" and that she was raised in foster homes herself as a child.

The school nurse indicated that Johnnie comes to school dirty and unwashed. Although he is a good athlete, he doesn't get along with other children. She stated that Johnnie is a bully at school and does get into fights. However, the school nurse pointed out that she didn't think he was in a fight the day the bruises were observed.

Statement of the Mother

Mrs. S. told me on October 3, 1996 that her husband never beats Johnnie and that she had no idea where the welts came from. She said she was not at home the day Johnnie says he was hit.

She implied that the welts may have come from a school fight. On October 6, 1996, Mrs. S. refused to talk to me. I can only assume that she disagrees with the recommendations that Johnnie be placed in a foster home. Earlier, she threatened to sue if Johnnie was not returned to her care.

Statement of the Father

On October 3, 1996, Mr. S. said that he was not sure how the minor got the welts. He further stated that he loved Johnnie and wants him home.

On October 4, 1996, Mr. S. refused to see me and indicated "I don't want you coming out to try to visit at our home." He also stated that he will sue.

Based on Mr. S.'s statements, it is safe to assume that he doesn't agree with the recommendations and that this case will be contested.

Statement of the Minor

On the October 3, 1996 contact, Johnnie told me "My dad beat me with his belt and he hit me a lot."

On October 4, 1996, I visited the minor at the Cresthaven Receiving Home. I asked Johnnie if he wanted to go home. He responded "I guess so."

Evaluation

I believe that Johnnie is in need of the protection of the Juvenile Court and out-of-home placement for the following reasons:

1. The Case County records may indicate that this is more than an "excessive discipline" case. The alleged unexplained fractures (one of which was a pelvic fracture) could indicate a long-standing, serious history of severe child physical abuse.
2. Johnnie indicates his father beats him "every day." Additionally, on my last contact, Johnnie did not seem anxious to go home. When asked if he wanted to return home, he answered

(Continued)

Exhibit 23-2 (*Continued*)

"I guess so." I believe the child's ambivalence about going home is significant.

3. Because the parents have turned uncooperative, there is no way for me to assess their family support systems or their willingness to use treatment resources.

4. The school nurse stated that she was concerned for the minor's safety, and an anonymous complaint also stated that Johnnie was in danger and that he was treated differently than his siblings.

5. There has been no history of allegations of physical abuse in relation to Johnnie's siblings, so I am not recommending court intervention on their behalf.

Recommendations

Based on indications that this 6-year-old could be a target of selective, serious physical abuse in his own home, I am making the following recommendations.

1. That Johnnie S. be declared a Dependent Child of the Freemount Juvenile Court under the care, custody, and control of the Department of Social Services pursuant to Section 300(d) of the Welfare and Institutions Code;

2. that said minor be detained in Cresthaven Receiving Home pending placement in a licensed foster home when available;

3. that the County Treasurer shall be authorized to pay for care and maintenance, clothing, and incidentals at the prevailing rate pending granting or reinstatement of AFDC funds through the Department of Social Services, and that nothing in this order shall be construed to relieve the responsible relatives of their legal obligation to support said minor;

4. that the mother and the father undergo psychological evaluations;

5. that the mother and the father participate in a program of counseling as directed by the Department of Social Services;

6. that the mother and the father participate in a program of parenting classes as directed by the Department of Social Services;

7. that the other two children be evaluated immediately to see whether they have been abused and that they be evaluated periodically;

8. that the Court order the parents to sign Release of Information Forms for parenting, psychological, and therapy reports from Case County, Toledo;

9. that the six-month review hearing date in this matter be set for April 17, 1997.

Respectfully submitted,
Frank L., Director
Department of Social Services

By:
_____
(Signature)

Helen F.
Social Worker

Approved:
_____
(Signature)

Virginia V.
Senior Social Work Supervisor

---

6. How much do you think this offender could benefit from psychological treatment? (1 = not at all, 7 = greatly)
1 2 3 4 5 6 7

7. To what extent would you say that this offender is responsible for his actions? (1 = not at all responsible, 7 = totally responsible)
1 2 3 4 5 6 7

8. To what extent would you say that this child is responsible for her actions? (1 = not at all responsible, 7 = totally responsible)
1 2 3 4 5 6 7

9. To what extent would you say that these parents were responsible for what happened? (1 = not at all responsible, 7 = totally responsible) 1 2 3 4 5 6 7

According to ratings given to the case by 35 college students in 1994 at San Diego State University, (1) the crime was serious ($M = 6.80$), (2) the situation was a relatively common one ($M = 4.94$), (3) the situation was extremely harmful for the child ($M = 6.49$), (4) the offender was likely to commit a similar offense in the future ($M = 6.40$), (5) the offender was psychologically disturbed ($M = 5.26$), (6) the offender could benefit from psychological treatment ($M = 5.37$), (7) the offender was highly responsible for his actions ($M = 6.83$), (8) the child had little, if any, responsibility for her actions ($M = 1.11$), and (9) the parents were somewhat responsible for what happened to the child ($M = 2.97$). Ratings on the last question showed the most variability, ranging from 1 to 7. The college students were almost equally split as to whether the parents were responsible for what happened.

If your classmates also did this exercise, compare your ratings with their ratings. How are the ratings similar and how are they different? Why do you think the last question showed the most variability among the students at San Diego State University? Did your classmates also have variable ratings on the last question?

Recognition [of child sexual abuse] is rarely straightforward. Evidence is often inaccessible and open to varying interpretation and evaluation. Despite the language of diagnosis sometimes used, sexual abuse is not a disease with clearly identifiable characteristics, but an interaction between individuals. Discovery is the product of further interactions, between social workers and other professionals, and between professionals, different members of the family and others. Reality is constructed through this interaction and the complexity of communication surrounding child sexual abuse means it is often precarious and uncertain, for workers as well as for mothers.

—Carol-Ann Hooper

EVALUATING FACILITIES, INSTITUTIONS, AND FOSTER HOMES

When children are alleged to have been maltreated in a facility, institution, or foster home, you may want to inspect the site. Inspecting the site may give you valuable information about the physical plant and the staff that will help you understand the allegation and make recommendations, if needed.

Evaluating Facilities and Institutions

In evaluating a child care facility or institution when there has been a report of child maltreatment, consider the following (Garbarino et al., 1987):

- the condition of the children (for example, their degree of nourishment and cleanliness and their overall behavior and mood)
- the types of children who are at the facility (for example, children with handicaps, state wards, delinquents, or infants)
- the location of the facility (for example, in a city or in a remote area)
- the layout of the facility (for example, whether some areas of the facility are off limits)
- the condition of the facility (for example, well or poorly maintained)
- the quality of the staff (for example, trained or untrained)
- the quality of the interactions of staff with children (for example, caring or uncaring, warm or cold, friendly or hostile)
- the history of reports of maltreatment at the facility (for example, no prior reports or several prior reports)

The following signs indicate that the child care facility or institution may be deficient in caring for children (Koralek, 1992).

1. The children do not seem healthy, well cared for, or well supervised.
2. The physical condition of the building(s) is poor.
3. The facility is overcrowded.
4. There have been several prior reports of maltreatment, some of which have been substantiated.
5. The staff is uncooperative.
6. Some areas of the facility are off limits to the investigators.
7. The staff yells or screams at the children.
8. The staff grabs or jerks the children.
9. The staff fails to let the children speak.
10. The staff controls activities without allowing the children to choose what they want to do or what materials they want to use.
11. The staff insists that the children be obedient and not question authority.

12. The staff shows satisfaction over winning a power struggle with the children.
13. The staff has no sense of humor.
14. The staff has unrealistic expectations for the children's stages of development.
15. The staff uses negative techniques to guide the children's behavior.
16. The staff is unwilling to play with the children.
17. The staff fails to comfort children who are distressed.
18. The staff members do not support each other.
19. The staff is not comfortable in caring for young children and seems not to enjoy the children.
20. The staff uses the same disciplinary technique with all children and in every situation.
21. The staff watches the children from a distance rather than interacting with them.
22. The staff takes unusual or inappropriate interest in one child.
23. The staff shows no respect for the children's rights to privacy or their refusal to be touched by an adult.

Evaluating Family Foster Homes

The guidelines for evaluating child care facilities and institutions and for observing staff behaviors also pertain, for the most part, to family foster homes—or to any home, for that matter. Let's now consider how faulty evaluations of foster homes may occur when homes are certified and recertified and when children with special problems are placed in foster homes.

Certification.   Agency representatives should conduct an in-depth home evaluation *before* they place a child in a foster home. If they fail to obtain critical information and ask critical questions, they may make a wrong placement. The following two cases illustrate how superficial home studies failed to uncover serious problems (McFadden & Ryan, 1991).

CASE 23-5. MRS. Q

Mrs. Q, the single parent of an adolescent daughter, had two adult sons living out of the home. One was a drug dealer, and the other was in a halfway house for the mentally ill. Both of these men were in and out of the home regularly, but the agency did not know of their existence until the mentally ill son was accused of beating a 10-year-old foster boy for disobeying Mrs. Q. In this case, the social worker did not attempt to learn about the adult children and the extent to which their current life situations might reflect either unperceived difficulties in the foster family or environmental risks for children who might be placed there.

CASE 23-6. MR. L

Mr. L was a divorced single father who specialized in taking care of school-aged boys under the age of 12 years. He was noted for his devotion to the children. The agency staff was shocked when allegations of sexual abuse were filed. Only later did they learn that he never saw the children of either of his marriages, having lost custody in both divorces due to the children's allegations that he had sexually abused them. The agency staff should have contacted all children living out of the home as part of the home study. If, as required in many states, they had required fingerprinting and a thorough police check of Mr. L, they would have discovered that he was a pedophile. Had the staff been adequately trained, they might have recognized several indicators of his problem. (p. 214, with changes in notation)

Recertification. When a foster home is being considered for recertification, all members of the family, including children placed in the home, should be interviewed and observed (McFadden & Ryan, 1991). The social worker should note and assess changes in family composition, verify the family's economic resources, discuss health issues and verify medical problems, if necessary, and reassess the healthfulness and safety of the home environment. In addition, all earlier family studies and recertifications should be reviewed to assess changes in the family.

The following case illustrates what can happen when the recertification study is inadequate (McFadden & Ryan, 1991).

CASE 23-7. MRS. R

Mrs. R had been a foster care mother for over 12 years when a charge of neglect was filed. The prior recertification study noted severe problems in housekeeping. Earlier studies had indicated that Mrs. R was an immaculate housekeeper and was a nurturing, high-energy woman. After her husband's untimely death 5 years ago, the quality of home care declined. Mrs. R became particularly upset after her husband's death when twin boys who were staying with her were returned to their parents against her advice. Mrs. R had reported headaches that would force her to lie down. However, the agency continued to place preschool children in her home, despite Mrs. R's statement that she was getting "too old to chase little ones around." Following the death of Mrs. R's only daughter, the licensing social worker noted her depression and the poor housekeeping. A homemaker was sent to help her clean the house. Mrs. R continued to complain of health problems and became more upset each time a child left. Finally, a complaint of neglect was substantiated due to her poor housekeeping and the chronically dirty condition of the children. (p. 216, with changes in notation)

Placement of special children. Placement of a child with special needs in a foster home requires special care (McFadden & Ryan, 1991). If an agency is desperate to place a child with special needs, it may ask a foster family to take the child even though the family is not prepared for the responsibility. In such cases, the child may be maltreated. Foster families that take children with special needs should receive training and ongoing support to help them with the care of the children.

It is ironic that children removed from their families and placed in foster care for their own protection should be further subjected to maltreatment in a system which calls itself child welfare. It is also ironic that competent and dedicated foster families who give fully of themselves to help children should be suspect.

—Emily Jean McFadden and Patricia Ryan

RISK ASSESSMENT

Your decisions about whether a child has been maltreated and whether the child is at risk for further maltreatment are two of the most important ones you will ever make as a human services provider, mental health professional, or law enforcement officer. What you decide will be critical for the health and welfare of the child and his or her family. An incorrect decision may have extremely harmful consequences.

Social workers, clinicians, and law enforcement officers working with cases of child maltreatment or in Child Protective Services must walk a fine line between protecting children and protecting the rights of parents and other people. If they leave the child (and possibly siblings) in a setting dangerous for his or her development, the child may suffer irreparable harm. But removing the child also has costs. Separation from the family may cause the child to feel anxious, unworthy, guilty, rejected, and unloved. Questioning the actions and motives of parents, relatives, or others suspected of maltreatment may cause grief and harm to those who are innocent. Any actions you take (or recommend) that have serious consequences for the child, family, and others must be based on a careful analysis of all of the available information. Where needed, unimpeachable forensic procedures should be used in the investigation (for example, blood typing, semen analysis, and so forth). *However, if you believe that the child is in danger, take immediate action to protect the child.*

Here is how one father felt about being falsely accused of child sexual abuse (Jim, 1991, reprinted with permission of Jim).

CASE 23-8. JIM

Jim, a 20-year Navy veteran, and his wife, Denise, learned that Alicia, their 8-year-old daughter, had been brutally raped and sodomized. The father was accused of the crime, convicted, sent to jail, and the child was taken away from the family. Approximately two and one-half years later, DNA evidence overlooked by police investigators in the initial investigations proved that he didn't rape his daughter. Jim (whose last name is not being used to protect his privacy) was totally exonerated and the family—Jim, Denise, Joshua (age 8) and Alicia (11)—were reunited. This is Jim's perspective on his family's ordeal.

On Friday, San Diego County gave me back a shred of my dignity. I was cleared of all charges relating to the brutal rape of my daughter 2½ years ago. At last, I won the battle, but I lost the war.

There were not apologies for separating me from my daughter for 2½ precious years of her life.

For badgering Alicia for 13 months until she finally said "my daddy did it," just to please them.

No apologies for sending my wife to the brink of suicide and sentencing me to a personal hell.

No apologies for the more than $125,000 in legal fees that robbed me and my parents of our life savings.

No apologies for the smearing of my reputation.

For overlooking crucial evidence that proved beyond a doubt I was innocent.

For letting the real rapist, a known child abuser, go unpunished.

No apologies for making my entire family outcasts in my community where my neighbor's child was forbidden to play with the "son of a pervert."

No apologies for the sleepless nights, the accusatory stares, the unending tears, the strain on our family, the doubts planted in the minds of best friends.

No apologies from the district attorney, the social workers, the therapists. I have grown to expect none....

They fear no one because, when threatened by exposure, they invoke the holy words, "in the best interest of the child," wrap the cloak of confidentiality around themselves and promptly go on about their business. The irony and utter hypocrisy of this holy writ can only be fully appreciated when you hear it applied to your child, as I have, solely to protect the livelihood and reputation of those who have actually caused the most damage. (p. B7)

(*Editorial note.* Jim sued the therapist, San Diego County, and other organizations and settled for approximately $3.7 million, of which $1 million came from the therapist.)

Risk Assessment Protocols— New York State Model

Since the 1980s, several states in the United States have developed risk assessment protocols. Popular protocols include those developed by the states of Illinois, Washington, and New York. Risk assessment protocols are valuable because they allow you to rate the degree of deficit, pathology, or risk in several key areas that affect the child. Risk assessment rating scales are particularly useful in the early stages of training because they provide a framework for recognizing critical case factors (Gaudin, 1993). However, they should not be used in a rigid manner to make decisions about individual cases. *You always must use clinical judgment based on all the factors and information available to you.* In this part of the chapter, the New York State protocol will be used as an example of a structured risk assessment procedure.

According to the *New York State Risk Assessment and Services Planning Model—Field Guide* and The User Manual Series of the National Center on Child Abuse and

Neglect (DePanfilis & Salus, 1992), you may have to take immediate action to protect the child when you find any of the following conditions, either in the child or in the caregiver:

THE CHILD

- *Child is experiencing life-threatening conditions.*
- *Child has multiple injuries.*
- *Child needs immediate medical attention.*
- *Child is alone or abandoned and not competent to provide his or her own care.*
- *Child is suicidal.*
- *Child is justifiably fearful of people who are living in or frequenting the home.*
- *Child's physical living conditions are hazardous and may cause serious harm.*
- *Child's safety is of immediate concern.*

THE CAREGIVER

- *Caregiver's behavior is violent or out of control.*
- *Caregiver caused serious physical harm to the child or has made a plausible threat.*
- *Caregiver has not provided or will not provide sufficient supervision to protect the child from potentially serious harm.*
- *Caregiver has not met or is unable to meet the child's immediate needs for food, clothing, shelter, and/or medical care.*
- *Caregiver has previously maltreated a child, and the severity of the maltreatment or the caregiver's prior response to the incident suggests that the child's safety may be an immediate concern.*
- *Caregiver's drug or alcohol use seriously affects his or her ability to supervise, protect, or care for the child.*

In evaluating whether the child is at risk, consider the nature of the symptoms (including type, severity, duration, and cause), situational factors, and the interaction between the symptoms and situational factors. For example, factors that may place the child at risk for maltreatment include the following:

- family poverty
- poorly educated parents
- authoritarian child-rearing practices
- family insularity and social isolation
- parents who suffer from depression
- parents who abuse substances
- parents who are unemployed
- domestic violence in the home
- parents who were maltreated as children
- family environment that is in constant crisis and chaos
- little organization or structure to daily routines in the family (for example, meals are unplanned, and young children in the family roam the neighborhood unsupervised)

These factors are likely to cause stress in the family and influence the caregiver's ability to care for the children in the family (Pianta et al., 1989). *Of course, the presence of any or all of these factors does not indicate that the child has been maltreated.* However, it does provide warning signs, indicating that the child may be *at risk* for maltreatment.

Risk assessment protocols can aid you in making a decision, but they also require you to make judgments. Ideally, we should know the reliability and validity of each risk assessment protocol currently in use, but we don't.

Appendix D presents the eight sections of the New York State risk assessment protocol most pertinent to risk assessment. Here is a brief overview of those sections.

1. *Safety Assessment* covers several behaviors or conditions that indicate whether the child may be in immediate danger of serious harm.
2. *Caretaker Influence* covers six factors that indicate the likelihood of future maltreatment.
3. *Child Influence* covers five factors that describe the child's behavior and mental and physical development.
4. *Family Influence* covers five factors associated with family functioning and the family's ability to take care of the child.
5. *Intervention Influence* covers the caregiver's motivation and the caregiver's cooperation with the intervention.
6. *Abuse/Maltreatment Influence* covers the perpetrator's access to the child, the perpetrator's sense of responsibility, the severity of the maltreatment, and other maltreatment committed by the perpetrator.
7. *Risk Assessment Analysis* has spaces for the interviewer to write an analysis of important features of the case.
8. *Case Risk Rating Guidelines* requires an overall risk rating for the child.

The New York State risk assessment protocol uses quantitative and qualitative procedures, as both are equally important in conducting a risk assessment. The quantitative procedures require the use of checklists to make ratings. The qualitative procedures require summarization of the key risk assessment elements of the case. The risk scales alone are insufficient to formulate case decisions and intervention plans. Risk assessment protocols bring some uniformity to the assessment process, help you focus on relevant variables, ensure that you do not overlook important variables, allow you to compare your judgments across several cases, and allow you to compare your judgments with those of others. However, you should use all available sources of information in making a risk assessment.

Ongoing Risk Assessment

Risk assessment is not a one-time process. *Constant monitoring of the child and family is necessary until you believe that there is no more danger to the child.* Failure to take appropriate action may prove fatal to the child, as shown in the following incident reported by the Associated Press.

REPORT ON TOT'S DEATH FAULTS SYSTEM— ILLINOIS BOY, 3, RETURNED TO CARE OF MENTALLY ILL MOM

Chicago—The tragedy of 3-year-old Joseph Wallace began before he was born. It ended April 19 with his hanging, allegedly at the hands of his mentally ill mother.

Six months later, a task force looking into how Illinois' juvenile justice system failed Joseph said similar tragedies are possible. "It would be comfortable to believe the facts in this case are so exceptional that such cases are not likely to happen again," the task force said in a report to Cook County's chief circuit judge. "That hope is unfounded."

The report recommends a complete overhaul of a system that allowed four judges to remove Joseph from foster care and return him each time to his mother, who has been charged with murder.... The chief judge, Harry Comerford, said he will reassign 10 probation officers to serve as investigators for judges hearing abuse and neglect cases.

The task force report alternates between legal jargon and chilling biographical details on the life of 28-year-old Amanda Wallace, the suicidal woman who gave birth to Joseph on July 29, 1989, while she was in a mental health center. She had been institutionalized repeatedly since childhood. At age 2, she set her mother's Chicago apartment on fire; a brother died of smoke inhalation. In 1974, the state removed her from her mother's custody because of physical abuse. Later, the report said, she would abuse herself— swallowing broken glass, screws, and batteries.

And finally, the task force said, she fatally abused Joseph. The mother allegedly stood the boy on a chair, wrapped an electrical cord around his neck, tied the other end of the cord to a door and kicked the chair out from under him. (Associated Press, *San Diego Union-Tribune,* Nov. 12, 1993, p. A-36)

Exercise 23-2. Risk Assessment

Part 1

Read the following hypothetical case. Then evaluate it, using a copy of the New York State Risk Assessment and Services Planning Model—Field Guide shown in Appendix D. If you are not sure how to use a scale, review the relevant part of the field guide. Some scales may not be applicable to the case. In that event, write "N/A" ("Not Applicable") in the space below the name of the scale. If one parent or child would be rated high on a particular scale, please record the high rating. The case was obtained from John Nasuti (personal communication, May 1994).

The Green Family
Investigative Summary

Referral Source: School Nurse
Family: Father, unemployed, age 30
Mother, housewife, age 32
Michael, age 13 (from mother's previous marriage)
Billie, age 8
Sammie, age 4

Referral

Child Protective Services received the following child neglect referral from the school nurse because Michael, age 13 years, and Billie, age 8 years, attended school in clothes that were often muddy, torn, and never clean. Their faces were usually caked with dirt, and their body odor was extremely bad. The nurse stated that the children were absent from school at least three days a week. The school nurse said she had talked to the mother about the problem several times before, but it didn't seem to help matters. Mrs. Green told the nurse that the children were old enough to take care of themselves, and, if they seemed dirty, it was their own fault.

Social Worker Assessment

Before going to the school, the social worker from Child Protective Services contacted the records department and discovered that there had been two prior substantiated referrals for neglect. In addition, records showed that the children had been removed temporarily from their home. Two years ago, Mr. Green had lost control and had hit the children with a cutting board. As a result, the children were placed in the Emergency Crisis Center and later foster care for eight months. A second referral was made requesting temporary foster placement for the children when Mr. and Mrs. Green had left the children alone for two days. The children were placed in a foster home for another six months. The social worker went to the Greens' home to interview the family. The following is a brief account of what the social worker recorded in the case record after several meetings with the family.

Household Adequacy

The Green family lived in an extremely rural and isolated part of the state. Their community has a population of less than 1,000 people, and most residents have to travel a minimum of 30 miles to go shopping or receive assistance for most personal needs. Both parents were unemployed and spent their time around the house listening to the radio or doing errands away from the house. They had no telephone.

The social worker made three home visits before she was able to make contact with the parents. During the first two visits to the home, the social worker found the children in the care of Michael, the 13-year-old boy. Michael was hyperactive and could not say when his parents would be home. His manner of speech and level of maturity seemed to be those of a much younger child. He appeared to have attention-deficit/hyperactivity disorder. Michael stated that he took care of the kids three or four days a week for five to six hours each time while his parents were out. During the second visit to the home, the social worker found the youngest child wandering down the road by himself. She noticed that Michael and Billie had been trying to start a fire in the backyard. This time, the social worker left a note asking the parents to please contact her immediately.

The third time the social worker visited the home, Mrs. Green initially refused to let the social worker enter the house. The social worker was not actually invited into the house until she insisted that if she wasn't invited in to see the condition of the home and discuss the referral she'd have to call the police.

Once the social worker entered the home, she noticed that the living room was cluttered with dirty clothes and that there were piles of old trash left everywhere. In the bathroom, the toilet was stopped up, and there was a large pile of dirty clothes in the bathtub. None of the beds had sheets on them, and there were clothes strewn all over the floors, including the hallway.

In the kitchen, there was mold in the sink, and the stench was so bad that the social worker nearly gagged. The stove was not in working condition because old food was caked onto its surface. The kitchen cupboards were virtually empty and contained only small amounts of "junk" food. Mrs. Green reported that the kids often went hungry. She stated that she sometimes had to hide food so the children couldn't sneak into the refrigerator and eat it all. The two oldest children were extremely underweight for their ages.

The children's room was cluttered with construction materials that were left behind when the family tried to build an additional bedroom for the boys. These materials blocked the entrance to the room so that you had to climb over them just to enter the room. There were large pieces of broken glass and nails lying all over the floor. Mrs. Green stated that she didn't think they would be able to finish the room now that Mr. Green was not working. She added that they had applied for assistance with the Housing Authority, but that she was told the program had run out of money and was closing down.

Children

The children seemed hesitant to answer any questions. They kept their distance from the social worker, always looking toward their mother before they answered any questions. When they did answer, their bodies became tense and trembled. They constantly gave conflicting answers, looking at their mother each time. At one point, Mrs. Green screamed at the children to be seated or she would beat them with their father's belt or lock them in their room without dinner. The 4-year-old's left foot appeared to be swollen and infected. When asked about his condition, the mother simply replied that he had cut his foot three days ago playing near the construction materials in the bedroom and that she did not take him to the hospital because she thought it wasn't that serious.

When asked about her children's behavior, Mrs. Green responded that their behavior was terrible, and they never did what they were told to do. She claimed that it was difficult to get the children to go to school, and, on two occasions, Michael was expelled from school for fighting. She stated that Michael lives in a world of his own and keeps to himself. He has no friends and doesn't communicate well with the other children at school.

She further stated that one day last week the children had a food and water fight in the house. One of the children (Billie) had taken a water hose into the house and turned it on to splash his brother. In addition, Billie had been stealing money from his father, at least once a week for the past six months, and giving some of it to Michael for video games. One time, this behavior made Mr. Green so mad that he lost his control and spanked the children with a cutting board. He didn't mean to hurt the children, but he had hit them so hard that he broke Michael's right arm. She stated that things weren't getting any better around the house now that Mr. Green was unemployed and spending more time at home.

Parents

Mr. Green said that his father used to beat him with a belt every time he misbehaved. Mr. Green claims he has reoccurring nightmares about these beatings and can still see the anger in his father's face. He further stated that because his parents used beatings with a strap or paddle when he was a child, he thought that it was appropriate to use the same type of physical punishment as a way of keeping his children in line.

Mr. Green has been unemployed for over two years. Being unemployed used to frustrate him so much that on one occasion, when he had been drinking, he lost control of his temper. He paddled the children so hard with a cutting board that he broke Michael's arm and split Billie's lip so badly that it required several stitches to heal. Mr. Green appeared to become tense and restless every time he mentioned being fired from his job for fighting with another employee.

When asked if there were any family members or friends living in the area who would be willing to help with housework or care for the children, Mrs. Green responded that the only family member left in the community was her older sister, whom she hasn't spoken to for more than five years. She claimed that her sister in the past has tried to tell her how to take care of her children.

When the social worker asked the parents if they were willing to learn some new discipline methods, they became angry, claiming they knew how to take care of their children and didn't need some agency telling them what to do. Because of their rural location, parenting classes and therapeutic day care services are not readily available, but homemaker services are available on a monthly basis. When a homemaker service was offered to Mr. and Mrs. Green, they told the social worker to go "jump in the lake."

Part 2

After you have made your ratings, answer the following questions.

1. Did you have any problems making your ratings or understanding the scales? If so, which scales were difficult to use, and why do you think you had difficulty making some ratings?
2. What additional information would you have liked to have in the case to help you make your ratings?
3. How could the scales and the field guide be improved so that they could be used more effectively?
4. What were the risks to the social worker in this case, and what is her potential for burnout?

Now compare your ratings with those of your classmates and with those of nine Child Protective Services social workers, who also read the case and completed the scales (ratings to follow). How do your ratings compare with your classmates' ratings and with those of the Child Protective Services social workers? Which items show most disagreement? What are the possible reasons for the disagreements?

Safety Assessment:

1. 5 Y, 4 N	5. 9 Y, 0 N	9. 9 Y, 0 N
2. 9 Y, 0 N	6. 9 Y, 0 N	10. 0 Y, 9 N
3. 7 Y, 2 N	7. 9 Y, 0 N	11. 3 Y, 6 N
4. 0 Y, 9 N	8. 9 Y, 0 N	12. —

Caretaker Influence:

1. Five raters gave 4, three raters gave 3, and one rater gave 2.
2. One rater gave 3, seven raters gave 2, and one rater gave 9.
3. Two raters gave 4, and seven raters gave 3.
4. Seven raters gave 3, and two raters gave 2.
5. Eight raters gave 0, and one rater gave 9.
6. Two raters gave 3, three raters gave 2, one rater gave 1, two raters gave 0, and one rater gave 9.

Child Influence:

1. Six raters gave 3, and three raters gave 2.
2. Four raters gave 3, and five raters gave 2.
3. Four raters gave 3, and five raters gave 2.
4. Three raters gave 3, four raters gave 2, one rater gave 1, and one rater gave 9.
5. Two raters gave 4, one rater gave 3, one rater gave 2, three raters gave 1, one rater gave 0, and one rater gave 9.

Family Influence:

1. Three raters gave 4, three raters gave 2, and three raters gave 9.
2. Three raters gave 4, and six raters gave 3.
3. Nine raters gave 4.
4. Seven raters gave 4, and two raters gave 3.
5. Four raters gave 4, and five raters gave 3.

Intervention Influence:

1. Three raters gave 4, and six raters gave 3.
2. Eight raters gave 4, and one rater gave 3.

Abuse/Maltreatment Influence:

1. Six raters gave 4, and three raters gave 3.
2. Four raters gave 3, and five raters gave 2.
3. Eight raters gave 3, and one rater gave 2.
4. Three raters gave 4, four raters gave 3, and two raters gave 2.

Note that for the *Safety Assessment* scale, the Child Protective Services social workers generally gave similar ratings on items 2 through 10. However, on item 1 and item 11, there were disagreements. The social workers were split on whether the caretaker's behavior was violent or out of control and whether the caretaker's drug or alcohol use seriously affected his or her ability to supervise, protect, or care for the child.

For the *Caretaker Influence* scale, the social workers generally agreed on the first five items, but they did not agree on item 6 (whether the caretaker had the mental capacity to take care of the child).

For the *Child Influence* scale, the social workers generally agreed on the first four items, but they did not agree on item 5 (the severity of the child's physical illness).

For the *Family Influence* scale, the social workers generally agreed on items 2 through 5, but they did not agree on item 1 (the extent of domestic violence).

For the *Intervention Influence* scale, the social workers essentially agreed on both items.

For the *Abuse/Maltreatment Influence* scale, the social workers generally agreed on the first three items, but they did not agree on item 4 (the history of maltreatment committed by the caretakers).

Do you have an explanation for the social workers' patterns of agreements and disagreements? What about the case may have led to their patterns of agreements and disagreements?

INTERVENTIONS

The ability of the child, parents, siblings, and known offender to recover from the maltreatment in large part will depend on how each was functioning *before* the maltreatment occurred. Other factors that will affect the recovery process include the age of the child, the type of maltreatment, the length of the maltreatment, the prior relationship between the child and the offender, their relationship after the maltreatment, the supports available to each individual involved, and the court orders. Let's look first at intervention efforts and the court and then at interventions with maltreated children, their families, and known offenders.

Intervention Efforts and the Court

After consultation with Child Protective Services and law enforcement personnel, as needed, and after a review of all the case material, the county district or state attorney will decide whether to petition the court for a hearing. Although the offender may be prosecuted criminally, this section considers only what may occur in juvenile courts. The purpose of the juvenile court is to determine whether the child was maltreated and to protect the child and help the family, whereas the purpose of the criminal court is to determine whether a crime has been committed and, if so, to punish the known offender for the wrongdoing.

Information needed by the court. Courts usually will want specific information from Child Protective Services in cases of child maltreatment. Table 23-5 lists some important questions about the family and child that the court will want answered. Answers to the court's questions, in part, will be based on information obtained during the interviews with the child, parents, alleged or known offenders, and other interested parties. Unfortunately, once the court becomes involved in a child maltreatment case, it may take months or even several years to resolve the case (Bishop, Murphy, Jellinek, & Quinn, 1992).

If you have information about the known offender, questions the courts typically will ask you to answer include the following (Burgess et al., 1978; Groth, 1979):

1. What were some reasons for the known offender's actions?
2. How dangerous is the known offender to the victim or to other children?
3. How likely is it that the known offender will repeat the offense?
4. Under what environmental conditions is the known offender likely to repeat the offense?
5. What is the likelihood that these environmental conditions will occur or reoccur?
6. What should be done with the known offender?
7. What can be done to help the known offender?

To answer these and related questions, you need to conduct a thorough assessment, including a study of police and hospital records, court transcripts, and reports given by the child and witnesses of the maltreatment. In some cases, alleged offenders will admit to the allegations; in others, they may deny the allegations and request a trial. Evaluations of known or alleged offenders should be performed by highly trained professionals with expertise in forensic interviewing.

Possible decisions made by the court. After the court has heard the facts, it must decide first whether there is probable cause to believe that the facts alleged are true and then whether those facts, if true, constitute maltreatment under state statutes (Duquette, 1990). If the court decides that child maltreatment did occur, it will consider three important guidelines in making its decision: (a) *family autonomy,* (b) *the best interests of the child,* and (c) *the least detrimental alternative.* Although these guidelines are useful in helping the court make its decision, the court is not required to follow them.

Family autonomy refers to the rights of parents to raise their children as they deem appropriate, without intrusion of the state. This concept assumes that the child's best interests generally are most adequately provided for within the context of strong family ties....

The "best interests test," however, subordinates family autonomy when the state establishes that there is child abuse or neglect. In utilizing this test, the court compares the parental environment with existing alternatives and makes a judgment regarding which situation is more likely to promote the child's well-being....

In contrast to the "best interests test," the concept of the least detrimental alternative suggests that the court weigh its choices for child care on the basis of a realistic appraisal of existing resources rather than in the abstract with little direct knowledge of the specific alternative environments available. (Kamen & Gewirtz, 1989, p. 180)

The court may seek advice from Child Protective Services, law enforcement personnel, and clinicians involved in the case, through questions like the following (Plumer, 1992):

1. Is the child safe at home?
2. Does the child have a reasonable chance for growth and development in the home?
3. Are services available that can help the family alleviate the problems that led to the maltreatment? If so, who will provide the needed services?
4. What placement is available that best provides for the child's needs?
5. Who will monitor this placement?
6. When will a final decision be made about permanent resolution of the problem, such as reunion of the family, termination of parental rights, or some other plan?

The court then may decide to do one or more of the following (Duquette, 1990; Kamen & Gewirtz, 1989):

- return the child home immediately
- return the child home only if specific conditions are met

Table 23-5
Questions About the Family and Child That the Court Usually Will Want Answered in Cases of Child Maltreatment

Present Problem
1. What happened?
2. Where did it happen?
3. When did it happen?
4. Who was the offender?
5. How serious is the harm suffered by the child?
6. Does the child remain at risk for physical or emotional harm?
7. What are the options for protecting the child from further harm?

Family Background
8. What is the family composition?
9. What is the family's immediate home environment like?
10. Do the children in the family have adequate food, clothing, housing, medical care, guidance, and supervision?
11. Does the family have community support systems?
12. Have the parents made all reasonable efforts to protect the child in the home?
13. What are the parents like?
14. How do they get along?
15. What are their strengths and weaknesses?
16. Were they maltreated by their parents?
17. Do they have substance abuse problems?
18. Do they have psychiatric problems?
19. How are the other children in the family getting along?
20. Do the parents have a history of maltreating children?
21. Do the parents have a prior criminal history?
22. Have other children in the family been abused?
23. Can at least one parent protect the child from further maltreatment?

Child Background
24. What symptoms is the child showing?
25. What is the child like?
26. Is the child's development normal?
27. How is the child doing in school?
28. Have there been any changes in the child's behavior or school performance since the maltreatment began?
29. Does the child have any special needs?
30. What is the quality of the child's relationship with her or his parents, siblings, neighbors, and friends?
31. Has the child contributed to the abuse or neglect in any way?
32. (If so) In what way?

Opinion of Social Worker (or Clinician)
33. What do you think the major problems are at this point?

34. What are your recommendations?
35. What do the parents think the major problems are at this point?
36. What do the parents want done?
37. What does the child think the major problems are at this point?
38. What does the child want done?
39. What do other professionals involved in the case think the major problems are?
40. What do they think should be done?
41. How confident are you of your opinion?
42. What questions remain to be answered?
43. What other assessments or evaluations are needed to get a more comprehensive picture of the child and family?
44. Who should do them, and when can they be done?

Intervention Efforts
45. What should be done at this time?
46. Is the child's home safe, or can the home be made safe pending further proceedings?
47. What reasonable efforts can be made to prevent out-of-home placement?
48. If the child must be placed outside the home, what placement will be least disruptive to the child (such as sending the child to a relative, family friend, or neighbor who can care for her or him)?
49. What would be the most family-like setting (often referred to as the "least-restrictive setting")?
50. What steps can be taken to ensure that the child's normal life pattern is disrupted as little as possible?
51. Will the parents be permitted to visit the child?
52. (If yes) Under what conditions?
53. Will the child be permitted to visit the family?
54. (If yes) Under what conditions?
55. Will services be provided for the family?
56. (If yes) What kinds of services?
57. For how long will the temporary placement be necessary?

Child's Needs and Desires
58. What questions does the child have about the court process?
59. What does the child think about the options that have been discussed?
60. What does the child want to see happen as a result of the court proceedings?
61. Where does the child want to live now?
62. What other preferences does the child have about placement, visitation, school, and so on?
63. What other questions does the child have?

Source: Adapted from Duquette (1990).

- require that the family be involved in services intended to alleviate or prevent future maltreatment
- adjourn the case for a specified time but place the family under active treatment (time frames vary, depending on individual state policy)
- place the child under the formal supervision of Child Protective Services or another agency
- place the child in the custody of the child welfare authority
- give a relative or other interested party temporary custody of the child (usually physical, not legal, custody)
- issue an order of protection to safeguard the custodial parent or child from actions of another person
- return the child to his or her family on a certain date only if specific conditions are met
- arrange daily, weekly, overnight, or weekend visitations (supervised or unsupervised) only if specific conditions are met
- sever parental rights (it usually takes a minimum of six months of court supervision before the court will sever parental rights, and generally there must be parental abandonment, lack of cooperation with treatment, or failure to provide an adequate home)

You may be asked to testify as an expert witness in a case of child maltreatment. To prepare for your testimony, review the material in Chapter 6.

Interventions with Maltreated Children and Their Families

After you complete your evaluation, you may need to develop an intervention plan. Intervention plans may focus on the following:

- helping the child cope with the maltreatment
- enhancing the child's development
- reducing the factors contributing to the family's vulnerability
- decreasing the likelihood that stressful events will occur
- helping family members understand and deal with their own feelings about the maltreatment
- improving the family's coping mechanisms

Information needed to formulate an intervention plan.   You want to review all available information in formulating your intervention plan. Answering the questions in Tables 23-1, 23-2, and 23-4 will help you accomplish this task. Information about the following areas will be particularly crucial (Elton, 1988):

1. *The maltreatment.* Consider when the maltreatment took place, over what period, the type of maltreatment, the severity of the maltreatment, what adults were involved in the maltreatment, whether other children were involved, and so forth. Also consider what you know about the disclosure, such as to whom the disclosure was made, when it was

made, what happened as a result of the disclosure, and what the family did as a result of the disclosure.

2. *The victim.* Consider the effects of the maltreatment on the victim's current functioning; the victim's health, developmental, and educational history; the victim's relationship with parents, siblings, and extended family; and so forth. What was the reaction of the victim after the disclosure was made?

3. *The perpetrator.* Consider the perpetrator's relationship to the child, age, background, previous history of maltreating children, reaction to being accused (for example, accepting responsibility, scapegoating or blaming the victim, anger, hostility, or denial), and so forth. Also consider the type of maltreatment engaged in by the perpetrator, as well as the method used to induce the child to keep the maltreatment secret (if any).

4. *The family.* Consider the household and the family members, including members of the extended family. What are the family's supports, interpersonal relationships, communication patterns, roles, and so forth? Consider any history either parent may have of being maltreated, of experiencing violence in his or her own family, and of substance use and abuse. Evaluate the home environment, especially its suitability for raising children. What were the reactions of the family members after the disclosure was made? Consider who cares for the children, custody arrangements (if any), and visitation rights. Also consider each family member's views about the maltreatment—whether it occurred, why it may have occurred, and whose responsibility it was to protect the child from the abuse.

Formulating an intervention plan.   You want to develop intervention plans for the maltreated child *and* the entire family. If only the child is seen in therapy, the parents may not be able to deal with changes in the child's behavior. Therefore, the mother, father, and siblings also should receive services.

In formulating an intervention plan, consider the structure of the family, family dynamics, the family's resources, availability of extended family members, changes needed in the parents and family, interventions needed by the family, agencies or practitioners available to provide services, ability of the family to pay for services, and the individuals in the family who need the services. You want to get the victim to resume his or her usual activities as quickly as possible and to get the nonsuspect family members to support the victim (Burge, 1983). Do this by encouraging open expression of feelings by the family members, providing education about the maltreatment, encouraging the family to listen to and respect the victim's feelings, and allowing and encouraging the victim to reestablish his or her autonomy. Recognize, however, that some family members may be suffering from their own crisis precipitated by the maltreatment. You will need to consider how the family structure has changed and how the family should mobilize its strengths to help the maltreated victim.

Your intervention plan also might include helping the parents (a) understand normal child development, (b) develop skills in observing their child's growth and development, (c) set realistic goals for their child and themselves, (d) plan activities to help them reach their goals, (e) cope better with feelings of anxiety, hostility, and depression, and (f) develop the family's resources. These and related activities may come under a "family preservation plan" involving the provision of services, including emotional support, needed to help the family function more adequately.

Removal of the child from the home. On the basis of your evaluation, you may recommend that the child be removed from the home. This is one of the most serious steps that you can take. "Only the decision to terminate parental rights has more serious implications" (Jones, 1993, p. 252). Removing the child even temporarily from the home may stigmatize the family and threaten the parent-child relationship, particularly with young children. *Consider removing the child from the home primarily when the child is at risk for further maltreatment or is in immediate danger.*

The potential for further maltreatment is greater when the offender (Jones, 1993)

- is living at home and has committed a serious offense
- refuses to acknowledge the maltreatment
- has a history of abusing the child or other children
- is psychologically or medically incompetent to be a parent
- refuses to meet minimal caregiving expectations
- has multiple problems
- is experiencing severe environmental stress
- has a life style that conflicts with being a parent
- or is unable to hold a job

You also should consider removing the child from the home when the nonsuspect parent cannot keep the child safe from the abusing parent. Any one or combination of these factors may indicate that the parent is unable to fulfill his or her parenting responsibilities. In 1994, 35 states reported that 126,117 victims of child maltreatment were removed from their homes (National Center on Child Abuse and Neglect, 1996). This figure represents about 15% of the victims of child maltreatment in these states.

When a parent or caregiver is the perpetrator, consider allowing the child to remain at home (a) when the maltreatment was minor and the parent poses no immediate danger to the child, (b) when the parent appears able to stop any further maltreatment, or (c) when the abusive parent has been removed from the home and the nonsuspect parent can take care of the child. One or more of the following conditions should be present if you are considering allowing the child to remain at home with the offending parent: The parent is remorseful, is nurturing, has a strong attachment to the child, and has a support system, and there is another person in the home not involved in the maltreatment who is mature and responsible and can monitor the situation (Jones, 1993).

When the perpetrator is someone other than the parents, there usually is little reason to remove the child from the home. Exceptions are when the perpetrator who is not a parent is living in the home, when the parents cannot protect the child from further maltreatment, and when the parents deny or minimize the maltreatment.

Surveys suggest that children younger than 6 years are likely to be removed from the home more frequently than adolescents (Jones, 1993). The theory is that adolescents are more able to take care of themselves. Removal is likely to be recommended when the adolescent is delinquent or has mental health problems or when the maltreatment was dangerous or life threatening to the adolescent.

Earlier in the chapter, you read about Joseph Wallace, who was killed by his mother; in retrospect, removal from the home was clearly necessary for the child's survival. The following newspaper report from the *Los Angeles Times* tells of a case in which a social service agency removed a child from his home when it should not have; however, the court rectified the situation (Maharaj, 1995).

COURT ASSAILS BOY'S REMOVAL FROM FAMILY

An appellate court has assailed Orange County's Social Services Agency for removing a 4-year-old boy from his home because his parents were poor housekeepers. The case involved a possibly autistic boy, identified as Paul E., who was placed in a foster home in May 1995 after social workers reported that his parents kept a messy house. Children are usually removed from their homes when they are seriously maltreated or when they face great harm.

The 4th District Court of Appeals criticized the social services agency for separating the boy from his home, holding that "mere chronic messiness in housekeeping" does not justify a child's removal from his parents. On a visit to the youngster's residence, social workers said they found a lamp socket with an electrical short, a propeller protruding from a boat outside the house, and a small child's plastic wading pool filled with dirty water in the backyard. But Justice David Sills said the hazards cited by the county agency were "trivial to the point of being pretextual…. A shorted lamp socket could occur in the White House," Justice Sills wrote for a unanimous three-judge panel. "Motorboats normally have propellers on them. Children's plastic wading pools do not come with filtration systems on them, and if they are filled with water for any amount of time, the water is going to get dirty. Worse hazards than these may be found on practically every farm in America," he continued. "If such conditions were sufficient for removal from the home, generations of Americans who grew up on farms and ranches would have spent their childhoods in foster care."

Justice Sills said the appellate panel was "not sympathetic" to the social service agency's concerns and recognized that removal of a child "represents perhaps the biggest stick the agency can wield in getting recalcitrant parents to clean up their act—in this case, by literally cleaning up their house…. While we certainly hope conditions improve in Paul's household, chronic messiness by itself and apart from any unsanitary conditions or resulting illness or accident is just not clear and convincing evidence" to remove the child, the court said. The petition by county social workers to place Paul in a foster home was initially approved by an Orange County

Superior Court judge. If the petition were upheld by the appellate court, the boy could have been permanently separated from his parents. (pp. A3, A32, with changes in notation)

Domestic violence in the home complicates the picture of child maltreatment (McKay, 1994). Instead of removing the children from homes where there is domestic violence, a better solution might be to remove the batterer from the home. Furthermore, when the mother is being battered or experiencing symptoms of posttraumatic stress disorder, it is difficult to assess her capacity to care for her children. In cases of domestic violence when the father (or partner) is the batterer, offer to arrange shelter services for the mother and children, if these services are needed. In a home where there is domestic violence, removing the children instead of the batterer may endanger the woman's life by increasing her vulnerability and isolating her from others (McKay, 1994).

Reuniting the family or terminating parental rights.

Once a child has been removed from the home, you will have to decide if and when he or she should return home. Here are some questions for you to consider:

1. How cooperative have the parents been in carrying out the intervention plan, assuming one has been required?
2. How successful have the parents been in meeting the goals of the intervention plan?
3. What problems did the child have before he or she was removed from the home?
4. How have these problems changed since the child left home?
5. If there are other children in the family, what problems do they have?
6. What would have to be different for the child to return home?
7. Have significant changes been made in the child's family?
8. In what way did the child's parents contribute to the child's problems?
9. If the parents have problems, how severe are their problems?
10. How would things be different if the parents' problems were resolved or diminished?
11. What new skills do the parents need to develop?
12. How would you go about helping the parents develop these skills?

Reunification may not be feasible if any of the following conditions are present (County of San Diego, 1992):

- the caregiver is actively psychotic, suicidal, and/or a danger to himself or herself or others
- the caregiver has psychotic delusions that involve the child
- the caregiver is of extremely low functioning, has no positive family support system, and is not capable of learning to care for the child
- the caregiver has a history of maltreatment that resulted in the death of a child

- the caregiver has Munchausen's Syndrome by Proxy (see Chapter 20)
- the caregiver inflicted physical trauma to the child that, if untreated, would cause permanent physical disfigurement, permanent physical disability, or death
- the caregiver inflicted severe internal injuries on the child, such as a subdural hematoma, perforated bowel, or ruptured liver
- the caregiver inflicted multiple or healing fractures in young infants
- the caregiver is responsible for the child's failure to thrive
- the caregiver deliberately poisoned the child
- the caregiver inflicted burns on the child for punitive purposes
- the caregiver sexually abused the child and, in the process, caused significant bleeding, deep bruising, significant external or internal swelling, bone fracture, or unconsciousness
- the caregiver engaged in sadistic abuse of the child

The following report in the *San Diego Union* describes the tragic consequences of returning an infant to a dangerous environment which proved to be lethal (Callahan, 1994).

JUDGE SENTENCES PARENTS
FOR KILLING TOT, RAPS AGENCY

The slaying of "Baby George," who was beaten to death by his parents, so outraged a San Diego judge yesterday that the jurist blasted the county agency charged with protecting children. The judge's critical remarks came after an emotional hearing in which he sentenced the child's parents to 15-years-to-life prison terms.

Although both parents blamed each other for their 19-month-old son's death, the judge placed part of the responsibility on bureaucratic procedures. Particularly upsetting was that Child Protective Services workers returned the infant to the couple after taking him away from them at birth because the mother was on probation for abusing another of the couple's children. "Not only did his parents let [him down], the system also let him down. The system, in my opinion, presently places far too much emphasis on protecting the rights of the parents and on reunification at almost any cost and places far too little emphasis on protecting the child and on doing what is best for the child. It is all too clear that the cost of reunification in this case was far too high," the judge said.

According to medical testimony, the infant died of brain damage and internal injuries suffered during daily beatings over the last two months of his life. The child had more than a dozen broken bones in various stages of healing at the time of his death.

The director of Child Protective Services said that this case is "a heartache for the worker involved and the entire department. The first consideration of a social worker should always be the safety of the child. If the worker feels the child is in imminent danger, the child should be removed. However, that is often a difficult call to make. There is an old adage that it takes a whole village to raise a child and I think it also takes that whole village to protect its children." (adapted from pp. B-1, B-4)

Courts sometimes will recommend involuntary termination of parental rights, and parents sometimes will request voluntary termination of their parental rights (Kaye & Westman, 1991).

The voluntary termination of parental rights can provide relief for overtaxed parents who make this painful decision in their children's interests. The involuntary termination of parental rights can relieve parental guilt, because an external authority has made the decision. For the child, the benefits are early adoption and the avoidance of an uncertain future resulting from multiple foster placements. The careful and methodical assessment of parenting capacities provides a structure for formulating treatment goals and monitoring progress. This saves anguish, prolonged indecisiveness, and futile efforts. Last, for society, facilitating the adoption of abused and neglected children reduces the ultimate burden on everyone imposed by "children of the state." (p. 264)

In the following case, a social services worker helped a parent enhance her parenting skills but still recommended termination of parental rights because of the best interests of the children (Kaye & Westman, 1991).

CASE 23-9. KATHY

One-year-old Kathy was brought to an emergency room after being dropped on her head by her 23-year-old mother's live-in boyfriend, Mr. G. Kathy had two sisters, who were 4 and 5 years old, respectively. Each child was fathered by a different man, none of whom was married to the mother. Shortly after Kathy returned home from the hospital, a neighbor reported Mr. G to the police, alleging that he sexually abused the three girls. He was subsequently arrested and convicted. At that time, all three children were removed from the home and placed in foster care.

Investigation by the Department of Social Services revealed grossly inadequate food, clothing, shelter, and supervision. Kathy's 5-year-old sister provided supervision and guidance for the two younger children and was called "mom" by her 4-year-old sister. A physical examination revealed that Kathy was filthy, anemic, and malnourished, and that she had feces in her vagina. The children were placed in a foster home.

The mother denied that there were any problems at home and wished to have her children returned home. The Department of Social Services recommended that the mother receive a psychological evaluation, homemaker services, counseling, and parent training with indefinite foster placement of the children. Over the next 1-½ years, numerous specialized services were offered to the mother. After a few meetings, she typically dismissed the services, saying that she "knew everything already." Despite her claims, however, she made few, if any, improvements. The Department of Social Services filed for the termination of her parental rights. The attorney for the mother fought this recommendation, claiming that the mother was an unfortunate person who was being unfairly punished by society.

After 6 months of therapy, with the children in foster care and the possibility of an involuntary termination of her parental rights facing her, the mother stopped drinking, solidified her relationship with her boyfriend, and began to look for employment. Still, her parenting skills remained grossly inadequate. When the children came for a supervised home visit, she smiled and greeted them verbally but made no physical contact with them. Mr. G watched cartoons on television and did not acknowledge the children's presence or interact with

them during the visit. The children appeared wary of him and stayed away from him. The mother's only words were instructions to the children such as "Eat your vegetables." When the children left, there were no good-byes and no expressions of parting from the mother. Mr. G continued watching television. After a subsequent unsupervised visit, the 4-year-old had an unexplained burn on her hand.

Because of the mother's failure to improve her parenting skills in spite of vigorous treatment efforts, the child advocacy team decided to pursue involuntary termination of her parental rights. Several dramatic last-minute occurrences followed, including the mother's failure to retain legal counsel until a few days before the scheduled hearing. Her first attorney resigned from the case soon after the team was formed. Because of her tardiness in pursuing new legal aid, she was refused representation by the Public Defender. Her initial attorney agreed to take up the case again. He encouraged her to terminate voluntarily her rights to all three children, which she agreed to do. She apparently recognized that the responsibility of raising three young children would jeopardize the progress she had made in improving her personal life adjustment. (adapted from pp. 262–263)

What would maltreated children say about reuniting with their families if they were asked to speak for themselves? This question led Yarborough (1996b) to interview a 26-year-old woman, one of six children, who was raised by an abusive, schizophrenic mother. The woman's statement follows (with permission of Trin Yarborough).

Often when Mother would beat us or stomp on us or throw us downstairs, so that sometimes our faces would swell with bruises or we'd get concussions and broken bones, she'd tell us kids that Satan or demons made her do it. Other times she'd blame us, saying our badness had driven her to hurt us. "Look what you made me do!" she'd say when she'd look at our bodies covered with purple bruises.

Mom told us that when she was 13 she was at a baseball game when Satan spoke to her and told her he was taking over her body. She never again let anyone look into her eyes, because she believed they would see the Devil there. But from the time I was 3, she would make me stare into her eyes and ask me over and over if I could see the Devil staring back. She has scary, evil-looking, tormented greenish eyes, and as a child I believed I did see Satan there. I was terrified by all this, but never imagined that it wasn't a normal way of life because it was all I knew.

This is the story of my family and the theory of family reunification—keeping families together no matter what. My mother is a paranoid schizophrenic. Her first stint in a mental hospital came when she was 13, and she had her first baby when she was 15. An aunt adopted him and would never let Mom see him. Mom married at 18 and had four kids—my brother, me and my twin sisters—in less than three years before my Dad left. Another child, my sister, was born when I was 7.

Over and over again we kids were removed from Mom and put in foster homes for a few days or longer. But we always got sent back except for the twins, who were put up for adoption when they were 4. That day we knew the social workers were coming to take them. I was 5, and I'd always helped take care of the twins, sheltering them from Mom when I could. We sisters hid in a closet, all of us crying. When the workers found us, the twins clung to me, begging: "Please don't let them take us!" I didn't see them again for 22 years. When I was small I was always scared to be taken away. Life with Mom was the only life I knew. But by the time I was 10 I didn't want to go back to her. It's sad because many times I had the chance to be adopted. Once an aunt wanted to take me, but Mom backed out of the adoption. A lot of the foster parents were mean, but one foster mother who was really nice wanted to keep me. I begged the social workers to let me stay with her, but they said they'd promised Mom to bring me back if she attended parenting classes, had counseling, and looked for work, and she'd done that.

I began to understand that although the social workers pretended to care, no matter what happened I would always be sent back. I was angry because they never really listened to me. They'd say "Oh, that's impossible," or "You must have done something to cause it." So I stopped telling them I didn't want to go back, and tried to act loving to Mom when I got sent home. Otherwise she'd go into a so-called demon-possessed rage. She'd say she'd just seen Satan, that he'd told her we must be punished, and that he was coming to get us some night while we slept. Sometimes I'd wake at night and find her sitting at the end of my bed in the darkness, staring at me. She also said demons would come out of the TV and enter our minds unless we truly had faith in God. So I always prayed when I watched television.

Over the years I had many concussions and hairline fractures, and shattered shoulder blades, wrists and an arm. The worst was when I lost our house keys when I was 7. She had hallucinated that a certain neighbor was evil and would break in and rape all of us. During the night she broke one of my ankles by throwing me downstairs over and over again, then making me walk back up to her. Later at the hospital she acted very loving. She would tell the doctors I fell off a bike, that I was clumsy. I never disagreed because I was afraid. As a teenager I was hospitalized for anorexia and twice I tried to commit suicide. My brother also tried several times—once I came in and found him hanging, already unconscious, but paramedics saved him. He ran away over and over again. I don't know where he is now.

My mother joined several churches that held exorcisms. At her first exorcism when I was 3, church members told us kids to duck behind the sofa, because exorcised demons "shoot out like black bullets" and might enter our minds. One preacher gave us family counseling, which he said was according to the Bible. He'd tell us to "obey your parents" and he'd tell Mom not to hit us. She'd act very sweet, and cry that all she'd ever done was slap us.

When my youngest sister was born when I was 7, I became very protective of her. Once she cried while Mom was washing her hair, and Mom bit her like an animal, all over her head and arms. I washed her hair myself from then on. Mom sort of favored me because I tried to be a mediator, helped her around the house and acted loving to her. She even went to court several times to get us back. Maybe one reason was the AFDC she drew, but more important, she was terrified of being alone. I hid the worst things from everybody. But social workers should be smart enough, or trained enough, to understand how kids act in that situation.

Family reunification is total nonsense. Parents and relatives should be held to the same standards as nonrelatives, and have the same psychological testing and background checks. Social workers need more training in understanding abuse. And my mother should have gotten evaluation and treatment before she had her first baby. Doctors did try for years to give her medication, but she would never take it. She's lived her whole life in torment, and her disease has

made her horribly torture her kids. Maybe someone like her should have their tubes tied, so they can't keep having children they abuse. But then I wouldn't have been born, and I wouldn't have my sisters.

As for me, I should have been taken away from her for good when I was 3 and my face and body turned purple with bruises. While workers were banging on our doors to take me, she was frantically trying to cover my bruises with makeup. She hid me in a closet, but they found me and took me away—for a few days. When they returned me to her, many of the bruises still hadn't faded.

My husband has helped me a lot with my feelings and fears from those years. Mom lives in another state. I've never mentioned demons to my own little girl and never spanked her. But sometimes, when I'm alone at night and hear a strange sound or see a curtain move, my same childish fear of demons can come back. (p. B7)

Gibson (1996), in response to this article, wrote that, although mistakes happen, social workers do care.

[This woman's statement] leaves the distinct impression that a social worker's involvement is superficial, even deceptive toward a child in crisis.

I'm in no way denying this story of abuse and neglect of a child [by her mother] or her commentary on how the system works. It's all too real. What I am taking issue with is the assumption regarding social workers.

As a volunteer child advocate for more than seven years, my observation is that social workers tirelessly put themselves on the line every day on behalf of abused children. They are knowledgeable and caring.

They work in a system where the mandate is for children to be returned to their parents whenever possible, despite unresolved neglect and abuse issues. Social workers do not make the rules. They, more often than not, attempt to do everything possible in a child's best interest—without "pretending" in any sense of the word.

This report is heartbreaking. But to cast blame on the very people who're trying to make things better for children is a slap in the face to those who deserve much more honor and respect. (p. B9)

Exercise 23-3. Perceptions of Child Welfare Services and Policies with Respect to Child Maltreatment

The National Committee to Prevent Child Abuse (1996) commissioned a national public opinion poll in 1995 to determine public attitudes about child maltreatment. A nationwide sample of 1,000 parents were interviewed by the Gallup organization. Your first task in this exercise is to answer the questions the respondents were asked about child welfare services and policies. Answer each question with one of the following: *agree, unsure,* or *disagree.*

1. Child welfare workers should always try to keep a child at home with his or her parents, regardless of how the parents behave.
2. Some families are simply too dangerous to be trusted with the care of their young children.
3. It is possible for child welfare workers to preserve families and protect a child's physical safety.

4. Child welfare services provided in the home can successfully protect abused children from further abuse by their parents.
5. A child should always be removed from the home in cases of child sexual abuse in which the person accused remains in the home.
6. Parents who have seriously injured their child should have their children taken away for good.
7. Parents who fail to provide for their child's basic food, clothing and shelter should have their children taken away from them.
8. Too many children are harmed or die because public agencies do not fully investigate reports of abuse or neglect.
9. The vast majority of the cases investigated by public child welfare agencies are false reports that do not involve truly abused or neglected children.

Now compare your answers with those of the respondents:

1. agree, 16%; unsure, 10%; disagree, 73%
2. agree, 82%; unsure, 13%; disagree, 6%
3. agree, 67%; unsure, 17%; disagree, 16%
4. agree, 51%; unsure, 21%; disagree, 28%
5. agree, 88%; unsure, 6%; disagree, 7%
6. agree, 73%; unsure, 13%; disagree, 13%
7. agree, 61%; unsure, 17%; disagree, 21%
8. agree, 69%; unsure, 22%; disagree, 9%
9. agree, 27%; unsure, 40%; disagree, 33%

Finally, answer the following questions.

1. How did your answers compare with those of the respondents?
2. If you disagreed with the majority opinion on any statement, what might account for the disagreement?
3. The respondents' answers were most divergent on statement 9, which focused on false reports of child maltreatment. Why do you think they differed on this item?
4. On item 4, a bare majority of the respondents agreed with the statement that child welfare services in the home could protect children from further abuse by their parents. Why do you think the respondents were not more confident of the value of child welfare services in protecting children?

Whenever a child's safety is in serious jeopardy, that child must be removed from the custody of the parents—temporarily, if it appears that safe reunification with the parents is feasible in the foreseeable future, and permanently, if there is no reasonable likelihood of safe reunification.

—U.S. Advisory Board on Child Abuse and Neglect (1995)

Interventions to Prevent Child Sexual Abuse

Although sex offenders may seem like an unlikely source of information on prevention of child sexual abuse, they can make valuable suggestions. Table 23-6 shows the suggestions of 91 sex offenders for helping children, parents, and teachers prevent child sexual abuse. The sex offenders "gained access to children through caretaking, such as babysitting; targeted children by using bribes, gifts and games; used force, anger, threats, and bribes to ensure their compliance; and systematically desensitized children through touch, talk about sex, and persuasion" (Elliott, Browne, & Kilcoyne, 1995, p. 579). Their suggestions, in part, are aimed at helping children guard themselves from unwanted approaches that may lead to child sexual abuse and helping parents and teachers teach children how to protect themselves from becoming victims of child sexual abuse.

Interventions with Maltreated Children with a Disability

Children with a disability may be particularly vulnerable to maltreatment because they are extremely dependent on their caregivers and they may be devalued and perceived as powerless by their perpetrators. Possible interventions include helping the children understand what situations increase their risk of maltreatment, enlightening their caregivers about the sexual needs of adolescents with disabilities, and promoting societal norms and attitudes that show respect for body integrity and the right of all individuals to protection (Andrews & Veronen, 1993).

Interventions with Maltreated Children in Schools

Those of you who will be or who are working in schools can help maltreated children by implementing the following 10 recommendations (Cicchetti, Toth, & Hennessy, 1993):

1. Obtain an individual, comprehensive assessment of maltreated children.
2. Begin intervention efforts with the children as soon as possible after the maltreatment has been confirmed.
3. Recommend the most appropriate educational setting possible for the children.
4. Involve the nonsuspect parent(s) in the intervention and treatment process, when feasible.
5. Encourage teachers to focus on the whole child and not merely on academic growth.
6. Help teachers understand how children are affected by maltreatment.
7. Help teachers learn how best to relate to maltreated children.
8. Work toward coordinating the services of the child welfare system, special education system, legal system, and child mental health system to help maltreated children.
9. Encourage researchers to conduct studies on how maltreated children function in schools.
10. Encourage schools to develop programs that can identify maltreated children.

Table 23-6
Offenders' Suggestions for Preventing Child Sexual Abuse

Children

- need a guidebook and programs to give them information about prevention—"Kids are easy to trick when they don't have a clue about what I'm trying to do."
- should avoid secluded, remote places—"Children place themselves at risk by playing in quiet places. Don't play in deserted stairways or streets at night; don't ever play hide and seek alone—hide in groups."
- are too trusting and need to be told that not everyone is trustworthy—"It is probably the last person you would suspect."
- should tell if anyone tries to trick them or "makes strange suggestions or talks about sexual things or seems to touch or brush up against them accidentally."
- should make up a fib and get away to tell a neighbor or someone if a babysitter tries or suggests anything—"Children always fall for the idea that you will let them stay up late if they'll play a secret game with you. Parents should tell kids that if the babysitter tries to do them a special favor, they should not be fooled."
- should try to go out with other children—"I never approach children in groups; there are plenty of children on their own. It just isn't worth the risk when there are several kids together because you can't control them all."
- should be wary of public toilets and never go into them alone—"A great place to hang out is in a toilet in a kiddies' hamburger-type restaurant. Little boys, especially, go into the toilets alone and they aren't expecting someone to try

to touch them. Most of the time they are too embarrassed even to shout. I would teach kids to run out of the toilets yelling the minute anyone tries to help them zip up or touch them."
- should walk to school with other people—"The best time of the day to get at children is when they are walking home from school alone."
- should never accept lifts or talk to anyone who comes up to them—"Children are so trusting. A good way to approach is to ask the time. Seems innocent enough, but once you get them in conversation, it's hard for them to get away. If you look respectable, they figure you can't be a nasty stranger."
- should knock on the door of a nearby house if they are being followed—"This really put me off following the child, so that child didn't get abused."
- should always tell parents where they are going.
- should tell if anyone, including a relative, is abusing them—"Don't pretend that nothing is happening and hide it from everyone, it will only get worse. That's what happened to me."
- should tell a friend—"Sometimes kids don't have a grown-up to trust, so they can have the friend come with them to tell a teacher or a school nurse or someone else."
- need to be especially wary if a man on his own tries to approach—in light of the information that many of the abusers operate alone.

Parents need to

- be suspicious if someone seems more interested in their children than in them—"Watch out for someone who offers to take your child on holiday or who tells you to take a break while they watch the kids—why would this man want to hang around your children?"
- be aware that "over-loving or over-affectionate type people are potentially dangerous."
- be told that "our offenses can occur gently and subtly and that children need to be prompted to get help early."
- realize that there are some people, even family members and friends, who could ask their children to do something sexual—"Parents are so naive; they're worried about strangers and should be worried about their brother-in-law. They just don't realize how devious we can be. I used to abuse children in the same room with their parents and they couldn't see it or didn't know it was happening."
- know that we will use any way we can to get to children—"I was disabled and spent months grooming the parents, so they would tell their child to take me out and help me. No one thought that disabled people could be abusers."
- teach their children that they should never keep secrets or feel they are to blame if they are maltreated—"Secrecy and blame were my best weapons. Most kids worry that they are to blame for the abuse and that they should keep

it a secret." Indeed, parents should emphasize openness and a "no secrets" attitude throughout their children's upbringing.
- teach children about sex, different parts of the body, and "right and wrong" touches—"Parents are partly to blame if they don't tell their children about these things [sexual matters]; I used it to my advantage by teaching the child myself."
- know that children hold adults in high esteem and will do what they say—"Don't teach your kids to do everything adults tell them; otherwise they'll be too frightened of adult status."
- have family discussions about preventing abuse—"Parents shouldn't be embarrassed to talk about things like this; it's harder to abuse or trick a child who knows what you're up to."
- tell children that they have rights and that if they aren't "comfortable with someone, they don't have to be with him or her."
- know that it is a dangerous age when girls are "transforming into women and might be sexually curious—I used that curiosity to trap them into sex."
- be aware of children's behavior changing—"Notice if your child becomes different or seems to feel bad or is with-

(Continued)

Table 23-6 (*Continued*)

drawn; ask why. Examine small children for physical signs."
- not be too hard on children—"Kids who felt unloved or not appreciated were easiest to victimize; they needed the *love* I gave."

- realize that single-parent families are a good target for pedophiles—"The mothers are stressed, overworked and are grateful for someone taking one of the children out for a while."

Teachers and schools should

- have prevention programs for all kids from a very young age—"In the same way that we groom children from a young age to be victims, schools should groom them to tell automatically."
- have the children role play what to do—"It's no good just lecturing to kids, they probably aren't paying attention. Get them to run and yell, so they'll do it automatically."
- go to courses to learn the signs of maltreatment—"Teachers think the child is just messing around, when they might be crying for help. I was and no one saw it. In the past people didn't want to know and didn't have the experience to understand what kids were going through."
- make sure the programs don't concentrate on stranger danger and stereotypes—"Children never considered me a stranger if I dressed alright and seemed nice. Stereotyp-

ing people as bad, mean strangers makes kids more at risk from people like us."
- have discussions in school to prompt children to tell—"Kids who are being abused sometimes need to tell someone outside the family, like a teacher or nurse."
- believe children if they say maltreatment is happening—"Children need to feel confident that someone will do something before they will tell."
- have advertisements in school about being safe—"The abuse is happening anyway; it should be publicized."
- teach sex education—"Make sure children have sex education that makes them aware of the emotional and physical side of sex. They need information to know what's happening."

Source: Reprinted from pp. 588–591, with changes in notation, with permission from *Child Abuse and Neglect*, M. Elliott, K. Browne and J. Kilcoyne, "Child Sexual Abuse Prevention: What Offenders Tell Us," copyright 1995, Elsevier Science Ltd, Oxford, England.

Interventions with Maltreated Children in Institutions, Residential Settings, and Foster Homes

The causes of child maltreatment in institutions, residential settings, and foster homes are multidimensional, as they are in society at large. Following are some guidelines that may reduce child maltreatment in institutions and residential settings (Andrews & Veronen, 1993; Blatt, 1992):

1. Identify the environmental factors that cause distress for staff and children.
2. Institute changes in programming to meet the needs of the children.
3. Hire the most competent staff possible, and screen all employees for histories of maltreating children.
4. Provide fair salaries for personnel working in an institutional or residential setting.
5. Educate all staff regarding child maltreatment.
6. Enforce all policies and laws regarding mistreatment of residents.
7. Recognize individual characteristics that might make particular children more difficult to care for, and provide the services necessary to help these children.
8. Increase security procedures, including surveillance of isolated areas.
9. Offer crisis management training for the direct care staff.

10. Reassign staff members to positions that they are most capable of handling.
11. Arrange for the professional staff to work split shifts or to have flexible work hours, thereby making the professional staff more accessible to the direct care staff and reducing the direct care staff's sense of isolation, frustration, and anger.

Foster parents may need training in understanding the needs of foster children. The following guidelines may reduce child maltreatment in foster care (Steinhauer, 1991):

1. Evaluate carefully the foster family and foster home before placing children in the home.
2. Be sure that the foster home can provide for the physical and emotional needs of the foster child.
3. Help the foster parents understand that foster children have special needs stemming from their experiences before coming to the home. These experiences may include abandonment, neglect, physical or sexual abuse, and placements in other foster homes.
4. Help the foster parents understand that foster children may be anxious and fearful because of past trauma, uncertainty about the future, helplessness and lack of control over the future, concern about the stigma of being foster children, and the need to contend with several different adults, including the foster parents, social workers, and, in some cases, their natural parents and relatives as well.

5. Inform the foster children of any plans that are being made about them, and enlist their participation in planning to the extent possible, considering their developmental level.

6. Place foster children in settings that protect as much as possible their major attachment relationships, such as those with natural parents, siblings, and other relatives.

7. Maintain the foster children's sense of historical continuity by protecting their relationships with key attachment figures (as noted in the previous guideline), minimizing the number of moves to which they are exposed, minimizing changes in social workers and foster homes, and keeping them aware of their life stories through discussions and use of life books that contain pictures and other information about their past.

8. Ensure that the children's natural parents, the foster parents, the social workers, and the agency staff work together in the best interests of the children.

Interventions with Convicted Offenders

Interventions with offenders who commit any type of abuse.
Interventions with individuals convicted of maltreating children may be more successful when the following conditions are present (Burgess et al., 1978; Elton, 1988; Groth, 1982; Powell & Ilett, 1992). The convicted offender

- accepts responsibility for the maltreatment
- acknowledges the child's needs as primary
- is concerned about the impact of the maltreatment on the child
- is attached to his or her child (in cases of intrafamilial maltreatment)
- is distressed about his or her actions
- acknowledges his or her need to change and accepts the need for treatment
- is willing to change his or her attitudes
- used minimal or no force
- did not threaten to harm the child
- committed the maltreatment only one time under stress
- acknowledges that there are problems in the family
- is willing to change his or her communication patterns within the family
- is willing to work with mental health professionals to develop the ability to detect early warning signs that might lead him or her to maltreat a child and to develop more appropriate modes of self-expression, need gratification, and impulse management
- is willing to make restitution
- lives in a family in which the members do not scapegoat or blame the child
- lives in a family that has a sound family structure and good relationships among its members
- has adequate social and occupational skills
- has no major psychopathology or substance abuse problem

Interventions with individuals convicted of maltreating children may be more difficult when any of the following conditions are present (Knopp, 1985; Powell & Ilett, 1992). The convicted offender

- scapegoats or blames the child or someone else for the abusive act
- has been treated for previous offenses and continues to repeat the offenses
- has a history of extensive antisocial behavior or alcohol or drug addiction or has many problem behaviors, including a severe personality disorder or psychosis
- continues to have a substance abuse problem
- used violence, physical force, or a weapon or threatened to use a weapon
- used progressively more force to commit repeated offenses
- used predatory or ritualistic methods that continued despite the victim's expressions of distress
- has significant intellectual deficits that limit his or her ability to learn from the consequences of his or her behavior

Behavioral and cognitive-behavioral programs for parents who have physically abused or neglected their children typically involve some form of skills training that focuses on child management skills, anger-control skills, and/or general stress management (Wolfe & Wekerle, 1993). Parents may be taught how to use contingency management principles (such as reinforcement, punishment, and consistency) in dealing with their children, how to use new ways to solve problems and increase child compliance, how to replace anger-producing thoughts with more appropriate ones, how to develop self-control skills to lessen the likelihood of emotional outbursts and the expression of rage, and how to increase their awareness and coping skills.

Interventions with offenders who neglect their children.
Following are examples of interventions that might be used with parents who neglect their children (Crittenden, 1993; Gaudin, 1993):

- providing parents with information about child development and how meeting their child's needs will help the child become more independent
- helping parents identify and attend to children's signals that parental attention is required
- helping parents improve their living conditions
- teaching parents better home management, budgeting, and shopping skills
- recommending that parents obtain psychotherapy for depression or negative, dysfunctional self-images
- providing help with other conditions that interfere with parents' ability to adequately care for their children (for example, providing instruction in job-seeking skills, job training, or education, if parents are unemployed or need to upgrade their skills)

Two cases illustrating the prognosis for convicted offenders. Let's now look at two cases of convicted offenders. The case of Margaret illustrates a favorable prognosis for family reunification (Elton, 1988).

CASE 23-10. MARGARET

Margaret, aged 12, told her mother that her father had sexually abused her, involving her in oral sex. The mother confronted the father and told him to seek psychiatric treatment. Two months later, he again abused Margaret and Margaret again told her mother. The mother then took the matter to the police. After a court hearing, the father was required to see a therapist and to leave the home.

At the first meeting with the therapist, the family showed many hopeful signs. The father acknowledged that he was totally responsible for the maltreatment and even showed some real distress. The mother also acknowledged responsibility, both because she had distanced herself from her husband, being burdened with child care, and because she had somewhat undermined him after he became unemployed. She recognized that she had expected Margaret to be too responsible.

Both parents recognized some marital difficulties. They also saw that the generation boundaries were rather confused, in that they alternatively made demands on Margaret and her 11-year-old brother to be substitute parents to the younger children, and in other ways had real problems in being firm enough with them.

There was a marked lack of scapegoating in the family; indeed, quite open communication and considerable affective warmth was present between all members. The parents accepted without question the need for the father to live away for a period—the mother made it clear that she would insist on this even if the law did not. The mother continued for many months to think that it was not yet time for her husband to return home, although she missed his sharing in the care of the children. She maintained this view despite the fact that she became pregnant by him during his absence. The pregnancy itself constituted evidence of improvement in the marital relationship and a reestablishment of appropriate generation boundaries.

Despite very real and practical problems, the whole family, led by the parents, cooperated actively in the treatment. Although there were worrying and difficult moments during the treatment, the family repeatedly demonstrated the strengths that were noted in the original assessment. The first was an openness in communication of worries within the family and to the professionals involved. The second was that even when the family ran into difficulties when trying to establish the best living and child-care arrangements, they never scapegoated any member; rather, the difficulties arose from each trying too hard to help the others. (pp. 175–176, with changes in notation)

The case of Holly and Aileen illustrates an unfavorable prognosis for family reunification (Elton, 1988).

CASE 23-11. HOLLY AND AILEEN

Holly and Aileen were sisters who were 15 and 11 years old, respectively. They were taken into care following a disclosure of sexual abuse by their uncle toward one of their school friends. During this investigation, it was discovered that this uncle, a man with a known, long history of serious sexual offenses, was living with the mother and the girls despite an injunction that he should not do so. Although the parents were at that point living apart, they, together with the uncle and other men, had been known to engage in various group sexual practices. The two girls, especially Holly, were noted to be showing disturbing sexual provocativeness themselves. The mother was in fact rejecting Holly, scapegoating her, but clinging to the younger girl, Aileen. Aileen initially appeared as a frozen little girl, unable to speak for herself, but highly aware of her mother's needs and distress. At the point of assessment, the parents were engaged in a bitter marital battle, part of which was fighting for custody of the girls. However, it was also known that at times they joined together to fight for joint custody against the social services department, since this was the only way in which they related amicably. Both parents acknowledged the risk the uncle presented to the girls. Ostensibly, the mother had denied to the professionals that she was continuing to live with him, but during the assessment she made it clear that she would break down without him. Her daughters were able to hear this. In acknowledging her own paramount need for the uncle, she allowed the professionals to make alternative permanent arrangements for the girls. Holly was subsequently able to disclose that she had been sexually abused and made it clear that she herself did not wish to have any further contact with her family. The younger sister, Aileen, was sad that her mother had chosen her uncle rather than her but was able to begin separating emotionally from her mother. After several months, she too was wishing to find a new family. (p. 180, with changes in notation)

Children are our most precious gift; they are our hope for the future. Surely, psychology has a responsibility to help prevent the tragedy of traumatized and violated children. This means using our scientific methodology to uncover the causes of human-caused traumas, apply those psychological principles for prevention, and ameliorate the social conditions that facilitate abuse being passed down from one generation to another. It is not an individual's pathology nor is it a problem within a dysfunctional family; rather, child traumatization is a systemic problem that requires a social solution.

—Lenore E. Walker

Interventions with domestic violence offenders. Psychotherapeutic approaches are based on the premise that domestic violence is learned and can be controlled by teaching batterers better conflict resolution skills; therapy aims to help batterers change their violent behavior (Tifft, 1993). The focus is on anger control, anger management, stress management, communication skills training, and training in emotional awareness. Programs focusing on batterers may aim to decrease their isolation; develop support systems; increase their feelings of self-esteem; help them recognize their responsibility for their actions, the potential dangerousness of their violent behavior, and the consequences of their actions; increase their communication skills, assertiveness skills, stress reduction skills, ability to empathize with their partner, and understanding of the relationship between violence and sex-role behavior; and develop control over alcohol and/or drug use, if present (Tifft, 1993). Batterers may be trained to monitor, evaluate, and challenge the interpretations and assumptions they make about their partners.

Interventions at a Societal Level in Cases of Child Maltreatment and Domestic Violence

There is much that we can do as a society to prevent and remediate child maltreatment (Belsky, 1993). We need to support programs that provide the following:

- fertility planning and encouragement for adolescents to defer parenthood
- education and strong incentives for at-risk youth to remain in school and complete their education
- employment opportunities
- economic assistance, such as guaranteed minimal incomes, child allowances, and housing benefits
- professional home visits designed to provide emotional support, reduce social isolation, and provide alternative child-rearing strategies that may, for example, help parents and at-risk youth deal with anxiety, hostility, and depression
- parenting education classes during and after pregnancy
- affordable or free high-quality child care

These programs will be difficult to implement, given that the United States is struggling with a huge budget deficit and a child poverty rate of 20% (Belsky, 1993). Although some of these programs are operating in portions of the country, they have not been implemented nationwide. What judgment will be made about our society if we cannot protect our nation's children? And do we as a nation have the will to carry out the tasks needed to prevent child maltreatment?

Similarly, there are no easy ways to prevent domestic violence. However, acting on the following recommendations of Murray Straus, Suzanne Steinmetz, and Richard J. Gelles would help stem the tide of domestic violence and child maltreatment in our society (adapted from Gelles, 1993, p. 20):

1. *Eliminate the norms that legitimize and glorify violence in society and the family.* The elimination of spanking as a child-rearing technique and corporal punishment in schools, the institution of gun control to get deadly weapons out of the home, the elimination of the death penalty, and the elimination of media violence that glorifies and legitimizes violence are all necessary steps.

2. *Reduce violence-provoking stress created by society.* Reducing poverty, inequality, and unemployment and pro-

viding for adequate housing, nutrition, medical and dental care, and educational opportunities are steps that could reduce stress in families.

3. *Integrate families into a network of kin and community.* Reducing social isolation would significantly reduce stress and increase the abilities of family members to manage stress and support each other.

4. *Change the sexist character of society.* Sexual inequality, perhaps more than economic inequality, makes violence possible in homes. Eliminating the distinction between men's roles and women's roles would be a major step toward equality in and out of the home.

5. *Break the cycle of violence in the family.* This step repeats the message of step 1: Violence cannot be prevented as long as there are individuals who believe that it is appropriate to hit the people they love. Physical punishment of children is perhaps the most effective means of teaching violence, and eliminating it would be an important step in violence prevention. Schools should be encouraged to offer parenting classes that stress nonviolent forms of discipline.

As these authors acknowledge, "these proposals call for such fundamental changes in society and family life that many people resist them and argue that they could not work. But not making such changes continues the harmful and deadly tradition of family violence" (p. 20). These recommendations complement those offered by Belsky (1993).

Exercise 23-4. Values Clarification

Read the statement below, rate it using the scale that follows, and then write some reasons to support your rating. Then take the opposing position—that is, if you initially strongly disagreed or disagreed with the statement, take the position "strongly agree" or "agree"—and write some reasons to justify this position. Check your reasons with those in the Comments section. This exercise was adapted with permission, from J. S. Rycus, R. C. Hughes, and J. K. Garrison (1989), *Child Protective Services: A Training Manual,* Institute for Human Services, pp. 14, 18–19.

Although it is generally accepted that children have basic rights, this should not mean that society can interfere with the parents' basic right to teach, discipline, and guide their children according to their own values and beliefs.

Scale:
Strongly disagree—Disagree—Agree—Strongly agree

Comments
Following are some reasons for supporting the "strongly agree" or "agree" position:

1. Society must always respect the rights of parents. There must be a limit to society's dictation of child-rearing standards. Otherwise, it would be possible for all of us to lose our children. For example, if the government declared that it was in our children's best interests if one parent stayed

home, it could decide to take our children away if both parents worked outside the home.

2. People and their situations are so different that there can't be a single rule that applies to everyone in all circumstances. People must be able to make their own decisions about their own lives. Individual decisions will probably be better suited to the individual situation. We assume that people make decisions in their own best interests—that they know themselves best.

3. If we really believe in the value and viability of different cultures, then we must allow people to express themselves and live according to their cultural mores and customs. We can't give lip service to cultural diversity and then expect everyone to live by a single standard of parenting that represents "mainstream" society.

Following are some reasons for supporting the "strongly disagree" and "disagree" positions:

1. Preserving the rights of parents is what created a need for child protection in the first place, because it allowed parents to seriously harm their children without societal interference. Society has both a right and a responsibility to intervene when parents act in ways that are detrimental to their children's welfare.

2. Children aren't able to look out for themselves. They are entitled to the same basic rights as everyone else, but they need advocates to assure that their rights are preserved.

3. The purpose of organizing any society is to make rules that protect all its citizens. Children are members of that society. The society establishes police and courts to protect citizens from harm; it must establish mechanisms to protect children, as well.

4. Parents who harm their children should have no rights, because they have not lived up to their responsibility. People must earn the right to freedom by behaving responsibly. If they cannot do so, they should lose their right to make free decisions.

Every day you come to work knowing that a child will be saved from pain or want…because you were there…. Countless tragedies do not occur because you are there to prevent them.

—Peter Digre in a memo
to Los Angeles County social workers

CONCLUDING COMMENT ABOUT INTERVIEWING CHILDREN WHO MAY HAVE BEEN MALTREATED

The field of child maltreatment is truly interdisciplinary. Professionals representing social work, law enforcement, medicine, psychology, education, psychiatry, and other disciplines all may be involved in a case. Failure to do a competent job anywhere in the investigatory process may mean that a child's life is endangered, that innocent people's lives

are ruined, and that the public's trust is breached. I believe that, with proper training, we can make a difference by protecting children whose lives may be endangered and by assuring that those who are accused receive the fairest treatment possible. We all will make mistakes, but that makes it even more urgent that we mobilize our resources to the fullest so that we can avoid every *preventable* error. *In the final analysis, the community is responsible for children—no one agency or person can do it alone.*

Family preservation will truly occur when many families with children no longer struggle to exist at less than subsistence level, when poor parents are freed from anxiety and depression generated by raising children in hostile environments, and when it is widely acknowledged that the real cause of family breakdown is the failure of our society to value and support the parenting role.

—Martha Morrison Dore

THINKING THROUGH THE ISSUES

What do you think of your ability to evaluate and summarize complex and potentially conflicting information?

Will you be able to work effectively within designated, and often limited, time frames for the completion of your report?

How will your feelings about child maltreatment affect the recommendations you make?

How will you handle situations in which a parent will not believe that his or her child has been maltreated, despite clear evidence?

What role do you believe law enforcement should have in cases of child maltreatment?

What skills will you need to communicate effectively with professionals of diverse backgrounds involved in child maltreatment cases?

How will you feel about child sexual abuse victims if they behave seductively or appear to have willingly participated in sexual contact with the offender? Will you then partly blame the victim for the sexual abuse?

Do you have fantasies of rescuing children while reacting with hostility toward perpetrators?

What clues might alert you to the possibility that the alleged maltreatment did not occur?

Do you believe that young children cannot accurately report what happened to them or that their stories are merely fabrications developed to gain some favor or to seek revenge?

Which has more serious consequences: falsely labeling a person as an abuser or missing a true case of maltreatment? What is the basis for your answer?

How valuable are risk assessment protocols?

What changes would you make in the current child protective laws and procedures?

How successful do you believe interventions can be with individuals convicted of child maltreatment?

Do you believe that a person who engages in child maltreatment should serve a jail term? What is the basis for your belief?

If you were setting up child sexual abuse prevention programs for (a) preschool children, (b) elementary school children, (c) junior high school students, and (d) high school students, what would you include in the program for each age group? How difficult do you believe it would be to obtain permission from the parents to conduct the programs? How would the four programs be similar, and how would they be different?

What are your thoughts about family reunification?

How do your present views of child maltreatment differ from those you had when you began studying this book?

If you were designing a training unit on child maltreatment for teachers, health professionals, law enforcement personnel, or another professional group, what information would you include in the unit?

SUMMARY

1. If you are working or in training in a child protective agency or in a law enforcement agency, you will need to evaluate the findings and make decisions after you have completed your interviews and reviewed relevant records and reports.

2. Critical questions that you may need to decide after you complete the assessment include whether the source of information is credible; whether the alleged maltreatment constitutes child maltreatment as defined by state statute; whether the child is at risk for further maltreatment and what the level of risk is; if the child is at risk, what type of agency or community response will ensure the child's safety; if the child's safety cannot be ensured within the family, what type and level of care the child needs; how quick the response must be to ensure the safety of the child; whether the family has emergency needs that must be met; and whether ongoing agency services should be offered to the family.

3. The signs of child physical abuse or neglect often will be evident to you or to those who reported the maltreatment.

4. Evaluating cases of alleged child sexual abuse may be particularly difficult if there are no physical signs of sexual abuse. In such cases, you will have to base your decision about whether the alleged sexual abuse occurred primarily on the child's statements (and the statements of other informants, as applicable).

5. Evaluation of alleged emotional abuse can be difficult because signs associated with this type of maltreatment are difficult to verify.

6. A false negative error occurs when you conclude that no maltreatment occurred when, in fact, maltreatment did occur.

7. A false positive error occurs when you conclude that maltreatment did occur when, in fact, no maltreatment occurred.

Evaluating Allegations of Child Maltreatment

8. It is useful to think of gradations of certainty about child maltreatment unless you are absolutely positive that maltreatment has or has not occurred.

9. In preparing for your evaluation of a case, review such information as the description of the victim, description of the family, description of the alleged maltreatment, description of the suspected perpetrator, and description of any witnesses.

10. As a result of your evaluation of the child, you should have information about the following areas: background information; type of alleged maltreatment: details of disclosure; child's feelings about the alleged abusive event; child's credibility; alleged offender; conditions under which the alleged maltreatment occurred; medical examinations; behavior, affect, personality, and temperament of the child; and future actions and needs.

11. In evaluating the child's credibility, use everything you know about the case. Indices useful for evaluating child maltreatment center on physical signs of abuse, quality of the child's communications and verbal report, consistency of the child's report, environmental pressures on the child, reasons for any misinformation given by the child, the child's affect, reports from others, explanations given by caregivers, and caregivers' interactions with the child.

12. Statement Validity Analysis is a potentially useful way to evaluate allegations of child sexual abuse; however, insufficient research at present precludes use of the method in forensic work.

13. When an infant dies suddenly—a condition referred to as Sudden Infant Death Syndrome (SIDS)—it may be difficult to distinguish between death due to unexplained causes and death due to fatal child abuse.

14. In evaluating SIDS, look at the history surrounding the death; the physical examination; the history of the pregnancy, delivery, and infancy; the death scene investigation; previous infant injuries or deaths; the autopsy findings; and previous involvement of Child Protective Services or law enforcement.

15. The evaluation of the family should help you learn about the personality and temperament of the family members; family environment; family members' reactions to the possible maltreatment, including whether they can corroborate the child's story; strengths and weaknesses of the family; and family members who may be called on to help in the intervention.

16. Recognize that alleged offenders only become offenders in the eyes of the court when they confess or are judged to be guilty.

17. Don't use the interview to decide whether the alleged offender committed the offense.

18. Neither the interview nor psychological tests can tell you whether someone is a perpetrator. This determination is best left to law enforcement agencies and to the courts.

19. In evaluating alleged or known offenders, you want to review all sources of information to arrive at a clinical impression of their temperament, personality, and adjustment.

20. In evaluating the known offender, you will want to consider his or her frame of mind, precipitating stressors, motivational intent, perception of the victim, style of maltreatment, type of maltreatment, physiological response, and attitude toward the victim at the time of the maltreatment.

21. You will also want to consider how the offense can be understood in light of the known offender's developmental and family history, the social-environmental context of his or her early life, the environmental-situational context of the maltreatment, and the known offender's current psychological and emotional life.

22. Caregiver behaviors that should raise suspicions of child maltreatment include the following: caregiver shows little concern

for the child; denies that the child has problems or blames the child for the child's problems; delays in getting an injured child medical attention; offers a report of the injury that does not accord with the injury observed in the child; provides no explanation for the child's injury; explains the injury differently than another caregiver; describes behavior inconsistent with the child's developmental level; gives a report of the injury different from that of the child; changes the report about the child's injury or gives inconsistent reports; does not provide information voluntarily about the child's injury; is the only one who had access to the child at the time of the injuries; attributes the injuries to the child's sibling when there is little likelihood that the sibling could have carried out the behavior; does not show concern about the child's injury, treatment, or prognosis; does not follow medical advice about the child; does not bring the child in for routine medical health checks; brings the child to different medical providers for different injuries; gives limited, if any, physical or emotional support to the child or shows inappropriate or no response to the child when the child is crying; is not available for questioning about the alleged maltreatment; is involved in domestic violence; says that he or she knows little about basic child care and child development; says that he or she has little patience with the child; is constantly criticizing the child; says that he or she fears that he or she might hurt the child or cannot take care of the child; says that he or she is frequently drunk or high on drugs; says that he or she has little energy to take care of the child; says that he or she has violent temper outbursts; and makes excuses for the child's condition—such as bruises, burns, or other injuries—or minimizes the child's condition.

23. As a practical matter in cases of physical abuse involving infants and toddlers, if there isn't a confession or eyewitness, it will be difficult to identify the offender.

24. Evaluating the family and protecting the victim can be especially challenging when no one accepts responsibility for the physical abuse.

Evaluating Facilities, Institutions, and Foster Homes

25. When children are alleged to have been maltreated in a facility, institution, or foster home, you may want to inspect the site. Inspecting the site may give you valuable information about the physical plant and the staff that will help you understand the allegation and make recommendations, if needed.

26. In evaluating a child care facility or institution when there has been a report of child maltreatment, consider the condition of the children, the types of children who are at the facility, the location of the facility, the layout of the facility, the condition of the facility, the quality of the staff, the interactions of staff with children, and the history of reports of maltreatment.

27. Following are indications that an institution or a facility is deficient in caring for children: children are in poor health, building is in poor condition, institution or facility is overcrowded, there have been prior reports of maltreatment, staff is uncooperative, negative interactions occur between the staff and children, staff exhibits authoritarian traits, staff members do not support each other, staff has unusual or inappropriate interests in one child, and staff shows no respect for children's right to privacy or refusal to be touched by an adult.

28. Agency representatives should conduct an in-depth home evaluation before they place a child in a foster home. If they fail to

obtain critical information and ask critical questions, they may make a wrong placement.

29. In conducting a recertification of a foster home, interview and observe all family members living in the home.

30. Placement of a child with special needs in a foster home requires special care.

Risk Assessment

31. Your decisions about whether a child has been maltreated and whether the child is at risk for further maltreatment are two of the most important ones you will ever make as a human services provider, mental health professional, or law enforcement officer. What you decide will be critical for the health and welfare of the child and his or her family. An incorrect decision may have extremely harmful consequences.

32. Social workers, clinicians, and law enforcement officers working with cases of child maltreatment or in Child Protective Services must walk a fine line between protecting children and protecting the rights of parents and other people.

33. Any of the following conditions may indicate that you should take immediate action to protect the child: The child is experiencing life-threatening conditions, has multiple injuries, needs immediate medical attention, has been abandoned, is suicidal, is fearful of people in the home, is living in physically hazardous conditions, and may be in immediate danger. In addition, immediate action may be needed when the caregiver exhibits behavior that is violent or out of control; has caused serious physical harm to the child or has made a plausible threat; has not provided or will not provide sufficient supervision to protect the child from potentially serious harm; has not met or is unable to meet the child's immediate needs for food, clothing, shelter, and/or medical care; has previously maltreated a child; or has a drug or alcohol problem that seriously affects his or her ability to supervise, protect, or care for the child.

34. Factors that may place the child at risk for maltreatment include family poverty, poorly educated parents, authoritarian child-rearing practices, family insularity and social isolation, parents who suffer from depression, parents who abuse substances, parents who are unemployed, domestic violence in the home, parents who were maltreated as children, family environment that is in constant crisis and chaos, and little organization or structure to daily routines in the family. These factors are likely to cause stress in the family and influence the caregiver's ability to take care of the children in the family. However, the presence of any or all of these factors does not indicate that the child has been maltreated.

35. Risk assessment protocols can aid you in making a decision, but they also require you to make judgments.

36. Risk assessment protocols bring some uniformity to the assessment process, help you focus on relevant variables, ensure that you do not overlook important variables, allow you to compare your judgments across several cases, and allow you to compare your judgments with those of others.

37. Risk assessment is not a one-time process. Constant monitoring of the child and family is necessary until you believe that there is no more danger to the child.

Interventions

38. The ability of the child, parents, siblings, and known offender to recover from the maltreatment in large part will

depend on how each was functioning before the maltreatment occurred.

39. Other factors that will affect the recovery process include the age of the child, the type of maltreatment, the length of the maltreatment, the prior relationship between the child and the offender, their relationship after the maltreatment, the supports available to each individual involved, and the court orders.

40. After consultation with Child Protective Services and law enforcement personnel, as needed, and after a review of all the case material, the county district or state attorney will decide whether to petition the court for a hearing.

41. Once the court becomes involved in a child maltreatment case, it may take months or even several years to resolve the case.

42. If the court decides that child maltreatment did occur, it will consider three important guidelines in making its decision—family autonomy, the best interests of the child, and the least detrimental alternative.

43. After you complete your evaluation, you may want to develop an intervention plan. Direct your plan to ways of helping the child cope with the maltreatment, enhancing the child's development, reducing the factors contributing to the family's vulnerability, decreasing the likelihood that stressful events will occur, helping family members understand and deal with their own feelings about the maltreatment, and improving the family's coping mechanisms.

44. In developing your intervention plan, consider the information you have about the maltreatment, the victim, the perpetrator, and the family. For example, consider the structure of the family, family dynamics, the family's resources, availability of extended family members, changes needed in the parents and family, interventions needed by the family, agencies or practitioners available to provide services, ability of the family to pay for services, and the individuals who need the services.

45. Consider removing the child from the home primarily when the child is at risk for further maltreatment or is in immediate danger.

46. Instead of removing the children from homes where there is domestic violence, a better solution might be to remove the batterer from the home.

47. Once a child has been removed from the home, you will have to decide if and when he or she should return home.

48. Reunification may not be feasible if the caregiver is actively psychotic, suicidal, and/or a danger to himself or herself or others; has psychotic delusions that involve the child; is of extremely low functioning, has no positive family support system, and is not capable of learning to care for the child; has a history of maltreatment that resulted in the death of a child; has Munchausen's Syndrome by Proxy; inflicted physical trauma to the child that, if untreated, would cause permanent physical disfigurement, permanent physical disability, or death; inflicted severe internal injuries on the child; inflicted multiple or healing fractures in young infants; is responsible for the child's failure to thrive; deliberately poisoned the child; inflicted burns on the child for punitive purposes; sexually abused the child and, in the process, caused significant bleeding, deep bruising, significant external or internal swelling, bone fracture, or unconsciousness; or engaged in sadistic abuse of the child.

49. Interventions to help maltreated children with a disability include helping them understand what situations increase their risk of maltreatment, enlightening their caregivers about the

sexual needs of adolescents with disabilities, and promoting societal norms and attitudes that show respect for body integrity and the right of all individuals to protection.

50. Interventions to help maltreated children in schools include recommending the most appropriate educational setting, involving the nonsuspect parent(s) in the treatment process, helping teachers understand the needs of children who have been maltreated, coordinating services for the maltreated children, encouraging researchers to conduct studies of how maltreated children function in schools, and encouraging schools to develop programs that can identify maltreated children.

51. Interventions to help maltreated children in institutions and residential settings include identifying stressful factors, instituting program changes to meet the needs of the children, hiring competent staff, providing fair salaries for residential personnel, educating staff regarding maltreatment, enforcing policies regarding mistreatment of residents, increasing security procedures, offering crisis management training, reassigning staff, and making the professional staff more accessible to the direct care staff.

52. Interventions to help maltreated children in foster homes include carefully evaluating the families and homes before placing the children in the homes; helping foster parents understand the needs of foster children, especially those with special needs; informing the children of any plans that involve them; protecting the children's major attachment relationships; maintaining foster children's sense of historical continuity, and coordinating efforts among foster parents, natural parents, social workers, and agency staff.

53. Intervention efforts with an individual convicted of maltreating children may be more successful when the convicted offender accepts responsibility for the maltreatment; acknowledges the child's needs as primary; is concerned about the impact of the maltreatment on the child; is attached to his or her child (in cases of intrafamilial maltreatment); is distressed about his or her actions; acknowledges his or her need to change and accepts the need for treatment; is willing to change his or her attitudes; used minimal or no force; did not threaten to harm the child; committed the maltreatment only one time under stress; acknowledges that there are problems in the family; is willing to change his or her communication patterns within the family; is willing to work with mental health professionals to develop the ability to detect early warning signs that might lead him or her to maltreat a child and to develop more appropriate modes of self-expression, need gratification, and impulse management; is willing to make restitution; lives in a family in which the members do not scapegoat or blame the child; lives in a family that has a sound family structure and good relationships among its members; has adequate social and occupational skills; and has no major psychopathology or substance abuse problem.

54. Intervention efforts with a convicted offender will likely be more difficult when he or she scapegoats or blames the child or someone else for the abusive act; has been treated for previous offenses and continues to repeat the same offenses; has a history of extensive antisocial behavior, or alcohol or drug addiction or has many problem behaviors; continues to have a substance abuse problem; used violence, physical force, or a weapon or threatened to use a weapon; used progressively more force to commit repeated offenses; used predatory or ritualistic methods that continued despite the victim's expres-

sions of distress; and has significant intellectual deficits that limit his or her ability to learn from the consequences of his or her behavior.

55. Behavioral and cognitive-behavioral programs for parents who have physically abused or neglected their children typically involve some form of skills training that focuses on child management skills, anger-control skills, and/or general stress management.

56. Examples of interventions with parents who neglect their children are providing parents with information about child development and how meeting their child's needs will help the child become more independent; helping parents identify and attend to children's signals that parental attention is required; helping parents improve their living conditions; teaching parents better home management, budgeting, and shopping skills; recommending that parents obtain psychotherapy for depression or negative, dysfunctional self-images; and providing help with other conditions that interfere with the parents' ability to adequately care for their children.

57. In cases of domestic violence, psychotherapeutic approaches are based on the premise that domestic violence is learned and can be controlled by teaching batterers better conflict resolution skills; therapy aims to help batterers change their violent behavior.

58. There is much that we can do as a society to prevent and remediate child maltreatment, including supporting programs that provide fertility planning and encouragement for adolescents to defer parenthood; education and strong incentives for at-risk youth to remain in school and complete their education; employment opportunities; economic assistance, such as guaranteed minimal incomes, child allowances, and housing benefits; professional home visits designed to provide emotional support, reduce social isolation, and provide alternative childrearing strategies; parenting education classes during and after pregnancy; and affordable or free high-quality child care.

59. The tide of domestic violence could be stemmed if we as a society would eliminate the norms that legitimize and glorify violence in society and the family, reduce violence-provoking stress created by society, integrate families into a network of kin and community, change the sexist character of society, and break the cycle of violence in the family.

Concluding Comment About Interviewing Children Who May Have Been Maltreated

60. The field of child maltreatment is truly interdisciplinary. Professionals representing social work, law enforcement, medicine, psychology, education, psychiatry, and other disciplines all may be involved in a case. Failure to do a competent job anywhere in the investigatory process may mean that a child's life is endangered, that innocent people's lives are ruined, and that the public's trust is breached.

61. In the final analysis, the community is responsible for children—no one agency or person can assume responsibility alone.

KEY TERMS, CONCEPTS, AND NAMES

STUDY QUESTIONS

1. What are some of the critical questions that you may need to decide after you evaluate the findings in cases of child maltreatment? Include in your discussion the types of errors that can be made in evaluating cases of child maltreatment.

2. In preparing for your evaluation of a case of child maltreatment, what types of basic information do you need?

3. How would you go about evaluating the interview findings obtained from a child in a case of child maltreatment?

4. Describe how you would go about evaluating the credibility of a child's report in a case of child maltreatment. Include in your discussion general indices of credibility, as well as additional specific indices of credibility in allegations of (a) physical abuse, (b) neglect, (c) emotional abuse, and (d) sexual abuse.

5. Describe how you would evaluate cases of Sudden Infant Death Syndrome.

6. Discuss how you would evaluate families in cases of child maltreatment.

7. Discuss how you would evaluate the alleged offender in cases of child maltreatment. Include in your discussion indices in the caregiver of possible child maltreatment.

8. Discuss how you would evaluate a known offender in cases of child maltreatment. Include in your discussion some questions that the court typically will want you to answer about the convicted offender.

9. Discuss how you would evaluate a facility, institution, or foster home in cases of child maltreatment. Include in your discussion signs suggesting that the facility or institution may be deficient in caring for children.

10. Describe how you would conduct a risk assessment. Include in your discussion some critical decisions that you might need to make and risk assessment protocols. What conditions in the child and in the caregiver would prompt you to take immediate action? What are some strengths and weaknesses of risk assessment?

11. Describe the New York State risk assessment protocol.

12. In cases of child maltreatment, the court will want specific information about the case in order to arrive at an intervention decision. Describe what information the court will want, some possible decisions that the court can make, and what will guide the court in making its decision.

13. Discuss intervention efforts with maltreated children and their families. Include in your discussion arguments in favor of and against family reunification. When would you recommend family reunification, and when would you not recommend family reunification?

14. Discuss interventions to prevent child sexual abuse.

15. Discuss interventions to help maltreated children with a disability.

16. Discuss interventions to help maltreated children in schools.

17. Discuss interventions to help maltreated children in institutions, residential settings, and foster homes.

18. Discuss intervention efforts to help convicted offenders. Include a discussion of prognosis for offenders.

19. Discuss interventions to help domestic violence offenders.

20. Discuss interventions at a societal level in cases of child maltreatment and domestic violence.

EPILOGUE

I would like to close with a poem from *The Prophet,* written by Kahil Gibran. The poem richly illustrates the interdependence between parent and child and the need for all of us to recognize the uniqueness of each child.

Your children are not your children.
They are the sons and daughters of Life's longing for itself.
They came through you, but not from you,
And though they are with you yet they belong not to you.
You can give them your love but not your thoughts.
For they have their own thoughts.
You can house their bodies but not their souls,
For their souls dwell in the house of tomorrow, which you cannot visit, not even in your dreams.
You can strive to be like them, but seek not to make them like you.
For life goes not backward nor tarries with yesterday.
You are the bows from which your children as living arrows are sent forth.
The archer sees the mark upon the path of the infinite, and He bends you with His might that
   His arrows may go swift and far.
Let your bending in the archer's hand be for gladness;
For even as He loves the arrow that flies, so He loves also
The bow that is stable.

APPENDIX A

LIST OF NATIONAL ORGANIZATIONS FOR FAMILIES WITH SPECIAL NEEDS

Action for Child Protection
2101 Sardis Road N, Suite 204
Charlotte, NC 28227
(704)845-2121
FAX (704)845-8577

Adam Walsh Child Resource Center
9176 Alternate A1A, N100
Lake Park, FL 33403
(407)820-9000
FAX (407)835-8628

Adults Molested as Children United
(AMACU)
Giarretto Institute
232 E. Gish Road, 1st Floor
San Jose, CA 95112
(408)453-7616
FAX (408)453-9064

Alexander Graham Bell Association for
the Deaf (AGBAD)
3417 Volta Place NW
Washington, DC 20007
(202)337-5220
FAX (202)337-8314

American Academy of Pediatrics
141 Northwest Point Boulevard
P.O. Box 927
Elk Grove Village, IL 60009-0927
(847)228-5005
FAX (847)228-5097

American Bar Association, Center on
Children and the Law (ABACCL)
750 15th Street NW, 9th Floor
Washington, DC 20005
(202)662-1720
FAX (202)662-1755

American College of Obstetricians and
Gynecologists (ACOG)
409 12th Street SW
Washington, DC 20024-2188
(202)638-5577
FAX (202)484-8107

American Foundation for the Blind
(AFB)
11 Penn Plaza, Suite 300
New York, NY 10011
(212)502-7600
(800)232-5463
FAX (212)502-7777

American Humane Association (AHA)
63 Inverness Drive E
Englewood, CO 80122-5117
(303)792-9900
FAX (303)792-5333

American Medical Association (AMA)
515 N. State Street
Chicago, IL 60610
(312)464-5000
FAX (312)464-4184

American Professional Society on
Abuse and Children (APSAC)
407 S. Dearborn Street, Suite 1300
Chicago, IL 60605
(312)554-0166
FAX (312)554-0919

American Psychiatric Association
(APA)
1400 K Street NW
Washington, DC 20005
(202)682-6000
FAX (202)682-6114

American Psychological Association
(APA)
750 First Street NE
Washington, DC 20002-4242
(202)336-5500
FAX (202)336-5568

American Public Welfare Association
(APWA)
810 First Street NE, Suite 500
Washington, DC 20002-4267
(202)682-0100
(202)682-2384
FAX (202)289-6555

ARC
500 E. Border Street, Suite 300
Arlington, TX 76010
(817)261-6003
FAX (817)277-3491

Arthritis Foundation (AF)
1314 Spring Street NW
Atlanta, GA 30309
(404)872-7100
(800)283-7800
FAX (404)872-0457

Association for the Education and
Rehabilitation of the Blind and
Visually Impaired (AER)
206 N. Washington Street, Suite 320
Alexandria, VA 22314
(703)548-1884
FAX (703)683-2926

Attention Deficit Disorder Association
(National ADDA)
P.O. Box 972
Mentor, OH 44061
(800)487-2282

Autism Society of America (ASA)
7910 Woodmont Avenue, Suite 650
Bethesda, MD 20814
(301)657-0881
(800)328-8476
FAX (301)657-0869

Boys and Girls Clubs of America
    (BGCA)
1230 W. Peachtree Street NW
Atlanta, GA 3030
(404)815-5700
(800)854-2582
FAX (404)815-5757

Candlelighters Childhood Cancer
    Foundation (CCCF)
7910 Woodmont Avenue, Suite 460
Bethesda, MD 20814
(301)657-8401
(800)366-2223
FAX (301)718-2686

Center for Women Policy Studies
2000 P Street NW, Suite 508
Washington, DC 20036
(202)872-1770
FAX (202)872-8962

Child Welfare Institute (CWI)
1349 W. Peachtree Street NE, Suite 900
Atlanta, GA 30390
(404)876-1934
FAX (404)876-7949

Child Welfare League of America
    (CWLA)
440 First Street NW, Suite 310
Washington, DC 20001-2085
(202)638-2952
FAX (202)638-4004

Childhelp USA
PO Box 630
Los Angeles, CA 90028
(800)422-4453

Children and Adults with Attention
    Deficit Disorders (CH. A. D. D.)
499 NW 70th Avenue, Suite 101
Plantation, FL 33317
(305)587-3700
FAX (305)587-4599

Children's Defense Fund (CDF)
25 E Street NW
Washington, DC 20001
(202)628-8787
(800)233-1200
FAX (202)662-3530

Committee for Children (CFC)
2203 Airport Way S, Suite 500
Seattle, WA 98134
(206)343-1223
(800)634-4449
FAX (206)343-1445

Council for Exceptional Children (CEC)
1920 Association Drive
Reston, VA 22091
(703)620-3660
(703)264-9462
FAX (703)264-9494

Cystic Fibrosis Foundation (CFF)
6931 Arlington Road, No. 200
Bethesda, MD 20814
(301)951-4422
(800)344-4823
FAX (301)951-6378

Daughters and Sons United (DSU)
232 E. Gish Road, 1st Floor
San Jose, CA 95112
(408)453-7611 ext. 124
FAX (408)453-9064

EMERGE: Counseling and Education to
    Stop Male Violence
2380 Massachusetts Avenue, Suite 101
Cambridge, MA 02140
(617)547-9879
FAX (617)547-0904

Epilepsy Foundation of America (EFA)
4351 Garden City Drive
Landover, MD 20785
(301)459-3700
(800)332-1000
FAX (301)577-2684

Family Violence Prevention Fund's
    Health Resource Center on Domestic
    Violence
383 Rhode Island Street, Suite 304
San Francisco, CA 94103-5133
(415)252-8900
(888)792-2873
FAX (415)252-8991

Juvenile Diabetes Foundation
    International (JDFI)
120 Wall Street
New York, NY 10005
(212)889-7575
(800)533-2873
FAX (212)725-7259

Learning Disabilities Association of
    America (LDA)
4156 Library Road
Pittsburgh, PA 15234
(412)341-1515
FAX (412)344-0224

National Association of Counsel for
    Children (NACC)
1205 Oneida Street
Denver, CO 80220
(303)322-2260
FAX (303)327-3523

National Association of Social Workers
    (NASW)
750 First Street NE, Suite 700
Washington, DC 20002
(202)408-8600
(800)638-8799
FAX (202)336-8312

National Association of the Deaf (NAD)
814 Thayer Avenue
Silver Springs, MD 20910
(301)587-1788
FAX (301)587-1791

National Black Child Development
    Institute (NBCDI)
1023 15th Street NW, Suite 600
Washington, DC 20005
(202)387-1281
FAX (202)234-1738

National Center for Assault Prevention
606 Delsea Drive
Sewell, NJ 08080
(609)582-7000
(800)258-3189
FAX (609)582-3588

National Center for Education in
    Maternal and Child Health
    (NCEMCH)
2000 15th Street N, Suite 701
Arlington, VA 22201-2617
(703)524-7802
FAX (703)524-9335

National Center for Learning Disabilities
    (NCLD)
381 Park Avenue S, Suite 1420
New York, NY 10016
(212)545-7510
FAX (212)545-9665

National Center for Missing and
   Exploited Children and Hotline
   (NCMEC)
2101 Wilson Boulevard, Suite 550
Arlington, VA 22201-3052
(800)843-5678
(703)235-3900
FAX (703)235-4067

National Center for Prosecution of Child
   Abuse (NCPCA)
99 Canal Center Plaza, Suite 510
Alexandria, VA 22314
(703)739-0321
FAX (703)549-6259

National Center on Child Abuse and
   Neglect (NCCAN)
P.O. Box 1182
Washington, DC 20013-1182
(800)394-3366
FAX (703)385-3206

National Children's Advocacy Center
200 Westside Square, Suite 700
Huntsville, AL 35801
(205)534-6868
FAX (205)534-6883

National Clearinghouse for Alcohol and
   Drug Information (NCADI)
P.O. Box 2345
Rockville, MD 20847-2345
(800)729-6686
FAX (301)468-6433

National Coalition Against Domestic
   Violence
P.O. Box 18749
Denver, CO 80218
(303)839-1852
FAX (303)831-9251

National Coalition Against Sexual
   Assault
912 N. Second Street
Harrisburg, PA 17102
(717)232-6745
(717)232-7460
FAX (717)232-6771

National Coalition of Hispanic Health
   and Human Services Organizations
   (COSSMHO)
1501 16th Street NW
Washington, DC 20036
(202)387-5000
FAX (202)797-4353

National Committee to Prevent Child
   Abuse (NCPCA)
332 S. Michigan Avenue, Suite 1600
Chicago, IL 60604-4357
(312)663-3520
(800)244-5373
FAX (312)939-8962

National Council of Juvenile and Family
   Court Judges (NCJFCJ)
P.O. Box 8970
University of Nevada
Reno, NV 89507
(702)784-6012
FAX (702)784-6628

National Council on Child Abuse and
   Family Violence (NCCAFV)
1155 Connecticut Avenue NW
Suite 400
Washington, DC 20036
(202)429-6695
(800)222-2000

National Court Appointed Special
   Advocate Association (NCASAA)
100 W. Harrison Street, North Tower
Suite 500
Seattle, WA 98119
(206)270-0072
(800)628-3233
FAX (206)270-0078

National Crime Prevention Council
   (NCPC)
1700 K Street NW, 2nd Floor
Washington, DC 20006-3817
(202)466-6272
FAX (202)296-1356

National Criminal Justice Reference
   Service (NCJRS)
P.O. Box 6000
Rockville, MD 20849-6000
(301)251-5500
(800)627-6872
FAX (410)792-4358

National Domestic Violence Hotline
(800)799-7233

National Down Syndrome Congress
   (NDSC)
1605 Chantilly Drive, Suite 250
Atlanta, GA 30324
(404)633-1555
(800)323-6372
FAX (404)633-2817

National Easter Seal Society (NESS)
230 W. Monroe
Chicago, IL 60606
(312)726-6200
(800)221-6827
FAX (312)726-1494

National Education Association (NEA)
1201 16th Street NW
Washington, DC 20036
(202)833-4000
FAX (202)822-7974

National Exchange Club Foundation for
   Prevention of Child Abuse (NECF)
3050 Central Avenue
Toledo, OH 43606
(419)535-3232
(800)760-3413
FAX (419)535-1989

National Federation of the Blind (NFB)
1800 Johnson Street
Baltimore, MD 21230
(410)659-9314
(800)638-7518
FAX (410)685-5653

National Hemophilia Foundation (NHF)
110 Greene Street, Suite 303
New York, NY 10012
(212)219-8180
FAX (212)431-0906

National Indian Child Welfare
   Association (NICWA)
3611 S.W. Hood Street, Suite 201
Portland, OR 97201
(503)222-4044
FAX (503)222-4007

National Indian Justice Center
7 Fourth Street, Suite 46
Petaluma, CA 94952
(707)762-8113
FAX (707)762-7681

National Information Center for Children
   and Youth with Disabilities (NICHCY)
P.O. Box 1492
Washington, DC 20013-1492
(202)884-8200
(800)695-0285
FAX (202)884-8441

National Information Clearinghouse for Infants with Disabilities and Life-Threatening Conditions (NIC)
University of South Carolina
Center for Developmental Disabilities
Benson Building, 1st Floor
Columbia, SC 29208
(803)777-4435
(800)922-9234
FAX (803)777-6058

National Maternal and Child Health Clearinghouse (NMCHC)
2070 Chain Bridge Road, Suite 450
Vienna, VA 22182
(703)821-8955
FAX (703)821-2098

National Mental Health Association (NMHA)
1021 Prince Street
Alexandria, VA 22314-2971
(703)684-7722
(800)969-6642
FAX (703)684-5968

National Organization for Men (NOM)
11 Park Place
New York, NY 10007
(212)686-6253
FAX (212)766-4030

National Organization for Victims Assistance (NOVA)
1757 Park Road NW
Washington, DC 20010
(202)232-6682
(800)879-6682
FAX (202)462-2255

National Organization for Women (NOW)
1000 16th Street NW, Suite 700
Washington, DC 20036
(202)331-0066
FAX (202)785-8576

National Runaway Switchboard
3080 N. Lincoln
Chicago, IL 60657
(800)621-4000
FAX (773)929-5150

National SIDS Resource Center (NSRC)
8201 Greensboro Drive, Suite 600
McLean, Va 22102-3843
(703)821-8955
FAX (703)821-2098

National Tay-Sachs and Allied Diseases Association (NTSAD)
2001 Beacon Street
Brookline, MA 02146
(617)277-4463
(800)906-8723
FAX (617)277-0134

National Victim Center (NVC)
2111 Wilson Boulevard, Suite 300
Arlington, VA 22201
(703)276-2880
FAX (703)276-2889

National Youth Crisis Hotline
(800)448-4663

New York State Coalition Against Domestic Violence
79 Central Avenue
Albany, NY 12206
(518)432-4864
(800)942-6906 (New York State only)
FAX (518)432-4864

Orton Dyslexia Society (ODS)
800 LaSalle Road
Baltimore, MD 21286
(410)296-0232
(800)222-3123
FAX (410)321-5069

Parents Anonymous (PA)
675 W. Foothill Boulevard
Claremont, CA 91711
(909)621-6184
FAX (909)625-6304

Parents United International (PU)
615 15th Street
Modesto, CA 95354
(408)453-7616
FAX (408)453-9064

Society of Teachers of Family Medicine (STFM)
8880 Ward Parkway
Kansas City, MO 64114
(800)274-2237
(816)333-9700
FAX (816)333-3884

Spina Bifida Association of America
4590 MacArthur Boulevard NW
Suite 250
Washington, DC 20007
(202)944-3285
(800)621-3141
FAX (202)944-3295

Survivors of Incest Anonymous (SIA)
P.O. Box 21817
Baltimore, MD 21222-6817
(410)282-3400

United Cerebral Palsy Associations
1522 K Street NW, Suite 1112
Washington, DC 20003
(202)776-0406
FAX (202)776-0414

Victims of Child Abuse Laws (VOCAL)
11625 East Old Spanish Trail
Tucson, AZ 85730-5615
(520)722-1968
FAX (520)722-1968

VOICES in Action (Victims of Incest Can Emerge Survivors)
P.O. Box 148309
Chicago, IL 60614
(312)327-1500
(800)786-4232
FAX (312)327-4592

WomanKind (Worldwide) (WW)
3/4 Albion Place
Galena Road
London W6 OLT
England
44 181 5638 607
44 181 5638 608
FAX 44 181 5638 611

Women's Bureau Clearinghouse
U.S. Department of Labor
Room S3317
200 Constitution Avenue NW
Washington, DC 20210-0002
(202)219-4486
(800)827-5335
FAX (202)219-5529

Youth Development International
P.O. Box 178408
San Diego, CA 92177-8408
(619)759-5683
FAX (619)759-1460

GENERAL SOURCES OF INFORMATION FOR FAMILIES WITH SPECIAL NEEDS

BOOKS FOR PARENTS

Adoption

Gilman, L. (1992). *The adoption resource book* (3rd ed.). New York: HarperCollins. (This book explores issues involved in adoption.)

Jewett, C. L. (1978). *Adopting the older child.* Boston: Harvard Common Press. (Case histories are used to illustrate the emotional and practical aspects of adopting an older child.)

Johnston, P. I. (1992). *Adopting after infertility.* Indianapolis: Perspectives Press. (This book is designed to help infertile couples determine if adoption is the right choice for them.)

Komar, M. (1991). *Communicating with the adopted child.* New York: Walker. (This book addresses how to give information to an adopted child about his or her past. It stresses the importance of acknowledging the child's legitimate concerns about his or her origins.)

Melina, L. R. (1986). *Raising adopted children: A manual for adoptive parents.* New York: Harper & Row. (This book, designed for parents, gives practical, reassuring advice about adoption. It addresses becoming an instant family, concerns that arise as the adoptee grows up, and other special issues in adoption.)

Melina, L. R. (1989). *Making sense of adoption: A parent's guide.* New York: HarperCollins. (This book focuses on the importance of clear and open communication in the adoptive family.)

Register, C. (1990). *"Are those kids yours?": American families with children adopted from other countries.* New York: Free Press. (This sensitive and compassionate inquiry into the many ethical and psychosocial issues associated with cross-cultural adoptions is important reading for anyone who has adopted internationally or is considering doing so.)

Schaffer, J., & Lindstrom, C. (1989). *How to raise an adopted child: A guide to help your child flourish from infancy through adolescence.* New York: Plume. (This book discusses issues that might arise during an adopted child's development, from infancy through the teen years.)

Takas, M., & Warner, E. (1992). *To love a child: A complete guide to adoption, foster parenting, and other ways to share your life with children.* Reading, MA: Addison-Wesley. (This book covers several topics related to adoption, including the process of adoption, adoption by a foster parent, and international adoption.)

Watkins, M., & Fisher, S. (1993). *Talking with young children about adoption.* New Haven: Yale University Press. (This sensitive book should be of interest to adoptive parents and family therapists who work with adoptive families.)

Asthma

Plaut, T. F. (1988). *Children with asthma: A manual for parents.* Amherst, MA: Pedipress. (This book gives parents much useful information about asthma in children.)

Attention-Deficit/Hyperactivity Disorder

Bain, L. J. (1991). *A parent's guide to attention deficit disorders.* New York: Dell. (This book discusses ADHD, including definitions and treatments.)

Barkley, R. A. (1995). *Taking charge of ADHD: The complete, authoritative guide for parents.* New York: Guilford Press. (This book gives excellent suggestions to parents for managing children with ADHD and for enhancing children's school performance.)

Coleman, W. S. (1988). *Attention deficit disorders, hyperactivity and associated disorders: A handbook for parents and professionals* (5th ed.). Madison, WI: Calliope Books. (This book is designed to help parents and professionals understand the causes and treatment of attention-deficit disorders.)

Dendy, C. A. Z. (1995). *Teenagers with ADD: A parent's guide.* Bethesda, MD: Woodbine House. (This book takes a comprehensive look at the issues and challenges faced by teenagers with ADHD, their families, teachers, and professionals.)

Fowler, M. C. (1990). *Maybe you know my kid: A parent's guide to identifying, understanding, and helping your child with attention-deficit hyperactivity disorder.* Secaucus, NJ:

Carol Publishing Group. (This book is written by a parent about understanding children with ADHD.)

Friedman, R. J., & Doyal, G. T. (1987). *Attention deficit disorder and hyperactivity* (2nd ed.). Danville, IL: Interstate. (This book provides a good overview of attention deficit-disorder and hyperactivity for parents and teachers.)

Garber, S. W., Garber, M. D., & Spizman, R. F. (1990). *If your child is hyperactive, inattentive, impulsive, distractible....* New York: Villard Books. (This book provides a step-by-step program to improve children's attention span, concentration, and self-control.)

Gordon, M. (1991). *ADHD/hyperactivity: A consumer's guide for parents and teachers.* New York: GSI Publications. (This book presents 30 principles designed to help parents understand attention-deficit/hyperactivity disorder.)

Greenberg, G. S., & Horn, W. F. (1991). *Attention deficit hyperactivity disorder: Questions and answers for parents.* Champaign, IL: Research Press.

Ingersoll, B. (1988). *Your hyperactive child: A parent's guide to coping with attention deficit disorder.* New York: Doubleday. (This book provides information about symptoms and causes of attention-deficit disorder.)

Ingersoll, B., & Goldstein, M. (1993). *Attention deficit disorder and learning disabilities: Realities, myths, and controversial treatments.* New York: Doubleday. (This book reviews treatments for ADHD.)

Johnson, D. D. (1992). *I can't sit still; educating and affirming inattentive and hyperactive children.* Santa Cruz, CA: ETR Associates. (This book provides suggestions to parents and teachers for managing children with ADHD.)

Jones, C. B. (1991). *Source book for children with attention deficit disorder: A management guide for early childhood professionals and parents.* Tucson: Communication Skill Builders.

Kennedy, P., Terdal, L., & Fusetti, L. (1993). *The hyperactive child book.* New York: St. Martin's Press. (This book discusses ADHD and ways parents can deal with professionals.)

Moss, R. A. (1990). *Why Johnnie can't concentrate: Coping with attention deficit disorder.* New York: Bantam. (This book presents information about children, adolescents, and adults who have an attention-deficit disorder.)

Neuville, M. B. (1991). *Sometimes I get all scribbly: Living with attention deficit/hyperactivity disorder.* Lacrosse, WI: Crystal Press. (This book provides a mother's account of her experiences with her own child with attention-deficit/hyperactivity disorder.)

Parker, H. C. (1988). *The ADD hyperactivity workbook for parents, teachers, and kids* (2nd ed.). Plantation, FL: Specialty Press. (This book provides strategies for helping children with ADHD at home.)

Umansky, W., & Smalley, B. S. (1994). *ADD: Helping your child.* New York: Warner. (This book provides good examples of how ADHD affects children at school and at home. It gives practical strategies to help parents work with their ADHD children.)

Wodrich, D. L. (1994). *Attention deficit hyperactivity disorder: What every parent wants to know.* Baltimore: Paul H. Brookes. (This book provides answers to questions and concerns that parents and educators may have about children with an attention-deficit/hyperactivity disorder.)

Autistic Disorder

Baron-Cohen, S., & Bolton, P. (1993). *Autism: The facts.* New York: Oxford University Press. (This book provides answers to basic questions regarding autism.)

Greenfield, J. (1973). *A child called Noah.* New York: Warner Paperback. (A father writes of the family's experiences in coping with an autistic son.)

Greenfield, J. (1978). *A place for Noah.* New York: Holt, Rinehart & Winston. (This is a sequel to Greenfield's earlier book.)

Harris, S. L. (1994). *Siblings of children with autism: A guide for families.* Bethesda, MD: Woodbine House. (This book will be useful in helping parents of children with an autistic disorder deal with the needs of other family members.)

Park, C. C. (1983). *The siege: The first eight years of an autistic child: With an epilogue, 15 years later.* London: Hutchinson. (A mother writes sensitively about raising her autistic daughter.)

Behavior Disorders

Love, H. D. (1987). *Behavior disorders in children: A book for parents.* Springfield, IL: Charles C Thomas. (This book outlines the assessment process for children with behavior problems, the role of the psychologist, causes of common disorders, and behavioral treatment.)

Blindness

Harrison, F., & Crow, M. (1993). *Living and learning with blind children.* Toronto: University of Toronto Press. (This general guide for parents and teachers of visually impaired children has many practical suggestions for working with visually impaired children.)

Lowenfeld, B. (1971). *Our blind children.* Springfield, IL: Charles C. Thomas. (Written primarily for parents, this comprehensive treatment of the situation of blind children from birth through adolescence provides helpful suggestions on a variety of topics.)

Scott, E. P., Jan, J. E., & Freeman, R. D. (1977). *Can't your child see? A guide for parents and professionals.* Baltimore: University Park Press. (This general guide for parents of visually handicapped children covers various aspects of blindness and offers suggestions for both parents and professionals.)

Ulrich, S. (with Wolf, A. W. M.). (1972). *Elizabeth.* Ann Arbor: University of Michigan Press. (A mother describes the first five years of her blind child's life and provides many useful ideas for home care.)

Cancer

Adams, D. W., & Deveau, E. J. (1984). *Coping with childhood cancer: Where do we go from here?* Reston, VA: Reston. (The book stresses hope in dealing with childhood cancer and discusses what can and cannot be done to cure cancer.)

Bearlson, D. J. (1991). *They never want to tell you: Child talk about cancer.* Cambridge, MA: Harvard University Press. (This valuable book for parents, professionals, and older children presents narratives of eight children who have cancer. It includes common themes about children who face cancer.)

Bracken, J. M. (1986). *Children with cancer: A comprehensive reference guide for parents.* New York: Oxford. (The book describes the range of childhood cancers, how cancer can affect the child, treatments for cancer, and other useful topics.)

Lilleyman, J. S. (1994). *Childhood leukaemia: The facts.* Oxford, England: Oxford University Press. (The book answers parents' questions about childhood leukemia in a clearly written manner.)

Child Maltreatment

Crowley, P. (1990). *Not my child: A mother confronts her child's sexual abuse.* New York: Doubleday. (This book examines emotional and behavioral problems associated with children who have been maltreated.)

Hagans-Sharp, K. B., & Case, J. (1988). *When your child has been molested: A parent's guide to healing and recovery.* Lexington, MA: Lexington Books. (This book offers suggestions regarding therapy for children who have been sexually molested.)

Hillman, D., & Solek-Tefft, J. (1990). *Spiders and flies: Help for parents and teachers of sexually abused children.* New York: Free Press. (This book gives parents, teachers, and counselors suggestions when they suspect or discover that a child has been abused.)

Child Rearing

General

Bettelheim, B. (1987). *The good enough parent: A book on child-rearing.* New York: Knopf. (This book focuses on raising children as individuals. Subjects include developing self-hood in children, parental expectations, and children's school performance.)

Crystal, D. (1986). *Listen to your child: A parent's guide to children's language.* New York: Penguin Books. (This book is designed to help parents understand their child's language development.)

Griffore, R. J., & Boger, R. P. (1986). *Child rearing in the home and school.* New York: Plenum Press. (This book on child-rearing is designed for parents, teachers, and health-care workers. Issues discussed include special problems of ethnic minority families and the interrelations between home and school and their effects on ability and achievement.)

Williamson, P. (1990). *Good kids, bad behavior: Helping children learn self-discipline.* New York: Simon & Schuster. (This book discusses the use of discipline as a teaching tool and emphasizes self-discipline for children. It offers guidance to parents whose children get out of control and who need help in establishing routines and rituals.)

Infants, Toddlers, and Preschoolers

American Academy of Pediatrics. (1991). *Caring for your baby and young child: Birth to age five.* New York: Bantam. (This book provides detailed information on specific health problems in young children.)

Brazelton, T. B. (1989). *Toddlers and parents: A declaration of independence* (Rev. ed.). New York: Dell. (This book examines the struggle for independence and self-mastery that every child goes through between the ages of 1 and 3 years. The cases, which illustrate events at various ages and in diverse family settings, are presented with commentary and referrals to relevant research.)

Brazelton, T. B. (1992). *Touchpoints: Your child's emotional and behavioral development; the essential reference.* Reading, MA: Addison-Wesley. (This introductory book surveys a child's development during the first three years of life and discusses common emotional and behavioral problems that children have during the first six years of life.)

Devine, M. (1991). *Baby talk: The art of communicating with infants and toddlers.* New York: Plenum Press. (This book, written for both parents and early childhood staff educators, explores the communication process from birth to 3 years of age. It also describes games and activities that can help adults communicate with children.)

Driscoll, J., & Walker, M. (1989). *Taking care of your new baby: A guide to infant care.* Garden City Park, NY: Avery Publishing Group. (This sourcebook covers issues in basic care of an infant, including feeding, elimination, crying, and bathing, and examines postpartum adjustment in both the mother and the father.)

Kopp, C. B. (1994). *Baby steps: The "whys" of your child's behavior in the first two years.* New York: W. H. Freeman. (This book provides a detailed account of the first two years of development.)

Leach, P. (1989). *Your baby and child: From birth to age five* (2nd rev. ed.). New York: Knopf. (This book is a detailed account of the developmental stages between birth and age 5 and how developmental accomplishments are expressed in a child's behavior.)

Lief, N. R., & Fohs, M. E. (1991). *The first year of life* (Rev. ed.). New York: Walker. (This book gives advice on child-rearing methods from birth to age 1 year.)

Lief, N. R., & Thomas, R. M. (1991). *The second year of life* (Rev. ed.). New York: Walker. (This book give advice on child-rearing methods for ages 1 to 2 years.)

Lief, N. R., with Thomas, R. M. (1992). *The third year of life.* New York: Walker. (This book gives advice on child-rearing methods for ages 2 to 3 years.)

Rosemond, J. (1990). *Parent power!: A common-sense approach to parenting in the '90s and beyond* (Rev. ed.). Kansas City, MO: Andrews & McMeel. (This book provides a commonsense approach to parenting.)

Spock, B., & Rothenberg, M. B. (1992). *Dr. Spock's baby and child care* (6th ed.). New York: Dutton. (This is an enduring standard in the field of child care.)

School-Aged Children and Adolescents

American Academy of Pediatrics. (1991). *Caring for your adolescent: Ages 12–21.* New York: Bantam. (This book covers adolescent development, including psychological, social, and sexual development.)

Elkind, D. (1993). *Parenting your teenager in the '90s: Practical information and advice about adolescent development and contemporary issues.* Rosemont, NJ: Modern Learning Press. (This book addresses some of the pressing issues affecting teens and parents today. It emphasizes the adolescent's need for a compassionate parent, who can set limits and yet understand teen life in the 1990s.)

Kelly, M. (1989). *The mother's almanac II: Your child from six to twelve.* New York: Doubleday. (This book looks at the changes of the middle years through the lenses of developmental cycles, family life, and the outside world.)

Patterson, G., & Forgatch, M. (1987). *Parents and adolescents living together—Part 1: The basics.* Eugene, OR: Castalia Publishing. (This book is designed to help parents cope with problems that they typically encounter with raising adolescents.)

Shalov, J., Sollinger, I., Spotts, J., Steinbrecher, P. S., & Thorpe, D. W. (1991). *You can say no to your teenager, and other strategies for effective parenting in the 1990s.* Reading, MA: Addison-Wesley. (This book examines how parents can clarify their values and thoughtfully guide adolescents to develop their own identity and beliefs.)

Steinberg, L., & Levine, A. (1990). *You and your adolescent: A parent's guide for ages 10–20.* New York: HarperCollins. (This book provides a comprehensive review of developmental changes by age group, a survey of psychological health and development, and an examination of social relations, school, and the transition to adulthood in the life of an average adolescent.)

Deafness and Hearing Impairments

Medwid, D., & Weston, D. C. (1995). *Kid-friendly parents with deaf and hard of hearing children.* Washington, DC: Gallaudet University Press. (Designed for parents of deaf or hard-of-hearing children who are between the ages of 3 and 12 years, this book provides guidelines that focus on play activities, special resources, and support services.)

Spradley, T. S., & Spradley, J. P. (1978). *Deaf like me.* New York: Random House. (In this true account of a family's experiences with a deaf daughter, including the search for an appropriate education, the authors advocate a total communication approach to language development.)

West, P. (1970). *Words for a deaf daughter.* New York: Harper & Row. (A novelist-poet-critic tells the story of his deaf and brain-damaged daughter.)

Death

Arnstein, H. (1960). *What to tell your children.* Indianapolis: Bobbs Merrill. (This guide helps parents explain death to children.)

Bloom, L. A. (1986). *Mourning after suicide.* New York: Pilgrim Press. (This book is for survivors of suicide.)

Bolton, I., & Mitchell, C. (1983). *My son…my son: A guide to healing after death, loss, or suicide.* Atlanta: Bolton Press. (This book is for survivors of suicide.)

Buckingham, R. W. (1983). *A special kind of love: Care of the dying child.* New York: Continuum. (This book was written to help parents understand and care for a terminally ill child. Issues discussed include fear of dying, children's ideas of death, and parental guilt. Also included is a listing of information and support agencies, children's hospice programs, and home care programs.)

Crenshaw, D. A. (1990). *Bereavement.* New York: Continuum. (Written for a general audience, this book presents information about grieving children and adults at different developmental stages. The author discusses reactions to different deaths [e.g., that of siblings, classmates, and parents], coping strategies, and counseling needs of preschoolers, school-aged children, adolescents, and adults.)

Donnelly, N. H. (1987). *I never know what to say: How to help your family and friends cope with tragedy.* New York: Ballantine. (Written by a hospital chaplain and based on her personal experiences with death and with relatives and friends of dying and deceased children, this book describes well the grieving process of children and teenagers and gives concrete suggestions for what to do and say to the bereaved.)

Gaffney, D. A. (1988). *The seasons of grief: Helping children grow through loss.* New York: Plume.

Grollman, E. A. (1967). *Explaining death to children.* Boston: Beacon Press. (This book is designed to help parents discuss the subject of death with their children.)

Grollman, E. A. (1976). *Talking about death.* Boston: Beacon Press. (This book explains the concept of death to children and lays the groundwork for future support in times of bereavement.)

Hewett, J. H. (1980). *After suicide.* Philadelphia: Westminister Press. (This book is designed to help families who have a member who recently has committed suicide.)

Jackson, E. N. (1965). *Telling a child about death.* New York: Hawthorne. (This book explores ways to discuss death with children.)

Kolehmainen, J., & Handwerk, S. (1986). *Teen suicide, a book for friends, family, and classmates.* Minneapolis: Lerner. (In this easy-to-read book for survivors and those who know a potentially suicidal teen, the authors use fictionalized vignettes from the lives of hurting teens to illustrate facts and myths about suicide.)

Lombardo, V. S., & Lombardo, E. F. (1986). *Kids grieve too!* Springfield, IL: Charles C Thomas. (This book is intended to help parents understand how children view death, deal with death, and react to a death.)

Lukas, C., & Seiden, H. (1987). *Silent grief.* New York: Charles Scribner's Sons. (This book is for survivors of suicide.)

Nuttall, D. (1991). *The early days of grieving.* Beaconsfield, England: Beaconsfield Publishers. (This clear, reassuring, and practical book for people who are recently bereaved covers the common questions that recently bereaved people ask themselves.)

Rosenfeld, L., & Prupas, M. (1984). *Left alive: After a suicide in the family.* Springfield, IL: Charles C Thomas. (This book is for family members and friends and for the helping professionals who work with them following a suicide.)

Schaefer, D., & Lyons, C. (1988). *How do we tell the children? Helping children understand and cope when someone dies.* New York: Newmarket. (This book discusses children's understanding of and reactions to death at different ages. It provides scripts for explaining death from many causes, including suicide, homicide, and old age. This is an excellent resource for parents, teachers, and counselors who work with very young children and teachers of high school child development courses.)

Schif, H. S. (1977). *The bereaved parent.* New York: Crown. (This book is designed to help parents work through the death of their child.)

Stein, S. B. (1972). *About dying.* New York: Walker & Co. (This book presents the idea of the cycle of life and death to children.)

Tatelbaum, J. (1980). *The courage to grieve.* New York: Harper & Row. (This book presents various aspects of grief and grief resolution, including important ideas about self-help, avenues for finishing unfinished business, and how to let go.)

Veninga, R. (1985). *The gift of hope: How we survive our tragedies.* Boston: Little, Brown. (This book guides readers through grief and goes to the spiritual and emotional core of heartbreak. Its last sections deal specifically with suicide.)

Wolf, W. (1973). *Helping your child to understand death.* Springfield, IL: Charles C Thomas.

Depression

Cytryn, L., & McKnew, D. H., Jr. (1996). *Growing up sad.* New York: Norton. (An excellent overview of childhood depression, useful for both parents and professionals.)

Herskowitz, J. (1988). *Is your child depressed?* New York: Pharos. (The book will help parents recognize depression in children and learn how to help depressed children.)

Oster, G. D. (1995). *Helping your depressed teenager: A guide for parents and caregivers.* New York: Wiley. (This book provides suggestions for helping depressed teenagers. Topics include understanding depression, suicide, and interventions.)

Shamoo, T. K., & Patros, P. G. (1996). *Helping your child cope with suicide and suicidal thoughts.* San Francisco: Jossey-Bass. (This is a guide for parents of depressed teenagers. It shows what signs of suicide to watch for; how to talk to, listen to, and communicate with depressed teenagers; and how to intervene in cases of potential suicide.)

Diabetes

Elliott, J. (1990). *If your child has diabetes—An answer book for parents.* New York: Perigee. (This book will help parents understand how to care for children with diabetes.)

Johnson, R. W., Johnson, S., & Kleinman, S. (1992). *Managing your child's diabetes.* New York: MasterMedia. (Filled with important facts and compassionate advice, this book will help families cope better with their diabetic child.)

Loring, G. (1991). *Parenting a diabetic child.* Los Angeles: Lowell House. (A down-to-earth, practical guide to help parents learn to care for their diabetic child, taking into consideration the overall family dynamics.)

Siminerio, L., & Betschart, J. (1995). *Raising a child with diabetes.* Alexandria, VA: American Diabetes Association. (This book provides guidelines for parents and family members to help them raise children with diabetes.)

Divorce

Ahrons, C. R. (1994). *The good divorce: Keeping your family together when you marriage comes apart.* New York: HarperCollins. (This scholarly and comprehensive resource for therapists and laypeople offers hope to divorcing couples, as well as guidance through the transition from a nuclear to a "binuclear" family.)

Ahrons, C. R., & Rodgers, R. H. (1989). *Divorced families: Meeting the challenge of divorce and remarriage.* New York: Norton.

Benedek, E. P., & Brown, C. F. (1995). *How to help your child overcome your divorce.* Washington, DC: American Psychiatric Press. (This book is designed to aid parents in helping children under age 12 adjust to separation and divorce.)

Cohen, M. G. (1989). *Long distance parenting.* New York: New American Library. (This guidebook specifically focuses on keeping the long-distance connections intact and growing.)

Diamond, S. A. (1985). *Helping children of divorce: A handbook for parents and teachers.* New York: Schocken. (This book is designed to help parents and teachers work with children of divorce.)

Ferrara, F. (1985). *On being a father: A divorced man talks about sharing the new responsibilities of parenthood.* New York: Doubleday/Dolphin. (This book shows how divorced fathers can maintain a productive relationship with their children.)

Jewitt, C. (1982). *Helping children cope with separation and loss.* Boston: Harvard Common. (This book offers information about the expected behaviors and mourning processes of children and techniques that help children process their losses.)

Kalter, N. (1989). *Growing up with divorce: Helping your child avoid immediate and later emotional problems.* New York: Free Press. (This book offers information on helping children whose parents are divorced become better adjusted.)

Lansky, V. (1991). *Vicki Lansky's divorce book for parents: Helping your children cope with divorce and its aftermath.* New York: New American Library. (This comprehensive, down-to-earth, and affordable book is written by a divorced parent.)

Neuman, G. (1983). *101 ways to be a long distance superdad.* Mountain View, CA: Blossom Valley Press. (This concise paperback gives lots of helpful tips and ideas.)

Plumb, G. B., & Lindley, M. E. (1990). *Humanizing child custody disputes: The family's team.* Springfield, IL: Charles C Thomas. (Intended for parents, legislators, and mental health and legal professionals, this book gives information on meeting children's emotional and psychological needs in child custody situations and explores ethical principles, custody criteria, the psychological evaluation, and visitation rights.)

Ricci, I. (1980). *Mom's house, Dad's house: Making shared custody work.* New York: Macmillan. (This book helps with the everyday considerations that make joint custody a successful option.)

Wallerstein, J. S., & Blakeslee, S. (1990). *Second changes: Men, women, and children a decade after divorce.* Boston: Houghton Mifflin. (This book is insightful and clearly written. It describes the risks that adolescence poses to children of divorce.)

Weitzman, L. J. (1985). *The divorce revolution: The unexpected social and economic consequences for women and children in America.* New York: Free Press. (This book examines the social and economic consequences of divorce.)

Eating Disorders

Romeo, F. F. (1986). *Understanding anorexia nervosa.* Springfield, IL: Charles C Thomas. (This book explains anorexia nervosa in a clear, readable manner and explores the causes, effects, treatment, and prevention of the disorder.)

Sherman, R. T., & Thompson, R. A. (1996). *Bulimia: A guide for family and friends.* San Francisco: Jossey-Bass. (This book, which answers questions most frequently asked by the families and friends of individuals with bulimia, offers practical information and advice.)

Learning Disabilities

Brutten, M., Richardson, S., & Mangel, C. (1973). *Something's wrong with my child.* New York: Harcourt Brace Jovanovich. (This book offers practical information on various aspects of raising a child with learning disabilities.)

Clarke, L. (1973). *Can't read, can't write, can't talk too good either: How to recognize and overcome dyslexia in your child.* New York: Penguin Books. (A mother writes about her experiences with her learning-disabled child.)

Cronin, E. M. (1994). *Helping your dyslexic child: A guide to improving your child's reading, writing, spelling, comprehension, and self-esteem.* Rocklin, CA: Prima. (A book designed for parents who want to help their children overcome dyslexia and build the children's self-esteem.)

Grabow, B. W. (1978). *Your child has a learning disability... What is it? A guide for parents and teachers.* Chicago: National Easter Seal Society for Crippled Children and Adults. (This inexpensive booklet provides parents and teachers with basic information concerning the nature of learning disabilities, as well as practical tips for coping with the problem.)

Kronick, D. (Compiler). (1970). *They too can succeed: A practical guide for parents of learning-disabled children.* San Rafael, CA: Academic Therapy Publications. (The collected articles, written for parents of learning-disabled children, cover a wide variety of topics related to child management and offer practical ways for parents to help their children overcome learning problems.)

Kronick, D. (1975). *What about me? The L. D. adolescent.* San Rafael, CA: Academic Therapy Publications. (This book is about the particular problems experienced by learning-disabled adolescents, their parents and teachers, and other professionals working with them. It is particularly sensitive to the questions of parents and to questions the developing adolescent asks about himself or herself.)

Nowicki, S., Jr., & Duke, M. P. (1992). *Helping the child who doesn't fit in.* Atlanta, GA: Peachtree Publishers. (This book is written for teachers, caregivers, parents, and other professionals to help them understand dysemmia—difficulty in understanding and reacting appropriately to nonverbal language.)

Osman, B. B. (1979). *Learning disabilities: A family affair.* New York: Random House. (The book briefly covers the diagnostic process and then focuses on parents' feelings, on parents' acceptance of their child, and on the child's behavior at home, at school, and with friends. Clinical case examples are used liberally, making reading easier.)

Osman, B. B. (1982). *No one to play with: The social side of learning disabilities.* New York: Random House. (This book deals sensitively with the social dilemmas of the learning-disabled child and how the learning problems and sensory and attention deficits cause social problems. Case examples offer helpful, concrete suggestions for facilitating social and emotional development. It also includes helpful

lists of legal resources, college programs, and state support groups.)

Rosalie, M. Y., & Savage, H. H. (1989). *How to help students overcome learning problems and learning disabilities: Better learning for all ages.* Danville, IL: Interstate. (Written for parents, teachers, volunteers, and therapists, this book focuses on understanding and helping students who have learning problems and children who are not ready for school learning.)

Schoonover, R. J. (1983). *Handbook for parents of children with learning disabilities.* Danville, IL: Interstate. (This short, concise, and easy-to-read book is packed with useful information.)

Stevens, S. H. (1980). *The learning-disabled child: Ways that parents can help.* Winston-Salem, NC: John F. Blair. (This book contains much useful information, especially on what teachers can offer learning-disabled youngsters and their parents. It also provides helpful guidelines for parents regarding management of homework, teacher-parent conferences, tutoring, and how to obtain appropriate professional help.)

Wallbrown, J. D., & Wallbrown, F. H. (1981). *So your child has a learning problem, now what?* Brandon, VT: Clinical Psychology Publications. (This book is helpful in understanding the nature and diagnosis of learning disabilities and how parents and teachers can help the learning-disabled child. It is recommended primarily for parents who have a child with auditory-processing problems.)

Weiss, M. S., & Weiss, H. G. (1976). *Home is a learning place: A parent's guide to learning disabilities.* Boston: Little, Brown. (This practical volume explains the many ramifications of learning disabilities and offers advice to parents concerning ways they can help their children.)

Mental Retardation

Cunningham, C. (1996). *Understanding Down syndrome: An introduction for parents.* Cambridge, MA: Brookline Books. (This book is designed for parents, as well as professionals, and provides an excellent overview of children with Down syndrome.)

Dolce, L. (1994). *Mental retardation.* New York: Chelsea House. (This book discusses types of mental retardation, the origins of mental retardation, and treatments for mental retardation, along with information on how to ensure the best education for mentally retarded children.)

Kumin, L. (1994). *Communication skills in children with Down syndrome.* Rockville, MD: Woodbine House. (The book offers many practical suggestions that parents can use to help their children with Down syndrome develop better speech and language skills.)

Peuschel, S. M. (1990). *A parent's guide to Down syndrome.* Baltimore: Paul H. Brookes. (This book provides useful information to parents about important developmental stages in the life of a child with Down syndrome.)

Schaefer, N. (1982). *Does she know she's there?* Toronto: Fitzhenry & Whiteside. (A mother describes her development in becoming an advocate for her severely retarded daughter.)

Smith, R. (Ed.). (1993). *Children with mental retardation: A parent's guide.* Rockville, MD: Woodbine House. (This edited volume covers medical, therapeutic, and educational needs of children who are mentally retarded.)

Strauss, S. (1975). *Is it well with the child? A parent's guide to raising a mentally handicapped child.* New York: Doubleday. (A professional writer tells of her own experiences as the parent of a mentally handicapped child and gives general advice for parents and professionals.)

Miscellaneous

Arnberg, L. (1987). *Raising children bilingually: The preschool years.* Clevedon, England: Multilingual Matters. (This book is designed for parents who speak languages other than English and who are looking for information about whether to raise their children bilingually.)

Bornstein, A. C. (1989). *Yours, mine, and ours: How families change when remarried parents have a child together.* New York: Scribner. (Written for remarried couples who have children from previous marriages or who anticipate having a child, this book is an introduction to possible concerns and problems that family members may have.)

Brans, J. (1987). *Mother, I have something to tell you: Understand your child's chosen life-style.* Garden City, NY: Doubleday. (This book is designed to help parents understand their older child's life style. It provides real-life examples of mother-child crises, including teenage pregnancy, drug abuse, homosexuality, and anorexia.)

Clark, L. (1989). *The time-out solution: A practical guide for handling common everyday behavior problems.* Chicago: Contemporary Books.

Cutler, B. C. (1993). *You, your child, and "special" education: A guide to making the system work.* Baltimore: Brookes. (This sound and practical book is designed to help parents who have children in special education become better advocates for their children.)

Faber, A., & Mazlish, E. (1982). *How to talk so kids will listen and listen so kids will talk.* New York: Avon.

McCue, K., with Bonn, R. (1994). *How to help children through a parent's serious illness.* New York: St. Martin's Press. (This practical book is designed to help adults help children cope with a parent's serious illness.)

McKay, G. D., & Dinkmeyer, D. C. (1989). *Systematic training for effective parenting: Parents' handbook.* Circle Pines, MN: American Guidance.

Monahon, C. (1993). *Children and trauma: A parent's guide to helping children heal.* New York: Lexington Books. (This practical book is designed to help parents cope with children who have faced crises.)

Schaefer, C. E., & Millman, H. L. (1989). *How to help children with common problems.* New York: Nal-Dutton.

Shore, M. F., Brice, P. J., & Love, B. G. (1992). *When your child needs testing: What parents, teachers, and other helpers need to know about psychological testing.* New York: Crossroad. (This book is designed to help parents understand and become involved in their child's psychological testing.)

Williamson, P. (1991). *Good kids, bad behavior: Helping children learn self-discipline.* New York: Simon & Schuster.

Other Physical and Medical Disabilities

Affleck, G., Tennen, H., & Rowe, J. (1991). *Infants in crisis: How parents cope with newborn intensive care and its aftermath.* New York: Springer-Verlag. (This book provides coping strategies for parents to help them deal with newborns in intensive care units.)

Aspar, V., & Beck, J. (1972). *Is my baby all right?* New York: Pocket Books.

Ayrault, E. V. (1971). *Helping the handicapped teenager mature.* New York: Association Press. (This guide to common problems includes directories of rehabilitation services, camps, colleges, and universities accepting the physically handicapped.)

Brown, H. (1976). *Yesterday's child.* New York: New American Library. (A mother writes openly about the emotions and realities she faced in raising her multiply handicapped daughter.)

Burks, H. F. (1978). *School and homework together.* Huntington Beach, CA: Arden Press. (This manual contains numerous practical suggestions on a variety of topics, most of which directly concern handicapped students. Most ideas can be implemented both in the classroom and at home.)

Featherstone, H. A. (1980). *A difference in the family: Living with a disabled child.* New York: Basic Books. (A parent writes about her profoundly handicapped child and her experiences with other parents who have similar problems.)

Ferber, R. (1985). *Solving your child's sleep problems.* New York: Simon & Schuster. (A physician describes sleep problems in children and gives advice to parents.)

Finnie, N. R. (1975). *Handling the young cerebral palsied child at home.* New York: Dutton. (This book gives excellent suggestions for parents, teachers, and therapists on working with cerebral palsied children, especially those between 1 and 5 years of age.)

Guide to resources for parents of the handicapped child. (1978). In *Yearbook of special education.* Chicago: Marquis Academic Media. (This is an excellent annotated resource list for parents, including books, self-help resources, and miscellaneous materials.)

Heisler, V. A. (1972). *A handicapped child in the family: A guide for parents.* New York: Grune & Stratton. (A handicapped professional author frankly and perceptively discusses what it means to be the parent of a handicapped child.)

Henderson, M., & Synhorst, D. (1975). *Care of the infant with myelomeningocele and hydrocephalus: A guide for parents.* Iowa City: University of Iowa Press.

Mantle, M. (1985). *Some just clap their hands: Raising a handicapped child.* New York: Adama Books. (This account of raising handicapped children is based on interviews and case histories. Its three parts cover discovering the handicap, coping with it, and placement outside the home.)

Mapes, M. K., Mapes, J. C., & Lian, M. G. J. (1988). *Education of children with disabilities from birth to three: A handbook for parents, teachers and other care providers.* Springfield, IL: Charles C Thomas. (This book addresses programs for children with disabilities. It includes information on teaching activities, rehabilitation services, and parental involvement.)

Massie, R., & Massie, S. (1975). *Journey.* New York: Knopf. (The authors write of their son's hemophilia and have much to say to families of children with other handicapping conditions.)

McNamara, J., & McNamara, B. (1977). *The special child handbook*. New York: Hawthorn. (The authors have directed their book toward parents of exceptional children. They cover practical information on topics such as helpful organizations and agencies, communicating with doctors, and selecting appropriate schools.)

Parent's Campaign for Handicapped Children and Youth. *Closer Look*. Box 1492, Washington, DC 20013. (Published by an organization for parents that is sponsored by the U.S. Department of Education, this extremely informative newsletter is appropriate for professionals, as well as for handicapped people and their parents. *Closer Look* and other publications of the organization are free.)

Phillips, R. H. (1984). *Coping with lupus: A guide to living with lupus for you and your family*. Wayne, NJ: Avery. (This book provides basic information on lupus and offers suggestions about emotional reactions to diagnosis and symptoms.)

Schimmel, D., & Fischer, L. (1977). *The rights of parents in the education of their children*. National Committee for Citizens in Education, Suite 410, Wilde Lake Village Green, Columbia, MD 21044. (This book covers many legal questions of interest to parents of handicapped children. One chapter is devoted to special education.)

Siegel, B., & Silverstein, S. (1994). *What about me? Growing up with a developmentally disabled sibling*. New York: Insight Books/Plenum Press. (This book will be of interest to parents, siblings, and professionals who work with children with special needs, as it focuses on how siblings of a disabled brother or sister cope.)

Tasker, M. (1992). *How can I tell you?* Bethesda, MD: Association for Care of Children's Health. (This book was written to help families and professionals understand the complex issues surrounding the disclosure of HIV infection to children.)

Turnbull, A., & Turnbull, H. (1978). *Parents speak out: Views from the other side of the two way mirror*. Columbus, OH: Charles Merrill. (This book offers insights from professionals who are parents of handicapped children.)

White, R. (1972). *Be not afraid*. New York: The Dial Press. (A father chronicles his family's experiences for 14 years, following the diagnosis of epilepsy in his 8-year-old son.)

Wright, B. (1983). *Physical disability—A psychosocial approach* (2nd ed.). New York: Harper & Row. (This excellent survey of physical disability was written both for parents and professionals.)

Sex Education

Berstein, A. C. (1978). *Flight of the stork*. New York: Delacorte. (This book presents research into children's ideas concerning human conception and birth. It is surprising and humorous and discusses the misconceptions often given to children by adults about sexuality.)

Sudden Infant Death Syndrome

Defrain, J., Ernst, L., Jakub, D., & Taylor, J. (1991). *Sudden infant death*. Lexington, MA: Lexington Books. (This insightful book, designed to help bereaved families of SIDS children, presents a positive approach to coping with this crisis.)

Horchler, J. N., & Morris, R. R. (1994). *The SIDS survival guide: Information and comfort for grieving family and friends and professionals who seek to help them*. Hyattsville, MD: SIDS Educational Services. (This useful collection of articles is for parents whose children died of sudden infant death syndrome.)

Sears, W. (1995). *SIDS: A parent's guide to understanding and preventing sudden infant death syndrome*. Boston: Little, Brown. (By providing clear and concise information about SIDS, this book raises parents' awareness about SIDS and promotes steps to reduce the risk of SIDS.)

BOOKS FOR CHILDREN

Books in this section are classified by level. *Preschool* books can be read aloud to children ages 2 to 5 years and usually have pictures that also tell the story. *Primary* books can be read aloud or by beginning readers, are of interest to kindergarteners through third graders, and are usually illustrated. *Elementary* books are on third- to eighth-grade levels of interest and reading. *Intermediate* books are on approximately a seventh- to ninth-grade reading level. *Youth* books are of interest to those of high school age (and often to adults) and have a relatively uncomplicated literary style; some youth books may be of interest to younger readers.

Adoption

Bloomquist, G. M. (1990). *Zachary's new home: A story for foster and adopted children*. New York: Magination Press. (Primary)

Dorris, M. (1989). *The broken cord*. New York: Harper and Row. (This book, a result of Dorris's research on the affliction of his 3-year-old Native American adopted son, is a combination of personal narrative and factual information on fetal alcohol syndrome. The final chapter is Adam's story, at age 21, in his own words.) (Youth)

Dunn, L. (1983). *Adopting children with special needs: A sequel*. Riverside, CA: North American Council on Adoptable Children. (This collection of short narratives by people involved in the adoption of special needs children deals with children who are emotionally impaired, mentally handicapped, and physically handicapped.) (Intermediate)

Girard, L. (1986). *Adoption is for always*. Morton Grove, IL: Albert Whitman. (Primary and Elementary)

Krementz, J. (1988). *How it feels to be adopted*. New York: Knopf. (This book features first-person narratives by adopted children, ages 8 to 16, from a variety of backgrounds.) (Elementary, Intermediate, and Youth)

Sandness, G. L. (1978). *Brimming over*. Minneapolis: Mini-World Publication. (The author, who is a quadriplegic, writes about her adoption of two children with disabilities. One child, a 4-year-old Korean-Caucasian girl, has cerebral palsy; the other child, 3-year-old Jennifer, is a victim of polio. The book, through photos and text, realistically depicts adopting children with disabilities.) (Youth)

Sandness, G. L. (1984). *Commitment: The reality of adoption*. Maple Grove, MN: Mini-World Publication. (The author provides short stories of special needs children and the families that adopt them.) (Intermediate)

Welch, S. K. (1990). *Don't call me Marda.* Wayne, PA: Our Child Press. (Eleven-year-old Marsha, who is an only child, has mixed emotions when her parents tell her that they are considering adopting a mentally handicapped child. After a homestudy, the parents adopt Wendy, a pretty 7-year-old who is mentally retarded. Marsha is initially embarrassed by Wendy's inappropriate behavior but in time learns to love Wendy. The book, a combination of narrative and Marsha's diary entries, reveals her change of heart and personal growth.) (Elementary and Intermediate)

Wheeler, K. (1979). *Tanya: The building of a family through adoption.* New York: North American Center on Adoption, Child Welfare League of America. (The author, who adopted a 6-year-old girl with a bone disease, describes the problems surrounding the adoption. The book covers the educational and medical needs of the child and also the adjustments that the family unit must make to meet the needs of a child with a disability.) (Youth)

AIDS

Ford, M. T. (1992). *100 questions and answers about AIDS: A guide for young people.* New York: New Discovery Books. (This book looks at questions most often asked about AIDS and gives straightforward, honest answers about what AIDS is and about issues related to transmission and prevention.) (Youth)

Sirimarco, E. (1994). *AIDS.* North Bellmore, NY: Marshall Cavendish. (This book, with excellent photos, will help teenagers learn about AIDS and how to prevent it.) (Youth)

Taylor, B. (1995). *Everything you need to know about AIDS.* New York: Rosen. (This short book, filled with photos, provides an introduction to AIDS, including information on how to prevent it and how to interact with those who have it.) (Youth)

Alcohol and Drugs

Allen, W. A., Piccone, N. L., & D'Amanda, C. (Eds.). (1987). *How drugs can affect your life: The effects of drugs on safety and well-being—with special emphasis on prevention of drug use* (2nd ed.). Springfield, IL: Charles C Thomas. (This easy-to-read book is aimed at adolescents, young adults, parents, and teachers. It discusses alcohol and drug abuse, including smoking, and provides guidelines for prevention and treatment.) (Youth)

Childress, A. (1973). *A hero ain't nothing but a sandwich.* New York: Coward, McCann, and Geoghegan. (This book discusses the life of a 13-year-old black heroin addict, who lives with his grandmother and stepfather. After initially denying that he has a problem, he gradually recognizes his problem and receives treatment.) (Intermediate and Youth)

Fishman, R. (1986). *Alcohol and alcoholism.* New York: Chelsea House. (This book was written for junior high students who need detailed information on the problems of alcohol use and alcoholism.) (Intermediate and Youth)

Greene, S. M. (1979). *The boy who drank too much.* New York: Viking. (This book is about a child who wrestles with his own drinking problem, as well as his father's. He finds support in the friendship of several peers and of an older recovered alcoholic.) (Youth)

Hawkes, N. (1986). *The heroin trail.* New York: Gloucester Press. (This excellent discussion of heroin pulls no punches. The book includes a pictorial presentation on heroin abuse.) (Intermediate and Youth)

Hyde, O. (1986). *Mind drugs.* New York: Dodd. (This volume provides information about the seriousness of the drug abuse problem. Counselors will find it extremely helpful.) (Intermediate and Youth)

Mohn, N. (1977). *In Nueva York.* New York: Dial Press. (This book tells the stories of many different people in a poor ethnic neighborhood in New York City whose lives intersect at Rudi's Diner. Alcohol and drugs are problems for several of the characters.) (Youth)

Newman, S. (1986). *You can say no to a drink or a drug.* New York: Putnam/Perigee. (Ten vignettes offer strategies for saying no to drugs and alcohol, even in the face of strong peer pressure.) (Intermediate and Youth)

Strasser, T. (1979). *Angel dust blues.* New York: Coward, McCann, and Geoghegan. (This book tells the story of a wealthy 17-year-old who becomes bored with life and turns to the drug culture for excitement.) (Intermediate and Youth)

Anger and Other Emotions

Anderson, M. (1978). *Step on a crack.* New York: Atheneum. (This story is about a girl who finds out that frequent nightmares in which she hurts someone are related to emotional strain she is experiencing.) (Youth)

Brett, D. (1992). *More Annie stories: Therapeutic storytelling techniques.* New York: Brunner/Mazel. (This sequel offers stories to help children cope with several problems, such as fear of the dark.) (Preschool and Elementary)

Danziger, P. (1985). *It's an aardvark-eat-turtle world.* New York: Delacorte. (In this story of the child of a white mother and black father, Rosie experiences the joys of first love and must deal with a racist who does not like seeing her with a boy who is white.) (Intermediate and Youth)

Galvin, M. (1988). *Robby really transforms: A story about grown-ups helping children.* New York: Magination Press. (This story-picture book is designed for young children to read by themselves or with adults. It gives children an understanding of how an adult therapist can help a depressed child or a withdrawn child.) (Elementary)

Philips, B. (1980). *Don't call me fatso.* Milwaukee: Raintree Children's Books. (This book illustrates how a child deals with emotional problems related to being overweight.) (Elementary)

Thomas, B. (1986). *Who stole Mrs. Wick's self-esteem?* Chicago: National Committee for Prevention of Child Abuse. (This educational pamphlet, written in storybook form, provides easy ways to improve self-esteem. Characters solve "mysteries" of why people have poor self-esteem.) (Preschool, Primary, and Elementary)

Asthma

Carter, A. R., & Carter, S. M. (1996). *I'm tougher than asthma!* Morton Grove, IL: Albert Whitman. (This beautifully illustrated book will help build self-confidence in elementary school–aged children who have asthma.) (Elementary)

Attention-Deficit/Hyperactivity Disorder

Corman, C., & Trevino, E. (1995). *Eulcee the jumpy jumpy elephant.* Plantation, FL: Specialty Press. (Primary and Elementary)

Galvin, M. (1988). *Otto learns about his medicine: A story about medication for hyperactive children.* New York: Magination Press. (This story-picture book is designed for young children to read by themselves or with adults. It gives children an understanding of how taking medicine helps hyperactivity.) (Elementary)

Gordon, M. (1992). *I would if I could.* De Witt, NY: GSI. (Elementary)

Moss, D. (1989). *Shelly the hyperactive turtle.* Rockville, MD: Woodbine House. (Elementary)

Parker, R. (1992). *Making the grade.* Plantation, FL: Specialty Press. (Youth)

Quinn, P. O. (1992). *Putting on the brakes.* New York: Magination Press. (This book is designed to help children understand ADHD and provides suggestions for managing the disorder.) (Youth)

Blindness

Hickok, L. A. (1958). *The story of Helen Keller.* New York: Grosset & Dunlap. (This is a biography of the accomplished and famous blind and deaf woman.) (Elementary and Intermediate)

Krents, H. (1972). *To race the wind.* New York: G. P. Pulnarus. (This autobiography of an undaunted blind young man is both moving and humorous.) (Youth)

Radin, R. Y. (1990). *Carver.* New York: Macmillan. (This book shows that, with determination, blind persons can avoid being helpless.) (Elementary)

Child Maltreatment

Adler, C. S. (1984). *Fly free.* Rutherford, NJ: Coward-MaCann. (This book is about a girl who learns to cope with the reality of the situation that has driven her mother to hate her.) (Elementary, Intermediate, and Youth)

Anderson, D., & Finne, M. (1986). *Liza's story: Neglect and the police.* Minneapolis, MN: Dillon Press. (This book is about a girl, neglected by her widowed father and in danger of becoming delinquent, who is helped by a therapist.) (Elementary and Intermediate)

Anderson, D., & Finne, M. (1986). *Margaret's story: Sexual abuse and going to court.* Minneapolis: Dillon Press. (This book is about sexual abuse and how a child confronts her perpetrator and successfully gets through the experience of going to court.) (Primary)

Anderson, D., & Finne, M. (1986). *Michael's story: Emotional abuse and working with a counselor.* Minneapolis: Dillon Press. (This book deals with emotional abuse. A boy whose parents continually berate him believes himself to be stupid and unloved. A supportive counselor suggests that he and his parents undergo family therapy.) (Elementary and Intermediate)

Anderson, D., & Finne, M. (1986). *Robin's story: Physical abuse and seeing the doctor.* Minneapolis: Dillon Press. (This book deals with a girl who is physically abused by her mother. A teacher puts the girl in touch with a therapist, and, after her mother gets counseling, the relationship between mother and daughter improves.) (Elementary and Intermediate)

Bawden, N. (1982). *Squib.* New York: Lothrop. (This suspenseful story portrays an abused child who is rescued by her friends.) (Intermediate and Youth)

Gil, E. (1983). *Outgrowing the pain.* San Francisco: Launch Press. (Youth)

Gil, E. (1986). *A book for kids who were abused.* San Francisco: Launch Press. (Elementary)

Girard, L. W. (1984). *My body is private.* Morton Grove, IL: Albert Whitman. (This book addresses ways for parents to talk about sexual abuse with their children and what to do when it occurs.) (Primary)

Hunter, M. (1990). *Abused boys: The neglected victims of sexual abuse.* Lexington, MA: Lexington Books/Heath. (Written for boys who are recovering from sexual abuse, this book addresses general issues of sexual abuse and issues related to recovery. It also will be helpful to therapists treating male victims of sexual abuse.) (Youth)

Kehoe, P. (1987). *Something happened and I'm scared to tell: A book for young victims of abuse.* Seattle, WA: Parenting Press. (Primary)

McGovern, K. (1985). *Alice doesn't babysit anymore.* Portland, OR: McGovern and Mulbacker Books. (Primary and Elementary)

Napier, N. J. (1993). *Getting through the day: Strategies for adults hurt as children.* New York: Norton. (This book is written for adult survivors of abuse but also can be used by older adolescents. It will help guide them through the journey of healing from abuse.) (Youth)

Sweet, P. (1985). *Something happened to me.* Racine, WI: Mother Courage. (Elementary)

Wachter, O. (1983). *No more secrets for me.* Boston: Little, Brown. (Primary)

Deafness and Hearing Impairments

Aseltine, L. (1986). *I'm deaf and it's okay.* Niles, IL: Albert Whitman. (A narrator describes the frustrations caused by his deafness and explains how he copes. The narrator's dilemma is presented in a realistic fashion and can be used as a starting point for discussion of disabilities.) (Elementary)

Peterson, J. W. (1977). *I have a sister, my sister is deaf.* New York: Harper & Row. (This book is a realistic portrait of an independent and happy child who happens to be deaf.) (Primary)

Robinson, V. (1966). *David in silence.* Philadelphia: Lippincott. (In this story, a deaf boy in industrial Birmingham, England has many adventures; his thoughts and feelings are sensitively chronicled.) (Intermediate and Youth)

Scott, V. (1986). *Belonging.* Washington, DC: Gallaudet University Press. (This book is the story of a popular girl, struck by meningitis at 15, who is physically devastated by her illness. She slowly gets her strength back, but she loses her hearing.) (Intermediate)

Warfield, F. (1957). *Keep listening.* New York: Viking Press. (The author tells of her struggles as a hard-of-hearing adolescent.) (Youth)

Death

Agee, J. (1969). *A death in the family.* New York: Bantam. (This Pulitzer Prize–winning novel provides insight into how death affects a family, including the misunderstandings that often occur.) (Youth)

Braithwaite, A. (1982). *When Uncle Bob died.* London: Dinosaur Publications. (This excellent booklet for children and young adolescents helps them understand and gain perspective on dying and associated issues.) (Elementary, Intermediate, Youth)

Brown, M. W. (1958). *The dead bird.* Reading, MA: Childrens Addison-Wesley Publishing Co. (This book can help very young children understand death.) (Preschool)

Bunting, E. (1982). *The happy funeral.* New York: Harper & Row. (This story of a young Chinese girl who grieves for her grandfather tells of how she helps prepare for his funeral and is comforted by cultural rituals.) (Elementary, Intermediate, and Youth)

Clardy, A. F. (1984). *Dusty was my friend.* New York: Human Sciences. (This book shows how sharing memories of the deceased alleviates the pain of grieving, as a young boy tells about his friend who was killed in an automobile accident.) (Elementary, Intermediate, and Youth)

Coutant, H. (1974). *First snow.* New York: Random House. (This book helps very young children understand death by describing the unfolding process of life and death.) (Preschool)

Crawford, C. P. (1974). *Three-legged race.* New York: Harper & Row. (This book helps older children understand the death of a friend. It is a story of three teenagers who form an unusual friendship.) (Intermediate and Youth)

De Paola, T. A. (1973). *Nana upstairs and Nana downstairs.* New York: Penguin. (This tender and unpretentious story describes a 4-year-old's first contact with death.) (Preschool and Primary)

Fassler, J. (1971). *My grandpa died today.* New York: Human Sciences Press. (This is the story of an ailing grandfather who tries to prepare his grandson for his imminent death. Although his grandfather's death saddens him greatly, the child is able to resume his usual pursuits rather quickly—a normal reaction for a child his age.) (Primary and Elementary)

Greene, C. C. (1976). *Beat the turtle drum.* New York: Viking. (After her younger sister dies when she falls from a tree, the girl in this book experiences emotions common after a sibling death—loneliness, anger, confusion over her parents' reactions, and deep sadness.) (Intermediate and Youth)

Hammond, J. (1981). *When my daddy died and when my mommy died.* Cincinnati: Cranbrook. (This is a book of simple drawings and text.) (Preschool and Primary)

Koch, R. (1975). *Goodbye grandpa.* Minneapolis: Augsburg Publishing House. (This book helps children understand death.) (Primary)

Krementz, J. (1981). *How it feels when a parent dies.* New York: Knopf. (This book has several first-person accounts by children aged 7 to 16 years who have suffered the death of a parent.) (Intermediate and Youth)

Lee, V. (1972). *The magic moth.* New York: Seabury Press. (Explained from a child's point of view, this is an excellent story about how a family copes with the loss of a child.) (Elementary)

LeShan, E. (1988). *Learning to say goodbye: When a parent dies.* New York: Avon. (This book describes common feelings after the death of a parent and offers suggestions on how to work through the grief.) (Elementary, Intermediate, and Youth)

Miles, M. (1971). *Annie and the old one.* Boston: Little, Brown. (This classic, fictional story depicts a Native American grandmother explaining death to a young child. The grandmother believes that she will die when she finishes the rug she is weaving. The book teaches that death is a natural part of the life cycle.) (Primary, Elementary, and Intermediate)

Powell, E. S. (1990). *Geranium morning.* Minneapolis: Carolrhoda Books. (This book tells about Timothy, whose dad was killed in a car accident, and Frannie, whose mother is dying.) (Elementary)

Richter, E. (1986). *Losing someone you love: When a brother or sister dies.* New York: Putnam. (Young people ages 10 to 24 discuss candidly their experiences following the death of a sibling.) (Intermediate and Youth)

Rofes, E. (Ed.). (1985). *Kid's book about death and dying.* Boston: Little, Brown. (Students, ages 11 to 14, explore their feelings and thoughts about death and grief, discussing topics ranging from causes of death, euthanasia, and funerals to graveyards.) (Intermediate and Youth)

Saint-Exupery, A. (1943). *The little prince.* New York: Harcourt Brace. (This book helps children understand death.) (Primary and Elementary)

Sanders, P. (1990). *Let's talk about death and dying.* London: Aladdin Books. (This helpful book, with photographs of everyday situations, is designed to be read by an adolescent thinking about death and dying either in relation to his or her own circumstances or as part of an education program.) (Intermediate and Youth)

Silverstein, S. (1964). *The giving tree.* New York: Harper & Row. (This book helps children understand death by using a simple parable to describe the passage from youth to old age.) (Primary and Elementary)

Slote, A. (1973). *Hang tough Paul Mather.* Philadelphia: Lippincott. (This book helps children understand death by describing how a child with leukemia faces death.) (Elementary)

Smith, D. B. (1973). *A taste of blackberries.* New York: Thomas Crowell. (This book helps children understand death through a sensitive portrayal of the sudden, violent death of a child's close friend and the death's affect on the child.) (Elementary)

Stigney, D. (1984). *Water-bugs and dragonflies: Explaining death to children.* London: Mowbray. (This famous allegorical tale explains dying—and the failure of the dead to return—in terms of water-bugs turning into dragonflies. It is best read to young children and followed by discussion about the death of the person they have lost.) (Preschool)

Viorst, J. (1972). *The tenth good thing about Barney.* New York: Atheneum. (This book helps children understand death through an account of the death of a family pet.) (Preschool, Primary, and Elementary)

White, E. B. (1952). *Charlotte's web.* New York: Harper & Row. (This book is about how one copes with the death of a friend.) (Elementary)

Williams, M. (1958). *The velveteen rabbit.* New York: Doubleday. (This book may help young children understand that a deceased loved one can live on in the children's hearts and through their memories.) (Primary and Elementary)

Zolotow, C. (1974). *My grandson Lew.* New York: Harper. (A 6-year-old boy and his mother share their memories of the boy's beloved grandfather. The child's memories comfort his mother in her grief.) (Primary, Elementary, Intermediate, and Youth)

Diabetes

Alvin, V., & Silverstein, R. (1994). *Diabetes.* Hillsdale, NJ: Enslow. (This book covers a useful range of topics associated with diabetes, including types and causes of diabetes, how to test and treat diabetes, how to live with it, and how to prevent it.) (Youth)

Betschart, M. N., & Thom, S. (1995). *In control: A guide for teens with diabetes.* Minneapolis: Chronimed Publishing. (This book is designed to help teenagers cope with diabetes.) (Youth)

Landau, E. (1994). *Diabetes.* New York: Twenty-First Century Books. (This book offers a useful overview of diabetes for teenagers.) (Youth)

Pirner, C. W. (1991). *Even little kids get diabetes.* Morton Grove, IL: Albert Whitman. (Parents can read this picture book about children who have diabetes to their young children.) (Preschool and Primary)

Divorce

Banks, A. (1990). *When your parents get a divorce.* New York: Puffin/Penguin. (Elementary and Intermediate)

Barnwell, R. D. (1972). *Shadow on the water.* New York: David McKay. (A 13-year-old girl responds to the painful situation between her parents.) (Intermediate)

Bawden, N. M. K. (1969). *The runaway summer.* Philadelphia: Lippincott. (This book discusses many aspects of divorce, including displacement of aggression, meanings of friendship, honesty/dishonesty, parental rejection, and living in the home of relatives.) (Elementary)

Boegehold, B. (1985). *Dad doesn't live here anymore.* Racine, WI: Western Publishing. (This book is about a young girl who acts out her family's problems with her dolls. She eventually realizes that she will still see her father, just not as often.) (Preschool and Primary)

Cameron, E. (1975). *To the green mountain.* New York: Dutton. (This story is about a young girl whose mother makes the painful decision to divorce her dad.) (Youth)

Cleary, B. (1986). *Dear Mr. Henshaw.* New York: Morrow Junior Books. (This serious story about divorce is told through letters from a sixth-grade boy to his favorite author.) (Elementary)

Dolmetsch, P., & Shih, A. (Eds.). (1985). *The kids' book about single-parent families.* Garden City, NY: Doubleday. (This book was written to help adolescents deal with living in a single-parent family. Topics discussed include the different stages of divorce, discipline, and parental dating.) (Youth)

Goff, B. (1988). *Where is Daddy? The story of divorce.* Boston: Beacon Press. (This book was written to help pre-schoolers cope with grief, loneliness, and confusion after parental separation.) (Preschool)

Grunsell, A. (1990). *Divorce.* New York: Gloucester. (This book, written in a question-and-answer format, discusses how children may cope with divorced parents.) (Elementary)

Hazen, B. S. (1978). *Two homes to live in: A child's eye-view of divorce.* New York: Human Sciences. (This picture book presents divorce issues from a child's viewpoint.) (Primary)

Holland, I. (1973). *Heads you win, tails I lose.* Philadelphia: Lippincott. (This story is about an overweight 15-year-old whose parents battle constantly and finally separate.) (Intermediate)

Hunter, E. (1976). *Me and Mr. Stenner.* New York: Atheneum. (This book deal with a child's learning that she can love both her stepfather and her real father.) (Elementary)

Jukes, M. (1984). *Like Jake and me.* New York: Knopf. (This book is about a young boy who is unsure of his feelings about his mother's being pregnant until he is able to forge a bond with his stepfather.) (Preschool and Primary)

Lexan, J. M. (1972). *Emily and the klunky baby and the next door dog.* New York: Dial Press. (This story is about a child who feels neglected after her parents divorce.) (Primary)

List, J. (1980). *The day the loving stopped: A daughter's view of her parents' divorce.* New York: Seaview. (Julie tells how she felt when her father left and how she copes with having to live two lives—one with Mum and one with Dad.) (Youth)

Mann, P. (1973). *My dad lives in a downtown hotel.* New York: Scholastic Press. (A boy who feels that he is responsible for his parents' divorce shows how he deals with these feelings.) (Intermediate)

Newfield, M. (1975). *A book for Jordan.* New York: Atheneum. (This book tells the story of a young girl, shaken by parental separation, who questions whether her parents still love her and whether she is to blame for their separation.) (Elementary)

Prokop, M. S. (1986). *Divorce happens to the nicest kids: A self-help book for kids (3–15) and adults.* Warren, OH: Alegra House. (This book was written for children going through divorce. It answers many questions that children have and offers positive suggestions for dealing with the consequences of a divorce.) (Preschool, Primary, Elementary, Intermediate, and Youth)

Schuchman, J. (1979). *Two places to sleep.* Minneapolis: Carolrhoda Books. (Nice drawings by Jim LaMarche illustrate the story of 7-year-old David, who lives with his father in their original house and visits his mother in her apartment on weekends. It emphasizes his happiness with each parent and that he is loved as much as ever and that the divorce is not his fault.) (Elementary)

Sobol, D. B. (1984). *The first hard times.* New York: Dell. (This book is about a girl who is devoted to the memory of her father, missing in action in Vietnam for more than 10 years, and who has difficulty accepting her new stepfather.) (Elementary and Intermediate)

Sullivan, M. (1988). *The parent/child manual of divorce.* New York: RGA Publishing Group. (This manual is meant to be read to very young children by their parents to teach them that the world is not as frightening as they might think and that they are not alone in facing life's difficulties.) (Preschool)

Vigna, J. (1984). *Grandma without me.* Niles, IL: Whitman. (This story is of a young boy, struggling with the divorce of his parents, whose grandmother provides support to him during this crisis.) (Preschool, Primary, Elementary, and Intermediate)

Eating Disorders

Sirimarco, E. (1994). *Eating disorders.* North Bellmore, NY: Marshall Cavendish. (This book, which contains interesting photographs, discusses anorexia nervosa, bulimia, and being overweight and provides useful suggestions for recognizing eating disorders and getting help.) (Youth)

Epilepsy

Landau, E. (1994). *Epilepsy.* New York: Twenty-First Century Books. (This book offers a brief overview of epilepsy, including how it is diagnosed and treated.) (Youth)

Family Violence

Burby, L. N. (1996). *Family violence.* San Diego: Lucent. (This book discusses several topics related to family violence, including child maltreatment, domestic violence, and victims killing the abusers.) (Youth)

Learning Disabilities

Gilson, J. (1980). *Do bananas chew gum?* New York: Lothrop, Lee & Shepard. (This fictional story is about a sixth-grade boy with a learning disability, whose thoughts and feelings about himself are sensitively presented.) (Youth)

Hayes, M. L. (1974). *The tuned-in, turned-on book about learning problems.* Novato, CA: Academic Therapy Publications. (This book will give learning-disabled children a better understanding of their problems and will help them develop some coping skills.) (Youth)

Morton, J. (1979). *Running scared.* Wheaton, IL: Elsevier/ Nelson Books. (This book is about a learning-disabled boy's frustration and inability to communicate. A counselor helps the boy deal with issues related to his disabilities.) (Elementary and Intermediate)

Pevsner, S. (1977). *Keep stompin' till the music stops.* New York: Clarion Books. (This fictional story is about a 12-year-old who has a learning disability. It is generally upbeat, and the vocabulary and humor are fairly sophisticated.) (Youth)

Mental Retardation

Ominsky, E. (1977). *Jon O. A special boy.* Englewood Cliffs, NJ: Prentice-Hall. (Photographs and text describe the life of a young boy with Down syndrome.) (Preschool and Primary)

Sobol, H. L. (1977). *My brother Steven is retarded.* New York: Macmillan. (The photographs and text tell a poignant and sensitive story from the perspective of a younger sister.) (Elementary)

Miscellaneous

Adams, B. (1979). *Like it is: Facts and feelings about handicaps from kids who know.* New York: Walker. (This book presents children discussing their disabilities and the problems that often accompany them. A range of disabilities are discussed, from mental retardation to physical disabilities.) (Intermediate)

Brandenberg, F. (1985). *Otto is different.* New York: Greenwillow. (This story is about an octopus who feels he is different from his friends because he has eight arms. However, he discovers that having eight arms can sometimes be to his advantage.) (Preschool and Primary)

Brown, T. (1984). *Someone special, just like you.* New York: Holt, Rinehart & Winston. (Through black-and-white photos, this book tells of children with disabilities playing and learning together.) (Primary)

Galvin, M. (1988). *Ignatius finds help: A story about psychotherapy for children.* New York: Magination Press. (This story-picture book is designed for young children to read

by themselves or with adults. It helps a child understand his or her family's first psychotherapy session.) (Elementary)

Goldman, M. N. (1994). *Emotional disorders.* North Bellmore, NY: Marshall Cavendish. (This book offers useful introduction to a range of emotional problems that teenagers may experience, including depression, anxiety, schizophrenia, substance abuse, alcoholism, eating disorders, and suicide. Excellent photographs enrich the book.) (Youth)

Kamien, J. (1979). *What if you couldn't…? A book about special needs.* New York: Scribner's. (This book explains the causes and characteristics of impaired mobility, blindness, dyslexia, deafness, and emotional problems.) (Elementary)

Other Physical and Medical Problems

Campanella, R. (1959). *It's good to be alive.* Boston: Little, Brown. (The baseball star tells of his life after being paralyzed as a result of an automobile accident.) (Youth)

Fassler, J. (1975). *Howie helps himself.* Chicago: Albert Whitman & Co. (This book is appropriate to share with a child in a wheelchair, who may appreciate reading about another child who is disabled.) (Primary)

Gordon, S. (1975). *Living fully: A guide for young people with a handicap, their parents, their teachers and professionals.* New York: John Day. (This special educator has a no-nonsense and compassionate approach to disabled kids.) (Youth)

Griese, A. A. (1969). *At the mouth of the luckiest river.* New York: Crowell. (Tatlek, the hero, is an Athabascan child in Alaska who has an orthopedic handicap but deals with it in a natural, pragmatic fashion.) (Elementary)

Harries, J. (1981). *They triumphed over their handicaps.* New York: Franklin Watts. (This book is a profile of six disabled people who have achieved in sports, music, and careers. Among the more famous disabled individuals included in the book are Ray Charles, a blind musician; Kathy Miller, who, although physically handicapped, won the International Valor in Sports Award for her running; Ted Kennedy, Jr., who skis, swims, and scuba dives in spite of having had one leg amputated; and Kitty O'Neil, who, after becoming deaf in childhood and then discovering she had cancer at age 25, became the women's 1964 10-meter diving champion. The reader learns about the inspirational experiences in each individual's life and how the handicap was overcome.) (Elementary and Intermediate)

Hill, E. (1987). *Spot visits the hospital.* New York: G. P. Putnam's Sons. (This story is about a monkey who has a broken leg and goes to the hospital, where he is visited by his animal friends.) (Primary)

Kellogg, M. (1968). *Tell me that you love me Junie Moon.* New York: Farrar, Straus, & Giroux. (This story is about a group of "rejects" who leave a rehabilitation institution and learn to live and love in the real world.) (Youth)

Meyer, D. J., Vadasy, P. F., & Fewell, R. R. (1985). *Living with a brother or sister with special needs: A book for sibs.* Seattle: University of Washington Press. (This book, written for siblings, describes the most common handicaps, including mental retardation; handicaps of vision, speech, hearing, learning, and behavior; birth defects; and neurological problems. The appendix includes a list of books about handicaps for young readers.) (Elementary and Intermediate)

Southall, I. (1985). *Let the balloon go.* New York: Bradbury Press. (This compelling story portrays an intelligent, imaginative Australian boy with cerebral palsy as he learns to assert himself and overcome the expectations of family and peers.) (Elementary and Intermediate)

White, P. (1978). *Janet at school.* New York: Crowell. (Text and photographs portray appealing 5-year-old Janet, who has spina bifida, having many school experiences.) (Preschool and Primary)

Wolf, B. (1974). *Don't feel sorry for Paul.* Philadelphia: Lippincott. (This photo-journalistic documentary is about a child who wears a prosthesis. It will inspire children, disabled or not, to work hard to accomplish what they want, even if the odds seem to be against them.) (Elementary and Intermediate)

Sex Education

Johnson, E. W. (1985). *People, love, sex, and families: Answers to questions that preteens ask.* New York: Walker. (This book is the result of a survey conducted by Johnson, who polled 1,000 young people on what they really wanted to know about people, love, sex, and families.) (Intermediate and Youth)

McCoy, K., & Wibbelsman, C. (1987). *Growing and changing: A handbook for preteens.* New York: Putman/Perigee. (Aimed at youngsters on the verge of adolescence, this guide to the pre-teen and early teen years offers a wealth of information on physical development, health and hygiene, and the emotional changes that accompany adolescence.) (Intermediate and Youth)

Miles, B. (1979). *The trouble with thirteen.* New York: Knopf. (A young girl who hates changes details the feelings of young teenage girls facing traumatic alterations in their lives, including menstruation, divorce, changes in friends, the death of a pet, and separations from best friends.) (Elementary, Intermediate, and Youth)

Pomeroy, W. B. (1981). *Boys and sex.* New York: Delacorte. (This book makes a straightforward attempt to clear up the myths, fears, and inhibitions that plague the healthy sexual development of the average boy.) (Intermediate)

Substance Abuse

Hjelmeland, A. (1990). *The facts about drinking and driving.* New York: Crestwood House. (This book presents information about drinking and driving and real-life stories of accidents that resulted from drunk driving.) (Intermediate and Youth)

Monroe, J. (1988). *The facts about stimulants and hallucinogens.* New York: Crestwood House. (Intermediate and Youth)

Turck, M. (1990). *The facts about crack and cocaine.* New York: Crestwood Books. (This book presents short vignettes about different aspects of crack use, as well as facts about crack and cocaine.) (Intermediate and Youth)

Note. Portions reprinted with permission of the publishers and authors from J. H. Lombana, *Guidance for Handicapped Students* (Springfield, IL: Courtesy of Charles C Thomas, 1982), pp. 382–384; S. K. Maul-Mellott and J. N. Adams, *Childhood Cancer* (Boston: Jones & Bartlett, © 1987, reprinted with permission), p. 176; and J. B. Mullins, "The uses of bibliotherapy in counseling families confronted with handicaps," in M. Seligman (Ed.), *The Family with a Handicapped Child: Understanding and Treatment* (San Diego: Grune & Stratton, 1983), pp. 257–259.

Source: Adapted, in part, from Ayalon and Flasher (1993); Carpenter (1992); Carr (1994); Cullum (1994); Dunne, McIntosh, and Maxim (1987); Franck and Brownstone (1991); Grossman (1983); Lombana (1982); Maul-Mellot and Adams (1987); Monahon (1993); Mullins (1983); Oates (1993); Pardeck (1991, 1992, 1993); Rasinski and Gillespie (1992); Reed (1985); and Van Dongen (1991).

APPENDIX C

MISCELLANEOUS TABLES

Table C-1
Sources for Obtaining Highly Structured Interviews

Child Adolescent Schedule (CAS)[a]
Kay Hodges, Ph.D.
Eastern Michigan University
Department of Psychology
537 Mark Jefferson
Ypsilanti, MI 48197

Child and Adolescent Psychiatric Assessment (CAPA):
Version 4.2—Child Version [a]
Adrian Angold, MRC Psych
Developmental Epidemiology Program
Duke Medical Center
P.O. Box 3454
Durham, NC 27710

Diagnostic Interview for Children and
Adolescents—Revised (DICA-R) 8.0[a]
Wendy Reich (Ed.), Ph.D.
Washington University
School of Medicine, Department of Psychiatry
4940 Children's Place
St. Louis, MO 63110

Diagnostic Interview Schedule for Children (DISC-IV)[a]
David Shaffer, M.D.
Division of Child Psychiatry
New York State Psychiatric Institute
722 W. 168th Street
New York, NY 10032

Revised Schedule for Affective Disorders and
Schizophrenia for School Aged Children:
Present and Lifetime Version (K-SADS-PL)
Joan Kaufman, Ph.D.
Western Psychiatric Institute and Clinic
University of Pittsburgh School of Medicine
3811 O'Hara Street
Pittsburgh, PA 15213

Schedule for Affective Disorders & Schizophrenia
for School-Age Children (K-SADS-IVR)
Paul Ambrosini, M.D.
Allegheny University of the Health Sciences
2900 Queen Lane
Philadelphia, PA 19129

Schedule for Affective Disorders and Schizophrenia
for School-Age Children, Epidemiological Version 5
(K-SADS-E5)[b]
Helen Orvaschel, Ph.D.
NOVA Southeastern University
Center for Psychological Studies
3301 College Avenue
Fort Lauderdale, FL 33314

[a]Parent version also available.
[b]Parent and child versions are contained within the same interview.
Source: Adapted and updated from Hodges (1993).

Table C-2
Sample Background Questionnaire Used in a Child Guidance Clinic or School

BACKGROUND QUESTIONNAIRE

FAMILY DATA

Child's name _____ Today's date _____

Birthdate _____ Age ____ Sex: ☐ Male ☐ Female

Home address _____ Phone _____

_____

School _____

Person filling out this form: ☐ Mother ☐ Father ☐ Stepmother ☐ Stepfather ☐ Both together ☐ Caregiver

☐ Other (please explain) _____

Mother's name _____ Age ____ Education _____

Occupation _____ Phone: Home _____ Business_____

Father's name _____ Age ____ Education _____

Occupation _____ Phone: Home _____ Business_____

Stepparent's name _____ Age ____ Education _____

Occupation _____ Phone: Home _____ Business_____

Marital status of parents _____ If separated or divorced, how old was the child when the separation occurred? _____

If remarried, how old was the child when the stepparent entered the family? _____

List all people living in the household:

Name	Relationship to Child	Age
_____	_____	_____
_____	_____	_____
_____	_____	_____
_____	_____	_____
_____	_____	_____
_____	_____	_____

If any brothers, sisters, or other significant people are living outside the home, list their names, ages, and relationships: _____

_____

Primary language spoken in the home _____ Other languages spoken in the home _____

Was the child adopted? ☐ Yes ☐ No If yes, at what age? _____ Does the child know? ☐ Yes ☐ No

Name of medical coverage group or insurance company (If none, write "none") _____

Name of medical provider _____

If insured, insured's name _____ ID/Group # _____

If referred, who referred you here? _____

PRESENTING PROBLEM

Briefly describe your child's current difficulties: _____

_____

_____

How long has this problem been of concern to you? _____

When was the problem first noticed? _____

What seems to help the problem? _____

What seems to make the problem worse? _____

Have you noticed changes in the child's abilities? ☐ Yes   ☐ No

If yes, please describe: _____

Have you noticed changes in the child's behavior? ☐ Yes   ☐ No

If yes, please describe: _____

Has the child received evaluation or treatment for the current problem or similar problems? ☐ Yes   ☐ No

If yes, when and with whom? _____

Is the child being treated for a medical illness? ☐ Yes   ☐ No

If yes, for what condition is the child being treated? _____

Is the child on any medication at this time? ☐ Yes   ☐ No   If yes, please note kind of medication: _____

SOCIAL AND BEHAVIOR CHECKLIST

Place a check next to any behavior or problem that your child currently exhibits.

☐ Has difficulty with speech
☐ Has difficulty with hearing
☐ Has difficulty with language
☐ Has difficulty with vision
☐ Has difficulty with coordination
☐ Has difficulty making friends
☐ Has difficulty keeping friends
☐ Refuses to share
☐ Prefers to be alone
☐ Does not get along well with brothers/sisters
☐ Does not get along well with other children
☐ Is aggressive
☐ Is shy or timid
☐ Tires easily, has little energy
☐ Is more interested in things (objects) than in people
☐ Engages in behavior that could be dangerous to self or others

   (describe)_____

_____

☐ Lies
☐ Steals
☐ Injures self often
☐ Runs away
☐ Has low self-esteem
☐ Blames others for his or her troubles
☐ Is argumentative
☐ Fights with other children
☐ Shows wide mood swings

☐ Has unusual or special fears, habits, or mannerisms (describe)

_____

☐ Wets bed
☐ Bites nails
☐ Sucks thumb
☐ Has frequent temper tantrums
☐ Has frequent nightmares
☐ Has trouble sleeping (describe)

_____

☐ Rocks back and forth
☐ Bangs head
☐ Holds breath
☐ Eats poorly
☐ Is stubborn
☐ Has poor bowel control (soils self)
☐ Is much too active
☐ Is fidgety
☐ Is easily distracted
☐ Is disorganized
☐ Is clumsy
☐ Has blank spells
☐ Daydreams too much
☐ Worries a lot
☐ Is impulsive
☐ Takes unnecessary risks
☐ Gets hurt frequently
☐ Has too many accidents
☐ Doesn't learn from experience
☐ Feels that he or she is bad
☐ Is slow to learn

☐ Does not understand other people's feelings
☐ Has difficulty following directions
☐ Gives up easily
☐ Takes drugs (describe) _____

_____

☐ Complains of aches or pains
☐ Is disobedient
☐ Constantly seeks attention
☐ Is restless
☐ Is jealous
☐ Feels hopeless
☐ Is nervous
☐ Does not show feelings
☐ Is immature
☐ Is easily frustrated
☐ Requires constant supervision
☐ Has difficulty resisting peer pressure
☐ Shows anger easily
☐ Has difficulty accepting criticism
☐ Feels sad, unhappy
☐ Has poor attention span
☐ Has poor memory
☐ Sets fires
☐ Is afraid of new situations
☐ Eats inedible objects
☐ Is not toilet trained
☐ Other problem(s) (describe)_____

_____

_____

Place a check next to any behavior or problem that your child has shown within the last three months.

- ☐ Shows sexually provocative behavior
- ☐ Has extreme fear of bathroom or bathing
- ☐ Has anxiety when separated from parents
- ☐ Has extreme anxiety about going to school
- ☐ Has fear at bedtime

- ☐ Refuses to sleep alone
- ☐ Refuses to go to bed
- ☐ Has loss of bladder control
- ☐ Is fearful of visiting a relative or going to a babysitter
- ☐ Is fearful of strangers
- ☐ (In cases of divorce) Is fearful of visiting a parent or caregiver

- ☐ (In cases of divorce) Appears dazed, drugged, or groggy when returning from visiting a parent or caregiver
- ☐ Other recent behaviors or problems

  (describe)_____

  _____

EDUCATIONAL HISTORY

Place a check next to any educational problem that your child currently exhibits.

- ☐ Has difficulty reading
- ☐ Has difficulty with arithmetic
- ☐ Has difficulty with spelling
- ☐ Has difficulty with writing
- ☐ Has difficulty with other subjects

  (please list) _____

- ☐ Has difficulty paying attention
- ☐ Has difficulty sitting still
- ☐ Has difficulty waiting turn
- ☐ Has difficulty respecting others' rights
- ☐ Has difficulty remembering things

- ☐ Has difficulty getting along with teacher
- ☐ Has difficulty getting along with other children
- ☐ Dislikes school

At what age did your child begin kindergarten? _____ What is his/her current grade? _____

Is your child in a special education class? ☐ Yes ☐ No If yes, what type of class? _____

Has your child been held back in a grade? ☐ Yes ☐ No

If yes, what grade and why? _____

Has your child ever received special tutoring or therapy in school? ☐ Yes ☐ No

If yes, please describe: _____

Has your child's school performance become poorer recently? ☐ Yes ☐ No

If yes, please describe: _____

Has your child missed a lot of school? ☐ Yes ☐ No

If yes, please indicate reasons: _____

DEVELOPMENTAL HISTORY

Pregnancy

Were there any problems during pregnancy? ☐ Yes ☐ No

If yes, what kind? _____

How old was the mother when she became pregnant? _____

Was this a first pregnancy? ☐ Yes ☐ No

(If no) How many times was mother previously pregnant? _____

During pregnancy, did mother smoke? ☐ Yes ☐ No If yes, how many cigarettes each day?_____

During pregnancy, did mother drink alcoholic beverages? ☐ Yes ☐ No

If yes, what did she drink? _____ Approximately how much alcohol was consumed each day?_____

During which part of pregnancy—1st trimester, 2nd trimester, 3rd trimester—was the alcohol consumed? _____

Were there times when 5 or more drinks were consumed at one time during pregnancy? ☐ Yes ☐ No

If yes, during which trimester—1st trimester, 2nd trimester, 3rd trimester? _____

During pregnancy, did mother use drugs (including prescription, over-the-counter, and recreational)? ☐ Yes ☐ No

If yes, what kind? _____

During pregnancy, was mother exposed to any x-rays or chemicals? ☐ Yes ☐ No

If yes, what kind? _____

During pregnancy, was mother exposed to any infectious disease? ☐ Yes ☐ No

If yes, what kind? _____

During pregnancy, did mother receive prenatal care? ☐ Yes ☐ No

Was delivery induced? ☐ Yes ☐ No

How long was labor? _____ Were forceps used during delivery? ☐ Yes ☐ No

Was a Caesarean section performed? ☐ Yes ☐ No If yes, for what reason? _____

Were there any complications associated with the delivery? ☐ Yes ☐ No

If yes, what kind? _____

Was the child premature? ☐ Yes ☐ No If yes, by how many weeks? _____

Infancy

What was the child's birthweight? _____ Were there any birth defects or complications? ☐ Yes ☐ No

If yes, please describe: _____

Were there any feeding problems? ☐ Yes ☐ No

If yes, please describe: _____

Were there any sleeping problems? ☐ Yes ☐ No

If yes, please describe: _____

Were there any other problems? ☐ Yes ☐ No

If yes, please describe: _____

As an infant, was the child quiet? ☐ Yes ☐ No As an infant, did the child like to be held? ☐ Yes ☐ No

As an infant, was the child alert? ☐ Yes ☐ No As an infant, did he or she grow normally? ☐ Yes ☐ No

If no, please describe: _____

As an infant, was he or she different in any way from siblings? ☐ Yes ☐ No ☐ Not Applicable

If yes, please describe: _____

First Years

During your child's first years, did he or she show any of the following behaviors? Place a check next to each one that he or she showed.

☐ Did not enjoy cuddling   ☐ Excessive restlessness   ☐ Constantly into everything
☐ Was not calmed by being held ☐ Poor sleep patterns   ☐ Excessive number of accidents
☐ Colic   ☐ Frequent head banging

Were there any other special problems in the growth and development of the child during the first few years? ☐ Yes ☐ No

If yes, please describe: _____

The following is a list of infant and preschool behaviors. Please indicate the age at which your child first demonstrated each behavior. If you are not certain of the age but have some idea, write the age followed by a question mark. If you don't remember the age at which the behavior occurred, please write a question mark.

Behavior	Age	Behavior	Age
Showed response to mother	_____	Stood alone	_____
Held head erect	_____	Walked alone	_____
Rolled over	_____	Ran with good control	_____
Sat alone	_____	Babbled	_____
Crawled	_____	Spoke first word	_____

Behavior	*Age*	*Behavior*	*Age*
Showed fear of strangers	_____	Took off clothing alone	_____
Put several words together	_____	Put on clothing alone	_____
Became toilet trained	_____	Tied shoelaces	_____
Stayed dry at night	_____	Rode tricycle	_____
Drank from cup	_____	Named colors	_____
Fed self	_____	Said alphabet in order	_____
Played pat-a-cake, peek-a-boo, or bye-bye	_____		

CHILD'S MEDICAL HISTORY

Place a check next to any illness or condition that your child has had. When you check an item, also note the approximate age of the child when he or she had the illness or condition.

Illness or condition	*Age*	*Illness or condition*	*Age*	*Illness or condition*	*Age*
☐ Measles	_____	☐ Hospitalizations	_____	☐ Epilepsy	_____
☐ German measles	_____	☐ Operations	_____	☐ Tuberculosis	_____
☐ Mumps	_____	☐ Ear problems	_____	☐ Bone or joint disease	_____
☐ Chicken pox	_____	☐ Eye problems	_____	☐ Gonorrhea or syphilis	_____
☐ Whooping cough	_____	☐ Fainting spells	_____	☐ Anemia	_____
☐ Diphtheria	_____	☐ Loss of consciousness	_____	☐ Jaundice/hepatitis	_____
☐ Scarlet fever	_____	☐ Paralysis	_____	☐ Diabetes	_____
☐ Meningitis	_____	☐ Dizziness	_____	☐ Cancer	_____
☐ Encephalitis	_____	☐ Frequent or severe headaches	_____	☐ High blood pressure	_____
☐ High fever	_____	☐ Difficulty concentrating	_____	☐ Heart disease	_____
☐ Convulsions	_____	☐ Memory problems	_____	☐ Asthma	_____
☐ Allergy	_____	☐ Extreme tiredness or weakness	_____	☐ Bleeding problems	_____
☐ Hay fever	_____			☐ Eczema or hives	_____
☐ Injuries to head	_____			☐ Suicide attempt(s)	_____
☐ Broken bones	_____	☐ Rheumatic fever	_____	☐ Sleeping problems	_____

Has your child had any other serious illnesses? ☐ Yes ☐ No   If yes, what illness?_____

Has your child been hospitalized? ☐ Yes ☐ No   If yes, please list reasons: _____

Has your child had any operations? ☐ Yes ☐ No   If yes, please list reasons: _____

Has your child had any accidents? ☐ Yes ☐ No   If yes, please describe: _____

Are your child's immunizations up to date? ☐ Yes ☐ No   Child's height _____   Child's weight _____

FAMILY MEDICAL HISTORY

Place a check next to any illness or condition that any member of the immediate family has had. When you check an item, please note the family member's relationship to the child.

Relationship of family member to child   *Relationship of family member to child*

☐ Academic problem   _____   ☐ Emotional problem   _____

☐ Alcoholism   _____   ☐ Epilepsy   _____

☐ Cancer   _____   ☐ Heart trouble   _____

☐ Depression   _____   ☐ Neurological disease   _____

☐ Developmental problem   _____   ☐ Suicide attempt   _____

☐ Diabetes   _____   ☐ Other problems (please list)

☐ Drug problem   _____   _____   _____

OTHER INFORMATION

Child's Activities

What are your child's favorite activities?

1. _____   2. _____   3. _____

4. _____   5. _____   6. _____

What activities would your child like to engage in more often than he/she does at present?

1. _____   2. _____   3. _____

What activities does your child like least?

1. _____   2. _____   3. _____

What chores does your child do around the house? _____

Has there been any recent change in his or her ability to carry out these chores? ☐ Yes   ☐ No

If yes, please describe the change: _____

What time does your child usually go to bed on weekdays? _____ On weekends? _____

Trouble with the Law

Has your child ever been in trouble with the law? ☐ Yes   ☐ No

If yes, please describe briefly: _____

Your Use of Disciplinary Techniques

What disciplinary techniques do you usually use when your child behaves inappropriately? Place a check next to each technique that you usually use. There also is space for writing in any other disciplinary techniques that you use.

☐ Ignore problem behavior   ☐ Redirect child's interest   ☐ Other technique (describe) _____
☐ Scold child   ☐ Tell child to sit on chair
☐ Spank child   ☐ Send child to his or her room   _____
☐ Threaten child   ☐ Take away some activity or food   ☐ Don't use any technique
☐ Reason with child

Which disciplinary techniques are usually effective? _____

_____

With what type of problem(s)? _____

_____

Which disciplinary techniques are usually ineffective? _____

_____

With what type of problem(s)? _____

_____

Which parent usually administers discipline? _____

Child's Responsibilities

Can your child be trusted to care for a pet? ☐ Yes   ☐ No

If no, why not?_____

Does your child handle his/her personal finances? ☐ Yes   ☐ No

If no, why not?_____

Does your child take responsibility for his/her personal hygiene? ☐ Yes   ☐ No

If no, why not?_____

Is the child's behavior generally age appropriate? ☐ Yes   ☐ No

If no, please describe in what ways it is not age appropriate:_____

_____

Other Areas

What do you enjoy doing with your child?_____

_____

What have you found to be the most satisfactory ways of helping your child? _____

_____

What are your child's assets or strengths? _____

_____

Is there any other information that you think may help us in working with your child? ____

_____

_____

What prompted you to seek help at this time? _____

_____

Family Stress Survey

Every family sometimes experiences some form of stress. Please put a check next to each event that your family has experienced *in the last 12 months*. There also is a place for listing other types of stresses that your family experienced in the last 12 months.

☐ Child's mother died.
☐ Child's father died.
☐ Child's brother died.
☐ Child's sister died.
☐ Parents divorced.
☐ Parents separated.
☐ Grandparent died.
☐ Someone in family was seriously injured or became ill (list person):

_____

☐ Parent remarried.
☐ Father lost job.
☐ Mother lost job.
☐ Family moved to another city.

☐ Family moved to another part of town.
☐ Someone in family was in trouble with the law or police (list person):

_____

☐ Family's financial condition changed.
☐ Member of family was accused of child abuse or neglect (list person):

_____

☐ Neighborhood was changing for the worse.
☐ Child started having trouble with parents.

☐ Child started having trouble with sisters/brothers.
☐ Child started having trouble in school.
☐ Child changed schools.
☐ Child's close friend moved away.
☐ Child's pet died.
☐ Other forms of stress _____

_____

_____

_____

_____

Parent Needs Survey[a]

Listed below are some needs commonly expressed by parents. Please put a check next to each item if you need help in that area.

- ☐ More information about my child's abilities.
- ☐ Someone who can help me feel better about myself.
- ☐ Help with child care.
- ☐ More money/financial help.
- ☐ Someone who can babysit for a day or evening so that I can get away.
- ☐ Better medical/dental care for my child.
- ☐ More information about child development.
- ☐ More information about behavior problems.
- ☐ More information about programs that can help my child.
- ☐ Someone to help with household chores.

- ☐ Counseling to help me cope with my situation.
- ☐ Better/more frequent teaching or therapy services for my child.
- ☐ Day care so that I can get a job.
- ☐ A bigger or better house or apartment.
- ☐ More information about how I can help my child.
- ☐ More information about nutrition or feeding.
- ☐ Assistance in handling my other children's jealousy of their brother or sister.
- ☐ Assistance in dealing with problems with in-laws or other relatives.
- ☐ Assistance in dealing with problems with friends or neighbors.

- ☐ Special equipment to meet my child's needs.
- ☐ More friends who have a child like mine.
- ☐ Someone to talk to about my problems.
- ☐ Assistance in dealing with problems with my husband/wife.
- ☐ A car or other form of transportation.
- ☐ Medical care for myself.
- ☐ More time for myself.
- ☐ More time to be with my child.
- ☐ More time to be with my spouse or other adults.
- ☐ Any other needs (list)_____

_____

_____

Thank you.

[a]These items are modifications of items included in the Parent Needs Survey by M. Seligman and R. B. Darling (1989) in *Ordinary Families, Special Children: A Systems Approach to Childhood Disability*, New York: Guilford Press. The Parent Needs Survey is an instrument designed to identify the priorities and concerns of parents of young children with disabilities. Reprinted and adapted with permission of the publisher and author.

Table C-3
Sample Personal Data Questionnaire

PERSONAL DATA QUESTIONNAIRE

Please complete this questionnaire as carefully as you can. All information will be treated confidentially. Please print clearly.

Name _____
              First   Middle   Last

Address _____
                                              Street

_____
              City   State   Zip Code

School_____ Grade ____ Age _____ Birthdate_____

Phone _____Sex _____ Today's date _____

School information:

	Name of school	Grades attended	Years attended	Course of study or special classes
Elementary				
Middle school				
High school				
Other				

Best-liked subjects _____

Least-liked subjects _____

Easiest subjects _____

Hardest subjects_____

Leisure-time (or free-time) activities _____

Hobbies_____

Do you read magazines? ☐ Yes   ☐ No   If yes, which ones? _____

Do you read books? ☐ Yes   ☐ No   If yes, what types? _____

(If you read books) Approximately how many books have you read in the last month? _____

Do you participate in sports or athletic activities? ☐ Yes   ☐ No   If yes, which ones? _____

School activities:

School Activity	Number of years of participation	Positions held	Describe activity

Please note any awards received or class offices held: _____

Work experience:

	Job held	When	What did you like best about your job?	What did you like least about your job?
1.	_____	_____	_____	_____
2.	_____	_____	_____	_____
3.	_____	_____	_____	_____
4.	_____	_____	_____	_____

Family and home:

	Name First	Last	Does this person live at your home? (yes or no)	Age	Occupation	Years of School
Father	_____		_____	___	_____	_____
Mother	_____		_____	___	_____	_____
Brother/Sister	_____		_____	___	_____	_____
	_____		_____	___	_____	_____
	_____		_____	___	_____	_____
	_____		_____	___	_____	_____

Health:

Current height _____ Current weight_____

Do you have normal eyesight? ☐ Yes ☐ No Normal hearing? ☐ Yes ☐ No

Do you eat a healthy diet? ☐ Yes ☐ No (If no) Briefly indicate in what way your diet is not healthy: _____

_____

_____

Briefly summarize important factors in your health history, including any serious illnesses or hospitalizations: _____

_____

_____

List any health problems you are now having: _____

_____

Are you taking any medications? ☐ Yes   ☐ No   (If yes) List the medications and what you are taking them for: _____

_____

Personal characteristics:

Circle any of the following words that seem to describe you fairly well:

active, ambitious, self-confident, persistent, hard working, nervous, impatient, impulsive, quick-tempered, excitable,

imaginative, original, witty, calm, easily discouraged, serious, easy-going, good-natured, unemotional, shy, submissive,

absent-minded, methodical, timid, lazy, frequently gloomy, hard-boiled, dependable, reliable, cheerful, sarcastic, jittery,

likeable, leader, sociable, quiet, retiring, self-conscious, often feel lonely, fearful

What do you like best about yourself? _____

What do you like least about yourself? _____

Do you use drugs? _____   (If yes) What kinds? _____

How often? _____

Do you use alcohol? _____   (If yes) What kinds? _____

How often? _____

Do you smoke? _____   (If yes) How many cigarettes per day do you smoke? _____

List the stressful events that you have experienced in the past year: _____

_____

Stress:

Circle Y (yes) if the item generally causes you stress, or circle N (no) if the item does not generally cause you stress.

Y N   1. Examinations and tests

Y N   2. Parents who don't understand what it's like to be a student today

Y N   3. Too much work required to prepare for class

Y N   4. Poor relations with other students

Y N   5. Picked out by teacher for poor work

Y N   6. Disciplined in school for doing things wrong

Y N   7. Teased by other students

Y N   8. Ignored by other students

Y N   9. Shortage of money

Y N   10. Too many things to study

Y N   11. Cost of books and equipment

Y N   12. Cost of clothes I need

Y N   13. Wishing my parents were richer

Y N   14. Difficulty with exams

Y N   15. Difficulty with a boy/girl relationship

Y N   16. No place to study at home

Y N   17. No time to relax between classes

Y N   18. Nobody to talk to about personal problems

Y N   19. Difficulties in travel to school

Y N   20. Unable to really talk to my mother

Y N   21. Unable to really talk to my father

Y N   22. Not knowing how to study properly

Y N   23. No time for leisure activities

Y N   24. Being asked to read aloud or talk in front of the class

Y N   25. Teachers who talk to other students, rather than me

Y N   26. Sexual problems

Y N   27. Watching too much TV so that it affects my homework

Y N   28. Neglected or abused emotionally at home

Y N   29. Abused physically or subjected to excessive physical punishment at home

Y N   30. Abused sexually by an older person

Y N   31. Unable to relate to people my own age

Y N   32. Fear of asking teachers about school work

Y N   33. Worry about part-time employment

Y N   34. Worry about finding a job after leaving school

Y N   35. Worry about entering senior high school

Y N   36. Worry about entering junior high school

Y N   37. Adults who treat me like a child

Y N   38. Pressure to behave in a way my parents won't approve of

Y N   39. Feelings of loneliness

Y N   40. What others think of me

Y N   41. Mother's drinking habit

Y N   42. Father's drinking habit

Y N   43. My own drinking habit

Y N   44. Worry that I may not get a good job when I leave school

Y N   45. Unemployment generally

Y N   46. Pressure to smoke cigarettes

Y N   47. Pressure to take alcoholic drinks

Y N   48. Unable to keep up with others in school work

Y N   49. Pressure to take drugs

Y N   50. My parents being divorced or separated

Y N   51. My smoking habit

Y N   52. Experience with drugs

Y N   53. School classes that are too large

Y N 54. Classmates jealous of my success in school

Y N 55. Problems of self-concept

Y N 56. Demands by parents on after-school time

Y N 57. My shyness in social situations

Y N 58. Sexual abuse by someone close in age

Y N 59. Adults who don't listen when I talk about problems

Y N 60. Uncertainty about what values are the correct ones

Y N 61. Lack of self-confidence

Y N 62. Rejection by a group I want to belong to

Y N 63. Doubts about my religious beliefs

Y N 64. Lack of privacy at home

Y N 65. Arguments between my parents

Y N 66. Concern about my health

Y N 67. Pressure from parents to get on in life

Y N 68. Appearing foolish to others

Relationship with parents:

Circle Y (yes) if the item generally describes your parents, or circle N (no) if the item does not generally describe your parents.

Y N 1. My parents are very affectionate with me.

Y N 2. My parents enjoy talking things over with me.

Y N 3. My parents comfort me and help me when I have troubles.

Y N 4. My parents are happy when they are with me.

Y N 5. My parents smile at me very often.

Y N 6. My parents punish me by making me do extra work.

Y N 7. My parents scold and yell at me.

Y N 8. My parents threaten to spank me.

Y N 9. My parents lose their temper with me when I don't help around the house.

Y N 10. When I am bad, my parents forbid me to do things I especially enjoy.

Y N 11. My parents won't let me roam around because something might happen to me.

Y N 12. My parents worry that I can't take care of myself.

Y N 13. My parents worry about me when I am away.

Y N 14. My parents do not approve of my spending a lot of time away from home.

Y N 15. My parents ask me to tell them everything that happens when I am away from home.

Y N 16. My parents let me off easy when I misbehave.

Y N 17. My parents are consistent about punishing me when they feel I deserve it.

Y N 18. My parents let me get away without doing work they tell me to do.

Y N 19. My parents find it difficult to punish me.

Y N 20. My parents excuse my bad conduct.

Family:

Circle Y (yes) if the item generally describes your family, or circle N (no) if the item does not generally describe your family.

Y N 1. Family members pay attention to each other's feelings.

Y N 2. Our family would rather do things together than with other people.

Y N 3. We all have a say in family plans.

Y N 4. The grownups in this family understand and agree on family decisions.

Y N 5. Grownups in the family compete and fight with each other.

Y N 6. There is closeness in my family but each person is allowed to be special and different.

Y N 7. We accept each other's friends.

Y N 8. There is confusion in our family because there is no leader.

Y N 9. Our family members touch and hug each other.

Y N 10. Family members put each other down.

Y N 11. We speak our minds, no matter what.

Y N 12. In our home, we feel loved.

Y N 13. Even when we feel close, our family is embarrassed to admit it.

Y N 14. We argue a lot and never solve problems.

Y N 15. Our happiest times are at home.

Y N 16. The grownups in this family are strong leaders.

Y N 17. The future looks good to our family.

Y N 18. We usually blame one person in our family when things aren't going right.

Y N 19. Family members go their own way most of the time.

Y N 20. Our family is proud of being close.

Y N 21. Our family is good at solving problems together.

Y N 22. Family members easily express warmth and caring towards each other.

Y N 23. It's okay to fight and yell in our family.

Y N 24. One of the adults in this family has a favorite child.

Y N 25. When things go wrong, we blame each other.

Y N 26. We say what we think and feel.

Y N 27. Our family members would rather do things with other people than together.

Y N 28. Family members pay attention to each other and listen to what is said.

Y N 29. We worry about hurting each other's feelings.

Y N 30. The mood in my family is usually sad and blue.

Y N 31. We argue a lot.

Y N 32. One person controls and leads our family.

Y N 33. My family is happy most of the time.

Y N 34. Each person takes responsibility for his/her behavior.

Plans:

What are your plans for the future? _____

_____

What occupation would you like to have?_____

_____

Are there issues bothering you that you would like to discuss with a professional? ☐ Yes   ☐ No   If yes, what are they? ____

_____

Any other comments?_____

_____

_____

_____

_____

Note. The 20 items in the section "Relationship with parents" fall into the following categories: Items 1–5 measure *affection,* 6–10 measure *punitiveness,* 11–15 measure *control,* and 16–20 measure *lax discipline.* The 34 items in the "Family" section fall into the following categories: Items 2, 3, 4, 6, 12, 15, 16, 17, 18(R), 19(R), 20, 21, 24(R), 25(R), 27(R), 28, and 33 measure *health/competence;* 5(R), 6(R), 7(R), 8(R), 10(R), 14(R), 18(R), 24(R), 25(R), 30(R), 31(R), and 34 measure *conflict;* 2, 15, 19(R), and 27(R) measure *cohesion;* 8(R), 16, and 32 measure *leadership;* and 1, 9, 13(R), 20, and 22 measure *expressiveness.* Items 11, 23, 26, and 29 do not fall into any of these categories. R refers to reversed scoring for negative indicators.

Source: The section on stress adapted from "Life Stress: A Questionnaire" by C. Bagley (1992); the section on relationship with parents adapted from "A Brief Scale for Assessing Parental Child-Rearing Style" by B. L. Bloom and E. R. Levergood (unpublished manuscript); and the section on family adapted from pp. 205–206, from SUCCESSFUL FAMILIES: Assessment and Intervention by W. Robert Beavers and Robert B. Hampson. Copyright © by W. Robert Beavers, M. D. and Robert C. Hampson, Ph.D. Reprinted by permission of W. W. Norton & Company, Inc.

Table C-4
Developmental Trends in Cognitive Development

Age	Developmental trend
Birth–2 yrs.	Focus on senses and motor abilities Realize that objects exist even when they can't be seen Remember and imagine ideas and experiences
3–6 yrs.	Think symbolically, using pretend play and language Focus on one aspect of a problem at a time Think concretely and deal with specific content Remember by recalling prior knowledge, rather than specific details of the materials presented
7–11 yrs.	Assume multiple perspectives Take on the role of another Reason simultaneously about a subclass and the whole class Give relatively more weight to language than to contextual cues Think more logically and objectively Continue to tie thinking to concrete experiences
12 yrs. and on	Engage in abstract thought Develop problem-solving strategies Develop personal characteristics, values, and relationships Consider how several different aspects of a problem might affect other people Separate the real from the impossible Recognize a hypothetical problem Think sequentially Consider events in relation to one another Separate one's own point of view from that of others Recognize how one's opinions affect others See from another's perspective Detect inconsistent logic Understand metaphors Generalize

Source: Adapted, in part, from Hughes (1988) and Worchel (1988).

Table C-5
Developmental Trends in Language Acquisition

Age	Developmental trend
0–9 mos.	Progress from crying to cooing to babbling to patterned speech
9–13 mos.	Use gestures or sounds to communicate Speak first meaningful words
13–18 mos.	Increase use of gesturing for communication (for example, pointing, waving) Develop vocabulary of approximately 50 words Understand that words represent objects that can be acted upon Overextend word meanings (for example, call all adult males "Daddy") Underextend word meanings (for example, call only a red ball a ball)
18–30 mos.	Increase vocabulary from a few dozen to several hundred words Use imitation Engage in conversation Develop syntactical skills needed to create two- or three-word sentences (for example, "I want milk")
30 mos.–5 yrs.	Use strings of sounds that convey meaning (grammatical morphemes), including plurals, prepositions, irregular verb endings, articles, possessives, auxiliary verbs, and verb contractions Develop vocabulary of approximately 900 words by 3 yrs. Use language competently in a meaningful context Use simple sentences
5–8 yrs.	Structure language much as adults do, using an awareness of grammar and language structure and meaning Continue to increase vocabulary rapidly, from approximately 10,000 words at 6 yrs. to approximately 20,000 words at 8 yrs. Use concrete word definitions, referring to functions and appearance Improve language awareness
8–11 yrs.	Develop vocabulary of approximately 40,000 words by 10 yrs. Use word definitions that emphasize synonyms and categorical relations Understand complex grammatical forms Grasp double meanings of words, as in metaphors and humor Consider needs of listeners in complex communicative situations Refine conversational strategies

Source: Adapted from Anglin (1993), Berk (1993), Hughes (1988), Prizant and Wetherby (1993), and Stone and Lemanek (1990).

Table C-6
Developmental Trends in Concept of Self

Age	Developmental trend
9–12 mos.	Begin to show self-recognition
15–18 mos.	Differentiate between pictures of oneself and others
18–24 mos.	Refer to oneself by name
28 mos.	Describe physical states (for example, thirsty, tired)
3–6 yrs.	Conceptualize oneself primarily in physical terms (for example, "I have black hair") Make distinctions between oneself and others primarily on the basis of observable behaviors and characteristics (for example, "Bill is tall") Have overly positive perceptions of one's own abilities, despite feedback to the contrary
7–8 yrs.	Realize that one has better access to one's own thoughts than others do Use information about one's own performance, as well as that of peers, in evaluating oneself Change from "all-or-none" thinking to being able to distinguish between one situation and another (for example, "I'm good in reading but not good in drawing") Distinguish between mental and physical aspects of self Recognize that discrepancies may exist between psychological experiences and physical appearance (for example, one can act one way and feel another way) Adjust self-perceptions on the basis of feedback and past experiences with success and failure
10 yrs.	Realize that one can be smart and ignorant in the same area
12 yrs.	Realize that one knows oneself better than one's parents do Incorporate abstract conceptions (such as temperament), beliefs, attitudes, and values (for example, "I'm stubborn," "I'm a liberal") in self-descriptions Engage in self-reflection, self-monitoring, and self-evaluation Exhibit self-consciousness, self-centeredness, and preoccupation with one's own thoughts Imagine that one is the center of attention (or the focus of other people's attention) Overreact to criticism Become susceptible to shame and self-doubt Think that one is special Think that no one else is capable of experiencing similar events or feelings Believe that unfortunate consequences will happen to others but not to oneself

Source: Adapted from Stone and Lemanek (1990).

Table C-7
Developmental Trends in Person Perception

Age	Developmental trend
3–6 yrs.	Differentiate oneself from others but fail to distinguish between one's own social perspective (thoughts, feelings) and those of others Label others' overt feelings but fail to see the cause-and-effect relationship between reasons and social actions Describe others primarily in terms of concrete, observable characteristics, such as clothes, possessions, hair color, and size (for example, "Ray is tall") View others as good or bad (that is, use "all-or-none" reasoning) Equate effort with ability, regardless of outcome Describe others in global, highly evaluative, egocentric, and subjective terms (for example, "He is nice because he gave me a toy") Report one's own misdeeds honestly (because of an inability to deceive, which requires taking another's perspective) Exhibit eagerness for adult approval
4 yrs.	Assume that all acts and outcomes are intended (because of an inability to differentiate accidental from intended actions or outcomes)
5–6 yrs.	Distinguish accidental from intended acts and outcomes Assume that others in similar situations will have perceptions similar to one's own Reflect on thoughts and feelings from another's perspective Understand that another's perspective is different
7–12 yrs.	Describe others in more differentiated, individualized, and detailed ways, using traits, dispositions, and attitudes (for example, "Alice is nice," "Henry is stubborn") Describe others in "all-or-none" fashion (that is, as possessing either desirable or undesirable traits) Understand that effort influences outcome Realize that individuals are aware of others' perspectives and that this awareness influences them and others' views of them Put oneself in others' places as a way of judging others' intentions, purposes, and actions
12–13 yrs. and on	View behavior of others as an interaction between personal characteristics and situational factors Use psychological constructs to reflect consistent traits in describing others ("Bill is smarter than Frank") Understand how personal characteristics relate to each other Differentiate among specific courses of behavior Develop more advanced, less hedonistic concepts of morality Understand that others may have simultaneously both desirable and undesirable traits

Source: Adapted from Selman (1976) and Stone and Lemanek (1990).

Table C-8
Developmental Trends in Moral Judgment

Age	Developmental trend
3–6 yrs.	Base judgments of right and wrong on good or bad consequences and not on intentions Base moral choices on wishes that good things would happen to oneself Simply assert choices rather than attempting to justify choices
6–8 yrs.	Define morality by resort to authority figures, whose rules must be obeyed Understand that good actions are based on good intentions Develop a sense of fairness
8–10 yrs.	Realize that others have a different point of view and that others are aware that one has one's own particular point of view Recognize that if someone has a mean intention toward one, it may be right to act in kind Define right by what one values
10–12 yrs.	Focus on conforming to what people believe is the right behavior Define right in terms of the Golden Rule: "Do unto others as you would have others do unto you" Obey rules to obtain the approval of people one cares about
12–15 yrs. and on	View morality from the perspective of the social system and what is necessary to keep it working Consider individual needs less important than maintaining the social order Base morality on protecting each individual's human rights View behavior that harms society as wrong

Note. Not all children reach the highest level of moral development.
Source: Adapted from Kohlberg (1976) and Selman (1976).

Table C-9
Developmental Trends in Temporal Concepts

Age	Developmental trend
2–3½ yrs.	Focus primarily on the present
3½–5 yrs.	Understand time in a rudimentary way, but have difficulty distinguishing morning from afternoon and remembering days of the week Measure time by special events or identified routines, such as time to get up instead of "morning"
6–8 yrs.	Master clock time, days of the week, and then months of the year Give temporal information about symptoms and their duration (for example, how long it takes to fall asleep or how long a headache has been present)
8–9 yrs.	Understand temporal concepts, such as temporal order (succession of events) and temporal duration (length of intervals between events)
9–11 yrs.	Comprehend years, as well as dates Estimate adults' ages Develop a grasp of historical chronology
12–14 yrs.	Develop a more complete sense of personal and historical time, making it possible to report on the duration of one symptom relative to others and on the persistence of symptoms
14 yrs. and on	Develop greater understanding of and preoccupation with the future

Source: Adapted from Clarizio (1994) and Helms and Turner (1976).

Table C-10
Developmental Trends in Recognition of Emotion

Age	Developmental trend
7 mos.	Distinguish facial expressions
12 mos.	Use expressive information from mother's face to guide behavior
3–5 yrs.	Reliably identify sad, angry, and happy Communicate about simple emotions in everyday situations Deny the presence of simultaneous emotions Identify feelings in stories based on situational cues Base judgments of affect on facial expressions Use idiosyncratic body cues (for example, a smile) or situational cues (for example, a birthday party) to identify one's own emotions See feelings as global and "all-or-none" (either good or bad), rather than mixed Believe that an event causes the same feelings in all people
5–6 yrs.	Believe that one is the cause of other people's emotions
6–8 yrs.	Identify fear, disgust, and other more difficult emotions Accept the possibility of simultaneous feelings only if they are separated temporally (for example, feeling happy when eating an ice cream cone and sad when some of the ice cream falls to the ground) Use inner experiences and mental cues to identify emotions Understand that one can change and hide one's feelings See oneself as the primary cause of parental emotions, but at the same time identify causes that are more appropriate Recognize one's own emotions but have difficulty describing them, often associating physiological or behavioral cues with feelings (for example, saying "I have a stomachache" when feeling bad or "I kicked the door" when feeling angry)
8–10 yrs.	Use content cues in judging a story character's feelings Base judgments of affect on situational cues Accept the simultaneous co-occurrence of two emotions (for example, feeling happy and sad at the same time) Recognize that events in one's parents' lives cause the parents' emotions
10–12 yrs.	Understand that internal emotional experiences and external affective expressions need not correspond Recognize that the sources of one's parents' emotions can include people and events unrelated to oneself Recognize that emotions come from "inner experiences"

Source: Adapted from Hughes (1988) and Stone and Lemanek (1990).

Table C-11
Percentile Ranks for Height (in centimeters) of Children from Birth to 18.0 Years

Age	Male Percentile							Female Percentile						
	5th	10th	25th	50th	75th	90th	95th	5th	10th	25th	50th	75th	90th	95th
Birth	46.4	47.5	49.0	50.5	51.8	53.5	54.4	45.4	46.5	48.2	49.9	51.0	52.0	52.9
1 mo.	50.4	51.3	53.0	54.6	56.2	57.7	58.6	49.2	50.2	51.9	53.5	54.9	56.1	56.9
3 mos.	56.7	57.7	59.4	61.1	63.0	64.5	65.4	55.4	56.2	57.8	59.5	61.2	62.7	63.4
6 mos.	63.4	64.4	66.1	67.8	69.7	71.3	72.3	61.8	62.6	64.2	65.9	67.8	69.4	70.2
9 mos.	68.0	69.1	70.6	72.3	74.0	75.9	77.1	66.1	67.0	68.7	70.4	72.4	74.0	75.0
12 mos.	71.7	72.8	74.3	76.1	77.7	79.8	81.2	69.8	70.8	72.4	74.3	76.3	78.0	79.1
18 mos.	77.5	78.7	80.5	82.4	84.3	86.6	88.1	76.0	77.2	78.8	80.9	83.0	85.0	86.1
24 mos.	82.3	83.5	85.6	87.6	89.9	92.2	93.8	81.3	82.5	84.2	86.5	88.7	90.8	92.0
30 mos.	87.0	88.2	90.1	92.3	94.6	97.0	98.7	86.0	87.0	88.9	91.3	93.7	95.6	96.9
3.0 yrs.	89.0	90.3	92.6	94.9	97.5	100.1	102.0	88.3	89.3	91.4	94.1	96.6	99.0	100.6
3.5 yrs.	92.5	93.9	96.4	99.1	101.7	104.3	106.1	91.7	93.0	95.2	97.9	100.5	102.8	104.5
4.0 yrs.	95.8	97.3	100.0	102.9	105.7	108.2	109.9	95.0	96.4	98.8	101.6	104.3	106.6	108.3
4.5 yrs.	98.9	100.6	103.4	106.6	109.4	111.9	113.5	98.1	99.7	102.2	105.0	107.9	110.2	112.0
5.0 yrs.	102.0	103.7	106.5	109.9	112.8	115.4	117.0	101.1	102.7	105.4	108.4	111.4	113.8	115.6
5.5 yrs.	104.9	106.7	109.6	113.1	116.1	118.7	120.3	103.9	105.6	108.4	111.6	114.8	117.4	119.2
6.0 yrs.	107.7	109.6	112.5	116.1	119.2	121.9	123.5	106.6	108.4	111.3	114.6	118.1	120.8	122.7
6.5 yrs.	110.4	112.3	115.3	119.0	122.2	124.9	126.6	109.2	111.0	114.1	117.6	121.3	124.2	126.1
7.0 yrs.	113.0	115.0	118.0	121.7	125.0	127.9	129.7	111.8	113.6	116.8	120.6	124.4	127.6	129.5
7.5 yrs.	115.6	117.6	120.6	124.4	127.8	130.8	132.7	114.4	116.2	119.5	123.5	127.5	130.9	132.9
8.0 yrs.	118.1	120.2	123.2	127.0	130.5	133.6	135.7	116.9	118.7	122.2	126.4	130.6	134.2	136.2
8.5 yrs.	120.5	122.7	125.7	129.6	133.2	136.5	138.8	119.5	121.3	124.9	129.3	133.6	137.4	139.6
9.0 yrs.	122.9	125.2	128.2	132.2	136.0	139.4	141.8	122.1	123.9	127.7	132.2	136.7	140.7	142.9
9.5 yrs.	125.3	127.6	130.8	134.8	138.8	142.4	144.9	124.8	126.6	130.6	135.2	139.8	143.9	146.2
10.0 yrs.	127.7	130.1	133.4	137.5	141.6	145.5	148.1	127.5	129.5	133.6	138.3	142.9	147.2	149.5
10.5 yrs.	130.1	132.6	136.0	140.3	144.6	148.7	151.5	130.4	132.5	136.7	141.5	146.1	150.4	152.8
11.0 yrs.	132.6	135.1	138.7	143.3	147.8	152.1	154.9	133.5	135.6	140.0	144.8	149.3	153.7	156.2
11.5 yrs.	135.0	137.7	141.5	146.4	151.1	155.6	158.5	136.6	139.0	143.5	148.2	152.6	156.9	159.5
12.0 yrs.	137.6	140.3	144.4	149.7	154.6	159.4	162.3	139.8	142.3	147.0	151.5	155.8	160.0	162.7
12.5 yrs.	140.2	143.0	147.4	153.0	158.2	163.2	166.1	142.7	145.4	150.1	154.6	158.8	162.9	165.6
13.0 yrs.	142.9	145.8	150.5	156.5	161.8	167.0	169.8	145.2	148.0	152.8	157.1	161.3	165.3	168.1
13.5 yrs.	145.7	148.7	153.6	159.9	165.3	170.5	173.4	147.2	150.0	154.7	159.0	163.2	167.3	170.0
14.0 yrs.	148.8	151.8	156.9	163.1	168.5	173.8	176.7	148.7	151.5	155.9	160.4	164.6	168.7	171.3
14.5 yrs.	152.0	155.0	160.1	166.2	171.5	176.6	179.5	149.7	152.5	156.8	161.2	165.6	169.8	172.2
15.0 yrs.	155.2	158.2	163.3	169.0	174.1	178.9	181.9	150.5	153.2	157.2	161.8	166.3	170.5	172.8
15.5 yrs.	158.3	161.2	166.2	171.5	176.3	180.8	183.9	151.1	153.6	157.5	162.1	166.7	170.9	173.1
16.0 yrs.	161.1	163.9	168.7	173.5	178.1	182.4	185.4	151.6	154.1	157.8	162.4	166.9	171.1	173.3
16.5 yrs.	163.4	166.1	170.6	175.2	179.5	183.6	186.6	152.2	154.6	158.2	162.7	167.1	171.2	173.4
17.0 yrs.	164.9	167.7	171.9	176.2	180.5	184.4	187.3	152.7	155.1	158.7	163.1	167.3	171.2	173.5
17.5 yrs.	165.6	168.5	172.4	176.7	181.0	185.0	187.6	153.2	155.6	159.1	163.4	167.5	171.1	173.5
18.0 yrs.	165.7	168.7	172.3	176.8	181.2	185.3	187.6	153.6	156.0	159.6	163.7	167.6	171.0	173.6

Note. Recumbent length or height is in centimeters. To convert to inches, multiply by 0.39.
Source: P. V. Hamill (1977). NCHS Growth Curves for Children. Vital and Health Statistics 11, Data from the National Health Survey, No. 165. Washington, DC: U.S. Government Printing Office (DWEH No. 78-1650).

Table C-12
Percentile Ranks for Weight (in kilograms) of Children from Birth to 18.0 Years

Age	Male Percentile							Female Percentile							Age
	5th	10th	25th	50th	75th	90th	95th	5th	10th	25th	50th	75th	90th	95th	
Birth	2.54	2.78	3.00	3.27	3.64	3.82	4.15	2.36	2.58	2.93	3.23	3.52	3.64	3.81	Birth
1 mo.	3.16	3.43	3.82	4.29	4.75	5.14	5.38	2.97	3.22	3.59	3.98	4.36	4.65	4.92	1 mo.
3 mos.	4.43	4.78	5.32	5.98	6.56	7.14	7.37	4.18	4.47	4.88	5.40	5.90	6.39	6.74	3 mos.
6 mos.	6.20	6.61	7.20	7.85	8.49	9.10	9.46	5.79	6.12	6.60	7.21	7.83	8.38	8.73	6 mos.
9 mos.	7.52	7.95	8.56	9.18	9.88	10.49	10.93	7.00	7.34	7.89	8.56	9.24	9.83	10.17	9 mos.
12 mos.	8.43	8.84	9.49	10.15	10.91	11.54	11.99	7.84	8.19	8.81	9.53	10.23	10.87	11.24	12 mos.
18 mos.	9.59	9.92	10.67	11.47	12.31	13.05	13.44	8.92	9.30	10.04	10.82	11.55	12.30	12.76	18 mos.
24 mos.	10.54	10.85	11.65	12.59	13.44	14.29	14.70	9.87	10.26	11.10	11.90	12.74	13.57	14.08	24 mos.
30 mos.	11.44	11.80	12.63	13.67	14.51	15.47	15.97	10.78	11.21	12.11	12.93	13.93	14.81	15.35	30 mos.
3.0 yrs.	12.05	12.58	13.52	14.62	15.78	16.95	17.77	11.61	12.26	13.11	14.10	15.50	16.54	17.22	3.0 yrs.
3.5 yrs.	12.84	13.41	14.46	15.68	16.90	18.15	18.98	12.37	13.08	14.00	15.07	16.59	17.77	18.59	3.5 yrs.
4.0 yrs.	13.64	14.24	15.39	16.69	17.99	19.32	20.27	13.11	13.84	14.80	15.96	17.56	18.93	19.91	4.0 yrs.
4.5 yrs.	14.45	15.10	16.30	17.69	19.06	20.50	21.63	13.83	14.56	15.55	16.81	18.48	20.06	21.24	4.5 yrs.
5.0 yrs.	15.27	15.96	17.22	18.67	20.14	21.70	23.09	14.55	15.26	16.29	17.66	19.39	21.23	22.62	5.0 yrs.
5.5 yrs.	16.09	16.83	18.14	19.67	21.25	22.96	24.66	15.29	15.97	17.05	18.56	20.36	22.48	24.11	5.5 yrs.
6.0 yrs.	16.93	17.72	19.07	20.69	22.40	24.31	26.34	16.05	16.72	17.86	19.52	21.44	23.89	25.75	6.0 yrs.
6.5 yrs.	17.78	18.62	20.02	21.74	23.62	25.76	28.16	16.85	17.51	18.76	20.61	22.68	25.50	27.59	6.5 yrs.
7.0 yrs.	18.64	19.53	21.00	22.85	24.94	27.36	30.12	17.71	18.39	19.78	21.84	24.16	27.39	29.68	7.0 yrs.
7.5 yrs.	19.52	20.45	22.02	24.03	26.36	29.11	32.73	18.62	19.37	20.95	23.26	25.90	29.57	32.07	7.5 yrs.
8.0 yrs.	20.40	21.39	23.09	25.30	27.91	31.06	34.51	19.62	20.45	22.26	24.84	27.88	32.04	34.71	8.0 yrs.
8.5 yrs.	21.31	22.34	24.21	26.66	29.61	33.22	36.96	20.68	21.64	23.70	26.58	30.08	34.73	37.58	8.5 yrs.
9.0 yrs.	22.25	23.33	25.40	28.13	31.46	35.57	39.58	21.82	22.92	25.27	28.46	32.44	37.60	40.64	9.0 yrs.
9.5 yrs.	23.25	24.38	26.68	29.73	33.46	38.11	42.35	23.05	24.29	26.94	30.45	34.94	40.61	43.85	9.5 yrs.
10.0 yrs.	24.33	25.52	28.07	31.44	35.61	40.80	45.27	24.36	25.76	28.71	32.55	37.53	43.70	47.17	10.0 yrs.
10.5 yrs.	25.51	26.78	29.59	33.30	37.92	43.63	48.31	25.75	27.32	30.57	34.72	40.17	46.84	50.57	10.5 yrs.
11.0 yrs.	26.80	28.17	31.25	35.30	40.38	46.57	51.47	27.24	28.97	32.49	36.95	42.84	49.96	54.00	11.0 yrs.
11.5 yrs.	28.24	29.72	33.08	37.46	43.00	49.61	54.73	28.83	30.71	34.48	39.23	45.48	53.03	57.42	11.5 yrs.
12.0 yrs.	29.85	31.46	35.09	39.78	45.77	52.73	58.09	30.52	32.53	36.52	41.53	48.07	55.99	60.81	12.0 yrs.
12.5 yrs.	31.64	33.41	37.31	42.27	48.70	55.91	61.52	32.30	34.42	38.59	43.84	50.56	58.81	64.12	12.5 yrs.
13.0 yrs.	33.64	35.60	39.74	44.95	51.79	59.12	65.02	34.14	36.35	40.65	46.10	52.91	61.45	67.30	13.0 yrs.
13.5 yrs.	35.85	38.03	42.40	47.81	55.02	62.35	68.51	35.98	38.26	42.65	48.26	55.11	63.87	70.30	13.5 yrs.
14.0 yrs.	38.22	40.64	45.21	50.77	58.31	65.57	72.13	37.76	40.11	44.54	50.28	57.09	66.04	73.08	14.0 yrs.
14.5 yrs.	40.66	43.34	48.08	53.46	61.58	68.76	75.66	39.45	41.83	46.28	52.10	58.84	67.95	75.59	14.5 yrs.
15.0 yrs.	43.11	46.06	50.92	56.71	64.72	71.91	79.12	40.99	43.38	47.82	53.68	60.32	69.54	77.78	15.0 yrs.
15.5 yrs.	45.50	48.69	53.64	59.51	67.64	74.98	82.45	42.32	44.72	49.10	54.96	61.48	70.79	79.59	15.5 yrs.
16.0 yrs.	47.74	51.16	56.16	62.10	70.26	77.97	85.62	43.41	45.78	50.09	55.89	62.29	71.68	80.99	16.0 yrs.
16.5 yrs.	49.76	53.39	58.38	64.39	72.46	80.84	88.59	44.20	46.54	50.75	56.44	62.75	72.18	81.93	16.5 yrs.
17.0 yrs.	51.50	55.28	60.22	66.31	74.17	83.58	91.31	44.74	47.04	51.14	56.69	62.91	72.38	82.46	17.0 yrs.
17.5 yrs.	52.89	56.78	61.61	67.78	75.32	86.14	93.73	45.08	47.33	51.33	56.71	62.89	72.37	82.62	17.5 yrs.
18.0 yrs.	53.97	57.89	62.61	68.88	76.04	88.41	95.76	45.26	47.47	51.39	56.62	62.78	72.25	82.47	18.0 yrs.

Note. Weight is in kilograms. To convert to pounds, multiply by 2.2.
Source: P. V. Hamill (1977). NCHS Growth Curves for Children. Vital and Health Statistics 11, Data from the National Health Survey, No. 165. Washington, DC: U.S. Government Printing Office (DWEH No. 78-1650).

Table C-13
Sample School Referral Questionnaire

SCHOOL REFERRAL QUESTIONNAIRE

Student's name_____   Date_____

School_____

Teacher_____

Grade _____   Sex _____

PRESENTING PROBLEM

Briefly describe student's current problem:_____

_____

_____

How long has this problem been of concern to you? _____

When did you first notice the problem? _____

What seems to help the problem? _____

What seems to make the problem worse? _____

Have you noticed changes in the student's abilities? ☐ Yes   ☐ No

If yes, please describe: _____

Have you noticed changes in the student's behavior? ☐ Yes   ☐ No

If yes, please describe: _____

Has the student received evaluation or treatment for the current problem or similar problems? ☐ Yes   ☐ No

If yes, when and with whom? _____

What are the student's current school grades? _____

CHECKLIST

Directions: Place a check mark next to each item that accurately describes the student. If you can't evaluate an item, please write a question mark next to the box by the item number.

Cognitive

☐   1. Has poor comprehension of material
☐   2. Has poor short-term memory of verbal stimuli
☐   3. Has poor short-term memory of nonverbal stimuli
☐   4. Has limited attention span
☐   5. Has difficulty in understanding and following directions
☐   6. Has difficulty in following a sequence of directions
☐   7. Has difficulty in shifting mental sets
☐   8. Has difficulty in reasoning abstractly
☐   9. Has difficulty in conceptualizing material
☐   10. Uses problem-solving strategies inefficiently
☐   11. Learns very slowly
☐   12. Has poor long-term memory

Language/Academic

☐   13. Has difficulty in decoding words
☐   14. Has poor reading comprehension

☐   15. Has poor expressive language
☐   16. Has poor listening comprehension
☐   17. Has difficulty in rapidly naming objects
☐   18. Has difficulty in rapidly naming words
☐   19. Has speech impairment
☐   20. Has difficulty in producing rhymes
☐   21. Has difficulty in recognizing similar phonemes
☐   22. Has difficulty in arranging phonemes into words
☐   23. Has difficulty in using verbal coding as an aid in memory
☐   24. Has difficulty in using verbal coding as an aid in rehearsal
☐   25. Has poor grammar
☐   26. Has poor math skills
☐   27. Has poor spelling
☐   28. Has fluctuating performance
☐   29. Has difficulty in writing composition

Perceptual/Motor

- ☐ 30. Has poor auditory perception
- ☐ 31. Has poor visual perception
- ☐ 32. Has poor tactile discrimination
- ☐ 33. Has poor handwriting
- ☐ 34. Has clumsy and awkward movements
- ☐ 35. Has poor speech communication
- ☐ 36. Has difficulty in putting objects in correct sequence
- ☐ 37. Has difficulty in remembering sequence of objects
- ☐ 38. Has right-left confusion
- ☐ 39. Has poor gross motor coordination
- ☐ 40. Has poor fine motor coordination

Social/Behavioral

- ☐ 41. Avoids doing work in class
- ☐ 42. Does not get along with other children
- ☐ 43. Is easily frustrated
- ☐ 44. Gives up easily
- ☐ 45. Has difficulty in finishing tasks
- ☐ 46. Shows anger quickly
- ☐ 47. Has limited motivation
- ☐ 48. Is immature
- ☐ 49. Is stubborn
- ☐ 50. Is often anxious
- ☐ 51. Has low self-esteem
- ☐ 52. Is socially isolated
- ☐ 53. Has low popularity
- ☐ 54. Has difficulty in communicating interests
- ☐ 55. Has difficulty in accepting criticism
- ☐ 56. Asks questions constantly
- ☐ 57. Has low expectation for success
- ☐ 58. Has limited social perceptiveness
- ☐ 59. Is depressed or unhappy
- ☐ 60. Is impulsive
- ☐ 61. Has difficulty waiting turn
- ☐ 62. Has trouble starting and continuing tasks
- ☐ 63. Shifts often to other activities
- ☐ 64. Has difficulty in functioning independently
- ☐ 65. Has difficulty in playing quietly
- ☐ 66. Is easily distracted
- ☐ 67. Doesn't seem to listen
- ☐ 68. Has disorganized approach to tasks
- ☐ 69. Shows aggressive behavior
- ☐ 70. Shows disruptive behavior
- ☐ 71. Talks excessively

- ☐ 72. Interrupts others often
- ☐ 73. Speaks out of turn (often blurts out answers)
- ☐ 74. Has difficulty remaining seated
- ☐ 75. Fidgets often when seated
- ☐ 76. Fails to return on time to class
- ☐ 77. Gives in to peer pressure
- ☐ 78. Has limited persistence
- ☐ 79. Fails to do homework
- ☐ 80. Has low interest in school work
- ☐ 81. Is self-critical
- ☐ 82. Seeks attention constantly
- ☐ 83. Is unorganized
- ☐ 84. Uses immature vocabulary
- ☐ 85. Is overexcitable
- ☐ 86. Is hyperactive
- ☐ 87. Is uncooperative
- ☐ 88. Behaves inappropriately
- ☐ 89. Has poor skills on playground
- ☐ 90. Is upset by changes in routine
- ☐ 91. Daydreams
- ☐ 92. Tires easily
- ☐ 93. Has wide mood changes
- ☐ 94. Tells lies
- ☐ 95. Steals things
- ☐ 96. Has numerous physical complaints
- ☐ 97. Blames others for problems
- ☐ 98. Is frequently absent
- ☐ 99. Has poor eye contact
- ☐ 100. Requires constant supervision
- ☐ 101. Engages in dangerous situations

Self-Care Skills

- ☐ 102. Has poor personal hygiene
- ☐ 103. Has disheveled and unclean personal appearance
- ☐ 104. Fails to dress appropriately for weather
- ☐ 105. Has poor table manners in cafeteria
- ☐ 106. Fails to use free time appropriately
- ☐ 107. Engages in self-stimulating behaviors

Other problems _____

_____

_____

_____

Assets

Please list the child's assets or strengths in each of the following areas.

Cognitive_____

Language/academic _____

Perceptual/motor _____

Social/behavioral _____

Other Comments

Please list anything else about the child that you think may be helpful. _____

Thank you!

APPENDIX D

NEW YORK STATE RISK ASSESSMENT AND SERVICES PLANNING MODEL

KEY FEATURES

1. The Model's primary goal is to promote and support a structured and rational decision-making approach to case practice, without replacing professional judgment.
2. The Model supports a process of information gathering and analysis that examines the inter-relatedness of risk influences and individual elements affecting family functioning.
3. The Model's conceptual framework facilitates a rehabilitative approach to working with families and helps to guide the selection of rehabilitative services in order to reduce risk of future abuse and maltreatment.
4. The Model's structure has the capacity to assist the supervisor in evaluating and supporting staff, as well as promoting a shared responsibility for case decision-making.
5. One key component of the Model is a thorough and timely evaluation of child safety, including an analysis of selected safety factors and circumstances that may suggest there is an immediate threat to a child that, if not controlled or alleviated, will likely cause serious harm.
6. To ensure the protection of each child judged unsafe, the Model's safety assessment and response process promotes the implementation of immediate interventions that can control the dangerous situation.
7. Model implementation assists in the decision whether to keep a case open following an indicated determination.
8. For cases which have been opened for service, the Model's implementation helps decide when, and under what circumstances, a case should be closed. This decision is based on the present safety of each child, risk reduction, and the development of family strengths and resources.
9. Risk assessment applies to all active CPS cases regardless of service provider or case planner. Model implementation supports a common focus and communication mechanism among all service providers and planners involved in the case.
10. Risk assessment is not a static activity; therefore, The New York State Risk Assessment and Services Planning Model is equally applicable at all stages in the life of a case.

SAFETY ASSESSMENT

The first priority after receiving a report from the State Central Register (SCR) is to focus on the safety of each child. A child is considered to be safe when an assessment of available information concludes that children in the household or custodial setting are not in immediate danger of serious harm. If any child is assessed to be unsafe, then appropriate interventions must be immediately taken to protect that child. Assessing a child's safety, and taking necessary actions to protect unsafe children, are a CPS caseworker's first priority. When child safety has been assured, then a more comprehensive assessment of family functioning and investigation of reported allegations can proceed.

Whenever a new CPS report is registered, this safety decision process is documented by completing the Preliminary Assessment of Safety (PAS). The purpose of this form is to help assess whether any children are likely to be in immediate danger of serious harm, and to determine what interventions can be initiated or should be maintained to provide appropriate protection.

The Preliminary Assessment of Safety (PAS) is completed no later than seven days following receipt of an SCR report. A new PAS is required in response to any subsequent reports. In child fatality cases, the due date is within 24 hours following receipt of the SCR report, if there are surviving siblings. When safety related decisions are necessary in situations where a new SCR report has not been received, case circumstances and interventions are documented in the Progress Notes, and at the next scheduled risk assessment and services planning period.

To support the safety assessment process, eleven safety factors are listed on the PAS form and in this Field Guide. These eleven factors identify behaviors and conditions that are frequently associated with a child being in immediate danger of serious harm. The presence of these specific factors, and any other information known about a particular case, can provide a useful framework for reaching a safety decision.

The safety decision is one of the most critical decisions made in the family and children's services profession. It is critical insofar as one must decide, often with limited information available, whether any child requires immediate protection from serious harm.

The safety decision is framed by incorporating three criteria. The first is based on **"immediacy."** In other words, one must assess whether a dangerous situation is already present or would likely occur in the immediate future.

Another criterion is **"seriousness."** While not always easy to define, these are typically dangerous situations that must be addressed to avoid the likelihood of harm to a child's life or health.

The last criterion is **"protection."** This specifies that for a child to be considered "Unsafe," the situation requires the continuation or initiation of an intervention that protects the child. In other words, without a safety intervention, the dangerous behaviors or conditions would still be present or would immediately return. Therefore, the child is considered to be in an "Unsafe" status.

If after considering all three safety criteria, the safety decision concludes that any child is in an "Unsafe" status, it is the caseworker's responsibility to identify, provide, facilitate, or arrange for appropriate interventions that control those factors that jeopardize a child's safety. The actions taken are intended to ensure that a child will not be seriously harmed while the complete risk assessment and investigation of allegations is being completed.

Safety interventions are not expected to provide rehabilitation or change behaviors or conditions. The interventions are specifically employed to control the situation until more permanent change can take place. Listed below are some of the commonly used safety interventions, although, depending on the particular case, others may be appropriate.

- Emergency Shelter
- Emergency Cash/Goods
- Legal/Court
- Crisis Intervention Casework
- Intensive Home-Based Family Preservation Services
- Foster Care
- Health Related
- Family, Friend, Volunteer Assistance
- Domestic Violence Services
- Homemaker

SAFETY FACTORS

(The examples following each safety factor were obtained from a supplemental report issued by the New York State Department of Social Services [undated]. The examples should not be considered complete descriptions of all possible circumstances related to the factors. Other behaviors or conditions may be associated with each listed factor and may also be indicative of the **possibility of immediate danger of serious harm.** Recency of the behavior or condition should also be considered; that is, is the situation currently present, would it likely occur in the immediate future, or has it occurred in the recent past. The examples should not be construed as necessarily equating with an "Unsafe" decision but rather as "red flag alerts" to the possibility that the child may be unsafe.)

1. Caretaker's behavior is violent or out of control.

    - extreme physical or verbal angry or hostile outbursts at child
    - use of brutal or bizarre punishment (that is, scalding with hot water, burning with cigarettes, forced feeding)
    - domestic violence likely to negatively impact on the child
    - use of guns, knives, or other instruments in a violent way
    - violently shaking or choking baby or young child to stop a particular behavior
    - behavior that seems out of touch with reality, fanatical, or bizarre
    - behavior that seems to indicate a serious lack of self-control (that is, reckless, unstable, raving, explosive)

2. Caretaker describes or acts toward child in predominantly negative terms or has extremely unrealistic expectations.

    - caretaker describes child as evil, stupid, ugly or in some other demeaning or degrading manner
    - caretaker curses and/or repeatedly puts child down
    - caretaker scapegoats a particular child in the family
    - caretaker expects a child to perform or act in a way that is impossible or improbable for the child's age (that is, babies and young children expected not to cry, expected to be still for extended periods, be toilet trained, or eat neatly)

3. Caretaker caused, or has made a plausible threat that has or would result in, serious physical harm to the child.

    - other than accidentally, caretaker caused serious abuse or injury (that is, fractures, poisoning, suffocating, shooting, burns, bruises/welts, bite marks, choke marks, etc.)
    - caretaker directly or indirectly threatens to cause serious harm in a believable manner (that is, kill, starve, lock out of home, etc.)
    - caretaker plans to retaliate against child for CPS investigation
    - caretaker has used torture or physical force which bears no resemblance to reasonable discipline, or punished child beyond the duration of the child's endurance

4. Child's whereabouts cannot be ascertained and/or there is reason to believe that the family is about to flee or refuse access to the child.

    - family has previously fled in response to a CPS investigation
    - family has removed child from a hospital against medical advice
    - family has history of keeping child at home, away from peers, school, other outsiders for extended periods

5. Caretaker has not provided, or will not provide, sufficient supervision to protect the child from potentially serious harm.

    - caretaker does not attend to child to the extent that need for adequate care goes unnoticed or unmet (that is, although caretaker is present, child can wander

outdoors alone, play with dangerous objects, play on unprotected window ledge, or be exposed to other serious hazards)
- caretaker leaves child alone (time period varies with age and developmental stage)
- caretaker makes inadequate and/or inappropriate baby-sitting or child care arrangements or demonstrates very poor planning for child's care

6. Caretaker has not met, or is unable to meet, the child's immediate needs for food, clothing, shelter, and/or medical care.

- no food provided or available to child, or child starved or deprived of food or drink for prolonged periods
- child without minimally warm clothing in cold months; clothing extremely dirty
- no housing or emergency shelter; child must, or is forced to, sleep in street, car, etc.; housing is unsafe, without heat, etc.
- caretaker does not seek treatment for child's immediate and dangerous medical condition(s) or does not follow prescribed treatment for such condition(s)
- child appears malnourished

7. Caretaker has previously abused or maltreated a child, and the severity of the abuse or maltreatment, or the caretaker's prior response to the incident, suggests that child safety may be an immediate concern.

- previous abuse or maltreatment was serious enough to cause, or could have caused, severe injury or harm
- caretaker has retaliated or threatened retribution against child for past incidents
- escalating pattern of maltreatment
- caretaker does not acknowledge or take responsibility for prior inflicted harm to the child or explains incident(s) as deliberate

8. Child is fearful of people living in or frequenting the home.

- child cries, cowers, cringes, trembles, or otherwise exhibits fear in the presence of certain individuals or verbalizes such fear
- child exhibits severe anxiety (that is, nightmares, insomnia) related to situation associated with a person(s) in the home
- child reasonably expects retribution or retaliation from caretakers

9. The child's physical living conditions are hazardous and may cause serious harm to the child.

- leaking gas from stove or heating unit
- dangerous substances or objects stored in unlocked lower shelves or cabinets, under sink, or in open
- lack of water or utilities (heat, plumbing, electricity) and no alternative provisions made
- peeling lead-base paint accessible to young child
- hot water/steam leaks from radiator
- no guards on open/broken/missing windows
- garbage not disposed of properly
- perishable food not properly stored or already rotted or spoiled

- evidence of human or animal waste throughout living quarters
- serious illness or significant injury has occurred due to living conditions and these conditions still exist

10. Child sexual abuse is suspected and circumstances suggest that child safety may be an immediate concern.

- it appears that caretaker has committed rape or sodomy or has had other sexual contact with child
- child has been forced or encouraged to sexually gratify caretaker or others or engage in sexual performances or activities
- access by possible or confirmed perpetrator to child continues to exist

11. Caretaker's drug or alcohol use seriously affects his/her ability to supervise, protect, or care for the child.

- caretaker has misused a drug(s) or alcoholic beverages to the extent that control of his or her actions is lost or significantly impaired. As a result, the caretaker is unable, or will likely be unable, to care for the child, or has harmed the child, or is likely to harm the child

12. Other.

- child's behavior is likely to provoke caretaker to harm the child
- unexplained injuries
- abuse or neglect related child death, or unexplained child death
- serious allegations with significant discrepancies or contradictions by caretaker, or between caretaker and collateral contacts
- caretaker refuses to cooperate or is evasive
- criminal behavior is occurring in the presence of the child, or the child is forced to commit a crime(s) or engage in criminal behavior

RISK ASSESSMENT

Risk assessment is an analysis of risk related elements, the family's own perceptions, an identification and examination of a family's strengths, and any other significant case circumstances that may affect family functioning. The analysis should help evaluate the likelihood that a child may be abused or maltreated in the future. It should also help determine what services are needed, if any, to *reduce identified risk, build family strengths,* and *resolve identified problems.*

In contrast to the time limited and control oriented focus of the safety assessments and safety responses, the Initial Risk Assessment and all future risk assessments cover the time period through the next scheduled (re)assessment of risk. Highly rated risk elements, or combinations of elements, which may place one or more children at an unacceptable level of risk, should be addressed in the service plan.

Unlike safety interventions which control unsafe situations, service plans are oriented toward long-term risk reduction and the resolution of identified problems that create risk. The emphasis of the service plan is on facilitating behavior change and/or altering the conditions affecting a family so that risk reduction can take place.

The Risk Assessment Model includes a collection of assessment categories called **Influences.** The five influences are related to the Caretaker, Child, Family, Intervention, and Abuse/Maltreatment. Within each one of these influences are related risk **Elements,** which have been derived from child welfare theory, research studies, and field experience. Grouping risk elements within a set of risk influences facilitates a sharper focus on the specific elements within an influence, as well as a broader examination of the interactions of more diverse risk elements.

There are 22 risk elements examined the first time the scales are used and 20 risk elements at subsequent assessments. Each risk element includes five scales of severity ranging from zero (0) to four (4). The scale headings are present on the UCR forms. These scales are further defined by descriptions called **Anchors.** The anchors offer a standard for assigning a rating by providing a narrative description which helps to define the status or functioning of a child, caretaker, or family.

This Field Guide contains expanded and more detailed descriptions of the anchors in order to help you complete your assessment of each individual risk element in an accurate and reliable manner. You are encouraged to refer to these expanded descriptions whenever assigning a risk element rating. In order to choose the anchor best suited to describe or define the particular case situation, the following guidelines should be kept in mind:

- Choose the anchor where the description most closely reflects your assessment of that particular risk element. It does *not* have to match exactly.
- If there is more than one description within an anchor, not all parts need apply in order to select that particular anchor.
- Not all anchors will be mutually exclusive. Partial descriptions from more than one anchor may reflect your particular case. Again, choose the risk element level that seems to fit *most closely.*
- When multiple children and/or caretakers are associated with different risk levels for a particular risk element, select the rating that reflects the highest appropriate risk level. Next, specifically identify the particular child or caretaker in the Summary Description.
- When services are being provided, select the most appropriate anchor that would apply if services were withdrawn. This method best reflects the *actual risk* that would be present without services' support.

RISK ASSESSMENT SCALE ANCHOR DESCRIPTIONS

Caretaker Influence

CT1. Abuse/Maltreatment of Caretaker

4. Severe abuse/maltreatment as a child. Severe abuse/maltreatment as a child resulted in serious emotional disturbance and/or physical scars/disability.

3. Recurrent but not severe abuse/maltreatment as a child. Recurrent abuse/maltreatment as a child; may have resulted in emotional or physical impairment.

2. Episodes of abuse/maltreatment as a child. Recounts being abused or maltreated as a child, but not severely or recurrently; no apparent impairment.

1. Perceived maltreatment as a child with no specific incidents. Does not recount being abused or maltreated.

Expresses dissatisfaction with the care or treatment s/he received when young.

0. No perceived maltreatment as a child. Recounts being loved and well cared for with no incidents of maltreatment or abuse.

CT2. Alcohol or Drug Use

4. Substance use with severe social/behavioral consequences. Compulsion to use substance, loss of control over use, and continued use despite adverse consequences. Suspected sale and/or manufacture of drugs; dropout from social responsibilities (unemployment, spouse has left, child is abandoned); or severe behavioral problems (extreme aggression or passivity, no concern for future, confusion much of time).

3. Substance use with serious social/behavioral consequences. Regular and heavy abuse of one or more substances: alcohol or drugs. High risk of not meeting social responsibilities (danger of losing job, financial problems, spouse threatens to leave, child care suffers).

2. Occasional substance use with negative effects on behavior. Uses drugs other than marijuana or alcohol occasionally or binges on alcohol or marijuana. Negative effects on social behavior (job absenteeism, constant arguments at home, dangerous driving) and on child care. Short-term stupor impairs performance.

1. Occasional substance use. Occasionally smokes marijuana or drinks alcohol to point of impairment. Mild effects on child caring ability or everyday functioning.

0. No misuse of alcohol or use of drugs. May drink but in moderation. No use of illegal drugs or drug-related activity. No observable effects on everyday functioning.

CT3. Caretaker's Expectations of Child

4. Unrealistic expectations with violent punishment. Unrealistic, not age-appropriate expectations may result in violent behavior or punishment for child's failure to meet expectations. Physical discipline is the caretaker's only response to child's misconduct and pattern of physical discipline is escalating in severity.

3. Unrealistic expectations with angry conflicts. Unrealistic expectations may lead to regular conflicts and anger toward child over behavior. Caretaker frequently administers excessive physical discipline. Verbal discipline is frequently inappropriate and excessive in response to child's age and misconduct.

2. Inconsistent expectations leading to confusion. Has knowledge of age-appropriate behavior but is inconsistent in expectations. Child is left frustrated and confused by inconsistency. Verbal and physical discipline are inconsistently administered and are often not appropriate to child's age and misconduct.

1. Realistic expectations with minimal support. Good knowledge of age-appropriate behaviors with realistic standards most of the time. May not encourage or assist child with tasks when necessary to meet standards. Verbal discipline is generally controlled and appropriate to child's age and misconduct.

0. Realistic expectations with strong support. Good knowledge of age-appropriate behavior with consistent and realistic standards. Sets safe and reasonable limits with appropriate consequences. Has flexible demands and provides child with options. Encourages and helps child with tasks when needed. Verbal discipline is controlled and appropriate to child's age and misconduct.

CT4. Caretaker's Acceptance of Child

4. **Rejects and is hostile to child.** Child is viewed as evil or bad. Child is consistently deprecated and put down. Child is resented and even hated. Caretaker is hostile to child.

3. **Disapproves of and resents child.** Child is seen as disruptive and the cause of many problems. Caretaker disapproves of or criticizes child constantly and is resentful of child.

2. **Indifferent and aloof to child.** Caretaker is neither accepting nor rejecting. Relates to child in matter-of-fact, functional terms but has little emotional involvement and rarely demonstrates acceptance.

1. **Limited acceptance of child.** Describes child positively most of the time, but only when asked; only occasionally does so spontaneously.

0. **Very accepting of child.** Frequently and spontaneously speaks about accomplishments of child with approval. Accepts child even when disapproves of behavior.

CT5. Physical Capacity to Care for Child (Consider presence of substance use withdrawal symptoms, such as insomnia, chronic fatigue, irritability, severe headaches, seizures, nausea, and vomiting in assessing presence of physical illness or disability.)

4. **Incapacitated due to chronic illness or disability resulting in inability to care for child.** Acute or chronic illness or disability or experience of severe pain critically impairs caretaker's ability to perform child caring role.

3. **Physical impairment or illness which seriously impairs child caring capacity.** Physical illness or disability seriously restricts or interferes with caretaker's ability to care for child. Child care may be at risk because of communicable disease that endangers health, or terminal illness that will impair child caring capacity of caretaker.

2. **Moderate physical impairment or illnesses resulting in only limited impact on child caring capacity.** Generally healthy but has one or more physical illnesses or disabilities which have a mild impact on child caring capacity.

1. **Very limited physical impairment or illness with virtually no impact on child caring capacity.** Caretaker has limited physical illness or has a debilitating disease (e.g., MS, arthritis, diabetes, or hypertension) that has not progressed to stage of sustained impairment. Limited impairment of motor functioning has little or no effect on child caring capacity.

0. **Healthy with no identifiable risks to child caring capacity.** Caretaker in generally good health with no identifiable illnesses, disabilities, or inadequate health habits that would impact child caring.

CT6. Mental Capacity to Care for Child

4. **Incapacitated due to mental/emotional disturbance or developmental disability resulting in inability to care**

for child. Caretaker has serious mental/emotional disturbance and behavior may be affected by delusions or hallucinations. Psychological state may exhibit severe impairment in communication (incoherent, unresponsive) or judgment. Illness critically impairs ability to provide child care. Caretaker could be dangerous to self and others; suicidal preoccupations. Caretaker has severe intellectual limitations (that is, has severe developmental disability), emotional instability, and/or has very poor reasoning abilities which severely affect his/her ability to protect or care for child.

3. **Serious mental/emotional disturbance or developmental disability which seriously impairs child caring capacity.** Symptoms may include serious disturbances in judgment, thinking, or emotions that may frequently affect caretaker's ability to perform child care tasks. Caretaker is not a danger to others or self. Caretaker has intellectual limitations which adversely affect his/her ability to care for child.

2. **Moderate mental/emotional disturbance or developmental disability with limited impairment of child caring capacity.** Symptoms such as feelings of powerlessness, low self-esteem, anxiety attacks, or mood swings have only a mild impact on the child caring capacity of caretaker. Caretaker has some intellectual limitations or developmental disability which somewhat restricts ability to protect/care for child.

1. **Symptoms of mental/emotional disturbance or developmental disability with no impact on child caring capacity.** Caretaker suffers from transient symptoms of psychological stress, emotional problems, or from mental illnesses with little or no impairment of child caring capacity. Caretaker may have some intellectual limitations which do not affect his/her ability to care for child.

0. **No identifiable mental/emotional disturbance.** Caretaker has no symptoms of mental illness, psychological disturbance, or intellectual limitations. Appears to be emotionally stable.

Child Influence

C1. Child's Vulnerability

4. **Child younger than 2 years old, or older child with special needs.** Child is an infant or toddler under the age of 2, or an older child with special needs.

3. **Child older than 2 years old, not regularly accessible to community oversight.** Child is older than 2 years of age and is generally cared for in the family home; public exposure is minimal; or child may be cared for outside the home, but scheduled periods of absence are greater than two days at a time.

2. **Child is under 12 years old, attends school, day care, or early childhood development program.** Child is under the age of 12, regularly attends school or other child care program at least three days a week, with no more than two days between days of attendance.

1. **Child is over 12 years old and younger than 18 years old.** Child is between the ages of 12 and 18, is regularly in the community and/or school environment.

0. **Child is 16 years old or older, with adequate self-sufficiency skills.** Child can care for self independently.

Is able, when necessary, to prepare food for self and dress appropriately for conditions. Can negotiate transportation system and knows how to access emergency services.

C2. Child's Response to Caretaker

4. Extremely anxious with uncontrolled fear, withdrawal, or passivity. No interaction between child and caretaker. Child is extremely fearful, shakes or cowers hysterically, or cries uncontrollably from fear. Child is extremely passive, withdrawn, or aloof toward caretaker. Persistently crying infant not soothed or comforted by caretaker. Minimal eye contact between caretaker and infant. Physical response may be rigidity or pulling away from caretaker.

3. Very anxious with negative, disruptive, and possibly violent interaction. Child/caretaker interaction is very negative. Interaction is disruptive, unpredictable, or possibly violent. Child may deny knowledge, tell conflicting stories, refuse to answer questions, or use rehearsed answers in response to questions about caretaker or injuries. Child does not respond, over-responds, or withdraws if caretaker displays affection or anger.

2. Moderately anxious with apprehension and suspicion toward caretaker. Child is apprehensive and suspicious toward caretaker; appears inappropriately fearful of caretaker. Asks caseworker not to tell caretaker what s/he says. Claims no problems but demeanor does not match statement. Afraid to answer questions and checks caretaker's response after answering. Overly compliant with or mistrustful of caretaker. Child does not respond to caretaker's affection.

1. Marginally anxious with some hesitancy towards caretaker. Child is sometimes cautious around caretaker. Hesitant to talk; exhibits excessive shyness. Child may fail to elicit affection, or respond to caretaker's affection on occasion.

0. Child trusts and responds to caretaker in age-appropriate way. Child trusts and responds to caretaker in age-appropriate, positive way. Minor conflicts with caretaker are resolved and are seldom long-term. Child is calm, relaxed, and self-assured. Child engages positively with caretaker and elicits affection, and responds with facial expression, posture, and behavior.

C3. Child's Behavior

4. Dangerous behavior problems. Is violent and dangerous to others or self (suicidal thoughts or attempts) or has a history of violent, delinquent, or criminal behavior. Incidents of exhibitionism or voyeurism. Age-inappropriate, violent, or intimidating sexual behavior; admits to or is diagnosed as chemically dependent or associates with peers who are. Inappropriately wary of adult contacts; behavioral extremes. Exaggerated fear of closeness or physical contact. Infant or young child is rigid, nonresponsive, or listless.

3. Serious behavior problems. Occasionally violent and dangerous to others. Evidences some self-destructive or self-abusive behaviors. Destructive of objects or possessions, and/or animals. May be chemically dependent. Isolated or scapegoated by peers/siblings. Withdrawal from

social interaction; lack of trust, particularly with significant others. Sleep disorders such as insomnia or nightmares. Runs away frequently or exhibits regular truancy from school. Difficult infant (colic, hyperactive); fussy, sleeps very little.

2. Moderate but pervasive behavior problems. Significant pattern of aggression or withdrawal at school, with friends, or siblings. Periodic truancy from school or runs away for short periods of time. Child may act much younger than age appropriate; use behavior to gain attention; or be having behavior problems at school, in the community, or at home. Difficulty in concentrating at school; overeating, loss of appetite, or other changes in diet. Repeated use of alcohol or other substances.

1. Minor behavior problems. Mild symptoms of hyperactivity or depression. Possible minor school problems or truancy. Experimentation with alcohol or other substances. Generally exhibits age-appropriate behavior.

0. No significant behavior problems. Behavior seems age-appropriate with acceptable school attendance and school/community/home behavior. No use of alcohol or other substances.

C4. Child's Mental Health and Development

4. Incapacitated due to mental/emotional disturbance or developmental delay and unable to function independently. Child has severe mental/emotional disturbance (including possible delusions, hallucinations)and/or developmental delay that makes him/her unable to function age appropriately. May be dangerous to self (suicidal) or others. Psychological state shows severely impaired communications (incoherent, unresponsive, chronic depression) and judgment (grossly inappropriate acts). Child has diagnosed mental illness (autism, schizophrenia, conduct disorder, etc.) or emotional instability.

3. Serious mental/emotional disturbance or developmental delay impairs ability to function in most daily activities. Child exhibits a serious mental/emotional disturbance or developmental delay. This often is characterized by poor judgment, disturbances in thinking or mood (severely depressed, talks of suicide) that effectively prevent child from functioning in most daily activities: attending school, successfully interacting with family or friends, going out in public. Child appears to act in a hyperactive manner.

2. Moderate mental/emotional disturbance or developmental delay impairs ability to perform some daily activities. Emotional disturbance (self-doubt or anxiety attacks) or moderate developmental delay impairs ability of child to function in some daily activities but not others. Symptoms include refusal to attend school, bed-wetting, aggression, or withdrawal from others. Child has diagnosed learning disability (dyslexia, attention deficit disorder, etc.) which impacts negatively on school performance without aggression or withdrawal.

1. Symptoms of mental/emotional disturbance or developmental delay with minimal impact on daily activities. Child suffers from transient symptoms of emotional stress (difficulty concentrating, loss of appetite, frequent fatigue, nightmares) or mild developmental delay which has minimal impact on school or socialization. May be anxious or have some conflict around peer relations; child may be slightly immature.

0. **No identifiable mental/emotional disturbance or developmental delay.** Child has no symptoms of illness or developmental delay. Is emotionally stable and exhibits age-appropriate emotional behavior and intellectual development.

C5. Child's Physical Health and Development

4. **Severe physical illness, disability, or lack of physical development; requires medical care.** Severe/chronic physical illness, substance use having serious effect on child's health and development, drug withdrawal or positive toxicology, disability or handicap, or severe pain/discomfort from condition severely restricts child's activities or school performance. Special efforts unable to restore such activities. Child's weight and height are below 5th percentile for age; reason unknown or attributed to quality of care. Child is listless and needs medical care. Diagnosis of Fetal Alcohol Syndrome. Child diagnosed with Sexually Transmitted Disease or other physical indications of sexual activity inappropriate to age.

3. **Serious physical illness, disability, or lack of physical development; restricts activities without special care.** Physical illness or disability seriously restricts activities and school performance and requires special care which caretaker views as burdensome. Child's weight and height are below 5th percentile for age; reason unknown, but parent is cooperative and willing to learn.

2. **Moderate physical illness, disability, or lack of physical development; restricts activities somewhat but overcome with special care.** Moderate physical illness or disability or moderate pain/discomfort restricts child somewhat. Activities and school performance achieved with special care and treatment. Child's weight and height are below 5th percentile for age; medical reasons are known.

1. **Mild physical illness, disability, or lack of physical development; does not restrict activities.** Mild physical illness or disability that does not restrict child's activities or school performance. Child's height and weight are between 5th and 10th percentile; reason is known.

0. **Healthy and no obvious physical illness, disability, or lack of physical development.** Child is healthy and has no or only minor illness or disability which does not restrict child's activities or school performance. Child's weight and height are at or above the 10th percentile.

Family Influence

F1. Domestic Violence (Household member could include adults in the household; siblings; any other individuals who may be included in the family constellation, regardless of residence, such as a batterer who may be in and out of the home over time.)

4. **Repeated or serious physical violence or substantial risk of serious physical violence in household.** Household member required medical treatment for injuries sustained, or medical attention required but not sought.

Unexplained injuries. Recurring or frequent requests for police intervention; order of protection may exist. Threats or use of weapons by one household member against another. Absolute domination of emotional, financial, and sexual spheres by one member; other member submissive. Caretaker is pregnant, incidents of physical violence have occurred since pregnancy.

3. **Incidents of physical violence in household; imbalance of power and control.** Household member physically assaulted by another member but no medical attention required. Threats (to kill or seriously injure) expressed between members. Previous requests have been made to police for assistance. Emotional and financial control maintained by one member; possible sexual abuse of one household member by another. Incidents of violence occur in presence of children.

2. **Isolation and intimidation; threats of harm.** Household members controlled through limited access to financial resources, intimidation, and/or isolation. Other member attempts to control activities, movement, and contacts with other people. Member put in fear by looks, actions, gestures, destruction of property. Threats of harm and/or pushing and shoving of one household member by another.

1. **Verbal aggression.** Household member's activities constrained through verbal aggression. Member may exhibit anxiety or apprehension in the presence of other member. Caretaker has experienced prior abusive relationships.

0. **Mutual tolerance.** There is mutual communication. Conflicts between household members are handled without physical threats, intimidation, or violence. One adult in household—no domestic violence issues. No experience with prior abusive relationships.

F2. Ability to Cope with Stress (Stressors may include, but are not limited to, pregnancy or recent birth, unemployment or other employment changes, financial hardship, death of a spouse or family member, recent mobility, change in marital relationships, prolonged illness or serious injury, inconsistent child care arrangements, overcrowding, blended families, chaotic lifestyle or consistent conflict, acute psychiatric episode, or loss of housing. May also include other events not listed, but perceived by family as major stressors.)

4. **Chronic crisis with limited coping.** One or more stressors have caused caretaker to act severely depressed or immobilized. Crisis is adversely affecting child caring on a chronic basis; caretaker exhibits inappropriate, very limited, or no coping skills.

3. **Prolonged crisis strains coping skills.** One or more stressors have occurred which resulted in a prolonged or current crisis. Caretaker's coping strategies are strained and adversely affect child caring capacity.

2. **Stabilized after period of crisis.** One or more stressors have occurred, but the family has stabilized after crisis. Child caring capacity adversely affected during periods of crisis.

1. **Resolution without adverse effect.** One or more stressors have occurred, but the family has resolved any associated crisis with no adverse effect on child caring capacity.

0. Free from stress influence. Family is currently, and has been, free from the influence of any major stressors during the last year.

F3. Availability of Social Supports

4. Effectively isolated. Geographically and/or socially isolated from community supports. Alienated from, or ongoing conflict with, extended family, friends, or neighbors.

3. Some support, but unreliable. Support from family/friends is inconsistent/unreliable. Limited community services available; transportation/mobility difficulty.

2. Some reliable support, but limited usefulness. Family supportive, but not close by. Some support from friends. Community services available but difficult to access.

1. Some reliable and useful support. Satisfactory relationships with family and friends. May participate in one or more community, church, or other social groups. Community services available and accessible.

0. Multiple sources of reliable and useful support. Strong relationships with family, friends, and neighbors; available for necessary support. Caretakers are involved with activities outside the home.

F4. Living Conditions

4. Extremely unsafe: multiple hazardous conditions that are dangerous to children and have caused physical injury or illness. Dangerous conditions in the home have caused physical injury or illness in children. There have been episodes of eviction and/or homelessness or severe overcrowding that have created anxiety in children, disruption of schooling, etc.

3. Very unsafe: multiple hazardous conditions that are dangerous to children.

2. Unsafe: one hazardous condition that is dangerous to children.

1. Fairly safe: one possibly hazardous condition that may harm children.

0. Safe: no hazardous conditions apparent.

F5. Family Identity and Interactions

4. Negative family interactions. One or both caretakers fail to provide children with emotional nurturance. Vacating of roles by adults; interaction between household members primarily negative. Serious disruption of family functioning resulting from significant change in family composition.

3. Family interactions generally indifferent. One or both adult caretakers rely on support in daily living; provide only limited emotional nurturance to children. Roles and responsibilities are confused and misunderstood. Limited positive family interactions. Some members isolated from family functioning, through means including scapegoating of the child. Change in family composition disrupting functioning of one or more household members.

2. Inconsistent family interactions. Adult caretakers expect a disproportionate amount of emotional support and comfort from children during periods of stress or crisis. Caretakers provide inconsistent emotional support for children. Interactions between members unsupportive or

indifferent. Family is adapting poorly to change in family composition.

1. Family interactions usually positive. Child and caretaker roles are normally distributed and fulfilled with only occasional minor exceptions. Family roles are sometimes confused and ineffective. Interaction between family members usually positive with only occasional relationship problems within household; or family is adapting to recent alteration or breakdown in family structure.

0. Family interactions typically supportive. Child and caretaker roles are appropriate. Adult caretakers provide appropriate amounts of emotional nurturance and support to the child. Caretaker has stable marriage or relationship with paramour; household members appear close, supportive, and caring.

Intervention Influence

I1. Caretaker's Motivation

4. No motivation to meet child's needs. Rejects caretaking role, taking a hostile attitude towards child care responsibilities; denies it's his/her job. Denies family problems.

3. Very little motivation to meet child's needs. Does not reject caretaking role but is indifferent or apathetic to child's needs; not concerned enough to resist competing demands on money, time, and attention; takes no responsibility for child's unmet needs.

2. Motivated to meet child's needs, but caretaker has multiple impediments to solving problems. Caretaker is motivated to meet the needs of the child but there are serious impediments (e.g., problem recognition, parenting ability, parenting confidence, willingness and ability to seek help) that may limit progress.

1. Motivated to meet child's needs, but caretaker has some impediments to solving problems. Caretaker is motivated to meet the needs of the child, but there are some impediments (e.g., problem recognition, parenting ability, parenting confidence, willingness/ability to seek and utilize help) that may interfere with progress.

0. Motivated to meet child's needs, and caretaker has no impediments to solving problems. Caretaker is motivated to meet the needs of the child and there are no impediments that will significantly affect progress.

I2. Caretaker's Cooperation with Intervention

4. Refuses to cooperate. Refuses to accept agency involvement. Actively resists and sabotages agency efforts (e.g., by making it impossible to contact family).

3. Cooperates minimally, but resists intervention. May verbally accept agency involvement. May resist utilization of services. Requires constant prodding/assistance from agency to use services, or participates in service in a minimally acceptable manner.

2. Cooperates, but poor response to intervention. Accepts agency involvement and utilizes services, but utilization is poor. Accepts referrals but may delay action; may postpone or not keep appointments; may drop services too soon.

1. **Cooperates, with generally appropriate response to intervention.** Accepts agency involvement and utilizes services in manner that will benefit client, but full service benefits not always realized due to various factors such as ambivalence, disorganization, etc. May require support and active encouragement from agency to properly utilize services.
0. **Cooperates with intervention.** Accepts agency involvement. Actively participates in services, if needed.

Abuse/Maltreatment Influence

A1. Access to Child by Perpetrator

4. **Open access with no adult supervision.** Victim and perpetrator live together with no other adult supervision.
3. **Open access with ineffective adult supervision.** Victim and perpetrator live together with other adult who sometimes leaves them alone. There is uncertainty whether other adult in household can or will protect child. Perpetrator lives elsewhere, but has unrestricted visitation without supervision.
2. **Open access with effective adult supervision.** Lives with victim or frequently visits, but effectively supervised (e.g., other adult almost always present, other adult willing and able to protect child).
1. **Limited access with effective adult supervision.** Perpetrator lives outside the home and visits victim infrequently and only with other effective adult supervision.
0. **No access to child.** Perpetrator lives outside the home and never visits, or is totally prevented from gaining access due to incarceration or by the effective barring of access by another caretaker.

A2. Intent and Acknowledgment of Responsibility

4. **Deliberate or premeditated abuse/maltreatment.** Caretaker explains occurrences of abuse/maltreatment as deliberate or premeditated and blames victim for their occurrence.
3. **Hides or denies responsibility for abuse/maltreatment.** Caretaker refuses to offer explanation despite evidence and/or denies role in and responsibility for occurrences.
2. **Rationalizes abuse/maltreatment or doesn't understand role.** Caretaker justifies or rationalizes role, assumes little responsibility, or is confused or unaware about his/her role.
1. **Understands role in abuse/maltreatment; accepts responsibility.** Caretaker acknowledges role in occurrences, takes responsibility, and feels guilty.
0. **Abuse/maltreatment accidental.** Incident appears accidental and caretaker appears sorry and remorseful.

A3. Severity of Abuse/Maltreatment

4. **Extreme harm or substantial danger of extreme harm.** Severe or bizarre maltreatment resulting in death, disfigurement, or dysfunction of organ or limb; or intentional acts that created a substantial danger of death, disfigurement, or dysfunction of organ or limb; or tortuous disciplinary practices; or sexual abuse accompanied by violence or exploitation (that is, prostitution, pornography); or life threatening failure to meet child's needs (e.g., failure to thrive).
3. **Serious harm or substantial danger of serious harm.** Nonaccidental serious physical injury requiring immediate medical attention; or intentional acts or disciplinary practices that created a substantial danger of serious physical injury; or sexual abuse; or failure to meet minimum needs of child (food, clothing, shelter, medical, supervision, emotional care) has caused or has created a substantial danger of causing serious physical injury or serious disease requiring immediate medical attention.
2. **Moderate harm or substantial danger of moderate harm.** Moderate harm to less sensitive parts of the child's body, which may require medical attention, or substantial danger thereof, as a result of intentional actions or disciplinary practices; or moderate harm or substantial danger thereof created as a result of failing to meet a child's minimum needs in one or several areas.
1. **Minor harm or substantial danger of minor harm.** Minor injury or substantial danger of minor harm, clearly not requiring medical attention, caused by intentional acts or disciplinary practices; or failure to meet a child's minimum need(s) resulting in minor harm or substantial danger of minor harm.

A4. History of Abuse/Maltreatment Committed by Present Caretakers

4. **Severe or escalating pattern of past abuse/maltreatment.** Severe past abuse/maltreatment or an escalating pattern of seriousness.
3. **Serious recent incident or a pattern of maltreatment.** There has been recent serious abuse/maltreatment or there exists a nonescalating pattern of maltreatment.
2. **Previous maltreatment.** There are disclosures of previous maltreatment of a specific nature.
1. **Maltreatment concerns.** Children or other sources provide information that raises concerns about possible past maltreatment, but there is no real clarity about the nature of such maltreatment.
0. **No history of abuse or maltreatment.** There is no information available that previous maltreatment has occurred.

CASE RISK RATING GUIDELINES

(5) High Risk

- Cases assigned a high risk rating reflect situations which pose the most danger and highest likelihood of future abuse or maltreatment to a child.
- It is likely that most of the risk element ratings are "3" or "4." If many risk elements have lower ratings, one or more particular elements are significant enough to warrant a high case risk rating.
- It is expected that these cases will be opened in the State Central Register unless clear justification can be provided. Services are essential to decrease identified risk.

(4) Moderately High Risk

- Cases assigned a moderately high risk rating reflect situations where there is substantial risk of future abuse or maltreatment to a child.
- It is likely that several of the risk element ratings are "3" or "4." If many risk elements have lower ratings, one or more particular elements are significant enough to warrant a moderately high case risk rating.
- It is expected that these cases will be opened in the State Central Register unless clear justification can be provided. There is a high likelihood that these cases need services to decrease identified risk.

(3) Intermediate Risk

- Cases assigned an intermediate risk rating reflect situations where there is significant risk of future abuse or maltreatment to a child.
- It is likely that several of the risk element ratings are "3" or "2." If many risk elements have lower ratings, one or more particular elements are significant enough to warrant an intermediate case risk rating.
- It is expected that these cases will be opened in the State Central Register unless clear justification can be provided. These cases are likely to benefit from services to decrease identified risk.

(2) Moderately Low Risk

- Cases assigned a moderately low risk rating reflect situations where the risk of future abuse or maltreatment to a child is relatively low.
- It is likely that most of the risk elements are rated "2" or lower. If there are any risk elements rated higher, these risk elements are likely to be offset by lower rated elements and family or individual strengths.
- Some of these cases may have family or child needs which are appropriate for local district and/or agency services provision.

(1) No/Low Risk

- Cases assigned no/low case risk rating reflect situations where the risk of future abuse or maltreatment to a child is low or insignificant.
- It is likely that most of the risk elements are rated "1" or "0." If there are any risk elements rated higher, these risk elements are likely to be offset by lower rated elements and family or individual strengths.
- Few of these cases are likely to have family or child needs which are appropriate for local district and/or agency services provision.

GUIDELINES FOR CASE CLOSING

Once a CPS case has been opened for service, it is important to work toward the time when the case can be appropriately closed. Family members, the case planner, and all service providers should clearly understand what needs to be accomplished in order to reach this milestone. Each individual case will have its own set of Outcomes that family members are working to achieve. It is against these Outcomes that progress will be measured and assessed. The following list of general guidelines for case closing may be useful in conjunction with your specific evaluation of a particular case. Consider closing a CPS case when:

- All children can remain safe despite withdrawal of controlling interventions that have protected each child.
- Risk element ratings and your risk assessment analysis lead you to conclude that future risk of abuse or maltreatment is not likely, or is significantly less likely, due to a less dangerous combination of risk elements, increasing family strengths, a more realistic viewpoint by family members, or other ameliorating factors.
- The overall Case Risk Rating has reached an acceptable level.
- The service plan review shows an acceptable level of outcome achievement for the most significant identified problems.

Then additionally consider:

- Whether case progress has been consistent over a long enough period of time.
- Whether improvements can likely be maintained despite withdrawal of services.
- Whether additional services could further reduce risk, whether these services are available, and whether the family has a reasonably strong ability to benefit if services were maintained or provided.

There are several circumstances which may require a CPS case closing whether or not risk has been reduced. Some of these circumstances are listed below:

- All children in the case have been freed for adoption.
- All children are in foster care and have permanency planning goals of independent living or in adult residential care.
- Caretakers refuse to accept offered services **and** Family Court intervention is unwarranted or a Family Court petition has been dismissed.
- Death of one or more caretakers or all children.
- Family moves out of state or cannot be located.
- All children in the case are over 18 years of age.

Source: Reprinted, with changes in notation, with permission of the New York State Department of Social Services, from *New York State Risk Assessment and Services Planning Model—Field Guide* (2nd ed.), 1994.

PRELIMINARY ASSESSMENT OF SAFETY

Case name _____ Report date _____

District_____ Report # _____ Case # _____

PURPOSE: To help assess whether any children are likely to be in immediate danger of serious harm, and to determine what interventions should be maintained or initiated to provide appropriate protection.

General Instructions: Complete this form within 7 days of the receipt of *each* report (including *each* subsequent report) received from the State Central Register. If a fatality is reported, complete this form within 24 hours if there are surviving children.

SAFETY ASSESSMENT

Part A. Safety Factor Identification

Directions: The following factors are behaviors or conditions that may be associated with a child being in immediate danger of serious harm. Identify the presence or absence of each factor by checking either "yes" or "no." *Note: "Caretaker" may refer to anyone who meets the legal definition of "Subject of a Report."*

1. Yes ☐ No ☐ Caretaker's behavior is violent or out of control.
2. Yes ☐ No ☐ Caretaker describes or acts toward child in predominantly negative terms or has extremely unrealistic expectations.
3. Yes ☐ No ☐ Caretaker caused, or has made a plausible threat that has or would result in, serious physical harm to the child.
4. Yes ☐ No ☐ Child's whereabouts cannot be ascertained and/or there is reason to believe that the family is about to flee or refuse access to the child.
5. Yes ☐ No ☐ Caretaker has not provided, or will not provide, sufficient supervision to protect the child from potentially serious harm.
6. Yes ☐ No ☐ Caretaker has not met, or is unable to meet, the child's immediate needs for food, clothing, shelter, and/or medical care.
7. Yes ☐ No ☐ Caretaker has previously abused or maltreated a child, and the severity of the abuse or maltreatment, or the caretaker's prior response to the incident, suggests that child safety may be an immediate concern.
8. Yes ☐ No ☐ Child is fearful of people living in or frequenting the home.
9. Yes ☐ No ☐ The child's physical living conditions are hazardous and may cause serious harm to the child.
10. Yes ☐ No ☐ Child sexual abuse is suspected and circumstances suggest that child safety may be an immediate concern.
11. Yes ☐ No ☐ Caretaker's drug or alcohol use seriously affects his/her ability to supervise, protect, or care for the child.
12. Yes ☐ No ☐ Other (specify) _____

Part B. Safety Factor Description

Directions: For all safety factors which are checked "Yes," note the applicable safety factor number and then briefly describe the specific individuals, behaviors, conditions, and/or circumstances associated with that particular safety factor.

_____

_____

_____

_____

_____

_____

_____

_____

Case name _____ Case # _____

RISK ASSESSMENT SCALES

Directions: Listed below are risk elements which may affect the likelihood of future abuse or maltreatment and which may be used to help assess case progress. **Record the rating that best describes what the risk level would be without the provision of services.** If you are unsure which rating applies best, consult the detailed anchor descriptions found in the Risk Assessment Field Guide. After completing the ratings of all risk elements within a particular Influence, complete the corresponding Summary Description. *Note. Record the highest rating applicable to a particular family member and explain differences in the Summary Description section. "Insufficient Information Available" may be recorded with a rating of "9" with supervisory approval.*

Caretaker Influence

CT1 Abuse/Maltreatment of Caretaker
- ☐ 4. Severe abuse/maltreatment as a child
- ☐ 3. Recurrent but not severe abuse/maltreatment as a child
- ☐ 2. Episodes of abuse/maltreatment as a child
- ☐ 1. Perceived maltreatment as a child with no specific incidents
- ☐ 0. No perceived maltreatment as a child
- ☐ 9. Insufficient information available

CT2 Alcohol or Drug Use
- ☐ 4. Substance use with severe social/behavioral consequences
- ☐ 3. Substance use with serious social/behavioral consequences
- ☐ 2. Occasional substance use with negative effects on behavior
- ☐ 1. Occasional substance use
- ☐ 0. No misuse of alcohol or use of drugs
- ☐ 9. Insufficient information available

CT3 Caretaker's Expectations of Child
- ☐ 4. Unrealistic expectations with violent punishment
- ☐ 3. Unrealistic expectations with angry conflicts
- ☐ 2. Inconsistent expectations leading to confusion
- ☐ 1. Realistic expectations with minimal support
- ☐ 0. Realistic expectations with strong support
- ☐ 9. Insufficient information available

CT4 Caretaker's Acceptance of Child
- ☐ 4. Rejects and is hostile to child
- ☐ 3. Disapproves of and resents child
- ☐ 2. Indifferent and aloof to child
- ☐ 1. Limited acceptance of child
- ☐ 0. Very accepting of child
- ☐ 9. Insufficient information available

CT5 Physical Capacity to Care for Child
- ☐ 4. Incapacitated due to chronic illness or disability resulting in inability to care for child
- ☐ 3. Physical impairment or illness which seriously impairs child caring capacity
- ☐ 2. Moderate physical impairment or illness resulting in only limited impact on child caring capacity
- ☐ 1. Very limited physical impairment or illness with virtually no impact on child caring capacity
- ☐ 0. Healthy with no identifiable risks to child caring capacity
- ☐ 9. Insufficient information available

CT6 Mental Capacity to Care for Child
- ☐ 4. Incapacitated due to mental/emotional disturbance or developmental disability resulting in inability to care for child
- ☐ 3. Serious mental/emotional disturbance or developmental disability which seriously impairs child caring capacity
- ☐ 2. Moderate mental/emotional disturbance or developmental disability with limited impairment of child caring capacity
- ☐ 1. Symptoms of mental/emotional disturbance or developmental disability with no impact on child caring capacity
- ☐ 0. No identifiable mental/emotional disturbance
- ☐ 9. Insufficient information available

Summary Description
Describe the most significant risk elements related to the Caretaker Influence. Use specific examples to justify your risk ratings. **Explain circumstances in which different caretakers or children may have different levels of risk associated with a particular risk element.**

_____

_____

_____

Case name _____ Case # _____

Child Influence

C1 Child's Vulnerability
☐ 4. Child younger than 2 years old, or older child with special needs
☐ 3. Child older than 2 years old, not regularly accessible to community oversight
☐ 2. Child is under 12 years old, attends school, day care, or early childhood development program
☐ 1. Child is over 12 years old and younger than 18 years old
☐ 0. Child is 16 years old or older, with adequate self-sufficiency skills

C2 Child's Response to Caretaker
☐ 4. Extremely anxious with uncontrolled fear, withdrawal, or passivity
☐ 3. Very anxious with negative, disruptive, and possibly violent interaction
☐ 2. Moderately anxious with apprehension and suspicion towards caretaker
☐ 1. Marginally anxious with some hesitancy towards caretaker
☐ 0. Child trusts and responds to caretaker in age-appropriate way
☐ 9. Insufficient information available

C3 Child's Behavior
☐ 4. Dangerous behavior problems
☐ 3. Serious behavior problems
☐ 2. Moderate but pervasive behavior problems
☐ 1. Minor behavior problems
☐ 0. No significant behavior problems
☐ 9. Insufficient information available

C4 Child's Mental Health and Development
☐ 4. Incapacitated due to mental/emotional disturbance or developmental delay and unable to function independently
☐ 3. Serious mental/emotional disturbance or developmental delay impairs ability to function in most daily activities
☐ 2. Moderate mental/emotional disturbance or developmental delay impairs ability to perform some daily activities
☐ 1. Symptoms of mental/emotional disturbance or developmental delay with minimal impact on daily activities
☐ 0. No identifiable mental/emotional disturbance or developmental delay
☐ 9. Insufficient information available

C5 Child's Physical Health and Development
☐ 4. Severe physical illness, disability, or lack of physical development; requires medical care
☐ 3. Serious physical illness, disability, or lack of physical development; restricts activities without special care
☐ 2. Moderate physical illness, disability, or lack of physical development; restricts activities somewhat but overcome with special care
☐ 1. Mild physical illness, disability, or lack of physical development; does not restrict activities
☐ 0. Healthy and no obvious physical illness, disability, or lack of physical development
☐ 9. Insufficient information available

Summary Description
Describe the most significant risk elements related to the Child Influence. Use specific examples to justify your risk ratings. **Explain circumstances in which different caretakers or children may have different levels of risk associated with a particular risk element.**

_____

_____

_____

_____

_____

_____

Case name _____   Case # _____

Family Influence

F1 Domestic Violence
- ☐ 4. Repeated or serious physical violence or substantial risk of serious physical violence in household
- ☐ 3. Incidents of physical violence in household; imbalance of power and control
- ☐ 2. Isolation and intimidation; threats of harm
- ☐ 1. Verbal aggression
- ☐ 0. Mutual tolerance
- ☐ 9. Insufficient information available

F2 Ability to Cope with Stress
- ☐ 4. Chronic crisis with limited coping
- ☐ 3. Prolonged crisis strains coping skills
- ☐ 2. Stabilized after period of crisis
- ☐ 1. Resolution without adverse effect
- ☐ 0. Free from stress influence
- ☐ 9. Insufficient information available

F3 Availability of Social Supports
- ☐ 4. Effectively isolated
- ☐ 3. Some support, but unreliable
- ☐ 2. Some reliable support, but limited usefulness
- ☐ 1. Some reliable and useful support
- ☐ 0. Multiple sources of reliable and useful support
- ☐ 9. Insufficient information available

F4 Living Conditions
- ☐ 4. Extremely unsafe: multiple hazardous conditions that are dangerous to children and have caused physical injury or illness
- ☐ 3. Very unsafe: multiple hazardous conditions that are dangerous to children
- ☐ 2. Unsafe: one hazardous condition that is dangerous to children
- ☐ 1. Fairly safe: one possibly hazardous condition that may harm children
- ☐ 0. Safe: no hazardous conditions apparent
- ☐ 9. Insufficient information available

F5 Family Identity and Interactions
- ☐ 4. Negative family interactions
- ☐ 3. Family interactions generally indifferent
- ☐ 2. Inconsistent family interactions
- ☐ 1. Family interactions usually positive
- ☐ 0. Family interactions typically supportive

Summary Description
Describe the most significant risk elements related to the Family Influence. Use specific examples to justify your risk ratings. **Explain circumstances in which different caretakers or children may have different levels of risk associated with a particular risk element.**

_____

_____

_____

_____

_____

_____

Case name _____ Case # _____

Intervention Influence

I1 Caretaker's Motivation
- ☐ 4. No motivation to meet child's needs
- ☐ 3. Very little motivation to meet child's needs
- ☐ 2. Motivated to meet child's needs, but caretaker has multiple impediments to solving problems
- ☐ 1. Motivated to meet child's needs, but caretaker has some impediments to solving problems
- ☐ 0. Motivated to meet child's needs, and caretaker has no impediments to solving problems
- ☐ 9. Insufficient information available

I2 Caretaker's Cooperation with Intervention
- ☐ 4. Refuses to cooperate
- ☐ 3. Cooperates minimally, but resists intervention
- ☐ 2. Cooperates, but poor response to intervention
- ☐ 1. Cooperates, with generally appropriate response to intervention
- ☐ 0. Cooperates with intervention

Summary Description
Describe the most significant risk elements related to the Intervention Influence. Use specific examples to justify your risk ratings. **Explain circumstances in which different caretakers or children may have different levels of risk associated with a particular risk element.**

_____

_____

_____

_____

Abuse/Maltreatment Influence

A1 Access to Child by Perpetrator
- ☐ 4. Open access with no adult supervision
- ☐ 3. Open access with ineffective adult supervision
- ☐ 2. Open access with effective adult supervision
- ☐ 1. Limited access with effective adult supervision
- ☐ 0. No access to child

A2 Intent and Acknowledgment of Responsibility
- ☐ 4. Deliberate or premeditated abuse/maltreatment
- ☐ 3. Hides or denies responsibility for abuse/maltreatment
- ☐ 2. Rationalizes abuse/maltreatment or doesn't understand role
- ☐ 1. Understands role in abuse/maltreatment; accepts responsibility
- ☐ 0. Abuse/maltreatment accidental

A3 Severity of Abuse/Maltreatment
- ☐ 4. Extreme harm or substantial danger of extreme harm
- ☐ 3. Serious harm or substantial danger of serious harm
- ☐ 2. Moderate harm or substantial danger of moderate harm
- ☐ 1. Minor harm or substantial danger of minor harm

A4 History of Abuse/Maltreatment Committed by Present Caretakers
- ☐ 4. Severe or escalating pattern of past abuse/maltreatment
- ☐ 3. Serious recent incident or a pattern of maltreatment
- ☐ 2. Previous maltreatment
- ☐ 1. Maltreatment concerns
- ☐ 0. No history of abuse or maltreatment

Summary Description
Describe the most significant risk elements related to the Abuse/Maltreatment Influence. Use specific examples to justify your risk ratings. **Explain circumstances in which different caretakers or children may have different levels of risk associated with a particular risk element.**

_____

_____

_____

_____

Case name _____   Case # _____

RISK ASSESSMENT ANALYSIS

A. Identify and evaluate the significance and interaction of the key risk elements and any other relevant areas of family functioning that should be addressed before the case is closed. Use additional paper as needed.

_____

_____

_____

_____

_____

_____

_____

_____

_____

B. Describe how relevant family members view the identified risk elements and any other areas of family functioning identified above.

_____

_____

_____

_____

C. Describe significant family or individual strengths that have been identified that may be used as part of the service plan to reduce future risk.

_____

_____

_____

_____

_____

_____

CASE RISK RATING

Assign an overall level of risk of future abuse or maltreatment by checking one of the case risk levels listed below. Consider all information available, including risks and strengths. **Guidelines for each case risk level are provided in the Risk Assessment Field Guide.**

☐   5. High Risk
☐   4. Moderately High Risk
☐   3. Intermediate Risk
☐   2. Moderately Low Risk
☐   1. No/Low Risk

APPENDIX E

HIGHLIGHTS OF THE THIRD NATIONAL INCIDENCE STUDY OF CHILD ABUSE AND NEGLECT (NIS-3)

Data on the incidence of child maltreatment in relationship to several demographic variables appear in the Third National Incidence Study of Child Abuse and Neglect (NIS-3; Sedlak & Broadhurst, 1996). In this study, 1,533,800 cases of reported or observed and suspected child maltreatment for the 1993 year were examined. The cases include those reported to agencies, as well as those reported from other sources. The NIS-3 provides definitions of child abuse and neglect in order to classify incidence figures of maltreatment (see Table E-1). These definitions overlap with those presented in Chapter 20. The other tables in this appendix use the definitions provided in Table E-1.

Incidence of Child Maltreatment as a Function of Gender

In the NIS-3 study, the incidence of child maltreatment was generally the same for boys and girls for all categories of maltreatment, except for sexual abuse (see Table E-2). The incidence of sexual abuse was three times higher for girls than for boys: 4.9 per 1,000 girls versus 1.6 per 1,000 boys.

Incidence of Child Maltreatment as a Function of Family Income

A strong relationship exists between family income and rate of maltreatment. Table E-3 shows that children in families with the lowest income level had the highest rate of maltreatment. The rate of all maltreatment was 2.23 times greater in families with incomes below $15,000 per year than in families with incomes between $15,000 and $29,999 (47 per 1,000 versus 20 per 1,000) and 22 times greater for children in the lowest bracket than for children in families with incomes over $30,000 per year (2.1 per 1,000).

The rate of neglect, in particular, shows the largest differences among the three income groups. The rate of neglect in families with incomes below $15,000 was 2.4 times greater than that in families with incomes between $15,000 and $29,000 per year (27.2 per 1,000 versus 11.3 per 1,000) and 45 times higher than that in families with incomes above $30,000 per year (0.6 per 1,000). The rate of neglect for chil-

dren in families with incomes between $15,000 and $29,999 per year was 9.5 times higher than that for children in families with incomes above $30,000 per year.

Incidence of Child Maltreatment as a Function of Family Size

Table E-4 shows that there is a relationship between family size and child maltreatment. Children in families with four or more children in 1993 were (a) nearly twice as likely to be maltreated as children in families with two or three children (34.5 per 1,000 versus 17.7 per 1,000, respectively) and (b) somewhat more likely to be maltreated than children in families with one child only (22 per 1,000). Of all the maltreatment categories, neglect, in particular, shows the largest difference associated with family size. The incidence rate for children from larger families (21.5 per 1,000) is almost 1.75 times the rate for only children (12.6 per 1,000), and it is almost 2.5 times the rate for children who have one or two siblings (8.8 per 1,000).

Incidence of Child Maltreatment as a Function of Family Structure

Table E-5 shows the relationship between the incidence of child maltreatment and the number of parents living in the child's household. The rate of maltreatment among children living with a single parent was more than 1.75 times the rate for children living with both parents (27.3 per 1,000 versus 15.5 per 1,000). The incidence of overall neglect was 2.2 times higher for children living with a single parent than for children in two-parent households (17.3 per 1,000 versus 7.9 per 1,000).

Perpetrators' Characteristics

Highlights of the NIS-3 study on perpetrators follow:

1. Natural parents committed the most offenses against children, 78%; followed by other parents and parent-substitutes (includes stepparents, foster parents, adoptive parents, separated spouse of in-home parent, and parent's boyfriend or girlfriend), 14%; and others (includes

913

Table E-1
Types of Child Maltreatment Defined in the Third National Incidence Study of Child Abuse and Neglect (NIS-3) in 1993

Physical Abuse

Acts constituting physical abuse include hitting with a hand, stick, strap, or other object; punching; kicking; shaking; throwing; burning; stabbing; or choking a child.

Sexual Abuse

Intrusion: Oral, anal, or genital penile penetration or anal or genital digital or other penetration.

Molestation with Genital Contact: Acts where there is some form of actual genital contact, without intrusion.

Other or Unknown Sexual Abuse: Unspecified acts not known to have involved actual genital contact (for example, fondling of breasts or buttocks, exposure) and inadequate or inappropriate supervision of a child's voluntary sexual activities.

Emotional Abuse

Close Confinement (Tying or Binding and Other Forms): Tortuous restriction of movement, as by tying a child's arms or legs together or binding a child to a chair, bed, or other object, or confining a child to an enclosed area (such as a closet) as a means of punishment (does not include use of safety harness on toddlers, swaddling of infants, or discipline involving "grounding" a child or restricting a child to his or her room).

Verbal or Emotional Assault: Habitual patterns of belittling, denigrating, scapegoating, or other nonphysical forms of overtly hostile or rejecting treatment, as well as threats of other forms of maltreatment (such as threats of beating, sexual assault, abandonment, and so forth).

Other or Unknown Abuse: Overtly punitive, exploitative, or abusive treatment (for example, attempted or potential physical or sexual assault, deliberate withholding of food, shelter, sleep, or other necessities as a form of punishment, economic exploitation, and unspecified abusive actions).

Physical Neglect

Refusal of Health Care: Failure to provide or allow needed care in accord with recommendations of a competent health care professional for a physical injury, illness, medical condition, or impairment.

Delay in Health Care: Failure to seek timely and appropriate medical care for a serious health problem that any reasonable layperson would have recognized as requiring professional medical attention.

Abandonment: Desertion of a child without arranging for reasonable care and supervision.

Expulsion: Other blatant refusals of custody, such as permanent or indefinite expulsion of a child from the home without adequate arrangement for care by others or refusal to accept custody of a returned runaway.

Other Custody Issues: Includes other issues, such as repeated shuttling of a child from one household to another, due to apparent unwillingness to maintain custody, or chronically and repeatedly leaving a child with others for days or weeks at a time.

Inadequate Supervision: Child left unsupervised or inadequately supervised for extended periods of time or allowed to remain away from home overnight without the parent or caregiver knowing (or attempting to determine) the child's whereabouts, or when the child is temporarily locked out of the home.

Other Physical Neglect: Conspicuous inattention to avoidable hazards in the home; inadequate nutrition, clothing, or hygiene; and other forms of reckless disregard of the child's safety and welfare, such as driving with the child while intoxicated, leaving a young child unattended in a motor vehicle, and so forth.

Educational Neglect

Permitted Chronic Truancy: Habitual truancy averaging at least 5 days a month when the parent has been informed of the problem and has not attempted to intervene.

Failure to Enroll/Other Truancy: Failure to register or enroll a child of mandatory school age, causing the child to miss at least 1 month of school; or a pattern of keeping a school-age child home for nonlegitimate reasons (for example, to work, to care for siblings,and so forth) an average of at least 3 days a month.

Inattention to Special Education Need: Refusal to allow or failure to obtain recommended remedial education services, or neglect in obtaining or following through with treatment for a child's diagnosed learning disorder or other special education need without reasonable cause.

Emotional Neglect

Inadequate Nurturance/Affection: Marked inattention to the child's needs for affection, emotional support, attention, or competence (includes nonorganic failure to thrive).

Chronic/Extreme Spouse Abuse: Chronic or extreme spouse abuse or other domestic violence in the child's presence.

Permitted Drug/Alcohol Abuse: Encouragement or permitting of drug or alcohol use by the child.

Permitted Other Maladaptive Behavior: Encouragement or permitting of other maladaptive behavior (for example, severe assaultiveness, chronic delinquency) under circumstances where the parent had reason to be aware of the existence and seriousness of the problem but did not attempt to intervene.

Refusal of Psychological Care: Refusal to allow needed and available treatment for a child's emotional or behavioral impairment or problem in accord with competent professional recommendation.

Delay in Psychological Care: Failure to seek or provide needed treatment for a child's emotional or behavioral impairment or problem that any reasonable layperson would have recognized as needing professional psychological attention (for example, severe depression, suicide attempt).

Other Emotional Neglect: Other inattention to the child's developmental/emotional needs (for example, markedly overprotective restrictions that foster immaturity or emotional overdependence, chronically applying expectation clearly inappropriate in relation to the child's age or level of development, and so forth).

Source: Sedlak and Broadhurst (1996).

Table E-2
Incidence Rates per 1,000 Children for Maltreatment in the NIS-3 (1993) Study for Males and Females

Maltreatment category	Males	Females
All Maltreatment	21.7	24.5
All Abuse	9.5	12.6
Physical Abuse	5.8	5.6
Sexual Abuse	1.6	4.9
Emotional Abuse	2.9	3.1
All Neglect	13.3	12.9
Physical Neglect	5.5	4.5
Emotional Neglect	3.5	2.8
Educational Neglect	5.5	6.4

Source: Sedlak and Broadhurst (1996).

Table E-3
Incidence Rates per 1,000 Children for Maltreatment in the NIS-3 (1993) Study for Different Levels of Family Income

Maltreatment category	Yearly income		
	<$15,000	$15,000–$29,999	≥$30,000
All Maltreatment	47.0	20.0	2.1
All Abuse	22.2	9.7	1.6
Physical Abuse	11.0	5.0	0.7
Sexual Abuse	7.0	2.8	0.4
Emotional Abuse	6.5	2.5	0.5
All Neglect	27.2	11.3	0.6
Physical Neglect	12.0	2.9	0.3
Emotional Neglect	5.9	4.3	0.2
Educational Neglect	11.1	4.8	0.2

Source: Sedlak and Broadhurst (1996).

other family members, other unrelated adults, and others), 9%. Table E-6 shows the type of maltreatment as a function of the perpetrator's relationship to the child and of the sex of the perpetrator.

2. The majority of children who were maltreated by their birth parents were maltreated by their mothers (75%); a sizable minority were maltreated by their fathers (46%).

3. Children who were maltreated by other parents and parent-substitutes were more likely to have been maltreated by a male (85% by males and 41% by females).

4. "Children tended to suffer neglect from female perpetrators—87% of those neglected in any way were neglected by a female" (pp. 6-8, 6-10). Female perpetrators predominate in the neglect category because they are the primary caregivers and are usually held accountable when the children are not taken care of.

5. Children were more often abused by males than by females (67% of all abused children were abused by males versus 40% by females).

6. Children were most often sexually abused by a male perpetrator (in 89% of the cases).

7. "Among all abused children, those abused by their birth parents were about equally likely to have been abused by mothers (55%) as by fathers (56%), but those abused by other parents and parent-substitutes or by others were much more likely to be abused by males (90% versus 15% and 80% versus 14%, respectively)" (p. 6-10).

8. "For emotional abuse, the pattern is largely congruent with the overall abuse pattern" (p. 6-10).

9. "For physical abuse, the pattern is slightly different, with children more likely to be physically abused by their mothers than by their fathers (60% versus 48%), but much more likely to be abused by a male when the perpetrator was another parent or parent-substitute (90% versus 19%), and somewhat more likely to be abused by a male when the perpetrator was related to them in some other way (57% versus 39%)" (p. 6-10).

Table E-4
Incidence Rates per 1,000 Children for Maltreatment in the NIS-3 (1993) Study for Different Levels of Family Size

Maltreatment category	Number of children		
	1	2–3	4+
All Maltreatment	22.0	17.7	34.5
All Abuse	10.5	9.9	13.9
Physical Abuse	5.1	5.2	6.4
Sexual Abuse	3.2	2.5	5.8
Emotional Abuse	3.2	2.8	3.4
All Neglect	12.6	8.8	21.5
Physical Neglect	4.4	3.8	9.1
Emotional Neglect	3.9	2.4	3.7
Educational Neglect	6.0	3.2	9.2

Source: Sedlak and Broadhurst (1996).

Table E-5
Incidence Rates per 1,000 Children for Maltreatment in the NIS-3 (1993) Study for Different Family Structures

		Single parent			
Maltreatment category	Both parents	Either mother or father	Mother only	Father only	Neither parent
All Maltreatment	15.5	27.3	26.1	36.6	22.9
All Abuse	8.4	11.4	10.5	17.7	13.7
Physical Abuse	3.9	6.9	6.4	10.5	7.0
Sexual Abuse	2.6	2.5	2.5	2.6	6.3
Emotional Abuse	2.6	2.5	2.1	5.7	5.4
All Neglect	7.9	17.3	16.7	21.9	10.3
Physical Neglect	3.1	5.8	5.9	4.7	4.3
Emotional Neglect	2.3	4.0	3.4	8.8	3.1
Educational Neglect	3.0	9.6	9.5	10.8	3.1

Source: Sedlak and Broadhurst (1996).

Table E-6
Distribution of Perpetrator's Sex by Type of Maltreatment and Perpetrator's Relationship to Child in the NIS-3 (1993) Study

Category and perpetrator[a]	Maltreated children		Sex of perpetrator		Category and perpetrator[a]	Maltreated children		Sex of perpetrator	
	Number	%[b]	M[c] %	F[d] %		Number	%[b]	M[c] %	F[d] %
All Abuse	743,200	100	67	40	All Neglect	879,000	100	43	87
Natural parents	461,800	62	56	55	Natural parents	800,600	91	40	87
Other parents	144,900	19	90	15	Other parents	78,400	9	76	88
Others	136,600	18	80	14	Others	—	—	—	—
Physical Abuse	381,700	100	58	50	Physical Neglect	338,900	100	35	93
Natural parents	273,200	72	48	60	Natural parents	320,400	95	34	93
Other parents	78,700	21	90	19	Other parents	18,400	5	—	90
Others	29,700	8	57	39	Others	—	—	—	—
Sexual Abuse	217,700	100	89	12	Emotional Neglect	212,800	100	47	77
Natural parents	63,300	29	87	28	Natural parents	194,600	91	44	78
Other parents	53,800	25	97	—	Other parents	18,200	9	—	—
Others	100,500	46	86	8	Others	—	—	—	—
Emotional Abuse	204,500	100	63	50	Educational Neglect	397,300	100	47	88
Natural parents	166,500	81	60	55	Natural parents	354,300	89	43	86
Other parents	27,400	13	74	—	Other parents	43,000	11	82	100
Others	10,600	5	—	—	Others	—	—	—	—
					All Maltreatment	1,553,800	100	54	65
					Natural parents	1,208,100	78	46	75
					Other parents	211,200	14	85	41
					Others	134,500	9	80	14

[a]Other parents category includes non-natural parents and parent-substitutes.
[b]% refers to the percentage of children in the maltreatment category.
[c]M% refers to the percentage of the total number of maltreated children in that category who were abused by a male perpetrator.
[d]F% refers to the percentage of the total number of maltreated children in that category who were abused by a female perpetrator.
Note. The percentages for males and females can sum to more than 100% because children who were abused by both a mother and a father were included in both classifications.
Source: Sedlak and Broadhurst (1996).

APPENDIX F

SEMISTRUCTURED INTERVIEW QUESTIONS

Note. The semistructured interview questions in this Appendix are designed to help interviewers obtain information from interviewees. The questions in the tables are neither psychometric devices nor standardized instruments—their reliability and validity are unknown. Furthermore, they are not designed to cover every contingency. Rather, they should be seen as guidelines to be modified as needed for each individual case.

Throughout this Appendix, you can use questions preceded by the words "If needed" when the more general question does not elicit sufficient information. "If needed" questions reflect more detailed probes.

Table F-1
Semistructured Interview Questions for an Adolescent (or Older Child) with a Drug Abuse Problem

Introduction
1. Hi! I'm Dr. [Ms., Mr.] _____. Dr. _____ asked me to see you. I'd like to talk to you about how you're getting along. OK?
2. When you don't understand a question that I ask, please say "I don't understand." When you tell me that, I'll try to ask it better. OK?

Background Information
3. Tell me about your being here today.
   (If the child does not mention problems with drug use, go to question 4; if the child does mention problems with drug use, go to question 5.)
4. I understand that you are using drugs. Is that right?
   (Respond as needed. After the child acknowledges drug use, go to question 5.)
5. Tell me about the drug[s] you use.
6. Where do you get it [them]?

7. How much does it [do they] cost?
8. About how much money do you spend each week on [cite drug]?
9. How do you pay for it?
10. Are you having financial problems because of your drug use?
11. (If yes) Tell me about that.
12. Have you ever done things you otherwise wouldn't do to get [cite drug]?
13. (If yes) Tell me about that.
14. (If needed) What do you do to get [cite drug]?
15. Do you have trouble turning down [cite drug] when it is offered to you?
16. Tell me about that.
17. Does the sight, thought, or mention of [cite drug] trigger urges and craving for [cite drug]?
18. (If yes) Tell me about that.
19. Do you think about [cite drug] much of the time?
20. (If yes) Tell me about these thoughts.
21. Do you have any concerns about your drug use?
22. (If yes) Tell me about your concerns.
23. (If needed) Are you frightened by the strength of your drug habit?
24. Do you feel you are dependent on [cite drug]?
25. Tell me about that.

Exposure to Drugs
26. Does anyone else in your family drink alcohol too much or use drugs?
27. (If yes) Tell me about that.
28. Do any of your friends regularly use alcohol or drugs?
29. (If yes) Tell me about that.
30. Do any of your friends sell or give drugs to other kids?
31. (If yes) Tell me about that.
32. When did you first learn about [cite drug]?
33. Who told you about [cite drug]?
34. What did he [she] tell you?
35. How old were you when you first tried [cite drug]?
36. Where were you when you first tried [cite drug]?
37. Was anyone else there?

38. (If yes) Tell me about who was there.
39. How much [cite drug] did you take?
40. How did you feel after you took [cite drug]?
41. As you look back on your first experience with [cite drug], how does it seem now?

Drug Usage

42. How old were you when you first started using [cite drug] on a regular basis?
43. How do you go about taking [cite drug]?
44. (If needed) Do you smoke it…eat it…inject it…snort it…inhale it?
45. How much [cite drug] do you take?
    (If drug is injected, go to question 46; if not, go to question 48.)
46. Do you use a sterile needle?
47. Do you share needles with other people?
48. Where are you when you take [cite drug]?
49. (If needed) Do you take it at home…school…the park…friends' houses…other places?
50. At what times during the day do you take [cite drug]?
51. Are you with anyone else when you take [cite drug]?
52. (If yes) Tell me about whom you're with.
53. About how many times have you used [cite drug]?
54. When was the last time you used [cite drug]?
55. How often do you use [cite drug]?
56. (If needed) On the average, how many days per week do you use [cite drug]?
57. How long have you been doing this?
58. Do you tend to use all the [cite drug] that you have on hand, even though you want to save some for another time?
59. Was there a time when you began to use [cite drug] more often?
    (If yes, go to question 60; if no, go to question 62.)
60. When was that?
61. Why do you think you started to use [cite drug] more often?
62. How do you feel when you don't have [cite drug]?
63. What do you do about it when you don't have [cite drug]?
64. Did you ever find you needed larger amounts of [cite drug] because you couldn't get high on the amount you were using?
65. (If yes) Tell me more about that.
66. (If needed) When did that begin to happen?
67. Would you use even more [cite drug] if you could get it?
68. Have you ever woken up the morning after taking [cite drug] and found you couldn't remember a part of what happened the night before, even though your friends tell you that you didn't pass out?
69. Do you often wish you could keep taking [cite drug], even after your friends have had enough?
70. (If yes) Tell me about that.

Drug Binges

71. Do you go on drug binges—that is, use a drug or drugs continually for a period of time?
    (If yes, go to question 72; if no, go to question 79.)

72. How many times have you gone on binges?
73. When was the last time you went on a binge?
74. What was happening in your life at that time?
75. How long does the binge last?
76. How much [cite drug] do you take during the binge?
77. How do you feel during the binge?
78. How do you feel after the binge?

Attempts to Stop Drug Usage

79. Has a friend or member of your family ever gone to anyone for help about your drug use?
80. (If yes) Tell me about that.
81. Have you ever attended Alcoholics Anonymous or Narcotics Anonymous?
82. (If yes) Tell me about what happened.
83. Have you ever tried to stop taking [cite drug]?
    (If yes, go to question 84; if no, go to question 91.)
84. What did you do to try to stop taking [cite drug]?
85. How long did you go without taking [cite drug]?
86. What happened that you started taking [cite drug] again?
87. About how many times have you tried to stop taking [cite drug]?
88. What happened when you tried to stop?
89. (If needed) Did you have withdrawal symptoms—that is, feel sick because you stopped or cut down on [cite drug]?
90. (If yes) Tell me about your symptoms.
91. Do you have any idea about why you haven't stopped using [cite drug]?
92. (If yes) Tell me about that.
93. Does your drug habit frighten you?
94. (If yes) In what way does your drug habit frighten you?
95. Have you ever tried to limit your drug use to only certain times or certain situations?
96. (If yes) Tell me about that.
97. Have you ever thought that you were "hooked" on drugs?
98. (If yes) Tell me about that.

Symptoms Associated with Drug Usage

99. Do you have any health problems because of using [cite drug]?
100. (If yes) Tell me about your health problems.
101. How is your appetite?
102. Have you gained or lost weight recently?
103. (If yes) Tell me about that.
104. Tell me about what you ate yesterday and today.
105. Is that the usual amount you would eat?
106. (If no) How did it differ from what you would eat other times?
107. When you are taking [cite drug] regularly, do you miss meals?
108. (If yes) Tell me more about that.
109. Have you ever gone to a doctor about these problems?
110. (If yes) What did the doctor do?
111. Have you ever been hospitalized for using [cite drug]?
112. (If yes) Tell me about that.
113. Have you ever overdosed on a drug?

114. (If yes) Tell me about that.
115. Have you ever had blackouts as a result of drug use?
116. (If yes) Tell me about that.
117. Has your use of [cite drug] caused you to miss school…do poorly in school…get into trouble with your teacher or principal…get into an accident… lose control…get the shakes or become depressed…get into trouble with your family…get into trouble with your friends…get into trouble with the police…have sex with someone…be sexually abused by someone?
118. (If yes to any of these areas) Tell me about the problems [cite drug] caused with [name area]. (Ask about the problems for each area mentioned by interviewee.)
119. Do people tell you that your behavior or personality has changed, even though they might not know it's because of drugs?
120. Have your parents talked to you about your drug use?
121. Tell me about that.
122. (If adolescent has a driver's license) Do you ever drive a car when you're high on [cite drug]?
123. (If yes) Tell me about that.
124. (If needed) Have you neglected your schoolwork or any important responsibilities because of your drug habit?
125. (If yes) Tell me about that.
126. Have your values and priorities changed because of your drug use?
127. (If yes) Tell me about that.
128. Do you feel guilty and ashamed of using [cite drug]?
129. Do you like yourself less for using [cite drug]?
130. Do you tend to spend time with certain people or go to certain places because you know that [cite drug] will be available?
131. Do you deal drugs to support your habit?
132. (If yes) Tell me about that.
133. Do you have any strange or scary feelings or thoughts when you use [cite drug]?
134. (If yes) Tell me about them.
135. (If needed) Do you find yourself lying and making excuses because of your drug use?
136. Tell me about that.
137. Do you ever deny or downplay the severity of your drug problem?
138. Has taking [cite drug] interfered with your life or activities a lot?
139. (If yes) Tell me about how taking [cite drug] has interfered.
140. Have you been spending less time with "straight" people since you've been using more [cite drug]?

Reasons for Taking Drugs

141. People have different reasons for taking drugs. What reasons do you have?
142. (If needed) Is it because you like the feeling it gives you…you need it to have a good time…you're afraid

of being bored or unhappy without it…it makes you feel less nervous or tense…you feel lonely and sad… your friends take drugs…you feel you couldn't function well without it?
143. Has your reason for taking [cite drug] changed since you began using it [them]?
144. (If yes) Tell me about that.

Involvement with Other Drugs

145. Are you taking other drugs or drinking alcohol along with taking [cite drug]?
(If yes, go to question 146; if no, go to question 151.)
146. Tell me about what else you are taking or drinking.
147. How does it [do they] make you feel?
148. Do you use it [them] at the same time you use [cite drug]?
149. Are you concerned about how these drugs [drugs and alcohol] interact with each other?
150. (If yes) Tell me about your concerns.

Attitude Toward Treatment

151. Do you think you have a problem with drugs?
(If yes, go to question 152; if no, go to question 156.)
152. Do you want help for your problem?
153. (If yes) What kind of help do you want?
154. How long do you think it will take to help you?
155. Are you prepared to work with people trained to help you?
156. If you became drug free, what would you miss most about [cite drug]?
157. And if you became drug free, what would be the best thing about being clean?
158. How would your friends react if you became drug free?
159. And how would your family react if you became drug free?

Other Questions

160. Is there anything else you'd like to tell me about your drug use?
161. (If yes) Go ahead.
162. Do you have any questions that you would like to ask me?
163. (If yes) Go ahead.
164. Thank you for talking with me. If you have any questions or if you want to talk to me, please call me. Here is my card.

Note. With modifications, these questions also can be used for a parent. You would need to substitute the child's name for "you" or "your" and make the appropriate grammatical changes.

Table F-2 in this Appendix contains a semistructured interview useful for inquiring about alcohol abuse or dependence.

Source: Adapted, in part, from Roffman and George (1988) and Washton, Stone, and Hendrickson (1988).

Table F-2
Semistructured Interview Questions for an Adolescent (or Older Child) Being Screened for Alcohol Abuse or Dependence

Introduction
1. Hi. I'm Dr. [Ms., Mr.] _____. Your doctor, Dr. _____, asked me to see you. I'd like to talk to you about how you're getting along. OK?
2. When you don't understand a question that I ask, please say "I don't understand." When you tell me that, I'll try to ask it better. OK?

Background Information
3. Do you know the reason why Dr. _____ asked me to see you?
4. (If yes) Tell me about what you know.
   (Clarify what interviewee says, if needed, and go to question 5, or say "That is right" if the interviewee knows the reason for the referral and go to question 7.)
5. (Tell interviewee the reason.) Dr. _____ said that you are having a problem with drinking too much alcohol. Is that right?
   (If adolescent says no, go to question 6; if adolescent says yes, go to question 7.)
6. Well, do you have any idea why your physician referred you to me [the clinic, the hospital, the center, etc.]?
   (If adolescent refuses to acknowledge that he or she has a problem with alcohol, you may not be able to continue with this interview. Instead, consider asking the questions in Table F-13 in this Appendix that focus on general issues associated with children's adjustment.)
7. Tell me about your drinking.
   (Ask questions 8 to 30, as needed.)
8. What do you drink?
9. How much do you drink?
10. How often do you drink?
11. At what times during the day do you drink?
12. Do you ever drink just after you get up in the morning?
13. (If yes) Tell me about when this happens.
14. Can you stop drinking after you've had one or two drinks if you want to?
15. (If needed) Where do you do your drinking?
16. Are you alone when you drink or are you with other people?
17. (If with others) Tell me something about the people you drink with.
18. Where do you get the alcohol?
19. (If purchased) Where do you get the money to buy the alcohol?
20. At what age did you first start drinking?
21. What did you drink when you first started?
22. How much did you drink at that time?
23. Have you ever been drunk?
24. (If yes) Tell me about the times you have been drunk.
25. How old were you the first time you ever drank enough to get drunk?
26. How has your drinking changed since you first began to drink?
27. Do you think you are losing control over your drinking?
28. (If yes) Tell me about that.
29. Do you think you have a serious drinking problem?
30. (If yes) Tell me about that.

Symptoms and Related Issues
31. Do you ever have hangovers?
32. (If yes) Tell me about the times you get hangovers.
33. Have you ever had blackouts while drinking—that is, drunk enough so that you couldn't remember the next day what you said or did?
34. (If yes) Tell me about your blackouts.
35. Have you ever had the shakes after cutting down on your drinking or when you stopped drinking?
   (If yes, go to question 36; if no, go to question 39.)
36. Tell me about when you had the shakes.
37. How often have you had them?
38. And what did you do about them?
39. Have you ever had health problems because of your drinking, such as liver disease or stomach problems?
40. (If yes) Tell me about them.
41. Have you ever made any rules about drinking, like not drinking before 5 o'clock in the evening or never drinking alone?
42. (If yes) Tell me about them.
43. Have you ever continued to drink when you knew you had a problem that might be made worse by drinking, such as drinking when you were taking medicine?
44. (If yes) Tell me about these times.
45. Have you ever gone on binges where you kept drinking for a couple days or more without sobering up?
46. (If yes) Tell me about these times.
47. Have your parents said anything to you about your drinking?
   (If yes, go to question 48; if no, go to question 51.)
48. What did they say?
49. When did they say this to you?
50. And what did you do about it?
51. Have other people said anything to you about your drinking?
   (If yes, go to question 52; if no, go to question 54.)
52. When did they say this to you?
53. And what did you do about it?

Reasons for Drinking
54. People have different reasons for drinking. What reasons do you have for drinking?
55. (If needed) Is it because you like the taste…you are celebrating special occasions…your friends drink…you feel nervous and tense…you are upset…you feel lonely or sad…you want to get high? Are there other reasons?
56. Does alcohol ever allow you to do things that you wouldn't do if you weren't drinking?
57. (If yes) Tell me about these things.
58. Have you ever felt bad or guilty about your drinking?
59. (If yes) Tell me about your feelings.

Problems as a Result of Drinking

60. Have you ever gotten into fights while drinking?
61. (If yes) Tell me about these times.
62. Have you ever been arrested because of your drinking?
63. (If yes) Tell me about that.
64. (If relevant) Have you ever been arrested for drunk driving?
65. (If yes) Tell me about that.
66. Have you ever had an accident because of drinking?
67. (If yes) Tell me about that.
68. Have you ever had school troubles because of drinking—like missing too much school, coming in late for classes, or not paying attention in class?
69. (If yes) Tell me about these times.
70. (If relevant) Have you ever had trouble on a job because of drinking—like missing work or coming in late for work?
71. (If yes) Tell me about these times.
72. Have you lost any friends because of your drinking?
73. (If yes) Tell me about what happened.
74. Has there ever been a period of your life when you could not do your daily work unless you had something to drink?
75. (If yes) Tell me about that.

Family and Friends

76. Does your father drink alcohol?
77. (If yes) Tell me about that.
78. Does your mother drink alcohol?
79. (If yes) Tell me about that.
80. (If relevant) Do any of your sisters and brothers drink alcohol?
81. (If yes) Tell me about that.
82. Does anyone else in the family drink alcohol?
83. (If yes) Who?
84. Do your friends drink alcohol?
    (If yes, go to question 85; if no, go to question 87.)
85. Tell me about their drinking.
86. When you are drinking with your friends, do you try to drink a few extras and hide it from them?
87. Does anyone in your family use drugs?
88. (If yes) Tell me about that.
89. Do your friends use drugs?
90. (If yes) Tell me about that.

Attempts to Seek Help

91. Have you ever felt the need to cut down your drinking?
92. (If yes) Tell me about that.
93. Have you ever talked to your parents…your friends…your doctor…your clergyman…your teachers…any other professional about your drinking too much?
    (If yes, go to question 94; if no, go to question 97.)
94. Tell me about whom you talked to.

95. What did you say?
96. And what did he [she, they] say?
97. Have you ever tried to stop drinking?
98. (If yes) Tell me about the times when you tried to stop drinking.
99. Do you think you have a serious drinking problem?
100. (If yes) Tell me about that.
101. Have you ever been in an alcohol treatment program? (If yes, go to question 102; if no, go to question 104.)
102. Tell me about when you were in the program.
103. Did it help?
104. What is your goal—what would you like to see happen with regard to your drinking right now?

Attitude Toward Treatment

(If adolescent has said that he or she has a problem with alcohol, go to question 105; if not, go to question 109.)
105. Do you want help for your problem?
     (If yes, go to question 106; if no, go to question 109.)
106. What kind of help do you want?
107. How long do you think it will take to help you?
108. Are you prepared to work with the people who are trained to help you?
109. If you did not drink alcohol, what would you miss most about it?
110. And what would be the best thing about not drinking alcohol?
111. How would your friends react if you did not drink alcohol?
112. And how would your family react if you did not drink alcohol?
113. How then do you see the role of alcohol in your life—that is, what part should alcohol play in your life?

Other Questions

114. Is there anything else you would like to tell me about your alcohol use?
115. (If yes) Go ahead.
116. Do you also use drugs?
117. (If yes) Tell me about the drugs you use.
118. Do you have any questions that you would like to ask me?
119. (If yes) Go ahead.
     (Tell adolescent what will happen next, as needed.)
120. Thank you for talking with me. If you have any questions or if you want to talk to me, please call me. Here is my card.

Note. With modifications, these questions also can be used for a parent. You would need to substitute the child's name for "you" or "your" and make the appropriate grammatical changes.

Table F-1 in this Appendix contains a semistructured interview useful for inquiring about drug use.

Source: Adapted in part from Robins and Marcus (1987).

Table F-3
Semistructured Interview Questions for an Adolescent (or Older Child) Who Smokes

For questions involving rating scales (such as questions 69–72, 75, 86, and 89), consider making the appropriate scales on a sheet of paper and showing them to the interviewee.

Introduction
1. Hi! I'm Dr. [Ms., Mr.] _____. And you are [cite adolescent's name]. How are you today?
2. When you don't understand a question that I ask, please say "I don't understand." When you tell me that, I'll try to ask it better. OK?
3. What did your parents tell you about why you're here?
4. How old are you?
5. When is your birthday?
6. What is your present weight?
7. Have you lost or gained weight in the past year?
8. (If yes) Tell me about that.
9. What is your present height?

Smoking History
10. I'd like to talk about your smoking. OK?
11. How old were you when you started smoking?
12. Why did you begin to smoke?
13. How old were you when you began smoking a pack a week or more regularly?
14. What brand do you smoke?
15. In an average day, about how many cigarettes do you smoke?
16. How many cigarettes do you think you smoked per day over the past week?
17. On the average, how much of a cigarette do you smoke?
18. Do you inhale?
19. How soon after you wake up do you smoke your first cigarette?
20. When do you do most of your smoking?
21. Which cigarette in the day would you most hate to give up?
22. Where do you do most of your smoking?
23. Is it hard for you to not smoke in places where it's not allowed?
24. (If yes) Tell me about that.
25. Do you smoke even when you have a bad cold?
26. Do you smoke even when you are so sick that you are in bed most of the day?
27. In the past year, have you changed the number of cigarettes you smoke?
28. (If yes) In what way?
29. In the past year, have you changed the way you inhale?
30. (If yes) In what way?
31. In the past year, have you changed your smoking habits in any other way?
32. (If yes) Tell me about that.
33. Are you concerned about your smoking?

34. Tell me about that.
35. Are others concerned about your smoking? (If yes, go to question 36; if no, go to question 38.)
36. Who is concerned about your smoking?
37. What are their concerns?
38. What's the best thing about smoking for you?
39. (If needed) Does it help you relax…release stress… be part of a group? Do you have some other reason for smoking?

Quitting History
40. How many times have you tried to quit smoking and succeeded for at least 24 hours? (If adolescent has tried to quit, go to question 41; if adolescent hasn't tried to quit, go to question 53.)
41. How long ago was your most recent serious attempt to quit smoking?
42. What have you tried in the past to help you quit cigarettes?
43. (If needed) Have you gone to a clinic…seen a doctor…read self-help books?
44. What is the longest period of time you were able to stay off cigarettes after quitting on your own?
45. In your past quitting attempts, what happened that made you go back to smoking? (If needed, ask questions 46 to 52.)
46. Did you go back to smoking when you were irritated or angry about something…were sad…were happy… were anxious…gained weight?
47. In your past quitting attempts, were you most likely to go back to smoking in the morning…around lunch time…in the late afternoon…in the night?
48. In your past quitting attempts, were you most likely to go back to smoking while drinking alcohol, coffee, or anything else?
49. (If yes) What were you drinking?
50. In your past quitting attempts, were you most likely to go back to smoking when you were alone or when you were with others?
51. In your past quitting attempts, were you most likely to go back to smoking when you were at home or some other place?
52. (If at some other place) What place was that?

Social Support
53. Does your mother smoke?
54. Does your father smoke?
55. (If relevant) Do any of your brothers and sisters smoke?
56. Do you have a boyfriend [girlfriend]?
57. (If yes) Does your boyfriend [girlfriend] smoke?
58. Does your closest friend smoke?
59. (If relevant) Does your closest coworker smoke?
60. How many people who live in your house smoke?
61. How many people who live in your house used to smoke?
62. How many people who live in your house have never smoked?
63. About how many of your close friends smoke?

64. About how many of your close friends used to smoke?
65. About how many of your close friends have never smoked?
66. How many children 13 years old or younger are living in your home?
67. Are there any people who have been trying to get you to quit smoking?
68. (If yes) Who?
69. On a scale of 1 to 10, with 1 being none and 10 being very, very much, how much support and understanding do you expect to get from family and friends for your effort to quit smoking?

Ability to Quit Smoking

70. On a scale of 1 to 10, with 1 being not at all and 10 being very, very much, how much do you want to quit smoking?
71. On a scale of 1 to 10, with 1 being no chance and 10 being can't fail, how much of a chance do you have to quit smoking soon?
72. On a scale of 1 to 10, with 1 being poor and 10 being excellent, what are the chances that you will not be smoking in six months?
73. If you are successful in quitting cigarettes, do you foresee any problems that you might have? (If adolescent doesn't understand question, provide list of problems, such as problems with eating or with getting along with people.)
74. (If yes) What problems?

Health

75. On a scale of 1 to 10, with 1 being not at all and 10 being very, very much, do you believe smoking can harm your health?
76. Do you believe that your health has been harmed by your smoking?
77. (If yes) In what way?
78. Has the health of any of your close friends been harmed by smoking?
79. (If yes) Tell me about that.
80. Has the health of any of your relatives been harmed by smoking?
81. (If yes) Tell me about that.
82. Has any doctor ever asked you to quit smoking?
83. (If yes) Tell me about that.
84. I'm going to list some physical problems. Please tell me if you ever had any of these problems. Have you ever had…heart problems…high blood pressure… tuberculosis…bronchitis…diabetes…asthma… anemia?
85. (For females) Are you pregnant at this time?
86. On a scale of never, rarely (less than once a week), often (once or twice a week), or frequently (two or more times a week), how often over the past month have you suffered from headaches…sleep problems…stomach upset…tight muscles… dizziness…pain…heart racing or palpitations… nervous sweating?
87. Have you seen a mental health professional in the past two years?
88. (If yes) Tell me about that.

89. Using a scale of 1 to 10, with 1 being not at all characteristic of you and 10 being very characteristic of you, rate how much each of the following applies to you:

— Wheezing
— Coughing
— Short of breath
— Good energy level
— Able to get lots of things done
— Good appetite
— Restless
— Tense
— Impatient
— Irritable
— Sociable
— Overeating
— Getting enough exercise
— Sharp sense of smell and taste
— Sad
— Depressed
— In control of your life
— Able to get things done in an efficient way
— Good concentration
— Addicted to tobacco
— Physically healthy
— Good self-esteem
— Tired

Other Habits

90. Do you use other forms of tobacco, such as snuff, chewing tobacco, pipes, or cigars?
    (If yes, go to question 91; if no, go to question 93.)
91. What kind?
92. Tell me about your use of [cite other form of tobacco].
93. Do you drink any caffeinated beverages, such as coffee, tea, or cola?
    (If yes, go to question 94; if no, go to question 96.)
94. What do you drink?
95. How much [cite beverage] do you drink each day?
96. Do you drink alcohol?
    (If yes, go to question 97; if no, go to question 100.)
97. What do you drink?
98. How much do you drink each day [week]?
99. What's the best thing about drinking for you?
100. Do you take any drugs?
    (If yes, go to question 101; if no, go to question 117.)
101. (If yes) Tell me about that.
102. (If needed) What is the name of the drug you take?… What is the strength or dosage of the drug you take?…How do you take the drug?…How much do you take each day?…What do you get out of taking [cite drug]?
    (Ask questions 103 to 116, as needed.)
103. Do you use cocaine or crack?
104. (If yes) Tell me about your use of crack [cocaine].
105. Do you use marijuana?
106. (If yes) Tell me about your use of marijuana.
107. Do you take any tranquilizers?
108. (If yes) Tell me about your use of tranquilizers.
109. Do you take any stimulants?

110. (If yes) Tell me about your use of stimulants.
111. Do you take over-the-counter pills?
112. (If yes) Tell me about your use of pills.
113. Do you take any prescription drugs?
114. (If yes) Tell me about your use of prescription drugs.
115. Do you use any other drugs that I haven't mentioned?
116. (If yes) Tell me about your use of it [them].

Attitude Toward Treatment

117. Do you think you have a problem with smoking?
     (If yes, go to question 118; if no, go to question 127.)
118. Do you want help for your problem?
     (If yes, go to question 119; if no, go to question 127.)
119. What kind of help do you want?
120. How long do you think it will take to help you?
121. Are you prepared to work with the people who are trained to help you?
122. If you did not smoke, what would you miss most about it?
123. And what would be the best thing about not smoking?
124. How would your friends react if you did not smoke?
125. And how would your family react if you did not smoke?
126. How then do you see the role of cigarettes in your life—that is, what part should cigarettes play in your life?

Other Questions

127. Do you have any questions that you would like to ask me?
128. (If yes) Go ahead.
129. Thank you for talking with me. If you have any questions or if you want to talk to me, please call me. Here is my card.

Note. With modifications, these questions also can be used for a parent. You would need to substitute the child's name for "you" or "your" and make the appropriate grammatical changes.

If you need to ask additional questions about possible drug abuse and possible alcohol abuse, see Table F-1 and Table F-2, respectively, in this Appendix.
Source: Adapted from Orleans and Shipley (1982).

Table F-4
Semistructured Interview Questions for a Child (or Adolescent) Alleged to Have Been Physically or Emotionally Abused

---

If the child describes the abuse, be sure to repeat what he or she says. Also repeat what the child says if he or she corrects you. This is especially important if a videotape is being made.

Introduction

1. Hi! I'm Dr. [Ms., Mr.] _____. And you are [cite child's name]. How are you today?
   (You can establish rapport in different ways, depending on the child's age and any other relevant factors. For preschool and young school-aged children, go to question 2; for older children and adolescents, go to question 61.)

Rapport Building

2. [Cite child's name], let's do something together. I'm going to draw a tree, and I'd like you to help me color it. OK? (Draw an outline of a tree.)
3. Here are some crayons. What color do you want to make the leaves?
4. Go ahead and color the leaves.
5. And now this part, the trunk of the tree (point to the trunk). What color do you want to make the trunk?
6. Go ahead. You're doing a good job.
7. Is there anything else you want to put on our tree?
8. (If yes) Go ahead.

Background Questions

9. (If relevant) I want to tell you something special about my room. Behind the mirror is a video camera, and we make videotapes of all the boys and girls who come in here. That way I can remember everything we talk about. OK?
10. Now I'd like to ask you some questions. When you don't understand a question that I ask, please say "I don't understand." When you tell me that, I'll try to ask it better. OK?
11. How old are you?
12. When is your birthday?
13. Where do you live?
14. Do you know your address?
15. (If yes) What is it?
16. Who lives at your house?
17. (If relevant) What do you call your mother?
18. (If relevant) What do you call your father?
19. Do you know your phone number?
20. (If yes) What is it?
21. Do you know what city you live in?
22. (If yes) What is the name of the city you live in?
23. Do you know what state you live in?
24. (If yes) What is the name of the state you live in?
25. Who are the people you like to be with? (Inquire about each person.)
26. Who are the people you don't like to be with? (Inquire about each person.)
27. Do you have a favorite toy?
28. (If yes) Tell me about it.
29. Do you have something you really like to do?
30. (If yes) Tell me about it.
31. Do you go to school?
    (If yes, go to question 32; if no, go to question 39.)
32. What school do you go to?
33. What do you do at school?
34. Do you know what time you get home from school?
35. Do you come home right after school?
    (If no, go to question 36; if yes, go to question 39.)
36. Where do you go after school?
37. Which days do you go to [cite place where child goes after school]?
38. What is the name of the person who takes care of you at [cite place where child goes after school]?

Concepts

39. Now, [cite child's name], I'd like to see what colors you know. If you don't know a color, just say "I don't know." That's OK.
40. (Take out a box of crayons. Hold up a crayon.) What color is this? (Repeat same procedure for several colors—namely, orange, red, blue, brown, black, purple, and green.)
41. [Cite child's name], I'm going to ask you some more questions, and if there's something you don't know, just say "I don't know," because that's all right. OK?
42. How about counting? Can you count?
43. (If yes) Go ahead.
44. (Hand a crayon, a piece of paper, and a crayon box to child.) Please put the crayon on top of the paper.
45. Now put it under the paper.
46. Now put it behind the paper.
47. How about putting it under the table?
48. Can you put it on top of your head?
49. Now put it inside the crayon box.
50. And now put it outside the box.

Difference Between Truth and Lie

51. (Hold up a stuffed cat or similar animal.) Do you know what this is?
52. (If yes) Tell me what it is.
    (If child does not know) It's a cat.
53. Is it a real cat or a pretend cat?
54. How do you know that?
55. Can you think of any other reason?
56. [Cite child's name], do you know what a lie is?
57. (If yes) Give me an example of what a lie might be.
58. So, if I told you this was a red crayon (holding up a black one), would that be the truth or a lie?
59. And if I said this was an orange crayon (holding up an orange crayon), would that be the truth or a lie?
60. And if I said that I'm a woman [man], would that be the truth or a lie?
    (Go to question 62.)

Inquiry About Recent Event

61. (If relevant) I want to tell you something special about my room. Behind the mirror is a video camera, and we make videotapes of all the kids [children, teenagers] who come in here. That way I can remember everything we talk about. OK?
62. Remember, when you don't understand a question that I ask, please say "I don't understand." When you tell me that, I'll try to ask it better. OK?
63. One of the things that I do when I talk to kids [children, teenagers] is to get them to promise to tell the truth. Would you promise me to tell the truth today while we talk?
64. Can we shake on it?
65. [Cite child's name], do you know why you came here today?
    (If child doesn't know, tell child in simple terms why he or she is there—for example, "I'd like to talk to you to see how you are getting along. OK?")
66. Has anything happened to you that you would like to tell me about?

67. (If yes) What happened?
    (See directions following question 68.)
68. [Cite person who reported alleged act] told me that something happened to you recently. I'd really like to talk to you about it. OK? What happened?
    (Ask questions 69 to 88, as needed; then go to question 89.)
69. Who [cite act]? (Make sure you know the person the child is referring to and what was done.)
70. How did it begin?
71. And what happened next?
72. What did [cite alleged perpetrator] say to you?
73. And what did you say?
74. (If needed) Did you ask [cite alleged perpetrator] to stop?
75. (If yes) What did [cite alleged perpetrator] say or do?
76. What were you doing the day [cite alleged perpetrator] [cite act]?
77. Do you remember what the weather was like?
78. (If yes) What was the weather like?
79. Where were you when it happened?
80. (If needed) Were you playing inside or outside?
81. When did it happen?
82. (If needed) Was it during the morning or the afternoon or at nighttime?
83. (If needed) Was it during the summer, winter, spring, or fall?
84. What were you doing right before [cite alleged perpetrator] [cite act]?
85. (If needed) Tell me about your being at [cite place where event occurred].
86. What else was going on at that time?
87. Did anything else happen?
88. (If yes) Tell me about that.

Whereabouts of Relatives During Event

89. (If relevant) Where was [were] [cite nonoffending caregiver(s)] when this happened?
90. (If relevant) Where were your brothers and sisters?

Others Adults Present During Event

91. Were any other grown-ups there?
92. (If yes) Who was there?
93. And what did [cite names of other adults who were there] do? (Inquire about the actions of each person child names.)
94. Were any other children there?
95. (If yes) Who was there?
96. And what did they do?
97. Did anyone else see what happened?
98. (If yes) Who else saw what happened?

Secrecy

99. What did [cite alleged perpetrator] tell you about what he [she] was doing?
100. Did [cite alleged perpetrator] tell you not to tell anybody about what was happening?
     (If yes, go to question 101; if no, go to question 112.)
101. What did [cite alleged perpetrator] say?
102. What did you think would happen if you told?
     (Ask questions 103 to 111, as needed. These ques-

tions are more direct and leading and should be used only if necessary.)

103. Did [cite alleged perpetrator] say that it would cause trouble for him [her] if you told anybody?
104. (If yes) What kind of trouble did he [she] say it would cause?
105. Did [cite alleged perpetrator] say that he [she] would hurt someone else if you told anybody?
106. (If yes) Who would be hurt?
107. Did [cite alleged perpetrator] say that he [she] would go to jail if you told anybody?
108. Did [cite alleged perpetrator] say that he [she] would never be able to see you again if you told anybody?
109. (If relevant) Did [cite alleged perpetrator] say that he [she] would be divorced if you told anybody?
110. Did [cite alleged perpetrator] say that you would be taken away from your family if you told anybody?
111. Did [cite alleged perpetrator] say that he [she] would hurt you if you told anybody?

Inquiry About Similar Events
112. Did this happen one time or more than one time?
(If more than one time, go to question 113; if child says it happened only one time, go to question 123.)
113. Tell me about the other time[s] it happened.
114. How many times did it happen before?
115. When was the very first time it happened?
116. When was the very last time it happened?
117. How long has this been going on?
118. What happened to you at these other times?
119. Were these other times different from the most recent time?
120. (If yes) In what way?
121. Have you ever seen anyone else [cite act]?
122. (If yes) Tell me about it.
(Repeat questions 70 to 111 for each incident, as needed.)

Others Who Know About the Abuse
123. Did you tell anyone about what was going on?
(If yes, go to question 124; if no, go to question 131.)
124. Whom did you tell?
(Ask questions 125 and 126 for each person child mentions, as needed.)
125. What did you tell [cite person] about what happened?
126. What did [cite person] say or do after you told him [her]?
127. Did anyone else know what was going on?
(If yes, go to question 128; if no, go to question 132.)
128. Who knew about it?
(Ask questions 129 and 130 for each person child mentions, as needed.)
129. How did [cite person] find out about it?
130. What did [cite person] say or do?
(Go to question 132.)
131. Did anyone know what was going on?
(If yes, go to question 128; if no, go to question 132.)

Alleged Perpetrator's Actions with Others
132. Do you think [cite alleged perpetrator] has [cite act] to anyone else?
133. (If yes) To whom has he [she] done this?
134. How do you know?

Relationship with and Feelings About the Alleged Perpetrator
135. What is [cite alleged perpetrator] like?
136. What did [cite alleged perpetrator] do to get you to [cite act]?
137. How did you feel when [cite alleged perpetrator] [cite act]?
138. Did [cite alleged perpetrator] promise you anything or give you anything afterwards?
139. (If yes) What did [cite alleged perpetrator] promise you or give you?
140. Did you do it because you were afraid?
141. Did [cite alleged perpetrator] ever threaten to hurt you if you did not do it?
142. (If yes) Tell me more about that.
143. How did you feel about [cite alleged perpetrator] before this happened?
144. How do you feel now about him [her]?
(Ask optional questions 145 to 211 if you want to inquire about how the child is functioning. If you do not, go to question 212.)

Sleeping (Optional)
145. You did a good job in talking to me. Now I'd like to ask you about how you are doing. OK?
146. How are you sleeping?
147. (If needed) Are you sleeping well?
148. (If no) Tell me about that.
149. What kinds of dreams are you having?
150. Are you having more of these dreams lately?
151. And how about bad or scary dreams? Do you have any bad or scary dreams?
152. (If yes) Tell me about them.

Eating (Optional)
153. How are you eating?
154. (If needed) Are you eating well?
155. (If no) Tell me about that.
156. Have there been any changes in how you are eating since this happened?
157. (If yes) Tell me about what has changed.

School (Optional)
158. How are you doing in school?
(Ask questions 159 to 162, as needed.)
159. How have your grades been?
160. Can you pay attention?
161. How are you getting along with your teachers?
162. And how are you getting along with other children at school?

Affect (Optional)
163. How are you feeling these days?
(Ask questions 164 to 177, as needed.)
164. Are you worrying about anything?
165. (If yes) What are you worrying about?
166. Are you happy?
167. (If no) Why aren't you happy?
168. Are you sad?
169. (If yes) Tell me why you are sad.
170. Are you afraid of things?
171. (If yes) What are you afraid of?

172. Are you afraid of people?
173. (If yes) Whom are you afraid of?
174. Do you feel guilty about anything?
175. (If yes) What do you feel guilty about?
176. How often do you think about what happened to you?
177. How does that make you feel?

Physical Symptoms (Optional)
178. Does your body hurt anywhere?
179. (If yes) Tell me where it hurts.
180. Do you have stomachaches?
181. (If yes) Tell me about them.
182. Do you have headaches?
183. (If yes) Tell me about them.
184. Do you have problems going to the bathroom?
185. (If yes) Tell me about the problems you're having.
186. Do you have problems breathing?
187. (If yes) Tell me about the problems you're having.
188. Do you feel tired all the time?
189. (If yes) Tell me about your feeling tired.
190. Do you feel restless?
191. (If yes) Tell me about your feeling restless.
192. Have you been sick since this happened?
193. (If yes) What sickness have you had?
194. Did you see a doctor?
(If yes, go to question 195; if no, go to question 200.)
195. What did the doctor tell you?
196. (If needed) Did the doctor give you anything to take or want you to do anything?
(If yes, go to question 197; if no, go to question 201.)
197. What did the doctor give you or want you to do?
198. Did you do what the doctor wanted you to do?
199. Did it help?
(Go to question 201.)
200. What was the reason that you didn't go to the doctor?

Family and Friends (Optional)
201. How have you been getting along with your family since this happened?
202. Has your relationship with your mother [stepmother, female caregiver] changed in any way since this happened?
203. (If yes) In what way has it changed?
204. Has your relationship with your father [stepfather, male caregiver] changed in any way since this happened?
205. (If yes) In what way has it changed?
206. (If relevant) And has your relationship with your sisters and brothers changed since this happened?
207. (If yes) In what way has it changed?
208. Has your relationship with your other relatives changed since this happened?
209. (If yes) Tell me, in what way has it changed?
210. Has your relationship with your friends changed since this happened?
211. (If yes) Tell me, in what way has it changed?

Concluding Questions
212. [Cite child's name], did anyone tell you what to say to me?
(If yes, go to question 213; if no, go to question 215.)
213. Who told you?
214. What did he [she, they] tell you to say?
215. [Cite child's name], do you remember when we talked about telling the truth?
216. Is everything you told me today the truth?
217. (If not) What did you tell me that wasn't the truth?
218. (If you have any doubts about whether the abuse occurred) Did [cite alleged perpetrator] really do that to you?
219. Is there anything else you want to tell me?
220. (If yes) Go ahead.
221. Is there anything you want to ask me?
222. (If yes) Go ahead.
223. [Cite child's name], if someone does something to hurt you, what can you do?
224. (If the child fails to mention telling someone) Is there someone you could tell?
225. (If child fails to mention anyone) You could tell your mom [dad, caregiver, neighbor, relative, friend's parent].
226. (If relevant) Do you go to day care, [cite child's name]?
227. (If yes) It's OK to tell your day care person, too.
228. Well, I really appreciate your coming in and talking to me today and telling me about what happened. Here's a card for you with my name and phone number on it. If you think of anything else that you want to tell me about, you can give me a call or have [cite nonsuspect parent or caregiver] call me so that I can talk to you. OK?
(Spend additional time to wind down the interview, as needed.)

Additional Focused Questions (Optional)
(If you have not been successful with the previous open-ended and focused questions, you may need to ask additional questions about the alleged physical or emotional abuse. The suggested questions will need to be followed up with appropriate probing questions.)
229. Has anyone hurt you?
230. Has anyone yelled at you in a way that you didn't like?
231. Has anyone taken food away from you when you didn't want him or her to do it?

Note. If the child is having behavior problems, also consider asking the questions in Table F-13 in this Appendix.
Source: Adapted, in part, from Burgess, Groth, Holmstrom, and Sgroi (1978); Cage (1988); Faller (1988); Sgroi, Porter, and Blick (1982); and White, Strom, Santilli, and Quinn (1987).

Table F-5
Semistructured Interview Questions for a Child (or Adolescent) Alleged to Have Been Sexually Abused

If the child describes the abuse, be sure to repeat what he or she says. Also repeat what the child says if he or she corrects you. This is especially important if a videotape is being made.

Introduction
1. Hi! I'm Dr. [Ms., Mr.] _____. And you are [cite child's name]. How are you today?
   (You can establish rapport in different ways, depending on the child's age and any other relevant factors. For preschool and young school-aged children, go to question 2; for older children and adolescents, go to question 83. You can use the section on names of body parts, questions 51 to 72, for older children and adolescents if you are having difficulty understanding their terminology for body parts.)

Rapport Building
2. [Cite child' name], let's do something together. I'm going to draw a tree, and I'd like you to help me color it. OK? (Draw an outline of a tree.)
3. Here are some crayons. What color do you want to make the leaves?
4. Go ahead and color the leaves.
5. And now this part, the trunk of the tree (point to trunk). What color do you want to make the trunk?
6. Go ahead. You're doing a good job.
7. Is there anything else you want to put on our tree?
8. (If yes) Go ahead.

Background Questions
9. (If relevant) I want to tell you something special about my room. Behind the mirror is a video camera, and we make videotapes of all the boys and girls who come in here. That way I can remember everything we talk about. OK?
10. Now I'd like to ask you some questions. When you don't understand a question that I ask, please say "I don't understand." When you tell me that, I'll try to ask it better. OK?
11. How old are you?
12. When is your birthday?
13. Where do you live?
14. Do you know your address?
15. (If yes) What is it?
16. Who lives at your house?
17. Do you know your phone number?
18. (If yes) What is it?
19. Do you know what city you live in?
20. (If yes) What is the name of the city you live in?
21. Do you know what state you live in?
22. (If yes) What is the name of the state you live in?
23. (If relevant) What do you call your mother?
24. (If relevant) What do you call your father?
25. Who are the people you like to be with? (Inquire about each person.)
26. Who are the people you don't like to be with? (Inquire about each person.)
27. Do you have a favorite toy?
28. (If yes) Tell me about it.
29. Do you have something you really like to do?
30. (If yes) Tell me about it.
31. Do you go to school?
    (If yes, go to question 32; if no, go to question 39.)
32. What school do you go to?
33. What do you do at school?
34. Do you know what time you get home from school?
35. Do you come home right after school?
    (If no, go to question 36; if yes, go to question 39.)
36. Where do you go after school?
37. Which days do you go to [cite place where child goes after school]?
38. What is the name of the person who takes care of you at [cite place where child goes after school]?

Concepts
39. Now, [cite child's name], I'd like to see what colors you know. If you don't know a color, just say "I don't know." That's OK.
40. (Take out a box of crayons. Hold up a crayon.) What color is this? (Repeat same procedure for several colors—namely, orange, red, blue, brown, black, purple, green, and yellow.)
41. [Cite child's name], I'm going to ask you some more questions, and if there's something you don't know, just say "I don't know," because that's all right. OK?
42. How about counting? Can you count?
43. (If yes) Go ahead.
44. (Hand a crayon, a piece of paper, and a crayon box to child.) Please put the crayon on top of the paper.
45. Now put it under the paper.
46. Now put it behind the paper.
47. How about putting it under the table?
48. Can you put it on top of your head?
49. Now put it inside the crayon box.
50. And now put it outside the box.

Body Parts
51. I have some pictures to show you, [cite child's name]. (Show child a picture of a girl and a picture of a boy. You can use the pictures in Figures 17-1 and 17-2 in Chapter 17.) Can you look at these pictures for me, [cite child's name]? (Point to pictures.)
52. OK. I have pictures of a girl and a boy. Which one's the girl?
53. Which one's the boy?
54. Which one are you, the girl or the boy?
55. (Repeat child's description of gender.) I'm going to put this picture up here, [cite child's name]. (Pin picture of girl or boy, whichever represents the child's gender, on wall or leave on desk.) OK. And I want to see what you call the body parts. OK? What's this up here? What's this stuff? (Point to hair.)
56. (Repeat child's description.) What's this? (Point to nose.)

57. (Repeat child's description.) What are these? (Point to breasts.)
58. (Repeat child's description.) This? (Point to hand.)
59. (Repeat child's description.) What's that? (Point to belly button.)
60. (Repeat child's description.) What's that? (Point to vagina or penis.)
61. (Repeat child's description.) What's that? (Point to toes.)
62. (Repeat child's description.) How about this? (Point to buttocks.)
63. (Repeat child's description.) How about this? (Point to back.)
64. (Repeat child's description.) Good. You know all [most, some] of your body parts. Do you have all of these parts on you?
65. Let's put your name here. (Write child's name above drawing.) Who else in your family is a girl [boy], like this picture?
66. OK. (Point to the other picture.) Who's a boy [girl], like this picture?
67. OK. I'm going to put this picture here, too. (Put picture of boy or girl on wall or place picture on desk, as you did the other one.) What's this on the boy [girl]? (Point to breasts.)
68. (Repeat child's description.) What's this long part right here? (Point to arm.)
69. (Repeat child's description.) What's that? (Point to belly button.)
70. (Repeat child's description.) What's this? (Point to penis or vagina.)
71. (Repeat child's description.) What's this? (Point to buttocks.)
72. (Repeat child's description.) And what's this? (Point to hair on head.)

Difference Between Truth and Lie

73. (Repeat child's description.) Good. You know all [most, some] of the body parts on the boy [girl]. (Hold up a stuffed cat or similar animal.) Do you know what this is?
74. (If yes) Tell me what it is.
    (If child does not know say) It's a cat.
75. Is it a real cat or a pretend cat?
76. How do you know that?
77. Can you think of any other reason?
78. [Cite child's name], do you know what a lie is?
79. (If yes) Give me an example of what a lie might be.
80. So, if I told you this was a red crayon (holding up a black one), would that be the truth or a lie?
81. And if I said this was an orange crayon (holding up an orange crayon), would that be the truth or a lie?
82. And if I said that I'm a woman [man], would that be the truth or a lie?
    (Go to question 84.)

Inquiry About Recent Event

83. (If relevant) I want to tell you something special about my room. Behind the mirror is a video camera, and we make videotapes of all the kids [children, teenagers]

who come in here. That way I can remember everything we talk about. OK?
84. Remember, when you don't understand a question that I ask, please say "I don't understand." When you tell me that, I'll try to ask it better. OK?
85. One of the things that I do when I talk to kids [children, teenagers] is to get them to promise to tell the truth. Would you promise me to tell the truth today while we talk?
86. Can we shake on it?
87. [Cite child's name], do you know why you came here today? (If child doesn't know, tell child in simple terms why he or she is there—for example, "I'd like to talk to you to see how you are getting along. OK?")
88. Has anything happened to you that you would like to tell me about?
89. (If yes) What happened?
    (See directions following question 90.)
90. [Cite the person who reported alleged act] told me that something happened to you recently. I'd really like to talk to you about it. OK? What happened?
    (Ask questions 91 to 175, as needed; then go to question 176. If child is reluctant to tell you about what happened, ask questions 91 to 106 to inquire about different kinds of touches. If child said at any time that he or she [a] was touched in a way that made him or her feel uncomfortable, ask questions 108 to 125; [b] was asked to touch someone in a way that made him or her feel uncomfortable, ask questions 126 to 130; [c] had a finger stuck inside him or her, ask questions 131 to 137; [d] was touched or penetrated by a penis, ask questions 138 to 156; [e] was forced to touch or penetrate a vagina, ask questions 157 to 161; or [f] observed someone play with his or her genitals, ask questions 162 to 175.)

Different Kinds of Touches

91. [Cite child's name], let's talk about different kind of touches. OK?
92. Do you ever get touches that you like, like hugs or kisses?
    (If yes, go to question 93; if no, go to question 103.)
93. Who gives you the hugs and kisses? (Make sure you know whom child is referring to.)
94. (If needed) Does [cite person child mentioned] have another name?
95. (If yes) What is it?
96. (Repeat child's description.) Where does [cite person] hug or kiss you?
97. (If child points) What is that called?
98. When does [cite person] hug or kiss you?
99. Do you ever get hugs or kisses from anybody else, [cite child's name]?
    (If yes, go to question 100, repeating questions 100 to 102 for each person mentioned; if no, go to question 103.)
100. Where does [cite person child mentioned] hug or kiss you on your body?
101. How often does [cite person] kiss or hug you on [cite part of body child mentioned]?

102. How do you feel when [cite person] [cite act and place on body]?

103. How about tickles, [cite child's name]? Do you ever get tickles?
(If yes, go to question 104, repeating questions 105 and 106 for each person mentioned; if no, go to question 107.)

104. Who gives you tickles?

105. Where does [cite person child mentioned] tickle you?

106. Do you like to get tickles from [cite person child mentioned]?

Touches on Body Not Liked

107. Are there places on your body that you don't like to get touched?
(If yes, go to question 108; if no, be prepared to end interview if the child will not discuss the alleged sexual abuse, or you can go to optional areas needing inquiry, such as sleeping, eating, and so forth [see questions 258 on].)

108. [Cite child's name], tell me where you don't like to get touched.

109. Did anyone ever touch you [cite place child mentioned]?
(If yes, go to question 110; if no, be prepared to end interview if the child will not discuss the alleged sexual abuse, or you can go to optional areas needing inquiry, such as sleeping, eating, and so forth [see questions 258 on].)

110. Who touched you there? (Make sure you know whom the child is referring to.) (If needed) Does [cite person child mentioned] have another name?

111. (If yes) What is it?

112. How did [cite act] start?

113. What happened next?

114. (Take out a drawing or picture of a girl or boy, depending on the child's sex.) Could you look at this drawing and take my pen and make a circle around where [cite alleged perpetrator] touched you?

115. What part of [cite alleged perpetrator's] body did he [she] use to touch you?

116. What did [cite alleged perpetrator] do after he [she] touched you?

117. How did it make you feel?

118. Did [cite alleged perpetrator] touch you anywhere else?

119. (If yes) Where else did [cite alleged perpetrator] touch you?

120. Did [cite alleged perpetrator] touch you with anything else?

121. (If yes) What was it?

122. Did [cite alleged perpetrator] talk to you when he [she] touched you?

123. (If yes) What did [cite alleged perpetrator] say?

124. Did you tell [cite alleged perpetrator] to stop?

125. (If yes) What did [cite alleged perpetrator] do or say when you told him [her] to stop?
(Ask questions 126 to 175, as needed; if not, go to question 176.)

Touched Someone
(Ask questions 126 to 130 if child said at any time that he or she was asked to touch someone in a way that he or she didn't like.)

126. [Cite child's name], you said that someone asked you to touch him [her] in a way that made you feel uncomfortable. Where did you touch him [her]?

127. (If needed) Who wanted you to do this?

128. How did you touch [cite alleged perpetrator]?

129. Did you tell [cite alleged perpetrator] that you didn't want to do it?

130. (If yes) What did [cite alleged perpetrator] do or say?

Had Finger Stuck Inside Him or Her
(Ask questions 131 to 137 if child said at any time that someone tried to stick his or her fingers inside him or her.)

131. [Cite child's name], you said that someone tried to stick his [her] fingers inside you. Is that right?

132. (If needed) Who tried to stick a finger inside you?

133. What did [cite alleged perpetrator] do?

134. Where did [cite alleged perpetrator] [cite act]?

135. When did [cite alleged perpetrator] [cite act]?

136. Did you ask [cite alleged perpetrator] to stop?

137. (If yes) What did [cite alleged perpetrator] do or say when you asked him [her] to stop?

Touched or Penetrated by a Penis
(Ask questions 138 to 156 if child said at any time that someone's penis touched or penetrated him or her or that he or she touched a penis.)

138. [Cite child's name], you said that someone put his [cite child's word for penis] on [in] your body. Tell me what happened.

139. (If needed) Who did this?

140. What did his [cite child's word for penis] look like?

141. How long or big around was it?

142. Was it hard or soft?

143. (If hard) Did it get soft?

144. What did [cite alleged perpetrator] do with his [cite child's word for penis]?

145. Did [cite alleged perpetrator] put anything on his [cite child's word for penis]?

146. Did anything come out of it?
(If yes, go to question 147; if no, go to question 155.)

147. What came out of it?

148. Where did the [cite child's name for semen] that came out go? (If the child says "In the toilet," you need to question further to determine whether the alleged perpetrator was simply urinating. If the child says "In my mouth," you might then ask what it tasted like.)

149. What did it look like?

150. Did you feel it?

151. (If yes) What did it feel like?

152. Did anybody clean it up?
(If yes, ask questions 153 and 154; if no, go to question 155.)

153. Who cleaned it up?

154. How was it cleaned up?

155. Did you ask [cite alleged perpetrator] to stop?

156. (If yes) What did [cite alleged perpetrator] do or say?

Forced to Touch or Penetrate a Vagina

(Ask questions 157 to 161 if child said at any time that someone's vagina touched him or her or that he or she was forced to penetrate or touch a vagina.)

157. [Cite child's name], you said that someone asked you to touch her [cite child's term for vagina] or put your [cite child's term or penis or vagina, as applicable] on her [cite child's term for vagina]. Tell me what happened.
158. (If needed) Who did this?
159. How did you feel when it was going on?
160. Did you ask [cite alleged perpetrator] to stop?
161. (If yes) What did [cite alleged perpetrator] do or say when you asked her to stop?

Observed Someone Touch His or Her Own Genitals

(Ask questions 162 to 175 if child said at any time that he or she saw someone touching himself or herself.)

162. [Cite child's name], did you ever see [cite alleged perpetrator] touch himself [herself] anywhere?
(If yes, go to question 163; if no, go to question 176.)
163. Where did [cite alleged perpetrator] touch himself [herself]?
164. Did [cite alleged perpetrator] say anything to you when he [she] did that?
165. (If yes) What did [cite alleged perpetrator] say?
166. Where would [cite alleged perpetrator] [cite act as described by child]?
167. Would anyone else be there when [cite alleged perpetrator] touched himself [herself]?
168. (If yes) Who was there?
169. (If the alleged perpetrator is male and if the child said he or she saw the alleged perpetrator touch his penis) Did you see anything come out of [cite alleged perpetrator]'s [cite child's name for penis] when he touched it?
(If yes, go to question 170; if no, go to question 174.)
170. What came out?
171. What did it look like?
172. Where did it go?
173. And then what did he do?
174. Did you ask [cite alleged perpetrator] to stop?
175. (If yes) What did [cite alleged perpetrator] do or say when you asked him to stop?

Other Information About Event

176. How were you dressed when [cite act] happened?
177. (If needed) Did you always have your clothes on?
178. (If no) Tell me about that.
179. How was [cite alleged perpetrator] dressed?
180. (If needed) Did [cite alleged perpetrator] always have his [her] clothes on?
181. (If no) Tell me about that.
182. Did anything else happen?
183. (If yes) Tell me about that.
184. What were you doing the day [cite alleged perpetrator] [cite act]?
185. Do you remember what the weather was like?
186. (If yes) What was the weather like?
187. Where were you when it happened?

188. (If needed) Were you playing inside or outside?
189. When did it happen?
190. (If needed) Was it during the morning or the afternoon or at nighttime?
191. (If needed) Was it during the summer, winter, spring, or fall?
192. What were you doing right before [cite alleged perpetrator] [cite act]?
193. (If needed) Tell me about your being at [cite place where event happened].
194. What else was going on at that time?

Other Actions of Perpetrator

195. Did [cite alleged perpetrator] show you anything?
196. (If needed) Did he [she] show you any books… magazines…pictures…special objects…other things?
197. (If yes) What did [cite object child saw] look like?
198. Did [cite alleged perpetrator] take pictures of you?
(If yes, go to question 199; if no, go to question 202.)
199. What were you doing when [cite alleged perpetrator] took the pictures? (Or use alternative wording) What did [cite alleged perpetrator] want you to do when he [she] took the pictures?
200. What did [cite alleged perpetrator] take the pictures with—a regular camera or a video camera?
201. Did [cite alleged perpetrator] show you the pictures [video]?

Whereabouts of Relatives During Event

202. Where was your [cite nonoffending caregivers] when this happened?
203. (If relevant) Where were your brothers and sisters?

Other Adults Present During Event

204. Were any other grown-ups there?
205. (If yes) Who was there?
206. And what did [cite names of other adults who were there] do? (Inquire about the actions of each person the child names.)
207. Were there any other children there?
208. (If yes) Who was there?
209. And what did they do?
210. Did anyone else see what happened?
211. (If yes) Who else saw what happened?

Secrecy

212. What did [cite alleged perpetrator] tell you about what he [she] was doing?
213. Did [cite alleged perpetrator] tell you not to tell anybody about what was happening?
(If yes, go to question 214; if no, go to question 225.)
214. What did [cite alleged perpetrator] say?
215. What did you think would happen if you told?
(Ask questions 216 to 224, as needed. These questions are more direct and leading and should be used only if necessary.)
216. Did [cite alleged perpetrator] say that it would cause trouble for him [her] if you told anybody?
217. (If yes) What kind of trouble did he [she] say it would cause?

218. Did [cite alleged perpetrator] say that he [she] would hurt someone else if you told anybody?
219. (If yes) Who would be hurt?
220. Did [cite alleged perpetrator] say that he [she] would go to jail if you told anybody?
221. Did [cite alleged perpetrator] say that he [she] would never be able to see you again if you told anybody?
222. (If relevant) Did [cite alleged perpetrator] say that he [she] would be divorced if you told anybody?
223. Did [cite alleged perpetrator] say that you would be taken away from your family if you told anybody?
224. Did [cite alleged perpetrator] say that he [she] would hurt you if you told anybody?

Inquiry About Similar Events

225. Did this happen one time or more than one time?
     (If more than one time, go to question 226; if child says it happened only one time, go to question 236.)
226. Tell me about the other time[s] it happened.
227. How many times did it happen before?
228. When was the very first time it happened?
229. When was the very last time it happened?
230. How long has this been going on?
231. What happened to you at these other times?
232. Were these other times different from the most recent time?
233. (If yes) In what way?
234. Have you ever seen anyone else [cite act]?
235. (If yes) Tell me about it.
     (Repeat questions 110 to 224, as needed, for each incident.)

Others Who Know About the Sexual Abuse

236. Did you tell anyone about what was going on?
     (If yes, go to question 237; if no, go to question 244.)
237. Whom did you tell?
     (Ask questions 238 and 239 for each person child mentions, as needed.)
238. What did you tell [cite person] about what happened?
239. What did [cite person] say or do after you told him [her]?
240. Did anyone else know what was going on?
     (If yes, go to question 241; if no, go to question 245.)
241. Who knew about it?
     (Ask questions 242 and 243 for each person child mentions, as needed.)
242. How did [cite person] find out about it?
243. What did [cite person] say or do?
     (Go to question 245.)
244. Did anyone know what was going on?
     (If yes, go to question 241; if no, go to question 245.)

Alleged Perpetrator's Actions with Others

245. Do you think [cite alleged perpetrator] has [cite act] anyone else?
246. (If yes) To whom has he [she] done this?
247. How do you know?

**Relationship with and Feelings
About the Alleged Perpetrator**

248. What is [cite alleged perpetrator] like?
249. What did [cite alleged perpetrator] do to get you to [cite act]?

250. How did you feel when [cite alleged perpetrator] [cite act]?
251. Did [cite alleged perpetrator] promise you anything or give you anything afterwards?
252. (If yes) What did [cite alleged perpetrator] promise you or give you?
253. Did you do it because you were afraid?
254. Did [cite alleged perpetrator] ever threaten to hurt you if you did not do it?
255. (If yes) Tell me more about that.
256. How did you feel about [cite alleged perpetrator] before this happened?
257. How do you feel now about him [her]?
     (Ask optional questions 258 to 329 if you want to inquire about how the child is functioning. If not, go to question 330.)

Sleeping (Optional)

258. You did a good job in talking to me. Now I'd like to ask you about how you are doing. OK?
259. How are you sleeping?
260. (If needed) Are you sleeping well?
261. (If no) Tell me about that.
262. What kinds of dreams are you having?
263. Are you having more of these dreams lately?
264. And how about bad or scary dreams? Do you have any bad or scary dreams?
265. (If yes) Tell me about them.

Eating (Optional)

266. How are you eating?
267. (If needed) Are you eating well?
268. (If no) Tell me about that.
269. Have there been any changes in how you are eating since this happened?
270. (If yes) Tell me about what has changed.

School (Optional)

271. How are you doing in school?
     (Ask questions 272 to 275, as needed.)
272. How have your grades been?
273. Can you pay attention?
274. How are you getting along with your teachers?
275. And how are you getting along with other children at school?

Friends (Optional)

276. How are you getting along with your friends?
277. Tell me about that.
278. (If needed) What do you do together?
279. (If needed) Are you still friends?
280. (If no) Tell me why you're not getting along.

Affect (Optional)

281. How are you feeling these days?
     (Ask questions 282 to 295, as needed.)
282. Are you worrying about anything?
283. (If yes) What are you worrying about?
284. Are you happy?
285. (If no) Why aren't you happy?
286. Are you sad?
287. (If yes) Tell me why you are sad.

288. Are you afraid of things?
289. (If yes) What are you afraid of?
290. Are you afraid of people?
291. (If yes) Whom are you afraid of?
292. Do you feel guilty about anything?
293. (If yes) What do you feel guilty about?
294. How often do you think about what happened to you?
295. How does that make you feel?

Physical Symptoms (Optional)
296. Does your body hurt anywhere?
297. (If yes) Tell me where it hurts.
298. Do you have stomachaches?
299. (If yes) Tell me about them.
300. Do you have headaches?
301. (If yes) Tell me about them.
302. Do you have problems going to the bathroom?
303. (If yes) Tell me about the problems you're having.
304. Do you have problems breathing?
305. (If yes) Tell me about the problems you're having.
306. Do you feel tired all the time?
307. (If yes) Tell me about your feeling tired.
308. Do you feel restless?
309. (If yes) Tell me about your feeling restless.
310. Have you been sick since this happened?
311. (If yes) What sickness have you had?
312. Did you see a doctor?
    (If yes, go to question 313; if no, go to question 319.)
313. What did the doctor tell you?
314. (If needed) Did the doctor give you anything to take or want you to do anything?
    (If yes, go to question 315; if no, go to question 318.)
315. What did the doctor give you or want you to do?
316. Did you do what the doctor wanted you to do?
317. (If yes) Did it help?
    (Go to question 319.)
318. What was the reason you didn't go to the doctor?

Family and Friends (Optional)
319. How have you been getting along with your family since this happened?
320. Has your relationship with your mother [stepmother, female caregiver] changed in any way since this happened?
321. (If yes) In what way has it changed?
322. Has your relationship with your father [stepfather, male caregiver] changed in any way since this happened?
323. (If yes) In what way has it changed?
324. (If relevant) And has your relationship with your sisters and brothers changed since this happened?
325. (If yes) In what way has it changed?
326. Has your relationship with your other relatives changed since this happened?
327. (If yes) Tell me, in what way has it changed?
328. Has your relationship with your friends changed since this happened?

329. (If yes) Tell me, in what way has it changed?

Concluding Questions
330. [Cite child's name], did anyone tell you what to say to me?
    (If yes, go to question 331; if no, go to question 333.)
331. Who told you?
332. What did he [she, they] tell you to say?
333. [Cite child's name], do you remember when we talked about telling the truth?
334. Is everything you told me today the truth?
335. (If not) What did you tell me that wasn't the truth?
336. Is there anything else you want to tell me?
337. (If yes) Go ahead.
338. Is there anything you want to ask me?
339. (If yes) Go ahead.
340. [Cite child's name], if someone touches you in a way that you don't like or in a way that is wrong, what can you do?
341. (If the child fails to mention telling someone) Is there someone you could tell?
342. (If child fails to mention anyone) You could tell your mom [dad, caregiver, neighbor, relative, friend's parent].
343. (If relevant) Do you go to day care, [cite child's name]?
344. (If yes) It's OK to tell your day care person, too.
345. Well, I really appreciate your coming in and talking to me today and telling me about what happened. Here's a card for you with my name and phone number on it. If you think of anything else that you want to tell me about, you can give me a call or have [cite nonsuspect parent or caregiver] call me so that I can talk to you. OK? (Spend additional time to wind down the interview, as needed.)

Additional Focused Questions (Optional)
(If you have not been successful with the previous open-ended and focused questions, you may need to ask additional questions about the alleged sexual abuse. The suggested questions will need to be followed up with appropriate probing questions.)
346. Has anyone touched you in a way that you didn't like?
347. Has anyone asked you to touch him [her] in a way that you didn't like?
348. Sometimes people kiss different parts of children's bodies. Has anyone done this to you in a way that you didn't like?

Note. If the child is having behavior problems, also consider asking the questions in Table F-13 in this Appendix.
Source: Adapted, in part, from Burgess, Groth, Holmstrom, and Sgroi (1978); Cage (1988); Faller (1988); Sgroi, Porter, and Blick (1982); Toth and Whalen (1987); and White, Strom, Santilli, and Quinn (1987).

Table F-6
**Semistructured Interview Questions for a Child
(or Adolescent) with Asthma**

Introduction

1. Hi. I'm Dr. [Ms., Mr.] _____. Your doctor, Dr. _____, asked me to see you. I'd like to talk to you about how you're getting along. OK?
2. When you don't understand a question that I ask, please say "I don't understand." When you tell me that, I'll try to ask it better. OK?
3. I understand that you have asthma. Is that right?
4. Tell me about the difficulties you have in breathing.

Description of Asthmatic Attacks

5. How often do you have an attack of asthma?
6. (If needed) How many attacks do you have each week?
7. What happens when you have an attack?
8. Where do the attacks happen?
9. When during the day or night do the attacks occur?
10. How bad are the attacks?
11. (If needed) Are they mild (that is, just a nuisance), moderate, severe, or very severe (that is, seriously interfere with your daily activities)?
12. How long do they last?
13. What do you do when you have an attack?
14. What do your parents do when you have an attack?
15. How does it help?
16. Have you ever gone to a hospital emergency room for treatment of your asthma?
17. (If yes) Tell me about it.
18. Have you ever had to stay in the hospital because your asthma was so bad?
19. (If yes) Tell me about it.
20. How do you feel after an attack?
21. (If needed) Do you feel frustrated…angry…upset… fearful?
22. Tell me about those feelings.
23. Do you have any trouble sleeping through the night?
24. (If yes) Tell me about that.
25. What do you do the day after you've had an attack?

Factors That May Trigger an Attack

26. How do you know when an attack is coming?
27. Tell me about that.
28. (If needed) Do any of the following behaviors cause you to have an asthma attack: crying…laughing… coughing…sneezing…yelling…holding your breath… breathing very fast…choking or gasping?
29. (If yes to any of the above behaviors) Tell me about what happens.
30. Do any of the following feelings cause you to have an asthma attack: anger…anxiety…excitement… fear… frustration…panic…irritation…tension?
31. (If yes to any of the above feelings) Tell me what happens.
32. Do you avoid things that might make your condition worse?
    (If yes, go to question 33; if no, go to question 35.)
33. What do you do?

34. How does it help?
35. Is your asthma worse at certain times of the year?
36. (If yes) What times of the year is it worse?
37. What seems to make your asthma worse?
38. What seems to make your asthma better?

Medication and Treatment Regimen

39. Are you taking any medicine for the asthma?
    (If yes, go to question 40; if no, go to question 51.)
40. What medicine are you taking?
41. How is it helping?
42. Do you take your medicine when you are supposed to?
43. (If no) Tell me about that.
44. Do you take your medicine the way you are supposed to?
45. (If no) Tell me about that.
46. Have you ever had any bad effects when you take the medicine?
47. (If needed) Have you ever had weight gain…weight loss…trouble with your memory…loss of appetite?
48. (If yes) Tell me about that.
49. Have you ever talked with your doctor about changing the amount of medication you take?
50. (If yes) Tell me about that.
51. Are you taking any other treatments for your asthma?
52. (If yes) Tell me about the other treatments you are taking.
53. Has your doctor or anyone else explained to you what you should do when you have an asthma attack?
54. (If yes) What are you supposed to do?
55. Do you think it would help you to know more about what to do when you have an asthma attack?

How Asthma Affects Family Relationships

56. How do your parents treat you at home?
57. Do you think they treat you differently because you have asthma?
58. How do you feel about the way they treat you?
59. And how do they treat you after an attack?
60. How do you feel about what they do?
61. Tell me more about your answer.
62. (If relevant) Do your parents treat you any differently than your brothers and sisters?
    (If yes, go to question 63; if no, go to question 65.)
63. Tell me about that.
64. How does that make you feel?

How Asthma Affects Other Relationships

65. Are you treated differently at school by your teacher because of your asthma?
66. (If yes) In what way?
67. Are you treated differently by your friends because of your asthma?
68. (If yes) In what way?
69. (If relevant) And at work, are you treated differently because of your asthma?
70. (If yes) In what way?

Reactions to Having Asthma

71. Do you ever feel sad or all alone because you have asthma?
72. (If yes) Tell me about your feelings.

73. Does asthma limit the kinds of things you can do?
74. (If yes) Tell me about that.
75. Have you ever avoided your family or friends because of your asthma?
    (If yes, go to question 76; if no, go to question 78.)
76. Whom did you avoid?
77. How did you feel after avoiding [cite person's name]?

Concluding Questions
78. Is there anything else you would like to tell me?
79. (If yes) Go ahead.
80. Is there anything you want to ask me?
81. (If yes) Go ahead.
82. Thank you for talking with me. If you have any questions or if you want to talk to me, please call me. Here is my card.

Note. With modifications, these questions also can be used for a parent. You would need to substitute the child's name for "you" or "your" and make the appropriate grammatical changes.
Source: Adapted from T. L. Creer, J. K. Wigal, D. L. Tobin, H. Kostes, S. E. Snyder, and J. A. Winder (1989), The Revised Asthma Problem Behavior Checklist, *Journal of Asthma, 26,* 17–29.

Table F-7
Semistructured Interview Questions for a Child (or Adolescent) Being Discharged from a Hospital and at Follow-Up

Introduction
1. Hi. I'm Dr. [Ms., Mr.] _____. Your doctor, Dr. _____, asked me to see you. I'd like to talk to you about how you feel about leaving the hospital. OK?
2. When you don't understand a question that I ask, please say "I don't understand." When you tell me that, I'll try to ask it better. OK?

At Discharge from Hospital
3. How do you feel about leaving the hospital?
4. (If needed) Tell me more about your feelings.
5. Do you think you'll have any problems when you go home?
6. (If yes) Tell me what problems you think you might have.
7. What is it going to be like to go back home?
8. Who is going to take care of you while you're at home?
9. Tell me about your illness.
10. Do you have to take any medicine or special treatments when you're at home?
11. (If yes) Tell me about it [them].
12. Can you think of anything you might need help with at home?
13. (If yes) Tell me what you might need.

Follow-Up After Child Returns Home
14. How have things been since you've been home?
15. What problems have you had?

16. (If needed) Tell me about these problems.
17. How has your family changed since you've been at home?
18. How have you been since your last visit?
19. Are you taking any medicine?
    (If yes, go to question 20; if no, go to question 27.)
20. What medicine are you taking?
21. Have you had any difficulty taking the medicine?
22. (If yes) Tell me about the difficulty you're having.
23. How has the medicine helped you?
24. Do your parents help you take the medicine?
25. Have you had any bad effects from taking the medicine?
26. (If yes) What bad effects are you having?
27. Have you seen any other doctors, specialists, or therapists?
    (If yes, go to question 28; if no, go to question 31.)
28. (If yes) Whom have you seen?
29. What medical services are you getting now?
30. (If needed) Are you getting physical therapy, speech therapy, or occupational therapy?
31. What do you do during the day?
32. How are you sleeping?
33. How are you eating?
34. Has there been any change in your appetite?
35. (If yes) Tell me about the change in your appetite.
36. Has there been any change in your energy level?
37. (If yes) Tell me about the change.
38. Has there been any change in the way you are feeling?
39. (If yes) Tell me about the change.
40. How are you getting along at school?
41. And how is your schoolwork?
42. How are you getting along at home?
43. How are you getting along with your friends?
    (Ask questions 44 to 49 for adolescents; for younger children, go to question 50.)
44. (If relevant) How are you getting along at work?
45. (If relevant) How much are you smoking?
46. (If relevant) How much are you drinking?
47. (If relevant) Are you taking any drugs?
48. (If yes to any of the above) Tell me about that.
49. What plans do you have for the future?
50. Can I help you in any way?
51. Is there any other kind of help that you think you need now?
52. Do you have any questions you'd like to ask me?
53. (If yes) Go ahead.
54. Thank you for talking with me. If you have any questions or if you want to talk to me, please call me. Here is my card.

Note. With modifications, these questions also can be used for a parent. You would need to substitute the child's name for "you" or "your" and make the appropriate grammatical changes.
Source: Adapted from Enelow and Swisher (1986) and Power (1988).

Table F-8
Semistructured Interview Questions for a Child
(or Adolescent) in a Child Custody Dispute

Introduction

1. Hi. I'm Dr. [Ms., Mr.] _____. We're going to spend some time together. I'd like to get to know you better. When you don't understand a question that I ask, please say "I don't understand." When you tell me that, I'll try to ask it better. OK?
2. Perhaps we can begin with your telling me what your mother or father told you about your coming to see me.
3. (If the child doesn't know) I'm here to help you and your parents decide on the best way to take care of you. In order to do this, I need to learn about you and also learn about your parents. OK?

School and Friends

4. How old are you?
5. What grade are you in at school?
6. What school do you go to?
7. What's your favorite subject in school?
8. What's your least favorite subject in school?
9. Do you have friends?
   (If yes, go to question 10; if no, go to question 17.)
10. What do you and your friends like to do?
11. How does your mother feel about your friends?
12. How does she feel about their coming to your house?
13. And your father. How does he feel about your friends?
14. And how does he feel about their coming to your house?
15. How do your friends feel about your mother?
16. And how do your friends feel about your father?
    (Go to question 18.)
17. Tell me about your not having friends.

Home

18. Tell me about your home.
19. What things in your home do you like?
20. What things in your home don't you like?
21. (If relevant) And what about your dad's [mom's] home when you visit there? Tell me about the things you like in your dad's [mom's] home.
22. Tell me about the things you don't like in your dad's [mom's] home.
23. Does anybody else live at home with you other than your mom [dad]?
24. (If yes) Tell me about who else lives at home.
25. Does anybody else live at your dad's [mom's] home where you visit?
26. (If yes) Tell me about who else lives there.

Parents

27. Tell me about your mother.
28. Tell me about your father.
29. All people have things about them that you like and some things that you don't like. No one is perfect. Tell me what you like about your mother.
30. Now, as I mentioned before, no one is perfect. Tell me what you don't like about your mother.

31. And how about your father? Tell me what you like about your father.
32. As I mentioned before, no one is perfect. Tell me what you don't like about your father.

Extended Family

33. Do you have grandparents?
    (If yes, go to question 34; if no, go to question 40.)
34. Tell me about them.
    (Ask questions 35 to 39, as needed.)
35. Where do they live?
36. When do you see them?
37. What kinds of things do you do with them when you see them?
38. How do you get along with them?
39. When did you see them last?
40. Do you have any other relatives whom you like a lot or are close to?
41. (If yes) Tell me about him [her, them].

Preference for Parent

42. When you have a problem, whom do you talk to about it?
43. When you are sick, whom do you ask for help?
44. When you wake up in the middle of the night with a nightmare, whom do you ask for help?
45. Do you play games with anyone at home?
    (If yes, go to question 46; if no, go to question 48.)
46. Whom do you play with?
47. Which games do you play with her [him, them]?
48. Do you have any hobbies or things you especially like to do?
49. (If yes) Does your mom or dad help you with the hobby?
50. If you were happy—if you had fun at school or got a good grade—whom would you tell?
51. If you were sad, whom would you tell?

Medical Care

52. If you have to go to the doctor, who takes you?
53. If you get sick and have to stay home from school, who stays home with you?
54. Who takes you to the dentist?
55. Do you remember the last time you went to the dentist?
56. (If yes) When was that?

Religion

57. Does your family practice a religion?
    (If yes, go to question 58; if no, go to question 69.)
58. Tell me about that.
    (Ask questions 59 to 68, as needed.)
59. What religion is your mother?
60. What religion is your father?
61. What religion are you?
62. Does your mother go to church [synagogue, etc.]?
63. Does your father go to church [synagogue, etc.]?
64. Do you go to church [synagogue, etc.]?
65. (If yes) Who takes you there?
66. Do you go to Sunday School or religious classes?
    (If yes, go to question 67; if no, go to question 69.)

67. How often?
68. (If needed) When did you go last?

Day Care/Babysitting (If relevant)

69. When you are staying with your mother [father], who takes care of you if she [he] has to go out?
70. How do you feel about that?
71. Where do you go after school?
72. Who else is there?
73. How do you feel about going there?

Punishment

74. When your mom gets angry, what does she do?
75. When your dad gets angry, what does he do?
76. When you get angry, what do you do?
77. Do you ever get punished?
    (If yes, go to question 78; if no, go to question 84.)
78. What do you get punished for?
79. Who does the punishing?
80. How are you punished?
81. How do you feel about it?
82. Do your mom and dad punish you in different ways?
83. (If yes) Tell me about that.

Daily Routine

84. Tell me about a typical day in your [choose mother's or father's—whichever is the primary residence] house.
85. (If needed) Who gets you up, helps you get dressed, gets you breakfast, gets you off to school, and so on?
86. Do you buy lunch or pack it?
87. Who cooks dinner?
88. Who helps you with your homework?
89. (For a very young child) Who gives you a bath?
90. What happens at bedtime?
91. Where do you sleep?
92. Tell me about a typical day in your [choose mother's or father's—whichever is the secondary residence] house.
93. (If needed) Who gets you up, helps you get dressed, gets you breakfast, gets you off to school, and so on?
94. Do you buy lunch or pack it?
95. Who cooks dinner?
96. Who helps you with your homework?
97. (For a very young child) Who gives you a bath?
98. What happens at bedtime?
99. Where do you sleep?

Rules

100. What kinds of rules are there at your mother's house?
101. What kinds of rules are there at your father's house?
102. (If needed) What about rules about watching TV… time to go to bed…where you can go…how late you can stay out…what friends you can be with?
103. (If needed) How do the rules in your mother's house differ from those in your father's house?

Visitation Rights Issues

104. Does your dad [mom] show up on time to pick you up when you are going to visit him [her]?
105. (If no) Tell me about that.

106. Does your dad [mom] come to get you when he [she] says he [she] will?
107. (If no) How do you feel when he [she] doesn't come?
108. Do you look forward to your dad's [mom's] coming to see you?
109. Tell me about that.
110. How often does he [she] come to see you?
111. What do you do together?
112. Do you enjoy the things you do together?
113. (If no) Tell me about that.

Feelings About the Divorce

114. How do you feel about your parents' getting a divorce?
115. Do you have any ideas about why they're getting a divorce?
     (Follow up any leads. For example, if child says father was mean to mother, ask what kinds of mean things the father did. Also address any concerns child may have about the divorce being his or her fault.)
116. What kinds of problems were they having?
117. How did their problems affect you?
118. (If relevant) How did the problems affect your sisters and brothers?
119. Do you feel caught between your mother and your father?
120. (If yes) Tell me about that.
121. How is your life different now since the divorce [separation]?
122. (If needed) How is it better?
123. (If needed) How is it worse?
124. How do your mother and father get along now?

Possible Living Arrangements

125. What do you imagine it would be like if you spent weekdays with your mother and weekends with your father?
126. And what do you imagine it would be like if you spent weekdays with your father and weekends with your mother?
127. Would you like to spend school nights at your mom's house or your dad's house?
128. Tell me about your answer.
129. Would you like to spend weekends at your mom's house or your dad's house?
130. Tell me about your answer.
131. (Try to find out whether the child prefers to live in mom's or dad's home because of its facilities or because of who lives there.) Would you still want to live with your mom [dad] even if she [he] didn't have [cite facility mentioned, such as big backyard, swimming pool, or extra bedroom]?
132. Where would you like to live?
133. Tell me about your answer.

Sibling Preference

134. (If relevant) How do your parents get along with your brothers and sisters?
135. Whom do you think your brothers and sisters would like to live with?
136. Tell me about your answer.

Concluding Questions

137. If there was one thing you could change about yourself, what would it be?
138. If you could have three wishes for anything in the world, what would you wish for?
139. Did either of your parents tell you what to say to me?
140. (If yes) What did he [she, they] tell you?
141. Do you have anything else you would like to share with me?
142. (If yes) Go ahead.
143. Do you have any questions that you would like to ask me?
144. (If yes) Go ahead.
145. Thank you for talking with me. If you have any questions or if you want to talk to me, please call me. Here is my card.

Note. If you want to inquire about any problems that the child is having or if you want to explore other areas in detail, see Table F-13 in this Appendix.
Source: The questions in this exhibit were obtained from Gardner (1982, pp. 156–169), Hodges (1991, p. 138), and Schutz, Dixon, Lindenberger, and Ruther (1989, pp. 155–161).

Table F-9
Semistructured Interview Questions for a Child (or Adolescent) with an Eating Problem

---

Introduction

1. Hi! I'm Dr. [Ms., Mr.] _____. Dr. _____ asked me to see you. I'd like to talk to you about how you're getting along. OK?
2. When you don't understand a question that I ask, please say "I don't understand." When you tell me that, I'll try to ask it better. OK?

Current Eating Patterns

3. Let's begin by talking about your eating patterns. Do your eating habits vary from day to day?
4. (If yes) Tell me about how they vary.
5. Do you eat differently on weekdays than on weekends?
6. (If yes) How do you eat differently?
7. What foods do you like to eat?
8. And what foods do you try to avoid?
9. What are your favorite drinks?
10. Do you enjoy trying new foods?
11. Tell me about that.
12. Tell me what you eat in a typical day.
13. Do you enjoy eating sweet foods?
14. Tell me about that.
15. Tell me what you usually eat for breakfast.
16. What do you usually eat for lunch?
17. And for dinner. What do you usually eat for dinner?
18. And how much do you eat when you have a snack?
19. What times of the day do you eat your meals?

20. And when do you eat your snacks?
21. Where do you eat your meals?
22. And where do you eat your snacks?
23. How long does each meal usually last?
24. And how long does each snack usually last?
25. Whom do you usually eat with?
26. Do you do anything else while you are eating, such as watching TV or reading?
27. (If yes) Tell me about that.
28. Do you eat when you are upset or under stress?
29. (If yes) Does eating help you feel better?
30. Do you ever go a whole day without eating?
31. (If yes) Tell me about that.
32. (If needed) How often do you go a whole day without eating? When does it happen?
33. Do you ever overeat?
    (If yes, go to question 34; if no, go to question 36.)
34. Tell me about it.
35. When you feel you have overeaten, do others agree that you ate too much?
36. Do you ever feel that the way you eat is different from the way others eat?
37. (If yes) Tell me about that.

Specific Eating Problems

38. Now I'd like to ask you about some specific problems that you may be having. OK?
39. Do you avoid eating foods you like?
    (If yes, go to question 40; if no, go to question 42.)
40. What foods do you avoid?
41. How often do you avoid eating them?
42. Are there any types of food that are particularly appealing to you?
43. (If yes) Tell me about these foods.
44. Do you hold off as long as possible before coming to the dinner table?
45. (If yes) Tell me about that.
46. Do you feel tense during mealtimes?
47. (If yes) How do you show your tension?
48. Do you pick at the food on your plate without eating very much?
49. Would you say that you eat only certain foods?
50. (If yes) Tell me about these foods.
51. Do you dispose of food in any other ways besides eating it?
52. (If yes) In what other ways do you dispose of food?
53. Do you ever eat in secret?
54. (If yes) Tell me about it.
55. Do you hide food in your room so that nobody will find it?
56. (If yes) Tell me about that.
57. Do you eat a reasonable amount of food in front of others and then stuff yourself when you are alone?
58. (If yes) Tell me about that.
    (Ask questions 59–61 for older children and adolescents.)
59. What do you think a nutritious meal consists of?
60. Do you believe that you eat a balanced diet?
61. Tell me about that.
62. Tell me how you know when you are hungry.
63. Tell me how you know when you are full.

64. Did anything happen in your life just before your eating problem began?
65. (If yes) What happened?

Attitude Toward Eating and Food

66. How do you feel after eating?
67. (If needed) Do you ever feel guilty after eating?
68. (If yes) Tell me about your feelings.
69. Do you think you can control your eating?
70. Tell me about your answer.
71. Do you spend a lot of time thinking about food?
    (If yes, go to question 72; if no, go to question 75.)
72. How much time do you spend between meals thinking about food?
73. Has thinking about food interfered with your doing other things?
74. (If yes) Tell me about that.
75. Do you try to follow any rules about what you should or shouldn't eat?
76. (If yes) Tell me about your rules.
77. Do you think food controls your life?
78. (If yes) In what way does food control your life?

Body Image

79. How do you feel about your body?
80. Tell me more about that.
81. (If needed) Are you satisfied with the shape of your body?
82. (If no) Tell me about that.
83. (If needed) Do you always think about wanting to be thinner?
84. (If yes) Tell me about that.
85. (If needed) How do you feel when you see your body—that is, when you look in a mirror or see your reflection in a shop window?
86. How do you feel when other people see your body?
87. How do you feel about your weight?
88. Are you scared of being overweight?
89. (If yes) Tell me about that.
90. How do you feel about the word *fat?*
91. Have you ever been teased about your weight?
92. (If yes) How do you feel when you are teased?
93. Do you weigh yourself regularly?
94. (If yes) How often?
95. How often do you take your body measurements?
96. What is the largest size of clothing that you feel comfortable in?

Weight

97. How much do you weigh now?
98. Has your weight changed in the last three months?
99. (If yes) By how much?
100. What has been your lowest weight since the problem began?
101. What has been your highest weight since the problem began?
102. How much would you like to weigh?
103. How do you feel about your weight?
104. Are you now trying to lose weight or are you on a diet to lose weight?
    (If yes, go to question 105; if no, go to question 114.)

105. What is the reason that you want to lose weight?
106. Tell me what you are doing to lose weight.
107. (If needed) Are you cutting down on sweets… exercising more…using diet pills…using laxatives… using water pills? (*Note.* You will need to ask questions 184 to 194 if interviewee says that she or he exercises.)
108. How long have you been doing [cite method mentioned]?
109. Are you satisfied with your progress?
110. Tell me about that.
111. (If needed) How much have you lost since you started on the diet?
112. Are you good at sticking to your diet?
113. Tell me about that.
114. Have you been on diets to lose weight before?
    (If yes, go to question 115; if no, go to question 131.)
115. Tell me about the other diets you went on to lose weight.
    (Ask questions 116 to 120, as needed.)
116. How did you try to lose weight on the other diets?
117. Were you successful?
118. How much weight did you lose?
119. (If lost weight) How long did the weight stay off?
120. How old were you when you first tried to lose weight?
121. Are you now trying to gain weight or on a diet to gain weight?
    (If yes, go to question 122; if no, go to question 131.)
122. What is the reason that you want to gain weight?
123. Tell me what you are doing to gain weight.
124. (If needed) Are you eating more at meals…eating more snacks…eating foods that are high in calories… drinking liquids high in calories?
125. How long have you been [cite method mentioned]?
126. Are you satisfied with your progress?
127. Tell me about that.
128. (If needed) Tell me how much you have gained since you started on the diet.
129. Are you good at sticking to your diet to gain weight?
130. Tell me about that.
131. Have you been on diets before to gain weight?
    (If yes, go to question 132; if no, go to question 138.)
132. Tell me about the other diets you went on to gain weight.
    (Ask questions 133 to 137, as needed.)
133. How did you try to gain weight on the other diets?
134. Were you successful?
135. How much weight did you gain?
136. (If gained weight) How long did the weight stay on?
137. How old were you when you first tried to gain weight?

Binge Eating

138. Have you ever been unable to control the amount or type of food you ate?
    (If yes, go to question 139; if no, go to question 160.)
139. Tell me everything you can about the times when you have been unable to control the amount or type of food you ate.
    (Ask questions 140 to 159, as needed.)
140. When did it happen last?
141. When this happens, what are you usually eating?

142. About how often are you unable to control what you eat?
143. What is the highest number of times in one day you have been unable to control what you ate?
144. In the last month, how many days have you gone without this happening?
145. About how long does your eating without control last?
146. At what time during the day are you most likely to eat like this?
147. Where do you eat like this?
148. Is anyone with you when you eat like this?
149. (If yes) Who is with you?
150. How do you feel after you eat lots of food quickly?
151. (If needed) Do you feel as if you have lost control when you eat lots of food quickly?
152. Do you have any concerns about eating lots of food quickly and being unable to stop?
153. (If yes) What are your concerns?
154. Do you ever plan to overeat?
155. (If yes) Tell me about that.
156. How old were you when you began to eat lots of food quickly?
157. After you started eating lots of food quickly, was there a time when you were able to stop?
   (If yes, go to question 158; if no, go to question 160.)
158. When was that?
159. And for how long were you able to stop eating like this?

Purging Behavior

160. Do you deliberately try to vomit after you eat?
   (If yes, go to question 161; if no, go to question 174.)
161. How do you go about getting yourself to vomit?
162. How often do you vomit?
163. After what meals do you vomit?
164. How do you feel about your vomiting?
165. What first made you think of vomiting after eating?
166. Are you concerned about your vomiting?
167. (If yes) What are your concerns?
168. How old were you when you began vomiting after meals?
169. What is the highest number of times in one day you have vomited?
170. In the last month, how many days in a row have you gone without vomiting?
171. After you started vomiting, was there a time when you stopped vomiting?
172. (If yes) When was that?
173. And for how long were you able to stop vomiting after meals?

Other Methods Used to Control Weight

174. Do you take laxatives, ipecac syrup, diuretics, diet pills, or anything else to control your weight?
   (If yes, go to question 175; if no, go to directions preceding question 184.)
175. What do you take?
176. How often do you take [cite substance]?
177. How do you feel about taking [cite substance]?
178. Are you concerned about taking [cite substance]?
179. (If yes) What are your concerns?

180. How old were you when you began taking [cite substance]?
181. After you started taking [cite substance], was there a time when you stopped taking [cite substance]?
182. (If yes) When was that?
183. And for how long were you able to stop taking [cite substance]?

Exercise and Activity Patterns

(If interviewee has mentioned that she or he exercises, ask questions 184 to 194. If exercise was not mentioned, go to question 195.)
184. You mentioned that you exercise. What kind of exercise do you do?
185. How often do you [cite exercise]?
186. How long do you [cite exercise]?
187. When do you [cite exercise]?
188. How do you feel about exercising?
189. Is your exercise connected with your eating in any way?
190. (If yes) Tell me about that.
191. Do you keep busy all the time—more than you think is average?
192. (If needed) Do you spend an unusual amount of time clearing the table, cleaning your room, and so on?
193. (If yes) Tell me about what you do.
194. When you are outside, do you walk as fast as possible or run whenever possible?

Personality and Interpersonal Relations

195. Tell me how you feel about yourself.
196. Is your weight important in how you feel about yourself?
197. (If yes) Tell me about that.
198. How important is it for you to be perfect in everything you do?
199. How do you get along with your friends?
200. (If needed) Have you told anyone about your eating problems?
201. Tell me about that.

Health Status

202. How have you been feeling recently?
203. (If problems mentioned) Tell me about [cite problems].
204. Do you get tired easily?
205. (If yes) Tell me about that.
206. Do you often feel cold?
207. (If yes) Tell me about that.
208. How are your teeth?
209. (If problems mentioned) Tell me about [cite problems].
210. Have you noticed more hair lately on your face or body?
211. (If yes) Tell me about that.
   (For female adolescents, go to question 212; for male adolescents, go to question 217.)
212. Tell me about your menstrual periods.
213. Do you feel bloated or fat before or during them?
214. Do you eat more before or during them?
215. (If needed) Has there been any change in them—that is, have they been irregular or have you missed any?
216. (If yes) Tell me more about that.

Family Characteristics

217. Do your parents know about your eating problem?
     (If yes, go to question 218; if no, go to question 234.)
218. How did they find out about your eating problem?
219. How long ago did they find out?
220. How long had you had the eating problem when they found out?
221. (If needed) Do you know how they felt when they found out (such as angry, guilty, or sad)?
222. Did your parents say anything to you about your eating problem?
     (If yes, go to question 223; if no, go to question 228.)
223. What did they say?
224. And how did you react to what they said?
225. (If needed) Did talking with them about it help you at all?
226. (If needed) Have they tried to do anything to help you with your problem?
227. (If yes) Tell me about that.
228. How has your eating problem affected your family?
229. How has your eating problem affected your relationship with your parents?
230. Have your parents changed anything at home because of your eating problem?
231. (If yes) What have they changed?
232. Has your problem affected your parents' eating patterns?
233. Has your problem affected the rest of your family's eating patterns?
234. What has been the most frustrating thing for you about having an eating problem?
235. Have your parents played a part in your eating problem?
236. (If yes) Tell me about that.
237. Do you believe that your parents' eating habits have affected you in any way?
238. (If yes) In what way?
239. Do you believe that your parent's weight has affected you in any way?
240. (If yes) In what way?
241. Does anyone in your family have an eating or weight problem?
242. (If yes) Tell me about the problem.

Interventions

243. What do you think caused your eating problem?
244. (If needed) What do you think contributes to your eating problem?
245. What did you know about your type of eating problem before you found out that you had one?
246. What do you know about your type of problem now?
247. Do you believe that you could beat your eating problem by yourself if you really wanted to?
248. Tell me about that.
249. What goals do you have about your weight?
250. Have you ever been treated for your problem, including any hospitalizations?
251. (If yes) Tell me about the treatment.
252. Do you want to be treated for your problem?
     (If yes, go to question 253; if no, go to question 257.)
253. What kind of treatment do you want?

254. If you enter a treatment program to get help for your eating problem, do you think your parents will help you?
255. Tell me about that.
256. Do you think you will get better?
     (Go to question 258.)
257. Tell me about why you don't want treatment.

Concluding Questions

258. Do you have any other types of problems that we didn't discuss?
259. (If yes) Tell me about your other problems.
260. Is there anything else you would like to tell me?
261. (If yes) Go ahead.
262. Do you have any questions that you would like to ask me?
263. (If yes) Go ahead.
264. Thank you for talking with me. If you have any questions or if you want to talk to me, please call me. Here is my card.

Note. With modifications, these questions also can be used for a parent. You would need to substitute the child's name for "you" or "your" and make the appropriate grammatical changes.
Source: Adapted in part from Fairburn and Cooper (1993), Loro and Orleans (1982), and Reiff and Reiff (1992).

Table F-10
Semistructured Interview Questions for a Child (or Adolescent) with Headaches

---

Introduction
1. Hi! I'm Dr. [Ms., Mr.] _____. Dr. _____ asked me to see you. I'd like to talk to you about how you're getting along. OK?
2. When you don't understand a question that I ask, please say "I don't understand." When you tell me that, I'll try to ask it better. OK?

Description of Headaches

3. I understand that you have headaches. Please tell me about them.
4. How often do you get the headaches?
5. (If needed) How many times a day [a week, a month] do you get the headaches?
6. Where is the headache located?
7. Does the headache occur in the same place each time?
8. (If no) Where does it occur?
9. At what time of the day does your headache begin?
10. Does it come on gradually or suddenly?
11. How long does the headache usually last?
12. Do you ever wake up with a headache?
13. (If yes) Tell me about that.
14. Do you get the headaches on weekdays or weekends or both?
15. Do you get headaches all through the year or only during some months?

16. (If some months only) During what months do you get headaches?
17. In what situations do your headaches usually occur?
18. How do you feel just before the headache begins?
19. (If needed) Are you under stress before the headache begins?
20. Do you have any unusual sensations before the headache begins, such as seeing flashing lights?
21. (If yes) Tell me about them.
22. Does your mood change before the headache begins?
23. (If yes) Tell me about the mood change.
24. Do you lose your appetite before the headache begins?
25. (If yes) Tell me about your loss of appetite.
26. How old were you when the headaches first began?
27. Do you have different types of headaches?
28. (If yes) Tell me about them.
29. Are the headaches becoming worse, staying the same, or getting better?
30. Tell me about that.
31. Do you see a doctor for your headaches?
32. (If yes) How often?

Type of Headache Pain and Symptoms
33. Please describe the pain and symptoms you're having. (Ask questions 34 to 45, as needed.)
34. Is the pain mild, severe, or excruciating?
35. (If severe or excruciating) Is it so bad that you have thought of committing suicide?
36. Is the pain throbbing or stabbing?
37. Is it a band-like pressure around your head?
38. Do you have tingling sensations?
39. Does the pain leave you feeling numb?
40. Do you have stomach pain…nausea…vomiting?
41. Are you sensitive to light?
42. Are there changes in your vision?
43. Do you have dizziness…fevers?
44. What do you do to make the pain better?
45. What makes it worse?

Affects of Headaches
46. Do the headaches often interfere with your activities [play time]?
47. (If yes) Tell me about that.
48. Have you missed school because of your headaches?
49. (If yes) About how many days of school have you missed this year?
50. What do your parents usually do when you have a headache?

Family Factors
51. Do other members of your family have regular headaches?
 (If yes, go to question 52; if no, go to question 54.)
52. Who else in your family has headaches?
53. (Ask for each member of the family named) What type of headache does he [she] have?

Temperament and Personality Variables
54. Now I'd like to talk about some other things. Do you have trouble talking about your feelings?
55. (If yes) Tell me about that.

56. When you are angry, how do you handle your anger?
57. Do you want things to be as perfect as possible?
58. (If yes) Tell me about that.
59. Do you think about things for a long time before you decide to act?
60. (If yes) Tell me about that.
61. Do you feel that once you have decided something, no one can change your mind?
62. (If yes) Tell me about that.
63. Do you think that you depend too much on other people to do things for you?
64. (If yes) Tell me about that.
65. Do you have goals that you have set for yourself? (If yes, go to question 66; if no, go to question 68.)
66. Tell me about them.
67. (If needed) How do you try to meet your goals?
68. Do you have any questions that you would like to ask me?
69. (If yes) Go ahead.
70. Thank you for talking with me. If you have any questions or if you want to talk to me, please call me. Here is my card.

Note. With modifications, these questions also can be used for a parent. You would need to substitute the child's name for "you" or "your" and make the appropriate grammatical changes.
Source: Adapted from Boudewyns (1982) and Wickramasekera (1988).

Table F-11
Semistructured Interview Questions for a Child (or Adolescent) with a Learning Disability

Introduction
1. Hi! I'm Dr. [Ms., Mr.] _____. I'd like to talk to you about how you are getting along. OK?
2. When you don't understand a question that I ask, please say "I don't understand." When you tell me that, I'll try to ask it better. OK?

Attitude Toward School
3. How are you getting along in school?
4. What do you like about school?
5. What don't you like about school?
6. What are your favorite subjects?
7. What are your least favorite subjects?
8. Which subjects are easiest for you?
9. Which subjects are hardest for you?
10. Now I'd like to talk to you about some specific subjects. OK?

Reading
11. How well do you read?
12. Do you like to read?
13. Tell me about that.
14. When you read, do you make mistakes like skipping words or lines, reading the same lines twice, or reading letters backwards?

15. (If needed) Tell me about the mistakes you make when you read.
16. Do you find that you can read each line of every paragraph, but, when you finish the page or chapter, you don't remember what you've just read?

Writing

17. How good is your handwriting?
18. Do you find that you cannot write as fast as you think?
19. (If yes) Do you run one word into another when you're writing because you're thinking of the next word rather than the one you're writing?
20. How good is your spelling?
21. Tell me about that.
22. How good is your grammar?
23. Tell me about that.
24. How good is your punctuation?
25. Tell me about that.
26. Do you have difficulty copying from the blackboard?
27. Tell me about that.

Math

28. Do you know the multiplication tables?
29. (If no) Tell me about that.
30. When you do math, do you make mistakes like writing "21" when you mean to write "12," mixing up columns of numbers, or adding when you mean to subtract?
31. Tell me about the mistakes you make when you do math.
32. Do you sometimes start a math problem but halfway through forget what you are trying to do?

Sequencing

33. When you speak or write, do you sometimes find it hard to get everything in the right order—that is, do you start in the middle, go to the beginning, and then jump to the end?
34. Do you have trouble saying the alphabet in order?
35. (If yes) Tell me about that.
36. Do you have to start from the beginning each time you say the alphabet?

Abstraction

37. Do you understand jokes when your friends tell them?
38. (If no) Tell me about that.
39. Do you sometimes find that people seem to say one thing yet tell you that they meant something else?
40. (If yes) Tell me about that.

Organization

41. What does your notebook look like?
42. (If needed) Is it pretty neat and organized, or is it a mess, with papers in the wrong place or falling out?
43. Is it hard for you to organize your thoughts or to organize the facts you're learning into the bigger idea that the teacher is trying to teach you?
44. Can you read a chapter and answer the questions at the end of the chapter but still not be sure what the chapter is about?

45. (If yes) Tell me about that.
46. Do you have trouble planning your time so that things get done on time?
47. (If yes) Tell me about that.
48. What does your bedroom at home look like?

Memory

49. How is your memory?
50. Has it changed in any way?
   (Ask questions 51 to 54, as needed.)
51. Do you find that you can learn something at night but, when you go to school the next day, you don't remember what you learned?
52. When talking, do you sometimes forget what you are saying halfway through?
53. (If yes) What do you do when this happens?
54. (If needed) Do you cover up by saying things like "Oh, forget it" or "It's not important"?

Language

55. When the teacher is speaking in class, do you have trouble understanding or keeping up?
56. (If yes) Tell me about that.
57. Do you sometimes misunderstand people and, therefore, give the wrong answer?
58. (If yes) Tell me when this happens.
59. Do you sometimes lose track of what people are saying?
60. (If yes) Does this sometimes cause you to lose your concentration in class?
61. Do you sometimes have trouble organizing your thoughts when you speak?
62. (If yes) Tell me about that.
63. Do you often have a problem finding the word you want to use?
64. (If yes) When this happens, what do you do?

Study Habits

65. Now I'd like to ask you about your learning and study habits. Tell me about what happens when you study.
66. Do you learn better alone, with one friend, or in a group?
67. Tell me more about that.
68. When you study, do you like to have adults help you, be available to help you, or leave you alone?
69. Tell me about that.

Time Rhythm

70. At what time of day do you learn best?
71. (If needed) Do you learn best early in the morning, right before lunch, after lunch, after school, or right before bedtime?
72. After you wake up in the morning, how long does it take you to feel really awake?
73. Do you sometimes have trouble staying awake after lunch or dinner?
74. (If yes) Tell me more about that.
75. Do you like to get up early?
76. If you stay up late, do you feel "foggy" the next day—as if your head's in a cloud?

Environment

77. Where is the best place for you to study?
78. Tell me more about that.
79. Do you like to study in a room with bright lighting or low lighting?
80. Do you think you feel cold or hot more often than other people?
81. Tell me about your answer.
82. Do you like the room you're in to be warm or cool?

Attention and Concentration

83. Do you prefer noise or silence when you are studying?
84. Can you study if you hear a radio or television in the background?
85. Are you distracted if you hear people talking or children playing?
86. Do you like to study with music playing?
87. (If yes) What kind of music?
88. Do you daydream a lot when you are in class?
89. (If yes) Tell me about that.
90. Do you have trouble sitting still or staying in your seat at school?
91. (If yes) Tell me about the trouble you're having.
92. And at home, do you have trouble sitting still or staying in your seat?
93. (If yes) Tell me about that.
94. How is your concentration?
95. Can you complete your assignments or are you easily distracted?
96. (If distracted) What seems to distract you?
97. Do you like to leave your studies to go see what's going on, get a drink, or change rooms or positions?
98. (If yes) Tell me more about that.
99. Do you like to keep at your work until it's done?
100. Tell me more about that.

Eating Habits

101. Do you like to eat, chew gum, or have a drink while you are studying?
102. (If yes) How does it help?
103. Do you overeat while you are studying?
104. (If yes) How does it help?
105. Do you have any nervous habits while you're studying, such as chewing your fingernails or a pencil?
106. (If yes) Tell me about your habits.

Motivation

107. How important is it for you to get good grades?
108. Tell me about that.
109. Do you think your grades are important to your parents?
110. Tell me about that.
111. Do you think your grades are important to your teachers?
112. Tell me about that.

113. When you try to get good grades, is it more to please adults or to please yourself?
114. Tell me about that.
115. Do you think that getting a good education is one of the most important things in life?
116. Tell me about that.
117. Do you think reading is important for more things in life than just school?
118. Tell me about that.
119. Do you let things go until the last minute?
120. Tell me about that.
121. Do you feel responsible for your learning?
122. Tell me about that.
123. How do you feel when you don't do well in school?
124. How do you feel when you turn in an assignment late?
125. How do you feel when you don't finish an assignment?
126. Do you like solving problems on your own, or do you prefer being told exactly what is expected and how to do it?
127. Do you get upset easily when you are learning?
128. (If yes) Tell me about that.
129. Do you like to learn and find out things, even when you aren't in school and don't have to?
130. Tell me about that.
131. How do you feel when someone criticizes your schoolwork?
132. Tell me about that.
133. Do you usually try to do your very best in school?
134. Tell me about that.

Anxiety

135. Do you think that you worry more about school or tests than other kids do?
136. (If yes) Tell me about that.
137. Do you feel shaky when the teacher asks you to read aloud, get up in front of the class, or write on the board?
138. (If yes) Tell me about that.
139. How do you feel about surprise tests?

Concluding Comments

140. Is there anything else you would like to tell me or talk about?
141. Do you have any questions that you would like to ask me?
142. (If yes) Go ahead.
143. Thank you for talking with me. If you have any questions or if you want to talk to me, please call me. Here is my card.

Note. With modifications, these questions also can be used for a parent. You would need to substitute the child's name for "you" or "your" and make the appropriate grammatical changes.
Source: Adapted from Dunn and Dunn (1977) and Silver (1992).

Table F-12
Semistructured Interview Questions for a Child (or Adolescent) with Obsessive Tendencies

These questions complement those in Table F-13 in this Appendix. If you want to get a detailed history from the child, also use Table F-13.

1. Hi! I'm Dr. [Ms., Mr.] _____. I'd like to talk to you about how you're getting along. OK?
2. When you don't understand a question that I ask, please say "I don't understand." When you tell me that, I'll try to ask it better. OK?
3. Do you often feel as if you have to do certain things even though you know you really don't have to do them?
4. (If yes) Tell me more about that.
5. Do thoughts or words ever keep repeating over and over in your mind?
6. (If yes) Tell me more about that.
7. Do you have to check things several times?
8. (If yes) Tell me more about that.
9. Do you hate dirt and dirty things?
10. (If yes) Tell me more about that.
11. Do you ever feel that if something has been used or touched by someone else it is spoiled for you?
12. (If yes) Tell me more about that.
13. Do you ever worry about being clean enough?
14. (If yes) Tell me more about that.
15. Are you fussy about keeping your hands clean?
16. (If yes) Tell me more about that.
17. When you put things away at night, do they have to be put away just right?
18. (If yes) Tell me more about that.
19. Do you get angry if other students mess up your desk?
20. (If yes) Tell me more about that.
21. Do you spend a lot of extra time checking your homework to make sure that it's just right?
22. (If yes) Tell me more about that.
23. Do you ever have to do things over and over a certain number of times before they seem quite right?
24. (If yes) Tell me more about that.
25. Do you ever have to count things several times or say certain numbers to yourself?
26. (If yes) Tell me more about that.
27. Do you ever have trouble finishing your schoolwork or chores because you have to do something over and over again?
28. (If yes) Tell me more about that.
29. Do you have a favorite or special number that you like to count up to or that determines just how many times you do things?
30. (If yes) Tell me more about that.
31. Do you often feel bad about something you've done, even though no one else thinks it's bad?
32. (If yes) Tell me more about that.
33. Do you worry a lot if you haven't done something exactly the way you would like to have done it?
34. (If yes) Tell me more about that.
35. Do you have trouble making up your mind?
36. (If yes) Tell me more about that.
37. Do you think a lot about things that you have done because you aren't sure that they were the right things to do?
38. (If yes) Tell me more about that.
39. Do you move or talk in a special way to avoid bad luck?
40. (If yes) Tell me more about that.
41. Do you have special numbers or words you say just because they keep bad luck or bad things away?
42. (If yes) Tell me more about that.
43. Do you have any questions that you would like to ask me?
44. (If yes) Go ahead.
45. Thank you for talking with me. If you have any questions or if you want to talk to me, please call me. Here is my card.

Note. With modifications, these questions also can be used for a parent. You would need to substitute the child's name for "you" or "your" and make the appropriate grammatical changes.
Source: Adapted from Berg, Whitaker, Davies, Flament, and Rapoport (1988), with permission.

Table F-13
Semistructured Interview Questions for a Child (or Adolescent) of School Age

Introduction
1. Hi! I'm Dr. [Ms., Mr.] _____. And you are [cite child's name]. How are you today?
2. When you don't understand a question that I ask, please say "I don't understand." When you tell me that, I'll try to ask it better. OK?
3. Please tell me how old you are.
4. When is your birthday?
5. What is your address?
6. And what is your telephone number?

Information About Problem
7. Has anyone told you why you are here today?
   (If yes, go to question 8; if no, go to question 10.)
8. Who told you?
9. What did he [she] tell you?
10. Tell me why *you* think you are here.
    (If child mentions a problem or a concern, explore it in detail. Ask questions 11 to 39, as needed.)
11. Tell me about [cite problem child mentioned].
12. When did you first notice [cite problem]?
13. How long has it been going on?
14. (If relevant) Where does [cite problem] happen?
15. (If needed) Does it occur at home…at school…when you're traveling…at a friend's house?
16. (If relevant) When does [cite problem] happen?
17. (If needed) Does it happen when you first get up in the morning…during the day…at night before bedtime…at mealtimes?…Does it happen when you are with

your mother…your father…brothers and sisters…
other children…other relatives…the whole family
together…friends…at school?

18. (If relevant) How long does [cite problem] last?
19. How often does [cite problem] occur?
20. (If relevant) Do your brothers and sisters also have [cite problem]?
21. (If yes) Is your [cite problem] worse than or not as bad as theirs?
22. In what way?
23. What happens just before [cite problem] begins?
24. What happens just after [cite problem] begins?
25. What makes [cite problem] worse?
26. What makes [cite problem] better?
27. What do you do when you have [cite problem]?
28. What seems to work best?
29. What do you think caused [cite problem]?
30. Was anything happening in your family when [cite problem] first started?
31. (If needed) Did your parents get separated or divorced …you move to another city or school…your dad or mom lose a job…someone in your family go into the hospital?
32. (If some event occurred) How did you feel when [cite event] happened?
33. How do your parents help you with [cite problem]?
34. (If relevant) How do your brothers and sisters help you with [cite problem]?
35. And your friends, do they help in any way?
36. Have you seen anybody for help with [cite problem]?
     (If yes, go to question 37; if no, go to question 40.)
37. What kind of help did you get?
38. Has it helped?
39. (If needed) In what way?

School
40. Let's talk about school. What grade are you in?
41. What is your teacher's name [are your teachers' names]?
42. How do you get along with your teacher[s]?
43. Who is your favorite teacher?
44. Tell me about him [her].
45. Who is the teacher you like the least?
46. Tell me about him [her]?
47. What subjects do you like best?
48. What is it about these subjects that you like?
49. And what subjects do you like least?
50. What is it about these subjects that you don't like?
51. What grades are you getting?
52. Are you in any activities at school?
53. (If yes) What activities are you in at school?
54. How do you get along with your classmates?
55. Tell me how you spend a usual day at school.

Attention and Concentration at School
56. Do you have any trouble following what your teacher says [teachers say]?
57. (If yes) What kind of trouble do you have?
58. Do you daydream a lot when you are in class?
59. (If yes) Tell me about that.

60. Can you complete your assignments, or are you easily distracted?
61. (If distracted) What seems to distract you?
62. Do you have trouble sitting still or staying in your seat at school?
63. (If yes) Tell me about the trouble you're having.
64. Do you find it hard to sit still for a long time and need a lot of breaks while studying?
65. Do you like to leave your studies to go see what's going on, get a drink, or change rooms or positions?
66. (If yes) Tell me more about that.
67. Do you have any trouble copying what your teacher writes on the blackboard?
68. (If yes) What kind of trouble do you have?
69. Do you have any trouble remembering things?
70. (If yes) Tell me about the trouble you're having.
71. How is your concentration?
72. Do you like to keep at your work until it's done?
73. Tell me more about that.

Home
74. Now let's talk about your home. Who lives with you at home?
     (Many questions from 75 to 104 assume that the child lives in a family with two caregivers. Ask those questions that apply to the child or modify them as needed.)
75. Tell me a little about [cite persons child mentioned].
76. (If needed) What does your father do for work?
77. (If needed) What does your mother do for work?
78. Tell me what your home is like.
79. Do you have your own room at home?
     (If no, go to question 80; if yes, go to question 82.)
80. Whom do you share it with?
81. How do you get along?
82. What chores do you do at home?
83. How do you get along with your father?
84. What does he do that you like?
85. What does he do that you don't like?
86. How do you get along with your mother?
87. What does she do that you like?
88. What does she do that you don't like?
     (If child has one or more siblings, go to question 89 and modify questions accordingly; if child has no siblings, go to question 96.)
89. How do you get along with your brothers and sisters?
90. What do they do that you like?
91. What do they do that you don't like?
92. What do you argue or fight with your brothers and sisters about?
93. What does your mother or father do when you argue or fight with your brothers and sisters?
94. Do your parents treat you and your brothers and sisters the same?
95. (If no) Tell me about that.
96. Are there rules you must follow at home?
97. Tell me about that.
98. When you get in trouble at home, who disciplines you?
99. Tell me about how your father [mother] disciplines you.
100. How do your parents tell you or show you that they like what you have done?

101. When you have a problem, whom do you talk to about it?
102. How does he [she] help you?
103. Do you think your parents are worried about you?
104. (If yes) What are their worries about you?
105. Is there anyone else in your family that you are close to, like a grandparent or other relative?
106. (If yes) Tell me about him [her, them].
107. Do you spend much time at home alone?
108. (If yes) Tell me about that.
109. In general, how would you describe your family?

Interests
110. Now let's talk about what you like to do. What hobbies and interests do you have?
111. What do you do in the afternoons after school?
112. Tell me what you usually do on Saturdays and Sundays.
113. Do you play any sports?
114. (If yes) Tell me what sports you play.
115. Of all the things you do, what do you like doing best?
116. And what do you like doing least?
117. Do you belong to any group like the Boy Scouts [Girl Scouts] or a church group?
118. (If yes) Tell me about the group you belong to.
119. How much TV do you watch in a day?
120. Would you like to watch more TV?
121. (If yes) About how much more would you like to watch?
122. What are your favorite programs?
123. What do you like about them?
124. Do you play Nintendo or some similar game? (If yes, go to question 125; if no, go to question 128.)
125. Where do you play the game?
126. How many hours a day do you play it?
127. What are your favorite Nintendo [Sega, etc.] games?

Friends
128. Do you have friends? (If yes, go to question 129; if no, go to question 138.)
129. Tell me about your friends. (Ask questions 130 to 137, as needed.)
130. (If needed) What do you like to do with your friends?
131. (If needed) Are you spending as much time with your friends now as you used to?
132. (If needed) When you are with your friends, how do you feel?
133. (If needed) How are your friends treating you?
134. Who is your best friend?
135. Tell me about him [her].
136. What do you like to do together?
137. How many of your friends do your parents know? (Go to question 139.)
138. Tell me about your not having friends.

Mood/Feelings
139. Tell me about how you've been feeling lately.
140. Do you have different feelings in the same day?
141. (If yes) Tell me about these different feelings.
142. Have you been feeling more nervous over the past couple of days, as though you can't relax?
143. (If yes) Tell me about that.

144. Nearly everybody feels happy at times. What kinds of things make you feel happiest?
145. And sometimes people feel sad. What makes you feel sad?
146. What do you do when you're sad?
147. Sometimes children [teenagers] begin to get less pleasure from things that they used to enjoy. Has this happened to you?
148. (If yes) Tell me about that.
149. Have there been times lasting more than a day when you felt very cheerful in a way that was different from your normal feelings?
150. (If yes) Tell me about these feelings.
151. Almost everybody gets angry at times. What kinds of things make you angriest?
152. What do you do when you are angry?
153. Do you ever get into fights?
154. (If yes) Tell me about the fights.

Fears/Worries
155. Most children [teenagers] get scared sometimes about some things. What do you do when you are scared?
156. Tell me what scares you.
157. Does anything else scare you?
158. Are you startled by noises?
159. (If yes) Tell me more about that.
160. Do you have any special worries?
161. (If yes) Tell me about what you are worried about.

Self-Concept
162. What do you like best about yourself?
163. Anything else?
164. Tell me about the best thing that ever happened to you.
165. What do you like least about yourself?
166. Anything else?
167. Tell me about the worst thing that ever happened to you.

Somatic Concerns
168. Tell me how you feel about your body.
169. How have you been feeling lately?
170. Do you have any problems with not having enough energy to do the things you want to do?
171. (If yes) Tell me what problems you're having.
172. Tell me how you feel about eating.
173. Are you having problems sleeping enough?
174. (If yes) Tell me about your problems getting enough sleep.
175. Are you sleeping too much?
176. (If yes) Tell me about your problems with sleeping too much.
177. Tell me about your health.
178. (If needed) Have you been sick a lot?
179. (If yes) Tell me about that. (Follow up as needed.)
180. Do you ever get headaches?
181. (If yes) Tell me about them.
182. (If needed) How often do you get them?…What do you usually do?
183. Do you get stomachaches?
184. (If yes) Tell me about them.

185. (If needed) How often do you get them?…What do you usually do?
186. Do you get any other kinds of body pains?
187. (If yes) Tell me about them.
188. Do you have any trouble seeing things?
189. (If yes) Tell me about the trouble you're having seeing.
190. Do you have any trouble hearing things?
191. (If yes) Tell me about the trouble you're having hearing.
192. Do you take medicine every day?
    (If yes, go to question 193; if no, go to question 197.)
193. What do you take the medicine for?
194. What medicine do you take?
195. How often do you take the medicine?
196. How does the medicine make you feel?

Obsessions and Compulsions

197. Some children [teenagers] have thoughts that they think are silly or unpleasant or do not make sense, but these thoughts keep repeating over and over in their minds. Have you had thoughts like this?
198. (If yes) Tell me about these thoughts.
199. Some children [teenagers] are bothered by a feeling that they have to do something over and over even when they don't want to do it. For example, they might keep washing their hands or check over and over again whether the door is locked or the stove is turned off. Is this a problem for you?
200. (If yes) Tell me about it.

Thought Disorder

201. Do you ever hear things no one else hears that seem funny or unusual?
202. (If yes) Tell me about them.
203. (If a voice) What does it say?…How often do you hear it?…How do you feel about the voice?…What do you usually do?
204. Do you ever see things no one else sees that seem funny or unreal?
205. (If yes) Tell me about them.
206. (If needed) How often do you see them?…How do you feel about them?…What do you usually do?
207. Do you ever feel as if someone's spying on you or plotting to hurt you?
208. (If yes) Tell me about these feelings.
209. Does your thinking seem to speed up or slow down at times?
210. (If yes) Tell me about it.
211. Is it hard for you to make decisions?
212. (If yes) Tell me about it.
213. Is it hard for you to concentrate on your reading?
214. (If yes) Tell me about it.
215. Is it hard for you to understand people when they talk?
216. (If yes) Tell me about it.
217. Does it seem as if your thoughts are getting more mixed up or jumbled lately?
218. (If yes) Tell me more about that.
219. Have you had experiences that seemed odd or frightening to you?
220. (If yes) Tell me about them.

Memories/Fantasy

221. What's the first thing you can remember from the time you were a little baby?
222. How old were you then?
223. Tell me about your dreams.
224. Do you ever have the same dream over and over again?
225. (If yes) Tell me about that.
226. Who are your favorite television characters?
227. Tell me about them.
228. What animals do you like best?
229. Tell me what you like about these animals.
230. What animals do you like least?
231. Tell me what you don't like about these animals.
232. What is your happiest memory?
233. What is your saddest memory?
234. If you could change places with anyone in the whole world, who would it be?
235. Tell me about that.
236. If you could go anywhere you wanted to right now, where would you go?
237. Tell me about that.
238. If you could have three wishes, what would they be?
239. What things do you think you might need to take with you if you were to go to the moon and stay there for six months?

Aspirations

240. What do you plan on doing when you're grown up?
241. Do you think you will have any problem doing that?
242. If you could do anything you wanted when you became an adult, what would it be?
    (If interviewee is an adolescent, go to questions following question 245.)

Concluding Questions

243. Do you have anything else that you would like to tell me about yourself?
244. Do you have any questions that you would like to ask me?
245. Thank you for talking with me. If you have any questions or if you want to talk to me, please call me. Here is my card.

For Adolescents

Jobs

1. Do you have an after-school job or a summer job?
2. (If yes) Tell me about your job.

Heterosexual Relations

3. Do you have a special girlfriend [boyfriend]?
4. (If yes) Tell me about her [him].
5. Have you had any sexual experiences?
6. (If yes) Tell me about them.
7. Do you have any sexual concerns?
8. (If yes) Tell me about them.
9. Are you concerned about getting a sexual disease?
10. Tell me about that.
11. Are you sexually active now?
    (If yes, go to question 12; if no, go to directions after question 16.)
12. Tell me about it.

13. Do you use birth control?
    (If yes, go to question 14; if no, go to question 16.)
14. What type?
15. (If needed) Do you [Does your partner] use a condom?
16. Tell me about your not using birth control.
    (If adolescent is a female, go to question 17; if adolescent is a male, go to question 51.)

Questions for Adolescent Females Only

17. Have you ever been pregnant?
    (If yes, go to question 18; if no, go to question 86.)
18. Tell me about it.
    (Ask questions 19 to 50, as needed.)
19. How many times have you been pregnant?
    (Ask questions for each pregnancy, as needed.)
20. How old were you when you first became pregnant?
21. Did you have the baby?
    (If yes, go to question 22; if no, go to question 44.)
22. When was the baby born?
23. Did you have a boy or a girl?
24. How is the child?
25. Who helped you during the pregnancy?
26. Did you see a doctor for care during your pregnancy?
27. Were there any problems during your pregnancy?
28. And were there any complications while you were in labor?
29. And during delivery, were there any problems?
30. Did you have any problems soon after the baby was born?
31. How did you feel during the pregnancy?
32. How do you feel about your baby?
33. How did your family react to your being pregnant?
34. And how did the baby's father react to your being pregnant?
35. Are you raising the baby?
    (If yes, go to question 36; if no, go to question 40.)
36. What is it like being a mother?
37. What kind of help are you getting?
38. Does the baby's father contribute money?
39. Does the baby's father see the baby?
    (Go to question 86.)
40. Who is raising the baby?
41. How do you feel about that?
42. Do you ever see the baby?
43. (If yes) Tell me about that.
    (Go to question 86.)
44. What happened during your pregnancy that you didn't have the baby?
    (If interviewee had an abortion, go to question 45; otherwise, go to question 86.)
45. Tell me about the abortion.
    (Ask questions 46 to 50, as needed.)
46. What were your feelings about the abortion before it was performed?
47. And how did you feel afterwards?
48. What would having a baby have meant for your future?
49. Would your family have helped you if you had had the baby?
50. Tell me about that.
    (Go to question 86.)

Questions for Adolescent Males Only

51. Have you ever gotten anyone pregnant?
    (If yes, go to question 52; if no, go to question 86.)
52. Tell me about it.
    (Ask questions 53 to 55, as needed.)
53. How many times have you gotten someone pregnant?
    (Ask questions for each time interviewee got someone pregnant.)
54. How old were you when you first got someone pregnant?
55. Did she have the baby?
    (If yes, go to question 56; if no, go to question 81.)
56. When was the baby born?
57. Did you have a boy or a girl?
58. How is the child?
59. Who helped the mother during the pregnancy?
60. Did she see a doctor for care during her pregnancy?
61. Were there any problems during her pregnancy?
62. And were there any problems while she was in labor?
63. And during her delivery, were there any problems?
64. And were there any problems soon after the baby was born?
65. How did she feel during her pregnancy?
66. How did she feel about the baby?
67. And how did you react to her being pregnant?
68. Do your parents know that you got someone pregnant?
69. (If yes) How did your parents react to her being pregnant?
70. Who is raising the baby?
    (If the baby is being raised by the mother or by someone else the father knows, go to question 71; if the baby is being raised by the father, go to question 76; if the baby was given up for adoption, go to question 78.)
71. How is the baby doing?
72. Do you see the baby?
73. (If yes) Tell me about that.
74. Do you contribute to the baby's support?
75. Tell me about that.
    (Go to question 86.)
76. How is the baby doing?
77. What is it like being a father?
    (Go to question 86.)
78. How do you feel about the baby's being adopted?
79. Is there anything else you want to tell me about your feelings about the adoption?
80. (If yes) Go ahead.
    (Go to question 86.)
81. What happened during her pregnancy that she didn't have the baby?
    (If she had an abortion, go to question 82; otherwise, go to question 86.)
82. Tell me about the abortion.
    (Ask questions 83 to 85, as needed.)
83. What were your feelings about the abortion before it was performed?
84. And how did you feel afterwards?
85. What would having a baby have meant for your future?
    (Go to question 86.)

Eating Habits

86. Now I'm going to ask some questions about your eating habits. Have you ever gone on eating binges—that is, eaten an abnormally large amount of food over a short period of time?
87. (If yes) Tell me about these eating binges.
88. Has there ever been a time when people gave you a hard time about being too thin or losing too much weight?
89. (If yes) Tell me about that.

Drug/Alcohol Use

90. Do your parents drink alcohol?
91. (If yes) Tell me about their drinking.
92. (If needed) How much do they drink?…How frequently do they drink?…Where do they drink?
93. Do your friends drink alcohol?
94. (If yes) Tell me about their drinking.
95. Do you drink alcohol?
96. (If yes) Tell me about your drinking.
97. Was there ever a time when you drank too much?
98. (If yes) Tell me about the time[s] when you drank too much.
99. Has anyone in your family, a friend, a doctor, or anyone else ever said that you drank too much?
100. (If yes) Tell me about that.
101. Has alcohol ever caused problems for you?
102. (If yes) Tell me about that.
103. Do your parents use drugs?
104. (If yes) Tell me about the drugs they use.
105. (If needed) How much of the drugs do they take?… How frequently do they take them?…Why do they take them?
106. Do your friends use drugs?
107. (If yes) Tell me about the drugs they use.
108. Do you use drugs?
109. (If yes) Tell me about the drugs you use.
110. Have you or has anyone else ever thought that you used drugs too much?
111. (If yes) Tell me about that.
    (Go to question 243 in the main interview.)

Note. Table F-2 in this Appendix contains a more detailed interview on alcohol use, and Table F-1 in this Appendix contains a more detailed interview on drug use.

Table F-14
Semistructured Interview Questions for a Child (or Adolescent) with a Sleep Disorder

Introduction

1. Hi! I'm Dr. [Ms., Mr.] _____. [Cite referral source] asked me to see you. I'd like to talk to you about how you are getting along. OK?
2. When you don't understand a question that I ask, please say "I don't understand." When you tell me that, I'll try to ask it better. OK?

Nature of Sleep-Awake Problem

3. [Cite referral source] tells me that you are having trouble sleeping. Tell me about the trouble you're having.
4. Do you have trouble falling asleep?
    (If yes, go to question 5; if no, go to question 7.)
5. How many nights a week do you have trouble falling asleep?
6. How long does it usually take you to fall asleep after you go to bed?
7. Do you have a problem staying asleep?
    (If yes, go to question 8; if no, go to question 15.)
8. Tell me about the problem you have staying asleep.
9. During the past month, about how many times did you wake up in the night?
10. What time is it generally when you wake up in the night?
11. What causes you to wake up?
12. Do you wake up quickly?
13. What do you do while you are awake?
14. On a typical night during the last month, how long were you awake during the night?
15. Do you have a problem with waking up too early in the morning?
16. (If yes) Tell me about it.
17. Do you have a problem with staying awake during the day?
18. (If yes) Tell me about it.
19. When you are not having sleeping problems, how many hours of sleep do you usually get?
20. When you are having sleep problems, how many hours of sleep do you usually get?
21. After sleeping poorly, what kinds of problems do you have?
22. (If needed) Are you tired…sleepy…washed out?…Do you have problems at school…memory problems… problems doing chores?…Do you have mood problems—that is, are you irritable, nervous, groggy, depressed, anxious, grouchy, hostile, angry, or confused?…Do you have physical symptoms—that is, muscle aches or pains, light-headedness, headache, nausea, or stomachache?
23. Is your sleep problem getting worse?
24. (If yes) How is it getting worse?

First Occurrence of Problem

25. When was the first time you had trouble sleeping?
26. Was anything happening in your life when the problem started?
27. (If yes) Tell me about that.
28. Had any changes been made in your bedroom?
29. (If yes) Tell me about the changes.
30. Had any changes occurred in your family?
31. (If yes) Tell me about the changes.
32. Had any changes been made in your activities during the day?
33. (If yes) Tell me about the changes.
34. Had anything happened that upset you?
35. (If yes) Tell me what upset you.
36. Did you lose a friend or did someone close to you go away?
37. (If yes) Tell me about it.

Concerns of Family

38. Do you think your family is worried about your sleeping problem?
39. (If yes) Tell me about how they are worried.
40. How do your parents act when you have this sleeping problem?
41. Do you think your mom and dad pay more attention to you if you have a hard time sleeping?
42. (If yes) How do they pay more attention to you?
43. Are you as worried about your sleep as your parents are?

Other Sleep Parameters

44. What do you do before going to bed?
45. Do you do the same thing every night?
46. What do you do if you can't fall asleep or can't go back to sleep after waking up?
47. How do you sleep when you're away from home?
48. How do you sleep on weekends?
49. What things make your sleeping problem worse?
50. What things make your sleeping problem better?
51. How does your sleeping problem affect the things you do or feel?
52. What do you do when you feel this way?
53. Has anyone tried to help you with your sleeping problem before?
54. (If yes) Tell me about how they tried to help you.
55. Have you ever been hurt because of something that happened when you were having sleeping problem?
56. (If yes) Tell me about how you were hurt.
57. Can you remember anything that happens when you have a sleeping problem?
58. (If yes) What do you remember?
59. Are you having any other sleeping problems that you haven't told me about?
60. (If yes) Tell me about these problems.
61. What time do you usually go to bed on weekdays?
62. What time do you usually wake up on weekdays?
63. What time do you usually go to bed on weekends?
64. What time do you usually wake up on weekends?
65. Do you take naps?
    (If yes, go to question 66; if no, go to question 69.)
66. What time of day do you nap?
67. How often do you take naps?
68. What days of the week do you take naps?
69. Do you ever fall asleep when you should be awake?
    (If yes, go to question 70; if no, go to question 72.)
70. Tell me about these times.
71. Where do you fall asleep when you should be awake?

Sleep Aids

72. Do you have a special stuffed animal or blanket or anything else that you sleep with?
73. (If yes) What do you take to bed with you?
74. Do you have to be in a special place or position to fall asleep?
75. (If yes) Tell me about that.
76. Do you take anything to help you sleep?
    (If yes, go to question 77; if no, go to question 79.)
77. What do you take?
78. How often do you take it?

Bedroom Environment

79. How would you describe your bedroom?
80. Do you share a room with anyone?
    (If yes, go to question 81; if no, go to question 83.)
81. Whom do you share your room with?
82. Where does [cite person] sleep?
83. Is your mattress comfortable?
84. (If no) Tell me about that.
85. Is the bedroom quiet?
86. (If no) Tell me about that.
87. Is there a TV, radio, or phone in your bedroom?
    (If yes, go to question 88; if no, go to question 90.)
88. Do you use it [them] before you go to bed?
89. (If yes) Tell me about that.
90. Do you ever read in bed before you go to sleep?
91. Is your room too hot or too cold at night or just right?

Eating, Drinking, and Exercise

92. Do you play a lot of ball or get a lot of exercise?
    (If yes, go to question 93; if no, go to question 98.)
93. Tell me about the things you do.
94. How often do you do them?
95. Do you sometimes exercise before you go to bed?
    (If yes, go to question 96; if no, go to question 98.)
96. What kinds of exercise do you do before going to bed?
97. How much time do you spend exercising before going to bed?
98. Do you drink anything before going to bed that might keep you awake?
    (If yes, go to question 99; if no, go to question 102.)
99. What do you like to drink before going to bed?
100. How much do you drink?
101. When do you drink [cite drink child named]?
102. How many glasses of liquid, such as water, juice, or soda, do you drink during the day?
103. How many glasses of liquid do you drink at night?
104. How long before bedtime do you drink your last glass of liquid?
    (If the interviewee is an adolescent, go to question 105; if not, go to question 110.)

Additional Questions for Adolescents

105. (If needed) Do you ever drink alcohol to help you go to sleep?
    (If yes, go to question 106; if no, go to question 110.)
106. Tell me about your drinking alcohol.
107. (If needed) What kind of alcohol do you drink?… How much do you drink?…How often do you drink alcohol?
108. Do you smoke cigarettes?
109. How many cigarettes do you smoke a day?

Family

110. Does anyone else in the family have a sleeping problem like yours?
    (If yes, go to question 111; if no, go to question 114.)
111. Who has the problem?
112. What has been done to help [cite person child named]?
113. How has it helped?

Other Questions

114. Do you feel healthy?
115. (If no) Tell me about your not feeling healthy.
116. Do you take any medicine?
    (If yes, go to question 117; if no, go to question 119.)
117. What medicine are you taking?
118. What do you take the medicine for?
119. Did something happen that made you come to see me at this time?
120. (If yes) Tell me about that.
121. Do you have any questions that you would like to ask me?
122. (If yes) Go ahead.
123. Thank you for talking with me. If you have any questions or if you want to talk to me, please call me. Here is my card.

Note. With modifications, these questions also can be used for a parent. You would need to substitute the child's name for "you" or "your" and make the appropriate grammatical changes.
Source: Adapted from Morin (1993).

Table F-15
Semistructured Interview Questions for a Child (or Adolescent) Who Is Homeless

Introduction

1. Hi. I'm Dr. [Ms., Mr.] _____. I'd like to talk to you about how you're getting along. OK?
2. When you don't understand a question that I ask, please say "I don't understand." When you tell me that, I'll try to ask it better. OK?
3. Whom do you live with?
    (If the child lives with a parent, go to question 4; if the child lives alone, go to question 30.)

Living with Family

4. Tell me a little about each member of your family.
    (If child lives with his or her mother only, go to question 5. If child lives with his or her father only, go to question 8. If child lives with both parents, go to question 11.)
5. Tell me about your mother.
6. (If needed) What does your mother do during the day?
7. How do you get along with your mother?
    (Go to question 17 if child has siblings; if not, go to question 22.)
8. Tell me about your father.
9. (If needed) What does your father do during the day?
10. How do you get along with your father?
    (Go to question 17 if child has siblings; if not, go to question 22.)
11. Tell me about your mother.
12. (If needed) What does your mother do during the day?
13. How do you get along with your mother?

14. Tell me about your father.
15. (If needed) What does your father do during the day?
16. How do you get along with your father?
    (Go to question 17 if child has siblings; if not, go to question 22.)
17. Tell me about your brothers and sisters.
18. How are they getting along?
19. Do they have any problems?
20. (If yes) Tell me about their problems.
21. How do you get along with them? (Follow up, as needed.)
22. Where do you live right now?
23. How long have you been living there?
24. How do you like living there?
25. What is the best thing about living there?
26. What is the worst thing about living there?
27. What would you change to make the place you live in now better?
28. Tell me about other places you've lived.
29. When do you think your family will get its own place to live?
    (Go to question 62.)

Living Alone

30. How old were you when you began living on your own?
31. Where were you living before you left home?
32. What was the reason you left?
33. What did you like best about living there?
34. What did you like least about living there?
35. What makes a place seem like home?
36. Where do you live right now?
37. How long have you been living there?
38. How do you like living there?
39. What is the best thing about living there?
40. What is the worst thing about living there?
41. What would you change to make the place you live in now better?
42. Tell me about other places you've lived.
43. When do you think you will get your own place to live?
44. How do you support yourself?
45. Do you do anything else for money?
46. (If yes) Tell me what else you do.
47. Are you responsible for taking care of anyone else?
48. (If yes) Who is that?
49. Is anyone responsible for you?
50. (If yes) Who is that?
51. How do you usually spend your time during the day?
52. Whom do you go to when you need help?
    (Ask questions 53 to 61, as needed.)
53. Tell me about your family.
54. Tell me about your mother.
55. How do you get along with her?
56. And tell me about your father.
57. How do you get along with him?
58. Tell me about your brothers and sisters.
59. How do you get along with them?
60. Would you like to go back home?
61. What would have to change at home for you to go back?

School

62. Are you going to school?
(If yes, go to question 63; if no, go to question 78.)
63. What grade are you in?
64. How are you doing in school?
65. What are your favorite subjects?
66. What do you like best about school?
67. What do you like least about school?
68. Have you missed a lot of school?
69. (If yes) Tell me how much school you have missed.
70. Have you ever repeated a grade in school?
71. (If yes) Tell me about that.
72. How long have you been going to this school?
73. Do you have friends at school?
74. (If yes) Tell me about your friends.
(Go to question 76.)
75. Tell me about your not having friends at school.
76. Have you gone to any other schools?
77. (If yes) Tell me about the other schools. (Probe for dates, length of time attended, number of schools, etc.)
(Go to question 80.)
78. Do you plan to go back to school?
79. Tell me more about that.

Health

80. Tell me about your health.
(If child has health problems, go to question 81; if child does not have health problems, go to question 86.)
81. Tell me about the health problems you're having.
82. Have you been to a doctor for the problem[s]?
(If yes, go to question 83; if no, go to question 86.)
83. What did the doctor say about your problem[s]?
84. What did he [she] say that you should do for the problem[s]?
85. (Follow up any leads, as needed. For example, if the interviewee is taking medicine) What medicines do you take?…How do you get the medicine you need?…Who pays for the medicine?…Do you have another appointment to see the doctor about your problem?…Do you need to continue to take the medicine for a long time?

Coping

86. How do you feel about not having your own place to live?
87. Do you know the reason why your family doesn't [you don't] have a home now?
88. (If yes) Tell me about that.
89. Has not having your own place to live changed how you get along with your parents?
90. (If relevant) Has not having your own place to live changed how you get along with your brothers and sisters?
91. What do you think can be done to get you back into your own place?

Aspirations

92. In the future, how do you see your life?
93. What do you plan on doing when you become an adult?
94. Do you think you will have your own place to live when you are an adult?
95. Do you have any questions that you would like to ask me?

96. (If yes) Go ahead.
97. Thank you for talking with me. If you have any questions or if you want to talk to me, please call me. Here is my card.

Note. This semistructured interview does not probe problem behavior. If the child has psychological problems, see Table F-13 in this Appendix for relevant questions.
Source: Adapted from Masten, Miliotis, Graham-Bermann, Ramirez, and Neemann (1993).

Table F-16
Semistructured Interview Questions for a Child (or Adolescent) Who May Have a Dissociative Identity Disorder

Introduction

1. Hello. I'm Dr. [Ms., Mr.] _____. (If relevant) I work [cite place]. I'd like to talk with you about how you're getting along. OK?
2. When you don't understand a question that I ask, please say "I don't understand." When you tell me that, I'll try to ask it better. OK?

General Problems

3. Could you please tell me how you're feeling?
4. Have you had any medical problems recently?
5. (If yes) Tell me about them.
6. Have you been treated before for an emotional problem?
7. (If yes) Tell me about that.

Attention and Concentration Difficulties

8. Is it easy or hard for you to pay attention to things?
9. Tell me about that.
(Ask questions 10 to 15, as needed.)
10. Are you easily distracted?
11. (If yes) Give me some examples of how you are easily distracted.
12. Do you ever go from one thing to another and not remember what you started out to do?
13. (If yes) Give me an example of when this happened.
14. Do you have difficulty understanding the teacher's instructions or instructions that other people give you?
15. (If yes) Tell me about the difficulty you are having understanding instructions.

Mood Symptoms

(Ask questions 16 to 25 if the information wasn't covered earlier. If the information was covered earlier, go to question 26.)
16. Do you feel sad much of the time?
17. (If yes) Tell me about your feeling sad.
18. Do your moods change a lot?
19. (If yes) Tell me about these changes.
20. Are you ever quiet one minute and active the next minute?
21. (If yes) Tell me about these changes in your behavior.

22. Have you ever thought of suicide?
23. (If yes) Tell me about these thoughts.
24. Have you ever tried to hurt yourself?
25. (If yes) Tell me about the time[s] that you tried to hurt yourself.

Somatoform Symptoms

26. Do you sometimes notice that you have no feeling in part of your body but can't explain why?
27. (If yes) Tell me about when this has happened.
28. Sometimes, when you want to do one thing, does it seem as if your body wants to do another?
29. (If yes) Tell me about this feeling.
30. Do you do lots of things at the same time without understanding how you can do that?
31. (If yes) Tell me about when this happens.
32. Do you find that your vision changes all the time but nobody believes you when you tell them about it?
33. (If yes) Tell me about these changes in your vision.
34. Do you sleepwalk?
35. (If yes) Tell me about your sleepwalking.
36. Do you have nightmares?
37. (If yes) Tell me about them.
38. Are you afraid to go to sleep?
39. (If yes) Tell me about your fears of going to sleep.

Dissociative Symptoms

40. Do you find that you have no memory about things that happened in the past?
41. (If yes) Tell me about the times this has happened.
42. Do you find yourself sometimes in a daze or a trance?
43. (If yes) Tell me about that.
44. Do you sometimes have to try to figure out what has happened to you or where you are?
45. (If yes) Tell me about the times this has happened.
46. Do you daydream often?
47. (If yes) Tell me about when this happens.
48. Do you have a pretend playmate?
49. (If yes) Tell me about that.
50. Do you get lost easily?
51. (If yes) Tell me about your getting lost easily.

Symptoms in Common with Other Disorders

52. Do you hear voices inside your head?
53. (If yes) Tell me about the voices you hear.
54. Do you have any unusual experiences with smells… pictures…touching things…feeling things?

Acting-Out Problems

55. Have you had any trouble with the police?
56. (If yes) What trouble have you had with the police?
57. Do you ever see yourself getting into trouble but you can't stop yourself?
58. (If yes) Give me an example of when this happened.
59. Have you ever used drugs?
60. (If yes) Tell me about the drugs you have used.
61. Is there a part of you that wants to use drugs, but you try to keep that part under control?
62. (If yes) Tell me about that.

63. Have you ever been accused of stealing?
64. (If yes) Tell me about how that happened.
65. Has anyone told you that you lie a lot?
66. (If yes) Tell me about that.
67. (If needed) Do you think you lie a lot?
68. How do you get along with other teenagers and adults?
69. Do you like to cause trouble for people?
70. (If yes) Tell me about that.
71. Do you feel that a part of you is violent?
72. (If yes) Tell me about this feeling.
73. Do you feel that you have lost control over yourself?
74. (If yes) Tell me about that.

School

75. I'd like to talk to you now about school. How are you getting along in school?
    (Ask questions 76 to 99, as needed.)
76. Have you missed much school?
77. (If yes) Tell me about your missing school.
78. Tell me about your schoolwork.
79. (If needed) Do you seem to do well in school sometimes and poorly at other times?
80. (If yes) Do you have any idea about why this happens?
81. How do you get along with the other kids in school?
82. (If needed) Do other kids tease or ignore you?
83. (If yes) Tell me about how you feel when this happens.
84. Have you noticed any changes in your handwriting?
85. (If yes) Tell me about these changes.
86. Have you noticed that sometimes you can do things and other times you can't do them?
87. (If yes) Tell me about this.
88. Do you find yourself forgetting things, like the names of your teacher or friends or the dates of important events?
89. (If yes) Tell me about that.
90. Do you have a bad memory for subjects that you thought you knew well?
91. (If yes) Tell me about that.
92. Do you answer questions on exams without knowing sometimes where the answers come from?
93. (If yes) Tell me about the last time this happened.
94. Have you had any trouble at school with the authorities?
95. (If yes) Please tell me about the trouble you've had.
96. How do you think you're being treated by the school staff?
97. (If needed) Tell me about that.
98. Have you seen a school psychologist or guidance counselor?
99. (If yes) Tell me about what happened when you went to see him or her.

Identity

100. How do you feel about being a boy [girl]?
101. (If needed) Tell me more about that.

102. (For males) Do you ever feel yourself becoming more like a female? (For females) Do you ever feel yourself becoming more like a male?
103. (If yes) Tell me about these feelings.
104. Are there times when you aren't sure who you are or even what your name is?
105. (If yes) Tell me about this.
106. Do you ever call yourself by another name?
107. (If yes) Tell me about that.

Supernatural/ESP Experiences/Possession/Cults

108. Have you ever had any kind of supernatural experience?
109. (If yes) Tell me about the experience.
110. Have you ever had any extrasensory perception experiences, such as mental telepathy, seeing the future while awake, or seeing the future in dreams?
111. (If yes) Tell me about these experiences.
112. Have you ever thought that you were possessed by a demon, a dead person, a living person, or some other power or force?
113. (If yes) Tell me about your being possessed.
114. Have you ever had contact with ghosts or spirits?
115. (If yes) Tell me about these contacts.
116. Have you ever thought that you had a past life or lives?
117. (If yes) Tell me about your past life or lives.
118. Have you ever been involved with a cult?
119. (If yes) Tell me about how you were involved.

Attitude Toward Professionals

120. Have you seen any other mental health professionals in the past?
(If yes, go to question 121; if no, go to question 125.)
121. Tell me whom you've seen.
122. How do you feel about how [cite name of person or persons mentioned by child] tried to help you?
123. Would you say that most people who have tried to help you in the past have asked the right questions?
124. (If no) Tell me about what you believe are the right questions to ask you.
125. Have I asked you the right questions today?
126. (If no) What questions do you think I should have asked?

Concluding Questions

127. Is there anything else you would like to tell me?
128. (If yes) Go ahead.
129. Is there anything that you would like to ask me?
130. (If yes) Go ahead.
131. Thank you for talking with me. If you have any questions or if you want to talk to me, please call me. Here is my card.

Note. With modifications, these questions also can be used for a parent. You would need to substitute the child's name for "you" or "your" and make the appropriate grammatical changes.
Source: Adapted from Dean (1985) and Steinberg, Rousaville, and Cicchetti (1990).

Table F-17
Semistructured Interview Questions for a Family

---

1. Hi! I'm Dr. [Ms., Mr.] _____. We are all here today to try to work out the problems you're having as a family. I'd like to hear from everyone about what's going on. OK?
2. (Looking at the family members present) Would you like to tell me why you are here today?

Perception of Problem

3. What do you see as the problem? (Obtain each member's view, if possible.)
4. When did the problem start?
5. How did the problem start?
6. What is the problem like now?
7. How has the problem affected all of you? (Obtain each member's view, if possible.)
8. How have you dealt with the problem? (Obtain each member's view, if possible.)
9. To what degree have your attempts been successful?
10. Have you had any previous professional help?
(If yes, go to question 11; if no, go to question 15.)
11. What kind of help did you receive?
12. What do you think about the help you received?
13. Was it successful?
14. Tell me in what way it was successful [unsuccessful].

Description of Family

15. What words would you use to describe your family?
16. How do you think other people would describe your family?
17. What's it like when you are all together?
18. (Looking at the family members) What kind of a person is Mr. [cite father's last name]?
19. (Looking at the family members) What kind of a person is Mrs. [cite mother's last name]?
20. (Looking at the family members) What kind of son is [cite each son's name in turn]?
21. (Looking at the family members) What kind of daughter is [cite each daughter's name in turn]?
22. Do you agree with the description of yourself given by the other family members? (Obtain a response from each member.)
23. Which parent deals more with the children?
24. Do the children have any specific chores to do at home?
25. Are these arrangements satisfactory and fair?
26. (If no) How could they be better?
27. Do you find it easy to talk with others in your family? (Obtain a response from each member; explore any difficulties, including who is involved and what the problem is.)
28. What's it like when you discuss something together as a family?
29. Who talks the most?
30. Who talks the least?
31. Does everybody get a chance to have a say?
32. (Looking at the family members) Do you find you have to be careful about what you say in your family?
33. Who are the good listeners in your family?

34. Is it helpful to talk things over with the family, or does it seem to be a waste of time?
35. Is it easy to express your feelings in your family?
36. Do you generally know how the others in your family are feeling?
37. How can you tell how they are feeling?
38. How much time do you spend together as a family?
39. What sorts of things do you do together?
40. Who does what with whom?
41. Is this okay with everybody?
42. Who is closest to whom in the family?
43. How are decisions made in your family?
44. Is this satisfactory?
45. (If no) What would be preferable?
46. Do you have disagreements in your family?
    (If yes, go to question 47; if no, go to question 53.)
47. Who has disagreements?
48. What are they about?
49. What are the disagreements like?
50. What happens?
51. How do they end up?
52. Do they get worked out?
53. What kind of work does Mr. [cite father's last name] do?
54. What kind of work does Mrs. [cite mother's last name] do?

Extended Family
55. Are there any other relatives or close friends living at home or nearby?
    (If yes, go to question 56; if no, go to question 58.)
56. Who are they?
57. How do all of you get along with him [her, them]?

Concluding Questions
58. How might each of you change in order to improve the family situation?
59. Is there anything else that you would like to discuss?
60. Are there any questions that any of you would like to ask me?
61. (If yes) Go ahead.
62. Thank you for talking with me. If you have any questions or if you want to talk to me, please call me. Here is my card.

Note. This table is based on the Family Assessment Interview, which was prepared by Dr. Peter Loader for the Family Research Programme at Brunel—The University of West London. Work related to the interview schedule was published by Kinston and Loader (1984). *Source:* Adapted from Kinston and Loader, unpublished manuscript, 1984.

Table F-18
Semistructured Interview Questions for a Healthy Sibling of a Child (or Adolescent) Who Has a Health-Related Disorder

1. Hi! I'm Dr. [Ms., Mr.] _____. I'd like to talk to you about how you're getting along. OK?
2. When you don't understand a question that I ask, please say "I don't understand." When you tell me that, I'll try to ask it better. OK?
3. Tell me what you know about [cite sibling' name]'s illness.
4. Who told you about [cite sibling's name]'s illness?
5. How often do you think about [cite sibling's name]'s illness?
6. How do you feel when you think about [cite sibling's name]'s illness?
7. If you have any questions about [cite sibling's name]'s illness or treatment, whom do you ask?
8. Can you talk to [cite sibling's name] about his [her] illness?
9. Tell me about that.
10. Can you talk to your parents about [cite sibling's name]'s illness?
11. Tell me about that.
12. Are you able to talk to anyone else about [cite sibling's name]'s illness?
13. Tell me about that.
14. Do you worry that you may get the same illness?
15. (If yes) Tell me about that.
16. Would you like to know more about [cite sibling's name]'s illness?
    (If yes, go to question 17; if no, go to question 19.)
17. What would you like to know?
18. Whom would you like to tell you these things?
19. Has anything changed for you since [cite sibling's name] got ill?
    (If yes, go to question 20; if no, go to question 23.)
20. What kinds of things have changed?
21. How have they changed?
22. How do these changes make you feel?
23. What's the hardest thing about having a brother [sister] who is ill?
24. Since [cite sibling's name]'s illness, has anything changed about the way others act around you?
    (If yes, go to question 25; if no, go to question 27.)
25. Tell me about who treats you differently.
26. In what way do they treat you differently?
27. How has [cite sibling's name]'s illness changed your relationship with your parents?
28. (If relevant) How has [cite sibling's name]'s illness changed your relationship with your other brothers and sisters?
29. Who has been the biggest help to you since your brother [sister] got sick?
30. Tell me about that.
31. If you could talk to other kids whose brother or sister is sick, would you like to do that?
32. Tell me about that.

33. Do you have any questions that you would like to ask me?
34. (If yes) Go ahead.
35. Thank you for talking with me. If you have any questions or if you want to talk to me, please call me. Here is my card.

Source: Adapted, in part, from Evans, Stevens, Cushway, and Houghton (1992) and Menke (1987).

Table F-19
Semistructured Interview Questions for an Individual Who May Be Experiencing or Who Is Experiencing Domestic Violence

---

Introduction

1. Hi! I'm Dr. [Ms., Mr.] _____. (If relevant) I'm a member of the staff at [cite place]. I'd like to talk to you about how you are getting along. OK? Let's begin.
2. Who lives at your home?
3. Tell me about how things are going at home.
   (Ask questions 4 to 6, as needed.)
4. Are you having any problems in your relationship with your husband [wife, partner, friend, etc.]?
5. (If yes) Tell me about the problems you are having.
   (Go to question 7.)
6. You were referred because of [cite incident]. Could you tell me about that?

Inquiry About Being Abused

7. Have you ever been physically hurt or sexually abused by your husband [wife, partner, friend, etc.]?
   (If yes, go to question 8; if no, go to directions preceding question 40.)
8. Tell me about how you were hurt or abused.
   (Ask questions 9 to 17, as needed.)
9. Where did it happen?
10. When did it happen?
11. What did your husband [wife, partner, friend, etc.] say to you during the incident?
12. How did you feel when it happened?
13. And how do you feel now?
14. Was your husband [wife, partner, friend, etc.] using alcohol or drugs?
15. (If yes) Tell me about that.
16. Was a weapon involved?
17. (If yes) Tell me about it.
18. Is there a weapon in the house?
    (If yes, go to question 19; if no, go to question 22.)
19. What kind of weapon is in the house?
20. (If a gun or rifle) Is it loaded?
21. (If a gun or rifle) Is it locked up?
22. Did you say anything to your husband [wife, partner, friend, etc.] during the incident?
23. (If yes) What did you say?

24. Did you or anyone else report the incident to the police?
    (If yes, go to question 25; if no, go to question 29.)
25. Who reported it?
26. (If someone else reported it) Tell me about him [her].
27. What happened after it was reported?
28. What did the police do?
29. (If needed) Did you get any kind of help?
    (If yes, go to question 30, if no, go to question 34.)
30. Tell me about the help you got.
31. (If needed) Who helped you?
32. (If needed) What did he [she, they] do?
33. (If needed) What did he [she, they] say to you?
    (Go to question 35.)
34. Tell me about your not reporting it or getting help.
35. Have you ever obtained a protective [restraining] order?
    (If yes, go to question 36; if no, go to question 38.)
36. Tell me about the order.
37. Did your husband [wife, partner, friend, etc.] follow the order?
38. Have you ever tried to press charges against your husband [wife, partner, friend, etc.]?
39. (If yes) Tell me about that.

Children in the Home
(If children are in the home, go to question 40; if no children are in the home, go to question 54.)

40. What are the ages of the children living in your home?
41. How do they get along with their father [their mother, your partner, your friend, etc.]?
42. Have the children been involved in or observed any violent episodes between you and your husband [wife, partner, friend, etc.]?
    (If yes, go to question 43; if no, go to question 46.)
43. What have they seen?
44. How did they react?
45. How did you handle their reactions?
46. Has your husband [wife, partner, friend, etc.] ever hit, hurt, or abused the children?
    (If yes, go to question 47; if no, go to question 52.)
47. Tell me about what your husband [wife, partner, friend, etc.] has done to the children.
48. Do you think the children are in danger?
49. (If yes) Tell me about the danger they are in.
50. Has Child Protective Services ever been contacted?
51. (If yes) Tell me about what happened.
52. Have the children ever been removed from the home or moved to another place?
53. (If yes) Tell me about that.

Threats
54. Has your husband [wife, partner, friend, etc.] ever threatened you?
55. (If yes) Tell me about these threats.
56. Do you feel safe with your husband [wife, partner, friend, etc.]?
57. Tell me about your feelings.
58. (If needed) Are you afraid to go home?
59. (If yes) Tell me about your fears.

60. Are you in any type of danger?
61. (If yes) Tell me about that.
62. Do you ever feel overwhelmed?
63. (If yes) Tell me about your feelings.

Medication and Drugs
64. Are you taking any medication?
65. (If yes) Tell me about the medication you are taking.
66. Do you use drugs?
67. (If yes) Tell me about the drugs you use.
68. Do you drink alcohol?
69. (If yes) Tell me about your drinking.

Past Events
70. Has [cite incident] or something similar happened before?
    (If yes, go to question 71; if no, go to question 84.)
71. What happened before?
72. Who was involved?
73. When did it first happen?
74. Was a weapon involved?
75. (If yes) Tell me about the weapon that was used.
76. How often has this happened to you?
77. How badly have you been hurt in the past?
78. (For females) Were you ever pregnant when he tried to hurt you?
79. (If yes) Tell me about that.
80. Have you ever told anyone that your husband [wife, partner, friend, etc.] hurt you before?
81. (If yes) Whom did you tell?
82. What have you done in the past to protect yourself?
83. What have you done in the past to get help?
84. Have you ever called the police in the past because of what your husband [wife, partner, friend, etc.] did to you?
    (If yes, go to question 85; if no, go to question 90.)
85. What did you call them about?
86. When did you call them?
87. How did you report the incident?
88. What happened after you reported it?
89. What did the police do?
90. Are there any past incidents that you could have reported but decided not to?
91. (If yes) Tell me about that.
92. Did you ever obtain a protective [restraining] order?
    (If yes, go to question 93; if no, go to question 95.)
93. Tell me about the order.
94. Did your husband [wife, partner, friend, etc.] follow the order?
95. Did you ever try to press charges against your husband [wife, partner, friend, etc.] before the present incident occurred?
96. (If yes) Tell me about that.
97. (If needed) Have you ever gone to a shelter or safe house for victims?
98. (If yes) Tell me about that.

Progression of Violence
99. How soon after you met your husband [wife, partner, friend, etc.] did the physical violence begin?

100. Have you noticed that the violence is happening more often lately?
101. (If yes) Tell me about that.
102. Have you noticed that the violence is getting more severe lately?
103. (If yes) Tell me about that.

Other Family Members' and Friends' Awareness of Abuse
104. Do any of your relatives or friends know about your being abused?
     (If yes, go to question 105; if no, go to question 109.)
105. Who knows?
106. What did you tell him [her, them]?
107. How did he [she, they] react?
108. (If needed) What kind of support did he [she, they] give you?
     (Go to question 113.)
109. Do you think that you could tell any of your relatives or friends?
110. What do you think would happen if you did tell them?
111. Do you think that if you told them they would give you support?
112. Tell me about that.

Description of Offender
113. What kind of work does your husband [wife, partner, friend, etc.] do?
114. Does your husband [wife, partner, friend, etc.] have a criminal record?
115. (If yes) Tell me about your husband's [wife's, partner's, friend's, etc.] criminal record.
116. Has your husband [wife, partner, friend, etc.] ever beaten up or hurt other people?
117. (If yes) Tell me about what your husband [wife, partner, friend, etc.] has done.
118. What does your husband [wife, partner, friend, etc.] do or say after the physical violence?
119. (If needed) For example, does he [she] apologize, try to make things right, or ask for forgiveness?
120. (If yes) Tell me about what he [she] does.

Emergency Plan
121. Do you have a safe place to go in case of an emergency?
122. (If yes) Where would you go?
123. Would you like help in locating a shelter?
124. Would you like to talk with me about developing an emergency plan?
125. (If yes) What kind of plan do you think you need?
     (You may need to assist the victim because he or she may be unable to develop a plan by herself or himself. See Exhibit 22-1 on page 787 in Chapter 22 for some guidelines.)
126. (If relevant) Do you need any help for your children?
     (If yes, discuss what options are available in the community for the victim and the children.)

Prosecution of Offender
127. Would you like to see your husband [wife, partner, friend, etc.] prosecuted?

128. (If yes) Explain how you would like him [her] prosecuted.
(Go to question 130.)
129. Tell me about why you don't want him [her] prosecuted.

Concluding Questions

130. Is there anything else you would like to tell me or talk about?
131. (If yes) Go ahead.
132. Thank you for talking with me. If you want to speak to me at any time, please call this number. (Give interviewee your number.) If it is an emergency situation, please call 911. You also may want to call an emergency shelter or crisis hotline. Here are some numbers that might be helpful to you. (Give interviewee shelter and hotline numbers.)

Note. If the interviewee is reluctant to talk to you about the abuse, consider using the following questions: People in marriages [relationships] sometimes disagree or fight. What happens when you and your husband [wife, partner, friend, etc.] disagree or fight?…Have there been times in your relationship when you have been afraid of your husband [wife, partner, friend, etc.]?…(If yes) Tell me about these times.
Source: Adapted from Hatchett-Jones et al. (1994), Johann (1994), and Sonkin, Martin, and Walker (1985). A variant of this interview was developed by the Emergency Medicine Department of the Medical College of Pennsylvania.

Table F-20
Semistructured Interview Questions for a Known Offender

The questions in this table are designed to be used by human service providers to get an in-depth picture of a known offender's background. The questions in this table should not be used for investigatory purposes.

Introduction

1. Hi! I'm Dr. [Ms., Mr.] _____. (If relevant) I'm a member of the staff at [cite agency]. I'd like to talk to you about your background and get to know you better. OK? (If needed, explain the purpose of the interview.)

Family Background

2. I'd like to begin by learning about your family. Where did you grow up?
3. What was your home like?
4. And your neighborhood. What was it like?
5. Who was mainly responsible for you?
6. Do you have any sisters and brothers?
(If yes, go to question 7; if no, go to question 18.)
7. How many sisters and brothers do you have?
8. Tell me about them.
9. (If needed) How old are they?
10. (If needed) Where do they live?
11. (If needed) What do they do?
12. (If needed) How are they getting along?
13. Did you get along with them when you were growing up?
14. What kind of relationship did you have with them?
15. How do you get along with them now?
16. Is there anything else you want to tell me about your sisters and brothers?
17. (If yes) Go ahead.
18. Tell me about your parents.
19. (If needed) Are they still living?
(If no, go to question 20; if yes, go to question 22.)
20. When did they die?
21. How did they die?
(Go to question 26.)
22. How old are they?
23. Are they married to each other?
24. (If no) Tell me about that.
25. (If divorced) How old were you when they got divorced?
26. Do you remember hearing your parents argue?
(If yes, go to question 27; if no, go to question 31.)
27. What did your parents argue about?
28. Tell me more about their arguments.
29. (If needed) Did your parents ever quarrel about money?
30. (If yes) Tell me about that.
31. Did your father ever hurt your mother?
32. (If yes) How did he hurt her?
33. Did your mother ever hurt your father?
34. (If yes) How did she hurt him?
35. What type of work did [does] your father do?
36. Was your father ever unemployed?
37. (If yes) What was it like when he wasn't working?
38. Was your family ever on welfare?
39. (If yes) What was it like getting financial assistance from the government?
40. What type of work did [does] your mother do?
41. (If relevant) Was your mother ever unemployed?
42. (If yes) What was it like when she wasn't working?
43. Did you practice a religion at home?
44. Tell me about that.
45. (If needed) Did you go to church when you were growing up?…What religion was the church associated with?
46. Did your father drink too much alcohol?
47. (If yes) What was it like when he was drinking alcohol?
48. And how about drugs? Did he use drugs?
49. (If yes) What was it like when he was using drugs?
50. Did your mother drink too much alcohol?
51. (If yes) What was it like when she was drinking alcohol?
52. And how about drugs? Did she use drugs?
53. (If yes) What was it like when she was using drugs?
54. Did anyone in your family have any psychological or emotional problems?
(If yes, go to question 55; if no, go to question 59.)
55. Who in your family had these problems?
56. What problems did they have?
57. Were they ever treated by a specialist or hospitalized for treatment for their problems?

58. (If yes) Did the treatment help?
59. Did anyone in your family ever commit suicide?
    (If yes, go to question 60; if no, go to question 62.)
60. Who in your family committed suicide?
61. How did it affect you?
62. Were any of the members of your family ever in trouble with the police?
    (If yes, go to question 63; if no, go to question 65.)
63. Who in the family was in trouble with the police?
64. What kind of trouble were they in?
65. (If relevant) Did your parents have sexual affairs with other people when they were married [living together]?
66. (If yes) Tell me what you know about the sexual affairs they had.
67. Is there anything else you want to tell me about the problems your family had?
68. (If yes) Go ahead.
69. How did you get along with your mother?
70. (If needed) Tell me more about how you got along with her.
71. (If relevant) And how do you get along with your mother now?
72. What do you like about your mother?
73. What do you dislike about your mother?
74. How did you get along with your father?
75. (If needed) Tell me more about how you got along with him.
76. (If relevant) And how do you get along with your father now?
77. What do you like about your father?
78. What do you dislike about your father?
79. Were you ever physically punished?
80. (If yes) Tell me about that.
81. What sort of physical or sexual contact occurred in your family?
82. (If needed) Were any of your brothers or sisters physically or sexually abused?
83. (If yes) Tell me about that.
84. (If needed) Were you ever physically or sexually abused by a family member or anyone else?
85. (If yes) Tell me about who abused you.
86. (If needed) And how were you abused?
87. Were you ever placed in a foster home?
    (If yes, go to question 88; if no, go to question 91.)
88. What was it like to be there?
89. How old were you when you first went into a foster home?
90. How many years did you spend in the foster home[s]?
91. Have you ever lived in other types of places, like a group home or a residential treatment facility?
92. (If yes) Tell me about that.
93. Were you ever a ward of the court?
94. (If yes) Tell me about that.
95. Is there anything else you want to tell me about your parents?
96. (If yes) Go ahead.

Friends

97. Did you have friends when you were a child?
    (If yes, go to question 98; if no, go to question 105.)
98. How did you get along with your friends?
99. How did your parents accept your friends?
100. Tell me about your best friend, if you had one.
101. Were you ever in a gang?
102. (If yes) Tell me about the gang.
103. Is there anything else you want to tell me about your friends?
104. (If yes) Go ahead.
    (Go to question 106.)
105. Tell me why you didn't have friends.

Acting-Out Behavior

106. Did you ever get into trouble with the police?
107. (If yes) What kind of trouble did you get into?
108. Did you ever run away from home?
109. (If yes) Tell me about your running away from home.
110. Were you ever placed in a juvenile hall or other institution?
    (If yes, go to question 111; if no, go to question 114.)
111. What happened?
112. What kind of institution were you in?
113. What was it like to be there?

Medical and Psychiatric History

114. Now I'd like to ask you about any problems you had growing up and your medical history. First, did you have nightmares as a child?
115. (If yes) Tell me about your nightmares.
116. Were you afraid of anything in particular when you were a child?
117. (If yes) Tell me about what you were afraid of.
118. Did you have problems with wetting the bed when you were growing up?
    (If yes, go to question 119; if no, go to question 122.)
119. Were your parents concerned about your wetting the bed?
120. And what did they do about your bed-wetting?
121. At what age did you stay dry all night?
122. Did you have any serious physical illnesses when you were growing up?
123. (If yes) Tell me about them.
124. And did you have any serious accidents when you were growing up?
125. (If yes) Tell me about them. (Pay particular attention to head injuries, unconsciousness, loss of memory, etc.)
126. (If needed) Did you ever injure your head?
127. (If yes) Tell me about your head injury.
128. (If needed) Have you ever had seizures?
129. (If yes) Tell me about your seizures.
130. (If needed) Have you ever had blackouts?
131. (If yes) Tell me about your blackouts.
132. Have you ever been hospitalized?
133. (If yes) Tell me about it.
134. (If needed) When were you hospitalized?…For how long?…For what condition?
135. Did you have any other problems that we didn't talk about?
136. (If yes) Tell me about them.
137. How did your parents treat you when you were sick?
138. Now I'd like to talk about problems that you may have had as an adolescent and as an adult. Tell me about any serious illness or accidents that you had.

139. (If needed) What was your condition?...When did it happen?...For how long were you sick [hurt]?...What kind of treatment did you receive?
140. (If needed) Have you ever had a venereal disease?
141. (If yes) Tell me about the venereal disease you had.
142. (If needed) Are you HIV positive?
143. (If yes) Tell me about that.
144. Do you have trouble sleeping at night now?
145. (If yes) Tell me about your difficulty in sleeping.
146. Do you have any nightmares now?
147. (If yes) Tell me about your nightmares.
148. Have you ever had any physical problems for which doctors couldn't find a cause?
149. (If yes) Tell me about these problems.

Use of Drugs
150. Have you ever used drugs?
     (If yes, go to question 151; if no, go to question 166.)
151. Tell me about your use of drugs.
     (Ask questions 152 to 156, as needed.)
152. What drugs did you use?
153. Have you ever been in a drug rehabilitation program?
154. (If yes) Tell me about the program.
155. (If needed) Did the program help you?
156. Do you use drugs now?
     (If yes, go to question 157; if no, go to question 166.)
157. Tell me about your current use of drugs.
     (Ask questions 158 to 165, as needed.)
158. What drugs do you use?
159. How often do you use them?
160. How much do they cost you each week?
161. How do you pay for them?
162. How do you get them when you need them?
163. Do you think of yourself as being dependent on the drugs?
164. Has the use of drugs interfered with your relationship with your family...with your work...with your friendships?
165. (If yes) Tell me about that.

Use of Alcohol
166. Did you ever drink alcohol?
     (If yes, go to question 167; if no, go to question 186.)
167. Tell me about your use of alcohol.
     (Ask questions 168 to 176, as needed.)
168. What do you drink?
169. How much alcohol did you drink daily [weekly]?
170. Did you have problems handling alcohol?
171. (If yes) What problems did you have?
172. Has the use of alcohol ever interfered with your relationship with your family...with your work...with your friendships?
173. (If yes) Tell me about that.
174. (If relevant) Have you ever been in an alcohol rehabilitation program?
175. (If yes) Tell me about the program.
176. (If needed) Did it help you?
177. Do you use alcohol now?
     (If yes, go to question 178; if no, go to question 186.)
178. Tell me about your current use of alcohol.
     (Ask questions 179 to 185, as needed.)

179. What do you drink now?
180. How often do you drink?
181. How much does your drinking cost you each week?
182. How do you pay for the alcohol?
183. Do you think of yourself as being dependent on the alcohol?
184. Does the use of alcohol now interfere with your relationship with your family...with your work...with your friendships?
185. (If yes) Tell me about that.

Gambling
186. Did you ever gamble?
     (If yes, go to question 187; if no, go to question 206.)
187. Tell me about your gambling.
     (Ask questions 188 to 196, as needed.)
188. What did you gamble on?
189. Where did you gamble?
190. How often did you gamble each week?
191. How much did you usually win or lose each week [each time you gamble]?
192. Did you get restless or irritable if you couldn't gamble?
193. Have you ever spent time gambling when you should have been doing something else?
194. (If yes) Tell me about that.
195. Has your gambling led to debt, family problems, or legal problems?
196. (If yes) Tell me about the problems you've had.
197. Do you gamble now?
     (If yes, go to question 198; if no, go to question 206.)
198. Tell me about your current gambling.
     (Ask questions 199 to 205, as needed.)
199. What kind of gambling do you do now?
200. How often do you gamble now?
201. How much does your gambling cost you each week?
202. How do you pay for the gambling?
203. Do you think of yourself as being dependent on gambling?
204. Does gambling now interfere with your relationship with your family...with your work...with your friendships?
205. (If yes) Tell me about that.

Treatment for Emotional Problems
206. Have you ever been treated for emotional problems?
     (If yes, go to question 207; if no, go to question 210.)
207. What problems have you been treated for?
208. Who treated you?
209. What treatment did you get?
210. Have you ever tried to commit suicide?
211. (If yes) Tell me about your attempt[s] to commit suicide.
212. Do you think about committing suicide?
213. (If yes) Tell me about these thoughts.
214. Do you have a plan to kill yourself?
215. (If yes) Tell me about it.
216. Do you ever have the urge to hurt or harm others?
217. (If yes) Tell me about these feelings.
218. Do you feel that you're accident prone?
219. (If yes) Tell me about that.
220. In general, how are you getting along now?

221. Tell me more about that.
222. What kind of stresses are you under now?
223. Are you now being treated by a psychologist or psychiatrist?
   (If yes, go to question 224; if no, go to question 228.)
224. For what conditions?
225. What treatment are you getting?
226. Are you following your treatment plan—taking medications, attending therapy sessions, etc.?
227. (If no) Tell me about why you're not following the treatment plan.
228. Are you now being treated by a medical doctor?
   (If yes, go to question 229; if no, go to question 233.)
229. For what conditions?
230. What treatment are you getting?
231. Are you following your treatment plan—taking medications, not smoking, etc.?
232. (If no) Tell me about why you're not following the treatment plan.
233. Whom can you turn to for help when you are under stress?
234. (If needed) How do you feel about going to others for help?
235. What changes would you like to make in your life?
236. Is there anything else you want to tell me about your medical and psychiatric history?
237. (If yes) Go ahead.

Educational History

238. I'd now like to discuss your schooling. Tell me about your education.
239. (If needed) What was the highest grade of school you finished?
240. What grades did you get in elementary school?
241. What grades did you get in high school?
242. (If relevant) What grades did you get in college?
243. Were you ever placed in special classes?
244. (If yes) Tell me about the classes.
245. Did you ever repeat a grade?
246. (If yes) Tell me about that.
247. Were you ever told that you had a learning disability?
   (If yes, go to question 248; if no, go to question 251.)
248. Tell me about that.
249. What type of help did you get, if any?
250. (If help obtained) How did it help?
251. How did you do on standardized tests you took in school?
252. Did you ever have an intelligence test?
253. (If yes) How did you do?
254. Did you have any problems in school?
255. (If yes) What problems did you have?
256. Did you skip a lot of days of school?
257. (If yes) Tell me about your skipping school.
258. Were you ever suspended from school?
259. (If yes) Tell me about your suspension[s].
260. Were you ever expelled from school?
261. (If yes) Tell me about it.
262. When you were growing up, were you afraid to go to school?
263. (If yes) What about school made you afraid?

264. Did you ever see a school psychologist, school counselor, or anyone else about school problems?
   (If yes, go to question 265; if no, go to question 267.)
265. What happened when you saw this person?
266. (If needed) Did it help?
267. Is there anything else you want to tell me about your schooling?
268. (If yes) Go ahead.

Military History

269. I'd now like to ask you about another topic. Were you ever in the military?
   (If yes, go to question 270; if no, go to question 288.)
270. What branch of the service were you in?
271. What was your job in the [cite service]?
272. How long were you in the [cite service]?
273. Were you ever hospitalized while you were in the military?
274. (If yes) Tell me about your hospitalization.
275. Were you ever disciplined while you were in the military?
276. (If yes) What kind of disciplinary actions did you face?
277. (If needed) Were you ever court-martialed?
278. (If yes) Tell me about the court martial.
279. Were you in combat?
280. (If yes) Tell me about it.
281. (If needed) Were you injured in combat?
282. (If yes) Tell me about your injury.
283. (If relevant) Did any of your comrades get injured or die during combat?
284. (If yes) Tell me about their injuries or deaths.
285. What type of discharge did you receive?
286. Is there anything else you want to tell me about your military history?
287. (If yes) Go ahead.

Vocational History

288. Let's turn to your job history. What is your occupation?
289. Are you employed?
   (If yes, go to question 290; if no, go to question 295.)
290. What kind of work are you doing?
291. How do you like your work?
292. How do you get along with your bosses?
293. How do you get along with your coworkers?
294. And what is your salary?
   (Go to question 298.)
295. Since you're not working, how do you support yourself?
296. How do you feel about not working?
297. How do you spend your time?
298. When you were growing up, what did you want to be?
299. If you could do anything you wanted, what would that be?
300. What jobs have you had in the past?
   (If interviewee had previous jobs, go to question 301; if interviewee had no previous jobs, go to question 313.)
301. How did you feel about these jobs?
302. On your previous jobs, how did you get along with your supervisors?
303. And how did you get along with your coworkers?
304. How much did you earn on your previous jobs?
305. Were you ever fired from a job?

306. (If yes) What happened?
307. Have you ever been injured on a job?
308. (If yes) Tell me about your injury.
309. Have you ever received unemployment or welfare checks?
310. (If yes) Tell me about that.
311. Is there anything else you want to tell me about your work history?
312. (If yes) Go ahead.

Marital History

313. I'd like to talk to you about relationships. Are you married or in a relationship?
    (If yes, go to question 314; if no, go to question 412.)
314. Which one?
315. Tell me about your present marriage [relationship].
316. (If needed) When did you get married [start your relationship]?
317. (If needed) Tell me about the reason you got married [started the relationship].
318. (If needed) How would you describe your marriage [relationship] at this time?
319. What is your husband [wife, partner, friend, etc.] like?
320. What about him [her] pleases you?
321. What about him [her] displeases you?
322. What is the best thing about your marriage [relationship]?
323. What is there about your marriage [relationship] that could be better?
324. What kinds of things do you do together?
325. How do you feel about the things you do together?
326. Are there things about your husband [wife, partner, friend, etc.] that you would like changed?
327. (If yes) What things would you like changed?
328. How do you show your affection for your husband [wife, partner, friend, etc.]?
329. How does your husband [wife, partner, friend, etc.] show his [her] affection for you?
330. Does your husband [wife, partner, friend, etc.] know when you are upset?
    (If yes, go to question 331; if no, go to question 333.)
331. What does your husband [wife, partner, friend, etc.] do when you are upset?
332. How do you feel about that?
333. Do you know when your husband [wife, partner, friend, etc.] is upset?
334. What do you do when your husband [wife, partner, friend, etc.] is upset?
335. Can you depend on your husband [wife, partner, friend, etc.]?
336. Tell me more about that.

Perpetration of Physical Violence

337. Have you ever been physically violent with your present husband [wife, partner, friend, etc.]?
    (If yes, go to question 338; if no, go to question 366.)
338. Tell me more about that.
    (Ask questions 339 to 365, as needed.)
339. What happens when you're physically violent with your husband [wife, partner, friend, etc.]?

340. How many times did you [cite act] your husband [wife, partner, friend, etc.] in the past year?
341. Did you ever use any weapons?
342. (If yes) What weapons did you use?
343. When was the first time you were physically violent with your husband [wife, partner, friend, etc.]?
344. When was the last time you were physically violent with your husband [wife, partner, friend, etc.]?
345. What is the worst thing you have ever done to your husband [wife, partner, friend, etc.]?
346. What happens that sets things off?
347. (If needed) Were you ever using alcohol or drugs before an incident began?
348. (If yes) Tell me about what you used.
349. How does your husband [wife, partner, friend, etc.] react to the physical violence?
350. Tell me about the reason you do it.
351. How do you feel after the physical violence has taken place?
352. Has anybody ever tried to stop what was happening?
    (If yes, go to question 353; if no, go to question 357.)
353. Who tried to stop it?
354. What did he [she, they] do?
355. (If needed) Were the police ever called?
356. (If yes) What did they do?
357. How soon after you met your present husband [wife, partner, friend, etc.] did the physical violence begin?
358. Have you noticed that the violence is happening more often lately?
359. (If yes) Tell me about that.
360. Have you noticed that the violence is getting worse lately?
361. (If yes) Tell me about that.
362. What kinds of injuries has your husband [wife, partner, friend, etc.] had as a result of your [cite act]?
363. (If male) Was your wife [partner, friend, etc.] pregnant when you [cite act]?
364. Have you ever received help or undergone treatment for this problem?
365. (If yes) Tell me about that.

Reactions to Physical Violence

366. Has your present husband [wife, partner, friend, etc.] ever been physically violent with you?
    (If yes, go to question 367; if no, go to question 397.)
367. Tell me more about that.
    (Ask questions 368 to 396, as needed.)
368. What happens that sets things off?
369. (If needed) What do you and your husband [wife, partner, friend, etc.] argue over most?
370. What happens when your husband [wife, partner, friend, etc.] is physically violent with you?
371. How many times has your husband [wife, partner, friend, etc.] been physically violent with you in the past year?
372. Did your husband [wife, partner, friend, etc.] ever use any weapons?
373. (If yes) What weapons did you your husband [wife, partner, friend, etc.] use?
374. When was the first time your husband [wife, partner, friend, etc.] was physically violent with you?

375. When was the last time your husband [wife, partner, friend, etc.] was physically violent with you?
376. What is the worst thing your husband [wife, partner, friend, etc.] has ever done to you?
377. (If needed) Does your husband [wife, partner, friend, etc.] ever use alcohol or drugs before an incident begins?
378. (If yes) Tell me about what your husband [wife, partner, friend, etc.] uses.
379. How do you react to your his [her] physical violence?
380. Tell me about the reason you think your husband [wife, partner, friend, etc.] does it.
381. Has anybody ever tried to stop what was happening? (If yes, go to question 382; if no, go to question 386.)
382. Who tried to stop it?
383. What did he [she, they] do?
384. (If needed) Were the police ever called?
385. (If yes) What did they do?
386. (If needed) Have you tried to stop the violence by obtaining a restraining order, moving to a shelter, or taking any other action?
387. (If yes) Tell me what you did.
388. How soon after you met your present husband [wife, partner, friend, etc.] did the physical violence begin?
389. Have you noticed that the violence is happening more often lately?
390. (If yes) Tell me about that.
391. Have you noticed that the violence is getting worse lately?
392. (If yes) Tell me about that.
393. What kinds of injuries have you had as a result of your husband's [wife's, partner's, friend's, etc.] [cite act]?
394. (If female) Were you pregnant when your husband [partner, friend, etc.] [cite act]?
395. Have you ever had to be hospitalized as a result of your husband's [wife's, partner's, friend's, etc.] [cite act]?
396. (If yes) Tell me about that.

Extramarital Sexual Relations
397. Have you ever had sex with someone other than your present husband [wife, partner, friend, etc.] since your marriage [relationship] began?
398. (If yes) With whom did you have sex?
399. Has your husband [wife, partner, friend, etc.] ever had sex with someone other than you since your marriage [relationship] began?
400. (If yes) With whom did he [she] have sex?

Feelings About Separation
401. How would you feel if your present husband [wife, partner, friend, etc.] left you?
402. Tell me about these feelings.
403. Have you ever been legally separated from your husband [wife, partner, friend, etc.]?
404. (If yes) Tell me about your separation.

Divorce
405. Have you ever been divorced? (If yes, go to question 406; if no, go to question 412.)
406. Tell me about your divorce[s].

407. What type of relationship do you have with your ex-husband [ex-wife]?
408. Was there any physical violence between you and your ex-husband [ex-wife]?
409. (If yes) Tell me about the physical violence.
410. Is there anything else you want to tell me about your marriage[s]?
411. (If yes) Go ahead.
     (Ask questions 315 to 409 about prior marriages or relationships, as needed, substituting the appropriate words to refer to the prior marriages.)

Religious Development
412. Let's talk about your religious development. Did your family practice a religion when you were growing up? (If yes, go to question 413; if no, go to question 416.)
413. Tell me about your family's religious practices.
414. Did you also practice this religion?
415. Tell me about that.
416. Do you practice a religion today?
417. (If yes) Tell me about that.
418. What do you think about religion?

Sexual Development
419. Let's turn to your sexual development. First, how did you learn about sex?
420. (If needed) What did your parents tell you about sex when you were growing up?
421. (If needed) Did you ever take a sex education course in school?
422. (If yes) What did you think of it?
423. What concerns about sex did you have when you were growing up?
424. What kind of sexual fantasies did you have when you were growing up?
425. What kind of sexual fantasies do you have now?
426. Did any member of your family ever make any sexual advances toward you when you were a child?
427. (If yes) Tell me about what happened.
428. Did you have a special boyfriend [girlfriend] when you were growing up?
429. (If yes) Tell me about that person.
430. How old were you when you had your first boyfriend [girlfriend]?
431. What sexual experiences did you have when you were growing up?
432. Do you feel sexually attracted to members of the opposite sex?
433. (If yes) Tell me about your attraction.
434. Do you feel sexually attracted to members of your own sex?
435. (If yes) Tell me about your attraction.
436. Do you feel sexually attracted to children?
437. (If yes) Tell me about your attraction to children.
438. Is there anything else that arouses you sexually?
439. (If yes) Tell me about that.
440. What, if any, concerns about sex do you have now?
441. Do you have any fears about sex?
442. (If yes) What fears do you have about sex?

443. What sexual experiences have you had since you became an adult?
(If interviewee had sexual experiences, go to question 444; if interviewee had no sexual experiences, go to question 455.)
444. How many partners have you had?
445. (If relevant) In how many years?
446. How old was the oldest person with whom you ever had sexual relations?
447. How old was the youngest person with whom you ever had sexual relations?
448. Have you ever felt that you needed to force someone to have sex with you against his [her] will?
449. (If yes) Tell me about these feelings.
450. On average, how often do you have sex?
451. Do you have one or more steady sexual partners at this time?
(If yes, go to question 452; if no, go to question 454.)
452. Tell me about your partner[s].
453. Are you satisfied with the relationship[s]? (Ask about each relationship.)
(Go to question 455.)
454. How do you feel about not having a steady sex partner?
455. Have you ever been treated for any sexual problems?
456. (If yes) Tell me about these treatments.
457. Did you ever make any sexual advances toward any member of your family when you were a child?
458. (If yes) Tell me about what happened.
459. What are your feelings about sexual relationships between family members?
460. Have you ever been sexually assaulted?
461. (If yes) Tell me about the time[s] this happened.
462. Is there anything else you want to tell me about how you feel about sex?
463. (If yes) Go ahead.

Current Family History
464. Do you have any children?
(If yes, go to question 465; if no, go to question 549.)
465. Tell me about your children.
466. How is your relationship with your children?
467. Do you get frustrated with your children?
468. (If yes) Tell me about your frustrations.
469. What kinds of things do your children do that make you upset?
470. What do you do when these things happen?
471. Whom do you turn to when you are upset with your children?
472. Do you expect your children to do things that they can't seem to do?
473. (If yes) What do you expect your children to do that they can't seem to do?

Discipline
474. How do you discipline your children?
475. (If relevant) Does your present husband [wife, partner, friend, etc.] agree with your methods of discipline?
476. (If relevant) Does your husband [wife, partner, friend, etc.] support you when you discipline your children?

477. Do you ever lose your temper when you try to discipline your children?
(If yes, go to question 478; if no, go to question 491.)
478. What do you do when you lose your temper?
479. Whom do you turn to after you lose your temper with your children?
480. What might be the reason that you lose your temper?
481. Are you violent when you lose your temper?
(If yes, go to question 482; if no, go to question 485.)
482. What do you do when you are violent?
483. Do you feel that you can control your children without resorting to violence?
484. Tell me about that.
485. (If interviewee drinks alcohol) Does drinking alcohol contribute to your losing your temper with your children?
486. (If yes) What do you do at these times?
487. (If interviewee uses drugs) Does your drug use contribute to your losing your temper with your children?
488. (If yes) What do you do at these times?
489. Are there other times when you lose your temper?
490. (If yes) Tell me about these times.

Children's Behavior Problems
491. Are your children having any problems in school?
(If yes, go to question 492; if no, go to question 494.)
492. What problems are your children having in school?
493. What is being done about these problems?
494. Are your children having problems outside the home, such as problems with friends, with the law, or with joining gangs?
495. (If yes) Tell me about that.
496. Are your children having problems at home?
(If yes, go to question 497; if no, go to question 499.)
497. What problems are your children having at home?
498. What is being done about these problems?

Children's Understanding of Feelings
499. How well do your children understand your feelings?
500. Can your children tell when you're upset?
(If yes, go to question 501; if no, go to question 503.)
501. What do your children do or say when you are upset?
502. How does that make you feel?
503. How have your children been of help to you?
504. When you're upset, do your children comfort you?
505. How does that make you feel?

Children's Emotional Problems
506. Have your children ever been treated for psychological or emotional problems?
507. (If yes) Tell me about their treatment.
508. Do your children use drugs?
509. (If yes) Tell me about their use of drugs.
510. Do your children use alcohol?
511. (If yes) Tell me about their use of alcohol.

View of Privacy and Nudity
512. Families have different views about privacy and nudity. First, I'd like to talk to you about how your family deals with privacy. Could you tell me something about that?

513. (If needed) Do you agree with what your family does?
514. And how about nudity? What is your family's attitude about nudity in the home?
515. (If needed) Do you agree with your family's attitude?

Sleeping Arrangements

516. Now I'd like to talk to you about sleeping arrangements. Where do your children sleep?
517. Did your [child, children] ever sleep in the same room with you?
518. (If yes) Tell me about that.

Discussion of Sex

(Ask questions 519 to 523, as needed; if not, go to question 524. Discussion of sex can include names and functions of body parts, as well as intercourse and pregnancy. These questions are not appropriate for parents of infants.)

519. Have you talked about sex with your children?
(If yes, to question 520; if no, go to question 523.)
520. What did you discuss?
521. How old were your children when you discussed sex with them?
522. How did they feel about the discussion?
(Go to question 524.)
523. Tell me about your decision to not discuss sex with your children.

Other Family Matters

524. (If relevant) What happens when you and your present husband [wife, partner, friend, etc.] disagree on how to handle your children?...How do you feel about that?
525. (If relevant) How does your husband [wife, partner, friend, etc.] get along with the children?
526. How important is your family to you?
527. (If needed) Tell me more about that.
528. Is there anything else you want to tell me about your family?
529. (If yes) Go ahead.

Relationship with Alleged Victim

(If alleged victim is the offender's child, ask questions 530 to 540.)

530. What about [cite alleged victim] pleases you?
531. And what displeases you about [cite alleged victim]?
532. What do you and [cite alleged victim] do together?
533. How do you know when [cite alleged victim] is happy?
534. And how do you know when [cite alleged victim] is sad?
535. What are [cite alleged victim]'s strengths?
536. And what are [cite alleged victim]'s weaknesses?
(If there is more than one child in family, go to question 537; if there is only one child, go to question 549.)
537. Is [cite alleged victim] different from the other children?
538. (If yes) In what way?
539. Do you treat [cite alleged victim] differently?
540. (If yes) How do you treat [cite alleged victim] differently than the other children?

Involvement of Children in Domestic Violence

(Ask questions 541 to 548 if there have been incidents of domestic violence in the family; if not, go to question 549.)

541. Have any of your children been involved in or observed any violent episodes between you and your present husband [wife, partner, friend, etc.]?
(If yes, go to question 542; if no, go to question 549.)
542. What have they observed?
543. How did they react?
544. How did you handle their reactions?
545. Did anyone contact Child Protective Services?
546. (If yes) Tell me about that.
547. Were the children ever removed from your home and moved to another place?
548. (If yes) Tell me about that.

Social-Recreational History

549. Let's talk about what you do in your spare time. First, how much spare time do you have?
550. What do you do in your spare time?
551. How much time do you spend doing this?
552. (If needed) What sports do you participate in?
553. (If any) Tell me about these activities.
554. Do you belong to any social clubs?
555. (If yes) Tell me about the club[s].
556. Do you have any hobbies?
557. (If yes) Tell me about them.
558. Do you belong to any professional organizations?
559. (If yes) Tell me about the organization[s].
560. Do you have friends?
(If yes, go to question 561; if no, go to question 568.)
561. Tell me about them.
562. What do you like to do together?
563. How do you get along with your friends?
564. Are you easily influenced by your friends?
565. (If yes) How do they influence you?
566. If you had a choice between being alone during your spare time and being with your friends, which would you choose?
567. Tell me about that.
(Go to question 569.)
568. Tell me why you don't have friends.
569. Do you like to do things that are dangerous?
570. (If yes) What do you like to do that is dangerous?
571. Is there anything else you want to tell me about what you do in your spare time?
572. (If yes) Go ahead.

Criminal History

573. I'd like to ask you about any criminal history you might have. Have you ever been arrested?
(If yes, go to question 574; if no, go to instructions following question 598.)
574. Tell me about your arrest[s].
575. (If needed) What did you do to get arrested?
576. How old were you when you first were arrested?
577. Have you ever been convicted of a crime?
(If yes, go to question 578; if no, go to question 597.)
578. Tell me about it.
579. Have you ever been in prison or in jail?
(If yes, go to question 580; if no, go to question 590.)
580. Tell me about your going to prison or jail.
581. (If needed) What did you do to get put in prison [jail]?
582. What was your sentence?

583. Did you serve it out, or were you released early for good behavior?
584. (If needed) What was prison [jail] like?
585. Have you ever been on parole?
    (If yes, go to question 586; if no, go to question 590.)
586. Tell me about your parole.
587. (If needed) Did you ever violate parole?
588. (If yes) How did you violate parole?
589. (If needed) Was the parole ever canceled?
590. Have you ever been on probation?
    (If yes, go to question 591; if no, go to question 597.)
591. Tell me about your probation.
592. (If needed) Why were you on probation?
593. (If needed) Did you ever violate your probation?
594. (If yes) How did you violate your probation?
595. (If needed) Was the probation ever canceled?
596. (If yes) What did you do to have your probation canceled?
597. Is there anything else you want to tell me about your criminal history?
598. (If yes) Go ahead.
    (Go to question 599 for an offender who has sexually abused one or more children; go to question 659 for an offender who has physically or psychologically abused or neglected one or more children.)

Offense History Related to Sexual Abuse
599. Tell me about why you're here today.
600. (If needed) What exactly did you do?
601. How long did [cite act] last?
602. When did it take place?
603. Where did it take place?
604. What started it?
605. Were any other children involved in [cite act]?
606. (If yes) Tell me about the other children.
607. Were any other adults involved in [cite act]?
608. (If yes) Tell me about the other adults.
609. Have you done anything like [cite act] with other children in the past?
    (If yes, go to question 610; if no, go to question 613.)
610. How often have you done this in the past?
611. How long have you been doing this with children?
612. What made you continue to do it?
613. When did you first begin [cite act] with [cite child's name]?
614. Do you prefer girls or boys?
615. Do you prefer children of any particular age?
616. Tell me about your preference.
617. Do you prefer any particular type of child?
618. (If yes) Tell me about your preference.
619. Now I'd like to learn about how you're feeling and what is going on when you [cite act]. First, how do you feel just before you do it?
620. And what is going on at that time?
621. (If needed) Are you drinking alcohol?
622. (If yes) Tell me about your drinking.
623. (If needed) Are you using drugs?
624. (If yes) Tell me about the drugs you use.
625. (If needed) Are you looking at pornographic material, like magazines or videos?

626. (If yes) Tell me about the pornographic material you look at.
627. And how do you feel when you [cite act]?
628. And when it's over, how do you feel?
629. Is there anything else you can tell me about what you are experiencing when you [cite act]?
630. (If yes) What else are you experiencing?
631. Now I'd like to ask you about the child. How do you get the child to go along with you?
    (Ask questions 632 to 638, as needed.)
632. I'm going to name different things that people might say or do to children. Let me know if you have said or done these things. OK?
633. Do you bribe the child?
634. (If yes) With what?
635. Do you threaten the child?
636. (If yes) With what?
637. Do you force the child to [cite act]?
638. (If yes) What kind of force do you use?
639. How do you think the child feels when you [cite act]?
640. And afterwards. How do you think the child feels then?
641. Do you tell the child not to say anything to anybody about what happened?
642. (If yes) What do you tell the child?
    (Ask questions 643 to 648, as needed.)
643. Do you tell the child that you will go to jail if he [she] tells anyone?
644. Do you tell the child that you will never be able to see him [her] again if he [she] tells anyone?
645. Do you tell the child that you will get into a lot of trouble if he [she] tells anyone?
646. Do you tell the child that he [she] will be taken away from his [her] family if he [she] tells anyone?
647. Do you tell the child that his [her] mother [father] will get divorced if he [she] tells anyone?
648. Do you tell the child that if people find out they will think that he [she] is bad because he [she] did these things?
649. How do you feel about [cite act] with the child?
650. (If needed) Do you feel sexual pleasure… disappointment…disgust?
651. Do you think that it is okay to [cite act]?
652. Tell me more about that.
653. Do you think you will continue to [cite act] in the future?
654. Tell me about your answer.
655. Do you want to stop [cite act]?
656. (If yes) What will help you stop [cite act]?
657. Is there anything else you want to tell me about why you are here today?
658. (If yes) Go ahead.
    (Go to question 699.)

Offense History Related to Physical Abuse, Psychological Abuse, or Neglect
659. Tell me about why you are here today.
660. (If needed) What exactly did you do?
661. How long did [cite act] last?
662. When did it take place?
663. Where did it take place?
664. What started it?

665. Were any other children there when it happened?
666. (If yes) Tell me about the other children.
667. Were any other adults there when it happened?
668. (If yes) Tell me about the other adults.
669. Have you done anything like [cite act] with other children in the past?
    (If yes, go to question 670; if no, go to question 674.)
670. To whom did you do it?
671. How often have you done this in the past?
672. How long have you been doing this with children?
673. What made you continue to do it?
674. When did you first begin [cite act] with [cite child's name]?
675. Now I'd like to learn about how you're feeling and what is going on when you [cite act]. First, how do you feel just before you do it?
676. And what is going on at that time?
677. (If needed) Are you drinking alcohol?
678. (If yes) Tell me about your drinking.
679. (If needed) Are you taking drugs?
680. (If yes) Tell me about the drugs you use.
681. And how do you feel when you [cite act]?
682. And when it's over, how do you feel?
683. Is there anything else you can tell me about what you are experiencing when you [cite act]?
684. (If yes) What else are you experiencing?
685. Now I'd like to ask you about the child. How do you think the child feels when you [cite act]?
686. And afterwards. How do you think the child feels then?
687. Do you tell the child not to say anything to anybody about what happened?
688. (If yes) What do you tell the child?
    (Ask questions 689 to 693, as needed.)
689. Do you tell the child that you will go to jail if he [she] tells anyone?
690. Do you tell the child that you will never be able to see him [her] again if he [she] tells anyone?
691. Do you tell the child that you will get into a lot of trouble if he [she] tells anyone?
692. Do you tell the child that he [she] will be taken away from his [her] family if he [she] tells anyone?
693. Do you tell the child that his [her] mother [father] will get divorced if he [she] tells anyone?
694. How do you feel about [cite act] with the child?
695. Do you think you will continue to [cite act] in the future?
696. Tell me about your answer.
697. Is there anything else you want to tell me about why you are here today?
698. (If yes) Go ahead.

Attitude Toward Treatment
699. Do you think that you have a problem?
    (If yes, go to question 700; if no, go to question 705.)
700. Tell me about your answer.
701. Do you want any help for your problem?
702. Tell me about that.
703. Is there anything else you want to tell me about getting help for your problem?
704. (If yes) Go ahead.
    (Go to question 706.)
705. Tell me why you think you don't have a problem.

Concluding Questions
706. Is there anything I haven't asked you that you think is important?
707. (If yes) Tell me about what I left out.
708. Is there anything else you would like to tell me?
709. (If yes) Go ahead.
710. Is there anything you would like to ask me?
711. (If yes) Go ahead.
712. Thank you for talking with me. If you have any questions or if you want to talk to me again, please call me. Here is my card.

Note. Table F-19 in this Appendix contains a more detailed interview for individuals who are experiencing domestic violence.
Source: Adapted, in part, from Burgess, Groth, Holmstrom, and Sgroi (1978), Faller (1988), and Sonkin, Martin, and Walker (1985).

Table F-21

Semistructured Interview Questions for a Mother to Obtain a Detailed Developmental History Covering Her Child's Early Years and to Evaluate Her Parenting Skills

The questions in this semistructured interview supplement those in Table F-36 in this Appendix, which should be used first. You then have the choice of following up in areas related to infancy and toddler/preschool years. The questions are designed not only to obtain information about the child but also to evaluate parenting skills. Select the questions that you believe are applicable to the specific case and that complement those in Table F-36. If you want information about the mother's obstetric history, you can say, for example, "I'd now like to get some more information about [cite child's name] development. I would first like to learn about the time before [cite child's name] was born." If you decide to begin the semistructured interview with another section, use an appropriate introduction. The questions can be used to inquire about an infant or toddler/preschooler. Sections that pertain specifically to infants or toddlers/preschoolers are so identified in the section headings.

Additional Questions About Maternal Obstetric History
1. How old were you when [cite child's name] was born?
2. Have you had any other pregnancies?
    (If yes, go to question 3; if no, go to question 9.)
3. Tell me about them. (Pay particular attention to miscarriages, abortions, and premature births and their outcomes.)
4. How many living children do you have?
5. (If more than one child) How old are they now?
6. (If any child died) How did your child die?
7. (If needed) Tell me about what happened.
8. (If needed) How old was your child when he [she] died?
9. I'd like to talk to you about your pregnancy with [cite child's name]. What was your pregnancy like?
    (Ask questions 10 to 13, as needed.)
10. Was it planned?

11. (If yes) How long did it take you to become pregnant?
12. Did you have any illnesses or problems during pregnancy? (Pay particular attention to vaginal bleeding, fevers, rashes, hospitalizations, weight gain, weight loss, vomiting, hypertension, proteinuria [the presence of an excess of protein in the urine; also called albuminuria], preeclampsia [a toxemia of late pregnancy characterized by hypertension, albuminuria, and edema], general infections, and urinary tract infections.)
13. Were one or more sonograms performed?
(If yes, go to question 14; if no, go to question 16.)
14. How many were performed?
15. What did it [they] show?
16. Was your blood type incompatible with that of [cite child's name]?
17. (If yes) Tell me about that.
18. Did you take any medications or street drugs during pregnancy?
19. (If yes) What did you take? (Pay particular attention to prescription drugs; over-the-counter pills; cocaine/crack; marijuana/pot; hallucinogens, such as LSD, PCP, DMT, mescaline, and mushrooms; stimulants, such as uppers, speed, amphetamines, crystal, crank, and Dexedrine; tranquilizers, such as downers, Valium, Elavil, quaaludes, Stelazine, barbiturates, and thorazine; opiates, such as morphine, Demerol, Percodan, codeine, Darvon, Darvocet, heroin, and methadone; *and other drugs that may affect the development of the fetus.* If the medicine or drug is listed here or if it is any drug that may affect the development of the fetus, go to question 20; if not, go to question 25.)
20. How often did you take it?
21. When during your pregnancy did you take it?
22. How did it make you feel?
23. Did you tell your health care provider that you were taking [cite drug]?
24. (If yes) Tell me about that.
25. Did you drink alcohol during your pregnancy?
(If yes, go to question 26; if no, go to question 32.)
26. What did you drink?
27. How often did you drink alcohol?
28. And how much did you drink each time?
29. When during your pregnancy did you start drinking?
30. Did you drink throughout your pregnancy?
31. Did you tell your health care provider that you were drinking alcohol during your pregnancy?
32. Did you smoke cigarettes during your pregnancy?
(If yes, go to question 33; if no, go to question 37.)
33. And how many cigarettes did you smoke each day?
34. When during your pregnancy did you start smoking?
35. Did you smoke throughout your pregnancy?
36. Did you tell your health care provider that you were smoking during your pregnancy?
37. Did you have x-rays taken during your pregnancy?
38. (If yes) Tell me about them.
39. Were you exposed to chemicals or other potentially harmful substances during your pregnancy?
40. (If yes) Tell me about what you were exposed to.
41. Did you see a health care provider during your pregnancy?
(If yes, go to question 42; if no, go to question 44.)

42. What kind of health care provider did you see during your pregnancy?
43. How many visits did you make?
(Go to question 45.)
44. What was the reason you did not see a health care provider?
45. Did you see anyone else for care during your pregnancy?
46. (If yes) Tell me about whom you saw.
47. Overall, was your pregnancy with [cite child's name] a good experience or a bad experience?
48. Tell me about your answer.
49. In general, how would you rate your health during your pregnancy with [cite child's name]?
50. Tell me about your answer.

Additional Questions About Labor, Delivery, Infant's Condition at Birth, and Immediate Postpartum Period for Mother
1. Now I'd like to talk to you about your labor and delivery. Tell me about your labor and delivery.
(Ask questions 2 to 14, as needed.)
2. What were your thoughts and feelings during labor?
3. Was [cite child's name] born on time?
4. (If early) How early was [cite child's name] born?
5. (If late) How late was [cite child's name] born?
6. How long did the labor last?
7. What kind of delivery did you have?
8. (If needed) Was it normal…breech…Caesarean… forceps…induced?
9. (If delivery was breech, Caesarean, forceps, or induced) Why was this type of delivery needed?
10. How did the delivery go?
11. (If needed) Were there any complications at delivery?
12. (If yes) Tell me about them.
13. Were you given anything for pain during labor?
14. (If yes) Tell me about it.
15. Were labor and delivery what you expected?
16. What were your first impressions of your new baby?
17. Was the baby's father present during delivery?
18. (If yes) What were his first impressions of the new baby?
19. How was [cite child's name] right after he [she] was born?
20. What was [cite child's name]'s weight at birth?
21. What was [cite child's name]'s length at birth?
22. What was [cite child's name]'s skin color?
23. Did [cite child's name] cry soon after birth?
24. Do you know [cite child's name]'s Apgar score?
25. (If yes) What was it?
26. Did you want to hold [cite child's name] right away?
27. Were you allowed to hold [cite child's name]?
28. (If father was present) Was the baby's father allowed to hold [cite child's name]?
29. Did you have any physical problems immediately after [cite child's name] was born?
30. (If yes) Tell me about them.
31. Did you have any psychological problems after [cite child's name] was born?
32. (If yes) Tell me about them.
33. Did you have a rooming-in arrangement with the baby?

34. (If yes) What was it like to have the baby in the room with you?
    (Go to question 36.)
35. Tell me your reason for not having a rooming-in arrangement.
36. How did you spend your time at home with [cite child's name] in the first few days after he [she] was born?
37. After the first few days, how much time did you spend at home with [cite child's name]?
38. Was [cite child's name] breastfed or bottlefed?
39. How did that go?
    (If the father is in the picture, go to question 40; if not, go to question 45.)
40. Did [cite child's name]'s father also spend time with him [her]?
41. What was their relationship like at this time?
42. (If needed) How did he feel about the baby?
43. Did the baby's father help you during this time?
44. Tell me about that.
45. Did [cite child's name] have any health problems following birth?
46. (If yes) Tell me about them.
47. Was [cite child's name] in a special care nursery in the hospital for observation or treatment?
    (If yes, go to question 48; if no, go to next section, as needed.)
48. Tell me about the reason that [cite child's name] was in a special care nursery.
49. Did you visit [cite child's name] when he [she] was in the special care nursery?
50. Did you feed [cite child's name] when he [she] was in the special care nursery?
51. How did you feel about having [cite child's name] stay in the special care nursery?
52. And how many days old was [cite child's name] when he [she] went home from the special care nursery?
    (If the father is in the picture, go to question 53; if not, end this section.)
53. Did the baby's father visit [cite child's name] when he [she] was in the special care nursery?
54. Did the baby's father feed [cite child's name] when he [she] was in the special care nursery?
55. How did the baby's father feel about having [cite child's name] stay in the special care nursery?

Additional Questions About Infant's Attachment
1. When [cite child's name] came home from the hospital, what was it like to have him [her] home?
2. Did you feel you knew the baby?
3. Tell me about that.
4. Did you feel the baby knew you?
5. Tell me about that.
6. How was [cite child's name]'s first few weeks of life at home?
7. Did [cite child's name] have any problems?
8. (If needed) Did [cite child's name] have problems with eating…drinking…sleeping…alertness…irritability?
9. (If yes) Tell me about [cite child's name]'s problems. (Inquire about the types of problems, their severity, what the parent did, treatment, outcomes, and so forth.)
10. Was it easy or difficult to comfort [cite child's name]?

11. How did you go about comforting [cite child's name]?
12. Was [cite child's name] too good—that is, did he [she] demand little or no care?
13. (If yes) What did you think about this?
14. Was [cite child's name] alert as a baby?
15. (If no) Tell me about how [cite child's name] reacted.
16. What was [cite child's name]'s mood generally?
17. How well did he [she] adjust to new things or routines?
18. How did he [she] respond to new people?
19. Was he [she] cuddly or rigid?
20. Was he [she] overactive or underactive?
21. Did he [she] engage in any tantrums…rocking behavior …head banging?
22. Did [cite child's name] develop a regular pattern of eating and sleeping?
23. (If no) Tell me about that.
24. Were there any surprises during [cite child's name]'s first weeks of life at home?
25. What was most enjoyable about taking care of [cite child's name]?
26. And what was least enjoyable about taking care of [cite child's name]?
27. What was most difficult about taking care of [cite child's name]?
28. What was easiest about taking care of [cite child's name]?
29. How did you feel about [cite child's name] during his [her] first few weeks of life at home?
30. (If father is in the picture) How did his [her] father feel about [cite child's name] during his [her] first few weeks of life?
31. (If other children in family) How did the other children in the family react to [cite child's name]?
32. (If needed) Did the other children show any signs of jealousy?
33. (If yes) How did they demonstrate their jealousy?
34. And how did you [you and your husband, you and the baby's father] handle the jealousy?
35. Did you have confidence in yourself as a parent during the first six months of [cite child's name]'s life?
36. Tell me about that.
37. What kind of adjustments did you [you and your family] have to make?
38. How did your extended family react to [cite child's name]?

Additional Questions About Infant's Responsiveness (if infant is focus of interview)
1. Does [cite child's name] respond to your voice?
2. When you pick [cite child's name] up, does he [she] become quiet?
3. Does [cite child's name] smile?
4. Does [cite child's name] look at you when you try to talk to or play with him [her]?
5. (If no) What does [cite child's name] do instead?
6. What sounds does [cite child's name] make?
7. Can [cite child's name] reach out and grasp a person's face or finger?
8. Can [cite child's name] tell the difference between strangers and familiar people?
9. Can [cite child's name] play with other people?
10. How does [cite child's name] respond to new people?

11. How does [cite child's name] respond to being in a new place?
12. How often does [cite child's name] want to be held?
13. Does [cite child's name] like physical contact, such as when you gently touch his [her] face, hands, and arms?
14. Is there any physical activity that [cite child's name] seems to enjoy especially?

Additional Questions About Infant's Crying, Adjustment to Caregiving Situation, Behavior in Public, and Unusual Behavior (if infant is focus of interview)
1. When does [cite child's name] cry?
2. What do you do when [cite child's name] cries?
3. Why do you think [cite child's name] cries?
4. (If needed) When [cite child's name] cries, does it usually mean that something is really wrong or is it that something is bothering him [her] only a little bit and he [she] wants attention?
5. Can you tell the difference between the types of crying [cite child's name] does?
6. (If yes) How?
7. (If no) What does he [she] do that makes it difficult to know what his [her] crying means?
8. With whom do you leave [cite child's name] when you go out?
9. How do you feel about leaving [cite child's name]?
10. Do you leave [cite child's name] at a day care center, at somebody's house, or at your house with a sitter during any part of the week?
    (If yes, go to question 11; if no, go to question 28.)
11. Where do you leave him [her]?
12. Tell me about the reason you leave [cite child's name] there.
13. (If day care center or someone's house) How did you find out about [cite place where child is cared for]?
14. Are you satisfied with the way [cite child's name] is cared for there?
15. How is [cite child's name] getting along at [cite place where child is cared for]?
16. (If needed) Is [cite child's name] having any problems there?
17. (If yes) Tell me about them.
18. (If needed) How does [cite child's name] get along with the child care provider[s]?
19. And how does [cite child's name] get along with the other children?
20. Do you have a chance to talk regularly about [cite child's name] with the person[s] taking care of him [her]?
21. How long does it take you to get to [cite place where child is cared for]?
22. How does [cite child's name] act when you leave him [her] at [cite place where child is cared for]?
    (If behavior is not satisfactory, go to question 23; if behavior is satisfactory, go to question 27.)
23. How do you feel when [cite child's name] acts this way?
24. Does [cite child's name] always show that he [she] is upset in the same way?
25. What do you do when [cite child's name] is upset to quiet him [her]?
26. How does it help?

27. How does [cite child's name] react when you pick him [her] up from the [cite place where child is cared for]?
28. How do you feel about taking [cite child's name] out in public?
29. How does [cite child's name] behave when he [she] is outside the home?
30. How does [cite child's name] react when you take him [her] to a friend's home?
    (If there are problems or concerns, go to question 31; otherwise, go to question 33.)
31. How do you handle these problems?
32. What seems to work best?
33. Does [cite child's name] have any unusual behaviors?
    (If yes, go to question 34; if no, end this section.)
34. What unusual behaviors does [cite child's name] have?
35. How often does [cite child's name] [cite unusual behavior]?
36. What is most likely to bring on [cite unusual behavior]?
37. What situations seem to make [cite child's name]'s [cite unusual behavior] worse?
38. What do you do at these times?
39. What works best?
40. Is there any connection between what [cite child's name] eats and [cite unusual behavior]?
41. How do you feel about taking care of [cite child's name] when he [she] behaves in this way?

Additional Questions About Infant's Play, Language, Communication, and Problem-Solving Skills (if infant is focus of interview)
1. What does [cite child's name] play?
2. What toys does [cite child's name] like to play with?
3. What is [cite child's name]'s favorite toy?
4. Does [cite child's name] like to do the same activity over and over again?
5. What sounds does [cite child's name] make?
6. How long has he [she] been making these sounds?
7. In which situations does [cite child's name] make sounds?
8. (If needed) Does he [she] makes sounds early in the morning in his [her] crib…while riding in the car…when other children are around…when playing by himself [herself]…when adults are talking…when someone is talking on the phone…when in a quiet room?
9. At what times during the day does [cite child's name] make the most sounds?
10. What is happening at these times?
11. Does [cite child's name] seem to be trying to tell you something as he [she] babbles or makes sounds?
12. Do you have any idea what [cite child's name] is trying to say when he [she] makes sounds?
13. How does [cite child's name] let you know that he [she] wants something?
14. How does [cite child's name] let you know how he [she] feels?
15. (If relevant) About how many words does [cite child's name] understand?
16. (If relevant) Tell me about [cite child's name]'s ability to gesture or point.
17. Do you ever hear [cite child's name] making sounds a few minutes after an adult speaks to him [her]?

18. Was there a time when [cite child's name] made more sounds or babbled more?
    (If yes, go to question 19; if no, go to question 21.)
19. When did he [she] babble more?
20. How long has it been since he [she] stopped babbling as much?
21. Has [cite child's name] had any recent illness with fever and earache?
22. Is [cite child's name] exhibiting any other behavior that concerns you?
23. (If yes) What is this behavior?
24. Have there been any changes or stressful events in your home recently?
25. (If yes) Tell me about them.
26. Does [cite child's name] say any words?
27. (If yes) How old was [cite child's name] when he [she] spoke his [her] first words?
28. How does [cite child's name] use his [her] hands, eyes, and body to solve problems?
29. Is [cite child's name] able to transfer small objects from hand to hand?
30. Does [cite child's name] help you hold the bottle?
31. Is [cite child's name] able to follow an object or face with his [her] eyes?
32. Does [cite child's name] use his [her] eyes to examine his [her] hands?
33. Does [cite child's name] reach for objects?
34. Tell me about [cite child's name]'s attention span.

Additional Questions About Infant's Motor Skills (if infant is focus of interview)
(Note that these questions are arranged in developmental sequence. If the child has not mastered a motor skill, it is unlikely that he or she will be able to perform the next motor skill. Therefore, you can stop your inquiry after you find that the child has not mastered a skill.)
1. Can [cite child's name] roll over?
2. (If yes) How old was he [she] when he [she] first rolled over?
   (Go to question 4.)
3. What progress is [cite child's name] making in rolling over?
4. Can [cite child's name] crawl?
5. (If yes) How old was he [she] when he [she] began to crawl?
   (Go to question 7.)
6. What progress is [cite child's name] making in crawling?
7. Can [cite child's name] sit up?
8. (If yes) How old was he [she] when he [she] first sat up?
   (Go to question 10.)
9. What progress is [cite child's name] making in sitting up?
10. Can [cite child's name] pull himself [herself] up to a standing position?
    (If yes, go to question 11; if no, go to question 13.)
11. How old was he [she] when he [she] first pulled himself [herself] up to a standing position?
12. Does [cite child's name] sometimes remain standing for a short time after he [she] has pulled himself [herself] up?
    (Go to question 14.)

13. What progress is he [she] making in pulling himself [herself] up to a standing position?
14. Can [cite child's name] walk?
15. (If yes) How old was he [she] when he [she] first walked?
    (Go to question 18.)
16. What progress is he [she] making in walking?
17. (If needed) Does [cite child's name] seem to want to move and explore on his [her] own?
18. In what situations is [cite child's name] most active physically?
19. (If needed) Is he [she] most active when someone plays with him [her]…when other children are around… when he [she] is outdoors?
20. Tell me about [cite child's name]'s ability to do things that require small motor movements, such as his [her] ability to grasp things, pick things up, hold onto things, and release things.

Additional Questions About Infant's Temperament and Activity Level (if infant is focus of interview)
1. How would you describe [cite child's name] to someone who did not know him [her] well?
2. What moods does [cite child's name] have?
3. How would you describe [cite child's name]'s activity level?
4. Are there times when [cite child's name] engages in quiet activities?
5. (If yes) Tell me about these times.
6. When does [cite child's name] get overexcited?
7. When [cite child's name] gets overexcited, what do you do to calm him [her] down?
8. What kinds of comforting make [cite child's name] feel better?
9. How does [cite child's name] respond to new situations?
10. How does [cite child's name] respond to separation from you?
11. (If relevant) And how does [cite child's name] respond to separation from his [her] father?
12. (If child has trouble separating) How long does [cite response] last?
13. What do you do to help [cite child's name] with difficult changes?
14. (If responses to questions in this section do not give you the information you want about the child's temperament, ask more direct questions, such as the following.) Would any of the following terms be helpful in describing [cite child's name]—even-tempered… moody… independent…clinging…stubborn… flexible…active… calm…happy…sad…serious…carefree?

Additional Questions About Infant's Eating (if infant is focus of interview)
1. I'd like to learn about [cite child's name]'s eating. How is [cite child's name] eating?
2. What does [cite child's name] like to eat?
3. Is [cite child's name] a messy eater?
4. (If yes) Tell me about that.
5. How does [cite child's name] let you know that he [she] is hungry?

6. How does [cite child's name] show that he [she] likes certain foods?
7. How does [cite child's name] show his [her] dislike for certain foods?
8. Is [cite child's name] able to tolerate most foods?
9. Does [cite child's name] like warm foods or cold foods?
10. Does [cite child's name] like foods with any special flavors…special smells…special colors?
11. What does [cite child's name] seem to enjoy about being fed?
12. (If needed) Does [cite child's name] enjoy having you pay attention to him [her]…being at eye level with you while he [she] is in the high chair…having you talk to him [her] while he [she] eats…playing with the spoon?
13. What meals does [cite child's name] eat during the day?
14. What snacks does [cite child's name] eat during the day?
15. Are there certain times during the day when [cite child's name] makes excessive demands for food?
(If yes, go to question 16; if no, go to question 18.)
16. At what times does this happen?
17. Do you think [cite child's name] is truly hungry, or is he [she] just asking for attention?
18. Does [cite child's name] skip meals and not ask to eat?
19. (If yes) Tell me about that.
20. Does [cite child's name] eat when you do or at a different time?
21. (If at different time) Tell me about the reason [cite child's name] eats at a different time.
22. How often does [cite child's name] see adults in the family eat?
23. Does [cite child's name] eat what he [she] is given at mealtimes?
24. Does [cite child's name] have any problems with eating?
25. (If yes) What are the problems?
26. Does [cite child's name] drink from a cup or bottle?
27. Does [cite child's name] have any problem with drinking from a cup [bottle]?
28. (If yes) What are the problems?
(If child has problem with eating, drinking, or both, go to question 29; otherwise, end this section.)
29. How do you handle the problems?
30. Do your methods work?
31. (If father is in the picture) What does [cite child's name]'s father think about how you handle the problems?

Additional Questions About Infant's Sleeping (if infant is the focus of the interview)
1. How is [cite child's name] sleeping at night?
2. About how many hours of sleep does he [she] get at night?
3. Tell me what happens at night before bedtime.
4. (If needed) Does [cite child's name] go to sleep on his [her] own, or does he [she] need to be rocked, patted, or given some other kind of help from you?
5. Does [cite child's name] take a daytime nap or naps?
6. (If yes) Around what time[s] does he [she] nap?
7. And for how long?
8. Do you think that [cite child's name] is tired enough at bedtime to go to sleep easily?

9. (If child naps) Is there any connection between the amount of time he [she] sleeps during the day and his [her] sleeping at night?
10. What kind of routine do you have at night for putting [cite child's name] to bed?
11. What parts of the nighttime routine do you think [cite child's name] likes?
12. What parts of the nighttime routine do you think [cite child's name] dislikes?
13. What parts of the routine do you like?
14. And what parts of the routine do you dislike?
15. Does [cite child's name] wake up during the night? (If yes, go to question 16; if no, go to question 24.)
16. How often does [cite child's name] wake up during the night?
17. How does [cite child's name] act when he [she] wakes up?
18. (If needed) Does he [she] moan…scream…whisper occasionally…call you?
19. What do you do when [cite child's name] gets up during the night?
20. What seems to work the best?
21. Have you noticed any changes in [cite child's name]'s behavior during the daytime since he [she] began to wake up at night?
22. Have you noticed any signs of physical discomfort, such as teething, earache, congestion from a cold, or general fussiness, during the day?
23. (If yes) What have you noticed?
24. Have there been any changes recently in your home or in the child's routine related to bedtime?
25. (If yes) Tell me about these changes.
26. Does anyone share [cite child's name]'s bedroom?
27. (If yes) Who shares his [her] bedroom?
28. Does [cite child's name] have any difficulties falling asleep?
29. (If yes) Tell me about them.
30. Does [cite child's name] have his [her] own bed?
31. (If no) With whom does [cite child's name] sleep?
32. When does [cite child's name] usually go to bed?
33. How do you know when [cite child's name] is tired?

Additional Questions About Toddler's/Preschooler's Personal-Social-Affective Behavior (if toddler/preschooler is focus of interview)
1. Can [cite child's name] take turns?
2. Can [cite child's name] point to body parts on a doll?
3. Can [cite child's name] name his [her] own body parts?
4. Can [cite child's name] identify himself [herself] in a mirror?
5. Can [cite child's name] use words like *I, me,* and *them* correctly?
6. Can [cite child's name] feed himself [herself]?
7. Can [cite child's name] use a spoon or a fork?
8. Can [cite child's name] imitate things you do, like sweeping the floor and making a bed?
9. Can [cite child's name] play with a doll and do such things as feed, hug, and scold the doll?
10. How does [cite child's name] handle common dangers?

11. How does [cite child's name] behave when he [she] plays with another child?
12. Does [cite child's name] share his [her] toys?
    (If yes, go to question 13; if no, go to question 15.)
13. What toys does he [she] share?
14. And with whom does he [she] share them?
    (Go to question 16.)
15. What have you done to help him [her] learn how to share?
16. Does [cite child's name] have temper tantrums?
    (If yes, go to question 17; if no, go to question 26.)
17. Tell me about the temper tantrums.
18. What sets off the temper tantrums?
19. Are the temper tantrums more frequent at certain times of the day than at other times?
20. (If yes) Tell me about these times.
21. Where do the temper tantrums occur?
22. What happens when [cite child's name] has a temper tantrum?
23. How do you feel about the temper tantrums?
24. How do you deal with [cite child's name]'s temper tantrums?
25. Which methods seem to be most effective?
26. How does [cite child's name] get along with other children?
27. Is [cite child's name] stubborn at times?
    (If yes, go to question 28; if no, go to question 31.)
28. In what way is [cite child's name] stubborn?
29. How do you handle his [her] stubbornness?
30. Has it worked?
31. Does [cite child's name] hit, bite, or try to hurt other children?
    (If yes, go to question 32; if no, go to question 36.)
32. How does he [she] hurt other children?
33. Why do you think he [she] acts this way?
34. How do you handle these situations?
35. What seems to work best?
36. Does [cite child's name] have any fears?
    (If yes, go to question 37; if no, go to question 45.)
37. What fears does he [she] have?
38. What kinds of situations tend to make [cite child's name] fearful?
39. Are these new situations or old ones?
40. What does [cite child's name] do when he [she] is fearful?
41. How long has [cite child's name] been fearful?
42. What do you do when [cite child's name] shows fear?
43. How does it work?
44. Have you found that some methods are more effective than others?
45. How do you handle [cite child's name] demands for your attention?
46. What situations seem to cause [cite child's name] to demand your attention?
47. What kinds of things does [cite child's name] seem to want when he [she] asks for attention?
48. Does he [she] demand your attention for a long time, or will a short time do?
49. Have you noticed any changes during the past few months in how much attention [cite child's name] has demanded?

50. (If yes) Tell me about the changes you've noticed.
51. How does [cite child's name] react when he [she] meets new people?
52. How do you feel about [cite child's name]'s behavior when he [she] meets new people?
53. (If needed) Is there anything you can do to make [cite child's name] more comfortable when he [she] meets new people?
54. When does [cite child's name] cry?
55. What do you do when [cite child's name] cries?
56. Why do you think [cite child's name] cries?
57. (If needed) When [cite child's name] cries, does it usually mean that something is really wrong or is it that something is bothering him [her] only a little bit and he [she] wants attention?
58. How can you tell the difference between the types of crying [cite child's name] does?
59. Does [cite child's name] play with his [her] private parts?
    (If yes, go to question 60; if no, go to question 65.)
60. When does [cite child's name] play with his [her] private parts?
61. (If needed) Does this occur during any particular situations?
62. (If yes) In what situation[s] does he [she] play with his [her] private parts?
63. How do you feel about his [her] doing this?
64. And what do you do when you find [cite child's name] playing with his [her] private parts?
65. What kinds of activities does [cite child's name] seem to be interested in?
66. What does [cite child's name] like to do on his [her] own?
67. What difficulties are you having with [cite child's name] about performing daily routines, such as washing hands…dressing…picking up clothes…putting away toys?
68. Does [cite child's name] let you do things *with* him [her]?
69. Tell me about that.
70. Does [cite child's name] let you do things *for* him [her]?
71. Tell me about that.
72. How does [cite child's name] get along with adults?
73. Is [cite child's name] interested in people?
74. Tell me more about that.
75. How does [cite child's name] spend his [her] time during a typical weekday?
76. And on weekends, how does [cite child's name] spend his [her] time?
77. How does [cite child's name] feel about himself [herself]?
78. (If there are other siblings in family) How does [cite child's name] compare with his [her] sisters and brothers?
79. Is [cite child's name] interested in animals?
80. Tell me more about that.
81. Is [cite child's name] generally interested in things?
82. (If no) Tell me more about that.
83. At what time of the day is [cite child's name] most active?

84. When [cite child's name] needs to do things, like get dressed or put things away, does he [she] do them too fast, too slowly, or at just about the right pace? (If too fast, go to question 85; if too slowly, go to question 89; otherwise, go to question 93.)

85. What happens when you try to make [cite child's name] move more slowly?

86. What other things does [cite child's name] do too fast?

87. (If needed) Does [cite child's name] eat too fast…get ready for bed too fast?

88. Are you concerned that [cite child's name] may be hyperactive?

89. What happens when you try to make [cite child's name] move faster?

90. What other things does [cite child's name] do slowly?

91. (If needed) Does he [she] eat slowly…get ready for bed slowly?

92. Are you concerned that [cite child's name] may be generally slow?

93. How does [cite child's name] react when his [her] play is interrupted?

94. How does [cite child's name] let you know when he [she] wants to stay with an activity longer than you had planned?

95. Does [cite child's name] have any unusual behaviors? (If yes, go to question 96; if no, end this section.)

96. What unusual behaviors does [cite child's name] have?

97. How often does [cite child's name] [cite unusual behavior]?

98. What is most likely to bring on [cite unusual behavior]?

99. What situations seem to make [cite child's name]'s [cite unusual behavior] worse?

100. What do you do at these times?

101. What works best?

102. Is there any connection between what [cite child's name] eats and [cite unusual behavior]?

103. How do you feel about taking care of [cite child's name] when he [she] behaves in this way?

Additional Questions About Toddler's/Preschooler's Play and Cognitive Ability (if toddler/preschooler is focus of interview)

1. How does [cite child's name] occupy himself [herself] during the day?

2. What does [cite child's name] like to play?

3. How would you describe [cite child's name]'s play?

4. (If needed) Is it quiet play…active play?…Does he [she] build things…color?

5. What toys or other objects does [cite child's name] play with?

6. What kinds of things does [cite child's name] do with the toys or other objects that he [she] plays with?

7. What toys seem to be particularly interesting to [cite child's name]?

8. And how does [cite child's name] play with the toys he [she] especially likes?

9. Is [cite child's name] interested in exploring objects?

10. (If yes) Tell me more about what [cite child's name] does.

11. What happens when [cite child's name] is left on his [her] own to play?

12. How long does [cite child's name] usually stay with an activity?

13. Does [cite child's name] seem to play better at certain times of the day than at others?

14. What is particularly distracting to [cite child's name]?

15. In what situations does [cite child's name] get the most out of his [her] play?

16. How does [cite child's name] let you know what he [she] is interested in?

17. Tell me more about that.

18. (If relevant) Can [cite child's name] find his [her] toys when they are mixed up with those of his [her] brothers and sisters?

19. Is [cite child's name] more interested in watching others play than in playing himself [herself]?

20. Do you think that [cite child's name]'s play is about the same as that of other children of his [her] age?

21. (If no) In what way is it different?

22. What changes have you noticed over the last few months in the way [cite child's name] plays?

23. Where does [cite child's name] play at home?

24. (If needed) Does he [she] play in different rooms?

25. Does he [she] have enough space to play?

26. (If no) What have you done to get more space for [cite child's name] to play in?

27. How long does [cite child's name] stay in his [her] own room to play?

28. Is this amount of time OK with you?

29. Does [cite child's name] prefer playing outside or inside?

30. Does [cite child's name] prefer playing alone or with someone?

31. With whom does he [she] like to play?

32. Does [cite child's name] prefer quiet activities, such as arts and crafts or board games, to more physical games, or does he [she] enjoy both types of activities?

33. Does [cite child's name] engage in any pretend play?

34. (If needed) Does he [she] play house…play school… play doctor?

35. Does [cite child's name] have any imaginary friends?

36. (If yes) Who are they?

37. How does [cite child's name]'s play change when an adult plays with him [her]?

38. What kinds of things does [cite child's name] like to do with you?

39. How does [cite child's name] react when you try to show him [her] how to use a toy?

40. How much fun is [cite child's name] to play with?

41. Have you ever wondered whether [cite child's name] enjoys playing with you?

42. Tell me about that.

43. How much time do you spend playing with [cite child's name]?

44. Does having [cite child's name]'s toys underfoot in the house bother you?

45. (If yes) Tell me about that.

46. Does [cite child's name] look at you when you try to talk to or play with him [her]?

47. (If no) What does he [she] do instead?

48. Is [cite child's name] responsive to you?
49. Is [cite child's name] responsive to other adults?
50. Does [cite child's name] like physical contact, such as when you gently touch his [her] face, hands, and arms?
51. (If no) Tell me about that.
52. Is there any physical activity that [cite child's name] seems to enjoy especially?
53. Does [cite child's name] like doing the same activity over and over again?
54. Does [cite child's name] like to spin objects?
55. (If yes) Tell me about that.
56. Does [cite child's name] play outdoors?
    (If yes, go to question 57; if no, go to question 62.)
57. Where does he [she] play outdoors?
58. (If needed) Do you take [cite child's name] to any parks or playgrounds?
59. How does [cite child's name] react when you take him [her] outdoors to play?
60. Does [cite child's name] behave differently outdoors than indoors?
61. (If yes) In what way?
62. Does [cite child's name] seem to be in constant motion?
63. (If yes) How do you handle that?
64. Tell me about [cite child's name]'s ability to pay attention.
65. Does [cite child's name] like to put puzzles together?
66. Tell me about that.
67. Can [cite child's name] construct things out of blocks?
68. Tell me about that.

Additional Questions About Toddler's/Preschooler's Adjustment to Caregiving Situation (if toddler/preschooler is focus of interview)

1. Do you leave [cite child's name] at a day care center, preschool, at somebody's house, or at your house with a sitter during any part of the week?
   (If yes, go to question 2; if no, go to question 20.)
2. Where do you leave him [her]?
3. Tell me about the reason you leave [cite child's name] there.
4. How do you feel about leaving [cite child's name]?
5. (If day care center, preschool, or someone's house) How did you find out about [cite place where child is cared for]?
6. Are you satisfied with the way [cite child's name] is cared for there?
7. How is [cite child's name] getting along at [cite place where child is cared for]?
8. (If needed) Is [cite child's name] having any problems there?
9. (If yes) Tell me about them.
10. (If needed) How does [cite child's name] get along with the caregiver[s]?
11. And how does he [she] get along with the other children?
12. Do you have a chance to talk regularly about [cite child's name] with the person[s] taking care of him [her]?
13. How long does it take you to get to [cite place where child is cared for]?

14. How does [cite child's name] act when you leave him [her] at [cite place where child is cared for]?
    (If behavior is not satisfactory, go to question 15; if behavior is satisfactory, go to question 19.)
15. How do you feel when [cite child's name] acts this way?
16. Does [cite child's name] always show that he [she] is upset in the same way?
17. What have you done to try to help him [her]?
18. How does it help?
19. How does [cite child's name] react when you pick him [her] up from [cite place where child is cared for]?
20. How do you feel about taking [cite child's name] out in public?
21. How does [cite child's name] behave when he [she] is outside the home?
22. How does [cite child's name] react when you take him [her] to a friend's home?
    (If there are problems or concerns, go to question 23; otherwise, end section.)
23. How do you handle these problems?
24. What seems to work best?

Additional Questions About Toddler's/Preschooler's Self-Help Skills (if toddler/preschooler is focus of interview)

1. Is [cite child's name] toilet trained?
   (If yes, go to question 2; if no, go to question 5.)
2. How old was [cite child's name] when he [she] was toilet trained?
3. Does [cite child's name] have toilet accidents once in a while?
4. (If yes) Tell me about the toilet accidents [cite child's name] has.
   (Go to question 13.)
5. Have you begun to toilet train [cite child's name]?
6. (If no) At what age do you think [cite child's name] should be toilet trained?
   (Go to question 13.)
7. Tell me how it's going.
   (Ask questions 8 to 10, as needed.)
8. Are you having any problems with the toilet training?
9. (If yes) Tell me about the problems you're having.
10. What training methods are you using?
11. What did [cite child's name] do to make you think that he [she] was ready to be toilet trained?
12. (If needed) Did he [she] come to you to be changed? Was he [she] interested in watching others in the bathroom…imitating others…staying dry?
13. Tell me about how [cite child's name] dresses and undresses himself [herself].
    (Ask questions 14 to 17, as needed.)
14. What clothing can [cite child's name] put on?
15. What clothing can [cite child's name] take off?
16. (If child is older than 4 years) Can [cite child's name] tie his [her] shoes?
17. How much supervision does [cite child's name] need in dressing and undressing?
18. Tell me about [cite child's name] bath time.
19. (If needed) Does [cite child's name] wash himself [herself]?

20. Does [cite child's name] wash his [her] hands when necessary, such as when he [she] is dirty or after he [she] goes to the toilet?
21. (If no) Tell me about [cite child's name]'s not washing his [her] hands when necessary.
22. Does [cite child's name] brush his [her] teeth?
23. (If no) Tell me about [cite child's name]'s not brushing his [her] teeth.
24. Does [cite child's name] brush or comb his [her] hair?
25. (If no) Tell me about [cite child's name]'s not brushing his [her] hair.

Additional Questions About Toddler's/Preschooler's Language, Communication, Speech, Comprehension, and Problem-Solving Skills (if toddler/preschooler is focus of interview)

1. Does [cite child's name] talk?
   (If yes, go to question 2; if no, go to question 20.)
2. When did [cite child's name] begin to talk?
3. Does [cite child's name] have any problems with his [her] speech?
4. (If yes) Tell me about [cite child's name]'s problems with speech.
5. (If needed) Is [cite child's name] having problems speaking clearly…forming grammatically correct sentences…saying the right words in order… stuttering?
6. About how many words can [cite child's name] say?
7. What kinds of words does [cite child's name] usually say?
8. Does [cite child's name] have any pet phrases?
9. (If yes) What are they?
10. Does [cite child's name] use action words?
11. Can [cite child's name] speak in sentences?
12. (If yes) How old was [cite child's name] when he [she] first combined words to make sentences?
13. Did [cite child's name] have any problems with speech in the past?
14. (If yes) Tell me about that.
15. Do you understand what [cite child's name] says?
16. (If no) Tell me more about that.
17. Do other people also understand [cite child's name]'s speech?
18. (If no) Tell me more about that.
19. What kinds of things does [cite child's name] talk about?
    (Go to question 25.)
20. How is [cite child's name] able to tell you about what he [she] needs?
21. (If needed) Does [cite child's name] make any sounds?
22. (If yes) Tell me about the sounds that [cite child's name] makes.
23. Did [cite child's name] ever talk?
24. (If yes) Tell me about when he [she] talked.
25. Does [cite child's name] understand most things?
26. (If no) What problems does [cite child's name] have in understanding things?
27. Can [cite child's name] follow directions?
28. (If no) What problems does [cite child's name] have in following directions?

Additional Questions About Toddler's/Preschooler's Motor Skills (if toddler/preschooler is focus of interview)

1. Tell me about [cite child's name]'s ability to do things that require small motor movements, such as his [her] ability to grasp things, pick up things, hold onto things, and release things.
2. (If needed) Tell me about [cite child's name]'s ability to open doors…turn pages in a book…use scissors to cut paper…fold paper…build objects with blocks…use pencils…use crayons…draw… copy circles or squares …screw things…unscrew things…button…tie shoes…use a zipper…play with Lego-type toys…print letters.
3. What types of toys are most frustrating to [cite child's name]?
4. Tell me about [cite child's name]'s other motor skills, such as his [her] ability to walk, run, jump, skip, and play ball.
5. (If needed) Tell me about [cite child's name]'s ability to walk up steps…walk down steps…hop…roll a ball… throw a ball…climb…ride a tricycle…use a slide…use a jungle gym.

Additional Questions for Pregnant Mother About Toddler's/Preschooler's Acceptance of the Arrival of a New Baby (if toddler/preschooler is focus of interview)

1. How do you think [cite child's name] will handle the coming of the new baby?
2. What do you think will be most difficult for [cite child's name] to handle?
3. What might you do to help [cite child's name] adjust to the new baby?
4. Have you told [cite child's name] about the new baby?
   (If yes, ask questions 5 and 6; if no, end this section.)
5. What did you say to him [her]?
6. And how did he [she] react?

Additional Questions for Mother About the Family Environment and Family Relationships

1. I'd now like to ask you about life at home. OK?
2. How does [cite child's name] get along with you?
3. (For older child) How did [cite child's name] get along with you when he [she] was younger?
4. Who else lives at home?
   (If father or other adult male is in the picture, go to question 5; otherwise, go to question 7.)
5. How does [cite child's name] get along with [cite name of father or other adult male]?
6. With whom does [cite child's name] get along better, you or [cite name of father or other adult male]?
7. (If child has sister or brother) How does [cite child's name] get along with his [her] sisters and brothers?
   (Ask questions 8 to 11, as needed.)
8. What situations tend to cause conflict between [cite child's name] and the other children?
9. What do you do when the children argue?
10. What have you found that works?
11. What do you think would happen if you let the children settle their arguments themselves—except when you thought that one child might hurt the other?
12. What relatives live in your home or nearby?

13. (If any relatives mentioned) Where do they live?
14. (If child has grandparents) How does [cite child's name] get along with his [her] grandparents?
15. (If child has other relatives at home or living nearby) How does [cite child's name] get along with his [her] other relatives?
16. How does everyone get along at home?
    (If mother has a husband or partner, go to question 17; otherwise, see directions preceding question 19.)
17. How are you getting along with your husband [partner]?
18. (If needed) Is there anything bothering you about your relationship with your husband [partner]?
    (If in-laws or friends are staying at child's home, go to question 19; otherwise, end this section.)
19. How are things working out with your mother-in-law [father-in-law, mother, father, etc.] staying at your home?
20. Are there any problems with having her [him, them] there?

Additional Questions to Evaluate Parent's Ability to Set Limits and Discipline Child

1. How do you make [cite child's name] mind you?
2. Do you feel that you are spoiling [cite child's name]?
3. Tell me about your answer.
4. Does anyone tell you that you are spoiling [cite child's name]?
5. (If yes) Tell me about that.
6. Do you believe that [cite child's name] acts spoiled?
7. (If yes) In what ways does he [she] act spoiled?
8. Do you ever give in to [cite child's name]?
    (If yes, go to question 9; if no, go to question 14.)
9. Give me some examples of how you give in to [cite child's name].
10. How often do you give in to [cite child's name]?
11. How do you feel about giving in?
12. Which things are you sorry you gave in to?
13. Which of the things you gave in to do you feel are disruptive to the family?
14. Do you believe that you are too easy with [cite child's name], too strict, or just about right?
15. Tell me about that.
16. Which of [cite child's name]'s behaviors are particularly irritating to you?
17. In which areas would you most like to set limits?
18. What things won't you let [cite child's name] do?
19. Overall, how satisfied are you with [cite child's name]'s behavior?
20. Are there times when [cite child's name] doesn't mind you or gets into trouble?
    (If yes, go to question 21; if no, go to question 31.)
21. Tell me about these times.
22. (If needed) What kind of trouble does [cite child's name] get into?
23. What do you do when [cite child's name] doesn't mind [gets into trouble]?
24. (If relevant) How does [cite child's name] react when he [she] is punished?
25. Which methods of discipline work best?
26. Which methods don't work?

27. How do you feel when you have to discipline [cite child's name]?
28. What problems are you most concerned about?
29. What does [cite child's name] do that makes you most angry?
30. Does [cite child's name] usually understand what is expected of him [her]?
31. How do you expect [cite child's name] to behave?
32. What does [cite child's name] do that leads you to think that he [she] can live up to your expectations?
    (If child's father lives at home or has visitation rights, go to question 33; otherwise, end this section.)
33. What about [cite child's name] makes his [her] father most angry?
34. What does his [her] father discipline him [her] for?
35. How does his [her] father discipline him [her]?
36. Does his method work?
37. How does [cite child's name]'s father feel when he has to discipline him [her]?
38. How does [cite child's name] respond to his [her] father's discipline?
39. Do you and [cite child's name]'s father agree about how to discipline him [her]?
40. (If no) How do you handle the disagreements?
41. How do you feel about what [cite child's name]'s father does when he is angry with him [her]?
42. Do you do anything about your feelings?

Additional Questions to Evaluate Environmental Safeguards and Neighborhood

1. What have you done to make the house safe for [cite child's name] and to keep him [her] from getting into things?
2. (If needed) Have you put covers on electric outlets?… Have you put safety latches on any drawers or cupboards that contain cleaning products or other poisons, knives, guns, or other dangerous things?
3. Does [cite child's name] get into things at home that he [she] is not supposed to?
    (If yes, go to question 4; if no, go to question 8.)
4. What does he [she] get into?
5. Have you been teaching [cite child's name] not to get into these things?
6. (If yes) How has it been going?
7. How do you feel when [cite child's name] wants to get into everything he [she] sees?
8. Does [cite child's name] ever break things?
9. (If yes) How do you feel when this happens?
10. (If yes) And what do you do when he [she] breaks things?
11. Does [cite child's name] seem to understand when you tell him [her] not to touch objects?
12. (If yes) Do you think that he [she] can remember not to get into things?
13. Which objects seem to be particularly attractive to [cite child's name]?
14. Why do you think [cite child's name] likes them so much?
15. How do you stop [cite child's name] when he [she] is about to do something dangerous?

16. How long have you lived in your present house [apartment]?
17. How do you like living there?
18. (If needed) Tell me about that.
19. How do you get along with your neighbors?
20. (If needed) Tell me about that.
21. Are there any problems in the neighborhood?
22. (If yes) Tell me about that.

Additional Questions to Evaluate Mother's Resources and Occupation

1. Do you have any living relatives?
   (If yes, go to question 2; if no, go to question 8.)
2. Tell me about who your living relatives are.
3. How often do you see your relatives?
4. And how do you get along?
5. Do they give you help when you need it?
   (If yes, go to question 6; if no, go to question 8.)
6. Which relatives give you help when you need it?
7. How do they help you?
8. Do you have any close friends?
9. Tell me about that.
10. Have you ever turned to them for help?
11. (If yes) And how did they respond?
12. To whom would you turn for help if your family needed it?
13. Do you have someone to talk to when you have a problem or are feeling frustrated and upset?
14. Tell me about it.
15. Do you have medical insurance?
16. (If no) How do you plan to take care of any hospitalizations?
17. Have you been in contact with any social agencies?
18. (If yes) Tell me about your contacts.
19. Are you a member of a religious group?
20. (If yes) Tell me about it.
21. What is your occupation?
22. How do you like your job?
23. (If needed) Tell me more about that.
   (If father is in the picture, go to question 24; otherwise, end this section.)
24. What is [cite child's name]'s father's occupation?
25. And [cite child's name]'s father, how does he like his job?
26. (If needed) Tell me more about that.

Additional Questions to Evaluate a Mother Who Stays at Home

1. What do you enjoy about being a full-time parent?
2. What do you find most difficult about being a full-time parent?
3. What made you decide to be a full-time parent?
4. (If needed) What were you doing before your child was [children were] born?
5. Are you occasionally able to get out of the house with [cite child's name]?
6. Are you able to get some time for yourself on a regular basis?
7. Tell me about your answer.
8. (If needed) Do you get a babysitter occasionally and go out by yourself or with a friend [with your husband]?

9. Do you know other parents with young children in the neighborhood?
10. (If yes) Have you worked out any cooperative babysitting arrangements with them?

Additional Questions About Spending Time with Child
(for mother who works)

1. How much time do you spend with [cite child's name]?
2. How do you feel about the amount of time you spend with [cite child's name]?
3. How do you spend time with [cite child's name] before you go to work?
4. And when you come home, how do you spend time together?
5. And on weekends, how do you spend time together?
6. Which times seem to be the most enjoyable for you and [cite child's name]?
7. Which times seem to be the most rushed and tense for you and [cite child's name]?
8. How do you feel about taking care of [cite child's name] when you return home from work?
9. What do you usually do when you pick [cite child's name] up after work?
10. Do you have any time alone when you come home after work?
11. How do you deal with [cite child's name] if he [she] cries and fusses in the evening?
12. How do you get [cite child's name] to relax when you get home after work?
13. How do you get to relax when you get home after work?

Additional Questions About Family Medical History

1. I'd like to know about your health history. Have you had any serious illnesses, accidents, or diseases?
2. (If yes) Tell me about them.
3. (If needed) How was the diagnosis established?...Tell me about the course of your illness, its treatment, and the prognosis.
4. (If father is in the picture) And how about [cite child's name]'s father. Has he had any serious illnesses, accidents, or diseases?
5. (If yes) Tell me about them.
6. (If needed) How was the diagnosis established?...Tell me about the course of his illness, its treatment, and the prognosis.
7. (If child has siblings) And [cite child's name]'s sisters and brothers. Have they had any serious illnesses, accidents, or diseases?
8. (If yes) Tell me about them.
9. (If needed) How was the diagnosis established? Tell me about the course of the illness, its treatment, and the prognosis.

Additional General Questions About Infant or Toddler/Preschooler and Mother

1. We've covered a lot of areas. Before we finish, I have just a few more questions I'd like to ask you. OK?
2. What experiences did you have with young children before you had a child?
3. What do you like about being a parent?
4. What do you dislike about being a parent?

5. Is being a parent what you expected?
6. Tell me about that.
7. (If needed) What is the same as what you expected? What is different from what you expected?
8. What would it take to make it easier for you to be a parent?
9. What about [cite child's name] gives you the most pleasure?
10. What kinds of things do you do together that are fun?
11. Do you have quiet times when you relax together?
12. (If yes) Tell me about them.
13. (If mother has other children) Do you spend about the same amount of time with [cite child's name] that you do with the other children?
14. (If no) Tell me about that.
    (If child's father lives at home or has visitation rights, go to question 15; otherwise, go to question 19.)
15. What kinds of things does [cite child's name] do with his [her] father?
16. How much time do they spend together?
17. (If father has other children) Is this about the same amount of time he spends with the other children in the family?
18. (If no) Tell me about that.
19. In general, does [cite child's name] act like other children of his [her] age?
20. (If not) In what way doesn't he [she] act like other children of his [her] age?
21. Is there anything else about [cite child's name] that you would like to tell me?
22. (If yes) Go ahead.
23. Is [cite child's name] having any problems that we didn't discuss?
24. (If yes) What are they?
25. (If not asked previously) Do you have any reason to think that [cite child's name] is under any particular stress at this time?
26. (If yes) Tell me about that.
27. (If not asked previously) Have there been any changes in the home or in [cite child's name]'s routine recently?
28. (If yes) Tell me about that.
29. Have you discussed your concerns about [cite child's name]'s problems with a health care provider?
30. (If yes) What did the health care provider say?
31. Is there anything else about your role as a parent that you would like to tell me?
32. (If yes) Go ahead.
33. Do you have any questions that you would like to ask me?
34. (If yes) Go ahead.
35. Thank you for talking with me. If you have any questions or if you want to talk to me, please call me. Here is my card.

Note. This table is designed for interviewing mothers about their young children. With some alterations, it also can be used to interview fathers or other caregivers. Use Table F-35 in this Appendix to interview a parent who has a child with a pervasive developmental disorder.
Source: Adapted from Bromwich (1981) and Ferholt (1980).

Table F-22
Semistructured Interview Questions for a Nonsuspect Parent of Child Who Was Allegedly Maltreated

Because child maltreatment covers a wide area, several questions in this table may not be applicable for specific cases, especially those involving psychological abuse. Select those questions that are most appropriate to the case, and use follow-up questions, as needed. In situations where the parent is reluctant to talk about the maltreatment, ask general background questions first, such as those covering the nonsuspect parent's background. Interview the nonsuspect parent alone.

Introduction
1. Hi, I'm Dr. [Ms., Mr.] _____. I understand that something may have happened to your child. I'd like to talk to you about it. OK?
2. Your child's name is…?
3. How old is [cite child's name]?
4. Are there other children in the family?
5. (If yes) What are their names and ages?

Incidents of Maltreatment
6. Tell me what happened to [cite child's name].
7. How did you learn about what happened?
8. (If needed) What did [cite child's name] tell you happened to him [her]?
   (If child told parent about the maltreatment, go to question 9; if not, go to directions preceding question 12.)
9. What were the exact words your child used to tell you about what happened to him [her]?
10. Did your child show any emotions when he [she] told you about what happened?
11. (If yes) What emotions did [cite child's name] show?
    (Ask questions 12 to 25, as needed.)
12. Who [cite act] your child?
13. When did it happen?
14. Where did [cite act] take place?
15. What time did [cite act] take place?
16. What was [cite child's name] wearing at the time?
17. Were other children there at the time?
18. (If yes) Who are the other children who were there?
19. Were other adults there at the time?
20. (If yes) Who are the adults who were there?
21. What physical signs indicated that something had happened to [cite child's name]?
22. (If sexual abuse) How did [cite alleged perpetrator] get your child to participate in [cite act]?
23. Do you have any idea why [cite act] happened to [cite child's name]?
24. (If yes) Tell me about it.
25. Did [cite act] happen more than once?
    (If yes, go to question 26; if no, go to question 31.)
26. How many times did [cite alleged perpetrator] [cite act]?
27. Over how long a period of time did this happen?
28. Where did [cite act] usually take place?
29. Was there a certain time when [cite act] usually took place?
30. (If yes) When was that?

31. Has any agency been notified, such as the police or Child Protective Services?
(If yes, go to question 32; if no, go to question 36.)
32. Who was notified?
33. When were they notified?
34. What did they do?
35. What did they tell you?
(Go to directions preceding question 37.)
36. What was the reason an agency wasn't notified?

Information About Offender
(If a family member was the offender, go to question 37; if a non–family member was the offender, go to question 49.)
37. Do you have any idea why [cite family member] did it?
38. (If yes) Tell me about your idea.
39. (If needed) When did you first think this might be happening?
40. (If needed) Before this time did you ever see [cite family member] doing anything wrong with [cite child's name]?
41. What is [cite family member] like?
42. How do you get along with [cite family member]?
43. Has he [she] done anything like this before?
44. (If yes) What did he [she] do?
45. What has happened to [cite family member] since [cite act] was discovered?
46. (If needed and relevant) Will [cite family member] continue to live in the home?
47. (If yes) Do you think that [cite child's name] should continue to live with [cite family member]?
48. Tell me about your answer.
(Go to question 54.)
49. What do you know about [cite alleged offender]?
50. What do you think about [cite alleged offender] doing [cite act]?
51. What has happened to [cite alleged offender] since the incident?
52. Do you think [cite child's name] should continue to live at home?
53. Tell me about your answer.

Behavior of Maltreated Child
54. How did [cite child's name] react immediately after [cite act] took place?
55. (If needed) What did you notice about [cite child's name] that was different or out of the ordinary after [cite act] took place?
56. What did you say to or do for [cite child's name] when you found out?
57. How is [cite child's name] getting along now?
58. How was [cite child's name] getting along before the incident took place?
59. (If needed) What, if any, emotional or behavioral problems did [cite child's name] have before the incident took place?
60. What changes have you noticed in [cite child's name]'s behavior since the incident occurred?
61. (If needed) Have you noticed any changes in [cite child's name]'s sleeping habits…eating habits…mood …level of anxiety…fears…friendship patterns… school performance…physical complaints?

62. How does [cite child's name] typically handle stress?
63. How do you think [cite child's name] will do in the future?

Family's Reaction to the Maltreatment
64. How do you feel about what happened?
65. How has the family reacted to [cite child's name] since [cite act] happened?
66. How have family members reacted to each other since [cite act] happened?
67. (If needed) How has it affected your relationship with your husband [wife, partner, friend, etc.]?
68. How has it affected the way the family is functioning?
69. (If needed) Has anything changed in your family since the incident happened?
70. (If yes) Tell me about the changes that have taken place.
71. How is the family getting along?
72. Is where you live somehow connected to the maltreatment?
73. (If yes) In what way?

Family's Reaction to the Alleged Offender
74. How do you feel about [cite alleged offender]?
75. What would you like to see happen to [cite alleged offender]?
76. Is there anything you could do to prevent something like this from happening again?

Maltreatment of Other Children
(If there are other children in the family, go to question 77; otherwise, go to directions preceding question 83.)
77. Have any of your other children been abused or maltreated?
(If yes, go to question 78; if no, go to directions preceding question 83.)
78. Tell me about it.
(Ask detailed questions, as needed. See "Incidents of Maltreatment" section, which follows the introduction, for possible questions; also include the following questions.)
79. How old were the children when it happened?
80. How long ago did it happen?
81. What happened to the children as a result of [cite act]?
82. How are the children getting along now?

Description of Child Who Has Allegedly Been Maltreated
(Ask the questions in this section for each child who has allegedly been maltreated.)
83. Now I'd like to learn a little more about [cite child's name]. How would you describe him [her]?
(Ask questions 84 to 92, as needed and as relevant.)
84. How has [cite child's name]'s health been—any illnesses or accidents?
85. What was he [she] like as an infant?
86. And as a toddler. What was [cite child's name] like from 2 to 5 years of age?
87. How do you get along with [cite child's name]?
88. (If relevant) And how does your husband [wife, partner, friend, etc.] get along with [cite child's name]?
(If child is of school age, go to question 89; if child is of preschool age, go to question 99.)
89. How is [cite child's name] doing in school?

90. How are his [her] grades?
91. Does [cite child's name] have any problems in school?
92. (If yes) What problems is he [she] having?
93. Has [cite child's name] ever gotten into trouble with the law?
    (If yes, go to question 94; if no, go to question 97.)
94. What kind of trouble has [cite child's name] gotten into?
95. (If needed) Was [cite child's name] involved in a gang when he [she] got into trouble with the law?
96. (If yes) Tell me about that.
97. Has [cite child's name] had any problems with drugs or alcohol?
98. (If yes) What kinds of problems has [cite child's name] had?
99. How does [cite child's name] get along with other children?
100. Does [cite child's name] have friends?
    (If yes, go to question 101; if no, go to question 104.)
101. Tell me about his [her] friends.
102. How do you feel about [cite child's name]'s friends?
103. (If needed) What does [cite child's name] do with his [her] friends?
    (Go to question 105.)
104. Tell me about [cite child's name]'s not having friends.
105. With whom does [cite child's name] spend time besides his [her] family?
106. Is [cite child's name] frequently alone only with males or only with females?
107. (If yes) Tell me about that.
108. (If needed and relevant) Is there any possibility that [cite child's name] is participating in sexual activities?
109. (If yes) What kind of sexual activities might [cite child's name] be participating in?
110. Now I'd like to turn to the topic of discipline. What does [cite child's name] do that causes you to discipline him [her]?
111. How do you discipline [cite child's name]?
112. How often do you discipline [cite child's name]?
113. Do you have any problems in disciplining [cite child's name]?
114. (If yes) What kind of problems do you have?
    (If interviewee has significant other, go to question 115; otherwise, go to question 121.)
115. And what about your husband [wife, partner, friend, etc.]? What type of discipline does he [she] use with [cite child's name]?
116. Who seems to be more effective in getting [cite child's name] to listen or obey—you or your husband [wife, partner, friend, etc.]?
117. Tell me about that.
118. Does your husband [wife, partner, friend, etc.] have any problems disciplining [cite child's name]?
119. (If yes) What kinds of problems does he [she] have?
120. What complaints does your husband [wife, partner, friend, etc.] have about the way you handle [cite child's name]?
121. How do you spend time with [cite child's name]?
122. (If needed) What activities do you like to do with [cite child's name]?
123. What activities with [cite child's name] don't you like or bore you the most?

124. How do you express your affection for [cite child's name]?
125. (If relevant) And how does your husband [wife, partner, friend, etc.] express affection for [cite child's name]?
126. What would you like [cite child's name]'s future to be?
127. What kinds of needs does [cite child's name] have now?
128. Families have different views about privacy and nudity. I'd like to talk to you about how your family deals with privacy and nudity. First, could you tell me about privacy in your family?
129. (If needed) Do you agree with what your family does?
130. And how about nudity? What is your family's attitude about nudity in the home?
131. (If needed) Do you agree with your family's practices?
132. Now I'd like to talk to you about sleeping arrangements. Where does [cite child's name] sleep?
133. Did [cite child's name] ever sleep in the same room with you?
134. (If yes) Tell me about that.
    (If relevant, ask questions 135 to 139; if not, go to directions preceding question 140. Discussion of sex can include names and functions of body parts, as well as intercourse and pregnancy. These questions are not appropriate to ask parents of infants.)
135. Please tell me if you have talked about sex with [cite child's name].
    (If yes, go to question 136; if no, go to question 139.)
136. What did you discuss?
137. How old was [cite child's name] when you discussed sex with him [her]?
138. How did [cite child's name] feel about the discussion?
    (Go to instructions preceding question 140.)
139. Tell me about your decision not to discuss sex with [cite child's name].

Description of Other Children in Family
(Ask these questions if there are other children in the family; otherwise, go to question 180.)
140. Now I'd like to learn about the other children in your family. Tell me about them.
    (Ask questions 141 to 160, as needed.)
141. How has their health been—any illnesses and accidents?
142. What were they like as infants?
143. And as toddlers. What were they like when they were 2 to 5 years old?
144. And when they went to school. What were they like?
145. How were their grades?
146. Did they have any problems in school?
147. (If yes) What problems did they have?
148. Do they have friends?
149. (If yes) Tell me about their friends.
    (Go to question 151.)
150. Tell me about their not having friends.
151. How do you get along with the children?
152. And how does your husband [wife, partner, friend, etc.] get along with them?
153. Did they ever get into trouble with the law?
154. (If yes) What trouble did they get into?
155. Did they have any problems with drugs or alcohol?

156. (If yes) What problems did they have?
157. Are any of your children frequently alone only with males or only with females?
158. (If yes) Tell me about that.
159. (If needed and relevant) Is there any possibility that any of your children are participating in sexual activities?
160. (If yes) What kind of sexual activity might they be participating in?
161. Now I'd like to discuss discipline. What do they do that makes you discipline them?
162. How do you discipline them?
163. How often do you discipline them?
164. Do you have any problems disciplining them?
165. (If yes) What problems do you have?
     (If interviewee has significant other, go to question 166; otherwise, go to question 172.)
166. And what about your husband [wife, partner, friend, etc.]? What type of discipline does he [she] use?
167. Who seems to be more effective in getting the kids to listen—you or your husband [wife, partner, friend, etc.]?
168. Tell me about that.
169. Does your husband [wife, partner, friend, etc.] have any problems disciplining the children?
170. (If yes) What problems does he [she] have?
171. What complaints does your husband [wife, partner, friend, etc.] have about the way you handle the children?
172. How do you spend time with your children?
173. (If needed) What activities do you like to do with your children?
174. What activities with the children bore you the most?
175. How do you feel about your children's friends?
176. How do you treat your children's friends?
177. (If relevant) And how does your husband [wife, partner, friend, etc.] treat them?
178. What kinds of needs does each of your children have now?
179. What would you like your children's future to be?

Social Supports
180. When you are having problems, to whom can you turn?
181. (If needed) Do you have any relatives or friends to whom you can turn?
182. (If yes) How do they help you?
183. And how about agencies? Have you contacted any agencies?
184. (If yes) How have they helped you?
185. Can you turn to any religious group for help?
186. (If yes) Tell me about that.
187. (If relevant) Is there any place that you and your children can go during this time of crisis?
188. (If yes) Where can you go?
189. Have you ever had a financial crisis?
     (If yes, go to question 190; if no, go to question 194.)
190. Do you have someone to turn to when you are having a financial crisis?
     (If yes, go to question 191; if no, go to question 193.)
191. To whom do you turn?

192. How do they [does he, does she] help?
     (Go to question 194.)
193. If you had no one to turn to, how did you manage the financial crisis?
194. To whom do you turn when you are having problems with your children?
195. How can they [he, she] help?
196. If you were unable to take care of your children, who would take care of them?
197. Tell me about that.

Concluding Questions
198. Is there anything else you would like to tell me?
199. (If yes) Go ahead.
200. Do you have any questions that you would like to ask me?
201. (If yes) Go ahead.
202. Thank you for talking with me. If you have any questions or if you want to talk to me, please call me. Here is my card.

Note. To obtain information about the child's psychological problems, see Table F-36 in this Appendix. To obtain a more detailed developmental history of the child, see Table F-21 in this Appendix.
Source: Adapted, in part, from Burgess, Groth, Holmstrom, and Sgroi (1978), Faller (1988), and Hodges (1986).

Table F-23
Semistructured Interview Questions for an Older Child or Adolescent in a Crisis Associated with an Event

---

This interview assumes that the child may be in a crisis precipitated by some event, such as a natural disaster, fire, shooting, or suicide.

Introduction
1. Hi. I'm Dr. [Mr., Ms.] _____. I work at _____. I'd like to talk to you about how you are getting along. OK?
2. When you don't understand a question that I ask, please say "I don't understand." When you tell me that, I'll try to ask it better. OK?
3. What brought you to see me at this time?
4. (If child does not talk about the event and you know about the event, consider mentioning it at this time.) I understand that something recently happened in your family. I'd like to know more about it, if you could share your thoughts with me. (Or) I'm talking to boys and girls about [cite event] that recently happened. I'd like to talk to you about it. OK?
5. How are you getting along?
6. Tell me what happened.
   (Ask questions 7 to 20, as needed.)
7. What did you see?
8. Where were you when it happened?
9. Whom were you with?
10. What were you doing?

11. How did it make you feel?
12. What was your first thought when it happened?
13. What were you thinking while it was happening?
14. What did other people do while it was happening?
15. What did you do after it happened?
16. Were you injured, or was anyone you know injured?
17. (If yes) Tell me about that.
18. And how do you feel now when you think about what happened?
19. (If needed) Are you having any problems?
20. Tell me about that.
21. Do you feel any different now than you did before [cite event]?
22. Tell me about that.
23. Do you keep thinking about [cite event]?
24. (If yes) Tell me about it.
25. (If needed) How do you feel when you think about [cite event]?

Symptoms

(If child does not describe any problems or if you want to ask about specific symptoms, go to question 26; if not, go to question 63.)

26. Do you feel scared?
27. (If yes) Tell me about your feeling scared.
28. How are you sleeping?
29. (If sleep is disturbed) Tell me more about that.
30. Do you have any scary dreams?
31. (If yes) Tell me about your scary dreams.
32. Do you have more scary dreams now than you did before [cite event] happened?
33. And how about scary thoughts during the day? Do you have any scary thoughts during the day?
34. (If yes) Tell me about them.
35. Do you have more scary thoughts during the day now than you did before [cite event] happened?
36. Is there anything that you are afraid of lately?
37. (If yes) Tell me about it.
38. Have you developed any new habits that you don't like or that your parents don't like?
39. (If yes) Tell me about these habits.
40. Do you think about [cite event] even when you don't want to?
41. (If yes) How do you feel when you think about it?
42. Have you lost interest in things since [cite event] happened?
43. (If yes) Tell me about the things you've lost interest in.
44. Do you find that sometimes you can't remember some important things about [cite event]?
45. (If yes) Tell me about that.
46. Do you have trouble paying attention to your schoolwork?
47. (If yes) Tell me about your difficulties paying attention.
48. Do you feel as though you can't talk about your feelings as easily as you did before [cite event] happened?
49. (If yes) Tell me about that.
50. Do you lose your temper or get mad more easily than you did before [cite event] happened?
51. (If yes) Tell me about that.
52. Do you get startled more easily now than you did before [cite event] happened?
53. Tell me more about that.

54. Do you feel sick more often now than you did before [cite event] happened?
55. (If needed) Do you have more headaches or stomachaches?
56. (If yes) Tell me about these problems you're having.
57. Have you felt as if life is not worth living?
58. (If yes) Tell me about that.
59. (If needed) Are you able to carry on your normal activities?
60. (If no) In what way can't you carry on your normal activities?
61. Are you worried that you might die soon?
62. (If yes) Tell me about your worries.

Coping with Crisis and Getting Help

63. When before in your life have you felt most like you have been feeling lately?
64. Tell me about that time.
65. (If needed) How did you handle those feelings then?
66. What could you do now to make yourself feel better?
67. Do you have anyone you can talk to about what you have been through?
68. (If yes) Tell me about him [her, them].
69. What kind of help do you think you need?
70. What kind of help have you gotten?
71. (If receiving help) Are you satisfied with the help you're getting?
72. Whom else can you turn to for help?
73. How is your family treating you?
74. Have they given you any advice?
75. (If yes) Tell me about that.

Concluding Questions

76. How has this event affected your life?
77. How do you think [cite event] will affect your future?
78. How has this event affected your family?
79. Is there anything you would do differently if it happened again?
80. On the basis of what we've talked about, what do you think we can do about [cite problems or feelings]?
81. Is there anything else you want to tell me or you think I should know?
82. (If yes) Go ahead.
83. Do you have any questions for me?
84. (If yes) Go ahead.
85. Thank you for talking with me. If you have any questions or if you want to talk to me, please call me. Here is my card.

Note. With modifications, these questions also can be used for a parent. You would need to substitute the child's name for "you" or "your" and make the appropriate grammatical changes.

Phrase question 4 appropriately, depending on the type of crisis. After you learn about how the child is handling the crisis, do the following, as needed: (a) help the child work through his or her feelings about the crisis, (b) help the child realistically evaluate his or her situation, and (c) encourage the child to seek appropriate support groups. If you find a potential for suicide, consider using the semistructured interview in Table F-30 in this Appendix. If you need to interview the child about a problem area or concern in more detail, use the questions in Table F-13 in this Appendix.

Table F-24
Semistructured Interview Questions for an Older Child or Adolescent with Depression

Introduction

1. Hi! I'm Dr. [Ms., Mr.] _____. I'd like to talk to you about how you're getting along. OK?
2. When you don't understand a question that I ask, please say "I don't understand." When you tell me that, I'll try to ask it better. OK?

Dysphoric Mood

3. Tell me how you're feeling.
   (If needed, ask questions 4 through 24; otherwise, go to directions preceding question 25.)
4. I'm going to name some feelings and reactions. Please tell me if you often feel this way. OK?
5. Sad. Do you feel sad?
6. (If yes) Tell me about your feeling sad.
7. Lonely. Do you feel lonely?
8. (If yes) Tell me about your feeling lonely.
9. Unhappy. Do you feel unhappy?
10. (If yes) Tell me about your feeling unhappy.
11. Hopeless. Do you feel hopeless?
12. (If yes) Tell me about your feeling hopeless.
13. Depressed. Do you feel depressed?
14. (If yes) Tell me about your feeling depressed.
15. Pessimistic. Do you feel pessimistic?
16. (If yes) Tell me about your feeling pessimistic.
17. Do you get moody?
18. (If yes) Tell me about the times you get moody.
19. Do you get easily annoyed?
20. (If yes) Give me some examples of what gets you easily annoyed.
21. Do you cry easily?
22. (If yes) Tell me about the times you cry easily.
23. Are you hard to please?
24. (If yes) Give me some examples of how you are hard to please.
   (Ask questions 25 to 32 separately for each feeling or reaction mentioned by interviewee, as needed.)
25. In the last week, how often have you felt [cite feeling or reaction]?
26. When did you first notice being troubled by [cite feeling or reaction]?
27. Does this feeling ever go away for some time—say, for a few days or weeks?
28. (If yes) How do you feel when [cite feeling or reaction] goes away?
29. How does [cite feeling or reaction] start—does it start suddenly, or is there a slow build-up of feelings?
30. Is your [cite feeling or reaction] connected in some way with what you are doing at a particular time?
31. (If yes) Tell me about that.
32. Do you have any idea about why this feeling [or reaction] comes about?
33. Has anything happened to you lately that might be important to mention now?
34. When do you feel best during the day?
35. When do you feel worst during the day?
36. How much change do you notice in the way you feel from day to day?
37. (If relevant) When you are feeling really down, is there anything that can cheer you up?
38. (If yes) Tell me what can cheer you up.

Self-Deprecatory Ideation

39. How do you feel about yourself?
   (Ask questions 40 to 53, as needed.)
40. Do you feel that you are worthless?
41. (If yes) Tell me about your feelings of being worthless.
42. Do you feel that you are useless?
43. (If yes) Give me some examples of how you feel useless.
44. Do you feel that you are dumb or stupid?
45. (If yes) Give me some examples of when you feel dumb or stupid.
46. Do you feel that you are ugly?
47. (If yes) Tell me about these feelings of being ugly.
48. Do you feel guilty?
49. (If yes) Give me some examples of when you feel guilty.
50. Do you feel that you are to blame for something that happened?
51. (If yes) Tell me about this feeling.
52. Do you believe that you are being harassed or picked on?
53. (If yes) Tell me about these feelings of being harassed or picked on.
54. Do you feel that you want to die?
55. (If yes) Tell me about these feelings of wanting to die.
56. Have you thought about committing suicide?
57. (If yes) Tell me about these thoughts.
58. Have you attempted suicide?
59. (If yes) Tell me about your suicide attempt[s].
60. Have you thought about running away from home?
61. (If yes) Tell me about these thoughts of wanting to run away from home.

Aggressive Behavior (Agitation)

62. Do you think that you're difficult to get along with?
63. (If yes) Give me some examples of how you're difficult to get along with.
64. Do you argue a lot with anyone?
   (If yes, go to question 65; if no, go to question 67.)
65. With whom do you argue?
66. What do you argue about?
67. Do you have trouble getting along with people in authority, such as teachers, the school principal, or the police?
   (If yes, go to question 68; if no, go to question 70.)
68. With whom do you have trouble getting along?
69. Give me some examples of the trouble you have getting along with [cite person or persons named by interviewee].
70. Do you get into fights with people?
   (If yes, go to question 71; if no, go to question 73.)
71. With whom do you fight?
72. What do you fight about?
73. Do you feel angry sometimes?
   (If yes, go to question 74; if no, go to question 76.)

74. What do you feel angry about?
75. What do you do when you feel angry?

Sleep Disturbances
76. Do you need more sleep than usual lately?
77. (If yes) Tell me about that.
78. Do you have trouble sleeping?
79. (If yes) Tell me about your trouble sleeping.
80. (If needed) How many nights this week have you had trouble falling asleep?
81. Are you restless when you sleep?
82. (If yes) Tell me about your restlessness when you sleep.
83. Is it hard for you to wake up in the morning?
84. (If yes) Tell me about the difficulty you have waking up in the morning.

Change in School Performance and Attitude
85. How do you feel about school?
86. Has your attitude toward school changed recently?
87. (If yes) How has your attitude toward school changed?
88. Do you daydream in school?
89. (If yes) Give me some examples of when you daydream.
90. Do you have trouble concentrating in school?
91. (If yes) Tell me about your trouble concentrating in school.
92. How have your grades been?
93. Do you have a good memory or a poor memory for your schoolwork?
94. (If poor) Give me some examples of your poor memory for schoolwork.
95. Do you find that you usually get your homework done or that you have a lot of homework that you don't get done?
96. Have there been changes recently in your ability to do your school work?
97. (If yes) Tell me about these changes.
98. Have you ever refused to go to school?
99. (If yes) Tell me about that.

Diminished Socialization
100. How are you getting along with your friends?
101. Do you have any close friends to whom you can talk?
102. Tell me about that.
103. Have there been any changes in your relationships with your friends?
104. (If yes) Tell me about these changes.
105. And how about school? How do you get along with other students at school?
106. (If needed) Have you lost interest in doing things with other people?
107. (If yes) Tell me about that.
108. How much time do you spend alone?
109. How do you feel about the time you spend alone?
110. And how do you feel when you are alone?
111. Do you feel a need to be alone?
112. (If yes) Tell me about that.

Somatic Complaints
113. Tell me about your health.
     (Ask questions 114 to 121, as needed.)
114. Do you get headaches?
115. (If yes) Tell me about your headaches.
116. Do you get pains in your stomach?
117. (If yes) Tell me about the pains in your stomach.
118. Do you get muscle aches or pains?
119. (If yes) Tell me about your muscle aches or pains.
120. Do you have any other pains or physical problems?
121. (If yes) Tell me about these pains or physical problems.

Loss of Usual Energy
122. Have you lost interest in doing things, like your hobbies?
123. (If yes) Give me some examples of your loss of interest.
124. Do you feel as though you have less energy to do things?
125. (If yes) Give me some examples of your loss of energy.
126. Have you stopped doing anything you used to do?
127. (If yes) Tell me about that.
128. Do you often feel tired?
129. (If yes) Give me some examples of your feeling tired.
130. Is there anything you look forward to?
131. (If yes) Tell me what you look forward to.

Unusual Change in Appetite and/or Weight
132. Has there been a change in your appetite?
133. (If yes) Tell me about the change in your appetite. (If needed, ask questions 134 to 139.)
134. Have you had to force yourself to eat?
135. (If yes) Tell me about that.
136. Do you find yourself eating too much?
137. (If yes) Tell me about that.
138. Has there been a change in your weight?
139. (If yes) Tell me about the change in your weight.

Concluding Questions
140. Is there anything else you would like to talk about or tell me?
141. (If yes) Go ahead.
142. Is there anything you would like to ask me?
143. (If yes) Go ahead.
144. Thank you for talking with me. If you have any questions or if you want to talk to me, please call me. Here is my card.

Note. With modifications, these questions also can be used for a parent. You would need to substitute the child's name for "you" or "your" and make the appropriate grammatical changes.

If interviewee expresses suicidal thoughts, consider asking questions in Table F-30 in this Appendix.

Source: Adapted from Weinberg, Rutman, Sullivan, Penick, and Dietz (1973) and Wilson, Spence, and Kavanaugh (1989).

Table F-25
**Semistructured Interview Questions
for an Older Child or Adolescent in a
Mental Status Examination**

1. Hi! I'm Dr. [Ms., Mr.] _____. I'd like to ask you some questions. OK?

General Orientation to Time, Place, and Person
2. What is your name?
3. How old are you?
4. What is today's date?
5. What day of the week is it?
6. What is the season?
7. What time of day is it?
8. Where are you?
9. What is the name of the state we are in?
10. What is the name of this city?
11. What is the name of this place?

Recent and Remote Memory
12. And your telephone number is…?
13. What is your address?
14. What do you do?
15. What is my name?
16. What did you have for breakfast?
17. What did you do in school [at the hospital, at home] yesterday?
18. Who is the president of the United States?
19. Who was the president before him?
20. (If relevant) Where did you live before you moved to [cite city]?
21. Name three major cities in the United States.
22. What are two major news events that happened in the last month?
23. How did you get to this hospital [clinic, office]?
24. What is your father's name?
25. What is your mother's name?
26. When is your birthday?
27. Where were you born?
28. What school do you go to?
29. (If relevant) When did you finish elementary school?
30. (If relevant) When did you finish high school?

Immediate Memory
31. Say these numbers after me: 6-9-5…4-3-8-1… 2-9-8-5-7.
32. Say these numbers backwards: 8-3-7…9-4-6-1… 7-3-2-5-8.
33. Say these words after me: pencil, chair, stone, plate.

Insight and Judgment
34. What does this saying mean: "Too many cooks spoil the broth"?
35. What does this saying mean: "A stitch in time saves nine"?
36. How are a banana, peach, and pear alike?
37. How are a bicycle, wagon, and car alike?

Reading, Writing, and Spelling
38. Read these words. (Give interviewee a piece of paper with the following words on it: pat, father, setting, intervention.)
39. Now write these same words. (Give interviewee blank piece of paper on which to write; show same words as in question 38.)
40. Spell these words: spoon…cover…attitude… procedure.

Arithmetical Concentration
41. (For children between 7 and 12 years) Subtract by 3s, starting with 30.
42. (For adolescents) Subtract by 7s, starting with 50.

Concluding Questions
43. Are there any questions that you would like to ask me?
44. (If yes) Go ahead.
45. Thank you for talking with me. If you have any questions or if you want to talk to me, please call me. Here is my card.

Table F-26
Semistructured Interview Questions for an Older Child or Adolescent with Traumatic Brain Damage

These questions supplement those in Table F-13 in this Appendix.

Introduction
1. Hi, I'm Dr. [Ms., Mr.] _____. And your name is…? I'm going to be asking you some questions. When you don't understand a question that I ask, please say "I don't understand." When you tell me that, I'll try to ask it better. OK?
2. Has anyone told you why you are here today? (If yes, go to question 3; if no, go to question 5.)
3. Who told you?
4. What did he [she, they] tell you? (Go to question 6.)
5. Tell me why you think you are here. (If interviewee doesn't know, explain to her or him that you want to find out how she or he is getting along or something similar.)

General Problems
6. Please tell me anything you can about how you are getting along.
7. (If needed) Are you having any problems? (If child says that he or she is having problems, go to question 8; otherwise, go to question 19.)
8. Tell me about [cite problems mentioned by child].
9. How do you feel about [cite problems]?
10. What changes have you noticed since [cite problems] began?
11. In what situations do you have the most difficulty with [cite problems]?

12. What do you do in these situations?
13. Is there anything that helps?
14. (If yes) How does it help?
15. What kind of help would you like?
16. How do your parents feel about the problems you are having?
17. How do your friends feel about the problems you are having?
18. And how do your teachers feel about the problems you are having?

Specific Current Problems and Complaints

19. I'm going to name some other areas in which you may have problems. If you have problems or complaints in any of these areas, please let me know by saying yes. After we finish the list, we'll go back to the beginning and I'll ask you more about these problems. OK?

(*If the child previously told you about a problem, do not mention it again now.* Pause after you name each problem or complaint. From time to time, remind the child of the task by prefacing the name of the problem with "Are you having a problem with…" or "Do you have any complaints about…")

General Physical Problems
— bowel or bladder control
— seizures
— headaches
— dizziness
— pain
— sleeping
— numbness
— loss of feeling
— blackouts
— muscle strength

Sensory-Motor Problems
— seeing
— hearing
— smelling
— speaking
— balance
— movements you can't control or stop
— standing
— walking
— running
— drawing
— handwriting
— eating
— dressing
— recognizing objects
— building or constructing things
— hearing ringing sounds
— changes in taste
— tingling in your fingertips or toes

Cognitive Problems
— thinking
— planning
— concentrating
— remembering
— paying attention
— understanding directions
— giving directions
— learning
— judging
— reading
— writing stories, poems, and other things
— spelling
— doing simple arithmetic problems
— understanding what is read to you
— handling money
— finding your way around

Psychosocial-Affective Problems
— keeping up with your responsibilities at home
— staying interested in things
— bathing
— organizing things
— getting along with other children [teenagers]
— getting along with friends and family members
— getting along with teachers
— controlling your temper
— feeling sad
— feeling anxious
— showing initiative
— doing things too fast or too slowly
— realizing that another person is upset
— controlling your laughter
— being inconsiderate of others
— being impatient
— being inflexible
— becoming angry without cause
— changing moods easily
— being irritable
— being aggressive
— being uncooperative
— being negative
— lying
— stealing
— having to do things exactly the same way each time
— changes in your personality
— failing to recognize problems in yourself
— being insecure
— changing from one activity to another
— visiting friends
— keeping friends
— going shopping

Language and Communication Problems
— talking too much
— talking too little
— using the right word
— using peculiar words
— saying embarrassing things
— reversing what you hear
— defining words
— naming objects that are shown to you
— counting
— naming the days of the week
— repeating names
— carrying on a conversation
— recognizing mistakes that you make in speaking or writing or reading

— using the telephone
— watching television
— looking up telephone numbers
— remembering telephone numbers

Consciousness Problems
— feeling disoriented
— feeling that you are losing your body
— feeling that some unknown danger is lurking
— doing things that you are unaware of
— starting to do one thing and then finding yourself doing something else
— feeling that the size of your hands or feet or head is changing

(If the child responded "yes" to any area, go to question 20; otherwise, go to question 24.)

20. You told me that you have a problem with [cite area]. Tell me more about your difficulty with [cite area]. (Repeat for each problem.)
21. Which problems bother you most?
22. How do you deal with these problems?
23. How do your parents deal with these problems?

Accident or Injury
24. I'd like to learn about the accident [injury]. Please tell me about it.
(Ask questions 25 to 36 as needed.)
25. What happened?
26. What were you doing at the time of the accident [injury]?
27. Who else was involved in the accident [injury]?
28. Were you unconscious?
(If yes, go to question 29; if no, go to question 31.)
29. How long were you unconscious?
30. Where did you wake up?
31. What kind of treatment did you get?
32. How did the treatment help?
33. What kind of treatment are you receiving now?
34. What was your behavior like right after the accident [injury] happened?
35. What was your behavior like several days later?
36. And what is your behavior like now?

Adjustment to Brain Injury and Typical Activities
37. Have you noticed any changes since the accident [injury] in how you are getting along with your parents?
38. (If yes) Tell me what you have noticed.
39. (If relevant) Have you noticed any changes since the accident [injury] in how you are getting along with your brothers and sisters?
40. (If yes) Tell me what you have noticed.
41. Have you noticed any changes since the accident [injury] in how you are getting along with your friends?
42. (If yes) Tell me what you have noticed.
43. Have there been any changes in your schoolwork since the accident [injury]?
44. (If yes) Tell me about the changes in your schoolwork.
45. (If relevant) Have there been any changes in your work habits since the accident [injury]?
46. (If yes) Tell me about the changes in your work habits.

Concluding Questions
47. Is there anything else that you want to tell me or that you think I should know?
48. (If yes) Go ahead.
49. Do you have any questions that you would like to ask me?
50. (If yes) Go ahead.
51. Thank you for talking with me. If you have any questions or if you want to talk to me, please call me. Here is my card.

Note. With modifications, these questions also can be used for a parent. You would need to substitute the child's name for "you" or "your" and make the appropriate grammatical changes.

Guidelines for conducting a more extensive interview with the child are shown in Table F-13 in this Appendix.

Table F-27
Semistructured Interview Questions for an Older Child or Adolescent Who Has a Health-Related Disorder

Introduction
1. Hi. I'm Dr. [Ms., Mr.] _____. Your doctor, Dr. _____, asked me to see you. I'd like to talk to you about how you're getting along. OK?
2. When you don't understand a question that I ask, please say "I don't understand." When you tell me that, I'll try to ask it better. OK?

Knowledge of Problem
3. Do you know why Dr. _____ asked me to see you?
4. (If yes) Tell me about what you know. (Clarify what interviewee says, if necessary, or say, "That's right" if interviewee knows why he or she was referred. Then go to question 6.)
5. Dr. _____ said [tell interviewee the reason].
6. Tell me about [cite problem, illness, concern, etc., that doctor mentioned].
7. (If needed) Tell me anything else you know about [cite problem, illness, concern, etc.].
8. How do you feel about [cite problem, illness, concern, etc.]?
9. Tell me about your feelings.
10. Who told you about [cite problem, illness, concern, etc.]?
11. (If needed) Are you worried about [cite problem, illness, concern, etc.]?
12. (If yes) Tell me about your worries.
13. What do you think caused [cite problem, illness, concern, etc.]?
14. (If relevant) Do you believe that your doctor has told you everything you should know about [cite problem, illness, concern, etc.]?
15. Tell me about that.
16. Have you learned anything else about [cite problem, illness, concern, etc.] from anyone else?

17. (If yes) Tell me who told you things about [cite problem, illness, concern, etc.] and what they told you.
18. When you want to know something about [cite problem, illness, concern, etc.], what do you do?
19. (If needed) Whom do you ask? Do you ask your parents about [cite problem, illness, concern, etc.]?
20. Tell me about that.
21. Do they [does he, does she] answer all your questions?
22. (If no) Tell me about that.
23. What do you talk about?
24. Have they [has he, has she] told you what you want to know about [cite problem, illness, concern, etc.]?
25. (If no) Tell me about that.

Symptoms
26. When did you first notice that you had [cite problem, illness, concern, etc.]?
27. (If child has not mentioned symptoms) What were the first things that bothered you?
28. What did you do after [cite symptoms mentioned by child] began?
29. How long did you wait before you told anyone about [cite symptoms]?
30. (If a long delay) Tell me about the reason that you didn't tell anyone for a while.
   (If pain is the major problem or concern, go to question 31; if not, go to question 79.)

Pain
31. How would you describe your pain?
32. (If needed) Would you say that your pain is dull… sharp…cutting…aching…throbbing… grinding… pressure-like…crushing?
33. Do you feel anything else when you have the pain? For example, do you also have nausea, vomiting, dizziness, or rapid breathing, or do you feel faint or anxious?
34. (If yes) Tell me about what else you feel when you have the pain.
35. How bad is the pain?
36. Where do you have the pain?
37. Look at this diagram (show Figure 17-1 for a male or Figure 17-2 for a female in Chapter 17). Please put an X on the exact place where you feel you are having pain now. If there is more than one painful place, mark those places 1, 2, 3, 4, and so forth, starting with the most painful place as 1.
   (Questions 38 to 40 are designed to produce a quantitative rating of the child's pain. To use this procedure, make a card on which the numbers 0, 1, 2, 3, 4, 5, 6, 7, 8, 9, and 10 appear below a horizontal line. Write "no pain" under the 0, "medium pain" under the 5, and "very bad pain" under the 10. Show the card to the child, and ask him or her to point to a position on the line after you ask each question. If you prefer, you can modify the instructions so that the questions can be answered without using a card. If you prefer to use another procedure to obtain a quantitative rating of the child's pain, use it in place of questions 38 to 40.)

38. On a scale from 0 to 10, please show me how much pain you are having right now. Remember, 0 means no pain at all and 10 means very bad pain. You can put your finger anywhere you want on the line to show how much pain you are having right now. (Show card.)
39. On a scale from 0 to 10, please show me how much pain you have on a usual day. Remember, 0 means no pain at all and 10 means very bad pain. You can put your finger anywhere you want on the line to show how much pain you feel on a usual day. (Show card.)
40. On a scale from 0 to 10, please show me the worst pain you had in the past week. Remember, 0 means no pain at all and 10 means very bad pain. You can put your finger anywhere you want on the line to show the worst pain you had in the past week. (Show card.)
41. What time of day do you feel the worst pain?
42. (If needed) Is it in the morning…at noon…at night… before you go to bed?
43. What time of day do you feel the least amount of pain?
44. (If needed) Is it in the morning…at noon…at night… before you go to bed?
45. Is your pain there all the time, or does it come and go?
46. Tell me about that.
   (If the pain comes and goes, go to question 47; if the pain is there all the time, go to question 60.)
47. Do you know when the pain is coming?
48. (If yes) Tell me how you know.
49. What seems to bring on the pain?
50. How do you feel before the pain begins?
51. And after?
52. (If needed) Have you ever noticed any sign that the pain is about to come, such as stiffness, a particular thought or statement, some other feeling in your body, or irritability?
53. (If yes) What have you noticed?
54. Does your pain go away suddenly or slowly drift away?
55. How many hours a day do you have pain now?
56. How long does one episode of pain usually last?
   (If child has more than one type of pain, ask this question for each type of pain.)
57. Where are you usually when you have the pain?
58. (If needed) Are you at home…at school…playing with friends?
59. What are you usually doing before the pain begins?
60. What makes your pain worse?
61. (If needed) Does your pain seem worse when you are feeling a certain way, such as tired, angry, happy, lonely, or upset?
62. (If yes) Tell me about these feelings.
63. Are there any other times when your pain is particularly bad?
64. (If yes) When?
65. How does stress in your life [worry] change the pain you are having?
66. How is the pain on weekends?
67. On vacations?
68. How does a change in your daily routine affect the pain?
69. Do you have other problems or difficulties at the same time you are having the pain?
70. (If yes) What are they?

71. When you have the pain, how do you react?
72. (If needed) Does the pain ever make you angry, irritable, or hard to be with?
73. What kinds of things can't you do because of the pain? (Ask questions 74 to 78, as needed.)
74. During the past three months, did the pain stop you from doing things that you wanted to do?
75. (If yes) Tell me about these things.
76. During the past three months, how often did the pain stop you from doing activities that require a lot of energy, such as running, bicycling, lifting heavy objects, or participating in sports?
77. During the past three months, how often did the pain stop you from doing activities that require a medium amount of energy, such as climbing several flights of stairs, bending, walking several blocks, lifting something, or stooping?
78. During the past three months, how often did the pain stop you from doing light activities, such as walking one block, climbing one flight of stairs, sitting, or standing?

Relationship with Parents, Family, and Friends

79. How do your parents feel about [cite problem, illness, concern, etc.]?
80. Do you tell your parents how you feel about [cite problem, illness, concern, etc.]?
81. (If yes) What do they say when you tell them your feelings?
82. Do your parents talk to other people about your [cite problem, illness, concern, etc.] when you are present?
83. (If yes) How do you feel about their talking to other people about your [cite problem, illness, concern, etc.]?
84. Since you became ill, have your parents changed the way they treat you?
85. (If yes) Tell me about how they've changed.
86. (If relevant) Do your parents treat you differently than they do your brothers and sisters?
87. (If yes) In what way?
88. (If relevant) How do your brothers and sisters feel about your problem?
89. And do your friends know about your problem?
90. (If yes) How do they feel about your problem? (Go to question 92.)
91. What makes it difficult to tell your friends?

Communication with Doctor

92. How are you getting along with your doctor?
93. Do you have any problems talking to your doctor?
94. (If yes) Tell me about the problems you're having talking with your doctor.
95. Do you discuss your symptoms with your doctor?
96. (If no) Tell me about that.

Treatment and Management Issues

97. What treatment are you getting?
98. How is it helping?
99. Do you have any bad effects from the treatment?
100. (If yes) Tell me about them.
101. How much do your parents help you with your treatment?

102. Who told you about how to take care of your problem?
103. Do you understand what to do? (If no, go to question 104; if yes, go to question 106.)
104. What problems are you having understanding what to do?
105. What makes it hard to follow the treatment?
106. Sometimes things happen in a family that affect a kid's ability to follow the treatment. Has anything like that happened in your family?
107. (If yes) Tell me about that.
108. Sometimes things happen at school or with friends that affect a kid's ability to follow the treatment. Has anything like that happened to you?
109. (If yes) Tell me about that.
110. What things make you go off your treatment?
111. Tell me about how that happens.
112. Do you have any say in how you can carry out your treatment?
113. Tell me about that.
114. What do you think might happen if you didn't follow the treatment?
115. Do you have any questions about the treatment?
116. (If yes) What are they?
117. Do you have any questions about how to follow the treatment?
118. (If yes) What are they?
119. Have you ever been in a hospital for [cite problem, illness, concern, etc.]?
120. (If yes) What was it like being in a hospital?
121. Do you keep your appointments with your doctor?
122. (If no) What makes it difficult to keep your appointments?
123. Has your doctor told you that you should exercise? (If yes, go to question 124; if no, go to question 130.)
124. What kinds of exercises did your doctor tell you to do?
125. How often should you exercise?
126. How often do you exercise?
127. (If child does not follow exercise schedule) What makes it hard to do the exercises?
128. Do you think that the exercises help you?
129. Tell me about that.
130. Has your doctor given you a special diet? (If yes, go to question 131; if no, go to question 139.)
131. What kind of diet did your doctor give you?
132. Are you able to follow it most of the time?
133. (If no) What part of the diet is hard to follow?
134. What makes it hard to follow the diet?
135. Does anyone help you with your diet?
136. Tell me about that.
137. Do you think that following the diet helps you?
138. Tell me about your answer.
139. Has your doctor prescribed any medicines for you? (If yes, go to question 140; if no, go to question 156.)
140. What medicine has the doctor prescribed?
141. Do you take the medicine that the doctor has prescribed? (If yes, go to question 142; if no, go to question 153.)
142. What do you think about taking your medicine?
143. Do you take all the pills [liquids, shots, etc.] that the doctor has prescribed?
144. (If no) What makes it difficult to take the medicine?

145. Do you take the pills [liquids, shots, etc.] at the right times during the day?
146. (If no) What makes it difficult to take the pills [liquids, shots, etc.] at the right times?
(Ask questions 147 to 152, if not covered previously.)
147. How does the medicine help you?
148. Have you had any bad effects from taking the medicine?
149. (If yes) Tell me about them.
150. Does anyone help you remember to take your pills [liquids, shots, etc.]?
151. Tell me about that.
152. (If relevant) Do you check the expiration dates on your medicine?
(Go to question 156.)
153. Tell me about the reasons you don't want to take the pills [liquids, shots, etc.].
154. (If needed) Are you concerned about possible side effects taking the medicine?
155. (If yes) Tell me about your answer.
156. Has the doctor recommended any special treatments for your condition that we haven't discussed?
(If yes, go to question 157; if no, go to question 166.)
157. What special treatments has your doctor recommended?
158. Have you been following his [her] recommendation?
(If no, go to question 159; if yes, go to question 161.)
159. What makes it difficult to follow your doctor's recommendation?
160. In what way are you not following your doctor's recommendation?
161. (If relevant) Who helps you with these treatments?
162. What do you think about these treatments?
163. How much time does each treatment take?
164. Do you think these treatments help you?
165. Tell me about that.

Adjustment to Problem

166. How has [cite problem, illness, concern, etc.] changed your life?
167. What do you do differently since you've had [cite problem, illness, concern, etc.]?
168. How much control over [cite problem, illness, concern, etc.] do you have?
169. How does having [cite problem, illness, concern, etc.] make it hard to plan?
170. Do you think [cite problem, illness, concern, etc.] is going to get worse or better in the next couple of years?
171. Tell me about that.
172. How are you managing [cite problem, illness, concern, etc.]?
173. How does [cite problem, illness, concern, etc.] get in the way of your thinking about the future?
174. How does [cite problem, illness, concern, etc.] affect the things you can do?
175. Tell me about that.
176. Have you missed school because of [cite problem, illness, concern, etc.]?
177. (If yes) How are you keeping up with your classes?

178. Are you ever teased about [cite problem, illness, concern, etc.]?
179. (If yes) Tell me about that.
180. How bad do you think [cite problem, illness, concern, etc.] is?
181. Tell me about that.
182. Has [cite problem, illness, concern, etc.] caused any particular problems with your family or friends?
183. (If yes) Tell me about these problems.
184. Have your family and friends had problems getting used to your having [cite problem, illness, concern, etc.]?
185. (If yes) Tell me about the problems they're having.

Interest in More Information

186. Would you like to learn more about your [cite problem, illness, concern, etc.]?
187. (If yes) What would you like to learn about?
188. Are there any other areas you would like to have more information about, such as following the treatment plan, medicines, diet, exercise, or getting along with your family and friends?
189. (If yes) What areas would you like to have more information about?
190. Do you think that your family would like to have more information about [cite problem, illness, concern, etc.]?
191. Would you like to meet other children [teenagers] with [cite problem, illness, concern, etc.] at a support group?

Concluding Questions

192. Is there anything else that you would like to talk about?
193. (If yes) Go ahead.
194. Do you have any questions that you would like to ask me?
195. (If yes) Go ahead.
196. Thank you for talking with me. If you have any questions or if you want to talk to me, please call me. Here is my card.

Source: Adapted from McLaughlin and Sliepcevich (1985).

Table F-28
Semistructured Interview Questions for an Older Child or Adolescent Who Is Having Difficulty Following His or Her Diabetes Regimen

Introduction

1. Hi. I'm Dr. [Ms., Mr.] _____. Your physician, Dr. _____, referred you to me. I'd like to talk to you about how you're getting along. OK?
2. When you don't understand a question that I ask, please say "I don't understand." When you tell me that, I'll try to ask it better. OK?

Effects of Diabetes on Normal Activities

3. Tell me about your understanding of what diabetes is.
4. What is it like to have diabetes?

5. How does having diabetes interfere with your life?
6. Do you have to miss school [work] because of your diabetes?
7. (If yes) Tell me about that.
8. Does your diabetes interfere with the activities you'd like to do in your spare time?
9. (If yes) Tell me about that.
10. Does stress [worry] have an impact on how you take care of your diabetes?
11. (If yes) What kind of stress [worry] has an effect on you?

Symptoms of Diabetes

12. One of the things people have to do when they have diabetes is control their blood sugar level. Do you know what that means?
13. (If yes) Tell me about that.
    (If child does not know about blood sugar levels, you will need to revise the following sections.)
14. Do you know whether your blood sugar is *too low* without testing it?
15. (If yes) How do you know?
    (Go to question 17.)
16. Have you ever had a low blood sugar level that caused symptoms like sweating, weakness, tiredness, anxiety, trembling, hunger, headache, or unconsciousness or for which you had to go to the hospital?
    (If yes, go to question 17; if no, go to question 21.)
17. How often do you have [cite symptoms]?
18. When did you last have [cite symptoms]?
19. What was going on that caused this to happen?
20. What did you do about it?
21. Have you ever had a low blood sugar reaction while sleeping?
22. (If yes) Tell me about that.
23. How much do you worry about having a really bad low blood sugar reaction?
24. Do you know whether your blood sugar is *too high* without testing it?
25. (If yes) How do you know?
    (Go to question 27.)
26. Have you ever had such high blood sugar that you had symptoms like thirst, dry mouth and skin, loss of appetite, nausea, or fatigue?
    (If yes, go to question 27; if no, go to question 31.)
27. How often do you have [cite symptoms]?
28. When did you last have [cite symptoms]?
29. What was going on that caused this to happen?
30. What did you do about it?

Management of Diabetes

31. I'm going to ask you about some things that people with diabetes may have to do.
32. Do you take insulin regularly?
    (If yes, go to question 33; if no, go to question 44.)
33. How many shots of insulin do you take each day?
34. Who gives you the shots?
    (If child gives shots, go to question 35; if somebody else gives shots, go to question 43.)
35. Do you ever have problems measuring the amount of insulin you need?

36. How do you decide how much insulin to give yourself?
37. Do you always remember to give yourself your insulin injections?
38. (If no) Tell me about that.
39. Does anyone help you remember to take your insulin?
40. Tell me about that.
41. Do you change your injection sites?
42. (If no) Tell me about that.
    (Go to question 44.)
43. How do you feel about having [cite person giving shots] give you shots?
44. Do you test your blood sugar regularly?
    (If yes, go to question 45; if no, go to question 52.)
45. How often do you test your blood sugar level on a typical day?
46. Do you always remember to test your blood sugar level?
47. (If no) Tell me about that.
48. Does anyone help you test your blood sugar level?
49. Tell me about that.
50. What values do you usually get when you test your blood sugar level?
51. (If needed) What values do you get before breakfast… before lunch…before dinner…before bed?
52. Do you check your urine for sugar or ketones or both?
    (If yes, go to question 53; if no, go to question 57.)
53. How often do you do this?
54. Does anyone help you test your urine?
55. (If yes) Tell me about that.
56. What values do you usually get?
57. Do you follow any type of special diet?
    (If yes, go to question 58; if no, go to question 61.)
58. Tell me about the diet.
59. Does anyone help you follow your diet?
60. (If yes) Tell me about that.
61. Do you avoid foods that are high in sugar?
62. Tell me about that.
63. Do you avoid foods that are high in fat?
64. Tell me about that.
65. Do you eat meals regularly?
66. Tell me about that.
67. Do you eat regular snacks?
68. Tell me about that.
69. Do you sometimes eat when you're not hungry?
70. (If yes) Tell me about that.
71. Do you sometimes eat something you shouldn't rather than tell someone that you have diabetes?
72. (If yes) Tell me about that.
73. How often do you eat something you shouldn't eat?
74. Do you often gain or lose weight?
75. (If yes) Tell me about that.
76. Do you watch your weight?
77. (If yes) Tell me about that.
78. Do family members eat foods that are different from the foods you eat?
79. (If yes) How do you feel about that?
80. Do you sometimes eat at a restaurant or friend's house?
81. (If yes) How do you decide what to eat?
82. Do you have trouble keeping to your meal schedule when you are away from home?

83. (If yes) Tell me about that.
84. Do you exercise?
    (If yes, go to question 85; if no, go to question 93.)
85. Tell me about that.
86. How often do you exercise?
87. What type of exercise do you do?
88. How do you feel about exercising?
89. Do you ever get a low blood sugar reaction when you exercise?
90. (If yes) What do you do when this happens?
91. Do you adjust your diet or insulin according to how much exercise you do?
92. Tell me about that.
93. Do you do anything different for your diabetes when you are sick?
94. (If yes) Tell me about what you do.
95. How do you take care of any injuries you get?
96. Tell me about that.
97. Do you carry food or glucose tablets with you?
98. Tell me about that.

Reactions to Managing Diabetes
99. How do you feel about the things you have to do to control your diabetes?
100. What is the hardest thing you have to do to control your diabetes?
101. What is the easiest thing you have to do to control your diabetes?
102. How would you rate the control of your diabetes?
103. (If needed) Would you rate the control of your diabetes as not very good, below average, average, above average, or very good?
104. Has your management of the diabetes changed over time?
105. (If yes) What caused you to change your management of the diabetes?
106. What interferes with your taking care of the diabetes?
107. How hard is it for you to do the things you must do to take care of the diabetes?
108. Is there anything that would make taking care of the diabetes easier for you?
109. (If yes) Tell me about that.
110. How involved are you in making decisions about care of the diabetes?
111. Is there anything going on in your life now that interferes with your ability to take care of the diabetes?
112. When you disagree with [cite person who helps child with management], what do you do?
113. When things happen in your family that affect the diabetes and how you control it, such as an argument between your parents about something, how do you handle these things?
114. Sometimes things happen at school or with friends that affect your diabetes or how you control your diabetes, such as being offered candy by someone. How do you handle things like that?

Attitude Toward Diabetes
115. How serious do you think diabetes is as an illness?
116. Tell me about that.

117. Do you think that your diabetes will lead to other problems?
118. Tell me about that.
119. Is there anything else you want to tell me?
120. (If yes) Go ahead.
121. Do you have anything that you want to ask me?
122. (If yes) Go ahead.
123. Thank you for talking with me. If you have any questions or if you want to talk to me, please call me. Here is my card.

Note. With modifications, these questions also can be used for a parent. You would need to substitute the child's name for "you" or "your" and make the appropriate grammatical changes.

Table F-29
Semistructured Interview Questions for an Older Child or Adolescent Who Is an Immigrant

Before you begin the formal interview, inquire about the interviewee's proficiency in English. Use an interpreter for interviewees who have a poor command of English. See Chapter 8 for information about using an interpreter.

Introduction
1. Hi. I'm Dr. [Ms., Mr.] _____. You must be [cite child's name]. Come in.
2. Has anyone told you why you are here today?
   (If yes, go to question 3; if no, go to question 5.)
3. Who told you?
4. What did he [she, they] say?
   (Go to question 6.)
5. Tell me why you think you are here today.
   (If child does not know or refuses to say why he or she is being seen, tell him or her the reason why, such as "Your teacher is concerned about how you are doing in school" or "Your mother is concerned about _____.")

Description of Problem
6. Tell me about the problem you're having.
7. When did you first notice [cite problem]?
8. How long has [cite problem] been going on?
9. Where does [cite problem] occur?
10. (If needed) Does it occur at home…at school…when you're traveling…at a friend's house?
11. When does [cite problem] occur?
12. (If needed) Does it occur when you first get up… during the day…at night before bedtime…at meal times? Does it happen when you are with your mother …father…brothers and sisters…other children… other relatives…the whole family together?
13. How long does [cite problem] last?
14. How often does [cite problem] occur?
15. (If relevant) Do your brothers and sisters also have this problem?
16. (If yes) How does your problem compare with theirs?

17. What happens just before [cite problem] begins?
18. What happens just after [cite problem] begins?
19. What makes [cite problem] worse?
20. What makes [cite problem] better?
21. What do you do when you have this problem?
22. What seems to work best?
23. What do you believe caused [cite problem]?
24. Was anything significant happening in your family when [cite problem] first started?
25. (If needed) For example, had your parents separated or divorced…you moved to another city or school… your dad or mom lost a job…someone in your family become very ill?
26. (If some event occurred) How did you feel when [cite event] happened?
27. How do your parents help you with [cite problem]?
28. (If relevant) How do your brothers and sisters help you with [cite problem]?
29. And your friends, do they help in any way?

Reasons for and Description of Leaving Native Country
30. What country were you born in?
31. What were your family's reasons for wanting to come to the United States?
32. Where were you before you came to the United States?
33. How did you get to the United States?
34. When did you leave?
35. Tell me about the way you left.
36. How long did it take you to get here?
37. When did you arrive in the United States?
38. Did you come here with just your family or with other people too?
    (If interviewee came with other people, go to question 39; otherwise, go to question 41.)
39. How many other people did you come with?
40. And who were these people?
41. How did you live while you were getting here?
42. How did you get food during this time?
43. How do you feel about the people who were left behind?
44. (If needed) Do you feel guilty?
45. Tell me more about these feelings.
46. Who made the decision to come to the United States?
47. (If needed) Were you able to leave freely, or did you have to escape?
    (If family had to escape, go to question 48; if not, go to question 57.)

Inquiry About Escape
48. Tell me about your escape.
    (Ask questions 49 to 56, as needed.)
49. How did you escape?
50. How long did it take?
51. With whom did you escape?
52. How did you survive during your escape?
53. Were there any periods in which you were separated from your family?
54. (If yes) Tell me about that.
55. Did anything terrible happen to you while you were try-ing to get here?
56. (If yes) Could you talk some more about that?

Inquiry About Refugee Camp
57. Were you ever in a refugee camp?
    (If yes, go to question 58; if no, go to question 68.)
58. What was your experience like in the refugee camp? (Ask questions 59 to 67, as needed.)
59. What did you do there?
60. Did you have enough food?
61. (If no) How did you manage to survive?
62. What were the living conditions like?
63. What were your sleeping arrangements?
64. Did you have enough clothing to wear?
65. Did you go to school?
66. How did you get along in the camp?
67. And how did your family get along in the camp?

Death of Family Member
68. Did anybody close to you die either before you left your country or during your journey?
    (If yes, go to question 69; if no, go to question 74.)
69. Tell me about that.
70. (If needed) How did you find out about his [her] death?
71. (If needed) How did he [she] die?
72. How did you feel when you found out about his [her] death?
73. Do you have any other thoughts or feelings about his [her] death at this time?

Life in Country of Origin
74. What was your life like before you left your home country?
    (Ask questions 75 to 92, as needed.)
75. Where did you live in [cite country]?
76. What did you do there?
77. How many years did you go to school there?
78. What did you study in school?
79. And how did you do in school?
80. How old were you when you were in your last year in school there?
81. What were your future plans?
82. What did your parents do there?
83. What relatives lived with you or nearby?
84. How did you all get along?
85. Did you practice a religion?
86. (If yes) Tell me about that.
87. Did you have any problems when you were living in [cite country]?
88. (If yes) Tell me about them.
89. (If child has siblings) Did any of your brothers or sis-ters have problems?
90. (If yes) Tell me about them.
91. Did your mother or father have any problems?
92. (If yes) Tell me about them.

Solving Problems in Former Country
93. How would you try to solve the problems you're having now if you were back in your home country?
    (Ask questions 94 to 100, as needed.)
94. To whom would you go for help?
95. (If needed) Would you go to a doctor, priest, or some other type of healer?
96. Tell me about that.

97. What medicines would you use?
98. (If needed) Would these medicines include herbal medicines?
99. Are there any other healing practices that you would use?
100. (If yes) Tell me about that.

Adjustment in the United States

101. Since you arrived in the United States, what have you been doing?
102. What did you think you would find when you came here?
103. Has your life in the United States been the way you thought it would be?
104. Tell me more about this.
105. How does your life in the United States compare with the life you had before you came here?
106. Do you have any regrets about leaving your home country?
107. (If yes) Tell me about that.

Interpersonal Relations

108. How are you getting along with your parents?
109. Tell me about that.
110. Are you able to talk about things with your parents?
111. What language do you speak with your parents?
112. (If needed) Do you have problems knowing what language to use when you talk to your parents?
113. (If yes) Tell me about that.
     (If child has siblings, go to question 114; otherwise, go to question 117.)
114. How are you getting along with your sisters and brothers?
115. Tell me about that.
116. What language do you speak with your sisters and brothers?
117. Do you have friends?
     (If yes, go to question 118; if no, go to question 122.)
118. Tell me about that.
119. What language do you speak with your friends?
120. Do you prefer hanging around with friends from your own culture or friends from other cultures, or doesn't it matter?
121. Tell me more about that.
     (Go to question 123.)
122. Tell me about your not having friends.
123. (If needed) Do your parents give you enough freedom?
124. (If not) Tell me about that.

Schooling

(If child is going to school, ask the questions in this section.)
125. What grade are you in?
126. What is your teacher's name [are your teachers' names]?
127. How do you get along with your teacher [teachers]?
     (If child has more than one teacher, go to question 128; otherwise, go to question 132.)
128. Who is your favorite teacher [are your favorite teachers]?
129. Tell me about him [her, them].

130. Who is the teacher you like least?
131. Tell me about him [her].
132. What subjects do you like best?
133. What about these subjects do you like?
134. What subjects do you like least?
135. What about these subjects do you like least?
136. What grades are you getting?
137. Are you in any activities at school?
138. (If yes) What activities are you in at school?
139. How do you get along with the other children in your school?
140. Tell me how you spend a usual day at school.
     (For older children, go to question 141; for younger children, go to question 144.)
141. Do you plan to go to college?
142. (If yes) What do you plan to major in?
143. (If relevant) And what career goals do you have?

Solving Problems in United States

144. What do you see as keeping you from solving your problems?
145. (If needed) Tell me which of the following you see as keeping you from solving your problems:

     — limited ability to speak English
     — poor study habits
     — lack of job skills
     — lack of transportation
     — lack of understanding of American culture
     — your parents' lack of understanding of American culture
     — lack of support from relatives
     — lack of money
     — inability to get along with other children [teenagers]
     — belonging to a gang
     — use of drugs
     — use of alcohol

146. What can you do about these things?

Parents

(If child is living with parents, go to question 147; if not, go to directions preceding question 156.)
147. And how are your parents getting along?
148. Tell me about that.
149. What kind of work is your father doing?
150. Tell me about his work [lack of work].
151. And your mother. Is she working?
152. Tell me more about that.
153. Are there any financial problems at home?
154. (If yes) Tell me about that.
155. What do your parents do for relaxation?

Other Children in Family

(If child has siblings, go to question 156; otherwise, go to question 160.)
156. Do your parents treat you about the same way they do your brothers and sisters?
157. Tell me about that.
158. And how are your brothers and sisters getting along?
159. Tell me about that.

Life Style

160. What do you do for relaxation?
161. Do you practice a religion in the United States?
162. (If yes) Tell me about that.
163. Are there conflicts between the culture of your native country and the American culture?
164. (If yes) Tell me about that.
165. (If relevant) Do you have any problems speaking English?
166. (If yes) Tell me about that.
167. (If relevant) Do you have any problems reading English?
168. (If yes) Tell me about that.

Contacting Utilities and Agencies

169. Do you know where to go for help when you need it?
170. Tell me about that.
171. (If needed) Do you know how to get to a doctor…get to a hospital…contact the police…call the fire station…contact the school principal?
172. Do you know how to get around in this city?
173. Tell me about that.
174. (If needed) Do you have a driver's license…know how to use the buses…have other means of transportation?

Concluding Questions

175. Is there anything else you would like to tell me?
176. (If yes) Go ahead.
177. Are there any questions that you would like to ask me?
178. (If yes) Go ahead.
179. Thank you for talking with me. If you have any questions or if you want to talk to me, please call me. Here is my card.

Note. See Table F-13 in this Appendix for a semistructured interview useful in obtaining a detailed history from a child.
Source: This table was adapted from material provided by Walter Philips, personal communication, March 1991.

Table F-30
Semistructured Interview Questions for an Older Child or Adolescent Who May Be Suicidal

Introduction

1. Hello. I'm Dr. [Ms., Mr.] _____. I work at _____. I'd like to talk with you about how you're getting along. OK?
2. When you don't understand a question that I ask, please say "I don't understand." When you tell me that, I'll try to ask it better. OK?

Changes in Behavior and Feelings

3. Have you noticed any changes in the way you've been feeling or acting recently?
4. (If yes) What changes have you noticed? (Ask questions 5 to 41, as needed.)
5. Do you feel that life is pretty hopeless? (If yes, go to question 6; if no, go to question 8.)

6. In what way?
7. What has happened to make you feel that life is hopeless?
8. Do you often feel so frustrated that you just want to lie down and quit struggling altogether?
9. (If yes) Tell me more about that.
10. Do you ever feel that you are worthless?
11. (If yes) Tell me about these feelings.
12. Have you become quieter lately?
13. (If yes) Tell me about that.
14. Do you find yourself losing interest in things?
15. (If yes) What are you losing interest in?
16. And do you tend to stay by yourself?
17. (If yes) Tell me about that.
18. And how about crying? Do you find yourself crying often?
19. (If yes) Tell me about that.
20. Do you find that you blame yourself for bad things that have happened? (If yes, go to question 21; if no, go to question 24.)
21. What do you blame yourself for?
22. (If needed) Do you blame yourself for family problems?
23. (If yes) What family problems do you blame yourself for?
24. Have you become more irritable lately?
25. (If yes) Tell me about it.
26. Do you find that you get angry very easily?
27. (If yes) Tell me about it.
28. Have you been worried about losing your mother [father, sister, brother, etc.]?
29. (If yes) Tell me about your worries.
30. Have you been worried about losing a close friend?
31. (If yes) Tell me about your worries about losing a close friend.
32. Have you recently changed the way you eat?
33. (If yes) In what way?
34. Have your sleep patterns recently changed?
35. (If yes) In what way?
36. Have your school grades recently changed?
37. (If yes) In what way?
38. Has your personality changed in any way recently?
39. (If yes) In what way?
40. Have you begun to use drugs or alcohol recently?
41. (If yes) Tell me about that.

Loss of Interest in Living

42. Have you recently given away things that are very special to you?
43. (If yes) What have you given away?
44. Have you done anything to hurt yourself?
45. (If yes) Tell me what you've done.
46. Do you tend to do dangerous things now?
47. (If yes) What sorts of things are you doing?
48. Have you eaten or drunk anything that might harm you?
49. (If yes) What have you eaten or drunk?
50. Have you done anything that might have caused you to die?
51. (If yes) What have you done?
52. Have you written anything that you think might be the last thing you will ever write?
53. (If yes) What have you written?

Traumatic Events

54. Have you been seriously ill recently?
55. (If yes) Tell me about your illness.
56. Has someone close to you been seriously ill?
57. (If yes) Tell me about that.
58. Has someone close to you been hospitalized?
59. (If yes) Tell me about his [her] hospitalization.
60. Have you lost a pet recently?
61. (If yes) Tell me about how you lost your pet.
62. Did you recently break up with a good friend?
63. (If yes) Tell me about the breakup.
64. Has someone close to you died recently?
65. (If yes) Tell me about who died.
66. Has anyone in your family attempted or committed suicide?
    (If yes, go to question 67; if no, go to question 69.)
67. Who was it?
68. Please tell me about it.
69. Have any of your friends attempted or committed suicide?
    (If yes, go to question 70; if no, go to question 72.)
70. Who was it?
71. Please tell me about it.
72. Is there anyone else you like or admire who has attempted or committed suicide?
    (If yes, go to question 73; if no, go to question 75.)
73. Who was it?
74. Please tell me about it.
75. Is there anything else that has happened to you or someone close to you that you are concerned about?
76. (If yes) Tell me about what happened.

Preoccupation with Death

77. Do you think about dying?
78. (If yes) What do you think about?
79. Do you dream about dying?
80. (If yes) What do you dream about?
81. Have you ever seen a dead person?
82. (If yes) Tell me about that.
83. Do you dream about any of your relatives who are dead?
84. (If yes) What do you dream about?
85. What do you think happens to people when they die?
86. How would others feel if you were dead?
87. Does the idea of endless sleep appeal to you?
88. (If yes) Tell me more about that.

Family

89. How does your family feel about the way you have been feeling?
90. How are you getting along with your parents?
91. Do your parents fight a lot?
    (If yes, go to question 92; if no, go to question 94.)
92. What do they fight about?
93. How does their fighting make you feel?
94. Do your parents give you the help and encouragement you need?
95. Do you feel pressured to do more or better than you are able to?
96. (If yes) Tell me about that.
97. (If relevant) How have you been getting along with your sisters and brothers?

98. Have you or anyone else one in your family been abused?
99. (If yes) Tell me about that.

Thoughts and Actions Related to Suicide

100. Have you recently thought about killing yourself?
     (If yes, ask questions 101 to 109 as needed; if no, go to question 110.)
101. How much do you want to die?
102. How serious are you about wanting to die?
103. Do you have a plan as to how you would kill yourself?
     (If yes, go to question 104; if no, go to question 108.)
104. Tell me about your plan.
105. Do you have a way to carry out your plan?
106. (If needed) Would you use a gun…a knife…pills…hanging?
107. (If yes) Tell me about that.
108. How do you think your family and friends would feel if you tried to take your life?
109. Tell me about that.
110. Have you wished that you were dead?
111. (If yes) Tell me about that.
112. Have you talked to anyone about killing yourself?
113. (If yes) Tell me about that.
114. Have you ever tried to commit suicide?
     (If yes, go to question 115; if no, go to question 121.)
115. Tell me about your suicide attempt[s].
     (Ask questions 116 to 120, as needed.)
116. What happened?
117. When did it happen?
118. Who found you?
119. What happened after he [she, they] found you?
120. How do you feel about what you did?
121. Do you want to live?
122. Tell me about how you feel about living.

Concluding Questions

123. What are your future plans?
124. Is there anything else you would like to tell me?
125. (If yes) Go ahead.
126. How does talking about all this make you feel?
127. Can anyone do anything to make you feel better?
128. Tell me about that.
129. Do you have anyone with whom you can talk about your problems?
130. (If yes) Who is that?
131. Is there anything else you would like to talk about?
132. (If yes) Go ahead.
133. Is there anything you would like to ask me?
134. (If yes) Go ahead.
135. Can you promise me that you won't hurt yourself at least until you meet with me again?
136. Thank you for talking with me. If you have any questions or if you want to talk to me, please call me. Here is my card.

Note. With modifications, these questions also can be used for a parent. You would need to substitute the child's name for "you" or "your" and make the appropriate grammatical changes.
Source: Adapted, in part, from Pfeffer (1986).

Table F-31
Semistructured Interview Questions for an Older Child or Adolescent Whose Relative Has Died

Introduction

1. Hi! I'm Dr. [Ms., Mr.] _____. I'd like to talk to you about how you're getting along. OK?
2. When you don't understand a question that I ask, please say "I don't understand." When you tell me that, I'll try to ask it better. OK?
3. I know this is a very difficult time for you, and I am sorry this happened. Could you tell me how you are feeling?
4. Is there anything you would like to talk about?
5. (If yes) Go ahead.
6. (If needed) Your mother [father, caregiver, etc.] is concerned about how you are handling the death of [cite relative's name]. What are you most worried about?

Relationship with Deceased Relative

7. I have talked to other children who had a [cite relative's relationship to child] die, and some of them are worried that they might have done something to cause the death. Does this worry you?
8. (If yes) Tell me about how this worries you.
9. Can you tell me a little about [cite relative's name]'s death?
10. (If needed) What happened?
11. What was your relationship like with [cite relative's name]?
12. Before [cite relative's name] died, were you able to say goodbye to each other?
13. (If no) What happened that you weren't able to say goodbye?
14. Before [cite relative's name] died, were you able to tell him [her] the things you wanted to say?
15. (If no) What happened that you weren't able to say the things you wanted to say?

Adjustment After Death of Relative

16. Since [cite relative's name]'s death, what has life been like for you?
17. And for your family. What has life been like for them since [cite relative's name]'s death?
18. Have you been through any other bad times like this lately?
19. (If yes) Tell me about them—what helped you get through those times?
20. And what about in the past? Have you been through any times like this before?
21. (If yes) Tell me about them—what helped you get through those times?
22. And how are you getting along with your friends?
23. Now could you tell me about how you've been eating?
24. And sleeping. How have you been sleeping?
25. How is your schoolwork?
26. Have you been seeing a physician?
27. (If yes) Tell me about that.
28. Is there anything else that you want to talk about?
29. Is there anything else you think I should know about how you are getting along?
30. (If yes) Tell me about that.
31. Do you have any questions that you would like to ask me?
32. (If yes) Go ahead.
33. Thank you for talking with me. If you have any questions or if you want to talk to me, please call me. Here is my card.

Note. If the child is depressed, consider using Table F-24 in this Appendix to inquire about his or her symptoms. If the child appears to be suicidal, consider using Table F-30 in this Appendix. If the child has other problems, consider using Table F-13 in this Appendix.
Source: Adapted from Schroeder and Gordon (1991).

Table F-32
Semistructured Interview Questions for a Parent in a Child Custody Dispute

Introduction

1. Hi. I'm Dr. [Ms., Mr.] _____. I've been asked by _____ to talk to you about the custody of [cite children's names]. In order to give a recommendation, I need to learn about you and about the children's father [mother]. I'm going to ask you about yourself, your family, and related topics. OK?
2. Let's begin by your telling me how you're getting along. Go ahead.
3. (If needed) Are you under any kind of stress?
4. (f yes) Tell me about it.
5. What changes would you like to make in your life?

Parent's Developmental History/Schooling

6. I'd like to know what it was like for you growing up. Perhaps we can begin with your telling me about your childhood. Where did you grow up?
7. What do you remember about the first five years of your life?
8. What do you remember about your early school years?
9. And junior high. What was that like?
10. And high school. What was that like?
11. (If relevant) And college. What was that like? (Ask questions 12 to 20 as needed.)
12. How did you get along in school?
13. Did you have problems with any subjects?
14. (If yes) Tell me about that.
15. Did you have any problems with the teachers?
16. (If yes) Tell me about that.
17. Did you have any problems with other children?
18. (If yes) Tell me about that.
19. Were you in any special classes?
20. (If yes) Tell me about the classes.

Parent's Friends

21. Tell me about the friends you had when you were a child.
22. (If no friends) Tell me about your not having friends.

23. Did you date as a teenager or young adult?
24. Tell me about that.

Parent's Family

25. Now I'd like to turn to your family. What were your parents like when you were growing up?
26. Did you have any problems with your parents?
27. (If yes) Tell me about the problems you had.
28. How would you describe your family when you were growing up?
29. (If relevant) How did you get along with your brothers and sisters?
30. As you look back on your family, what were some of the best things about growing up in your family?
31. And what were some of the worst things about growing up in your family?
32. (If relevant) How do you get along with your parents now?

Parent's Health

33. How was your health as a youngster?
34. Did you ever have any serious illnesses or accidents?
35. (If yes) Tell me about that.
36. Did you ever receive any professional counseling or therapy as a child?
37. (If yes) Tell me about that.

Parent's Work History

38. When you finished school, what did you do?
39. Tell me about your job history.
40. Are you working now?
    (If yes, go to question 41; if no, go to question 43.)
41. Tell me about your present job.
42. Are you satisfied with your job?
    (Go to question 45.)
43. When was the last time you worked?
44. What happened that you're not working now?
45. What would you like to be doing in five years?
46. Were you ever in the military?
    (If yes, go to question 47; if no, go to question 51.)
47. Tell me about that.
48. (If needed) What did you do in the Army [Navy, Air Force, etc.]?
49. What type of discharge did you get?
50. (If needed) Tell me about that.

Parent's Religious History

51. What is your religion?
52. What religion is the father [mother] of your children?
53. Have you and your children's father [mother] ever had serious disagreements over the children's religious training?
54. (If yes) Tell me about the disagreements.

Parent's Social-Recreational History

55. I'd like to ask you about your social and recreational activities. What do you do for relaxation?
56. Tell me about your hobbies.
57. Do you belong to any social clubs?
58. (If yes) Tell me about that.
59. Tell me about your friends.

60. Do you like to drink alcohol or take drugs?
    (If yes, go to question 61; if no, go to question 64.)
61. Tell me about that.
62. Have you ever been treated for alcoholism or drug addiction?
63. (If yes) Tell me about that.
64. Whom do you confide in if you have a personal problem?
65. How does it help?

Parent's Criminal History

66. Have you had any trouble with the law?
67. (If yes) Tell me about that.

Parent's Marital History

68. Have you been married before this marriage? (Note that "this marriage" refers to the marriage that produced the children involved in the custody dispute.) (If yes, go to question 69; if no, go to directions preceding question 75.)
69. Tell me about your former marriage[s].
70. What type of relationship do you now have with your former husband [wife]?
71. Did you have children in your former marriage[s]? (If yes, go to question 72; if no, go to directions preceding question 75.)
72. Tell me about the children from your former marriage[s].
73. What type of custody arrangement was made for the children of your former marriage[s]?
74. (If needed) What is your current relationship with your children from your former marriage[s]?

Parent's Marriage/Relationship That Produced the Children Involved in the Custody Dispute
(If interviewee was in a relationship and not married to the children's father or mother, you will need to substitute appropriate terms.)

75. Now I'd like to learn about your marriage to the children's father [mother]. When did you get married?
76. How did you meet him [her]?
77. What was your relationship like before you were married?
78. Did your relationship change after you were married?
79. (If yes) In what way?
80. Tell me about the marriage.
81. (If needed) How did you get along with your husband [wife]?
82. When did the problems in your marriage first begin?
83. What problems did you have?
84. How did you usually settle the problems?
85. When did you decide to separate?
86. Tell me about the separation.
87. Where are you living?
88. And your spouse [ex-spouse], where does he [she] live?
89. Where are the children living?
90. (If relevant) How often do you see them?
91. What problems have you and your husband [wife, former husband, former wife] had since the separation?

92. (If needed) When will the divorce be final?
93. Have either you or your husband [wife, former husband, former wife] started to date other people yet or remarried?
(If yes, go to question 94; if no, go to question 97.)
94. Has that affected the arrangements for your children in any way?
95. (If yes) How?
96. How does the new person get along with your children?

Description of Family
97. I'd like to learn about your family before the separation. What was your family like before the separation?
98. Is there anything else you want to tell me about what your family was like before the separation?
99. (If yes) Go ahead.
100. Who wanted to have the children?
101. And after the babies were born, how did you both feel?
102. Now let's talk about the children. Tell me about each of the children.
(Ask questions 103 to 119, as needed. Some questions concern older children only, such as questions 110 to 113.)
103. Tell me about their health, including any illnesses and accidents.
104. What were the children like as infants?
105. And as toddlers. What were the children like during the ages of 2 to 5 years?
106. And when they went to school. What were they like?
107. How were their grades?
108. Did they have any problems in school?
109. (If yes) Tell me about that.
110. Did they ever get into trouble with the law?
111. (If yes) Tell me about that.
112. Did they have any problems with drugs or alcohol?
113. (If yes) Tell me about that.
114. Tell me about your children's daily routine.
115. Generally, who helps your children with their routine, if they need help?
116. What chores do your children have to do at home?
117. How do you feel about your children's friends?
118. Before the separation, how did you get along with your children?
119. And now, how do you get along them?
120. Is your mother living?
121. (If yes) Tell me about your children's relationship with your mother.
122. Is your father living?
123. (If yes) Tell me about your children's relationship with your father.
124. Is your husband's [wife's, ex-husband's, ex-wife's] mother living?
125. (If yes) Tell me about your children's relationship with your husband's [wife's, ex-husband's, ex-wife's] mother.
126. Is your husband's [wife's, ex-husband's, ex-wife's] father living?
127. (If yes) Tell me about your children's relationship with your husband's [wife's, ex-husband's, ex-wife's] father.

128. (If needed) How often last year did your children see their grandparents?
129. Do your children have close relationships with any other members of your family?
130. (If yes) Tell me about that.
131. Do your children have close relationships with any other members of your husband's [wife's, ex-husband's, ex-wife's] family?
132. (If yes) Tell me about that.
133. How did you express affection for your husband [wife]?
134. And for your children? How do you express your affection for them?
135. How did your husband [wife] express affection for you?
136. And for your children? How does your husband [wife, ex-husband, ex-wife] express affection for them?
137. Now I'd like to turn to the topic of discipline. How do you discipline your children?
138. What do they do that causes you to have to discipline them?
139. How often do you discipline them?
140. Do you have any problems disciplining your children?
141. (If yes) Tell me about that.
142. Who disciplined the children before the separation?
143. And what about your husband [wife, ex-husband, ex-wife]? What type of discipline does he [she] use?
144. Who seems to be more effective in getting your children to listen—you or your husband [wife, ex-husband, ex-wife]?
145. Tell me about that.
146. Does your husband [wife, ex-husband, ex-wife] have any problems disciplining your children?
147. (If yes) Tell me about that.
148. Are the rules in both households the same or different?
149. What complaints does your husband [wife, ex-husband, ex-wife] have about the way you handle your children?
150. How do you spend time with your children?
151. What activities do you most like to do with your children?
152. What activities with the children bore you most?
153. How do you think your children have been affected by the separation?
154. What would you like your children's future to be?
155. What kinds of needs does each of your children have now?
156. How will these needs change as a result of the divorce?
157. Do you argue with your husband [wife, ex-husband, ex-wife] in front of your children?
(If yes, go to question 158; if no, go to question 161.)
158. What do you argue about?
159. How do your children feel when you argue?
160. How does your arguing affect your children?
161. What kinds of financial problems will your husband [wife, ex-husband, ex-wife] have as a result of the divorce?
162. And how will these problems affect raising the children?
163. Are you and your husband [wife, ex-husband, ex-wife] able to talk to each other?

164. When you get together or talk to each other, what happens?
165. How does important information regarding your children get relayed to your husband [wife, ex-husband, ex-wife]?
166. (If needed) Does he [she] get it in writing…over the phone…through the children…not at all?
167. What do you believe are your strongest qualities as a parent?
168. And what do you see as your weakest qualities as a parent?
169. And how about your husband [wife, ex-husband, ex-wife]? What do you see as his [her] strongest qualities as a parent?
170. And what are his [her] weakest qualities as a parent?
171. What do you think your husband [wife, ex-husband, ex-wife] would say are your strongest qualities as a parent?
172. And your weakest qualities?
173. Do you expect your husband [wife, ex-husband, ex-wife] to make any statements about you that are not true?
174. (If yes) Tell me about that.

Custody Questions
175. I'd like to turn to the area of custody. Tell me about why you would like custody of [cite children's names].
176. Have your children told you their feelings and ideas about custody and visitation arrangements?
177. (If yes) What did they say?
178. Did you ask your children or did they volunteer their feelings and ideas about custody and visitation?
179. Have your children told anyone else about their feelings about custody and visitation arrangements?
180. (If yes) Whom did they tell?
181. How would it affect you if your husband [wife, ex-husband, ex-wife] got custody of [cite children's names]?
182. What do you think is the ideal custody arrangement for your family?
183. Tell me why you think so.
184. What do you think about joint custody?
185. What would be the benefits of joint custody?
186. And the drawbacks of joint custody?
187. What aspects of your ideal arrangement are you willing to negotiate?
188. If you got custody, what type of arrangements would you make for your husband [wife, ex-husband, ex-wife] to see your children?

Future Plans
189. How do you see yourself in the future?
190. (If needed) Do you plan on remarrying?
191. (Any answer) How would this affect your ability to raise your children?
192. And how about moving from this area? Do you have any such plans?
193. (If yes) How would this affect your husband [wife]?

Concluding Questions
194. Is there anything else you would like to tell me?
195. (If yes) Go ahead.

196. Is there anything you would like to ask me?
197. (If yes) Go ahead.
198. Thank you for talking with me. If you have any questions or if you want to talk to me, please call me. Here is my card.

Source: Adapted from Hodges (1991) and Skafte (1985).

Table F-33
Semistructured Interview Questions for a Parent of a Child Who May Have a Health-Related Disorder

Introduction
1. Hi! I'm Dr. [Ms., Mr.] _____. Your physician, Dr. _____, referred you to me. I'd like to talk to you about how your child is getting along. OK?

Knowledge About Child's Illness
2. What has your physician told you about [cite child's name]'s illness?
3. (If needed) What was the diagnosis?…And what is the prognosis?
4. When did you first suspect [cite child's name] had a problem?
5. When was the diagnosis first made?
6. (If relevant) How long has the illness stayed in remission?
7. (If relevant) What relapses or recurrences of the illness has [cite child's name] had?
8. What type of treatment has [cite child's name] received?
9. How is the treatment helping?
10. Does the treatment have any side effects?
11. (If yes) Tell me about them.
12. How long has [cite child's name] been getting the treatment?
13. How often does [cite child's name] see a physician?
14. How many times has [cite child's name] been admitted to a hospital for treatment of his [her] illness?
15. How many days has [cite child's name] spent in the hospital for treatment of his [her] illness?
16. Does [cite child's name] have any outward scars or any deformities from the illness?
17. (If yes) Tell me about them.

Feelings About and Reactions to Child's Illness
18. How did you feel about [cite child's name]'s illness when you first found out about it?
19. How do you feel about [cite child's name]'s illness now?
20. (If needed) Would you say you are pessimistic, neither pessimistic nor optimistic, or optimistic about the illness?
21. Tell me about your answer.
22. What do you think will happen in the future?
23. How has [cite child's name]'s illness affected your family?

24. How has [cite child's name]'s illness affected your job?
25. How has [cite child's name]'s illness affected your social life?
26. How has [cite child's name]'s illness affected your health?
27. How has [cite child's name]'s illness affected your eating and sleeping?
28. Do you ever feel very angry or very irritable about [cite child's name]'s becoming ill?
29. (If yes) Tell me about those times.
30. Do you ever find yourself doing unusual things or having unusual thoughts since [cite child's name] became ill?
31. (If yes) Tell me about that.
32. How has the illness affected [cite child's name]'s life?
33. In what ways has [cite child's name] been able to return to a normal life?
34. How is [cite child's name] doing now?
35. Have you changed the way you treat [cite child's name] since he [she] became ill?
36. (If yes) In what way?

Communication with Child

37. Has anyone discussed with you what to say to your child about his [her] illness?
38. (If yes) Tell me about that.
39. (If needed) Who told you?…What did he [she, they] say?
40. What have you told [cite child's name] about his [her] illness?
41. What do you want [cite child's name] to know about the illness?
42. And what don't you want [cite child's name] to know about the illness?
43. What do you think [cite child's name] knows about the illness at this time?
44. When did [cite child's name] first become aware of how ill he [she] was?
45. Have you said anything to [cite child's name] about his [her] getting well?
46. (If relevant) Have you discussed the possibility of his [her] dying with [cite child's name]?
47. Does [cite child's name] know how you feel about his [her] illness?
48. Do you show your feelings about the illness when you are around [cite child's name]?
49. Have you asked [cite child's name] how he [she] feels about the illness?
50. What have you said to [cite child's name] that you feel was useful in helping him [her] understand the illness?
51. Does [cite child's name] ever talk to you about his [her] illness?
52. Tell me about that.

Communication with Siblings (if applicable)

53. What have you told [cite child's name]'s sisters and brothers about the illness?
54. How do they feel about [cite child's name]'s illness?
55. How are they affected by [cite child's name]'s illness?
56. Do they talk to you about [cite child's name]'s illness?

57. Tell me about that.
58. Have you noticed any changes in the behavior of [cite child's name]'s sisters and brothers since he [she] became ill?
59. (If yes) Tell me about the changes.

Communication with Spouse

60. Do you talk to your spouse about [cite child's name]'s illness?
61. (If yes) Tell me what you say to each other when you talk about [cite child's name]'s illness.
62. (If needed) How does your spouse feel about [cite child's name]'s illness?
63. How has [cite child's name]'s illness affected your spouse's ability to work?
64. Do you know what your spouse has told [cite child's name] about his [her] disease?
65. Do you belong to any parents' support group?
66. (If yes) Tell me about the group.
67. How has [cite child's name]'s illness affected your relationship with your spouse?

Management Issues

68. Does [cite child's name] get any special treats when he [she] isn't feeling well?
69. (If yes) Tell me about that.
70. Do you encourage [cite child's name] to go to school when he [she] is feeling just a little sick?
71. (If no) Tell me about that.
72. What aspects of managing [cite child's name]'s illness have been most difficult for him [her]?
73. What aspects of managing [cite child's name]'s illness have been least difficult for him [her]?
74. What aspects of managing [cite child's name]'s illness have been most difficult for you?
75. What aspects of managing [cite child's name]'s illness have been least difficult for you?
76. Is there any conflict between you and [cite child's name] about managing his [her] illness?
77. (If yes) Tell me about that.
78. Is there anything special going on in [cite child's name]'s life that might affect how he [she] takes care of his [her] illness?
79. (If yes) Tell me about that.
80. How would you rate how you are able to control [cite child's name]'s illness?
81. (If needed) Do you think that you have not very good control, good control, or very good control?
82. How has your management of [cite child's name]'s illness changed over time?
83. What would help you manage [cite child's name]'s illness better?
84. What interferes with your taking care of [cite child's name]'s illness?
85. How hard is it for you to do the things you must do to take care of [cite child's name]'s illness?
86. What could be done to make it easier for you to take care of [cite child's name]?
87. Tell me about that.
88. How satisfied are you with your involvement in making decisions about [cite child's name]'s care?

Parental Needs

89. What has been a source of support for you and your husband [wife, family] throughout [cite child's name]'s illness?
90. Tell me about that.
91. Do you need more support from your family or friends or someone else?
92. (If yes) Tell me about that.
93. Is it hard to talk about [cite child's name]'s illness with people?
94. (If yes) Tell me about that.
95. Do you think that [cite child's name] will be cured?
96. Do you need any specific information at this time about how to help or work with [cite child's name]?
97. (If yes) Tell me about that.
    (Ask questions 98 to 108, as needed.)
98. Do you need more information about his [her] condition?
99. (If yes) Tell me about that.
100. What have you done so far to learn more about his [her] illness?
101. Do you need help in explaining his [her] condition to other family members or to other people in general?
102. (If yes) Tell me about that.
103. Do you need help in obtaining services for [cite child's name], such as medical or child care facilities?
104. (If yes) Tell me about that.
105. Do you need financial help?
106. (If yes) Tell me about that.
107. Do you need help for family problems?
108. (If yes) Tell me about that.
109. Do you have any questions that you would like to ask me?
110. (If yes) Go ahead.
111. Thank you for talking with me. If you have any questions or if you want to talk to me, please call me. Here is my card.

Note. If you want to obtain more information about the child from the parent, see Tables F-21 and F-36 in this Appendix.

Table F-34
Semistructured Interview Questions for a Parent of a Child Who May Have a Hearing Impairment

---

1. Hi. I'm Dr. [Ms., Mr.] _____. I'd like to talk to you about [cite child's name]. I understand that [cite child's name] has a hearing loss. Is that right?
2. When was the hearing loss first suspected?
3. Who first suspected the hearing loss?
4. What caused [cite person] to suspect a hearing loss?
5. What did you do when you learned that [cite child's name] might have a problem?
6. (If needed) Have you consulted other professionals?

7. (If yes) What did they tell you?
8. How did you feel when you were told that [cite child's name] might have a problem?
9. Does anyone else in the family have hearing loss?
10. (If yes) Tell me about it.
11. Describe [cite child's name]'s speech and language development.
    (If child speaks, go to question 12; if child does not speak, go to question 14.)
12. At what age did [cite child's name] begin to use words…phrases…sentences?
13. Is [cite child's name]'s speech intelligible?
    (Go to question 16.)
14. How does [cite child's name] communicate her [his] needs to others?
15. (If needed) Does she [he] use gestures to communicate?
16. How do others communicate with [cite child's name]?
17. Does [cite child's name] respond to loud sounds…soft sounds…vibrations?
18. Can [cite child's name] understand what is said to her [him] without gestures…with gestures?
19. Does [cite child's name] watch the face of the speaker?
20. Does [cite child's name] read lips?
21. Are there words that [cite child's name] seems to understand but cannot say?
22. About how many hearing tests has [cite child's name] had?
23. What do the tests show?
24. Has [cite child's name] ever worn a hearing aid?
    (If yes, go to question 25; if no, go to question 35.)
25. How old was [cite child's name] when she [he] started wearing it?
26. How has the hearing aid improved [cite child's name]'s hearing?
27. Who recommended it?
28. What model is the hearing aid?
29. Who is the manufacturer?
30. When was it purchased?
31. Has it been satisfactory?
32. Describe [cite child's name]'s reactions to wearing the hearing aid.
33. Does [cite child's name] wear it in one or both ears?
34. How consistently does, she [he] wear it?
35. What do you see as [cite child's name]'s limits in functioning in a hearing world?
36. Are you more overprotective of [cite child's name] than you believe you should be?
37. (If yes) Tell me about that.
38. Is there anything else you want to share with me at this time?
39. (If yes) Go ahead.
40. Are there any questions that you would like to ask me?
41. (If yes) Go ahead.
42. Thank you for talking with me. If you have any questions or if you want to talk to me, please call me. Here is my card.

Table F-35
Semistructured Interview Questions for a Parent of a Child Who May Have a Pervasive Developmental Disorder

The questions in this table primarily apply to children who are at least toddler-age. If the child is an infant, use only those questions that are appropriate.

Introduction

1. Hi! I'm Dr. [Ms., Mr.] _____. I'd like to get from you a fairly complete picture of [cite child's name]'s development. OK?

Developmental History

2. Did you experience any problems during your pregnancy?
3. (If yes) Tell me about the problems.
4. Did you experience any difficulties during labor and delivery?
5. (If yes) Tell me about those difficulties.
6. After [cite child's name] was born, did you sometimes wonder whether he [she] might have problems?
7. (If needed) Did you sometimes wonder whether he [she] might be deaf or blind?
8. (If yes) Tell me what you were concerned about.
9. Do you recall when [cite child's name] sat unassisted for the first time?
10. (If yes) When was that?
11. Do you recall how old [cite child's name] was when he [she] took his [her] first steps?
12. (If yes) When was that?
13. How would you describe [cite child's name]'s emotional responses during infancy?

Social Behavior as Infant

14. Now please tell me how [cite child's name] responded to you when he [she] was an infant.
(Ask questions 15 to 21, as needed.)
15. Was [cite child's name] overly rigid when you held him [her]?
16. Was [cite child's name] ever overly limp when you held him [her]?
17. Did [cite child's name] seem to resist being held closely?
18. Did [cite child's name] seem indifferent to being held?
19. Did [cite child's name] look at you when you spoke to him [her]?
20. Was [cite child's name] content to be alone?
21. (If no) Did [cite child's name] cry and demand attention if he [she] was left alone?
22. And now please tell me how [cite child's name] responded to other adults.
(Ask questions 23 to 26, as needed.)
23. Was [cite child's name] frightened of other people?
24. (If yes) Tell me more about that.
25. Did [cite child's name] withdraw from people?
26. (If yes) Tell me more about that.

Social Behavior as Toddler, Preschooler, or School-Aged Child

27. How does [cite child's name] interact with you now? (Ask questions 28 to 46, as needed.)
28. Does [cite child's name] look at you while you are playing with him [her]?
29. (If no) What does he [she] do?
30. Does [cite child's name] look at you when you are talking to him [her]?
31. (If no) What does he [she] do?
32. What does [cite child's name] do when you smile at him [her]?
33. Does [cite child's name] look through you as if you weren't there?
34. Does [cite child's name] seem to be hard to reach or in his [her] own world?
35. (If yes) Give me some examples.
36. Does [cite child's name] want you for comfort when he [she] is sick or hurt?
37. (If no) Tell me more about that.
38. Does [cite child's name] enjoy being held or cuddled?
39. Does [cite child's name] hug or kiss you back when you hug or kiss him [her]?
40. Does [cite child's name] come to you for a kiss or hug on his [her] own, without your asking him [her] to?
41. Does [cite child's name] enjoy being kissed?
42. Is [cite child's name] particular about when or how he [she] likes affection?
43. (If yes) Give me some examples of this.
44. Does [cite child's name] go limp when you hold or hug him [her]?
45. Does [cite child's name] pull away from you when you are being affectionate with him [her]?
46. Does [cite child's name] smile back at you when you smile at him [her]?
47. And how does [cite child's name] interact with adults? (Ask questions 48 to 52, as needed.)
48. Does [cite child's name] ignore people who try to interact with him [her]?
49. (If yes) Tell me more about that.
50. Does [cite child's name] actively avoid looking at people during interactions with them?
51. (If yes) Tell me more about that.
52. Does [cite child's name] look at people more when they are far away than when they are interacting with him [her]?

Peer Interactions

53. Now I'd like to talk to you about how [cite child's name] gets along with other children. Please tell me about that. (Ask questions 54 to 63, as needed.)
54. Does [cite child's name] prefer to play alone rather than with other children?
55. Does [cite child's name] like to watch other children while they are playing?
56. Will [cite child's name] ever join in play with other children?
57. Do other children invite [cite child's name] to play with them?

58. Does [cite child's name] play games with other children in which they each take turns?
59. (If yes) What games does he [she] play with other children?
60. Does [cite child's name] enjoy playing with other children?
61. How does [cite child's name] show his [her] feelings toward other children?
62. Does [cite child's name] seem to be interested in making friends with other children?
63. (If yes) How does [cite child's name] show this interest?

Affective Responses

64. Now I'd like to ask you about [cite child's name]'s feelings. Does [cite child's name] seem to understand how others are feeling?
65. (If yes) Please give me some examples.
66. Does [cite child's name] understand the expressions on people's faces?
67. Is it difficult to tell what [cite child's name] is feeling from his [her] facial expressions?
68. (If yes) What makes it hard to tell?
69. Does [cite child's name] smile during his [her] favorite activities?
70. Does [cite child's name] smile, laugh, and cry when you expect him [her] to?
71. Do [cite child's name]'s moods change quickly, without warning?
72. (If yes) Please give me some examples of these changes.
73. Does [cite child's name] become very frightened of harmless things?
74. (If yes) What does he [she] become frightened of?
75. Does [cite child's name] laugh for no obvious reason?
76. Does [cite child's name] cry for no obvious reason?
77. Does [cite child's name] shed tears when he [she] cries?
78. Does [cite child's name] make unusual facial expressions?
79. (If yes) Please describe them.

Communication Ability

80. Now I'd like to talk to you about [cite child's name]'s language. Does [cite child's name] currently speak or attempt to speak?
    (If yes, go to question 81; if no, go to question 87.)
81. Tell me about his [her] speech.
82. Does [cite child's name] repeat words or phrases spoken by others?
83. Does [cite child's name] refer to himself [herself] as "you" or by his [her] name?
84. Does [cite child's name] have any problems when he [she] speaks?
85. (If yes) Tell me about that.
86. Overall, how would you describe [cite child's name]'s language abilities?
    (Go to question 95.)
87. Has he [she] ever spoken in the past?
    (If yes, go to question 88; if no, go to question 95.)
88. When did [cite child's name] speak in the past?

89. What did he [she] say?
90. How old was [cite child's name] when he [she] stopped speaking?
91. Did anything happen at the time he [she] stopped speaking?
92. (If yes) Tell me about what happened.
93. Were you concerned when [cite child's name] stopped speaking?
94. Tell me about that.
95. In addition to talking, there are lots of other ways that children can communicate their needs and wants, such as making sounds, pointing, or gesturing. Does [cite child's name] communicate by any other method?
96. (If yes) Tell me about that.
97. Does [cite child's name] have a range of facial expressions?
98. (If yes) Tell me about them.
99. Does [cite child's name] nod or shake his [her] head, clearly meaning yes or no?
100. Does he [she] use other gestures such as "thumbs up" to indicate success or approval?
101. Can you understand what [cite child's name] is trying to communicate?
102. Can other people understand him [her]?
103. Does [cite child's name] become frustrated when he [she] tries to communicate?
104. (If yes) What does [cite child's name] do when he [she] is frustrated?
105. Does [cite child's name] respond when you say his [her] name?
106. Does [cite child's name] understand what you say to him [her]?
107. How can you tell?
108. Does [cite child's name] seem interested in the conversations other people are having?
109. (If yes) Tell me more about that.
110. Does [cite child's name] follow simple directions, such as "Get your coat"?
111. Does [cite child's name] respond to only one word in a sentence rather than to the whole meaning of the sentence?
112. (If yes) Please give me some examples of this.
113. Does [cite child's name] take some speech literally? For example, would [cite child's name] think that the saying "It's raining cats and dogs" literally means that cats and dogs are falling from the sky?
114. Does [cite child's name] listen to you when you read him [her] short stories?
115. Do you ever send [cite child's name] out of the room to get one object?
116. Could [cite child's name] be sent to get two or three things?
117. Can [cite child's name] follow a sequence of commands, such as "First do this, then this, then this"?
118. Can [cite child's name] understand the past tense… the future tense…the present tense?
119. Does [cite child's name] have any problems with spatial words, such as "under," "in," or "above"?
120. Does [cite child's name] understand better if instructions are sung to a tune instead of spoken?

121. Do you have to point or use gestures to help [cite child's name] understand what you say?
122. (If yes) Please give me some examples of what you do.
123. Does [cite child's name] understand that a nod or a shake of the head means yes or no?
124. Does [cite child's name] understand other gestures you use?
125. (If yes) Please give me some examples.
126. When you point to something, does [cite child's name] look in the direction you point?

Using Senses and Responding to Environment
127. Now I'd like to ask you about the way [cite child's name] uses his [her] senses and how he [she] responds to the environment. First, how does he [she]react to painful events, such as falling down or bumping his [her] head?
128. Is [cite child's name] overly sensitive to being touched?
129. (If yes) How does he [she] show this?
130. Does [cite child's name] examine objects by sniffing or smelling them?
131. (If yes) Please give me some examples of this.
132. Does [cite child's name] put inedible objects in his [her] mouth?
133. (If yes) What are some of the inedible objects he [she] puts in his [her] mouth?
134. Does [cite child's name] examine objects by licking or tasting them?
135. (If yes) Please give me some examples of this.
136. Is [cite child's name] overly interested in the way things feel?
137. (If yes) Tell me about this.
138. Does [cite child's name] enjoy touching or rubbing certain surfaces?
139. (If yes) Give me some examples of this.
140. Is [cite child's name] oversensitive to sounds or noises?
141. (If yes) Give me some examples of his [her] oversensitivity.
142. Does [cite child's name] cover his [her] ears at certain sounds?
143. (If yes) Please give me some examples of when he [she] does this.
144. Does [cite child's name] become agitated or upset at sudden or loud noises?
145. (If yes) Give me some examples of when this happens.
146. Does it seem to you that [cite child's name] does not hear well?
147. (If yes) Tell me more about this.
148. Does [cite child's name] ever ignore loud noises?
149. (If yes) Give me some examples of when he [she] ignores loud noises.
150. Does [cite child's name] stare into space for long periods of time?
151. (If yes) When might he [she] do this?
152. Is [cite child's name] overly interested in looking at small details or parts of objects?
153. (If yes) Please give me some examples of this.

154. Does [cite child's name] hold objects close to his [her] eyes to look at them?
155. Is [cite child's name] overly interested in watching the movements of his [her] hands or fingers?
156. Is [cite child's name] overly interested in watching objects that spin?
157. (If yes) Give me some examples of what he [she] likes to watch spin.
158. Is [cite child's name] overly interested in looking at lights or shiny objects?
159. (If yes) Give me some examples of this.
160. Is [cite child's name] overly sensitive to bright lights?
161. (If yes) Tell me more about this.
162. Does [cite child's name] look at things out of the corner of his [her] eyes?
163. (If yes) Give me some examples of this.
164. Does [cite child's name] do things without looking at what he [she] is doing?
165. (If yes) Give me some examples of what he [she] does without looking.
166. Is [cite child's name] aware of dangers, such as from hot things or sharp things?
167. Tell me about that.

Movement, Gait, and Posture
168. The next topic I'd like to cover is the way [cite child's name] moves and uses his [her] body. First, does [cite child's name] walk?
(If yes, go to question 169; if no, go to question 176.)
169. How does [cite child's name] walk?
170. (If needed) Does he [she] walk with swinging arms… on tip toe…oddly and awkwardly…gracefully?
171. Can [cite child's name] walk upstairs without help?
172. Can [cite child's name] walk downstairs without help?
173. Is [cite child's name] able to climb well?
174. Can [cite child's name] pedal a tricycle or a bicycle?
175. Can [cite child's name] run as well as other children of his [her] age?
176. Is [cite child's name]'s posture odd or awkward in any way?
177. (If yes) Tell me in what way his [her] posture is odd or awkward.
178. Can [cite child's name] copy other people's movements?
179. Does [cite child's name] wave goodbye?
180. Does [cite child's name] clap his [her] hands?
181. Are [cite child's name]'s movements easy, or are they stiff and awkward?
182. How easily does he [she] learn gymnastic exercises, dances, or miming games?
183. Does he [she] confuse up/down, back/front, or right/left when trying to imitate others?
184. How does he [she] behave when excited?
185. Does excitement produce movements of his [her] whole body, including face, arms, and legs?
186. Does [cite child's name] spin or whirl himself [herself] around for long periods of time?
187. (If yes) Tell me more about that.
188. Does [cite child's name] rock back and forth for long periods of time?
189. (If yes) Tell me more about that.

190. Does [cite child's name] move his [her] hands or fingers in unusual or repetitive ways, such as flapping or twisting them?
191. (If yes) Please give me some examples.
192. How well does [cite child's name] use his [her] fingers?
193. Tell me about that.
194. Does [cite child's name] move his [her] body in unusual or repetitive ways?
195. (If yes) Please give me some examples.
196. Would you say that [cite child's name] is more active or less active than other children of his [her] age?
197. Tell me about that.

Need for Sameness

198. Now I'd like to talk to you about [cite child's name]'s flexibility in adapting to change. Tell me how [cite child's name] responds when something out of the ordinary happens and his [her] routines must be changed.
199. Does [cite child's name] insist on certain routines or rituals, such as insisting on wearing only certain clothes or types of clothing?
200. (If yes) Tell me more about that.
201. Does [cite child's name] become upset if changes are made in his [her] daily routines?
202. (If yes) Please give me some examples of how he [she] becomes upset.
203. Does [cite child's name] become upset if his [her] belongings are moved or disturbed?
204. (If yes) Please give me some examples of how he [she] becomes upset.
205. Does [cite child's name] become upset if changes are made in the household, such as by moving furniture?
206. (If yes) Please give me some examples of how he [she] becomes upset.
207. Does [cite child's name] have certain favorite objects or toys that he [she] insists on carrying around?
208. (If yes) Tell me more about that.
209. Does [cite child's name] become upset when things don't look right, such as when the rug has a spot on it or books on a shelf lean to the side?
210. (If yes) Please give me some examples of this.
211. Does [cite child's name] become upset when he [she] is interrupted before he [she] has finished doing something?
212. (If yes) Give me some examples of this.
213. Does [cite child's name] become agitated or upset by new people, places, or activities?
214. (If yes) Please give me some examples of this.
215. Does [cite child's name] insist on performing certain activities over and over again?
216. (If yes) Tell me more about these activities.
217. Does [cite child's name] become upset when he [she] puts on new clothes?
218. (If yes) Tell me more about that.
219. Does [cite child's name] have certain mealtime rituals, such as eating from only one specific plate?
220. (If yes) Tell me about [cite child's name]'s mealtime rituals.

221. Does [cite child's name] have unusual food preferences, such as foods of a certain color or texture?
222. (If yes) Please give me some examples of what foods he [she] prefers.

Play and Amusements

223. Now I'd like to talk to you about [cite child's name]'s play. What kinds of games does [cite child's name] play?
224. Does [cite child's name] like to play with toys?
225. Does [cite child's name] roll things along the floor?
226. How many blocks can [cite child's name] use to build a tower?
227. Can [cite child's name] put puzzles together?
228. (If yes) How large a puzzle—how many pieces—can he [she] put together?
229. Does [cite child's name] make things with Legos, Tinker Toys, or similar toys?
230. (If yes) Can [cite child's name] follow the printed diagrams that come with such toys?
231. Does [cite child's name] use toys in unusual ways, such as spinning them, or lining them up over and over again?
232. (If yes) Tell me how he [she] uses the toys in unusual ways.
233. Is [cite child's name] destructive with toys?
234. (If yes) Tell me about that.
235. Does [cite child's name] play with toys or other objects in the same exact way each time?
236. Does [cite child's name] imitate what you do when you play with him [her]?
237. (If yes) Tell me about that.
238. Does [cite child's name] imitate what other children do in their play?
239. (If yes) Tell me about that.
240. Does [cite child's name] engage in make believe or pretend play?
241. (If needed) Does he [she] pretend to be a cowboy [cowgirl], policeman [policewoman], or doctor while acting out an imaginary game?
242. (If yes) Tell me about that.
243. Does [cite child's name] play with cars or trains as if they were real, such as by putting cars into a garage or moving trains around on a track?
244. Does [cite child's name] play with toy animals, dolls, or tea sets as if they were real?
245. Does [cite child's name] kiss the toy animals and dolls, put them to bed, hold tea parties for them, or play school with them?
246. Does [cite child's name] engage in imaginative play with other children, such as doctor and nurse, mother and father, or teacher and student?
247. Does [cite child's name] take an active part, or is he [she] always passive and not contributing to the play fantasy?
248. Does [cite child's name] join in cooperative play that does not incorporate fantasy, such as tag, hide-and-seek, ball games, and table games?
249. What types of outings does [cite child's name] enjoy?
250. What does [cite child's name] watch on television?
251. Does [cite child's name] enjoy listening to music?

252. Can [cite child's name] sing in tune?
253. Can [cite child's name] play a musical instrument?
254. (If yes) What instrument?

Special Skills

255. I'd like to learn whether [cite child's name] is especially good at something. Does he [she] have any special skills?
256. (If yes) Tell me about his [her] skills.
257. (If needed) We talked earlier about working with puzzles. Now can you tell me whether [cite child's name] has an unusual talent for assembling puzzles?
258. (If yes) Tell me about that.
259. Does [cite child's name] show any unusual abilities in music?
260. (If yes) Tell me about his [her] unusual abilities in music.
261. Does [cite child's name] have a very good memory?
262. (If yes) Tell me about his [her] memory.

Self-Care

(Modify the following questions based on the child's age.)
263. Now I'd like to talk to you about how [cite child's name] can take care of himself [herself]. First, does [cite child's name] have to be fed, or can he [she] feed himself [herself] with his [her] fingers, a spoon, a spoon and a fork, or a knife and a fork?
264. Does [cite child's name] need a special diet?
265. (If yes) Tell me about his [her] special diet.
266. Can [cite child's name] help himself [herself] to food when at the table?
267. Can [cite child's name] cut a slice of bread from a loaf?
268. How good are [cite child's name]'s table manners?
269. Does [cite child's name] have any problems with chewing?
270. Does [cite child's name] drink from a cup?
271. Does [cite child's name] dribble?
272. Can [cite child's name] wash and dry his [her] hands?
273. Can [cite child's name] bathe himself [herself] without help?
274. Is [cite child's name] aware when his [her] hands or face is dirty?
275. Can [cite child's name] dress himself [herself]?
276. (If yes) Tell me what [cite child's name] can do.
277. Can [cite child's name] undress himself [herself]?
278. (If yes) Tell me what [cite child's name] can do.
279. Can [cite child's name] brush or comb his [her] own hair?
280. Can [cite child's name] brush his [her] own teeth?
281. Is [cite child's name] concerned if his [her] clothes are dirty or untidy?
282. What stage has [cite child's name] reached in his [her] toilet training in the daytime?
283. (If dry during the day) And at nighttime, does [cite child's name] stay dry at night?
284. (If no) Tell me more about this.
285. Can [cite child's name] get objects that he [she] wants for himself [herself]?
286. Does [cite child's name] look for things that are hidden?
287. Does [cite child's name] climb on a chair to reach things?
288. Can [cite child's name] open doors?
289. Can [cite child's name] open locks?
290. Is [cite child's name] aware of the danger of heights or of deep water?
291. Is [cite child's name] aware that traffic is dangerous?
292. Does [cite child's name] know how to cross a road safely?
293. How much does [cite child's name] have to be supervised?
294. Is [cite child's name] allowed to go alone into another room…outside…in the neighborhood…farther away?
295. (If child is older than 11 or 12 years) Can [cite child's name] travel on a bus or train alone?

Sleep

296. Let's now talk about [cite child's name]'s sleeping habits. What are [cite child's name]'s sleeping habits? (Ask questions 297 to 300, as needed.)
297. What time does [cite child's name] go to sleep?
298. Does [cite child's name] have any rituals before going to sleep?
299. (If yes) Tell me about them.
300. What time does [cite child's name] get up?

Behavior Problems

(Modify the following questions based on the child's age.)
301. Let's now talk about [cite child's name]'s behavior. Does [cite child's name] run away or wander?
302. (If yes) Tell me about that.
303. Is [cite child's name] destructive with toys or other things?
304. (If yes) Tell me about that.
305. Does [cite child's name] have severe temper tantrums?
306. (If yes) Tell me about them.
307. (If needed) When do they occur?…Where do they occur?…How long do they last?
308. Does [cite child's name] hurt other children by biting, hitting, or kicking them?
309. (If yes) Give me some examples of how [cite child's name] hurts other children.
310. Does [cite child's name] try to hurt adults by biting, hitting, or kicking them?
311. (If yes) Give me some examples of how [cite child's name] tries to hurt adults.
312. How does [cite child's name] behave in public?
313. (If needed) Does [cite child's name] grab things in shops…scream in the street…make nasty remarks… feel people's clothing, hair, or skin… do anything else that is annoying?
314. Does [cite child's name] resist whatever you try to do for him [her]?
315. Does [cite child's name] automatically say "no" to any suggestion?
316. Is [cite child's name] generally aggressive?
317. (If yes) Tell me about his [her] aggressiveness.
318. Is [cite child's name] generally manipulative?
319. (If yes) Tell me about that.

320. Does [cite child's name] comply with rules or requests?
321. (If yes) Tell me about what he [she] does.
322. Does [cite child's name] hurt himself [herself] on purpose, such as by banging his [her] head, biting his [her] hand, or hitting any part of his [her] body?
323. (If yes) Please give me some examples.
324. How would you describe [cite child's name]'s overall behavior at home?

School and Learning Ability
325. (If relevant) Now I'd like to talk about school. Does [cite child's name] go to school?
(If yes, go to question 326; if no, go to question 330. Modify questions 330 to 342 based on the child's age.)
326. Where does [cite child's name] go to school?
327. How is [cite child's name] doing in school?
328. What subjects does [cite child's name] study in school?
329. (If subjects named) Tell me about how [cite child's name] is doing in these subjects.
330. Tell me about [cite child's name]'s ability to recognize objects in pictures.
331. (If needed) What kinds of pictures does [cite child's name] recognize?
332. Tell me about [cite child's name]'s ability to read.
333. (If needed) What kinds of things does [cite child's name] read?
334. Tell me about [cite child's name]'s ability to write.
335. (If needed) What does [cite child's name] write?
336. Tell me about [cite child's name]'s ability to do arithmetic.
337. (If needed) What kind of arithmetic problems can [cite child's name] do?
338. Can [cite child's name] tell time?
339. Does [cite child's name] know the days of the week?
340. Does [cite child's name] know the months of the year?
341. Does [cite child's name] know dates?
342. Can [cite child's name] draw?

Domestic and Practical Skills
(Modify the following questions based on the child's age.)
343. Now let's talk about how [cite child's name] functions at home. Does [cite child's name] have any chores to do around the house?
344. (If yes) Tell me about what [cite child's name] does. (Ask questions 345 and 346, as needed.)
345. Does [cite child's name] help set the table…clean the table?
346. Does [cite child's name] straighten up his [her] room…wash his [her] clothes…help with washing dishes…use a vacuum cleaner…help with shopping…help prepare food…cook…knit or sew…do woodwork…help with gardening…do any other kind of craft work?

Concluding Questions
347. Is there anything else you would like to discuss?
348. (If yes) Go ahead.
349. Does [cite child's name] have any problems that we didn't discuss?
350. (If yes) Go ahead.

351. Do you have any questions that you would like to ask me?
352. (If yes) Go ahead.
353. Thank you for talking with me. If you have any questions later or if you want to talk to me, please call me. Here is my card.

Source: Adapted from Schreibman (1988), Stone and Hogan (1993), and Wing (1976). Permission to use questions from the "Parent Interview for Autism" was obtained from W. L. Stone.

Table F-36
Semistructured Interview Questions for a Parent of a Child Who May Have a Psychological or Educational Problem or Disorder

Some of the questions in this table (for example, those dealing with peer relationships, interests and hobbies, and academic functioning) are not applicable to infants, and other questions (for example, those dealing with academic functioning) may not be applicable to toddlers. Therefore, use your judgment in selecting appropriate questions to use. This table can be used in conjunction with Table F-21 in this Appendix, which contains additional questions concerning specific areas of child development in infancy and the toddler/preschool years. This table also contains additional questions that you can use to inquire about adolescents.

Introduction
1. Hi! I'm Dr. [Ms., Mr.] _____. I'd like to talk to you about [cite child's name]'s adjustment and functioning. OK?

Parent's Perception of Problem Behavior
2. Please tell me your concerns about [cite child's name].
3. (If needed) Can you describe these concerns a little more?
4. Is there anything else that you are concerned about?
5. What concerns you most?
6. You mentioned that [cite problem] is troubling you most. Let's discuss [cite problem] in more detail. How serious do you consider [cite problem] to be?
7. When did you first notice [cite problem]?
8. How long has [cite problem] been going on?
9. Where does [cite problem] occur?
10. (If needed) Tell me about how [cite child's name] behaves at school…in stores or other public places…in a car…at friends' houses…with visitors at home.
11. When does [cite problem] occur?
12. (If needed) Does it happen in the morning…in the afternoon…at bedtime?…Does it occur when [cite child's name] is with you…his [her] father…his [her] brothers and sisters…other children…other relatives?
13. How long does [cite problem] last?
14. How often does [cite problem] occur?
15. What happens just before [cite problem] begins?
16. What happens just after [cite problem] begins?

17. What makes [cite problem] worse?
18. What makes [cite problem] better?
19. What do you do when [cite problem] occurs?
20. Has this been successful?
21. What do you think is causing [cite problem]?
22. Was anything significant happening in your family when [cite problem] first started?
23. (If needed) For example, had you recently separated or divorced…moved to another city or school district…had financial problems…dealt with the serious illness of a family member?
24. (If some event occurred) What was [cite child's name]'s reaction to [cite event]?
25. How does [cite child's name] deal with [cite problem]?
26. Do any other children in your family also have [cite problem]?
27. (If yes) How does [cite child's name]'s [cite problem] compare with theirs?
28. Has [cite child's name] been evaluated or received any help for [cite problem]?
    (If yes, go to question 29; if no, go to question 31.)
29. What type of evaluation or help has he [she] received?
30. And what progress has been made?
31. Why do you think [cite child's name] has [cite problem]?
32. How do you deal with [cite problem]?
33. How do family members react to [cite child's name]'s [cite problem]?

Home Environment
34. Tell me what your home is like.
35. Where does [cite child's name] sleep?
36. Where does [cite child's name] play?
37. Who lives at your home?
38. (If needed) Do you have a husband [wife] or partner?
39. (If relevant) Tell me about your husband [wife, partner].

Neighborhood
40. Tell me about your neighborhood.
41. Do you know your neighbors?
42. (If yes) What do you think of your neighbors?
43. (If needed) How do you get along with them?

Sibling Relations (if relevant)
44. How does [cite child's name] get along with his [her] brothers and sisters?
45. What do they do that [cite child's name] likes?
46. What do they do that [cite child's name] dislikes?
47. How do they get along when you aren't around?
48. Is it different when you are there?

Peer Relations
49. Does [cite child's name] have friends?
    (If yes, go to question 50; if no, go to question 58.)
50. Tell me about [cite child's name]'s friends.
51. (If needed) About how many friends does he [she] have?
52. (If needed) What are their ages?
53. How does he [she] get along with his [her] friends?
54. What does [cite child's name] do with his [her] friends?
55. How does he [she] get along with friends of the opposite sex?

56. Do you approve of his [her] friends?
57. Does [cite child's name] usually go along with what his [her] friends want to do, or is [cite child's name] more likely to do what he [she] wants to do?
    (Go to question 62.)
58. Tell me about [cite child's name]'s not having friends.
59. Does [cite child's name] have normal opportunities to meet other children?
60. (If needed) Tell me more about that.
61. Does [cite child's name] seem to want to have friends?
62. Does [cite child's name] have a problem keeping friends?
63. (If yes) Tell me about that.
64. How do other children react to [cite child's name]?

Child's Relations with Parents and Other Adults
65. How does [cite child's name] get along with you?
66. What does [cite child's name] do with you on a regular basis?
67. How does [cite child's name] express his [her] affection for you?
68. What are the good times like for [cite child's name] and you?
69. What are the bad times like for [cite child's name] and you?
70. Are there times when both you and [cite child's name] end up feeling angry or frustrated with each other?
71. (If yes) Tell me more about that.
    (If there are other adults in the household, repeat questions 65 to 71 for each adult, substituting the adult's name, and then go to question 72; otherwise, go to question 78.)
72. When something is bothering [cite child's name], whom does he [she] confide in most often?
73. Who is responsible for discipline?
74. Who is most protective of [cite child's name]?
75. Do you have any concerns about how other adults interact with [cite child's name]?
76. (If yes) Tell me about your concerns.
77. (If needed) About whom do you have concerns?
78. Does [cite child's name] listen to what he [she] is told to do?
79. How is [cite child's name] disciplined?
80. Which techniques are effective?
81. Which are ineffective?
82. What have you found to be the most satisfactory ways of helping your child?
83. How do you express your affection for [cite child's name]?

Child's Interests and Hobbies
84. What does [cite child's name] like to do in his [her] spare time?
85. What types of games does [cite child's name] like to play?
86. How skilled is [cite child's name] at sports or other games?
87. Is [cite child's name] involved in any extracurricular activities?
88. (If yes) Tell me about that.

89. What does [cite child's name] like to do alone...with friends...with family members?
90. What activities does [cite child's name] like least?
91. How much television does [cite child's name] watch each day?
92. Do you think that is the right amount of television?
93. (If no) Tell me about that.
94. What are his [her] favorite programs?
95. How do you feel about the programs he [she] watches?
96. Does [cite child's name] play video or computer games?
97. (If yes) How much time does [cite child's name] spend every day playing these games?
98. Do you think that is the right amount of time?
99. (If no) Tell me about that.
100. (If needed) And how about listening to music? Does [cite child's name] listen to music?
    (If yes, go to question 101; if no, go to question 103.)
101. What kind of music does [cite child's name] listen to?
102. How do you feel about the music [cite child's name] listens to?

Child's Routine Daily Activities

103. How does [cite child's name] behave when he [she] wakes up?
104. What changes occur in [cite child's name]'s behavior during the course of a day?
105. (If needed) Does he [she] become more fidgety or restless as the day proceeds, or does he [she] become more calm and relaxed?
106. Does [cite child's name] do household chores?
107. (If yes) What chores does he [she] do?
108. What does [cite child's name] do before bedtime?
109. How does [cite child's name] behave when he [she] goes to bed?

Child's Cognitive Functioning

110. How well does [cite child's name] learn things?
111. Does [cite child's name] seem to understand things that are said to him [her]?
112. Does [cite child's name] seem to be quick or slow to catch on?
113. Does [cite child's name] stick with tasks that he [she] is trying to learn?

Child's Academic Functioning

114. How is [cite child's name] getting along in school?
115. What does he [she] like best about school?
116. What does he [she] like least about school?
117. What grades does [cite child's name] get?
118. What are [cite child's name]'s best subjects?
119. What are [cite child's name]'s worst subjects?
120. Are you generally satisfied with [cite child's name]'s achievement in school?
121. How does [cite child's name] feel about his [her] schoolwork?
122. How does [cite child's name] get along with the other children at school?
123. How does [cite child's name] get along with his [her] teacher[s]?

124. What do you think about [cite child's name]'s school?
125. What do you think about [cite child's name]'s teacher[s]?
126. What do you think about the principal of the school?
127. Has [cite child's name] ever repeated a grade?
128. (If yes) Tell me about that.
129. Has any teacher recommended special help or special education services for [cite child's name]?
    (If yes, go to question 130; if no, go to question 135.)
130. Tell me about the help that was recommended.
131. Please describe what help, if any, he [she] has received.
132. Does [cite child's name] attend a special class?
133. Have you needed to attend specially scheduled parent-teacher meetings because of [cite child's name]'s behavior?
134. (If yes) What did you learn at the meeting[s]?

Child's Behavior

135. Tell me about [cite child's name]'s attention span.
136. What kind of self-control does [cite child's name] have?
137. How well does [cite child's name] follow directions?
138. Tell me about [cite child's name]'s activity level.
139. Is [cite child's name] impulsive?
140. (If yes) Tell me about his [her] impulsiveness.

Child's Affective Life

141. What kinds of things make [cite child's name] happy?
142. What makes him [her] sad?
143. What does [cite child's name] do when he [she] is sad?
144. What kinds of things make [cite child's name] angry?
145. What does [cite child's name] do when he [she] is angry?
146. What kinds of things make [cite child's name] afraid?
147. What does [cite child's name] do when he [she] is afraid?
148. What kinds of things does [cite child's name] worry about?
149. What kinds of things does [cite child's name] think about a lot?
150. What sorts of things does [cite child's name] ask questions about?
151. How does [cite child's name] typically react to a painful or uncomfortable event, such as when he [she] gets an injection or has to take pills?
152. How does [cite child's name] feel about himself [herself]?
153. How does [cite child's name] behave when faced with a difficult problem?
154. What makes [cite child's name] frustrated?
155. What does [cite child's name] do when he [she] is frustrated?
156. Does [cite child's name] ever become annoyed when you try to help him [her] with something?
157. (If yes) Tell me about that.
158. What things does [cite child's name] do well?
159. What things does [cite child's name] really enjoy doing?

160. Tell me what [cite child's name] is really willing to work to obtain.
161. What do you do when [cite child's name] is sad...is angry...is afraid...worries a lot...is in pain?

Child's Motor Skills

162. Tell me about [cite child's name]'s ability to do things that require small motor movements, such as turning pages of a book, using scissors, and folding paper.
163. Tell me about [cite child's name]'s general coordination, such as his [her] ability to walk, jump, skip, and roll a ball.

Child's Health History

164. I'd like to ask you about [cite child's name]'s health history. What common childhood illnesses has [cite child's name] had?
165. And has [cite child's name] had any serious illnesses?
166. (If yes) Tell me about them.
167. Has he [she] had surgical procedures?
168. (If yes) Tell me about them.
169. How would you describe [cite child's name]'s usual state of health?
170. Do you believe that [cite child's name] has been growing adequately?
171. (If no) Tell me more about that.
172. How is [cite child's name]'s hearing?
173. How is [cite child's name]'s vision?
174. Did [cite child's name] ever have any serious accidents or injuries?
175. (If yes) Tell me about them.
176. Did [cite child's name] ever go to an emergency room for an accident or illness?
177. (If yes) Tell me about it.
178. Did [cite child's name] ever need any stitches?
179. (If yes) Tell me about it.
180. Has [cite child's name] ever had any broken bones?
181. (If yes) Tell me about it.
182. Did [cite child's name] ever swallow anything dangerous?
183. (If yes) Tell me about what happened.
184. Does [cite child's name] have any allergies?
185. (If yes) Tell me about them.
186. What immunizations has [cite child's name] had?
187. Does [cite child's name] eat well?
188. (If no) Tell me about that.
189. Does [cite child's name] sleep well?
190. (If no) Tell me about that.
191. Does [cite child's name] have nightmares or other sleep problems?
192. (If yes) Tell me about that.
193. Does [cite child's name] have problems with bowel or bladder control?
194. (If yes) Tell me about that.
195. Does [cite child's name] take any medicine regularly? (If yes, go to question 196; if no, go to question 202.)
196. What medicine does he [she] take regularly?
197. What does [cite child's name] take the medicine for?
198. Does [cite child's name] report any side effects from taking the medicine? (If yes, go to question 199; if no, go to question 202.)

199. What are the side effects?
200. Have you discussed them with your doctor?
201. (If yes) What did the doctor say?

Family

202. Tell me about your family. Does anyone in your immediate or extended family have any major problems?
203. (If yes) Tell me about them.
204. (If relevant) How are you getting along with your husband [wife, partner]?
205. (If relevant) How do you see your relationship with your husband [wife, partner] affecting [cite child's name]'s problem?
206. What kinds of serious medical or psychological difficulties have you or members of your family had?
207. Has anyone in the family that [cite child's name] was close to died?
208. (If yes) Tell me about that.
209. How about a close friend? Have any of [cite child's name]'s friends died?
210. (If yes) Tell me about that.
211. Has the family lost a pet?
212. (If yes) Tell me about the loss.
213. Has anyone in your family been the victim of a crime?
214. (If yes) Please tell me about what happened.
215. Have you recently changed your place of residence?
216. (If yes) Tell me about your move.
217. (If relevant) Has [cite child's name]'s caregiver recently changed?
218. (If yes) Tell me about that.
219. In addition to [cite child's name], is any other family member currently having a problem at school or work?
220. (If yes) Tell me about him [her, them].
221. Have any members of your family had a problem similar to [cite child's name]'s problem?
222. (If yes) Tell me about that.
223. Has anyone in the family shown a major change in behavior within the past year?
224. (If yes) Tell me about that.
225. (If needed) Do any members of your family have a problem with drugs or alcohol?
226. (If yes) Tell me about that.
227. Do you have any concerns about your child's having been physically abused or sexually abused?
228. (If yes) Tell me about your concerns.

Parent's Expectations

229. Do you think that [cite child's name] needs treatment, special education, or special services?
230. What do you expect such services to do for [cite child's name]?
231. What are your goals for [cite child's name]?
232. How would your life be different if [cite child's name]'s problems were resolved?
233. (If relevant) Do you desire treatment for your own difficulties? (If there are other adult members of the household, go to question 234; otherwise, go to instructions following question 239.)
234. Who in the family is most concerned about [cite child's name]'s problem?

235. Who is least concerned?
236. Who is most affected by the problem?
237. Who is least affected?
238. How does your view of [cite child's name]'s problem compare with that of [cite other adult members of household]?
239. How does your view about what should be done to help [cite child's name] compare with that of [cite other adult members of household]?
(Before concluding the interview, ask the questions below about the development of an adolescent or those in Table F-21 in this Appendix about the development of an infant or toddler/preschooler, as needed.)

Concluding Questions

240. Overall, what do you see as [cite child's name]'s strong points?
241. And overall, what do you see as [cite child's name]'s weak points?
242. Is there any other information about [cite child's name] that I should know?
243. Where do you see [cite child's name] five years from now?
244. Thank you for talking with me. If you have any questions or if you want to talk to me, please call me. Here is my card.

Additional Questions About Adolescent's Development

1. Is [cite child's name] involved in any dating activities?
2. (If yes) What kind of dating activities?
3. Are there any restrictions on his [her] dating activities?
4. (If yes) How does he [she] feel about them?
5. Have you talked with [cite child's name] about sexual behaviors?
(If yes, go to question 6; if no, go to question 10.)
6. Tell me what you've talked about.
7. What kinds of sexual concerns does [cite child's name] have?
8. Do you and [cite child's name] agree or disagree about appropriate sexual behavior?
9. Tell me about that.
10. Does [cite child's name] use drugs?
(If yes, go to question 11; if no, go to question 20.)
11. Tell me about his [her] drug use.
(Ask questions 12 to 19, as needed.)
12. What kind of drugs does [cite child's name] use?
13. How does [cite child's name] get the drugs?
14. How does [cite child's name] pay for the drugs?
15. Has [cite child's name] ever gotten into trouble because of his [her] drug use?
16. (If yes) Tell me about that.
17. Has [cite child's name] received any treatment for his [her] drug use?
18. (If yes) Tell me about what treatment he [she] has received.
19. Is there anything else you want to tell me about [cite child's name]'s drug use?
20. Does [cite child's name] drink alcohol?
(If yes, go to question 21; if no, go to question 30.)
21. Tell me about his [her] drinking.
(Ask questions 22 to 29, as needed.)
22. What kind of alcohol does [cite child's name] drink?

23. How does [cite child's name] get the alcohol?
24. (If relevant) How does [cite child's name] pay for the alcohol?
25. Has [cite child's name] ever gotten into trouble because of his [her] drinking?
26. (If yes) Tell me about that.
27. Has [cite child's name] received any treatment for his [her] use of alcohol?
28. (If yes) Tell me about what treatment he [she] has received.
29. Is there anything else you want to tell me about [cite child's name]'s drinking?
30. Does [cite child's name] get high by using other things besides drugs or alcohol?
(If yes, go to question 31; if no, go to question 240 in main interview.)
31. What does [cite child's name] use to get high?
32. Tell me about that.
(Ask questions 33 to 39, as needed.)
33. How does [cite child's name] get [cite substance]?
34. (If relevant) How does [cite child's name] pay for [cite substance]?
35. Has [cite child's name] ever gotten into trouble because of his [her] use of [cite substance]?
36. (If yes) Tell me about that.
37. Has [cite child's name] received any treatment for his [her] use of [cite substance]?
38. (If yes) Tell me about what treatment he [she] has received.
39. Is there anything else you want to tell me about [cite child's name]'s use of [cite substance]?
(Go to question 240 in main interview.)

Note. If you want to obtain information about other problems, repeat questions 7 through 33 in the main interview. Any responses given to questions in this interview can be probed further. If you want to ask additional questions about maternal obstetric history, pregnancy, or labor and delivery or if you suspect that the parent has minimal parenting skills, see Table F-21 in this Appendix. If you suspect that the child has a specific disorder or problems associated with life or living (such as suicide or bereavement), go to the semistructured interview questionnaire that is most closely related to the disorder or problem area. See the inside back cover of this book for an index of the semistructured interviews.

Table F-37
Semistructured Interview Questions for a Parent of a Child Who May Have a Visual Impairment

---

The questions in this table complement those in Table F-34 in this Appendix. In most cases, the questions in Table F-34 should be asked first. If you begin with this table, introduce yourself to the parent.

1. When did you first suspect that [cite child's name] was having problems seeing?
2. What did you notice about his [her] seeing that didn't seem quite right?

3. What did you do about your concerns?
   (If a physician or optometrist was consulted, go to question 4; otherwise, go to question 7.)
4. What did the physician or [optometrist] tell you?
5. Did you follow his [her] advice?
6. (If no) Tell me why you didn't follow his [her] advice. (Go to question 8.)
7. Tell me about your decision not to go to a physician or optometrist.
8. Do other people in the family have problems with their vision?
9. (If yes) Tell me about their problems.
10. (If child wears glasses) What can [cite child's name] see without glasses?
11. How have [cite child's name]'s problems seeing affected the way he [she] gets along?
12. Is there anything else you want to tell me about [cite child's name]?
13. (If yes) Go ahead.
14. Do you have any questions that you would like to ask me?
15. (If yes) Go ahead.
16. Thank you for talking with me. If you have any questions or if you want to talk to me, please call me. Here is my card.

16. (If yes) What are your concerns?
17. How well does [cite child's name] get along with other children…with adults…with his [her] brothers or sisters …with you [you and your spouse]?
18. How well does [cite child's name] feed himself [herself]…dress himself [herself]…go to the toilet by himself [herself]?
19. Is there anything else about [cite child's name] that you wonder or worry about?
20. Did [cite child's name] have any difficulties during his [her] first two years of life?
21. (If yes) Tell me about that.
22. Does [cite child's name] have any problems that we did not cover?
23. Do you have any questions that you would like to ask me?
24. (If yes) Go ahead.
25. Thank you for talking with me. If you have any questions or if you want to talk to me, please call me. Here is my card.

Note. You can use probing questions to follow up on any problem areas mentioned by the parent.
Source: Adapted from Lichtenstein and Ireton (1984).

Table F-38
Semistructured Interview Questions for a Parent Regarding a Brief Screening of Her or His Preschool-Aged Child

1. Hi! I'm Dr. [Ms., Mr.] _____. I'd like to talk to you about [cite child's name]. Tell me a little bit about him [her].
2. Please tell me what [cite child's name] has been doing and learning lately.
3. How well do you think [cite child's name] is doing now?
4. Do you have any concerns about [cite child's name]'s health?
5. (If yes) What are your concerns?
6. Are you concerned about [cite child's name]'s general physical coordination or his [her] ability to run, climb, or do other motor activities?
7. (If yes) What are your concerns?
8. How well does [cite child's name] seem to understand things that are said to him [her]?
9. How well does [cite child's name] let you know what he [she] needs?
10. How would you describe [cite child's name]'s speech?
11. Does [cite child's name] speak in sentences?
12. Does [cite child's name] have any unusual speech behaviors?
    (If yes, go to question 13; if no, go to question 15.)
13. Tell me what seems to be unusual about his [her] speech.
14. (If needed) Is [cite child's name]'s speech intelligible?
15. Do you have any concerns about [cite child's name]'s behavior?

Table F-39
Semistructured Interview Questions for a Parent Regarding How Her or His Preschool-Aged or Elementary School–Aged Child Spends a Typical Day

Introduction
1. Hi! I'm Dr. [Ms., Mr.] _____. I'd like to know how [cite child's name] spends a typical day. I'll be asking you about how [cite child's name] spends the morning, afternoon, and evening. OK? Let's begin.

Early Morning
2. What time does [cite child's name] usually wake up?
3. Does [cite child's name] wake up by himself [herself]?
4. How do you know [cite child's name] is awake?
5. What does [cite child's name] do after he [she] wakes up?
6. Where are the other members of the family at that time?
7. What is [cite child's name]'s mood when he [she] wakes up?
8. How does [cite child's name] get along with other members of the family soon after he [she] wakes up?
9. When does [cite child's name] get dressed?
10. Does [cite child's name] dress himself [herself]?
11. (If no) What kind of help does [cite child's name] need? (Go to question 13.)
12. Can [cite child's name] manage buttons…manage zippers…tie his [her] shoes?
13. Does [cite child's name] choose his [her] own clothes?
14. Are there any conflicts over dressing?
15. (If yes) Tell me about that.

Breakfast

16. Does [cite child's name] usually eat breakfast?
    (If yes, go to question 17; if no, go to question 22.)
17. When does [cite child's name] usually eat breakfast?
18. What does [cite child's name] usually have for breakfast?
19. With whom does [cite child's name] eat breakfast?
20. Are there any problems at breakfast?
21. (If yes) Tell me about them.
    (Go to question 23.)
22. Tell me about [cite child's name]'s not eating breakfast.

Morning

23. What does [cite child's name] do after breakfast [in the morning]?
24. (If needed) Does [cite child's name] go to a day care center or preschool, a regular school, or a sitter's house, or does he [she] stay at home?
    (For children who stay at home, go to question 25; for children who go to a sitter's house, go to question 30; for children who go to a day care center or preschool, go to question 43; for children who go to a regular school, go to question 78.)

Stays at Home

25. Who is at home with [cite child's name]?
26. (If parent stays at home with child) How do you feel about being at home with him [her] during the day?
27. How does [cite child's name] spend his [her] time at home?
28. Does [cite child's name] have any problems at home during the day?
29. (If yes) Tell me about them.
    (Go to question 109.)

Goes to Sitter's House

30. Tell me about the sitter who watches [cite child's name].
31. How long does it take you to get to the sitter's house?
32. What time does [cite child's name] go there?
33. What time does [cite child's name] leave the sitter's?
34. How many other children are at the sitter's house when [cite child's name] is there?
35. (If one or more children) Tell me about the other children.
36. (If needed) How old are the other children at the sitter's?
37. How does [cite child's name] like it at the sitter's?
38. What kinds of things does [cite child's name] do there?
39. How is [cite child's name] doing at the sitter's?
40. Are you satisfied with [cite child's name]'s care at the sitter's?
41. (If no) Tell me about why you're not satisfied.
42. What changes have you noticed in [cite child's name]'s behavior since he [she] has been at the sitter's?
    (Go to question 109.)

Goes to Day Care Center or Preschool

43. Tell me about the day care center [preschool] that [cite child's name] goes to.
44. How long does it take you to get there?

45. What time does [cite child's name] go there?
46. What time does [cite child's name] leave the center [preschool]?
47. How old are the other children at the center [preschool]?
48. How many children are in [cite child's name]'s group?
49. And how many caregivers are in [cite child's name]'s group?
50. How does [cite child's name] like it at the center [preschool]?
51. What kinds of things does [cite child's name] do there?
52. How is [cite child's name] doing at the center [preschool]?
53. Are you satisfied with the center [preschool]?
54. (If no) Tell me about why you're not satisfied.
55. What changes have you noticed in [cite child's name]'s behavior since he [she] has been at the center [preschool]?
56. How did you decide to send [cite child's name] to this center [preschool]?
57. Have you met with [cite child's name]'s teacher?
58. (If yes) Tell me what you learned in talking with the teacher.
    (Go to question 61.)
59. Do you believe that you need to meet with [cite child's name]'s teacher?
60. (If yes) Tell me about the reason you want to meet with [cite child's name]'s teacher.
61. Do you participate in any activities at the center [preschool]?
62. (If yes) Tell me about them.
63. Is [cite child's name] having any problems at the center [preschool]?
    (If yes, go to question 64; if no, go to question 109.)
64. Tell me about [cite child's name]'s problem[s].
65. What is being done about it [them]?
66. Is anything being accomplished?
67. (If needed) Have you discussed the problem[s] with the teacher?
68. (If yes) What did the teacher say?
69. How do you feel about how the center [preschool] is handling the problem[s]?
70. Has [cite child's name] had problems in a center [preschool] before?
    (If yes, go to question 71; if no, go to question 74.)
71. Tell me about them.
72. What did you do about the problems then?
73. How did it turn out?
74. (If relevant) Have any of your other children had problems in a center [preschool]?
75. (If yes) Tell me about that.
76. Is there anything you would like to ask me about [cite child's name]'s problem[s] at the center [preschool]?
77. Is there anything you think I might do to help you with [cite child's name]'s problem[s] at the center [preschool]?
    (Go to question 109.)

Goes to Regular School

78. Tell me about [cite child's name]'s school.
79. How is [cite child's name] doing at school?

80. What are [cite child's name]'s best subjects?
81. What are his [her] poorest subjects?
82. What activities does [cite child's name] like best at school?
83. How does [cite child's name] get along with the other children?
84. How does [cite child's name] get along with the teachers?
85. Are you satisfied with the school?
86. (If no) Tell me about that.
87. How did you decide to send [cite child's name] to this school?
88. Have you met with [cite child's name]'s teacher?
89. (If yes) Tell me what you learned in talking with the teacher.
    (Go to question 92.)
90. Do you believe that you need to meet with [cite child's name]'s teacher?
91. (If yes) Tell me about the reason you want to meet with [cite child's name]'s teacher.
92. Are you involved in any school activities?
93. Tell me about that.
94. Is [cite child's name] having any problems at school?
    (If yes, go to question 95; if no, go to question 101.)
95. Tell me about [cite child's name]'s problem[s].
96. What is being done about it [them]?
97. Is anything being accomplished?
98. (If needed) Have you discussed the problem[s] with the teacher?
99. (If yes) What did the teacher say?
100. How do you feel about how the school is handling the problem[s]?
101. Has [cite child's name] had problems in school before?
    (If yes, go to question 102; if no, go to question 109.)
102. Tell me about them.
103. What did you do about the problems then?
104. How did it turn out?
105. (If relevant) Have any of your other children had problems in school?
106. (If yes) Tell me about that.
107. Is there anything you would like to ask me about [cite child's name]'s problem[s] at school?
108. Is there anything you think I might do to help you with [cite child's name]'s problem[s] at school?

Lunch
109. When does [cite child's name] usually eat lunch?
110. What does [cite child's name] usually have for lunch?
111. Does [cite child's name] usually eat his [her] lunch?
112. Who eats with [cite child's name] at lunchtime?
113. Are there any problems at lunchtime?
114. (If yes) Tell me about the problems.

Afternoon
115. How does [cite child's name] spend his [her] afternoons?
116. Are there any problems in the afternoon?
117. (If yes) Tell me about them.

Related Areas
(Ask about any of the following areas, as needed.)
118. Before we get to supper and the end of the day, I'd like to ask you about [cite child's name]'s eating, friends, play activities, TV watching, and behavior outside the home. Let's first turn to [cite child's name]'s eating. OK?

Eating
119. How is [cite child's name]'s diet in general?
120. What are [cite child's name]'s likes and dislikes in food?
121. What is [cite child's name]'s behavior like when he [she] refuses to eat something?
122. How do you handle that kind of situation?
123. What does [cite child's name] usually have for snacks?
124. Are there any problems about snacks?
125. (If yes) Tell me about that.

Friends
126. Tell me about [cite child's name]'s friends.
127. (If needed) How old are they?
128. Where do the children play?
129. What do they do together?
130. How do they get along?
131. Are they able to take turns and share toys?
132. (If no) Tell me about that.
133. Who supervises them?
134. What kind of supervision do they need?

Play Activities
135. Does [cite child's name] ride a tricycle or bicycle?
136. (If yes) How well does [cite child's name] ride the tricycle [bicycle]?
137. Is [cite child's name] reckless in his [her] play?
138. (If yes) Tell me about that.
139. Does [cite child's name] have any fears about climbing?
140. (If yes) Tell me about that.
141. What are some of [cite child's name]'s favorite toys?
142. What does [cite child's name] like to do with them?
143. Is [cite child's name] able to play alone?
144. (If no) Tell me about that.

TV Watching
145. Does [cite child's name] watch television?
    (If yes, go to question 146; if no, go to question 156.)
146. What TV programs does [cite child's name] watch?
147. How much time does [cite child's name] spend watching television in an average day?
148. Does anyone in the family watch television with him [her]?
149. Does [cite child's name] watch any adult shows?
150. (If yes) Which adult shows does he [she] watch?
151. Has [cite child's name] ever been frightened by any shows?
152. (If yes) Tell me about that.
153. How did you handle his [her] fright?
154. Do you supervise [cite child's name]'s TV viewing?
155. (If yes) Tell me about that.

Behavior Outside the Home

156. I'd like to know how [cite child's name] gets along when you go out, such as to a store, friend's house, church or synagogue, or restaurant. First, does [cite child's name] go shopping with you?
(If yes, go to question 157; if no, go to question 161.)
157. How does [cite child's name] behave in the stores?
158. Does [cite child's name] like to choose things to buy?
159. What happens if [cite child's name] wants things he [she] cannot have?
160. How do you handle it?
161. How does [cite child's name] behave at a friend's house?
162. And how does [cite child's name] behave at church or synagogue, if you go there?
163. And how about at a restaurant? How does [cite child's name] behave there?

Supper

164. When does [cite child's name] usually eat supper?
165. What does [cite child's name] usually have for supper?
166. Does [cite child's name] usually eat all his [her] food?
167. Who eats with [cite child's name] at supper?
168. Are there any problems at suppertime?
169. (If yes) Tell me about them.

Evening

170. What does [cite child's name] usually do in the evening?
171. When does [cite child's name] usually go to bed?
172. Does [cite child's name] have any routines associated with going to bed?
173. (If yes) Tell me about them.
174. Does [cite child's name] have any problems around bedtime?
175. (If yes) Tell me about them.
176. How much sleep does [cite child's name] usually get?
177. Does [cite child's name] sleep through the night?
178. (If no) How often does [cite child's name] wake up?
179. What does [cite child's name] do when he [she] wakes up?
180. How do you handle it?
181. Where does [cite child's name] sleep?
182. Does [cite child's name] share a room with anyone?
183. (If yes) With whom?
184. How does that arrangement work out?

Concluding Questions

185. Is there anything that we have left out about how [cite child's name] spends a typical day?
186. (If yes) Please tell me about that.
187. Is there anything that you would like to ask me?
188. (If yes) Go ahead.
189. Thank you for talking with me. If you have any questions or if you want to talk to me, please call me. Here is my card.

Source: Adapted from Ferholt (1980).

Table F-40
Semistructured Interview Questions
for a Parent Who Is Considering Adoption

1. Hi! I'm Dr. [Ms., Mr.] _____. I understand that you are interested in adopting a child. Tell me about your interests in adopting a child.
2. How did you make the decision to adopt?
3. How does each member of the family feel about the idea of adopting a child?
4. How did everyone feel about the final decision to go ahead?
5. How will the child fit in with your family?
6. What changes will you need to make to take care of the child?
7. (If needed) And what changes do you think your family will need to make when you adopt a child?
8. What will be the financial impact of having the child join your family?
9. What characteristics would you like in the child you adopt (for example, age and sex)?
10. What would you like to know about the birth parents?
11. And how about the child's brothers, sisters, or other relatives? What would you like to know about them?
12. Have you ever applied for adoption before?
13. (If yes) Tell me about your experiences.
14. And what about a special needs child? Have you considered adopting a child with a handicap?
15. How do you think you would handle being turned down for adoption?
16. Have you thought about whether you would tell your adopted child that he or she was adopted?
(If yes, go to question 17; if no, go to question 19.)
17. Tell me about your thoughts.
18. What do you think you will do?
19. Have you thought about whether you would tell the child about his [her] birth family?
20. (If needed) Tell me about that.
21. Do you have any questions that you would like to ask me?
22. (If yes) Go ahead.
23. Thank you for talking with me. If you have any questions or if you want to talk to me, please call me. Here is my card.

Table F-41
Semistructured Interview Questions
for a Parent Who Is Homeless

These questions are designed to supplement those in Table F-36 in this Appendix. If you need more in-depth information about the child's development, also see Table F-21.

Introduction

1. Hi. I'm Dr. [Ms., Mr.] _____. I'd like to talk to you about how [cite child's name] is getting along. OK?
2. When you don't understand a question that I ask, please say "I don't understand." When you tell me that, I'll try to ask it better. OK?
3. Can you tell me what happened that led to your becoming homeless?
4. When did you first become homeless? (Probe for sequence of events.)
5. Since you first became homeless, where have you been living?
6. (If needed) Have you been living in a car…in a motel… on the street…in a shelter…with friends…with relatives?
7. How long have you lived there? (Inquire about each place.)
8. What has it been like to live there? (Inquire about each place.)
9. What have been some of your worst experiences since becoming homeless?
10. And what about [cite child's name]? What have been his [her] worst experiences since becoming homeless?
11. Have you been able to care for [cite child's name] since you became homeless?
12. (If no) Tell me about who cares for him [her].

Assistance/Employment

13. Where have you gotten money since you became homeless?
14. How have you been able to feed yourself and your family?
15. Is there anybody who can help you?
16. (If needed) How about a group or service? Is there any group or service that you can count on to help you?

Coping

17. How have you been feeling since you became homeless?
18. How has [cite child's name] been feeling?
19. Has your situation caused strains in your family?
20. (If yes) Tell me about that.
21. How have you and [cite child's name] been getting along?

Background

22. Tell me what growing up was like for [cite child's name] before you became homeless.
23. What kind of house [apartment] did you live in?
24. (If needed) When did money become a problem for you?
25. Is this the first time you've been homeless?

Sibling Relations (if relevant)

26. Do you have any other children?
    (If yes, go to question 27; if no, go to question 33.)
27. Tell me about your other children.
28. (If needed) How are they getting along?
29. How does [cite child's name] get along with them?
30. (If needed) Are they living with you?
    (If no, go to question 31; if yes, go to question 33.)
31. Where are they living?
32. How often do you see them?

Peer Relations

33. How have [cite child's name]'s friends changed since you became homeless?
34. Has [cite child's name] lost any significant friends because of homelessness?

Child's Interests and Hobbies

35. What activities has [cite child's name] had to give up because of homelessness?
36. Has [cite child's name] started any new activities or developed any new interests since becoming homeless?

Child's Academic Functioning

37. How many schools has [cite child's name] gone to since you became homeless?
38. (If more than one) For how long did he [she] go to each one?
39. How is [cite child's name] doing in school?
40. Has [cite child's name] missed a lot of school?
41. Has [cite child's name] repeated a grade?

Health

42. Does [cite child's name] have any health problems now?
43. (If yes) What health problems does he [she] have?
44. How long has [cite child's name] had these problems?
45. (If relevant) How is the health of your other children?
46. How about your health?
47. (If relevant) And how about the health of your husband [wife, partner]?
48. (If anyone is ill) What sort of treatment has [cite person] been getting?
49. Has it been a problem to get or pay for medical treatment?

Parent's Adjustment

50. How are you getting along?
51. Tell me about that.
52. Do you use alcohol or drugs?
53. (If yes) Tell me about what types of alcohol [drugs] you use.
54. Do you believe that using alcohol [drugs] is a problem for you?
55. (If yes) Tell me about that.

Future

56. What are your immediate plans?
57. Do you have any specific plans for getting housing?
58. When you think about the future, what do you imagine things will be like for you in five years…in ten years?

Concluding Questions
59. Do you have any questions that you would like to ask me?
60. (If yes) Go ahead.
61. Thank you for talking with me. If you have any questions or if you want to talk to me, please call me. Here is my card.

Source: Adapted from Seltser and Miller (1993).

Table F-42
Semistructured Interview Questions for a Parent Who Is an Immigrant

---

Before you begin the formal interview, inquire about the interviewee's proficiency in English. Use an interpreter with interviewees who have a poor command of English. See Chapter 8 for information about using an interpreter.

Introduction
1. Hi. I'm Dr. [Ms., Mr.] _____. I understand that your child is having some problems. I'd like to talk to you about your child, yourself, and your family. OK?
2. Your child's name is…?
3. And [cite child's name]'s date of birth is…?
4. Are there other children in the family?
5. (If yes) What are their names and ages?
6. What country were you born in?
7. And what country was [cite child's name] born in?
8. Are you married?
   (If yes, go to question 9; if no, go to question 13.)
9. Do you live with your husband [wife]?
10. What is your husband's [wife's] name?
11. What country was your husband [wife] born in?
12. How did you and your husband [wife] meet?

Description of Problem
13. Please tell me your concerns about [cite child's name].
14. (If needed) Can you describe these concerns a little more?
15. Is there anything else that you are concerned about?
16. Which concerns bother you most?
17. Which one is bothering you most right now?
18. You mentioned that [cite problem] is troubling you most. Let's discuss this problem in more detail. How serious do you consider [cite problem] to be?
19. When did you first notice [cite problem]?
20. How long has [cite problem] been going on?
21. Where does [cite problem] occur?
22. (If needed) Tell me about how [cite child's name] behaves at school…in stores or other public places… in a car…at friends' houses…with visitors at home.
23. When does [cite problem] occur?
24. (If needed) Does it happen in the morning…in the afternoon…at bedtime?…Does it occur more often when [cite child's name] is with you…his [her] father

[mother]…his [her] brothers and sisters…other children…other relatives?
25. How long does [cite problem] last?
26. How often does [cite problem] occur?
27. (If relevant) Do any other children in your family also have [cite problem]?
28. (If yes) How does [cite child's name]'s problem compare with theirs?
29. What happens just before [cite problem] begins?
30. What happens just after [cite problem] begins?
31. What makes [cite problem] worse?
32. What makes [cite problem] better?
33. How do family members react to [cite child's name]'s [cite problem]?
34. What do you do when [cite problem] occurs?
35. How does [cite child's name] deal with [cite problem]?
36. Tell me about anything you've done that has been even partially successful in making [cite problem] better.
37. What do you think is causing [cite problem]?
38. Was anything significant happening in your family when [cite problem] first started?
39. (If needed) For example, had you recently separated or divorced…moved to another city or school district…had financial problems…dealt with the serious illness of a family member?
40. (If some event occurred) What was [cite child's name]'s reaction to the event?
41. Has [cite child's name] been evaluated or received any help for [cite problem]?
    (If yes, go to question 42; if no, go to question 44.)
42. What type of evaluation or help has he [she] received?
43. And what progress has been made?
44. Why do you think [cite child's name] has [cite problem]?

Reasons for and Description of Leaving Native Country
45. What were your reasons for leaving [cite country]?
46. Who made the decision to come to the United States?
47. Where were you just before you came to the United States?
48. When did you leave?
49. Tell me about how you left.
50. (If needed) Were you able to leave freely, or did you have to escape?
    (If family had to escape, go to question 51; if not, go to question 58.)

Inquiry About Escape
51. Tell me about your escape.
    (Ask questions 52 to 57, as needed.)
52. How did you escape?
53. How long did it take?
54. With whom did you escape?
55. How did you survive during your escape?
56. Were there any periods in which you were separated from your family?
57. (If yes) Tell me about that.

Inquiry About Refugee Camp

58. Were you ever in a refugee camp?
    (If yes, go to question 59; if no, go to question 70.)
59. What was your experience like in the refugee camp?
    (Ask questions 60 to 69, as needed.)
60. What did you do there?
61. Did you have enough food?
62. (If no) How did you manage to survive?
63. What were the living conditions like?
64. What were the sleeping arrangements?
65. Did you have adequate clothing?
66. What type of schooling was available for [cite child's name]?
67. How did [cite child's name] get along in the camp?
68. (If other children) And how did your other children get along in the camp?
69. (If relevant) And how did you and your husband [wife] get along in the camp?

Arrival in the United States

70. When did you arrive in the United States?
71. What were your reasons for wanting to come to the United States?
72. How did you get to the United States?
73. How long did it take you to get here?
74. (If referred child was born overseas) How did [cite child's name] do on the journey here?
75. (If other children were born overseas) And how about the other children? How did they do?
76. Did you come here with just your family or with other people too?
    (If interviewee came with other people, go to question 77; otherwise, go to question 79.)
77. How many other people did you come with?
78. And who were these people?
79. Does some of your family still live in [cite country of origin]?
80. (If yes) Tell me about which members of your family still live there.
81. How do you feel about the people who were left behind?
82. (If needed) Could you tell me more about these feelings?
83. How did you live while you were getting here?
84. How did you get food during this time?
85. Were you ever separated from your family during your journey?
86. (If yes) Tell me about that.
87. Did anything terrible happen to you while you were trying to get here?
88. (If yes) Could you talk some more about that?

Death of Family Member

89. Did anybody close to you die either before you left your country or during your journey?
    (If yes, go to question 90; if no, go to question 95.)
90. Tell me about that.
91. (If needed) How did you find out about his [her] death?
92. (If needed) How did he [she] die?
93. How did you feel when you found out about his [her] death?
94. Do you have any other thoughts or feelings about his [her] death at this time?

Life in Country of Origin

95. What was your life like before you left your home country?
    (Ask questions 96 to 103, as needed.)
96. Where did you live in [cite country]?
97. (If needed) Did you live in a city or a small village?
98. How did you like living there?
99. What did you do there?
100. (If needed) What kind of job did you have?
101. Were you satisfied with your work?
102. Did you have any future plans?
103. (If yes) Tell me about them.
    (If married in country of origin, go to question 104; if not, go to question 107.)
104. And how about your husband [wife]? What did he [she] do there?
105. (If relevant) Was he [she] satisfied with his [her] work?
106. (If no) Tell me more about that.
107. What relatives lived with you or nearby?
108. How did you all get along?
109. Did you practice a religion?
110. (If yes) Tell me about that.
111. (If referred child was born overseas) Did you have any problems with [cite child's name] when you were living in [cite country]?
112. (If yes) Tell me about them.
113. (If other children were born overseas) Did any of your other children have problems when you were living in [cite country]?
114. (If yes) Tell me about them.

Schooling for Child

(If child is going to school, ask the questions in this section.)
115. How is [cite child's name] getting along in school?
116. What does he [she] like best about school?
117. What does he [she] like least about school?
118. What grades does [cite child's name] get?
119. What are [cite child's name]'s best subjects?
120. What are [cite child's name]'s worst subjects?
121. Are you generally satisfied with [cite child's name]'s achievement in school?
122. How does [cite child's name] feel about his [her] schoolwork?
123. How does [cite child's name] get along with the other children at school?
124. How does [cite child's name] get along with his [her] teacher[s]?
125. What do you think about [cite child's name]'s teacher[s]?
126. What do you think about the principal of the school?
127. What do you think about the school overall?
128. Has [cite child's name] ever repeated a grade?
129. (If yes) Tell me about that.
130. Has any teacher recommended special help or special education services for [cite child's name]?
    (If yes, go to question 131; if no, go to question 135.)
131. Tell me about that.
132. Please describe what help, if any, he [she] has received.
133. Does [cite child's name] attend a special class?
134. (If yes) Tell me about the special class.

135. Have you needed to attend any specially scheduled parent-teacher meetings because of [cite child's name]'s behavior?
136. (If yes) What did you learn at the meeting[s]?

Solving Problems in Former Country

137. How would you try to solve the problems you're having with your child if you were back in your home country? (Ask questions 138 to 144, as needed.)
138. To whom would you go for help?
139. (If needed) Would you go to a doctor, priest, or other kind of healer?
140. Tell me about that.
141. What medicines would you use?
142. (If needed) Would these medicines include herbal medicines?
143. Are there any other healing practices that you would use?
144. (If yes) Tell me about that.

Adjustment in the United States

145. Since you arrived in the United States, what have you been doing?
146. What did you expect to find when you came here?
147. Has your life in the United States met these expectations?
148. Tell me more about this.
149. How does your life in the United States compare with the life you had before you came here?
150. Do you have any regrets about leaving your home country?
151. (If yes) Tell me about that.

Work

152. Have you been able to get a job?
    (If yes, go to question 153; if no, go to question 156.)
153. Tell me about your job.
154. How satisfied are you with your job?
155. What are your future job plans?
    (Go to question 159.)
156. How do you feel about not having a job?
157. (If needed) What can you do about getting a job?
158. (If needed) What is making it difficult for you to get a job?

Relationships with Others

159. How are you getting along with [cite child's name]?
160. Tell me about that.
161. (If other children) Tell me about how you are getting along with the other children.
162. (If relatives nearby) Tell me about how you are getting along with your relatives.
163. And with your neighbors. How are you getting along with them?
164. Tell me about that.
165. And friends. Do you have any friends?
166. Tell me about that.

Husband [Wife]

(If interviewee has a spouse, go to question 167; otherwise, go to question 173.)

167. How about your husband [wife]. How is he [she] doing?
168. Has he [she] been able to get a job?
169. (If yes) Tell me about how he [she] is getting along on the job.
170. How are you getting along with your husband [wife]?
171. And how is your husband [wife] getting along with [cite child's name]?
172. (If other children) How does he [she] get along with the other children?

Referred Child

173. Does [cite child's name] have any friends at school?
174. Tell me about that.
175. And in your neighborhood. Does [cite child's name] have any friends there?
176. Tell me about that.
177. (If other children) Tell me about how [cite child's name] gets along with his [her] brothers and sisters.
178. How much freedom do you give [cite child's name]?
179. Is [cite child's name] satisfied with this amount of freedom?
180. Do you treat [cite child's name] as you would in your former country or in the same way that American parents treat their children?
181. Tell me about that.
182. What do you see as keeping you from solving your child's problems?
183. (If needed) Tell me which of the following you see as contributing to your child's problems:

    — limited ability to speak English
    — poor study habits
    — lack of job skills
    — lack of transportation
    — unfamiliarity with American culture
    — lack of support from relatives
    — lack of money
    — inability to get along with other children [teenagers]
    — belonging to a gang
    — use of drugs
    — use of alcohol
    — becoming too Americanized and losing traditional values

184. What can you do about these things?

Other Children in Family

(If there are other children, go to question 185; otherwise, go to question 189.)

185. How about your other children? How are they doing? Tell me about each one.
186. (If needed) How are they getting along in school?
187. Do you treat your other children the same way as you treat [cite child's name]?
188. Tell me about that.

Contacting Utilities and Agencies

189. Do you understand how to get things done for your home, such as getting a phone, gas and electricity, and a bank account?
190. Do you know where to go for help when you need it?

191. Tell me about that.
192. (If needed) Do you know how to get to a doctor…get to a hospital…contact the police…call the fire station…contact the school principal?
193. Do you know how to get around in this city?
194. Tell me about that.
195. (If needed) Do you have a driver's license…know how to use the buses…have other means of transportation?

Life Style

196. Are there any financial problems at home?
197. (If yes) Tell me about that.
198. What do you do for relaxation?
199. Do you practice a religion in the United States?
200. (If yes) Tell me about that.
201. Are there conflicts between the culture of your native country and the American culture?
202. (If yes) Tell me about that.
    (Ask questions 203 to 208, as needed.)
203. Do you have any problems reading English?
204. (If yes) Tell me about that.
205. Are you going to school to study English?
206. (If yes) Tell me about that.
207. Do you have any problems talking to [cite child's name], either in English or in your native language?
208. (If yes) Tell me about that.

Concluding Questions

209. Is there anything else you would like to tell me?
210. (If yes) Go ahead.
211. Are there any questions that you would like to ask me?
212. (If yes) Go ahead.
213. Thank you for talking with me. If you have any questions or if you want to talk with me, please call me. Here is my card.

Note. See Table F-36 in this Appendix for questions useful in interviewing a parent to obtain information about a child's problems and Table F-21 in this Appendix to obtain information from a mother about a child's early development.
Source: This table was adapted from material provided by Walter Philips, personal communication, March 1991.

Table F-43
Semistructured Interview Questions for a Teacher of a Child Referred for School Difficulties

Introduction

1. Hi! I'm Dr. [Ms., Mr.] _____. Please tell me why you referred [cite child's name].
2. Before we talk about these problems, I'd like to ask you about how [cite child's name] functions in some general areas. Does [cite child's name] have any auditory problems that you have noticed?
3. Does he [she] have any problems in the visual area… in the motor area…with speech…with attention…

with concentration…in getting along with other children…in getting along with you or other teachers?
4. How about [cite child's name]'s energy level? Does he [she] tire easily?
5. And how is [cite child's name]'s motivation?
6. How does [cite child's name] handle assignments that require organization…that require planning…that require independent effort?
7. Does [cite child's name] attend class regularly?
8. (If no) Tell me about that.
9. Does [cite child's name] arrive in class on time, or is he [she] frequently late?
10. (If late) Do you know why he [she] is late?
    (If child has primarily academic problems, go to item 11 and then go to specific sections for problems in reading, mathematics, spelling, use of language, attention and memory, perception, and motor skills. If child has primarily behavioral problems, go to item 127.)

Academic Problems

11. What types of academic problems is [cite child's name] having in the classroom?

Reading Difficulties

12. What type of reading difficulty does [cite child's name] have?
    (Ask questions 13 to 21, as needed.)
13. Does [cite child's name] have any problems with… silent reading…oral reading…reading comprehension …listening?
14. Does [cite child's name] have difficulty reading single letters…words…sentences…paragraphs… stories?
15. Does [cite child's name] have difficulty with specific parts of words, such as prefixes…suffixes…middle sound units…vowels…or consonants?
16. How does [cite child's name] go about attacking words?
17. Does [cite child's name] have receptive difficulties, such as difficulty in understanding what he [she] reads?
18. Does [cite child's name] have expressive difficulties, such as difficulty in telling you about what he [she] has read?
19. Is there a discrepancy between [cite child's name]'s silent and oral reading?
20. (If yes) Tell me about the discrepancy.
21. What do you think should be done to help [cite child's name] master reading skills?

Mathematics Difficulties

22. What types of mathematical difficulties does [cite child's name] have?
23. Tell me about [cite child's name]'s problem with [cite mathematical difficulty].
24. (Include only relevant items, based on the child's grade level and the information obtained in questions 22 and 23.) Does [cite child's name] have difficulty with addition…subtraction…multiplication…division… word problems…oral problems…fractions…decimals …percents…measurement concepts such as

length…area…liquid measures…dry measures…
temperature…time…and money…exponents…
numerical reasoning…numerical application…
algebra…geometry?

25. Is [cite child's name] careless when he [she] does mathematical problems?

26. Is [cite child's name] impulsive when he [she] does mathematical problems?

27. Is [cite child's name] unmotivated when he [she] does mathematical problems?

28. What do you think should be done to help [cite child's name] master mathematical skills?

Spelling Difficulties

29. What types of spelling difficulties does [cite child's name] have?

30. Tell me more about [cite child's name]'s problem with [cite spelling difficulty].

31. (If needed) Does [cite child's name] tend to insert extra letters…omit letters…substitute one letter for another one…spell phonetically…reverse sequences of letters…put letters in wrong order?

32. What do you think should be done to help [cite child's name] master spelling skills?

Language Skill Difficulties

33. What types of language difficulties does [cite child's name] have?

34. Tell me more about [cite child's name]'s problem in [cite language skill difficulty].
(Ask questions 35 to 47, as needed.)

35. Does [cite child's name] have oral expressive language difficulties?

36. (If yes) Tell me about them.

37. Does [cite child's name] have difficulty in speaking in complete sentences…using correct words in speaking …writing expressive language?

38. (If yes) Tell me about his [her] difficulties.

39. Does [cite child's name] have difficulty writing complete sentences…using correct words in writing… generating ideas…with grammar…with punctuation…with writing organized compositions?

40. How would you compare [cite child's name]'s oral and written language?

41. Does [cite child's name] have difficulty using nonverbal gestures or signs?

42. Does [cite child's name] have difficulty speaking?

43. (If yes) What kinds of difficulty does he [she] have speaking?

44. (If needed) Does [cite child's name] have problems with pronunciation…speed of talking…vocal tone… intonation?

45. Does [cite child's name] have receptive language difficulties, such as difficulty in understanding what others say…what he [she] reads…gestures?

46. How well does [cite child's name] recognize pictures… environmental sounds…nonverbal signs?

47. What do you think should be done to help [cite child's name] master language skills?

Attention and Memory Difficulties

48. What types of attention and/or memory difficulties does [cite child's name] have?

49. Tell me more about [cite child's name]'s problem with [cite attention and/or memory difficulty].
(Ask questions 50 to 89, as needed.)

General Attention

50. Under what conditions does [cite child's name] have difficulty attending to things?

51. Is [cite child's name] able to concentrate for a time period commensurate with his [her] chronological age?

52. Can [cite child's name] focus on a specific task?

53. Is [cite child's name] able to sustain attention for the duration of a typical assignment?

54. Is [cite child's name] distractible?

55. Does [cite child's name] talk excessively…have difficulty working or playing quietly…often fail to finish things or follow through…often seem to not listen… often act before thinking…excessively shift from one activity to another?

56. Does [cite child's name] have difficulty organizing work …often lose things necessary for activities at school or home, such as toys, pencils, books, or assignments?

57. Does [cite child's name] need a lot of supervision?

58. Does [cite child's name] call out in class or blurt out answers?

59. Is [cite child's name] able to filter out surrounding noises—such as pencil sharpening or noises in the hall—so that he [she] can concentrate on the assigned task?

60. Does [cite child's name] stare into space for relatively long periods of time…doodle frequently?

61. Can [cite child's name] sit still for a long period of time?

62. (If no) Tell me what he [she] does.

63. Can [cite child's name] sit still for a short period of time?

64. (If no) Tell me what he [she] does.

65. Does [cite child's name] repeatedly say "What" or "Huh"?

66. Does [cite child's name] seek quiet places to work… become very upset in noisy, crowded places?

67. Is [cite child's name] constantly in motion?

68. What is [cite child's name]'s tolerance for frustration like?

69. Is [cite child's name] impulsive in his [her] behavior?

Auditory Attention

70. How does [cite child's name] attend to sounds… lectures…class discussions?

71. Can [cite child's name] shift his [her] attention from one sound to another?

72. Does [cite child's name] have difficulty maintaining his [her] focus on sounds?

73. (If yes) Are there any specific types of sounds that he [she] has difficulty focusing on?

74. Is it easier for [cite child's name] to attend to rhythmic sounds, like music, than to spoken language sounds?

75. Does [cite child's name] mistake words he [she] hears, like *rat* for *ran*?
76. Can [cite child's name] attend better when you speak slowly to him [her]?

Auditory Memory

77. Does [cite child's name] have a good memory for things that happened recently…for things that happened in the distant past…for present events?
78. Can [cite child's name] recall the names of people easily?
79. Does [cite child's name] have difficulty learning telephone numbers…addresses…the ABCs?
80. Does [cite child's name] call common objects, such as buttons and zippers, by their correct names?
81. Does [cite child's name] hesitate to name objects when he [she] is asked to do so?
82. Does [cite child's name] often ask to have questions repeated?

Visual Attention

83. How does [cite child's name] attend to visual stimuli?
84. (If needed) How does he [she] attend to…pictures… words in print…TV presentations…movie presentations…actions on a computer screen?

Visual Memory

85. Does [cite child's name] remember things that he [she] saw recently…things that he [she] saw in the distant past…present events?
86. Can [cite child's name] recall the names of people he [she] has seen?
87. Does [cite child's name] have difficulty associating names with pictures?
88. Does [cite child's name] have difficulty in recognizing letters…numbers…shapes?
89. What do you think should be done to help [cite child's name] master attention and memory skills?

Perceptual Difficulties

90. What types of perceptual difficulties does [cite child's name] have?
91. Tell me more about [cite child's name]'s problem with [cite perceptual difficulties].
    (Ask questions 92 to 106, as needed.)
92. Does [cite child's name] have difficulty in auditory perception?
93. Does he [she] have difficulty with localizing sounds… identifying sounds…distinguishing between sounds… auditory sequencing…sound blending…figure-ground identification of sounds—that is, identifying only the most important sounds and ignoring other potentially useful sounds?
94. Does [cite child's name] have difficulty in visual perception?
95. Does he [she] have difficulty with identifying visual stimuli…matching forms…figure-ground discrimination of shapes—that is, identifying only the key letter, shape, or form on a page…recognizing letters or words in different forms, such as

lowercase versus uppercase or standard type versus italics?
96. Does [cite child's name] have difficulty in spatial perception?
97. Does he [she] have difficulty recognizing the position or location of an object on a page…in a room…in a building…on the playground?
98. Does [cite child's name] have difficulty with appreciating relative sizes…depth perception…perspective… recognizing whether objects differ in size?
99. Does [cite child's name] have difficulty distinguishing right from left?
100. Which modality—visual or auditory—does [cite child's name] prefer?
101. Does [cite child's name] prefer to look at pictures or at graphs?
102. Does [cite child's name] prefer making oral or written presentations?
103. Does [cite child's name] seem to have difficulty processing visual information…auditory information?
104. Can [cite child's name] copy material from a blackboard…from dictation?
105. Can [cite child's name] keep his [her] place on a page while reading?
106. Can [cite child's name] find his [her] way around a school building?
107. What do you think should be done to help [cite child's name] master perceptual skills?

Motor Skill Difficulties

108. What types of motor difficulties does [cite child's name] have?
109. Tell me more about [cite child's name]'s problem with [cite motor difficulties].
     (Ask questions 110 to 125, as needed.)
110. Does [cite child's name] have gross motor problems?
111. (If yes) Please describe them.
112. Do they involve walking…running…sitting… throwing…balance?
113. Does [cite child's name] have fine motor problems?
114. (If yes) Tell me about them.
115. Do they involve drawing…handwriting…coloring … tracing…cutting…pencil grip…hand dexterity?
116. Tell me more about these problems.
117. (If there are handwriting problems) Does [cite child's name] have problems in sequencing, such as transposing letters…spatial orientation, such as placing a letter of one word at the end of the preceding word (for example, using "goh ome" for "go home")…writing letters or words on the same line…writing letters of appropriate size?
118. Does [cite child's name] scrawl?
119. Does [cite child's name] make tiny compressed letters?
120. Are [cite child's name]'s papers messy or neat?
121. How would you compare how [cite child's name] writes on a spelling test with how he [she] writes spontaneously?
122. Is [cite child's name] able to write clearly single letters …uppercase letters…lower case letters… words… sentences…paragraphs…short stories or themes?

123. Is [cite child's name]'s problem in remembering shapes or in reproducing letter shapes?
124. Does [cite child's name] have visual-motor integration difficulties?
125. (If yes) Tell me about them.
126. What do you think should be done to help [cite child's name] master motor skills?

Behavioral Difficulties

127. Now I'd like to talk with you about [cite child's name]'s behaviors that bother you most. I'd like to discuss these behaviors, when they occur, how often they occur, and what occurs in your classroom that might influence the behaviors. I also would like to discuss some other matters related to [cite child's name] that will help us develop useful interventions. Please describe exactly what [cite child's name] does that causes you concern.
128. Which behaviors bother you most?
129. Which of these behaviors are of most pressing concern to you now?
130. Which behaviors, in order of most to least pressing, would you like to work on now?
131. Let's look into the first problem in more detail. How serious is the problem behavior?
132. How long has it been going on?
133. When does the problem behavior occur?
134. (If needed) Does it occur when the children are just arriving at school…at their desks in the classroom…in small groups…at recess…at lunch…on a field trip…at an assembly…working on a reading assignment…working on a math assignment…working on a history assignment…working on a writing assignment…working on a spelling assignment…working on an art assignment…working on a music assignment…working on a social studies assignment?
135. What classroom activity is generally taking place at the time the problem behavior occurs?
136. (If needed) Does the problem occur when the child is involved in a lecture…unstructured play…independent work…interaction with you… interaction with other children?
137. How does the problem behavior affect the other children in the class?
138. How long does the problem behavior last?
139. How often does the problem behavior occur?
140. How many other children in the class also have this problem?
141. How does [cite child's name]'s problem behavior compare with that of other children in the class who show the same behavior?
142. What happens just before the problem behavior begins?
143. What happens just after the problem behavior begins?
144. What makes the problem behavior worse?
145. What makes the problem behavior better?

Teacher's Reactions to Problem Behavior and Child

146. What do you do when the problem behavior occurs?
147. What does [cite child's name] do then?

148. What have you done that has been even partially successful in dealing with the problem behavior?
149. What do you think is causing the problem behavior?
150. What is your reaction to [cite child's name] in general?

Child's Relationship with Peers

151. How does [cite child's name] get along with his [her] classmates?
152. Does [cite child's name] have many friends?
153. Do the children include [cite child's name] in their games and activities?
154. Is [cite child's name] disliked by other children?
155. (If yes) Tell me why other children dislike [cite child's name].
156. How do other children contribute to [cite child's name]'s problem?
157. What do they do when [cite child's name] engages in the problem behavior?
158. How do other children help reduce the problem behavior?
159. How do other children react to [cite child's name] in general?
160. (If relevant) How do other teachers perceive and react to [cite child's name]?

Child's Social-Interpersonal Difficulties

(If social-interpersonal difficulties were not discussed, use this section.)

161. Does [cite child's name] have social and interpersonal problems?
162. (If yes) Tell me more about [cite child's name]'s problem in [cite social-interpersonal difficulties]. (Ask questions 163 to 170, as needed. Whenever there is a "yes" response, you might say "Please tell me more about that.")
163. Does [cite child's name] cry easily…give up easily…fly into a rage with no obvious cause…fear trying new games or activities…lie or cheat in games…have problems with losing…show overcontrolling tendencies…prefer the company of younger children…prefer to be alone?
164. Does [cite child's name] have difficulty waiting for his [her] turn in games or group situations?
165. Does [cite child's name] fight, hit, or punch other children?
166. Does [cite child's name] frequently interrupt other children's activities?
167. Is [cite child's name] bossy, always telling other children what to do?
168. Does [cite child's name] tease or call other children names?
169. Does [cite child's name] refuse to participate in group activities?
170. Does [cite child's name] lose his [her] temper often and easily?

Child's Strengths

171. What are [cite child's name]'s strengths?
172. In what situations does [cite child's name] display these strengths?

173. How can these strengths be used in helping [cite child's name]?

Teacher's View of Child's Family

174. How much contact have you had with [cite child's name]'s family?
175. What impressions do you have about [cite child's name]'s family?

Teacher's Expectations and Suggestions

176. For what part of the day is [cite child's name]'s behavior acceptable?
177. What do you consider to be an acceptable level of frequency for the problem behavior?
178. What expectations do you have for [cite child's name]?
179. What suggestions do you have for remedying the problem behavior?

180. What would you like to see done?
181. How would your life be different if [cite child's name]'s problems were resolved?

Concluding Questions

182. Are there any questions that you would like to ask me?
183. (If yes) Go ahead.
184. Thank you for talking with me. If you have any questions or if you want to talk to me further, please call me. Here is my card.

Note. Questions 131 through 145 can be repeated for additional problem areas.
Source: Some questions in this table were adapted from McMahon and Forehand (1988) and Witt and Elliott (1983).

GLOSSARY

Many of the terms in the Glossary are important terms that appeared in italics when they were first introduced in the text. The Glossary also includes other terms related to exceptional children, forensics, special education, and child psychopathology. Many of the terms in the Glossary have several meanings. In most cases, only those meanings most pertinent to clinical assessment and forensic interviewing are included. You are encouraged to use the Glossary as a general reference tool and as a study aid as you learn about clinical assessment and forensic interviewing of children and families.

AAMD. American Association on Mental Deficiency.

AAMR. American Association on Mental Retardation.

AAP. American Academy of Pediatrics.

ABA. American Bar Association.

Abandonment. A parent's or caregiver's leaving a child without adequate supervision or provision for his or her needs for an excessive period. State laws vary in defining adequacy of supervision and the length of time a child may be left alone or in the care of another before abandonment is determined to have occurred. The age of the child also is an important factor.

ABDC. Association for Birth Defect Children.

Aberration. Unexpected or severe departure from the normal.

Abnormal prosody. Changes in pitch, intonation, stress, phrasing, or rhythm that are unrelated to the content of the communication. Examples are using a "question-like melody" (rising inflection) for statements, chanting, using a sing-song melody, and having hollow-sounding speech.

Abrasion. Wound in which skin or mucous membrane is scraped off an area of the body.

Abruptio placenta. Premature separation of a normally implanted placenta. It can cause asphyxia, premature labor, hemorrhage, and shock.

Abstract ability. Ability to comprehend nonconcrete ideas and relationships.

Abused child. Any person under the age of 18 years, in the charge of a caregiver, who is physically or emotionally harmed by the caregiver's act or omission; also known as maltreated child.

Acalculia. Impaired ability to perform arithmetical operations.

Acceptance of communication. Acknowledgment and appreciation by the interviewer of the interviewee's point of view.

Accessible. Easy for disabled individuals to enter, use, or communicate with; in the case of information and services, easily obtained. Accessibility is enhanced by buildings and vehicles (for example, buses) designed so that people with limited mobility can move in and out without help, picture labels, nonauditory telephone devices, interpreters, and presenting information in various formats (multiple languages, large print, Braille, audiotape, diskette, etc.).

ACCH. Association for the Care of Children's Health.

Accommodation, visual. Adjusting or focusing of the eye's lens.

Accommodation to sexual maltreatment. Process by which a child attempts to cope with sexual maltreatment. The child may dissociate from her or his body, pretend that nothing has happened, fail to disclose the maltreatment, deny the maltreatment, delay disclosing the maltreatment, or recant a disclosure.

Acculturation. Modification of the culture of a group or individual as a result of contact with a different culture.

ACF. Administration on Children and Families.

Acquiescent response style. Tendency on the part of an interviewee to agree with all or most of the questions asked of her or him by the interviewer.

Acquired aphasia. Language dysfunction resulting from brain injury following normal language development.

Acquired brain injury. Traumatic or nontraumatic brain injury occurring after birth. Examples of traumatic brain injury include a blow to the head and a gunshot wound to the brain. Examples of nontraumatic brain injury include strokes, tumors, and infections attacking the brain.

Acquired immune deficiency syndrome (AIDS). Currently fatal disease that results from infection by the HIV-1 virus. The disease compromises a person's immune system to such a degree that he or she ultimately dies from complications of the disease, notably infections.

Action (legal). Lawsuit brought by one or more individuals seeking redress for or prevention of a wrong or protection of a right.

Activities of daily living (ADL). Processes such as dressing, eating, washing, and toileting.

Activity level. In infants, amount of physical motion during sleeping, eating, playing, dressing, bathing, and so forth.

Acuity. (1) Extent to which a given sensory modality can make accurate discriminations between similar stimuli. (2) Clarity or sharpness.

Acupuncture. Method of treatment, developed in China, in which the skin is punctured with needles in an effort to cure illness or relieve pain.

Acute illness. Serious medical condition that needs immediate care. It contrasts with chronic illness, which requires care over time.

Acute lymphocytic leukemia. The most common type of leukemia. Symptoms include lethargy, fatigue, anorexia, abdominal discomfort, signs of hemorrhaging (such as easy bruising), headache, and bone and joint pain.

Acute pain. Severe discomfort that is present for a limited period of time.

Acute stress disorder. Condition that is characterized by symptoms similar to those of posttraumatic stress disorder but that can be diagnosed within four weeks after an extremely traumatic event.

ACYF. Administration on Children, Youth, and Families.

ADA. Americans with Disabilities Act.

Adaptability. In infants, ease or difficulty with which reactions to stimuli can be modified in an appropriate way. An adaptable infant adjusts easily to unexpected company, warms up to new people, and tries new foods with interest.

Adapted physical education (APE). Program of physical activity for students who are precluded from participation in regular or modified physical education classes.

Adaptive behavior. Ability of an individual to interact appropriately and effectively with her or his environment.

ADC. Adult disabled children.

ADD. (1) Attention deficit disorder. (2) Administration on Developmental Disabilities. (3) See *Anatomically detailed dolls*.

ADHD. See *Attention-deficit/hyperactivity disorder.*

Adherence to a medical regimen. Extent to which a person's behavior—such as taking medication, following a diet, or making changes in his or her life style—coincides with medical advice; also known as compliance.

Adjudicated father. Man determined by the court to be the father, usually through a court action and genetic testing. See also *Paternity.*

Adjudication. Decision made by a court or administrative agency with respect to a case.

Adjudicatory hearing. See *Adjudication.*

Adjustment sleep disorder. Form of insomnia related to emotional arousal and caused by acute stress, conflict, or an environmental change.

ADL. See *Activities of daily living.*

Admissible evidence. Evidence determined by a court to satisfy applicable rules and laws.

Admission (legal). Voluntary statement that a certain fact is true.

Admonition. In court, advice, instruction, or caution by a judge to jury members about what is and is not admissible or about their duties, conduct, or alternatives of verdict. Also, warnings by a judge to a defendant or convicted felon of the consequences of future misconduct. Also, caution or reprimand by a judge of an attorney.

Adnexa. Appendages or accessory parts adjoining an organ or structure, such as ovaries and oviducts in relation to the uterus.

Adoption. Legal proceeding in which an adult takes, as his or her lawful child, an individual (usually a minor) who is not the adoptive parent's natural offspring. The adopted child may lose all legal connection to the previous parent(s), and the adoptive parent undertakes the responsibility of providing for the child until he or she becomes an adult.

Adoption Assistance & Child Welfare Act of 1980 (PL 96-272). Federal act that requires states to comply with certain mandates in order to be eligible for federal funds for child welfare. For example, states must document that they have made reasonable efforts to provide preventive and reunification services to families when children have been placed out of the home and to provide written case plans and a case review system. Removal of children from their home must be pursuant to a judicial determination, and there must be periodic reviews of the case.

Adoptive parents. Adults who legally become parents of a child not born to them.

Adversarial system. Trial process whereby the trier of fact, either a judge or a jury, after listening to the defense and plaintiff argue their cases, decides which side has proven its claim.

Adversary parties. Individuals or groups in litigation whose interests are opposed to each other.

Advocacy. Speaking, acting, or intervening on behalf of another individual or group.

AFDC. Aid to Families with Dependent Children; a U.S. financial entitlement system.

Affect. Emotion; feeling.

Affect labels technique. Procedure used by interviewers to help a child express his or her feelings. The interviewer might ask the child to point to the line drawing that depicts how the child is feeling.

Affidavit. Written statement, usually signed in the presence of a public official who swears in the signer and informs the signer that the contents are stated under penalty of perjury. Affidavits are frequently used in the initiation of juvenile and criminal court cases and may be presented to the court as evidence.

Affirm (legal). To approve the judgment of a lower court; to state that the judgment is legally proper or correct and should stand.

AGA. Appropriate for gestational age. The term usually refers to intrauterine growth normal for gestational age.

Against medical advice. Contrary to the orders of a physician. In cases of child abuse or neglect, the term often refers to removal of a child from a hospital without the physician's consent or refusal to comply with medical advice (by, for example, failing to keep appointments or give prescribed immunizations or medication).

Age norm. In testing, average score on an aptitude or achievement test earned by children of a given chronological age.

Agitation. Repeated, nonproductive motor activity that is out of proportion to the surroundings. Agitation may include screaming and abusive language, pacing, pulling at tubing or restraints, and extreme restlessness.

Agnosia. Impairment or loss, associated with brain injury, of the ability to recognize or comprehend the meaning of stimuli, including familiar objects and symbols. See also specific types of agnosia.

Agoraphobia. Disorder characterized by anxiety about being in places or situations from which escape might be difficult or embarrassing.

Agrammatism. Omission of adjectives and adverbs in speech, giving it a telegraphic quality. Agrammatism may be due to brain injury or severe mental disturbance, especially schizophrenia.

Agraphia. Loss or impairment, associated with brain injury, of the ability to express language in written or printed form.

AH. Auditory (or hearing) handicap.

AHA. American Hospital Association.

AIDS. See *Acquired immune deficiency syndrome.*

AIDS/HIV-1 encephalopathy. Extremely serious condition, associated with AIDS or HIV infection, that affects motor and mental functions.

Akathesia. Motor restlessness shown by pacing or continual movement.

Akinesia. Lowered level of muscle activity.

Albinism. Condition in which an individual has defective pigmentation of the skin, hair, and eyes.

Alexia. Disturbance of the ability to read or interpret written symbols, despite adequate vision and intelligence; also known as word blindness.

ALJ. Administrative law judge.

Allegation (legal). Charge or complaint to be proven true or false at a hearing or trial. In a child maltreatment case, an allegation is made in the form of a petition or complaint containing statements about specific acts of the respondent or defendant that the petitioner or complainant anticipates proving at trial.

Allergen. Substance that can cause an allergic reaction.

Alternative communication. See *Augmentative communication.*

Alters. Alternative personalities seen in dissociative identity disorder.

AMA. American Medical Association.

Amaurotic family idiocy. See *Tay-Sachs disease.*

Amblyopia. Refractive defect resulting in dim vision, sometimes associated with cerebral palsy; also known as lazy eye.

Amicus curiae. Friend of the court. The court may grant permission for a person or organization with an interest in a lawsuit to appear in court, file briefs, and present oral arguments, even though this person or organization is not party to the action.

Amnesia. Partial or total loss of memory for past experiences. See also specific types of amnesia.

Amnesic aphasia. Disturbance of the ability to retrieve words needed for the spoken form of language.

Amniocentesis. Diagnostic procedure, used for genetic assessment, in which embryonic cells are withdrawn from the amniotic fluid to permit a chromosomal analysis.

Amotivational. Lacking in motivation.

Amphetamines. Drugs that serve as central nervous system stimulants by increasing activity and suppressing appetite. They may create a feeling of well-being. Some are used in a paradoxical fashion in the treatment of hyperactivity to increase attention. Types of amphetamines include cocaine, benzedrine, dexedrine, and methedrine.

Amusia. Loss of the ability to produce or to comprehend musical sounds.

Anaclitic depression. Profound sadness of an infant when separated from his or her mother for a prolonged period.

Analytical listening. Type of listening in which the interviewer critically analyzes the responses of the interviewee.

Anarthria. Loss of the ability to form words accurately, caused by brain lesion or damage to peripheral nerves that carry impulses to the articulatory muscles.

Anatomically detailed dolls (ADD). Dolls that show various explicit anatomical details of some body parts, such as genitals, breasts, and/or open mouth and rectal orifices. Their use in child abuse investigations is controversial.

Anencephaly. Defect in the development of the brain, in which the cerebral hemispheres and the overlying bones of the skull are absent.

Anger. Intense feeling of displeasure and antagonism.

Angiogram. See *Cerebral angiography.*

Anhedonia. Condition in which the intensity of experienced pain and pleasure is diminished. It decreases responsiveness to negative and positive reinforcement.

Anomia. Difficulty in naming objects, finding the right word, or recalling names; also known as anomic aphasia or nominal aphasia.

Anomic aphasia. See *Anomia.*

Anorexia nervosa. Eating disorder characterized by a refusal to maintain a minimally normal body weight, leading to a body weight of less than 85% of that expected. It may be accompanied by intense fear of gaining weight or becoming fat, disturbance in the perception of body weight and shape, and, in females, amenorrhea (absence of expected menstrual cycles).

Anoscopy. Examination of the anus and lower rectum by means of an anoscope.

Anosognosia. Failure or refusal to recognize that one has a deficit or a disease.

Anoxia. Deficiency in or lack of oxygen. It may occur in newborns during the transition from the maternal supply of oxygenated cord blood to independent breathing. Brain cells are particularly vulnerable to continued anoxia.

Answer (legal). Defendant's response to the plaintiff's allegations.

Antecedent events. Events that preceded the behavior in question.

Anterograde amnesia. Inability to remember events after some trauma to the brain.

Anticipatory grief. Form of grief in which individuals, aware of the impending loss of a loved one, attempt to relinquish their attachment to the dying person. They may become depressed, have a heightened concern for the dying person, and attempt to adjust to the consequences of the person's death.

Antisocial. Exhibiting attitudes and overt behavior contrary to accepted customs, standards, or moral principles of a society.

Anus. Opening to the rectum.

Anxiety. Generalized feeling of uneasiness, fear, and apprehension.

APA. (1) American Psychological Association. (2) American Psychiatric Association.

APE. See *Adapted physical education.*

Apgar score. General measure taken one minute after birth and then again five minutes later, based on evaluation of the neonate's heart rate, respiratory effort, color, muscle tone, and cry. A score from 0 to 2 is assigned to each of these factors, for a maximum score of 10; the ideal score is between 7 and 10.

Aphasia. Central nervous system dysfunction manifested through disorders in the perception, production, and symbolic use of language. See also specific types of aphasia.

Aphonia. Loss or impairment of voice resulting from a laryngeal defect or emotional disorder.

Apnea. Cessation of breathing, usually of a temporary nature.

Appeal (legal). (1) Request to a higher court to change the decision of a trial court. Usually appeals are made and decided on questions of law only; issues of fact are left to the trial judge's or jury's discretion. (2) Request to a higher authority to review the facts and possibly reverse a decision. For example, parents may appeal a denial of services.

Appeals court. Court that hears an appeal after a trial court has made a judgment. The appeal is usually based on the contention that the trial judge misinterpreted the law or misused judicial authority when rendering a decision.

Appellant. Party who initiates an appeal from one court to a higher court.

Appellee. Party in a lawsuit against whom an appeal is made.

Appointed counsel. Attorney appointed by the court to render legal assistance to a person unable, for any of various reasons, to obtain counsel.

Appraisal-focused strategy. Plan designed to evaluate a situation. See also *Logical analysis, Cognitive redefinition, Cognitive avoidance.*

Approach tendency. In infants, positive initial responses to new stimuli, including people, situations, places, foods, toys, and procedures.

Apraxia. Loss, caused by lesions in the cerebral cortex, of the ability to perform purposeful movements in the absence of paralysis or sensory disturbance. See also specific types of apraxia.

APWA. American Public Welfare Association.

ARC. Formerly, Association for Retarded Citizens. Now, the official name of the organization is the ARC.

ARCH. Access to respite care and health.

Arraignment. Process of bringing persons accused of crimes before the court to be advised of the charges against them and their rights and, in certain cases, to give them an opportunity to state their answers to the charges (to plead guilty or not guilty); also known as first appearance or initial appearance.

Arrest. Process of taking a person into custody. Peace officers must have probable cause to arrest individuals.

Arteries. Blood vessels that carry blood from the heart to various parts of the body.

Articulation. Production of speech sounds.

Asafetida. In traditional medicine practiced by some Black Americans, rotted flesh that looks like a dried-out sponge and is worn around the neck to prevent the contraction of contagious diseases.

Asceticism. Renunciation of pleasures.

Asphyxia. Lack of oxygen or excess of carbon dioxide in the body. Asphyxia may lead to unconsciousness, seizures, damage to various sensory systems, and death.

Assault, physical. Demonstration of intent by one person to inflict physical injury on another person. Even though physical contact is not an essential element of assault, violence—threatened or offered—is essential.

Assessment. Collection of information with which to rate development and performance. Assessment may include observing a child, interviewing, and using formal tests to measure specific skills and determine strengths and needs. Results may be used to plan for appropriate services.

Assimilation. Form of acculturation in which individuals embrace traditions of the new culture and reject cultural practices and customs of the country of origin.

Assisted living. Inhabiting a structured, supervised living environment, such as a group home.

Assistive device. Item, equipment, or product used as an external aid to functioning. In communication, items such as a notebook, computer, typewriter, or board with pictures or words may be used to help individuals express daily needs. In physical therapy, aids may be a brace, walker, or cane. In occupational therapy, aids may be plate rails, hand splints, or adapted clothing fasteners.

Assistive technology (AT). Devices and services used to maintain or improve a person's ability to function. Examples of AT devices include medical equipment and mobility, sensory, daily living, and communication aids. AT services include any service that helps a person select, obtain, or use an assistive technology device. Examples of AT services are evaluation, financial assistance, training, and repair.

Associated words. Terms that commonly go together, such as *salt* and *pepper, black* and *white, eat* and *drink.* These words are often substituted for each other by persons with cognitive or language problems—for example, *left* for *right, knife* for *fork,* and *yes* for *no.*

Association of ideas. Mental connections that an interviewee exhibits when he or she deviates from a particular topic and begins to speak freely.

Astereognosis. Form of agnosia thought to be caused by lesions in the central parietal lobe, characterized by an inability to recognize objects or geometric forms by touch.

Asthma. Respiratory disorder characterized by intermittent and reversible attacks of difficulty in breathing.

Astrocytomas. The most prevalent form of brain tumor in children. Symptoms include irritability, lethargy, headache, vomiting, decreased appetite, and withdrawn behavior.

Asymbolia. Loss of the ability to use or understand symbols, such as those used in mathematics, language, chemistry, and music.

AT. See *Assistive technology.*

At-rest tremors. Trembling that appears when a person is still.

At risk. Vulnerable to psychological, physical, and adaptive difficulties during developmental years and later in life, as well. This statistical, epidemiological concept is usually used to refer to children with certain types of life experiences or from certain social or ethnic groups.

Ataque. In Puerto Rican traditional medicine, symptoms of screaming, falling to the ground, and wildly moving arms and legs.

Ataxia. Muscle coordination problem that results in a jerky pattern of movement or a lurching walk, which can interfere with daily life functioning.

Athetoid movements. See *Athetosis.*

Athetosis. Slow, recurring, writhing movements of arms and legs and facial grimaces, resulting primarily from brain damage or brain immaturity; also known as athetoid movements.

Atonia. Lack of muscle tone.

Atresia. Absence or closure of a normal body passage or opening at birth. Examples include esophageal atresia and intestinal atresia.

Atrophy. Wasting away of flesh, tissue, cells, or organs.

Attachment bond. Strong emotional relationship that develops between two people. The term is often used to describe the relationship between an infant and his or her caregiver.

Attachment theory. Proposal, evolved from both psychodynamic and cognitive science perspectives, that infants develop internal working models of their self and their caregiver. These models help infants forecast and interpret the caregiver's behavior and plan their own behavior in response to that of the caregiver.

Attention. Ability to focus on incoming stimulation.

Attention-deficit/hyperactivity disorder (ADHD). Behavioral syndrome marked by inattention, impulsivity, and hyperactivity; also known as minimal brain dysfunction.

Attention span. Length of time for which particular activities are pursued.

Audiologist. Health care professional who specializes in the area of hearing and its disorders and is qualified to diagnose hearing disorders, fit hearing aids, and train a person to use his or her remaining hearing.

Audiology. Science of the measurement of hearing.

Audiometry. Measurement of sound, especially in the human speech ranges.

Auditory agnosia. Impaired ability to identify sounds.

Auditory aphasia. Impaired ability to comprehend the meaning of spoken words; also known as word deafness. The problem is with comprehension; the individual's ability to hear remains intact. See also *Receptive aphasia.*

Auditory comprehension. Ability to understand what is heard.

Auditory discrimination. Ability to identify differences among sounds.

Auditory memory. Ability to recall spoken words, digits, etc., in a meaningful manner. It includes memory for meaning.

Auditory perception. Hearing and interpretation of sounds.

Augmentative communication. Procedure through which people with severe expressive difficulties compensate for their communication limitations by using a device such as a computer or a keyboard; also known as alternative communication.

Aura. Subjective experience, such as a taste, sound, sight, or smell, that precedes and marks the onset of an epileptic seizure or a migraine headache.

Autism. Mental introversion in which thinking is governed by personal needs and the world is perceived in terms of wishes rather than reality; extreme preoccupation with one's own thoughts and fantasies. See also *Autistic disorder.*

Autistic disorder. Severe and chronic disturbance in children that affects communication and behavior; also known as early infantile autism, childhood autism, or Kanner's syndrome. Symptoms include withdrawal from contact with others, limited social responses, language disturbances, ritualistic behavior and insistence on sameness, abnormalities in response to the sensory environment, self-stimulatory behavior, self-injurious behavior, inappropriate affect, limited intellectual functioning, and repetitive body movements.

Automatic language. See *Automatic speaking.*

Automatic speaking. Speaking without voluntary control; also known as automatic language. Often, there is no apparent meaning to the communication.

Autonomic nervous system. Involuntary system of the body that regulates smooth muscles, glands, and heart.

Autosomal. Associated with an ordinary paired chromosome, as distinguished from a sex chromosome.

Autosome. Any chromosome other than a sex (X or Y) chromosome.

Autotopagnosia. Disturbance in recognition of body parts; body-image agnosia.

Aversive conditioning. Form of learning brought about through use of punishment (negative consequences) or removal of positive reinforcers.

Babbling. Incoherent vocalization; random articulation; unintelligible jabber. Babbling is a normal stage in an infant's development.

Babinski reflex. Involuntary response involving upward movement of the big toe and fanning of the other toes when the sole of the foot is stimulated. It is usually absent by 12 to 24 months of age, unless there is specific neurological dysfunction.

Ballismus. Rapid, forceful, purposeless, unilateral movements that may affect the proximal portion of limbs, with face and trunk usually spared.

Barbiturates. Drugs that act as central nervous system depressants, inducing sleep and muscular relaxation. Examples include Nembutal, Seconal, and phenobarbital.

Barrier free. Allowing complete access. For example, buildings, sidewalks, telephones, and services that are totally accessible to persons with all disabilities are barrier free.

Basal ganglia. Collection of subcortical nuclei in the forebrain, involved in motor and cognitive functions.

Base rate. Proportion of people in a population who possess a characteristic of interest. The base rate must be taken into account to determine the effectiveness of a test in identifying people having the characteristic.

Baseline. Characteristic level of performance before the implementation of treatment. It may be used to assess changes in behavior resulting from rehabilitation or intervention.

Battered child syndrome. Medical condition, occurring in infants and young children, in which there is evidence of repeated injury inflicted by others to the nervous system, skin, or skeletal system. Frequently, the child's medical history, as given by the caregiver, does not adequately explain the injuries. Many courts recognize this syndrome as an accepted medical diagnosis.

Battery (legal). Unauthorized touching of another person. Battery may be the basis for criminal prosecution, a civil lawsuit, or both.

BD. See *Behavior disorder.*

Behavior disorder (BD). General term used for any aberrant or maladaptive pattern of behavior.

Behavior modification. Use of learning theory principles to bring about changes in specified target behaviors.

Behavioral analysis. Analytical approaches that focus on specific observable behaviors and on observable environmental events, objects, and conditions that affect those specific behaviors.

Behavioral indicators of child maltreatment. Symptoms manifested in a child's behavior that reveal possible maltreatment, including fears and anxieties, extremely aggressive or passive behavior, changes in appetite, regressive behavior, hyperalertness, feelings of inferiority and self-blame, suspiciousness, inappropriate social responses, and secretive behavior. Behavioral indicators of child maltreatment also are associated with other conditions.

Behavioral medicine. Multidisciplinary field that integrates behavioral science approaches with biomedical knowledge and techniques.

Being-in-becoming orientation. Value orientation of a cultural group that emphasizes what a person is and developing aspects of the self.

Being orientation. Value orientation of a cultural group that emphasizes cooperation, seeking harmony with nature, concern with what a person is, and spontaneous self-expression.

Benign. (1) Mild. (2) Nonmalignant and, therefore, having a favorable prognosis.

Bereavement. Psychological, physiological, or behavioral responses associated with loss or death.

Best interests test. Consideration of what is best for the child, divorced from any consideration of welfare, claims, or interests of the parents or others.

Beyond a reasonable doubt. See *Proof beyond a reasonable doubt.*

BIA. Bureau of Indian Affairs.

Biculturalism. Form of acculturation in which individuals integrate practices of both the old and the new culture by selectively adapting new customs and maintaining former ones without losing their sense of identity.

Bifurcated (legal). Divided into two parts or sections. A hearing held in two parts, with separate issues to be decided at each hearing, is called a bifurcated hearing.

Bilateral. On both sides. The term is especially related to hemispheric functioning and the two sides of the body.

Bilateral hearing loss. Loss of hearing in both ears.

Bilateral simultaneous stimulation. Touching of both sides of the body at the same time.

Bilingual education. Schooling in which those not fluent in English are taught subjects in their own language, as well as in English.

Bilirubin. Red pigment contained in bile secreted by the liver, which in large amounts causes jaundice, as well as tissue and brain damage.

Binge eating. Rapid eating, with little chewing, of tremendous amounts of highly caloric foods by an individual with an eating disorder.

Binge-eating/purging subtype of anorexia nervosa. Form of anorexia nervosa experienced by those who attempt to limit food intake and those who have episodes of binge eating, purging, or both.

Biopsy. Process of removing a piece of tissue from a living organism for diagnostic examination.

Bipolar questions. Queries that present two alternatives. They are a useful compromise between open-ended and "yes-no" questions when an interviewer wants to find out what the interviewee believes about a specific issue.

Birth families. Families to which children are biologically related as a result of being born into them.

Birth parents. Parents who conceive and give birth to a child.

Black dialect. See *Black English.*

Black English. Variant of English spoken by Black Americans; also known as nonstandard Black English, Black dialect, or Ebonics.

Blindness. Visual impairment that restricts an individual from seeing any more at a distance of 20 feet than someone with normal vision can see at a distance of 200 feet.

Blocking. Interruption of words or thoughts before an idea has been completed.

Blood-glucose monitoring. Procedure performed by individuals with diabetes to test their blood glucose level at various times during the day.

Blunted affect. Restricted range and intensity of emotional expression, sometimes accompanied by an immobile facial expression or monotonous voice.

Body asymmetry. Lack of correspondence between the two sides of the body, such as when one arm is longer or stronger than the other.

Body image. Awareness of one's own body and its orientation, position, and movement in space and time.

Body language. Nonverbal communications associated with posture, facial expressions, and mannerisms.

Bonding. Psychological attachment between mother and infant. Courts may consider bonding in making decisions about children's placements.

Bone marrow aspiration. Obtaining a sample of bone marrow by use of a needle.

Bone scan. Procedure used to examine bone tissue by means of a scanning device.

BPD. See *Bronchopulmonary dysplasia.*

Bradycardia. In infants, heart rate dangerously below the developmental norm.

Brain damage. Any anatomical or physiological change of a pathological nature in the nerve tissue of the brain.

Brain disorder. Organic syndrome characterized by impairment of orientation, memory, intellectual function, or emotional stability.

Brain lesion. Localized damage to the brain; destruction of brain tissue.

Brain stem. Part of the brain from the medulla to the midbrain, excluding the cerebellum. The brain stem is the main control center of breathing, blood pressure, swallowing, and consciousness. It connects the cerebral hemispheres with the spinal cord.

Brain waves. Rhythmic, spontaneous electrical discharges of the living brain, principally the cortex.

Brief (legal). Written statement of the propositions of law that attorneys submit to the court to advance the case of their clients.

Brightness. Visual sensation of intensity or amplitude of light.

Broad open-ended questions. General queries that cannot be answered by a yes or no. They are useful in discovering the interviewee's associations, values, perspectives, and perception of facts.

Broca's speech area. Portion of the left cerebral hemisphere said to control motor speech.

Bronchodilator. Type of drug that relaxes and opens the airways in the lungs, thereby facilitating breathing.

Bronchopulmonary dysplasia (BPD). Lung disease in infants that causes thickening and degeneration in the lungs. BPD results from the use of high oxygen concentrations and high-pressure respirators. High concentrations of inspired oxygen are toxic to lung tissue and can cause damage to the trachea, bronchi, bronchioli, and alveoli.

Brujeria. Form of witchcraft practiced by some Cubans.

Brujo. Mexican American traditional healer who practices witchcraft and uses hexes to solve problems of love and illness believed to be caused by hatred, jealousy, or envy.

Bulimia nervosa. Eating disorder characterized by repeated episodes of binge eating followed by inappropriate compensatory behaviors such as self-induced vomiting; misuse of laxatives, diuretics, enemas, or other medications; fasting; and excessive exercise. The episodes usually occur at least twice a week for three months, in individuals whose self-evaluation is influenced by body shape and weight.

Burden of proof. Duty (usually falling on the state as petitioner or complainant) of proving allegations against an alleged offender or opposing party at trial. It is the petitioner's or complainant's responsibility to prove the case; neither the victim nor the alleged offender is required to explain the allegations.

Burn. Wound resulting from the application of too much heat. Burns are classified by the degree of damage caused: 1st degree—scorching or painful redness of the skin; 2nd degree—formation of blisters; and 3rd degree—destruction of outer layers of the skin.

Burnout. Apathy and frustration experienced by persons who are overworked, undertrained, distressed by work-related duties, and/or lacking employer or supervisory support. Symptoms include not looking forward to going to work; being absent frequently; being less productive; making more mistakes; drinking alcohol more often; using drugs; exhibiting anxiety, sleeplessness, tiredness, and fatigue; losing temper more easily; and other similar symptoms associated with stress.

Burr holes. Small holes made in the skull in order to place an intracranial pressure monitor, access the brain so as to evacuate blood clots, or reduce spinal fluid pressure.

C-section. See *Caesarean section.*

CA. See *Chronological age.*

Caesarian section (C-section). Procedure by which a baby is delivered by surgery through the abdomen.

Caida de la mollera. Ailment, commonly treated by Mexican American traditional healers, in which the infant's anterior fontanelle is depressed below the contour of the skull. It is caused by some trauma, such as a fall or blow to the head. Symptoms include inability of the infant to grasp firmly with her or his mouth when eating or drinking, diarrhea, crying spells, and restlessness.

Cancer. Disease in which malignant cells destroy normal cells in various regions of the body.

Candidiasis. Local or general cutaneous infection or severe systemic infection caused by a yeast-like fungus; also known as moniliasis.

Cannabis sativa. See *Marijuana.*

CAP. Client assistance program.

Caregiver. Person responsible for another's health and welfare, such as a parent or guardian, another person within the home, or a person in a relative's home, foster care home, or residential institution. A caregiver is responsible for meeting an individual's basic physical and psychological needs and for providing protection and supervision.

CARF. Commission on the Accreditation of Rehabilitation Facilities.

CARS. See *Childhood Autism Rating Scale.*

CASA. See *Court-appointed special advocate.* See also *Guardian ad litem.*

Case law. Law formed by cases decided by courts rather than by statute.

Case management. Coordination of the several services required by an individual, such as a child who has been maltreated or a child with special needs. See also *Service coordination.*

Cataplexy. Condition characterized by lack of response to external stimuli and by muscular rigidity, with the limbs remaining in whatever position they are placed in.

Cataract. Clouded lens in the eye that prevents light from entering.

Catastrophic reaction. Sudden outbreak of inappropriate behavior as a result of stress, fear, or frustration.

Catharsis. Release of tension and anxiety by emotionally reliving or talking about incidents of the past.

Catheter. Tubing used to introduce fluids (such as an IV line), to provide monitoring of the body, or to drain fluids from the body.

CBC. Complete blood count.

CCANI. Clearinghouse for Child Abuse and Neglect Information.

CCP. Crippled Children's Program.

CDB. Childhood disability benefit.

CDC. Centers for Disease Control and Prevention.

CDF. Children's Defense Fund.

CDH. Congenital diaphragmatic hernia.

CEC. Council for Exceptional Children.

Celiac disease. Chronic nutritional disturbance, usually of young children, caused by the inability to metabolize gluten and resulting in malnutrition, a distended abdomen, muscle wasting, and the passage of stools having a high fat content. The disorder can be controlled by a special diet that eliminates all foods containing gluten.

Central directory. Centralized source of information about services for infants and toddlers (0–36 months) with various disabilities and their families, required by federal education laws. These laws require that each state have a central directory that includes information on public and private early intervention services, state resources, experts on disabilities, state research and demonstration projects, professional groups, and other groups that provide assistance to eligible children and their families. Central directory formats vary from state to state.

Central nervous system (CNS). The brain and spinal cord.

Central registry for child maltreatment. Records of child maltreatment reports collected from various agencies under state law or voluntary agreement. The purposes of central registries are to alert authorities to families with a prior history of maltreatment, to assist agencies in planning for abusive families, and to provide data for statistical analysis of child maltreatment. Not all states have a central registry.

Central tendency error. Error occurring when the interviewer is unable to form judgments and opts for the middle ground, thereby taking a neutral position and failing to probe valuable leads in the interview.

Cerebellum. Portion of the brain consisting of two hemispheres located behind and above the medulla. It coordinates motor activities, maintains bodily equilibrium, and has recently been implicated in some cognitive tasks.

Cerebral angiography. Procedure involving radiographic recording of internal structures of the vascular system of the brain. Recordings are produced by action of x-rays or gamma rays on a specially sensitive film after injection of contrast material (for example, iodinated compounds) into the arterial blood system.

Cerebral contusion. Bruising of brain tissue, marked by swelling and hemorrhage and resulting in loss of consciousness.

Cerebral cortex. Convoluted outer layer of gray matter of the cerebral hemispheres which, together with the corpus callosum, comprises the cerebrum.

Cerebral dominance. Assumption that one cerebral hemisphere of the brain generally leads the other in governing an individual's functions.

Cerebral hemisphere. Either of the two halves that make up the cerebrum.

Cerebral hemorrhage. Bleeding onto brain tissue from a ruptured blood vessel.

Cerebral palsy (CP). Disability caused by damage to centers of the brain during or after birth, resulting in imperfect control of the muscles and marked by muscular incoordination, spastic paralysis, and speech disturbances.

Cerebral plasticity. Theory that the brain can change in various ways to compensate for loss of function due to damage.

Cerebral trauma. Brain injury resulting from some type of physical force—for example, a concussion.

Cerebral vascular disease. Disease of the blood vessels of the brain.

Cerebrospinal fluid (CSF). Specialized body fluid that surrounds the brain and spinal cord, providing cushioning and protection from injury.

Cerebrum. Main portion of the brain, occupying the upper part of the cranium and consisting of the two cerebral hemispheres, which are united by the corpus callosum. The cerebrum forms the largest part of the central nervous system.

Cervical os. Opening to the cervix.

CF. See *Cystic fibrosis.*

CFR. Code of Federal Regulations.

CHADD. Children with attention-deficit/hyperactivity disorder.

Challenging. Asking direct questions designed to clarify incongruencies in the interviewee's communication and to elicit more complete information.

Character disorder. Term once used for a personality disorder.

CHD. See *Congenital heart disease.*

Child. Person from birth to legal age of maturity; also known as minor.

Child abuse. Act of commission by a parent or caregiver that is not accidental and that harms or threatens to harm a child's physical or mental health or welfare.

Child Abuse Prevention and Treatment Act (PL 93-247). Act, introduced and promoted in Congress by then U.S. Senator Walter Mondale and signed into law on January 31, 1974, establishing the National Center on Child Abuse and Neglect in the Health, Education, and Welfare Children's Bureau. The purpose of the National Center is to conduct research, compile and publish training materials, provide technical assistance, investigate national incidence, and fund demonstration projects related to prevention, identification, and treatment of child abuse and neglect. The law also provides minimum standards for protection of children from abuse, which states must meet to be eligible for federal funding.

Child Find. Part of the federal education laws that requires each state to identify all children with disabilities who would be eligible for early intervention or special education services; also known as search and serve.

Child in need of supervision (CHINS). Juvenile who has committed a delinquent act and has been found by a children's court judge to require further court supervision, often through probation or transfer of custody of the child to a relative or public or private welfare agency for a period usually not to exceed one year; known as person in need of supervision (PINS) or minor in need of supervision (MINS) in some states.

Child neglect. Failure of a parent or other person legally responsible for a child's welfare to provide for the child's basic needs and a proper level of care with respect to food, clothing, shelter, hygiene, medical attention, or supervision. Child neglect is an act of omission.

Child pornography. Pictures or other visual media portraying a child involved in sexual activity.

Child prostitution. Form of sexual exploitation in which a child is solicited for sexual conduct or contact.

Child Protective Services (CPS). Public social services agency designated in most states to receive reports of child maltreatment, investigate, and provide rehabilitation services to children and families. Frequently, this agency is located within a larger public social services agency such as the Department of Social Services, Human Services, or Public Welfare. CPS workers look for a certain amount of evidence, such as "clear and convincing evidence," in order to decide whether maltreatment occurred and whether services are needed.

Childhood autism. See *Autistic disorder.*

Childhood Autism Rating Scale (CARS). Measure that evaluates 15 dimensions of behavior in children with an autistic disorder.

Childhood psychosis. Disorder characterized by disturbed social relationships, impairment of speech, bizarre motor behavior, daydreaming, and irritability in children.

Childhood schizophrenia. Disorder that manifests itself, after a period of normal development, in severe disturbances in the child's social adjustment and contact with reality.

CHINS. See *Child in need of supervision.*

CHIPS. Child in need of protection or services. In some states, CHIPS refers to a child who needs protection or services because of parental abuse or neglect.

Chlamydia trachomatis. Sexually transmitted organism that can cause nongonococcal urethritis and pelvic inflammatory disease.

Chlorpromazine. Generic term for one of the most widely used major tranquilizers, sold under the name Thorazine.

Chorea. Rapid, irregular, jerky, purposeless contraction and relaxation of random muscle groups affecting face, neck, or limbs.

Chorea gait. Uneven manner of walking in which one or two normal steps are followed by several long, hopping steps.

Choreiform movements. Spasmodic or jerky movements that occur quite irregularly and arrhythmically in different muscles.

Chromosomal abnormalities. Hereditary malfunctions of an individual's chromosomal structure. They may involve either the loss of a chromosome or the addition of one or more chromosomes.

Chronic brain disorder. Relatively permanent and usually irreversible condition resulting from diffuse impairment of brain tissue.

Chronic condition. Disability or illness that persists for a long time or for a person's entire life; also known as chronic illness.

Chronic illness. See *Chronic condition.*

Chronic pain. Unpleasant sensation that is long lasting.

Chronological age (CA). Number of years and months a person has lived.

Circular migration. Among immigrants to the United States, traveling back and forth between the United States and their countries of origin.

Circumlocution. Indirect or round-about expression; use of superfluous words.

Circumstantial evidence. Fact from which another fact can be reasonably inferred. For example, proof that a parent kept a broken appliance cord may connect the parent to the infliction of unique marks on a child's body.

Circumstantiality. Indirect conversation characterized by many tedious, irrelevant details and additions.

Civil action. See *Civil proceeding.*

Civil complaint. See *Complaint, civil.*

Civil proceeding. Any legal action other than a criminal prosecution; also known as civil action. Parties bringing such actions need not meet the "beyond a reasonable doubt" standard required in criminal proceedings; the standard is a preponderance of evidence. Juvenile and family court cases are considered to be civil proceedings.

Civil rights. Rights guaranteed to all citizens by the U.S. Constitution and relevant acts of Congress.

Clang association. Pattern of speech in which sounds rather than meaningful relationships appear to govern word choice—for example, "How are you Don, pawn, gone?"; also known as clanging. The intelligibility of the speech is impaired, and redundant words are introduced.

Clanging. See *Clang association.*

Clarification. Probing technique used when the interviewer does not understand what the interviewee is saying.

Class action. Lawsuit filed by one or a few people on behalf of a larger number of persons with a grievance against the same party.

Classic migraine headaches. Severe, recurrent, often unilateral, paroxysmal headaches that occur with prodromal symptoms. The prodromal symptoms typically precede the actual headache by 10 to 30 minutes and usually involve transient visual, motor, and/or sensory disturbances.

Clear and convincing evidence. Evidence that produces, in the mind of the judge or jury, a conviction that the allegations are very likely true.

Cleft lip. Condition in which the upper lip is separated, leaving an opening between the nose and the mouth.

Cleft palate. Condition in which there is a large opening in the roof of the mouth.

Climate, interview. Physical setting, social setting, time dimension, and psychological characteristics of the interview.

Clinging behavior. Behavior characterized by excessive physical contact with others and a demand for constant attention and direction.

Clinical assessment interview. Interview designed to obtain relevant information in order to make an informed decision about the interviewee, such as for screening, classification/placement, program planning/remediation, or program evaluation.

Clitoris. Erectile tissue in female analogous to a male penis, located above the urethra and covered by the clitoral hood.

Clonic. Relating to the rapid alternation between muscular rigidity and relaxation that characterizes epileptic contractions.

Closed-ended questions. Queries that can be answered by yes or no.

Closed-head injury. Injury to the head with no penetrating wound or fracture to the skull.

Closing argument. Attorney's final statement to the court summing up the case and the points proven as well as those points not proven by opposing counsel; also known as final argument.

Closure. Process of achieving completion of a visual, behavioral, or mental act.

Closure stage of coping. Final stage of coping, after a parent learns that she or he has a child with special needs. It is characterized by returning to precrisis behavior, calmness, working toward new goals, and acceptance of the child and the situation.

CMS. Children's medical services.

CMV. See *Cytomegalovirus.*

CNS. See *Central nervous system.*

Co-occurring disorder. Psychological disorder that tends to occur with another psychological disorder; also known as comorbid disorder.

COBRA. See *Consolidated Omnibus Budget Reconciliation Act.*

Cocaine. Stimulating and pain-reducing psychoactive drug that is addicting. Long-term abuse is associated with toxic psychosis.

Code. Collection of laws or statutes classified according to subject matter.

Coercive questioning. Asking questions designed to force the interviewee to see things as the interviewer sees them. Such questions are avoided in objective, neutral interviews.

Cognition. Processes involved in thinking, including perceiving, recognizing, conceiving, judging, and reasoning.

Cognitive. Related to the process used for remembering, reasoning, understanding, thinking, or using judgment.

Cognitive appraisal. Evaluation by an individual of situations, affects, and thoughts, such as the meaning of an illness for a person's life.

Cognitive avoidance. Strategy that focuses on trying to forget a situation, distracting oneself to keep from thinking about a situation, or blaming someone else for one's predicament.

Cognitive-behavioral perspective. Outlook that focuses on the importance of cognitions, the role that cognitions play in the development of maladaptive behavior, and the individual and environmental influences that may shape and control behavior.

Cognitive-behavioral rehabilitation. Form of rehabilitation in which the goal is to reduce or eliminate dysfunctional thoughts and cognitive distortions.

Cognitive interview. Guided memory search, using techniques designed to enhance a witness's memory of an event by facilitating complete and accurate reporting.

Cognitive redefinition. Strategy that focuses on redefining a situation by accepting it and finding something favorable in it.

Cognitive style. Individual's characteristic approach to problem solving and cognitive tasks.

Coherence (in Statement Validity Analysis). Consistency of a person's statements. Coherence requires that the various parts of the person's allegation fit together—it must be physically possible for the event to have happened. See also *Statement Validity Analysis.*

COHI. See *Crippled and other health impaired.*

Coining. Traditional healing procedure, used by Asians, that involves applying oil and rubbing the affected area with the edge of a coin. The treatment may result in bruises.

Colitis. Inflammation of the colon.

Collateral orientation. Value orientation of a cultural group that emphasizes collective decision making.

Colostomy. Surgical creation of an opening between the colon and the surface of the body.

Colposcope. Instrument for examination of tissues of the vagina and cervix by means of a magnifying glass.

Coma. State of unconsciousness from which a person cannot be aroused, even by powerful stimulation.

Commission. Willful or volitional act.

Commitment (legal). In juvenile law, court order placing children in a mental health facility or correctional facility when they are declared delinquent, neglected, dependent, or uncared for.

Common law. Body of law based on judicial decision (precedents or customs and usages), generally derived from justice, reason, and common sense rather than legislative enactments.

Common migraine headaches. Severe, recurrent headaches that occur without prodromal symptoms.

Community-based care. Provision of services in the community so as to allow a child to participate as fully as possible in all aspects of family and community life.

Community neglect. Failure of a community to provide adequate support and social services for families and children; lack of community control over illegal or discriminatory activities with respect to families and children.

Community re-entry. Person's return to the mainstream of life, requiring the appropriate social, educational, emotional, vocational, and independent living skills.

Comorbid disorder. See *Co-occurring disorder.*

Compadrazgo. Hispanic American term referring to godparents.

Compensation. (1) Use of other than normal means to achieve a goal. (2) Remuneration for loss or damages. (3) Psychological mechanism used to make up for a psychological defect.

Compensatory damages. Remuneration awarded to a party based on the actual loss suffered, such as medical expenses.

Compensatory use of substances. Relying on substances to cope with stress and uncomfortable feelings.

Competency. In the law of evidence, possession of characteristics that qualify a witness to observe, recall, and testify under oath; personal qualifications of the witness to give testimony, which differ from the witness's ability to tell the truth. See also *Credibility.*

Complainant. Party who initiates the complaint in an action; also known as plaintiff or petitioner.

Complaint, civil. Legal document submitted to the court by plaintiffs, in which they inform the court and the defendants that they are bringing a lawsuit and set out the reasons they are suing and the relief they want.

Complaint, criminal. Legal document that initiates the criminal court process; written statement by the investigating officer(s), outlining the facts in a particular criminal violation and charging the suspect with the crime. The complaint must include facts to support a finding that probable cause exists to believe a crime has been committed and the defendant suspect committed it, and it must outline the elements of the crime. Although the officer is called the complainant, ordinarily the district or county attorney's office will prepare the complaint, using the officer's written report, and have the officer sign it.

Compliance. See *Adherence to a medical regimen.*

Compulsions. Irrational and repetitive impulses to perform some type of action.

Compulsive stage of substance abuse. Fifth stage of substance abuse, in which substance use becomes compulsive and addictive. At this stage, the addict is preoccupied with thoughts of getting high; other concerns become nonexistent. The use of the substance is out of control.

Computed tomography (CT). Imaging technique in which an array of detectors is used to collect information from an x-ray beam that has passed through a portion of the brain or another body part. The beam is rotated to produce the equivalent of a "slice" through the area of interest. A computer reconstructs the internal structure from the information collected and displays it on a screen.

Concealed meanings. Special patterns of communication revealed by slips of the tongue, hidden agendas, and rationalizations. They may suggest areas needing further exploration in the interview.

Conciliation court. Civil court, found in many states, that aids in resolving marital disputes and provides counseling services for couples considering divorce.

Concrete mode. (1) Style of cognitive functioning used by a child to solve problems at a simple, elementary level. (2) Use of tangible objects in instruction, as opposed to purely verbal instruction.

Concrete referents. Techniques used by an interviewer to help a child understand what the interviewer is saying.

Concur (legal). To agree with the judgment of another. When one court concurs with another, it agrees with or follows the precedent set by that court's decision.

Concurrent validity. See *Validity*.

Concussion. Sudden shock to or jarring of the brain, which may or may not cause a loss of consciousness.

Condensation. Combining fragments of two or more ideas and expressing them in the pattern of a single phrase; telescoping of thoughts.

Conduct disorder. Condition characterized by a pattern of antisocial behavior, rule-breaking, or aggressive behavior that creates difficulties for children, their families, their school systems, and their communities; repetitive and persistent pattern of behavior in which the basic rights of others or major age-appropriate societal norms or rules are violated.

Conductive hearing loss. Decreased ability to perceive sounds, characterized by damage to or obstruction of the auditory (ear) canal, tympanic membrane (eardrum), or ossicular chain (ear bones in the middle ear). It can often be treated successfully by removal of ear wax, antibiotics, or surgery.

Confabulation. Type of thinking characterized by the filling of memory gaps with false and irrelevant information and details.

Confidential communication. Statement made under circumstances indicating that the speaker intended the statement only for the person addressed. If the communication is made in the presence of a third party whose presence is not reasonably necessary for the communication, it is not confidential. See also *Privileged communication*.

Confidentiality. Ethical obligation of a professional not to reveal information obtained through professional contact with a client without specific consent. It protects the client from any unauthorized disclosures of information given in confidence to a professional. Confidentiality must be broken when the client threatens another person, talks about abusing children or about having been abused, or says he or she wants to harm himself or herself.

Confrontation. Probing technique used to clarify incongruities in the interviewee's statements or contradictions between what the interviewee says and does. Confrontation should be done in a nonthreatening manner.

Confused behavior. Behavior characterized by bewilderment, perplexity, and puzzlement.

Confusion. Inability of a person to make sense of the environment, reflected in agitated behavior, disorganized language, incorrect memories, or poor memories.

Confusional arousals. Sleep disorder characterized by cloudiness of conscious behavior during and after arousal from sleep, mainly occurring in the first part of the night and lasting from several minutes to hours. Children are often disoriented and show slowed speech and slowed response to commands or ques-

tions. Typically, treatment is not recommended, as children outgrow this sleep problem.

Congenital. (1) Existing at or before birth. (2) Acquired at birth or during uterine development as a result of either hereditary or environmental influences.

Congenital anomalies. Abnormalities that are present at birth. Congenital anomalies are not necessarily inherited.

Congenital aphasia. Language dysfunction marked by almost complete failure to acquire language.

Congenital diaphragmatic hernia. Protrusion of an organ within the abdomen through an opening in the diaphragm, present at birth. The extent of herniation determines the severity of symptoms, but some degree of respiratory distress is usually present.

Congenital glaucoma. Disease of the eye that is marked by increased pressure within the eyeball, damage to the optic disk, and gradual loss of vision and is acquired during development in the uterus, not through heredity.

Congenital heart disease (CHD). Incomplete or poor development of the heart in utero (in the womb), resulting in deformities of the heart or large vessels arising from the heart.

Congenital infections. Diseases acquired either before birth or during birth through exposure to viral, bacterial, or protozoal organisms. They may result in chronic physical, sensory, and mental disabilities for the newborn. The congenital infections that most often cause developmental disabilities include syphilis, herpes, chicken pox, and German measles (rubella). A test called TORCH or STORCH (syphilis, toxoplasmosis, other agents, rubella, cytomegalovirus, and herpes simplex) is often used to diagnose these congenital infections.

Conjunctiva. Transparent lining covering the white of the eye and eyelids. Bleeding beneath the conjunctiva can occur spontaneously or from accidental or nonaccidental injury.

Consent decree. Agreement reached by the parties to a lawsuit out of court and then formally approved by the court.

Consequent events. Events that occurred after the behavior in question.

Consolidated Omnibus Budget Reconciliation Act (COBRA). Bill passed by the U.S. Congress to deal with a number of subjects related to the budget. Past COBRAs have addressed the provisions of health insurance to terminated employees and the need for hospitals to care for indigent persons.

Constructional apraxia. Impaired ability to construct objects, manifested, for example, through an inability to construct a pattern with blocks.

Contempt (legal). Act calculated to inhibit, hinder, or affront the court in the administration of justice; obstruction of the court's work. Disobedience of a judge's order is one type of contempt.

Contextual embedding (in Statement Validity Analysis). Placing the alleged event in the context of routine life experiences. The abusive incident(s) should not seem to appear in a vacuum but should be connected in some way to the child's everyday life. Thus, the child may be encouraged to make statements about everyday occurrences, habits, the family, acquaintances, and relationships with people living at his or her residence and provide details about the time and place of the event.

Continuance (legal). Court order that postpones legal action, such as a court hearing, until a later time.

Continuous positive airway pressure (CPAP). Procedure used to help individuals with some types of respiratory problems breathe better. It improves the functioning of the lungs by holding the alveoli open, thereby making more oxygen available to the individual.

Contracture. Abnormal tightness of a muscle, due to spasm or paralysis, that limits the range of motion of the joint.

Contralateral. Pertaining to the opposite side.

Contrast and similarity error. Error occurring when the interviewer constantly compares his or her values to those of the interviewee and finds the interviewee's values lacking.

Contrecoup. Damage occurring opposite the point of impact.

Contusion. Bruise. When it occurs on the brain, a contusion can cause tissue damage and bleeding.

Convergence. In physiology, coordinated turning of the eyes inward to focus on an object at close range.

Convergent thinking. Generation of ideas and facts from known information where the emphasis is on finding a single, logical solution to a problem.

Conversion reactions. Psychological responses, not intentionally produced, that generate symptoms of organic illness in the absence of any related organic pathology.

Convulsion. Violent, extensive, involuntary, and pathological paroxysmal muscle contraction.

Convulsive disorder. Clinical syndrome, the central feature of which is recurrent muscular seizures. Also, recurrent disturbances of consciousness, with or without muscular components and accompanied by changes in the electrical potential of the brain.

Coping. Ways in which individuals deal with anxiety, stress, illness, and other forms of tension and adversity.

Coping strategies. Behaviors, cognitions, and perceptions employed by a person to maintain equilibrium when faced with stress or illness.

Coping styles. Relatively enduring and characteristic ways in which individuals respond to stressful situations, such as illness.

Corporal punishment. Physical punishment inflicted directly upon the body.

Corpus callosum. Large band of white fiber connecting the two cerebral hemispheres.

Correlation. Statistical procedure for determining the degree of relationship between two variables.

Cortex. Upper, outer layer of the brain, which controls sensation and movement and thinking and behavior, as well as the association of these functions.

Cortical. Pertaining to the cortex.

Cortical evoked potential. Electrical activity in response to a stimulus, as recorded from the cerebral cortex.

Coup. Damage localized to the area under the point of impact.

Court-appointed special advocate (CASA). Individual (usually a volunteer) who serves to ensure that the needs and best interests of a child in judicial proceedings are fully protected.

Court order. Directive, issued by the court, that has the authority of the court and is enforceable as law; written command or directive given by the judge.

CP. See *Cerebral palsy.*

CPAP. See *Continuous positive airway pressure.*

CPS. See *Child Protective Services.*

Crack cocaine. Almost pure form of the drug cocaine hydrochloride, obtained from a shrub native to Bolivia and Peru. It can cause increased alertness and energy, runny nose, and decreased appetite when snorted, injected, or smoked. It is a highly addictive type of cocaine.

Craniotomy. Operation in which a portion of the skull is removed to allow surgical access to the brain.

Credibility (legal). Worthiness of belief; quality of witnesses that makes their testimony believable. Once the competency of a witness has been established, the witness is able to testify; it is at this point that the court or jury considers whether the witness is truthful or credible. See also *Competency.*

Credible evidence. Evidence that is worthy of belief.

Cretinism. Abnormal condition resulting from thyroid insufficiency in childhood and characterized by severe mental retardation, stunted growth, patchy hair, a protruding abdomen, and a severely underdeveloped personality. See also *Hypothyroidism.*

Criminal complaint. See *Complaint, criminal.*

Criminal court. Court that has jurisdiction over cases alleging violations of criminal law. Some judicial districts do not distinguish between the types of cases a particular judge will hear; in other jurisdictions, specific judges are assigned to criminal court.

Criminal investigators. In child maltreatment investigations, individuals (usually members of a police or sheriff's department) who look for evidence that can be used in criminal court to prove their case "beyond a reasonable doubt."

Criminal justice system interviewer. Interviewer whose goal is to obtain objective, verifiable information from the child, the parents, and the offender that will meet legal standards for admissibility in court.

Criminal prosecution. Process that begins with the filing of charges against a person who has allegedly violated criminal law and includes the arraignment and trial of the defendant. Criminal prosecution may result in fines, restitution, imprisonment, or probation. Most criminal defendants are entitled to a jury trial.

Crippled and other health impaired (COHI). Individuals with physical and health handicaps.

Crisis intervention. Action to relieve a specific stressful situation or series of problems that is immediately threatening to a person's health or welfare.

Criteria-based content analysis (in Statement Validity Analysis). Evaluation of a person's statements in order to distinguish statements about actually experienced events from those based on fantasy, fiction, or coercion. See also *Statement Validity Analysis.*

Critical period hypothesis. Theory that there are critical times in a child's development during which certain functions can develop.

Cross-dominance. Sensorimotor functioning, characterized by right-handed and left-eyed—or left-handed and right-eyed—dominance. Occasionally, the term refers to dominance of ear or foot, as well.

Cross-examination (legal). Interrogation of a witness who has already been questioned by the opposing party.

Cross-generational effect. Result of parents' treating their children as they were treated by their parents.

Cross-modality perception. Process by which a certain stimulus acquires meaning through the use of more than one sensory modality.

CRS. Children's rehabilitative services.

CSF. See *Cerebrospinal fluid.*

CSHN. Children with special health needs. The term varies from state to state; other forms are CCP, CMS, CRS, and CSN.

CSN. Children with special needs.

CT. See *Computerized tomography.*

Cultural deprivation. Hindering effect that a person's past learning and life experiences may have on her or his adaptive and intellectual functioning when another cultural orientation is encountered.

Cultural-familial retardation. Mental retardation in the absence of indications of cerebral pathology, but where there is a history of familial intellectual subnormality.

Culture. Human-made part of the environment, consisting of highly variable systems of meaning learned and shared by a people or an identifiable segment of a population; designs and ways of life normally transmitted from one generation to another.

Cupping. Traditional healing procedure, used by Asians, in which a vacuum is created by burning a material in a cup and then the cup is immediately placed on selected areas of the body. The procedure sometimes leaves circular burns.

Curanderismo. Health care belief and practice system followed by some Mexican Americans.

Curandero. Mexican American traditional healer who is believed to have a gift from God for healing and who treats serious illnesses with prayers, teas, poultices (substances applied to the body), and herbs.

Custodial parent. Parent who has the physical control, care, and custody of a minor child.

Custody. Right to care for and control a child; duty to provide food, clothing, shelter, ordinary medical care, education, and discipline for a child. Permanent legal custody may be taken from a parent or given up by a parent through court action. Temporary legal custody of child is granted for a limited time only, usually pending further action or review by the court; it may be granted for hours, days, months, or years. Upon divorce, one parent is often given physical (residential) custody of the child, or physical custody may be shared. Generally, both parents receive joint legal custody if there is no abuse or neglect of the child.

Custody evaluation. Investigative procedure to gather and analyze facts about the family for the purpose of making a recommendation to the court regarding child custody and/or visitation. A custody evaluation may be initiated by order of the court or by stipulation of the parties involved, pursuant to local court rules.

Custody hearing. Legal process, usually in family or juvenile court, to determine who has the right of legal or physical custody of a minor. It may involve one parent against the other, a parent against a third party, or a parent against a social services agency seeking protective custody in juvenile court.

Cutaneous. Pertaining to the skin or sense organs in the skin.

CWLA. Child Welfare League of America.

Cyanosis. Blueness of the skin due to insufficient oxygen in the blood, poor circulation, or, especially in a newborn, delayed or insufficient breathing. It is present in many heart and respiratory conditions.

Cystic fibrosis (CF). A hereditary disease of the exocrine glands (externally secreting glands, such as the salivary glands or sweat glands, that release their secretions directly or through a duct), usually developing during early childhood and affecting mainly the pancreas, respiratory system, and sweat glands. The disease is characterized by the production of abnormally viscous mucus by the affected glands, usually resulting in chronic respiratory infections and impaired pancreatic function.

Cytomegalovirus (CMV). Systemic illness caused by exposure to the virus as the baby passes through the infected birth canal. It may be transmitted prenatally or postnatally through infected urine, saliva, breast milk, and, perhaps, feces, tears, or blood transfusions from infected donors. The effects of CMV vary from severe central nervous system destruction to asymptomatic carrying of the virus. In its most severe form, CMV causes global central nervous system infection involving the cerebral cortex, brain stem, cochlear nuclei, cranial nerves, and inner ear. See also *Congenital infections.*

D&E. Diagnosis and evaluation.

DAC. Disabled adult child.

Damages (legal). Remuneration awarded by a court to someone who has been injured (the plaintiff), to be paid by the one who is responsible for the injury (the defendant).

db. See *Decibel.*

D/BL. Deaf/blind. Individuals with both hearing and visual disabilities.

DCP. Disabled Children's Program.

DD. Developmental disabilities.

DDC/DDPC. Developmental Disabilities (Planning) Council.

De facto. In fact; in deed; actually. This phrase is used to characterize a past action or a state of affairs that must be accepted for all practical purposes but is not necessarily legal or legitimate.

De jure. By right; according to law. This phrase is used in contrast to *de facto.*

De minimus. Insignificant; not sufficiently important to be dealt with judicially.

Deaf children. Children whose hearing disability prevents successful processing of auditory information.

DEC. Developmental evaluation clinic.

Decibel (db). Unit of measure for the intensity or loudness of sound.

Decile. Score in a frequency distribution below which 10% (1st decile), 20% (2nd decile), …, 90% (9th decile), or 100% (10th decile) of the total number of scores fall.

Declaration of parentage. A judicial decision stating who the parents of a child are.

Declaratory judgment. Judicial statement that establishes rights of the parties involved or expresses the opinion of the court on a question of law without ordering anything to be done.

Decoding. Process by which a receiver translates signals into messages, as in reading.

Default (legal). Failure of an individual to appear for a hearing when he or she has been given legally sufficient information regarding the action (including the date and place of the court hearing), resulting in a decision by the court that the party who appeared at the hearing has won the case. For example, the court may grant a county child protection agency's petition by default if parents do not attend a hearing of which they were given notice.

Defendant. Person against whom an action (either civil or criminal) is brought.

Defense mechanisms. In the psychodynamic perspective, techniques used by individuals to try to avoid awareness of unpleasant or anxiety-arousing feelings and thoughts.

Degenerative brain disease. Illness or condition that results in progressive deterioration of the brain.

Delayed echolalia. Speech pattern in which the speaker repeats another person's words after a delay.

Delinquency. Behavior on the part of a minor that would, if performed by an adult, constitute criminal conduct.

Delusion. False, but persistent, belief.

Demographic variables. Vital statistics on a human population, such as age, gender, ethnicity, and socioeconomic status.

Demyelinating disease. Any of the disorders of the central nervous system that result in progressive deterioration of the myelin sheath that surrounds and insulates nerve fibers.

Dendrite. Receiving branch of the neuron.

Dendritic expansion. Growth of interconnected dendrites (nerve connectors) along which messages are transmitted electrochemically. The dendrites of short-axon neurons are said to be susceptible to such expansion when there is appropriate stimulation from the environment early in life.

Denial. Process of protecting oneself from unpleasant or traumatic aspects of reality by refusing to acknowledge them; a defense mechanism.

Denial stage of coping. Second stage of coping, after a parent learns that she or he has a child with special needs. It is characterized by mood swings, seeking people who support one's view, and distorted expectations.

Dependency/neglect petition. Request on the part of Child Protective Services, filed by the county or district attorney, to remove a child from an allegedly abusive home for a period of time longer than the initial 48-hour emergency period.

Dependent child. Child who is homeless, destitute, or without proper care or support through no fault of his or her parent, guardian, or custodian; who lacks proper care or support by reason of the mental or physical condition of his or her parent, guardian, or custodian; or whose condition or environment is such as to warrant that the state, in the interests of the child, assume guardianship.

Depersonalization disorder. Dissociative condition in which an individual feels estranged from the self and perhaps separated from the body, but his or her reality testing ability remains intact.

Deposition. Questioning of a party or witness, under oath, outside of the courtroom, usually in the offices of one of the lawyers.

Depressant. Class of drugs, including alcohol, barbiturates, and benzodiazepines, the major effect of which is to reduce neurological activity.

Depression. Feelings of sadness, self-deprecation, loss of hope, and often apprehension, associated with difficulty in thinking and conducting usual activities and responsibilities, lowered energy level, and self-preoccupation.

Derailment. Thought pattern in which associations are loose or obliquely related to the topic under discussion; reasons for the shift of topics are obscure, idiosyncratic, or unexplained; and connections are illogical.

Dermatology. Branch of science dealing with the skin and its structure, functions, and diseases.

Descriptive comments. Statements made by an interviewer about a child's appearance, behavior, or demeanor. They provide a simple way of giving attention to the child and encouraging the child to continue with appropriate behavior.

Desert island technique. Interview method used with children in which the interviewer asks the child whom he or she would want to be with on a desert island.

Designated instructional services (DIS). Additional support services for handicapped students enrolled in either special education classes or regular classes.

Designer drugs. Drugs that are produced illicitly by means of chemical technology. They can cause uncontrollable tremors, chills, or sweating and faintness and paranoia when injected or taken in pill form.

Detention (legal). Temporary confinement of a person by a public authority; also known as placement. See also *Arrest.*

Detention hearing. Court session conducted to determine whether a child should be held in the legal custody of the local child protection agency or a correctional facility until a hearing on the allegations of a child protection or delinquency petition can take place; also known as placement hearing.

Developmental aphasia. Impairment of or failure to develop language due to brain injury that occurred before language usually is acquired.

Developmental deficit. Deficiency in using a particular function relative to expectations for an individual of a particular age.

Developmental delay. Lag in the development of a function relative to expectations for an individual of a particular age.

Developmental (delay) theory of retardation. Premise that a mentally retarded individual goes through the same sequence of developmental stages as a nonretarded individual, but at a slower rate, and ultimately reaches a comparatively lower level.

Developmental disability. Chronic, severe disability that (a) results from a mental or physical impairment, (b) begins before age 22, (c) is likely to be life-long, (d) results in major limitations in everyday functioning, such as self-care, language, learning, mobility, self-direction, capacity for independent living, and economic self-sufficiency, and (e) reflects a need for special services that are individually planned and coordinated. Examples of developmental disabilities are cerebral palsy, mental retardation, Down syndrome, autism, epilepsy, deafness, blindness, serious learning disabilities, and spina bifida.

Developmental history interview. Interview with a parent to obtain a history of the child's development.

Developmental language disorder. Disorder in children in which language is late in onset.

Developmental perspective. Theoretical view that many behaviors are genetically programmed. The programming gives development a definite, nonrandom direction and assures that development proceeds toward specific goals.

Developmental variables. Measures of level of development, such as measures of language, motor, social, and self-help skills.

Developmentally handicapped (DH). Individuals who are severely delayed in their physical and mental development and may require assistance with physical health care, such as feeding, toileting, and positioning.

Deviant locomotion. Walking on toes, whirling on one's own longitudinal axis, or running in small circles.

Deviation IQ. Intelligence quotient derived from a statistical table comparing an individual's score with scores of other individuals of the same age.

Dexedrine. Stimulant drug, sometimes used to control attention-deficit/hyperactivity disorder behavior in children; also known as dextroamphetamine.

Dextral. Consistently right-sided in lateral preference.

Dextroamphetamine. See *Dexedrine.*

DH. See *Developmentally handicapped.*

D/HH. Deaf/hard of hearing. Individuals who have a measurable hearing loss—conductive or sensorineural—that limits the normal acquisition of speech and language through the ear.

DHHS/HSS. U.S. Department of Health and Human Services.

Diabetes control. Maintenance of blood glucose level in the normal range by adherence to diet, exercise, and proper medication.

Diabetes mellitus. Metabolic disorder caused by insufficient production of or response to insulin from the pancreas, which leads to excessive amounts of unmetabolized sugar in the blood. Diabetes mellitus in the mother can lead to the infant's having heart defects, skeletal deformities, respiratory distress, and neurological problems.

Diabetic coma. Coma resulting from an excessive amount of unmetabolized sugar in the blood, which leads initially to symptoms of thirst, hunger, and weakness.

Diabetic ketoacidosis (DKA). Toxic condition, associated with diabetes, that occurs when the blood does not have enough insulin and glucose accumulates in the bloodstream. Caused by illness or nonadherence to diet and proper medication, it requires emergency treatment. As blood glucose levels increase, the body uses stored fat for energy and ketone bodies (acids) build up in the blood. Signs of DKA include nausea and vomiting, dehydration, stomach pain, and deep and rapid breathing. If fluids and insulin are not given immediately, ketoacidosis can lead to coma and even death.

Diabetic retinopathy. Disease of the small blood vessels in the retina that can occur after long-term uncontrolled diabetes.

Diadochokinesia. Ability to perform alternating movements, such as flexion and extension of a limb.

Diagnosis. Determination of the nature and extent of a specific disorder.

Diagnostic classification. Identification made when an interviewee's set of symptoms or problems indicates a particular disorder, usually with reference to the *Diagnostic and Statistical Manual of Mental Disorders—Fourth Edition (DSM-IV).*

Diagnostician. In traditional Native American culture, healer who diagnoses illness or disharmony.

Dialect. Regional variation of a spoken language.

Dichotic. Affecting the two ears.

Dichotic stimulation. Concurrent stimulation of both ears with distinctly different stimuli.

DID. See *Dissociated identity disorder.*

Differential diagnosis. Diagnosis aimed at distinguishing which of two or more similar diseases or disorders an individual has.

Difficult child. Child who is predominantly negative and intense in mood, not very adaptable, and arrhythmic.

Dilantin. Trade name for phenytoin sodium, an anticonvulsant drug used for epilepsy.

Diplegia. Paralysis affecting like parts on both sides of the body.

Direct evidence. Information offered by witnesses who testify about their own knowledge of the facts. In cases of child maltreatment, for example, it might consist of a neighbor's testimony that he saw the parent strike the child with an appliance cord.

Direct examination. Initial interrogation of a witness on the merits of a case by the party on whose behalf she or he is called.

Direct questions. Queries that are phrased in a positive and confident manner, are stated clearly, and address the topic in a forthright manner.

Direct service providers. (1) Groups and individuals who directly interact with clients and patients in the delivery of health, education, and welfare services. (2) Agencies that employ these groups and individuals.

Directional confusion. Tendency to make reversals and substitutions because of a left-right or laterality orientation disorder.

Directionality. Ability to distinguish right from left, forward from backward, and up from down.

DIS. See *Designated instructional services.*

Disability. Any lack of ability to perform an activity in a manner or within the range considered normal for a person of the same age

and similar circumstances. A disability may be temporary or permanent and can occur in any component of human functioning. Different impairments may result in similar disabilities; the same impairments do not necessarily result in similar disabilities. Not all impairments result in disability. An example of a disability is the inability to climb stairs.

Discovery (legal). System of pretrial procedures that enables the parties involved in a court proceeding to find out about the evidence supporting the positions taken by the other parties, including facts that those parties believe support their positions.

Discrimination. See *Auditory discrimination, Visual discrimination.*

Disease model. See *Medical model.*

Disenfranchised grief. Form of grief experienced by individuals who are denied the opportunity to grieve or are discouraged by others from grieving.

Disfluency. Part-word, whole-word, or phrase repetitions, revisions, and interjections; incomplete phrases that occur in conversational speech.

Disinhibition. Lack of ability to restrain oneself from responding to distracting stimuli. A motor disinhibition is an unplanned or meaningless motor response, such as responding to a given stimulus with inappropriate or excessive motor activity.

Dislocation. Displacement of a bone, usually disrupting a joint, that may accompany a fracture or may occur alone.

Dismissal (legal). Action by the court that removes the court's jurisdiction over a given case.

Disorganized behavior. Behavior that is inconsistent, changes abruptly, or has no coherent goal direction.

Disposition (legal). In child protection matters, order of a court, issued at a hearing, that determines whether a minor, already found to be in need of protection or services or delinquent, should continue in or return to the parental home, be under a particular type of supervision, or be placed out of home (and, if so, in what kind of setting). Also considered are the conditions that must exist or services that must be accepted or provided before the court will dismiss its jurisdiction. Disposition in a child protection matter parallels sentencing in a criminal case.

Dissociative amnesia. Condition in which an individual has memory loss of psychological origin. A loss of memory for important personal information may occur as a reaction to an intolerable traumatic situation.

Dissociative fugue. Psychological condition in which an individual not only is amnesic but also wanders away from home, often assuming a completely new identity.

Dissociative identity disorder. Condition in which an individual develops two or more distinct identities or personality states that recurrently take control of his or her behavior; formerly known as multiple personality disorder. The individual is unable to recall important personal information; this cannot be explained by ordinary forgetfulness or by direct physiological effects of a substance or a medical condition. In children, dissociative identity disorder cannot be attributed to imaginary playmates or other fantasy play.

Dissolution of marriage. Act of terminating a marriage through a legal proceeding; divorce.

Distal. Far from any point of reference; opposed to proximal.

Distortion of ideas. Use of hyperbole, exaggeration, or incorrect details; misrepresentation of fact.

Distractibility. Difficulty in maintaining focused attention because of the influence of extraneous stimuli.

Distractible speech. Speech in which the speaker stops repeatedly in the middle of a sentence or idea and changes the subject in response to a nearby stimulus, such as an object on a desk or the interviewer's clothing or appearance.

Divergent thinking. (1) Ability to generate several possible alternative solutions to a problem presented. (2) Thought processes required to produce a novel response.

Divided custody. See *Joint custody.*

Dizygotic twins. Twins originating from two fertilized ova and thus having different genetic makeups; also known as fraternal twins.

DKA. See *Diabetic ketoacidosis.*

DMH. Department of Mental Health.

DMR. Department of Mental Retardation.

DNA. Deoxyribonucleic acid, a complex molecule that is found in the genes and contains the chemical blueprint to regulate the functioning and development of an organism.

Docket. Schedule of cases on the calendar to be heard by a court.

DOE. Department of Education.

Doing orientation. Value orientation of a cultural group that emphasizes achievement, competitiveness, striving for upward mobility in jobs, and controlling feelings.

Domestic relations (legal). Branch of the law that deals with matters of the household or family, which may include divorce, separation, custody, support, domestic violence, and adoption.

Domestic violence. Physical or mental abuse of a family member or partner.

Dorsiflexion. Lifting of the foot up toward the body.

Double-barreled questions. Queries that ask about two things at the same time. Such questions should be avoided in clinical assessment and forensic interviews.

Double bind. Situation in which faulty communication causes a child to receive contradictory messages from a parent. For example, the parent may communicate warmth but then be cold and withdrawn when the child approaches.

Down syndrome. Chromosomal abnormality that arises from the presence of an extra chromosome 21; also known as mongolism or Trisomy 21. Many children with Down syndrome are mentally retarded, with delays in physical, psychomotor, and language development. The children usually have a flat skull, thickened skin on the eyelids, stubby fingers, and a short, stocky body.

Dozens. Word game, most commonly engaged in by young Black males, in which close members of the family are degraded.

Dressing apraxia. Impaired ability to dress oneself.

DSM-IV. *Diagnostic and Statistical Manual of Mental Disorders—Fourth Edition,* which presents the diagnostic classification system officially adopted by the American Psychiatric Association.

DSS. Department of Social Services.

Due process. (1) Rights of a person involved in legal proceedings to be treated with fairness. These rights may include the right to adequate notice in advance of a hearing, the right to notice of allegations of misconduct, the right to the assistance of a lawyer, the right to confront and cross-examine witnesses, and the right to refuse to give self-incriminating testimony. (2) In federal education law, steps and rules established to ensure fairness in providing educational opportunities to all children.

Duration. In behavioral assessment, how long the behavior lasts.

DVR. Department of Vocational Rehabilitation.

Dx. Diagnosis.

Dynamometer. Device for measuring the strength of a muscular response.

Dysarthria. Speech difficulties due to interference with the peripheral speech mechanisms, larynx, pharynx, and tongue.

Dyscalculia. Partial inability to calculate, to manipulate number symbols, or to do simple arithmetic; also known as mathematics disorder.

Dysdiadochokinesia. Inability to perform rapid alternating movements.

Dysfunctional family coping methods. In cases of maltreatment, adjustment strategies, such as patronization and protective silence, that may interfere with the maltreated child's recovery.

Dysfunctional family strategies. See *Dysfunctional family coping methods.*

Dysgenesis. Failure to mature. For example, cerebral dysgenesis is failure of parts of the brain to mature as expected.

Dysgraphethesia. Inability to recognize figures or numbers traced on the skin when blindfolded.

Dysgraphia. Partial inability to express ideas by means of writing or written symbols, usually associated with brain dysfunction.

Dyskinesia. Impairment of voluntary movement, resulting in poor coordination.

Dyslalia. Impaired speech ability caused by functional or unknown factors.

Dyslexia. Impaired ability to read or to understand what one reads, either silently or aloud.

Dysnomia. Impaired ability to recall names of objects or words.

Dyspareunia. (1) Lack of capacity to enjoy sexual intercourse. (2) Painful intercourse.

Dysphagia. Difficulty in swallowing, often found in children with cerebral palsy.

Dysphasia. Impairment of speech that is characterized by difficulty in arranging words in their proper sequence and results from central nervous system damage.

Dysphemia. Defective articulation of speech in the absence of structural abnormality.

Dysphonia. Impairment of voice quality.

Dysphoria. Generalized feeling of anxiety, restlessness, and depression.

Dysphoric/borderline domestic violence batterers. Abusers who engage in moderate to severe spousal abuse, are psychologically distressed, and may evidence borderline and schizoidal personality characteristics.

Dyspraxia. Partial loss of ability to perform coordinated movements.

Dysprosody. Speech that is unmelodic and dysrhythmic.

Dysrhythmia. (1) Abnormal speech fluency, characterized by defective stress, breath control, and intonation. (2) Disruption of rhythm, as in abnormal EEG wave patterns.

Dyssomnias. Sleep disorders characterized by abnormalities in the amount, quality, or timing of sleep leading to excessive sleepiness or insomnia.

Dystonia. Disordered muscle tone.

Dystrophy. (1) Degenerative disorder caused by inadequate or defective nutrition. (2) Any of several disorders, especially muscular dystrophy, in which the muscles weaken and atrophy.

Early infantile autism. See *Autistic disorder.*

Early intervention (EI). (1) Services provided to infants and young children during the period of most rapid growth and development, designed to help them develop to their greatest potential. These services may be home-based, center-based, or both; they may include family training and counseling, special instruction, speech pathology/audiology, physical therapy, occupational therapy, psychological therapy, vision services, assistive technology, service coordination, health services, evaluation, screening, and assessment. (2) Services provided to families who are at risk for maltreating their children.

Easy child. Child who is mild and predominantly positive in mood, approachable, adaptable, and rhythmic.

Eating disorders. See *Anorexia nervosa, Bulimia nervosa, Obesity.*

Ebonics. See *Black English.*

Eccentric/odd behavior. Behavior characterized by preoccupation with unusual objects or activities.

Ecchymosis. Bruise.

ECG. See *Electrocardiogram.*

Echolalia. Inappropriate repetition of speech previously uttered by another speaker.

Echopraxia. Imitation of the movements and gestures of others.

ECI. Early childhood initiative.

Eclectic perspective. View that combines features from diverse sources or theories and draws on the strengths of each for understanding behavior.

ECMO. Extracorporeal membrane oxygenation.

Ecological intervention. Intervention strategies that emphasize the interaction between the individual and the environment.

Ecological validity. In evaluating interview findings, type of validity that takes into account the child's environment, which includes the immediate and extended family, neighborhood and school, and larger community.

ED/EH. Emotional disorder/emotionally handicapped.

Edema. Swelling caused by extra fluid in the tissues.

Educable mentally retarded/handicapped (EMR/ER/EMH). Mentally retarded children who are capable of some degree of school achievement and have IQs in the 50 to 70 range.

Educational neglect. Failure to provide for a child's educational needs, as by failing to enroll the child in school or tolerating truancy.

Educational systems interviewer. Clinician whose goal is to elicit information about the factors contributing to a child's school performance.

Edward's syndrome. See *Trisomy 18.*

EEG. See *Electroencephalogram.*

EFA. Epilepsy Foundation of America.

Ego. In psychoanalytic theory, predominantly conscious part of the personality, responsible for making decisions and for dealing with reality.

EHA. Education for All Handicapped Children Act. **EI.** See *Early intervention.*

Elaboration. (1) In interviewing, probing technique designed to encourage the interviewee to provide additional information. (2) Embellishment by the addition of associated ideas, movements, or drawings.

Electrocardiogram (EKG/ECG). Recording of the electrical activity of the heart, created by placing electrodes on the chest.

Electroencephalogram (EEG). Recording of the electrical potentials from the brain, created by placing electrodes on the scalp or in the brain.

Electromyographic (EMG) feedback. Type of biofeedback used for tension headaches. An electron amplifier measures muscle contractions and provides visual or auditory information concerning increases or decreases in muscle tension.

Electrophysiological abnormalities. Abnormalities in the electrical phenomena involved in physiological processes.

Elevated bilirubin. See *Hyperbilirubinemia.*

Emancipation. Legal process whereby a child is released from all of the restraints of childhood and receives the duties, privileges, and responsibilities of an adult.

Embarrassing questions. Queries that may embarrass or offend the interviewee. Such questions should be rephrased in more neutral terms or avoided entirely.

Embolism. Sudden blocking of an artery by a blood clot or foreign material that originated elsewhere in the body and was carried by the blood stream to the site of blockage.

Emergency custody. See *Protective custody.*

Emergency hearings (legal). In juvenile and family court, hearings held to determine the need for emergency protection of a child who may have been a victim of maltreatment.

EMG. See *Electromyographic (EMG) feedback.*

Emotion-focused strategy. Plan designed to release, reduce, or manage emotional tensions, through such means as revealing of feelings, reversal of affect, fatalism, self-pity, tension reduction, and acting out.

Emotional abuse. Form of child maltreatment in which parents or other persons engage in acts or omissions that cause or could cause emotional, behavioral, cognitive, or mental disorders; also known as emotional/psychological maltreatment or psychological abuse. Emotional abuse is found in a continuum of habitual behavioral interactions, such as belittling through comments, comparisons, and name-calling; scapegoating; humiliating; isolating; raging and terrorizing (by verbally assaulting the child, threatening the child, and creating a climate of fear); rejecting (by refusing to acknowledge the child's worth and the legitimacy of the child's needs); ignoring (by depriving the child of essential stimulation and responsiveness); and corrupting (by stimulating the child to engage in destructive antisocial behavior).

Emotional lability. Easy arousal and rapid shifts from one emotion to another.

Emotional neglect. Failure to provide the emotional and psychological nurturance necessary for a child's emotional and psychological growth and development; also known as emotional/ psychological neglect or psychological neglect.

Emotional/psychological maltreatment. See *Emotional abuse.*

Empacho. Ailment, commonly treated by Mexican American traditional healers, that is caused by undigested food. Common symptoms are stomach pains, diarrhea, and vomiting.

EMR/ER/EMH. See *Educable mentally retarded/handicapped.*

Encephalitis. Acute inflammation of the brain or its meninges, resulting from any of a wide variety of infections and toxins; also known as encephalopathy.

Encephalomyelitis. Inflammation involving both the brain and the spinal cord.

Encephalopathy. See *Encephalitis.*

Encoding. Translating information into a communicable form, as in the process of expressing knowledge or intention through written, oral, or body language.

Encoding process. Registering of events in memory.

Encopresis. Involuntary passage of feces; loss of stool (bowel movement) control; fecal staining.

Encouraging appropriate replies. Use of techniques such as nodding, maintaining eye contact, or giving prompts to encourage the speaker to elaborate or to ease the speaker's anxieties.

Endangerment. Form of neglect that puts the child at risk, such as failing to use seat belts or a car seat for the child or keeping loaded firearms within reach of the child.

Endogenous. Arising from causes within the individual; attributable to internal causes associated with hereditary factors.

Endorsement of communication. Agreement by the listener that the speaker's perspective is accurate.

Enjoin (legal). To issue a court order commanding a person to perform or abstain from performing a specified act.

ENT. Ear, nose, and throat.

Enuresis. Involuntary passage of urine, resulting in daytime or nighttime wetting.

Envidia. Ailment, commonly treated by Mexican American traditional healers, that occurs when a person's success provokes the envy of friends and neighbors.

Environmental toxins. Poisons from the environment that can have a detrimental effect on physiological processes.

Epicanthus. Prolonged fold of skin of the upper eyelid over the inner angle or both angles of the eye.

Epidemiology. Science that deals with the incidence, distribution, and control of disease in a population.

Epididymis. Tube that passes from the testes to the vas deferens.

Epilepsy. Organic disorder characterized by irregularly occurring transitory disturbances in consciousness, often accompanied by seizures or convulsion.

EPSDT. Early periodic screening, diagnosis, and treatment.

Equal protection of the law. The right, guaranteed under the Fourteenth Amendment (and by state constitution or state law), not to be discriminated against for any unjustifiable reason, such as race or handicap.

Escape theory. Theory of suicide that postulates nine steps—experiencing major disappointment or stress, attributing primary responsibility to self, high self-awareness, emotional distress, distorted thinking, mental narrowing, becoming receptive to suicide, having the opportunity to commit suicide, and committing the act of suicide.

ESEA. Elementary and Secondary Education Act.

Esophageal candidiasis. Fungal infection in the esophagus that is commonly associated with AIDS.

ESP. See *Extrasensory perception.*

Espiritismo. Hispanic American belief in spirits and spiritualism.

Espiritualisto. Hispanic American traditional healer who analyzes dreams and fears, foretells the future, and treats some supernatural or magical diseases.

Ethnic identity. Sense of belonging to an ethnic group; part of one's thinking, perceptions, feelings, and behavior that is related to ethnic group membership.

Ethnicity. Affiliation with a group characterized by a common nationality, culture, or language.

Etiology. Origins or causes of a disease or condition. Some are environmental; others are organic.

Eugenics. Science that deals with the improvement of hereditary qualities of race or breed by, for example, controlling human mating.

Euglycemia. Normal level of glucose in the blood.

Evidence. Any sort of proof submitted to a court to influence its decision. See also *Circumstantial evidence, Direct evidence, Hearsay, Opinion, Physical evidence.*

Evidence code. Section of state law that governs what evidence can be introduced in a legal proceeding.

Evidentiary standards (legal). Guidelines used in examining evidence to determine whether it has been legally collected and whether it is factual and legally proves or is relevant to the case

being heard. See also *Clear and convincing evidence, Preponderance of evidence, Proof beyond a reasonable doubt.*

Evil orientation. Cultural belief that people are born with evil inclinations that must be controlled.

Evoked potential. See *Cortical evoked potential.*

Ex parte. Involving only one party. An *ex parte* judicial proceeding is one brought by one party, without notice to or opportunity for challenge by an adverse party.

Ex rel. On behalf of. This term may be used in the title of a case when one party is bringing an action on behalf of another party.

Exceptional child. Child who deviates significantly from the norm by virtue of, for example, unusually high or low intelligence, physical disability, or emotional difficulties.

Exculpatory. Clearing or tending to clear from an alleged fault or guilt; excusing.

Executive functioning. Ability to set goals, develop a plan, and effectively follow through with the plan.

Exhibit (legal). Item produced during a trial or hearing that is connected with the subject matter before the court and that, upon acceptance by the court, is marked for identification and made a part of the case. Physical evidence offered to the court for inspection may be accepted as an exhibit. An exhibit also may be attached to a document, such as an affidavit, and made a part of that document.

Exit interview. Interview designed to present findings and recommendations to parents, the child (in some cases), teachers, or the referral source; also known as post-assessment interview or interpretive interview.

Exogenous. Attributable to external causes.

Expectancy effect. Influence of a person's expectations on another person's behavior.

Experimental stage of substance abuse. First stage of substance abuse, in which substance use is related to curiosity, risk-taking, and, at times, peer pressure. At this stage, the mood-altering effects of the substance are secondary to the adventure of using the substance.

Expert testimony. Statements given to the court by witnesses with special skills or knowledge in some art, science, profession, or technical area. Experts educate the court or jury by assisting them in understanding the evidence or in determining an issue of fact. Experts are initially questioned in court about their education or experience to ascertain their qualifications to give professional opinions about the matter in question.

Expert witness. Individual who, by reason of education or specialized experience, possesses superior knowledge of a subject and is therefore determined by the court to be qualified to give an opinion on a specific area, such as child custody.

Exploitation of children. (1) Involving children in illegal or immoral activities—including child pornography, child prostitution, sexual maltreatment, and stealing—for the benefit of a parent or caregiver. (2) Forcing workloads on children inside or outside the home that interfere with their health, education, and well-being.

Expressive aphasia. Inability, caused by brain damage, to remember the pattern of movement required to speak, write, or use signs, even though the individual knows what she or he wants to say.

Expressive language skills. Skills required to communicate ideas through writing, gesturing, and speaking.

Expunge. To strike out, obliterate, or mark for deletion from the court record.

Expungement (legal). (1) Destruction of records. Expungement may be ordered by the court after a specified number of years or when the juvenile, parent, or defendant applies for expungement and shows that his or her conduct has improved. (2) Removal of an unverified report of abuse or neglect that has been made to a central registry.

Extended family. Individuals who are related to members of a nuclear family, such as the grandparents, aunts, and uncles of a child.

External factors and atmosphere. In an interview, physical aspects that may affect the interviewee's and the interviewer's behavior.

Externalizing disorders. Conditions whose symptoms are outer-directed and primarily associated with undercontrolled behaviors. Examples are conduct disorder, oppositional defiant disorder, attention-deficit/hyperactivity disorder, aggression, and adjustment disorder.

Extrafamilial crises. Crises associated with major hazardous events that occur outside the family and are not under the family's control. Examples are war, terrorist activity, economic recession, witnessing violence, kidnapping, natural disasters (such as hurricanes, tornadoes, fires, earthquakes, and floods), and people-made disasters (such as plane crashes, mine disasters, and shipwrecks).

Extrafamilial maltreatment. Maltreatment perpetrated by someone who is not part of the child's family.

Extrasensory perception (ESP). Perception that occurs outside the use of any known senses.

Extrinsic tumor. Growth having its origin outside the limb or organ in which it is found.

Eye-hand coordination. Cooperative functioning of eyes and hands in performing motor tasks.

Facial apraxia. Impairment of ability to carry out facial movements on command (whistle, pucker, protrude tongue), although facial movements can be done spontaneously.

Facilitated communication. Procedure in which a facilitator (aide) guides a disabled individual's hand, wrist, or arm across a keyboard or keyboard facsimile to help the person type a message or point to letters. This is an extremely controversial procedure, which current research indicates is not valid.

Fact finder (legal). Judge or jury.

Failure to thrive (FTT). Disorder that results in poor growth or a significant deceleration in rate of weight gain. This potentially life-threatening problem may have an organic cause or may result from a disturbed parent-child relationship; it is most often seen in children under 1 year of age. Children identified as suffering from FTT usually weigh below the 5th percentile for their age.

False negative conclusion. In child maltreatment, finding that no maltreatment occurred when, in fact, maltreatment did occur. As a result, the child will remain in a home or situation in which maltreatment has occurred or is occurring, and the perpetrator may victimize other children, as well.

False negatives. Individuals wrongly excluded from a group through application of a certain standard or criterion. An example is examinees whose test scores indicate that they will not succeed on the criterion, but who actually do succeed.

False positive conclusion. In child maltreatment, finding that maltreatment occurred when, in fact, no maltreatment occurred. As a result, an innocent person is wrongly accused, the person's reputation is damaged, parental rights may be taken away if the falsely accused is a parent, and a prison term is possible.

False positives. Individuals wrongly included in a group through application of a certain standard or criterion. An example is examinees whose test scores indicate that they will succeed on the criterion, but who actually do not succeed.

Familial retardation. Condition of mild mental retardation having no known cause, found in members of the same family.

Families at risk. Families that evidence high potential for child maltreatment or neglect or other problems because of environmental or parental problems, such as criminal behavior, poverty, substance abuse, mental retardation, or psychosis. Family problems also may be less conspicuous, but multiple.

Family assigned roles. Prescribed responsibilities, expectations, and rights of individual family members. For example, one family member may be designated breadwinner, another overseer of health care, and still another manager of household operations. Roles do not have to be mutually exclusive, and they seldom are. For example, the mother may oversee family health care and manage the household.

Family autonomy. Right of parents to raise their children as they deem appropriate, without intrusion of the state. This concept assumes that the child's best interests generally are most adequately provided for within the context of a strong family environment.

Family-centered care. Care based on the recognition that the family is the constant in the child's life. It acknowledges family differences and strengths and emphasizes family-to-family support, networking, and families and professionals working together. The focus is on the entire family.

Family court. Civil court, found in some states, that combines the functions of domestic relations, juvenile, and probate courts.

Family foster care. Full-time care provided by nonbiological parents in their home, usually with supervision and financial support from a social services child placement agency.

Family functions. Tasks the family performs for society and its members, such as education and reproduction.

Family history. Description of how the family functioned in the past, including past illnesses of members and their modes of coping with stress. The family history affects the ways families interpret and respond to various events.

Family law. Field of law involving family issues, such as divorce, paternity, guardianship, dependency, adoption, and domestic violence.

Family life cycle. Pattern of family development that changes over time. The family progresses through a reasonably well defined set of phases of development, beginning with courtship and ending with the death of parents or parental figures. Each phase is associated with certain developmental tasks, the successful completion of which leads to a higher level of family functioning.

Family mode of interaction. Style adopted by family members to deal with the environment and with one another in both problem solving and decision making.

Family preservation services. Activities of social services agencies intended to keep families together when the children are at risk of removal. Usually, family preservation services are crisis oriented, short term, and offered in the home on an on-call basis.

Family resources. All the resources of a family, including general health of members, social support and skills, personality characteristics, and financial support. These resources influence the way the family interprets events.

Family reunification. Return of children who have been in substitute care to their family of origin.

Family structure. Configuration of a family, based on the number and characteristics of its individual members, including gender and age.

Family support services. Services that enable families to provide the extra care needed to keep their child with a disability at home. Examples include respite care, counseling, adaptive equipment, specialized transportation, financial assistance, support groups, information, and training.

Family systems perspective. Theoretical view, helpful in evaluating the behavior of individuals in families, that focuses on the family's structure, functions, assigned roles, modes of interacting, resources, history, and life cycle and its individual members' unique histories.

Fantasy technique. Procedure used by interviewers to draw out middle childhood-aged children and adolescent children who are reluctant to speak. Examples are the three wishes technique and the desert island technique.

FAPE. Free appropriate public education.

FAS. See *Fetal alcohol syndrome.*

Fatigue. (1) Physical or mental weariness resulting from exertion. (2) In Puerto Rican traditional medicine, asthma-like symptoms.

Fear. Feeling of extreme apprehension or dread associated with a potential or real threat to the well-being of an individual.

Feedback. Listener's paraphrasing of the speaker's thoughts and feelings to show him or her that the listener understood what was said.

Feeding disorder of infancy or early childhood. Eating disorder characterized by persistent failure to eat adequately, as reflected in significant failure to gain weight or significant weight loss during a period of at least one month.

Felony. Serious crime for which the punishment may be lengthy imprisonment and/or a significant fine.

Fetal alcohol syndrome (FAS). Group of symptoms appearing in infants born to women who abuse alcohol. The main characteristics of this syndrome are low birthweight, growth retardation, organic anomalies (including cleft palate, neural tube defect, hearing loss, and heart defects), and neurobehavioral deficits (including mental retardation, speech and language disorders, and attention-deficit/hyperactivity disorder).

FHR. Fetal heart rate.

Fifth Amendment to the U.S. Constitution. Amendment providing that no person will be compelled to present self-incriminating testimony, that no person will be required to answer for crimes without an indictment or grand jury decision, that no person will be subjected to double jeopardy, and that no person shall be deprived of life, liberty, or property without due process.

Figure-ground disturbance. Inability to differentiate the central stimulus or figure from its background.

Figure-ground perception. Ability to attend to one aspect of a sensory field (figure) while perceiving it in relation to the rest of the field (ground).

Final argument. See *Closing argument.*

Finding (legal). Determination of fact by a court based on the evidence presented.

Fine motor coordination. Fine muscle control required to do precise movements, as in writing and drawing.

Finger agnosia. Inability to recognize the names of or identify the individual fingers of one's own hand or the hands of others, usually associated with brain damage.

Fingerspelling. Communicating by means of the manual alphabet, in which words are spelled out on the fingers.

First appearance (legal). See *Arraignment.*

First generation. Refers to (1) persons who have left one country and settled in another or (2) persons whose parents are immigrants.

Fistula. Abnormal passage that forms between body structures or from a normal body structure to the body surface. An example is a tracheoesophageal fistula. Fistulas and atresias often occur together.

Flaccid paralysis. Paralysis in which the muscles become weak, soft, or atrophied.

Flaccidity. Condition characterized by slumping, letting the arms dangle limply, or having slack facial muscles.

Flapping. Oscillating the hands or wiggling or bizarrely positioning the fingers.

Flexion. Bending of any part of the body, especially joints.

Fluent aphasia. Central nervous system dysfunction in which verbal expression remains normal in speed, grammar, and intonation but lacks content and auditory comprehension is markedly reduced. The afflicted person often is unaware of the extent of his or her language deficits.

Focal effects. Effects of brain damage that are in a circumscribed area.

Focal lesion. Injury to a small definite area.

Focused question. In interviews, query that focuses on a specific topic.

Focusing outward stage of coping. Fourth stage of coping, after a parent learns that she or he has a child with special needs. It is characterized by information seeking, regaining of confidence, renewed energy, talking about options with others, and increased awareness of reality.

Follow-up interview. Interview designed to obtain information about how the child and family are coping after the initial assessment has been completed. It also may be designed to measure outcomes of treatment or intervention and to gauge the appropriateness of the assessment findings and recommendations.

Forensic. Relating to courts of law. Forensic psychology refers to psychological methods or knowledge applied to the resolution of legal disputes. A forensic evaluation is a medical or psychological evaluation that interprets or establishes the facts in civil or criminal law cases.

Forensic interview. Interview that interprets or helps establish the facts in a civil or criminal case.

Foster care. Form of substitute care for children who need to be removed from their own homes. Usually, this is a temporary placement in which a child lives with a licensed foster family or caregiver until he or she either can return to his or her own home or reaches the age of majority.

Foster parents. Adults who assume, usually for a limited period of time, the day-to-day care of a child not born to them and for whom they do not have full legal parental rights.

Founded. See *Substantiated.*

Fracture. Broken bone. This is one of the injuries most commonly found among battered children.

Fragile X syndrome. Condition characterized by a physical abnormality on the X chromosome. It is one of the more common genetic causes of mental retardation, especially in males.

Fraternal twins. See *Dizygotic twins.*

Free narrative account phase. In child maltreatment, second stage of the interview, which focuses on helping the child tell what happened to him or her and stresses open-ended questions.

Frequency. In behavioral assessment, how often the behavior occurs.

Frontal lobe. Roughly, upper or forward half of the cerebral hemisphere; lobe of the cerebral cortex responsible for planning, performance, and execution of all voluntary behavior.

Frustration. Feeling that occurs when a need or action is blocked.

FTE. Full-time equivalent. (1) Number of hours that must be worked for a job to be equivalent to a full-time position. (2) Number of course units required by a school for a student to be considered a full-time student.

FTT. See *Failure to thrive.*

Functional. Serving a useful purpose.

Functional analysis. In cognitive and behavioral assessment, process of learning about the antecedents and consequences associated with a particular behavior.

Functional family coping methods. In cases of maltreatment, adaptive family techniques, such as open communication and role flexibility, that may help the maltreated child recover.

Functional family strategies. See *Functional family coping methods.*

Functional limitations. Behavior or conditions in an individual that impair his or her ability to participate in and perform the minimal activities of daily living required to secure and maintain proper food, clothing, shelter, health care, or safety.

Functional status. Normal or characteristic performance of the individual. Functional status can be conceptually divided into four categories: (a) physical function—sensory-motor performance, (b) mental function—intellectual, cognitive, or reasoning capabilities of the individual, (c) emotional function—affect and effectiveness in coping psychologically with life stresses, and (d) social function—performance of social roles or obligations.

g. Term used to represent general intellectual ability.

Gait. Manner or style of walking.

GAL. See *Guardian ad litem.*

Galactosemia. Metabolic disorder that results from the inability to metabolize galactose, which is a sugar found in milk. If untreated, it may result in jaundice, poor weight gain, and mental retardation.

Gardnerella vaginalis. Sexually transmitted pathologic bacteria.

Gastroesophageal reflux. Condition caused by stomach acids backing up into the lower esophagus; also known as heartburn.

Gastrostomy tube (G-tube). Tube placed into the stomach through the abdominal wall to permit feeding directly into the stomach when the person is unable to eat by mouth.

Gault decision. Landmark 1967 Supreme Court decision affirming that juveniles are entitled to the same due process rights as adults: the right to counsel, the right to notice of specific charges of the offense, the right to confront and cross-examine a witness, the right to remain silent, and the right to subpoena witnesses in defense. The right to trial by jury was not included.

Gavage feeding. Feeding through a tube (catheter). The tube may be passed from the mouth, nose, or esophagus into the stomach or intestine for the purpose of giving nutrition.

Generalization. Process of forming an idea or judgment applicable to an entire class of objects, people, or events.

Generalization effect error. Error that occurs when the interviewer generalizes from one behavior to others, although there is little evidence to support these generalizations.

Generalized anxiety disorder. Condition characterized by at least six months of persistent and excessive anxiety and worry.

Generic. (1) Relating to or descriptive of an entire group or class; general. (2) Commonly available; not protected by trademark; nonproprietary (as in reference to drugs).

Genes. Fundamental transmitters of hereditary characteristics, located on chromosomes.

Genetic services. Screening, testing, counseling, and providing information related to disabilities caused by genetic, external, or hereditary factors. These services help families determine the chance that a genetic condition may occur in their family.

Genetics. Study of the nature and mechanisms of heredity and variation in biological systems.

Genital herpes. Viral disease that is generally transmitted sexually.

Genotype. (1) Genetic makeup of an individual. (2) Qualities or traits shared by members of a biologically defined group.

Gerstmann syndrome. Group of symptoms (agraphia, acalculia, right-left disorientation, and finger agnosia) indicating a disturbance of laterality and of body image.

Gestalt. Any unified whole whose properties cannot be derived just by adding the parts and their relationships because the whole is different from the sum of its parts.

GI. Gastrointestinal.

Gifted. Having an IQ above about 130; talented.

Glasgow Coma Scale. Observational method used to monitor levels of consciousness based on eye opening, motor (movement) response, and talking.

Glasgow Outcome Scale. Observational method used to predict improvement or late outcome from head injury, based on the degree of maintained independence and functioning.

Glaucoma. Increased pressure in the eye, resulting in hardening of the eyeball.

Global. Perceived as a whole, without distinguishing separate parts or functions.

Global aphasia. Central nervous system dysfunction that involves both expressive and receptive domains of language.

Global-diffuse effects. Effects that pervade the entire area and are not restricted to any one part.

Glucose. Simple sugar, found in the blood, that is the body's main source of energy.

Glycemic. Concerning blood glucose.

Glycosylated hemoglobin test. See *Hemoglobin A1C.*

Goal directedness. In interviewing, ability of the interviewer to remain aware of the purpose of the interview and stay on task.

Good faith. Standard used to determine whether a reporter has reason to suspect that child maltreatment or neglect has occurred. In general, good faith applies if any reasonable person, given the same information, would draw a conclusion that the child may have been abused or neglected.

Good orientation. Cultural belief that people are born good.

Grand mal seizure. The most common and most dramatic of the epileptic seizures, involving widespread and abnormal electrical activity in the brain, violent convulsions, and loss of consciousness.

Graphesthesia. Sense by which outlines, numbers, words, or symbols traced or written on the skin are recognized.

Grief. Feeling of sorrow or anguish resulting from the loss of someone through death; often accompanied by crying.

Grief stage of coping. Third stage of coping, after a parent learns that she or he has a child with special needs. It is characterized by sleeplessness, anger, helplessness, anxiety, retreating from others, and questioning the meaning of life.

Grimacing. Making bizarre facial movements.

Gris-gris. Symbols of voodoo used to prevent illness or to give illness to others. Examples are powders and oils that are highly and pleasantly scented or have a vile odor and colored candles designed for special intentions.

Gross motor skills. Large muscle-dependent activities such as walking, running, and throwing.

Guardian. Adult charged lawfully with the responsibility for a child. A guardian has almost all the rights and powers of a natural parent, but the relationship is subject to termination or change. A guardian may or may not also have custody and, therefore, may not actually care for and supervise the child.

Guardian ad litem (GAL). Lawyer, mental health professional, or (in some states) layperson, appointed by the court, who represents a child in juvenile or family court. This person may perform a variety of roles in the best interest of the child, including independent investigator, advocate, advisor, and guardian for the child. A volunteer is sometimes known as a court-appointed special advocate or CASA.

Guardianship (legal). Legal responsibility to provide for the protection, care, and management of a person considered unable to take care of his or her own affairs.

Guilt. Feeling that one has done something wrong. Also, realization that one has violated principles, accompanied by regretful feeling of lessened personal worth on that account.

Habeas corpus. You have the body. A writ of habeus corpus requires that a person be brought before a court or a judge. It usually alleges that the person is illegally imprisoned.

Habitual stage of substance abuse. Fourth phase of substance abuse, in which the substance use becomes habit forming. Symptoms of dependency start to appear at this stage. The focus of life centers around substance use as a means of coping and being.

Hallucination. Perception in the absence of real external stimulation.

Hallucinogens. Drugs or chemicals capable of producing hallucinations.

Halo effect. Tendency in rating to let one of an individual's traits influence ratings on other traits.

Handedness. Hand preference of an individual.

Handicap. Disadvantage, resulting from an impairment or a disability, that limits or prevents the fulfillment of a role that is normal for that individual. A handicap is characterized by a difference between what an individual appears to be able to do and the expectations of the particular group of which he or she is a member. The state of being handicapped is strongly influenced by societal values.

Haptic. Pertaining to the sense of touch.

Hard-of-hearing children. Children who have residual hearing sufficient for successful processing of auditory information, generally with the use of a hearing aid.

Hard signs. Fairly definitive indicators of cerebral dysfunction, such as abnormalities in reflexes, cranial nerves, and motor organization and asymmetrical failures in sensory and motor responses. These are usually correlated with other independent evidence of brain damage, such as that obtained from CT scans or EEGs.

Harmony orientation. Cultural belief that people can achieve a partnership with nature.

Hashish. Purified resin prepared from the flowering tops of the female cannabis plant and smoked or chewed as a narcotic or an intoxicant.

HCFA. U.S. Health Care Financing Administration.

Head injury. Brain injury as a result of an accident. See also *Brain damage, Brain disorder, Brain lesion.*

Hearing (legal). Judicial or legal examination of the issues of law and fact between parties. Also, a formal proceeding where evidence is taken for the purpose of determining an issue of fact and reaching a decision on the basis of that evidence.

Hearing impairment. Difficulty with hearing but not to the point of being deaf.

Hearsay (legal). Testimony concerning statements of someone who is not in court and therefore not subject to cross-examination; second-hand evidence. Such evidence is usually excluded because it is considered unreliable and because the person making the original statement cannot be cross-examined.

Heart defects. Abnormalities of the heart structure.

Heartburn. See *Gastroesophageal reflux.*

Hebephilia. Sexual behavior directed toward pubescent children.

Hedonism. Pursuit of instant gratification.

Hedonistic use of substances. Use of substances in pursuit of pleasure, such as a desire to get high or to do things that are normally not done.

Hematemesis. Vomiting of blood from the stomach, often resulting from internal injuries.

Hematology. Branch of biology that deals with blood and blood-forming organs.

Hematoma. Collection of blood in an organ, space, or tissue.

Hemianopsia. Loss of visual recognition and possibly vision itself in one half of the field of vision because of brain injury.

Hemiopia. Condition in which one has only one-half of the field of vision in one or both eyes.

Hemiparesis. Weakness of one side of the body.

Hemiplegia. Paralysis of one side of the body.

Hemisphere of the brain. One side of the brain.

Hemispherectomy. Removal of an entire cerebral hemisphere.

Hemispheric dominance. View that certain functions are controlled by one of the cerebral hemispheres.

Hemoglobin A1C (HBA1C). Substance of red blood cells that carries oxygen to the cells and sometimes joins with glucose. Because the glucose stays attached for the life of the cell (about four months), a test of hemoglobin A1C, also known as glycosylated hemoglobin test, shows the average blood glucose level for that period of time.

Hemorrhage. Escape of blood from the vessels; bleeding.

Herbalist. In traditional Native American culture, healer who uses herbs to treat illnesses.

Herniation. Rupture of tissue into an adjacent space due to internal pressure or swelling.

Herpes simplex virus (HSV). Virus that may be transmitted to the fetus during the birth process if the mother is actively infected and may cause a severe generalized disease in the neonate, with high mortality and devastating sequelae, including brain infections, respiratory difficulties, convulsions, hepatitis, and hearing impairments.

Heterogeneous. Consisting of dissimilar ingredients or parts; mixed.

HHS. U.S. Department of Health and Human Services.

High-risk period. For parents of disabled child, time period during which they may face particular stress, such as when the child receives the initial diagnosis, is supposed to walk, is supposed to talk, falls behind other children in growth, enters school, graduates from elementary school, reaches puberty, graduates from high school, reaches his or her 21st birthday, and needs to be given a guardian.

Higher-level cognitive processes. Thinking or information processing that goes beyond simple sensation or perception.

Highly structured interview. Interview in which the exact order and wording of each question and the coding of responses are specified and little room is left for follow-up questions.

HI/HH. Hearing impaired/handicapped.

HIV-1. See *Human immunodeficiency virus type I.*

Hodgkin's disease. Type of cancer characterized by painless lymph node enlargement. Symptoms may include fever, sweating, itching, weight loss, and malaise.

Holistic. (1) Emphasizing the importance of the whole and the interdependence of its parts. (2) Concerned with the whole rather than analysis or separation into parts.

Home health services. Provision of health care, such as nursing, nutrition, and respiratory services, in the child's home.

Homeless. People who lack a fixed, regular, and adequate nighttime residence.

Homicide. Killing of one human being by another.

Homogeneity. Similarity or likeness among members of any group, data, or variables.

Homolateral. Occurring on the same side; ipsilateral.

Honeymoon period. In diabetes, time period during which a diabetic experiences partial insulin secretion due to some residual pancreatic beta cell functioning. It usually takes about one year from the time of diagnosis and the onset of symptoms before the beta cells cease producing insulin completely.

Hostility. Tendency to feel anger toward and to seek to inflict harm on a person.

HSV. See *Herpes simplex virus.*

Human immunodeficiency virus type 1 (HIV-1). Retrovirus that infects white blood cells, the brain, the bowel, the skin, and other tissues.

Human nature. The characteristics of human beings that develop from the interaction of innate and cultural influences.

Humanistic-phenomenological perspective. View that emphasizes an individual's perception of the world. Behavior is seen as a reflection of how the individual views the world at a particular moment in time; the emphasis is on the here and now. Individuals are seen as active, thinking people who are responsible for their behavior and capable of making choices.

Humanitarian admission. Process by which immigrants are allowed to enter the United States for humanitarian reasons, such as having suffered human rights abuses in the country of origin.

Hx. History.

Hyaline membrane disease. See *Respiratory distress syndrome.*

Hydramnios. Amniotic fluid that accumulates progressively throughout the pregnancy; also known as polyhydramnios.

Hydrocephalus. Increased accumulation of fluid within the ventricles of the brain.

Hymen. Thin membrane, in females, that separates the external genitalia from the vagina. The outer surface is a dry, squamous epithelium, and the inner surface is a moist mucous membrane.

Hyperactivity. Exceedingly active behavior not typical of most children, characterized by overactivity, restlessness, distractibility, and limited attention span; also known as hyperkinesis.

Hyperal. See *Hyperalimentation.*

Hyperalimentation (HA). Special-formula fluid for intravenous therapy, prescribed only when adequate nutrition cannot be taken orally; also known as hyperal.

Hyperbilirubinemia. Condition that occurs when there is an excessive amount of bilirubin in the blood; also known as elevated bilirubin. Bilirubin is formed from the metabolism of red blood cells. High levels of bilirubin can cause jaundice, and very high levels can lead to kernicterus, causing brain and spinal cord damage and hearing impairment. Initial treatment of hyperbilirubinemia is by light (photo) therapy. Exchange transfusions may be needed in severe cases.

Hyperglycemia. High blood glucose levels, which occur when the body does not have enough insulin. This is an indication that diabetes is out of control. Signs of hyperglycemia are great thirst, a dry mouth, and a need to urinate often. Hyperglycemia may lead to diabetic ketoacidosis.

Hyperkinesis. See *Hyperactivity.*

Hyperthyroidism. Oversecretion of the thyroid gland. The condition is potentially life-threatening in infants if left untreated.

Hypertonia. Sustained high muscle tension.

Hyphema. Hemorrhage within the anterior chamber of the eye, often appearing as a bloodshot eye. The cause could be a blow to the head or violent shaking.

Hypoactivity. Exceedingly inactive behavior not typical of most children; also known as hypokinesis. The condition is characterized by lethargy, frequent sleepiness, and little movement.

Hypoglycemia. Low blood sugar, which occurs when a person has injected too much insulin, eaten too little food, or exercised without extra food. A person with hypoglycemia may feel jittery, weak, or sweaty and have a headache, blurred vision, and hunger. This can be compensated for within about 15 minutes by taking small amounts of sugar, juice, or food with sugar.

Hypokinesis. See *Hypoactivity.*

Hypotension. Reduced blood pressure.

Hypothermia. Body temperature below 98.6°F.

Hypothyroidism. Deficiency in thyroid secretion or activity. If untreated, hypothyroidism can cause delays in brain development. See also *Cretinism.*

Hypotonia. Low muscle tension.

Hypovitaminosis. Condition due to a deficiency of one or more essential vitamins.

Hypoxia. Deficiency of oxygen reaching the tissues of the body.

I&O. Intake and output. The term generally refers to a measurement of bodily functioning, such as fluid intake and urine output.

I&R. Information and referral; method of connecting a person needing a service to the service. I&R is provided in several ways at the local, state, and national level.

IBC. Infant bioethics committee.

ICC. Interagency coordinative council.

ICF/MR. Intermediate care facility for the mentally retarded.

Iconic memory. Very short-term, image-like memory; visual-spatial imagery characteristic of the second stage of a child's linguistic development.

ICP monitor. Intracranial pressure monitor; device inserted through the skull to measure pressure being exerted on the brain.

ICRC. See *Infant care review committee.*

ICWA. See *Indian Child Welfare Act.*

ID. Immune deficiency.

IDDM. See *Insulin-dependent diabetes mellitus.*

IDEA. Individuals with Disabilities Education Act. See *Part H of IDEA.*

Ideational agnosia. Inability to visualize or recall construction of words.

Ideational apraxia. Impaired ability to execute a series of acts, though the individual may be able to perform each step correctly.

Ideational fluency. Flow and number of ideas generated by an individual.

Identical twins. See *Monozygotic twins.*

Ideomotor apraxia. Impaired ability to carry out an action on verbal command, although the action can be performed automatically.

Idiopathic. (1) Self-originated. (2) Of unknown origin.

IDT. Interdisciplinary team.

IEP. See *Individualized education plan.*

IFSP. See *Individual family service plan.*

IH. Infantile hydrocephalus.

IHP. Individualized habilitation plan.

Illegal immigrant. Person from another country who enters the United States illegally (that is, without an invitation) or without inspection or who enters legally (as a visitor, student, or temporary employee) but then fails to leave when her or his visa expires; also known as undocumented immigrant. See also *Visa overstayer.*

Illogicality. Quality of speech characterized by illogical conclusions—for example, "I like cats because my name is Fred."

Immediate echolalia. Speech pattern in which the speaker immediately repeats another person's words.

Immobility. Limitation of movement.

Immunity from prosecution (legal). Exemption from legal prosecution provided to certain individuals or categories of individuals. For example, to protect reporters from civil lawsuits and criminal prosecution resulting from the filing of a report of child abuse and neglect, child maltreatment laws provide immunity as long as the report is made in good faith.

Impact stage of coping. Initial stage of coping, after a parent learns that she or he has a child with special needs. It is characterized by agitation, support seeking, and possible disorientation.

Impeachment of witness. Attack on the truthfulness or credibility of a witness.

Impetigo. Highly contagious, rapidly spreading skin disorder, caused by staphylococcus or streptococcus and characterized by red blisters. Impetigo sometimes occurs as a result of poor hygiene.

Impulsive. Characterized by rapid movement or decision making without benefit of judgment; characterized by a tendency to act quickly without thinking; hasty; rash.

In camera. In chambers; in a judge's chambers or another private location, where the public is not present. For example, a judge may inspect particular records *in camera,* to determine whether the records should be given to an opposing party, admitted into evidence, or made public. In child custody litigation, the judge may interview the child *in camera.*

In loco parentis. In the place of a parent. A guardian or other non-parental custodian or authority acts *in loco parentis.*

In re. In the matter of. The term may be used in the title of a case in which there are no adversaries, such as a child custody case.

In utero. In the uterus.

Inappropriate posturing. Maintaining uncomfortable or inappropriate positions of the trunk or extremities.

Inborn error of metabolism. Innate disorder in which the baby's chemical reactions are disrupted, usually by an enzymatic defect.

Incest. Sexual conduct between persons who are closely related by blood. Laws in a number of states define incest as marriage or sexual relationships between relatives who are closer than second (or sometimes more distant) cousins. The most common form of incest is between fathers and daughters.

Incoherence. Lack of continuity in speech that makes it incomprehensible at times—for example, "I feel trow the happy."

Incoherent language. Incomprehensible language, including confused sentences and distorted syntax.

Incongruous affect. Emotion or feeling that is not in keeping with concurrent verbal content or the context of the interview.

Inconsistencies and gaps. In interviews, pattern of lack of agreement and lack of completeness in the information provided, which may suggest guilt, confusion, or ambivalence.

Indian Child Welfare Act (ICWA). Federal law granting special rights to eligible American Indian children. States must follow prescribed procedures when handling matters involving protection and custody of American Indian children.

Indictment (legal). Report of a grand jury charging an adult with criminal conduct. The process of indictment by grand jury bypasses the filing of a criminal complaint and the holding of a preliminary hearing, so prosecution begins immediately.

Individual family service plan (IFSP). Written plan documenting a child's and family's strengths and needs and the services to be provided to meet those needs. It is developed by the family and a team of early intervention professionals. Part H of the Individuals with Disabilities Education Act (IDEA) mandates that an IFSP be developed for all families with infants or toddlers (ages 0 through 2) who are eligible for early intervention services.

Individual orientation. Value orientation of a cultural group that emphasizes individuality and autonomy over group goals.

Individual with exceptional needs (IWEN). Special education student.

Individualized education plan (IEP). Written plan that identifies a child's strengths, weaknesses, educational needs, and needs for related service. The Individuals with Disabilities Education Act (IDEA) mandates that an IEP be developed for all school-aged children (beginning at age 3) who are eligible for special education and related services and that the plan be reviewed at least annually.

Infant care review committee (ICRC). Internal hospital group that reviews cases and decides when life-preserving medical treatment may or may not be withheld from infants with disabilities. These committees are often operated as part of the hospital's ethics or bioethics committee.

Infanticide. Killing of an infant or infants.

Infarct. Tissue area deprived of blood flow.

Information-processing model. In cases of neglect, model that accounts for parental neglect by dividing parental behavior into four stages: perception, interpretation, selection of a response, and implementation of the response. It is at the two earliest stages that neglectful parents have most of their problems. They may not be able to perceive the essential aspects of their children's states, or, if they are able to perceive their children's states, they may not be able to interpret accurately the implications of their perceptions.

Informed consent. Permission granted with knowledge of the potential risks or consequences. Professionals have legal and ethical responsibilities to fully inform their clients of these risks before the clients agree to receive services.

Inhalant. Drug that is inhaled or sniffed, sometimes by using a paper bag, rag, gauze, or ampoule. It can cause, for example, impaired coordination, nosebleeds, and disorientation.

Initial appearance (legal). See *Arraignment.*

Initial interview. Interview designed to obtain information relevant to diagnosis, treatment, remediation, or placement in special programs.

Injunctive relief. Remedy granted by the court forbidding or requiring some action by the defendant.

Innate intelligence. Genetically determined intelligence.

Inner ear. Fluid-filled cavity containing the end organs of hearing (cochlea) and balance (vestibule). The inner ear converts sound vibrations into electrochemical impulses.

Inpatient. Individual who receives services while staying in a facility or hospital.

Insanity. Form of mental illness that qualifies individuals for special treatment under the law. Legally, insanity is defined by federal and state statute in various ways.

Institutional maltreatment. (1) Abuse and neglect resulting from social or institutional policies, practices, or conditions. The widespread practice of detaining children in adult jails is one example. (2) Child abuse or neglect committed by an employee of a public or private institution or group home against a child in the institution or group home.

Instrumental stage of substance abuse. Third phase of substance abuse, in which a substance is used to manipulate emotions and behavior, such as to suppress or embrace feelings or to inhibit or disinhibit behavior. Intoxication and other mood-altering or behavioral effects are sought at this stage.

Insulin. Protein hormone, produced by the pancreas, that regulates the metabolism of sugar.

Insulin-dependent diabetes mellitus of childhood (IDDM). Chronic metabolic disease of childhood involving glucose utilization and storage; also known as Type I diabetes or juvenile onset diabetes. It affects about 1 in every 600 children under the age of 10 years.

Insulin reaction. Dizziness, nausea, and, perhaps, loss of consciousness due to excessive insulin.

Intake. In human services fields, process by which cases are introduced to an agency.

Integrated day care. Daily care program in which both children with disabilities and children without disabilities are served together.

Intelligence. Ability to deal with abstractions, to learn, and to cope with novel situations.

Intelligence quotient (IQ). Index of rate of development of certain aspects of intelligence during childhood. Although preferred current practice is to compute a deviation IQ, IQ was originally found by obtaining the ratio between mental age (MA) and chronological age (CA): $IQ = MA/CA \times 100$. See also *Deviation IQ.*

Intelligence test. Psychological test designed to measure cognitive functions, such as reasoning, comprehension, and judgment.

Intensity. In behavioral assessment, degree of severity or mildness of the behavior.

Intensity of reaction. In infants, energy level of responses, whatever the quality or direction. An infant with a high level of intensity reacts vigorously with pleasure or displeasure.

Intention tremor. See *Tremor.*

Inter alia. Among other things. The term is used to refer to one of several issues involved.

Interdisciplinary team. Group of individuals from different disciplines who perform their assessments and other tasks separately and then meet as a team to share information, develop plans, and work together. Communication between team members and inclusion of families are emphasized in the team process.

Interindividual comparison. Contrasting of one person with another or with a group of individuals.

Interinterviewer agreement. See *Interobserver agreement.*

Interinterviewer reliability. See *Interobserver agreement.*

Interlocutory (legal). Temporary; provisional; not final.

Intermittently supportive family. In cases of maltreatment, family that is ambivalent about the child, the circumstances surrounding the maltreatment, and the child's role in the maltreatment.

Internal consistency. In interviews, degree to which the information given by the interviewee agrees with other information given by the interviewee in the same interview.

Internalizing disorders. Conditions in which the symptoms are inner-directed and primarily associated with overcontrolled behaviors. Examples are anxiety disorders, depressive disorders, social withdrawal, psychophysiological disorders, eating disorders, gender identity disorder, and psychotic disorders.

Interobserver agreement. Degree to which information obtained from one observer, rater, or interviewer is consistent with information obtained from another observer, rater, or interviewer; also known as interrater agreement, interinterviewer agreement, or interinterviewer reliability. See also *Method error.*

Interpretive interview. See *Exit interview.*

Interrater agreement. See *Interobserver agreement.*

Interrogatories. Formal written questions presented by one party to another, requiring answers written under oath.

Intersensory integration. Combining information from more than one sensory modality to form a perception about a certain object.

Interstate compact re children. Agreement entered into by a number of states governing interstate placements of children, defining state financial and supervisory responsibilities, and guaranteeing certain constitutional protections for children.

Intervention strategy. Rationale, methods, and materials on which instruction, treatment, or rehabilitation is based.

Interview climate. See *Climate, interview.*

Interviewer bias. Tendency of the interviewer's actions to influence, directly or indirectly, the interviewee to respond in a way that he or she did not intend or to distort his or her communications to please the interviewer.

Interviewer/interviewee characteristics. Physical, cognitive, and affective traits of the interviewer and interviewee that influence the interview process.

Intonation. Pattern of pitch, stress, and juncture in language.

Intracerebral. Situated within the cerebrum.

Intracerebral hematoma. Mass of blood, usually wholly or partially clotted, within the cerebrum.

Intracranial. Within the brain.

Intracranial hemorrhage. See *Intraventricular hemorrhage.*

Intracranial neoplasm. New or abnormal growth, such as a tumor, located within the cranium.

Intrafamilial crises. Crisis events that take place within a family, such as physical/sexual abuse, abandonment, substance abuse, suicide, teenage pregnancy, and divorce. Crises often emerge gradually, with the stresses shared among the family members primarily, and may last a long time, depending on the child, the family, and the type of crisis.

Intrafamilial maltreatment. Abuse in which the perpetrator is part of the child's family.

Intraindividual. Pertaining to different characteristics within an individual.

Intrauterine growth retardation (IUGR). Failure of the fetus to grow at the expected rate during pregnancy.

Intrauterine insult. Injury to the uterus during the gestation period (particularly during the first trimester) that interferes with proper fetal development.

Intraventricular hemorrhage (IVH). Bleeding into the ventricles of the brain; sometimes called by the more general term intracranial hemorrhage.

Intrinsic tumor. Growth located entirely within the limb or organ of origin.

Investigation. Process of inquiring into or tracing through inquiry.

Investigative interview. In child maltreatment, interview designed to obtain information about possible maltreatment. Perhaps the most stringent type of adult interview of children, it may play an important role in the criminal indictment of another human being or other types of court proceedings.

Involuntary client. Person who has been referred for services, often through court order, but who has not asked for help. Most abusive and neglectful parents are initially involuntary clients and may not accept the need for services. They may deny that there is a problem and resist assistance. Motivation for change may be minimal or nonexistent; however, skillful workers have demonstrated that motivation can be developed in involuntary clients and treatment can be effective.

Involuntary placement. (1) Court-ordered assignment of custody to an agency and placement of a child, often against the parents' wishes, after a formal court proceeding. (2) Taking of emergency or protective custody of a child against the parents' wishes preceding a custody hearing.

Ipsilateral. Occurring on the same side; homolateral.

IQ. See *Intelligence quotient.*

Irrelevancies. Words or ideas out of context with the issues being considered.

Irrelevant language. Out-of-context language, unrelated to the theme of play or conversation.

Irreparable harm (legal). Any damage or wrong resulting from a violation of a legal right for which money damages would be inadequate compensation. The threat of irreparable harm may require some form of equitable intervention, such as an injunction.

Irritable bowel syndrome. Functional bowel disorder characterized by alternating diarrhea and constipation.

IS. Infant stimulation.

IUGR. See *Intrauterine growth retardation.*

IV. Intravenous.

IVH. See *Intraventricular hemorrhage.*

IWEN. See *Individual with exceptional needs.*

Jacksonian epilepsy. Form of epilepsy, caused by irritation of the cerebral cortex, in which muscle spasms are limited to a particular part of the body, usually without loss of consciousness.

Jargon. (1) Nonsensical words or sounds used in place of real words. (2) Fluent speech with neologisms, circumlocutions, and semantic or phonemic paraphasias.

Joint custody. Custodial arrangement in which both parents share the rights and responsibilities to make decisions regarding the health, education, and welfare of a child. See also *Joint physical custody.*

Joint physical custody. Custodial arrangement in which the child spends significant periods of time with each parent.

Judgment. (1) Evaluation or decision. (2) Order by a court after a verdict has been reached; judicial decision.

Jurisdiction (legal). Inherent power and authority of a particular court to hear and determine cases, usually involving certain categories of persons or allegations. Jurisdiction should be distinguished from venue, which is the particular county or district where a court with jurisdiction may hear and determine a case.

Jury. Group of adult citizens who serve as fact finders, judging the truth of allegations made in a legal proceeding. Jurors are sworn to inquire into certain matters of fact; the judge will rule on matters of law. Trial by jury is available in most criminal cases. In some states, cases of juvenile delinquency can be tried before a jury, but most are decided by the court.

Juvenile. In a majority of states, youth under the age of 18 years; minor.

Juvenile court. Court with jurisdiction over minors. It usually handles cases of suspected delinquency, as well as cases involving suspected child maltreatment or termination of parental rights.

Juvenile court judge. Presiding officer in a juvenile court.

Juvenile delinquent. Minor who has been determined by a court to have violated a federal, state, or local criminal law.

Juvenile onset diabetes. See *Insulin-dependent diabetes mellitus of childhood.*

Juvenile rheumatoid arthritis. Inflammatory process affecting the muscle joints.

Kanner's syndrome. See *Autistic disorder.*

Kernicterus. Condition with severe neurological symptoms associated with high levels of bile secretion in the blood, often associated with jaundice.

Ketoacidosis. See *Diabetic ketoacidosis.*

Ketone bodies. Chemicals produced by the body if insulin is insufficient and the body metabolizes fat for energy. When ketones accumulate in the bloodstream, they spill over into the urine or are passed through the lungs as acetone, producing a fruity breath odor. Ketone bodies can poison and even kill body cells. If ketones build up in the body over a long time, they can cause serious illness and coma.

Ketonuria. Condition evidenced by ketone bodies in the urine; in diabetics, a warning sign of ketoacidosis.

Kinesics. Aspects of nonverbal communication that involve bodily movements, such as facial expression, posture, gesture, characteristics of movement, and eye contact.

Kinesthesia. Sensation of bodily position, presence, or movement resulting chiefly from stimulation of sensory nerve endings in muscles, tendons, and joints.

Kinesthetic method. Approach to treating reading disability through the systematic incorporation of muscle movement (as by tracing the outlines of words) to supplement visual and auditory stimuli.

Kinetic reversal. Transposing letters within words or numerals within number groups—for example, *aet* for *ate* or *749* for *794.*

Kinship care. Form of foster care in which members of a child's extended birth family formally become his or her foster parents; also known as relative foster care.

Kinship network. Group of people one considers one's "relatives," on the basis of blood ties, legal action, function, or mutual affection and agreement. The boundaries of such a network are flexibly determined by law, culture, and individual choice.

Kleinfelter's syndrome. Chromosomal abnormality characterized by small genitalia, infertility, and scant facial and pubic hair. Approximately 20% of individuals with this condition are mentally retarded.

Kwashiorkor. Nutritional deficiency in young children resulting from severe protein deprivation and characterized by edema, dermatitis, growth failure, and liver damage.

Labeling. Describing people using terms based on categories of exceptionality, such as mentally retarded, learning disabled, and emotionally disturbed.

Labia majora. Outer lips to the vagina, which are covered by pubic hair after menarche (onset of menstruation).

Labia minora. Inner lips to the vagina.

Labile affect. Tendency to change suddenly from one mood to another.

Lability. Sudden appearance of uncontrolled crying or laughing inappropriate to the situation; sudden changeability of mood.

Laceration. Jagged cut or wound.

Lag. See *Maturational lag.*

Language. System that gives meaning to speech sounds or written configurations. Understanding, thinking, talking, reading, and writing all involve language.

Language and speech (LAS) program. Program for students who have articulation, voice, fluency, or language disorders.

Larynx. Part of the respiratory tract containing the vocal cords.

LAS. See *Language and speech program.*

Lateral. Toward the side.

Lateral confusion. Inability to distinguish left from right.

Lateral dominance. Preferential dominance and use of the parts of one side of the body.

Laterality. Preference for use of the left or right side of body, determined by hemispheric dominance.

Lateralization. Localization of function attributed to either the right or the left side of the brain.

Lazy eye. See *Amblyopia.*

LBW. See *Low birthweight.*

LD. See *Learning disability.*

LDA. Learning Disabilities Association.

LEA. Local educational agency; public board of education or other public authority legally constituted within a state to administer or to perform a service function for public elementary or secondary schools.

Leading case (legal). Precedent often cited as an authoritative or controlling guide for subsequent cases.

Leading questions. (1) Queries that direct the interviewee to talk about an area that he or she did not intend to talk about. A leading question may engender in the mind of the listener a specific visual image that would not have been produced had the question not been asked. (2) Queries with implied directions that lead the witness toward a conclusion that supports the argument of the attorney asking the question. Leading questions are usually prohibited during direct examination.

Learning. Relatively permanent change in behavior occurring as the result of practice.

Learning disability (LD). Disorder in one or more of the basic psychological processes involved in understanding or using spoken or written language. A learning disability may manifest itself in an impaired ability to listen, think, speak, read, write, spell, or do mathematical calculations. Students with a learning disability have a severe discrepancy between intellectual ability and achievement in one or more academic areas.

Least detrimental alternative. In cases of child abuse and neglect, choice of child care that is determined by the court to be least damaging to the child, based on a realistic appraisal of existing resources.

Least restrictive environment (LRE). Educational setting that gives the child as much involvement in regular education as is appropriate to his or her abilities, is challenging, allows for success and failure, and results in growth for the child.

Left cerebral hemisphere. Left half of the cerebrum.

Left-to-right progression. Ability to recognize letter or word sequences. It can be disturbed if laterality has not been established.

Legal custody. Right and responsibility to make the decisions regarding the health, education, and welfare of a child.

Legal immigrant. Person from another country who enters the United States as a legal permanent resident. After five years of continuous residence, a legal immigrant is eligible to apply for citizenship.

Leniency effect error. Error that occurs when the interviewer tends to excuse behaviors shown by the interviewee because of the interviewer's preconceived ideas.

LEP. See *Limited English proficiency.*

Lesion. Injury to tissue from wound, disease, or surgical procedures.

Leukemia. Any of various acute or chronic neoplastic diseases of the bone marrow in which unrestrained proliferation of white blood cells occurs, usually accompanied by anemia, impaired blood clotting, and enlargement of the lymph nodes, liver, and spleen.

LH. Learning handicapped. See also *Learning disability.*

Liability. Legal responsibility.

Liability for failure to report. Legal responsibility of mandated reporters to report cases of suspected child abuse or neglect. Some states impose a penalty, fine, and/or imprisonment on those who fail to report. See also *Mandated reporters.*

Libel. Defamation of a person's character in any type of printed material. See also *Slander.*

Libido. (1) Psychic energy. (2) Sexual desire.

Life-threatening condition. Medical condition that, in the treating physician's reasonable medical judgment, threatens the person's life.

Limb-kinetic apraxia. Apraxia localized to a single limb, resulting in clumsiness or inability to carry out fine motor acts with the affected limb.

Limit-setting sleep disorder. Condition involving difficulty in initiating sleep, typically characterized by stalling or refusing to go to bed.

Limited English proficiency (LEP). Linguistic ability of students who have difficulty in reading, writing, speaking, and/or understanding English.

Limp. To walk with abnormal, jerky movements.

Lineal orientation. Value orientation of a cultural group that emphasizes clearly established lines of authority.

Litigation. Judicial contest through which a party seeks to determine and enforce legal rights.

Lobectomy. Surgical excision of any lobe of an organ or gland; in reference to the brain, usually surgical excision of the prefrontal or temporal lobes.

Lobes of the brain. The four divisions of the brain. See also *Frontal lobe, Occipital lobe, Parietal lobe, Temporal lobe.*

Local agency or authority. In child maltreatment, (1) social service agency designated by the state and authorized by state law to handle child maltreatment cases or (2) local law enforcement agency.

Local rules of court. Rules adopted by individual courts to define more specifically the procedural rules that are set out in the various state rules of court.

Locomotion. Movement from one location to another, such as walking, crawling, and rolling.

Logbook. Written record of daily events used to stimulate orientation and memory.

Logical analysis. Strategy that focuses on putting things into perspective and rationalizing or reinterpreting a situation.

Logical rating error. In interviews, error occurring when the interviewer rates one area the same as another because the two seem to be logically related.

Long-term memory. Storage system that enables individuals to retain information for relatively long periods of time.

Long-term treatment. In child maltreatment, supportive and therapeutic services provided over a period of time, perhaps as long as a year or more, to restore the parent(s) of an abused or neglected child or the child himself or herself to adequate levels of functioning and to prevent recurrence of child maltreatment.

Loose association. Aspect of thought disorder wherein the patient has difficulty sticking to one topic and drifts off on a train of associations evoked by an idea.

Loss of goal. Failure to follow a chain of thought through to its natural conclusion. The child begins with a particular subject and then wanders away from it, never to return to it.

Low birthweight (LBW). Weight of less than 5.5 pounds at birth, regardless of length of gestation.

Lower-level functions. Functions, such as those of the motor system and reflexes, that do not involve higher-order thinking.

LRE. See *Least restrictive environment.*

LSD. Lysergic acid diethylamide; type of hallucinogen that is odorless, colorless, and tasteless and can produce intoxication with an amount smaller than a grain of salt.

Lumbar puncture. Insertion of a hollow needle into the lumbar region of the spinal cord to withdraw cerebrospinal fluid for diagnostic purposes or to administer medication.

Lymphoma. Type of cancer in which the lymph nodes are enlarged.

MA. See *Mental age.*

Machismo. Life pattern in which masculine behaviors are emphasized.

Macular degeneration. Deterioration of the central viewing area of the eye where vision is sharpest.

Magnetic resonance imaging (MRI). Diagnostic tool that provides a two-dimensional intensity plot of a cross-sectional slice of any part of the body. The plot is an image of the anatomy at the cross section.

Mainstreaming. Placing special education students in the least restrictive environment that meets their needs and enhances their instruction. Mainstreaming does not mean enrolling all special education students in regular classes.

Majority group. In the United States, White Americans, Anglo-Americans, or people of Western-European ancestry.

Mal de ojo. Evil eye or powerful eye; ailment, treated by Mexican American traditional healers, caused when one person glances or stares at another person. Symptoms include general malaise, sleepiness, fatigue, high fever, and severe headache.

Malapropism. Misapplication of a word that sounds somewhat like the one intended but is ludicrously wrong in context.

Malfeasance. Commission of an act in violation of legal duty. A mental health professional who breaches confidentiality unlawfully commits an act of malfeasance. See also *Nonfeasance.*

Malingering. Conscious fabrication or gross exaggeration of physical or psychological symptoms in pursuit of a recognizable goal.

Malpractice. Professional misconduct or improper practice. The professional's actions or lack thereof must be below the minimum standards for the profession, and the patient or client must be harmed because of the professional's actions or failure to act.

Maltreated child. See *Abused child.*

Maltreatment, child. Treatment that is abusive, neglectful, or otherwise threatening to a child's welfare; child abuse and neglect.

Mandamus. We command. A writ of mandamus is an order from a superior court to a lower court or other body commanding that a specified act be done.

Mandated agency. Agency designated by state statutes as responsible for receiving and investigating certain types of reports. In cases of suspected child abuse and neglect, the mandated agency may be a department of social services, a Child Protective Services unit within that department, or a police or sheriff's department.

Mandated reporters. In child maltreatment, persons legally required to report suspected cases of child maltreatment to the mandated agency. These persons are usually professionals, such as physicians, nurses, school personnel, social workers, psychologists, and clergy (or their delegates), who have frequent contact with children and families.

Manual communication. All gestural methods of communicating, including natural gestures, conceptually accurate signs, manually coded English, facial expressions, fingerspelling, and body language.

Maple syrup urine disease. Metabolic disorder involving anomalies in amino acid metabolism that may result in retardation, neurologic symptoms (such as reflex changes or hypertonicity), convulsions, coma, and death.

Marginality. Form of acculturation in which individuals try to meet all the demands of both the old and the new culture, developing anxiety and becoming isolated from both cultures in the process.

Marijuana. Popular name for the dried flowers and leaves of Cannabis sativa.

Mastery orientation. Cultural belief that people can gain mastery over nature.

Mathematics disorder. See *Dyscalculia.*

Maturation. (1) Attainment of complete psychobiological development. (2) Process whereby this state of development is reached.

Maturational lag. Delay in physiological, mental, or neurological development without apparent structural defect.

Maturational processes. Biological processes leading to maturity.

MBD. See *Minimal brain dysfunction.*

MCH. Maternal and child health.

MD. Muscular dystrophy.

MDT. Multidisciplinary team.

Meconium aspiration. Respiratory problem in newborns, caused by the passage into the amniotic fluid of meconium (the infant's first stool), which is then aspirated by the child during labor. Often a result of fetal distress during labor and delivery, it can lead to pneumonia.

Medial. Toward the middle or midline.

Mediation. Process by which individuals voluntarily discuss and try to settle disputes, often with the assistance of an attorney or mental health professional trained in mediation skills. Mediation is commonly used with parents to resolve issues related to child custody and visitation.

Medical model. Conceptualization of abnormal behaviors as diseases, analogous to organic diseases; also known as disease model.

Medical neglect. Failure to seek medical or dental treatment for a health problem or condition that, if untreated, could become severe enough to represent a danger to the individual.

Medically fragile children. Children who are born vulnerable as a result of genetic or congenital difficulties or poor prenatal care or who develop illnesses that necessitate special medical observation or care to assure their continued well-being.

Melting pot. Place where individuals from different cultures and countries form an integrated society.

Memory. Ability to mentally record and store events, feelings, reactions, and actions and then to recall them, as needed.

Memory span. Number of items that can be recalled mentally immediately after presentation.

Meningitis. Brain infection involving an acute inflammation of the membranes that cover the brain and spinal cord, characterized by drowsiness, confusion, irritability, and sensory impairments.

Meningocele. Protrusion of the membranes of the brain or spinal cord through a defect in the skull or spinal column.

Meningomyelocele. See *Spina bifida.*

Mens rea. Guilty mind; guilty or wrongful purpose; criminal intent. In most cases, *mens rea* must be present for a crime to have been committed.

Mental ability. Intelligence or cognitive ability.

Mental age (MA). Chronological age that an average child with that particular degree of mental ability would possess.

Mental deficiency. See *Mental retardation.*

Mental health interviewer. Clinician with expertise in mental health whose goals are to elicit the child's or adult's feelings, thoughts, and experiences in order to obtain information about the child's problem and family and to obtain a developmental history.

Mental injury. Injury to the intellectual or psychological capacity of an individual, as evidenced by observable and substantial impairment in his or her ability to function within a normal range of performance and behavior, with due regard to his or her culture.

Mental retardation (MR). Condition characterized by subaverage general intellectual functioning existing concurrently with deficits in adaptive behavior. Individuals with mental retardation have difficulty learning and then applying what they learn in different situations. There are four levels of mental retardation: *mild*—range of IQs between 52 and 67 (Stanford-Binet Intelligence Scale) or 55 and 69 (Wechsler Scale); *moderate*—range of IQs between 36 and 51 (Stanford-Binet Intelligence Scale) or 40 and 54 (Wechsler Scale); *severe*—range of IQs between 20 and 35 (Stanford-Binet Intelligence Scale) or 25 and 39 (Wechsler Scale, extrapolated); and *profound*—range of IQs 19 and below (Stanford-Binet Intelligence Scale) or 24 and below (Wechsler Scale, extrapolated).

Mental status evaluation. Assessment by an interviewer of a child's competence in such areas as general orientation to time, place, and person; recent and remote memory; immediate memory; insight and judgment; reading, writing, and spelling; and

arithmetical concentration. Such an evaluation may be conducted in cases of brain injury, when a child appears confused, or when the interviewer simply wants to obtain some indication of the child's general mental functioning. All areas assessed should be interpreted within a developmental framework, using age-appropriate norms or age-appropriate expectations.

Mental status interview. Interview that evaluates appearance and behavior, speech and communications, content of thought, sensory and motor functioning, cognitive functioning, temperament and emotional functioning, and insight and judgment. It may be conducted as part of the intake interview.

Meridians. In Chinese medicine, specific points of the body extending internally throughout the body in a fixed network.

Message components. Language characteristics, nonverbal characteristics, and sensory channels associated with the communications that take place in an interview.

Metabolic disorders. Hereditary (inborn) disorders or glandular dysfunctions that prevent the proper breaking down of one or more nutritive elements, such as protein, carbohydrates, fats, or lactose.

Metabolic dysfunction. Dysfunction in the chemical processes of the body.

Metacognition. Awareness of one's own cognitive processes and self-regulatory processes.

Method error. In interviews, degree to which information obtained by one interviewer is not consistent with that obtained by another interviewer from the same interviewee. See also *Interobserver agreement.*

Methylphenidate. Ritalin; psychostimulant medication most often used in treatment of attention-deficit/hyperactivity disorder.

MH. See *Multihandicapped.*

MHLP. Mental Health Law Project; now known as the Brazelton Center.

Microcephaly. Abnormally small head size, often seen in conjunction with mental retardation.

Midbrain. Smallest of the three principal divisions of the vertebrate brain, concerned mainly with eye movement and reflexes, as well as the relay of auditory impulses to the auditory cortex of the temporal lobes.

Migraine headaches. Recurrent, severe headaches that are typically unilateral in nature and are often accompanied by nausea and vomiting. See also *Classic migraine headaches, Common migraine headaches.*

Migration experience. The set of experiences that people have when they leave their native country to resettle in another country. It may influence their self-concept and how they adapt to the new country.

Mild hearing loss. Hearing loss of 20–40 decibels.

Mild learning disabilities. Slight perceptual-conceptual deviations that impair the ability of children to process information effectively, thereby serving as barriers to appropriate academic adaptation.

Mild malingering. Conscious exaggeration or fabrication of symptoms on the part of the interviewee, modest enough to have little or no bearing on the diagnosis or disposition.

Mild mental retardation. See *Mental retardation.*

Minimal brain dysfunction (MBD). See *Attention-deficit/hyperactivity disorder.*

Minimally acceptable environment. Minimal emotional climate and physical surroundings necessary for children to grow physically, mentally, socially, and emotionally.

Minor. See *Child.*

Minor in need of supervision (MINS). See *Child in need of supervision.*

Minority group. Group of people subordinated in terms of power and privilege to the majority group.

Miranda warning. Law enforcement procedure that forewarns suspects of their right to remain silent when in police custody. A statement or confession made by the suspect is usually inadmissible as evidence in court proceedings if the suspect was not informed of this right before the confession was disclosed.

Misdemeanor. Relatively minor offense punishable by a small fine or a short jail sentence.

Mistrial. Trial declared invalid because of procedural errors.

Mitigating circumstance (legal). Circumstance that lessens the degree of moral culpability of an offense but does not justify the offense.

Mixed dominance theory. Hypothesis that language disorders may be due wholly or partly to the fact that one cerebral hemisphere does not consistently lead the other in the control of sensorimotor functioning, perception, or body movements—that is, hemispheric dominance is not adequately established.

Mixed laterality. Tendency to perform some acts with a right-side preference and others with a left-side preference. Also, shifting from right to left for certain activities.

Mixed orientation. Cultural belief that people are born with both evil and good inclinations.

Mixed type of aphasia. Impaired ability in both expressive and receptive domains of language.

Mixed type of headache. Headache reflecting a combination of symptoms associated with both migraine and muscle contraction headaches.

Mnemonics. Art of assisting or improving memory with the aid of artificial systems.

Modality. In physiology, any of the various types of sensations, such as vision, hearing, taste, smell, or touch.

Mode. In statistics, most frequently occurring score in a group of scores.

Moderate hearing loss. Hearing loss of 41–60 decibels.

Moderate malingering. Clear pattern of exaggeration or fabrication of symptoms on the part of an interviewee, making it difficult to arrive at a diagnosis or a disposition.

Moderate mental retardation. See *Mental retardation.*

Moderately focused questions. Questions that address a specific topic but give some latitude to the interviewee.

Modification (legal). Changing of the prior orders of a court.

Mongolian spots. Birthmarks that can appear anywhere on a child's body but are seen most frequently on the lower back. These dark spots, which usually fade by the age of 5 years, can be mistaken for bruises.

Mongolism. See *Down syndrome.*

Moniliasis. See *Candidiasis.*

Monoplegia. Paralysis of one limb.

Monozygotic twins. Twins originating from a single fertilized ovum and having identical genetic makeup; also known as identical twins. By definition, these twins must be of the same sex.

Moral neglect. Failure to give a child adequate guidance in developing positive social values.

Motion (legal). Application made to a court for an order or ruling.

Motion to modify. Request that the court change its prior order.

Motor area of the cerebral cortex. Portion of the frontal lobe that controls voluntary movement.

Motor retardation. Condition characterized by unusual stillness; sluggishness; slow, feeble, or labored movements; slow walking; or delays in performing movements.

Mourning. Act or social expression of deprivation associated with the loss of someone through death. Mourning includes rituals and behaviors specific to various cultures and religions.

Moxibustion. Traditional healing procedure, used by Asians, in which the moxa plant is ignited and placed near specific areas of the body, leaving tiny craters on the skin.

MPD. Multiple personality disorder. See *Dissociative identity disorder.*

MR. See *Mental retardation.*

MRI. See *Magnetic resonance imaging.*

MRRC. Mental Retardation Research Center.

MS. See *Multiple sclerosis.*

Multidisciplinary team. (1) In child maltreatment, group of professionals, such as Child Protective Services workers, law enforcement officers, and district or county attorneys, who interact and coordinate their efforts to address child maltreatment cases. (2) Group of individuals from various disciplines who work together at all levels; also known as transdisciplinary team. Roles are often blended to enhance communication, and families are made an active, integral part of the process.

Multifocal effects. See *Global-diffuse effects.*

Multihandicapped (MH). Individuals with a combination of at least two handicapping conditions.

Multiple personality disorder (MPD). See *Dissociative identity disorder.*

Multiple questions. Queries that ask several different things in one statement. Because they allow the interviewee to answer one part and ignore the other parts, such questions should generally be avoided.

Multiple sclerosis (MS). Chronic degenerative disease of the central nervous system in which gradual destruction of myelin occurs in patches throughout the brain or spinal cord or both, interfering with the nerve pathways and causing muscular weakness, loss of coordination, and speech and visual disturbances. It occurs chiefly in young adults and is thought to be caused by a defect in the immune system that may be of genetic or viral origin.

Multisensory approaches. Educational techniques in which several sensory modalities are employed simultaneously or successively to facilitate learning.

MUMS. Mothers United for Moral Support.

Munchausen Syndrome by Proxy. Form of child maltreatment in which the child's illness is simulated, feigned, or produced by a caregiver. Generally, the caregiver makes repeated requests for medical evaluation and care of the child and denies any knowledge of the etiology of the child's illness; the child's symptoms quickly cease when the child and caregiver are separated.

Muscular dystrophy. Disease characterized by progressive atrophy of the muscles, resulting in neuromuscular impairment and weakness. It is caused by one or more genes that control muscle function.

Mushroom. Umbrella-shaped fungus, some varieties of which contain a drug that can cause hyperventilation, tremors, and hyperactivity when the fungus is chewed, smoked, or ground and infused in water and drunk as a tea. See also *Peyote.*

Mutism. (1) Refusal or inability to talk due to severe emotional conflicts. (2) Lack of speech, resulting from congenital deafness or poor development of the speech organs.

Myelination. Process of insulating or coating the axon of the neuron.

Myelomenigocele. See *Spina bifida*.

Myopia. Condition in which visual images can be seen distinctly only when they are close to the eye, resulting in defective vision of distant objects; also known as nearsightedness.

Myxedema. Acute condition caused by deficiency in thyroid hormone secretion and characterized by poor emotional control, fatigability, frequent skin disorders, and hair loss in adults. See also *Cretinism*.

NACHRI. National Association of Children's Hospitals and Related Institutions.

Narcolepsy. Sleep disorder often involving excessive sleepiness. It typically appears in adolescence.

Narcotic. See *Opiate*.

Narrow open-ended questions. Queries addressed to a specific area. Such questions are useful in eliciting specific information and speeding up the interview.

National hysteria. In child maltreatment, general feeling people have that they must not touch or help children because they may be accused of abusing the children or that they will be falsely accused of child maltreatment when children accidentally hurt themselves.

Naturalistic observation. Examination of behavior under normal or unstructured conditions.

NCCA. National Center for Child Advocacy.

NCCAN. National Center on Child Abuse and Neglect.

NCCIP. National Center for Clinical Infant Programs; now known as Zero to Three.

Nearsightedness. See *Myopia*.

NEC. See *Necrotizing enterocolitis*.

Necrotizing enterocolitis (NEC). Inflammation—and sometimes death—of the intestinal wall tissue. This potentially life-threatening condition is commonly found in premature infants.

Needs assessment. Formal or informal evaluation of the services needed by children with special needs and their families.

Negative behavior. Behavior characterized by active opposition and resistance to the interviewer's suggestions, evasive replies, deliberate silence, and refusal to cooperate.

Neglect. Form of child maltreatment characterized by failure to provide for the child's basic needs. Neglect can be physical, educational, or emotional/psychological. See also *Physical neglect, Educational neglect, Emotional neglect*.

Negligence. Failure to use the degree of care and skill that an ordinarily prudent person would use in the same circumstances.

Neologism. Word that does not resemble any legitimate word in a given language. Also, coinage of new words of the individual's own making.

Neonatal intensive care unit (NICU). Special hospital unit caring for infants with life-threatening conditions or severe medical problems; also known as intensive care nursery (ICN). Care is given from immediately after birth until the child is stable, transferred to another unit such as a pediatric intensive care unit, or released to go home.

Neonatal period. First four weeks after birth.

Neonate. Newborn infant.

Neoplasm. See *Tumor*.

Neovascularization. See *Diabetic retinopathy*.

Nephritis. Inflammation of the kidneys.

Nephropathy. Disease of the kidneys, common in persons who have had diabetes for a long time. Nephropathy is caused by damage to the small blood vessels or to the units in the kidney that clean the blood.

Networking. For children with special needs, formal or informal linking of individuals, families, or other groups with similar social, educational, medical, or other service needs with public or private agencies, organizations, or individuals who can provide such services within their locale. Many parents network with other parents by working with support groups, reading newsletters, and attending conferences.

Neural tube defect (NTD). Congenital defect in the formation of the brain or spinal cord. Defects include anencephaly and spina bifida.

Neuroblastomas. Virulent tumors that can arise anywhere along the sympathetic nervous system, with the most common sites being the adrenal gland and the paraspinal ganglion. A common symptom is a fixed mass in the chest, abdomen, or neck; less common symptoms include weakness, pallor, weight loss, shortness of breath, and cough.

Neurofibromatosis. Genetic disorder characterized by skin and neural tumors that result in mild intellectual impairment.

Neurological. Pertaining to the nervous system. Neurological problems are those arising from disease, damage, or dysfunction of the nervous system.

Neurological examination. Assessment of sensory and motor responses, especially reflexes, to determine whether the nervous system is impaired.

Neurological handicap. Impairment of the central nervous system.

Neurological insult. Damage to the brain or spinal cord caused by prenatal, perinatal, or postnatal factors.

Neurological lag. Delay in nervous system development relative to physical development.

Neurologically based communication disorders. Speech, language, or voice disorders caused by injury or illness affecting the brain or other portions of the nervous system.

Neurologist. Physician specializing in diseases of the nervous system.

Neurology. Discipline that studies the structure and function of the nervous system.

Neuromuscular. Relating to interaction between nerves and muscles.

Neuromuscular dysfunction. Inadequate functioning of the nerves and muscles.

Neuron. Individual nerve cell; basic unit of the nervous system.

Neuropathy. Disease of the nervous system, common in individuals with long-term diabetes, that causes peripheral nerve damage. Although it typically affects the feet and hands, neuropathy also can cause double vision, diarrhea, paralysis of the bladder, and loss of sexual responsiveness.

Neuropsychological evaluation. Assessment designed to draw inferences about the organic integrity of the cerebral hemispheres and to identify the adaptive strengths and weaknesses of brain-injured children. It complements a neurological examination by providing a profile of cognitive ability, sensorimotor functioning, and affective reactions.

Neuropsychologist. Psychologist specially trained in assessing behavioral aspects of brain function.

Neuropsychology. Branch of psychology that deals with the nervous system's impact on behavior or brain-behavior relationships.

Neurotoxin. Toxic substance that affects the brain and its neural pathways, causing psychological and physical problems.

Neurotransmitter. Chemical substance that transmits nerve impulses across a synapse.

Neutral phrases. Probing technique in which such statements such as "Uh huh," "I see," and "OK" are used to encourage the interviewee to keep talking.

NIC. National Information Clearinghouse for Infants with Disabilities and Life-Threatening Conditions.

NICHCY. National Information Center for Children and Youth with Disabilities.

NICU. See *Neonatal intensive care unit.*

NIDRR. National Institute on Disability and Rehabilitation Research.

Nightmares. Sleep disorder characterized by fears of attack, falling, or death. Nightmares generally should not be considered a sign of a psychological disturbance, unless they are frequent or severe.

NIH. National Institutes of Health.

Nocturnal eating (drinking) syndrome. Sleep disorder in which children wake in the night and cannot go back to sleep without eating or drinking.

Nocturnal enuresis. See *Sleep enuresis.*

Nolo contendre. I will not contest it. A plea of *nolo contendre* in a criminal action has the same legal effect as a plea of guilty relative to the specific proceedings at hand. A *nolo* plea cannot be used against the defendant in a later civil suit regarding the same issues, however.

Nominal aphasia. See *Anomia.*

Non-Hodgkin's lymphomas. Heterogeneous group of malignancies with varied symptoms, such as malaise, cough, dyspnea, or colitis-like symptoms.

Nonaccidental injury. Injury that occurs other than by chance.

Nonadherence. Failure to follow the prescribed medical regimen, including refusing treatment, failing to take medication as prescribed, failing to keep appointments, and choosing alternative unorthodox treatments; also known as noncompliance.

Noncategorical program. In special education, program for preschool children (usually between 3 and 5.9 years) who have disabilities but who have not been given a specific label or diagnosis.

Noncompliance. See *Nonadherence.*

Noncustodial parent. Parent who does not have physical custody of a child.

Nondisabled. Having no disabilities. This term is preferred over "able-bodied," which implies that persons with disabilities are less able; "normal" is appropriate only in reference to statistical norms.

Nonfeasance. Failure to complete an act that is part of a legal duty. A mental health professional who fails to act to protect a third party from imminent danger from a patient may be guilty of nonfeasance in some states.

Nonfluent aphasia. Type of aphasia in which auditory comprehension is better than verbal expression. Correct grammar is reduced to its simplest forms. A person with nonfluent aphasia may be able to use only one or two words when speaking.

Noninsulin-dependent diabetes mellitus (NIDDM). Form of diabetes that occurs in adults, usually after the age of 40, and involves insufficient insulin production or resistance to insulin; also known as Type II diabetes.

Nonleading questioning phase. In child maltreatment interviews, third phase of the interview, in which the interviewer attempts to learn more about what happened to the child by asking focused, but nonleading, questions.

Nonpurging subtype of bulimia nervosa. Type of eating disorder in which individuals use inappropriate compensatory behaviors, such as fasting or excessive exercise.

Nonstandard Black English. See *Black English.*

Nonsupportive family. In cases of child maltreatment, family that fails to support a maltreated child because the members feel overburdened with their own crises and have little energy to handle anything besides daily needs. In some cases, the family may believe that the maltreatment was the child's fault.

Nonverbal. Unable to communicate with the spoken word. Many people who are nonverbal communicate using sign language, communication boards, or computers.

NORD. National Organization for Rare Diseases.

Normal curve. Theoretical frequency distribution for a set of data, represented by a bell-shaped curve symmetrical about the mean; also known as normal distribution.

Normal distribution. See *Normal curve.*

Normalization. Providing disabled individuals with services and opportunities that are similar to or the same as those provided to nondisabled individuals.

Normative-developmental perspective. View that emphasizes a child's cognitions, affect, and behavior in relation to a norm group and that attempts to account for changes as the child grows older.

Norms. Scores and the corresponding percentile ranks, standard scores, or other transformed scores of a group of examinees on whom a test was standardized.

Notice. Directive from an authentic source requiring someone to act or to refrain from acting.

NPND. National Parent Network on Disability.

NPO. Nothing by mouth. This notation indicates that a patient may not take fluids.

NRCCAN. National Resource Center on Child Abuse and Neglect.

NRCCSA. National Resource Center for Child Sexual Abuse.

NSVD. Normal spontaneous vaginal delivery.

NTD. See *Neural tube defect.*

Nurture. Affectionate care and attention provided by a parent, parent substitute, or caregiver to promote the well-being of a child and encourage healthy emotional and physical development.

Nystagmus. Rapid, jerky, involuntary movement of the eyes, followed by a slower return to a normal position.

Obesity. Eating disorder defined as an excessive accumulation of body fat.

Objection (legal). Contention by a party to a court proceeding that a question asked by the examining attorney is improper. When an objection is made during testimony, the judge will either sustain or overrule the objection. If the judge overrules the objection, the witness may answer the question. If the judge sustains the objection, the witness may not answer the question.

Objectivity. Degree to which interviewers are open to what they see, hear, and feel during the interview and do not prejudge the interviewee.

OBRA. Omnibus Budget Reconciliation Act.

Obsessions. Persistent ideas or thoughts that an individual recognizes as irrational but cannot get rid of.

Obsessive-compulsive disorder. Disorder characterized by obsessions, which cause marked anxiety or distress, and/or compulsions, which serve to neutralize anxiety.

Obstructive sleep apnea. Sleep disorder characterized by repetitive episodes of upper airway obstruction during sleep, often causing a reduction in blood oxygen saturation.

Occipital lobe. One of the four lobes making up the cerebral cortex; lobe responsible for processing information from the visual system.

Occupational therapist. Health-care professional who works to improve a disabled individual's strength, with special emphasis on the arms, and to retrain the individual in such living skills as feeding, bathing, dressing, and homemaking so as to allow him or her to become more independent. These activities are referred to as occupational therapy (OT).

OCR. Office of Civil Rights.

Ocular. Pertaining to the eye.

Ocular albinism. Hereditary condition involving a lack of pigment in the eye. Persons with this condition should wear UV sunglasses to shield the eyes from ultraviolet rays.

Ocular pursuit. Visually following a moving target by successive fixations of the eye.

Oculomotor. Pertaining to eye movements.

Odd communication. Speech that is tangential, digressive, vague, overelaborate, circumstantial, or metaphorical.

Odd mannerisms. Unusual stylized movements or actions, complex idiosyncratic motor rituals, or peculiar forms of darting and lunging.

Offender. See *Perpetrator.*

OH. Orthopedically handicapped.

OHDS. U.S. Office of Human Development Services.

Olfactory. Pertaining to the sense of smell.

OM. See *Otitis media.*

Omission, acts of. In child maltreatment, failure of a parent or caregiver to provide for a child's physical or emotional well-being, due to unwillingness or inability.

Omnibus hearing (legal). Hearing held in criminal court to dispose of appropriate issues, such as whether evidence is admissible, before trial so as to ensure a fair and expeditious trial and avoid a multiplicity of court appearances.

OMRDD. Office of Mental Retardation and Developmental Disabilities.

Ontogeny. Developmental history of an organism.

Open adoption. Adoption in which there is contact between the birth family and the adoptive family. The contact may range from an exchange of written information at the time of placement to regular, face-to-face meetings between the two families throughout the child's lifetime.

Open-ended questions. Queries that cannot be answered by yes or no. They give the interviewee some responsibility for sharing his or her concerns, allow the interviewee the opportunity to describe events in his or her own words, and may help the interviewer appreciate the interviewee's perspective.

Open-head injury. Injury in which the brain tissue is penetrated from the outside.

Opening and closing sentences. In interviews, initial and ending remarks made by the interviewee, which may be of special significance.

Opening statement (legal). Speech made by an attorney at the start of the trial or at the beginning of his or her presentation in court, summarizing the attorney's case, what he or she plans to prove, and the evidence to be presented.

Operant components. Circumstances under which a behavior occurs and the consequences that follow from the behavior.

Operational definition. Definition expressed in terms of the procedures (operations) used to measure a trait, object, or process.

Opiate. Drug that contains or is derived from opium. It can cause sleepiness, constricted pupils, and vomiting when injected, snorted, or smoked.

Opinion (legal). (1) Conclusion reported by a witness who qualifies as an expert on a given subject—for example, "Based upon these marks, it is my opinion as a physician that the child must have been struck with a flexible instrument very much like this appliance cord." Lawyers are sometimes allowed to ask qualified experts hypothetical questions, in which the witness is asked to assume the truth of certain facts and to express an opinion based on those facts. (2) Judge's statement of the reason for a court's judgment, as opposed to the judgment itself.

Opium. Narcotic drug, derived from the juice of the unripe capsule of the poppy, that leads to physiological dependence and the build up of tolerance. Its derivatives are morphine, heroin, paregoric, and codeine.

Oppositional defiant disorder. Developmental disorder characterized by behavior that is negativistic, defiant, disobedient, and hostile but does not seriously violate others' rights or age-appropriate societal norms and rules.

Optic atrophy. Progressive deterioration of the optic nerve.

Optic nerve. Nerve fibers beginning at the back of the retina that converge and connect the retina with the brain's visual centers.

Optic nerve atrophy. Wasting away of the second cranial nerve, which connects the retina with the visual centers in the brain.

Orchitis. Infection of the testes.

Order (legal). Any written directive of a court or judge other than a judgment.

Order to show cause (OSC). Order to appear in court and present reasons why a particular order should not be executed. If the party fails to appear or to give sufficient reasons why the court should desist, the court will take the action requested.

Ordinary conversation. Relatively spontaneous, informal, and minimally structured verbal interaction.

Organic. Pertaining to the biological, as opposed to the functional, aspects of an organism.

Organic brain damage (OBD). See *Brain damage.*

Organicity. Impairment of the central nervous system.

Orientation. Ability to know one's location in time, space, and relationship to other people.

ORT-OHI. See *Orthopedically handicapped and other health impaired.*

Orthopedically handicapped and other health impaired (ORT-OHI). Individuals with specific orthopedic or health problems that adversely affect their educational performance. These problems include but are not limited to congenital anomalies, cerebral palsy, asthma, and diabetes.

OSC. See *Order to show cause.*

OSEP. Office of Special Education Programs.

OSERS. Office of Special Education and Rehabilitation Services.

Osteogenic sarcoma. The most common type of bone tumor. Symptoms include bone pain with or without a palpable overlying mass, pain with increased activity, a limited range of motion, swelling and, rarely, a pathological fracture.

Osteoporosis. Softening of the bones.

OT. Occupational therapy. See also *Occupational therapist.*

Otitis media (OM). Inflammatory disease of the middle ear, common in children under the age of 6 years. Otitis media may result in varying degrees of hearing loss if untreated.

Out-of-home care. Child care, foster care, or residential care provided by persons, organizations, and institutions to children who are placed outside their families, usually under the jurisdiction of juvenile/family courts.

Outpatient. Individual who receives services during a short (partial day) visit to a hospital, clinic, or other facility, without being admitted as an inpatient.

Overarousal. Level of arousal above what is expected.

Overcompliant behavior. Behavior characterized by a tendency to go along with other people passively, rather than asserting oneself in a reasonable manner.

P&A. See *Protection and advocacy.*

Pain. Unpleasant sensation or emotional experience, which may be acute, recurrent, or chronic.

Palliative care. Care provided not to cure, but to keep comfortable. Examples include providing warmth, pain control measures, and appropriate nutrition, hydration, and medications. These must be provided to all infants in spite of their disabilities, anticipated quality of life, state of consciousness, odds of survival, or the projected effectiveness of other medical treatment.

Panic attack. Disorder characterized by a discrete period in which there is a sudden onset of intense apprehension, fearfulness, or terror, often associated with feelings of impending doom. During these attacks, symptoms such as shortness of breath, palpitations, chest pain or discomfort, choking or smothering sensations, and fear of going crazy or losing control are present.

Panic disorder. Disorder characterized by the presence of recurrent, unexpected panic attacks, worry about the possible implications or consequences of the panic attacks, or a significant behavioral change related to the attacks.

Paragrammatism. Incorrect use of verbs, clauses, or prepositional phrases.

Paralinguistics. Aspects of communication that are not purely linguistic; specifically, meanings conveyed by tone of voice, pacing, pausing, emphasis, hems and haws, snorting, and so forth.

Paralysis. Loss of muscle strength as a result of damage to the nerves or muscles. See also specific types of paralysis.

Paraphasia. Substitution of incorrect words for other words—for example, "We get milk from a spoon, I mean cow," or "The flower is on the garden" instead of "The flower is in the garden"; also known as semantic (verbal) paraphasia.

Paraplegia. Paralysis of the lower limbs of the body, caused by injury to the spinal cord.

Parapodium. Device that supports a child's trunk and legs in a standing position.

Paraprofessional. Worker trained to a limited extent in a particular profession.

Parasomnias. Sleep disorders characterized by abnormal behavioral or physiological events occurring in association with sleep, during specific sleep stages, or during sleep-wake transitions.

Parens patriae. Country as parent; state's power to act on behalf of persons who cannot act in their own behalf, such as minors, persons who are incompetent, and some developmentally disabled persons.

Parent-to-parent support. Informational and one-on-one support provided by parents of children with disabilities to other parents, especially parents whose children have just been diagnosed with a disability.

Parent training. Planned teaching for parents to help them interact with, teach, and advocate for their child.

Parenterally. Situated or occurring outside of the intestines. When a medication is injected parenterally, it is injected outside the alimentary canal (the tubular passage that extends from the mouth to anus).

Parenting skills. Parent's competencies in providing physical care, protection, supervision, and psychological nurturance appropriate to a child's age and stage of development.

Paresis. (1) Slight or partial paralysis. (2) Dementia associated with syphilitic infection of the brain.

Paresthesia. Sensation such as burning, pricking, or tingling of the skin without objective cause.

Parietal lobe. One of the four lobes making up the cerebral cortex; lobe responsible for processing somatosensory and visuospatial input from the body.

Parkinsonian gait. Shuffling walk, with speed often increasing gradually.

Paroxysmal. Related to a sudden recurrence or intensification of the symptoms of a disease.

Part H of IDEA. Section of the Individuals with Disabilities Education Act (IDEA) that requires states to develop a coordinated, complete system of early intervention services for infants and toddlers with developmental delays and their families. Part H applies to every state and is often used to refer to a state's early intervention program.

Partially hearing. Hard of hearing; individuals on the mild to moderate end of the continuum of auditory impairment who can usually understand conversational speech, though some require the help of a hearing aid.

Partially sighted. Individuals with visual acuity of 20/70 or less in the better eye with correcting glasses, but still with some functional sight; those with seriously defective vision.

Pasmo. Paralysis-like symptoms of the face or limbs, referred to in Puerto Rican traditional medicine.

PASS. Plan for achieving self-support.

Patau's syndrome. See *Trisomy 13.*

Paternity. Being the father of the child. The law presumes that a man is a child's father under specified circumstances. See also *Adjudicated father.*

Pathognomic. Characteristic of a disease. A pathognomic sign or symptom is one from which a diagnosis can be made.

PCA. Personal care attendant.

PCP. Phencyclidine, also known as angel dust. It may produce stuporous conditions and, at times, prolonged comas or psychoses.

PDD. See *Pervasive developmental disorder.*

Peculiar rhythmic movements. Rocking, swaying, banging the head, repetitive jumping, or any other odd, regular movements.

Pediatric health systems interviewer. Clinician whose goal is to obtain information about a child's health, including stresses, life style, and compliance with medical regimens.

Pediatric intensive care unit (PICU). Special hospital unit that provides constant monitoring and treatment for seriously ill or injured children.

Pedophile. Adult who has a preference for obtaining sexual gratification through contact with children.

Pedophilia. Sexual behavior directed toward prepubertal children.

Pelvic inflammatory disease (PID). Infection of the fallopian tubes or ovaries.

Penis. Male sex organ composed of erectile tissue through which the urethra passes.

Percentile rank. Score indicating the percentage of cases that fall at or below that point in the distribution. Thus, a score in the 84th percentile equals or surpasses those of 84% of the persons in the group and is exceeded by those of 16% of the persons in the group.

Perception. Process whereby sensory stimuli are organized, interpreted, and imbued with a meaning dependent on the past experiences of the individual.

Perceptual disorder. Disturbance in the ability to interpret sensory stimulation accurately.

Perceptual handicap. Inadequate ability to attend to, recognize, discriminate, and integrate information seen, heard, or touched, resulting in conceptual (cognitive) difficulties.

Perceptual-motor. Relating to the interaction of the various channels of perception with motor activity.

Perceptual-motor match. Process of comparing the input data received through the motor system and the input data received through other avenues of perception.

Peremptory challenge. Procedure used by an attorney to reject a prospective juror without explaining the reason for doing so. A designated number of such challenges are available to attorneys on both sides during jury selection.

Perinatal period. Time period from shortly before birth to shortly after birth.

Perinatally. Pertaining to the period from shortly before birth to shortly after birth.

Periodic summaries. Probing technique in which the interviewer summarizes key pieces of information. Especially valuable at the end of the interview, such a summary conveys the interviewer's understanding of the problem, allows the interviewee to comment on the interviewer's interpretation and clarify earlier statements, shows the interviewee that the interviewer has been listening, and builds a transition from one topic to the next.

Peripheral vision. Seeing by means of the outer portions of the retina.

Peritonitis. Inflammation, caused by infection, of the membrane lining the abdomen.

Perjury. Knowingly making false statements under oath or affirmation; intentionally providing inaccurate testimony. Perjury may be punishable as a felony.

Permanency planning. Planning of actions and services that have the potential to provide stability for children coming into substitute care by anchoring them in a family that can lend continuity to their care.

Perpetrator. Person who abuses a child or commits some other illegal or antisocial act; also known as offender.

Perseveration. Persistent repetition of the same thought or response.

Persistence. The extent to which activities are continued in the face of obstacles.

Person in need of supervision (PINS). See *Child in need of supervision.*

Personality disorder. Behavioral condition characterized by inflexible and maladaptive behaviors.

Pervasive developmental disorder (PDD). Condition, similar to autism, that includes inappropriate social responses, strong anxiety responses, sensitivity to sensory stimuli, and resistance to change.

PET. See *Positron emission tomography.*

Petechia. Singular or multiple hemorrhage, about pinhead size.

Petit mal seizures. Epileptic episodes marked by brief, frequent attacks of impaired consciousness, staring, disinterest, loss of attention, blinking of the eyes, or loss of normal posture.

Petition (legal). Formal application to the court for judicial action on a certain matter, stating allegations that, if true, form the basis for court intervention. A petition may be filed in juvenile or family court at the beginning of cases involving neglect, abuse, termination of parental rights, and/or delinquency.

Petitioner (legal). See *Complainant.*

Peyote. Hallucinogen obtained from the root of the peyote cactus. Its active ingredient is mescaline.

PH. See *Physically handicapped.*

Pharynx. Part of the alimentary canal that extends from the mouth and nasal cavities to the larynx.

Phenotype. Individual's observable traits.

Phenylketonuria (PKU). Chromosomal abnormality that arises from a recessive gene coming from both parents and causes a child to be unable to metabolize the protein phenylalanine. Untreated PKU results in severe mental retardation; it also may cause convulsions, behavioral problems, severe skin rash, and a musty odor of the body and urine.

Phenytoin sodium. See *Dilantin.*

Phobia. Persistent and abnormal fear.

Phonation. Production of speech sounds by vibration of the vocal cords.

Phoneme. Smallest unit of sound in spoken language, such as |b| in "boy."

Phonemic paraphasia. Recognizable mispronunciation of a word in which sounds or syllables are out of sequence—for example, "psghetti" for "spaghetti."

Phonetic decoding. Ability to read visually presented words.

Phonetics. Study of articulatory and acoustic specification of speech sounds.

Phonological processing. Detecting and interpreting the phonemes, or speech sounds, that comprise oral language.

Photophobia. Abnormal visual intolerance of light, often associated with pediatric headaches.

Physiatrist. Physician who specializes in physical rehabilitation.

Physical abuse. Maltreatment that results in physical injury. Physical abuse can be related as mild (a few bruises, welts, scratches, cuts, scars), moderate (numerous bruises, minor burns, a single fracture), severe (large burns, central nervous system injury, multiple fractures, any life-threatening maltreatment), or extreme (maltreatment that results in death).

Physical custody. Right of a person to have a child reside with him or her and to make the day-to-day decisions regarding the child's care during the time the child is in his or her care.

Physical evidence. Any tangible piece of proof, such as a document, an x-ray, a photograph, or a weapon used to inflict an injury; also known as exhibit. Physical evidence must usually be authenticated by a witness who testifies to the connection of the evidence with other facts in the case.

Physical indicators of child maltreatment. Injuries to the skin or bones, burns, rashes, bites, and other signs suggestive of physical injuries or neglect. Physical injuries need to be evaluated for their shape, location, and type; the force needed to produce the injury; and the number of new and old injuries. Physical indicators of child maltreatment also may be associated with other conditions.

Physical neglect. Failure to provide for a child's basic survival needs, such as food, clothing, shelter, and supervision, to the extent that the failure represents a hazard to the child's health or safety. Whether lack of supervision constitutes neglect depends on the child's age and competence, the amount of parental planning for the unsupervised time, and the time of day when the child is unsupervised.

Physical therapist. Health-care professional who works toward maximizing physical mobility, function, relief of pain, and independence.

Physical therapy (PT). Therapy concerned with restoring function and preventing disability following disease, injury, or loss of a body part. Different methods are used to improve circulation, strengthen muscles, encourage movement, and train or retrain an individual to perform activities of daily living.

Physically handicapped (PH). Individuals with physical disabilities, many of whom are educated through special services or special day class programs.

Physiognomy. Facial features, especially when regarded as revealing character.

Pica. Eating disorder characterized by the persistent eating of non-nutritive substances for at least 1 month. These substances include paint, plaster, string, hair, and cloth for infants and young children and animal droppings, sand, leaves, and pebbles for older children. The behavior is considered developmentally inappropriate and is not culturally sanctioned.

Picture question technique. Interview technique used with children, in which the interviewer shows the child a picture that the interviewer thinks will engage the child and help the child talk about his or her feelings. Pictures may serve as a less intrusive and more concrete way of getting information about children's feelings than questions alone.

PICU. See *Pediatric intensive care unit.*

PID. See *Pelvic inflammatory disease.*

PINS. Person in need of supervision. See also *Child in need of supervision.*

PKU. See *Phenylketonuria.*

PL. See *Public Law.*

PL 94-142. Education for All Handicapped Children Act of 1975.

Placebo. Inert (harmless) substance used in drug experiments as a control.

Placement. See *Detention.*

Placement hearing. See *Detention hearing.*

Placenta. Organ that develops in females during pregnancy, to supply oxygen, nutrients, and antibodies to the fetus and remove waste products.

Plaintiff. See *Complainant.*

Plantar reflex. Flexion of the toes when the sole of the foot is lightly stroked.

Plasticity of development. Ability of an organism to be flexible and adapt to conditions encountered during its development.

Plea bargaining. In criminal cases, negotiation by the prosecutor (on behalf of the state) and the defendant of a mutually agreed upon disposition of the case, which is then submitted to the court for approval.

Pleadings (legal). Statements, in logical and legal form, of each side of a case.

PMR/PMH. Profoundly mentally retarded/profoundly mentally handicapped.

Pneumocystis carinii pneumonia. Type of pneumonia in which blood appears in the lung tissue.

Pneumoencephalography. Radiographic visualization of the fluid-containing structures of the brain after cerebrospinal fluid is intermittently withdrawn by lumbar puncture and replaced by air, oxygen, or helium.

Pochismos. English words given Spanish pronunciations and endings.

Polygenic. Relating to the interaction of many genes, each of which adds to the development of a trait.

Polyhydramnios. See *Hydramnios.*

Poor gross motor coordination. Awkward, stiff, clumsy, or stumbling movements.

Positron emission tomography (PET). Scanning procedure that produces a cross-sectional image of radioactivity following intravenous injection of a radioactive substance.

Post-assessment interview. See *Exit interview.*

Posterior fornix. Vaginal cavity located beneath the cervix.

Posterior fourchette. External tissue extending from the hymen toward the anus, contained within the labia majora.

Postlingual deafness. Deafness occurring after speech and language have developed.

Postnatal period. Time period immediately after birth.

Posttraumatic amnesia (PTA). Loss of memory following a brain injury. Also, loss of memory following a traumatic event or a disturbing psychological experience.

Posttraumatic epilepsy. Recurring convulsions associated with brain injury.

Posttraumatic stress disorder (PTSD). Development of symptoms following a psychologically distressing event, such as a natural disaster, an accident, war, rape, and the like. Symptoms include intrusive memories of the traumatic event, emotional withdrawal, estrangement from others, a tendency to be easily startled, and nightmares and otherwise disturbed sleep.

Poverty of content. Restriction in the information conveyed by speech. Long replies convey little information. Language tends to be vague, overabstract or overconcrete, repetitive, and stereotyped.

Powerlessness. Perceived or real lack of control over one's body, mind, environment, or life.

Pragmatic. Practical; functional.

Precedent (legal). Prior court decisions relied upon to decide a similar subsequent legal problem.

Preconscious behavior. Behavior not present in consciousness at a given moment, but readily recallable.

Predictive validity. See *Validity.*

Preferred interviewer-interviewee model. Interviewing situation characterized by an open and responsible relationship between the interviewer and interviewee, in which each party shows respect for the other.

Prelingual deafness. Deafness present at birth or occurring at an age before the development of speech and language.

Premature infant. Infant born before the 37th week of gestation.

Premature nursery. Special hospital-based unit used only to care for premature infants.

Premorbid. Existing prior to the onset of the disorder.

Prenatal cataracts. In the fetus, clouding of the lens of the eye or its capsule, obstructing the passage of light.

Prenatal factors. Factors present during pregnancy (before the birth of the child).

Prenatal period. Time period before birth.

Preponderance of evidence. Standard usually used in civil court, requiring that the evidence be of greater weight or more convincing than the evidence offered in opposition. On the whole, it shows that the fact to be proved is more probable than not (has at least a 51% probability).

Preschool intervention. Programs designed to improve basic academic and personal-social skills in preschool children, who are usually between the ages of 3 and 6 years.

Presentence investigation report. Document, prepared by a probation officer for the court's consideration at the time of disposition or sentencing in a case, that details the subject's prior legal entanglements and other relevant factors and recommends a particular disposition or sentence.

Pressured speech. Speech that is overabundant, accelerated, loud, or difficult to interrupt.

Presumption (legal). Assumption of fact based on another fact or group of facts. It is either conclusive (not subject to opposition) or rebuttable (capable of being rebutted by presentation of contrary proof).

Pretrial diversion. Decision of a district or county attorney's office not to issue charges in a criminal case where those charges would likely be provable. The decision is usually made on the condition that the defendant agree to participate in rehabilitative services.

Prevalence. Number of cases of a condition or disease identified in a population at a given time.

Prevention. Measures designed to remove the causes of disabilities or problem behaviors, keep the disabilities or problem behaviors from occurring, or lessen the extent to which the disabilities or problem behaviors occur.

Prima facie. On its face; on the first appearance. A *prima facie* case is one that has been proven sufficiently to sustain a finding in favor of the complaining party unless the opposing party can rebut the evidence.

Primary enuresis. Failure to master bladder control. An individual with primary enuresis has never mastered bladder control.

Privileged communication. Disclosures made by clients to certain professionals, such as social workers, psychologists, marriage and family counselors, attorneys, clergy, psychiatrists, and other physicians, that cannot be revealed during legal proceedings without their informed consent. See also *Confidentiality.*

PRN. Whenever necessary.

Pro bono. For the public good. Attorneys' or other professionals' services rendered at no charge are said to be performed *pro bono.*

Pro se. In one's own behalf. In a *pro se* lawsuit, a party acts on his or her own behalf, without an attorney.

Probability. Likelihood that an event will occur.

Probable cause. Legal standard requiring reasonable grounds for believing in the existence of facts supporting the proceedings brought before the court.

Probation. Sentencing alternative in which a convicted criminal defendant or a juvenile found to be delinquent is allowed to remain at liberty, generally under the supervision of a probation officer and under threat of imprisonment if he or she fails to meet certain conditions.

Probing questions. Queries used by an interviewer to elicit more detailed responses from the interviewee.

Problem-focused strategy. Plan that involves using rational means to modify stressors.

Problem solving. Logically thinking one's way through a problem to arrive at a reasonable and acceptable solution.

Proceeding (legal). Events comprising the process by which administrative or judicial action is initiated and resolved.

Proctoscopy. Inspection of the rectum with a proctoscope.

Prodromal symptoms. Symptoms that occur before an attack or before the outbreak of a condition.

Profound hearing loss. Hearing loss of greater than 90 decibels.

Profound mental retardation. See *Mental retardation.*

Prognosis. Prediction of the likely duration, course, and outcome of a certain condition.

Projection. Unwittingly attributing one's traits, attitudes, or subjective processes to others.

Projective technique. Method of personality study in which ambiguous stimuli are used to elicit subjective responses of an associative or fantasy nature.

Pronoun reversal. Symptom of autism in which children reverse pronouns—for example, a child refers to himself or herself as "you" and to other people as "I."

Proof beyond a reasonable doubt. Stringent standard that must be met in criminal cases to prove that the alleged offender violated the law. The evidence presented must not leave any significant doubt in the court's or jury's mind as to the guilt of the accused and must fully satisfy the fact finder as to its factualness. The facts proven must, by virtue of their probative force (that is, by the evidence they furnish), establish guilt.

Proprioceptive stimulation activities. Activities that stimulate receptors in joints, tendons, or muscles.

Prosecutor. Attorney for the local, state, or federal government in a criminal case.

Prosody. Variation in stress, pitch, and rhythm of speech by which different shades of emotionality are conveyed.

Prosopagnosia. Impaired ability to recognize faces.

Prostate. Gland that produces part of the seminal fluid and stimulates production of sperm.

Prosthesis. Artificial body part, such as a palatal lift, artificial leg, or dentures.

Protection and advocacy (P&A). System created by the Developmental Disabilities Assistance and Bill of Rights Act to protect the individual rights of persons with developmental disabilities.

Protective custody (legal). Detainment of a child on an emergency basis until a written detention request can be filed; also known as emergency custody. For example, police and Child Protective Services (in some states) may have the authority to detain a minor when they reasonably believe the child is in surroundings or conditions that endanger the child's health or welfare. The standard for protective custody varies by state.

Protective order (legal). Order of the court generally issued in emergencies. A judge may issue a protective order to hold a child in a hospital until an alleged maltreatment situation is assessed or to restrain or control the conduct of the alleged perpetrator or any other person who might harm the child or interfere with the disposition.

Protective services. See *Child Protective Services.*

Protocol. Set of rules or guidelines prescribing procedures and responsibilities.

Provider. Individual, organization, or agency that delivers services to persons and their families.

Proxemics. Aspects of nonverbal communication that involve the perception and use of personal and interpersonal space.

Proximal. Near. Used in opposition to distal, the term refers to the object closer to the point of reference.

Psychic numbing. Condition, usually caused by a traumatic event, characterized by inability to remember parts of an event or erosion of interest in life. Symptoms include loss of interest in school, constricted affect, interpersonal detachment, pessimism about the future, and suppression of thoughts, feelings, and actions associated with an event.

Psychodiagnostic workup. Evaluation of a client, usually including a clinical assessment interview and sometimes involving the administration of a battery of psychological tests.

Psychodynamic perspective. View that stresses early childhood experiences and emphasizes intrapsychic factors, such as thoughts, feelings, impulses, desires, motives, and conflicts that influence behavior.

Psychoeducational diagnostician. Specialist in education who diagnoses and evaluates a child who is having difficulty in learning.

Psychogenic. Pertaining to emotional conditions that have no clearcut organic foundations.

Psycholinguistics. Study of language and communication processes from the shared viewpoint of the disciplines of psychology and linguistics.

Psychological abuse. See *Emotional abuse.*

Psychological autopsy. Profile developed after an individual's death, from a retrospective analysis of the individual's letters and writings and interviews with family members and friends.

Psychological evaluation. Assessment of an individual, usually consisting of a clinical assessment interview plus the administration of a battery of psychological tests.

Psychological neglect. See *Emotional neglect.*

Psychometrics. (1) Measurement of psychological variables, such as intelligence, aptitude, and emotional disturbance. (2) Mathematical, especially statistical, design of psychological tests and measures.

Psychometrician. Also known as psychometrist. (1) Person who administers psychological tests. (2) Specialist in the statistical analysis of psychological data.

Psychomotor. Pertaining to the motor effects of psychological processes. Psychomotor tests are tests of motor skill that depend on sensory or perceptual-motor coordination.

Psychomotor seizure. Form of epileptic seizure characterized by loss of contact with the environment, during which the individual may engage in well-organized and normal-appearing behavioral sequences.

Psychosexual development. In psychoanalytic theory, progress through the five critical stages of growth characterized by interaction between biological drives and environmental forces—the oral, anal, phallic, latency, and genital stages.

Psychosis. Severe mental disorder characterized by disturbances in cognitive, perceptual, and emotional processes.

Psychotherapeutic interview. Interview designed to foster behavioral, cognitive, and affective change.

Psychotherapy. Techniques derived from psychological principles and used by trained mental health professionals to help individuals with mental problems, emotional problems, or problems of living.

Psychotropic drug. Substance that affects mental activity.

PT. See *Physical therapy.*

PTA. See *Posttraumatic amnesia.*

PTI. Parent training and information center.

PTSD. See *Posttraumatic stress disorder.*

Public defender. Attorney paid with public funds to plead the cause of an indigent defendant. Public defenders are appointed by the court and work for a government agency.

Public Law (PL). Federal law passed by the United States Congress.

Pull-out services. Special services provided to children with disabilities in a special class different from the children's regular classroom.

Purging subtype of bulimia nervosa. Type of eating disorder in which individuals regularly engage in self-induced vomiting or misuse laxatives, diuretics, or enemas.

Quadriplegia. Paralysis of all four limbs.

Quality. In behavioral assessment, how good or poor the behavior is.

Quality of mood. In infants, amount of pleasant, joyful, and friendly behavior or the amount of unpleasant, unhappy, and unfriendly behavior.

Questionnaire. List of questions asked to obtain information about such subjects as an individual's or a group's preferences, beliefs, interests, and behavior.

Quid pro quo. Something for something. A *quid pro quo* exists when something is exchanged for something else in a transaction between parties to a contract or agreement.

Rabies. Acute viral disease of the nervous system transmitted through the bite of an infected (rabid) animal.

Race. Population united by common physical characteristics, such as skin color, facial features, and hair type.

Rancho Los Amigos Levels of Cognitive Recovery. Observational scale of behaviors developed by Rancho Los Amigos Hospital in Downey, California. The scale can be used to describe the condition of a head-injured person and assist in developing treatment goals. The eight levels of the scale range from coma to nearly complete recovery.

Random probing. In an interview, asking questions in a hit-or-miss fashion in the hope of stumbling on a useful topic. This approach is avoided in careful interviewing.

Rapport. Relationship of mutual trust or emotional affinity.

Rapport phase. In an interview, initial phase designed to establish a good relationship with the interviewee.

Rational-intellectual strategy. Problem-focused strategy in which information or advice is used to modify psychological stressors.

Rationalization. Process of thinking up good reasons to justify one's actions.

RDS. See *Respiratory distress syndrome.*

Reactive effects. Changes in one's behavior as a result of being observed or knowing that one's products may be observed.

Reading comprehension. Ability to understand the printed or written word.

Reading disorder. The most frequent form of learning disability, characterized by difficulty in reading. See also *Dyslexia.*

Real evidence. Evidence addressed directly to the senses without intervention of testimony, such as bloody underpants.

Reasonable cause or suspicion (legal). Standard requiring facts that would lead a person of ordinary care and prudence to believe or conscientiously entertain an honest and strong suspicion that the suspect was guilty of a crime.

Reasonable doubt (legal). Doubt that arises from evidence or lack thereof and would be entertained by a reasonable or prudent person. Reasonable doubt requires acquittal.

Reasonable efforts (legal). Under state law, plausible attempts by Child Protective Services or a similar agency to keep the family together or, if the child has already been removed, to reunify the family. Before a state can receive federal financial support for the costs of out-of-home care resulting from a child's removal from her or his home, a judge must determine that reasonable efforts have been made to keep the family together. Similarly, continued federal support for the placement requires a finding by the judge that reasonable efforts have been made to reunite the family.

Reasonable medical judgment. Determination made by a reasonable, prudent physician who is knowledgeable about the cause of the illness and its treatment possibilities.

Reauditorization. Ability to recall the names or sounds of visual symbols (letters).

Rebuttal (legal). (1) Refuting of statements made and evidence introduced. (2) Stage of a trial during which such refuting is appropriate.

Receptive aphasia. Inability to understand spoken or written language, even though there is no auditory or visual damage. Receptive aphasia is associated with brain damage. See also *Auditory aphasia.*

Receptive language. Language spoken, written, or signed by one or more persons and received by another.

Recessive gene. Gene that requires another gene like itself in order for a trait to be manifest; opposite of dominant gene.

Recidivism. Relapse into a previous condition or mode of illegal behavior.

Recommendation conference (legal). In some jurisdictions, hearing at which the judge and attorneys review the recommendations of a custody evaluator and try to reach settlement on the issues.

Recounting technique. Process by which the interviewee is asked to relate the details of a specific episode.

Rectum. Terminal area of the colon.

Recurrent pain. Unpleasant sensation that is experienced on repeated occasions.

Recurrent references. Major themes that run throughout an interview and may provide clues about significant attitudes of the interviewee.

Redirect examination (legal). Additional questioning conducted by the attorney who originally requested the testimony. It follows cross-examination.

Referral question. Stated reason for referring the child for evaluation.

Reflection. Interviewing technique of paraphrasing the thoughts and feelings of the interviewee to obtain more information. See also *Reflective statements.*

Reflective statements. Comments designed both to provide feedback to the interviewee and to get the interviewee to expand on a topic.

Reflex. Automatic elicitation of a specific response without involving higher brain functions.

Refreshing recollection. See *Refreshing the memory.*

Refreshing the memory (legal). Act on the part of an individual of checking back into documents in order to remember details related to testimony; also known as refreshing recollection.

Refugee. Person who is unable or unwilling to return to his or her country of origin because of persecution or a well-founded fear of persecution. Persecution or the fear of persecution may be based on the person's race, religion, nationality, membership in a particular social group, or political opinion. Refugees are exempt from numerical limitations and are eligible to receive lawful permanent resident status after one year of continuous presence in the United States.

Regression. Return to earlier and less mature behavior.

Rehabilitation. Course of treatment directed toward improvement of an impaired function or functions.

Relative foster care. See *Kinship care.*

Relevancy (legal). Degree to which evidence addresses the issue before the court. Evidence not relevant to the issue before the court is usually not admissible.

Reliability. Degree to which a test or interview is consistent in its measurements. See also *Internal consistency, Interobserver agreement, Method error, Test-retest reliability.*

Relief (legal). Remedy, requested by a plaintiff, for some legal wrong. Relief is granted by a court or jury against a defendant. Examples include monetary damages, specific performance of a contractual obligation, temporary restraining orders, and preliminary injunctions.

Remand (legal). Order from an appellate court sending a lawsuit back to a lower court with specific instructions on handling the case.

Remediation. Procedures used to increase a child's competence in various skills.

Repetition. In an interview, probing technique that consists of repeating the same question, perhaps with slight modification, when the interviewee did not answer it the first time it was asked.

Reporting laws. In child maltreatment, laws that require specified categories of persons, such as professionals involved with children, to notify public authorities of cases of suspected child maltreatment. All 50 states have reporting laws.

Representative sample. Group of people or objects that matches the population of which it is a sample with respect to characteristics important for the purposes under investigation.

Res ipsa loquitur. The thing speaks for itself; doctrine in negligence law under which no proof is needed other than the incident itself.

Residential treatment facility. Institution that provides housing, 24-hour supervision, education, and behavioral assistance for children needing these services.

Residual. That which is left over; remainder.

Resonation. Vibration of air in cavities as it passes through the voice and speech mechanism. It produces the melodic and enriching features of individual human voices.

Resource room. Designated room in a school, other than the regular classroom, in which special education instruction is offered.

Resource specialist program (RSP). Classes for students who have specific learning disabilities or other health-related problems that interfere with learning, but who spend the majority of the school day in a regular program.

Resource specialist program teacher (RSPT). Specialist who works with children with specific learning disabilities or other health-related problems that interfere with learning. This teacher acts as a consultant to other teachers, providing materials and methods to help children who are having difficulty within the regular classroom.

Respiratory distress syndrome (RDS). Disease that occurs in premature infants, resulting in difficulty in breathing; also known as hyaline membrane disease. Severe cases may require a respirator to keep the infant alive.

Respite care. Short-term, temporary care for persons with a disability, provided in or out of the home. Companions are paid to provide short-term relief ranging from a few hours to a few days for the primary caretaker of a disabled person.

Respondent (legal). Person who answers a petition.

Response set. Relatively fixed or stereotyped ways in which individuals tend to respond, such as guessing, always answering "true," or giving socially desirable answers; also known as response style.

Response style. See *Response set.*

Restraining order (legal). Order of the court forbidding a party from committing particular acts, either until a hearing can be held (temporary) or for a specific period of time.

Restricting subtype of anorexia nervosa. Form of anorexia nervosa in which weight is lost by restricting food intake or engaging in excessive exercise.

Restrictive interviewer-interviewee models. Interviewer-interviewee models that are less open than the preferred model and limit the interviewee's responsibility. These models include the active interviewer/passive interviewee model, the "pure" scientist model, the paternalistic model, and the collegial model. All of these models have disadvantages that keep them from being effective.

Retinitis pigmentosa. Disease, frequently hereditary, that is marked by progressive deterioration of the rods of the retina. The person is able to see centrally (tunnel vision); peripheral vision and night vision are impaired.

Retinoblastomas. Tumors that arise from the tissue within the retina in the eye. Symptoms include eye abnormality (for example, a whitish appearance of the pupil) and strabismus (that is, cross-eyedness).

Retinopathy of prematurity. In a premature infant, condition in which the retina (the innermost part of the eye, comparable to the film in a camera), because of underdevelopment, is unable to activate the nerve fibers necessary to produce a visual image. See also *Diabetic retinopathy.*

Retrieval processes. Series of actions used to recall events from memory.

Retrograde amnesia. Inability to remember events that occurred prior to the onset of the amnesia.

Retrolental fibroplasia (RLF). Disease of the retina in which a mass of scar tissue fills the space between the back of the lens and the retina. It occurs mainly in infants born prematurely who receive excessive oxygen. Both eyes are affected in most cases.

Reversal. (1) In reading, transposition of letters. (2) In law, decision of an appellate court that the judgment of a lower court or other body should be set aside, vacated, or changed.

Reversibility. Ability to move backward in thinking about a sequence of ideas or actions.

Review hearing (legal). Hearing held by juvenile or family court to reexamine dispositions (usually every 6 months) and to determine the need to maintain placement in out-of-home care and/or court jurisdiction over a child.

Revisualization. Ability to retrieve a visual image of a stimulus (for example, letter or word or object) that was seen before.

Rh incompatibility. Condition in which the mother has Rh negative blood and the fetus has Rh positive blood. When blood from the fetus mixes in the placenta with the mother's blood, antibodies may be produced that will destroy the red blood cells of the fetus in subsequent pregnancies. If this condition is not treated, it can cause such pathologies as abortion, stillbirth, jaundice, or mental retardation.

Rhythm. Tempo or pattern of speech flow.

Rhythmicity. In infants, regularity of physiological functions. An infant with rhythmicity has regular feeding times, sleeping times, and times for bowel movements. Rhythmicity also may refer to the infant's emotional states and ability to make transitions.

Rickets. Condition caused by a deficiency of vitamin D, which disturbs the normal development of bones.

Right cerebral hemisphere. Right half of the brain.

Right-left disorientation. Inability to distinguish right from left; confused directionality.

Rigid interviewer style. Manner of interviewing that yields information but makes the interviewee feel distant from the interviewer.

Rigidity. In behavior, maintenance of a stiff attitude or unyielding behavior set when it is no longer appropriate.

Risk assessment. Process leading to a determination by Child Protective Services workers or law enforcement personnel about whether a child is in danger of maltreatment and needs to be removed from the home or needs protective services.

Ritalin. See *Methylphenidate.*

RLF. See *Retrolental fibroplasia.*

Roseola. Rose-colored skin rash, sometimes occurring with diseases such as measles, syphilis, or scarlet fever.

RR. Resource room.

RSA. U.S. Rehabilitation Services Administration.

RSP. See *Resource specialist program.*

RST. See *Resource specialist teacher.*

RT. Recreational therapy.

Rubella. Infectious disease that, if contracted by the mother during the first three months of pregnancy, has a high risk of causing congenital anomalies, including deafness, cataracts, cardiac malformation, and mental retardation; also known as German measles. On reaching adulthood, children with congenital rubella syndrome may have diabetes, glaucoma, endocrine pathology, and central nervous system infections.

Rubeola. Measles.

Rumination disorder. Eating disorder, characterized by repeated regurgitation and rechewing of food, that develops in an infant or child after a period of normal functioning and lasts for at least 1 month. Partially digested food is brought up into the mouth without apparent nausea, retching, disgust, or associated gastrointestinal disorder. The food is then either ejected from the mouth or, more frequently, rechewed and reswallowed.

Runaways. Youths who have left home without parental consent.

Rx. Prescription.

Saccadic movements. Jerky movements of the eyes from one fixation point to another, as while reading.

Santeria. Form of witchcraft practiced by some Cubans.

SCAN. Suspected child abuse and neglect.

Scapegoating. Casting blame for a problem on one who is innocent or only partially responsible. For example, a parent or caregiver might abuse or neglect a child as punishment for family problems unrelated to the child.

Schizophrenia. Any of a group of psychotic disorders usually characterized by withdrawal from reality, illogical patterns of thinking, delusions, and hallucinations and accompanied in varying degrees by other emotional, behavioral, or intellectual disturbances.

Schizophrenogenic. Causing or contributing to the development of schizophrenia.

School phobia. Irrational inability to attend school, usually accompanied by somatic complaints and separation issues. Often diagnosed as separation anxiety, it is the most common phobia of childhood. See also *Separation anxiety disorder.*

Scissor gait. Manner of walking in which legs cross in an "X" form.

Scotoma. Area in the visual field in which vision is absent or depressed.

Screening. (1) Use of basic, standard procedures (health, hearing, vision, developmental, and behavioral) to identify children with or at risk of disabilities. (2) Procedures used by Child Protective

Services to determine whether a report of child maltreatment should be investigated further.

Screening evaluation. Initial assessment to determine whether the interviewee has a psychological disturbance or needs special services.

Scrotum. Sac containing the testes.

Scurvy. Condition caused by a deficiency of vitamin C and characterized by weakness, anemia, spongy gums, and other symptoms.

SD. See *Standard deviation*.

SDC. See *Special day class*.

SEA. State education agency.

Sealing (legal). In juvenile court or criminal court practice, process of closing court records to inspection by all but the subject of the records.

Search and serve. See *Child Find*.

Second generation. Refers to (1) a person or persons whose parents are immigrants or (2) a person or persons whose parents are citizens by birth and whose grandparents are immigrants.

Second interview. Interview that occurs when all needed information is not obtained in the first session and the interviewer wants to pursue unclear details or resolve incongruities in interview, observational, and test findings.

Secondary enuresis. Loss of bladder control by an individual who previously had mastered it.

Secondary gains. Benefits that accrue to an individual as a function of an illness, such as increased attention from family and the medical community, reduced work load, and lowered expectations on the part of others.

Section 504. Federal statute prohibiting discrimination against individuals with disabilities by institutions receiving or benefiting from federal funds; part of the Rehabilitation Act of 1973.

SED. See *Seriously emotionally disturbed*.

Sedative. Drug that slows bodily activities, especially those of the central nervous system. It is used to reduce pain and tension and to induce relaxation and sleep.

Seizure. Disturbance in the electrical activity of the brain as a result of damage or electrolyte imbalance, characterized by involuntary motor activity or a change in consciousness or behavior. Convulsions of varying degrees of severity are caused by abnormal electrochemical discharges in the brain. See also *Grand mal seizure, Petit mal seizure, Psychomotor seizure*.

Selective attention. Ability to choose from an array of competing stimuli those that are relevant to the task or purpose at hand.

Selective migration. Movement to a new country of a large number of immigrants who are not representative of the full spectrum of citizens in their county of origin because of the specific factors, such as higher (or lower) education level, that influenced their decision to migrate.

Self-actualization. Process of fulfilling one's potential as a human being.

Self-concept. Person's sense of his or her own identity, worth, or capabilities.

Self-fulfilling prophecy. Attitude held by one person (the believer) about another person that determines how the believer interacts with that other person and eventually may lead the other person to change her or his behavior so as to reflect the believer's attitude. It also can apply to an attitude of a person about himself or herself.

Self-monitoring. Procedure in which an individual systematically observes and records aspects of his or her behavior over a speci-

fied period of time. Self-monitoring procedures may involve symptom diaries, rating scales, use of counters, daily charting, or portable monitoring devices.

Self-reference. Speech pattern in which the speaker repeatedly refers the subject under discussion back to himself or herself.

Semantic aphasia. Inability to understand the meaning of words or phrases.

Semantic (verbal) paraphasia. See *Paraphasia*.

Semantics. Study of meaning within a language.

Semicoma. See *Stupor*.

Semistructured interview. Interview in which the topics covered are specified in advance, but there is some latitude in how the questions are asked, as well as in how the questions are followed up.

Sensation. Conscious reception of information from one of the sense organs (eyes, ears, tongue, nose, or skin).

Sensorimotor. Relating to a combination of the functions of the sensory and motor activities.

Sensorineural hearing loss. Hearing impairment that is characterized by pathology in the inner ear (cochlea) or somewhere along the eighth cranial nerve and that cannot be corrected by surgery. Loss may be partial or complete. When loss is partial, there is distortion of sound, making speech discrimination difficult even with a hearing aid.

Sensory. Relating to the reception of sensation.

Sensory deprivation. Decreased sensory input from the external or internal environment.

Sensory overload. Excessive sensory experiences perceived as confusing, bothersome, meaningless, and extremely stressful.

Sentence completion technique. Interview technique used with children, in which the interviewer orally gives a sentence stem and the child finishes it—for example, "I like...."

Sentencing (legal). Last stage of criminal prosecution, in which a convicted defendant is imprisoned, fined, ordered to pay restitution, or granted a conditional release from custody. Sentencing is the equivalent of disposition in a juvenile case.

Separation anxiety. Fear experienced when a person is separated from someone on whom he or she is very dependent.

Separation anxiety disorder. Condition characterized by excessive anxiety concerning separation from the home or from those to whom the child is attached. This anxiety is beyond that expected for the child's developmental level and causes clinically significant distress or impairment in social, academic, occupational, or other important areas of functioning.

Separation distress. Form of grief in which individuals have the urge to find, recover, and reunite with a deceased loved one.

Sepsis. Serious condition resulting from overwhelming infection that spreads to the blood; also known as septicemia.

Septicemia. See *Sepsis*.

Sequential development. Step-by-step progression, wherein competency at any given stage implies having achieved competency in all earlier stages.

Seriously emotionally disturbed (SED). Individuals who have emotional problems that interfere with learning.

Service coordination. Process of harmonizing all services to meet the needs of the child and family. Formal service coordination includes analyzing strengths and needs, developing an individualized plan, coordinating services and agencies, and monitoring service delivery and progress. See also *Case management*.

SES. See *Socioeconomic status*.

Settlement (legal). Determination of a disputed matter by agreement of all parties. It sometimes requires approval by the court, resulting in a court order outlining the parties' agreement.

Severe hearing loss. Hearing loss of 61–90 decibels.

Severe malingering. Overwhelming pattern of fabrication of symptoms. The interviewee may appear severely disturbed, produce rare and improbable symptoms, or manifest symptoms uncorroborated by clinical observations.

Severe mental retardation. See *Mental retardation.*

Severely handicapped (SH). People who are seriously emotionally disturbed, developmentally handicapped, trainable mentally retarded, or autistic.

Sex-linked characteristics. Inherited traits carried by the genes of the X and Y chromosomes.

Sexual abuse, child. Form of child maltreatment that includes a wide range of conduct including genital exposure; masturbation between adult and child; fondling of breasts, genitals, buttocks, and thighs; oral copulation; vaginal or anal penetration by finger, penis, or foreign object; dry intercourse (rubbing the penis between the child's thighs or on anal-genital areas); forcing the child to fondle an adult; and commercial exploitation of the child through prostitution or the production of pornographic materials.

Sexual assault. Unlawful actions of a sexual nature committed against persons forcibly and usually against their will; criminal sexual conduct. Various degrees of sexual assault are established by state law and distinguished by the age of the perpetrator in relationship to the victim, the amount of force used, and the type of sexual contact or conduct.

Sexual exploitation. Involvement of children and adolescents in sexual activities that they do not usually fully comprehend, that they are unable to give informed consent to, and that violate social taboos.

Sexually transmitted disease (STD). See *Venereal disease.*

SGA. See *Small for gestational age.*

SH. See *Severely handicapped.*

Shaken baby syndrome. See *Whiplash-shaken infant syndrome.*

Shaping. Form of operant conditioning that begins with reinforcing all responses similar to the desired one, then reinforces only successively closer approximations until the desired response is attained.

Shearing. Tearing of nerve fibers in the brain at the microscopic level because of movement of the brain during a head injury.

Sheltered workshop. Facility that provides occupational training or protective employment for handicapped, retarded, or disturbed individuals.

Shifts in conversation. Abrupt changes in topic.

Shopping for diagnosis. Behavior of parents who visit several professionals in the hope of obtaining a diagnosis that is acceptable to them.

Short-term memory. Temporary retention of information (usually 30–60 seconds).

Show cause (legal). See *Order to show cause.*

Shuffle. To slide the feet along the floor or ground while walking.

Shunt. Tube used to divert fluid from one place to another. A shunt is commonly used to treat hydrocephalus.

Sickle cell anemia. Hereditary disorder, governed by a recessive gene, that causes red blood cells to assume a sickle shape, with resultant obstruction of capillaries.

SIDS. See *Sudden infant death syndrome.*

Sign language. Natural or formal hand-signing system, through which units of thought can be communicated.

Silence. Period of time without speech or noise. On the part of the interviewee, it may indicate resentment at being at the interview, fear, or not knowing what to say. The interviewer may use it as a probing technique, to allow the interviewee more time to reflect or think, or to communicate that he or she expects more of the interviewee.

Singer. In traditional Native American culture, healer who performs or directs healing ceremonies.

Single photon emission computed tomography (SPECT). Medical procedure that provides a three-dimensional representation of regional cerebral blood flow. SPECT brings together tomographic techniques for imaging brain structure with methods for measuring brain blood flow.

Situation. In behavioral assessment, circumstances under which the behavior occurs.

Situational bias. Unreliability arising from the interview setting itself. It may result from external noise, delay in starting the interview, the location of the interview, the time of the interview, the chance assignment of an interviewee to an interviewer, or temporary fluctuations in the behavior of the interviewer and interviewee.

Situational child abuse and neglect. Instances of child maltreatment—particularly of child neglect—in which the major causative factors cannot be readily eliminated because they relate to problems over which the parents have little control, such as limited or no income.

Skin scraping. See *Coining.*

Slander. Verbal defamation. See also *Libel.*

SLD. See *Specific learning disability.*

Sleep bruxism. Sleep disorder characterized by grinding or clenching of the teeth during sleep. Bruxism may cause dental problems, such as abnormal wear of the teeth or periodontal tissue damage, and may be related to headaches or jaw pain.

Sleep enuresis. Sleep disorder, characterized by bedwetting, that affects approximately 5% to 17% of children 3 to 15 years old; also referred to as nocturnal enuresis. There are two subtypes: primary, where the child has always wet the bed, and secondary, where the child has learned bladder control but then loses control.

Sleep-onset association disorder. Sleep disorder in children in which the onset of sleep is impaired by the absence of a certain set of objects or circumstances, such as a bottle or pacifier or being rocked to sleep. When these objects or circumstances are present, sleep is normal.

Sleep terrors. Sleep disorder in children characterized by a sudden arousal from slow wave sleep with a piercing scream or cry, accompanied by autonomic and behavioral manifestations of intense fear. The children are often amnesic for the arousal period.

Sleepwalking. Sleep disorder characterized by behavior that ranges from simply sitting up in bed to walking while asleep. Children are often difficult to awaken and, on wakening, appear confused.

Slight hearing loss. Hearing loss of less than 20 decibels.

Slow learner. Child who is performing below grade level.

Slow-to-warm-up child. Child who is low in activity level, approach tendency, and adaptability; variable in rhythm; and somewhat negative.

SMA. See *Spinal muscular atrophy.*

Small for gestational age (SGA). Refers to any infant whose weight falls below the tenth percentile for gestational age, whether premature, full-term, or postmature. Despite her or his small size, a full-term SGA infant does not have the problems related to organ system immaturity that the premature infant has.

SNF. Skilled nursing facility.

SOBRA. Sixth Omnibus Budget Reconciliation Act.

Social class. Society-wide group defined by employment status, family income, or education.

Social history. Information compiled by a human services worker about an individual and his or her family.

Social isolation. Condition in which families have limited contact with relatives, friends, and community resources.

Social learning and interaction theory. Proposition that intrafamilial violence results from psychosocial interaction processes within the family and between the family and its social environment.

Social phobia. Disorder characterized by clinically significant anxiety provoked by exposure to certain types of social or performance situations, often leading to avoidance behavior.

Social quotient (SQ). Index of a person's ability to look after his or her own needs and to take responsibility for himself or herself.

Social stage of substance abuse. Second stage of substance abuse, in which the primary motivation for using the substance is social acceptance, although curiosity, thrill-seeking, and defiance also may play a role.

Societal child abuse and neglect. Failure of a society to provide social policies or funding to support the well-being of all families and children or to provide sufficient resources to prevent and treat child abuse and neglect.

Socioeconomic status (SES). Individual's position in a given society as determined by wealth, occupation, and social class.

Sociogram. Diagram depicting preferred or actual interactions among members of a given group.

Sociometric. Pertaining to a technique for assessing the degree to which an individual is liked or respected by his or her peers.

Sociometry. Quantitative method for determining and describing the pattern of acceptances and rejections in a group of people.

Sodomy. Anal intercourse. The term is used in some state statutes to cover unconventional sex in general.

Soft neurological signs. Symptoms associated with deficiencies in complex behaviors that are considered uncertain indicators of brain damage. Representative soft neurological signs are poor balance, impaired fine motor coordination, clumsiness, slight reflex asymmetries, and choreiform (irregular, jerky) limb movements.

Soft signs of brain damage. Symptoms suggestive of mild and equivocal neurological irregularities or developmental immaturities in sensorimotor functions.

Sole legal custody. Custodial arrangement in which one parent has all the rights and responsibilities to make the decisions regarding the health, education, and welfare of a child.

Sole physical custody. Custodial arrangement in which a child resides primarily with one parent, with specific visitation rights by the other parent.

Somatosensory. Pertaining to bodily sensations, including those of touch, pain, pressure, and temperature.

Sound blending. Ability to integrate separate word sounds into a meaningful whole.

Space perception. Awareness of the spatial properties of an object, including position, direction, size, form, and distance.

Spasm. Sudden involuntary contraction in the muscles or blood vessels that disrupts function.

Spastic. Characterized by sudden, violent, involuntary contractions of a muscle or a group of muscles, attended by pain and interference with function, producing involuntary movement and distortion.

Spastic gait. Manner of walking in which a person holds her or his legs together while flexing hip and knee joints; choppy and stiff walk.

Spasticity. State of increased tension in a muscle; heightened resistance to the extension or flexion of a joint.

Special class. See *Special day class.*

Special class approach. Intervention alternative for exceptional children that involves the placement of children with similar instructional needs in a special class.

Special day class (SDC). Special education class in which a student with special needs is enrolled for the majority of the school day; also known as special class.

Special education. Education provided to children whose abilities (physical, mental, and social) and learning styles require alternative teaching methods or related support services to enable them to benefit from the education program.

Special needs adoption. Adoption of a child with a disability or special health care need. Usually, public financial assistance is available to help the adopting family meet the child's needs.

Special needs child. Child who has a disability or health condition that requires special care and supportive services.

Specific language disability. Disorder of children with adequate intelligence who have difficulty in learning to read, write, spell, or communicate.

Specific learning disability (SLD). Disorder in one or more of the basic psychological processes involved in understanding or using language, spoken or written. It may manifest itself in an imperfect ability to listen, think, speak, read, write, spell, or do mathematical calculations.

Specific phobia. Disorder characterized by clinically significant anxiety provoked by exposure to a specific feared object or situation, often leading to avoidance behavior.

SPECT. See *Single photon emission computed tomography.*

Speech. Mechanical production and molding of human sound into words, using the muscles of the chest, throat, and mouth. It involves breathing, voicing, resonation, and rhythm.

Speech and language therapy. Treatment of difficulties affecting the voice or production of spoken and written communication. It is designed to improve communication skills of children with language or speech impairments arising from physiological difficulties in articulation or dialect.

Spermatozoa. Mature male reproductive cells.

Spina bifida. Developmental anomaly characterized by defective closure of the bony encasement of the spinal cord, through which the cord and meninges may or may not protrude, and often associated with lower body paralysis; also known as myelomeningocele or meningomyelocele. It results in mild to severe mental retardation in about 25% of the cases.

Spinal muscular atrophy (SMA). Degenerative disease of the nerves that control muscles, causing generalized weakness and decreased muscular activity of varying degrees of severity.

Split custody. Custodial arrangement in which each parent has physical custody of at least one child of the marriage and specific visitation rights with the other child or children.

Spontaneous reproduction (in Statement Validity Analysis). Voluntary, impulsive, and somewhat disorganized account, which does not have a rigid feel or an overly strict chronology. In retelling the account, the child may drop out some peripheral details and add new ones. A fabricated account, in contrast, is likely to have a more rigid structure and be repeated in the same fashion a second time. However, if the child makes the same disclosure many times, even a credible account is unlikely to appear spontaneous.

Spooning. Traditional healing procedure, used by Asians, that involves applying salt solution or water to the back, neck, shoulders, chest, or forehead; pinching or massaging the area until it reddens; and then scratching the area with a porcelain spoon until bruises appear.

Spousal abuse. Nonaccidental physical or psychological injury inflicted on either the husband or the wife by the marital partner.

SQ. See *Social quotient.*

Squirming. Engaging in wriggling movements; shifting restlessly in one's chair.

SSA. Social Security Administration.

SSDI. Social Security Disability Income.

SSI. Supplemental Security Income.

ST. Speech therapy.

Standard deviation (SD). Measure of the variability or dispersion of a distribution of scores, based on the square of the deviation of each score from the mean. The SD is sometimes called "sigma" and represented by the symbol σ.

Standard of proof (legal). Burden of proof that a party must satisfy in order to prevail in a particular type of case. See also *Clear and convincing evidence, Preponderance of evidence, Proof beyond a reasonable doubt.*

Stare decisis. Let the decision stand; to abide by or adhere to decided cases; policy of courts of following previously established precedent. A court establishes legal doctrines to apply to a certain body of facts, and it will generally follow the same principles in subsequent cases where the controlling facts are similar.

Statement Validity Analysis. Procedure designed for examining case material and the content of the interview in cases of child maltreatment. It has five parts: careful analysis of relevant information; a semistructured interview that stresses rapport building, open-ended questions, and follow-up questions as needed; criteria-based content analysis, which focuses on analyzing the child's statements in order to distinguish statements about actually experienced events from those based on fantasy, fiction, or coercion; application of validity checks to the child's statements; and systematic summarization of the content analysis and validity checks.

Status offender. Minor who has committed an act that would not be a crime if committed by an adult but is illegal under the laws of the state, such as truancy, running away from home, or being beyond the reasonable control of his or her parents.

Status offense. Act prohibited by law only when it is committed by a person of a particular status, such as a minor. Because of the person's condition, age, or character, the act is prohibited; if an "ordinary" adult did the same thing, it would *not* be an offense.

Statute (legal). Law established by a legislature.

Statute of limitation. Statute specifying the time within which a lawsuit must be initiated. After the time expires, the claimant is forever barred from bringing the action.

Statutory right. Right based on a statute passed by a unit of federal, state, or local government.

Stay (legal). To stop, hold, or restrain; to suspend a case or part of it.

STD. Sexually transmitted disease. See also *Venereal disease.*

Steppage. High-stepping gait in which the thigh is raised very high and the toes slap down before the rest of the foot.

Stereognosis. Ability to perceive and understand objects or forms by touch.

Stereotypic movements. Repeated movements that are not goal directed.

Steroid hormones. Group of hormones including testosterone, estrogen, progesterone, and corticosteroids.

Stigma. Mark of disgrace; feeling of being devalued or unable to meet minimum societal norms.

Stilted speech. Speech that has an excessively formal quality, seems quaint or outdated, or appears pompous, distant, or overly polite.

Stimulant. Drug that increases alertness and motor activity and, at the same time, reduces fatigue, allowing an individual to remain awake for an extended period of time. It can cause weight loss, increased respiration and heart rate, blurred vision, and anxiety when snorted, injected, smoked, or swallowed in capsule, tablet, or pill form.

Stimulant pharmacotherapy. Type of therapy that involves the use of stimulant drugs, such as Ritalin or Dexedrine, to help children with attention-deficit/hyperactivity disorder.

Stipulate (legal). To agree.

Stipulation (legal). Statement, either oral or written, that establishes certain facts agreed on by all parties in a court case.

Stock phrases. Stereotyped expressions of more or less common use that are employed as pet responses, often out of context.

Story completion technique. Interview technique used with children, in which the interviewer begins a sentence and asks the child to complete the sentence.

Strabismus. Failure of the eyes to focus properly on the same points, leading to a squint, cross-eye, or wall-eye.

Strauss syndrome. Cluster of symptoms, including hyperactivity, distractibility, and impulsivity, characterizing a type of brain-injured child.

Street youths. Youths who have left home with the knowledge of their parents or guardians.

Strephosymbolia. Reading difficulty involving reversal in perception of left-right order, especially in letters or words—for example, the use of *was* for *saw;* sometimes called twisted symbols.

Strict construction (legal). Interpreting laws narrowly so that the letter of the law is followed; using little or no leeway in interpreting the law.

Structured interview. Interview in which the topics and questions and their order are predetermined.

Structuring statements. Comments that help move the interviewee to a desired topic.

Stupor. Condition similar to a coma but less severe, in which the individual shows loss of orientation and minimum activity and is inaccessible to stimuli, though not unconscious; also known as semicoma.

Stuttering. Speech impediment characterized by hesitations, rapid repetition of elements, and breathing or vocal muscle spasm.

Subarachnoid hemorrhage. Hemorrhage located between the outer connective tissue and the brain.

Subaverage intellectual functioning. Level of mental performance indicated by a score of 70 to 75 or below on an individually administered intelligence test.

Subconjunctival. Situated or occurring beneath the conjunctiva, which is the delicate membrane that lines the eyelids and covers the eyeball. Hemorrhages may be subconjunctival.

Subcortical. Beneath the cortex.

Subdural hematoma. Blood clot between the outer and inner linings of the brain. In cases of child maltreatment, the hematoma may be caused by a blow to the head or by shaking a baby or small child.

Subgaleal. Located on the inner lining of the scalp. Subgaleal hemorrhage is frequently secondary to hair pulling.

Subjugation orientation. Cultural belief that people are subject to natural forces that cannot be controlled.

Subjunctive mood. Hypothetical form that may be useful in getting an uncooperative child to speak, such as "Suppose you were…," "What if you…," or "Let's pretend that…."

Subpoena. Document issued by a court requiring a person to appear at a certain time to give testimony in a specified case. Failure to obey a subpoena may subject the person to contempt proceedings.

Subpoena duces tecum. Under penalty you shall bring with you; document requiring a person to bring specified records in his or her control or possession to the court.

Substance abuse. Use of alcohol or drugs that results in adverse effects on the user. Substance abuse is a major health and social problem in the United States among adolescents. See also specific stages of substance abuse.

Substantiated (legal). Determined to be supported by credible evidence; also known as founded. An allegation of abuse or neglect may or may not be substantiated.

Substantive right. Right usually granted by statutes and constitutions, such as the right to an education.

Substitute care. Means of meeting children's daily caretaking and developmental needs outside their home.

Substitute parents. Adults who agree to provide substitute care for a child in their home, either formally or informally and on a temporary or long-term basis.

Sudden infant death syndrome (SIDS). Sudden, unexpected death of an infant or young child, for which no apparent cause can be determined; also known as crib death. Death often occurs during sleep.

Summary judgment (legal). Decision made by a trial court based on written documentation submitted before any trial occurs. Summary judgments can be granted only when there are no genuine issues of material fact.

Summons (legal). Document issued by a court clerk and usually delivered by a process server or law enforcement officer, notifying a person of the filing of a lawsuit against him or her and of the deadline for answering the suit. In criminal matters, a summons includes a copy of the complaint against the defendant and requires the person summoned to attend court. If the defendant fails to appear in court, an arrest warrant is issued.

Supervised visitation. Arrangement under which a court allows a parent to visit a child only in the presence of a designated third person.

Supportive family. In cases of maltreatment, family that is loyal to the child, shows positive regard and concern, and does not blame the child for the maltreatment.

Survey research interview. Interview conducted to learn about the attitudes and opinions of the interviewee about a topic. The interviewer initiates the interview and encourages the interviewee to reply only to the questions asked. The consequences for the interviewee are minimal.

Susto. Ailment, treated by Mexican American traditional healers, that results from a frightening experience associated with a stressful event or traumatic experience. It is believed that a person's soul or spirit leaves the body. Symptoms include restlessness during sleep, anorexia, depression, listlessness, and disinterest in personal appearance.

Syllabication. Word-attack skill consisting of breaking a word down into its syllables.

Symbiotic infantile psychosis. Severe childhood mental disorder that appears when the child is threatened with separation from the mother.

Syndrome. Constellation of symptoms and signs that, when occurring together, characterize a particular disorder or disease.

Synkinesia. Involuntary and useless movements accompanying a voluntary movement.

Syntactic. Pertaining to grammar and the rules governing sentence structure and sequence.

Syntactic errors. Unconventional ordering of words—for example, "My house, well, I live in, well, my house, uh, I live in" for "I live in my house."

Syntax. System of rules defining the ways in which different parts of speech may be legitimately combined to form sentences.

Syphilis. Sexually transmitted bacterial infection that may result in central nervous system abnormalities, including hearing loss, vestibular dysfunction, and heart conditions. Mental retardation also may result, depending on the severity of the neurologic damage.

System kids. Youths who leave social service placements.

Systematic desensitization. Procedure used to teach individuals to relax or to behave in ways that are inconsistent with anxiety.

TA. Technical assistance.

Tactile. Pertaining to the sense of touch.

Tactile agnosia. Impaired ability to identify, without looking, familiar objects placed in the hand.

Tactile-kinesthetic. Combining sensory impressions of touch and muscle movement.

Tactile perception. Interpreting and giving meaning to stimuli that are experienced through the sense of touch.

TANF. Temporary Aid to Needy Families. Public Law 104-193 passed by Congress in 1996 to replace Aid to Families with Dependent Children (AFDC). It provides fixed block grants to states to help them establish programs for needy children and families, conditioned in part on requirements that recipients of the aid obtain work.

Tangentiality. Replying to questions or statements in an oblique or even irrelevant way—for example, picking up the blue car and saying "car" when asked to pick up the blue notebook.

Taoism. Chinese religion and philosophy that maintains that people have no control over nature and therefore must adjust to the physical world and not attempt to change it.

Target behavior. In the behavioral view, specific and explicitly described observable behavior to be changed.

Task analysis. Examination and description of an instructional task to determine its component parts or steps.

Tay-Sachs disease. Disorder of lipoid metabolism, caused by a recessive gene, that results in a progressive degenerative disease characterized by severe mental retardation, seizures, paralysis, and death.

TDD. Telecommunications device for the deaf.

Tech Act. Technology Related Assistance for Individuals with Disabilities Act.

TEFRA. Tax Equity and Fiscal Responsibility Act.

Telegraphic speech. Utterances that contain a subject, main verb, and object, but no function words or other "small" words—for example, "I got tricycle" for "I've got a tricycle."

Temperament. Style in which infants (or any individuals) react to their environment.

Temporal. (1) Pertaining to time or time relationships. (2) Pertaining to or near the temples of the skull.

Temporal lobe. One of the four lobes making up the cerebral cortex; lobe responsible for processing information from the auditory system. It is closely associated with the limbic system, which has a variety of functions, including regulation of hormones and memory.

Temporal lobectomy. Surgical excision of a temporal lobe.

Temporary placement. Voluntary or involuntary short-term placement of a child outside his or her own home, primarily when a child's safety or well-being is threatened or endangered or when a family crisis can be averted by such action.

Temporary restraining order (TRO) (legal). Emergency remedy of brief duration, issued by a court under exceptional circumstances, to protect a potential victim from the alleged behavior of another person until a hearing can be held on the matter.

Tender years doctrine. Outmoded presumption that custody of children of "tender years" (usually under 7 years old) should automatically be awarded to the mother.

Tension headaches. Headaches believed to result from a sustained level of tension in the skeletal muscles. These headaches often occur after prolonged stress. The pain is typically described as a feeling of tightness, pressure, or constriction of the skull.

Teratogens. Agents in the environment of a developing embryo and fetus that can cause structural and functional abnormalities. Examples include alcohol, radiation, pathogens causing intrauterine infection, drugs and environmental chemicals, and untreated maternal metabolic imbalances like PKU.

Termination of parental rights. Ending of the rights of a parent because the parent has failed to provide proper care for a child, abandoned the child, physically or sexually abused the child, or failed to cooperate with a proposed case plan designed to reunify the parent and child. If a court, after trial, determines that neither parent can provide the proper care and support for the child in the foreseeable future, the court may terminate parental rights and grant permanent custody to either a relative or an appropriate state agency, which may assume custody for purposes of adoptive placement.

Test. Series of questions, problems, or physical responses designed to determine knowledge, intelligence, or ability.

Test anxiety. Individual's feeling of fear or great concern that he or she will not do well on a test.

Test-retest reliability. Degree to which scores correlate when the same test is administered to the same group of examinees on two different occasions.

Testes. Male sex organs that produce spermatozoa.

Testimony (legal). Statements made by a witness, usually under oath in court. See also *Expert testimony*.

Theory of conflict-prone institution. Proposition that family structures and family norms that foster conflict may encourage violence within families.

Thorazine. Chlorpromazine; major tranquilizer, often used in the treatment of psychosis, that decreases autonomic and motor activity, attention span, and anxiety.

Thought disorder. Impaired thinking in psychotic individuals.

Three wishes technique. Interview technique used with children, in which the interviewer asks the child to state three wishes.

Threshold of responsiveness. In infants, amount of stimulation, such as sound or light, necessary to evoke discernible responses. An infant with a good threshold of responsiveness adjusts well to noises, textures of clothing, heat, cold, and environmental sounds such as the telephone and a siren.

Throwaways. Youths who have been thrown out of their homes.

Tic. Nervous twitching that cannot be voluntarily controlled, especially small, stereotyped movements of the face or voice.

Time. In behavioral assessment, when the behavior occurs.

Timing questions. Interjecting queries and comments at appropriate moments so that they are in harmony with the flow of thoughts of the interviewee.

Tinnitus. Ringing in the ears and other head noises caused by physiological activities in the sensory mechanism, in the absence of any corresponding external stimulus. It frequently follows exposure to a loud sound.

TMR/TMH. See *Trainable mentally retarded/trainable mentally handicapped*.

Token economy. Behavior modification system under which artificial rewards given for socially desirable behavior can be exchanged for desired objects and activities.

Token reinforcement. Use of objects, such as poker chips, stars, or check marks, to reinforce target behaviors, such as completion of assigned work, use of manners, and proper grooming.

Toluidine blue dye. Chemical put on the genitals to highlight injuries not visible to the naked eye. It is used in cases of child sexual maltreatment.

Tonic. Pertaining to a continuing slight stretching usually present in muscles when they are not in active movement.

Tonic phase. In seizures, unremitting muscular contraction.

Topical or referential identification problems. Difficulties in selecting the appropriate referent, such as the topic, in a conversation—for example, responding "My desk is clean" when asked "Did you put the book on my desk?"

Tort (legal). Any legally recognized private injury or wrong that does not arise out of a breach of contract.

Total communication approach. Method of teaching communication skills to the deaf that involves the combining of manual signs and oral language.

Toxemia. Any condition of blood poisoning, especially that caused by bacterial toxins transported through the bloodstream from a focus of infection.

Toxicity. Quality of being poisonous.

Toxoplasmosis, maternal. Parasitic infection transmitted by pregnant women to developing fetuses. Symptoms include blindness, central nervous system damage, jaundice, hydrocephalus, and mental retardation.

TPN. Total parental nutrition.

TPR. See *Termination of parental rights*.

Tracheotomy. Surgical procedure in which an external entrance to the airway (windpipe) is created through the neck to aid breathing.

Tracking. In education, placing pupils into ability levels, or "tracks," for the purpose of instruction.

Traditionalism. Form of acculturation in which individuals maintain and practice mainly the traditions of their culture of origin.

Trainable mentally retarded/trainable mentally handicapped (TMR/TMH). Individuals with severe mental disabilities who may require assistance with personal activities such as feeding, toileting, and grooming, as well as with motor or social development. IQ is in the 30 to 50 range.

Trait. Physical, mental, or behavioral characteristic that distinguishes one person from another.

Transcript (legal). Verbatim copy of the record of a trial or hearing.

Transdisciplinary team. See *Multidisciplinary team.*

Transfer. Shifting information, skills, or strategies learned in one situation to a new situation.

Transfer anxiety. Increased anxiety and feelings of insecurity experienced by children with special needs when they are moved from one unit of a facility to another.

Transition services. Assistance provided to a child who is moving from one program to another. Major transitions include moving from the hospital to home, from early intervention to preschool, from preschool to school, and from high school to employment, postsecondary education, adult services, or community activities.

Transition words. In report writing, words that provide continuity, including time links (*then, next, after, while, since*), cause-effect links (*therefore, consequently, as a result*), addition links (*in addition, moreover, furthermore, similarly*), and contrast links (*however, but, conversely, nevertheless, although, whereas*).

Transitional acculturation. Form of acculturation in which individuals partake of both the old and the new culture but question basic traditional values, as well as those of the new culture.

Transitional living programs. Programs in various settings, such as small group homes, rehabilitation hospitals, and outpatient centers, that prepare a disabled person for maximum independence in activities of daily living.

Transitional period. In acculturation, period during which an individual partakes of both the old and the new culture but questions basic traditional values and also those of the new culture.

Trauma. Wound or injury, either mental or physical, that inflicts serious damage on the individual.

Traumatic brain injury. Injury to the brain that is a result of some trauma, such as a gunshot or missile wound or a blow to the head.

Treatment, medical. Medical or surgical procedure(s) designed to improve or correct a physical condition.

Tremor. Continual, uncontrollable, and involuntary rhythmic muscular motion. An intention tremor may occur when a brain-injured patient reaches for an object; it increases as movement continues and may affect arms, hands, legs, and feet. A postural tremor may occur when a brain-injured patient holds a limb, such as an arm or leg, in a fixed position. A resting tremor may occur when a brain-injured patient is relaxed and not moving fingers, hands, proximal portions of arms or legs, or the head trunk; it may decrease or disappear when the body part is moved.

Trial. Judicial examination and determination of issues of law and fact disputed by parties to a lawsuit.

Trial court. Local court that initially hears all cases in dispute. If an attorney or party believes that a trial court judge has exceeded judicial authority or inappropriately applied the law, an appeal can be made to the appeals court.

Trichomonas vaginalis. Sexually transmitted disease caused by a single-cell protozoan.

Triplegia. Paralysis of three extremities, most often both legs and one arm.

Trisomy. In genetics, having three homologous chromosomes per cell instead of two.

Trisomy 13. Trisomy of the 13th chromosome; also known as Patau's syndrome. Symptoms include failure to thrive, mental retardation, and various other defects.

Trisomy 18. Trisomy of the 18th chromosome; also known as Edward's syndrome. Symptoms include mental retardation, serious deformities, failure to thrive, and hypertonia. Death occurs early, often within the first year of life.

Trisomy 21. See *Down syndrome.*

TRO. See *Temporary restraining order.*

Tuberous sclerosis. Congenital familial disease characterized by tumors on the surfaces of parts of the brain and marked by progressive mental deterioration and seizures.

Tumor. Abnormal growth of tissue in which cell multiplication is uncontrolled and progressive; also known as neoplasm.

Twenty-four-hour recall interview. Interview in which the interviewee is asked to focus on the specific behaviors she or he engaged in during the preceding 24 hours. The interview focuses on the period beginning when the interviewee woke up and ending when the interviewee went to bed.

Twisted symbols. See *Strephosymbolia.*

Tx. Treatment.

Type I diabetes. See *Insulin-dependent diabetes mellitus of childhood.*

Type II diabetes. See *Noninsulin-dependent diabetes mellitus.*

UAP/UAF. University affiliated program/university affiliated facilities.

UCP. United Cerebral Palsy Association.

Ultrasound. Medical procedure in which sound waves are used to obtain images.

Underachievement. Performance below that predicted by an aptitude measurement.

Underarousal. Level of arousal below what is expected.

Underproductive speech. Monosyllabic speech characteristic of individuals who fail to answer questions, need to be pressured for answers, and fail to elaborate their responses.

Understanding. In interviews, possession of a knowledgeable, helpful, and empathic attitude. A good interviewer conveys understanding to the interviewee.

Undocumented immigrant. See *Illegal immigrant.*

Undue influence. Any wrongful insistence, maneuvering, or threats used by one person to overpower the free will of another and coerce him or her to perform acts against his or her own wishes.

Unfounded report. In child maltreatment, any report of suspected abuse or neglect that the mandated agency is unable to substantiate upon investigation.

Unilateral. Pertaining to one side only.

Unintelligible speech. Speech characterized by a lack of recognizable words, babbling, or jargon.

Unresponsive. Failing to produce a reaction or producing an inadequate or delayed reaction in the presence of stimuli that usually elicit a reaction.

Unspontaneous behavior. Behavior characterized by failure to initiate or sustain social or verbal interchange, lack of spontaneity, and inhibition.

Unstructured interview. Interview in which the topics covered are unspecified at the outset and are dependent on the unfolding interaction between the interviewer and interviewee.

Unsubstantiated (legal). Determined not to be supported by credible evidence; also known as unfounded. When an allegation of abuse or neglect is unsubstantiated, some states say that it is denied or unsupported.

Urethra. Canal through which urine is discharged from the bladder.

Urethritis. Inflammation of the urethra.

URI. Upper respiratory infection.

USC. United States Code; official compilation of the laws enacted by the United States Congress.

Uterus. Reproductive organ composed of the cervix, corpus, and fundus.

UTI. Urinary tract infection.

Vacate (legal). To rescind a decree or judgment.

Vagina. Tubular anatomical structure that stretches from the hymen to the cervix.

Vaginitis. Inflammation of the vagina.

Validity. Extent to which an instrument or procedure, such as a test, interview, or observation, actually measures what it purports to measure. Concurrent validity measures the extent to which interview information corresponds to that obtained through other methods, and predictive validity measures the degree to which interview information predicts either the treatment plan or the treatment outcome.

Validity checks (in Statement Validity Analysis). Procedure whereby the interviewer evaluates and weighs all the material to arrive at an estimate of the credibility of the child's allegation of maltreatment.

Variability. Spread, or dispersion, of test scores around their average value, best indicated by their standard deviation.

Vas deferens. Tube that transports the sperm from each testis to the urethra.

Vascular. Relating to the body's blood vessels (arteries, veins, capillaries).

Venereal disease. Any disease transmitted by sexual contact; also known as sexually transmitted disease or STD. The two most common forms are gonorrhea and syphilis. Presence of a venereal disease in a child may indicate that the mother was infected with the disease during pregnancy or that the child was sexually maltreated.

Ventricular septal defect (VSD). Defect or small opening between the walls of the right and left ventricle (the lower pumping chambers of the heart). Symptoms and treatment depend on the severity of the defect.

Venue (legal). Particular district, county, or state where a case may be heard and decided. Determination of where a child maltreatment case may be initiated is based on such factors as where the parents reside, where the child resides, and where the child is found.

Verbal abuse. Particular form of emotional maltreatment characterized by constant verbal harassment and denigration.

Verbal expression. Use of words to convey a thought, feeling, or experience.

Verdict (legal). Decision by a judge or a jury in favor of one side or the other in a case.

Verification of maltreatment. Finding that maltreatment occurred, following an investigation of a suspected case by mandated agency workers or law enforcement officers.

Vertigo. Illusion of movement; dizziness. An individual may sense that the external world is revolving around him or her or that he or she is revolving in space.

Very low birthweight (VLBW). Weight of less than 1,000 grams (slightly more than 2 pounds) at birth.

VH. See *Visually handicapped.*

VI. Visually impaired. See also *Visually handicapped.*

Violent-antisocial domestic violence batterers. Abusers who engage in moderate to severe marital violence, may have a history of extrafamilial aggression, and may have an antisocial personality disorder.

Visa overstayer. Noncitizen who enters the country on a visa that allows him or her to stay for a limited period of time and then overstays that limit. See also *Illegal immigrant, Undocumented immigrant.*

Vision screening. Sampling of visual skills for the purpose of assessing visual problems.

Visitation rights. Permission to visit children, granted by the court to parents and other persons having an interest in the welfare of the child, including but not limited to grandparents, stepparents, and other relatives.

Visual accommodation. See *Accommodation, visual.*

Visual acuity. Clarity or sharpness of vision.

Visual agnosia. Impaired ability to recognize familiar objects by sight.

Visual closure. Identification of a visual stimulus from an incomplete visual presentation.

Visual discrimination. Ability to recognize differences among visual stimuli.

Visual evoked potential. Brain waves generated by nerve impulses to the cortex in response to visual stimuli.

Visual field. The area a person can see at a given time with one eye without moving that eye.

Visual field defects. Difficulty in seeing parts of the visual field. See also *Visual field restriction.*

Visual field restriction. Condition of impaired peripheral vision in which the field of vision subtends an angle no greater than 20 degrees. See also *Visual field defects.*

Visual impairment. Difficulty with vision, but not to the point of being blind.

Visual-motor coordination. Ability to perform skills involving visual perception and an integrated motor response. It often involves spatial relations and tactile perception.

Visual motor memory. Ability to reproduce by drawing previously seen objects or designs.

Visual perception. Identification, organization, and interpretation of visual stimuli.

Visual sequential memory. Ability to reproduce sequences of visual items from memory.

Visual-spatial agnosia. Impaired ability to follow directions, to understand spatial details such as left-right positions or the floor plan of a house, and to understand other types of visual-spatial factors.

Visually handicapped (VH). Individuals whose visual impairment, even with correction, adversely affects educational performance; also known as visually impaired (VI). This includes blind and low vision students.

Visually impaired (VI). See *Visually handicapped.*

Visuoconstructional skills. Skills involving use of vision to build or construct objects.

Vital signs (VS). Indicators of life, such as respiratory rate, heartbeat, pulse, blood pressure, and eye responses.

VLBW. See *Very low birthweight.*

Vocal inflection. Changes in the pitch of the voice to give additional emotion or meaning to words or sentences.

Voir dire. To speak the truth. (1) Procedure whereby lawyers question prospective jurors to determine their biases, competency, and interests. (2) Procedure whereby the court or lawyers question witnesses regarding their interests, qualifications, etc., before they give testimony.

Voluntary placement. In child custody, act of the parent whereby he or she relinquishes custody of the child without a formal court proceeding.

Voodoo. Type of traditional medicine and religion, practiced mainly in Caribbean countries, that involves the use of magic in rituals.

VR. Vocational rehabilitation.

VS. See *Vital signs.*

VSD. See *Ventricular septal defect.*

Vulvitis. Inflammation of the labia.

Waddling gait. Short, wide-based steps, resulting in swaying from side to side.

Waiver. Intentional and voluntary relinquishment of a known right.

Wanton (legal). Characterized by reckless disregard of consequences and the safety and welfare of others; malicious or immoral; undisciplined, unruly, or unjustified.

Ward of the court. Person (such as a minor child or someone who is psychotic) who, by reason of incapacity, is under protection of a court either directly or through a guardian appointed by the court.

Warrant (legal). Document issued by a judge, authorizing a peace officer to arrest or detain a person or search a place and seize specified items in that place. The judge must be given probable cause to believe that a crime has occurred and that the warrant is necessary for the apprehension of a criminal or to obtain evidence of a crime.

Whiplash-shaken infant syndrome. Injury to an infant or child that results from the child's being shaken, usually as a misguided means of discipline; also known as shaken baby syndrome. The most common symptoms, which can be inflicted by seemingly harmless shaking, are bleeding inside the head, detached retinas, and other bleeding. Shaking and the resultant injuries may cause mental and developmental disabilities and death.

White matter. Those parts of the brain or spinal cord that are very light gray because they are primarily communication tracts containing myelin, which is white.

Whole word reading ability. Ability to recognize words based on their visual features.

Why questions. Queries that begin with "why." The interviewee may react defensively to such questions because they are perceived as a request to explain or justify his or her behavior. Why questions should be avoided; questions should be rephrased without the use of the word "why."

WIC. Women, Infants, and Children Program.

Widening the circle of inquiry. Branching out, by an interviewer, from the topic being discussed to obtain additional information.

Willful (legal). Carried out with voluntary intent, not carelessly or inadvertently.

Withdrawal tendency. In infants, negative initial responses to new stimuli, including people, situations, places, foods, toys, and procedures.

Withdrawn behavior. Behavior characterized by preoccupation, avoidance of eye contact, aloofness, mechanical responsiveness, and limited or no sustained emotional relatedness.

Withholding of medically indicated treatment. Failure to respond to an individual's life-threatening condition by providing treatment that, in the treating physician's judgment, will most likely be effective in improving or correcting the condition.

Witness (legal). Person whose declaration under oath is received as evidence for any purpose. See also *Expert witness.*

Wood's Lamp. Light source used by physicians to detect various substances, including semen stains. It may be used in cases of suspected child sexual maltreatment.

Word approximation. (1) Use of old words in a new and unconventional way. (2) Development of new words by using conventional rules of word formation.

Word-attack skills. Ability to analyze unfamiliar words in terms of syllables and phonic elements so as to pronounce them correctly.

Word blindness. See *Alexia.*

Word deafness. See *Auditory aphasia.*

Word finding. See *Word retrieval.*

Word retrieval. Ability to locate words from learned vocabulary when they are needed; also known as word finding.

Word salad. Speech pattern in which words and phrases are combined in a disorganized fashion, seemingly devoid of logic and meaning.

Writ (legal). Court order requiring performance of a specified act.

Yang. Chinese concept representing the positive, active, or "male" force that regulates the universe and exists within the body, as well as in food. Yang also reflects light, warmth, and fullness.

Yerbero. Mexican American traditional healer who specializes in using herbs and spices for healing and prevention.

Yes-no questions. Queries that ask the interviewee to either confirm or negate a statement, as opposed to requesting information. They are not as useful as open-ended questions because they elicit less information and require the interviewer to ask additional questions.

Yin. Chinese concept representing the negative, inactive, or "female" force that regulates the universe and exists within the body, as well as in food. Yin also reflects darkness, cold, and emptiness.

Zero to Three. Center previously known as the National Center for Clinical Infant Programs.

Source: Adapted, in part, from Center for Developmental Disabilities (1993a, 1993b, 1993c, 1993d); Filip, Schene, and McDaniel (1991); Holmes and Sellars (1991); Knapp and VandeCreek (1985); Stahl (1994); Turnbull (1993); Underwood and Mead (1995); and Wyne and O'Connor (1979). The 89 terms from Filip et al. (1991), *Helping in Child Protective Services—A Casework Handbook* (Revised Edition), are reprinted with permission of the American Humane Association. The 212 terms from Holmes and Sellars (1991), *Coordination of Child Protection Cases: A Guide for Child Protection Services, Law Enforcement, and County Attorneys in Minnesota,* are reprinted with permission of Children's Services Division of the Minnesota Department of Human Services. The 42 terms from Knapp and VandeCreek (1985), "An Annotated Glossary of Legal Terms for Mental Health Clinicians," in Keller and Ritt (Eds.), *Innovations in Clinical Practice: A Source Book* (Vol. 4), are reprinted with permission of the authors and publisher, copyright 1985, Professional Resource Exchange.

REFERENCES

Abbott, D. A., & Meredith, W. H. (1986). Strengths of parents with retarded children. *Family Relations: Journal of Applied Family & Child Studies, 35,* 371–375.

Abcarian, R. (1995, April 16). Yes, abuse claims must be investigated…but then what? *Los Angeles Times,* pp. E1, E2.

Abel, E. L., & Sokol, R. J. (1991). A revised estimate of the economic impact of fetal alcohol syndrome. In M. Galanter, H. Begleiter, R. Deitrich, D. M. Gallant, D. Goodwin, E. Gottheil, A. Paredes, M. Rothschild, D. H. Van Thiel, & D. Cancellare (Eds.), *Recent developments in alcoholism: Vol. 9. Children of alcoholics* (pp. 117–125). New York: Plenum.

Abikoff, H., & Gittelman, R. (1985). Classroom observation code: A modification of the Stony Brook Code. *Psychopharmacology Bulletin, 21,* 901–909.

Abraham, S., & Llewellyn-Jones, D. (1992). *Eating disorders: The facts* (3rd ed.). Oxford, England: Oxford University Press.

Adams, D. W., & Deveau, E. J. (1987). When a brother or sister is dying of cancer: The vulnerability of the adolescent sibling. *Death Studies, 11,* 279–295.

Adams, J. (1991). Family crisis intervention and psychosocial care for children and adolescents. In C. S. Austad & W. H. Berman (Eds.), *Psychotherapy in managed health care: The optimal use of time and resources* (pp. 111–125). Washington, DC: American Psychological Association.

Adams, R. L., Parsons, O. A., Culbertson, J. L., & Nixon, S. J. (1996) (Eds.), *Neuropsychology for clinical practice: Etiology, assessment, and treatment of common neurological disorders.* Washington, DC: American Psychological Association.

Adams, R. L., & Rankin, E. J. (1996). A practical guide to forensic neuropsychological evaluations and testimony. In R. L. Adams, O. A. Parsons, J. L. Culbertson, & S. J. Nixon (Eds.), *Neuropsychology for clinical practice: Etiology, assessment, and treatment of common neurological disorders* (pp. 455–487). Washington, DC: American Psychological Association.

Adams-Greenly, M. (1989). Psychosocial interventions in childhood cancer. In J. C. Holland & J. H. Rowland (Eds.), *Handbook of psychooncology: Psychological care of the patient with cancer* (pp. 562–572). New York: Oxford University Press.

Adams-Greenly, M. (1991). Psychosocial assessment and intervention at initial diagnosis. *Pediatrician, 18,* 3–10.

Afolayan, J. A. (1993). Consequences of domestic violence on elementary school education. *Child & Family Behavior Therapy, 15,* 55–58.

Ahlburg, D. A., & DeVita, C. J. (1992). New realities of the American family. *Population Bulletin, 47*(2), 1–44.

Ainsworth, M. D. S., Bell, S. M., & Stayton, D. (1974). Infant-mother attachment and social development. In M. P. Richards (Ed.), *The introduction of the child into a social world* (pp. 99–135). London: Cambridge University Press.

Albano, A. M., Chorpita, B. F., & Barlow, D. H. (1996). Childhood anxiety disorders. In E. J. Mash & R. A. Barkley (Eds.), *Child psychopathology* (pp. 196–241). New York: Guilford.

Alexander, P. C. (1992). Application of attachment theory to the study of sexual abuse. *Journal of Consulting and Clinical Psychology, 60,* 185–195.

Alexander, R. C. (1993). To team or not to team: Approaches to child abuse. *Journal of Child Sexual Abuse, 2,* 95–97.

Aljazireh, L. (1993). Historical, environmental, and behavioral correlates of sexual offending by male adolescents: A critical review. *Behavioral Sciences & the Law, 11,* 423–440.

Altmaier, E. M., & Johnson, B. D. (1992). Health-related applications of counseling psychology: Toward health promotion and disease prevention across the life span. In S. D. Brown & R. W. Lent (Eds.), *Handbook of counseling psychology* (2nd ed., pp. 315–347). New York: Wiley.

Ambrosini, P., & Dixon, J. F. (1996). *Schedule for Affective Disorders & Schizophrenia for School-Age Children (K-SADS-IVR).* Philadelphia: Allegheny University of the Health Sciences.

American Association on Mental Retardation. (1992). *Mental retardation: Definition, classification, and systems of supports* (9th ed.). Washington, DC: Author.

American Humane Association. (1989). *Highlights of official aggregate child neglect and abuse reporting 1987.* Denver, CO: Author.

American Professional Society on the Abuse of Children. (1995). *Practice guidelines: Use of anatomical dolls in child sexual abuse assessments.* Chicago: Author.

American Prosecutors Research Institute. (Undated). *Questions to ask caregivers in failure to thrive cases.* Washington, DC: Author.

American Prosecutors Research Institute. (1993). *Investigation and prosecution of child abuse* (2nd ed.). Alexandria, VA: Author.

American Prosecutors Research Institute. (1996). Batterers charged with mental suffering of child witnesses. *Update: National Center for Prosecution of Child Abuse, 9*(3), 1.

American Psychiatric Association. (1994). *Diagnostic and statistical manual of mental disorders* (4th ed.). Washington, DC: Author.

American Psychological Association. (1994a). *Guidelines for child custody evaluations in divorce proceedings.* Washington, DC: Author.

American Psychological Association. (1994b). *Publication manual of the American Psychological Association* (4th ed.). Washington, DC: Author.

American Psychological Association. (1996). *Violence and the family.* Washington, DC: Author.

Anderson, B. G., Toledo, J. R., & Hazam, N. (1982). An approach to the resolution of Mexican-American resistance to diagnostic and remedial pediatric heart care. In N. J. Chrisman & T. W. Maretzki (Eds.), *Clinically applied anthropology* (pp. 325–350). Dordrecht, The Netherlands: Reidel.

Anderson, B. J., Auslander, W. F., Jung, K. C., Miller, J. P., & Santiago, J. V. (1990). Assessing family sharing of diabetes responsibilities. *Journal of Pediatric Psychology, 15,* 477–492.

Anderson, C. M., & Stewart, S. (1983). *Mastering resistance: A practical guide to family therapy.* New York: Guilford.

Anderson, E., Levine, M., Sharma, A., Ferretti, L., Steinberg, K., & Wallach, L. (1993). Coercive uses of mandatory reporting in therapeutic relationships. *Behavioral Sciences & the Law, 11,* 335–345.

Anderson, S., Piantanida, M., & Anderson, C. M. (1993). Normal processes in adoptive families. In F. Walsh (Ed.), *Normal family processes* (2nd ed., pp. 254–281). New York: Guilford.

Andrews, A. B., & Veronen, L. J. (1993). Sexual assault and people with disabilities. *Journal of Social Work & Human Sexuality, 8,* 137–159.

Andrews, M. A. (1986). Application of family therapy techniques to the treatment of language disorders. *Seminars in Speech and Language, 7,* 347–358.

Angelou, M. (1969). *I know why the caged bird sings.* New York: Random House.

Anglin, J. M. (1993). Vocabulary development: A morphological analysis. *Monographs of the Society for Research in Development, Serial No. 238, 58*(10).

Angold, A., Cox, A., Rutter, M., & Siminoff, E. (1996). *Child and Adolescent Psychiatric Assessment (CAPA): Version 4.2—Child version.* Durham, NC: Duke Medical Center.

Annie E. Casey Foundation. (1993). *Kids count data book: State profiles of child well-being.* Baltimore: Author.

Ariel, A. (1992). *Education of children and adolescents with learning disabilities.* New York: Merrill.

Armstrong, F. D., Seidel, J. F., & Swales, T. P. (1993). Pediatric HIV infection: A neuropsychological and educational challenge. *Journal of Learning Disabilities, 26,* 92–103.

Arnett, E. C. (1995, November 25). Black collegians excel as key to survival. *San Diego Union-Tribune,* pp. A30, A31.

Arredondo-Dowd, P. (1981). Personal loss and grief as a result of immigration. *Personnel and Guidance Journal, 59,* 376–378.

Asarnow, J. R. (1988). Children at risk for schizophrenia: Converging lines of evidence. *Schizophrenia Bulletin, 14,* 613–631.

Associated Press. (1993, November 12). Report on tot's death faults system. *San Diego Union-Tribune,* p. A36.

Associated Press. (1996a, June 21). Clinton announces $46 million in aid to fight domestic violence. *San Diego Union-Tribune,* p. A6.

Associated Press. (1996b, April 2). Racism makes student drop out. *San Diego Union-Tribune,* p. A3.

Atakan, Z., & Cooper, J. E. (1989). Behavioural Observation Schedule (BOS), PIRS 2nd edition: A revised edition of the PIRS (WHO, Geneva, March 1978). *British Journal of Psychiatry, 155,* 78–80.

Athey, J. L., & Ahearn, F. L. (1991). The mental health of refugee children: An overview. In F. L. Ahearn, Jr. & J. L. Athey (Eds.), *Refugee children: Theory, research, and services* (pp. 3–19). Baltimore: Johns Hopkins University Press.

Auslander, W. F. (1993). Brief family interventions to improve family communication and cooperation regarding diabetes management. *Diabetes Spectrum, 6,* 330–333.

Auslander, W. F., Bubb, J., Rogge, M., & Santiago, J. V. (1993). Family stress and resources: Potential areas of intervention in children recently diagnosed with diabetes. *Health & Social Work, 18,* 101–113.

Austin, G. A., & Gilbert, M. J. (1989). *Substance abuse among Latino youth* [Prevention Research Update No. 3]. Los Alamitos, CA: SWIRL.

Ayalon, O., & Flasher, A. (1993). *Chain reaction: Children and divorce.* Bristol, PA: Jessica Kingsley Publishers.

Bagley, C. (1992). Development of an adolescent stress scale for use by school counsellors: Construct validity in terms of depression, self-esteem and suicidal ideation. *School Psychology International, 13,* 31–49.

Bagley, C., & Shewchuk-Dann, D. (1991). Characteristics of 60 children and adolescents who have a history of sexual assault against others: Evidence from a controlled study. *Journal of Child & Youth Care, 6,* 43–52.

Bailey, D. B., Jr. (1989). Issues and directions in preparing professionals to work with young handicapped children and their families. In J. J. Gallagher, P. L. Trohanis, & R. M. Clifford (Eds.), *Policy implementation & PL 99–457: Planning for young children with special needs* (pp. 97–132). Baltimore: Brookes.

Baird, S. M., Haas, L., McCormick, K., Carruth, C., & Turner, K. D. (1992). Approaching an objective system for observation and measurement: Infant-Parent Social Interaction Code. *Topics in Early Childhood Special Education, 12,* 544–571.

Baker, A. F. (1983). Psychological assessment of autistic children. *Clinical Psychology Review, 3,* 41–59.

Baker, L. S. (1992). The perspective of families. In M. L. Stuber (Ed.), *Children and AIDS* (pp. 147–161). Washington, DC: American Psychiatric Press.

Baldwin, L. C. (1990). Child abuse as an antecedent of multiple personality disorder. *American Journal of Occupational Therapy, 44,* 978–983.

Barbarin, O. A., & Chesler, M. A. (1986). The medical context of parental coping with childhood cancer. *American Journal of Community Psychology, 14,* 221–235.

Barker, P. (1990). *Clinical interviews with children and adolescents.* New York: Norton.

Barkley, R. A. (1981). *Hyperactive children: A handbook for diagnosis and treatment.* New York: Guilford.

Barkley, R. A. (1988). Attention deficit disorder with hyperactivity. In E. J. Mash & L. G. Terdal (Eds.), *Behavioral assessment of childhood disorders* (2nd ed., pp. 69–104). New York: Guilford.

Barkley, R. A. (1991). *Attention-deficit hyperactivity disorder: A clinical workbook.* New York: The Guilford Press.

Barkley, R. A. (1995). *Taking charge of ADHD: The complete, authoritative guide for parents.* New York: Guilford.

Barlow, D. H. (Ed.). (1993). *Clinical handbook of psychological disorders: A step-by-step treatment manual* (2nd ed.). New York: Guilford.

Barnett, O. W., & LaViolette, A. D. (1993). *It could happen to anyone: Why battered women stay.* Newbury Park, CA: Sage.

Barnett, O. W., & Lopez-Real, D. I. (1985, November). *Women's reactions to battering and why they stay.* Paper presented at the annual meeting of the American Society of Criminology, San Diego, CA.

Barrett, T. (1985). *Youth in crisis: Seeking solutions to self-destructive behavior.* Longmont, CO: Sopris West.

Bassuk, E. L. (1993). Social and economic hardships of homeless and other poor women. *American Journal of Orthopsychiatry, 63,* 340–347.

Bassuk, E. L., & Weinreb, L. (1994). The plight of homeless children. In J. Blacher (Ed.), *When there's no place like home: Options for children living apart from their natural families* (pp. 37–62). Baltimore: Brookes.

Bates, J. D. (1985). *Writing with precision* (Rev. ed.). Washington, DC: Acropolis Books.

Bates, K. G. (1996, May 1). Is the race cup half full? Or half empty? *Los Angeles Times,* p. B9.

Baugher, E., & Lamison-White, L. (1996). *Poverty in the United States: 1995* (U.S. Bureau of the Census, Current Population Reports, Series P60–194). Washington DC: U.S. Government Printing Office.

Baum, C. G. (1989). Conduct disorders. In T. H. Ollendick & M. Hersen (Eds.), *Handbook of child psychopathology* (2nd ed., pp. 171–196). New York: Plenum.

Bauman, M. K. (1974). Blind and partially sighted. In M. V. Wisland (Ed.), *Psychoeducational diagnosis of exceptional children* (pp. 159–189). Springfield, IL: Charles C Thomas.

Baumeister, R. F. (1993). Suicide attempts. In C. G. Costello (Ed.), *Symptoms of depression* (pp. 259–589). New York: Wiley.

Bayley, N. (1993). *Bayley Scales of Infant Development* (2nd ed.). San Antonio, TX: The Psychological Corporation.

Beard, H., & Cerf, C. (1992). *The official politically correct dictionary and handbook.* New York: Villard Books.

Beavers, W. R., & Hampson, R. B. (1990). *Successful families: Assessment and intervention.* New York: Norton.

Beck, A. T., Wright, F. D., Newman, C. F., & Liese, B. S. (1993). *Cognitive therapy of substance abuse.* New York: Guilford.

Bellack, A. S., & Hersen, M. (1980). *Introduction to clinical psychology.* New York: Oxford University Press.

Belsky, J. (1993). Etiology of child maltreatment: A developmental-ecological analysis. *Psychological Bulletin, 114,* 413–434.

Belson, P. (1993). Children in hospital. *Children & Society, 7,* 196–210.

Bene, C. R., Klesges, R. C., & Meyers, A. W. (1990). Obesity in childhood. In S. B. Morgan & T. M. Okwumabua (Eds.), *Child and adolescent disorders: Developmental and health psychology perspectives* (pp. 175–200). Hillsdale, NJ: Erlbaum.

Benjamin, A. (1981). *The helping interview* (3rd ed.). Boston: Houghton Mifflin.

Bentovim, A., & Boston, P. (1988). Sexual abuse—Basic issues—Characteristics of children and families. In A. Bentovim, A. Elton, J. Hilderbrand, M. Tranter, & E. Vizard (Eds.), *Child sexual abuse within the family—Assessment and treatment* (pp. 16–39). Bristol, England: John Wright.

Berg, C. Z., Whitaker, A., Davies, M., Flament, M. F., & Rapoport, J. L. (1988). The survey form of the Leyton Obsessional Inventory—Child Version: Norms from an epidemiological study. *Journal of the American Academy of Child & Adolescent Psychiatry, 27,* 759–763.

Bergan, J. R. (1977). *Behavioral consultation.* Columbus, OH: Merrill.

Bergland, M. M., & Thomas, K. R. (1991). Psychosocial issues following severe head injury in adolescence: Individual and family perceptions. *Rehabilitation Counseling Bulletin, 35,* 5–22.

Berk, L. E. (1993). *Infants, children, and adolescents.* Boston: Allyn and Bacon.

Berkman, L. (1993, July 19). Cancer therapy's troubling legacy. *Los Angeles Times,* pp. A3, A17.

Berkow, R. (Ed.). (1992). *The Merck manual of diagnosis and therapy* (16th ed.). Rahway, NJ: Merck.

Berliner, L., & Loftus, E. F. (1992). Sexual abuse accusations: Desperately seeking reconciliation. *Journal of Interpersonal Violence, 7,* 570–578.

Berman, A. L., & Jobes, D. A. (1991). *Adolescent suicide: Assessment and intervention.* Washington, DC: American Psychological Association.

Berman, A. L., & Jobes, D. A. (1992). Suicidal behavior of adolescents. In B. Bongar (Ed.), *Suicide: Guidelines for assessment,* management, and treatment (pp. 84–105). New York: Oxford University Press.

Bernet, W. (1993). False statements and the differential diagnosis of abuse allegations. *Journal of the American Academy of Child & Adolescent Psychiatry, 32,* 903–910.

Bernstein, G. A., & Borchardt, C. M. (1991). Anxiety disorders of childhood and adolescence: A critical review. *Journal of the American Academy of Child & Adolescent Psychiatry, 30,* 519–532.

Besharov, D. J. (1990). *Recognizing child abuse: A guide for the concerned.* New York: Free Press.

Betancourt, H., & López, S. R. (1993). The study of culture, ethnicity, and race in American psychology. *American Psychologist, 48,* 629–637.

Beukelman, D. R., & Mirenda, P. (1992). *Augmentative and alternative communication: Management of severe communication disorders in children and adults.* Baltimore: Brookes.

Bibace, R., & Walsh, M. (1980). Development of children's concepts of illness. *Pediatrics, 66,* 912–917.

Bierman, K. L. (1983). Cognitive development and clinical interviews with children. *Advances in Clinical Child Psychology, 6,* 217–250.

Bierman, K. L. (1990). Using the clinical interview to assess children's interpersonal reasoning and emotional understanding. In C. R. Reynolds & R. W. Kamphaus (Eds.), *Handbook of psychological and educational assessment of children: Personality, behavior, and context* (pp. 204–219). New York: Guilford.

Bierman, K. L., & Schwartz, L. A. (1986). Clinical child interviews: Approaches and developmental considerations. *Journal of Child and Adolescent Psychotherapy, 3,* 267–278.

Bigler, E. D. (1988). The role of neuropsychological assessment in relation to other types of assessment with children. In M. G. Tramontana & S. R. Hooper (Eds.), *Assessment issues in child neuropsychology* (pp. 67–91). New York: Plenum.

Biklen, D. (1992). Typing to talk: Facilitated communication. *American Journal of Speech-Language Pathology, 1*(2), 15–17.

Biklen, D., Morton, M. W., Gold, D., Berrigan, C., Swaminatham, S. (1992). Facilitated communication: Implications for individuals with autism. *Topics in Language Disorders, 12,* 1–28.

Bishop, S. J., Murphy, J. M., Jellinek, M. S., & Quinn, D. (1992). Protecting seriously mistreated children: Time delays in a court sample. *Child Abuse & Neglect, 16,* 465–474.

Blacher, J. (1984). A dynamic perspective on the impact of a severely handicapped child on the family. In J. Blacher (Ed.), *Severely handicapped young children and their families: Research in review* (pp. 3–50). Orlando, FL: Academic Press.

Blacher, J. (1994). Placement and its consequences for families with children who have mental retardation. In J. Blacher (Ed.), *When there's no place like home: Options for children living apart from their natural families* (pp. 213–243). Baltimore: Brookes.

Blacher, J., & Bromley, B. E. (1990). Correlates of out-of-home placement of handicapped children: Who places and why? *Journal of Children in Contemporary Society, 21,* 3–40.

Black, D. (1993). Causes of disorder, I. Theoretical perspectives. In D. Black & D. Cottrell (Eds.), *Seminars in child and adolescent psychiatry* (pp. 28–38). London: Gaskell/Royal College of Psychiatrists.

Black, M., & Dubowitz, H. (1991). Failure-to-thrive: Lessons from animal models and developing countries. *Journal of Developmental and Behavioral Pediatrics, 12,* 259–267.

Blair, J. (1995, March 11). Teen depression: "Even elite students suffer." *Los Angeles Times,* p. B7.

Blatt, E. R. (1992). Factors associated with child abuse and neglect in residential care settings. *Children & Youth Services Review, 14,* 493–517.

Bloch, B. (1983). Bloch's assessment guide for ethnic/cultural variations. In M. S. Orque, B. Bloch, & L. S. A. Monrroy (Eds.), *Ethnic nursing care: A multicultural approach* (pp. 49–75). St. Louis: Mosby.

Bloch, J. P. (1991). *Assessment and treatment of multiple personality and dissociative disorders.* Sarasota, FL: Professional Resource Press.

Bloom, B. L., & Levergood, E. R. (1995). *A brief scale for assessing parental child-rearing style: Psychometric properties and psychosocial correlates.* Unpublished manuscript.

Blosser, J. L., & DePompei, R. (1989). The head-injured student returns to school: Recognizing and treating deficits. *Topics in Language Disorders, 9,* 67–77.

Board of Children and Families. (1995). Immigrant children and their families: Issues for research and policy. *Critical Issues for Children and Youths, 5,* 72–89.

Boat, B. W., & Everson, M. D. (1988). Use of anatomical dolls among professionals in sexual abuse evaluations. *Child Abuse & Neglect, 12,* 171–179.

Boat, B. W., & Everson, M. D. (1996). Concerning practices of interviewers when using anatomical dolls in Child Protective Services investigations. *Child Maltreatment: Journal of the American Professional Society of the Abuse of Children, 1,* 96–104.

Boeck, M. A. (1992). Obesity. In S. B. Friedman, M. Fisher, & S. K. Schonberg (Eds.), *Comprehensive adolescent health care* (pp. 238–249). Ontario: Prentice Hall.

Bogdan, R. C., & Biklen, S. K. (1982). *Qualitative research for education: An introduction to theory and methods.* Boston: Allyn and Bacon.

Boggs, S. R., & Eyberg, S. (1990). Interview techniques and establishing rapport. In A. M. La Greca (Ed.), *Through the eyes of the child: Obtaining self-reports from children and adolescents* (pp. 85–108). Boston: Allyn and Bacon.

Boland, M. G., Czarniecki, L., & Haiken, H. J. (1992). Coordinated care for children with HIV infection. In M. L. Stuber (Ed.), *Children and AIDS* (pp. 165–181). Washington, DC: American Psychiatric Press.

Bolton, I. M. (1987). Beyond surviving: Suggestions for survivors. In E. J. Dunne, J. L. McIntosh, & K. D. Maxim (Eds.), *Suicide and its aftermath: Understanding and counseling the survivors* (pp. 289–290). New York: Norton.

Bond, M. H., & Lai, T. M. (1986). Embarrassment and code-switching into a second language. *Journal of Social Psychology, 126,* 179–186.

Boney-McCoy, S., & Finkelhor, D. (1995). Psychosocial sequelae of violent victimization in a national youth sample. *Journal of Consulting and Clinical Psychology, 63,* 726–736.

Bor, R., & Miller, R. (1989). The interface between counseling and neuropsychological assessment of patients with AIDS/HIV. *Counseling Psychology Quarterly, 2,* 481–491.

Bor, R., Miller, R., & Goldman, E. (1993). *Theory and practice of HIV counselling: A systemic approach.* New York: Brunner/Mazel.

Bordarampe, J., Ehrenberg, P., Foran, S., & Oksman, A. (1991). Innovative approaches in child custody evaluations: The joint office interview and client feedback. *Family & Conciliation Courts Review, 29,* 160–171.

Borkowski, J. G., Day, J. D., Saenz, D., Dietmeyer, D., Estrada, T. M., & Groteluschen, A. (1992). Expanding the boundaries of cognitive interventions. In B. Y. L. Wong (Ed.), *Contemporary intervention research in learning disabilities: An international perspective* (pp. 1–21). New York: Springer-Verlag.

Bornstein, P. H., Hamilton, S. B., & Bornstein, M. T. (1986). Self-monitoring procedures. In A. R. Ciminero, K. S. Calhoun, & H. E. Adams (Eds.), *Handbook of behavioral assessment* (2nd ed., pp. 176–222). New York: Wiley.

Bottoms, B. L., & Lantinga, S. B. (1995, June). Hearsay evidence in child sex-abuse cases. *APA Monitor,* p. 7.

Boudewyns, P. A. (1982). Assessment of headache. In F. J. Keefe & J. A. Blumenthal (Eds.), *Assessment strategies in behavioral medicine* (pp. 167–180). New York: Grune & Stratton.

Bowen, J. (1985). Helping children and their families cope with congenital heart disease. *Critical Care Quarterly, 8,* 65–74.

Bowlby, J. (1958). The child's tie to his mother. *International Journal of Psycho-Analysis, 39,* 1–23.

Bowlby, J. (1969). *Attachment and loss: Vol. 1. Attachment.* New York: Basic Books.

Bowman, E. S., Blix, S., & Coons, P. M. (1985). Multiple personality in adolescence: Relationship to incestual experiences. *Journal of the American Academy of Child Psychiatry, 24,* 109–114.

Boyer, P., & Chesteen, H. (1992). Professional helpfulness? The experiences of parents of handicapped children with counsellors and social workers. *Journal of Child & Youth Care, 7,* 37–48.

Boykin, A. W. (1983). The academic performance of Afro-American children. In J. T. Spence (Ed.), *Achievement and achievement motives: Psychological and sociological approaches* (pp. 321–371). San Francisco: Freeman.

Boykin, M. R. (1996, December 28). Ebonics vs. English: "Nobody goes to a wedding dressed in sweats." *Los Angeles Times,* p. B7.

Brasseur, J. W. (1994, October). The battered woman. *Clinician Reviews,* pp. 45–74.

Breen, M. J., & Fiedler, C. R. (Eds.). (1996). *Behavioral approach to assessment of youth with emotional/behavioral disorders: A handbook for school-based practitioners.* Austin, TX: Pro-Ed.

Bregman, J. D. (1991). Current developments in the understanding of mental retardation: II. Psychopathology. *Journal of the American Academy of Child & Adolescent Psychiatry, 30,* 861–872.

Brent, D. A., Perper, J., Moritz, G., Allman, C., Liotus, L., Schweers, J., Roth, C., Balach, L., & Canobbio, R. (1993). Bereavement or depression? The impact of the loss of a friend to suicide. *Journal of the American Academy of Child & Adolescent Psychiatry, 32,* 1189–1197.

Brent, D. A., Perper, J., Moritz, G., Friend, A., Schweers, J., Allman, C., McQuiston, L., Boylan, M. B., Roth, C., & Balach, L. (1993). Adolescent witnesses to a peer suicide. *Journal of the American Academy of Child & Adolescent Psychiatry, 32,* 1184–1188.

Brent, D. A., Perper, J. A., Moritz, G., Liotus, L., Schweers, J., Roth, C., Balach, L., & Allman, C. (1993). Psychiatric impact of the loss of an adolescent sibling to suicide. *Journal of Affective Disorders, 28,* 249–256.

Breslau, N. (1987). Inquiring about the bizarre: False positives in Diagnostic Interview Schedule for Children (DISC) ascertainment of obsessions, compulsions, and psychotic symptoms. *Journal of the American Academy of Child & Adolescent Psychiatry, 26,* 639–644.

Bretherton, I. (1993). Theoretical contributions from developmental psychology. In P. G. Boss, W. J. Doherty, R. LaRossa, W. R. Schumm, & S. K. Steinmetz (Eds.), *Sourcebook of family theories and methods: A contextual approach* (pp. 275–297). New York: Plenum.

Briggs, S. E. (1991). Medical issues with child victims of family violence. In R. T. Ammerman & M. Hersen (Eds.), *Case studies in family violence* (pp. 87–96). New York: Plenum.

Bristol, M. M., & Schopler, E. (1984). A developmental perspective on stress and coping in families of autistic children. In J. Blacher (Ed.), *Severely handicapped young children and their families: Research in review* (pp. 91–141). Orlando, FL: Academic Press.

Brockway, B. S. (1978). Evaluating physician competency: What difference does it make? *Evaluation and Program Planning, 1,* 211.

Brodsky, S. (1991). *Testifying in court: Guidelines and maxims for the expert witness.* Washington, DC: American Psychological Association.

Brodzinsky, D. M., Schechter, M. D., & Henig, R. M. (1992). *Being adopted: The lifelong search for self.* New York: Doubleday.

Bromwich, R. M. (1981). *Working with parents and infants: An interactional approach.* Baltimore: University Park Press.

Brooks, D. N. (1991). The head-injured family. *Journal of Clinical & Experimental Neuropsychology, 13,* 155–188.

Brooks, N. R. (1994, May 19). Study of Asians in U.S. finds many struggling. *Los Angeles Times,* pp. A1, A25.

Brown, P. G. (1989). Families who have a child diagnosed with cancer: What the medical caregiver can do to help them and themselves. *Issues in Comprehensive Pediatric Nursing, 12,* 247–260.

Brown, S. A., Mott, M. A., & Stewart, M. A. (1992). Adolescent alcohol and drug abuse. In C. E. Walker & M. C. Roberts (Eds.), *Handbook of clinical child psychology* (2nd ed., pp. 677–693). New York: Wiley.

Bryant, D., Kessler, J., & Shirar, L. (1992). *The family inside: Working with the multiple.* New York: Norton.

Bugental, D. B. (1992). Affective and cognitive processes within threat-oriented family systems. In I. E. Sigel, A. V. McGillicuddy-DeLisi, & J. J. Goodnow (Eds.), *Parental belief systems: The psychological consequences for children* (2nd ed., pp. 219–248). Hillsdale, NJ: Erlbaum.

Bureau of Justice Statistics (1994). *Crime rape victims, 1992.* Washington, DC: U.S. Department of Justice.

Burge, S. K. (1983). Rape: Individual and family reactions. In C. R. Figley & H. I. McCubbin (Eds.), *Stress and the family: Vol. II. Coping with catastrophe* (pp. 103–119). New York: Brunner/Mazel.

Burgess, A. W., Groth, A. N., Holmstrom, L. L., & Sgroi, S. M. (Eds.). (1978). *Sexual assault of children and adolescents.* Lexington, MA: Lexington Books.

Busch, B. (1993). Attention deficits: Current concepts, controversies, management, and approaches to classroom instruction. *Annals of Dyslexia, 43,* 5–25.

Bussey, K. (1992). Children's lying and truthfulness: Implications for children's testimony. In S. J. Ceci, M. D. Leichtman, & M. Putnick (Eds.), *Cognitive and social factors in early deception* (pp. 89–109). Hillsdale, NJ: Erlbaum.

Bussey, K., & Grimbeek, E. J. (1995). Disclosure processes: Issues for child sexual abuse victims. In K. J. Rotenberg (Ed.), *Disclosure processes in children and adolescents* (pp. 166–203). New York: Cambridge University Press.

Byrd, M. (1994, August 19). Mixed couples. *Los Angeles Times,* p. B6.

Cage, R. L. (1988). Criminal investigation of child sexual abuse cases. In S. M. Sgroi (Ed.), *Vulnerable populations: Evaluation and treatment of sexually abused children and adult survivors* (Vol. 1, pp. 187–227). Lexington, MA: Lexington Books.

Calculator, S. N., & Singer, K. M. (1992). Preliminary validation of facilitated communication. *Topics in Language Disorders, 13,* ix–xvi.

California Attorney General's Office. (1994, July). *Child victim witness investigative pilot projects—Research and evaluation final report.* Sacramento, CA: Author.

Callahan, B. (1994, November 4). Judge sentences parents for killing tot, raps agency. *San Diego Union-Tribune,* pp. B1, B4.

Cambor, R., & Millman, R. B. (1991). Alcohol and drug abuse in adolescents. In M. Lewis (Ed.), *Child and adolescent psychiatry: A comprehensive textbook* (pp. 736–755). Baltimore: Williams & Wilkins.

Campbell, S. B. (1989). Developmental perspectives. In T. H. Ollendick & M. Hersen (Eds.), *Handbook of child psychopathology* (pp. 5–28). New York: Plenum.

Canino, I. A. (1985). Taking a history. In D. Shaffer, A. A. Erhardt, & L. L. Greenhill (Eds.), *The clinical guide to child psychiatry* (pp. 393–407). New York: Free Press.

Canino, I. A., & Canino, G. (1980). Impact of stress on the Puerto Rican family: Treatment considerations. *American Journal of Orthopsychiatry, 50,* 535–541.

Carlton, T. O., & Stephenson, M. D. G. (1990). Social work and the management of severe head injury. *Social Science & Medicine, 31,* 5–11.

Carmody, M. (1991). Invisible victims: Sexual assault of people with an intellectual disability. *Australia & New Zealand Journal of Developmental Disabilities, 17,* 229–236.

Carnegie Corporation of New York. (April, 1994). *Starting points: Meeting the needs of our youngest children.* Waldorf, MD: Author.

Carpenter, K. H. (1992). Childcare selections to grow on. *Library Journal, 117,* 67–71.

Carr, T. (1994). Bereavement, dying and terminal care. *British Journal of Clinical Psychology, 33,* 243–245.

Carruth, G. (1993). *The encyclopedia of American facts and dates* (9th ed.). New York: HarperCollins.

Carskadon, M. A., Anders, T. F., & Hole, W. (1988). Sleep disturbances in childhood and adolescence. In H. E. Fitzgerald, B. M. Lester, & M. W. Yogman (Eds.), *Theory and research in behavioral pediatrics* (Vol. 4, pp. 221–247). New York: Plenum.

Casey, R., Levy, S. E., Brown, K., & Brooks-Gunn, J. (1992). Impaired emotional health in children with mild reading disability. *Journal of Developmental and Behavioral Pediatrics, 13,* 256–260.

Catherall, D. R. (1988). Interviewing in family therapy: The problem-centered approach. *Therapy Collections, 24,* 49–69.

Caton, C. L. (1990). *Homeless in America.* New York: Oxford University Press.

Ceci, S. J., & Bruck, M. (1993). Suggestibility of the child witness: A historical review and synthesis. *Psychological Bulletin, 113,* 403–439.

Ceci, S. J., & Bruck, M. (1995). *Jeopardy in the courtroom: A scientific analysis of children's testimony.* Washington, DC: American Psychological Association.

Center for Developmental Disabilities. (1993a, November). *Acronyms/abbreviations: Disabilities, health conditions and related services.* Columbia, SC: Author.

Center for Developmental Disabilities. (1993b, November). *Acronyms/abbreviations: Disability related agencies and legal terms.* Columbia, SC: Author.

Center for Developmental Disabilities. (1993c, November). *Primer of disabilities, health conditions, and medical terminology related to infants with disabilities.* Columbia, SC: Author.

Center for Developmental Disabilities. (1993d, November). *Primer of disability related terms.* Columbia, SC: Author.

Centers for Disease Control and Prevention. (1995). *HIV/AIDS Surveillance Report, 7*(2).

Centers for Disease Control and Prevention. (1996a). *HIV/AIDS Surveillance Report, 8*(1).

Centers for Disease Control and Prevention. (1996b). *Suicide death and rates per 100,000, United States, 1988–1994 (E950-E959).* Atlanta: Author.

Centers for Disease Control and Prevention. (1997). Update: Prevalence of overweight among children, adolescents, and adults—United States, 1988–1994. *Morbidity and Mortality Weekly Report, 46*(9), 199–202.

Chapman, S. L. (1991). Psychological assessment and treatment. In J. J. Sweet, R. H. Rozensky, & S. M. Tovian (Eds.), *Handbook of clinical psychology in medical settings* (pp. 401–420). New York: Plenum.

Charles, G., Coleman, H., & Matheson, J. (1993). Staff reactions to young people who have been sexually abused. *Residential Treatment for Children & Youth, 11*, 9–21.

Chesler, M. A., Allswede, J., & Barbarin, O. O. (1991). Voices from the margin of the family: Siblings of children with cancer. *Journal of Psychosocial Oncology, 9*, 19–42.

Chesler, M. A., & Barbarin, O. A. (1984). Difficulties of providing help in a crisis: Relationships between parents of children with cancer and their friends. *Journal of Social Issues, 40*, 113–134.

Chesler, M. A., & Barbarin, O. A. (1987). *Childhood cancer and the family: Meeting the challenge of stress and support.* New York: Brunner/Mazel.

Chesler, P. (1986). *Mothers on trial: The battle for children and custody.* New York: McGraw-Hill.

Chess, S., & Thomas, A. (1986). *Temperament in clinical practice.* New York: Guilford.

Chochinov, H., & Holland, J. C. (1989). Bereavement: A special issue in oncology. In J. C. Holland & J. H. Rowland (Eds.), *Handbook of psychooncology: Psychological care of the patient with cancer* (pp. 612–627). New York: Oxford University Press.

Christ, G. H., & Adams, M. A. (1984). Therapeutic stages at psycho-social crisis points in the treatment of childhood cancer. In A. E. Christ & K. Flomenhaft (Eds.), *Childhood cancer: Impact on the family* (pp. 109–130). New York: Plenum.

Christ, G. H., Siegel, K., Freund, B., Langosch, D., Hendersen, S., Sperber, D., & Weinstein, L. (1993). Impact of parental terminal cancer on latency-age children. *American Journal of Orthopsychiatry, 63*, 417–425.

Christophersen, E. R. (1994). *Pediatric compliance: A guide for the primary care physician. Critical issues in developmental and behavioral pediatrics.* New York: Plenum.

Chung, R. C.-Y., & Lin, K.-M. (1994). Help-seeking behavior among Southeast Asian refugees. *Journal of Community Psychology, 22*, 109–120.

Cicchetti, D., & Carlson, V. (1989). Preface. In D. Cicchetti & V. Carlson (Eds.), *Child maltreatment: Theory and research on the causes and consequences of child abuse and neglect* (pp. xiii–xx). New York: Cambridge University Press.

Cicchetti, D., Toth, S. L., & Hennessy, K. (1993). Child maltreatment and school adaptation: Problems and promises. In D. Cicchetti & S. L. Toth (Eds.), *Child abuse, child development, and social policy* (pp. 301–330). Norwood, NJ: Ablex.

Clarizio, H. F. (1994). *Assessment and treatment of depressions in children and adolescents* (2nd ed.). Brandon, VT: Clinical Psychology Publishing Company.

Clark, C. R. (1988). Sociopathy, malingering, and defensiveness. In R. Rogers (Ed.), *Clinical assessment of malingering and deception* (pp. 54–64). New York: Guilford.

Clark, H. H. (1985). Language use and language users. In G. Lindzey & E. Aronson (Eds.), *Handbook of social psychology* (3rd ed., Vol. 2, pp. 179–231). New York: Random House.

Clarke, A. M., & Clarke, A. D. B. (1994). Variations, deviations, risks, and uncertainties in human development. In W. B. Carey & S. C. McDevitt (Eds.), *Prevention and early intervention: Individual differences as risk factors for the mental health of children: A festschrift for Stella Chess and Alexander Thomas* (pp. 83–91). New York: Brunner/Mazel.

Claussen, A. H., & Crittenden, P. M. (1991). Physical and psychological maltreatment: Relations among types of maltreatment. *Child Abuse & Neglect, 15*, 5–18.

Cobb, H. C. (1989). Counseling and psychotherapy with handicapped children and adolescents. In D. T. Brown & H. T. Prout (Eds.), *Counseling and psychotherapy with children and adolescents: Theory and practice for school and clinic settings* (2nd ed., pp. 467–501). Brandon, VT: Clinical Psychology Publishing Company.

Cohen, H. J., & Diamond, G. W. (1992). Developmental assessment of children with HIV infection. In A. C. Crocker, H. J. Cohen, & T. A. Kastner (Eds.), *HIV infection and developmental disabilities: A resource for service providers* (pp. 53–61). Baltimore: Brookes.

Cohen, J. A., & Mannarino, A. P. (1991). Incest. In R. T. Ammerman & M. Hersen (Eds.), *Case studies in family violence* (pp. 171–186). New York: Plenum.

Cohen, R. (1995, November 21). The perilous game of stereotyping. *San Diego Union-Tribune*, p. B6.

Cohen, S., & Erwin, E. J. (1994). Characteristics of children with prenatal drug exposure being served in preschool special education programs in New York City. *Topics in Early Childhood Special Education, 14*, 232–253.

Cohen, S. B. (1991). Adapting educational programs for students with head injuries. *Journal of Head Trauma Rehabilitation, 6*(1), 56–63.

Coll, C. T. G., & Meyer, E. C. (1993). The sociocultural context of infant development. In C. H. Zeanah, Jr. (Ed.), *Handbook of infant mental health* (pp. 56–69). New York: Guilford.

Coller, D. R. (1988). Joint custody: Research, theory, and policy. *Family Process, 27*, 459–469.

Compas, B. E., & Hammen, C. L. (1994). Child and adolescent depression: Covariation and comorbidity in development. In R. J. Haggerty, L. R. Sherrod, N. Garmezy, & M. Rutter (Eds.), *Stress, risk, and resilience in children and adolescents: Processes, mechanisms, and interventions* (pp. 225–267). New York: Cambridge University Press.

Compas, B. E., Hinden, B. R., & Gerhardt, C. A. (1995). Adolescent development: Pathways and processes of risk and resilience. *Annual Review of Psychology, 46*, 265–293.

Conduct Problems Prevention Research Group. (1992). A developmental and clinical model for the prevention of conduct disorder: The FAST Track Program. *Development and Psychopathology, 4,* 509–527.

Connaway, S. (1996). ABCs for teachers who suspect child abuse. *NRCCSA News, 5*(4), 4–5.

Conte, J. R., Sorenson, E., Fogarty, L., & Rosa, J. D. (1991). Evaluating children's reports of sexual abuse: Results from a survey of professionals. *American Journal of Orthopsychiatry, 61,* 428–437.

Cook, A. S., & Dworkin, D. S. (1992). *Helping the bereaved: Therapeutic interventions for children, adolescents, and adults.* New York: Basic Books.

Cope, D. N., & Wolfson, B. (1994). Crisis intervention with the family in the trauma setting. *Journal of Head Trauma Rehabilitation, 9,* 67–81.

Corey, G., Corey, M. S., & Callanan, P. (1993). *Issues and ethics in the helping professions* (4th ed.). Pacific Grove, CA: Brooks/Cole.

Corey, M. R. (1987). A comprehensive model for psychosocial assessment of individuals with closed head injury. *Cognitive Rehabilitation, 5,* 28–33.

Cormier, W. H., & Cormier, L. S. (1979). *Interviewing strategies for helpers: A guide to assessment, treatment, and evaluation.* Monterey, CA: Brooks/Cole.

Cornell, D. G. (1993). Juvenile homicide: A growing national problem. *Behavioral Sciences & the Law, 11,* 389–396.

Costello, A. J., Dulcan, M. K., & Kalas, R. (1991). A checklist of hospitalization criteria for use with children. *Hospital & Community Psychiatry, 42,* 823–828.

Counts, D. R., & Counts, D. A. (1991). Conclusions: Coping with the final tragedy. In D. R. Counts & D. A. Counts (Eds.), *Coping with the final tragedy: Cultural variation in dying and grieving* (pp. 277–291). Amityville, NY: Baywood.

County of San Diego Department of Social Services. (1992, November 25). *Children's services special notice #49-92.* San Diego: County of San Diego.

Coupey, S. M. (1992). Anorexia nervosa. In S. B. Friedman, M. Fisher, & S. K. Schonberg (Eds.), *Comprehensive adolescent health care* (pp. 217–231). Ontario: Prentice Hall.

Cox, D. J., & Gonder-Frederick, L. (1992). Major developments in behavioral diabetes research. *Journal of Consulting and Clinical Psychology, 60,* 628–638.

Craft, J. L., & Staudt, M. M. (1991). Reporting and founding of child neglect in urban and rural communities. *Child Welfare, 70,* 359–370.

Craine, M. H., Hanks, R., & Stevens, H. (1992). Mapping family stress: The application of family adaptation theory to post-traumatic stress disorder. *American Journal of Family Therapy, 20,* 195–203.

Cranberg, L. D., Filley, C. M., Hart, E. J., & Alexander, M. P. (1987). Acquired aphasia in childhood: Clinical and CT investigations. *Neurology, 37,* 1165–1172.

Crary, W. G., & Johnson, C. W. (1975). Mental status examination. In C. W. Johnson, J. R. Snibbe, & L. A. Evans (Eds.), *Basic psychopathology: A programmed text* (pp. 50–89). New York: Spectrum.

Craske, M. G., & Barlow, D. H. (1993). Panic disorder and agoraphobia. In D. H. Barlow (Ed.), *Clinical handbook of psychological disorders: A step-by-step treatment manual* (2nd ed., pp. 1–47). New York: Guilford.

Creer, T. L. (1991). The application of behavioral procedures to childhood asthma: Current and future perspectives. *Patient Education & Counseling, 17,* 9–22.

Creer, T. L., & Bender, B. G. (1995). Recent trends in asthma research. In A. J. Goreczny (Ed.), *Handbook of health and rehabilitation psychology* (pp. 31–53). New York: Plenum.

Creer, T. L., Harm, D. L., & Marion, R. J. (1988). Childhood asthma. In D. K. Routh (Ed.), *Handbook of pediatric psychology* (pp. 162–189). New York: Guilford.

Creer, T. L., Kotses, H., & Reynolds, R. V. C. (1989). Living with asthma: Part II. Beyond CARIH. *Journal of Asthma, 26,* 31–51.

Creer, T. L., Renne, C. M., & Chai, H. (1982). The application of behavioral techniques to childhood asthma. In D. C. Russo & J. W. Varni (Eds.), *Behavioral pediatrics: Research and practice* (pp. 27–66). New York: Plenum.

Creer, T. L., & Reynolds, R. V. C. (1990). Asthma. In A. M. Gross & R. S. Drabman (Eds.), *Handbook of clinical behavioral pediatrics* (pp. 183–203). New York: Plenum.

Creer, T. L., Wigal, J. K., Tobin, D. L., Kotses, H., Snyder, S. E., & Winder, J. A. (1989). The Revised Asthma Problem Behavior Checklist. *Journal of Asthma, 26,* 17–29.

Creighton, A., with Kivel, P. (1992). *Helping teens stop violence: A practical guide for counselors, educators, and parents.* Alameda, CA: Hunter House.

Crittenden, P. M. (1993). An information-processing perspective on the behavior of neglectful parents. *Criminal Justice & Behavior, 20,* 27–48.

Crittenden, P. M. (1996). Research on maltreating families: Implications for intervention. In J. Briere, L. Berliner, J. A. Bulkley, C. Jenny, & T. Reid (Eds.), *The APSAC handbook on child maltreatment* (pp. 158–174). Thousand Oaks, CA: Sage.

Crosby, J. F., & Jose, N. L. (1983). Death: Family adjustment to loss. In C. R. Figley & H. I. McCubbin (Eds.), *Stress and the family: Vol. II. Coping with catastrophe* (pp. 76–89). New York: Brunner/Mazel.

Crossley, R. (1992). Getting the words out: Case studies in facilitated communication training. *Topics in Language Disorders, 12,* 46–59.

Culbertson, J. L., & Willis, D. J. (1988). Acute loss and grieving reactions: Treatment issues. In J. L. Culbertson, H. F. Krows, & G. D. Bendell (Eds.), *Sudden infant death syndrome* (pp. 157–181). Baltimore: Johns Hopkins University Press.

Culebras, A. (1992). Update on disorders of sleep and the sleep-wake cycle. *Psychiatric Clinics of North America, 15,* 467–489.

Cullum, L. (1994). Considering the options: Infertility and adoption books. *Library Journal, 119,* 73–76.

Cunnien, A. J. (1988). Psychiatric and medical syndromes associated with deception. In R. Rogers (Ed.), *Clinical assessment of malingering and deception* (pp. 13–33). New York: Guilford.

Cunningham, R. (1992). Developmentally appropriate psychosocial care for children affected by parental chemical dependence. *Journal of Health Care for the Poor & Underserved, 3,* 208–221.

Curran, D. K. (1987). *Adolescent suicidal behavior.* Washington, DC: Hemisphere.

Cutter, A. V., & Miller, E. A. (1971). The interpretive and summing up process with parents during and after diagnostic studies of children. In R. L. Noland (Ed.), *Counseling parents of the ill and the handicapped* (pp. 62–77). Springfield, IL: Charles C Thomas.

Dahl, R. (1993). Parasomnias. In R. T. Ammerman, C. G. Last, & M. Hersen (Eds.), *Handbook of prescriptive treatments for children and adolescents* (pp. 281–299). Boston: Allyn and Bacon.

Daly, L. W. (1992). Child sexual abuse allegations: Investigative approaches to identifying "alternative hypotheses." *Issues in Child Abuse Accusations, 4,* 125–131.

Danek, M. (1988). Deafness and family impact. In P. W. Power, A. E. Dell Orto, & M. B. Gibbons (Eds.), *Family interventions throughout chronic illness and disability* (pp. 120–135). New York: Springer.

Darley, F. L. (1978). A philosophy of appraisal and diagnosis. In F. L. Darley & D. C. Spriestersbach (Eds.), *Diagnostic methods in speech pathology* (pp. 1–60). New York: Harper & Row.

Darling, R. B. (1991). Initial and continuing adaptation to the birth of a disabled child. In M. Seligman (Ed.), *The family with a handicapped child* (2nd ed., pp. 55–89). Boston: Allyn and Bacon.

Davies, B. (1993). After a child dies: Helping the siblings. In A. Armstrong-Dailey & S. Z. Goltzer (Eds.), *Hospice care for children* (pp. 140–153). New York: Oxford University Press.

Davis, H. (1993). *Counselling parents of children with chronic illness or disability. Communication and counselling in health care.* Leicester, England: British Psychological Society.

Davis, J. K., & Wasserman, E. (1992). Behavioral aspects of asthma in children. *Clinical Pediatrics, 31,* 678–681.

Dean, G. L. (1985). *Dean Adolescent Inventory Scale/D.* Unpublished manuscript.

Dean, G. L., Dean, M., Giem, D., Guerra, G., & Leark, R. (1989, October). *Child and adolescent MPD symptoms in common with other disorders (A structured interview symptoms checklist for MPD).* Paper presented at the Sixth International Conference on Multiple Personality and Dissociative States, Chicago, IL.

Deasy-Spinetta, P. (1981). The adolescent with cancer: A view from the inside. In J. J. Spinetta & P. Deasy-Spinetta (Eds.), *Living with childhood cancer* (pp. 189–197). St. Louis: Mosby.

Deaton, A. V. (1987). Behavioral change strategies for children and adolescents with severe brain injury. *Journal of Learning Disability, 20,* 581–589.

Deaton, W. S., & Hertica, M. (1993). Developmental considerations in forensic interviews with adolescents. *APSAC Advisor, 6*(1), 5–8.

DeBlassie, R. R. (1990). Alcohol abuse in childhood. In M. Hersen & C. G. Last (Eds.), *Handbook of child and adult psychopathology* (pp. 355–364). New York: Pergamon.

DeLipsey, J. M., & James, S. K. (1988). Videotaping the sexually abused child: The Texas experience, 1983–1987. In J. M. Sgroi (Ed.), *Vulnerable populations: Evaluation and treatment of sexually abused children and adult survivors* (Vol. 1, pp. 220–264). Lexington, MA: Lexington Books.

DeLoach, J. S. (1995). The use of dolls in interviewing young children. In M. S. Zaragoza, J. R. Graham, G. C. N. Hall, R. Hirschman, & Y. S. Ben-Porath (Eds.), *Memory and testimony in the child witness* (pp. 160–178). Thousand Oaks, CA: Sage.

De Monchy, M. L. (1991). Recovery and rebuilding: The challenge for refugee children and service providers. In F. L. Ahearn, Jr. & J. L. Athey (Eds.), *Refugee children: Theory, research, and services* (pp. 163–180). Baltimore: Johns Hopkins University Press.

Dempster, H. L. (1993). The aftermath of child sexual abuse: Women's perspectives. In L. Waterhouse (Ed.), *Child abuse and child abusers: Protection and prevention* (pp. 58–72). Bristol, PA: Jessica Kingsley Publishers.

DeMyer, M. K. (1979). *Parents and children in autism.* Washington, DC: Winston.

Denholm, C. (1991). Preparing adolescents for hospitalization: The role of the school counselor. *School Counselor, 38,* 352–357.

Denton, R. (1986). An occupational therapy protocol for assessing infants and toddlers who fail to thrive. *American Journal of Occupational Therapy, 40,* 352–358.

DePanfilis, D., & Salus, M. K. (1992). *Child protective services: A guide for caseworkers.* Washington, DC: National Center on Child Abuse and Neglect.

DePompei, R., & Blosser, J. L. (1987). Strategies for helping head-injured children successfully return to school. *Language, Speech, and Hearing Services in Schools, 18,* 292–300.

DePompei, R., Blosser, J. L., & Zarski, J. F. (1989, November). *The path less traveled: Counseling family and friends of T. B. I. survivors.* Paper presented at the American Speech-Language-Hearing Association National Convention, St. Louis, MO.

DePompei, R., Zarski, J. F., & Hall, D. E. (1988). Cognitive communication impairments: A family-focused viewpoint. *Journal of Head Trauma Rehabilitation, 3*(2), 13–22.

DeSpelder, L. A., & Strickland, A. L. (1992). *The last dance: Encountering death and dying* (3rd ed.). Mountain View, CA: Mayfield.

deYoung, M. (1994). Immediate maternal reactions to the disclosure or discovery of incest. *Journal of Family Violence, 9,* 21–33.

Diagnostic Classification Steering Committee. (1990). *The international classification of sleep disorders: Diagnostic and coding manual.* Rochester, MN: American Sleep Disorder Association.

Diamond, G. W., & Cohen, H. J. (1992). Developmental disabilities in children with HIV infection. In A. C. Crocker, H. J. Cohen, & T. A. Kastner (Eds.), *HIV infection and developmental disabilities: A resource for service providers* (pp. 33–41). Baltimore: Brookes.

Diehl, S. F., Moffitt, K. A., & Wade, S. M. (1991). Focus group interview with parents of children with medically complex needs: An intimate look at their perceptions and feelings. *Children's Health Care, 20,* 170–178.

Dillon, K. M. (1993). Facilitated communication, autism, and ouija. *Skeptical Inquirer, 17,* 281–287.

DiNicola, V. F., Roberts, N., & Oke, L. (1989). Eating and mood disorders in young children. *Psychiatric Clinics of North America, 12,* 873–893.

Doe, S. (1994, August 22). Anorexic teen: "We need help, not insults." *Los Angeles Times,* p. B5.

Doka, K. J. (1989). Disenfranchised grief. In K. J. Doka (Ed.), *Disenfranchised grief* (pp. 3–11). Lexington, MA: Lexington Books.

Domek, D. (1994). Failure to thrive: Medical issues. In R. A. Olson, L. L. Mullins, J. B. Gillman, & J. M. Chaney (Eds.), *The sourcebook of pediatric psychology* (pp. 26–28). Boston: Allyn and Bacon.

Donaghy, W. C. (1984). *The interview: Skills and applications.* Glenview, IL: Scott, Foresman.

Donders, J. (1993). Bereavement and mourning in pediatric rehabilitation settings. *Death Studies, 17,* 517–527.

Donovan, J. E., Jessor, R., & Costa, F. M. (1988). Syndrome of problem behavior in adolescence: A replication. *Journal of Consulting and Clinical Psychology, 56,* 762–765.

Douglas, M. A. (1987). The battered woman syndrome. In D. J. Sonkin (Ed.), *Domestic violence on trial: Psychological and legal dimensions of family violence* (pp. 39–54). New York: Springer.

Douglas, V. I. (1988). Cognitive deficits in children with attention deficit disorder with hyperactivity. In L. M. Bloomindale & J. Sergeant (Eds.), *Attention deficit disorder: Criteria, cognition, and intervention* [A book supplement of the *Journal of Child Psychology and Psychiatry* (No. 5)] (pp. 65–81). New York: Pergamon.

Downs, C. W., Smeyak, G. P., & Martin, E. (1980). *Professional interviewing.* New York: Harper & Row.

Doyle, J. S., & Bauer, S. K. (1989). Post-traumatic stress disorder in children: Its identification and treatment in a residential setting for emotionally disturbed youth. *Journal of Traumatic Stress, 2,* 275–288.

Dozier, M. (1990). Attachment organization and treatment use for adults with serious psychopathological disorders. *Development and Psychopathology, 2,* 47–60.

Drake, E. A., & Bardon, J. I. (1978). Confidentiality and inter-agency communication: Effect of the Buckley Amendment. *Hospital and Community Psychiatry, 29,* 312–315.

Draucker, C. B. (1993). Childhood sexual abuse: Sources of trauma. *Issues in Mental Health Nursing, 14,* 249–262.

Drell, M. J., Siegel, C. H., & Gaensbauer, T. J. (1993). Post-traumatic stress disorder. In C. H. Zeanah, Jr. (Ed.), *Handbook of infant mental health* (pp. 291–304). New York: Guilford.

Dresser, N. (1994, October 24). Recognizing death as a part of life. *Los Angeles Times,* p. B6.

Dresser, N. (1996a). *Multicultural manners.* New York: Wiley.

Dresser, N. (1996b, April 20). Remaining safe from the remains. *Los Angeles Times,* p. B7.

Drotar, D., Baskiewicz, A., Irvin, N., Kennell, J., & Klaus, M. (1975). The adaptation of parents to the birth of an infant with a congenital malformation: A hypothetical model. *Pediatrics, 56,* 710–717.

Drotar, D., & Sturm, L. (1994). Failure to thrive: Psychological issues. In R. A. Olson, L. L. Mullins, J. B. Gillman, & J. M. Chaney (Eds.), *The sourcebook of pediatric psychology* (pp. 29–41). Boston: Allyn and Bacon.

Drugge, J. E. (1992). Perceptions of child sexual assault: The effects of victim and offender characteristics and behavior. *Journal of Offender Rehabilitation, 18,* 141–165.

Dunbar, J., & Waszak, L. (1990). Patient compliance: Pediatric and adolescent populations. In A. M. Gross & R. S. Drabman (Eds.), *Handbook of clinical behavioral pediatrics* (pp. 365–382). New York: Plenum.

Dunn, R., & Dunn, K. (1977). *How to raise independent and professionally successful daughters.* Englewood Cliffs, NJ: Prentice Hall.

Dunne, E. J., McIntosh, J. L., & Maxim, K. D. (1987). Suggested reading list for survivors of suicide. In E. J. Dunne, J. L. McIntosh, & K. D. Maxim (Eds.), *Suicide and its aftermath: Understanding and counseling the survivors* (pp. 287–288). New York: Norton.

Dunne-Maxim, K., Dunne, E. J., & Hauser, M. J. (1987). When children are suicide survivors. In E. J. Dunne, J. L. McIntosh, & K. D. Maxim (Eds.), *Suicide and its aftermath: Understanding and counseling the survivors* (pp. 234–244). New York: Norton.

DuPaul, G. J., & Stoner, G. (1994). *ADHD in the schools: Assessment and intervention strategies.* New York: Guilford.

Duquette, D. N. (1990). *Advocating for the child in protection proceedings: A handbook for lawyers and court appointed special advocates.* Lexington, MA: Lexington Books/D. C. Heath.

Dutton, D. G., & Painter, S. (1993). The battered woman syndrome: Effects of severity and intermittency of abuse. *American Journal of Orthopsychiatry, 63,* 614–622.

Duwa, S. M., Wells, C., & Lalinde, P. (1993). Creating family-centered programs and policies. In D. M. Bryant & M. A. Graham (Eds.), *Implementing early intervention: From research to effective practice* (pp. 92–123). New York: Guilford.

Ebonics at a glance. (1997, January 19). *Los Angeles Times,* p. 22.

Edelbrock, C. S. (1984). Developmental considerations. In T. H. Ollendick & M. Hersen (Eds.), *Child behavioral assessment: Principles and procedures* (pp. 20–37). New York: Pergamon.

Edelbrock, C. S., & Costello, A. J. (1988). Structured psychiatric interviews for children. In M. Rutter, A. H. Tuma, & I. Lann (Eds.), *Assessment diagnosis in child psychopathology* (pp. 87–112). New York: Guilford.

Edelbrock, C. S., Costello, A. J., Dulcan, M. K., Conover, N. C., & Kalas, R. (1986). Parent-child agreement on child psychiatric symptoms assessed via structured interview. *Journal of Child Psychology and Psychiatry, 27,* 181–190.

Edelbrock, C. S., Costello, A. J., Dulcan, M. K., Kalas, R., & Conover, N. C. (1985). Age differences in the reliability of the psychiatric interview of the child. *Child Development, 56,* 265–275.

Edwards, G., & Starr, M. (1996). Internalizing disorders: Mood and anxiety disorders. In M. J. Breen & C. R. Fiedler (Eds.), *Behavioral approach to assessment of youth with emotional/behavioral disorders: A handbook for school-based practitioners* (pp. 361–412). Austin, TX: Pro-Ed.

Egeland, B., & Abery, B. (1991). A longitudinal study of high-risk children: Educational outcomes. *International Journal of Disability, Development & Education, 38,* 271–287.

Eisen, A. R., & Kearney, C. A. (1995). *Practitioner's guide to treating fear and anxiety in children and adolescents: A cognitive-behavioral approach.* Northvale, NJ: Aronson.

Eisenbruch, M. (1991). From post-traumatic stress disorder to cultural bereavement: Diagnosis of Southeast Asian refugees. *Social Science and Medicine, 33,* 673–680.

Eiser, C. (1993). *Growing up with a chronic disease: The impact on children and their families.* Bristol, PA: Jessica Kingsley Publishers.

Elkin, M. (1991). Joint custody: In the best interest of the family. In J. Folberg (Ed.), *Joint custody and shared parenting* (2nd ed., pp. 11–25). New York: Guilford.

Elliott, M. (1993). Men survivors' stories. In M. Elliott (Ed.), *Female sexual abuse of children* (pp. 153–197). New York: Guilford.

Elliott, M., Browne, K., & Kilcoyne, J. (1995). Child sexual abuse prevention: What offenders tell us. *Child Abuse & Neglect, 19,* 579–594.

Elton, A. (1988). Assessment of families for treatment. In A. Bentovim, A. Elton, J. Hildegrand, M. Tranter, & E. Vizard (Eds.), *Child sexual abuse within the family, assessment and treatment* (pp. 153–181). Bristol, England: John Wright.

Emmons, R. (1996, December 27). Black English has its place. *Los Angeles Times,* p. B9.

Enelow, A. J., & Swisher, S. N. (1986). *Interviewing and patient care* (3rd ed.). New York: Oxford University Press.

Engel, G. L. (1977). The need for a new medical model: A challenge for biomedicine. *Science, 196,* 129–136.

Epstein, N. B., & Bishop, D. S. (1981). Problem-centered systems therapy of the family. In A. Gurman & D. Kiniskern (Eds.), *Handbook of family therapy* (pp. 444–482). New York: Brunner/Mazel.

Erickson, M. F., & Egeland, B. (1996). Child neglect. In J. Briere, L. Berliner, J. A. Bulkley, C. Jenny, & T. Reid (Eds.), *The*

APSAC handbook on child maltreatment (pp. 4–20). Thousand Oaks, CA: Sage.

Eth, S. (1990). Post-traumatic stress disorder in childhood. In M. Hersen & C. G. Last (Eds.), *Handbook of child and adult psychopathology* (pp. 263–274). New York: Pergamon.

Evans, C. A., Stevens, M., Cushway, D., & Houghton, J. (1992). Sibling response to childhood cancer: A new approach. *Child: Care, Health & Development, 18,* 229–244.

Evans, D., Hearn, M., Uhleman, M. R., & Ivey, A. E. (1979). *Essential interviewing: A programmed approach to effective communication.* Monterey, CA: Brooks/Cole.

Evans, H. L., & Sullivan, M. A. (1993). Children and the use of self-monitoring, self-evaluation, and self-reinforcement. In A. J. Finch, Jr., W. M. Nelson, III, & E. S. Ott (Eds.), *Cognitive-behavioral procedures with children and adolescents: A practical guide* (pp. 67–89). Boston: Allyn and Bacon.

Everett, F., Proctor, N., & Cartmell, B. (1983). Providing psychological services to American Indian children and families. *Professional Psychology: Research and Practice, 14,* 588–603.

Everson, M. D., & Boat, B. W. (1994). Putting the anatomical doll controversy in perspective: An examination of the major uses and criticisms of the dolls in child sexual abuse evaluations. *Child Abuse & Neglect, 18,* 113–129.

Ewing-Cobbs, L., Levin, H. S., Eisenberg, H. M., & Fletcher, J. M. (1987). Language functions following closed-head injury in children and adolescents. *Journal of Clinical & Experimental Neuropsychology, 9,* 575–592.

Fairburn, C. G., & Cooper, Z. (1993). The Eating Disorder Examination (12th ed.). In C. G. Fairburn & G. T. Wilson (Eds.), *Binge eating: Nature, assessment and treatment* (pp. 317–360). New York: Guilford.

Falicov, C. J. (1982). Mexican families. In M. McGoldrick, J. K. Pearce, & J. Giordano (Eds.), *Ethnicity and family therapy* (pp. 134–163). New York: Guilford.

Faller, K. C. (1988). *Child sexual abuse: An interdisciplinary manual for diagnosis, case management, and treatment.* New York: Columbia University Press.

Faller, K. C., Froning, M. L., & Lipovsky, J. A. (1991). The parent-child interview: Use in evaluating child allegations of sexual abuse by the parent. *American Journal of Orthopsychiatry, 61,* 552–557.

Fals-Stewart, W., & Schafer, J. (1992). Using neuropsychological assessment with adolescent substance abusers: A review of findings and treatment implications. *Comprehensive Mental Health Care, 2,* 179–199.

Famighetti, R. (Ed.). (1995). *The world almanac: And book of facts.* Mahwah, NJ: Funk & Wagnalls.

Famularo, R., Kinscherff, R., & Fenton, T. (1990). Symptom differences in acute and chronic presentation of childhood post-traumatic stress disorder. *Child Abuse & Neglect, 14,* 439–444.

Fantuzzo, J., Boruch, R., Beriama, A., Atkins, M., & Marcus, S. (1997). Domestic violence and children: Prevalence and risk in five major U.S. cities. *Journal of the American Academy of Child & Adolescent Psychiatry, 36,* 116–122.

Farberow, N., & Gordon, N. (1981). *Manual for child health workers in major disasters* [DHHS Publication No. (ADM) 81-1071]. Washington, DC: U.S. Government Printing Office.

Federal Emergency Management Agency. (1992). *Helping children cope with disaster.* Washington, DC: Author.

Feinstein, S. (1986, October 9). Computers are replacing interviewers for personnel and marketing tasks. *Wall Street Journal,* p. 37.

Felner, R. D., & Terre, L. (1987). Child custody dispositions and children's adaptation following divorce. In L. A. Weithorn (Ed.), *Psychology and child custody determinations: Knowledge, roles, and expertise* (pp. 106–153). Lincoln: University of Nebraska Press.

Fenster, R. G. (1988). The effect of the deaf child upon the family. *Australian Journal of Sex, Marriage & Family, 9,* 225–234.

Ferber, R. (1985). Sleep, sleeplessness, and sleep disruptions in infants and young children. *Annals of Clinical Research, 17,* 227–234.

Ferholt, J. D. L. (1980). *Clinical assessment of children: A comprehensive approach to primary pediatric care.* Philadelphia: Lippincott.

Figley, C. R. (1983). Catastrophes: An overview of family reactions. In C. R. Figley & H. I. McCubbin (Eds.), *Stress and the family: Vol. II. Coping with catastrophe* (pp. 3–20). New York: Brunner/Mazel.

Filip, J., Schene, P., & McDaniel, N. (Eds.). (1991). *Helping in Child Protective Services—A casework handbook* (Rev. ed.). Englewood, CO: American Humane Association.

Filley, C. M., Cranberg, L. D., Alexander, M. P., & Hart, E. J. (1987). Neurobehavioral outcome after closed head injury in childhood and adolescence. *Archives of Neurology, 44,* 194–198.

Filley, C. M., Heaton, R. K., & Rosenberg, N. C. (1990). White matter dementia in chronic toluene abuse. *Neurology, 40,* 532–534.

Fine, M. J. (1991). The handicapped child and the family: Implications for professionals. In M. J. Fine (Ed.), *Collaboration with parents of exceptional children* (pp. 3–24). Brandon, VT: Clinical Psychology Publishing Co.

Finkelhor, D. (1984). *Child sexual abuse: New theory and research.* New York: Free Press.

Finkelhor, D. (1988). The trauma of child sexual abuse. In G. E. Wyatt & G. J. Powell (Eds.), *Lasting effects of child sexual abuse* (pp. 61–82). Beverly Hills: Sage.

Finkelhor, D. (1990). Early and long-term effects of child sexual abuse: An update. *Professional Psychology: Research and Practice, 21,* 325–330.

Finkelhor, D. (1993). The main problem is still underreporting, not overreporting. In R. J. Gelles & D. R. Loseke (Eds.), *Current controversies on family violence* (pp. 273–287). Newbury Park, CA: Sage.

Finkelhor, D. (1995). The victimization of children: A developmental perspective. *American Journal of Orthopsychiatry, 65,* 177–193.

Finlayson, L. M., & Koocher, G. P. (1991). Professional judgment and child abuse reporting in sexual abuse cases. *Professional Psychology: Research and Practice, 22,* 464–472.

Fish, B. (1985). Children's Psychiatric Rating Scale—A. *Psychopharmacology Bulletin, 21,* 753, 764.

Fisher, R. P., & Geiselman, R. E. (1992). *Memory-enhancing techniques for investigative interviewing: The cognitive interview.* Springfield, IL: Charles C Thomas.

Fivush, R., & Shukat, J. R. (1995). Content, consistency, and coherence of early autobiographical recall. In M. S. Zaragoza, J. R. Graham, G. C. N. Hall, R. Hirschman, & Y. S. Ben-Porath (Eds.), *Memory and testimony in the child witness* (pp. 5–23). Thousand Oaks, CA: Sage.

Fixico, M. (1986). The road to middle class Indian America. In C. E. Tratzer (Ed.), *American Indian identity: Today's changing perspectives* (pp. 29–37). Sacramento, CA: Sierra Oaks.

Florian, V., Katz, S., & Lahav, V. (1989). Impact of traumatic brain damage on family dynamics and functioning: A review. *Brain Injury, 3,* 219–233.

Foddy, W. H. (1993). *Constructing questions for interviews and questionnaires: Theory and practice in social research.* New York: Cambridge University Press.

Fontana, V. J., & Besharov, D. J. (1996). *The maltreated child: The maltreatment syndrome in children—A medical, legal and social guide* (5th ed.). Springfield, IL: Charles C Thomas.

Fontes, L. A. (1993). Disclosures of sexual abuse by Puerto Rican children: Oppression and cultural barriers. *Journal of Child Sexual Abuse, 2,* 21–35.

Foreyt, J. P., & Goodrick, G. K. (1988). Childhood obesity. In E. J. Mash & L. G. Terdal (Eds.), *Behavioral assessment of childhood disorders* (2nd ed., pp. 528–551). New York: Guilford.

Forness, S. R., Kavale, K. A., & Lopez, M. (1993). Conduct disorders in school: Special education eligibility and comorbidity. *Journal of Emotional & Behavioral Disorders, 1,* 101–108.

Fortier, L. M., & Wanlass, R. L. (1984). Family crisis following the diagnosis of a handicapped child. *Family Relations, 33,* 13–24.

France, K., & Kish, M. (1995). *Supportive interviewing in human service organizations: Fundamental skills for gathering information and encouraging productive change.* Springfield, IL: Charles C Thomas.

France, K. G., & Hudson, S. M. (1993). Management of infant sleep disturbance: A review. *Clinical Psychology Review, 13,* 635–647.

Franck, I. M., & Brownstone, D. (1991). *The parent's desk reference.* New York: Prentice Hall.

Frank, M. G. (1992). Commentary: On the structure of lies and deception experiments. In S. J. Ceci, M. D. Leichtman, & M. Putnick (Eds.), *Cognitive and social factors in early deception* (pp. 127–146). Hillsdale, NJ: Erlbaum.

Fraser, B. G. (1981). Sexual child abuse: The legislation and the law in the United States. In P. B. Mrazek & C. H. Kempe (Eds.), *Sexually abused children and their families* (pp. 55–74). New York: Pergamon.

Freedman, D. A., Feinstein, C., & Berger, K. (1988). The blind child and adolescent. In C. J. Kestenbaum & D. T. Williams (Eds.), *Handbook of clinical assessment of children and adolescents* (Vol. 2, pp. 864–878). New York: New York University Press.

Freedman, M. R., Rosenberg, S. J., Gettman-Felzien, D., & Van Scoyk, S. (1993). Evaluator countertransference in child custody evaluations. *American Journal of Forensic Psychology, 11,* 61–73.

Freeman, B. J., & Ritvo, E. A. (1984). The syndrome of autism: Establishing diagnosis and principles of management. *Pediatric Annals, 13,* 284–296.

Fremouw, W. J., de Perczel, M., & Ellis, T. E. (1990). *Suicide risk: Assessment and response guidelines.* Elmsford, NY: Pergamon.

Frick, P. J. (1993). Childhood conduct problems in a family context. *School Psychology Review, 22,* 376–385.

Frick, P. J., Silverthorn, P., & Evans, C. (1994). Assessment of childhood anxiety using structured interviews: Patterns of agreement among informants and association with maternal anxiety. *Psychological Assessment, 6,* 372–379.

Frick, P. J., Strauss, C. C., Lahey, B. B., & Christ, M. A. G. (1992). Behavior disorders of children. In P. B. Sutker (Ed.), *Comprehensive handbook of psychopathology* (pp. 765–789). New York: Plenum.

Friedman, M. M. (1986). *Family nursing: Theory and assessment* (2nd ed.). Norwalk, CT: Appleton-Century-Crofts.

Friedrich, W. N., Greenberg, M. T., & Crnic, K. (1983). A short-form of the Questionnaire on Resources and Stress. *American Journal of Mental Deficiency, 88,* 41–48.

Fritz, G. K., & Overholser, J. C. (1989). Patterns of response to childhood asthma. *Psychosomatic Medicine, 51,* 347–355.

Frude, N. (1991). *Understanding family problems: A psychological approach.* New York: Wiley.

Fulwood, S., III. (1995a, October 30). Black attitudes shift away from goal of inclusion. *Los Angeles Times,* pp. A1, A16.

Fulwood, S., III. (1995b, November 25). U.S. Blacks: A divided experience. *Los Angeles Times,* pp. A1, A30.

Furniss, T. (1991). *The multi-professional handbook of child sexual abuse: Integrated management, therapy, and legal intervention.* London: Routledge.

Fyfe, A. (1989). *Child labour.* Cambridge, England: Polity Press.

Gadow, K. D. (1991). Clinical issues in child and adolescent psychopharmacology. *Journal of Consulting and Clinical Psychology, 59,* 842–852.

Gaffney, A., & Dunne, E. A. (1986). Developmental aspects of children's definitions of pain. *Pain, 26,* 105–117.

Gans, B. M., Mann, N. R., & Ylvisaker, M. (1990). Rehabilitation management approaches. In M. Rosenthal, E. R. Griffith, M. R. Bond, & J. D. Miller (Eds.), *Rehabilitation of the adult and child with traumatic brain injury* (2nd ed., pp. 593–615). Philadelphia: Davis.

Garbarino, J. K., Guttman, E., & Seeley, J. W. (1987). *The psychologically battered child: Strategies for identification, assessment and intervention.* San Francisco: Jossey-Bass.

Garbarino, J. K., & Stott, F. M. (1989). *What children can tell us: Eliciting, interpreting, and evaluating information from children.* San Francisco: Jossey-Bass.

Garcia, J. M., Garrett, K., Stetz, M., Emanuel, L., & Brandt, J. (1990). Early behavioral responses in severe head injury. *Cognitive Rehabilitation, 8,* 30–36.

Gardner, F. E. (1992). Parent-child interaction and conduct disorder. *Educational Psychology Review, 4,* 135–163.

Gardner, R. A. (1982). *Family evaluation in child custody litigation.* Cresskill, NJ: Creative Therapeutics.

Garner, D. M., Olmsted, M. P., & Polivy, J. (1983). Development and validation of a multidimensional eating disorder inventory for anorexia nervosa and bulimia. *International Journal of Eating Disorders, 2,* 15–34.

Garner, D. M., & Parker, P. (1993). Eating disorders. In T. H. Ollendick & M. Hersen (Eds.), *Handbook of child and adolescent assessment* (pp. 384–399). New York: Pergamon.

Garner, R. (1987). *Metacognition and reading comprehension.* Norwood, NJ: Ablex.

Garrett, A. M. (1982). *Interviewing: Its principles and methods* (3rd ed.). New York: Family Service Association of America.

Garrison, W. T., & McQuiston, S. (1989). *Chronic illness during childhood and adolescence: Psychological aspects.* Newbury Park, CA: Sage.

Gaudin, J. M. (1993). Effective intervention with neglectful families. *Criminal Justice and Behavior, 20,* 66–89.

Gearheart, B. R., & Willenberg, E. P. (1980). *Application of pupil assessment information* (3rd ed.). Denver: Love.

Geffken, G., & Johnson, S. B. (1994). Diabetes: Psychological issues. In R. A. Olson, L. L. Mullins, J. B. Gillman, & J. M. Chaney (Eds.), *The sourcebook of pediatric psychology* (pp. 118–129). Boston: Allyn and Bacon.

Gellert, G. A., Berkowitz, C. D., & Durfee, M. J. (1993). Testing the sexually abused child for HIV: Reducing uncertainty in clinical decision-making. *Journal of Child Sexual Abuse, 2,* 83–93.

Gelles, R. J. (1993). Family violence. In R. L. Hampton, T. P. Gullotta, G. R. Adams, E. H. Potter, & R. Weissberg (Eds.), *Family violence: Prevention and treatment* (pp. 1–24). Thousand Oaks, CA: Sage.

Gibbs, J. C., Basinger, K. S., & Fuller, K. (1992). *Moral maturity: Measuring the development of sociomoral reflection.* Hillsdale, NJ: Erlbaum.

Gibbs, J. T. (1990). Mental health issues of black adolescents: Implications for policy and practice. In A. R. Stiffman & L. E. Davis (Eds.), *Ethnic issues in adolescent mental health* (pp. 21–52). Newbury Park, CA: Sage.

Gibbs, J. T., & Huang, L. N. (1989). A conceptual framework for assessing and treating minority youth. In J. T. Gibbs & L. N. Huang (Eds.), *Children of color: Psychological interventions with minority children* (pp. 1–29). San Francisco: Jossey-Bass.

Gibson, E. (1996, September 21). Social workers and abused children. *Los Angeles Times,* p. B9.

Giger, J. N., & Davidhizar, R. F. (Eds.). (1991). *Transcultural nursing: Assessment and intervention.* St. Louis: Mosby.

Gilliland, B. E., & James, R. K. (1993). *Crisis intervention strategies* (2nd ed.). Pacific Grove, CA: Brooks/Cole.

Gillis, H. M. (1993). Individual and small-group psychotherapy for children involved in trauma and disaster. In C. F. Saylor (Ed.), *Children and disasters* (pp. 165–186). New York: Plenum.

Gilmore, S. K. (1973). *The counselor-in-training.* New York: Appleton-Century-Crofts.

Gilsig, L. D. (1993). *To a 12-year-old whose name I never knew.* Unpublished manuscript (Reprinted in the book review section of the *Los Angeles Times,* August 1, 1993, p. 6).

Giordano, G. (1987). Diagnosing specific math disabilities. *Academic Therapy, 23,* 69–74.

Gleaves, D. H. (1996). The sociocognitive model of dissociative identity disorder: A reexamination of the evidence. *Psychological Bulletin, 120,* 42–59.

Glick, P. C. (1988). The role of divorce in the changing family structure: Trends and variations. In S. A. Wolchik & P. Karoly (Eds.), *Children of divorce: Empirical perspectives on adjustment* (pp. 3–34). New York: Gardner.

Glidden, L. M. (1994). Not under my heart, but in it: Families by adoption. In J. Blacher (Ed.), *When there's no place like home: Options for children living apart from their natural families* (pp. 181–209). Baltimore: Brookes.

Goetting, A., & Goetting, M. G. (1993). Adoptive parents to children with severe developmental disabilities: A profile. *Children & Youth Services Review, 15,* 489–506.

Goldberg, R. J., & Tull, R. M. (1983). *The psychosocial dimensions of cancer: A practical guide for healthcare providers.* New York: Free Press.

Goldenberg, H. (1983). *Contemporary clinical psychology* (2nd ed.). Monterey, CA: Brooks/Cole.

Goodman, J. D., & Sours, J. A. (1967). *The child mental status examination.* New York: Basic Books.

Goodman, L. A. (1991). The prevalence of abuse among homeless and housed poor mothers: A comparison study. *American Journal of Orthopsychiatry, 61,* 489–500.

Goodman, L. A., Saxe, L., & Harvey, M. (1991). Homelessness as psychological trauma: Broadening perspectives. *American Psychologist, 46,* 1219–1225.

Gorden, R. L. (1975). *Interviewing: Strategy, techniques and tactics* (Rev. ed.). Homewood, IL: Dorsey.

Gordon, B. N., Schroeder, C. S., Ornstein, P. A., & Baker-Ward, L. E. (1995). Clinical implications of research on memory development. In T. Ney (Ed.), *True and false allegations of child sexual abuse: Assessment and case management* (pp. 99–124). New York: Brunner/Mazel.

Gorman, T. (1995, February 23). Two teen-age girls, "tired of life," die in suicide pact. *Los Angeles Times,* pp. A3, A21.

Gorney, C. (1988, May 18). The community of fear. *Washington Post,* p. D1.

Goswami, U. (1992). Phonological factors in spelling development. *Journal of Child Psychology and Psychiatry, 33,* 967–975.

Gotlib, I. H., & Hammen, C. L. (1992). *Psychological aspects of depression: Toward a cognitive-interpersonal integration. The Wiley series in clinical psychology.* Chichester, England: Wiley.

Gratus, J. (1988). *Successful interviewing.* Harmondsworth, England: Penguin Books.

Gray, J., Cutler, C., Dean, J., & Kempe, C. H. (1976). Perinatal assessment of mother-baby interaction. In R. Helfer & C. H. Kempe (Eds.), *Child abuse and neglect: The family and the community* (pp. 377–392). Cambridge, MA: Ballinger.

Green, B. L., Korol, M., Grace, M. C., Vary, M. G., Leonard, A. C., Gleser, G. C., & Smitson-Cohen, S. (1991). Children and disaster: Age, gender, and parental effects on PTSD symptoms. *Journal of the American Academy of Child & Adolescent Psychiatry, 30,* 945–951.

Green, P. (1994, April 30). An adoption can be a trying experience. *San Diego Union-Tribune,* p. B9.

Greenbaum, A. (1982). Conducting effective parent conferences. *Communiqué, 10*(6), 4–5.

Greenberg, S. A. (1990). Conducting unbiased sexual abuse evaluations. Some suggestions for conducting interviews of sex abuse victims. *Preventing Sexual Abuse, 2,* 8–14.

Greenfield, D. (1987). Feigned psychosis in a 14-year-old girl. *Hospital and Community Psychiatry, 38,* 73–75.

Greenspan, S. I., & Greenspan, N. T. (1981). *The clinical interview of the child.* New York: McGraw-Hill.

Greer, D. (1995, April). Failure to thrive: Guidelines for investigation. *Update—National Center for Prosecution of Child Abuse, 8*(4).

Gregory, S. (1976). *The deaf child and his family.* London: Allen and Unwin.

Gresham, F. M. (1984). Behavioral interviews in school psychology: Issues in psychometric adequacy and research. *School Psychology Review, 13,* 17–25.

Grevious, C. (1985). The role of the family therapist with low-income Black families. *Family Therapy, 12,* 115–122.

Grollman, E. A. (1974). Children and death. In E. A. Grollman (Ed.), *Concerning death: A practical guide for the living* (pp. 65–79). Boston: Beacon.

Grollman, E. A. (1990). *Talking about death: A dialogue between parent and child.* Boston: Beacon.

Grosch, W. N., & Olsen, D. C. (1994). *When helping starts to hurt: A new look at burnout among psychotherapists.* New York: Norton.

Gross, A. M. (1990). Behavioral management of the child with diabetes. In A. M. Gross & R. S. Drabman (Eds.), *Handbook of clinical behavioral pediatrics* (pp. 147–163). New York: Plenum.

Gross, J. (1996, February 26). Front-line fighter for children. *Los Angeles Times,* pp. A1, A10.

Grossman, C. S. (1983). Children's books: Developing positive attitudes by and toward the handicapped. *Clinical Pediatrics, 23,* 448–463.

Grossman, H. J. (Ed.). (1983). *Classification in mental retardation.* Washington, DC: American Association on Mental Deficiency.

Grossman, T. B. (1986). *Mothers and children facing divorce.* Ann Arbor, MI: UMI Press.

Groth, A. N. (1979). *Men who rape: The psychology of the offender.* New York: Plenum.

Groth, A. N. (1982). The incest offender. In S. M. Sgroi (Ed.), *Handbook of clinical intervention in child sexual abuse* (pp. 215–239). Lexington, MA: Lexington Books.

Grych, J. H., & Fincham, F. D. (1990). Marital conflict and children's adjustment: A cognitive contextual framework. *Psychological Bulletin, 108,* 267–290.

Gudas, L. J. (1993). Concepts of death and loss in childhood and adolescence: A developmental perspective. In C. F. Saylor (Ed.), *Children and disasters* (pp. 67–84). New York: Plenum.

Gudas, L. J., Koocher, G. P., & Wypij, D. (1991). Perceptions of medical compliance in children and adolescents with cystic fibrosis. *Journal of Developmental and Behavioral Pediatrics, 12,* 236–242.

Guernsey, T. F., & Klare, K. (1993). *Special education law.* Durham, NC: Carolina Academic Press.

Gutheil, I. A. (1992). Considering the physical environment: An essential component of good practice. *Social Work, 37,* 391–396.

Guttmann, J. (1993). *Divorce in psychosocial perspective: Theory and research.* Hillsdale, NJ: Erlbaum.

Hafen, B. Q., & Frandsen, J. K. (1985). *Psychological emergencies and crisis intervention.* Englewood, CO: Morton.

Hagerty, B. K. (1984). *Psychiatric–mental health assessment.* St. Louis: Mosby.

Hagopian, L. P., & Ollendick, T. H. (1993). Simple phobia in children. In R. T. Ammerman & M. Hersen (Eds.), *Handbook of behavior therapy with children and adults: A developmental and longitudinal perspective* (pp. 123–136). Boston: Allyn and Bacon.

Hahn, W. K. (1987). Cerebral lateralization of function: From infancy through childhood. *Psychological Bulletin, 101,* 376–392.

Haldane, D. (1988, September 24). Asian girls: A cultural tug of war. *Los Angeles Times,* pp. I1, I22, I23.

Haley, J. (1987). *Problem solving therapy* (2nd ed.). San Francisco: Jossey-Bass.

Hall, L. A., Sachs, B., Rayens, M. K., & Lutenbacher, M. (1993). Childhood physical and sexual abuse: Their relationship with depressive symptoms in adulthood. *IMAGE: Journal of Nursing Scholarship, 25,* 317–323.

Hamill, P. V. V. (1977). NCHS growth curves for children. *Vital and Health Statistics, 11,* No. 165. Washington, DC: U.S. Government Printing Office (DWEH No. 78–1650).

Hammen, C. L., & Rudolph, K. D. (1996). Childhood depression. In E. J. Mash & R. A. Barkley (Eds.), *Child psychopathology* (pp. 153–195). New York: Guilford.

Hancock, K., Wilgosh, L., & McDonald, L. (1990). Parenting a visually impaired child: The mother's perspective. *Journal of Visual Impairment & Blindness, 84,* 411–413.

Handleman, J. S. (1990). Providing effective consultation to students with severe developmental disabilities and their families. *Journal of Educational & Psychological Consultation, 1,* 137–147.

Hanson, C. L., & Onikul-Ross, S. R. (1990). Developmental issues in the lives of youths with insulin-dependent diabetes mellitus. In S. B. Morgan & T. M. Okwumabua (Eds.), *Child and adolescent disorders: Developmental and health psychology perspectives* (pp. 201–240). Hillsdale, NJ: Erlbaum.

Harris, J. C. (1995). *Developmental neuropsychiatry: Vol. 2. Assessment, diagnosis, and treatment of developmental disorders.* Cary, NC: Oxford University Press.

Harris, R. (1991, May 15). Homeless boy's life a series of moving days, schools. *Los Angeles Times,* pp. A1, A16–A17.

Harris, R. J., & Cook, C. A. (1994). Attributions about spouse abuse: It matters who the batterers and victims are. *Sex Roles, 30,* 553–565.

Harris, S. L. (1994). *Siblings of children with autism: A guide for families.* Bethesda, MD: Woodbine House.

Harry, B. (1986). Interview, diagnostic, and legal aspects in the forensic psychiatric assessments of deaf persons. *Bulletin of the American Academy of Psychiatry & the Law, 14,* 147–162.

Hart, S. N., Brassard, M. R., & Karlson, H. C. (1996). Psychological maltreatment. In J. Briere, L. Berliner, J. A. Bulkley, C. Jenny, & T. Reid (Eds.), *The APSAC handbook on child maltreatment* (pp. 72–89). Thousand Oaks, CA: Sage.

Hartley, L. L. (1990). Assessment of functional communication. In D. E. Tupper & K. D. Cicerone (Eds.), *The neuropsychology of everyday life: Assessment of basic competencies* (pp. 125–168). Boston: Kluwer.

Hartley, R. E., Frank, L. K., & Goldenson, R. M. (1952). *Understanding children's play.* New York: Columbia University Press.

Haskew, P., & Donnellan, A. M. (1993). *Emotional maturity and well-being: Psychological lessons of facilitated communication.* Madison, WI: DRI Press.

Hatchett-Jones, A., McClosky, L., Muzic, J., Shapiro, M., Tadros, W., & Tomita, M. (1994, June). *Domestic violence: Recognizing the epidemic.* Unpublished manuscript, Kaiser Permanente, Southern California Region.

Haugaard, J. J., & Reppucci, N. D. (1988). *The sexual abuse of children: A comprehensive guide to current knowledge and intervention strategies.* San Francisco: Jossey-Bass.

Hauser, M. J. (1987). Special aspects of grief after a suicide. In E. J. Dunne, J. L. McIntosh, & K. D. Maxim (Eds.), *Suicide and its aftermath: Understanding and counseling the survivors* (pp. 57–70). New York: Norton.

Hautman, M. A. (1979). Folk health and illness beliefs. *The Nurse Practitioner: American Journal of Primary Health Care, 4*(4), 23, 26, 27, 31, 34.

Haynes, R. B., Wang, E., & Da Mota Gomes, M. (1987). A critical review of interventions to improve compliance with prescribed medications. *Patient Education and Counseling, 10,* 155–166.

Heath, S. B. (1989). Oral and literate traditions among Black Americans living in poverty. *American Psychologist, 44,* 367–373.

Hécaen, H. (1983). Acquired aphasia in children: Revisited. *Neuropsychologia, 21,* 581–587.

Hechtman, L. (1994). Genetic and neurobiological aspects of attention hyperactive disorder: A review. *Journal of Psychiatry & Neuroscience, 19,* 193–201.

Heide, K. M. (1995). *Why kids kill parents: Child abuse and adolescent homicide.* Thousand Oaks, CA: Sage.

Heiman, M. L. (1992). Putting the puzzle together: Validating allegations of child sexual abuse. *Journal of Child Psychology and Psychiatry, 33,* 311–329.

Helfand, D., & Steinberg, S. (1995, November 22). Suit accuses Beverly Hills of racism. *Los Angeles Times,* pp. B1, B3.

Helms, D. B., & Turner, J. S. (1976). *Exploring child behavior.* Philadelphia: Saunders.

Hepworth, D. H., & Larsen, J. (1990). *Direct social work practice: Theory and skills* (3rd ed). Belmont, CA: Wadsworth.

Herrenkohl, E. C., Herrenkohl, R. C., & Egolf, B. (1994). Resilient early school-age children from maltreating homes: Outcomes in late adolescence. *American Journal of Orthopsychiatry, 64,* 301–309.

Herring, R. D. (1992). Biracial children: An increasing concern for elementary and middle school counselors. *Elementary School Guidance & Counseling, 27,* 123–130.

Hester, N. O., Foster, R. L., & Kristensen, K. (1990). Measurement of pain in children: Generalizability and validity of the pain ladder and poker chip tool. In D. C. Tyler & E. J. Krane (Eds.), *Advances in pain research and therapy* (Vol. 15, pp. 79–84). New York: Raven.

Hetherington, E. M., Law, T. C., & O'Connor, T. G. (1993). Divorce: Challenges, changes, and new chances. In F. Walsh (Ed.), *Normal family processes* (2nd ed., pp. 208–234). New York: Guilford.

Hickey, J. V. (1992). *The clinical practice of neurological and neurosurgical nursing* (3rd ed.). Philadelphia: Lippincott.

Hiegel, S. M., & Hipple, J. (1990). Survivors of suicide; victims left behind: An overview. *TACD Journal, 18,* 55–67.

Hinshaw, S. P. (1994, winter). *Attention deficits and hyperactivity in children.* Thousand Oaks, CA: Sage.

Hirshberg, L. M. (1993). Clinical interviews with infants and their families. In C. H. Zeanah, Jr. (Ed.), *Handbook of infant mental health* (pp. 173–190). New York: Guilford.

Hjern, A., Angel, B., & Höjer, B. (1991). Persecution and behavior: A report of refugee children from Chile. *Child Abuse & Neglect, 15,* 239–248.

Hodges, K. (1993). Structured interviews for assessing children. *Journal of Child Psychology and Psychiatry, 34,* 49–68.

Hodges, K. (1997). *Child Adolescent Schedule (CAS).* Ypsilanti, MI: Eastern Michigan University.

Hodges, W. F. (1986). *Interventions for children of divorce: Custody, access, and psychotherapy.* New York: Wiley.

Hodges, W. F. (1991). *Interventions for children of divorce: Custody, access, and psychotherapy* (2nd ed.). New York: Wiley.

Hodnicki, D. R., & Horner, S. D. (1993). Homeless mothers' caring for children in a shelter. *Issues in Mental Health Nursing, 14,* 349–356.

Hoghughi, M. (1992). *Assessing child and adolescent disorders: A practical manual.* Newbury Park, CA: Sage.

Holden, P., & Serrano, A. C. (1989). Language barriers in pediatric care. *Clinical Pediatrics, 28,* 193–194.

Holinger, P. C., Offer, D., Barter, J. T., & Bell, C. C. (1994). *Suicide and homicide among adolescents.* New York: Guilford.

Holland, J. C. (1989a). Anxiety and cancer: The patient and the family. *Journal of Clinical Psychiatry, 50,* 20–25.

Holland, J. C. (1989b). Stresses on mental health professionals. In J. C. Holland & J. H. Rowland (Eds.), *Handbook of psychooncology: Psychological care of the patient with cancer* (pp. 678–682). New York: Oxford University Press.

Holmes, L. S., & Sellars, I. M. (1991). *Coordination of child protection cases: A guide for child protection services, law enforcement, and county attorneys in Minnesota.* St. Paul: Children's Services Division of Minnesota Department of Human Services.

Holroyd, J. (1974). The Questionnaire on Resources and Stress: An instrument to measure family response to a handicapped family member. *Journal of Community Psychology, 2,* 92–94.

Holtzworth-Munroe, A., & Stuart, G. L. (1994). Typologies of male batterers: Three subtypes and the differences among them. *Psychological Bulletin, 116,* 476–497.

Home Office (1992). *Memorandum of good practice: On video recorded interview with child witnesses for criminal proceedings.* London: HMSO.

Hooper, S. R., Boyd, T. A., Hynd, G. W., & Rubin, J. (1993). Definitional issues and neurobiological foundations of selected severe neurodevelopmental disorders. *Archives of Clinical Neuropsychology, 8,* 279–307.

Hornstein, N. L., & Putnam, F. W. (1992). Clinical phenomenology of child and adolescent dissociative disorders. *Journal of the American Academy of Child & Adolescent Psychiatry, 31,* 1077–1085.

Hornstein, N. L., & Tyson, S. (1991). Inpatient treatment of children with multiple personality/dissociative disorders and their families. *Psychiatric Clinics of North America, 14,* 631–648.

Horton, C. B., & Kochurka, K. A. (1995). The assessment of children with disabilities who report sexual abuse: A special look at those most vulnerable. In T. Ney (Ed.), *True and false allegations of child sexual abuse: Assessment and case management* (pp. 275–289). New York: Brunner/Mazel.

Hotz, R. L. (1996a, October 13). Deciphering the miracles of the mind. *Los Angeles Times,* pp. A1, A20–A22.

Hotz, R. L. (1996b, October 16). Unraveling the riddle of identity. *Los Angeles Times,* pp. A1, A10–A11.

Howard, M. E. (1988). Behavior management in the acute care rehabilitation setting. *Journal of Head Trauma Rehabilitation, 3*(3), 14–22.

Hozman, T. L., & Froiland, D. J. (1976). Families in divorce: A proposed model for counseling the children. *The Family Coordinator, 25,* 271–276.

Huang, L. N., & Ying, Y. W. (1989). Chinese American children and adolescents. In J. T. Gibbs & L. N. Huang (Eds.), *Children of color: Psychological interventions with minority children* (pp. 30–66). San Francisco: Jossey-Bass.

Hughes, J. N. (1988). Interviewing children. In J. M. Dillard & R. R. Reilly (Eds.), *Systematic interviewing: Communication skills for professional effectiveness* (pp. 90–113). Columbus, OH: Merrill.

Hughs, I. (1995). *A prayer for children.* New York: William Morrow.

Human Resources Administration (1993). *1992 Child fatality report—Executive summary.* New York: Author.

Hunt, P. L. (1987). Black clients: Implications for supervision of trainees. *Psychotherapy, 24,* 114–119.

Hunter, J., & Schaecher, R. (1992). Adolescents and AIDS: Coping issues. In P. I. Ahmed & N. Ahmed (Eds.), *Living and dying with AIDS* (pp. 35–45). New York: Plenum.

Huszti, H. C., & Walker, C. E. (1991). Critical issues in consultation and liaison: Pediatrics. In J. J. Sweet, R. H. Rozensky, & S. M. Tovian (Eds.), *Handbook of clinical psychology in medical settings* (pp. 165–185). New York: Plenum.

Hutto, S. C. (1994). Pediatric HIV infection and AIDS: Medical issues. In R. A. Olson, L. L. Mullins, J. B. Gillman, & J. M. Chaney (Eds.), *The sourcebook of pediatric psychology* (pp. 218–224). Boston: Allyn and Bacon.

An infant-care lifesaver. (1996, June 26). *Los Angeles Times,* p. B8.

Jacobs, M. P. (1993). Limited understanding of deficit in children with brain dysfunction. *Neuropsychological Rehabilitation, 3,* 341–365.

Jacobson, J. W., & Mulick, J. A. (1994). Facilitated communication: Better education through applied ideology. *Journal of Behavioral Education, 4,* 95–107.

Jaffe, A. C., & Singer, L. T. (1989). Atypical eating disorders in young children. *International Journal of Eating Disorders, 8,* 575–582.

Jaffe, P., Wolfe, D. A., & Wilson, S. K. (1990). *Children of battered women.* Newbury Park, CA: Sage.

Jahiel, R. I. (1987). The situation of homelessness. In R. Bingham, R. Green, & S. White (Eds.), *The homeless in contemporary society* (pp. 99–118). Newbury Park, CA: Sage.

Jahiel, R. I. (1992). Empirical studies of homeless populations in the 1980s. In R. I. Jahiel (Ed.), *Homelessness: A prevention-oriented approach.* Baltimore: Johns Hopkins University Press.

James, L. A., & Wherry, J. N. (1991). Suicide in residential treatment: Causes, assessment, and treatment issues. *Residential Treatment for Children & Youth, 9,* 23–36.

Jameson, M. (1996, May 5). A place to awaken from the nightmare. *Los Angeles Times,* pp. E2, E6.

Jay, S. M., & Elliott, C. H. (1984). Behavioral observation scales for measuring children's distress: The effects of increased methodological rigor. *Journal of Consulting and Clinical Psychology, 52,* 1106–1107.

Jay, S. M., Elliott, C. H., & Varni, J. W. (1986). Acute and chronic pain in adults and children with cancer. *Journal of Consulting and Clinical Psychology, 54,* 601–607.

Jenkins, R. (1995, November 19). Make room for the changing face of America. *Los Angeles Times,* p. M5.

Jennett, B., & Bond, M. R. (1975). Assessment of outcome after severe brain damage. *Lancet, 1,* 480–484.

Jennings, R. L. (1982). *Handbook for basic considerations in interviewing children.* Unpublished manuscript, Counseling and Assessment Service, Independence, IA.

Jim. (1991, November 19). A father falsely accused reflects on his ruin by perverse system. *San Diego Union,* p. B7.

Joanette, Y., Lafond, D., & Lecours, A. R. (1993). The person and aphasia. In D. Lafond, Y. Joanette, J. Ponzio, R. Jacques, & M. T. Sarno (Eds.), *Living with aphasia: Psychosocial issues* (pp. 17–36). San Diego: Singular.

Johann, S. L. (1994). *Domestic abusers: Terrorists in our homes.* Springfield, IL: Charles C Thomas.

Johansen, B. O. (1988). Care of the dying adolescent and the bereaved family. *Loss, Grief & Care, 2,* 59–67.

Johnson, B. H., Jeppson, E. S., & Redburn, L. (1992). *Caring for children and families: Guidelines for hospitals.* Bethesda, MD: Association for the Care of Children's Health.

Johnson, D. A. (1992). Head injured children and education: A need for greater delineation and understanding. *British Journal of Educational Psychology, 62,* 404–409.

Johnson, D. A., Uttley, D., & Wyke, M. (Eds.). (1989). *Head injured children: Who cares?* Philadelphia: Falmer Press.

Johnson, S. B. (1991). Compliance with complex medical regimens: Assessing daily management of childhood diabetes. *Advances in Behavioral Assessment of Children and Families: A Research Annual, 5,* 113–137.

Johnson, T. C. (1996). *Understanding children's sexual behaviors: What's natural and healthy.* South Pasadena, CA: Author.

Johnston, L. D., O'Malley, P. M., & Bachman, J. G. (1994). *National survey results on drug use from the monitoring the future study, 1975–1993: Vol. 2. College students and young adults.* Washington, DC: U.S. Department of Health and Human Services.

Johnston, L. D., O'Malley, P. M., & Bachman, J. G. (1995a, December 11). *Cigarette smoking among American teens rises again in 1995* [University of Michigan News and Information Services News Release]. Ann Arbor, MI: Author.

Johnston, L. D., O'Malley, P. M., & Bachman, J. G. (1995b, December 11). *Drug use rises again in 1995 among American teens.* [University of Michigan News and Information Services News Release]. Ann Arbor, MI. Author.

Jones, A. C. (1992). Self-esteem and identity in psychotherapy with adolescents from upwardly mobile middle-class African American families. In L. A. Vargas & J. D. Koss-Chioino (Eds.), *Working with culture: Psychotherapeutic interventions with ethnic minority children and adolescents* (pp. 25–42). San Francisco: Jossey-Bass.

Jones, D. P. H., & McQuiston, M. G. (1989). *Interviewing the sexually abused child* (3rd ed.). London: Gaskell/Royal College of Psychiatrists.

Jones, L. (1993). Decision making in child welfare: A critical review of the literature. *Child & Adolescent Social Work Journal, 10,* 241–262.

Jones, R. W., & Peterson, L. W. (1993). Post-traumatic stress disorder in a child following an automobile accident. *Journal of Family Practice, 36,* 223–225.

Jorgensen, E. C. (1990). *Child abuse: A practical guide for those who help others.* New York: Continuum.

Kachur, S. P., Potter, L. B., James, S. P., & Powell, K. E. (1995). *Suicide in the United States, 1980–1992* (Violence Surveillance Summary Series, No. 1). Atlanta: Centers for Disease Control and Prevention, National Center for Injury Prevention and Control.

Kadushin, A. (1983). *The social work interview* (2nd. ed.). New York: Columbia University Press.

Kadushin, A., & Martin, J. A. (1981). *Child abuse: An interactional event.* New York: Columbia University Press.

Kagan, J. (1991). Etiologies of adolescents at risk. *Journal of Adolescent Health, 12,* 591–596.

Kaiser Permanente. (1994). Domestic violence. *Planning for Health* (Issue 2), 8–14.

Kaiser Permanente. (1995, Spring). Managing your medication. *Planning for Health Member News* (Issue 2), 3.

Kalichman, S. C. (1993). *Mandated reporting of suspected child abuse: Ethics, law, and policy.* Hyattsville, MD: American Psychological Association.

Kalichman, S. C. (1996). *Understanding AIDS: A guide for mental health professionals.* Hyattsville, MD: American Psychological Association.

Kamen, B., & Gewirtz, B. (1989). Child maltreatment and the court. In S. M. Ehrenkranz, E. G. Goldstein, L. Goodman, & J. Seinfeld (Eds.), *Clinical social work with maltreated children and their families: An introduction to practice* (pp. 178–201). New York: New York University Press.

Kamphaus, R. W., & Frick, P. J. (1996). *Clinical assessment of child and adolescent personality and behavior.* Boston: Allyn & Bacon.

Kanfer, F. H., & Saslow, G. (1969). Behavioral diagnosis. In C. M. Franks (Ed.), *Behavior therapy: Appraisal and status* (pp. 430–437). New York: McGraw-Hill.

Kanfer, R., Eyberg, S. M., & Krahn, G. L. (1983). Interviewing strategies in child assessment. In C. E. Walker & M. C. Roberts (Eds.), *Handbook of clinical child psychology* (pp. 95–108). New York: Wiley.

Kanfer, R., Eyberg, S. M., & Krahn, G. L. (1992). Interviewing strategies in child assessment. In C. E. Walker & M. C. Roberts (Eds.), *Handbook of clinical child psychology* (2nd ed., pp. 49–62). New York: Wiley.

Kann, L., Warren, C. W., Harris, W. A., Collins, J. L., Williams, B. I., Ross, J. G., & Kolbe, L. J. (1996). Youth risk behavior surveillance—United States, 1995. *Morbidity and Mortality Weekly Report, 45*(4), pp. 1–84.

Kaplan, L., Hennon, C. B., & Ade-Ridder, L. (1993). Splitting custody of children between parents: Impact on the sibling system. *Families in Society, 74,* 131–144.

Karoly, P. (1981). Self-management problems in children. In E. J. Mash & L. G. Terdal (Eds.), *Behavioral assessment of childhood disorders* (pp. 79–126). New York: Guilford.

Karpel, M. A., & Strauss, E. S. (1983). *Family evaluation.* New York: Gardner.

Kash, K. M., & Holland, J. C. (1989). Special problems of physicians and house staff in oncology. In J. C. Holland & J. H. Rowland (Eds.), *Handbook of psychooncology: Psychological care of the patient with cancer* (pp. 647–657). New York: Oxford University Press.

Kaslow, F. (1991). The sociocultural context of divorce. *Contemporary Family Therapy: An International Journal, 13,* 583–607.

Katz, E. R., Dolgin, M. J., & Varni, J. W. (1990). Cancer in children and adolescents. In A. M. Gross & R. S. Drabman (Eds.), *Handbook of clinical behavioral pediatrics* (pp. 129–146). New York: Plenum.

Kaufman, J., Birmaher, B., Brent, D. A., Rao, U., & Ryan N. (1996). *Revised Schedule for Affective Disorders and Schizophrenia for School Aged Children: Present and Lifetime version (K-SADS-PL).* Pittsburgh: Western Psychiatric Institute and Clinic.

Kaufman, K. L. (1994). Munchausen syndrome by proxy: Psychological issues. In R. A. Olson, L. L. Mullins, J. B. Gillman, & J. M. Chaney (Eds.), *The sourcebook of pediatric psychology* (pp. 361–374). Boston: Allyn and Bacon.

Kavanagh, K. H., & Kennedy, P. H. (1992). *Promoting cultural diversity: Strategies for health care professionals.* Newbury Park, CA: Sage.

Kay, T., & Silver, S. M. (1989). Closed head trauma: Assessment for rehabilitation. In M. D. Lezak (Ed.), *Assessment of the behavioral consequences of head trauma* (pp. 145–170). New York: Liss.

Kaye, D. L., & Westman, J. C. (1991). The termination of parental rights as a therapeutic option. In J. C. Westman (Ed.), *Who speaks for the children? The handbook of individual and class advocacy* (pp. 251–266). Sarasota, FL: Professional Resource Exchange.

Kazdin, A. E. (1988). Childhood depression. In E. J. Mash & L. G. Terdal (Eds.), *Behavioral assessment of childhood disorders* (2nd ed., pp. 157–195). New York: Guilford.

Kazdin, A. E. (1990). Childhood depression. *Journal of Child Psychology & Psychiatry & Allied Disciplines, 31,* 121–160.

Keane, K. J. (1987). Assessing deaf children. In C. S. Lidz (Ed.), *Dynamic assessment: An interactional approach to evaluating learning potential* (pp. 360–376). New York: Guilford.

Kelley, M. L., & Heffer, R. W. (1990). Eating disorders: Food refusal and failure to thrive. In A. M. Gross & R. S. Drabman (Eds.), *Handbook of clinical behavioral pediatrics* (pp. 111–128). New York: Plenum.

Kelly, J. A. (1983). *Treating child-abusive families.* New York: Plenum.

Kelly, J. A., St. Lawrence, J. S., Hood, H. V., & Brasfield, T. L. (1989). An objective test of AIDS risk behavior knowledge: Scale development, validation, and norms. *Journal of Behavior Therapy & Experimental Psychiatry, 20,* 227–234.

Kemper, D. W. (Ed.). (1994). *Kaiser Permanente healthwise handbook.* Boise, ID: Healthwise, 1994.

Kendall-Tackett, K. A., & Watson, M. W. (1992). Use of anatomical dolls by Boston-area professionals. *Child Abuse & Neglect, 16,* 423–428.

Kendall-Tackett, K. A., Williams, L. M., & Finkelhor, D. (1993). Impact of sexual abuse on children: A review and synthesis of recent empirical studies. *Psychological Bulletin, 113,* 164–180.

Kendziora, K. T., & O'Leary, S. G. (1992). Dysfunctional parenting as a focus for prevention and treatment of child behavior problems. *Advances in Clinical Child Psychology, 15,* 175–206.

Kerr, J. K., Skok, R. L., & McLaughin, T. F. (1991). Characteristics common to females exhibiting anorexic or bulimic behavior: A review of the current literature. *Journal of Clinical Psychology, 47,* 846–853.

Kessler, J. W. (1988). *Psychopathology of childhood* (2nd ed.). Englewood Cliffs, NJ: Prentice Hall.

Kiecolt-Glaser, J. K., & Glaser, R. (1992). Psychoneuroimmunology: Can psychological interventions modulate immunity? *Journal of Consulting and Clinical Psychology, 60,* 569–575.

Kiesler, C. A. (1991). Homelessness and public policy priorities. *American Psychologist, 46,* 1245–1252.

King, C. A., Segal, G. H., Naylor, M., & Evans, T. (1993). Family functioning and suicidal behavior in adolescent inpatients with mood disorders. *Journal of the American Academy of Child & Adolescent Psychiatry, 32,* 1198–1206.

Kinsbourne, M., & Caplan, P. J. (1979). *Children's learning and attention problems.* Boston: Little, Brown.

Kinston, W., & Loader, P. (1984). Eliciting whole-family interaction with a standardized clinical interview. *Journal of Family Therapy, 6,* 347–363.

Kinzie, J. D., & Sack, W. (1991). Severely traumatized Cambodian children: Research findings and clinical implications. In F. L. Ahearn, Jr. & J. L. Athey (Eds.), *Refugee children: Theory, research, and services* (pp. 92–105). Baltimore: Johns Hopkins University Press.

Kirkwood, C. (1993). *Leaving abusive partners: From the scars of survival to the wisdom for change.* London: Sage.

Kleber, R. J., Brom, D., & Defares, P. B. (1992). *Coping with trauma: Theory, prevention and treatment.* Amsterdam, The Netherlands: Swets & Zeitlinger.

Klein, R. G. (1991). Parent-child agreement in clinical assessment of anxiety and other psychopathology: A review. *Journal of Anxiety Disorders, 5,* 187–198.

Klein, R. G., & Slomkowski, C. (1993). Treatment of psychiatric disorders in children and adolescents. *Psychopharmacology Bulletin, 29,* 525–535.

Klein, S. D., & Schleifer, M. J. (Eds.) (1993). My special brother. In *It isn't fair! Siblings of children with disabilities* (pp. 107–108). Westport, CT: Bergin & Garvey.

Kleinmuntz, B. (1967). *Personality measurement: An introduction.* Homewood, IL: Dorsey.

Kleinmuntz, B. (1982). *Personality and psychological assessment.* New York: St. Martin's Press.

Klonoff, H., Clark, C., & Klonoff, P. S. (1993). Long-term outcome of head injuries: A 23 year follow up study of children with head injuries. *Journal of Neurology, Neurosurgery & Psychiatry, 56,* 410–415.

Klopovich, P., Vats, T. S., Butterfield, G., Cairns, N. U., & Lansky, S. B. (1981). School phobia. *Journal of Kansas Medical Society, 82,* 125–127.

Kluckhohn, F. R. (1958). Family diagnosis: 1. Variations in the basic values of family systems. *Social Casework, 39,* 63–72.

Kluft, R. P. (1985). Childhood multiple personality disorder: Predictors, clinical findings, and treatment results. In R. P. Kluft (Ed.), *Childhood antecedents of multiple personality* (pp. 167–196). Washington, DC: American Psychiatric Press.

Kluft, R. P. (1987). The dissociative disorders. In J. S. Talbott, R. E. Hales, & S. C. Yudofsky (Eds.), *The American Psychiatric Press textbook of psychiatry* (pp. 569–578). Washington, DC: American Psychiatric Press.

Kluft, R. P., Braun, B. G., & Sachs, R. (1984). Multiple personality, intrafamilial abuse, and family psychiatry. *International Journal of Family Psychiatry, 5,* 283–301.

Knapp, S., & VandeCreek, L. (1985). An annotated glossary of legal terms for mental health clinicians. In P. A. Keller & L. G. Ritt (Eds.), *Innovations in clinical practice: A source book* (Vol. 4, pp. 459–466). Sarasota, FL: Professional Resource Exchange.

Knopp, F. H. (1985). *The youthful sex offender: The rationale and goals of early intervention and treatment.* Syracuse, NY: Safer Society Press.

Knox, J. M. (1989). *Learning disabilities.* New York: Chelsea House Publishers.

Koch, A. (1985). "If only it could be me": The families of pediatric cancer patients. *Family Relations: Journal of Applied Family & Child Studies, 34,* 63–70.

Koch-Hattem, A. (1986). Siblings' experience of pediatric cancer: Interviews with children. *Health & Social Work, 11,* 107–117.

Kochman, T. (1972). Black American speech events and a language program for the classroom. In C. B. Cazden, V. P. John, & D. Hymes (Eds.), *Functions of language in the classroom* (pp. 211–261). New York: Teachers College Press.

Kohlberg, L. (1976). Moral stages and moralization: The cognitive-developmental approach. In T. Lickona (Ed.), *Moral development and behavior: Theory, research, and social issues* (pp. 31–53). New York: Holt, Rinehart and Winston.

Kolb, B., & Whishaw, I. Q. (1990). *Fundamentals of human neuropsychology* (3rd ed.). New York: Freeman.

Kolin, P. C., & Kolin, J. L. (1980). *Professional writing for nurses in education, practice, and research.* St. Louis: Mosby.

Kondratas, A. (1991). Ending homelessness: Policy changes. *American Psychologist, 46,* 1226–1231.

Koocher, G. P. (1985). Psychosocial care of the child cured of cancer. *Pediatric Nursing, 11,* 91–93.

Koocher, G. P. (1986a). Coping with a death from cancer. *Journal of Consulting and Clinical Psychology, 54,* 623–631.

Koocher, G. P. (1986b). Psychosocial issues during the acute treatment of pediatric cancer. *Cancer, 58,* 468–472.

Koocher, G. P., Goodman, G. S., White, C. S., Friedrich, W. N., Sivan, A. B., & Reynolds, C. R. (1995). Psychological science and the use of anatomically detailed dolls in child sexual-abuse assessments. *Psychological Bulletin, 118,* 199–222.

Koocher, G. P., & Keith-Spiegel, P. C. (1990). *Children, ethics, and the law: Professional issues and cases.* Lincoln: University of Nebraska Press.

Koocher, G. P., & MacDonald, B. L. (1992). Preventive intervention and family coping with a child's life-threatening or terminal illness. In T. J. Akamatsu, M. A. P. Stephens, S. E. Hobfoll, & J. H. Crowther (Eds.), *Family health psychology* (pp. 67–86). Washington, DC: Hemisphere.

Koralek, D. (1992). *Caregivers of young children: Preventing and responding to child maltreatment.* Washington, DC: U.S. Department of Health and Human Services.

Kowal, A., & Pritchard, D. W. (1990). Psychological characteristics of children who suffer from headache: A research note. *Journal of Child Psychology and Psychiatry, 31,* 637–649.

Krahn, G. L., Eisert, D., & Fifield, B. (1990). Obtaining parental perceptions of the quality of services for children with special health needs. *Journal of Pediatric Psychology, 15,* 761–774.

Krajewski-Jaime, E. R. (1991). Folk-healing among Mexican-American families as a consideration in the delivery of child welfare and child health care services. *Child Welfare, 70,* 157–167.

Krehbiel, R., & Kroth, R. L. (1991). Communicating with families of children with disabilities or chronic illness. In M. J. Fine (Ed.), *Collaboration with parents of exceptional children* (pp. 103–127). Brandon, VT: Clinical Psychology Publishing Company.

Kropenske, V., & Howard, J. (1994). *Protecting child in substance-abusing families.* Washington, DC: U.S. Department of Health and Human Services.

Kübler-Ross, E. (1969). *On death and dying.* New York: Macmillan.

Kumabe, K. T., Nishida, C., & Hepworth, D. H. (1985). *Bridging ethnocultural diversities in social work and health.* Honolulu: University of Hawaii.

Lacks, P. (1987). *Behavioral treatment for persistent insomnia.* New York: Pergamon.

LaFromboise, T. D. (1988). American Indian mental health policy. *American Psychologist, 43,* 388–397.

LaFromboise, T. D., Choney, S. B., James, A., & Running Wolf, P. (1995). American Indian women and psychology. In H. Landrine (Ed.), *Bringing cultural diversity to feminist psychology: Theory, research, and practice* (pp. 197–239). Washington, DC: American Psychological Association.

LaFromboise, T. D., & Low, K. G. (1989). American Indian children and adolescents. In J. T. Gibbs & L. N. Huang (Eds.), *Children of color: Psychological interventions with minority youth* (pp. 114–147). San Francisco: Jossey-Bass.

LaFromboise, T. D., Trimble, J. E., & Mohatt, G. V. (1990). Counseling intervention and American Indian tradition: An integrative approach. *Counseling Psychologist, 18,* 628–654.

La Greca, A. M. (1983). Interviewing and behavioral observations. In C. E. Walker & M. C. Roberts (Eds.), *Handbook of clinical child psychology* (pp. 109–131). New York: Wiley.

La Greca, A. M. (1990). Issues in adherence with pediatric regimens. *Journal of Pediatric Psychology, 15,* 423–436.

La Greca, A. M., & Spetter, D. S. (1992). Psychosocial aspects of childhood diabetes: A multivariate framework. In N. Schneiderman, P. McCabe, & A. Baum (Eds.), *Stress and disease processes. Perspectives in behavioral medicine* (pp. 249–273). Hillsdale, NJ: Erlbaum.

Lahey, B. B., & Loeber, R. (1994). Framework for a developmental model of oppositional defiant disorder and conduct disorder. In D. K. Routh (Ed.), *Disruptive behavior disorders in childhood* (pp. 139–180). New York: Plenum.

Lamb, M. E., Sternberg, K. J., & Esplin, P. W. (1995). Making children into competent witnesses: Reactions to the amicus brief *In re Michales. Psychology, Public Policy, and Law, 1,* 438–449.

Landers, A. (1991, January 21). Dear Ann Landers—Mary in Michigan. *Los Angeles Times,* p. E6.

Landers, A. (1996, July 8). Dear Ann Landers: Mother's kids are abuse victims, too. *San Diego Union-Tribune,* p. E2.

Lansky, S. B., List, M. A., Lansky, L. L., Ritter-Sterr, C., & Miller, D. R. (1987). The measurement of performance in childhood cancer patients. *Cancer, 62,* 1651–1656.

LaRoche, C. (1986). Prevention in high risk children of depressed parents. *Canadian Journal of Psychiatry, 31,* 161–165.

Larson, D. G. (1993). *The helper's journey: Working with people facing grief, loss, and life-threatening illness.* Champaign, IL: Research Press.

Lash, M., & Licenziato, V. (1995). *When an Asian child needs health care: Tips for health care professionals on cultural beliefs.* Boston: New England Medical Center.

Lask, B., & Bryant-Waugh, R. (1992). Early-onset anorexia nervosa and related eating disorders. *Journal of Child Psychology and Psychiatry, 33,* 281–300.

Lask, B., & Fosson, A. (1989). *Childhood illness: The psychosomatic approach.* New York: Wiley.

Lazare, A. (1979). Unresolved grief. In A. Lazare (Ed.), *Outpatient psychiatry: Diagnosis and treatment* (pp. 498–512). Baltimore: Williams & Wilkins.

Lazarus, R. S., & Folkman, S. (1984). *Stress, appraisal, and coping.* New York: Springer.

Lederberg, M. (1989). Psychological problems of staff and their management. In J. C. Holland & J. H. Rowland (Eds.), *Handbook of psychooncology: Psychological care of the patient with cancer* (pp. 631–646). New York: Oxford University Press.

Lee, C. C., & Richardson, B. L. (1991). The Latino American experience. In C. C. Lee & B. L. Richardson (Eds.), *Multicultural issues in counseling: New approaches to diversity* (p. 141). Alexandria, VA: American Association for Counseling and Development.

Leff, P. T., & Walizer, E. H. (1992). The uncommon wisdom of parents at the moment of diagnosis. *Family Systems Medicine, 10,* 147–168.

Lehr, E. (1990). *Psychological management of traumatic brain injuries in children and adolescents.* Rockville, MD: Aspen.

Leon, G. R., & Dinklage, D. (1989). Obesity and anorexia nervosa. In T. H. Ollendick & M. Ilersen (Eds.), *Handbook of child psychopathology* (2nd ed., pp. 247–264). New York: Plenum.

Lerner, E., & Murphy, L. B. (1941). Methods for the study of personality in young children. *Monographs of the Society for Research in Child Development, 6*(4, Serial No. 30).

Levenson, R. L., Jr., & Mellins, C. A. (1992). Pediatric HIV disease: What psychologists need to know. *Professional Psychology: Research and Practice, 23,* 410–415.

Levin, H. S. (1981). Assessment in closed head injury. In M. T. Sarno (Ed.), *Acquired aphasia* (pp. 427–463). New York: Academic Press.

Levin, H. S., Ewing-Cobbs, L., & Fletcher, J. M. (1989). Neurobehavioral outcome of mild head injury in children. In H. S. Levin, H. M. Eisenberg, & A. L. Benton (Eds.), *Mild head injury* (pp. 189–213). New York: Oxford University Press.

Levine, B. (1993, November 18). The forbidden touch. *Los Angeles Times,* pp. E1–E2.

Levine, M., Anderson, E., Ferretti, L., & Steinberg, K. (1992). Legal and ethical issues affecting clinical child psychology. *Advances in Clinical Child Psychology, 15,* 81–120.

Levy, A. (1989). Recommendations of the Cleveland report. In A. Levy (Ed.), *Focus on child abuse: Medical, legal and social work perspectives* (pp. 165–184). Over Wallop, England: Hawksmere.

Levy, R. J. (1989). Using "scientific" testimony to prove child sexual abuse. *Family Law Quarterly, 23,* 383–409.

Lewis, D. O. (1991a). Conduct disorder. In M. Lewis (Ed.), *Child and adolescent psychiatry: A comprehensive textbook* (pp. 561–573). Baltimore: Williams & Wilkins.

Lewis, D. O. (1991b). Multiple personality. In M. Lewis (Ed.), *Child and adolescent psychiatry: A comprehensive textbook* (pp. 707–715). Baltimore: Williams & Wilkins.

Lewis, M. (1991). Psychiatric assessment of infants, children, and adolescents. In M. Lewis (Ed.), *Child and adolescent psychiatry: A comprehensive textbook* (pp. 447–463). Baltimore: Williams & Wilkins.

Lewis, M. (1994). Chronic illness as a psychological risk factor in children. In W. B. Carey & S. C. McDevitt (Eds.), *Prevention and early intervention: Individual differences as risk factors for the mental health of children: A festschrift for Stella Chess and Alexander Thomas* (pp. 103–112). New York: Brunner/Mazel.

Lewis, M., Lewis, D. O., & Schonfeld, D. J. (1991). Dying and death in childhood and adolescence. In M. Lewis (Ed.), *Child and adolescent psychiatry: A comprehensive textbook* (pp. 1051–1059). Baltimore: Williams & Wilkins.

Lewkowicz, D. J., & Turkewitz, G. (1982). Influence of hemispheric specialization in sensory processing on reaching in infants: Age and gender related effects. *Developmental Psychology, 18,* 301–308.

Lezak, M. D. (1978). Living with the characterologically altered brain-injured patient. *Journal of Clinical Psychiatry, 39,* 592–598.

Lezak, M. D. (1995). *Neuropsychological assessment* (3rd ed.). New York: Oxford University Press.

Lichtenstein, R., & Ireton, H. (1984). *Preschool screening: Identifying young children with developmental and educational problems.* Orlando, FL: Grune & Stratton.

Light, M. J., & Sheridan, M. S. (1990). Munchausen syndrome by proxy and apnea (MBPA). *Clinical Pediatrics, 29,* 162–168.

Lindsay, D. S., & Read, J. D. (1994). Psychotherapy and memories of childhood sexual abuse: A cognitive perspective. *Applied Cognitive Psychology, 8,* 281–338.

Lindsay, J., & Monserrat, C. (1989). *Adoption awareness: A guide for teachers, counselors, nurses and caring others.* Buena Park, CA: Morning Glory Press.

Linscheid, T. R. (1992). Eating problems in children. In C. E. Walker & M. C. Roberts (Eds.), *Handbook of clinical child psychology* (2nd ed., pp. 451–473). New York: Wiley.

Linscheid, T. R., Tarnowski, K. J., & Richmond, D. A. (1988). Behavioral approaches to anorexia nervosa, bulimia and obesity. In D. K. Routh (Ed.), *Handbook of pediatric psychology* (pp. 332–362). New York: Guilford.

Lipovsky, J. A. (1991). Disclosure of father-child sexual abuse: Dilemmas for families and therapists. *Contemporary Family Therapy: An International Journal, 13,* 85–101.

Livneh, H. (1984). On the origins of negative attitudes toward people with disabilities. In R. P. Marinelli & A. E. Dell Orto (Eds.), *The psychological and social impact of physical disability* (2nd ed., pp. 167–184). New York: Springer-Verlag.

Locust, C. (1988). Wounding the spirit: Discrimination and traditional American Indian belief systems. *Harvard Educational Review, 58,* 315–330.

Loftus, E. F., & Ketcham, K. (1994). *The myth of repressed memory: False memories and allegations of sexual abuse.* New York: St. Martin's Press.

Lombana, J. H. (1982). *Guidance for handicapped students.* Springfield, IL: Charles C Thomas.

López, S. R., Blacher, J. B., & Shapiro, J. (1998). The interplay of culture and disability in Latino families. In I. T. Mink, M. L. Siantz, & P. W. Berman (Eds.), *Culture, disability, and family in the United States.* Washington, DC: American Association on Mental Retardation.

López, S. R., Grover, K. P., Holland, D., Johnson, M. J., Kain, C. D., Kanel, K., Mellins, C. A., & Rhyne, M. C. (1989). Development of culturally sensitive psychotherapists. *Professional Psychology: Research and Practice, 20,* 369–376.

Lord, C., & Baker, A. F. (1977). Communicating with autistic children. *Journal of Pediatric Psychology, 2,* 181–186.

Loro, A., & Orleans, C. S. (1982). The behavioral assessment of obesity. In F. J. Keefe & J. A. Blumenthal (Eds.), *Assessment strategies in behavioral medicine* (pp. 225–259). New York: Grune & Stratton.

Lowenstein, R. J., & Putnam, F. W. (1990). The clinical phenomenology of males with MPD: A report of 21 cases. *Dissociation, 3,* 135–143.

Lubinski, R. (1981). Environmental language intervention. In R. Chapey (Ed.), *Language intervention strategies in adult aphasia* (pp. 223–245). Baltimore: Williams & Wilkins.

Luiselli, J. K. (1989). Health-threatening behaviors. In J. K. Luiselli (Ed.), *Behavioral medicine and developmental disabilities* (pp. 114–151). New York: Springer-Verlag.

Lukas, C., & Seiden, H. (1987). *Silent grief: Living in the wake of suicide.* New York: Bantam Books.

Lung, C., & Daro, D. (1996, April). *Current trends in child abuse reporting and fatalities: The results of the 1995 annual fifty state survey.* Chicago: National Committee to Prevent Child Abuse.

Lynch, E. W., & Hanson, M. J. (Eds.). (1992). *Developing cross-cultural competence: A guide for working with young children and their families.* Baltimore: Brookes.

Lyon, E. (1993). Hospital staff reactions to accounts by survivors of childhood abuse. *American Journal of Orthopsychiatry, 63,* 410–416.

Lyon, G. R. (1996). Learning disabilities. *The Future of Children, 6*(1), 54–76.

Lyon, G. R., & Moats, L. C. (1988). Critical issues in the instruction of the learning disabled. *Journal of Consulting and Clinical Psychology, 56,*830–835.

Lyon, G. R., Moats, L. C., & Flynn, J. M. (1988). From assessment to treatment: Linkage to intervention with children. In M. G. Tramontana & S. R. Hooper (Eds.), *Assessment issues in child neuropsychology* (pp. 113–142). New York: Plenum.

Lyon, T. D. (1995). False allegations and false denials in child sexual abuse. *Psychology, Public Policy, and Law, 1,* 429–437.

Lyons, J. A. (1987). Posttraumatic stress disorder in children and adolescents: A review of the literature. *Journal of Developmental and Behavioral Pediatrics, 8,*349–356.

Lyons, J. A. (1988). Posttraumatic stress disorder in children and adolescents: A review of the literature. *Annual Progress in Child Psychiatry & Child Development,* 451–467.

Lytle-Vieria, J. (1987). Kramer v. Kramer revisited: The social work role in child custody cases. *Social Work, 32*(1), 6–9.

MacFarlane, K., & Feldmeth, J. (1988). *Response to child sexual abuse: The clinical interview.* New York: Guilford.

MacFarlane, K., & Krebs, S. (1986). Techniques for interviewing and evidence gathering. In K. MacFarlane & J. Waterman (with S. Conerly, L. Damon, M. Durfee, & S. Long) (Eds.), *Sexual abuse of young children* (pp. 67–100). New York: Guilford.

MacKenzie, R. G., & Kipke, M. D. (1992). Substance use and abuse. In S. B. Friedman, M. Fisher, & S. K. Schonberg (Eds.), *Comprehensive adolescent health care* (pp. 765–786). Ontario: Prentice Hall.

Magrab, P. R. (1984). A developmental framework for psychological assessment of pediatric conditions. In P. R. Magrab (Ed.), *Psychological and behavioral assessment: Impact on pediatric care* (pp. 3–21). New York: Plenum.

Maharaj, D. (1995, October 27). Court assails boy's removal from family. *Los Angeles Times,* pp. A3, A32.

Mahoney, G., Powell, A., & Finger, I. (1986). The Maternal Behavior Rating Scale. *Topics in Early Childhood Special Education, 6,* 44–56.

Maier, S. F., Watkins, L. R., & Fleshner, M. (1994). Psychoneuroimmunology: The interface between behavior, brain, and immunity. *American Psychologist, 49,* 1004–1017.

Main, M., & Solomon, J. (1986). Discovery of a disorganized/disoriented attachment pattern. In T. B. Brazelton & M. W. Yogman (Eds.), *Affective development in infancy* (pp. 95–124). Norwood, NJ: Ablex.

Mainstream English is the key. (1996, December 22). *Los Angeles Times,* p. M4.

Manio, E. B., & Hall, R. R. (1987). Asian family traditions and their influence in transcultural health care delivery. *Children's Health Care, 15,* 172–177.

Manne, S. L., & Andersen, B. L. (1991). Pain and pain-related distress in children with cancer. In J. P. Bush & S. W. Harkins (Eds.), *Children in pain: Clinical and research issues from a developmental perspective* (pp. 337–371). New York: Springer-Verlag.

Mannuzza, S., Fyer, A. J., & Klein, D. F. (1993). Assessing psychopathology. *International Journal of Methods in Psychiatric Research, 3,* 157–165.

Mapes, B. E. (1995). *Child eyewitness testimony in sexual abuse investigations.* Brandon, VT: Clinical Psychology Publishing Company.

Mapou, R. L. (1995). A cognitive framework for neuropsychological assessment. In R. L. Mapou & J. Spector (Eds.), *Clinical neuropsychological assessment: A cognitive approach* (pp. 295–337). New York: Plenum.

Marcenko, M. O., & Smith, L. K. (1991). Post-adoption needs of families adopting children with developmental disabilities. *Child & Youth Services Review, 13,* 413–424.

Marcos, L. R. (1979). Effects of interpreters on the evaluation of psychopathology in non-English-speaking patients. *American Journal of Psychiatry, 136,* 171–174.

Marin, G., & Marin, B. V. (1991). *Research with Hispanic populations.* Newbury Park, CA: Sage.

Maron, M., & Bush, J. P. (1991). Burn injury and treatment pain. In J. P. Bush & S. W. Harkins (Eds.), *Children in pain: Clinical and research issues from a developmental perspective* (pp. 275–295). New York: Springer-Verlag.

Marquardt, T. P., Stoll, J., & Sussman, H. (1988). Disorders of communication in acquired cerebral trauma. *Journal of Learning Disabilities, 21,* 340–351.

Marsh, D. T. (1992). *Families and mental retardation: New directions in professional practice.* New York: Praeger.

Marshall, W. L. (1993). The role of attachments, intimacy, and loneliness in the etiology and maintenance of sexual offending. *Sexual and Marital Therapy, 8,* 109–121.

Martin, D. A. (1988). Children and adolescents with traumatic brain injury: Impact on the family. *Journal of Learning Disabilities, 21,* 464–470.

Martin, J. E. (1989). Bulimia: A literature review. *British Journal of Occupational Therapy, 52,* 138–142.

Martinson, I. M., & Campos, R. G. (1991). Adolescent bereavement: Long-term responses to a sibling's death from cancer. *Journal of Adolescent Research, 6,* 54–69.

Martinson, I. M., & Cohen, M. H. (1988). Themes from a longitudinal study of family reaction to childhood cancer. *Journal of Psychosocial Oncology, 6,* 81–98.

Martinson, I. M., McClowry, S. G., Davies, B., & Kuhlenkamp, E. J. (1994). Changes over time: A study of family bereavement following childhood cancer. *Journal of Palliative Care, 10,* 19–25.

Masek, B. J., & Hoag, N. L. (1990). Headache. In A. M. Gross & R. S. Drabman (Eds.), *Handbook of clinical behavioral pediatrics* (pp. 99–109). New York: Plenum.

Masek, B. J., Russo, D. C., & Varni, J. W. (1984). Behavioral approaches to the management of chronic pain in children. *Pediatric Clinics of North America, 31,* 1113–1131.

Mash, E. J., & Dozois, D. J. A. (1996). Child psychopathology: A developmental-systems perspective. In E. J. Mash & R. A. Barkley (Eds.), *Child psychopathology* (pp. 3–60). New York: Guilford.

Mash, E. J., & Johnston, C. (1983). Parental perceptions of child behavior problems, parenting self-esteem, and mothers' reported stress in younger and older hyperactive and normal children. *Journal of Consulting and Clinical Psychology, 51,* 86–99.

Mash, E. J., & Terdal, L. G. (1981). Behavioral assessment of childhood disturbance. In E. J. Mash & L. G. Terdal (Eds.), *Behavioral assessment of childhood disorders* (pp. 3–76). New York: Guilford.

Mash, E. J., & Terdal, L. G. (1988). Behavioral assessment of child and family disturbance. In E. J. Mash & L. G. Terdal (Eds.), *Behavioral assessment of childhood disorders* (2nd ed., pp. 3–65). New York: Guilford.

Mash, E. J., & Terdal, L. G. (1990). Assessment strategies in clinical behavioral pediatrics. In A. M. Gross & R. S. Drabman (Eds.), *Handbook of clinical behavioral pediatrics* (pp. 49–79). New York: Plenum.

Maslach, C., & Schaufeli, W. B. (1993). Historical and conceptual development of burnout. In W. B. Schaufeli, C. Maslach, & T. Marek (Eds.), *Professional burnout: Recent developments in theory and research* (pp. 1–18). Washington, DC: Taylor & Francis.

Masten, A. S. (1992). Homeless children in the United States: Mark of a nation at risk. *Current Directions in Psychological Science, 1,* 41–44.

Masten, A. S. (1994). Resilience in individual development: Successful adaptation despite risk and adversity. In M. C. Wang & E. W. Gordon (Eds.), *Educational resilience in inner-city America* (pp. 3–25). Hillsdale, NJ: Erlbaum.

Masten, A. S., & Braswell, L. (1991). Developmental psychopathology: An integrative framework. In P. R. Martin (Ed.), *Handbook of behavior therapy and psychological science: An integrative approach* (pp. 35–56). New York: Pergamon.

Masten, A. S., Miliotis, D., Graham-Bermann, S. A., Ramirez, M. L., & Neemann, J. (1993). Children in homeless families: Risks to mental health and development. *Journal of Consulting and Clinical Psychology, 61,* 335–343.

Mateer, C. A., & Williams, D. (1991). Effects of frontal lobe injury in childhood. *Developmental Neuropsychology, 7,* 359–376.

Matheny, K. B., Aycock, D. W., Pugh, J. L., Curlett, W. L., & Cannella, K. A. (1986). Stress coping: A qualitative and quantitative synthesis with implications for treatment. *Counseling Psychologist, 14,* 499–549.

Matthews, J. R., Bowen, J. M., & Matthews, R. W. (1996). *Successful scientific writing: A step-by-step guide for the biological and medical sciences.* New York: Cambridge University Press.

Mauk, G. W. (1991, April). *Adolescent suicide postvention in schools: Managing grief of peer survivors.* Paper presented at the Annual Convention of the Western Psychological Association, San Francisco.

Mauk, G. W., & Mauk, P. P. (1992). Somewhere, out there: Preschool children with hearing impairment and learning disabilities. *Topics in Early Childhood Special Education, 12,* 174–195.

Mauk, G. W., & Weber, C. (1991). Peer survivors of adolescent suicide: Perspectives on grieving and postvention. *Journal of Adolescent Research, 6,* 113–131.

Maul-Mellott, S. K., & Adams, J. N. (1987). *Childhood cancer: A nursing overview.* Boston: Jones & Bartlett.

Max, L. (1985). Parents' views of provisions, services and research. In N. N. Singh & K. M. Wilton (Eds.), *Mental retardation in New Zealand* (pp. 250–262). Christchurch, New Zealand: Whitoculls.

Mayer, D. D. (1996, January 18, Segment 15). Rolling Stones tune helps woman turn life's corner. National Public Radio, *All Things Considered,* Transcript pp. 26–28.

Mays, V. M. (1986). Identity development of Black Americans: The role of history and the importance of ethnicity. *American Journal of Psychotherapy, 40,* 582–593.

Maza, P. L., & Hall, J. H. (1988). *Homeless children and their families: A preliminary study.* New York: Child Welfare League of America.

McClain, L. (1980, October 13). The middle-class black's burden. *Newsweek,* p. 21.

McConaughy, S. H. (1996). The interview process. In M. Breen & C. Fiedler (Eds.), *Behavioral approach to the assessment of emotionally/behaviorally disordered youth: A handbook for school-based practitioners* (pp. 181–223). Austin, TX: Pro-Ed.

McConaughy, S. H., & Achenbach, T. M. (1994). *Manual for the Semistructured Clinical Interview for Children and Adolescents.* Burlington, VT: University Associates in Psychiatry.

McCubbin, H. I., & Figley, C. R. (1983). Bridging normative and catastrophic family stress. In H. I. McCubbin & C. R. Figley (Eds.), *Stress and the family: Vol. 1. Coping with normative transitions* (pp. 218–228). New York: Brunner/Mazel.

McCubbin, H. I., & Patterson, J. M. (1983). Family transitions: Adaptation to stress. In H. I. McCubbin & C. R. Figley (Eds.), *Stress and the family: Vol. 1. Coping with normative transitions* (pp. 5–25). New York: Brunner/Mazel.

McCue, K. (1994). *How to help children through a parent's serious illness.* New York: St. Martin's Press.

McFadden, E. J., & Ryan, P. (1991). Maltreatment in family foster homes: Dynamics and dimensions. *Child & Youth Services, 15,* 209–231.

McGoldrick, M. (1993). Ethnicity, cultural diversity, and normality. In F. Walsh (Ed.), *Normal family processes* (2nd ed., pp. 331–360). New York: Guilford.

McGovern, K., & Peters, J. (1988). Guidelines for assessing sex offenders. In L. E. A. Walker (Ed.), *Handbook on sexual abuse of children* (pp. 216–246). New York: Springer.

McGrath, P. A. (1989). *Pain in children: Nature, assessment and treatment.* New York: Guilford.

McGrath, P. A., & Brigham, M. C. (1992). The assessment of pain in children and adolescents. In D. C. Turk & R. Melzack (Eds.), *Handbook of pain assessment* (pp. 295–314). New York: Guilford.

McGrath, P. A., & Hillier, L. M. (1989). The enigma of pain in children: An overview. *Pediatrician, 16,* 6–15.

McGraw, J. M., & Smith, H. A. (1992). Child sexual abuse allegations amidst divorce and custody proceedings: Refining the validation process. *Journal of Child Sexual Abuse, 1,* 49–62.

McIntosh, J. L. (1987). Survivor family relationships: Literature review. In E. J. Dunne, J. L. McIntosh, & K. D. Maxim (Eds.), *Suicide and its aftermath: Understanding and counseling the survivors* (pp. 73–84). New York: Norton.

McKay, M. M. (1994). The link between domestic violence and child abuse: Assessment and treatment considerations. *Child Welfare, 73,* 29–39.

McKenna, M. S. (1989). Assessment of the eating disordered patient. *Psychiatric Annals, 19,* 467–472.

McKnew, D. H., Jr., Cytryn, L., & Yahraes, H. (1983). *Why isn't Johnny crying? Coping with depression in children.* New York: Norton.

McLaughlin, J., & Sliepcevich, E. M. (1985). The Self-Care Behavior Inventory: A model for behavioral instrument development. *Patient Education & Counseling, 7,* 289–301.

McMahon, R. J., & Forehand, R. (1988). Conduct disorders. In E. J. Mash & L. G. Terdal (Eds.), *Behavioral Assessment of Childhood Disorders* (2nd ed., pp. 105–153). New York: Guilford.

McWhirter, J. J., McWhirter, B., McWhirter, A. M., & McWhirter, E. H. (1993). *At-risk youth: A comprehensive response.* Pacific Grove, CA: Brooks/Cole.

Medoff-Cooper, B., Carey, W. B., & McDevitt, S. C. (1993). The Early Infancy Temperament Questionnaire. *Journal of Developmental and Behavioral Pediatrics, 14,* 230–235.

Meichenbaum, D., & Turk, D. C. (1987). *Facilitating treatment adherence: A practitioner's guidebook.* New York: Plenum.

Meinhold, P. (1994). A clinical method for testing claims of facilitated communication. *Psychology in Mental Retardation and Developmental Disabilities, 19,* 3–7.

Mellins, C. A., Levenson, R. L. Jr., Zawadzki, R., Kairam, R., & Weston, M. (1994). Effects of pediatric HIV infection and prenatal drug exposure on mental and psychomotor development. *Journal of Pediatric Psychology, 19,* 617–628.

Melton, G. B. (1994). Doing justice and doing good: Conflicts for mental health professionals. *The Future of Children: Sexual Abuse of Children, 4,* 102–118.

Melzack, R., & Torgerson, W. W. (1971). On the language of pain. *Anesthesiology, 34,* 54–55.

Menke, E. M. (1987). The impact of a child's chronic illness on school-aged siblings. *Children's Health Care, 15,* 132–140.

Mercer, S. O., & Perdue, J. D. (1993). Munchausen syndrome by proxy: Social work's role. *Social Work, 38,* 74–81.

Meshot, C. M., & Leitner, L. M. (1992–93). Adolescent mourning and parental death. *Omega: Journal of Death & Dying, 26,* 287–299.

Mian, M. (1995). A multidisciplinary approach. In A. V. Levin & M. S. Sheridan (Eds.), *Munchausen syndrome by proxy: Issues in diagnosis and treatment* (pp. 271–286). New York: Lexington Books.

Miller, B. A., Downs, W. R., & Testa, M. (1990, August). *Relationship between women's alcohol problems and experiences of childhood violence.* Paper presented at the Annual Convention of the American Psychological Association, Boston.

Miller, L. (1989). Neuropsychology, personality and substance abuse: Implications for head injury rehabilitation. *Cognitive Rehabilitation, 7,* 26–31.

Miller, L. (1991). Significant others: Treating brain injury in the family context. *Cognitive Rehabilitation, 9,* 16–25.

Miller, L. (1992). Neuropsychology, personality, and substance abuse in the head injury case: Clinical and forensic issues. *International Journal of Law & Psychiatry, 15,* 303–316.

Miller, L. (1993). Family therapy of brain injury: Syndromes, strategies, and solutions. *American Journal of Family Therapy, 21,* 111–121.

Miller, N. B. (1979). Parents of children with neurological disorders: Concerns and counseling. *Journal of Pediatric Psychology, 4,* 297–306.

Miller, P. M., & Mastria, M. A. (1977). *Alternatives to alcohol abuse: A social learning model.* Champaign, IL: Research Press.

Miller, W. R., & Rollnick, S. (1991). *Motivational interviewing: Preparing people to change addictive behavior.* New York: Guilford.

Millon, T. (1987). On the nature of taxonomy in psychopathology. In C. G. Last & M. Hersen (Eds.), *Issues in diagnostic research* (pp. 3–85). New York: Plenum.

Milton, S. B. (1988). Management of subtle cognitive communication deficits. *Journal of Head Trauma Rehabilitation, 3*(2), 1–11.

Mindell, J. A. (1993). Sleep disorders in children. *Health Psychology, 12,* 151–162.

Minnes, P. M. (1988). Family stress associated with a developmentally handicapped child. *International Review of Research in Mental Retardation, 15,* 195–226.

Mohatt, G. V., McDiarmid, G. W., & Montoya, V. C. (1988). Societies, families, and change: The Alaskan example. *Behavioral Health Issues Among American Indians and Alaska Natives: Indian and Alaska Native Mental Health Research* [Monograph No. 1] (pp. 325–365).

Molyneaux, D., & Lane, V. W. (1982). *Effective interviewing: Techniques and analysis.* Boston: Allyn and Bacon.

Monahon, C. (1993). *Children and trauma: A parent's guide to helping children heal.* New York: Lexington Books.

Moody, R. A., & Moody, C. P. (1991). A family perspective: Helping children acknowledge and express grief following the death of a parent. *Death Studies, 15,* 587–602.

Moore, D. J., & Klonoff, E. A. (1986). Assessment of compliance: A systems perspective. In K. D. Gadow & A. Poling (Eds.), *Advances in learning and behavioral disabilities: Supplement I.*

Methodological issues in human psychopharmacology (pp. 223–245). Greenwich, CT: JAI Press.

Moore, M. V. (1969). Pathological writing. *Asha, 11,* 535–538.

Moos, R. (Ed.). (1977). *Coping with physical illness.* New York: Plenum.

Moreno, S. (1992). A parent's view of more able people with autism. In E. Schopler & G. B. Mesibov (Eds.), *High-functioning individuals with autism* (pp. 91–103). New York: Plenum.

Morgan, S. B. (1984). Helping parents understand the diagnosis of autism. *Journal of Developmental and Behavioral Pediatrics, 5,* 78–85.

Morgan, S. R. (1994). *At-risk youth in crises: A team approach in the schools* (2nd ed.). Austin, TX: Pro-Ed.

Morin, C. M. (1993). *Insomnia: Psychological assessment and management.* New York: Guilford.

Moritz, B., Van Nes, H., & Brouwer, W. (1989). The professional helper as a concerned party in suicide cases. In R. F. W. Diekstra, R. Maris, S. Platt, A. Schmidtke, & G. Sonneck (Eds.), *Suicide and its prevention* (pp. 199–210). New York: Brill.

Morris, R. D. (1988). Classification of learning disabilities: Old problems and new approaches. *Journal of Consulting and Clinical Psychology, 56,* 789–794.

Morsbach, H. (1988). The importance of silence and stillness in Japanese nonverbal communication: A cross-cultural approach. In P. Fernando (Ed.), *Cross-cultural perspectives in nonverbal communication* (pp. 201–216). Gîttingen, Germany: Hogrefe.

Moscovitch, M. (1981). Right-hemisphere language. *Topics in Language Disorders, 1*(4), 41–61.

Moses, J. M. (1992, September 25). Autistic youths "speak" in court with aid. *Wall Street Journal,* p. B2.

Motto, J. A. (1991). An integrated approach to estimating suicide risk. *Suicide & Life Threatening Behavior, 21,* 74–89.

Mrazek, D. A. (1991). Chronic pediatric illness and multiple hospitalizations. In M. Lewis (Ed.), *Child and adolescent psychiatry: A comprehensive textbook* (pp. 1041–1050). Baltimore: Williams & Wilkins.

Mueller, B. U., & Pizzo, P. A. (1992). Medical treatment of children with HIV infection. In A. C. Crocker, H. J. Cohen, & T. A. Kastner (Eds.), *HIV infection and developmental disabilities: A resource for service providers* (pp. 63–73). Baltimore: Brookes.

Mulick, J. A. (1993, August). *Facilitated communication.* Paper presented at the 101st Convention of the American Psychological Association, Toronto.

Mulick, J. A., Jacobson, J. W., & Kobe, F. H. (1993). Anguished silence and helping hands: Autism and facilitated communication. *Skeptical Inquirer, 17,* 270–280.

Mullen, P. E., Martin, J. L., Anderson, J. C., Romans, S. E., & Herbison, G. P. (1994). The effect of child sexual abuse on social, interpersonal and sexual function in adult life. *British Journal of Psychiatry, 165,* 35–47.

Mullins, J. B. (1983). The uses of bibliotherapy in counseling families confronted with handicaps. In M. Seligman (Ed.), *The family with a handicapped child: Understanding and treatment* (pp. 235–259). New York: Grune & Stratton.

Muñoz, E. (1996, November 2). A brother's keeper spurns the newest drug-war slogan. *Los Angeles Times,* p. B7.

Munro, J. D. (1985). Counseling severely dysfunctional families of mentally and physically disabled persons. *Clinical Social Work Journal, 13,* 18–31.

Murphy, W., Rau, T., & Worley, P. (1994). The perils and pitfalls of profiling child sex abusers. *APSAC Advisor, 7*(3–4), 28–29.

Myers, J. E. B. (1993). Expert testimony regarding child sexual abuse. *Child Abuse & Neglect, 17,* 175–185.

Nashio, K., & Bilmes, M. (1987). Psychotherapy with Southeast Asian American clients. *Professional Psychology: Research and Practice, 18,* 342–346.

National Alliance to End Homelessness. (1995). *Annual report, 1995.* Washington, DC: Author.

National Center for Clinical Infant Programs. (1994). *Diagnostic classification: 0–3.* Richmond, VA: Author.

National Center on Child Abuse and Neglect (U.S. Department of Health and Human Services). (1989). *Child abuse and neglect: A shared community concern.* Washington, DC: U.S. Government Printing Office.

National Center on Child Abuse and Neglect (U.S. Department of Health and Human Services). (1991). *Family violence: An overview.* Washington, DC: U.S. Government Printing Office.

National Center on Child Abuse and Neglect (U.S. Department of Health and Human Services). (1993). *A report on the maltreatment of children with disabilities.* Washington, DC: U.S. Government Printing Office.

National Center on Child Abuse and Neglect (U.S. Department of Health and Human Services). (1994). *Child Abuse Prevention and Treatment Act, as amended November 4, 1992.* Washington, DC: U.S. Government Printing Office.

National Center on Child Abuse and Neglect (U.S. Department of Health and Human Services). (1996). *Child maltreatment 1994: Reports from the states to the National Center on Child Abuse and Neglect.* Washington, DC: U.S. Government Printing Office.

National Committee to Prevent Child Abuse. (1994). *Building a healthy families America system: A summary of costs and benefits.* Chicago: Author.

National Committee to Prevent Child Abuse. (1995, September). Focus on prevention: Understanding and preventing maltreatment of children with disabilities. *National Committee to Prevent Child Abuse Memorandum, 2,* 2.

National Committee to Prevent Child Abuse. (1996, January). *Focus on prevention: Poll indicates public perceptions of child welfare services and policies.* Chicago: Author.

National Joint Committee on Learning Disabilities (1987). *Issues in learning disabilities: Assessment and diagnosis.* Unpublished manuscript.

Nay, W. R. (1979). *Multimethod clinical assessment.* New York: Gardner.

Needle, R. H., Glynn, T. J., & Needle, M. P. (1983). Drug abuse: Adolescent addictions and the family. In C. R. Figley & H. I. McCubbin (Eds.), *Stress and the family: Vol. II. Coping with catastrophe* (pp. 37–52). New York: Brunner/Mazel.

Neidigh, L., & Krop, H. (1992). Cognitive distortions among child sexual offenders. *Journal of Sex Education & Therapy, 18,* 208–215.

Newacheck, P. (1994). Poverty and childhood illness. *Archives of Pediatric and Adolescent Medicine, 148,* 1143–1149.

Newcomb, M. D., & Bentler, P. M. (1989). Substance use and abuse among children and teenagers. *American Psychologist, 44,* 242–248.

Newman, R. (1991). The role of the psychologist expert witness: Provider of perspective and input. *Neuropsychology Review, 2,* 241–249.

New York State Department of Social Services. (1994). *New York State Risk Assessment and Services Planning Model: Field Guide* (2nd ed.). Albany, NY: Author.

North, C. S., Ryall, J.-E. M., Ricci, D. A., & Wetzel, R. D. (1993). *Multiple personalities, multiple disorders: Psychiatric classification and media influence.* [Oxford monographs on psychiatry, 1.] New York: Oxford University Press.

Northern, J. L., & Downs, M. P. (1991). *Hearing in children* (4th ed.). Baltimore: Williams & Wilkins.

Northouse, P. G., & Northouse, L. L. (1987). Communication and cancer: Issues confronting patients, health professionals, and family members. *Journal of Psychosocial Oncology, 5,* 17–46.

Nottelmann, E. D., & Jensen, P. S. (1995). Comorbidity of disorders in children and adolescents: Developmental perspectives. *Advances in Clinical Child Psychology, 17,* 109–155.

Novacek, J., Raskin, R., & Hogan, R. (1991). Why do adolescents use drugs? Age, sex, and user differences. *Journal of Youth & Adolescence, 20,* 475–492.

Novick, B. Z., & Arnold, M. M. (1988). *Fundamentals of clinical child neuropsychology.* Philadelphia: Grune & Stratton/Saunders.

Nowinski, J. (1990). *Substance abuse in adolescents and young adults: A guide to treatment.* New York: Norton.

Nurcombe, B. (1986). The child as witness: Competency and credibility. *Journal of the American Academy of Child Psychiatry, 25,* 473–480.

Nursey, A. D., Rohde, J. R., & Farmer, R. D. (1991). Ways of telling new parents about their child and his or her mental handicap: A comparison of doctors' and parents' views. *Journal of Mental Deficiency Research, 35,* 48–57.

Oates, M. D. (1993). *Death in the school community: A handbook for counselors, teachers, and administrators.* Alexandria, VA: American Counseling Association.

Ochberg, F. M. (1988). Post-traumatic therapy and victims of violence. In F. M. Ochberg (Ed.), *Post-traumatic therapy and victims of violence* (pp. 196–212). New York: Brunner/Mazel.

O'Dougherty, M., & Brown, R. T. (1990). The stress of childhood illness. In L. E. Arnold (Ed.), *Childhood stress* (pp. 325–349). New York: Wiley.

Office of National AIDS Policy. (1996). *Youth & HIV/AIDS: An American agenda.* Washington, DC: Author.

Okazaki, S., & Sue, S. (1995). Methodological issues in assessment research with ethnic minorities. *Psychological Assessment, 7,* 367–375.

Oktay, J. S. (1992). Burnout in hospital social workers who work with AIDS patients. *Social Work, 37,* 432–439.

Okun, B. (1982). *Effective helping interviewing and counseling techniques* (2nd ed.). Monterey, CA: Brooks/Cole.

Ollendick, T. H., & Huntzinger, R. M. (1990). Separation anxiety disorder in childhood. In M. Hersen & C. G. Last (Eds.), *Handbook of child and adult psychopathology* (pp. 133–149). New York: Pergamon.

Ollendick, T. H., Oswald, D. P., & Ollendick, D. G. (1993). Anxiety disorders in mentally retarded persons. In J. L. Matson & R. P. Barrett (Eds.), *Psychopathology in the mentally retarded* (2nd ed., pp. 41–85). Boston: Allyn and Bacon.

Olsen, K. (1994). *Chronology of women's history.* Westport, CT: Greenwood.

Olson, D. H., & Portner, J. (1983). Family Adaptability and Cohesion Evaluation Scales. In E. E. Filsinger (Ed.), *Marriage and family assessment: A source book for family therapy* (pp. 299–315). Beverly Hills: Sage.

O'Malley, J. E., & Koocher, G. P. (1977). Psychological consultation to a pediatric oncology unit: Obstacles to effective intervention. *Journal of Pediatric Psychology, 2,* 54–57.

Oppenheim, L. (1992). The first interview in child protection: Social work method and process. *Children & Society, 6,* 132–150.

Orleans, C. S., & Shipley, R. H. (1982). Assessment in smoking cessation research: Some practical guidelines. In F. J. Keefe & J. A. Blumenthal (Eds.), *Assessment strategies in behavioral medicine* (pp. 261–317). New York: Grune & Stratton.

Ornstein, P. A., Larus, D. M., & Clubb, P. A. (1991). Understanding children's testimony: Implications of research on the development of memory. In R. Vasta (Ed.), *Annals of child development* (Vol. 8, pp. 145–176). London: Kingsley.

Orvaschel, H. (1995). *Schedule for Affective Disorders and Schizophrenia for School-Age Children—Epidemiological Version 5 (K-SADS-E5).* Ft. Lauderdale, FL: NOVA Southeastern University.

Oster, G. D., Caro, J. E., Eagen, D. R., & Lillo, M. A. (1988). *Assessing adolescents.* New York: Pergamon.

Oster, G. D., & Montgomery, S. S. (1995). *Helping your depressed teenager: A guide for parents and caregivers.* New York: Wiley.

Overcast, T. D., Sales, B. D., & Kesler, J. A. (1983). Psychological evaluation of children at the request of noncustodial parents. *Psychotherapy in Private Practice, 1,* 65–74.

Pain Management Guideline Panel. (1992). Clinicians' quick reference guide to acute pain management in infants, children, and adolescents: Operative and medical procedures. *Journal of Pain & Symptom Management, 7,* 229–242.

Paluszny, M. J., DeBeukelaer, M. M., & Rowane, W. A. (1991). Families coping with the multiple crises of chronic illness. *Loss, Grief & Care, 5,* 15–26.

Paquier, P., & Van Dongen, H. R. (1993). Current trends in acquired childhood aphasia: An introduction. *Aphasiology, 7,* 421–440.

Pardeck, J. T. (1991). Using books to prevent and treat adolescent chemical dependency. *Adolescence, 26,* 201–208.

Pardeck, J. T. (1992). Using bibliotherapy in treatment with children in residential care. *Residential Treatment for Children & Youth, 9,* 73–90.

Pardeck, J. T. (1993). Literature and adoptive children with disabilities. *Early Child Development & Care, 91,* 33–39.

Passler, M. A., Isaac, W., & Hynd, G. W. (1985). Neuropsychological development of behavior attributed to frontal lobe functioning in children. *Developmental Neuropsychology, 1,* 349–370.

Pataki, C. S., & Carlson, G. A. (1990). Major depression in childhood. In M. Hersen & C. G. Last (Eds.), *Handbook of child and adult psychopathology* (pp. 35–50). New York: Pergamon.

Patrick, D. (1996, September 2). Have Americans forgotten who they are? *Los Angeles Times,* p. B5.

Patterson, J. M., & McCubbin, H. I. (1983). Chronic illness: Family stress and coping. In C. R. Figley & H. I. McCubbin (Eds.), *Stress and the family: Vol. II. Coping with catastrophe* (pp. 21–36). New York: Brunner/Mazel.

Peach, L., & Reddick, T. L. (1991). Counselors can make a difference in preventing adolescent suicide. *School Counselor, 39,* 107–110.

Pearson, H. (1994, November 23). The black academic environment. *Wall Street Journal,* p. A14.

Peckham, V. C. (1989). Learning disabilities in long-term survivors of childhood cancer: Concerns for parents and teachers. *Journal of Reading, Writing, & Learning Disabilities International, 5,* 313–325.

Pence, D., & Wilson, C. (1994). *Team investigation of child sexual abuse: The uneasy alliance.* Thousand Oaks, CA: Sage.

Pendler, B. (1993). The sibling situation. In S. D. Klein & M. J. Schleifer (Eds.), *It isn't fair! Siblings of children with disabilities* (pp. 79–86). Westport, CT: Bergin & Garvey.

Pessar, L. F., Coad, M. L., Linn, R. T., & Willer, B. S. (1993). The effects of parental traumatic brain injury on the behaviour of parents and children. *Brain Injury, 7,* 231–240.

Peterson, G. (1991). Children coping with trauma: Diagnosis of "dissociation identity disorder." *Dissociation, 4,* 152–164.

Peterson, G., & Putnam, F. W. (1994). Preliminary results of the field trial of proposed criteria for dissociative disorder of childhood. *Dissociation, 8,* 212–220.

Peterson, L., Farmer, J., Harbeck, C., & Chaney, J. (1990). Preparing children for hospitalization and threatening medical procedures. In A. M. Gross & R. S. Drabman (Eds.), *Handbook of clinical behavioral pediatrics* (pp. 349–364). New York: Plenum.

Peterson, M. S., & Urquiza, A. J. (1993). *The role of mental health professionals in the prevention and treatment of child abuse and neglect.* Washington, DC: U.S. Government Printing Office.

Petraitis, J., Flay, B. R., & Miller, T. Q. (1995). Reviewing theories of adolescent substance use: Organizing pieces in the puzzle. *Psychological Bulletin, 117,* 67–86.

Pezdek, K., & Banks, W. P. (Eds.) (1996). *The recovered memory/ false memory debate.* San Diego: Academic Press.

Pfeffer, C. R. (1986). *The suicidal child.* New York: Guilford.

Pfefferbaum, B. (1989). Common psychiatric disorders in childhood cancer and their management. In J. C. Holland & J. H. Rowland (Eds.), *Handbook of psychooncology: Psychological care of the patient with cancer* (pp. 544–561). New York: Oxford University Press.

Phelps, L., & Cox, D. (1993). Children with prenatal cocaine exposure: Resilient or handicapped? *School Psychology Review, 22,* 710–724.

Phinney, J. S. (1989). Stages of ethnic identity development in minority group adolescents. *Journal of Early Adolescence, 9,* 34–49.

Pianta, R., Egeland, B., & Erickson, M. F. (1989). The antecedents of maltreatment: Results of the Mother-Child Interaction Research Project. In D. Cicchetti & V. Carlson (Eds.), *Child maltreatment: Theory and research on the causes and consequences of child abuse and neglect* (pp. 203–253). New York: Cambridge University Press.

Pitcher, G. D., & Poland, S. (1992). *Crisis intervention in the schools.* New York: Guilford.

Plumer, E. H. (1992). *When you place a child....* Springfield, IL: Charles C Thomas.

Poirier, J. G. (1991). Disputed custody and concerns of parental violence. *Psychotherapy in Private Practice, 9,* 7–23.

Poland, S. (1989). *Suicide intervention in the schools.* New York: Guilford.

Polansky, N. A., Ammons, P. W., & Gaudin, J. M. (1985). Loneliness and isolation in child neglect. *Social Casework, 66,* 38–47.

Polansky, N. A., Borgman, R. D., & De Saix, C. (1972). *Roots of futility.* San Francisco: Jossey-Bass.

Polivy, J., Herman, C. P., & Garner, D. M. (1988). Cognitive assessment. In D. M. Donovan & G. A. Marlatt (Eds.), *Assessment of addictive behaviors* (pp. 274–295). New York: Guilford.

Pollak, J. M. (1988). The feedback process to parents in child and adolescent assessment. *Psychology in the Schools, 25,* 143–153.

Pollock, N. L., & Hashmall, J. M. (1991). The excuses of child molesters. *Behavioral Sciences & the Law, 9,* 53–59.

Ponton, L. E. (1996). Disordered eating. In R. J. DiClemente, W. B. Hansen, & L. E. Ponton (Eds.), *Handbook of adolescent health risk behavior* (pp. 83–113). New York: Plenum.

Pope, K. S., Brown, L. S. (1996). *Recovered memories of abuse: Assessment, therapy, forensics.* Washington, DC: American Psychological Association.

Pope, K. S., Butcher, J. N., & Seelen, J. (1993). *The MMPI, MMPI-2, and MMPI-A in court: Assessment, testimony, and cross-examination for expert witnesses and attorneys.* Washington, DC: American Psychological Association.

Porcher, L. T. (1995, November 17–19). Reader asserts Brooks should face real discrimination. *The Daily Aztec,* p. 7.

Powell, G. F., & Low, J. L. (1983). Behavior in nonorganic failure to thrive. *Journal of Developmental and Behavioral Pediatrics, 4,* 26–33.

Powell, G. F., Low, J. L., & Speers, M. A. (1987). Behavior as a diagnostic aid in failure-to-thrive. *Journal of Developmental and Behavioral Pediatrics, 8,* 18–24.

Powell, M. B. (1991). Investigating and reporting child sexual abuse: Review and recommendations for clinical practice. *Australian Psychologist, 26,* 77–83.

Powell, M. B., & Ilett, M. J. (1992). Assessing the incestuous family's readiness for reconstruction. *Families in Society, 73,* 417–423.

Power, P. W. (1988). An assessment approach to family intervention. In P. W. Power, A. E. Dell Orto, & M. B. Gibbons (Eds.), *Family interventions throughout chronic illness and disability* (pp. 5–23). New York: Springer.

Poythress, N. G. (1992). Expert testimony on violence and dangerousness: Roles for mental health professionals. *Forensic Reports, 5,* 135–150.

Prigatano, G. P., Fordyce, D. J., Zeiner, H. K., Roueche, J. R., Pepping, M., & Wood, B. C. (1986). *Neuropsychological rehabilitation after brain injury.* Baltimore: Johns Hopkins University Press.

Prizant, B. M., & Wetherby, A. M. (1993). Communication in preschool autistic children. In E. Schopler, M. E. Van Bourgondien, & M. M. Bristol (Eds.), *Preschool issues in autism* (pp. 95–128). New York: Plenum.

Prout, H. T. (1989). Counseling and psychotherapy with children and adolescents: An overview. In D. T. Brown & H. T. Prout (Eds.), *Counseling and psychotherapy with children and adolescents: Theory and practice for school and clinic settings* (2nd ed., pp. 3–36). Brandon, VT: Clinical Psychology Publishing Company.

Putnam, F. W. (1991). Dissociative disorders in children and adolescents: A developmental perspective. *Psychiatric Clinics of North America, 14,* 519–531.

Putnam, F. W., Guroff, J. J., Silberman, E. K., Barban, L., & Post, R. M. (1986). The clinical phenomenology of multiple personality disorder: Review of 100 recent cases. *Journal of Clinical Psychiatry, 47,* 285–293.

Pynoos, R. S., & Nader, K. (1989). Children who witness the sexual assaults of their mothers. *Annual Progress in Child Psychiatry & Child Development,* 165–178.

Quay, H. D., Routh, D. K., & Shapiro, S. K. (1987). Psychopathology of childhood: From description to validation. *Annual Review of Psychology, 38,* 491–532.

Quinn, K. M. (1988). Children and deception. In R. Rogers (Ed.), *Clinical assessment of malingering and deception* (pp. 104–119). New York: Guilford.

Quinsey, V. L., & Lalumière, M. L. (1995). *Assessment of sexual offenders against children.* Thousand Oaks, CA: Sage.

Quintanilla, M. (1995, November 17). The great divide. *Los Angeles Times,* pp. E1, E7.

Rafferty, Y., & Rollins, N. (1989). *Learning in limbo: The educational deprivation of homeless children.* New York: Advocates for Children of New York.

Rafferty, Y., & Shinn, M. (1991). The impact of homelessness on children. *American Psychologist, 46,* 1170–1179.

Rainey, L. C., Wellisch, D. K., Fawzy, F. I., Wolcott, D., & Pasnau, R. O. (1983). Training health professionals in psychosocial aspects of cancer: A continuing education model. *Journal of Psychosocial Oncology, 1,* 41–59.

Rainey, R., & Dinsmore, J. (1994). Medical examiners in child homicide cases. *Update—National Center for Prosecution of Child Abuse, 7*(Fall), pp. 1–2.

Rait, D., & Lederberg, M. (1989). The family of the cancer patient. In J. C. Holland & J. H. Rowland (Eds.), *Handbook of psychooncology: Psychological care of the patient with cancer* (pp. 585–597). New York: Oxford University Press.

Ramirez, D. N. (1978). *College of the Desert guide: Education of handicapped adults.* Palm Desert, CA: College of the Desert.

Ramos-McKay, J. M., Comas-Diaz, L., & Rivera, L. A. (1988). Puerto Ricans. In L. Comas-Diaz & E. Griffith (Eds.), *Clinical guidelines in cross cultural mental health* (pp. 204–232). New York: Wiley.

Rando, T. A. (1984). *Grief, dying, and death.* Champaign, IL: Research Press.

Rapoff, M. A., Lindsley, C. B., & Christophersen, E. R. (1985). Parent perceptions of problems experienced by their children in complying with treatments for juvenile rheumatoid arthritis. *Archives of Physical Medicine and Rehabilitation, 66,* 427–429.

Rapoport, J. L., Swedo, S. E., & Leonard, H. L. (1992). Childhood obsessive compulsive disorder. *Journal of Clinical Psychiatry, 53,* 11–16.

Rapport, M. D. (1994). Attention-deficit hyperactivity disorder. In V. B. Van Hasselt & M. Hersen (Eds.), *Advanced abnormal psychology* (pp. 189–206). New York: Plenum.

Rasinski, T. V., & Gillespie, C. S. (1992). *Sensitive issues: An annotated guide to children's literature K–6.* Phoenix: Oryx Press.

Raskin, D. C., & Steller, M. (1989). Assessing credibility of allegations of child sexual abuse: Polygraph examinations and statement analysis. In H. Wegener, F. Loesel, & J. Haisch (Eds.), *Criminal behavior and the justice system* (pp. 290–302). New York: Springer-Verlag.

Rawlins, R. P., & Drake, V. K. (1993). Therapy with victims of abuse. In R. P. Rawlins, S. R. Williams, & C. K. Beck (Eds.), *Mental health–psychiatric nursing: A holistic life-cycle approach* (3rd ed., pp. 671–693). St. Louis: Mosby.

Read, J. D., & Lindsay, D. S. (1994). Moving toward a middle ground on the "false memory debate": Reply to commentaries on Lindsay and Read. *Applied Cognitive Psychology, 8,* 407–435.

Reagor, P. A., Kasten, J. D., & Morelli, N. (1992). A checklist for screening dissociative disorders in children and adolescents. *Dissociation: Progress in the Dissociative Disorders, 5,* 4–19.

Reavis, D. (1990). *Assessing students with multiple disabilities: Practical guidelines for practitioners.* Springfield, IL: Charles C Thomas.

Redd, W. (1989). Behavioral interventions to reduce child distress. In J. C. Holland & J. H. Rowland (Eds.), *Handbook of psycho-*

oncology: Psychological care of the patient with cancer* (pp. 573–581). New York: Oxford University Press.

Reder, P., Lucey, C., & Fredman, G. (1991). The challenge of deliberate self-harm by young adolescents. *Journal of Adolescence, 14,* 135–148.

Red Horse, Y. (1982). A cultural network model: Perspectives for adolescent services and paraprofessional training. In S. M. Manson (Ed.), *New directions in prevention among American Indian and Alaska native communities* (pp. 173–184). Portland: Oregon Health Sciences University.

Reece, R. M. (1994). Fatal child abuse and sudden infant death syndrome. In R. M. Reece (Ed.), *Child abuse: Medical diagnosis and management* (pp. 107–137). Baltimore: Williams & Wilkins.

Reed, L. D. (1993). Enhancing children's resistance to misleading questions during forensic interviews. *APSAC Advisor, 6*(2), 3–8.

Reed, L. J., Carter, B. D., & Miller, L. C. (1992). Fear and anxiety in children. In C. E. Walker & R. C. Roberts (Eds.), *Handbook of clinical child psychology* (2nd ed., pp. 237–260). New York: Wiley.

Reed, M. (1985). Books for parents and children on learning disabilities. *Journal of Clinical Child Psychology, 14,* 257–263.

Rees, R. (1988). How some families cope and why some families do not. *Journal of Head Trauma Rehabilitation, 3,* 72–77.

Reich, W. (Ed.) (1996). *Diagnostic Interview for Children and Adolescents—Revised (DICA-R) 8.0.* St. Louis: Washington University.

Reiff, D. W., & Reiff, K. K. L. (1992). *Eating disorders: Nutrition therapy in the recovery process.* Gaithersburg, MD: Aspen.

Reisman, J. M. (1973). *Principles of psychotherapy with children.* New York: Wiley.

Reitz, M., & Watson, K. W. (1992). *Adoption and the family system: Strategies for treatment.* New York: Guilford.

Retterstöl, N. (1993). *Suicide: A European perspective.* Cambridge, England: Cambridge University Press.

Reviere, S. L. (1996). *Memory of childhood trauma: A clinician's guide to the literature.* New York: Guilford.

Reynolds, W. M. (1992). Depression in children and adolescents. In W. M. Reynolds (Ed.), *Internalizing disorders in children and adolescents* (pp. 149–253). New York: Wiley.

Rich, C. L., Sherman, M., & Fowler, R. C. (1990). San Diego Suicide Study: The adolescents. *Adolescence, 25,* 855–865.

Rich, D., & Taylor, H. G. (1993). Attention deficit hyperactivity disorder. In M. Singer, L. Singer, & T. Anglin (Eds.), *Handbook for screening adolescents at psychosocial risk* (pp. 333–374). New York: Lexington Books.

Richard, M. (1993, December). Ask CH.A.D.D. *CH.A.D.D.er,* p. 10.

Rief, S. F. (1993). *How to reach and teach ADD/ADHD children: Practical techniques, strategies, and interventions for helping children with attention problems and hyperactivity.* West Nyack, NY: Center for Applied Research in Education.

Rigdon, J. E. (1991, July 10). Asian-American youth suffer a rising toll from heavy pressures. *Wall Street Journal,* pp. A1, A5.

Riley, R. L., & Mead, J. (1988). The development of symptoms of multiple personality disorder in a child of three. *Dissociation: Progress in the Dissociative Disorders, 1,* 41–46.

Roach, S. S., & Nieto, B. C. (1997). *Healing and the grief process.* Albany, NY: Delmar.

Roberts, J., & Taylor, C. (1993). Sexually abused children and young people speak out. In L. Waterhouse (Ed.), *Child abuse and child abusers: Protection and prevention* (pp. 13–37). Bristol, PA: Jessica Kingsley Publishers.

Robin, M. (1991). Beyond validation interviews: An assessment approach to evaluating sexual abuse allegations. *Child & Youth Services, 15,* 93–114.

Robins, L. N., & Marcus, S. C. (1987). The Diagnostic Screening Procedure Writer: A tool to develop individualized screening procedures. *Medical Care, 25,* S106–S122.

Roffman, R. A., & George, W. H. (1988). Cannabis abuse. In D. M. Donovan & G. A. Marlatt (Eds.), *Assessment of addictive behaviors* (pp. 325–363). New York: Guilford.

Rogers, R. (1988a). Current status of clinical methods. In R. Rogers (Ed.), *Clinical assessment of malingering and deception* (pp. 293–308). New York: Guilford.

Rogers, R. (1988b). Introduction. In R. Rogers (Ed.), *Clinical assessment of malingering and deception* (pp. 1–9). New York: Guilford.

Rolland, J. S. (1994). *Families, illness, and disability: An integrative treatment model.* New York: Basic Books.

Rollin, W. J. (1987). *The psychology of communication disorders in individuals and their families.* Englewood Cliffs, NJ: Prentice Hall.

Romano, M. D. (1989). Ethical issues and families of brain-injured persons. *Journal of Head Trauma Rehabilitation, 4*(1), 33–41.

Rosado, J. W. (1986). Toward an interfacing of Hispanic cultural variables with school psychology service delivery systems. *Professional Psychology: Research and Practice, 17,* 191–199.

Rosenberg, D. A. (1987). Web of deceit: A literature review of Munchausen syndrome by proxy. *Child Abuse & Neglect, 11,* 547–563.

Rosenberg, D. A. (1995). From lying to homicide: The spectrum of Munchausen syndrome by proxy. In A. V. Levin & M. S. Sheridan (Eds.), *Munchausen syndrome by proxy: Issues in diagnosis and treatment* (pp. 13–37). New York: Lexington Books.

Rosenberg, L. A. (1990). Interviewing children: Psychological considerations. In L. S. Wissow, *Child advocacy for the clinician: An approach to child abuse and neglect* (pp. 23–39). Baltimore: Williams & Wilkins.

Rosenblatt, R. A. (1996, March 14). Latinos, Asians to lead rise in U.S. population. *Los Angeles Times,* pp. A1, A4.

Rosenstock, H. A., Rosenstock, J. D., & Weiner, J. (1988). *Journey through divorce.* New York: Human Sciences Press.

Rosenthal, J. A., Motz, J. K., Edmonson, D. A., & Groze, V. (1991). A descriptive study of abuse and neglect in out-of-home placement. *Child Abuse & Neglect, 15,* 249–260.

Rosenthal, M., & Young, T. (1988). Effective family intervention after traumatic brain injury: Theory and practice. *Journal of Head Trauma Rehabilitation, 3,* 42–50.

Ross, C. A. (1989). *Multiple personality disorder: Diagnosis, clinical features and treatment.* New York: Wiley.

Ross, C. A., Anderson, G., Fleisher, W. P., & Norton, G. R. (1991). The frequency of multiple personality disorder among psychiatric inpatients. *American Journal of Psychiatry, 148,* 1717–1720.

Ross, C. A., Miller, S. C., Bjornson, L., Reagor, P. A., Fraser, G. A., & Anderson, G. (1991). Abuse histories in 102 cases of multiple personality disorder. *Canadian Journal of Psychiatry, 36,* 97–101.

Ross, D. M., & Ross, S. A. (1984). The importance of type of question, psychological climate and subject set in interviewing children about pain. *Pain, 19,* 71–79.

Ross, D. M., & Ross, S. A. (1988). Assessment of pediatric pain: An overview. *Issues in Comprehensive Pediatric Nursing, 11,* 73–91.

Roter, D. L., & Hall, J. A. (1992). *Doctors talking with patients/patients talking with doctors: Improving communication in medical visits.* Westport, CT: Auburn House.

Rotheram, M. J., & Phinney, J. S. (1986). Introduction: Definitions and perspectives in the study of children's ethnic socialization. In J. S. Phinney & M. J. Rotheram (Eds.), *Children's ethnic socialization: Pluralism and development* (pp. 10–28). Newbury Park, CA: Sage.

Rotheram-Borus, M. J., & Koopman, C. (1992). Adolescents. In M. L. Stuber (Ed.), *Children and AIDS* (pp. 45–67). Washington, DC: American Psychiatric Press.

Rotheram-Borus, M. J., Koopman, C., & Ehrhardt, A. A. (1991). Homeless youths and HIV infection. *American Psychologist, 46,* 1188–1197.

Rounds, K. A. (1991). Early intervention services for very young children and their families under P. L. 99–457. *Child & Adolescent Social Work Journal, 8,* 489–499.

Roundy, L. M., & Horton, A. L. (1991). Professional and treatment issues for clinicians who intervene with incest perpetrators. In A. L. Horton, B. L. Johnson, L. M. Roundy, & D. Williams (Eds.), *The incest perpetrator: A family member no one wants to treat* (pp. 164–189). Newbury Park, CA: Sage.

Rourke, B. P. (1993). Arithmetic disabilities, specific and otherwise: A neuropsychological perspective. *Journal of Learning Disabilities, 26,* 214–226.

Rovet, J. F., Ehrlich, R. M., Czuchta, D., & Akler, M. (1993). Psychoeducational characteristics of children and adolescents with insulin-dependent diabetes mellitus. *Journal of Learning Disabilities, 26,* 7–22.

Rowland, J. H. (1989a). Developmental stage and adaptation: Child and adolescent model. In J. C. Holland & J. H. Rowland (Eds.), *Handbook of psychooncology: Psychological care of the patient with cancer* (pp. 519–543). New York: Oxford University Press.

Rowland, J. H. (1989b). Intrapersonal resources: Coping. In J. C. Holland & J. H. Rowland (Eds.), *Handbook of psychooncology: Psychological care of the patient with cancer* (pp. 44–57). New York: Oxford University Press.

Rudel, R. G. (1988). *Assessment of developmental learning disorders: A neuropsychological approach.* New York: Basic Books.

Ruiz, P. (1985). Cultural barriers to effective medical care among Hispanic-American patients. *Annual Review of Medicine, 36,* 63–71.

Russell, D. M. (1988). Language and psychotherapy: The influence of nonstandard English in clinical practice. In L. Comas-Diaz & E. E. H. Griffith (Eds.), *Clinical guidelines in cross-cultural mental health* (pp. 33–68). New York: Wiley.

Russo, D. C., Lehn, B. M., & Berde, C. B. (1993). Pain. In T. H. Ollendick & M. Hersen (Eds.), *Handbook of child and adolescent assessment* (pp. 413–438). Boston: Allyn and Bacon.

Rutter, M. (1982). Developmental neuropsychiatry: Concepts, issues, and prospects. *Journal of Clinical Neuropsychology, 4,* 91–115.

Rycus, J. S., Hughes, R. C., & Garrison, J. K. (1989). *Child Protective Services: A training manual.* Columbus, OH: Institute for Human Services.

Ryland, D. H., & Kruesi, M. J. (1992). Suicide among adolescents. *International Review of Psychiatry, 4,* 185–195.

Sabotta, E. E., & Davis, R. L. (1992). Fatality after report to a child abuse registry in Washington State, 1973–1986. *Child Abuse & Neglect, 16,* 627–635.

Sachs, P. R. (1991). *Treating families of brain-injury survivors.* New York: Springer.

Sales, B. D., Manber, R., & Rohman, L. (1992). Social science research and child-custody decision making. *Applied & Preventive Psychology, 1,* 23–40.

San Diego County Grand Jury. (1994). *Analysis of child molestation issues (Report No. 7).* San Diego: Author.

Sandler, A. D., Footo, M., Levine, M. D., Coleman, W. L., & Hooper, S. R. (1992). Neurodevelopmental study of writing disorders in middle childhood. *Developmental and Behavioral Pediatrics, 13,* 17–23.

Sarafino, E. P. (1994). *Health psychology: Biopsychosocial interactions* (2nd ed.). New York: Wiley.

Sattler, J. M. (1992). *Assessment of children: Revised and updated third edition.* San Diego: Author.

Savage, D. G. (1994, April 26). High court lets stand social worker immunity. *Los Angeles Times,* p. A26.

Savage, R. C. (1987). Educational issues for the head-injured adolescent and young adult. *Journal of Head Trauma Rehabilitation, 2,* 1–10.

Savage, R. C. (1993). Children with traumatic brain injury. *TBI Challenge! 1,* 4–5.

Savage, R. C., & Carter, R. (1988). Transitioning pediatric patients into educational systems: Guidelines for rehabilitation professionals. *Cognitive Rehabilitation, 6,* 10–14.

Savedra, M. C., & Tesler, M. D. (1989). Assessing children's and adolescents' pain. *Pediatrician, 16,* 24–29.

Savedra, M. C., Tesler, M. D., Holzemer, W. L., & Ward, J. A. (1989). *Adolescent Pediatric Pain Tool (APPT): Preliminary user's manual.* San Francisco: University of California.

Saywitz, K. J. (1990). Developmental considerations for forensic interviewing. *The Advisor, 3,* 2, 5, 15.

Saywitz, K. J. (1994). Questioning child witnesses. *Violence UpDate, 4*(7), 3, 6, 8.

Saywitz, K. J., Geiselman, R. E., & Bornstein, G. K. (1992). Effects of cognitive interviewing and practice on children's recall performance. *Journal of Applied Psychology, 77,* 744–756.

Sbordone, R. J. (1988). Assessment and treatment of cognitive-communicative impairments in the closed-head-injury patient: A neurobehavioral-systems approach. *Journal of Head Trauma Rehabilitation, 3*(2), 55–62.

Sbriglio, R., Hartman, N., Millman, R. B., & Khuri, E. T. (1988). Drug and alcohol abuse in children and adolescents. In C. J. Kestenbaun & D. T. William (Eds.), *Handbook of clinical assessment of children and adolescents* (Vol. 2, pp. 915–937). New York: New York University Press.

Schachter, J. E., & Romano, B. A. (1993). Developmental issues in childhood and adolescent depression. In H. S. Koplewicz & E. Klass (Eds.), *Depression in children and adolescents: Monographs in clinical pediatrics* (Vol. 6, pp. 1–13). Philadelphia: Harwood Academic Publishers.

Scheer, R. (1993, October 11). Asian-Americans: "We are still treated like foreigners." *Los Angeles Times,* p. B5.

Schmitz, T. A. (1988). Environmental assessment. In S. B. O'Sullivan & T. J. Schmitz (Eds.), *Physical rehabilitation: Assessment and treatment* (2nd ed., pp. 237–251). Philadelphia: Davis.

Schneider, H. J. (1993). Violence in the family. *Studies on Crime & Crime Prevention, 2,* 34–44.

Schopler, E. (1992). Facilitated communication—Hope or hype? *Autism Society of North Carolina, 8*(3), 6.

Schopler, E., Reichler, R. J., & Renner, B. R. (1986). *The Childhood Autism Rating Scale* (CARS). New York: Irvington.

Schopler, E., Van Bourgondien, M. E., & Bristol, M. M. (Eds.). (1993). *Preschool issues in autism. Current issues in autism.* New York: Plenum.

Schowalter, J. E. (1970). The child's reaction to his own terminal illness. In B. Schoenberg, A. C. Carr, D. Peretz, & A. H. Kutscher (Eds.), *Loss and grief: Psychological management in medical practice* (pp. 51–69). New York: Columbia University Press.

Schreiber, M. (1993). Forgotten children. In S. D. Klein & M. J. Schleifer (Eds.), *It isn't fair! Siblings of children with disabilities* (pp. 33–40). Westport, CT: Bergin & Garvey.

Schreibman, L. (1988). Diagnostic features of autism. *Journal of Child Neurology, 3,* 57–64.

Schreibman, L., & Charlop, M. H. (1989). Infantile autism. In T. H. Ollendick & M. Hersen (Eds.), *Handbook of child psychopathology* (pp. 105–129). New York: Plenum.

Schreier, H. A., & Libow, J. A. (1993). *Hurting for love: Munchausen by proxy syndrome.* New York: Guilford.

Schroeder, C. S., & Gordon, B. N. (1991). *Assessment and treatment of childhood problems: A clinician's guidebook.* New York: Guilford.

Schultz, L. G. (1990). Social workers as expert witnesses in child abuse cases: A format. *Journal of Independent Social Work, 5,* 69–87.

Schutz, B. M., Dixon, E. B., Lindenberger, J. C., & Ruther, N. J. (1989). *Solomon's sword: A practical guide to conducting child custody evaluations.* San Francisco: Jossey-Bass.

Schwab-Stone, M., Fallon, T., Briggs, M., & Crowther, B. (1994). Reliability of diagnostic reporting for children aged 6–11 years: A test-retest study of the Diagnostic Interview Schedule for Children—Revised. *American Journal of Psychiatry, 151,* 1048–1054.

Schwab-Stone, M., Fisher, P., Piacentini, J., Shaffer, D., Davies, M., & Briggs, M. (1993). The Diagnostic Interview Schedule for Children—Revised version (DISC-R): II. Test-retest reliability. *Journal of the American Academy of Child & Adolescent Psychiatry, 32,* 651–657.

Schwartz, M. L. (1987). Limitations on neuropsychological testimony by the Florida appellate decisions: Action, reaction, and counteraction. *Clinical Neuropsychologist, 1,* 51–60.

Schwartz, R. C., & Barrett, M. J. (1987). Women and eating disorders. *Journal of Psychotherapy & the Family, 3,* 131–144.

Scott, E. S., & Emery, R. (1987). Child custody dispute resolution: The adversarial system and divorce mediation. In L. A. Weithorn (Ed.), *Psychology and child custody determinations: Knowledge, roles, and expertise* (pp. 23–56). Lincoln: University of Nebraska Press.

Scully, R. (1990). Adolescent suicide. In M. E. Connal & B. A. Johnson (Eds.), *Pediatric emergencies: A handbook for nurses.* Rockville, MD: Aspen.

Sedlak, A. J., & Broadhurst, D. D. (1996). *Third national incidence study of child abuse and neglect.* Washington, DC: U.S. Department of Health and Human Services, National Center on Child Abuse and Neglect.

Seligman, M., & Darling, R. B. (1989). *Ordinary families, special children: A systems approach to childhood disability.* New York: Guilford.

Seligmann, J., & Chideya, F. (1992, September 21). Horror story or big hoax? A new technique gives voice to abuse charges. *Newsweek, 120,* 75.

Selman, R. L. (1976). Social-cognitive understanding: A guide to educational and clinical practice. In T. Lickona (Ed.), *Moral development and behavior: Theory, research, and social issues* (pp. 299–316). New York: Holt, Rinehart and Winston.

Seltser, B. J., & Miller, D. E. (1993). *Homeless families: The struggle for dignity.* Chicago: University of Illinois Press.

Seltzer, M. M., & Krauss, M. W. (1984). Placement alternatives for mentally retarded children and their families. In J. Blacher (Ed.), *Severely handicapped young children and their families: Research in review* (pp. 143–175). Orlando, FL: Academic Press.

Sgroi, S. M. (1982). Family treatment. In S. M. Sgroi (Ed.), *Handbook of clinical intervention in child sexual abuse* (pp. 241–267). Lexington, MA: Lexington Books.

Sgroi, S. M., Porter, F. S., & Blick, L. C. (1982). Validation of child sexual abuse. In S. M. Sgroi (Ed.), *Handbook of clinical intervention in child sexual abuse* (pp. 39–80). Lexington, MA: Lexington Books.

Shaffer, D. (1996). *Diagnostic Interview Schedule for Children (DISC-IV).* New York: New York State Psychiatric Institute.

Shaheen, S. J. (1984). Neuromaturation and behavior development: The case of childhood lead poisoning. *Developmental Psychology, 20,* 542–550.

Shane, H. C. (1993). The dark side of facilitated communication. *Topics in Language Disorders, 13,* ix–xv.

Shapiro, B. K. (1991). The pediatric neurodevelopmental assessment of infants and young children. In A. J. Capute & P. J. Accardo (Eds.), *Developmental disabilities in infancy and childhood* (pp. 139–164). Baltimore: Brookes.

Shapiro, D. E., & Koocher, G. P. (1996). Goals and practical considerations in outpatient medical crises intervention. *Professional Psychology: Research and Practice, 27,* 109–120.

Shapiro, E. S. (1984). Self-monitoring procedures. In T. H. Ollendick & M. Hersen (Eds.), *Child behavioral assessment: Principles and procedures* (pp. 148–165). New York: Pergamon.

Shaw, D. S. (1991). The effects of divorce on children's adjustment: Review and implications. *Behavior Modification, 15,* 456–485.

Shaw, D. S., & Bell, R. Q. (1993). Developmental theories of parental contributors to antisocial behavior. *Journal of Abnormal Child Psychology, 21,* 493–518.

Shea, S. C. (1988). *Psychiatric interviewing: The art of understanding.* Philadelphia: Saunders.

Shedler, J., & Block, J. (1990). Adolescent drug use and psychological health: A longitudinal inquiry. *American Psychologist, 45,* 612–630.

Sheridan, C. L., & Radmacher, S. A. (1992). *Health psychology: Challenging the biomedical model.* New York: Wiley.

Sheridan, K. (1991). Psychosocial services for persons with human immunodeficiency virus disease. In J. J. Sweet, R. H. Rozensky, & S. M. Tovian (Eds.), *Handbook of clinical psychology in medical settings* (pp. 587–600). New York: Plenum.

Sheridan, M. S., & Levin, A. V. (1995). Summary. In A. V. Levin & M. S. Sheridan (Eds.), *Munchausen syndrome by proxy: Issues in diagnosis and treatment* (pp. 433–443). New York: Lexington Books.

Shinn, M., Knickman, J. R., & Weitzman, B. C. (1991). Social relationships and vulnerability to becoming homeless among poor families. *American Psychologist, 46,* 1180–1187.

Shontz, F. C. (1977). Six principles relating disability and psychological adjustment. *Rehabilitation Psychology, 24,* 207–210.

Shuster, S., Guskin, S., Hawkins, B., & Okolo, C. (1986). Views of health and development: Six mothers and their infants. *Journal of the Division for Early Childhood, 11,* 18–27.

Siegel, L. J. (1993). Children's understanding of AIDS: Implications for preventive interventions. *Journal of Pediatric Psychology, 18,* 173–176.

Siegel, L. J., & Smith, K. E. (1989). Children's strategies for coping with pain. *Pediatrician, 16,* 110–118.

Silcner, N. A., & Hanson, S. R. (1989). Guidelines for videotape interviews in child sexual abuse cases. *American Journal of Forensic Psychology, 7,* 61–74.

Silver, L. B. (1992). *Attention-deficit hyperactivity disorder: A clinical guide to diagnosis and treatment.* Washington, DC: American Psychiatric Press.

Simkins, L., Ward, W., Bowman, S., Rinck, C., & DeSouza, E. (1990). Predicting treatment outcome for child sexual abusers. *Annals of Sex Research 3,* 21–57.

Simmons, J. E. (1987). *Psychiatric examination of children* (4th ed.). Philadelphia: Lea and Febiger.

Simonds, R. J., & Rogers, M. F. (1992). Epidemiology of HIV in children and other populations. In A. C. Crocker, H. J. Cohen, & T. A. Kastner (Eds.), *HIV infection and developmental disabilities: A resource for service providers* (pp. 3–13). Baltimore: Brookes.

Sincoff, M. Z., & Goyer, R. S. (1984). *Interviewing.* New York: Macmillan.

Sisson, L. A., & Van Hasselt, V. B. (1987). Visual impairment. In V. B. Van Hasselt & M. Hersen (Eds.), *Psychological evaluation of the developmentally and physically disabled* (pp. 115–153). New York: Plenum.

Skafte, D. (1985). *Child custody evaluations.* Beverly Hills: Sage.

Skinner, L. J., & Berry, K. K. (1993). Anatomically detailed dolls and the evaluation of child sexual abuse allegations: Psychometric considerations. *Law and Human Behavior, 17,* 399–421.

Smith, C. A., & Lazarus, R. S. (1990). Emotion and adaptation. In L. A. Pervin (Ed.), *Handbook of personality: Theory and research* (pp. 609–637). New York: Guilford.

Smith, L. (1995, January 11). Facing the issue head-on. *Los Angeles Times,* pp. E1, E2.

Smith, M. D., & Belcher, R. G. (1994). Facilitated communication and autism: Separating fact from fiction. *Journal of Vocational Rehabilitation, 4,* 66–74.

Smith, M. S., Tyler, R. C., Womack, W. M., & Chen, A. C. (1989). Assessment and management of recurrent pain in adolescence. *Pediatrician, 16,* 85–93.

Smith, P. (1993). *Munchausen syndrome by proxy: A concept paper.* Unpublished manuscript.

Smith, R. (Ed.). (1993). *Children with mental retardation: A parents' guide.* Rockville, MD: Woodbine House.

Smith, S. M. (1983). Disaster: Family disruption in the wake of natural disaster. In C. R. Figley & H. I. McCubbin (Eds.), *Stress and the family: Vol. II. Coping with catastrophe* (pp. 120–147). New York: Brunner/Mazel.

Snyder, J., Rains, J., & Popejoy, J. (1988). Assessing aggressive and violent parent-child interaction. In P. Karoly (Ed.), *Handbook of child health assessment: Biopsychosocial perspectives* (pp. 579–607). New York: Wiley.

Sobell, M. B., & Sobell, L. C. (1978). *Behavioral treatment of alcohol problems: Individualized therapy and controlled drinking.* New York: Plenum.

Somers, A. (1992). Domestic violence survivors. In M. J. Robertson & M. Greenblatt (Eds.), *Homelessness: A national perspective* (pp. 265–272). New York: Plenum.

Sonkin, D. J., Martin, D., & Walker, L. E. A. (1985). *The male batterer: A treatment approach.* New York: Springer.

Sourkes, B. M. (1987). Siblings of the child with a life-threatening illness. *Journal of Children in Contemporary Society, 19,* 159–184.

Spano, S. L. (1994). The miracle of Michael. In R. B. Darling & M. I. Peter (Eds.), *Families, physicians, and children with special health needs: Collaborative medical education models* (pp. 29–50). Westport, CT: Auburn House.

Spanos, N. P. (1994). Multiple identity enactments and multiple personality disorder: A sociocognitive perspective. *Psychological Bulletin, 116,* 143–165.

Spector, R. E. (1991). *Cultural diversity in health and illness* (3rd ed.). Norwalk, CT: Appleton & Lange.

Spencer, J. R., & Flin, R. H. (1990). *The evidence of children: The law and the psychology.* London: Blackstone Press.

Spencer, M. B., & Markstrom-Adams, C. (1990). Identity processes among racial and ethnic minority children in America. *Child Development, 61,* 290–310.

Spencer, T., Biederman, J., Wilens, T., Harding, M., O'Donnell, D., & Griffin, S. (1996). Pharmacotherapy of attention-deficit hyperactivity disorder across the life cycle. *Journal of the American Academy of Child & Adolescent Psychiatry, 35,* 409–432.

Spiegel, J. (1982). An ecological model of ethnic families. In M. McGoldrick, J. Pearce, & L. Giordano (Eds.), *Ethnicity and family therapy* (pp. 31–51). New York: Guilford.

Spinetta, J. J. (1980). Disease-related communication: How to tell. In J. Kellerman (Ed.), *Psychological aspects of childhood cancer* (pp. 257–269). Springfield, IL: Charles C Thomas.

Spitzer, R. L., Gibbon, M., Skodol, A. E., Williams, J. B. W., & First, M. B. (1989). *DSM-III-R case book.* Washington, DC: American Psychiatric Press.

Spreen, O. (1988). Prognosis of learning disability. *Journal of Consulting and Clinical Psychology, 56,* 836–842.

Spreen, O., Risser, A. H., & Edgell, D. (1995). *Developmental neuropsychology.* New York: Oxford University Press.

Sprenkle, D. H., & Cyrus, C. L. (1983). Abandonment: The stress of sudden divorce. In C. R. Figley & H. I. McCubbin (Eds.), *Stress and the family: Vol. II. Coping with catastrophe* (pp. 53–75). New York: Brunner/Mazel.

St. James-Roberts, I. (1981). A reinterpretation of hemispherectomy data without functional plasticity of the brain. *Brain and Language, 13,* 31–53.

Stacey, W., & Shupe, A. (1983). *The family secret: Domestic violence in America.* Boston: Beacon.

Stahl, P. M. (1994). *Conducting child custody evaluations: A comprehensive guide.* Thousand Oaks, CA: Sage.

Stanovich, K. E. (1988). Explaining the differences between the dyslexic and the garden-variety poor reader: The phonological-core variable-difference model. *Journal of Learning Disability, 21,* 590–604, 612.

Staples, R. (1991). Health issues: Substance abuse and the Black family crisis: An overview. In R. Staples (Ed.), *Black family: Essays and studies* (4th ed., pp. 257–267). Belmont, CA: Wadsworth.

Steele, W., & Raider, M. (1991). *Working with families in crisis: School-based intervention.* New York: Guilford.

Stein, T. J., Gambrill, E. D., & Wiltse, K. T. (1978). *Children in foster homes: Achieving continuity of care.* New York: Praeger.

Steinberg, M., Rounsaville, B., & Cicchetti, D. V. (1990). The Structured Clinical Interview for *DSM-III-R* dissociative disorders: Preliminary report on a new diagnostic instrument. *American Journal of Psychiatry, 147,* 76–82.

Steinhauer, P. D. (1991). *The least detrimental alternative: A systematic guide to case planning and decision making for children in care.* Toronto: University of Toronto Press.

Steinmetz, M. (1996). Intervening with non-offending parents during an abuse investigation. *NRCCSA News, 5*(3), 4–5.

Steller, M., & Boychuk, T. (1992). Children as witnesses in sexual abuse cases: Investigative interview and assessment techniques. In H. Dent & R. Flin (Eds.), *Children as witnesses* (pp. 47–71). Chichester, England: Wiley.

Stelmachers, Z. T. (1995). Assessing suicidal clients. In J. N. Butcher (Ed.), *Clinical personality assessment: Practical approaches* (pp. 367–379). New York: Oxford University Press.

The stereotyping habit: Young people try to fight it. (1992, November 30). *Los Angeles Times,* p. B7.

Sternberg, K. J., Lamb, M. E., Hershkowitz, I., Esplin, P. W., Redlich, A., & Sunshine, N. (1996). The relationship between investigative utterance types and the informativeness of child witnesses. *Journal of Applied Developmental Psychology, 17,* 439–451.

Stevenson, I. (1960). *Medical history-taking.* New York: Hoeber.

Stevenson, I. (1974). The psychiatric interview. In S. Arieti (Ed.), *American handbook of psychiatry* (2nd ed., Vol. 1, pp. 1138–1156). New York: Basic Books.

Stevenson, M. R., & Black, K. N. (1995). *How divorce affects offspring: A research approach.* Dubuque, IA: Brown & Benchmark.

Stewart B. McKinney Homeless Assistance Act of 1987, §11301 *et seq.* 42 U.S.C. (1987; amended, 1988).

Stillion, J. M., McDowell, E. E., & May, J. H. (1989). *Suicide across the life span: Premature exits.* New York: Hemisphere.

Stone, W. L., & Hogan, K. L. (1993). A structured parent interview for identifying young children with autism. *Journal of Autism & Developmental Disorders, 23,* 639–652.

Stone, W. L., & Lemanek, K. L. (1990). Developmental issues in children's self-reports. In A. M. La Greca (Ed.), *Through the eyes of the child: Obtaining self-reports from children and adolescents* (pp. 18–56). Boston: Allyn and Bacon.

Stout, C. E. (1992). Substance abuse and teenagers: A review. In C. E. Stout, J. L. Levitt, & D. H. Ruben (Eds.), *Handbook for assessing and treating addictive disorders* (pp. 287–298). New York: Greenwood.

Stout, C. E. (1993). Child and adolescent issues in transition. In D. H. Rubin & C. E. Stout (Eds.), *Transitions: Handbook of managed care for inpatient to outpatient treatment* (pp. 59–71). Westport, CT: Praeger.

Stouthamer-Loeber, M. (1986). Lying as problem behavior in children: A review. *Clinical Psychology Review, 6,* 267–289.

Sue, D., & Sue, S. (1987). Cultural factors in the clinical assessment of Asian Americans. *Journal of Consulting and Clinical Psychology, 55,* 479–487.

Sue, D. W. (1990). Culture-specific strategies in counseling: A conceptual framework. *Professional Psychology: Research and Practice, 21,* 424–433.

Summit, R. C. (1983). The child sexual abuse accommodations syndrome. *Child Abuse & Neglect, 7,* 177–193.

Sundberg, N. D., Taplin, J. R., & Tyler, L. E. (1983). *Introduction to clinical psychology: Perspectives, issues, and contributions to human service.* Englewood Cliffs, NJ: Prentice Hall.

Sussman, A. N. (1977). *The rights of young people: The basic ACLU guide to a young person's rights.* New York: Avon Books.

Swanson, F. L. (1970). *Psychotherapists and children: A procedural guide.* New York: Pitman.

Swanson, J., McBurnett, K., Christian, D., & Wigal, T. (1995). Stimulant medication and the treatment of children with ADHD. *Advances in Clinical Child Psychology, 17,* 265–322.

Sweet, E. S. (1991). What do adolescents want? What do adolescents need? Treating the chronic relapser. *Journal of Adolescent Chemical Dependency, 1,* 1–8.

Swoboda, F. (1995, November 25). Law, education failing to break glass ceiling: Panel reports boardrooms remain "overwhelmingly" white, male. *Washington Post,* pp. C1-C2.

Szapocznik, J., & Kurtines, W. M. (1989). *Breakthroughs in family therapy with drug abusing and problem youth.* New York: Springer.

Szapocznik, J., Perez-Vidal, A., Brickman, A. L., Foote, F. H., Santisteban, D., Hervis, O., & Kurtines, W. M. (1988). Engaging adolescent drug abusers and their families in treatment: A strategic structural systems approach. *Journal of Consulting and Clinical Psychology, 56,* 552–557.

Szekeres, S. F. (1989). Clinical illustration: Cognitive-communicative problem. *Journal of Children in Contemporary Society, 21,* 167–172.

Szempruch, J., & Jacobson, J. W. (1993). Evaluating facilitated communications of people with developmental disabilities. *Research in Developmental Disabilities, 14,* 253–264.

Szymanski, L. S., & Crocker, A. C. (1985). Mental retardation. In H. I. Kaplan & B. J. Sadock (Eds.), *Comprehensive book of psychiatry/IV* (Vol. 2, 4th ed., pp. 1635–1671). Baltimore: Williams & Wilkins.

Tanguay, P. E., & Russell, A. T. (1991). Mental retardation. In M. Lewis (Ed.), *Child and adolescent psychiatry: A comprehensive textbook* (pp. 508–516). Baltimore: Williams & Wilkins.

Tarbell, S. E., Cohen, I. T., & Marsh, J. L. (1992). The Toddler-Preschooler Postoperative Pain Scale: An observational scale for measuring postoperative pain in children aged 1–5: Preliminary report. *Pain, 50,* 273–280.

Tarnowski, K. J., & Kaufman, K. L. (1988). Behavioral assessment of pediatric pain. *Advances in Behavioral Assessment of Children and Families, 4,* 119–158.

Tarnowski, K. J., & Rohrbeck, C. A. (1993). Disadvantaged children and families. *Advances in Clinical Child Psychology, 15,* 41–79.

Tarter, R., Ott, P., & Mezzich, A. (1991). Psychometric assessment. In R. J. Frances & S. I. Miller (Eds.), *Clinical textbook of addictive disorders* (pp. 237–267). New York: Guilford.

Tasker, M. (1992). *How can I tell you?* Bethesda, MD: Association for Care of Children's Health.

Taylor, H. G. (1988a). Learning disabilities. In E. J. Mash & L. G. Terdal (Eds.), *Behavioral assessment of childhood disorders* (2nd ed., pp. 402–450). New York: Guilford.

Taylor, H. G. (1988b). Neuropsychological testing: Relevance for assessing children's learning disabilities. *Journal of Consulting and Clinical Psychology, 56,* 795–800.

Taylor, R. L. (1990). *Distinguishing psychological from organic disorders: Screening for psychological masquerade.* New York: Springer.

Terry, G. P. (1995, October 22). Peter Digre: Trying to protect children enmeshed in the welfare-reform plans. *Los Angeles Times,* p. M3.

Tharp, R. G. (1989). Psychocultural variables and constants: Effects on teaching and learning in schools. *American Psychologist, 44,* 349–359.

Tharp, R. G., & Wetzel, R. J. (1969). *Behavior modification in the natural environment.* New York: Academic Press.

Thoennes, N., & Tjaden, P. (1990). The extent, nature, and validity of sexual abuse allegations in custody/visitation disputes. *Child Abuse & Neglect, 14,* 151–163.

Thompson, J. W., Walker, R. D., & Silk-Walker, P. (1993). Psychiatric care of American Indians and Alaska natives. In A. C. Gaw (Ed.), *Culture, ethnicity, and mental illness* (pp. 189–243). Washington, DC: American Psychiatric Press.

Thompson, R. A. (1993). Developmental research and legal policy: Toward a two-way street. In D. Cicchetti & S. L. Toth (Eds.), *Child abuse, child development, and social policy* (pp. 75–115). Norwood, NJ: Ablex.

Thompson, R. J., & Gustafson, K. E. (1996). *Adaptation to chronic childhood illness.* Hyattsville, MD: American Psychological Association.

Thompson, R. J., Merritt, K. A., Keith, B. R., Murphy, L. B., & Johndrow, D. A. (1993). Mother-child agreement on the Child Assessment Schedule with nonreferred children: A research note. *Journal of Child Psychology and Psychiatry, 34,* 813–820.

Thornton, K. (1994, February 2). Parents jailed after tot is locked in closet. *San Diego Union-Tribune,* p. B3.

Tifft, L. L. (1993). *Battering of women: The failure of intervention and the case for prevention.* Boulder, CO: Westview.

Tobin, D. L., Johnson, C., & Franke, K. (1991). Development of an eating-disorder program. In J. J. Sweet, R. H. Rozensky, & S. M. Tovian (Eds.), *Handbook of clinical psychology in medical settings* (pp. 315–330). New York: Plenum.

Todis, B., & Singer, G. (1991). Stress and stress management in families with adopted children who have severe disabilities. *Journal of the Association of Speech & Hearing, 16,* 3–13.

Toledo, J. R., Hughes, H., & Sims, J. (1979). Management of noncompliance to medical regimen: A suggested methodological approach. *International Journal of Health Services, 22,* 232–241.

Toth, J. (1991, May 21). Asian-Americans find being ethnic "model" has downside. *Los Angeles Times,* p. A5.

Toth, P., & Whalen, M. (1987). *Investigation and prosecution of child abuse.* Alexandria, VA: American Prosecutors Research Institute.

Towers, R. L. (1987). *Student drug and alcohol abuse.* Washington, DC: National Education Association.

Tracy, E. M., Bean, N., Gwatkin, S., & Hill, B. (1992). Family preservation workers: Sources of job satisfaction and job stress. *Research on Social Work Practice, 2,* 465–478.

Tramontana, M. G., & Hooper, S. R. (1988). Child neuropsychological assessment: Overview of current status. In M. G. Tramontana & S. R. Hooper (Eds.), *Assessment issues in child neuropsychology* (pp. 3–38). New York: Plenum.

Trautman, P. D., Rotheram-Borus, M. J., Dopkins, S., & Lewin, N. (1991). Psychiatric diagnoses in minority female adolescent suicide attempters. *Journal of the American Academy of Child & Adolescent Psychiatry, 30,* 617–622.

Trotter, R. T. (1991). A survey of four illnesses and their relationship to intracultural variation in a Mexican-American community. *American Anthropologist, 93,* 115–125.

Trupin, E. W., Forsyth-Stephens, A., & Low, B. P. (1991). Service needs of severely disturbed children. *American Journal of Public Health, 81,* 975–980.

Tunks, E., & Bellissimo, A. (1991). *Behavioral medicine: Concepts and procedures.* New York: Pergamon.

Turk, D. C., & Kerns, R. D. (1985). The family in health and illness. In D. C. Turk & R. D. Kerns (Eds.), *Health, illness and families: A life-span perspective* (pp. 1–22). New York: Wiley.

Turnbull, H. R., III. (1993). *Free appropriate public education: The law and children with disabilities* (4th ed.). Denver: Love.

Tyson, G. M. (1992). Childhood MPD/dissociation identity disorder: Applying and extending current diagnostic checklists. *Dissociation: Progress in the Dissociative Disorders, 5,* 20–27.

Tzeng, O. C. S., Jackson, J. W., & Karlson, H. C. (1991). *Theories of child abuse and neglect: Differential perspectives, summaries, and evaluations.* New York: Praeger.

Uba, L. (1994). *Asian Americans: Personality patterns, identity, and mental health.* New York: Guilford.

Underwood, J. K., & Mead, J. F. (1995). *Legal aspects of special education and pupil services.* Boston: Allyn and Bacon.

Uniform Marriage and Divorce Act. (1970). *Uniform Laws Annotated, 9A,* p. 147.

United States Conference of Mayors. (1995). *A status report on hunger and homelessness in America's cities.* Washington, DC: Author.

U.S. Advisory Board on Child Abuse and Neglect. (1995, April). *A nation's shame: Fatal child abuse and neglect in the United States.* Washington, DC: Author.

U.S. Bureau of the Census. (1993a). *The foreign-born population in the United States: 1990 census of population.* Washington, DC: U.S. Department of Commerce.

U.S. Bureau of the Census. (1993b). *We the American…Asians.* Washington, DC: U.S. Department of Commerce.

U.S. Bureau of the Census. (1993c). *We the American…children.* Washington, DC: U.S. Department of Commerce.

U.S. Bureau of the Census. (1993d). *We the American…Hispanics.* Washington, DC: U.S. Department of Commerce.

U.S. Bureau of the Census. (1993e). *We the…first Americans.* Washington, DC: U.S. Department of Commerce.

U.S. Bureau of the Census. (1996a). *Income, poverty, and valuation of noncash benefits* (Current population reports, series P60–189). Washington, DC: U.S. Government Printing Office.

U.S. Bureau of the Census. (1996b). *Statistical Abstracts of the United States: 1996* (116th Edition). Washington, DC: U.S. Government Printing Office.

U.S. Department of Agriculture. (1986). *Cross-cultural counseling: A guide for nutrition and health counselors.* Washington, DC: U.S. Government Printing Office.

U.S. Department of Education. (1991). *Growing up drug free.* Washington, DC: Author.

U.S. Department of Education. (1995). *To assure the free appropriate public education of all children with disabilities: Seventeenth annual report to Congress on the implementation of the Individuals with Disabilities Education Act.* Washington, DC: Author.

U.S. General Accounting Office. (1990). *Asian Americans: A status report* (#GAO/HRD-90–36FS). Washington, DC: Author.

University of Chicago Press. (1993). *The Chicago manual of style* (14th ed.). Chicago: Author.

Urbach, J. R., & Culbert, J. P. (1991). Head-injured parents and their children: Psychosocial consequences of a traumatic syndrome. *Psychosomatics, 32,* 24–33.

Valenti-Hein, D. C., & Schwartz, L. D. (1993). Witness competency in people with mental retardation: Implications for prosecution of sexual abuse. *Sexuality & Disability, 11,* 287–294.

Van der Hart, O., Faure, H., Van Gerven, M., & Goodwin, J. (1991). Unawareness and denial of pregnancy in patients with multiple personality disorder. *Dissociation, 4,* 65–73.

Vanderheiden, G. C., & Lloyd, L. L. (1986). Communication systems and their components. In S. W. Blackston (Ed.), *Augmentative communication: An introduction* (pp. 49–161). Rockville, MD: American Speech-Language-Hearing Association.

Van Dongen, C. J. (1990). Agonizing questioning: Experiences of survivors of suicide victims. *Nursing Research, 39,* 224–229.

Van Dongen, C. J. (1991). Experiences of family members after a suicide. *Journal of Family Practice, 33,* 375–380.

Van Dongen-Melman, J. E. W. M. (1992). Quality of life in childhood cancer. In R. Zittoun (Ed.), *Quality of life of cancer patients: A review* (pp. 115–120). France: Laboratoire Roger Bellou.

Van Dongen-Melman, J. E. W. M., & Sanders-Woudstra, J. A. R. (1986). Psychosocial aspects of childhood cancer: A review of the literature. *Journal of Child Psychology and Psychiatry, 27,* 145–180.

Van Heeswyk, D., & Hibbert, J. (1989). Workshops for Black women on eliminating internalized racism. *Black Re-emergence, 5,* 11–21.

van Veldhuizen, A. M., & Last, B. F. (1991). *Children with cancer: Communication and emotions.* Amsterdam, The Netherlands: Swets & Zeitlinger.

Vasquez, C., & Javier, R. A. (1991). The problem with interpreters: Communicating with Spanish-speaking patients. *Hospital & Community Psychiatry, 42,* 163–165.

Vernberg, E. M., & Vogel, J. M. (1993). Psychological responses of children to natural and human-made disasters: II. Interventions with children after disasters. *Journal of Clinical Child Psychology, 22,* 485–498.

Vizard, E., & Tranter, M. (1988). Helping young children to describe experiences of child sexual abuse—General issues. In A. Bentovim, A. Elton, J. Hildegrand, M. Tranter, & E. Vizard (Eds.), *Child sexual abuse within the family, assessment and treatment* (pp. 84–104). Bristol, England: John Wright.

Vlaeyen, J. W. S., Pernot, D. F. M., Kole-Snijders, A. M. J., Schuerman, J. A., Van Eek, H., & Groenman, N. H. (1990). Assessment of the components of observed chronic pain behavior: The Checklist for Interpersonal Pain Behavior (CHIP). *Pain, 43,* 337–347.

Voeller, K. K. (1991). Clinical management of attention deficit hyperactivity disorder. *Journal of Child Neurology, 6,* S51-S67.

Walker, C. E., Bonner, B. L., & Kaufman, K. L. (1988). *The physically and sexually abused child: Evaluation and treatment.* New York: Pergamon.

Walker, D. K., Epstein, S. G., Taylor, A. B., Crocker, A. C., & Tuttle, G. A. (1989). Perceived needs of families with children who have chronic health conditions. *Children's Health Care, 18,* 196–201.

Walker, L. E. A. (1990). Psychological assessment of sexually abused children for legal evaluation and expert witness testimony. *Professional Psychology: Research and Practice, 21,* 344–353.

Walker, L. E. A. (1992). Helping heal violated children's trauma. [Review]. *Contemporary Psychology, 37,* 46–48.

Wallace, J. M., & Bachman, J. G. (1991). Explaining racial/ethnic differences in adolescent drug use: The impact of background and lifestyle. *Social Problems, 38,* 333–357.

Wallerstein, J. S. (1983). Children of divorce: Stress and developmental tasks. In N. Garmezy & M. Rutter (Eds.), *Stress coping and development in children* (pp. 265–302). New York: McGraw-Hill.

Ware, J. C., & Orr, W. C. (1992). Evaluation and treatment of sleep disorders in children. In C. E. Walker & M. C. Roberts (Eds.), *Handbook of clinical child psychology* (2nd ed., pp. 261–282). New York: Wiley.

Warner, J. E., & Hansen, D. J. (1994). The identification and reporting of physical abuse by physicians: A review and implications for research. *Child Abuse & Neglect, 18,* 11–25.

Washton, A. M., Stone, N. S., & Hendrickson, E. C. (1988). Cocaine abuse. In D. M. Donovan & G. A. Marlatt (Eds.), *Assessment of addictive behaviors* (pp. 364–389). New York: Guilford.

Webb, N. B. (1993). Assessment of the bereaved child. In N. B. Webb (Ed.), *Helping bereaved children: A handbook for practitioners* (pp. 19–42). New York: Guilford.

Webster-Stratton, C., & Herbert, M. (1994). *Troubled families— Problem children: Working with parents: A collaborative process.* Chichester, England: Wiley.

Weikel, D. (1996, April 7). Meth labs: How young lives are put in peril. *Los Angeles Times,* pp. A1, A18, A19.

Weinberg, W. A., Rutman, J., Sullivan, L., Penick, E. C., & Dietz, S. G. (1973). Depression in children referred to an educational diagnostic center: Diagnosis and treatment. *Journal of Pediatrics, 83,* 1066.

Weinberg, W. A., & Emslie, G. J. (1991). Attention deficit hyperactivity disorder: The differential diagnosis. *Journal of Child Neurology, 6,* S23-S36.

Weiner, B. A., Simons, V. A., & Cavanaugh, J. L., Jr. (1985). The child custody dispute. In D. Schetky & E. Benedek (Eds.), *Emerging issues in child psychiatry and the law.* New York: Brunner/Mazel.

Weiner, I. B. (1982). *Child and adolescent psychopathology.* New York: Wiley.

Weiner, I. B. (1992). *Psychological disturbance in adolescence* (2nd ed.). New York: Wiley.

Weisman, A. D., & Worden, J. W. (1976–1977). The existential plight in cancer: Significance of the first 100 days. *International Journal of Psychiatry in Medicine, 7,* 1–15.

Weiss, R., & Hardy, L. (1990). HIV infection and health policy. *Journal of Consulting and Clinical Psychology, 58,* 70–76.

Weiss, S. J. (1991). Stressors experienced by family caregivers of children with pervasive developmental disorders. *Child Psychiatry & Human Development, 21,* 203–216.

Weithorn, L. A., & Grisso, T. (1987). Psychological evaluations in divorce custody: Problems, principles, and procedures. In L. A. Weithorn (Ed.), *Psychology and child custody determinations: Knowledge, roles, and expertise* (pp. 157–181). Lincoln: University of Nebraska Press.

Weller, E. B., Weller, R. A., Fristad, M. A., Cain, S. E., & Bowes, J. M. (1988). Should children attend their parent's funeral? *Journal of the American Academy of Child & Adolescent Psychiatry, 27,* 559–562.

Wellman, M. M. (1993). Child sexual abuse and gender differences: Attitudes and prevalence. *Child Abuse & Neglect, 17,* 539–547.

Wells, K. B., Benson, M. C., & Hoff, P. (1985). A model for teaching the brief psychosocial interview. *Journal of Medical Education, 60,* 181–188.

Werner, E. E. (1990). Protective factors and individual resilience. In S. J. Meisels & J. P. Shonkoff (Eds.), *Handbook of early childhood intervention* (pp. 97–116). New York: Cambridge University Press.

Wertlieb, D. (1991). Children and divorce: Stress and coping in developmental perspective. In J. Eckenrode (Ed.), *The social context of coping* (pp. 31–54). New York: Plenum.

Westcott, H. (1991). The abuse of disabled children: A review of the literature. *Child: Care, Health & Development, 17,* 243–258.

Wetherby, A. M., & Prizant, B. M. (1992). Facilitating language and communication development in autism: Assessment and intervention guidelines. In D. E. Berkell (Ed.), *Autism: Identification, education, and treatment* (pp. 107–134). Hillsdale, NJ: Erlbaum.

Whalen, C. K. (1989). Attention deficit and hyperactivity disorders. In T. H. Ollendick & M. Hersen (Eds.), *Handbook of child psychopathology* (pp. 131–169). New York: Plenum.

White, D. R. (1983). *The official lawyer's handbook.* New York: Wallaby Books.

White, G. W., & White, N. L. (1993). The adoptive process: Challenges and opportunities for people with disabilities. *Sexuality & Disability, 11,* 211–219.

White, S., Strom, G. A., Santilli, G., & Quinn, K. M. (1987). *Guidelines for interviewing preschoolers with sexually anatomically detailed dolls.* Unpublished manuscript, Case Western Reserve University.

Whitman, B. Y., & Munkel, W. (1991). Multiple personality disorder: A risk indicator, diagnostic marker and psychiatric outcome for severe child abuse. *Clinical Pediatrics, 30,* 422–428.

Wickramasekera, I. E. (1988). *Clinical behavioral medicine: Some concepts and procedures.* New York: Plenum.

Wideman, J. C. (1990). Investigative procedures in allegations of child sexual abuse: Part II. Victim and subject interviews. *Issues in Child Abuse Accusations, 2,* 7–14.

Wiener, L. S., Fair, C. D., & Granowsky, R. T. (1993). HIV infection in infants, children, and adolescents: Implications for social work practice. In V. J. Lynch, G. A. Lloyd, & M. F. Finbres (Eds.), *The changing face of AIDS: Implications for social work practice* (pp. 105–121). Westport, CT: Auburn House/Greenwood.

Wiener, L. S., Fair, C. D., & Pizzo, P. A. (1993). Care for the child with HIV infection and AIDS. In A. Armstrong-Dailey & S. Z. Goltzer (Eds.), *Hospice care for children* (pp. 85–104). New York: Oxford University Press.

Wiener, L. S., Moss, H., Davidson, R., & Fair, C. D. (1992). Pediatrics: The emerging psychosocial challenges of the AIDS epidemic. *Child & Adolescent Social Work Journal, 9,* 381–407.

Wiese, D., & Daro, D. (1995, April). *Current trends in child abuse reporting and fatalities: The results of the 1994 annual fifty state survey.* Chicago: National Committee to Prevent Child Abuse.

Wikler, L., Wasow, M., & Hatfield, E. (1981). Chronic sorrow revisited: Parent vs. professional depiction of the adjustment of parents of mentally retarded children. *American Journal of Orthopsychiatry, 51,* 63–70.

Wilkie, D. J., Holzemer, W. L., Tesler, M. D., Ward, J. A., Paul, S. M., & Savedra, M. C. (1990). Measuring pain quality: Validity and reliability of children's and adolescents' pain language. *Pain, 41,* 151–159.

Wilkinson, S. R. (1988). *The child's world of illness: The development of health and illness behaviour.* Cambridge, England: Cambridge University Press.

Williams, C. L. (1991). Toward the development of preventive interventions for youth traumatized by war and refugee flight. In F. L. Ahearn, Jr., & J. L. Athey (Eds.), *Refugee children: Theory, research, and services* (pp. 201–217). Baltimore: Johns Hopkins University Press.

Williamson, D. A., Baker, J. D., & Cubic, B. A. (1992). Advances in pediatric headache research. *Advances in Clinical Child Psychology, 15,* 275–304.

Williamson, D. A., Head, S. B., & Baker, J. D. (1993). Behavioral treatment. In V. B. Van Hasselt & M. Hersen (Eds.), *Handbook of behavior therapy and pharmacotherapy for children: A comparative analysis* (pp. 195–212). Boston: Allyn and Bacon.

Williamson, D. A., Sebastian, S. B., & Varnado, P. J. (1995). Anorexia and bulimia nervosa. In A. J. Goreczny (Ed.), *Handbook of health and rehabilitation psychology* (pp. 175–196). New York: Plenum.

Willis, D. J., Elliott, C. H., & Jay, S. M. (1982). Psychological effects of physical illness and its concomitant. In J. M. Tuma (Ed.), *Handbook for the practice of pediatric psychology* (pp. 28–66). New York: Wiley.

Willis, D. J., & Walker, C. E. (1989). Etiology. In T. H. Ollendick & M. Hersen (Eds.), *Handbook of child psychopathology* (2nd ed., pp. 29–51). New York: Plenum.

Wilson, B. (1991). Theory, assessment, and treatment in neuropsychological rehabilitation. *Neuropsychology, 5,* 281–291.

Wilson, C., & Steppe, S. C. (1994). Backlash and Child Protective Services from the perspective of state CPS administrators. In J. E. B. Myers (Ed.), *The backlash: Child protection under fire* (pp. 60–69). Thousand Oaks, CA: Sage.

Wilson, P. H., Spence, S. H., & Kavanagh, D. J. (1989). *Cognitive-behavioral interviewing for adult disorders: A practical handbook.* London: Routledge.

Windle, M., Miller-Tutzauer, C., Barnes, G. M., & Welte, J. (1991). Adolescent perceptions of help-seeking resources for substance abuse. *Child Development, 62,* 179–189.

Winer-Bernheimer, L. (1994, August 8). Whoopi: Bruised but unbowed. *Los Angeles Times,* pp. F1, F5.

Wing, L. (1976). Assessment: The role of the teacher. In M. P. Everard (Ed.), *An approach to teaching autistic children* (pp. 15–30). New York: Pergamon.

Winton, P. J. (1992). *Communicating with families in early intervention: A training module.* Chapel Hill, NC: Frank Porter Graham Child Development Center.

Witchel, R. I. (1991). College-student survivors of incest and other child sexual abuse. *New Directions for Student Services, 54,* 63–76.

Witt, J. C., & Elliott, S. N. (1983). Assessment in behavioral consultation: The initial interview. *School Psychology Review, 12,* 42–49.

Wolfe, D. A. (1987). *Child abuse: Implications for child development and psychopathology.* Newbury Park, CA: Sage.

Wolfe, D. A., & Wekerle, C. (1993). Treatment strategies for child physical abuse and neglect: A critical progress report. *Clinical Psychology Review, 13,* 473–500.

Wolfe, V. V., & Birt, J. (1995). The psychological sequelae of child sexual abuse. *Advances in Clinical Child Psychology, 17,* 233–263.

Wolfner, G., Faust, D., & Dawes, R. (1993). The use of anatomical dolls in sexual abuse evaluations: The state of the science. *Applied and Preventative Psychology, 2,* 1–11.

Wonderlich, S. (1994). Bulimia nervosa: Psychological issues. In R. A. Olson, L. L. Mullins, J. B. Gillman, & J. M. Chaney (Eds.), *The sourcebook of pediatric psychology* (pp. 340–354). Boston: Allyn and Bacon.

Wong, D. L. (1988). False allegations of child abuse: The other side of the tragedy. *Annual Progress in Child Psychiatry & Child Development 13,* 615–626.

Wood, D. J. (1982). Talking to young children. *Developmental Medicine & Child Neurology, 24,* 856–859.

Wood, R. L. (1987). *Brain injury rehabilitation: A neurobehavioral approach.* London: Croom Helm.

Worchel, F. F. (1988). Interviewing adolescents. In J. M. Dillard & R. R. Reilly (Eds.), *Systematic interviewing: Communication skills for professional effectiveness* (pp. 114–138). Columbus, OH: Merrill.

Worden, J. W., & Monahan, J. R. (1993). Caring for bereaved parents. In A. Armstrong-Dailey & S. Z. Goltzer (Eds.), *Hospice care for children* (pp. 122–139). New York: Oxford University Press.

Wright, B., & Tierney, W. G. (1991). American Indian in higher education: A history of cultural conflict. *Change, 23*(2), 11–18.

Wright, B. A. P. (1983). *Physical disability—A psychosocial approach* (2nd ed.). New York: Harper & Row.

Wright, M. O'D., & Masten, A. S. (1997). Vulnerability and resilience in young children. In J. O. Noshpitz (Series Ed.) & S. I. Greenspan, S. Weider, & J. D. Osofsky (Vol. Eds.), *Handbook of child and adolescent psychiatry: Vol 1. Infants and preschoolers: Development and syndromes* (pp. 202–224). New York: Wiley.

Wyer, M. M., Gaylord, S. J., & Grove, E. T. (1987). The legal context of child custody evaluations. In L. A. Weithorn (Ed.), *Psychology and child custody determinations: Knowledge, roles, and expertise* (pp. 3–22). Lincoln: University of Nebraska Press.

Wyne, M. D., & O'Connor, P. D. (1979). *Exceptional children: A developmental view.* Lexington, MA: D. C. Heath.

Yap, J. N. (1988). The effects of hospitalization and surgery on children: A critical review. *Journal of Applied Developmental Psychology, 9,* 349–358.

Yarborough, T. (1996a, March 2). "I saw women go to school and have jobs." *Los Angeles Times,* p. B7.

Yarborough, T. (1996b, September 14). "Social workers pretended to care, but I was always sent back." *Los Angeles Times,* p. B7.

Yarrow, L. J. (1960). Interviewing children. In P. H. Mussen (Ed.), *Handbook of research methods in child development* (pp. 561–602). New York: Wiley.

Yates, J. L., & Musty, W. (1993). Dissociation, affect, and network models of memory: An integrative proposal. *Journal of Traumatic Stress, 6,* 305–326.

Yeates, K. O. (1994). Head injuries: Psychological issues. In R. A. Olson, L. L. Mullins, J. B. Gillman, & J. M. Chaney (Eds.), *The sourcebook of pediatric psychology* (pp. 262–281). Boston: Allyn and Bacon.

Ying, Y. W., & Hu, L. (1994). Public outpatient mental health services: Use and outcome among Asian Americans. *American Journal of Orthopsychiatry, 64,* 448–455.

Yllî, K. (1993). Through a feminist lens: Gender, power, and violence. In R. J. Gelles & D. R. Loseke (Eds.), *Current controversies on family violence* (pp. 47–62). Newbury Park, CA: Sage.

Ylvisaker, M. (1986). Language and communication disorders following pediatric head injury. *Journal of Head Trauma Rehabilitation, 1*(4), 48–56.

Ylvisaker, M., Chorazy, A. J. L., Cohen, S. B., Mastrilli, J. P., Molitor, C. B., Nelson, J., Szekeres, S. F., Valko, A. S., & Jaffe, K. M. (1990). Rehabilitative assessment following head injury in children. In M. Rosenthal, E. R. Griffith, M. R. Bond, & J. D. Miller (Eds.), *Rehabilitation of the adult and child with traumatic brain injury* (pp. 558–592). Philadelphia: Davis.

Ylvisaker, M., Hartwick, P., & Stevens, M. (1991). School reentry following head injury: Managing the transition from hospital to school. *Journal of Head Trauma Rehabilitation, 6*(1), 10–22.

Young, T. J. (1992). Native Americans and substance abuse. In C. E. Stout, J. L. Levitt, & D. H. Ruben (Eds.), *Handbook for assessing and treating addictive disorders* (pp. 203–213). New York: Greenwood.

Young, T. J. (1993). Alcoholism prevention among Native-American youth. *Child Psychiatry & Human Development, 24*, 41–47.

Young, V. H. (1974). A black American socialization pattern. *American Ethnologist, 1*, 405–413.

Zahn-Waxler, C., Iannotti, R. J., Cummings, E. M., & Denham, S. (1990). Antecedents of problem behaviors in children of depressed mothers. *Development & Psychopathology, 2*, 271–291.

Zambrana, R. E., & Silva-Palacios, V. (1989). Gender differences in stress among Mexican immigrant adolescents in Los Angeles, California. *Journal of Adolescent Research, 4*, 426–442.

Zane, M. D., & Milt, H. (1984). *Your phobia: Understanding your fears through contextual therapy.* Washington, DC: American Psychiatric Press.

Zaslow, M. J. (1988). Sex differences in children's response to parental divorce: Research methodology and postdivorce family forms. *American Journal of Orthopsychiatry, 58*, 355–378.

Zayas, L. H. (1992). Childrearing, social stress, and child abuse: Clinical considerations with Hispanic families. *Journal of Social Distress and the Homeless, 1*, 291–309.

Zehnder, M. M. (1994). *Using expert witnesses in child abuse and neglect cases.* St. Paul: Minnesota County Attorneys Association.

Zellman, G. L. (1992). The impact of case characteristics on child abuse reporting decisions. *Child Abuse & Neglect, 16*, 57–74.

Zima, J. P. (1983). *Interviewing: Key to effective management.* Chicago: Science Research Associates.

Zimring, F. E. (1996, November 11). Paranoia on the playground. *Los Angeles Times*, p. B5.

Zintz, M. V. (1962). Problems of classroom adjustment of Indian children in public elementary schools in the Southwest. *Science Education, 46*, 261–269.

NAME INDEX

SUBJECT INDEX

Abuse. See *Maltreatment, child*
Abuser, 665. See also *Domestic violence; Maltreatment, child; Offender; Perpetrator*
Abusive interviewees, 79
Academic difficulties, and anxiety disorders, 364
Academic underachievers, 350
Acalculia, 623
Acculturation, 264–266, 305, 314, 316–317. See also *Culture; Ethnic minority groups;* specific ethnic groups
Acquiescent response style, 52
Acquired aphasia, 623
Acquired immune deficiency syndrome (AIDS), 428, 558–568. See also *Human immune deficiency syndrome; Pediatric acquired immune deficiency syndrome*
   books for children on, 867
   semistructured interview for, 989–992
Acting out, 490
Active-interviewer/passive-interviewee model, 22
Activity level, of infants, 103
Acupuncture, 302
Acute lymphoblastic leukemia, 556
Acute lymphocytic leukemia, 556
Acute stress disorder, 366
Adaptability, of infants, 103
Adaptive behavior, of Black adolescents, 283
Addiction, 586. See also *Substance abuse*
Adherence, 488, 495–501, 502–503
   in asthmatic children, 551
   to diabetic regimen, 553–554
   encouraging, 533
Adjustment disorder, 437
Adjustment problem, semistructured interviews for, 945–950, 1010–1014
Adjustment sleep disorder, 579
Adolescents
   acculturation of, 265
   ADHD in, 352
   adherence by, 496
   American Indian, 266
   aphasic, 625
   Asian American, 266, 298, 299
   biracial American, 267
   Black American, 261–262, 266, 283–284
   books for parents on, 861–862
   brain injury in, 618–619, 620–621, 642, 644
   with cancer, 557
   cigarette smoking among, 588
   concept of death among, 430
   conduct disorders in, 357, 359
   confidentiality and, 760

depression in, 364–365
divorce and, 459
effects of domestic violence on, 702
Hispanic American, 266
HIV/AIDS and, 559, 561–562
homeless, 475
homosexual, 562
hospitalization of, 486, 521–522
independence in, 109
insomnia in, 581
of low socioeconomic status, 34
pain and, 542
parenthood and, 32
as perpetrators of child sexual abuse, 708–709
personal data questionnaire for, 110, 882–886
PTSD in, 369, 370
reaction to crisis by, 370
resistance in, 110
separation anxiety disorder in, 368
sexual abuse and, 719
sleep diary for, 582–583
with substance-abusing mothers, 328
substance use and abuse among, 587, 588, 591–592, 593–597, 599
suicide in, 326–327, 435, 437, 439–440, 446
transition to adult services of, 524
understanding of medical illness among, 486–487
unemployment and, 32
use of fantasy techniques with, 116
violent death and, 32
Adoption, 452–457, 458
   books for children on, 866–867
   books for parents on, 859
   report on, 458–459
   semistructured interview for, 1018
Adversarial system, 218
Affect, 12, 325
   of Black adolescent, 283
   of child during play, 107
   of infant, 104, 164
   of interviewee, 57–59, 208
   of interviewer, 768
   of school-aged child, 167
   of toddler, 167
   types of, 59
Affective aspect of post-assessment interview, 186
Affective disorder, suicide and, 437
Affective responses, of family, 170, 172, 173
Affect labels, 113
African cultural perspective, 284. See also *Black Americans*

Aggression
   of alters in dissociative identity disorder, 379
   in conduct disorder, 359, 360
Agnosia, 621, 622, 624
Agoraphobia, 366
Agrammatism, 623
Agraphia, 623
AIDS. See *Acquired immune deficiency syndrome*
AIDS/HIV-1 encephalopathy, 560
AIDS risk behavior knowledge test, 567–568
Aid to Families with Dependent Children (AFDC), 471
Akathesia, 635
Akinesia, 635
Alateen, 599
Albinism, 412
Alcohol abuse, 327, 588, 589, 591, 592, 619
   ADHD and, 351
   books for children on, 867
   brain injury and, 642
   custody evaluation and, 466
   domestic violence and, 698, 699, 701
   Native Americans and, 305
   pregnant mothers and, 328, 403
   semistructured interview for, 920–921
   suicide and, 437, 446
Alcoholics Anonymous, 599
Alexia, 623
Allergens, 550
Altered states of consciousness, 723
Alternative communication procedures, 338
Alternative rewards, 488
Alters, 377, 378–379. See also *Dissociative identity disorder*
Alzheimer's disease, 615
American Medical Association, 698
American Sign Language, 415
Amnesia, 383, 384
   anterograde, 632
   dissociative, 377
   in psychological disorders, 326
   retrograde, 632
Amniocentesis, 403
Amphetamines, 588, 589, 590
Amulets, 302
Amyl nitrite, 589
Anabolic steroids, 590
Analytical listening, 50–53
Anatomically detailed dolls, 770–771. See also *Maltreatment, child*
Anger
   books for children on, 867
   at law, 726
   at offender, 733

1120

Index for Semistructured Interview Questions

[a]These semistructured interview questions, with minor modifications, also can be used with parents.